HISTORICAL STATISTICS
OF THE
UNITED STATES

HISTORICAL STATISTICS
OF THE
UNITED STATES

Earliest Times to the Present

MILLENNIAL EDITION

VOLUME ONE

PART A
POPULATION

Editors in Chief

Susan B. Carter

Scott Sigmund Gartner

Michael R. Haines

Alan L. Olmstead

Richard Sutch

Gavin Wright

CAMBRIDGE
UNIVERSITY PRESS

CAMBRIDGE UNIVERSITY PRESS
Cambridge, New York, Melbourne, Madrid, Cape Town, Singapore, São Paulo

Cambridge University Press
40 West 20th Street, New York, NY 10011-4211, USA

http://www.cambridge.org
Information on this title: www.cambridge.org/9780521817912

First published 2006

Printed in the United States of America

A catalog record for this publication is available from the British Library.

Library of Congress Cataloging in Publication Data

Historical statistics of the United States : earliest times to the present / Susan B. Carter ... [et al.]. – Millennial ed.
    p. cm.
   Rev. update of: Historical statistics of the United States, colonial times to 1970. Bicentennial ed. Washington : U.S. Dept. of Commerce, Bureau of the Census, 1975.
   Includes bibliographical references and index.
   ISBN 0-521-81791-9 (set)
   1. United States – Statistics.   I. Carter, Susan B.   II. Historical statistics of the United States, colonial times to 1970.   III. Title.

HA202.H57 2006
317.3 – dc22   2005027089

ISBN-13 978-0-521-81791-2 (set of five volumes hardback)
ISBN-10 0-521-81791-9 (set of five volumes hardback)

ISBN-13 978-0-521-58496-8 (volume 1 hardback)
ISBN-10 0-521-58496-5 (volume 1 hardback)

ISBN-13 978-0-521-58540-8 (volume 2 hardback)
ISBN-10 0-521-58540-6 (volume 2 hardback)

ISBN-13 978-0-521-81790-5 (volume 3 hardback)
ISBN-10 0-521-81790-0 (volume 3 hardback)

ISBN-13 978-0-521-85389-7 (volume 4 hardback)
ISBN-10 0-521-85389-3 (volume 4 hardback)

ISBN-13 978-0-521-85390-3 (volume 5 hardback)
ISBN-10 0-521-85390-7 (volume 5 hardback)

ISBN-13 978-0-511-13297-1 (on-line edition)
ISBN-10 0-511-13297-2 (on-line edition)

SUMMARY CONTENTS

DETAILED CONTENTS
OF VOLUME ONE

PART A. POPULATION

Tables

EDITORS' PREFACE

Historical Statistics of the United States has long been the standard source for quantitative indicators of American history. It has not been revised, however, since the Bicentennial Edition, which was published in 1975 and provided data through 1970. The period since then has witnessed an explosion of quantitative scholarship and the general expansion of the government's statistical record keeping. By one estimate, more than three fourths of the data output of the U.S. government and more than 80 percent of the historical data series generated by scholars have been produced since 1970. No subject area and few data series have remained untouched by this phenomenal growth of the American quantitative record.

The revised, updated, and expanded Millennial Edition contains considerably more information than its immediate predecessor: five volumes rather than two, more than twice as many pages of data and documentation, and a tripling of the number of data series – 37,339 in the new edition. This expansion occurred along several dimensions. Most series from the previous edition were extended by roughly thirty years, and the coverage of most topics was enhanced. More than a dozen new topics were added: American Indians, slavery, outlying areas, poverty, nonprofit organizations, and the Confederate States of America, to list a few examples. Finally, the chapters in the new edition are preceded by essays that introduce the quantitative history of their subject, provide a guide to the sources, and offer expert advice on the reliability of the data and the limits that might be placed on their interpretation.

Unlike the previous three editions of *Historical Statistics of the United States*, the Millennial Edition was not produced by the U.S. Bureau of the Census.* Representatives of three academic organizations (the Economic History Association, the Cliometrics Society, and the Social Science History Association) met with Census Bureau officials in November 1993 to urge the Bureau to compile and issue a fourth edition of *Historical Statistics of the United States*. Despite agreement that a new edition was both long overdue and vitally important, it became clear that such a project could not be a priority for the Bureau in the foreseeable future. Instead, more than eighty scholars contributed their efforts and expertise to assemble and document the data, to write the introductory essays, and to raise funds as needed to support their work. As a consequence, we have no single sponsor, but rather more than seventy separate funding sources, public as well as private. The donation of time, energy, and funding resources by so many testifies to the status of the project as a landmark of collaborative scholarship.

Although the Census Bureau indicated clearly that it was not going to publish another edition, it authorized us to treat this edition as an approved successor to the previous editions. At the same time, it gave us encouragement, advice, and permission to draw freely from previous editions, a privilege of which we have taken full advantage. For all of these courtesies, we are extremely grateful.

This work is also available in electronic form from Cambridge University Press. The data are readily available for charting, or statistical analysis, or regrouping across tables, which should greatly facilitate the efforts of scholars, journalists, students, and other researchers.

Work on this project exposed many lacunas in the statistical record and revealed opportunities to make existing data series more reliable by reworking information in the original sources. Although we asked our contributors to confine their efforts to compiling and verifying previously published data, many could not resist the temptation and submitted newly developed historical data series to these volumes. We hope that this new edition will encourage a continued expansion of quantitative history: research deploying data from the Millennial Edition to revise historical interpretations; efforts to improve and perhaps render obsolete the statistics presented here; and ultimately the need for a revision of *Historical Statistics of the United States* in far less time than has elapsed since the publication of the Bicentennial Edition.

SUSAN B. CARTER
SCOTT SIGMUND GARTNER
MICHAEL R. HAINES
ALAN L. OLMSTEAD
RICHARD SUTCH
GAVIN WRIGHT

---

* For a discussion of the origin and early history of *Historical Statistics of the United States* at the Census Bureau, see Appendix 3.

ACKNOWLEDGMENTS

We have been occupied with the Millennial Edition of *Historical Statistics of the United States* for more than eleven years. This long effort, launched in March 1994, has proven to be more complicated and time-consuming than we anticipated, but we have been sustained throughout by the assistance and support of many colleagues. The Millennial Edition is truly a collaborative product of the community of researchers and scholars who generate and use historical statistics.

The following few pages can list only the most obvious of those who have contributed. We begin with the names of the eighty-three individuals who wrote the essays or selected and documented the tables of data. Most contributed both. We owe these experts a great debt. They raised the financial support required and added their own considerable effort to ours to assemble this work. Yet we should also note that a great deal that is reported by our contributors builds on the work of those who preceded them. These include the previous editions of *Historical Statistics of the United States,* upon which we have drawn when appropriate, and the original contributions of the scholars and government researchers whom we have acknowledged through the citations recorded in the source notes to the tables.

The Historical Statistics Project received financial and material support from many institutions and foundations. Without the promise of such support, acknowledged on page 1-xix, we would not have dared to begin. Expending the financial support received, we employed over the years a total of sixty-five research assistants (some graduate students, some undergraduate students) and two staff members. Their names are listed on page 1-xxi. During the project's eleven-year gestation, we freely asked for and received assistance, advice, and critical review from many people and institutions – too many, indeed, to name them all. Two hundred ninety-nine individuals are formally listed here as "consultants," but they were also enthusiastic supporters of the effort. Their willingness to be involved added immeasurably more than the perfunctory documentation of their assistance suggests.

Beyond these formal contacts, we held five planning conferences with a combined attendance of more than 150 scholars and historical statisticians. Coordination and numerous opportunities for review and feedback were provided through more than eighteen meetings of the University of California Group in Economic History. Without the support of the All-UC Group, managing the project would have been immeasurably more difficult. Many of the essays were first presented at the meetings of the Social Science History Association in 1999, where comments by discussants and members of the audience helped improve the final product. Other chapters were presented at special gatherings, both in the United States and abroad. Librarians and government officers at many locations were of enormous assistance in guiding us both to the original data and to its proper interpretation.

The research required to select, assemble, explain, and contextualize the historical statistics contained in these five volumes was only half the project. After all that work, the manuscript had to be converted to both print and electronic media. In that undertaking Cambridge University Press became our collaborator. Frank Smith, our editor and champion at the Press, recognized the value of the work from the beginning and has stood behind us with unwavering optimism and commitment for more than ten years. Thank you, Frank.

The New York staff at Cambridge University Press has been fantastic. We owe special thanks to Shari Chappell, Eric Crahan, Anna Curry, Laura Dorfman, Pauline Ireland, and Alia Winters. Their professionalism never obscured their personal interest in and genuine understanding of an effort that might strike many as boring and obscurely technical. Cathy Felgar, also in New York but working with compositors in India and cartographers in Wisconsin, saw the volumes through the tortuous production process with skill, perseverance, and uncommon patience.

Madeleine Adams was responsible for preparing the manuscript for publication. She coordinated the efforts of a small army of copy editors and proofreaders and applied her own considerable editorial talent and knowledge of history and statistics to keep an otherwise unwieldy monster as error-free and user-friendly as possible. We are appreciative beyond words that she sustained this concentrated effort with good humor, unflagging attention to detail, and a genuine concern for the researchers who will come to rely on the data presented here. Every user owes her a nod of thanks.

Anthony Angiletta of Stanford Libraries has been an invaluable advisor concerning the requirements and expectations of reference librarians, the rapidly changing field of electronic publishing, and the evolving needs of students and scholars who come looking for historical statistics in the library or on the Web.

Finally, we acknowledge the excellent work of our three Managing Editors. Robert Barde was with us at the beginning and served until the headquarters of the project moved from Berkeley to Riverside in 1998. He played a major role in our initial fund-raising efforts and coordinated our individual meetings with the primary contributors. Matthew Sobek joined the project in Riverside and served as a project manager through 2001. He organized both the routine and the unexpected. He devised systems to keep track of everything from intertextual cross references to our far-flung team of contributors. Matt also refined and then enforced the "technical protocol" that guided the preparation of the spreadsheets and text files. Monty Hindman took over as Managing Editor in 2001 and took charge of the final stage of manuscript preparation. Monty wrote the computer algorithms that processed the raw data and, when necessary, flagged questionable numbers. He formatted the spreadsheets, with their often complex heading structure, for transmission to the compositors. Each of these fine Managing Editors left their personal mark on the project. As scholars they believed in the importance of the quantitative approach to history and social science, they worked diligently to ensure the fidelity and accuracy of the data, and they insisted on clarity in the documentation.

We asked the most distinguished and busy people to join us as contributors and collaborators. At every turn we were gratified by the enthusiasm and selfless willingness of our colleagues. We can record our thanks publicly here, but we trust that the real reward for these many people will be the value that the Millennial Edition will bring to future scholarship.

CONTRIBUTORS TO THE MILLENNIAL EDITION

Albert K. A. Acquaye
Department of Agricultural Economics and
　Rural Sociology
Auburn University
Auburn, Alabama

Richard Alba
Department of Sociology
State University of New York
Albany, New York

Julian M. Alston
Department of Agricultural and Resource
　Economics
University of California
Davis, California

Richard G. Anderson
Federal Reserve Bank of St. Louis
St. Louis, Missouri

Jeremy Atack
Departments of Economics and History
Vanderbilt University
Nashville, Tennessee

Robert Barde
Institute of Business and Economic
　Research
University of California
Berkeley, California

Linda Barrington
The Conference Board
New York, New York

Fred Bateman
Department of Economics
University of Georgia
Athens, Georgia

Peter Berck
Department of Agricultural and Resource
　Economics
University of California
Berkeley, California

Howard Bodenhorn
Department of Economics
Lafayette College
Easton, Pennsylvania

Michael D. Bordo
Department of Economics
Rutgers University
New Brunswick, New Jersey

Susan Brower
Department of History
University of Minnesota
Minneapolis, Minnesota

Colin B. Burke
Department of History
University of Maryland, Baltimore County
Baltimore, Maryland

Michelle L. Butler
Department of History
University of Texas
Austin, Texas

Louis P. Cain
Graduate School of Business
Loyola University
Chicago, Illinois

Susan B. Carter
Department of Economics
University of California
Riverside, California

Dustin L. Chambers
Department of Economics
University of California
Riverside, California

Carmel Ullman Chiswick
Department of Economics
University of Illinois
Chicago, Illinois

William J. Collins
Department of Economics
Vanderbilt University
Nashville, Tennessee

Lee A. Craig
Department of Economics
North Carolina State University
Raleigh, North Carolina

Douglas Eckberg
Department of Sociology
Winthrop University
Rock Hill, South Carolina

Michael Edelstein
Department of Economics
City University of New York, Queens
　College and the Graduate School
Flushing, New York

Stanley L. Engerman
Department of Economics
University of Rochester
Rochester, New York

Reynolds Farley
Department of Sociology
University of Michigan
Ann Arbor, Michigan

Scott Farrow
H. J. Heinz III School of Public Policy
   and Management
Carnegie Mellon University
Pittsburgh, Pennsylvania

Joseph P. Ferrie
Department of Economics
Northwestern University
Evanston, Illinois

Alexander J. Field
Department of Economics
Santa Clara University
Santa Clara, California

Price V. Fishback
Department of Economics
University of Arizona
Tucson, Arizona

Gordon M. Fisher
Office of the Assistant Secretary for
   Planning and Evaluation
U.S. Department of Health and Human
   Services
Washington, D.C.

Catherine Fitch
Minnesota Population Center
University of Minnesota
Minneapolis, Minnesota

Bruce L. Gardner
Department of Agricultural and Resource
   Economics
University of Maryland
College Park, Maryland

Todd K. Gardner
U.S. Census Bureau
Washington, D.C.

Scott Sigmund Gartner
Department of Political Science
University of California
Davis, California

Claudia Goldin
Department of Economics
Harvard University
Cambridge, Massachusetts

Brian Gratton
Department of History
Arizona State University
Tempe, Arizona

Myron P. Gutmann
Inter-University Consortium for
   Political and Social Research
University of Michigan
Ann Arbor, Michigan

Michael R. Haines
Department of Economics
Colgate University
Hamilton, New York

Peter Dobkin Hall
John F. Kennedy School of
   Government
Harvard University
Cambridge, Massachusetts

Christopher Hanes
Department of Economics
State University of New York
Binghamton, New York

Joan Underhill Hannon
Department of Economics
Saint Mary's College of California
Moraga, California

Monty Hindman
Center for Social and Economic
   Policy
University of California
Riverside, California

Charles Hirschman
Department of Sociology
University of Washington
Seattle, Washington

Douglas A. Irwin
Department of Economics
Dartmouth College
Hanover, New Hampshire

John A. James
Department of Economics
University of Virginia
Charlottesville, Virginia

Daniel K. N. Johnson
Department of Economics
Wellesley College
Wellesley, Massachusetts

Sukkoo Kim
Department of Economics
Washington University
St. Louis, Missouri

Timothy G. F. Kittel
Climate and Global Dynamics Division
National Center for Atmospheric
   Research
Boulder, Colorado

Sumner J. La Croix
Department of Economics
University of Hawai'i
Honolulu, Hawai'i

Naomi R. Lamoreaux
Departments of Economics and History
University of California
Los Angeles, California

Peter H. Lindert
Department of Economics
University of California
Davis, California

Robert A. Margo
Departments of Economics and
   History
Vanderbilt University
Nashville, Tennessee

John J. McCusker
Departments of History and Economics
Trinity University
San Antonio, Texas

John P. McIver
Department of Political Science
University of Colorado
Boulder, Colorado

Lawrence H. Officer
Department of Economics
University of Illinois
Chicago, Illinois

Alan L. Olmstead
Department of Economics
University of California
Davis, California

Philip G. Pardey
Department of Applied Economics
University of Minnesota
Minneapolis, Minnesota

Daniel M. G. Raff
Wharton School
University of Pennsylvania
Philadelphia, Pennsylvania

Roger L. Ransom
Department of History
University of California
Riverside, California

Paul W. Rhode
Department of Economics
University of North Carolina
Chapel Hill, North Carolina

Eric W. Rise
Department of Sociology and Criminal
  Justice
University of Delaware
Newark, Delaware

Hugh Rockoff
Department of Economics
Rutgers University
New Brunswick, New Jersey

Joshua L. Rosenbloom
Department of Economics
University of Kansas
Lawrence, Kansas

Peter L. Rousseau
Department of Economics
Vanderbilt University
Nashville, Tennessee

Steven Ruggles
Minnesota Population Center
University of Minnesota
Minneapolis, Minnesota

C. Matthew Snipp
Department of Sociology
Stanford University
Stanford, California

Kenneth A. Snowden
Department of Economics
University of North Carolina
Greensboro, North Carolina

Matthew Sobek
Center for Social and Economic
  Policy
University of California
Riverside, California

Richard H. Steckel
Departments of Economics and
  Anthropology
Ohio State University
Columbus, Ohio

Daniel A. Sumner
Department of Agricultural and Resource
  Economics
University of California
Davis, California

William A. Sundstrom
Department of Economics
Santa Clara University
Santa Clara, California

Richard Sutch
Department of Economics
University of California
Riverside, California

Richard Sylla
Department of Economics
New York University
New York, New York

Ben Tausig
Department of History
University of Michigan
Ann Arbor, Michigan

Melissa A. Thomasson
Department of Economics
Miami University
Oxford, Ohio

John Joseph Wallis
Department of Economics
University of Maryland
College Park, Maryland

David F. Weiman
Department of Economics
Barnard College, Columbia University
New York, New York

Thomas Weiss
Department of Economics
University of Kansas
Lawrence, Kansas

David C. Wheelock
Federal Reserve Bank of St. Louis
St. Louis, Missouri

Eugene N. White
Department of Economics
Rutgers University
New Brunswick, New Jersey

Elizabeth Wildsmith
Department of Sociology
University of Texas
Austin, Texas

Christie S. Wilson
Department of History
St. Edward's University
Austin, Texas

Gavin Wright
Department of Economics
Stanford University
Stanford, California

Stephen T. Ziliak
School of Policy Studies
Roosevelt University
Chicago, Illinois

SUPPORT FOR THE MILLENNIAL EDITION

With the cooperation of the U.S. Bureau of the Census:
Martha Farnsworth Riche, Director (1994–1998)
Kenneth Prewitt, Director (1998–2001)
John Haltiwanger, Chief Economist (1998–2001)
Glenn W. King, Chief, Statistical Compendium Staff

With the initial support of:
University of California – Berkeley, Davis, and Riverside
University of California, Office of the President
Cambridge University Press
Colgate University
Alfred P. Sloan Foundation
Stanford University and Stanford Libraries

With continuing support from:
U.S. National Science Foundation
University of California, All-UC Group in Economic History
University of California, Office of the President
University of California, Riverside, Center for Social and Economic Policy

With additional support from:
U.S. Department of Agriculture
American Association of Fundraising Counsel Trust for Philanthropy
American Council of Learned Societies
American Philosophical Society
University of Arizona:
   College of Business and Public Administration
   Department of Economics
Aspen Institute, Nonprofit Sector Research Fund
Bibliographical Society of America and the Bibliographical Society of Great Britain
Bowling Green State University, Office of Sponsored Programs
British Library
University of California, Berkeley:
   Center for Real Estate and Urban Economics
   Institute for Business and Economic Research
University of California, Davis:
   Agricultural Issues Center
   Department of Agricultural and Resource Economics
   Division of Social Science
   Institute of Governmental Affairs
University of California, Riverside:
   Center for Social and Behavioral Science Research
   College of Humanities, Arts, and Sciences
University of California, San Diego, Institute for Global Conflict and Cooperation
University of California, Washington, D.C. Center
California Institute of Technology, Division of Humanities and Social Sciences
University of Cambridge, Girton College
University of Canterbury, New Zealand, Department of Political Science
Farm Foundation
Federal Reserve Bank of St. Louis
The Ford Foundation
The Fulbright Foundation
John Simon Guggenheim Memorial Foundation
Ewing Halsell Foundation
Harvard University, Hauser Center for Nonprofit Organizations

International Centre for Economic Research, Turin, Italy
University of Iowa, Department of Political Science
Robert Wood Johnson Foundation
University of Kansas, Department of Economics
Leverhulme Trust of Great Britain
Lilly Endowment, Incorporated
University of London, Institute of United States Studies
University of Minnesota, Minnesota Population Center
National Endowment for the Humanities
National Institute of Aging
National Institute of Child Health and Human Development
National Institutes of Health
North Carolina State University:
   College of Agriculture and Life Sciences
   College of Management
University of North Carolina, Greensboro, Joseph M. Bryan School of Business and Economics
Northwestern University:
   University Research Grants Committee
   Weinberg College of Arts and Sciences
University of Pennsylvania, Wharton School:
   Huntsman Emerging Technologies Management Research Program
   Jones Center for Management Policy, Strategy, and Organization
   Mack Center for Technological Innovation
Rockefeller Center
Russell Sage Foundation
Rutgers University, Department of Economics
Saint Mary's College of California
Santa Clara University, Leavey School of Business
The Spencer Foundation
Stanford University, Office of Technology Licensing
Trinity University
Wellesley College
Winthrop University
Yale University:
   Institution for Social and Policy Studies
   Program on Non-Profit Organizations

RESEARCH ASSISTANCE FOR THE MILLENNIAL EDITION

Historical Statistics Project Staff

Monica Barzak, Postdoctoral Research Fellow
Shelagh Mackay, Librarian

Research Assistants

Bethany Barratt
Kari Beardsley
Heidi Beyer
Mousumi Bhakta
Deepa Bhat
Lyda Bigelow
Simone Peart Boyce

Lisa Cappellari
Molly Cooper

Catherine V. DeLuca

Amanda Ebel
Jeannette Espinoza

Nicolas Fawzi

Alka Gandhi
Manu Gayatrinath
Thomas Geraghty

Nora Gordon
Bernard Gress
Courtney M. Grey
Sumi Gupta

Daniel Hallstrom

Faye Iosotaluno
Susana Iranzo
Kristine Ishii

Marina Jovanovic

Liam Kavanagh
Christopher Kingston
Randi Kirtman
Michael Koch
Nicolai Kuminoff

Michelle Lee
Juliette Levy

Xian Li
Max Lin

Andrea Macstrejuan
Astrid Marschatz
Mishuku Matsuda
Leslie Maulhardt
Christopher Meissner
Peter Meyer
Raymond Mikus
Erin Mooney
Bernadette Moton
Antu Murshid

Sriniketh Nagavarapu
Victoria Nayak
Stephen James Noll

Laura Phillips
Michael Pisetsky

Susan Pozzanghera

Claudio Robles
Preeta Roy

Alicia Sasser
Phillip Schuler
Ritesh Shah
Slavi Trifonov Slavov
Patricia Sullivan

Min Min Thaw

Kavita Vashi

William White
Janine L. F. Wilson
Kwok-Chung Wong
Lee Wright

Luning Yu

Jian Zhang

CONSULTANTS TO THE MILLENNIAL EDITION

Alan Abramson
Rikki Abzug
Jeffrey Adler
Dauril Alden
Margo Anderson
Walter Armbruster

Christopher L. Bach
Bernard Bailyn
Richard Beaumont
E. M. Beck
Robert A. Becker
Stephen D. Behrendt
Ira Berlin
Lisa Berlinger
Ann Bixby
Scott Blashek
Ruth Bloch
Christine Bose
Clair Brown
W. Fitzhugh Brundage
Richard Buel Jr.
Trevor G. Burnard

Henry Caplan
Caroline Carbaugh
David Card
George Carlson
Leonard A. Carlson
Jason Carr
Lois Green Carr
Cary Carson
James W. Chamberlin
John Whiteclay Chambers II
Joyce E. Chaplin
Mark Chaves
Barry Chiswick
John Church
Gregory Clark
Sally Clarke
Paul G. E. Clemens
Converse D. Clowse
Peter A. Coclanis
Sherry Compton
Nicholas F. R. Crafts
Barbara Craig

François M. Crouzet
Timothy Cuff
Louis Cullen
Carroll Curtis

Joe Dalaker
Elizabeth Dale
Paul A. David
K. G. Davies
Joseph Davis
Lance E. Davis
George Day
J. Bradford DeLong
Trevor Dick
Paul DiMaggio
Thomas M. Doerflinger
Alan Dye

Carville V. Earle
Richard A. Easterlin
Cheryl Eavey
Christopher R. Eck
Barry Edmonston
Marc M. Egnal
Barry Eichengreen
Howard Elitzak
David Eltis
Ken Erickson
Joseph A. Ernst
Karl Eschbach
Robert E. Evenson

Robert Fairlee
Daniel Feenberg
Bruce Fetter
Charles H. Fine
Roger Finke
Mike Finucan
Robert Flanagan
David J. Fleck
Robert William Fogel
Nancy Folbre
Daniel M. Fox

Louis Galambos
Joseph Galaskiewicz
David W. Galenson
Matthew Gallman

Robert E. Gallman
Gerald Gamm
Millicent Hall Gauderi
Roger Geiger
Henry A. Gemery
Campbell Gibson
Frances Goldscheider
Robert J. Gordon
Chris Grandy
Bradford Gray
Jack P. Greene
Steve Greer
Kirsten Gronbjerg
Farley Grubb

Stephen Haber
Alastair Hall
Gwendolyn Midlo Hall
Thomas D. Hall
Dan Hallstrom
John Haltiwanger
Daniel Hamermesh
Annette Hamilton
David C. Hammack
John Hammer
Janice H. Hammond
David J. Hancock
Henry Hansman
John Hanson
Stephen G. Hardy
Tamara Hareven
Charles Knickerbacher Harley
Lawrence A. Harper
P. M. G. Harris
William J. Hausman
John M. Hemphill II
Ruth Wallis Herndon
Josiah Heyman
Barry W. Higman
Barry T. Hirsch
Donna Hirsch
Ronald Hoffman
Dean Hoge
Paul Hohenberg
Mark Holliday
Caroline Hoxby

Marla Huddleston
Michael Hurd
Stephen Innes
Sanford M. Jacoby
Dwight Jaffee
Charles Janini
Michael J. Jarvis
Rupert C. Jarvis
Shelia Ryan Johansson
Louis Johnston
Warren Johnston
Alice Hanson Jones
Dwyryd W. Jones

Laura Croghan Kamoie
Shawn Kantor
Glenn W. King
Gary Kleck
Herbert Klein
Anne Knowles
Liesl Koch
John Komlos
Barbara Koostra
Allan L. Kulikoff

David Lamoreaux
Roger Lane
John Langbein
Jonathan Leonard
William Letwin
Kenneth Lipartito
Robert E. Lipsey
Leonard M. Lodish

David A. Macpherson
Gloria L. Main
Jackson T. Main
John Majewski
Peter C. Mancall
Kathleen Mangold
Gregory Mark
Phillip Martin
Peter Mathias
Cathy D. Matson
Charles R. Mayberry
Marvin McInnis
James McPherson

James Meier
Chris Meissner
William G. Melchior Jr.
Russell R. Menard
Ellen Merry
Peter Meyer
Ronald W. Michener
David Middaugh
Sally Milano
Annie M. Millard
Mark Miller
Robert Milton
Jeffrey A. Miron
Franco Modigliani
Carolyn Moehling
Eric Monkkonen
Alexander Moore
Georgina Moreno
Kenneth J. Morgan
Philip D. Morgan
Tom Mroz
John Murray
Antu Panini Murshid

Gary B. Nash
Robert C. Nash
Max Neiman
Margaret Ellen Newell
Daniel Newlon
Eric P. Newman
Andrea Norris
Douglass C. North

Patrick K. O'Brien

Paul F. Paskoff
Brad Patterson
Dan Peed
Marie Pees
John Pencavel
Edwin J. Perkins
Peter Philips
Thomas Pollak
Giulio Pontecorvo
Emie Portwood
Jacob M. Price
Robert D. Putnam

Wayne Rassmussen
David J. Reibstein
Jan Reiff
David Richardson
Gary Richardson
James C. Riley
Donna J. Rilling
Christine Rodriguez
Moises Rodriguez
Christina D. Romer
Adam Rose
Nathan Rosenberg
Nan A. Rosenbloom
Jean-Laurent Rosenthal
Elyce Rotella
Winifred B. Rothenberg
Mort Rothstein
Anne Royalty
J. Andrew Royle
Jean Elliott Russo

Anita H. Rutman
Darrett B. Rutman
Vernon Ruttan

Neal Salisbury
Walter J. Salmon
Kay Lehman Schlozman
Jürgen Schneider
Roger Schofield
Anna Schwartz
Stacy Schwartz
Stuart Schwartz
John E. Schwarz
Mary McKinney Schweitzer
Carole Shammas
William F. Shaw
James F. Shepherd
David Sicilia
John G. Simon
Theda Skocpol
Billy G. Smith
Bruce Smith
Daniel Scott Smith
George Smith
Hayden W. Smith
Marian Smith
Shirley Smith
Simon D. Smith
Eugene Smolensky
T. C. Smout
Tom Snyder
Jerome Stam
Roger Strickland

Joel Tarr
Dora Teimouri
Michael S. Teitelbaum
Peter Temin
Jeff Thomas
Russell Thornton
James Tippett
Stewart Tolnay
Clifford Trafzer
Werner Troesken
Thomas M. Truxes

Stephanie J. Ventura
Sidney Verba
Daniel F. Vickers

Christopher Waldrep
Lorena S. Walsh
Gary M. Walton
Michael Wells
Elmus Wicker
Jeffrey G. Williamson
Samuel Williamson
Sidney G. Winter
James Woodard
Robert E. Wright
Henry Wulf

Peter Xenos

Mary Yeager

Nuala B. Zahedieh
Aklilu Zegeye
David Zilberman

GUIDE TO THE MILLENNIAL EDITION

Monty Hindman and Richard Sutch

Editions and Copyright

Previous editions. This is the fourth edition of *Historical Statistics of the United States*. The U.S. Bureau of the Census published the prior editions in 1949, 1960, and 1975, the last known as the Bicentennial Edition. Cambridge University Press publishes this, the Millennial Edition, with the permission of the Census Bureau. Some of the data and table documentation presented here are used without explicit quotation, but with permission, from the earlier editions. The Census Bureau takes no responsibility for the design of this edition or the accuracy of its content, which rests solely with the contributors, the editors, and Cambridge University Press.

Electronic edition. This edition of *Historical Statistics of the United States* is available in electronic form from Cambridge University Press. A compact disk containing the Bicentennial Edition of *Historical Statistics of the United States* is also available from the Press.

Copyright. Permission to quote or reprint copyright material should be obtained directly from the copyright owner. Much of the data reproduced in this work were originally published by agencies of the U.S. government and are in the public domain. Generally speaking, original data that have been published elsewhere under copyright protection may be freely used for educational, scholarly, or journalistic purposes (but not commercial purposes) with proper citation to the original source under the fair use provision of U.S. copyright law. Cambridge University Press has made every effort to secure, where necessary, permission to reproduce protected material. In almost every case the permission requested was freely granted. In a few instances, however, the copyright owner requested a specific citation. These citations may be found in the listing of Copyright Citations at the end of Volume 5.

Data Revisions and Updates

Reproduction and revision of data from prior editions. Although this volume provides many data series from prior editions of *Historical Statistics of the United States*, users should be aware that some data from these editions have subsequently been revised. Our contributors sought to present the most recently available data, and thus users probably will wish to use the data presented here rather than that in previous editions. In some cases, data from the earlier editions were judged to be unreliable or obsolete and were not reproduced.

Data updates. The data series in *Historical Statistics of the United States* do not have a uniform end date; instead, each table reports the data available at the time the contributor compiled the data. Many series in these volumes are continued on a regular basis with periodic updates and revisions by the agency, group, or individual responsible for the original data. Figures for many of the current series are presented in the *Statistical Abstract of the United States*, published annually by the U.S. Bureau of the Census. The updating of industrial statistics will be complicated by the switch in 1997 from the Standard Industrial Classification (SIC) system to the North American Industrial Classification System (NAICS); see the Introduction to Part D.

Additional data. In many cases, additional data can be found in the source documents, in references mentioned in the table documentation or chapter essays, and through the Internet sites of the groups or agencies noted in the sources for the data presented here.

Errors. In a work as large as this, errors of both commission and omission are likely to have occurred. Users who discover errors are urged to communicate them to Cambridge University Press, 40 West 20th Street, New York, New York 10011-4211, USA.

Data Selection

General principles. The criteria for the selection of data to be included in this edition varied broadly, depending on the particular subject matter. Generally, summary measures or aggregates at gross levels and immediately below were given highest priority for inclusion. Below such levels, selection was governed by the interplay of the following: the amount of space already devoted to a particular subject; the attempt to achieve a relatively balanced presentation among subject fields; whether other data already covered a particular topic; the quantity and quality of the data available; and the extent to which the data might enhance the value of other material in the book. During the early phases of the project these selection criteria were conveyed to our contributors, upon whose judgment we ultimately relied.

Data reliability. Our contributors have attempted to select data that they consider to be generally reliable and to reproduce faithfully the data reported in their sources. They have also provided citations and technical descriptions to assist users in making independent assessments of both the data's reliability and their suitability for a project at hand.

Original versus derived data. Primary emphasis was placed on the presentation of original, unmodified figures rather than derived data because they offer greater flexibility to users. Derived data – for example, averages, percentages, ratios, and index numbers – were provided if they were the accepted standard for presentation (for example, unemployment rates), if the table contributor judged that the derived data would be particularly helpful, or if the use of derived data saved a significant amount of space.

Topical coverage. Because the last thirty years have witnessed the expansion of data collection into areas that were only inadequately covered, if at all, in the 1970s, this edition has a broader topical scope than its predecessors. A tentative list of topics emerged after extensive discussions between the project's editors in chief and Cambridge University Press. The outline was widely circulated to scholars, reference librarians, and government statistical bureaus. After a revision of that outline, the project recruited contributors, who offered additional suggestions. What emerged from this process was an outline for the project that was both designed by the profession and feasible to accomplish.

Temporal coverage. Contributors were asked to take the data series under their charge as far backward and forward in time as possible. They were also encouraged to include important lapsed series – those that begin and terminate in the past – because such series are sometimes available only in out-of-print documents. Most data series in *Historical Statistics of the United States* provide annual or decennial data spanning at least twenty years, with the main exceptions being for special topics (the colonial period and the Confederate States of America), for newly developed series providing the only data available to represent an important subject field, and for short series that served as important extensions of longer series.

Data frequency. Annual data were given preference for inclusion, but certain series are presented only for years in which a national census was conducted and, in some instances, only for scattered dates, as dictated by data availability. When both annual figures and benchmark data exist, both series are sometimes shown. A major exception was made for Chapter Cb, which presents many of its series on a monthly or quarterly basis. Although this volume mainly provides annual data, underlying data are sometimes available more frequently from the original sources.

Geographical coverage. The data in *Historical Statistics of the United States* generally cover the nation as a whole, defined by the recognized borders of the country for the year in question. As new states were admitted to the Union, the coverage of the typical statistical series in this volume expands to include the new additions, without any special notation in the table documentation. The documentation should be consulted to determine if such changes in the boundaries of the United States are likely to have affected the series. When the year of a state's inclusion in a series differs significantly from its year of statehood, this fact was noted in the documentation whenever possible. Refer to Appendix 2 for the dates of statehood.

Subnational data. Because of limitations of space, data are generally not shown for regions, states, or localities. The underlying sources sometimes provide data in finer geographical detail than shown here. Some tables provide data for U.S. census regions or divisions; see Appendix 2 for more information on such regional classifications.

Outlying areas. In almost all cases, outlying areas are not included in the national totals reported here. Refer to Chapter Ef for additional information on such areas.

Organization of the Volume

Arrangement of the data. In this edition of *Historical Statistics of the United States,* data are arranged by broad subjects in five parts, each published in a separate volume and each volume containing several chapters. The tables in most chapters are further organized into various subsections (see the Detailed Table of Contents in each volume).

Essays. Each chapter is introduced by one or more essays that provide a general guide to the data, the sources, and the historical trends that have been emphasized in the scholarly literature. They contain a list of references that may be consulted by those interested in more detail.

Series identifiers. Each data series is assigned a unique alphanumeric identifier. The two letters in the identifier indicate the chapter in which the series resides. Within a chapter, series are numbered sequentially. Sets of contiguous series are identified by means of a series range (for example, series Da42–47). Source citations and table documentation are linked to the data series by means of such identifiers, which may be preferred over page numbers for use in reference citations.

Table identifiers. An entire table is identified by the range of series that it contains. For example, the first two tables in the chapter on vital statistics contain ten and twenty series, respectively; thus, they are identified as Table Ab1–10 and Table Ab11–30. Similarly, a group of contiguous tables is identified by a series range. Using the same example, these two tables could be referred to jointly as Tables Ab1–30.

Table Documentation

Table contributors. Each table provides the names of the contributors who selected, collected, and described the data. The editorial staff also reviewed the data and table documentation for accuracy, completeness, and clarity of presentation.

Sources. In most cases, full citations are given for data sources; however, when numerous issues of a publication were used, the source citations are usually limited to "annual issues" or similar notations. When data are reproduced from the Bicentennial Edition, the source citation lists the original source rather than the Bicentennial Edition, except under special circumstances.

Unpublished data. Nearly all the data reported here have been previously published or accepted for publication. Rare exceptions for previously unpublished data were allowed if a contributor felt that the data were particularly important and if peer review accepted the data for inclusion.

Integrated Public Use Microdata Series. A number of series reported in this edition are extracted from the Integrated Public Use Microdata Series (IPUMS). The IPUMS is composed of representative samples drawn from the returns of the decennial censuses of the population. All censuses from 1850 to 1990 are included, with the exception of 1930, which is under development, and 1890, the manuscripts for which were destroyed by fire. The IPUMS data and documentation are available over the Internet.*

Internet sources. Some data series in *Historical Statistics of the United States* are based on electronic sources; however, owing to the fleeting nature of specific Internet addresses or Web-based

---

* Steven Ruggles, Matthew Sobek, et al., *Integrated Public Use Microdata Series: Version 2.0* (Historical Census Projects, University of Minnesota, 1997).

file names, we do not use them when identifying sources. Instead, we use more general phrasing to direct users to the Internet source.

Table documentation. Most tables are accompanied by documentation defining relevant terms and concepts, providing methodological and historical background, noting unusual values or comparability issues, explaining methods used to calculate derived data, and providing references to sources containing more detailed data or more extensive discussion. Unlike prior editions, which consolidated table documentation at the beginning of chapters, this edition locates the documentation with the tables, the intent being to increase its visibility, convenience, and thus use. Many tables are fully self-documenting, without cross references to other parts of this work; however, when cross references to other tables or essays are provided, the user is encouraged to follow those references.

Footnotes. There is no sharp demarcation between the type of information conveyed in the ordinary table documentation and that conveyed in the footnotes. Roughly speaking, footnotes are used for two purposes: to draw attention to issues of particular importance (footnotes as warnings) or to comment on matters related to specific columns, rows, or cells in a table.

Footnote order. Within a table, footnotes are numbered sequentially as follows: first the general footnotes that apply to the entire table; then left-to-right across the table header (the footnotes governing specific series); and finally footnotes attached to the table stub and the data area, proceeding in top-to-bottom, then left-to-right fashion (as used here, the directional terms apply to tables with standard page orientation). A footnote's first appearance within a table determines its position within the sequential numbering.

Total and subtotals. In most cases, a table's header structure will clearly indicate the total–subtotal relationships among the series. The typical practice in this volume is to provide the total series first, followed by its components. Often the sum of the components will equal the total, perhaps with small deviations attributable to rounding or other causes; however, sometimes the breakdowns provided in a table are not exhaustive, and the components will add to an amount less than the total. Users should consult the table documentation and exercise caution in this regard.

Race and ethnicity. Many tables provide disaggregations by race or ethnicity. This volume typically uses the terms "white," "black," "Asian" (or "Asian American"), "Indian" (or "Amerindian" or "Native American"), and "Hispanic." Note that a person identified as Hispanic may be of any race. See the essay on definitions and measurement of race and ethnicity in the Introduction to Part A for a discussion of racial classification and identification as it applies to the collection of historical statistics in the United States.

Dates

Date ranges. Throughout the table documentation and the chapter essays, date ranges are inclusive: for example, 1964–1987 includes both 1964 and 1987.

Year of record. The identification of the year of record – in other words, the precise meaning of the years shown in a table stub – was complicated by the failure of some sources to state whether the data were prepared on a calendar year, fiscal year, or some other basis; by changes in the year of record over time; and, in some instances, by imprecision or silence in the source concerning the beginning or ending date for the year of record. Table contributors

attempted to clarify such matters, but ambiguity remains in some tables.

Transition quarters. Sometimes the year of record changes in the middle of a table, and values are provided for the "transition quarter" – the gap between the end of the old year of record and beginning of the new. In such cases, users will see a (TQ) designation in the table stub. Nearly all transition quarters in this volume are associated with the year 1976, when the federal government changed the end of its fiscal year from June 30 to September 30. In rare cases, the (TQ) designation will be for a transition period that is not actually a quarter, but some other fraction of a year.

Units, Measures, and Monetary Values

Units of measure. Series are usually expressed in the units reported in the original source. In some cases, however, units were converted to make two or more data series comparable, or to create a single series when splicing data from multiple sources. The approach taken in these volumes was to restrict the units information to true *measures* and to rely on the table title and layered headers to convey other details about the things being counted or measured. Sometimes series are expressed in units too complex for pithy statement; in these rare cases, a generic unit of measure is given, with further elaboration left to the table documentation.

Billion and trillion. The American and Canadian definitions of billion (10^9) and trillion (10^{12}) are used throughout, not the definitions used in England, Germany, and many other countries.

Index numbers. Some series are expressed in terms of index numbers. In such cases, the base period of the index is provided where the unit of measure would normally be found. For a discussion of index numbers, see the essay on prices and price indexes in Chapter Cc and the essay on national income and product in Chapter Ca.

Weights and measures. Most data series are expressed in American units (the U.S. Customary System) rather than metric units (the International System). For a discussion of these two systems and for conversion information, see Appendix 1.

Monetary values. Unless otherwise noted, monetary values are expressed in current or nominal terms – in other words, the actual historical values (usually U.S. dollars), not adjusted for previous or subsequent changes in prices. This standard was adopted to avoid attaching the word "current" or "nominal" to every reference to a monetary unit. When monetary values have been adjusted in some fashion, this is stated explicitly and the relevant base period is given. For a discussion of monetary values, see Appendix 1 and the essay on prices and price indexes in Chapter Cc.

Data Values

Data precision and significant digits. In making decisions regarding the precision with which data values should be presented, fidelity to sources was our primary consideration. Thus, the underlying data files for *Historical Statistics of the United States* – available in the electronic edition – retain the full precision provided by table contributors, even though this level of detail might be deemed excessive by scientific standards for the reporting of significant digits. In most cases, the detail comes straight from the sources themselves; therefore, exact reproduction provides a valuable check for researchers wanting to trace the provenance of a number or hunt down an anomaly. In other cases, excessive precision comes from spreadsheet calculations made by table contributors (for example, in the computation of derived data). Here, too, we did not impose our judgments concerning the appropriate precision and instead retained the full detail provided by contributors. Users should note that historical sources sometimes change the precision with which they report data over time. Also, some tables contain series reported in the sources at different levels of detail but that, for ease of comparison, are provided here in consistent units. The usual indication of varying precision – whether in a single series or across multiple series within a table – is a run of data values with trailing zeros, either before or after the decimal point. In such cases, users will need to exercise judgment concerning the precision of the data.

Decimal precision for display purposes. While the underlying data files retain all of the detail provided by table contributors, the data displayed in the print edition of *Historical Statistics of the United States* are shown in rounded fashion, typically with no more than three digits following the decimal point. Similarly, tables generated for display purposes by the electronic edition are formatted using the same rounding conventions; however, the underlying files available for downloading provide the values at full precision.

Zero values and (Z). A zero in a data series means exactly that: a reported value of zero. In some cases, an underlying data value may be so small that it rounds to zero when displayed at the level of decimal precision chosen for the series. In such cases, a (Z) marker is used rather than a zero value. Stated more precisely, the (Z) notation indicates a *nonzero value that is not shown or possibly not known*. In the former case – a nonzero value not shown – (Z) means that the value falls below the threshold of our rounding convention: the number rounds to zero, as displayed in this volume (full precision for such values is available through the electronic edition). In the latter case – a nonzero value not known – (Z) means that the original source did not provide a specific value. Owing to these complexities, the meaning of the (Z) marker is specifically documented in every table that uses the device.

Dash as a data value. The "—" marker means that a value is not being reported. There are several possible reasons: the data are not available anywhere; the data were not provided in the source but conceivably could be found with sufficient research; the data were available in the source but the table contributor decided that they should not be reported (for example, unreliable data); or the data might conceivably be reported as a zero, but the table contributor decided for conceptual reasons to represent it as "no value reported" (for example, if a category or program covered by the series did not yet exist). Some sources do not carefully distinguish between zero values and missing data. Table contributors attempted to eliminate such confusion, but in some cases the "—" marker could mean that the value, if shown, would be zero.

Historical Statistics
of the
United States

Millennial Edition
Volume 1

Part A
Population

Introduction

POPULATION CHANGE

Michael R. Haines and Richard Sutch

The most basic historical statistic about any country is its "national population." The national population as defined by the U.S. Census Bureau is the resident population of the country including noncitizens who are permanent residents and, during major foreign wars, the armed forces abroad. For the nineteenth century and through to 1912, it is conventional to include the population of territorial possessions that would eventually become part of the forty-eight contiguous states. The populations of Hawai'i and Alaska are traditionally included only after their admission to statehood in 1959 (see Table Ap-E in Appendix 2). The national population excludes the population of outlying areas of the United States such as Puerto Rico.

The national population is counted only once every ten years at the constitutionally mandated decennial census (see Article I, Section 2 of the U.S. Constitution). The first such census was conducted in 1790, and it has been repeated each decade since then. See series Aa2 for the enumerated populations at each census. The U.S. Bureau of the Census has made estimates of the national population for the intervening years using linear interpolation for the period 1790–1900. First, the census data were adjusted to put the population in the census year at its level on July 1. Next, a constant numerical increase in each year is calculated to exactly connect the populations at two adjacent census dates. These annual increases are used to estimate the population on July 1 for each of the intervening years. If these data were plotted on a graph, a straight line would connect each census date figure.

For the period 1900–1930, the Census Bureau made intercensal interpolations by a more eclectic and complicated interpolation procedure that exploited detailed data on the age, sex, and racial breakdown of the population at each of the four censuses conducted during that period. Since 1930, the annual interpolations have been made by the components of change method described next.

Population Change

As a mathematical proposition, the population one year from now is equal to the population today plus the births that occur over the course of the year, minus the deaths, plus net immigration from abroad. Net immigration is calculated as the number of immigrants who arrived during the year less the number of departures. In its simplest realization, the components of change method begins with a national census count. It then derives annual estimates of the change in the population in the succeeding year by summing the three components of change: births, deaths (a negative number), and net immigration (positive or negative). Birth and death statistics are taken from vital records, and estimates of net immigration are based on administrative data collected (for the most part) by the U.S. Immigration and Naturalization Service.

After ten successive calculations, the next census date is reached. If all of the data were perfect – without error – then the effect of cumulating the components of change would bring the count to exactly the number enumerated at the second census. Perfect counts are unlikely, of course, and the population estimated by the components of change method usually will not exactly match the population enumerated at the second census. The difference between the actual enumerated population and the estimated population is called the "error of closure." This difference is attributable to some combination of errors in counting the components of change or incomplete or imperfect enumeration at the two censuses.

For this edition of *Historical Statistics of the United States* we have made new intercensal estimates of the national population for 1790–1900 using the components of change approach rather than the linear interpolations used in the previous editions. For the period 1900–1930, we have added the components of change and calculated an error of closure consistent with the official totals published by the Census Bureau. These are linked to the official census figures for the twentieth century. See Table Aa9–14 for the data and the description of these new estimates. Figure Pa-A plots the rate of net population change.

The unusually high values of the rate of population change for the 1840s were caused primarily by the influx of immigrants from Ireland escaping the devastation of the Irish potato famine. The unusually low value for 1918 is attributed to the high mortality during the influenza epidemic. The low values during the Great Depression of the 1930s are attributed by scholars to the reduction in fertility brought on by hardship and the net out-migration from the United States. The high levels of population change exhibited for the late 1940s and the 1950s reflect the postwar "baby boom."

All of the ingredients for making estimates of the population are to be found in Part A. The chapter on population characteristics (Chapter Aa) presents statistics on the size and composition of the population with detailed information by age, sex, race, marital status, nativity, and place of residence. The chapter on vital statistics (Chapter Ab) contains statistics on fertility and mortality, the two

Acknowledgments

Michael Haines and Richard Sutch thank Susan B. Carter and Nancy Folbre for advice.

The essay by Charles Hirschman, Richard Alba, and Reynolds Farley is an abbreviated and revised version of "The Meaning and Measurement of Race in the U.S. Census: Glimpses into the Future," *Demography* 37 (August 2000): 381–93. The authors gratefully acknowledge Susan Carter's advice and assistance in revising the article for publication in this volume.

FIGURE Pa-A   Rate of net population change: 1790–1999

Source

Series Aa10 as a percentage of series Aa9.

components of the natural increase of a population, and Chapter Ad, on international migration, presents data on immigration and emigration, the other two sources of national population change. Chapter Ac, on internal migration, presents information on movements of the population within the United States, which can be a significant element in the population growth (or decline) of a state or region of the country.

Completing Part A are three chapters that examine the characteristics of the population from different perspectives. Chapter Ae examines marriage, family composition, and living arrangements. Chapter Af presents data for population cohorts organized by year of birth. Finally, Chapter Ag presents the available data on American Indians, a unique segment of the American population.

Characteristics of the Population

The Millennial Edition of *Historical Statistics* is organized around functional categories rather than by the characteristics of the population. That fact, however, should not distract the user from the importance of the changing composition of the population. Although some would consider the population counts presented here rather dry information of interest only to demographers, in reality these counts are the starting place for examining almost any subject from an historical perspective. Particularly notable in this regard are the social and economic issues that revolve around race, ethnicity, and gender. Because of the importance of these issues, many of the tables in *Historical Statistics* report figures separately for men and women and for separate races, variously defined. We have no separate chapters on gender or race.[1] Nonetheless, these distinctions are so important that they require some discussion at the outset.

Table Pa-B provides a chronology of important events relating to race, ethnicity, and gender. The second essay in this introduction to Part A charts changes over time in the definition of race and ethnicity from the first federal census of 1790 to the present. The third essay describes the evolution of race and ethnic distinctions in American life as influenced by the institution of slavery, the

changing magnitude and character of immigration from abroad, internal migration, economic development, and other factors.

Gender is the other preeminent social category in American life. Because sex – the biological correlate of gender – is a key component of personal identification, gender identification is requested in almost all official records, including census counts, birth and death registers, school enrollment, and more. Many governmental agencies publish the data they collect in a format that is disaggregated by sex. The rich availability of these sex distinctions in the quantitative historical record makes it possible to illuminate the many differences in the experience of men and women both today and in times past. These gender differences are pronounced, and they cut across most aspects of life. Gender distinctions appear in virtually every chapter of *Historical Statistics*. The changing salience of gender in America is also the subject of a large scholarly literature. Important works of synthesis include Smuts (1959); Baxandall, Gordon, and Reverby (1976); Brownlee and Brownlee (1976); Cott (1977, 1987); Degler (1980); Kessler-Harris (1982); Woloch (1984); Jones (1985); Bergman (1986); Goldin (1990); Sklar and Dublin (1991); and Folbre (1994).

References

Baxandall, Rosalyn, Linda Gordon, and Susan Reverby, editors. 1976. *America's Working Women: A Documentary History – 1600 to the Present.* Vintage Books.

Bergman, Barbara R. 1986. *The Economic Emergence of Women.* Basic Books.

Brownlee, W. Elliot, and Mary M. Brownlee. 1976. *Women in the American Economy: A Documentary History, 1675 to 1929.* Yale University Press.

Cott, Nancy F. 1977. *The Bonds of Womanhood: "Woman's Sphere" in New England, 1750–1835.* Yale University Press.

Cott, Nancy F. 1987. *The Grounding of Modern Feminism.* Yale University Press.

Degler, Carl N. 1980. *At Odds: Women and the Family in America from the Revolution to the Present.* Oxford University Press.

Folbre, Nancy. 1994. *Who Pays for the Kids? Gender and the Structures of Constraint.* Routledge.

Goldin, Claudia. 1990. *Understanding the Gender Gap: An Economic History of American Women.* Oxford University Press.

Jones, Jacqueline. 1985. *Labor of Love, Labor of Sorrow: Black Women, Work, and the Family from Slavery to the Present.* Basic Books.

Kessler-Harris, Alice. 1982. *Out to Work: A History of Wage-Earning Women in the United States.* Oxford University Press.

Sklar, Katherine Kish, and Thomas Dublin, editors. 1991. *Women and Power in American History: A Reader.* Prentice Hall, 2002 [originally published in 1991].

Smuts, Robert W. 1959. *Women and Work in America.* Columbia University Press.

Woloch, Nancy. 1984. *Women and the American Experience.* Knopf.

RACE AND ETHNICITY: DEFINITIONS AND MEASUREMENT

Charles Hirschman with Richard Alba and Reynolds Farley

For 200 years, race has been a standard item in the decennial censuses of the United States. These official statistics on the population by race are displayed in Table Aa145–184. For much of this period, there was no popular debate and apparently no major problem in the

---

[1] Chapter Aa on population characteristics has a separate section on the Hispanic population and Chapter Ag is on American Indians. Hispanic origin or identification is not considered to be a race.

TABLE Pa-B   Important events in the history of race, ethnicity, and gender: 1619–2003

1619	The first slaves are imported into Jamestown, Virginia. They were treated as indentured servants and freed after a fixed period of service.
1637	Anne Hutchinson is expelled by Massachusetts Bay Colony for preaching to men.
1692	Witchcraft trials take place in Salem, Massachusetts.
1705	Virginia law defines slaves as real estate and allows slave owners to kill fugitive slaves.
1790	An act of Congress limits naturalization of immigrants to free whites.
1793	The Fugitive Slave Act is passed, making it illegal to give aid or comfort to runaway slaves.
1808	England and the United States prohibit engagement in the international slave trade.
1814	The first textile mill opens in Waltham, Massachusetts, and offers employment to young women.
1822	Denmark Vesey organizes a slave revolt in Charleston, South Carolina. The slaves are betrayed by an informer. Thirty-seven, including Vesey, are executed.
1830	Robert Dale Owen's *Moral Physiology* is the first tract on birth control to be published in America.
1831	Nat Turner leads a slave revolt that kills fifty-seven whites before the slaves are cut down by an overwhelming force.
1833	Oberlin College becomes the first college to open its doors to both blacks and whites, women as well as men.
1837	Mount Holyoke College is established as the first college for women.
1839	Mississippi becomes the first state to grant limited property rights to married women (largely involving control over slaves), but only with their husbands' permission.
1843	The nativistic Know-Nothing political movement founds the American Republican Party to combat foreign influences and to uphold American values. The party is disbanded after the presidential election of 1856.
1845	Massachusetts becomes the first state to recognize the right of married women to manage and otherwise control their own estates without their husbands' permission.
1845	The Great Irish Potato Famine (1845–1849) stimulates the immigration of large numbers of Irish to the United States.
1848	The first Women's Rights Convention takes place at Seneca Falls, New York.
1852	Harriet Beecher Stowe publishes *Uncle Tom's Cabin,* providing momentum to abolitionism.
1857	The U.S. Supreme Court rules in the *Dred Scott* decision that a black person is not entitled to citizenship rights.
1859	John Brown raids Harper's Ferry, Virginia, to obtain arms for slaves to help them fight for their freedom. He is hanged for treason.
1865	President Abraham Lincoln signs the Emancipation Proclamation, which frees slaves in territory under Confederate control as of January 1.
1865	Slavery is abolished in the United States by the ratification of the Thirteenth Amendment to the Constitution after the end of the Civil War.
1866	The Fourteenth Amendment to the Constitution (ratified in 1868) confers citizenship on emancipated slaves. The Civil Rights Act of 1866 grants citizenship to all native-born persons except Indians.
1868	Elizabeth Cady Stanton and Susan B. Anthony found the feminist newspaper *The Revolution.*
1870	The Fifteenth Amendment to the Constitution grants blacks the right to vote.
1870	The Naturalization Act of July 14, 1870, is enacted. It extends the naturalization laws to aliens of African nativity and to persons of African descent and overturns the 1790 restriction on the naturalization of nonwhites.
1873	The Comstock Law forbids sending birth control information and devices through the U.S. mail.
1882	The Chinese Exclusion Act of May 6, 1882, is enacted. It outlaws the immigration of Chinese laborers to the United States for a period of ten years, bars Chinese from naturalization, provides for the deportation of Chinese living illegally in the United States, and permits the entry of Chinese students, teachers, merchants, and tourists. The provisions of the Act are continued in a series of laws. The Act is repealed in 1943.
1889	Wyoming becomes the first state to give women the vote in state and municipal elections.
1890	The Second Morrill Land Grant Act becomes law. Congress institutes regular appropriations for the land-grant colleges; the "historically black" institutions were set up in response to the demands of this Act that nonwhite students be provided facilities.
1896	In *Plessy v. Ferguson,* the Supreme Court validates the separation of black and white pupils and establishes the "separate but equal" doctrine.
1906	The Naturalization Act of June 29, 1906, is enacted. It makes knowledge of the English language a requirement for naturalization.
1907	The United States and Japan sign the "Gentlemen's Agreement," according to which Japan agrees to halt the emigration of Japanese laborers to the United States and the United States agrees to end discrimination against Japanese nationals living in the United States. Later, the Quota Act of 1924 excludes immigration from Japan.
1908	In *Muller v. Oregon,* the Supreme Court upholds an Oregon law limiting women's workday to ten hours.
1909	W. E. B. DuBois founds the National Association for the Advancement of Colored People (NAACP) to fight for civil rights for blacks through legal action.
1909	Women shirtwaist dressmakers in New York stage a general strike, the "Uprising of the Twenty Thousand."
1911	Illinois passes the first "mothers' pension" law.
1915	Margaret Sanger coins the term "birth control."
1915	The "Great Migration" begins. Between 1900 and 1960, more than 4.8 million African Americans flee the South's oppressive conditions. The vast majority of these migrants settle in Northern cities such as Chicago, Cleveland, Detroit, Pittsburgh, and New York. Both world wars create greater economic opportunities for blacks in Northern-based industries as military demands for manufactured items coincide with wartime labor shortages.

(continued)

TABLE Pa-B   Important events in the history of race, ethnicity, and gender: 1619–2003   *Continued*

1920	Nicola Sacco and Bartolomeo Vanzetti, immigrant anarchists, are arrested for murder in a bungled robbery. After a long trial, they are executed in 1927. The case stirs xenophobic feeling among Americans.
1920	The Nineteenth Amendment to the Constitution, giving women the right to vote, is ratified.
1924	The Indian Citizenship Act gives Indians the right to vote.
1924	The Immigration Act of May 26, 1924, becomes law. It establishes the National Origins Quota System. In conjunction with the Immigration Act of 1917, it governs American immigration policy until 1952. This important law radically reduces the level of immigration to the United States and sets restrictive quotas on immigration by country of origin of the immigrants.
1930	State and municipal governments begin pressuring married women to leave civil service in order to provide more jobs for men at the onset of the Great Depression.
1930s	Mexican and Philippine repatriations. A large number of Mexican and Philippine agricultural laborers who migrated to the western United States to work in seasonal agriculture during the 1920s are unable to find work after the onset of the Great Depression. Strong anti-Mexican and anti-Filipino demonstrations by native-born whites prompt the federal government to pay the transportation costs to return these workers to their home countries.
1935	The Social Security Act, which provides the basis for public assistance to mothers with dependent children, is passed by Congress.
1942	Japanese internment begins. Approximately 110,000 Japanese and Japanese Americans, most of them U.S. citizens, are interned in relocation centers during World War II. Most remain in internment through December 1944.
1943	The Act of December 17, 1943, which in effect repeals the Chinese Exclusion Act of 1882, becomes law. China is an ally of the United States against Japan in World War II.
1943	A Fair Employment Practices Committee is established by the government to eliminate discrimination in war industries based on race, creed, or national origins. Women enter war industries in large numbers, and symbols such as "Rosie the Riveter" assert, "We can do it!" – women can do the jobs of men in the world of work.
1945	The Equal Pay Act is first introduced in Congress.
1948	President Harry S Truman ends segregation in the U.S. military.
1954	In *Brown v. Board of Education,* the Supreme Court holds unconstitutional the deliberate segregation of schools by law on account of race.
1955	The Montgomery bus boycott begins after Rosa Parks refuses to give up her seat to comply with racial segregation laws. The boycott is led by the Reverend Martin Luther King Jr. and continues for almost a year. It ends when the Supreme Court declares racial segregation on public transportation unconstitutional.
1957	U.S. Army troops are sent to Little Rock, Arkansas, to enforce the desegregation of public schools.
1959	During the Cuban revolution, thousands of Cubans fleeing the government of Fidel Castro are granted nonimmigrant visas and enter the United States. Many are later granted permanent resident status with the passage of the Act of November 2, 1966.
1960	The federal Food and Drug Administration approves the use of norethynodrel (Enovid) as an oral contraceptive.
1963	The Equal Pay Act, requiring equal pay for persons performing the same work, is passed by Congress.
1963	The University of Alabama is desegregated. After a long period of litigation, a major battle of the campaign to end racial segregation in American higher education takes place on the campus of the University of Alabama. In June 1963, the stalemate between the state and federal governments over the admission of two black students to the university ends when President Kennedy federalizes part of the Alabama National Guard and orders it to safeguard the students' entry into the university, by force if necessary.
1964	The Civil Rights Act of 1964 outlaws discrimination in employment or public accommodations on the basis of race or sex.
1965	The Voting Rights Act of 1965 nullifies state and local laws and practices, such as literacy tests, that prevent blacks and other minorities from voting. The Act authorizes federal examiners to register qualified voters.
1965	The Immigration and Nationality Act Amendments of October 3, 1965, abolish the National Origins Quota System of 1924, eliminating national origin, race, or ancestry as a basis for immigration to the United States, and establish the Preference System.
1965	A Connecticut law prohibiting married couples from using contraception is ruled unconstitutional.
1966	Farm workers led by Cesar Chavez join the AFL-CIO and march 300 miles from Delano to Sacramento to dramatize their grievances. The United Farm Workers–led boycott of grapes picked by nonunion workers involves more Americans than any previous consumer boycott.
1966	The National Organization of Women is founded.
1968	Martin Luther King Jr. is assassinated while in Memphis to support a sanitation workers' strike. A wave of civil unrest follows in many urban areas.
1969	The Stonewall Riots inaugurate the Gay and Lesbian Liberation movement.
1970	California passes the nation's first "no-fault" divorce law.
1970s	The formerly all-male Ivy League colleges and universities become coeducational.
1972	The Equal Rights Amendment (ERA) is approved by Congress. The amendment is not ratified.
1972	Title IX of the Educational Amendments Act of 1972 mandates equal resources for women and men in educational institutions receiving federal support.
1973	In *Roe v. Wade,* the Supreme Court loosens restrictions on abortion.
1975	The Indochina Migration and Refugee Assistance Act of May 23, 1975, establishes a program of domestic resettlement assistance for refugees from Cambodia and Vietnam. Laotians are made eligible the following year.

TABLE Pa-B   Important events in the history of race, ethnicity, and gender: 1619–2003 *Continued*

1978	The United States agrees to admit 47,000 "Boat People" fleeing Vietnam and Cambodia.
1978	In *University of California Regents v. Bakke,* the Supreme Court rules that the University of California, Davis, medical school discriminated against Allan Bakke, a white applicant, by maintaining a quota for minority admissions. The court holds, however, that race can be one of the factors considered in university admissions decisions.
1980	The United States agrees to admit approximately 125,000 Cubans fleeing Castro's Cuba in the Mariel Boat Lift.
1982	The ERA fails to achieve ratification by the states within the prescribed time period.
1986	The Immigration Reform and Control Act of 1986 (IRCA) becomes law. This comprehensive immigration legislation authorizes legalization for certain aliens who had resided in the United States in an unlawful status and increases employer sanctions and border enforcement.
1996	Changes in welfare rules impose strict time limits and work requirements.
1997	The Office of Management and Budget revises standard categories into five major racial groups (American Indian or Alaskan Native; Asian; black or African American; native Hawaiian or other Pacific Islander; and white) and two ethnic categories (Hispanic or Latino; and non-Hispanic, non-Latino).
2000	Individuals are allowed to self-identify with more than one race in the U.S. census.
2003	The Supreme Court upholds *Roe v. Wade.*
2003	In a case involving the University of Michigan Law School (*Grutter v. Bollinger*), the Supreme Court upholds the principle that race may be a factor in admissions decisions, under the rationale that there is a compelling state interest in racial diversity. However, in a separate case (*Gratz v. Bollinger*), the court rules against the University of Michigan's undergraduate admissions policy, particularly its use of a mechanical point system that failed to meet the requirement for individualized consideration of applicants, as laid out in the court's 1978 *Bakke* decision.

measurement of race – either for those in charge of collecting government statistics or for those who responded to census inquiries. It is likely that at least some problems arose in assigning persons to specific racial categories. Some individuals probably felt that the race classification did not acknowledge their true identities, especially if they were of mixed ancestry or if their appearance did not meet stereotypical expectations (Forbes 1990). Indeed, some persons "passed" from one racial identity to another as a means of individual social mobility (Myrdal 1944, pp. 129–30, 683–8). Nonetheless, the system worked in the sense that the categories used in the race question agreed with popular perceptions. As a consequence, the measurement of race in the census met with only minor challenges over this long period.

In spite of this seeming stability, the conceptual content and the meaning of race have undergone a sea change over time, and a new concept – that of ethnicity – has arisen (Glazer and Moynihan 1975; Anderson and Fienberg 1999). A hundred years ago, most people, including a significant share of intellectuals, thought of racial classifications as biological groups akin to species (Gould 1996; Lott 1998). Over the course of the twentieth century, however, both the scientific and the popular understandings of race shifted gradually. Today, races are generally defined as social categories (Omi and Winant 1994; Hollinger 1995).

Although the standard sociological approach was to apply the term "race" to distinctions based on people's appearance and the term "ethnicity" to distinctions based on culture or language (van den Berghe 1967), "ethnicity" came to be used increasingly as an inclusive term for all groups believed to share common descent. In a 1987 decision giving an Iraqi the right to sue under provisions of the Civil Rights Act of 1964, the Supreme Court ruled that ethnic groups could be considered races because of the historical meaning of these terms (*St. Francis College v. Al-Khazraji* 1987). Conventional and scientific usage of terms such as "race" and "ethnicity" will undoubtedly be subject to further change, as they have in the past, but "race" remains the term officially used in population censuses as well as in popular discourse.

The social science conception of race and ethnicity underlying contemporary census measurements has moved far from the popular beliefs that motivated the original inclusion of race (Cornell and Hartmann 1998). In 1790, at the time of the first census of the United States, race or color was assumed to be part of the natural order, with differential entitlements for citizenship and legal standing. The first naturalization law, passed in 1790, stipulated that only those who were "free and white" could become citizens (Heer 1996). The Constitution required that each enslaved individual be counted as 60 percent of a person to determine population and electoral apportionment. Indians who did not pay taxes were excluded altogether.

Toward the end of the nineteenth century, with the development of pseudoscientific social Darwinism, "race" became a defining category in Western thought (Harris 1968). At that time, race was equated with biologically based divisions among humans; these divisions, according to a view shared by many social scientists of the period, determined fundamental capacities, such as intelligence, of the members of different races. This view led to attempts, in the late nineteenth century, to gather more detailed racial data. Color had been added as a census classification in 1850, with the categories of white, black, and mulatto; in 1870, Chinese and (American) Indian were added. By 1890, the search for racial (that is, biological) precision led to census categories based on degrees of African ancestry (mulatto, quadroon, and octoroon). In 1900, categories included the proportion of "white blood" (none, $1/2$, $1/4$, $1/8$) for each enumerated Indian.[1]

In the 1930 Census, Mexicans were included as a category in the race classification. The stigmatizing effect of being listed as a nonwhite group in the census was understood clearly (the other groups were Negro, Indian, Chinese, Japanese, Filipino, Hindu, and

---

[1] The full text of census questionnaires is reproduced in U.S. Bureau of the Census (1973); for a review of the evolution of American censuses, see Anderson (1990).

Korean). Therefore, after protests by the Mexican-American community and the Mexican government, the Census Bureau agreed to discontinue the practice (Cortes 1980, p. 697).

Over the second half of the twentieth century, race came to be viewed widely as a social construction lacking a universal, inherent meaning (Nagel 1994; Omi and Winant 1994). The recognition that race is not a "natural" category whose meaning can be taken for granted has raised the issue of how best to measure race so as to capture its contemporary social significance. This issue also has become salient because of the growth in interracial marriage, especially after the Supreme Court invalidated the last state laws against miscegenation in 1967 (Sandefur 1986; Kalmijn 1993; Shinagawa and Pang 1996; Qian 1997). The increase in the number of mixed-race Americans has blurred what formerly were viewed as clear-cut boundaries separating major racial groups (Root 1992, 1996).

Questions about the measurement of race and ethnicity also have arisen because of the increasing politicization of racial and ethnic census data. Census data are widely used to measure social and economic problems; these are generally presented in terms of the numbers of persons affected, especially by racial and ethnic divisions. Moreover, census numbers show the potential size of a political constituency: in interethnic politics, increases in population numbers can be used to make a case for increased governmental attention, changes in electoral districts, and the allocation of resources.

In 1960, the census shifted to a self-enumeration format, in which respondents could specify their own race as they wished (Taeuber and Hansen 1966). Prior to this time, enumerators assigned individuals to racial categories. In most cases, these enumerators probably did not even ask respondents about their race because the racial characteristics were thought to be readily observable. With the new method of data collection, respondents could say how they wished to be identified. It is something of a surprise that the practical consequences of this fundamental change in measurement methods were minor. There was an increase in persons who reported themselves as American Indians (Eschbach 1993, 1995), and more persons checked the "other race" category because they thought their identity was not included in the list of races on the census questionnaire (Harrison and Bennett 1995). The overall patterns of racial composition, however, suggest that in 1960 most Americans identified themselves by race largely as census enumerators had classified them in earlier censuses.

Ethnic political mobilization was directly responsible for the addition of a separate census question on Hispanic identity, beginning in the 1970 Census, and for the separate listing of numerous Asian nationality groups under the race question (see Table Aa2189–2215) (Choldin 1986; U.S. Bureau of the Census 1990; Espiritu 1992, Chapter 5; Lott 1998). Hispanic origin has been conceptualized as an ethnic category independent of a person's racial classification. Administrative actions and popular understanding, however, have created a social position for Hispanics almost equivalent to that of one of the major racial categories. The result is a five-category racial and ethnic scheme that has been used widely to describe American society (non-Hispanic whites, non-Hispanic blacks, non-Hispanic Asians, non-Hispanic Indians, and Hispanics), and is characterized by the historian David Hollinger (1995) as the ethnoracial "pentagon." This five-category classification was formally created in 1977 in Statistical Directive 15 from the Office of Management and Budget (OMB) (Office of Management and Budget 1997a, Appendix 1). Although Hispanic origin and race

officially are independent classifications, the popular assumption is that virtually everyone can be fit into one, and only one, of these five OMB categories.

In the 1980 Census, a new question on ancestry (or ethnic origins) was added to supplement the data on race and Hispanic identity and to replace the question on parents' place of birth that had been asked since 1870 (for statistics on the native-born population of foreign parentage, by parents' country of origin, see Table Ad319–353). The richness of new data on race, Hispanic origin, and ancestry might have led to a greater understanding of the racial and ethnic roots of the American population; instead it created a crisis. Problems in measuring and interpreting information on race and ethnicity that had been obscured with limited data were now painfully evident (Levin and Farley 1982; Lieberson and Waters 1988; Alba 1990). Investigations found ambiguity and inconsistency across the various measures of race and ethnic classifications (Lieberson and Santi 1985; Farley 1991); studies of reliability were not encouraging (Johnson 1974).

The increase in marriages across racial and ethnic boundaries has contributed greatly to doubts about the use of race as an ascriptive category, that is, as a characteristic that is assigned to an individual in some official tabulation. The offspring of these unions do not fit neatly into the standard census categories (Xie and Goyette 1997). Examination of census data along the three dimensions of race, Hispanic origin, and ancestry shows a significant number of persons who are black and Hispanic, persons who are white (by race) and American Indian (by ancestry), and persons with other blended and mixed ethnic origins. Although the numbers are not so large as to change the findings based on the conventional ethnic comparisons, and although ad hoc rules can be devised to handle inconsistent cases (del Pinal 1992), a major flaw is evident in the conceptual framework of mutually exclusive and exhaustive racial and ethnic categories.

The underlying problems are evident in the contentious task of revising Statistical Directive 15, the set of OMB rules that defines racial and ethnic categories for government agencies' collection and presentation of data (Edmonston, Goldstein, and Lott 1996; Office of Management and Budget 1997a; Lott 1998). Members of some groups (for example, religious groups) do not find the primary source of their group identity in any of the census questions. A growing number of persons either do not answer the questions or write in that they are "American" (Lieberson and Waters 1993). Because classifications reflect a variety of criteria (physical appearance, language, treaty status, national or regional ancestry) that are determined solely by individual, subjective choice, it is not surprising that many persons find the census questions difficult to answer and that government agencies find the logic behind them difficult to explain (Perlmann 1997). The arrival of immigrants with mixed backgrounds, such as Afro-Dominicans, Spanish-speaking Filipinos, Chinese from Thailand, and Indians from Guatemala, further challenges the traditional classification system.

After deliberate study and efforts to bring stakeholders into the process, the OMB revised Statistical Directive 15 (Office of Management and Budget 1997b). There are now five major racial categories (American Indian or Alaskan Native; Asian; black or African American; native Hawaiian or other Pacific Islander – Filipinos and Samoans dominate this "other" group; and white) and two ethnic categories (Hispanic or Latino, and not Hispanic or Latino).

The greatest change in the government's classification of individuals by race took place in the 2000 Census, when persons were allowed for the first time to identify themselves as belonging to more than one race. This change in the measurement of race has occurred in a social and political climate very different from that of the past. Indeed, it is a direct response to the challenge from individuals and groups who wish the census to reflect more accurately the growing multiracial portion of the population (Statistics Canada and U.S. Bureau of the Census 1993; Wright 1994; Edmonston, Goldstein, and Lott 1996).

This change has created concern about the effects of the new inquiry on the country's racial composition. Some minority-group leaders believe that the new methods may reduce the number of persons identifying themselves as members of their respective groups. Statisticians and public officials fear that continuity in one of the most important series of census data will be disrupted and that data mandated for important public purposes, such as electoral redistricting, will shift in unexpected ways.

The preliminary results from the 2000 Census that are available to us as this edition of *Historical Statistics of the United States* is going to press suggest that none of these potentially important problems have materialized. Only 2.4 percent of the population claimed two or more races. Individuals who did so were highly concentrated geographically and racially.

Hawai'i led the nation, with 21.4 percent of the population claiming their origins from two or more races. Alaska and California were the distant second- and third-ranked states, with 5.4 and 4.7 percent of their populations, respectively. The sparsely populated fourth- and fifth-ranked states, Nevada, New Mexico, and Washington (two tied for fifth place), had only 3.8 and 3.6 percent of their populations claiming two or more races.

Multiple racial identities were highly concentrated among native peoples and Hispanics. 54.4 percent of native Hawaiians and other Pacific Islanders and 39.9 percent of American Indian and Alaska Natives reported two or more races. Hispanics accounted for 6.3 percent of the total population nationwide, yet their share of the population reporting two or more races was 32.6 percent.

An interesting statistic that portends change in the very near future in the United States has to do with reports of racial identity by age group. While only 1.9 percent of the population 18 years of age and older claimed two or more racial identities, more than double that percentage (4.0 percent) of those younger than 18 years of age did so. The proximate cause of this substantial change is the growing share of Hispanics in the population, for whom multiple racial identities are closer to the norm.

In conclusion, for the most part, the racial categorization of Americans that was established in 1790 remains a reasonably reliable guide to racial distinctions to the 2000 Census. In the near future, however, we can expect substantial changes in racial self-identification as marriage partnerships increasingly cross traditionally defined racial boundaries.

References

Alba, Richard. 1990. *Ethnic Identity: The Transformation of White America*. Yale University Press.

Anderson, Margo J. 1990. *The American Census: A Social History*. Yale University Press.

Anderson, Margo J., and Stephen E. Fienberg. 1999. *Who Counts? The Politics of Census-Taking in Contemporary America*. Russell Sage Foundation.

Choldin, Harvey M. 1986. "Statistics and Politics: The 'Hispanic Issue' in the 1980 Census." *Demography* 23: 403–18.

Cornell, Stephen, and Douglass Hartmann. 1998. *Ethnicity and Race: Making Identities in a Changing World*. Pine Forge Press.

Cortes, Carlos E. 1980. "Mexicans." In Stephan Thernstrom, editor. *The Harvard Encyclopedia of American Ethnic Groups*. Harvard University Press.

del Pinal, Jorge H. 1992. *Exploring Alternative Race–Ethnic Comparison Groups in Current Population Surveys. Current Population Reports*, Series P23-182. U.S. Bureau of the Census.

Edmonston, Barry, Joshua Goldstein, and Juanita T. Lott, editors. 1996. *Spotlight on Heterogeneity: The Federal Standards for Racial and Ethnic Classification: Summary of a Workshop*. National Academy Press.

Eschbach, Karl. 1993. "Changing Identification among American Indians and Alaskan Natives." *Demography* 30: 635–52.

Eschbach, Karl. 1995. "The Enduring and Vanishing American Indian." *Ethnic and Racial Studies* 18: 89–108.

Espiritu, Yen Le. 1992. *Asia American Panethnicity: Bridging Institutions and Identities*. Temple University Press.

Farley, Reynolds. 1991. "The New Census Question about Ancestry: What Did It Tell Us?" *Demography* 28: 411–30.

Forbes, Jack D. 1990. "The Manipulation of Race, Caste, and Identity: Classifying AfroAmericans, Native Americans, and Red-Black Peoples." *Journal of Ethnic Studies* 17: 1–51.

Glazer, Nathan, and Daniel Patrick Moynihan, editors. 1975. *Ethnicity: Theory and Experience*. Harvard University Press.

Gould, Stephen Jay. 1996. *The Mismeasure of Man*. Revised and expanded edition. Norton.

Harris, Marvin. 1968. "Race." In David L. Sills, editor. *International Encyclopedia of the Social Sciences*, volume 13. Free Press.

Harrison, Roderick J., and Claudette E. Bennett. 1995. "Racial and Ethnic Diversity." In Reynolds Farley, editor. *State of the Union: America in the 1990's*, volume 2, *Social Trends*. Russell Sage Foundation.

Heer, David. 1996. *Immigration in America's Future: Social Science Findings and the Policy Debate*. Westview.

Hollinger, David. 1995. *Postethnic America: Beyond Multiculturalism*. Basic Books.

Johnson, Charles E., Jr. 1974. "Consistency of Reporting of Ethnic Origin in the Current Population Survey." U.S. Bureau of the Census, Technical Paper number 31.

Kalmijn, Matthijs. 1993. "Trends in Black/White Intermarriage." *Social Forces* 72: 119–46.

Levin, Michael J., and Reynolds Farley. 1982. "Historical Comparability of Ethnic Designations in the United States." In *Proceedings of the American Statistical Association, 1982: Social Statistics Section*. American Statistical Association.

Lieberson, Stanley, and Lawrence Santi. 1985. "The Use of Nativity Data to Estimate Ethnic Characteristics and Patterns." *Social Science Research* 14: 31–46.

Lieberson, Stanley, and Mary C. Waters. 1988. *From Many Strands: Ethnic and Racial Groups in Contemporary America*. Russell Sage Foundation.

Lieberson, Stanley, and Mary C. Waters. 1993. "The Ethnic Responses of Whites: What Causes Their Instability, Simplification, and Inconsistency?" *Social Forces* 72: 421–50.

Lott, Juanita Tamago. 1998. *Asian Americans: From Racial Categories to Multiple Identities*. Altamira.

Myrdal, Gunnar. 1944. *An American Dilemma: The Negro Problem and Modern Democracy*. Harper & Row, 1962 [original edition 1944].

Nagel, Joane. 1994. "Constructing Ethnicity: Creating and Recreating Ethnic Identity and Culture." *Social Problems* 41: 152–76.

Office of Management and Budget. 1997a. "Recommendations from the Interagency Committee for the Review of the Race and Ethnic Standards to the Office of Management and Budget Concerning Changes to the Standards for the Classification of Federal Data on Race and Ethnicity." *Federal Register* 62 (131) (July 9): 36874–946.

Office of Management and Budget. 1997b. "Revisions to the Standards for the Classification of Federal Data on Race and Ethnicity." *Federal Register* 62 (210) (October 30): 58782–90.

Omi, Michael, and Howard Winant. 1994. *Racial Formation in the United States: From the 1960s to the 1990s*. 2nd edition. Routledge.

Perlmann, Joel. 1997. *Reflecting the Changing Face of America: Multiracials, Racial Classification, and American Intermarriage*. Jerome Levy Economics Institute of Bard College.

Qian, Zhenchao. 1997. "Breaking the Racial Barriers: Variants in Interracial Marriage between 1980 and 1990." *Demography* 34: 263–76.

Root, Maria P. P., editor. 1992. *Racially Mixed Peoples in America*. Sage.

Root, Maria P. P. 1996. *The Multiracial Experience: Racial Borders as the New Frontier*. Sage.

Sandefur, Gary D. 1986. "American Indian Intermarriage." *Social Science Research* 15: 347–71.

Shinagawa, Larry H., and Gin Yong Pang. 1996. "Asian American Panethnicity and Intermarriage." *Amerasia Journal* 22: 12–52.

St. Francis College v. Al-Khazraji. 1987. 481 U.S., 604.

Statistics Canada and U.S. Bureau of the Census. 1993. *Challenges of Measuring an Ethnic World: Science, Politics and Reality*. U.S. Government Printing Office.

Taeuber, Conrad, and Morris H. Hansen. 1966. "Self-Enumeration as a Census Method." *Demography* 3: 289–95.

U.S. Bureau of the Census. 1973. "Population and Housing Inquiries in the U.S. Decennial Censuses, 1790–1970." U.S. Bureau of the Census, Working Paper number 39.

U.S. Bureau of the Census. 1990. *Census of Population and Housing (1990), Content Determination Reports, 1990 CDR-6: Race and Ethnic Origin*. U.S. Government Printing Office.

van den Berghe, Pierre. 1967. *Race and Racism: A Comparative Perspective*. Wiley.

Wright, Lawrence. 1994. "One Drop of Blood." *New Yorker*, July 24, pp. 46–50.

Xie, Yu, and Kimberly Goyette. 1997. "The Racial Identification of Biracial Children with One Asian Parent: Evidence from the 1990 Census." *Social Forces* 76 (December): 547–70.

RACE AND ETHNICITY: POPULATION, VITAL PROCESSES, AND EDUCATION

Susan B. Carter, Michael R. Haines,
Richard Sutch, and Gavin Wright

At the beginning of the Republic, about four fifths of the population was white and one fifth black.[1] Most of the blacks at that time were slaves in the South. Importantly, people of no other race were enslaved in the United States at this time. For this reason, the presumptive status of blacks was enslaved. In 1820, the first census that distinguished slaves from free blacks, the free black population was 13 percent of the total black population. By 1860, this proportion had fallen to about 11 percent. The decline was largely due to the higher fertility of slaves relative to free blacks, but it also reflected the very low rate of manumissions.

The massive influx of European immigrants beginning in the 1840s caused the nonwhite share of the population to decline from about 20 percent in 1800 to just over 10 percent by 1930. Immigration from Asia began in the 1850s, but later was strictly limited, first by the Chinese Exclusion Act of 1882 and then by a series

---

[1] The racial and ethnic characteristics of the population and the impact of these characteristics on the growth and development of the American economy are subjects of a large scholarly literature. Key works of synthesis include Thompson and Welpton (1933); Taeuber and Taeuber (1958); Bean and Frisbee (1978); and Haines and Steckel (2000). Useful statistical compendia include Cummings (1918) and Smith and Horton (1995).

of additional laws that expanded the geographic areas in Asia to which exclusion applied. These exclusionary laws culminated in 1924 with the passage of the Quotas Act, which imposed strict numerical limitations on immigration and plugged the last loopholes on all immigration from the Eastern Hemisphere (see the essay in Chapter Ad). Following the adoption of this Quota System, the white share of the population remained stable at about 89 percent until the mid-1960s.

The ethnicity of the white population changed considerably during the period of mass immigration from the 1880s through the adoption of the Quota System in 1924. The geographic source of immigration shifted away from Northern and Western Europe toward Southern and Eastern Europe (Table Ad90–97). This produced a large shift in the country of origin of the foreign-born population. Thus in 1850, 59.7 percent of the foreign-born originated in the British Isles and only 0.4 percent from Southern and Eastern Europe. By 1920, the percentages were 15.6 and 40.7, respectively (Table Ad354–443).

In 1965, the Congress replaced the Quota System with a new set of immigration laws called the Preference System. The Preference System raised the limit on the number of immigrants and shifted the criterion of admission from country of origin to family reunification. The number of immigrants increased and, unexpectedly, the country of origin of immigrants shifted away from Europe toward Asia and Latin America (see the essay in Chapter Ad). These legal changes in immigration law were reflected in an increase in the Asian and Pacific Islander share of the population from less than 1 percent in 1960 to almost 3 percent by 1990 (Table Aa145–184).

American Indians are another nonwhite group that displayed unusually rapid growth during the last years of the twentieth century. The growth in their numbers is due almost exclusively to ethnic reidentification (see Chapter Ag).

The Hispanic population comprises various races and is considered an ethnic, not a racial, category. This population has grown at rates of from 4 to 6 percent per year in the decades since 1940. A great deal of that growth more recently has been from persons of Mexican origin, who now comprise 58 percent of the Hispanic-origin population. The other important components are those of Puerto Rican and Cuban origin (9.6 and 3.5 percent of the Hispanic population, respectively) and, recently, a rapidly growing representation from Central and South America, including individuals from non-Spanish-speaking backgrounds.

The growth of the Mexican American population was stimulated by a migrant agricultural labor program, which was developed during World War II and continued into the 1950s and 1960s. Data on those engaged in this work during the World War II years are not available, but the number participating in the 1950s and through 1964 is included in series Ad1022 and constitutes most of the nonimmigrants reported in that series. During the peak years of this Braceros Program in the late 1950s, almost a half million people entered the country annually under its auspices – more than the number who entered as immigrants from all countries during these years. At the conclusion of the Braceros Program in 1964, the annual flow of migrant agricultural labor became undocumented. By the mid-1980s, the undocumented population was so large as to prompt legislation that legalized the status of this group while at the same time implementing controls to slow the future stream of such workers (see the essay in Chapter Ad).

The growth of the Cuban American population can be traced to the passage of the Cuban Refugees Act of 1966. Fidel Castro's 1959 overthrow of the Cuban government produced a large number of Cuban refugees to the United States. The 1966 Act allowed Cuban refugees to adjust their status to permanent resident, but the shift in status was not automatic (for the numbers admitted under this program, see series Ad1000).

Puerto Rico is a self-governing commonwealth of the United States, and its citizens are American citizens who are free to enter and leave the United States proper as they please. (For the population of Puerto Rico, see series Aa100.) The movement of Puerto Ricans to the United States is thought to be a response to the relatively more favorable economic opportunities in the States. This population moves into and out of the United States on a regular basis.

Geographic Distribution

The geographic distribution of the population has a strong racial and ethnic character. At the time of the first census in 1790, more than 90 percent of all blacks (but only 40 percent of all whites) lived in the South.

The end of slavery did not immediately end this geographic concentration, as illiteracy, lack of savings, and racial violence made long-distance travel difficult and dangerous for ex-slaves (for evidence on these factors, see Tables Ae97–127, Bc793–797, Ec251–289, and Ec343–357). It wasn't until the boll weevil infestation – which began in the first decade of the twentieth century and which, over a fifteen-year period, ultimately destroyed much of the cotton crop – that large numbers of blacks began the "Great Migration" out of the South, mostly into Northern industrial cities (see Tables Ac1–42 and Ac206–413) (Ransom and Sutch 2001). At the end of that tumultuous half century of movement, there were no longer any black-majority states, as there had been in 1900, and this form of geographic concentration had become far less distinct. Beginning in the 1960s, many blacks living in the North and West migrated to the South. By the decade of the 1990s, net migration of blacks to the South was the predominate direction of the migration flow (see Table Ac206–413) (Wright 1986; Frey 2001).

The migration of blacks out of the South during the first part of the twentieth century had a profound effect on the rural–urban distribution of the races. In 1880, when statistics on urban residence by race first become available, blacks were only half as likely as whites to live in an urban environment (12.9 percent for blacks compared with 28.3 percent for whites). By 1950, the likelihood of urban residence was similar for whites and blacks (at about 43 percent), but then, following 1950, the black propensity for urban living grew so rapidly that by 1990 blacks were far more likely than whites to live in urban areas (87.2 percent versus 72.0 percent; see Table Aa776–823). This concentration of the black population in the urban centers occurred at a time when the white population and the better-paying jobs were moving to suburbia. A number of analysts point to this central-city concentration of blacks as a root of many of the social and economic difficulties that blacks experience today (Wilson 1987).

For immigrants, the key geographic distinctions have been urban living and, until the 1960s (which brought the large Cuban immigration), an avoidance of the South. When statistics on urban residence by nativity first become available in 1890, the percentage of the foreign-born living in cities (places of 2,500 persons or more) was almost double that for the native-born (61.4 versus 31.3 percent). In 1990, the latest year for which we have data, the foreign-born continue to outpace the native-born in urban living by a 30 percentage-point margin (see Table Ad707–710). The Hispanic population has an especially strong geographic concentration, with Mexicans in California and Texas, Cubans in Florida, and Puerto Ricans in New York. This geographic distinctiveness of the population distribution by race and ethnicity has had numerous implications for vital processes and for educational, employment, occupational, and income differentials that run along race and ethnic lines.

Fertility

Evidence on fertility by race is presented in Tables Ab40–117 and Ab315–346, which report the crude birth rate, the general fertility rate, the total fertility rate, and the census-based child–woman ratio (see the table documentation for definitions of these terms). These tables reveal two distinctive features of the demography of the early Republic. One is the high fertility of white women. As Table Ab40–51 shows, the crude birth rate is estimated at 55 per thousand in 1800, which implies a total fertility rate of about seven live births per woman in her reproductive lifetime. A second feature is the even higher fertility of the black population. Information for the black population becomes available in 1820 in the form of a child–woman ratio (Table Ab315–346) and in 1850 in the form of the crude birth rate and the total fertility rate (Tables Ab40–117). All of these fertility measures suggest that black women's fertility in the mid-nineteenth century was even higher than that of white women. In fact, these high rates are close to what demographers have calculated as "maximum" fertility for large heterogeneous populations.

Beginning in 1800, white fertility declined fairly steadily until the onset of the "baby boom" in the 1940s, while black fertility remained rather stable up to the Civil War. The standard explanation for the high level and the constancy over time of the black fertility rate emphasizes the financial incentives to slave owners for slave-breeding and the power of the slaveholder, even in such intimate matters as reproduction. Evidence suggests that slave owners implemented a variety of measures that enhanced the fertility of their female slaves and that they did so consciously in an effort to enhance their profits (Gutman and Sutch 1976).

The total fertility rate, shown in Table Ab52–117 and in Figure Pa-C, indicates that in 1880 the rate for blacks was more than 70 percent higher than that for whites. The two rates declined and converged until about 1920. Over the next forty years there was some widening of the racial gap in fertility to about one birth per woman by the end of the baby boom in the early 1960s. Since about 1960, the gap has once again begun to close, with much of the decline occurring in the 1990s. Some of the decline has come from declines in birth rates among very young black women. For instance, birth rates for black women aged 15–17 declined from 82.3 per 1,000 in 1990 to 56.8 in 1998, and from 152.9 to 126.8 for black women aged 18–19 (see series Ab88–89). There has been some decline in age-specific rates at older ages as well.

The comparative fertility of native- and foreign-born women is shown in Table Ad744–751. In 1900, when the first statistics become available, they reveal considerably higher fertility among the foreign-born (almost entirely white) population relative to that of native-born whites. The statistics in Table Ad744–751 show that the fertility of foreign-born women remained substantially higher than that of native-born white women throughout the period of

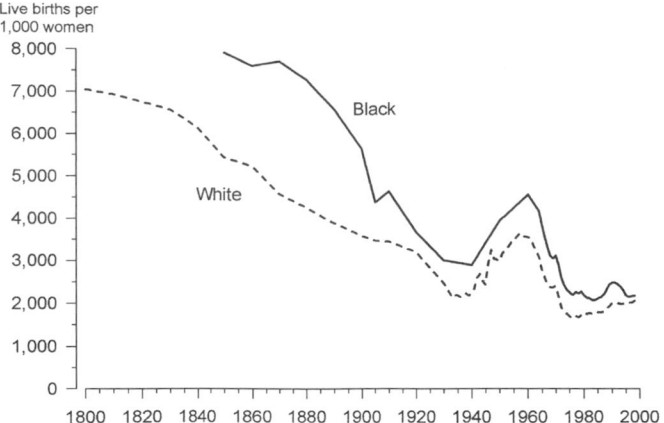

FIGURE Pa-C   Total fertility rate, by race: 1800–1998

Sources
Series Ab63 and Ab85.

mass migration around the turn of the twentieth century, although research by King and Ruggles reveals that the fertility of the second generation was considerably *below* that of other native-born whites (King and Ruggles 1990). During the period of severely restricted migration in the middle of the twentieth century, the fertility of the foreign-born was indistinguishable from that of native-born whites. The resumption of mass migration at the end of the twentieth century is associated with a slight rise in the relative fertility of the foreign-born.

Vital statistics for American Indian and Asian populations are available from 1980 onward; they are available from 1989 onward for the Hispanic-origin population. These statistics show initially higher fertility for these groups as compared with native-born whites, but more rapid rates of decline. This means that convergence between the fertility of these groups and the white population has been taking place. Indeed, the fertility of Asian and Pacific Islanders is now below that for the white population, and the fertility of the Hispanic-origin population is very close to that of non-Hispanic whites (see Table Ab40–51). Total fertility rates stabilized in the 1970s and began a slow increase to more than two births per woman (or 2,000 per 1,000 women) in the late 1990s. The increased representation of the somewhat higher-fertility Hispanic women in the white population was certainly playing some role. Simultaneously, the total fertility rates for black, American Indian, and Asian women declined a bit. Finally, the fertility of Hispanic-origin women has remained roughly stable since 1989.

It remains an open question why minorities should have different fertility from the non-Hispanic white population. We know that blacks, Hispanics, and the American Indian populations have lower incomes, less wealth, less stable employment, and less education on average than the majority white population. These factors are often associated with higher birth rates. But there is also the "minority group status hypothesis," which conjectures that minority groups strive to improve their status (Bean and Marcum 1978). This may be achieved using the labor of children, thus providing parents with an incentive for higher birth rates. A competing view holds that the desire to be upwardly mobile may spur more efforts to limit family size in order to conserve family resources and invest more human capital in each child. Thus, the predicted direction of the differential is unclear. The American case would seem to support the view that lower socioeconomic status has had the effect of raising fertility, but this effect is diminishing over time, as birth rates come close to replacement levels.

Mortality

In contrast to the trends in fertility, racial differences in mortality have not converged. Although there have been absolute improvements for both whites and blacks, the racial differential in mortality remained quite substantial at the end of the twentieth century. Indeed, some mortality measures display a *relative* growth in the racial differential over time. For example, while the difference between blacks and whites in the number of infant deaths per 1,000 live births has been reduced from 46 in 1910 to 8.3 in 1998, the relative situation has deteriorated. In 1910, black infant mortality was 42 percent higher than that for whites, whereas in 1998 it was 137 percent higher. The record for neonatal mortality and low-birth-weight infants is similar (Tables Ab912–927 and Bd688–693; Preston and Haines 1991, 1997; Haines 1998).

Maternal mortality for both whites and nonwhites also declined significantly over the first half of the twentieth century, with the absolute decline for nonwhites even greater than that for whites (see Table Ab912–927). Nonetheless, at the end of the twentieth century, maternal mortality was still more than three times higher in the black population than in the white population. Relative progress for blacks ended about 1960; since then the racial differential in rates shows no trend.

Table Ab644–655 demonstrates that overall mortality for blacks, as measured by the expectation of life at birth, was higher than that for whites throughout the period 1900 to 1998. Although real progress has been made, in 1998 black males still had an estimated life expectancy at birth that was 6.9 years below that for white males. Black females showed a deficit of 5.2 years. The racial difference in 1900 had been 8.1 and 7.4 years, respectively.

Table Ab952–987 provides data on age-adjusted death rates by race and sex from 1900 to 1998. The record indicates only modest progress for the African American population (the overwhelming share of the "other race" category until the 1950s). In 1998, the age-adjusted death rate for blacks was 53 percent higher than that for whites. Outcomes for the American Indian and Asian populations were better. Indeed, the younger populations of those groups did relatively well, with the rates for American Indians close to those for whites and the rates for Asians and Pacific Islanders substantially below those for the white population (58 percent of the rates for whites).

To some extent, racial differences in mortality appear to reflect racial differences in overall health. Blacks endure more "restricted activity," "bed-disability," and "work-loss" days per person than whites despite the fact that the black population is younger and the number of such days per person rises with age. For a fraction of the black population greater than that of the white population, chronic medical conditions mean a major limitation in some physical activity. Blacks are also more likely than whites to be afflicted with acute digestive conditions. The only areas where blacks appear to have a health advantage is in afflictions from acute infective and parasitic conditions and in acute respiratory conditions (Tables Bd694–1085).

Homicide accounts for another portion of the racial differential in mortality. Blacks are far more likely than whites to be victims of homicide (but not suicide). This is true despite the fact that blacks are less likely than whites to own firearms (Table Ec1139–1158).

The current mortality disadvantage of the black population is due in significant part to their low income and relatively poor coverage by health insurance (see Table Bd306–317). For example, the excess infant and maternal mortality of the black population could be largely prevented with proper health care.

Nuptiality

Relative racial and ethnic differentials in nuptiality are presented in Tables Ae481–506. The statistic in Table Ae481–488 is the median age at first marriage, defined here as the age at which half of the never-married population is older and half is younger. The statistic in Table Ae489–506 is the singulate mean age at marriage, an estimate of the mean number of years lived by a cohort before its first marriage. Both statistics are widely used indicators of age at first marriage.

These rates suggest a complex pattern of change in marriage behavior over the last two hundred years (see Figure Pa-D). From the mid-nineteenth century (and possibly earlier) the age at first marriage rose, as did the fraction of the population never marrying, with marriage age and nonmarriage among whites noticeably higher than among blacks. Over the first half of the twentieth century, marriages were increasingly at younger ages, and nonmarriage became less common for all groups, but especially for whites. In fact, the decline in the age of marriage for whites was so dramatic that by the mid-twentieth century, whites were marrying earlier than blacks and forgoing marriage less frequently. Then, beginning about 1960, age at marriage rose dramatically for all groups. By the end of the twentieth century, age at first marriage for all groups, but especially among blacks, were at all-time highs. Analysts explain this development in terms of improved employment opportunities for women, which made it possible for women to delay marriage if they wished. For the black population, scholars also cite the high and growing rate of incarceration of young black men, a situation that has left black women without eligible marriage partners (for racial differences in incarceration, see Tables Ae97–127 and Ec309–327, and Figure Pa-E).

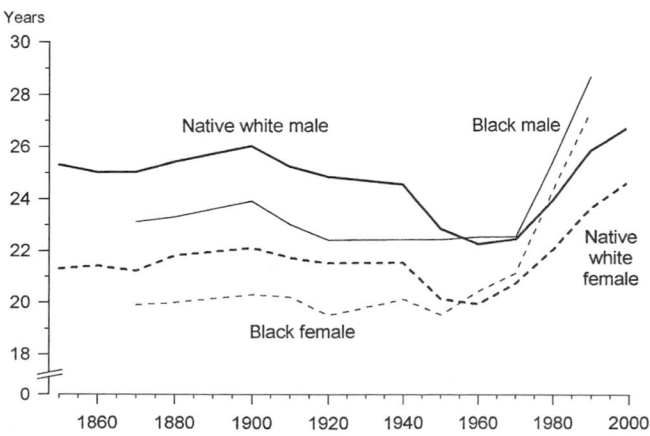

FIGURE Pa-D   Median age at first marriage, by sex and race: 1850–1999

Sources

Series Ae485–488.

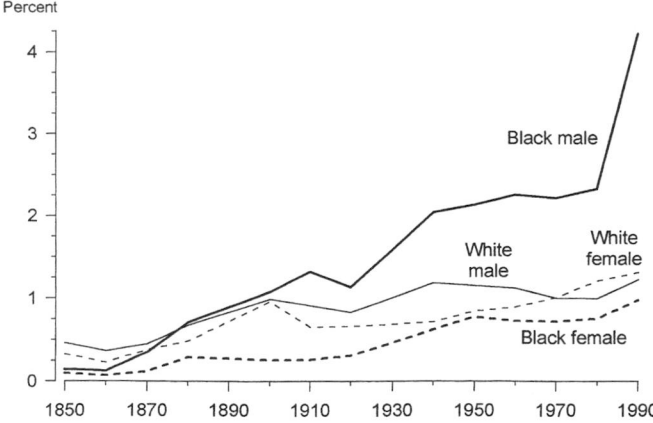

FIGURE Pa-E   Institutional inmates as a percentage of the population, by sex and race: 1850–1990

Sources

Series Ae106–107 expressed as a percentage of series Aa160–161, and series Ae112–113 expressed as a percentage of Aa173–174.

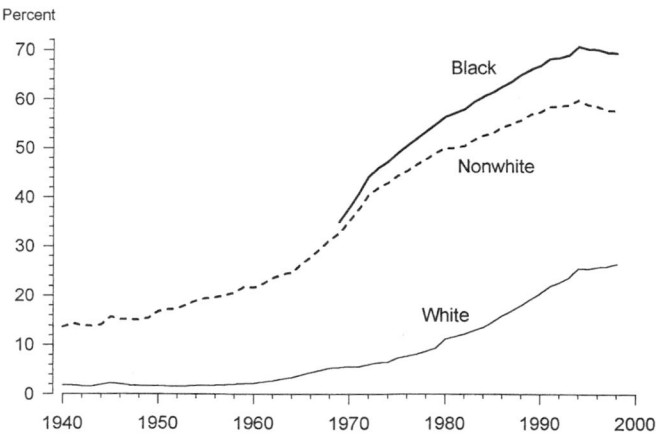

FIGURE Pa-F   Live births to unmarried women as a percentage of all live births, by race: 1940–1998

Sources

Series Ab274, Ab285, and Ab296, each as a percentage of series Ab12–14, respectively.

The recent increase in age at first marriage for whites and blacks has been associated with an increase in births to unmarried women and a marked widening of the gap between blacks and whites in this regard. By the late twentieth century, nearly 70 percent of all births among blacks were to unmarried women. This compares with 26 percent of births among whites (see Tables Ab11–30 and Ab264–305, and Figure Pa-F). This widening of the racial differential in the marital status of mothers has implications for racial differences in many aspects of the American economy and society. Perhaps the most important has to do with the experience of children. In recent years, only 33 percent of black children younger than five years of age have been living with both parents; the comparable figure for white children is 80 percent (Table Ae128–190). The overwhelming majority of these single-parent children live with their mothers. They are at much greater risk of poverty than are children who live in two-parent families. Female-headed households are almost six times more likely to be in poverty than are married-couple households (series Be298 and

Be300). The substantial increase in the proportion of black children living in households headed by women has contributed to the large and stable racial differential in children living in poverty (Table Be323–342). Despite the decline in poverty overall, the poverty of black children has remained high and stubbornly persistent over time.

Education

Educational opportunities differed greatly by race in nineteenth-century America. American whites enjoyed unusually high rates of schooling opportunities. Boys and girls, rich and poor, children of natives and children of foreigners, city dwellers and frontiersmen, all had access to schooling and did in fact attend. By the middle of the century, literacy was almost universal among whites. No other country in the world at the time could match this achievement. Schooling was less accessible in the rural South, yet even this region showed substantial progress in literacy among whites beginning in the 1840s (see Table Bc793–797, the essay in Chapter Bc, and Fishlow 1966).

By contrast, literacy was rare in the black population. This was because approximately 90 percent of the black population was enslaved, and in most slave states masters were forbidden to educate their slaves. Despite this obstacle, a few slaves managed to learn to read and write. We know, for example, that Nat Turner, the leader of a famous slave revolt in Virginia in 1831, was literate (see Table Bb252–254). But such individuals were rare (Bullock 1970). Roger Ransom and Richard Sutch estimate that on the eve of the Civil War, illiteracy was practically universal among slaves in the countryside and no more than 2–5 percent of urban slaves could read and write (Ransom and Sutch 2001, p. 15).

Education emerged as one of the foremost goals of the newly emancipated freedmen, and it is remarkable how successful they were in achieving it. From an estimated level of 80 percent of the black population illiterate in 1870, the rate dropped to less than half (44.2 percent) by 1900 (Table Bc793–797). This improvement was achieved through a variety of strategies. One was the educational commitment of black parents who withdrew children and mothers from field labor to allow them time to devote to education (Tables Ba11–24 and Ba50–63) (Ransom and Sutch 2001). Others were the establishment of special segregated schools for blacks, the recruitment of teachers from the North, and the development of institutions for training black teachers. In addition, many black adults who had been denied educational opportunities in their youth learned to read alongside their children.

In the late nineteenth century, political forces in the South began to limit blacks' further educational progress. Southern blacks were increasingly disenfranchised, and public educational funds were diverted from segregated schools for blacks to those for whites (Kousser 1974). Robert Margo measures substantial declines in the relative quality of education for black children between 1890 and 1910. These include reductions in the black–white ratio of per-pupil expenditures on instruction, length of the school year, and teacher salaries and substantial increases in class size (Margo 1990, Tables 2.5, 2.6, 4.1, 2.7, pp. 21–22, 26, 54, 27). These findings suggest that the statistics on racial differences in school enrollment shown in Table Bc438–446 may overstate the relative quality of improvement in the education of blacks around the turn of the twentieth century.

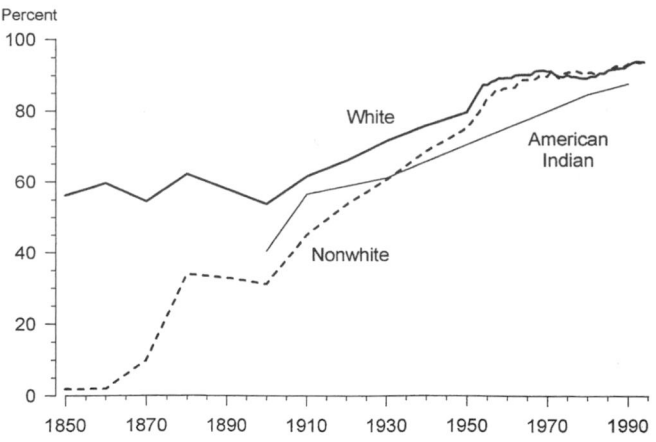

FIGURE Pa-G School enrollment rates, by race: 1850–1994

Sources

Series Ag917 and Bc439–440.

In the twentieth century, three major developments altered racial differences in educational attainment. The Great Migration of blacks out of the rural South into Northern cities from the 1910s through the 1960s provided the children of black migrants with access to better-quality Northern schools and also prompted Southern school boards to improve their services to black children in an effort to stem the outward tide (Margo 1990). By 1954, when the Supreme Court ruled against the "separate but equal" doctrine that had legitimized segregated schools for close to a half century, the racial differential in school attendance had already narrowed considerably. The black school enrollment rate for 5- to 19-year-olds was 80.8 percent, as compared with 87.0 percent for whites. After the Supreme Court ruling against segregated schools, the racial gap in education through high school closed further still (see Table Bc438–446 and Figure Pa-G). Nonetheless, the quality of Southern schools – as measured by class size, qualifications of teachers, and other similar measures – remained below that of schools in other parts of the country at the close of the twentieth century (Card and Krueger 1992).

The second development was the "high school movement," the effort to make high school completion the norm among youths. Among the birth cohort of 1900, only about 10 percent eventually graduated from high school; among the birth cohort of 1930, the high school graduation rate was more than 50 percent (Tables Bc468–479 and Bc492–500). There are only limited data available on high school graduation rates by race for the early twentieth century. Available data suggest that although blacks were less likely than whites to graduate from high school, they experienced more dramatic improvements in high school graduation rates over time. In 1940, when statistics on the educational attainment of the population by race first become available, whites reported high school completion rates of 24.2 and 28.0 percent for males and females, respectively; the comparable numbers for blacks were 6.9 and 8.4 percent. The racial differential in these rates is smaller than were illiteracy rates fifty years earlier. While blacks still remained at a substantial educational disadvantage, these data suggest that they benefited differentially from the high school movement. Nonetheless, at the end of the twentieth century, a racial gap in high school completion rates still remained (see Table Bc737–792 and Figure Pa-H).

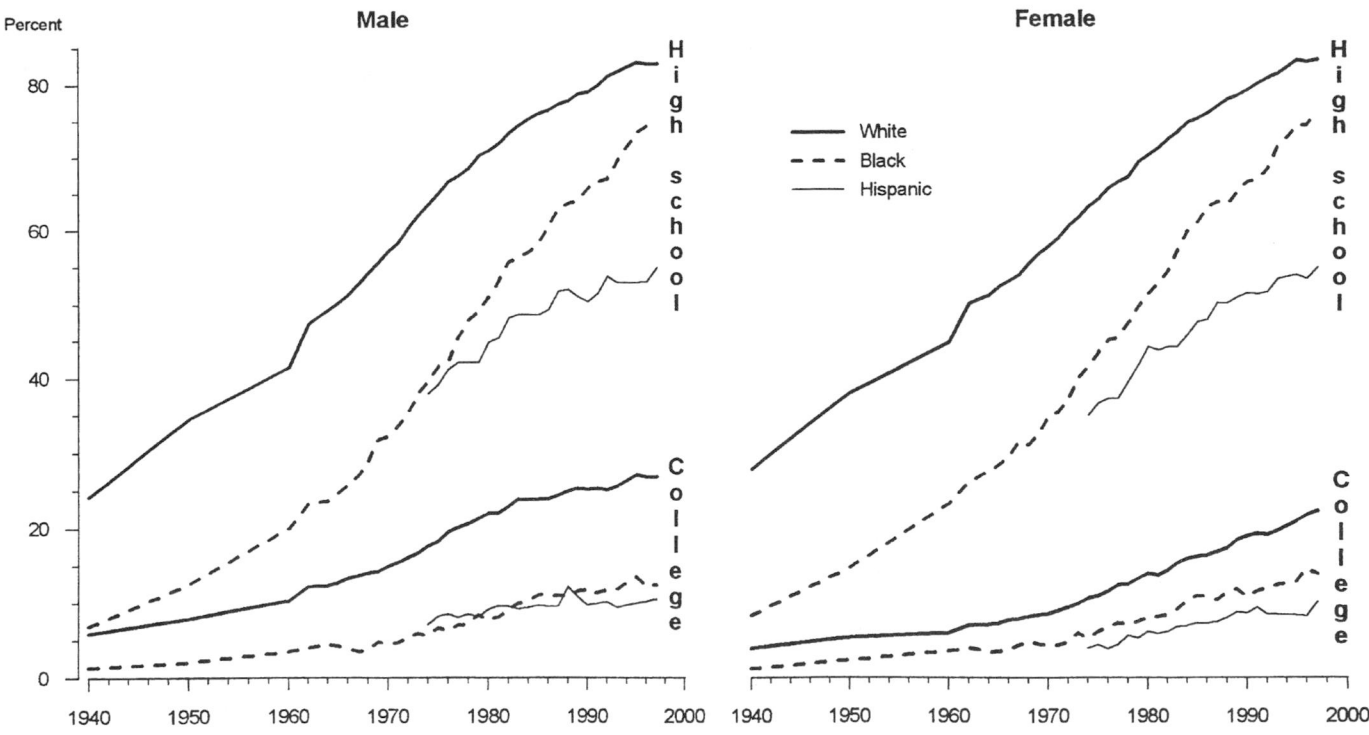

FIGURE Pa-H   Educational attainment, by sex, race, and ethnicity: 1940–1997

Source

Calculated from Table Bc737–792.

Documentation

The figures indicate the percentage of the given population (age 25 or older) that completed four years of high school or at least four years of college.

The third development was the movement to mass higher education, which began following World War II. In 1950, only 1.9 percent of black males and 2.6 percent of black females 25–64 years of age were college graduates, as compared with 8.8 and 6.1 percent of native-born white males and females, respectively. By 1997, the rates had climbed to 16.3 and 16.5 percent for blacks and 30.1 and 26.6 percent for native-born whites. Thus, while the percentage gains for blacks were greater than for native-born whites, the proportionate gap was larger at the end of the century than it was in 1950.

There remain stubborn racial differentials in educational accomplishments by race. Since 1971, when national statistics on proficiency levels in different subjects become available by race and age, we observe large and stable differences in children's academic achievement by race and ethnicity. These differentials extend across all age groups. Table Bc273–428 indicates, for example, a 15 percentage-point differential in the percentage of non-Hispanic white nine-year-olds scoring in the top reading level compared with black and Hispanic nine-year-olds. The race and ethnic differentials for math are even greater. Although there is some year-to-year variation in these differentials, there is no discernible trend over the three decades following 1971.

Literacy and educational attainment differ by ethnicity as well as by race. For the years 1880 through 1940, we can compare the literacy of native- and foreign-born whites (Table Bc793–797). In 1880, when data first become available, the native-born show only a slight advantage over the foreign-born in literacy rates (Perlmann 1988). Over time up through 1940, the literacy of the foreign-born remained essentially unchanged, while the literacy rate of the native-born population improved considerably. The literacy differential began to be reversed in the 1930s, when the composition of immigration from abroad changed to reflect a new flow of refugees fleeing the fascist governments that were taking over in Europe at that time. Refugees admitted to the United States as immigrants at that time were primarily of middle-class origins, and they worked in business and the professions. Twelve of these immigrants had already received the Nobel Prize, most famously Albert Einstein. Many others who immigrated at this time went on to win the Nobel Prize after their arrival in the United States (see Table Ad938–949). A large number of less well connected refugees who wished to emigrate to the United States were not permitted to enter (Gemery 1994). One consequence of this change in policy preferences was that the educational attainment of the foreign-born grew rapidly, not only absolutely but also relative to the native-born population.

After the replacement of the Quota System with the Preference System in 1965, the educational attainment of the immigrant population changed once again. Instead of uniformity, a bimodal pattern emerged. On the one hand, there was a large fraction of immigrants with educational levels above the national average. These were the scientists, engineers, and graduate students who remained in the country after completing their advanced degrees in order to teach and do research. At the opposite end of the spectrum were colleagues, family, and friends of agricultural workers and political refugees whose educational levels averaged at about the elementary school level.

One of the most poorly educated of the numerically important immigrant groups in the second half of the twentieth century were the Mexicans. Data on their educational attainment are available beginning in the mid-1970s. These data reveal low rates of educational attainment compared with the native-born population, white and black. By the mid-twentieth century, when the vast majority of Americans were high school graduates, the majority of Mexican immigrants to the United States had barely completed the sixth grade. The impact of this educational differential shows up in a variety of areas, including the occupational distribution of the Hispanic population and the educational achievement of Hispanic children born in the United States (Table Bc 737–792).

The role of the public school as a tool of democracy and as an "Americanizer" has a large and complex history. The high rates of public school attendance throughout the period of rapid immigration played a large role in assimilating the children of the foreign-born into American society and culture. Public schools have been the educators of the majority of the population at least since the 1840s. When statistics become available in 1890, they indicate that a little more than 90 percent of kindergarten through eighth-grade enrollments were in these public schools. That proportion declined slightly over the twentieth century, and recent data indicate a share of about 87 percent today. When high school attendance was relatively rare, as it was throughout the nineteenth century, many high school students attended private institutions. However, the high school revolution of the first half of the twentieth century was accomplished by the expansion of public high schools and a consequent shift in high school enrollment share out of the private sector. There was a rapid increase in the public school share of high school enrollment up to about 1920 and relative stability since then. The overwhelming majority of private high schools are Catholic.

At the end of the twentieth century, and despite notable improvements along a variety of dimensions, American race and ethnic differences remained pronounced in the areas covered by this essay – population, vital processes, and education. Racial and ethnic differences were also prominent in other areas of American life. For additional discussions of racial and ethnic difference in opportunities and outcomes, see Chapters Ba, Be, Dc, and Ed.

References

Bean, Frank D., and W. Parker Frisbee, editors. 1978. *The Demography of Racial and Ethnic Groups*. Academic Press.

Bean, Frank D., and John P. Marcum. 1978. "Differential Fertility and the Minority Group Status Hypothesis: An Assessment and Review." In Frank D. Bean and W. Parker Frisbee, editors. *The Demography of Racial and Ethnic Groups*. Academic Press.

Bullock, Henry Allen. 1970. *A History of Negro Education in the South: From 1619 to the Present*. Praeger.

Card, David, and Alan Krueger. 1992. "School Quality and Black/White Relative Earnings." *Quarterly Journal of Economics* 107: 151–200.

Cummings, John. 1918. *Negro Population: 1790–1915*. U.S. Bureau of the Census.

Fishlow, Albert. 1966. "The American Common School Revival: Fact or Fancy?" In Henry Rosovsky, editor. *Industrialization in Two Systems: Essays in Honor of Alexander Gerschenkron*. Wiley.

Frey, William H. 2001. "Census 2000 Shows Large Black Return to the South, Reinforcing the Region's 'Black–White' Demographic Profile." PSC Research Report number 01-473, Population Studies Center, University of Michigan (May).

Gemery, Henry A. 1994. "Immigrants and Emigrants: International Migration and the US Labor Market in the Great Depression." In Timothy J. Hatton and Jeffrey G. Williamson, editors. *Migration and the International Labor Market, 1850–1939*. Routledge.

Gutman, Herbert, and Richard Sutch. 1976. "Victorians All? The Sexual Mores and Conduct of Slaves and Their Masters." In Paul A. David, Herbert Gutman, et al., editors. *Reckoning with Slavery: A Critical Study in the Quantitative History of American Negro Slavery*. Oxford University Press.

Haines, Michael R. 1998. "Estimated Life Tables for the United States, 1850–1910." *Historical Methods* 31 (4): 149–69.

Haines, Michael R. 2002. "Ethnic Differences in Demographic Behavior in the United States: Has There Been Convergence?" Paper prepared for the "Workshop on the Historical Demography of Ethnicity: Population Processes and Their Genetic Implications," California Institute of Technology, Pasadena, California, May 13–14.

Haines, Michael R., and Samuel H. Preston. 1997. "The Use of the Census to Estimate Childhood Mortality: Comparisons from the 1900 and 1910 United States Census Public Use Samples." *Historical Methods* 30 (2): 77–97.

Haines, Michael R., and Richard H. Steckel, editors. 2000. *A Population History of North America*. Cambridge University Press.

King, Miriam, and Steven Ruggles. 1990. "American Immigration, Fertility Differentials, and the Ideology of Race Suicide at the Turn of the Century." *Journal of Interdisciplinary History* 20 (3): 347–69.

Kousser, J. Morgan. 1974. *The Shaping of Southern Politics: Suffrage Restriction and the Establishment of the One-Party South, 1880–1910*. Yale University Press.

Margo, Robert A. 1990. *Race and Schooling in the South, 1880–1950: An Economic History*. University of Chicago Press.

Perlmann, Joel. 1988. *Ethnic Differences: Schooling and Social Structure among the Irish, Italians, Jews and Blacks in an American City, 1880–1935*. Cambridge University Press.

Preston, Samuel H., and Michael R. Haines. 1991. *Fatal Years: Child Mortality in Late Nineteenth-Century America*. Princeton University Press.

Ransom, Roger L., and Richard Sutch. 2001. *One Kind of Freedom: The Economic Consequences of Emancipation*. 2d edition. Cambridge University Press.

Smith, Jessie Carney, and Carrell Peterson Horton, editors. 1995. *Historical Statistics of Black America*. Gale Research.

Taeuber, Conrad, and Irene B. Taeuber. 1958. *The Changing Population of the United States*. Wiley.

Thompson, Warren S., and P. K. Whelpton. 1933. *Population Trends in the United States*. McGraw-Hill.

Wilson, William J. 1987. *The Truly Disadvantaged: The Inner City, the Underclass, and Public Policy*. University of Chicago Press.

Wright, Gavin. 1986. *Old South, New South: Revolutions in the Southern Economy since the Civil War*. Basic Books.

CHAPTER Aa
Population Characteristics

Editor: Michael R. Haines

POPULATION CHARACTERISTICS

Michael R. Haines

The human population of a nation is the stock of resident persons, at any given time, of various ages, sexes, marital statuses, races, ethnic origins, religions, residences, and socioeconomic statuses (such as occupation, income, and wealth). These persons are spread across the area of the nation in distinctive patterns, living in central cities, suburban areas, or rural regions. The study of population is crucial because it is important to know such things as how legislative bodies are apportioned; what the stock of actual and potential workers in the labor force with various skills and education levels in different places is; what the base of income, property, sales, and excise taxpayers is; what the stock of citizens potentially eligible for military service is; how many children will need places in public and private schools; how many older citizens will be collecting retirement benefits and will be in need of medical care both now and in the future; and where the population is located (central cities, suburbs, or rural areas) so demand for public services (roads, schools, post offices, water and sewer systems, electricity, and telephone and cable services) can be predicted. The human resources of a nation are as important as anything it possesses. This essay describes the population of the United States since the date of the first federal census in 1790: the components of its growth; composition by age, sex, race, and ethnic group; and location (rural–urban residence, suburbanization, and regional shifts). The population prior to 1790 is treated in Chapter Eg, on colonial statistics. Although reference is made in this essay to the American Indian population, Chapter Ag is specifically devoted to American Indians. Finally, this essay includes a discussion on the Hispanic population.

Sources and Methods

A difficulty in the study of American historical demography is the lack of some types of data for the calculation of standard demographic measures. The principal source of population data is the decennial census of population, a house-by-house count made by the Census Bureau. In accordance with a constitutional provision for a decennial canvass of the population, the first census enumeration was made in 1790 (see Anderson 1988 for a recent history of the census). The primary reason for the census of population,

as set forth in the Constitution, is to provide a basis for the apportionment of members of the House of Representatives among the several states. Until 1902, the census organization was temporary. It was assembled before each decennial census and disbanded after the work was finished. In 1902, the Census Bureau was established as a permanent agency of the government, charged with responsibility for the decennial census and for compiling statistics on other subjects as needed. Currently, this bureau provides population data based on surveys and estimates in addition to making the comprehensive decennial census enumerations.

In accordance with census practice dating back to 1790, each person is counted as an inhabitant of his or her usual place of residence or usual place of abode, that is, the place where he or she lives and sleeps most of the time. This place is not necessarily the same as his or her legal residence, voting residence, or domicile, although, in the vast majority of cases, the use of these different bases of classification would produce identical results. Indians living in Indian Territory or on reservations were not included in the population count until 1890, and in earlier censuses large tracts of unorganized and sparsely settled territory were not covered by enumerators. Alaska and Hawai'i were territories through 1950 and were first included in the United States in the 1960 Census.[1] The totals simply include the two new states for 1960 and later. Through 1930, the data presented are based on complete counts. Some of the data shown from Censuses of 1940 and later are based on sample tabulations (ranging from 3.33 percent to 25 percent), as indicated in the documentation to the tables.

Several tables present estimates from the Current Population Survey (CPS), a survey that is conducted monthly by the Bureau of the Census since 1947 (for example, Tables Aa6–8 and Aa110–124). These data allow estimates of population size and composition on a more frequent basis without resorting to the costly and complex process of a full census count. Originally, the CPS covered a representative sample of approximately 21,000 interviewed households in areas throughout the United States. This sample size was increased to approximately 35,000 in May 1956 and to approximately 50,000 in January 1967. The sample covered 754 areas comprising 2,121 counties (of the approximately 3,300 counties in the United States), independent cities, and minor civil divisions with coverage in every state and the District of Columbia.

---

[1] They were, however, separately enumerated – Alaska since 1880 and Hawai'i since 1900.

Acknowledgments

Michael R. Haines wishes to thank Todd K. Gardner and Campbell Gibson of the U.S. Bureau of the Census for advice and assistance. The collection of the data for the tables in this chapter was supported in part by the National Institute of Aging through Grant 1 R01 HD 10120 (Michael R. Haines). The

preparation of data for Tables Aa2189–2243 was partly supported by the National Institute of Child Health and Human Development, through Grants 1 F33 HD08147-0 (Brian Gratton), 5 R01 HD32325 (Myron P. Gutmann), and HD37824-02 (Brian Gratton).

Estimates of population characteristics based on the CPS will not agree with those from the census because of differences in procedures for collecting and processing data on subgroups of the populations (for example, racial and ethnic groups).

Exact agreement is not to be expected among the various samples, nor between them and the complete census count; however, the sample data may be used with confidence where large numbers are involved, and may be assumed to indicate patterns and relationships where small numbers are involved. Detailed statements regarding the sampling errors are given in the original sources.

Many errors appear in the census publications of 1790–1840. The data for these censuses were adjusted by county and race, and the revised figures were published in the 1840 and 1870 Censuses. Revised figures for the U.S. population by sex and race for 1790–1840 were published in the 1910 Census. Official revisions by age have not been made, and thus the 1790–1840 age data in this chapter for most race–sex groups add up to totals that differ slightly from the revised figures for race–sex groups. The data for individual states generally reflect the corrected 1840 results, except for 1790, for which corrected data given by Rossiter are used (U.S. Census Bureau 1909).

The Census Bureau has always been concerned about the degree of completeness of enumeration in the decennial censuses, although public interest in census coverage and statistical techniques for estimating coverage was quite limited prior to 1950. Discussions of coverage in earlier censuses were limited mostly to qualitative statements. The quantitative evaluation of census coverage can be done at the individual and aggregate levels. At the individual level, the approaches include re-interview (for example, postenumeration surveys) and record checks (for example, matching of census records and birth records). At the aggregate level, the approaches include demographic analysis (the use of data on births, deaths, and migration, and of life tables, expected sex ratios, etc.) and the use of aggregated data from administrative records (for example, comparing the enrollment in Medicare with the census count of the aged population).

In 1950, the postenumeration survey was thought to be a satisfactory method of determining net census underenumeration. The number of persons missed in the 1950 Census was estimated at about 2.1 million, or 1.4 percent, with corresponding estimates of 1.6 percent for 1940 and 0.7 percent for 1930. Demographers now generally believe, however, that postenumeration surveys tend to understate census omissions because persons missed in a census have an above-average probability of being missed in a postenumeration survey.

Evaluations of census coverage now rely heavily on demographic analysis. Analyses of coverage conducted by the Census Bureau and using demographic analysis show the following estimates and revisions of net census underenumeration (Edmonston and Schultze 1995, Table 2.1):

1940	7.0 million	5.4 percent
1950	6.3 million	4.1 percent
1960	5.6 million	3.1 percent
1970	5.5 million	2.7 percent
1980	2.8 million	1.2 percent
1990	4.7 million	1.8 percent

Studies back to 1880 show general improvement over time (Coale and Zelnik 1963; Coale and Rives 1973). There are also substantial differentials in undercount among groups and regions. For example, the postenumeration survey results for 1990 indicate the following differences in undercount by racial and ethnic groups: 0.7 percent for whites; 4.4 percent for blacks; 5.0 percent for Hispanics; and 4.5 percent for Amerindians. Analyses of census coverage are subject to revision on the basis of additional information and research.

A number of studies have been done on the U.S. census and on various systems that collected vital data in the nineteenth and twentieth centuries (Coale and Zelnik 1963; Condran and Crimmins 1979; *Social Science History* 1991). Overall, it seems that censuses in the mid-nineteenth century missed anywhere from 5 percent to 25 percent of the population. A careful analysis of the white population from 1880 to 1960 indicates overall underenumeration of 6.1 percent in 1880, declining to 5.7 percent by 1920 and 2.1 percent by 1960. Results varied by age and sex, with the very young and the elderly being least well enumerated. Blacks were more likely to be missed than whites. A summary of recent work on the mid-nineteenth-century federal census notes that those more likely to be counted were older, native-born heads of more complex households, with moderate wealth and better-paying occupations, in the political mainstream, and living in smaller communities or rural areas having slow economic and population growths. Those less likely to be enumerated were younger, native-born sons or foreign-born male boarders, living in smaller households, working in low-wage occupations in large, rapidly growing urban areas, and not in the political mainstream (Shryock, Siegel, and Associates 1971, p. 109; Parkerson 1991).

Another technique is the comparison of rates of change with respect to consistency and reasonableness. On this basis, it is believed that figures for the South showed unreasonably low rates of increase for the decade 1860–1870 and abnormally high rates of increase for 1870–1880. The differences are so great that it appears evident that the enumeration of 1870 in this area was seriously incomplete, undoubtedly as a result of the unsettled conditions of the Reconstruction period. For the portion of the United States outside the South, the rate of increase for 1860–1870 was about the same as that for 1870–1880. Therefore, the number initially enumerated in 1870 for the South was revised upward.[2] This chapter generally reports the "official" published totals in the census volumes.

Nonetheless, many of these deficiencies do not affect overall results too dramatically. Calculation of rates involves canceling errors. The extent of the errors usually did not change too much from census to census or year to year. In addition, demographic estimates often involve some corrections to the data. Many of the tabular results presented here use uncorrected data; however, some of the estimates do make adjustments.

Although originally the census was intended to provide the basis for allocating seats in the U.S. House of Representatives, the published material grew from a modest one-volume compilation of spare aggregated statistics in 1790 to multiple-volume descriptions of the population, economy, and society by the late nineteenth and early twentieth centuries. Original manuscript returns exist

---

[2] For a detailed discussion of the adjustment, see *U.S. Census of Population: 1890*, volume 1, pp. xi–xii. For analyses of the completeness of census enumerations from 1880 to 1990, see Coale and Zelnik (1963), Coale and Rives (1973), Siegel (1974), Robinson, Ahmed, et al. (1993), and Edmonston and Schultze (1995), Chapter 2.

for all dates except 1890, opening great analytical opportunities.[3] The census has been *the* major source for the study of population growth, structure, and redistribution, as well as fertility prior to the twentieth century. Some states also took censuses, usually in years between the federal censuses. A number have been published and some also exist in manuscript form (Dubester 1948). Vital registration was left, however, to state and local governments and, in consequence, it was instituted unevenly. The entire United States was not covered until 1933.[4]

The federal census has consistently inquired about age, sex, and race, although the nonwhite population was not categorized by sex and age until 1820. The Censuses of 1790 through 1840 were taken by households using forms with spaces for counts by age, sex, and race categories. The first nominal census, in which each individual was enumerated on a separate line, was not taken until 1850 (for a description of the enumerator's schedules and instructions, see U.S. Census Bureau 1979 and 2002). Even then, the Censuses of 1850 and 1860 had special schedules for slaves, for whom less detailed information was taken than for whites and free blacks. The American Indian and Asian-origin populations were not separately designated until 1860. The 1850 Census was also the first to ask explicitly about the occupation of each person, although this was done only for males ages 15 and older.[5] Females were asked about their occupations from 1860 onward, and children were asked from 1870 onward. Economic questions then began to multiply. Questions on unemployment began in 1880; on employment status, industry, and class of worker (employer, employee, working on own account) in 1910; on wage and salary income in 1940; and on personal income in 1950. Questions on real wealth were asked in 1850–1870 and on personal wealth in 1860–1870.

Interest in education dates back to the 1840 Census, with questions on schools, school attendance, and adult literacy. Questions on literacy continued up through the 1930 Census, after which the literacy question was replaced with a query on the number of years of formal schooling completed. Other personal characteristics were also included in the census over time. Marital status and relationship to the head of the household were first asked about in 1880; children ever born in 1890 (and children surviving in 1890–1910); duration of current marriage in 1910; number of times married in 1910; age at first marriage in 1940; and veteran status in 1910. Some questions were not asked in all censuses, and some have been dropped.

The U.S. census also provided, from 1850, information on a person's place of birth and, after 1870, on the nativity of each person's parents. This was either state of birth for the native-born or country of birth for the foreign-born. These data permit study of international migration (for example, the geographic distribution of the foreign-born) and also analysis of internal migration by providing cross-classification of the native-born by birth and current residence (from 1860 onward).[6] Internal migration is a rather difficult issue because of lack of evidence on date of change of residence between the time of birth and current residence. For the foreign-born, questions on duration of residence in the United States were asked in the Censuses of 1890–1930 and again in 1970–2000, but a question about duration of current residence was not asked of all inhabitants until 1940 (when a question was asked concerning a person's place of residence five years prior to the census). Also of interest have been a person's mother tongue (1910–1940, 1960–1970) and language customarily spoken (1910, 1980–2000). An ambiguous question of self-identification of ancestry was introduced in 1980.

Demography, the study of human populations, depends heavily on measurement and estimation techniques. Most of the results presented in this chapter are simple tabulations or standard demographic rates. However, a number of the newer findings arise from rather sophisticated techniques (Haines 1998; Haines and Preston 1997). Estimation of better demographic information is of importance for research in social, demographic, and economic history. Basic demographic structures and events, reflected in birth and death rates, population size and structure, growth rates, the composition and growth of the labor force, marriage rates and patterns, household composition, the levels and nature of migration flows, causes of death, urbanization and spatial population distribution, and so forth, determine the human capital of society as producers and consumers and also how that human capital reproduces, relocates, and depreciates. Demographic events are important both as indicators of social and economic change and as integral components of modern economic growth.

Population in the United States, 1790–1990

Every modern, economically developed nation has undergone a demographic transition from high to low levels of fertility and mortality. This was certainly true for the United States, which has experienced a sustained fertility decline from at least about 1800 (see Tables Ab1–10 and Ab40–117). Around that time, the typical American woman had about seven or eight live births during her reproductive years, and the average person had an expectation of life at birth of 39–40 years, an outcome greatly affected by high infant mortality. However, the American pattern was distinctive. First, the American fertility transition was under way from at least the beginning of the nineteenth century, and some evidence indicates that family size was declining in older settled areas from the late eighteenth century on. Other Western developed nations, with the exception of France, began their sustained, irreversible decline in birth rates only in the late nineteenth or early twentieth century (Coale and Watkins 1986). It is perhaps not coincidental that both France and the United States experienced important political revolutions in the late eighteenth century and were then characterized by small-scale, owner-occupier agriculture. Second, it appears that fertility in America was in sustained decline long before mortality. This is in contrast to the stylized view of the demographic transition, in which mortality decline precedes or occurs simultaneously

---

[3] The 1890 Census returns were destroyed in a fire in 1921. The population schedules are available on microfilm from the National Archives now up through 1920. This permitted construction of machine-readable public use microdata samples for 1900, 1910, and 1940–1980. Consistent national public use samples have now been constructed for 1850, 1880, 1900, 1910, and 1940–1990. Samples are currently under way for 1860, 1870, and 1920. These are the Integrated Public Use Microsamples (IPUMS) created by Steven Ruggles and his colleagues at the University of Minnesota (see Ruggles and Hall 1999). Some results in the tables in this and other chapters have been derived using these samples.

[4] A discussion of vital registration can be found in Chapter Ab, on vital statistics.

[5] The Censuses of 1820 and 1840 had asked about the sector of employment of the head of household.

[6] For internal migration, see Chapter Ac, and for international migration, see Chapter Ad.

with fertility decline. Mortality in the United States did not stabilize and begin a consistent decline until about the 1870s. Third, these demographic processes were influenced by both the large volume of international net in-migration and significant internal population redistribution to frontier areas and to cities, towns, and (later) suburbs.

Although the American case may be, in many respects, sui generis, it furnishes a long-term view of a completed demographic transition with accompanying urbanization. The United States was a demographic laboratory in which natives and migrants, different racial and ethnic groups, and varying occupational and socioeconomic strata experienced these significant behavioral changes in a fertile, land-abundant, resource-rich country.

Table Aa15–21 provides summary measures of population growth and its components by decades from 1790 to 2000.[7] This table (as is Table Aa9–14) is organized around the demographic balancing equation, which states that the decade rate of population growth (RTI) equals the crude birth rate (CBR) minus the crude death rate (CDR) plus the rate of net migration (RNM). The difference between the birth rate and the death rate is the rate of natural increase (RNI) (that is, RTI = CBR – CDR + RNM, and CBR – CDR = RNI). Table Aa9–14 provides entirely new annual estimates of the population as of July 1 for the nineteenth century.

Several features of the American demographic transition can be discerned from Tables Aa9–35 and Ab1–10 (see also Figure Aa-A). The United States experienced a truly remarkable population increase during its transition. From a modest 4 million inhabitants in 1790, the population grew to more than 281 million in 2000, an average annual growth rate of about 2 percent per year. In the early years of the republic, population growth rates were even higher, more than 3 percent per annum for the period 1790–1810 and again in the 1840s and 1850s. Such rapid growth is historically rather unusual and is comparable to the recent experience of some developing nations. Growth rates of this magnitude would lead to a doubling of the population in slightly more than two decades (approximately twenty-three years). The surge of growth in the 1840s and 1850s was particularly caused by a significant increase in migration from abroad – the now familiar story of Irish, Germans, and others from Western and Northern Europe fleeing the great potato famine, the "Hungry Forties," and political upheaval and seeking better farming, business, and employment opportunities in the Western Hemisphere. Natural increase had been declining from the early 1800s, largely because of a decline in birth rates for both white and black populations. Some of the decline in natural increase in the 1840s and 1850s was also likely attributable to *rising* mortality in those decades. Table Ab1–10 indicates, however, that mortality did decline steadily from the 1870s onward.

Another feature notable in Tables Aa9–21 is the dominant role played by natural increase in overall population growth. In the decades before 1840, less than one sixth or one seventh of total growth originated from net migration. With the surge in overseas migration after 1840, however, the share of net migration in total

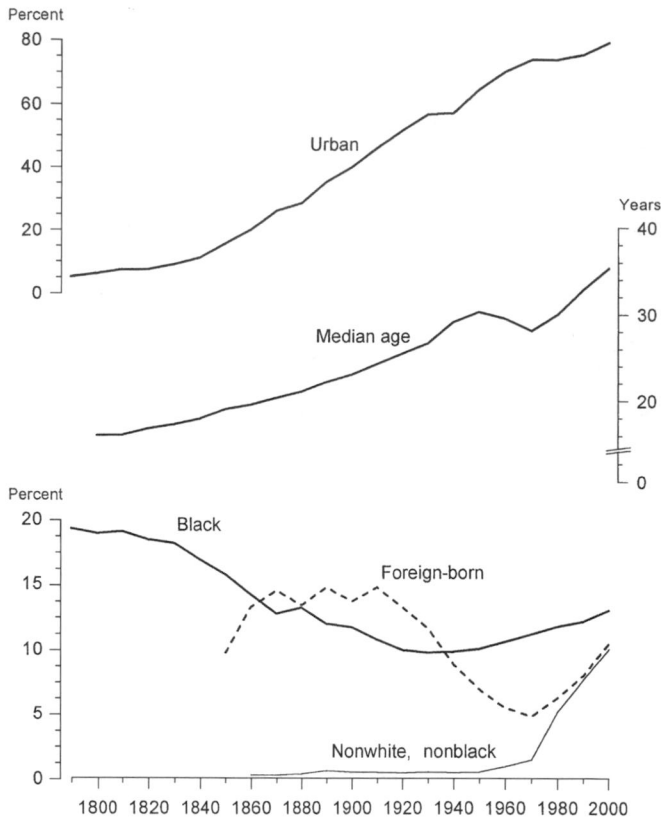

FIGURE Aa-A   Selected population characteristics: 1790–2000

Source
Table Aa22–35.

increase rose to between one fourth and one third. Notably, the share of labor force growth accounted for by migration was higher because migration was selective of persons of an age to participate in the labor force. Nonetheless, despite declining birth rates, the American population grew rapidly in the nineteenth century, principally from an excess of births over deaths, although it must be recognized that the births to the foreign-born and their descendants contributed importantly. If it could be assumed that no immigration occurred after 1790 and that the natural increase of the colonial stock population had been what it actually was (with no effect of immigration on the natural increase of the native-born), then the white population would have been about 52 million in 1920, or about 55 percent of what it actually was. The surge in migration after 1840 can also be recognized in the rise in the proportion of the population that was foreign-born from less than 10 percent in 1850 (the first census for which such data were available) to nearly 15 percent in 1890 and 1910 (see Table Aa1884–1895).

The effects of immigration restriction after World War I are apparent in the reduced rate of net migration after 1920. The Great Depression had a dramatic damping effect on both fertility and migration from abroad, resulting in the only decade of net out-migration since the first census in 1790. The post–World War II "baby boom" is apparent in the higher crude birth rates in the 1940s and 1950s. More recent changes in immigration regulations clearly affected the surge in net in-migrants, when 37 percent and 47 percent of population growth in the 1970s and 1990s, respectively, were attributable to this source. These proportions are larger than those in the decades preceding both the Civil War and World War I.

---

[7] The results in this table differ somewhat from those in Haines and Steckel (2000), Table 8.3, p. 315; and Table A.3, p. 700. The differences stem from small corrections to the rate of natural increase and rate of net migration from 1820 to 1870, and revising the results from 1900 to 2000 to accord with current Census Bureau estimates of mid-decade populations and of decadal births and deaths. The results also differ from those in Table Aa9–14 because of different assumptions (see text to Tables Aa9–21).

Table Aa22–35 provides some summary information about the changing composition of the American population by race and ethnicity, sex, and age since 1790 (for a discussion of the problems of defining race and ethnicity, see Haines 2003). The share of the white population in the total increased fairly steadily between 1790 and 1930 (from 80.7 percent to 89.8 percent), largely as a result of the substantial net immigration of white Europeans up through the 1920s. The restriction of migration after World War I, combined with the higher natural increase in the black population, led to a slow rise in the representation of the black population in the total. In recent decades, this has been accelerated by a rising net in-migration of individuals from sub-Saharan Africa, the Caribbean, and other areas with a large proportion of persons of African descent. Really dramatic, however, was the rising share of other ethnic groups in the late twentieth century. From less than 1 percent of the population in 1960, this share rose to 12.6 percent in the 2000 Census. This had its origins mostly in a heavy immigration of persons from East and South Asia; however, it also stems in part from the rapid increase in the American Indian population. The latter was the result of a large amount of ethnic self-reidentification. The political, social, and economic consequences of the changing racial and ethnic composition of the American population are already apparent and are likely to be profound in the future.

The median age of the population has been steadily rising since 1800, from about 16 in 1800 to about 23 in 1900 to more than 35 in 2000.[8] This is mostly a function of the decline in birth rates (see Table Ab1–10). Birth rates (and not death rates) are the major determinants of the age structure of a population not subject to significant migration flows. Although the effects of migration on age structure are an issue for the United States, the fall in birth rates has dominated the aging of the American population in the last two centuries. A similar result holds for sex composition. Table Aa22–35 gives the sex ratio (males per 100 females) since 1790. Slightly more males than females are born to most human populations (about 5 percent more); however, male mortality usually tends to exceed female mortality at all ages (see Table Ab988–1047). For a high-fertility population with a young age structure, such as the United States in the early nineteenth century, this leads to a majority of the population being male. As birth rates fall and the population ages, however, the older age groups with a majority being women come to dominate. This was offset in the nineteenth and early twentieth centuries by immigration, in which migrant selectivity favored males.[9] However, the sex ratio declined between 1910 and 1980 as the population aged. More recently, the effects of male selective migration have again been seen in the rising sex ratio.

Another notable feature in Table Aa22–35 is the share of the foreign-born in the population. As already mentioned, the Census of 1850 was the first to ask about the place of birth of all persons. Already in 1850, almost 10 percent of the American population was born abroad, in this case overwhelmingly in Europe (more than 90 percent; see Table Ad354–443). This rose to almost 15 percent in the Census of 1910, based on the huge immigration from the 1840s up through World War I. Immigration restriction from the 1920s onward, largely in the form of quotas by national origin, led to a reduction in net immigration (see Table Aa9–14) and a

drop in the proportion of the foreign-born to 4.7 percent in 1970. However, recent changes in immigration legislation and a surge in immigration, now from Asia, Latin America, the Caribbean, and Africa, have once again raised the share of the foreign-born in the American population to more than 10 percent in the 2000 Census. We continue to be a nation of immigrants.

Table Aa22–35 also demonstrates that the United States experienced a transition from a predominantly rural society to a largely urban one. In 1790, only 5 percent of the population was living in officially classified urban areas. This rose to about 20 percent on the eve of the Civil War in 1860. It was not until 1920 that more than half of the population was enumerated as urban. Currently, more than three fourths of the American population is classified as urban; however, this understates the urban population because there are "rural" areas at the edges of metropolitan areas that will soon be placed in the urban category.

The urban population is currently defined as comprising all persons living in urbanized areas and in places of 2,500 inhabitants or more outside urbanized areas (for details, see the text for Table Aa684–698). In addition, the Census Bureau has, since 1950, provided information on metropolitan statistical areas (MSAs), consolidated metropolitan statistical areas, and primary metropolitan statistical areas. The general concept of a metropolitan area (MA) is that of a core area containing a large population nucleus, together with adjacent communities having a high degree of economic and social integration with that core. Currently defined MAs are based on application of 1999 standards (which were effective in 1996) to 1990 decennial census data. These MA definitions were announced by the Office of Management and Budget effective June 30, 1996. Tables Aa824–1033 provide some information on MAs, using the different boundaries and definitions that have evolved since 1950. These data indicate that, at present, about one fourth of the population lives in areas that are classified as central cities, about one half in suburbs (non–central city portions of MSAs), and about one fourth in rural places.

The effects of regional differences in population growth are also apparent. The 4.5 million inhabitants in 1790 were clustered along the Atlantic coast, about evenly divided between North (New England and Middle Atlantic regions) and South (South Atlantic region). By 1860 only 51 percent of the 31 million Americans were still living in these regions, but this had fallen to 41 percent in 1920 and 38 percent by 1990. Regions of earliest settlement grew at an average rate of 1.6 percent per annum over the whole period 1790–1990, while the entire United States was growing at 2 percent. This regional disparity was driven, of course, by the relentless westward movement of population, agriculture, and industry. Much of the growth that did occur on the Atlantic coast was in yet another "frontier" – urban areas. In the regions of original European settlement, cities and towns grew from just 5 percent of the population in 1790 to 28 percent in 1860, 61 percent in 1920, and 74 percent in 1990, an annual growth rate of 2.9 percent per annum, while the growth of the rural population was merely 1 percent per annum. For the nation as a whole, this led to the large increase in the share of national urban population.

Not surprisingly, the demographic "center" of the nation has moved from the Atlantic coastal states (New England, Middle Atlantic, and South Atlantic regions) to the Midwest (East North Central and West North Central) and western South (East South Central and West South Central). By 1920, the Mountain and Pacific states were still relatively small demographically,

---

[8] Many of the tables in this chapter contain tabulations by age and sex, as well as race.

[9] Between 1820 and 1917, 62.9 percent of all recorded immigrants were male.

comprising less than 10 percent of the total population (as opposed to 21 percent in 1990). Two migrations, thus, were driving the numbers – the movement from east to west and the movement from rural to urban areas. The average annual growth rate over that period was 3.4 percent for the urban population, in contrast to only 1.4 percent for rural dwellers. As we have every indication that the birth rates were lower and death rates higher in urban relative to rural areas, the more rapid growth of urban areas originated in population redistribution and not differences in natural increase. This rural-to-urban shift reflects, of course, labor market conditions as the economy changed its structure of opportunities from a rural population of smallholder agricultural proprietors to an urban, industrial, and service-based economy made up predominantly of employees. This is certainly exemplified by the increase in the nonfarm share of the labor force from 25.6 percent in 1800 to 44.2 percent in 1860, 74.1 percent in 1920, and 97.3 percent in 1990 (Weiss 1992, Table 1.1). A primary motive for migration in ordinary times is to take advantage of wage and income differences across space, which substitutes factor mobility for interregional trade in goods and services.

Urbanization did spread across regions, albeit unevenly. The Northeast was the urban–industrial center of the nation in the nineteenth century. By 1860, New England and the Middle Atlantic regions had 61 percent of the nation's urban inhabitants but only 33 percent of the overall population. Conversely, the South had 17 percent of the urban population but 36 percent of the overall total. Even in 1920, the Northeast still had 41 percent of urban dwellers, with the Midwest close behind at 33 percent. The South still had only 17 percent. However, by 1990 the Northeast had only 21.5 percent of America's urban dwellers, with the Midwest at 23 percent. The South now had 31.4 percent and the West 24 percent. The "Sunbelt" is not an illusion.

From 1850 onward we are able to examine migration by place of birth and current residence (also see Chapter Ac, on internal migration). The proportion of the native-born population residing outside the state of birth ("lifetime" migrants) was relatively stable from the middle of the nineteenth century – 23.3 percent of the white population in 1850, 23.5 percent in 1890, 23.9 percent in 1920, and 32 percent in 1990. The nonwhite population had lower rates of lifetime mobility in this period, about 15–20 percent until after 1920. In the nineteenth century, much of this interstate movement was on an east–west axis until the closing of the frontier at the end of the nineteenth century. For instance, in 1850, of those born in Pennsylvania but residing elsewhere, 67 percent could be found in Ohio, Indiana, or Illinois, whereas 77 percent of those born in South Carolina but residing outside that state were found in Georgia, Alabama, Mississippi, and Tennessee. A variety of explanations has been advanced for the migration along latitudes, but recently it has been shown that real and human capital invested in seed, livestock, implements, and farming techniques made movement along climatic bands highly rational. This also provides a partial explanation for the greater preference of the bulk of the nineteenth-century immigrants from Northern and Western Europe for the Northeast and the Midwest: their human capital matched that climatic band better. This was true for those going to rural areas at least. The remainder of the explanation was largely the greater opportunities in the more rapidly urbanizing and industrializing North, as well as the tendency of migration streams, once established, to grow along familiar paths. This has largely disappeared, as the varied opportunities of cities have drawn people in many directions, especially to the South and West regions.

Agrarian motives for migration diminished as the frontier closed in the late nineteenth century and as rural population growth slowed dramatically (to only 0.4 percent per year over the period 1890–1990). For most of the nineteenth century, migration flows westward were consistent with the land availability hypothesis discussed in connection with the fertility transition (see Chapter Ab, on vital statistics). Rural migrants moved west to secure cheaper, good-quality land. Frederick Jackson Turner's thesis that the frontier was a demographic "safety valve" in nineteenth-century America remains a durable view. Nevertheless, late in the century, rural-to-urban flows assumed the dominant role. However, much of the rural–urban migration was within regions or along an east–west axis because the bulk of urban and industrial growth from the Civil War to 1920 was in the Northeast or Midwest. Notably, the South failed to increase its share of urban population over this period. The major shift to a south-to-north movement began on a large scale only with the radical shifts in demand for labor accompanying World War I and the restriction, after 1921, of cheap immigrant labor. The shift to the Sunbelt came even later, largely after World War II. Changes in transportation technology, particularly electric street and underground railways and later the automobile and motorized bus, led to a movement out of central cities and into suburban communities. This process was under way in parts of the Northeast by the end of the nineteenth century, but really accelerated after World War I, and again after 1945. So, for instance, during the 1920s the rural part of metropolitan districts (as defined by the Census Bureau) increased by 55 percent, faster than any part of the metropolitan population except for small cities. This development was suburbanization.

The urbanization process was accompanied by a filling out in the city size hierarchy. Large cities did tend to grow most rapidly. In 1810 there were only two cities with populations of more than 50,000 (New York and Philadelphia), and together they made up 29 percent of the total urban population. By 1860, there were sixteen places with populations of more than 50,000, containing 50 percent of urban inhabitants. In 1920, in the first census when more than half of the American population was urban, 144 cities exceeded 50,000 persons (with 25 cities of more than 250,000 inhabitants), and they had 60 percent of city dwellers. The three largest cities with populations of more than one million each (New York, Chicago, Philadelphia) together had 19 percent of America's urbanites. In 1990, with three fourths of the population being urban, 555 places had populations of more than 50,000, 64 had more than 250,000, and 8 places had more than one million. The share of the urban population in those cities with populations of 50,000 and more was still only 62 percent of the urban population. However, the urban size hierarchy did not become distorted, as it has in some developing nations. That is, large cities did not grow such that medium and smaller urban places became unimportant. There were 213 places with populations of 5,000–50,000 in 1860, accounting for 41 percent of the urban inhabitants. In 1920 this number had risen to a total of 1,323 places, with 32 percent of the urban population. These places numbered 4,929 in 1990, with 41 percent of urban dwellers (see Tables Aa684–715). And this urban growth had powerful economic linkages. Considerable industrial output of the period 1865–1920 was devoted to providing infrastructure and materials for housing, transportation, and public services for this massive population shift to towns and cities. Iron and steel for sewer and water pipes, bridges, rails, structural pieces, and nails; concrete, stone, brick, and asphalt for roads and structures; cut timber; transport equipment; glass; and so forth were demanded in huge quantities to build the cities.

Migration patterns, both internal and international, did affect regional population growth rates and shares. In 1790 the North and South had about 50 percent of the total population. But differential migration, and not differential natural increase, began to drive the share in the North upward as slower population growth in New England was balanced by more rapid growth in New York, Pennsylvania, and later the Midwest. The Northeast and Midwest together accounted for 56 percent of the nation's inhabitants in 1830 and 62 percent in 1860, compared to 35 percent for the South at the latter date. This demographic shift alone was instrumental in the political crisis leading up to the Civil War, as southern representation in the Congress slowly ebbed.

The regional preference of migrants from abroad, once they had landed in the United States, was strongly in favor of the Northeast and Midwest and not the South. For instance, in 1860 a mere 5.6 percent of the South's white population was foreign-born, whereas the proportion was 19.3 percent in the Northeast and 17.4 percent in the Midwest. For 1910, the proportion of foreign-born living in the Northeast had risen to 26.2 percent. It had fallen to 3.5 percent in the South and held at 17.4 percent in the Midwest. Further, at the latter date, only 6.1 percent of Southern whites had one or both parents foreign-born, whereas 30.1 percent of white residents of the Northeast were first-generation native-born. This had profound political implications in terms of regional growth both before and after the Civil War. Not only did it change the Congressional balance of power, but it also limited the labor supply in the South for industrial and agricultural development throughout the nineteenth and early twentieth centuries. The Southern share slipped even further, to 31 percent in 1920, whereas the Northeast and Midwest held about steady at 60 percent. These population realignments were both cause and effect of rapid industrial growth in the postbellum era, as many of the rural migrants and most of the later immigrants were destined for northern cities. By the late twentieth century, however, the South had managed to raise its share in the national total to 34 percent, whereas the Northeast and Midwest had slipped to 44 percent, as the movement to the Sunbelt became a dominant feature of the American migration story.

The census also makes it possible to study aspects such as marriage and household structure. Census-based measures of nuptiality, such as the median age at first marriage and the singulate mean age at first marriage, are among the most revealing indexes of marriage and changes in marriage age over time (see Tables Ae481–506). Similarly, the census offers data on marriage incidence (for example, percentage single or married by age) and also information about widowhood and divorce. The census began to ask a question about the marital status of individuals in 1880 and began publishing tabulations of this in 1890.[10] These data permit the study of long-term trends in marriage (see Table Aa614–683). From this and other information, we find that the age at marriage for both men and women was rising from the late nineteenth century (and likely from about 1800) until it reached a peak in 1900

(Haines 1996). Even at that point, however, the American age at marriage and the proportion of persons still single at ages 45–54 were low by the standards of Western and Northern Europe, the origins of much of the American white population (Coale and Watkins 1986). Thereafter, marriage age declined slowly until about 1970, after which there was a sharp rise in age at first marriage for both men and women, and whites and nonwhites. Similarly, divorce rates have been on the rise in recent decades (see Table Ae507–513).

Household composition and its change over time are also discernible from census documents. It is especially important to have the Integrated Public Use Microdata Series (IPUMS) because the published documents often gave very little detail on this topic.[11] Newer theoretical and methodological perspectives have changed our views on how household and family structure should be analyzed. This is dealt with in Chapter Ae, on family and household composition.

The Hispanic Population

Estimating the size and composition of the Hispanic population or those of its subgroups prior to 1970 is difficult because the census rarely collected information other than birthplace variables that could allow such measurement.[12] In 1930, for example, the Census attempted to classify the Mexicans as a "race," but this effort officially added nothing to previous information using birthplace variables: enumerators were to record as Mexican "all persons born in Mexico, or having parents born in Mexico, who are not definitely white, Negro." The race clause actually restricted Mexican descent because persons whose appearances met enumerators' standards for white, black, or other race categories were not to be recorded as Mexican, and variations in enumerator policies leave the meaning of published results unclear. Additional variables have sometimes offered the means for identifying Hispanics, especially the intermittent recording of language characteristics beginning with the 1910 Census.

In 1950 the Census first experimented with a more general Hispanic indicator, one that identified individuals beyond the second generation. The census recorded white persons with Spanish *surnames* in Arizona, California, Colorado, New Mexico, and Texas. Undoubtedly designed to focus on Mexican-origin Hispanics who lived in the Southwest, the surname variable did not provide any information outside the region, nor did it distinguish among subgroups. Although the Census Bureau knew that the Spanish surname lists omitted certain persons who were Hispanic, the opportunity to reach beyond the second generation encouraged the use of such indicators. More extensive lists were employed in the 1960, 1970, and 1980 Censuses, still limited to the five Southwestern states.

The 1970 Census marked an important change. In that year, two new efforts were made to classify the population. The first relied on a combination of variables that located "Spanish Americans," including Spanish as a mother tongue, Puerto Rican family background in three Northeastern states, and Spanish surname in

---

[10] The IPUMS file for the 1880 Census has allowed us to make use of these untabulated data.

[11] See the Guide to the Millennial Edition for information on IPUMS.

[12] The material in this section is based on the work of Brian Gratton and Myron Gutmann (2000), who have made the estimates of the Hispanic population of the United States dating back to 1850. For Hispanic fertility, mortality, and infant mortality, see Chapter Ab, on vital statistics.

five Southwestern states. The second effort asked respondents to identify themselves in four "Spanish origin" categories (Mexican, Cuban, Puerto Rican, others). Although the 1970 origin question did not produce satisfactory results, self-identification of Hispanic origin became increasingly detailed and accurate in the 1980 and 1990 Censuses and has allowed estimates of the Hispanic population and its subgroups to be made with much greater confidence (Bean and Tienda 1987).

For years prior to 1980, the estimates provided in Table Aa2189–2215 make use of individual-level census sample data from the IPUMS project (Ruggles and Hall 1999).[13] Hispanic origin is determined by place of birth, parents' place of birth, and Spanish surname; these data are available for all census years considered and produce consistent estimates; the methodology for these estimates can be found in Gratton and Gutmann (2000). Other variables, such as language spoken, are available in certain censuses and lead to more complete and accurate estimates; these are not, however, consistent in their coverage from year to year. For 1980 and 1990, the estimates reported use the results published in the census, based on the Hispanic identity question asked of all persons. The foreign-born estimates, however, are based on a question only asked of a sample of census respondents and the totals vary from the complete count data.

A notable feature of the Hispanic population of the United States has been its rapid growth, from high rates of both natural increase and net in-migration. In recent years there has also been some significant ethnic reidentification of the existing resident population toward Hispanic identity, which has further enhanced the apparent growth rate. The percentage share of the Hispanic population has grown from an estimated 0.6 percent in 1850 to 0.9 percent in 1910 to 4.4 percent in 1970 and 8.7 percent in 1990 (Gratton and Gutmann 2000, Table 2). In short, the Hispanic population has been growing faster than the American population as a whole over the past 150 years.[14] The largest groups in the Hispanic population have been of Mexican origin (58.5 percent in 2000) and Puerto Rican origin (9.6 percent in 2000), although the shares have been shifting toward other national-origin groups. The Mexican-origin population has retained its dominant share, however, based on continued large net in-migration.

The sex ratio of the Hispanic population slightly favors males (103.8 males per 100 females), well above the overall sex ratio for the native-born non-Hispanic population (95.1 in 1990). Differential net immigration of males accounts for this, as it did for other foreign-born groups historically. The Hispanic population is overwhelmingly urban (92 percent in 1990), and a majority (63 percent in 1990) was born in the United States. Most Hispanics are concentrated in a few states in the West and Southwest (California, Texas, Arizona, New Mexico) and the Northeast (New York, New Jersey) and in Florida; however, a large number are now found in other areas (such as Illinois) and indeed they are distributing themselves throughout the nation where work can be found. A slight majority of Hispanics identify themselves as white (51.7 percent in 1990), but only 3.4 percent self-identify as black. Many (42.7 percent) classed themselves as "other race" in 1990, likely because of issues of mixed racial categories.

---

[13] See the Guide to the Millennial Edition for information on IPUMS.

[14] The 2000 Census indicated that the Hispanic population was about 35.3 and nearly equal in size to the black population at about 35.7 million.

Conclusions

This essay has focused on the evolution of the American population over the period 1790 to the present. The discussion has perforce covered the nature of demographic data and measurement and the size, growth, and structure of the population. It has also dealt with urbanization with some treatment of both internal and international migration. The relatively rapid population growth over this period (averaging about 2 percent per year) was driven largely by high (though declining) birth rates and moderate levels of mortality; however, immigration was also significant. About three fourths of the overall growth was the result of natural increase and about one fourth was attributable to net in-migration. More than 34 million persons entered the United States between the 1790s and 1920 and an additional 29.4 million between 1921 and the present.

The population has experienced substantial changes over these two centuries. The population has aged significantly, moving from a median age of about 16 in 1800 to about 35 in 2000. Accompanying this has been a shift from a majority male to a majority female population. In 1800, about 51 percent of the population was male, but in 2000 it was only about 49 percent. American men and women now marry at the oldest ages in history, and an increasing number have experienced divorce.

Further, Americans have moved from predominantly rural and small-town life (5 percent of the population was urban in 1790) to become a nation of urban dwellers and suburbanites. At least three fourths of the population was living in officially designated urban places in 1990. Americans are extremely mobile, and migration has been a fact of life. In recent years, about 15–20 percent of the population has moved to a different house each year. Within the nation's boundaries, there has been significant movement from east to west, following the frontier (until the late nineteenth century); from rural to urban areas; and, later, from central cities to suburbs, from south to north, and ultimately to the Sunbelt. These developments have been responsible for changing the United States from a rural to an urban nation and then to a suburban nation.

The population of the United States shifted from the original areas of settlement on the Atlantic coast to the center of the nation and later to the Pacific and Mountain states. Migration from abroad, first from Western and Northern Europe and then, after about 1890, from Central, Eastern, and Southern Europe, occurred in waves in response to upswings in business cycles and the expansion of economic opportunities. This flood of immigrants both directly augmented population growth rates and indirectly acted to raise birth rates before immigration was severely restricted in the 1920s by legislation and subsequently by the Great Depression. However, it left an indelible stamp on the economy, society, and culture.

References

Anderson, Margo J. 1988. *The American Census: A Social History.* Yale University Press.

Bean, Frank D., and Marta Tienda. 1987. *The Hispanic Population of the United States.* National Committee for Research on the 1980 Census. Russell Sage.

Coale, Ansley J., and Norfleet W. Rives Jr. 1973. "A Statistical Reconstruction of the Black Population of the United States, 1880–1970: Estimates of True Numbers by Age and Sex." *Population Index* 39 (1): 3–36.

Coale, Ansley J., and Susan Cotts Watkins, editors. 1986. *The Decline of Fertility in Europe.* Princeton University Press.

Coale, Ansley J., and Melvin Zelnik. 1963. *New Estimates of Fertility and Population in the United States: A Study of Annual White Births from 1855 to 1960 and of Completeness of Enumeration in the Censuses from 1880 to 1960*. Princeton University Press.

Condran, Gretchen A., and Eileen Crimmins. 1979. "A Description and Evaluation of Mortality Data in the Federal Census: 1850–1900." *Historical Methods* 12 (1): 1–23.

Dubester, Henry J. 1948. *State Censuses: An Annotated Bibliography of Censuses of Population Taken after the Year 1790 by States and Territories of the United States*. U.S. Government Printing Office.

Edmonston, Barry, and Charles Schultze, editors. 1995. *Modernizing the U.S. Census*. National Academy Press.

Gratton, Brian, and Myron P. Gutmann. 2000. "Hispanics in the United States, 1850–1990: Estimates of Population Size and National Origin." *Historical Methods* 33 (2): 137–53.

Haines, Michael R. 1996. "Long Term Marriage Patterns in the United States from Colonial Times to the Present." *The History of the Family: An International Quarterly* 1 (1): 15–39.

Haines, Michael R. 1998. "Estimated Life Tables for the United States, 1850–1910." *Historical Methods* 31 (4): 149–69.

Haines, Michael R. 2003. "Ethnic Differences in Demographic Behavior in the United States: Has There Been Convergence?" *Historical Methods* 36 (4): 155–92.

Haines, Michael R., and Samuel H. Preston. 1997. "The Use of the Census to Estimate Childhood Mortality: Comparisons from the 1900 and 1910 United States Census Public Use Samples." *Historical Methods* 30 (2): 77–96.

Haines, Michael R., and Richard H. Steckel, editors. 2000. *A Population History of North America*. Cambridge University Press.

Parkerson, Donald H. 1991. "Comments on the Underenumeration of the U.S. Census, 1850–1880." *Social Science History* 15 (4): 509–15.

Robinson, J. G., B. Ahmed, et al. 1993. "Estimation of Population Coverage in the 1990 U.S. Census Based on Demographic Analysis." *Journal of the American Statistical Association* 88 (42): 1061–79.

Ruggles, Steven, and Patricia Kelly Hall, editors. 1999. "IPUMS: Integrated Public Use Microdata Series." *Historical Methods* 32 (3): 102–58.

Shryock, Henry S., Jacob S. Siegel, and Associates. 1971. *The Methods and Materials of Demography*. U.S. Government Printing Office.

Siegel, Jacob S. 1974. "Estimates of Coverage of the Population by Sex, Race, and Age in the 1970 Census." *Demography* 11 (1): 1–23.

Social Science History. 1991. 15 (4).

U.S. Census Bureau. 1909. *A Century of Population Growth from the First Census of the United States to the Twelfth, 1790–1900*. U.S. Government Printing Office.

U.S. Census Bureau. 1979. *Twenty Censuses: Population and Housing Questions, 1790–1980*. U.S. Government Printing Office.

U.S. Census Bureau. 2002. *Measuring America: The Decennial Censuses from 1790 to 2000*. U.S. Government Printing Office.

Weiss, Thomas. 1992. "U.S. Labor Force Estimates and Economic Growth, 1800–1860." In Robert E. Gallman and John Joseph Wallis, editors. *American Economic Growth and Standards of Living before the Civil War*. University of Chicago Press.

AREA AND POPULATION

Michael R. Haines

TABLE Aa1–5   Population, population density, and land area: 1790–2000   [Original counts for census dates]

Contributed by Michael R. Haines

Date	Land area	Population		Population increase from previous census	
	Aa1	Aa2	Aa3	Aa4	Aa5
	Square miles	Total	Per square mile	Number	Percentage
		Number	Number	Number	Percent
Aug 2, 1790	864,746	3,929,625	4.5	—	—
Aug 4, 1800	864,746	5,308,483	6.1	1,378,858	35.1
Aug 6, 1810	1,681,828	7,239,881	4.3	1,931,398	36.4
Aug 7, 1820	1,749,462	9,638,453	5.5	2,398,572	33.1
June 1, 1830	1,749,462	12,866,020	7.4	3,227,567	33.5
June 1, 1840	1,749,462	17,069,453	9.8	4,203,433	32.7
June 1, 1850	2,940,042	23,191,876	7.9	6,122,423	35.9
June 1, 1860	2,969,640	31,443,321	10.6	8,251,445	35.6
June 1, 1870 [1]	2,969,640	38,558,371	13.0	7,115,050	22.6
June 1, 1880	2,969,640	50,155,783	16.9	11,597,412	30.1
June 1, 1890	2,969,640	62,947,714	21.2	12,791,931	25.5
June 1, 1900	2,969,834	75,994,575	25.6	13,046,861	20.7
Apr 15, 1910	2,969,565	91,972,266	31.0	15,977,691	21.0
Jan 1, 1920	2,969,451	105,710,620	35.6	13,738,354	14.9
Apr 1, 1930	2,977,128	122,775,046	41.2	17,064,426	16.1
Apr 1, 1940	2,977,128	131,669,275	44.2	8,894,229	7.2
Apr 1, 1950	2,974,726	150,697,361	50.7	19,028,086	14.5
Apr 1, 1960	3,540,911	179,323,175	50.6	28,625,814	19.0
Apr 1, 1970 [2]	3,540,023	203,211,926	57.4	23,888,751	13.3
Apr 1, 1980 [3]	3,539,289	226,545,805	64.0	23,333,879	11.5
Apr 1, 1990 [4]	3,536,278	248,709,873	70.3	22,164,068	9.8
Apr 1, 2000 [5]	3,537,438	281,422,426	79.6	32,704,124	13.2

[1] Population later revised to include adjustment of 1,260,078 for underenumeration in the Southern states. Revised census count is 39,818,449.

[2] Figures corrected after the 1970 final reports were issued.

[3] Total population has been revised since the 1980 Census publications. Data by age, race, Hispanic origin, and sex have not been revised.

[4] Includes count question resolution corrections processed through December 1997 and does not include adjustments for census coverage errors.

[5] The revised April 1, 2000, Census count includes count question resolution corrections processed through May 2002 and does not include adjustments for census coverage errors.

Sources

1790: U.S. Bureau of the Census, *A Century of Population Growth from the First Census of the United States to the Twelfth, 1790–1900* (1909), p. 49. 1800–2000: U.S. Bureau of the Census, *Statistical Abstract of the United States* (2002), Table 1, p. 8.

Documentation

The principal source of population data is the decennial census of population, a house-by-house enumeration made by the Bureau of the Census. In accordance with a constitutional provision for a decennial canvass of the population, the first census enumeration was made in 1790. The primary reason for the census of population, as set forth in the Constitution, is to provide a basis for the apportionment of members of the House of Representatives among the states. Until 1902, the census organization was temporary. It was assembled before each decennial census and disbanded after the work was finished. In 1902, the Bureau of the Census was established as a permanent agency of the federal government, charged with the responsibility for conducting the decennial census and compiling statistics on other subjects as needed. The Bureau of the Census now also provides population data based on surveys and estimates in addition to making the comprehensive decennial census enumeration.

In accordance with census practice dating back to 1790, each person is counted as an inhabitant of his or her usual place of residence or usual place of abode – that is, the place where the person lives and sleeps most of the time. This place is not necessarily the same as that person's legal residence, voting residence, or domicile, although in the vast majority of cases the use of these different bases of classification would produce identical results. Indians living in Indian Territory or on reservations were not included in the population count until 1890, and in earlier censuses large tracts of unorganized and sparsely settled territory were not covered by enumerators. Territories were routinely included in the census as part of the United States, with the exception of Alaska and Hawai'i. They were territories through 1950 and were first included in the United States in the 1960 Census.

Through 1930, the data presented are based on complete counts. Since 1940, some of the data are based on sample tabulations (ranging from $3\frac{1}{3}$ percent to 25 percent), as indicated in the text for particular tables in this chapter. In the 1990 and 2000 Censuses, one in every six households received the long form or sample questionnaire in most of the country. In minor civil divisions estimated to have fewer than 2,500 inhabitants, 50 percent of the households received the sample questionnaire to improve the reliability of the sample estimates. Exact agreement is not to be expected among the various samples, nor between them and the complete census count; however, the sample data may be used with confidence where large numbers are involved, and may be assumed to indicate patterns and relationships where small numbers are involved. Detailed statements regarding the sampling errors are given in the original sources.

Some tables in this chapter present data from the Current Population Survey (CPS), conducted monthly by the Bureau of the Census since 1947. Originally, the survey covered a representative sample of approximately 21,000 interviewed households in areas throughout the United States. This sample was increased to approximately 35,000 in May 1956, and to approximately 50,000 in January 1967. It is currently taken in 754 areas comprising 2,121

TABLE Aa1–5   Population, population density, and land area: 1790–2000   [Original counts for census dates]
  Continued

counties, independent cities, and minor civil divisions, with coverage in every state and the District of Columbia. It is subject to sampling error. At present, about 50,000 occupied households are eligible for interview each month. Of these, about 4–5 percent are, for a variety of reasons, unavailable for the interview. Estimates of population characteristics based on the CPS will not agree with counts based on the census, because the CPS and the census use different sampling procedures, different samples, and different procedures for racial groups, the Hispanic population, and other topics. Caution should also be used when comparing estimates from various years of the CPS because of the periodic introduction of changes in the CPS. In particular, beginning in January 1994, a number of changes were introduced in the CPS that affect comparability with all previous years. These changes include the results of a major redesign of the survey questionnaire and collection methodology and the introduction of 1990 Census population controls, adjusted for the estimated undercount. This change in population controls had relatively little impact on derived measures such as means, medians, and percentage distributions, but did have a significant impact on levels.

Many tabulation errors appear in the census publications of 1790–1840. The data for these censuses were adjusted by county and race, and the revised figures were published in the 1870 Census. Revised figures for the U.S. population by sex and race for 1790–1840 were published in the 1910 Census. Official revisions by age have not been made, and thus the 1790–1840 age data in this chapter for most race-sex groups add to totals that differ slightly from the revised figures for race-sex groups.

The Bureau of the Census has always been concerned about the degree of completeness of enumeration in the decennial censuses, although public interest in census coverage and statistical techniques for estimating coverage were quite limited prior to 1950. Discussions of coverage in earlier censuses were limited mostly to qualitative statements.

The quantitative evaluation of census coverage can be done at the individual and aggregate levels. At the individual level, the approaches include re-interview (for example, postenumeration surveys) and record checks (for example, matching of census records and birth records). At the aggregate level, the approaches include demographic analysis (that is, the use of data on births, deaths, and migration, and of life tables, expected sex ratios, etc.) and the use of aggregated data from administrative records (for example, comparing the enrollment in Medicare with the census count of the aged population).

In 1950 the postenumeration survey (PES) was thought to be a satisfactory method of determining net census underenumeration. The number missed in the 1950 Census was estimated at about 2.1 million, or 1.4 percent, with corresponding estimates of 1.6 percent for 1940 and 0.7 percent for 1930. However, demographers now generally believe that PESs tend to understate census omissions because persons missed in a census have an above-average probability of being missed in a PES. Evaluations of census coverage now rely heavily on demographic analysis (DA). An analysis of coverage conducted in conjunction with the 1970 Census shows the following estimates and revisions of net census underenumeration: 5.3 million, or 2.5 percent, for 1970; 5.1 million, or 2.7 percent, for 1960; 5.1 million, or 3.3 percent, for 1950. Results from the evaluation program for the 1990 Census indicate that the overall national undercount was between 1 and 2 percent. The estimate from the PES was 1.6 percent, and the estimate from DA was 1.8 percent. Both the PES and the DA estimates showed disproportionately large undercounts among some demographic groups. For instance, the PES

estimates of undercount for blacks (4.4 percent), Hispanics (5.0 percent), and American Indians (4.5 percent) were significantly higher than the estimated undercount of the non-Hispanic white population (0.7 percent). Historical DA estimates demonstrate that the overall undercount rate in the census has declined over the past fifty years from an estimated 5.4 percent in 1940 to an estimated 1.8 percent in 1990. Yet the estimated undercount of blacks has remained disproportionately high. Analyses of census coverage are subject to revision on the basis of additional information and research.

Although the earlier censuses no doubt were characterized by under-enumeration, the amounts generally are difficult to determine. One technique is the comparison of rates of change with respect to consistency and reasonableness. On this basis, it is believed that figures for the South show unreasonably low rates of increase for the decade 1860–1870 and abnormally high rates of increase for 1870–1880. The differences are so great that it appears evident that the enumeration of 1870 in this area was seriously incomplete, undoubtedly as a result of the unsettled conditions of the Reconstruction period. For the portion of the United States outside the South, the rate of increase for 1860–1870 was about the same as that for 1870–1880. Therefore, the number initially enumerated in 1870 for the South was revised upward, as indicated in the footnotes.

For analyses of the completeness of census enumerations from 1880 to 1970, see the following sources: Ansley J. Coale and Melvin Zelnik, *New Estimates of Fertility and Population in the United States* (Princeton University Press, 1963); Jacob S. Siegel, "Estimates of Coverage of the Population by Sex, Race, and Age in the 1970 Census," *Demography* 11 (1) (1974): 1–23; Ansley J. Coale and Norfleet W. Rives Jr., "A Statistical Reconstruction of the Black Population of the United States, 1880–1970: Estimates of True Numbers by Age and Sex, Birth Rates, and Total Fertility," *Population Index* 39 (1) (1973): 3–36.

Series Aa1. The land area of the United States excludes inland water (gross area, including inland water, is available in the source). In 1990 the figure also excludes the Great Lakes and coastal waters. Figures for each census year represent the conterminous area under the jurisdiction of the United States, with the addition of Alaska and Hawai'i beginning in 1960. In some years, large areas are included that were not yet settled or covered by the census. Area figures prior to 1940 have been adjusted to bring them into agreement with remeasurements made in 1940. For area measurements, see the text for Table Cf8–64. For a further discussion of areas covered by the censuses, see *U.S. Census of Population: 1940*, Areas of the United States: 1940; and *U.S. Census of Population: 1950*, volume I, p. xi.

Series Aa2. The figures are for the resident population of the United States as enumerated at each census and initially reported by the Census Bureau. Armed forces abroad are excluded. For 1870 and 1970–1990, revisions to the initial count were subsequently released (see the footnotes). For a discussion of the revision of the 1870 Census of Population, see *U.S. Census of Population: 1890*, volume I, pp. xi–xii.

Series Aa3. The population density is defined as series Aa2 divided by series Aa1.

Series Aa4–5. Series Aa4 gives the increase in the population enumerated over the preceding census, which is not always exactly ten years, and series Aa5 expresses this change as a percentage.

TABLE Aa6–8   Population: 1790–2000   [Annual estimates]

Contributed by Michael R. Haines and Richard Sutch

Year	Total, including armed forces overseas	Resident population		Year	Total, including armed forces overseas	Resident population	
		Total	Civilian			Total	Civilian
	Aa6	Aa7	Aa8		Aa6	Aa7	Aa8
	Thousand	Thousand	Thousand		Thousand	Thousand	Thousand
1790	—	3,929	—	1850	—	23,261	—
1791	—	4,048	—	1851	—	24,095	—
1792	—	4,172	—	1852	—	24,999	—
1793	—	4,299	—	1853	—	25,911	—
1794	—	4,429	—	1854	—	26,856	—
1795	—	4,563	—	1855	—	27,727	—
1796	—	4,701	—	1856	—	28,497	—
1797	—	4,844	—	1857	—	29,298	—
1798	—	4,990	—	1858	—	30,068	—
1799	—	5,141	—	1859	—	30,780	—
1800	—	5,297	—	1860	—	31,513	—
1801	—	5,461	—	1861	—	32,215	—
1802	—	5,632	—	1862	—	32,889	—
1803	—	5,809	—	1863	—	33,607	—
1804	—	5,991	—	1864	—	34,376	—
1805	—	6,180	—	1865	—	35,182	—
1806	—	6,379	—	1866	—	36,052	—
1807	—	6,588	—	1867	—	36,970	—
1808	—	6,797	—	1868	—	37,885	—
1809	—	7,009	—	1869	—	38,870	—
1810	—	7,224	—	1870	—	39,905	—
1811	—	7,436	—	1871	—	41,010	—
1812	—	7,651	—	1872	—	42,066	—
1813	—	7,867	—	1873	—	43,225	—
1814	—	8,085	—	1874	—	44,429	—
1815	—	8,308	—	1875	—	45,492	—
1816	—	8,540	—	1876	—	46,459	—
1817	—	8,790	—	1877	—	47,400	—
1818	—	9,057	—	1878	—	48,319	—
1819	—	9,335	—	1879	—	49,264	—
1820	—	9,618	—	1880	—	50,262	—
1821	—	9,899	—	1881	—	51,466	—
1822	—	10,189	—	1882	—	52,893	—
1823	—	10,488	—	1883	—	54,435	—
1824	—	10,795	—	1884	—	55,826	—
1825	—	11,115	—	1885	—	57,128	—
1826	—	11,449	—	1886	—	58,258	—
1827	—	11,797	—	1887	—	59,357	—
1828	—	12,158	—	1888	—	60,614	—
1829	—	12,525	—	1889	—	61,893	—
1830	—	12,901	—	1890	—	63,056	—
1831	—	13,277	—	1891	—	64,432	—
1832	—	13,676	—	1892	—	65,920	—
1833	—	14,086	—	1893	—	67,470	—
1834	—	14,504	—	1894	—	68,910	—
1835	—	14,917	—	1895	—	70,076	—
1836	—	15,340	—	1896	—	71,188	—
1837	—	15,790	—	1897	—	72,441	—
1838	—	16,224	—	1898	—	73,600	—
1839	—	16,656	—	1899	—	74,793	—
1840	—	17,120	—	1900	—	76,094	—
1841	—	17,612	—	1901	—	77,584	—
1842	—	18,124	—	1902	—	79,163	—
1843	—	18,641	—	1903	—	80,632	—
1844	—	19,157	—	1904	—	82,166	—
1845	—	19,708	—	1905	—	83,822	—
1846	—	20,313	—	1906	—	85,450	—
1847	—	20,987	—	1907	—	87,008	—
1848	—	21,706	—	1908	—	88,710	—
1849	—	22,464	—	1909	—	90,490	—

TABLE Aa6–8   Population: 1790–2000   [Annual estimates]   *Continued*

Year	Total, including armed forces overseas	Resident population		Year	Total, including armed forces overseas	Resident population	
		Total	Civilian			Total	Civilian
	Aa6	Aa7	Aa8		Aa6	Aa7	Aa8
	Thousand	Thousand	Thousand		Thousand	Thousand	Thousand
1910	—	92,407	—	1960	180,671	179,979	178,140
1911	—	93,863	—	1961	183,691	182,992	181,143
1912	—	95,335	—	1962	186,538	185,771	183,677
1913	—	97,225	—	1963	189,242	188,483	186,493
1914	—	99,111	—	1964	191,889	191,141	189,141
1915	—	100,546	—	1965	194,303	193,526	191,605
1916	—	101,961	—	1966	196,560	195,576	193,420
1917	103,414	103,268	102,796	1967	198,712	197,457	195,264
1918	104,550	103,208	101,488	1968	200,706	199,399	197,113
1919	105,063	104,514	104,158	1969	202,677	201,385	199,145
1920	—	106,461	—	1970	205,052	203,984	201,895
1921	—	108,538	—	1971	207,661	206,827	204,866
1922	—	110,049	—	1972	209,896	209,284	207,511
1923	—	111,947	—	1973	211,909	211,357	209,600
1924	—	114,109	—	1974	213,854	213,342	211,636
1925	—	115,829	—	1975	215,973	215,465	213,789
1926	—	117,397	—	1976	218,035	217,563	215,894
1927	—	119,035	—	1977	220,239	219,760	218,106
1928	—	120,509	—	1978	222,585	222,095	220,467
1929	—	121,767	—	1979	225,055	224,567	222,969
1930	123,188	123,077	122,923	1980	227,726	227,225	225,621
1931	124,149	124,040	123,686	1981	229,966	229,466	227,818
1932	124,949	124,840	124,694	1982	232,188	231,664	229,995
1933	125,690	125,579	125,436	1983	234,307	233,792	232,097
1934	126,485	126,374	126,228	1984	236,348	235,825	234,110
1935	127,362	127,250	127,099	1985	238,466	237,924	236,219
1936	128,181	128,053	127,879	1986	240,651	240,133	238,412
1937	128,961	128,825	128,639	1987	242,804	242,289	240,550
1938	129,969	129,825	129,635	1988	245,021	244,499	242,817
1939	131,028	130,880	130,683	1989	247,342	246,819	245,131
1940	132,122	131,954	131,658	1990	250,132	249,623	247,983
1941	133,402	133,121	131,595	1991	253,493	252,981	251,370
1942	134,860	133,920	130,942	1992	256,894	256,514	254,929
1943	136,739	134,245	127,499	1993	260,255	259,919	258,446
1944	138,397	132,885	126,708	1994	263,436	263,126	261,714
1945	139,928	132,481	127,573	1995	266,557	266,278	264,927
1946	141,389	140,054	138,385	1996	269,667	269,394	268,108
1947	144,126	143,446	142,566	1997	272,912	272,647	271,394
1948	146,631	146,093	145,168	1998	276,115	275,854	274,633
1949	149,188	148,665	147,578	1999	279,295	279,040	277,841
1950	152,271	151,868	150,790	2000	282,339	282,125	280,939
1951	154,878	153,982	151,599				
1952	157,553	156,393	153,892				
1953	160,184	158,956	156,595				
1954	163,026	161,884	159,695				
1955	165,931	165,069	162,967				
1956	168,903	168,088	166,055				
1957	171,984	171,187	169,110				
1958	174,882	174,149	172,226				
1959	177,830	177,135	175,277				

Sources

1790–1899: see Table Aa9–14. 1900–1989: U.S. Bureau of the Census, Current Population Reports, series P-25, numbers 499, 1045, and 1126. 1990–2000: U.S. Bureau of the Census, *Statistical Abstract of the United States, 2002*, Table 2.

Documentation

Estimates for 1790–1899 are based on the methodology described in the text for Table Aa9–14. Estimates for the 1900–1919 period are based on interpolation techniques applied to census age data. Estimates for subsequent years are based on census data and information on births, deaths, and international migration. Annual national population estimates start with decennial census data as benchmarks and add annual population component of change data. Component of change data are obtained from various agencies: births and deaths (National Center for Health Statistics), legal immigrants (Immigration and Naturalization Service), refugees (Office of Refugee Resettlement), net movement between Puerto Rico and the U.S. mainland (U.S. Census Bureau's International Programs Center), and movement of military and civilian citizens abroad (Department of Defense and Office of Personnel Management). Emigration and net undocumented immigration are projected based on research using census data.

The estimates are as of July 1, and thus figures for the resident population for census years differ from decennial census populations.

(continued)

TABLE Aa6–8   Population: 1790–2000   [Annual estimates]   *Continued*

Alaska and Hawai'i are included beginning in 1950.

Estimates subsequent to the 1990 Census reflect the final results of the 2000 Census.

Population estimates are published in the P-25 series of Current Population Reports and as Population Paper Listings (PPLs). These estimates are generally consistent with official decennial census figures and do not reflect the amount of estimated census underenumeration. The estimates by race,

however, have been modified and are not necessarily comparable to the census race categories.

For a discussion of the methodology, see the following: for 1940–1949 and 1950–1959, Bureau of the Census, Current Population Reports, series P-25, number 311, pp. 1–3; for 1960–1969, number 519, pp. 1–11; for 1970–1979, number 917, pp. 1–7; for 1980–1989, number 1095, pp. v–xxi, and Frederick W. Hollmann, Lisa B. Kuzmekus, et al., "U.S. Population by Age, Sex, Race, and Hispanic Origin: 1990 to 1997," U.S. Bureau of the Census PPL-91 and appendixes.

TABLE Aa9–14   National population and the demographic components of change: 1790–2000   [Annual estimates]

Contributed by Michael R. Haines and Richard Sutch

	Population (July 1)	Population change (July 1 to June 30 of subsequent year)				
		Net change	Births	Deaths	Net immigration	Error of closure
	Aa9	Aa10	Aa11	Aa12	Aa13	Aa14
Year	Thousand	Thousand	Thousand	Thousand	Thousand	Thousand
1790	3,929	119	—	—	4	—
1791	4,048	124	—	—	5	—
1792	4,172	127	—	—	4	—
1793	4,299	130	—	—	4	—
1794	4,429	134	—	—	4	—
1795	4,563	138	—	—	4	—
1796	4,701	142	—	—	4	—
1797	4,844	146	—	—	4	—
1798	4,990	151	—	—	4	—
1799	5,141	156	—	—	4	—
1800	5,297	164	290	138	12	0
1801	5,461	171	299	141	14	0
1802	5,632	176	308	145	14	0
1803	5,809	182	317	149	15	0
1804	5,991	189	327	153	16	0
1805	6,180	199	337	157	19	0
1806	6,379	209	347	163	25	0
1807	6,588	209	358	170	21	0
1808	6,797	211	369	176	19	0
1809	7,009	215	380	183	18	0
1810	7,224	212	391	192	13	0
1811	7,436	215	401	198	12	0
1812	7,651	216	411	204	9	0
1813	7,867	219	421	210	8	0
1814	8,085	223	431	216	8	0
1815	8,308	231	441	222	12	0
1816	8,540	251	452	224	23	0
1817	8,790	267	463	226	30	0
1818	9,057	278	476	229	32	0
1819	9,335	283	488	233	27	0
1820	9,618	281	501	242	21	0
1821	9,899	290	516	247	21	0
1822	10,189	299	532	252	19	0
1823	10,488	308	548	258	18	0
1824	10,795	320	564	263	19	0
1825	11,115	334	581	269	22	0
1826	11,449	348	599	281	30	0
1827	11,797	360	618	294	37	0
1828	12,158	367	637	308	38	0
1829	12,525	376	657	322	41	0
1830	12,901	376	677	355	54	0
1831	13,277	399	692	366	73	0
1832	13,676	410	708	376	78	0
1833	14,086	418	724	387	80	0
1834	14,504	414	740	398	71	0

TABLE Aa9–14   National population and the demographic components of change: 1790–2000   [Annual estimates]   Continued

	Population (July 1)	Population change (July 1 to June 30 of subsequent year)				Error of closure
		Net change	Births	Deaths	Net immigration	
	Aa9	Aa10	Aa11	Aa12	Aa13	Aa14
Year	Thousand	Thousand	Thousand	Thousand	Thousand	Thousand
1835	14,917	423	756	409	75	0
1836	15,340	450	772	417	95	0
1837	15,790	433	789	425	69	0
1838	16,224	432	805	432	60	0
1839	16,656	465	820	440	84	0
1840	17,120	492	837	437	91	0
1841	17,612	512	852	442	102	0
1842	18,124	517	867	448	97	0
1843	18,641	516	883	453	86	0
1844	19,157	551	897	458	112	0
1845	19,708	606	913	462	155	0
1846	20,313	674	930	469	212	0
1847	20,987	719	950	477	245	0
1848	21,706	758	972	485	272	0
1849	22,464	796	994	494	297	0
1850	23,261	835	1,017	513	330	0
1851	24,095	903	1,050	532	385	0
1852	24,999	913	1,086	553	379	0
1853	25,911	944	1,122	574	396	0
1854	26,856	871	1,160	597	308	0
1855	27,727	770	1,193	618	194	0
1856	28,497	802	1,223	640	220	0
1857	29,298	770	1,253	664	181	0
1858	30,068	711	1,282	688	117	0
1859	30,780	733	1,308	710	135	0
1860	31,513	702	1,335	756	123	0
1861	32,215	675	1,362	779	92	0
1862	32,889	717	1,388	805	134	0
1863	33,607	769	1,415	831	185	0
1864	34,376	806	1,445	859	221	0
1865	35,182	870	1,476	889	283	0
1866	36,052	918	1,510	909	317	0
1867	36,970	914	1,545	928	297	0
1868	37,885	985	1,581	948	353	0
1869	38,870	1,036	1,619	970	387	0
1870	39,905	1,105	1,658	920	366	0
1871	41,010	1,056	1,701	945	300	0
1872	42,066	1,158	1,742	962	379	0
1873	43,225	1,204	1,786	984	402	0
1874	44,429	1,063	1,832	1,014	245	0
1875	45,492	967	1,872	1,076	133	38
1876	46,459	941	1,893	1,088	100	36
1877	47,400	919	1,912	1,099	71	35
1878	48,319	945	1,929	1,110	89	37
1879	49,264	997	1,946	1,120	132	39
1880	50,262	1,205	1,965	1,131	424	−53
1881	51,466	1,426	1,991	1,146	645	−64
1882	52,893	1,542	2,024	1,166	752	−68
1883	54,435	1,391	2,061	1,187	579	−62
1884	55,826	1,302	2,090	1,204	474	−58
1885	57,128	1,130	2,115	1,219	284	−50
1886	58,258	1,098	2,129	1,232	250	−49
1887	59,357	1,257	2,141	1,244	416	−56
1888	60,614	1,279	2,157	1,259	438	−57
1889	61,893	1,162	2,173	1,274	315	−52
1890	63,056	1,377	2,183	1,286	328	152
1891	64,432	1,488	2,200	1,302	426	164
1892	65,920	1,550	2,219	1,319	480	170
1893	67,470	1,441	2,239	1,337	381	158
1894	68,910	1,166	2,253	1,353	137	129

(continued)

TABLE Aa9–14   National population and the demographic components of change: 1790–2000   [Annual estimates]   *Continued*

		Population change (July 1 to June 30 of subsequent year)				
	Population (July 1)	Net change	Births	Deaths	Net immigration	Error of closure
	Aa9	Aa10	Aa11	Aa12	Aa13	Aa14
Year	Thousand	Thousand	Thousand	Thousand	Thousand	Thousand
1895	70,076	1,113	2,258	1,362	95	122
1896	71,188	1,253	2,279	1,368	205	137
1897	72,441	1,159	2,303	1,377	105	128
1898	73,600	1,194	2,325	1,383	121	131
1899	74,793	1,301	2,346	1,389	201	143
1900	76,094	1,490	2,371	1,397	385	131
1901	77,584	1,579	2,401	1,407	288	297
1902	79,163	1,469	2,433	1,419	386	69
1903	80,632	1,534	2,461	1,428	532	−31
1904	82,166	1,656	2,491	1,437	530	72
1905	83,822	1,628	2,523	1,448	662	−109
1906	85,450	1,558	2,547	1,462	697	−224
1907	87,008	1,702	2,568	1,475	767	−158
1908	88,710	1,780	2,592	1,490	210	468
1909	90,490	1,917	2,617	1,506	544	262
1910	92,407	1,456	2,645	1,523	818	−484
1911	93,863	1,472	2,659	1,533	512	−166
1912	95,335	1,890	2,673	1,542	402	357
1913	97,225	1,886	2,697	1,557	815	−69
1914	99,111	1,435	2,720	1,572	769	−482
1915	100,546	1,415	2,730	1,579	50	214
1916	101,961	1,453	2,730	1,554	126	151
1917	103,414	1,136	2,730	1,528	217	−283
1918	104,550	513	2,721	1,497	19	−730
1919	105,063	1,398	2,695	1,455	21	137
1920	106,461	2,077	2,691	1,426	194	618
1921	108,538	1,511	2,703	1,403	552	−341
1922	110,049	1,898	2,699	1,372	87	484
1923	111,947	2,162	2,704	1,344	472	330
1924	114,109	1,720	2,713	1,317	662	−338
1925	115,829	1,568	2,710	1,283	232	−91
1926	117,397	1,638	2,688	1,302	268	−16
1927	119,035	1,474	2,666	1,321	284	−155
1928	120,509	1,258	2,639	1,339	227	−269
1929	121,767	1,310	2,605	1,354	227	−168
1930	123,077	963	2,572	1,370	174	−413
1931	124,040	800	2,530	1,382	−10	−338
1932	124,840	739	2,483	1,392	−113	−239
1933	125,579	795	2,435	1,401	−93	−146
1934	126,374	876	2,387	1,412	−13	−86
1935	127,250	803	2,340	1,423	−9	−105
1936	128,053	772	2,407	1,430	−2	−203
1937	128,825	1,000	2,474	1,437	8	−45
1938	129,825	1,055	2,547	1,447	30	−75
1939	130,880	1,714	2,621	1,457	66	484
1940	132,594	1,300	2,631	1,425	72	22
1941	133,894	1,467	2,789	1,389	45	22
1942	135,361	1,889	3,168	1,451	129	43
1943	137,250	1,666	2,989	1,520	170	27
1944	138,916	1,552	2,937	1,639	231	23
1945	140,468	1,468	2,873	1,443	88	−50
1946	141,936	2,762	3,948	1,429	217	26
1947	144,698	2,510	3,658	1,457	263	46
1948	147,208	2,559	3,660	1,440	313	26
1949	149,767	2,504	3,638	1,465	308	23
1950	152,271	2,607	3,771	1,485	306	15
1951	154,878	2,675	3,859	1,510	323	3
1952	157,553	2,631	3,951	1,530	211	−1
1953	160,184	2,842	4,045	1,487	285	−1
1954	163,026	2,905	4,119	1,505	294	−3

TABLE Aa9–14   National population and the demographic components of change: 1790–2000   [Annual estimates]   *Continued*

Year	Population (July 1)	Population change (July 1 to June 30 of subsequent year)				
		Net change	Births	Deaths	Net immigration	Error of closure
	Aa9	Aa10	Aa11	Aa12	Aa13	Aa14
	Thousand	Thousand	Thousand	Thousand	Thousand	Thousand
1955	165,931	2,972	4,167	1,570	376	−1
1956	168,903	3,081	4,312	1,581	350	0
1957	171,984	2,898	4,313	1,683	269	−1
1958	174,882	2,948	4,298	1,647	298	−1
1959	177,830	2,841	4,279	1,697	270	−11
1960	180,671	3,020	4,350	1,683	385	−32
1961	183,691	2,847	4,259	1,744	365	−33
1962	186,538	2,704	4,185	1,804	356	−33
1963	189,242	2,647	4,119	1,782	341	−31
1964	191,889	2,414	3,940	1,821	323	−28
1965	194,303	2,257	3,716	1,851	425	−33
1966	196,560	2,152	3,608	1,852	429	−33
1967	198,712	1,994	3,520	1,911	420	−35
1968	200,706	1,971	3,583	1,946	383	−49
1969	202,677	2,375	3,676	1,930	505	124
1970	205,052	2,609	3,713	1,927	395	428
1971	207,661	2,235	3,393	1,947	343	446
1972	209,896	2,013	3,195	1,973	339	452
1973	211,909	1,945	3,111	1,951	329	456
1974	213,854	2,119	3,181	1,925	402	461
1975	215,973	2,062	3,127	1,909	376	468
1976	218,035	2,204	3,274	1,882	335	477
1977	220,239	2,346	3,304	1,932	496	478
1978	222,585	2,470	3,415	1,902	486	471
1979	225,055	2,170	3,563	1,955	750	−188
1980	227,225	2,241	3,619	1,998	757	−137
1981	229,466	2,198	3,666	1,968	683	−183
1982	231,664	2,128	3,681	1,999	597	−151
1983	233,792	2,033	3,614	2,033	621	−169
1984	235,825	2,099	3,731	2,069	613	−176
1985	237,924	2,209	3,766	2,091	673	−139
1986	240,133	2,156	3,782	2,105	639	−160
1987	242,289	2,210	3,849	2,164	714	−189
1988	244,499	2,320	3,948	2,162	664	−130
1989	246,819	2,804	4,114	2,155	687	158
1990	249,623	3,358	4,133	2,139	694	670
1991	252,981	3,533	4,106	2,180	951	656
1992	256,514	3,405	4,027	2,226	952	652
1993	259,919	3,207	3,971	2,283	856	663
1994	263,126	3,152	3,927	2,284	834	675
1995	266,278	3,116	3,882	2,318	861	691
1996	269,394	3,253	3,892	2,322	985	698
1997	272,647	3,207	3,906	2,320	879	742
1998	275,854	3,186	3,938	2,345	849	744
1999	279,040	3,085	4,020	2,380	858	587
2000	282,125	—	—	—	—	—

Sources

Series Aa9. 1790–1899: figures for years ending in zero are reported in U.S. Bureau of the Census, *Historical Statistics of the United States: Colonial Times to 1957* (1960), p. 7; for all other years, figures are calculated as described below. 1900–1989: U.S. Census Bureau, "Historical National Population Estimates," Population Estimates Program, April 11, 2000, downloaded from U.S. Census Bureau's Internet site. 1990–2000: U.S. Census Bureau, *Statistical Abstract of the United States, 2002,* Table 2, p. 8.

Series Aa10. 1790–1899: calculated as described below. 1900–1999: calculated from series Aa9.

Series Aa11–13. 1800–1939: calculated as described below. 1940–1980: Frederick W. Hollmann, U.S. Bureau of the Census, "United States Population Estimates, by Age, Sex, Race, and Hispanic Origin: 1980 to 1988,"

Current Population Reports, series P-25, number 1045, Table 6, p. 80. 1981–1989, births and deaths: U.S. Census Bureau, "1981 to 1989 Intercensal Estimates of the Resident Population of States, and Year-to-Year Components of Change" (release date: September 1995), downloaded from the Internet site of the Census Bureau, August 2003. 1981–1987, net migration: same source used for 1940–1980. 1988–1989, net migration: calculated as the average of adjacent calendar-year estimates from U.S. Bureau of the Census, *Statistical Abstract of the United States: 2001,* Table 4, p. 9. 1990–1998: U.S. Census Bureau, "State Population Estimates and Demographic Components of Population Change: Annual Time Series, April 1, 1990 to July 1, 1999," Table ST-99-7 (release date: December 29, 1999), downloaded from the Internet site of the Census Bureau, August 2003. 1999, births and deaths: *National Vital Statistics Reports,* using monthly data for 1999 and 2000. 1999, net migration: same source used for 1988–1989.

(continued)

TABLE Aa9–14   National population and the demographic components of change: 1790–2000   [Annual estimates]
    Continued

Series Aa14. Calculated as a residual: series Aa10, minus series Aa11, plus series Aa12, minus series Aa13.

Documentation

This table is based on the basic demographic identity that links the population count in one year to that of the next. If all elements were measured perfectly, then the population on July 1 of any year, plus the number of births over the coming year, less the number of deaths, plus net immigration (immigration minus emigration) should equal the population on July 1 of the following year. Because all the elements are not measured perfectly, there is a residual element called the "error of closure." Generally speaking, there is no way to distribute the error of closure over the ten years between census dates except arbitrarily. Before 1875, the error of closure is included in the series for deaths.

Alaska and Hawai'i and armed forces abroad are included beginning in 1940, accounting for 472,000 of the increase between 1939 and 1940 and thus the large error of closure given for 1939.

Series Aa9 Population

The national population is the resident population of the United States, including the armed forces. For 1917–1919 and for 1940–1979, the national population includes armed forces abroad.

For nondecennial years during the 1790–1899 period and for 2000, figures are computed as the sum of the population and the net change (series Aa10) shown for the previous year.

For the years 1790–1900, the figures for the census years (ending in zero) coincide with the July 1 estimates of the resident population reported in the source and thus differ from decennial census population figures given in Table Aa1–5.

Series Aa10 Net Change

The net change in population from July 1 of the year indicated to June 30 of the subsequent year is distributed among births, deaths, net immigration, and the error of closure, a residual balancing item that accumulates the errors in the other series.

For 1790–1899, figures are the population on July 1 multiplied by the estimated rate of natural increase, plus net immigration (series Aa13), plus an adjustment factor described below. The rate of natural increase has been estimated by Michael R. Haines for decade-long periods. These are reported in Michael R. Haines and Richard H. Steckel, editors, *A Population History of North America* (Cambridge University Press, 2000), Table 8.3, p. 315.

Haines's estimates of the rate of natural increase were centered on the years ending in five, and annual estimates were made by linear interpolation between these benchmarks. The estimated series was then adjusted by a multiplication factor to ensure that cumulated changes between decennial census years summed to the official census figure indicated by series Aa9 at the end of each decade.

Haines has subsequently corrected and revised his figures for the decades spanning 1820–1870. The revised figures are as follows:

Decade	Rate of natural increase per 1,000 midperiod population per year
1820–1830	26.82
1830–1840	23.50
1840–1850	22.37
1850–1860	20.61
1860–1870	17.36

Series Aa11 Births

For years ending in zero during the period 1800–1874, births were calculated as series Aa9 multiplied by the crude birth rate of the population for that year. The crude birth rate was estimated as the weighted average of the white crude birth rate and the black crude birth rate. The weights were based on the white and black populations at each census as reported in Table Aa145–184. Estimates of white crude birth rates are obtained from the following: for 1800–1850, Warren S. Thompson and P. K. Whelpton, *Population Trends in the United States* (McGraw Hill, 1933), p. 263; and for 1860, Ansley J. Coale and Melvin Zelnik, *New Estimates of Fertility and Population in the United States* (Princeton University Press, 1963), p. 21. Estimates of the black birth rate are obtained from Peter D. McClelland and Richard J. Zeckhauser, *Demographic Dimensions of the New Republic: American Interregional Migration, Vital Statistics, and Manumissions, 1800–1860* (Cambridge University Press, 1982), Table D-27, p. 186. The crude birth rates for the total population were linearly interpolated between census dates.

For the period 1875–1939, a similar procedure was employed; however, the total crude birth rate was taken from Haines and Steckel (2000), Table 8.3, p. 315. Linear interpolations were used to span the years between those ending in five.

Series Aa12, Deaths

For 1800–1874, deaths were estimated as a residual: births plus net immigration minus net change. For 1875–1939, deaths were estimated by applying an estimate of the crude death rate to the national population in series Aa9. The crude death rates were obtained from Haines and Steckel (2000), Table 8.3, p. 315, and were linearly interpolated between years ending in five.

Series Aa13, Net Immigration

For 1790–1939, figures are based on the following series, with averaging used to convert from a calendar-year to a July 1–June 30 basis: 1790–1799, series Ad19; 1800–1849, series Ad16; 1850–1858, series Ad20; 1859–1869, series Ad1–2; and 1870–1939, series Ad22.

TABLE Aa15–21   Components of population growth, by decade: 1790–2000

Contributed by Michael R. Haines

Decade	Average mid-decade population	Rate of total increase	Crude birth rate	Crude death rate	Rate of natural increase	Rate of net migration	
						Rate	As a percentage of rate of total increase
	Aa15	Aa16	Aa17	Aa18	Aa19	Aa20	Aa21
	Thousand	Per 1,000	Per 1,000	Per 1,000	Per 1,000	Per 1,000	Percent
1790–1800	4,520	30.08	—	—	26.49	3.59	11.9
1800–1810	6,132	31.04	—	—	26.85	4.19	13.5
1810–1820	8,276	28.62	—	—	24.70	3.92	13.7
1820–1830	11,031	28.88	—	—	26.82	2.06	7.1
1830–1840	14,685	28.27	—	—	23.50	4.77	16.9
1840–1850	19,686	30.65	—	—	22.37	8.28	27.0
1850–1860	26,721	30.44	—	—	20.61	9.83	32.3
1860–1870	35,156	23.62	—	—	17.36	6.26	26.5
1870–1880	44,414	23.08	41.16	23.66	17.50	5.58	24.2
1880–1890	55,853	22.72	37.03	21.34	15.69	7.03	30.9
1890–1900	68,876	18.97	32.22	19.44	12.78	6.19	32.6
1900–1910	83,822	19.42	29.83	17.26	12.57	6.85	35.3
1910–1920	100,546	14.16	26.85	15.26	11.59	2.57	18.1
1920–1930	115,829	14.50	23.15	11.62	11.53	2.97	20.5
1930–1940	127,250	7.34	19.49	11.12	8.37	−1.03	−14.0
1940–1950	139,928	13.94	23.08	10.48	12.60	1.34	9.6
1950–1960	165,931	17.10	24.78	9.46	15.32	1.78	10.4
1960–1970	194,303	12.66	20.05	9.43	10.62	2.04	16.1
1970–1980	215,973	10.27	15.41	8.94	6.47	3.80	37.0
1980–1990	238,466	9.91	15.84	8.69	7.15	2.76	27.9
1990–2000	266,557	11.14	14.90	8.54	6.36	4.78	42.9

Sources

Estimated population. 1790–1900: taken as the mid-decade point from the unadjusted census populations, using exponential interpolation; population figures are taken from U.S. Census Bureau, *Statistical Abstract of the United States, 2001,* Table 1. 1900–1980: July 1 populations from U.S. Census Bureau, "Historical Population Estimates: July 1, 1900 to July 1, 1999," downloaded from the Census Bureau's Internet site. 1980–2000: July 1 populations taken from U.S. Bureau of the Census, *Statistical Abstract of the United States, 2002,* Table 2.

Births. 1870–1899: Simon Kuznets, "Long Swings in the Growth of Population and Related Economic Variables," *Proceedings of the American Philosophical Society* 102 (1) (1958): 25–52. 1900–1998: estimated from series Aa11. 1999–2000: U.S. Bureau of the Census, *Statistical Abstract of the United States, 2002,* Table 66.

Deaths. 1870–1899: same source used for births. 1900–1932: estimated from the crude death rate for the Death Registration Area (from Table Ab929–951) and the annual estimated population for the United States (source provided above). 1933–1998: series Ab17. 1999–2000: same source used for births.

Net migration. 1790–1820: Henry A. Gemery, "European Emigration to North America: Numbers and Quasi-Numbers," *Perspectives in American History,* new series 1 (1984): 283–342, supplemented by estimates of slave

imports from Philip Curtin, *The Atlantic Slave Trade: A Census* (University of Wisconsin Press, 1969). 1820–1860: Peter D. McClelland and Richard J. Zeckhauser, *Demographic Dimensions of the New Republic: American Interregional Migration, Vital Statistics and Manumissions, 1800–1860* (Cambridge University Press, 1982), also supplemented by estimates of slave imports from Curtin, *Atlantic Slave Trade,* Table 67. 1860–1870: series Ad90. 1870–2000: calculated as described below.

Documentation

Series Aa16. Calculated as the exponential population growth rate over the decade.

Series Aa17–18. For 1900–2000, birth and death totals for decades were adjusted for census dates. The crude birth rate is live births per 1,000 mid-period population per year. The crude death rate is deaths per 1,000 midperiod population per year.

Series Aa19. The rate of natural increase is equal to the crude birth rate minus the crude death rate (for 1870–2000). Prior to 1870, the rate of natural increase is calculated as the difference between the rate of total increase and the rate of net migration.

Series Aa20. For 1790–1860, the rate of net migration was calculated directly from net migrants. Gross migrants were used for 1860–1870. For 1870–2000, the rate of net migration is equal to the rate of total increase minus the rate of natural increase.

TABLE Aa22–35 Selected population characteristics – median age, sex ratio, annual growth rate, and number, by race, urban residence, and nativity: 1790–2000

Contributed by Michael R. Haines

	Total		By race						Urban		Foreign-born		Median age	Sex ratio: males per 100 females
	Number	Percentage per annum growth since previous census	White		Black		Other						Aa34 [1]	Aa35 [1]
			Number	Percentage	Number	Percentage	Number	Percentage	Number	Percentage	Number	Percentage		
Year	Aa22	Aa23	Aa24	Aa25	Aa26	Aa27	Aa28	Aa29	Aa30	Aa31	Aa32	Aa33	Years	Per 100
	Number	Percent	Number	Percent	Number	Percent	Number	Percent	Number	Percent	Number	Percent		
1790	3,929,625	—	3,172,444	80.7	757,181	19.3	—	—	201,655	5.1	—	—	—	103.8
1800	5,308,483	3.0	4,306,446	81.1	1,002,037	18.9	—	—	322,371	6.1	—	—	16.0	104.0
1810	7,239,881	3.1	5,862,073	81.0	1,377,808	19.0	—	—	525,459	7.3	—	—	16.0	104.0
1820	9,638,453	2.9	7,866,797	81.6	1,771,656	18.4	—	—	693,255	7.2	—	—	16.7	103.3
1830	12,866,020	2.9	10,532,060	81.9	2,328,642	18.1	—	—	1,127,247	8.8	—	—	17.2	103.1
1840	17,069,453	2.8	14,189,705	83.1	2,873,648	16.8	—	—	1,845,055	10.8	—	—	17.8	103.7
1850	23,191,876	3.1	19,553,068	84.3	3,638,808	15.7	—	—	3,574,496	15.4	2,244,602	9.7	18.9	104.3
1860	31,443,321	3.0	26,922,537	85.6	4,441,830	14.1	78,954	0.3	6,216,518	19.8	4,138,697	13.2	19.4	104.7
1870	38,558,321	2.0	33,589,377	87.1	4,880,009	12.7	88,985	0.2	9,902,361	25.7	5,567,229	14.4	20.2	102.2
1880	50,155,783	2.6	43,402,970	86.5	6,580,793	13.1	172,020	0.3	14,129,735	28.2	6,679,943	13.3	20.9	103.6
1890	62,947,714	2.3	55,101,258	87.5	7,488,676	11.9	357,780	0.6	22,106,265	35.1	9,249,547	14.7	22.0	105.0
1900	75,994,575	1.9	66,809,196	87.9	8,833,994	11.6	351,385	0.5	30,214,832	39.8	10,341,276	13.6	22.9	104.4
1910	91,972,266	1.9	81,731,957	88.9	9,827,763	10.7	412,546	0.4	42,064,001	45.7	13,515,886	14.7	24.1	106.0
1920	105,710,620	1.4	94,820,915	89.7	10,463,131	9.9	426,574	0.4	54,253,282	51.3	13,920,692	13.2	25.3	104.0
1930	122,775,046	1.5	110,286,740	89.8	11,891,143	9.7	597,163	0.5	69,160,599	56.3	14,204,149	11.6	26.5	102.5
1940	131,669,275	0.7	118,214,870	89.8	12,865,518	9.8	588,887	0.4	74,705,338	56.7	11,594,896	8.8	29.0	100.7
1950	150,697,361	1.3	134,942,028	89.5	15,042,286	10.0	713,047	0.5	96,846,817	64.3	10,347,395	6.9	30.2	98.6
1960	179,323,175	1.7	158,831,732	88.6	18,871,831	10.5	1,619,612	0.9	125,268,750	69.9	9,738,091	5.4	29.5	97.1
1970	203,302,031	1.3	177,748,975	87.4	22,580,289	11.1	2,882,662	1.4	149,646,617	73.6	9,619,302	4.7	28.1	94.8
1980	226,542,199	1.1	188,371,622	83.2	26,495,025	11.7	11,679,158	5.2	167,050,992	73.7	14,079,906	6.2	30.0	94.5
1990	248,718,301	0.9	199,686,070	80.3	29,986,060	12.1	19,037,743	7.7	187,053,487	75.2	19,767,316	7.9	32.8	95.1
2000	281,421,906	1.2	216,930,975	77.1	36,419,434	12.9	28,071,497	10.0	222,360,539	79.0	28,379,000	10.4	35.3	96.3

[1] Through 1810, white population only.

Sources

1790–1990: Tables Aa1–5, Aa145–184, Aa599–613, Aa699–715, and Aa1896–1921.

2000: "American Fact Finder," available from the U.S. Census Bureau's Internet site. Foreign-born population: U.S. Bureau of the Census, *Statistical Abstract of the United States 2001*, Table 45.

Documentation

This table presents selected summary measures of data found in other tables within the chapter.

TABLE Aa36–92 Population, by region and urban–rural residence: 1790–1990

Contributed by Michael R. Haines

Total population

Year	United States	New England	Middle Atlantic	East North Central	West North Central	South Atlantic	East South Central	West South Central	Mountain	Pacific
	Aa36	Aa37	Aa38	Aa39	Aa40	Aa41	Aa42	Aa43	Aa44	Aa45
	Number	Number	Number	Number	Number	Number	Number	Number	Number	Number
1790	3,929,214	1,009,408	958,632	—	—	1,851,806	109,368	—	—	—
1830	12,860,702	1,954,717	3,587,664	1,470,018	140,455	3,645,752	1,815,969	246,127	—	—
1860	31,443,321	3,135,283	7,458,985	6,926,884	2,169,832	5,364,703	4,020,991	1,747,667	174,923	444,053
1890	62,979,766	4,700,749	12,706,220	13,478,305	8,932,112	8,857,922	6,429,154	4,740,983	1,213,935	1,920,386
1920	106,021,537	7,400,909	22,261,144	21,475,543	12,544,249	13,990,272	8,893,307	10,242,224	3,336,101	5,877,788
1950	151,325,798	9,314,453	30,163,533	30,399,368	14,061,394	21,182,335	11,477,181	14,537,572	5,074,998	15,114,964
1990	248,709,873	13,206,943	37,602,286	42,008,942	17,659,690	43,566,853	15,176,284	26,702,793	13,658,776	39,127,306

Urban population

Year	United States	New England	Middle Atlantic	East North Central	West North Central	South Atlantic	East South Central	West South Central	Mountain	Pacific
	Aa46	Aa47	Aa48	Aa49	Aa50	Aa51	Aa52	Aa53	Aa54	Aa55
	Number	Number	Number	Number	Number	Number	Number	Number	Number	Number
1790	201,655	76,188	83,309	—	—	42,158	—	—	—	—
1830	1,127,247	273,949	510,915	36,658	4,977	226,750	27,916	46,082	—	—
1860	6,216,518	1,148,489	2,638,848	973,459	289,783	614,671	236,755	215,368	17,620	81,525
1890	22,106,265	2,893,860	7,372,218	5,111,944	2,306,157	1,728,019	817,308	715,999	355,627	805,133
1920	54,253,282	5,620,384	16,783,474	13,050,086	4,725,880	4,336,482	1,994,207	2,969,366	1,217,988	3,555,415
1950	96,846,817	7,101,511	24,271,689	21,185,713	7,305,219	10,391,163	4,484,771	8,079,828	2,785,888	11,241,035
1990	187,053,487	9,829,175	30,262,562	31,073,858	11,700,338	30,231,280	8,530,551	19,894,436	10,881,341	34,649,946

Rural population

Year	United States	New England	Middle Atlantic	East North Central	West North Central	South Atlantic	East South Central	West South Central	Mountain	Pacific
	Aa56	Aa57	Aa58	Aa59	Aa60	Aa61	Aa62	Aa63	Aa64	Aa65
	Number	Number	Number	Number	Number	Number	Number	Number	Number	Number
1790	3,727,559	933,220	875,323	—	—	1,809,648	109,368	—	—	—
1830	11,733,455	1,680,768	3,076,749	1,433,360	135,478	3,419,002	1,788,053	200,045	—	—
1860	25,226,803	1,986,794	4,820,137	5,953,425	1,880,049	4,750,032	3,784,236	1,532,299	157,303	362,528
1890	40,873,501	1,806,889	5,334,002	8,366,361	6,625,955	7,129,903	5,611,846	4,024,984	858,308	1,115,253
1920	51,768,255	1,780,525	5,477,670	8,425,457	7,818,369	9,653,790	6,899,100	7,272,858	2,118,113	2,322,373
1950	54,478,981	2,212,942	5,891,844	9,213,655	6,756,175	10,791,172	6,992,410	6,457,744	2,289,110	3,873,929
1990	61,656,386	3,377,768	7,339,724	10,935,084	5,959,352	13,335,573	6,645,733	6,808,357	2,777,435	4,477,360

(continued)

TABLE Aa36-92   Population, by region and urban–rural residence: 1790–1990   Continued

Percentage of total population

Year	New England Aa66 Percent	Middle Atlantic Aa67 Percent	East North Central Aa68 Percent	West North Central Aa69 Percent	South Atlantic Aa70 Percent	East South Central Aa71 Percent	West South Central Aa72 Percent	Mountain Aa73 Percent	Pacific Aa74 Percent
1790	25.7	24.4	—	—	47.1	2.8	—	—	—
1830	15.2	27.9	11.4	1.1	28.3	14.1	1.9	—	—
1860	10.0	23.7	22.0	6.9	17.1	12.8	5.6	0.6	1.4
1890	7.5	20.2	21.4	14.2	14.1	10.2	7.5	1.9	3.0
1920	7.0	21.0	20.3	11.8	13.2	8.4	9.7	3.1	5.5
1950	6.2	19.9	20.1	9.3	14.0	7.6	9.6	3.4	10.0
1990	5.3	15.1	16.9	7.1	17.5	6.1	10.7	5.5	15.7

Percentage of urban population

Year	New England Aa75 Percent	Middle Atlantic Aa76 Percent	East North Central Aa77 Percent	West North Central Aa78 Percent	South Atlantic Aa79 Percent	East South Central Aa80 Percent	West South Central Aa81 Percent	Mountain Aa82 Percent	Pacific Aa83 Percent
1790	37.8	41.3	—	—	20.9	—	—	—	—
1830	24.3	45.3	3.3	0.4	20.1	2.5	4.1	—	—
1860	18.5	42.4	15.7	4.7	9.9	3.8	3.5	0.3	1.3
1890	13.1	33.3	23.1	10.4	7.8	3.7	3.2	1.6	3.6
1920	10.4	30.9	24.1	8.7	8.0	3.7	5.5	2.2	6.6
1950	7.3	25.1	21.9	7.5	10.7	4.6	8.3	2.9	11.6
1990	5.3	16.2	16.6	6.3	16.2	4.6	10.6	5.8	18.5

Percentage of rural population

Year	New England Aa84 Percent	Middle Atlantic Aa85 Percent	East North Central Aa86 Percent	West North Central Aa87 Percent	South Atlantic Aa88 Percent	East South Central Aa89 Percent	West South Central Aa90 Percent	Mountain Aa91 Percent	Pacific Aa92 Percent
1790	25.0	23.5	—	—	48.5	—	—	—	—
1830	14.3	26.2	12.2	1.2	29.1	15.2	1.7	—	—
1860	7.9	19.1	23.6	7.5	18.8	15.0	6.1	0.6	1.4
1890	4.4	13.1	20.5	16.2	17.4	13.7	9.8	2.1	2.7
1920	3.4	10.6	16.3	15.1	18.6	13.3	14.0	4.1	4.5
1950	4.1	10.8	16.9	12.4	19.8	12.8	11.9	4.2	7.1
1990	5.5	11.9	17.7	9.7	21.6	10.8	11.0	4.5	7.3

(continued)

Source

U.S. Bureau of the Census, *U.S. Census of Population: 1990*, 1990 CPH-2-1, Tables 16 and 23.

Documentation

On the composition of the census regions, see Appendix 2.

TABLE Aa93–109 Population – United States and outlying areas: 1880–1990

Contributed by Michael R. Haines and Sumner J. La Croix

Year	Total Aa93	United States proper Aa94	Abroad Aa95	Total Aa96	Alaska Aa97	Hawai'i Aa98	Philippines Aa99	Puerto Rico Aa100	Guam Aa101	American Samoa Aa102	Canal Zone Aa103	Virgin Islands Aa104	Northern Mariana Islands Aa105	Federated States of Micronesia Aa106	Marshall Islands Aa107	Palau Aa108	Minor outlying islands Aa109
	Number	Number	Number	Number	Number	Number	Number	Number	Number	Number	Number	Number	Number	Number	Number	Number	Number
1880	50,189,209	50,155,783	—	33,426	33,426	—	—	—	—	—	—	—	—	—	—	—	—
1890	62,979,766	62,947,714	—	32,052	32,052	—	—	—	—	—	—	—	—	—	—	—	—
1900	84,371,985	75,994,575	91,219	8,375,910	63,592	54,001	7,189,719	953,243 [6]	9,676 [7]	5,679	—	—	—	—	—	—	—
1910	102,370,018	91,972,266	55,608	10,241,981	64,356	191,874	8,785,837	1,118,012	11,806	7,251 [8]	62,810 [8]	—	—	—	—	—	35
1920	118,107,855	105,710,620	117,238	12,435,762	55,036	255,881	10,754,765	1,299,809	13,275	8,056	22,858	26,051 [9]	—	—	—	—	31
1930	138,439,069	122,775,046	89,453	15,317,334	59,278 [5]	368,300	13,255,764	1,543,913	18,509	10,055	39,467	22,012	—	—	—	—	36
1940	150,622,754	131,669,275	118,933	18,816,911	72,524 [5]	422,770	16,338,365	1,869,255	22,290	12,908	51,827	24,889	—	—	—	—	2,083
1950	154,233,234	150,697,361	481,545 [3]	3,054,328	128,643	499,794	—	2,210,703	59,498	18,937	52,822	26,665	6,286	29,735	13,220	5,602	2,423
1960	183,285,009	179,323,175	1,374,421	2,587,540	—	—	—	2,349,544	67,044	20,051	42,122	32,099	8,290	39,289	13,928	9,344	5,829
1970	208,066,557	203,302,031 [2]	1,737,836	3,025,697	—	—	—	2,712,033	84,996	27,159	44,198	62,468	9,640	50,172	18,925	11,210	4,896
1980	231,106,727	226,545,805	995,546	3,564,293	—	—	—	3,196,520	105,979	32,297	—	96,569	16,780 [10]	73,159	30,873	12,116	—
1990	248,718,301	248,718,301	—[4]	4,004,438	—	—	—	3,522,037	133,152	46,773	—	101,809	43,345	96,000	46,200	15,122	—

Columns Aa101–Aa109 fall under the heading **Outlying areas**.

1 Figures 1950–1970 are from the following: for 1950, estimated civilian population as of June 30, 1950; for 1960, population as of the 1958 Census; and for 1970, the census taken in 1967.

2 Official 1970 resident population; see text for Table Aa1–5.

3 Estimate based on 20 percent sample of reports received.

4 Population enumerated at place of usual U.S. residence.

5 Census taken as of October 1 of preceding year.

6 Census taken November 10, 1899, by the Department of War.

7 Population as of 1901 Census.

8 Census taken February 1, 1912.

9 Census taken November 1, 1917, after purchase by the United States.

10 Northern Mariana Islands separate from the Pacific Island Trust Territory.

Sources

United States. U.S. Bureau of the Census, *Statistical Abstract of the United States, 2000*, Table 1.

Population abroad and other. U.S. Bureau of the Census, *U.S. Census of Population: 1990*, CP-1, parts 1, 53, 55, volume 1, *Characteristics of the Population: American Samoa*, Table 1; Guam, Table 1; Northern Mariana Islands, Table 1; Puerto Rico, Table 1.

Virgin Islands. *U.S. Census of Population and Housing: 1990, Population and Housing Unit Counts: Virgin Islands of the United States*, Table 1.

Federated States of Micronesia. Office of Planning and Statistics, Federated States of Micronesia, *1994 Census of Population and Housing* (Office of Planning and Statistics, 1996), Table 1.1.

Marshall Islands. *Republic of the Marshall Islands: Census of Population and Housing, 1988.* (Republic of the Marshall Islands, Office of Planning and Statistics, 1989), Table 3.1; and World Bank, *World Development Indicators, 2000* (World Bank, 2000).

Palau. Republic of Palau, *1990 Census Monograph: Population and Housing Characteristics, 1993* (1993), Tables 2.1 and 3.1; J. Useem, *Report on Yap and Palau* (U.S. Commercial Company, 1946); World Bank, *World Development Indicators, 2000*.

Canal Zone. U.S. Bureau of the Census, *1960 Census of Population*, volume 1, *Characteristics of the Population: Outlying Areas*, Table 5; U.S. Bureau of the Census, *1970 Census of Population*, volume 1, *Characteristics of the Population: Outlying Areas*.

Philippines. Philippines National Census and Statistics Office, *1970 Census of Population and Housing* (Philippine National Statistics Office, 1973), Table 1.

Documentation

Series Aa94 and Aa97–98. Alaska and Hawai'i are included with outlying areas through 1950 and with the United States thereafter. Although Alaska became a U.S. possession in 1867, the population was not enumerated in the 1870 Census.

Series Aa95. Excludes U.S. citizens temporarily abroad on private business, travel, and so forth.

Series Aa99. Estimates are derived by extrapolation and interpolation of Censuses of 1903 (7,635,426), 1918 (10,314,310), and 1939 (16,000,303). The Philippines became independent in 1946.

Series Aa101. In 1920, includes native men enlisted in U.S. Navy, but excludes U.S. naval station personnel, numbering 309. In 1930, includes population on U.S. naval reservations and persons on U.S. ships stationed at Guam (1,118). In 1940, includes 213 persons on U.S. naval vessels stationed at Guam.

Series Aa102. Through 1920, census does not include population of Swain's Island, annexed in 1925.

Series Aa109. Through 1930, figures are the population of Midway Islands. The 1940 figure includes Corn (1,523), Midway (437), Johnston (69), Canton and Enderbury (44), and Baker, Howland, and Jarvis (10) islands. The 1950 figure includes Corn (1,304), Midway (416), Wake (349), Canton (272), Johnston (46), and Swan (36) islands. The 1960 figure includes Midway (2,356), Corn (1,872), Wake (1,097), Canton (320), Johnston (156), and Swan (28) islands. The 1960 figure includes Midway (2,220), Wake (1,647), Johnston (1,007), and Swan (22) islands.

SEX, AGE, RACE, AND MARITAL STATUS

Michael R. Haines

TABLE Aa110–124   Population, by race and sex: 1900–1997   [Annual estimates][1]

Contributed by Michael R. Haines

	All races			White		
	Total	Males	Females	Total	Males	Females
	Aa110	Aa111	Aa112	Aa113	Aa114	Aa115
Year	Number	Number	Number	Number	Number	Number
1900	76,094,000	38,867,000	37,227,000	66,900,000	34,249,000	32,651,000
1901	77,584,000	39,649,000	37,935,000	68,267,000	34,971,000	33,296,000
1902	79,163,000	40,483,000	38,680,000	69,722,000	35,745,000	33,977,000
1903	80,632,000	41,262,000	39,370,000	71,084,000	36,471,000	34,613,000
1904	82,166,000	42,089,000	40,077,000	72,520,000	37,249,000	35,271,000
1905	83,822,000	42,965,000	40,857,000	74,059,000	38,072,000	35,987,000
1906	85,450,000	43,841,000	41,609,000	75,583,000	38,890,000	36,693,000
1907	87,008,000	44,682,000	42,326,000	77,055,000	39,683,000	37,372,000
1908	88,710,000	45,594,000	43,116,000	78,658,000	40,542,000	38,116,000
1909	90,490,000	46,545,000	43,945,000	80,339,000	41,438,000	38,901,000
1910	92,407,000	47,554,000	44,853,000	82,137,000	42,385,000	39,752,000
1911	93,863,000	48,290,000	45,573,000	83,524,000	43,088,000	40,436,000
1912	95,335,000	49,025,000	46,310,000	84,928,000	43,786,000	41,142,000
1913	97,225,000	49,957,000	47,268,000	86,705,000	44,663,000	42,042,000
1914	99,111,000	50,883,000	48,228,000	88,480,000	45,532,000	42,948,000
1915	100,546,000	51,573,000	48,973,000	89,848,000	46,188,000	43,660,000
1916	101,961,000 [2]	52,234,000 [3]	49,727,000	91,196,000	46,819,000	44,377,000
1917	103,268,000 [2]	52,788,000 [3]	50,480,000	92,435,000	47,339,000	45,096,000
1918	103,208,000 [2]	51,974,000 [3]	51,234,000	92,352,000	46,540,000	45,812,000
1919	104,514,000	53,103,000	51,411,000	93,684,000	47,672,000	46,012,000
1920	106,461,000	54,291,000	52,170,000	95,510,000	48,787,000	46,723,000
1921	108,538,000	55,292,000	53,246,000	97,416,000	49,710,000	47,706,000
1922	110,049,000	55,886,000	54,163,000	98,768,000	50,228,000	48,540,000
1923	111,947,000	56,861,000	55,086,000	100,510,000	51,131,000	49,379,000
1924	114,109,000	57,985,000	56,124,000	102,512,000	52,177,000	50,335,000
1925	115,829,000	58,813,000	57,016,000	104,061,000	52,931,000	51,130,000
1926	117,397,000	59,588,000	57,809,000	105,468,000	53,628,000	51,840,000
1927	119,035,000	60,397,000	58,638,000	106,941,000	54,358,000	52,583,000
1928	120,509,000	61,101,000	59,408,000	108,244,000	54,982,000	53,262,000
1929	121,767,000	61,680,000	60,087,000	109,383,000	55,509,000	53,874,000
1930	123,076,741	62,296,517	60,780,224	110,558,880	56,069,079	54,489,801
1931	124,039,648	62,725,503	61,314,145	111,433,404	56,462,405	54,970,999
1932	124,840,471	63,070,137	61,770,334	112,154,442	56,775,715	55,378,727
1933	125,578,763	63,384,009	62,194,754	112,815,249	57,059,471	55,755,778
1934	126,373,773	63,726,196	62,647,577	113,527,128	57,369,149	56,157,979
1935	127,250,232	64,109,888	63,140,344	114,309,177	57,714,338	56,594,839
1936	128,053,180	64,459,383	63,593,797	115,022,229	58,026,634	56,995,595
1937	128,824,829	64,789,797	64,035,032	115,706,360	58,322,024	57,384,336
1938	129,824,939	65,235,361	64,589,578	116,591,855	58,718,342	57,873,513
1939	130,879,718	65,713,339	65,166,379	117,524,368	59,142,657	58,381,711
1940	132,122,446	66,352,363	65,770,083	118,628,858	59,718,338	58,910,520
1941	133,402,471	66,920,133	66,482,338	119,731,465	60,196,094	59,535,371
1942	134,859,553	67,596,729	67,262,824	120,991,519	60,774,953	60,216,566
1943	136,739,353	68,545,741	68,193,612	122,605,238	61,567,825	61,037,413
1944	138,397,345	69,377,719	69,019,626	124,009,212	62,249,895	61,759,317
1945	139,928,165	70,035,073	69,893,092	125,266,471	62,748,059	62,518,412
1946	141,388,566	70,631,171	70,757,395	126,564,527	63,287,081	63,277,446
1947	144,126,071	71,945,892	72,180,179	129,059,434	64,507,124	64,552,310
1948	146,631,302	73,129,684	73,501,618	131,308,208	65,582,129	65,726,079
1949	149,188,130	74,335,435	74,852,695	133,598,298	66,677,722	66,920,576

Notes appear at end of table

TABLE Aa110–124 Population, by race and sex: 1900–1997 [Annual estimates] *Continued*

	All races			White		
	Total	Males	Females	Total	Males	Females
	Aa110	Aa111	Aa112	Aa113	Aa114	Aa115
Year	Number	Number	Number	Number	Number	Number
1950	152,271,417	75,849,012	76,422,405	135,983,517	67,848,105	68,135,412
1951	154,877,889	77,101,263	77,776,626	138,220,962	68,924,398	69,296,564
1952	157,552,740	78,372,190	79,180,550	140,526,418	70,023,125	70,503,293
1953	160,184,192	79,614,310	80,569,882	142,772,988	71,083,397	71,689,591
1954	163,025,854	80,972,704	82,053,150	145,193,083	72,241,638	72,951,445
1955	165,931,202	82,363,638	83,567,564	147,652,501	73,419,797	74,232,704
1956	168,903,031	83,779,505	85,123,526	150,163,163	74,616,342	75,546,821
1957	171,984,130	85,248,426	86,735,704	152,768,656	75,859,479	76,909,177
1958	174,881,904	86,605,105	88,276,799	155,199,538	76,996,151	78,203,387
1959	177,829,628	87,995,434	89,834,194	157,654,929	78,153,703	79,501,226
1960	180,671,158	89,319,511	91,351,647	160,022,673	79,256,987	80,765,686
1961	183,691,481	90,739,919	92,951,562	162,533,035	80,441,245	82,091,790
1962	186,537,737	92,066,119	94,471,618	164,884,753	81,538,592	83,346,161
1963	189,241,798	93,302,933	95,938,865	167,104,323	82,552,723	84,551,600
1964	191,888,791	94,517,752	97,371,039	169,256,724	83,539,369	85,717,355
1965	194,302,963	95,608,501	98,694,462	171,204,758	84,417,662	86,787,096
1966	196,560,338	96,619,711	99,940,627	172,997,665	85,217,766	87,779,899
1967	198,712,056	97,563,882	101,148,174	174,695,114	85,960,615	88,734,499
1968	200,706,052	98,426,257	102,279,795	176,245,903	86,630,989	89,614,914
1969	202,676,946	99,286,946	103,390,000	177,781,859	87,303,138	90,478,721
1970	205,052,174	100,353,876	104,698,298	179,644,033	88,138,613	91,505,420
1971	207,660,677	101,567,006	106,093,671	181,663,094	89,080,570	92,582,524
1972	209,896,021	102,590,732	107,305,289	183,325,614	89,843,389	93,482,225
1973	211,908,788	103,506,451	108,402,337	184,781,915	90,506,843	94,275,072
1974	213,853,928	104,391,110	109,462,818	186,169,616	91,137,841	95,031,775
1975	215,973,199	105,365,965	110,607,234	187,628,887	91,806,171	95,822,716
1976	218,035,164	106,308,604	111,726,560	189,074,304	92,466,252	96,608,052
1977	220,239,425	107,334,548	112,904,877	190,648,946	93,202,287	97,446,659
1978	222,584,545	108,423,580	114,160,965	192,334,700	93,985,772	98,348,928
1979	225,055,487	109,583,961	115,471,526	194,097,556	94,817,729	99,279,827
1980	227,726,463	110,859,060	116,867,403	195,555,548	95,510,072	100,045,476
1981	229,966,237	111,955,857	118,010,380	197,002,810	96,225,291	100,777,519
1982	232,187,835	113,052,446	119,135,389	198,424,512	96,936,901	101,487,611
1983	234,307,207	114,112,509	120,194,698	199,800,063	97,637,647	102,162,416
1984	236,348,292	115,142,137	121,206,155	201,096,244	98,306,482	102,789,762
1985	238,466,283	116,217,185	122,249,098	202,435,866	99,003,838	103,432,028
1986	240,650,755	117,324,112	123,326,643	203,812,644	99,718,634	104,094,010
1987	242,803,533	118,415,937	124,387,596	205,149,981	100,414,883	104,735,098
1988	245,021,414	119,549,752	125,471,662	206,513,109	101,132,984	105,380,125
1989	247,341,697	120,739,045	126,602,652	207,918,890	101,874,830	106,044,060
1990	249,948,625	122,072,626	127,875,999	209,551,584	102,732,162	106,819,422
1991	252,635,924	123,446,851	129,189,073	211,341,387	103,675,807	107,665,580
1992	255,381,792	124,838,732	130,543,060	213,162,121	104,626,470	108,535,651
1993	258,089,466	126,208,697	131,880,769	214,962,030	105,565,963	109,396,067
1994	260,602,289	127,487,847	133,114,442	216,642,023	106,451,938	110,190,085
1995	263,039,337	128,743,203	134,296,134	218,272,152	107,325,622	110,946,530
1996	265,452,518	129,984,089	135,468,429	219,887,580	108,187,075	111,700,505
1997	267,900,896	131,246,804	136,654,092	221,528,318	109,065,506	112,462,812

(continued)

TABLE Aa110–124   Population, by race and sex: 1900–1997   [Annual estimates]   *Continued*

				Nonwhite					
				Black			Other nonwhite		
Year	Total	Males	Females	Total	Males	Females	Total	Males	Females
	Aa116	Aa117	Aa118	Aa119	Aa120	Aa121	Aa122	Aa123	Aa124
	Number	Number	Number	Number	Number	Number	Number	Number	Number
1900	9,194,000	4,618,000	4,576,000	—	—	—	—	—	—
1901	9,317,000	4,678,000	4,639,000	—	—	—	—	—	—
1902	9,441,000	4,738,000	4,703,000	—	—	—	—	—	—
1903	9,548,000	4,791,000	4,757,000	—	—	—	—	—	—
1904	9,646,000	4,840,000	4,806,000	—	—	—	—	—	—
1905	9,763,000	4,893,000	4,870,000	—	—	—	—	—	—
1906	9,867,000	4,951,000	4,916,000	—	—	—	—	—	—
1907	9,953,000	4,999,000	4,954,000	—	—	—	—	—	—
1908	10,052,000	5,052,000	5,000,000	—	—	—	—	—	—
1909	10,151,000	5,107,000	5,044,000	—	—	—	—	—	—
1910	10,270,000	5,169,000	5,101,000	—	—	—	—	—	—
1911	10,339,000	5,202,000	5,137,000	—	—	—	—	—	—
1912	10,407,000	5,239,000	5,168,000	—	—	—	—	—	—
1913	10,520,000	5,294,000	5,226,000	—	—	—	—	—	—
1914	10,631,000	5,351,000	5,280,000	—	—	—	—	—	—
1915	10,698,000	5,385,000	5,313,000	—	—	—	—	—	—
1916	10,765,000	5,415,000	5,350,000	—	—	—	—	—	—
1917	10,833,000	5,449,000	5,384,000	—	—	—	—	—	—
1918	10,856,000	5,434,000	5,422,000	—	—	—	—	—	—
1919	10,830,000	5,431,000	5,399,000	—	—	—	—	—	—
1920	10,951,000	5,504,000	5,447,000	—	—	—	—	—	—
1921	11,122,000	5,582,000	5,540,000	—	—	—	—	—	—
1922	11,281,000	5,658,000	5,623,000	—	—	—	—	—	—
1923	11,437,000	5,730,000	5,707,000	—	—	—	—	—	—
1924	11,597,000	5,808,000	5,789,000	—	—	—	—	—	—
1925	11,768,000	5,882,000	5,886,000	—	—	—	—	—	—
1926	11,929,000	5,960,000	5,969,000	—	—	—	—	—	—
1927	12,094,000	6,039,000	6,055,000	—	—	—	—	—	—
1928	12,265,000	6,119,000	6,146,000	—	—	—	—	—	—
1929	12,384,000	6,171,000	6,213,000	—	—	—	—	—	—
1930	12,517,861	6,227,438	6,290,423	—	—	—	—	—	—
1931	12,606,244	6,263,098	6,343,146	—	—	—	—	—	—
1932	12,686,029	6,294,422	6,391,607	—	—	—	—	—	—
1933	12,763,514	6,324,538	6,438,976	—	—	—	—	—	—
1934	12,846,645	6,357,047	6,489,598	—	—	—	—	—	—
1935	12,941,055	6,395,550	6,545,505	—	—	—	—	—	—
1936	13,030,951	6,432,749	6,598,202	—	—	—	—	—	—
1937	13,118,469	6,467,773	6,650,696	—	—	—	—	—	—
1938	13,233,084	6,517,019	6,716,065	—	—	—	—	—	—
1939	13,355,350	6,570,682	6,784,668	—	—	—	—	—	—
1940	13,493,588	6,634,025	6,859,563	—	—	—	—	—	—
1941	13,671,006	6,724,039	6,946,967	—	—	—	—	—	—
1942	13,868,034	6,821,776	7,046,258	—	—	—	—	—	—
1943	14,134,115	6,977,916	7,156,199	—	—	—	—	—	—
1944	14,388,133	7,127,824	7,260,309	—	—	—	—	—	—
1945	14,661,694	7,287,014	7,374,680	—	—	—	—	—	—
1946	14,824,039	7,344,090	7,479,949	—	—	—	—	—	—
1947	15,066,637	7,438,768	7,627,869	—	—	—	—	—	—
1948	15,323,094	7,547,555	7,775,539	—	—	—	—	—	—
1949	15,589,832	7,657,713	7,932,119	—	—	—	—	—	—
1950	16,287,900	8,000,907	8,286,993	—	—	—	—	—	—
1951	16,656,927	8,176,865	8,480,062	—	—	—	—	—	—
1952	17,026,322	8,349,065	8,677,257	—	—	—	—	—	—
1953	17,411,204	8,530,913	8,880,291	—	—	—	—	—	—
1954	17,832,771	8,731,066	9,101,705	—	—	—	—	—	—
1955	18,278,701	8,943,841	9,334,860	—	—	—	—	—	—
1956	18,739,868	9,163,163	9,576,705	—	—	—	—	—	—
1957	19,215,474	9,388,947	9,826,527	—	—	—	—	—	—
1958	19,682,366	9,608,954	10,073,412	—	—	—	—	—	—
1959	20,174,699	9,841,731	10,332,968	—	—	—	—	—	—

TABLE Aa110–124   Population, by race and sex: 1900–1997   [Annual estimates]   *Continued*

				Nonwhite					
				Black			Other nonwhite		
	Total	Males	Females	Total	Males	Females	Total	Males	Females
	Aa116	Aa117	Aa118	Aa119	Aa120	Aa121	Aa122	Aa123	Aa124
Year	Number	Number	Number	Number	Number	Number	Number	Number	Number
1960	20,648,485	10,062,524	10,585,961	19,006,281	9,199,339	9,806,942	1,642,204	863,185	779,019
1961	21,158,446	10,298,674	10,859,772	19,437,319	9,400,167	10,037,152	1,721,127	898,507	822,620
1962	21,652,984	10,527,527	11,125,457	19,852,037	9,593,142	10,258,895	1,800,947	934,385	866,562
1963	22,137,475	10,750,210	11,387,265	20,255,067	9,779,461	10,475,606	1,882,408	970,749	911,659
1964	22,632,067	10,978,383	11,653,684	20,671,914	9,972,854	10,699,060	1,960,153	1,005,529	954,624
1965	23,098,205	11,190,839	11,907,366	21,063,732	10,152,077	10,911,655	2,034,473	1,038,762	995,711
1966	23,562,673	11,401,945	12,160,728	21,434,066	10,319,583	11,114,483	2,128,607	1,082,362	1,046,245
1967	24,016,942	11,603,267	12,413,675	21,780,162	10,470,302	11,309,860	2,236,780	1,132,965	1,103,815
1968	24,460,149	11,795,268	12,664,881	22,116,847	10,613,989	11,502,858	2,343,302	1,181,279	1,162,023
1969	24,895,087	11,983,808	12,911,279	22,431,263	10,747,881	11,683,382	2,463,824	1,235,927	1,227,897
1970	25,408,141	12,215,263	13,192,878	22,801,214	10,913,011	11,888,203	2,606,927	1,302,252	1,304,675
1971	25,997,583	12,486,436	13,511,147	23,239,524	11,114,200	12,125,324	2,758,059	1,372,236	1,385,823
1972	26,570,407	12,747,343	13,823,064	23,646,177	11,297,893	12,348,284	2,924,230	1,449,450	1,474,780
1973	27,126,873	12,999,608	14,127,265	24,028,815	11,469,853	12,558,962	3,098,058	1,529,755	1,568,303
1974	27,684,312	13,253,269	14,431,043	24,402,325	11,638,204	12,764,121	3,281,987	1,615,065	1,666,922
1975	28,344,312	13,559,794	14,784,518	24,777,554	11,805,791	12,971,763	3,566,758	1,754,003	1,812,755
1976	28,960,860	13,842,352	15,118,508	25,157,029	11,975,906	13,181,123	3,803,831	1,866,446	1,937,385
1977	29,590,479	14,132,261	15,458,218	25,559,193	12,158,361	13,400,832	4,031,286	1,973,900	2,057,386
1978	30,249,845	14,437,808	15,812,037	25,983,680	12,351,427	13,632,253	4,266,165	2,086,381	2,179,784
1979	30,957,931	14,766,232	16,191,699	26,417,364	12,546,873	13,870,491	4,540,567	2,219,359	2,321,208
1980	32,170,915	15,348,988	16,821,927	26,890,093	12,761,599	14,128,494	5,280,822	2,587,389	2,693,433
1981	32,963,427	15,730,566	17,232,861	27,254,771	12,932,199	14,322,572	5,708,656	2,798,367	2,910,289
1982	33,763,323	16,115,545	17,647,778	27,631,606	13,107,942	14,523,664	6,131,717	3,007,603	3,124,114
1983	34,507,144	16,474,862	18,032,282	27,990,243	13,278,197	14,712,046	6,516,901	3,196,665	3,320,236
1984	35,252,048	16,835,655	18,416,393	28,334,903	13,441,179	14,893,724	6,917,145	3,394,476	3,522,669
1985	36,030,417	17,213,347	18,817,070	28,693,129	13,611,711	15,081,418	7,337,288	3,601,636	3,735,652
1986	36,838,111	17,605,478	19,232,633	29,062,867	13,787,796	15,275,071	7,775,244	3,817,682	3,957,562
1987	37,653,552	18,001,054	19,652,498	29,445,325	13,969,363	15,475,962	8,208,227	4,031,691	4,176,536
1988	38,508,305	18,416,768	20,091,537	29,846,347	14,160,162	15,686,185	8,661,958	4,256,606	4,405,352
1989	39,422,807	18,864,215	20,558,592	30,271,776	14,364,978	15,906,798	9,151,031	4,499,237	4,651,794
1990	40,397,041	19,340,464	21,056,577	30,750,048	14,597,886	16,152,162	9,646,993	4,742,578	4,904,415
1991	41,294,537	19,771,044	21,523,493	31,255,566	14,842,331	16,413,235	10,038,971	4,928,713	5,110,258
1992	42,219,671	20,212,262	22,007,409	31,761,293	15,086,312	16,674,981	10,458,378	5,125,950	5,332,428
1993	43,127,436	20,642,734	22,484,702	32,257,868	15,324,873	16,932,995	10,869,568	5,317,861	5,551,707
1994	43,960,266	21,035,909	22,924,357	32,722,820	15,547,055	17,175,765	11,237,446	5,488,854	5,748,592
1995	44,767,185	21,417,581	23,349,604	33,155,310	15,755,164	17,400,146	11,611,875	5,662,417	5,949,458
1996	45,564,938	21,797,014	23,767,924	33,575,149	15,957,757	17,617,392	11,989,789	5,839,257	6,150,532
1997	46,372,578	22,181,298	24,191,280	34,006,188	16,167,301	17,838,887	12,366,390	6,013,997	6,352,393

[1] As of July 1. 1900–1939, resident population; 1940–1989, total population, including armed forces overseas; 1990–1997, preliminary.

[2] Estimates including armed forces overseas, in thousands: 1917 – 103,414; 1918 – 104,550; 1919 – 105,063.

[3] Estimates including armed forces overseas, in thousands: 1917 – 52,934; 1918 – 53,316; 1919 – 53,658.

Sources

U.S. Bureau of the Census. 1900–1949, Current Population Reports, series P-25, number 311, pp. 24–123; 1950–1959, Current Population Reports, series P-25, number 310, pp. 14–15, 30–31. 1960–1969, Current Population Reports, series P-25, number 519, pp. 15–25. 1970–1979, Current Population Reports, series P-25, number 917, pp. 8–64. 1980–1991, Current Population Reports, series P-25, number 1095, pp. 2–29. Machine-readable data were obtained from U.S. Bureau of the Census, 1900–1979, PE-11 (POP 3987); 1980–1990, PE-10 (POP 3988–3990); 1990–1997, PE-61 (POP 3991–3998).

Documentation

For a discussion of race, see the text for Table Aa145–184. For a discussion of methodology, see the text for Table Aa6–8. See also Frederick W. Hollmann, Lisa B. Kuzmekus, et al., "U.S. Population by Age, Sex, Race, and Hispanic Origin: 1990 to 1997," U.S. Bureau of the Census PPL-91 and appendixes.

These series have not been updated to be consistent with the 2000 Census because the Bureau of the Census has not yet produced a reconciliation between the racial categories in the 1990 and 2000 Censuses.

TABLE Aa125–144 Population, by age: 1900–2000 [Annual estimates][1]

Contributed by Michael R. Haines

	Total	Age 0–4	5–9	10–14	15–19	20–24	25–29	30–34	35–39	40–44
	Aa125	Aa126	Aa127	Aa128	Aa129	Aa130	Aa131	Aa132	Aa133	Aa134
Year	Number	Number	Number	Number	Number	Number	Number	Number	Number	Number
1900	76,094,000	9,181,000	8,880,000	8,086,000	7,568,000	7,383,000	6,572,000	5,589,000	4,996,000	4,277,000
1901	77,584,000	9,336,000	8,977,000	8,181,000	7,698,000	7,544,000	6,729,000	5,713,000	5,126,000	4,378,000
1902	79,163,000	9,502,000	9,079,000	8,281,000	7,842,000	7,713,000	6,890,000	5,847,000	5,261,000	4,484,000
1903	80,632,000	9,645,000	9,155,000	8,369,000	7,982,000	7,876,000	7,048,000	5,971,000	5,394,000	4,580,000
1904	82,166,000	9,791,000	9,237,000	8,460,000	8,131,000	8,047,000	7,210,000	6,105,000	5,530,000	4,681,000
1905	83,822,000	9,944,000	9,326,000	8,562,000	8,289,000	8,237,000	7,382,000	6,249,000	5,677,000	4,784,000
1906	85,450,000	10,092,000	9,405,000	8,662,000	8,450,000	8,414,000	7,553,000	6,399,000	5,823,000	4,882,000
1907	87,008,000	10,220,000	9,480,000	8,759,000	8,600,000	8,584,000	7,715,000	6,542,000	5,967,000	4,978,000
1908	88,710,000	10,364,000	9,569,000	8,871,000	8,762,000	8,764,000	7,888,000	6,697,000	6,121,000	5,081,000
1909	90,490,000	10,509,000	9,670,000	9,000,000	8,928,000	8,943,000	8,063,000	6,860,000	6,281,000	5,190,000
1910	92,407,000	10,671,000	9,803,000	9,147,000	9,095,000	9,117,000	8,243,000	7,031,000	6,453,000	5,306,000
1911	93,863,000	10,796,000	9,934,000	9,280,000	9,163,000	9,192,000	8,371,000	7,159,000	6,598,000	5,405,000
1912	95,335,000	10,915,000	10,077,000	9,426,000	9,228,000	9,249,000	8,491,000	7,281,000	6,742,000	5,510,000
1913	97,225,000	11,082,000	10,285,000	9,619,000	9,316,000	9,333,000	8,634,000	7,436,000	6,920,000	5,642,000
1914	99,111,000	11,244,000	10,498,000	9,818,000	9,392,000	9,404,000	8,779,000	7,591,000	7,097,000	5,778,000
1915	100,546,000	11,347,000	10,674,000	9,986,000	9,428,000	9,416,000	8,873,000	7,707,000	7,241,000	5,889,000
1916	101,961,000	11,442,000	10,858,000	10,150,000	9,449,000	9,423,000	8,959,000	7,817,000	7,383,000	6,005,000
1917	103,268,000 [2]	11,527,000	11,045,000	10,324,000	9,466,000	9,370,000	8,997,000	7,916,000	7,526,000	6,121,000
1918	103,208,000 [2]	11,606,000	11,233,000	10,499,000	9,429,000	8,642,000	8,573,000	7,872,000	7,648,000	6,231,000
1919	104,514,000 [2]	11,536,000	11,298,000	10,551,000	9,394,000	9,071,000	8,918,000	7,994,000	7,715,000	6,293,000
1920	106,461,000	11,631,000	11,523,000	10,635,000	9,582,000	9,239,000	9,321,000	8,095,000	7,843,000	6,539,000
1921	108,538,000	11,879,000	11,636,000	10,879,000	9,817,000	9,323,000	9,505,000	8,242,000	7,942,000	6,723,000
1922	110,049,000	12,031,000	11,728,000	11,060,000	10,029,000	9,373,000	9,502,000	8,422,000	7,914,000	6,909,000
1923	111,947,000	12,119,000	11,844,000	11,245,000	10,274,000	9,524,000	9,458,000	8,773,000	7,929,000	7,137,000
1924	114,109,000	12,269,000	11,939,000	11,419,000	10,563,000	9,751,000	9,415,000	9,142,000	7,992,000	7,345,000
1925	115,829,000	12,316,000	12,087,000	11,527,000	10,784,000	9,907,000	9,350,000	9,370,000	8,076,000	7,500,000
1926	117,397,000	12,189,000	12,290,000	11,616,000	10,973,000	10,064,000	9,387,000	9,480,000	8,195,000	7,652,000
1927	119,035,000	12,111,000	12,436,000	11,716,000	11,172,000	10,258,000	9,473,000	9,475,000	8,424,000	7,748,000
1928	120,509,000	11,978,000	12,496,000	11,824,000	11,339,000	10,472,000	9,584,000	9,369,000	8,732,000	7,808,000
1929	121,767,000	11,734,000	12,587,000	11,883,000	11,457,000	10,694,000	9,729,000	9,212,000	9,032,000	7,889,000
1930	123,076,741	11,372,115	12,590,170	12,040,620	11,572,129	10,915,220	9,894,030	9,144,806	9,218,464	8,052,099
1931	124,039,648	11,179,407	12,468,736	12,160,190	11,614,368	11,003,403	10,050,628	9,191,170	9,170,428	8,241,540
1932	124,840,471	10,903,103	12,318,969	12,295,227	11,639,411	11,076,535	10,194,926	9,289,495	9,068,537	8,434,608
1933	125,578,763	10,612,152	12,176,481	12,355,034	11,667,638	11,152,144	10,325,604	9,423,967	8,974,240	8,595,478
1934	126,373,773	10,330,791	11,981,207	12,420,564	11,724,759	11,237,709	10,447,553	9,574,173	8,941,393	8,698,714
1935	127,250,232	10,170,377	11,788,568	12,424,094	11,812,771	11,316,920	10,557,834	9,717,063	8,973,399	8,738,999
1936	128,053,180	10,043,792	11,594,107	12,347,888	11,933,977	11,375,296	10,660,480	9,844,799	9,050,530	8,732,348
1937	128,824,829	10,008,673	11,334,821	12,229,373	12,075,857	11,410,691	10,767,647	9,955,178	9,164,264	8,702,095
1938	129,824,939	10,176,429	11,055,752	12,090,133	12,201,962	11,453,098	10,891,755	10,060,757	9,305,802	8,695,116
1939	130,879,718	10,418,326	10,795,035	11,905,678	12,300,027	11,518,863	11,013,377	10,163,259	9,445,834	8,731,544
1940	132,122,446	10,578,643	10,648,297	11,714,958	12,342,637	11,690,361	11,156,261	10,289,688	9,596,675	8,824,991
1941	133,402,471	10,849,632	10,523,040	11,566,173	12,267,309	11,807,338	11,277,517	10,413,194	9,738,707	8,953,365
1942	134,859,553	11,301,496	10,412,401	11,411,193	12,138,180	11,955,482	11,372,978	10,538,269	9,869,741	9,080,016
1943	136,739,353	12,016,357	10,438,842	11,259,817	12,000,573	12,064,392	11,510,311	10,684,273	10,008,416	9,217,955
1944	138,397,345	12,523,814	10,621,984	10,951,158	11,936,856	12,062,241	11,673,750	10,837,346	10,155,979	9,348,737
1945	139,928,165	12,978,811	10,822,136	10,776,794	11,668,891	12,036,202	11,797,101	10,936,606	10,312,804	9,474,038
1946	141,388,566	13,243,923	11,096,213	10,747,700	11,378,439	12,004,312	11,892,509	11,061,168	10,458,622	9,614,195
1947	144,126,071	14,405,735	11,551,130	10,706,119	11,308,080	11,814,354	12,039,007	11,196,868	10,657,485	9,763,822
1948	146,631,302	14,918,931	12,280,312	10,808,867	11,071,850	11,793,817	12,155,044	11,339,095	10,871,882	9,921,887
1949	149,188,130	15,607,096	12,802,534	10,967,378	10,870,047	11,699,991	12,252,869	11,475,526	11,098,010	10,089,244
1950	152,271,417	16,409,955	13,374,537	11,212,659	10,675,405	11,680,392	12,361,596	11,674,177	11,346,649	10,289,820
1951	154,877,889	17,333,447	13,667,630	11,499,983	10,557,360	11,552,184	12,294,867	11,894,513	11,462,184	10,451,492
1952	157,552,740	17,312,258	14,810,804	11,962,333	10,535,179	11,350,086	12,187,349	12,114,392	11,572,130	10,620,674
1953	160,184,192	17,638,336	15,332,413	12,671,001	10,683,767	11,062,145	12,131,813	12,208,194	11,664,248	10,781,531
1954	163,025,854	18,057,457	16,031,707	13,190,678	10,894,141	10,832,415	11,982,369	12,357,659	11,740,758	10,920,707
1955	165,931,202	18,566,313	16,748,917	13,637,838	11,039,170	10,713,668	11,834,567	12,447,663	11,856,643	11,054,896
1956	168,903,031	19,003,397	17,652,183	13,917,539	11,340,462	10,615,739	11,722,691	12,399,044	12,062,681	11,194,519
1957	171,984,130	19,493,808	17,624,418	15,045,275	11,798,149	10,602,967	11,539,820	12,303,958	12,268,531	11,327,939
1958	174,881,904	19,886,602	17,940,912	15,545,886	12,501,223	10,755,798	11,272,165	12,266,153	12,351,895	11,446,313
1959	177,829,628	20,175,118	18,344,095	16,220,010	13,018,941	10,968,960	11,046,962	12,121,784	12,478,150	11,544,617

Notes appear at end of table

TABLE Aa125–144   Population, by age: 1900–2000   [Annual estimates]   *Continued*

		Age								
	Total	0–4	5–9	10–14	15–19	20–24	25–29	30–34	35–39	40–44
	Aa125	Aa126	Aa127	Aa128	Aa129	Aa130	Aa131	Aa132	Aa133	Aa134
Year	Number	Number	Number	Number	Number	Number	Number	Number	Number	Number
1960	180,671,158	20,341,249	18,810,017	16,925,481	13,442,177	11,134,177	10,935,627	11,982,903	12,542,472	11,678,891
1961	183,691,481	20,522,270	19,195,946	17,835,463	13,759,149	11,482,571	10,869,740	11,821,862	12,540,484	11,851,939
1962	186,537,737	20,468,793	19,641,124	17,793,934	14,950,359	11,959,117	10,857,229	11,636,937	12,473,576	12,045,211
1963	189,241,798	20,341,531	19,995,900	18,127,789	15,509,040	12,713,513	10,973,952	11,436,030	12,353,180	12,231,166
1964	191,888,791	20,164,865	20,235,872	18,546,960	16,250,213	13,268,550	11,167,969	11,228,332	12,195,540	12,366,102
1965	194,302,963	19,823,841	20,377,572	19,048,875	17,026,731	13,746,439	11,340,210	11,124,787	12,020,684	12,426,362
1966	196,560,338	19,207,974	20,573,496	19,477,689	17,961,799	14,050,419	11,661,757	11,063,412	11,846,556	12,428,961
1967	198,712,056	18,562,509	20,533,100	19,962,834	17,947,775	15,247,873	12,093,274	11,062,934	11,662,848	12,375,308
1968	200,706,052	17,913,415	20,414,346	20,357,244	18,303,342	15,786,164	12,799,887	11,189,864	11,459,844	12,270,867
1969	202,676,946	17,375,513	20,242,725	20,641,025	18,756,219	16,479,793	13,290,478	11,390,192	11,251,513	12,131,538
1970	205,052,174	17,166,191	19,919,437	20,852,843	19,333,097	17,202,106	13,736,148	11,587,384	11,154,676	11,994,976
1971	207,660,677	17,243,968	19,395,287	21,095,181	19,788,508	18,159,035	14,041,352	11,916,942	11,119,869	11,858,178
1972	209,896,021	17,101,353	18,846,825	21,098,690	20,295,914	18,153,093	15,240,474	12,383,463	11,158,422	11,701,085
1973	211,908,788	16,850,846	18,278,834	21,029,600	20,718,843	18,521,423	15,786,244	13,152,833	11,269,992	11,540,075
1974	213,853,928	16,486,729	17,805,201	20,910,552	21,041,598	18,975,407	16,521,117	13,704,283	11,448,920	11,376,569
1975	215,973,199	16,121,483	17,594,132	20,645,886	21,284,826	19,526,836	17,280,356	14,190,906	11,633,670	11,197,160
1976	218,035,164	15,617,115	17,671,273	20,087,589	21,534,141	19,986,149	18,274,285	14,484,571	11,927,493	11,166,358
1977	220,239,425	15,563,659	17,529,735	19,503,932	21,540,319	20,499,222	18,277,493	15,720,733	12,353,724	11,208,747
1978	222,584,545	15,735,004	17,300,027	18,919,562	21,496,126	20,945,960	18,683,006	16,280,097	13,096,865	11,339,956
1979	225,055,487	16,062,882	16,946,625	18,445,149	21,401,910	21,296,573	19,177,693	17,024,931	13,635,505	11,540,494
1980	227,726,463	16,451,184	16,602,353	18,236,335	21,165,372	21,589,949	19,792,494	17,810,424	14,120,501	11,746,798
1981	229,966,237	16,892,719	16,060,121	18,300,407	20,595,350	21,869,467	20,274,915	18,798,322	14,408,117	12,046,266
1982	232,187,835	17,227,829	15,957,945	18,144,578	20,013,757	21,901,906	20,815,645	18,781,492	15,612,347	12,482,941
1983	234,307,207	17,546,883	16,053,251	17,868,526	19,426,912	21,843,802	21,259,485	19,137,308	16,165,983	13,170,116
1984	236,348,292	17,694,905	16,337,925	17,450,275	18,968,146	21,737,408	21,584,268	19,575,550	16,919,105	13,656,309
1985	238,466,283	17,841,621	16,664,857	17,027,433	18,762,678	21,478,486	21,804,381	20,101,924	17,657,680	14,108,907
1986	240,650,755	17,962,501	17,098,398	16,474,234	18,855,347	20,942,250	22,018,123	20,551,705	18,663,191	14,417,570
1987	242,803,533	18,052,205	17,430,258	16,376,846	18,740,544	20,385,338	21,981,550	21,057,923	18,669,377	15,629,533
1988	245,021,414	18,195,420	17,759,302	16,496,237	18,534,705	19,845,846	21,868,413	21,469,540	19,045,890	16,211,626
1989	247,341,697	18,508,058	17,916,793	16,796,836	18,171,750	19,441,753	21,689,979	21,758,369	19,509,367	16,984,937
1990	250,131,894	18,856,447	18,076,746	17,212,887	17,808,617	19,322,710	21,402,276	22,022,763	20,046,900	17,818,792
1991	253,492,503	19,208,046	18,281,130	17,755,955	17,303,542	19,413,800	21,044,294	22,386,796	20,634,869	18,778,279
1992	256,894,189	19,528,041	18,431,104	18,245,763	17,264,839	19,313,978	20,591,139	22,564,396	21,232,648	18,812,899
1993	260,255,352	19,729,275	18,645,956	18,721,403	17,489,864	19,101,455	20,145,747	22,645,815	21,771,092	19,203,765
1994	263,435,673	19,776,862	19,024,679	19,001,286	17,891,676	18,758,285	19,808,545	22,648,049	22,176,001	19,701,422
1995	266,557,091	19,626,505	19,438,171	19,207,049	18,386,355	18,390,552	19,742,392	22,425,455	22,530,059	20,235,070
1996	269,667,391	19,408,272	19,860,530	19,435,109	18,932,862	17,964,682	19,926,646	21,995,775	22,824,013	20,780,743
1997	272,911,760	19,232,671	20,254,032	19,600,697	19,410,995	17,992,291	19,959,808	21,494,424	22,942,112	21,340,265
1998	276,115,288	19,144,923	20,510,328	19,825,181	19,853,214	18,250,115	19,862,981	20,998,635	22,964,161	21,837,576
1999	279,294,713	19,135,544	20,606,460	20,213,364	20,098,823	18,672,082	19,631,967	20,646,545	22,920,443	22,209,417
2000	282,124,631	19,211,515	20,470,322	20,594,433	20,216,249	19,133,226	19,246,866	20,568,087	22,604,380	22,526,928

		Age								
	45–49	50–54	55–59	60–64	65 and older	14 and older	16 and older	18 and older	21 and older	62 and older
	Aa135	Aa136	Aa137	Aa138	Aa139	Aa140	Aa141	Aa142	Aa143	Aa144
Year	Number	Number	Number	Number	Number	Number	Number	Number	Number	Number
1900	3,475,000	2,962,000	2,224,000	1,802,000	3,099,000	51,511,000	48,403,000	45,379,000	40,879,000	4,130,000
1901	3,561,000	3,045,000	2,279,000	1,843,000	3,174,000	52,676,000	49,523,000	46,448,000	41,862,000	4,229,000
1902	3,654,000	3,134,000	2,338,000	1,882,000	3,256,000	53,911,000	50,710,000	47,578,000	42,896,000	4,333,000
1903	3,744,000	3,220,000	2,390,000	1,923,000	3,335,000	55,094,000	51,848,000	48,661,000	43,886,000	4,436,000
1904	3,837,000	3,313,000	2,444,000	1,966,000	3,414,000	56,331,000	53,038,000	49,792,000	44,919,000	4,541,000
1905	3,940,000	3,410,000	2,504,000	2,013,000	3,505,000	57,668,000	54,322,000	51,014,000	46,036,000	4,658,000
1906	4,043,000	3,511,000	2,558,000	2,063,000	3,595,000	58,993,000	55,595,000	52,224,000	47,142,000	4,778,000
1907	4,146,000	3,609,000	2,615,000	2,109,000	3,684,000	60,275,000	56,828,000	53,397,000	48,216,000	4,894,000
1908	4,262,000	3,712,000	2,676,000	2,164,000	3,779,000	61,659,000	58,157,000	54,660,000	49,375,000	5,021,000
1909	4,381,000	3,823,000	2,741,000	2,223,000	3,878,000	63,093,000	59,531,000	55,970,000	50,579,000	5,155,000

(continued)

TABLE Aa125–144 Population, by age: 1900–2000 [Annual estimates] *Continued*

	Age									
	45–49	50–54	55–59	60–64	65 and older	14 and older	16 and older	18 and older	21 and older	62 and older
	Aa135	Aa136	Aa137	Aa138	Aa139	Aa140	Aa141	Aa142	Aa143	Aa144
Year	Number	Number	Number	Number	Number	Number	Number	Number	Number	Number
1910	4,516,000	3,938,000	2,813,000	2,288,000	3,986,000	64,598,000	60,974,000	57,346,000	51,852,000	5,301,000
1911	4,633,000	4,024,000	2,880,000	2,354,000	4,074,000	65,688,000	62,022,000	58,369,000	52,839,000	5,427,000
1912	4,762,000	4,113,000	2,950,000	2,422,000	4,169,000	66,775,000	63,068,000	59,387,000	53,828,000	5,562,000
1913	4,913,000	4,222,000	3,040,000	2,502,000	4,281,000	68,127,000	64,364,000	60,650,000	55,048,000	5,719,000
1914	5,073,000	4,325,000	3,127,000	2,584,000	4,401,000	69,470,000	65,652,000	61,907,000	56,272,000	5,887,000
1915	5,209,000	4,409,000	3,206,000	2,660,000	4,501,000	70,482,000	66,623,000	62,863,000	57,224,000	6,029,000
1916	5,350,000	4,496,000	3,288,000	2,738,000	4,603,000	71,476,000	67,579,000	63,811,000	58,176,000	6,176,000
1917	5,488,000	4,580,000	3,377,000	2,817,000	4,714,000	72,361,000	68,425,000	64,646,000	59,030,000	6,332,000
1918	5,628,000	4,665,000	3,458,000	2,898,000	4,826,000	71,886,000	67,899,000	64,092,000	58,670,000	6,490,000
1919	5,704,000	4,698,000	3,510,000	2,946,000	4,886,000	73,144,000	69,170,000	65,407,000	59,911,000	6,577,000
1920	5,693,000	4,812,000	3,596,000	3,023,000	4,929,000	74,708,000	70,683,000	66,839,000	61,235,000	6,663,000
1921	5,769,000	4,952,000	3,710,000	3,081,000	5,080,000	76,233,000	72,102,000	68,154,000	62,446,000	6,847,000
1922	5,829,000	5,070,000	3,857,000	3,094,000	5,231,000	77,362,000	73,144,000	69,102,000	63,297,000	6,998,000
1923	5,941,000	5,127,000	4,045,000	3,120,000	5,411,000	78,915,000	74,606,000	70,461,000	64,518,000	7,184,000
1924	6,111,000	5,167,000	4,221,000	3,166,000	5,609,000	80,704,000	76,297,000	72,035,000	65,914,000	7,399,000
1925	6,304,000	5,217,000	4,362,000	3,243,000	5,786,000	82,149,000	77,677,000	73,324,000	67,068,000	7,615,000
1926	6,466,000	5,320,000	4,473,000	3,332,000	5,960,000	83,575,000	79,050,000	74,619,000	68,244,000	7,840,000
1927	6,649,000	5,443,000	4,554,000	3,449,000	6,127,000	85,071,000	80,489,000	75,978,000	69,472,000	8,076,000
1928	6,835,000	5,595,000	4,600,000	3,578,000	6,299,000	86,536,000	81,898,000	77,323,000	70,701,000	8,328,000
1929	6,976,000	5,785,000	4,625,000	3,690,000	6,474,000	87,902,000	83,233,000	78,619,000	71,897,000	8,576,000
1930	7,075,624	6,019,607	4,697,531	3,778,507	6,705,819	89,438,490	84,722,188	80,068,980	73,256,057	8,867,567
1931	7,160,356	6,135,969	4,869,778	3,864,996	6,928,679	90,597,151	85,876,693	81,209,172	74,358,417	9,144,886
1932	7,253,691	6,227,182	5,040,141	3,952,428	7,146,218	91,699,349	86,968,603	82,294,743	75,411,088	9,410,368
1933	7,374,471	6,310,477	5,194,023	4,054,610	7,362,444	92,836,633	88,069,074	83,392,142	76,481,625	9,678,346
1934	7,529,044	6,403,533	5,324,698	4,177,097	7,582,538	94,079,346	89,246,720	84,552,935	77,619,744	9,960,988
1935	7,698,260	6,510,031	5,430,629	4,307,803	7,803,484	95,349,817	90,435,495	85,698,080	78,750,594	10,254,777
1936	7,863,748	6,630,944	5,517,244	4,431,504	8,026,523	96,574,992	91,594,471	86,791,801	79,826,583	10,553,306
1937	8,012,386	6,773,355	5,593,391	4,539,478	8,257,620	97,734,276	92,754,348	87,876,551	80,868,525	10,853,394
1938	8,132,728	6,944,254	5,677,875	4,631,583	8,507,695	98,980,822	94,017,278	89,072,692	81,977,414	11,162,637
1939	8,212,368	7,124,393	5,779,159	4,707,579	8,764,276	100,208,989	95,282,988	90,311,164	83,103,866	11,466,611
1940	8,273,732	7,280,886	5,903,498	4,790,688	9,031,131	101,607,263	96,732,352	91,764,122	84,430,228	11,781,284
1941	8,371,035	7,388,341	6,036,757	4,922,382	9,287,681	102,878,207	98,036,754	93,135,825	85,766,601	12,113,985
1942	8,476,329	7,499,687	6,165,978	5,054,319	9,583,484	104,130,002	99,325,984	94,486,828	87,148,033	12,498,092
1943	8,587,730	7,611,230	6,289,651	5,182,115	9,867,691	105,404,276	100,630,642	95,837,053	88,593,729	12,872,155
1944	8,700,054	7,719,415	6,410,786	5,307,702	10,147,523	106,627,079	101,924,329	97,153,352	89,976,667	13,234,275
1945	8,810,434	7,832,292	6,543,537	5,444,460	10,494,059	107,623,408	103,042,444	98,372,755	91,327,263	13,662,747
1946	8,889,838	7,929,954	6,673,330	5,570,913	10,827,450	108,519,397	104,042,198	99,500,869	92,595,214	14,067,108
1947	8,949,475	8,021,192	6,820,687	5,706,685	11,185,432	109,601,625	105,251,946	100,723,315	93,869,865	14,498,153
1948	8,996,728	8,110,100	6,977,622	5,846,143	11,539,024	110,722,108	106,503,407	102,066,436	95,265,442	14,926,100
1949	9,049,910	8,210,203	7,149,431	5,995,617	11,920,274	111,947,294	107,728,759	103,444,722	96,683,704	15,385,907
1950	9,141,999	8,310,945	7,293,084	6,103,023	12,397,176	113,437,998	109,141,664	104,994,301	98,340,618	15,930,038
1951	9,312,990	8,363,831	7,448,701	6,236,146	12,802,561	114,546,605	110,266,005	106,048,368	99,592,717	16,427,700
1952	9,533,927	8,401,096	7,546,983	6,402,138	13,203,391	115,739,300	111,345,916	107,054,753	100,791,872	16,916,791
1953	9,735,136	8,492,362	7,600,379	6,565,808	13,617,059	116,844,468	112,318,804	108,053,025	101,798,764	17,396,904
1954	9,950,490	8,609,326	7,678,142	6,704,176	14,075,829	118,081,916	113,488,920	109,122,793	102,818,741	17,942,553
1955	10,159,845	8,724,570	7,787,751	6,833,891	14,525,470	119,439,718	114,683,584	110,192,874	103,803,223	18,499,373
1956	10,323,825	8,882,094	7,893,622	6,957,576	14,937,659	120,970,614	115,906,232	111,353,676	104,874,669	19,006,864
1957	10,493,176	9,086,347	7,986,881	7,025,041	15,387,820	122,817,476	117,217,470	112,514,204	105,900,070	19,503,150
1958	10,656,799	9,270,436	8,135,955	7,045,691	15,806,076	124,344,589	118,550,783	113,558,478	106,788,632	19,940,644
1959	10,796,038	9,465,880	8,309,275	7,091,875	16,247,923	125,887,773	120,286,005	114,779,195	107,823,591	20,401,193
1960	10,914,008	9,664,114	8,470,898	7,154,113	16,675,031	127,364,812	121,835,069	116,145,687	108,856,440	20,835,901
1961	10,999,165	9,876,334	8,646,496	7,200,852	17,089,210	129,952,215	123,403,725	117,900,175	109,926,376	21,277,072
1962	11,072,357	10,051,259	8,870,722	7,260,516	17,456,603	132,171,780	124,864,216	119,412,390	111,063,131	21,681,909
1963	11,150,213	10,195,686	9,105,949	7,330,192	17,777,657	134,322,467	127,275,039	120,822,242	112,273,796	22,039,221
1964	11,249,863	10,330,268	9,324,873	7,432,686	18,126,698	136,479,513	129,427,151	122,205,737	113,844,141	22,426,410
1965	11,380,135	10,459,044	9,505,017	7,571,873	18,451,393	138,725,536	131,542,151	124,572,108	115,197,547	22,799,653
1966	11,544,529	10,580,584	9,652,979	7,755,052	18,755,131	141,069,470	133,650,570	126,664,717	116,522,798	23,183,690
1967	11,740,037	10,699,780	9,765,655	7,986,714	19,071,415	143,520,111	135,905,135	128,784,895	117,822,897	23,625,010
1968	11,931,194	10,826,841	9,851,119	8,236,808	19,365,117	145,988,147	138,170,507	130,814,842	120,097,811	24,072,729
1969	12,072,471	10,974,617	9,922,992	8,467,405	19,680,465	148,465,066	140,461,687	132,904,639	122,019,056	24,551,933

TABLE Aa125–144   Population, by age: 1900–2000   [Annual estimates]   *Continued*

	Age									
	45–49	50–54	55–59	60–64	65 and over	14 and over	16 and over	18 and over	21 and over	62 and over
	Aa135	Aa136	Aa137	Aa138	Aa139	Aa140	Aa141	Aa142	Aa143	Aa144
Year	Number	Number	Number	Number	Number	Number	Number	Number	Number	Number
1970	12,150,627	11,165,775	10,006,476	8,675,709	20,106,729	151,213,954	143,069,848	135,290,289	124,127,118	25,078,742
1971	12,141,906	11,376,668	10,089,821	8,872,502	20,561,460	154,180,686	145,825,445	137,852,263	126,341,128	25,691,274
1972	12,032,621	11,653,511	10,153,941	9,056,808	21,019,821	157,115,665	148,592,093	140,476,487	128,657,450	26,366,534
1973	11,960,173	11,846,845	10,228,957	9,199,189	21,524,934	160,011,581	151,476,403	143,144,603	131,032,292	26,961,357
1974	11,848,693	11,960,053	10,385,884	9,327,439	22,061,483	162,902,527	154,378,180	145,867,315	133,507,295	27,574,956
1975	11,784,362	11,972,279	10,645,757	9,399,251	22,696,295	165,932,854	157,343,227	148,805,353	136,138,986	28,236,186
1976	11,652,055	11,970,041	10,884,113	9,501,880	23,278,101	168,902,195	160,319,125	151,783,587	138,881,967	28,908,437
1977	11,501,147	11,869,208	11,191,600	9,588,061	23,891,845	171,821,065	163,377,933	154,776,287	141,701,283	29,631,238
1978	11,357,929	11,815,672	11,425,441	9,686,849	24,502,051	174,756,005	166,421,661	157,810,346	144,716,017	30,289,836
1979	11,217,085	11,724,940	11,581,791	9,866,165	25,133,744	177,561,152	169,441,037	160,950,041	147,779,440	30,956,659
1980	11,053,414	11,695,953	11,611,552	10,142,678	25,707,456	180,186,088	172,437,763	164,041,304	150,847,156	31,583,457
1981	10,989,929	11,595,812	11,554,606	10,359,409	26,220,797	182,362,782	174,929,422	166,753,445	153,605,500	32,182,530
1982	11,016,782	11,415,022	11,462,769	10,567,341	26,787,481	184,432,504	177,176,075	169,374,534	156,406,152	32,839,671
1983	11,206,391	11,155,763	11,457,152	10,654,962	27,360,673	186,481,425	179,234,271	171,741,042	159,028,868	33,539,971
1984	11,434,573	10,957,900	11,351,764	10,802,657	27,877,507	188,591,381	181,192,313	173,865,591	161,555,003	34,235,778
1985	11,611,814	10,854,915	11,228,901	10,906,507	28,416,179	190,731,757	183,174,968	175,842,487	163,984,490	34,842,986
1986	11,883,424	10,782,288	11,135,261	10,858,866	29,007,597	192,609,940	185,284,415	177,785,002	166,277,965	35,460,538
1987	12,299,992	10,802,878	10,968,316	10,782,607	29,626,166	194,249,244	187,418,805	179,747,130	168,306,944	36,066,527
1988	12,960,892	10,995,955	10,722,674	10,791,307	30,123,607	195,797,754	189,233,284	181,774,324	170,195,556	36,557,224
1989	13,427,716	11,213,100	10,533,992	10,707,291	30,681,756	197,421,032	190,861,476	183,885,403	172,010,424	37,074,669
1990	13,835,587	11,378,970	10,478,385	10,623,535	31,247,279	199,245,891	192,643,286	185,916,304	174,088,399	37,624,737
1991	14,135,766	11,692,293	10,442,986	10,603,123	31,811,624	201,675,387	194,935,553	188,184,628	176,835,961	38,178,217
1992	15,418,956	12,136,113	10,521,122	10,477,197	32,355,994	204,167,037	197,204,992	190,392,429	179,601,532	38,708,646
1993	16,018,909	12,851,587	10,736,415	10,292,258	32,901,811	206,765,467	199,622,152	192,669,718	182,052,316	39,181,969
1994	16,795,682	13,363,079	11,009,104	10,150,200	33,330,803	209,441,540	201,969,503	194,804,126	184,193,009	39,505,004
1995	17,628,665	13,857,336	11,182,428	10,137,750	33,769,304	212,105,790	204,420,624	197,093,059	186,261,138	39,805,799
1996	18,615,263	14,190,306	11,480,824	10,109,317	34,143,049	214,884,499	207,087,438	199,441,923	188,428,133	40,045,505
1997	18,691,506	15,491,912	11,905,236	10,194,250	34,401,561	217,764,571	209,846,278	201,995,309	190,639,009	40,397,195
1998	19,119,045	16,118,836	12,589,605	10,421,529	34,619,159	220,516,048	212,638,134	204,686,760	192,964,840	40,706,728
1999	19,659,233	16,924,789	13,084,979	10,693,226	34,797,841	223,355,599	215,404,601	207,348,336	195,304,015	41,001,347
2000	20,224,397	17,820,336	13,568,708	10,868,514	35,070,670	225,885,853	217,818,993	209,794,486	—	—

[1] Figures are as of July 1. Through 1939, figures cover the resident population; thereafter, total population, including armed forces overseas.

[2] Estimates including armed forces overseas, in thousands: 1917 – 103,414; 1918 – 104,550; 1919 – 105,063.

Sources

U.S. Bureau of the Census. 1900–1949: Current Population Reports, series P-25, number 311, pp. 24–123. 1950–1959, Current Population Reports, series P-25, number 310, pp. 14–15, 30–31. 1960–1969: Current Population Reports, series P-25, number 519, pp. 15–25. 1970–1979: Current Population Reports, series P-25, number 917, pp. 8–64. 1980–1989, Current Population Reports, series P-25, number 1095, pp. 2–29. 1990–2000: U.S. Census Bureau's Internet site. Machine-readable data were obtained from censuses: 1900–1979, PE-11 (POP 3987); 1980–1989, PE-10 (POP 3988–3990); 1990–2000, downloaded from the U.S. Census Bureau's Internet site.

Documentation

For a discussion of methodology, see the text for Table Aa6–8. See also Frederick W. Hollmann, Lisa B. Kuzmekus, et al., "U.S. Population by Age, Sex, Race, and Hispanic Origin: 1990 to 1997," U.S. Bureau of the Census PPL-91 and appendixes.

TABLE Aa145–184   Population, by sex and race: 1790–1990

Contributed by Michael R. Haines

			Both sexes					
			Black			Other races		
	All races	White	Total	Slave	Free colored	Total	Race and sex unknown	American Indian
	Aa145	Aa146	Aa147	Aa148	Aa149	Aa150	Aa151	Aa152
Year	Number	Number	Number	Number	Number	Number	Number	Number
1790 [1]	3,929,625	3,172,444	757,181	697,624	59,557	—	—	—
1800 [1]	5,308,483	4,306,446	1,002,037	893,602	108,435	—	—	—
1810 [1]	7,239,881	5,862,073	1,377,808	1,191,362	186,446	—	—	—
1820	9,638,453	7,866,797	1,771,656	1,538,022	233,634	—	—	—
1830	12,866,020	10,532,060	2,328,642	2,009,043	319,599	—	5,318 [6]	—
1840	17,069,453	14,189,705	2,873,648	2,487,355	386,293	—	6,100 [6]	—
1850	23,191,876	19,553,068	3,638,808	3,204,313	434,495	—	—	—
1860	31,443,321	26,922,537	4,441,830	3,953,760	488,070	78,954	—	44,021
1870 [2]	38,558,371	33,589,377	4,880,009	—	—	88,985	—	25,731
1880	50,155,783	43,402,970	6,580,793	—	—	172,020	—	66,407
1890	62,947,714	55,101,258	7,488,676	—	—	357,780	—	248,253
1900	75,994,575	66,809,196	8,833,994	—	—	351,385	—	237,196
1910	91,972,266	81,731,957	9,827,763	—	—	412,546	—	265,683
1920	105,710,620	94,820,915	10,463,131	—	—	426,574	—	244,437
1930 [3]	122,775,046	110,286,740	11,891,143	—	—	597,163	—	332,397
1940	131,669,275	118,214,870	12,865,518	—	—	588,887	—	333,969
1950	150,697,361	134,942,028	15,042,286	—	—	713,047	—	343,410
1960	179,323,175	158,831,732	18,871,831	—	—	1,619,612	—	523,591
1970 [4]	203,211,926	177,748,975	22,580,289	—	—	2,882,662	—	792,730
1980 [5]	226,545,805	188,371,622	26,495,025	—	—	11,679,158	—	1,364,033
1990 [5]	248,709,873	199,686,070	29,986,060	—	—	19,037,743	—	—

			Both sexes					Male	
			Other races						
	American Indian, Eskimo, or Aleut	Asian or Pacific islander	Japanese	Chinese	Filipino	Other		All races	White
	Aa153	Aa154	Aa155	Aa156	Aa157	Aa158		Aa159	Aa160
Year	Number	Number	Number	Number	Number	Number		Number	Number
1790 [1]	—	—	—	—	—	—		—	1,615,761
1800 [1]	—	—	—	—	—	—		—	2,195,305
1810 [1]	—	—	—	—	—	—		—	2,988,130
1820	—	—	—	—	—	—		4,896,605	3,995,809
1830	—	—	—	—	—	—		6,532,489	5,360,895
1840	—	—	—	—	—	—		8,683,214	7,249,444
1850	—	—	—	—	—	—		11,831,560	10,026,402
1860	44,021	34,933	—	34,933	—	—		16,085,204	13,811,387
1870 [2]	25,731	63,254	55	63,199	—	—		19,493,565	17,029,088
1880	66,407	105,613	148	105,465	—	—		25,518,820	22,130,900
1890	248,253	109,527	2,039	107,488	—	—		32,237,101	28,270,379
1900	237,196	114,189	24,326	89,863	—	—		38,816,448	34,201,735
1910	265,683	146,863	72,157	71,531	160	3,015		47,332,277	42,178,245
1920	244,437	182,137	111,010	61,639	5,603	3,885		53,900,431	48,430,655
1930 [3]	332,397	264,766	138,834	74,954	45,208	5,770		62,137,080	55,922,528
1940	333,969	254,918	126,947	77,504	45,563	4,904		66,061,592	59,448,548
1950	343,410	321,033	141,768	117,629	61,636	48,604		74,833,239	67,129,192
1960	551,669	980,337	464,332	237,292	176,310	218,087		88,331,494	78,367,149
1970 [4]	827,255	1,538,721	591,290	435,062	343,060	720,520		98,912,192	86,720,987
1980 [5]	1,420,400	3,500,439	700,974	806,040	774,652	8,033,459		110,053,161	91,685,333
1990 [5]	1,959,234	7,273,662	—	—	—	9,804,847		121,239,418	97,475,880

Notes appear at end of table

TABLE Aa145–184   Population, by sex and race: 1790–1990   *Continued*

	Male							
	Black			Other races				
	Total	Slave	Free colored	Total	American Indian	American Indian, Eskimo, or Aleut	Asian or Pacific islander	Japanese
	Aa161	Aa162	Aa163	Aa164	Aa165	Aa166	Aa167	Aa168
Year	Number	Number	Number	Number	Number	Number	Number	Number
1790 [1]	—	—	—	—	—	—	—	—
1800 [1]	—	—	—	—	—	—	—	—
1810 [1]	—	—	—	—	—	—	—	—
1820	900,796	788,028	112,734	—	—	—	—	—
1830	1,166,276	1,012,823	153,453	—	—	—	—	—
1840	1,432,988	1,246,517	186,481	—	—	—	—	—
1850	1,811,258	1,602,534	208,724	—	—	—	—	—
1860	2,216,744	1,982,625	234,119	57,073	23,924	—	—	—
1870 [2]	2,393,263	—	—	71,214	12,534	—	—	47
1880	3,253,115	—	—	134,805	33,985	—	—	134
1890	3,735,603	—	—	231,119	125,719	—	—	1,780
1900	4,386,547	—	—	228,166	119,484	—	—	23,341
1910	4,885,881	—	—	268,151	135,133	—	—	63,070
1920	5,209,436	—	—	260,340	125,068	—	—	72,707
1930 [3]	5,855,669	—	—	358,883	170,350	—	—	81,771
1940	6,269,038	—	—	344,006	171,427	—	—	71,967
1950	7,298,722	—	—	405,325	178,824	—	—	76,649
1960	9,113,408	—	—	850,937	263,369	—	—	224,828
1970 [4]	10,748,316	—	—	1,442,889	388,691	—	—	271,300
1980 [5]	12,519,189	—	—	5,848,639	673,517	702,228	1,693,312	320,941
1990 [5]	14,170,151	—	—	9,593,387	—	967,186	3,558,038	—

	Male			Female				
	Other races					Black		
	Chinese	Filipino	Other	All races	White	Total	Slave	Free colored
	Aa169	Aa170	Aa171	Aa172	Aa173	Aa174	Aa175	Aa176
Year	Number	Number	Number	Number	Number	Number	Number	Number
1790 [1]	—	—	—	—	1,556,683	—	—	—
1800 [1]	—	—	—	—	2,111,141	—	—	—
1810 [1]	—	—	—	—	2,873,943	—	—	—
1820	—	—	—	4,741,848	3,870,988	870,860	750,010	120,790
1830	—	—	—	6,333,531	5,171,165	1,162,366	996,220	166,146
1840	—	—	—	8,380,921	6,940,261	1,440,660	1,240,938	199,822
1850	—	—	—	11,354,216	9,526,666	1,827,550	1,601,779	225,771
1860	33,149	—	—	15,358,117	13,111,150	2,225,086	1,971,135	253,951
1870 [2]	58,633	—	—	19,064,806	16,560,289	2,486,746	—	—
1880	100,686	—	—	24,636,963	21,272,070	3,327,678	—	—
1890	103,620	—	—	30,710,613	26,830,879	3,753,073	—	—
1900	85,341	—	—	37,178,127	32,607,461	4,447,447	—	—
1910	66,856	144	2,948	44,639,989	39,553,712	4,941,882	—	—
1920	53,891	5,232	3,442	51,810,189	46,390,260	5,253,695	—	—
1930 [3]	59,802	42,268	4,692	60,637,966	54,364,212	6,035,474	—	—
1940	57,389	39,723	3,500	65,607,683	58,766,322	6,596,480	—	—
1950	77,008	46,101	26,743	75,864,122	67,812,836	7,743,564	—	—
1960	135,549	112,286	114,905	90,991,681	80,464,583	9,758,423	—	—
1970 [4]	228,565	189,498	364,835	104,299,734	91,027,988	11,831,973	—	—
1980 [5]	407,544	374,191	4,072,446	116,492,644	96,686,289	13,975,836	—	—
1990 [5]	—	—	5,068,163	127,470,455	102,210,190	15,815,909	—	—

Notes appear at end of table

(continued)

TABLE Aa145–184   Population, by sex and race: 1790–1990   *Continued*

				Female				
				Other races				
	Total	American Indian	American Indian, Eskimo, or Aleut	Asian or Pacific islander	Japanese	Chinese	Filipino	Other
	Aa177	Aa178	Aa179	Aa180	Aa181	Aa182	Aa183	Aa184
Year	Number	Number	Number	Number	Number	Number	Number	Number
1790 [1]	—	—	—	—	—	—	—	—
1800 [1]	—	—	—	—	—	—	—	—
1810 [1]	—	—	—	—	—	—	—	—
1820	—	—	—	—	—	—	—	—
1830	—	—	—	—	—	—	—	—
1840	—	—	—	—	—	—	—	—
1850	—	—	—	—	—	—	—	—
1860	21,881	20,097	—	—	—	1,784	—	—
1870 [2]	17,771	13,197	—	—	8	4,566	—	—
1880	37,215	32,422	—	—	14	4,779	—	—
1890	126,661	122,534	—	—	259	3,868	—	—
1900	123,219	117,712	—	—	985	4,522	—	—
1910	144,395	130,550	—	—	9,087	4,675	16	67
1920	166,234	119,369	—	—	38,303	7,748	371	443
1930 [3]	238,280	162,047	—	—	57,063	15,152	2,940	1,078
1940	244,881	162,542	—	—	54,980	20,115	5,840	1,404
1950	307,722	164,586	—	—	65,119	40,621	15,535	21,861
1960	768,675	260,222	—	—	239,504	101,743	64,024	103,182
1970 [4]	1,439,773	404,039	—	—	319,990	206,497	153,562	355,685
1980 [5]	5,830,519	690,516	718,172	1,807,127	380,033	398,496	400,461	3,961,013
1990 [5]	9,444,356	—	992,048	3,715,624	—	—	—	4,736,684

[1] Data by sex not available.

[2] Revisions to include adjustments for underenumeration in the Southern states show a total (both sexes) of 34,337,292 for whites and 5,392,172 for blacks.

[3] In 1930, Mexicans were classified as nonwhites. This decision was changed by 1940, and revised tabulations were published. The revised population estimates are given here. The actual 1930 figures are: white (108,864,207), all other races (1,428,303).

[4] The population of other races (that is, neither white nor black) was overstated by about 327,000 in the 1970 Census; see the documentation. Figures exclude 23,372 persons for whom sex and race data are not available; see text for Table Aa1–5.

[5] In 1980, there were 7,279,831 males and 7,328,842 females of Spanish origin (any race). In 1990, there were 11,388,059 males and 10,966,000 females of Hispanic origin (any race), and 91,656,591 males and 96,471,705 females who were white, not of Hispanic origin.

[6] In 1830, 5,318 persons were enumerated as "on board public ships in the service of the United States on the 1st of June, 1830," without distinction of race or sex. In 1840, 6,100 persons were enumerated as "on board vessels of war in the United States naval service, June 1, 1840," without distinction of race or sex.

Sources

1790: W. S. Rossiter, *A Century of Population Growth* (1909), Table 108.

1800–1920: U.S. Bureau of the Census, *U.S. Census of Population: 1920*, volume 2, p. 107. Slave population: *U.S. Census of Population: 1870*, volume 1, p. 7. Race and sex unknown: *U.S. Census of Population: 1830*, p. 163; *U.S. Census of Population: 1840*, "Compendium," p. 102.

1930–1960: U.S. Bureau of the Census, *U.S. Census of Population: 1960*, volume 1, part 1, pp. 144–5.

1970: U.S. Bureau of the Census, *U.S. Census of Population: 1970*, volume I, part 1, section 1, p. 262.

1980: U.S. Bureau of the Census, *U.S. Census of Population: 1980*, volume 1, *Characteristics of the Population*, Chapter B "General Population Characteristics," part 1 "United States Summary," PC80-1-B1, Tables 40, 41.

1990: U.S. Bureau of the Census, *U.S. Census of Population: 1990*, *General Population Characteristics, United States*, CP-1-1, Table 13.

1860–1970: for "American Indian, Eskimo, or Aleut" and "Asian or Pacific Islander." Campbell Gibson and Kay Jung, "Historical Census Statistics on Population Totals by Race, 1790–1990, and by Hispanic Origin, 1970 to 1990, for the United States, Regions, Divisions, and States," U.S. Census

Bureau, Population Division, Working Paper number 56 (September 2002), Table 1.

Documentation

The U.S. Census Bureau currently collects and publishes racial statistics as defined in *Statistical Policy Directive No. 15*, issued by the U.S. Office of Management and Budget. This directive provides standards on ethnic and racial categories for statistical reporting to be used by all federal agencies. According to this directive, the basic racial categories are American Indian or Alaska Native; Asian and Pacific Islander; black; and white. The directive identifies Hispanic as an ethnic category. The concept of race used by the Census Bureau reflects self-identification by respondents – that is, the individual's perception of his or her racial identity. The concept is not intended to reflect any biological or anthropological definition. It is also recognized that some persons do not identify with a specific racial group. The 1990 Census race question included the category "other race" with provision for a write-in response for such persons. The race categories include racial, national origin, and sociocultural groups.

Differences between the 1990 Census and earlier censuses affect the comparability of data for certain racial groups and American Indian tribes. The lack of comparability is due to changes in the way some respondents reported their race as well as changes in 1990 Census procedures related to the racial classification. See *U.S. Census of Population: 1990, General Population Characteristics, United States*, 1990 CP-1-1.

In the Current Population Survey and other household sample surveys in which data are obtained through personal interview, respondents are asked to classify their race as (1) white; (2) black; (3) American Indian, Aleut, or Eskimo; or (4) Asian or Pacific Islander. The procedures for classifying persons of mixed races who could not provide a single response to the race question are generally similar to those used in the census.

In the 1980 Census, fifteen groups were listed in the race item on the census questionnaire: white, black, American Indian, Eskimo, Aleut, Chinese, Filipino, Japanese, Asian Indian, Korean, Vietnamese, Hawaiian, Samoan, Guamian, and other. The procedure was self-identification. If persons of mixed racial parentage could not provide a single response to the race question, the race of the person's mother was used. If a single response could not be provided for the mother, however, then the first race reported by the

TABLE Aa145–184   Population, by sex and race: 1790–1990   *Continued*

person was used. This was a modification of the 1970 procedure in which the race of the person's father was used. The categories for "white" and "other" for 1980 are not precisely comparable to previous censuses. This was due to changes in the way some respondents reported their race as well as changes in the census procedures of racial classification; see *U.S. Census of Population: 1980*, volume 1, *General Population Characteristics*, PC80-1-B.

The historical classification of the population by race has reflected common usage rather than an attempt to define biological stock. As a result, the white and black populations usually have not been divided into racial subgroups (although the white population has been classified by ethnic origin), but American Indians and some Asian groups (for example, Japanese, Chinese, Filipino, Korean, etc.) have typically been identified with country of origin.

Through 1950, the classification of the population by race was usually obtained by the enumerator's observation. Persons of mixed white and other parentage were usually classified with the other race. A person of mixed parentage other than white was usually classified by the race of his father, except that mixtures of black and American Indian were classified as black unless the American Indian stock was clearly predominant or unless the individual was accepted in the community in which he or she resided as an American Indian.

The category Indian included unmixed American Indians together with persons who were of mixed white and Indian ancestry if they were enrolled on an Indian reservation or agency roll. Persons who were part Indian were included as Indian if they were one fourth or more Indian, or if they were regarded as Indians in the community in which they resided.

In the 1960 Census, data on race were collected by a combination of self-classification, direct interview, and observation by the enumerator; the classification rules were essentially the same as in 1950.

In the 1970 Census, data on race were obtained primarily through self-classification. In a change from earlier censuses, persons of mixed white and other parentage who were in doubt as to their classification were classified according to the race of their fathers. It is believed that self-identification of race may lead to a somewhat higher proportion of the population being classed in the "other races" category than does observation by the enumerator. In the Censuses of 1980 and 1990, self-classification was used.

In the 1930 Census, persons of Mexican origin were included with "other races"; however, the tables in this volume have been revised to include Mexicans in the white population.

In the 1970 Census, the editing and review of questionnaires were not completed when the complete-count data were processed. As a result, some information that pertained to nationality or ethnicity was accepted as identifying race. For example, some persons who classified themselves in the race item as Mexican or Spanish American were included in the "other races" population but should have been included in the white population. In the tabulation of sample data, this error was corrected. The result in the case of 20 percent sample data was that the population of "other races" was reduced from 2,882,662 to 2,555,872 (1,270,625 males and 1,285,247 females), or by 326,790, which is roughly the number added to the white population in the sample tabulations.

The Census of 1860 was the first in which American Indians were distinguished from other classes in the population. Prior to 1890, enumeration of American Indians was limited to American Indians living in the general population of the various states; American Indians in Indian Territory and on Indian reservations were excluded. In 1910, a special effort was made to secure a complete enumeration of persons with any perceptible amount of American Indian ancestry. This probably resulted in the enumeration as American Indians of a considerable number of persons who would have been reported as white in earlier censuses. There were no special efforts in 1920, and the returns showed a much smaller number of American Indians than in 1910. Again in 1930, emphasis was placed on securing a complete count of American Indians, with the result that the returns probably overstated the decennial increase in the number of American Indians.

For a discussion of the historical evolution of census racial statistics, see Sharon M. Lee, "Racial Classification in the U.S. Census: 1890–1990," *Ethnic and Racial Studies* 16 (1) (1993): 75–94; Michael R. Haines, "Ethnic Differences in Demographic Behavior in the United States: Has There Been Convergence?" National Bureau of Economic Research, Working Paper number 9042 (July 2002); and the essay on definitions and measurement of race and ethnicity in the introduction to Part A. For further discussion of race in census statistics, see *U.S. Census of Population: 1950*, volume 2, part 1, pp. 35–36; 1960, volume 1, part 1, pp. xli–xliii; 1970, volume 1, part 1, section 2, pp. App. 15–16.

Series Aa158, Aa171, and Aa184. Includes races other than white and black not shown separately.

TABLE Aa185–286   Total population, by sex and age: 1850–1990[1]

Contributed by Michael R. Haines

		Both sexes									
		Age									
	Total	0–4	5–9	10–14	15–19	20–29	20–24	25–29	30–39	30–34	35–39
	Aa185	Aa186	Aa187	Aa188	Aa189	Aa190	Aa191	Aa192	Aa193	Aa194	Aa195
Year	Number	Number	Number	Number	Number	Number	Number	Number	Number	Number	Number
1850	23,191,876	3,497,773	3,241,268	2,890,629	2,529,792	4,277,318	—	—	2,825,819	—	—
1860	31,443,321	4,842,496	4,171,200	3,720,780	3,361,495	5,726,400	—	—	4,021,248	—	—
1870	38,558,371	5,514,713	4,814,713	4,786,189	4,040,588	—	3,748,299	3,075,118	—	2,562,829	2,314,976
1880	50,155,783	6,914,516	6,479,660	5,715,186	5,011,415	—	5,087,772	4,080,621	—	3,368,943	3,000,419
1890	62,622,250	7,634,693	7,573,998	7,033,509	6,557,563	—	6,196,676	5,227,777	—	4,578,630	3,866,161
1900	75,994,575	9,170,628	8,874,123	8,080,234	7,556,089	—	7,335,016	6,529,441	—	5,556,039	4,964,781
1910	91,972,266	10,631,364	9,760,632	9,107,140	9,063,603	—	9,056,984	8,180,003	—	6,972,185	6,396,100
1920	105,710,620	11,573,230	11,398,075	10,641,137	9,430,556	—	9,277,021	9,086,491	—	8,071,193	7,775,281
1930	122,775,046	11,444,390	12,607,609	12,004,877	11,552,115	—	10,870,378	9,833,608	—	9,120,421	9,208,645
1940	131,669,275	10,541,524	10,684,622	11,745,935	12,333,523	—	11,587,835	11,096,638	—	10,242,388	9,545,377
1950	150,697,361	16,163,571	13,199,685	11,119,268	10,616,598	—	11,481,828	12,242,260	—	11,517,007	11,246,386
1960	179,323,175	20,320,901	18,691,780	16,773,492	13,219,243	—	10,800,761	10,869,124	—	11,949,186	12,481,109
1970 [2]	203,211,926	17,154,337	19,956,247	20,789,468	19,070,348	—	16,371,021	13,476,993	—	11,430,436	11,106,851
1980	226,545,805	16,348,254	16,699,956	18,242,129	21,168,124	—	21,318,704	19,520,919	—	17,560,920	13,965,302
1990	248,709,873	18,354,443	18,099,179	17,114,249	17,754,015	—	19,020,312	21,313,045	—	21,862,887	19,963,117

Notes appear at end of table

(continued)

TABLE Aa185–286   Total population, by sex and age: 1850–1990   *Continued*

	Both sexes										
	Age										
	40–49	40–44	45–49	50–59	50–54	55–59	60–69	60–64	65–69	70–79	70–74
	Aa196	Aa197	Aa198	Aa199	Aa200	Aa201	Aa202	Aa203	Aa204	Aa205	Aa206
Year	Number	Number	Number	Number	Number	Number	Number	Number	Number	Number	Number
1850	1,846,660	—	—	1,109,540	—	—	609,926	—	—	257,234	—
1860	2,614,330	—	—	1,585,879	—	—	888,809	—	—	348,890	—
1870	—	1,939,712	1,578,932	—	1,367,969	876,552	—	778,971	484,353	—	344,358
1880	—	2,468,811	2,089,445	—	1,839,883	1,271,434	—	1,104,219	725,876	—	495,442
1890	—	3,185,518	2,731,640	—	2,326,262	1,672,336	—	1,458,034	1,010,110	—	701,751
1900	—	4,247,166	3,454,612	—	2,942,829	2,211,172	—	1,791,363	1,302,926	—	883,841
1910	—	5,261,587	4,469,197	—	3,900,791	2,786,951	—	2,267,150	1,679,503	—	1,113,728
1920	—	6,345,557	5,763,620	—	4,734,873	3,549,124	—	2,982,548	2,068,475	—	1,395,036
1930	—	7,990,195	7,042,279	—	5,975,804	4,645,677	—	3,751,221	2,770,605	—	1,950,004
1940	—	8,787,843	8,255,225	—	7,256,846	5,843,865	—	4,728,340	3,806,657	—	2,569,532
1950	—	10,203,973	9,070,465	—	8,272,188	7,235,120	—	6,059,475	5,002,936	—	3,411,949
1960	—	11,600,243	10,879,485	—	9,605,954	8,429,865	—	7,142,452	6,257,910	—	4,738,932
1970 [2]	—	11,980,954	12,115,939	—	11,104,018	9,973,028	—	8,616,784	6,991,625	—	5,443,831
1980	—	11,669,408	11,089,755	—	11,710,032	11,615,254	—	10,087,621	8,782,481	—	6,798,124
1990	—	17,615,786	13,872,573	—	11,350,513	10,531,756	—	10,616,167	10,111,735	—	7,994,823

	Both sexes									
	Age									
	75–79	80–89	80–84	85–89	90–99	90–94	95–99	100 and older	75 and older	85 and older
	Aa207	Aa208	Aa209	Aa210	Aa211	Aa212	Aa213	Aa214	Aa215	Aa216
Year	Number	Number	Number	Number	Number	Number	Number	Number	Number	Number
1850	—	77,382	—	—	11,695	—	—	2,555	—	—
1860	—	93,552	—	—	13,778	—	—	2,953	—	—
1870	175,686	—	94,602	34,475	—	12,671	3,982	3,522	—	—
1880	281,065	—	146,362	49,835	—	16,100	4,763	4,016	—	—
1890	393,062	—	203,851	75,240	—	23,645	5,648	3,981	—	—
1900	519,857	—	251,512	88,600	—	23,992	6,266	3,504	—	—
1910	667,302	—	321,754	122,818	—	33,473	7,391	3,555	—	—
1920	856,560	—	402,779	156,539	—	39,980	9,579	4,267	—	—
1930	1,106,390	—	534,676	205,469	—	51,664	11,033	3,964	—	—
1940	1,503,982	—	774,391	277,012	—	69,598	14,463	3,679	—	—
1950	—	—	—	—	—	—	—	—	3,854,652	—
1960	3,053,559	—	1,579,927	—	—	—	—	—	—	929,252
1970 [2]	3,834,834	—	2,284,311	1,018,147	—	313,237	73,076	106,441	—	—
1980	4,793,722	—	2,935,033	1,520,202	—	556,592	131,079	32,194	—	—
1990	6,121,369	—	3,933,739	2,060,247	—	769,481	213,131	37,306	—	—

Notes appear at end of table

TABLE Aa185–286   Total population, by sex and age: 1850–1990   *Continued*

	Both sexes		Male								
	Age						Age				
	65 and older	Not stated	Total	0–4	5–9	10–14	15–19	20–29	20–24	25–29
	Aa217	Aa218	Aa219	Aa220	Aa221	Aa222	Aa223	Aa224	Aa225	Aa226
Year	Number	Number	Number	Number	Number	Number	Number	Number	Number	Number
1850	—	14,285	11,837,660	1,769,460	1,640,407	1,473,116	1,237,680	2,194,469	—	—
1860	—	51,511	16,085,204	2,449,547	2,109,545	1,900,868	1,650,012	2,911,558	—	—
1870	1,153,649	5,161	19,493,565	2,797,257	2,437,442	2,435,585	1,989,695	—	1,835,946	1,515,671
1880	1,723,459	—	25,518,820	3,507,709	3,275,131	2,907,481	2,476,088	—	2,554,684	2,109,741
1890	2,417,288	162,165	32,067,880	3,884,869	3,830,352	3,574,787	3,248,711	—	3,104,893	2,698,311
1900	3,080,498	200,584	38,816,448	4,633,612	4,479,396	4,083,041	3,750,451	—	3,624,580	3,323,543
1910	3,949,524	169,055	47,332,277	5,380,596	4,924,123	4,601,753	4,527,282	—	4,580,290	4,244,348
1920	4,933,215	148,699	53,900,431	5,857,461	5,753,001	5,369,306	4,673,792	—	4,527,045	4,538,233
1930	6,633,805	94,022	62,137,080	5,806,174	6,381,108	6,068,777	5,757,825	—	5,336,815	4,860,180
1940	9,019,314	—	66,061,592	5,354,808	5,418,823	5,952,329	6,180,153	—	5,692,392	5,450,662
1950	12,269,537	—	74,833,239	8,236,164	6,714,555	5,660,399	5,311,342	—	5,606,293	5,972,078
1960	16,559,580	—	88,331,494	10,329,729	9,504,368	8,524,289	6,633,661	—	5,272,340	5,333,075
1970 [2]	—	—	98,912,192	8,745,499	10,168,496	10,590,737	9,633,847	—	7,917,269	6,621,567
1980	25,549,427	—	110,053,161	8,362,009	8,539,080	9,316,221	10,755,409	—	10,663,231	9,705,107
1990	31,241,831	—	121,239,418	9,392,409	9,262,527	8,767,167	9,102,698	—	9,675,596	10,695,936

	Male									
	Age									
	30–39	30–34	35–39	40–49	40–44	45–49	50–59	50–54	55–59	60–69
	Aa227	Aa228	Aa229	Aa230	Aa231	Aa232	Aa233	Aa234	Aa235	Aa236
Year	Number	Number	Number	Number	Number	Number	Number	Number	Number	Number
1850	1,490,135	—	—	967,573	—	—	575,685	—	—	309,515
1860	2,129,017	—	—	1,392,223	—	—	835,350	—	—	455,754
1870	—	1,273,633	1,179,366	—	990,021	839,578	—	740,360	469,495	—
1880	—	1,744,308	1,527,159	—	1,243,773	1,078,695	—	966,702	674,927	—
1890	—	2,425,664	2,051,044	—	1,654,604	1,418,102	—	1,208,922	871,663	—
1900	—	2,901,321	2,616,865	—	2,255,916	1,837,836	—	1,564,622	1,145,257	—
1910	—	3,656,768	3,367,016	—	2,786,350	2,378,916	—	2,110,013	1,488,437	—
1920	—	4,130,783	4,074,361	—	3,285,543	3,117,550	—	2,535,545	1,880,065	—
1930	—	4,561,786	4,679,860	—	4,136,459	3,671,924	—	3,131,645	2,425,992	—
1940	—	5,070,312	4,745,659	—	4,419,135	4,209,269	—	3,752,750	3,011,364	—
1950	—	5,624,723	5,517,544	—	5,070,269	4,526,366	—	4,128,648	3,630,046	—
1960	—	5,846,224	6,079,512	—	5,675,881	5,357,925	—	4,734,829	4,127,245	—
1970 [2]	—	5,595,790	5,412,423	—	5,818,813	5,851,334	—	5,347,916	4,765,821	—
1980	—	8,676,796	6,861,509	—	5,708,210	5,388,249	—	5,620,670	5,481,863	—
1990	—	10,876,933	9,902,243	—	8,691,984	6,810,597	—	5,514,738	5,034,370	—

Notes appear at end of table

(continued)

TABLE Aa185–286   Total population, by sex and age: 1850–1990   *Continued*

					Male					
					Age					
Year	60–64	65–69	70–79	70–74	75–79	80–89	80–84	85–89	90–99	90–94
	Aa237	Aa238	Aa239	Aa240	Aa241	Aa242	Aa243	Aa244	Aa245	Aa246
	Number	Number	Number	Number	Number	Number	Number	Number	Number	Number
1850	—	—	127,460	—	—	36,727	—	—	5,183	—
1860	—	—	172,563	—	—	43,790	—	—	5,854	—
1870	407,491	250,662	—	173,036	86,282	—	44,529	15,513	—	5,317
1880	584,858	379,498	—	250,001	138,601	—	67,941	21,908	—	6,351
1890	758,710	525,627	—	363,642	199,093	—	97,862	34,063	—	9,848
1900	917,167	667,669	—	449,609	261,579	—	122,273	40,742	—	9,858
1910	1,185,966	863,994	—	561,644	331,280	—	153,745	56,335	—	14,553
1920	1,581,800	1,079,817	—	706,301	419,965	—	185,903	69,272	—	16,383
1930	1,941,508	1,417,812	—	991,647	547,604	—	251,138	90,893	—	20,431
1940	2,397,816	1,896,088	—	1,270,967	723,680	—	359,011	121,455	—	27,965
1950	3,037,838	2,424,561	—	1,628,829	—	—	—	—	—	—
1960	3,409,319	2,931,088	—	2,185,216	1,359,424	—	665,093	—	—	—
1970 [2]	4,026,972	3,122,084	—	2,315,000	1,560,661	—	875,584	362,063	—	103,649
1980	4,669,892	3,902,955	—	2,853,547	1,847,661	—	1,019,227	477,185	—	159,077
1990	4,947,047	4,532,307	—	3,409,306	2,399,768	—	1,366,094	614,036	—	190,089

			Male					Female			
			Age						Age		
Year	95–99	100 and older	75 and older	85 and older	65 and older	Not stated	Total	0–4	5–9	10–14
	Aa247	Aa248	Aa249	Aa250	Aa251	Aa252	Aa253	Aa254	Aa255	Aa256
	Number	Number	Number	Number	Number	Number	Number	Number	Number	Number
1850	—	1,077	—	—	479,962	9,173	11,354,216	1,728,313	1,600,861	1,417,513
1860	—	1,233	—	—	679,194	27,890	15,358,117	2,392,949	2,061,655	1,819,912
1870	1,605	1,286	—	—	578,230	3,795	19,064,806	2,717,456	2,377,271	2,350,604
1880	1,855	1,409	—	—	867,564	—	24,636,963	3,406,807	3,204,529	2,807,705
1890	2,186	1,398	—	—	1,233,719	103,529	30,554,370	3,749,824	3,743,646	3,458,722
1900	2,417	1,271	—	—	1,555,418	127,423	37,178,127	4,537,016	4,394,727	3,997,193
1910	3,045	1,380	—	—	1,985,976	114,443	44,639,989	5,250,768	4,836,509	4,505,387
1920	3,869	1,561	—	—	2,483,071	92,875	51,810,189	5,715,769	5,645,074	5,271,831
1930	4,283	1,403	—	—	3,325,211	51,816	60,637,966	5,638,216	6,226,501	5,936,100
1940	5,616	1,338	—	—	4,406,120	—	65,607,683	5,186,716	5,265,799	5,793,606
1950	—	—	1,743,584	—	5,796,974	—	75,864,122	7,927,407	6,485,130	5,458,869
1960	—	—	—	362,276	7,503,097	—	90,991,681	9,991,172	9,187,412	8,249,203
1970 [2]	22,329	54,338	—	—	8,415,708	—	104,299,734	8,408,838	9,787,751	10,198,731
1980	34,961	10,302	—	—	10,304,915	—	116,492,644	7,986,245	8,160,876	8,925,908
1990	45,672	7,901	—	—	12,565,173	—	127,470,455	8,962,034	8,836,652	8,347,082

Notes appear at end of table

TABLE Aa185–286   Total population, by sex and age: 1850–1990   *Continued*

	Female									
	Age									
	15–19	20–29	20–24	25–29	30–39	30–34	35–39	40–49	40–44	45–49
	Aa257	Aa258	Aa259	Aa260	Aa261	Aa262	Aa263	Aa264	Aa265	Aa266
Year	Number	Number	Number	Number	Number	Number	Number	Number	Number	Number
1850	1,292,112	2,082,849	—	—	1,335,684	—	—	879,087	—	—
1860	1,711,483	2,814,842	—	—	1,892,231	—	—	1,222,107	—	—
1870	2,050,893	—	1,912,353	1,559,447	—	1,289,196	1,135,610	—	949,691	739,354
1880	2,535,327	—	2,533,088	1,970,880	—	1,624,635	1,473,260	—	1,225,038	1,010,750
1890	3,308,852	—	3,091,783	2,529,466	—	2,152,966	1,815,117	—	1,530,914	1,313,538
1900	3,805,638	—	3,710,436	3,205,898	—	2,654,718	2,347,916	—	1,991,250	1,616,776
1910	4,536,321	—	4,476,694	3,935,655	—	3,315,417	3,029,084	—	2,475,237	2,090,281
1920	4,756,764	—	4,749,976	4,548,258	—	3,940,410	3,700,920	—	3,060,014	2,646,070
1930	5,794,290	—	5,533,563	4,973,428	—	4,558,635	4,528,785	—	3,853,736	3,370,355
1940	6,153,370	—	5,895,443	5,645,976	—	5,172,076	4,799,718	—	4,368,708	4,045,956
1950	5,305,256	—	5,875,535	6,270,182	—	5,892,284	5,728,842	—	5,133,704	4,544,099
1960	6,585,582	—	5,528,421	5,536,049	—	6,102,962	6,401,597	—	5,924,362	5,521,560
1970 [2]	9,436,501	—	8,453,752	6,855,426	—	5,834,646	5,694,428	—	6,162,141	6,264,605
1980	10,412,715	—	10,655,473	9,815,812	—	8,884,124	7,103,793	—	5,961,198	5,701,506
1990	8,651,317	—	9,344,716	10,617,109	—	10,985,954	10,060,874	—	8,923,802	7,061,976

	Female									
	Age									
	50–59	50–54	55–59	60–69	60–64	65–69	70–79	70–74	75–79	80–89
	Aa267	Aa268	Aa269	Aa270	Aa271	Aa272	Aa273	Aa274	Aa275	Aa276
Year	Number	Number	Number	Number	Number	Number	Number	Number	Number	Number
1850	533,855	—	—	300,411	—	—	129,774	—	—	40,655
1860	750,529	—	—	433,055	—	—	176,327	—	—	49,762
1870	—	627,609	407,057	—	371,480	233,691	—	171,322	89,404	—
1880	—	873,181	596,507	—	519,361	346,378	—	245,441	142,464	—
1890	—	1,117,340	800,673	—	699,324	484,483	—	338,109	193,969	—
1900	—	1,378,207	1,065,915	—	874,196	635,257	—	434,232	258,278	—
1910	—	1,790,778	1,298,514	—	1,081,184	815,509	—	552,084	336,022	—
1920	—	2,199,328	1,669,059	—	1,400,748	988,658	—	688,735	436,595	—
1930	—	2,844,159	2,219,685	—	1,809,713	1,352,793	—	958,357	558,786	—
1940	—	3,504,096	2,832,501	—	2,330,524	1,910,569	—	1,298,565	780,302	—
1950	—	4,143,540	3,605,074	—	3,021,637	2,578,375	—	1,783,120	—	—
1960	—	4,871,125	4,302,620	—	3,733,133	3,326,822	—	2,553,716	1,694,135	—
1970 [2]	—	5,756,102	5,207,207	—	4,589,812	3,869,541	—	3,128,831	2,274,173	—
1980	—	6,089,362	6,133,391	—	5,417,729	4,879,526	—	3,944,577	2,946,061	—
1990	—	5,835,775	5,497,386	—	5,669,120	5,579,428	—	4,585,517	3,721,601	—

Notes appear at end of table

(continued)

TABLE Aa185–286   Total population, by sex and age: 1850–1990   *Continued*

	Female									
	Age									
	80–84	85–89	90–99	90–94	95–99	100 and older	75 and older	85 and older	65 and older	Not stated
	Aa277	Aa278	Aa279	Aa280	Aa281	Aa282	Aa283	Aa284	Aa285	Aa286
Year	Number	Number	Number	Number	Number	Number	Number	Number	Number	Number
1850	—	—	6,512	—	—	1,478	—	—	478,830	5,112
1860	—	—	7,924	—	—	1,720	—	—	668,788	23,621
1870	50,073	18,962	—	7,354	2,377	2,236	—	—	575,419	1,366
1880	78,421	27,927	—	9,749	2,908	2,607	—	—	855,895	—
1890	105,989	41,177	—	13,797	3,462	2,583	—	—	1,183,569	58,636
1900	129,239	47,858	—	14,134	3,849	2,233	—	—	1,525,080	73,161
1910	168,009	66,483	—	18,920	4,346	2,175	—	—	1,963,548	54,612
1920	216,876	87,267	—	23,597	5,710	2,706	—	—	2,450,144	55,824
1930	283,538	114,576	—	31,233	6,750	2,561	—	—	3,308,594	42,206
1940	415,380	155,557	—	41,633	8,847	2,341	—	—	4,613,194	—
1950	—	—	—	—	—	—	2,111,068	—	6,472,563	—
1960	914,834	—	—	—	—	—	—	566,976	9,056,483	—
1970 [2]	1,408,727	656,084	—	209,588	50,747	52,103	—	—	11,649,794	—
1980	1,915,806	1,043,017	—	397,515	96,118	21,892	—	—	15,244,512	—
1990	2,567,645	1,446,211	—	579,392	167,459	29,405	—	—	18,676,658	—

[1] For changes in age and racial categorization, as well as exclusions in particular years, see the essay in this chapter.

[2] Figures for persons ages 100 and older are greatly overstated; see the essay in this chapter.

Sources

U.S. Bureau of the Census. 1850–1870, *U.S. Census of Population: 1870*, volume 2, pp. 552–8. 1880, *U.S. Census of Population: 1880*, volume 1, pp. 548–51. 1890, *U.S. Census of Population: 1890*, volume 1, part 2, pp. 2–5. 1900, *U.S. Census of Population: 1900*, volume 2, part 2, pp. xxxvi–xli. 1910, *U.S. Census of Population: 1910*, Abstract of the Census, p. 122. 1920, *U.S. Census of Population: 1920*, Abstract of the Fourteenth Census of the United States 1920, pp. 140–1. 1930–1940, *U.S. Census of Population: 1940*, volume 4, part 1, pp. 8–14; Population: Second Series, Characteristics of the Population, United States Summary, pp. 16–20. 1950, *U.S. Census of Population: 1950*, volume 2, part 1, pp. 93–4. 1960, *U.S. Census of Population: 1960*, volume 1, part 1, pp. 153–4, 349–58; parts 3 and 13, pp. 23–4. 1970, *U.S. Census of Population: 1970*, volume 1, part 1, section 1, pp. 265–96. 1980, *U.S. Census of Population: 1980*, volume 1, Chapter B, part 1, PC80-1-B1, pp. 23, 27–36. 1990, *U.S. Census of Population: 1990*, 1990 CP-1-1, pp. 17–18, 23–34.

Documentation

For additional information see the text for Table Aa1–5. For definitions of race and nativity, see the text for Tables Aa145–184 and Aa1896–1921.

The Censuses of 1790–1840 contain numerous inconsistencies and other errors. Total population by race (including a division of the Negro population into free and slave) for each state and county was corrected in *U.S. Census of Population: 1870*, volume 1, pp. xliv–xlix, 3–8. Adjusted totals by sex appear in *U.S. Census of Population: 1920*, volume 2, p. 107; however, the age data were not adjusted, and thus the totals in Tables Aa185–598, Aa1922–2077, and Aa2093–2188, which are consistent with the age data shown, differ slightly in some cases from the totals in Table Aa145–184.

Age is age at last birthday, except for 1890, which is based on age at nearest birthday.

Nonwhite population (titled in some censuses colored) was derived as the difference between the total and the white populations.

Other nonwhite population (titled in some censuses other races) was derived as the difference between the total nonwhite population and the black population. It includes Asians, Amerindians, and other groups.

Data for 1870 exclude 1,260,078 persons (747,915 white and 512,163 Negro) for whom age is not available.

For 1880, population by age is available only for all races, white, and for Negro and other races.

Data for 1890 exclude 325,464 persons enumerated in the Indian Territory and on Indian reservations.

Data for 1970 exclude 23,372 persons for whom age data are not available.

Data for 1930 were adjusted in the 1940 Census to reallocate Mexicans back to the category of white population. They had been classified as nonwhite in 1930.

For 1940–1970, age not reported was allocated on the basis of other characteristics.

The number of persons shown as 100 years and over in the 1970 census is overstated, apparently because of a misunderstanding by some persons in filling the age portion of the census questionnaire. This kind of reporting error appears to have affected the count of persons 100 years and over in varying degrees in all of the states. Available evidence suggests that the true number of persons 100 years old and over in the United States does not exceed several thousand and is possibly less than 5,000, as compared with the tabulated figure of 106,441. (U.S. Bureau of the Census, *U.S. Census of Population: 1970*, volume 1, part 1, section 2, Appendix B, pp. App. 13–14.) An effort was made to estimate the true number of centenarians in 1970 using a variety of demographic techniques and alternative data sources: Jacob S. Siegel and Jeffrey S. Passel, "New Estimates of the Number of Centenarians in the United States," *Journal of the American Statistical Association* 71 (355) (1976): 559–66. Their preferred estimate is 4,800 total persons, of which 1,550 were males and 3,250 were females.

TABLE Aa287–364   White population, by sex and age: 1790–1990[1]

Contributed by Michael R. Haines

		Male										
			Age									
	Total	0–9	0–4	5–9	10–15	10–14	16–25	15–19	26–44	20–29	20–24	25–29
	Aa287	Aa288	Aa289	Aa290	Aa291	Aa292	Aa293	Aa294	Aa295	Aa296	Aa297	Aa298
Year	Number	Number	Number	Number	Number	Number	Number	Number	Number	Number	Number	Number
1790	1,615,625	—	—	—	—	—	—	—	—	—	—	—
1800	2,204,421	764,118	—	—	353,071	—	393,156	—	431,589	—	—	—
1810	2,987,571	1,035,058	—	—	468,083	—	547,597	—	571,997	—	—	—
1820	3,995,113	1,345,220	—	—	612,515	—	776,030	—	766,283	—	—	—
1830	5,360,451	—	972,980	782,075	—	669,734	—	573,196	—	956,487		—
1840	7,255,534	—	1,270,743	1,024,050	—	879,530	—	756,106	—	1,322,453	—	—
1850	10,026,402	—	1,472,053	1,372,438	—	1,225,575	—	1,041,116	—	1,869,092	—	—
1860	13,811,387	—	2,091,460	1,788,711	—	1,590,472	—	1,400,536	—	2,497,210	—	—
1870	17,029,088	—	2,398,615	2,103,986	—	2,103,425	—	1,731,015	—	—	1,591,909	1,328,232
1880	22,130,900	—	2,949,449	2,756,201	—	2,482,572	—	2,150,068	—	—	2,219,317	1,838,054
1890	28,206,332	—	3,351,104	3,276,983	—	3,044,058	—	2,818,914	—	—	2,740,864	2,407,153
1900	34,201,735	—	4,011,455	3,862,349	—	3,519,303	—	3,258,090	—	—	3,145,481	2,942,882
1910	42,178,245	—	4,728,650	4,285,366	—	4,006,104	—	3,999,143	—	—	4,070,955	3,792,224
1920	48,430,655	—	5,260,714	5,099,205	—	4,735,150	—	4,141,831	—	—	4,018,576	4,094,301
1930	55,922,528	—	5,158,439	5,662,102	—	5,415,256	—	5,132,461	—	—	4,746,792	4,324,314
1940	59,448,548	—	4,701,470	4,744,537	—	5,259,007	—	5,515,920	—	—	5,113,642	4,892,013
1950	67,129,192	—	7,244,211	5,915,130	—	4,944,535	—	4,685,825	—	—	5,002,782	5,349,707
1960	78,367,149	—	8,849,181	8,202,157	—	7,456,573	—	5,837,093	—	—	4,645,822	4,721,783
1970 [2]	86,720,987	—	7,374,333	8,633,093	—	9,033,725	—	8,291,270	—	—	6,940,820	5,849,792
1980	91,685,333	—	6,484,021	6,685,142	—	7,408,443	—	8,634,142	—	—	8,683,292	8,005,295
1990	97,475,880	—	7,004,481	6,990,531	—	6,606,726	—	6,845,571	—	—	7,388,380	8,384,815

	Male										
	Age										
	30–39	30–34	35–39	40–49	40–44	45–49	50–59	50–54	55–59	60–69	60–64
	Aa299	Aa300	Aa301	Aa302	Aa303	Aa304	Aa305	Aa306	Aa307	Aa308	Aa309
Year	Number	Number	Number	Number	Number	Number	Number	Number	Number	Number	Number
1790	—	—	—	—	—	—	—	—	—	—	—
1800	—	—	—	—	—	—	—	—	—	—	—
1810	—	—	—	—	—	—	—	—	—	—	—
1820	—	—	—	—	—	—	—	—	—	—	—
1830	592,535	—	—	367,840	—	—	229,284	—	—	135,082	—
1840	866,452	—	—	536,606	—	—	314,528	—	—	174,238	—
1850	1,288,682	—	—	840,222	—	—	498,660	—	—	264,742	—
1860	1,867,378	—	—	1,224,086	—	—	740,429	—	—	400,862	—
1870	—	1,131,799	1,048,443	—	881,637	751,745	—	654,500	424,553	—	358,940
1880	—	1,548,077	1,353,221	—	1,111,763	962,027	—	856,178	610,080	—	516,416
1890	—	2,200,973	1,831,443	—	1,495,923	1,271,113	—	1,083,091	793,301	—	686,462
1900	—	2,619,446	2,360,348	—	2,055,176	1,651,972	—	1,396,035	1,040,235	—	825,213
1910	—	3,297,169	3,024,002	—	2,537,219	2,161,848	—	1,915,860	1,363,821	—	1,076,753
1920	—	3,776,266	3,665,341	—	2,987,412	2,779,175	—	2,293,604	1,740,661	—	1,461,619
1930	—	4,116,726	4,225,332	—	3,772,619	3,327,142	—	2,835,808	2,239,604	—	1,799,730
1940	—	4,573,316	4,254,368	—	3,995,190	3,842,613	—	3,451,717	2,790,046	—	2,232,453
1950	—	5,080,610	4,955,941	—	4,573,529	4,080,174	—	3,756,125	3,350,888	—	2,829,399
1960	—	5,218,188	5,446,833	—	5,117,038	4,828,179	—	4,286,023	3,728,599	—	3,121,664
1970 [2]	—	4,925,069	4,784,375	—	5,194,497	5,257,619	—	4,832,555	4,310,921	—	3,647,243
1980	—	7,299,659	5,831,107	—	4,849,516	4,638,737	—	4,918,060	4,852,744	—	4,173,113
1990	—	8,699,545	8,054,129	—	7,227,231	5,736,583	—	4,657,384	4,330,811	—	4,334,784

Notes appear at end of table

(continued)

TABLE Aa287–364   White population, by sex and age: 1790–1990   *Continued*

	Male										
	Age										
	65–69	70–79	70–74	75–79	80–89	80–84	85–89	90–99	90–94	95–99	100 and older
	Aa310	Aa311	Aa312	Aa313	Aa314	Aa315	Aa316	Aa317	Aa318	Aa319	Aa320
Year	Number	Number	Number	Number	Number	Number	Number	Number	Number	Number	Number
1790	—	—	—	—	—	—	—	—	—	—	—
1800	—	—	—	—	—	—	—	—	—	—	—
1810	—	—	—	—	—	—	—	—	—	—	—
1820	—	—	—	—	—	—	—	—	—	—	—
1830	—	57,772	—	—	15,806	—	—	2,041	—	—	301
1840	—	80,067	—	—	21,677	—	—	2,508	—	—	476
1850	—	111,416	—	—	31,243	—	—	3,653	—	—	357
1860	—	153,649	—	—	38,001	—	—	4,135	—	—	385
1870	226,814	—	155,225	78,213	—	38,709	13,726	—	3,939	1,070	394
1880	341,831	—	224,652	125,704	—	59,648	19,277	—	4,756	1,216	393
1890	479,479	—	333,325	182,768	—	88,648	30,305	—	7,920	1,446	413
1900	608,715	—	411,658	240,284	—	110,087	35,838	—	7,607	1,405	330
1910	792,310	—	518,888	307,446	—	141,301	50,843	—	11,970	1,935	326
1920	998,779	—	655,916	391,383	—	172,064	63,308	—	13,852	2,706	467
1930	1,329,539	—	937,275	516,409	—	234,690	83,536	—	17,698	3,121	559
1940	1,736,937	—	1,183,283	681,397	—	339,291	112,091	—	24,498	4,224	535
1950	2,223,014	—	1,513,308	—	—	—	—	—	—	—	—
1960	2,684,132	—	2,018,350	1,255,281	—	619,338	—	—	—	—	—
1970 [2]	2,807,974	—	2,107,552	1,437,628	—	805,564	330,213	—	92,024	18,705	46,015
1980	3,481,640	—	2,552,321	1,650,386	—	923,308	434,949	—	142,518	29,614	7,326
1990	4,013,229	—	3,055,729	2,154,399	—	1,227,102	548,370	—	170,311	39,970	5,799

	Male					Female					
	Age						Age				
	45 and older	75 and older	85 and older	65 and older	Not stated	Total	0–9	0–4	5–9	10–15	10–14
	Aa321	Aa322	Aa323	Aa324	Aa325	Aa326	Aa327	Aa328	Aa329	Aa330	Aa331
Year	Number	Number	Number	Number	Number	Number	Number	Number	Number	Number	Number
1790	—	—	—	—	—	1,556,839	—	—	—	—	—
1800	262,487	—	—	—	—	2,100,068	715,197	—	—	323,648	—
1810	364,836	—	—	—	—	2,874,433	981,421	—	—	448,322	—
1820	495,065	—	—	—	—	3,866,804	1,280,570	—	—	605,375	—
1830	—	—	—	—	5,318	5,171,115	—	921,934	750,741	—	638,856
1840	—	—	—	—	6,100	6,940,161	—	1,203,319	986,940	—	836,630
1850	—	—	—	—	7,153	9,526,666	—	1,424,405	1,331,690	—	1,176,554
1860	—	—	—	—	14,073	13,111,150	—	2,025,985	1,739,387	—	1,523,281
1870	—	—	—	518,090	2,199	16,560,289	—	2,321,177	2,047,729	—	2,033,036
1880	—	—	—	777,477	—	21,272,070	—	2,850,702	2,686,218	—	2,397,959
1890	—	—	—	1,124,304	80,646	26,777,558	—	3,228,544	3,196,185	—	2,947,914
1900	—	—	—	1,415,924	97,826	32,607,461	—	3,908,497	3,775,977	—	3,439,935
1910	—	—	—	1,825,019	94,112	39,553,712	—	4,594,264	4,189,807	—	3,912,304
1920	—	—	—	2,298,475	78,325	46,390,260	—	5,113,207	4,988,040	—	4,634,172
1930	—	—	—	3,122,827	43,376	54,364,212	—	4,983,730	5,499,561	—	5,279,168
1940	—	—	—	4,082,256	—	58,766,322	—	4,528,035	4,584,414	—	5,093,688
1950	—	1,624,014	—	5,360,336	—	67,812,836	—	6,940,293	5,681,442	—	4,749,994
1960	—	—	330,915	6,908,016	—	80,464,583	—	8,509,371	7,885,385	—	7,182,319
1970 [2]	—	—	—	7,645,675	—	91,027,988	—	7,048,807	8,264,333	—	8,647,392
1980	—	—	—	9,222,062	—	96,686,289	—	6,150,054	6,347,824	—	7,052,479
1990	—	—	—	11,214,909	—	102,210,190	—	6,645,009	6,625,737	—	6,246,832

Notes appear at end of table

TABLE Aa287–364   White population, by sex and age: 1790–1990   *Continued*

	Female										
	Age										
	16–25	15–19	26–44	20–29	20–24	25–29	30–39	30–34	35–39	40–49	40–44
	Aa332	Aa333	Aa334	Aa335	Aa336	Aa337	Aa338	Aa339	Aa340	Aa341	Aa342
Year	Number	Number	Number	Number	Number	Number	Number	Number	Number	Number	Number
1790	—	—	—	—	—	—	—	—	—	—	—
1800	401,499	—	411,694	—	—	—	—	—	—	—	—
1810	561,956	—	544,256	—	—	—	—	—	—	—	—
1820	781,371	—	736,600	—	—	—	—	—	—	—	—
1830	—	596,254	—	918,411	—	—	555,531	—	—	356,046	—
1840	—	792,223	—	1,253,490	—	—	779,120	—	—	502,183	—
1850	—	1,087,600	—	1,758,469	—	—	1,128,257	—	—	748,566	—
1860	—	1,452,045	—	2,420,139	—	—	1,636,213	—	—	1,058,246	—
1870	—	1,780,021	—	—	1,643,119	1,353,320	—	1,133,266	998,877	—	833,618
1880	—	2,201,582	—	—	2,183,155	1,703,647	—	1,431,177	1,295,271	—	1,078,972
1890	—	2,856,433	—	—	2,707,603	2,239,534	—	1,943,859	1,608,487	—	1,369,725
1900	—	3,285,099	—	—	3,189,563	2,820,098	—	2,384,998	2,100,227	—	1,796,967
1910	—	3,969,248	—	—	3,915,456	3,464,912	—	2,970,107	2,707,843	—	2,243,053
1920	—	4,172,324	—	—	4,166,765	4,047,389	—	3,562,524	3,300,464	—	2,768,135
1930	—	5,116,318	—	—	4,865,877	4,384,684	—	4,094,186	4,052,936	—	3,494,273
1940	—	5,448,127	—	—	5,226,507	5,012,257	—	4,633,162	4,262,292	—	3,940,893
1950	—	4,644,695	—	—	5,176,405	5,575,097	—	5,275,721	5,102,532	—	4,616,761
1960	—	5,771,136	—	—	4,824,957	4,833,802	—	5,370,642	5,694,008	—	5,305,982
1970 [2]	—	8,079,090	—	—	7,341,007	5,962,122	—	5,042,368	4,936,494	—	5,412,335
1980	—	8,327,960	—	—	8,605,482	7,979,535	—	7,345,140	5,930,000	—	4,976,317
1990	—	6,497,132	—	—	7,135,532	8,253,729	—	8,651,968	8,027,477	—	7,279,159

	Female										
	Age										
	45–49	50–59	50–54	55–59	60–69	60–64	65–69	70–79	70–74	75–79	80–89
	Aa343	Aa344	Aa345	Aa346	Aa347	Aa348	Aa349	Aa350	Aa351	Aa352	Aa353
Year	Number	Number	Number	Number	Number	Number	Number	Number	Number	Number	Number
1790	—	—	—	—	—	—	—	—	—	—	—
1800	—	—	—	—	—	—	—	—	—	—	—
1810	—	—	—	—	—	—	—	—	—	—	—
1820	—	—	—	—	—	—	—	—	—	—	—
1830	—	223,504	—	—	131,307	—	—	58,336	—	—	17,434
1840	—	304,852	—	—	173,329	—	—	80,565	—	—	23,962
1850	—	459,511	—	—	256,480	—	—	112,648	—	—	34,403
1860	—	659,246	—	—	380,011	—	—	156,583	—	—	42,753
1870	654,870	—	549,743	370,218	—	327,739	212,557	—	152,510	80,756	—
1880	899,865	—	771,714	544,835	—	460,892	315,578	—	219,495	129,164	—
1890	1,178,107	—	1,007,858	738,358	—	636,648	446,045	—	308,626	178,057	—
1900	1,453,706	—	1,237,946	980,982	—	795,445	586,580	—	396,439	237,436	—
1910	1,899,214	—	1,639,453	1,200,385	—	992,570	757,644	—	511,996	313,546	—
1920	2,408,865	—	2,023,662	1,565,010	—	1,309,814	925,517	—	642,822	410,295	—
1930	3,054,428	—	2,609,935	2,079,697	—	1,697,047	1,277,594	—	908,047	527,901	—
1940	3,690,143	—	3,228,590	2,636,799	—	2,184,240	1,762,109	—	1,217,262	736,959	—
1950	4,089,180	—	3,779,314	3,344,844	—	2,823,207	2,362,572	—	1,668,267	—	—
1960	4,956,983	—	4,407,505	3,897,612	—	3,429,009	3,055,092	—	2,372,692	1,580,037	—
1970 [2]	5,587,023	—	5,169,302	4,695,581	—	4,157,467	3,491,080	—	2,874,531	2,114,943	—
1980	4,818,254	—	5,239,501	5,385,014	—	4,802,598	4,330,607	—	3,543,031	2,659,898	—
1990	5,849,120	—	4,847,487	4,637,605	—	4,876,339	4,886,408	—	4,070,835	3,330,626	—

Notes appear at end of table

(continued)

TABLE Aa287–364   White population, by sex and age: 1790–1990   *Continued*

	Female										
	Age										
	80–84	85–89	90–99	90–94	95–99	100 and older	45 and older	75 and older	85 and older	65 and older	Not stated
	Aa354	Aa355	Aa356	Aa357	Aa358	Aa359	Aa360	Aa361	Aa362	Aa363	Aa364
Year	Number	Number	Number	Number	Number	Number	Number	Number	Number	Number	Number
1790	—	—	—	—	—	—	—	—	—	—	—
1800	—	—	—	—	—	—	248,030	—	—	—	—
1810	—	—	—	—	—	—	338,478	—	—	—	—
1820	—	—	—	—	—	—	462,888	—	—	—	—
1830	—	—	2,523	—	—	238	—	—	—	—	—
1840	—	—	3,232	—	—	316	—	—	—	—	—
1850	—	—	4,499	—	—	430	—	—	—	—	3,154
1860	—	—	5,634	—	—	542	—	—	—	—	11,085
1870	42,945	16,643	—	5,185	1,526	570	—	—	—	512,692	864
1880	67,879	24,521	—	7,047	1,835	562	—	—	—	766,081	—
1890	94,647	36,710	—	10,846	2,236	641	—	—	—	1,077,808	40,495
1900	114,630	42,189	—	10,712	2,302	507	—	—	—	1,390,795	47,226
1910	153,254	60,093	—	15,191	2,822	438	—	—	—	1,814,984	40,112
1920	201,002	80,228	—	19,861	4,125	701	—	—	—	2,284,551	45,338
1930	264,558	106,003	—	27,154	5,102	787	—	—	—	3,117,146	35,226
1940	392,854	143,838	—	36,563	6,714	876	—	—	—	4,297,175	—
1950	—	—	—	—	—	—	—	1,982,512	—	6,013,351	—
1960	861,351	—	—	—	—	—	—	—	526,700	8,395,872	—
1970 [2]	1,314,258	609,149	—	193,048	44,693	42,965	—	—	—	10,684,667	—
1980	1,762,041	964,400	—	364,437	84,878	16,839	—	—	—	13,726,131	—
1990	2,325,593	1,316,183	—	531,945	151,168	24,306	—	—	—	16,637,064	—

[1] For changes in age and racial categorization, as well as exclusions in particular years, see the text for Table Aa185–286.

[2] Figures for persons ages 100 and older are greatly overstated; see the text for Table Aa185–286.

Sources

U.S. Bureau of the Census. 1790–1840, *U.S. Census of Population: 1840, Compendium* (Thomas Allen), pp. 100–3, 366–75. 1850–1870, *U.S. Census of Population: 1870*, volume 2, pp. 552–8, 673. 1880, *U.S. Census of Population: 1880*, volume 1, pp. 548–51. 1890, *U.S. Census of Population: 1890*, volume 1, part 2, pp. 2–5. 1900, *U.S. Census of Population: 1900*, volume 2, part 2, pp. xxxvi–xli. 1910, *U.S. Census of Population: 1910*, "Abstract of the Census," p. 122. 1920, *U.S. Census of Population: 1920*, "Abstract of the Fourteenth Census of the United States 1920," pp. 140–1. 1930–1940, *U.S. Census of Population: 1940*, volume 4, part 1, pp. 8–14; "Population: Second Series, Characteristics of the Population, United States Summary," pp. 16–20. 1950, *U.S. Census of Population: 1950*, volume 2, part 1, pp. 93–4. 1960, *U.S. Census of Population: 1960*, volume 1, part 1, pp. 153–4, 349–58; parts 3 and 13, pp. 23–4. 1970, *U.S. Census of Population: 1970*, volume 1, part 1, section 1, pp. 265–96. 1980, *U.S. Census of Population: 1980*, volume 1, Chapter B, part 1, PC80-1-B1, pp. 23, 30. 1990, *U.S. Census of Population: 1990*, 1990 CP-1-1, pp. 17, 25.

Documentation

See the text for Table Aa185–286. For 1790, only broad age categories for males were given: age 0–15, 802, 327; age 16 and older, 813, 298. No age data for females were given.

TABLE Aa365–456   Black population, by sex and age: 1820–1990[1]

Contributed by Michael R. Haines

		Male										
			Age									
	Total	0–13	0–9	0–4	5–9	14–25	10–23	10–14	15–19	20–29	20–24
	Aa365	Aa366	Aa367	Aa368	Aa369	Aa370	Aa371	Aa372	Aa373	Aa374	Aa375
Year	Number	Number	Number	Number	Number	Number	Number	Number	Number	Number	Number
1820	900,762	391,511	—	—	—	227,100	—	—	—	—	—
1830	1,166,276	—	402,173	—	—	—	355,646	—	—	—	—
1840	1,432,998	—	478,868	—	—	—	444,011	—	—	—	—
1850	1,811,258	—	—	297,407	267,969	—	—	247,541	196,564	325,377	—
1860	2,216,744	—	—	354,999	317,999	—	—	307,374	245,104	394,185	—
1870	2,393,263	—	—	396,812	331,795	—	—	329,339	251,822	—	232,490
1880	3,253,115	—	—	—	—	—	—	—	—	—	—
1890	3,725,561	—	—	529985 [5]	549405 [5]	—	—	526450 [5]	422,258	—	350,392
1900	4,386,547	—	—	604,487	600,410	—	—	548,642	473,750	—	458,921
1910	4,885,881	—	—	629,320	619,175	—	—	578,074	507,945	—	482,157
1920	5,209,436	—	—	568,633	631,341	—	—	616,251	513,416	—	487,169
1930	5,855,669	—	—	611,231	679,748	—	—	623,228	595,646	—	553,622
1940	6,269,038	—	—	621,689	643,781	—	—	661,351	630,079	—	550,193
1950 [2]	7,269,170	—	—	947,740	761,430	—	—	674,480	591,550	—	563,730
1960 [3]	9,097,704	—	—	1,362,831	1,195,123	—	—	989,360	740,971	—	569,398
1970 [4]	10,748,316	—	—	1,219,567	1,377,355	—	—	1,406,715	1,201,605	—	839,848
1980	12,519,189	—	—	1,227,900	1,255,253	—	—	1,344,324	1,489,065	—	1,300,253
1990	14,170,151	—	—	1,408,495	1,350,265	—	—	1,314,408	1,342,263	—	1,258,626

	Male										
	Age										
	24–35	25–29	26–44	30–39	30–34	35–44	35–39	36–54	40–49	40–44	45–49
	Aa376	Aa377	Aa378	Aa379	Aa380	Aa381	Aa382	Aa383	Aa384	Aa385	Aa386
Year	Number	Number	Number	Number	Number	Number	Number	Number	Number	Number	Number
1820	—	—	187,173	—	—	—	—	—	—	—	—
1830	213,235	—	—	—	—	—	—	141,151	—	—	—
1840	270,707	—	—	—	—	—	—	173,534	—	—	—
1850	—	—	—	201,453	—	—	—	—	127,351	—	—
1860	—	—	—	247,378	—	—	—	—	162,220	—	—
1870	—	175,068	—	—	130,517	—	123,129	—	—	101,580	85,010
1880	—	—	—	—	—	—	—	—	—	—	—
1890	—	272,044	—	—	203,361	343,858	—	—	—	—	—
1900	—	360,597	—	—	262,130	—	233,371	—	—	179,090	168,495
1910	—	421,805	—	—	332,163	—	320,450	—	—	229,680	199,928
1920	—	424,352	—	—	331,579	—	383,587	—	—	275,926	320,506
1930	—	500,520	—	—	416,869	—	430,472	—	—	339,329	323,162
1940	—	529,613	—	—	467,887	—	462,559	—	—	400,249	348,251
1950 [2]	—	579,880	—	—	510,970	—	530,210	—	—	468,595	418,690
1960 [3]	—	547,941	—	—	563,502	—	569,133	—	—	508,082	479,629
1970 [4]	—	657,544	—	—	568,086	—	540,539	—	—	543,737	520,095
1980	—	1,084,442	—	—	870,997	—	662,338	—	—	566,539	515,277
1990	—	1,285,760	—	—	1,250,610	—	1,083,051	—	—	865,660	642,441

Notes appear at end of table   (continued)

TABLE Aa365–456   Black population, by sex and age: 1820–1990 *Continued*

					Male				
					Age				
45–54	50–59	50–54	55–59	55–64	55–59	60–69	60–64	65–69	70–79
Aa387	Aa388	Aa389	Aa390	Aa391	Aa392	Aa393	Aa394	Aa395	Aa396
Year Number	Number	Number	Number	Number	Number	Number	Number	Number	Number
1820 —	—	—	—	—	—	—	—	—	—
1830 —	—	—	—	—	53,054	—	—	—	—
1840 —	—	—	—	—	64,844	—	—	—	—
1850 —	77,025	—	—	—	—	44,773	—	—	16,044
1860 —	93,106	—	—	—	—	53,909	—	—	18,631
1870 —	—	83,941	44,237	—	—	—	47,811	23,649	—
1880 —	—	—	—	—	—	—	—	—	—
1890 257,301	—	—	—	144,761	—	—	—	—	—
1900 —	—	155,188	97,323	—	—	—	85,961	56,018	—
1910 —	—	179,387	115,090	—	—	—	101,149	67,956	—
1920 —	—	227,995	129,153	—	—	—	112,137	76,184	—
1930 —	—	277,532	174,367	—	—	—	133,349	82,843	—
1940 —	—	283,120	207,220	—	—	—	154,245	151,990	—
1950 [2] —	—	350,255	264,085	—	—	—	195,155	191,435	—
1960 [3] —	—	406,991	365,302	—	—	—	258,918	229,067	—
1970 [4] —	—	458,526	404,704	—	—	—	334,425	277,117	—
1980 —	—	504,531	466,506	—	—	—	385,052	331,725	—
1990 —	—	531,976	456,919	—	—	—	414,245	362,942	—

				Male					
				Age					
70–74	75–79	80–89	80–84	85–89	90–99	90–94	95–99	100 and older	45 and older
Aa397	Aa398	Aa399	Aa400	Aa401	Aa402	Aa403	Aa404	Aa405	Aa406
Year Number	Number	Number	Number	Number	Number	Number	Number	Number	Number
1820 —	—	—	—	—	—	—	—	—	94,978
1830 —	—	—	—	—	—	—	—	1,017	—
1840 —	—	—	—	—	—	—	—	1,034	—
1850 —	—	5,484	—	—	1,530	—	—	720	—
1860 —	—	5,632	—	—	1,644	—	—	799	—
1870 17,700	8,014	—	5,779	1,774	—	1,371	529	885	—
1880 —	—	—	—	—	—	—	—	—	—
1890 —	—	—	—	—	—	—	—	—	—
1900 36,235	20,475	—	11,655	4,713	—	2,085	958	886	—
1910 40,584	22,667	—	11,696	5,164	—	2,394	1,017	1,004	—
1920 47,411	27,172	—	13,049	5,620	—	2,340	1,087	1,018	—
1930 50,896	29,219	—	15,343	6,864	—	2,516	1,073	776	—
1940 83,835	—	—	—	—	—	—	—	—	—
1950 [2] 108,390	64,885	—	30,825	—	—	—	—	—	—
1960 [3] 151,112	94,216	—	39,841	—	—	—	—	—	—
1970 [4] 183,822	109,959	—	58,674	26,658	—	8,812	3,182	7,346	—
1980 234,315	152,755	—	74,951	33,487	—	12,752	4,309	2,418	—
1990 254,699	178,540	—	100,659	47,842	—	14,698	4,465	1,587	—

Notes appear at end of table

TABLE Aa365–456   Black population, by sex and age: 1820–1990   *Continued*

	Male				Female					
	Age					Age				
	75 and older	85 and older	65 and older	Not stated	Total	0–13	0–9	0–4	5–9	14–25
	Aa407	Aa408	Aa409	Aa410	Aa411	Aa412	Aa413	Aa414	Aa415	Aa416
Year	Number	Number	Number	Number	Number	Number	Number	Number	Number	Number
1820	—	—	—	—	870,800	370,242	—	—	—	231,186
1830	—	—	—	—	1,162,366	—	394,994	—	—	—
1840	—	—	—	—	1,440,760	—	476,527	—	—	—
1850	—	—	—	2,020	1,827,550	—	—	303,908	269,171	—
1860	—	—	—	13,764	2,225,086	—	—	364,085	319,807	—
1870	—	—	59,701	11	2,486,746	—	—	394,609	328,036	—
1880	—	—	—	—	3,327,678	—	—	—	—	—
1890	—	—	107,311	18,435	3,744,479	—	—	517589[5]	544089[5]	—
1900	—	—	133,025	25,157	4,447,447	—	—	611,168	602,348	—
1910	—	—	152,482	17,076	4,941,882	—	—	633,968	627,378	—
1920	—	—	173,881	13,510	5,253,695	—	—	575,066	634,866	—
1930	—	—	189,530	7,064	6,035,474	—	—	618,975	688,633	—
1940	72,976	—	308,801	—	6,596,480	—	—	627,391	650,765	—
1950 [2]	—	16,865	412,400	—	7,757,505	—	—	942,880	768,400	—
1960 [3]	—	26,287	540,523	—	9,750,915	—	—	1,359,569	1,195,515	—
1970 [4]	—	—	675,570	—	11,831,973	—	—	1,213,071	1,370,073	—
1980	—	—	846,712	—	13,975,836	—	—	1,208,269	1,235,464	—
1990	—	—	965,432	—	15,815,909	—	—	1,377,407	1,320,844	—

	Female									
	Age									
	10–23	10–14	15–19	20–29	20–24	24–35	25–29	26–44	30–39	30–34
	Aa417	Aa418	Aa419	Aa420	Aa421	Aa422	Aa423	Aa424	Aa425	Aa426
Year	Number	Number	Number	Number	Number	Number	Number	Number	Number	Number
1820	—	—	—	—	—	—	—	179,874	—	—
1830	356,908	—	—	—	—	218,327	—	—	—	—
1840	446,709	—	—	—	—	281,507	—	—	—	—
1850	—	240,959	204,512	324,380	—	—	—	—	207,427	—
1860	—	294,273	256,489	389,418	—	—	—	—	253,220	—
1870	—	315,972	268,728	—	266,364	—	203,980	—	—	154,232
1880	—	—	—	—	—	—	—	—	—	—
1890	—	507251 [5]	448,860	—	381,156	—	287,507	—	—	206,616
1900	—	543,348	508,272	—	510,251	—	376,882	—	—	262,477
1910	—	577,192	552,471	—	548,638	—	459,422	—	—	335,926
1920	—	620,663	569,799	—	567,678	—	485,387	—	—	366,286
1930	—	628,314	654,882	—	649,569	—	571,267	—	—	447,645
1940	—	669,309	674,527	—	645,034	—	615,671	—	—	524,992
1950 [2]	—	677,965	634,585	—	667,815	—	669,295	—	—	592,570
1960 [3]	—	983,572	756,020	—	642,315	—	630,858	—	—	663,092
1970 [4]	—	1,403,154	1,221,440	—	974,372	—	770,713	—	—	684,849
1980	—	1,328,948	1,495,798	—	1,424,553	—	1,236,877	—	—	1,017,716
1990	—	1,287,182	1,316,230	—	1,320,327	—	1,422,005	—	—	1,431,114

Notes appear at end of table

(continued)

TABLE Aa365–456 Black population, by sex and age: 1820–1990 *Continued*

	Female									
	Age									
	35–44	35–39	36–54	40–49	40–44	45–49	45–54	50–59	50–54	55–59
	Aa427	Aa428	Aa429	Aa430	Aa431	Aa432	Aa433	Aa434	Aa435	Aa436
Year	Number	Number	Number	Number	Number	Number	Number	Number	Number	Number
1820	—	—	—	—	—	—	—	—	—	—
1830	—	—	136,214	—	—	—	—	—	—	—
1840	—	—	169,575	—	—	—	—	—	—	—
1850	—	—	—	130,521	—	—	—	74,344	—	—
1860	—	—	—	162,299	—	—	—	90,587	—	—
1870	—	135,709	—	—	115,240	83,958	—	—	77,421	36,620
1880	—	—	—	—	—	—	—	—	—	—
1890	363,723	—	—	—	—	—	242,378	—	—	—
1900	—	241,316	—	—	188,126	157,889	—	—	135,799	81,853
1910	—	312,999	—	—	225,733	185,981	—	—	146,683	94,532
1920	—	390,344	—	—	283,775	231,083	—	—	171,115	100,827
1930	—	460,428	—	—	348,094	306,903	—	—	227,058	135,030
1940	—	523,274	—	—	414,847	344,556	—	—	267,315	189,999
1950 [2]	—	608,650	—	—	503,960	444,215	—	—	351,980	251,280
1960 [3]	—	652,195	—	—	578,429	533,714	—	—	444,591	393,439
1970 [4]	—	655,188	—	—	654,128	602,684	—	—	530,941	468,824
1980	—	795,409	—	—	684,528	627,671	—	—	624,395	570,278
1990	—	1,253,715	—	—	1,010,402	763,325	—	—	647,035	575,830

	Female									
	Age									
	55–64	55–59	60–69	60–64	65–69	70–79	70–74	75–79	80–89	80–84
	Aa437	Aa438	Aa439	Aa440	Aa441	Aa442	Aa443	Aa444	Aa445	Aa446
Year	Number	Number	Number	Number	Number	Number	Number	Number	Number	Number
1820	—	—	—	—	—	—	—	—	—	—
1830	—	54,861	—	—	—	—	—	—	—	—
1840	—	65,499	—	—	—	—	—	—	—	—
1850	—	—	43,931	—	—	17,126	—	—	6,252	—
1860	—	—	52,566	—	—	19,562	—	—	6,904	—
1870	—	—	—	43,503	21,015	—	18,686	8,606	—	7,902
1880	—	—	—	—	—	—	—	—	—	—
1890	123,559	—	—	—	—	—	—	—	—	—
1900	—	—	—	75,726	46,653	—	36,147	19,945	—	13,872
1910	—	—	—	85,353	55,594	—	38,255	21,351	—	13,883
1920	—	—	—	87,981	60,851	—	44,168	25,180	—	15,073
1930	—	—	—	108,820	72,334	—	48,200	29,492	—	18,034
1940	—	—	—	141,659	144,747	—	79,113	—	—	—
1950 [2]	—	—	—	189,685	215,495	—	112,260	65,720	—	34,500
1960 [3]	—	—	—	290,249	258,339	—	173,208	108,903	—	50,558
1970 [4]	—	—	—	399,352	349,800	—	232,081	144,528	—	85,389
1980	—	—	—	485,784	445,272	—	329,252	234,644	—	125,024
1990	—	—	—	547,374	500,103	—	385,716	302,730	—	192,979

Notes appear at end of table

TABLE Aa365–456   Black population, by sex and age: 1820–1990   *Continued*

	Female									
	Age									
	85–89	90–99	90–94	95–99	100 and older	45 and older	75 and older	85 and older	65 and older	Not stated
	Aa447	Aa448	Aa449	Aa450	Aa451	Aa452	Aa453	Aa454	Aa455	Aa456
Year	Number	Number	Number	Number	Number	Number	Number	Number	Number	Number
1820	—	—	—	—	—	89,498	—	—	—	—
1830	—	—	—	—	1,062	—	—	—	—	—
1840	—	—	—	—	943	—	—	—	—	—
1850	—	2,013	—	—	1,048	—	—	—	—	1,958
1860	—	2,241	—	—	1,141	—	—	—	—	12,494
1870	2,306	—	2,151	849	1,652	—	—	—	62,357	17
1880	—	—	—	—	—	—	—	—	—	—
1890	—	—	—	—	—	—	—	—	104,373	17,378
1900	5,370	—	3,208	1,476	1,667	—	—	—	128,338	23,654
1910	6,002	—	3,456	1,430	1,671	—	—	—	141,642	13,964
1920	6,661	—	3,507	1,475	1,917	—	—	—	158,832	9,993
1930	8,084	—	3,816	1,538	1,691	—	—	—	183,189	6,667
1940	—	—	—	—	—	—	83,281	—	307,141	—
1950 [2]	—	—	—	—	—	—	—	26,250	454,225	—
1960 [3]	—	—	—	—	—	—	—	36,349	627,357	—
1970 [4]	42,722	—	14,853	5,565	8,246	—	—	—	883,184	—
1980	64,261	—	27,695	9,662	4,336	—	—	—	1,240,146	—
1990	105,132	—	38,693	13,479	4,287	—	—	—	1,543,119	—

[1] For changes in age and racial categorization, as well as exclusions in particular years, see the text for Table Aa185–286.

[2] 20 percent sample data.

[3] 25 percent sample data.

[4] Figures for persons ages 100 and older are greatly overstated; see the text for Table Aa185–286.

[5] Estimates based on population younger than 15 years old and age distribution of Negro and other races.

Sources

U.S. Bureau of the Census. 1820–1840, *U.S. Census of Population: 1840, Compendium* (Thomas Allen), pp. 100–3, 366–75. 1850–1870, *U.S. Census of Population: 1870,* volume 2, pp. 552–8, 673. 1880, *U.S. Census of Population: 1920,* volume 2, p. 107. 1890–1930, *U.S. Census of Population: 1930,* volume 2, p. 580. 1940, *U.S. Census of Population: 1940,* volume 2, part 1, p. 22. 1950, *U.S. Census of Population: 1950,* volume 2, part 1, p. 172. 1960, *U.S. Census of Population: 1960,* volume 1, part 1, p. 359; part 3, p. 117; part 13, p. 113. 1970, *U.S. Census of Population: 1970,* volume 1, part 1, section 1, pp. 269–96. 1980, *U.S. Census of Population: 1980,* Chapter B, part 1, PC80-1-B1, pp. 23, 31–2. 1990, *U.S. Census of Population: 1990,* 1990 CP-1-1, pp. 17, 26.

Documentation

See the text for Table Aa185–286.

TABLE Aa457–524   Nonwhite population, by sex and age: 1860–1990[1]

Contributed by Michael R. Haines

		Male										
	Total	Age										
		0–4	5–9	10–14	15–19	20–29	20–24	25–29	30–39	30–34	35–39	40–49
	Aa457	Aa458	Aa459	Aa460	Aa461	Aa462	Aa463	Aa464	Aa465	Aa466	Aa467	Aa468
Year	Number	Number	Number	Number	Number	Number	Number	Number	Number	Number	Number	Number
1860	2,273,817	358,087	320,834	310,396	249,476	414,348	—	—	261,639	—	—	168,137
1870	2,464,477	398,642	333,456	332,160	258,680	—	244,037	187,439	—	141,834	130,923	—
1880	3,387,920	558,260	518,930	424,909	326,020	—	335,367	271,687	—	196,231	173,938	—
1890	3,861,548	533,765	553,369	530,729	429,797	—	364,029	291,158	—	224,691	219,601	—
1900	4,614,713	622,157	617,047	563,738	492,361	—	479,099	380,661	—	281,875	256,517	—
1910	5,154,032	651,946	638,757	595,649	528,139	—	509,335	452,124	—	359,599	343,014	—
1920	5,469,776	596,747	653,796	634,156	531,961	—	508,469	443,932	—	354,517	409,020	—
1930	6,214,552	647,735	719,006	653,521	625,364	—	590,023	535,866	—	445,060	454,528	—
1940	6,613,044	653,338	674,286	693,322	664,233	—	578,750	558,649	—	496,996	491,291	—
1950	7,931,615	1,021,229	824,146	735,565	645,524	—	623,136	642,036	—	560,772	579,570	—
1960	9,964,345	1,480,548	1,302,211	1,067,716	796,568	—	626,518	611,292	—	628,036	632,679	—
1970 [2]	12,191,205	1,371,166	1,535,403	1,557,012	1,342,577	—	976,449	771,775	—	670,721	628,048	—
1980	18,367,828	1,877,988	1,853,938	1,907,778	2,121,267	—	1,979,939	1,699,812	—	1,377,137	1,030,402	—
1990	23,763,538	2,387,928	2,271,996	2,160,441	2,257,127	—	2,287,216	2,311,121	—	2,177,388	1,848,114	—

Notes appear at end of table

(continued)

TABLE Aa457-524   Nonwhite population, by sex and age: 1860-1990   *Continued*

Male

	Age											
	40-44	45-49	50-59	50-54	55-59	60-69	60-64	65-69	70-79	70-74	75-79	80-89
	Aa469	Aa470	Aa471	Aa472	Aa473	Aa474	Aa475	Aa476	Aa477	Aa478	Aa479	Aa480
Year	Number	Number	Number	Number	Number	Number	Number	Number	Number	Number	Number	Number
1860	—	—	94,921	—	—	54,892	—	—	18,914	—	—	5,789
1870	108,384	87,833	—	85,860	44,942	—	48,551	23,848	—	17,811	8,069	—
1880	132,010	116,668	—	110,524	64,847	—	68,442	37,667	—	25,349	12,897	—
1890	158,681	146,989	—	125,831	78,362	—	72,248	46,148	—	30,317	16,325	—
1900	200,740	185,864	—	168,587	105,022	—	91,954	58,954	—	37,951	21,295	—
1910	249,131	217,068	—	194,153	124,616	—	109,213	71,684	—	42,756	23,834	—
1920	298,131	338,375	—	241,941	139,404	—	120,181	81,038	—	50,385	28,582	—
1930	363,840	344,782	—	295,837	186,388	—	141,778	88,273	—	54,372	31,195	—
1940	423,945	366,656	—	301,033	221,318	—	165,363	159,151	—	87,684	42,283	—
1950	511,437	459,049	—	381,332	285,123	—	214,884	205,962	—	118,852	—	—
1960	558,843	529,746	—	448,806	398,646	—	287,655	246,956	—	166,866	104,143	—
1970 ²	624,316	593,715	—	515,361	454,900	—	379,729	314,110	—	207,448	123,033	—
1980	858,694	749,512	—	702,610	629,119	—	496,779	421,315	—	301,226	197,275	—
1990	1,464,753	1,074,014	—	857,354	703,559	—	612,263	519,078	—	353,577	245,369	—

Male

	Age									
	80-84	85-89	90-99	90-94	95-99	100 and older	75 and older	85 and older	65 and older	Not stated
	Aa481	Aa482	Aa483	Aa484	Aa485	Aa486	Aa487	Aa488	Aa489	Aa490
Year	Number	Number	Number	Number	Number	Number	Number	Number	Number	Number
1860	—	—	1,719	—	—	848	—	—	679,194	13,817
1870	5,820	1,787	—	1,378	535	892	—	—	60,140	1,596
1880	8,293	2,631	—	1,595	639	1,016	—	—	90,087	—
1890	9,214	3,758	—	1,928	740	985	—	—	109,415	22,883
1900	12,186	4,904	—	2,251	1,012	941	—	—	139,494	29,597
1910	12,444	5,492	—	2,583	1,110	1,054	—	—	160,957	20,331
1920	13,839	5,964	—	2,531	1,163	1,094	—	—	184,596	14,550
1930	16,448	7,357	—	2,733	1,162	844	—	—	202,384	8,440
1940	19,720	9,364	—	3,467	1,392	803	—	—	323,864	—
1950	—	—	—	—	—	—	122,998	—	447,812	—
1960	45,755	—	—	—	—	—	—	31,361	595,081	—
1970 ²	70,020	31,850	—	11,625	3,624	8,323	—	—	770,033	—
1980	95,919	42,236	—	16,559	5,347	2,976	—	—	1,082,853	—
1990	138,992	65,666	—	19,778	5,702	2,102	—	—	1,350,264	—

Female

		Age										
	Total	0-4	5-9	10-14	15-19	20-29	20-24	25-29	30-39	30-34	35-39	40-49
	Aa491	Aa492	Aa493	Aa494	Aa495	Aa496	Aa497	Aa498	Aa499	Aa500	Aa501	Aa502
Year	Number	Number	Number	Number	Number	Number	Number	Number	Number	Number	Number	Number
1860	2,246,967	366,964	322,268	296,631	259,438	394,703	—	—	256,018	—	—	163,861
1870	2,504,517	396,279	329,542	317,568	270,872	—	269,234	206,127	—	155,930	136,733	—
1880	3,364,893	556,105	518,311	409,746	333,745	—	349,933	267,233	—	193,458	177,989	—
1890	3,776,812	521,280	547,461	510,808	452,419	—	384,180	289,932	—	209,107	206,630	—
1900	4,570,666	628,519	618,750	557,258	520,539	—	520,873	385,800	—	269,720	247,689	—
1910	5,086,277	656,504	646,702	593,083	567,073	—	561,238	470,743	—	345,310	321,241	—
1920	5,419,929	602,562	657,034	637,659	584,440	—	583,211	500,869	—	377,886	400,456	—
1930	6,273,754	654,486	726,940	656,932	677,972	—	667,686	588,744	—	464,449	475,849	—
1940	6,841,361	658,681	681,385	699,918	705,243	—	668,936	633,719	—	538,914	537,426	—
1950	8,244,554	1,015,174	826,952	728,018	680,365	—	719,300	713,911	—	631,865	637,747	—
1960	10,527,098	1,481,801	1,302,027	1,066,844	814,446	—	703,464	702,247	—	732,320	707,589	—
1970 ²	13,271,746	1,360,031	1,523,418	1,551,339	1,357,411	—	1,112,745	893,304	—	792,278	757,934	—
1980	19,806,355	1,836,191	1,813,052	1,873,429	2,084,755	—	2,049,991	1,836,277	—	1,538,984	1,173,793	—
1990	25,260,265	2,317,025	2,210,915	2,100,250	2,154,185	—	2,209,184	2,363,380	—	2,333,986	2,033,397	—

Notes appear at end of table

TABLE Aa457–524 Nonwhite population, by sex and age: 1860–1990 *Continued*

	Female											
	Age											
	40–44	45–49	50–59	50–54	55–59	60–69	60–64	65–69	70–79	70–74	75–79	80–89
	Aa503	Aa504	Aa505	Aa506	Aa507	Aa508	Aa509	Aa510	Aa511	Aa512	Aa513	Aa514
Year	Number	Number	Number	Number	Number	Number	Number	Number	Number	Number	Number	Number
1860	—	—	91,283	—	—	53,044	—	—	19,744	—	—	7,009
1870	116,073	84,484	—	77,866	36,839	—	43,741	21,134	—	18,812	8,648	—
1880	146,066	110,885	—	101,467	51,672	—	58,469	30,800	—	25,946	13,300	—
1890	161,189	135,431	—	109,482	62,315	—	62,676	38,438	—	29,483	15,912	—
1900	194,283	163,070	—	140,261	84,933	—	78,751	48,677	—	37,793	20,842	—
1910	232,184	191,067	—	151,325	98,129	—	88,614	57,865	—	40,088	22,476	—
1920	291,879	237,205	—	175,666	104,049	—	90,934	63,141	—	45,913	26,300	—
1930	359,463	315,927	—	234,224	139,988	—	112,666	75,199	—	50,310	30,885	—
1940	427,815	355,813	—	275,506	195,702	—	146,284	148,460	—	81,303	43,343	—
1950	524,916	462,537	—	370,598	265,364	—	202,103	218,533	—	116,786	—	—
1960	618,380	564,577	—	463,620	405,008	—	304,124	271,730	—	181,024	114,098	—
1970	749,806	677,582	—	586,800	511,626	—	432,345	378,461	—	254,300	159,230	—
1980	984,881	883,252	—	849,861	748,377	—	615,131	548,919	—	401,546	286,163	—
1990	1,644,643	1,212,856	—	988,288	859,781	—	792,781	693,020	—	514,682	390,975	—

	Female									
	Age									
	80–84	85–89	90–99	90–94	95–99	100 and older	75 and older	85 and older	65 and older	Not stated
	Aa515	Aa516	Aa517	Aa518	Aa519	Aa520	Aa521	Aa522	Aa523	Aa524
Year	Number	Number	Number	Number	Number	Number	Number	Number	Number	Number
1860	—	—	2,290	—	—	1,178	—	—	668,788	12,536
1870	7,128	2,319	—	2,169	851	1,666	—	—	62,727	502
1880	10,542	3,406	—	2,702	1,073	2,045	—	—	89,814	—
1890	11,342	4,467	—	2,951	1,226	1,942	—	—	105,761	18,141
1900	14,609	5,669	—	3,422	1,547	1,726	—	—	134,285	25,935
1910	14,755	6,390	—	3,729	1,524	1,737	—	—	148,564	14,500
1920	15,874	7,039	—	3,736	1,585	2,005	—	—	165,593	10,486
1930	18,980	8,573	—	4,079	1,648	1,774	—	—	191,448	6,980
1940	22,526	11,719	—	5,070	2,133	1,465	—	—	316,019	—
1950	—	—	—	—	—	—	130,385	—	459,212	—
1960	53,483	—	—	—	—	—	—	40,276	660,611	—
1970	94,469	46,935	—	16,540	6,054	9,138	—	—	965,127	—
1980	153,765	78,617	—	33,078	11,240	5,053	—	—	1,518,381	—
1990	242,052	130,028	—	47,447	16,291	5,099	—	—	2,039,594	—

[1] For changes in age and racial categorization, as well as exclusions in particular years, see the text for Table Aa185–286.

[2] Figures for persons ages 100 and older are greatly overstated; see the text for Table Aa185–286.

Sources

U.S. Bureau of the Census. 1860–1870, *U.S. Census of Population: 1870*, volume 2, pp. 552–8. 1880, *U.S. Census of Population: 1880*, volume 1, pp. 548–51. 1890, *U.S. Census of Population: 1890*, volume 1, part 2, pp. 2–5. 1900, *U.S. Census of Population: 1900*, volume 2, part 2, pp. xxxvi–xli. 1910, *U.S. Census of Population: 1910*, "Abstract of the Census," p. 122. 1920, *U.S. Census of Population: 1920*, "Abstract of the Fourteenth Census of the United States 1920" pp. 140–1. 1930–1940, *U.S. Census of Population: 1940*, volume 4, part 1, pp. 8–14; "Population: Second Series, Characteristics of the Population, United States Summary," pp. 16–20. 1950, *U.S. Census of Population: 1950*, volume 2, part 1, pp. 93–4. 1960, *U.S. Census of Population: 1960*, volume 1, part 1, pp. 153–4, 349–58; parts 3 and 13, pp. 23–4. 1970, *U.S. Census of Population: 1970*, volume 1, part 1, section 1, pp. 265–96. 1980, *U.S. Census of Population: 1980*, volume 1, Chapter B, part 1, PC80-1-B1, pp. 23, 27–36. 1990, *U.S. Census of Population: 1990*, 1990 CP-1-1, pp. 17, 23–4.

Documentation

See the text for Table Aa185–286.

TABLE Aa525–598 Other nonwhite population, by sex and age: 1860–1990[1]

Contributed by Michael R. Haines

Male

						Age				
	Total	0–4	5–9	10–14	15–19	20–29	20–24	25–29	30–39	30–34
	Aa525	Aa526	Aa527	Aa528	Aa529	Aa530	Aa531	Aa532	Aa533	Aa534
Year	Number	Number	Number	Number	Number	Number	Number	Number	Number	Number
1860	57,073	3,088	2,835	3,022	4,372	20,163	—	—	14,261	—
1870	71,214	1,830	1,661	2,821	6,858	—	11,547	12,371	—	11,317
1880	134,805	—	—	—	—	—	—	—	—	—
1890	135,987	3,780 [5]	3,964 [5]	4,279 [5]	7,539	—	13,637	19,114	—	21,330
1900	228,166	17,670	16,637	15,096	18,611	—	20,178	20,064	—	19,745
1910	268,151	22,626	19,582	17,575	20,194	—	27,178	30,319	—	27,436
1920	260,340	28,114	22,455	17,905	18,545	—	21,300	19,580	—	22,938
1930	358,883	36,504	39,258	30,293	29,718	—	36,401	35,346	—	28,191
1940	344,006	31,649	30,505	31,971	34,154	—	28,557	29,036	—	29,109
1950 [2]	401,525	48,045	36,145	36,690	30,440	—	35,930	34,690	—	25,985
1960 [3]	857,707	118,812	102,276	84,592	63,920	—	56,364	59,861	—	60,361
1970 [4]	1,442,889	151,599	158,048	150,297	140,972	—	136,601	114,231	—	102,635
1980	5,848,639	650,088	598,685	563,454	632,202	—	679,686	615,370	—	506,140
1990	9,593,387	979,433	921,731	846,033	914,864	—	1,028,590	1,025,361	—	926,778

Male

					Age					
	35–39	35–44	40–49	40–44	45–49	45–54	50–59	50–54	55–59	55–64
	Aa535	Aa536	Aa537	Aa538	Aa539	Aa540	Aa541	Aa542	Aa543	Aa544
Year	Number	Number	Number	Number	Number	Number	Number	Number	Number	Number
1860	—	—	5,917	—	—	—	1,815	—	—	—
1870	7,794	—	—	6,804	2,823	—	—	1,919	705	—
1880	—	—	—	—	—	—	—	—	—	—
1890	—	34,424	—	—	—	15,519	—	—	—	5,849
1900	23,146	—	—	21,650	17,369	—	—	13,399	7,699	—
1910	22,564	—	—	19,451	17,140	—	—	14,766	9,526	—
1920	25,433	—	—	22,205	17,869	—	—	13,946	10,251	—
1930	24,056	—	—	24,511	21,620	—	—	18,305	12,021	—
1940	28,732	—	—	23,696	18,405	—	—	17,913	14,098	—
1950 [2]	26,985	—	—	27,470	25,300	—	—	20,370	14,655	—
1960 [3]	59,119	—	—	46,508	44,820	—	—	42,769	44,732	—
1970 [4]	87,509	—	—	80,579	73,620	—	—	56,835	50,196	—
1980	368,064	—	—	292,155	234,235	—	—	198,079	162,613	—
1990	765,063	—	—	599,093	431,573	—	—	325,378	246,640	—

Male

					Age					
	60–69	60–64	65–69	70–79	70–74	75–79	80–89	80–84	85–89	90–99
	Aa545	Aa546	Aa547	Aa548	Aa549	Aa550	Aa551	Aa552	Aa553	Aa554
Year	Number	Number	Number	Number	Number	Number	Number	Number	Number	Number
1860	983	—	—	283	—	—	157	—	—	75
1870	—	740	199	—	111	55	—	41	13	—
1880	—	—	—	—	—	—	—	—	—	—
1890	—	—	—	—	—	—	—	—	—	—
1900	—	5,993	2,936	—	1,716	820	—	531	191	—
1910	—	8,064	3,728	—	2,172	1,167	—	748	328	—
1920	—	8,044	4,854	—	2,974	1,410	—	790	344	—
1930	—	8,429	5,430	—	3,476	—	—	—	—	—
1940	—	11,118	7,161	—	3,849	—	—	—	—	—
1950 [2]	—	14,310	11,175	—	6,940	3,545	—	1,610	—	—
1960 [3]	—	25,533	17,322	—	14,918	9,235	—	4,072	—	—
1970 [4]	—	45,304	36,993	—	23,626	13,074	—	11,346	5,192	—
1980	—	111,727	89,590	—	66,911	44,520	—	20,968	8,749	—
1990	—	198,018	156,136	—	98,878	66,829	—	38,333	17,824	—

Notes appear at end of table

TABLE Aa525–598 Other nonwhite population, by sex and age: 1860–1990 *Continued*

	Male							Female		
	Age								Age	
	90–94	95–99	100 and older	75 and older	85 and older	65 and older	Not stated	Total	0–4	5–9
	Aa555	Aa556	Aa557	Aa558	Aa559	Aa560	Aa561	Aa562	Aa563	Aa564
Year	Number	Number	Number	Number	Number	Number	Number	Number	Number	Number
1860	—	—	49	—	—	—	53	21,881	2,879	2,461
1870	7	—	7	—	—	439	1,585	17,771	1,670	1,506
1880	—	—	—	—	—	—	—	37,215	—	—
1890	—	—	—	—	—	2,104	4,448	82,333	3,691[5]	3,372[5]
1900	166	54	55	—	—	6,469	4,440	123,219	17,351	16,402
1910	189	93	50	—	—	8,475	3,255	144,445	22,536	19,374
1920	191	76	76	—	—	10,715	1,040	166,234	27,496	22,168
1930	—	—	—	3,948	—	12,854	1,376	238,280	35,511	38,307
1940	—	—	—	4,053	—	15,063	—	244,881	31,290	30,620
1950 [2]	—	—	—	—	1,240	24,510	—	309,545	47,195	35,875
1960 [3]	—	—	—	—	2,493	48,040	—	781,670	115,094	98,834
1970 [4]	2,813	442	977	—	—	94,463	—	1,439,773	146,960	153,345
1980	3,807	1,038	558	—	—	236,141	—	5,830,519	627,922	577,588
1990	5,080	1,237	515	—	—	384,832	—	9,444,356	939,618	890,071

	Female									
	Age									
	10–14	15–19	20–29	20–24	25–29	30–39	30–34	35–39	35–44	40–49
	Aa565	Aa566	Aa567	Aa568	Aa569	Aa570	Aa571	Aa572	Aa573	Aa574
Year	Number	Number	Number	Number	Number	Number	Number	Number	Number	Number
1860	2,358	2,949	5,285	—	—	2,798	—	—	—	1,562
1870	1,596	2,144	—	2,870	2,147	—	1,698	1,024	—	—
1880	—	—	—	—	—	—	—	—	—	—
1890	3,557[5]	3,559	—	3,024	52,425	—	2,491	—	4,096	—
1900	13,910	12,267	—	10,622	8,918	—	7,243	6,373	—	—
1910	15,891	14,602	—	12,600	11,321	—	9,384	8,242	—	—
1920	16,996	14,641	—	15,533	15,482	—	11,600	10,112	—	—
1930	28,618	23,090	—	18,117	17,477	—	16,804	15,421	—	—
1940	30,609	30,716	—	23,902	18,048	—	13,922	14,152	—	—
1950 [2]	31,480	28,725	—	31,950	29,140	—	21,820	17,480	—	—
1960 [3]	81,118	60,161	—	55,245	66,264	—	68,690	57,439	—	—
1970 [4]	148,185	135,971	—	138,373	122,591	—	107,429	102,746	—	—
1980	544,481	588,957	—	625,438	599,400	—	521,268	378,384	—	—
1990	813,068	837,955	—	888,857	941,375	—	902,872	779,682	—	—

	Female									
	Age									
	40–44	45–49	45–54	50–59	50–54	55–59	55–64	60–69	60–64	65–69
	Aa575	Aa576	Aa577	Aa578	Aa579	Aa580	Aa581	Aa582	Aa583	Aa584
Year	Number	Number	Number	Number	Number	Number	Number	Number	Number	Number
1860	—	—	—	696	—	—	—	478	—	—
1870	833	526	—	—	445	219	—	—	238	119
1880	—	—	—	—	—	—	—	—	—	—
1890	—	—	2,535	—	—	—	1,432	—	—	—
1900	6,157	5,181	—	—	4,462	3,080	—	—	3,025	2,024
1910	6,451	5,086	—	—	4,642	3,597	—	—	3,261	2,271
1920	8,104	6,122	—	—	4,551	3,222	—	—	2,953	2,290
1930	11,369	9,024	—	—	7,166	4,958	—	—	3,846	2,865
1940	12,968	11,257	—	—	8,191	5,703	—	—	4,625	3,713
1950 [2]	13,665	12,615	—	—	11,460	8,855	—	—	6,460	5,345
1960 [3]	41,103	31,736	—	—	25,027	31,021	—	—	17,568	13,715
1970 [4]	95,678	74,898	—	—	55,859	42,802	—	—	32,993	28,661
1980	300,353	255,581	—	—	225,466	178,099	—	—	129,347	103,647
1990	634,241	449,531	—	—	341,253	283,951	—	—	245,407	192,917

Notes appear at end of table   (continued)

TABLE Aa525–598   Other nonwhite population, by sex and age: 1860–1990   *Continued*

	Female													
	Age													
	70–79	70–74	75–79	80–89	80–84	85–89	90–99	90–94	95–99	100 and older	75 and older	85 and older	65 and older	Not stated
	Aa585	Aa586	Aa587	Aa588	Aa589	Aa590	Aa591	Aa592	Aa593	Aa594	Aa595	Aa596	Aa597	Aa598
Year	Number	Number	Number	Number	Number	Number	Number	Number	Number	Number	Number	Number	Number	Number
1860	182	—	—	105	—	—	49	—	—	37	—	—	851	42
1870	—	126	42	—	36	13	—	18	2	14	—	—	370	485
1880	—	—	—	—	—	—	—	—	—	—	—	—	—	—
1890	—	—	—	—	—	—	—	—	—	—	—	—	1,388	763
1900	—	1,646	897	—	737	299	—	214	71	59	—	—	5,947	2,281
1910	—	1,833	1,125	—	872	388	—	273	94	66	—	—	6,922	536
1920	—	1,745	1,120	—	801	378	—	229	110	88	—	—	6,761	493
1930	—	2,110	—	—	—	—	—	—	—	—	3,284	—	8,259	313
1940	—	2,190	—	—	—	—	—	—	—	—	2,975	—	8,878	—
1950 [2]	—	3,410	1,940	—	1,170	—	—	—	—	—	—	960	12,825	—
1960 [3]	—	9,035	5,038	—	2,748	—	—	—	—	—	—	1,834	32,370	—
1970 [4]	—	22,219	14,702	—	9,080	4,213	—	1,687	489	892	—	—	81,943	—
1980	—	72,294	51,519	—	28,741	14,356	—	5,383	1,578	717	—	—	278,235	—
1990	—	128,966	88,245	—	49,073	24,896	—	8,754	2,812	812	—	—	496,475	—

[1] For changes in age and racial categorization, as well as exclusions in particular years, see the text for Table Aa185–286.

[2] 20 percent sample data.

[3] 25 percent sample data.

[4] Figures for persons ages 100 and older are greatly overstated; see the text for Table Aa185–286.

[5] Estimates based on population less than fifteen years old and age distribution of Negro and other races.

Sources

U.S. Bureau of the Census. 1860–1870, *U.S. Census of Population: 1870*, volume 2, pp. 552–8. 1880–1950, all races and white, *U.S. Census of Population: 1950*, volume 2, part 1, pp. 93–4. 1890–1930, Negro, *U.S. Census of Population: 1930*, volume 2, p. 580. 1890–1930, other races by subtraction of Negro (as cited) from Negro and other races, *U.S. Census of Population: 1950*, volume 2, part 1, pp. 93–4. 1940, Negro and other races, *U.S. Census of Population: 1940*, volume 2, part 1, p. 22. 1950, Negro and other races, *U.S. Census of Population: 1950*, volume 2, part 1, p. 172. 1960, all races and white, *U.S. Census of Population: 1960*, volume 1, part 1, pp. 153–4; parts 3 and 13, pp. 23–4. 1960, Negro and other races, *U.S. Census of Population: 1960*, volume 1, part 1, p. 359; part 3, p. 117; part 13, p. 113. 1970, *U.S. Census of Population: 1970*, volume 1, part 1, section 1, pp. 269–96. 1980, *U.S. Census of Population: 1980*, volume 1, Chapter B, part 1, PC80-1-B1, pp. 23, 27–36. 1990, *U.S. Census of Population: 1990*, 1990 CP-1-1, pp. 17–8, 23–34.

Documentation

See the text for Table Aa185–286.

TABLE Aa599–613　Median age, by race, sex, and nativity: 1800–1990

Contributed by Michael R. Haines

	Race												Foreign-born whites		
	All races			White			Black			Other races			Total	Male	Female
	Total	Male	Female	Total	Male	Female	Total	Male	Female	Total	Male	Female			
	Aa599	Aa600	Aa601	Aa602	Aa603	Aa604	Aa605	Aa606	Aa607	Aa608	Aa609	Aa610	Aa611	Aa612	Aa613
Year	Years	Years	Years	Years	Years	Years	Years	Years	Years	Years	Years	Years	Years	Years	Years
1800	—	—	—	16.0	15.7	16.3	—	—	—	—	—	—	—	—	—
1810	—	—	—	16.0	15.9	16.1	—	—	—	—	—	—	—	—	—
1820	16.7	16.6	16.8	16.6	16.5	16.6	17.2	17.1	17.4	—	—	—	—	—	—
1830	17.2	17.2	17.3	17.3	17.2	17.3	17.2	17.1	17.3	—	—	—	—	—	—
1840	17.8	17.9	17.8	17.9	18.0	17.8	17.6	17.5	17.6	—	—	—	—	—	—
1850	18.9	19.2	18.6	19.2	19.5	18.8	17.4	17.3	17.4	—	—	—	—	—	—
1860	19.4	19.8	19.1	19.7	20.1	19.3	17.5	17.5	17.5	26.1	27.5	20.5	—	—	—
1870	20.2	20.2	20.1	20.4	20.6	20.3	18.3	17.8	18.8	28.1	29.1	23.0	34.6	35.3	33.9
1880	20.9	21.2	20.7	21.4	21.6	21.1	—	—	—	—	—	—	38.3	38.5	38.0
1890	22.0	22.3	21.6	22.5	22.9	22.1	18.1	17.9	18.3	28.9	33.2	27.2	37.1	37.1	37.0
1900	22.9	23.3	22.4	23.4	23.8	22.9	19.5	19.5	19.5	27.3	30.9	20.3	38.5	38.8	38.1
1910	24.1	24.6	23.5	24.5	24.9	23.9	20.8	21.0	20.7	26.5	29.2	19.8	37.2	36.9	37.6
1920	25.3	25.8	24.7	25.6	26.1	25.1	22.3	22.8	22.0	26.1	30.4	20.5	40.0	40.1	39.9
1930	26.5	26.7	26.2	26.9	27.1	26.6	23.5	23.7	23.3	23.3	25.9	18.6	43.9	44.1	43.7
1940	29.0	29.1	29.0	29.5	29.5	29.5	25.3	25.3	25.3	24.1	27.6	19.9	51.0	51.4	50.5
1950	30.2	29.9	30.5	30.8	30.4	31.1	26.1	25.8	26.4	24.5	26.9	21.8	56.1	59.0	55.5
1960	29.5	28.7	30.3	30.3	29.4	31.1	23.5	22.3	24.5	24.3	25.2	23.2	57.7	58.4	57.1
1970	28.1	26.8	29.3	28.9	27.6	30.2	22.4	21.0	23.6	24.7	24.4	24.9	54.6	54.5	54.7
1980	30.0	28.8	31.2	31.3	30.0	32.5	24.9	23.5	26.1	23.5	22.5	23.6	—	—	—
1990	32.9	31.7	34.1	34.4	33.1	35.6	28.1	26.6	29.5	24.1	24.5	25.9	—	—	—

Sources

Derived from data underlying Tables Aa185–598 and Aa1922–2025.

Documentation

The median age is that age that divides the population into two equal groups, one half being older and the other half being younger. Medians have been computed on the basis of the population for which age is available and on the assumption that population is evenly distributed within the age groups shown in Tables Aa185–598 and Aa1922–2025. In most cases, the median falls in a five-year age group, and the assumption of linearity introduces little error. In cases where the median falls near the center of a large age span (for example, black population in 1830 and 1840), this assumption may introduce considerable error. The fluctuations in median ages for the "other races" population are caused in part by the changing composition of this group (for example, the majority of the American Indian population was not included in tabulations by age until 1900).

TABLE Aa614–683   Population, by marital status, sex, and race: 1880–1990

Contributed by Michael R. Haines and Richard Sutch

All races

Males

Year and age	Total	Never married	Married Total	Married Spouse present	Married Spouse absent Total	Married Spouse absent Separated	Married Spouse absent Other	Married Spouse absent Not separated	Widowed	Divorced	Marital status unknown
	Aa614	Aa615	Aa616	Aa617	Aa618	Aa619 [1]	Aa620	Aa621	Aa622	Aa623	Aa624
	Number	Number	Number	Number	Number	Number	Number	Number	Number	Number	Number
1880											
total	25,551,807	16,084,299	8,841,797	8,456,811	384,986	—	—	—	593,185	32,526	—
0–14	9,743,089	9,742,290	599	0	599	—	—	—	200	0	—
15–19	2,457,734	2,428,706	26,330	20,747	5,583	—	—	—	2,498	200	—
20–24	2,547,780	1,968,401	566,120	525,726	40,394	—	—	—	11,863	1,396	—
25–29	2,119,393	870,221	1,219,948	1,159,298	60,650	—	—	—	25,135	4,089	—
30–34	1,749,107	416,131	1,292,081	1,236,119	55,962	—	—	—	37,003	3,892	—
35–39	1,540,772	229,113	1,262,167	1,213,563	48,604	—	—	—	44,500	4,992	—
40–44	1,237,347	143,928	1,042,163	997,154	45,009	—	—	—	48,463	2,793	—
45–49	1,065,973	92,672	918,048	883,724	34,324	—	—	—	50,965	4,288	—
50–54	964,484	71,332	824,821	792,796	32,025	—	—	—	64,937	3,394	—
55–59	679,147	39,403	584,683	566,433	18,250	—	—	—	52,966	2,095	—
60–64	580,298	34,020	479,757	462,498	17,259	—	—	—	64,228	2,293	—
65–69	369,398	20,942	291,491	282,013	9,478	—	—	—	55,070	1,895	—
70–74	255,422	13,273	191,079	182,101	8,978	—	—	—	50,270	800	—
75+	241,863	13,867	142,510	134,639	7,871	—	—	—	85,087	399	—
1890											
total	32,067,880	19,945,576	11,205,228	—	—	—	—	—	815,437	49,101	52,538
0–14	11,290,008	11,289,865	23	—	—	—	—	—	0	1	119
15–19	3,248,711	3,230,835	16,746	—	—	—	—	—	137	28	965
20–24	3,104,893	2,505,460	585,748	—	—	—	—	—	7,610	1,468	4,607
25–29	2,698,311	1,240,797	1,421,407	—	—	—	—	—	26,601	4,340	5,166
30–34	2,425,664	642,827	1,728,930	—	—	—	—	—	43,777	5,832	4,298
35–44	3,705,648	568,511	2,997,030	—	—	—	—	—	120,796	12,837	6,474
45–54	2,627,024	239,928	2,213,901	—	—	—	—	—	157,920	11,393	3,882
55–64	1,630,373	111,144	1,342,414	—	—	—	—	—	166,686	7,835	2,294
65+	1,233,719	69,100	869,925	—	—	—	—	—	287,583	4,974	2,137
unknown	103,529	47,109	29,104	—	—	—	—	—	4,327	393	22,596
1900											
total	39,059,242	23,666,836	14,003,798	—	—	—	—	—	1,182,293	84,903	121,412
0–14	13,219,756	13,218,683	667	—	—	—	—	—	33	7	366
15–19	3,765,980	3,721,374	38,124	—	—	—	—	—	882	195	5,405
20–24	3,684,373	2,867,395	786,295	—	—	—	—	—	14,470	3,380	12,833
25–29	3,369,077	1,557,014	1,754,896	—	—	—	—	—	39,119	8,362	9,686
30–34	2,931,037	820,323	2,034,813	—	—	—	—	—	58,842	10,453	6,606
35–44	4,905,206	842,275	3,855,382	—	—	—	—	—	175,507	22,826	9,216
45–54	3,414,508	353,912	2,803,878	—	—	—	—	—	231,439	19,565	5,714
55–64	2,067,455	158,217	1,647,178	—	—	—	—	—	246,139	12,329	3,592
65+	1,557,634	89,512	1,045,136	—	—	—	—	—	411,281	7,368	4,337
unknown	144,216	38,131	37,429	—	—	—	—	—	4,581	418	63,657

All races

Males

Married

Year and age	Total	Never married	Married Total	Spouse present	Spouse absent Total	Separated	Other	Not separated	Widowed	Divorced	Marital status unknown
	Aa614	Aa615	Aa616	Aa617	Aa618	Aa619 ¹	Aa620	Aa621	Aa622	Aa623	Aa624
	Number	Number	Number	Number	Number	Number	Number	Number	Number	Number	Number
1910											
total	47,332,277	27,455,607	18,093,498	—	—	—	—	—	1,471,472	156,176	155,524
0–14	14,906,472	14,905,478	898	—	—	—	—	—	82	14	0
15–17	2,688,370	2,667,874	4,990	—	—	—	—	—	252	70	15,184
18–19	1,838,912	1,780,193	46,887	—	—	—	—	—	858	277	10,697
15–19	4,527,282	4,448,067	51,877	—	—	—	—	—	1,110	347	25,881
20–24	4,580,290	3,432,161	1,100,093	—	—	—	—	—	18,815	6,732	22,489
25–29	4,244,348	1,816,137	2,353,525	—	—	—	—	—	45,092	15,503	14,091
30–34	3,656,768	951,820	2,611,244	—	—	—	—	—	65,339	19,068	9,297
35–44	6,153,366	1,026,502	4,873,153	—	—	—	—	—	198,701	42,688	12,322
45–54	4,488,929	499,751	3,658,931	—	—	—	—	—	286,222	36,502	7,523
55–64	2,674,403	222,950	2,112,699	—	—	—	—	—	312,420	21,675	4,659
65+	1,985,976	123,322	1,303,768	—	—	—	—	—	539,058	13,075	6,753
unknown	114,443	29,419	27,310	—	—	—	—	—	4,633	572	52,509
1920											
total	53,900,431	29,944,007	21,852,439	—	—	—	—	—	1,758,426	235,319	110,240
0–14	16,979,768	16,976,442	3,173	—	—	—	—	—	118	35	0
15–17	2,828,546	2,815,533	12,521	—	—	—	—	—	384	108	0
18–19	1,845,246	1,752,237	83,853	—	—	—	—	—	1,446	651	7,059
15–19	4,673,792	4,567,770	96,374	—	—	—	—	—	1,830	759	7,059
20–24	4,527,045	3,200,623	1,280,318	—	—	—	—	—	20,511	10,280	15,313
25–29	4,538,233	1,789,721	2,662,124	—	—	—	—	—	51,470	22,856	12,062
30–34	4,130,783	995,869	3,023,357	—	—	—	—	—	74,454	28,080	9,023
35–44	7,359,904	1,188,586	5,873,308	—	—	—	—	—	220,700	63,592	13,718
45–54	5,653,095	677,420	4,580,056	—	—	—	—	—	329,976	56,162	9,481
55–64	3,461,865	337,592	2,697,429	—	—	—	—	—	386,587	34,249	6,008
65+	2,483,071	182,211	1,607,187	—	—	—	—	—	668,656	18,506	6,511
unknown	92,875	27,773	29,113	—	—	—	—	—	4,124	800	31,065
1930											
total	62,137,080	33,208,947	26,327,870	—	—	—	—	—	2,025,078	489,499	85,686
0–14	18,256,059	18,255,235	761	—	—	—	—	—	42	21	0
15–17	3,493,718	3,482,706	10,553	—	—	—	—	—	281	178	0
18–19	2,264,107	2,162,653	89,809	—	—	—	—	—	1,232	1,170	9,243
15–19	5,757,825	5,645,359	100,362	—	—	—	—	—	1,513	1,348	9,243
20–24	5,336,815	3,779,443	1,500,493	—	—	—	—	—	17,657	21,900	17,322
25–29	4,860,180	1,785,413	2,977,004	—	—	—	—	—	39,013	50,229	8,521
30–34	4,561,786	965,945	3,468,176	—	—	—	—	—	59,493	62,669	5,503
35–39	4,679,860	718,396	3,792,614	—	—	—	—	—	93,204	70,765	4,881
40–44	4,136,459	543,309	3,396,838	—	—	—	—	—	125,677	66,415	4,220
45–49	3,671,924	435,252	3,013,521	—	—	—	—	—	158,561	60,850	3,740
50–54	3,131,645	341,611	2,537,625	—	—	—	—	—	198,486	50,621	3,302
55–59	2,425,992	251,017	1,929,201	—	—	—	—	—	204,742	38,220	2,812
60–64	1,941,508	191,488	1,478,550	—	—	—	—	—	240,520	28,279	2,671
65–69	1,417,812	131,451	1,013,226	—	—	—	—	—	252,072	18,783	2,280
70–74	991,647	84,851	641,628	—	—	—	—	—	251,970	11,157	2,041
75+	915,752	64,315	461,683	—	—	—	—	—	379,638	7,431	2,685
unknown	51,816	15,862	16,188	—	—	—	—	—	2,490	811	16,465

Note appears at end of table   (continued)

TABLE Aa614–683   Population, by marital status, sex, and race: 1880–1990   *Continued*

					All races						
					Males						
			Married								
					Spouse absent						
	Total	Never married	Total	Spouse present	Total	Separated [1]	Other	Not separated	Widowed	Divorced	Marital status unknown
	Aa614	Aa615	Aa616	Aa617	Aa618	Aa619	Aa620	Aa621	Aa622	Aa623	Aa624
Year and age	Number	Number	Number	Number	Number	Number	Number	Number	Number	Number	Number
1940											
total	50,553,748	17,593,379	30,192,334	28,657,376	1,533,711	—	—	—	2,143,612	624,423	—
14	1,218,116	1,216,784	1,247	—	—	—	—	—	60	25	—
15–17	3,684,780	3,670,287	14,002	—	—	—	—	—	311	180	—
18–19	2,495,373	2,402,878	90,933	—	—	—	—	—	720	842	—
15–19	6,180,153	6,073,165	104,935	82,219	22,716	—	—	—	1,031	1,022	—
20–24	5,692,392	4,109,304	1,557,104	1,450,696	106,408	—	—	—	8,394	17,590	—
25–29	5,450,662	1,964,118	3,417,046	3,254,819	162,227	—	—	—	20,973	48,525	—
30–34	5,070,312	1,050,199	3,912,820	3,742,054	170,766	—	—	—	36,714	70,579	—
35–39	4,745,659	725,987	3,874,210	3,693,534	180,676	—	—	—	60,759	84,703	—
40–44	4,419,135	558,007	3,677,764	3,495,812	181,952	—	—	—	94,646	88,718	—
45–49	4,209,269	471,982	3,517,891	3,344,383	173,508	—	—	—	135,957	83,439	—
50–54	3,752,750	413,022	3,073,063	2,916,399	156,664	—	—	—	192,173	74,492	—
55–59	3,011,364	325,220	2,407,253	2,284,884	122,369	—	—	—	222,202	56,689	—
60–64	2,397,816	251,950	1,838,174	1,742,766	95,408	—	—	—	266,418	41,274	—
65–69	1,896,088	195,007	1,363,456	1,290,127	73,329	—	—	—	308,000	29,625	—
70–74	1,270,967	126,322	825,326	780,171	45,155	—	—	—	302,921	16,398	—
75–79	723,680	68,573	406,148	381,161	24,987	—	—	—	241,285	7,674	—
80–84	359,011	31,333	164,315	152,237	12,078	—	—	—	160,631	2,732	—
85+	156,374	12,406	51,582	46,114	5,468	—	—	—	91,448	938	—
1950											
total	54,601,105	14,399,840	36,866,055	34,975,900	1,890,155	851,930	1,038,225	—	2,263,850	1,071,360	—
14	1,090,020	1,080,370	6,660	3,540	3,120	1,195	1,925	—	1,670	1,320	—
15–17	3,187,510	3,151,360	30,410	18,325	12,085	3,085	9,000	—	3,460	2,280	—
18–19	2,135,960	1,995,250	136,545	115,245	21,300	5,870	15,430	—	1,535	2,630	—
15–19	5,323,470	5,146,610	166,955	133,570	33,385	8,955	24,430	—	4,995	4,910	—
20–24	5,559,265	3,281,540	2,217,810	2,056,605	161,205	65,730	95,475	—	9,060	50,855	—
25–29	5,904,975	1,404,860	4,381,375	4,147,425	233,950	94,040	139,910	—	15,485	103,255	—
30–34	5,562,315	734,195	4,690,995	4,477,120	213,875	92,215	121,660	—	20,945	116,180	—
35–39	5,432,630	549,180	4,717,260	4,503,160	214,100	100,725	113,375	—	36,215	129,975	—
40–44	4,969,565	447,390	4,329,415	4,127,705	201,710	96,805	104,905	—	58,650	134,110	—
45–49	4,444,195	388,205	3,832,980	3,641,885	191,095	92,165	98,930	—	92,070	130,940	—
50–54	4,040,320	337,150	3,434,635	3,260,165	174,470	81,550	92,920	—	148,685	119,850	—
55–59	3,557,555	294,220	2,955,480	2,815,645	139,835	67,050	72,785	—	210,065	97,790	—
60–64	2,982,545	256,965	2,365,190	2,248,370	116,820	55,850	60,970	—	285,075	75,315	—
65–69	2,399,645	209,960	1,776,810	1,686,200	90,610	45,835	44,775	—	358,880	53,995	—
70–74	1,607,185	133,945	1,085,310	1,027,875	57,435	26,470	30,965	—	357,560	30,370	—
75–79	992,645	80,110	585,475	551,025	34,450	15,265	19,185	—	312,160	14,900	—
80–84	500,345	37,090	240,970	224,400	16,570	5,885	10,685	—	216,625	5,660	—
85+	234,430	18,050	78,735	71,210	7,525	2,195	5,330	—	135,710	1,935	—

All races — Males

Year and age	Total	Never married	Married Total	Spouse present	Spouse absent Total	Separated[1]	Other	Not separated	Widowed	Divorced	Marital status unknown
	Aa614	Aa615	Aa616	Aa617	Aa618	Aa619	Aa620	Aa621	Aa622	Aa623	Aa624
	Number	Number	Number	Number	Number	Number	Number	Number	Number	Number	Number
1960											
total	61,315,358	15,313,822	42,630,422	40,473,195	2,157,227	873,471	1,283,756	—	2,071,910	1,299,204	—
14	1,402,724	1,394,426	7,756	1,771	5,985	554	5,431	—	163	379	—
15–17	4,341,635	4,290,310	48,850	25,514	23,336	2,759	20,577	—	897	1,578	—
18–19	2,357,202	2,146,876	205,527	166,061	39,466	6,824	32,642	—	887	3,912	—
15–19	6,698,837	6,437,186	254,377	191,575	62,802	9,583	53,219	—	1,784	5,490	—
20–24	5,283,228	2,807,784	2,417,552	2,191,739	225,813	59,398	166,415	—	4,780	53,112	—
25–29	5,333,282	1,111,768	4,117,072	3,891,307	225,765	82,337	143,428	—	9,548	94,894	—
30–34	5,840,287	694,924	5,000,763	4,767,193	233,570	97,046	136,524	—	17,246	127,354	—
35–39	6,089,780	534,350	5,376,707	5,141,093	235,614	103,859	131,755	—	29,446	149,277	—
40–44	5,649,411	414,434	5,033,384	4,822,853	210,531	98,383	112,148	—	46,990	154,603	—
45–49	5,374,935	385,408	4,754,204	4,551,514	202,690	98,014	104,676	—	73,981	161,342	—
50–54	4,764,736	363,982	4,142,564	3,962,082	180,482	84,602	95,880	—	108,279	149,911	—
55–59	4,184,657	346,176	3,546,065	3,382,993	163,072	76,030	87,042	—	160,729	131,687	—
60–64	3,384,496	259,011	2,805,343	2,675,474	129,869	56,292	73,577	—	219,779	100,363	—
65–69	2,883,433	222,027	2,289,201	2,181,016	108,185	46,520	61,665	—	294,901	77,304	—
70–74	2,138,977	167,016	1,562,813	1,483,718	79,095	31,218	47,877	—	358,546	50,602	—
75–79	1,318,028	104,233	852,659	801,038	51,621	18,541	33,080	—	333,550	27,586	—
80–84	635,164	47,313	340,886	313,965	26,921	7,642	19,279	—	236,303	10,662	—
85+	333,383	23,784	129,076	113,864	15,212	3,452	11,760	—	175,885	4,638	—
1970											
total	71,485,878	20,426,937	47,001,412	44,597,574	2,403,838	1,046,142	1,357,696	—	2,130,932	1,926,597	—
14	2,136,818	2,111,778	20,768	15,042	5,726	2,115	3,611	—	2,451	1,821	—
15–17	6,071,485	5,986,895	74,740	56,486	18,254	5,682	12,572	—	5,057	4,793	—
18–19	3,646,704	3,328,546	306,760	252,244	54,516	11,730	42,786	—	3,472	7,926	—
15–19	9,718,189	9,315,441	381,500	308,730	72,770	17,412	55,358	—	8,529	12,719	—
20–24	7,761,209	4,307,592	3,329,772	2,995,836	333,936	96,015	237,921	—	12,878	110,967	—
25–29	6,569,934	1,288,594	5,066,314	4,792,193	274,121	123,161	150,960	—	19,196	195,830	—
30–34	5,607,593	601,868	4,803,203	4,577,716	225,487	105,230	120,257	—	19,574	182,948	—
35–39	5,431,809	447,460	4,772,338	4,560,686	211,652	100,815	110,837	—	27,586	184,425	—
40–44	5,829,922	436,912	5,123,593	4,903,583	220,010	112,310	107,700	—	47,960	221,457	—
45–49	5,808,783	381,353	5,131,288	4,919,580	211,708	110,904	100,804	—	74,526	221,616	—
50–54	5,329,398	329,746	4,682,225	4,492,422	189,803	98,502	91,301	—	111,618	205,809	—
55–59	4,800,385	305,561	4,156,178	3,988,816	167,362	86,451	80,911	—	153,163	185,483	—
60–64	4,058,508	268,864	3,430,907	3,285,721	145,186	68,675	76,511	—	211,502	147,235	—
65–69	3,116,348	221,999	2,511,965	2,397,729	114,236	51,103	63,133	—	273,861	108,523	—
70–74	2,324,327	169,511	1,762,886	1,674,712	88,174	33,709	54,465	—	320,653	71,277	—
75–79	1,579,915	115,116	1,087,208	1,018,878	68,330	21,636	46,694	—	334,647	42,944	—
80–84	876,058	66,914	508,525	463,687	44,838	11,193	33,645	—	280,008	20,611	—
85+	536,682	58,228	232,742	202,243	30,499	6,911	23,588	—	232,780	12,932	—

Note appears at end of table

(continued)

TABLE Aa614–683 Population, by marital status, sex, and race: 1880–1990 *Continued*

All races

Males

			Married								Marital status unknown
						Spouse absent					
Year and age	Total	Never married	Total	Spouse present	Total	Separated	Other	Not separated	Widowed	Divorced	
	Aa614	Aa615	Aa616	Aa617	Aa618	Aa619 [1]	Aa620	Aa621	Aa622	Aa623	Aa624
	Number	Number	Number	Number	Number	Number	Number	Number	Number	Number	Number
1980											
total	83,824,951	24,887,632	52,427,195	49,545,413	2,881,782	1,563,066	1,318,716	—	2,104,821	4,405,303	—
15–17	6,420,149	6,367,474	48,917	20,700	28,217	4,357	23,860	—	992	2,766	—
18–19	4,349,036	4,101,040	237,709	182,732	54,977	11,889	43,088	—	1,089	9,198	—
15–19	10,769,185	10,468,514	286,626	203,432	83,194	16,246	66,948	—	2,081	11,964	—
20–24	10,639,312	7,255,520	3,140,110	2,795,679	344,431	143,934	200,497	—	5,970	237,712	—
25–29	9,678,198	3,106,296	5,915,237	5,475,347	439,890	247,007	192,883	—	11,759	644,906	—
30–34	8,755,937	1,303,972	6,677,112	6,290,853	386,259	241,829	144,430	—	16,531	758,322	—
35–39	6,862,568	595,951	5,656,541	5,371,676	284,865	182,561	102,304	—	22,337	587,739	—
40–44	5,707,639	383,571	4,834,421	4,600,578	233,843	151,594	82,249	—	31,037	458,610	—
45–49	5,345,908	319,592	4,574,853	4,372,559	202,294	129,739	72,555	—	52,711	398,752	—
50–54	5,611,240	338,030	4,793,715	4,596,283	197,432	126,693	70,739	—	99,713	379,782	—
55–59	5,497,675	307,557	4,716,683	4,537,844	178,839	106,794	72,045	—	153,611	319,824	—
60–64	4,694,721	244,679	4,002,814	3,859,912	142,902	79,744	63,158	—	213,638	233,590	—
65–69	3,880,624	208,751	3,220,514	3,102,364	118,150	59,814	58,336	—	282,545	168,814	—
70–74	2,859,530	156,171	2,277,135	2,182,258	94,877	38,716	56,161	—	320,245	105,979	—
75–79	1,842,694	104,110	1,356,101	1,282,689	73,412	22,849	50,563	—	323,432	59,051	—
80–84	1,011,742	57,253	651,876	599,576	52,300	9,701	42,599	—	276,386	26,227	—
85+	667,978	37,665	323,457	274,363	49,094	5,845	43,249	—	292,825	14,031	—
1990											
total	93,817,315	28,804,618	55,677,642	—	—	1,896,397	—	53,781,245	2,377,589	6,957,466	—
15–17	5,162,175	5,108,499	47,302	—	—	4,983	—	42,319	1,584	4,790	—
18–19	3,940,523	3,786,268	144,955	—	—	9,567	—	135,388	2,098	7,202	—
15–19	9,102,698	8,894,767	192,257	—	—	14,550	—	177,707	3,682	11,992	—
20–24	9,675,596	7,622,622	1,899,114	—	—	104,121	—	1,794,993	6,471	147,389	—
25–29	10,695,936	4,924,494	5,165,645	—	—	241,725	—	4,923,920	12,167	593,630	—
30–34	10,876,933	2,855,846	7,019,414	—	—	300,180	—	6,719,234	20,250	981,423	—
35–44	18,594,227	2,493,033	13,771,496	—	—	542,942	—	13,228,554	71,894	2,257,804	—
45–54	12,325,335	838,551	9,864,133	—	—	330,459	—	9,533,674	134,155	1,488,496	—
55–59	5,034,370	280,511	4,146,439	—	—	109,312	—	4,037,127	126,670	480,750	—
60–64	4,947,047	275,901	4,059,736	—	—	92,372	—	3,967,364	220,798	390,612	—
65–74	7,941,613	392,314	6,401,337	—	—	113,819	—	6,287,518	701,651	446,311	—
75–84	3,765,862	181,886	2,714,210	—	—	39,825	—	2,674,385	732,438	137,328	—
85+	857,698	44,693	443,861	—	—	7,092	—	436,769	347,413	21,731	—

All races

Females

			Married								
						Spouse absent					
Year and age	Total	Never married	Total	Spouse present	Total	Separated	Other	Not separated	Widowed	Divorced	Marital status unknown
	Aa625	Aa626	Aa627	Aa628	Aa629	Aa630 [1]	Aa631	Aa632	Aa633	Aa634	Aa635
	Number	Number	Number	Number	Number	Number	Number	Number	Number	Number	Number
1880											
total	24,603,241	14,063,489	8,773,849	8,456,911	316,938	—	—	—	1,707,267	58,636	—
0–14	9,414,289	9,410,497	3,593	1,997	1,596	—	—	—	199	0	—
15–19	2,527,818	2,223,900	296,037	277,380	18,657	—	—	—	5,989	1,892	—
20–24	2,512,803	1,215,600	1,253,015	1,197,869	55,146	—	—	—	36,706	7,482	—
25–29	1,974,241	458,750	1,444,266	1,392,687	51,579	—	—	—	60,658	10,567	—
30–34	1,596,772	228,691	1,276,220	1,238,326	37,894	—	—	—	83,777	8,084	—
35–39	1,483,717	160,274	1,193,282	1,160,080	33,202	—	—	—	121,783	8,378	—
40–44	1,239,435	110,627	968,227	938,721	29,506	—	—	—	154,399	6,182	—
45–49	1,003,711	74,517	759,723	731,892	27,831	—	—	—	165,781	3,690	—
50–54	863,012	55,353	597,566	576,825	20,741	—	—	—	205,310	4,783	—
55–59	594,843	33,512	386,481	371,421	15,060	—	—	—	171,760	3,090	—
60–64	526,956	33,320	297,036	285,866	11,170	—	—	—	195,104	1,496	—
65–69	346,303	21,446	162,079	154,905	7,174	—	—	—	160,882	1,896	—
70–74	251,860	17,855	82,078	78,187	3,891	—	—	—	151,130	797	—
75+	267,481	19,147	54,246	50,755	3,491	—	—	—	193,789	299	—
1890											
total	30,554,370	17,183,988	11,126,196	—	—	—	—	—	2,154,615	71,895	17,676
0–14	10,952,192	10,950,672	1,411	—	—	—	—	—	17	12	80
15–19	3,308,852	2,987,949	313,983	—	—	—	—	—	4,845	1,101	974
20–24	3,091,783	1,601,266	1,444,712	—	—	—	—	—	36,456	6,931	2,418
25–29	2,529,466	641,988	1,805,064	—	—	—	—	—	69,965	10,588	1,861
30–34	2,152,966	326,306	1,717,204	—	—	—	—	—	96,797	11,161	1,498
35–44	3,346,031	330,139	2,698,266	—	—	—	—	—	296,302	18,899	2,425
45–54	2,430,878	171,454	1,796,979	—	—	—	—	—	447,370	13,080	1,995
55–64	1,499,997	86,573	905,627	—	—	—	—	—	499,420	6,721	1,656
65+	1,183,569	66,758	418,399	—	—	—	—	—	693,324	3,091	1,997
unknown	58,636	20,883	24,551	—	—	—	—	—	10,119	311	2,772
1900											
total	37,244,145	20,520,319	13,845,963	—	—	—	—	—	2,721,564	114,965	41,334
0–14	12,950,982	12,946,500	3,783	—	—	—	—	—	126	30	543
15–19	3,811,344	3,378,373	417,773	—	—	—	—	—	9,363	2,427	3,408
20–24	3,718,110	1,914,812	1,732,525	—	—	—	—	—	52,666	13,175	4,932
25–29	3,214,129	883,521	2,076,553	—	—	—	—	—	92,161	18,524	3,370
30–34	2,660,508	441,743	2,076,822	—	—	—	—	—	122,221	17,426	2,296
35–44	4,346,344	481,997	3,457,528	—	—	—	—	—	373,309	30,005	3,505
45–54	2,998,613	234,528	2,214,957	—	—	—	—	—	527,197	19,138	2,793
55–64	1,941,821	129,011	1,173,910	—	—	—	—	—	626,904	9,574	2,422
65+	1,526,321	90,900	521,661	—	—	—	—	—	905,881	4,130	3,749
unknown	75,973	18,934	30,451	—	—	—	—	—	11,736	536	14,316

Note appears at end of table

(continued)

TABLE Aa614–683   Population, by marital status, sex, and race: 1880–1990 *Continued*

All races — Females

Year and age	Total Aa625 Number	Never married Aa626 Number	Married Total Aa627 Number	Married Spouse present Aa628 Number	Married Spouse absent Total Aa629 Number	Married Spouse absent Separated Aa630 [1] Number	Married Spouse absent Other Aa631 Number	Not separated Aa632 Number	Widowed Aa633 Number	Divorced Aa634 Number	Marital status unknown Aa635 Number
1910											
total	44,639,989	23,522,121	17,688,169	—	—	—	—	—	3,176,426	185,101	68,172
0–14	14,592,664	14,588,951	3,482	—	—	—	—	—	198	33	0
15–17	2,683,806	2,543,264	121,803	—	—	—	—	—	2,697	867	15,175
18–19	1,852,515	1,442,500	391,436	—	—	—	—	—	7,564	2,783	8,232
15–19	4,536,321	3,985,764	513,239	—	—	—	—	—	10,261	3,650	23,407
20–24	4,476,694	2,163,683	2,225,362	—	—	—	—	—	55,354	20,370	11,925
25–29	3,935,655	981,556	2,823,935	—	—	—	—	—	95,385	29,153	5,626
30–34	3,315,417	535,170	2,619,959	—	—	—	—	—	128,942	28,109	3,237
35–44	5,504,321	628,516	4,410,310	—	—	—	—	—	411,896	49,269	4,330
45–54	3,881,059	331,573	2,904,043	—	—	—	—	—	610,386	31,934	3,123
55–64	2,379,698	167,991	1,479,454	—	—	—	—	—	714,452	15,200	2,601
65+	1,963,548	124,223	687,335	—	—	—	—	—	1,140,558	6,903	4,529
unknown	54,612	14,694	21,050	—	—	—	—	—	8,994	480	9,394
1920											
total	51,810,189	26,243,696	21,324,487	—	—	—	—	—	3,917,894	273,361	50,751
0–14	16,632,674	16,626,794	5,554	—	—	—	—	—	269	57	0
15–17	2,861,030	2,711,081	145,390	—	—	—	—	—	3,091	1,468	0
18–19	1,895,734	1,426,569	451,152	—	—	—	—	—	9,148	4,549	4,316
15–19	4,756,764	4,137,650	596,542	—	—	—	—	—	12,239	6,017	4,316
20–24	4,749,976	2,164,051	2,483,697	—	—	—	—	—	65,414	28,582	8,232
25–29	4,548,258	1,048,285	3,336,501	—	—	—	—	—	117,387	41,243	4,842
30–34	3,940,410	588,119	3,155,854	—	—	—	—	—	152,893	40,188	3,356
35–44	6,760,934	767,882	5,426,434	—	—	—	—	—	485,493	75,027	6,098
45–54	4,845,398	464,838	3,587,794	—	—	—	—	—	739,058	48,562	5,146
55–64	3,069,807	257,029	1,878,478	—	—	—	—	—	906,362	23,451	4,487
65+	2,450,144	173,442	830,160	—	—	—	—	—	1,430,621	9,609	6,312
unknown	55,824	15,606	23,473	—	—	—	—	—	8,158	625	7,962
1930											
total	60,637,966	29,102,964	26,174,997	—	—	—	—	—	4,734,374	573,246	52,385
0–14	17,800,817	17,796,311	4,241	—	—	—	—	—	167	98	0
15–17	3,465,118	3,279,560	179,404	—	—	—	—	—	3,284	2,870	0
18–19	2,329,172	1,752,614	552,563	—	—	—	—	—	9,053	9,501	5,441
15–19	5,794,290	5,032,174	731,967	—	—	—	—	—	12,337	12,371	5,441
20–24	5,533,563	2,547,057	2,857,665	—	—	—	—	—	56,375	62,464	10,002
25–29	4,973,428	1,079,923	3,697,645	—	—	—	—	—	102,041	89,124	4,695
30–34	4,558,635	603,048	3,715,648	—	—	—	—	—	148,571	88,219	3,149
35–39	4,528,785	472,053	3,725,680	—	—	—	—	—	240,604	87,533	2,915
40–44	3,853,736	367,077	3,106,901	—	—	—	—	—	306,958	70,117	2,683
45–49	3,370,355	303,864	2,616,213	—	—	—	—	—	391,342	56,446	2,490
50–54	2,844,159	260,602	2,057,326	—	—	—	—	—	481,334	42,428	2,469
55–59	2,219,685	199,569	1,469,931	—	—	—	—	—	520,158	27,898	2,129

All races

Females

Year and age	Total	Never married	Married						Widowed	Divorced	Marital status unknown
			Total	Spouse present	Spouse absent						
					Total	Separated	Other	Not separated			
	Aa625	Aa626	Aa627	Aa628	Aa629	Aa630 [1]	Aa631	Aa632	Aa633	Aa634	Aa635
	Number	Number	Number	Number	Number	Number	Number	Number	Number	Number	Number
60–64	1,809,713	160,619	1,029,354	—	—	—	—	—	599,644	17,983	2,113
65–69	1,352,793	114,186	630,293	—	—	—	—	—	596,224	10,204	1,886
70–74	958,357	80,918	334,963	—	—	—	—	—	536,003	4,830	1,643
75+	997,444	73,312	181,944	—	—	—	—	—	736,807	2,859	2,522
unknown	42,206	12,251	15,226	—	—	—	—	—	5,809	672	8,248
1940											
total	50,549,176	13,935,866	30,090,488	28,514,359	1,572,776	—	—	—	5,700,202	822,620	—
14	1,187,614	1,184,094	3,353	—	—	—	—	—	110	57	—
15–17	3,629,909	3,461,246	165,131	—	—	—	—	—	1,729	1,803	—
18–19	2,523,461	1,962,777	548,809	—	—	—	—	—	4,694	7,181	—
15–19	6,153,370	5,424,023	713,940	653,103	60,837	—	—	—	6,423	8,984	—
20–24	5,895,443	2,781,001	3,025,923	2,850,306	175,617	—	—	—	32,751	55,768	—
25–29	5,645,976	1,288,092	4,185,325	3,977,450	207,875	—	—	—	71,878	100,681	—
30–34	5,172,076	761,698	4,155,872	3,955,695	200,177	—	—	—	128,256	126,250	—
35–39	4,799,718	536,205	3,911,529	3,714,510	197,019	—	—	—	219,608	132,376	—
40–44	4,368,708	414,671	3,519,262	3,345,033	174,229	—	—	—	317,976	116,799	—
45–49	4,045,956	349,238	3,167,650	3,012,651	154,999	—	—	—	432,856	96,212	—
50–54	3,504,096	305,074	2,568,964	2,440,627	128,337	—	—	—	558,592	71,466	—
55–59	2,832,501	246,099	1,902,259	1,806,196	96,063	—	—	—	634,932	49,211	—
60–64	2,330,524	216,308	1,352,509	1,282,642	69,867	—	—	—	730,112	31,595	—
65–69	1,910,569	179,086	888,691	836,840	51,851	—	—	—	823,196	19,596	—
70–74	1,298,565	123,512	445,966	416,946	29,020	—	—	—	720,414	8,673	—
75–79	780,302	72,036	179,353	163,657	15,696	—	—	—	525,501	3,412	—
80–84	415,380	38,064	55,985	48,399	7,586	—	—	—	320,184	1,147	—
85+	208,378	16,665	13,907	10,304	3,603	—	—	—	177,413	393	—
1950											
total	57,102,295	11,418,335	37,576,800	35,568,810	2,007,990	1,168,730	839,260	—	6,734,275	1,372,885	—
14	1,047,370	1,039,610	6,980	4,525	2,455	635	1,820	—	565	215	—
15–17	3,116,230	2,893,350	217,325	187,865	29,460	11,785	17,675	—	2,055	3,500	—
18–19	2,205,525	1,519,215	670,290	612,385	57,905	27,755	30,150	—	3,205	12,815	—
15–19	5,321,755	4,412,565	887,615	800,250	87,365	39,540	47,825	—	5,260	16,315	—
20–24	5,878,040	1,898,910	3,856,760	3,620,775	235,985	132,570	103,415	—	25,280	97,090	—
25–29	6,277,480	833,040	5,227,960	4,962,485	265,475	159,840	105,635	—	57,490	158,990	—
30–34	5,896,625	546,245	5,082,260	4,847,690	234,570	149,485	85,085	—	91,945	176,175	—
35–39	5,712,555	477,035	4,882,565	4,645,605	236,960	154,690	82,270	—	155,500	197,455	—
40–44	5,125,095	423,445	4,257,490	4,045,825	211,665	134,820	76,845	—	253,750	190,410	—
45–49	4,553,255	360,110	3,635,340	3,446,745	188,595	116,530	72,065	—	391,825	165,980	—
50–54	4,134,350	320,040	3,102,335	2,939,880	162,455	93,845	68,610	—	575,770	136,205	—
55–59	3,604,960	278,500	2,491,385	2,366,775	124,610	70,790	53,820	—	738,245	96,830	—
60–64	3,028,210	246,905	1,818,775	1,722,245	96,530	50,655	45,875	—	898,415	64,115	—
65–69	2,598,145	218,510	1,270,475	1,196,350	74,125	36,980	37,145	—	1,068,905	40,255	—
70–74	1,799,480	162,460	658,660	614,805	43,855	17,165	26,690	—	958,730	19,630	—
75–79	1,157,730	109,390	285,610	260,215	25,395	7,915	17,480	—	754,200	8,530	—
80–84	624,225	58,375	88,625	76,580	12,045	2,520	9,525	—	474,045	3,180	—
85+	343,020	33,195	23,965	18,060	5,905	750	5,155	—	284,350	1,510	—

Note appears at end of table   (continued)

TABLE Aa614–683 Population, by marital status, sex, and race: 1880–1990 *Continued*

All races

Females

Year and age	Total	Never married	Married Total	Spouse present	Spouse absent Total	Separated[1]	Other	Not separated	Widowed	Divorced	Marital status unknown
	Aa625	Aa626	Aa627	Aa628	Aa629	Aa630	Aa631	Aa632	Aa633	Aa634	Aa635
	Number	Number	Number	Number	Number	Number	Number	Number	Number	Number	Number
1960											
total	64,961,189	12,320,199	42,905,285	40,334,785	2,570,500	1,317,620	1,252,880	—	7,880,607	1,855,098	—
14	1,345,136	1,330,089	14,250	7,357	6,893	889	6,004	—	391	406	—
15–17	4,171,262	3,886,610	277,151	219,116	58,035	12,946	45,089	—	1,874	5,627	—
18–19	2,417,335	1,642,135	756,653	657,837	98,816	27,541	71,275	—	2,877	15,670	—
15–19	6,588,597	5,528,745	1,033,804	876,953	156,851	40,487	116,364	—	4,751	21,297	—
20–24	5,519,937	1,567,622	3,833,956	3,520,133	313,823	126,773	187,050	—	17,252	101,107	—
25–29	5,537,104	582,114	4,772,006	4,488,307	283,699	152,221	131,478	—	37,047	145,937	—
30–34	6,111,422	422,915	5,423,228	5,127,882	295,346	174,236	121,110	—	74,109	191,170	—
35–39	6,418,536	389,524	5,658,013	5,366,757	291,256	175,349	115,907	—	138,383	232,616	—
40–44	5,917,805	359,242	5,083,593	4,827,259	256,334	156,025	100,309	—	235,833	239,137	—
45–49	5,553,943	362,948	4,579,971	4,345,688	234,283	139,178	95,105	—	372,811	238,213	—
50–54	4,931,766	375,318	3,799,854	3,600,607	199,247	112,444	86,803	—	548,447	208,147	—
55–59	4,411,290	363,072	3,085,057	2,918,015	167,042	88,864	78,178	—	791,240	171,921	—
60–64	3,727,401	285,192	2,290,305	2,165,866	124,439	61,028	63,411	—	1,027,803	124,101	—
65–69	3,303,330	260,368	1,703,279	1,602,440	100,839	45,307	55,532	—	1,250,898	88,785	—
70–74	2,522,159	212,109	986,041	917,110	68,931	25,968	42,963	—	1,271,577	52,432	—
75–79	1,659,319	145,853	455,313	413,817	41,496	12,741	28,755	—	1,032,827	25,326	—
80–84	883,042	84,116	143,128	122,997	20,131	4,420	15,711	—	645,702	10,096	—
85+	530,402	50,972	43,487	33,597	9,890	1,690	8,200	—	431,536	4,407	—
1970											
total	77,910,094	17,624,105	47,666,431	44,481,843	3,184,588	1,740,328	1,444,260	—	9,615,280	3,004,278	—
14	2,049,056	2,019,680	22,010	13,515	8,495	2,285	6,210	—	5,421	1,945	—
15–17	5,825,133	5,553,582	250,529	193,093	57,436	14,254	43,182	—	12,382	8,640	—
18–19	3,660,096	2,804,666	822,618	683,629	138,989	37,824	101,165	—	10,656	22,156	—
15–19	9,485,229	8,358,248	1,073,147	876,722	196,425	52,078	144,347	—	23,038	30,796	—
20–24	8,354,509	3,030,876	5,054,321	4,543,058	511,263	216,706	294,557	—	56,508	212,804	—
25–29	6,810,076	827,906	5,616,300	5,242,673	373,627	225,992	147,635	—	71,530	294,340	—
30–34	5,868,858	435,897	5,055,678	4,730,613	325,065	204,205	120,860	—	86,494	290,789	—
35–39	5,710,623	337,144	4,944,969	4,639,467	305,502	194,021	111,481	—	124,615	303,895	—
40–44	6,149,692	335,111	5,242,784	4,939,106	303,678	199,552	104,126	—	229,145	342,652	—
45–49	6,255,178	334,549	5,207,386	4,932,125	275,261	178,032	97,229	—	366,406	346,837	—
50–54	5,741,230	327,957	4,520,709	4,288,196	232,513	146,005	86,508	—	576,390	316,174	—
55–59	5,228,025	338,912	3,776,995	3,582,919	194,076	114,248	79,828	—	841,602	270,516	—
60–64	4,599,123	330,139	2,900,860	2,746,981	153,879	85,660	68,219	—	1,146,494	221,630	—
65–69	3,897,364	289,111	2,026,280	1,912,992	113,288	56,662	56,626	—	1,420,898	161,075	—
70–74	3,115,737	241,493	1,244,819	1,164,105	80,714	32,909	47,805	—	1,525,353	104,072	—
75–79	2,284,301	190,934	636,342	580,634	55,708	18,540	37,168	—	1,395,378	61,647	—
80–84	1,399,774	123,463	240,526	207,143	33,383	7,994	25,389	—	1,006,613	29,172	—
85+	961,319	102,685	103,305	81,594	21,711	5,439	16,272	—	739,395	15,934	—

All races

Females

Married

Year and age	Total	Never married	Married Total	Spouse present	Spouse absent				Widowed	Divorced	Marital status unknown
					Total	Separated	Other	Not separated			
	Aa625	Aa626	Aa627	Aa628	Aa629	Aa630 [1]	Aa631	Aa632	Aa633	Aa634	Aa635
	Number	Number	Number	Number	Number	Number	Number	Number	Number	Number	Number
1980											
total	91,482,678	20,927,318	52,850,784	49,382,444	3,468,340	2,358,636	1,109,704	—	11,240,418	6,464,158	—
15–17	6,134,000	5,932,023	191,452	141,598	49,854	12,332	37,522	—	2,757	7,768	—
18–19	4,274,943	3,557,993	679,507	583,207	96,300	39,897	56,403	—	3,691	33,752	—
15–19	10,408,943	9,490,016	870,959	724,805	146,154	52,229	93,925	—	6,448	41,520	—
20–24	10,654,502	5,450,056	4,732,727	4,268,094	464,633	285,965	178,668	—	24,746	446,973	—
25–29	9,793,296	2,111,744	6,739,235	6,222,973	516,262	377,355	138,907	—	51,751	890,566	—
30–34	8,953,943	951,028	6,917,901	6,461,432	456,469	355,089	101,380	—	79,480	1,005,534	—
35–39	7,109,659	479,202	5,691,415	5,331,604	359,811	283,669	76,142	—	111,579	827,463	—
40–44	5,957,689	314,845	4,812,272	4,518,974	293,298	230,623	62,675	—	167,725	662,847	—
45–49	5,679,017	265,239	4,553,757	4,302,139	251,618	193,125	58,493	—	285,345	574,676	—
50–54	6,096,136	282,463	4,737,284	4,495,303	241,981	179,197	62,784	—	530,289	546,100	—
55–59	6,153,592	288,465	4,515,936	4,305,399	210,537	145,908	64,629	—	873,312	475,879	—
60–64	5,440,083	280,375	3,572,778	3,412,572	160,206	103,045	57,161	—	1,231,668	355,262	—
65–69	4,887,335	287,669	2,679,906	2,553,352	126,554	71,873	54,681	—	1,651,807	267,953	—
70–74	3,962,619	262,012	1,690,340	1,597,204	93,136	42,729	50,407	—	1,830,220	180,047	—
75–79	2,952,351	205,390	870,270	801,640	68,630	22,607	46,023	—	1,770,105	106,586	—
80–84	1,908,812	138,827	338,278	293,383	44,895	9,525	35,370	—	1,379,391	52,316	—
85+	1,524,701	119,987	127,726	93,570	34,156	5,697	28,459	—	1,246,552	30,436	—
1990											
total	101,324,687	23,755,235	55,820,936	—	—	2,676,840	—	53,144,096	12,121,939	9,626,577	—
15–17	4,874,386	4,762,086	101,293	—	—	8,485	—	92,808	4,439	6,568	—
18–19	3,776,931	3,399,406	353,056	—	—	24,784	—	328,272	5,619	18,850	—
15–19	8,651,317	8,161,492	454,349	—	—	33,269	—	421,080	10,058	25,418	—
20–24	9,344,716	6,032,648	3,002,021	—	—	209,254	—	2,792,767	18,346	291,701	—
25–29	10,617,109	3,400,696	6,322,074	—	—	385,669	—	5,936,405	42,091	852,248	—
30–34	10,985,954	2,002,228	7,649,157	—	—	442,850	—	7,206,307	78,946	1,255,623	—
35–44	18,984,676	1,904,185	13,857,915	—	—	747,333	—	13,110,582	304,050	2,918,526	—
45–54	12,897,751	719,994	9,488,986	—	—	428,274	—	9,060,712	665,565	2,023,206	—
55–59	5,497,386	251,599	3,913,674	—	—	139,383	—	3,774,291	658,724	673,389	—
60–64	5,669,120	256,449	3,734,899	—	—	110,965	—	3,623,934	1,118,169	559,603	—
65–74	10,164,945	489,966	5,383,874	—	—	129,986	—	5,253,888	3,587,808	703,297	—
75–84	6,289,246	379,334	1,811,074	—	—	42,309	—	1,768,765	3,832,368	266,470	—
85+	2,222,467	156,644	202,913	—	—	7,548	—	195,365	1,805,814	57,096	—

Note appears at end of table

(continued)

TABLE Aa614–683   Population, by marital status, sex, and race: 1880–1990   *Continued*

White

Males

	Total	Never married	Married Total	Spouse present	Married Spouse absent Total	Separated	Other	Not separated	Widowed and divorced	Widowed	Divorced	Marital status unknown
	Aa636	Aa637	Aa638	Aa639	Aa640	Aa641 [1]	Aa642	Aa643	Aa644	Aa645	Aa646	Aa647
Year and age	Number	Number	Number	Number	Number	Number	Number	Number	Number	Number	Number	Number
1880												
total	22,137,410	13,836,694	7,753,406	7,461,483	291,923	—	—	—	—	519,671	27,639	—
0–14	8,221,078	8,220,379	499	0	499	—	—	—	—	200	0	—
15–19	2,131,367	2,108,628	20,241	16,355	3,886	—	—	—	—	2,298	200	—
20–24	2,214,729	1,761,509	444,549	416,122	28,427	—	—	—	—	7,674	997	—
25–29	1,844,858	783,040	1,040,175	998,385	41,790	—	—	—	—	18,451	3,192	—
30–34	1,548,032	373,223	1,140,598	1,102,088	38,510	—	—	—	—	30,619	3,592	—
35–39	1,368,174	206,469	1,119,798	1,082,468	37,330	—	—	—	—	37,913	3,994	—
40–44	1,102,720	125,678	933,063	898,729	34,334	—	—	—	—	41,783	2,196	—
45–49	948,682	84,989	814,128	786,388	27,740	—	—	—	—	45,676	3,889	—
50–54	855,273	64,545	731,972	705,231	26,741	—	—	—	—	56,061	2,695	—
55–59	613,218	35,413	528,329	513,068	15,261	—	—	—	—	47,680	1,796	—
60–64	509,966	30,827	420,494	406,030	14,464	—	—	—	—	56,551	2,094	—
65–69	335,788	18,450	264,466	256,380	8,086	—	—	—	—	51,077	1,795	—
70–74	229,480	11,673	170,529	162,750	7,779	—	—	—	—	46,478	800	—
75+	214,045	11,871	124,565	117,489	7,076	—	—	—	—	77,210	399	—
1890												
total	28,206,332	17,404,880	9,992,921	—	—	—	—	—	—	721,971	43,829	42,731
0–14	9,672,145	9,672,048	11	—	—	—	—	—	—	0	0	86
15–19	2,818,914	2,805,397	12,734	—	—	—	—	—	—	85	15	683
20–24	2,740,864	2,264,012	466,877	—	—	—	—	—	—	5,253	1,091	3,631
25–29	2,407,153	1,144,597	1,234,233	—	—	—	—	—	—	20,709	3,547	4,067
30–34	2,200,973	590,836	1,564,904	—	—	—	—	—	—	36,894	5,088	3,251
35–44	3,327,366	509,320	2,699,336	—	—	—	—	—	—	102,517	11,387	4,806
45–54	2,354,204	216,251	1,987,488	—	—	—	—	—	—	137,032	10,392	3,041
55–64	1,479,763	101,459	1,219,090	—	—	—	—	—	—	149,988	7,345	1,881
65+	1,124,304	62,777	788,954	—	—	—	—	—	—	266,108	4,658	1,807
unknown	80,646	38,183	19,294	—	—	—	—	—	—	3,385	306	19,478
1900												
total	34,349,007	20,675,809	12,476,851	—	—	—	—	—	—	1,023,289	73,235	99,823
0–14	11,406,742	11,405,947	493	—	—	—	—	—	—	19	5	278
15–19	3,268,697	3,234,841	29,265	—	—	—	—	—	—	580	132	3,879
20–24	3,188,443	2,542,353	624,893	—	—	—	—	—	—	9,211	2,444	9,542
25–29	2,968,526	1,412,663	1,513,157	—	—	—	—	—	—	28,638	6,505	7,563
30–34	2,634,676	747,801	1,826,024	—	—	—	—	—	—	46,857	8,773	5,221
35–44	4,431,038	760,013	3,497,772	—	—	—	—	—	—	146,034	19,862	7,357
45–54	3,054,820	317,556	2,519,574	—	—	—	—	—	—	195,838	17,248	4,604
55–64	1,868,409	143,728	1,493,763	—	—	—	—	—	—	216,737	11,196	2,985
65+	1,417,610	82,307	948,372	—	—	—	—	—	—	376,361	6,779	3,791
unknown	110,046	28,600	23,538	—	—	—	—	—	—	3,014	291	54,603

White

Males

Year and age	Total	Never married	Married: Total	Married: Spouse present	Married: Spouse absent, Total	Married: Spouse absent, Separated[1]	Married: Spouse absent, Other	Married: Not separated	Widowed and divorced	Widowed	Divorced	Marital status unknown
	Aa636	Aa637	Aa638	Aa639	Aa640	Aa641	Aa642	Aa643	Aa644	Aa645	Aa646	Aa647
	Number	Number	Number	Number	Number	Number	Number	Number	Number	Number	Number	Number
1910												
total	42,178,245	24,379,558	16,254,696	—	—	—	—	—	—	1,274,464	135,215	134,312
0–14	13,020,120	13,019,276	756	—	—	—	—	—	—	76	12	0
15–17	2,368,842	2,352,379	3,787	—	—	—	—	—	219	—	—	12,457
18–19	1,630,301	1,584,171	36,517	—	—	—	—	—	691	—	—	8,922
15–19	3,999,143	3,936,550	40,304	—	—	—	—	—	—	680	230	21,379
20–24	4,070,955	3,122,440	913,059	—	—	—	—	—	—	11,506	4,856	19,094
25–29	3,792,224	1,670,927	2,065,898	—	—	—	—	—	—	31,290	12,101	12,008
30–34	3,297,169	874,513	2,348,874	—	—	—	—	—	—	50,039	15,819	7,924
35–44	5,561,221	944,724	4,407,687	—	—	—	—	—	—	161,346	37,007	10,457
45–54	4,077,708	463,510	3,330,529	—	—	—	—	—	—	244,431	32,828	6,410
55–64	2,440,574	206,976	1,933,201	—	—	—	—	—	—	276,500	19,888	4,009
65+	1,825,019	115,719	1,195,982	—	—	—	—	—	—	495,282	12,019	6,017
unknown	94,112	24,923	18,406	—	—	—	—	—	—	3,314	455	47,014
1920												
total	48,430,655	26,874,811	19,700,899	—	—	—	—	—	—	1,549,269	207,695	97,981
0–14	15,095,069	15,092,146	2,786	—	—	—	—	—	—	105	32	0
15–17	2,509,043	2,498,616	10,027	—	—	—	—	—	1,423	—	—	0
18–19	1,632,788	1,559,528	65,827	—	—	—	—	—	1,823	—	—	6,010
15–19	4,141,831	4,058,144	75,854	—	—	—	—	—	—	376	24	6,010
20–24	4,018,576	2,916,983	1,066,140	—	—	—	—	—	—	14,402	7,808	13,243
25–29	4,094,301	1,655,994	2,368,084	—	—	—	—	—	—	40,782	18,965	10,476
30–34	3,776,266	920,897	2,760,747	—	—	—	—	—	—	62,336	24,405	7,881
35–44	6,652,753	1,088,203	5,312,851	—	—	—	—	—	—	183,604	56,103	11,992
45–54	5,072,779	627,420	4,107,564	—	—	—	—	—	—	279,270	50,191	8,334
55–64	3,202,280	319,371	2,497,936	—	—	—	—	—	—	347,739	31,826	5,408
65+	2,298,475	171,704	1,487,186	—	—	—	—	—	—	616,530	17,168	5,887
unknown	78,325	23,949	21,751	—	—	—	—	—	—	3,226	649	28,750
1930												
total	55,163,854	29,313,557	23,603,919	—	—	—	—	—	—	1,745,239	428,090	73,049
0–14	15,949,698	15,949,048	607	—	—	—	—	—	—	26	17	0
15–17	3,075,551	3,067,438	7,818	—	—	—	—	—	—	183	112	8,313
18–19	1,988,424	1,910,065	68,647	—	—	—	—	—	—	650	749	6,869
15–19	5,063,975	4,977,503	76,465	—	—	—	—	—	—	833	861	15,182
20–24	4,666,016	3,389,842	1,234,723	—	—	—	—	—	—	9,882	16,387	6,821
25–29	4,246,957	1,592,650	2,581,163	—	—	—	—	—	—	25,045	41,278	4,356
30–34	4,059,179	859,861	3,099,125	—	—	—	—	—	—	42,246	53,591	3,872
35–39	4,171,206	639,880	3,397,317	—	—	—	—	—	—	69,273	60,864	3,386
40–44	3,733,591	491,575	3,081,779	—	—	—	—	—	—	98,256	58,595	3,057
45–49	3,293,779	397,943	2,712,488	—	—	—	—	—	—	126,327	53,964	2,803
50–54	2,815,281	315,948	2,287,972	—	—	—	—	—	—	162,975	45,583	2,465
55–59	2,225,068	236,505	1,772,722	—	—	—	—	—	—	178,255	35,121	2,379
60–64	1,789,010	181,762	1,365,713	—	—	—	—	—	—	213,058	26,098	2,102
65–69	1,322,823	125,560	947,545	—	—	—	—	—	—	230,050	17,566	1,890
70–74	933,348	81,389	605,085	—	—	—	—	—	—	234,449	10,535	2,473
75+	851,414	60,645	428,812	—	—	—	—	—	—	352,576	6,908	8,313
unknown	42,509	13,446	12,403	—	—	—	—	—	—	1,988	722	13,950

Note appears at end of table

(continued)

TABLE Aa614–683   Population, by marital status, sex, and race: 1880–1990   Continued

White — Males

Year and age	Total	Never married	Married Total	Married Spouse present	Married Spouse absent Total	Married Spouse absent Separated [1]	Married Spouse absent Other	Married Spouse absent Not separated	Widowed and divorced	Widowed	Divorced	Marital status unknown
	Aa636	Aa637	Aa638	Aa639	Aa640	Aa641	Aa642	Aa643	Aa644	Aa645	Aa646	Aa647
	Number	Number	Number	Number	Number	Number	Number	Number	Number	Number	Number	Number
1940												
total	45,823,031	15,915,844	27,438,595	26,236,779	1,200,767	—	—	—	—	1,891,536	577,056	—
14	1,079,497	1,078,374	1,049	—	—	—	—	—	—	52	22	—
15–17	3,283,502	3,272,026	11,090	—	—	—	—	—	—	249	137	—
18–19	2,232,418	2,158,061	73,159	—	—	—	—	—	—	509	689	—
15–19	5,515,920	5,430,087	84,249	66,444	17,805	—	—	—	—	758	826	—
20–24	5,113,642	3,759,539	1,333,140	1,254,440	78,700	—	—	—	—	5,532	15,431	—
25–29	4,892,013	1,793,729	3,039,523	2,922,002	117,521	—	—	—	—	14,886	43,875	—
30–34	4,573,316	944,493	3,536,995	3,413,184	123,811	—	—	—	—	27,412	64,416	—
35–39	4,254,368	643,064	3,487,701	3,357,283	130,418	—	—	—	—	46,311	77,292	—
40–44	3,995,190	499,085	3,340,449	3,203,700	136,749	—	—	—	—	74,108	81,548	—
45–49	3,842,613	430,435	3,223,350	3,086,558	136,792	—	—	—	—	111,729	77,099	—
50–54	3,451,717	382,516	2,835,951	2,706,503	129,448	—	—	—	—	163,555	69,695	—
55–59	2,790,046	305,233	2,236,093	2,131,583	104,510	—	—	—	—	195,223	53,497	—
60–64	2,232,453	238,370	1,715,598	1,632,402	83,196	—	—	—	—	239,348	39,137	—
65–69	1,736,937	183,654	1,251,409	1,188,342	63,067	—	—	—	—	274,018	27,856	—
70–74	1,183,283	120,319	770,024	729,936	40,088	—	—	—	—	277,357	15,583	—
75–79	681,397	65,565	382,395	359,593	22,802	—	—	—	—	226,131	7,306	—
80–84	339,291	29,937	154,901	143,803	11,098	—	—	—	—	151,841	2,612	—
85+	141,348	11,444	45,768	41,006	4,762	—	—	—	—	83,275	861	—
1950												
total	49,301,825	12,892,040	33,451,380	32,065,355	1,386,025	536,190	849,835	—	—	1,985,970	972,435	—
14	956,905	947,870	6,195	3,285	2,910	1,155	1,755	—	—	1,600	1,240	—
15–17	2,805,300	2,774,005	25,920	15,480	10,440	2,570	7,870	—	—	3,190	2,185	—
18–19	1,896,180	1,777,765	114,735	98,345	16,390	3,555	12,835	—	—	1,265	2,415	—
15–19	4,701,480	4,551,770	140,655	113,825	26,830	6,125	20,705	—	—	4,455	4,600	—
20–24	4,959,605	2,953,380	1,954,655	1,841,075	113,580	38,540	75,040	—	—	5,980	45,590	—
25–29	5,290,405	1,250,075	3,936,390	3,775,200	161,190	51,765	109,425	—	—	11,260	92,680	—
30–34	5,025,360	657,010	4,249,810	4,104,115	145,695	49,930	95,765	—	—	15,105	103,435	—
35–39	4,875,435	491,100	4,243,570	4,100,635	142,935	53,810	89,125	—	—	25,890	114,875	—
40–44	4,473,500	402,650	3,907,145	3,766,865	140,280	56,215	84,065	—	—	43,595	120,110	—
45–49	4,000,205	351,355	3,459,735	3,322,775	136,960	56,780	80,180	—	—	70,385	118,730	—
50–54	3,669,695	311,070	3,129,510	2,998,160	131,350	54,135	77,215	—	—	119,460	109,655	—
55–59	3,278,815	276,940	2,731,330	2,620,915	110,415	48,035	62,380	—	—	180,050	90,495	—
60–64	2,773,080	243,790	2,206,375	2,108,995	97,380	43,665	53,715	—	—	252,315	70,600	—
65–69	2,197,035	198,560	1,632,890	1,557,875	75,015	35,290	39,725	—	—	315,145	50,440	—
70–74	1,491,855	128,065	1,010,830	961,015	49,815	21,700	28,115	—	—	324,300	28,660	—
75–79	924,215	76,695	545,165	515,050	30,115	12,515	17,600	—	—	288,185	14,170	—
80–84	467,910	35,495	224,850	210,070	14,780	4,730	10,050	—	—	202,190	5,375	—
85+	216,325	16,215	72,275	65,500	6,775	1,800	4,975	—	—	126,055	1,780	—

White

Males

Year and age	Total	Never married	Married							Widowed	Divorced	Marital status unknown
			Total	Spouse present	Spouse absent				Widowed and divorced			
					Total	Separated	Other	Not separated				
	Aa636	Aa637	Aa638	Aa639	Aa640	Aa641 [1]	Aa642	Aa643	Aa644	Aa645	Aa646	Aa647
	Number	Number	Number	Number	Number	Number	Number	Number	Number	Number	Number	Number
1960												
total	55,036,177	13,405,226	38,696,538	37,143,042	1,553,496	536,206	1,017,290	—	—	1,787,199	1,147,214	—
14	1,225,956	1,218,696	6,871	1,378	5,493	405	5,088	—	—	101	288	—
15–17	3,819,651	3,775,235	42,480	22,112	20,368	1,892	18,476	—	—	612	1,324	—
18–19	2,074,295	1,887,869	182,147	149,849	32,298	5,044	27,254	—	—	668	3,611	—
15–19	5,893,946	5,663,104	224,627	171,961	52,666	6,936	45,730	—	—	1,280	4,935	—
20–24	4,657,470	2,450,464	2,154,622	1,982,512	172,110	39,808	132,302	—	—	3,514	48,870	—
25–29	4,725,480	943,736	3,690,406	3,536,162	154,244	48,509	105,735	—	—	6,963	84,375	—
30–34	5,216,424	587,491	4,507,044	4,353,361	153,683	53,152	100,531	—	—	12,346	109,543	—
35–39	5,461,528	454,734	4,858,753	4,703,513	155,240	55,501	99,739	—	—	20,933	127,108	—
40–44	5,094,821	360,726	4,566,236	4,424,508	141,728	54,713	87,015	—	—	34,110	133,749	—
45–49	4,850,486	339,279	4,314,328	4,175,673	138,655	57,057	81,598	—	—	56,065	140,814	—
50–54	4,314,976	322,390	3,775,814	3,647,198	128,616	52,145	76,471	—	—	84,005	132,767	—
55–59	3,774,623	302,732	3,227,120	3,109,800	117,320	48,312	69,008	—	—	127,498	117,273	—
60–64	3,100,045	236,434	2,587,769	2,487,662	100,107	39,197	60,910	—	—	184,661	91,181	—
65–69	2,637,044	204,549	2,109,659	2,023,886	85,773	33,173	52,600	—	—	252,566	70,270	—
70–74	1,972,947	156,315	1,449,897	1,383,815	66,082	23,982	42,100	—	—	320,087	46,648	—
75–79	1,214,577	97,807	789,326	744,969	44,357	14,560	29,797	—	—	302,029	25,415	—
80–84	591,251	44,728	317,345	293,268	24,077	6,173	17,904	—	—	219,457	9,721	—
85+	304,603	22,041	116,721	103,376	13,345	2,583	10,762	—	—	161,584	4,257	—
1970												
total	63,573,807	17,602,671	42,495,670	40,740,647	1,755,023	664,778	1,090,245	—	—	1,801,685	1,673,781	—
14	1,826,237	1,806,427	16,118	11,819	4,299	1,494	2,805	—	—	2,146	1,546	—
15–17	5,219,565	5,151,626	59,947	45,375	14,572	4,069	10,503	—	—	4,045	3,947	—
18–19	3,166,488	2,891,320	265,717	224,047	41,670	8,340	33,330	—	—	2,675	6,776	—
15–19	8,386,053	8,042,946	325,664	269,422	56,242	12,409	43,833	—	—	6,720	10,723	—
20–24	6,839,742	3,754,339	2,973,470	2,713,140	260,330	70,178	190,152	—	—	9,954	101,979	—
25–29	5,826,536	1,088,031	4,546,878	4,349,534	197,344	83,706	113,638	—	—	15,189	176,438	—
30–34	4,948,318	493,236	4,282,119	4,126,674	155,445	64,685	90,760	—	—	14,660	158,303	—
35–39	4,807,899	364,773	4,266,376	4,122,549	143,827	59,105	84,722	—	—	20,379	156,371	—
40–44	5,215,482	366,351	4,624,459	4,474,295	150,164	66,330	83,834	—	—	35,038	189,634	—
45–49	5,227,719	325,406	4,656,836	4,510,059	146,777	65,779	80,998	—	—	56,223	189,254	—
50–54	4,818,742	287,700	4,268,331	4,134,575	133,756	59,236	74,520	—	—	85,491	177,220	—
55–59	4,338,440	270,066	3,788,800	3,668,842	119,958	53,452	66,506	—	—	120,605	158,969	—
60–64	3,677,779	238,689	3,139,779	3,032,116	107,663	43,891	63,772	—	—	171,803	127,508	—
65–69	2,803,469	196,360	2,292,463	2,207,017	85,446	32,596	52,850	—	—	219,832	94,814	—
70–74	2,112,482	151,661	1,621,871	1,551,812	70,059	23,018	47,041	—	—	276,299	62,651	—
75–79	1,452,801	104,731	1,011,319	953,646	57,673	15,548	42,125	—	—	298,035	38,716	—
80–84	808,569	61,487	471,972	432,132	39,840	8,752	31,088	—	—	256,505	18,605	—
85+	483,539	50,468	209,215	183,015	26,200	4,599	21,601	—	—	212,806	11,050	—

Note appears at end of table

(continued)

TABLE Aa614–683 Population, by marital status, sex, and race: 1880–1990 *Continued*

White

Males

Year and age	Total	Never married	Married Total	Married Spouse present	Married Spouse absent Total	Married Spouse absent Separated [1]	Married Spouse absent Other	Married Spouse absent Not separated	Widowed and divorced	Widowed	Divorced	Marital status unknown
	Aa636	Aa637	Aa638	Aa639	Aa640	Aa641	Aa642	Aa643	Aa644	Aa645	Aa646	Aa647
	Number	Number	Number	Number	Number	Number	Number	Number	Number	Number	Number	Number
1980												
total	71,348,399	19,983,643	45,941,723	44,063,066	1,878,657	972,401	906,256	—	—	1,732,398	3,690,635	—
15–17	5,153,640	5,115,357	35,740	16,908	18,832	2,464	16,368	—	—	547	1,996	—
18–19	3,526,721	3,318,876	199,630	160,869	38,761	8,741	30,020	—	—	508	7,707	—
15–19	8,680,361	8,434,233	235,370	177,777	57,593	11,205	46,388	—	—	1,055	9,703	—
20–24	8,726,875	5,839,573	2,672,794	2,437,714	235,080	105,782	129,298	—	—	4,143	210,365	—
25–29	8,013,599	2,442,500	5,013,602	4,737,473	276,129	161,641	114,488	—	—	8,038	549,459	—
30–34	7,386,562	1,017,141	5,720,676	5,480,835	239,841	152,150	87,691	—	—	11,137	637,608	—
35–39	5,848,891	461,612	4,882,550	4,705,940	176,610	112,669	63,941	—	—	14,876	489,853	—
40–44	4,862,473	294,654	4,169,866	4,026,806	143,060	90,712	52,348	—	—	20,484	377,469	—
45–49	4,616,347	252,388	3,999,393	3,874,655	124,738	75,910	48,828	—	—	36,831	327,735	—
50–54	4,925,489	277,707	4,259,842	4,136,138	123,704	73,176	50,528	—	—	72,959	314,981	—
55–59	4,877,635	257,872	4,235,692	4,122,013	113,679	60,856	52,823	—	—	118,153	265,918	—
60–64	4,199,446	210,087	3,626,019	3,532,921	93,098	45,168	47,930	—	—	168,285	195,055	—
65–69	3,470,295	181,831	2,921,688	2,841,863	79,825	34,737	45,088	—	—	226,656	140,120	—
70–74	2,565,929	137,062	2,073,996	2,004,622	69,374	23,753	45,621	—	—	266,028	88,843	—
75–79	1,652,668	91,778	1,235,915	1,178,134	57,781	14,455	43,326	—	—	275,739	49,236	—
80–84	918,166	51,613	599,834	555,084	44,750	6,337	38,413	—	—	244,305	22,414	—
85+	603,663	33,592	294,486	251,091	43,395	3,850	39,545	—	—	263,709	11,876	—
1990												
total	76,874,142	21,578,604	47,554,648	—	—	1,181,969	—	46,372,679	—	1,955,833	5,785,057	—
15–17	3,868,387	3,832,943	31,447	—	—	2,380	—	29,067	—	818	3,179	—
18–19	2,977,184	2,859,815	110,734	—	—	6,081	—	104,653	—	1,224	5,411	—
15–19	6,845,571	6,692,758	142,181	—	—	8,461	—	133,720	—	2,042	8,590	—
20–24	7,388,380	5,747,631	1,510,995	—	—	72,608	—	1,438,387	—	3,741	126,013	—
25–29	8,384,815	3,639,210	4,233,367	—	—	161,981	—	4,071,386	—	7,750	504,488	—
30–34	8,699,545	2,066,357	5,797,171	—	—	189,860	—	5,607,311	—	13,797	822,220	—
35–44	15,281,360	1,834,420	11,535,620	—	—	334,083	—	11,201,537	—	49,114	1,862,206	—
45–54	10,393,967	629,879	8,433,586	—	—	201,181	—	8,232,405	—	95,284	1,235,218	—
55–59	4,330,811	218,498	3,619,608	—	—	64,033	—	3,555,575	—	95,158	397,547	—
60–64	4,334,784	223,469	3,613,391	—	—	53,986	—	3,559,405	—	172,817	325,107	—
65–74	7,068,958	329,574	5,790,134	—	—	66,627	—	5,723,507	—	577,846	371,404	—
75–84	3,381,501	158,520	2,477,362	—	—	24,785	—	2,452,577	—	631,144	114,475	—
85+	764,450	38,288	401,233	—	—	4,364	—	396,869	—	307,140	17,789	—

White

Females

	Total	Never married	Married						Widowed and divorced	Widowed	Divorced	Marital status unknown
			Total	Spouse present	Married Spouse absent			Not separated				
					Total	Separated [1]	Other					
Year and age	Aa648	Aa649	Aa650	Aa651	Aa652	Aa653	Aa654	Aa655	Aa656	Aa657	Aa658	Aa659
	Number	Number	Number	Number	Number	Number	Number	Number	Number	Number	Number	Number
1880												
total	21,239,224	12,068,078	7,703,325	7,461,985	241,340	—	—	—	—	1,420,852	46,969	—
0–14	7,942,416	7,939,522	2,695	1,598	1,097	—	—	—	—	199	0	—
15–19	2,190,594	1,949,019	235,888	223,414	12,474	—	—	—	—	4,292	1,395	—
20–24	2,165,513	1,095,300	1,042,880	1,005,082	37,798	—	—	—	—	22,046	5,287	—
25–29	1,704,978	407,376	1,249,126	1,211,324	37,802	—	—	—	—	40,700	7,776	—
30–34	1,404,256	204,557	1,132,181	1,102,863	29,318	—	—	—	—	61,132	6,386	—
35–39	1,301,608	142,225	1,056,857	1,031,230	25,627	—	—	—	—	95,644	6,882	—
40–44	1,090,928	99,053	862,017	839,487	22,530	—	—	—	—	124,772	5,086	—
45–49	893,421	67,538	681,054	659,007	22,047	—	—	—	—	141,838	2,991	—
50–54	763,540	50,570	537,905	521,352	16,553	—	—	—	—	170,681	4,384	—
55–59	541,767	30,418	356,358	342,895	13,463	—	—	—	—	152,099	2,892	—
60–64	467,415	29,534	272,695	262,825	9,870	—	—	—	—	163,889	1,297	—
65–69	313,289	19,452	149,211	142,737	6,474	—	—	—	—	142,830	1,796	—
70–74	225,725	16,158	76,296	73,002	3,294	—	—	—	—	132,773	498	—
75+	233,774	17,356	48,162	45,169	2,993	—	—	—	—	167,957	299	—
1890												
total	26,777,558	14,946,572	9,925,915	—	—	—	—	—	—	1,831,778	61,131	12,162
0–14	9,372,643	9,371,429	1,130	—	—	—	—	—	—	6	6	72
15–19	2,856,433	2,604,070	248,468	—	—	—	—	—	—	2,519	802	574
20–24	2,707,603	1,455,162	1,224,572	—	—	—	—	—	—	21,135	5,243	1,491
25–29	2,239,534	591,276	1,591,385	—	—	—	—	—	—	47,357	8,383	1,133
30–34	1,943,859	302,038	1,557,516	—	—	—	—	—	—	74,003	9,366	936
35–44	2,978,212	303,001	2,423,665	—	—	—	—	—	—	233,882	16,119	1,545
45–54	2,185,965	159,679	1,634,516	—	—	—	—	—	—	378,516	11,832	1,422
55–64	1,375,006	81,451	841,087	—	—	—	—	—	—	444,907	6,288	1,273
65+	1,077,808	62,183	387,660	—	—	—	—	—	—	623,528	2,900	1,537
unknown	40,495	16,283	15,916	—	—	—	—	—	—	5,925	192	2,179
1900												
total	32,641,781	17,885,978	12,337,002	—	—	—	—	—	—	2,293,856	91,889	33,056
0–14	11,137,399	11,133,950	2,956	—	—	—	—	—	—	77	17	399
15–19	3,288,538	2,945,066	334,357	—	—	—	—	—	—	4,865	1,651	2,599
20–24	3,192,701	1,708,306	1,443,343	—	—	—	—	—	—	28,149	9,062	3,841
25–29	2,823,260	804,659	1,943,162	—	—	—	—	—	—	59,059	13,684	2,696
30–34	2,387,461	407,316	1,875,627	—	—	—	—	—	—	89,009	13,654	1,855
35–44	3,901,178	447,311	3,133,743	—	—	—	—	—	—	292,665	24,628	2,831
45–54	2,694,045	219,298	2,015,067	—	—	—	—	—	—	440,847	16,550	2,283
55–64	1,777,639	122,345	1,088,333	—	—	—	—	—	—	556,269	8,680	2,012
65+	1,391,730	85,167	482,642	—	—	—	—	—	—	817,081	3,738	3,102
unknown	47,830	12,560	17,772	—	—	—	—	—	—	5,835	225	11,438

Note appears at end of table   (continued)

TABLE Aa614–683   Population, by marital status, sex, and race: 1880–1990   Continued

White

Females

Year and age	Total	Never married	Married Total	Spouse present	Spouse absent Total	Separated[1]	Other	Not separated	Widowed and divorced	Widowed	Divorced	Marital status unknown
	Aa648	Aa649	Aa650	Aa651	Aa652	Aa653	Aa654	Aa655	Aa656	Aa657	Aa658	Aa659
	Number	Number	Number	Number	Number	Number	Number	Number	Number	Number	Number	Number
1910												
total	39,553,712	20,784,712	15,854,757	—	—	—	—	—	—	2,706,127	150,830	57,286
0–14	12,696,375	12,693,463	2,746	—	—	—	—	—	—	137	29	0
15–17	2,348,162	2,236,408	97,177	—	—	—	—	—	1,991	—	—	12,586
18–19	1,621,086	1,289,580	319,001	—	—	—	—	—	5,622	—	—	6,883
15–19	3,969,248	3,525,988	416,178	—	—	—	—	—	—	5,233	2,380	19,469
20–24	3,915,456	1,968,679	1,893,144	—	—	—	—	—	—	29,260	14,330	10,043
25–29	3,464,912	901,520	2,478,162	—	—	—	—	—	—	58,617	21,881	4,732
30–34	2,970,107	497,585	2,355,630	—	—	—	—	—	—	91,490	22,649	2,753
35–44	4,950,896	589,925	3,996,443	—	—	—	—	—	—	319,868	41,029	3,631
45–54	3,538,667	315,788	2,675,528	—	—	—	—	—	—	516,596	28,137	2,618
55–64	2,192,955	160,891	1,380,018	—	—	—	—	—	—	636,007	13,836	2,203
65+	1,814,984	118,826	642,347	—	—	—	—	—	—	1,043,632	6,274	3,905
unknown	40,112	12,047	14,561	—	—	—	—	—	—	5,287	285	7,932
1920												
total	46,390,260	23,503,448	19,214,680	—	—	—	—	—	—	3,399,884	228,604	43,644
0–14	14,735,419	14,730,716	4,442	—	—	—	—	—	—	222	39	0
15–17	2,516,621	2,398,571	115,227	—	—	—	—	—	2,823	—	—	0
18–19	1,655,703	1,279,249	364,325	—	—	—	—	—	8,522	—	—	3,607
15–19	4,172,324	3,677,820	479,552	—	—	—	—	—	—	7,180	4,165	3,607
20–24	4,166,765	1,980,872	2,115,727	—	—	—	—	—	—	41,979	21,258	6,929
25–29	4,047,389	970,746	2,956,906	—	—	—	—	—	—	83,030	32,620	4,087
30–34	3,562,524	549,172	2,861,120	—	—	—	—	—	—	116,013	33,396	2,823
35–44	6,068,599	720,176	4,901,943	—	—	—	—	—	—	378,031	63,326	5,123
45–54	4,432,527	444,810	3,313,121	—	—	—	—	—	—	627,200	42,949	4,447
55–64	2,874,824	248,842	1,778,768	—	—	—	—	—	—	821,658	21,581	3,975
65+	2,284,551	166,673	784,359	—	—	—	—	—	—	1,319,140	8,810	5,569
unknown	45,338	13,621	18,742	—	—	—	—	—	—	5,431	460	7,084
1930												
total	53,700,353	25,706,178	23,447,330	—	—	—	—	—	—	4,023,477	477,684	45,684
0–14	15,480,124	15,476,872	3,087	—	—	—	—	—	—	105	60	0
15–17	3,029,478	2,887,948	138,238	—	—	—	—	—	—	1,528	1,764	0
18–19	2,018,131	1,561,377	441,266	—	—	—	—	—	—	4,304	6,264	4,920
15–19	5,047,609	4,449,325	579,504	—	—	—	—	—	—	5,832	8,028	4,920
20–24	4,800,139	2,304,549	2,412,268	—	—	—	—	—	—	28,387	45,931	9,004
25–29	4,326,739	979,382	3,216,233	—	—	—	—	—	—	57,175	69,974	3,975
30–34	4,050,587	554,453	3,323,466	—	—	—	—	—	—	97,089	72,978	2,601
35–39	4,012,414	437,404	3,331,898	—	—	—	—	—	—	167,550	73,153	2,409
40–44	3,464,916	345,230	2,826,591	—	—	—	—	—	—	230,337	60,528	2,230
45–49	3,029,210	288,425	2,382,342	—	—	—	—	—	—	306,961	49,392	2,090
50–54	2,593,775	249,506	1,905,135	—	—	—	—	—	—	398,865	38,157	2,112

White — Females

Year and age	Total	Never married	Married Total	Married Spouse present	Married Spouse absent Total	Separated [1]	Other	Not separated	Widowed and divorced	Widowed	Divorced	Marital status unknown
	Aa648	Aa649	Aa650	Aa651	Aa652	Aa653	Aa654	Aa655	Aa656	Aa657	Aa658	Aa659
	Number	Number	Number	Number	Number	Number	Number	Number	Number	Number	Number	Number
55–59	2,068,039	193,675	1,385,758	—	—	—	—	—	—	461,044	25,682	1,880
60–64	1,687,983	155,781	975,776	—	—	—	—	—	—	537,884	16,654	1,888
65–69	1,272,017	111,177	600,998	—	—	—	—	—	—	548,662	9,458	1,722
70–74	904,702	78,816	320,929	—	—	—	—	—	—	498,930	4,529	1,498
75+	927,279	70,781	171,097	—	—	—	—	—	—	680,529	2,621	2,251
unknown	34,820	10,802	12,248	—	—	—	—	—	—	4,127	539	7,104
1940												
total	45,605,134	12,645,291	27,279,080	26,106,430	1,170,266	—	—	—	—	4,940,037	740,726	—
14	1,044,949	1,042,439	2,384	—	—	—	—	—	—	81	45	—
15–17	3,211,989	3,080,078	129,584	—	—	—	—	—	—	996	1,331	—
18–19	2,236,138	1,772,616	455,099	—	42,078	—	—	—	—	2,660	5,763	—
15–19	5,448,127	4,852,694	584,683	542,605	42,078	—	—	—	—	3,656	7,094	—
20–24	5,226,507	2,531,997	2,627,520	2,508,418	119,102	—	—	—	—	19,527	47,463	—
25–29	5,012,257	1,165,281	3,714,518	3,577,645	136,873	—	—	—	—	45,321	87,137	—
30–34	4,633,162	693,790	3,740,699	3,606,351	134,348	—	—	—	—	86,728	111,945	—
35–39	4,262,292	488,801	3,502,949	3,369,321	133,628	—	—	—	—	152,641	117,901	—
40–44	3,940,893	385,439	3,210,801	3,081,402	129,399	—	—	—	—	238,529	106,124	—
45–49	3,690,143	329,791	2,924,576	2,801,283	123,293	—	—	—	—	347,308	88,468	—
50–54	3,228,590	291,445	2,398,502	2,290,497	108,005	—	—	—	—	471,754	66,889	—
55–59	2,636,799	237,498	1,792,098	1,708,303	83,795	—	—	—	—	560,803	46,400	—
60–64	2,184,240	209,616	1,282,960	1,220,312	62,648	—	—	—	—	661,667	29,997	—
65–69	1,762,109	172,901	834,991	789,180	45,811	—	—	—	—	735,873	18,344	—
70–74	1,217,262	120,210	425,264	398,691	26,573	—	—	—	—	663,540	8,248	—
75–79	736,959	70,272	171,296	156,812	14,484	—	—	—	—	492,155	3,236	—
80–84	392,854	37,164	53,393	46,316	7,077	—	—	—	—	301,210	1,087	—
85+	187,991	15,953	12,446	9,294	3,152	—	—	—	—	159,244	348	—
1950												
total	51,404,020	10,240,550	34,042,410	32,671,095	1,371,315	677,765	693,550	—	—	5,901,950	1,219,110	—
14	912,350	906,175	5,515	3,660	1,855	425	1,430	—	—	485	175	—
15–17	2,718,285	2,536,405	177,380	156,975	20,405	6,560	13,845	—	—	1,500	3,000	—
18–19	1,940,160	1,352,935	573,615	535,150	38,465	14,955	23,510	—	—	2,165	11,445	—
15–19	4,658,445	3,889,340	750,995	692,125	58,870	21,515	37,355	—	—	3,665	14,445	—
20–24	5,178,275	1,680,345	3,397,090	3,252,610	144,480	66,780	77,700	—	—	17,245	83,595	—
25–29	5,579,045	734,450	4,667,640	4,510,870	156,770	75,075	81,695	—	—	41,410	135,545	—
30–34	5,282,235	491,770	4,571,455	4,429,845	141,610	74,480	67,130	—	—	66,760	152,250	—
35–39	5,086,425	433,795	4,370,970	4,226,135	144,835	79,460	65,375	—	—	111,100	170,560	—
40–44	4,607,470	394,030	3,854,490	3,714,880	139,610	76,500	63,110	—	—	189,690	169,260	—
45–49	4,096,425	337,515	3,305,320	3,173,515	131,805	71,250	60,555	—	—	304,515	149,075	—
50–54	3,770,910	305,095	2,864,565	2,740,190	124,375	64,715	59,660	—	—	476,300	124,950	—
55–59	3,344,825	267,610	2,339,885	2,237,285	102,600	53,865	48,735	—	—	646,830	90,500	—
60–64	2,832,065	238,905	1,722,375	1,639,305	83,070	41,125	41,945	—	—	810,265	60,520	—
65–69	2,377,305	209,970	1,186,360	1,123,820	62,540	28,830	33,710	—	—	943,775	37,200	—
70–74	1,683,810	157,995	627,230	587,935	39,295	14,415	24,880	—	—	880,040	18,545	—
75–79	1,090,070	106,035	272,195	248,960	23,235	6,700	16,535	—	—	703,745	8,095	—
80–84	588,555	56,955	84,145	73,060	11,085	2,060	9,025	—	—	444,460	2,995	—
85+	315,810	30,565	22,180	16,900	5,280	570	4,710	—	—	261,665	1,400	—

Note appears at end of table

(continued)

TABLE Aa614–683   Population, by marital status, sex, and race: 1880–1990   *Continued*

White — Females

Year and age	Total	Never married	Married Total	Spouse present	Spouse absent Total	Separated [1]	Other	Not separated	Widowed and divorced	Widowed	Divorced	Marital status unknown
	Aa648	Aa649	Aa650	Aa651	Aa652	Aa653	Aa654	Aa655	Aa656	Aa657	Aa658	Aa659
	Number	Number	Number	Number	Number	Number	Number	Number	Number	Number	Number	Number
1960												
total	58,086,725	10,809,133	38,739,192	36,992,324	1,746,868	739,824	1,007,044	—	—	6,931,623	1,606,777	—
14	1,169,550	1,156,909	12,010	6,136	5,874	569	5,305	—	—	291	340	—
15–17	3,656,350	3,411,197	238,727	191,950	46,777	8,914	37,863	—	—	1,383	5,043	—
18–19	2,116,071	1,433,834	665,751	589,051	76,700	18,352	58,348	—	—	2,148	14,338	—
15–19	5,772,421	4,845,031	904,478	781,001	123,477	27,266	96,211	—	—	3,531	19,381	—
20–24	4,822,377	1,320,862	3,400,183	3,184,351	215,832	71,696	144,136	—	—	12,186	89,146	—
25–29	4,839,982	472,759	4,221,733	4,054,148	167,585	71,345	96,240	—	—	24,613	120,877	—
30–34	5,379,640	352,540	4,820,728	4,651,205	169,523	79,850	89,673	—	—	50,319	156,053	—
35–39	5,708,902	335,923	5,078,136	4,903,142	174,994	85,431	89,563	—	—	101,414	193,429	—
40–44	5,298,273	319,555	4,594,033	4,430,945	163,088	83,883	79,205	—	—	181,674	203,011	—
45–49	4,988,493	329,726	4,155,047	3,998,978	156,069	79,986	76,083	—	—	298,240	205,480	—
50–54	4,462,148	346,523	3,476,268	3,334,396	141,872	69,925	71,947	—	—	455,625	183,732	—
55–59	3,986,830	333,909	2,827,528	2,704,843	122,685	57,132	65,553	—	—	671,702	153,691	—
60–64	3,419,584	270,773	2,130,147	2,030,568	99,579	43,964	55,615	—	—	904,854	113,810	—
65–69	3,031,276	248,586	1,587,562	1,504,732	82,830	33,698	49,132	—	—	1,113,276	81,852	—
70–74	2,339,916	204,139	926,946	867,435	59,511	20,168	39,343	—	—	1,160,101	48,730	—
75–79	1,545,378	140,828	429,221	392,371	36,850	10,122	26,728	—	—	951,599	23,730	—
80–84	829,736	81,743	135,217	116,961	18,256	3,546	14,710	—	—	603,289	9,487	—
85+	492,219	49,327	39,955	31,112	8,843	1,243	7,600	—	—	398,909	4,028	—
1970												
total	68,874,544	15,048,138	42,804,008	40,627,831	2,176,177	995,788	1,180,389	—	—	8,463,052	2,559,346	—
14	1,742,981	1,719,278	17,610	10,974	6,636	1,599	5,037	—	—	4,471	1,622	—
15–17	4,982,975	4,753,084	212,206	167,451	44,755	10,113	34,642	—	—	10,333	7,352	—
18–19	3,154,754	2,410,507	715,620	607,164	108,456	26,472	81,984	—	—	8,520	20,107	—
15–19	8,137,729	7,163,591	927,826	774,615	153,211	36,585	116,626	—	—	18,853	27,459	—
20–24	7,281,251	2,558,246	4,491,545	4,110,857	380,688	139,779	240,909	—	—	44,117	187,343	—
25–29	5,942,246	646,466	4,992,785	4,753,486	239,299	123,838	115,461	—	—	54,513	248,482	—
30–34	5,083,029	338,370	4,446,096	4,252,537	193,559	101,080	92,479	—	—	63,010	235,553	—
35–39	4,965,486	267,297	4,361,698	4,179,163	182,535	95,849	86,686	—	—	90,365	246,126	—
40–44	5,404,173	278,857	4,671,134	4,486,871	184,263	102,497	81,766	—	—	171,948	282,234	—
45–49	5,588,715	289,137	4,713,535	4,533,892	179,643	99,958	79,685	—	—	293,296	292,747	—
50–54	5,157,803	290,376	4,121,117	3,962,722	158,395	85,726	72,669	—	—	476,196	270,114	—
55–59	4,713,614	306,052	3,454,577	3,317,836	136,741	70,311	66,430	—	—	717,670	235,315	—
60–64	4,165,869	302,187	2,668,777	2,556,118	112,659	54,907	57,752	—	—	998,448	196,457	—
65–69	3,513,525	266,865	1,860,017	1,774,674	85,343	36,581	48,762	—	—	1,242,920	143,723	—
70–74	2,865,593	227,369	1,160,809	1,094,334	66,475	23,527	42,948	—	—	1,382,984	94,431	—
75–79	2,124,860	181,004	597,823	549,383	48,440	14,019	34,421	—	—	1,289,399	56,634	—
80–84	1,305,966	117,280	225,531	195,892	29,639	5,814	23,825	—	—	936,158	26,997	—
85+	881,704	95,763	93,128	74,477	18,651	3,718	14,933	—	—	678,704	14,109	—

White

Females

Year and age	Total	Never married	Married						Widowed and divorced	Widowed	Divorced	Marital status unknown
			Total	Spouse present	Spouse absent							
					Total	Separated	Other	Not separated				
	Aa648	Aa649	Aa650	Aa651	Aa652	Aa653 [1]	Aa654	Aa655	Aa656	Aa657	Aa658	Aa659
	Number	Number	Number	Number	Number	Number	Number	Number	Number	Number	Number	Number
1980												
total	77,346,203	16,376,983	46,010,536	43,896,708	2,113,828	1,323,852	789,976	—	—	9,674,535	5,284,149	—
15–17	4,905,583	4,740,167	157,116	121,711	35,405	8,494	26,911	—	—	1,833	6,467	—
18–19	3,454,028	2,840,529	580,837	510,917	69,920	30,303	39,617	—	—	2,659	30,003	—
15–19	8,359,611	7,580,696	737,953	632,628	105,325	38,797	66,528	—	—	4,492	36,470	—
20–24	8,637,371	4,201,810	4,030,232	3,718,849	311,383	195,092	116,291	—	—	17,809	387,520	—
25–29	7,983,618	1,529,431	5,693,353	5,384,936	308,417	221,078	87,339	—	—	34,058	726,776	—
30–34	7,411,223	671,202	5,886,122	5,625,280	260,842	196,071	64,771	—	—	50,172	803,727	—
35–39	5,949,670	335,022	4,881,560	4,680,965	200,595	149,827	50,768	—	—	73,559	659,529	—
40–44	4,981,237	221,284	4,124,393	3,966,012	158,381	115,890	42,491	—	—	112,680	522,880	—
45–49	4,807,473	198,070	3,949,990	3,813,375	136,615	95,982	40,633	—	—	204,307	455,106	—
50–54	5,249,428	224,515	4,178,614	4,044,239	134,375	89,909	44,466	—	—	404,584	441,715	—
55–59	5,409,320	241,395	4,059,770	3,935,962	123,808	76,119	47,689	—	—	711,861	396,294	—
60–64	4,826,403	243,408	3,241,943	3,143,342	98,601	55,977	42,624	—	—	1,040,636	300,416	—
65–69	4,344,316	256,485	2,440,021	2,356,132	83,889	40,614	43,275	—	—	1,419,289	228,521	—
70–74	3,562,454	239,683	1,552,396	1,484,572	67,824	24,923	42,901	—	—	1,613,230	157,145	—
75–79	2,667,233	189,861	802,246	747,380	54,866	13,670	41,196	—	—	1,581,482	93,644	—
80–84	1,756,793	130,914	315,174	276,178	38,996	6,223	32,773	—	—	1,263,395	47,310	—
85+	1,400,053	113,207	116,769	86,858	29,911	3,680	26,231	—	—	1,142,981	27,096	—
1990												
total	82,692,612	17,175,748	47,457,526	—	—	1,525,724	—	45,931,802	—	10,279,559	7,779,779	—
15–17	3,640,526	3,559,361	73,511	—	—	5,081	—	68,430	—	2,952	4,702	—
18–19	2,856,606	2,553,819	282,992	—	—	18,152	—	264,840	—	3,954	15,841	—
15–19	6,497,132	6,113,180	356,503	—	—	23,233	—	333,270	—	6,906	20,543	—
20–24	7,135,532	4,436,391	2,436,737	—	—	145,084	—	2,291,653	—	12,528	249,876	—
25–29	8,253,729	2,312,627	5,202,313	—	—	242,970	—	4,959,343	—	29,387	709,402	—
30–34	8,651,968	1,287,398	6,309,186	—	—	254,194	—	6,054,992	—	53,180	1,002,204	—
35–44	15,306,636	1,249,773	11,560,378	—	—	410,486	—	11,149,892	—	199,355	2,297,130	—
45–54	10,696,607	491,672	8,108,357	—	—	225,157	—	7,883,200	—	472,731	1,623,847	—
55–59	4,637,605	183,834	3,411,138	—	—	69,450	—	3,341,688	—	500,692	541,941	—
60–64	4,876,339	201,123	3,321,554	—	—	56,031	—	3,265,523	—	894,137	459,525	—
65–74	8,957,243	413,371	4,898,171	—	—	69,667	—	4,828,504	—	3,052,569	593,132	—
75–84	5,656,219	341,597	1,668,018	—	—	24,802	—	1,643,216	—	3,415,057	231,547	—
85+	2,023,602	144,782	185,171	—	—	4,650	—	180,521	—	1,643,017	50,632	—

Note appears at end of table

(continued)

TABLE Aa614–683   Population, by marital status, sex, and race: 1880–1990   Continued

Nonwhite

Males

Year and age	Total	Never married	Married Total	Spouse present	Married Total	Spouse absent Separated[1]	Other	Not separated	Widowed and divorced	Widowed	Divorced	Marital status unknown
	Aa660	Aa661	Aa662	Aa663	Aa664	Aa665	Aa666	Aa667	Aa668	Aa669	Aa670	Aa671
	Number	Number	Number	Number	Number	Number	Number	Number	Number	Number	Number	Number
1880												
total	3,414,397	2,247,605	1,088,391	995,328	93,063	—	—	—	—	73,514	4,887	—
0–14	1,522,011	1,521,911	100	0	100	—	—	—	—	0	0	—
15–19	326,367	320,078	6,089	4,392	1,697	—	—	—	—	200	0	—
20–24	333,051	206,892	121,571	109,604	11,967	—	—	—	—	4,189	399	—
25–29	274,535	87,181	179,773	160,913	18,860	—	—	—	—	6,684	897	—
30–34	201,075	42,908	151,483	134,031	17,452	—	—	—	—	6,384	300	—
35–39	172,598	22,644	142,369	131,095	11,274	—	—	—	—	6,587	998	—
40–44	134,627	18,250	109,100	98,425	10,675	—	—	—	—	6,680	597	—
45–49	117,291	7,683	103,920	97,336	6,584	—	—	—	—	5,289	399	—
50–54	109,211	6,787	92,849	87,565	5,284	—	—	—	—	8,876	699	—
55–59	65,929	3,990	56,354	53,365	2,989	—	—	—	—	5,286	299	—
60–64	70,332	3,193	59,263	56,468	2,795	—	—	—	—	7,677	199	—
65–69	33,610	2,492	27,025	25,633	1,392	—	—	—	—	3,993	100	—
70–74	25,942	1,600	20,550	19,351	1,199	—	—	—	—	3,792	0	—
75+	27,818	1,996	17,945	17,150	795	—	—	—	—	7,877	0	—
1890												
total	3,861,548	2,540,696	1,212,307	—	—	—	—	—	—	93,466	5,272	9,807
0–14	1,617,863	1,617,817	12	—	—	—	—	—	—	0	1	33
15–19	429,797	425,438	4,012	—	—	—	—	—	—	52	13	282
20–24	364,029	241,448	118,871	—	—	—	—	—	—	2,357	377	976
25–29	291,158	96,200	187,174	—	—	—	—	—	—	5,892	793	1,099
30–34	224,691	51,991	164,026	—	—	—	—	—	—	6,883	744	1,047
35–44	378,282	59,191	297,694	—	—	—	—	—	—	18,279	1,450	1,668
45–54	272,820	23,677	226,413	—	—	—	—	—	—	20,888	1,001	841
55–64	150,610	9,685	123,324	—	—	—	—	—	—	16,698	490	413
65+	109,415	6,323	80,971	—	—	—	—	—	—	21,475	316	330
unknown	22,883	8,926	9,810	—	—	—	—	—	—	942	87	3,118
1900												
total	4,710,235	2,991,027	1,526,947	—	—	—	—	—	—	159,004	11,668	21,589
0–14	1,813,014	1,812,736	174	—	—	—	—	—	—	14	2	88
15–19	497,283	486,533	8,859	—	—	—	—	—	—	302	63	1,526
20–24	495,930	325,042	161,402	—	—	—	—	—	—	5,259	936	3,291
25–29	400,551	144,351	241,739	—	—	—	—	—	—	10,481	1,857	2,123
30–34	296,361	72,522	208,789	—	—	—	—	—	—	11,985	1,680	1,385
35–44	474,168	82,262	357,610	—	—	—	—	—	—	29,473	2,964	1,859
45–54	359,688	36,356	284,304	—	—	—	—	—	—	35,601	2,317	1,110
55–64	199,046	14,489	153,415	—	—	—	—	—	—	29,402	1,133	607
65+	140,024	7,205	96,764	—	—	—	—	—	—	34,920	589	546
unknown	34,170	9,531	13,891	—	—	—	—	—	—	1,567	127	9,054

Nonwhite

Males

Year and age	Total	Never married	Married: Total	Married: Spouse present	Married: Spouse absent: Total	Married: Spouse absent: Separated [1]	Married: Spouse absent: Other	Married: Not separated	Widowed and divorced	Widowed	Divorced	Marital status unknown
	Aa660	Aa661	Aa662	Aa663	Aa664	Aa665	Aa666	Aa667	Aa668	Aa669	Aa670	Aa671
	Number	Number	Number	Number	Number	Number	Number	Number	Number	Number	Number	Number
1910												
total	5,154,032	3,076,049	1,838,802	—	—	—	—	—	—	197,008	20,961	21,212
0–14	1,886,352	1,886,202	142	—	—	—	—	—	—	6	2	0
15–17	319,528	315,495	1,203	—	—	—	—	—	103	—	—	2,727
18–19	208,611	196,022	10,370	—	—	—	—	—	444	—	—	1,775
15–19	528,139	511,517	11,573	—	—	—	—	—	—	430	117	4,502
20–24	509,335	309,721	187,034	—	—	—	—	—	—	7,309	1,876	3,395
25–29	452,124	145,210	287,627	—	—	—	—	—	—	13,802	3,402	2,083
30–34	359,599	77,307	262,370	—	—	—	—	—	—	15,300	3,249	1,373
35–44	592,145	81,778	465,466	—	—	—	—	—	—	37,355	5,681	1,865
45–54	411,221	36,241	328,402	—	—	—	—	—	—	41,791	3,674	1,113
55–64	233,829	15,974	179,498	—	—	—	—	—	—	35,920	1,787	650
65+	160,957	7,603	107,786	—	—	—	—	—	—	43,776	1,056	736
unknown	20,331	4,496	8,904	—	—	—	—	—	—	1,319	117	5,495
1920												
total	5,469,776	3,069,196	2,151,540	—	—	—	—	—	—	209,157	27,624	12,259
0–14	1,884,699	1,884,296	387	—	—	—	—	—	—	13	3	0
15–17	319,503	316,917	2,494	—	—	—	—	—	92	—	—	0
18–19	212,458	192,709	18,026	—	—	—	—	—	674	—	—	1,049
15–19	531,961	509,626	20,520	—	—	—	—	—	—	555	211	1,049
20–24	508,469	283,640	214,178	—	—	—	—	—	—	6,109	2,472	2,070
25–29	443,932	133,727	294,040	—	—	—	—	—	—	10,688	3,891	1,586
30–34	354,517	74,972	262,610	—	—	—	—	—	—	12,118	3,675	1,142
35–44	707,151	100,383	560,457	—	—	—	—	—	—	37,096	7,489	1,726
45–54	580,316	50,000	472,492	—	—	—	—	—	—	50,706	5,971	1,147
55–64	259,585	18,221	199,493	—	—	—	—	—	—	38,848	2,423	600
65+	184,596	10,507	120,001	—	—	—	—	—	—	52,126	1,338	624
unknown	14,550	3,824	7,362	—	—	—	—	—	—	898	151	2,315
1930												
total	6,973,226	3,895,390	2,723,951	—	—	—	—	—	—	279,839	61,409	12,637
0–14	2,306,361	2,306,187	154	—	—	—	—	—	—	16	4	0
15–17	418,167	415,268	2,735	—	—	—	—	—	—	98	66	0
18–19	275,683	252,588	21,162	—	—	—	—	—	—	582	421	930
15–19	693,850	667,856	23,897	—	—	—	—	—	—	680	487	930
20–24	670,799	389,601	265,770	—	—	—	—	—	—	7,775	5,513	2,140
25–29	613,223	192,763	395,841	—	—	—	—	—	—	13,968	8,951	1,700
30–34	502,607	106,084	369,051	—	—	—	—	—	—	17,247	9,078	1,147
35–39	508,654	78,516	395,297	—	—	—	—	—	—	23,931	9,901	1,009
40–44	402,868	51,734	315,059	—	—	—	—	—	—	27,421	7,820	834
45–49	378,145	37,309	301,033	—	—	—	—	—	—	32,234	6,886	683
50–54	316,364	25,663	249,653	—	—	—	—	—	—	35,511	5,038	499
55–59	200,924	14,512	156,479	—	—	—	—	—	—	26,487	3,099	347
60–64	152,498	9,726	112,837	—	—	—	—	—	—	27,462	2,181	292
65–69	94,989	5,891	65,681	—	—	—	—	—	—	22,022	1,217	178
70–74	58,299	3,462	36,543	—	—	—	—	—	—	17,521	622	151
75+	64,338	3,670	32,871	—	—	—	—	—	—	27,062	523	212
unknown	9,307	2,416	3,785	—	—	—	—	—	—	502	89	2,515

Note appears at end of table

(continued)

TABLE Aa614–683   Population, by marital status, sex, and race: 1880–1990   *Continued*

Nonwhite

Males

Year and age	Total	Never married	Married		Spouse absent				Widowed and divorced	Widowed	Divorced	Marital status unknown
			Total	Spouse present	Total	Separated	Other	Not separated				
	Aa660	Aa661	Aa662	Aa663	Aa664	Aa665 [1]	Aa666	Aa667	Aa668	Aa669	Aa670	Aa671
	Number	Number	Number	Number	Number	Number	Number	Number	Number	Number	Number	Number
1940												
total	4,730,717	1,677,535	2,753,739	2,420,597	332,944	—	—	—	—	252,076	47,367	—
14	138,619	138,410	198	—		—	—	—	—	8	3	—
15–17	401,278	398,261	2,912	—		—	—	—	—	62	43	—
18–19	262,955	244,817	17,774			—	—	—	—	211	153	—
15–19	664,233	643,078	20,686	15,775	4,911	—	—	—	—	273	196	—
20–24	578,750	349,765	223,964	196,256	27,708	—	—	—	—	2,862	2,159	—
25–29	558,649	170,389	377,523	332,817	44,706	—	—	—	—	6,087	4,650	—
30–34	496,996	105,706	375,825	328,870	46,955	—	—	—	—	9,302	6,163	—
35–39	491,291	82,923	386,509	336,251	50,258	—	—	—	—	14,448	7,411	—
40–44	423,945	58,922	337,315	292,112	45,203	—	—	—	—	20,538	7,170	—
45–49	366,656	41,547	294,541	257,825	36,716	—	—	—	—	24,228	6,340	—
50–54	301,033	30,506	237,112	209,896	27,216	—	—	—	—	28,618	4,797	—
55–59	221,318	19,987	171,160	153,301	17,859	—	—	—	—	26,979	3,192	—
60–64	165,363	13,580	122,576	110,364	12,212	—	—	—	—	27,070	2,137	—
65–69	159,151	11,353	112,047	101,785	10,262	—	—	—	—	33,982	1,769	—
70–74	87,684	6,003	55,302	50,235	5,067	—	—	—	—	25,564	815	—
75–79	42,283	3,008	23,753	21,568	2,185	—	—	—	—	15,154	368	—
80–84	19,720	1,396	9,414	8,434	980	—	—	—	—	8,790	120	—
85+	15,026	962	5,814	5,108	706	—	—	—	—	8,173	77	—
1950												
total	5,299,280	1,507,800	3,414,675	2,910,545	504,130	315,740	188,390	—	—	277,880	98,925	—
14	133,115	132,500	465	255	210	40	170	—	—	70	80	—
15–17	382,210	377,355	4,490	2,845	1,645	515	1,130	—	—	270	95	—
18–19	239,780	217,485	21,810	16,900	4,910	2,315	2,595	—	—	270	215	—
15–19	621,990	594,840	26,300	19,745	6,555	2,830	3,725	—	—	540	310	—
20–24	599,660	328,160	263,155	215,530	47,625	27,190	20,435	—	—	3,080	5,265	—
25–29	614,570	154,785	444,985	372,225	72,760	42,275	30,485	—	—	4,225	10,575	—
30–34	536,955	77,185	441,185	373,005	68,180	42,285	25,895	—	—	5,840	12,745	—
35–39	557,195	58,080	473,690	402,525	71,165	46,915	24,250	—	—	10,325	15,100	—
40–44	496,065	44,740	422,270	360,840	61,430	40,590	20,840	—	—	15,055	14,000	—
45–49	443,990	36,850	373,245	319,110	54,135	35,385	18,750	—	—	21,685	12,210	—
50–54	370,625	26,080	305,125	262,005	43,120	27,415	15,705	—	—	29,225	10,195	—
55–59	278,740	17,280	224,150	194,730	29,420	19,015	10,405	—	—	30,015	7,295	—
60–64	209,465	13,175	158,815	139,375	19,440	12,185	7,255	—	—	32,760	4,715	—
65–69	202,610	11,400	143,920	128,325	15,595	10,545	5,050	—	—	43,735	3,555	—
70–74	115,330	5,880	74,480	66,860	7,620	4,770	2,850	—	—	33,260	1,710	—
75–79	68,430	3,415	40,310	35,975	4,335	2,750	1,585	—	—	23,975	730	—
80–84	32,435	1,595	16,120	14,330	1,790	1,155	635	—	—	14,435	285	—
85+	18,105	1,835	6,460	5,710	750	395	355	—	—	9,655	155	—

Nonwhite

Males

Year and age	Total	Never married	Married		Spouse absent				Widowed and divorced	Widowed	Divorced	Marital status unknown
			Total	Spouse present	Total	Separated	Other	Not separated				
	Aa660	Aa661	Aa662	Aa663	Aa664	Aa665 [1]	Aa666	Aa667	Aa668	Aa669	Aa670	Aa671
	Number	Number	Number	Number	Number	Number	Number	Number	Number	Number	Number	Number
1960												
total	6,279,181	1,908,596	3,933,884	3,330,153	603,731	337,265	266,466	—	—	284,711	151,990	—
14	176,768	175,730	885	393	492	149	343	—	—	62	91	—
15–17	521,984	515,075	6,370	3,402	2,968	867	2,101	—	—	285	254	—
18–19	282,907	259,007	23,380	16,212	7,168	1,780	5,388	—	—	219	301	—
15–19	804,891	774,082	29,750	19,614	10,136	2,647	7,489	—	—	504	555	—
20–24	625,758	357,320	262,930	209,227	53,703	19,590	34,113	—	—	1,266	4,242	—
25–29	607,802	168,032	426,666	355,145	71,521	33,828	37,693	—	—	2,585	10,519	—
30–34	623,863	107,433	493,719	413,832	79,887	43,894	35,993	—	—	4,900	17,811	—
35–39	628,252	79,616	517,954	437,580	80,374	48,358	32,016	—	—	8,513	22,169	—
40–44	554,590	53,708	467,148	398,345	68,803	43,670	25,133	—	—	12,880	20,854	—
45–49	524,449	46,129	439,876	375,841	64,035	40,957	23,078	—	—	17,916	20,528	—
50–54	449,760	41,592	366,750	314,884	51,866	32,457	19,409	—	—	24,274	17,144	—
55–59	410,034	43,444	318,945	273,193	45,752	27,718	18,034	—	—	33,231	14,414	—
60–64	284,451	22,577	217,574	187,812	29,762	17,095	12,667	—	—	35,118	9,182	—
65–69	246,389	17,478	179,542	157,130	22,412	13,347	9,065	—	—	42,335	7,034	—
70–74	166,030	10,701	112,916	99,903	13,013	7,236	5,777	—	—	38,459	3,954	—
75–79	103,451	6,426	63,333	56,069	7,264	3,981	3,283	—	—	31,521	2,171	—
80–84	43,913	2,585	23,541	20,697	2,844	1,469	1,375	—	—	16,846	941	—
85+	28,780	1,743	12,355	10,488	1,867	869	998	—	—	14,301	381	—
1970												
total	7,912,071	2,824,266	4,505,742	3,856,927	648,815	381,364	267,451	—	—	329,247	252,816	—
14	310,581	305,351	4,650	3,223	1,427	621	806	—	—	305	275	—
15–17	851,920	835,269	14,793	11,111	3,682	1,613	2,069	—	—	1,012	846	—
18–19	480,216	437,226	41,043	28,197	12,846	3,390	9,456	—	—	797	1,150	—
15–19	1,332,136	1,272,495	55,836	39,308	16,528	5,003	11,525	—	—	1,809	1,996	—
20–24	921,467	553,253	356,302	282,696	73,606	25,837	47,769	—	—	2,924	8,988	—
25–29	743,398	200,563	519,436	442,659	76,777	39,455	37,322	—	—	4,007	19,392	—
30–34	659,275	108,632	521,084	451,042	70,042	40,545	29,497	—	—	4,914	24,645	—
35–39	623,910	82,687	505,962	438,137	67,825	41,710	26,115	—	—	7,207	28,054	—
40–44	614,440	70,561	499,134	429,288	69,846	45,980	23,866	—	—	12,922	31,823	—
45–49	581,064	55,947	474,452	409,521	64,931	45,125	19,806	—	—	18,303	32,362	—
50–54	510,656	42,046	413,894	357,847	56,047	39,266	16,781	—	—	26,127	28,589	—
55–59	461,945	35,495	367,378	319,974	47,404	32,999	14,405	—	—	32,558	26,514	—
60–64	380,729	30,175	291,128	253,605	37,523	24,784	12,739	—	—	39,699	19,727	—
65–69	312,879	25,639	219,502	190,712	28,790	18,507	10,283	—	—	54,029	13,709	—
70–74	211,845	17,850	141,015	122,900	18,115	10,691	7,424	—	—	44,354	8,626	—
75–79	127,114	10,385	75,889	65,232	10,657	6,088	4,569	—	—	36,612	4,228	—
80–84	67,489	5,427	36,553	31,555	4,998	2,441	2,557	—	—	23,503	2,006	—
85+	53,143	7,760	23,527	19,228	4,299	2,312	1,987	—	—	19,974	1,882	—

Note appears at end of table   (continued)

TABLE Aa614–683   Population, by marital status, sex, and race: 1880–1990   *Continued*

Nonwhite

Males

	Total	Never married	Married						Widowed and divorced	Widowed	Divorced	Marital status unknown
			Total	Spouse present	Spouse absent							
					Total	Separated[1]	Other	Not separated				
	Aa660	Aa661	Aa662	Aa663	Aa664	Aa665	Aa666	Aa667	Aa668	Aa669	Aa670	Aa671
Year and age	Number	Number	Number	Number	Number	Number	Number	Number	Number	Number	Number	Number
1980												
total	12,476,552	4,903,989	6,485,472	5,482,347	1,003,125	590,665	412,460	—	—	372,423	714,668	—
15–17	1,266,509	1,252,117	13,177	3,792	9,385	1,893	7,492	—	—	445	770	—
18–19	822,315	782,164	38,079	21,863	16,216	3,148	13,068	—	—	581	1,491	—
15–19	2,088,824	2,034,281	51,256	25,655	25,601	5,041	20,560	—	—	1,026	2,261	—
20–24	1,912,437	1,415,947	467,316	357,965	109,351	38,152	71,199	—	—	1,827	27,347	—
25–29	1,664,599	663,796	901,635	737,874	163,761	85,366	78,395	—	—	3,721	95,447	—
30–34	1,369,375	286,831	956,436	810,018	146,418	89,679	56,739	—	—	5,394	120,714	—
35–39	1,013,677	134,339	773,991	665,736	108,255	69,892	38,363	—	—	7,461	97,886	—
40–44	845,166	88,917	664,555	573,772	90,783	60,882	29,901	—	—	10,553	81,141	—
45–49	729,561	67,204	575,460	497,904	77,556	53,829	23,727	—	—	15,880	71,017	—
50–54	685,751	60,323	533,873	460,145	73,728	53,517	20,211	—	—	26,754	64,801	—
55–59	620,040	49,685	480,991	415,831	65,160	45,938	19,222	—	—	35,458	53,906	—
60–64	495,275	34,592	376,795	326,991	49,804	34,576	15,228	—	—	45,353	38,535	—
65–69	410,329	26,920	298,826	260,501	38,325	25,077	13,248	—	—	55,889	28,694	—
70–74	293,601	19,109	203,139	177,636	25,503	14,963	10,540	—	—	54,217	17,136	—
75–79	190,026	12,332	120,186	104,555	15,631	8,394	7,237	—	—	47,693	9,815	—
80–84	93,576	5,640	52,042	44,492	7,550	3,364	4,186	—	—	32,081	3,813	—
85+	64,315	4,073	28,971	23,272	5,699	1,995	3,704	—	—	29,116	2,155	—
1990												
total	16,943,173	7,226,014	8,122,994	—	—	714,428	—	7,408,566	—	421,756	1,172,409	—
15–17	1,293,788	1,275,556	15,855	—	—	2,603	—	13,252	—	766	1,611	—
18–19	963,339	926,453	34,221	—	—	3,486	—	30,735	—	874	1,791	—
15–19	2,257,127	2,202,009	50,076	—	—	6,089	—	43,987	—	1,640	3,402	—
20–24	2,287,216	1,874,991	388,119	—	—	31,513	—	356,606	—	2,730	21,376	—
25–29	2,311,121	1,285,284	932,278	—	—	79,744	—	852,534	—	4,417	89,142	—
30–34	2,177,388	789,489	1,222,243	—	—	110,320	—	1,111,923	—	6,453	159,203	—
35–44	3,312,867	658,613	2,235,876	—	—	208,859	—	2,027,017	—	22,780	395,598	—
45–54	1,931,368	208,672	1,430,547	—	—	129,278	—	1,301,269	—	38,871	253,278	—
55–59	703,559	62,013	526,831	—	—	45,279	—	481,552	—	31,512	83,203	—
60–64	612,263	52,432	446,345	—	—	38,386	—	407,959	—	47,981	65,505	—
65–74	872,655	62,740	611,203	—	—	47,192	—	564,011	—	123,805	74,907	—
75–84	384,361	23,366	236,848	—	—	15,040	—	221,808	—	101,294	22,853	—
85+	93,248	6,405	42,628	—	—	2,728	—	39,900	—	40,273	3,942	—

Nonwhite

Females

Year and age	Total	Never married	Married						Widowed and divorced	Widowed	Divorced	Marital status unknown
			Total	Spouse present	\[Spouse absent\] Total	\[Spouse absent\] Separated [1]	\[Spouse absent\] Other	\[Spouse absent\] Not separated				
	Aa672	Aa673	Aa674	Aa675	Aa676	Aa677	Aa678	Aa679	Aa680	Aa681	Aa682	Aa683
	Number	Number	Number	Number	Number	Number	Number	Number	Number	Number	Number	Number
1880												
total	3,364,017	1,995,411	1,070,524	994,926	75,598	—	—	—	—	286,415	11,667	—
0–14	1,471,873	1,470,975	898	399	499	—	—	—	—	0	0	—
15–19	337,224	274,881	60,149	53,966	6,183	—	—	—	—	1,697	497	—
20–24	347,290	120,300	210,135	192,787	17,348	—	—	—	—	14,660	2,195	—
25–29	269,263	51,374	195,140	181,363	13,777	—	—	—	—	19,958	2,791	—
30–34	192,516	24,134	144,039	135,463	8,576	—	—	—	—	22,645	1,698	—
35–39	182,109	18,049	136,425	128,850	7,575	—	—	—	—	26,139	1,496	—
40–44	148,507	11,574	106,210	99,234	6,976	—	—	—	—	29,627	1,096	—
45–49	110,290	6,979	78,669	72,885	5,784	—	—	—	—	23,943	699	—
50–54	99,472	4,783	59,661	55,473	4,188	—	—	—	—	34,629	399	—
55–59	53,076	3,094	30,123	28,526	1,597	—	—	—	—	19,661	198	—
60–64	59,541	3,786	24,341	23,041	1,300	—	—	—	—	31,215	199	—
65–69	33,014	1,994	12,868	12,168	700	—	—	—	—	18,052	100	—
70–74	26,135	1,697	5,782	5,185	597	—	—	—	—	18,357	299	—
75+	33,707	1,791	6,084	5,586	498	—	—	—	—	25,832	0	—
1890												
total	3,776,812	2,237,416	1,200,281	—	—	—	—	—	—	322,837	10,764	5,514
0–14	1,579,549	1,579,243	281	—	—	—	—	—	—	11	6	8
15–19	452,419	383,879	65,515	—	—	—	—	—	—	2,326	299	400
20–24	384,180	146,104	220,140	—	—	—	—	—	—	15,321	1,688	927
25–29	289,932	50,712	213,679	—	—	—	—	—	—	22,608	2,205	728
30–34	209,107	24,268	159,688	—	—	—	—	—	—	22,794	1,795	562
35–44	367,819	27,138	274,601	—	—	—	—	—	—	62,420	2,780	880
45–54	244,913	11,775	162,463	—	—	—	—	—	—	68,854	1,248	573
55–64	124,991	5,122	64,540	—	—	—	—	—	—	54,513	433	383
65+	105,761	4,575	30,739	—	—	—	—	—	—	69,796	191	460
unknown	18,141	4,600	8,635	—	—	—	—	—	—	4,194	119	593
1900												
total	4,602,364	2,634,341	1,508,961	—	—	—	—	—	—	427,708	23,076	8,278
0–14	1,813,583	1,812,550	827	—	—	—	—	—	—	49	13	144
15–19	522,806	433,307	83,416	—	—	—	—	—	—	4,498	776	809
20–24	525,409	206,506	289,182	—	—	—	—	—	—	24,517	4,113	1,091
25–29	390,869	78,862	273,391	—	—	—	—	—	—	33,102	4,840	674
30–34	273,047	34,427	201,195	—	—	—	—	—	—	33,212	3,772	441
35–44	445,166	34,686	323,785	—	—	—	—	—	—	80,644	5,377	674
45–54	304,568	15,230	199,890	—	—	—	—	—	—	86,350	2,588	510
55–64	164,182	6,666	85,577	—	—	—	—	—	—	70,635	894	410
65+	134,591	5,733	39,019	—	—	—	—	—	—	88,800	392	647
unknown	28,143	6,374	12,679	—	—	—	—	—	—	5,901	311	2,878

Note appears at end of table

(continued)

TABLE Aa614–683   Population, by marital status, sex, and race: 1880–1990   *Continued*

Nonwhite

Females

Year and age	Total	Never married	Married Total	Spouse present	Spouse absent Total	Separated [1]	Other	Not separated	Widowed and divorced	Widowed	Divorced	Marital status unknown
	Aa672	Aa673	Aa674	Aa675	Aa676	Aa677	Aa678	Aa679	Aa680	Aa681	Aa682	Aa683
	Number	Number	Number	Number	Number	Number	Number	Number	Number	Number	Number	Number
1910												
total	5,086,277	2,737,409	1,833,412	—	—	—	—	—	—	470,299	34,271	10,886
0–14	1,896,289	1,895,488	736	—	—	—	—	—	—	61	4	0
15–17	335,644	306,856	24,626	—	—	—	—	—	1,573	—	—	2,589
18–19	231,429	152,920	72,435	—	—	—	—	—	4,725	—	—	1,349
15–19	567,073	459,776	97,061	—	—	—	—	—	—	5,028	1,270	3,938
20–24	561,238	195,004	332,218	—	—	—	—	—	—	26,094	6,040	1,882
25–29	470,743	80,036	345,773	—	—	—	—	—	—	36,768	7,272	894
30–34	345,310	37,585	264,329	—	—	—	—	—	—	37,452	5,460	484
35–44	553,425	38,591	413,867	—	—	—	—	—	—	92,028	8,240	699
45–54	342,392	15,785	228,515	—	—	—	—	—	—	93,790	3,797	505
55–64	186,743	7,100	99,436	—	—	—	—	—	—	78,445	1,364	398
65+	148,564	5,397	44,988	—	—	—	—	—	—	96,926	629	624
unknown	14,500	2,647	6,489	—	—	—	—	—	—	3,707	195	1,462
1920												
total	5,419,929	2,740,248	2,109,807	—	—	—	—	—	—	518,010	44,757	7,107
0–14	1,897,255	1,896,078	1,112	—	—	—	—	—	—	47	18	0
15–17	344,409	312,510	30,163	—	—	—	—	—	1,736	—	—	709
18–19	240,031	147,320	86,827	—	—	—	—	—	5,175	—	—	709
15–19	584,440	459,830	116,990	—	—	—	—	—	—	5,059	1,852	709
20–24	583,211	183,179	367,970	—	—	—	—	—	—	23,435	7,324	1,303
25–29	500,869	77,539	379,595	—	—	—	—	—	—	34,357	8,623	755
30–34	377,886	38,947	294,734	—	—	—	—	—	—	36,880	6,792	533
35–44	692,335	47,706	524,491	—	—	—	—	—	—	107,462	11,701	975
45–54	412,871	20,028	274,673	—	—	—	—	—	—	111,858	5,613	699
55–64	194,983	8,187	99,710	—	—	—	—	—	—	84,704	1,870	512
65+	165,593	6,769	45,801	—	—	—	—	—	—	111,481	799	743
unknown	10,486	1,985	4,731	—	—	—	—	—	—	2,727	165	878
1930												
total	6,937,613	3,396,786	2,727,667	—	—	—	—	—	—	710,897	95,562	6,701
0–14	2,320,693	2,319,439	1,154	—	—	—	—	—	—	62	38	0
15–17	435,640	391,612	41,166	—	—	—	—	—	—	1,756	1,106	521
18–19	311,041	191,237	111,297	—	—	—	—	—	—	4,749	3,237	521
15–19	746,681	582,849	152,463	—	—	—	—	—	—	6,505	4,343	998
20–24	733,424	242,508	445,397	—	—	—	—	—	—	27,988	16,533	720
25–29	646,689	100,541	481,412	—	—	—	—	—	—	44,866	19,150	548
30–34	508,048	48,595	392,182	—	—	—	—	—	—	51,482	15,241	506
35–39	516,371	34,649	393,782	—	—	—	—	—	—	73,054	14,380	453
40–44	388,820	21,847	280,310	—	—	—	—	—	—	76,621	9,589	400
45–49	341,145	15,439	233,871	—	—	—	—	—	—	84,381	7,054	357
50–54	250,384	11,096	152,191	—	—	—	—	—	—	82,469	4,271	

Nonwhite

Females

Year and age	Total	Never married	Married						Widowed and divorced	Widowed	Divorced	Marital status unknown
			Total	Spouse present	Spouse absent							
					Total	Separated[1]	Other	Not separated				
	Aa672	Aa673	Aa674	Aa675	Aa676	Aa677	Aa678	Aa679	Aa680	Aa681	Aa682	Aa683
	Number	Number	Number	Number	Number	Number	Number	Number	Number	Number	Number	Number
55–59	151,646	5,894	84,173	—	—	—	—	—	—	59,114	2,216	249
60–64	121,730	4,838	53,578	—	—	—	—	—	—	61,760	1,329	225
65–69	80,776	3,009	29,295	—	—	—	—	—	—	47,562	746	164
70–74	53,655	2,102	14,034	—	—	—	—	—	—	37,073	301	145
75+	70,165	2,531	10,847	—	—	—	—	—	—	56,278	238	271
unknown	7,386	1,449	2,978	—	—	—	—	—	—	1,682	133	1,144
1940												
total	4,944,042	1,290,575	2,811,408	2,407,929	402,510	—	—	—	—	760,165	81,894	—
14	142,665	141,655	969	—	—	—	—	—	—	29	12	—
15–17	417,920	381,168	35,547	—	—	—	—	—	—	733	472	—
18–19	287,323	190,161	93,710	—	—	—	—	—	—	2,034	1,418	—
15–19	705,243	571,329	129,257	110,498	18,759	—	—	—	—	2,767	1,890	—
20–24	668,936	249,004	398,403	341,888	56,515	—	—	—	—	13,224	8,305	—
25–29	633,719	122,811	470,807	399,805	71,002	—	—	—	—	26,557	13,544	—
30–34	538,914	67,908	415,173	349,344	65,829	—	—	—	—	41,528	14,305	—
35–39	537,426	47,404	408,580	345,189	63,391	—	—	—	—	66,967	14,475	—
40–44	427,815	29,232	308,461	263,631	44,830	—	—	—	—	79,447	10,675	—
45–49	355,813	19,447	243,074	211,368	31,706	—	—	—	—	85,548	7,744	—
50–54	275,506	13,629	170,462	150,130	20,332	—	—	—	—	86,838	4,577	—
55–59	195,702	8,601	110,161	97,893	12,268	—	—	—	—	74,129	2,811	—
60–64	146,284	6,692	69,549	62,330	7,219	—	—	—	—	68,445	1,598	—
65–69	148,460	6,185	53,700	47,660	6,040	—	—	—	—	87,323	1,252	—
70–74	81,303	3,302	20,702	18,255	2,447	—	—	—	—	56,874	425	—
75–79	43,343	1,764	8,057	6,845	1,212	—	—	—	—	33,346	176	—
80–84	22,526	900	2,592	2,083	509	—	—	—	—	18,974	60	—
85+	20,387	712	1,461	1,010	451	—	—	—	—	18,169	45	—
1950												
total	5,698,275	1,177,785	3,534,390	2,897,715	636,675	490,965	145,710	—	—	832,325	153,775	—
14	135,020	133,435	1,465	865	600	210	390	—	—	80	40	—
15–17	397,945	356,945	39,945	30,890	9,055	5,225	3,830	—	—	555	500	—
18–19	265,365	166,280	96,675	77,235	19,440	12,800	6,640	—	—	1,040	1,370	—
15–19	663,310	523,225	136,620	108,125	28,495	18,025	10,470	—	—	1,595	1,870	—
20–24	699,765	218,565	459,670	368,165	91,505	65,790	25,715	—	—	8,035	13,495	—
25–29	698,435	98,590	560,320	451,615	108,705	84,765	23,940	—	—	16,080	23,445	—
30–34	614,390	54,475	510,805	417,845	92,960	75,005	17,955	—	—	25,185	23,925	—
35–39	626,130	43,240	511,595	419,470	92,125	75,230	16,895	—	—	44,400	26,895	—
40–44	517,625	29,415	403,000	330,945	72,055	58,320	13,735	—	—	64,060	21,150	—
45–49	456,830	22,595	330,020	273,230	56,790	45,280	11,510	—	—	87,310	16,905	—
50–54	363,440	14,945	237,770	199,690	38,080	29,130	8,950	—	—	99,470	11,255	—
55–59	260,135	10,890	151,500	129,490	22,010	16,925	5,085	—	—	91,415	6,330	—
60–64	196,145	8,000	96,400	82,940	13,460	9,530	3,930	—	—	88,150	3,595	—
65–69	220,840	8,540	84,115	72,530	11,585	8,150	3,435	—	—	125,130	3,055	—
70–74	115,670	4,465	31,430	26,870	4,560	2,750	1,810	—	—	78,690	1,085	—
75–79	67,660	3,355	13,415	11,255	2,160	1,215	945	—	—	50,455	435	—
80–84	35,670	1,420	4,480	3,520	960	460	500	—	—	29,585	185	—
85+	27,210	2,630	1,785	1,160	625	180	445	—	—	22,685	110	—

Note appears at end of table

(continued)

TABLE Aa614–683   Population, by marital status, sex, and race: 1880–1990   Continued

Nonwhite — Females

Year and age	Total	Never married	Married Total	Spouse present	Spouse absent Total	Separated [1]	Other	Not separated	Widowed and divorced	Widowed	Divorced	Marital status unknown
	Aa672	Aa673	Aa674	Aa675	Aa676	Aa677	Aa678	Aa679	Aa680	Aa681	Aa682	Aa683
	Number	Number	Number	Number	Number	Number	Number	Number	Number	Number	Number	Number
1960												
total	6,874,464	1,511,066	4,166,093	3,342,461	823,632	577,796	245,836	—	—	948,984	248,321	—
14	175,586	173,180	2,240	1,221	1,019	320	699	—	—	100	66	—
15–17	514,912	475,413	38,424	27,166	11,258	4,032	7,226	—	—	491	584	—
18–19	301,264	208,301	90,902	68,786	22,116	9,189	12,927	—	—	729	1,332	—
15–19	816,176	683,714	129,326	95,952	33,374	13,221	20,153	—	—	1,220	1,916	—
20–24	697,560	246,760	433,773	335,782	97,991	55,077	42,914	—	—	5,066	11,961	—
25–29	697,122	109,355	550,273	434,159	116,114	80,876	35,238	—	—	12,434	25,060	—
30–34	731,782	70,375	602,500	476,677	125,823	94,386	31,437	—	—	23,790	35,117	—
35–39	709,634	53,601	579,877	463,615	116,262	89,918	26,344	—	—	36,969	39,187	—
40–44	619,532	39,687	489,560	396,314	93,246	72,142	21,104	—	—	54,159	36,126	—
45–49	565,450	33,222	424,924	346,710	78,214	59,192	19,022	—	—	74,571	32,733	—
50–54	469,618	28,795	323,586	266,211	57,375	42,519	14,856	—	—	92,822	24,415	—
55–59	424,460	29,163	257,529	213,172	44,357	31,732	12,625	—	—	119,538	18,230	—
60–64	307,817	14,419	160,158	135,298	24,860	17,064	7,796	—	—	122,949	10,291	—
65–69	272,054	11,782	115,717	97,708	18,009	11,609	6,400	—	—	137,622	6,933	—
70–74	182,243	7,970	59,095	49,675	9,420	5,800	3,620	—	—	111,476	3,702	—
75–79	113,941	5,025	26,092	21,446	4,646	2,619	2,027	—	—	81,228	1,596	—
80–84	53,306	2,373	7,911	6,036	1,875	874	1,001	—	—	42,413	609	—
85+	38,183	1,645	3,532	2,485	1,047	447	600	—	—	32,627	379	—
1970												
total	9,035,550	2,575,967	4,862,423	3,854,012	1,008,411	744,540	263,871	—	—	1,152,228	444,932	—
14	306,075	300,402	4,400	2,541	1,859	686	1,173	—	—	950	323	—
15–17	842,158	800,498	38,323	25,642	12,681	4,141	8,540	—	—	2,049	1,288	—
18–19	505,342	394,159	106,998	76,465	30,533	11,352	19,181	—	—	2,136	2,049	—
15–19	1,347,500	1,194,657	145,321	102,107	43,214	15,493	27,721	—	—	4,185	3,337	—
20–24	1,073,258	472,630	562,776	432,201	130,575	76,927	53,648	—	—	12,391	25,461	—
25–29	867,830	181,440	623,515	489,187	134,328	102,154	32,174	—	—	17,017	45,858	—
30–34	785,829	97,527	609,582	478,076	131,506	103,125	28,381	—	—	23,484	55,236	—
35–39	745,137	69,847	583,271	460,304	122,967	98,172	24,795	—	—	34,250	57,769	—
40–44	745,519	56,254	571,650	452,235	119,415	97,055	22,360	—	—	57,197	60,418	—
45–49	666,463	45,412	493,851	398,233	95,618	78,074	17,544	—	—	73,110	54,090	—
50–54	583,427	37,581	399,592	325,474	74,118	60,279	13,839	—	—	100,194	46,060	—
55–59	514,411	32,860	322,418	265,083	57,335	43,937	13,398	—	—	123,932	35,201	—
60–64	433,254	27,952	232,083	190,863	41,220	30,753	10,467	—	—	148,046	25,173	—
65–69	383,839	22,246	166,263	138,318	27,945	20,081	7,864	—	—	177,978	17,352	—
70–74	250,144	14,124	84,010	69,771	14,239	9,382	4,857	—	—	142,369	9,641	—
75–79	159,441	9,930	38,519	31,251	7,268	4,521	2,747	—	—	105,979	5,013	—
80–84	93,808	6,183	14,995	11,251	3,744	2,180	1,564	—	—	70,455	2,175	—
85+	79,615	6,922	10,177	7,117	3,060	1,721	1,339	—	—	60,691	1,825	—

Nonwhite

Females

Year and age	Total	Never married	Married		Spouse absent				Widowed and divorced	Widowed	Divorced	Marital status unknown
			Total	Spouse present	Total	Separated [1]	Other	Not separated				
	Aa672	Aa673	Aa674	Aa675	Aa676	Aa677	Aa678	Aa679	Aa680	Aa681	Aa682	Aa683
	Number	Number	Number	Number	Number	Number	Number	Number	Number	Number	Number	Number
1980												
total	14,136,475	4,550,335	6,840,248	5,485,736	1,354,512	1,034,784	319,728	—	—	1,565,883	1,180,009	—
15–17	1,228,417	1,191,856	34,336	19,887	14,449	3,838	10,611	—	—	924	1,301	—
18–19	820,915	717,464	98,670	72,290	26,380	9,594	16,786	—	—	1,032	3,749	—
15–19	2,049,332	1,909,320	133,006	92,177	40,829	13,432	27,397	—	—	1,956	5,050	—
20–24	2,017,131	1,248,246	702,495	549,245	153,250	90,873	62,377	—	—	6,937	59,453	—
25–29	1,809,678	582,313	1,045,882	838,037	207,845	156,277	51,568	—	—	17,693	163,790	—
30–34	1,542,720	279,826	1,031,779	836,152	195,627	159,018	36,609	—	—	29,308	201,807	—
35–39	1,159,989	144,180	809,855	650,639	159,216	133,842	25,374	—	—	38,020	167,934	—
40–44	976,452	93,561	687,879	552,962	134,917	114,733	20,184	—	—	55,045	139,967	—
45–49	871,544	67,169	603,767	488,764	115,003	97,143	17,860	—	—	81,038	119,570	—
50–54	846,708	57,948	558,670	451,064	107,606	89,288	18,318	—	—	125,705	104,385	—
55–59	744,272	47,070	456,166	369,437	86,729	69,789	16,940	—	—	161,451	79,585	—
60–64	613,680	36,967	330,835	269,230	61,605	47,068	14,537	—	—	191,032	54,846	—
65–69	543,019	31,184	239,885	197,220	42,665	31,259	11,406	—	—	232,518	39,432	—
70–74	400,165	22,329	137,944	112,632	25,312	17,806	7,506	—	—	216,990	22,902	—
75–79	285,118	15,529	68,024	54,260	13,764	8,937	4,827	—	—	188,623	12,942	—
80–84	152,019	7,913	23,104	17,205	5,899	3,302	2,597	—	—	115,996	5,006	—
85+	124,648	6,780	10,957	6,712	4,245	2,017	2,228	—	—	103,571	3,340	—
1990												
total	18,632,075	6,579,487	8,363,410	—	—	1,151,116	—	7,212,294	—	1,842,380	1,846,798	—
15–17	1,233,860	1,202,725	27,782	—	—	3,404	—	24,378	—	1,487	1,866	—
18–19	920,325	845,587	70,064	—	—	6,632	—	63,432	—	1,665	3,009	—
15–19	2,154,185	2,048,312	97,846	—	—	10,036	—	87,810	—	3,152	4,875	—
20–24	2,209,184	1,596,257	565,284	—	—	64,170	—	501,114	—	5,818	41,825	—
25–29	2,363,380	1,088,069	1,119,761	—	—	142,699	—	977,062	—	12,704	142,846	—
30–34	2,333,986	714,830	1,339,971	—	—	188,656	—	1,151,315	—	25,766	253,419	—
35–44	3,678,040	654,412	2,297,537	—	—	336,847	—	1,960,690	—	104,695	621,396	—
45–54	2,201,144	228,322	1,380,629	—	—	203,117	—	1,177,512	—	192,834	399,359	—
55–59	859,781	67,765	502,536	—	—	69,933	—	432,603	—	158,032	131,448	—
60–64	792,781	55,326	413,345	—	—	54,934	—	358,411	—	224,032	100,078	—
65–74	1,207,702	76,595	485,703	—	—	60,319	—	425,384	—	535,239	110,165	—
75–84	633,027	37,737	143,056	—	—	17,507	—	125,549	—	417,311	34,923	—
85+	198,865	11,862	17,742	—	—	2,898	—	14,844	—	162,797	6,464	—

[1] For 1990, "separated" could be either spouse absent or spouse present.

Sources

U.S. Census of Population. 1880, Integrated Public Use Microsample Series (IPUMS) of the 1880 Census (see the Guide to the Millennial Edition for information on IPUMS). 1890, *U.S. Census of Population: 1890*, volume 1, part 1, pp. 830–1. 1900, *U.S. Census of Population: 1900*, volume 2, part 2, pp. 254–5. 1910, *U.S. Census of Population: 1910*, volume 1, pp. 517–8. 1910–1920, *U.S. Census of Population: 1920*, volume 2, pp. 388–93. 1930, *U.S. Census of Population: 1930*, volume 2, pp. 843–7. 1940, *U.S. Census of Population: 1940*, volume 4, part 1, pp. 17–22. 1950, *U.S. Census of Population: 1950*, volume 2, part 1, pp. 179–83. 1960, *U.S. Census of Population: 1960*, volume 1, part 1, pp. 424–8. 1970, *U.S. Census of Population: 1970*, volume 1, part 1, section 2, pp. 640–8. 1980, *U.S. Census of Population: 1980*, volume 1,

Chapter D, part 1, PC80-1-D1-A, pp. 67–79. 1990, *U.S. Census of Population: 1990*, volume 1, 1990 CP-1-1, pp. 45–7.

Documentation

Marital status (single, married, widowed, and divorced) represents the status of persons at the time of the enumeration. Persons classified as "married" include those who have been married only once, those who have been remarried after having been widowed or divorced, those who are separated, and those living in common-law marriages. Persons reported as never married or with annulled marriages are classified as single. Because it is probable that some divorced persons are reported as single, married, or widowed, the census figures may understate somewhat the actual number of divorced persons who have not remarried.

RURAL AND URBAN PLACES

Michael R. Haines

TABLE Aa684–698   Urban and rural territory – number of places, by size of place: 1790–1990

Contributed by Michael R. Haines

	Total	2,500 or more	1,000,000 or more	500,000–999,999	250,000–499,999	100,000–249,999	50,000–99,999	25,000–49,999
	Aa684	Aa685	Aa686	Aa687	Aa688	Aa689	Aa690	Aa691
Year	Number	Number	Number	Number	Number	Number	Number	Number
1790	24	24	0	0	0	0	0	2
1800	33	33	0	0	0	0	1	2
1810	46	46	0	0	0	0	2	2
1820	61	61	0	0	0	1	2	2
1830	90	90	0	0	0	1	3	3
1840	131	131	0	0	1	2	2	7
1850	237	237	0	1	0	5	4	17
1860	392	392	0	2	1	6	7	19
1870	663	663	0	2	5	7	11	27
1880	939	939	1	3	4	12	15	42
1890	1,348	1,348	3	1	7	17	30	66
1900	1,740	1,740	3	3	9	23	40	83
1910	2,266	2,266	3	5	11	31	60	119
1920	2,725	2,725	3	9	13	43	77	143
1930 [1]	3,183	3,183	5	8	24	57	98	186
1940	3,485	3,485	5	9	23	56	107	213
1950 [2]	4,764	4,306	5	13	23	65	126	253
1960	6,041	5,445	5	16	30	81	201	432
1970	7,128	6,433	6	20	30	100	240	520
1980	8,765	7,749	6	16	34	117	290	675
1990	9,421	8,510	8	15	41	136	355	741

	Urban territory				Rural territory		
	Population size					Population size	
	10,000–24,999	5,000–9,999	2,500–4,999	Less than 2,500	Total	1,000–2,499	Less than 1,000
	Aa692	Aa693	Aa694	Aa695	Aa696	Aa697	Aa698
Year	Number	Number	Number	Number	Number	Number	Number
1790	3	7	12	—	—	—	—
1800	3	15	12	—	—	—	—
1810	7	17	18	—	—	—	—
1820	8	22	26	—	—	—	—
1830	16	33	34	—	—	—	—
1840	25	48	46	—	—	—	—
1850	36	85	89	—	—	—	—
1860	58	136	163	—	—	—	—
1870	116	186	309	—	—	—	—
1880	146	249	467	—	—	—	—
1890	230	340	654	—	6,490	1,603	4,887
1900	281	465	833	—	8,933	2,130	6,803
1910	369	606	1,062	—	11,843	2,723	9,120
1920	466	715	1,256	—	12,872	3,034	9,838
1930 [1]	609	853	1,343	—	13,468	3,111	10,357
1940	666	970	1,436	—	13,328	3,233	10,095
1950 [2]	779	1,184	1,858	457	13,851	4,186	9,665
1960	1,134	1,394	2,152	596	13,749	4,151	9,598
1970	1,385	1,838	2,294	695	13,639	4,128	9,511
1980	1,765	2,181	2,665	1,016	13,764	4,434	9,330
1990	1,852	2,336	3,026	911	14,014	4,424	9,590

TABLE Aa684–698   Urban and rural territory – number of places, by size of place: 1790–1990   *Continued*

[1] In 1930, several pairs of places were counted as single places. See documentation.

[2] 1950 urban definition. According to the 1940 urban definition, in 1950 there were 4,077 urban places. See documentation for details.

Sources

U.S. Bureau of the Census. 1790–1990, *1990 Census of Population and Housing*, "Population and Housing Unit Counts, United States," 1990 CPH-2-1, Table 7.

Documentation

The U.S. Census Bureau has used several definitions of urban population. According to the definition adopted for use in the 1990 Census, the urban population comprises all persons living in urbanized areas and in places of 2,500 or more inhabitants outside of urbanized areas. More specifically, the urban population consists of all persons living in (a) places of 2,500 or more inhabitants incorporated as cities, villages, boroughs (except Alaska and New York), and towns (except in the New England states, New York, and Wisconsin), but excluding those persons living in the rural portions of extended cities (places with low population density in one or more large parts of their area); (b) census-designated places (previously termed "unincorporated") of 2,500 or more inhabitants; and (c) other territory, incorporated or unincorporated, included in urbanized areas.

In censuses prior to 1950, the urban population comprised all persons living in incorporated places of 2,500 or more and areas (usually minor civil divisions) classified as urban under special rules relating to population size and density. The most important component of the urban territory in any definition is the group of incorporated places having 2,500 or more inhabitants. A definition of urban territory restricted to such places, however, would exclude a number of large and densely settled areas merely because they are not considered "incorporated places." Prior to 1950, an effort was made to avoid some of the more obvious omissions by inclusion of selected areas that were classified as urban under special rules. Even with these rules, however, many large and closely built-up areas were excluded from the urban territory.

To improve its measure of the urban population, the Census Bureau adopted, in 1950, the concept of the urbanized area and delineated, in advance of enumeration, boundaries for unincorporated places. With the adoption of the urbanized area and unincorporated place concepts for the 1950 Census, the urban population was defined as all persons residing in urbanized areas and, outside these areas, in all places, incorporated or unincorporated, that had 2,500 or more inhabitants. With the following exception, the 1950 definition of urban was continued substantially unchanged to 1960 and 1970. In 1960 (but not in 1970), certain towns in the New England states, townships in New Jersey and Pennsylvania, and counties

elsewhere were designated as urban. However, most of the population of these "special rule" areas would have been classified as urban in any event because they were residents of an urbanized area or an unincorporated place of 2,500 or more inhabitants.

In all urban and rural definitions, the population not classified as urban constitutes the rural population.

The first official publication of figures formally presenting the urban population was made following the Census of 1870 in U.S. Census Office, Ninth Census, 1870, *Statistical Atlas of the United States* (Julius Bien, 1874). The population of cities and towns of 8,000 or more inhabitants was presented as the "urban population." In the reports of the 1880, 1890, and 1900 Censuses, the urban population was variously defined as the population living in places of 4,000 or more inhabitants, or 8,000 or more inhabitants. The first publication in which the population of places having 2,500 or more inhabitants was officially designated as urban was the *Supplementary Analysis of the Twelfth Census* (U.S. Census, 1900), published in 1906. This definition, with minor modifications, was used in later censuses up to and including 1940. For purposes of comparison, the data for 1950 were also tabulated in accordance with this urban definition.

A time series on the urban population since 1790 according to the 1940 definition of urban was published in the 1940 Census. Data on the urban population by selected characteristics are not always available on this basis, and thus the total urban populations shown in other tables may differ slightly.

For detailed discussions of the urban definitions used up to 1940 and of the major changes implemented in 1950, see U.S. Bureau of the Census, *Current Population Reports*, series P-23, number 1, "The Development of the Urban–Rural Classification in the United States: 1874 to 1949," and *U.S. Census of Population: 1950*, volume 1, pp. xv–xviii.

If the 1940 urban definition is imposed on the 1950 data, there were 4,077 urban places of the following sizes in 1950: 1,000,000 or more inhabitants (5), 500,000–999,999 (13), 250,000–499,999 (23), 100,000–249,999 (68), 50,000–99,999 (129), 25,000–49,999 (284), 10,000–24,999 (832), 5,000–9,999 (1,137), 2,500–4,999 (1,586), total rural places (13,279), rural places with 1,000–2,499 inhabitants (3,436), and rural places with fewer than 1,000 inhabitants (9,843).

In 1930, each pair of the following was counted as a single place: Bluefield, Virginia, and Bluefield, West Virginia; Bristol, Tennessee, and Bristol, Virginia; Delmar, Delaware, and Delmar, Maryland; Harrison, Ohio, and West Harrison, Indiana; Junction City, Arkansas, and Junction City, Louisiana; Texarkana, Arkansas, and Texarkana, Texas; Texhoma, Oklahoma, and Texhoma, Texas; and Union City, Indiana, and Union City, Ohio. In all other years they were counted as separate incorporated places.

TABLE Aa699–715   Urban and rural territory – population, by size of place: 1790–1990

Contributed by Michael R. Haines

		Urban territory						
		Places with population size						
	Total	2,500 or more	1,000,000 or more	500,000–999,999	250,000–499,999	100,000–249,999	50,000–99,999	25,000–49,999
	Aa699	Aa700	Aa701	Aa702	Aa703	Aa704	Aa705	Aa706
Year	Number	Number	Number	Number	Number	Number	Number	Number
1790	201,655	201,655	0	0	0	0	0	61,653
1800	322,371	322,371	0	0	0	0	60,515	67,734
1810	525,459	525,459	0	0	0	0	150,095	80,342
1820	693,255	693,255	0	0	0	123,706	126,540	70,474
1830	1,127,247	1,127,247	0	0	0	202,589	222,474	105,243
1840	1,845,055	1,845,055	0	0	312,710	204,506	187,048	235,424
1850	3,574,496	3,574,496	0	515,547	0	659,121	284,355	642,108
1860	6,216,518	6,216,518	0	1,379,198	266,661	992,922	452,060	670,293
1870 [1]	9,902,361	9,902,361	0	1,616,314	1,523,820	989,855	768,238	930,119
1880	14,129,735	14,129,735	1,206,299	1,917,018	1,300,809	1,786,783	947,918	1,446,366

Notes appear at end of table

(continued)

TABLE Aa699–715   Urban and rural territory – population, by size of place: 1790–1990   *Continued*

				Urban territory			
				Places with population size			
	Total	2,500 or more	1,000,000 or more	500,000–999,999	250,000–499,999	100,000–249,999	50,000–99,999	25,000–49,999
	Aa699	Aa700	Aa701	Aa702	Aa703	Aa704	Aa705	Aa706
Year	Number	Number	Number	Number	Number	Number	Number	Number
1890	22,106,265	22,106,265	3,662,115	806,343	2,447,608	2,781,894	2,027,569	2,268,786
1900	30,214,832	30,214,832	6,429,474	1,645,087	2,861,296	3,272,490	2,709,338	2,839,933
1910	42,064,001	42,064,001	8,501,174	3,010,667	3,949,839	4,840,458	4,231,098	4,023,397
1920	54,253,282	54,253,282	10,145,532	6,223,769	4,540,838	6,519,187	5,347,228	5,075,041
1930	69,160,599	69,160,599	15,064,555	5,763,987	7,956,228	7,678,548	6,491,448	6,425,693
1940	74,705,338	74,705,338	15,910,866	6,456,959	7,827,514	7,971,976	7,343,917	7,417,093
1950 [2]	96,846,817	88,924,799	17,404,450	9,186,945	8,241,560	9,726,696	8,930,823	8,834,919
1960	125,268,750	114,727,899	17,484,059	11,110,991	10,765,881	11,652,426	13,835,902	14,950,612
1970 [3]	149,646,617	133,415,871	18,769,365	12,966,746	10,441,689	14,286,033	16,723,878	17,860,912
1980	167,050,992	153,128,028	17,530,248	10,834,121	12,157,578	17,015,074	19,786,487	23,435,654
1990	187,053,487	170,417,870	19,952,631	10,107,184	14,585,006	19,702,834	24,027,445	25,701,046

	Urban territory					Rural territory			
	Places with population size				Other urban territory		Places with population size		Other rural territory
	10,000–24,999	5,000–9,999	2,500–4,999	Less than 2,500		Total	1,000–2,499	Less than 1,000	
	Aa707	Aa708	Aa709	Aa710	Aa711	Aa712	Aa713	Aa714	Aa715
Year	Number	Number	Number	Number	Number	Number	Number	Number	Number
1790	48,182	47,569	44,251	—	—	3,727,559	—	—	—
1800	54,479	94,394	45,249	—	—	4,986,112	—	—	—
1810	108,980	116,271	69,771	—	—	6,714,422	—	—	—
1820	121,613	155,035	95,887	—	—	8,945,198	—	—	—
1830	240,371	230,859	125,711	—	—	11,733,455	—	—	—
1840	404,822	328,744	171,801	—	—	15,218,298	—	—	—
1850	560,783	596,086	316,496	—	—	19,617,380	—	—	—
1860	884,433	976,436	594,515	—	—	25,226,803	—	—	—
1870 [1]	1,709,541	1,278,145	1,086,329	—	—	28,656,010	—	—	—
1880	2,189,447	1,717,146	1,617,949	—	—	36,059,474	—	—	—
1890	3,451,258	2,383,685	2,277,007	—	—	40,873,501	2,511,085	2,250,909	36,112,326
1900	4,350,738	3,204,195	2,902,281	—	—	45,779,743	3,301,314	3,003,479	39,692,543
1910	5,548,868	4,224,165	3,734,335	—	—	49,908,265	4,242,798	3,933,993	41,987,704
1920	7,045,099	4,970,683	4,385,905	—	—	51,457,338	4,718,651	4,262,255	42,787,349
1930	9,116,668	5,910,028	4,753,444	—	—	53,614,447	4,851,746	4,368,170	44,822,109
1940	9,990,251	6,712,485	5,074,277	—	—	56,963,937	5,067,057	4,321,471	48,070,703
1950 [2]	11,877,759	8,192,636	6,529,011	577,992	7,344,026	54,478,981	6,515,474	4,036,760	43,926,747
1960	17,568,286	9,779,714	7,580,028	689,746	9,851,105	54,054,425	6,496,788	3,893,090	43,664,547
1970 [3]	21,414,545	12,914,296	8,038,407	835,318	15,395,428	53,565,309	6,551,504	3,849,112	43,164,693
1980	27,644,903	15,356,137	9,367,826	1,260,246	12,662,718	59,494,813	7,037,840	3,863,470	48,593,503
1990	29,041,164	16,599,341	10,701,219	1,078,903	15,556,714	61,656,386	7,050,858	3,801,051	50,804,477

[1] Excludes 1,260,078 persons for whom urban–rural residence data are not available.

[2] 1950 urban definition. By the 1940 urban definition, in 1950 there were 90,128,194 persons in urban areas. See the documentation for details.

[3] In 1970, relatively sparsely settled portions of certain incorporated places were classified as rural. The population of these portions was excluded from the items under "urban" and included in "other rural." The size class to which these places were assigned, however, was based on the population of the places within their legal boundaries. Excludes 23,377 persons for whom urban–rural residence data are not available.

Source
U.S. Bureau of the Census. 1790–1990, *1990 Census of Population and Housing*, "Population and Housing Unit Counts: United States ," 1990 CPH-2-1, Table 7.

Documentation
See the text for Table Aa684–698.

In determining residence, the Census Bureau counts each person as an inhabitant of a usual place of residence (that is, the place where that person usually sleeps). Although this place is not necessarily a person's legal residence or voting residence, the use of these different bases of classification would produce the same results in the majority of cases.

If the 1940 urban definition is imposed on the 1950 data, there were 90,128,194 persons in urban areas of the following sizes: 1,000,000 or more inhabitants (17,404,450), 500,000–999,999 (9,186,945), 250,000–499,999 (8,241,560), 100,000–249,999 (9,971,804), 50,000–99,999 (9,137,541), 25,000–49,999 (9,903,043), 10,000–24,999 (12,779,084), 5,000–9,999 (7,885,742), 2,500–4,999 (5,618,025), rural places (61,997,604), rural places with 1,000–2,499 inhabitants (4,134,661), and rural places with fewer than 1,000 inhabitants (51,638,147).

TABLE Aa716-775   Population, by race, sex, and urban-rural residence: 1880-1990[1]

Contributed by Michael R. Haines

Total

Year	All races Total	Male	Female	White Total	Male	Female	Black Total	Male	Female	Other races Total	Male	Female
	Aa716	Aa717	Aa718	Aa719	Aa720	Aa721	Aa722	Aa723	Aa724	Aa725	Aa726	Aa727
	Number	Number	Number	Number	Number	Number	Number	Number	Number	Number	Number	Number
1880 [2,3]	50,155,783	—	—	43,402,970	—	—	6,580,793	—	—	172,020	—	—
1890 [2,3]	62,947,714	32,237,101	30,710,613	55,101,258	28,270,379	26,830,879	7,488,676	—	—	357,780	—	—
1900 [2,3]	75,994,575	38,816,448	37,178,127	66,809,196	34,201,735	32,607,461	8,833,994	4,386,547	4,447,447	351,385	228,166	123,219
1910	91,972,266	47,332,277	44,639,989	81,731,957	42,178,245	39,553,712	9,827,763	4,885,881	4,941,882	412,546	268,151	144,395
1920	105,710,620	53,900,431	51,810,189	94,820,915	48,430,655	46,390,260	10,463,131	5,209,436	5,253,695	426,574	260,340	166,234
1930	122,775,046	62,137,080	60,637,966	110,286,740	55,922,528	54,364,212	11,891,143	5,855,669	6,035,474	597,163	358,883	238,280
1940	131,669,275	66,061,592	65,607,683	118,214,870	59,448,548	58,766,322	12,865,518	6,269,038	6,596,480	588,887	344,006	244,881
1950 [4]	150,697,361	74,833,239	75,864,122	134,942,028	67,129,192	67,812,836	15,042,286	7,298,722	7,743,564	713,047	405,325	307,722
1950 [5]	150,697,361	74,833,239	75,864,122	134,942,028	67,129,192	67,812,836	15,042,286	7,298,722	7,743,564	713,047	405,325	307,722
1960 [6]	179,323,175	88,331,494	90,991,681	158,831,732	78,367,149	80,464,583	18,871,831	9,113,408	9,758,423	1,619,612	850,937	768,675
1970 [7]	203,211,926	98,912,192	104,299,734	177,748,975	86,720,987	91,027,988	22,580,289	10,748,316	11,831,973	2,882,662	1,442,889	1,439,773
1980	226,545,805	110,053,161	116,492,644	188,371,622	91,685,333	96,686,289	26,495,025	12,519,189	13,975,836	11,679,158	5,848,639	5,830,519
1990	248,709,873	121,239,418	127,470,455	199,686,070	97,475,880	102,210,190	29,986,060	14,170,151	15,815,909	19,037,743	9,593,387	9,444,356

Urban

Year	All races Total	Male	Female	White Total	Male	Female	Black Total	Male	Female	Other races Total	Male	Female
	Aa728	Aa729	Aa730	Aa731	Aa732	Aa733	Aa734	Aa735	Aa736	Aa737	Aa738	Aa739
	Number	Number	Number	Number	Number	Number	Number	Number	Number	Number	Number	Number
1880 [2,3]	13,184,902	—	—	12,297,612	—	—	849,721	—	—	37,569	—	—
1890 [2,3]	20,693,924	10,349,963	10,343,961	19,317,550	9,676,685	9,640,865	1,317,062	—	—	59,312	—	—
1900 [2,3]	28,372,392	14,083,330	14,289,062	26,494,130	13,176,238	13,317,892	1,810,250	844,797	965,453	68,012	62,295	5,717
1910	42,623,383	21,496,181	21,127,202	39,831,913	20,129,679	19,702,234	2,689,229	1,279,484	1,409,745	102,241	87,018	15,223
1920	54,304,603	27,203,312	27,101,291	50,620,084	25,373,627	25,246,457	3,559,473	1,737,820	1,821,653	125,046	91,865	33,181
1930	68,954,823	34,154,760	34,800,063	63,560,033	31,538,288	32,021,745	5,193,913	2,479,158	2,714,755	200,877	137,314	63,563
1940	74,423,702	36,363,706	38,059,996	67,972,823	33,304,701	34,668,122	6,253,588	2,929,423	3,324,165	197,291	129,582	67,709
1950 [4]	88,927,464	43,117,270	45,810,194	79,667,864	38,697,282	40,970,582	—	—	—	—	—	—
1950 [5]	96,467,686	46,891,782	49,575,904	86,756,435	42,249,894	44,506,541	9,392,608	4,449,766	4,942,842	318,643	192,122	126,521
1960 [6]	125,268,750	60,733,005	64,535,745	110,428,332	53,631,145	56,797,187	13,807,640	6,557,123	7,250,517	1,032,778	544,737	488,041
1970 [7]	149,324,930	71,958,564	77,366,366	128,773,240	62,210,243	66,562,997	18,367,318	8,657,231	9,710,087	2,184,372	1,091,090	1,093,282
1980	167,050,992	80,292,291	86,758,701	134,321,744	64,638,068	69,683,676	22,594,016	10,596,862	11,997,154	10,135,232	5,057,361	5,077,871
1990	187,053,487	90,386,114	96,667,373	143,807,279	69,549,285	74,257,994	26,153,444	12,246,371	13,907,073	17,092,764	8,590,458	8,502,306

Rural

Total

Year	All races Total	Male	Female	White Total	Male	Female	Black Total	Male	Female	Other races Total	Male	Female
	Aa740	Aa741	Aa742	Aa743	Aa744	Aa745	Aa746	Aa747	Aa748	Aa749	Aa750	Aa751
	Number	Number	Number	Number	Number	Number	Number	Number	Number	Number	Number	Number
1880 [2,3]	36,970,881	—	—	31,105,358	—	—	5,731,072	—	—	134,451	—	—
1890 [2,3]	42,253,790	21,887,138	20,366,652	35,783,708	18,593,694	17,190,014	6,171,614	—	—	298,468	—	—
1900 [2,3]	47,622,183	24,733,118	22,889,065	40,315,066	21,025,497	19,289,569	7,023,744	3,541,750	3,481,994	283,373	165,871	117,502
1910	49,348,883	25,836,096	23,512,787	41,900,044	22,048,566	19,851,478	7,138,534	3,606,397	3,532,137	310,305	181,133	129,172
1920	51,406,017	26,697,119	24,708,898	44,200,831	23,057,028	21,143,803	6,903,658	3,471,616	3,432,042	301,528	168,475	133,053
1930	53,820,223	27,982,320	25,837,903	46,726,707	24,384,240	22,342,467	6,697,230	3,376,511	3,320,719	396,286	221,569	174,717
1940	57,245,573	29,697,886	27,547,687	50,242,047	26,143,847	24,098,200	6,611,930	3,339,615	3,272,315	391,596	214,424	177,172
1950 [4]	61,769,897	31,715,969	30,053,928	55,274,164	28,431,910	26,842,254	—	—	—	—	—	—
1950 [5]	54,229,675	27,941,457	26,288,218	48,185,593	24,879,298	23,306,295	5,649,678	2,848,956	2,800,722	394,404	213,203	181,201
1960 [6]	54,054,425	27,598,489	26,455,936	48,403,400	24,736,004	23,667,396	5,064,191	2,556,285	2,507,906	586,834	306,200	280,634
1970 [7]	53,886,996	26,953,628	26,933,368	48,975,735	24,510,744	24,464,991	4,212,971	2,091,085	2,121,886	698,290	351,799	346,491
1980	59,494,813	29,760,870	29,733,943	54,049,878	27,047,265	27,002,613	3,901,009	1,922,327	1,978,682	1,543,926	791,278	752,648
1990	61,656,386	30,853,304	30,803,082	55,878,791	27,926,595	27,952,196	3,832,616	1,923,780	1,908,836	1,944,979	1,002,929	942,050

Notes appear at end of table   (continued)

TABLE Aa716–775   Population, by race, sex, and urban-rural residence: 1880–1990 *Continued*

Rural

Nonfarm

Year	All races Total	Male	Female	White Total	Male	Female	Black Total	Male	Female	Other races Total	Male	Female
	Aa752	Aa753	Aa754	Aa755	Aa756	Aa757	Aa758	Aa759	Aa760	Aa761	Aa762	Aa763
	Number	Number	Number	Number	Number	Number	Number	Number	Number	Number	Number	Number
1880 [2,3]	—	—	—	—	—	—	—	—	—	—	—	—
1890 [2,3]	—	—	—	—	—	—	—	—	—	—	—	—
1900 [2,3]	—	—	—	—	—	—	—	—	—	—	—	—
1910	—	—	—	—	—	—	—	—	—	—	—	—
1920	20,047,377	10,337,060	9,710,317	18,128,031	9,352,304	8,775,727	1,803,695	918,382	885,313	115,651	66,374	49,277
1930	23,662,710	12,117,945	11,544,765	21,500,462	11,012,799	10,487,663	2,016,707	1,022,066	994,641	145,541	83,080	62,461
1940	27,029,385	13,757,516	13,271,869	24,778,585	12,627,240	12,151,345	2,109,630	1,053,699	1,055,931	141,170	76,577	64,593
1950 [4]	31,181,325	15,862,847	15,318,478	28,470,339	14,489,275	13,981,064	2,491,377	1,256,115	1,235,262	219,609	117,457	102,152
1950 [5]	38,693,358	19,622,272	19,071,086	35,534,215	18,028,680	17,505,535	—	—	—	—	—	—
1960 [6]	40,567,121	20,598,091	19,969,030	36,518,676	18,547,804	17,970,872	3,574,677	1,804,715	1,769,962	473,768	245,572	228,196
1970 [7]	45,586,707	22,683,834	22,902,873	41,260,864	20,537,870	20,722,994	3,764,285	1,865,126	1,899,159	561,558	280,838	280,720
1980	—	—	—	—	—	—	—	—	—	—	—	—
1990	—	—	—	—	—	—	—	—	—	—	—	—

Rural

Farm

Year	All races Total	Male	Female	White Total	Male	Female	Black Total	Male	Female	Other races Total	Male	Female
	Aa764	Aa765	Aa766	Aa767	Aa768	Aa769	Aa770	Aa771	Aa772	Aa773	Aa774	Aa775
	Number	Number	Number	Number	Number	Number	Number	Number	Number	Number	Number	Number
1880 [2,3]	—	—	—	—	—	—	—	—	—	—	—	—
1890 [2,3]	—	—	—	—	—	—	—	—	—	—	—	—
1900 [2,3]	—	—	—	—	—	—	—	—	—	—	—	—
1910	—	—	—	—	—	—	—	—	—	—	—	—
1920	31,358,640	16,360,059	14,998,581	26,072,800	13,704,724	12,368,076	5,099,963	2,553,234	2,546,729	185,877	102,101	83,776
1930	30,157,513	15,864,375	14,293,138	25,226,245	13,371,441	11,854,804	4,680,523	2,354,445	2,326,078	250,745	138,489	112,256
1940	30,216,188	15,940,370	14,275,818	25,463,462	13,516,607	11,946,855	4,502,300	2,285,916	2,216,384	250,426	137,847	112,579
1950 [4]	23,048,350	12,078,610	10,969,740	19,715,254	10,390,023	9,325,231	3,158,301	1,592,841	1,565,460	174,795	95,746	79,049
1950 [5]	23,076,539	12,093,697	10,982,842	19,739,949	10,403,230	9,336,719	—	—	—	—	—	—
1960 [6]	13,474,771	6,986,175	6,488,596	11,876,333	6,177,614	5,698,719	1,481,985	747,075	734,910	116,453	61,486	54,967
1970 [7]	8,292,150	4,260,965	4,031,185	7,776,577	4,002,398	3,774,179	447,109	223,241	223,868	68,464	35,326	33,138
1980	—	—	—	—	—	—	—	—	—	—	—	—
1990	—	—	—	—	—	—	—	—	—	—	—	—

[1] The urban definition used is the one operative for that census year, except where indicated.

[2] Definition modified to exclude population in incorporated places and New England towns in the 2,500–3,999 size range.

[3] 1906 urban definition.

[4] 1940 urban definition.

[5] 1950 urban definition.

[6] Complete-count data for total, urban, and rural; 25 percent sample data for rural nonfarm and rural farm.

[7] Complete-count data for total, urban, and rural; 20 percent sample data for rural nonfarm and rural farm. See text for Table Aa145–184 for discussion of 1970 data by race. Complete-count figures exclude 23,372 persons for whom data are not available.

Sources

U.S. Bureau of the Census. 1880–1900, *Supplementary Analysis of the Twelfth Census* (1900), pp. 597–607, 632–42. 1910–1940, *U.S. Census of Population: 1940*, volume 2, part 1, pp. 19–20. 1950, *U.S. Census of Population: 1950*, volume 2, part 1, pp. 88, 91. 1960, *U.S. Census of Population: 1960*, volume 1, part 1, pp. 144, 359; part 3, pp. 17, 117–18; part 13, pp. 17, 113–14. 1970, *U.S. Census of Population: 1970*, volume 1, part 1, section 1, pp. 262, 380–1. 1980, *U.S. Census of Population: 1980*, volume 1, Chapter B, part 1, p. 20. 1990, *U.S. Census of Population: 1990*, 1990 CP-1-1, pp. 3, 19–20, 23–6.

Documentation

See the text for Table Aa684–698.

Between 1920 and 1970, the rural population was subdivided into rural farm and rural nonfarm components. In 1960 and 1970, the farm population was defined as persons living on places of ten or more acres from which sales of farm products amounted to $50 or more in the preceding calendar year or on places of fewer than ten acres from which sales of farm products amounted to $250 or more in the preceding year. In 1950, the farm population was defined as all persons living on farms and depended on the respondent's conception of farm (or ranch), with the exception that persons living on what might have been considered farmland were classified as nonfarm if they paid cash rent for their homes and yards only. In 1930 and 1940, the farm population comprised all persons living on farms and depended primarily on the interviewer's conception of what was meant by the word "farm." In 1920, the farm population comprised all persons living on farms and those farm laborers (and their families) who, although not living on a farm, lived in rural, unincorporated territory. Farms were defined in 1920 (as in the Census of Agriculture) to include all tracts of three acres or more used for agricultural purposes and smaller tracts that produced as much as $250 worth of farm products in 1919 or required for their agricultural operations the continuous services of at least one person.

For further discussion, see *U.S. Census of Population: 1930*, volume 2, p. 8; *U.S. Census of Population: 1950*, volume 2, part 1, pp. 33–5; *U.S. Census of Population: 1960*, volume 1, part 1, pp. xxxvii–xxxviii. See the text for Table Aa684–698 for the definitions of urban and rural. See the text for Table Aa145–184 for the definition of race.

TABLE Aa776-823   Urban population, by race, sex, and type of urban residence: 1950-1990

Contributed by Michael R. Haines

Urbanized areas

Total

Year	All races Total	Male	Female	White Total	Male	Female	Black Total	Male	Female	Other races Total	Male	Female
	Aa776	Aa777	Aa778	Aa779	Aa780	Aa781	Aa782	Aa783	Aa784	Aa785	Aa786	Aa787
	Number	Number	Number	Number	Number	Number	Number	Number	Number	Number	Number	Number
1950 [1]	69,249,148	33,670,714	35,578,434	61,925,036	30,160,082	31,764,954	7,053,900	3,338,340	3,715,560	258,000	154,320	103,680
1960	95,848,487	46,494,210	49,354,277	83,769,935	40,706,094	43,063,841	11,257,567	5,352,291	5,905,276	820,985	435,825	385,160
1970 [2]	118,446,566	57,035,148	61,411,418	100,951,502	48,751,475	52,200,027	15,692,685	7,384,180	8,308,505	1,802,379	899,493	902,886
1980	139,170,683	66,975,219	72,195,464	110,148,772	53,114,020	57,034,752	20,106,051	9,420,120	10,685,931	8,915,860	4,441,079	4,474,781
1990	158,258,878	76,628,073	81,630,805	119,359,248	57,900,997	61,458,251	23,533,536	11,012,916	12,520,620	15,366,094	7,714,160	7,651,934

Urbanized areas

Central cities

Year	All races Total	Male	Female	White Total	Male	Female	Black Total	Male	Female	Other races Total	Male	Female
	Aa788	Aa789	Aa790	Aa791	Aa792	Aa793	Aa794	Aa795	Aa796	Aa797	Aa798	Aa799
	Number	Number	Number	Number	Number	Number	Number	Number	Number	Number	Number	Number
1950 [1]	48,377,240	23,432,038	24,945,202	42,041,968	20,402,408	21,639,560	6,107,730	2,886,420	3,221,310	215,190	129,690	85,500
1960	57,975,132	27,927,624	30,047,508	47,627,232	22,976,282	24,650,950	9,702,112	4,606,147	5,095,965	645,788	345,195	300,593
1970 [2]	63,921,684	30,409,942	33,511,742	49,546,571	23,642,104	25,904,467	13,144,798	6,151,899	6,992,899	1,230,315	615,939	614,376
1980	67,035,302	31,899,486	35,135,816	46,408,745	22,152,755	24,255,990	15,143,702	7,022,482	8,121,220	5,482,855	2,724,249	2,758,606
1990	78,847,406	37,947,570	40,899,836	52,192,735	25,230,721	26,962,014	17,308,291	8,017,149	9,291,142	9,346,380	4,699,700	4,646,680

Urbanized areas

Urban fringe

Year	All races Total	Male	Female	White Total	Male	Female	Black Total	Male	Female	Other races Total	Male	Female
	Aa800	Aa801	Aa802	Aa803	Aa804	Aa805	Aa806	Aa807	Aa808	Aa809	Aa810	Aa811
	Number	Number	Number	Number	Number	Number	Number	Number	Number	Number	Number	Number
1950 [1]	20,871,908	10,238,676	10,633,232	19,883,068	9,757,674	10,125,394	946,170	451,920	494,250	42,810	24,630	18,180
1960	37,873,355	18,566,586	19,306,769	36,142,703	17,729,812	18,412,891	1,555,455	746,144	809,311	175,197	90,630	84,567
1970 [2]	54,524,882	26,625,206	27,899,676	51,404,931	25,109,371	26,295,560	2,547,887	1,232,281	1,315,606	572,064	283,554	288,510
1980	72,135,381	35,075,733	37,059,648	63,740,027	30,961,265	32,778,762	4,962,349	2,397,638	2,564,711	3,433,005	1,716,830	1,716,175
1990	79,411,472	38,680,503	40,730,969	67,166,513	32,670,276	34,496,237	6,225,245	2,995,767	3,229,478	6,019,714	3,014,460	3,005,254

Other urban

Year	All races Total	Male	Female	White Total	Male	Female	Black Total	Male	Female	Other races Total	Male	Female
	Aa812	Aa813	Aa814	Aa815	Aa816	Aa817	Aa818	Aa819	Aa820	Aa821	Aa822	Aa823
	Number	Number	Number	Number	Number	Number	Number	Number	Number	Number	Number	Number
1950 [1]	27,218,538	13,221,068	13,997,470	24,831,399	12,089,812	12,741,587	2,316,990	1,090,110	1,226,880	62,010	34,950	27,060
1960	29,420,263	14,238,795	15,181,468	26,658,397	12,925,051	13,733,346	2,550,073	1,204,832	1,345,241	211,793	108,912	102,881
1970 [2]	30,878,364	14,923,416	15,954,948	27,821,738	13,458,768	14,362,970	2,674,633	1,273,051	1,401,582	381,993	191,597	190,396
1980	27,880,309	13,317,072	14,563,237	24,172,972	11,524,048	12,648,924	2,487,965	1,176,742	1,311,223	1,219,372	616,282	603,090
1990	28,794,609	13,758,041	15,036,568	24,448,031	11,648,288	12,799,743	2,619,908	1,233,455	1,386,453	1,726,670	876,298	850,372

[1] Complete-count data for all races and for white; $3\frac{1}{3}$ percent sample for Negro and for other races.

[2] See text for Table Aa145-184 for discussion of 1970 data by race. Excludes 23,372 persons for whom data are not available.

Sources

U.S. Bureau of the Census. 1950, all races and white, *U.S. Census of the Population: 1960*, volume 1, part 1, p. 143; 1950, Negro and other races, *U.S. Census of Population: 1950*, volume 4, part 5, Chapter A, pp. 15-16. 1960, *U.S. Census of Population: 1960*, volume 1, part 1, p. 144; parts 3 and 13, p. 17. 1970, *U.S. Census of Population: 1970*, volume 1, part 1, section 1, p. 262. 1980, *U.S. Census of Population: 1980*, volume 1, Chapter B, part 1, PC80-1-B1, p. 20. 1990, *U.S. Census of Population: 1990*, 1990 CP-1-1, pp. 19-20, 25-6.

Documentation

The first systematic attempt to define the metropolitan population of the United States was presented in the 1910 Census in which metropolitan districts were defined for cities of 200,000 or more inhabitants. Each metropolitan district included contiguous minor civil divisions that met certain rules of proximity and population density. The metropolitan district concept was

(continued)

TABLE Aa776–823 Urban population, by race, sex, and type of urban residence: 1950–1990 *Continued*

used with changes in definition up through the 1940 Census, when metropolitan districts were defined for cities with populations of 50,000 or more. Metropolitan districts were seldom cross-tabulated with census data on social and economic characteristics and thus were of limited usefulness.

In 1950, metropolitan districts were replaced in census reports by standard metropolitan areas (see the text for Table Aa824–831) and urbanized areas. Urbanized areas, with minor changes in definition, were delineated in the 1950 through 1990 Censuses. In general, an urbanized area comprises one or more places and the adjacent densely settled surrounding territory that together have a minimum population of 50,000 or more persons. The

urban population can be divided into the urbanized area population and the other urban population. The urbanized area population can be further divided into central city and urban fringe components.

For a further discussion, see the following sources: *U.S. Census of Population: 1910*, volume 1, pp. 73–7; *U.S. Census of Population: 1930, Metropolitan Districts*; *U.S. Census of Population: 1940, The Growth of Metropolitan Districts in the United States: 1900–1940*; *U.S. Census of Population: 1950*, volume 1, pp. xxvii–xxviii; *U.S. Census of Population: 1970*, volume 1, part A, section 1, p. xiii.

See the text for Table Aa684–698 for the definitions of urban and rural. See the text for Table Aa145–184 for the definition of race.

TABLE Aa824–831 Metropolitan areas as defined at specified dates – number, population, and land area: 1952–1993[1, 2]

Contributed by Michael R. Haines

Year of definition	Metropolitan areas	Total population						Total land area, 1990
		1950	1960	1970	1980	1990	1992	
	Aa824	Aa825	Aa826	Aa827	Aa828	Aa829	Aa830	Aa831
	Number	Number	Number	Number	Number	Number	Number	Square miles
1952 [3]	169 [15]	84,853,700	106,344,548	122,184,836	128,839,422	139,837,352	—	206,802
1960 [4]	212	89,316,903 [17]	112,885,139	130,982,661	140,793,427	155,088,626	—	308,742
1964 [5]	217	91,644,188	115,876,343	134,700,911	145,503,863	160,500,956	—	348,400
1968 [6]	230	93,629,986	118,413,604	137,976,252	149,811,057	165,707,672	—	377,042
1971 [7]	243	94,579,008 [18]	119,593,498 [20]	139,479,806	151,662,221	167,896,646	—	386,241
1974 [8]	265 [16]	100,219,707 [19]	126,613,710	148,198,993	162,753,335	181,125,276	—	490,551
1977 [9]	277	101,109,145	127,674,818	149,482,664	164,383,496	182,989,860	—	509,841
1981 [10]	318	104,172,853	131,318,714	153,693,767	169,430,623	188,759,597	—	565,288
1983	275	105,214,471	132,633,988	155,411,328	171,776,970	191,634,355	—	559,752
1984	277	105,269,301	132,707,748	155,519,340	171,955,900	191,903,497	—	563,796
1985	280	105,411,428	132,887,134	155,700,823	172,169,456	192,135,964	—	569,816
1986	281	105,481,211	132,977,580	155,805,452	172,304,016	192,314,367	—	571,745
1987 [11]	281	105,502,909	133,003,445	155,832,688	172,334,547	192,345,395	—	572,284
1988 [12]	282	105,582,961	133,088,400	155,937,275	172,454,948	192,476,951	—	573,560
1989 [12]	283	105,718,150	133,233,777	156,084,580	172,601,873	192,618,846	—	574,622
1990 [12, 13]	284	105,742,856	133,275,412	156,137,337	172,679,870	192,725,741	—	580,136
1992 [12]	268	—	—	—	176,662,797	197,466,567	202,903,519	669,927
1993 [12, 14]	268	—	—	—	176,892,735	197,724,892	203,172,185	673,057

[1] Census population data through 1980 include corrections made since publication. The area data for the 1950, 1960, 1970, and 1980 Census definitions of metropolitan areas (MAs) differ from the data published in those censuses because of subsequent remeasurement of land areas and changes in inland water area occurring for the 1990 Census.

[2] Beginning 1983, all figures refer to metropolitan statistical areas (MSAs) and consolidated metropolitan statistical areas (CMSAs). See documentation.

[3] MAs as defined for the 1950 Census.

[4] MAs as defined for the 1960 Census.

[5] MAs as defined for the 1963 economic censuses.

[6] MAs as defined for the 1967 economic censuses.

[7] MAs as defined for the 1970 Census.

[8] MAs as defined for the 1972 economic censuses.

[9] MAs as defined for the 1977 economic censuses.

[10] MAs as defined for the 1982 economic censuses.

[11] MAs as defined for the 1987 economic censuses.

[12] Data exclude the portion of Sullivan city in Crawford County, Missouri (1990 population, 1,116) added to the St. Louis, Missouri–Illinois MSA by Congressional action effective December 22, 1987.

[13] MAs as defined for the 1990 Census.

[14] MAs as defined for the 1992 economic censuses.

[15] Corresponds to total MA population for 1950 Census (84,500,680) plus the Honolulu MA.

[16] Includes estimated 1950 population (32,060) of the Anchorage census division, as defined in 1970.

[17] Corresponds to the total MA population for 1960 published in the 1960 Census (112,885,178), corrected by subtracting population (39) erroneously included in Franklin County, Ohio (Columbus MA).

[18] Corresponds to the total 1960 population for 1970 MAs published in the 1970 Census (119,594,754), corrected by subtracting 1,256 population from Lawrence–Haverhill MA; this represented an addition to the 1960 population of Andover town MA made subsequent to the original census tabulations, and therefore not reflected in state or national totals.

[19] Includes 1960 population (82,833) of the Anchorage census division, as defined in 1970.

[20] Corresponds to the total MA population for 1970 published in the 1970 Census (139,418,811), plus net corrections to the MA population made subsequent to publication.

Sources

U.S. Bureau of the Census, *Statistical Abstract of the United States: 1997* (1997), Appendix 2, Table A. Originally taken from: U.S. Bureau of the Census, *1950, U.S. Census of Population*, volume 1; U.S. Bureau of the Census, *1960, U.S. Census of Population*, volume 1; U.S. Bureau of the Census, *1970, U.S. Census of Population*, volume 1; *1980 Census of Population*, volume 1, Chapters A and B and Supplementary Report, Metropolitan Statistical Areas, PC80-S1-18; 1990 Census of Population and Housing Data Paper Listing, CPH-L-10 and CPH-L-118; 1990 Census of Population and Housing, Supplementary Reports, Metropolitan Areas as Defined by the Office of Management and Budget, June 30, 1993, 1990 CPH-S-1-1; and Population Paper Listing, PPL-2.

TABLE Aa824–831   Metropolitan areas as defined at specified dates – number, population, and land area: 1952–1993   *Continued*

Documentation

This table presents historical summary information for MAs as defined on certain dates. For example, series Aa827 shows what the 1970 total population of MAs would be under various historical definitions. For such series, the differences in population – running down a column – result entirely from net expansion of metropolitan territory through changes in the MA definition. The differences in population over time – running across a row – result entirely from population changes within that territory, unaffected by changes in MA definitions. Similarly, the changes in 1990 land area, series Aa831, result entirely from net change in MA territory. Subtraction of any line of the table from the line below will show the net effect of change in population and land area undergone by the MAs as the result of changes in definitions between the specified dates. Such changes may have occurred throughout the period, not on any single date, and may have included reductions in, as well as additions to, MA territory.

Statistics for MAs shown in the *Statistical Abstract* represent areas designated by the U.S. Office of Management and Budget (OMB) as MSAs, CMSAs, and primary metropolitan statistical areas (PMSAs).

The general concept of an MA is that of a core area having a large population nucleus, together with adjacent communities having a high degree of economic and social integration with this core. Currently defined MAs are based on application of 1999 standards (which appeared in the *Federal Register* on March 30, 1990) to 1990 decennial census data. These MA definitions were announced by the OMB effective June 30, 1996. As of the June 1996 OMB announcement, there were 255 MSAs and 18 CMSAs comprising 73 PMSAs in the United States.

Standard definitions of MAs were first issued in 1949 by the then Bureau of the Budget (predecessor of the OMB), under the designation "standard metropolitan area" (SMA). The term was changed to "standard metropolitan statistical area" (SMSA) in 1959, and to "metropolitan statistical area" (MSA) in 1983. The current collective term "metropolitan area" (MA) became effective in 1990. OMB has been responsible for the official metropolitan areas since they were first defined, except for the period 1977–1981, when they were the responsibility of the Office of Federal Statistical Policy and Standards, Department of Commerce.

The standards for defining metropolitan areas were modified in 1958, 1971, 1975, 1980, and 1990. The current standards provide that each MSA must include at least: (1) one city with 50,000 or more inhabitants, or (2) a Census Bureau–defined urbanized area (of at least 50,000 inhabitants) and a total metropolitan population of at least 100,000 (75,000 in New England). Under these standards the county (or counties) that contains the largest city becomes the central county (counties), along with any adjacent counties that have at least 50 percent of their population in the urbanized area surrounding the largest city. Additional "outlying counties" are included in the MSA if they meet specified requirements of commuting to the central counties and other selected requirements of metropolitan character (such as population density and percent urban). In New England, the MSAs are defined in terms of cities and towns rather than counties. An area that meets these requirements for recognition as an MSA and also has a population of one million or more may be recognized as a CMSA if: (1) separate component areas can be identified within the entire area by meeting statistical criteria specified in the standards, and (2) local opinion indicates there is support for the component areas. If recognized, the component areas are designated PMSAs, and the entire area becomes a CMSA. (PMSAs, like the CMSAs that contain them, are composed of individual or groups of counties outside New England, and cities and towns within New England.) If no PMSAs are recognized, the entire area is designated as an MSA. The largest city in each MSA/CMSA is designated a "central city," and additional cities qualify if specified requirements are met concerning population size and commuting patterns. The title of each MSA consists of the names of up to three of its central cities and the name of each state into which the MSA extends. However, a central city with less than one third of the population of the area's largest city is not included in an MSA title unless local opinion desires its inclusion. Titles of PMSAs typically are also based on central city names but in certain cases consist of county names. Generally, titles of CMSAs are based on the names of their component PMSAs.

The OMB defines New England consolidated metropolitan areas (NECMAs) as a county-based alternative for the county- and town-based New England MSAs and CMSAs. The NECMA for an MSA or CMSA includes: (1) the county containing the first-named city in that MSA/CMSA title (this county may include the first-named cities of other MSAs/CMSAs as well), and (2) each additional county having at least half its population in the MSAs/CMSAs whose first-named cities are in the previously identified county. NECMAs are not identified for individual PMSAs. There are twelve NECMAs, including one for the Boston–Worcester–Lawrence CMSA and one for the portion of the New York–Northern New Jersey–Long Island CMSA in Connecticut. Central cities of a NECMA are those cities in the NECMA that qualify as central cities of an MSA or a CMSA. NECMA titles derive from names of central cities of MSAs/CMSAs.

Changes in the definitions of MAs since the 1950 Census have consisted chiefly of (1) the recognition of new areas as they reached the minimum required city or area population; and (2) the addition of counties or New England cities and towns to existing areas as new census data showed them to qualify. Also, former separate MAs have been merged with other areas, and occasionally territory has been transferred from one MA to another or from an MA to nonmetropolitan territory. The large majority of changes have taken place on the basis of decennial census data, although the MA standards specify the bases for intercensal updates. Because of these changes in definition, caution must be used in comparing MA data from different dates. For some purposes, comparisons of data for MAs as defined at given dates may be appropriate. To facilitate constant-area comparisons, data for earlier dates have been revised in tables where possible to reflect the MA boundaries of the more recent date. In this table, data are given for MAs as defined for specific dates, thereby indicating the extent of change in population and land area resulting from revisions in definitions.

The dates for MA revisions are as follows: 1952, March; 1960, November; 1964, August 31; 1968, January 31; 1971, February 28; 1974, April 30; 1977, December 31; 1981–1990 and 1993, June 30; and 1992, December 31. The census and survey dates for population and area figures are as follows: 1950–1990, April 1; and 1992, July 1.

All data include Alaska and Hawai'i and exclude Puerto Rico.

TABLE Aa832–1033   Population of cities with at least 100,000 population in 1990: 1790–1990

Contributed by Michael R. Haines

	New York, NY					Los Angeles, CA	Chicago, IL	Houston, TX	Philadelphia, PA	San Diego, CA	Detroit, MI
	Total, five boroughs	Bronx borough	Brooklyn borough	Manhattan borough	Queens borough	Richmond borough						
	Aa832	Aa833	Aa834	Aa835	Aa836	Aa837	Aa838	Aa839	Aa840	Aa841	Aa842	Aa843
Year	Number	Number	Number	Number	Number	Number	Number	Number	Number	Number	Number	Number
1790	49,401	1,781	4,495	33,131	6,159	3,835	—	—	—	28,522	—	—
1800	79,216	1,755	5,740	60,515	6,642	4,564	—	—	—	41,220	—	—
1810	119,734	2,267	8,303	96,373	7,444	5,347	—	—	—	53,722	—	—
1820	152,056	2,782	11,187	123,706	8,246	6,135	—	—	—	63,802	—	1,422
1830	242,278	3,023	20,535	202,589	9,049	7,082	—	—	—	80,462	—	2,222
1840	391,114	5,346	47,613	312,710	14,480	10,965	—	4,470	—	93,665	—	9,102
1850	696,115	8,032	138,882	515,547	18,593	15,061	1,610	29,963	2,396	121,376	—	21,019
1860	1,174,779	23,593	279,122	813,669	32,903	25,492	4,385	112,172	4,845	565,529	731	45,619
1870	1,478,103	37,393	419,921	942,292	45,468	33,029	5,728	298,977	9,382	674,022	2,300	79,577
1880	1,911,698	51,980	599,495	1,164,673	56,559	38,991	11,183	503,185	16,513	847,170	2,637	116,340
1890	2,507,414	88,908	838,547	1,441,216	87,050	51,693	50,395	1,099,850	27,557	1,046,964	16,159	205,876
1900	3,437,202	200,507	1,166,582	1,850,093	152,999	67,021	102,479	1,698,575	44,633	1,293,697	17,700	285,704
1910	4,766,883	430,980	1,634,351	2,331,542	284,041	85,969	319,198	2,185,283	78,800	1,549,008	39,578	465,766
1920	5,620,048	732,016	2,018,356	2,284,103	469,042	116,531	576,673	2,701,705	138,276	1,823,779	74,361	993,678
1930	6,930,446	1,265,258	2,560,401	1,867,312	1,079,129	158,346	1,238,048	3,376,438	292,352	1,950,961	147,995	1,568,662
1940	7,454,995	1,394,711	2,698,285	1,889,924	1,297,634	174,441	1,504,277	3,396,808	384,514	1,931,334	203,341	1,623,452
1950	7,891,957	1,451,277	2,738,175	1,960,101	1,550,849	191,555	1,970,358	3,620,962	596,163	2,071,805	334,387	1,849,568
1960	7,781,984	1,424,815	2,627,319	1,698,281	1,809,578	221,991	2,479,015	3,550,404	938,219	2,002,512	573,224	1,670,144
1970	7,894,862	1,471,701	2,602,012	1,539,233	1,986,473	295,443	2,811,801	3,369,357	1,233,535	1,949,996	697,741	1,514,063
1980	7,071,639	1,168,972	2,230,936	1,428,285	1,891,325	352,121	2,968,528	3,005,072	1,595,138	1,688,210	875,538	1,203,368
1990	7,322,564	1,203,789	2,300,664	1,487,536	1,951,598	378,977	3,485,398	2,783,726	1,630,553	1,585,577	1,110,549	1,027,974

	Dallas, TX	Phoenix, AZ	San Antonio, TX	San Jose, CA	Indianapolis, IN	Baltimore, MD	San Francisco, CA	Jacksonville, FL	Columbus, OH	Milwaukee, WI	Memphis, TN	Washington, DC
	Aa844	Aa845	Aa846	Aa847	Aa848	Aa849	Aa850	Aa851	Aa852	Aa853	Aa854	Aa855
Year	Number	Number	Number	Number	Number	Number	Number	Number	Number	Number	Number	Number
1790	—	—	—	—	—	13,503	—	—	—	—	—	—
1800	—	—	—	—	—	26,514	—	—	—	—	—	3,210
1810	—	—	—	—	—	46,555	—	—	—	—	—	8,208
1820	—	—	—	—	—	62,738	—	—	—	—	—	13,247
1830	—	—	—	—	—	80,620	—	—	2,435	—	—	18,826
1840	—	—	—	—	2,692	102,313	—	—	6,048	1,712	—	23,364
1850	—	—	3,488	—	8,091	169,054	34,776	1,045	17,882	20,061	8,841	40,001
1860	—	—	8,235	—	18,611	212,418	56,802	2,118	18,554	45,246	22,623	61,122
1870	—	—	12,256	9,089	48,244	267,354	149,473	6,912	31,274	71,440	40,226	109,199
1880	10,358	—	20,550	12,567	75,056	332,313	233,959	7,650	51,647	115,587	33,592	147,293
1890	38,067	3,152	37,673	18,060	105,436	434,439	298,997	17,201	88,150	204,468	64,495	188,932
1900	42,638	5,544	53,321	21,500	169,164	508,957	342,782	28,429	125,560	285,315	102,320	278,718
1910	92,104	11,134	96,614	28,946	233,650	558,485	416,912	57,699	181,511	373,857	131,105	331,069
1920	158,976	29,053	161,379	39,642	314,194	733,826	506,676	91,558	237,031	457,147	162,351	437,571
1930	260,475	48,118	231,542	57,651	364,161	804,874	634,394	129,549	290,564	578,249	253,143	486,869
1940	294,734	65,414	253,854	68,457	386,972	859,100	634,536	173,065	306,087	587,472	292,942	663,091
1950	434,462	106,818	408,442	95,280	427,173	949,708	775,357	204,517	375,901	637,392	396,000	802,178
1960	679,684	439,170	587,718	204,196	476,258	939,024	740,316	201,030	471,316	741,324	497,524	763,956
1970	844,401	584,303	654,153	459,913	736,856	905,787	715,674	504,265	540,025	717,372	623,988	756,668
1980	904,599	789,704	785,940	629,400	711,539	786,741	678,974	571,003	565,021	636,297	646,174	638,432
1990	1,006,877	983,403	935,933	782,248	741,952	736,014	723,959	672,971	632,910	628,088	610,337	606,900

TABLE Aa832–1033   Population of cities with at least 100,000 population in 1990: 1790–1990   *Continued*

Year	Boston, MA	Seattle, WA	El Paso, TX	Nashville, TN	Cleveland, OH	New Orleans, LA	Denver, CO	Austin, TX	Fort Worth, TX	Oklahoma City, OK	Portland, OR	Kansas City, MO
	Aa856	Aa857	Aa858	Aa859	Aa860	Aa861	Aa862	Aa863	Aa864	Aa865	Aa866	Aa867
	Number	Number	Number	Number	Number	Number	Number	Number	Number	Number	Number	Number
1790	18,320	—	—	—	—	—	—	—	—	—	—	—
1800	24,937	—	—	345	—	—	—	—	—	—	—	—
1810	33,787	—	—	—	—	17,242	—	—	—	—	—	—
1820	43,298	—	—	—	606	27,176	—	—	—	—	—	—
1830	61,392	—	—	5,566	1,076	46,082	—	—	—	—	—	—
1840	93,383	—	—	6,929	6,071	102,193	—	—	—	—	—	—
1850	136,881	—	—	10,165	17,034	116,375	—	629	—	—	—	—
1860	177,840	—	—	16,988	43,417	168,675	4,749	3,494	—	—	2,874	4,418
1870	250,526	1,107	—	25,865	92,829	191,418	4,759	4,428	—	—	8,293	32,260
1880	362,839	3,533	736	43,350	160,146	216,090	35,629	11,013	6,663	—	17,577	55,785
1890	448,477	42,837	10,338	76,168	261,353	242,039	106,713	14,575	23,076	4,151	46,385	132,716
1900	560,892	80,671	15,906	80,865	381,768	287,104	133,859	22,258	26,688	10,037	90,426	163,752
1910	670,585	237,194	39,279	110,364	560,663	339,075	213,381	29,860	73,312	64,205	207,214	248,381
1920	748,060	315,312	77,560	118,342	796,841	387,219	256,491	34,876	106,482	91,295	258,288	324,410
1930	781,188	365,583	102,421	153,866	900,429	458,762	287,861	53,120	163,447	185,389	301,815	399,746
1940	770,816	368,302	96,810	167,402	878,336	494,537	322,412	87,930	117,662	204,424	305,394	399,178
1950	801,444	467,591	130,485	174,307	914,808	570,445	415,786	132,459	278,778	243,504	373,628	456,622
1960	697,197	557,087	276,687	154,563	876,050	627,525	493,887	186,545	356,268	324,253	372,676	475,539
1970	641,071	530,831	322,261	426,029	750,879	593,471	514,678	253,539	393,455	368,164	379,967	507,330
1980	562,994	493,846	425,259	477,811	573,822	557,927	492,686	345,890	385,164	404,014	368,148	448,028
1990	574,283	516,259	515,342	510,784	505,616	496,938	467,610	465,622	447,619	444,719	437,319	435,146

Year	Long Beach, CA	Tucson, AZ	St. Louis, MO	Charlotte, NC	Atlanta, GA	Virginia Beach, VA	Albuquerque, NM	Oakland, CA	Pittsburgh, PA Total	Pittsburgh, before consolidation	Allegheny, before consolidation	Sacramento, CA
	Aa868	Aa869	Aa870	Aa871	Aa872	Aa873	Aa874	Aa875	Aa876	Aa877	Aa878	Aa879
	Number	Number	Number	Number	Number	Number	Number	Number	Number	Number	Number	Number
1790	—	—	—	—	—	—	—	—	—	—	—	—
1800	—	—	—	—	—	—	—	—	1,565	1,565	—	—
1810	—	—	—	—	—	—	—	—	4,768	4,768	—	—
1820	—	—	—	—	—	—	—	—	7,248	7,248	—	—
1830	—	—	4,977	—	—	—	—	—	15,369	12,568	2,801	—
1840	—	—	16,469	—	—	—	—	—	31,204	21,115	10,089	—
1850	—	—	77,860	1,065	2,572	—	—	—	67,863	46,601	21,262	6,820
1860	—	—	160,773	2,265	9,554	—	—	1,543	77,923	49,221	28,702	13,785
1870	—	3,224	310,864	4,473	21,789	—	—	10,500	139,256	86,076	53,180	16,283
1880	—	7,007	350,518	7,094	37,409	—	—	34,555	235,071	156,389	78,682	21,420
1890	564	5,150	451,770	11,557	65,533	—	3,785	48,682	343,904	238,617	105,287	26,386
1900	2,252	7,531	575,238	18,091	89,872	—	6,238	66,960	451,512	321,616	129,896	29,282
1910	17,809	13,193	687,029	34,014	154,839	320	11,020	150,174	533,905	533,905	—	44,696
1920	55,593	20,292	772,897	46,338	200,616	846	15,157	216,261	588,343	588,343	—	65,908
1930	142,032	32,506	821,960	82,675	270,366	1,719	26,570	284,063	669,817	669,817	—	93,750
1940	164,271	35,752	816,048	100,899	302,288	2,600	35,449	302,163	671,659	671,659	—	105,958
1950	250,767	45,454	856,796	134,042	331,314	5,390	96,815	384,575	676,806	676,806	—	137,572
1960	344,168	212,892	750,026	201,564	487,455	8,091	201,189	367,548	604,332	604,332	—	191,667
1970	358,879	262,933	622,236	241,420	495,039	172,106	244,501	361,561	520,089	520,089	—	257,105
1980	361,498	330,537	452,801	315,474	425,022	262,199	332,920	339,337	423,959	423,959	—	275,741
1990	429,433	405,390	396,685	395,934	394,017	393,069	384,736	372,242	369,879	369,879	—	369,365

(continued)

TABLE Aa832–1033   Population of cities with at least 100,000 population in 1990: 1790–1990   *Continued*

Year	Minneapolis, MN	Tulsa, OK	Honolulu, HI	Cincinnati, OH	Miami, FL	Fresno, CA	Omaha, NE	Toledo, OH	Buffalo, NY	Wichita, KS	Santa Ana, CA	Mesa City, AZ
	Aa880	Aa881	Aa882	Aa883	Aa884	Aa885	Aa886	Aa887	Aa888	Aa889	Aa890	Aa891
	Number	Number	Number	Number	Number	Number	Number	Number	Number	Number	Number	Number
1790	—	—	—	—	—	—	—	—	—	—	—	—
1800	—	—	—	—	—	—	—	—	—	—	—	—
1810	—	—	—	2,540	—	—	—	—	1,508	—	—	—
1820	—	—	—	9,642	—	—	—	—	2,095	—	—	—
1830	—	—	—	24,831	—	—	—	—	8,668	—	—	—
1840	—	—	—	46,338	—	—	—	1,222	18,213	—	—	—
1850	—	—	—	115,435	—	—	—	3,829	42,261	—	—	—
1860	2,564	—	—	161,044	—	—	1,883	13,768	81,129	—	—	—
1870	13,066	—	—	216,239	—	—	16,083	31,584	117,714	—	—	—
1880	46,887	—	—	255,139	—	1,112	30,518	50,137	155,134	4,911	—	—
1890	164,738	—	22,907	296,908	—	10,818	140,452	81,434	255,664	23,853	3,628	—
1900	202,718	1,390	39,306	325,902	1,681	12,470	102,555	131,822	352,387	24,671	4,933	722
1910	301,408	18,182	52,183	363,591	5,471	24,892	124,096	168,497	423,715	52,450	8,429	1,692
1920	380,582	72,075	83,327	401,247	29,571	45,086	191,601	243,164	506,775	72,217	15,485	3,036
1930	464,356	141,258	137,582	451,160	110,637	52,513	214,006	290,718	573,076	111,110	30,322	3,711
1940	492,370	142,157	179,326	455,610	172,172	60,685	223,844	282,349	575,901	114,966	31,921	7,224
1950	521,718	182,740	248,034	503,998	249,276	91,669	251,117	303,616	580,122	168,279	45,533	16,790
1960	482,872	261,685	294,194	502,550	291,688	133,929	301,598	318,003	532,759	254,698	100,350	33,772
1970	434,400	330,350	324,871	453,514	334,859	165,655	346,929	383,062	462,768	276,554	155,710	63,049
1980	370,951	360,919	365,048	385,409	346,681	217,491	313,939	354,635	357,870	279,838	204,023	152,404
1990	368,383	367,302	365,272	364,040	358,548	354,202	335,795	332,943	328,123	304,011	293,742	288,091

Year	Colorado Springs, CO	Tampa, FL	Newark, NJ	St. Paul, MN	Louisville, KY	Anaheim, CA	Birmingham, AL	Arlington, TX	Norfolk, VA	Las Vegas, NV	Corpus Christi, TX	St. Petersburg, FL
	Aa892	Aa893	Aa894	Aa895	Aa896	Aa897	Aa898	Aa899	Aa900	Aa901	Aa902	Aa903
	Number	Number	Number	Number	Number	Number	Number	Number	Number	Number	Number	Number
1790	—	—	—	—	200	—	—	—	2,959	—	—	—
1800	—	—	—	—	359	—	—	—	6,926	—	—	—
1810	—	—	—	—	1,357	—	—	—	9,193	—	—	—
1820	—	—	—	—	4,012	—	—	—	8,478	—	—	—
1830	—	—	10,953	—	10,341	—	—	—	9,814	—	—	—
1840	—	—	17,290	—	21,210	—	—	—	10,920	—	—	—
1850	—	—	38,894	1,112	43,194	—	—	—	14,326	—	—	—
1860	—	—	71,941	10,401	68,033	—	—	—	14,620	—	175	—
1870	—	796	105,059	20,030	100,753	881	—	—	19,229	—	2,140	—
1880	4,226	720	136,508	41,473	123,758	833	3,086	—	21,966	—	3,257	—
1890	11,140	5,532	181,830	133,156	161,129	1,273	26,178	664	34,871	—	4,387	273
1900	21,085	15,839	246,070	163,065	204,731	1,456	38,415	1,079	46,624	—	4,703	1,575
1910	29,078	37,782	347,469	214,744	223,928	2,628	132,685	1,794	67,452	—	8,222	4,127
1920	30,105	51,608	414,524	234,698	234,891	5,526	178,806	3,031	115,777	2,304	10,522	14,237
1930	33,237	101,161	442,337	271,606	307,745	10,995	259,678	3,661	129,710	5,165	27,741	40,425
1940	36,789	108,391	429,760	287,736	319,077	11,031	267,583	4,240	144,332	8,422	57,301	60,812
1950	45,472	124,681	438,776	311,349	369,129	14,556	326,037	7,692	213,513	24,624	108,287	96,738
1960	70,194	274,970	405,220	313,411	390,639	104,184	340,887	44,775	304,869	64,405	167,690	181,298
1970	135,517	277,714	381,930	309,866	361,706	166,408	300,910	90,229	307,951	125,787	204,525	216,159
1980	215,105	271,577	329,248	270,230	298,694	219,494	284,413	160,113	266,979	164,674	232,134	238,647
1990	281,140	280,015	275,221	272,235	269,063	266,406	265,968	261,721	261,229	258,295	257,453	238,629

TABLE Aa832–1033   Population of cities with at least 100,000 population in 1990: 1790–1990 *Continued*

	Rochester, NY	Jersey City, NJ	Riverside, CA	Anchorage, AK	Lexington–Fayette, KY	Akron, OH	Aurora, CO	Baton Rouge, LA	Stockton, CA	Raleigh, NC	Richmond, VA	Shreveport, LA
	Aa904	Aa905	Aa906	Aa907	Aa908	Aa909	Aa910	Aa911	Aa912	Aa913	Aa914	Aa915
Year	Number	Number	Number	Number	Number	Number	Number	Number	Number	Number	Number	Number
1790	—	—	—	—	834	—	—	—	—	—	3,761	—
1800	—	—	—	—	1,795	—	—	—	—	669	5,737	—
1810	—	—	—	—	4,326	—	—	—	—	—	9,735	—
1820	—	—	—	—	5,279	—	—	—	—	2,674	12,067	—
1830	9,207	—	—	—	6,026	—	—	—	—	1,700	16,060	—
1840	20,191	3,072	—	—	6,997	—	—	2,269	—	2,244	20,153	—
1850	36,403	6,856	—	—	8,159	3,266	—	3,905	—	4,518	27,570	1,728
1860	48,204	29,226	—	—	9,321	3,477	—	5,428	3,679	4,780	37,910	2,190
1870	62,386	82,546	—	—	14,801	10,006	—	6,498	10,066	7,790	51,038	4,607
1880	89,366	120,722	—	—	16,656	16,512	—	7,197	10,282	9,265	63,600	8,009
1890	133,896	163,003	4,683	—	21,567	27,601	—	10,478	14,424	12,678	81,388	11,979
1900	162,608	206,433	7,973	—	26,369	42,728	202	11,269	17,506	13,643	85,050	16,013
1910	218,149	267,779	15,212	—	35,099	69,067	679	14,897	23,253	19,218	127,628	28,015
1920	295,750	298,103	19,341	1,856	41,534	208,435	983	21,782	40,296	24,418	171,667	43,874
1930	328,132	316,715	29,696	2,277	45,736	255,040	2,295	30,729	47,963	37,379	182,929	76,655
1940	324,975	301,173	34,696	3,495	49,304	244,791	3,437	34,719	54,714	46,897	193,042	98,167
1950	332,488	299,017	46,764	11,254	55,534	274,605	11,421	125,629	70,853	65,679	230,310	127,206
1960	318,611	276,101	84,332	44,237	62,810	290,351	48,548	152,419	86,321	93,931	219,958	164,372
1970	295,011	260,350	140,089	48,081	108,137	275,425	74,974	165,291	109,963	122,830	249,332	182,064
1980	241,741	223,532	170,591	174,431	204,165	237,177	158,588	220,394	148,283	150,255	219,214	206,989
1990	231,636	228,537	226,505	226,338	225,366	223,019	222,103	219,531	210,943	207,951	203,056	198,525

	Jackson, MS	Mobile, AL	Des Moines, IA	Lincoln, NE	Madison, WI	Grand Rapids, MI	Yonkers, NY	Hialeah, FL	Montgomery, AL	Lubbock, TX	Greensboro, NC	Dayton, OH
	Aa916	Aa917	Aa918	Aa919	Aa920	Aa921	Aa922	Aa923	Aa924	Aa925	Aa926	Aa927
Year	Number	Number	Number	Number	Number	Number	Number	Number	Number	Number	Number	Number
1790	—	—	—	—	—	—	—	—	—	—	—	—
1800	—	—	—	—	—	—	—	—	—	—	—	—
1810	—	—	—	—	—	—	—	—	—	—	—	383
1820	—	—	—	—	—	—	—	—	—	—	—	1,000
1830	—	3,194	—	—	—	—	—	—	—	—	—	2,950
1840	—	12,672	—	—	—	—	—	—	2,179	—	—	6,067
1850	1,881	20,515	—	—	1,525	2,686	—	—	8,728	—	—	10,977
1860	3,191	29,258	3,965	—	6,611	8,085	8,218	—	8,843	—	—	20,081
1870	4,234	32,034	12,035	—	9,176	16,507	12,733	—	10,588	—	497	30,473
1880	5,204	29,132	22,408	13,003	10,324	32,016	18,892	—	16,713	—	2,105	38,678
1890	5,920	31,076	50,093	55,154	13,426	60,278	32,033	—	21,883	—	3,317	61,220
1900	7,816	38,469	62,139	40,169	19,164	87,565	47,931	—	30,346	—	10,035	85,333
1910	21,262	51,521	86,368	43,973	25,531	112,571	79,803	—	38,136	1,938	15,895	116,577
1920	22,817	60,777	126,468	54,948	38,378	137,634	100,176	—	43,464	4,051	19,861	152,559
1930	48,282	68,202	142,559	75,933	57,899	168,592	134,646	2,600	66,079	20,520	53,569	200,982
1940	62,107	78,720	158,819	81,984	67,447	164,292	142,598	3,958	78,084	31,853	59,319	210,718
1950	98,271	129,009	177,965	98,884	96,056	176,515	152,798	19,676	106,525	71,747	74,389	243,872
1960	144,422	194,856	208,982	128,521	126,706	177,313	190,634	66,972	134,393	128,691	119,574	262,332
1970	153,968	190,026	210,404	149,518	171,809	197,649	204,297	102,452	133,386	149,101	144,076	243,023
1980	202,895	200,452	191,003	171,932	170,616	181,843	195,351	145,254	177,857	174,361	155,642	193,536
1990	196,637	196,278	193,187	191,972	191,262	189,126	188,082	188,004	187,106	186,206	183,521	182,044

(continued)

TABLE Aa832–1033   Population of cities with at least 100,000 population in 1990: 1790–1990   *Continued*

Year	Huntington Beach, CA Aa928 Number	Garland, TX Aa929 Number	Glendale, CA Aa930 Number	Columbus, GA Aa931 Number	Spokane, WA Aa932 Number	Tacoma, WA Aa933 Number	Little Rock, AR Aa934 Number	Bakersfield, CA Aa935 Number	Fremont, CA Aa936 Number	Fort Wayne, IN Aa937 Number	Newport News, VA Aa938 Number	Worcester, MA Aa939 Number
1790	—	—	—	—	—	—	—	—	—	—	—	2,095
1800	—	—	—	—	—	—	—	—	—	—	—	2,411
1810	—	—	—	—	—	—	—	—	—	—	—	2,577
1820	—	—	—	—	—	—	—	—	—	—	—	2,962
1830	—	—	—	—	—	—	—	—	—	—	—	4,173
1840	—	—	—	3,114	—	—	—	—	—	—	—	7,497
1850	—	—	—	5,942	—	—	2,167	—	—	4,282	—	17,049
1860	—	—	—	9,621	—	—	3,727	—	—	9,121	—	24,960
1870	—	—	—	7,401	—	—	12,380	—	—	17,718	—	41,105
1880	—	—	—	10,123	—	—	13,138	—	—	26,880	—	58,291
1890	—	478	—	17,303	19,922	36,006	25,874	2,626	—	35,393	4,449	84,655
1900	—	819	—	17,614	36,848	37,714	38,307	4,836	—	45,115	19,635	118,421
1910	—	804	2,746	20,554	104,402	83,743	45,941	12,727	—	63,933	20,205	145,986
1920	—	1,421	13,536	31,125	104,437	96,965	65,142	18,638	—	86,549	35,596	179,754
1930	3,690	1,584	62,736	43,131	115,514	106,817	81,679	26,015	—	114,946	34,417	195,311
1940	3,738	2,233	82,582	53,280	122,001	109,408	88,039	29,252	—	118,410	37,067	193,694
1950	5,237	10,571	95,702	79,611	161,721	143,673	102,213	34,784	—	133,607	42,358	203,486
1960	11,492	38,501	119,442	116,779	181,608	147,979	107,813	56,848	43,790	161,776	113,662	186,587
1970	115,960	81,437	132,664	155,028	170,516	154,407	132,483	69,515	100,869	178,269	138,177	176,572
1980	170,505	138,857	139,060	170,108	171,300	158,501	159,159	105,611	131,945	172,391	144,903	161,799
1990	181,519	180,650	180,038	179,278	177,196	176,664	175,795	174,820	173,339	173,072	170,045	169,759

Year	Knoxville, TN Aa940 Number	Modesto, CA Aa941 Number	Orlando, FL Aa942 Number	San Bernardino, CA Aa943 Number	Syracuse, NY Aa944 Number	Providence, RI Aa945 Number	Salt Lake City, UT Aa946 Number	Huntsville, AL Aa947 Number	Amarillo, TX Aa948 Number	Springfield, MA Aa949 Number	Irving, TX Aa950 Number	Chattanooga, TN Aa951 Number
1790	—	—	—	—	—	6,380	—	—	—	1,574	—	—
1800	—	—	—	—	—	7,614	—	—	—	2,312	—	—
1810	—	—	—	—	—	10,071	—	—	—	2,767	—	—
1820	—	—	—	—	—	11,767	—	—	—	3,914	—	—
1830	—	—	—	—	—	16,833	—	—	—	6,784	—	—
1840	—	—	—	—	—	23,171	—	—	—	10,985	—	—
1850	2,076	—	—	—	22,271	41,513	—	2,863	—	11,766	—	—
1860	—	—	—	—	28,119	50,666	8,236	3,634	—	15,199	—	—
1870	8,682	—	—	—	43,051	68,904	12,854	4,907	—	26,703	—	6,093
1880	9,693	—	—	1,673	51,792	104,857	20,768	4,977	—	33,340	—	12,892
1890	22,535	2,402	2,856	4,012	88,143	132,146	44,843	7,995	482	44,179	—	29,100
1900	32,637	2,024	2,481	6,150	108,374	175,597	53,531	8,068	1,442	62,059	—	30,154
1910	36,346	4,034	3,894	12,779	137,249	224,326	92,777	7,611	9,957	88,926	—	44,604
1920	77,818	9,241	9,282	18,721	171,717	237,595	118,110	8,018	15,494	129,614	357	57,895
1930	105,802	13,842	27,330	37,481	209,326	252,981	140,267	11,554	43,132	149,900	731	119,798
1940	111,580	16,379	36,736	43,646	205,967	253,504	149,934	13,050	51,686	149,554	1,089	128,613
1950	124,769	17,389	52,367	63,058	220,583	248,674	182,121	16,437	74,246	162,399	2,621	131,041
1960	111,827	36,585	88,135	91,922	216,038	207,498	189,454	72,365	137,969	174,463	45,985	130,009
1970	174,587	61,712	99,006	106,869	197,297	179,116	175,885	139,282	127,010	163,905	97,260	119,923
1980	175,045	106,963	128,291	118,794	170,105	156,804	163,034	142,513	149,230	152,319	109,943	169,514
1990	165,121	164,730	164,693	164,164	163,860	160,728	159,936	159,789	157,615	156,983	155,037	152,466

TABLE Aa832–1033　Population of cities with at least 100,000 population in 1990: 1790–1990　*Continued*

Year	Chesapeake, VA	Kansas City, KS	Fort Lauderdale, FL	Glendale, AZ	Warren, MI	Winston-Salem, NC	Garden Grove, CA	Oxnard, CA	Tempe, AZ	Bridgeport, CT	Paterson, NJ	Flint, MI
	Aa952	Aa953	Aa954	Aa955	Aa956	Aa957	Aa958	Aa959	Aa960	Aa961	Aa962	Aa963
	Number	Number	Number	Number	Number	Number	Number	Number	Number	Number	Number	Number
1790	—	—	—	—	—	—	—	—	—	—	—	—
1800	—	—	—	—	—	—	—	—	—	—	—	—
1810	—	—	—	—	—	—	—	—	—	—	—	—
1820	—	—	—	—	—	—	—	—	—	—	—	—
1830	—	—	—	—	—	—	—	—	—	—	—	—
1840	—	—	—	—	—	—	—	—	—	3,294	7,596	—
1850	—	—	—	—	—	—	—	—	—	6,080	11,334	—
1860	—	—	—	—	—	—	—	—	—	12,106	19,586	2,950
1870	—	—	—	—	—	443	—	—	—	18,969	33,579	5,386
1880	—	3,200	—	—	—	4,194	—	—	—	27,643	51,031	8,409
1890	—	38,316	—	—	—	10,729	—	—	—	48,866	78,347	9,803
1900	—	51,418	—	—	350	13,650	—	—	885	70,996	105,171	13,103
1910	—	82,331	—	—	297	22,700	—	2,555	1,473	102,054	125,600	38,550
1920	—	101,177	2,065	2,737	326	48,395	—	4,417	1,963	143,555	135,875	91,599
1930	—	121,857	8,666	3,665	515	75,274	—	6,285	2,495	146,716	138,513	156,492
1940	—	121,458	17,996	4,855	582	79,815	—	8,519	2,906	147,121	139,656	151,543
1950	—	129,553	36,328	8,179	727	87,811	—	21,567	7,684	158,709	139,336	163,413
1960	—	121,901	83,648	15,893	89,246	111,135	84,238	40,265	24,897	156,748	143,663	196,940
1970	89,580	168,213	139,590	36,228	179,260	133,683	121,155	71,225	63,550	156,542	144,824	193,317
1980	114,486	161,148	153,249	97,172	161,134	131,885	123,307	108,195	106,919	142,546	137,970	159,611
1990	151,976	149,767	149,377	148,134	144,864	143,485	143,050	142,216	141,865	141,686	140,891	140,761

Year	Springfield, MO	Hartford, CT	Rockford, IL	Savannah, GA	Durham, NC	Chula Vista, CA	Reno, NV	Hampton, VA	Ontario, CA	Torrance, CA	Pomona, CA	Pasadena, CA
	Aa964	Aa965	Aa966	Aa967	Aa968	Aa969	Aa970	Aa971	Aa972	Aa973	Aa974	Aa975
	Number	Number	Number	Number	Number	Number	Number	Number	Number	Number	Number	Number
1790	—	2,683	—	—	—	—	—	—	—	—	—	—
1800	—	3,523	—	5,146	—	—	—	—	—	—	—	—
1810	—	3,955	—	5,215	—	—	—	—	—	—	—	—
1820	—	4,726	—	7,523	—	—	—	—	—	—	—	—
1830	—	7,074	—	7,303	—	—	—	—	—	—	—	—
1840	—	9,468	—	11,214	—	—	—	—	—	—	—	—
1850	415	13,555	—	15,312	—	—	—	—	—	—	—	—
1860	—	26,917	6,979	22,292	—	—	—	—	—	—	—	—
1870	5,555	37,180	11,049	28,235	—	—	1,035	—	—	—	—	—
1880	6,522	42,015	13,129	30,709	2,041	—	1,302	—	—	—	—	—
1890	21,850	53,230	23,584	43,189	5,485	—	3,563	2,513	683	—	3,634	4,882
1900	23,267	79,850	31,051	54,244	6,679	—	4,500	2,764	722	—	5,526	9,117
1910	35,201	98,915	45,401	65,064	18,241	—	10,867	5,505	4,274	—	10,207	30,291
1920	39,631	138,036	65,651	83,252	21,719	1,718	12,016	6,138	7,280	—	13,505	45,354
1930	57,527	164,072	85,864	85,024	52,037	3,869	18,529	6,382	13,583	7,271	20,804	76,086
1940	61,238	166,267	84,637	95,996	60,195	5,138	21,317	5,898	14,197	9,950	23,539	81,864
1950	66,731	177,397	92,927	119,638	71,311	15,927	32,497	5,966	22,872	22,241	35,405	104,577
1960	95,865	162,178	126,706	149,245	78,302	42,034	51,470	89,258	46,617	100,991	67,157	116,407
1970	120,096	158,017	147,370	118,349	95,438	67,901	72,863	120,779	64,118	134,968	87,384	112,951
1980	133,116	136,392	139,712	141,654	101,149	83,927	100,756	122,617	88,820	129,881	92,742	118,072
1990	140,494	139,739	139,426	137,560	136,611	135,163	133,850	133,793	133,179	133,107	131,723	131,591

(continued)

TABLE Aa832–1033   Population of cities with at least 100,000 population in 1990: 1790–1990   *Continued*

	New Haven, CT	Scottsdale, AZ	Plano, TX	Oceanside, CA	Lansing, MI	Lakewood, CO	Evansville, IN	Boise City, ID	Tallahassee, FL	Laredo, TX	Hollywood, FL	Topeka, KS
	Aa976	Aa977	Aa978	Aa979	Aa980	Aa981	Aa982	Aa983	Aa984	Aa985	Aa986	Aa987
Year	Number	Number	Number	Number	Number	Number	Number	Number	Number	Number	Number	Number
1790	4,487	—	—	—	—	—	—	—	—	—	—	—
1800	4,049	—	—	—	—	—	—	—	—	—	—	—
1810	5,772	—	—	—	—	—	—	—	—	—	—	—
1820	7,147	—	—	—	—	—	—	—	—	—	—	—
1830	10,180	—	—	—	—	—	—	—	—	—	—	—
1840	12,960	—	—	—	—	—	—	—	1,616	—	—	—
1850	20,345	—	—	—	—	—	3,235	—	—	—	—	—
1860	38,267	—	—	3,074	—	11,484	—	1,932	1,256	—	759
1870	50,840	—	155	—	5,241	—	21,830	995	2,023	2,046	—	5,790
1880	62,882	—	556	—	8,319	—	29,280	1,899	2,494	3,521	—	15,452
1890	86,045	—	842	—	13,102	—	50,756	2,311	2,934	11,319	—	31,007
1900	108,027	—	1,304	330	16,485	—	59,007	5,957	2,981	13,429	—	33,608
1910	133,605	—	1,258	673	31,229	—	69,647	17,358	5,018	14,855	—	43,684
1920	162,537	—	1,715	1,161	57,327	—	85,264	21,393	5,637	22,710	—	50,022
1930	162,655	—	1,554	3,508	78,397	—	102,249	21,554	10,700	32,618	2,869	64,120
1940	160,605	—	1,582	4,651	78,753	—	97,062	26,130	16,240	39,274	6,239	67,833
1950	164,443	—	2,126	12,881	92,129	—	128,636	34,393	27,237	51,910	14,351	78,791
1960	152,048	10,026	3,695	24,971	107,807	—	141,543	34,481	48,174	60,678	35,237	119,484
1970	137,707	67,823	17,872	40,494	131,403	92,743	138,764	74,990	72,624	69,024	106,873	125,011
1980	126,089	88,622	72,331	76,698	130,414	113,808	130,496	102,249	81,548	91,449	121,323	118,690
1990	130,474	130,069	128,713	128,398	127,321	126,481	126,272	125,738	124,773	122,899	121,697	119,883

	Pasadena, TX	Moreno Valley, CA	Sterling Heights, MI	Sunnyvale, CA	Gary, IN	Beaumont, TX	Fullerton, CA	Peoria, IL	Santa Rosa, CA	Eugene, OR	Independence, MO	Overland Park, KS
	Aa988	Aa989	Aa990	Aa991	Aa992	Aa993	Aa994	Aa995	Aa996	Aa997	Aa998	Aa999
Year	Number	Number	Number	Number	Number	Number	Number	Number	Number	Number	Number	Number
1790	—	—	—	—	—	—	—	—	—	—	—	—
1800	—	—	—	—	—	—	—	—	—	—	—	—
1810	—	—	—	—	—	—	—	—	—	—	—	—
1820	—	—	—	—	—	—	—	—	—	—	—	—
1830	—	—	—	—	—	—	—	—	—	—	—	—
1840	—	—	—	—	—	—	—	1,467	—	—	—	—
1850	—	—	—	—	—	—	—	5,095	—	—	—	—
1860	—	—	—	—	—	—	—	14,045	425	—	3,164	—
1870	—	—	—	—	—	—	—	22,849	—	861	3,184	—
1880	—	—	—	—	—	—	—	29,259	3,616	1,117	3,146	—
1890	—	—	—	—	—	3,296	—	41,024	5,220	—	6,380	—
1900	—	—	—	—	—	9,427	—	56,100	6,673	3,236	6,974	—
1910	—	—	—	—	16,802	20,640	1,725	66,950	7,817	9,009	9,859	—
1920	—	—	—	—	55,378	40,422	4,415	76,121	8,758	10,593	11,686	—
1930	1,647	—	—	3,094	100,426	57,732	10,860	104,969	10,636	18,901	15,296	—
1940	3,436	—	—	4,373	111,719	59,061	10,442	105,087	12,605	20,838	16,066	—
1950	22,483	—	—	9,829	133,911	94,014	13,958	111,856	17,902	35,879	36,963	—
1960	58,737	—	—	52,898	178,320	119,175	56,180	103,162	31,027	50,977	62,328	—
1970	89,957	—	61,365	95,976	175,415	117,548	85,987	126,963	50,006	79,028	111,630	77,934
1980	112,560	—	108,999	106,618	151,968	118,102	102,246	124,160	82,658	105,664	111,797	81,784
1990	119,363	118,779	117,810	117,229	116,646	114,323	114,144	113,504	113,313	112,669	112,301	111,790

TABLE Aa832–1033   Population of cities with at least 100,000 population in 1990: 1790–1990   *Continued*

Year	Hayward, CA	Concord, CA	Alexandria, VA	Orange, CA	Santa Clarita, CA	Irvine, CA	Elizabeth, NJ	Inglewood, CA	Ann Arbor, MI	Vallejo, CA	Waterbury, CT	Salinas, CA
	Aa1000	Aa1001	Aa1002	Aa1003	Aa1004	Aa1005	Aa1006	Aa1007	Aa1008	Aa1009	Aa1010	Aa1011
	Number	Number	Number	Number	Number	Number	Number	Number	Number	Number	Number	Number
1790	—	—	2,748	—	—	—	—	—	—	—	—	—
1800	—	—	4,971	—	—	—	—	—	—	—	—	—
1810	—	—	7,227	—	—	—	2,977	—	—	—	—	—
1820	—	—	8,218	—	—	—	3,515	—	—	—	—	—
1830	—	—	8,241	—	—	—	3,455	—	—	—	—	—
1840	—	—	8,459	—	—	—	4,184	—	—	—	—	—
1850	—	—	8,734	—	—	—	5,583	—	—	—	—	—
1860	—	—	12,652	—	—	—	11,567	—	5,097	—	10,004	—
1870	504	—	13,570	—	—	—	20,832	—	7,363	—	10,826	—
1880	1,231	—	13,659	679	—	—	28,229	—	8,061	5,987	17,806	—
1890	1,419	—	14,339	866	—	—	37,764	—	9,431	6,343	28,646	2,339
1900	1,965	—	14,528	1,216	—	—	52,130	—	14,509	7,965	45,859	3,304
1910	2,746	703	15,329	2,920	—	—	73,409	1,536	14,817	11,340	73,141	3,736
1920	3,487	912	18,060	4,884	—	—	95,783	3,286	19,516	21,107	91,715	4,308
1930	5,530	1,125	24,149	8,066	—	—	114,589	19,480	26,944	16,072	99,902	10,263
1940	6,736	1,373	33,523	7,901	—	—	109,912	30,114	29,815	20,072	99,314	11,586
1950	14,272	6,953	61,787	10,027	—	—	112,817	46,185	48,251	26,038	104,477	13,917
1960	72,700	36,000	91,023	26,444	—	—	107,698	63,390	67,340	60,877	107,310	28,957
1970	93,058	85,164	110,927	77,365	—	—	112,654	89,985	100,035	71,710	108,033	58,896
1980	93,585	103,763	103,217	91,450	—	62,134	106,201	94,162	107,969	80,303	103,266	80,479
1990	111,498	111,348	111,183	110,658	110,642	110,330	110,002	109,602	109,592	109,199	108,961	108,777

Year	Cedar Rapids, IA	Erie, PA	Escondido, CA	Stamford, CT	Salem, OR	Abilene, TX	Macon, GA	El Monte, CA	South Bend, IN	Springfield, IL	Allentown, PA	Thousand Oaks, CA
	Aa1012	Aa1013	Aa1014	Aa1015	Aa1016	Aa1017	Aa1018	Aa1019	Aa1020	Aa1021	Aa1022	Aa1023
	Number	Number	Number	Number	Number	Number	Number	Number	Number	Number	Number	Number
1790	—	—	—	—	—	—	—	—	—	—	—	—
1800	—	81	—	—	—	—	—	—	—	—	—	—
1810	—	394	—	—	—	—	—	—	—	—	—	—
1820	—	635	—	—	—	—	—	—	—	—	—	—
1830	—	1,465	—	—	—	—	—	—	—	—	1,544	—
1840	—	3,412	—	—	—	—	3,927	—	—	2,579	2,493	—
1850	—	5,858	—	—	—	—	5,720	—	1,652	4,533	3,779	—
1860	1,830	9,419	—	—	1,139	—	8,247	—	3,832	9,320	8,025	—
1870	5,940	19,646	—	—	1,139	—	10,810	—	7,206	17,364	13,884	—
1880	10,104	27,737	—	2,540	2,538	—	12,749	—	13,280	19,743	18,063	—
1890	18,020	40,634	—	10,396	3,398	3,194	22,746	—	21,819	24,963	25,228	—
1900	26,656	52,733	—	15,997	4,258	3,411	23,272	—	35,999	34,159	35,416	—
1910	32,811	66,525	—	25,138	14,094	9,204	40,665	—	53,684	51,678	51,913	—
1920	45,566	93,372	—	35,096	17,679	10,274	52,995	—	70,983	59,183	73,502	—
1930	56,097	115,967	3,421	46,346	26,266	23,175	53,829	3,479	104,193	71,864	92,563	—
1940	62,120	116,955	4,560	47,938	30,908	26,612	57,865	4,746	101,268	75,503	96,904	—
1950	72,296	130,803	6,544	74,293	43,140	45,570	70,252	8,101	115,911	81,628	106,756	—
1960	92,035	138,440	16,377	92,713	49,142	90,368	69,764	13,163	132,445	83,271	108,347	—
1970	110,642	129,265	36,792	108,798	68,725	89,653	122,423	69,892	125,580	91,753	109,871	35,873
1980	110,243	119,123	64,355	102,466	89,091	98,315	116,896	79,494	109,727	100,054	103,758	77,072
1990	108,751	108,718	108,635	108,056	107,786	106,654	106,612	106,209	105,511	105,227	105,090	104,352

(continued)

TABLE Aa832–1033 Population of cities with at least 100,000 population in 1990: 1790–1990 *Continued*

	Portsmouth, VA	Waco, TX	Lowell, MA	Berkeley, CA	Mesquite, TX	Rancho Cucamonga, CA	Albany, NY	Livonia, MI	Sioux Falls, SD	Simi Valley, CA
	Aa1024	Aa1025	Aa1026	Aa1027	Aa1028	Aa1029	Aa1030	Aa1031	Aa1032	Aa1033
Year	Number	Number	Number	Number	Number	Number	Number	Number	Number	Number
1790	—	—	—	—	—	—	3,498	—	—	—
1800	—	—	—	—	—	—	5,349	—	—	—
1810	—	—	—	—	—	—	10,762	—	—	—
1820	—	—	—	—	—	—	12,630	—	—	—
1830	—	—	6,474	—	—	—	24,209	—	—	—
1840	6,477	—	20,796	—	—	—	33,721	—	—	—
1850	8,326	—	33,383	—	—	—	50,763	—	—	—
1860	9,496	—	36,827	—	—	—	62,367	—	—	—
1870	10,590	3,008	40,928	—	—	—	69,422	—	—	—
1880	11,390	7,295	59,475	—	—	—	90,758	—	2,164	—
1890	13,268	14,445	77,696	5,101	135	—	94,923	—	10,177	—
1900	17,427	20,686	94,969	13,214	406	—	94,151	—	10,266	—
1910	33,190	26,425	106,294	40,434	687	—	100,253	—	14,094	—
1920	54,387	38,500	112,759	56,036	674	—	113,344	—	25,202	—
1930	45,704	52,848	100,234	82,109	729	—	127,412	—	33,362	—
1940	50,745	55,982	101,389	85,547	1,045	—	130,577	—	40,832	—
1950	80,039	84,706	97,249	113,805	1,696	—	134,995	17,534	52,696	—
1960	114,773	97,808	92,107	111,268	27,526	—	129,726	66,702	65,466	—
1970	110,963	95,326	94,239	114,091	55,131	—	115,781	110,109	72,488	59,832
1980	104,577	101,261	92,418	103,328	67,053	55,250	101,727	104,814	81,343	77,500
1990	103,907	103,590	103,439	102,724	101,484	101,409	101,082	100,850	100,814	100,217

Source

U.S. Bureau of the Census, *1990 Census of Population and Housing*, "Population and Housing Unit Counts," CPH-2-1, Table 46.

Documentation

Population is given for 1990 boundaries. Cities are defined as incorporated places.

Series Aa877–878. Series present separate figures for Pittsburgh City and Allegheny City prior to their consolidation in 1907.

TABLE Aa1034–1178 Metropolitan areas – population: 1800–1990 [Part 1]

Contributed by Todd K. Gardner and Michael R. Haines

	New York–Northern New Jersey–Long Island											
	Historically defined metropolitan area											
	Total	Bergen–Passaic, NJ	Bridgeport–Milford, CT	Danbury, CT	Jersey City, NJ	Long Branch–Asbury Park, NJ	Middlesex County, NJ	Middlesex–Somerset–Hunterdon, NJ	Monmouth–Ocean, NJ	Nassau–Suffolk, NY	New Brunswick–Perth Amboy–Sayreville, NJ	New York, NY
	Aa1034	Aa1035	Aa1036	Aa1037	Aa1038	Aa1039	Aa1040	Aa1041	Aa1042	Aa1043	Aa1044	Aa1045
Year	Number	Number	Number	Number	Number	Number	Number	Number	Number	Number	Number	Number
1800	—	—	—	—	—	—	—	—	—	—	—	—
1810	—	—	—	—	—	—	—	—	—	—	—	—
1820	—	—	—	—	—	—	—	—	—	—	—	—
1830	—	—	—	—	—	—	—	—	—	—	—	—
1840	—	—	—	—	—	—	—	—	—	—	—	—
1850	—	—	—	—	—	—	—	—	—	—	—	—
1860	—	—	—	—	—	—	—	—	—	—	—	—
1870	—	—	—	—	—	—	—	—	—	—	—	—
1880	—	—	—	—	—	—	—	—	—	—	—	—
1890	—	—	—	—	—	—	—	—	—	—	—	—
1900	—	—	—	—	—	—	—	—	—	—	—	—
1910	—	—	—	—	—	—	—	—	—	—	—	—
1920	—	—	—	—	—	—	—	—	—	—	—	—
1930	—	—	—	—	—	—	—	—	—	—	—	—
1940	—	—	—	—	—	—	—	—	—	—	—	—
1950	—	—	—	—	—	—	—	—	—	—	—	—
1960	14,759,429	—	—	—	610,734	—	433,856	—	—	—	—	10,694,633
1970	16,178,700	—	—	—	609,266	—	583,813	—	—	—	—	11,571,899
1980	16,121,297	—	—	—	556,972	503,173	—	—	—	2,605,813	595,893	9,120,346
1990	18,087,251	1,278,440	443,722	187,867	553,099	—	—	1,019,835	986,327	2,609,212	—	8,546,846

TABLE Aa1034–1178   Metropolitan areas – population: 1800–1990   [Part 1]   *Continued*

New York–Northern New Jersey–Long Island

	Historically defined metropolitan area						New York–Northeastern New Jersey, NY–NJ	Bridgeport, CT	Stamford, CT	Danbury, CT	Norwalk, CT
	Newark, NJ	Norwalk, CT	Orange County, NY	Paterson–Clifton–Passaic, NJ	Somerset County, NJ	Stamford, CT					
	Aa1046	Aa1047	Aa1048	Aa1049	Aa1050	Aa1051	Aa1052	Aa1053	Aa1054	Aa1055	Aa1056
Year	Number	Number	Number	Number	Number	Number	Number	Number	Number	Number	Number
1800	—	—	—	—	—	—	60,515	—	—	—	—
1810	—	—	—	—	—	—	96,373	—	—	—	—
1820	—	—	—	—	—	—	134,893	—	—	—	—
1830	—	—	—	—	—	—	223,124	—	—	—	—
1840	—	—	—	—	—	—	425,392	—	—	—	—
1850	—	—	—	—	—	—	765,262	—	—	—	—
1860	—	—	—	—	—	—	1,379,050	—	—	—	—
1870	—	—	—	—	—	—	1,887,771	—	—	—	—
1880	—	—	—	—	—	—	2,492,863	—	—	—	—
1890	—	—	—	—	—	—	3,552,190	—	—	—	—
1900	—	—	—	—	—	—	4,882,772	83,159	—	—	—
1910	—	—	—	—	—	—	6,952,909	118,159	—	—	—
1920	—	—	—	—	—	—	8,380,448	172,491	—	—	—
1930	—	—	—	—	—	—	10,859,443	202,956	—	—	—
1940	—	—	—	—	—	—	11,660,839	215,539	—	—	—
1950	—	—	—	—	—	—	12,911,994	258,137	126,895	—	—
1960	1,689,420	—	—	1,186,873	143,913	—	—	334,576	178,409	—	96,756
1970	1,856,556	—	—	1,358,794	198,372	—	—	389,153	206,419	78,405	120,099
1980	1,965,969	126,692	—	447,585	—	198,854	—	395,455	—	146,405	—
1990	1,824,321	127,378	307,647	—	—	202,557	—	—	—	—	—

Los Angeles–Anaheim–Riverside / Chicago–Gary–Lake County

	Historically defined metropolitan area					Los Angeles–Long Beach, CA	San Bernardino–Riverside–Ontario, CA	Anaheim–Santa Ana–Garden Grove, CA	Oxnard–Ventura, CA	Historically defined metropolitan area		
	Total	Anaheim–Santa Ana, CA	Los Angeles–Long Beach, CA	Oxnard–Ventura, CA	Riverside–San Bernardino, CA					Total	Aurora–Elgin, IL	Chicago, IL
	Aa1057	Aa1058	Aa1059	Aa1060	Aa1061	Aa1062	Aa1063	Aa1064	Aa1065	Aa1066	Aa1067	Aa1068
Year	Number	Number	Number	Number	Number	Number	Number	Number	Number	Number	Number	Number
1800	—	—	—	—	—	—	—	—	—	—	—	—
1810	—	—	—	—	—	—	—	—	—	—	—	—
1820	—	—	—	—	—	—	—	—	—	—	—	—
1830	—	—	—	—	—	—	—	—	—	—	—	—
1840	—	—	—	—	—	—	—	—	—	—	—	—
1850	—	—	—	—	—	—	—	—	—	—	—	—
1860	—	—	—	—	—	—	—	—	—	—	—	—
1870	—	—	—	—	—	—	—	—	—	—	—	—
1880	—	—	—	—	—	—	—	—	—	—	—	—
1890	—	—	—	—	—	101,454	—	—	—	—	—	—
1900	—	—	—	—	—	170,298	—	—	—	—	—	—
1910	—	—	—	—	—	504,131	—	—	—	—	—	—
1920	—	—	—	—	—	936,455	—	—	—	—	—	—
1930	—	—	—	—	—	2,327,166	—	—	—	—	—	—
1940	—	—	—	—	—	2,916,403	—	—	—	—	—	—
1950	—	—	—	—	—	4,367,911	281,642	—	—	—	—	—
1960	—	—	—	—	—	6,742,696	809,782	—	—	6,794,461	—	6,220,913
1970	—	—	—	—	—	7,032,075	1,143,146	1,420,386	376,430	7,612,314	—	6,978,947
1980	11,497,568	1,932,709	7,477,503	529,174	1,558,182	—	—	—	—	7,869,542	—	7,103,624
1990	14,531,529	2,410,556	8,863,164	669,016	2,588,793	—	—	—	—	8,065,633	356,884	6,069,974

(continued)

TABLE Aa1034–1178   Metropolitan areas – population: 1800–1990   [Part 1]   *Continued*

	Chicago–Gary–Lake County						San Francisco–Oakland–San Jose				
	Historically defined metropolitan area						Historically defined metropolitan area				
	Gary–Hammond, IN	Joliet, IL	Kenosha, WI	Lake County, IL	Chicago, IL–IN	Kenosha, WI	Total	Oakland, CA	San Francisco, CA	San Francisco–Oakland, CA	San Jose, CA
	Aa1069	Aa1070	Aa1071	Aa1072	Aa1073	Aa1074	Aa1075	Aa1076	Aa1077	Aa1078	Aa1079
Year	Number	Number	Number	Number	Number	Number	Number	Number	Number	Number	Number
1800	—	—	—	—	—	—	—	—	—	—	—
1810	—	—	—	—	—	—	—	—	—	—	—
1820	—	—	—	—	—	—	—	—	—	—	—
1830	—	—	—	—	—	—	—	—	—	—	—
1840	—	—	—	—	—	—	—	—	—	—	—
1850	—	—	—	—	—	—	—	—	—	—	—
1860	—	—	—	—	144,900	—	—	—	—	—	—
1870	—	—	—	—	349,966	—	—	—	—	—	—
1880	—	—	—	—	607,524	—	—	—	—	—	—
1890	—	—	—	—	1,191,922	—	—	—	—	—	—
1900	—	—	—	—	1,911,131	—	—	—	—	—	—
1910	—	—	—	—	2,543,155	—	—	—	—	—	—
1920	—	—	—	—	3,329,379	—	—	—	—	—	—
1930	—	—	—	—	4,439,818	63,277	—	—	—	—	—
1940	—	—	—	—	4,581,111	63,505	—	—	—	—	—
1950	—	—	—	—	5,495,364	75,238	—	—	—	—	—
1960	573,548	—	—	—	—	100,615	—	—	—	—	—
1970	633,367	—	—	—	—	117,917	—	—	—	—	—
1980	642,781	—	123,137	—	—	—	5,179,784	—	—	3,250,630	1,295,071
1990	604,526	389,650	128,181	516,418	—	—	6,253,311	2,082,914	1,603,678	—	1,497,577

	San Francisco–Oakland–San Jose								Philadelphia–Wilmington–Trenton		
	Historically defined metropolitan area								Historically defined metropolitan area		
	Santa Cruz, CA	Santa Rosa–Petaluma, CA	Vallejo–Fairfield–Napa, CA	San Francisco–Oakland, CA	San Jose, CA	Vallejo–Napa, CA	Santa Rosa, CA	Santa Cruz, CA	Total	Philadelphia, PA–NJ	Trenton, NJ
	Aa1080	Aa1081	Aa1082	Aa1083	Aa1084	Aa1085	Aa1086	Aa1087	Aa1088	Aa1089	Aa1090
Year	Number	Number	Number	Number	Number	Number	Number	Number	Number	Number	Number
1800	—	—	—	—	—	—	—	—	—	—	—
1810	—	—	—	—	—	—	—	—	—	—	—
1820	—	—	—	—	—	—	—	—	—	—	—
1830	—	—	—	—	—	—	—	—	—	—	—
1840	—	—	—	—	—	—	—	—	—	—	—
1850	—	—	—	—	—	—	—	—	—	—	—
1860	—	—	—	56,766	—	—	—	—	—	—	—
1870	—	—	—	173,710	—	—	—	—	—	—	—
1880	—	—	—	296,935	—	—	—	—	—	—	—
1890	—	—	—	392,861	—	—	—	—	—	—	—
1900	—	—	—	472,979	—	—	—	—	—	—	—
1910	—	—	—	688,157	—	—	—	—	—	—	—
1920	—	—	—	968,865	—	—	—	—	—	—	—
1930	—	—	—	1,306,938	145,118	—	—	—	—	—	—
1940	—	—	—	1,412,686	174,949	—	—	—	—	—	—
1950	—	—	—	2,240,767	290,547	—	—	—	—	—	—
1960	—	—	—	2,783,359	642,315	—	—	—	—	—	—
1970	—	—	—	3,109,519	1,064,714	249,081	204,885	—	—	—	—
1980	—	299,681	334,402	—	—	—	—	188,141	5,547,902	4,716,818	307,863
1990	229,734	388,222	451,186	—	—	—	—	—	5,899,345	4,856,881	325,824

TABLE Aa1034–1178   Metropolitan areas – population: 1800–1990   [Part 1]   *Continued*

Philadelphia–Wilmington–Trenton

	Historically defined metropolitan area					
Year	Vineland–Millville–Bridgeton, NJ	Wilmington, DE–NJ–MD	Philadelphia, PA–NJ	Trenton, NJ	Vineland–Millville–Bridgeton, NJ	Wilmington, DE–NJ–MD
	Aa1091	Aa1092	Aa1093	Aa1094	Aa1095	Aa1096
	Number	Number	Number	Number	Number	Number
1800	—	—	—	—	—	—
1810	—	—	111,210	—	—	—
1820	—	—	137,097	—	—	—
1830	—	—	188,797	—	—	—
1840	—	—	258,037	—	—	—
1850	—	—	492,475	—	—	—
1860	—	—	670,324	—	—	—
1870	—	—	841,230	—	—	—
1880	—	—	1,062,707	—	—	—
1890	—	—	1,391,152	79,978	—	97,182
1900	—	—	1,693,338	95,365	—	109,697
1910	—	—	2,045,098	125,657	—	123,188
1920	—	—	2,599,151	159,881	—	184,811
1930	—	—	3,010,411	187,143	—	197,866
1940	—	—	3,064,011	197,318	—	221,836
1950	—	—	3,671,048	229,781	—	268,387
1960	—	—	4,342,897	266,392	—	366,157
1970	—	—	4,817,914	303,968	121,374	499,493
1980	—	523,221	—	—	132,866	—
1990	138,053	578,587	—	—	—	—

Detroit–Ann Arbor

	Historically defined metropolitan area					
Year	Total	Ann Arbor, MI	Detroit, MI	Detroit, MI	Pontiac, MI	Ann Arbor, MI
	Aa1097	Aa1098	Aa1099	Aa1100	Aa1101	Aa1102
	Number	Number	Number	Number	Number	Number
1800	—	—	—	—	—	—
1810	—	—	—	—	—	—
1820	—	—	—	—	—	—
1830	—	—	—	—	—	—
1840	—	—	—	—	—	—
1850	—	—	—	—	—	—
1860	—	—	—	—	—	—
1870	—	—	—	119,038	—	—
1880	—	—	—	166,444	—	—
1890	—	—	—	257,114	—	—
1900	—	—	—	348,793	—	—
1910	—	—	—	531,591	—	—
1920	—	—	—	1,177,645	—	—
1930	—	—	—	1,966,092	211,251	—
1940	—	—	—	2,123,261	254,068	—
1950	—	—	—	3,016,197	—	—
1960	—	—	—	3,762,360	—	172,440
1970	—	—	—	4,199,931	—	234,103
1980	4,618,161	264,748	4,353,413	—	—	—
1990	4,665,236	282,937	4,382,299	—	—	—

Boston–Lawrence–Salem

	Historically defined metropolitan area									
Year	Total	Boston, MA	Brockton, MA	Lawrence–Haverhill, MA–NH	Lowell, MA–NH	Nashua, NH	Salem–Gloucester, MA	Boston, MA	Lawrence–Haverhill, MA–NH	Lowell, MA
	Aa1103	Aa1104	Aa1105	Aa1106	Aa1107	Aa1108	Aa1109	Aa1110	Aa1111	Aa1112
	Number	Number	Number	Number	Number	Number	Number	Number	Number	Number
1800	—	—	—	—	—	—	—	—	—	—
1810	—	—	—	—	—	—	—	—	—	—
1820	—	—	—	—	—	—	—	—	—	—
1830	—	—	—	—	—	—	—	92,989	—	—
1840	—	—	—	—	—	—	—	150,950	—	—
1850	—	—	—	—	—	—	—	274,388	—	—
1860	—	—	—	—	—	—	—	398,388	—	—
1870	—	—	—	—	—	—	—	508,861	—	—
1880	—	—	—	—	—	—	—	647,987	—	59,475
1890	—	—	—	—	—	—	—	978,344	—	77,696
1900	—	—	—	—	—	—	—	1,271,287	81,127	105,889
1910	—	—	—	—	—	—	—	1,552,493	110,170	118,515
1920	—	—	—	—	—	—	—	1,799,640	123,992	128,171
1930	—	—	—	—	—	—	—	2,106,093	123,067	125,633
1940	—	—	—	—	—	—	—	2,140,399	124,849	130,999
1950	—	—	—	—	—	—	—	2,369,986	125,935	133,928
1960	—	—	—	—	—	—	—	2,589,301	187,601	157,982
1970	—	—	—	—	—	—	—	2,753,700	232,415	212,860
1980	3,448,122	2,763,357	169,374	281,981	233,410	—	—	—	—	—
1990	4,171,643	2,870,669	189,478	393,516	273,067	180,557	264,356	—	—	—

(continued)

TABLE Aa1034–1178 Metropolitan areas – population: 1800–1990 [Part 1] *Continued*

	Boston–Lawrence–Salem			Dallas–Fort Worth							Houston–Galveston–Brazoria	
				Historically defined metropolitan area							Historically defined metropolitan area	
	Brockton, MA	Nashua, NH	Washington, DC–MD–VA	Total	Dallas, TX	Fort Worth–Arlington, TX	Dallas–Fort Worth, TX	Dallas, TX	Fort Worth, TX	Total	Brazoria, TX
	Aa1113	Aa1114	Aa1115	Aa1116	Aa1117	Aa1118	Aa1119	Aa1120	Aa1121	Aa1122	Aa1123
Year	Number	Number	Number	Number	Number	Number	Number	Number	Number	Number	Number
1800	—	—	—	—	—	—	—	—	—	—	—
1810	—	—	—	—	—	—	—	—	—	—	—
1820	—	—	—	—	—	—	—	—	—	—	—
1830	—	—	—	—	—	—	—	—	—	—	—
1840	—	—	—	—	—	—	—	—	—	—	—
1850	—	—	—	—	—	—	—	—	—	—	—
1860	—	—	73,738	—	—	—	—	—	—	—	—
1870	—	—	125,954	—	—	—	—	—	—	—	—
1880	—	—	195,170	—	—	—	—	—	—	—	—
1890	—	—	248,989	—	—	—	—	—	—	—	—
1900	—	—	299,676	—	—	—	—	—	—	—	—
1910	113,628	—	356,629	—	—	—	—	135,748	108,572	—	—
1920	54,236	—	471,671	—	—	—	—	210,551	152,800	—	—
1930	129,124	—	646,934	—	—	—	—	325,691	197,553	—	—
1940	131,285	—	967,985	—	—	—	—	398,564	225,521	—	—
1950	129,428	—	1,464,089	—	—	—	—	614,799	361,253	—	—
1960	149,458	—	2,001,897	—	—	—	—	1,083,601	573,215	—	—
1970	189,820	66,458	2,861,123	—	—	—	—	1,555,950	762,086	—	—
1980	—	114,221	3,060,922	—	—	—	2,974,805	—	—	3,101,293	—
1990	—	—	3,923,574	3,885,415	2,553,362	1,332,053	—	—	—	3,711,043	191,707

	Houston–Galveston–Brazoria				Miami–Fort Lauderdale					
	Historically defined metropolitan area				Historically defined metropolitan area					
	Galveston–Texas City, TX	Houston, TX	Houston, TX	Galveston–Texas City, TX	Total	Fort Lauderdale–Hollywood–Pompano Beach, FL	Miami–Hialeah, FL	Miami, FL	Fort Lauderdale–Hollywood, FL	Atlanta, GA
	Aa1124	Aa1125	Aa1126	Aa1127	Aa1128	Aa1129	Aa1130	Aa1131	Aa1132	Aa1133
Year	Number	Number	Number	Number	Number	Number	Number	Number	Number	Number
1800	—	—	—	—	—	—	—	—	—	—
1810	—	—	—	—	—	—	—	—	—	—
1820	—	—	—	—	—	—	—	—	—	—
1830	—	—	—	—	—	—	—	—	—	—
1840	—	—	—	—	—	—	—	—	—	—
1850	—	—	—	—	—	—	—	—	—	—
1860	—	—	—	—	—	—	—	—	—	—
1870	—	—	—	—	—	—	—	—	—	—
1880	—	—	—	—	—	—	—	—	—	—
1890	—	—	—	—	—	—	—	—	—	84,655
1900	—	—	—	—	—	—	—	—	—	117,363
1910	—	—	115,693	—	—	—	—	—	—	205,614
1920	—	—	186,667	—	—	—	—	—	—	276,657
1930	—	—	359,328	64,401	—	—	—	142,955	—	388,865
1940	—	—	528,961	81,173	—	—	—	267,739	—	479,828
1950	—	—	806,701	113,066	—	—	—	495,084	—	671,797
1960	—	—	1,243,158	140,364	—	—	—	935,047	333,946	1,017,188
1970	—	—	1,985,031	169,812	—	—	—	1,267,792	620,100	1,390,164
1980	195,940	2,905,353	—	—	2,643,981	1,018,200	1,625,781	—	—	2,029,710
1990	217,399	3,301,937	—	—	3,192,582	1,255,488	1,937,094	—	—	2,833,511

TABLE Aa1034–1178   Metropolitan areas – population: 1800–1990   [Part 1]   *Continued*

	Cleveland–Akron–Lorain							Seattle–Tacoma				
	Historically defined metropolitan area							Historically defined metropolitan area				
	Total	Akron, OH	Cleveland, OH	Lorain–Elyria, OH	Cleveland, OH	Akron, OH	Lorain–Elyria, OH	Total	Seattle, WA	Tacoma, WA	Seattle–Everett, WA	Tacoma, WA
	1134	Aa1135	Aa1136	Aa1137	Aa1138	Aa1139	Aa1140	Aa1141	Aa1142	Aa1143	Aa1144	Aa1145
Year	Number	Number	Number	Number	Number	Number	Number	Number	Number	Number	Number	Number
1800	—	—	—	—	—	—	—	—	—	—	—	—
1810	—	—	—	—	—	—	—	—	—	—	—	—
1820	—	—	—	—	—	—	—	—	—	—	—	—
1830	—	—	—	—	—	—	—	—	—	—	—	—
1840	—	—	—	—	—	—	—	—	—	—	—	—
1850	—	—	—	—	—	—	—	—	—	—	—	—
1860	—	—	—	—	—	—	—	—	—	—	—	—
1870	—	—	—	—	132,010	—	—	—	—	—	—	—
1880	—	—	—	—	196,943	—	—	—	—	—	—	—
1890	—	—	—	—	309,970	—	—	—	—	—	—	—
1900	—	—	—	—	439,120	—	—	—	—	—	110,053	—
1910	—	—	—	—	637,425	108,253	—	—	—	—	284,638	120,812
1920	—	—	—	—	943,495	286,065	—	—	—	—	389,273	144,127
1930	—	—	—	—	1,243,129	344,131	—	—	—	—	463,517	163,842
1940	—	—	—	—	1,267,270	339,405	—	—	—	—	504,980	182,081
1950	—	—	—	—	1,465,511	410,032	148,162	—	—	—	732,992	275,876
1960	—	—	—	—	1,796,595	513,569	217,500	—	—	—	1,107,213	321,590
1970	—	—	—	—	2,064,194	679,239	256,843	—	—	—	1,421,869	411,027
1980	2,834,062	660,328	1,898,825	274,909	—	—	—	2,093,112	1,607,469	485,643	—	—
1990	2,759,823	657,575	1,831,122	271,126	—	—	—	2,559,164	1,972,961	586,203	—	—

	San Diego, CA	Minneapolis– St. Paul, MN–WI	St. Louis, MO–IL	Baltimore, MD	Pittsburgh–Beaver Valley			Pittsburgh, PA	Phoenix, AZ	Tampa–St. Petersburg– Clearwater, FL
					Historically defined metropolitan area					
					Total	Beaver County, PA	Pittsburgh, PA			
	Aa1146	Aa1147	Aa1148	Aa1149	Aa1150	Aa1151	Aa1152	Aa1153	Aa1154	Aa1155
Year	Number	Number	Number	Number	Number	Number	Number	Number	Number	Number
1800	—	—	—	—	—	—	—	—	—	—
1810	—	—	—	—	—	—	—	—	—	—
1820	—	—	—	—	—	—	—	—	—	—
1830	—	—	—	120,870	—	—	—	—	—	—
1840	—	—	—	134,379	—	—	—	—	—	—
1850	—	—	104,978	210,646	—	—	—	138,290	—	—
1860	—	—	190,488	266,445	—	—	—	178,777	—	—
1870	—	—	351,159	330,741	—	—	—	262,204	—	—
1880	—	—	350,518	415,649	—	—	—	355,869	—	—
1890	—	325,090	451,770	507,348	—	—	—	664,778	—	—
1900	—	398,894	661,923	599,712	—	—	—	935,233	—	—
1910	—	557,155	979,163	680,834	—	—	—	1,249,767	—	—
1920	112,248	659,973	1,117,049	808,643	—	—	—	1,570,997	—	88,257
1930	209,659	804,506	1,335,158	929,439	—	—	—	1,818,467	—	153,519
1940	289,348	878,834	1,406,526	1,014,925	—	—	—	1,871,704	186,193	272,000
1950	556,808	1,116,509	1,681,281	1,337,373	—	—	—	2,213,236	331,770	409,143
1960	1,033,011	1,482,030	2,060,103	1,727,023	—	—	—	2,405,435	663,510	772,453
1970	1,357,854	1,813,647	2,363,017	2,070,670	—	—	—	2,401,245	967,522	1,012,594
1980	1,861,846	2,113,533	2,356,460	2,174,023	—	—	—	2,263,894	1,509,052	1,569,134
1990	2,498,016	2,464,124	2,444,099	2,382,172	2,242,798	186,093	2,056,705	—	2,122,101	2,067,959

(continued)

TABLE Aa1034–1178 Metropolitan areas – population: 1800–1990 [Part 1] *Continued*

	Denver–Boulder				Cincinnati–Hamilton					Milwaukee–Racine		
	Historically defined metropolitan area				Historically defined metropolitan area					Historically defined metropolitan area		
	Total	Boulder–Longmont, CO	Denver, CO	Denver–Boulder, CO	Total	Cincinnati, OH–KY–IN	Hamilton–Middletown, OH	Cincinnati, OH–KY–IN	Hamilton–Middletown, OH	Total	Milwaukee, WI	Racine, WI
	Aa1156	Aa1157	Aa1158	Aa1159	Aa1160	Aa1161	Aa1162	Aa1163	Aa1164	Aa1165	Aa1166	Aa1167
Year	Number	Number	Number	Number	Number	Number	Number	Number	Number	Number	Number	Number
1800	—	—	—	—	—	—	—	—	—	—	—	—
1810	—	—	—	—	—	—	—	—	—	—	—	—
1820	—	—	—	—	—	—	—	—	—	—	—	—
1830	—	—	—	—	—	—	—	—	—	—	—	—
1840	—	—	—	—	—	—	—	—	—	—	—	—
1850	—	—	—	—	—	—	—	173,882	—	—	—	—
1860	—	—	—	—	—	—	—	241,787	—	—	—	—
1870	—	—	—	—	—	—	—	323,872	—	—	—	—
1880	—	—	—	—	—	—	—	394,797	—	—	—	—
1890	—	—	—	132,135	—	—	—	472,942	—	—	—	—
1900	—	—	—	153,017	—	—	—	527,293	—	—	—	—
1910	—	—	—	213,381	—	—	—	590,456	—	—	—	—
1920	—	—	—	256,491	—	—	—	628,999	—	—	—	—
1930	—	—	—	332,318	—	—	—	756,281	114,084	—	—	—
1940	—	—	—	385,287	—	—	—	787,044	120,249	—	—	—
1950	—	—	—	563,832	—	—	—	904,402	147,203	—	—	—
1960	—	—	—	929,383	—	—	—	1,071,624	199,076	—	—	—
1970	—	—	—	1,227,529	—	—	—	1,384,851	226,207	—	—	—
1980	—	—	—	1,620,902	1,660,278	1,401,491	258,787	—	—	1,570,275	1,397,143	173,132
1990	1,848,319	225,339	1,622,980	—	1,744,124	1,452,645	291,479	—	—	1,607,183	1,432,149	175,034

	Milwaukee–Racine				Portland–Vancouver						
					Historically defined metropolitan area						
	Milwaukee, WI	Racine, WI	Kansas City, MO–KS	Sacramento, CA	Total	Portland, OR	Vancouver, WA	Portland, OR–WA	Norfolk–Virginia Beach, VA	Newport News–Hampton, VA	Columbus, OH
	Aa1168	Aa1169	Aa1170	Aa1171	Aa1172	Aa1173	Aa1174	Aa1175	Aa1176	Aa1177	Aa1178
Year	Number	Number	Number	Number	Number	Number	Number	Number	Number	Number	Number
1800	—	—	—	—	—	—	—	—	—	—	—
1810	—	—	—	—	—	—	—	—	—	—	—
1820	—	—	—	—	—	—	—	—	—	—	—
1830	—	—	—	—	—	—	—	—	—	—	—
1840	—	—	—	—	—	—	—	—	—	—	—
1850	—	—	—	—	—	—	—	—	—	—	—
1860	—	—	—	—	—	—	—	—	—	—	—
1870	89,930	—	—	—	—	—	—	—	—	—	—
1880	138,537	—	101,468	—	—	—	—	—	—	—	86,797
1890	236,101	—	214,917	—	—	—	—	—	—	—	124,087
1900	330,017	—	268,420	—	—	—	—	103,167	—	—	164,460
1910	433,187	—	383,590	—	—	—	—	226,261	153,386	—	221,567
1920	539,449	78,961	490,064	91,029	—	—	—	275,898	227,522	—	283,951
1930	725,263	90,217	611,665	141,999	—	—	—	384,446	213,353	—	361,055
1940	766,885	94,047	656,226	170,333	—	—	—	462,081	238,943	—	388,712
1950	871,047	109,585	814,357	277,140	—	—	—	704,829	446,200	—	503,410
1960	1,194,290	141,781	1,039,493	502,778	—	—	—	821,897	578,507	224,503	682,962
1970	1,403,688	170,838	1,253,916	800,592	—	—	—	1,009,129	680,600	292,159	916,228
1980	—	—	1,327,106	1,014,002	—	—	—	1,242,594	806,951	364,449	1,093,316
1990	—	—	1,566,280	1,481,102	1,477,895	1,239,842	238,053	—	1,396,107	—	1,377,419

Sources

1800–1940: Todd Gardner, "The Metropolitan Fringe: Suburbanization in the United States before World War II" (Ph.D. dissertation, University of Minnesota, 1998), pp. 269–85.

1950: U.S. Bureau of the Census, *Census of Population: 1950,* volume 2, *Characteristics of the Population* (1953), Table 27, "Population Inside and Outside Central City or Cities of Standard Metropolitan Areas in Continental United States, Hawaii, and Puerto Rico: 1950 and 1940," pp. 1–69 to 1–73.

1960: U.S. Bureau of the Census, *Census of Population: 1960,* volume 1, *Characteristics of the Population* (1961), Table 63, "Summary of Population Characteristics, for Standard Metropolitan Statistical Areas, Urbanized Areas, and Urban Places of 50,000 or More: 1960," pp. 1–176 to 1–178.

1970: U.S. Bureau of the Census, *1970 Census of the Population: Characteristics of the Population, Number of Inhabitants* (1972), Table 32, "Population of Standard Metropolitan Statistical Areas: 1950 to 1970," pp. 1–171 to 1–179.

TABLE Aa1034–1178 Metropolitan areas – population: 1800–1990   [Part 1]   *Continued*

1980: U.S. Bureau of the Census, *1980 Census of the Population: Characteristics of the Population, Number of Inhabitants* (1983), Table 29, "Population of Standard Consolidated Statistical Areas (SCSAs): 1960 to 1980," and Table 30, "Land Area, Population, and Population Density for Standard Metropolitan Statistical Areas (SMSA's): 1960 to 1980," pp. 1–236 to 1–248.

1990: U.S. Bureau of the Census, *1990 Census of Population: General Population Characteristics, Metropolitan Areas* (1992), Table 1, "Summary of General Characteristics of Persons: 1990," pp. 1–29.

Documentation

For 1800 through 1940, the numbers are estimates made by Gardner to be as consistent as possible with the definition of a standard metropolitan area (SMA) adopted in 1950. Thus, the populations of the metropolitan areas will not necessarily agree with the enumerations given at each individual census and reported in Table Aa832–1033. For a full discussion of Gardner's estimation technique, see Todd Gardner, "Metropolitan Classification for Census Years before World War II," *Historical Methods* 32 (3) (1999): 139–50.

For 1950 through 1990, the population is given for the statistical boundaries current at the time of each census. Care should be taken in using these numbers because the boundaries are not necessarily consistent over time either geographically or politically. Subsequent adjustments to account for underenumeration, annexations, separations, and the like have been made from time to time by the Census Bureau. Those adjusted results were published at various times in the *Statistical Abstract of the United States* and other official publications, and these will not agree with the numbers in this table. For concepts and definitions of metropolitan areas, see the text for Table Aa824–831. See also U.S. Bureau of the Census, *Statistical Abstract of the United States, 1997*, Appendix II.

Metropolitan areas are presented in the table in order of population rank in 1990. As an aid to those looking for a specific city or metropolitan area we provide the following index. See Table Ap-E in the Appendix for the state names corresponding to each two-letter abbreviation. Some cities are represented in more than one series because of the changing definitions used at different census dates between 1950 and 1990. For example, Rock Hill, South Carolina, is included as part of the Charlotte–Gastonia–Rock Hill consolidated metropolitan area from 1930 to 1990 (series Aa1187) but is enumerated as a separate entity as well in 1980 (series Aa1470).

Abilene, Texas	Aa1417	
Akron, Ohio	Aa1135	Aa1139
Albany, Georgia	Aa1430	
Albany, New York	Aa1220	Aa1221
Albuquerque, New Mexico	Aa1257	
Alexandria, Louisiana	Aa1392	
Allentown, Pennsylvania	Aa1236	
Altoona, Pennsylvania	Aa1401	
Amarillo, Texas	Aa1346	
Anaheim, California	Aa1058	Aa1064
Anchorage, Alaska	Aa1325	
Anderson, Indiana	Aa1399	
Anderson, South Carolina	Aa1379	
Ann Arbor, Michigan	Aa1098	Aa1102
Anniston, Alabama	Aa1423	
Appleton, Wisconsin	Aa1296	
Arlington, Texas	Aa1118	
Asbury Park, New Jersey	Aa1039	
Asheville, North Carolina	Aa1353	
Ashland, Kentucky	Aa1297	
Athens, Georgia	Aa1364	
Atlanta, Georgia	Aa1133	
Atlantic City, New Jersey	Aa1294	
Attleboro, Rhode Island	Aa1190	
Auburn, Maine	Aa1451	
Augusta, Georgia	Aa1273	
Aurora, Illinois	Aa1067	
Austin, Texas	Aa1226	

Bakersfield, California	Aa1246	
Baltimore, Maryland	Aa1149	
Bangor, Maine	Aa1450	
Baton Rouge, Louisiana	Aa1251	
Battle Creek, Michigan	Aa1387	
Bay City, Michigan	Aa1268	Aa1270
Beaumont, Texas	Aa1284	
Beaver County, Pennsylvania	Aa1151	
Bellingham, Washington	Aa1403	
Beloit, Wisconsin	Aa1385	
Benton Harbor, Michigan	Aa1359	
Bergen, New Jersey	Aa1035	
Bethlehem, Pennsylvania	Aa1236	
Billings, Montana	Aa1428	
Biloxi, Mississippi	Aa1338	
Binghamton, New York	Aa1309	
Birmingham, Alabama	Aa1218	
Bismarck, North Dakota	Aa1455	
Bloomington, Illinois	Aa1402	
Bloomington, Indiana	Aa1433	
Boca Raton, Florida	Aa1224	
Boise City, Idaho	Aa1336	
Boston, Massachusetts	Aa1123	
Bremerton, Washington	Aa1342	
Bridgeport, Connecticut	Aa1036	Aa1053
Bridgeton, New Jersey	Aa1091	Aa1095
Bristol, Connecticut	Aa1196	Aa1202
Bristol, Tennessee	Aa1261	
Bristol, Virginia	Aa1261	
Brockton, Massachusetts	Aa1105	Aa1113
Brownsville, Texas	Aa1311	
Bryan, Texas	Aa1411	
Buffalo, New York	Aa1183	Aa1185
Burlington, North Carolina	Aa1435	
Burlington, Vermont	Aa1394	
Canton, Ohio	Aa1275	
Cape Coral, Florida	Aa1292	
Carlisle, Pennsylvania	Aa1245	
Casper, Wyoming	Aa1465	
Cedar Falls, Iowa	Aa1377	
Cedar Rapids, Iowa	Aa1356	
Champaign, Illinois	Aa1354	
Charleston, South Carolina	Aa1253	
Charleston, West Virginia	Aa1316	
Charlotte, North Carolina	Aa1187	
Charlottesville, Virginia	Aa1396	
Chattanooga, Tennessee	Aa1262	
Cheyenne, Wyoming	Aa1463	
Chicago, Illinois	Aa1068	Aa1073
Chico, California	Aa1349	
Cincinnati, Ohio	Aa1161	Aa1163
Clarksville, Tennessee	Aa1355	
Clearwater, Florida	Aa1155	
Cleveland, Ohio	Aa1136	Aa1138
Clifton, New Jersey	Aa1049	
College Station, Texas	Aa1411	
Colonial Heights, Virginia	Aa1469	
Colorado Springs, Colorado	Aa1272	
Columbia, Missouri	Aa1431	
Columbia, South Carolina	Aa1259	
Columbus, Georgia	Aa1318	
Columbus, Ohio	Aa1178	
Concord, North Carolina	Aa1468	
Corpus Christi, Texas	Aa1287	
Cumberland, Maryland	Aa1441	

(continued)

TABLE Aa1034–1178   Metropolitan areas – population: 1800–1990   [Part 1]   *Continued*

Dallas, Texas	Aa1117	Aa1119	Aa1120	Green Bay, Wisconsin	Aa1340		
Danbury, Connecticut	Aa1037	Aa1055		Greensboro, North Carolina	Aa1215	Aa1216	
Danville, Virginia	Aa1434			Greenville, South Carolina	Aa1240		
Davenport, Iowa	Aa1286			Gulfport, Mississippi	Aa1338		
Dayton, Ohio	Aa1212	Aa1213					
Daytona Beach, Florida	Aa1278			Hagerstown, Maryland	Aa1412		
Decatur, Alabama	Aa1393			Hamilton, Ohio	Aa1162	Aa1164	
Decatur, Illinois	Aa1421			Hammond, Indiana	Aa1069		
Delray Beach, Florida	Aa1224			Hampton, Virginia	Aa1177		
Denison, Texas	Aa1449			Harlingen, Texas	Aa1311		
Denver, Colorado	Aa1158	Aa1159		Harrisburg, Pennsylvania	Aa1245		
Des Moines, Iowa	Aa1276			Hartford, Connecticut	Aa1197	Aa1200	
Detroit, Michigan	Aa1099	Aa1100		Haverhill, Massachusetts	Aa1106	Aa1111	
Dothan, Alabama	Aa1397			Hazleton, Pennsylvania	Aa1233		
Dover, New Hampshire	Aa1327			Hialeah, Florida	Aa1130		
Dubuque, Iowa	Aa1453			Hickory, North Carolina	Aa1330		
Duluth, Minnesota	Aa1322			High Point, North Carolina	Aa1215	Aa1216	
Dunkirk, New York	Aa1384			Hollywood, Florida	Aa1129	Aa1132	
Durham, North Carolina	Aa1228	Aa1230		Honolulu, Hawai'i	Aa1225		
				Hopewell, Virginia	Aa1469		
East Lansing, Michigan	Aa1263			Hopkinsville, Kentucky	Aa1355		
Easton, Pennsylvania	Aa1236			Houma, Louisiana	Aa1348		
Eau Claire, Wisconsin	Aa1386			Houston, Texas	Aa1125	Aa1126	
Edinburg, Texas	Aa1277			Hunterdon, New Jersey	Aa1041		
El Paso, Texas	Aa1244			Huntington, West Virginia	Aa1297		
Elgin, Illinois	Aa1067			Huntsville, Alabama	Aa1323		
Elkhart, Indiana	Aa1365						
Elmira, New York	Aa1448			Indianapolis, Indiana	Aa1180		
Elyria, Ohio	Aa1137	Aa1140		Iowa City, Iowa	Aa1447		
Enid, Oklahoma	Aa1466						
Erie, Pennsylvania	Aa1306			Jackson, Michigan	Aa1373		
Eugene, Oregon	Aa1301			Jackson, Mississippi	Aa1274		
Evansville, Indiana	Aa1303			Jackson, Tennessee	Aa1460		
Everett, Washington	Aa1144			Jacksonville, Florida	Aa1219		
				Jacksonville, North Carolina	Aa1372		
Fairfield, California	Aa1082			Jamestown, New York	Aa1384		
Fall River, Massachusetts	Aa1189	Aa1194		Janesville, Wisconsin	Aa1385		
Fargo, North Dakota	Aa1367			Jersey City, New Jersey	Aa1038		
Fayette, Kentucky	Aa1288			Johnson City, Tennessee	Aa1261		
Fayetteville, Arkansas	Aa1429			Johnstown, Pennsylvania	Aa1320		
Fayetteville, North Carolina	Aa1307			Joliet, Illinois	Aa1070		
Fitchburg, Massachusetts	Aa1440			Joplin, Missouri	Aa1389		
Flint, Michigan	Aa1264						
Florence, Alabama	Aa1395			Kalamazoo, Michigan	Aa1328		
Florence, South Carolina	Aa1427			Kankakee, Illinois	Aa1446		
Fort Collins, Colorado	Aa1347			Kansas City, Kansas	Aa1170		
Fort Lauderdale, Florida	Aa1129	Aa1132		Kansas City, Missouri	Aa1170		
Fort Myers, Florida	Aa1292			Kennewick, Washington	Aa1371		
Fort Pierce, Florida	Aa1315			Kenosha, Wisconsin	Aa1071	Aa1074	
Fort Smith, Arkansas	Aa1351			Killeen, Texas	Aa1313		
Fort Walton Beach, Florida	Aa1380			Kingsport, Tennessee	Aa1261		
Fort Wayne, Indiana	Aa1282			Knoxville, Tennessee	Aa1243		
Fort Worth, Texas	Aa1118	Aa1119	Aa1121	Kokomo, Indiana	Aa1445		
Fresno, California	Aa1237						
				La Crosse, Wisconsin	Aa1444		
Gadsden, Alabama	Aa1442			Lafayette, Indiana	Aa1400		
Gainesville, Florida	Aa1337			Lafayette, Louisiana	Aa1335		
Galveston, Texas	Aa1124	Aa1127		Lake Charles, Louisiana	Aa1357		
Garden Grove, California	Aa1064			Lake County, Illinois	Aa1072		
Gary, Indiana	Aa1069			Lakeland, Florida	Aa1267		
Gastonia, North Carolina	Aa1187			Lancaster, Pennsylvania	Aa1265		
Glens Falls, New York	Aa1420			Lansing, Michigan	Aa1263		
Gloucester, Massachusetts	Aa1109			Laredo, Texas	Aa1390		
Goshen, Indiana	Aa1365			Las Cruces, New Mexico	Aa1388		
Grand Forks, North Dakota	Aa1464			Las Vegas, Nevada	Aa1227		
Grand Rapids, Michigan	Aa1235			Lawrence, Kansas	Aa1457		
Great Falls, Montana	Aa1461			Lawrence, Massachusetts	Aa1106	Aa1111	
Greeley, Colorado	Aa1391			Lawton, Oklahoma	Aa1432		
				Lebanon, Pennsylvania	Aa1245		

TABLE Aa1034–1178   Metropolitan areas – population: 1800–1990   [Part 1]   *Continued*

Leominster, Massachusetts	Aa1440		
Lewiston, Maine	Aa1451		
Lexington, Kentucky	Aa1288		
Lima, Ohio	Aa1366		
Lincoln, Nebraska	Aa1333		
Little Rock, Arkansas	Aa1252		
Lompoc, California	Aa1280		
Long Beach, California	Aa1059	Aa1062	
Long Branch, New Jersey	Aa1039		
Longmont, Colorado	Aa1157		
Longview, Texas	Aa1358		
Lorain, Ohio	Aa1137	Aa1140	
Los Angeles, California	Aa1059	Aa1062	
Louisville, Kentucky	Aa1211		
Loveland, Colorado	Aa1347		
Lowell, Massachusetts	Aa1107	Aa1112	
Lubbock, Texas	Aa1329		
Lynchburg, Virginia	Aa1382		
Macon, Georgia	Aa1302		
Madison, Wisconsin	Aa1281		
Manchester, New Hampshire	Aa1375		
Mansfield, Ohio	Aa1405		
Marietta, Ohio	Aa1374		
Marshall, Texas	Aa1358		
McAllen, Texas	Aa1277		
Medford, Oregon	Aa1378		
Melbourne, Florida	Aa1271		
Memphis, Tennessee	Aa1209		
Merced, California	Aa1350		
Meriden, Connecticut	Aa1247	Aa1249	
Miami, Florida	Aa1130	Aa1131	
Middlesex, New Jersey	Aa1040	Aa1041	
Middletown, Connecticut	Aa1198		
Middletown, New York	Aa1467		
Middletown, Ohio	Aa1162	Aa1164	
Midland, Michigan	Aa1268		
Midland, Texas	Aa1437		
Milford, Connecticut	Aa1036		
Millville, New Jersey	Aa1091	Aa1095	
Milwaukee, Wisconsin	Aa1166	Aa1168	
Minneapolis, Minnesota	Aa1147		
Mishawaka, Indiana	Aa1317		
Mission, Texas	Aa1277		
Mobile, Alabama	Aa1258		
Modesto, California	Aa1279		
Moline, Illinois	Aa1286		
Monmouth, New Jersey	Aa1042		
Monroe, Louisiana	Aa1383		
Monterey, California	Aa1285		
Montgomery, Alabama	Aa1299		
Moorhead, Minnesota	Aa1367		
Morgantown, North Carolina	Aa1330		
Muncie, Indiana	Aa1416		
Muskegon, Michigan	Aa1363		
Napa, California	Aa1082	Aa1085	
Naples, Florida	Aa1368		
Nashua, New Hampshire	Aa1108	Aa1114	
Nashville, Tennessee	Aa1208		
Nassau, New York	Aa1043		
Neenah, Wisconsin	Aa1296		
New Bedford, Massachusetts	Aa1352		
New Britain, Connecticut	Aa1199	Aa1201	
New Brunswick, New Jersey	Aa1044		
New Haven, Connecticut	Aa1247	Aa1248	
New London, Connecticut	Aa1308		
New Orleans, Louisiana	Aa1181		
New York, New York	Aa1045	Aa1052	
Newark, New Jersey	Aa1046		
Newburgh, New York	Aa1467		
Newport News, Virginia	Aa1177		
Niagara Falls, New York	Aa1184	Aa1186	
Norfolk, Virginia	Aa1176		
Normal, Illinois	Aa1402		
North Little Rock, Arkansas	Aa1252		
Norwalk, Connecticut	Aa1047	Aa1056	
Norwich, Rhode Island	Aa1308		
Oakland, California	Aa1076	Aa1078	Aa1083
Ocala, Florida	Aa1339		
Ocean, New Jersey	Aa1042		
Odessa, Texas	Aa1418		
Ogden, Utah	Aa1204	Aa1206	
Oklahoma City, Oklahoma	Aa1210		
Olympia, Washington	Aa1360		
Omaha, Nebraska	Aa1241		
Ontario, California	Aa1063		
Orange County, New York	Aa1048		
Orem, Utah	Aa1310		
Orlando, Florida	Aa1203		
Oshkosh, Wisconsin	Aa1296		
Owensboro, Kentucky	Aa1452		
Oxnard, California	Aa1060	Aa1065	
Palm Bay, Florida	Aa1271		
Panama City, Florida	Aa1404		
Parkersburg, West Virginia	Aa1374		
Pascagoula, Mississippi	Aa1425		
Pasco, Washington	Aa1371		
Passaic, New Jersey	Aa1035	Aa1049	
Paterson, New Jersey	Aa1049		
Pawtucket, Rhode Island	Aa1190	Aa1192	Aa1193
Pensacola, Florida	Aa1289		
Peoria, Illinois	Aa1290		
Perth Amboy, New Jersey	Aa1044		
Petaluma, California	Aa1081		
Petersburg, Virginia	Aa1223	Aa1469	
Philadelphia, Pennsylvania	Aa1089	Aa1093	
Phoenix, Arizona	Aa1154		
Pine Bluff, Arkansas	Aa1454		
Pittsburgh, Pennsylvania	Aa1152	Aa1153	
Pittsfield, Massachusetts	Aa1459		
Pompano Beach, Florida	Aa1129		
Pontiac, Michigan	Aa1101		
Port Arthur, Texas	Aa1284		
Porterville, California	Aa1298		
Portland, Maine	Aa1332		
Portland, Oregon	Aa1173	Aa1175	
Portsmouth, New Hampshire	Aa1327		
Poughkeepsie, New York	Aa1312		
Providence, Rhode Island	Aa1191	Aa1192	Aa1193
Provo, Utah	Aa1310		
Pueblo, Colorado	Aa1408		
Racine, Wisconsin	Aa1167	Aa1169	
Raleigh, North Carolina	Aa1228	Aa1229	
Rantoul, Illinois	Aa1354		
Rapid City, South Dakota	Aa1458		
Reading, Pennsylvania	Aa1291		
Redding, California	Aa1376		
Reno, Nevada	Aa1314		
Richland, Washington	Aa1371		
Richmond, Virginia	Aa1223		
Riverside, California	Aa1061	Aa1063	

(continued)

TABLE Aa1034–1178   Metropolitan areas – population: 1800–1990   [Part 1]   *Continued*

Roanoke, Virginia	Aa1326			Superior, Wisconsin	Aa1322	
Rochester, Maine	Aa1327			Syracuse, New York	Aa1239	
Rochester, Minnesota	Aa1438					
Rochester, New York	Aa1207			Tacoma, Washington	Aa1143	Aa1145
Rock Hill, South Carolina	Aa1187	Aa1470		Tallahassee, Florida	Aa1324	
Rock Island, Illinois	Aa1286			Tampa, Florida	Aa1155	
Rockford, Illinois	Aa1300			Temple, Texas	Aa1313	
Rome, New York	Aa1295			Terre Haute, Indiana	Aa1398	
				Texarkana, Arkansas	Aa1415	
Sacramento, California	Aa1171			Texarkana, Texas	Aa1415	
Saginaw, Michigan	Aa1268	Aa1269		Texas City, Texas	Aa1124	Aa1127
Salem, Massachusetts	Aa1109			Thibodaux, Louisiana	Aa1348	
Salem, Oregon	Aa1304			Titusville, Florida	Aa1271	
Salinas, California	Aa1285			Toledo, Ohio	Aa1242	
Salisbury, North Carolina	Aa1468			Topeka, Kansas	Aa1361	
Salt Lake City, Utah	Aa1204	Aa1205		Trenton, New Jersey	Aa1090	Aa1094
San Angelo, Texas	Aa1443			Troy, New York	Aa1220	Aa1221
San Antonio, Texas	Aa1179			Tucson, Arizona	Aa1238	
San Bernardino, California	Aa1061	Aa1063		Tulare, California	Aa1298	
San Diego, California	Aa1146			Tulsa, Oklahoma	Aa1234	
San Francisco, California	Aa1077	Aa1078	Aa1083	Tuscaloosa, Alabama	Aa1370	
San Jose, California	Aa1079	Aa1084		Tyler, Texas	Aa1369	
Santa Ana, California	Aa1058	Aa1064				
Santa Barbara, California	Aa1280			Urbana, Illinois	Aa1354	
Santa Cruz, California	Aa1080	Aa1087		Utica, New York	Aa1295	
Santa Fe, New Mexico	Aa1422					
Santa Maria, California	Aa1280			Vallejo, California	Aa1082	Aa1085
Santa Rosa, California	Aa1081	Aa1086		Vancouver, Washington	Aa1174	
Sarasota, Florida	Aa1305			Ventura, California	Aa1060	Aa1065
Savannah, Georgia	Aa1319			Victoria, Texas	Aa1462	
Sayreville, New Jersey	Aa1044			Vineland, New Jersey	Aa1091	Aa1095
Schenectady, New York	Aa1220	Aa1222		Virginia Beach, Virginia	Aa1176	
Scranton, Pennsylvania	Aa1231	Aa1232		Visalia, California	Aa1298	
Seaside, California	Aa1285					
Seattle, Washington	Aa1142	Aa1144		Waco, Texas	Aa1344	
Sharon, Pennsylvania	Aa1413			Warner Robins, Georgia	Aa1302	
Sheboygan, Wisconsin	Aa1439			Warren, Ohio	Aa1254	
Sherman, Texas	Aa1449			Warwick, Rhode Island	Aa1192	Aa1193
Shreveport, Louisiana	Aa1293			Washington, District of Columbia	Aa1115	
Sioux City, Iowa	Aa1426			Waterbury, Connecticut	Aa1331	
Sioux Falls, South Dakota	Aa1406			Waterloo, Iowa	Aa1377	
Somerset, New Jersey	Aa1041	Aa1050		Wausau, Wisconsin	Aa1424	
South Bend, Indiana	Aa1317			Weirton, West Virginia	Aa1381	
Spartanburg, South Carolina	Aa1240			West Haven, Connecticut	Aa1248	
Spokane, Washington	Aa1283			West Lafayette, Indiana	Aa1400	
Springdale, Arkansas	Aa1429			West Palm Beach, Florida	Aa1224	
Springfield, Illinois	Aa1343			Wheeling, West Virginia	Aa1362	
Springfield, Massachusetts	Aa1250			Wichita Falls, Texas	Aa1410	
Springfield, Missouri	Aa1321			Wichita, Kansas	Aa1255	
Springfield, Ohio	Aa1212	Aa1214		Wilkes-Barre, Pennsylvania	Aa1231	Aa1233
Springfield, Oregon	Aa1301			Williamsport, Pennsylvania	Aa1419	
St. Cloud, Minnesota	Aa1341			Wilmington, Delaware	Aa1092	Aa1096
St. Joseph, Missouri	Aa1456			Wilmington, North Carolina	Aa1414	
St. Louis, Missouri	Aa1148			Winston-Salem, North Carolina	Aa1215	Aa1217
St. Paul, Minnesota	Aa1147			Winter Haven, Florida	Aa1267	
St. Petersburg, Florida	Aa1155			Woonsocket, Rhode Island	Aa1190	
Stamford, Connecticut	Aa1051	Aa1054		Worcester, Massachusetts	Aa1260	
State College, Pennsylvania	Aa1407					
Steubenville, Ohio	Aa1381			Yakima, Washington	Aa1345	
Stockton, California	Aa1256			York, Pennsylvania	Aa1266	
Suffolk, New York	Aa1043			Youngstown, Ohio	Aa1254	
				Yuba City, California	Aa1409	
				Yuma, Arizona	Aa1436	

TABLE Aa1179–1322   Metropolitan areas – population: 1840–1990   [Part 2]

Contributed by Todd K. Gardner and Michael R. Haines

			Buffalo–Niagara Falls					Charlotte–Gastonia–Rock Hill, NC–SC
			Historically defined metropolitan area					
	San Antonio, TX	Indianapolis, IN	New Orleans, LA	Total	Buffalo, NY	Niagara Falls, NY	Buffalo, NY	Niagara Falls, NY	
	Aa1179	Aa1180	Aa1181	Aa1182	Aa1183	Aa1184	Aa1185	Aa1186	Aa1187
Year	Number	Number	Number	Number	Number	Number	Number	Number	Number
1840	—	—	102,193	—	—	—	—	—	—
1850	—	—	144,553	—	—	—	—	—	—
1860	—	—	174,455	—	—	—	141,917	—	—
1870	—	—	191,418	—	—	—	178,699	—	—
1880	—	102,782	228,256	—	—	—	219,884	—	—
1890	—	141,156	255,260	—	—	—	322,981	—	—
1900	69,422	197,227	287,104	—	—	—	433,686	—	—
1910	119,676	263,661	339,075	—	—	—	528,985	—	—
1920	202,096	348,061	387,219	—	—	—	634,688	118,705	—
1930	292,533	422,666	498,794	—	—	—	762,408	149,329	127,971
1940	338,176	460,926	544,964	—	—	—	798,377	160,110	151,826
1950	500,460	551,777	685,405	—	—	—	1,089,230	—	197,052
1960	687,151	697,567	868,480	—	—	—	1,306,957	—	272,111
1970	864,014	1,109,882	1,045,809	—	—	—	1,349,211	—	409,370
1980	1,071,954	1,166,575	1,187,073	—	—	—	1,242,826	—	637,218
1990	1,302,099	1,249,822	1,238,816	1,189,288	968,532	220,756	—	—	1,162,093

Providence–Pawtucket–Fall River

	Historically defined metropolitan area						
	Total	Fall River, MA–RI	Pawtucket–Woonsocket–Attleboro, RI–MA	Providence, RI	Providence–Warwick–Pawtucket, RI	Providence–Pawtucket–Warwick, RI–MA	Fall River, MA–RI
	Aa1188	Aa1189	Aa1190	Aa1191	Aa1192	Aa1193	Aa1194
Year	Number	Number	Number	Number	Number	Number	Number
1840	—	—	—	—	—	—	—
1850	—	—	—	—	—	—	—
1860	—	—	—	—	—	94,321	—
1870	—	—	—	—	—	132,584	—
1880	—	—	—	—	—	199,881	—
1890	—	—	—	—	—	263,227	76,504
1900	—	—	—	—	—	339,482	107,104
1910	—	—	—	—	—	440,319	122,093
1920	—	—	—	—	—	498,604	124,005
1930	—	—	—	—	—	580,462	129,191
1940	—	—	—	—	—	596,117	131,003
1950	—	—	—	—	—	737,203	137,298
1960	—	—	—	—	—	816,148	138,156
1970	—	—	—	—	—	910,781	149,976
1980	1,096,047	176,831	—	—	919,216	—	—
1990	1,141,510	157,272	329,384	654,854	—	—	—

(continued)

TABLE Aa1179–1322   Metropolitan areas – population: 1840–1990   [Part 2]   *Continued*

	Hartford–New Britain–Middletown								Orlando, FL	Salt Lake City–Ogden			Rochester, NY
	Historically defined metropolitan area				Hartford, CT	New Britain, CT	Bristol, CT		Salt Lake City–Ogden, UT	Salt Lake City, UT	Ogden, UT	
	Total	Bristol, CT	Hartford, CT	Middletown, CT	New Britain, CT								
	Aa1195	Aa1196	Aa1197	Aa1198	Aa1199	Aa1200	Aa1201	Aa1202	Aa1203	Aa1204	Aa1205	Aa1206	Aa1207
Year	Number	Number	Number	Number	Number	Number	Number	Number	Number	Number	Number	Number	Number
1840	—	—	—	—	—	—	—	—	—	—	—	—	—
1850	—	—	—	—	—	—	—	—	—	—	—	—	—
1860	—	—	—	—	—	—	—	—	—	—	—	—	—
1870	—	—	—	—	—	—	—	—	—	—	—	—	117,868
1880	—	—	—	—	—	—	—	—	—	—	—	—	144,903
1890	—	—	—	—	—	68,178	—	—	—	—	—	—	189,586
1900	—	—	—	—	—	102,680	—	—	—	—	77,725	—	217,854
1910	—	—	—	—	—	128,650	—	—	—	—	131,426	—	283,212
1920	—	—	—	—	—	190,424	78,549	—	—	—	159,282	—	352,034
1930	—	—	—	—	—	247,986	93,113	—	—	—	194,102	—	423,881
1940	—	—	—	—	—	273,504	95,948	—	—	—	211,623	—	438,230
1950	—	—	—	—	—	358,081	111,022	—	114,950	—	274,895	83,319	487,632
1960	—	—	—	—	—	525,207	129,397	—	318,487	—	383,035	110,744	586,387
1970	—	—	—	—	—	663,891	145,269	65,808	428,003	—	557,635	126,278	882,667
1980	—	—	—	—	—	726,114	142,241	73,762	700,055	936,255	—	—	971,230
1990	1,085,837	79,488	767,841	90,320	148,188	—	—	—	1,072,748	1,072,227	—	—	1,002,410

	Nashville, TN	Memphis, TN-AR-MS	Oklahoma City, OK	Louisville, KY-IN	Dayton–Springfield			Greensboro–Winston-Salem–High Point		
					Dayton–Springfield, OH	Dayton, OH	Springfield, OH	Greensboro–Winston-Salem–High Point, NC	Greensboro–High Point, NC	Winston-Salem, NC
	Aa1208	Aa1209	Aa1210	Aa1211	Aa1212	Aa1213	Aa1214	Aa1215	Aa1216	Aa1217
Year	Number	Number	Number	Number	Number	Number	Number	Number	Number	Number
1840	—	—	—	—	—	—	—	—	—	—
1850	—	—	—	—	—	—	—	—	—	—
1860	—	—	—	129,945	—	—	—	—	—	—
1870	—	—	—	167,023	—	—	—	—	—	—
1880	—	—	—	199,210	—	—	—	—	—	—
1890	108,174	112,740	—	248,315	—	100,852	—	—	—	—
1900	122,815	153,557	—	294,502	—	130,146	—	—	—	—
1910	149,478	191,439	85,232	323,473	—	163,763	—	—	—	—
1920	167,815	223,216	116,307	346,411	—	209,532	80,728	—	—	—
1930	222,854	306,482	221,738	420,769	—	273,481	90,936	—	133,010	111,681
1940	257,267	358,250	244,159	451,473	—	295,480	95,647	—	153,916	126,475
1950	321,758	482,393	325,352	576,900	—	457,333	111,661	—	191,057	146,135
1960	399,743	627,019	511,833	725,139	—	694,623	131,440	—	246,520	189,428
1970	541,108	770,120	640,889	826,553	—	850,266	157,115	603,895	—	—
1980	850,505	913,472	834,088	906,152	1,013,955	—	—	827,252	—	—
1990	985,026	981,747	958,839	952,662	951,270	—	—	942,091	—	—

TABLE Aa1179–1322   Metropolitan areas – population: 1840–1990   [Part 2]   *Continued*

	Birmingham, AL	Jacksonville, FL	Albany–Schenectady–Troy			Richmond–Petersburg, VA	West Palm Beach–Boca Raton–Delray Beach, FL	Honolulu, HI	Austin, TX	Las Vegas, NV
			Albany–Schenectady–Troy, NY	Albany–Troy, NY	Schenectady, NY					
	Aa1218	Aa1219	Aa1220	Aa1221	Aa1222	Aa1223	Aa1224	Aa1225	Aa1226	Aa1227
Year	Number	Number	Number	Number	Number	Number	Number	Number	Number	Number
1840	—	—	—	—	—	—	—	—	—	—
1850	—	—	—	166,642	—	—	—	—	—	—
1860	—	—	—	200,137	—	—	—	—	—	—
1870	—	—	—	232,601	—	66,179	—	—	—	—
1880	—	—	—	270,218	—	107,788	—	—	—	—
1890	—	—	—	289,066	—	129,605	—	—	—	—
1900	—	—	—	287,268	—	133,916	—	—	—	—
1910	226,476	75,163	—	295,942	88,235	151,065	—	—	—	—
1920	310,054	113,540	—	299,235	109,363	171,667	—	—	—	—
1930	431,493	155,503	—	331,734	125,021	239,288	—	—	77,777	—
1940	459,930	210,143	—	343,149	122,494	266,185	—	—	111,053	—
1950	558,928	304,029	514,490	—	—	328,050	—	—	160,980	—
1960	634,864	455,411	657,503	—	—	408,494	228,106	500,409	212,136	127,016
1970	739,274	528,865	721,910	—	—	518,319	348,753	629,176	295,516	273,288
1980	847,487	737,541	795,019	—	—	632,015	576,863	762,565	536,688	463,087
1990	907,810	906,727	874,304	—	—	865,640	863,518	836,231	781,572	741,459

	Raleigh–Durham			Scranton–Wilkes-Barre			Tulsa, OK	Grand Rapids, MI	Allentown–Bethlehem–Easton, PA–NJ	Fresno, CA
	Raleigh–Durham, NC	Raleigh, NC	Durham, NC	Scranton–Wilkes-Barre, PA	Scranton, PA	Wilkes-Barre–Hazleton, PA				
	Aa1228	Aa1229	Aa1230	Aa1231	Aa1232	Aa1233	Aa1234	Aa1235	Aa1236	Aa1237
Year	Number	Number	Number	Number	Number	Number	Number	Number	Number	Number
1840	—	—	—	—	—	—	—	—	—	—
1850	—	—	—	—	—	—	—	—	—	—
1860	—	—	—	—	—	—	—	—	—	—
1870	—	—	—	—	—	—	—	—	—	—
1880	—	—	—	—	—	—	—	—	—	—
1890	—	—	—	—	142,088	—	—	109,922	—	—
1900	—	—	—	—	193,831	257,121	—	129,714	—	—
1910	—	—	—	—	259,570	343,186	—	159,145	246,499	—
1920	—	—	—	—	286,311	390,991	109,023	183,041	301,607	—
1930	—	—	67,196	—	310,397	445,109	187,574	240,511	342,197	144,379
1940	—	—	80,244	—	301,243	441,518	193,363	246,338	346,492	178,565
1950	—	136,450	101,639	—	257,396	392,241	251,686	288,292	437,824	276,515
1960	—	169,082	111,995	—	234,531	346,972	418,974	363,187	492,168	365,945
1970	—	228,453	190,388	—	234,107	342,301	476,945	539,225	543,551	413,053
1980	531,167	—	—	640,396	—	—	689,434	601,680	635,481	514,621
1990	735,480	—	—	734,175	—	—	708,954	688,399	686,688	667,490

(continued)

TABLE Aa1179–1322   Metropolitan areas – population: 1840–1990   [Part 2]   *Continued*

Year	Tucson, AZ	Syracuse, NY	Greenville–Spartanburg, SC	Omaha, NE–IA	Toledo, OH	Knoxville, TN	El Paso, TX	Harrisburg–Lebanon–Carlisle, PA	Bakersfield, CA
	Aa1238	Aa1239	Aa1240	Aa1241	Aa1242	Aa1243	Aa1244	Aa1245	Aa1246
	Number	Number	Number	Number	Number	Number	Number	Number	Number
1840	—	—	—	—	—	—	—	—	—
1850	—	—	—	—	—	—	—	—	—
1860	—	—	—	—	—	—	—	—	—
1870	—	—	—	—	—	—	—	—	—
1880	—	117,893	—	—	67,377	—	—	—	—
1890	—	146,247	—	158,008	102,296	—	—	—	—
1900	—	168,735	—	140,590	153,559	—	—	114,443	—
1910	—	200,298	—	168,546	192,728	—	—	136,152	—
1920	—	241,465	—	266,074	275,721	112,926	101,877	211,694	—
1930	—	291,606	—	302,870	347,709	155,902	131,597	233,467	—
1940	—	295,108	—	325,153	344,333	178,468	131,067	252,216	—
1950	—	341,719	168,152	366,395	395,551	337,105	194,968	292,241	—
1960	265,660	563,781	209,776	457,873	456,931	368,080	314,070	345,071	291,984
1970	351,667	636,507	299,502	540,142	692,571	400,337	359,291	410,626	329,162
1980	531,443	642,971	569,066	569,614	791,599	476,517	479,899	446,576	403,089
1990	666,880	659,864	640,861	618,262	614,128	604,816	591,610	587,986	543,477

	New Haven–Meriden									
Year	New Haven–Meriden, CT	New Haven–West Haven, CT	Meriden, CT	Springfield, MA	Baton Rouge, LA	Little Rock–North Little Rock, AR	Charleston, SC	Youngstown–Warren, OH	Wichita, KS	Stockton, CA
	Aa1247	Aa1248	Aa1249	Aa1250	Aa1251	Aa1252	Aa1253	Aa1254	Aa1255	Aa1256
	Number	Number	Number	Number	Number	Number	Number	Number	Number	Number
1840	—	—	—	—	—	—	—	—	—	—
1850	—	—	—	—	—	—	—	—	—	—
1860	—	—	—	—	—	—	—	—	—	—
1870	—	53,554	—	—	—	—	—	—	—	—
1880	—	65,939	—	—	—	—	—	—	—	—
1890	—	94,393	—	—	—	—	59,903	—	—	—
1900	—	118,805	—	175,125	—	—	88,006	—	—	—
1910	—	162,935	—	238,623	—	—	88,594	168,917	73,095	—
1920	—	208,102	—	325,999	—	109,464	108,450	270,230	92,234	—
1930	—	254,518	—	366,442	—	137,727	101,050	359,205	136,330	—
1940	—	269,715	—	361,639	—	156,085	121,105	372,566	143,311	134,207
1950	—	264,622	—	407,255	158,236	196,685	164,856	528,498	222,290	200,750
1960	—	311,681	51,850	478,592	230,058	242,980	216,382	509,006	343,231	249,989
1970	—	355,538	55,959	529,922	285,167	323,296	303,849	536,003	389,352	290,208
1980	—	417,592	57,118	530,668	494,151	393,774	430,462	531,350	411,313	347,342
1990	530,180	—	—	529,519	528,264	513,117	506,875	492,619	485,270	480,628

Year	Albuquerque, NM	Mobile, AL	Columbia, SC	Worcester, MA	Johnson City–Kingsport–Bristol, TN–VA	Chattanooga, TN–GA	Lansing–East Lansing, MI	Flint, MI	Lancaster, PA	York, PA	Lakeland–Winter Haven, FL
	Aa1257	Aa1258	Aa1259	Aa1260	Aa1261	Aa1262	Aa1263	Aa1264	Aa1265	Aa1266	Aa1267
	Number	Number	Number	Number	Number	Number	Number	Number	Number	Number	Number
1840	—	—	—	—	—	—	—	—	—	—	—
1850	—	—	—	—	—	—	—	—	—	—	—
1860	—	—	—	—	—	—	—	—	—	—	—
1870	—	—	—	—	—	—	—	—	—	—	—
1880	—	—	—	76,329	—	—	—	—	—	—	—
1890	—	—	—	103,883	—	—	—	—	—	—	—
1900	—	—	—	140,186	—	—	—	—	—	—	—
1910	—	80,854	—	173,104	—	—	—	—	—	—	—
1920	—	100,117	—	225,421	—	115,954	81,554	125,668	173,797	—	—
1930	—	118,363	87,667	249,194	—	185,703	116,587	211,641	196,882	167,135	—
1940	—	141,974	104,843	250,546	—	211,502	130,616	227,944	212,504	178,022	—
1950	145,673	231,105	142,565	276,336	—	246,453	172,941	270,963	234,717	202,737	—
1960	262,199	314,301	260,828	323,306	—	283,169	298,949	374,313	278,359	238,336	—
1970	315,774	376,690	322,880	344,320	—	304,927	378,423	496,658	319,693	329,540	—
1980	454,499	443,536	410,088	372,940	433,638	426,540	471,565	521,589	362,346	381,255	321,652
1990	480,577	476,923	453,331	436,905	436,047	433,210	432,674	430,459	422,822	417,848	405,382

TABLE Aa1179–1322　Metropolitan areas – population: 1840–1990　[Part 2]　*Continued*

	Saginaw–Bay City–Midland									
	Saginaw–Bay City–Midland, MI	Saginaw, MI	Bay City, MI	Melbourne–Titusville–Palm Bay, FL	Colorado Springs, CO	Augusta, GA–SC	Jackson, MS	Canton, OH	Des Moines, IA	McAllen–Edinburg–Mission, TX
	Aa1268	Aa1269	Aa1270	Aa1271	Aa1272	Aa1273	Aa1274	Aa1275	Aa1276	Aa1277
Year	Number	Number	Number	Number	Number	Number	Number	Number	Number	Number
1840	—	—	—	—	—	—	—	—	—	—
1850	—	—	—	—	—	—	—	—	—	—
1860	—	—	—	—	—	—	—	—	—	—
1870	—	—	—	—	—	—	—	—	—	—
1880	—	—	—	—	—	—	—	—	—	—
1890	—	—	—	—	—	—	—	—	65,410	—
1900	—	—	—	—	—	—	—	—	82,624	—
1910	—	89,290	—	—	—	—	—	122,987	110,438	—
1920	—	100,286	—	—	—	63,692	—	177,218	154,029	—
1930	—	120,717	—	—	—	72,990	—	221,784	172,837	—
1940	—	130,468	—	—	—	81,863	107,273	234,887	195,835	—
1950	—	153,515	88,461	—	—	162,013	142,164	283,194	226,010	—
1960	—	190,752	107,042	—	143,742	216,639	187,045	340,345	266,315	—
1970	—	219,743	117,339	—	235,972	253,460	258,906	372,210	286,101	181,535
1980	—	228,059	119,881	272,959	317,458	327,372	320,425	404,421	338,048	283,229
1990	399,320	—	—	398,978	397,014	396,809	395,396	394,106	392,928	383,545

	Daytona Beach, FL	Modesto, CA	Santa Barbara–Santa Maria–Lompoc, CA	Madison, WI	Fort Wayne, IN	Spokane, WA	Beaumont–Port Arthur, TX	Salinas–Seaside–Monterey, CA	Davenport–Rock Island–Moline, IA–IL	Corpus Christi, TX	Lexington–Fayette, KY
	Aa1278	Aa1279	Aa1280	Aa1281	Aa1282	Aa1283	Aa1284	Aa1285	Aa1286	Aa1287	Aa1288
Year	Number	Number	Number	Number	Number	Number	Number	Number	Number	Number	Number
1840	—	—	—	—	—	—	—	—	—	—	—
1850	—	—	—	—	—	—	—	—	—	—	—
1860	—	—	—	—	—	—	—	—	—	—	—
1870	—	—	—	—	—	—	—	—	—	—	—
1880	—	—	—	—	—	—	—	—	—	—	—
1890	—	—	—	—	—	—	—	—	—	—	—
1900	—	—	—	—	—	—	—	—	—	—	—
1910	—	—	—	—	93,386	139,404	—	—	—	—	—
1920	—	—	—	—	114,303	141,289	—	—	166,249	—	—
1930	—	—	—	112,737	146,743	150,477	133,391	—	175,523	—	—
1940	—	—	—	130,660	155,084	164,652	145,329	—	198,071	92,661	—
1950	—	—	—	169,357	183,722	221,561	195,083	—	234,256	165,471	100,746
1960	—	—	168,962	222,095	232,196	278,333	306,016	—	270,058	221,573	131,906
1970	—	194,506	264,324	290,272	280,455	287,487	315,943	250,071	362,638	284,832	174,323
1980	258,762	265,900	298,694	323,545	382,961	341,835	375,497	290,444	383,958	326,228	317,629
1990	370,712	370,522	369,608	367,085	363,811	361,364	361,226	355,660	350,861	349,894	348,428

	Pensacola, FL	Peoria, IL	Reading, PA	Fort Myers–Cape Coral, FL	Shreveport, LA	Atlantic City, NJ	Utica–Rome, NY	Appleton–Oshkosh–Neenah, WI	Huntington–Ashland, WV–KY–OH	Visalia–Tulare–Porterville, CA	Montgomery, AL
	Aa1289	Aa1290	Aa1291	Aa1292	Aa1293	Aa1294	Aa1295	Aa1296	Aa1297	Aa1298	Aa1299
Year	Number	Number	Number	Number	Number	Number	Number	Number	Number	Number	Number
1840	—	—	—	—	—	—	—	—	—	—	—
1850	—	—	—	—	—	—	—	—	—	—	—
1860	—	—	—	—	—	—	—	—	—	—	—
1870	—	—	—	—	—	—	—	—	—	—	—
1880	—	—	—	—	—	—	—	—	—	—	—
1890	—	—	137,327	—	—	—	—	—	—	—	—
1900	—	88,608	159,615	—	—	—	132,800	—	—	—	—
1910	—	100,255	183,222	—	—	—	154,157	—	—	—	—
1920	—	150,250	200,854	—	—	83,914	247,795	—	65,746	—	—
1930	—	187,426	231,717	—	124,670	124,823	262,769	—	210,382	—	98,671
1940	—	211,736	241,884	—	150,203	124,066	263,163	—	225,668	—	114,420
1950	—	250,512	255,740	—	176,547	132,399	284,262	—	245,795	—	138,965
1960	203,376	288,833	275,414	—	281,481	160,880	330,771	—	254,780	—	169,210
1970	243,075	341,979	296,382	—	294,703	175,043	340,670	276,891	253,743	—	201,325
1980	289,782	365,864	312,509	205,266	376,710	194,119	320,180	291,369	311,350	245,738	272,687
1990	344,406	339,172	336,523	335,113	334,341	319,416	316,633	315,121	312,529	311,921	292,517

(continued)

TABLE Aa1179–1322   Metropolitan areas – population: 1840–1990   [Part 2]   *Continued*

Year	Rockford, IL Aa1300 Number	Eugene–Springfield, OR Aa1301 Number	Macon–Warner Robins, GA Aa1302 Number	Evansville, IN–KY Aa1303 Number	Salem, OR Aa1304 Number	Sarasota, FL Aa1305 Number	Erie, PA Aa1306 Number	Fayetteville, NC Aa1307 Number	New London–Norwich, CT–RI Aa1308 Number	Binghamton, NY Aa1309 Number	Provo–Orem, UT Aa1310 Number	Brownsville–Harlingen, TX Aa1311 Number
1840	—	—	—	—	—	—	—	—	—	—	—	—
1850	—	—	—	—	—	—	—	—	—	—	—	—
1860	—	—	—	—	—	—	—	—	—	—	—	—
1870	—	—	—	—	—	—	—	—	—	—	—	—
1880	—	—	—	—	—	—	—	—	—	—	—	—
1890	—	—	—	59,809	—	—	—	—	—	—	—	—
1900	—	—	—	71,769	—	—	98,473	—	—	—	—	—
1910	—	—	—	77,438	—	—	115,517	—	—	—	—	—
1920	90,929	—	71,304	92,293	—	—	153,536	—	—	113,610	—	—
1930	117,373	—	77,042	113,320	—	—	175,277	—	—	147,022	—	—
1940	121,178	—	83,783	130,783	—	—	180,889	—	—	165,749	—	—
1950	152,385	—	135,043	160,422	—	—	219,388	—	—	184,698	—	—
1960	209,765	162,890	180,403	199,313	—	—	250,682	—	156,913	212,661	106,991	151,098
1970	272,063	213,358	206,342	232,775	186,658	—	263,654	212,042	208,412	302,672	137,776	140,368
1980	279,514	275,226	253,794	309,408	249,895	202,251	279,780	247,160	248,554	301,336	218,106	209,727
1990	283,719	282,912	281,103	278,990	278,024	277,776	275,572	274,566	266,819	264,497	263,590	260,120

Year	Poughkeepsie, NY Aa1312 Number	Killeen–Temple, TX Aa1313 Number	Reno, NV Aa1314 Number	Fort Pierce, FL Aa1315 Number	Charleston, WV Aa1316 Number	South Bend–Mishawaka, IN Aa1317 Number	Columbus, GA–AL Aa1318 Number	Savannah, GA Aa1319 Number	Johnstown, PA Aa1320 Number	Springfield, MO Aa1321 Number	Duluth–Superior, MN–WI Aa1322 Number
1840	—	—	—	—	—	—	—	—	—	—	—
1850	—	—	—	—	—	—	—	—	—	—	—
1860	—	—	—	—	—	—	—	—	—	—	—
1870	—	—	—	—	—	—	—	—	—	—	—
1880	—	—	—	—	—	—	—	—	—	—	—
1890	—	—	—	—	—	—	—	—	—	—	—
1900	—	—	—	—	—	—	—	71,239	—	—	119,267
1910	—	—	—	—	—	84,312	—	79,690	166,131	—	210,696
1920	—	—	—	—	—	103,304	—	100,032	197,839	—	256,162
1930	—	—	—	—	157,667	160,033	—	105,431	283,910	82,929	251,179
1940	—	—	—	—	195,619	161,823	75,494	117,970	298,416	90,541	254,036
1950	—	—	—	—	322,072	205,058	170,541	151,481	291,354	104,823	252,777
1960	—	—	84,743	—	252,925	238,614	217,985	188,299	280,733	126,276	276,596
1970	—	—	121,068	—	229,515	280,031	238,584	187,767	262,822	152,929	265,350
1980	245,055	214,656	193,623	—	269,595	280,772	239,196	230,728	264,506	207,704	266,650
1990	259,462	255,301	254,667	251,071	250,454	247,052	243,072	242,622	241,247	240,593	239,971

Sources

See the sources for Table Aa1034–1178.

Documentation

This table continues Table Aa1034–1178. See the text for Table Aa1034–1178.

TABLE Aa1323–1470   Metropolitan areas – population: 1890–1990   [Part 3]

Contributed by Todd K. Gardner and Michael R. Haines

	Huntsville, AL	Tallahassee, FL	Anchorage, AK	Roanoke, VA	Portsmouth–Dover–Rochester, NH–ME	Kalamazoo, MI	Lubbock, TX	Hickory–Morgantown, NC	Waterbury, CT	Portland, ME
	Aa1323	Aa1324	Aa1325	Aa1326	Aa1327	Aa1328	Aa1329	Aa1330	Aa1331	Aa1332
Year	Number	Number	Number	Number	Number	Number	Number	Number	Number	Number
1890	—	—	—	—	—	—	—	—	—	—
1900	—	—	—	—	—	—	—	—	—	63,715
1910	—	—	—	—	—	—	—	—	94,417	74,323
1920	—	—	—	73,237	—	—	—	—	124,344	87,979
1930	—	—	—	104,495	—	91,368	—	—	134,360	97,833
1940	—	—	—	112,184	—	100,085	—	—	135,526	103,683
1950	—	—	—	133,407	—	126,707	101,048	—	154,656	119,942
1960	117,348	—	—	158,803	—	169,712	156,271	—	181,638	120,655
1970	228,239	103,047	—	181,436	—	201,550	179,295	—	208,956	141,625
1980	308,593	159,542	174,431	224,341	163,880	279,192	211,651	130,207	228,178	183,625
1990	238,912	233,598	226,338	224,477	223,578	223,411	222,636	221,700	221,629	215,281

	Lincoln, NE	Bradenton, FL	Lafayette, LA	Boise City, ID	Gainesville, FL	Biloxi–Gulfport, MS	Ocala, FL	Green Bay, WI	St. Cloud, MN	Bremerton, WA
	Aa1333	Aa1334	Aa1335	Aa1336	Aa1337	Aa1338	Aa1339	Aa1340	Aa1341	Aa1342
Year	Number	Number	Number	Number	Number	Number	Number	Number	Number	Number
1890	76,395	—	—	—	—	—	—	—	—	—
1900	64,835	—	—	—	—	—	—	—	—	—
1910	73,793	—	—	—	—	—	—	—	—	—
1920	85,902	—	—	—	—	—	—	—	—	—
1930	100,324	—	—	—	—	—	—	—	—	—
1940	100,585	—	—	—	—	—	—	—	—	—
1950	119,742	—	—	—	—	—	—	98,314	—	—
1960	155,272	—	—	—	—	—	—	125,082	—	—
1970	167,972	—	109,716	112,230	104,764	134,582	—	158,244	—	—
1980	192,884	148,442	150,017	173,036	151,348	191,918	122,488	175,280	163,256	147,152
1990	213,641	211,707	208,740	205,775	204,111	197,125	194,833	194,594	190,921	189,731

	Springfield, IL	Waco, TX	Yakima, WA	Amarillo, TX	Fort Collins–Loveland, CO	Houma–Thibodaux, LA	Chico, CA	Merced, CA	Fort Smith, AR–OK	New Bedford, MA
	Aa1343	Aa1344	Aa1345	Aa1346	Aa1347	Aa1348	Aa1349	Aa1350	Aa1351	Aa1352
Year	Number	Number	Number	Number	Number	Number	Number	Number	Number	Number
1890	—	—	—	—	—	—	—	—	—	—
1900	—	—	—	—	—	—	—	—	—	66,009
1910	91,024	—	—	—	—	—	—	—	—	101,774
1920	100,262	—	—	—	—	—	—	—	—	131,583
1930	111,733	98,682	—	—	—	—	—	—	—	136,418
1940	117,912	101,898	—	61,450	—	—	—	—	—	134,435
1950	131,484	130,194	—	87,140	—	—	—	—	—	137,469
1960	146,539	150,091	—	149,493	—	—	—	—	66,685	143,176
1970	161,335	147,553	—	144,396	—	—	—	—	160,421	152,642
1980	187,789	170,755	172,508	173,699	149,184	—	143,851	—	203,511	169,425
1990	189,550	189,123	188,823	187,547	186,136	182,842	182,120	178,403	175,911	175,641

(continued)

TABLE Aa1323–1470 Metropolitan areas – population: 1890–1990 [Part 3] *Continued*

Year	Asheville, NC	Champaign–Urbana–Rantoul, IL	Clarksville–Hopkinsville, TN–KY	Cedar Rapids, IA	Lake Charles, LA	Longview–Marshall, TX	Benton Harbor, MI	Olympia, WA	Topeka, KS	Wheeling, WV–OH
	Aa1353	Aa1354	Aa1355	Aa1356	Aa1357	Aa1358	Aa1359	Aa1360	Aa1361	Aa1362
	Number	Number	Number	Number	Number	Number	Number	Number	Number	Number
1890	—	—	—	—	—	—	—	—	—	—
1900	—	—	—	—	—	—	—	—	—	—
1910	—	—	—	—	—	—	—	—	—	—
1920	—	—	—	—	—	—	—	—	69,159	189,766
1930	97,937	—	—	82,336	—	—	—	—	85,200	206,627
1940	108,755	—	—	89,142	—	—	—	—	91,247	208,918
1950	124,403	—	—	104,274	—	—	—	—	105,160	354,092
1960	130,074	132,436	—	136,899	145,475	—	—	—	141,286	190,342
1970	145,056	163,281	—	163,213	145,415	—	—	—	155,322	182,712
1980	177,761	168,392	150,220	169,775	167,223	151,752	171,276	124,264	185,442	185,566
1990	174,821	173,025	169,439	168,767	168,134	162,431	161,378	161,238	160,976	159,301

Year	Muskegon, MI	Athens, GA	Elkhart–Goshen, IN	Lima, OH	Fargo–Moorhead, ND–MN	Naples, FL	Tyler, TX	Tuscaloosa, AL	Richland–Kennewick–Pasco, WA	Jacksonville, NC
	Aa1363	Aa1364	Aa1365	Aa1366	Aa1367	Aa1368	Aa1369	Aa1370	Aa1371	Aa1372
	Number	Number	Number	Number	Number	Number	Number	Number	Number	Number
1890	—	—	—	—	—	—	—	—	—	—
1900	—	—	—	—	—	—	—	—	—	—
1910	—	—	—	—	—	—	—	—	—	—
1920	—	—	—	—	—	—	—	—	—	—
1930	—	—	—	—	—	—	—	—	—	—
1940	—	—	—	—	—	—	—	—	—	—
1950	—	—	—	88,183	—	—	—	—	—	—
1960	149,943	—	—	103,691	106,027	—	86,350	109,047	—	—
1970	157,426	—	—	171,472	120,238	—	97,096	116,029	—	—
1980	179,591	130,015	137,330	218,244	137,574	—	128,366	137,541	144,469	112,784
1990	158,983	156,267	156,198	154,340	153,296	152,099	151,309	150,522	150,033	149,838

Year	Jackson, MI	Parkersburg–Marietta, WV–OH	Manchester, NH	Redding, CA	Waterloo–Cedar Falls, IA	Medford, OR	Anderson, SC	Fort Walton Beach, FL	Steubenville–Weirton, OH–WV	Lynchburg, VA
	Aa1373	Aa1374	Aa1375	Aa1376	Aa1377	Aa1378	Aa1379	Aa1380	Aa1381	Aa1382
	Number	Number	Number	Number	Number	Number	Number	Number	Number	Number
1890	—	—	—	—	—	—	—	—	—	—
1900	—	—	56,987	—	—	—	—	—	—	—
1910	—	—	70,063	—	—	—	—	—	—	—
1920	—	—	78,384	—	—	—	—	—	—	—
1930	92,304	—	76,834	—	—	—	—	—	—	—
1940	93,108	—	77,685	—	79,946	—	—	—	—	—
1950	107,925	—	88,370	—	100,448	—	—	—	—	—
1960	131,994	—	95,512	—	122,482	—	—	—	167,756	110,701
1970	143,274	—	108,461	—	132,916	—	—	—	165,627	123,474
1980	151,495	162,836	160,767	115,715	137,961	132,456	133,235	109,920	163,099	153,260
1990	149,756	149,169	147,809	147,036	146,611	146,389	145,196	143,776	142,523	142,199

TABLE Aa1323–1470 Metropolitan areas – population: 1890–1990 [Part 3] *Continued*

Year	Monroe, LA	Jamestown–Dunkirk, NY	Janesville–Beloit, WI	Eau Claire, WI	Battle Creek, MI	Las Cruces, NM	Joplin, MO	Laredo, TX	Greeley, CO	Alexandria, LA
	Aa1383	Aa1384	Aa1385	Aa1386	Aa1387	Aa1388	Aa1389	Aa1390	Aa1391	Aa1392
	Number	Number	Number	Number	Number	Number	Number	Number	Number	Number
1890	—	—	—	—	—	—	—	—	—	—
1900	—	—	—	—	—	—	—	—	—	—
1910	—	—	—	—	—	—	—	—	—	—
1920	—	—	—	—	—	—	—	—	—	—
1930	—	—	—	—	—	—	—	—	—	—
1940	—	—	—	—	—	—	—	—	—	—
1950	—	—	—	—	—	—	—	56,141	—	—
1960	101,663	—	—	—	—	—	—	64,791	—	—
1970	115,387	—	—	—	—	—	—	72,859	—	—
1980	139,241	—	139,420	130,932	187,338	96,340	127,513	99,258	123,438	151,985
1990	142,191	141,895	139,510	137,543	135,982	135,510	134,910	133,239	131,821	131,556

Year	Decatur, AL	Burlington, VT	Florence, AL	Charlottesville, VA	Dothan, AL	Terre Haute, IN	Anderson, IN	Lafayette–West Lafayette, IN	Altoona, PA	Bloomington–Normal, IL
	Aa1393	Aa1394	Aa1395	Aa1396	Aa1397	Aa1398	Aa1399	Aa1400	Aa1401	Aa1402
	Number	Number	Number	Number	Number	Number	Number	Number	Number	Number
1890	—	—	—	—	—	—	—	—	—	—
1900	—	—	—	—	—	—	—	—	—	—
1910	—	—	—	—	—	87,930	—	—	108,858	—
1920	—	—	—	—	—	100,212	—	—	128,334	—
1930	—	—	—	—	—	98,861	—	—	139,840	—
1940	—	—	—	—	—	99,709	—	—	140,358	—
1950	—	—	—	—	—	105,160	—	—	139,514	—
1960	—	—	—	—	—	108,458	—	—	137,270	—
1970	—	—	—	—	—	175,143	138,451	109,378	135,356	104,389
1980	—	114,070	135,065	113,568	—	176,583	139,336	121,702	136,621	119,149
1990	131,556	131,439	131,327	131,107	130,964	130,812	130,669	130,598	130,542	129,180

Year	Bellingham, WA	Panama City, FL	Mansfield, OH	Sioux Falls, SD	State College, PA	Pueblo, CO	Yuba City, CA	Wichita Falls, TX	Bryan–College Station, TX	Hagerstown, MD
	Aa1403	Aa1404	Aa1405	Aa1406	Aa1407	Aa1408	Aa1409	Aa1410	Aa1411	Aa1412
	Number	Number	Number	Number	Number	Number	Number	Number	Number	Number
1890	—	—	—	—	—	—	—	—	—	—
1900	—	—	—	—	—	—	—	—	—	—
1910	—	—	—	—	—	—	—	—	—	—
1920	—	—	—	—	—	—	—	—	—	—
1930	—	—	—	—	—	66,038	—	—	—	—
1940	—	—	—	—	—	68,870	—	—	—	—
1950	—	—	—	70,910	—	90,188	—	98,493	—	—
1960	—	—	—	86,575	—	118,707	—	129,638	—	—
1970	—	—	129,997	95,209	—	118,238	—	127,621	57,978	—
1980	106,701	97,740	131,205	109,435	112,760	125,972	101,979	130,664	93,588	113,086
1990	127,780	126,994	126,137	123,809	123,786	123,051	122,643	122,378	121,862	121,393

(continued)

TABLE Aa1323–1470 Metropolitan areas – population: 1890–1990 [Part 3] *Continued*

Year	Sharon, PA	Wilmington, NC	Texarkana, TX–AR	Muncie, IN	Abilene, TX	Odessa, TX	Williamsport, PA	Glens Falls, NY	Decatur, IL	Santa Fe, NM
	Aa1413	Aa1414	Aa1415	Aa1416	Aa1417	Aa1418	Aa1419	Aa1420	Aa1421	Aa1422
	Number	Number	Number	Number	Number	Number	Number	Number	Number	Number
1890	—	—	—	—	—	—	—	—	—	—
1900	—	—	—	—	—	—	—	—	—	—
1910	—	—	—	—	—	—	—	—	—	—
1920	—	—	—	—	—	—	—	—	—	—
1930	—	—	—	—	—	—	—	—	81,731	—
1940	—	—	—	—	—	—	—	—	84,693	—
1950	—	—	—	90,252	—	—	—	—	98,853	—
1960	—	—	91,657	110,938	120,377	90,995	—	—	118,257	—
1970	—	107,219	101,198	129,219	113,959	91,805	—	—	125,010	—
1980	128,299	139,248	127,019	128,587	139,192	115,374	118,416	109,649	131,375	—
1990	121,003	120,284	120,132	119,659	119,655	118,934	118,710	118,539	117,206	117,043

Year	Anniston, AL	Wausau, WI	Pascagoula, MS	Sioux City, IA–NE	Florence, SC	Billings, MT	Fayetteville–Springdale, AR	Albany, GA	Columbia, MO	Lawton, OK
	Aa1423	Aa1424	Aa1425	Aa1426	Aa1427	Aa1428	Aa1429	Aa1430	Aa1431	Aa1432
	Number	Number	Number	Number	Number	Number	Number	Number	Number	Number
1890	—	—	—	—	—	—	—	—	—	—
1900	—	—	—	—	—	—	—	—	—	—
1910	—	—	—	—	—	—	—	—	—	—
1920	—	—	—	92,171	—	—	—	—	—	—
1930	—	—	—	101,669	—	—	—	—	—	—
1940	—	—	—	103,627	—	—	—	—	—	—
1950	—	—	—	103,917	—	—	—	—	—	—
1960	—	—	107,849	—	79,016	—	75,680	—	90,803	
1970	—	—	—	116,189	—	87,367	—	89,639	80,911	108,144
1980	119,761	111,270	118,015	117,457	110,163	108,035	178,609	112,402	100,376	112,456
1990	116,034	115,400	115,243	115,018	114,344	113,419	113,409	112,561	112,379	111,486

Year	Bloomington, IN	Danville, VA	Burlington, NC	Yuma, AZ	Midland, TX	Rochester, MN	Sheboygan, WI	Fitchburg–Leominster, MA	Cumberland, MD–WV	Gadsden, AL
	Aa1433	Aa1434	Aa1435	Aa1436	Aa1437	Aa1438	Aa1439	Aa1440	Aa1441	Aa1442
	Number	Number	Number	Number	Number	Number	Number	Number	Number	Number
1890	—	—	—	—	—	—	—	—	—	—
1900	—	—	—	—	—	—	—	—	—	—
1910	—	—	—	—	—	—	—	—	—	—
1920	—	—	—	—	—	—	—	—	—	—
1930	—	—	—	—	—	—	—	—	—	—
1940	—	—	—	—	—	—	—	—	—	—
1950	—	—	—	—	—	—	—	—	—	93,892
1960	—	—	—	—	67,707	—	—	82,486	—	96,980
1970	—	—	—	—	65,433	84,104	—	97,164	—	94,144
1980	98,785	111,789	99,319	—	82,636	92,006	100,935	99,957	107,782	103,057
1990	108,978	108,711	108,213	106,895	106,611	106,470	103,877	102,797	101,643	99,840

TABLE Aa1323–1470   Metropolitan areas – population: 1890–1990   [Part 3]   *Continued*

	San Angelo, TX	La Crosse, WI	Kokomo, IN	Kankakee, IL	Iowa City, IA	Elmira, NY	Sherman–Denison, TX	Bangor, ME	Lewiston–Auburn, ME	Owensboro, KY
	Aa1443	Aa1444	Aa1445	Aa1446	Aa1447	Aa1448	Aa1449	Aa1450	Aa1451	Aa1452
Year	Number	Number	Number	Number	Number	Number	Number	Number	Number	Number
1890	—	—	—	—	—	—	—	—	—	—
1900	—	—	—	—	—	—	—	—	—	—
1910	—	—	—	—	—	—	—	—	—	—
1920	—	—	—	—	—	—	—	—	—	—
1930	—	—	—	—	—	—	—	—	—	—
1940	—	—	—	—	—	—	—	—	—	—
1950	58,929	—	—	—	—	—	—	—	—	—
1960	64,630	—	—	—	—	—	—	—	70,295	—
1970	71,047	80,468	—	—	—	—	83,225	—	72,474	79,486
1980	84,784	91,056	103,715	102,926	81,717	97,656	89,796	83,919	72,378	85,949
1990	98,458	97,904	96,946	96,255	96,119	95,195	95,021	88,745	88,141	87,189

	Dubuque, IA	Pine Bluff, AR	Bismarck, ND	St. Joseph, MO	Lawrence, KS	Rapid City, SD	Pittsfield, MA	Jackson, TN	Great Falls, MT	Victoria, TX
	Aa1453	Aa1454	Aa1455	Aa1456	Aa1457	Aa1458	Aa1459	Aa1460	Aa1461	Aa1462
Year	Number	Number	Number	Number	Number	Number	Number	Number	Number	Number
1890	—	—	—	70,100	—	—	—	—	—	—
1900	—	—	—	121,838	—	—	—	—	—	—
1910	—	—	—	93,020	—	—	—	—	—	—
1920	—	—	—	93,684	—	—	—	—	—	—
1930	—	—	—	98,633	—	—	—	—	—	—
1940	—	—	—	94,067	—	—	—	—	—	—
1950	—	—	—	96,826	—	—	66,567	—	—	—
1960	80,048	—	—	90,581	—	—	73,839	—	73,418	—
1970	90,609	85,329	—	86,915	—	—	79,727	—	81,804	—
1980	93,745	90,718	79,988	101,868	67,640	—	90,505	—	80,696	68,807
1990	86,403	85,487	83,831	83,083	81,798	81,343	79,250	77,982	77,691	74,361

	Cheyenne, WY	Grand Forks, ND	Casper, WY	Enid, OK	Newburgh–Middletown, NY	Salisbury–Concord, NC	Petersburg–Colonial Heights–Hopewell, VA	Rock Hill, SC
	Aa1463	Aa1464	Aa1465	Aa1466	Aa1467	Aa1468	Aa1469	Aa1470
Year	Number	Number	Number	Number	Number	Number	Number	Number
1890	—	—	—	—	—	—	—	—
1900	—	—	—	—	—	—	—	—
1910	—	—	—	—	—	—	—	—
1920	—	—	—	—	—	—	—	—
1930	—	—	—	—	—	—	—	—
1940	—	—	—	—	—	—	—	—
1950	—	—	—	—	—	—	—	—
1960	—	—	—	—	—	—	—	—
1970	—	—	—	—	—	—	128,809	—
1980	—	100,944	71,856	62,820	259,603	185,081	129,296	106,720
1990	73,142	70,683	61,226	56,735	—	—	—	—

Sources

See the sources for Table Aa1034–1178.

Documentation

This table is a continuation of the previous two tables. See the text for Table Aa1034–1178.

TABLE Aa1471–1663   Urbanized areas – population: 1800–1990   [Part 1]

Contributed by Todd K. Gardner and Michael R. Haines

	New York, NY–Northeastern New Jersey	Los Angeles, CA	Chicago, IL–Northwestern Indiana	Philadelphia, PA–NJ	Detroit				Dallas–Fort Worth		
					Detroit, MI	Pontiac, MI	San Francisco–Oakland, CA	Washington, DC–MD–VA	Dallas–Fort Worth, TX	Dallas, TX	Fort Worth, TX
	Aa1471 [1]	Aa1472 [2]	Aa1473 [3]	Aa1474 [4]	Aa1475 [5]	Aa1476	Aa1477 [6]	Aa1478 [7]	Aa1479 [8]	Aa1480	Aa1481
Year	Number	Number	Number	Number	Number	Number	Number	Number	Number	Number	Number
1800	60,515	—	—	61,559	—	—	—	—	—	—	—
1810	96,373	—	—	90,190	—	—	—	—	—	—	—
1820	123,706	—	—	112,772	—	—	—	—	—	—	—
1830	209,518	—	—	161,271	—	—	—	—	—	—	—
1840	357,109	—	—	223,319	—	—	—	—	—	—	—
1850	661,045	—	—	376,015	—	—	—	—	—	—	—
1860	1,223,288	—	109,260	579,887	—	—	56,802	69,855	—	—	—
1870	1,642,527	—	298,977	702,504	79,577	—	159,973	120,583	—	—	—
1880	2,278,058	—	503,185	894,176	116,340	—	274,222	159,871	—	—	—
1890	3,051,998	50,395	1,133,737	1,115,888	205,876	—	358,844	244,731	—	—	—
1900	4,503,594	102,479	1,753,519	1,388,910	285,704	—	426,206	293,246	—	—	—
1910	6,409,569	379,714	2,366,239	1,695,823	473,445	—	638,706	348,372	—	92,104	73,312
1920	7,746,873	761,986	3,093,502	2,175,731	1,097,439	—	827,654	466,927	—	161,297	111,536
1930	9,866,002	1,961,839	4,159,984	2,517,963	1,929,314	64,928	1,075,130	556,586	—	273,097	163,447
1940	10,595,881	2,390,609	4,243,534	2,537,088	2,039,027	66,626	1,106,608	817,865	—	319,480	177,662
1950	12,296,117	3,996,946	4,920,816	2,922,470	2,659,398	92,573	2,022,078	1,287,333	—	538,924	315,578
1960	14,114,927	6,675,338	5,959,213	3,635,228	3,537,709	—	2,430,663	1,808,423	—	832,349	502,682
1970	16,206,841	8,351,266	6,714,578	4,021,066	3,970,584	—	2,987,850	2,481,489	—	1,338,684	676,944
1980	15,590,274	9,479,436	6,779,799	4,112,933	3,809,327	—	3,190,698	2,763,105	2,451,390	—	—
1990	16,044,012	11,402,946	6,792,087	4,222,211	3,697,529	—	3,629,516	3,363,031	3,198,259	—	—

| | Houston, TX | Boston, MA | San Diego, CA | Atlanta, GA | Minneapolis–St. Paul, MN | Phoenix, AZ | St. Louis, MO–IL | Miami, FL | Baltimore, MD | Seattle, WA |
| | Aa1482 | Aa1483 | Aa1484 | Aa1485 | Aa1486 | Aa1487 | Aa1488 [9] | Aa1489 [10] | Aa1490 | Aa1491 [11] |
Year	Number	Number	Number	Number	Number	Number	Number	Number	Number	Number
1800	—	—	—	—	—	—	—	—	—	—
1810	—	—	—	—	—	—	—	—	—	—
1820	—	—	—	—	—	—	—	—	62,738	—
1830	—	70,175	—	—	—	—	—	—	80,620	—
1840	—	113,276	—	—	—	—	—	—	102,313	—
1850	—	202,346	—	—	—	—	77,860	—	169,054	—
1860	—	285,291	—	—	—	—	164,766	—	212,418	—
1870	—	361,008	—	—	—	—	316,508	—	267,354	—
1880	—	515,965	—	—	—	—	359,703	—	332,313	—
1890	—	861,046	—	65,533	297,894	—	466,939	—	434,439	—
1900	—	1,155,231	—	89,872	365,783	—	613,463	—	523,882	85,239
1910	85,784	1,412,921	—	154,839	523,322	—	795,790	—	584,468	237,194
1920	142,356	1,657,518	87,958	214,644	628,070	—	905,368	—	733,826	319,399
1930	292,352	1,957,349	168,153	298,184	776,403	—	1,118,399	122,828	816,430	378,051
1940	399,996	2,021,070	231,151	339,652	835,460	65,414	1,145,565	231,320	887,902	398,071
1950	700,508	2,233,448	432,974	507,887	985,101	216,038	1,400,058	458,647	1,161,852	621,509
1960	1,139,678	2,413,236	836,175	758,125	1,377,143	552,043	1,667,693	852,705	1,418,948	864,109
1970	1,677,863	2,652,575	1,198,323	1,172,778	1,704,423	863,357	1,882,944	1,219,661	1,579,781	1,238,107
1980	2,412,664	2,678,762	1,704,352	1,613,357	1,787,564	1,409,279	1,848,590	1,608,159	1,755,477	1,391,535
1990	2,901,851	2,775,370	2,348,417	2,157,806	2,079,676	2,006,239	1,946,526	1,914,660	1,889,873	1,744,086

Notes appear at end of table

TABLE Aa1471–1663　　Urbanized areas – population: 1800–1990　[Part 1]　*Continued*

	Tampa–St. Petersburg–Clearwater							Norfolk–Virginia Beach–Newport News		
	Tampa–St. Petersburg–Clearwater, FL	Tampa, FL	St. Petersburg, FL	Pittsburgh, PA	Cleveland, OH	Denver, CO	San Jose, CA	Norfolk–Virginia Beach–Newport News, VA	Norfolk–Portsmouth, VA	Newport News–Hampton, VA
	Aa1492 [12]	Aa1493	Aa1494	Aa1495 [13]	Aa1496	Aa1497	Aa1498	Aa1499 [14]	Aa1500	Aa1501
Year	Number	Number	Number	Number	Number	Number	Number	Number	Number	Number
1800	—	—	—	—	—	—	—	—	—	—
1810	—	—	—	—	—	—	—	—	—	—
1820	—	—	—	—	—	—	—	—	—	—
1830	—	—	—	—	—	—	—	—	—	—
1840	—	—	—	—	—	—	—	—	—	—
1850	—	—	—	81,508	—	—	—	—	—	—
1860	—	—	—	103,748	—	—	—	—	—	—
1870	—	—	—	183,439	93,477	—	—	—	—	—
1880	—	—	—	249,578	161,441	—	—	—	—	—
1890	—	—	—	409,952	270,055	111,874	—	—	—	—
1900	—	—	—	573,260	399,377	137,435	—	—	64,051	—
1910	—	—	—	763,840	602,940	216,364	—	—	100,642	—
1920	—	60,071	—	975,207	901,413	260,847	—	—	177,888	—
1930	—	105,259	—	1,111,009	1,131,012	295,841	68,120	—	183,271	—
1940	—	118,388	60,812	1,133,803	1,150,331	342,009	75,118	—	203,115	—
1950	—	179,335	114,596	1,532,953	1,383,599	498,743	176,473	—	385,111	—
1960	—	301,790	324,842	1,804,400	1,784,491	803,624	602,805	—	507,825	208,874
1970	—	368,742	495,159	1,846,042	1,959,880	1,047,311	1,025,273	—	668,259	268,263
1980	—	520,912	833,337	1,810,038	1,752,424	1,352,070	1,243,952	—	770,784	328,576
1990	1,708,710	—	—	1,678,745	1,677,492	1,517,977	1,435,019	1,323,098	—	—

	Kansas City, MO–KS	Fort Lauderdale–Hollywood, FL	Milwaukee, WI	Cincinnati, OH–KY	Portland, OR–WA	Riverside–San Bernardino, CA	San Antonio, TX	Sacramento, CA	New Orleans, LA
	Aa1502	Aa1503 [15]	Aa1504	Aa1505	Aa1506 [16]	Aa1507 [17]	Aa1508	Aa1509	Aa1510
Year	Number	Number	Number	Number	Number	Number	Number	Number	Number
1800	—	—	—	—	—	—	—	—	—
1810	—	—	—	—	—	—	—	—	—
1820	—	—	—	—	—	—	—	—	—
1830	—	—	—	—	—	—	—	—	—
1840	—	—	—	—	—	—	—	—	105,400
1850	—	—	—	133,962	—	—	—	—	133,650
1860	—	—	—	191,423	—	—	—	—	179,598
1870	—	—	71,440	256,936	—	—	—	—	197,913
1880	65,134	—	115,587	328,043	—	—	—	—	216,090
1890	178,040	—	204,468	407,923	—	—	—	—	242,039
1900	225,311	—	285,315	463,862	90,426	—	53,321	—	287,104
1910	336,672	—	386,555	528,278	212,086	—	96,614	—	339,075
1920	433,261	—	482,343	573,033	259,399	—	161,379	65,908	394,416
1930	524,177	—	657,597	673,450	315,000	—	235,416	95,847	472,333
1940	523,324	—	682,630	675,724	329,815	53,332	262,612	109,011	510,506
1950	698,350	—	829,495	813,292	512,643	135,770	449,521	211,777	659,768
1960	921,121	319,951	1,149,997	993,568	651,685	377,531	641,965	451,920	845,237
1970	1,101,787	613,797	1,252,457	1,110,514	824,926	593,597	772,513	633,732	961,728
1980	1,097,793	1,008,526	1,207,008	1,123,412	1,026,144	705,175	944,893	796,266	1,078,299
1990	1,275,317	1,238,134	1,226,293	1,212,675	1,172,158	1,170,196	1,129,154	1,097,005	1,040,226

Notes appear at end of table　　　　　　　　　　　　　　　　　　　　　　　　　　　(continued)

TABLE Aa1471–1663   Urbanized areas – population: 1800–1990   [Part 1]   *Continued*

	Buffalo–Niagara Falls										
	Buffalo–Niagara Falls, NY	Buffalo, NY	Niagara Falls, NY	Columbus, OH	Indianapolis, IN	Orlando, FL	Providence–Pawtucket, RI–MA	Memphis, TN–AR–MS	West Palm Beach, FL	Salt Lake City, UT	Oklahoma City, OK
	Aa1511 [18]	Aa1512	Aa1513	Aa1514	Aa1515	Aa1516	Aa1517 [19]	Aa1518 [20]	Aa1519 [21]	Aa1520	Aa1521
Year	Number	Number	Number	Number	Number	Number	Number	Number	Number	Number	Number
1800	—	—	—	—	—	—	—	—	—	—	—
1810	—	—	—	—	—	—	—	—	—	—	—
1820	—	—	—	—	—	—	—	—	—	—	—
1830	—	—	—	—	—	—	—	—	—	—	—
1840	—	—	—	—	—	—	—	—	—	—	—
1850	—	—	—	—	—	—	—	—	—	—	—
1860	—	81,129	—	—	—	—	62,484	—	—	—	—
1870	—	117,714	—	—	—	—	89,399	—	—	—	—
1880	—	155,134	—	51,647	75,056	—	123,887	—	—	—	—
1890	—	255,664	—	88,150	111,990	—	159,779	64,495	—	—	—
1900	—	353,260	—	125,560	169,651	—	232,995	102,320	—	53,531	—
1910	—	440,372	—	182,502	235,923	—	335,617	132,778	—	92,777	64,205
1920	—	531,045	54,573	240,887	318,845	—	420,106	162,351	—	118,110	91,295
1930	—	619,003	75,460	307,915	373,274	—	479,503	253,143	—	140,267	185,389
1940	—	624,729	78,029	327,676	398,893	—	514,971	292,942	—	155,635	205,366
1950	—	798,043	97,620	437,707	502,375	73,163	583,346	406,034	—	227,368	275,091
1960	1,054,370	—	—	616,743	639,340	200,995	659,542	544,505	172,835	348,661	429,188
1970	1,086,594	—	—	790,019	820,259	305,479	795,311	663,976	287,561	479,342	579,788
1980	1,002,285	—	—	833,648	836,472	577,235	796,250	774,551	487,044	674,201	674,322
1990	954,332	—	—	945,237	914,761	887,126	846,293	825,193	794,848	789,447	784,425

	Louisville, KY–IN	Jacksonville, FL	Las Vegas, NV	Honolulu, HI	Birmingham, AL	Rochester, NY	Dayton, OH	Richmond, VA	Tucson, AZ	Nashville, TN	El Paso, TX
	Aa1522	Aa1523	Aa1524	Aa1525	Aa1526	Aa1527	Aa1528	Aa1529	Aa1530	Aa1531 [22]	Aa1532 [23]
Year	Number	Number	Number	Number	Number	Number	Number	Number	Number	Number	Number
1800	—	—	—	—	—	—	—	—	—	—	—
1810	—	—	—	—	—	—	—	—	—	—	—
1820	—	—	—	—	—	—	—	—	—	—	—
1830	—	—	—	—	—	—	—	—	—	—	—
1840	—	—	—	—	—	—	—	—	—	—	—
1850	53,497	—	—	—	—	—	—	—	—	—	—
1860	84,700	—	—	—	—	—	—	—	—	—	—
1870	123,403	—	—	—	—	62,386	—	53,637	—	—	—
1880	151,635	—	—	—	—	89,366	—	69,329	—	—	—
1890	197,432	—	—	—	—	134,601	61,220	90,634	—	76,168	—
1900	239,720	—	—	—	—	163,496	85,333	94,765	—	80,865	—
1910	259,152	57,699	—	—	136,076	220,087	116,577	127,628	—	110,364	—
1920	271,711	94,333	—	—	190,691	295,750	152,559	171,667	—	118,342	77,560
1930	348,368	135,146	—	—	289,525	346,156	207,476	182,929	—	153,866	102,421
1940	358,967	173,065	—	—	295,473	348,351	218,370	193,042	—	167,402	96,810
1950	472,736	242,909	—	—	445,314	409,149	346,864	257,995	—	258,887	136,918
1960	606,659	372,569	89,427	351,336	521,330	493,402	501,664	333,438	227,433	346,729	277,128
1970	739,396	529,585	236,681	442,397	558,099	601,361	685,942	416,563	294,184	448,444	337,471
1980	761,002	598,015	432,874	582,463	606,085	606,070	595,059	491,627	450,059	518,325	454,159
1990	754,956	738,413	697,348	632,603	622,074	619,653	613,467	589,980	579,235	573,294	571,019

Notes appear at end of table

TABLE Aa1471–1663   Urbanized areas – population: 1800–1990   [Part 1]   *Continued*

Year	Austin, TX	Hartford, CT	Omaha, NE–IA	Akron, OH	Springfield, MA–CT	Albany–Schenectady–Troy			Tacoma, WA	Albuquerque, NM	Toledo, OH–MI
						Albany–Schenectady–Troy, NY	Albany–Troy, NY	Schenectady, NY			
	Aa1533	Aa1534 [24]	Aa1535	Aa1536	Aa1537 [25]	Aa1538 [26]	Aa1539	Aa1540	Aa1541	Aa1542	Aa1543 [27]
	Number	Number	Number	Number	Number	Number	Number	Number	Number	Number	Number
1800	—	—	—	—	—	—	—	—	—	—	—
1810	—	—	—	—	—	—	—	—	—	—	—
1820	—	—	—	—	—	—	—	—	—	—	—
1830	—	—	—	—	—	—	—	—	—	—	—
1840	—	—	—	—	—	—	—	—	—	—	—
1850	—	—	—	—	—	—	91,341	—	—	—	—
1860	—	—	—	—	—	—	120,822	—	—	—	—
1870	—	—	—	—	—	—	154,515	—	—	—	—
1880	—	—	—	—	—	—	194,496	—	—	—	50,137
1890	—	53,230	169,988	—	—	—	216,068	—	—	—	81,434
1900	—	79,850	154,488	—	126,938	—	223,858	—	—	—	131,822
1910	—	98,915	180,878	69,067	172,057	—	235,542	75,783	84,523	—	168,497
1920	—	138,036	227,988	218,635	226,031	—	242,288	93,081	98,093	—	243,164
1930	53,120	189,013	257,046	301,943	286,826	—	257,959	103,129	107,635	—	295,306
1940	87,930	218,658	265,283	296,907	280,896	—	256,609	95,509	110,473	—	289,011
1950	135,971	300,788	310,291	366,765	356,908	—	291,897	123,273	167,667	—	364,344
1960	187,157	381,619	389,881	458,253	449,777	455,447	—	—	214,930	241,216	438,283
1970	264,499	465,001	491,776	542,775	514,308	486,525	—	—	332,521	297,451	487,789
1980	379,560	510,034	512,438	515,720	505,822	490,015	—	—	402,077	418,206	485,440
1990	562,008	546,198	544,292	527,863	522,747	509,106	—	—	497,210	497,120	489,155

Year	Oxnard–Ventura, CA	Tulsa, OK	Charlotte, NC	Fresno, CA	New Haven–Meriden			Wilmington, DE–NJ–MD–PA	Sarasota–Bradenton, FL	Grand Rapids, MI	Bridgeport, CT
					New Haven–Meriden, CT	New Haven, CT	Meriden, CT				
	Aa1544 [28]	Aa1545	Aa1546	Aa1547	Aa1548 [29]	Aa1549	Aa1550	Aa1551 [30]	Aa1552	Aa1553	Aa1554 [31]
	Number	Number	Number	Number	Number	Number	Number	Number	Number	Number	Number
1800	—	—	—	—	—	—	—	—	—	—	—
1810	—	—	—	—	—	—	—	—	—	—	—
1820	—	—	—	—	—	—	—	—	—	—	—
1830	—	—	—	—	—	—	—	—	—	—	—
1840	—	—	—	—	—	—	—	—	—	—	—
1850	—	—	—	—	—	—	—	—	—	—	—
1860	—	—	—	—	—	—	—	—	—	—	—
1870	—	—	—	—	—	50,840	—	—	—	—	—
1880	—	—	—	—	—	62,882	—	—	—	—	—
1890	—	—	—	—	—	81,298	—	61,431	—	60,278	—
1900	—	—	—	—	—	113,274	—	78,334	—	87,565	70,996
1910	—	—	—	—	—	142,148	—	89,529	—	112,571	102,054
1920	—	72,075	—	—	—	162,537	—	116,228	—	137,634	143,555
1930	—	141,258	82,675	52,513	—	188,463	—	112,492	—	172,616	176,041
1940	—	142,157	100,899	60,685	—	190,626	—	118,992	—	169,191	180,672
1950	—	206,311	140,930	130,592	—	244,836	—	187,359	—	226,817	237,435
1960	—	298,922	209,551	213,444	—	278,794	51,850	283,667	—	294,230	366,654
1970	244,653	371,499	279,530	262,908	—	348,341	98,454	371,267	—	352,703	413,366
1980	377,695	443,350	350,715	331,551	—	368,061	57,118	406,112	305,431	374,744	410,998
1990	480,482	474,668	455,597	453,388	451,486	—	—	449,616	444,385	436,336	413,863

Notes appear at end of table

(continued)

TABLE Aa1471–1663   Urbanized areas – population: 1800–1990   [Part 1]   *Continued*

			Scranton–Wilkes-Barre							
Year	Allentown–Bethlehem–Easton, PA–NJ	Charleston, SC	Syracuse, NY	Scranton–Wilkes-Barre, PA	Scranton, PA	Wilkes-Barre, PA	Baton Rouge, LA	Youngstown–Warren, OH	Colorado Springs, CO	Wichita, KS	Columbia, SC
	Aa1555 [32]	Aa1556	Aa1557	Aa1558 [33]	Aa1559	Aa1560	Aa1561	Aa1562 [34]	Aa1563	Aa1564	Aa1565
	Number	Number	Number	Number	Number	Number	Number	Number	Number	Number	Number
1800	—	—	—	—	—	—	—	—	—	—	—
1810	—	—	—	—	—	—	—	—	—	—	—
1820	—	—	—	—	—	—	—	—	—	—	—
1830	—	—	—	—	—	—	—	—	—	—	—
1840	—	—	—	—	—	—	—	—	—	—	—
1850	—	—	—	—	—	—	—	—	—	—	—
1860	—	—	—	—	—	—	—	—	—	—	—
1870	—	—	—	—	—	—	—	—	—	—	—
1880	—	—	56,877	—	51,001	—	—	—	—	—	—
1890	—	54,955	90,374	—	94,972	65,390	—	—	—	—	—
1900	65,933	55,807	114,717	—	145,171	133,881	—	54,983	—	—	—
1910	109,423	58,833	146,472	—	201,460	201,946	—	99,505	—	52,450	—
1920	155,979	67,957	185,369	—	222,250	234,572	—	169,699	—	72,217	—
1930	181,320	62,265	221,958	—	237,082	273,413	—	223,811	—	111,110	57,205
1940	185,982	79,675	218,688	—	228,661	247,105	—	220,851	—	114,966	68,835
1950	225,962	120,289	265,286	—	236,076	271,589	138,864	298,051	—	194,047	120,808
1960	256,016	160,113	333,286	—	210,676	233,932	193,485	372,748	100,220	292,138	162,601
1970	363,517	228,399	376,169	—	204,205	222,830	249,463	395,540	204,766	302,334	241,781
1980	381,734	328,572	379,284	406,517	—	—	350,657	383,398	276,872	305,752	311,561
1990	410,436	393,956	388,918	388,225	—	—	365,943	361,627	352,989	338,789	328,349

| Year | Flint, MI | Worcester, MA | Melbourne–Palm Bay, FL | Raleigh, NC | Little Rock–North Little Rock, AR | Knoxville, TN | Bakersfield, CA | Mobile, AL | Trenton, NJ–PA | Chattanooga, TN–GA | Des Moines, IA |
| | Aa1566 | Aa1567 [35] | Aa1568 [36] | Aa1569 | Aa1570 [37] | Aa1571 | Aa1572 | Aa1573 | Aa1574 [38] | Aa1575 | Aa1576 |
	Number	Number	Number	Number	Number	Number	Number	Number	Number	Number	Number
1800	—	—	—	—	—	—	—	—	—	—	—
1810	—	—	—	—	—	—	—	—	—	—	—
1820	—	—	—	—	—	—	—	—	—	—	—
1830	—	—	—	—	—	—	—	—	—	—	—
1840	—	—	—	—	—	—	—	—	—	—	—
1850	—	—	—	—	—	—	—	—	—	—	—
1860	—	—	—	—	—	—	—	—	—	—	—
1870	—	—	—	—	—	—	—	—	—	—	—
1880	—	58,291	—	—	—	—	—	—	—	—	—
1890	—	84,655	—	—	—	—	—	—	57,458	—	50,093
1900	—	118,421	—	—	—	—	—	—	75,392	—	62,139
1910	—	145,986	—	—	57,079	—	—	51,521	99,711	—	88,941
1920	91,599	179,754	—	—	79,190	77,818	—	60,777	124,190	73,148	130,568
1930	156,492	195,311	—	—	101,097	105,802	—	82,120	130,032	126,211	147,127
1940	151,543	193,694	—	—	109,176	111,580	—	100,493	131,649	136,628	164,397
1950	197,631	219,330	—	68,743	153,643	148,166	—	182,963	189,321	167,764	199,934
1960	277,786	225,446	—	93,931	185,017	172,734	141,763	268,139	242,401	205,143	241,115
1970	330,128	247,416	—	152,289	222,616	190,502	176,155	257,816	274,148	223,580	255,824
1980	331,931	276,022	212,917	206,597	295,133	284,708	222,236	295,493	260,751	301,515	267,192
1990	326,023	315,666	305,978	305,925	305,353	304,466	302,605	300,912	298,602	296,955	293,666

Notes appear at end of table

TABLE Aa1471–1663   Urbanized areas – population: 1800–1990   [Part 1]   *Continued*

Year	Harrisburg, PA	Jackson, MS	Augusta, GA–SC	Spokane, WA	Corpus Christi, TX	Lansing, MI	Davenport–Rock Island–Moline, IA–IL	McAllen–Edinburg–Mission, TX	Stockton, CA	Ogden, UT	Shreveport, LA
	Aa1577	Aa1578	Aa1579	Aa1580	Aa1581	Aa1582 [39]	Aa1583	Aa1584 [40]	Aa1585	Aa1586	Aa1587
	Number	Number	Number	Number	Number	Number	Number	Number	Number	Number	Number
1800	—	—	—	—	—	—	—	—	—	—	—
1810	—	—	—	—	—	—	—	—	—	—	—
1820	—	—	—	—	—	—	—	—	—	—	—
1830	—	—	—	—	—	—	—	—	—	—	—
1840	—	—	—	—	—	—	—	—	—	—	—
1850	—	—	—	—	—	—	—	—	—	—	—
1860	—	—	—	—	—	—	—	—	—	—	—
1870	—	—	—	—	—	—	—	—	—	—	—
1880	—	—	—	—	—	—	—	—	—	—	—
1890	—	—	—	—	—	—	52,506	—	—	—	—
1900	63,117	—	—	—	—	—	73,849	—	—	—	—
1910	86,112	—	—	107,678	—	—	98,490	—	—	—	—
1920	102,088	—	54,290	108,379	—	57,327	133,854	—	—	—	—
1930	115,881	—	62,345	115,514	—	78,397	146,465	—	—	—	80,658
1940	120,500	62,107	68,548	122,001	57,301	78,753	161,914	—	54,714	—	103,953
1950	169,646	100,261	87,733	176,004	122,956	134,052	194,925	—	112,834	—	150,208
1960	209,501	147,480	123,698	226,938	177,380	169,325	227,176	—	141,604	121,927	208,583
1970	240,751	190,060	148,953	229,620	212,820	229,518	266,119	91,141	160,373	149,727	234,564
1980	278,296	265,051	251,250	266,709	245,854	254,704	285,024	157,423	197,052	205,744	263,827
1990	292,904	289,285	286,539	279,038	270,006	265,095	264,018	263,192	262,046	259,147	256,489

Year	Pensacola, FL	Fort Wayne, IN	Greenville, SC	Canton, OH	Madison, WI	Peoria, IL	Fayetteville, NC	South Bend–Mishawaka, IN–MI	Lawrence–Haverhill, MA–NH	Modesto, CA	Lorain–Elyria, OH
	Aa1588	Aa1589	Aa1590	Aa1591	Aa1592	Aa1593	Aa1594	Aa1595 [41]	Aa1596 [42]	Aa1597	Aa1598
	Number	Number	Number	Number	Number	Number	Number	Number	Number	Number	Number
1800	—	—	—	—	—	—	—	—	—	—	—
1810	—	—	—	—	—	—	—	—	—	—	—
1820	—	—	—	—	—	—	—	—	—	—	—
1830	—	—	—	—	—	—	—	—	—	—	—
1840	—	—	—	—	—	—	—	—	—	—	—
1850	—	—	—	—	—	—	—	—	—	—	—
1860	—	—	—	—	—	—	—	—	—	—	—
1870	—	—	—	—	—	—	—	—	—	—	—
1880	—	—	—	—	—	—	—	—	—	—	—
1890	—	—	—	—	—	—	—	—	—	—	—
1900	—	—	—	—	—	60,031	—	—	62,559	—	—
1910	—	63,933	—	64,096	—	71,154	—	55,189	85,892	—	—
1920	—	86,549	—	104,519	—	81,524	—	70,983	109,459	—	—
1930	—	114,946	—	131,306	57,899	115,161	—	104,193	106,137	—	—
1940	—	118,410	—	135,045	67,447	126,286	—	101,268	106,203	—	—
1950	—	140,314	—	173,917	110,111	154,539	—	168,165	112,309	—	—
1960	128,049	179,571	126,887	213,574	157,814	181,432	—	218,933	166,125	—	142,860
1970	166,619	225,184	157,073	244,279	205,457	247,121	161,370	288,572	200,280	106,107	192,265
1980	215,995	236,479	229,303	244,888	213,675	261,418	215,839	226,331	211,428	159,538	225,331
1990	253,558	248,424	248,173	244,576	244,336	242,353	241,763	237,932	237,362	230,609	224,087

Notes appear at end of table

(continued)

TABLE Aa1471–1663   Urbanized areas – population: 1800–1990   [Part 1]   *Continued*

Year	Ann Arbor, MI	Anchorage, AK	Daytona Beach, FL	Lexington, KY	Columbus, GA–AL	Provo–Orem, UT	Fort Myers, FL	Reno, NV	Montgomery, AL	Rockford, IL	Durham, NC
	Aa1599	Aa1600	Aa1601	Aa1602 [43]	Aa1603	Aa1604	Aa1605 [44]	Aa1606	Aa1607	Aa1608	Aa1609
	Number	Number	Number	Number	Number	Number	Number	Number	Number	Number	Number
1800	—	—	—	—	—	—	—	—	—	—	—
1810	—	—	—	—	—	—	—	—	—	—	—
1820	—	—	—	—	—	—	—	—	—	—	—
1830	—	—	—	—	—	—	—	—	—	—	—
1840	—	—	—	—	—	—	—	—	—	—	—
1850	—	—	—	—	—	—	—	—	—	—	—
1860	—	—	—	—	—	—	—	—	—	—	—
1870	—	—	—	—	—	—	—	—	—	—	—
1880	—	—	—	—	—	—	—	—	—	—	—
1890	—	—	—	—	—	—	—	—	—	—	—
1900	—	—	—	—	—	—	—	—	—	—	—
1910	—	—	—	—	—	—	—	—	—	—	—
1920	—	—	—	—	—	—	—	—	—	65,651	—
1930	—	—	—	—	58,700	—	—	—	66,079	85,864	52,037
1940	—	—	—	—	70,262	—	—	—	78,084	84,637	60,195
1950	—	—	—	—	118,485	—	—	—	109,468	122,226	73,368
1960	115,282	—	—	111,940	158,382	60,795	—	70,189	142,893	171,681	84,862
1970	178,605	—	—	159,538	208,616	104,110	—	99,687	138,983	206,084	100,764
1980	208,782	170,247	170,749	194,093	214,591	169,699	140,958	162,286	196,947	204,304	157,287
1990	222,061	221,883	221,341	220,701	220,698	220,556	220,552	213,747	210,007	207,826	205,355

Year	Savannah, GA	Santa Rosa, CA	Greensboro, NC	Lancaster, PA	Lincoln, NE	Aurora, IL	Eugene, OR	Lubbock, TX	Stamford, CT	Lancaster, CA	Reading, PA
	Aa1610	Aa1611	Aa1612	Aa1613	Aa1614	Aa1615 [45]	Aa1616 [46]	Aa1617	Aa1618 [47]	Aa1619 [48]	Aa1620
	Number	Number	Number	Number	Number	Number	Number	Number	Number	Number	Number
1800	—	—	—	—	—	—	—	—	—	—	—
1810	—	—	—	—	—	—	—	—	—	—	—
1820	—	—	—	—	—	—	—	—	—	—	—
1830	—	—	—	—	—	—	—	—	—	—	—
1840	—	—	—	—	—	—	—	—	—	—	—
1850	—	—	—	—	—	—	—	—	—	—	—
1860	—	—	—	—	—	—	—	—	—	—	—
1870	—	—	—	—	—	—	—	—	—	—	—
1880	—	—	—	—	—	—	—	—	—	—	—
1890	—	—	—	—	55,154	—	—	—	—	—	58,661
1900	54,244	—	—	—	40,169	—	—	—	—	—	78,961
1910	65,064	—	—	—	49,853	—	—	—	—	—	99,905
1920	83,252	—	—	53,150	64,911	—	—	—	—	—	114,137
1930	85,024	—	53,569	59,949	79,592	—	—	—	—	—	124,699
1940	95,996	—	59,319	61,345	81,984	—	—	—	—	—	125,326
1950	128,196	—	83,412	76,280	99,509	—	—	—	113,890	—	154,931
1960	169,887	—	123,334	93,855	136,220	85,522	95,686	129,289	166,990	—	160,297
1970	163,753	75,083	152,252	117,097	153,443	134,982	139,255	150,135	184,898	—	167,932
1980	186,546	137,019	170,457	157,385	173,550	158,911	182,495	175,479	182,978	56,328	173,450
1990	198,630	194,560	194,508	193,583	192,558	192,043	189,192	187,906	187,200	187,190	186,267

Notes appear at end of table

TABLE Aa1471–1663   Urbanized areas – population: 1800–1990   [Part 1]   *Continued*

Year	Winston-Salem, NC	Evansville, IN–KY	Santa Barbara, CA	Lowell, MA–NH	Huntsville, AL	Biloxi– Gulfport, MS	Roanoke, VA	Erie, PA	Waterbury, CT	Joliet, IL	Atlantic City, NJ
	Aa1621	Aa1622 [49]	Aa1623	Aa1624 [50]	Aa1625	Aa1626	Aa1627	Aa1628	Aa1629	Aa1630	Aa1631
	Number	Number	Number	Number	Number	Number	Number	Number	Number	Number	Number
1800	—	—	—	—	—	—	—	—	—	—	—
1810	—	—	—	—	—	—	—	—	—	—	—
1820	—	—	—	—	—	—	—	—	—	—	—
1830	—	—	—	—	—	—	—	—	—	—	—
1840	—	—	—	—	—	—	—	—	—	—	—
1850	—	—	—	—	—	—	—	—	—	—	—
1860	—	—	—	—	—	—	—	—	—	—	—
1870	—	—	—	—	—	—	—	—	—	—	—
1880	—	—	—	59,475	—	—	—	—	—	—	—
1890	—	50,756	—	77,696	—	—	—	—	—	—	—
1900	—	59,007	—	94,969	—	—	—	52,733	56,400	—	—
1910	—	69,647	—	106,294	—	—	—	66,525	85,863	—	52,026
1920	—	85,264	—	112,759	—	—	53,621	94,829	106,766	—	60,163
1930	75,274	102,249	—	100,234	—	—	72,816	122,062	114,217	—	90,169
1940	79,815	97,062	—	101,389	—	—	72,742	122,993	114,702	—	89,163
1950	92,477	137,573	—	106,661	—	—	106,682	151,710	131,707	—	105,083
1960	128,176	143,660	72,740	118,547	74,970	—	124,752	177,433	141,626	116,585	124,902
1970	142,584	142,476	129,774	182,731	146,565	121,601	156,621	175,263	156,986	155,500	134,016
1980	171,530	180,089	150,173	157,412	153,841	179,280	117,475	178,338	160,249	167,475	146,034
1990	185,184	183,087	182,163	181,651	180,315	179,643	178,277	177,668	175,067	170,717	169,993

Year	Huntington–Ashland, WV–KY–OH	Boise City, ID	Kalamazoo, MI	Charleston, WV	Green Bay, WI	Appleton, WI	Brockton, MA	Springfield, MO	Utica-Rome, NY	Binghamton, NY	Amarillo, TX
	Aa1632 [51]	Aa1633	Aa1634	Aa1635	Aa1636	Aa1637 [52]	Aa1638	Aa1639	Aa1640 [53]	Aa1641	Aa1642
	Number	Number	Number	Number	Number	Number	Number	Number	Number	Number	Number
1800	—	—	—	—	—	—	—	—	—	—	—
1810	—	—	—	—	—	—	—	—	—	—	—
1820	—	—	—	—	—	—	—	—	—	—	—
1830	—	—	—	—	—	—	—	—	—	—	—
1840	—	—	—	—	—	—	—	—	—	—	—
1850	—	—	—	—	—	—	—	—	—	—	—
1860	—	—	—	—	—	—	—	—	—	—	—
1870	—	—	—	—	—	—	—	—	—	—	—
1880	—	—	—	—	—	—	—	—	—	—	—
1890	—	—	—	—	—	—	—	—	—	—	—
1900	—	—	—	—	—	—	—	—	57,390	—	—
1910	—	—	—	—	—	—	64,170	—	78,680	52,218	—
1920	51,627	—	—	—	—	—	73,401	—	100,327	75,387	—
1930	139,101	—	54,786	66,312	—	—	71,435	57,527	114,412	92,131	—
1940	141,820	—	54,097	83,557	—	—	70,102	61,238	112,874	99,054	51,686
1950	156,288	—	83,332	130,914	—	—	92,116	75,549	117,424	144,011	74,443
1960	165,732	—	115,659	169,500	97,162	—	111,315	97,224	187,779	158,141	137,969
1970	167,583	85,187	152,083	157,662	129,105	129,532	148,844	121,340	180,355	167,224	127,010
1980	179,840	134,848	154,990	153,618	142,747	142,151	177,784	139,030	155,238	161,312	149,230
1990	169,594	167,941	164,430	164,418	161,931	160,918	160,910	159,086	158,553	158,405	157,934

Notes appear at end of table

(continued)

TABLE Aa1471–1663   Urbanized areas – population: 1800–1990   [Part 1]   *Continued*

Year	Salem, OR	New London–Norwich, CT	Tallahassee, FL	Antioch–Pittsburg, CA	Hesperia–Apple Valley–Victorville, CA	Santa Cruz, CA	Poughkeepsie, NY	Lakeland, FL	Waco, TX	Fall River, MA–RI	New Britain, CT
	Aa1643	Aa1644	Aa1645	Aa1646	Aa1647	Aa1648	Aa1649	Aa1650	Aa1651	Aa1652	Aa1653 [54]
	Number	Number	Number	Number	Number	Number	Number	Number	Number	Number	Number
1800	—	—	—	—	—	—	—	—	—	—	—
1810	—	—	—	—	—	—	—	—	—	—	—
1820	—	—	—	—	—	—	—	—	—	—	—
1830	—	—	—	—	—	—	—	—	—	—	—
1840	—	—	—	—	—	—	—	—	—	—	—
1850	—	—	—	—	—	—	—	—	—	—	—
1860	—	—	—	—	—	—	—	—	—	—	—
1870	—	—	—	—	—	—	—	—	—	—	—
1880	—	—	—	—	—	—	—	—	—	—	—
1890	—	—	—	—	—	—	—	—	—	74,398	—
1900	—	—	—	—	—	—	—	—	—	104,863	—
1910	—	—	—	—	—	—	—	—	—	119,295	—
1920	—	—	—	—	—	—	—	—	—	120,485	59,316
1930	—	—	—	—	—	—	—	—	52,848	115,274	68,128
1940	—	—	—	—	—	—	—	—	55,982	115,428	68,685
1950	—	—	—	—	—	—	—	—	92,834	118,120	87,118
1960	—	—	—	—	—	—	—	—	116,163	123,951	99,894
1970	93,041	—	77,851	—	—	—	—	—	118,843	139,392	131,349
1980	135,747	148,829	119,341	86,435	—	123,226	136,571	114,360	134,491	141,510	135,817
1990	157,079	156,286	155,884	153,768	153,176	152,355	148,527	147,628	144,372	144,358	143,064

Year	York, PA	Saginaw, MI	New Bedford, MA	Killeen, TX	Cedar Rapids, IA	Seaside–Monterey, CA	Topeka, KS	Lafayette LA	Macon, GA	Palm Springs, CA
	Aa1654	Aa1655	Aa1656	Aa1657	Aa1658	Aa1659	Aa1660	Aa1661	Aa1662	Aa1663
	Number	Number	Number	Number	Number	Number	Number	Number	Number	Number
1800	—	—	—	—	—	—	—	—	—	—
1810	—	—	—	—	—	—	—	—	—	—
1820	—	—	—	—	—	—	—	—	—	—
1830	—	—	—	—	—	—	—	—	—	—
1840	—	—	—	—	—	—	—	—	—	—
1850	—	—	—	—	—	—	—	—	—	—
1860	—	—	—	—	—	—	—	—	—	—
1870	—	—	—	—	—	—	—	—	—	—
1880	—	—	—	—	—	—	—	—	—	—
1890	—	—	—	—	—	—	—	—	—	—
1900	—	—	62,442	—	—	—	—	—	—	—
1910	—	50,510	96,652	—	—	—	—	—	—	—
1920	53,071	61,903	121,217	—	—	—	51,743	—	52,995	—
1930	63,051	80,715	112,597	—	56,097	—	64,120	—	53,829	—
1940	64,718	82,794	110,341	—	62,120	—	67,833	—	57,865	—
1950	78,796	105,939	125,495	—	78,212	—	89,104	—	93,499	—
1960	100,872	129,215	126,657	—	105,118	—	119,500	—	114,161	—
1970	123,106	147,552	133,667	—	132,008	93,284	132,108	78,544	128,065	—
1980	129,336	146,769	133,274	88,145	135,798	115,418	125,936	113,999	130,871	66,431
1990	142,675	140,079	139,082	137,876	136,190	133,188	132,711	129,592	129,496	129,025

[1] 1840–1850: New York, New York–New Jersey; 1800–1830: New York, New York.

[2] 1960–1980: Los Angeles–Long Beach, California; 1890–1950: Los Angeles, California. The Census Bureau listed the Pomona–Ontario, California, urbanized area (UA) separately in 1960 (population 186,547). Combined with the Los Angeles–Long Beach, California, UA in this table.

[3] 1860–1880: Chicago, Illinois.

[4] 1800–1840: Philadelphia, Pennsylvania.

[5] Detroit, Michigan, UA and Pontiac, Michigan, UA combined after 1950.

[6] 1860–1900: San Francisco, California.

[7] 1890–1900: Washington, D.C.–Virginia; 1860–1880: Washington, D.C.

[8] Dallas, Texas, UA and Fort Worth, Texas, UA combined after 1970.

[9] 1850–1860: St. Louis, Missouri.

[10] 1990: Miami–Hialeah, Florida.

[11] 1970–1980: Seattle–Everett, Washington.

[12] Tampa, Florida, UA and St. Petersburg, Florida, UA combined after 1980.

[13] 1850–1900: Pittsburgh–Allegheny, Pennsylvania.

[14] Norfolk–Portsmouth, Virginia, UA and Newport News–Hampton, Virginia, UA combined after 1980.

[15] 1990: Fort Lauderdale–Hollywood–Pompano Beach, Florida.

[16] 1990: Portland–Vancouver, Oregon–Washington.

[17] 1960–1980: San Bernardino–Riverside, California; 1940–1950: San Bernardino, California.

[18] Buffalo, New York, UA and Niagara Falls, New York, UA combined after 1950; 1950–1980: Buffalo, New York.

[19] 1970–1980: Providence–Pawtucket–Warwick, Rhode Island–Massachusetts; 1960: Providence–Pawtucket, Rhode Island–Massachusetts; 1860–1950: Providence, Rhode Island–Massachusetts.

[20] 1970: Memphis, Tennessee–Arkansas; 1890–1960: Memphis, Tennessee.

TABLE Aa1471–1663   Urbanized areas – population: 1800–1990   [Part 1]   *Continued*

21 1990: West Palm Beach-Boca Raton-Delray Beach, Florida.

22 1970-1980: Nashville-Davidson, Tennessee; 1890-1960: Nashville, Tennessee.

23 1990: El Paso, Texas-New Mexico.

24 1990: Hartford-Middletown, Connecticut.

25 1960-1980: Springfield-Chicopee-Holyoke, Massachusetts-Connecticut; 1900-1950: Springfield-Holyoke, Massachusetts.

26 Albany-Troy, New York, UA and Schenectady, New York, UA combined after 1950.

27 1880-1960: Toledo, Ohio.

28 1970-1980: Oxnard-Ventura-Thousand Oaks, California.

29 New Haven, Connecticut, UA and Meriden, Connecticut, UA combined after 1980.

30 1980: Wilmington, Delaware-New Jersey-Maryland; 1900-1970: Wilmington, Delaware-New Jersey; 1890: Wilmington, Delaware.

31 1990: Bridgeport-Milford, Connecticut.

32 1920-1960: Allentown-Bethlehem, Pennsylvania; 1900-1910: Allentown, Pennsylvania.

33 Scranton, Pennsylvania, UA and Wilkes-Barre, Pennsylvania, UA combined after 1970.

34 1900-1950: Youngstown, Ohio.

35 1990: Worcester, Massachusetts-Connecticut.

36 1980: Melbourne-Cocoa, Florida.

37 1910-1940: Little Rock, Arkansas.

38 1890: Trenton, New Jersey.

39 1990: Lansing-East Lansing, Michigan.

40 1970-1980: McAllen-Pharr-Edinburg, Texas.

41 1990: South Bend-Mishawaka, Indiana-Michigan; 1950-1980: South Bend, Indiana-Michigan; 1910-1940: South Bend, Indiana.

42 1900-1950: Lawrence, Massachusetts.

43 1990: Lexington-Fayette, Kentucky.

44 1990: Fort Myers-Cape Coral, Florida.

45 Census Bureau combined Aurora, Illinois, UA and Elgin, Illinois, UA in 1970. Separated in this table.

46 1990: Eugene-Springfield, Oregon.

47 1990: Stamford, Connecticut-New York. Census Bureau combined Stamford, Connecticut, UA and Norwalk, Connecticut, UA in 1950. Separated in this table.

48 1990: Lancaster-Palmdale, California.

49 1890-1970: Evansville, Indiana.

50 1880-1970: Lowell, Massachusetts.

51 1920: Huntington, West Virginia-Ohio.

52 1990: Appleton-Neewah, Wisconsin.

53 1900-1950: Utica, New York.

54 Census Bureau combined New Britain, Connecticut, UA and Bristol, Connecticut, UA in 1950. Bristol removed in this table.

Sources

1800-1940: Todd Gardner, "The Metropolitan Fringe: Suburbanization in the United States before World War II" (Ph.D. dissertation, University of Minnesota, 1998), pp. 286–357.

1950: U.S. Bureau of the Census, *Census of Population: 1950,* volume 2, *Characteristics of the Population*, Table 17, "Population and Land Area or Urbanized Areas: 1950," pp. 1-26 to 1-29.

1960: U.S. Bureau of the Census, *Census of Population: 1960,* volume 1, *Characteristics of the Population*, Table 63, "Summary of Population Characteristics, for Standard Metropolitan Statistical Areas, Urbanized Areas, and Urban Places of 50,000 or More: 1960," pp. 1-178 to 1-181.

1970: U.S. Bureau of the Census, *1970 Census of the Population: Characteristics of the Population, Number of Inhabitants*, Table 20, "Population and Land Area of Urbanized Areas: 1970 and 1960," pp. 1-74 to 1-86.

1980: U.S. Bureau of the Census, *1980 Census of the Population: Characteristics of the Population, Number of Inhabitants*, Table 34, "Population, Land Area, and Population Density of Urbanized Areas, 1980," pp. 1-236 to 1-248.

1990: U.S. Bureau of the Census, *1990 Census of Population: General Population Characteristics, Urbanized Areas*, Table 1, "Summary of General Characteristics of Persons: 1990," pp. 1-24.

Documentation

Population is given for current boundaries.

The Census Bureau delineates urbanized areas (UAs) to provide a better separation of urban and rural territories, population, and housing in the vicinity of large places. A UA comprises one or more places ("central place") and the adjacent densely settled surrounding territory ("urban fringe") that together have a minimum of 50,000 inhabitants. The urban fringe generally consists of contiguous territory having a density of at least 1,000 persons per square mile. The urban fringe also includes outlying territory of such density if it was connected to the core of the contiguous area by road and is within one and one-half road miles of this core, or within five road miles of the core but separated by water or other undevelopable territory. Other territory with a population density of fewer than 1,000 persons per square mile is included in the urban fringe if it eliminates an enclave or closes an indentation in the boundary of the urbanized area. The population density is determined by (1) outside of a place, one or more census blocks with a population density of at least 1,000 persons per square mile, or (2) inclusion of a place containing census blocks that have at least 50 percent of the population of the place and a density of at least 1,000 persons per square mile. See U.S. Bureau of the Census, *1990 Census of Population: General Population Characteristics, Urbanized Areas*, 1990 CP-1-1C, Appendix A, "Area Classifications," p. A-12.

For census years before 1950, only entire minor civil divisions were included in UAs. The Census Bureau includes areas smaller than minor civil divisions in UAs; however, such information is not available before 1950.

The series in this table are arranged according to 1990 population rank. Urbanized areas for which a 1990 population value is not shown are not part of this rank ordering.

TABLE Aa1664–1883   Urbanized areas – population: 1890–1990   [Part 2]

Contributed by Todd K. Gardner and Michael R. Haines

Year	Texas City, TX Aa1664 [1] Number	Simi Valley, CA Aa1665 Number	Fort Pierce, FL Aa1666 Number	Gainesville, FL Aa1667 Number	Springfield, IL Aa1668 Number	Elgin, IL Aa1669 [2] Number	Laredo, TX Aa1670 Number	Duluth–Superior, MN–WI Aa1671 [3] Number	Beaumont, TX Aa1672 Number	Salinas, CA Aa1673 [4] Number	Racine, WI Aa1674 Number
1890	—	—	—	—	—	—	—	—	—	—	—
1900	—	—	—	—	—	—	—	84,060	—	—	—
1910	—	—	—	—	51,678	—	—	121,093	—	—	—
1920	—	—	—	—	59,183	—	—	140,966	—	—	58,593
1930	—	—	—	—	71,864	—	—	140,097	57,732	—	67,542
1940	—	—	—	—	75,503	—	—	138,669	59,061	—	67,195
1950	—	—	—	—	97,371	—	—	143,028	94,169	—	76,537
1960	—	—	—	—	111,403	—	60,678	144,763	119,178	—	95,862
1970	84,054	56,936	—	69,329	120,794	97,935	70,197	138,352	116,350	62,456	117,408
1980	109,193	79,921	70,450	103,768	122,806	106,593	94,961	132,585	123,729	82,600	118,987
1990	128,211	128,043	126,342	126,215	124,524	123,899	123,651	122,971	122,841	122,225	121,788

Year	Fargo–Moorhead, ND–MN Aa1675 Number	Portland, ME Aa1676 Number	Lake Charles, LA Aa1677 Number	Hamilton, OH Aa1678 Number	Brownsville, TX Aa1679 Number	Danbury, CT–NY Aa1680 [5] Number	Richland–Kennewick–Pasco, WA Aa1681 [6] Number	Champaign–Urbana, IL Aa1682 Number	Portsmouth–Dover–Rochester, NH–ME Aa1683 Number	Manchester, NH Aa1684 Number	Kailua, HI Aa1685 [7] Number
1890	—	—	—	—	—	—	—	—	—	—	—
1900	—	63,715	—	—	—	—	—	—	—	56,987	—
1910	—	74,323	—	—	—	—	—	—	—	70,063	—
1920	—	87,979	—	—	—	—	—	—	—	78,384	—
1930	—	95,457	—	53,465	—	—	—	—	—	76,834	—
1940	—	100,511	—	52,035	—	—	—	—	—	77,685	—
1950	—	113,499	—	63,270	—	—	—	—	—	84,918	—
1960	72,730	111,701	89,115	89,778	—	—	—	78,014	—	91,698	—
1970	85,446	106,599	88,260	90,912	52,627	66,651	—	100,417	—	95,140	—
1980	104,643	107,099	123,820	105,026	91,611	95,371	112,171	109,278	103,722	102,844	105,712
1990	121,336	120,220	119,067	118,315	117,676	116,240	116,118	115,524	114,960	114,918	114,506

Year	Odessa, TX Aa1686 Number	Gastonia, NC Aa1687 Number	Bremerton, WA Aa1688 Number	Round Lake Beach, IL Aa1689 [8] Number	Fort Walton Beach, FL Aa1690 Number	Monroe, LA Aa1691 Number	Asheville, NC Aa1692 Number	Port Arthur, TX Aa1693 Number	Norwalk, CT Aa1694 [9] Number	High Point, NC Aa1695 Number	Waterloo–Cedar Falls, IA Aa1696 [10] Number
1890	—	—	—	—	—	—	—	—	—	—	—
1900	—	—	—	—	—	—	—	—	—	—	—
1910	—	—	—	—	—	—	—	—	—	—	—
1920	—	—	—	—	—	—	—	—	—	—	—
1930	—	—	—	—	—	—	50,193	50,902	—	—	—
1940	—	—	—	—	—	—	51,310	46,140	—	—	51,743
1950	—	—	—	—	—	—	58,437	82,150	59,646	—	84,386
1960	84,285	—	—	—	—	80,546	68,592	116,365	82,270	66,543	102,827
1970	81,645	—	—	—	—	90,567	72,451	116,474	106,707	93,547	112,881
1980	101,518	106,884	64,536	65,676	85,318	112,537	102,400	118,562	107,550	100,089	120,290
1990	113,672	113,637	112,977	112,693	112,522	110,737	110,429	109,560	108,888	108,686	108,260

Notes appear at end of table

TABLE Aa1664–1883 Urbanized areas – population: 1890–1990 [Part 2] *Continued*

	Abilene, TX	Bryan–College Station, TX	Tuscaloosa, AL	Muskegon, MI	Pueblo, CO	Fort Collins, CO	Spartanburg, SC	Panama City, FL	Petersburg, VA	Wilmington, NC	Jacksonville, NC
	Aa1697	Aa1698	Aa1699	Aa1700 [11]	Aa1701	Aa1702	Aa1703	Aa1704	Aa1705 [12]	Aa1706	Aa1707
Year	Number	Number	Number	Number	Number	Number	Number	Number	Number	Number	Number
1890	—	—	—	—	—	—	—	—	—	—	—
1900	—	—	—	—	—	—	—	—	—	—	—
1910	—	—	—	—	—	—	—	—	—	—	—
1920	—	—	—	—	—	—	—	—	—	—	—
1930	—	—	—	56,974	51,517	—	—	—	—	—	—
1940	—	—	—	63,744	54,133	—	—	—	—	—	—
1950	—	—	—	85,245	73,247	—	—	—	—	—	—
1960	91,566	—	76,815	95,350	103,336	—	—	—	—	—	—
1970	90,571	51,395	85,875	105,716	103,300	—	—	—	100,617	57,645	—
1980	99,763	83,036	99,554	105,634	109,444	78,287	100,706	78,886	106,582	88,763	72,891
1990	107,836	107,599	106,428	106,252	106,155	105,809	104,801	103,667	103,526	101,357	101,297

	Sioux Falls, SD	Lafayette–West Lafayette, IN	Fairfield, CA	Boulder, CO	Middletown, OH	Elkhart–Goshen, IN	Lynchburg, VA	Clarksville, TN–KY	Wichita Falls, TX	Nashua, NH	Sioux City, IA–NE–SD
	Aa1708	Aa1709	Aa1710	Aa1711	Aa1712	Aa1713	Aa1714	Aa1715	Aa1716	Aa1717	Aa1718
Year	Number	Number	Number	Number	Number	Number	Number	Number	Number	Number	Number
1890	—	—	—	—	—	—	—	—	—	—	—
1900	—	—	—	—	—	—	—	—	—	—	—
1910	—	—	—	—	—	—	—	—	—	—	—
1920	—	—	—	—	—	—	—	—	—	—	71,227
1930	—	—	—	—	—	—	—	—	—	—	83,110
1940	—	—	—	—	—	—	—	—	—	—	86,920
1950	52,696	—	—	—	—	—	—	—	—	—	90,101
1960	66,582	—	—	—	—	—	59,319	—	102,104	—	97,926
1970	75,146	79,117	—	68,634	—	—	70,842	—	97,564	60,961	95,937
1980	85,834	91,380	69,255	81,239	91,730	83,920	93,921	77,535	94,716	75,299	96,746
1990	100,843	100,103	99,964	98,910	98,822	98,787	98,138	97,581	97,151	96,791	96,211

	Decatur, IL	Olympia, WA	Fort Smith, AR–OK	Naples, FL	Kenosha, WI	Vineland–Millville, NJ	Bloomington–Normal, IL	Lawton, OK	Bristol, CT	Midland, TX	Hemet, CA
	Aa1719	Aa1720	Aa1721	Aa1722	Aa1723	Aa1724	Aa1725	Aa1726	Aa1727	Aa1728	Aa1729 [13]
Year	Number	Number	Number	Number	Number	Number	Number	Number	Number	Number	Number
1890	—	—	—	—	—	—	—	—	—	—	—
1900	—	—	—	—	—	—	—	—	—	—	—
1910	—	—	—	—	—	—	—	—	—	—	—
1920	—	—	—	—	—	—	—	—	—	—	—
1930	57,510	—	—	—	50,262	—	—	—	—	—	—
1940	59,305	—	—	—	48,765	—	—	—	—	—	—
1950	73,713	—	56,046	—	54,368	—	—	—	—	—	—
1960	89,516	—	61,640	—	72,852	—	—	61,941	—	63,274	—
1970	99,693	—	75,517	—	84,262	73,579	69,392	95,687	71,732	60,371	—
1980	107,864	68,616	90,021	53,675	85,742	88,822	82,397	96,134	83,601	71,606	55,377
1990	96,039	95,471	94,486	94,344	94,292	94,236	94,186	92,634	92,418	91,999	90,929

Notes appear at end of table

(continued)

TABLE Aa1664–1883   Urbanized areas – population: 1890–1990   [Part 2]   *Continued*

Year	Santa Maria, CA Aa1730 Number	Springfield, OH Aa1731 Number	Billings, MT Aa1732 Number	Muncie, IN Aa1733 Number	Yakima, WA Aa1734 Number	Kingsport, TN–VA Aa1735 Number	Albany, GA Aa1736 Number	Burlington, VT Aa1737 Number	Winter Haven, FL Aa1738 Number	Alton, IL Aa1739 Number	Alexandria, LA Aa1740 Number
1890	—	—	—	—	—	—	—	—	—	—	—
1900	—	—	—	—	—	—	—	—	—	—	—
1910	—	—	—	—	—	—	—	—	—	—	—
1920	—	60,840	—	—	—	—	—	—	—	—	—
1930	—	68,743	—	—	—	—	—	—	—	—	—
1940	—	70,662	—	—	—	—	—	—	—	—	—
1950	—	82,284	—	—	—	—	—	—	—	—	—
1960	—	90,157	60,712	77,504	—	—	58,353	—	—	—	—
1970	—	93,653	71,197	90,427	—	—	76,512	—	—	—	—
1980	57,237	86,742	84,328	91,479	81,085	89,760	88,716	76,528	72,560	88,994	92,742
1990	88,989	88,649	88,181	88,073	88,054	87,403	87,223	87,088	86,427	86,236	86,001

Year	San Angelo, TX Aa1741 Number	Wheeling, WV–OH Aa1742 Number	Visalia, CA Aa1743 Number	Johnson City, TN Aa1744 Number	Fitchburg–Leominster, MA Aa1745 Number	Las Cruces, NM Aa1746 Number	Eau Claire, WI Aa1747 Number	Stuart, FL Aa1748 Number	Tyler, TX Aa1749 Number	Lewisville, TX Aa1750 Number	Harlingen, TX Aa1751 [14] Number
1890	—	—	—	—	—	—	—	—	—	—	—
1900	—	—	—	—	—	—	—	—	—	—	—
1910	—	—	—	—	—	—	—	—	—	—	—
1920	—	80,374	—	—	—	—	—	—	—	—	—
1930	—	89,380	—	—	—	—	—	—	—	—	—
1940	—	88,990	—	—	—	—	—	—	—	—	—
1950	—	106,650	—	—	—	—	—	—	—	—	—
1960	58,815	98,951	—	—	72,347	—	—	—	51,739	—	61,658
1970	63,884	92,944	—	—	78,053	—	—	—	59,781	—	50,469
1980	73,994	101,049	58,957	78,473	76,652	55,072	72,317	—	72,927	—	66,702
1990	85,408	84,507	83,594	82,382	82,249	81,471	80,293	80,069	79,703	79,433	79,309

Year	La Crosse, WI–MN Aa1752 Number	Annapolis, MD Aa1753 Number	Redding, CA Aa1754 Number	Kannapolis, NC Aa1755 Number	Jackson, MI Aa1756 Number	Battle Creek, MI Aa1757 Number	Johnstown, PA Aa1758 Number	Yuba City, CA Aa1759 Number	Terre Haute, IN Aa1760 Number	Altoona, PA Aa1761 Number	Mansfield, OH Aa1762 Number
1890	—	—	—	—	—	—	—	—	—	—	—
1900	—	—	—	—	—	—	—	—	—	—	—
1910	—	—	—	—	—	—	67,530	—	61,240	57,412	—
1920	—	—	—	—	—	—	82,495	—	70,393	67,991	—
1930	—	—	—	—	55,187	—	89,049	—	66,398	82,054	—
1940	—	—	—	—	49,656	—	89,050	—	66,422	80,214	—
1950	—	—	—	—	51,088	—	93,354	—	78,028	86,614	—
1960	—	—	—	—	71,412	—	96,474	—	81,415	83,058	—
1970	63,373	—	—	—	78,572	—	96,146	—	80,908	81,795	77,599
1980	67,966	64,447	52,867	—	81,178	77,789	90,254	61,107	74,736	78,802	78,948
1990	78,928	78,590	78,364	78,177	78,126	77,921	77,841	77,167	77,019	76,551	76,521

Notes appear at end of table

TABLE Aa1664–1883 Urbanized areas – population: 1890–1990 [Part 2] *Continued*

Year	Longview, TX	Columbia, MO	St. Joseph, MO–KS	Fayetteville–Springdale, AR	Bay City, MI	Burlington, NC	St. Cloud, MN	Anderson, IN	Rochester, MN	Athens, GA	Crystal Lake, IL
	Aa1763	Aa1764	Aa1765	Aa1766	Aa1767	Aa1768	Aa1769	Aa1770	Aa1771	Aa1772	Aa1773
	Number	Number	Number	Number	Number	Number	Number	Number	Number	Number	Number
1890	—	—	52,324	—	—	—	—	—	—	—	—
1900	—	—	102,979	—	—	—	—	—	—	—	—
1910	—	—	77,403	—	—	—	—	—	—	—	—
1920	—	—	77,939	—	—	—	—	—	—	—	—
1930	—	—	80,935	—	—	—	—	—	—	—	—
1940	—	—	75,711	—	50,346	—	—	—	—	—	—
1950	—	—	82,290	—	55,690	—	—	—	—	—	—
1960	—	—	81,187	—	72,763	—	—	—	—	—	—
1970	—	59,231	77,223	—	78,097	—	—	80,704	56,604	—	—
1980	69,757	65,380	79,936	62,703	77,678	66,580	58,375	78,581	60,473	62,896	—
1990	76,429	75,854	75,395	74,880	74,118	74,053	74,037	74,037	73,563	73,282	72,498

Year	Grand Junction, CO	Chico, CA	Gadsden, AL	Lewiston–Auburn, ME	Newburgh, NY	Greeley, CO	Vacaville, CA	Bloomington, IN	Iowa City, IA	Yuma, AZ–CA	Hagerstown, MD–PA–WV
	Aa1774	Aa1775	Aa1776	Aa1777	Aa1778	Aa1779	Aa1780	Aa1781	Aa1782	Aa1783	Aa1784 [15]
	Number	Number	Number	Number	Number	Number	Number	Number	Number	Number	Number
1890	—	—	—	—	—	—	—	—	—	—	—
1900	—	—	—	—	—	—	—	—	—	—	—
1910	—	—	—	—	—	—	—	—	—	—	—
1920	—	—	—	—	—	—	—	—	—	—	—
1930	—	—	—	—	—	—	—	—	—	—	—
1940	—	—	—	—	—	—	—	—	—	—	—
1950	—	—	—	—	—	—	—	—	—	—	—
1960	—	—	68,944	65,253	—	—	—	—	—	—	—
1970	—	—	67,706	65,212	—	—	—	—	—	—	—
1980	56,854	51,914	74,730	70,108	65,711	62,297	—	63,513	59,295	54,657	66,277
1990	71,938	71,831	71,630	71,598	71,584	71,578	71,535	71,440	71,372	70,955	70,206

Year	Hickory, NC	Florence, AL	Steubenville–Weirton, OH–WV–PA	Lima, OH	Anniston, AL	Napa, CA	Ocala, FL	Charlottesville, VA	Punta Gorda, FL	Medford, OR	Hyannis, MA
	Aa1785	Aa1786	Aa1787	Aa1788	Aa1789	Aa1790	Aa1791	Aa1792	Aa1793	Aa1794	Aa1795
	Number	Number	Number	Number	Number	Number	Number	Number	Number	Number	Number
1890	—	—	—	—	—	—	—	—	—	—	—
1900	—	—	—	—	—	—	—	—	—	—	—
1910	—	—	—	—	—	—	—	—	—	—	—
1920	—	—	—	—	—	—	—	—	—	—	—
1930	—	—	—	—	—	—	—	—	—	—	—
1940	—	—	—	—	—	—	—	—	—	—	—
1950	—	—	—	—	—	—	—	—	—	—	—
1960	—	—	81,613	62,963	—	—	—	—	—	—	—
1970	—	—	85,492	70,295	—	—	—	—	—	—	—
1980	62,329	72,669	77,651	70,104	75,614	59,277	50,860	59,422	—	52,469	—
1990	69,914	69,186	69,118	68,621	68,150	68,049	68,004	67,553	67,033	66,974	66,713

Notes appear at end of table

(continued)

TABLE Aa1664–1883   Urbanized areas – population: 1890–1990   [Part 2]   *Continued*

Year	Elmira, NY	Bismarck, ND	Denton, TX	Houma, LA	Lawrence, KS	Texarkana, TX–Texarkana, AR	Monessen, PA	Merced, CA	Vero Beach, FL	Dubuque, IA–IL	Decatur, AL
	Aa1796	Aa1797 [16]	Aa1798	Aa1799	Aa1800	Aa1801	Aa1802	Aa1803	Aa1804	Aa1805	Aa1806
	Number	Number	Number	Number	Number	Number	Number	Number	Number	Number	Number
1890	—	—	—	—	—	—	—	—	—	—	—
1900	—	—	—	—	—	—	—	—	—	—	—
1910	—	—	—	—	—	—	—	—	—	—	—
1920	—	—	—	—	—	—	—	—	—	—	—
1930	—	—	—	—	—	—	—	—	—	—	—
1940	—	—	—	—	—	—	—	—	—	—	—
1950	—	—	—	—	—	—	—	—	—	—	—
1960	—	—	—	—	—	53,420	—	—	—	—	—
1970	—	—	—	—	—	58,570	—	—	—	65,550	—
1980	68,227	61,105	—	65,780	52,810	63,474	65,884	—	—	68,149	54,710
1990	66,612	66,476	66,445	65,879	65,755	65,086	65,072	64,742	64,707	63,705	63,541

Year	Great Falls, MT	Santa Fe, NM	Port Huron, MI	Holland, MI	Pine Bluff, AR	Cheyenne, WY	Bangor, ME	State College, PA	Rapid City, SD	Sheboygan, WI	Warner Robins, GA
	Aa1807	Aa1808	Aa1809	Aa1810	Aa1811	Aa1812	Aa1813	Aa1814	Aa1815	Aa1816	Aa1817
	Number	Number	Number	Number	Number	Number	Number	Number	Number	Number	Number
1890	—	—	—	—	—	—	—	—	—	—	—
1900	—	—	—	—	—	—	—	—	—	—	—
1910	—	—	—	—	—	—	—	—	—	—	—
1920	—	—	—	—	—	—	—	—	—	—	—
1930	—	—	—	—	—	—	—	—	—	—	—
1940	—	—	—	—	—	—	—	—	—	—	—
1950	—	—	—	—	—	—	—	—	—	—	—
1960	57,629	—	—	—	—	—	—	—	—	—	—
1970	70,905	—	—	—	60,907	—	—	—	—	—	—
1980	66,256	52,042	59,647	—	62,817	58,429	60,003	51,298	50,882	58,531	54,923
1990	63,506	63,023	62,774	62,418	61,941	61,890	61,402	61,239	61,124	61,012	60,976

Year	Owensboro, KY	Goldsboro, NC	Joplin, MO	Hattiesburg, MS	Kankakee, IL	Bellingham, WA	Oshkosh, WI	Dothan, AL	Taunton, MA	Rock Hill, SC	Temple, TX
	Aa1818	Aa1819	Aa1820	Aa1821	Aa1822	Aa1823	Aa1824	Aa1825	Aa1826	Aa1827	Aa1828
	Number	Number	Number	Number	Number	Number	Number	Number	Number	Number	Number
1890	—	—	—	—	—	—	—	—	—	—	—
1900	—	—	—	—	—	—	—	—	—	—	—
1910	—	—	—	—	—	—	—	—	—	—	—
1920	—	—	—	—	—	—	—	—	—	—	—
1930	—	—	—	—	—	—	—	—	—	—	—
1940	—	—	—	—	—	—	—	—	—	—	—
1950	—	—	—	—	—	—	—	—	—	—	—
1960	—	—	—	—	—	—	—	—	—	—	—
1970	53,133	—	—	—	—	—	55,480	—	—	—	—
1980	57,549	57,670	57,658	56,542	61,451	51,025	52,958	51,976	52,334	50,846	53,191
1990	60,645	60,230	60,208	59,757	59,695	59,317	58,935	58,925	58,884	58,757	58,710

Notes appear at end of table

TABLE Aa1664–1883   Urbanized areas – population: 1890–1990   [Part 2]   *Continued*

Year	Parkersburg, WV–OH	Frederick, MD	Pascagoula, MS	Myrtle Beach, SC	Galveston, TX	Grand Forks, ND–MN	Deltona, FL	Benton Harbor, MI	Sumter, SC	Williamsport, PA	Wausau, WI
	Aa1829	Aa1830	Aa1831 [17]	Aa1832	Aa1833 [1]	Aa1834	Aa1835	Aa1836	Aa1837	Aa1838	Aa1839
	Number	Number	Number	Number	Number	Number	Number	Number	Number	Number	Number
1890	—	—	—	—	—	—	—	—	—	—	—
1900	—	—	—	—	—	—	—	—	—	—	—
1910	—	—	—	—	—	—	—	—	—	—	—
1920	—	—	—	—	—	—	—	—	—	—	—
1930	—	—	—	—	52,938	—	—	—	—	—	—
1940	—	—	—	—	60,862	—	—	—	—	—	—
1950	—	—	—	—	71,527	—	—	—	—	—	—
1960	—	—	—	—	67,175	—	—	—	—	—	—
1970	—	—	—	—	61,809	—	—	—	—	—	—
1980	63,181	—	65,174	—	61,382	52,310	—	60,639	—	58,650	52,990
1990	58,683	58,393	58,386	58,384	58,263	58,103	58,053	57,744	57,632	57,425	57,352

Year	Missoula, MT	Kokomo, IN	Longview, WA–OR	Fredericksburg, VA	Lompoc, CA	Auburn–Opelika, AL	Glens Falls, NY	Idaho Falls, ID	Beloit, WI–IL	Indio–Coachella, CA	Greenville, NC
	Aa1840	Aa1841	Aa1842	Aa1843	Aa1844	Aa1845	Aa1846	Aa1847	Aa1848	Aa1849	Aa1850
	Number	Number	Number	Number	Number	Number	Number	Number	Number	Number	Number
1890	—	—	—	—	—	—	—	—	—	—	—
1900	—	—	—	—	—	—	—	—	—	—	—
1910	—	—	—	—	—	—	—	—	—	—	—
1920	—	—	—	—	—	—	—	—	—	—	—
1930	—	—	—	—	—	—	—	—	—	—	—
1940	—	—	—	—	—	—	—	—	—	—	—
1950	—	—	—	—	—	—	—	—	—	—	—
1960	—	—	—	—	—	—	—	—	—	—	—
1970	—	—	—	—	—	—	—	—	—	—	—
1980	58,035	61,224	55,076	—	—	51,823	51,382	—	50,834	—	—
1990	57,196	57,146	57,123	56,718	56,591	56,510	56,475	56,356	56,076	56,038	55,884

Year	Lodi, CA	Sherman–Denison, TX	Kissimmee, FL	Victoria, TX	Pittsfield, MA	Florence, SC	Cumberland, MD–WV	Danville, VA	Slidell, LA	Newark, OH	Pocatello, ID
	Aa1851	Aa1852	Aa1853	Aa1854	Aa1855	Aa1856	Aa1857	Aa1858	Aa1859	Aa1860	Aa1861
	Number	Number	Number	Number	Number	Number	Number	Number	Number	Number	Number
1890	—	—	—	—	—	—	—	—	—	—	—
1900	—	—	—	—	—	—	—	—	—	—	—
1910	—	—	—	—	—	—	—	—	—	—	—
1920	—	—	—	—	—	—	—	—	—	—	—
1930	—	—	—	—	—	—	—	—	—	—	—
1940	—	—	—	—	—	—	—	—	—	—	—
1950	—	—	—	—	—	—	—	—	—	—	—
1960	—	—	—	—	62,306	—	—	—	—	—	—
1970	—	55,343	—	—	62,872	—	—	—	—	—	—
1980	—	56,441	—	50,725	57,554	56,240	59,331	54,815	—	50,839	53,401
1990	55,590	55,522	55,419	55,122	55,047	54,659	54,655	54,315	54,084	54,063	53,903

Notes appear at end of table

(continued)

TABLE Aa1664–1883   Urbanized areas – population: 1890–1990   [Part 2]   *Continued*

Year	Newport, RI	Pottstown, PA	Jackson, TN	Janesville, WI	Sharon, PA–OH	Davis, CA	Bristol, TN–VA	Anderson, SC	Longmont, CO	Casper, WY	Spring Hill, FL
	Aa1862	Aa1863	Aa1864	Aa1865	Aa1866	Aa1867	Aa1868	Aa1869	Aa1870	Aa1871	Aa1872
	Number	Number	Number	Number	Number	Number	Number	Number	Number	Number	Number
1890	—	—	—	—	—	—	—	—	—	—	—
1900	—	—	—	—	—	—	—	—	—	—	—
1910	—	—	—	—	—	—	—	—	—	—	—
1920	—	—	—	—	—	—	—	—	—	—	—
1930	—	—	—	—	—	—	—	—	—	—	—
1940	—	—	—	—	—	—	—	—	—	—	—
1950	—	—	—	—	—	—	—	—	—	—	—
1960	—	—	—	—	—	—	—	—	—	—	—
1970	—	—	—	—	—	—	—	—	—	—	—
1980	51,381	—	50,338	51,643	50,933	—	53,537	51,014	—	59,287	—
1990	53,481	53,371	53,031	52,995	52,816	52,711	52,563	52,492	52,464	52,248	52,056

Year	Rome, GA	Titusville, FL	Watsonville, CA	Rocky Mount, NC	Logan, UT	San Luis Obispo, CA	Ithaca, NY	Brunswick, GA	Concord, NC	Danville, IL	Enid, OK
	Aa1873	Aa1874	Aa1875	Aa1876	Aa1877	Aa1878	Aa1879	Aa1880	Aa1881	Aa1882	Aa1883
	Number	Number	Number	Number	Number	Number	Number	Number	Number	Number	Number
1890	—	—	—	—	—	—	—	—	—	—	—
1900	—	—	—	—	—	—	—	—	—	—	—
1910	—	—	—	—	—	—	—	—	—	—	—
1920	—	—	—	—	—	—	—	—	—	—	—
1930	—	—	—	—	—	—	—	—	—	—	—
1940	—	—	—	—	—	—	—	—	—	—	—
1950	—	—	—	—	—	—	—	—	—	—	—
1960	—	—	—	—	—	—	—	—	—	—	—
1970	—	—	—	—	—	—	—	—	—	—	—
1980	51,082	—	—	—	—	—	—	—	71,994	52,243	50,601
1990	51,589	51,549	51,378	50,870	50,401	50,305	50,132	50,066	—	—	—

1 1970–1980: Texas City-La Marque, Texas. Census Bureau combined Galveston, Texas, urbanized area (UA) and Texas City, Texas, UA in 1960. Separated in this table.

2 Census Bureau combined Aurora, Illinois, UA and Elgin, Illinois, UA in 1970. Separated in this table.

3 1990: Duluth, Minnesota-Wisconsin.

4 1990: Salinas-Seaside, California.

5 1970: Danbury, Connecticut.

6 1980: Richland-Kennewick, Washington.

7 1980: Kailua-Kaneohe, Hawai'i.

8 1990: Round Lake Beach-McHenry, Illinois-Wisconsin.

9 1990: Stamford, Connecticut-New York. Census Bureau combined Stamford, Connecticut, UA and Norwalk, Connecticut, UA in 1950. Separated in this table.

10 1990: Waterloo–Cedar Falls, Iowa.

11 1960–1980: Muskegon-Muskegon Heights, Michigan; 1930–1950: Muskegon, Michigan.

12 1970–1980: Petersburg-Colonial Heights, Virginia.

13 1990: Hemet-San Jacinto, California.

14 1960–1980: Harlingen-San Benito, Texas.

15 1980: Hagerstown, Maryland-Pennsylvania.

16 1980: Bismarck-Mandan, North Dakota.

17 1980: Pascagoula-Moss Point, Mississippi.

Sources
See the sources for Table Aa1471–1663.

Documentation
See the text for Table Aa1471–1663.

TABLE Aa1884–1895 Metropolitan areas – population, density, land area, international migration, and natural increase: 1980–1997

Contributed by Michael R. Haines

Metropolitan area	FIPS code	Population 1980	Population 1990	Population 1996	Population 1997	Rank 1990	Rank 1997	Net change, 1990–1997	Natural increase, 1990–1997	Net international migration, 1990–1997	Density, 1997	Land area, 1990
	Aa1884	Aa1885	Aa1886 [1]	Aa1887	Aa1888	Aa1889	Aa1890	Aa1891	Aa1892	Aa1893	Aa1894 [2]	Aa1895
	—	Number	Number	Number	Number	Number	Number	Number	Number	Number	Persons per square mile	Square miles
Abilene, TX MSA	0040	110,932	119,655	121,404	121,456	223	232	1,801	7,301	1,423	132.6	915.7
Albany, GA MSA	0120	112,394	112,571	117,074	117,674	182	237	5,103	6,963	227	171.7	685.5
Albany–Schenectady–Troy, NY MSA	0160	824,729	861,623	879,051	876,420	221	54	14,797	25,517	8,127	272.0	3,222.4
Albuquerque, NM MSA	0200	485,429	589,131 [3]	668,507	674,837	52	62	85,706	42,054	11,331	113.5	5,943.5
Alexandria, LA MSA	0220	135,282	131,556	126,025	126,491	268	222	−5,065	4,909	660	95.6	1,322.7
Allentown–Bethlehem–Easton, PA MSA	0240	551,052	595,081	612,421	613,836	202	67	18,755	10,944	4,408	556.4	1,103.2
Altoona, PA MSA	0280	136,621	130,542	131,327	130,923	237	219	381	149	226	249.0	525.8
Amarillo, TX MSA	0320	173,699	187,514	206,321	208,165	73	156	20,651	11,540	3,775	114.1	1,823.9
Anchorage, AK MSA	0380	174,431	226,338	249,377	251,047	76	141	24,709	27,284	3,503	147.9	1,697.6
Anniston, AL MSA	0450	119,761	116,032	116,513	117,092	228	239	1,060	3,393	110	192.4	608.5
Appleton–Oshkosh–Neenah, WI MSA	0460	291,369	315,121	339,493	342,154	120	115	27,033	15,207	961	244.6	1,398.9
Asheville, NC MSA	0480	177,761	191,772	209,568	211,284	84	154	19,512	2,484	505	191.1	1,105.7
Athens, GA MSA	0500	104,672	126,262	136,932	138,523	96	209	12,261	6,738	1,200	234.4	591.0
Atlanta, GA MSA	0520	2,233,229	2,959,500	3,531,203	3,627,184	13	11	667,684	233,406	54,892	592.1	6,126.2
Augusta–Aiken, GA–SC MSA	0600	363,451	415,220	453,049	457,228	86	85	42,008	24,570	1,774	186.7	2,448.9
Austin–San Marcos, TX MSA	0640	585,051	846,227	1,040,709	1,071,023	8	42	224,796	74,578	21,583	253.4	4,226.0
Bakersfield, CA MSA	0680	403,089	544,981	621,719	628,605	47	64	83,624	59,828	23,106	77.2	8,141.6
Bangor, ME NECMA	0733	137,015	146,601	143,895	143,300	260	202	−3,301	2,991	225	42.2	3,396.0
Barnstable–Yarmouth, MA NECMA	0743	147,925	186,605	202,339	205,128	93	158	18,523	−1,558	1,264	518.3	395.8
Baton Rouge, LA MSA	0760	494,151	528,261	566,114	570,165	126	71	41,904	35,822	3,217	359.4	1,586.6
Beaumont–Port Arthur, TX MSA	0840	373,211	361,218	374,440	374,991	193	105	13,773	14,850	3,657	174.1	2,154.4
Bellingham, WA MSA	0860	106,701	127,780	152,217	154,249	20	191	26,469	6,011	3,238	72.8	2,120.1
Benton Harbor, MI MSA	0870	171,276	161,378	161,175	160,713	243	187	−665	5,229	711	281.5	571.0
Billings, MT MSA	0880	108,035	113,419	125,514	125,771	77	223	12,352	4,934	189	47.7	2,635.2
Biloxi–Gulfport–Pascagoula, MS MSA	0920	300,176	312,368	341,166	343,423	92	114	31,055	16,772	857	192.4	1,784.5
Binghamton, NY MSA	0960	263,460	264,497	253,987	251,698	272	139	−12,799	6,602	3,982	205.4	1,225.6
Birmingham, AL MSA	1000	815,333	839,942	894,024	900,029	151	53	60,087	29,315	2,705	282.4	3,187.3
Bismarck, ND MSA	1010	79,988	83,831	90,162	91,044	118	262	7,213	3,865	388	25.6	3,559.6
Bloomington, IN MSA	1020	98,783	108,978	115,917	116,653	153	240	7,675	3,932	752	295.8	394.4
Bloomington–Normal, IL MSA	1040	119,149	129,180	139,577	140,797	111	205	11,617	6,820	684	119.0	1,183.6
Boise City, ID MSA	1080	256,881	295,851	372,816	383,843	4	103	87,992	23,260	3,893	233.4	1,644.8
Boston–Worcester–Lawrence–Brockton, MA–NH NECMA	1123	5,336,242	5,685,763	5,788,380	5,827,654	207	7	141,891	241,159	104,750	903.5	6,450.0
Brownsville–Harlingen–San Benito, TX MSA	1240	209,727	260,120	313,835	320,801	12	118	60,681	41,271	21,254	354.2	905.6
Bryan–College Station, TX MSA	1260	93,588	121,862	131,494	133,008	106	216	11,146	9,465	3,024	227.1	585.8
Buffalo–Niagara Falls, NY MSA	1280	1,242,826	1,189,340	1,173,350	1,164,721	258	36	−24,619	27,208	7,675	742.9	1,567.7
Burlington, VT NECMA	1303	154,935	177,059	189,497	191,088	127	168	14,029	10,468	1,625	151.8	1,258.7
Canton–Massillon, OH MSA	1320	404,421	394,106	402,677	402,644	211	97	8,538	10,736	415	414.7	970.9
Casper, WY MSA	1350	71,856	61,226	63,647	63,638	192	272	2,412	3,264	134	11.9	5,340.1
Cedar Rapids, IA MSA	1360	169,775	168,767	179,941	181,704	135	171	12,937	9,418	1,220	253.2	717.5
Champaign–Urbana, IL MSA	1400	168,392	173,025	167,971	168,473	263	178	−4,552	9,097	1,702	168.9	997.2

Notes appear at end of table

(continued)

TABLE Aa1884–1895 Metropolitan areas – population, density, land area, international migration, and natural increase: 1980–1997 *Continued*

Metropolitan area	FIPS code	1980	1990[1]	1996	1997	Rank 1990	Rank 1997	Net change, 1990–1997	Natural increase, 1990–1997	Net international migration, 1990–1997	Density, 1997[2]	Land area, 1990
	Aa1884	Aa1885	Aa1886	Aa1887	Aa1888	Aa1889	Aa1890	Aa1891	Aa1892	Aa1893	Aa1894	Aa1895
	—	Number	Number	Number	Number	Number	Number	Number	Number	Number	Persons per square mile	Square miles
Charleston–North Charleston, SC MSA	1440	430,346	506,877	502,536	509,856	234	78	2,979	35,836	1,976	196.7	2,591.7
Charleston, WV MSA	1480	269,595	250,454	254,390	253,850	225	137	3,396	3,720	686	203.2	1,249.5
Charlotte–Gastonia–Rock Hill, NC–SC MSA	1520	971,447	1,162,140	1,318,718	1,350,243	40	32	188,103	63,220	9,939	399.7	3,378.4
Charlottesville, VA MSA	1540	113,568	131,373	144,599	146,617	67	198	15,244	5,420	1,396	124.6	1,177.1
Chattanooga, TN–GA MSA	1560	417,838	424,347	444,514	447,488	170	88	23,141	12,442	1,567	245.2	1,824.7
Cheyenne, WY MSA	1580	68,649	73,142	78,703	78,473	149	269	5,331	4,669	292	29.2	2,686.2
Chicago–Gary–Kenosha, IL–IN–WI CMSA	1602	8,114,844	8,239,820	8,590,176	8,642,175	175	3	402,355	551,711	258,603	1,247.0	6,930.5
Chicago, IL PMSA	1600	7,246,048	7,410,858	7,726,089	7,773,896	—	—	363,038	515,656	255,140	1,534.8	5,065.0
Gary, IN PMSA	2960	642,733	604,526	621,132	623,423	—	—	18,897	25,552	2,622	681.2	915.2
Kankakee, IL PMSA	3740	102,926	96,255	101,560	101,984	—	—	5,729	3,962	541	150.5	677.5
Kenosha, WI PMSA	3800	123,137	128,181	141,395	142,872	160	165	14,691	6,541	300	523.7	272.8
Chico–Paradise, CA MSA	1620	143,851	182,120	192,953	194,160	163	23	12,040	3,857	3,174	118.4	1,639.6
Cincinnati–Hamilton, OH–KY–IN CMSA	1642	1,726,430	1,817,569	1,919,010	1,934,145			116,576	87,121	6,470	507.7	3,809.6
Cincinnati, OH–KY–IN PMSA	1640	1,467,643	1,526,090	1,595,652	1,607,396	—	—	81,306	71,907	5,369	480.9	3,342.3
Hamilton–Middletown, OH PMSA	3200	258,787	291,479	323,358	326,749	—	—	35,270	15,214	1,101	699.2	467.3
Clarksville–Hopkinsville, TN–KY MSA	1660	150,220	150,439	194,103	197,481	38	162	28,042	16,941	553	156.7	1,260.6
Cleveland–Akron, OH CMSA	1692	2,938,277	2,859,644	2,909,182	2,908,439	222	14	48,795	98,370	14,301	805.1	3,612.7
Akron, OH PMSA	0080	660,328	657,575	679,586	682,442	—	—	24,867	24,451	2,164	753.9	905.2
Cleveland–Lorain–Elyria, OH PMSA	1680	2,277,949	2,202,069	2,229,596	2,225,997	—	—	23,928	73,919	12,137	822.2	2,707.5
Colorado Springs, CO MSA	1720	309,424	397,014	472,393	480,041	19	80	83,027	38,100	1,821	225.7	2,126.7
Columbia, MO MSA	1740	100,376	112,379	125,943	128,309	53	221	15,930	7,113	1,110	187.2	685.4
Columbia, SC MSA	1760	409,953	453,932	497,671	503,948	72	79	50,016	25,546	1,977	345.8	1,457.3
Columbus, GA–AL MSA	1800	254,660	260,862	271,418	272,035	188	133	11,173	15,192	741	173.3	1,570.0
Columbus, OH MSA	1840	1,214,291	1,345,450	1,446,583	1,460,242	122	31	114,792	79,633	8,234	464.7	3,142.1
Corpus Christi, TX MSA	1880	326,228	349,894	382,754	387,100	79	101	37,206	27,593	4,060	253.4	1,527.7
Cumberland, MD–WV MSA	1900	107,782	101,643	100,107	99,122	261	258	-2,521	-1,095	238	131.6	753.1
Dallas–Fort Worth, TX CMSA	1922	3,046,136	4,037,282	4,565,324	4,683,013	41	9	645,731	350,476	137,762	514.4	9,104.7
Dallas, TX PMSA	1920	2,055,284	2,676,248	3,043,684	3,126,613	—	—	450,365	242,833	103,271	505.4	6,186.6
Fort Worth–Arlington, TX PMSA	2800	990,852	1,361,034	1,521,640	1,556,400	—	—	195,366	107,643	34,491	533.4	2,918.1
Danville, VA MSA	1950	111,789	108,728	108,958	108,602	239	248	-126	79	194	107.1	1,014.0
Davenport–Moline–Rock Island, IA–IL MSA	1960	384,749	350,855	357,072	357,163	217	109	6,308	11,678	2,333	209.1	1,708.0
Dayton–Springfield, OH MSA	2000	942,083	951,270	949,591	944,934	245	49	-6,336	34,724	3,257	561.3	1,683.6
Daytona Beach, FL MSA	2020	269,675	399,438	457,918	465,925	36	82	66,487	-4,817	5,986	292.9	1,590.9
Decatur, AL MSA	2030	120,401	131,556	140,579	141,690	133	204	10,134	5,267	208	111.1	1,275.6
Decatur, IL MSA	2040	131,375	117,206	115,310	114,265	262	242	-2,941	3,371	432	196.8	580.6
Denver–Boulder–Greeley, CO CMSA	2082	1,741,899	1,980,140	2,271,732	2,318,355	33	20	338,215	144,337	36,547	272.9	8,496.2
Boulder–Longmont, CO PMSA	1125	189,625	225,339	257,557	261,617	—	—	36,278	14,526	4,935	352.3	742.5
Denver, CO PMSA	2080	1,428,836	1,622,980	1,862,554	1,901,156	—	—	278,176	119,965	28,805	505.5	3,760.9
Greeley, CO PMSA	3060	123,438	131,821	151,621	155,582	—	—	23,761	9,846	2,807	39.0	3,992.8
Des Moines, IA MSA	2120	367,561	392,928	426,992	429,717	101	92	36,789	23,275	4,218	248.7	1,727.7

Metropolitan area	FIPS code	Population 1980	Population 1990 [1]	Population 1996	Population 1997	Rank 1990	Rank 1997	Net change, 1990–1997	Natural increase, 1990–1997	Net international migration, 1990–1997	Density, 1997 [2] (Persons per square mile)	Land area, 1990 (Square miles)
	Aa1884	Aa1885	Aa1886	Aa1887	Aa1888	Aa1889	Aa1890	Aa1891	Aa1892	Aa1893	Aa1894	Aa1895
	—	Number	Number	Number	Number	Number	Number	Number	Number	Number		
Detroit–Ann Arbor–Flint, MI CMSA	2162	5,293,161	5,187,171	5,423,379	5,438,756	176	8	251,585	256,342	50,466	828.3	6,565.9
Ann Arbor, MI PMSA	0440	454,977	490,058	530,735	539,415	—	—	49,357	27,834	5,556	265.8	2,029.1
Detroit, MI PMSA	2160	4,387,735	4,266,654	4,457,136	4,463,948	—	—	197,294	205,112	43,696	1,145.5	3,897.1
Flint, MI PMSA	2640	450,449	430,459	435,508	435,393	—	—	4,934	23,396	1,214	680.6	639.7
Dothan, AL MSA	2180	122,453	130,964	133,387	134,270	206	213	3,306	6,460	241	117.6	1,141.5
Dover, DE MSA	2190	98,219	110,993	121,752	122,709	80	226	11,716	6,808	615	207.7	590.7
Dubuque, IA MSA	2200	93,745	86,403	88,329	88,084	214	264	1,681	2,553	154	144.8	608.2
Duluth–Superior, MN–WI MSA	2240	266,650	239,971	237,625	238,184	246	143	-1,787	-22	486	31.6	7,535.0
Eau Claire, WI MSA	2290	130,932	137,543	142,804	143,486	187	201	5,943	4,528	358	87.1	1,648.2
El Paso, TX MSA	2320	479,899	591,610	685,018	701,576	26	60	109,966	87,348	62,298	692.5	1,013.1
Elkhart–Goshen, IN MSA	2330	137,330	156,198	168,811	170,725	103	176	14,527	10,361	1,083	368.1	463.8
Elmira, NY MSA	2335	97,656	95,195	93,596	93,088	259	260	-2,107	1,929	855	228.0	408.2
Enid, OK MSA	2340	62,820	56,735	56,878	56,699	238	273	-36	1,112	206	53.6	1,058.5
Erie, PA MSA	2360	279,780	275,572	280,027	279,401	224	132	3,829	9,576	1,407	348.4	802.0
Eugene–Springfield, OR MSA	2400	275,226	282,912	306,529	311,356	90	123	28,444	8,599	1,933	68.4	4,554.2
Evansville–Henderson, IN–KY MSA	2440	276,252	278,990	288,004	288,929	196	129	9,939	7,399	658	196.9	1,467.4
Fargo–Moorhead, ND–MN MSA	2520	137,574	153,296	164,752	166,396	121	182	13,100	8,421	2,147	59.2	2,811.0
Fayetteville, NC MSA	2560	247,160	274,713	283,737	284,047	200	131	9,334	29,272	1,435	434.9	653.1
Fayetteville–Springdale–Rogers, AR MSA	2580	178,609	210,908	261,283	266,980	7	134	56,072	11,361	1,540	148.9	1,793.5
Flagstaff, AZ–UT MSA	2620	79,032	101,760	117,943	119,547	30	235	17,787	10,398	779	5.3	22,611.3
Florence, AL MSA	2650	135,065	131,327	136,749	137,288	181	210	5,961	2,775	292	108.6	1,264.1
Florence, SC MSA	2655	110,163	114,344	123,224	124,379	117	224	10,035	4,314	258	155.6	799.2
Fort Collins–Loveland, CO MSA	2670	149,184	186,136	221,454	226,021	18	150	39,885	11,569	1,509	86.9	2,601.4
Fort Myers–Cape Coral, FL MSA	2700	205,266	335,113	380,919	387,091	45	102	51,978	1,004	4,689	481.7	803.6
Fort Pierce–Port St.Lucie, FL MSA	2710	151,196	251,071	289,731	295,646	29	128	44,575	2,048	6,387	262.1	1,128.2
Fort Smith, AR–OK MSA	2720	162,813	175,911	191,008	192,395	100	166	16,484	7,245	828	106.5	1,805.8
Fort Walton Beach, FL MSA	2750	109,920	143,777	165,633	167,580	37	180	23,803	10,295	714	179.1	935.8
Fort Wayne, IN MSA	2760	444,772	456,281	474,156	477,536	178	81	21,255	26,303	1,533	195.1	2,447.7
Fresno, CA MSA	2840	577,737	755,580	859,551	868,703	51	56	113,123	84,413	43,400	107.2	8,101.6
Gadsden, AL MSA	2880	103,057	99,840	102,327	104,313	183	250	4,473	727	127	195.1	534.8
Gainesville, FL MSA	2900	151,369	181,596	197,429	198,326	104	161	16,730	9,476	3,122	226.8	874.3
Glens Falls, NY MSA	2975	109,649	118,539	122,409	122,582	198	227	4,043	3,213	770	71.9	1,705.2
Goldsboro, NC MSA	2980	97,054	104,666	111,801	111,801	154	244	7,315	4,875	444	202.6	552.6
Grand Forks, ND–MN MSA	2985	100,944	103,272	103,482	101,700	253	253	-1,572	5,362	554	29.8	3,408.4
Grand Junction, CO MSA	2995	81,530	93,145	108,324	110,681	25	245	17,536	2,912	327	33.3	3,327.9
Grand Rapids–Muskegon–Holland, MI MSA	3000	840,824	937,891	1,015,273	1,026,295	97	46	88,404	64,009	6,851	372.0	2,758.6
Great Falls, MT MSA	3040	80,696	77,691	80,787	79,134	215	268	1,443	4,168	97	29.3	2,698.0
Green Bay, WI MSA	3080	175,280	194,594	212,443	214,244	88	152	19,650	11,427	776	405.2	528.7
Greensboro–Winston-Salem–High Point, NC MSA	3120	950,763	1,050,304	1,139,359	1,152,779	95	37	102,475	38,666	6,363	296.9	3,882.9
Greenville, NC MSA	3150	90,146	108,480	119,117	121,057	68	233	12,577	5,608	455	185.8	651.6
Greenville–Spartanburg–Anderson, SC MSA	3160	744,428	830,539	894,789	904,729	114	52	74,190	30,065	3,049	281.8	3,210.7
Harrisburg–Lebanon–Carlisle, PA MSA	3240	556,242	587,986	613,658	615,025	179	66	27,039	16,476	4,065	308.9	1,990.9
Hartford, CT NECMA	3283	1,051,606	1,123,678	1,106,322	1,105,174	254	39	-18,504	40,663	17,470	729.5	1,514.9
Hattiesburg, MS MSA	3285	89,839	98,738	107,914	109,584	74	247	10,846	4,374	208	113.7	964.1
Hickory–Morganton–Lenoir, NC MSA	3290	270,457	292,405	314,378	318,368	116	120	25,963	10,969	1,192	194.3	1,638.7

TABLE Aa1884–1895   Metropolitan areas – population, density, land area, international migration, and natural increase: 1980–1997   *Continued*

Metropolitan area	FIPS code	Population				Rank		Net change, 1990–1997	Natural increase, 1990–1997	Net international migration, 1990–1997	Density, 1997	Land area, 1990
		1980	1990 [1]	1996	1997	1990	1997					
	Aa1884	Aa1885	Aa1886	Aa1887	Aa1888	Aa1889	Aa1890	Aa1891	Aa1892	Aa1893	Aa1894 [2]	Aa1895
	—	Number	Number	Number	Number	Number	Number	Number	Number	Number	Persons per square mile	Square miles
Honolulu, HI MSA	3320	762,565	836,231	869,343	869,857	190	55	33,626	66,814	30,622	1,449.3	600.2
Houma, LA MSA	3350	176,876	182,842	189,386	191,227	180	167	8,385	11,613	405	81.7	2,339.9
Houston–Galveston–Brazoria, TX CMSA	3362	3,118,480	3,731,029	4,239,927	4,320,041	42	10	589,012	357,651	173,821	560.6	7,706.7
Brazoria, TX PMSA	1145	169,587	191,707	220,410	225,406	—	—	33,699	15,840	3,263	162.5	1,386.9
Galveston–Texas City, TX PMSA	2920	195,738	217,396	240,213	242,979	—	—	25,583	12,760	3,983	609.4	398.7
Houston, TX PMSA	3360	2,753,155	3,321,926	3,779,304	3,851,656	—	—	529,730	329,051	166,575	650.5	5,921.1
Huntington–Ashland, WV–KY–OH MSA	3400	336,410	312,529	315,973	315,204	230	122	2,675	3,263	393	145.9	2,159.8
Huntsville, AL MSA	3440	242,971	293,047	329,975	332,993	58	116	39,946	18,119	1,655	242.5	1,373.1
Indianapolis, IN MSA	3480	1,305,911	1,380,491	1,488,837	1,503,468	115	29	122,977	78,997	6,195	426.7	3,523.3
Iowa City, IA MSA	3500	81,717	96,119	101,589	102,318	162	252	6,199	6,306	1,256	166.5	614.5
Jackson, MI MSA	3520	151,495	149,756	154,448	155,346	194	189	5,590	5,659	299	219.8	706.6
Jackson, MS MSA	3560	362,038	395,396	421,683	425,383	140	93	29,987	23,229	1,123	180.0	2,363.0
Jackson, TN MSA	3580	87,273	90,801	98,320	99,319	99	257	8,518	3,110	197	117.5	845.6
Jacksonville, FL MSA	3600	722,252	906,727	1,015,271	1,034,604	54	44	127,877	55,184	11,964	392.5	2,635.6
Jacksonville, NC MSA	3605	112,784	149,838	142,899	143,013	271	203	-6,825	19,025	437	186.5	766.9
Jamestown, NY MSA	3610	146,925	141,895	141,110	140,015	250	207	-1,880	1,966	729	131.8	1,062.1
Janesville–Beloit, WI MSA	3620	139,420	139,510	149,958	150,332	132	194	10,822	5,946	386	208.6	720.5
Johnson City–Kingsport–Bristol, TN–VA MSA	3660	433,638	436,047	456,957	460,147	169	84	24,100	4,264	1,135	160.6	2,865.5
Johnstown, PA MSA	3680	264,506	241,280	239,138	237,674	252	144	-3,606	-919	496	134.8	1,762.9
Jonesboro, AR MSA	3700	63,239	68,956	76,099	76,932	69	270	7,976	2,909	173	108.2	710.8
Joplin, MO MSA	3710	127,513	134,910	145,668	147,127	110	196	12,217	4,086	425	116.2	1,266.3
Kalamazoo–Battle Creek, MI MSA	3720	420,771	429,453	444,389	446,699	190	90	17,246	19,254	1,736	237.4	1,881.8
Kansas City, MO–KS MSA	3760	1,449,380	1,582,874	1,688,301	1,709,273	125	24	126,399	79,810	11,442	316.1	5,406.8
Killeen–Temple, TX MSA	3810	214,587	255,299	298,765	299,740	32	126	44,441	29,748	2,166	142.0	2,110.9
Knoxville, TN MSA	3840	546,488	585,960	648,150	654,181	66	63	68,221	16,675	2,688	267.1	2,449.1
Kokomo, IN MSA	3850	103,715	96,946	100,250	99,981	203	256	3,035	3,862	303	180.6	553.5
La Crosse, WI–MN MSA	3870	109,438	116,401	121,179	121,507	185	230	5,106	3,930	465	120.2	1,011.2
Lafayette, LA MSA	3880	330,786	345,053	368,149	372,027	130	106	26,974	22,343	1,060	143.4	2,593.8
Lafayette, IN MSA	3920	153,247	161,572	171,084	171,539	165	174	9,967	6,998	1,153	189.6	904.9
Lake Charles, LA MSA	3960	167,223	168,134	178,094	178,874	164	172	10,740	8,959	601	167.0	1,071.2
Lakeland–Winter Haven, FL MSA	3980	321,652	405,382	441,966	448,646	78	87	43,264	12,517	5,618	239.3	1,874.9
Lancaster, PA MSA	4000	362,346	422,822	450,347	454,063	147	86	31,241	22,292	2,863	478.4	949.1
Lansing–East Lansing, MI MSA	4040	419,750	432,684	446,820	447,349	201	89	14,665	23,353	3,856	262.0	1,707.2
Laredo, TX MSA	4080	99,258	133,239	177,029	183,219	2	169	49,980	28,520	15,994	54.6	3,357.0
Las Cruces, NM MSA	4100	96,340	135,510	164,029	168,470	11	179	32,960	16,116	9,866	44.2	3,807.4
Las Vegas, NV–AZ MSA	4120	528,000	852,646	1,197,613	1,262,099	1	34	409,453	63,217	22,557	32.1	39,370.3
Lawrence, KS MSA	4150	67,640	81,798	89,674	91,093	71	261	9,295	4,480	874	199.3	457.0
Lawton, OK MSA	4200	112,456	111,486	114,954	113,957	209	243	2,471	9,630	359	106.6	1,069.4
Lewiston–Auburn, ME NECMA	4243	99,509	105,259	101,572	101,045	269	255	-4,214	2,239	-153	214.9	470.3
Lexington, KY MSA	4280	370,900	405,936	439,719	444,073	98	91	38,137	19,809	2,450	231.3	1,920.0
Lima, OH MSA	4320	154,795	154,340	155,469	154,944	236	190	604	5,633	311	192.3	805.8
Lincoln, NE MSA	4360	192,884	213,641	231,080	233,319	104	146	19,678	11,810	2,982	278.1	838.9
Little Rock–North Little Rock, AR MSA	4400	474,463	513,026	547,639	552,194	137	72	39,168	26,436	1,767	189.8	2,908.7
Longview–Marshall, TX MSA	4420	180,355	193,801	206,235	208,250	144	155	14,449	6,460	1,890	118.3	1,760.6

Population

Metropolitan area	FIPS code	1980	1990	1996	1997	Rank 1990	Rank 1997	Net change, 1990–1997	Natural increase, 1990–1997	Net international migration, 1990–1997	Density, 1997	Land area, 1990
	Aa1884	Aa1885	Aa1886 [1]	Aa1887	Aa1888	Aa1889	Aa1890	Aa1891	Aa1892	Aa1893	Aa1894 [2]	Aa1895
	—	Number	Number	Number	Number	Number	Number	Number	Number	Number	Persons per square mile	Square miles
Los Angeles–Riverside–Orange, CA CMSA		11,497,548	14,531,529	15,426,907	15,608,886	146	2	1,077,357	1,487,406	1,027,717	459.5	33,966.0
Los Angeles–Long Beach, CA PMSA	4472	7,477,238	8,863,052	9,083,596	9,145,219	—	—	282,167	912,187	712,578	2,252.5	4,060.0
Orange, CA PMSA	5945	1,932,921	2,410,668	2,619,358	2,674,091	—	—	263,423	255,240	184,603	3,386.2	789.7
Riverside–San Bernardino, CA PMSA	6780	1,558,215	2,588,793	3,009,260	3,063,608	—	—	474,815	260,820	97,917	112.3	27,270.4
Ventura, CA PMSA	8735	529,174	669,016	714,693	725,968	—	—	56,952	59,159	32,619	393.3	1,845.9
Louisville, KY-IN MSA	4520	953,520	949,012	988,802	993,369	177	48	44,357	33,436	3,805	479.4	2,072.3
Lubbock, TX MSA	4600	211,651	222,636	231,399	230,672	195	148	8,036	15,311	2,089	256.4	899.6
Lynchburg, VA MSA	4640	182,207	193,928	205,578	207,426	155	157	13,498	4,338	577	115.8	1,790.8
Macon, GA MSA	4680	272,945	291,079	312,035	316,077	119	121	24,998	14,483	1,136	206.3	1,532.1
Madison, WI MSA	4720	323,545	367,085	394,487	397,511	123	98	30,426	20,031	3,171	330.7	1,202.2
Mansfield, OH MSA	4800	181,280	174,007	175,282	174,851	235	173	844	4,680	−21	194.4	899.3
McAllen–Edinburg–Mission, TX MSA	4880	283,323	383,545	494,890	510,922	3	77	127,377	73,247	41,389	325.6	1,569.1
Medford–Ashland, OR MSA	4890	132,456	146,387	168,392	170,960	35	175	24,573	3,515	1,357	61.4	2,785.4
Melbourne–Titusville–Palm Bay, FL MSA	4900	272,959	398,978	454,514	460,977	44	83	61,999	9,300	4,142	452.6	1,018.5
Memphis, TN–AR–MS MSA	4920	938,777	1,007,306	1,075,386	1,083,186	141	41	75,880	65,820	4,980	360.1	3,007.6
Merced, CA MSA	4940	134,558	178,403	193,039	196,123	93	163	17,720	21,939	10,799	101.7	1,928.9
Miami–Fort Lauderdale, FL CMSA	4992	2,643,766	3,192,725	3,478,051	3,515,358	87	12	322,633	134,177	218,429	1,114.7	3,153.6
Fort Lauderdale, FL PMSA	2680	1,018,257	1,255,531	1,440,542	1,470,758	—	—	215,227	27,172	55,812	1,216.6	1,208.9
Miami, FL PMSA	5000	1,625,509	1,937,194	2,037,509	2,044,600	—	—	107,406	107,005	162,617	1,051.4	1,944.7
Milwaukee–Racine, WI CMSA	5082	1,570,152	1,607,183	1,637,539	1,636,572	216	26	29,389	78,341	7,877	912.7	1,793.1
Milwaukee–Waukesha, WI PMSA	5080	1,397,020	1,432,149	1,453,050	1,451,179	—	—	19,030	70,088	7,314	994.0	1,460.0
Racine, WI PMSA	6600	173,132	175,034	184,489	185,393	—	—	10,359	8,253	563	556.6	333.1
Minneapolis–St.Paul, MN–WI MSA	5120	2,198,190	2,538,776	2,760,404	2,792,137	91	16	253,361	174,676	29,948	460.4	6,064.4
Mobile, AL MSA	5160	443,536	476,923	520,622	527,118	81	76	50,195	24,464	1,815	186.3	2,829.9
Modesto, CA MSA	5170	265,900	370,522	415,977	421,818	57	94	51,296	32,296	14,688	282.2	1,494.6
Monroe, LA MSA	5200	139,241	142,191	146,839	147,055	197	197	4,864	7,358	300	240.7	611.0
Montgomery, AL MSA	5240	272,687	292,517	316,566	319,175	108	119	26,658	15,541	496	159.0	2,007.5
Muncie, IN MSA	5280	128,587	119,659	118,274	117,625	255	238	−2,034	2,549	249	299.1	393.3
Myrtle Beach, SC MSA	5330	101,419	144,053	163,661	169,178	31	177	25,125	4,922	590	149.2	1,133.7
Naples, FL MSA	5345	85,971	152,099	188,820	195,731	5	164	43,632	5,647	8,091	96.6	2,025.5
Nashville, TN MSA	5360	850,505	985,026	1,114,380	1,134,524	49	38	149,498	51,990	7,940	278.5	4,073.1
New London–Norwich, CT NECMA	5523	238,409	254,957	252,948	252,958	247	138	−1,999	11,300	1,272	379.8	666.1
New Orleans, LA MSA	5560	1,304,212	1,285,262	1,308,472	1,307,758	220	33	22,496	65,923	10,954	384.7	3,399.4
New York–Northern New Jersey–Long Island, NY–NJ–CT–PA CMSA/NECMA	5602	18,829,146	19,480,012	19,799,710	19,876,488	212	1	396,476	958,005	1,081,307	1,955.3	10,165.7
Bergen–Passaic, NJ PMSA	0875	1,292,970	1,296,244	1,327,151	1,335,393	—	—	39,149	49,281	72,877	3,185.6	419.2
Dutchess, NY PMSA	2281	245,055	259,462	262,968	264,687	—	—	5,225	11,016	2,799	330.2	801.7
Jersey City, NJ PMSA	3640	556,972	553,099	549,257	551,451	—	—	−1,648	28,535	52,094	11,808.4	46.7
Middlesex–Somerset–Hunterdon, NJ PMSA	5015	886,383	1,019,858	1,090,408	1,105,522	—	—	85,664	56,885	44,876	1,057.5	1,045.4
Monmouth–Ocean, NJ PMSA	5190	849,211	986,296	1,063,268	1,076,971	—	—	90,675	21,436	10,731	971.8	1,108.2
Nassau–Suffolk, NY PMSA	5380	2,605,813	2,609,212	2,657,422	2,666,302	—	—	57,090	121,524	55,859	2,225.6	1,198.0

Notes appear at end of table

(continued)

TABLE Aa1884–1895 Metropolitan areas – population, density, land area, international migration, and natural increase: 1980–1997   Continued

Metropolitan area	FIPS code	Population 1980	Population 1990	Population 1996	Population 1997	Rank 1990	Rank 1997	Net change, 1990–1997	Natural increase, 1990–1997	Net international migration, 1990–1997	Density, 1997	Land area, 1990
	Aa1884	Aa1885	Aa1886 [1]	Aa1887	Aa1888	Aa1889	Aa1890	Aa1891	Aa1892	Aa1893	Aa1894 [2]	Aa1895
	—	Number	Number	Number	Number	Number	Number	Number	Number	Number	Persons per square mile	Square miles
New Haven–Bridgeport–Stamford–Waterbury–Danbury, CT NECMA	5483	1,568,468	1,631,864	1,623,353	1,625,515	—	—	−6,349	66,812	31,313	1,319.7	1,231.7
New York, NY PMSA	5600	8,274,961	8,546,846	8,596,656	8,611,099	—	—	64,253	480,976	719,649	7,504.2	1,147.5
Newark, NJ PMSA	5640	1,963,576	1,915,694	1,937,648	1,943,494	—	—	27,800	88,321	79,170	1,231.8	1,577.8
Newburgh, NY–PA PMSA	5660	277,874	335,613	362,168	366,268	—	—	30,655	21,000	3,439	268.6	1,363.5
Trenton, NJ PMSA	8480	307,863	325,824	329,411	329,786	—	—	3,962	12,219	8,500	1,459.2	226.0
Norfolk–Virginia Beach–Newport News, VA–NC MSA	5720	1,200,998	1,444,710	1,535,679	1,544,945	28	27	100,235	104,448	8,857	657.8	2,348.6
Ocala, FL MSA	5790	122,488	194,835	231,483	237,308	156	145	42,473	799	1,949	150.3	1,579.0
Odessa–Midland, TX MSA	5800	198,010	225,545	239,722	243,389	135	142	17,844	18,825	5,832	135.1	1,801.4
Oklahoma City, OK MSA	5880	860,969	958,839	1,022,327	1,030,504	45	45	71,665	46,289	10,423	242.6	4,247.5
Omaha, NE–IA MSA	5920	605,419	639,580	680,307	687,454	60	61	47,874	40,760	3,709	277.7	2,475.8
Orlando, FL MSA	5960	804,774	1,224,844	1,426,408	1,467,045	36	30	242,201	70,175	33,982	420.2	3,490.9
Owensboro, KY MSA	5990	85,949	87,189	90,726	91,011	265	263	3,822	3,064	197	196.8	462.4
Panama City, FL MSA	6015	97,740	126,994	144,659	146,223	220	199	19,229	6,507	560	191.5	763.7
Parkersburg–Marietta, WV–OH MSA	6020	157,893	149,169	151,292	150,641	197	193	1,472	2,729	234	150.3	1,002.6
Pensacola, FL MSA	6080	289,782	344,406	386,978	397,085	102	99	52,679	18,123	3,672	236.4	1,679.4
Peoria–Pekin, IL MSA	6120	365,864	339,172	346,282	345,954	104	113	6,782	12,065	1,269	192.6	1,796.5
Philadelphia–Wilmington–Atlantic City, PA–NJ–DE–MD CMSA	6162	5,649,031	5,893,019	5,973,281	5,971,860	6	6	78,841	225,139	75,701	1,006.0	5,936.0
Atlantic–Cape May, NJ PMSA	0560	276,385	319,416	333,025	334,694	—	—	15,278	10,401	6,490	410.0	816.4
Philadelphia, PA–NJ PMSA	6160	4,781,235	4,922,257	4,949,301	4,940,653	—	—	18,396	182,975	62,997	1,281.4	3,855.8
Vineland–Millville–Bridgeton, NJ PMSA	8760	132,866	138,053	141,230	140,907	—	—	2,854	5,443	1,294	288.0	489.3
Wilmington–Newark, DE–MD PMSA	9160	458,545	513,293	549,725	555,606	—	—	42,313	26,320	4,920	717.4	774.5
Phoenix–Mesa, AZ MSA	6200	1,600,093	2,238,498	2,753,043	2,839,539	20	15	601,041	179,536	49,788	194.8	14,574.0
Pine Bluff, AR MSA	6240	90,718	85,487	82,905	82,259	266	266	−3,228	3,011	205	93.0	884.8
Pittsburgh, PA MSA	6280	2,571,223	2,394,811	2,373,640	2,361,019	19	19	−33,792	13,573	7,211	510.6	4,623.9
Pittsfield, MA NECMA	6323	145,110	139,352	134,711	134,244	205	214	−5,108	476	846	144.1	931.4
Pocatello, ID MSA	6340	65,421	66,026	73,379	73,850	281	271	7,824	5,679	309	66.3	1,113.2
Portland, ME NECMA	6403	215,789	243,135	249,784	251,438	135	140	8,303	7,319	1,372	300.9	835.6
Portland–Salem, OR–WA CMSA	6442	1,583,518	1,793,476	2,072,805	2,112,802	24	22	319,326	97,140	38,715	303.8	6,953.8
Portland–Vancouver, OR–WA PMSA	6440	1,333,623	1,515,452	1,753,760	1,787,549	—	—	272,097	82,873	31,977	355.5	5,027.7
Salem, OR PMSA	7080	249,895	278,024	319,045	325,253	—	—	47,229	14,267	6,738	168.9	1,926.1
Providence–Warwick–Pawtucket, RI NECMA	6483	865,771	916,270	905,806	904,831	47	51	−11,439	34,488	11,672	961.6	941.0
Provo–Orem, UT MSA	6520	218,106	263,590	320,241	328,142	124	117	64,552	45,378	4,132	164.2	1,998.4
Pueblo, CO MSA	6560	125,972	123,051	130,991	132,901	224	218	9,850	3,550	419	55.6	2,388.8
Punta Gorda, FL MSA	6580	58,460	110,975	131,298	133,681	237	215	22,706	−5,763	2,269	192.7	693.7
Raleigh–Durham–Chapel Hill, NC MSA	6640	664,788	858,485	1,022,413	1,050,054	52	43	191,569	55,514	10,959	300.8	3,491.0
Rapid City, SD MSA	6660	70,361	81,343	86,906	87,190	270	265	5,847	6,499	322	31.4	2,776.4
Reading, PA MSA	6680	312,509	336,523	352,099	354,057	105	111	17,534	8,387	3,291	412.1	859.2
Redding, CA MSA	6690	115,613	147,036	161,944	163,178	199	184	16,142	4,710	1,302	43.1	3,785.7
Reno, NV MSA	6720	193,623	254,667	298,665	305,792	128	124	51,125	17,031	8,367	48.2	6,342.5

Metropolitan area	FIPS code	Population 1980	Population 1990 [1]	Population 1996	Population 1997	Rank 1990	Rank 1997	Net change, 1990–1997	Natural increase, 1990–1997	Net international migration, 1990–1997	Density, 1997	Land area, 1990
	Aa1884	Aa1885	Aa1886	Aa1887	Aa1888	Aa1889	Aa1890	Aa1891	Aa1892	Aa1893	Aa1894 [2]	Aa1895
	—	Number	Number	Number	Number	Number	Number	Number	Number	Number	Persons per square mile	Square miles
Richland–Kennewick–Pasco, WA MSA	6740	144,469	150,033	180,302	182,799	15	170	32,766	13,535	7,147	62.1	2,945.3
Richmond–Petersburg, VA MSA	6760	761,311	865,640	934,727	943,264	113	50	77,624	39,986	6,578	320.3	2,944.8
Roanoke, VA MSA	6800	220,393	224,592	228,634	228,534	218	149	3,942	2,479	1,295	268.6	850.9
Rochester, MN MSA	6820	92,006	106,470	113,158	114,619	136	241	8,149	8,127	1,572	175.5	653.0
Rochester, NY MSA	6840	1,030,630	1,062,470	1,086,439	1,086,082	209	40	23,612	48,667	10,653	317.0	3,425.6
Rockford, IL MSA	6880	325,852	329,676	352,561	354,774	138	110	25,098	15,618	3,888	228.3	1,554.1
Rocky Mount, NC MSA	6895	123,141	133,369	143,822	145,571	106	200	12,202	5,337	519	139.2	1,045.4
Sacramento–Yolo, CA CMSA	6922	1,099,814	1,481,220	1,631,232	1,655,866	65	25	174,646	104,332	45,362	325.1	5,094.0
Sacramento, CA PMSA	6920	986,440	1,340,010	1,480,973	1,503,069	—	—	163,059	94,871	37,748	368.3	4,081.6
Yolo, CA PMSA	9270	113,374	141,210	150,259	152,797	—	—	11,587	9,461	7,614	150.9	1,012.4
Saginaw–Bay City–Midland, MI MSA	6960	421,518	399,320	402,993	402,949	228	96	3,629	17,545	1,606	227.1	1,774.5
St. Cloud, MN MSA	6980	133,348	149,509	159,820	161,211	129	185	11,702	8,487	562	92.0	1,752.9
St. Joseph, MO MSA	7000	101,868	97,715	97,096	97,111	244	259	-604	1,628	93	114.9	845.0
St. Louis, MO–IL MSA	7040	2,414,061	2,492,348	2,548,410	2,557,806	205	18	65,458	103,337	15,833	400.1	6,393.0
Salinas, CA MSA	7120	290,444	355,660	350,018	361,907	218	108	6,247	37,429	22,684	108.9	3,321.9
Salt Lake City–Ogden, UT MSA	7160	910,222	1,072,227	1,226,277	1,247,554	39	35	175,327	120,516	13,799	771.3	1,617.5
San Angelo, TX MSA	7200	84,784	98,458	102,024	102,648	189	251	4,190	4,586	1,222	67.4	1,522.2
San Antonio, TX MSA	7240	1,088,881	1,324,749	1,485,811	1,511,386	55	28	186,637	106,213	30,642	454.3	3,326.8
San Diego, CA MSA	7320	1,861,846	2,498,016	2,677,203	2,722,650	111	17	224,634	218,627	129,997	647.6	4,204.5
San Francisco–Oakland–San Jose, CA CMSA	7362	5,367,900	6,277,525	6,616,009	6,700,753	159	5	423,228	385,053	354,028	909.4	7,368.6
Oakland, CA PMSA	5775	1,761,710	2,108,078	2,236,006	2,270,325	—	—	162,247	135,607	91,519	1,557.4	1,457.8
San Francisco, CA PMSA	7360	1,488,895	1,603,678	1,648,258	1,662,005	—	—	58,327	55,188	116,930	1,636.5	1,015.6
San Jose, CA PMSA	7400	1,295,071	1,497,577	1,588,282	1,609,037	—	—	111,460	132,115	107,578	1,246.2	1,291.2
Santa Cruz–Watsonville, CA PMSA	7485	188,141	229,734	237,717	240,488	—	—	10,754	15,403	11,449	539.6	445.7
Santa Rosa, CA PMSA	7500	299,681	388,222	421,324	428,609	—	—	40,387	16,310	10,492	271.9	1,576.2
Vallejo–Fairfield–Napa, CA PMSA	8720	334,402	450,236	484,422	490,289	145	147	40,053	30,430	16,060	309.9	1,582.1
San Luis Obispo–Atascadero–Paso Robles, CA MSA	7460	155,435	217,162	229,982	233,291	168	100	16,129	6,804	4,443	70.6	3,304.5
Santa Barbara–Santa Maria–Lompoc, CA MSA	7480	298,694	369,608	384,959	390,199	24	206	20,591	25,847	20,021	142.5	2,738.5
Santa Fe, NM MSA	7490	93,118	117,043	137,161	140,066	89	74	23,023	6,494	2,587	69.4	2,018.8
Sarasota–Bradenton, FL MSA	7510	350,696	489,483	531,586	538,783	85	130	49,300	-14,073	7,784	410.3	1,313.0
Savannah, GA MSA	7520	230,728	257,899	281,175	284,090	264	65	26,191	16,099	1,453	208.6	1,361.7
Scranton–Wilkes-Barre–Hazleton, PA MSA	7560	659,387	638,524	627,150	621,641	60	13	-16,883	-7,512	2,143	278.4	2,232.6
Seattle–Tacoma–Bremerton, WA CMSA	7602	2,408,749	2,970,300	3,309,180	3,367,872	—	—	397,572	181,142	54,700	466.2	7,223.5
Bremerton, WA PMSA	1150	147,152	189,731	231,156	234,608	—	—	44,877	14,215	1,845	592.4	396.0
Olympia, WA PMSA	5910	124,264	161,238	196,709	200,362	—	—	39,124	8,246	1,774	275.6	727.1
Seattle–Bellevue–Everett, WA PMSA	7600	1,651,666	2,033,128	2,226,300	2,268,126	—	—	234,998	119,995	46,331	512.6	4,424.9
Tacoma, WA PMSA	8200	485,667	586,203	655,015	664,776	—	—	78,573	38,686	4,750	396.8	1,675.5
Sharon, PA MSA	7610	128,299	121,003	122,243	122,045	230	229	1,042	547	109	181.6	671.9
Sheboygan, WI MSA	7620	100,935	103,877	109,440	109,896	167	246	6,019	2,887	528	213.9	513.7
Sherman–Denison, TX MSA	7640	89,796	95,019	100,306	101,541	157	254	6,522	1,437	790	108.8	933.7
Shreveport–Bossier City, LA MSA	7680	376,789	376,330	378,898	378,738	232	104	2,408	14,707	838	163.5	2,316.5
Sioux City, IA–NE MSA	7720	117,457	115,018	121,024	120,823	174	234	5,805	6,204	2,426	106.3	1,136.7
Sioux Falls, SD MSA	7760	123,377	139,236	159,138	160,670	46	188	21,434	8,498	1,673	115.8	1,387.3
South Bend, IN MSA	7800	241,617	247,052	257,338	258,056	184	136	11,004	10,510	1,060	564.3	457.3
Spokane, WA MSA	7840	341,835	361,333	403,669	404,650	63	95	43,317	16,334	2,610	229.4	1,763.8

Notes appear at end of table   (continued)

TABLE Aa1884–1895 Metropolitan areas – population, density, land area, international migration, and natural increase: 1980–1997 *Continued*

Metropolitan area	FIPS code	Population 1980	1990 [1]	1996	1997	Rank 1990	Rank 1997	Net change, 1990–1997	Natural increase, 1990–1997	Net international migration, 1990–1997	Density, 1997 [2]	Land area, 1990
	Aa1884	Aa1885	Aa1886	Aa1887	Aa1888	Aa1889	Aa1890	Aa1891	Aa1892	Aa1893	Aa1894	Aa1895
	—	Number	Number	Number	Number	Number	Number	Number	Number	Number	Persons per square mile	Square miles
Springfield, IL MSA	7880	187,770	189,550	203,908	203,942	139	159	14,392	6,766	1,030	172.5	1,182.6
Springfield, MO MSA	7920	228,118	264,346	296,902	300,980	56	125	36,634	10,010	843	164.3	1,831.6
Springfield, MA NECMA	8003	581,831	602,878	591,045	591,110	257	70	-11,768	16,663	7,640	515.1	1,147.5
State College, PA MSA	8050	112,760	124,812	132,216	132,993	161	217	8,181	4,527	1,073	120.1	1,107.6
Steubenville–Weirton, OH–WV MSA	8080	163,734	142,523	138,214	136,725	270	212	-5,798	-1,209	-33	235.1	581.5
Stockton–Lodi, CA MSA	8120	347,342	480,628	533,005	542,504	62	73	61,876	39,567	22,026	387.7	1,399.3
Sumter, SC MSA	8140	88,243	101,276	106,589	106,589	171	249	5,313	6,235	199	160.2	665.5
Syracuse, NY MSA	8160	722,865	742,237	745,115	740,771	240	59	-1,466	31,412	6,391	240.3	3,082.8
Tallahassee, FL MSA	8240	190,329	233,609	259,713	260,611	70	135	27,002	13,941	3,359	220.3	1,183.0
Tampa–St. Petersburg–Clearwater, FL MSA	8280	1,613,600	2,067,959	2,198,898	2,227,000	134	21	159,041	9,453	29,537	871.8	2,554.5
Terre Haute, IN MSA	8320	155,476	147,585	149,364	148,468	233	195	883	2,311	432	145.9	1,017.8
Texarkana, AR–TX MSA	8360	113,067	120,132	123,522	123,380	204	225	3,248	3,520	439	81.6	1,512.0
Toledo, OH MSA	8400	616,864	614,128	610,624	611,805	242	68	-2,323	26,056	2,705	448.3	1,364.6
Topeka, KS MSA	8440	154,916	160,976	164,761	164,932	208	183	3,956	5,734	727	299.9	549.9
Tucson, AZ MSA	8520	531,443	666,957	767,743	780,150	34	57	113,193	36,735	16,192	84.9	9,187.0
Tulsa, OK MSA	8560	657,173	708,954	754,323	764,396	130	58	55,442	36,284	4,604	152.4	5,015.0
Tuscaloosa, AL MSA	8600	137,541	150,522	158,872	160,760	158	186	10,238	6,223	431	121.3	1,325.3
Tyler, TX MSA	8640	128,366	151,309	164,654	166,723	83	181	15,414	6,752	2,670	179.6	928.5
Utica–Rome, NY MSA	8680	320,180	316,645	301,719	298,878	273	127	-17,767	6,508	4,078	113.9	2,624.6
Victoria, TX MSA	8750	68,807	74,361	81,624	82,024	82	267	7,663	5,204	743	92.9	882.6
Visalia–Tulare–Porterville, CA MSA	8780	245,738	311,921	350,053	353,175	61	112	41,254	34,282	18,075	73.2	4,824.3
Waco, TX MSA	8800	170,755	189,123	201,493	202,983	148	160	13,860	8,811	2,242	194.8	1,041.9
Washington–Baltimore, DC–MD–VA–WV CMSA	8872	5,790,555	6,726,395	7,145,947	7,206,517	152	4	480,122	412,441	195,900	752.4	9,578.3
Baltimore, MD PMSA	0720	2,199,497	2,382,172	2,468,790	2,475,332	—	—	93,160	102,079	23,030	948.6	2,609.4
Hagerstown, MD PMSA	3180	113,086	121,393	127,287	128,155	—	—	6,762	3,049	542	279.7	458.2
Washington, DC–MD–VA–WV PMSA	8840	3,477,972	4,222,830	4,549,870	4,603,030	—	—	380,200	307,313	172,328	707.0	6,510.7
Waterloo–Cedar Falls, IA MSA	8920	137,961	123,798	122,245	121,502	256	231	-2,296	3,464	431	214.1	567.4
Wausau, WI MSA	8940	111,270	115,400	121,475	122,450	166	228	7,050	5,643	632	79.3	1,545.1
West Palm Beach–Boca Raton, FL MSA	8960	576,758	863,503	996,125	1,018,524	27	47	155,021	9,596	36,017	515.9	1,974.2
Wheeling, WV–OH MSA	9000	185,566	159,301	155,175	154,153	265	192	-5,148	-1,419	96	162.2	950.5
Wichita, KS MSA	9040	442,401	485,270	523,278	530,508	102	75	45,238	31,733	4,960	178.8	2,967.8
Wichita Falls, TX MSA	9080	128,348	130,351	137,608	137,103	173	211	6,752	5,096	960	89.2	1,537.5
Williamsport, PA MSA	9140	118,416	118,710	118,991	118,405	241	236	-305	2,333	393	95.9	1,234.9
Wilmington, NC MSA	9200	139,248	171,269	207,099	213,580	9	153	42,311	5,976	490	202.7	1,053.8
Yakima, WA MSA	9260	172,508	188,823	216,110	218,318	43	151	29,495	18,652	11,321	50.8	4,296.1
York, PA MSA	9280	313,024	339,574	367,906	370,518	108	107	30,944	11,290	1,213	409.6	904.6
Youngstown–Warren, OH MSA	9320	644,922	600,895	597,870	595,215	248	69	-5,680	9,322	691	380.7	1,563.6
Yuba City, CA MSA	9340	101,979	122,643	137,898	139,315	59	208	16,672	10,154	7,697	113.0	1,233.2
Yuma, AZ MSA	9360	76,205	106,895 [3]	125,404	130,016	17	220	23,121	15,172	10,326	23.6	5,514.4

TABLE Aa1884–1895   Metropolitan areas – population, density, land area, international migration, and natural increase: 1980–1997   *Continued*

[1] Includes count resolution corrections through December 1996.

[2] Based on 1990 land area.

[3] 1980 population based on 1990 boundaries.

Sources

U.S. Bureau of the Census, *State and Metropolitan Area Data Book 1997–98* (5th edition) (1998), Table B-1. Land area: U.S. Bureau of the Census, data file from Geography Division based on the TIGER/GICS computer file. Related information available from the Census Bureau's Internet site, "Density Using Land Area for States, Counties, Metropolitan Areas, and Places." 1980 population: U.S. Bureau of the Census, "1980–1990 Intercensal Population Estimates by County," on diskette. 1996 population: U.S. Bureau of the Census, "Estimates of the Population of Counties, Annual Time Series, July 1, 1990 to July 1, 1997," CO-97-4, from the Census Bureau's Internet site, accessed March 30, 1998. 1990 and 1997 population: U.S. Bureau of the Census, "Estimates of the Population of Counties and Demographic Components of Population Change: April 1, 1990 to July 1, 1997," CO-97-5, from the Census Bureau's Internet site, accessed March 30, 1998.

Documentation

This table includes 245 metropolitan statistical areas (MSAs), 17 consolidated MSAs (CMSAs), and 58 primary MSAs (PMSAs) not in New England, as well as 12 New England county metropolitan areas (NECMAs). It excludes 10 MSAs, 1 CMSA, and 15 PMSAs in New England. All areas are defined as of June 30, 1996.

Population, rank, and density are as of April 1 for 1980–1990 and July 1 for 1990–1997.

Series Aa1884. Federal Information Processing Standards (FIPS) codes for metropolitan areas defined as of June 30, 1996.

Series Aa1889–1890. Based on 273 metropolitan areas (245 MSAs, 17 CMSAs, and 11 NECMAs). When metropolitan areas share the same rank, the next lower rank is omitted.

Series Aa1891. Includes net domestic migration, net federal movement, and residual not shown separately.

Series Aa1892. Equals the difference between the number of births and the number of deaths.

Series Aa1893. "Net international migration is the difference between migration to an area from outside the United States (immigration) and migration from the area to outside the United States (emigration) during the period. More specifically, net international migration consists of (1) legal immigration to the United States as reported by the Immigration and Naturalization Service, (2) an estimate of net undocumented immigration from abroad, (3) an estimate of emigration from the United States, and (4) net movement between Puerto Rico and the United States." (U.S. Bureau of the Census, *State and Metropolitan Area Data Book 1997–98*, p. A-35)

Series Aa1895. Includes dry land and land temporarily or partially covered by water.

NATIVITY

Michael R. Haines

TABLE Aa1896–1921   Foreign-born population, by sex and race: 1850–1990

Contributed by Michael R. Haines

					Both sexes					
							Other races			
	All races	White	Nonwhite	Black	Total	Indian	Asian and Pacific islander	Japanese	Chinese	Filipinos
	Aa1896	Aa1897	Aa1898	Aa1899	Aa1900 [1]	Aa1901	Aa1902	Aa1903	Aa1904	Aa1905
Year	Number	Number	Number	Number	Number	Number	Number	Number	Number	Number
1850	—	2,240,535	—	4,067 [7]	—	—	—	—	—	—
1860	—	4,096,753	—	7,011 [7]	34,933	—	—	—	—	—
1870 [2]	5,567,229	5,493,712	73,517	9,645	63,872	1,136	—	54	62,682	—
1880	6,679,943	6,559,679	120,264	14,017	106,247	1,820	—	145	104,282	—
1890 [3]	9,249,547	9,121,867	127,680	19,979	107,701	1,235	—	1,921	104,545	—
1900	10,341,276	10,213,817	127,459	20,336	107,123	2,213	—	24,057	80,853	—
1910	13,515,886	13,345,545	170,341	40,339	130,002	2,753	—	67,655	56,596	5
1920	13,920,692	13,712,754	207,938	73,803	134,135	6,299	—	81,338	43,107	10
1930	14,204,149	13,983,405	220,744	98,620	122,124	3,552	—	70,477	44,086	182
1940	11,594,896	11,419,138	175,758	83,941	91,817	4,491	—	47,305	37,242	—
1950 [4]	10,347,395	10,095,415	251,980	—	—	—	—	—	—	—
1960 [5]	9,738,091	9,293,992	444,099	125,322	318,777	—	—	101,656	93,288	88,805
1970 [6]	9,619,302	8,733,770	885,532	253,458	632,074	14,488	—	122,500	204,232	178,970
1980	14,079,906	9,323,946	4,755,960	815,720	3,940,240	38,190	2,182,639	—	—	—
1990	19,767,316	10,022,812	9,744,504	1,455,294	8,289,210	46,919	4,558,744	—	—	—

				Males				
						Other races		
	All races	White	Nonwhite	Black	Total	Indian	Japanese	Chinese
	Aa1906	Aa1907	Aa1908	Aa1909	Aa1910 [2]	Aa1911	Aa1912	Aa1913
Year	Number	Number	Number	Number	Number	Number	Number	Number
1850	—	1,239,434	—	2,015 [7]	—	—	—	—
1860	—	2,192,230	—	3,512 [7]	33,149	—	—	—
1870 [2]	3,006,943	2,942,579	64,364	5,346	59,018	647	46	58,325
1880	3,630,566	3,521,635	108,931	7,758	101,173	1,002	133	100,038
1890 [3]	5,067,130	4,951,858	115,272	—	—	—	—	—
1900	5,630,190	5,515,285	114,905	11,829	103,076	1,207	23,185	78,684
1910	7,667,748	7,523,788	143,960	23,888	120,072	1,464	60,730	54,935
1920	7,675,435	7,528,322	147,113	42,641	104,472	3,539	57,213	40,573
1930	7,647,090	7,502,491	144,599	54,081	90,518	1,888	45,897	39,109
1940	6,121,647	6,011,015	110,632	44,488	66,144	2,463	29,651	31,687
1950 [4]	5,258,255	5,098,370	159,885	—	—	—	—	—
1960 [5]	4,760,432	4,507,502	252,930	65,952	186,978	—	40,709	59,083
1970 [6]	4,403,687	3,982,797	420,890	115,406	305,484	7,153	39,375	105,907
1980	6,581,094	—	—	—	—	—	—	—
1990	9,670,861	—	—	—	—	—	—	—

Notes appear at end of table

TABLE Aa1896–1921   Foreign-born population, by sex and race: 1850–1990   *Continued*

	Females							
	All races	White	Nonwhite	Black	Other races			
					Total	Indian	Japanese	Chinese
	Aa1914	Aa1915	Aa1916	Aa1917	Aa1918 [2]	Aa1919	Aa1920	Aa1921
Year	Number	Number	Number	Number	Number	Number	Number	Number
1850	—	1,001,101	—	2,052 [7]	—	—	—	—
1860	—	1,904,523	—	3,499 [7]	1,784	—	—	—
1870 [2]	2,560,286	2,551,133	9,153	4,299	4,854	489	8	4,357
1880	3,049,377	3,038,044	11,333	6,259	5,074	818	12	4,244
1890 [3]	4,182,417	4,170,009	12,408	—	—	—	—	—
1900	4,711,086	4,698,532	12,554	8,507	4,047	1,006	872	2,169
1910	5,848,138	5,821,757	26,381	16,451	9,930	1,289	6,925	1,661
1920	6,245,257	6,184,432	60,825	31,162	29,663	2,760	24,125	2,534
1930	6,557,059	6,480,914	76,145	44,539	31,606	1,664	24,580	4,977
1940	5,473,249	5,408,123	65,126	39,453	25,673	2,028	17,654	5,555
1950 [4]	5,089,140	4,997,045	92,095	92,095	92,095	—	—	—
1960 [5]	4,977,659	4,786,490	191,169	59,370	131,799	—	60,947	34,205
1970 [6]	5,215,615	4,750,973	464,642	138,052	326,590	7,335	83,125	98,325
1980	7,498,812	—	—	—	—	—	—	—
1990	10,096,455	—	—	—	—	—	—	—

[1] Includes races not shown separately.

[2] Excludes 1,260,078 persons for whom data on nativity are not available. See text for Table Aa1–5.

[3] Data by sex for blacks and other races not available. Excludes population enumerated in the Indian Territory and on Indian reservations (totaling 325,464) that was not classified by nativity. Totals by race and sex: males – 169,221; females – 156,243; white males – 64,047; white females – 53,321; Negro males – 10,042; Negro females – 8,594; Indian males – 95,119; Indian females – 94,328; Chinese males – 13.

[4] 20 percent sample data. Complete-count data available only for the white population: Total – 10,161,168; males – 5,176,390; females – 4,984,778. Data for specific races in the Negro and other races grouping are based on various samples and are extremely unreliable. See U.S. Bureau of the Census, *Census of Population: 1950*, volume 4, part 3, Chapter B.

[5] 25 percent sample data.

[6] 15 percent sample data. These data vary in degree of comparability with data on total population by race. See text for Table Aa145–184.

[7] Free blacks only; data on nativity were not collected for slaves.

Sources

U.S. Bureau of the Census. 1850 and 1870, *U.S. Census of Population: 1870*, volume 1, pp. 606-9, 614–15. 1860, white, *U.S. Census of Population: 1930*, volume 2, p. 97. 1860, all races and Negro, *U.S. Census of Population: 1870*, volume 1, pp. 610-13. 1880, *U.S. Census of Population: 1880*, volume 1, pp. 542-5. 1890, all races and white, *U.S. Census of Population: 1890*, volume 1, part 1, pp. 486-7. 1890, other races, *U.S. Census of Population: 1900*, volume 2, part 2, p. xvii. 1900-1940, *U.S. Census of Population: 1940*, volume 2, p. 19. 1950, *U.S. Census of Population: 1950*, volume 2, part 1, p. 171. 1960, *U.S. Census of Population: 1960*, volume 1, part 1, p. 354; part 3, p. 118; part 13, p. 115. 1970, *U.S. Census of Population: 1970*, volume 1, part 1, section 2, pp. 593-6. 1980, *U.S. Census of Population: 1980*, volume 1, chapter D, part 1, PC80-1-D1-A, pp. 7-8. 1990, *U.S. Census of Population: 1990*, "The Foreign-Born Population in the United States," 1990 CP-3-1, p. 1. Campbell Gibson and Emily Lennon, "Historical Census Statistics on the Foreign-Born Population of the United States: 1850 to 1990," U.S. Bureau of the Census, Population Division, Working Paper number 29 (February 1999).

Documentation

The 1850 decennial census was the first census in which data were collected on the nativity of the population. Data on the total foreign-born population of the United States are generally comparable from 1850 to 1990, although the definition of foreign-born has been refined. Since 1890, individuals who were born in a foreign country, but who had at least one parent who was an American citizen, have been defined as native rather than as foreign-born. In the 1990 Census, the population was classified by nativity as follows: The native population included all U.S. residents who were born in the United States or an outlying area of the United States (for example, Puerto Rico), or who were born in a foreign country, but who had at least one parent who was an American citizen. All other residents of the United States were classified as foreign-born. Through 1950, persons for whom place of birth was not reported were included in the native population. For 1960 through 1990, such persons were classified as native unless their census report contained contradictory information, such as an entry of a language spoken prior to coming to the United States.

The outlying areas are as defined at each census. Thus, for example, individuals born in the Philippines (which was granted independence in 1946) were classified as native in 1940 and as foreign-born in 1950. The primary outlying areas in censuses of the United States include Alaska (1880-1950), Hawai'i (1900-1950), the Philippines (1900-1940), Puerto Rico (1900-1990), Guam (1900-1990), American Samoa (1900-1990), the Canal Zone (1900-1970), Virgin Islands of the United States (1920-1990), and Trust Territory of the Pacific Islands (1950-1980). See Table Cf1.

TABLE Aa1922–1973   Native-born white population, by sex and age: 1870–1970[1]

Contributed by Michael R. Haines

Males

	Total	0–4	5–9	10–14	15–19	20–24	25–29	30–34	35–39	40–44	45–49	50–54	55–59
	Aa1922	Aa1923	Aa1924	Aa1925	Aa1926	Aa1927	Aa1928	Aa1929	Aa1930	Aa1931	Aa1932	Aa1933	Aa1934
Year	Number	Number	Number	Number	Number	Number	Number	Number	Number	Number	Number	Number	Number
1870	14,086,509	2,356,293	2,015,664	1,998,699	1,573,965	1,285,174	948,655	763,379	688,959	553,617	490,940	438,783	309,000
1880	18,609,265	2,918,193	2,694,398	2,361,832	1,965,748	1,945,279	1,472,960	1,128,308	920,264	726,832	621,164	538,133	403,260
1890	23,254,474	3,307,064	3,150,913	2,842,899	2,561,256	2,264,640	1,804,608	1,651,874	1,337,972	1,020,817	837,647	700,104	514,816
1900	28,686,450	3,984,888	3,788,622	3,361,671	2,986,709	2,689,295	2,353,361	1,958,744	1,687,544	1,497,876	1,183,506	955,956	694,994
1910	34,654,457	4,676,710	4,134,714	3,824,801	3,647,389	3,247,035	2,801,648	2,408,501	2,211,995	1,785,700	1,505,393	1,389,604	983,711
1920	40,902,333	5,237,857	5,013,431	4,567,998	3,882,561	3,561,588	3,302,213	2,829,448	2,656,664	2,184,217	2,034,752	1,642,058	1,236,872
1930	48,420,037	5,141,207	5,590,230	5,325,152	4,949,246	4,378,161	3,753,275	3,422,875	3,291,333	2,780,484	2,419,605	2,097,986	1,674,270
1940	53,437,533	4,697,251	4,733,600	5,231,893	5,433,529	5,014,725	4,698,366	4,230,325	3,724,204	3,338,408	3,025,658	2,568,375	2,054,198
1950 [2]	61,431,020	7,246,820	5,898,645	4,942,910	4,653,840	4,873,460	5,135,855	4,878,085	4,630,965	4,090,275	3,465,810	3,042,480	2,575,345
1960 [3]	73,840,267	8,811,521	8,114,197	7,376,422	5,801,340	4,536,263	4,575,970	5,031,475	5,217,959	4,890,642	4,556,616	3,918,175	3,260,430
1970 [4,5]	82,910,031	7,343,472	8,587,720	8,952,771	8,238,958	6,647,675	5,612,749	4,706,376	4,588,964	4,962,895	4,986,437	4,611,795	4,034,355

Males

	60–64	65–69	70–74	75–79	80–84	85–89	90–94	95–99	100 and older	75 and older	85 and older	65 and older	Not stated
	Aa1935	Aa1936	Aa1937	Aa1938	Aa1939	Aa1940	Aa1941	Aa1942	Aa1943	Aa1944	Aa1945	Aa1946	Aa1947
Year	Number	Number	Number	Number	Number	Number	Number	Number	Number	Number	Number	Number	Number
1870	260,237	174,516	118,823	62,729	31,040	11,035	3,074	757	259	—	—	402,233	911
1880	345,575	243,803	165,062	94,598	44,492	14,858	3,486	783	237	—	—	567,319	—
1890	432,361	312,734	226,961	129,601	65,305	22,110	5,612	930	234	—	—	763,487	64,016
1900	539,430	395,274	263,590	157,351	74,697	25,036	5,268	796	152	—	—	922,164	81,690
1910	744,839	536,894	346,137	202,034	91,039	32,762	7,777	1,168	200	—	—	1,218,011	74,406
1920	1,068,990	723,379	461,184	267,213	115,363	41,304	8,729	1,657	262	—	—	1,619,091	64,593
1930	1,307,887	946,404	690,941	—	—	—	—	—	340	614,272	—	2,251,617	36,709
1940	1,659,153	1,314,177	873,177	487,767	250,401	81,790	17,331	2,865	520	—	—	3,027,848	—
1950 [2]	2,057,895	1,615,625	1,115,670	703,345	348,260	118,905	30,810	5,500	2,265	—	—	3,938,635	—
1960 [3]	2,578,250	2,084,917	1,481,137	915,116	453,113	183,666	43,524	7,269	—	—	—	5,171,007	—
1970 [4,5]	3,308,016	2,406,948	1,753,478	1,165,059	617,056	—	—	—	—	—	385,307	6,327,848	—

Females

	Total	0–4	5–9	10–14	15–19	20–24	25–29	30–34	35–39	40–44	45–49	50–54	55–59
	Aa1948	Aa1949	Aa1950	Aa1951	Aa1952	Aa1953	Aa1954	Aa1955	Aa1956	Aa1957	Aa1958	Aa1959	Aa1960
Year	Number	Number	Number	Number	Number	Number	Number	Number	Number	Number	Number	Number	Number
1870	14,009,156	2,279,587	1,961,818	1,932,224	1,611,645	1,340,786	1,024,371	812,091	690,369	560,889	462,849	395,682	282,255
1880	18,234,026	2,819,587	2,625,324	2,280,260	2,007,090	1,928,938	1,397,625	1,088,315	938,963	751,013	609,787	512,672	378,541
1890	22,607,549	3,185,955	3,073,904	2,752,694	2,592,796	2,266,453	1,769,840	1,550,638	1,231,366	984,877	823,758	681,625	491,712
1900	27,908,929	3,882,695	3,702,512	3,286,002	2,994,734	2,726,267	2,312,390	1,872,017	1,595,465	1,388,155	1,081,952	874,633	683,220
1910	33,731,955	4,543,697	4,041,950	3,735,277	3,647,241	3,308,995	2,792,792	2,353,060	2,111,757	1,691,097	1,409,309	1,240,654	886,975
1920	40,205,828	5,091,080	4,903,930	4,469,962	3,903,652	3,696,909	3,385,114	2,857,867	2,571,336	2,143,231	1,853,613	1,507,831	1,160,077
1930	47,883,298	4,966,953	5,429,060	5,190,738	4,922,427	4,487,320	3,840,791	3,467,227	3,284,504	2,740,508	2,351,913	2,002,627	1,596,555
1940	53,358,199	4,523,933	4,573,767	5,067,051	5,365,733	5,115,915	4,781,628	4,267,062	3,744,061	3,334,605	3,003,193	2,546,364	2,053,897
1950 [2]	62,951,930	6,943,695	5,672,145	4,748,715	4,613,840	5,056,860	5,380,955	5,107,255	4,803,860	4,203,675	3,573,345	3,172,720	2,723,280
1960 [3]	75,703,420	8,462,708	7,800,966	7,078,705	5,673,801	4,666,412	4,650,093	5,131,265	5,415,880	5,071,441	4,669,791	4,048,307	3,479,254
1970 [4,5]	86,475,420	7,020,958	8,247,244	8,574,171	7,984,897	7,050,949	5,675,672	4,770,378	4,676,399	5,096,719	5,249,680	4,901,714	4,392,853

Females

	60–64	65–69	70–74	75–79	80–84	85–89	90–94	95–99	100 and older	75 and older	85 and older	65 and older	Not stated
	Aa1961	Aa1962	Aa1963	Aa1964	Aa1965	Aa1966	Aa1967	Aa1968	Aa1969	Aa1970	Aa1971	Aa1972	Aa1973
Year	Number	Number	Number	Number	Number	Number	Number	Number	Number	Number	Number	Number	Number
1870	245,511	167,617	119,616	66,518	35,058	13,955	4,234	1,139	383	—	—	408,520	559
1880	321,270	232,245	164,476	99,574	51,949	19,425	5,357	1,260	355	—	—	574,641	—
1890	413,102	301,216	215,984	130,009	71,137	27,980	8,028	1,547	420	—	—	756,321	32,508
1900	536,197	389,281	262,182	161,453	80,945	30,824	7,730	1,499	294	—	—	934,208	38,482
1910	696,901	524,663	347,780	210,746	102,226	40,741	10,350	1,866	271	—	—	1,238,643	33,607
1920	986,712	681,691	456,229	287,978	138,768	54,759	13,267	2,595	421	—	—	1,635,708	38,806
1930	1,262,997	938,830	688,030	551,340	302,852	108,798	26,615	4,642	—	681,641	—	2,308,501	31,177
1940	1,688,665	1,372,341	925,209	861,470	456,745	177,015	51,775	9,000	528	—	—	3,292,325	—
1950 [2]	2,232,445	1,848,375	1,314,000	1,241,207	668,633	298,676	81,399	15,402	760	—	—	4,719,140	—
1960 [3]	2,880,635	2,490,332	1,874,624	1,775,470	1,077,674	—	—	—	3,889	—	—	6,674,162	—
1970 [4,5]	3,777,113	3,028,265	2,435,500	—	—	—	—	—	—	—	739,764	9,056,673	—

1 For changes in age and racial categorization, as well as exclusions in particular years, see the text for Table Aa185–286.

2 20 percent sample data.

3 25 percent sample data.

4 15 percent sample data.

5 Figures for persons ages 100 and older are greatly overstated; see the text for Table Aa185–286.

Sources

U.S. Bureau of the Census. 1870, *U.S. Census of Population: 1870*, volume 2, p. 553, 673. 1880, *U.S. Census of Population: 1880*, volume 1, pp. 549, 551. 1890, *U.S. Census of Population: 1890*, volume 1, part 2, pp. 2–5. 1900, *U.S. Census of Population: 1900*, volume 2, part 2, pp. xxxvi–xli. 1910, *U.S. Census of Population: 1910*, "Abstract of the Census," p. 122. 1920, *U.S. Census of Population: 1920*, "Abstract of the Fourteenth Census of the United States 1920," pp. 140–1. 1930–1940, *U.S. Census of Population: 1940*, "Population: Second Series; Characteristics of the Population, United States Summary," pp. 16–20; volume 4, part 1, p. 13. 1950, *U.S. Census of Population: 1950*, volume 2, part 1, pp. 165, 172; volume 4, part 3, Chapter A, p. 16. 1960, *U.S. Census of Population: 1960*, volume 1, part 1, pp. 354. 1970, *U.S. Census of Population: 1970*, volume 1, part 1, section 2, pp. 591.

Documentation

See the text for Table Aa185–286.

TABLE Aa1974–2025   Foreign-born white population, by sex and age: 1870–1970[1]
Contributed by Michael R. Haines

Males

	Total								Age				
Year	Aa1974	Aa1975	Aa1976	Aa1977	Aa1978	Aa1979	Aa1980	Aa1981	Aa1982	Aa1983	Aa1984	Aa1985	Aa1986
		0–4	5–9	10–14	15–19	20–24	25–29	30–34	35–39	40–44	45–49	50–54	55–59
	Number	Number	Number	Number	Number	Number	Number	Number	Number	Number	Number	Number	Number
1870	2,942,579	42,322	88,322	104,726	157,050	306,735	379,577	368,420	359,484	328,020	260,805	215,717	115,553
1880	3,521,635	31,256	61,803	120,740	184,320	274,038	365,094	419,769	432,957	384,931	340,863	318,045	206,820
1890	4,951,858	44,040	126,070	201,159	257,658	476,224	602,545	549,099	493,471	475,106	433,466	382,987	278,485
1900	5,515,285	26,567	73,727	157,632	271,381	456,186	589,521	660,702	672,804	557,300	468,466	440,079	345,241
1910	7,523,788	51,940	150,652	181,303	351,754	823,920	990,576	888,668	812,007	751,519	656,455	526,256	380,110
1920	7,528,322	22,857	85,774	167,152	259,270	456,988	792,088	946,818	1,008,677	803,195	744,423	651,546	503,789
1930	7,502,491	17,232	71,872	90,104	183,215	368,631	571,039	693,851	933,999	992,135	907,537	737,822	565,334
1940	6,011,015	4,219	10,937	27,114	82,391	98,917	193,647	342,991	530,164	656,782	816,955	883,342	735,848
1950 [2]	5,098,370	31,735	31,430	32,930	47,640	86,140	154,555	147,275	244,470	383,225	534,395	627,215	703,470
1960 [3]	4,507,502	46,307	76,961	112,140	92,606	121,207	149,510	184,949	243,569	204,179	293,870	396,801	514,193
1970 [4,5]	3,982,797	41,809	94,967	122,194	149,214	184,966	212,082	236,906	232,179	247,359	272,021	219,606	282,728

Males

								Age					Not stated or not available
Year	Aa1987	Aa1988	Aa1989	Aa1990	Aa1991	Aa1992	Aa1993	Aa1994	Aa1995	Aa1996	Aa1997	Aa1998	Aa1999
	60–64	65–69	70–74	75–79	80–84	85–89	90–94	95–99	100 and older	75 and older	85 and older	65 and older	
	Number	Number	Number	Number	Number	Number	Number	Number	Number	Number	Number	Number	Number
1870	98,703	52,298	36,402	15,484	7,669	2,691	865	313	135	—	—	115,857	1,288
1880	170,841	98,028	59,590	31,106	15,156	4,419	1,270	433	156	—	—	210,158	—
1890	254,101	166,745	106,364	53,167	23,343	8,195	2,308	516	179	—	—	360,817	16,630
1900	285,783	213,441	148,068	82,933	35,390	10,802	2,339	609	178	—	—	493,760	16,136
1910	331,914	255,416	172,751	105,412	50,262	18,081	4,193	767	126	—	—	607,008	19,706
1920	392,629	275,400	194,732	124,170	56,701	22,004	5,123	1,049	205	—	—	679,384	13,732
1930	491,843	383,135	246,334	—	—	—	—	—	—	241,741	—	871,210	6,667
1940	573,300	422,760	310,106	193,630	88,890	30,301	7,167	1,359	195	—	—	1,054,408	—
1950 [2]	715,185	581,410	376,185	220,870	119,650	47,100	11,145	2,065	280	—	—	1,358,705	—
1960 [3]	521,795	552,127	491,810	299,461	138,138	51,900	13,180	2,309	490	—	—	1,549,415	—
1970 [4,5]	351,105	390,545	353,545	294,647	191,107	—	—	—	—	—	105,817	1,335,661	—

Females

	Age												
	Total	**0–4**	**5–9**	**10–14**	**15–19**	**20–24**	**25–29**	**30–34**	**35–39**	**40–44**	**45–49**	**50–54**	**55–59**
	Aa2000	Aa2001	Aa2002	Aa2003	Aa2004	Aa2005	Aa2006	Aa2007	Aa2008	Aa2009	Aa2010	Aa2011	Aa2012
Year	Number	Number	Number	Number	Number	Number	Number	Number	Number	Number	Number	Number	Number
1870	2,551,133	41,590	85,911	100,812	168,376	302,333	328,949	321,175	308,508	272,729	192,021	154,061	87,963
1880	3,038,044	31,115	60,894	117,699	194,492	254,217	306,022	342,862	356,308	327,959	290,078	259,042	166,294
1890	4,170,009	42,589	122,281	195,220	263,637	441,150	469,694	393,221	377,121	384,848	354,349	326,233	246,646
1900	4,698,532	25,802	73,465	153,933	290,365	463,296	507,708	512,981	504,762	408,812	371,754	363,313	297,762
1910	5,821,757	50,567	147,857	177,027	322,007	606,461	672,120	617,047	596,086	551,956	489,905	398,799	313,410
1920	6,184,432	22,127	84,110	164,210	268,672	469,856	662,275	704,657	729,128	624,904	555,252	515,831	404,933
1930	6,480,914	16,777	70,501	88,430	193,891	378,557	543,893	626,959	768,432	753,765	702,515	607,308	483,142
1940	5,408,123	4,102	10,647	26,637	82,394	110,592	230,629	366,100	518,231	606,288	686,950	682,226	582,902
1950 [2]	4,997,045	31,815	30,605	30,330	44,605	121,415	198,090	174,980	282,565	403,795	523,080	598,190	621,545
1960 [3]	4,786,490	45,022	75,273	110,061	98,620	155,965	189,889	248,375	293,022	226,832	318,702	413,841	507,576
1970 [4,5]	4,750,973	40,097	89,354	120,721	149,534	229,069	277,961	299,307	282,098	317,950	333,321	250,963	323,164

Females

	Age												
	60–64	**65–69**	**70–74**	**75–79**	**80–84**	**85–89**	**90–94**	**95–99**	**100 and older**	**75 and older**	**85 and older**	**65 and older**	**Not stated**
	Aa2013	Aa2014	Aa2015	Aa2016	Aa2017	Aa2018	Aa2019	Aa2020	Aa2021	Aa2022	Aa2023	Aa2024	Aa2025
Year	Number	Number	Number	Number	Number	Number	Number	Number	Number	Number	Number	Number	Number
1870	82,228	44,940	32,894	14,238	7,887	2,688	951	387	187	—	—	104,172	305
1880	139,622	83,333	55,019	29,590	15,930	5,096	1,690	575	207	—	—	191,440	—
1890	223,546	144,829	92,642	48,048	23,510	8,730	2,818	689	221	—	—	321,487	7,987
1900	259,248	197,299	134,257	75,983	33,685	11,365	2,982	803	213	—	—	456,587	8,744
1910	295,669	232,981	164,216	102,800	51,028	19,352	4,841	956	167	—	—	576,341	6,505
1920	323,102	243,826	186,593	122,317	62,234	25,469	6,594	1,530	280	—	—	648,843	6,532
1930	434,050	338,764	220,017	—	—	—	—	—	—	249,864	—	808,645	4,049
1940	495,575	389,768	292,053	185,619	90,002	35,040	9,948	2,072	348	—	—	1,004,850	—
1950 [2]	599,620	528,930	369,810	228,600	131,810	58,695	15,115	3,005	445	—	—	1,336,410	—
1960 [3]	538,949	540,944	465,292	304,171	161,103	68,862	18,951	4,146	894	—	—	1,564,363	—
1970 [4,5]	398,068	464,533	442,988	346,776	234,265	—	—	—	—	—	150,804	1,639,366	—

1 For changes in age and racial categorization, as well as exclusions in particular years, see the text for Table Aa185–286.

2 20 percent sample data.

3 25 percent sample data.

4 15 percent sample data.

5 Figures for persons ages 100 and older are greatly overstated; see the text for Table Aa185–286.

Sources

U.S. Bureau of the Census. 1870, *U.S. Census of Population: 1870*, volume 2, pp. 553, 673. 1880, *U.S. Census of Population: 1880*, volume 1, pp. 549, 551. 1890, *U.S. Census of Population: 1890*, volume 1, part 2, pp. 2–5. 1900, *U.S. Census of Population: 1900*, volume 2, part 2, pp. xxxvi–xli. 1910, *U.S. Census of Population: 1910*, "Abstract of the Census," p. 122. 1920, *U.S. Census of Population: 1920*, "Abstract of the Fourteenth Census of the United States 1920," pp. 140–1. 1930–1940, *U.S. Census of Population: 1940* "Population: Second Series; Characteristics of the Population, United States Summary," pp. 16–20; volume 4, part 1, p. 13. 1950, *U.S. Census of Population: 1950*, volume 2, part 1, pp. 165, 172; volume 4, part 3, Chapter A, p. 16. 1960, *U.S. Census of Population: 1960*, volume 1, part 1, pp. 354. 1970, *U.S. Census of Population: 1970*, volume 1, part 1, section 2, p. 591.

Documentation

See the text for Table Aa185–286.

TABLE Aa2026–2077 Foreign-born population, by sex and age: 1870–1990[1,2]
Contributed by Michael R. Haines

Males

Year	Total	Age 0–4	5–9	10–14	15–19	20–24	25–29	30–34	35–39	40–44	45–49	50–54	55–59
	Aa2026	Aa2027	Aa2028	Aa2029	Aa2030	Aa2031	Aa2032	Aa2033	Aa2034	Aa2035	Aa2036	Aa2037	Aa2038
	Number	Number	Number	Number	Number	Number	Number	Number	Number	Number	Number	Number	Number
1870	3,006,943	42,529	88,754	106,139	162,942	317,832	391,721	379,445	367,113	334,598	263,473	217,493	116,216
1880	3,630,566	31,256	61,803	120,740	184,320	274,038	365,094	419,769	432,957	384,931	340,863	318,045	206,820
1890	5,067,130	44,040	126,070	201,159	257,658	476,224	602,545	549,099	493,471	475,106	433,466	382,987	278,485
1900	5,630,190	26,696	73,999	158,238	277,243	465,989	601,812	674,974	691,211	574,293	481,780	449,875	350,498
1910	7,667,748	51,940	150,652	181,303	351,754	823,920	990,576	888,668	812,007	751,519	656,455	526,256	380,110
1920	7,675,435	22,857	85,774	167,152	259,270	456,988	792,088	946,818	1,008,677	803,195	744,423	651,546	503,789
1930	7,647,090	17,232	71,872	90,104	183,215	368,631	571,039	693,851	933,999	992,135	907,537	737,822	565,334
1940	6,121,647	4,219	10,937	27,114	82,391	98,917	193,647	342,991	530,164	656,782	816,955	883,342	735,848
1950[3]	5,258,255	32,895	32,435	35,890	50,610	94,065	165,695	156,730	259,040	403,305	555,815	647,580	717,930
1960[4]	4,760,432	51,442	84,098	119,935	98,724	137,519	171,310	204,769	262,716	219,307	315,526	422,367	541,383
1970[5,6]	4,403,687	52,581	112,954	141,941	173,640	225,048	259,025	285,459	270,735	277,423	297,134	238,495	304,699
1980[7]	6,581,094	111,303	225,619	299,821	458,465	627,268	658,419	643,054	514,454	460,209	383,657	355,372	354,864
1990[7]	9,670,861	134,079	249,438	380,340	628,491	997,074	1,197,162	1,189,686	1,008,317	854,453	653,597	540,321	421,206

Males

Year	Age 60–64	65–69	70–74	75–79	80–84	85–89	90–94	95–99	100 and older	75 and older	85 and older	65 and older	Not stated or not available
	Aa2039	Aa2040	Aa2041	Aa2042	Aa2043	Aa2044	Aa2045	Aa2046	Aa2047	Aa2048	Aa2049	Aa2050	Aa2051
	Number	Number	Number	Number	Number	Number	Number	Number	Number	Number	Number	Number	Number
1870	99,394	52,493	36,579	15,616	7,821	2,771	980	351	288	—	—	116,899	2,395
1880	170,841	98,028	59,590	31,106	15,156	4,419	1,270	433	156	—	—	210,158	108,931
1890	254,101	166,745	106,364	53,167	23,343	8,195	2,308	516	179	—	—	360,817	131,902
1900	289,456	214,792	148,537	83,099	35,462	10,823	2,358	616	190	—	—	495,877	18,249
1910	331,914	255,416	172,751	105,412	50,262	18,081	4,193	767	126	—	—	607,008	163,666
1920	392,629	275,400	194,732	124,170	56,701	22,004	5,123	1,049	205	—	—	679,384	160,845
1930	491,843	383,135	246,334	—	—	—	—	—	—	241,741	—	871,210	151,266
1940	573,300	422,760	310,106	193,630	88,890	30,301	7,167	1,359	195	—	—	1,054,408	110,632
1950[3]	728,515	591,040	381,535	223,175	—	—	—	—	—	—	120,505	1,316,255	61,495
1960[4]	542,483	566,414	504,663	306,872	141,429	53,115	13,489	2,349	522	—	—	1,588,853	0
1970[5,6]	375,377	411,562	368,503	303,070	196,637	—	—	—	—	—	109,404	1,389,176	0
1980[7]	264,191	301,778	309,328	280,426	181,612	—	—	—	—	—	151,254	1,224,398	0
1990[7]	363,634	330,058	218,183	204,011	155,326	—	—	—	—	—	145,485	1,053,063	0

Females

Year	Total	0–4	5–9	10–14	15–19	20–24	25–29	30–34	35–39	40–44	45–49	50–54	55–59
	Aa2052	Aa2053	Aa2054	Aa2055	Aa2056	Aa2057	Aa2058	Aa2059	Aa2060	Aa2061	Aa2062	Aa2063	Aa2064
	Number	Number	Number	Number	Number	Number	Number	Number	Number	Number	Number	Number	Number
1870	2,560,286	41,787	86,272	101,308	169,400	304,257	330,402	322,192	309,170	273,122	192,282	154,279	88,091
1880	3,049,377	31,115	60,894	117,699	194,492	254,217	306,022	342,862	356,308	327,959	290,078	259,042	166,294
1890	4,182,417	42,589	122,281	195,220	263,637	441,150	469,694	393,221	377,121	384,848	354,349	326,233	246,646
1900	4,711,086	25,945	73,724	154,353	291,265	465,189	509,666	514,578	506,146	409,893	372,694	363,995	298,173
1910	5,848,138	50,567	147,857	177,027	322,007	606,461	672,120	617,047	596,086	551,956	489,905	398,799	313,410
1920	6,245,257	22,127	84,110	164,210	268,672	469,856	662,275	704,657	729,128	624,904	555,252	515,831	404,933
1930	6,557,059	16,777	70,501	88,430	193,891	378,557	543,893	626,959	768,432	753,765	702,515	607,308	483,142
1940	5,473,249	4,102	10,647	26,637	82,394	110,592	230,629	366,100	518,231	606,288	686,950	682,226	582,902
1950 [3]	5,089,140	32,965	32,005	32,255	46,990	128,270	205,070	181,010	289,910	412,310	534,715	610,265	630,600
1960 [4]	4,977,659	50,444	81,760	117,107	104,175	169,846	215,994	274,047	308,769	238,437	328,865	423,946	521,864
1970 [5,6]	5,215,615	50,345	107,523	141,497	174,866	277,481	338,362	356,811	335,799	362,998	361,398	270,281	339,504
1980 [7]	7,498,812	109,544	211,271	287,573	414,470	571,126	648,142	688,804	587,044	536,528	460,333	463,910	440,186
1990 [7]	10,096,455	126,999	237,416	355,894	533,506	800,346	1,040,868	1,093,950	992,072	898,465	726,979	631,462	520,005

Females

Year	60–64	65–69	70–74	75–79	80–84	85–89	90–94	95–99	100 and older	75 and older	85 and older	65 and older	Not stated or not available
	Aa2065	Aa2066	Aa2067	Aa2068	Aa2069	Aa2070	Aa2071	Aa2072	Aa2073	Aa2074	Aa2075	Aa2076	Aa2077
	Number	Number	Number	Number	Number	Number	Number	Number	Number	Number	Number	Number	Number
1870	82,388	45,050	33,048	14,342	7,993	2,754	1,040	431	317	—	—	104,975	361
1880	139,622	83,333	55,019	29,590	15,930	5,096	1,690	575	207	—	—	191,440	11,333
1890	223,546	144,829	92,642	48,048	23,510	8,730	2,818	689	221	—	—	321,487	20,395
1900	259,544	197,496	134,378	76,062	33,746	11,388	2,998	812	228	—	—	457,108	8,813
1910	295,669	232,981	164,216	102,800	51,028	19,352	4,841	956	167	—	—	576,341	32,886
1920	323,102	243,826	186,593	122,317	62,234	25,469	6,594	1,530	280	—	—	648,843	67,357
1930	434,050	338,764	220,017	185,619	90,002	35,040	9,948	2,072	348	—	—	808,645	80,194
1940	495,575	389,768	292,053	230,230	—	—	—	—	—	249,864	—	1,004,850	65,126
1950 [3]	605,860	533,695	372,110	308,044	163,051	—	—	—	—	—	132,365	1,268,400	78,515
1960 [4]	553,213	551,776	472,503	355,837	238,930	69,575	19,126	4,192	925	—	—	1,589,192	0
1970 [5,6]	412,769	480,548	456,780	406,413	297,110	—	—	—	—	—	153,886	1,685,981	0
1980 [7]	323,925	385,923	410,826	311,617	265,576	—	—	—	—	—	255,684	1,755,956	0
1990 [7]	495,958	455,531	304,427	—	—	—	—	—	—	—	305,384	1,642,535	0

[1] For changes in age and racial categorization, as well as exclusions in particular years, see the text for Table Aa185–286.

[2] For 1880–1890 and 1910–1940, foreign-born white population only. Age by sex is not available for the overall foreign-born population.

[3] 20 percent sample data.

[4] 25 percent sample data.

[5] 15 percent sample data.

[6] Figures for persons ages 100 and older are greatly overstated; see the text for Table Aa185–286.

[7] 17 percent sample data.

Sources

U.S. Bureau of the Census. 1870, *U.S. Census of Population: 1870*, volume 2, pp. 553, 673. 1880, *U.S. Census of Population: 1880*, volume 1, pp. 549, 551. 1890, *U.S. Census of Population: 1890*, volume 1, part 2, pp. 2–5. 1900, *U.S. Census of Population: 1900*, volume 2, part 2, pp. xxxvi–xli. 1910, *U.S. Census of Population: 1910*, "Abstract of the Census," p. 122. 1920, *U.S. Census of Population: 1920*, "Abstract of

(continued)

TABLE Aa2026–2077 Foreign-born population, by sex and age: 1870–1990 Continued

the Census," p. 122. 1920, U.S. Census of Population: 1920, "Abstract of the Fourteenth Census of the United States 1920," pp. 140–1. 1930–1940, U.S. Census of Population: 1940, "Population: Second Series; Characteristics of the Population, United States Summary," pp. 16–20; volume IV, part 1, p. 13. 1950, U.S. Census of Population: 1950, volume 2, part 1, pp. 165, 172; volume 4, part 3, Chapter A, p. 16. 1960, U.S. Census of Population: 1960, volume 1, part 1, p. 354. 1970, U.S. Census of Population: 1970, volume 1, part 1, section 2, p. 591. 1980–1990, Campbell Gibson and Emily Lennon, "Historical Census Statistics on the Foreign-Born Population of the United States: 1850 to 1990," U.S. Bureau of the Census, Population Division, Working Paper number 29 (February 1999), Table 7.

Documentation

See the text for Table Aa185–286.

TABLE Aa2078–2092 Native-born white population, by sex and parentage: 1850–1970

Contributed by Michael R. Haines

	Both sexes					Males					Females				
	Total	Native parentage	Foreign or mixed parentage			Total	Native parentage	Foreign or mixed parentage			Total	Native parentage	Foreign or mixed parentage		
			Total	Foreign parentage	Mixed parentage			Total	Foreign parentage	Mixed parentage			Total	Foreign parentage	Mixed parentage
Year	Aa2078	Aa2079	Aa2080	Aa2081	Aa2082	Aa2083	Aa2084	Aa2085	Aa2086	Aa2087	Aa2088	Aa2089	Aa2090	Aa2091	Aa2092
	Number	Number	Number	Number	Number	Number	Number	Number	Number	Number	Number	Number	Number	Number	Number
1850	17,312,533	—	—	—	—	8,786,968	—	—	—	—	8,525,565	—	—	—	—
1860	22,825,784	—	—	—	—	11,619,157	—	—	—	—	11,206,627	—	—	—	—
1870 [1]	28,095,665	22,771,397	5,324,268	4,167,098	1,157,170	14,086,509	—	—	—	—	14,009,156	—	—	—	—
1880	36,843,291	28,568,424	8,274,867	6,363,769	1,911,098	18,609,265	—	—	—	—	18,234,026	—	—	—	—
1890 [2]	45,979,391	34,475,716	11,503,675	8,085,019	3,418,656	23,318,521	17,536,950	5,781,571	—	—	22,660,870	16,938,766	5,722,104	—	—
1900	56,595,379	40,949,362	15,646,017	10,632,280	5,013,737	28,686,450	20,849,847	7,836,603	5,341,350	2,495,253	27,908,929	20,099,515	7,809,414	5,290,930	2,518,484
1910	68,386,412	49,488,575	18,897,837	12,916,311	5,981,526	34,654,457	25,229,218	9,425,239	6,456,793	2,968,446	33,731,955	24,259,357	9,472,598	6,459,518	3,013,080
1920	81,108,161	58,421,957	22,686,204	15,694,539	6,991,665	40,902,333	29,636,781	11,265,552	7,810,531	3,455,021	40,205,828	28,785,176	11,420,652	7,884,008	3,536,644
1930	96,303,335	70,400,952	25,902,383	17,407,527	8,494,856	48,420,037	35,595,286	12,824,751	8,645,951	4,178,800	47,883,298	34,805,666	13,077,632	8,761,576	4,316,056
1940 [3]	106,795,732	84,124,840	23,157,580	15,183,740	7,973,840	53,437,533	42,126,520	11,558,280	7,613,220	3,945,060	53,358,199	41,998,320	11,599,300	7,570,520	4,028,780
1950 [4]	124,382,950	100,804,575	23,578,375	14,815,760	8,762,615	61,431,020	50,004,910	11,426,110	7,195,325	4,230,785	62,951,930	50,799,665	12,152,265	7,620,435	4,531,830
1960 [5]	149,543,687	125,759,263	23,784,371	13,790,446	9,993,925	73,840,267	62,271,351	11,568,884	6,674,831	4,894,053	75,703,420	63,487,912	12,215,487	7,115,615	5,099,872
1970 [6]	169,385,451	146,231,286	23,154,165	—	—	82,910,031	71,823,652	11,086,379	—	—	86,475,420	74,407,634	12,067,786	—	—

[1] Excludes 747,915 white persons for whom data on nativity are not available. See text for Tables Aa1–5 and Aa145–184.

[2] Excludes population enumerated in the Indian Territory and on Indian reservations (including 64,047 white males and 53,321 white females) not classified by nativity.

[3] Complete-count data for totals by sex; 5 percent sample data for parentage.

[4] 20 percent sample data.

[5] 25 percent sample data. Total native, and data by parentage, are from different tabulations.

[6] 15 percent sample data. These data are not entirely comparable with data on total white population, by sex. See text for Table Aa145–184.

Sources

U.S. Bureau of the Census. 1850–1880, U.S. Census of Population: 1930, volume 2, pp. 33, 97. 1890–1930, U.S. Census of Population: 1950, volume 4, part 3, Chapter A, p. 11. 1940, parentage, U.S. Census of Population: 1940, "Nativity and Parentage of the White Population," p. 7; total native population, U.S. Census of Population: 1950, volume 2, part 1, p. 19. 1950, U.S. Census of Population: 1950, volume 4, part 3, Chapter A, p. 11. 1960, parentage, U.S. Census of Population: 1960, PC(2)-1A, p. 2; total native population, U.S. Census of Population: 1960, volume 1, part 1, pp. 354, 359. 1970, U.S. Census of Population: 1970, Final Report PC (2)-1A, "National Origin and Language," p. 1.

Documentation

The procedures for determining the nativity of parents are generally the same as those for determining the nativity of the individual. The native-born population can be subdivided into native-born of native (American) parents, native-born of mixed parentage (one American parent and one foreign-born parent), and native-born of foreign parentage (both parents foreign-born).

The figures for total native-born population in Table Aa2078–2092 and the figures for foreign-born population in Table Aa1896–1921 for each year are from the same census count or sample. For 1850–1940, these are complete-count data that add to the totals in Table Aa145–184. For 1950–1970, these are sample data that do not agree with the totals in Table Aa145–184.

Similarly, the figures by parentage in Table Aa2078–2092 for each year are from the same census count or sample. For 1870–1930, these are complete-count data that add to the totals in Table Aa2078–2092. For 1940–1970, these are sample data that add to the totals in Table Aa2078–2092. For 1940–1970, these are sample data only when all figures are from the same tabulation of the same sample.

SLAVE POPULATION

Michael R. Haines

TABLE Aa2093–2140   Slave population, by sex and age: 1820–1860[1]

Contributed by Michael R. Haines

	Males											
						Age						
	Total	0–13	0–9	0–4	5–9	14–25	10–23	10–14	15–19	20–29	24–35	26–44
	Aa2093	Aa2094	Aa2095	Aa2096	Aa2097	Aa2098	Aa2099	Aa2100	Aa2101	Aa2102	Aa2103	Aa2104
Year	Number	Number	Number	Number	Number	Number	Number	Number	Number	Number	Number	Number
1820	788,028	343,852	—	—	—	203,088	—	—	—	—	—	163,723
1830	1,012,823	—	353,498	—	—	—	312,567	—	—	—	185,585	—
1840	1,246,517	—	422,584	—	—	—	391,206	—	—	—	235,386	—
1850	1,602,534	—	—	267,088	239,163	—	—	221,480	176,169	289,595	—	—
1860	1,982,625	—	—	322,156	287,299	—	—	276,928	220,365	355,018	—	—

	Males											
						Age						
	30–39	36–54	40–49	50–59	55–59	60–69	70–79	80–89	90–99	100 and older	45 and older	Not stated
	Aa2105	Aa2106	Aa2107	Aa2108	Aa2109	Aa2110	Aa2111	Aa2112	Aa2113	Aa2114	Aa2115	Aa2116
Year	Number	Number	Number	Number	Number	Number	Number	Number	Number	Number	Number	Number
1820	—	—	—	—	—	—	—	—	—	—	77,365	—
1830	—	118,880	—	—	41,545	—	—	—	—	748	—	—
1840	—	145,260	—	—	51,331	—	—	—	—	750	—	—
1850	175,300	—	109,152	65,254	—	38,102	13,166	4,378	1,211	606	—	1,870
1860	218,346	—	140,791	79,776	—	46,219	15,433	4,627	1,317	671	—	13,679

	Females											
						Age						
	Total	0–13	0–9	0–4	5–9	14–25	10–23	10–14	15–19	20–29	24–35	26–44
	Aa2117	Aa2118	Aa2119	Aa2120	Aa2121	Aa2122	Aa2123	Aa2124	Aa2125	Aa2126	Aa2127	Aa2128
Year	Number	Number	Number	Number	Number	Number	Number	Number	Number	Number	Number	Number
1820	750,010	324,344	—	—	—	202,336	—	—	—	—	—	152,693
1830	996,220	—	347,665	—	—	—	308,770	—	—	—	185,786	—
1840	1,240,938	—	421,465	—	—	—	390,117	—	—	—	239,825	—
1850	1,601,779	—	—	273,406	239,925	—	—	214,712	181,113	282,615	—	—
1860	1,971,135	—	—	331,010	288,650	—	—	264,320	228,481	343,023	—	—

	Females											
						Age						
	30–39	36–54	40–49	50–59	55–59	60–69	70–79	80–89	90–99	100 and older	45 and older	Not stated
	Aa2129	Aa2130	Aa2131	Aa2132	Aa2133	Aa2134	Aa2135	Aa2136	Aa2137	Aa2138	Aa2139	Aa2140
Year	Number	Number	Number	Number	Number	Number	Number	Number	Number	Number	Number	Number
1820	—	—	—	—	—	—	—	—	—	—	70,637	—
1830	—	111,887	—	—	41,436	—	—	—	—	676	—	—
1840	—	139,204	—	—	49,746	—	—	—	—	581	—	—
1850	178,355	—	110,780	61,762	—	36,569	13,688	4,740	1,473	819	—	1,822
1860	220,520	—	139,002	75,926	—	44,124	15,724	5,334	1,714	900	—	12,407

[1] For changes in age and racial categorization, as well as exclusions in particular years, see the text for Table Aa185–286.

Sources

U.S. Bureau of the Census. 1820–1840, *U.S. Census of Population: 1840, Compendium* (Thomas Allen), pp. 100–3, 366–75. 1850–1860, *U.S. Census of Population: 1870*, volume 2, pp. 552–8.

Documentation

See the text for Table Aa185–286.

TABLE Aa2141–2188   Free black population, by sex and age: 1820–1860[1]

Contributed by Michael R. Haines

Males

		Age										
Year	Total	0–13	0–9	0–4	5–9	14–25	10–23	10–14	15–19	20–29	24–35	26–44
	Aa2141	Aa2142	Aa2143	Aa2144	Aa2145	Aa2146	Aa2147	Aa2148	Aa2149	Aa2150	Aa2151	Aa2152
	Number	Number	Number	Number	Number	Number	Number	Number	Number	Number	Number	Number
1820	112,734	47,659	—	—	—	24,012	—	—	—	—	—	23,450
1830	153,453	—	48,675	—	—	—	43,079	—	—	—	27,650	—
1840	186,481	—	56,284	—	—	—	52,805	—	—	—	35,321	—
1850	208,724	—	—	30,319	28,806	—	—	26,061	20,395	35,782	—	—
1860	234,119	—	—	32,843	30,700	—	—	30,446	24,739	39,167	—	—

Males

	Age											
Year	30–39	36–54	40–49	50–59	55–59	60–69	70–79	80–89	90–99	100 and older	45 and older	Not stated
	Aa2153	Aa2154	Aa2155	Aa2156	Aa2157	Aa2158	Aa2159	Aa2160	Aa2161	Aa2162	Aa2163	Aa2164
	Number	Number	Number	Number	Number	Number	Number	Number	Number	Number	Number	Number
1820	—	—	—	—	—	—	—	—	—	—	17,613	—
1830	—	22,271	—	—	11,509	—	—	—	—	269	—	—
1840	—	28,274	—	—	13,513	—	—	—	—	284	—	—
1850	26,153	—	18,199	11,771	—	6,671	2,878	1,106	319	114	—	150
1860	29,032	—	21,429	13,330	—	7,690	3,198	1,005	327	128	—	85

Females

		Age										
Year	Total	0–13	0–9	0–4	5–9	14–25	10–23	10–14	15–19	20–29	24–35	26–44
	Aa2165	Aa2166	Aa2167	Aa2168	Aa2169	Aa2170	Aa2171	Aa2172	Aa2173	Aa2174	Aa2175	Aa2176
	Number	Number	Number	Number	Number	Number	Number	Number	Number	Number	Number	Number
1820	120,790	45,898	—	—	—	28,850	—	—	—	—	—	27,181
1830	166,146	—	47,329	—	—	—	48,138	—	—	—	32,541	—
1840	199,822	—	55,062	—	—	—	56,592	—	—	—	41,682	—
1850	225,771	—	—	30,502	29,246	—	—	26,247	23,399	41,765	—	—
1860	253,951	—	—	33,075	31,157	—	—	29,953	28,008	46,395	—	—

Females

	Age											
Year	30–39	36–54	40–49	50–59	55–59	60–69	70–79	80–89	90–99	100 and older	45 and older	Not stated
	Aa2177	Aa2178	Aa2179	Aa2180	Aa2181	Aa2182	Aa2183	Aa2184	Aa2185	Aa2186	Aa2187	Aa2188
	Number	Number	Number	Number	Number	Number	Number	Number	Number	Number	Number	Number
1820	—	—	—	—	—	—	—	—	—	—	18,861	—
1830	—	24,327	—	—	13,425	—	—	—	—	386	—	—
1840	—	30,371	—	—	15,753	—	—	—	—	362	—	—
1850	29,072	—	19,741	12,582	—	7,362	3,438	1,512	540	229	—	136
1860	32,700	—	23,297	14,661	—	8,442	3,838	1,570	527	241	—	87

[1] For changes in age and racial categorization, as well as exclusions in particular years, see the text for Table Aa185–286.

Sources

U.S. Bureau of the Census. 1820–1840, *U.S. Census of Population: 1840, Compendium* (Thomas Allen), pp. 100–3, 366–75. 1850–1860, *U.S. Census of Population: 1870*, volume 2, pp. 552–8.

Documentation

See the text for Table Aa185–286.

HISPANIC POPULATION

Brian Gratton and Myron P. Gutmann

TABLE Aa2189–2215   Hispanic population estimates, by sex, race, Hispanic origin, residence, nativity: 1850–1990[1]

Contributed by Brian Gratton, Myron P. Gutmann, and Elizabeth Wildsmith

	Total	Sex		Urban–rural residence			Country of birth		
		Male	Female	Urban	Rural	Unknown	United States	Foreign-born		
								Total	Hispanic countries
	Aa2189	Aa2190	Aa2191	Aa2192	Aa2193	Aa2194	Aa2195	Aa2196	Aa2197
Year	Number	Number	Number	Number	Number	Number	Number	Number	Number
1850	116,943	64,282	52,661	16,377	100,566	—	39,724	78,128	77,219
1880	393,555	202,062	191,493	88,070	305,485	—	251,710	141,845	134,961
1900	503,189	263,359	239,830	151,029	352,160	—	311,181	192,008	182,141
1910	797,994	425,283	372,711	299,991	498,003	—	495,531	302,463	291,295
1920	1,286,154	698,258	587,896	618,661	667,493	—	684,224	601,930	587,595
1940	2,021,820	1,028,777	993,043	—	—	—	1,501,168	520,652	512,969
1950	3,231,409	1,621,765	1,609,644	—	—	—	2,620,532	610,877	598,453
1960	5,814,784	2,920,424	2,894,360	4,777,647	980,673	56,464	4,911,090	903,694	840,638
1970	8,920,940	4,365,937	4,555,003	7,892,753	934,101	94,086	6,929,772	1,991,168	1,818,288
1980	14,608,673	7,279,831	7,328,842	13,133,865	1,474,808	—	10,430,832 [2]	4,172,851 [2]	—
1990	22,354,059	11,388,059	10,966,000	20,426,228	1,927,831	—	14,058,439 [2]	7,841,650 [2]	—

	Region					Hispanic origin			
	Northeast	Midwest	South	West	Military base or state unknown	Mexican	Spanish	Puerto Rican	Cuban
	Aa2198	Aa2199	Aa2200	Aa2201	Aa2202	Aa2203	Aa2204	Aa2205	Aa2206
Year	Number	Number	Number	Number	Number	Number	Number	Number	Number
1850	9,704	6,262	29,919	71,058	—	80,959	4,955	0	2,124
1880	30,101	25,119	129,681	208,654	—	290,642	32,504	0	12,267
1900	22,011	17,457	245,891	214,794	3,036	401,491	47,055	0	22,006
1910	44,589	33,336	349,410	370,659	—	640,104	69,020	2,937	34,903
1920	107,775	74,663	577,602	526,114	—	999,535	120,042	20,384	35,809
1940	246,274	134,772	752,550	888,224	—	1,567,596	150,332	95,129	49,938
1950	476,220	205,579	1,154,385	1,395,225	—	2,489,477	134,659	326,186	70,919
1960	1,147,001	384,718	1,817,399	2,465,666	—	4,087,546	202,822	1,027,338	163,241
1970	1,968,339	679,127	2,537,969	3,735,505	—	5,641,956	248,439	1,620,777	637,931
1980	2,604,289	1,276,545	4,473,966	6,253,873	—	8,740,439	—	2,013,945	803,226
1990	3,754,389	1,726,509	6,767,021	10,106,140	—	13,495,938	—	2,727,754	1,043,932

	Hispanic origin		Race						
	Other identifiable Hispanic	Unidentifiable origin	White	Black	American Indian	Chinese	Japanese	Other Asian or Pacific Islander	Other
	Aa2207	Aa2208	Aa2209	Aa2210	Aa2211	Aa2212	Aa2213	Aa2214	Aa2215
Year	Number	Number	Number	Number	Number	Number	Number	Number	Number
1850	1,112	27,793	114,617	2,326	0	0	0	0	0
1880	11,373	46,769	337,291	35,319	20,845	100	0	0	0
1900	18,216	14,421	434,879	18,216	25,047	0	0	0	25,047
1910	29,616	21,414	688,709	23,792	27,318	58	0	0	58,117
1920	39,465	70,919	1,216,303	36,330	17,268	403	101	1,009	14,740
1940	86,636	72,189	1,953,681	45,996	18,804	708	0	1,923	708
1950	117,023	93,145	3,136,623	70,599	16,994	981	1,962	2,942	1,308
1960	272,972	60,865	5,614,234	135,389	35,471	3,387	3,285	15,146	7,872
1970	704,798	67,039	8,496,628	253,835	54,574	6,416	5,210	19,457	84,820
1980	3,051,063	—	8,115,256	390,852	—	—	—	—	6,102,565
1990	5,086,435	—	11,557,774	769,767	165,461	—	—	305,303	9,555,754

Notes appear on next page

(continued)

TABLE Aa2189–2215   Hispanic population estimates, by sex, race, Hispanic origin, residence, nativity: 1850–1990
Continued

[1] Figures through 1970 are derived from sample data in the Integrated Public Use Microdata Series (IPUMS) data base. See text and the Guide to the Millennial Edition for information on IPUMS. Estimates for 1940–1950 are based on sample-line record data; 1970 estimates are based on 15 percent state sample data. 1980–1990 figures are from published census sources, except as indicated.

[2] Based on sample data.

Sources

1850–1970: Brian Gratton and Myron P. Gutmann, "Hispanics in the United States, 1850–1990: Estimates of Population Size and National Origin," *Historical Methods* 33 (2000): 137–53, plus additional calculations using the samples described in Gratton and Gutmann (2000).

1980: U.S. Bureau of the Census, *1980 Census of Population, General Population Characteristics: United States Summary*, PC80-1-B1. U.S. Bureau of the Census, *1980 Census of Population, Detailed Population Characteristics: United States Summary*, PC80-1-D1-A.

1990: U.S. Bureau of the Census, *1990 Census of Population, General Population Characteristics, United States*, 1990 CP-1-1. U.S. Bureau of the Census, *1990 Census of Population, Social and Economic Characteristics, United States*, 1990 CP-2-1.

Documentation

Tables Aa2189–2243 provide estimates of Hispanic population size and composition for the United States from 1850 to 1990, based on U.S. Census publications and on data drawn from Public Use Samples of the United States Census for various years. Much of the text that follows was published originally in Gratton and Gutmann (2000).

Before 1970, estimating the size of the Hispanic population or that of its subgroups was problematic because the census rarely collected information other than birthplace variables (even these results were not published fully). In 1930, for example, the Census attempted to classify Mexican as a "race"; however, this effort officially added nothing to previous information using birthplace variables: enumerators were to record as Mexican "all persons born in Mexico, or having parents born in Mexico, who are not definitely white, Negro . . . ." The race clause actually restricted Mexican descent, as persons whose appearance met enumerators' standards for white, black, or other race categories were not to be recorded as Mexican. In any case, variations in enumerator policies leave the meaning of published results in 1930 unclear. See T. W. Longmore and H. L. Hitt, "A Demographic Analysis of the First and Second Generation Mexican Population of the United States: 1930," *Southwestern Social Science Quarterly* 24 (1943): 138–48; and J. Samora and P. V. Simon, *A History of the Mexican American People* (University of Notre Dame Press, 1977).

In 1950, the Census first experimented with a more general Hispanic indicator, one that identified individuals beyond the second generation. Census Bureau personnel recorded white persons of Spanish *surname* in Arizona, California, Colorado, New Mexico, and Texas. Undoubtedly designed to focus on Mexican-origin Hispanics who lived in the Southwest, the surname variable did not provide any information outside the region, nor did it distinguish other national subgroups. Although the Census Bureau knew that the Spanish surname lists omitted certain persons who were Hispanic (U.S. Bureau of the Census, *United States Census of Population: 1950*, volume 4, *Special Reports, No. 3C Persons of Spanish Surname*), the opportunity to reach beyond the second generation encouraged the use of such indicators. More extensive lists were employed in the 1960, 1970, and 1980 Censuses, still limited to the five Southwestern states (R. M. Ito II, B. Gratton, and J. Wycoff, "Using the 1940 and 1950 Public Use Microdata Samples: A Cautionary Tale," *Historical Methods* 30 (1997): 137–47).

Additional variables in the census offered alternative means for identifying Hispanics, especially the intermittent recording of language characteristics beginning in the 1910 Census. The 1970 Census marked a more decisive change. In that year, two new efforts were made to classify the population. The first relied on a combination of variables that located "Spanish Americans," including Spanish as a mother tongue, Puerto Rican family background in three Northeastern states, and Spanish surname in the five Southwestern states. The second effort asked respondents to identify themselves in four "Spanish origin" categories (Mexican, Cuban, Puerto Rican, other). Although the 1970 origin question did not produce satisfactory results, self-identification of Hispanic origin became increasingly detailed and accurate in the 1980 and 1990 Censuses and has allowed estimates of the Hispanic population and its subgroups to be made with much greater confidence (F. D. Bean and M. Tienda, *The Hispanic Population of the United States* (National Committee for Research on the 1980 Census, Russell Sage, 1987)).

For years prior to 1980, the estimates provided here made use of individual-level census sample data made available through the IPUMS project (see the Guide to the Millennial Edition for information on IPUMS). The methodology for use of these data can be found in Gratton and Gutmann (2000). The IPUMS data sets contain samples of U.S. census enumeration records, which can be tabulated to produce population estimates not published by the Census Bureau. Hispanic origin is determined by place of birth, parents' place of birth, and Spanish surname; places of birth, both in foreign countries and in regions of the United States, allowed estimates for subdivision of the Hispanic population into national origin groups. These data are available for all census years considered and produce consistent estimates; however, they constitute *lower end* estimates. Additional variables available in certain censuses (such as language spoken) allow more complete and accurate estimates. Results based on these additional variables can be found in Gratton and Gutmann (2000); these are not, however, consistent in their coverage from year to year. For 1980 and 1990, the estimates reported make use of results published by the U.S. Bureau of the Census, based on the Hispanic identity question asked of all persons. The foreign-born estimates, however, are based on a question asked of only a sample of census respondents and the totals may vary.

See Table Ap-G in Appendix 2 regarding the composition of census regions and divisions.

TABLE Aa2216–2229 Hispanic female population estimates, by age: 1850–1990[1]

Contributed by Brian Gratton, Myron P. Gutmann, and Elizabeth Wildsmith

	0–4	5–9	10–14	15–19	20–24	25–29	30–34	35–39	40–44	45–49	50–54	55–59	60–64	65 and older
	Aa2216	Aa2217	Aa2218	Aa2219	Aa2220	Aa2221	Aa2222	Aa2223	Aa2224	Aa2225	Aa2226	Aa2227	Aa2228	Aa2229
Year	Number	Number	Number	Number	Number	Number	Number	Number	Number	Number	Number	Number	Number	Number
1850	7,078	6,666	6,167	6,872	6,166	4,752	3,234	2,224	2,729	1,719	1,920	708	1,516	910
1880	26,323	25,022	23,134	19,459	21,644	14,564	15,761	11,367	10,669	7,384	4,993	2,892	3,891	4,387
1900	22,008	37,190	28,081	27,321	22,769	18,216	18,974	17,457	11,384	6,831	9,108	5,312	3,794	11,385
1910	49,769	50,483	41,255	46,648	36,019	30,919	20,774	22,255	16,510	17,280	13,082	7,292	8,013	12,412
1920	79,016	79,821	71,637	65,595	60,947	55,607	35,016	39,347	27,044	22,809	16,143	10,693	9,284	14,937
1940	132,540	128,080	128,300	115,959	82,287	81,685	67,234	65,812	46,891	43,673	31,736	22,844	17,994	28,008
1950	241,869	189,554	156,871	150,665	167,978	145,116	108,841	99,029	93,803	72,228	56,540	43,476	31,380	52,294
1960	463,139	386,670	321,161	254,207	234,213	229,943	218,552	194,141	139,850	120,345	96,058	80,073	54,895	101,113
1970	533,963	612,518	554,482	467,788	389,280	341,017	316,129	284,042	257,537	212,376	152,049	131,616	103,794	198,412
1980	815,130	754,226	728,023	779,603	766,674	678,543	570,374	438,416	367,481	321,449	294,306	237,175	173,766	403,676
1990	1,169,330	1,075,119	978,234	970,064	1,042,941	1,090,881	987,846	814,565	644,100	485,653	391,770	336,937	298,686	679,874

[1] Figures through 1970 are derived from sample data in the Integrated Public Use Microdata Series (IPUMS) data base (see the Guide to the Millennial Edition for information on IPUMS; also see the text for Table Aa2189–2215). Estimates for 1940–1950 are based on sample-line record data; 1970 estimates are based on 15 percent state sample data. 1980–1990 figures are from published census sources.

Sources
See the sources for Table Aa2189–2215.

Documentation
See the text for Table Aa2189–2215.

TABLE Aa2230–2243 Hispanic male population estimates, by age: 1850–1990[1]

Contributed by Brian Gratton, Myron P. Gutmann, and Elizabeth Wildsmith

	0–4	5–9	10–14	15–19	20–24	25–29	30–34	35–39	40–44	45–49	50–54	55–59	60–64	65 and older
	Aa2230	Aa2231	Aa2232	Aa2233	Aa2234	Aa2235	Aa2236	Aa2237	Aa2238	Aa2239	Aa2240	Aa2241	Aa2242	Aa2243
Year	Number	Number	Number	Number	Number	Number	Number	Number	Number	Number	Number	Number	Number	Number
1850	8,393	7,074	6,670	7,275	7,275	7,582	4,548	4,044	2,932	2,729	2,526	404	1,213	1,617
1880	26,632	24,537	23,630	18,348	18,645	18,350	15,758	14,866	10,873	9,076	7,083	4,090	4,690	5,484
1900	28,082	27,323	27,322	25,804	27,324	24,287	14,420	18,973	19,733	15,938	9,107	4,554	6,831	13,661
1910	52,714	42,961	42,810	38,900	52,630	39,140	30,923	28,910	19,943	17,892	19,626	12,788	10,498	15,548
1920	82,542	81,020	68,614	65,581	81,740	76,174	55,902	49,855	37,031	32,602	24,816	12,112	13,013	17,256
1940	132,534	115,751	120,720	113,337	85,738	77,242	71,977	77,744	70,471	56,201	41,251	21,433	16,172	28,206
1950	243,153	199,694	165,061	148,706	149,706	153,613	102,963	93,794	94,446	78,123	55,557	50,003	31,704	55,242
1960	495,011	381,844	329,925	240,310	214,180	236,994	221,559	195,718	143,840	116,051	102,211	91,755	55,301	95,725
1970	549,245	617,577	571,521	449,859	348,974	294,590	278,263	274,674	247,897	202,121	141,754	116,204	93,768	179,490
1980	848,043	782,955	746,975	826,725	819,189	697,371	558,171	415,802	344,790	300,140	270,070	217,193	147,203	305,204
1990	1,218,194	1,118,733	1,023,383	1,083,893	1,261,500	1,250,358	1,074,457	846,161	640,168	468,257	364,219	302,371	254,956	481,409

[1] Figures through 1970 are derived from sample data in the Integrated Public Use Microdata Series (IPUMS) data base (see the Guide to the Millennial Edition for information on IPUMS; also see the text for Table Aa2189–2215). Estimates for 1940–1950 are based on sample-line record data; 1970 estimates are based on 15 percent state sample data. 1980–1990 figures are from published census sources.

Sources
See the sources for Table Aa2189–2215.

Documentation
See the text for Table Aa2189–2215.

STATE POPULATIONS

Michael R. Haines

TABLE Aa2244–2340   Alabama population, by race, sex, age, nativity, and urban–rural residence: 1800–1990

Contributed by Michael R. Haines

			Population									
				Race				Residence		Nativity	
	Area	Population density	Total	White	Nonwhite	Black	Other nonwhite	Urban	Rural	Native-born	Foreign-born
	Aa2244	Aa2245	Aa2246	Aa2247	Aa2248	Aa2249	Aa2250	Aa2251	Aa2252	Aa2253	Aa2254
Year	Square miles	Persons per square mile	Number	Number	Number	Number	Number	Number	Number	Number	Number
1800	—	—	1,250	733	517	517	—	0	1,250	—	—
1810	—	—	9,046	6,422	2,624	2,624	—	0	9,046	—	—
1820	51,279	2.49	127,901	85,451	42,450	42,450	0	0	127,901	—	—
1830	51,279	6.04	309,527	190,406	119,121	119,121	—	3,194	306,333	—	—
1840	51,279	11.52	590,756	335,185	255,571	255,571	—	12,672	578,084	—	—
1850	51,279	15.05	771,623	426,514	345,109	345,109	—	35,179	736,444	764,114	7,509
1860	51,279	18.80	964,201	526,271	437,930	437,770	160	48,901	915,300	951,849	12,352
1870	51,279	19.44	996,992	521,384	475,608	475,510	98	62,700	934,292	987,030	9,962
1880	51,279	24.62	1,262,505	662,185	600,320	600,103	217	68,518	1,193,987	1,252,771	9,734
1890 [1]	51,279	29.51	1,513,401	833,718	679,299	678,489	810	152,235	1,361,166	1,498,240	14,777
1900	51,279	35.66	1,828,697	1,001,152	827,545	827,307	238	216,714	1,611,983	1,814,105	14,592
1910	51,279	41.70	2,138,093	1,228,832	909,261	908,282	979	370,431	1,767,662	2,118,807	19,286
1920	51,279	45.79	2,348,174	1,447,032	901,142	900,652	490	509,317	1,838,857	2,330,147	18,027
1930	51,279	51.60	2,646,248	1,700,844	945,404	944,834	570	744,273	1,901,975	2,630,187	16,061
1940	51,078	55.46	2,832,961	1,849,097	983,864	983,290	574	855,941	1,977,020	2,820,797	12,164
1950	51,078	59.94	3,061,743	2,079,591	982,152	979,617	2,535	1,340,937	1,720,806	3,042,805	13,405
1960	50,851	64.24	3,266,740	2,283,609	983,131	980,271	2,860	1,791,721	1,475,019	3,251,785	14,955
1970	50,708	67.92	3,444,165	2,533,831	910,334	903,467	6,867	2,017,485	1,426,680	3,428,160	15,988
1980	50,767	76.70	3,893,888	2,872,621	1,021,267	996,335	24,932	2,337,713	1,556,175	3,854,886	39,002
1990	50,750	79.62	4,040,587	2,975,797	1,064,790	1,020,705	44,085	2,439,549	1,601,038	3,997,054	43,533

	Population											
	Sex		Male, by age									
	Male	Female	0	1–4	5–9	10–14	15–19	20–29	20–24	25–29	30–39	30–34
	Aa2255	Aa2256	Aa2257	Aa2258	Aa2259	Aa2260	Aa2261	Aa2262	Aa2263	Aa2264	Aa2265	Aa2266
Year	Number	Number	Number	Number	Number	Number	Number	Number	Number	Number	Number	Number
1800	—	—	—	—	—	—	—	—	—	—	—	—
1810	—	—	—	—	—	—	—	—	—	—	—	—
1820	67,937	59,964	—	—	—	—	—	—	—	—	—	—
1830	160,860	148,667	—	—	—	—	—	—	—	—	—	—
1840	305,082	285,674	—	—	—	—	—	—	—	—	—	—
1850	392,343	379,280	10,301	55,855	60,089	53,482	43,652	68,160	—	—	44,587	—
1860	489,291	474,910	14,712	65,239	71,866	68,133	54,254	87,758	—	—	54,505	—
1870	488,738	508,254	15,396	64,545	67,813	71,359	55,640	—	48,288	32,972	—	24,902
1880	622,629	639,876	22,483	86,715	99,336	79,782	61,319	—	61,560	46,337	—	33,972
1890 [1]	757,456	755,561	22,431	89,539	113,545	106,742	86,485	—	68,706	52,108	—	44,320
1900	916,764	911,933	27,438	107,707	130,096	116,236	101,647	—	91,861	70,838	—	50,992
1910	1,074,209	1,063,884	32,438	124,944	143,412	129,025	112,318	—	101,563	86,627	—	68,072
1920	1,173,105	1,175,069	31,476	119,766	160,519	151,115	118,000	—	98,277	84,952	—	69,258
1930	1,315,009	1,331,239	30,722	127,659	167,749	153,633	144,433	—	122,173	98,999	—	78,702
1940	1,399,901	1,433,060	28,236	121,370	153,593	158,869	148,677	—	124,596	116,162	—	102,209
1950	1,502,640	1,559,103	37,421	155,138	165,565	148,691	130,236	—	114,007	112,183	—	102,408
1960	1,591,709	1,675,031	40,139	157,792	186,248	177,448	139,709	—	99,655	92,990	—	96,538
1970	1,661,941	1,782,224	31,730	121,605	176,751	189,466	171,457	—	132,169	105,422	—	91,439
1980	1,871,534	2,022,354	31,888	118,462	160,615	167,885	190,792	—	177,550	154,658	—	138,949
1990	1,936,162	2,104,425	24,867	120,532	149,894	152,852	162,510	—	150,906	157,212	—	159,598

Note appears at end of table

TABLE Aa2244–2340   Alabama population, by race, sex, age, nativity, and urban–rural residence: 1800–1990
Continued

						Population							
						Male, by age							
	35–39	40–49	40–44	45–49	50–59	50–54	55–59	60–69	60–64	65–69	70–79	70–74
	Aa2267	Aa2268	Aa2269	Aa2270	Aa2271	Aa2272	Aa2273	Aa2274	Aa2275	Aa2276	Aa2277	Aa2278
Year	Number	Number	Number	Number	Number	Number	Number	Number	Number	Number	Number	Number
1800	—	—	—	—	—	—	—	—	—	—	—	—
1810	—	—	—	—	—	—	—	—	—	—	—	—
1820	—	—	—	—	—	—	—	—	—	—	—	—
1830	—	—	—	—	—	—	—	—	—	—	—	—
1840	—	—	—	—	—	—	—	—	—	—	—	—
1850	—	27,504	—	—	16,273	—	—	8,361	—	—	2,908	—
1860	—	35,935	—	—	20,154	—	—	11,731	—	—	3,688	—
1870	23,482	—	17,803	18,494	—	17,710	8,975	—	9,593	5,030	—	3,434
1880	26,465	—	18,419	25,076	—	19,705	12,622	—	11,496	7,348	—	5,016
1890 [1]	39,914	—	27,017	32,751	—	22,153	15,140	—	13,118	8,730	—	5,912
1900	42,602	—	33,865	46,035	—	32,256	19,600	—	15,655	11,212	—	7,447
1910	62,038	—	41,544	49,077	—	38,872	28,181	—	22,169	13,992	—	8,552
1920	73,617	—	53,313	68,102	—	44,408	29,481	—	27,107	19,092	—	12,150
1930	77,868	—	61,534	74,858	—	56,451	39,839	—	29,970	20,438	—	14,808
1940	90,272	—	73,215	69,061	—	60,037	47,657	—	38,094	31,702	—	18,876
1950	104,383	—	94,134	79,284	—	65,773	54,904	—	44,087	41,434	—	26,484
1960	99,198	—	93,756	92,207	—	81,123	67,291	—	50,570	45,444	—	33,563
1970	88,578	—	92,945	91,938	—	85,386	79,091	—	68,558	53,311	—	36,215
1980	111,298	—	95,998	91,518	—	92,262	87,747	—	76,539	67,931	—	50,261
1990	148,622	—	135,558	108,997	—	92,239	86,192	—	81,862	73,630	—	54,938

							Population						
	Male, by age			Female, by age									
	75–79	80 and older	Unknown age	0	1–4	5–9	10–14	15–19	20–29	20–24	25–29	30–39
	Aa2279	Aa2280	Aa2281	Aa2282	Aa2283	Aa2284	Aa2285	Aa2286	Aa2287	Aa2288	Aa2289	Aa2290
Year	Number	Number	Number	Number	Number	Number	Number	Number	Number	Number	Number	Number
1800	—	—	—	—	—	—	—	—	—	—	—	—
1810	—	—	—	—	—	—	—	—	—	—	—	—
1820	—	—	—	—	—	—	—	—	—	—	—	—
1830	—	—	—	—	—	—	—	—	—	—	—	—
1840	—	—	—	—	—	—	—	—	—	—	—	—
1850	—	1,113	58	10,074	54,813	59,300	51,473	45,213	67,166	—	—	40,702
1860	—	1,251	65	14,944	64,238	70,854	64,949	57,212	84,926	—	—	52,326
1870	1,631	1,671	0	14,974	61,549	65,913	68,408	58,484	—	55,973	41,153	—
1880	2,638	2,340	—	21,792	83,209	97,190	75,036	63,449	—	67,172	50,010	—
1890 [1]	3,480	3,069	2,296	21,079	85,940	110,938	101,786	88,108	—	71,472	53,992	—
1900	4,164	3,608	3,505	26,963	105,192	126,598	112,449	103,175	—	97,775	71,832	—
1910	4,972	4,205	2,208	32,074	122,260	141,390	124,171	117,199	—	109,842	90,930	—
1920	6,097	4,780	1,595	31,074	117,206	157,712	148,297	126,993	—	112,998	95,889	—
1930	8,616	5,956	601	30,308	125,193	163,964	149,807	149,735	—	137,188	109,955	—
1940	9,449	7,826	—	27,628	120,085	150,905	155,472	151,614	—	137,180	126,686	—
1950	18,271	8,237	—	36,418	151,147	161,238	144,749	135,004	—	128,999	122,059	—
1960	21,989	16,049	—	39,062	153,410	181,610	172,843	139,772	—	107,979	101,889	—
1970	23,451	22,429	—	30,217	117,479	170,554	182,356	170,294	—	142,375	111,525	—
1980	31,608	25,573	—	30,918	115,144	153,535	160,211	186,614	—	183,637	160,802	—
1990	39,683	36,070	—	23,590	114,306	143,693	146,561	157,916	—	154,496	162,350	—

Note appears at end of table

(continued)

TABLE Aa2244–2340   Alabama population, by race, sex, age, nativity, and urban–rural residence: 1800–1990
Continued

	Population											
	Female, by age											
	30–34	35–39	40–49	40–44	45–49	50–59	50–54	55–59	60–69	60–64	65–69	70–79
	Aa2291	Aa2292	Aa2293	Aa2294	Aa2295	Aa2296	Aa2297	Aa2298	Aa2299	Aa2300	Aa2301	Aa2302
Year	Number	Number	Number	Number	Number	Number	Number	Number	Number	Number	Number	Number
1800	—	—	—	—	—	—	—	—	—	—	—	—
1810	—	—	—	—	—	—	—	—	—	—	—	—
1820	—	—	—	—	—	—	—	—	—	—	—	—
1830	—	—	—	—	—	—	—	—	—	—	—	—
1840	—	—	—	—	—	—	—	—	—	—	—	—
1850	—	—	25,598	—	—	13,934	—	—	7,282	—	—	2,570
1860	—	—	32,674	—	—	17,926	—	—	10,098	—	—	3,371
1870	31,713	27,374	—	23,213	17,569	—	15,033	7,782	—	8,333	4,159	—
1880	38,537	33,817	—	28,402	23,408	—	19,728	11,060	—	10,754	6,356	—
1890 [1]	44,337	40,682	—	33,602	29,760	—	23,408	14,394	—	13,628	8,303	—
1900	50,953	45,162	—	39,907	35,137	—	29,082	19,644	—	16,977	11,312	—
1910	68,817	61,804	—	44,146	38,675	—	32,990	23,390	—	20,669	13,969	—
1920	75,233	76,717	—	58,000	49,093	—	35,371	24,607	—	23,388	16,686	—
1930	86,131	86,123	—	69,337	63,545	—	50,008	33,877	—	25,978	18,808	—
1940	108,687	97,214	—	78,228	70,053	—	58,593	45,660	—	36,699	30,339	—
1950	111,029	113,277	—	97,840	82,372	—	69,733	55,870	—	45,146	45,543	—
1960	108,211	108,969	—	101,635	98,145	—	86,286	73,070	—	58,048	54,577	—
1970	99,609	97,844	—	103,574	101,415	—	94,234	89,425	—	80,768	68,843	—
1980	144,343	117,622	—	104,796	100,411	—	104,804	102,315	—	92,560	88,364	—
1990	169,320	157,225	—	142,182	115,865	—	102,320	97,485	—	98,448	94,679	—

	Population											
	Female, by age				White							
							Male, by age					
	70–74	75–79	80 and older	Unknown age	Male	Female	0–4	5–9	10–14	15–19	20–29	30–39
	Aa2303	Aa2304	Aa2305	Aa2306	Aa2307	Aa2308	Aa2309	Aa2310	Aa2311	Aa2312	Aa2313	Aa2314
Year	Number	Number	Number	Number	Number	Number	Number	Number	Number	Number	Number	Number
1800	—	—	—	—	389	344	—	—	—	—	—	—
1810	—	—	—	—	3,481	2,941	—	—	—	—	—	—
1820	—	—	—	—	45,839	39,612	—	—	—	—	—	—
1830	—	—	—	—	100,846	89,560	22,764	15,482	12,129	9,509	17,440	11,399
1840	—	—	—	—	176,692	158,493	36,611	28,215	22,819	16,222	31,455	19,340
1850	—	—	1,113	42	—	—	—	—	—	—	—	—
1860	—	—	1,348	44	—	—	—	—	—	—	—	—
1870	3,254	1,430	1,940	0	—	—	—	—	—	—	—	—
1880	4,751	2,448	2,757	—	—	—	—	—	—	—	—	—
1890 [1]	5,784	3,187	3,426	1,735	—	—	—	—	—	—	—	—
1900	7,985	4,340	4,238	3,212	—	—	—	—	—	—	—	—
1910	9,246	5,204	5,223	1,885	—	—	—	—	—	—	—	—
1920	11,774	6,955	5,964	1,112	—	—	—	—	—	—	—	—
1930	14,376	8,627	7,611	668	—	—	—	—	—	—	—	—
1940	18,027	10,157	9,833	0	—	—	—	—	—	—	—	—
1950	28,115	20,385	10,179	0	—	—	—	—	—	—	—	—
1960	40,206	27,061	22,258	0	—	—	—	—	—	—	—	—
1970	49,535	35,292	36,885	0	—	—	—	—	—	—	—	—
1980	71,826	51,018	53,434	0	—	—	—	—	—	—	—	—
1990	77,971	65,888	80,130	0	—	—	—	—	—	—	—	—

Note appears at end of table

TABLE Aa2244–2340   Alabama population, by race, sex, age, nativity, and urban–rural residence: 1800–1990
Continued

		Population										
		White										
	Male, by age					Female, by age						
	40–49	50–59	60–69	70–79	80 and older	0–4	5–9	10–14	15–19	20–29	30–39	40–49	50–59
	Aa2315	Aa2316	Aa2317	Aa2318	Aa2319	Aa2320	Aa2321	Aa2322	Aa2323	Aa2324	Aa2325	Aa2326	Aa2327
Year	Number	Number	Number	Number	Number	Number	Number	Number	Number	Number	Number	Number	Number
1800	—	—	—	—	—	—	—	—	—	—	—	—	—
1810	—	—	—	—	—	—	—	—	—	—	—	—	—
1820	—	—	—	—	—	—	—	—	—	—	—	—	—
1830	6,029	3,593	1,741	591	169	21,340	14,801	11,092	9,951	14,457	8,559	4,695	2,731
1840	11,783	6,024	2,886	997	340	33,917	26,804	21,786	17,911	25,574	15,152	9,184	4,647
1850	—	—	—	—	—	—	—	—	—	—	—	—	—
1860	—	—	—	—	—	—	—	—	—	—	—	—	—
1870	—	—	—	—	—	—	—	—	—	—	—	—	—
1880	—	—	—	—	—	—	—	—	—	—	—	—	—
1890 [1]	—	—	—	—	—	—	—	—	—	—	—	—	—
1900	—	—	—	—	—	—	—	—	—	—	—	—	—
1910	—	—	—	—	—	—	—	—	—	—	—	—	—
1920	—	—	—	—	—	—	—	—	—	—	—	—	—
1930	—	—	—	—	—	—	—	—	—	—	—	—	—
1940	—	—	—	—	—	—	—	—	—	—	—	—	—
1950	—	—	—	—	—	—	—	—	—	—	—	—	—
1960	—	—	—	—	—	—	—	—	—	—	—	—	—
1970	—	—	—	—	—	—	—	—	—	—	—	—	—
1980	—	—	—	—	—	—	—	—	—	—	—	—	—
1990	—	—	—	—	—	—	—	—	—	—	—	—	—

		Population										
		White										
	Female, by age			Male, by age					Female, by age				
	60–69	70–79	80 and older	0–9	10–15	16–25	26–44	45 and older	0–9	10–15	16–25	26–44	45 and older
	Aa2328	Aa2329	Aa2330	Aa2331	Aa2332	Aa2333	Aa2334	Aa2335	Aa2336	Aa2337	Aa2338	Aa2339	Aa2340
Year	Number	Number	Number	Number	Number	Number	Number	Number	Number	Number	Number	Number	Number
1800	—	—	—	139	49	53	100	48	141	61	60	56	26
1810	—	—	—	1,297	466	694	741	283	1,197	443	598	514	189
1820	—	—	—	17,103	6,281	9,336	9,055	4,064	15,810	6,289	7,993	6,625	2,895
1830	1,319	432	183	—	—	—	—	—	—	—	—	—	—
1840	2,407	847	264	—	—	—	—	—	—	—	—	—	—
1850	—	—	—	—	—	—	—	—	—	—	—	—	—
1860	—	—	—	—	—	—	—	—	—	—	—	—	—
1870	—	—	—	—	—	—	—	—	—	—	—	—	—
1880	—	—	—	—	—	—	—	—	—	—	—	—	—
1890 [1]	—	—	—	—	—	—	—	—	—	—	—	—	—
1900	—	—	—	—	—	—	—	—	—	—	—	—	—
1910	—	—	—	—	—	—	—	—	—	—	—	—	—
1920	—	—	—	—	—	—	—	—	—	—	—	—	—
1930	—	—	—	—	—	—	—	—	—	—	—	—	—
1940	—	—	—	—	—	—	—	—	—	—	—	—	—
1950	—	—	—	—	—	—	—	—	—	—	—	—	—
1960	—	—	—	—	—	—	—	—	—	—	—	—	—
1970	—	—	—	—	—	—	—	—	—	—	—	—	—
1980	—	—	—	—	—	—	—	—	—	—	—	—	—
1990	—	—	—	—	—	—	—	—	—	—	—	—	—

[1] Includes 384 American Indians not counted in the general enumeration; see the documentation.

Sources

Except where noted otherwise for Alaska and Hawai'i, the source for Tables Aa2244–6550 is the U.S. Bureau of the Census. Details are provided below.

For 1790, total population, population by race (white, nonwhite, black), and white population by sex and age. W. S. Rossiter, *A Century of Popula-tion Growth from the First Census of the United States to the Twelfth 1790–1900* (1909).

Total population (except 1790) and population by urban–rural residence. *U.S. Census of Population and Housing: 1990*, volume CPH-2-1, Tables 16 and 23.

Area. 1790-1920: *Fourteenth Census of the United States: 1920*, volume 1, *Population*, Table 14. 1930: *Fifteenth Census of the United States, 1930*, volume 1, *Population*, Table 7. 1940: *Sixteenth Census of the United States: 1940, Areas of the United States, 1940*, Table 1. 1950: *Census of Population: 1950*, volume 2,

(continued)

TABLE Aa2244–2340   Alabama population, by race, sex, age, nativity, and urban–rural residence: 1800–1990
Continued

Characteristics of the Population, part 1, U.S. Summary, Table 9. 1960: *Area Measurement Reports, 1960*, series GE-20. 1970: *U.S. Census of Population: 1970*, volume 1, part 1, section 1, Table 11. 1980: *U.S. Census of Population: 1980*, volume 1, part 1, Chapter A (PC80-1-A1), Table 11. 1990: *U.S. Census of Population: 1990*, 1990 CPH-2-1, Table 22.

Persons per square mile. Equals total population divided by area.

Except 1790, population by race (white, nonwhite, black, other nonwhite), population by sex and age, and white population by sex and age. 1800–1830: *Compendium of the Sixth Census of the United States: 1840*, calculated from pp. 370–5. 1840: *Sixth Census of the United States: 1840*, calculated from pp. 474–5. 1850: *Seventh Census of the United States: 1850*, calculated from Tables XXI–XXIII. 1860: *Eighth Census of the United States: 1860*, calculated from pp. 592–9. 1870: *Ninth Census of the United States: 1870*, "The Vital Statistics of the United States Embracing the Tables of Deaths, Births, Sex, and Age," pp. 560–74. 1880: *Tenth Census of the United States: 1880*, "Statistics of the Population of the United States at the Tenth Census," pp. 548–645. 1890: *Eleventh Census of the United States: 1890*, "Report on the Population of the United States at the Eleventh Census: 1890," part 2, Tables 1 and 2. 1900: *Twelfth Census of the United States: 1900*, volume 2, part 2, "Population," Tables 1 and 2. 1910: *Thirteenth Census of the United States: 1910*, volume 1, "Population 1910," Tables 29 and 43. 1920: *Fourteenth Census of the United States: 1920*, volume 2, "Population, 1920: General Report and Analytical Tables," Tables 9 and 13. 1930: *Fifteenth Census of the United States: 1930*, volume 2, "Population: General Report. Statistics by Subjects," Tables 24 and 28. 1940–1980: *U.S. Census of Population: 1980*, state volumes, "General Population Characteristics," Table 20. 1990: *U.S. Census of Population: 1990*, 1990 CP-1-1, state volumes, "General Population Characteristics," Table 16. The division of population into the age groups 75–79 and 80 and older was estimated for 1950 from the 20 percent sample.

Population by nativity (native-born, foreign-born). 1850–1870: *Ninth Census of the United States: 1870*, volume 1, Table XXII. 1880–1890: *Abstract of the Eleventh Census of the United States: 1890*, Table 5. 1900–1910: *Thirteenth Census of the United States: 1910*, "Abstract of the Census," Table 13. 1920–1930: *Fifteenth Census of the United States: 1930*, "Abstract of the Census," Tables 30 and 59. 1940: *Sixteenth Census of the United States: 1940*, volume 2, *Characteristics of the Population*, parts 1–7, Table 2 (for the United States and each state). 1950: *U.S. Census of Population: 1950*, state volumes "General Population Characteristics," Table 15, and "Detailed Population Characteristics," Table 52 (20

percent sample). 1960: *U.S. Census of Population: 1960*, volume 1, *Characteristics of the Population*, part 1 "United States Summary," Table 108. 1970: *U.S. Census of Population: 1970*, volume 1, *Characteristics of the Population*, part 1, "United States Summary," section 1, Table 143 (15 percent sample). 1980: *U.S. Census of Population: 1980*, volume 1, *Characteristics of the Population*, Chapter C, "General Social and Economic Characteristics," part 1 "United States Summary" (PC80-1-C1) Table 236 (approximately a 19 percent sample). 1990: *U.S. Census of Population: 1990*, "Social and Economic Characteristics: United States," 1990 CP-2-1, Table 143 (a one in six sample). See especially Campbell Gibson and Emily Lennon, *Historical Census Statistics on the Foreign-Born Population of the United States: 1850 to 1990*, Working Paper number 29, Population Division, U.S. Bureau of the Census (February 1999), Table 13.

Documentation

For 1890, age is age at nearest birthday. For all other censuses, it is age at last birthday.

For definitions of residence, race, and nativity, see the text for Tables Aa145–184, Aa684–698, and Aa1896–1921. See also the text for Table Aa1–5.

For 1930, Mexicans were classified as nonwhite. They were reclassified as white in 1940, and a retabulation of the 1930 Census was done for some variables in the 1940 Census.

For a discussion of changes in state boundaries, see *U.S. Census of Population: 1960*, volume 1, part 1, pp. xvi–xviii. A helpful guide to the boundaries of states and territories and the regions enumerated at each census is William Thorndale and William Dollarhide, *Map Guide to the U.S. Federal Censuses, 1790–1920* (Genealogical Publishing Company, 1987).

For some states in Tables Aa2244–6550, total population figures for 1890 include American Indians not counted in the general enumeration. See U.S. Bureau of the Census, *Eleventh Census of the United States: 1890*, "Report on Indians Taxed and Indians Not Taxed in the United States at the Eleventh Census: 1890," part 2, p. 27. The data by sex, age, race, and nativity do not add up to this total; the data for rural and urban residence do.

Alabama was part of Georgia, the Mississippi Territory, and Spanish Florida in 1800, and part of the Mississippi Territory and disputed territory in Spanish Florida in 1810. The populations in 1800 and 1810 represent those counties (Washington in 1800 and Baldwin, Madison, and Washington in 1810) later placed in Alabama at statehood in 1819.

TABLE Aa2341–2391   Alaska population, by race, sex, age, nativity, and urban–rural residence: 1880–1990

Contributed by Michael R. Haines

			Population									
				Race				Residence		Nativity	
	Area	Population density	Total	White	Nonwhite	Black	Other nonwhite	Urban	Rural	Native-born	Foreign-born
	Aa2341	Aa2342	Aa2343	Aa2344	Aa2345	Aa2346	Aa2347	Aa2348	Aa2349	Aa2350	Aa2351
Year	Square miles	Persons per square mile	Number	Number	Number	Number	Number	Number	Number	Number	Number
1880	571,065	0.06	33,426	430	32,996	—	32,996	0	33,426	—	—
1890	571,065	0.06	32,052	4,298	27,784	112	27,642	0	32,052	15,381	16,671
1900	571,065	0.11	63,592	30,493	33,099	168	32,931	15,605	47,987	50,931	12,661
1910	571,065	0.11	64,356	36,400	27,956	209	27,747	6,141	58,215	43,921	20,435
1920	571,065	0.10	55,036	27,883	27,153	128	27,025	3,058	51,978	42,766	12,270
1929	571,065	0.10	59,278	28,640	30,638	136	30,502	7,839	51,439	48,709	10,569
1939	571,065	0.13	72,524	39,170	33,354	—	—	17,374	55,150	63,392	9,132
1950	571,065	0.23	128,643	92,808	35,835	—	—	34,262	94,381	121,565	7,078
1960	566,432	0.40	226,167	174,546	51,621	6,771	44,850	85,767	140,400	217,940	8,227
1970	566,432	0.53	300,382	236,767	63,615	8,911	54,704	171,030	129,352	292,619	7,763
1980	570,833	0.70	401,851	309,728	92,123	13,643	78,480	258,567	143,284	385,635	16,216
1990	570,374	0.96	550,043	415,492	134,551	22,451	112,100	371,235	178,808	525,229	24,814

Notes appear at end of table

TABLE Aa2341–2391   Alaska population, by race, sex, age, nativity, and urban–rural residence: 1880–1990
Continued

						Population				
	Sex		Male, by age							
	Male	Female	0	1–4	5–9	10–14	15–19	20–24	25–29	30–34
	Aa2352	Aa2353	Aa2354	Aa2355	Aa2356	Aa2357	Aa2358	Aa2359	Aa2360	Aa2361
Year	Number	Number	Number	Number	Number	Number	Number	Number	Number	Number
1880	—	12,804	—	—	—	—	—	—	—	—
1890	19,248	12,804	264	1,517	1,648	1,505	1,538	2,039	2,509	2,306
1900	45,872	17,720	332	1,535	2,037	1,749	1,692	3,122	4,140	4,307
1910	45,857	18,499	557	2,148	2,044	1,510	2,001	4,570	6,238	6,323
1920	34,539	20,497	564	2,274	2,757	2,169	1,687	2,049	2,563	3,137
1929	35,764	23,514	710	2,530	3,096	2,619	2,395	2,301	2,363	2,197
1939	43,003	29,521	—	3,889 [1]	3,497	3,123	2,920	3,633	3,986	3,482
1950	79,472	49,171	1,790	6,181	5,387	4,121	7,481	12,867	8,475	7,672
1960	128,811	97,356	3,571	13,926	13,607	10,012	10,824	15,997	11,851	10,890
1970	163,258	137,124	3,555	12,917	18,760	17,533	14,186	22,419	14,149	12,178
1980	213,041	188,810	4,452	15,588	17,943	17,720	19,819	24,186	25,564	22,676
1990	289,867	260,176	5,076	23,113	26,635	22,503	19,689	22,783	28,185	30,718

						Population				
	Male, by age									
	35–39	40–44	45–49	50–54	55–59	60–64	65–69	70–74	75–79	80 and older
	Aa2362	Aa2363	Aa2364	Aa2365	Aa2366	Aa2367	Aa2368	Aa2369	Aa2370	Aa2371
Year	Number	Number	Number	Number	Number	Number	Number	Number	Number	Number
1880	—	—	—	—	—	—	—	—	—	—
1890	1,943	1,446	971	662	405	286	102	59	30	18
1900	4,077	3,254	2,092	1,466	782	499	220	112	58	67
1910	5,643	4,895	3,752	2,697	1,407	815	423	204	91	66
1920	3,715	3,242	3,112	2,648	1,908	1,255	707	280	157	89
1929	2,706	2,911	2,845	2,725	2,176	1,778	1,233	656	431 [2]	—
1939	3,109	2,524	2,528	2,668	2,474	1,894	1,497	890	726 [2]	—
1950	6,377	4,821	3,887	2,925	2,270	1,883	1,495	888	952 [2]	—
1960	9,860	8,159	6,389	4,691	3,514	2,175	1,360	958	586	441
1970	11,363	9,726	8,263	6,483	4,881	2,989	1,798	853	485	720
1980	17,077	12,484	9,982	8,711	6,777	4,303	2,740	1,538	883	598
1990	30,720	24,652	17,578	11,945	8,817	6,901	4,780	2,826	1,692	1,254

						Population				
	Male, by age	Female, by age								
	Unknown age	0	1–4	5–9	10–14	15–19	20–24	25–29	30–34	35–39
	Aa2372	Aa2373	Aa2374	Aa2375	Aa2376	Aa2377	Aa2378	Aa2379	Aa2380	Aa2381
Year	Number	Number	Number	Number	Number	Number	Number	Number	Number	Number
1880	—	—	—	—	—	—	—	—	—	—
1890	—	262	1,395	1,477	1,279	1,622	1,308	1,210	1,000	923
1900	14,331	315	1,452	1,940	1,461	1,462	1,582	1,566	1,317	1,084
1910	473	551	2,107	1,982	1,366	1,533	1,747	1,883	1,818	1,580
1920	226	588	2,243	2,842	2,123	1,592	1,440	1,772	1,704	1,707
1929	92	629	2,487	2,982	2,476	2,340	1,958	1,808	1,565	1,753
1939	163	—	3,722 [1]	3,302	2,974	2,690	2,639	2,788	2,405	2,056
1950	—	1,670	5,938	5,257	3,737	3,334	4,304	5,532	4,768	4,188
1960	—	3,530	13,166	12,982	9,509	6,375	7,526	8,743	8,188	7,913
1970	—	3,414	12,189	17,949	16,715	12,582	13,157	12,562	10,410	9,198
1980	—	4,301	14,608	17,100	16,562	17,335	20,904	23,081	19,487	14,239
1990	—	4,718	21,990	25,101	20,676	17,462	18,445	25,156	28,906	27,048

Notes appear at end of table   (continued)

TABLE Aa2341-2391   Alaska population, by race, sex, age, nativity, and urban-rural residence: 1880-1990
Continued

					Population					
					Female, by age					
	40-44	45-49	50-54	55-59	60-64	65-69	70-74	75-79	80 and older	Unknown age
	Aa2382	Aa2383	Aa2384	Aa2385	Aa2386	Aa2387	Aa2388	Aa2389	Aa2390	Aa2391
Year	Number	Number	Number	Number	Number	Number	Number	Number	Number	Number
1880	—	—	—	—	—	—	—	—	—	—
1890	748	528	391	271	206	97	45	20	22	—
1900	886	658	592	275	243	113	82	55	57	2,580
1910	1,273	832	566	378	335	159	115	51	74	149
1920	1,347	1,071	744	403	356	197	132	64	101	71
1929	1,474	1,266	995	652	467	266	168	181 [2]	—	47
1939	1,515	1,519	1,233	928	674	536	242	210 [2]	—	88
1950	3,131	2,283	1,561	1,209	852	631	400	376 [2]	—	—
1960	6,049	4,613	3,264	2,207	1,250	877	550	338	276	—
1970	7,734	6,869	5,324	3,669	2,321	1,333	720	438	540	—
1980	10,222	8,422	7,128	5,840	3,793	2,466	1,568	962	792	—
1990	20,677	14,539	9,867	7,778	5,996	4,846	3,096	1,947	1,928	—

[1] Ages 0-4 years.

[2] Ages 75 and older.

Sources

Except as noted below, see the sources for Table Aa2244-2340.

Series Aa2344-2347 and Aa2352-2391. 1880: *Tenth Census of the United States: 1880*, "Statistics of the Population of the United States at the Tenth Census," pp. 695-9. 1890: *Eleventh Census of the United States: 1890*, "Report on the Population and Resources of Alaska at the Eleventh Census: 1890," pp. 3, 178. 1900: *Twelfth Census of the United States: 1900*, volume 2, part 2, "Population," Table 2. 1910, *Thirteenth Census of the United States: 1910*, volume 3, "Population 1910. Reports by States," Table 11. 1920: *Fourteenth Census of the United States: 1920*, volume 2, "Population, 1920: Composition and Characteristics of the Population by States," pp. 1157-69. 1929: *Fifteenth Census of the United States: 1929*, volume 2, "Outlying Territories and Possessions," pp. 7-27. 1939: *Sixteenth Census of the United States: 1940*,

"Population. Characteristics of the Population. Alaska." 1950: *U.S. Census of Population: 1950*, volume 2, "Characteristics of the Population," part 51, Tables 6 and 7.

Series Aa2350-2351. 1890: *Eleventh Census of the United States: 1890*, "Report on the Population and Resources of Alaska at the Eleventh Census: 1890," p. 3. 1900-1910: *Thirteenth Census of the United States: 1910*, volume 3, "Population 1910. Reports by States," Table 18. 1920-1929: *Fifteenth Census of the United States: 1930*, volume 2, "Outlying Territories and Possessions," pp. 7-27. 1939: *Sixteenth Census of the United States: 1940*, "Population. Characteristics of the Population. Alaska." 1950: *U.S. Census of Population: 1950*, volume 2, "Characteristics of the Population," part 51, Table 39.

Documentation

See the text for Table Aa2244-2340.

For Alaska, censuses were taken in 1929 and 1939 instead of 1930 and 1940, respectively.

TABLE Aa2392-2442   Arizona population by race, sex, age, nativity, and urban-rural residence: 1870-1990

Contributed by Michael R. Haines

				Population								
					Race				Residence		Nativity	
	Area	Population density	Total	White	Nonwhite	Black	Other nonwhite		Urban	Rural	Native-born	Foreign-born
	Aa2392	Aa2393	Aa2394	Aa2395	Aa2396	Aa2397	Aa2398		Aa2399	Aa2400	Aa2401	Aa2402
Year	Square miles	Persons per square mile	Number	Number	Number	Number	Number		Number	Number	Number	Number
1870	113,840	0.08	9,658	9,581	77	26	51		3,224	6,434	3,849	5,809
1880	113,840	0.36	40,440	35,160	5,280	155	5,125		7,007	33,433	24,391	16,049
1890 [1]	113,840	0.78	88,243	55,580	4,040	1,357	2,683		8,302	79,941	40,825	18,795
1900	113,840	1.08	122,931	92,903	30,028	1,848	28,180		19,495	103,436	98,698	24,233
1910	113,810	1.80	204,354	171,468	32,886	2,009	30,877		63,260	141,094	155,589	48,765
1920	113,810	2.94	334,162	291,449	42,713	8,005	34,708		120,788	213,374	253,596	80,566
1930	113,810	3.83	435,573	378,551	57,022	10,749	46,273		149,856	285,717	369,817	65,756
1940	113,580	4.40	499,261	426,792	72,469	14,993	57,476		173,981	325,280	460,568	38,693
1950	113,575	6.60	749,587	654,511	95,076	25,974	69,102		416,000	333,587	699,280	47,375
1960	113,563	11.47	1,302,161	1,169,517	132,644	43,403	89,241		970,616	331,545	1,231,843	70,318
1970	113,417	15.61	1,770,900	1,604,948	165,952	53,344	112,608		1,408,864	362,036	1,694,323	76,570
1980	113,508	23.95	2,718,215	2,240,761	477,454	74,977	402,477		2,278,728	439,487	2,555,409	162,806
1990	113,642	32.25	3,665,228	2,963,186	702,042	110,524	591,518		3,206,973	458,255	3,387,023	278,205

Note appears at end of table

(continued)

TABLE Aa2392–2442   Arizona population by race, sex, age, nativity, and urban–rural residence: 1870–1990
Continued

	Sex		Population								
			Male, by age								
	Male	Female	0	1–4	5–9	10–14	15–19	20–24	25–29	30–34
	Aa2403	Aa2404	Aa2405	Aa2406	Aa2407	Aa2408	Aa2409	Aa2410	Aa2411	Aa2412
Year	Number	Number	Number	Number	Number	Number	Number	Number	Number	Number
1870	6,887	2,771	93	306	340	343	289	1,280	1,483	973
1880	28,202	12,238	361	1,675	1,899	1,535	1,724	3,311	4,304	4,022
1890 [1]	36,571	23,049	704	2,776	3,355	3,005	2,497	3,653	4,171	4,038
1900	71,795	51,136	1,629	5,986	7,153	6,013	5,447	6,758	7,120	6,589
1910	118,574	85,780	2,586	9,985	11,191	9,426	9,002	12,249	13,480	11,401
1920	183,602	150,560	4,408	16,400	19,143	16,534	14,424	17,685	17,679	15,978
1930	231,304	204,269	5,388	19,928	25,622	21,745	20,251	21,099	19,820	17,775
1940	258,170	241,091	5,424	21,399	25,608	25,361	24,039	22,197	21,953	19,890
1950	379,059	370,528	9,384	37,786	40,146	34,601	28,311	28,243	28,778	27,557
1960	654,928	647,233	17,530	67,255	77,284	67,926	49,984	44,105	42,438	42,639
1970	871,006	899,894	16,890	63,735	94,338	98,362	85,867	73,106	57,389	48,928
1980	1,337,942	1,380,273	24,340	84,735	107,650	111,583	128,283	133,486	119,140	104,855
1990	1,810,691	1,854,537	26,229	123,413	143,978	132,160	134,271	145,249	162,127	159,973

	Population									
	Male, by age									
	35–39	40–44	45–49	50–54	55–59	60–64	65–69	70–74	75–79	80 and older
	Aa2413	Aa2414	Aa2415	Aa2416	Aa2417	Aa2418	Aa2419	Aa2420	Aa2421	Aa2422
Year	Number	Number	Number	Number	Number	Number	Number	Number	Number	Number
1870	807	473	215	156	52	44	13	9	2	9
1880	3,106	2,538	1,496	1,225	479	328	104	54	23	18
1890 [1]	3,387	2,776	2,003	1,624	996	886	376	175	53	51
1900	6,093	5,294	3,917	3,294	1,937	1,665	947	589	282	232
1910	10,062	7,855	6,237	5,127	3,292	2,695	1,540	976	563	450
1920	15,495	11,787	10,647	7,467	5,174	4,042	2,620	1,760	851	719
1930	17,871	15,081	13,216	10,406	7,674	5,875	3,953	2,628	1,538	1,116
1940	18,063	15,723	14,650	12,492	10,070	7,933	5,989	3,684	2,095	1,600
1950	27,811	25,394	21,543	18,068	15,726	12,712	9,957	6,505	4,286	2,251
1960	45,016	41,040	37,377	31,393	25,942	20,141	19,086	13,189	7,385	5,198
1970	47,549	47,830	47,703	43,428	37,591	33,729	29,042	21,604	13,455	10,460
1980	80,333	66,836	61,538	60,295	61,155	57,682	53,009	39,867	24,236	18,919
1990	141,870	122,852	94,547	75,955	70,240	70,890	72,823	58,748	40,594	34,772

	Male, by age	Population								
		Female, by age								
	Unknown age	0	1–4	5–9	10–14	15–19	20–24	25–29	30–34	35–39
	Aa2423	Aa2424	Aa2425	Aa2426	Aa2427	Aa2428	Aa2429	Aa2430	Aa2431	Aa2432
Year	Number	Number	Number	Number	Number	Number	Number	Number	Number	Number
1870	0	85	265	332	271	281	405	368	288	166
1880	—	372	1,534	1,677	1,243	1,247	1,315	1,296	1,150	787
1890 [1]	45	732	2,687	3,290	2,755	2,405	2,164	2,066	1,774	1,466
1900	850	1,524	5,646	6,846	5,658	4,965	5,023	4,579	3,863	3,202
1910	457	2,530	9,677	10,726	8,665	8,387	8,507	8,495	7,045	6,015
1920	789	4,144	15,855	18,751	16,139	14,011	14,153	14,419	12,376	11,143
1930	318	5,160	19,611	24,835	21,116	19,730	19,354	17,813	15,675	15,068
1940	—	5,215	21,095	25,303	24,529	24,031	21,938	20,808	18,652	16,983
1950	—	9,077	36,478	38,811	32,794	28,936	28,675	30,295	28,843	28,595
1960	—	17,069	65,112	74,985	65,635	50,692	42,008	41,056	43,745	46,035
1970	—	16,295	61,755	91,176	94,980	85,501	73,449	59,004	51,522	49,218
1980	—	23,205	81,603	103,417	107,990	123,734	130,297	116,911	102,909	82,540
1990	—	25,184	118,033	137,755	126,204	126,651	134,672	155,921	156,878	140,895

Note appears at end of table

(continued)

TABLE Aa2392–2442   Arizona population by race, sex, age, nativity, and urban–rural residence: 1870–1990
Continued

	Population									
	Female, by age									
	40–44	45–49	50–54	55–59	60–64	65–69	70–74	75–79	80 and older	Unknown age
	Aa2433	Aa2434	Aa2435	Aa2436	Aa2437	Aa2438	Aa2439	Aa2440	Aa2441	Aa2442
Year	Number	Number	Number	Number	Number	Number	Number	Number	Number	Number
1870	139	55	55	18	26	4	8	3	2	0
1880	639	376	291	108	103	38	29	14	19	—
1890 [1]	1,196	818	692	372	318	127	83	30	50	24
1900	2,597	1,955	1,644	1,002	915	492	394	162	230	439
1910	4,395	3,247	2,584	1,566	1,496	899	654	344	368	180
1920	8,429	6,321	4,819	3,117	2,620	1,635	1,118	625	649	236
1930	11,972	10,079	7,707	5,363	4,046	2,697	1,845	1,075	916	207
1940	14,416	12,704	10,430	8,313	6,133	4,631	2,882	1,640	1,388	—
1950	24,391	20,043	17,105	13,996	11,247	9,206	5,779	4,026	2,231	—
1960	40,938	37,125	30,678	25,449	21,339	18,484	12,875	7,890	6,118	—
1970	50,726	52,208	46,534	42,087	38,526	32,785	24,309	15,685	14,134	—
1980	68,279	63,533	66,454	71,352	66,718	61,835	47,409	31,249	30,838	—
1990	123,091	98,024	80,990	76,418	81,984	87,340	71,133	54,175	59,189	—

[1] Includes 28,623 American Indians not counted in the general enumeration; see text for Table Aa2244–2340.

Sources
See the sources for Table Aa2244–2340.

Documentation
See the text for Table Aa2244–2340.

Arizona was originally part of the Mexican Cession of 1848 and was augmented by the Gadsden Purchase of 1853. It was part of the New Mexico Territory from 1850 and was organized as a separate territory in 1863. It became a state in 1912.

TABLE Aa2443–2539   Arkansas population by race, sex, age, nativity, and urban–rural residence: 1810–1990
Contributed by Michael R. Haines

			Population										
				Race				Residence		Nativity		Sex	
	Area	Population density	Total	White	Nonwhite	Black	Other nonwhite	Urban	Rural	Native-born	Foreign-born	Male	Female
	Aa2443	Aa2444	Aa2445	Aa2446	Aa2447	Aa2448	Aa2449	Aa2450	Aa2451	Aa2452	Aa2453	Aa2454	Aa2455
Year	Square miles	Persons per square mile	Number	Number	Number	Number	Number	Number	Number	Number	Number	Number	Number
1810	—	—	1,062	924	138	138	—	0	1,062	—	—	—	—
1820	105,275	0.14	14,273	12,579	1,694	1,676	18	0	14,273	—	—	7,835	6,420
1830	52,525	0.58	30,388	25,671	4,717	4,717	—	0	30,388	—	—	16,576	13,812
1840	52,525	1.86	97,574	77,174	20,400	20,400	—	0	97,574	—	—	52,578	44,996
1850	52,525	4.00	209,897	162,189	47,708	47,708	—	0	209,897	208,426	1,471	109,846	100,051
1860	52,525	8.29	435,450	324,143	111,307	111,259	48	3,727	431,723	431,850	3,600	227,747	207,703
1870	52,525	9.22	484,471	362,115	122,356	122,169	187	12,380	472,091	479,445	5,026	248,261	236,210
1880	52,525	15.28	802,525	591,531	210,994	210,666	328	32,020	770,505	792,175	10,350	416,279	386,246
1890 [1]	52,525	21.48	1,128,211	818,752	309,427	309,117	310	73,159	1,055,052	1,113,915	14,264	585,755	542,424
1900	52,525	24.97	1,311,564	944,580	366,984	366,856	128	111,733	1,199,831	1,297,275	14,289	675,312	636,252
1910	52,525	29.98	1,574,449	1,131,026	443,423	442,891	532	202,681	1,371,768	1,557,403	17,046	810,026	764,423
1920	52,525	33.36	1,752,204	1,279,757	472,447	472,220	227	290,497	1,461,707	1,738,067	14,137	895,228	856,976
1930	52,525	35.31	1,854,482	1,375,315	479,167	478,463	704	382,878	1,471,604	1,843,850	10,632	939,843	914,639
1940	52,725	36.97	1,949,387	1,466,084	483,303	482,578	725	431,910	1,517,477	1,941,461	7,926	982,916	966,471
1950	52,675	36.25	1,909,511	1,481,507	428,004	426,639	1,365	630,591	1,278,920	1,896,210	9,495	951,534	957,977
1960	52,175	34.24	1,786,272	1,395,703	390,569	388,787	1,782	765,303	1,020,969	1,778,815	7,457	878,987	907,285
1970	51,945	37.03	1,923,295	1,565,915	357,380	352,445	4,935	960,865	962,430	1,914,953	8,287	932,310	990,985
1980	52,078	43.90	2,286,435	1,890,322	396,113	373,768	22,345	1,179,556	1,106,879	2,264,064	22,371	1,104,688	1,181,747
1990	52,075	45.14	2,350,725	1,944,744	405,981	373,912	32,069	1,258,021	1,092,704	2,325,858	24,867	1,133,076	1,217,649

Note appears at end of table

TABLE Aa2443–2539   Arkansas population by race, sex, age, nativity, and urban–rural residence: 1810–1990
Continued

	Population											
	Male, by age											
	0	1–4	5–9	10–14	15–19	20–29	20–24	25–29	30–39	30–34	35–39	40–49
	Aa2456	Aa2457	Aa2458	Aa2459	Aa2460	Aa2461	Aa2462	Aa2463	Aa2464	Aa2465	Aa2466	Aa2467
Year	Number	Number	Number	Number	Number	Number	Number	Number	Number	Number	Number	Number
1810	—	—	—	—	—	—	—	—	—	—	—	—
1820	—	—	—	—	—	—	—	—	—	—	—	—
1830	—	—	—	—	—	—	—	—	—	—	—	—
1840	—	—	—	—	—	—	—	—	—	—	—	—
1850	3,363	15,958	16,991	15,356	11,828	20,166	—	—	12,610	—	—	7,512
1860	7,130	31,166	35,187	31,110	24,309	43,536	—	—	26,199	—	—	15,672
1870	8,732	33,404	30,931	35,358	29,583	—	28,129	18,520	—	14,517	12,589	—
1880	16,108	56,726	65,260	50,479	36,652	—	42,955	37,043	—	28,043	20,579	—
1890 [1]	18,563	69,789	85,176	78,706	66,375	—	52,878	40,024	—	37,521	34,184	—
1900	19,837	76,098	94,776	84,334	72,904	—	65,210	53,668	—	40,508	33,645	—
1910	24,247	92,247	105,399	90,951	86,350	—	74,812	64,900	—	54,173	49,582	—
1920	23,116	88,427	115,713	112,015	90,122	—	73,007	66,445	—	55,105	58,223	—
1930	20,434	84,767	114,170	106,667	101,209	—	84,488	68,276	—	56,934	58,845	—
1940	18,931	80,675	101,165	104,424	102,405	—	83,847	77,659	—	70,117	62,649	—
1950	21,813	94,014	102,665	91,546	79,188	—	64,287	62,901	—	59,982	62,902	—
1960	19,911	78,419	95,496	95,466	76,407	—	48,630	43,632	—	45,935	49,148	—
1970	16,636	63,928	94,844	99,819	91,678	—	68,431	56,563	—	47,889	45,442	—
1980	19,298	70,840	92,287	94,932	108,641	—	95,013	85,136	—	78,989	64,914	—
1990	14,482	69,817	89,592	90,639	92,092	—	80,831	88,116	—	87,784	82,637	—

	Population											
	Male, by age											
	40–44	45–49	50–59	50–54	55–59	60–69	60–64	65–69	70–79	70–74	75–79	80 and older
	Aa2468	Aa2469	Aa2470	Aa2471	Aa2472	Aa2473	Aa2474	Aa2475	Aa2476	Aa2477	Aa2478	Aa2479
Year	Number	Number	Number	Number	Number	Number	Number	Number	Number	Number	Number	Number
1810	—	—	—	—	—	—	—	—	—	—	—	—
1820	—	—	—	—	—	—	—	—	—	—	—	—
1830	—	—	—	—	—	—	—	—	—	—	—	—
1840	—	—	—	—	—	—	—	—	—	—	—	—
1850	—	—	3,714	—	—	1,694	—	—	501	—	—	135
1860	—	—	8,065	—	—	3,886	—	—	965	—	—	268
1870	9,891	8,121	—	7,284	4,338	—	3,321	1,735	—	997	413	398
1880	14,364	16,467	—	11,440	7,291	—	5,763	3,422	—	1,968	995	724
1890 [1]	24,140	26,149	—	17,037	11,637	—	8,970	5,705	—	3,453	1,868	1,302
1900	29,251	33,404	—	24,280	16,061	—	11,530	7,761	—	4,854	2,450	1,745
1910	34,571	37,435	—	30,208	22,659	—	16,985	11,244	—	6,701	3,650	2,491
1920	44,159	51,948	—	35,548	24,619	—	21,635	15,643	—	9,844	5,376	3,317
1930	48,936	52,202	—	43,175	33,240	—	24,650	16,883	—	12,392	7,113	5,021
1940	53,309	53,658	—	46,493	38,682	—	31,515	26,411	—	16,218	8,282	6,476
1950	59,514	53,297	—	45,962	42,470	—	34,925	31,781	—	21,475	15,787	7,025
1960	50,168	52,026	—	48,919	44,098	—	35,807	35,627	—	27,378	18,034	13,886
1970	48,255	49,637	—	49,398	48,330	—	45,320	38,701	—	28,242	20,127	19,070
1980	55,535	51,379	—	51,978	52,325	—	50,680	48,578	—	37,625	24,701	21,837
1990	76,891	64,336	—	53,671	49,746	—	49,572	47,930	—	38,618	28,792	27,530

Note appears at end of table   (continued)

TABLE Aa2443–2539   Arkansas population by race, sex, age, nativity, and urban–rural residence: 1810–1990
Continued

	Population											
Male, by age	Female, by age											
Unknown age	0	1–4	5–9	10–14	15–19	20–29	20–24	25–29	30–39	30–34	35–39
Aa2480	Aa2481	Aa2482	Aa2483	Aa2484	Aa2485	Aa2486	Aa2487	Aa2488	Aa2489	Aa2490	Aa2491
Year	Number	Number	Number	Number	Number	Number	Number	Number	Number	Number	Number	Number
1810	—	—	—	—	—	—	—	—	—	—	—	—
1820	—	—	—	—	—	—	—	—	—	—	—	—
1830	—	—	—	—	—	—	—	—	—	—	—	—
1840	—	—	—	—	—	—	—	—	—	—	—	—
1850	18	3,279	15,556	16,489	14,393	11,798	17,959	—	—	10,063	—	—
1860	254	7,129	29,749	33,287	29,022	25,259	38,150	—	—	21,961	—	—
1870	0	8,303	31,725	29,639	32,930	29,530	—	26,989	19,255	—	14,758	12,426
1880	—	15,548	54,068	62,939	47,469	36,550	—	40,129	31,313	—	23,866	20,093
1890 [1]	2,278	17,934	66,453	83,151	74,543	65,988	—	50,782	36,124	—	32,277	29,391
1900	2,996	19,444	74,432	92,645	82,147	74,009	—	66,457	51,142	—	36,412	29,674
1910	1,421	23,399	90,808	104,262	88,928	87,538	—	76,948	64,233	—	50,548	44,844
1920	966	22,628	86,640	112,775	109,456	93,730	—	78,999	70,651	—	56,676	55,506
1930	441	20,295	83,213	111,658	104,346	101,525	—	90,820	73,146	—	59,842	60,247
1940	—	18,564	79,332	99,108	101,916	102,508	—	88,226	80,398	—	72,953	65,808
1950	—	21,542	90,910	99,398	87,939	80,577	—	70,515	68,181	—	64,727	66,170
1960	—	19,497	76,616	92,617	91,637	74,748	—	51,222	48,015	—	52,000	54,880
1970	—	16,162	61,324	91,808	96,314	90,514	—	74,608	59,225	—	51,095	50,539
1980	—	18,248	67,206	88,078	90,559	105,681	—	98,756	89,177	—	82,035	68,722
1990	—	14,057	66,311	85,459	85,458	87,530	—	81,919	90,920	—	92,225	87,012

	Population											
	Female, by age											
40–49	40–44	45–49	50–59	50–54	55–59	60–69	60–64	65–69	70–79	70–74	75–79
Aa2492	Aa2493	Aa2494	Aa2495	Aa2496	Aa2497	Aa2498	Aa2499	Aa2500	Aa2501	Aa2502	Aa2503
Year	Number	Number	Number	Number	Number	Number	Number	Number	Number	Number	Number
1810	—	—	—	—	—	—	—	—	—	—	—	—
1820	—	—	—	—	—	—	—	—	—	—	—	—
1830	—	—	—	—	—	—	—	—	—	—	—	—
1840	—	—	—	—	—	—	—	—	—	—	—	—
1850	5,945	—	—	2,788	—	—	1,256	—	—	375	—	—
1860	12,812	—	—	6,316	—	—	2,868	—	—	745	—	—
1870	—	9,595	6,935	—	5,453	3,097	—	2,610	1,362	—	833	393
1880	—	15,661	12,678	—	9,660	5,629	—	4,618	2,718	—	1,663	848
1890 [1]	—	23,036	19,638	—	14,422	9,390	—	7,444	4,599	—	2,719	1,581
1900	—	27,251	23,759	—	18,841	13,241	—	10,086	6,566	—	4,080	2,152
1910	—	31,997	25,988	—	23,098	16,762	—	13,329	9,348	—	5,687	3,159
1920	—	43,592	36,611	—	26,564	18,271	—	16,247	12,073	—	7,884	4,549
1930	—	49,089	44,203	—	36,177	26,199	—	19,351	13,103	—	9,989	6,142
1940	—	54,368	50,193	—	41,768	34,284	—	27,172	22,526	—	13,645	7,155
1950	—	61,366	54,718	—	45,851	40,674	—	32,482	30,934	—	19,814	14,441
1960	—	54,554	54,704	—	51,632	47,142	—	38,574	37,092	—	27,424	19,048
1970	—	53,465	54,754	—	54,223	53,258	—	52,076	45,706	—	33,966	25,594
1980	—	58,244	55,945	—	58,457	61,252	—	59,651	57,721	—	48,523	35,727
1990	—	80,163	67,749	—	57,581	56,065	—	58,012	58,720	—	50,693	42,768

Note appears at end of table

TABLE Aa2443–2539   Arkansas population, by race, sex, age, nativity, and urban–rural residence: 1810–1990
Continued

				Population									
				White									
	Female, by age				Male, by age								
	80 and older	Unknown age	Male	Female	0–4	5–9	10–14	15–19	20–29	30–39	40–49	50–59
	Aa2504	Aa2505	Aa2506	Aa2507	Aa2508	Aa2509	Aa2510	Aa2511	Aa2512	Aa2513	Aa2514	Aa2515
Year	Number	Number	Number	Number	Number	Number	Number	Number	Number	Number	Number	Number
1810	—	—	553	371	—	—	—	—	—	—	—	—
1820	—	—	6,971	5,608	—	—	—	—	—	—	—	—
1830	—	—	14,195	11,476	3,020	2,021	1,626	1,272	2,835	1,820	876	434
1840	—	—	42,211	34,963	8,607	6,331	5,077	3,863	8,532	5,129	2,751	1,194
1850	137	13	—	—	—	—	—	—	—	—	—	—
1860	297	108	—	—	—	—	—	—	—	—	—	—
1870	377	0	—	—	—	—	—	—	—	—	—	—
1880	796	—	—	—	—	—	—	—	—	—	—	—
1890 [1]	1,367	1,585	—	—	—	—	—	—	—	—	—	—
1900	1,736	2,178	—	—	—	—	—	—	—	—	—	—
1910	2,618	929	—	—	—	—	—	—	—	—	—	—
1920	3,406	718	—	—	—	—	—	—	—	—	—	—
1930	4,957	337	—	—	—	—	—	—	—	—	—	—
1940	6,547	—	—	—	—	—	—	—	—	—	—	—
1950	7,738	—	—	—	—	—	—	—	—	—	—	—
1960	15,883	—	—	—	—	—	—	—	—	—	—	—
1970	26,354	—	—	—	—	—	—	—	—	—	—	—
1980	37,765	—	—	—	—	—	—	—	—	—	—	—
1990	55,007	—	—	—	—	—	—	—	—	—	—	—

				Population									
				White									
	Male, by age			Female, by age									
	60–69	70–79	80 and older	0–4	5–9	10–14	15–19	20–29	30–39	40–49	50–59	60–69
	Aa2516	Aa2517	Aa2518	Aa2519	Aa2520	Aa2521	Aa2522	Aa2523	Aa2524	Aa2525	Aa2526	Aa2527
Year	Number	Number	Number	Number	Number	Number	Number	Number	Number	Number	Number	Number
1810	—	—	—	—	—	—	—	—	—	—	—	—
1820	—	—	—	—	—	—	—	—	—	—	—	—
1830	209	69	13	2,782	1,897	1,494	1,225	2,012	1,087	528	301	107
1840	523	162	42	8,108	5,853	4,869	3,911	5,881	3,317	1,715	805	357
1850	—	—	—	—	—	—	—	—	—	—	—	—
1860	—	—	—	—	—	—	—	—	—	—	—	—
1870	—	—	—	—	—	—	—	—	—	—	—	—
1880	—	—	—	—	—	—	—	—	—	—	—	—
1890 [1]	—	—	—	—	—	—	—	—	—	—	—	—
1900	—	—	—	—	—	—	—	—	—	—	—	—
1910	—	—	—	—	—	—	—	—	—	—	—	—
1920	—	—	—	—	—	—	—	—	—	—	—	—
1930	—	—	—	—	—	—	—	—	—	—	—	—
1940	—	—	—	—	—	—	—	—	—	—	—	—
1950	—	—	—	—	—	—	—	—	—	—	—	—
1960	—	—	—	—	—	—	—	—	—	—	—	—
1970	—	—	—	—	—	—	—	—	—	—	—	—
1980	—	—	—	—	—	—	—	—	—	—	—	—
1990	—	—	—	—	—	—	—	—	—	—	—	—

Note appears at end of table   (continued)

TABLE Aa2443–2539   Arkansas population by race, sex, age, nativity, and urban–rural residence: 1810–1990
Continued

			Population									
			White									
Female, by age		Male, by age					Female, by age					
70–79	80 and older	0–9	10–15	16–25	26–44	45 and older	0–9	10–15	16–25	26–44	45 and older	
Aa2528	Aa2529	Aa2530	Aa2531	Aa2532	Aa2533	Aa2534	Aa2535	Aa2536	Aa2537	Aa2538	Aa2539	
Year	Number	Number	Number	Number	Number	Number	Number	Number	Number	Number	Number	Number
1810	—	—	161	84	90	148	70	149	59	72	78	13
1820	—	—	2,420	985	1,427	1,453	686	2,142	927	1,179	934	426
1830	31	12	—	—	—	—	—	—	—	—	—	—
1840	113	34	—	—	—	—	—	—	—	—	—	—
1850	—	—	—	—	—	—	—	—	—	—	—	—
1860	—	—	—	—	—	—	—	—	—	—	—	—
1870	—	—	—	—	—	—	—	—	—	—	—	—
1880	—	—	—	—	—	—	—	—	—	—	—	—
1890 [1]	—	—	—	—	—	—	—	—	—	—	—	—
1900	—	—	—	—	—	—	—	—	—	—	—	—
1910	—	—	—	—	—	—	—	—	—	—	—	—
1920	—	—	—	—	—	—	—	—	—	—	—	—
1930	—	—	—	—	—	—	—	—	—	—	—	—
1940	—	—	—	—	—	—	—	—	—	—	—	—
1950	—	—	—	—	—	—	—	—	—	—	—	—
1960	—	—	—	—	—	—	—	—	—	—	—	—
1970	—	—	—	—	—	—	—	—	—	—	—	—
1980	—	—	—	—	—	—	—	—	—	—	—	—
1990	—	—	—	—	—	—	—	—	—	—	—	—

[1] Includes thirty-two American Indians not counted in the general enumeration; see text for Table Aa2244–2340.

Sources
See the sources for Table Aa2244–2340.

Documentation
See the text for Table Aa2244–2340.

Arkansas was part of the Louisiana Territory in 1810 and became the Arkansas Territory in 1819, before becoming a state in 1836. It was enumerated with the Missouri Territory (created 1812) for 1810. For 1810, the population represents Arkansas county and the Hopefield and St. Francis settlements.

TABLE Aa2540–2602   California population by race, sex, age, nativity, and urban–rural residence: 1850–1990
Contributed by Michael R. Haines

				Population					
				Race				Residence	
	Area	Population density	Total	White	Nonwhite	Black	Other nonwhite	Urban	Rural
	Aa2540	Aa2541	Aa2542	Aa2543	Aa2544	Aa2545	Aa2546	Aa2547	Aa2548
Year	Square miles	Persons per square mile	Number	Number	Number	Number	Number	Number	Number
1850	155,900	0.59	92,597	91,635	962	962	—	6,820	85,777
1860	155,900	2.44	379,994	323,177	56,817	4,086	52,731	78,651	301,343
1870	155,900	3.59	560,247	499,424	60,823	4,272	56,551	208,438	351,809
1880	155,900	5.55	864,694	767,181	97,513	6,018	91,495	370,611	494,083
1890 [1]	155,900	7.78	1,213,398	1,111,672	96,458	11,322	85,136	589,464	623,934
1900	156,092	9.51	1,485,053	1,402,727	82,326	11,045	71,281	776,820	708,233
1910	155,652	15.27	2,377,549	2,259,672	117,877	21,645	96,232	1,468,419	909,130
1920	155,652	22.02	3,426,861	3,264,711	162,150	38,763	123,387	2,326,959	1,099,902
1930	155,652	36.47	5,677,251	5,408,260	268,991	81,048	187,943	4,160,596	1,516,655
1940	156,803	44.05	6,907,387	6,596,763	310,624	124,306	186,318	4,902,265	2,005,122
1950	156,740	67.54	10,586,223	9,915,173	671,050	462,172	208,878	8,539,420	2,046,803
1960	156,537	100.41	15,717,204	14,455,230	1,261,974	883,861	378,113	13,573,155	2,144,049
1970	156,361	127.61	19,953,134	17,761,032	2,192,102	1,400,143	791,959	18,144,552	1,808,582
1980	156,299	151.43	23,667,902	18,030,893	5,637,009	1,819,281	3,817,728	21,607,606	2,060,296
1990	155,973	190.80	29,760,021	20,524,327	9,235,694	2,208,801	7,026,893	27,571,321	2,188,700

Note appears at end of table

TABLE Aa2540–2602   California population by race, sex, age, nativity, and urban–rural residence: 1850–1990
Continued

	Population									
	Nativity		Sex		Male, by age					
	Native-born	Foreign-born	Male	Female	0	1–4	5–9	10–14	15–19	20–29
	Aa2549	Aa2550	Aa2551	Aa2552	Aa2553	Aa2554	Aa2555	Aa2556	Aa2557	Aa2558
Year	Number	Number	Number	Number	Number	Number	Number	Number	Number	Number
1850	70,795	21,802	85,580	7,017	149	843	1,084	1,145	4,641	45,144
1860	233,466	146,528	273,337	106,657	4,645	17,277	13,338	10,114	12,189	89,877
1870	350,416	209,831	349,479	210,768	6,792	27,662	31,285	26,973	22,333	—
1880	571,820	292,874	518,176	346,518	9,648	37,721	45,637	40,715	43,307	—
1890 [1]	841,821	366,309	700,059	508,071	11,213	42,972	56,622	56,107	57,268	—
1900	1,117,813	367,240	820,531	664,522	12,755	50,966	69,017	64,085	65,207	—
1910	1,791,117	586,432	1,322,978	1,054,571	20,626	77,764	89,099	87,896	102,000	—
1920	2,669,236	757,625	1,813,591	1,613,270	27,762	112,614	141,417	130,826	124,564	—
1930	4,603,287	1,073,964	2,942,595	2,734,656	38,641	167,489	236,016	214,715	215,304	—
1940	5,982,522	924,865	3,515,730	3,391,657	46,871	184,419	220,669	242,873	275,635	—
1950	9,498,550	1,060,375	5,295,629	5,290,594	110,985	449,001	430,680	332,014	326,160	—
1960	14,377,162	1,343,698	7,836,707	7,880,497	180,547	708,494	813,681	719,720	567,486	—
1970	18,199,314	1,757,990	9,816,685	10,136,449	173,822	663,481	975,981	998,536	930,884	—
1980	20,087,869	3,580,033	11,666,485	12,001,417	193,310	680,329	843,750	915,240	1,091,684	—
1990	23,301,196	6,458,825	14,897,627	14,862,394	217,039	1,010,554	1,138,181	1,013,849	1,077,682	—

	Population									
	Male, by age									
	20–24	25–29	30–39	30–34	35–39	40–49	40–44	45–49	50–59	50–54
	Aa2559	Aa2560	Aa2561	Aa2562	Aa2563	Aa2564	Aa2565	Aa2566	Aa2567	Aa2568
Year	Number	Number	Number	Number	Number	Number	Number	Number	Number	Number
1850	—	—	21,716	—	—	7,647	—	—	2,061	—
1860	—	—	83,210	—	—	28,913	—	—	9,697	—
1870	31,509	38,004	—	39,061	40,987	—	35,869	20,586	—	13,407
1880	50,527	52,536	—	50,778	42,986	—	40,714	33,306	—	30,551
1890 [1]	68,199	73,367	—	68,203	57,237	—	50,847	39,060	—	33,953
1900	70,039	71,739	—	73,248	73,111	—	63,424	49,750	—	41,324
1910	131,064	142,834	—	131,048	114,194	—	101,430	86,179	—	69,741
1920	140,432	157,214	—	163,653	171,308	—	143,108	130,234	—	107,354
1930	246,080	260,590	—	250,498	254,044	—	237,829	212,892	—	176,131
1940	291,552	312,809	—	299,597	289,978	—	268,575	250,394	—	231,579
1950	390,711	453,331	—	440,479	430,855	—	387,980	347,040	—	304,788
1960	503,508	515,818	—	555,623	596,662	—	535,960	487,566	—	412,116
1970	872,256	726,974	—	611,232	575,226	—	592,330	607,160	—	529,935
1980	1,213,068	1,132,811	—	1,008,606	776,545	—	629,452	578,420	—	578,795
1990	1,348,808	1,494,692	—	1,455,070	1,267,705	—	1,071,416	807,467	—	633,482

	Population								
	Male, by age								
	55–59	60–69	60–64	65–69	70–79	70–74	75–79	80 and older	Unknown age
	Aa2569	Aa2570	Aa2571	Aa2572	Aa2573	Aa2574	Aa2575	Aa2576	Aa2577
Year	Number	Number	Number	Number	Number	Number	Number	Number	Number
1850	—	394	—	—	66	—	—	21	669
1860	—	3,123	—	—	502	—	—	234	218
1870	6,091	—	4,772	2,023	—	1,044	375	277	429
1880	15,877	—	13,345	5,442	—	2,889	1,326	871	—
1890 [1]	26,159	—	26,690	13,569	—	7,225	3,069	1,891	6,408
1900	30,565	—	29,974	22,087	—	14,750	7,255	3,821	7,414
1910	47,290	—	43,840	29,840	—	20,239	12,690	8,465	6,739
1920	82,611	—	66,786	44,533	—	30,683	18,989	12,921	6,582
1930	133,385	—	106,334	79,150	—	54,709	29,759	20,690	8,339
1940	190,248	—	149,698	110,507	—	75,344	44,424	30,558	—
1950	259,365	—	223,232	176,277	—	115,053	77,283	40,395	—
1960	352,148	—	280,371	234,333	—	179,744	111,787	81,143	—
1970	451,259	—	363,840	278,585	—	202,534	134,280	128,370	—
1980	573,119	—	467,607	378,259	—	269,849	175,580	160,061	—
1990	551,968	—	513,915	476,557	—	350,804	244,198	224,240	—

Note appears at end of table

(continued)

TABLE Aa2540–2602   California population by race, sex, age, nativity, and urban–rural residence: 1850–1990
Continued

	Population								
	Female, by age								
	0	1–4	5–9	10–14	15–19	20–29	20–24	25–29	30–39
	Aa2578	Aa2579	Aa2580	Aa2581	Aa2582	Aa2583	Aa2584	Aa2585	Aa2586
Year	Number	Number	Number	Number	Number	Number	Number	Number	Number
1850	124	785	1,016	833	891	1,626	—	—	998
1860	4,530	16,317	12,734	8,956	9,300	25,781	—	—	17,813
1870	6,698	27,125	30,241	24,812	17,710	—	18,505	19,372	—
1880	9,140	36,917	44,569	40,094	37,049	—	33,885	27,614	—
1890 [1]	10,439	41,906	55,082	55,059	54,373	—	54,963	47,377	—
1900	12,382	49,834	67,988	62,804	62,877	—	66,510	62,530	—
1910	19,710	75,559	87,093	86,049	94,034	—	103,057	103,592	—
1920	26,158	109,193	138,862	128,450	118,762	—	134,336	150,221	—
1930	37,678	161,559	229,378	209,411	213,380	—	229,047	235,439	—
1940	44,829	177,375	214,423	235,842	268,966	—	283,378	300,040	—
1950	106,662	432,464	416,910	320,857	303,583	—	382,459	471,579	—
1960	172,442	684,316	786,471	698,024	528,536	—	480,152	500,265	—
1970	166,663	638,717	942,146	965,145	886,495	—	868,710	730,640	—
1980	184,402	650,359	806,598	880,779	1,038,781	—	1,142,897	1,100,153	—
1990	207,264	962,858	1,085,801	963,494	975,466	—	1,161,986	1,359,365	—

	Population								
	Female, by age								
	30–34	35–39	40–49	40–44	45–49	50–59	50–54	55–59	60–69
	Aa2587	Aa2588	Aa2589	Aa2590	Aa2591	Aa2592	Aa2593	Aa2594	Aa2595
Year	Number	Number	Number	Number	Number	Number	Number	Number	Number
1850	—	—	456	—	—	186	—	—	69
1860	—	—	6,861	—	—	2,781	—	—	1,077
1870	18,911	16,906	—	11,831	6,896	—	4,613	2,536	—
1880	25,419	24,241	—	21,136	16,007	—	12,388	6,551	—
1890 [1]	39,558	32,308	—	28,721	24,413	—	21,573	14,305	—
1900	55,855	50,011	—	40,790	32,189	—	28,206	21,939	—
1910	94,562	86,625	—	72,856	60,699	—	49,552	34,805	—
1920	142,935	138,749	—	119,245	101,927	—	87,086	66,602	—
1930	232,166	234,576	—	205,670	180,655	—	155,348	121,904	—
1940	281,152	267,542	—	251,049	234,805	—	211,582	176,239	—
1950	446,706	431,979	—	375,993	327,003	—	298,674	262,324	—
1960	558,514	608,699	—	536,677	484,455	—	409,154	354,774	—
1970	608,157	574,773	—	616,220	638,743	—	553,917	481,985	—
1980	1,001,445	775,899	—	633,042	585,714	—	617,005	629,021	—
1990	1,377,244	1,233,244	—	1,066,956	813,061	—	648,559	581,939	—

	Population						
	Female, by age						
	60–64	65–69	70–79	70–74	75–79	80 and older	Unknown age
	Aa2596	Aa2597	Aa2598	Aa2599	Aa2600	Aa2601	Aa2602
Year	Number	Number	Number	Number	Number	Number	Number
1850	—	—	19	—	—	10	4
1860	—	—	274	—	—	170	63
1870	2,076	1,095	—	713	276	175	277
1880	5,011	2,825	—	1,887	991	794	—
1890 [1]	11,912	6,636	—	4,096	2,109	1,709	1,532
1900	18,914	13,119	—	8,442	4,346	3,026	2,760
1910	30,727	22,725	—	15,328	9,454	6,522	1,622
1920	54,732	37,692	—	26,695	16,550	12,238	2,837
1930	101,228	76,596	—	52,855	29,714	22,652	5,400
1940	150,021	120,569	—	83,534	51,120	39,191	—
1950	227,404	192,102	—	134,993	99,571	59,331	—
1960	308,821	278,218	—	218,420	145,260	127,299	—
1970	406,930	342,220	—	281,897	207,817	225,274	—
1980	524,821	460,988	—	361,882	272,826	334,805	—
1990	585,404	578,617	—	451,243	357,611	452,282	—

TABLE Aa2540–2602   California population by race, sex, age, nativity, and urban–rural residence: 1850–1990
Continued

[1] Includes 5,268 American Indians not counted in the general enumeration; see text for Table Aa2244–2340.

Sources
See the sources for Table Aa2244–2340.

Documentation
See the text for Table Aa2244–2340.

The population presented for 1850 does not include the returns for San Francisco, Contra Costa, and Santa Clara counties, which were lost on their travel to Washington, DC. The state was enumerated again in a state census of 1852. The overall state population was 255,122 and the missing counties were enumerated as follows: San Francisco (36,154), Santa Clara (6,764), and Contra Costa (2,786). See U.S. Department of the Census, *Seventh Census of the United States: 1850*, pp. 965–85.

TABLE Aa2603–2665   Colorado population by race, sex, age, nativity, and urban–rural residence: 1860–1990
Contributed by Michael R. Haines

			Population						
				Race				Residence	
	Area	Population density	Total	White	Nonwhite	Black	Other nonwhite	Urban	Rural
	Aa2603	Aa2604	Aa2605	Aa2606	Aa2607	Aa2608	Aa2609	Aa2610	Aa2611
Year	Square miles	Persons per square mile	Number	Number	Number	Number	Number	Number	Number
1860	103,658	0.33	34,277	34,231	46	46	0	4,749	29,528
1870	103,658	0.38	39,864	39,221	643	456	187	4,759	35,105
1880	103,658	1.87	194,327	191,126	3,201	2,435	766	60,961	133,366
1890 [1]	103,658	3.99	413,249	404,468	7,730	6,215	1,515	185,905	227,344
1900	103,658	5.21	539,700	529,046	10,654	8,570	2,084	260,651	279,049
1910	103,658	7.71	799,024	783,415	15,609	11,453	4,156	402,192	396,832
1920	103,658	9.06	939,629	924,103	15,526	11,318	4,208	453,259	486,370
1930	103,658	9.99	1,035,791	1,018,793	16,998	11,828	5,170	519,882	515,909
1940	103,967	10.80	1,123,296	1,106,502	16,794	12,176	4,618	590,756	532,540
1950	103,922	12.75	1,325,089	1,296,653	28,436	20,177	8,259	831,318	493,771
1960	103,794	16.90	1,753,947	1,700,700	53,247	39,992	13,255	1,292,790	461,157
1970	103,766	21.27	2,207,259	2,112,352	94,907	66,411	28,496	1,733,311	473,948
1980	103,595	27.90	2,889,964	2,571,498	318,466	101,703	216,763	2,329,869	560,095
1990	103,729	31.76	3,294,394	2,905,474	388,920	133,146	255,774	2,715,517	578,877

			Population							
	Nativity		Sex		Male, by age					
	Native-born	Foreign-born	Male	Female	0	1–4	5–9	10–14	15–19
	Aa2612	Aa2613	Aa2614	Aa2615	Aa2616	Aa2617	Aa2618	Aa2619	Aa2620
Year	Number	Number	Number	Number	Number	Number	Number	Number	Number
1860	31,611	2,666	32,691	1,586	32	236	178	191	855
1870	33,265	6,599	24,820	15,044	526	2,250	2,113	1,699	1,501
1880	154,537	39,790	129,131	65,196	2,106	7,760	8,369	6,732	7,457
1890 [1]	328,208	83,990	245,247	166,951	4,924	17,603	20,001	16,848	16,716
1900	448,545	91,155	295,332	244,368	6,181	22,714	28,772	24,508	22,639
1910	669,437	129,587	430,697	368,327	8,726	33,093	38,194	35,262	35,980
1920	820,491	119,138	492,731	446,898	9,807	39,429	47,863	44,819	39,541
1930	935,916	99,875	530,752	505,039	9,836	38,458	52,960	50,333	47,319
1940	1,051,732	71,564	568,778	554,518	9,901	39,198	47,334	49,176	51,160
1950	1,260,340	60,565	665,149	659,940	15,507	59,861	59,176	50,938	49,110
1960	1,694,044	59,881	870,467	883,480	21,795	84,633	98,429	84,103	66,619
1970	2,146,948	60,311	1,089,377	1,117,882	19,999	75,044	114,126	119,055	110,406
1980	2,775,834	114,130	1,434,293	1,455,671	24,577	86,377	108,961	115,145	137,609
1990	3,151,960	142,434	1,631,295	1,663,099	21,891	107,227	130,000	116,738	116,134

Notes appear at end of table

(continued)

TABLE Aa2603–2665   Colorado population by race, sex, age, nativity, and urban–rural residence: 1860–1990
Continued

	Population								
	Male, by age								
	20–29	20–24	25–29	30–39	30–34	35–39	40–49	40–44	45–49
	Aa2621	Aa2622	Aa2623	Aa2624	Aa2625	Aa2626	Aa2627	Aa2628	Aa2629
Year	Number	Number	Number	Number	Number	Number	Number	Number	Number
1860	17,611	—	—	10,525	—	—	2,114	—	—
1870	—	3,389	4,019	—	3,296	2,276	—	1,478	862
1880	—	20,319	21,631	—	17,340	13,310	—	9,308	5,948
1890 [1]	—	29,219	34,078	—	29,809	22,790	—	16,843	11,937
1900	—	26,214	27,924	—	28,115	27,480	—	23,340	17,456
1910	—	42,842	43,544	—	38,159	34,171	—	30,146	26,323
1920	—	39,309	39,780	—	39,668	39,285	—	33,279	29,910
1930	—	43,337	38,321	—	37,144	39,691	—	36,424	32,937
1940	—	46,965	45,430	—	42,672	38,371	—	36,123	35,828
1950	—	51,283	54,565	—	49,659	46,935	—	43,058	37,228
1960	—	55,508	55,520	—	58,724	60,005	—	54,885	49,388
1970	—	103,921	77,414	—	66,025	63,028	—	63,072	60,961
1980	—	154,319	153,566	—	136,128	97,252	—	76,653	69,013
1990	—	122,928	144,666	—	161,457	154,242	—	131,915	94,642

	Population								
	Male, by age								
	50–59	50–54	55–59	60–69	60–64	65–69	70–79	70–74	75–79
	Aa2630	Aa2631	Aa2632	Aa2633	Aa2634	Aa2635	Aa2636	Aa2637	Aa2638
Year	Number	Number	Number	Number	Number	Number	Number	Number	Number
1860	388	—	—	80	—	—	6	—	—
1870	—	632	305	—	243	101	—	75	22
1880	—	4,335	2,030	—	1,358	613	—	302	126
1890 [1]	—	8,975	5,297	—	3,509	1,890	—	1,068	468
1900	—	13,403	9,075	—	6,216	4,017	—	2,114	1,067
1910	—	22,269	14,685	—	10,811	7,274	—	4,114	2,259
1920	—	25,311	20,068	—	16,444	10,386	—	6,535	3,579
1930	—	28,205	22,685	—	18,891	14,997	—	10,012	5,433
1940	—	32,389	27,504	—	22,533	17,810	—	13,024	7,886
1950	—	33,997	31,132	—	27,068	22,067	—	15,685	11,205
1960	—	42,986	35,816	—	29,841	26,570	—	20,704	13,753
1970	—	54,163	44,980	—	37,701	28,172	—	21,149	15,002
1980	—	64,918	60,307	—	48,894	37,868	—	27,687	17,641
1990	—	72,635	63,604	—	57,542	50,798	—	36,758	24,704

	Population								
	Male, by age		Female, by age						
	80 and older	Unknown age	0	1–4	5–9	10–14	15–19	20–29	20–24
	Aa2639	Aa2640	Aa2641	Aa2642	Aa2643	Aa2644	Aa2645	Aa2646	Aa2647
Year	Number	Number	Number	Number	Number	Number	Number	Number	Number
1860	4	471	17	170	137	107	160	532	—
1870	29	4	537	2,172	1,917	1,665	1,379	—	1,711
1880	87	—	1,904	7,530	8,438	6,475	5,650	—	7,428
1890 [1]	296	2,976	4,734	17,199	19,841	15,986	15,720	—	18,658
1900	546	3,551	5,769	22,335	28,505	24,363	22,375	—	23,386
1910	1,241	1,604	8,398	32,345	37,422	34,426	35,065	—	36,208
1920	2,102	5,616	9,437	38,385	47,223	44,395	39,091	—	39,029
1930	3,366	403	9,604	37,772	51,820	48,607	47,813	—	43,576
1940	5,474	—	9,530	38,031	46,371	48,442	50,984	—	48,268
1950	6,675	—	14,786	58,121	57,266	48,426	47,210	—	51,590
1960	11,188	—	20,765	81,915	94,775	82,643	64,107	—	56,689
1970	15,159	—	19,038	72,287	110,045	114,624	107,045	—	100,587
1980	17,378	—	23,457	82,084	104,174	111,002	130,979	—	148,287
1990	23,414	—	21,075	102,700	123,197	110,551	108,828	—	115,522

Note appears at end of table

TABLE Aa2603–2665   Colorado population by race, sex, age, nativity, and urban–rural residence: 1860–1990
Continued

	Population								
	Female, by age								
	25–29	30–39	30–34	35–39	40–49	40–44	45–49	50–59	50–54
	Aa2648	Aa2649	Aa2650	Aa2651	Aa2652	Aa2653	Aa2654	Aa2655	Aa2656
Year	Number	Number	Number	Number	Number	Number	Number	Number	Number
1860	—	281	—	—	96	—	—	21	—
1870	1,646	—	1,331	930	—	619	407	—	296
1880	7,291	—	6,220	4,854	—	3,399	2,149	—	1,578
1890 [1]	18,174	—	15,544	12,053	—	9,012	6,689	—	4,916
1900	23,411	—	21,823	19,556	—	15,315	11,303	—	8,727
1910	35,341	—	31,154	28,270	—	23,921	19,247	—	15,420
1920	39,125	—	35,157	33,659	—	28,205	24,525	—	20,678
1930	38,989	—	37,047	37,646	—	32,906	29,365	—	25,158
1940	46,440	—	41,907	38,026	—	35,096	33,667	—	29,584
1950	54,789	—	50,232	47,728	—	42,418	36,810	—	33,701
1960	57,158	—	60,451	61,994	—	55,131	49,777	—	42,790
1970	80,006	—	67,759	64,088	—	65,436	63,944	—	55,132
1980	149,035	—	130,816	96,257	—	76,791	68,869	—	68,060
1990	144,932	—	160,794	151,816	—	130,114	95,561	—	73,833

	Population								
	Female, by age								
	55–59	60–69	60–64	65–69	70–79	70–74	75–79	80 and older	Unknown age
	Aa2657	Aa2658	Aa2659	Aa2660	Aa2661	Aa2662	Aa2663	Aa2664	Aa2665
Year	Number	Number	Number	Number	Number	Number	Number	Number	Number
1860	—	2	—	—	1	—	—	0	62
1870	161	—	131	61	—	37	20	23	1
1880	862	—	670	332	—	243	91	82	—
1890 [1]	2,979	—	2,309	1,280	—	832	374	248	403
1900	6,244	—	4,355	2,823	—	1,667	872	540	999
1910	10,461	—	8,065	5,528	—	3,242	1,872	1,197	745
1920	15,447	—	12,043	7,874	—	5,254	3,130	2,203	2,038
1930	19,923	—	16,536	11,886	—	8,178	4,578	3,337	298
1940	24,881	—	21,047	17,117	—	12,403	7,281	5,443	—
1950	30,445	—	26,458	22,769	—	16,497	12,792	7,902	—
1960	37,059	—	32,281	29,679	—	23,778	16,844	15,644	—
1970	48,184	—	41,298	33,904	—	28,217	21,858	24,430	—
1980	65,404	—	53,705	46,240	—	36,871	27,283	36,357	—
1990	66,589	—	63,818	60,448	—	46,523	37,151	49,647	—

[1] Includes 1,051 American Indians not counted in the general enumeration; see text for Table Aa2244–2340.

Sources
See the sources for Table Aa2244–2340.

Documentation
See the text for Table Aa2244–2340.

The population of Colorado in 1860 represents Arapahoe County in the Kansas Territory. The Colorado Territory was created in 1861.

TABLE Aa2666–2766   Connecticut population by race, sex, age, nativity, and urban–rural residence: 1790–1990
Contributed by Michael R. Haines

				Population								
	Area	Population density	Total	White	Nonwhite	Black	Other nonwhite	Urban	Rural	Native-born	Foreign-born
				Race				Residence		Nativity	
	Aa2666	Aa2667	Aa2668	Aa2669	Aa2670	Aa2671	Aa2672	Aa2673	Aa2674	Aa2675	Aa2676
Year	Square miles	Persons per square mile	Number	Number	Number	Number	Number	Number	Number	Number	Number
1790	4,820	49.31	237,655	232,236	5,419	5,419	—	7,170	230,776	—	—
1800	4,820	52.08	251,002	244,721	6,281	6,281	—	12,722	238,280	—	—
1810	4,820	54.34	261,942	255,279	6,763	6,763	—	15,941	246,001	—	—
1820	4,820	57.11	275,248	267,181	8,067	7,941	100	20,804	254,444	—	—
1830	4,820	61.76	297,675	289,603	8,072	8,072	—	27,847	269,828	—	—
1840	4,820	64.31	309,978	301,856	8,159	8,159	—	38,952	271,026	—	—
1850	4,820	76.93	370,792	363,099	7,693	7,693	—	59,321	311,471	332,274	38,518
1860	4,820	95.47	460,147	451,504	8,643	8,627	16	122,121	338,026	379,451	80,696
1870	4,820	111.50	537,454	527,549	9,905	9,668	237	177,153	360,301	423,815	113,639
1880	4,820	129.19	622,700	610,769	11,931	11,547	384	260,718	361,982	492,708	129,992
1890	4,820	154.83	746,258	733,438	12,820	12,302	518	379,853	366,405	562,657	183,601
1900	4,820	188.47	908,420	892,424	15,996	15,226	770	543,755	364,665	670,210	238,210
1910	4,820	231.28	1,114,756	1,098,897	15,859	15,174	685	731,797	382,959	785,182	329,574
1920	4,820	286.44	1,380,631	1,358,732	21,899	21,046	853	936,339	444,292	1,002,192	378,439
1930	4,820	333.38	1,606,903	1,576,700	30,203	29,354	849	1,131,770	475,133	1,222,267	384,636
1940	4,899	348.90	1,709,242	1,675,407	33,835	32,992	843	1,158,162	551,080	1,379,945	329,297
1950	4,899	409.73	2,007,280	1,952,329	54,951	53,472	1,479	1,558,642	448,638	1,700,010	296,040
1960	4,870	520.58	2,535,234	2,423,816	111,418	107,449	3,969	1,985,567	549,667	2,259,711	275,523
1970	4,862	623.55	3,031,709	2,835,458	196,251	181,177	15,074	2,376,079	655,630	2,770,091	261,614
1980	4,872	637.84	3,107,576	2,799,420	308,156	217,433	90,723	2,449,774	657,802	2,839,770	267,806
1990	4,845	678.40	3,287,116	2,859,353	427,763	274,269	153,494	2,601,548	685,568	3,007,733	279,383

			Population									
	Sex		Male, by age									
	Male	Female	0	1–4	5–9	10–14	15–19	20–29	20–24	25–29	30–39	30–34
	Aa2677	Aa2678	Aa2679	Aa2680	Aa2681	Aa2682	Aa2683	Aa2684	Aa2685	Aa2686	Aa2687	Aa2688
Year	Number	Number	Number	Number	Number	Number	Number	Number	Number	Number	Number	Number
1790	—	—	—	—	—	—	—	—	—	—	—	—
1800	—	—	—	—	—	—	—	—	—	—	—	—
1810	—	—	—	—	—	—	—	—	—	—	—	—
1820	134,581	140,541	—	—	—	—	—	—	—	—	—	—
1830	146,905	150,770	—	—	—	—	—	—	—	—	—	—
1840	152,233	157,782	—	—	—	—	—	—	—	—	—	—
1850	183,704	187,088	3,925	16,540	19,726	19,770	18,888	36,054	—	—	25,621	—
1860	225,994	234,153	5,613	22,231	23,744	22,160	21,965	41,626	—	—	32,762	—
1870	265,270	272,184	6,167	23,496	26,487	28,103	25,211	—	24,851	22,272	—	19,387
1880	305,782	316,918	6,541	25,239	31,610	30,024	28,853	—	29,883	24,827	—	21,819
1890	369,538	376,720	7,328	27,649	33,886	33,524	35,637	—	37,971	33,895	—	29,908
1900	454,294	454,126	9,947	36,045	43,172	38,321	38,119	—	43,321	44,297	—	39,654
1910	563,642	551,114	12,253	44,386	51,056	47,849	49,822	—	54,491	52,570	—	47,171
1920	695,335	685,296	15,282	62,353	69,976	61,250	52,421	—	55,497	63,314	—	59,150
1930	801,303	805,600	12,695	55,147	76,993	80,679	73,343	—	63,931	58,679	—	59,324
1940	849,923	859,319	10,542	44,945	58,996	70,415	77,559	—	78,930	73,509	—	65,001
1950	988,497	1,018,783	18,542	81,296	82,229	62,292	60,848	—	70,189	80,728	—	83,725
1960	1,244,229	1,291,005	28,187	113,337	126,831	112,977	85,334	—	64,313	73,492	—	86,567
1970	1,470,487	1,561,222	25,101	103,473	150,957	154,760	133,184	—	108,196	101,552	—	82,904
1980	1,498,005	1,609,571	20,172	74,307	105,508	130,582	146,275	—	135,362	123,182	—	117,419
1990	1,592,873	1,694,243	20,421	96,600	107,119	99,164	108,683	—	127,549	144,054	—	147,196

TABLE Aa2666–2766   Connecticut population by race, sex, age, nativity, and urban–rural residence: 1790–1990
Continued

	Population											
	Male, by age											
	35–39	40–49	40–44	45–49	50–59	50–54	55–59	60–69	60–64	65–69	70–79	70–74
	Aa2689	Aa2690	Aa2691	Aa2692	Aa2693	Aa2694	Aa2695	Aa2696	Aa2697	Aa2698	Aa2699	Aa2700
Year	Number	Number	Number	Number	Number	Number	Number	Number	Number	Number	Number	Number
1790	—	—	—	—	—	—	—	—	—	—	—	—
1800	—	—	—	—	—	—	—	—	—	—	—	—
1810	—	—	—	—	—	—	—	—	—	—	—	—
1820	—	—	—	—	—	—	—	—	—	—	—	—
1830	—	—	—	—	—	—	—	—	—	—	—	—
1840	—	—	—	—	—	—	—	—	—	—	—	—
1850	—	18,269	—	—	12,082	—	—	7,555	—	—	3,759	—
1860	—	23,896	—	—	15,831	—	—	9,995	—	—	4,838	—
1870	17,740	—	15,637	14,419	—	12,212	8,660	—	7,659	5,229	—	3,924
1880	20,846	—	17,907	16,078	—	14,401	11,028	—	9,725	6,802	—	5,057
1890	25,176	—	22,117	19,542	—	16,902	12,375	—	11,450	8,326	—	6,245
1900	35,321	—	29,527	23,720	—	20,488	15,480	—	12,821	9,430	—	6,816
1910	44,929	—	38,057	32,087	—	26,486	18,526	—	15,442	11,469	—	7,902
1920	55,576	—	45,768	42,775	—	34,276	24,532	—	20,827	13,642	—	9,032
1930	64,944	—	58,892	50,468	—	41,697	32,159	—	28,308	19,397	—	12,686
1940	60,517	—	59,607	60,838	—	54,490	41,614	—	33,647	25,898	—	17,295
1950	79,226	—	69,452	61,250	—	58,158	54,691	—	45,484	33,985	—	22,498
1960	93,547	—	91,833	83,371	—	69,278	58,548	—	49,404	42,839	—	31,725
1970	81,649	—	91,984	95,087	—	89,662	76,085	—	59,099	42,198	—	31,665
1980	99,619	—	79,838	78,231	—	85,632	85,285	—	73,078	56,435	—	38,383
1990	131,465	—	119,611	98,066	—	75,675	70,912	—	70,010	62,886	—	48,896

	Population										
	Male, by age			Female, by age							
	75–79	80 and older	Unknown age	0	1–4	5–9	10–14	15–19	20–29	20–24	25–29
	Aa2701	Aa2702	Aa2703	Aa2704	Aa2705	Aa2706	Aa2707	Aa2708	Aa2709	Aa2710	Aa2711
Year	Number	Number	Number	Number	Number	Number	Number	Number	Number	Number	Number
1790	—	—	—	—	—	—	—	—	—	—	—
1800	—	—	—	—	—	—	—	—	—	—	—
1810	—	—	—	—	—	—	—	—	—	—	—
1820	—	—	—	—	—	—	—	—	—	—	—
1830	—	—	—	—	—	—	—	—	—	—	—
1840	—	—	—	—	—	—	—	—	—	—	—
1850	—	1,318	197	3,721	16,268	19,464	18,945	19,883	35,782	—	—
1860	—	1,314	19	5,522	21,749	23,726	21,527	23,482	45,461	—	—
1870	2,191	1,625	0	5,833	23,139	26,436	26,998	26,175	—	25,855	23,295
1880	2,933	2,209	—	6,338	24,753	30,916	29,438	30,037	—	31,326	26,152
1890	3,619	2,837	1,151	7,141	27,156	33,268	32,568	36,771	—	39,553	34,651
1900	4,222	2,865	728	9,827	35,973	43,002	38,034	39,218	—	44,715	43,294
1910	4,744	3,426	976	11,944	43,661	50,430	47,423	51,203	—	53,848	49,084
1920	5,267	3,606	791	14,815	61,388	69,020	60,741	54,411	—	60,743	63,221
1930	6,934	4,490	537	12,055	53,002	75,537	79,367	74,780	—	67,931	62,104
1940	9,653	6,467	—	10,244	42,930	56,789	67,846	77,321	—	81,232	75,019
1950	15,489	8,415	—	17,677	77,065	78,451	59,314	60,810	—	74,169	86,897
1960	18,438	14,208	—	27,202	109,562	120,944	108,234	85,077	—	70,818	76,905
1970	22,421	20,510	—	24,601	100,087	145,009	149,451	130,869	—	121,598	104,459
1980	24,333	24,364	—	18,989	71,720	100,250	125,701	142,108	—	137,020	126,078
1990	33,900	30,666	—	19,510	91,825	101,886	95,208	102,897	—	124,152	143,637

(continued)

TABLE Aa2666–2766 Connecticut population by race, sex, age, nativity, and urban–rural residence: 1790–1990
Continued

Population

Female, by age

Year	30–39	30–34	35–39	40–49	40–44	45–49	50–59	50–54	55–59	60–69	60–64
	Aa2712	Aa2713	Aa2714	Aa2715	Aa2716	Aa2717	Aa2718	Aa2719	Aa2720	Aa2721	Aa2722
	Number	Number	Number	Number	Number	Number	Number	Number	Number	Number	Number
1790	—	—	—	—	—	—	—	—	—	—	—
1800	—	—	—	—	—	—	—	—	—	—	—
1810	—	—	—	—	—	—	—	—	—	—	—
1820	—	—	—	—	—	—	—	—	—	—	—
1830	—	—	—	—	—	—	—	—	—	—	—
1840	—	—	—	—	—	—	—	—	—	—	—
1850	24,792	—	—	18,579	—	—	13,705	—	—	9,139	—
1860	32,711	—	—	23,298	—	—	16,737	—	—	11,680	—
1870	—	20,572	18,994	—	16,179	13,633	—	11,877	8,590	—	8,256
1880	—	22,773	21,789	—	19,520	16,930	—	14,952	11,250	—	10,252
1890	—	29,023	25,149	—	22,238	19,931	—	18,159	13,445	—	12,451
1900	—	37,127	33,024	—	27,658	23,207	—	20,070	16,690	—	14,333
1910	—	43,494	42,213	—	35,691	29,630	—	25,137	18,749	—	16,069
1920	—	54,428	50,637	—	42,877	38,290	—	32,705	24,136	—	20,292
1930	—	61,820	64,777	—	55,168	47,090	—	39,807	32,017	—	29,933
1940	—	68,008	63,168	—	61,318	60,107	—	51,221	39,681	—	35,194
1950	—	88,933	81,786	—	71,734	62,995	—	60,818	55,656	—	46,041
1960	—	89,256	98,182	—	95,507	84,763	—	71,492	62,049	—	55,609
1970	—	85,850	85,779	—	96,535	101,265	—	95,677	80,944	—	66,984
1980	—	124,454	104,860	—	84,985	83,418	—	91,620	93,427	—	83,592
1990	—	148,995	134,302	—	125,618	102,173	—	80,128	76,110	—	78,243

Population

							White				
	Female, by age								Male, by age		
Year	65–69	70–79	70–74	75–79	80 and older	Unknown age	Male	Female	0–4	5–9	10–14
	Aa2723	Aa2724	Aa2725	Aa2726	Aa2727	Aa2728	Aa2729	Aa2730	Aa2731	Aa2732	Aa2733
	Number	Number	Number	Number	Number	Number	Number	Number	Number	Number	Number
1790	—	—	—	—	—	—	115,028	117,208	—	—	—
1800	—	—	—	—	—	—	121,193	123,528	—	—	—
1810	—	—	—	—	—	—	126,373	128,906	—	—	—
1820	—	—	—	—	—	—	130,707	136,474	—	—	—
1830	—	—	—	—	—	—	143,047	146,556	19,033	17,891	17,788
1840	—	—	—	—	—	—	148,300	153,556	19,021	17,420	17,270
1850	—	4,843	—	—	1,904	63	—	—	—	—	—
1860	—	6,113	—	—	2,141	6	—	—	—	—	—
1870	6,040	—	4,811	2,844	2,656	1	—	—	—	—	—
1880	7,475	—	5,769	3,802	3,446	—	—	—	—	—	—
1890	9,042	—	6,894	4,233	4,232	815	—	—	—	—	—
1900	10,748	—	7,603	4,987	4,179	437	—	—	—	—	—
1910	12,542	—	9,148	5,669	4,688	491	—	—	—	—	—
1920	14,212	—	10,317	6,812	5,629	622	—	—	—	—	—
1930	20,730	—	14,089	8,192	6,801	400	—	—	—	—	—
1940	28,632	—	19,759	11,599	9,251	—	—	—	—	—	—
1950	37,257	—	26,484	20,586	12,110	—	—	—	—	—	—
1960	49,998	—	38,361	24,393	22,653	—	—	—	—	—	—
1970	54,761	—	46,186	34,737	36,430	—	—	—	—	—	—
1980	69,980	—	54,919	41,748	54,702	—	—	—	—	—	—
1990	77,473	—	66,982	53,454	71,650	—	—	—	—	—	—

TABLE Aa2666–2766   Connecticut population by race, sex, age, nativity, and urban–rural residence: 1790–1990
Continued

	Population										
	White										
	Male, by age								Female, by age		
	15–19	20–29	30–39	40–49	50–59	60–69	70–79	80 and older	0–4	5–9	10–14
	Aa2734	Aa2735	Aa2736	Aa2737	Aa2738	Aa2739	Aa2740	Aa2741	Aa2742	Aa2743	Aa2744
Year	Number	Number	Number	Number	Number	Number	Number	Number	Number	Number	Number
1790	—	—	—	—	—	—	—	—	—	—	—
1800	—	—	—	—	—	—	—	—	—	—	—
1810	—	—	—	—	—	—	—	—	—	—	—
1820	—	—	—	—	—	—	—	—	—	—	—
1830	16,509	26,166	16,608	11,595	7,851	5,495	3,154	957	18,270	16,943	16,575
1840	16,718	26,097	19,056	13,355	9,121	5,727	3,381	1,134	18,253	16,889	15,964
1850	—	—	—	—	—	—	—	—	—	—	—
1860	—	—	—	—	—	—	—	—	—	—	—
1870	—	—	—	—	—	—	—	—	—	—	—
1880	—	—	—	—	—	—	—	—	—	—	—
1890	—	—	—	—	—	—	—	—	—	—	—
1900	—	—	—	—	—	—	—	—	—	—	—
1910	—	—	—	—	—	—	—	—	—	—	—
1920	—	—	—	—	—	—	—	—	—	—	—
1930	—	—	—	—	—	—	—	—	—	—	—
1940	—	—	—	—	—	—	—	—	—	—	—
1950	—	—	—	—	—	—	—	—	—	—	—
1960	—	—	—	—	—	—	—	—	—	—	—
1970	—	—	—	—	—	—	—	—	—	—	—
1980	—	—	—	—	—	—	—	—	—	—	—
1990	—	—	—	—	—	—	—	—	—	—	—

	Population										
	White										
	Female, by age								Male, by age		
	15–19	20–29	30–39	40–49	50–59	60–69	70–79	80 and older	0–9	10–15	16–25
	Aa2745	Aa2746	Aa2747	Aa2748	Aa2749	Aa2750	Aa2751	Aa2752	Aa2753	Aa2754	Aa2755
Year	Number	Number	Number	Number	Number	Number	Number	Number	Number	Number	Number
1790	—	—	—	—	—	—	—	—	—	—	—
1800	—	—	—	—	—	—	—	—	37,946	19,408	21,683
1810	—	—	—	—	—	—	—	—	37,812	20,498	23,880
1820	—	—	—	—	—	—	—	—	36,848	20,682	25,731
1830	15,978	26,540	17,937	13,214	9,245	6,707	3,760	1,387	—	—	—
1840	16,478	27,120	20,110	14,863	10,792	7,220	4,274	1,593	—	—	—
1850	—	—	—	—	—	—	—	—	—	—	—
1860	—	—	—	—	—	—	—	—	—	—	—
1870	—	—	—	—	—	—	—	—	—	—	—
1880	—	—	—	—	—	—	—	—	—	—	—
1890	—	—	—	—	—	—	—	—	—	—	—
1900	—	—	—	—	—	—	—	—	—	—	—
1910	—	—	—	—	—	—	—	—	—	—	—
1920	—	—	—	—	—	—	—	—	—	—	—
1930	—	—	—	—	—	—	—	—	—	—	—
1940	—	—	—	—	—	—	—	—	—	—	—
1950	—	—	—	—	—	—	—	—	—	—	—
1960	—	—	—	—	—	—	—	—	—	—	—
1970	—	—	—	—	—	—	—	—	—	—	—
1980	—	—	—	—	—	—	—	—	—	—	—
1990	—	—	—	—	—	—	—	—	—	—	—

(continued)

TABLE Aa2666–2766   Connecticut population by race, sex, age, nativity, and urban–rural residence: 1790–1990
Continued

					Population						
					White						
	Male, by age		Female, by age					Male, by age		Female, by age	
	26–44	45 and older	0–9	10–15	16–25	26–44	45 and older	0–15	16 and older	0–15	16 and older
	Aa2756	Aa2757	Aa2758	Aa2759	Aa2760	Aa2761	Aa2762	Aa2763	Aa2764	Aa2765	Aa2766
Year	Number	Number	Number	Number	Number	Number	Number	Number	Number	Number	Number
1790	—	—	—	—	—	—	—	54,289	60,739	51,196	66,012
1800	23,180	18,976	35,736	18,218	23,561	25,186	20,827	—	—	—	—
1810	23,699	20,484	35,913	18,931	25,073	26,293	22,696	—	—	—	—
1820	25,632	21,814	35,289	19,833	27,205	29,069	25,078	—	—	—	—
1830	—	—	—	—	—	—	—	—	—	—	—
1840	—	—	—	—	—	—	—	—	—	—	—
1850	—	—	—	—	—	—	—	—	—	—	—
1860	—	—	—	—	—	—	—	—	—	—	—
1870	—	—	—	—	—	—	—	—	—	—	—
1880	—	—	—	—	—	—	—	—	—	—	—
1890	—	—	—	—	—	—	—	—	—	—	—
1900	—	—	—	—	—	—	—	—	—	—	—
1910	—	—	—	—	—	—	—	—	—	—	—
1920	—	—	—	—	—	—	—	—	—	—	—
1930	—	—	—	—	—	—	—	—	—	—	—
1940	—	—	—	—	—	—	—	—	—	—	—
1950	—	—	—	—	—	—	—	—	—	—	—
1960	—	—	—	—	—	—	—	—	—	—	—
1970	—	—	—	—	—	—	—	—	—	—	—
1980	—	—	—	—	—	—	—	—	—	—	—
1990	—	—	—	—	—	—	—	—	—	—	—

Sources
See the sources for Table Aa2244–2340.

Documentation
See the text for Table Aa2244–2340.

Connecticut was one of the original thirteen states, admitted to the Union in 1788.

TABLE Aa2767–2867   Delaware population by race, sex, age, nativity, and urban–rural residence: 1790–1990

Contributed by Michael R. Haines

				Population								
					Race				Residence		Nativity	
	Area	Population density	Total	White	Nonwhite	Black	Other nonwhite	Urban	Rural	Native-born	Foreign-born
	Aa2767	Aa2768	Aa2769	Aa2770	Aa2771	Aa2772	Aa2773	Aa2774	Aa2775	Aa2776	Aa2777
Year	Square miles	Persons per square mile	Number	Number	Number	Number	Number	Number	Number	Number	Number
1790	1,965	30.07	59,096	46,310	12,786	12,786	—	0	59,096	—	—
1800	1,965	32.71	64,273	49,852	14,421	14,421	—	0	64,273	—	—
1810	1,965	36.98	72,674	55,361	17,313	17,313	—	0	72,674	—	—
1820	1,965	37.02	72,749	55,282	17,467	17,467	0	0	72,749	—	—
1830	1,965	39.06	76,748	57,601	19,147	19,147	—	0	76,748	—	—
1840	1,965	39.74	78,085	58,561	19,524	19,524	—	8,367	69,718	—	—
1850	1,965	46.58	91,532	71,169	20,363	20,363	—	13,979	77,553	86,279	5,253
1860	1,965	57.11	112,216	90,589	21,627	21,627	0	21,258	90,958	103,051	9,165
1870	1,965	63.62	125,015	102,221	22,794	22,794	0	30,841	94,174	115,879	9,136
1880	1,965	74.61	146,608	120,160	26,448	26,442	6	48,989	97,619	137,140	9,468
1890	1,965	85.75	168,493	140,066	28,427	28,386	41	71,067	97,426	155,332	13,161
1900	1,965	94.01	184,735	153,977	30,758	30,697	61	85,717	99,018	170,925	13,810
1910	1,965	102.96	202,322	171,102	31,220	31,181	39	97,085	105,237	184,830	17,492
1920	1,965	113.49	223,003	192,615	30,388	30,335	53	120,767	102,236	203,102	19,901
1930	1,965	121.31	238,380	205,718	32,662	32,602	60	123,146	115,234	221,355	17,025
1940	1,978	134.73	266,505	230,528	35,977	35,876	101	139,432	127,073	251,592	14,913
1950	1,978	160.81	318,085	273,878	44,207	43,598	609	199,122	118,963	302,680	13,055
1960	1,982	225.17	446,292	384,327	61,965	60,688	1,277	292,788	153,504	431,642	14,650
1970	1,982	276.54	548,104	466,459	81,645	78,276	3,369	395,569	152,535	532,445	15,648
1980	1,932	307.63	594,338	487,817	106,521	95,845	10,676	419,819	174,519	575,509	18,829
1990	1,955	340.82	666,168	535,094	131,074	112,460	18,614	486,501	179,667	643,893	22,275

		Population									
	Sex		Male, by age							
	Male	Female	0	1–4	5–9	10–14	15–19	20–29	20–24	25–29
	Aa2778	Aa2779	Aa2780	Aa2781	Aa2782	Aa2783	Aa2784	Aa2785	Aa2786	Aa2787
Year	Number	Number	Number	Number	Number	Number	Number	Number	Number	Number
1790	—	—	—	—	—	—	—	—	—	—
1800	—	—	—	—	—	—	—	—	—	—
1810	—	—	—	—	—	—	—	—	—	—
1820	36,939	35,810	—	—	—	—	—	—	—	—
1830	38,533	38,215	—	—	—	—	—	—	—	—
1840	39,256	38,829	—	—	—	—	—	—	—	—
1850	45,955	45,577	1,281	5,491	6,650	6,018	5,066	7,894	—	—
1860	56,689	55,527	1,675	6,777	7,367	7,245	6,517	10,147	—	—
1870	62,628	62,387	1,783	6,658	7,913	8,055	6,862	—	6,142	4,754
1880	74,108	72,500	1,927	7,263	8,915	8,332	7,798	—	7,657	6,054
1890	85,573	82,920	1,944	7,090	9,230	9,566	8,854	—	8,207	7,261
1900	94,158	90,577	2,095	7,794	9,874	9,538	9,053	—	8,865	7,979
1910	103,435	98,887	2,085	7,913	9,650	9,889	10,022	—	9,889	8,946
1920	113,755	109,248	2,287	9,137	10,529	10,191	9,282	—	10,115	10,099
1930	121,257	117,123	1,866	7,791	11,383	11,331	10,743	—	10,352	9,347
1940	134,333	132,172	1,896	8,093	10,090	10,730	11,788	—	12,114	11,340
1950	157,344	160,741	3,235	13,735	13,659	11,289	10,327	—	10,900	12,891
1960	221,136	225,156	5,678	22,557	24,438	20,469	14,788	—	13,250	14,869
1970	267,332	280,772	4,975	19,839	29,316	30,260	25,481	—	20,682	18,622
1980	286,599	307,739	4,632	16,352	21,441	24,895	29,572	—	28,339	24,242
1990	322,968	343,200	4,355	20,679	24,034	21,995	23,086	—	26,913	29,483

(continued)

TABLE Aa2767–2867   Delaware population by race, sex, age, nativity, and urban–rural residence: 1790–1990
Continued

Population

Male, by age

Year	30–39	30–34	35–39	40–49	40–44	45–49	50–59	50–54	55–59	60–69
	Aa2788	Aa2789	Aa2790	Aa2791	Aa2792	Aa2793	Aa2794	Aa2795	Aa2796	Aa2797
	Number	Number	Number	Number	Number	Number	Number	Number	Number	Number
1790	—	—	—	—	—	—	—	—	—	—
1800	—	—	—	—	—	—	—	—	—	—
1810	—	—	—	—	—	—	—	—	—	—
1820	—	—	—	—	—	—	—	—	—	—
1830	—	—	—	—	—	—	—	—	—	—
1840	—	—	—	—	—	—	—	—	—	—
1850	5,647	—	—	3,820	—	—	2,183	—	—	1,199
1860	6,621	—	—	4,975	—	—	3,083	—	—	1,548
1870	—	3,833	3,670	—	2,974	2,644	—	2,487	1,562	—
1880	—	5,005	4,588	—	3,818	3,132	—	2,853	1,958	—
1890	—	6,502	5,816	—	4,711	4,151	—	3,422	2,471	—
1900	—	6,810	6,720	—	6,067	4,909	—	4,303	3,208	—
1910	—	7,743	7,517	—	6,456	5,775	—	5,318	3,829	—
1920	—	8,699	8,687	—	7,035	6,943	—	5,840	4,559	—
1930	—	9,078	9,448	—	8,201	7,228	—	6,691	5,186	—
1940	—	10,777	10,021	—	9,544	9,023	—	7,780	6,117	—
1950	—	13,107	12,269	—	11,133	9,673	—	9,015	7,736	—
1960	—	16,012	16,670	—	15,367	13,101	—	11,240	9,247	—
1970	—	15,786	16,092	—	16,213	16,271	—	14,745	11,826	—
1980	—	22,144	18,029	—	15,199	15,099	—	15,547	15,051	—
1990	—	29,575	25,735	—	22,831	18,211	—	14,810	14,337	—

Population

	Male, by age							Female, by age		
Year	60–64	65–69	70–79	70–74	75–79	80 and older	Unknown age	0	1–4	5–9
	Aa2798	Aa2799	Aa2800	Aa2801	Aa2802	Aa2803	Aa2804	Aa2805	Aa2806	Aa2807
	Number	Number	Number	Number	Number	Number	Number	Number	Number	Number
1790	—	—	—	—	—	—	—	—	—	—
1800	—	—	—	—	—	—	—	—	—	—
1810	—	—	—	—	—	—	—	—	—	—
1820	—	—	—	—	—	—	—	—	—	—
1830	—	—	—	—	—	—	—	—	—	—
1840	—	—	—	—	—	—	—	—	—	—
1850	—	—	522	—	—	145	39	1,273	5,408	6,421
1860	—	—	563	—	—	171	0	1,641	6,608	7,246
1870	1,419	896	—	555	225	196	0	1,661	6,611	7,803
1880	1,995	1,242	—	846	444	281	—	1,940	7,205	8,502
1890	2,197	1,487	—	1,171	587	378	528	1,842	7,081	9,339
1900	2,516	1,808	—	1,218	661	453	287	2,072	7,835	9,565
1910	3,143	2,270	—	1,484	771	529	206	2,095	7,952	9,547
1920	3,877	2,679	—	1,765	1,003	649	379	2,387	9,118	10,615
1930	4,321	3,424	—	2,456	1,414	898	99	1,837	7,789	10,938
1940	5,101	4,115	—	2,809	1,745	1,250	—	1,842	7,647	9,592
1950	6,236	4,890	—	3,371	2,456	1,422	—	3,054	13,213	13,186
1960	7,475	6,279	—	4,544	2,860	2,292	—	5,568	21,604	23,445
1970	9,411	6,695	—	4,952	3,235	2,931	—	4,661	18,997	28,366
1980	12,741	9,495	—	6,294	3,922	3,605	—	4,319	15,848	20,635
1990	14,137	12,877	—	9,228	5,837	4,845	—	4,159	19,631	22,915

TABLE Aa2767–2867   Delaware population by race, sex, age, nativity, and urban–rural residence: 1790–1990
Continued

					Population					
					Female, by age					
	10–14	15–19	20–29	20–24	25–29	30–39	30–34	35–39	40–49	40–44
	Aa2808	Aa2809	Aa2810	Aa2811	Aa2812	Aa2813	Aa2814	Aa2815	Aa2816	Aa2817
Year	Number	Number	Number	Number	Number	Number	Number	Number	Number	Number
1790	—	—	—	—	—	—	—	—	—	—
1800	—	—	—	—	—	—	—	—	—	—
1810	—	—	—	—	—	—	—	—	—	—
1820	—	—	—	—	—	—	—	—	—	—
1830	—	—	—	—	—	—	—	—	—	—
1840	—	—	—	—	—	—	—	—	—	—
1850	5,682	5,076	8,100	—	—	5,561	—	—	3,668	—
1860	6,670	6,290	10,046	—	—	6,557	—	—	4,759	—
1870	7,817	6,591	—	6,116	5,001	—	4,019	3,706	—	2,944
1880	7,921	7,711	—	7,544	5,791	—	4,853	4,507	—	3,787
1890	8,984	8,410	—	8,100	7,126	—	6,209	5,216	—	4,494
1900	9,208	8,820	—	8,705	7,608	—	6,574	6,317	—	5,462
1910	9,419	9,438	—	9,367	8,357	—	7,430	6,973	—	6,008
1920	10,023	9,290	—	9,841	9,352	—	8,141	7,772	—	6,909
1930	11,283	10,430	—	9,770	8,894	—	8,779	8,773	—	7,768
1940	10,622	11,509	—	12,154	11,482	—	10,535	9,751	—	9,287
1950	10,586	10,550	—	12,273	13,933	—	13,620	12,468	—	11,010
1960	19,809	15,411	—	13,754	14,976	—	16,463	17,119	—	15,300
1970	28,968	25,851	—	23,103	19,571	—	16,461	16,133	—	17,094
1980	23,975	30,176	—	29,784	25,380	—	23,270	19,071	—	15,969
1990	21,060	23,220	—	27,527	29,803	—	30,254	26,548	—	23,752

					Population					
					Female, by age					
	45–49	50–59	50–54	55–59	60–69	60–64	65–69	70–79	70–74	75–79
	Aa2818	Aa2819	Aa2820	Aa2821	Aa2822	Aa2823	Aa2824	Aa2825	Aa2826	Aa2827
Year	Number	Number	Number	Number	Number	Number	Number	Number	Number	Number
1790	—	—	—	—	—	—	—	—	—	—
1800	—	—	—	—	—	—	—	—	—	—
1810	—	—	—	—	—	—	—	—	—	—
1820	—	—	—	—	—	—	—	—	—	—
1830	—	—	—	—	—	—	—	—	—	—
1840	—	—	—	—	—	—	—	—	—	—
1850	—	2,308	—	—	1,285	—	—	579	—	—
1860	—	3,109	—	—	1,674	—	—	675	—	—
1870	2,588	—	2,312	1,574	—	1,422	966	—	620	345
1880	2,983	—	2,781	1,905	—	1,896	1,260	—	909	553
1890	3,824	—	3,445	2,364	—	2,011	1,548	—	1,226	660
1900	4,427	—	3,821	3,072	—	2,541	1,814	—	1,199	745
1910	5,511	—	4,780	3,388	—	3,052	2,207	—	1,578	922
1920	6,039	—	5,233	4,286	—	3,593	2,530	—	1,791	1,138
1930	6,932	—	6,310	4,838	—	4,257	3,420	—	2,431	1,479
1940	8,331	—	7,445	6,087	—	5,241	4,180	—	3,015	1,915
1950	9,711	—	8,946	7,566	—	6,444	5,514	—	3,930	2,902
1960	13,024	—	11,215	9,475	—	8,223	7,144	—	5,538	3,703
1970	17,278	—	15,128	12,570	—	10,571	8,507	—	7,028	5,081
1980	15,860	—	16,704	16,796	—	14,089	11,723	—	9,118	6,585
1990	19,277	—	15,816	15,524	—	15,766	15,597	—	11,894	8,977

(continued)

TABLE Aa2767–2867   Delaware population by race, sex, age, nativity, and urban–rural residence: 1790–1990
Continued

			Population							
			White							
Female, by age		Male	Female	Male, by age					
80 and older	Unknown age			0–4	5–9	10–14	15–19	20–29	30–39
Aa2828	Aa2829	Aa2830	Aa2831	Aa2832	Aa2833	Aa2834	Aa2835	Aa2836	Aa2837
Year	Number	Number	Number	Number	Number	Number	Number	Number	Number	Number
1790	—	—	23,926	22,384	—	—	—	—	—	—
1800	—	—	25,033	24,819	—	—	—	—	—	—
1810	—	—	28,006	27,355	—	—	—	—	—	—
1820	—	—	27,905	27,377	—	—	—	—	—	—
1830	—	—	28,845	28,756	4,744	4,099	3,919	3,184	5,508	3,206
1840	—	—	29,259	29,302	4,939	3,957	3,581	3,104	5,722	3,549
1850	197	19	—	—	—	—	—	—	—	—
1860	252	0	—	—	—	—	—	—	—	—
1870	291	0	—	—	—	—	—	—	—	—
1880	452	—	—	—	—	—	—	—	—	—
1890	585	456	—	—	—	—	—	—	—	—
1900	570	222	—	—	—	—	—	—	—	—
1910	704	159	—	—	—	—	—	—	—	—
1920	847	343	—	—	—	—	—	—	—	—
1930	1,156	39	—	—	—	—	—	—	—	—
1940	1,537	—	—	—	—	—	—	—	—	—
1950	1,835	—	—	—	—	—	—	—	—	—
1960	3,385	—	—	—	—	—	—	—	—	—
1970	5,404	—	—	—	—	—	—	—	—	—
1980	8,437	—	—	—	—	—	—	—	—	—
1990	11,480	—	—	—	—	—	—	—	—	—

				Population					
				White					
Male, by age					Female, by age				
40–49	50–59	60–69	70–79	80 and older	0–4	5–9	10–14	15–19	20–29
Aa2838	Aa2839	Aa2840	Aa2841	Aa2842	Aa2843	Aa2844	Aa2845	Aa2846	Aa2847
Year	Number	Number	Number	Number	Number	Number	Number	Number	Number	Number
1790	—	—	—	—	—	—	—	—	—	—
1800	—	—	—	—	—	—	—	—	—	—
1810	—	—	—	—	—	—	—	—	—	—
1820	—	—	—	—	—	—	—	—	—	—
1830	2,036	1,286	609	202	52	4,647	4,011	3,654	3,381	5,484
1840	2,117	1,270	682	268	70	4,751	3,859	3,404	3,337	5,707
1850	—	—	—	—	—	—	—	—	—	—
1860	—	—	—	—	—	—	—	—	—	—
1870	—	—	—	—	—	—	—	—	—	—
1880	—	—	—	—	—	—	—	—	—	—
1890	—	—	—	—	—	—	—	—	—	—
1900	—	—	—	—	—	—	—	—	—	—
1910	—	—	—	—	—	—	—	—	—	—
1920	—	—	—	—	—	—	—	—	—	—
1930	—	—	—	—	—	—	—	—	—	—
1940	—	—	—	—	—	—	—	—	—	—
1950	—	—	—	—	—	—	—	—	—	—
1960	—	—	—	—	—	—	—	—	—	—
1970	—	—	—	—	—	—	—	—	—	—
1980	—	—	—	—	—	—	—	—	—	—
1990	—	—	—	—	—	—	—	—	—	—

TABLE Aa2767–2867   Delaware population by race, sex, age, nativity, and urban–rural residence: 1790–1990
Continued

	Population									
	White									
	Female, by age						Male, by age			
	30–39	40–49	50–59	60–69	70–79	80 and older	0–9	10–15	16–25	26–44
	Aa2848	Aa2849	Aa2850	Aa2851	Aa2852	Aa2853	Aa2854	Aa2855	Aa2856	Aa2857
Year	Number	Number	Number	Number	Number	Number	Number	Number	Number	Number
1790	—	—	—	—	—	—	—	—	—	—
1800	—	—	—	—	—	—	8,250	4,437	5,121	5,012
1810	—	—	—	—	—	—	9,632	4,480	5,150	5,866
1820	—	—	—	—	—	—	9,071	4,448	5,516	5,607
1830	3,179	2,047	1,397	630	263	63	—	—	—	—
1840	3,469	2,173	1,341	837	320	104	—	—	—	—
1850	—	—	—	—	—	—	—	—	—	—
1860	—	—	—	—	—	—	—	—	—	—
1870	—	—	—	—	—	—	—	—	—	—
1880	—	—	—	—	—	—	—	—	—	—
1890	—	—	—	—	—	—	—	—	—	—
1900	—	—	—	—	—	—	—	—	—	—
1910	—	—	—	—	—	—	—	—	—	—
1920	—	—	—	—	—	—	—	—	—	—
1930	—	—	—	—	—	—	—	—	—	—
1940	—	—	—	—	—	—	—	—	—	—
1950	—	—	—	—	—	—	—	—	—	—
1960	—	—	—	—	—	—	—	—	—	—
1970	—	—	—	—	—	—	—	—	—	—
1980	—	—	—	—	—	—	—	—	—	—
1990	—	—	—	—	—	—	—	—	—	—

	Population									
	White									
	Male, by age	Female, by age					Male, by age		Female, by age	
	45 and older	0–9	10–15	16–25	26–44	45 and older	0–15	16 and over	0–15	16 and older
	Aa2858	Aa2859	Aa2860	Aa2861	Aa2862	Aa2863	Aa2864	Aa2865	Aa2866	Aa2867
Year	Number	Number	Number	Number	Number	Number	Number	Number	Number	Number
1790	—	—	—	—	—	—	12,143	11,783	10,737	11,647
1800	2,213	7,628	4,277	5,543	4,981	2,390	—	—	—	—
1810	2,878	9,041	4,370	5,541	5,527	2,876	—	—	—	—
1820	3,263	8,657	4,311	5,573	5,537	3,299	—	—	—	—
1830	—	—	—	—	—	—	—	—	—	—
1840	—	—	—	—	—	—	—	—	—	—
1850	—	—	—	—	—	—	—	—	—	—
1860	—	—	—	—	—	—	—	—	—	—
1870	—	—	—	—	—	—	—	—	—	—
1880	—	—	—	—	—	—	—	—	—	—
1890	—	—	—	—	—	—	—	—	—	—
1900	—	—	—	—	—	—	—	—	—	—
1910	—	—	—	—	—	—	—	—	—	—
1920	—	—	—	—	—	—	—	—	—	—
1930	—	—	—	—	—	—	—	—	—	—
1940	—	—	—	—	—	—	—	—	—	—
1950	—	—	—	—	—	—	—	—	—	—
1960	—	—	—	—	—	—	—	—	—	—
1970	—	—	—	—	—	—	—	—	—	—
1980	—	—	—	—	—	—	—	—	—	—
1990	—	—	—	—	—	—	—	—	—	—

Sources
See the sources for Table Aa2244–2340.

Documentation
See the text for Table Aa2244–2340.

Delaware was one of the original thirteen states, admitted to the Union in 1787.

TABLE Aa2868-2964   District of Columbia population by race, sex, age, nativity, and urban–rural residence: 1800–1990   [Present boundaries]

Contributed by Michael R. Haines

					Population							
					Race				Residence		Nativity	
	Area	Population density	Total	White	Nonwhite	Black	Other nonwhite	Urban	Rural	Native-born	Foreign-born
	Aa2868	Aa2869	Aa2870	Aa2871	Aa2872	Aa2873	Aa2874	Aa2875	Aa2876	Aa2877	Aa2878
Year	Square miles	Persons per square mile	Number	Number	Number	Number	Number	Number	Number	Number	Number
1800	58	140.41	8,144	5,672	2,472	2,472	0	6,203	1,941	—	—
1810	58	266.74	15,471	10,345	5,126	5,126	0	13,156	2,315	—	—
1820	58	402.34	23,336	16,058	7,278	7,278	0	20,607	2,729	—	—
1830	58	521.74	30,261	21,152	9,109	9,109	0	27,267	2,994	—	—
1840	58	581.81	33,745	23,926	9,819	9,819	0	30,676	3,069	—	—
1850	58	891.16	51,687	37,941	13,746	13,746	—	48,367	3,320	46,769	4,918
1860	58	1,294.48	75,080	60,763	14,317	14,316	1	69,855	5,225	62,596	12,484
1870	58	2,270.69	131,700	88,278	43,422	43,404	18	120,583	11,117	115,446	16,254
1880	58	3,062.48	177,624	118,006	59,618	59,596	22	159,871	17,753	160,502	17,122
1890	58	3,972.28	230,392	154,695	75,697	75,572	125	230,392	0	211,622	18,770
1900	60	4,645.30	278,718	191,532	87,186	86,702	484	278,718	0	258,599	20,119
1910	60	5,517.82	331,069	236,128	94,941	94,446	495	331,069	0	306,167	24,902
1920	60	7,292.85	437,571	326,860	110,711	109,966	745	437,571	0	408,206	29,365
1930	62	7,852.73	486,869	353,981	132,888	132,068	820	486,869	0	456,136	30,733
1940	61	10,870.34	663,091	474,326	188,765	187,266	1,499	663,091	0	628,175	34,916
1950	61	13,150.46	802,178	517,865	284,313	280,803	3,510	802,178	0	758,090	42,740
1960	61	12,523.87	763,956	345,263	418,693	411,737	6,956	763,956	0	724,985	38,971
1970	61	12,401.80	756,510	209,272	547,238	537,712	9,526	756,510	0	722,930	33,562
1980	63	10,132.27	638,333	171,768	466,565	448,906	17,659	638,333	0	597,774	40,559
1990	61	9,884.36	606,900	179,667	427,233	399,604	27,629	606,900	0	548,013	58,887

		Population												
	Sex		Male, by age											
	Male	Female	0	1–4	5–9	10–14	15–19	20–29	20–24	25–29	30–39	30–34	35–39
	Aa2879	Aa2880	Aa2881	Aa2882	Aa2883	Aa2884	Aa2885	Aa2886	Aa2887	Aa2888	Aa2889	Aa2890	Aa2891
Year	Number	Number	Number	Number	Number	Number	Number	Number	Number	Number	Number	Number	Number
1800	—	—	—	—	—	—	—	—	—	—	—	—	—
1810	—	—	—	—	—	—	—	—	—	—	—	—	—
1820	11,414	11,922	—	—	—	—	—	—	—	—	—	—	—
1830	14,789	15,472	—	—	—	—	—	—	—	—	—	—	—
1840	15,704	18,041	—	—	—	—	—	—	—	—	—	—	—
1850	24,164	27,523	648	2,769	3,316	2,929	2,430	4,434	—	—	3,337	—	—
1860	35,499	39,581	1,252	4,092	4,300	3,926	3,444	6,446	—	—	5,261	—	—
1870	62,192	69,508	1,873	6,990	6,677	6,884	5,522	—	5,302	5,729	—	5,107	4,922
1880	83,578	94,046	2,337	8,048	9,764	9,065	7,050	—	7,558	6,763	—	5,773	6,795
1890	109,584	120,808	2,208	7,945	10,728	11,217	10,760	—	11,604	9,227	—	8,254	7,682
1900	132,004	146,714	2,425	9,258	11,708	10,953	11,362	—	13,774	13,345	—	11,911	10,409
1910	158,050	173,019	2,732	10,669	12,666	12,151	13,232	—	16,066	16,517	—	14,685	13,931
1920	203,543	234,028	3,337	11,859	14,773	14,561	15,647	—	21,949	22,291	—	18,390	17,772
1930	231,883	254,986	3,136	13,262	17,797	16,015	16,899	—	22,909	23,401	—	21,411	20,724
1940	317,522	345,569	4,255	15,799	18,643	20,549	23,588	—	31,247	35,783	—	31,826	28,183
1950	377,918	424,260	7,542	28,547	24,588	19,934	22,189	—	34,532	39,692	—	34,721	33,059
1960	358,171	405,785	8,573	30,681	31,674	25,763	22,843	—	28,241	28,138	—	26,571	25,948
1970	351,491	405,019	6,356	23,730	32,233	32,296	30,819	—	35,249	31,085	—	23,513	20,524
1980	295,417	342,916	3,779	13,506	18,685	21,139	27,964	—	32,278	31,205	—	26,805	19,932
1990	282,970	323,930	3,597	15,333	16,299	14,752	20,084	—	27,842	30,224	—	28,320	25,123

TABLE Aa2868–2964   District of Columbia population by race, sex, age, nativity, and urban–rural residence: 1800–1990   [Present boundaries]   *Continued*

Population

Male, by age

Year	40–49	40–44	45–49	50–59	50–54	55–59	60–69	60–64	65–69	70–79	70–74	75–79
	Aa2892	Aa2893	Aa2894	Aa2895	Aa2896	Aa2897	Aa2898	Aa2899	Aa2900	Aa2901	Aa2902	Aa2903
	Number	Number	Number	Number	Number	Number	Number	Number	Number	Number	Number	Number
1800	—	—	—	—	—	—	—	—	—	—	—	—
1810	—	—	—	—	—	—	—	—	—	—	—	—
1820	—	—	—	—	—	—	—	—	—	—	—	—
1830	—	—	—	—	—	—	—	—	—	—	—	—
1840	—	—	—	—	—	—	—	—	—	—	—	—
1850	2,105	—	—	1,306	—	—	623	—	—	197	—	—
1860	3,502	—	—	1,875	—	—	957	—	—	344	—	—
1870	—	3,635	2,898	—	2,550	1,417	—	1,120	674	—	459	215
1880	—	5,687	4,408	—	3,752	2,272	—	1,916	1,091	—	715	356
1890	—	6,549	6,724	—	5,559	3,520	—	2,964	1,768	—	1,162	550
1900	—	8,679	6,876	—	6,371	5,285	—	4,123	2,431	—	1,611	796
1910	—	11,490	8,818	—	7,378	4,987	—	4,261	3,676	—	2,351	1,166
1920	—	15,120	14,438	—	10,956	6,928	—	5,761	3,488	—	2,488	1,644
1930	—	17,314	15,277	—	13,653	10,038	—	7,761	5,194	—	3,297	1,703
1940	—	25,853	22,630	—	18,268	13,436	—	10,772	7,730	—	4,777	2,492
1950	—	29,525	25,937	—	23,166	18,282	—	13,575	9,853	—	6,501	4,157
1960	—	23,160	23,286	—	21,925	18,966	—	15,159	11,523	—	7,598	4,537
1970	—	20,175	19,778	—	18,062	16,978	—	14,270	10,263	—	7,441	4,587
1980	—	15,763	14,122	—	15,148	15,209	—	12,651	10,769	—	7,592	4,664
1990	—	20,760	15,931	—	13,344	11,647	—	11,169	10,314	—	7,661	5,559

Population

	Male, by age		Female, by age									
Year	80 and older	Unknown age	0	1–4	5–9	10–14	15–19	20–29	20–24	25–29	30–39	30–34
	Aa2904	Aa2905	Aa2906	Aa2907	Aa2908	Aa2909	Aa2910	Aa2911	Aa2912	Aa2913	Aa2914	Aa2915
	Number	Number	Number	Number	Number	Number	Number	Number	Number	Number	Number	Number
1800	—	—	—	—	—	—	—	—	—	—	—	—
1810	—	—	—	—	—	—	—	—	—	—	—	—
1820	—	—	—	—	—	—	—	—	—	—	—	—
1830	—	—	—	—	—	—	—	—	—	—	—	—
1840	—	—	—	—	—	—	—	—	—	—	—	—
1850	67	3	671	2,659	3,415	3,190	3,176	5,531	—	—	3,607	—
1860	89	11	1,171	3,980	4,444	4,246	4,519	7,943	—	—	5,728	—
1870	218	0	1,906	7,009	6,792	7,452	7,488	—	7,699	6,945	—	5,431
1880	228	—	2,287	7,963	10,318	9,340	9,058	—	10,758	8,921	—	7,071
1890	396	767	2,259	7,891	10,794	11,635	13,500	—	14,527	11,454	—	9,398
1900	525	162	2,333	9,134	12,023	11,781	13,452	—	17,736	16,410	—	12,857
1910	764	510	2,757	10,511	12,646	12,498	14,880	—	18,358	18,596	—	16,344
1920	1,041	1,100	3,249	11,991	15,067	15,255	17,879	—	29,106	27,706	—	21,534
1930	1,277	815	3,000	12,906	17,827	16,697	18,907	—	25,478	24,719	—	23,684
1940	1,691	—	4,167	15,630	18,602	20,540	25,092	—	34,236	38,563	—	33,942
1950	2,118	—	7,493	27,771	24,881	20,105	23,222	—	37,189	44,857	—	39,656
1960	3,585	—	8,462	30,379	31,676	26,464	26,539	—	31,528	27,060	—	27,682
1970	4,132	—	6,194	23,455	31,989	32,128	34,790	—	44,389	33,815	—	24,112
1980	4,206	—	3,693	13,387	17,933	20,994	29,660	—	37,285	35,138	—	29,404
1990	5,011	—	3,453	14,968	15,698	14,566	21,193	—	31,865	32,905	—	29,827

(continued)

TABLE Aa2868-2964   District of Columbia population by race, sex, age, nativity, and urban-rural residence: 1800-1990   [Present boundaries]   *Continued*

Population

	Female, by age											
	35–39	40–49	40–44	45–49	50–59	50–54	55–59	60–69	60–64	65–69	70–79	70–74
	Aa2916	Aa2917	Aa2918	Aa2919	Aa2920	Aa2921	Aa2922	Aa2923	Aa2924	Aa2925	Aa2926	Aa2927
Year	Number	Number	Number	Number	Number	Number	Number	Number	Number	Number	Number	Number
1800	—	—	—	—	—	—	—	—	—	—	—	—
1810	—	—	—	—	—	—	—	—	—	—	—	—
1820	—	—	—	—	—	—	—	—	—	—	—	—
1830	—	—	—	—	—	—	—	—	—	—	—	—
1840	—	—	—	—	—	—	—	—	—	—	—	—
1850	—	2,421	—	—	1,538	—	—	810	—	—	334	—
1860	—	3,471	—	—	2,144	—	—	1,289	—	—	447	—
1870	4,784	—	3,672	2,848	—	2,445	1,478	—	1,330	845	—	669
1880	7,418	—	5,512	4,166	—	3,710	2,265	—	2,047	1,221	—	912
1890	8,797	—	7,239	6,430	—	5,262	3,272	—	2,913	1,915	—	1,337
1900	11,472	—	9,255	7,750	—	6,928	5,001	—	4,078	2,604	—	1,829
1910	15,731	—	12,082	9,747	—	8,133	5,764	—	5,187	3,992	—	2,577
1920	20,857	—	17,415	15,080	—	11,716	7,656	—	6,754	4,626	—	3,522
1930	22,863	—	19,012	17,297	—	15,079	11,571	—	9,197	6,518	—	4,397
1940	30,165	—	28,036	24,011	—	19,650	15,434	—	12,985	10,579	—	6,874
1950	38,634	—	33,735	28,855	—	26,512	21,042	—	16,250	13,485	—	9,250
1960	29,411	—	28,064	28,226	—	26,515	22,592	—	19,287	15,688	—	11,575
1970	21,813	—	22,462	23,520	—	22,316	21,016	—	18,640	15,038	—	12,107
1980	21,518	—	17,052	16,082	—	17,989	18,884	—	16,841	15,613	—	12,256
1990	26,276	—	23,037	17,941	—	14,815	13,794	—	14,290	14,527	—	12,051

Population

	Female, by age				White								
							Male, by age						
	75–79	80 and older	Unknown age	Male	Female	0–4	5–9	10–14	15–19	20–29	30–39	40–49
	Aa2928	Aa2929	Aa2930	Aa2931	Aa2932	Aa2933	Aa2934	Aa2935	Aa2936	Aa2937	Aa2938	Aa2939
Year	Number	Number	Number	Number	Number	Number	Number	Number	Number	Number	Number	Number
1800	—	—	—	3,038	2,634	—	—	—	—	—	—	—
1810	—	—	—	5,191	5,154	—	—	—	—	—	—	—
1820	—	—	—	8,028	8,030	—	—	—	—	—	—	—
1830	—	—	—	10,644	10,508	1,822	1,289	1,073	1,153	2,268	1,472	840
1840	—	—	—	11,584	12,342	1,837	1,359	1,395	1,282	2,289	1,530	975
1850	—	156	15	—	—	—	—	—	—	—	—	—
1860	—	178	21	—	—	—	—	—	—	—	—	—
1870	348	367	0	—	—	—	—	—	—	—	—	—
1880	550	529	—	—	—	—	—	—	—	—	—	—
1890	753	698	734	—	—	—	—	—	—	—	—	—
1900	1,049	889	133	—	—	—	—	—	—	—	—	—
1910	1,357	1,134	725	—	—	—	—	—	—	—	—	—
1920	2,227	1,599	789	—	—	—	—	—	—	—	—	—
1930	2,612	2,255	967	—	—	—	—	—	—	—	—	—
1940	3,888	3,175	—	—	—	—	—	—	—	—	—	—
1950	7,391	3,932	—	—	—	—	—	—	—	—	—	—
1960	7,572	7,065	—	—	—	—	—	—	—	—	—	—
1970	8,272	8,963	—	—	—	—	—	—	—	—	—	—
1980	8,772	10,415	—	—	—	—	—	—	—	—	—	—
1990	10,103	12,621	—	—	—	—	—	—	—	—	—	—

TABLE Aa2868-2964   District of Columbia population by race, sex, age, nativity, and urban–rural residence: 1800–1990   [Present boundaries]   Continued

	Population											
	White											
	Male, by age				Female, by age							
	50–59	60–69	70–79	80 and older	0–4	5–9	10–14	15–19	20–29	30–39	40–49	50–59
	Aa2940	Aa2941	Aa2942	Aa2943	Aa2944	Aa2945	Aa2946	Aa2947	Aa2948	Aa2949	Aa2950	Aa2951
Year	Number	Number	Number	Number	Number	Number	Number	Number	Number	Number	Number	Number
1800	—	—	—	—	—	—	—	—	—	—	—	—
1810	—	—	—	—	—	—	—	—	—	—	—	—
1820	—	—	—	—	—	—	—	—	—	—	—	—
1830	468	184	56	19	1,675	1,240	1,181	1,390	2,235	1,331	723	441
1840	561	246	89	21	1,772	1,394	1,511	1,607	2,341	1,591	1,032	625
1850	—	—	—	—	—	—	—	—	—	—	—	—
1860	—	—	—	—	—	—	—	—	—	—	—	—
1870	—	—	—	—	—	—	—	—	—	—	—	—
1880	—	—	—	—	—	—	—	—	—	—	—	—
1890	—	—	—	—	—	—	—	—	—	—	—	—
1900	—	—	—	—	—	—	—	—	—	—	—	—
1910	—	—	—	—	—	—	—	—	—	—	—	—
1920	—	—	—	—	—	—	—	—	—	—	—	—
1930*	—	—	—	—	—	—	—	—	—	—	—	—
1940	—	—	—	—	—	—	—	—	—	—	—	—
1950	—	—	—	—	—	—	—	—	—	—	—	—
1960	—	—	—	—	—	—	—	—	—	—	—	—
1970	—	—	—	—	—	—	—	—	—	—	—	—
1980	—	—	—	—	—	—	—	—	—	—	—	—
1990	—	—	—	—	—	—	—	—	—	—	—	—

	Population											
	White											
	Female, by age			Male, by age					Female, by age				
	60–69	70–79	80 and older	0–9	10–15	16–25	26–44	45 and older	0–9	10–15	16–25	26–44	45 and older
	Aa2952	Aa2953	Aa2954	Aa2955	Aa2956	Aa2957	Aa2958	Aa2959	Aa2960	Aa2961	Aa2962	Aa2963	Aa2964
Year	Number	Number	Number	Number	Number	Number	Number	Number	Number	Number	Number	Number	Number
1800	—	—	—	899	351	695	775	318	907	350	548	555	274
1810	—	—	—	1,606	706	956	1,333	590	1,660	742	1,127	1,106	519
1820	—	—	—	2,285	1,086	1,586	2,143	928	2,357	1,176	1,753	1,816	928
1830	201	59	32	—	—	—	—	—	—	—	—	—	—
1840	328	111	30	—	—	—	—	—	—	—	—	—	—
1850	—	—	—	—	—	—	—	—	—	—	—	—	—
1860	—	—	—	—	—	—	—	—	—	—	—	—	—
1870	—	—	—	—	—	—	—	—	—	—	—	—	—
1880	—	—	—	—	—	—	—	—	—	—	—	—	—
1890	—	—	—	—	—	—	—	—	—	—	—	—	—
1900	—	—	—	—	—	—	—	—	—	—	—	—	—
1910	—	—	—	—	—	—	—	—	—	—	—	—	—
1920	—	—	—	—	—	—	—	—	—	—	—	—	—
1930	—	—	—	—	—	—	—	—	—	—	—	—	—
1940	—	—	—	—	—	—	—	—	—	—	—	—	—
1950	—	—	—	—	—	—	—	—	—	—	—	—	—
1960	—	—	—	—	—	—	—	—	—	—	—	—	—
1970	—	—	—	—	—	—	—	—	—	—	—	—	—
1980	—	—	—	—	—	—	—	—	—	—	—	—	—
1990	—	—	—	—	—	—	—	—	—	—	—	—	—

Sources
See the sources for Table Aa2244–2340.

Documentation
See the text for Table Aa2244–2340.

The District of Columbia was created in 1790 by act of Congress. It became the seat of national government in 1800. Originally comprising territory on both the north and south banks of the Potomac River, the area south of the river, present-day Alexandria, Virginia, was retroceded to Virginia in 1846.

Table Aa2868–2964 is based on present-day boundaries, that is, as of 1850. Table Aa2965–3009 is based on the historical boundaries for the period 1800–1840.

TABLE Aa2965–3009   District of Columbia population by race, sex, age, nativity, and urban–rural residence: 1800–1840   [Historical boundaries]

Contributed by Michael R. Haines

		Population									
				Race				Residence		Sex	
Area	Population density	Total	White	Nonwhite	Black	Other nonwhite	Urban	Rural	Male	Female
Aa2965	Aa2966	Aa2967	Aa2968	Aa2969	Aa2970	Aa2971	Aa2972	Aa2973	Aa2974	Aa2975
Year	Square miles	Persons per square mile	Number	Number	Number	Number	Number	Number	Number	Number	Number
1800	90	156.59	14,093	10,066	4,027	4,027	—	11,174	2,919	—	—
1810	90	266.92	24,023	16,079	7,944	7,944	—	20,383	3,640	—	—
1820	90	367.10	33,039	22,614	10,425	10,425	0	28,825	4,214	15,909	17,130
1830	90	442.60	39,834	27,563	12,271	12,271	—	35,508	4,326	19,144	20,690
1840	90	485.69	43,712	30,657	13,055	13,055	—	39,135	4,577	20,333	23,379

		Population									
		White									
					Male, by age						
Male	Female	0–4	5–9	10–14	15–19	20–29	30–39	40–49	50–59	60–69
Aa2976	Aa2977	Aa2978	Aa2979	Aa2980	Aa2981	Aa2982	Aa2983	Aa2984	Aa2985	Aa2986
Year	Number	Number	Number	Number	Number	Number	Number	Number	Number	Number	Number
1800	5,308	4,758	—	—	—	—	—	—	—	—	—
1810	8,130	7,949	—	—	—	—	—	—	—	—	—
1820	11,171	11,443	—	—	—	—	—	—	—	—	—
1830	13,647	13,916	2,333	1,680	1,486	1,522	2,805	1,817	1,068	593	245
1840	14,822	15,835	2,354	1,755	1,764	1,728	2,891	1,953	1,201	724	312

		Population									
		White									
Male, by age		Female, by age									
70–79	80 and older	0–4	5–9	10–14	15–19	20–29	30–39	40–49	50–59	60–69
Aa2987	Aa2988	Aa2989	Aa2990	Aa2991	Aa2992	Aa2993	Aa2994	Aa2995	Aa2996	Aa2997
Year	Number	Number	Number	Number	Number	Number	Number	Number	Number	Number	Number
1800	—	—	—	—	—	—	—	—	—	—	—
1810	—	—	—	—	—	—	—	—	—	—	—
1820	—	—	—	—	—	—	—	—	—	—	—
1830	71	27	2,182	1,646	1,648	1,843	2,856	1,752	980	603	272
1840	115	25	2,294	1,771	1,899	2,077	3,030	2,026	1,338	795	413

		Population									
		White									
Female, by age		Male, by age					Female, by age				
70–79	80 and older	0–9	10–15	16–25	26–44	45 and older	0–9	10–15	16–25	26–44	45 and older
Aa2998	Aa2999	Aa3000	Aa3001	Aa3002	Aa3003	Aa3004	Aa3005	Aa3006	Aa3007	Aa3008	Aa3009
Year	Number	Number	Number	Number	Number	Number	Number	Number	Number	Number	Number	Number
1800	—	—	1,588	671	1,178	1,332	539	1,577	663	1,027	1,028	463
1810	—	—	2,479	1,158	1,520	2,107	866	2,538	1,192	1,653	1,734	832
1820	—	—	3,276	1,540	2,171	2,893	1,291	3,319	1,640	2,518	2,615	1,351
1830	98	36	—	—	—	—	—	—	—	—	—	—
1840	149	43	—	—	—	—	—	—	—	—	—	—

Sources

See the sources for Table Aa2244–2340.

Documentation

See the text for Tables Aa2244–2340 and Aa2868–2964.

TABLE Aa3010–3096 Florida population by race, sex, age, nativity, and urban–rural residence: 1830–1990

Contributed by Michael R. Haines

	Area	Population density	Population									
				Race				Residence		Nativity	
			Total	White	Nonwhite	Black	Other nonwhite	Urban	Rural	Native-born	Foreign-born
	Aa3010	Aa3011	Aa3012	Aa3013	Aa3014	Aa3015	Aa3016	Aa3017	Aa3018	Aa3019	Aa3020
Year	Square miles	Persons per square mile	Number	Number	Number	Number	Number	Number	Number	Number	Number
1830	54,861	0.63	34,730	18,385	16,345	16,345	—	0	34,730	—	—
1840	54,861	0.99	54,477	27,943	26,534	26,534	—	0	54,477	—	—
1850	54,861	1.59	87,445	47,203	40,242	40,242	—	0	87,445	84,676	2,769
1860	54,861	2.56	140,424	77,746	62,678	62,677	1	5,708	134,716	137,115	3,309
1870	54,861	3.42	187,748	96,057	91,691	91,689	2	15,275	172,473	182,781	4,967
1880	54,861	4.91	269,493	142,605	126,888	126,690	198	26,947	242,546	259,584	9,909
1890	54,861	7.13	391,422	224,949	166,473	166,180	293	77,358	314,064	368,490	22,932
1900	54,861	9.63	528,542	297,333	231,209	230,730	479	107,031	421,511	504,710	23,832
1910	54,861	13.72	752,619	443,634	308,985	308,669	316	219,080	533,539	711,986	40,633
1920	54,861	17.65	968,470	638,153	330,317	329,487	830	353,515	614,955	914,606	53,864
1930	54,861	26.76	1,468,211	1,035,390	432,821	431,828	993	759,778	708,433	1,398,464	69,747
1940	54,262	34.97	1,897,414	1,381,986	515,428	514,198	1,230	1,045,791	851,623	1,819,575	77,839
1950	54,262	51.07	2,771,305	2,166,051	605,254	603,101	2,153	1,813,890	957,415	2,631,800	131,065
1960	54,136	91.47	4,951,560	4,063,881	887,679	880,186	7,493	3,661,383	1,290,177	4,680,627	272,161
1970	54,090	125.52	6,789,443	5,719,343	1,070,100	1,041,651	28,449	5,544,551	1,244,892	6,249,099	540,284
1980	54,153	179.98	9,746,324	8,184,513	1,561,811	1,342,688	219,123	8,212,385	1,533,939	8,687,592	1,058,732
1990	53,997	239.60	12,937,926	10,749,285	2,188,641	1,759,534	429,107	10,967,328	1,970,598	11,275,325	1,662,601

	Population										
	Sex		Male, by age								
	Male	Female	0	1–4	5–9	10–14	15–19	20–29	20–24	25–29	30–39
	Aa3021	Aa3022	Aa3023	Aa3024	Aa3025	Aa3026	Aa3027	Aa3028	Aa3029	Aa3030	Aa3031
Year	Number	Number	Number	Number	Number	Number	Number	Number	Number	Number	Number
1830	18,604	16,126	—	—	—	—	—	—	—	—	—
1840	29,892	24,585	—	—	—	—	—	—	—	—	—
1850	45,927	41,518	1,123	6,260	6,770	5,646	4,348	8,714	—	—	5,879
1860	72,930	67,494	2,084	9,533	10,541	9,754	7,596	13,094	—	—	8,584
1870	94,548	93,200	2,655	12,800	13,420	13,293	10,218	—	9,551	7,053	—
1880	136,444	133,049	4,417	17,803	20,749	16,793	12,273	—	13,954	11,493	—
1890	201,947	189,475	5,375	22,364	27,341	25,824	21,278	—	18,852	16,167	—
1900	275,246	253,296	7,703	29,122	35,231	30,999	26,752	—	29,659	24,627	—
1910	394,166	358,453	10,149	38,836	46,072	40,616	37,140	—	39,855	36,090	—
1920	495,320	473,150	10,273	42,812	56,085	53,472	44,514	—	40,838	38,388	—
1930	737,675	730,536	12,777	59,042	76,239	71,834	66,894	—	64,820	61,953	—
1940	943,123	954,291	14,881	61,474	77,261	86,252	83,108	—	80,889	82,291	—
1950	1,366,917	1,404,388	28,640	118,897	120,765	99,664	91,060	—	104,596	107,897	—
1960	2,436,783	2,514,777	56,167	218,326	248,518	220,387	169,574	—	147,566	147,230	—
1970	3,275,571	3,513,872	52,546	203,304	308,295	326,969	292,261	—	244,660	195,443	—
1980	4,675,626	5,070,698	63,355	227,931	317,254	349,914	411,458	—	404,245	366,758	—
1990	6,261,719	6,676,207	72,878	362,373	416,447	383,021	410,413	—	441,504	530,513	—

(continued)

TABLE Aa3010–3096   Florida population by race, sex, age, nativity, and urban–rural residence: 1830–1990
Continued

Population

	Male, by age										
	30–34	35–39	40–49	40–44	45–49	50–59	50–54	55–59	60–69	60–64	65–69
	Aa3032	Aa3033	Aa3034	Aa3035	Aa3036	Aa3037	Aa3038	Aa3039	Aa3040	Aa3041	Aa3042
Year	Number	Number	Number	Number	Number	Number	Number	Number	Number	Number	Number
1830	—	—	—	—	—	—	—	—	—	—	—
1840	—	—	—	—	—	—	—	—	—	—	—
1850	—	—	3,449	—	—	2,180	—	—	1,038	—	—
1860	—	—	5,605	—	—	3,197	—	—	1,558	—	—
1870	5,171	4,802	—	3,904	3,279	—	2,912	1,926	—	1,619	887
1880	8,596	7,213	—	5,221	5,133	—	4,023	2,880	—	2,460	1,562
1890	13,603	12,461	—	9,329	8,967	—	6,234	4,325	—	3,546	2,405
1900	18,984	16,862	—	13,423	12,326	—	9,218	6,587	—	4,802	3,300
1910	30,154	28,547	—	21,648	18,582	—	13,948	10,830	—	7,909	5,507
1920	34,140	37,096	—	29,491	31,830	—	22,884	16,030	—	13,496	9,604
1930	53,882	54,983	—	47,211	43,159	—	36,370	27,996	—	21,791	16,150
1940	76,828	73,029	—	63,162	56,423	—	48,895	38,772	—	32,764	29,524
1950	103,605	103,184	—	96,189	86,222	—	74,524	62,995	—	52,708	47,828
1960	158,998	163,882	—	153,155	142,421	—	126,264	113,491	—	100,351	109,451
1970	173,171	171,599	—	186,840	187,117	—	173,526	156,056	—	155,896	160,748
1980	329,786	269,171	—	234,788	227,935	—	242,231	250,526	—	251,914	258,435
1990	532,185	475,078	—	420,576	339,471	—	284,206	275,935	—	307,929	333,477

Population

	Male, by age					Female, by age					
	70–79	70–74	75–79	80 and older	Unknown age	0	1–4	5–9	10–14	15–19	20–29
	Aa3043	Aa3044	Aa3045	Aa3046	Aa3047	Aa3048	Aa3049	Aa3050	Aa3051	Aa3052	Aa3053
Year	Number	Number	Number	Number	Number	Number	Number	Number	Number	Number	Number
1830	—	—	—	—	—	—	—	—	—	—	—
1840	—	—	—	—	—	—	—	—	—	—	—
1850	336	—	—	140	44	1,113	6,111	6,610	5,309	4,543	7,472
1860	508	—	—	191	685	2,121	9,264	9,891	9,290	7,918	11,815
1870	—	512	270	274	2	2,723	12,314	12,717	12,211	10,384	—
1880	—	965	477	432	—	4,496	17,132	20,246	16,182	13,305	—
1890	—	1,528	773	659	916	5,209	21,277	26,606	24,710	21,921	—
1900	—	1,996	1,099	894	1,662	7,361	28,507	35,128	29,976	27,501	—
1910	—	3,242	1,751	1,187	2,103	9,823	38,148	44,869	39,703	38,955	—
1920	—	6,405	3,858	2,386	1,718	10,272	41,906	55,335	52,839	47,323	—
1930	—	11,113	6,305	4,518	638	12,623	57,390	75,888	71,047	71,321	—
1940	—	19,657	10,536	7,377	—	14,329	60,794	75,707	84,831	86,672	—
1950	—	33,521	23,478	11,144	—	27,697	115,511	117,464	97,165	91,276	—
1960	—	82,678	47,304	31,020	—	54,467	212,141	242,012	214,796	167,913	—
1970	—	132,874	87,670	66,596	—	50,497	194,832	297,419	316,045	284,515	—
1980	—	212,018	141,044	116,863	—	60,214	218,724	304,280	335,102	399,882	—
1990	—	280,231	206,089	189,393	—	69,608	344,737	397,671	365,334	388,866	—

TABLE Aa3010–3096   Florida population by race, sex, age, nativity, and urban–rural residence: 1830–1990
Continued

	Population										
	Female, by age										
	20–24	25–29	30–39	30–34	35–39	40–49	40–44	45–49	50–59	50–54	55–59
	Aa3054	Aa3055	Aa3056	Aa3057	Aa3058	Aa3059	Aa3060	Aa3061	Aa3062	Aa3063	Aa3064
Year	Number	Number	Number	Number	Number	Number	Number	Number	Number	Number	Number
1830	—	—	—	—	—	—	—	—	—	—	—
1840	—	—	—	—	—	—	—	—	—	—	—
1850	—	—	4,730	—	—	2,797	—	—	1,635	—	—
1860	—	—	7,348	—	—	4,783	—	—	2,540	—	—
1870	10,427	7,661	—	5,853	5,040	—	4,063	3,078	—	2,495	1,344
1880	13,993	10,899	—	8,403	7,373	—	5,775	4,559	—	3,767	2,117
1890	18,620	14,654	—	11,738	10,774	—	8,903	7,508	—	5,655	3,535
1900	27,369	21,271	—	15,821	13,909	—	11,236	9,731	—	8,014	5,426
1910	38,743	33,087	—	25,851	22,800	—	16,642	13,521	—	10,780	7,687
1920	45,781	42,101	—	34,461	34,334	—	26,847	22,239	—	17,542	12,156
1930	72,994	66,346	—	56,237	55,769	—	44,564	38,488	—	31,595	23,593
1940	88,827	88,000	—	80,657	75,121	—	62,874	55,195	—	46,771	37,825
1950	108,095	117,009	—	112,114	112,464	—	100,316	87,263	—	76,198	64,514
1960	148,611	151,008	—	168,732	175,243	—	160,383	151,199	—	136,895	127,595
1970	251,857	207,653	—	185,494	183,813	—	204,615	207,323	—	194,021	191,281
1980	407,182	373,090	—	341,777	285,069	—	249,750	243,344	—	275,650	304,683
1990	429,042	521,593	—	531,953	482,350	—	433,152	357,852	—	310,082	312,617

	Population										
									White		
	Female, by age										Male, by age
	60–69	60–64	65–69	70–79	70–74	75–79	80 and older	Unknown age	Male	Female	0–4
	Aa3065	Aa3066	Aa3067	Aa3068	Aa3069	Aa3070	Aa3071	Aa3072	Aa3073	Aa3074	Aa3075
Year	Number	Number	Number	Number	Number	Number	Number	Number	Number	Number	Number
1830	—	—	—	—	—	—	—	—	10,236	8,149	1,932
1840	—	—	—	—	—	—	—	—	16,456	11,487	2,455
1850	796	—	—	262	—	—	139	1	—	—	—
1860	1,245	—	—	425	—	—	165	689	—	—	—
1870	—	1,323	602	—	461	221	282	1	—	—	—
1880	—	2,022	1,145	—	752	405	478	—	—	—	—
1890	—	3,118	1,879	—	1,277	687	688	716	—	—	—
1900	—	4,343	2,821	—	1,883	978	970	1,051	—	—	—
1910	—	6,690	4,464	—	2,779	1,516	1,351	1,044	—	—	—
1920	—	10,608	7,546	—	5,464	3,127	2,274	995	—	—	—
1930	—	18,966	13,635	—	9,596	5,412	4,473	599	—	—	—
1940	—	32,565	28,905	—	18,031	9,690	7,497	—	—	—	—
1950	—	55,799	51,662	—	34,044	23,899	11,898	—	—	—	—
1960	—	121,106	115,028	—	82,132	48,464	37,052	—	—	—	—
1970	—	203,029	196,795	—	156,264	100,548	87,871	—	—	—	—
1980	—	312,738	320,577	—	268,123	188,167	182,346	—	—	—	—
1990	—	371,109	407,748	—	348,196	279,304	324,993	—	—	—	—

(continued)

TABLE Aa3010–3096   Florida population by race, sex, age, nativity, and urban–rural residence: 1830–1990
Continued

	Population									
	White									
	Male, by age									
	5–9	10–14	15–19	20–29	30–39	40–49	50–59	60–69	70–79	80 and older
	Aa3076	Aa3077	Aa3078	Aa3079	Aa3080	Aa3081	Aa3082	Aa3083	Aa3084	Aa3085
Year	Number	Number	Number	Number	Number	Number	Number	Number	Number	Number
1830	1,333	1,015	789	2,171	1,536	760	436	194	57	13
1840	1,947	1,520	1,305	4,388	2,801	1,193	530	220	73	24
1850	—	—	—	—	—	—	—	—	—	—
1860	—	—	—	—	—	—	—	—	—	—
1870	—	—	—	—	—	—	—	—	—	—
1880	—	—	—	—	—	—	—	—	—	—
1890	—	—	—	—	—	—	—	—	—	—
1900	—	—	—	—	—	—	—	—	—	—
1910	—	—	—	—	—	—	—	—	—	—
1920	—	—	—	—	—	—	—	—	—	—
1930	—	—	—	—	—	—	—	—	—	—
1940	—	—	—	—	—	—	—	—	—	—
1950	—	—	—	—	—	—	—	—	—	—
1960	—	—	—	—	—	—	—	—	—	—
1970	—	—	—	—	—	—	—	—	—	—
1980	—	—	—	—	—	—	—	—	—	—
1990	—	—	—	—	—	—	—	—	—	—

	Population										
	White										
	Female, by age										
	0–4	5–9	10–14	15–19	20–29	30–39	40–49	50–59	60–69	70–79	80 and older
	Aa3086	Aa3087	Aa3088	Aa3089	Aa3090	Aa3091	Aa3092	Aa3093	Aa3094	Aa3095	Aa3096
Year	Number	Number	Number	Number	Number	Number	Number	Number	Number	Number	Number
1830	1,807	1,251	981	923	1,447	848	484	247	101	45	15
1840	2,241	1,761	1,448	1,322	2,220	1,219	704	354	156	49	13
1850	—	—	—	—	—	—	—	—	—	—	—
1860	—	—	—	—	—	—	—	—	—	—	—
1870	—	—	—	—	—	—	—	—	—	—	—
1880	—	—	—	—	—	—	—	—	—	—	—
1890	—	—	—	—	—	—	—	—	—	—	—
1900	—	—	—	—	—	—	—	—	—	—	—
1910	—	—	—	—	—	—	—	—	—	—	—
1920	—	—	—	—	—	—	—	—	—	—	—
1930	—	—	—	—	—	—	—	—	—	—	—
1940	—	—	—	—	—	—	—	—	—	—	—
1950	—	—	—	—	—	—	—	—	—	—	—
1960	—	—	—	—	—	—	—	—	—	—	—
1970	—	—	—	—	—	—	—	—	—	—	—
1980	—	—	—	—	—	—	—	—	—	—	—
1990	—	—	—	—	—	—	—	—	—	—	—

Sources
See the sources for Table Aa2244–2340.

Documentation
See the text for Table Aa2244–2340.

Florida was purchased from Spain in 1819, but treaty ratification and formal American possession were not completed until 1821. Thus, Florida was not enumerated in 1820. Florida became a territory in 1821 and a state in 1845.

TABLE Aa3097–3197   Georgia population by race, sex, age, nativity, and urban–rural residence: 1790–1990

Contributed by Michael R. Haines

				Population								
					Race				Residence		Nativity	
Year	Area	Population density	Total	White	Nonwhite	Black	Other nonwhite	Urban	Rural	Native-born	Foreign-born
	Aa3097	Aa3098	Aa3099	Aa3100	Aa3101	Aa3102	Aa3103	Aa3104	Aa3105	Aa3106	Aa3107
	Square miles	Persons per square mile	Number	Number	Number	Number	Number	Number	Number	Number	Number
1790	145,196	0.57	82,548	52,886	29,662	29,662	—	0	82,548	—	—
1800	111,877	1.45	162,686	101,678	60,423	60,423	—	5,146	157,540	—	—
1810	58,725	4.30	252,433	145,414	107,019	107,019	—	5,215	247,218	—	—
1820	58,725	5.81	340,989	189,566	151,423	151,419	4	7,523	333,466	—	—
1830	58,725	8.80	516,823	296,806	220,017	220,017	—	14,013	502,810	—	—
1840	58,725	11.77	691,392	407,695	283,697	283,697	—	24,658	666,734	—	—
1850	58,725	15.43	906,185	521,572	384,613	384,613	—	38,994	867,191	899,697	6,488
1860	58,725	18.00	1,057,286	591,550	465,736	465,698	38	75,466	981,820	1,045,615	11,671
1870	58,725	20.16	1,184,109	638,926	545,183	545,142	41	100,053	1,084,056	1,172,982	11,127
1880	58,725	26.26	1,542,180	816,906	725,274	725,133	141	145,090	1,397,090	1,531,616	10,564
1890	58,725	31.29	1,837,353	978,357	858,996	858,815	181	257,472	1,579,881	1,825,216	12,137
1900	58,725	37.74	2,216,331	1,181,294	1,035,037	1,034,813	224	346,382	1,869,949	2,203,928	12,403
1910	58,725	44.43	2,609,121	1,431,802	1,177,319	1,176,987	332	538,650	2,070,471	2,593,644	15,477
1920	58,725	49.31	2,895,832	1,689,114	1,206,718	1,206,365	353	727,859	2,167,973	2,879,268	16,564
1930	58,725	49.53	2,908,506	1,837,021	1,071,485	1,071,125	360	895,492	2,013,014	2,894,203	14,303
1940	58,518	53.38	3,123,723	2,038,278	1,085,445	1,084,927	518	1,073,808	2,049,915	3,111,542	12,181
1950	58,483	58.90	3,444,578	2,380,577	1,064,001	1,062,762	1,239	1,559,447	1,885,131	3,422,280	16,400
1960	58,197	67.75	3,943,116	2,817,223	1,125,893	1,122,596	3,297	2,180,236	1,762,880	3,917,636	25,300
1970	58,073	79.03	4,589,575	3,391,242	1,198,333	1,187,149	11,184	2,768,074	1,821,501	4,556,581	32,988
1980	58,056	94.10	5,463,105	3,947,135	1,515,970	1,465,181	50,789	3,409,081	2,054,024	5,371,625	91,480
1990	57,919	111.85	6,478,216	4,600,148	1,878,068	1,746,565	131,503	4,097,339	2,380,877	6,305,090	173,126

		Population									
	Sex		Male, by age								
Year	Male	Female	0	1–4	5–9	10–14	15–19	20–29	20–24	25–29
	Aa3108	Aa3109	Aa3110	Aa3111	Aa3112	Aa3113	Aa3114	Aa3115	Aa3116	Aa3117
	Number	Number	Number	Number	Number	Number	Number	Number	Number	Number
1790	—	—	—	—	—	—	—	—	—	—
1800	—	—	—	—	—	—	—	—	—	—
1810	—	—	—	—	—	—	—	—	—	—
1820	175,171	165,814	—	—	—	—	—	—	—	—
1830	263,366	253,457	—	—	—	—	—	—	—	—
1840	351,243	340,149	—	—	—	—	—	—	—	—
1850	456,465	449,720	12,668	66,006	71,804	64,112	50,509	79,025	—	—
1860	531,945	525,341	16,831	72,544	78,876	74,598	59,493	93,041	—	—
1870	578,955	605,154	18,659	77,937	80,812	84,683	66,248	—	57,843	38,094
1880	762,981	779,199	27,067	106,007	120,077	97,971	73,370	—	77,220	58,906
1890	919,925	917,428	26,787	109,228	135,988	130,642	102,605	—	85,225	63,842
1900	1,103,201	1,113,130	33,437	129,562	157,573	141,202	116,602	—	110,546	85,330
1910	1,305,019	1,304,102	39,459	151,306	174,463	160,007	134,719	—	124,619	103,427
1920	1,444,823	1,451,009	36,768	146,305	192,496	184,453	148,830	—	127,671	108,648
1930	1,434,527	1,473,979	30,382	128,996	177,258	171,020	164,961	—	136,061	104,210
1940	1,534,758	1,588,965	30,325	127,466	160,774	164,192	161,293	—	145,888	133,937
1950	1,688,667	1,755,911	41,875	172,323	179,499	157,309	147,552	—	133,076	132,746
1960	1,925,913	2,017,203	48,597	190,184	222,936	208,317	168,006	—	135,513	122,530
1970	2,230,696	2,358,879	44,387	170,198	239,079	244,813	223,312	—	208,153	163,425
1980	2,640,445	2,822,660	45,510	166,588	228,195	239,230	272,746	—	256,138	234,385
1990	3,144,503	3,333,713	44,771	208,904	247,095	238,812	255,202	—	262,818	293,492

(continued)

TABLE Aa3097–3197 Georgia population by race, sex, age, nativity, and urban–rural residence: 1790–1990
Continued

Population

	Male, by age									
	30–39	30–34	35–39	40–49	40–44	45–49	50–59	50–54	55–59	60–69
	Aa3118	Aa3119	Aa3120	Aa3121	Aa3122	Aa3123	Aa3124	Aa3125	Aa3126	Aa3127
Year	Number	Number	Number	Number	Number	Number	Number	Number	Number	Number
1790	—	—	—	—	—	—	—	—	—	—
1800	—	—	—	—	—	—	—	—	—	—
1810	—	—	—	—	—	—	—	—	—	—
1820	—	—	—	—	—	—	—	—	—	—
1830	—	—	—	—	—	—	—	—	—	—
1840	—	—	—	—	—	—	—	—	—	—
1850	47,339	—	—	31,027	—	—	17,537	—	—	10,831
1860	57,695	—	—	37,364	—	—	21,661	—	—	13,003
1870	—	30,078	27,897	—	22,944	18,316	—	17,577	10,293	—
1880	—	44,885	35,544	—	27,310	21,423	—	22,715	12,887	—
1890	—	56,771	52,010	—	39,111	27,564	—	28,180	16,246	—
1900	—	64,285	55,752	—	48,545	37,979	—	42,315	22,649	—
1910	—	84,575	77,318	—	55,428	40,555	—	54,497	32,871	—
1920	—	86,699	91,259	—	69,020	66,753	—	61,215	35,815	—
1930	—	86,672	88,698	—	71,870	62,314	—	72,420	45,562	—
1940	—	115,351	99,922	—	83,819	75,468	—	66,738	50,747	—
1950	—	123,850	123,364	—	107,515	87,711	—	73,745	60,983	—
1960	—	123,462	124,633	—	119,313	111,528	—	94,949	75,856	—
1970	—	133,969	124,606	—	125,061	120,832	—	111,513	97,611	—
1980	—	218,987	174,635	—	141,615	128,881	—	123,677	114,405	—
1990	—	287,097	259,118	—	236,163	184,425	—	143,070	123,637	—

Population

	Male, by age							Female, by age		
	60–64	65–69	70–79	70–74	75–79	80 and older	Unknown age	0	1–4	5–9
	Aa3128	Aa3129	Aa3130	Aa3131	Aa3132	Aa3133	Aa3134	Aa3135	Aa3136	Aa3137
Year	Number	Number	Number	Number	Number	Number	Number	Number	Number	Number
1790	—	—	—	—	—	—	—	—	—	—
1800	—	—	—	—	—	—	—	—	—	—
1810	—	—	—	—	—	—	—	—	—	—
1820	—	—	—	—	—	—	—	—	—	—
1830	—	—	—	—	—	—	—	—	—	—
1840	—	—	—	—	—	—	—	—	—	—
1850	—	—	3,881	—	—	1,594	132	12,190	63,933	70,031
1860	—	—	4,779	—	—	1,800	260	16,349	71,400	77,776
1870	12,419	6,593	—	4,397	2,084	2,081	0	18,233	74,579	77,960
1880	15,434	9,632	—	6,305	3,238	2,990	—	26,311	102,200	116,678
1890	17,449	10,932	—	7,529	4,130	3,733	1,953	26,358	104,644	132,140
1900	21,671	14,020	—	9,102	5,084	4,226	3,321	32,890	129,584	155,951
1910	30,094	18,155	—	10,469	5,973	4,748	2,336	38,278	147,598	172,906
1920	35,443	23,898	—	15,043	7,613	5,221	1,673	36,202	143,954	189,877
1930	36,691	23,401	—	16,989	9,507	6,535	980	30,036	126,990	176,652
1940	41,942	37,417	—	21,227	10,120	8,132	—	29,683	125,648	158,282
1950	47,521	43,488	—	27,824	19,794	8,492	—	40,944	167,344	175,709
1960	56,986	49,542	—	34,937	22,169	16,455	—	47,954	185,166	217,262
1970	79,702	58,105	—	38,798	24,742	22,390	—	42,473	164,651	231,232
1980	97,800	80,736	—	56,629	33,178	27,110	—	43,687	159,150	218,636
1990	109,382	94,771	—	69,331	46,719	39,696	—	42,891	198,969	236,857

TABLE Aa3097–3197   Georgia population by race, sex, age, nativity, and urban–rural residence: 1790–1990
Continued

	Population									
	Female, by age									
	10–14	15–19	20–29	20–24	25–29	30–39	30–34	35–39	40–49	40–44
	Aa3138	Aa3139	Aa3140	Aa3141	Aa3142	Aa3143	Aa3144	Aa3145	Aa3146	Aa3147
Year	Number	Number	Number	Number	Number	Number	Number	Number	Number	Number
1790	—	—	—	—	—	—	—	—	—	—
1800	—	—	—	—	—	—	—	—	—	—
1810	—	—	—	—	—	—	—	—	—	—
1820	—	—	—	—	—	—	—	—	—	—
1830	—	—	—	—	—	—	—	—	—	—
1840	—	—	—	—	—	—	—	—	—	—
1850	62,603	53,328	78,404	—	—	46,140	—	—	30,505	—
1860	71,522	61,713	92,385	—	—	57,660	—	—	36,146	—
1870	81,303	69,010	—	65,074	48,111	—	37,677	33,158	—	26,988
1880	92,688	76,332	—	80,422	61,158	—	47,805	41,500	—	34,684
1890	124,019	106,582	—	86,847	66,132	—	55,397	50,256	—	40,793
1900	136,663	124,876	—	118,653	87,489	—	63,497	55,959	—	48,711
1910	155,210	145,664	—	135,521	110,823	—	84,739	74,914	—	54,216
1920	180,859	158,719	—	145,143	121,725	—	94,050	94,241	—	71,457
1930	167,840	169,875	—	152,065	118,720	—	96,727	98,261	—	79,286
1940	160,817	167,117	—	158,750	143,563	—	120,787	109,623	—	90,301
1950	153,984	144,254	—	143,117	143,524	—	131,535	130,900	—	112,125
1960	203,333	163,548	—	135,698	129,240	—	132,889	135,430	—	125,668
1970	236,111	219,259	—	208,796	167,365	—	140,026	132,328	—	135,079
1980	230,368	258,027	—	259,946	246,891	—	229,778	181,628	—	149,454
1990	227,802	241,950	—	259,816	296,460	—	297,847	272,501	—	247,916

	Population									
	Female, by age									
	45–49	50–59	50–54	55–59	60–69	60–64	65–69	70–79	70–74	75–79
	Aa3148	Aa3149	Aa3150	Aa3151	Aa3152	Aa3153	Aa3154	Aa3155	Aa3156	Aa3157
Year	Number	Number	Number	Number	Number	Number	Number	Number	Number	Number
1790	—	—	—	—	—	—	—	—	—	—
1800	—	—	—	—	—	—	—	—	—	—
1810	—	—	—	—	—	—	—	—	—	—
1820	—	—	—	—	—	—	—	—	—	—
1830	—	—	—	—	—	—	—	—	—	—
1840	—	—	—	—	—	—	—	—	—	—
1850	—	16,784	—	—	10,119	—	—	3,803	—	—
1860	—	21,175	—	—	12,369	—	—	4,644	—	—
1870	20,179	—	17,361	9,948	—	10,386	5,781	—	4,539	2,197
1880	26,888	—	23,822	13,684	—	13,560	8,318	—	6,065	3,288
1890	33,439	—	28,571	17,423	—	16,692	10,479	—	7,187	4,056
1900	40,586	—	35,992	24,107	—	21,192	13,922	—	9,785	5,202
1910	45,295	—	41,743	28,571	—	25,432	17,314	—	11,442	6,711
1920	59,096	—	44,960	30,441	—	28,682	20,371	—	14,507	8,267
1930	70,840	—	59,035	39,071	—	30,871	21,741	—	16,749	9,998
1940	81,021	—	67,506	52,026	—	42,023	37,678	—	21,505	11,745
1950	95,144	—	79,373	65,326	—	52,575	52,068	—	32,782	23,431
1960	117,869	—	101,255	85,651	—	68,682	63,602	—	46,710	31,145
1970	131,446	—	121,312	109,515	—	95,863	79,639	—	58,564	41,199
1980	137,912	—	137,534	132,502	—	118,069	108,161	—	85,348	60,585
1990	190,493	—	150,963	136,098	—	129,397	123,307	—	100,642	81,807

(continued)

TABLE Aa3097-3197   Georgia population by race, sex, age, nativity, and urban-rural residence: 1790-1990
Continued

				Population							
				White							
	Female, by age		Male	Female	Male, by age					
	80 and older	Unknown age	Male	Female	0-4	5-9	10-14	15-19	20-29	30-39
	Aa3158	Aa3159	Aa3160	Aa3161	Aa3162	Aa3163	Aa3164	Aa3165	Aa3166	Aa3167
Year	Number	Number	Number	Number	Number	Number	Number	Number	Number	Number
1790	—	—	27,147	25,739	—	—	—	—	—	—
1800	—	—	53,380	48,298	—	—	—	—	—	—
1810	—	—	75,845	69,569	—	—	—	—	—	—
1820	—	—	98,404	91,162	—	—	—	—	—	—
1830	—	—	153,288	143,518	33,027	23,709	18,584	15,186	26,844	16,156
1840	—	—	210,534	197,161	43,759	33,899	27,136	20,897	34,696	22,196
1850	1,769	111	—	—	—	—	—	—	—	—
1860	2,014	188	—	—	—	—	—	—	—	—
1870	2,670	0	—	—	—	—	—	—	—	—
1880	3,796	—	—	—	—	—	—	—	—	—
1890	4,381	2,032	—	—	—	—	—	—	—	—
1900	5,035	3,036	—	—	—	—	—	—	—	—
1910	5,917	1,808	—	—	—	—	—	—	—	—
1920	7,191	1,267	—	—	—	—	—	—	—	—
1930	8,358	864	—	—	—	—	—	—	—	—
1940	10,890	—	—	—	—	—	—	—	—	—
1950	11,776	—	—	—	—	—	—	—	—	—
1960	26,101	—	—	—	—	—	—	—	—	—
1970	44,021	—	—	—	—	—	—	—	—	—
1980	64,984	—	—	—	—	—	—	—	—	—
1990	97,997	—	—	—	—	—	—	—	—	—

				Population					
				White					
	Male, by age					Female, by age			
	40-49	50-59	60-69	70-79	80 and older	0-4	5-9	10-14	15-19	20-29
	Aa3168	Aa3169	Aa3170	Aa3171	Aa3172	Aa3173	Aa3174	Aa3175	Aa3176	Aa3177
Year	Number	Number	Number	Number	Number	Number	Number	Number	Number	Number
1790	—	—	—	—	—	—	—	—	—	—
1800	—	—	—	—	—	—	—	—	—	—
1810	—	—	—	—	—	—	—	—	—	—
1820	—	—	—	—	—	—	—	—	—	—
1830	9,542	5,674	3,083	1,120	363	30,958	22,590	17,988	16,452	24,036
1840	13,886	7,623	4,240	1,641	561	40,579	32,080	25,993	22,395	31,705
1850	—	—	—	—	—	—	—	—	—	—
1860	—	—	—	—	—	—	—	—	—	—
1870	—	—	—	—	—	—	—	—	—	—
1880	—	—	—	—	—	—	—	—	—	—
1890	—	—	—	—	—	—	—	—	—	—
1900	—	—	—	—	—	—	—	—	—	—
1910	—	—	—	—	—	—	—	—	—	—
1920	—	—	—	—	—	—	—	—	—	—
1930	—	—	—	—	—	—	—	—	—	—
1940	—	—	—	—	—	—	—	—	—	—
1950	—	—	—	—	—	—	—	—	—	—
1960	—	—	—	—	—	—	—	—	—	—
1970	—	—	—	—	—	—	—	—	—	—
1980	—	—	—	—	—	—	—	—	—	—
1990	—	—	—	—	—	—	—	—	—	—

TABLE Aa3097–3197   Georgia population by race, sex, age, nativity, and urban–rural residence: 1790–1990
Continued

	Population									
	White									
	Female, by age						Male, by age			
	30–39	40–49	50–59	60–69	70–79	80 and older	0–9	10–15	16–25	26–44
	Aa3178	Aa3179	Aa3180	Aa3181	Aa3182	Aa3183	Aa3184	Aa3185	Aa3186	Aa3187
Year	Number	Number	Number	Number	Number	Number	Number	Number	Number	Number
1790	—	—	—	—	—	—	—	—	—	—
1800	—	—	—	—	—	—	19,841	8,470	9,787	10,325
1810	—	—	—	—	—	—	28,002	11,951	14,085	14,372
1820	—	—	—	—	—	—	35,444	14,743	19,483	17,874
1830	13,974	8,427	5,089	2,664	987	353	—	—	—	—
1840	19,603	12,300	6,795	3,679	1,485	547	—	—	—	—
1850	—	—	—	—	—	—	—	—	—	—
1860	—	—	—	—	—	—	—	—	—	—
1870	—	—	—	—	—	—	—	—	—	—
1880	—	—	—	—	—	—	—	—	—	—
1890	—	—	—	—	—	—	—	—	—	—
1900	—	—	—	—	—	—	—	—	—	—
1910	—	—	—	—	—	—	—	—	—	—
1920	—	—	—	—	—	—	—	—	—	—
1930	—	—	—	—	—	—	—	—	—	—
1940	—	—	—	—	—	—	—	—	—	—
1950	—	—	—	—	—	—	—	—	—	—
1960	—	—	—	—	—	—	—	—	—	—
1970	—	—	—	—	—	—	—	—	—	—
1980	—	—	—	—	—	—	—	—	—	—
1990	—	—	—	—	—	—	—	—	—	—

	Population									
	White									
	Male, by age	Female, by age					Male, by age		Female, by age	
	45 and older	0–9	10–15	16–25	26–44	45 and older	0–15	16 and older	0–15	16 and older
	Aa3188	Aa3189	Aa3190	Aa3191	Aa3192	Aa3193	Aa3194	Aa3195	Aa3196	Aa3197
Year	Number	Number	Number	Number	Number	Number	Number	Number	Number	Number
1790	—	—	—	—	—	—	14,044	13,103	14,028	11,711
1800	4,957	18,407	7,914	9,248	8,835	3,894	—	—	—	—
1810	7,435	26,283	11,237	13,461	12,350	6,238	—	—	—	—
1820	10,860	33,177	14,937	18,642	15,365	9,041	—	—	—	—
1830	—	—	—	—	—	—	—	—	—	—
1840	—	—	—	—	—	—	—	—	—	—
1850	—	—	—	—	—	—	—	—	—	—
1860	—	—	—	—	—	—	—	—	—	—
1870	—	—	—	—	—	—	—	—	—	—
1880	—	—	—	—	—	—	—	—	—	—
1890	—	—	—	—	—	—	—	—	—	—
1900	—	—	—	—	—	—	—	—	—	—
1910	—	—	—	—	—	—	—	—	—	—
1920	—	—	—	—	—	—	—	—	—	—
1930	—	—	—	—	—	—	—	—	—	—
1940	—	—	—	—	—	—	—	—	—	—
1950	—	—	—	—	—	—	—	—	—	—
1960	—	—	—	—	—	—	—	—	—	—
1970	—	—	—	—	—	—	—	—	—	—
1980	—	—	—	—	—	—	—	—	—	—
1990	—	—	—	—	—	—	—	—	—	—

Sources
See the sources for Table Aa2244–2340.

Documentation
See the text for Table Aa2244–2340.

Georgia was one of the original thirteen states, admitted to the Union in 1788.

TABLE Aa3198–3248   Hawai'i population by race, sex, age, nativity, and urban–rural residence: 1832–1990

Contributed by Michael R. Haines

			Population									
				Race				Residence		Nativity	
	Area	Population density	Total	White	Nonwhite	Black	Other nonwhite	Urban	Rural	Native-born	Foreign-born
	Aa3198	Aa3199	Aa3200	Aa3201	Aa3202	Aa3203	Aa3204	Aa3205	Aa3206	Aa3207	Aa3208
Year	Square miles	Persons per square mile	Number	Number	Number	Number	Number	Number	Number	Number	Number
1832	6,407	20.34	130,313	—	—	—	—	—	—	—	—
1836	6,407	16.95	108,579	—	—	—	—	—	—	—	—
1850	6,407	13.14	84,165	—	—	—	—	—	—	—	—
1860	6,407	6.21	39,800	—	—	—	—	—	—	—	—
1872	6,407	8.88	56,897	—	—	—	—	—	—	—	—
1884	6,407	12.58	80,578	—	—	—	—	—	—	—	—
1890	6,407	14.05	89,990	—	—	—	—	—	—	—	—
1900	6,407	24.04	154,001	28,819	125,182	233	124,949	39,306	114,695	63,221	90,780
1910	6,407	29.95	191,874	44,048	147,826	695	147,131	58,928	132,946	98,157	93,752
1920	6,407	39.94	255,881	54,742	201,139	348	200,791	92,251	163,630	168,671	87,241
1930	6,407	57.48	368,300	80,373	287,927	563	287,364	197,937	170,363	299,799	68,537
1940	6,420	65.85	422,770	103,791	318,979	255	319,284	264,262	158,508	370,717	52,613
1950	6,406	78.02	499,794	114,793	385,001	—	—	344,869	154,925	423,174	76,620
1960	6,425	98.49	632,772	202,230	430,542	4,943	425,599	483,961	148,811	563,872	68,900
1970	6,425	119.62	768,561	298,160	470,401	7,573	462,828	638,683	129,878	692,964	75,595
1980	6,425	150.15	964,691	318,770	645,921	17,364	628,557	834,592	130,099	827,675	137,016
1990	6,423	172.53	1,108,229	369,616	738,613	27,195	711,418	986,171	122,058	945,525	162,704

			Population							
	Sex		Male, by age							
	Male	Female	0	1–4	5–9	10–14	15–19	20–24	25–29	30–34
	Aa3209	Aa3210	Aa3211	Aa3212	Aa3213	Aa3214	Aa3215	Aa3216	Aa3217	Aa3218
Year	Number	Number	Number	Number	Number	Number	Number	Number	Number	Number
1832	—	—	—	—	—	—	—	—	—	—
1836	—	—	—	—	—	—	—	—	—	—
1850	—	—	—	—	—	—	—	—	—	—
1860	—	—	—	—	—	—	—	—	—	—
1872	—	—	—	—	—	—	—	—	—	—
1884	—	—	—	—	—	—	—	—	—	—
1890	—	—	—	—	—	—	—	—	—	—
1900	106,369	47,632	1,790	5,944	5,701	4,484	6,633	15,067	20,008	15,107
1910	123,099	68,810	2,784	9,386	9,642	7,109	7,865	13,608	13,451	15,071
1920	151,146	104,766	4,415	15,081	15,477	11,263	11,546	14,820	11,639	12,927
1930	222,640	145,696	4,891	19,639	23,894	19,235	19,324	31,778	25,333	17,263
1940	245,135	178,195	4,258	16,153	21,951	24,110	26,359	32,044	27,114	21,571
1950	273,895	225,899	6,444	26,373	26,626	20,402	23,467	27,539	25,967	23,143
1960	338,173	294,599	8,658	32,608	37,175	32,679	30,622	30,403	22,411	24,177
1970	399,205	369,356	7,821	28,435	40,990	40,791	37,275	46,807	30,358	23,846
1980	494,683	470,008	8,856	31,148	37,555	38,459	45,673	59,070	48,864	42,990
1990	563,891	544,338	7,867	34,881	41,579	38,144	38,097	50,552	52,738	51,325

TABLE Aa3198–3248   Hawai'i population by race, sex, age, nativity, and urban–rural residence: 1832–1990
Continued

	Population									
	Male, by age									
	35–39	40–44	45–49	50–54	55–59	60–64	65–69	70–74	75–79	80 and older
	Aa3219	Aa3220	Aa3221	Aa3222	Aa3223	Aa3224	Aa3225	Aa3226	Aa3227	Aa3228
Year	Number	Number	Number	Number	Number	Number	Number	Number	Number	Number
1832	—	—	—	—	—	—	—	—	—	—
1836	—	—	—	—	—	—	—	—	—	—
1850	—	—	—	—	—	—	—	—	—	—
1860	—	—	—	—	—	—	—	—	—	—
1872	—	—	—	—	—	—	—	—	—	—
1884	—	—	—	—	—	—	—	—	—	—
1890	—	—	—	—	—	—	—	—	—	—
1900	11,302	7,793	4,364	2,626	1,529	1,907	851	434	225	234
1910	14,257	10,593	7,529	4,635	2,648	2,296	1,073	567	295	253
1920	11,827	11,915	10,972	7,516	4,541	3,777	1,887	796	390	278
1930	12,844	12,082	10,077	8,968	6,882	4,966	2,849	1,438	1,115 [1]	—
1940	17,969	12,963	9,648	9,422	6,853	6,058	4,472	2,295	1,792 [1]	—
1950	22,644	17,915	15,353	10,704	7,445	7,491	4,979	3,665	2,543	1,195
1960	25,167	21,443	19,567	15,876	13,103	8,572	5,527	5,021	2,734	2,430
1970	23,084	23,749	23,347	19,620	17,037	13,791	9,671	5,781	3,062	3,740
1980	32,684	23,765	21,589	23,298	23,502	18,871	15,384	10,991	6,796	5,188
1990	48,955	42,368	31,253	23,019	21,087	22,651	21,848	15,696	11,255	10,576

	Population									
	Male, by age	Female, by age								
	Unknown age	0	1–4	5–9	10–14	15–19	20–24	25–29	30–34	35–39
	Aa3229	Aa3230	Aa3231	Aa3232	Aa3233	Aa3234	Aa3235	Aa3236	Aa3237	Aa3238
Year	Number	Number	Number	Number	Number	Number	Number	Number	Number	Number
1832	—	—	—	—	—	—	—	—	—	—
1836	—	—	—	—	—	—	—	—	—	—
1850	—	—	—	—	—	—	—	—	—	—
1860	—	—	—	—	—	—	—	—	—	—
1872	—	—	—	—	—	—	—	—	—	—
1884	—	—	—	—	—	—	—	—	—	—
1890	—	—	—	—	—	—	—	—	—	—
1900	370	1,641	5,709	5,448	3,954	4,211	6,003	6,533	4,371	3,102
1910	37	2,731	9,164	9,413	6,428	5,785	6,468	6,995	6,453	5,409
1920	79	4,164	14,890	14,718	10,797	9,099	9,943	9,856	7,758	7,085
1930	62	4,682	18,968	23,225	18,807	14,166	10,989	11,338	10,211	9,407
1940	103	4,055	15,619	21,480	23,384	21,979	19,033	15,215	11,816	10,919
1950	—	6,159	25,015	25,168	19,950	20,441	22,817	23,717	19,747	14,883
1960	—	8,196	31,500	35,603	31,339	24,199	20,203	22,142	24,759	24,078
1970	—	7,337	27,218	38,846	39,021	34,568	34,748	29,101	23,787	23,601
1980	—	8,373	29,471	35,502	36,411	40,773	46,612	46,423	41,324	31,264
1990	—	7,515	32,960	39,328	35,752	34,394	40,242	47,440	49,193	46,827

Note appears at end of table

(continued)

TABLE Aa3198-3248   Hawai'i population by race, sex, age, nativity, and urban-rural residence: 1832-1990
Continued

	Population									
	Female, by age									
	40-44	45-49	50-54	55-59	60-64	65-69	70-74	75-79	80 and older	Unknown age
	Aa3239	Aa3240	Aa3241	Aa3242	Aa3243	Aa3244	Aa3245	Aa3246	Aa3247	Aa3248
Year	Number	Number	Number	Number	Number	Number	Number	Number	Number	Number
1832	—	—	—	—	—	—	—	—	—	—
1836	—	—	—	—	—	—	—	—	—	—
1850	—	—	—	—	—	—	—	—	—	—
1860	—	—	—	—	—	—	—	—	—	—
1872	—	—	—	—	—	—	—	—	—	—
1884	—	—	—	—	—	—	—	—	—	—
1890	—	—	—	—	—	—	—	—	—	—
1900	2,004	1,447	900	617	566	332	263	140	198	193
1910	3,416	2,327	1,590	956	606	431	284	178	157	19
1920	5,646	4,144	2,550	1,540	1,098	651	365	209	219	34
1930	6,674	5,560	4,472	3,061	1,859	1,009	575	652 [1]	—	41
1940	9,148	7,839	5,694	4,275	3,332	2,193	1,152	1,010 [1]	—	52
1950	10,831	9,790	8,202	6,480	4,662	3,449	2,306	1,497	785	0
1960	18,915	13,918	10,189	8,909	7,199	5,432	3,667	2,356	1,995	0
1970	25,095	22,852	18,433	13,306	9,581	7,987	6,050	3,959	3,866	0
1980	23,703	23,651	25,906	23,881	18,923	13,769	9,231	6,877	7,914	0
1990	40,189	30,710	23,793	24,288	26,077	23,736	17,373	11,439	13,082	0

[1] Ages 75 and older.

Sources

Except as noted below, see the sources for Table Aa2244-2340.

Series Aa3200. 1832-1890: *Sixteenth Census of the United States: 1940*, "Number of Inhabitants. Hawaii," p. 1209.

Series Aa3201-3204 and Aa3209-3248. 1900, *Twelfth Census of the United States: 1900*, volume 2, part 2, "Population," Table 2. 1910, *Thirteenth Census of the United States: 1910*, volume 3, "Population 1910. Reports by States," Table 10. 1920: *Fourteenth Census of the United States: 1920*, volume 2, "Population, 1920: Composition and Characteristics of the Population by States," pp. 1171-93. 1930: *Fifteenth Census of the United States: 1930*, volume 2, "Outlying Territories and Possessions," pp. 35-104. 1930-1940: *Sixteenth Census of the United States: 1940*, "Population. Characteristics of the Population. Hawaii." 1950: *U.S. Census of Population: 1950*, volume 2, "Characteristics of the Population," part 52, Tables 8-15.

Series Aa3207-3208. 1900-1910: *Thirteenth Census of the United States: 1910*, volume 3, "Population 1910. Reports by States," Table 18. 1920-1930: *Fifteenth Census of the United States: 1930*, volume 2, "Outlying Territories and Possessions," p. 48. 1940: *Sixteenth Census of the United States: 1940*, "Population. Characteristics of the Population. Hawaii," p. 5. 1950: *U.S. Census of Population: 1950*, volume 2, "Characteristics of the Population," part 52, p. 52-13.

Documentation

See the text for Table Aa2244-2340. For 1900, the population given includes the population of the outlying Pacific islands: Baker, Canton, Enderbury, Howland, Jarvis, and Johnston. Censuses prior to 1900 were taken under the direction of the Hawaiian government.

TABLE Aa3249–3299   Idaho population by race, sex, age, nativity, and urban–rural residence: 1870–1990

Contributed by Michael R. Haines

				Population								
	Area	Population density	Total		Race				Residence		Nativity	
				White	Nonwhite	Black	Other nonwhite		Urban	Rural	Native-born	Foreign-born
	Aa3249	Aa3250	Aa3251	Aa3252	Aa3253	Aa3254	Aa3255		Aa3256	Aa3257	Aa3258	Aa3259
Year	Square miles	Persons per square mile	Number	Number	Number	Number	Number		Number	Number	Number	Number
1870	83,360	0.18	14,999	10,618	4,381	60	4,321		0	14,999	7,114	7,885
1880	83,354	0.39	32,610	29,013	3,597	53	3,544		0	32,610	22,636	9,974
1890 [1]	83,354	1.06	88,548	82,018	2,367	201	2,166		0	88,548	66,929	17,456
1900	83,354	1.94	161,772	154,495	7,277	293	6,984		10,003	151,769	137,168	24,604
1910	83,354	3.91	325,594	319,221	6,373	651	5,722		69,898	255,696	283,016	42,578
1920	83,354	5.18	431,866	425,668	6,198	920	5,278		119,037	312,829	391,119	40,747
1930	83,354	5.34	445,032	438,840	6,192	668	5,524		129,507	315,525	412,748	32,284
1940	82,808	6.34	524,873	519,292	5,581	595	4,986		176,708	348,165	500,161	24,712
1950	82,769	7.11	588,637	581,395	7,242	1,050	6,192		252,549	336,088	567,595	19,845
1960	82,677	8.07	667,191	657,383	9,808	1,502	8,306		317,097	350,094	651,649	15,542
1970	82,677	8.62	712,567	698,802	13,765	2,130	11,635		385,434	327,133	699,995	12,572
1980	82,412	11.45	943,935	901,641	42,294	2,716	39,578		509,702	434,233	920,531	23,404
1990	82,751	12.17	1,006,749	950,451	56,298	3,370	52,928		578,214	428,535	977,844	28,905

			Population								
	Sex		Male, by age								
	Male	Female	0	1–4	5–9	10–14	15–19	20–24	25–29	30–34
	Aa3260	Aa3261	Aa3262	Aa3263	Aa3264	Aa3265	Aa3266	Aa3267	Aa3268	Aa3269
Year	Number	Number	Number	Number	Number	Number	Number	Number	Number	Number
1870	12,184	2,815	111	431	372	310	393	1,254	2,171	2,299
1880	21,818	10,792	463	1,710	1,735	1,425	1,307	2,068	2,380	2,432
1890 [1]	51,290	33,095	1,123	4,520	5,371	4,213	3,656	4,965	5,401	5,258
1900	93,367	68,405	2,393	8,642	10,332	8,599	7,848	8,136	7,987	8,091
1910	185,546	140,048	4,293	16,251	18,219	16,533	15,951	18,551	18,648	16,288
1920	233,919	197,947	5,276	22,613	26,082	23,781	19,633	18,179	18,887	18,155
1930	237,347	207,685	4,602	18,728	25,379	25,484	22,839	19,442	16,113	15,164
1940	276,579	248,294	5,304	21,327	24,367	25,366	26,387	24,666	23,447	20,679
1950	303,237	285,400	7,271	29,643	31,342	26,929	22,462	20,473	21,871	22,153
1960	338,421	328,770	8,552	33,399	40,364	35,891	27,766	19,507	18,406	19,944
1970	355,750	356,817	6,857	25,807	37,065	40,798	37,633	26,238	22,216	19,207
1980	471,155	472,780	10,418	37,655	42,392	40,501	44,000	43,487	41,803	37,079
1990	500,956	505,793	7,354	33,728	46,183	46,328	40,845	34,083	36,247	40,257

				Population						
				Male, by age						
	35–39	40–44	45–49	50–54	55–59	60–64	65–69	70–74	75–79	80 and older
	Aa3270	Aa3271	Aa3272	Aa3273	Aa3274	Aa3275	Aa3276	Aa3277	Aa3278	Aa3279
Year	Number	Number	Number	Number	Number	Number	Number	Number	Number	Number
1870	2,102	1,427	619	419	116	99	31	14	2	4
1880	2,224	2,010	1,508	1,328	604	372	140	75	27	10
1890 [1]	4,194	3,376	2,484	2,503	1,623	1,236	607	298	125	63
1900	8,018	6,428	4,492	4,175	2,743	2,159	1,532	829	367	208
1910	13,991	12,144	9,927	9,046	5,453	3,902	2,506	1,549	873	572
1920	17,976	14,940	12,971	11,033	8,664	6,634	4,171	2,493	1,360	863
1930	15,998	15,583	14,383	12,415	9,663	7,850	6,005	4,083	2,071	1,412
1940	17,274	15,821	15,500	15,072	12,754	10,420	7,475	5,298	3,196	2,226
1950	21,807	19,730	16,325	14,517	13,054	12,001	9,780	6,816	4,500	2,563
1960	20,705	20,774	20,119	17,625	14,387	11,678	10,559	8,539	5,766	4,440
1970	18,100	18,968	19,158	19,167	17,786	15,324	11,165	8,224	5,999	6,038
1980	29,156	23,720	20,467	20,061	19,934	18,444	16,118	11,819	7,271	6,830
1990	40,123	35,254	27,547	22,309	19,292	18,626	17,854	14,461	10,692	9,773

Note appears at end of table

(continued)

TABLE Aa3249-3299   Idaho population by race, sex, age, nativity, and urban-rural residence: 1870-1990   *Continued*

	Population									
Male, by age	Female, by age									
Unknown age	0	1–4	5–9	10–14	15–19	20–24	25–29	30–34	35–39
Aa3280	Aa3281	Aa3282	Aa3283	Aa3284	Aa3285	Aa3286	Aa3287	Aa3288	Aa3289
Year	Number	Number	Number	Number	Number	Number	Number	Number	Number	Number
1870	10	110	423	363	290	240	324	276	280	201
1880	—	432	1,579	1,686	1,350	1,012	1,017	878	724	626
1890 [1]	274	1,093	4,426	5,131	4,043	3,262	3,216	2,789	2,337	1,791
1900	388	2,260	8,265	10,043	8,383	6,817	6,132	5,506	5,056	4,197
1910	849	3,995	15,905	17,913	15,369	14,319	13,446	12,407	10,719	9,279
1920	208	5,294	21,353	25,197	22,816	18,686	17,142	16,695	15,250	13,520
1930	133	4,357	18,127	24,691	24,356	21,726	18,016	14,915	13,895	14,113
1940	—	5,108	20,414	23,710	24,558	25,479	23,316	20,900	18,081	15,573
1950	—	7,135	28,584	30,237	25,528	22,363	20,909	22,232	21,893	20,356
1960	—	8,079	32,142	38,292	34,730	27,422	19,639	18,805	19,939	21,305
1970	—	6,594	24,582	35,896	38,699	36,432	27,088	22,144	19,402	18,689
1980	—	9,923	35,535	40,342	38,717	43,982	42,747	40,658	35,862	28,488
1990	—	6,849	32,262	43,860	43,858	39,593	31,709	35,820	40,476	39,771

	Population									
	Female, by age									
40–44	45–49	50–54	55–59	60–64	65–69	70–74	75–79	80 and older	Unknown age
Aa3290	Aa3291	Aa3292	Aa3293	Aa3294	Aa3295	Aa3296	Aa3297	Aa3298	Aa3299
Year	Number	Number	Number	Number	Number	Number	Number	Number	Number	Number
1870	115	67	51	33	19	12	8	1	1	1
1880	452	364	239	154	110	94	47	19	9	—
1890 [1]	1,428	1,086	890	588	427	257	160	80	36	55
1900	3,322	2,439	1,884	1,368	1,042	688	400	229	172	202
1910	7,452	5,741	4,576	3,009	2,222	1,551	966	549	374	256
1920	10,937	8,876	7,127	5,097	3,874	2,609	1,596	1,019	728	131
1930	12,830	10,847	8,828	6,756	5,408	3,725	2,546	1,413	1,055	81
1940	14,060	13,703	12,325	9,914	7,648	5,708	3,856	2,141	1,800	—
1950	17,304	14,381	12,704	11,727	10,169	8,239	5,530	3,820	2,289	—
1960	20,755	18,751	15,878	12,945	11,134	10,288	8,331	5,639	4,696	—
1970	19,176	20,000	19,529	17,373	14,863	11,479	9,368	7,354	8,149	—
1980	22,962	20,506	20,415	21,248	19,753	16,922	13,433	9,393	11,894	—
1990	34,020	27,000	22,051	20,115	19,924	20,132	17,308	13,837	17,208	—

[1] Includes 4,163 American Indians not counted in the general enumeration; see text for Table Aa2244-2340.

Sources

See the sources for Table Aa2244-2340.

Documentation

See the text for Table Aa2244-2340.

Idaho became a territory in 1863 and a state in 1890. In 1860, it had been part of the Washington and Utah Territories.

TABLE Aa3300–3396   Illinois population by race, sex, age, nativity, and urban–rural residence: 1800–1990

Contributed by Michael R. Haines

				Population								
					Race				Residence		Nativity	
	Area	Population density	Total	White	Nonwhite	Black	Other nonwhite	Urban	Rural	Native-born	Foreign-born
	Aa3300	Aa3301	Aa3302	Aa3303	Aa3304	Aa3305	Aa3306	Aa3307	Aa3308	Aa3309	Aa3310
Year	Square miles	Persons per square mile	Number	Number	Number	Number	Number	Number	Number	Number	Number
1800	—	—	2,458	2,175	183	183	—	0	2,458	—	—
1810	192,381	0.06	12,282	11,501	781	781	—	0	12,282	—	—
1820	56,002	0.99	55,211	53,788	1,423	1,374	49	0	55,211	—	—
1830	56,002	2.81	157,445	155,061	2,384	2,384	—	0	157,445	—	—
1840	56,002	8.50	476,183	472,254	3,929	3,929	—	9,607	466,576	—	—
1850	56,002	15.20	851,470	846,034	5,436	5,436	—	64,427	787,043	739,578	111,892
1860	56,002	30.57	1,711,951	1,704,291	7,660	7,628	32	245,545	1,466,406	1,387,308	324,643
1870	56,002	45.35	2,539,891	2,511,096	28,795	28,762	33	596,042	1,943,849	2,024,693	515,198
1880	56,002	54.96	3,077,871	3,031,151	46,720	46,368	352	940,504	2,137,367	2,494,295	583,576
1890 [1]	56,002	68.33	3,826,352	3,768,472	57,879	57,028	851	1,719,172	2,107,180	2,984,004	842,347
1900	56,002	86.10	4,821,550	4,734,873	86,677	85,078	1,599	2,616,368	2,205,182	3,854,803	966,747
1910	56,043	100.61	5,638,591	5,526,962	111,629	109,049	2,580	3,479,935	2,158,656	4,433,277	1,205,314
1920	56,043	115.72	6,485,280	6,299,333	185,947	182,274	3,673	4,403,677	2,081,603	5,274,696	1,210,584
1930	56,043	136.16	7,630,654	7,295,267	335,387	328,972	6,415	5,635,727	1,994,927	6,388,207	1,242,447
1940	55,947	141.16	7,897,241	7,504,202	393,039	387,446	5,593	5,809,650	2,087,591	6,924,846	972,395
1950	55,935	155.76	8,712,176	8,046,058	666,118	645,980	20,138	6,759,271	1,952,905	7,894,310	786,290
1960	55,875	180.42	10,081,158	9,010,252	1,070,906	1,037,470	33,436	8,140,315	1,940,843	9,395,555	686,009
1970	55,748	199.36	11,113,976	9,600,381	1,513,595	1,425,674	87,921	9,251,930	1,862,046	10,480,552	628,898
1980	55,645	205.35	11,426,518	9,233,327	2,193,191	1,675,398	517,793	9,518,039	1,908,479	10,602,822	823,696
1990	55,593	205.61	11,430,602	8,952,978	2,477,624	1,694,273	783,351	9,668,552	1,762,050	10,478,330	952,272

			Population									
	Sex		Male, by age									
	Male	Female	0	1–4	5–9	10–14	15–19	20–29	20–24	25–29	30–39
	Aa3311	Aa3312	Aa3313	Aa3314	Aa3315	Aa3316	Aa3317	Aa3318	Aa3319	Aa3320	Aa3321
Year	Number	Number	Number	Number	Number	Number	Number	Number	Number	Number	Number
1800	—	—	—	—	—	—	—	—	—	—	—
1810	—	—	—	—	—	—	—	—	—	—	—
1820	30,186	24,976	—	—	—	—	—	—	—	—	—
1830	83,219	74,226	—	—	—	—	—	—	—	—	—
1840	257,279	218,904	—	—	—	—	—	—	—	—	—
1850	448,321	403,149	13,621	58,714	66,768	58,871	47,244	80,016	—	—	57,531
1860	902,761	809,190	29,394	119,445	117,064	103,176	92,222	174,538	—	—	124,273
1870	1,316,537	1,223,354	40,181	157,930	171,709	164,254	130,862	—	123,536	106,473	—
1880	1,586,523	1,491,348	44,654	166,449	197,289	183,610	163,310	—	164,582	129,832	—
1890 [1]	1,972,308	1,854,043	50,382	188,754	226,013	202,051	194,461	—	202,045	182,555	—
1900	2,472,782	2,348,768	57,788	219,463	272,728	248,639	228,377	—	226,294	222,735	—
1910	2,911,674	2,726,917	63,255	239,447	275,742	262,007	270,700	—	293,502	279,166	—
1920	3,304,833	3,180,447	62,218	269,683	325,427	300,012	268,722	—	270,631	298,663	—
1930	3,873,457	3,757,197	60,345	252,682	346,414	344,669	336,166	—	331,377	325,151	—
1940	3,957,149	3,940,092	52,706	225,587	276,962	313,031	338,236	—	335,406	332,536	—
1950	4,319,251	4,392,925	84,648	344,964	348,021	287,417	272,554	—	310,549	347,749	—
1960	4,952,866	5,128,292	117,427	456,375	509,598	441,068	341,856	—	272,555	299,670	—
1970	5,391,836	5,722,140	96,106	381,107	559,898	576,422	511,016	—	392,724	364,828	—
1980	5,537,537	5,888,981	93,846	336,623	434,098	469,422	543,725	—	533,097	488,484	—
1990	5,552,233	5,878,369	76,769	356,606	428,589	407,375	423,448	—	436,863	491,782	—

Note appears at end of table

(continued)

TABLE Aa3300–3396   Illinois population by race, sex, age, nativity, and urban–rural residence: 1800–1990
Continued

Population

	Male, by age										
	30–34	35–39	40–49	40–44	45–49	50–59	50–54	55–59	60–69	60–64	65–69
	Aa3322	Aa3323	Aa3324	Aa3325	Aa3326	Aa3327	Aa3328	Aa3329	Aa3330	Aa3331	Aa3332
Year	Number	Number	Number	Number	Number	Number	Number	Number	Number	Number	Number
1800	—	—	—	—	—	—	—	—	—	—	—
1810	—	—	—	—	—	—	—	—	—	—	—
1820	—	—	—	—	—	—	—	—	—	—	—
1830	—	—	—	—	—	—	—	—	—	—	—
1840	—	—	—	—	—	—	—	—	—	—	—
1850	—	—	34,605	—	—	19,290	—	—	8,033	—	—
1860	—	—	73,326	—	—	42,475	—	—	19,512	—	—
1870	90,634	84,371	—	68,581	52,679	—	47,641	27,567	—	22,156	13,065
1880	108,720	97,739	—	81,039	66,927	—	63,045	41,175	—	33,090	21,024
1890 [1]	161,771	126,635	—	101,493	84,432	—	75,153	54,545	—	46,168	31,195
1900	208,831	188,322	—	157,456	115,087	—	95,345	71,028	—	56,361	42,328
1910	238,535	218,277	—	189,494	158,154	—	132,820	88,926	—	67,919	51,904
1920	285,266	272,165	—	216,170	196,848	—	165,294	123,337	—	98,276	62,621
1930	312,062	327,280	—	293,617	249,517	—	201,208	154,910	—	125,791	92,468
1940	315,030	304,148	—	291,236	286,763	—	257,129	201,280	—	153,565	115,735
1950	335,440	330,586	—	307,593	284,307	—	264,319	240,567	—	203,911	152,903
1960	335,973	348,110	—	329,891	316,558	—	282,215	253,476	—	208,999	173,751
1970	312,004	299,016	—	323,123	325,967	—	301,223	271,987	—	225,050	167,974
1980	427,350	342,300	—	289,497	272,240	—	291,318	283,082	—	236,521	189,786
1990	500,547	448,388	—	389,404	310,205	—	256,972	232,646	—	229,466	203,026

Population

	Male, by age					Female, by age					
	70–79	70–74	75–79	80 and older	Unknown age	0	1–4	5–9	10–14	15–19	20–29
	Aa3333	Aa3334	Aa3335	Aa3336	Aa3337	Aa3338	Aa3339	Aa3340	Aa3341	Aa3342	Aa3343
Year	Number	Number	Number	Number	Number	Number	Number	Number	Number	Number	Number
1800	—	—	—	—	—	—	—	—	—	—	—
1810	—	—	—	—	—	—	—	—	—	—	—
1820	—	—	—	—	—	—	—	—	—	—	—
1830	—	—	—	—	—	—	—	—	—	—	—
1840	—	—	—	—	—	—	—	—	—	—	—
1850	2,554	—	—	584	490	13,060	56,765	63,884	54,644	46,031	71,112
1860	5,832	—	—	1,304	200	28,568	115,782	113,991	97,391	90,271	150,256
1870	—	8,315	3,825	2,624	134	39,149	153,543	167,773	157,885	130,116	—
1880	—	12,915	6,893	4,230	—	43,205	162,006	194,953	179,341	165,827	—
1890 [1]	—	21,179	11,472	7,888	4,116	48,141	183,611	221,779	198,625	198,364	—
1900	—	28,457	16,150	10,216	7,177	56,604	216,180	271,042	246,241	231,791	—
1910	—	34,809	21,431	14,544	11,042	61,904	233,383	271,126	258,948	274,191	—
1920	—	41,124	25,813	17,454	5,109	60,833	262,339	319,837	295,318	271,830	—
1930	—	62,081	31,836	21,607	4,276	58,245	244,554	335,368	338,520	339,887	—
1940	—	80,727	46,143	30,929	—	51,223	217,446	265,797	305,249	334,760	—
1950	—	99,041	69,410	35,272	—	81,356	331,874	336,326	277,930	269,726	—
1960	—	129,549	78,387	57,408	—	114,092	442,352	493,204	427,302	344,707	—
1970	—	122,985	84,179	76,227	—	92,261	367,476	538,694	558,266	500,046	—
1980	—	134,564	88,236	83,348	—	90,179	321,593	415,515	449,963	523,270	—
1990	—	152,295	108,053	99,799	—	73,533	341,233	408,030	389,093	394,553	—

Note appears at end of table

TABLE Aa3300–3396   Illinois population by race, sex, age, nativity, and urban–rural residence: 1800–1990
Continued

	Population										
	Female, by age										
	20–24	25–29	30–39	30–34	35–39	40–49	40–44	45–49	50–59	50–54	55–59
	Aa3344	Aa3345	Aa3346	Aa3347	Aa3348	Aa3349	Aa3350	Aa3351	Aa3352	Aa3353	Aa3354
Year	Number	Number	Number	Number	Number	Number	Number	Number	Number	Number	Number
1800	—	—	—	—	—	—	—	—	—	—	—
1810	—	—	—	—	—	—	—	—	—	—	—
1820	—	—	—	—	—	—	—	—	—	—	—
1830	—	—	—	—	—	—	—	—	—	—	—
1840	—	—	—	—	—	—	—	—	—	—	—
1850	—	—	45,525	—	—	27,881	—	—	14,833	—	—
1860	—	—	99,162	—	—	58,169	—	—	33,132	—	—
1870	118,497	99,552	—	82,709	72,377	—	58,187	43,262	—	34,454	22,451
1880	156,439	116,204	—	97,327	88,233	—	73,032	60,520	—	50,529	34,643
1890 [1]	198,599	167,888	—	138,312	107,540	—	89,903	77,103	—	66,100	48,703
1900	228,688	213,746	—	188,065	164,053	—	131,444	100,519	—	84,061	65,568
1910	283,666	251,754	—	211,768	194,627	—	165,365	138,744	—	112,959	79,415
1920	290,485	303,929	—	267,132	239,402	—	195,625	171,109	—	146,248	112,606
1930	343,695	327,999	—	309,736	311,714	—	264,020	220,856	—	181,894	144,002
1940	352,436	351,020	—	328,146	308,769	—	288,549	274,810	—	236,010	184,231
1950	328,895	364,782	—	356,063	347,703	—	315,093	285,427	—	264,296	238,542
1960	309,193	309,222	—	343,529	361,054	—	346,380	327,074	—	289,805	260,280
1970	450,920	382,592	—	324,440	309,481	—	337,312	343,843	—	325,521	296,206
1980	539,911	497,135	—	441,894	358,299	—	303,599	286,889	—	310,994	310,078
1990	423,224	492,308	—	508,548	458,541	—	403,811	326,282	—	273,268	252,935

	Population								White	
	Female, by age									
	60–69	60–64	65–69	70–79	70–74	75–79	80 and older	Unknown age	Male	Female
	Aa3355	Aa3356	Aa3357	Aa3358	Aa3359	Aa3360	Aa3361	Aa3362	Aa3363	Aa3364
Year	Number	Number	Number	Number	Number	Number	Number	Number	Number	Number
1800	—	—	—	—	—	—	—	—	1,285	890
1810	—	—	—	—	—	—	—	—	6,380	5,121
1820	—	—	—	—	—	—	—	—	29,401	24,387
1830	—	—	—	—	—	—	—	—	82,048	73,013
1840	—	—	—	—	—	—	—	—	255,235	217,019
1850	6,515	—	—	2,084	—	—	510	305	—	—
1860	16,044	—	—	5,066	—	—	1,204	154	—	—
1870	—	18,720	11,392	—	7,359	3,470	2,398	60	—	—
1880	—	27,592	18,447	—	11,835	6,625	4,590	—	—	—
1890 [1]	—	41,627	28,486	—	18,772	10,660	8,055	1,775	—	—
1900	—	53,161	40,141	—	26,762	15,764	10,821	4,117	—	—
1910	—	64,548	49,711	—	33,881	21,275	15,819	3,833	—	—
1920	—	89,304	60,283	—	42,082	27,289	20,981	3,815	—	—
1930	—	120,519	90,728	—	61,485	34,379	26,489	3,107	—	—
1940	—	147,217	119,390	—	84,554	51,860	38,625	—	—	—
1950	—	197,237	158,320	—	108,677	82,542	48,136	—	—	—
1960	—	224,270	199,694	—	152,429	98,592	85,113	—	—	—
1970	—	252,793	209,885	—	171,442	129,315	131,647	—	—	—
1980	—	273,711	242,978	—	194,155	148,465	180,353	—	—	—
1990	—	259,638	252,726	—	213,893	176,227	230,526	—	—	—

Note appears at end of table   (continued)

TABLE Aa3300–3396   Illinois population by race, sex, age, nativity, and urban–rural residence: 1800–1990
Continued

	Population										
	White										
	Male, by age										
	0–4	5–9	10–14	15–19	20–29	30–39	40–49	50–59	60–69	70–79	80 and older
	Aa3365	Aa3366	Aa3367	Aa3368	Aa3369	Aa3370	Aa3371	Aa3372	Aa3373	Aa3374	Aa3375
Year	Number	Number	Number	Number	Number	Number	Number	Number	Number	Number	Number
1800	—	—	—	—	—	—	—	—	—	—	—
1810	—	—	—	—	—	—	—	—	—	—	—
1820	—	—	—	—	—	—	—	—	—	—	—
1830	18,834	12,753	10,024	7,770	14,706	8,825	4,627	2,853	1,172	384	100
1840	48,363	37,278	31,062	24,876	52,580	31,428	15,809	8,755	3,660	1,119	305
1850	—	—	—	—	—	—	—	—	—	—	—
1860	—	—	—	—	—	—	—	—	—	—	—
1870	—	—	—	—	—	—	—	—	—	—	—
1880	—	—	—	—	—	—	—	—	—	—	—
1890 [1]	—	—	—	—	—	—	—	—	—	—	—
1900	—	—	—	—	—	—	—	—	—	—	—
1910	—	—	—	—	—	—	—	—	—	—	—
1920	—	—	—	—	—	—	—	—	—	—	—
1930	—	—	—	—	—	—	—	—	—	—	—
1940	—	—	—	—	—	—	—	—	—	—	—
1950	—	—	—	—	—	—	—	—	—	—	—
1960	—	—	—	—	—	—	—	—	—	—	—
1970	—	—	—	—	—	—	—	—	—	—	—
1980	—	—	—	—	—	—	—	—	—	—	—
1990	—	—	—	—	—	—	—	—	—	—	—

	Population										
	White										
	Female, by age										
	0–4	5–9	10–14	15–19	20–29	30–39	40–49	50–59	60–69	70–79	80 and older
	Aa3376	Aa3377	Aa3378	Aa3379	Aa3380	Aa3381	Aa3382	Aa3383	Aa3384	Aa3385	Aa3386
Year	Number	Number	Number	Number	Number	Number	Number	Number	Number	Number	Number
1800	—	—	—	—	—	—	—	—	—	—	—
1810	—	—	—	—	—	—	—	—	—	—	—
1820	—	—	—	—	—	—	—	—	—	—	—
1830	17,429	12,000	9,246	8,053	12,461	6,850	3,750	2,047	812	273	92
1840	44,775	34,913	28,496	24,078	38,823	22,676	12,712	6,514	2,941	866	225
1850	—	—	—	—	—	—	—	—	—	—	—
1860	—	—	—	—	—	—	—	—	—	—	—
1870	—	—	—	—	—	—	—	—	—	—	—
1880	—	—	—	—	—	—	—	—	—	—	—
1890 [1]	—	—	—	—	—	—	—	—	—	—	—
1900	—	—	—	—	—	—	—	—	—	—	—
1910	—	—	—	—	—	—	—	—	—	—	—
1920	—	—	—	—	—	—	—	—	—	—	—
1930	—	—	—	—	—	—	—	—	—	—	—
1940	—	—	—	—	—	—	—	—	—	—	—
1950	—	—	—	—	—	—	—	—	—	—	—
1960	—	—	—	—	—	—	—	—	—	—	—
1970	—	—	—	—	—	—	—	—	—	—	—
1980	—	—	—	—	—	—	—	—	—	—	—
1990	—	—	—	—	—	—	—	—	—	—	—

Note appears at end of table

TABLE Aa3300–3396 Illinois population by race, sex, age, nativity, and urban–rural residence: 1800–1990
Continued

	Population									
	White									
	Male, by age					Female, by age				
	0–9	10–15	16–25	26–44	45 and older	0–9	10–15	16–25	26–44	45 and older
	Aa3387	Aa3388	Aa3389	Aa3390	Aa3391	Aa3392	Aa3393	Aa3394	Aa3395	Aa3396
Year	Number	Number	Number	Number	Number	Number	Number	Number	Number	Number
1800	418	152	231	345	139	353	117	190	179	51
1810	2,266	945	1,274	1,339	556	2,019	791	1,053	894	364
1820	10,554	4,227	6,224	5,755	2,641	9,558	4,018	4,842	4,166	1,803
1830	—	—	—	—	—	—	—	—	—	—
1840	—	—	—	—	—	—	—	—	—	—
1850	—	—	—	—	—	—	—	—	—	—
1860	—	—	—	—	—	—	—	—	—	—
1870	—	—	—	—	—	—	—	—	—	—
1880	—	—	—	—	—	—	—	—	—	—
1890 [1]	—	—	—	—	—	—	—	—	—	—
1900	—	—	—	—	—	—	—	—	—	—
1910	—	—	—	—	—	—	—	—	—	—
1920	—	—	—	—	—	—	—	—	—	—
1930	—	—	—	—	—	—	—	—	—	—
1940	—	—	—	—	—	—	—	—	—	—
1950	—	—	—	—	—	—	—	—	—	—
1960	—	—	—	—	—	—	—	—	—	—
1970	—	—	—	—	—	—	—	—	—	—
1980	—	—	—	—	—	—	—	—	—	—
1990	—	—	—	—	—	—	—	—	—	—

[1] Includes one American Indian not counted in the general enumeration; see text for Table Aa2244–2340.

Sources

See the sources for Table Aa2244–2340.

Documentation

See the text for Table Aa2244–2340.

Illinois was part of the Northwest Territory and became a separate territory only in 1809. The population in 1800 represents those counties (St. Clair, Randolph, and Jersey) later placed in Illinois in 1809. It became a state in 1818.

TABLE Aa3397–3493   Indiana population by race, sex, age, nativity, and urban–rural residence: 1800–1990

Contributed by Michael R. Haines

			Population							
					Race				Residence	
	Area	Population density	Total	White	Nonwhite	Black	Other nonwhite		Urban	Rural
	Aa3397	Aa3398	Aa3399	Aa3400	Aa3401	Aa3402	Aa3403		Aa3404	Aa3405
Year	Square miles	Persons per square mile	Number	Number	Number	Number	Number		Number	Number
1800	252,084	0.01	2,632	2,402	115	115	—		0	2,632
1810	42,933	0.57	24,520	23,890	630	630	—		0	24,520
1820	35,885	4.10	147,178	145,758	1,420	1,420	0		0	147,178
1830	35,885	9.56	343,031	339,399	3,632	3,632	—		0	343,031
1840	35,885	19.11	685,866	678,698	7,168	7,168	—		10,716	675,150
1850	35,885	27.54	988,416	977,154	11,262	11,262	—		44,632	943,784
1860	35,885	37.63	1,350,428	1,338,710	11,718	11,428	290		115,904	1,234,524
1870	35,885	46.83	1,680,637	1,655,837	24,800	24,560	240		247,657	1,432,980
1880	35,885	55.13	1,978,301	1,938,798	39,503	39,228	275		386,211	1,592,090
1890	35,885	61.10	2,192,404	2,146,736	45,668	45,215	453		590,039	1,602,365
1900	35,885	70.13	2,516,462	2,458,502	57,960	57,505	455		862,689	1,653,773
1910	36,045	74.93	2,700,876	2,639,961	60,915	60,320	595		1,143,835	1,557,041
1920	36,045	81.30	2,930,390	2,849,071	81,319	80,810	509		1,482,855	1,447,535
1930	36,045	89.85	3,238,503	3,125,778	112,725	111,982	743		1,795,892	1,442,611
1940	36,205	94.68	3,427,796	3,305,323	122,473	121,916	557		1,887,712	1,540,084
1950	36,205	108.67	3,934,224	3,758,512	175,712	174,168	1,544		2,357,196	1,577,028
1960	36,189	128.84	4,662,498	4,388,554	273,944	269,275	4,669		2,910,149	1,752,349
1970	36,097	143.88	5,193,669	4,820,324	373,345	357,464	15,881		3,372,060	1,821,609
1980	35,932	152.79	5,490,224	5,004,394	485,830	414,785	71,045		3,525,298	1,964,926
1990	35,870	154.56	5,544,159	5,020,700	523,459	432,092	91,367		3,598,099	1,946,060

	Population								
	Nativity		Sex		Male, by age				
	Native-born	Foreign-born	Male	Female	0	1–4	5–9	10–14	15–19
	Aa3406	Aa3407	Aa3408	Aa3409	Aa3410	Aa3411	Aa3412	Aa3413	Aa3414
Year	Number	Number	Number	Number	Number	Number	Number	Number	Number
1800	—	—	—	—	—	—	—	—	—
1810	—	—	—	—	—	—	—	—	—
1820	—	—	77,401	69,777	—	—	—	—	—
1830	—	—	177,742	165,289	—	—	—	—	—
1840	—	—	356,505	329,361	—	—	—	—	—
1850	932,844	55,572	511,893	476,523	16,505	69,066	80,430	69,063	56,104
1860	1,232,144	118,284	699,260	651,168	22,741	92,468	98,862	87,438	78,178
1870	1,539,163	141,474	857,994	822,643	25,919	102,700	116,543	113,762	93,476
1880	1,834,123	144,178	1,010,361	967,940	27,966	102,333	127,657	123,468	108,887
1890	2,046,199	146,205	1,118,347	1,074,057	27,041	102,665	133,273	123,170	116,358
1900	2,374,341	142,121	1,285,404	1,231,058	29,726	109,806	139,117	133,640	129,171
1910	2,541,213	159,663	1,383,295	1,317,581	28,345	111,746	134,437	129,203	131,143
1920	2,779,062	151,328	1,489,074	1,441,316	27,958	118,253	144,141	138,823	127,308
1930	3,095,504	142,999	1,640,061	1,598,442	27,690	117,138	159,595	150,104	142,886
1940	3,316,804	110,992	1,725,201	1,702,595	26,659	110,198	132,433	148,564	157,341
1950	3,818,365	99,275	1,958,516	1,975,708	42,491	172,881	175,111	147,094	133,134
1960	4,569,249	93,202	2,298,738	2,363,760	55,454	221,257	254,310	223,176	172,072
1970	5,110,467	83,198	2,531,170	2,662,499	46,856	185,623	268,759	278,959	253,127
1980	5,388,422	101,802	2,665,825	2,824,399	45,834	169,121	221,919	232,327	266,689
1990	5,449,896	94,263	2,688,281	2,855,878	36,447	167,537	210,824	208,811	217,475

TABLE Aa3397–3493   Indiana population by race, sex, age, nativity, and urban–rural residence: 1800–1990
Continued

	Population								
	Male, by age								
	20–29	20–24	25–29	30–39	30–34	35–39	40–49	40–44	45–49
	Aa3415	Aa3416	Aa3417	Aa3418	Aa3419	Aa3420	Aa3421	Aa3422	Aa3423
Year	Number	Number	Number	Number	Number	Number	Number	Number	Number
1800	—	—	—	—	—	—	—	—	—
1810	—	—	—	—	—	—	—	—	—
1820	—	—	—	—	—	—	—	—	—
1830	—	—	—	—	—	—	—	—	—
1840	—	—	—	—	—	—	—	—	—
1850	87,688	—	—	58,006	—	—	35,613	—	—
1860	123,097	—	—	83,428	—	—	52,429	—	—
1870	—	79,815	63,384	—	52,112	48,679	—	39,244	30,970
1880	—	106,077	83,284	—	66,452	58,770	—	46,979	38,345
1890	—	109,302	89,511	—	82,506	71,145	—	57,262	47,936
1900	—	115,676	106,305	—	96,208	86,165	—	76,939	63,091
1910	—	126,802	116,539	—	100,880	97,614	—	85,738	73,509
1920	—	120,277	119,524	—	111,150	110,313	—	91,413	88,365
1930	—	132,598	122,541	—	116,637	119,596	—	108,611	99,154
1940	—	142,979	137,108	—	127,465	120,562	—	112,446	108,384
1950	—	147,543	156,375	—	143,314	139,573	—	127,433	115,072
1960	—	136,052	138,988	—	152,671	155,975	—	142,722	134,614
1970	—	195,629	171,449	—	144,834	136,324	—	148,231	147,852
1980	—	256,924	229,755	—	202,401	163,201	—	138,100	129,714
1990	—	209,226	221,289	—	230,266	214,974	—	189,268	153,232

	Population								
	Male, by age								
	50–59	50–54	55–59	60–69	60–64	65–69	70–79	70–74	75–79
	Aa3424	Aa3425	Aa3426	Aa3427	Aa3428	Aa3429	Aa3430	Aa3431	Aa3432
Year	Number	Number	Number	Number	Number	Number	Number	Number	Number
1800	—	—	—	—	—	—	—	—	—
1810	—	—	—	—	—	—	—	—	—
1820	—	—	—	—	—	—	—	—	—
1830	—	—	—	—	—	—	—	—	—
1840	—	—	—	—	—	—	—	—	—
1850	23,884	—	—	10,561	—	—	3,729	—	—
1860	36,124	—	—	17,023	—	—	5,899	—	—
1870	—	32,931	20,655	—	15,660	10,284	—	6,492	3,135
1880	—	39,651	27,191	—	21,471	14,830	—	9,063	4,877
1890	—	45,938	33,878	—	28,080	20,213	—	14,014	8,044
1900	—	56,672	44,410	—	34,206	26,296	—	17,639	10,237
1910	—	71,298	52,950	—	43,337	33,520	—	22,048	13,170
1920	—	78,942	63,090	—	53,977	39,829	—	26,558	16,539
1930	—	87,936	74,202	—	62,413	48,283	—	35,360	20,423
1940	—	101,260	86,625	—	70,131	57,882	—	41,990	24,950
1950	—	106,496	96,554	—	83,138	68,509	—	48,136	36,377
1960	—	118,383	104,391	—	87,408	74,698	—	57,574	38,334
1970	—	132,652	118,207	—	98,179	74,348	—	55,881	38,238
1980	—	136,906	131,999	—	108,167	88,209	—	63,503	41,533
1990	—	126,878	114,684	—	113,169	100,717	—	73,502	51,786

(continued)

TABLE Aa3397–3493 Indiana population by race, sex, age, nativity, and urban–rural residence: 1800–1990
Continued

				Population						
	Male, by age		Female, by age							
	80 and older	Unknown age	0	1–4	5–9	10–14	15–19	20–29	20–24
	Aa3433	Aa3434	Aa3435	Aa3436	Aa3437	Aa3438	Aa3439	Aa3440	Aa3441
Year	Number	Number	Number	Number	Number	Number	Number	Number	Number
1800	—	—	—	—	—	—	—	—	—
1810	—	—	—	—	—	—	—	—	—
1820	—	—	—	—	—	—	—	—	—
1830	—	—	—	—	—	—	—	—	—
1840	—	—	—	—	—	—	—	—	—
1850	1,056	188	15,791	66,350	77,284	65,212	55,821	81,330	—
1860	1,447	126	22,286	89,437	96,158	82,975	77,331	113,947	—
1870	2,222	11	25,142	99,545	112,852	109,705	94,143	—	79,975
1880	3,060	—	27,387	99,947	124,916	119,069	110,208	—	103,464
1890	5,278	2,733	25,770	98,965	130,662	119,906	117,470	—	108,642
1900	6,594	3,506	28,267	107,000	134,331	131,182	128,239	—	115,959
1910	8,696	2,320	27,753	107,680	130,510	126,365	128,006	—	124,486
1920	10,484	2,130	27,398	115,586	140,840	135,577	126,896	—	122,848
1930	13,577	1,317	26,783	113,419	155,322	146,954	141,828	—	133,503
1940	18,224	—	25,509	106,169	128,919	144,097	154,571	—	145,953
1950	19,285	—	40,689	165,997	167,755	141,379	134,900	—	153,418
1960	30,659	—	53,356	212,883	245,083	216,049	173,285	—	147,364
1970	36,022	—	45,204	177,993	260,265	266,944	249,113	—	219,095
1980	39,523	—	43,371	160,438	211,134	222,501	262,939	—	261,737
1990	48,196	—	34,536	160,136	199,639	197,702	210,104	—	208,409

				Population					
	Female, by age								
	25–29	30–39	30–34	35–39	40–49	40–44	45–49	50–59	50–54
	Aa3442	Aa3443	Aa3444	Aa3445	Aa3446	Aa3447	Aa3448	Aa3449	Aa3450
Year	Number	Number	Number	Number	Number	Number	Number	Number	Number
1800	—	—	—	—	—	—	—	—	—
1810	—	—	—	—	—	—	—	—	—
1820	—	—	—	—	—	—	—	—	—
1830	—	—	—	—	—	—	—	—	—
1840	—	—	—	—	—	—	—	—	—
1850	—	50,413	—	—	32,381	—	—	18,718	—
1860	—	72,694	—	—	46,712	—	—	28,510	—
1870	64,460	—	51,702	45,546	—	36,563	29,090	—	24,206
1880	77,644	—	61,513	56,741	—	45,703	38,550	—	32,307
1890	88,134	—	77,087	64,860	—	53,914	47,789	—	40,116
1900	103,201	—	91,450	81,172	—	71,036	58,552	—	49,286
1910	112,955	—	97,306	91,246	—	79,870	69,884	—	62,244
1920	119,194	—	109,517	104,618	—	87,970	80,599	—	70,932
1930	123,231	—	116,213	115,385	—	104,490	95,625	—	82,102
1940	138,196	—	127,912	119,877	—	111,783	106,347	—	96,421
1950	163,346	—	149,655	140,439	—	127,475	115,440	—	106,287
1960	144,649	—	157,573	163,248	—	148,048	135,675	—	120,022
1970	174,413	—	148,775	143,141	—	154,703	156,684	—	141,669
1980	233,096	—	209,156	168,835	—	143,447	137,098	—	146,394
1990	226,787	—	236,767	218,989	—	195,930	157,856	—	132,825

TABLE Aa3397–3493   Indiana population by race, sex, age, nativity, and urban–rural residence: 1800–1990
Continued

	Population								
	Female, by age								
Year	55–59	60–69	60–64	65–69	70–79	70–74	75–79	80 and older	Unknown age
	Aa3451	Aa3452	Aa3453	Aa3454	Aa3455	Aa3456	Aa3457	Aa3458	Aa3459
	Number	Number	Number	Number	Number	Number	Number	Number	Number
1800	—	—	—	—	—	—	—	—	—
1810	—	—	—	—	—	—	—	—	—
1820	—	—	—	—	—	—	—	—	—
1830	—	—	—	—	—	—	—	—	—
1840	—	—	—	—	—	—	—	—	—
1850	—	8,970	—	—	3,143	—	—	964	146
1860	—	14,542	—	—	5,096	—	—	1,349	131
1870	16,771	—	13,486	8,743	—	5,683	2,915	2,108	8
1880	23,136	—	18,427	12,860	—	8,216	4,777	3,075	—
1890	30,559	—	25,078	18,109	—	12,453	7,147	5,396	2,000
1900	40,750	—	31,746	24,804	—	16,120	9,574	6,597	1,792
1910	47,663	—	38,386	30,681	—	20,071	12,563	8,725	1,187
1920	58,240	—	49,116	36,430	—	25,576	16,520	11,759	1,700
1930	69,104	—	58,387	46,078	—	33,787	20,241	15,038	952
1940	83,528	—	68,323	57,016	—	41,426	26,159	20,389	—
1950	96,371	—	83,838	72,955	—	51,424	39,965	24,375	—
1960	107,858	—	94,413	84,689	—	68,722	48,334	42,509	—
1970	125,775	—	109,405	92,145	—	76,349	57,775	63,051	—
1980	146,022	—	125,615	109,596	—	89,151	68,886	84,983	—
1990	125,008	—	129,195	125,218	—	102,604	82,954	111,219	—

	Population								
	White								
			Male, by age						
Year	Male	Female	0–4	5–9	10–14	15–19	20–29	30–39	40–49
	Aa3460	Aa3461	Aa3462	Aa3463	Aa3464	Aa3465	Aa3466	Aa3467	Aa3468
	Number	Number	Number	Number	Number	Number	Number	Number	Number
1800	1,289	1,113	—	—	—	—	—	—	—
1810	12,570	11,320	—	—	—	—	—	—	—
1820	76,649	69,109	—	—	—	—	—	—	—
1830	175,885	163,514	39,780	28,692	22,872	17,653	28,153	17,904	10,306
1840	352,773	325,925	70,468	57,457	46,129	36,599	60,002	37,565	21,678
1850	—	—	—	—	—	—	—	—	—
1860	—	—	—	—	—	—	—	—	—
1870	—	—	—	—	—	—	—	—	—
1880	—	—	—	—	—	—	—	—	—
1890	—	—	—	—	—	—	—	—	—
1900	—	—	—	—	—	—	—	—	—
1910	—	—	—	—	—	—	—	—	—
1920	—	—	—	—	—	—	—	—	—
1930	—	—	—	—	—	—	—	—	—
1940	—	—	—	—	—	—	—	—	—
1950	—	—	—	—	—	—	—	—	—
1960	—	—	—	—	—	—	—	—	—
1970	—	—	—	—	—	—	—	—	—
1980	—	—	—	—	—	—	—	—	—
1990	—	—	—	—	—	—	—	—	—

(continued)

TABLE Aa3397–3493   Indiana population by race, sex, age, nativity, and urban–rural residence: 1800–1990
Continued

	Population								
	White								
	Male, by age				Female, by age				
	50–59	60–69	70–79	80 and older	0–4	5–9	10–14	15–19	20–29
	Aa3469	Aa3470	Aa3471	Aa3472	Aa3473	Aa3474	Aa3475	Aa3476	Aa3477
Year	Number	Number	Number	Number	Number	Number	Number	Number	Number
1800	—	—	—	—	—	—	—	—	—
1810	—	—	—	—	—	—	—	—	—
1820	—	—	—	—	—	—	—	—	—
1830	6,004	3,160	1,059	302	37,505	27,313	21,072	18,087	26,702
1840	13,789	6,195	2,258	633	66,397	53,805	42,890	36,904	55,176
1850	—	—	—	—	—	—	—	—	—
1860	—	—	—	—	—	—	—	—	—
1870	—	—	—	—	—	—	—	—	—
1880	—	—	—	—	—	—	—	—	—
1890	—	—	—	—	—	—	—	—	—
1900	—	—	—	—	—	—	—	—	—
1910	—	—	—	—	—	—	—	—	—
1920	—	—	—	—	—	—	—	—	—
1930	—	—	—	—	—	—	—	—	—
1940	—	—	—	—	—	—	—	—	—
1950	—	—	—	—	—	—	—	—	—
1960	—	—	—	—	—	—	—	—	—
1970	—	—	—	—	—	—	—	—	—
1980	—	—	—	—	—	—	—	—	—
1990	—	—	—	—	—	—	—	—	—

	Population								
	White								
	Female, by age						Male, by age		
	30–39	40–49	50–59	60–69	70–79	80 and older	0–9	10–15	16–25
	Aa3478	Aa3479	Aa3480	Aa3481	Aa3482	Aa3483	Aa3484	Aa3485	Aa3486
Year	Number	Number	Number	Number	Number	Number	Number	Number	Number
1800	—	—	—	—	—	—	436	195	235
1810	—	—	—	—	—	—	4,923	1,922	2,284
1820	—	—	—	—	—	—	29,629	11,454	14,428
1830	15,703	9,028	4,808	2,275	780	241	—	—	—
1840	32,708	19,967	10,759	5,035	1,780	504	—	—	—
1850	—	—	—	—	—	—	—	—	—
1860	—	—	—	—	—	—	—	—	—
1870	—	—	—	—	—	—	—	—	—
1880	—	—	—	—	—	—	—	—	—
1890	—	—	—	—	—	—	—	—	—
1900	—	—	—	—	—	—	—	—	—
1910	—	—	—	—	—	—	—	—	—
1920	—	—	—	—	—	—	—	—	—
1930	—	—	—	—	—	—	—	—	—
1940	—	—	—	—	—	—	—	—	—
1950	—	—	—	—	—	—	—	—	—
1960	—	—	—	—	—	—	—	—	—
1970	—	—	—	—	—	—	—	—	—
1980	—	—	—	—	—	—	—	—	—
1990	—	—	—	—	—	—	—	—	—

TABLE Aa3397–3493   Indiana population by race, sex, age, nativity, and urban–rural residence: 1800–1990
Continued

	Population						
	White						
	Male, by age		Female, by age				
	26–44	45 and older	0–9	10–15	16–25	26–44	45 and older
	Aa3487	Aa3488	Aa3489	Aa3490	Aa3491	Aa3492	Aa3493
Year	Number	Number	Number	Number	Number	Number	Number
1800	300	123	438	163	234	214	64
1810	2,316	1,125	4,555	1,863	2,228	1,880	794
1820	14,072	7,066	27,684	10,707	13,635	12,009	5,074
1830	—	—	—	—	—	—	—
1840	—	—	—	—	—	—	—
1850	—	—	—	—	—	—	—
1860	—	—	—	—	—	—	—
1870	—	—	—	—	—	—	—
1880	—	—	—	—	—	—	—
1890	—	—	—	—	—	—	—
1900	—	—	—	—	—	—	—
1910	—	—	—	—	—	—	—
1920	—	—	—	—	—	—	—
1930	—	—	—	—	—	—	—
1940	—	—	—	—	—	—	—
1950	—	—	—	—	—	—	—
1960	—	—	—	—	—	—	—
1970	—	—	—	—	—	—	—
1980	—	—	—	—	—	—	—
1990	—	—	—	—	—	—	—

Sources
See the sources for Table Aa2244–2340.

Documentation
Indiana was part of the Northwest Territory and became a separate territory in 1800. It included, however, the territory that would later become Illinois, Wisconsin, and part of Michigan. The population in 1800 represents Knox County of the Indiana Territory, as well as Brown and Crawford Counties, which later became part of the Wisconsin Territory. The population in 1810 represents the Indiana Territory as given in the census. Indiana became a state in 1816.

TABLE Aa3494–3580   Iowa population by race, sex, age, nativity, and urban–rural residence: 1840–1990

Contributed by Michael R. Haines

			Population						
				Race				Residence	
	Area	Population density	Total	White	Nonwhite	Black	Other nonwhite	Urban	Rural
	Aa3494	Aa3495	Aa3496	Aa3497	Aa3498	Aa3499	Aa3500	Aa3501	Aa3502
Year	Square miles	Persons per square mile	Number	Number	Number	Number	Number	Number	Number
1840	191,656	0.22	43,112	42,924	188	188	—	0	43,112
1850	55,586	3.46	192,214	191,881	333	333	—	9,730	182,484
1860	55,586	12.14	674,913	673,779	1,134	1,069	65	60,028	614,885
1870	55,586	21.48	1,194,020	1,188,207	5,813	5,762	51	156,327	1,037,693
1880	55,586	29.23	1,624,615	1,614,600	10,015	9,516	499	247,427	1,377,188
1890 [1]	55,586	34.40	1,912,297	1,901,086	10,810	10,685	125	405,764	1,506,533
1900	55,586	40.15	2,231,853	2,218,667	13,186	12,693	493	572,386	1,659,467
1910	55,586	40.02	2,224,771	2,209,191	15,580	14,973	607	680,054	1,544,717
1920	55,586	43.25	2,404,021	2,384,181	19,840	19,005	835	875,495	1,528,526
1930	55,586	44.45	2,470,939	2,452,677	18,262	17,380	882	979,292	1,491,647
1940	55,986	45.34	2,538,268	2,520,691	17,577	16,694	883	1,084,231	1,454,037
1950	56,045	46.77	2,621,073	2,599,546	21,527	19,692	1,835	1,250,938	1,370,135
1960	56,043	49.20	2,757,537	2,728,709	28,828	25,354	3,474	1,462,512	1,295,025
1970	55,941	50.49	2,824,376	2,782,762	41,614	32,596	9,018	1,616,405	1,207,971
1980	55,965	52.06	2,913,808	2,839,225	74,583	41,700	32,883	1,708,232	1,205,576
1990	55,875	49.70	2,776,755	2,683,090	93,665	48,090	45,575	1,683,065	1,093,690

Note appears at end of table   (continued)

TABLE Aa3494–3580   Iowa population by race, sex, age, nativity, and urban–rural residence: 1840–1990   Continued

	Population								
	Nativity		Sex		Male, by age				
	Native-born	Foreign-born	Male	Female	0	1–4	5–9	10–14	15–19
	Aa3503	Aa3504	Aa3505	Aa3506	Aa3507	Aa3508	Aa3509	Aa3510	Aa3511
Year	Number	Number	Number	Number	Number	Number	Number	Number	Number
1840	—	—	24,355	18,757	—	—	—	—	—
1850	171,245	20,969	101,052	91,162	3,144	14,320	15,893	13,189	9,979
1860	568,836	106,077	354,493	320,420	12,585	50,943	49,870	41,094	35,056
1870	989,328	204,692	625,917	568,103	19,651	77,049	84,153	79,474	62,745
1880	1,362,965	261,650	848,136	776,479	24,533	92,532	107,396	99,993	88,481
1890 [1]	1,587,827	324,069	994,453	917,443	24,363	94,719	120,237	111,138	103,839
1900	1,925,933	305,920	1,156,849	1,075,004	27,900	105,721	129,316	121,662	114,876
1910	1,951,006	273,765	1,148,171	1,076,600	24,444	95,147	115,852	112,269	114,048
1920	2,178,027	225,994	1,229,392	1,174,629	23,874	103,600	121,558	114,953	107,374
1930	2,302,689	168,250	1,255,101	1,215,838	21,413	90,887	123,347	119,628	112,944
1940	2,420,903	117,365	1,280,494	1,257,774	20,457	85,333	101,507	110,385	117,166
1950	2,527,570	83,970	1,310,283	1,310,790	29,107	114,507	115,814	101,899	91,514
1960	2,701,259	56,278	1,359,047	1,398,490	31,889	124,877	149,086	132,287	100,914
1970	2,784,159	40,217	1,372,867	1,451,509	24,270	95,176	142,939	149,838	137,513
1980	2,866,149	47,659	1,416,390	1,497,418	24,736	88,569	107,877	118,841	140,188
1990	2,733,439	43,316	1,344,802	1,431,953	17,441	81,313	107,301	104,787	101,398

	Population								
	Male, by age								
	20–29	20–24	25–29	30–39	30–34	35–39	40–49	40–44	45–49
	Aa3512	Aa3513	Aa3514	Aa3515	Aa3516	Aa3517	Aa3518	Aa3519	Aa3520
Year	Number	Number	Number	Number	Number	Number	Number	Number	Number
1840	—	—	—	—	—	—	—	—	—
1850	16,737	—	—	13,637	—	—	7,798	—	—
1860	60,314	—	—	48,428	—	—	29,613	—	—
1870	—	58,452	48,510	—	40,049	37,857	—	31,060	25,602
1880	—	87,078	67,125	—	55,565	48,237	—	38,573	38,694
1890 [1]	—	98,538	81,452	—	72,230	58,425	—	46,806	45,023
1900	—	107,564	96,550	—	85,993	76,074	—	65,481	55,716
1910	—	108,172	94,593	—	82,199	77,393	—	66,980	62,544
1920	—	104,241	104,501	—	92,414	87,064	—	70,864	70,221
1930	—	100,005	89,205	—	87,317	90,556	—	80,196	74,753
1940	—	104,864	96,584	—	89,700	84,400	—	82,281	82,758
1950	—	93,886	96,100	—	89,454	86,810	—	81,524	75,625
1960	—	73,845	74,129	—	81,952	83,664	—	81,081	78,065
1970	—	95,553	82,954	—	72,614	68,957	—	76,491	77,170
1980	—	135,749	123,366	—	103,613	79,979	—	69,655	65,675
1990	—	99,442	102,258	—	110,293	106,553	—	91,436	72,161

Note appears at end of table

TABLE Aa3494–3580   Iowa population by race, sex, age, nativity, and urban–rural residence: 1840–1990 *Continued*

	Population										
	Male, by age										
	50–59	50–54	55–59	60–69	60–64	65–69	70–79	70–74	75–79	80 and older	Unknown age
	Aa3521	Aa3522	Aa3523	Aa3524	Aa3525	Aa3526	Aa3527	Aa3528	Aa3529	Aa3530	Aa3531
Year	Number	Number	Number	Number	Number	Number	Number	Number	Number	Number	Number
1840	—	—	—	—	—	—	—	—	—	—	—
1850	4,121	—	—	1,632	—	—	463	—	—	112	27
1860	16,416	—	—	7,616	—	—	2,097	—	—	401	60
1870	—	23,536	13,882	—	10,376	6,461	—	4,010	1,878	1,154	18
1880	—	31,910	23,631	—	18,730	11,971	—	7,141	3,959	2,587	—
1890 [1]	—	37,356	30,119	—	25,669	18,611	—	12,908	7,005	4,497	1,518
1900	—	44,283	36,297	—	29,238	23,546	—	16,389	10,194	6,696	3,353
1910	—	54,184	40,347	—	31,905	25,892	—	18,490	12,298	8,884	2,530
1920	—	60,996	49,033	—	42,197	30,268	—	20,698	13,581	10,091	1,864
1930	—	65,137	56,146	—	48,177	37,915	—	28,343	16,492	11,983	657
1940	—	74,698	63,181	—	53,333	44,472	—	33,300	20,297	15,778	—
1950	—	73,271	69,815	—	60,251	49,196	—	36,621	28,360	16,529	—
1960	—	72,170	65,904	—	59,943	54,355	—	42,479	28,299	24,108	—
1970	—	74,091	68,197	—	60,339	48,603	—	39,844	29,590	28,728	—
1980	—	71,343	69,954	—	62,177	53,196	—	41,052	28,875	31,545	—
1990	—	62,556	58,589	—	60,405	55,900	—	44,744	33,255	34,970	—

	Population								
	Female, by age								
	0	1–4	5–9	10–14	15–19	20–29	20–24	25–29	30–39
	Aa3532	Aa3533	Aa3534	Aa3535	Aa3536	Aa3537	Aa3538	Aa3539	Aa3540
Year	Number	Number	Number	Number	Number	Number	Number	Number	Number
1840	—	—	—	—	—	—	—	—	—
1850	2,955	13,871	15,123	12,157	10,151	15,683	—	—	10,468
1860	12,274	49,104	47,615	38,865	34,961	56,119	—	—	38,344
1870	19,324	74,677	81,207	75,589	59,927	—	53,371	44,252	—
1880	23,492	89,553	105,468	96,306	86,428	—	78,525	57,743	—
1890 [1]	23,692	90,738	116,839	107,043	100,980	—	93,348	73,329	—
1900	26,868	102,933	127,326	117,887	112,911	—	103,952	89,225	—
1910	23,746	92,726	112,570	110,308	110,962	—	103,232	89,400	—
1920	23,292	100,121	118,421	112,848	107,607	—	106,641	100,931	—
1930	20,687	87,290	119,616	116,192	110,598	—	101,162	91,152	—
1940	19,573	81,754	98,350	106,491	114,820	—	106,281	97,094	—
1950	27,425	109,230	110,560	97,326	92,654	—	95,902	96,743	—
1960	30,650	119,798	142,733	126,532	102,026	—	81,490	77,675	—
1970	22,822	90,944	137,162	143,602	135,962	—	108,138	84,551	—
1980	23,573	84,750	103,164	112,859	137,445	—	136,275	119,834	—
1990	16,860	77,589	102,037	99,430	98,018	—	96,977	104,358	—

Note appears at end of table   (continued)

TABLE Aa3494–3580   Iowa population by race, sex, age, nativity, and urban–rural residence: 1840–1990 *Continued*

					Population			
					Female, by age			
	30–34	35–39	40–49	40–44	45–49	50–59	50–54	55–59	60–69
	Aa3541	Aa3542	Aa3543	Aa3544	Aa3545	Aa3546	Aa3547	Aa3548	Aa3549
Year	Number	Number	Number	Number	Number	Number	Number	Number	Number
1840	—	—	—	—	—	—	—	—	—
1850	—	—	5,980	—	—	3,031	—	—	1,266
1860	—	—	22,649	—	—	12,556	—	—	5,813
1870	36,303	32,166	—	25,959	20,137	—	15,785	10,279	—
1880	48,858	44,071	—	35,929	30,956	—	25,411	18,322	—
1890 [1]	63,432	50,348	—	43,874	38,783	—	32,664	25,725	—
1900	76,543	66,474	—	57,643	45,300	—	38,572	32,495	—
1910	77,512	70,542	—	61,640	53,044	—	46,379	34,293	—
1920	87,488	80,964	—	69,386	61,597	—	53,920	43,552	—
1930	87,612	87,305	—	77,439	69,850	—	61,228	51,450	—
1940	89,151	84,911	—	82,153	79,458	—	70,969	61,080	—
1950	91,512	87,369	—	80,622	75,999	—	73,932	69,232	—
1960	83,100	86,529	—	83,831	79,327	—	72,941	69,014	—
1970	74,649	72,984	—	78,464	80,956	—	78,635	72,352	—
1980	102,341	81,267	—	71,796	69,845	—	74,559	75,900	—
1990	111,710	105,567	—	91,765	73,891	—	65,820	63,746	—

					Population				White	
										Male, by age
				Female, by age				Male	Female	0–4
	60–64	65–69	70–79	70–74	75–79	80 and older	Unknown age			
	Aa3550	Aa3551	Aa3552	Aa3553	Aa3554	Aa3555	Aa3556	Aa3557	Aa3558	Aa3559
Year	Number	Number	Number	Number	Number	Number	Number	Number	Number	Number
1840	—	—	—	—	—	—	—	24,256	18,668	4,380
1850	—	—	371	—	—	79	27	—	—	—
1860	—	—	1,730	—	—	352	38	—	—	—
1870	8,226	5,096	—	3,233	1,548	1,014	10	—	—	—
1880	14,347	9,501	—	6,038	3,265	2,266	—	—	—	—
1890 [1]	21,168	15,217	—	9,928	5,660	4,127	548	—	—	—
1900	25,916	20,616	—	13,945	8,705	5,825	1,868	—	—	—
1910	29,189	23,894	—	16,396	11,073	8,473	1,221	—	—	—
1920	36,534	26,404	—	19,498	13,324	10,528	1,573	—	—	—
1930	44,166	35,028	—	25,890	15,596	12,992	585	—	—	—
1940	51,769	42,847	—	32,644	21,013	17,416	—	—	—	—
1950	59,992	51,613	—	39,019	31,313	20,347	—	—	—	—
1960	64,400	60,005	—	48,829	35,410	34,200	—	—	—	—
1970	66,760	59,098	—	53,016	42,513	48,901	—	—	—	—
1980	70,894	64,709	—	55,897	46,229	66,081	—	—	—	—
1990	66,948	66,554	—	59,763	51,231	79,689	—	—	—	—

Note appears at end of table

TABLE Aa3494–3580   Iowa population by race, sex, age, nativity, and urban–rural residence: 1840–1990   *Continued*

	Population									
	White									
	Male, by age									
	5–9	10–14	15–19	20–29	30–39	40–49	50–59	60–69	70–79	80 and older
	Aa3560	Aa3561	Aa3562	Aa3563	Aa3564	Aa3565	Aa3566	Aa3567	Aa3568	Aa3569
Year	Number	Number	Number	Number	Number	Number	Number	Number	Number	Number
1840	3,138	2,475	2,179	6,207	3,310	1,512	698	272	73	12
1850	—	—	—	—	—	—	—	—	—	—
1860	—	—	—	—	—	—	—	—	—	—
1870	—	—	—	—	—	—	—	—	—	—
1880	—	—	—	—	—	—	—	—	—	—
1890 [1]	—	—	—	—	—	—	—	—	—	—
1900	—	—	—	—	—	—	—	—	—	—
1910	—	—	—	—	—	—	—	—	—	—
1920	—	—	—	—	—	—	—	—	—	—
1930	—	—	—	—	—	—	—	—	—	—
1940	—	—	—	—	—	—	—	—	—	—
1950	—	—	—	—	—	—	—	—	—	—
1960	—	—	—	—	—	—	—	—	—	—
1970	—	—	—	—	—	—	—	—	—	—
1980	—	—	—	—	—	—	—	—	—	—
1990	—	—	—	—	—	—	—	—	—	—

	Population										
	White										
	Female, by age										
	0–4	5–9	10–14	15–19	20–29	30–39	40–49	50–59	60–69	70–79	80 and older
	Aa3570	Aa3571	Aa3572	Aa3573	Aa3574	Aa3575	Aa3576	Aa3577	Aa3578	Aa3579	Aa3580
Year	Number	Number	Number	Number	Number	Number	Number	Number	Number	Number	Number
1840	4,082	2,962	2,188	2,064	3,789	1,865	979	494	187	51	7
1850	—	—	—	—	—	—	—	—	—	—	—
1860	—	—	—	—	—	—	—	—	—	—	—
1870	—	—	—	—	—	—	—	—	—	—	—
1880	—	—	—	—	—	—	—	—	—	—	—
1890 [1]	—	—	—	—	—	—	—	—	—	—	—
1900	—	—	—	—	—	—	—	—	—	—	—
1910	—	—	—	—	—	—	—	—	—	—	—
1920	—	—	—	—	—	—	—	—	—	—	—
1930	—	—	—	—	—	—	—	—	—	—	—
1940	—	—	—	—	—	—	—	—	—	—	—
1950	—	—	—	—	—	—	—	—	—	—	—
1960	—	—	—	—	—	—	—	—	—	—	—
1970	—	—	—	—	—	—	—	—	—	—	—
1980	—	—	—	—	—	—	—	—	—	—	—
1990	—	—	—	—	—	—	—	—	—	—	—

[1] Includes 401 American Indians and other people not counted in the general enumeration; see text for Table Aa2244–2340.

Sources

See the sources for Table Aa2244–2340.

Documentation

See the text for Table Aa2244–2340.

Iowa became a territory in 1838 and a state in 1846.

TABLE Aa3581–3643   Kansas population by race, sex, age, nativity, and urban–rural residence: 1860–1990

Contributed by Michael R. Haines

		Population										
			Race				Residence		Nativity	
	Area	Population density	Total	White	Nonwhite	Black	Other nonwhite	Urban	Rural	Native-born	Foreign-born
	Aa3581	Aa3582	Aa3583	Aa3584	Aa3585	Aa3586	Aa3587	Aa3588	Aa3589	Aa3590	Aa3591
Year	Square miles	Persons per square mile	Number	Number	Number	Number	Number	Number	Number	Number	Number
1860	81,774	1.31	107,206	106,390	816	627	189	10,045	97,161	94,515	12,691
1870	81,774	4.46	364,399	346,377	18,022	17,108	914	51,870	312,529	316,007	48,392
1880	81,774	12.18	996,096	952,155	43,941	43,107	834	104,956	891,140	886,010	110,086
1890 [1]	81,774	17.46	1,428,108	1,376,553	50,543	49,710	833	269,539	1,158,569	1,279,258	147,838
1900	81,774	17.98	1,470,495	1,416,319	54,176	52,003	2,173	329,696	1,140,799	1,343,810	126,685
1910	81,774	20.68	1,690,949	1,634,352	56,597	54,030	2,567	492,312	1,198,637	1,555,499	135,450
1920	81,774	21.64	1,769,257	1,708,906	60,351	57,925	2,426	616,485	1,152,772	1,658,290	110,967
1930	81,774	23.00	1,880,999	1,811,997	69,002	66,344	2,658	729,834	1,151,165	1,800,102	80,897
1940	82,113	21.93	1,801,028	1,734,496	66,532	65,138	1,394	753,941	1,047,087	1,749,398	51,630
1950	82,108	23.20	1,905,299	1,828,961	76,338	73,158	3,180	993,220	912,079	1,860,145	38,085
1960	82,056	26.55	2,178,611	2,078,666	99,945	91,445	8,500	1,328,741	849,870	2,145,350	33,268
1970	81,787	27.47	2,246,578	2,122,068	124,510	106,977	17,533	1,484,870	761,708	2,218,736	27,842
1980	81,778	28.90	2,363,679	2,168,221	195,458	126,127	69,331	1,575,899	787,780	2,315,788	47,891
1990	81,823	30.28	2,477,574	2,231,986	245,588	143,076	102,512	1,712,564	765,010	2,414,734	62,840

			Population									
	Sex		Male, by age									
	Male	Female	0	1–4	5–9	10–14	15–19	20–29	20–24	25–29	30–39
	Aa3592	Aa3593	Aa3594	Aa3595	Aa3596	Aa3597	Aa3598	Aa3599	Aa3600	Aa3601	Aa3602
Year	Number	Number	Number	Number	Number	Number	Number	Number	Number	Number	Number
1860	59,178	48,028	1,813	7,367	7,561	6,192	5,024	14,255	—	—	9,291
1870	202,224	162,175	6,507	23,693	23,872	21,504	17,258	—	24,593	22,081	—
1880	536,667	459,429	16,555	60,616	71,348	62,714	49,547	—	54,118	46,023	—
1890 [1]	752,112	674,984	19,931	74,700	94,465	87,311	78,896	—	69,463	58,440	—
1900	768,716	701,779	18,062	69,189	87,500	85,413	79,951	—	71,823	60,947	—
1910	885,912	805,037	19,566	77,404	89,758	85,169	87,235	—	87,617	76,077	—
1920	909,221	860,036	18,323	76,811	93,590	90,367	80,941	—	76,740	73,059	—
1930	961,291	919,708	16,788	70,433	96,822	92,134	87,971	—	81,183	69,771	—
1940	906,340	894,688	13,485	57,205	73,011	80,158	85,272	—	71,540	66,673	—
1950	953,534	951,765	19,967	82,303	82,606	70,206	69,246	—	70,307	74,220	—
1960	1,081,377	1,097,234	25,122	100,292	116,380	101,038	79,458	—	67,079	65,311	—
1970	1,101,573	1,145,005	18,482	70,877	108,291	116,059	109,720	—	97,263	70,078	—
1980	1,156,941	1,206,738	20,521	72,463	86,823	89,670	111,484	—	119,895	103,213	—
1990	1,214,645	1,262,929	17,001	79,836	100,504	92,409	88,466	—	93,256	101,772	—

Note appears at end of table

TABLE Aa3581–3643   Kansas population by race, sex, age, nativity, and urban–rural residence: 1860–1990   *Continued*

Population

Male, by age

Year	30–34	35–39	40–49	40–44	45–49	50–59	50–54	55–59	60–69	60–64	65–69
	Aa3603	Aa3604	Aa3605	Aa3606	Aa3607	Aa3608	Aa3609	Aa3610	Aa3611	Aa3612	Aa3613
	Number	Number	Number	Number	Number	Number	Number	Number	Number	Number	Number
1860	—	—	4,551	—	—	2,133	—	—	754	—	—
1870	17,003	14,380	—	9,980	7,487	—	5,706	3,366	—	2,387	1,263
1880	39,959	35,470	—	26,814	25,154	—	18,020	11,794	—	8,747	5,031
1890 [1]	54,148	45,071	—	37,433	38,911	—	30,206	22,299	—	16,850	10,766
1900	51,756	46,953	—	42,033	37,096	—	32,611	27,650	—	21,175	15,937
1910	64,174	58,568	—	48,225	43,319	—	40,672	30,440	—	25,550	21,638
1920	65,945	63,897	—	53,906	50,345	—	42,889	33,894	—	30,558	21,548
1930	66,389	67,620	—	61,681	55,581	—	50,573	41,996	—	33,866	26,650
1940	65,405	60,969	—	58,653	57,407	—	52,750	45,408	—	38,659	31,947
1950	67,000	64,844	—	61,247	55,278	—	52,231	48,118	—	42,342	35,462
1960	69,587	72,146	—	64,554	60,987	—	56,235	50,059	—	43,976	38,699
1970	58,448	57,839	—	62,080	63,279	—	57,531	53,046	—	47,544	37,474
1980	86,831	67,276	—	56,367	54,817	—	58,057	57,852	—	49,421	42,230
1990	106,272	99,030	—	83,474	63,799	—	52,345	49,887	—	49,909	46,434

Population

	Male, by age					Female, by age				
Year	70–79	70–74	75–79	80 and older	Unknown age	0	1–4	5–9	10–14	15–19
	Aa3614	Aa3615	Aa3616	Aa3617	Aa3618	Aa3619	Aa3620	Aa3621	Aa3622	Aa3623
	Number	Number	Number	Number	Number	Number	Number	Number	Number	Number
1860	145	—	—	27	65	1,786	7,284	7,085	5,709	5,172
1870	—	679	292	164	9	6,428	22,818	23,030	20,249	16,340
1880	—	2,715	1,344	698	—	15,992	58,541	68,747	57,750	46,763
1890 [1]	—	6,838	3,355	2,014	1,015	18,635	72,265	91,885	82,904	76,704
1900	—	9,974	5,304	3,293	2,049	17,767	67,104	84,840	82,864	77,628
1910	—	14,028	8,445	5,206	2,821	19,365	75,184	88,110	83,140	83,268
1920	—	16,246	11,329	7,148	1,685	17,971	74,157	91,680	88,944	81,750
1930	—	20,166	11,812	9,459	396	16,131	67,742	93,521	88,900	86,602
1940	—	22,671	13,966	11,161	—	13,154	54,466	70,404	77,582	83,518
1950	—	26,545	20,076	11,536	—	18,815	78,797	79,071	67,384	67,249
1960	—	30,913	20,987	18,554	—	24,529	96,179	111,779	96,993	77,912
1970	—	30,123	21,891	21,548	—	17,861	67,829	104,440	111,139	107,492
1980	—	33,338	22,630	24,053	—	19,293	68,600	82,192	85,693	106,237
1990	—	35,390	26,586	28,275	—	16,115	75,438	95,477	87,064	83,710

Population

Female, by age

Year	20–29	20–24	25–29	30–39	30–34	35–39	40–49	40–44	45–49	50–59
	Aa3624	Aa3625	Aa3626	Aa3627	Aa3628	Aa3629	Aa3630	Aa3631	Aa3632	Aa3633
	Number	Number	Number	Number	Number	Number	Number	Number	Number	Number
1860	10,325	—	—	5,762	—	—	2,883	—	—	1,379
1870	—	16,834	14,890	—	11,424	9,196	—	6,699	4,786	—
1880	—	44,452	36,142	—	31,706	27,663	—	21,073	16,672	—
1890 [1]	—	64,336	51,508	—	46,337	38,887	—	33,226	29,426	—
1900	—	68,287	56,913	—	47,055	40,742	—	36,375	30,378	—
1910	—	79,967	68,292	—	58,242	51,674	—	42,829	36,602	—
1920	—	76,516	71,534	—	64,214	59,155	—	50,355	44,080	—
1930	—	81,256	70,742	—	65,464	64,831	—	58,756	52,041	—
1940	—	73,415	69,248	—	66,677	62,779	—	58,424	56,026	—
1950	—	70,702	73,250	—	67,685	65,380	—	61,856	56,469	—
1960	—	65,473	65,474	—	69,794	71,922	—	65,732	62,006	—
1970	—	91,159	68,951	—	59,789	59,931	—	63,922	65,029	—
1980	—	112,893	99,458	—	85,116	67,933	—	58,064	57,698	—
1990	—	86,831	99,652	—	105,477	96,782	—	82,040	64,799	—

Note appears at end of table

(continued)

TABLE Aa3581–3643   Kansas population by race, sex, age, nativity, and urban–rural residence: 1860–1990   *Continued*

				Population					
				Female, by age					
	50–54	55–59	60–69	60–64	65–69	70–79	70–74	75–79	80 and older	Unknown age
	Aa3634	Aa3635	Aa3636	Aa3637	Aa3638	Aa3639	Aa3640	Aa3641	Aa3642	Aa3643
Year	Number	Number	Number	Number	Number	Number	Number	Number	Number	Number
1860	—	—	477	—	—	109	—	—	27	30
1870	3,661	2,291	—	1,659	969	—	535	224	139	3
1880	12,382	8,215	—	5,903	3,663	—	2,056	1,046	663	—
1890 [1]	22,712	16,239	—	12,107	8,070	—	4,832	2,669	1,806	436
1900	26,610	22,015	—	16,330	11,792	—	7,235	4,139	2,699	1,006
1910	32,585	25,242	—	20,943	16,816	—	10,826	6,431	4,566	955
1920	36,121	29,107	—	24,924	18,847	—	13,693	9,292	6,644	1,052
1930	45,243	36,793	—	29,982	23,077	—	17,625	11,227	9,452	323
1940	51,346	43,389	—	36,869	30,467	—	21,268	13,540	12,116	—
1950	52,719	48,627	—	43,162	37,273	—	27,730	22,200	13,396	—
1960	57,739	52,967	—	47,619	43,610	—	36,492	26,053	24,961	—
1970	61,333	57,165	—	53,800	46,615	—	40,206	31,478	36,866	—
1980	60,857	62,080	—	56,612	51,978	—	45,865	36,769	49,400	—
1990	54,445	53,934	—	55,279	54,987	—	47,853	41,034	62,012	—

[1] Includes 1,012 American Indians not counted in the general enumeration; see text for Table Aa2244–2340.

Sources

See the sources for Table Aa2244–2340.

Documentation

See the text for Table Aa2244–2340.

Kansas became a territory in 1854 and a state in 1861.

TABLE Aa3644–3744   Kentucky population by race, sex, age, nativity, and urban–rural residence: 1790–1990

Contributed by Michael R. Haines

				Population								
					Race				Residence		Nativity	
	Area	Population density	Total	White	Nonwhite	Black	Other nonwhite	Urban	Rural	Native-born	Foreign-born
	Aa3644	Aa3645	Aa3646	Aa3647	Aa3648	Aa3649	Aa3650	Aa3651	Aa3652	Aa3653	Aa3654
Year	Square miles	Persons per square mile	Number	Number	Number	Number	Number	Number	Number	Number	Number
1790	40,181	1.83	73,677	61,133	12,544	12,544	—	0	73,677	—	—
1800	40,181	5.50	220,955	179,871	41,084	41,084	—	0	220,955	—	—
1810	40,181	10.12	406,511	324,237	82,274	82,274	—	4,326	402,185	—	—
1820	40,181	14.04	564,317	434,644	129,673	129,491	182	9,291	555,026	—	—
1830	40,181	17.12	687,917	517,787	170,130	170,130	—	16,367	671,550	—	—
1840	40,181	19.41	779,828	590,253	189,575	189,575	—	30,948	748,880	—	—
1850	40,181	24.45	982,405	761,413	220,992	220,992	—	73,804	908,601	950,985	31,420
1860	40,181	28.76	1,155,684	919,484	236,200	236,167	33	120,624	1,035,060	1,095,885	59,799
1870	40,181	32.88	1,321,011	1,098,692	222,319	222,210	109	195,896	1,125,115	1,257,613	63,398
1880	40,181	41.03	1,648,690	1,377,179	271,511	271,451	60	249,923	1,398,767	1,589,173	59,517
1890	40,181	46.26	1,858,635	1,590,462	268,173	268,071	102	356,713	1,501,922	1,799,279	59,356
1900	40,181	53.44	2,147,174	1,862,309	284,865	284,706	159	467,668	1,679,506	2,096,925	50,249
1910	40,181	56.99	2,289,905	2,027,951	261,954	261,656	298	555,442	1,734,463	2,249,743	40,162
1920	40,181	60.14	2,416,630	2,180,560	236,070	235,938	132	633,543	1,783,087	2,385,724	30,906
1930	40,181	65.07	2,614,589	2,388,452	226,137	226,040	97	799,026	1,815,563	2,592,582	22,007
1940	40,109	70.95	2,845,627	2,631,425	214,202	214,031	171	849,327	1,996,300	2,829,883	15,744
1950	39,864	73.87	2,944,806	2,742,090	202,716	201,921	795	1,084,070	1,860,736	2,921,105	15,525
1960	39,851	76.24	3,038,156	2,820,083	218,073	215,949	2,124	1,353,215	1,684,941	3,021,326	16,830
1970	39,650	81.18	3,218,706	2,981,766	236,940	230,793	6,147	1,684,053	1,534,653	3,202,144	16,553
1980	39,669	92.28	3,660,777	3,379,006	281,771	259,477	22,294	1,862,183	1,798,594	3,626,215	34,562
1990	39,732	92.75	3,685,296	3,391,832	293,464	262,907	30,557	1,910,325	1,774,971	3,651,177	34,119

TABLE Aa3644–3744   Kentucky population by race, sex, age, nativity, and urban–rural residence: 1790–1990
Continued

					Population				
	Sex		Male, by age						
	Male	Female	0	1–4	5–9	10–14	15–19	20–29	20–24	25–29
	Aa3655	Aa3656	Aa3657	Aa3658	Aa3659	Aa3660	Aa3661	Aa3662	Aa3663	Aa3664
Year	Number	Number	Number	Number	Number	Number	Number	Number	Number	Number
1790	—	—	—	—	—	—	—	—	—	—
1800	—	—	—	—	—	—	—	—	—	—
1810	—	—	—	—	—	—	—	—	—	—
1820	289,103	275,032	—	—	—	—	—	—	—	—
1830	352,084	335,833	—	—	—	—	—	—	—	—
1840	400,088	379,740	—	—	—	—	—	—	—	—
1850	502,730	479,675	15,159	67,938	77,038	67,713	54,881	89,338	—	—
1860	592,321	563,363	19,324	78,807	85,769	77,401	64,688	102,912	—	—
1870	665,675	655,336	21,361	84,054	93,498	91,587	73,265	—	62,120	47,022
1880	832,590	816,100	26,771	99,470	119,925	105,641	87,503	—	82,706	63,437
1890	942,758	915,877	26,529	100,513	126,144	118,395	103,420	—	89,851	70,623
1900	1,090,227	1,056,947	31,294	113,055	138,722	127,657	114,145	—	103,492	87,732
1910	1,161,709	1,128,196	30,779	118,447	138,177	128,397	121,214	—	105,275	89,779
1920	1,227,494	1,189,136	29,513	118,707	146,099	137,673	117,986	—	103,323	93,649
1930	1,322,793	1,291,796	29,695	119,343	160,953	142,604	130,140	—	109,145	92,098
1940	1,435,812	1,409,815	27,897	116,727	144,907	149,415	148,395	—	123,431	111,504
1950	1,474,987	1,469,819	33,447	142,326	150,159	135,982	126,593	—	111,928	111,218
1960	1,508,448	1,529,708	35,609	139,039	165,553	158,156	131,485	—	98,523	85,347
1970	1,579,036	1,639,670	28,080	110,514	162,195	170,433	167,057	—	131,672	100,236
1980	1,789,039	1,871,738	30,424	114,355	148,353	154,689	183,893	—	174,464	153,713
1990	1,785,235	1,900,061	22,689	106,236	135,787	141,652	147,133	—	139,328	148,086

					Population				
					Male, by age				
	30–39	30–34	35–39	40–49	40–44	45–49	50–59	50–54	55–59	60–69
	Aa3665	Aa3666	Aa3667	Aa3668	Aa3669	Aa3670	Aa3671	Aa3672	Aa3673	Aa3674
Year	Number	Number	Number	Number	Number	Number	Number	Number	Number	Number
1790	—	—	—	—	—	—	—	—	—	—
1800	—	—	—	—	—	—	—	—	—	—
1810	—	—	—	—	—	—	—	—	—	—
1820	—	—	—	—	—	—	—	—	—	—
1830	—	—	—	—	—	—	—	—	—	—
1840	—	—	—	—	—	—	—	—	—	—
1850	56,162	—	—	35,567	—	—	21,197	—	—	11,058
1860	69,005	—	—	44,932	—	—	27,259	—	—	14,623
1870	—	38,199	35,625	—	28,658	25,007	—	22,245	14,023	—
1880	—	50,677	44,331	—	35,368	29,132	—	27,913	19,083	—
1890	—	62,485	54,409	—	43,445	36,297	—	31,994	22,558	—
1900	—	72,269	64,995	—	56,158	44,883	—	40,602	29,566	—
1910	—	77,939	75,426	—	61,757	52,063	—	49,259	35,332	—
1920	—	79,101	80,653	—	66,065	66,235	—	54,348	40,305	—
1930	—	84,880	85,760	—	74,163	67,660	—	62,736	50,041	—
1940	—	99,346	91,505	—	82,060	76,672	—	66,872	55,635	—
1950	—	99,274	97,666	—	88,447	78,978	—	70,833	62,453	—
1960	—	91,114	95,081	—	87,833	84,685	—	75,641	67,915	—
1970	—	85,942	81,721	—	87,635	88,294	—	80,478	74,105	—
1980	—	136,724	107,429	—	91,098	84,730	—	86,160	84,360	—
1990	—	151,212	141,713	—	127,918	101,316	—	84,877	77,667	—

(continued)

TABLE Aa3644–3744   Kentucky population by race, sex, age, nativity, and urban–rural residence: 1790–1990
Continued

Population

	Male, by age							Female, by age		
	60–64	65–69	70–79	70–74	75–79	80 and older	Unknown age	0	1–4	5–9
	Aa3675	Aa3676	Aa3677	Aa3678	Aa3679	Aa3680	Aa3681	Aa3682	Aa3683	Aa3684
Year	Number	Number	Number	Number	Number	Number	Number	Number	Number	Number
1790	—	—	—	—	—	—	—	—	—	—
1800	—	—	—	—	—	—	—	—	—	—
1810	—	—	—	—	—	—	—	—	—	—
1820	—	—	—	—	—	—	—	—	—	—
1830	—	—	—	—	—	—	—	—	—	—
1840	—	—	—	—	—	—	—	—	—	—
1850	—	—	4,793	—	—	1,766	120	14,914	65,981	74,791
1860	—	—	5,591	—	—	1,863	147	18,746	75,789	83,730
1870	11,856	7,416	—	5,019	2,583	2,132	5	20,659	80,916	90,387
1880	16,218	10,591	—	7,155	3,826	2,843	—	26,211	95,895	116,920
1890	19,505	14,155	—	9,760	5,286	4,008	3,381	25,486	96,627	123,305
1900	22,718	16,792	—	11,240	6,752	4,451	3,704	30,496	109,385	134,537
1910	27,913	21,113	—	13,702	8,041	5,401	1,695	30,327	114,950	134,581
1920	34,572	25,083	—	16,501	10,241	6,381	1,059	28,692	114,713	141,472
1930	40,066	29,832	—	22,086	12,381	8,502	708	28,766	115,062	155,278
1940	46,253	41,082	—	27,353	15,500	11,258	—	27,211	113,357	140,092
1950	51,809	45,188	—	32,146	24,549	11,991	—	32,264	137,969	145,224
1960	56,416	50,630	—	38,662	25,863	20,896	—	34,188	133,660	160,158
1970	65,344	52,693	—	39,616	27,088	25,933	—	26,770	105,735	155,048
1980	71,009	61,836	—	46,561	30,844	28,397	—	29,255	108,697	141,058
1990	74,363	67,346	—	49,077	35,172	33,663	—	21,366	100,580	129,670

Population

	Female, by age									
	10–14	15–19	20–29	20–24	25–29	30–39	30–34	35–39	40–49	40–44
	Aa3685	Aa3686	Aa3687	Aa3688	Aa3689	Aa3690	Aa3691	Aa3692	Aa3693	Aa3694
Year	Number	Number	Number	Number	Number	Number	Number	Number	Number	Number
1790	—	—	—	—	—	—	—	—	—	—
1800	—	—	—	—	—	—	—	—	—	—
1810	—	—	—	—	—	—	—	—	—	—
1820	—	—	—	—	—	—	—	—	—	—
1830	—	—	—	—	—	—	—	—	—	—
1840	—	—	—	—	—	—	—	—	—	—
1850	65,196	55,955	82,882	—	—	49,648	—	—	33,021	—
1860	74,802	66,125	96,242	—	—	62,407	—	—	40,156	—
1870	87,713	74,225	—	67,208	50,357	—	39,245	35,154	—	28,927
1880	101,739	88,590	—	85,167	62,675	—	49,549	44,636	—	35,721
1890	113,387	105,622	—	92,011	70,963	—	58,124	50,374	—	41,888
1900	123,996	114,622	—	106,756	87,207	—	69,303	60,824	—	51,163
1910	124,508	120,408	—	109,935	92,169	—	77,097	71,744	—	57,216
1920	133,564	117,838	—	106,715	93,872	—	80,440	78,307	—	64,785
1930	137,634	128,016	—	112,516	96,942	—	86,308	84,172	—	72,782
1940	144,443	146,412	—	122,411	111,344	—	99,934	92,340	—	81,034
1950	131,072	121,190	—	114,303	112,745	—	100,766	98,792	—	88,730
1960	153,394	122,244	—	94,620	90,123	—	96,510	99,758	—	91,070
1970	162,959	151,699	—	133,610	103,961	—	90,851	87,880	—	93,104
1980	147,056	170,546	—	171,655	155,625	—	139,564	110,539	—	95,454
1990	133,635	138,028	—	137,979	153,207	—	157,614	146,896	—	132,536

TABLE Aa3644–3744   Kentucky population by race, sex, age, nativity, and urban–rural residence: 1790–1990
Continued

	Population									
	Female, by age									
	45–49	50–59	50–54	55–59	60–69	60–64	65–69	70–79	70–74	75–79
	Aa3695	Aa3696	Aa3697	Aa3698	Aa3699	Aa3700	Aa3701	Aa3702	Aa3703	Aa3704
Year	Number	Number	Number	Number	Number	Number	Number	Number	Number	Number
1790	—	—	—	—	—	—	—	—	—	—
1800	—	—	—	—	—	—	—	—	—	—
1810	—	—	—	—	—	—	—	—	—	—
1820	—	—	—	—	—	—	—	—	—	—
1830	—	—	—	—	—	—	—	—	—	—
1840	—	—	—	—	—	—	—	—	—	—
1850	—	19,567	—	—	11,073	—	—	4,689	—	—
1860	—	23,698	—	—	13,680	—	—	5,733	—	—
1870	23,090	—	18,562	11,917	—	10,451	6,820	—	4,732	2,535
1880	29,521	—	25,407	16,711	—	14,337	9,516	—	6,482	3,667
1890	35,809	—	29,715	20,990	—	18,372	12,956	—	8,608	4,990
1900	41,995	—	36,234	27,684	—	21,783	15,974	—	10,856	6,495
1910	48,803	—	42,310	31,030	—	25,849	19,657	—	12,786	7,581
1920	58,138	—	47,173	36,584	—	30,418	22,620	—	15,805	9,926
1930	65,770	—	57,204	45,141	—	36,204	28,038	—	19,683	12,137
1940	73,958	—	64,474	54,163	—	44,551	39,869	—	25,991	15,710
1950	80,107	—	71,473	61,469	—	52,346	47,881	—	33,366	25,575
1960	87,074	—	78,086	71,379	—	61,172	55,393	—	43,618	30,661
1970	94,006	—	86,275	81,539	—	74,135	63,823	—	50,975	37,354
1980	89,692	—	93,670	93,973	—	82,764	77,102	—	63,489	47,927
1990	105,567	—	90,606	85,154	—	85,636	83,626	—	68,177	56,991

	Population									
	Female, by age		White							
					Male, by age					
	80 and older	Unknown age	Male	Female	0–4	5–9	10–14	15–19	20–29	30–39
	Aa3705	Aa3706	Aa3707	Aa3708	Aa3709	Aa3710	Aa3711	Aa3712	Aa3713	Aa3714
Year	Number	Number	Number	Number	Number	Number	Number	Number	Number	Number
1790	—	—	32,211	28,922	—	—	—	—	—	—
1800	—	—	93,956	85,915	—	—	—	—	—	—
1810	—	—	168,805	155,432	—	—	—	—	—	—
1820	—	—	223,696	210,948	—	—	—	—	—	—
1830	—	—	267,123	250,664	54,116	41,073	34,222	29,017	45,913	26,289
1840	—	—	305,323	284,930	59,290	46,242	39,190	32,611	53,265	32,206
1850	1,873	85	—	—	—	—	—	—	—	—
1860	2,119	136	—	—	—	—	—	—	—	—
1870	2,426	12	—	—	—	—	—	—	—	—
1880	3,356	—	—	—	—	—	—	—	—	—
1890	4,068	2,582	—	—	—	—	—	—	—	—
1900	4,567	3,070	—	—	—	—	—	—	—	—
1910	5,843	1,402	—	—	—	—	—	—	—	—
1920	7,215	859	—	—	—	—	—	—	—	—
1930	9,463	680	—	—	—	—	—	—	—	—
1940	12,521	—	—	—	—	—	—	—	—	—
1950	14,547	—	—	—	—	—	—	—	—	—
1960	26,600	—	—	—	—	—	—	—	—	—
1970	39,946	—	—	—	—	—	—	—	—	—
1980	53,672	—	—	—	—	—	—	—	—	—
1990	72,793	—	—	—	—	—	—	—	—	—

(continued)

TABLE Aa3644–3744   Kentucky population by race, sex, age, nativity, and urban–rural residence: 1790–1990
Continued

	Population									
	White									
	Male, by age					Female, by age				
	40–49	50–59	60–69	70–79	80 and older	0–4	5–9	10–14	15–19	20–29
	Aa3715	Aa3716	Aa3717	Aa3718	Aa3719	Aa3720	Aa3721	Aa3722	Aa3723	Aa3724
Year	Number	Number	Number	Number	Number	Number	Number	Number	Number	Number
1790	—	—	—	—	—	—	—	—	—	—
1800	—	—	—	—	—	—	—	—	—	—
1810	—	—	—	—	—	—	—	—	—	—
1820	—	—	—	—	—	—	—	—	—	—
1830	15,966	10,843	6,253	2,585	846	50,835	39,439	32,197	29,623	41,936
1840	19,958	11,809	6,639	3,092	1,021	55,419	44,022	37,298	33,207	47,970
1850	—	—	—	—	—	—	—	—	—	—
1860	—	—	—	—	—	—	—	—	—	—
1870	—	—	—	—	—	—	—	—	—	—
1880	—	—	—	—	—	—	—	—	—	—
1890	—	—	—	—	—	—	—	—	—	—
1900	—	—	—	—	—	—	—	—	—	—
1910	—	—	—	—	—	—	—	—	—	—
1920	—	—	—	—	—	—	—	—	—	—
1930	—	—	—	—	—	—	—	—	—	—
1940	—	—	—	—	—	—	—	—	—	—
1950	—	—	—	—	—	—	—	—	—	—
1960	—	—	—	—	—	—	—	—	—	—
1970	—	—	—	—	—	—	—	—	—	—
1980	—	—	—	—	—	—	—	—	—	—
1990	—	—	—	—	—	—	—	—	—	—

	Population									
	White									
	Female, by age						Male, by age			
	30–39	40–49	50–59	60–69	70–79	80 and older	0–9	10–15	16–25	26–44
	Aa3725	Aa3726	Aa3727	Aa3728	Aa3729	Aa3730	Aa3731	Aa3732	Aa3733	Aa3734
Year	Number	Number	Number	Number	Number	Number	Number	Number	Number	Number
1790	—	—	—	—	—	—	—	—	—	—
1800	—	—	—	—	—	—	37,274	14,045	15,705	17,699
1810	—	—	—	—	—	—	65,134	26,804	29,772	29,553
1820	—	—	—	—	—	—	83,050	36,004	41,328	38,178
1830	23,463	15,476	9,499	5,315	2,195	686	—	—	—	—
1840	28,608	18,050	10,907	6,029	2,525	895	—	—	—	—
1850	—	—	—	—	—	—	—	—	—	—
1860	—	—	—	—	—	—	—	—	—	—
1870	—	—	—	—	—	—	—	—	—	—
1880	—	—	—	—	—	—	—	—	—	—
1890	—	—	—	—	—	—	—	—	—	—
1900	—	—	—	—	—	—	—	—	—	—
1910	—	—	—	—	—	—	—	—	—	—
1920	—	—	—	—	—	—	—	—	—	—
1930	—	—	—	—	—	—	—	—	—	—
1940	—	—	—	—	—	—	—	—	—	—
1950	—	—	—	—	—	—	—	—	—	—
1960	—	—	—	—	—	—	—	—	—	—
1970	—	—	—	—	—	—	—	—	—	—
1980	—	—	—	—	—	—	—	—	—	—
1990	—	—	—	—	—	—	—	—	—	—

TABLE Aa3644–3744   Kentucky population by race, sex, age, nativity, and urban–rural residence: 1790–1990
Continued

			Population							
			White							
	Male, by age	Female, by age					Male, by age		Female, by age	
	45 and older	0–9	10–15	16–25	26–44	45 and older	0–15	16 and older	0–15	16 and older
	Aa3735	Aa3736	Aa3737	Aa3738	Aa3739	Aa3740	Aa3741	Aa3742	Aa3743	Aa3744
Year	Number	Number	Number	Number	Number	Number	Number	Number	Number	Number
1790	—	—	—	—	—	—	17,057	15,154	16,286	12,636
1800	9,233	34,949	13,433	15,524	14,934	7,075	—	—	—	—
1810	17,542	60,776	25,743	29,511	25,920	13,482	—	—	—	—
1820	25,136	77,641	35,120	41,905	35,483	20,799	—	—	—	—
1830	—	—	—	—	—	—	—	—	—	—
1840	—	—	—	—	—	—	—	—	—	—
1850	—	—	—	—	—	—	—	—	—	—
1860	—	—	—	—	—	—	—	—	—	—
1870	—	—	—	—	—	—	—	—	—	—
1880	—	—	—	—	—	—	—	—	—	—
1890	—	—	—	—	—	—	—	—	—	—
1900	—	—	—	—	—	—	—	—	—	—
1910	—	—	—	—	—	—	—	—	—	—
1920	—	—	—	—	—	—	—	—	—	—
1930	—	—	—	—	—	—	—	—	—	—
1940	—	—	—	—	—	—	—	—	—	—
1950	—	—	—	—	—	—	—	—	—	—
1960	—	—	—	—	—	—	—	—	—	—
1970	—	—	—	—	—	—	—	—	—	—
1980	—	—	—	—	—	—	—	—	—	—
1990	—	—	—	—	—	—	—	—	—	—

Sources
See the sources for Table Aa2244–2340.

Documentation
See the text for Table Aa2244–2340.

Kentucky was originally part of Virginia and was directly made a state in 1792. It was listed separately in the Census of 1790.

TABLE Aa3745–3841   Louisiana population by race, sex, age, nativity, and urban–rural residence: 1810–1990
Contributed by Michael R. Haines

				Population								
				Race				Residence		Nativity	
	Area	Population density	Total	White	Nonwhite	Black	Other nonwhite	Urban	Rural	Native-born	Foreign-born
	Aa3745	Aa3746	Aa3747	Aa3748	Aa3749	Aa3750	Aa3751	Aa3752	Aa3753	Aa3754	Aa3755
Year	Square miles	Persons per square mile	Number	Number	Number	Number	Number	Number	Number	Number	Number
1810	34,065	2.25	76,556	34,311	42,245	42,245	—	17,242	59,314	—	—
1820	45,409	3.38	153,407	73,383	80,024	79,540	484	27,176	126,231	—	—
1830	45,409	4.75	215,739	89,231	126,298	126,298	—	46,082	169,657	—	—
1840	45,409	7.76	352,411	158,457	193,954	193,954	—	105,400	247,011	—	—
1850	45,409	11.40	517,762	255,491	262,271	262,271	—	134,470	383,292	449,529	68,233
1860	45,409	15.59	708,002	357,456	350,546	350,373	173	185,026	522,976	627,027	80,975
1870	45,409	16.01	726,915	362,065	364,850	364,210	640	202,523	524,392	665,088	61,827
1880	45,409	20.70	939,946	454,954	484,992	483,655	1,337	239,390	700,556	885,800	54,146
1890 [1]	45,409	24.63	1,118,588	558,395	560,192	559,193	999	283,845	834,743	1,068,840	49,747
1900	45,409	30.43	1,381,625	729,612	652,013	650,804	1,209	366,288	1,015,337	1,328,722	52,903
1910	45,409	36.48	1,656,388	941,086	715,302	713,874	1,428	496,516	1,159,872	1,603,622	52,766
1920	45,409	39.61	1,798,509	1,096,611	701,898	700,257	1,641	628,163	1,170,346	1,752,082	46,427
1930	45,409	46.28	2,101,593	1,322,712	778,881	776,326	2,555	833,532	1,268,061	2,064,517	37,076
1940	45,177	52.32	2,363,880	1,511,739	852,141	849,303	2,838	980,439	1,383,441	2,335,907	27,973
1950	45,162	59.42	2,683,516	1,796,683	886,833	882,428	4,405	1,471,696	1,211,820	2,647,695	29,675
1960	45,131	72.17	3,257,022	2,211,715	1,045,307	1,039,207	6,100	2,060,606	1,196,416	3,226,465	30,557
1970	44,930	81.04	3,641,306	2,541,498	1,099,808	1,086,832	12,976	2,422,175	1,219,131	3,600,900	39,542
1980	44,521	94.47	4,205,900	2,912,172	1,293,728	1,238,241	55,487	2,887,309	1,318,591	4,120,398	85,502
1990	43,566	96.86	4,219,973	2,839,138	1,380,835	1,299,281	81,554	2,871,759	1,348,214	4,132,566	87,407

Note appears at end of table

(continued)

TABLE Aa3745–3841 Louisiana population by race, sex, age, nativity, and urban–rural residence: 1810–1990
Continued

	Sex		Population — Male, by age								
	Male	Female	0	1–4	5–9	10–14	15–19	20–29	20–24	25–29	30–39
	Aa3756	Aa3757	Aa3758	Aa3759	Aa3760	Aa3761	Aa3762	Aa3763	Aa3764	Aa3765	Aa3766
Year	Number	Number	Number	Number	Number	Number	Number	Number	Number	Number	Number
1810	—	—	—	—	—	—	—	—	—	—	—
1820	82,407	70,516	—	—	—	—	—	—	—	—	—
1830	114,856	100,673	—	—	—	—	—	—	—	—	—
1840	187,802	164,609	—	—	—	—	—	—	—	—	—
1850	274,596	243,166	6,007	30,550	32,993	29,027	22,475	57,923	—	—	48,601
1860	369,994	338,008	8,809	42,106	45,778	39,413	33,369	71,677	—	—	55,547
1870	362,165	364,750	10,936	44,593	45,466	45,581	34,770	—	33,463	27,670	—
1880	468,754	471,192	15,433	60,816	70,501	56,581	39,921	—	44,050	38,487	—
1890 [1]	559,350	559,237	15,811	67,512	81,212	74,107	59,408	—	51,125	39,755	—
1900	694,733	686,892	19,645	81,021	97,188	85,573	71,176	—	66,600	58,785	—
1910	835,275	821,113	22,468	90,109	110,164	97,545	84,902	—	79,383	70,552	—
1920	903,335	895,174	20,246	85,222	112,909	109,458	90,718	—	81,161	71,931	—
1930	1,047,823	1,053,770	21,982	94,282	124,903	114,496	106,048	—	98,240	85,931	—
1940	1,172,382	1,191,498	22,548	93,805	114,845	122,825	118,486	—	103,885	100,294	—
1950	1,319,166	1,364,350	33,632	136,031	138,549	119,123	102,401	—	100,991	102,697	—
1960	1,592,254	1,664,768	44,427	170,203	196,564	170,892	128,731	—	97,260	95,139	—
1970	1,771,484	1,869,822	35,625	141,224	201,210	208,870	191,193	—	146,900	113,594	—
1980	2,039,894	2,166,006	40,422	143,246	175,871	188,922	213,774	—	209,838	182,871	—
1990	2,031,386	2,188,587	29,202	141,412	182,631	174,425	167,273	—	160,254	167,974	—

	Population — Male, by age										
	30–34	35–39	40–49	40–44	45–49	50–59	50–54	55–59	60–69	60–64	65–69
	Aa3767	Aa3768	Aa3769	Aa3770	Aa3771	Aa3772	Aa3773	Aa3774	Aa3775	Aa3776	Aa3777
Year	Number	Number	Number	Number	Number	Number	Number	Number	Number	Number	Number
1810	—	—	—	—	—	—	—	—	—	—	—
1820	—	—	—	—	—	—	—	—	—	—	—
1830	—	—	—	—	—	—	—	—	—	—	—
1840	—	—	—	—	—	—	—	—	—	—	—
1850	—	—	27,197	—	—	11,964	—	—	5,259	—	—
1860	—	—	38,089	—	—	17,851	—	—	7,873	—	—
1870	22,179	21,848	—	18,296	17,910	—	14,937	8,482	—	7,417	3,535
1880	28,211	25,136	—	20,936	19,350	—	16,676	10,175	—	9,960	5,420
1890 [1]	33,692	32,670	—	24,489	21,457	—	18,223	12,287	—	10,407	6,791
1900	44,228	38,324	—	32,844	27,484	—	23,329	15,495	—	12,237	8,187
1910	58,104	55,170	—	41,721	32,154	—	28,608	20,609	—	16,265	10,644
1920	60,268	64,057	—	49,762	49,640	—	34,195	22,322	—	19,317	13,317
1930	72,653	73,012	—	60,256	56,100	—	45,144	33,117	—	24,426	15,664
1940	90,968	84,955	—	72,289	64,261	—	52,611	41,685	—	31,749	27,665
1950	92,900	93,639	—	86,032	76,235	—	63,024	51,438	—	40,044	37,245
1960	100,825	100,825	—	92,634	88,938	—	79,007	68,117	—	51,613	43,008
1970	95,896	90,757	—	97,043	93,850	—	84,850	77,035	—	65,805	51,570
1980	153,772	118,909	—	99,613	92,251	—	95,246	88,440	—	74,116	63,174
1990	174,677	158,939	—	135,781	106,609	—	88,013	80,199	—	78,390	68,767

Note appears at end of table

TABLE Aa3745–3841   Louisiana population by race, sex, age, nativity, and urban–rural residence: 1810–1990
Continued

	Population										
	Male, by age					Female, by age					
	70–79	70–74	75–79	80 and older	Unknown age	0	1–4	5–9	10–14	15–19	20–29
	Aa3778	Aa3779	Aa3780	Aa3781	Aa3782	Aa3783	Aa3784	Aa3785	Aa3786	Aa3787	Aa3788
Year	Number	Number	Number	Number	Number	Number	Number	Number	Number	Number	Number
1810	—	—	—	—	—	—	—	—	—	—	—
1820	—	—	—	—	—	—	—	—	—	—	—
1830	—	—	—	—	—	—	—	—	—	—	—
1840	—	—	—	—	—	—	—	—	—	—	—
1850	1,645	—	—	679	276	6,225	30,652	32,465	28,301	25,295	50,301
1860	2,315	—	—	866	6,301	9,069	41,888	45,111	37,627	36,776	65,604
1870	—	2,629	1,159	1,294	0	11,170	43,873	44,485	45,113	39,503	—
1880	—	3,592	1,721	1,788	—	15,513	59,321	69,292	55,405	44,456	—
1890 [1]	—	4,512	2,423	2,123	1,346	15,157	64,962	79,250	71,611	64,646	—
1900	—	5,373	3,061	2,519	1,664	19,439	79,301	94,667	83,812	74,558	—
1910	—	6,671	3,723	3,058	3,425	22,101	89,391	108,579	96,246	90,325	—
1920	—	8,044	4,609	3,414	2,745	20,014	83,731	110,321	109,769	97,587	—
1930	—	10,431	6,232	4,457	449	21,729	92,545	123,284	113,135	111,554	—
1940	—	15,615	7,729	6,167	—	22,124	92,150	113,131	121,011	121,912	—
1950	—	22,203	15,496	7,486	—	32,814	131,989	136,556	116,236	107,521	—
1960	—	29,801	19,513	14,757	—	43,485	164,608	191,329	166,484	133,031	—
1970	—	34,970	21,451	19,641	—	34,686	136,788	196,237	201,799	184,765	—
1980	—	46,295	29,138	23,996	—	39,220	138,645	170,095	182,873	212,383	—
1990	—	49,688	35,051	32,101	—	27,989	136,047	175,734	168,030	164,867	—

	Population										
	Female, by age										
	20–24	25–29	30–39	30–34	35–39	40–49	40–44	45–49	50–59	50–54	55–59
	Aa3789	Aa3790	Aa3791	Aa3792	Aa3793	Aa3794	Aa3795	Aa3796	Aa3797	Aa3798	Aa3799
Year	Number	Number	Number	Number	Number	Number	Number	Number	Number	Number	Number
1810	—	—	—	—	—	—	—	—	—	—	—
1820	—	—	—	—	—	—	—	—	—	—	—
1830	—	—	—	—	—	—	—	—	—	—	—
1840	—	—	—	—	—	—	—	—	—	—	—
1850	—	—	34,943	—	—	19,054	—	—	9,204	—	—
1860	—	—	45,424	—	—	28,199	—	—	13,617	—	—
1870	37,179	30,856	—	25,259	22,344	—	18,801	13,793	—	12,129	6,030
1880	48,391	37,667	—	28,440	26,299	—	22,591	17,859	—	16,068	8,469
1890 [1]	55,539	40,599	—	33,072	30,835	—	24,652	21,355	—	18,009	11,376
1900	72,481	58,501	—	41,494	35,712	—	30,456	25,223	—	21,361	14,445
1910	85,532	71,353	—	55,558	50,820	—	36,731	29,163	—	25,265	17,701
1920	90,126	77,737	—	61,893	61,091	—	46,688	39,451	—	28,636	19,261
1930	108,256	93,022	—	75,594	73,675	—	58,359	51,476	—	40,441	29,346
1940	112,511	106,727	—	95,486	89,194	—	72,092	62,424	—	49,658	39,639
1950	111,893	110,306	—	99,302	99,283	—	89,019	77,716	—	63,863	52,094
1960	108,067	102,981	—	109,445	108,504	—	97,752	92,536	—	83,149	71,920
1970	152,409	120,036	—	103,068	99,906	—	105,840	102,078	—	92,343	84,473
1980	210,438	185,861	—	158,255	125,336	—	106,361	100,920	—	105,489	100,838
1990	163,916	177,401	—	183,870	167,848	—	143,368	114,753	—	97,065	91,728

Note appears at end of table

(continued)

TABLE Aa3745–3841   Louisiana population by race, sex, age, nativity, and urban–rural residence: 1810–1990
Continued

					Population				White	
				Female, by age						
	60–69	60–64	65–69	70–79	70–74	75–79	80 and older	Unknown age	Male	Female
	Aa3800	Aa3801	Aa3802	Aa3803	Aa3804	Aa3805	Aa3806	Aa3807	Aa3808	Aa3809
Year	Number	Number	Number	Number	Number	Number	Number	Number	Number	Number
1810	—	—	—	—	—	—	—	—	18,940	15,371
1820	—	—	—	—	—	—	—	—	41,332	32,051
1830	—	—	—	—	—	—	—	—	49,715	39,516
1840	—	—	—	—	—	—	—	—	89,747	68,710
1850	4,486	—	—	1,500	—	—	693	47	—	—
1860	6,643	—	—	2,121	—	—	944	4,985	—	—
1870	—	6,289	3,020	—	2,339	1,021	1,546	0	—	—
1880	—	9,048	4,779	—	3,529	1,865	2,200	—	—	—
1890 [1]	—	10,579	6,486	—	4,548	2,586	2,900	1,075	—	—
1900	—	12,817	8,348	—	5,965	3,249	3,521	1,542	—	—
1910	—	15,150	10,424	—	7,125	4,126	3,962	1,561	—	—
1920	—	17,230	12,283	—	8,182	4,977	4,617	1,580	—	—
1930	—	21,932	15,260	—	10,969	6,797	6,040	356	—	—
1940	—	31,612	28,497	—	16,021	8,907	8,402	—	—	—
1950	—	41,339	41,716	—	24,484	18,354	9,865	—	—	—
1960	—	56,965	51,550	—	36,866	24,935	21,161	—	—	—
1970	—	76,319	65,768	—	47,413	32,354	33,540	—	—	—
1980	—	87,616	80,418	—	65,014	47,515	48,729	—	—	—
1990	—	92,587	87,092	—	69,461	56,343	70,488	—	—	—

					Population						
					White						
					Male, by age						
	0–4	5–9	10–14	15–19	20–29	30–39	40–49	50–59	60–69	70–79	80 and older
	Aa3810	Aa3811	Aa3812	Aa3813	Aa3814	Aa3815	Aa3816	Aa3817	Aa3818	Aa3819	Aa3820
Year	Number	Number	Number	Number	Number	Number	Number	Number	Number	Number	Number
1810	—	—	—	—	—	—	—	—	—	—	—
1820	—	—	—	—	—	—	—	—	—	—	—
1830	7,968	6,402	5,134	4,325	10,458	7,777	4,304	2,023	896	317	111
1840	13,835	10,736	7,848	7,218	20,795	16,304	7,940	3,309	1,206	410	146
1850	—	—	—	—	—	—	—	—	—	—	—
1860	—	—	—	—	—	—	—	—	—	—	—
1870	—	—	—	—	—	—	—	—	—	—	—
1880	—	—	—	—	—	—	—	—	—	—	—
1890 [1]	—	—	—	—	—	—	—	—	—	—	—
1900	—	—	—	—	—	—	—	—	—	—	—
1910	—	—	—	—	—	—	—	—	—	—	—
1920	—	—	—	—	—	—	—	—	—	—	—
1930	—	—	—	—	—	—	—	—	—	—	—
1940	—	—	—	—	—	—	—	—	—	—	—
1950	—	—	—	—	—	—	—	—	—	—	—
1960	—	—	—	—	—	—	—	—	—	—	—
1970	—	—	—	—	—	—	—	—	—	—	—
1980	—	—	—	—	—	—	—	—	—	—	—
1990	—	—	—	—	—	—	—	—	—	—	—

Note appears at end of table

TABLE Aa3745–3841   Louisiana population by race, sex, age, nativity, and urban–rural residence: 1810–1990
Continued

	Population										
	White										
	Female, by age										
	0–4	5–9	10–14	15–19	20–29	30–39	40–49	50–59	60–69	70–79	80 and older
	Aa3821	Aa3822	Aa3823	Aa3824	Aa3825	Aa3826	Aa3827	Aa3828	Aa3829	Aa3830	Aa3831
Year	Number	Number	Number	Number	Number	Number	Number	Number	Number	Number	Number
1810	—	—	—	—	—	—	—	—	—	—	—
1820	—	—	—	—	—	—	—	—	—	—	—
1830	7,800	6,193	5,140	4,709	6,930	4,204	2,310	1,257	660	222	91
1840	13,718	10,395	7,760	7,947	13,602	7,907	4,099	1,967	891	323	101
1850	—	—	—	—	—	—	—	—	—	—	—
1860	—	—	—	—	—	—	—	—	—	—	—
1870	—	—	—	—	—	—	—	—	—	—	—
1880	—	—	—	—	—	—	—	—	—	—	—
1890 [1]	—	—	—	—	—	—	—	—	—	—	—
1900	—	—	—	—	—	—	—	—	—	—	—
1910	—	—	—	—	—	—	—	—	—	—	—
1920	—	—	—	—	—	—	—	—	—	—	—
1930	—	—	—	—	—	—	—	—	—	—	—
1940	—	—	—	—	—	—	—	—	—	—	—
1950	—	—	—	—	—	—	—	—	—	—	—
1960	—	—	—	—	—	—	—	—	—	—	—
1970	—	—	—	—	—	—	—	—	—	—	—
1980	—	—	—	—	—	—	—	—	—	—	—
1990	—	—	—	—	—	—	—	—	—	—	—

	Population									
	White									
	Male, by age					Female, by age				
	0–9	10–15	16–25	26–44	45 and older	0–9	10–15	16–25	26–44	45 and older
	Aa3832	Aa3833	Aa3834	Aa3835	Aa3836	Aa3837	Aa3838	Aa3839	Aa3840	Aa3841
Year	Number	Number	Number	Number	Number	Number	Number	Number	Number	Number
1810	5,848	2,491	2,963	5,130	2,508	5,384	2,588	2,874	3,026	1,499
1820	11,817	4,710	8,747	11,236	4,822	11,062	5,484	6,708	5,695	3,102
1830	—	—	—	—	—	—	—	—	—	—
1840	—	—	—	—	—	—	—	—	—	—
1850	—	—	—	—	—	—	—	—	—	—
1860	—	—	—	—	—	—	—	—	—	—
1870	—	—	—	—	—	—	—	—	—	—
1880	—	—	—	—	—	—	—	—	—	—
1890 [1]	—	—	—	—	—	—	—	—	—	—
1900	—	—	—	—	—	—	—	—	—	—
1910	—	—	—	—	—	—	—	—	—	—
1920	—	—	—	—	—	—	—	—	—	—
1930	—	—	—	—	—	—	—	—	—	—
1940	—	—	—	—	—	—	—	—	—	—
1950	—	—	—	—	—	—	—	—	—	—
1960	—	—	—	—	—	—	—	—	—	—
1970	—	—	—	—	—	—	—	—	—	—
1980	—	—	—	—	—	—	—	—	—	—
1990	—	—	—	—	—	—	—	—	—	—

[1] Includes one American Indian not counted in the general enumeration; see text for Table Aa2244–2340.

Sources

See the sources for Table Aa2244–2340.

Documentation

See the text for Table Aa2244–2340.

Louisiana was originally part of the Louisiana Purchase of 1803. It was separated from the Louisiana Territory in 1804 and named the Orleans Territory. Orleans Territory became the state of Louisiana in 1812. Additional territory was added by 1812 from Spanish Florida in the east and in 1819 from Texas in the west as a result of the purchase of Florida from Spain and a treaty to establish the boundary with Mexico (ratified in 1821).

TABLE Aa3842–3942   Maine population by race, sex, age, nativity, and urban–rural residence: 1790–1990

Contributed by Michael R. Haines

			Population									
				Race				Residence		Nativity	
	Area	Population density	Total	White	Nonwhite	Black	Other nonwhite	Urban	Rural	Native-born	Foreign-born
	Aa3842	Aa3843	Aa3844	Aa3845	Aa3846	Aa3847	Aa3848	Aa3849	Aa3850	Aa3851	Aa3852
Year	Square miles	Persons per square mile	Number	Number	Number	Number	Number	Number	Number	Number	Number
1790	29,895	3.23	96,643	96,107	536	536	—	0	96,540	—	—
1800	29,895	5.08	151,719	150,901	818	818	—	3,704	148,015	—	—
1810	29,895	7.65	228,705	227,736	969	969	—	7,169	221,536	—	—
1820	29,895	9.98	298,335	297,340	995	929	66	8,581	289,754	—	—
1830	29,895	13.36	399,455	398,263	1,192	1,192	—	12,598	386,857	—	—
1840	29,895	16.79	501,793	500,438	1,355	1,355	—	39,342	462,451	—	—
1850	29,895	19.51	583,169	581,813	1,356	1,356	—	78,925	504,244	551,344	31,825
1860	29,895	21.02	628,279	626,947	1,332	1,327	5	104,373	523,906	590,826	37,453
1870	29,895	20.97	626,915	624,809	2,106	1,606	500	131,744	495,171	578,034	48,881
1880	29,895	21.71	648,936	646,852	2,084	1,451	633	146,608	502,328	590,053	58,883
1890	29,895	22.11	661,086	659,263	1,823	1,190	633	185,725	475,361	582,125	78,961
1900	29,895	23.23	694,466	692,226	2,240	1,319	921	232,827	461,639	601,136	93,330
1910	29,895	24.83	742,371	739,995	2,376	1,363	1,013	262,248	480,123	631,809	110,562
1920	29,895	25.69	768,014	765,695	2,319	1,310	1,009	299,569	468,445	660,200	107,814
1930	29,895	26.67	797,423	795,185	2,238	1,096	1,142	321,506	475,917	696,695	100,728
1940	31,040	27.29	847,226	844,543	2,683	1,304	1,379	343,057	504,169	763,233	83,993
1950	31,040	29.44	913,774	910,846	2,928	1,221	1,707	472,000	441,774	834,375	74,475
1960	30,933	31.33	969,265	963,291	5,974	3,318	2,656	497,114	472,151	908,862	60,403
1970	30,920	32.08	992,048	985,276	6,772	2,800	3,972	504,157	487,891	950,649	43,014
1980	30,995	36.29	1,124,660	1,109,850	14,810	3,128	11,682	534,072	590,588	1,081,258	43,402
1990	30,865	39.78	1,227,928	1,208,360	19,568	5,138	14,430	547,824	680,104	1,191,632	36,296

			Population									
	Sex		Male, by age									
	Male	Female	0	1–4	5–9	10–14	15–19	20–29	20–24	25–29	30–39
	Aa3853	Aa3854	Aa3855	Aa3856	Aa3857	Aa3858	Aa3859	Aa3860	Aa3861	Aa3862	Aa3863
Year	Number	Number	Number	Number	Number	Number	Number	Number	Number	Number	Number
1790	—	—	—	—	—	—	—	—	—	—	—
1800	—	—	—	—	—	—	—	—	—	—	—
1810	—	—	—	—	—	—	—	—	—	—	—
1820	149,632	148,637	—	—	—	—	—	—	—	—	—
1830	201,299	198,156	—	—	—	—	—	—	—	—	—
1840	253,709	248,084	—	—	—	—	—	—	—	—	—
1850	297,471	285,698	7,067	31,561	37,788	36,491	33,521	51,589	—	—	36,040
1860	317,189	311,090	7,552	32,255	37,423	36,587	35,285	54,152	—	—	37,512
1870	313,103	313,812	6,508	27,797	33,094	35,888	33,676	—	28,094	22,657	—
1880	324,058	324,878	6,411	26,249	32,811	33,249	31,639	—	30,683	25,398	—
1890	332,590	328,496	5,807	23,842	31,154	31,967	32,340	—	30,398	25,215	—
1900	350,995	343,471	6,761	26,186	31,934	30,782	31,274	—	30,580	27,859	—
1910	377,052	365,319	7,525	28,677	33,475	32,433	32,774	—	31,355	28,860	—
1920	388,752	379,262	7,501	30,576	36,100	35,097	31,774	—	30,081	28,622	—
1930	401,285	396,138	7,320	30,907	40,481	37,463	34,553	—	29,715	25,947	—
1940	425,821	421,405	6,638	28,834	37,494	39,252	39,941	—	33,310	30,827	—
1950	454,145	459,629	9,893	41,137	42,223	36,250	35,038	—	32,683	32,696	—
1960	479,054	490,211	11,167	43,895	49,895	47,698	38,315	—	29,959	28,103	—
1970	482,865	509,183	8,545	34,521	50,874	52,015	46,811	—	37,018	29,071	—
1980	546,235	578,425	8,556	31,621	43,264	48,258	54,741	—	48,900	45,334	—
1990	597,850	630,078	7,417	36,551	45,452	43,426	45,073	—	43,307	48,792	—

TABLE Aa3842–3942   Maine population by race, sex, age, nativity, and urban–rural residence: 1790–1990
Continued

	Population										
	Male, by age										
	30–34	35–39	40–49	40–44	45–49	50–59	50–54	55–59	60–69	60–64	65–69
	Aa3864	Aa3865	Aa3866	Aa3867	Aa3868	Aa3869	Aa3870	Aa3871	Aa3872	Aa3873	Aa3874
Year	Number	Number	Number	Number	Number	Number	Number	Number	Number	Number	Number
1790	—	—	—	—	—	—	—	—	—	—	—
1800	—	—	—	—	—	—	—	—	—	—	—
1810	—	—	—	—	—	—	—	—	—	—	—
1820	—	—	—	—	—	—	—	—	—	—	—
1830	—	—	—	—	—	—	—	—	—	—	—
1840	—	—	—	—	—	—	—	—	—	—	—
1850	—	—	27,505	—	—	17,687	—	—	10,522	—	—
1860	—	—	30,629	—	—	22,931	—	—	14,160	—	—
1870	19,566	18,819	—	16,379	15,427	—	14,241	11,635	—	10,134	7,840
1880	21,093	19,515	—	17,932	16,486	—	14,826	12,371	—	11,401	9,334
1890	23,508	21,924	—	18,844	17,460	—	16,674	13,977	—	12,265	9,544
1900	25,308	23,669	—	22,088	20,085	—	17,458	15,051	—	13,488	10,794
1910	27,016	26,689	—	24,049	21,832	—	20,604	16,546	—	13,916	11,993
1920	26,185	26,897	—	24,139	24,663	—	21,958	17,655	—	16,072	12,250
1930	25,789	26,389	—	24,624	23,733	—	22,355	20,203	—	17,342	13,454
1940	29,219	26,993	—	26,137	25,287	—	23,341	20,969	—	18,256	15,598
1950	30,547	29,984	—	28,276	25,491	—	24,498	21,814	—	19,157	16,575
1960	29,247	30,062	—	28,441	26,965	—	25,103	22,246	—	19,894	17,207
1970	25,242	25,584	—	27,445	27,456	—	25,820	23,580	—	21,261	16,927
1980	43,356	33,518	—	27,624	26,787	—	27,618	26,716	—	23,708	20,335
1990	52,301	50,300	—	46,301	34,577	—	27,433	26,205	—	25,534	22,964

	Population										
	Male, by age					Female, by age					
	70–79	70–74	75–79	80 and older	Unknown age	0	1–4	5–9	10–14	15–19	20–29
	Aa3875	Aa3876	Aa3877	Aa3878	Aa3879	Aa3880	Aa3881	Aa3882	Aa3883	Aa3884	Aa3885
Year	Number	Number	Number	Number	Number	Number	Number	Number	Number	Number	Number
1790	—	—	—	—	—	—	—	—	—	—	—
1800	—	—	—	—	—	—	—	—	—	—	—
1810	—	—	—	—	—	—	—	—	—	—	—
1820	—	—	—	—	—	—	—	—	—	—	—
1830	—	—	—	—	—	—	—	—	—	—	—
1840	—	—	—	—	—	—	—	—	—	—	—
1850	5,235	—	—	1,852	613	6,928	30,220	36,665	35,252	33,504	48,406
1860	6,674	—	—	2,029	0	7,279	31,328	36,075	34,395	35,399	56,096
1870	—	5,547	3,294	2,505	2	6,536	26,866	32,267	34,207	33,118	—
1880	—	6,923	4,489	3,248	—	6,401	25,326	32,069	31,722	32,108	—
1890	—	7,531	5,007	3,875	1,258	5,351	22,771	30,499	30,408	32,524	—
1900	—	7,861	4,966	3,755	1,096	6,742	26,001	31,402	29,525	31,201	—
1910	—	8,997	5,493	4,089	729	7,485	28,158	33,158	32,155	32,362	—
1920	—	8,870	5,650	4,090	572	7,199	29,864	35,541	34,894	32,086	—
1930	—	10,177	6,226	4,294	313	7,099	29,711	39,246	36,598	34,130	—
1940	—	11,565	6,953	5,207	—	6,442	28,080	36,360	38,207	38,838	—
1950	—	12,570	9,858	5,455	—	9,462	39,186	40,143	35,160	35,385	—
1960	—	13,627	9,181	8,049	—	10,929	42,722	49,023	45,649	36,774	—
1970	—	13,209	8,755	8,731	—	8,235	33,321	48,528	49,942	46,550	—
1980	—	15,581	10,402	9,916	—	8,090	30,247	40,915	46,019	52,671	—
1990	—	17,543	12,442	12,232	—	7,150	34,604	43,054	41,153	42,854	—

(continued)

TABLE Aa3842–3942   Maine population by race, sex, age, nativity, and urban–rural residence: 1790–1990
Continued

Population

	Female, by age										
	20–24	25–29	30–39	30–34	35–39	40–49	40–44	45–49	50–59	50–54	55–59
	Aa3886	Aa3887	Aa3888	Aa3889	Aa3890	Aa3891	Aa3892	Aa3893	Aa3894	Aa3895	Aa3896
Year	Number	Number	Number	Number	Number	Number	Number	Number	Number	Number	Number
1790	—	—	—	—	—	—	—	—	—	—	—
1800	—	—	—	—	—	—	—	—	—	—	—
1810	—	—	—	—	—	—	—	—	—	—	—
1820	—	—	—	—	—	—	—	—	—	—	—
1830	—	—	—	—	—	—	—	—	—	—	—
1840	—	—	—	—	—	—	—	—	—	—	—
1850	—	—	33,691	—	—	25,850	—	—	17,507	—	—
1860	—	—	36,699	—	—	28,573	—	—	21,758	—	—
1870	29,614	24,750	—	21,880	19,714	—	16,552	14,483	—	13,280	10,753
1880	31,720	25,183	—	21,784	20,889	—	19,261	16,672	—	14,587	11,848
1890	30,888	25,671	—	23,310	20,975	—	19,244	17,762	—	16,743	13,718
1900	30,913	27,702	—	24,339	22,907	—	21,145	18.313	—	16,914	14,824
1910	30,427	28,558	—	26,245	25,255	—	22,752	20,441	—	18,804	15,052
1920	30,987	28,861	—	25,775	25,570	—	23,756	21,845	—	19,914	16,583
1930	30,860	27,163	—	26,824	26,464	—	23,715	23,024	—	21,234	18,738
1940	33,063	30,630	—	29,513	27,433	—	26,581	24,903	—	22,375	20,209
1950	33,976	33,544	—	31,419	30,222	—	28,910	26,102	—	25,250	22,530
1960	28,351	28,062	—	30,427	31,286	—	29,171	27,508	—	26,236	23,736
1970	38,012	29,431	—	25,966	26,913	—	29,085	29,146	—	27,298	25,515
1980	49,538	46,908	—	43,201	33,436	—	28,147	27,937	—	29,679	29,850
1990	42,733	49,981	—	54,161	51,566	—	45,178	34,466	—	28,275	28,011

Population

	Female, by age								White		Male, by age
	60–69	60–64	65–69	70–79	70–74	75–79	80 and older	Unknown age	Male	Female	0–4
	Aa3897	Aa3898	Aa3899	Aa3900	Aa3901	Aa3902	Aa3903	Aa3904	Aa3905	Aa3906	Aa3907
Year	Number	Number	Number	Number	Number	Number	Number	Number	Number	Number	Number
1790	—	—	—	—	—	—	—	—	49,074	47,033	—
1800	—	—	—	—	—	—	—	—	76,832	74,069	—
1810	—	—	—	—	—	—	—	—	115,509	112,227	—
1820	—	—	—	—	—	—	—	—	149,195	148,145	—
1830	—	—	—	—	—	—	—	—	200,689	197,574	34,053
1840	—	—	—	—	—	—	—	—	252,989	247,449	40,532
1850	10,260	—	—	5,260	—	—	1,948	207	—	—	—
1860	14,280	—	—	6,789	—	—	2,419	0	—	—	—
1870	—	9,977	7,529	—	5,724	3,476	3,083	3	—	—	—
1880	—	10,796	8,887	—	6,967	4,573	4,085	—	—	—	—
1890	—	11,635	9,132	—	7,379	4,907	4,955	624	—	—	—
1900	—	13,251	10,618	—	7,636	5,026	4,466	546	—	—	—
1910	—	13,478	11,347	—	8,670	5,696	4,787	489	—	—	—
1920	—	14,823	11,316	—	8,578	6,013	5,334	323	—	—	—
1930	—	16,195	13,089	—	9,894	6,328	5,548	278	—	—	—
1940	—	17,769	15,521	—	11,578	7,405	6,498	—	—	—	—
1950	—	19,236	17,377	—	13,449	11,186	7,092	—	—	—	—
1960	—	21,857	19,601	—	15,739	11,557	11,583	—	—	—	—
1970	—	24,271	20,772	—	17,779	13,384	15,035	—	—	—	—
1980	—	27,103	24,787	—	21,585	16,554	21,758	—	—	—	—
1990	—	28,700	27,871	—	23,222	19,259	27,840	—	—	—	—

TABLE Aa3842–3942   Maine population by race, sex, age, nativity, and urban–rural residence: 1790–1990
Continued

	Population											
	White											
	Male, by age										Female, by age	
	5–9	10–14	15–19	20–29	30–39	40–49	50–59	60–69	70–79	80 and older	0–4	5–9
	Aa3908	Aa3909	Aa3910	Aa3911	Aa3912	Aa3913	Aa3914	Aa3915	Aa3916	Aa3917	Aa3918	Aa3919
Year	Number	Number	Number	Number	Number	Number	Number	Number	Number	Number	Number	Number
1790	—	—	—	—	—	—	—	—	—	—	—	—
1800	—	—	—	—	—	—	—	—	—	—	—	—
1810	—	—	—	—	—	—	—	—	—	—	—	—
1820	—	—	—	—	—	—	—	—	—	—	—	—
1830	28,742	25,522	22,400	34,985	21,701	14,547	9,228	5,956	2,637	918	32,471	27,676
1840	35,671	31,691	27,740	42,266	29,864	19,948	12,551	7,408	4,152	1,166	38,185	34,458
1850	—	—	—	—	—	—	—	—	—	—	—	—
1860	—	—	—	—	—	—	—	—	—	—	—	—
1870	—	—	—	—	—	—	—	—	—	—	—	—
1880	—	—	—	—	—	—	—	—	—	—	—	—
1890	—	—	—	—	—	—	—	—	—	—	—	—
1900	—	—	—	—	—	—	—	—	—	—	—	—
1910	—	—	—	—	—	—	—	—	—	—	—	—
1920	—	—	—	—	—	—	—	—	—	—	—	—
1930	—	—	—	—	—	—	—	—	—	—	—	—
1940	—	—	—	—	—	—	—	—	—	—	—	—
1950	—	—	—	—	—	—	—	—	—	—	—	—
1960	—	—	—	—	—	—	—	—	—	—	—	—
1970	—	—	—	—	—	—	—	—	—	—	—	—
1980	—	—	—	—	—	—	—	—	—	—	—	—
1990	—	—	—	—	—	—	—	—	—	—	—	—

	Population											
	White											
	Female, by age										Male, by age	
	10–14	15–19	20–29	30–39	40–49	50–59	60–69	70–79	80 and older	0–9	10–15
	Aa3920	Aa3921	Aa3922	Aa3923	Aa3924	Aa3925	Aa3926	Aa3927	Aa3928	Aa3929	Aa3930
Year	Number	Number	Number	Number	Number	Number	Number	Number	Number	Number	Number
1790	—	—	—	—	—	—	—	—	—	—	—
1800	—	—	—	—	—	—	—	—	—	27,970	12,305
1810	—	—	—	—	—	—	—	—	—	41,273	18,463
1820	—	—	—	—	—	—	—	—	—	49,217	24,528
1830	24,067	22,348	35,596	22,259	14,183	9,330	5,904	2,688	1,052	—	—
1840	30,044	27,940	42,165	29,046	20,024	12,304	7,703	4,122	1,458	—	—
1850	—	—	—	—	—	—	—	—	—	—	—
1860	—	—	—	—	—	—	—	—	—	—	—
1870	—	—	—	—	—	—	—	—	—	—	—
1880	—	—	—	—	—	—	—	—	—	—	—
1890	—	—	—	—	—	—	—	—	—	—	—
1900	—	—	—	—	—	—	—	—	—	—	—
1910	—	—	—	—	—	—	—	—	—	—	—
1920	—	—	—	—	—	—	—	—	—	—	—
1930	—	—	—	—	—	—	—	—	—	—	—
1940	—	—	—	—	—	—	—	—	—	—	—
1950	—	—	—	—	—	—	—	—	—	—	—
1960	—	—	—	—	—	—	—	—	—	—	—
1970	—	—	—	—	—	—	—	—	—	—	—
1980	—	—	—	—	—	—	—	—	—	—	—
1990	—	—	—	—	—	—	—	—	—	—	—

(continued)

TABLE Aa3842–3942 Maine population by race, sex, age, nativity, and urban–rural residence: 1790–1990
Continued

	Population											
	White											
	Male, by age			Female, by age					Male, by age		Female, by age	
	16–25	26–44	45 and older	0–9	10–15	16–25	26–44	45 and older	0–15	16 and older	0–15	16 and older
	Aa3931	Aa3932	Aa3933	Aa3934	Aa3935	Aa3936	Aa3937	Aa3938	Aa3939	Aa3940	Aa3941	Aa3942
Year	Number	Number	Number	Number	Number	Number	Number	Number	Number	Number	Number	Number
1790	—	—	—	—	—	—	—	—	24,733	24,341	24,020	23,013
1800	12,900	15,318	8,339	26,899	11,338	13,295	14,496	8,041	—	—	—	—
1810	20,403	22,079	13,291	39,131	17,827	21,290	21,464	12,515	—	—	—	—
1820	28,530	27,742	19,178	46,565	23,982	30,823	28,248	18,527	—	—	—	—
1830	—	—	—	—	—	—	—	—	—	—	—	—
1840	—	—	—	—	—	—	—	—	—	—	—	—
1850	—	—	—	—	—	—	—	—	—	—	—	—
1860	—	—	—	—	—	—	—	—	—	—	—	—
1870	—	—	—	—	—	—	—	—	—	—	—	—
1880	—	—	—	—	—	—	—	—	—	—	—	—
1890	—	—	—	—	—	—	—	—	—	—	—	—
1900	—	—	—	—	—	—	—	—	—	—	—	—
1910	—	—	—	—	—	—	—	—	—	—	—	—
1920	—	—	—	—	—	—	—	—	—	—	—	—
1930	—	—	—	—	—	—	—	—	—	—	—	—
1940	—	—	—	—	—	—	—	—	—	—	—	—
1950	—	—	—	—	—	—	—	—	—	—	—	—
1960	—	—	—	—	—	—	—	—	—	—	—	—
1970	—	—	—	—	—	—	—	—	—	—	—	—
1980	—	—	—	—	—	—	—	—	—	—	—	—
1990	—	—	—	—	—	—	—	—	—	—	—	—

Sources
See the sources for Table Aa2244–2340.
Documentation
See the text for Table Aa2244–2340.

Maine was originally part of Massachusetts, although tabulated separately in the early censuses. It became a state in 1820 without having been a territory. The present northern boundary was finally fixed by treaty with Great Britain in 1842.

TABLE Aa3943–4043   Maryland population by race, sex, age, nativity, and urban–rural residence: 1790–1990

Contributed by Michael R. Haines

	Area	Population density	Population									
				Race				Residence		Nativity	
			Total	White	Nonwhite	Black	Other nonwhite	Urban	Rural	Native-born	Foreign-born
	Aa3943	Aa3944	Aa3945	Aa3946	Aa3947	Aa3948	Aa3949	Aa3950	Aa3951	Aa3952	Aa3953
Year	Square miles	Persons per square mile	Number	Number	Number	Number	Number	Number	Number	Number	Number
1790	9,999	31.98	319,728	208,649	111,079	111,079	—	13,503	306,225	—	—
1800	9,941	34.36	341,548	216,326	125,222	125,222	—	26,514	315,034	—	—
1810	9,941	38.28	380,546	235,117	145,429	145,429	—	46,555	333,991	—	—
1820	9,941	40.98	407,350	260,222	147,128	147,128	0	66,378	340,972	—	—
1830	9,941	44.97	447,040	291,108	155,932	155,932	—	91,041	355,999	—	—
1840	9,941	47.28	470,019	318,204	151,573	151,573	—	113,912	356,107	—	—
1850	9,941	58.65	583,034	417,943	165,091	165,091	—	188,045	394,989	531,825	51,209
1860	9,941	69.11	687,049	515,918	171,131	171,131	—	233,300	453,749	609,520	77,529
1870	9,941	78.55	780,894	605,497	175,397	175,391	6	295,459	485,435	697,482	83,412
1880	9,941	94.05	934,943	724,693	210,250	210,230	20	375,843	559,100	852,137	82,806
1890	9,941	104.86	1,042,390	826,493	215,897	215,657	240	495,702	546,688	948,094	94,296
1900	9,941	119.51	1,188,044	952,424	235,620	235,064	556	591,206	596,838	1,094,110	93,934
1910	9,941	130.30	1,295,346	1,062,639	232,707	232,250	457	658,192	637,154	1,190,402	104,944
1920	9,941	145.83	1,449,661	1,204,737	244,924	244,479	445	869,422	580,239	1,346,482	103,179
1930	9,941	164.12	1,631,526	1,354,226	277,300	276,379	921	974,869	656,657	1,535,196	96,330
1940	9,887	184.21	1,821,244	1,518,481	302,763	301,931	832	1,080,351	740,893	1,738,653	82,591
1950	9,881	237.12	2,343,001	1,954,975	388,026	385,972	2,054	1,615,902	727,099	·2,248,080	85,165
1960	9,891	313.49	3,100,689	2,573,919	526,770	518,410	8,360	2,253,832	846,857	3,006,509	94,178
1970	9,891	396.56	3,922,399	3,194,888	727,511	699,479	28,032	3,003,935	918,464	3,798,046	124,345
1980	9,837	428.69	4,216,975	3,158,838	1,058,137	958,150	99,987	3,386,555	830,420	4,021,394	195,581
1990	9,775	489.17	4,781,468	3,393,964	1,387,504	1,189,899	197,605	3,888,429	893,039	4,467,974	313,494

	Population										
	Sex		Male, by age								
	Male	Female	0	1–4	5–9	10–14	15–19	20–29	20–24	25–29	30–39
	Aa3954	Aa3955	Aa3956	Aa3957	Aa3958	Aa3959	Aa3960	Aa3961	Aa3962	Aa3963	Aa3964
Year	Number	Number	Number	Number	Number	Number	Number	Number	Number	Number	Number
1790	—	—	—	—	—	—	—	—	—	—	—
1800	—	—	—	—	—	—	—	—	—	—	—
1810	—	—	—	—	—	—	—	—	—	—	—
1820	206,862	200,488	—	—	—	—	—	—	—	—	—
1830	225,688	221,352	—	—	—	—	—	—	—	—	—
1840	233,950	235,827	—	—	—	—	—	—	—	—	—
1850	292,323	290,711	8,319	34,692	39,410	36,786	29,806	53,693	—	—	38,073
1860	340,898	346,151	9,675	40,951	44,935	42,157	36,779	58,047	—	—	43,783
1870	384,984	395,910	11,031	43,434	49,225	48,909	40,546	—	34,429	29,387	—
1880	462,187	472,756	13,202	48,600	58,764	53,728	46,677	—	45,520	36,099	—
1890	515,691	526,699	12,451	48,840	61,915	58,426	54,204	—	48,289	40,590	—
1900	589,275	598,769	14,379	53,174	66,437	63,526	58,693	—	55,583	49,917	—
1910	644,225	651,121	14,243	55,379	67,182	65,122	62,871	—	60,357	53,800	—
1920	729,455	720,206	15,170	58,777	72,575	70,420	66,008	—	66,908	62,472	—
1930	821,009	810,517	13,442	59,669	82,088	76,915	74,031	—	73,992	66,653	—
1940	915,038	906,206	12,675	56,817	71,045	79,002	84,914	—	83,878	79,446	—
1950	1,166,603	1,176,398	24,802	106,923	104,772	81,864	78,113	—	92,854	104,111	—
1960	1,533,200	1,567,489	37,397	148,133	167,858	149,430	113,324	—	94,271	96,478	—
1970	1,916,321	2,006,078	34,308	141,052	205,742	208,448	178,039	—	157,219	140,082	—
1980	2,042,810	2,174,165	29,989	109,374	149,606	181,707	205,244	—	193,252	180,711	—
1990	2,318,671	2,462,797	32,787	150,403	168,911	152,048	158,929	—	184,252	221,623	—

(continued)

TABLE Aa3943–4043   Maryland population by race, sex, age, nativity, and urban–rural residence: 1790–1990
Continued

	Population										
	Male, by age										
	30–34	35–39	40–49	40–44	45–49	50–59	50–54	55–59	60–69	60–64	65–69
	Aa3965	Aa3966	Aa3967	Aa3968	Aa3969	Aa3970	Aa3971	Aa3972	Aa3973	Aa3974	Aa3975
Year	Number	Number	Number	Number	Number	Number	Number	Number	Number	Number	Number
1790	—	—	—	—	—	—	—	—	—	—	—
1800	—	—	—	—	—	—	—	—	—	—	—
1810	—	—	—	—	—	—	—	—	—	—	—
1820	—	—	—	—	—	—	—	—	—	—	—
1830	—	—	—	—	—	—	—	—	—	—	—
1840	—	—	—	—	—	—	—	—	—	—	—
1850	—	—	24,723	—	—	14,677	—	—	7,858	—	—
1860	—	—	31,159	—	—	18,581	—	—	9,949	—	—
1870	23,902	22,702	—	18,527	18,176	—	15,624	9,562	—	8,450	4,927
1880	29,636	28,502	—	23,790	19,863	—	17,900	12,384	—	11,396	7,345
1890	36,115	32,501	—	26,911	24,351	—	20,837	14,513	—	12,850	9,036
1900	41,848	39,200	—	34,664	28,166	—	24,195	18,501	—	14,957	10,569
1910	47,214	46,103	—	39,187	34,058	—	29,996	21,885	—	17,263	13,050
1920	55,176	53,445	—	44,570	43,980	—	35,692	26,503	—	22,238	15,289
1930	62,542	63,141	—	54,585	47,780	—	41,385	32,761	—	26,076	19,139
1940	75,064	70,311	—	65,031	58,876	—	50,762	38,631	—	31,321	25,217
1950	99,242	93,021	—	82,821	70,948	—	63,294	50,994	—	40,481	30,382
1960	110,797	117,591	—	108,232	95,499	—	79,742	65,826	—	51,277	40,362
1970	117,515	112,582	—	120,016	119,485	—	105,771	87,015	—	67,896	48,466
1980	172,115	141,427	—	116,118	107,307	—	110,853	104,727	—	84,809	62,872
1990	221,044	197,957	—	179,771	143,404	—	112,476	97,768	—	91,888	79,951

	Population										
	Male, by age					Female, by age					
	70–79	70–74	75–79	80 and older	Unknown age	0	1–4	5–9	10–14	15–19	20–29
	Aa3976	Aa3977	Aa3978	Aa3979	Aa3980	Aa3981	Aa3982	Aa3983	Aa3984	Aa3985	Aa3986
Year	Number	Number	Number	Number	Number	Number	Number	Number	Number	Number	Number
1790	—	—	—	—	—	—	—	—	—	—	—
1800	—	—	—	—	—	—	—	—	—	—	—
1810	—	—	—	—	—	—	—	—	—	—	—
1820	—	—	—	—	—	—	—	—	—	—	—
1830	—	—	—	—	—	—	—	—	—	—	—
1840	—	—	—	—	—	—	—	—	—	—	—
1850	3,213	—	—	1,064	9	8,163	34,470	38,859	35,590	31,942	52,432
1860	3,737	—	—	1,144	1	9,640	40,354	44,295	40,949	39,104	62,480
1870	—	3,261	1,661	1,228	3	11,055	42,947	47,763	47,570	43,308	—
1880	—	4,669	2,415	1,697	—	13,125	48,027	57,861	53,005	49,166	—
1890	—	6,359	3,218	2,305	1,980	12,066	47,619	60,894	57,600	56,233	—
1900	—	6,934	3,874	2,473	2,185	14,019	53,012	66,308	62,691	61,271	—
1910	—	8,480	4,523	2,800	712	13,621	54,471	66,500	64,483	65,102	—
1920	—	9,807	5,871	3,492	1,062	14,729	58,329	71,128	69,451	64,989	—
1930	—	13,208	7,165	4,518	1,919	13,245	58,273	80,568	75,698	71,773	—
1940	—	16,452	9,290	6,306	—	12,306	54,867	69,785	77,350	82,863	—
1950	—	20,315	13,780	7,886	—	23,887	102,640	101,125	79,839	77,507	—
1960	—	27,996	16,609	12,378	—	36,310	144,680	163,753	145,012	112,486	—
1970	—	33,828	20,855	18,002	—	32,620	136,287	198,750	201,480	178,100	—
1980	—	43,036	26,405	23,258	—	28,754	104,157	143,310	174,871	199,767	—
1990	—	56,867	36,837	31,755	—	30,942	143,686	163,462	145,116	151,721	—

TABLE Aa3943–4043   Maryland population by race, sex, age, nativity, and urban–rural residence: 1790–1990
Continued

	Population										
	Female, by age										
	20–24	25–29	30–39	30–34	35–39	40–49	40–44	45–49	50–59	50–54	55–59
	Aa3987	Aa3988	Aa3989	Aa3990	Aa3991	Aa3992	Aa3993	Aa3994	Aa3995	Aa3996	Aa3997
Year	Number	Number	Number	Number	Number	Number	Number	Number	Number	Number	Number
1790	—	—	—	—	—	—	—	—	—	—	—
1800	—	—	—	—	—	—	—	—	—	—	—
1810	—	—	—	—	—	—	—	—	—	—	—
1820	—	—	—	—	—	—	—	—	—	—	—
1830	—	—	—	—	—	—	—	—	—	—	—
1840	—	—	—	—	—	—	—	—	—	—	—
1850	—	—	36,458	—	—	23,970	—	—	14,904	—	—
1860	—	—	43,643	—	—	30,286	—	—	18,642	—	—
1870	38,841	32,213	—	26,330	23,583	—	20,213	16,374	—	14,838	9,270
1880	48,930	38,349	—	31,411	29,022	—	24,274	19,711	—	17,977	12,150
1890	53,409	44,292	—	37,438	32,795	—	27,617	23,782	—	20,949	14,372
1900	59,381	51,656	—	42,900	39,842	—	34,093	27,837	—	24,052	18,122
1910	62,883	56,205	—	48,572	46,006	—	39,361	33,667	—	28,948	21,185
1920	65,851	62,480	—	54,711	53,053	—	45,049	40,311	—	34,375	25,436
1930	71,854	65,595	—	61,816	61,164	—	52,782	47,099	—	41,081	31,915
1940	81,054	78,735	—	73,723	68,591	—	62,229	56,235	—	48,838	39,741
1950	94,418	109,774	—	100,067	91,708	—	80,109	69,102	—	61,912	51,070
1960	94,409	99,736	—	114,153	124,522	—	108,249	93,624	—	78,325	66,706
1970	168,236	146,343	—	120,490	115,142	—	124,147	128,669	—	109,968	91,454
1980	199,139	190,425	—	182,328	149,767	—	119,755	111,592	—	116,736	117,955
1990	185,357	227,573	—	229,858	209,041	—	190,237	149,830	—	116,091	104,402

	Population									White	
	Female, by age										Male, by age
	60–69	60–64	65–69	70–79	70–74	75–79	80 and older	Unknown age	Male	Female	0–4
	Aa3998	Aa3999	Aa4000	Aa4001	Aa4002	Aa4003	Aa4004	Aa4005	Aa4006	Aa4007	Aa4008
Year	Number	Number	Number	Number	Number	Number	Number	Number	Number	Number	Number
1790	—	—	—	—	—	—	—	—	107,254	101,395	—
1800	—	—	—	—	—	—	—	—	110,650	105,676	—
1810	—	—	—	—	—	—	—	—	120,210	114,907	—
1820	—	—	—	—	—	—	—	—	131,743	128,479	—
1830	—	—	—	—	—	—	—	—	147,340	143,768	23,737
1840	—	—	—	—	—	—	—	—	158,804	159,400	26,874
1850	8,597	—	—	3,746	—	—	1,571	9	—	—	—
1860	10,749	—	—	4,348	—	—	1,658	3	—	—	—
1870	—	8,540	5,222	—	4,034	1,920	1,888	1	—	—	—
1880	—	11,459	7,366	—	5,360	2,984	2,579	—	—	—	—
1890	—	13,449	9,189	—	6,838	3,728	3,213	1,216	—	—	—
1900	—	15,543	10,665	—	7,632	4,531	3,305	1,909	—	—	—
1910	—	17,608	13,440	—	9,074	5,283	4,017	695	—	—	—
1920	—	21,876	15,821	—	10,718	6,618	4,852	429	—	—	—
1930	—	26,825	20,153	—	14,211	8,265	6,313	1,887	—	—	—
1940	—	33,638	27,277	—	18,731	11,228	9,015	—	—	—	—
1950	—	42,089	36,157	—	25,044	19,286	10,664	—	—	—	—
1960	—	56,330	47,890	—	35,985	24,083	21,236	—	—	—	—
1970	—	75,861	61,251	—	48,449	33,681	35,150	—	—	—	—
1980	—	95,571	79,416	—	61,885	45,432	53,305	—	—	—	—
1990	—	103,409	100,253	—	77,420	59,491	74,908	—	—	—	—

(continued)

TABLE Aa3943–4043   Maryland population by race, sex, age, nativity, and urban–rural residence: 1790–1990
Continued

	Population										
	White										
	Male, by age										Female, by age
	5–9	10–14	15–19	20–29	30–39	40–49	50–59	60–69	70–79	80 and older	0–4
	Aa4009	Aa4010	Aa4011	Aa4012	Aa4013	Aa4014	Aa4015	Aa4016	Aa4017	Aa4018	Aa4019
Year	Number	Number	Number	Number	Number	Number	Number	Number	Number	Number	Number
1790	—	—	—	—	—	—	—	—	—	—	—
1800	—	—	—	—	—	—	—	—	—	—	—
1810	—	—	—	—	—	—	—	—	—	—	—
1820	—	—	—	—	—	—	—	—	—	—	—
1830	19,438	17,886	15,778	29,397	18,215	11,072	6,565	3,462	1,375	415	22,356
1840	20,551	18,382	16,302	30,041	20,753	12,664	7,281	3,911	1,549	496	25,650
1850	—	—	—	—	—	—	—	—	—	—	—
1860	—	—	—	—	—	—	—	—	—	—	—
1870	—	—	—	—	—	—	—	—	—	—	—
1880	—	—	—	—	—	—	—	—	—	—	—
1890	—	—	—	—	—	—	—	—	—	—	—
1900	—	—	—	—	—	—	—	—	—	—	—
1910	—	—	—	—	—	—	—	—	—	—	—
1920	—	—	—	—	—	—	—	—	—	—	—
1930	—	—	—	—	—	—	—	—	—	—	—
1940	—	—	—	—	—	—	—	—	—	—	—
1950	—	—	—	—	—	—	—	—	—	—	—
1960	—	—	—	—	—	—	—	—	—	—	—
1970	—	—	—	—	—	—	—	—	—	—	—
1980	—	—	—	—	—	—	—	—	—	—	—
1990	—	—	—	—	—	—	—	—	—	—	—

	Population											
	White											
	Female, by age										Male, by age	
	5–9	10–14	15–19	20–29	30–39	40–49	50–59	60–69	70–79	80 and older	0–9	10–15
	Aa4020	Aa4021	Aa4022	Aa4023	Aa4024	Aa4025	Aa4026	Aa4027	Aa4028	Aa4029	Aa4030	Aa4031
Year	Number	Number	Number	Number	Number	Number	Number	Number	Number	Number	Number	Number
1790	—	—	—	—	—	—	—	—	—	—	—	—
1800	—	—	—	—	—	—	—	—	—	—	35,852	17,392
1810	—	—	—	—	—	—	—	—	—	—	38,613	18,489
1820	—	—	—	—	—	—	—	—	—	—	41,511	18,952
1830	18,693	17,327	18,020	27,248	16,617	10,840	6,983	3,633	1,541	510	—	—
1840	19,997	17,602	18,404	31,116	19,366	12,517	7,901	4,406	1,804	637	—	—
1850	—	—	—	—	—	—	—	—	—	—	—	—
1860	—	—	—	—	—	—	—	—	—	—	—	—
1870	—	—	—	—	—	—	—	—	—	—	—	—
1880	—	—	—	—	—	—	—	—	—	—	—	—
1890	—	—	—	—	—	—	—	—	—	—	—	—
1900	—	—	—	—	—	—	—	—	—	—	—	—
1910	—	—	—	—	—	—	—	—	—	—	—	—
1920	—	—	—	—	—	—	—	—	—	—	—	—
1930	—	—	—	—	—	—	—	—	—	—	—	—
1940	—	—	—	—	—	—	—	—	—	—	—	—
1950	—	—	—	—	—	—	—	—	—	—	—	—
1960	—	—	—	—	—	—	—	—	—	—	—	—
1970	—	—	—	—	—	—	—	—	—	—	—	—
1980	—	—	—	—	—	—	—	—	—	—	—	—
1990	—	—	—	—	—	—	—	—	—	—	—	—

TABLE Aa3943–4043   Maryland population by race, sex, age, nativity, and urban–rural residence: 1790–1990
Continued

	Population											
	White											
	Male, by age			Female, by age					Male, by age		Female, by age	
	16–25	26–44	45 and older	0–9	10–15	16–25	26–44	45 and older	0–15	16 and older	0–15	16 and older
	Aa4032	Aa4033	Aa4034	Aa4035	Aa4036	Aa4037	Aa4038	Aa4039	Aa4040	Aa4041	Aa4042	Aa4043
Year	Number	Number	Number	Number	Number	Number	Number	Number	Number	Number	Number	Number
1790	—	—	—	—	—	—	—	—	51,339	55,915	42,504	58,891
1800	21,234	22,778	13,394	33,796	16,437	22,367	21,170	11,906	—	—	—	—
1810	22,688	25,255	15,165	36,137	17,833	23,875	22,908	14,154	—	—	—	—
1820	26,404	27,916	16,960	39,454	19,578	27,293	26,347	15,807	—	—	—	—
1830	—	—	—	—	—	—	—	—	—	—	—	—
1840	—	—	—	—	—	—	—	—	—	—	—	—
1850	—	—	—	—	—	—	—	—	—	—	—	—
1860	—	—	—	—	—	—	—	—	—	—	—	—
1870	—	—	—	—	—	—	—	—	—	—	—	—
1880	—	—	—	—	—	—	—	—	—	—	—	—
1890	—	—	—	—	—	—	—	—	—	—	—	—
1900	—	—	—	—	—	—	—	—	—	—	—	—
1910	—	—	—	—	—	—	—	—	—	—	—	—
1920	—	—	—	—	—	—	—	—	—	—	—	—
1930	—	—	—	—	—	—	—	—	—	—	—	—
1940	—	—	—	—	—	—	—	—	—	—	—	—
1950	—	—	—	—	—	—	—	—	—	—	—	—
1960	—	—	—	—	—	—	—	—	—	—	—	—
1970	—	—	—	—	—	—	—	—	—	—	—	—
1980	—	—	—	—	—	—	—	—	—	—	—	—
1990	—	—	—	—	—	—	—	—	—	—	—	—

Sources

See the sources for Table Aa2244–2340.

Documentation

See the text for Table Aa2244–2340.

Maryland was one of the original thirteen states, admitted to the Union in 1788.

TABLE Aa4044–4144   Massachusetts population by race, sex, age, nativity, and urban–rural residence: 1790–1990

Contributed by Michael R. Haines

						Population						
					Race				Residence		Nativity	
	Area	Population density	Total	White	Nonwhite	Black	Other nonwhite	Urban	Rural	Native-born	Foreign-born
	Aa4044	Aa4045	Aa4046	Aa4047	Aa4048	Aa4049	Aa4050	Aa4051	Aa4052	Aa4053	Aa4054
Year	Square miles	Persons per square mile	Number	Number	Number	Number	Number	Number	Number	Number	Number
1790	8,041	47.08	378,556	373,187	5,369	5,369	—	51,202	327,585	—	—
1800	8,041	52.59	422,845	416,793	6,452	6,452	—	65,300	357,545	—	—
1810	8,041	58.70	472,040	465,303	6,737	6,737	—	100,617	371,423	—	—
1820	8,041	65.08	523,287	516,419	6,868	6,740	128	119,187	404,100	—	—
1830	8,041	75.91	610,408	603,359	7,049	7,049	—	189,657	420,751	—	—
1840	8,041	91.74	737,699	729,030	8,669	8,669	—	279,454	458,245	—	—
1850	8,041	123.68	994,514	985,450	9,064	9,064	—	503,861	490,653	83,0490	164,024
1860	8,039	153.14	1,231,066	1,221,432	9,634	9,602	32	733,209	497,857	97,0960	260,106
1870	8,039	181.29	1,457,351	1,443,156	14,195	13,947	248	972,081	485,270	1,104,032	353,319
1880	8,039	221.80	1,783,085	1,763,782	19,303	18,697	606	1,331,580	451,505	1,339,594	443,491
1890 [1]	8,039	278.51	2,238,947	2,215,373	23,570	22,144	1,426	1,834,888	404,059	1,581,806	657,137
1900	8,039	348.97	2,805,346	2,769,764	35,582	31,974	3,608	2,411,877	393,469	1,959,022	846,324
1910	8,039	418.76	3,366,416	3,324,926	41,490	38,055	3,435	2,995,739	370,677	2,307,171	1,059,245
1920	8,039	479.21	3,852,356	3,803,524	48,832	45,466	3,366	3,468,916	383,440	2,763,808	1,088,548
1930	8,039	528.62	4,249,614	4,192,992	56,622	52,365	4,257	3,831,426	418,188	3,183,994	1,065,620
1940	7,907	545.94	4,316,721	4,257,596	59,125	55,391	3,734	3,859,476	457,245	3,459,063	857,658
1950	7,867	596.23	4,690,514	4,611,503	79,011	73,171	5,840	3,959,239	731,275	3,950,790	721,230
1960	7,833	657.29	5,148,578	5,023,144	125,434	111,842	13,592	4,302,530	846,048	4,572,865	576,452
1970	7,826	726.96	5,689,170	5,477,624	211,546	175,817	35,729	4,810,449	878,721	5,194,243	494,660
1980	7,824	733.26	5,737,037	5,362,836	374,201	221,279	152,922	4,808,339	928,698	5,236,055	500,982
1990	7,838	767.60	6,016,425	5,405,374	611,051	300,130	310,921	5,069,603	946,822	5,442,692	573,733

						Population						
	Sex		Male, by age									
	Male	Female	0	1–4	5–9	10–14	15–19	20–29	20–24	25–29	30–39
	Aa4055	Aa4056	Aa4057	Aa4058	Aa4059	Aa4060	Aa4061	Aa4062	Aa4063	Aa4064	Aa4065
Year	Number	Number	Number	Number	Number	Number	Number	Number	Number	Number	Number
1790	—	—	—	—	—	—	—	—	—	—	—
1800	—	—	—	—	—	—	—	—	—	—	—
1810	—	—	—	—	—	—	—	—	—	—	—
1820	255,462	267,697	—	—	—	—	—	—	—	—	—
1830	298,043	312,365	—	—	—	—	—	—	—	—	—
1840	365,334	372,365	—	—	—	—	—	—	—	—	—
1850	488,517	505,997	11,612	45,869	51,607	49,557	49,249	102,250	—	—	73,244
1860	596,713	634,353	15,869	60,059	64,476	57,544	57,070	112,413	—	—	90,246
1870	703,779	753,572	16,566	62,473	69,854	74,270	68,365	—	66,281	60,784	—
1880	858,440	924,645	19,012	71,635	86,007	81,035	80,445	—	84,573	75,212	—
1890 [1]	1,087,709	1,151,234	21,695	80,848	98,103	96,693	104,021	—	115,358	106,296	—
1900	1,367,474	1,437,872	30,266	111,507	128,120	114,122	115,258	—	129,363	136,438	—
1910	1,655,248	1,711,168	35,813	130,262	148,656	142,689	145,630	—	156,906	154,405	—
1920	1,890,014	1,962,342	37,401	157,135	180,574	167,116	147,742	—	154,178	165,852	—
1930	2,071,672	2,177,942	33,070	144,473	197,688	194,537	180,953	—	163,089	153,341	—
1940	2,102,479	2,214,242	26,759	116,876	154,991	179,575	192,892	—	180,111	167,530	—
1950	2,270,367	2,420,147	42,588	186,696	186,744	150,672	151,474	—	171,871	182,869	—
1960	2,486,235	2,662,343	56,567	222,832	248,916	226,583	178,500	—	143,553	147,715	—
1970	2,719,398	2,969,772	46,839	193,091	276,729	283,892	254,999	—	217,531	183,098	—
1980	2,730,893	3,006,144	36,771	136,258	191,602	235,669	274,859	—	270,713	239,341	—
1990	2,888,745	3,127,680	37,460	173,623	193,868	178,600	206,249	—	254,377	277,579	—

Note appears at end of table

TABLE Aa4044–4144   Massachusetts population by race, sex, age, nativity, and urban–rural residence: 1790–1990 *Continued*

						Population				
					Male, by age					
	30–34	35–39	40–49	40–44	45–49	50–59	50–54	55–59	60–69	60–64
	Aa4066	Aa4067	Aa4068	Aa4069	Aa4070	Aa4071	Aa4072	Aa4073	Aa4074	Aa4075
Year	Number	Number	Number	Number	Number	Number	Number	Number	Number	Number
1790	—	—	—	—	—	—	—	—	—	—
1800	—	—	—	—	—	—	—	—	—	—
1810	—	—	—	—	—	—	—	—	—	—
1820	—	—	—	—	—	—	—	—	—	—
1830	—	—	—	—	—	—	—	—	—	—
1840	—	—	—	—	—	—	—	—	—	—
1850	—	—	48,168	—	—	28,624	—	—	16,872	—
1860	—	—	63,826	—	—	39,430	—	—	22,715	—
1870	52,667	48,497	—	42,689	37,417	—	32,131	21,833	—	19,667
1880	65,773	60,554	—	52,646	44,796	—	39,328	28,867	—	25,881
1890 [1]	91,226	76,931	—	65,807	57,114	—	48,519	35,263	—	31,112
1900	121,794	108,467	—	88,875	71,238	—	60,678	45,130	—	36,814
1910	138,638	134,879	—	114,454	95,485	—	79,186	55,718	—	44,229
1920	153,699	149,182	—	126,906	122,933	—	101,687	74,244	—	58,914
1930	153,998	163,459	—	147,516	130,653	—	113,969	95,677	—	75,992
1940	154,751	148,346	—	147,919	146,594	—	131,099	106,246	—	86,647
1950	173,541	163,999	—	152,048	139,589	—	136,373	125,505	—	105,358
1960	164,055	172,059	—	165,039	153,047	—	137,410	123,067	—	107,917
1970	144,934	145,570	—	160,489	164,073	—	154,855	135,032	—	113,128
1980	217,649	169,502	—	134,925	134,444	—	146,211	145,603	—	126,323
1990	269,814	239,169	—	211,806	164,452	—	126,994	120,932	—	121,548

						Population				
		Male, by age					Female, by age			
	65–69	70–79	70–74	75–79	80 and older	Unknown age	0	1–4	5–9	10–14	15–19
	Aa4076	Aa4077	Aa4078	Aa4079	Aa4080	Aa4081	Aa4082	Aa4083	Aa4084	Aa4085	Aa4086
Year	Number	Number	Number	Number	Number	Number	Number	Number	Number	Number	Number
1790	—	—	—	—	—	—	—	—	—	—	—
1800	—	—	—	—	—	—	—	—	—	—	—
1810	—	—	—	—	—	—	—	—	—	—	—
1820	—	—	—	—	—	—	—	—	—	—	—
1830	—	—	—	—	—	—	—	—	—	—	—
1840	—	—	—	—	—	—	—	—	—	—	—
1850	—	7,845	—	—	2,575	1,045	11,580	44,984	51,190	48,467	56,492
1860	—	10,205	—	—	2,859	1	5,666	59,695	64,050	56,804	63,730
1870	12,760	—	9,024	4,821	3,664	16	16,421	61,429	69,942	74,101	73,819
1880	17,990	—	12,405	7,190	5,091	—	18,575	70,085	85,588	80,390	87,150
1890 [1]	22,427	—	16,099	9,442	6,934	3,821	21,348	79,867	97,475	95,535	110,592
1900	26,229	—	17,857	11,112	7,781	6,425	30,226	110,238	127,941	115,208	122,609
1910	32,486	—	21,739	12,744	9,214	2,115	34,921	127,890	146,190	142,271	150,931
1920	39,339	—	25,682	15,105	10,415	1,910	37,490	153,735	179,252	166,422	154,389
1930	54,579	—	35,453	18,968	12,628	1,629	31,964	140,133	192,969	192,466	185,196
1940	69,300	—	47,954	27,169	17,720	—	25,851	112,211	149,751	174,412	192,359
1950	81,710	—	56,171	41,732	21,427	—	41,215	178,009	178,017	144,835	157,032
1960	93,282	—	69,423	42,968	33,302	—	54,697	214,361	238,989	217,888	183,438
1970	87,197	—	67,491	47,160	43,290	—	44,915	185,221	265,635	271,501	259,557
1980	101,023	—	73,235	48,145	48,620	—	34,959	129,227	183,132	225,663	273,380
1990	111,013	—	85,747	59,416	56,098	—	35,975	165,415	184,167	169,493	203,685

Note appears at end of table

(continued)

TABLE Aa4044–4144 Massachusetts population by race, sex, age, nativity, and urban–rural residence: 1790–1990
Continued

	Population										
	Female, by age										
	20–29	20–24	25–29	30–39	30–34	35–39	40–49	40–44	45–49	50–59	50–54
	Aa4087	Aa4088	Aa4089	Aa4090	Aa4091	Aa4092	Aa4093	Aa4094	Aa4095	Aa4096	Aa4097
Year	Number	Number	Number	Number	Number	Number	Number	Number	Number	Number	Number
1790	—	—	—	—	—	—	—	—	—	—	—
1800	—	—	—	—	—	—	—	—	—	—	—
1810	—	—	—	—	—	—	—	—	—	—	—
1820	—	—	—	—	—	—	—	—	—	—	—
1830	—	—	—	—	—	—	—	—	—	—	—
1840	—	—	—	—	—	—	—	—	—	—	—
1850	108,747	—	—	70,687	—	—	48,098	—	—	31,630	—
1860	132,106	—	—	93,459	—	—	61,644	—	—	42,023	—
1870	—	78,293	69,501	—	59,175	53,812	—	46,164	36,419	—	31,861
1880	—	99,589	84,327	—	71,425	66,661	—	57,405	48,668	—	43,220
1890 [1]	—	129,401	114,332	—	94,026	79,439	—	69,729	60,531	—	54,076
1900	—	149,943	146,048	—	121,936	108,949	—	89,657	73,879	—	64,315
1910	—	168,476	158,664	—	142,143	136,370	—	114,646	96,490	—	81,602
1920	—	173,566	177,371	—	156,267	149,195	—	132,500	119,772	—	102,464
1930	—	182,484	170,794	—	167,501	171,982	—	148,488	134,757	—	120,283
1940	—	189,861	179,201	—	168,403	160,494	—	159,048	152,682	—	133,954
1950	—	179,741	190,888	—	184,415	178,258	—	165,802	152,177	—	150,547
1960	—	150,596	150,044	—	170,431	183,127	—	177,545	166,113	—	152,558
1970	—	246,874	188,499	—	150,316	151,253	—	170,370	178,504	—	171,325
1980	—	282,189	249,834	—	228,746	179,050	—	143,823	143,817	—	160,363
1990	—	259,262	279,341	—	274,627	245,224	—	222,257	172,217	—	136,432

	Population										
										White	
	Female, by age										
	55–59	60–69	60–64	65–69	70–79	70–74	75–79	80 and older	Unknown age	Male	Female
	Aa4098	Aa4099	Aa4100	Aa4101	Aa4102	Aa4103	Aa4104	Aa4105	Aa4106	Aa4107	Aa4108
Year	Number	Number	Number	Number	Number	Number	Number	Number	Number	Number	Number
1790	—	—	—	—	—	—	—	—	—	182,712	190,475
1800	—	—	—	—	—	—	—	—	—	205,494	211,299
1810	—	—	—	—	—	—	—	—	—	229,742	235,561
1820	—	—	—	—	—	—	—	—	—	252,154	264,265
1830	—	—	—	—	—	—	—	—	—	294,685	308,674
1840	—	—	—	—	—	—	—	—	—	360,679	368,351
1850	—	19,965	—	—	10,091	—	—	3,877	189	—	—
1860	—	27,158	—	—	13,331	—	—	4,687	0	—	—
1870	22,523	—	21,274	14,700	—	11,360	6,690	6,063	25	—	—
1880	30,638	—	27,850	19,898	—	15,259	9,483	8,434	—	—	—
1890 [1]	40,273	—	35,277	25,356	—	18,834	11,511	10,952	2,680	—	—
1900	50,268	—	43,424	32,127	—	22,359	14,027	11,615	3,103	—	—
1910	59,949	—	50,473	39,053	—	28,146	17,470	14,163	1,320	—	—
1920	78,381	—	64,410	45,182	—	32,297	21,011	17,416	1,222	—	—
1930	101,601	—	83,338	63,026	—	43,389	25,305	20,847	1,419	—	—
1940	111,414	—	97,770	83,180	—	58,688	36,296	28,667	—	—	—
1950	135,975	—	115,540	99,446	—	74,356	58,406	35,188	—	—	—
1960	139,478	—	130,444	117,630	—	92,925	62,290	59,789	—	—	—
1970	155,096	—	139,659	120,286	—	106,037	79,367	85,357	—	—	—
1980	165,392	—	151,061	134,551	—	113,806	89,683	117,468	—	—	—
1990	132,526	—	140,049	141,253	—	121,868	100,893	142,996	—	—	—

Note appears at end of table

TABLE Aa4044–4144   Massachusetts population by race, sex, age, nativity, and urban–rural residence: 1790–1990
Continued

	Population										
	White										
	Male, by age										
	0–4	5–9	10–14	15–19	20–29	30–39	40–49	50–59	60–69	70–79	80 and older
	Aa4109	Aa4110	Aa4111	Aa4112	Aa4113	Aa4114	Aa4115	Aa4116	Aa4117	Aa4118	Aa4119
Year	Number	Number	Number	Number	Number	Number	Number	Number	Number	Number	Number
1790	—	—	—	—	—	—	—	—	—	—	—
1800	—	—	—	—	—	—	—	—	—	—	—
1810	—	—	—	—	—	—	—	—	—	—	—
1820	—	—	—	—	—	—	—	—	—	—	—
1830	40,644	35,988	34,679	32,801	58,621	35,433	23,683	15,008	10,319	5,575	1,934
1840	47,313	40,296	37,971	37,069	76,285	52,283	30,161	19,270	11,432	6,473	2,126
1850	—	—	—	—	—	—	—	—	—	—	—
1860	—	—	—	—	—	—	—	—	—	—	—
1870	—	—	—	—	—	—	—	—	—	—	—
1880	—	—	—	—	—	—	—	—	—	—	—
1890 [1]	—	—	—	—	—	—	—	—	—	—	—
1900	—	—	—	—	—	—	—	—	—	—	—
1910	—	—	—	—	—	—	—	—	—	—	—
1920	—	—	—	—	—	—	—	—	—	—	—
1930	—	—	—	—	—	—	—	—	—	—	—
1940	—	—	—	—	—	—	—	—	—	—	—
1950	—	—	—	—	—	—	—	—	—	—	—
1960	—	—	—	—	—	—	—	—	—	—	—
1970	—	—	—	—	—	—	—	—	—	—	—
1980	—	—	—	—	—	—	—	—	—	—	—
1990	—	—	—	—	—	—	—	—	—	—	—

	Population											Male, by age
	White											
	Female, by age											0–9
	0–4	5–9	10–14	15–19	20–29	30–39	40–49	50–59	60–69	70–79	80 and older	0–9
	Aa4120	Aa4121	Aa4122	Aa4123	Aa4124	Aa4125	Aa4126	Aa4127	Aa4128	Aa4129	Aa4130	Aa4131
Year	Number	Number	Number	Number	Number	Number	Number	Number	Number	Number	Number	Number
1790	—	—	—	—	—	—	—	—	—	—	—	—
1800	—	—	—	—	—	—	—	—	—	—	—	63,646
1810	—	—	—	—	—	—	—	—	—	—	—	68,930
1820	—	—	—	—	—	—	—	—	—	—	—	70,993
1830	39,533	34,537	33,326	34,439	60,495	38,163	26,684	18,456	12,989	7,173	2,879	—
1840	45,313	40,115	36,832	40,360	74,250	49,324	33,109	22,684	14,645	8,387	3,332	—
1850	—	—	—	—	—	—	—	—	—	—	—	—
1860	—	—	—	—	—	—	—	—	—	—	—	—
1870	—	—	—	—	—	—	—	—	—	—	—	—
1880	—	—	—	—	—	—	—	—	—	—	—	—
1890 [1]	—	—	—	—	—	—	—	—	—	—	—	—
1900	—	—	—	—	—	—	—	—	—	—	—	—
1910	—	—	—	—	—	—	—	—	—	—	—	—
1920	—	—	—	—	—	—	—	—	—	—	—	—
1930	—	—	—	—	—	—	—	—	—	—	—	—
1940	—	—	—	—	—	—	—	—	—	—	—	—
1950	—	—	—	—	—	—	—	—	—	—	—	—
1960	—	—	—	—	—	—	—	—	—	—	—	—
1970	—	—	—	—	—	—	—	—	—	—	—	—
1980	—	—	—	—	—	—	—	—	—	—	—	—
1990	—	—	—	—	—	—	—	—	—	—	—	—

Note appears at end of table

(continued)

TABLE Aa4044–4144   Massachusetts population by race, sex, age, nativity, and urban–rural residence: 1790–1990
Continued

	Population													
	White													
	Male, by age				Female, by age					Male, by age		Female, by age	
	10–15	16–25	26–44	45 and older	0–9	10–15	16–25	26–44	45 and older	0–15	16 and older	0–15	16 and older
	Aa4132	Aa4133	Aa4134	Aa4135	Aa4136	Aa4137	Aa4138	Aa4139	Aa4140	Aa4141	Aa4142	Aa4143	Aa4144
Year	Number	Number	Number	Number	Number	Number	Number	Number	Number	Number	Number	Number	Number
1790	—	—	—	—	—	—	—	—	—	87,279	95,433	82,590	107,885
1800	32,498	38,305	39,729	31,316	60,920	30,674	40,491	43,833	35,381	—	—	—	—
1810	34,964	45,018	45,854	34,976	66,881	33,191	46,366	49,229	39,894	—	—	—	—
1820	38,573	49,506	54,414	38,668	69,260	38,308	52,805	57,721	46,171	—	—	—	—
1830	—	—	—	—	—	—	—	—	—	—	—	—	—
1840	—	—	—	—	—	—	—	—	—	—	—	—	—
1850	—	—	—	—	—	—	—	—	—	—	—	—	—
1860	—	—	—	—	—	—	—	—	—	—	—	—	—
1870	—	—	—	—	—	—	—	—	—	—	—	—	—
1880	—	—	—	—	—	—	—	—	—	—	—	—	—
1890 [1]	—	—	—	—	—	—	—	—	—	—	—	—	—
1900	—	—	—	—	—	—	—	—	—	—	—	—	—
1910	—	—	—	—	—	—	—	—	—	—	—	—	—
1920	—	—	—	—	—	—	—	—	—	—	—	—	—
1930	—	—	—	—	—	—	—	—	—	—	—	—	—
1940	—	—	—	—	—	—	—	—	—	—	—	—	—
1950	—	—	—	—	—	—	—	—	—	—	—	—	—
1960	—	—	—	—	—	—	—	—	—	—	—	—	—
1970	—	—	—	—	—	—	—	—	—	—	—	—	—
1980	—	—	—	—	—	—	—	—	—	—	—	—	—
1990	—	—	—	—	—	—	—	—	—	—	—	—	—

[1] Includes four American Indians not counted in the general enumeration; see text for Table Aa2244–2340.

Sources
See the sources for Table Aa2244–2340.

Documentation
See the text for Table Aa2244–2340.

Massachusetts was one of the original thirteen states, admitted to the Union in 1788. This table for 1790–1810 excludes the population of Maine, which was technically a part of Massachusetts before Maine became a state in 1820. For Maine, see Table Aa3842–3942.

TABLE Aa4145–4241   Michigan population, by race, sex, age, nativity, and urban–rural residence: 1800–1990
Contributed by Michael R. Haines

				Population								
					Race				Residence		Nativity	
	Area	Population density	Total	White	Nonwhite	Black	Other nonwhite	Urban	Rural	Native-born	Foreign-born
	Aa4145	Aa4146	Aa4147	Aa4148	Aa4149	Aa4150	Aa4151	Aa4152	Aa4153	Aa4154	Aa4155
Year	Square miles	Persons per square mile	Number	Number	Number	Number	Number	Number	Number	Number	Number
1800	—	—	3,757	3,067	139	139	—	0	3,757	—	—
1810	42,625	0.11	4,762	4,618	144	144	—	0	4,762	—	—
1820	186,052	0.05	8,896	8,591	305	174	131	0	8,896	—	—
1830	186,052	0.17	31,639	31,346	293	293	—	0	31,639	—	—
1840	57,480	3.69	212,267	211,560	707	707	—	9,102	203,165	—	—
1850	57,480	6.92	397,654	395,071	2,583	2,583	—	29,025	368,629	342,951	54,703
1860	57,480	13.03	749,113	736,142	12,971	6,799	6,172	99,701	649,412	600,020	149,093
1870	57,480	20.60	1,184,059	1,167,282	16,777	11,849	4,928	237,985	946,074	916,049	268,010
1880	57,480	28.48	1,636,937	1,614,560	22,377	15,100	7,277	405,412	1,231,525	1,248,429	388,508
1890 [1]	57,480	36.43	2,093,890	2,072,884	21,005	15,223	5,782	730,294	1,363,596	1,550,009	543,880
1900	57,480	42.12	2,420,982	2,398,563	22,419	15,816	6,603	952,323	1,468,659	1,879,329	541,653
1910	57,480	48.89	2,810,173	2,785,247	24,926	17,115	7,811	1,327,044	1,483,129	2,212,623	597,550
1920	57,480	63.82	3,668,412	3,601,627	66,785	60,082	6,703	2,241,560	1,426,852	2,939,120	729,292
1930	57,480	84.24	4,842,325	4,663,507	178,818	169,453	9,365	3,302,075	1,540,250	3,989,567	852,758
1940	57,022	92.18	5,256,106	5,039,643	216,463	208,345	8,118	3,454,867	1,801,239	4,569,921	686,185
1950	57,022	111.74	6,371,766	5,917,825	453,941	442,296	11,645	4,503,084	1,868,682	5,738,765	603,825
1960	56,817	137.69	7,823,194	7,085,865	737,329	717,581	19,748	5,739,132	2,084,062	7,295,341	529,624
1970	56,817	156.20	8,875,083	7,833,474	1,041,609	991,066	50,543	6,566,483	2,308,600	8,450,759	424,309
1980	56,954	162.62	9,262,078	7,872,241	1,389,837	1,199,023	190,814	6,551,551	2,710,527	8,844,926	417,152
1990	56,809	163.62	9,295,297	7,756,086	1,539,211	1,291,706	247,505	6,555,842	2,739,455	8,939,904	355,393

			Population									
	Sex		Male, by age								
	Male	Female	0	1–4	5–9	10–14	15–19	20–29	20–24	25–29	30–39
	Aa4156	Aa4157	Aa4158	Aa4159	Aa4160	Aa4161	Aa4162	Aa4163	Aa4164	Aa4165	Aa4166
Year	Number	Number	Number	Number	Number	Number	Number	Number	Number	Number	Number
1800	—	—	—	—	—	—	—	—	—	—	—
1810	—	—	—	—	—	—	—	—	—	—	—
1820	5,488	3,277	—	—	—	—	—	—	—	—	—
1830	18,349	13,290	—	—	—	—	—	—	—	—	—
1840	113,788	98,479	—	—	—	—	—	—	—	—	—
1850	209,896	187,758	5,501	25,193	30,560	25,624	21,321	36,467	—	—	28,372
1860	394,694	354,419	10,941	46,426	48,389	43,796	41,288	73,822	—	—	54,611
1870	617,745	566,314	16,639	66,805	73,893	71,649	60,211	—	60,118	52,898	—
1880	862,355	774,582	21,852	83,779	97,623	91,011	82,212	—	91,376	77,413	—
1890 [1]	1,091,780	1,002,109	25,187	95,648	119,782	111,438	102,882	—	104,012	94,681	—
1900	1,248,905	1,172,077	27,459	104,458	133,899	124,919	116,393	—	111,649	101,450	—
1910	1,454,534	1,355,639	31,418	119,834	139,447	130,746	135,439	—	136,012	125,670	—
1920	1,928,436	1,739,976	38,885	166,243	186,679	165,513	149,583	—	164,145	186,520	—
1930	2,519,309	2,323,016	45,463	190,607	246,844	229,865	209,141	—	212,341	217,402	—
1940	2,694,727	2,561,379	43,047	177,616	212,928	235,857	240,715	—	226,388	218,661	—
1950	3,212,119	3,159,647	72,356	287,233	289,560	241,321	212,575	—	239,117	263,471	—
1960	3,882,868	3,940,326	97,292	395,839	448,031	378,488	276,677	—	208,770	230,377	—
1970	4,348,648	4,526,435	82,759	327,337	471,266	498,844	436,420	—	328,837	293,503	—
1980	4,516,189	4,745,889	74,504	275,654	372,134	409,805	455,211	—	441,426	399,270	—
1990	4,512,781	4,782,516	65,970	293,209	354,276	341,138	354,213	—	349,570	376,794	—

Note appears at end of table   (continued)

TABLE Aa4145–4241   Michigan population, by race, sex, age, nativity, and urban–rural residence: 1800–1990
Continued

	Population										
	Male, by age										
	30–34	35–39	40–49	40–44	45–49	50–59	50–54	55–59	60–69	60–64	65–69
	Aa4167	Aa4168	Aa4169	Aa4170	Aa4171	Aa4172	Aa4173	Aa4174	Aa4175	Aa4176	Aa4177
Year	Number	Number	Number	Number	Number	Number	Number	Number	Number	Number	Number
1800	—	—	—	—	—	—	—	—	—	—	—
1810	—	—	—	—	—	—	—	—	—	—	—
1820	—	—	—	—	—	—	—	—	—	—	—
1830	—	—	—	—	—	—	—	—	—	—	—
1840	—	—	—	—	—	—	—	—	—	—	—
1850	—	—	19,558	—	—	10,434	—	—	4,834	—	—
1860	—	—	37,027	—	—	22,675	—	—	11,149	—	—
1870	43,212	39,980	—	32,666	28,081	—	24,212	16,296	—	13,044	8,277
1880	64,401	56,759	—	45,736	39,198	—	33,805	25,456	—	20,464	13,952
1890 [1]	87,670	73,452	—	62,014	53,688	—	45,195	34,441	—	28,576	21,273
1900	92,666	87,153	—	79,177	65,924	—	56,288	45,311	—	35,156	27,136
1910	109,909	100,130	—	89,198	80,289	—	72,639	55,690	—	44,135	34,994
1920	169,090	155,004	—	119,548	107,785	—	88,188	70,459	—	59,297	42,291
1930	207,425	215,071	—	183,010	150,402	—	117,908	90,184	—	71,101	54,962
1940	207,360	204,882	—	193,507	189,969	—	163,069	122,739	—	92,974	68,690
1950	247,214	236,471	—	215,835	200,456	—	182,249	165,257	—	133,656	97,076
1960	265,983	272,303	—	249,808	230,765	—	200,728	180,161	—	146,852	123,813
1970	239,490	230,493	—	259,354	257,814	—	231,567	201,328	—	162,083	123,237
1980	348,315	277,801	—	226,920	215,594	—	236,446	225,704	—	183,822	144,113
1990	396,653	368,243	—	322,860	257,695	—	206,904	188,020	—	190,306	166,321

	Population										
	Male, by age					Female, by age					
	70–79	70–74	75–79	80 and older	Unknown age	0	1–4	5–9	10–14	15–19	20–29
	Aa4178	Aa4179	Aa4180	Aa4181	Aa4182	Aa4183	Aa4184	Aa4185	Aa4186	Aa4187	Aa4188
Year	Number	Number	Number	Number	Number	Number	Number	Number	Number	Number	Number
1800	—	—	—	—	—	—	—	—	—	—	—
1810	—	—	—	—	—	—	—	—	—	—	—
1820	—	—	—	—	—	—	—	—	—	—	—
1830	—	—	—	—	—	—	—	—	—	—	—
1840	—	—	—	—	—	—	—	—	—	—	—
1850	1,603	—	—	366	63	5,397	23,950	29,016	24,162	21,342	32,734
1860	3,658	—	—	855	57	10,576	45,426	46,787	41,659	40,958	65,951
1870	—	5,465	2,556	1,736	7	15,990	64,768	72,201	68,846	59,098	—
1880	—	8,896	5,104	3,318	—	20,733	81,486	94,778	87,347	80,792	—
1890 [1]	—	14,591	8,333	5,834	3,083	23,767	92,787	117,683	108,789	102,749	—
1900	—	18,269	11,434	7,701	2,463	26,702	102,039	130,160	122,698	116,748	—
1910	—	22,965	14,124	9,692	2,203	30,632	116,670	135,920	127,734	131,391	—
1920	—	28,026	17,430	11,437	2,313	38,401	161,057	181,541	160,940	145,931	—
1930	—	38,881	22,131	14,846	1,725	43,856	183,515	240,126	225,604	207,745	—
1940	—	47,223	28,878	20,224	—	40,760	169,961	205,927	228,060	237,505	—
1950	—	62,637	42,880	22,755	—	68,938	275,334	279,126	230,650	218,531	—
1960	—	88,216	51,497	37,268	—	94,322	381,694	431,068	365,062	287,451	—
1970	—	89,288	61,889	53,139	—	79,616	314,751	452,552	480,421	436,204	—
1980	—	100,502	66,767	62,201	—	71,672	263,283	354,986	392,069	446,066	—
1990	—	121,386	83,061	76,162	—	63,285	280,090	337,971	325,232	342,590	—

Note appears at end of table

TABLE Aa4145–4241 Michigan population, by race, sex, age, nativity, and urban–rural residence: 1800–1990
Continued

	Population										
	Female, by age										
	20–24	25–29	30–39	30–34	35–39	40–49	40–44	45–49	50–59	50–54	55–59
	Aa4189	Aa4190	Aa4191	Aa4192	Aa4193	Aa4194	Aa4195	Aa4196	Aa4197	Aa4198	Aa4199
Year	Number	Number	Number	Number	Number	Number	Number	Number	Number	Number	Number
1800	—	—	—	—	—	—	—	—	—	—	—
1810	—	—	—	—	—	—	—	—	—	—	—
1820	—	—	—	—	—	—	—	—	—	—	—
1830	—	—	—	—	—	—	—	—	—	—	—
1840	—	—	—	—	—	—	—	—	—	—	—
1850	—	—	23,180	—	—	14,885	—	—	7,752	—	—
1860	—	—	44,427	—	—	28,816	—	—	17,423	—	—
1870	55,379	48,522	—	39,906	35,035	—	28,327	22,242	—	18,226	12,646
1880	78,550	62,431	—	54,585	49,708	—	40,327	33,426	—	27,596	20,272
1890 [1]	98,477	83,867	—	75,094	61,379	—	53,470	47,016	—	39,026	29,817
1900	110,763	96,736	—	85,744	77,908	—	68,552	56,324	—	47,922	40,369
1910	128,668	114,643	—	101,073	91,154	—	80,655	71,232	—	62,997	47,539
1920	152,148	160,044	—	141,050	124,442	—	102,778	88,507	—	76,470	62,207
1930	205,861	198,562	—	184,429	181,321	—	150,991	125,257	—	103,329	81,036
1940	230,763	219,705	—	203,122	190,475	—	174,769	163,330	—	137,979	107,529
1950	252,050	274,622	—	257,512	236,842	—	208,773	185,612	—	167,807	147,428
1960	238,363	243,411	—	272,879	283,295	—	258,967	230,432	—	197,571	172,426
1970	373,905	300,095	—	249,275	243,579	—	268,896	271,407	—	246,220	209,925
1980	453,004	407,648	—	360,054	286,626	—	237,652	229,920	—	248,971	245,707
1990	355,748	387,468	—	413,638	380,819	—	334,227	266,035	—	217,485	204,767

	Population										
									White		
	Female, by age										Male, by age
	60–69	60–64	65–69	70–79	70–74	75–79	80 and older	Unknown age	Male	Female	0–4
	Aa4200	Aa4201	Aa4202	Aa4203	Aa4204	Aa4205	Aa4206	Aa4207	Aa4208	Aa4209	Aa4210
Year	Number	Number	Number	Number	Number	Number	Number	Number	Number	Number	Number
1800	—	—	—	—	—	—	—	—	1,855	1,212	—
1810	—	—	—	—	—	—	—	—	2,837	1,781	—
1820	—	—	—	—	—	—	—	—	5,383	3,208	—
1830	—	—	—	—	—	—	—	—	18,168	13,178	3,023
1840	—	—	—	—	—	—	—	—	113,395	98,165	19,484
1850	3,797	—	—	1,213	—	—	270	60	—	—	—
1860	8,678	—	—	2,931	—	—	739	48	—	—	—
1870	—	10,644	6,572	—	4,202	2,163	1,542	5	—	—	—
1880	—	16,565	11,199	—	7,529	4,328	2,930	—	—	—	—
1890 [1]	—	24,618	17,690	—	12,037	7,094	5,405	1,344	—	—	—
1900	—	31,729	23,997	—	15,818	9,681	7,124	1,063	—	—	—
1910	—	39,343	31,377	—	20,913	12,985	9,469	1,244	—	—	—
1920	—	51,253	36,955	—	25,700	16,826	12,307	1,419	—	—	—
1930	—	66,163	51,076	—	36,198	20,956	15,841	1,150	—	—	—
1940	—	85,655	66,866	—	47,063	29,241	22,669	—	—	—	—
1950	—	120,120	94,897	—	65,043	46,984	29,378	—	—	—	—
1960	—	145,995	127,103	—	95,869	61,782	52,636	—	—	—	—
1970	—	174,187	140,340	—	113,757	84,670	86,635	—	—	—	—
1980	—	209,556	175,268	—	136,627	102,446	124,334	—	—	—	—
1990	—	211,630	202,790	—	165,341	129,433	163,967	—	—	—	—

Note appears at end of table   (continued)

TABLE Aa4145-4241   Michigan population, by race, sex, age, nativity, and urban-rural residence: 1800-1990
Continued

	Population										
	White										
	Male, by age										Female, by age
	5-9	10-14	15-19	20-29	30-39	40-49	50-59	60-69	70-79	80 and older	0-4
	Aa4211	Aa4212	Aa4213	Aa4214	Aa4215	Aa4216	Aa4217	Aa4218	Aa4219	Aa4220	Aa4221
Year	Number	Number	Number	Number	Number	Number	Number	Number	Number	Number	Number
1800	—	—	—	—	—	—	—	—	—	—	—
1810	—	—	—	—	—	—	—	—	—	—	—
1820	—	—	—	—	—	—	—	—	—	—	—
1830	2,326	1,905	1,543	4,389	2,739	1,232	658	264	64	25	2,743
1840	16,054	12,839	10,887	22,759	16,025	8,276	4,442	1,903	623	103	18,401
1850	—	—	—	—	—	—	—	—	—	—	—
1860	—	—	—	—	—	—	—	—	—	—	—
1870	—	—	—	—	—	—	—	—	—	—	—
1880	—	—	—	—	—	—	—	—	—	—	—
1890 [1]	—	—	—	—	—	—	—	—	—	—	—
1900	—	—	—	—	—	—	—	—	—	—	—
1910	—	—	—	—	—	—	—	—	—	—	—
1920	—	—	—	—	—	—	—	—	—	—	—
1930	—	—	—	—	—	—	—	—	—	—	—
1940	—	—	—	—	—	—	—	—	—	—	—
1950	—	—	—	—	—	—	—	—	—	—	—
1960	—	—	—	—	—	—	—	—	—	—	—
1970	—	—	—	—	—	—	—	—	—	—	—
1980	—	—	—	—	—	—	—	—	—	—	—
1990	—	—	—	—	—	—	—	—	—	—	—

	Population										
	White										
	Female, by age										Male, by age
	5-9	10-14	15-19	20-29	30-39	40-49	50-59	60-69	70-79	80 and older	0-9
	Aa4222	Aa4223	Aa4224	Aa4225	Aa4226	Aa4227	Aa4228	Aa4229	Aa4230	Aa4231	Aa4232
Year	Number	Number	Number	Number	Number	Number	Number	Number	Number	Number	Number
1800	—	—	—	—	—	—	—	—	—	—	540
1810	—	—	—	—	—	—	—	—	—	—	800
1820	—	—	—	—	—	—	—	—	—	—	1,220
1830	2,066	1,686	1,438	2,540	1,399	726	390	140	35	15	—
1840	15,089	11,798	10,819	18,706	11,864	6,109	3,394	1,441	451	93	—
1850	—	—	—	—	—	—	—	—	—	—	—
1860	—	—	—	—	—	—	—	—	—	—	—
1870	—	—	—	—	—	—	—	—	—	—	—
1880	—	—	—	—	—	—	—	—	—	—	—
1890 [1]	—	—	—	—	—	—	—	—	—	—	—
1900	—	—	—	—	—	—	—	—	—	—	—
1910	—	—	—	—	—	—	—	—	—	—	—
1920	—	—	—	—	—	—	—	—	—	—	—
1930	—	—	—	—	—	—	—	—	—	—	—
1940	—	—	—	—	—	—	—	—	—	—	—
1950	—	—	—	—	—	—	—	—	—	—	—
1960	—	—	—	—	—	—	—	—	—	—	—
1970	—	—	—	—	—	—	—	—	—	—	—
1980	—	—	—	—	—	—	—	—	—	—	—
1990	—	—	—	—	—	—	—	—	—	—	—

Note appears at end of table

TABLE Aa4145–4241   **Michigan population, by race, sex, age, nativity, and urban–rural residence: 1800–1990**
Continued

		Population							
		White							
	Male, by age				Female, by age				
	10–15	16–25	26–44	45 and older	0–9	10–15	16–25	26–44	45 and older
	Aa4233	Aa4234	Aa4235	Aa4236	Aa4237	Aa4238	Aa4239	Aa4240	Aa4241
Year	Number	Number	Number	Number	Number	Number	Number	Number	Number
1800	201	332	584	198	467	193	252	198	102
1810	351	583	763	340	640	332	368	311	130
1820	559	1,334	1,661	609	1,130	525	692	595	266
1830	—	—	—	—	—	—	—	—	—
1840	—	—	—	—	—	—	—	—	—
1850	—	—	—	—	—	—	—	—	—
1860	—	—	—	—	—	—	—	—	—
1870	—	—	—	—	—	—	—	—	—
1880	—	—	—	—	—	—	—	—	—
1890 [1]	—	—	—	—	—	—	—	—	—
1900	—	—	—	—	—	—	—	—	—
1910	—	—	—	—	—	—	—	—	—
1920	—	—	—	—	—	—	—	—	—
1930	—	—	—	—	—	—	—	—	—
1940	—	—	—	—	—	—	—	—	—
1950	—	—	—	—	—	—	—	—	—
1960	—	—	—	—	—	—	—	—	—
1970	—	—	—	—	—	—	—	—	—
1980	—	—	—	—	—	—	—	—	—
1990	—	—	—	—	—	—	—	—	—

[1] Includes one American Indian not counted in the general enumeration; see text for Table Aa2244–2340.

Sources

See the sources for Table Aa2244–2340.

Documentation

See the text for Table Aa2244–2340.

Michigan was part of the Northwest Territory and became a separate territory only in 1805, when it was separated from the Indiana Territory. The population in 1800 consists of the populations of Wayne County in the Ohio Territory and Michilimackinac County in the Indiana Territory. It became a state in 1837.

TABLE Aa4242–4304   **Minnesota population by race, sex, age, nativity, and urban–rural residence: 1850–1990**

Contributed by Michael R. Haines

			Population								
				Race				Residence		Nativity	
	Area	Population density	Total	White	Nonwhite	Black	Other nonwhite	Urban	Rural	Native-born	Foreign-born
	Aa4242	Aa4243	Aa4244	Aa4245	Aa4246	Aa4247	Aa4248	Aa4249	Aa4250	Aa4251	Aa4252
Year	Square miles	Persons per square mile	Number	Number	Number	Number	Number	Number	Number	Number	Number
1850	163,457	0.04	6,077	6,038	39	39	—	0	6,077	4,100	1,977
1860	80,858	2.13	172,023	169,395	2,628	259	2,369	16,223	155,800	113,295	58,728
1870	80,858	5.44	439,706	438,257	1,449	759	690	70,754	368,952	279,009	160,697
1880	80,858	9.66	780,773	776,884	3,889	1,564	2,325	148,758	632,015	513,097	267,676
1890 [1]	80,858	16.20	1,310,283	1,296,159	5,667	3,683	1,984	443,049	867,234	834,470	467,356
1900	80,858	21.66	1,751,394	1,737,036	14,358	4,959	9,399	598,100	1,153,294	1,246,076	505,318
1910	80,858	25.67	2,075,708	2,059,227	16,481	7,084	9,397	850,294	1,225,414	1,532,113	543,595
1920	80,858	29.52	2,387,125	2,368,936	18,189	8,809	9,380	1,051,593	1,335,532	1,900,330	486,795
1930	80,858	31.71	2,563,953	2,542,599	21,354	9,445	11,909	1,257,616	1,306,337	2,173,163	390,790
1940	80,009	34.90	2,792,300	2,768,982	23,318	9,928	13,390	1,390,098	1,402,202	2,496,927	295,373
1950	80,009	37.28	2,982,483	2,953,697	28,786	14,022	14,764	1,624,914	1,357,569	2,761,580	210,570
1960	79,289	43.06	3,413,864	3,371,603	42,261	22,263	19,998	2,122,566	1,291,298	3,269,986	143,878
1970	79,289	47.99	3,804,971	3,736,038	68,933	34,868	34,065	2,531,801	1,273,170	3,706,915	98,056
1980	79,548	51.24	4,075,970	3,935,770	140,200	53,344	86,856	2,725,202	1,350,768	3,968,496	107,474
1990	79,617	54.95	4,375,099	4,130,395	244,704	94,944	149,760	3,056,474	1,318,625	4,262,060	113,039

Note appears at end of table   (continued)

TABLE Aa4242–4304   Minnesota population by race, sex, age, nativity, and urban–rural residence: 1850–1990

Population

	Sex		Male, by age								
	Male	Female	0	1–4	5–9	10–14	15–19	20–29	20–24	25–29	30–39
	Aa4253	Aa4254	Aa4255	Aa4256	Aa4257	Aa4258	Aa4259	Aa4260	Aa4261	Aa4262	Aa4263
Year	Number	Number	Number	Number	Number	Number	Number	Number	Number	Number	Number
1850	3,716	2,361	66	388	363	302	229	1,161	—	—	724
1860	93,084	78,939	3,224	14,134	11,648	8,609	6,635	17,827	—	—	16,917
1870	235,299	204,407	7,069	28,657	32,117	28,304	20,053	—	20,639	18,869	—
1880	419,149	361,624	12,642	46,833	52,225	44,425	40,446	—	45,393	36,580	—
1890 [1]	695,321	606,505	18,735	71,413	81,831	70,094	64,045	—	69,621	69,194	—
1900	932,490	818,904	23,998	92,078	110,013	97,205	85,510	—	83,257	81,464	—
1910	1,108,511	967,197	23,250	91,572	111,643	108,763	108,316	—	115,241	104,395	—
1920	1,245,537	1,141,588	24,874	107,578	126,208	118,139	109,708	—	108,250	110,683	—
1930	1,316,571	1,247,382	22,642	94,925	130,495	128,714	120,379	—	105,569	94,824	—
1940	1,427,545	1,364,755	23,485	94,389	112,427	121,768	129,678	—	122,257	112,547	—
1950	1,501,208	1,481,275	34,832	135,012	136,844	114,280	102,770	—	103,314	110,005	—
1960	1,692,962	1,720,902	43,662	167,937	194,023	165,418	122,990	—	90,474	95,762	—
1970	1,863,810	1,941,161	34,072	135,573	206,012	211,803	185,668	—	133,440	123,848	—
1980	1,997,826	2,078,144	34,622	122,690	151,556	170,607	202,254	—	194,835	182,607	—
1990	2,145,183	2,229,916	30,611	141,444	177,049	160,702	151,359	—	157,244	190,480	—

Population

Male, by age

	30–34	35–39	40–49	40–44	45–49	50–59	50–54	55–59	60–69	60–64	65–69
	Aa4264	Aa4265	Aa4266	Aa4267	Aa4268	Aa4269	Aa4270	Aa4271	Aa4272	Aa4273	Aa4274
Year	Number	Number	Number	Number	Number	Number	Number	Number	Number	Number	Number
1850	—	—	293	—	—	129	—	—	39	—	—
1860	—	—	7,811	—	—	3,932	—	—	1,802	—	—
1870	16,497	16,503	—	13,913	10,725	—	9,073	4,713	—	3,563	2,133
1880	29,482	25,436	—	20,397	17,904	—	17,327	11,207	—	8,400	4,900
1890 [1]	60,801	44,663	—	34,161	27,884	—	23,936	18,100	—	15,680	10,450
1900	73,859	69,489	—	58,793	41,171	—	32,854	24,977	—	18,909	15,255
1910	84,847	76,098	—	66,143	59,572	—	51,124	33,484	—	24,968	18,864
1920	100,840	91,367	—	72,624	67,787	—	58,456	48,977	—	39,628	25,224
1930	94,973	99,717	—	91,578	78,506	—	65,180	54,361	—	45,965	37,798
1940	102,686	96,334	—	95,166	94,975	—	86,353	69,346	—	54,588	43,367
1950	105,664	102,432	—	95,211	88,090	—	86,420	80,975	—	70,317	53,686
1960	102,736	105,047	—	101,156	96,874	—	87,834	78,743	—	71,641	64,260
1970	103,114	95,850	—	100,748	100,592	—	94,618	86,181	—	74,314	59,592
1980	156,565	123,094	—	101,011	92,929	—	95,107	92,356	—	80,521	67,914
1990	199,447	182,163	—	152,870	118,342	—	94,635	85,014	—	82,224	74,123

Population

	Male, by age					Female, by age					
	70–79	70–74	75–79	80 and older	Unknown age	0	1–4	5–9	10–14	15–19	20–29
	Aa4275	Aa4276	Aa4277	Aa4278	Aa4279	Aa4280	Aa4281	Aa4282	Aa4283	Aa4284	Aa4285
Year	Number	Number	Number	Number	Number	Number	Number	Number	Number	Number	Number
1850	17	—	—	5	0	102	363	358	266	233	571
1860	451	—	—	91	3	3,114	13,691	11,278	7,684	6,877	15,463
1870	—	1,437	626	408	0	6,868	28,387	31,040	26,887	19,512	—
1880	—	2,862	1,591	1,099	—	12,182	45,552	51,362	43,357	39,743	—
1890 [1]	—	6,592	3,263	2,168	2,690	17,981	69,155	80,361	68,545	63,460	—
1900	—	10,555	6,202	3,819	3,082	23,058	89,156	107,434	94,859	84,667	—
1910	—	12,415	8,191	5,958	3,667	22,861	89,157	108,590	105,639	106,832	—
1920	—	16,191	10,141	7,192	1,670	24,217	104,725	122,391	115,822	109,901	—
1930	—	26,584	14,201	9,642	518	21,383	92,051	126,256	125,074	119,567	—
1940	—	32,236	20,862	15,081	—	22,286	89,897	107,749	117,150	127,671	—
1950	—	37,327	27,493	16,536	—	33,079	129,537	130,808	109,507	104,690	—
1960	—	49,560	30,616	24,229	—	42,106	162,300	186,627	159,292	128,362	—
1970	—	48,820	36,137	33,428	—	32,376	129,750	196,623	203,218	187,737	—
1980	—	52,201	36,637	40,320	—	32,801	117,136	144,739	162,771	197,564	—
1990	—	58,161	43,312	46,003	—	29,260	135,485	168,791	152,595	146,250	—

Note appears at end of table   (continued)

TABLE Aa4242–4304 Minnesota population by race, sex, age, nativity, and urban–rural residence: 1850–1990
Continued

	Population										
	Female, by age										
	20–24	25–29	30–39	30–34	35–39	40–49	40–44	45–49	50–59	50–54	55–59
	Aa4286	Aa4287	Aa4288	Aa4289	Aa4290	Aa4291	Aa4292	Aa4293	Aa4294	Aa4295	Aa4296
Year	Number	Number	Number	Number	Number	Number	Number	Number	Number	Number	Number
1850	—	—	255	—	—	132	—	—	53	—	—
1860	—	—	11,243	—	—	5,180	—	—	2,716	—	—
1870	16,938	15,287	—	13,907	12,796	—	10,274	7,373	—	5,436	3,228
1880	35,639	26,132	—	22,170	19,713	—	16,630	14,136	—	11,877	8,150
1890 [1]	61,197	53,488	—	44,060	33,044	—	26,426	22,435	—	19,044	14,725
1900	77,417	67,143	—	57,196	51,704	—	41,853	30,871	—	25,042	20,316
1910	101,429	83,043	—	68,348	59,514	—	51,113	45,717	—	36,986	25,788
1920	109,669	102,963	—	88,938	77,173	—	62,729	54,648	—	46,752	38,460
1930	108,863	98,645	—	94,732	93,217	—	81,402	68,637	—	56,991	46,452
1940	123,335	112,550	—	101,625	96,118	—	92,030	87,550	—	76,578	60,595
1950	110,398	110,775	—	107,101	103,015	—	94,518	88,122	—	84,385	76,715
1960	104,409	97,398	—	103,751	106,116	—	103,712	97,275	—	88,356	81,097
1970	158,597	125,668	—	103,655	97,013	—	101,962	102,312	—	99,338	90,830
1980	198,731	180,828	—	156,539	123,262	—	101,849	94,122	—	98,092	97,101
1990	158,802	191,279	—	198,537	179,111	—	151,940	118,708	—	96,775	88,052

	Population							
	Female, by age							
	60–69	60–64	65–69	70–79	70–74	75–79	80 and older	Unknown age
	Aa4297	Aa4298	Aa4299	Aa4300	Aa4301	Aa4302	Aa4303	Aa4304
Year	Number	Number	Number	Number	Number	Number	Number	Number
1850	23	—	—	3	—	—	2	0
1860	1,301	—	—	322	—	—	69	1
1870	—	2,769	1,797	—	1,040	506	362	0
1880	—	6,243	3,840	—	2,445	1,373	1,080	—
1890 [1]	—	12,506	8,607	—	5,487	2,901	2,101	982
1900	—	16,228	12,996	—	8,869	5,400	3,675	1,020
1910	—	20,220	15,961	—	11,121	7,539	6,008	1,331
1920	—	30,199	20,603	—	13,997	9,539	7,879	983
1930	—	38,407	31,281	—	21,672	12,427	9,875	450
1940	—	48,549	39,268	—	28,219	18,859	14,726	—
1950	—	64,537	51,502	—	36,378	28,030	18,178	—
1960	—	74,415	67,055	—	52,526	34,744	31,361	—
1970	—	81,140	70,563	—	61,431	47,306	51,642	—
1980	—	90,117	81,200	—	68,833	56,101	76,358	—
1990	—	88,996	85,913	—	76,325	65,121	97,976	—

[1] Includes 8,457 American Indians not counted in the general enumeration; see text for Table Aa2244–2340.

Sources
See the sources for Table Aa2244–340.

Documentation
See the text for Table Aa2244–2340.

The population enumerated in 1840 in Clayton County, Iowa Territory, included some persons in the precincts of Lake Pepin (present-day Wabasha) and St. Peter's (around Fort Snelling). Minnesota became a territory in 1849, created from parts of the Northwest Territory and the Louisiana Purchase. It became a state in 1858. The data for 1850 include the problem of present-day North and South Dakota east of the Missouri and the White Earth rivers.

TABLE Aa4305–4401   Mississippi population by race, sex, age, nativity, and urban–rural residence: 1800–1990
Contributed by Michael R. Haines

			Population									
				Race				Residence		Nativity	
	Area	Population density	Total	White	Nonwhite	Black	Other nonwhite	Urban	Rural	Native-born	Foreign-born
	Aa4305	Aa4306	Aa4307	Aa4308	Aa4309	Aa4310	Aa4311	Aa4312	Aa4313	Aa4314	Aa4315
Year	Square miles	Persons per square mile	Number	Number	Number	Number	Number	Number	Number	Number	Number
1800	33,319	0.23	7,600	4,446	3,154	3,154	—	0	7,600	—	—
1810	97,641	0.32	31,306	16,602	14,704	14,704	—	0	31,306	—	—
1820	46,362	1.63	75,448	42,176	33,272	33,272	0	0	75,448	—	—
1830	46,362	2.95	136,621	70,443	66,178	66,178	—	2,789	133,832	—	—
1840	46,362	8.10	375,651	179,074	196,577	196,577	—	3,612	372,039	—	—
1850	46,362	13.08	606,526	295,718	310,808	310,808	—	10,723	595,803	601,738	4,788
1860	46,362	17.07	791,305	353,899	437,406	437,404	2	20,689	770,616	782,747	8,558
1870	46,362	17.86	827,922	382,896	445,026	444,201	825	33,255	794,667	816,731	11,191
1880	46,362	24.41	1,131,597	479,398	652,199	650,291	1,908	34,581	1,097,016	1,122,388	9,209
1890	46,362	27.82	1,289,600	544,851	744,749	742,559	2,190	69,966	1,219,634	1,281,648	7,952
1900	46,362	33.46	1,551,270	641,200	910,070	907,630	2,440	120,035	1,431,235	1,543,289	7,981
1910	46,362	38.76	1,797,114	786,111	1,011,003	1,009,487	1,516	207,311	1,589,803	1,787,344	9,770
1920	46,362	38.62	1,790,618	853,962	936,656	935,184	1,472	240,121	1,550,497	1,782,210	8,408
1930	46,362	43.35	2,009,821	998,077	1,011,744	1,009,718	2,026	338,850	1,670,971	2,001,776	8,045
1940	47,420	46.05	2,183,796	1,106,327	1,077,469	1,074,578	2,891	432,882	1,750,914	2,177,324	6,472
1950	47,248	46.12	2,178,914	1,188,632	990,282	986,494	3,788	607,162	1,571,752	2,168,710	8,735
1960	47,358	45.99	2,178,141	1,257,546	920,595	915,743	4,852	820,805	1,357,336	2,170,083	8,058
1970	47,296	46.87	2,216,912	1,393,283	823,629	815,770	7,859	986,642	1,230,270	2,208,725	8,125
1980	47,233	53.37	2,520,638	1,615,190	905,448	887,206	18,242	1,192,805	1,327,833	2,497,111	23,527
1990	46,914	54.85	2,573,216	1,633,461	939,755	915,057	24,698	1,210,729	1,362,487	2,552,833	20,383

			Population									
	Sex		Male, by age									
	Male	Female	0	1–4	5–9	10–14	15–19	20–29	20–24	25–29	30–39
	Aa4316	Aa4317	Aa4318	Aa4319	Aa4320	Aa4321	Aa4322	Aa4323	Aa4324	Aa4325	Aa4326
Year	Number	Number	Number	Number	Number	Number	Number	Number	Number	Number	Number
1800	—	—	—	—	—	—	—	—	—	—	—
1810	—	—	—	—	—	—	—	—	—	—	—
1820	40,375	35,073	—	—	—	—	—	—	—	—	—
1830	71,853	64,768	—	—	—	—	—	—	—	—	—
1840	195,974	179,677	—	—	—	—	—	—	—	—	—
1850	311,724	294,802	8,083	44,808	47,701	41,827	32,502	57,169	—	—	37,675
1860	405,948	385,357	10,824	52,015	56,260	53,466	43,534	74,146	—	—	45,952
1870	413,421	414,501	14,331	55,565	55,340	57,945	45,794	—	43,351	29,697	—
1880	567,177	564,420	20,522	78,796	92,298	72,925	53,158	—	56,200	45,725	—
1890	649,687	639,913	19,118	79,231	99,550	93,475	75,654	—	57,574	43,572	—
1900	781,451	769,819	22,709	93,077	112,989	100,970	85,960	—	78,366	61,620	—
1910	905,760	891,354	26,385	105,308	122,676	111,939	96,487	—	84,135	72,529	—
1920	897,124	893,494	22,494	87,150	118,967	120,192	92,597	—	75,248	63,411	—
1930	1,005,141	1,004,680	22,310	95,832	125,871	116,451	109,700	—	94,254	75,405	—
1940	1,084,482	1,099,314	21,436	96,752	118,212	122,456	113,130	—	94,707	87,600	—
1950	1,076,791	1,102,123	27,821	115,502	120,840	110,320	97,999	—	81,067	72,584	—
1960	1,067,933	1,110,208	28,720	111,999	131,531	123,294	101,363	—	66,438	54,791	—
1970	1,074,217	1,142,695	22,319	83,900	120,292	128,897	117,980	—	84,986	61,773	—
1980	1,213,878	1,306,760	23,588	86,111	111,432	115,552	130,990	—	115,488	96,364	—
1990	1,230,617	1,342,599	17,160	82,355	108,214	109,073	112,919	—	96,793	95,405	—

TABLE Aa4305–4401   Mississippi population by race, sex, age, nativity, and urban–rural residence: 1800–1990
Continued

	Population										
	Male, by age										
	30–34	35–39	40–49	40–44	45–49	50–59	50–54	55–59	60–69	60–64	65–69
	Aa4327	Aa4328	Aa4329	Aa4330	Aa4331	Aa4332	Aa4333	Aa4334	Aa4335	Aa4336	Aa4337
Year	Number	Number	Number	Number	Number	Number	Number	Number	Number	Number	Number
1800	—	—	—	—	—	—	—	—	—	—	—
1810	—	—	—	—	—	—	—	—	—	—	—
1820	—	—	—	—	—	—	—	—	—	—	—
1830	—	—	—	—	—	—	—	—	—	—	—
1840	—	—	—	—	—	—	—	—	—	—	—
1850	—	—	21,409	—	—	11,552	—	—	6,011	—	—
1860	—	—	29,423	—	—	15,733	—	—	8,574	—	—
1870	22,342	20,264	—	16,377	13,324	—	11,413	10,020	—	8,218	4,208
1880	33,103	26,009	—	19,547	14,934	—	14,585	13,528	—	11,040	6,726
1890	36,874	35,499	—	26,837	19,046	—	16,721	15,042	—	11,309	7,786
1900	44,717	38,332	—	33,723	27,063	—	25,685	15,646	—	15,473	10,412
1910	59,269	54,992	—	39,444	28,589	—	31,138	21,964	—	20,521	12,692
1920	51,914	58,381	—	44,276	45,519	—	34,380	22,168	—	22,776	16,174
1930	60,977	60,827	—	51,381	45,929	—	46,534	32,767	—	25,971	16,408
1940	78,796	69,402	—	58,221	52,178	—	45,405	37,044	—	30,014	28,800
1950	65,450	68,908	—	65,212	56,347	—	47,614	39,894	—	32,349	32,284
1960	56,007	56,670	—	55,379	57,602	—	53,395	46,328	—	35,947	34,203
1970	54,596	51,075	—	53,812	52,364	—	50,803	49,482	—	45,887	37,173
1980	84,132	66,611	—	58,655	53,565	—	54,881	51,548	—	46,974	43,446
1990	96,955	89,441	—	79,776	63,480	—	54,999	49,891	—	48,233	43,303

	Population										
	Male, by age					Female, by age					
	70–79	70–74	75–79	80 and older	Unknown age	0	1–4	5–9	10–14	15–19	20–29
	Aa4338	Aa4339	Aa4340	Aa4341	Aa4342	Aa4343	Aa4344	Aa4345	Aa4346	Aa4347	Aa4348
Year	Number	Number	Number	Number	Number	Number	Number	Number	Number	Number	Number
1800	—	—	—	—	—	—	—	—	—	—	—
1810	—	—	—	—	—	—	—	—	—	—	—
1820	—	—	—	—	—	—	—	—	—	—	—
1830	—	—	—	—	—	—	—	—	—	—	—
1840	—	—	—	—	—	—	—	—	—	—	—
1850	1,810	—	—	694	483	8,003	44,167	46,654	39,953	33,282	53,721
1860	2,425	—	—	862	12,734	11,091	51,643	55,155	50,929	45,698	69,141
1870	—	2,642	1,175	1,285	130	13,628	53,779	54,073	54,863	47,300	—
1880	—	4,190	2,030	1,861	—	20,232	76,326	89,730	69,118	55,393	—
1890	—	5,205	2,848	2,598	1,748	18,007	75,459	96,207	89,229	77,650	—
1900	—	6,331	3,558	3,249	1,571	22,598	91,067	109,939	97,095	88,881	—
1910	—	7,421	4,378	3,571	2,322	25,723	102,245	121,597	107,975	99,754	—
1920	—	9,946	5,343	4,134	2,054	21,651	84,953	116,791	115,774	99,602	—
1930	—	11,770	7,005	5,343	406	21,786	94,367	123,527	111,893	112,702	—
1940	—	15,795	7,698	6,836	—	21,471	95,641	117,006	119,557	116,517	—
1950	—	20,658	15,306	6,636	—	27,480	112,546	118,229	107,123	97,089	—
1960	—	24,610	16,678	12,978	—	28,599	109,094	128,470	118,563	95,331	—
1970	—	25,661	16,989	16,228	—	21,733	81,654	117,480	123,530	114,991	—
1980	—	34,210	21,726	18,605	—	22,622	82,958	107,616	110,724	127,888	—
1990	—	33,221	24,748	24,651	—	16,876	78,974	103,704	104,232	109,960	—

(continued)

TABLE Aa4305–4401   Mississippi population by race, sex, age, nativity, and urban–rural residence: 1800–1990
Continued

Population

	Female, by age										
	20–24	25–29	30–39	30–34	35–39	40–49	40–44	45–49	50–59	50–54	55–59
	Aa4349	Aa4350	Aa4351	Aa4352	Aa4353	Aa4354	Aa4355	Aa4356	Aa4357	Aa4358	Aa4359
Year	Number	Number	Number	Number	Number	Number	Number	Number	Number	Number	Number
1800	—	—	—	—	—	—	—	—	—	—	—
1810	—	—	—	—	—	—	—	—	—	—	—
1820	—	—	—	—	—	—	—	—	—	—	—
1830	—	—	—	—	—	—	—	—	—	—	—
1840	—	—	—	—	—	—	—	—	—	—	—
1850	—	—	33,252	—	—	18,750	—	—	9,165	—	—
1860	—	—	41,591	—	—	25,479	—	—	12,697	—	—
1870	45,508	33,964	—	25,991	21,661	—	17,774	12,978	—	11,471	6,636
1880	58,087	44,566	—	33,577	28,639	—	24,134	17,573	—	15,885	9,264
1890	61,267	45,272	—	36,032	33,315	—	27,420	22,034	—	18,275	11,086
1900	83,949	61,704	—	42,962	37,466	—	32,039	26,558	—	23,386	15,309
1910	92,334	76,454	—	58,362	51,423	—	36,748	29,510	—	25,998	18,670
1920	87,606	72,352	—	57,658	58,492	—	45,437	37,017	—	27,923	18,474
1930	105,108	83,318	—	65,234	65,166	—	52,026	47,523	—	38,385	25,699
1940	103,327	95,580	—	82,041	75,339	—	60,002	51,784	—	43,229	33,826
1950	87,173	79,375	—	71,765	75,975	—	68,424	58,864	—	49,009	39,081
1960	68,322	60,987	—	64,416	64,620	—	62,069	62,153	—	56,262	49,503
1970	88,346	66,384	—	59,893	57,569	—	61,141	59,297	—	56,975	55,304
1980	118,017	100,765	—	88,278	71,478	—	63,761	60,097	—	63,276	61,220
1990	99,847	102,335	—	105,325	95,961	—	84,386	68,147	—	61,119	57,893

Population

	Female, by age								White		Male, by age
	60–69	60–64	65–69	70–79	70–74	75–79	80 and older	Unknown age	Male	Female	0–4
	Aa4360	Aa4361	Aa4362	Aa4363	Aa4364	Aa4365	Aa4366	Aa4367	Aa4368	Aa4369	Aa4370
Year	Number	Number	Number	Number	Number	Number Year	Number	Number	Number	Number	Number
1800	—	—	—	—	—	—	—	—	2,528	1,918	—
1810	—	—	—	—	—	—	—	—	9,369	7,233	—
1820	—	—	—	—	—	—	—	—	23,286	18,890	—
1830	—	—	—	—	—	—	—	—	38,466	31,977	7,918
1840	—	—	—	—	—	—	—	—	97,256	81,818	19,542
1850	5,110	—	—	1,596	—	—	678	471	—	—	—
1860	7,126	—	—	2,277	—	—	891	11,639	—	—	—
1870	—	6,491	3,206	—	2,390	1,149	1,509	130	—	—	—
1880	—	9,038	5,024	—	3,706	1,852	2,276	—	—	—	—
1890	—	10,383	6,445	—	4,668	2,521	2,804	1,839	—	—	—
1900	—	13,719	8,424	—	6,072	3,281	3,702	1,668	—	—	—
1910	—	16,271	10,797	—	7,318	4,095	4,066	2,014	—	—	—
1920	—	17,438	12,298	—	8,695	5,232	4,886	1,215	—	—	—
1930	—	20,626	13,779	—	10,406	6,563	6,169	403	—	—	—
1940	—	27,705	25,966	—	14,368	7,896	8,059	—	—	—	—
1950	—	31,910	33,840	—	20,602	15,263	8,375	—	—	—	—
1960	—	40,259	38,112	—	27,599	19,327	16,522	—	—	—	—
1970	—	52,129	45,721	—	32,849	22,983	24,716	—	—	—	—
1980	—	56,690	56,090	—	46,203	33,555	35,522	—	—	—	—
1990	—	58,479	56,474	—	47,151	40,641	51,095	—	—	—	—

TABLE Aa4305–4401   Mississippi population by race, sex, age, nativity, and urban–rural residence: 1800–1990
Continued

	Population										
	White										
	Male, by age										Female, by age
	5–9	10–14	15–19	20–29	30–39	40–49	50–59	60–69	70–79	80 and older	0–4
	Aa4371	Aa4372	Aa4373	Aa4374	Aa4375	Aa4376	Aa4377	Aa4378	Aa4379	Aa4380	Aa4381
Year	Number	Number	Number	Number	Number	Number	Number	Number	Number	Number	Number
1800	—	—	—	—	—	—	—	—	—	—	—
1810	—	—	—	—	—	—	—	—	—	—	—
1820	—	—	—	—	—	—	—	—	—	—	—
1830	5,572	4,591	3,623	7,237	4,632	2,419	1,595	632	189	58	7,319
1840	14,164	11,475	8,662	20,084	11,995	6,001	3,289	1,430	466	148	18,235
1850	—	—	—	—	—	—	—	—	—	—	—
1860	—	—	—	—	—	—	—	—	—	—	—
1870	—	—	—	—	—	—	—	—	—	—	—
1880	—	—	—	—	—	—	—	—	—	—	—
1890	—	—	—	—	—	—	—	—	—	—	—
1900	—	—	—	—	—	—	—	—	—	—	—
1910	—	—	—	—	—	—	—	—	—	—	—
1920	—	—	—	—	—	—	—	—	—	—	—
1930	—	—	—	—	—	—	—	—	—	—	—
1940	—	—	—	—	—	—	—	—	—	—	—
1950	—	—	—	—	—	—	—	—	—	—	—
1960	—	—	—	—	—	—	—	—	—	—	—
1970	—	—	—	—	—	—	—	—	—	—	—
1980	—	—	—	—	—	—	—	—	—	—	—
1990	—	—	—	—	—	—	—	—	—	—	—

	Population										
	White										
	Female, by age										Male, by age
	5–9	10–14	15–19	20–29	30–39	40–49	50–59	60–69	70–79	80 and older	0–9
	Aa4382	Aa4383	Aa4384	Aa4385	Aa4386	Aa4387	Aa4388	Aa4389	Aa4390	Aa4391	Aa4392
Year	Number	Number	Number	Number	Number	Number	Number	Number	Number	Number	Number
1800	—	—	—	—	—	—	—	—	—	—	870
1810	—	—	—	—	—	—	—	—	—	—	2,920
1820	—	—	—	—	—	—	—	—	—	—	8,104
1830	5,165	4,169	3,653	5,231	3,090	1,739	983	436	149	43	—
1840	13,328	10,919	8,911	14,464	7,847	4,284	2,250	1,075	381	124	—
1850	—	—	—	—	—	—	—	—	—	—	—
1860	—	—	—	—	—	—	—	—	—	—	—
1870	—	—	—	—	—	—	—	—	—	—	—
1880	—	—	—	—	—	—	—	—	—	—	—
1890	—	—	—	—	—	—	—	—	—	—	—
1900	—	—	—	—	—	—	—	—	—	—	—
1910	—	—	—	—	—	—	—	—	—	—	—
1920	—	—	—	—	—	—	—	—	—	—	—
1930	—	—	—	—	—	—	—	—	—	—	—
1940	—	—	—	—	—	—	—	—	—	—	—
1950	—	—	—	—	—	—	—	—	—	—	—
1960	—	—	—	—	—	—	—	—	—	—	—
1970	—	—	—	—	—	—	—	—	—	—	—
1980	—	—	—	—	—	—	—	—	—	—	—
1990	—	—	—	—	—	—	—	—	—	—	—

(continued)

TABLE Aa4305–4401   Mississippi population by race, sex, age, nativity, and urban–rural residence: 1800–1990
Continued

	Population								
	White								
	Male, by age				Female, by age				
	10–15	16–25	26–44	45 and older	0–9	10–15	16–25	26–44	45 and older
	Aa4393	Aa4394	Aa4395	Aa4396	Aa4397	Aa4398	Aa4399	Aa4400	Aa4401
Year	Number	Number	Number	Number	Number	Number	Number	Number	Number
1800	307	429	680	242	812	315	292	360	139
1810	1,171	1,998	2,419	861	2,818	1,101	1,589	1,239	486
1820	3,216	4,560	5,110	2,296	7,220	3,176	3,791	3,107	1,596
1830	—	—	—	—	—	—	—	—	—
1840	—	—	—	—	—	—	—	—	—
1850	—	—	—	—	—	—	—	—	—
1860	—	—	—	—	—	—	—	—	—
1870	—	—	—	—	—	—	—	—	—
1880	—	—	—	—	—	—	—	—	—
1890	—	—	—	—	—	—	—	—	—
1900	—	—	—	—	—	—	—	—	—
1910	—	—	—	—	—	—	—	—	—
1920	—	—	—	—	—	—	—	—	—
1930	—	—	—	—	—	—	—	—	—
1940	—	—	—	—	—	—	—	—	—
1950	—	—	—	—	—	—	—	—	—
1960	—	—	—	—	—	—	—	—	—
1970	—	—	—	—	—	—	—	—	—
1980	—	—	—	—	—	—	—	—	—
1990	—	—	—	—	—	—	—	—	—

Sources

See the sources for Table Aa2244–2340.

Documentation

See the text for Table Aa2244–2340.

Mississippi was part of Georgia, the Mississippi Territory (created in 1798), and Spanish West Florida in 1800. The population in 1800 represents those counties of Mississippi Territory (Pickering, renamed Jefferson in 1802, and Adams) later placed in Mississippi at statehood in 1817. Similarly, the population in 1810 represents the counties of Adams, Amite, Claiborne, Franklin, Jefferson, Warren, Wayne, and Wilkinson in Mississippi Territory and later part of the state.

TABLE Aa4402–4498   Missouri population by race, sex, age, nativity, and urban–rural residence: 1810–1990

Contributed by Michael R. Haines

			Population									
				Race				Residence		Nativity	
	Area	Population density	Total	White	Nonwhite	Black	Other nonwhite	Urban	Rural	Native-born	Foreign-born
	Aa4402	Aa4403	Aa4404	Aa4405	Aa4406	Aa4407	Aa4408	Aa4409	Aa4410	Aa4411	Aa4412
Year	Square miles	Persons per square mile	Number	Number	Number	Number	Number	Number	Number	Number	Number
1810	—	—	19,783	16,303	3,480	3,480	—	0	19,783	—	—
1820	65,618	1.01	66,586	55,988	10,598	10,569	29	0	66,586	—	—
1830	65,618	2.14	140,455	114,795	25,660	25,660	—	4,977	135,478	—	—
1840	68,727	5.58	383,702	323,888	59,814	59,814	—	16,469	367,233	—	—
1850	68,727	9.92	682,044	592,004	90,040	90,040	—	80,558	601,486	605,452	76,592
1860	68,727	17.20	1,182,012	1,063,489	118,523	118,503	20	203,487	978,525	1,021,471	160,541
1870	68,727	25.05	1,721,295	1,603,146	118,149	118,071	78	429,578	1,291,717	1,499,028	222,267
1880	68,727	31.55	2,168,380	2,022,826	145,554	145,350	204	545,993	1,622,387	1,956,802	211,578
1890 [1]	68,727	38.98	2,679,185	2,528,458	150,726	150,184	542	856,966	1,822,219	2,444,315	234,869
1900	68,727	45.20	3,106,665	2,944,843	161,822	161,234	588	1,128,104	1,978,561	2,890,286	216,379
1910	68,727	47.92	3,293,335	3,134,932	158,403	157,452	951	1,393,705	1,899,630	3,063,556	229,779
1920	68,727	49.53	3,404,055	3,225,044	179,011	178,241	770	1,586,903	1,817,152	3,217,220	186,835
1930	68,727	52.81	3,629,367	3,403,876	225,491	223,840	1,651	1,859,119	1,770,248	3,476,282	153,085
1940	69,270	54.64	3,784,664	3,539,187	245,477	244,386	1,091	1,960,696	1,823,968	3,670,131	114,533
1950	69,226	57.13	3,954,653	3,655,593	299,060	297,088	1,972	2,432,715	1,521,938	3,851,890	91,420
1960	69,046	62.56	4,319,813	3,922,967	396,846	390,853	5,993	2,876,557	1,443,256	4,243,018	77,756
1970	68,995	67.78	4,676,501	4,177,495	499,006	480,172	18,834	3,277,662	1,398,839	4,610,751	65,744
1980	68,945	71.31	4,916,686	4,345,521	571,165	514,276	56,889	3,349,588	1,567,098	4,831,070	85,616
1990	68,898	74.27	5,117,073	4,486,228	630,845	548,208	82,637	3,516,009	1,601,064	5,033,440	83,633

			Population									
	Sex		Male, by age									
	Male	Female	0	1–4	5–9	10–14	15–19	20–29	20–24	25–29	30–39
	Aa4413	Aa4414	Aa4415	Aa4416	Aa4417	Aa4418	Aa4419	Aa4420	Aa4421	Aa4422	Aa4423
Year	Number	Number	Number	Number	Number	Number	Number	Number	Number	Number	Number
1810	—	—	—	—	—	—	—	—	—	—	—
1820	36,528	30,029	—	—	—	—	—	—	—	—	—
1830	74,128	66,327	—	—	—	—	—	—	—	—	—
1840	203,095	180,607	—	—	—	—	—	—	—	—	—
1850	357,832	324,212	11,440	47,654	53,582	47,191	37,759	67,166	—	—	45,113
1860	622,201	559,811	20,474	83,386	86,394	76,516	64,375	119,437	—	—	81,151
1870	896,347	824,948	27,607	113,879	122,682	116,526	90,070	—	85,086	72,661	—
1880	1,127,187	1,041,193	33,035	124,727	152,463	137,041	115,380	—	115,937	93,454	—
1890 [1]	1,385,238	1,293,946	37,092	137,546	172,606	160,014	147,118	—	135,936	113,948	—
1900	1,595,710	1,510,955	38,262	146,316	187,964	175,600	160,730	—	146,875	135,851	—
1910	1,687,813	1,605,522	37,380	145,143	170,439	163,457	166,482	—	158,845	144,613	—
1920	1,723,319	1,680,736	31,640	134,647	171,285	169,504	151,139	—	140,924	140,470	—
1930	1,822,866	1,806,501	29,471	126,047	172,243	164,554	163,238	—	151,053	138,860	—
1940	1,881,252	1,903,412	27,744	114,259	147,274	160,353	167,860	—	146,818	146,155	—
1950	1,940,863	2,013,790	38,203	158,061	163,874	142,399	133,220	—	133,720	143,929	—
1960	2,108,279	2,211,534	48,549	188,686	214,526	191,721	154,440	—	123,557	120,849	—
1970	2,255,952	2,420,549	38,647	150,473	228,840	239,938	217,461	—	168,775	145,583	—
1980	2,365,487	2,551,199	39,217	142,480	181,730	195,538	234,870	—	219,935	196,248	—
1990	2,464,315	2,652,758	32,986	156,258	194,084	184,880	184,727	—	179,174	208,033	—

Note appears at end of table

(continued)

TABLE Aa4402–4498   Missouri population by race, sex, age, nativity, and urban–rural residence: 1810–1990
Continued

	Population										
	Male, by age										
	30–34	35–39	40–49	40–44	45–49	50–59	50–54	55–59	60–69	60–64	65–69
	Aa4424	Aa4425	Aa4426	Aa4427	Aa4428	Aa4429	Aa4430	Aa4431	Aa4432	Aa4433	Aa4434
Year	Number	Number	Number	Number	Number	Number	Number	Number	Number	Number	Number
1810	—	—	—	—	—	—	—	—	—	—	—
1820	—	—	—	—	—	—	—	—	—	—	—
1830	—	—	—	—	—	—	—	—	—	—	—
1840	—	—	—	—	—	—	—	—	—	—	—
1850	—	—	25,969	—	—	13,725	—	—	5,805	—	—
1860	—	—	48,661	—	—	25,662	—	—	11,646	—	—
1870	61,126	55,522	—	43,641	33,834	—	27,996	17,336	—	13,247	7,342
1880	77,329	67,868	—	55,175	43,578	—	39,719	25,022	—	20,551	12,639
1890 [1]	102,252	84,944	—	70,102	57,963	—	52,142	35,996	—	28,995	19,290
1900	119,260	106,486	—	92,450	72,120	—	63,112	48,165	—	37,560	26,927
1910	126,594	120,657	—	102,805	86,635	—	79,901	56,408	—	45,013	34,408
1920	128,201	128,925	—	108,450	105,193	—	87,998	68,325	—	58,619	40,163
1930	130,814	135,013	—	122,370	112,329	—	98,955	81,961	—	68,650	51,565
1940	142,392	135,343	—	126,201	122,565	—	111,052	94,656	—	77,772	65,260
1950	132,877	137,780	—	134,382	123,642	—	114,249	103,430	—	88,729	75,687
1960	129,000	134,359	—	126,218	127,655	—	120,322	109,780	—	92,881	82,354
1970	122,821	119,385	—	127,191	129,480	—	118,212	113,325	—	102,884	83,349
1980	173,204	141,811	—	120,901	117,508	—	121,583	120,188	—	103,253	91,914
1990	212,879	191,030	—	168,646	138,190	—	115,516	109,127	—	107,089	98,304

	Population										
	Male, by age					Female, by age					
	70–79	70–74	75–79	80 and older	Unknown age	0	1–4	5–9	10–14	15–19	20–29
	Aa4435	Aa4436	Aa4437	Aa4438	Aa4439	Aa4440	Aa4441	Aa4442	Aa4443	Aa4444	Aa4445
Year	Number	Number	Number	Number	Number	Number	Number	Number	Number	Number	Number
1810	—	—	—	—	—	—	—	—	—	—	—
1820	—	—	—	—	—	—	—	—	—	—	—
1830	—	—	—	—	—	—	—	—	—	—	—
1840	—	—	—	—	—	—	—	—	—	—	—
1850	1,795	—	—	538	95	10,891	46,293	51,594	45,153	37,778	58,168
1860	3,375	—	—	846	278	19,832	80,468	83,343	72,138	64,231	103,128
1870	—	4,517	1,920	1,345	10	26,643	108,233	116,683	111,101	90,977	—
1880	—	7,369	3,639	2,261	—	32,085	121,076	147,363	131,778	117,033	—
1890 [1]	—	12,889	6,752	4,172	5,481	35,623	132,521	168,158	155,489	149,504	—
1900	—	17,177	9,479	6,044	5,332	37,325	142,133	182,800	171,665	163,649	—
1910	—	22,306	13,056	8,480	5,191	36,549	141,431	167,793	160,734	167,591	—
1920	—	27,626	17,027	10,920	2,263	31,043	130,579	167,090	165,617	156,024	—
1930	—	37,451	21,378	15,339	1,575	28,845	121,499	166,894	160,504	163,317	—
1940	—	46,957	28,356	20,235	—	26,740	110,728	142,714	155,831	167,300	—
1950	—	53,740	41,312	21,629	—	36,731	151,396	158,414	137,135	139,110	—
1960	—	64,540	43,663	35,179	—	46,231	182,295	207,479	185,481	153,882	—
1970	—	63,517	43,698	42,373	—	37,258	144,694	219,761	230,816	212,192	—
1980	—	71,771	47,976	45,360	—	37,668	134,779	173,696	186,630	226,466	—
1990	—	73,572	55,187	54,633	—	32,024	147,976	184,766	175,601	178,090	—

Note appears at end of table

TABLE Aa4402–4498   Missouri population by race, sex, age, nativity, and urban–rural residence: 1810–1990
Continued

					Population						
					Female, by age						
	20–24	25–29	30–39	30–34	35–39	40–49	40–44	45–49	50–59	50–54	55–59
	Aa4446	Aa4447	Aa4448	Aa4449	Aa4450	Aa4451	Aa4452	Aa4453	Aa4454	Aa4455	Aa4456
Year	Number	Number	Number	Number	Number	Number	Number	Number	Number	Number	Number
1810	—	—	—	—	—	—	—	—	—	—	—
1820	—	—	—	—	—	—	—	—	—	—	—
1830	—	—	—	—	—	—	—	—	—	—	—
1840	—	—	—	—	—	—	—	—	—	—	—
1850	—	—	35,259	—	—	21,085	—	—	10,977	—	—
1860	—	—	64,393	—	—	38,092	—	—	20,541	—	—
1870	82,320	66,443	—	55,273	46,695	—	36,033	26,835	—	21,091	12,958
1880	109,944	80,195	—	65,904	59,318	—	47,677	37,707	—	31,242	20,783
1890 [1]	135,628	105,020	—	88,195	72,136	—	61,395	52,013	—	43,243	30,374
1900	152,391	131,495	—	109,342	93,567	—	78,546	62,574	—	53,892	42,469
1910	160,925	141,671	—	120,450	111,241	—	92,335	76,918	—	65,453	48,553
1920	150,799	147,271	—	129,475	123,400	—	104,975	93,610	—	78,789	60,362
1930	162,597	148,316	—	136,188	136,675	—	119,986	108,005	—	94,142	76,447
1940	157,301	154,707	—	150,600	142,420	—	128,832	122,782	—	108,556	92,722
1950	146,814	152,322	—	143,881	146,519	—	140,692	129,004	—	118,055	106,626
1960	128,772	127,474	—	136,805	143,721	—	136,648	134,375	—	128,283	118,924
1970	185,922	152,743	—	129,177	127,459	—	135,779	139,314	—	131,128	126,495
1980	225,507	202,150	—	181,135	149,932	—	127,922	125,367	—	132,094	134,769
1990	181,451	211,968	—	219,162	198,595	—	176,500	146,147	—	123,324	119,429

					Population					White		
					Female, by age							Male, by age
	60–69	60–64	65–69	70–79	70–74	75–79	80 and older	Unknown age		Male	Female	0–4
	Aa4457	Aa4458	Aa4459	Aa4460	Aa4461	Aa4462	Aa4463	Aa4464		Aa4465	Aa4466	Aa4467
Year	Number	Number	Number	Number	Number	Number	Number	Number		Number	Number	Number
1810	—	—	—	—	—	—	—	—		8,834	7,469	—
1820	—	—	—	—	—	—	—	—		31,001	24,987	—
1830	—	—	—	—	—	—	—	—		61,405	53,390	13,531
1840	—	—	—	—	—	—	—	—		173,470	150,418	34,597
1850	4,900	—	—	1,574	—	—	480	60		—	—	—
1860	9,724	—	—	2,951	—	—	816	154		—	—	—
1870	—	10,680	6,062	—	3,897	1,682	1,339	3		—	—	—
1880	—	16,452	10,344	—	6,397	3,423	2,472	—		—	—	—
1890 [1]	—	24,588	16,500	—	10,828	5,727	4,387	2,617		—	—	—
1900	—	32,978	23,580	—	14,989	8,692	5,794	3,074		—	—	—
1910	—	39,569	31,062	—	20,229	12,029	8,683	2,306		—	—	—
1920	—	49,988	35,668	—	25,384	16,534	12,180	1,948		—	—	—
1930	—	63,080	47,746	—	34,427	20,270	16,349	1,214		—	—	—
1940	—	77,242	64,937	—	47,772	29,221	23,007	—		—	—	—
1950	—	92,071	81,967	—	59,128	46,514	27,411	—		—	—	—
1960	—	103,489	95,869	—	77,108	54,610	50,088	—		—	—	—
1970	—	120,092	104,581	—	85,745	65,712	71,681	—		—	—	—
1980	—	121,979	116,032	—	101,343	79,312	94,418	—		—	—	—
1990	—	121,740	120,669	—	101,657	87,998	125,661	—		—	—	—

Note appears at end of table

(continued)

TABLE Aa4402–4498   Missouri population by race, sex, age, nativity, and urban–rural residence: 1810–1990
Continued

	Population										
	White										
	Male, by age										Female, by age
	5–9	10–14	15–19	20–29	30–39	40–49	50–59	60–69	70–79	80 and older	0–4
	Aa4468	Aa4469	Aa4470	Aa4471	Aa4472	Aa4473	Aa4474	Aa4475	Aa4476	Aa4477	Aa4478
Year	Number	Number	Number	Number	Number	Number	Number	Number	Number	Number	Number
1810	—	—	—	—	—	—	—	—	—	—	—
1820	—	—	—	—	—	—	—	—	—	—	—
1830	9,617	7,469	5,639	11,147	7,084	3,642	1,939	927	334	76	12,561
1840	26,054	21,222	16,784	33,772	20,568	11,384	5,620	2,439	814	216	32,600
1850	—	—	—	—	—	—	—	—	—	—	—
1860	—	—	—	—	—	—	—	—	—	—	—
1870	—	—	—	—	—	—	—	—	—	—	—
1880	—	—	—	—	—	—	—	—	—	—	—
1890 [1]	—	—	—	—	—	—	—	—	—	—	—
1900	—	—	—	—	—	—	—	—	—	—	—
1910	—	—	—	—	—	—	—	—	—	—	—
1920	—	—	—	—	—	—	—	—	—	—	—
1930	—	—	—	—	—	—	—	—	—	—	—
1940	—	—	—	—	—	—	—	—	—	—	—
1950	—	—	—	—	—	—	—	—	—	—	—
1960	—	—	—	—	—	—	—	—	—	—	—
1970	—	—	—	—	—	—	—	—	—	—	—
1980	—	—	—	—	—	—	—	—	—	—	—
1990	—	—	—	—	—	—	—	—	—	—	—

	Population										
	White										
	Female, by age										Male, by age
	5–9	10–14	15–19	20–29	30–39	40–49	50–59	60–69	70–79	80 and older	0–9
	Aa4479	Aa4480	Aa4481	Aa4482	Aa4483	Aa4484	Aa4485	Aa4486	Aa4487	Aa4488	Aa4489
Year	Number	Number	Number	Number	Number	Number	Number	Number	Number	Number	Number
1810	—	—	—	—	—	—	—	—	—	—	3,277
1820	—	—	—	—	—	—	—	—	—	—	10,677
1830	9,077	6,794	5,765	8,791	5,121	2,718	1,499	766	227	71	—
1840	24,321	19,679	16,952	26,330	14,889	8,580	4,259	2,019	634	155	—
1850	—	—	—	—	—	—	—	—	—	—	—
1860	—	—	—	—	—	—	—	—	—	—	—
1870	—	—	—	—	—	—	—	—	—	—	—
1880	—	—	—	—	—	—	—	—	—	—	—
1890 [1]	—	—	—	—	—	—	—	—	—	—	—
1900	—	—	—	—	—	—	—	—	—	—	—
1910	—	—	—	—	—	—	—	—	—	—	—
1920	—	—	—	—	—	—	—	—	—	—	—
1930	—	—	—	—	—	—	—	—	—	—	—
1940	—	—	—	—	—	—	—	—	—	—	—
1950	—	—	—	—	—	—	—	—	—	—	—
1960	—	—	—	—	—	—	—	—	—	—	—
1970	—	—	—	—	—	—	—	—	—	—	—
1980	—	—	—	—	—	—	—	—	—	—	—
1990	—	—	—	—	—	—	—	—	—	—	—

Note appears at end of table

TABLE Aa4402–4498   Missouri population by race, sex, age, nativity, and urban–rural residence: 1810–1990
Continued

	Population								
	White								
	Male, by age				Female, by age				
	10–15	16–25	26–44	45 and older	0–9	10–15	16–25	26–44	45 and older
	Aa4490	Aa4491	Aa4492	Aa4493	Aa4494	Aa4495	Aa4496	Aa4497	Aa4498
Year	Number	Number	Number	Number	Number	Number	Number	Number	Number
1810	1,261	1,478	1,921	897	3,064	1,206	1,359	1,291	549
1820	4,256	6,537	6,622	2,909	9,766	3,978	5,076	4,265	1,902
1830	—	—	—	—	—	—	—	—	—
1840	—	—	—	—	—	—	—	—	—
1850	—	—	—	—	—	—	—	—	—
1860	—	—	—	—	—	—	—	—	—
1870	—	—	—	—	—	—	—	—	—
1880	—	—	—	—	—	—	—	—	—
1890	—	—	—	—	—	—	—	—	—
1900	—	—	—	—	—	—	—	—	—
1910	—	—	—	—	—	—	—	—	—
1920	—	—	—	—	—	—	—	—	—
1930	—	—	—	—	—	—	—	—	—
1940	—	—	—	—	—	—	—	—	—
1950	—	—	—	—	—	—	—	—	—
1960	—	—	—	—	—	—	—	—	—
1970	—	—	—	—	—	—	—	—	—
1980	—	—	—	—	—	—	—	—	—
1990	—	—	—	—	—	—	—	—	—

[1] Includes one American Indian not counted in the general enumeration; see text for Table Aa2244–2340.

Sources
See the sources for Table Aa2244–2340.

Documentation
See the text for Table Aa2244–2340.

Missouri was originally part of the Louisiana Purchase of 1803. It was part of the Louisiana Territory from 1805, became the Missouri Territory in 1812, and became a state in 1821. The population in 1810 includes those districts (which became counties in 1812) that later became part of the state and excludes two districts (Arkansas and Hopefield/St. Francis) that were wholly within the area that would become the territory and state of Arkansas.

TABLE Aa4499–4549   Montana population by race, sex, age, nativity, and urban–rural residence: 1870–1990
Contributed by Michael R. Haines

			Population								
				Race				Residence		Nativity	
	Area	Population density	Total	White	Nonwhite	Black	Other nonwhite	Urban	Rural	Native-born	Foreign-born
	Aa4499	Aa4500	Aa4501	Aa4502	Aa4503	Aa4504	Aa4505	Aa4506	Aa4507	Aa4508	Aa4509
Year	Square miles	Persons per square mile	Number	Number	Number	Number	Number	Number	Number	Number	Number
1870	146,195	0.14	20,595	18,306	2,289	183	2,106	3,106	17,489	12,616	7,979
1880	146,201	0.27	39,159	35,385	3,774	346	3,428	6,987	32,172	27,638	11,521
1890 [1]	146,201	0.98	142,924	127,271	4,888	1,490	3,398	38,787	104,137	89,063	43,096
1900	146,201	1.66	243,329	226,283	17,046	1,523	15,523	84,554	158,775	176,262	67,067
1910	146,201	2.57	376,053	360,580	15,473	1,834	13,639	133,420	242,633	281,340	94,713
1920	146,131	3.76	548,889	534,260	14,629	1,658	12,971	172,011	376,878	453,298	95,591
1930	146,131	3.68	537,606	519,898	17,708	1,256	16,452	181,036	356,570	461,703	75,903
1940	146,316	3.82	559,456	540,468	18,988	1,120	17,868	211,535	347,921	503,092	56,364
1950	145,878	4.05	591,024	572,038	18,986	1,232	17,754	258,034	332,990	544,555	43,385
1960	145,603	4.63	674,767	650,738	24,029	1,467	22,562	338,457	336,310	644,121	30,646
1970	145,587	4.77	694,409	663,043	31,366	1,995	29,371	370,676	323,733	674,775	19,634
1980	145,388	5.41	786,690	740,148	46,542	1,786	44,756	416,402	370,288	768,371	18,319
1990	145,556	5.49	799,065	741,111	57,954	2,381	55,573	419,826	379,239	785,286	13,779

Note appears at end of table

(continued)

TABLE Aa4499–4549   Montana population by race, sex, age, nativity, and urban–rural residence: 1870–1990
Continued

	Population											
	Sex		Male, by age									
	Male	Female	0	1–4	5–9	10–14	15–19	20–24	25–29	30–34	35–39
	Aa4510	Aa4511	Aa4512	Aa4513	Aa4514	Aa4515	Aa4516	Aa4517	Aa4518	Aa4519	Aa4520
Year	Number	Number	Number	Number	Number	Number	Number	Number	Number	Number	Number
1870	16,771	3,824	153	593	508	406	422	2,098	3,186	3,078	2,390
1880	28,177	10,982	413	1,565	1,641	1,202	1,244	3,532	4,205	3,794	3,371
1890 [1]	87,882	44,277	1,512	5,211	5,563	4,256	4,386	11,215	14,808	12,944	8,634
1900	149,842	93,487	2,817	10,831	12,470	9,754	9,434	14,896	17,473	17,798	16,848
1910	226,872	149,181	4,071	15,338	17,200	15,043	15,939	27,140	28,966	23,768	19,916
1920	299,941	248,948	6,399	27,425	30,531	26,095	21,058	19,858	26,056	29,542	28,147
1930	293,228	244,378	4,988	20,166	27,541	28,623	25,540	23,211	20,155	18,831	22,137
1940	299,009	260,447	5,063	19,555	23,037	24,530	26,168	26,329	24,634	22,087	19,394
1950	309,423	281,601	6,754	27,788	28,305	23,796	20,533	21,355	22,732	23,032	22,347
1960	343,743	331,024	8,604	33,580	39,037	33,899	25,429	19,636	19,428	21,241	21,794
1970	347,005	347,404	5,936	23,184	36,959	39,728	35,512	25,529	21,171	18,626	17,958
1980	392,625	394,065	7,246	25,846	30,872	31,882	38,568	37,197	36,022	31,558	24,392
1990	395,769	403,296	5,220	25,189	33,493	32,363	29,473	24,249	27,742	32,773	34,185

	Population										
	Male, by age										Female, by age
	40–44	45–49	50–54	55–59	60–64	65–69	70–74	75–79	80 and older	Unknown age	0
	Aa4521	Aa4522	Aa4523	Aa4524	Aa4525	Aa4526	Aa4527	Aa4528	Aa4529	Aa4530	Aa4531
Year	Number	Number	Number	Number	Number	Number	Number	Number	Number	Number	Number
1870	1,464	730	423	177	91	30	10	6	0	1,006	161
1880	2,603	2,212	1,234	596	339	142	58	21	5	—	431
1890 [1]	5,743	4,938	3,391	2,005	1,126	570	292	113	69	1,106	1,403
1900	12,354	8,521	5,744	3,883	2,836	1,685	824	372	221	1,081	2,812
1910	16,359	13,668	10,679	6,187	4,236	2,704	1,627	984	461	2,586	3,831
1920	20,970	17,277	14,823	11,385	8,455	5,204	2,727	1,571	952	1,466	6,347
1930	24,479	21,437	16,859	12,346	10,208	7,669	4,946	2,451	1,427	214	4,845
1940	17,378	19,194	20,908	17,188	12,575	8,776	6,121	3,746	2,326	—	4,888
1950	20,196	17,376	15,245	15,530	15,901	12,574	7,839	5,254	2,866	—	6,704
1960	21,956	20,670	17,735	15,079	12,009	11,575	10,644	6,821	4,606	—	8,331
1970	19,406	19,535	19,638	17,443	14,585	10,820	7,728	6,166	7,081	—	5,771
1980	20,244	18,205	18,536	18,060	16,946	14,110	10,165	6,374	6,402	—	6,900
1990	30,034	22,947	18,561	16,756	16,730	15,571	12,882	9,111	8,490	—	4,974

	Population										
	Female, by age										
	1–4	5–9	10–14	15–19	20–24	25–29	30–34	35–39	40–44	45–49	50–54
	Aa4532	Aa4533	Aa4534	Aa4535	Aa4536	Aa4537	Aa4538	Aa4539	Aa4540	Aa4541	Aa4542
Year	Number	Number	Number	Number	Number	Number	Number	Number	Number	Number	Number
1870	562	448	363	291	447	493	376	248	173	88	64
1880	1,501	1,619	1,126	931	1,125	1,083	927	809	524	364	219
1890 [1]	5,140	5,519	4,138	3,862	5,287	5,394	4,259	2,831	2,047	1,510	1,040
1900	10,519	12,284	9,643	7,926	9,113	9,472	8,668	7,475	5,012	3,335	2,398
1910	15,083	16,979	14,643	13,925	16,007	15,298	12,933	11,060	8,774	6,899	4,903
1920	27,201	29,543	25,232	20,970	20,627	23,395	22,884	19,301	14,412	11,605	9,061
1930	19,264	26,451	27,773	24,595	20,542	18,040	16,645	18,422	17,648	14,197	10,975
1940	19,075	22,176	23,571	24,968	24,949	22,394	19,065	16,967	15,438	16,205	15,208
1950	26,955	27,052	22,738	20,107	20,361	21,449	22,258	20,716	17,356	14,784	13,469
1960	32,587	38,011	33,143	25,338	19,942	19,454	20,488	20,979	21,246	19,269	15,600
1970	22,163	35,299	38,890	34,834	25,993	21,031	19,051	18,305	19,329	19,127	19,537
1980	24,463	29,366	30,657	36,054	36,821	35,494	29,851	23,653	20,130	18,109	18,827
1990	23,874	31,884	30,536	27,340	23,520	28,369	34,186	33,987	28,550	22,186	18,612

Note appears at end of table

TABLE Aa4499–4549   Montana population by race, sex, age, nativity, and urban–rural residence: 1870–1990
Continued

	Population						
	Female, by age						
	55–59	60–64	65–69	70–74	75–79	80 and older	Unknown age
	Aa4543	Aa4544	Aa4545	Aa4546	Aa4547	Aa4548	Aa4549
Year	Number	Number	Number	Number	Number	Number	Number
1870	26	20	10	3	1	0	50
1880	134	87	56	24	14	8	—
1890 [1]	641	459	253	147	78	45	224
1900	1,669	1,254	797	484	249	213	164
1910	3,020	2,232	1,534	927	496	352	285
1920	6,806	4,739	3,087	1,679	921	667	471
1930	8,279	6,372	4,654	2,965	1,480	1,108	123
1940	11,600	8,655	6,580	4,289	2,589	1,830	—
1950	13,282	12,039	9,366	6,108	4,255	2,602	—
1960	13,413	11,449	11,222	9,555	6,122	4,875	—
1970	17,283	13,850	11,208	9,070	7,714	8,949	—
1980	18,497	17,735	15,499	11,754	8,548	11,707	—
1990	17,249	17,586	16,925	15,506	12,297	15,715	—

[1] Includes 10,765 American Indians not counted in the general enumeration; see text for Table Aa2244–2340.

Sources

See the sources for Table Aa2244–2340.

Documentation

See the text for Table Aa2244–2340.

In 1860, parts of what were to become the territory and state of Montana were in the Nebraska and Washington Territories. See Table Aa4550–4612 and Aa6249–6311. Montana became a territory in 1864 and a state in 1889.

TABLE Aa4550–4612   Nebraska population, by race, sex, age, nativity, and urban–rural residence: 1860–1990

Contributed by Michael R. Haines

			Population									
				Race					Residence		Nativity	
	Area	Population density	Total	White	Nonwhite	Black	Other nonwhite		Urban	Rural	Native-born	Foreign-born
	Aa4550	Aa4551	Aa4552	Aa4553	Aa4554	Aa4555	Aa4556		Aa4557	Aa4558	Aa4559	Aa4560
Year	Square miles	Persons per square mile	Number	Number	Number	Number	Number		Number	Number	Number	Number
1860	118,915	0.24	28,841	28,696	145	82	63		0	28,841	22,490	6,351
1870	76,172	1.61	122,993	122,117	876	789	87		22,133	100,860	92,245	30,748
1880	76,172	5.94	452,402	449,764	2,638	2,385	253		61,307	391,095	354,988	97,414
1890 [1]	76,808	13.84	1,062,656	1,046,888	12,022	8,913	3,109		291,641	771,015	856,368	202,542
1900	76,808	13.88	1,066,300	1,056,526	9,774	6,269	3,505		252,702	813,598	888,953	177,347
1910	76,808	15.52	1,192,214	1,180,293	11,921	7,689	4,232		310,852	881,362	1,015,552	176,662
1920	76,808	16.88	1,296,372	1,279,219	17,153	13,242	3,911		405,293	891,079	1,145,707	150,665
1930	76,808	17.94	1,377,963	1,360,023	17,940	13,752	4,188		486,107	891,856	1,258,764	119,199
1940	76,653	17.17	1,315,834	1,297,624	18,210	14,171	4,039		514,148	801,686	1,233,733	82,101
1950	76,663	17.29	1,325,510	1,301,328	24,182	19,234	4,948		621,905	703,605	1,261,415	57,600
1960	76,522	18.44	1,411,330	1,374,764	36,566	29,262	7,304		766,053	645,277	1,371,092	40,238
1970	76,483	19.40	1,483,493	1,432,867	50,626	39,911	10,715		912,598	570,895	1,453,616	28,796
1980	76,644	20.48	1,569,825	1,490,381	79,444	48,390	31,054		987,859	581,966	1,538,824	31,001
1990	76,878	20.53	1,578,385	1,480,558	97,827	57,404	40,423		1,043,984	534,401	1,550,187	28,198

Note appears at end of table

(continued)

TABLE Aa4550–4612   Nebraska population, by race, sex, age, nativity, and urban–rural residence: 1860–1990
Continued

Population

	Sex		Male, by age							
	Male	Female	0	1–4	5–9	10–14	15–19	20–29	20–24	25–29
	Aa4561	Aa4562	Aa4563	Aa4564	Aa4565	Aa4566	Aa4567	Aa4568	Aa4569	Aa4570
Year	Number	Number	Number	Number	Number	Number	Number	Number	Number	Number
1860	16,760	12,081	508	1,869	1,820	1,437	1,218	4,812	—	—
1870	70,425	52,568	2,065	7,971	7,801	6,815	5,407	—	9,020	9,056
1880	249,241	203,161	7,877	28,708	31,634	26,025	21,325	—	27,192	24,411
1890 [1]	572,824	486,086	14,975	60,274	70,760	59,877	54,237	—	58,542	58,129
1900	564,592	501,708	14,206	53,630	67,291	61,690	55,742	—	53,374	47,657
1910	627,782	564,432	14,747	56,401	64,928	61,594	63,188	—	64,722	56,370
1920	672,805	623,567	13,711	59,306	71,498	66,992	59,625	—	58,451	57,863
1930	706,348	671,615	12,907	53,835	71,931	69,173	66,788	—	60,298	52,163
1940	665,788	650,046	10,346	43,165	55,268	60,398	63,304	—	52,418	49,358
1950	667,332	658,178	14,444	57,019	56,549	50,332	48,605	—	49,437	50,478
1960	700,026	711,304	16,778	64,933	74,761	65,472	50,130	—	40,513	41,112
1970	724,455	759,038	12,429	48,759	74,811	78,362	71,377	—	55,167	44,302
1980	765,894	803,931	13,791	48,912	60,399	61,803	74,437	—	74,697	67,366
1990	769,439	808,946	11,073	50,334	64,659	60,239	57,530	—	54,477	62,702

Population

	Male, by age										
	30–39	30–34	35–39	40–49	40–44	45–49	50–59	50–54	55–59	60–69	60–64
	Aa4571	Aa4572	Aa4573	Aa4574	Aa4575	Aa4576	Aa4577	Aa4578	Aa4579	Aa4580	Aa4581
Year	Number	Number	Number	Number	Number	Number	Number	Number	Number	Number	Number
1860	2,918	—	—	1,293	—	—	611	—	—	215	—
1870	—	6,610	5,130	—	3,617	2,447	—	1,900	1,059	—	751
1880	—	21,099	17,673	—	13,038	9,634	—	7,672	4,999	—	3,737
1890 [1]	—	49,308	37,976	—	29,748	23,353	—	19,029	12,929	—	9,536
1900	—	40,930	38,246	—	33,722	25,569	—	22,302	17,168	—	12,396
1910	—	46,122	40,301	—	34,077	30,807	—	28,814	20,326	—	15,980
1920	—	52,355	48,252	—	38,489	34,617	—	29,779	24,653	—	20,864
1930	—	50,023	50,976	—	46,652	40,125	—	34,386	27,577	—	22,815
1940	—	47,518	44,236	—	43,017	42,757	—	40,001	33,023	—	26,405
1950	—	44,877	44,730	—	42,741	38,761	—	37,897	35,724	—	31,322
1960	—	43,529	44,088	—	40,929	39,518	—	37,378	33,768	—	30,766
1970	—	38,583	38,224	—	40,439	40,444	—	36,967	34,605	—	31,737
1980	—	57,398	44,229	—	37,445	36,065	—	37,910	36,566	—	31,490
1990	—	66,117	61,638	—	52,541	40,180	—	33,733	32,400	—	32,481

Population

	Male, by age						Female, by age				
	65–69	70–79	70–74	75–79	80 and older	Unknown age	0	1–4	5–9	10–14	15–19
	Aa4582	Aa4583	Aa4584	Aa4585	Aa4586	Aa4587	Aa4588	Aa4589	Aa4590	Aa4591	Aa4592
Year	Number	Number	Number	Number	Number	Number	Number	Number	Number	Number	Number
1860	—	52	—	—	6	1	498	1,873	1,664	1,299	1,233
1870	387	—	236	90	61	2	2,089	7,383	7,419	6,326	5,022
1880	2,170	—	1,117	580	350		7,788	27,783	30,341	23,946	19,760
1890 [1]	6,092	—	3,879	1,883	1,118	1,179	14,738	57,983	68,521	56,671	52,206
1900	9,079	—	5,501	3,045	1,884	1,160	13,587	52,324	65,507	60,053	54,535
1910	12,438	—	7,813	4,707	2,982	1,465	14,073	54,875	63,158	60,188	61,330
1920	14,239	—	10,025	6,385	4,076	1,625	13,103	57,120	69,082	65,116	59,427
1930	18,632	—	13,993	7,825	5,816	433	12,153	51,442	69,556	67,166	65,312
1940	21,276	—	15,433	9,932	7,933	—	9,823	41,212	53,284	58,035	61,797
1950	25,164	—	17,683	13,516	8,053	—	13,806	54,900	54,256	47,378	48,660
1960	27,872	—	22,196	14,424	11,859	—	16,249	62,247	72,650	62,735	50,153
1970	25,511	—	21,252	15,849	15,637	—	11,926	47,108	72,417	74,607	71,798
1980	27,847	—	22,608	15,678	17,253	—	13,108	47,135	57,646	59,104	72,812
1990	29,799	—	22,811	17,380	19,345	—	10,455	47,744	61,742	57,144	55,330

Note appears at end of table

TABLE Aa4550–4612   Nebraska population, by race, sex, age, nativity, and urban–rural residence: 1860–1990
Continued

	Population										
	Female, by age										
	20–29	20–24	25–29	30–39	30–34	35–39	40–49	40–44	45–49	50–59	50–54
	Aa4593	Aa4594	Aa4595	Aa4596	Aa4597	Aa4598	Aa4599	Aa4600	Aa4601	Aa4602	Aa4603
Year	Number	Number	Number	Number	Number	Number	Number	Number	Number	Number	Number
1860	2,659	—	—	1,543	—	—	734	—	—	405	—
1870	—	5,759	5,115	—	3,820	2,958	—	2,157	1,522	—	1,171
1880	—	19,495	16,866	—	14,835	12,326	—	8,823	6,755	—	5,065
1890 ¹	—	49,342	41,805	—	35,729	28,035	—	22,454	17,909	—	13,487
1900	—	48,879	40,497	—	34,185	30,080	—	25,866	20,329	—	17,017
1910	—	58,382	49,202	—	40,014	34,823	—	28,922	25,111	—	21,775
1920	—	58,364	55,625	—	48,408	41,866	—	34,486	29,493	—	24,516
1930	—	60,490	52,207	—	49,578	48,835	—	43,204	36,690	—	30,305
1940	—	54,921	50,687	—	48,035	44,506	—	42,925	41,321	—	37,718
1950	—	49,440	48,657	—	45,752	44,931	—	42,420	38,746	—	37,950
1960	—	42,461	41,513	—	43,290	43,751	—	41,875	40,176	—	38,358
1970	—	59,520	44,751	—	39,348	39,550	—	40,868	40,558	—	38,994
1980	—	74,037	67,428	—	57,009	44,195	—	37,905	37,732	—	38,946
1990	—	54,172	62,516	—	65,873	62,140	—	52,493	40,488	—	34,988

	Population								
	Female, by age								
	55–59	60–69	60–64	65–69	70–79	70–74	75–79	80 and older	Unknown age
	Aa4604	Aa4605	Aa4606	Aa4607	Aa4608	Aa4609	Aa4610	Aa4611	Aa4612
Year	Number	Number	Number	Number	Number	Number	Number	Number	Number
1860	—	135	—	—	32	—	—	6	0
1870	701	—	552	290	—	164	67	44	9
1880	3,563	—	2,539	1,571	—	920	502	283	—
1890 ¹	9,377	—	7,149	4,795	—	2,925	1,524	1,078	358
1900	13,370	—	9,732	6,755	—	4,430	2,417	1,643	502
1910	16,150	—	13,094	10,022	—	6,304	3,742	2,763	504
1920	19,869	—	16,555	11,881	—	8,404	5,484	3,847	921
1930	24,464	—	19,968	15,799	—	11,532	7,009	5,588	317
1940	30,222	—	24,502	19,976	—	14,131	9,119	7,832	—
1950	35,066	—	30,253	24,823	—	17,990	14,190	8,960	—
1960	35,065	—	32,976	30,602	—	24,479	17,045	15,679	—
1970	37,183	—	35,133	30,849	—	27,609	22,189	24,630	—
1980	38,538	—	36,038	33,634	—	29,932	24,309	34,423	—
1990	34,881	—	35,247	34,264	—	30,769	26,845	41,855	—

¹ Includes 3,746 American Indians not counted in the general enumeration; see text for Table Aa2244–2340.

Sources
See the sources for Table Aa2244–2340.

Documentation
See the text for Table Aa2244–2340.

Nebraska became a territory in 1854 and a state in 1867.

TABLE Aa4613–4675   Nevada population by race, sex, age, nativity, and urban–rural residence: 1860–1990

Contributed by Michael R. Haines

				Population								
				Race					Residence		Nativity	
	Area	Population density	Total	White	Nonwhite	Black	Other nonwhite	Urban	Rural	Native-born	Foreign-born
	Aa4613	Aa4614	Aa4615	Aa4616	Aa4617	Aa4618	Aa4619	Aa4620	Aa4621	Aa4622	Aa4623
Year	Square miles	Persons per square mile	Number	Number	Number	Number	Number	Number	Number	Number	Number
1860	61,260	0.11	6,857	6,812	45	45	0	0	6,857	4,793	2,064
1870	109,821	0.39	42,491	38,959	3,532	357	3,175	7,048	35,443	23,690	18,801
1880	109,821	0.57	62,266	53,556	8,710	488	8,222	19,353	42,913	36,613	25,653
1890 [1]	109,821	0.43	47,355	39,084	6,677	242	6,435	16,024	31,331	31,055	14,706
1900	109,821	0.39	42,335	35,405	6,930	134	6,796	7,195	35,140	32,242	10,093
1910	109,821	0.75	81,875	74,276	7,599	513	7,086	13,367	68,508	62,184	19,691
1920	109,821	0.70	77,407	70,699	6,708	346	6,362	15,254	62,153	61,404	16,003
1930	109,821	0.83	91,058	84,515	6,543	516	6,027	34,464	56,594	75,963	15,095
1940	109,802	1.00	110,247	104,030	6,217	664	5,553	43,291	66,956	99,206	11,041
1950	109,789	1.46	160,083	149,908	10,175	4,302	5,873	91,625	68,458	148,670	10,720
1960	109,889	2.60	285,278	263,443	21,835	13,484	8,351	200,704	84,574	272,145	13,133
1970	109,889	4.45	488,738	448,177	40,561	27,762	12,799	395,336	93,402	470,559	18,179
1980	109,894	7.28	800,493	700,345	100,148	50,999	49,149	682,947	117,546	746,709	53,784
1990	109,806	10.95	1,201,833	1,012,695	189,138	78,771	110,367	1,061,444	140,389	1,097,005	104,828

			Population									
	Sex		Male, by age									
	Male	Female	0	1–4	5–9	10–14	15–19	20–29	20–24	25–29	30–39
	Aa4624	Aa4625	Aa4626	Aa4627	Aa4628	Aa4629	Aa4630	Aa4631	Aa4632	Aa4633	Aa4634
Year	Number	Number	Number	Number	Number	Number	Number	Number	Number	Number	Number
1860	6,137	720	30	120	88	59	141	3,123	—	—	1,887
1870	32,379	10,112	295	1,337	1,317	943	1,094	—	3,214	5,393	—
1880	42,019	20,247	664	2,543	2,601	2,050	2,149	—	3,930	5,673	—
1890 [1]	29,214	16,547	345	1,540	1,959	2,061	1,936	—	2,427	2,796	—
1900	25,603	16,732	408	1,520	1,853	1,737	1,865	—	2,432	2,300	—
1910	52,551	29,324	739	2,567	2,837	2,563	2,927	—	5,169	6,263	—
1920	46,240	31,167	685	2,725	3,425	2,941	2,610	—	3,282	4,066	—
1930	53,161	37,897	719	2,940	3,968	3,619	3,601	—	4,001	4,490	—
1940	61,341	48,906	955	3,713	3,896	4,027	4,232	—	5,089	5,537	—
1950	85,017	75,066	1,713	6,893	6,930	5,665	4,921	—	5,681	6,423	—
1960	147,521	137,757	3,429	13,207	14,749	12,761	9,813	—	9,484	9,848	—
1970	247,798	240,940	4,459	17,807	25,784	25,101	20,244	—	19,267	18,614	—
1980	405,060	395,433	6,627	22,030	28,498	31,580	35,867	—	39,336	38,632	—
1990	611,880	589,953	8,604	38,764	43,840	38,820	38,254	—	45,306	58,212	—

Note appears at end of table

TABLE Aa4613–4675   Nevada population by race, sex, age, nativity, and urban–rural residence: 1860–1990 *Continued*

Population

	Male, by age										
	30–34	35–39	40–49	40–44	45–49	50–59	50–54	55–59	60–69	60–64	65–69
	Aa4635	Aa4636	Aa4637	Aa4638	Aa4639	Aa4640	Aa4641	Aa4642	Aa4643	Aa4644	Aa4645
Year	Number	Number	Number	Number	Number	Number	Number	Number	Number	Number	Number
1860	—	—	539	—	—	123	—	—	26	—	—
1870	6,245	5,395	—	3,923	1,690	—	910	302	—	193	67
1880	5,939	4,959	—	4,357	3,028	—	2,180	934	—	593	247
1890 ¹	2,948	2,730	—	2,827	2,277	—	1,964	1,345	—	1,071	468
1900	2,130	2,075	—	1,844	1,735	—	1,609	1,127	—	1,110	806
1910	6,233	5,624	—	4,658	3,822	—	3,033	1,959	—	1,605	933
1920	4,515	5,035	—	4,255	3,715	—	2,915	2,067	—	1,567	1,053
1930	4,212	4,757	—	4,627	4,412	—	3,777	2,737	—	2,189	1,418
1940	5,182	4,918	—	4,583	4,542	—	4,103	3,468	—	2,908	1,904
1950	6,899	7,107	—	6,700	6,108	—	5,359	4,496	—	3,764	2,767
1960	10,427	11,112	—	10,824	10,484	—	8,632	7,377	—	5,577	4,241
1970	17,408	16,070	—	15,917	15,629	—	14,474	12,305	—	9,413	6,611
1980	35,089	29,276	—	25,068	22,109	—	21,594	21,208	—	17,870	13,705
1990	57,680	52,367	—	46,670	38,188	—	31,841	28,017	—	26,746	24,702

Population

	Male, by age					Female, by age					
	70–79	70–74	75–79	80 and older	Unknown age	0	1–4	5–9	10–14	15–19	20–29
	Aa4646	Aa4647	Aa4648	Aa4649	Aa4650	Aa4651	Aa4652	Aa4653	Aa4654	Aa4655	Aa4656
Year	Number	Number	Number	Number	Number	Number	Number	Number	Number	Number	Number
1860	0	—	—	0	1	38	114	91	55	66	200
1870	—	26	5	9	21	343	1,322	1,222	949	728	—
1880	—	105	38	29	—	647	2,443	2,702	2,000	1,663	—
1890 ¹	—	223	80	53	164	376	1,439	1,877	2,000	1,768	—
1900	—	484	196	127	245	363	1,463	1,769	1,651	1,614	—
1910	—	579	346	240	454	621	2,456	2,833	2,373	2,336	—
1920	—	619	288	252	225	639	2,694	3,334	2,769	2,367	—
1930	—	873	453	339	29	723	2,741	3,882	3,443	3,274	—
1940	—	1,239	621	424	—	868	3,546	3,990	3,851	4,117	—
1950	—	1,896	1,214	481	—	1,592	6,760	6,593	5,279	4,523	—
1960	—	2,765	1,596	1,195	—	3,475	12,949	14,028	12,645	9,383	—
1970	—	4,189	2,485	2,021	—	4,346	17,232	24,868	24,459	19,941	—
1980	—	8,541	4,709	3,321	—	6,135	21,340	27,191	30,164	34,295	—
1990	—	17,042	9,985	6,842	—	8,076	36,773	41,722	37,188	35,906	—

Note appears at end of table

(continued)

TABLE Aa4613–4675   Nevada population by race, sex, age, nativity, and urban–rural residence: 1860–1990
Continued

	Population										
	Female, by age										
	20–24	25–29	30–39	30–34	35–39	40–49	40–44	45–49	50–59	50–54	55–59
	Aa4657	Aa4658	Aa4659	Aa4660	Aa4661	Aa4662	Aa4663	Aa4664	Aa4665	Aa4666	Aa4667
Year	Number	Number	Number	Number	Number	Number	Number	Number	Number	Number	Number
1860	—	—	108	—	—	30	—	—	17	—	—
1870	1,116	1,335	—	1,189	832	—	497	238	—	148	74
1880	1,937	2,066	—	1,981	1,684	—	1,237	764	—	514	230
1890 [1]	1,647	1,295	—	1,256	1,124	—	1,107	865	—	712	378
1900	1,679	1,482	—	1,242	1,082	—	947	809	—	725	561
1910	2,869	3,343	—	3,047	2,639	—	1,910	1,350	—	1,035	770
1920	2,516	2,952	—	2,870	2,849	—	2,186	1,768	—	1,266	874
1930	3,284	3,266	—	3,100	3,005	—	2,773	2,411	—	1,871	1,391
1940	4,495	4,807	—	4,301	3,736	—	3,289	2,992	—	2,628	2,073
1950	5,334	6,936	—	6,970	6,905	—	5,702	4,586	—	3,758	3,049
1960	9,142	9,650	—	10,297	11,098	—	10,315	9,259	—	7,379	5,663
1970	19,808	18,868	—	16,712	15,326	—	15,170	15,189	—	13,530	11,366
1980	38,106	37,319	—	34,108	27,840	—	23,127	20,743	—	20,964	20,908
1990	42,640	52,371	—	53,764	48,901	—	44,327	36,040	—	29,931	26,664

	Population							
	Female, by age							
	60–69	60–64	65–69	70–79	70–74	75–79	80 and older	Unknown age
	Aa4668	Aa4669	Aa4670	Aa4671	Aa4672	Aa4673	Aa4674	Aa4675
Year	Number	Number	Number	Number	Number	Number	Number	Number
1860	0	—	—	1	—	—	0	0
1870	—	61	24	—	17	2	6	9
1880	—	188	86	—	59	24	22	—
1890 [1]	—	319	135	—	81	42	36	90
1900	—	485	270	—	199	84	102	205
1910	—	650	440	—	313	147	122	70
1920	—	732	512	—	353	206	190	90
1930	—	981	661	—	487	309	274	21
1940	—	1,601	1,181	—	699	376	356	—
1950	—	2,451	1,980	—	1,264	961	423	—
1960	—	4,098	3,255	—	2,377	1,548	1,196	—
1970	—	8,463	6,202	—	4,089	2,681	2,690	—
1980	—	17,713	14,275	—	9,477	6,067	5,661	—
1990	—	26,590	25,410	—	18,631	12,579	12,440	—

[1] Includes 1,594 American Indians not counted in the general enumeration; see text for Table Aa2244–2340.

Sources

See the sources for Table Aa2244–2340.

Documentation

See the text for Table Aa2244–2340.

Nevada became a territory in 1861 and a state in 1864. It was part of the Mexican Cession of 1848. The data reported here for 1860 are the enumerated population of Carson, Humboldt, and St. Mary's Counties in Utah Territory. These portions of the territory were subsequently taken from Utah Territory in 1861.

TABLE Aa4676–4776   New Hampshire population by race, sex, age, nativity, and urban–rural residence: 1790–1990

Contributed by Michael R. Haines

			Population									
	Area	Population density	Total	Race				Residence		Nativity	
				White	Nonwhite	Black	Other nonwhite	Urban	Rural	Native-born	Foreign-born
	Aa4676	Aa4677	Aa4678	Aa4679	Aa4680	Aa4681	Aa4682	Aa4683	Aa4684	Aa4685	Aa4686
Year	Square miles	Persons per square mile	Number	Number	Number	Number	Number	Number	Number	Number	Number
1790	9,031	15.71	141,899	141,112	787	787	—	4,720	137,165	—	—
1800	9,031	20.36	183,858	182,898	864	864	—	5,339	178,519	—	—
1810	9,031	23.75	214,460	213,390	970	970	—	6,934	207,526	—	—
1820	9,031	27.04	244,161	243,236	925	786	139	7,327	236,834	—	—
1830	9,031	29.82	269,328	268,721	607	607	—	13,475	255,853	—	—
1840	9,031	31.51	284,574	284,036	538	538	—	28,531	256,043	—	—
1850	9,031	35.21	317,976	317,456	520	520	—	54,327	263,649	303,711	14,265
1860	9,031	36.11	326,073	325,579	494	494	0	72,038	254,035	305,135	20,938
1870	9,031	35.25	318,300	317,697	603	580	23	83,456	234,844	288,689	29,611
1880	9,031	38.42	346,991	346,229	762	685	77	104,105	242,886	300,697	46,294
1890	9,031	41.69	376,530	375,840	690	614	76	147,913	228,617	304,190	72,340
1900	9,031	45.58	411,588	410,791	797	662	135	192,240	219,348	323,481	88,107
1910	9,031	47.68	430,572	429,906	666	564	102	223,152	207,420	333,905	96,667
1920	9,031	49.06	443,083	442,331	752	621	131	250,438	192,645	351,686	91,397
1930	9,031	51.52	465,293	464,351	942	790	152	273,079	192,214	382,364	82,929
1940	9,024	54.47	491,524	490,989	535	414	121	283,225	208,299	423,131	68,393
1950	9,017	59.14	533,242	532,275	967	731	236	306,806	226,436	471,855	57,475
1960	9,033	67.19	606,921	604,334	2,587	1,903	684	353,766	253,155	562,149	44,772
1970	9,027	81.72	737,681	733,106	4,575	2,505	2,070	416,040	321,641	700,633	37,048
1980	8,993	102.37	920,610	910,099	10,511	3,990	6,521	480,325	440,285	879,649	40,961
1990	8,969	123.67	1,109,252	1,087,433	21,819	7,198	14,621	565,670	543,582	1,068,059	41,193

			Population								
	Sex		Male, by age								
	Male	Female	0	1–4	5–9	10–14	15–19	20–29	20–24	25–29	30–39
	Aa4687	Aa4688	Aa4689	Aa4690	Aa4691	Aa4692	Aa4693	Aa4694	Aa4695	Aa4696	Aa4697
Year	Number	Number	Number	Number	Number	Number	Number	Number	Number	Number	Number
1790	—	—	—	—	—	—	—	—	—	—	—
1800	—	—	—	—	—	—	—	—	—	—	—
1810	—	—	—	—	—	—	—	—	—	—	—
1820	119,582	124,440	—	—	—	—	—	—	—	—	—
1830	131,459	137,869	—	—	—	—	—	—	—	—	—
1840	139,252	145,322	—	—	—	—	—	—	—	—	—
1850	156,220	161,756	3,074	13,682	17,409	17,450	16,942	28,273	—	—	19,590
1860	159,816	166,257	3,452	14,523	16,430	16,532	16,776	27,184	—	—	20,446
1870	155,640	162,660	2,914	12,114	14,259	16,574	15,617	—	14,023	11,459	—
1880	170,526	176,465	3,137	12,367	15,215	15,505	15,623	—	17,267	14,183	—
1890	186,566	189,964	3,255	11,897	15,486	16,410	17,683	—	18,897	15,336	—
1900	205,379	206,209	4,054	15,024	17,818	16,350	17,097	—	19,038	18,017	—
1910	216,290	214,282	4,185	15,480	18,474	18,181	19,264	—	18,643	17,065	—
1920	222,112	220,971	4,002	16,916	19,908	19,355	17,381	—	17,142	17,143	—
1930	231,759	233,534	3,826	16,091	22,035	21,342	19,316	—	16,900	15,379	—
1940	244,909	246,615	3,582	14,674	19,097	21,144	21,794	—	19,689	18,364	—
1950	262,424	270,818	5,167	22,497	22,371	18,999	18,775	—	18,824	18,875	—
1960	298,107	308,814	6,848	26,866	30,716	28,653	22,429	—	17,741	17,100	—
1970	360,672	377,009	6,468	27,067	38,314	37,977	34,188	—	28,548	24,070	—
1980	448,462	472,148	6,818	25,065	34,800	39,684	44,217	—	41,075	39,156	—
1990	543,544	565,708	7,603	35,375	41,349	36,696	38,574	—	41,374	48,763	—

(continued)

TABLE Aa4676–4776   New Hampshire population by race, sex, age, nativity, and urban–rural residence: 1790–1990
Continued

Population

Male, by age

Year	30–34	35–39	40–49	40–44	45–49	50–59	50–54	55–59	60–69	60–64	65–69
	Aa4698	Aa4699	Aa4700	Aa4701	Aa4702	Aa4703	Aa4704	Aa4705	Aa4706	Aa4707	Aa4708
	Number	Number	Number	Number	Number	Number	Number	Number	Number	Number	Number
1790	—	—	—	—	—	—	—	—	—	—	—
1800	—	—	—	—	—	—	—	—	—	—	—
1810	—	—	—	—	—	—	—	—	—	—	—
1820	—	—	—	—	—	—	—	—	—	—	—
1830	—	—	—	—	—	—	—	—	—	—	—
1840	—	—	—	—	—	—	—	—	—	—	—
1850	—	—	15,863	—	—	11,321	—	—	7,188	—	—
1860	—	—	16,524	—	—	13,118	—	—	8,797	—	—
1870	9,824	9,843	—	9,158	8,311	—	7,791	6,218	—	5,827	4,456
1880	11,791	10,783	—	9,615	9,234	—	8,490	7,226	—	6,431	4,945
1890	14,374	12,622	—	11,074	9,986	—	9,066	7,863	—	6,920	5,495
1900	16,209	14,348	—	13,574	11,786	—	10,423	8,412	—	7,189	5,855
1910	15,968	15,990	—	14,609	12,688	—	12,136	9,481	—	7,839	6,023
1920	15,603	15,708	—	14,499	14,609	—	13,010	10,461	—	9,113	6,557
1930	15,595	15,985	—	14,795	14,197	—	13,415	12,171	—	10,495	7,958
1940	17,322	16,458	—	16,087	15,888	—	14,254	12,367	—	11,056	9,166
1950	18,447	17,914	—	17,075	15,915	—	15,366	13,898	—	11,731	9,789
1960	18,461	19,578	—	19,056	17,710	—	16,010	14,466	—	12,745	11,327
1970	20,402	19,640	—	20,555	20,534	—	19,280	16,784	—	14,795	11,642
1980	38,683	30,379	—	23,549	22,175	—	22,345	21,366	—	18,600	15,364
1990	52,940	48,391	—	43,064	32,333	—	24,264	22,119	—	20,769	18,118

Population

	Male, by age					Female, by age					
	70–79	70–74	75–79	80 and older	Unknown age	0	1–4	5–9	10–14	15–19	20–29
	Aa4709	Aa4710	Aa4711	Aa4712	Aa4713	Aa4714	Aa4715	Aa4716	Aa4717	Aa4718	Aa4719
Year	Number	Number	Number	Number	Number	Number	Number	Number	Number	Number	Number
1790	—	—	—	—	—	—	—	—	—	—	—
1800	—	—	—	—	—	—	—	—	—	—	—
1810	—	—	—	—	—	—	—	—	—	—	—
1820	—	—	—	—	—	—	—	—	—	—	—
1830	—	—	—	—	—	—	—	—	—	—	—
1840	—	—	—	—	—	—	—	—	—	—	—
1850	3,913	—	—	1,487	28	3,037	13,270	16,855	16,864	18,839	28,992
1860	4,635	—	—	1,399	0	3,238	13,801	16,134	15,621	17,674	30,325
1870	—	3,532	2,121	1,593	6	2,826	11,811	13,950	15,294	15,961	—
1880	—	4,170	2,597	1,947	—	3,004	12,065	15,015	15,164	16,432	—
1890	—	4,513	2,746	2,268	675	3,092	12,077	15,226	15,908	18,362	—
1900	—	4,512	2,812	2,124	737	3,994	15,159	17,646	16,547	17,623	—
1910	—	4,558	3,060	2,263	383	4,140	15,776	18,399	18,090	18,642	—
1920	—	5,039	3,052	2,160	454	3,918	16,555	19,854	19,436	17,771	—
1930	—	6,114	3,545	2,471	129	3,639	15,794	21,508	20,686	19,506	—
1940	—	6,951	4,143	2,873	—	3,368	14,181	18,399	20,452	21,555	—
1950	—	7,600	6,002	3,179	—	5,037	21,818	21,429	18,265	18,689	—
1960	—	8,341	5,428	4,632	—	6,635	25,771	29,229	27,791	21,931	—
1970	—	9,089	5,960	5,359	—	6,204	25,617	36,607	36,022	33,076	—
1980	—	11,291	7,227	6,668	—	6,482	24,147	33,197	37,079	43,559	—
1990	—	13,679	9,324	8,809	—	7,175	34,412	39,292	35,029	37,890	—

TABLE Aa4676–4776   New Hampshire population by race, sex, age, nativity, and urban–rural residence: 1790–1990
Continued

	Population										
	Female, by age										
	20–24	25–29	30–39	30–34	35–39	40–49	40–44	45–49	50–59	50–54	55–59
	Aa4720	Aa4721	Aa4722	Aa4723	Aa4724	Aa4725	Aa4726	Aa4727	Aa4728	Aa4729	Aa4730
Year	Number	Number	Number	Number	Number	Number	Number	Number	Number	Number	Number
1790	—	—	—	—	—	—	—	—	—	—	—
1800	—	—	—	—	—	—	—	—	—	—	—
1810	—	—	—	—	—	—	—	—	—	—	—
1820	—	—	—	—	—	—	—	—	—	—	—
1830	—	—	—	—	—	—	—	—	—	—	—
1840	—	—	—	—	—	—	—	—	—	—	—
1850	—	—	20,257	—	—	16,471	—	—	12,401	—	—
1860	—	—	21,203	—	—	17,089	—	—	13,851	—	—
1870	15,294	13,050	—	11,668	10,790	—	9,564	8,449	—	7,980	6,436
1880	17,484	14,318	—	12,183	11,775	—	10,849	9,646	—	8,838	7,444
1890	18,787	15,652	—	13,987	12,550	—	11,293	10,593	—	9,945	8,158
1900	19,110	17,827	—	15,581	14,196	—	12,873	11,365	—	10,087	8,934
1910	18,210	16,610	—	15,826	15,659	—	13,877	12,405	—	11,254	9,138
1920	18,303	17,332	—	15,395	15,102	—	14,374	13,524	—	12,031	9,980
1930	17,967	16,183	—	16,164	16,487	—	14,886	13,916	—	13,261	11,897
1940	19,830	18,688	—	17,690	16,663	—	16,594	15,843	—	14,090	12,353
1950	19,137	19,770	—	19,164	18,872	—	17,890	16,310	—	16,198	14,531
1960	16,930	17,388	—	19,317	20,626	—	19,423	18,462	—	17,224	15,441
1970	29,974	24,365	—	20,433	20,095	—	21,146	21,472	—	20,030	18,541
1980	42,549	40,312	—	39,245	29,712	—	23,388	22,120	—	23,481	23,383
1990	41,588	49,899	—	53,221	48,331	—	42,846	31,575	—	24,043	22,584

	Population									White	
	Female, by age										Male, by age
	60–69	60–64	65–69	70–79	70–74	75–79	80 and older	Unknown age	Male	Female	0–4
	Aa4731	Aa4732	Aa4733	Aa4734	Aa4735	Aa4736	Aa4737	Aa4738	Aa4739	Aa4740	Aa4741
Year	Number	Number	Number	Number	Number	Number	Number	Number	Number	Number	Number
1790	—	—	—	—	—	—	—	—	70,929	70,183	—
1800	—	—	—	—	—	—	—	—	91,158	91,740	—
1810	—	—	—	—	—	—	—	—	105,782	107,608	—
1820	—	—	—	—	—	—	—	—	119,210	124,026	—
1830	—	—	—	—	—	—	—	—	131,184	137,537	19,428
1840	—	—	—	—	—	—	—	—	139,004	145,032	18,435
1850	8,181	—	—	4,567	—	—	1,998	24	—	—	—
1860	9,966	—	—	5,346	—	—	2,009	0	—	—	—
1870	—	6,091	4,848	—	3,811	2,542	2,290	5	—	—	—
1880	—	6,711	5,330	—	4,476	2,984	2,747	—	—	—	—
1890	—	7,217	5,815	—	4,678	3,035	3,201	388	—	—	—
1900	—	7,835	6,401	—	4,622	3,186	2,832	391	—	—	—
1910	—	7,811	6,770	—	5,052	3,424	2,920	279	—	—	—
1920	—	8,656	6,760	—	4,972	3,551	3,119	338	—	—	—
1930	—	10,053	7,888	—	6,392	3,883	3,309	115	—	—	—
1940	—	11,322	9,490	—	7,385	4,674	4,038	—	—	—	—
1950	—	12,485	10,696	—	8,741	7,117	4,669	—	—	—	—
1960	—	14,669	13,028	—	10,286	7,202	7,461	—	—	—	—
1970	—	17,065	14,400	—	12,452	9,324	10,186	—	—	—	—
1980	—	21,077	19,002	—	16,131	12,014	15,270	—	—	—	—
1990	—	22,724	21,635	—	18,039	14,692	20,733	—	—	—	—

(continued)

TABLE Aa4676-4776   New Hampshire population by race, sex, age, nativity, and urban-rural residence: 1790-1990
Continued

	Population										
	White										
	Male, by age										Female, by age
	5-9	10-14	15-19	20-29	30-39	40-49	50-59	60-69	70-79	80 and older	0-4
	Aa4742	Aa4743	Aa4744	Aa4745	Aa4746	Aa4747	Aa4748	Aa4749	Aa4750	Aa4751	Aa4752
Year	Number	Number	Number	Number	Number	Number	Number	Number	Number	Number	Number
1790	—	—	—	—	—	—	—	—	—	—	—
1800	—	—	—	—	—	—	—	—	—	—	—
1810	—	—	—	—	—	—	—	—	—	—	—
1820	—	—	—	—	—	—	—	—	—	—	—
1830	17,521	16,737	14,847	21,191	14,696	10,772	7,218	5,059	2,786	929	18,538
1840	17,300	16,929	15,663	22,170	16,781	12,915	8,690	5,485	3,447	1,189	17,959
1850	—	—	—	—	—	—	—	—	—	—	—
1860	—	—	—	—	—	—	—	—	—	—	—
1870	—	—	—	—	—	—	—	—	—	—	—
1880	—	—	—	—	—	—	—	—	—	—	—
1890	—	—	—	—	—	—	—	—	—	—	—
1900	—	—	—	—	—	—	—	—	—	—	—
1910	—	—	—	—	—	—	—	—	—	—	—
1920	—	—	—	—	—	—	—	—	—	—	—
1930	—	—	—	—	—	—	—	—	—	—	—
1940	—	—	—	—	—	—	—	—	—	—	—
1950	—	—	—	—	—	—	—	—	—	—	—
1960	—	—	—	—	—	—	—	—	—	—	—
1970	—	—	—	—	—	—	—	—	—	—	—
1980	—	—	—	—	—	—	—	—	—	—	—
1990	—	—	—	—	—	—	—	—	—	—	—

	Population										
	White										
	Female, by age										Male, by age
	5-9	10-14	15-19	20-29	30-39	40-49	50-59	60-69	70-79	80 and older	0-9
	Aa4753	Aa4754	Aa4755	Aa4756	Aa4757	Aa4758	Aa4759	Aa4760	Aa4761	Aa4762	Aa4763
Year	Number	Number	Number	Number	Number	Number	Number	Number	Number	Number	Number
1790	—	—	—	—	—	—	—	—	—	—	—
1800	—	—	—	—	—	—	—	—	—	—	30,594
1810	—	—	—	—	—	—	—	—	—	—	34,084
1820	—	—	—	—	—	—	—	—	—	—	35,466
1830	16,790	15,525	14,823	24,564	16,690	11,896	8,448	5,888	3,110	1,265	—
1840	16,693	15,689	15,457	24,679	18,269	14,183	9,824	6,702	4,000	1,577	—
1850	—	—	—	—	—	—	—	—	—	—	—
1860	—	—	—	—	—	—	—	—	—	—	—
1870	—	—	—	—	—	—	—	—	—	—	—
1880	—	—	—	—	—	—	—	—	—	—	—
1890	—	—	—	—	—	—	—	—	—	—	—
1900	—	—	—	—	—	—	—	—	—	—	—
1910	—	—	—	—	—	—	—	—	—	—	—
1920	—	—	—	—	—	—	—	—	—	—	—
1930	—	—	—	—	—	—	—	—	—	—	—
1940	—	—	—	—	—	—	—	—	—	—	—
1950	—	—	—	—	—	—	—	—	—	—	—
1960	—	—	—	—	—	—	—	—	—	—	—
1970	—	—	—	—	—	—	—	—	—	—	—
1980	—	—	—	—	—	—	—	—	—	—	—
1990	—	—	—	—	—	—	—	—	—	—	—

TABLE Aa4676–4776   New Hampshire population by race, sex, age, nativity, and urban–rural residence: 1790–1990
Continued

	Population												
	White												
	Male, by age				Female, by age					Male, by age		Female, by age	
	10–15	16–25	26–44	45 and older	0–9	10–15	16–25	26–44	45 and older	0–15	16 and older	0–15	16 and older
	Aa4764	Aa4765	Aa4766	Aa4767	Aa4768	Aa4769	Aa4770	Aa4771	Aa4772	Aa4773	Aa4774	Aa4775	Aa4776
Year	Number	Number	Number	Number	Number	Number	Number	Number	Number	Number	Number	Number	Number
1790	—	—	—	—	—	—	—	—	—	34,855	36,074	3,709	36,474
1800	14,881	16,379	17,589	11,715	29,871	14,193	17,153	18,381	12,142	—	—	—	—
1810	17,840	18,865	20,531	14,462	32,313	17,259	20,792	22,040	15,204	—	—	—	—
1820	19,672	22,703	22,956	18,413	34,599	18,899	24,806	25,797	19,925	—	—	—	—
1830	—	—	—	—	—	—	—	—	—	—	—	—	—
1840	—	—	—	—	—	—	—	—	—	—	—	—	—
1850	—	—	—	—	—	—	—	—	—	—	—	—	—
1860	—	—	—	—	—	—	—	—	—	—	—	—	—
1870	—	—	—	—	—	—	—	—	—	—	—	—	—
1880	—	—	—	—	—	—	—	—	—	—	—	—	—
1890	—	—	—	—	—	—	—	—	—	—	—	—	—
1900	—	—	—	—	—	—	—	—	—	—	—	—	—
1910	—	—	—	—	—	—	—	—	—	—	—	—	—
1920	—	—	—	—	—	—	—	—	—	—	—	—	—
1930	—	—	—	—	—	—	—	—	—	—	—	—	—
1940	—	—	—	—	—	—	—	—	—	—	—	—	—
1950	—	—	—	—	—	—	—	—	—	—	—	—	—
1960	—	—	—	—	—	—	—	—	—	—	—	—	—
1970	—	—	—	—	—	—	—	—	—	—	—	—	—
1980	—	—	—	—	—	—	—	—	—	—	—	—	—
1990	—	—	—	—	—	—	—	—	—	—	—	—	—

Sources
See the sources for Table Aa2244–2340.

Documentation
See the text for Table Aa2244–2340.

New Hampshire was one of the original thirteen states, admitted to the Union in 1788.

TABLE Aa4777–4877   New Jersey population by race, sex, age, nativity, and urban–rural residence: 1790–1990

Contributed by Michael R. Haines

			Population									
				Race				Residence		Nativity	
	Area	Population density	Total	White	Nonwhite	Black	Other nonwhite	Urban	Rural	Native-born	Foreign-born
	Aa4777	Aa4778	Aa4779	Aa4780	Aa4781	Aa4782	Aa4783	Aa4784	Aa4785	Aa4786	Aa4787
Year	Square miles	Persons per square mile	Number	Number	Number	Number	Number	Number	Number	Number	Number
1790	7,514	24.51	184,139	169,954	14,185	14,185	—	0	184,139	—	—
1800	7,514	28.10	211,149	195,125	16,824	16,824	—	0	211,149	—	—
1810	7,514	32.68	245,562	226,861	18,694	18,694	—	5,979	239,583	—	—
1820	7,514	36.94	277,575	257,409	20,166	20,017	149	7,457	270,118	—	—
1830	7,514	42.70	320,823	300,266	20,557	20,557	—	18,333	302,490	—	—
1840	7,514	49.68	373,306	351,588	21,718	21,718	—	39,548	333,758	—	—
1850	7,514	65.15	489,555	465,509	24,046	24,046	—	86,195	403,360	429,607	59,948
1860	7,514	89.44	672,035	646,699	25,336	25,336	0	219,798	452,237	549,245	122,790
1870	7,514	120.59	906,096	875,407	30,689	30,658	31	396,012	510,084	717,153	188,943
1880	7,514	150.53	1,131,116	1,092,017	39,099	38,853	246	615,311	515,805	909,416	221,700
1890	7,514	192.30	1,444,933	1,396,581	48,352	47,638	714	904,543	540,390	1,115,958	328,975
1900	7,514	250.69	1,883,669	1,812,317	71,352	69,844	1,508	1,329,162	554,507	1,451,785	431,884
1910	7,514	337.66	2,537,167	2,445,894	91,273	89,760	1,513	1,938,612	598,555	1,876,379	660,788
1920	7,514	420.00	3,155,900	3,037,087	118,813	117,132	1,681	2,522,435	633,465	2,413,414	742,486
1930	7,514	537.84	4,041,334	3,829,663	211,671	208,828	2,843	3,339,244	702,090	3,191,296	850,038
1940	7,522	553.07	4,160,165	3,931,087	229,078	226,973	2,105	3,394,773	765,392	3,460,809	699,356
1950	7,522	642.82	4,835,329	4,511,585	323,744	318,565	5,179	4,186,207	649,122	4,181,355	635,080
1960	7,532	805.47	6,066,782	5,539,003	527,779	514,875	12,904	5,374,369	692,413	5,451,933	615,479
1970	7,521	953.09	7,168,164	6,349,908	818,256	770,292	47,964	6,373,405	794,759	6,533,325	634,818
1980	7,468	986.18	7,364,823	6,127,467	1,237,356	925,066	312,290	6,557,377	807,446	6,607,001	757,822
1990	7,419	1,041.97	7,730,188	6,130,465	1,599,723	1,036,825	562,898	6,910,220	819,968	6,763,578	966,610

			Population								
	Sex		Male, by age								
	Male	Female	0	1–4	5–9	10–14	15–19	20–29	20–24	25–29	30–39
	Aa4788	Aa4789	Aa4790	Aa4791	Aa4792	Aa4793	Aa4794	Aa4795	Aa4796	Aa4797	Aa4798
Year	Number	Number	Number	Number	Number	Number	Number	Number	Number	Number	Number
1790	—	—	—	—	—	—	—	—	—	—	—
1800	—	—	—	—	—	—	—	—	—	—	—
1810	—	—	—	—	—	—	—	—	—	—	—
1820	140,023	137,403	—	—	—	—	—	—	—	—	—
1830	163,089	157,734	—	—	—	—	—	—	—	—	—
1840	188,138	185,168	—	—	—	—	—	—	—	—	—
1850	245,346	244,209	6,762	27,746	32,099	29,713	25,473	44,221	—	—	31,707
1860	335,051	336,984	10,098	39,200	41,092	36,939	33,950	58,666	—	—	46,955
1870	449,672	456,424	12,626	47,838	53,389	52,398	43,065	—	39,780	36,558	—
1880	559,922	571,194	14,192	53,758	65,521	60,535	54,323	—	52,327	43,893	—
1890	720,819	724,114	16,325	61,139	74,770	71,861	70,081	—	71,069	64,773	—
1900	941,760	941,909	21,921	82,045	98,570	86,789	80,650	—	85,518	87,504	—
1910	1,286,463	1,250,704	28,467	106,432	121,915	114,881	115,644	—	125,183	121,720	—
1920	1,590,075	1,565,825	32,628	138,588	162,527	145,945	125,845	—	130,546	142,720	—
1930	2,030,644	2,010,690	31,189	136,255	192,990	194,051	180,997	—	172,891	165,246	—
1940	2,069,159	2,091,006	24,542	106,287	142,409	171,101	188,229	—	184,602	176,320	—
1950	2,382,744	2,452,585	43,493	191,376	189,523	148,150	150,753	—	169,197	196,172	—
1960	2,971,991	3,094,791	65,078	261,161	296,623	266,974	199,252	—	156,024	174,957	—
1970	3,467,373	3,700,791	58,637	241,893	354,242	361,478	310,254	—	241,859	221,527	—
1980	3,533,012	3,831,811	49,938	187,408	259,606	308,725	341,153	—	301,855	278,848	—
1990	3,735,685	3,994,503	46,935	225,398	252,235	246,555	259,249	—	285,807	334,651	—

TABLE Aa4777–4877   New Jersey population by race, sex, age, nativity, and urban–rural residence: 1790–1990
Continued

	Population										
	Male, by age										
	30–34	35–39	40–49	40–44	45–49	50–59	50–54	55–59	60–69	60–64	65–69
	Aa4799	Aa4800	Aa4801	Aa4802	Aa4803	Aa4804	Aa4805	Aa4806	Aa4807	Aa4808	Aa4809
Year	Number	Number	Number	Number	Number	Number	Number	Number	Number	Number	Number
1790	—	—	—	—	—	—	—	—	—	—	—
1800	—	—	—	—	—	—	—	—	—	—	—
1810	—	—	—	—	—	—	—	—	—	—	—
1820	—	—	—	—	—	—	—	—	—	—	—
1830	—	—	—	—	—	—	—	—	—	—	—
1840	—	—	—	—	—	—	—	—	—	—	—
1850	—	—	21,938	—	—	13,532	—	—	7,688	—	—
1860	—	—	32,541	—	—	19,443	—	—	10,672	—	—
1870	32,170	29,881	—	25,795	21,940	—	18,313	11,693	—	10,092	6,212
1880	39,416	39,217	—	32,995	27,201	—	23,938	16,808	—	14,553	9,374
1890	58,309	49,176	—	42,120	37,621	—	31,622	21,335	—	18,767	12,949
1900	81,535	74,661	—	61,674	46,987	—	40,110	30,128	—	23,941	16,262
1910	111,017	103,694	—	87,944	71,280	—	57,933	38,249	—	30,503	22,287
1920	135,386	131,730	—	106,771	98,197	—	78,546	55,059	—	42,857	26,924
1930	165,719	171,293	—	152,049	128,167	—	105,305	78,848	—	61,304	42,274
1940	167,548	159,442	—	156,875	150,281	—	133,506	101,657	—	78,334	56,640
1950	197,635	192,268	—	177,244	158,551	—	150,837	131,121	—	107,595	78,449
1960	210,829	228,632	—	217,076	200,775	—	173,641	149,927	—	124,069	102,096
1970	194,658	200,311	—	225,932	229,822	—	210,840	182,908	—	147,723	108,674
1980	270,274	230,157	—	193,465	189,797	—	207,573	203,380	—	170,391	133,579
1990	342,273	306,568	—	278,422	226,440	—	182,472	169,654	—	170,069	150,788

	Population										
	Male, by age					Female, by age					
	70–79	70–74	75–79	80 and older	Unknown age	0	1–4	5–9	10–14	15–19	20–29
	Aa4810	Aa4811	Aa4812	Aa4813	Aa4814	Aa4815	Aa4816	Aa4817	Aa4818	Aa4819	Aa4820
Year	Number	Number	Number	Number	Number	Number	Number	Number	Number	Number	Number
1790	—	—	—	—	—	—	—	—	—	—	—
1800	—	—	—	—	—	—	—	—	—	—	—
1810	—	—	—	—	—	—	—	—	—	—	—
1820	—	—	—	—	—	—	—	—	—	—	—
1830	—	—	—	—	—	—	—	—	—	—	—
1840	—	—	—	—	—	—	—	—	—	—	—
1850	3,309	—	—	1,064	94	6,794	27,082	31,662	28,336	26,951	45,254
1860	4,333	—	—	1,122	40	9,899	38,409	40,206	36,003	35,866	63,859
1870	—	4,215	2,149	1,557	1	12,260	46,899	52,397	51,406	45,549	—
1880	—	6,387	3,326	2,158	—	14,000	52,766	65,288	59,889	57,261	—
1890	—	8,795	4,685	3,210	2,212	15,762	60,272	73,542	70,904	74,160	—
1900	—	10,959	6,212	3,800	2,494	21,650	80,830	98,155	87,558	86,096	—
1910	—	14,651	7,877	5,162	1,624	27,731	104,312	120,364	113,814	120,897	—
1920	—	17,546	10,331	6,494	1,435	32,036	135,444	160,431	145,291	129,316	—
1930	—	27,729	14,003	8,868	1,466	30,065	132,159	187,928	190,291	183,399	—
1940	—	37,198	20,567	13,621	—	23,247	102,188	138,313	166,675	186,883	—
1950	—	50,242	32,960	17,178	—	41,400	182,637	182,303	142,394	145,106	—
1960	—	73,669	41,794	29,414	—	62,690	253,268	285,589	257,406	197,111	—
1970	—	79,734	51,943	44,938	—	56,493	232,203	338,406	348,931	301,577	—
1980	—	93,464	59,268	54,131	—	47,421	178,522	248,841	297,116	329,512	—
1990	—	112,627	77,390	68,152	—	45,634	214,670	240,809	234,428	246,139	—

(continued)

TABLE Aa4777–4877   New Jersey population by race, sex, age, nativity, and urban–rural residence: 1790–1990
Continued

	Population										
	Female, by age										
	20–24	25–29	30–39	30–34	35–39	40–49	40–44	45–49	50–59	50–54	55–59
	Aa4821	Aa4822	Aa4823	Aa4824	Aa4825	Aa4826	Aa4827	Aa4828	Aa4829	Aa4830	Aa4831
Year	Number	Number	Number	Number	Number	Number	Number	Number	Number	Number	Number
1790	—	—	—	—	—	—	—	—	—	—	—
1800	—	—	—	—	—	—	—	—	—	—	—
1810	—	—	—	—	—	—	—	—	—	—	—
1820	—	—	—	—	—	—	—	—	—	—	—
1830	—	—	—	—	—	—	—	—	—	—	—
1840	—	—	—	—	—	—	—	—	—	—	—
1850	—	—	30,389	—	—	20,640	—	—	13,759	—	—
1860	—	—	45,879	—	—	29,764	—	—	18,844	—	—
1870	44,287	39,899	—	33,831	30,321	—	25,319	19,715	—	17,064	11,136
1880	56,394	46,614	—	41,027	39,701	—	32,814	27,282	—	23,371	16,190
1890	76,408	66,307	—	56,195	47,587	—	41,631	35,713	—	31,205	21,616
1900	92,710	88,904	—	77,323	69,463	—	56,213	45,128	—	38,805	30,120
1910	125,430	114,452	—	102,065	95,953	—	78,694	65,015	—	54,070	37,490
1920	140,496	143,897	—	128,347	119,522	—	100,351	87,354	—	73,142	53,446
1930	177,511	167,564	—	165,613	166,929	—	139,822	118,221	—	100,129	78,280
1940	192,310	184,971	—	173,428	163,318	—	158,845	147,314	—	126,064	96,965
1950	181,206	213,718	—	211,799	201,649	—	180,516	159,953	—	154,398	132,395
1960	165,030	187,416	—	224,251	243,797	—	229,063	205,946	—	176,890	154,185
1970	267,339	241,637	—	208,817	213,618	—	239,560	248,156	—	228,263	197,769
1980	312,973	295,287	—	293,484	249,592	—	206,609	204,241	—	224,947	226,668
1990	280,787	334,266	—	349,461	316,395	—	295,274	240,041	—	194,056	186,023

	Population										
										White	
	Female, by age										Male, by age
	60–69	60–64	65–69	70–79	70–74	75–79	80 and older	Unknown age	Male	Female	0–4
	Aa4832	Aa4833	Aa4834	Aa4835	Aa4836	Aa4837	Aa4838	Aa4839	Aa4840	Aa4841	Aa4842
Year	Number	Number	Number	Number	Number	Number	Number	Number	Number	Number	Number
1790	—	—	—	—	—	—	—	—	86,667	83,287	—
1800	—	—	—	—	—	—	—	—	99,525	95,600	—
1810	—	—	—	—	—	—	—	—	115,357	111,504	—
1820	—	—	—	—	—	—	—	—	129,619	127,790	—
1830	—	—	—	—	—	—	—	—	152,529	147,737	25,071
1840	—	—	—	—	—	—	—	—	177,055	174,533	28,827
1850	8,186	—	—	3,673	—	—	1,402	81	—	—	—
1860	11,666	—	—	5,018	—	—	1,553	18	—	—	—
1870	—	10,217	6,505	—	4,747	2,636	2,236	0	—	—	—
1880	—	14,600	9,592	—	6,987	4,138	3,280	—	—	—	—
1890	—	19,453	12,936	—	9,524	5,297	4,555	1,047	—	—	—
1900	—	25,285	17,693	—	12,227	7,088	5,376	1,285	—	—	—
1910	—	32,175	23,661	—	16,542	9,698	7,209	1,132	—	—	—
1920	—	43,440	29,211	—	20,603	12,786	9,586	1,126	—	—	—
1930	—	63,372	46,175	—	31,222	17,429	13,343	1,238	—	—	—
1940	—	79,690	62,532	—	43,041	25,726	19,496	—	—	—	—
1950	—	107,951	86,472	—	59,199	44,089	25,400	—	—	—	—
1960	—	138,708	120,361	—	89,480	56,006	47,594	—	—	—	—
1970	—	166,322	137,083	—	114,378	80,524	79,715	—	—	—	—
1980	—	197,269	170,091	—	133,573	98,653	117,012	—	—	—	—
1990	—	193,452	189,444	—	157,333	124,051	152,240	—	—	—	—

TABLE Aa4777–4877   New Jersey population by race, sex, age, nativity, and urban–rural residence: 1790–1990
Continued

	Population										
	White										
	Male, by age										Female, by age
	5–9	10–14	15–19	20–29	30–39	40–49	50–59	60–69	70–79	80 and older	0–4
	Aa4843	Aa4844	Aa4845	Aa4846	Aa4847	Aa4848	Aa4849	Aa4850	Aa4851	Aa4852	Aa4853
Year	Number	Number	Number	Number	Number	Number	Number	Number	Number	Number	Number
1790	—	—	—	—	—	—	—	—	—	—	—
1800	—	—	—	—	—	—	—	—	—	—	—
1810	—	—	—	—	—	—	—	—	—	—	—
1820	—	—	—	—	—	—	—	—	—	—	—
1830	21,204	19,745	17,123	27,001	17,231	11,043	7,053	4,458	2,021	579	23,937
1840	23,809	21,951	19,308	31,052	21,553	13,949	8,526	4,887	2,459	734	27,505
1850	—	—	—	—	—	—	—	—	—	—	—
1860	—	—	—	—	—	—	—	—	—	—	—
1870	—	—	—	—	—	—	—	—	—	—	—
1880	—	—	—	—	—	—	—	—	—	—	—
1890	—	—	—	—	—	—	—	—	—	—	—
1900	—	—	—	—	—	—	—	—	—	—	—
1910	—	—	—	—	—	—	—	—	—	—	—
1920	—	—	—	—	—	—	—	—	—	—	—
1930	—	—	—	—	—	—	—	—	—	—	—
1940	—	—	—	—	—	—	—	—	—	—	—
1950	—	—	—	—	—	—	—	—	—	—	—
1960	—	—	—	—	—	—	—	—	—	—	—
1970	—	—	—	—	—	—	—	—	—	—	—
1980	—	—	—	—	—	—	—	—	—	—	—
1990	—	—	—	—	—	—	—	—	—	—	—

	Population											
	White											
	Female, by age										Male, by age	
	5–9	10–14	15–19	20–29	30–39	40–49	50–59	60–69	70–79	80 and older	0–9	10–15
	Aa4854	Aa4855	Aa4856	Aa4857	Aa4858	Aa4859	Aa4860	Aa4861	Aa4862	Aa4863	Aa4864	Aa4865
Year	Number	Number	Number	Number	Number	Number	Number	Number	Number	Number	Number	Number
1790	—	—	—	—	—	—	—	—	—	—	—	—
1800	—	—	—	—	—	—	—	—	—	—	34,780	15,859
1810	—	—	—	—	—	—	—	—	—	—	37,814	18,914
1820	—	—	—	—	—	—	—	—	—	—	42,055	19,970
1830	20,479	18,267	16,784	25,817	16,623	11,007	7,307	4,705	2,160	651	—	—
1840	23,161	20,362	19,701	31,514	20,530	14,009	8,841	5,253	2,769	888	—	—
1850	—	—	—	—	—	—	—	—	—	—	—	—
1860	—	—	—	—	—	—	—	—	—	—	—	—
1870	—	—	—	—	—	—	—	—	—	—	—	—
1880	—	—	—	—	—	—	—	—	—	—	—	—
1890	—	—	—	—	—	—	—	—	—	—	—	—
1900	—	—	—	—	—	—	—	—	—	—	—	—
1910	—	—	—	—	—	—	—	—	—	—	—	—
1920	—	—	—	—	—	—	—	—	—	—	—	—
1930	—	—	—	—	—	—	—	—	—	—	—	—
1940	—	—	—	—	—	—	—	—	—	—	—	—
1950	—	—	—	—	—	—	—	—	—	—	—	—
1960	—	—	—	—	—	—	—	—	—	—	—	—
1970	—	—	—	—	—	—	—	—	—	—	—	—
1980	—	—	—	—	—	—	—	—	—	—	—	—
1990	—	—	—	—	—	—	—	—	—	—	—	—

(continued)

TABLE Aa4777–4877   New Jersey population by race, sex, age, nativity, and urban–rural residence: 1790–1990
Continued

	Population											
	White											
	Male, by age			Female, by age					Male, by age		Female, by age	
	16–25	26–44	45 and older	0–9	10–15	16–25	26–44	45 and older	0–15	16 and older	0–15	16 and older
	Aa4866	Aa4867	Aa4868	Aa4869	Aa4870	Aa4871	Aa4872	Aa4873	Aa4874	Aa4875	Aa4876	Aa4877
Year	Number	Number	Number	Number	Number	Number	Number	Number	Number	Number	Number	Number
1790	—	—	—	—	—	—	—	—	41,416	45,251	41,335	41,952
1800	16,301	19,956	12,629	32,622	14,827	17,018	19,533	11,600	—	—	—	—
1810	21,231	21,394	16,004	36,065	17,787	21,184	21,359	15,109	—	—	—	—
1820	24,639	24,418	18,537	39,921	19,504	25,637	24,693	18,035	—	—	—	—
1830	—	—	—	—	—	—	—	—	—	—	—	—
1840	—	—	—	—	—	—	—	—	—	—	—	—
1850	—	—	—	—	—	—	—	—	—	—	—	—
1860	—	—	—	—	—	—	—	—	—	—	—	—
1870	—	—	—	—	—	—	—	—	—	—	—	—
1880	—	—	—	—	—	—	—	—	—	—	—	—
1890	—	—	—	—	—	—	—	—	—	—	—	—
1900	—	—	—	—	—	—	—	—	—	—	—	—
1910	—	—	—	—	—	—	—	—	—	—	—	—
1920	—	—	—	—	—	—	—	—	—	—	—	—
1930	—	—	—	—	—	—	—	—	—	—	—	—
1940	—	—	—	—	—	—	—	—	—	—	—	—
1950	—	—	—	—	—	—	—	—	—	—	—	—
1960	—	—	—	—	—	—	—	—	—	—	—	—
1970	—	—	—	—	—	—	—	—	—	—	—	—
1980	—	—	—	—	—	—	—	—	—	—	—	—
1990	—	—	—	—	—	—	—	—	—	—	—	—

Sources

See the sources for Table Aa2244–2340.

Documentation

See the text for Table Aa2244–2340.

New Jersey was one of the original thirteen states, admitted to the Union in 1787.

TABLE Aa4878–4940   New Mexico population by race, sex, age, nativity, and urban–rural residence: 1850–1990

Contributed by Michael R. Haines

						Population						
					Race				Residence		Nativity	
	Area	Population density	Total	White	Nonwhite	Black	Other nonwhite	Urban	Rural	Native-born	Foreign-born
	Aa4878	Aa4879	Aa4880	Aa4881	Aa4882	Aa4883	Aa4884	Aa4885	Aa4886	Aa4887	Aa4888
Year	Square miles	Persons per square mile	Number	Number	Number	Number	Number	Number	Number	Number	Number
1850	236,548	0.26	61,547	61,525	22	22	—	4,539	57,008	59,396	2,151
1860	247,782	0.38	93,516	82,924	10,592	85	10,507	4,635	88,881	86,793	6,723
1870	122,503	0.75	91,874	90,393	1,481	172	1,309	4,765	87,109	86,254	5,620
1880	122,503	0.98	119,565	108,721	10,844	1,015	9,829	6,635	112,930	111,514	8,051
1890 [1]	122,503	1.31	160,282	142,719	10,874	1,956	8,918	9,970	150,312	142,334	11,259
1900	122,503	1.59	195,310	180,207	15,103	1,610	13,493	27,381	167,929	181,685	13,625
1910	122,503	2.67	327,301	304,594	22,707	1,628	21,079	46,571	280,730	304,155	23,146
1920	122,503	2.94	360,350	334,673	25,677	5,733	19,944	64,960	295,390	330,542	29,808
1930	122,503	3.46	423,317	391,095	32,222	2,850	29,372	106,816	316,501	399,265	24,052
1940	121,511	4.38	531,818	492,312	39,506	4,672	34,834	176,401	355,417	516,416	15,402
1950	121,511	5.61	681,187	630,211	50,976	8,408	42,568	341,889	339,298	661,990	17,435
1960	121,445	7.83	951,023	875,763	75,260	17,063	58,197	626,479	324,544	929,615	21,408
1970	121,412	8.37	1,016,000	915,815	100,185	19,555	80,630	708,775	307,225	993,488	22,510
1980	121,335	10.74	1,302,894	977,587	325,307	24,020	301,287	939,963	362,931	1,250,489	52,405
1990	121,365	12.48	1,515,069	1,146,028	369,041	30,210	338,831	1,105,651	409,418	1,434,555	80,514

							Population					
	Sex						Male, by age					
	Male	Female	0	1–4	5–9	10–14	15–19	20–29	20–24	25–29	30–39
	Aa4889	Aa4890	Aa4891	Aa4892	Aa4893	Aa4894	Aa4895	Aa4896	Aa4897	Aa4898	Aa4899
Year	Number	Number	Number	Number	Number	Number	Number	Number	Number	Number	Number
1850	31,742	29,805	639	3,773	4,402	3,678	3,188	6,333	—	—	3,954
1860	49,091	44,425	1,354	5,819	6,836	5,548	4,040	10,363	—	—	7,011
1870	47,135	44,739	1,307	5,300	6,113	5,662	4,631	—	4,511	4,149	—
1880	64,496	55,069	1,831	6,435	7,964	7,075	5,651	—	6,548	6,270	—
1890 [1]	83,055	70,538	2,544	8,872	9,754	8,028	7,324	—	7,922	7,273	—
1900	104,228	91,082	3,094	10,691	13,624	11,164	8,808	—	8,730	8,448	—
1910	175,245	152,056	4,929	17,750	20,738	17,533	16,480	—	16,408	15,197	—
1920	190,456	169,894	4,846	18,436	23,348	20,659	17,276	—	17,173	16,225	—
1930	219,222	204,095	5,687	21,374	27,792	23,290	21,505	—	19,060	16,114	—
1940	271,846	259,972	6,453	25,790	30,692	29,443	26,884	—	23,063	22,040	—
1950	347,544	333,643	9,700	38,637	38,987	33,140	28,630	—	29,246	28,740	—
1960	479,770	471,253	14,515	54,323	61,310	52,445	38,228	—	34,488	33,485	—
1970	500,824	515,176	10,158	38,782	60,547	61,956	52,701	—	40,683	31,753	—
1980	642,157	660,737	13,145	45,392	55,704	58,030	66,969	—	62,568	57,567	—
1990	745,253	769,816	10,839	53,330	66,612	62,064	58,207	—	53,482	63,103	—

Note appears at end of table   (continued)

TABLE Aa4878–4940   New Mexico population by race, sex, age, nativity, and urban–rural residence: 1850–1990
Continued

	Population										
	Male, by age										
	30–34	35–39	40–49	40–44	45–49	50–59	50–54	55–59	60–69	60–64	65–69
	Aa4900	Aa4901	Aa4902	Aa4903	Aa4904	Aa4905	Aa4906	Aa4907	Aa4908	Aa4909	Aa4910
Year	Number	Number	Number	Number	Number	Number	Number	Number	Number	Number	Number
1850	—	—	2,411	—	—	1,627	—	—	1,010	—	—
1860	—	—	3,997	—	—	2,046	—	—	1,296	—	—
1870	3,614	3,241	—	2,589	1,714	—	1,498	774	—	976	330
1880	5,271	4,259	—	3,694	2,857	—	2,312	1,398	—	1,405	546
1890 [1]	6,688	6,293	—	4,797	3,895	—	3,241	2,271	—	1,802	976
1900	7,436	7,450	—	6,252	5,064	—	4,100	2,922	—	2,490	1,616
1910	12,690	12,379	—	9,650	8,530	—	7,168	5,151	—	4,471	2,636
1920	13,467	12,929	—	9,602	10,120	—	7,611	5,807	—	5,247	3,472
1930	14,220	14,923	—	12,347	11,030	—	8,758	7,141	—	5,956	4,292
1940	19,689	17,410	—	15,217	14,292	—	11,840	9,166	—	6,948	5,476
1950	25,335	23,828	—	20,350	17,180	—	14,175	12,228	—	9,881	7,502
1960	32,908	31,985	—	28,011	24,533	—	19,827	16,262	—	12,002	10,042
1970	28,565	28,415	—	28,152	26,495	—	23,172	20,401	—	16,667	12,424
1980	50,658	38,499	—	32,627	30,229	—	29,018	27,812	—	23,390	19,887
1990	64,626	60,113	—	52,641	39,676	—	32,162	29,842	—	28,002	25,744

	Population										
	Male, by age					Female, by age					
	70–79	70–74	75–79	80 and older	Unknown age	0	1–4	5–9	10–14	15–19	20–29
	Aa4911	Aa4912	Aa4913	Aa4914	Aa4915	Aa4916	Aa4917	Aa4918	Aa4919	Aa4920	Aa4921
Year	Number	Number	Number	Number	Number	Number	Number	Number	Number	Number	Number
1850	313	—	—	272	142	594	3,793	4,325	3,349	3,833	6,271
1860	442	—	—	328	11	1,355	5,846	6,655	5,169	4,548	9,446
1870	—	354	141	230	1	1,323	5,392	5,975	5,784	5,329	—
1880	—	468	195	317	—	1,766	6,117	7,486	6,560	5,679	—
1890 [1]	—	617	307	317	134	2,404	8,391	9,087	7,470	7,474	—
1900	—	947	500	453	439	3,065	10,377	13,177	10,685	8,666	—
1910	—	1,678	929	619	309	4,960	17,646	20,288	16,875	15,977	—
1920	—	2,047	1,087	853	251	4,583	18,534	23,008	20,266	17,384	—
1930	—	2,759	1,647	1,221	106	5,428	21,364	27,302	23,056	21,630	—
1940	—	3,693	2,117	1,633	—	6,408	25,350	30,464	28,992	27,417	—
1950	—	4,614	3,498	1,873	—	9,242	37,365	38,011	32,071	28,500	—
1960	—	7,496	4,551	3,359	—	14,212	53,110	59,757	51,017	38,008	—
1970	—	8,662	5,835	5,456	—	9,953	37,766	58,669	60,864	52,463	—
1980	—	14,332	8,753	7,577	—	12,758	43,436	53,911	56,071	65,337	—
1990	—	19,231	13,429	12,150	—	10,597	51,112	64,447	59,568	55,731	—

Note appears at end of table

TABLE Aa4878–4940   New Mexico population by race, sex, age, nativity, and urban–rural residence: 1850–1990
Continued

	Population									
	Female, by age									
	20–24	25–29	30–39	30–34	35–39	40–49	40–44	45–49	50–59	50–54
	Aa4922	Aa4923	Aa4924	Aa4925	Aa4926	Aa4927	Aa4928	Aa4929	Aa4930	Aa4931
Year	Number	Number	Number	Number	Number	Number	Number	Number	Number	Number
1850	—	—	3,296	—	—	1,981	—	—	1,245	—
1860	—	—	5,230	—	—	3,052	—	—	1,640	—
1870	4,433	3,715	—	3,223	2,572	—	2,139	1,454	—	1,252
1880	5,791	4,979	—	3,876	3,168	—	2,818	2,062	—	1,767
1890 [1]	7,152	6,035	—	5,022	4,712	—	3,412	2,789	—	2,217
1900	7,858	7,609	—	6,191	5,799	—	4,696	3,758	—	2,871
1910	14,523	12,726	—	10,303	9,656	—	7,430	6,015	—	5,199
1920	15,426	14,523	—	11,700	10,572	—	8,205	7,325	—	5,698
1930	18,737	16,218	—	13,764	13,594	—	10,543	8,676	—	6,933
1940	23,567	22,266	—	19,072	17,100	—	14,060	12,275	—	9,739
1950	28,380	28,686	—	24,798	23,440	—	19,222	16,102	—	13,133
1960	33,399	33,053	—	32,966	32,103	—	26,862	23,899	—	19,266
1970	42,012	33,404	—	31,004	30,000	—	29,497	28,041	—	24,062
1980	62,860	57,777	—	50,645	39,737	—	34,075	31,582	—	31,214
1990	52,576	62,980	—	66,040	61,850	—	53,113	41,114	—	34,496

	Population								
	Female, by age								
	55–59	60–69	60–64	65–69	70–79	70–74	75–79	80 and older	Unknown age
	Aa4932	Aa4933	Aa4934	Aa4935	Aa4936	Aa4937	Aa4938	Aa4939	Aa4940
Year	Number	Number	Number	Number	Number	Number	Number	Number	Number
1850	—	684	—	—	259	—	—	174	1
1860	—	900	—	—	347	—	—	233	4
1870	636	—	683	230	—	270	117	210	2
1880	867	—	1,017	426	—	342	111	237	—
1890 [1]	1,422	—	1,314	704	—	405	192	252	84
1900	1,983	—	1,726	1,031	—	634	295	370	291
1910	3,165	—	2,834	1,678	—	1,054	584	508	185
1920	4,234	—	3,447	2,139	—	1,289	685	672	204
1930	5,552	—	4,294	2,982	—	1,905	1,103	916	98
1940	7,306	—	5,591	4,565	—	2,805	1,610	1,385	—
1950	10,830	—	8,286	6,536	—	4,071	3,127	1,843	—
1960	15,861	—	11,918	10,169	—	7,241	4,549	3,863	—
1970	21,327	—	17,880	13,864	—	10,038	7,091	7,241	—
1980	30,612	—	25,365	23,188	—	17,325	12,168	12,676	—
1990	32,196	—	31,488	29,734	—	22,898	18,294	21,582	—

[1] Includes 6,689 American Indians not counted in the general enumeration; see text for Table Aa2244–2340.

Sources
See the sources for Table Aa2244–2340.

Documentation
See the text for Table Aa2244–2340.

New Mexico was part of the Mexican Cession of 1848. It was created a territory in 1850 and became a state in 1912. Some area was added with the Gadsden Purchase of 1853. Parts of the original territory were taken for Colorado, Arizona, and Nevada.

TABLE Aa4941–5041 New York population by race, sex, age, nativity, and urban–rural residence: 1790–1990

Contributed by Michael R. Haines

	Area	Population density	Population Total	Race White	Race Nonwhite	Race Black	Race Other nonwhite	Residence Urban	Residence Rural	Nativity Native-born	Nativity Foreign-born
	Aa4941	Aa4942	Aa4943	Aa4944	Aa4945	Aa4946	Aa4947	Aa4948	Aa4949	Aa4950	Aa4951
Year	Square miles	Persons per square mile	Number	Number	Number	Number	Number	Number	Number	Number	Number
1790	47,652	7.14	340,241	314,366	25,875	25,875	—	39,213	300,907	—	—
1800	47,652	12.36	589,051	556,039	30,717	30,717	—	74,757	514,294	—	—
1810	47,652	20.13	959,049	918,699	40,350	40,350	—	121,488	837,561	—	—
1820	47,652	28.81	1,372,812	1,332,724	40,088	39,367	701	160,996	1,211,816	—	—
1830	47,652	40.26	1,918,608	1,868,061	50,547	44,945	—	286,618	1,631,990	—	—
1840	47,652	50.97	2,428,921	2,378,890	50,031	50,031	—	471,266	1,957,655	—	—
1850	47,652	65.00	3,097,394	3,048,325	49,069	49,069	—	904,194	2,193,200	2,441,465	655,929
1860	47,654	81.44	3,880,735	3,831,590	49,145	49,005	140	1,524,344	2,356,391	2,879,455	1,001,280
1870	47,654	91.97	4,382,759	4,330,210	52,549	52,081	468	2,189,455	2,193,304	3,244,406	1,138,353
1880	47,654	106.66	5,082,871	5,016,022	66,849	65,104	1,745	2,868,529	2,214,342	3,871,492	1,211,379
1890 [1]	47,654	125.97	6,003,174	5,923,952	73,901	70,092	3,809	3,910,278	2,092,896	4,426,803	1,571,050
1900	47,654	152.53	7,268,894	7,156,881	112,013	99,232	12,781	5,298,111	1,970,783	5,368,469	1,900,425
1910	47,654	191.25	9,113,614	8,966,845	146,769	134,191	12,578	7,188,131	1,925,483	6,365,603	2,748,011
1920	47,654	217.93	10,385,227	10,172,027	213,200	198,483	14,717	8,588,586	1,796,641	7,559,852	2,825,375
1930	47,654	264.16	12,588,066	12,153,191	434,875	412,814	22,061	10,521,952	2,066,114	9,325,788	3,262,278
1940	47,929	281.23	13,479,142	12,879,546	599,596	571,221	28,375	11,165,893	2,313,249	10,562,497	2,916,645
1950	47,944	309.32	14,830,192	13,872,095	958,097	918,191	39,906	12,682,446	2,147,746	12,211,855	2,577,105
1960	47,869	350.59	16,782,304	15,287,071	1,495,233	1,417,511	77,722	14,331,925	2,450,379	14,494,290	2,289,314
1970	47,831	381.28	18,236,967	15,834,090	2,402,877	2,168,949	233,928	15,626,969	2,609,998	16,127,106	2,109,776
1980	47,377	370.60	17,558,072	13,960,868	3,597,204	2,402,006	1,195,198	14,858,068	2,700,004	15,169,134	2,388,938
1990	47,224	380.96	17,990,455	13,385,255	4,605,200	2,859,055	1,746,145	15,164,047	2,826,408	15,138,594	2,851,861

	Sex Male	Sex Female	Male, by age 0	1–4	5–9	10–14	15–19	20–29	20–24	25–29	30–39
	Aa4952	Aa4953	Aa4954	Aa4955	Aa4956	Aa4957	Aa4958	Aa4959	Aa4960	Aa4961	Aa4962
Year	Number	Number	Number	Number	Number	Number	Number	Number	Number	Number	Number
1790	—	—	—	—	—	—	—	—	—	—	—
1800	—	—	—	—	—	—	—	—	—	—	—
1810	—	—	—	—	—	—	—	—	—	—	—
1820	698,077	674,014	—	—	—	—	—	—	—	—	—
1830	972,920	940,086	—	—	—	—	—	—	—	—	—
1840	1,231,166	1,197,755	—	—	—	—	—	—	—	—	—
1850	1,567,941	1,529,453	38,672	164,872	190,500	172,560	159,196	313,372	—	—	220,261
1860	1,933,532	1,947,203	52,175	216,112	232,426	203,453	188,893	341,037	—	—	283,390
1870	2,163,229	2,219,530	52,457	210,284	241,984	243,363	208,951	—	191,688	173,983	—
1880	2,505,322	2,577,549	58,708	223,907	272,648	257,119	236,125	—	241,777	208,922	—
1890 [1]	2,976,893	3,020,960	63,298	239,844	288,129	279,909	282,105	—	293,672	278,470	—
1900	3,614,780	3,654,114	80,473	298,651	357,834	322,541	307,220	—	331,260	342,170	—
1910	4,584,597	4,529,017	97,245	356,618	403,516	393,939	408,962	—	460,053	450,570	—
1920	5,187,350	5,197,877	98,133	412,896	489,503	453,990	399,406	—	434,070	476,806	—
1930	6,312,520	6,275,546	94,573	408,220	549,866	545,253	530,085	—	551,650	553,736	—
1940	6,690,326	6,788,816	80,658	346,364	456,062	529,936	562,962	—	552,262	556,445	—
1950	7,239,944	7,590,248	131,400	565,177	558,105	455,858	443,027	—	511,308	573,974	—
1960	8,123,239	8,659,065	175,661	683,895	778,699	713,950	533,095	—	433,006	494,568	—
1970	8,715,339	9,521,628	152,398	605,950	857,010	872,857	779,471	—	633,202	584,775	—
1980	8,339,422	9,218,650	122,502	457,887	605,546	717,004	803,639	—	737,556	690,997	—
1990	8,625,673	9,364,782	110,680	532,068	603,086	582,620	626,761	—	705,729	774,559	—

Note appears at end of table

TABLE Aa4941–5041   New York population by race, sex, age, nativity, and urban–rural residence: 1790–1990
Continued

	Population										
	Male, by age										
	30–34	35–39	40–49	40–44	45–49	50–59	50–54	55–59	60–69	60–64	65–69
	Aa4963	Aa4964	Aa4965	Aa4966	Aa4967	Aa4968	Aa4969	Aa4970	Aa4971	Aa4972	Aa4973
Year	Number	Number	Number	Number	Number	Number	Number	Number	Number	Number	Number
1790	—	—	—	—	—	—	—	—	—	—	—
1800	—	—	—	—	—	—	—	—	—	—	—
1810	—	—	—	—	—	—	—	—	—	—	—
1820	—	—	—	—	—	—	—	—	—	—	—
1830	—	—	—	—	—	—	—	—	—	—	—
1840	—	—	—	—	—	—	—	—	—	—	—
1850	—	—	147,115	—	—	86,872	—	—	46,629	—	—
1860	—	—	195,713	—	—	117,829	—	—	67,457	—	—
1870	160,416	141,442	—	133,332	110,248	—	95,913	58,901	—	55,652	34,034
1880	182,720	171,034	—	148,391	124,442	—	112,714	81,491	—	72,105	46,760
1890 [1]	252,191	209,539	—	177,834	151,422	—	129,929	93,433	—	84,580	59,813
1900	315,586	288,203	—	240,758	186,599	—	157,474	118,115	—	95,717	67,957
1910	397,058	365,522	—	310,660	258,842	—	214,734	148,218	—	115,216	84,313
1920	452,985	433,860	—	356,411	320,442	—	270,271	195,523	—	156,361	101,780
1930	542,376	547,863	—	482,364	402,981	—	334,174	252,426	—	199,059	141,644
1940	560,230	553,202	—	537,892	498,388	—	439,121	333,401	—	258,341	188,113
1950	555,567	564,074	—	552,093	512,190	—	487,644	414,765	—	341,764	251,660
1960	561,884	581,053	—	545,530	533,008	—	500,933	453,826	—	383,798	310,591
1970	500,086	494,770	—	538,181	539,001	—	496,228	457,032	—	398,188	305,042
1980	649,344	526,286	—	446,856	433,243	—	469,110	456,018	—	382,502	312,502
1990	775,543	698,556	—	625,529	496,475	—	413,813	382,319	—	379,510	331,502

	Population										
	Male, by age					Female, by age					
	70–79	70–74	75–79	80 and older	Unknown age	0	1–4	5–9	10–14	15–19	20–29
	Aa4974	Aa4975	Aa4976	Aa4977	Aa4978	Aa4979	Aa4980	Aa4981	Aa4982	Aa4983	Aa4984
Year	Number	Number	Number	Number	Number	Number	Number	Number	Number	Number	Number
1790	—	—	—	—	—	—	—	—	—	—	—
1800	—	—	—	—	—	—	—	—	—	—	—
1810	—	—	—	—	—	—	—	—	—	—	—
1820	—	—	—	—	—	—	—	—	—	—	—
1830	—	—	—	—	—	—	—	—	—	—	—
1840	20,215	—	—	—	—	—	—	—	—	—	—
1850	27,246	—	—	6,496	1,181	37,665	162,221	187,105	170,091	174,133	313,672
1860	—	—	—	7,758	43	51,257	210,591	227,413	197,884	205,604	386,141
1870	—	25,632	13,059	10,050	1,840	51,421	206,366	241,288	240,310	224,913	—
1880	—	33,291	19,109	14,059	—	57,139	219,266	269,775	253,489	257,813	—
1890 [1]	—	43,399	23,773	18,079	7,474	61,679	236,010	286,501	275,269	300,865	—
1900	—	48,554	29,016	19,515	7,137	79,048	295,318	355,888	321,247	333,462	—
1910	—	56,428	32,129	22,827	7,747	94,308	350,756	400,352	391,887	433,487	—
1920	—	64,620	38,443	24,797	7,053	95,730	403,531	482,648	448,428	418,293	—
1930	—	92,933	48,028	30,003	5,286	91,161	395,340	534,973	532,933	541,228	—
1940	—	123,725	68,670	44,554	—	76,955	331,807	439,040	516,474	561,374	—
1950	—	161,749	107,083	52,506	—	126,934	541,210	536,920	436,326	461,007	—
1960	—	222,071	128,211	89,460	—	170,076	661,368	752,455	690,967	560,467	—
1970	—	225,996	147,845	127,307	—	146,156	582,239	822,025	838,787	783,708	—
1980	—	229,349	153,100	145,981	—	118,052	437,484	579,333	689,056	794,932	—
1990	—	244,199	174,121	168,603	—	105,395	507,621	574,920	557,557	603,366	—

Note appears at end of table

(continued)

TABLE Aa4941–5041   New York population by race, sex, age, nativity, and urban–rural residence: 1790–1990
Continued

	Population										
	Female, by age										
	20–24	25–29	30–39	30–34	35–39	40–49	40–44	45–49	50–59	50–54	55–59
	Aa4985	Aa4986	Aa4987	Aa4988	Aa4989	Aa4990	Aa4991	Aa4992	Aa4993	Aa4994	Aa4995
Year	Number	Number	Number	Number	Number	Number	Number	Number	Number	Number	Number
1790	—	—	—	—	—	—	—	—	—	—	—
1800	—	—	—	—	—	—	—	—	—	—	—
1810	—	—	—	—	—	—	—	—	—	—	—
1820	—	—	—	—	—	—	—	—	—	—	—
1830	—	—	—	—	—	—	—	—	—	—	—
1840	—	—	—	—	—	—	—	—	—	—	—
1850	—	—	201,244	—	—	131,196	—	—	80,387	—	—
1860	—	—	278,104	—	—	177,967	—	—	110,334	—	—
1870	223,315	192,905	—	172,932	148,390	—	133,902	100,281	—	88,657	55,500
1880	268,695	220,798	—	189,360	175,258	—	152,124	127,416	—	114,691	80,374
1890 [1]	327,002	287,285	—	239,806	200,775	—	175,612	150,634	—	134,470	98,265
1900	371,472	352,899	—	301,738	272,490	—	222,115	181,022	—	156,172	121,670
1910	478,888	429,273	—	371,246	346,687	—	289,306	244,836	—	203,579	145,942
1920	491,029	494,542	—	438,688	405,918	—	342,983	297,016	—	260,444	192,707
1930	587,379	569,143	—	538,753	524,522	—	442,594	377,680	—	321,023	251,838
1940	594,459	616,934	—	593,492	561,084	—	530,311	476,854	—	408,192	319,838
1950	573,504	632,949	—	617,700	625,838	—	579,851	521,730	—	494,247	413,652
1960	501,354	529,485	—	601,747	632,113	—	601,567	583,614	—	533,041	478,896
1970	749,174	641,434	—	538,278	532,769	—	586,772	597,132	—	562,028	522,590
1980	782,390	737,379	—	702,495	580,621	—	489,456	478,268	—	527,492	523,352
1990	703,170	790,058	—	798,028	727,905	—	672,695	545,842	—	457,790	429,538

	Population								White	
	Female, by age									
	60–69	60–64	65–69	70–79	70–74	75–79	80 and older	Unknown age	Male	Female
	Aa4996	Aa4997	Aa4998	Aa4999	Aa5000	Aa5001	Aa5002	Aa5003	Aa5004	Aa5005
Year	Number	Number	Number	Number	Number	Number	Number	Number	Number	Number
1790	—	—	—	—	—	—	—	—	162,073	152,293
1800	—	—	—	—	—	—	—	—	297,452	258,587
1810	—	—	—	—	—	—	—	—	474,281	444,418
1820	—	—	—	—	—	—	—	—	679,531	653,193
1830	—	—	—	—	—	—	—	—	951,441	916,620
1840	—	—	—	—	—	—	—	—	1,207,357	1,171,533
1850	44,740	—	—	19,619	—	—	6,848	532	—	—
1860	65,802	—	—	27,586	—	—	8,485	35	—	—
1870	—	54,023	33,724	—	25,977	13,481	11,486	659	—	—
1880	—	71,666	46,780	—	34,754	20,737	17,414	—	—	—
1890 [1]	—	88,613	61,709	—	44,524	25,007	21,741	5,193	—	—
1900	—	102,842	74,782	—	52,459	31,877	23,745	3,868	—	—
1910	—	122,673	90,734	—	63,493	38,712	29,519	3,339	—	—
1920	—	157,551	107,255	—	74,157	46,205	35,840	4,912	—	—
1930	—	206,982	151,803	—	102,735	57,134	43,045	5,280	—	—
1940	—	264,708	207,659	—	143,218	84,192	62,225	—	—	—
1950	—	342,921	278,443	—	190,690	138,384	77,942	—	—	—
1960	—	424,658	361,209	—	268,284	166,034	141,730	—	—	—
1970	—	463,974	391,864	—	321,531	221,956	219,211	—	—	—
1980	—	458,505	412,020	—	338,557	260,457	308,801	—	—	—
1990	—	445,600	423,840	—	348,738	287,759	384,960	—	—	—

Note appears at end of table

TABLE Aa4941–5041   New York population by race, sex, age, nativity, and urban–rural residence: 1790–1990 *Continued*

	Population								
	White								
	Male, by age								
	0–4	5–9	10–14	15–19	20–29	30–39	40–49	50–59	60–69
	Aa5006	Aa5007	Aa5008	Aa5009	Aa5010	Aa5011	Aa5012	Aa5013	Aa5014
Year	Number	Number	Number	Number	Number	Number	Number	Number	Number
1790	—	—	—	—	—	—	—	—	—
1800	—	—	—	—	—	—	—	—	—
1810	—	—	—	—	—	—	—	—	—
1820	—	—	—	—	—	—	—	—	—
1830	158,077	137,071	118,523	101,712	176,754	113,136	68,871	40,503	23,909
1840	187,730	158,107	139,752	130,094	230,981	158,194	97,542	54,975	30,869
1850	—	—	—	—	—	—	—	—	—
1860	—	—	—	—	—	—	—	—	—
1870	—	—	—	—	—	—	—	—	—
1880	—	—	—	—	—	—	—	—	—
1890 [1]	—	—	—	—	—	—	—	—	—
1900	—	—	—	—	—	—	—	—	—
1910	—	—	—	—	—	—	—	—	—
1920	—	—	—	—	—	—	—	—	—
1930	—	—	—	—	—	—	—	—	—
1940	—	—	—	—	—	—	—	—	—
1950	—	—	—	—	—	—	—	—	—
1960	—	—	—	—	—	—	—	—	—
1970	—	—	—	—	—	—	—	—	—
1980	—	—	—	—	—	—	—	—	—
1990	—	—	—	—	—	—	—	—	—

	Population								
	White								
	Male, by age		Female, by age						
	70–79	80 and older	0–4	5–9	10–14	15–19	20–29	30–39	40–49
	Aa5015	Aa5016	Aa5017	Aa5018	Aa5019	Aa5020	Aa5021	Aa5022	Aa5023
Year	Number	Number	Number	Number	Number	Number	Number	Number	Number
1790	—	—	—	—	—	—	—	—	—
1800	—	—	—	—	—	—	—	—	—
1810	—	—	—	—	—	—	—	—	—
1820	—	—	—	—	—	—	—	—	—
1830	10,034	2,851	151,868	133,084	115,166	105,196	168,897	104,522	64,315
1840	14,694	4,419	180,769	154,525	134,977	137,414	227,137	143,882	90,163
1850	—	—	—	—	—	—	—	—	—
1860	—	—	—	—	—	—	—	—	—
1870	—	—	—	—	—	—	—	—	—
1880	—	—	—	—	—	—	—	—	—
1890 [1]	—	—	—	—	—	—	—	—	—
1900	—	—	—	—	—	—	—	—	—
1910	—	—	—	—	—	—	—	—	—
1920	—	—	—	—	—	—	—	—	—
1930	—	—	—	—	—	—	—	—	—
1940	—	—	—	—	—	—	—	—	—
1950	—	—	—	—	—	—	—	—	—
1960	—	—	—	—	—	—	—	—	—
1970	—	—	—	—	—	—	—	—	—
1980	—	—	—	—	—	—	—	—	—
1990	—	—	—	—	—	—	—	—	—

Note appears at end of table

(continued)

TABLE Aa4941–5041   New York population by race, sex, age, nativity, and urban–rural residence: 1790–1990
Continued

					Population				
					White				
	Female, by age				Male, by age				
	50–59	60–69	70–79	80 and older	0–9	10–15	16–25	26–44	45 and older
	Aa5024	Aa5025	Aa5026	Aa5027	Aa5028	Aa5029	Aa5030	Aa5031	Aa5032
Year	Number	Number	Number	Number	Number	Number	Number	Number	Number
1790	—	—	—	—	—	—	—	—	—
1800	—	—	—	—	100,367	54,273	49,275	61,594	31,943
1810	—	—	—	—	165,933	73,702	85,779	94,882	53,985
1820	—	—	—	—	222,608	104,297	132,733	138,634	81,259
1830	38,344	22,589	9,645	2,994	—	—	—	—	—
1840	53,496	30,190	14,281	4,699	—	—	—	—	—
1850	—	—	—	—	—	—	—	—	—
1860	—	—	—	—	—	—	—	—	—
1870	—	—	—	—	—	—	—	—	—
1880	—	—	—	—	—	—	—	—	—
1890 [1]	—	—	—	—	—	—	—	—	—
1900	—	—	—	—	—	—	—	—	—
1910	—	—	—	—	—	—	—	—	—
1920	—	—	—	—	—	—	—	—	—
1930	—	—	—	—	—	—	—	—	—
1940	—	—	—	—	—	—	—	—	—
1950	—	—	—	—	—	—	—	—	—
1960	—	—	—	—	—	—	—	—	—
1970	—	—	—	—	—	—	—	—	—
1980	—	—	—	—	—	—	—	—	—
1990	—	—	—	—	—	—	—	—	—

					Population				
					White				
	Female, by age					Male, by age		Female, by age	
	0–9	10–15	16–25	26–44	45 and older	0–15	16 and older	0–15	16 and older
	Aa5033	Aa5034	Aa5035	Aa5036	Aa5037	Aa5038	Aa5039	Aa5040	Aa5041
Year	Number	Number	Number	Number	Number	Number	Number	Number	Number
1790	—	—	—	—	—	78,258	83,815	76,832	75,461
1800	85,473	39,876	48,176	56,411	28,651	—	—	—	—
1810	157,945	68,811	85,139	85,805	46,718	—	—	—	—
1820	216,513	101,904	132,492	129,899	72,385	—	—	—	—
1830	—	—	—	—	—	—	—	—	—
1840	—	—	—	—	—	—	—	—	—
1850	—	—	—	—	—	—	—	—	—
1860	—	—	—	—	—	—	—	—	—
1870	—	—	—	—	—	—	—	—	—
1880	—	—	—	—	—	—	—	—	—
1890 [1]	—	—	—	—	—	—	—	—	—
1900	—	—	—	—	—	—	—	—	—
1910	—	—	—	—	—	—	—	—	—
1920	—	—	—	—	—	—	—	—	—
1930	—	—	—	—	—	—	—	—	—
1940	—	—	—	—	—	—	—	—	—
1950	—	—	—	—	—	—	—	—	—
1960	—	—	—	—	—	—	—	—	—
1970	—	—	—	—	—	—	—	—	—
1980	—	—	—	—	—	—	—	—	—
1990	—	—	—	—	—	—	—	—	—

[1] Includes 5,321 American Indians not counted in the general enumeration; see text
for Table Aa2244–2340.

Sources

See the source for Table Aa2244–2340.

Documentation

See the text for Table Aa2244–2340.

New York was one of the original thirteen states, admitted to the Union
in 1788.

TABLE Aa5042–5142   North Carolina population by race, sex, age, nativity, and urban–rural residence: 1790–1990

Contributed by Michael R. Haines

				Population								
					Race				Residence		Nativity	
	Area	Population density	Total	White	Nonwhite	Black	Other nonwhite	Urban	Rural	Native-born	Foreign-born
	Aa5042	Aa5043	Aa5044	Aa5045	Aa5046	Aa5047	Aa5048	Aa5049	Aa5050	Aa5051	Aa5052
Year	Square miles	Persons per square mile	Number	Number	Number	Number	Number	Number	Number	Number	Number
1790	48,740	8.10	395,005	289,181	105,824	105,824	—	0	393,751	—	—
1800	48,740	9.81	478,103	337,764	140,339	140,339	—	0	478,103	—	—
1810	48,740	11.40	555,500	376,410	179,090	179,090	—	0	555,500	—	—
1820	48,740	13.11	638,829	419,200	219,629	219,629	0	12,502	626,327	—	—
1830	48,740	15.14	737,987	472,843	265,144	265,144	—	10,455	727,532	—	—
1840	48,740	15.46	753,419	484,870	268,549	268,549	—	13,310	740,109	—	—
1850	48,740	17.83	869,039	553,028	316,011	316,011	—	21,109	847,930	866,458	2,581
1860	48,740	20.37	992,622	629,942	362,680	361,522	1,158	24,554	968,068	989,324	3,298
1870	48,740	21.98	1,071,361	678,470	392,891	391,650	1,241	36,218	1,035,143	1,068,332	3,029
1880	48,740	28.72	1,399,750	867,242	532,508	531,277	1,231	55,116	1,344,634	1,396,008	3,742
1890 [1]	48,740	33.20	1,617,949	1,055,382	562,565	561,018	1,547	115,759	1,502,190	1,614,245	3,702
1900	48,740	38.86	1,893,810	1,263,603	630,207	624,469	5,738	186,790	1,707,020	1,889,318	4,492
1910	48,740	45.27	2,206,287	1,500,511	705,776	697,843	7,933	318,474	1,887,813	2,200,195	6,092
1920	48,740	52.51	2,559,123	1,783,779	775,344	763,407	11,937	490,370	2,068,753	2,551,851	7,272
1930	48,740	65.04	3,170,276	2,234,958	935,318	918,647	16,671	809,847	2,360,429	3,161,307	8,969
1940	49,142	72.68	3,571,623	2,567,635	1,003,988	981,298	22,690	974,175	2,597,448	3,562,411	9,212
1950	49,097	82.73	4,061,929	2,983,121	1,078,808	1,047,353	31,455	1,368,101	2,693,828	4,037,545	15,250
1960	48,880	93.21	4,556,155	3,399,285	1,156,870	1,116,021	40,849	1,801,921	2,754,234	4,534,177	21,978
1970	48,798	104.14	5,082,059	3,901,767	1,180,292	1,126,478	53,814	2,310,381	2,771,678	5,053,416	28,620
1980	48,843	120.42	5,881,766	4,457,507	1,424,259	1,318,857	105,402	2,822,852	3,058,914	5,803,408	78,358
1990	48,718	136.06	6,628,637	5,008,491	1,620,146	1,456,323	163,823	3,337,778	3,290,859	6,513,560	115,077

				Population								
	Sex						Male, by age					
	Male	Female	0	1–4	5–9	10–14	15–19	20–29	20–24	25–29	30–39
	Aa5053	Aa5054	Aa5055	Aa5056	Aa5057	Aa5058	Aa5059	Aa5060	Aa5061	Aa5062	Aa5063
Year	Number	Number	Number	Number	Number	Number	Number	Number	Number	Number	Number
1790	—	—	—	—	—	—	—	—	—	—	—
1800	—	—	—	—	—	—	—	—	—	—	—
1810	—	—	—	—	—	—	—	—	—	—	—
1820	323,590	315,239	—	—	—	—	—	—	—	—	—
1830	369,828	368,159	—	—	—	—	—	—	—	—	—
1840	374,820	378,599	—	—	—	—	—	—	—	—	—
1850	430,904	438,135	12,605	59,424	66,331	60,195	47,408	72,182	—	—	44,277
1860	495,616	497,006	14,535	65,247	73,702	69,871	54,209	83,051	—	—	53,275
1870	518,704	552,657	15,565	67,562	70,049	75,235	60,983	—	51,138	31,659	—
1880	687,908	711,842	23,919	93,894	104,827	86,532	69,144	—	68,028	51,287	—
1890 [1]	799,149	818,798	23,626	95,357	120,402	112,621	90,660	—	67,511	49,459	—
1900	938,677	955,133	30,313	113,175	133,458	119,436	105,565	—	87,901	65,226	—
1910	1,098,476	1,107,811	36,700	131,621	148,721	134,675	120,248	—	98,796	79,490	—
1920	1,279,062	1,280,061	36,512	145,170	179,497	161,252	131,828	—	109,480	89,245	—
1930	1,575,208	1,595,068	38,046	160,136	215,216	193,502	178,610	—	144,482	112,995	—
1940	1,772,990	1,798,633	35,629	154,195	193,654	202,911	201,254	—	172,910	153,139	—
1950	2,017,105	2,044,824	47,801	206,899	217,374	193,245	185,120	—	176,714	168,709	—
1960	2,247,069	2,309,086	53,964	212,674	257,546	247,186	210,617	—	160,721	142,676	—
1970	2,488,367	2,593,692	46,092	176,859	252,169	264,883	269,350	—	237,440	171,973	—
1980	2,855,385	3,026,381	43,216	163,067	229,002	246,258	291,140	—	298,630	249,262	—
1990	3,214,290	3,414,347	40,794	192,782	224,834	223,067	255,200	—	288,510	288,376	—

Note appears at end of table

(continued)

TABLE Aa5042–5142   North Carolina population by race, sex, age, nativity, and urban–rural residence: 1790–1990
Continued

Population

	Male, by age										
	30–34	35–39	40–49	40–44	45–49	50–59	50–54	55–59	60–69	60–64	65–69
	Aa5064	Aa5065	Aa5066	Aa5067	Aa5068	Aa5069	Aa5070	Aa5071	Aa5072	Aa5073	Aa5074
Year	Number	Number	Number	Number	Number	Number	Number	Number	Number	Number	Number
1790	—	—	—	—	—	—	—	—	—	—	—
1800	—	—	—	—	—	—	—	—	—	—	—
1810	—	—	—	—	—	—	—	—	—	—	—
1820	—	—	—	—	—	—	—	—	—	—	—
1830	—	—	—	—	—	—	—	—	—	—	—
1840	—	—	—	—	—	—	—	—	—	—	—
1850	—	—	29,552	—	—	20,536	—	—	11,143	—	—
1860	—	—	35,628	—	—	24,135	—	—	13,829	—	—
1870	25,027	23,962	—	19,193	17,562	—	21,368	12,132	—	10,790	6,813
1880	39,557	30,333	—	21,664	21,744	—	24,780	16,017	—	13,422	9,790
1890 [1]	46,664	43,651	—	31,930	27,074	—	26,055	19,069	—	15,234	11,293
1900	49,750	43,774	—	39,648	38,121	—	37,345	23,564	—	17,327	13,083
1910	65,177	59,636	—	43,133	39,136	—	44,045	33,376	—	24,866	16,261
1920	72,999	75,371	—	59,376	56,235	—	46,006	33,644	—	30,535	23,060
1930	95,156	91,831	—	75,219	68,391	—	63,238	45,697	—	33,448	23,612
1940	128,302	110,993	—	92,986	80,567	—	70,391	56,141	—	43,519	36,617
1950	148,455	141,945	—	120,206	99,133	—	84,804	67,850	—	53,546	45,975
1960	148,440	151,057	—	137,926	126,885	—	105,902	87,090	—	65,793	55,919
1970	144,593	138,724	—	144,958	142,485	—	127,351	111,292	—	90,206	67,537
1980	226,948	180,562	—	152,028	141,985	—	143,788	137,794	—	115,455	95,855
1990	282,072	258,741	—	235,204	186,750	—	152,039	138,660	—	133,553	120,981

Population

	Male, by age					Female, by age					
	70–79	70–74	75–79	80 and older	Unknown age	0	1–4	5–9	10–14	15–19	20–29
	Aa5075	Aa5076	Aa5077	Aa5078	Aa5079	Aa5080	Aa5081	Aa5082	Aa5083	Aa5084	Aa5085
Year	Number	Number	Number	Number	Number	Number	Number	Number	Number	Number	Number
1790	—	—	—	—	—	—	—	—	—	—	—
1800	—	—	—	—	—	—	—	—	—	—	—
1810	—	—	—	—	—	—	—	—	—	—	—
1820	—	—	—	—	—	—	—	—	—	—	—
1830	—	—	—	—	—	—	—	—	—	—	—
1840	—	—	—	—	—	—	—	—	—	—	—
1850	5,079	—	—	2,093	79	12,129	57,960	65,010	57,397	49,097	75,747
1860	5,637	—	—	2,149	348	14,097	64,314	71,319	65,495	54,991	86,206
1870	—	4,959	2,289	2,418	0	15,205	64,939	68,412	71,780	61,901	—
1880	—	6,367	3,612	2,991	—	23,974	91,330	101,855	81,758	69,523	—
1890 [1]	—	7,966	4,708	3,846	2,023	22,731	91,300	117,085	108,884	92,656	—
1900	—	9,004	5,282	4,142	2,563	29,912	110,312	129,906	115,889	108,332	—
1910	—	10,095	5,955	4,527	2,018	35,905	128,566	146,179	131,289	122,430	—
1920	—	14,728	7,313	4,985	1,826	35,546	141,580	176,145	157,605	136,370	—
1930	—	17,737	10,115	6,695	1,082	36,731	156,237	211,896	188,796	182,030	—
1940	—	20,654	10,684	8,444	—	34,815	151,359	190,187	198,458	203,596	—
1950	—	30,008	20,240	9,081	—	46,195	200,737	211,225	188,247	180,598	—
1960	—	39,688	24,707	18,278	—	52,660	207,168	250,513	239,396	197,516	—
1970	—	46,561	29,816	26,078	—	44,325	169,869	242,630	255,836	250,164	—
1980	—	66,274	40,271	33,850	—	41,544	156,249	218,686	235,970	275,182	—
1990	—	86,147	57,509	49,071	—	39,206	186,173	214,787	213,773	242,630	—

Note appears at end of table

TABLE Aa5042–5142   North Carolina population by race, sex, age, nativity, and urban–rural residence: 1790–1990
Continued

	Population										
	Female, by age										
	20–24	25–29	30–39	30–34	35–39	40–49	40–44	45–49	50–59	50–54	55–59
	Aa5086	Aa5087	Aa5088	Aa5089	Aa5090	Aa5091	Aa5092	Aa5093	Aa5094	Aa5095	Aa5096
Year	Number	Number	Number	Number	Number	Number	Number	Number	Number	Number	Number
1790	—	—	—	—	—	—	—	—	—	—	—
1800	—	—	—	—	—	—	—	—	—	—	—
1810	—	—	—	—	—	—	—	—	—	—	—
1820	—	—	—	—	—	—	—	—	—	—	—
1830	—	—	—	—	—	—	—	—	—	—	—
1840	—	—	—	—	—	—	—	—	—	—	—
1850	—	—	47,254	—	—	31,556	—	—	21,313	—	—
1860	—	—	55,058	—	—	37,054	—	—	24,395	—	—
1870	59,420	42,377	—	34,097	30,253	—	25,098	20,446	—	18,678	11,034
1880	73,117	54,259	—	42,844	38,275	—	31,735	26,446	—	23,614	14,729
1890 [1]	74,688	55,597	—	48,680	44,538	—	36,970	31,946	—	27,194	18,453
1900	98,050	70,284	—	52,579	47,135	—	43,216	36,808	—	32,856	23,183
1910	110,779	88,171	—	68,301	60,722	—	45,419	39,828	—	37,304	27,086
1920	122,541	98,733	—	78,276	75,901	—	62,631	50,089	—	39,111	28,746
1930	160,365	126,926	—	102,015	96,657	—	78,012	69,590	—	57,127	39,842
1940	182,824	160,115	—	133,659	117,359	—	96,068	82,413	—	69,721	54,703
1950	179,612	173,406	—	153,314	147,350	—	124,794	104,377	—	88,295	70,086
1960	156,891	150,221	—	157,841	159,878	—	144,080	133,295	—	113,412	95,524
1970	226,632	174,732	—	152,608	149,351	—	156,054	153,347	—	138,865	125,821
1980	280,882	253,317	—	234,221	187,930	—	162,114	154,954	—	160,608	158,116
1990	265,446	284,499	—	288,928	269,183	—	244,483	194,977	—	164,939	157,079

	Population								White	
	Female, by age								Male	Female
	60–69	60–64	65–69	70–79	70–74	75–79	80 and older	Unknown age		
	Aa5097	Aa5098	Aa5099	Aa5100	Aa5101	Aa5102	Aa5103	Aa5104	Aa5105	Aa5106
Year	Number	Number	Number	Number	Number	Number	Number	Number	Number	Number
1790	—	—	—	—	—	—	—	—	147,825	141,356
1800	—	—	—	—	—	—	—	—	171,648	166,116
1810	—	—	—	—	—	—	—	—	188,632	187,778
1820	—	—	—	—	—	—	—	—	209,644	209,556
1830	—	—	—	—	—	—	—	—	235,954	236,889
1840	—	—	—	—	—	—	—	—	240,047	244,823
1850	12,375	—	—	5,733	—	—	2,493	71	—	—
1860	14,802	—	—	6,222	—	—	2,755	298	—	—
1870	—	11,217	6,657	—	5,310	2,675	3,158	0	—	—
1880	—	13,923	9,445	—	6,904	3,934	4,177	—	—	—
1890 [1]	—	16,742	11,613	—	8,319	4,783	4,813	1,806	—	—
1900	—	19,731	13,925	—	9,989	5,679	5,044	2,303	—	—
1910	—	23,332	17,026	—	11,365	6,854	5,605	1,650	—	—
1920	—	26,774	19,941	—	13,877	8,124	6,688	1,383	—	—
1930	—	30,295	22,473	—	16,796	9,961	8,282	1,037	—	—
1940	—	43,204	37,020	—	20,973	11,694	10,454	—	—	—
1950	—	56,595	51,465	—	33,237	23,323	11,968	—	—	—
1960	—	77,116	66,329	—	48,518	32,228	26,500	—	—	—
1970	—	109,330	88,949	—	65,495	44,564	45,120	—	—	—
1980	—	139,677	126,841	—	98,617	68,855	72,618	—	—	—
1990	—	157,611	153,549	—	122,428	97,921	116,735	—	—	—

Note appears at end of table

(continued)

TABLE Aa5042-5142   North Carolina population by race, sex, age, nativity, and urban-rural residence: 1790-1990
Continued

	Population										
	White										
	Male, by age										
	0-4	5-9	10-14	15-19	20-29	30-39	40-49	50-59	60-69	70-79	80 and older
	Aa5107	Aa5108	Aa5109	Aa5110	Aa5111	Aa5112	Aa5113	Aa5114	Aa5115	Aa5116	Aa5117
Year	Number	Number	Number	Number	Number	Number	Number	Number	Number	Number	Number
1790	—	—	—	—	—	—	—	—	—	—	—
1800	—	—	—	—	—	—	—	—	—	—	—
1810	—	—	—	—	—	—	—	—	—	—	—
1820	—	—	—	—	—	—	—	—	—	—	—
1830	46,749	35,950	30,527	25,452	39,428	23,042	14,998	10,536	5,968	2,489	815
1840	46,413	37,011	31,473	24,819	38,756	24,254	16,799	10,432	6,365	2,830	895
1850	—	—	—	—	—	—	—	—	—	—	—
1860	—	—	—	—	—	—	—	—	—	—	—
1870	—	—	—	—	—	—	—	—	—	—	—
1880	—	—	—	—	—	—	—	—	—	—	—
1890 [1]	—	—	—	—	—	—	—	—	—	—	—
1900	—	—	—	—	—	—	—	—	—	—	—
1910	—	—	—	—	—	—	—	—	—	—	—
1920	—	—	—	—	—	—	—	—	—	—	—
1930	—	—	—	—	—	—	—	—	—	—	—
1940	—	—	—	—	—	—	—	—	—	—	—
1950	—	—	—	—	—	—	—	—	—	—	—
1960	—	—	—	—	—	—	—	—	—	—	—
1970	—	—	—	—	—	—	—	—	—	—	—
1980	—	—	—	—	—	—	—	—	—	—	—
1990	—	—	—	—	—	—	—	—	—	—	—

	Population										
	White										
	Female, by age										
	0-4	5-9	10-14	15-19	20-29	30-39	40-49	50-59	60-69	70-79	80 and older
	Aa5118	Aa5119	Aa5120	Aa5121	Aa5122	Aa5123	Aa5124	Aa5125	Aa5126	Aa5127	Aa5128
Year	Number	Number	Number	Number	Number	Number	Number	Number	Number	Number	Number
1790	—	—	—	—	—	—	—	—	—	—	—
1800	—	—	—	—	—	—	—	—	—	—	—
1810	—	—	—	—	—	—	—	—	—	—	—
1820	—	—	—	—	—	—	—	—	—	—	—
1830	43,775	34,264	28,842	27,398	41,636	24,534	16,428	10,601	5,980	2,496	935
1840	43,637	35,221	29,646	26,965	43,132	25,906	18,114	11,374	6,754	2,943	1,131
1850	—	—	—	—	—	—	—	—	—	—	—
1860	—	—	—	—	—	—	—	—	—	—	—
1870	—	—	—	—	—	—	—	—	—	—	—
1880	—	—	—	—	—	—	—	—	—	—	—
1890 [1]	—	—	—	—	—	—	—	—	—	—	—
1900	—	—	—	—	—	—	—	—	—	—	—
1910	—	—	—	—	—	—	—	—	—	—	—
1920	—	—	—	—	—	—	—	—	—	—	—
1930	—	—	—	—	—	—	—	—	—	—	—
1940	—	—	—	—	—	—	—	—	—	—	—
1950	—	—	—	—	—	—	—	—	—	—	—
1960	—	—	—	—	—	—	—	—	—	—	—
1970	—	—	—	—	—	—	—	—	—	—	—
1980	—	—	—	—	—	—	—	—	—	—	—
1990	—	—	—	—	—	—	—	—	—	—	—

Note appears at end of table

TABLE Aa5042-5142   North Carolina population by race, sex, age, nativity, and urban-rural residence: 1790-1990
Continued

	Population						
	White						
	Male, by age					Female, by age	
	0-9	10-15	16-25	26-44	45 and older	0-9	10-15
	Aa5129	Aa5130	Aa5131	Aa5132	Aa5133	Aa5134	Aa5135
Year	Number	Number	Number	Number	Number	Number	Number
1790	—	—	—	—	—	—	—
1800	63,118	27,073	31,560	31,209	18,688	59,074	25,874
1810	68,036	30,321	34,630	34,456	21,189	65,421	30,053
1820	75,448	32,912	39,527	36,264	25,453	70,998	33,101
1830	—	—	—	—	—	—	—
1840	—	—	—	—	—	—	—
1850	—	—	—	—	—	—	—
1860	—	—	—	—	—	—	—
1870	—	—	—	—	—	—	—
1880	—	—	—	—	—	—	—
1890 [1]	—	—	—	—	—	—	—
1900	—	—	—	—	—	—	—
1910	—	—	—	—	—	—	—
1920	—	—	—	—	—	—	—
1930	—	—	—	—	—	—	—
1940	—	—	—	—	—	—	—
1950	—	—	—	—	—	—	—
1960	—	—	—	—	—	—	—
1970	—	—	—	—	—	—	—
1980	—	—	—	—	—	—	—
1990	—	—	—	—	—	—	—

	Population						
	White						
	Female, by age			Male, by age		Female, by age	
	16-25	26-44	45 and older	0-15	16 and older	0-15	16 and older
	Aa5136	Aa5137	Aa5138	Aa5139	Aa5140	Aa5141	Aa5142
Year	Number	Number	Number	Number	Number	Number	Number
1790	—	—	—	77,653	70,172	72,289	69,067
1800	32,989	30,665	17,514	—	—	—	—
1810	37,933	33,944	20,427	—	—	—	—
1820	42,253	38,069	25,135	—	—	—	—
1830	—	—	—	—	—	—	—
1840	—	—	—	—	—	—	—
1850	—	—	—	—	—	—	—
1860	—	—	—	—	—	—	—
1870	—	—	—	—	—	—	—
1880	—	—	—	—	—	—	—
1890 [1]	—	—	—	—	—	—	—
1900	—	—	—	—	—	—	—
1910	—	—	—	—	—	—	—
1920	—	—	—	—	—	—	—
1930	—	—	—	—	—	—	—
1940	—	—	—	—	—	—	—
1950	—	—	—	—	—	—	—
1960	—	—	—	—	—	—	—
1970	—	—	—	—	—	—	—
1980	—	—	—	—	—	—	—
1990	—	—	—	—	—	—	—

[1] Includes two American Indians not counted in the general enumeration; see text for Table Aa2244-2340.

Sources
See the sources for Table Aa2244-2340.

Documentation
See the text for Table Aa2244-2340.

North Carolina was one of the original thirteen states, admitted to the Union in 1789.

TABLE Aa5143–5193 North Dakota population by race, sex, age, nativity, and urban–rural residence: 1890–1990
Contributed by Michael R. Haines

			Population						
					Race			Residence	
	Area	Population density	Total	White	Nonwhite	Black	Other nonwhite	Urban	Rural
	Aa5143	Aa5144	Aa5145	Aa5146	Aa5147	Aa5148	Aa5149	Aa5150	Aa5151
Year	Square miles	Persons per square mile	Number	Number	Number	Number	Number	Number	Number
1890 [1]	70,183	2.72	190,983	182,123	596	373	223	10,643	180,340
1900	70,183	4.55	319,146	311,712	7,434	286	7,148	23,413	295,733
1910	70,183	8.22	577,056	569,855	7,201	617	6,584	63,236	513,820
1920	70,183	9.22	646,872	639,954	6,918	467	6,451	88,239	558,633
1930	70,183	9.70	680,845	671,851	8,994	377	8,617	113,306	567,539
1940	70,054	9.16	641,935	631,464	10,471	201	10,270	131,923	510,012
1950	70,057	8.84	619,636	608,448	11,188	257	10,931	164,817	454,819
1960	69,280	9.13	632,446	619,538	12,908	777	12,131	222,708	409,738
1970	69,273	8.92	617,761	599,485	18,276	2,494	15,782	273,442	344,319
1980	69,300	9.42	652,717	625,557	27,160	2,568	24,592	318,310	334,407
1990	68,994	9.26	638,800	604,142	34,658	3,524	31,134	340,339	298,461

				Population					
	Nativity		Sex		Male, by age				
	Native-born	Foreign-born	Male	Female	0	1–4	5–9	10–14	15–19
	Aa5152	Aa5153	Aa5154	Aa5155	Aa5156	Aa5157	Aa5158	Aa5159	Aa5160
Year	Number	Number	Number	Number	Number	Number	Number	Number	Number
1890 [1]	101,258	81,461	101,590	81,129	3,303	11,721	12,124	9,303	7,561
1900	206,055	113,091	177,493	141,653	5,159	19,079	21,362	18,193	15,304
1910	420,402	156,654	317,554	259,502	8,765	32,959	35,172	30,466	29,656
1920	515,009	131,863	341,673	305,199	8,375	37,887	43,422	37,988	30,474
1930	574,974	105,871	359,615	321,230	7,748	30,594	39,447	40,476	38,368
1940	567,458	74,477	335,402	306,533	6,090	25,256	31,686	33,455	33,340
1950	569,500	48,205	322,944	296,692	7,576	30,823	31,850	27,682	25,804
1960	602,539	29,907	323,208	309,238	8,367	32,087	37,537	32,865	26,241
1970	599,324	18,437	311,609	306,152	5,405	20,924	32,744	35,855	33,050
1980	637,899	14,818	328,426	324,291	6,177	22,033	25,079	26,328	32,920
1990	629,412	9,388	318,201	320,599	4,362	20,051	26,724	25,165	24,368

				Population					
				Male, by age					
	20–24	25–29	30–34	35–39	40–44	45–49	50–54	55–59	60–64
	Aa5161	Aa5162	Aa5163	Aa5164	Aa5165	Aa5166	Aa5167	Aa5168	Aa5169
Year	Number	Number	Number	Number	Number	Number	Number	Number	Number
1890 [1]	10,206	11,318	10,948	7,727	5,196	3,611	2,752	1,932	1,584
1900	17,580	16,944	14,738	13,419	11,482	7,882	5,578	3,706	2,533
1910	34,151	32,744	26,591	22,207	17,312	14,048	12,197	7,868	5,065
1920	27,195	26,401	24,813	24,284	19,526	17,246	13,537	10,469	8,257
1930	32,048	25,490	22,912	23,076	21,371	19,866	16,925	13,322	10,217
1940	29,460	25,988	23,568	20,782	19,016	18,567	17,588	15,483	12,477
1950	24,560	23,385	22,203	21,885	20,176	17,318	15,720	14,615	12,855
1960	19,064	18,095	19,205	18,619	18,740	18,587	16,896	14,550	12,389
1970	25,388	17,823	15,202	15,667	16,543	16,240	16,169	15,652	13,883
1980	35,889	30,691	23,969	17,568	14,711	14,065	15,279	14,543	13,691
1990	25,187	25,613	27,065	25,869	20,619	15,520	12,960	12,704	13,225

Notes appear at end of table

TABLE Aa5143–5193   North Dakota population by race, sex, age, nativity, and urban–rural residence: 1890–1990
Continued

	Population							
	Male, by age					Female, by age		
	65–69	70–74	75–79	80 and older	Unknown age	0	1–4	5–9
	Aa5170	Aa5171	Aa5172	Aa5173	Aa5174	Aa5175	Aa5176	Aa5177
Year	Number	Number	Number	Number	Number	Number	Number	Number
1890 [1]	1,001	607	254	159	283	3,110	11,434	11,575
1900	1,811	1,138	639	378	568	5,039	18,506	20,840
1910	3,356	1,828	1,174	806	1,189	8,224	32,451	34,755
1920	5,331	2,940	1,688	1,051	789	8,225	36,402	42,351
1930	7,648	5,318	2,805	1,707	277	7,438	29,946	38,672
1940	9,575	6,435	3,871	2,765	—	5,890	24,557	30,736
1950	10,770	7,468	5,307	2,947	—	7,110	29,899	30,639
1960	10,742	8,708	5,846	4,670	—	8,048	31,041	36,034
1970	10,706	8,274	6,001	6,083	—	5,249	19,760	31,476
1980	12,315	9,715	6,635	6,818	—	5,842	20,700	23,937
1990	11,917	10,216	7,976	8,660	—	4,198	19,234	25,308

	Population							
	Female, by age							
	10–14	15–19	20–24	25–29	30–34	35–39	40–44	45–49
	Aa5178	Aa5179	Aa5180	Aa5181	Aa5182	Aa5183	Aa5184	Aa5185
Year	Number	Number	Number	Number	Number	Number	Number	Number
1890 [1]	8,326	7,277	7,697	7,750	6,986	4,745	3,344	2,472
1900	17,314	13,924	12,978	11,103	9,494	8,724	7,133	4,962
1910	28,926	27,043	27,480	23,982	18,405	14,899	11,030	9,524
1920	36,771	30,980	27,345	24,419	21,936	19,349	14,853	11,781
1930	39,410	36,975	29,805	23,498	20,429	19,855	18,198	15,767
1940	32,920	32,709	27,992	24,667	21,714	18,987	17,055	16,188
1950	26,597	25,409	23,258	21,115	20,204	19,995	17,782	15,552
1960	31,706	25,689	19,033	17,837	18,157	17,674	17,875	17,322
1970	34,479	31,719	23,379	16,780	15,647	15,704	16,284	15,628
1980	24,715	31,057	33,504	27,779	21,718	16,680	14,687	14,566
1990	23,655	22,300	22,686	24,541	26,796	24,264	19,268	15,115

	Population							
	Female, by age							
	50–54	55–59	60–64	65–69	70–74	75–79	80 and older	Unknown age
	Aa5186	Aa5187	Aa5188	Aa5189	Aa5190	Aa5191	Aa5192	Aa5193
Year	Number	Number	Number	Number	Number	Number	Number	Number
1890 [1]	1,892	1,476	1,231	821	471	238	166	118
1900	3,625	2,561	1,886	1,465	973	596	357	173
1910	7,875	5,102	3,662	2,453	1,504	1,007	770	410
1920	9,148	7,130	5,692	3,652	2,226	1,375	1,061	503
1930	12,310	9,103	6,906	5,371	3,794	2,121	1,516	116
1940	14,869	12,296	9,209	6,935	4,540	2,901	2,368	—
1950	13,927	12,502	10,999	9,045	5,874	4,306	2,479	—
1960	15,425	13,304	11,468	10,084	8,310	5,653	4,578	—
1970	15,910	15,271	13,562	11,047	9,137	7,019	8,101	—
1980	15,218	14,675	14,251	13,615	11,502	8,666	11,179	—
1990	13,489	13,564	13,895	13,033	12,375	11,014	15,864	—

[1] Includes 8,264 American Indians not counted in the general enumeration; see text for Table Aa2244–2340.

Sources
See the sources for Table Aa2244–2340.

Documentation
See the text for Table Aa2244–2340.

The portion of present-day North Dakota east of the Missouri and the White Earth rivers was part of Minnesota Territory in 1849 and the western portion was incorporated as part of Nebraska Territory in 1854. The population of the eastern portion in 1850 is included with Minnesota Territory in Table Aa4242–4304. Minnesota statehood in 1858 left the portion of Minnesota Territory west of the present Minnesota state border as unorganized territory. When Dakota Territory was organized in 1861, it comprised the present area of North and South Dakota. In 1860, the census reported the population of "Dakota Territory" even though it was not organized at the time of the census. North and South Dakota became separate states in 1889. The data for Dakota Territory, and hence for the area of present-day North Dakota, for 1860–1880 are reported in the Table 5708–5770 as the population of "South Dakota."

TABLE Aa5194–5290   Ohio population by race, sex, age, nativity, and urban–rural residence: 1800–1990

Contributed by Michael R. Haines

	Area	Population density	Population									
				Race				Residence		Nativity	
			Total	White	Nonwhite	Black	Other nonwhite	Urban	Rural	Native-born	Foreign-born
	Aa5194	Aa5195	Aa5196	Aa5197	Aa5198	Aa5199	Aa5200	Aa5201	Aa5202	Aa5203	Aa5204
Year	Square miles	Persons per square mile	Number	Number	Number	Number	Number	Number	Number	Number	Number
1800	40,228	1.05	42,159	41,961	198	198	—	0	42,159	—	—
1810	40,228	5.74	230,760	228,861	1,899	1,899	—	2,540	228,220	—	—
1820	40,228	14.45	581,434	576,572	4,862	4,723	139	9,642	571,792	—	—
1830	40,228	23.31	937,903	928,329	9,574	9,574	—	36,658	901,245	—	—
1840	40,740	37.30	1,519,467	1,502,122	17,345	17,345	—	83,491	1,435,976	—	—
1850	40,740	48.61	1,980,329	1,955,050	25,279	25,279	—	242,418	1,737,911	1,762,136	218,193
1860	40,740	57.43	2,339,511	2,302,808	36,703	36,673	30	400,435	1,939,076	2,011,262	328,249
1870	40,740	65.42	2,665,260	2,601,946	63,314	63,213	101	682,922	1,982,338	2,292,767	372,493
1880	40,740	78.50	3,198,062	3,117,920	80,142	79,900	242	1,030,769	2,167,293	2,803,119	394,943
1890 [1]	40,740	90.14	3,672,329	3,584,805	87,511	87,113	398	1,510,153	2,162,176	3,213,023	459,293
1900	40,740	102.05	4,157,545	4,060,204	97,341	96,901	440	1,998,382	2,159,163	3,698,811	458,734
1910	40,740	117.01	4,767,121	4,654,897	112,224	111,452	772	2,665,143	2,101,978	4,168,747	598,374
1920	40,740	141.37	5,759,394	5,571,893	187,501	186,187	1,314	3,677,136	2,082,258	5,078,942	680,452
1930	40,740	163.15	6,646,697	6,335,173	311,524	309,304	2,220	4,507,371	2,139,326	5,997,477	649,220
1940	41,122	167.98	6,907,612	6,566,531	341,081	339,461	1,620	4,612,986	2,294,626	6,386,839	520,773
1950	41,000	193.82	7,946,627	7,428,222	518,405	513,072	5,333	5,578,274	2,368,353	7,467,775	440,475
1960	41,018	236.64	9,706,397	8,909,698	796,699	786,097	10,602	7,123,162	2,583,235	9,310,522	396,614
1970	40,975	259.96	10,652,017	9,646,997	1,005,020	970,477	34,543	8,025,763	2,626,254	10,334,407	316,496
1980	41,004	263.33	10,797,630	9,597,458	1,200,172	1,076,748	123,424	7,918,259	2,879,371	10,495,445	302,185
1990	40,953	264.87	10,847,115	9,521,756	1,325,359	1,154,826	170,533	8,039,409	2,807,706	10,587,442	259,673

	Population										
	Sex		Male, by age								
	Male	Female	0	1–4	5–9	10–14	15–19	20–29	20–24	25–29	30–39
	Aa5205	Aa5206	Aa5207	Aa5208	Aa5209	Aa5210	Aa5211	Aa5212	Aa5213	Aa5214	Aa5215
Year	Number	Number	Number	Number	Number	Number	Number	Number	Number	Number	Number
1800	—	—	—	—	—	—	—	—	—	—	—
1810	—	—	—	—	—	—	—	—	—	—	—
1820	303,061	278,234	—	—	—	—	—	—	—	—	—
1830	484,503	453,400	—	—	—	—	—	—	—	—	—
1840	784,102	735,365	—	—	—	—	—	—	—	—	—
1850	1,016,808	963,521	28,858	128,601	147,751	129,676	108,421	181,101	—	—	122,068
1860	1,190,162	1,149,349	36,080	148,849	159,488	144,152	129,972	203,704	—	—	146,799
1870	1,337,550	1,327,710	38,568	152,103	170,291	169,152	140,524	—	123,591	100,014	—
1880	1,613,936	1,584,126	42,580	163,401	198,520	186,139	163,878	—	163,448	131,400	—
1890 [1]	1,855,736	1,816,580	42,050	161,041	210,215	201,062	191,344	—	180,483	151,457	—
1900	2,102,655	2,054,890	45,312	173,084	220,664	209,149	203,825	—	194,881	180,188	—
1910	2,434,758	2,332,363	49,903	193,418	221,410	214,364	225,299	—	230,390	219,813	—
1920	2,955,980	2,803,414	56,695	240,745	276,500	256,614	232,769	—	253,771	268,787	—
1930	3,361,141	3,285,556	55,525	235,758	323,602	309,571	287,102	—	278,498	259,905	—
1940	3,461,072	3,446,540	49,959	207,719	252,032	292,115	313,456	—	294,576	278,100	—
1950	3,928,534	4,018,093	86,283	345,739	334,596	278,927	247,691	—	283,493	320,487	—
1960	4,764,228	4,942,169	114,758	465,638	527,264	459,709	329,240	—	265,236	288,329	—
1970	5,163,373	5,488,644	94,955	375,449	540,381	574,349	505,516	—	384,908	337,735	—
1980	5,217,137	5,580,493	86,390	316,580	420,944	453,689	507,990	—	494,190	448,273	—
1990	5,226,340	5,620,775	71,349	330,773	406,612	393,130	403,489	—	393,624	426,245	—

Note appears at end of table

TABLE Aa5194–5290 Ohio population by race, sex, age, nativity, and urban–rural residence: 1800–1990 *Continued*

	Population										
	Male, by age										
	30–34	35–39	40–49	40–44	45–49	50–59	50–54	55–59	60–69	60–64	65–69
	Aa5216	Aa5217	Aa5218	Aa5219	Aa5220	Aa5221	Aa5222	Aa5223	Aa5224	Aa5225	Aa5226
Year	Number	Number	Number	Number	Number	Number	Number	Number	Number	Number	Number
1800	—	—	—	—	—	—	—	—	—	—	—
1810	—	—	—	—	—	—	—	—	—	—	—
1820	—	—	—	—	—	—	—	—	—	—	—
1830	—	—	—	—	—	—	—	—	—	—	—
1840	—	—	—	—	—	—	—	—	—	—	—
1850	—	—	81,184	—	—	46,920	—	—	27,875	—	—
1860	—	—	101,726	—	—	63,544	—	—	36,835	—	—
1870	82,532	75,992	—	65,120	57,635	—	47,295	38,063	—	29,815	20,269
1880	108,320	95,810	—	79,287	68,067	—	57,370	49,240	—	40,260	28,299
1890 [1]	141,031	119,495	—	99,828	85,914	—	71,351	56,494	—	49,307	36,902
1900	162,612	145,401	—	131,800	107,756	—	89,738	72,687	—	56,674	43,309
1910	195,886	182,116	—	156,229	133,716	—	117,485	90,282	—	70,386	55,847
1920	245,999	239,236	—	193,865	179,752	—	145,916	112,544	—	94,555	66,425
1930	254,249	269,415	—	238,778	211,801	—	178,288	141,358	—	113,496	84,764
1940	261,502	244,822	—	239,453	238,706	—	213,716	174,164	—	140,804	109,309
1950	303,353	287,397	—	264,365	237,678	—	224,600	206,248	—	173,716	137,116
1960	328,372	339,205	—	310,753	284,212	—	248,891	215,382	—	182,567	155,576
1970	291,574	282,051	—	313,556	316,163	—	285,142	246,309	—	201,356	149,439
1980	399,928	311,241	—	269,713	260,370	—	283,276	275,126	—	227,180	176,850
1990	454,019	419,243	—	372,323	291,042	—	246,989	229,688	—	232,280	207,546

	Population										
	Male, by age					Female, by age					
	70–79	70–74	75–79	80 and older	Unknown age	0	1–4	5–9	10–14	15–19	20–29
	Aa5227	Aa5228	Aa5229	Aa5230	Aa5231	Aa5232	Aa5233	Aa5234	Aa5235	Aa5236	Aa5237
Year	Number	Number	Number	Number	Number	Number	Number	Number	Number	Number	Number
1800	—	—	—	—	—	—	—	—	—	—	—
1810	—	—	—	—	—	—	—	—	—	—	—
1820	—	—	—	—	—	—	—	—	—	—	—
1830	—	—	—	—	—	—	—	—	—	—	—
1840	—	—	—	—	—	—	—	—	—	—	—
1850	10,927	—	—	3,068	358	28,026	124,841	143,535	125,245	112,639	170,830
1860	14,539	—	—	4,038	436	35,090	144,406	157,584	138,305	135,081	204,473
1870	—	13,788	7,321	5,395	82	37,089	147,652	166,183	165,247	148,243	—
1880	—	19,201	11,175	7,541	—	41,557	157,889	194,748	181,294	169,119	—
1890 [1]	—	26,801	15,356	11,269	4,336	40,893	155,633	203,825	195,470	195,303	—
1900	—	30,133	18,255	12,385	4,802	44,047	169,367	215,150	205,698	203,994	—
1910	—	36,907	21,884	14,960	4,463	48,873	187,281	217,489	211,238	221,613	—
1920	—	44,306	27,699	17,451	2,351	55,247	233,449	272,302	251,715	231,885	—
1930	—	60,917	34,131	22,157	1,826	53,409	228,472	315,670	303,197	291,031	—
1940	—	75,782	43,718	31,139	—	48,409	201,229	243,334	284,063	312,616	—
1950	—	94,236	67,673	34,936	—	82,715	332,012	323,268	270,054	258,412	—
1960	—	116,786	74,330	57,980	—	110,692	448,312	507,055	445,108	346,781	—
1970	—	113,016	78,937	72,537	—	91,257	359,369	519,093	552,836	506,705	—
1980	—	125,787	80,584	79,026	—	82,302	301,878	400,536	432,936	499,689	—
1990	—	152,217	102,363	93,408	—	68,355	314,672	388,523	373,692	390,430	—

Note appears at end of table

(continued)

TABLE Aa5194–5290 Ohio population by race, sex, age, nativity, and urban–rural residence: 1800–1990 *Continued*

	Population										
	Female, by age										
	20–24	25–29	30–39	30–34	35–39	40–49	40–44	45–49	50–59	50–54	55–59
	Aa5238	Aa5239	Aa5240	Aa5241	Aa5242	Aa5243	Aa5244	Aa5245	Aa5246	Aa5247	Aa5248
Year	Number	Number	Number	Number	Number	Number	Number	Number	Number	Number	Number
1800	—	—	—	—	—	—	—	—	—	—	—
1810	—	—	—	—	—	—	—	—	—	—	—
1820	—	—	—	—	—	—	—	—	—	—	—
1830	—	—	—	—	—	—	—	—	—	—	—
1840	—	—	—	—	—	—	—	—	—	—	—
1850	—	—	108,529	—	—	71,029	—	—	43,054	—	—
1860	—	—	135,831	—	—	90,919	—	—	57,197	—	—
1870	131,155	106,388	—	85,852	76,223	—	64,424	52,509	—	43,996	32,029
1880	163,974	127,724	—	105,052	95,823	—	79,634	66,493	—	57,839	43,868
1890 [1]	183,633	152,155	—	134,419	112,098	—	95,439	83,650	—	71,862	55,055
1900	198,496	179,595	—	156,258	138,885	—	121,707	100,577	—	85,274	71,180
1910	223,136	206,880	—	182,026	168,376	—	144,143	125,205	—	109,633	83,833
1920	246,888	251,437	—	223,903	209,386	—	176,591	156,115	—	133,015	106,601
1930	285,755	263,653	—	251,691	253,673	—	219,539	194,245	—	166,489	133,832
1940	304,186	288,956	—	268,394	249,693	—	237,152	226,805	—	199,274	165,368
1950	311,416	343,116	—	317,500	297,971	—	268,437	240,134	—	224,336	202,594
1960	306,039	303,742	—	339,957	355,738	—	321,826	290,687	—	254,875	223,165
1970	448,461	353,951	—	308,562	297,294	—	330,040	338,636	—	305,138	266,005
1980	510,729	459,406	—	415,769	329,353	—	289,516	278,348	—	304,613	306,822
1990	401,513	442,319	—	472,605	434,234	—	390,055	308,331	—	267,081	252,838

	Population								White	
	Female, by age									
	60–69	60–64	65–69	70–79	70–74	75–79	80 and older	Unknown age	Male	Female
	Aa5249	Aa5250	Aa5251	Aa5252	Aa5253	Aa5254	Aa5255	Aa5256	Aa5257	Aa5258
Year	Number	Number	Number	Number	Number	Number	Number	Number	Number	Number
1800	—	—	—	—	—	—	—	—	22,578	19,383
1810	—	—	—	—	—	—	—	—	119,657	109,204
1820	—	—	—	—	—	—	—	—	300,607	275,965
1830	—	—	—	—	—	—	—	—	479,713	448,616
1840	—	—	—	—	—	—	—	—	775,360	726,762
1850	23,518	—	—	9,295	—	—	2,712	268	—	—
1860	33,219	—	—	13,195	—	—	3,647	402	—	—
1870	—	26,964	18,332	—	12,953	6,929	5,475	67	—	—
1880	—	36,248	26,110	—	18,062	10,627	8,065	—	—	—
1890 [1]	—	47,773	35,251	—	25,160	14,821	11,594	2,546	—	—
1900	—	57,012	43,359	—	30,155	18,545	13,422	2,169	—	—
1910	—	68,585	54,856	—	37,087	23,062	17,207	1,840	—	—
1920	—	89,763	65,479	—	45,888	30,188	22,001	1,561	—	—
1930	—	110,672	85,701	—	62,226	37,182	27,758	1,361	—	—
1940	—	137,280	111,920	—	79,986	49,055	38,820	—	—	—
1950	—	171,114	144,689	—	103,709	78,926	47,690	—	—	—
1960	—	195,740	176,021	—	137,485	94,478	84,468	—	—	—
1970	—	227,532	186,492	—	155,633	117,547	124,093	—	—	—
1980	—	261,383	223,911	—	180,006	135,734	167,562	—	—	—
1990	—	264,700	258,567	—	209,698	166,534	216,628	—	—	—

Note appears at end of table

TABLE Aa5194–5290   Ohio population by race, sex, age, nativity, and urban–rural residence: 1800–1990   *Continued*

	Population										
	White										
	Male, by age										
	0–4	5–9	10–14	15–19	20–29	30–39	40–49	50–59	60–69	70–79	80 and older
	Aa5259	Aa5260	Aa5261	Aa5262	Aa5263	Aa5264	Aa5265	Aa5266	Aa5267	Aa5268	Aa5269
Year	Number	Number	Number	Number	Number	Number	Number	Number	Number	Number	Number
1800	—	—	—	—	—	—	—	—	—	—	—
1810	—	—	—	—	—	—	—	—	—	—	—
1820	—	—	—	—	—	—	—	—	—	—	—
1830	96,411	74,690	62,151	51,138	81,290	49,346	31,112	18,058	10,783	3,632	1,102
1840	144,582	115,832	96,697	81,431	138,755	85,944	54,992	30,298	18,182	6,778	1,869
1850	—	—	—	—	—	—	—	—	—	—	—
1860	—	—	—	—	—	—	—	—	—	—	—
1870	—	—	—	—	—	—	—	—	—	—	—
1880	—	—	—	—	—	—	—	—	—	—	—
1890 [1]	—	—	—	—	—	—	—	—	—	—	—
1900	—	—	—	—	—	—	—	—	—	—	—
1910	—	—	—	—	—	—	—	—	—	—	—
1920	—	—	—	—	—	—	—	—	—	—	—
1930	—	—	—	—	—	—	—	—	—	—	—
1940	—	—	—	—	—	—	—	—	—	—	—
1950	—	—	—	—	—	—	—	—	—	—	—
1960	—	—	—	—	—	—	—	—	—	—	—
1970	—	—	—	—	—	—	—	—	—	—	—
1980	—	—	—	—	—	—	—	—	—	—	—
1990	—	—	—	—	—	—	—	—	—	—	—

	Population										
	White										
	Female, by age										
	0–4	5–9	10–14	15–19	20–29	30–39	40–49	50–59	60–69	70–79	80 and older
	Aa5270	Aa5271	Aa5272	Aa5273	Aa5274	Aa5275	Aa5276	Aa5277	Aa5278	Aa5279	Aa5280
Year	Number	Number	Number	Number	Number	Number	Number	Number	Number	Number	Number
1800	—	—	—	—	—	—	—	—	—	—	—
1810	—	—	—	—	—	—	—	—	—	—	—
1820	—	—	—	—	—	—	—	—	—	—	—
1830	89,873	71,851	59,306	52,635	75,574	43,894	27,546	15,898	8,293	2,915	831
1840	137,725	110,949	91,294	84,872	127,730	75,799	48,588	28,037	14,636	5,592	1,540
1850	—	—	—	—	—	—	—	—	—	—	—
1860	—	—	—	—	—	—	—	—	—	—	—
1870	—	—	—	—	—	—	—	—	—	—	—
1880	—	—	—	—	—	—	—	—	—	—	—
1890 [1]	—	—	—	—	—	—	—	—	—	—	—
1900	—	—	—	—	—	—	—	—	—	—	—
1910	—	—	—	—	—	—	—	—	—	—	—
1920	—	—	—	—	—	—	—	—	—	—	—
1930	—	—	—	—	—	—	—	—	—	—	—
1940	—	—	—	—	—	—	—	—	—	—	—
1950	—	—	—	—	—	—	—	—	—	—	—
1960	—	—	—	—	—	—	—	—	—	—	—
1970	—	—	—	—	—	—	—	—	—	—	—
1980	—	—	—	—	—	—	—	—	—	—	—
1990	—	—	—	—	—	—	—	—	—	—	—

Note appears at end of table

(continued)

TABLE Aa5194–5290   Ohio population by race, sex, age, nativity, and urban–rural residence: 1800–1990 *Continued*

	Population									
	White									
	Male, by age					Female, by age				
	0–9	10–15	16–25	26–44	45 and older	0–9	10–15	16–25	26–44	45 and older
	Aa5281	Aa5282	Aa5283	Aa5284	Aa5285	Aa5286	Aa5287	Aa5288	Aa5289	Aa5290
Year	Number	Number	Number	Number	Number	Number	Number	Number	Number	Number
1800	8,822	3,446	4,304	4,249	1,757	8,177	3,160	3,609	3,144	1,293
1810	46,623	18,119	20,189	22,761	11,965	44,192	16,869	19,990	19,436	8,717
1820	111,683	45,858	57,008	54,432	31,626	106,036	44,106	53,337	48,797	23,689
1830	—	—	—	—	—	—	—	—	—	—
1840	—	—	—	—	—	—	—	—	—	—
1850	—	—	—	—	—	—	—	—	—	—
1860	—	—	—	—	—	—	—	—	—	—
1870	—	—	—	—	—	—	—	—	—	—
1880	—	—	—	—	—	—	—	—	—	—
1890 [1]	—	—	—	—	—	—	—	—	—	—
1900	—	—	—	—	—	—	—	—	—	—
1910	—	—	—	—	—	—	—	—	—	—
1920	—	—	—	—	—	—	—	—	—	—
1930	—	—	—	—	—	—	—	—	—	—
1940	—	—	—	—	—	—	—	—	—	—
1950	—	—	—	—	—	—	—	—	—	—
1960	—	—	—	—	—	—	—	—	—	—
1970	—	—	—	—	—	—	—	—	—	—
1980	—	—	—	—	—	—	—	—	—	—
1990	—	—	—	—	—	—	—	—	—	—

[1] Includes thirteen American Indians not counted in the general enumeration; see text for Table Aa2244–2340.

Sources

See the sources for Table Aa2244–2340.

Documentation

See the text for Table Aa2244–2340.

Ohio was part of the Northwest Territory. It was admitted directly to the Union in 1803 without having first been organized as a separate territory. The population for 1800 excludes the populations of what would later become Indiana, Illinois, Michigan, and Wisconsin.

TABLE Aa5291–5341   Oklahoma population by race, sex, age, nativity, and urban–rural residence: 1890–1990

Contributed by Michael R. Haines

			Population									
				Race				Residence		Nativity		
	Area	Population density	Total	White	Nonwhite	Black	Other nonwhite	Urban	Rural	Native-born	Foreign-born	
	Aa5291	Aa5292	Aa5293	Aa5294	Aa5295	Aa5296	Aa5297	Aa5298	Aa5299	Aa5300	Aa5301	
Year	Square miles	Persons per square mile	Number	Number	Number	Number	Number	Number	Number	Number	Number	
1890 [1]	38,624	6.70	258,657	58,826	3,008	2,973	35	9,484	249,173	59,094	2,740	
1900 [2]	69,414	11.39	790,391	670,204	120,187	55,684	64,503	58,417	731,974	769,853	20,538	
1910	69,414	23.87	1,657,155	1,444,531	212,624	137,612	75,012	318,975	1,338,180	1,616,713	40,442	
1920	69,414	29.22	2,028,283	1,821,194	207,089	149,408	57,681	538,017	1,490,266	1,987,851	40,432	
1930	69,414	34.52	2,396,040	2,130,778	265,262	172,198	93,064	821,681	1,574,359	2,365,482	30,558	
1940	69,283	33.72	2,336,434	2,104,228	232,206	168,849	63,357	879,663	1,456,771	2,315,889	20,545	
1950	69,031	32.35	2,233,351	2,032,526	200,825	145,503	55,322	1,139,481	1,093,870	2,211,395	18,270	
1960	68,983	33.75	2,328,284	2,107,900	220,384	153,084	67,300	1,464,786	863,498	2,308,281	20,003	
1970	68,782	37.21	2,559,229	2,280,362	278,867	171,892	106,975	1,740,137	819,092	2,539,015	20,160	
1980	68,655	44.07	3,025,290	2,597,791	427,499	204,674	222,825	2,035,082	990,208	2,968,996	56,294	
1990	68,679	45.80	3,145,585	2,583,512	562,073	233,801	328,272	2,130,139	1,015,446	3,080,096	65,489	

Notes appear at end of table

TABLE Aa5291–5341   Oklahoma population by race, sex, age, nativity, and urban–rural residence: 1890–1990
Continued

		Population										
	Sex						Male, by age					
	Male	Female	0	1–4	5–9	10–14	15–19	20–24	25–29	30–34	35–39	
	Aa5302	Aa5303	Aa5304	Aa5305	Aa5306	Aa5307	Aa5308	Aa5309	Aa5310	Aa5311	Aa5312	
Year	Number	Number	Number	Number	Number	Number	Number	Number	Number	Number	Number	
1890 [1]	34,733	27,101	811	3,752	4,359	3,557	2,673	3,130	3,344	3,100	2,552	
1900 [2]	423,311	367,080	12,764	47,122	56,197	49,941	42,784	38,519	34,874	29,613	25,718	
1910	881,578	775,577	25,224	97,630	110,608	95,090	89,067	81,593	73,531	63,007	58,677	
1920	1,058,044	970,239	25,085	103,229	131,977	125,918	104,457	91,079	83,829	71,092	71,486	
1930	1,233,264	1,162,776	26,200	107,990	145,130	130,886	126,490	114,425	98,301	85,588	82,521	
1940	1,181,892	1,154,542	21,784	89,827	114,975	120,361	121,588	98,531	92,269	87,741	80,098	
1950	1,115,555	1,117,796	23,510	98,949	107,857	96,003	90,324	82,619	83,354	74,816	75,317	
1960	1,147,851	1,180,433	24,986	98,288	119,742	111,787	93,774	74,358	66,555	69,270	72,635	
1970	1,246,355	1,312,874	21,357	79,577	121,518	129,338	122,876	104,687	80,874	67,753	66,492	
1980	1,476,705	1,548,585	25,721	93,903	117,801	118,628	144,127	144,884	127,185	110,659	89,761	
1990	1,530,819	1,614,766	19,720	96,069	125,027	119,525	120,064	113,803	124,659	129,568	118,626	

	Population									
	Male, by age									
	40–44	45–49	50–54	55–59	60–64	65–69	70–74	75–79	80 and older	Unknown age
	Aa5313	Aa5314	Aa5315	Aa5316	Aa5317	Aa5318	Aa5319	Aa5320	Aa5321	Aa5322
Year	Number	Number	Number	Number	Number	Number	Number	Number	Number	Number
1890 [1]	2,023	1,826	1,415	908	596	316	169	41	36	125
1900 [2]	22,745	18,443	15,460	10,446	7,234	4,728	2,431	1,108	715	2,469
1910	45,554	35,843	37,353	24,900	17,776	11,585	6,424	3,553	2,024	2,139
1920	56,680	53,637	43,781	31,023	25,504	17,373	10,571	5,768	3,407	2,148
1930	69,643	60,097	55,232	43,262	32,230	22,643	16,368	9,284	6,389	585
1940	70,290	64,495	55,944	46,922	38,910	34,158	22,297	12,375	9,327	—
1950	72,699	64,825	56,817	49,869	42,034	37,074	27,006	21,226	11,256	—
1960	67,685	67,172	63,496	56,626	47,060	41,377	31,979	21,942	19,119	—
1970	69,961	71,692	65,031	61,916	56,675	46,435	34,371	23,339	22,463	—
1980	76,010	72,138	72,247	71,471	60,557	54,179	42,904	28,637	25,893	—
1990	104,575	85,690	71,609	67,347	64,297	60,044	44,507	32,557	33,132	—

	Population											
	Female, by age											
	0	1–4	5–9	10–14	15–19	20–24	25–29	30–34	35–39	40–44	45–49	50–54
	Aa5323	Aa5324	Aa5325	Aa5326	Aa5327	Aa5328	Aa5329	Aa5330	Aa5331	Aa5332	Aa5333	Aa5334
Year	Number	Number	Number	Number	Number	Number	Number	Number	Number	Number	Number	Number
1890 [1]	786	3,401	4,024	3,341	2,733	2,727	2,359	1,940	1,586	1,301	1,025	779
1900 [2]	12,431	46,198	54,300	47,227	40,663	35,125	29,826	22,926	18,727	16,136	12,852	10,241
1910	24,571	94,479	107,167	90,979	85,335	77,416	65,678	53,011	46,361	34,808	26,713	22,785
1920	24,418	99,846	129,777	121,519	104,878	91,911	82,236	67,528	62,037	48,334	40,653	29,787
1930	25,434	104,913	140,716	127,144	126,265	116,466	98,955	83,149	78,151	63,434	54,027	43,774
1940	21,234	86,481	111,350	116,871	119,476	100,827	97,507	90,575	82,096	68,631	62,469	52,138
1950	22,712	95,287	103,365	91,698	88,548	83,803	85,319	77,946	79,692	74,729	66,890	57,171
1960	24,117	95,356	114,757	108,686	90,279	70,819	70,069	73,433	76,528	71,146	71,424	67,055
1970	20,227	76,108	116,357	124,029	118,659	102,763	81,981	71,860	71,907	74,695	75,718	69,865
1980	25,053	88,630	111,772	112,047	134,860	139,358	125,560	112,170	92,554	78,895	76,406	77,939
1990	19,208	91,526	119,095	112,367	113,029	108,963	123,950	131,142	120,917	108,123	89,528	76,148

Notes appear at end of table

(continued)

TABLE Aa5291-5341   Oklahoma population by race, sex, age, nativity, and urban–rural residence: 1890–1990
Continued

	Population						
	Female, by age						
	55–59	60–64	65–69	70–74	75–79	80 and older	Unknown age
	Aa5335	Aa5336	Aa5337	Aa5338	Aa5339	Aa5340	Aa5341
Year	Number	Number	Number	Number	Number	Number	Number
1890 [1]	450	274	171	90	38	32	44
1900 [2]	7,258	4,997	3,077	1,733	925	662	1,776
1910	16,061	11,776	8,255	4,665	2,632	1,907	978
1920	21,111	17,418	12,131	7,620	4,728	3,174	1,133
1930	33,520	24,170	17,033	12,214	7,364	5,593	454
1940	43,469	34,641	29,555	18,533	10,166	8,523	—
1950	50,607	42,669	38,186	26,985	20,835	11,354	—
1960	61,255	51,095	46,962	37,067	26,289	24,096	—
1970	69,707	65,850	57,116	44,839	33,786	37,407	—
1980	78,757	70,071	68,548	59,102	44,988	51,875	—
1990	73,867	72,930	71,511	59,073	52,298	71,091	—

[1] Includes 196,823 American Indians not counted in the general enumeration; see text for Table Aa2244–2340.

[2] Combines the populations of the Oklahoma Territory (398,331) and the Indian Territory (392,060).

Sources

See the sources for Table Aa2244–2340.

Documentation

See the text for Table Aa2244–2340.

Oklahoma was originally part of the Louisiana Purchase of 1803. It was part of the Missouri and Arkansas Territories from 1820. From 1828 it had an unofficial title as "Indian Territory," although there was no separate, unified territorial government. Part of the present state was organized as a separate territory in 1890. It became a state in 1907, when the Territory of Oklahoma and the Indian Territory were united.

TABLE Aa5342–5404   Oregon population by race, sex, age, nativity, and urban–rural residence: 1850–1990

Contributed by Michael R. Haines

			Population									
				Race					Residence		Nativity	
	Area	Population density	Total	White	Nonwhite	Black	Other nonwhite		Urban	Rural	Native-born	Foreign-born
	Aa5342	Aa5343	Aa5344	Aa5345	Aa5346	Aa5347	Aa5348		Aa5349	Aa5350	Aa5351	Aa5352
Year	Square miles	Persons per square mile	Number	Number	Number	Number	Number		Number	Number	Number	Number
1850	—	—	12,093	12,038	55	55	—		0	12,093	11,428	665
1860	95,607	0.55	52,465	52,160	305	128	177		2,874	49,591	47,342	5,123
1870	95,607	0.95	90,923	86,929	3,994	346	3,648		8,293	82,630	79,323	11,600
1880	95,607	1.83	174,768	163,075	11,693	487	11,206		25,852	148,916	144,265	30,503
1890 [1]	95,607	3.32	317,704	301,758	12,009	1,186	10,823		88,491	229,213	256,450	57,317
1900	95,607	4.33	413,536	394,582	18,954	1,105	17,849		133,180	280,356	347,788	65,748
1910	95,607	7.04	672,765	655,090	17,675	1,492	16,183		307,060	365,705	559,629	113,136
1920	95,607	8.19	783,389	769,146	14,243	2,144	12,099		390,346	393,043	675,745	107,644
1930	95,607	9.98	953,786	938,597	15,189	2,234	12,955		489,746	464,040	843,346	110,440
1940	96,350	11.31	1,089,684	1,075,731	13,953	2,565	11,388		531,675	558,009	999,491	90,193
1950	96,315	15.80	1,521,341	1,497,128	24,213	11,529	12,684		819,318	702,023	1,431,305	84,875
1960	96,209	18.38	1,768,687	1,732,037	36,650	18,133	18,517		1,100,122	668,565	1,697,361	71,314
1970	96,184	21.74	2,091,385	2,032,079	59,306	26,308	32,998		1,402,704	688,681	2,025,236	66,149
1980	96,184	27.38	2,633,105	2,490,610	142,495	37,060	105,435		1,788,354	844,751	2,525,300	107,805
1990	96,003	29.61	2,842,321	2,636,787	205,534	46,178	159,356		2,003,271	839,050	2,703,014	139,307

Note appears at end of table

TABLE Aa5342-5404   Oregon population by race, sex, age, nativity, and urban-rural residence: 1850-1990
Continued

			Population									
	Sex						Male, by age					
	Male	Female	0	1-4	5-9	10-14	15-19	20-29	20-24	25-29	30-39
	Aa5353	Aa5354	Aa5355	Aa5356	Aa5357	Aa5358	Aa5359	Aa5360	Aa5361	Aa5362	Aa5363
Year	Number	Number	Number	Number	Number	Number	Number	Number	Number	Number	Number
1850	7,332	4,761	159	867	856	692	645	1,948	—	—	1,185
1860	31,591	20,874	1,055	4,030	3,722	2,741	2,236	7,267	—	—	6,033
1870	53,131	37,792	1,289	5,686	6,295	5,893	4,468	—	4,369	4,580	—
1880	103,381	71,387	2,394	9,187	10,769	9,689	9,360	—	10,933	10,249	—
1890 [1]	181,840	131,927	3,532	14,059	17,843	16,359	15,157	—	18,681	19,114	—
1900	232,985	180,551	4,130	16,740	22,078	21,119	20,357	—	20,066	19,661	—
1910	384,265	288,500	6,274	24,367	28,907	28,349	31,796	—	40,225	42,069	—
1920	416,334	367,055	6,913	29,290	37,072	34,933	31,181	—	31,439	33,986	—
1930	499,672	454,114	6,482	28,592	41,276	41,793	41,796	—	39,397	36,417	—
1940	562,689	526,995	8,005	30,832	37,306	41,685	46,379	—	45,254	46,463	—
1950	772,776	748,565	16,704	66,910	67,244	55,528	47,652	—	51,469	57,940	—
1960	879,951	888,736	18,440	75,801	96,046	87,149	63,904	—	46,203	46,587	—
1970	1,023,952	1,067,433	17,335	66,501	99,274	107,664	100,952	—	75,549	68,827	—
1980	1,296,566	1,336,539	22,001	79,866	96,981	103,554	114,745	—	117,847	126,883	—
1990	1,397,073	1,445,248	18,192	84,834	107,486	103,460	97,288	—	96,097	106,931	—

			Population								
					Male, by age						
	30-34	35-39	40-49	40-44	45-49	50-59	50-54	55-59	60-69	60-64	65-69
	Aa5364	Aa5365	Aa5366	Aa5367	Aa5368	Aa5369	Aa5370	Aa5371	Aa5372	Aa5373	Aa5374
Year	Number	Number	Number	Number	Number	Number	Number	Number	Number	Number	Number
1850	—	—	539	—	—	285	—	—	99	—	—
1860	—	—	2,607	—	—	1,257	—	—	505	—	—
1870	4,762	4,776	—	3,851	2,486	—	1,953	1,098	—	780	419
1880	9,145	7,498	—	6,706	5,241	—	5,223	2,870	—	1,888	1,139
1890 [1]	17,927	14,429	—	11,273	8,438	—	8,115	5,652	—	4,634	2,710
1900	19,678	19,974	—	18,052	13,922	—	11,588	8,108	—	6,349	4,772
1910	35,582	31,154	—	27,727	23,750	—	21,432	14,183	—	10,379	7,063
1920	35,111	36,511	—	29,548	26,787	—	23,390	19,319	—	15,987	10,871
1930	36,165	39,140	—	39,017	36,503	—	30,549	24,188	—	20,481	15,872
1940	43,013	39,466	—	39,022	39,281	—	38,139	32,744	—	26,077	19,668
1950	57,930	59,391	—	54,452	48,574	—	44,802	40,426	—	36,027	28,498
1960	52,849	57,624	—	58,012	57,867	—	50,831	43,375	—	37,330	33,125
1970	57,764	52,738	—	57,790	60,407	—	58,563	54,576	—	45,809	35,886
1980	115,103	86,031	—	67,083	58,959	—	60,354	61,999	—	56,047	49,289
1990	119,014	125,067	—	112,168	84,182	—	64,343	56,179	—	56,845	56,463

Notes appear at end of table

(continued)

TABLE Aa5342–5404   Oregon population by race, sex, age, nativity, and urban–rural residence: 1850–1990
Continued

					Population					
	Male, by age					Female, by age				
70–79	70–74	75–79	80 and older	Unknown age	0	1–4	5–9	10–14	15–19	20–29
Aa5375	Aa5376	Aa5377	Aa5378	Aa5379	Aa5380	Aa5381	Aa5382	Aa5383	Aa5384	Aa5385
Year / Number	Number	Number	Number	Number	Number	Number	Number	Number	Number	Number
1850	16	—	—	3	38	147	795	907	669	509	758
1860	120	—	—	17	1	959	3,825	3,597	2,515	2,177	3,367
1870	—	250	99	76	1	1,343	5,490	6,135	5,576	4,154	—
1880	—	625	291	174	—	2,383	8,952	10,518	9,295	7,787	—
1890 [1]	—	1,593	806	486	1,032	3,301	13,345	17,313	16,139	14,591	—
1900	—	3,116	1,586	923	766	3,939	16,332	21,518	20,279	19,449	—
1910	—	4,754	2,937	1,902	1,415	6,115	23,455	28,016	27,427	28,953	—
1920	—	6,814	3,942	2,677	563	6,684	28,431	36,012	34,081	31,594	—
1930	—	11,490	6,217	4,021	276	6,263	27,521	40,244	40,867	41,574	—
1940	—	14,274	8,838	6,243	—	7,579	29,693	35,903	40,302	45,979	—
1950	—	19,085	13,080	7,064	—	16,226	64,075	64,352	52,612	49,086	—
1960	—	25,905	16,631	12,272	—	17,693	73,520	92,179	84,461	66,227	—
1970	—	26,956	18,946	18,415	—	16,534	63,690	95,071	103,620	102,410	—
1980	—	35,402	22,759	21,663	—	21,081	75,098	92,348	98,949	111,123	—
1990	—	45,484	32,987	30,053	—	17,046	81,349	102,289	97,905	92,667	—

					Population					
					Female, by age					
20–24	25–29	30–39	30–34	35–39	40–49	40–44	45–49	50–59	50–54	55–59
Aa5386	Aa5387	Aa5388	Aa5389	Aa5390	Aa5391	Aa5392	Aa5393	Aa5394	Aa5395	Aa5396
Year / Number	Number	Number	Number	Number	Number	Number	Number	Number	Number	Number
1850	—	—	521	—	—	265	—	—	117	—	—
1860	—	—	2,246	—	—	1,218	—	—	657	—	—
1870	3,174	2,765	—	2,247	2,045	—	1,496	1,071	—	840	544
1880	7,290	5,389	—	4,560	4,001	—	3,138	2,570	—	1,992	1,281
1890 [1]	13,924	11,358	—	10,116	7,715	—	6,451	5,145	—	4,148	2,821
1900	17,903	15,219	—	13,778	12,049	—	10,514	7,912	—	6,507	5,078
1910	30,203	27,661	—	23,681	20,888	—	17,682	14,767	—	12,445	8,623
1920	31,710	32,768	—	30,902	28,714	—	24,131	20,533	—	17,681	13,847
1930	38,589	35,636	—	34,937	35,879	—	32,959	29,160	—	24,747	19,681
1940	45,248	44,703	—	40,846	38,099	—	36,696	35,810	—	32,800	27,327
1950	53,601	59,766	—	58,870	57,970	—	51,123	44,654	—	41,316	37,417
1960	50,249	49,059	—	55,083	60,903	—	58,871	56,360	—	48,770	42,067
1970	87,089	70,151	—	57,835	55,094	—	60,160	63,988	—	60,433	56,163
1980	120,013	126,647	—	112,520	84,629	—	66,053	60,327	—	63,965	67,920
1990	93,045	105,050	—	120,549	126,128	—	111,488	83,196	—	64,874	59,832

Note appears at end of table

TABLE Aa5342-5404   Oregon population by race, sex, age, nativity, and urban–rural residence: 1850–1990
Continued

	Population							
	Female, by age							
	60–69	60–64	65–69	70–79	70–74	75–79	80 and older	Unknown age
	Aa5397	Aa5398	Aa5399	Aa5400	Aa5401	Aa5402	Aa5403	Aa5404
Year	Number	Number	Number	Number	Number	Number	Number	Number
1850	40	—	—	5	—	—	1	27
1860	252	—	—	50	—	—	9	2
1870	—	422	236	—	143	78	33	0
1880	—	895	595	—	410	189	142	—
1890 [1]	—	2,282	1,424	—	864	456	346	188
1900	—	3,830	2,730	—	1,739	969	640	166
1910	—	6,777	5,010	—	3,181	1,928	1,378	310
1920	—	11,397	7,567	—	5,195	3,244	2,273	291
1930	—	16,159	12,327	—	8,677	4,922	3,806	166
1940	—	22,305	17,417	—	12,376	7,743	6,169	—
1950	—	32,203	25,957	—	18,010	13,493	7,834	—
1960	—	37,574	33,869	—	27,657	18,239	15,955	—
1970	—	48,599	39,715	—	33,365	25,317	28,199	—
1980	—	61,643	55,894	—	43,969	32,583	41,777	—
1990	—	63,493	66,449	—	56,042	45,559	58,287	—

[1] Includes 3,937 American Indians not counted in the general enumeration; see text for Table Aa2244–2340.

Sources
See the sources for Table Aa2244–2340.

Documentation
See the text for Table Aa2244–2340.

The population in 1850 excludes Clark and Lewis Counties, which were placed in the Territory of Washington in 1853. Oregon became part of the United States officially after conclusion of settlement and treaty with Great Britain in 1846. It became a territory in 1848 and a state in 1859.

TABLE Aa5405-5505   Pennsylvania population by race, sex, age, nativity, and urban–rural residence: 1790–1990
Contributed by Michael R. Haines

			Population									
				Race				Residence		Nativity		
	Area	Population density	Total	White	Nonwhite	Black	Other nonwhite	Urban	Rural	Native-born	Foreign-born
	Aa5405	Aa5406	Aa5407	Aa5408	Aa5409	Aa5410	Aa5411	Aa5412	Aa5413	Aa5414	Aa5415
Year	Square miles	Persons per square mile	Number	Number	Number	Number	Number	Number	Number	Number	Number
1790	44,832	9.67	433,611	423,373	10,238	10,238	—	44,096	390,277	—	—
1800	44,832	13.44	602,365	586,094	16,267	16,267	—	68,354	534,011	—	—
1810	44,832	18.07	810,091	786,804	23,287	23,287	—	103,785	706,306	—	—
1820	44,832	23.41	1,049,458	1,017,094	32,364	30,413	1,951	136,465	912,993	—	—
1830	44,832	30.07	1,348,233	1,309,900	38,333	38,333	—	205,964	1,142,269	—	—
1840	44,832	38.46	1,724,033	1,676,115	47,918	47,918	—	307,977	1,416,056	—	—
1850	44,832	51.57	2,311,786	2,258,160	53,626	53,626	—	544,654	1,767,132	2,008,369	303,417
1860	44,832	64.82	2,906,215	2,849,259	56,956	56,949	7	894,706	2,011,509	2,475,710	430,505
1870	44,832	78.56	3,521,951	3,456,609	65,342	65,294	48	1,312,833	2,209,118	2,976,642	545,309
1880	44,832	95.53	4,282,891	4,197,016	85,875	85,535	340	1,783,378	2,499,513	3,695,062	587,829
1890 [1]	44,832	117.28	5,258,113	5,148,257	109,757	107,596	2,161	2,557,397	2,700,716	4,412,294	845,720
1900	44,832	140.57	6,302,115	6,141,664	160,451	156,845	3,606	3,448,610	2,853,505	5,316,865	985,250
1910	44,832	170.97	7,665,111	7,467,713	197,398	193,919	3,479	4,630,669	3,034,442	6,222,737	1,442,374
1920	44,832	194.50	8,720,017	8,432,726	287,291	284,568	2,723	5,672,453	3,047,564	7,327,460	1,392,557
1930	44,832	214.83	9,631,350	9,196,007	435,343	431,257	4,086	6,533,511	3,097,839	8,390,935	1,240,415
1940	45,045	219.78	9,900,180	9,426,989	473,191	470,172	3,019	6,586,877	3,313,303	8,923,607	976,573
1950	45,045	233.06	10,498,012	9,853,848	644,164	638,485	5,679	7,403,036	3,094,976	9,682,495	783,965
1960	45,025	251.40	11,319,366	10,454,004	865,362	852,750	12,612	8,102,051	3,217,315	10,717,090	603,490
1970	44,966	262.29	11,793,909	10,737,732	1,056,177	1,016,514	39,663	8,436,397	3,357,512	11,347,969	445,895
1980	44,888	264.30	11,863,895	10,652,320	1,211,575	1,046,810	164,765	8,220,851	3,643,044	11,462,879	401,016
1990	44,820	265.10	11,881,643	10,520,201	1,361,442	1,089,795	271,647	8,188,295	3,693,348	11,512,327	369,316

Note appears at end of table

(continued)

TABLE Aa5405–5505   Pennsylvania population by race, sex, age, nativity, and urban–rural residence: 1790–1990
Continued

		Population									
Sex		Male, by age									
Male	Female	0	1–4	5–9	10–14	15–19	20–29	20–24	25–29	30–39
Aa5416	Aa5417	Aa5418	Aa5419	Aa5420	Aa5421	Aa5422	Aa5423	Aa5424	Aa5425	Aa5426
Year	Number	Number	Number	Number	Number	Number	Number	Number	Number	Number	Number
1790	—	—	—	—	—	—	—	—	—	—	—
1800	—	—	—	—	—	—	—	—	—	—	—
1810	—	—	—	—	—	—	—	—	—	—	—
1820	531,507	516,000	—	—	—	—	—	—	—	—	—
1830	684,361	663,872	—	—	—	—	—	—	—	—	—
1840	867,557	856,476	—	—	—	—	—	—	—	—	—
1850	1,168,103	1,143,683	32,566	142,165	160,385	141,533	119,170	214,045	—	—	147,519
1860	1,454,419	1,451,796	44,167	179,253	194,258	171,262	149,531	246,343	—	—	187,514
1870	1,758,499	1,763,452	50,269	198,248	217,464	213,095	180,032	—	164,003	140,509	—
1880	2,136,655	2,146,236	58,635	221,196	265,768	243,266	211,489	—	204,328	172,635	—
1890 [1]	2,666,331	2,591,683	64,467	242,496	298,316	279,872	269,168	—	267,117	236,026	—
1900	3,204,541	3,097,574	78,516	289,300	345,718	314,966	299,530	—	300,469	295,786	—
1910	3,942,206	3,722,905	96,033	350,214	389,242	357,167	364,492	—	386,432	375,468	—
1920	4,429,020	4,290,997	98,881	407,555	475,245	427,052	368,950	—	356,519	374,855	—
1930	4,845,517	4,785,833	85,258	368,596	506,302	495,146	457,601	—	398,373	361,009	—
1940	4,951,207	4,948,973	68,148	300,981	387,066	458,539	484,035	—	443,237	410,690	—
1950	5,170,411	5,327,601	98,994	424,887	436,289	379,064	354,261	—	386,527	420,193	—
1960	5,509,851	5,809,515	119,621	484,530	560,646	511,795	391,968	—	285,718	311,659	—
1970	5,665,414	6,128,495	92,564	379,566	552,052	595,276	538,043	—	395,243	343,228	—
1980	5,682,590	6,181,305	80,893	301,378	412,460	476,210	545,210	—	522,900	468,512	—
1990	5,694,265	6,187,378	71,216	337,916	404,354	386,452	415,738	—	430,315	455,105	—

	Population										
	Male, by age										
30–34	35–39	40–49	40–44	45–49	50–59	50–54	55–59	60–69	60–64	65–69
Aa5427	Aa5428	Aa5429	Aa5430	Aa5431	Aa5432	Aa5433	Aa5434	Aa5435	Aa5436	Aa5437
Year	Number	Number	Number	Number	Number	Number	Number	Number	Number	Number	Number
1790	—	—	—	—	—	—	—	—	—	—	—
1800	—	—	—	—	—	—	—	—	—	—	—
1810	—	—	—	—	—	—	—	—	—	—	—
1820	—	—	—	—	—	—	—	—	—	—	—
1830	—	—	—	—	—	—	—	—	—	—	—
1840	—	—	—	—	—	—	—	—	—	—	—
1850	—	—	100,029	—	—	60,099	—	—	32,558	—	—
1860	—	—	132,039	—	—	81,157	—	—	46,093	—	—
1870	114,523	104,208	—	85,805	81,190	—	67,808	44,865	—	38,500	25,023
1880	147,258	134,399	—	108,417	93,798	—	81,161	60,373	—	52,118	35,719
1890 [1]	208,461	175,193	—	145,874	123,975	—	102,159	72,956	—	64,021	45,956
1900	262,310	232,724	—	196,164	155,746	—	128,954	96,724	—	75,705	53,603
1910	327,381	299,667	—	248,738	205,059	—	168,256	119,184	—	93,991	68,647
1920	351,094	345,993	—	282,378	264,229	—	209,250	152,795	—	122,758	82,915
1930	352,764	368,123	—	329,520	291,060	—	244,215	191,059	—	150,748	108,248
1940	372,292	343,267	—	330,542	321,829	—	288,921	233,573	—	185,269	141,080
1950	403,532	390,958	—	355,280	314,855	—	297,280	267,267	—	226,188	175,605
1960	370,465	394,703	—	382,518	361,294	—	317,503	275,427	—	234,391	201,204
1970	293,437	300,488	—	355,351	370,011	—	351,050	312,904	—	259,432	194,556
1980	416,215	330,811	—	284,324	286,858	—	329,850	332,033	—	289,152	235,802
1990	489,019	456,698	—	403,648	318,489	—	266,989	260,268	—	279,697	260,393

Note appears at end of table

TABLE Aa5405–5505   Pennsylvania population by race, sex, age, nativity, and urban–rural residence: 1790–1990
Continued

	Population										
	Male, by age					Female, by age					
	70–79	70–74	75–79	80 and older	Unknown age	0	1–4	5–9	10–14	15–19	20–29
	Aa5438	Aa5439	Aa5440	Aa5441	Aa5442	Aa5443	Aa5444	Aa5445	Aa5446	Aa5447	Aa5448
Year	Number	Number	Number	Number	Number	Number	Number	Number	Number	Number	Number
1790	—	—	—	—	—	—	—	—	—	—	—
1800	—	—	—	—	—	—	—	—	—	—	—
1810	—	—	—	—	—	—	—	—	—	—	—
1820	—	—	—	—	—	—	—	—	—	—	—
1830	—	—	—	—	—	—	—	—	—	—	—
1840	—	—	—	—	—	—	—	—	—	—	—
1850	13,485	—	—	3,850	699	31,765	138,901	157,841	136,379	127,458	212,588
1860	18,023	—	—	4,761	18	42,704	176,115	191,094	167,025	160,357	263,931
1870	—	17,645	8,954	6,358	0	48,992	194,832	214,337	209,450	188,319	—
1880	—	23,751	13,404	8,940	—	57,169	215,174	261,734	237,434	220,539	—
1890 [1]	—	32,837	17,604	12,255	7,578	62,107	235,095	292,399	272,484	271,988	—
1900	—	36,348	21,016	13,168	7,794	77,262	285,053	340,887	309,275	299,553	—
1910	—	44,744	24,706	15,784	7,001	93,469	344,554	383,849	354,398	357,987	—
1920	—	53,946	31,017	18,851	4,737	96,936	402,093	469,985	424,689	373,787	—
1930	—	72,077	38,805	23,882	2,731	82,188	359,801	498,145	489,618	460,906	—
1940	—	95,185	52,628	33,925	—	66,231	290,705	375,747	448,169	483,055	—
1950	—	117,565	80,947	40,719	—	95,429	407,135	421,769	365,686	368,400	—
1960	—	148,686	90,825	66,898	—	115,487	468,316	541,111	493,584	407,568	—
1970	—	146,346	99,287	86,580	—	89,019	365,038	530,703	573,278	537,387	—
1980	—	166,668	104,968	98,346	—	77,434	287,753	392,691	455,681	535,400	—
1990	—	199,559	137,547	120,862	—	67,992	319,934	383,947	368,709	402,320	—

	Population										
	Female, by age										
	20–24	25–29	30–39	30–34	35–39	40–49	40–44	45–49	50–59	50–54	55–59
	Aa5449	Aa5450	Aa5451	Aa5452	Aa5453	Aa5454	Aa5455	Aa5456	Aa5457	Aa5458	Aa5459
Year	Number	Number	Number	Number	Number	Number	Number	Number	Number	Number	Number
1790	—	—	—	—	—	—	—	—	—	—	—
1800	—	—	—	—	—	—	—	—	—	—	—
1810	—	—	—	—	—	—	—	—	—	—	—
1820	—	—	—	—	—	—	—	—	—	—	—
1830	—	—	—	—	—	—	—	—	—	—	—
1840	—	—	—	—	—	—	—	—	—	—	—
1850	—	—	136,864	—	—	92,040	—	—	57,432	—	—
1860	—	—	180,741	—	—	121,726	—	—	77,180	—	—
1870	174,134	144,828	—	117,169	105,044	—	89,199	72,419	—	62,720	43,075
1880	218,958	174,534	—	145,725	133,228	—	109,801	92,196	—	81,721	58,595
1890 [1]	266,272	223,584	—	192,655	161,090	—	136,166	118,026	—	100,819	73,850
1900	303,627	279,177	—	237,053	208,973	—	175,546	143,252	—	121,580	96,065
1910	363,921	331,214	—	285,350	263,819	—	218,703	183,723	—	156,713	114,450
1920	373,326	369,046	—	326,344	306,051	—	256,611	226,857	—	190,459	144,479
1930	415,535	371,276	—	350,656	354,460	—	304,954	268,892	—	229,338	183,322
1940	456,581	421,605	—	383,034	350,630	—	328,773	312,749	—	273,427	221,160
1950	421,471	449,186	—	431,144	408,497	—	365,878	323,258	—	302,721	268,954
1960	329,581	333,918	—	397,175	427,647	—	410,618	377,994	—	333,548	293,427
1970	457,182	362,595	—	315,937	325,778	—	386,170	406,563	—	387,701	345,782
1980	536,915	476,539	—	431,632	351,472	—	307,465	313,399	—	365,905	380,041
1990	432,692	465,112	—	503,220	466,320	—	418,201	337,594	—	290,773	292,110

Notes appear at end of table

(continued)

TABLE Aa5405–5505   Pennsylvania population by race, sex, age, nativity, and urban–rural residence: 1790–1990
Continued

Population

				Female, by age				White		Male, by age
	60–69	60–64	65–69	70–79	70–74	75–79	80 and older	Unknown age	Male	Female	0–4
	Aa5460	Aa5461	Aa5462	Aa5463	Aa5464	Aa5465	Aa5466	Aa5467	Aa5468	Aa5469	Aa5470
Year	Number	Number	Number	Number	Number	Number	Number	Number	Number	Number	Number
1790	—	—	—	—	—	—	—	—	217,487	205,886	—
1800	—	—	—	—	—	—	—	—	301,467	284,627	—
1810	—	—	—	—	—	—	—	—	401,466	385,338	—
1820	—	—	—	—	—	—	—	—	516,618	500,476	—
1830	—	—	—	—	—	—	—	—	665,812	644,088	117,853
1840	—	—	—	—	—	—	—	—	844,770	831,345	149,480
1850	33,014	—	—	14,226	—	—	4,699	476	—	—	—
1860	45,669	—	—	19,470	—	—	5,777	7	—	—	—
1870	—	37,794	24,819	—	18,423	9,844	8,054	0	—	—	—
1880	—	50,977	36,286	—	25,305	15,065	11,795	—	—	—	—
1890 [1]	—	65,695	46,515	—	33,362	19,581	15,678	4,317	—	—	—
1900	—	78,436	57,547	—	39,655	23,538	16,942	4,153	—	—	—
1910	—	94,930	71,992	—	49,504	29,255	21,286	3,788	—	—	—
1920	—	119,874	84,455	—	58,585	37,371	27,163	2,886	—	—	—
1930	—	149,133	110,325	—	76,810	44,805	33,326	2,343	—	—	—
1940	—	182,457	144,640	—	102,403	60,917	46,690	—	—	—	—
1950	—	226,084	186,919	—	130,811	97,992	56,267	—	—	—	—
1960	—	258,629	229,321	—	176,855	115,049	99,687	—	—	—	—
1970	—	300,005	246,773	—	202,440	147,096	149,048	—	—	—	—
1980	—	343,829	301,243	—	240,352	177,032	206,522	—	—	—	—
1990	—	327,709	330,164	—	279,905	223,759	276,917	—	—	—	—

Population

White

					Male, by age						Female, by age	
	5–9	10–14	15–19	20–29	30–39	40–49	50–59	60–69	70–79	80 and older	0–4	5–9
	Aa5471	Aa5472	Aa5473	Aa5474	Aa5475	Aa5476	Aa5477	Aa5478	Aa5479	Aa5480	Aa5481	Aa5482
Year	Number	Number	Number	Number	Number	Number	Number	Number	Number	Number	Number	Number
1790	—	—	—	—	—	—	—	—	—	—	—	—
1800	—	—	—	—	—	—	—	—	—	—	—	—
1810	—	—	—	—	—	—	—	—	—	—	—	—
1820	—	—	—	—	—	—	—	—	—	—	—	—
1830	96,199	82,375	73,113	121,359	75,172	46,600	28,032	16,085	6,979	2,045	111,947	92,719
1840	117,351	101,522	89,825	152,624	99,421	64,366	37,933	20,268	9,224	2,756	141,786	115,570
1850	—	—	—	—	—	—	—	—	—	—	—	—
1860	—	—	—	—	—	—	—	—	—	—	—	—
1870	—	—	—	—	—	—	—	—	—	—	—	—
1880	—	—	—	—	—	—	—	—	—	—	—	—
1890 [1]	—	—	—	—	—	—	—	—	—	—	—	—
1900	—	—	—	—	—	—	—	—	—	—	—	—
1910	—	—	—	—	—	—	—	—	—	—	—	—
1920	—	—	—	—	—	—	—	—	—	—	—	—
1930	—	—	—	—	—	—	—	—	—	—	—	—
1940	—	—	—	—	—	—	—	—	—	—	—	—
1950	—	—	—	—	—	—	—	—	—	—	—	—
1960	—	—	—	—	—	—	—	—	—	—	—	—
1970	—	—	—	—	—	—	—	—	—	—	—	—
1980	—	—	—	—	—	—	—	—	—	—	—	—
1990	—	—	—	—	—	—	—	—	—	—	—	—

Note appears at end of table

TABLE Aa5405–5505   Pennsylvania population by race, sex, age, nativity, and urban–rural residence: 1790–1990
Continued

	Population											
	White											
	Female, by age									Male, by age		
	10–14	15–19	20–29	30–39	40–49	50–59	60–69	70–79	80 and older	0–9	10–15	16–25
	Aa5483	Aa5484	Aa5485	Aa5486	Aa5487	Aa5488	Aa5489	Aa5490	Aa5491	Aa5492	Aa5493	Aa5494
Year	Number	Number	Number	Number	Number	Number	Number	Number	Number	Number	Number	Number
1790	—	—	—	—	—	—	—	—	—	—	—	—
1800	—	—	—	—	—	—	—	—	—	103,226	46,161	54,262
1810	—	—	—	—	—	—	—	—	—	138,464	62,506	74,203
1820	—	—	—	—	—	—	—	—	—	175,381	77,050	102,550
1830	80,087	75,976	115,898	69,604	44,485	27,882	16,221	7,084	2,185	—	—	—
1840	97,972	96,692	153,803	92,864	60,838	37,965	21,007	9,783	3,065	—	—	—
1850	—	—	—	—	—	—	—	—	—	—	—	—
1860	—	—	—	—	—	—	—	—	—	—	—	—
1870	—	—	—	—	—	—	—	—	—	—	—	—
1880	—	—	—	—	—	—	—	—	—	—	—	—
1890 [1]	—	—	—	—	—	—	—	—	—	—	—	—
1900	—	—	—	—	—	—	—	—	—	—	—	—
1910	—	—	—	—	—	—	—	—	—	—	—	—
1920	—	—	—	—	—	—	—	—	—	—	—	—
1930	—	—	—	—	—	—	—	—	—	—	—	—
1940	—	—	—	—	—	—	—	—	—	—	—	—
1950	—	—	—	—	—	—	—	—	—	—	—	—
1960	—	—	—	—	—	—	—	—	—	—	—	—
1970	—	—	—	—	—	—	—	—	—	—	—	—
1980	—	—	—	—	—	—	—	—	—	—	—	—
1990	—	—	—	—	—	—	—	—	—	—	—	—

	Population											
	White											
	Male, by age		Female, by age					Male, by age		Female, by age	
	26–44	45 and older	0–9	10–15	16–25	26–44	45 and older	0–15	16 and older	0–15	16 and older
	Aa5495	Aa5496	Aa5497	Aa5498	Aa5499	Aa5500	Aa5501	Aa5502	Aa5503	Aa5504	Aa5505
Year	Number	Number	Number	Number	Number	Number	Number	Number	Number	Number	Number
1790	—	—	—	—	—	—	—	106,928	110,559	103,746	102,140
1800	59,333	38,485	99,624	43,789	53,974	53,846	33,394	—	—	—	—
1810	74,193	52,100	131,769	60,943	75,960	70,826	45,840	—	—	—	—
1820	97,144	64,493	166,710	78,425	101,404	94,345	59,592	—	—	—	—
1830	—	—	—	—	—	—	—	—	—	—	—
1840	—	—	—	—	—	—	—	—	—	—	—
1850	—	—	—	—	—	—	—	—	—	—	—
1860	—	—	—	—	—	—	—	—	—	—	—
1870	—	—	—	—	—	—	—	—	—	—	—
1880	—	—	—	—	—	—	—	—	—	—	—
1890 [1]	—	—	—	—	—	—	—	—	—	—	—
1900	—	—	—	—	—	—	—	—	—	—	—
1910	—	—	—	—	—	—	—	—	—	—	—
1920	—	—	—	—	—	—	—	—	—	—	—
1930	—	—	—	—	—	—	—	—	—	—	—
1940	—	—	—	—	—	—	—	—	—	—	—
1950	—	—	—	—	—	—	—	—	—	—	—
1960	—	—	—	—	—	—	—	—	—	—	—
1970	—	—	—	—	—	—	—	—	—	—	—
1980	—	—	—	—	—	—	—	—	—	—	—
1990	—	—	—	—	—	—	—	—	—	—	—

[1] Includes ninety-nine American Indians not counted in the general enumeration; see text for Table Aa2244–2340.

Sources

See the sources for Table Aa2244–2340.

Documentation

See the text for Table Aa2244–2340.

Pennsylvania was one of the original thirteen states, admitted to the Union in 1788.

TABLE Aa5506–5606   Rhode Island population by race, sex, age, nativity, and urban–rural residence: 1790–1990

Contributed by Michael R. Haines

			Population									
				Race				Residence		Nativity	
Year	Area	Population density	Total	White	Nonwhite	Black	Other nonwhite	Urban	Rural	Native-born	Foreign-born
	Aa5506	Aa5507	Aa5508	Aa5509	Aa5510	Aa5511	Aa5512	Aa5513	Aa5514	Aa5515	Aa5516
	Square miles	Persons per square mile	Number	Number	Number	Number	Number	Number	Number	Number	Number
1790	1,067	64.77	69,112	64,670	4,442	4,442	—	13,096	55,729	—	—
1800	1,067	64.78	69,122	65,437	3,685	3,685	—	14,353	54,769	—	—
1810	1,067	72.10	76,931	73,314	3,717	3,717	—	17,978	58,953	—	—
1820	1,067	77.84	83,059	79,413	3,646	3,602	44	19,086	63,973	—	—
1830	1,067	91.10	97,199	93,621	3,578	3,578	—	30,372	66,827	—	—
1840	1,067	102.00	108,830	105,587	3,243	3,243	—	47,662	61,168	—	—
1850	1,067	138.28	147,545	143,875	3,670	3,670	—	82,084	65,461	123,643	23,902
1860	1,067	163.66	174,620	170,649	3,971	3,952	19	110,535	64,085	137,226	37,394
1870	1,067	203.70	217,353	212,219	5,134	4,980	154	162,107	55,246	161,957	55,396
1880	1,067	259.17	276,531	269,939	6,592	6,488	104	226,618	49,913	202,538	73,993
1890	1,067	323.81	345,506	337,859	7,647	7,393	254	294,843	50,663	239,201	106,305
1900	1,067	401.65	428,556	419,050	9,506	9,092	414	378,471	50,085	294,037	134,519
1910	1,067	508.54	542,610	532,492	10,118	9,529	589	493,938	48,672	363,469	179,141
1920	1,067	566.45	604,397	593,980	10,417	10,036	381	555,146	49,251	429,208	175,189
1930	1,067	644.33	687,497	677,026	10,471	9,913	558	635,429	52,068	515,568	171,929
1940	1,058	674.24	713,346	701,805	11,541	11,024	517	653,383	59,963	574,468	138,878
1950	1,058	748.48	791,896	777,015	14,881	13,903	978	667,212	124,684	674,775	113,395
1960	1,049	819.34	859,488	838,712	20,776	18,332	2,444	742,897	116,591	773,514	85,974
1970	1,049	902.50	946,725	914,757	31,968	25,338	6,630	824,930	121,795	874,470	74,374
1980	1,055	897.78	947,154	896,692	50,462	27,584	22,878	824,004	123,150	863,153	84,001
1990	1,045	960.25	1,003,464	917,375	86,089	38,861	47,228	863,381	140,083	908,376	95,088

		Population										
	Sex		Male, by age									
Year	Male	Female	0	1–4	5–9	10–14	15–19	20–29	20–24	25–29	30–39
	Aa5517	Aa5518	Aa5519	Aa5520	Aa5521	Aa5522	Aa5523	Aa5524	Aa5525	Aa5526	Aa5527
	Number	Number	Number	Number	Number	Number	Number	Number	Number	Number	Number
1790	—	—	—	—	—	—	—	—	—	—	—
1800	—	—	—	—	—	—	—	—	—	—	—
1810	—	—	—	—	—	—	—	—	—	—	—
1820	40,097	42,918	—	—	—	—	—	—	—	—	—
1830	46,884	50,315	—	—	—	—	—	—	—	—	—
1840	52,776	56,054	—	—	—	—	—	—	—	—	—
1850	72,078	75,467	1,777	7,103	7,786	7,524	7,325	15,015	—	—	10,622
1860	84,133	90,487	2,163	8,184	9,009	8,797	8,535	15,727	—	—	12,287
1870	104,756	112,597	2,494	9,223	10,215	11,387	10,494	—	10,343	9,134	—
1880	133,030	143,501	3,073	11,276	13,695	13,137	12,301	—	13,360	11,655	—
1890	168,025	177,481	3,548	12,482	16,040	15,918	16,827	—	17,584	15,196	—
1900	210,516	218,040	4,695	17,079	20,038	18,212	19,505	—	20,419	20,261	—
1910	270,314	272,296	5,918	20,953	24,222	23,490	26,522	—	26,977	24,878	—
1920	297,524	306,873	6,406	24,889	29,113	26,573	26,198	—	24,826	25,137	—
1930	335,372	352,125	5,476	24,641	34,113	32,468	30,933	—	26,834	24,560	—
1940	349,404	363,942	4,580	19,183	25,869	30,582	34,742	—	31,515	28,511	—
1950	390,583	401,313	7,349	32,040	30,435	24,815	28,462	—	35,431	34,199	—
1960	421,845	437,643	9,326	36,329	40,783	37,561	33,295	—	29,855	23,579	—
1970	464,291	482,434	7,712	31,166	43,903	44,935	44,181	—	49,076	30,154	—
1980	451,251	495,903	6,215	22,672	31,458	37,965	44,771	—	44,292	37,646	—
1990	481,496	521,968	5,977	28,407	32,916	30,261	35,764	—	42,946	42,980	—

TABLE Aa5506–5606   Rhode Island population by race, sex, age, nativity, and urban–rural residence: 1790–1990
Continued

Population

	Male, by age										
	30–34	35–39	40–49	40–44	45–49	50–59	50–54	55–59	60–69	60–64	65–69
	Aa5528	Aa5529	Aa5530	Aa5531	Aa5532	Aa5533	Aa5534	Aa5535	Aa5536	Aa5537	Aa5538
Year	Number	Number	Number	Number	Number	Number	Number	Number	Number	Number	Number
1790	—	—	—	—	—	—	—	—	—	—	—
1800	—	—	—	—	—	—	—	—	—	—	—
1810	—	—	—	—	—	—	—	—	—	—	—
1820	—	—	—	—	—	—	—	—	—	—	—
1830	—	—	—	—	—	—	—	—	—	—	—
1840	—	—	—	—	—	—	—	—	—	—	—
1850	—	—	6,816	—	—	4,130	—	—	2,501	—	—
1860	—	—	8,914	—	—	5,505	—	—	3,159	—	—
1870	7,605	6,988	—	6,045	5,665	—	4,737	3,253	—	2,811	1,817
1880	10,201	9,477	—	7,868	6,769	—	5,913	4,416	—	3,876	2,597
1890	13,484	11,813	—	10,381	9,060	—	7,523	5,298	—	4,667	3,272
1900	18,127	15,977	—	13,364	11,276	—	9,452	7,015	—	5,599	3,823
1910	22,573	21,055	—	18,466	15,029	—	12,460	8,994	—	7,083	5,018
1920	23,131	22,822	—	19,794	18,895	—	15,726	11,288	—	8,901	6,121
1930	24,488	25,422	—	22,843	20,614	—	18,035	14,698	—	12,021	8,205
1940	25,937	24,874	—	24,410	23,594	—	20,768	16,925	—	13,649	10,599
1950	30,733	28,530	—	25,484	23,306	—	22,117	20,293	—	16,677	12,647
1960	28,030	30,483	—	27,640	25,981	—	22,647	20,473	—	17,634	15,262
1970	23,586	23,374	—	27,220	28,677	—	26,266	23,523	—	19,278	14,947
1980	34,583	26,577	—	21,513	21,438	—	25,210	26,182	—	22,460	18,346
1990	43,387	38,891	—	34,329	25,984	—	20,597	19,842	—	21,571	20,821

Population

	Male, by age					Female, by age					
	70–79	70–74	75–79	80 and older	Unknown age	0	1–4	5–9	10–14	15–19	20–29
	Aa5539	Aa5540	Aa5541	Aa5542	Aa5543	Aa5544	Aa5545	Aa5546	Aa5547	Aa5548	Aa5549
Year	Number	Number	Number	Number	Number	Number	Number	Number	Number	Number	Number
1790	—	—	—	—	—	—	—	—	—	—	—
1800	—	—	—	—	—	—	—	—	—	—	—
1810	—	—	—	—	—	—	—	—	—	—	—
1820	—	—	—	—	—	—	—	—	—	—	—
1830	—	—	—	—	—	—	—	—	—	—	—
1840	—	—	—	—	—	—	—	—	—	—	—
1850	1,090	—	—	373	16	1,833	7,003	7,805	7,562	7,991	15,561
1860	1,463	—	—	390	0	2,227	8,060	9,133	8,549	9,332	18,048
1870	—	1,288	683	574	0	2,426	9,145	10,099	11,178	11,354	—
1880	—	1,752	962	702	—	3,059	11,177	13,790	12,981	13,484	—
1890	—	2,250	1,374	947	361	3,342	12,442	15,693	15,960	17,984	—
1900	—	2,530	1,531	1,009	604	4,673	17,005	20,242	18,527	19,787	—
1910	—	3,356	1,706	1,224	390	5,810	21,417	24,225	23,524	25,476	—
1920	—	3,886	2,240	1,427	151	6,340	24,721	29,140	27,263	25,457	—
1930	—	5,260	2,844	1,798	119	5,521	23,986	33,507	32,276	31,481	—
1940	—	7,287	3,883	2,496	—	4,421	18,433	24,690	30,042	33,439	—
1950	—	8,790	6,188	3,087	—	7,005	30,418	29,973	24,006	25,473	—
1960	—	11,149	6,668	5,150	—	9,011	35,105	39,444	36,269	29,912	—
1970	—	11,498	7,892	6,903	—	7,384	29,773	41,971	43,354	41,499	—
1980	—	12,994	8,619	8,310	—	5,860	21,945	30,007	36,205	45,002	—
1990	—	15,773	10,964	10,086	—	5,691	26,894	30,815	29,145	35,098	—

(continued)

TABLE Aa5506–5606   Rhode Island population by race, sex, age, nativity, and urban–rural residence: 1790–1990
Continued

	Population										
	Female, by age										
	20–24	25–29	30–39	30–34	35–39	40–49	40–44	45–49	50–59	50–54	55–59
	Aa5550	Aa5551	Aa5552	Aa5553	Aa5554	Aa5555	Aa5556	Aa5557	Aa5558	Aa5559	Aa5560
Year	Number	Number	Number	Number	Number	Number	Number	Number	Number	Number	Number
1790	—	—	—	—	—	—	—	—	—	—	—
1800	—	—	—	—	—	—	—	—	—	—	—
1810	—	—	—	—	—	—	—	—	—	—	—
1820	—	—	—	—	—	—	—	—	—	—	—
1830	—	—	—	—	—	—	—	—	—	—	—
1840	—	—	—	—	—	—	—	—	—	—	—
1850	—	—	10,500	—	—	7,211	—	—	4,793	—	—
1860	—	—	12,976	—	—	9,193	—	—	6,233	—	—
1870	11,670	10,241	—	8,728	7,894	—	6,834	5,577	—	4,903	3,476
1880	15,072	13,054	—	11,095	10,174	—	8,799	7,400	—	6,610	4,560
1890	19,129	16,547	—	14,159	12,486	—	11,032	9,282	—	8,421	5,975
1900	22,399	21,451	—	17,880	15,946	—	13,813	11,422	—	9,697	7,610
1910	26,661	25,247	—	22,140	21,047	—	18,081	14,747	—	12,837	9,271
1920	27,512	26,530	—	24,087	23,122	—	20,104	18,548	—	15,904	11,740
1930	29,843	27,130	—	26,886	26,677	—	23,725	21,567	—	19,027	15,588
1940	31,929	30,731	—	28,424	26,742	—	26,014	24,395	—	21,627	17,906
1950	31,324	34,161	—	31,599	30,388	—	27,812	25,183	—	24,354	21,675
1960	24,297	23,725	—	29,384	31,935	—	29,969	27,908	—	25,425	22,965
1970	38,887	29,165	—	23,690	24,091	—	29,017	30,880	—	29,332	26,745
1980	45,939	38,569	—	35,237	27,816	—	22,957	23,270	—	27,886	29,566
1990	42,134	42,872	—	44,385	39,685	—	34,712	27,399	—	22,445	22,235

	Population									White	
	Female, by age										Male, by age
	60–69	60–64	65–69	70–79	70–74	75–79	80 and older	Unknown age	Male	Female	0–4
	Aa5561	Aa5562	Aa5563	Aa5564	Aa5565	Aa5566	Aa5567	Aa5568	Aa5569	Aa5570	Aa5571
Year	Number	Number	Number	Number	Number	Number	Number	Number	Number	Number	Number
1790	—	—	—	—	—	—	—	—	31,801	32,869	—
1800	—	—	—	—	—	—	—	—	31,858	33,579	—
1810	—	—	—	—	—	—	—	—	35,843	37,471	—
1820	—	—	—	—	—	—	—	—	38,492	40,921	—
1830	—	—	—	—	—	—	—	—	45,333	48,288	6,733
1840	—	—	—	—	—	—	—	—	51,362	54,225	7,121
1850	3,073	—	—	1,561	—	—	573	1	—	—	—
1860	4,039	—	—	1,991	—	—	706	0	—	—	—
1870	—	3,320	2,153	—	1,714	980	905	0	—	—	—
1880	—	4,228	2,993	—	2,271	1,401	1,353	—	—	—	—
1890	—	5,185	3,704	—	2,659	1,685	1,506	290	—	—	—
1900	—	6,373	4,372	—	3,089	1,867	1,577	310	—	—	—
1910	—	7,624	5,649	—	3,958	2,280	1,829	473	—	—	—
1920	—	9,747	6,738	—	4,653	2,840	2,285	142	—	—	—
1930	—	12,963	9,193	—	6,361	3,597	2,695	102	—	—	—
1940	—	15,130	12,548	—	8,657	4,914	3,900	—	—	—	—
1950	—	18,236	15,440	—	10,914	8,500	4,852	—	—	—	—
1960	—	20,983	18,468	—	14,566	9,608	8,669	—	—	—	—
1970	—	23,954	20,304	—	17,167	12,376	12,845	—	—	—	—
1980	—	26,991	24,068	—	20,154	15,272	19,159	—	—	—	—
1990	—	25,555	26,389	—	22,633	18,705	25,176	—	—	—	—

TABLE Aa5506–5606   Rhode Island population by race, sex, age, nativity, and urban–rural residence: 1790–1990
Continued

	Population										
	White										
	Male, by age										Female, by age
	5–9	10–14	15–19	20–29	30–39	40–49	50–59	60–69	70–79	80 and older	0–4
	Aa5572	Aa5573	Aa5574	Aa5575	Aa5576	Aa5577	Aa5578	Aa5579	Aa5580	Aa5581	Aa5582
Year	Number	Number	Number	Number	Number	Number	Number	Number	Number	Number	Number
1790	—	—	—	—	—	—	—	—	—	—	—
1800	—	—	—	—	—	—	—	—	—	—	—
1810	—	—	—	—	—	—	—	—	—	—	—
1820	—	—	—	—	—	—	—	—	—	—	—
1830	5,786	5,400	5,354	8,425	5,379	3,512	2,157	1,444	854	289	6,623
1840	5,947	5,969	5,659	9,878	6,798	4,452	2,799	1,570	862	307	6,504
1850	—	—	—	—	—	—	—	—	—	—	—
1860	—	—	—	—	—	—	—	—	—	—	—
1870	—	—	—	—	—	—	—	—	—	—	—
1880	—	—	—	—	—	—	—	—	—	—	—
1890	—	—	—	—	—	—	—	—	—	—	—
1900	—	—	—	—	—	—	—	—	—	—	—
1910	—	—	—	—	—	—	—	—	—	—	—
1920	—	—	—	—	—	—	—	—	—	—	—
1930	—	—	—	—	—	—	—	—	—	—	—
1940	—	—	—	—	—	—	—	—	—	—	—
1950	—	—	—	—	—	—	—	—	—	—	—
1960	—	—	—	—	—	—	—	—	—	—	—
1970	—	—	—	—	—	—	—	—	—	—	—
1980	—	—	—	—	—	—	—	—	—	—	—
1990	—	—	—	—	—	—	—	—	—	—	—

	Population											
	White											
	Female, by age										Male, by age	
	5–9	10–14	15–19	20–29	30–39	40–49	50–59	60–69	70–79	80 and older	0–9	10–15
	Aa5583	Aa5584	Aa5585	Aa5586	Aa5587	Aa5588	Aa5589	Aa5590	Aa5591	Aa5592	Aa5593	Aa5594
Year	Number	Number	Number	Number	Number	Number	Number	Number	Number	Number	Number	Number
1790	—	—	—	—	—	—	—	—	—	—	—	—
1800	—	—	—	—	—	—	—	—	—	—	9,945	5,352
1810	—	—	—	—	—	—	—	—	—	—	10,735	5,554
1820	—	—	—	—	—	—	—	—	—	—	11,530	5,860
1830	5,642	5,213	5,584	9,203	5,756	4,024	2,826	1,939	1,058	420	—	—
1840	5,812	5,710	6,030	10,833	7,138	4,891	3,430	2,176	1,196	505	—	—
1850	—	—	—	—	—	—	—	—	—	—	—	—
1860	—	—	—	—	—	—	—	—	—	—	—	—
1870	—	—	—	—	—	—	—	—	—	—	—	—
1880	—	—	—	—	—	—	—	—	—	—	—	—
1890	—	—	—	—	—	—	—	—	—	—	—	—
1900	—	—	—	—	—	—	—	—	—	—	—	—
1910	—	—	—	—	—	—	—	—	—	—	—	—
1920	—	—	—	—	—	—	—	—	—	—	—	—
1930	—	—	—	—	—	—	—	—	—	—	—	—
1940	—	—	—	—	—	—	—	—	—	—	—	—
1950	—	—	—	—	—	—	—	—	—	—	—	—
1960	—	—	—	—	—	—	—	—	—	—	—	—
1970	—	—	—	—	—	—	—	—	—	—	—	—
1980	—	—	—	—	—	—	—	—	—	—	—	—
1990	—	—	—	—	—	—	—	—	—	—	—	—

(continued)

TABLE Aa5506–5606   Rhode Island population by race, sex, age, nativity, and urban–rural residence: 1790–1990
Continued

	Population											
	White											
	Male, by age			Female, by age					Male, by age		Female, by age	
	16–25	26–44	45 and older	0–9	10–15	16–25	26–44	45 and older	0–15	16 and older	0–15	16 and older
	Aa5595	Aa5596	Aa5597	Aa5598	Aa5599	Aa5600	Aa5601	Aa5602	Aa5603	Aa5604	Aa5605	Aa5606
Year	Number	Number	Number	Number	Number	Number	Number	Number	Number	Number	Number	Number
1790	—	—	—	—	—	—	—	—	15,745	16,056	14,242	18,627
1800	5,889	5,785	4,887	9,524	5,026	6,463	6,919	5,647	—	—	—	—
1810	7,250	6,765	5,539	10,555	5,389	7,520	7,635	6,372	—	—	—	—
1820	7,596	7,618	5,888	10,917	5,769	8,407	8,671	7,157	—	—	—	—
1830	—	—	—	—	—	—	—	—	—	—	—	—
1840	—	—	—	—	—	—	—	—	—	—	—	—
1850	—	—	—	—	—	—	—	—	—	—	—	—
1860	—	—	—	—	—	—	—	—	—	—	—	—
1870	—	—	—	—	—	—	—	—	—	—	—	—
1880	—	—	—	—	—	—	—	—	—	—	—	—
1890	—	—	—	—	—	—	—	—	—	—	—	—
1900	—	—	—	—	—	—	—	—	—	—	—	—
1910	—	—	—	—	—	—	—	—	—	—	—	—
1920	—	—	—	—	—	—	—	—	—	—	—	—
1930	—	—	—	—	—	—	—	—	—	—	—	—
1940	—	—	—	—	—	—	—	—	—	—	—	—
1950	—	—	—	—	—	—	—	—	—	—	—	—
1960	—	—	—	—	—	—	—	—	—	—	—	—
1970	—	—	—	—	—	—	—	—	—	—	—	—
1980	—	—	—	—	—	—	—	—	—	—	—	—
1990	—	—	—	—	—	—	—	—	—	—	—	—

Sources
See the text for Table Aa2244–2340.

Documentation
See the text for Table Aa2244–2340.

Rhode Island was one of the original thirteen states, admitted to the Union in 1790.

TABLE Aa5607–5707 South Carolina population by race, sex, age, nativity, and urban–rural residence: 1790–1990

Contributed by Michael R. Haines

				Population								
					Race				Residence		Nativity	
	Area	Population density	Total	White	Nonwhite	Black	Other nonwhite	Urban	Rural	Native-born	Foreign-born
	Aa5607	Aa5608	Aa5609	Aa5610	Aa5611	Aa5612	Aa5613	Aa5614	Aa5615	Aa5616	Aa5617
Year	Square miles	Persons per square mile	Number	Number	Number	Number	Number	Number	Number	Number	Number
1790	30,495	8.17	249,073	140,178	108,895	108,895	—	16,359	232,714	—	—
1800	30,495	11.33	345,591	196,255	149,336	149,336	—	18,824	326,767	—	—
1810	30,495	13.61	415,115	214,196	200,919	200,919	—	24,711	390,404	—	—
1820	30,495	16.49	502,741	237,440	265,301	265,301	0	24,780	477,961	—	—
1830	30,495	19.06	581,185	257,863	323,322	323,322	—	33,599	547,586	—	—
1840	30,495	19.49	594,398	259,084	335,314	335,314	—	33,601	560,797	—	—
1850	30,495	21.92	668,507	274,563	393,944	393,944	—	49,045	619,462	659,800	8,707
1860	30,495	23.08	703,708	291,300	412,408	412,320	88	48,574	655,134	693,722	9,986
1870	30,495	23.14	705,606	289,667	415,939	415,814	125	61,011	644,595	697,532	8,074
1880	30,495	32.65	995,577	391,105	604,472	604,332	140	74,539	921,038	987,891	7,686
1890	30,495	37.75	1,151,149	462,008	689,141	688,934	207	116,183	1,034,966	1,144,879	6,270
1900	30,495	43.95	1,340,316	557,807	782,509	782,321	188	171,256	1,169,060	1,334,788	5,528
1910	30,495	49.69	1,515,400	679,161	836,239	835,843	396	224,832	1,290,568	1,509,221	6,179
1920	30,495	55.21	1,683,724	818,538	865,186	864,719	467	293,987	1,389,737	1,677,142	6,582
1930	30,495	57.02	1,738,765	944,049	794,716	793,681	1,035	371,080	1,367,685	1,733,407	5,358
1940	30,594	62.10	1,899,804	1,084,308	815,496	814,164	1,332	466,111	1,433,693	1,894,825	4,979
1950	30,305	69.86	2,117,027	1,293,405	823,622	822,077	1,545	777,921	1,339,106	2,107,235	7,120
1960	30,280	78.69	2,382,594	1,551,022	831,572	829,291	2,281	981,386	1,401,208	2,371,454	11,140
1970	30,225	85.71	2,590,516	1,794,430	796,086	789,041	7,045	1,250,725	1,339,791	2,576,145	14,364
1980	30,203	103.36	3,121,820	2,147,224	974,596	948,623	25,973	1,689,253	1,432,567	3,075,740	46,080
1990	30,111	115.79	3,486,703	2,406,974	1,079,729	1,039,884	39,845	1,905,378	1,581,325	3,436,739	49,964

			Population									
	Sex		Male, by age									
	Male	Female	0	1–4	5–9	10–14	15–19	20–29	20–24	25–29	30–39
	Aa5618	Aa5619	Aa5620	Aa5621	Aa5622	Aa5623	Aa5624	Aa5625	Aa5626	Aa5627	Aa5628
Year	Number	Number	Number	Number	Number	Number	Number	Number	Number	Number	Number
1790	—	—	—	—	—	—	—	—	—	—	—
1800	—	—	—	—	—	—	—	—	—	—	—
1810	—	—	—	—	—	—	—	—	—	—	—
1820	254,702	248,039	—	—	—	—	—	—	—	—	—
1830	289,731	291,454	—	—	—	—	—	—	—	—	—
1840	293,038	301,360	—	—	—	—	—	—	—	—	—
1850	329,634	338,873	7,840	45,563	48,353	44,385	35,648	55,825	—	—	36,591
1860	347,320	356,388	9,805	45,340	49,543	48,576	38,202	58,337	—	—	38,729
1870	343,902	361,704	10,042	45,320	47,048	48,479	37,612	—	32,898	23,657	—
1880	490,408	505,169	17,753	70,229	78,062	62,307	45,870	—	47,254	36,804	—
1890	572,337	578,812	17,487	69,177	90,207	85,255	64,049	—	49,935	35,767	—
1900	664,895	675,421	21,460	80,564	97,849	88,697	76,992	—	66,311	46,137	—
1910	751,842	763,558	23,942	91,354	104,854	97,224	84,448	—	70,463	55,843	—
1920	838,293	845,431	22,693	92,808	118,568	111,996	88,816	—	74,678	59,445	—
1930	853,158	885,607	19,256	83,844	120,871	112,421	103,771	—	77,567	54,845	—
1940	935,239	964,565	20,135	85,783	107,496	109,379	110,830	—	93,495	77,719	—
1950	1,040,540	1,076,487	26,885	114,950	123,279	107,709	96,774	—	85,648	83,680	—
1960	1,175,818	1,206,776	30,239	119,246	144,940	136,408	121,254	—	86,495	71,450	—
1970	1,272,087	1,318,429	24,684	94,573	136,951	143,442	147,073	—	124,434	87,770	—
1980	1,518,013	1,603,807	25,913	95,853	129,490	135,477	163,108	—	159,883	135,275	—
1990	1,688,510	1,798,193	22,445	108,241	129,687	129,633	141,745	—	143,622	148,256	—

(continued)

TABLE Aa5607–5707   South Carolina population by race, sex, age, nativity, and urban–rural residence: 1790–1990
Continued

					Population					
					Male, by age					
30–34	35–39	40–49	40–44	45–49	50–59	50–54	55–59	60–69	60–64	65–69
Aa5629	Aa5630	Aa5631	Aa5632	Aa5633	Aa5634	Aa5635	Aa5636	Aa5637	Aa5638	Aa5639
Year Number	Number	Number	Number	Number	Number	Number	Number	Number	Number	Number
1790 —	—	—	—	—	—	—	—	—	—	—
1800 —	—	—	—	—	—	—	—	—	—	—
1810 —	—	—	—	—	—	—	—	—	—	—
1820 —	—	—	—	—	—	—	—	—	—	—
1830 —	—	—	—	—	—	—	—	—	—	—
1840 —	—	—	—	—	—	—	—	—	—	—
1850 —	—	23,994	—	—	15,854	—	—	9,190	—	—
1860 —	—	26,888	—	—	16,804	—	—	9,834	—	—
1870 17,863	16,659	—	14,444	12,218	—	11,989	6,549	—	8,548	4,259
1880 27,590	22,899	—	17,069	15,161	—	14,048	8,618	—	11,112	6,662
1890 32,098	31,456	—	23,091	17,171	—	17,145	10,953	—	10,432	7,184
1900 35,046	31,104	—	28,261	22,535	—	22,104	13,575	—	13,916	8,638
1910 45,086	41,596	—	30,934	23,097	—	24,890	17,099	—	18,040	10,531
1920 47,179	51,046	—	39,603	39,783	—	27,506	17,151	—	19,169	12,928
1930 46,149	49,227	—	41,683	38,051	—	33,620	23,349	—	19,761	12,186
1940 62,733	54,177	—	46,290	41,662	—	35,944	27,792	—	22,635	20,040
1950 72,840	70,940	—	58,912	47,847	—	40,019	32,923	—	26,015	23,734
1960 71,947	75,549	—	69,619	63,019	—	50,751	40,433	—	30,292	26,903
1970 70,928	67,866	—	69,205	70,105	—	63,062	53,632	—	42,671	31,401
1980 120,580	94,996	—	76,628	71,739	—	70,040	69,431	—	58,324	47,436
1990 144,836	134,650	—	121,517	96,134	—	76,399	69,756	—	65,772	61,581

					Population					
	Male, by age					Female, by age				
70–79	70–74	75–79	80 and older	Unknown age	0	1–4	5–9	10–14	15–19	20–29
Aa5640	Aa5641	Aa5642	Aa5643	Aa5644	Aa5645	Aa5646	Aa5647	Aa5648	Aa5649	Aa5650
Year Number	Number	Number	Number	Number	Number	Number	Number	Number	Number	Number
1790 —	—	—	—	—	—	—	—	—	—	—
1800 —	—	—	—	—	—	—	—	—	—	—
1810 —	—	—	—	—	—	—	—	—	—	—
1820 —	—	—	—	—	—	—	—	—	—	—
1830 —	—	—	—	—	—	—	—	—	—	—
1840 —	—	—	—	—	—	—	—	—	—	—
1850 3,602	—	—	1,461	1,328	7,961	45,854	48,831	43,591	37,900	58,117
1860 3,718	—	—	1,357	187	10,097	45,599	49,938	47,023	40,561	60,799
1870 —	3,190	1,423	1,704	0	9,859	44,101	45,473	46,082	39,699	—
1880 —	4,529	2,353	2,088	—	17,232	68,337	76,508	59,874	47,733	—
1890 —	4,852	2,696	2,367	1,015	16,502	66,775	88,595	80,827	67,450	—
1900 —	5,378	2,899	2,473	956	21,542	80,085	96,414	85,666	80,428	—
1910 —	5,833	2,984	2,301	1,323	23,463	89,700	103,926	95,182	88,226	—
1920 —	7,962	3,703	2,533	726	22,665	90,415	117,259	111,044	93,945	—
1930 —	8,570	4,614	3,116	257	19,125	82,851	119,879	110,387	107,574	—
1940 —	10,616	4,735	3,778	—	19,956	84,786	106,540	106,610	113,260	—
1950 —	14,855	9,652	3,878	—	26,517	111,251	120,765	104,591	97,501	—
1960 —	18,401	11,115	7,757	—	29,419	116,009	141,345	132,522	107,565	—
1970 —	20,592	12,854	10,844	—	23,991	92,516	132,291	139,261	133,808	—
1980 —	31,574	18,156	14,110	—	24,773	91,977	124,153	130,702	154,126	—
1990 —	44,251	27,953	22,032	—	21,556	104,095	126,389	124,086	135,889	—

TABLE Aa5607–5707   South Carolina population by race, sex, age, nativity, and urban–rural residence: 1790–1990
Continued

				Population						
				Female, by age						
20–24	25–29	30–39	30–34	35–39	40–49	40–44	45–49	50–59	50–54	55–59
Aa5651	Aa5652	Aa5653	Aa5654	Aa5655	Aa5656	Aa5657	Aa5658	Aa5659	Aa5660	Aa5661
Year Number	Number	Number	Number	Number	Number	Number	Number	Number	Number	Number
1790 —	—	—	—	—	—	—	—	—	—	—
1800 —	—	—	—	—	—	—	—	—	—	—
1810 —	—	—	—	—	—	—	—	—	—	—
1820 —	—	—	—	—	—	—	—	—	—	—
1830 —	—	—	—	—	—	—	—	—	—	—
1840 —	—	—	—	—	—	—	—	—	—	—
1850 —	—	38,846	—	—	25,472	—	—	15,809	—	—
1860 —	—	41,138	—	—	28,282	—	—	16,999	—	—
1870 39,176	28,795	—	22,850	19,670	—	17,193	12,793	—	11,855	6,383
1880 51,149	38,601	—	29,840	26,571	—	21,847	17,302	—	15,765	8,885
1890 54,164	39,672	—	32,229	30,927	—	24,689	20,557	—	17,281	10,518
1900 72,436	50,477	—	36,409	32,411	—	28,221	23,174	—	20,614	13,852
1910 81,007	62,474	—	46,664	41,938	—	30,534	24,999	—	22,271	15,196
1920 85,526	67,003	—	51,712	53,340	—	39,885	31,707	—	23,403	15,612
1930 88,787	65,623	—	52,710	55,533	—	44,906	40,087	—	31,751	20,969
1940 100,396	82,794	—	66,079	60,869	—	49,537	44,027	—	36,941	28,229
1950 91,366	88,753	—	76,487	75,553	—	62,015	52,121	—	43,412	34,729
1960 80,307	75,907	—	77,563	82,047	—	72,803	66,488	—	55,134	46,150
1970 113,768	87,134	—	74,413	73,654	—	75,275	76,060	—	67,892	60,456
1980 153,855	137,862	—	123,024	97,170	—	81,711	78,318	—	79,086	80,506
1990 139,345	148,508	—	149,748	141,033	—	126,095	99,969	—	83,108	79,006

				Population						
									White	
			Female, by age							Male, by age
60–69	60–64	65–69	70–79	70–74	75–79	80 and older	Unknown age	Male	Female	0–4
Aa5662	Aa5663	Aa5664	Aa5665	Aa5666	Aa5667	Aa5668	Aa5669	Aa5670	Aa5671	Aa5672
Year Number	Number	Number	Number	Number	Number	Number	Number	Number	Number	Number
1790 —	—	—	—	—	—	—	—	73,298	66,880	—
1800 —	—	—	—	—	—	—	—	100,916	95,339	—
1810 —	—	—	—	—	—	—	—	109,587	104,609	—
1820 —	—	—	—	—	—	—	—	120,934	116,506	—
1830 —	—	—	—	—	—	—	—	130,590	127,273	25,132
1840 —	—	—	—	—	—	—	—	130,496	128,588	24,828
1850 9,462	—	—	3,920	—	—	1,765	1,345	—	—	—
1860 9,992	—	—	4,062	—	—	1,720	178	—	—	—
1870 —	7,242	3,786	—	3,152	1,551	2,044	0	—	—	—
1880 —	9,640	5,879	—	4,865	2,342	2,799	—	—	—	—
1890 —	10,349	6,719	—	4,899	2,685	2,880	1,094	—	—	—
1900 —	12,609	8,152	—	5,949	3,166	2,968	848	—	—	—
1910 —	14,487	9,448	—	6,450	3,414	3,131	1,048	—	—	—
1920 —	15,056	10,711	—	7,563	4,307	3,668	610	—	—	—
1930 —	16,412	11,410	—	8,275	4,823	4,170	335	—	—	—
1940 —	22,396	20,379	—	10,957	5,695	5,114	—	—	—	—
1950 —	28,540	28,393	—	17,206	11,855	5,432	—	—	—	—
1960 —	37,094	33,758	—	24,367	15,670	12,628	—	—	—	—
1970 —	52,641	42,856	—	30,375	20,891	21,147	—	—	—	—
1980 —	70,492	62,799	—	47,718	32,301	33,234	—	—	—	—
1990 —	78,248	78,874	—	61,599	46,961	53,684	—	—	—	—

(continued)

TABLE Aa5607–5707   South Carolina population by race, sex, age, nativity, and urban–rural residence: 1790–1990
Continued

	Population										
	White										
	Male, by age										Female, by age
	5–9	10–14	15–19	20–29	30–39	40–49	50–59	60–69	70–79	80 and older	0–4
	Aa5673	Aa5674	Aa5675	Aa5676	Aa5677	Aa5678	Aa5679	Aa5680	Aa5681	Aa5682	Aa5683
Year	Number	Number	Number	Number	Number	Number	Number	Number	Number	Number	Number
1790	—	—	—	—	—	—	—	—	—	—	—
1800	—	—	—	—	—	—	—	—	—	—	—
1810	—	—	—	—	—	—	—	—	—	—	—
1820	—	—	—	—	—	—	—	—	—	—	—
1830	20,259	16,497	13,961	22,164	13,969	8,334	5,644	3,042	1,210	378	23,691
1840	19,360	16,621	13,719	22,489	13,774	9,132	5,615	3,059	1,418	481	23,639
1850	—	—	—	—	—	—	—	—	—	—	—
1860	—	—	—	—	—	—	—	—	—	—	—
1870	—	—	—	—	—	—	—	—	—	—	—
1880	—	—	—	—	—	—	—	—	—	—	—
1890	—	—	—	—	—	—	—	—	—	—	—
1900	—	—	—	—	—	—	—	—	—	—	—
1910	—	—	—	—	—	—	—	—	—	—	—
1920	—	—	—	—	—	—	—	—	—	—	—
1930	—	—	—	—	—	—	—	—	—	—	—
1940	—	—	—	—	—	—	—	—	—	—	—
1950	—	—	—	—	—	—	—	—	—	—	—
1960	—	—	—	—	—	—	—	—	—	—	—
1970	—	—	—	—	—	—	—	—	—	—	—
1980	—	—	—	—	—	—	—	—	—	—	—
1990	—	—	—	—	—	—	—	—	—	—	—

	Population										
	White										
	Female, by age										Male, by age	
	5–9	10–14	15–19	20–29	30–39	40–49	50–59	60–69	70–79	80 and older	0–9	10–15
	Aa5684	Aa5685	Aa5686	Aa5687	Aa5688	Aa5689	Aa5690	Aa5691	Aa5692	Aa5693	Aa5694	Aa5695
Year	Number	Number	Number	Number	Number	Number	Number	Number	Number	Number	Number	Number
1790	—	—	—	—	—	—	—	—	—	—	—	—
1800	—	—	—	—	—	—	—	—	—	—	37,411	16,156
1810	—	—	—	—	—	—	—	—	—	—	39,669	17,193
1820	—	—	—	—	—	—	—	—	—	—	42,658	18,258
1830	19,043	15,632	15,122	21,866	13,438	8,468	5,455	2,929	1,181	448	—	—
1840	18,741	15,822	14,691	22,392	13,471	9,145	5,551	3,168	1,443	525	—	—
1850	—	—	—	—	—	—	—	—	—	—	—	—
1860	—	—	—	—	—	—	—	—	—	—	—	—
1870	—	—	—	—	—	—	—	—	—	—	—	—
1880	—	—	—	—	—	—	—	—	—	—	—	—
1890	—	—	—	—	—	—	—	—	—	—	—	—
1900	—	—	—	—	—	—	—	—	—	—	—	—
1910	—	—	—	—	—	—	—	—	—	—	—	—
1920	—	—	—	—	—	—	—	—	—	—	—	—
1930	—	—	—	—	—	—	—	—	—	—	—	—
1940	—	—	—	—	—	—	—	—	—	—	—	—
1950	—	—	—	—	—	—	—	—	—	—	—	—
1960	—	—	—	—	—	—	—	—	—	—	—	—
1970	—	—	—	—	—	—	—	—	—	—	—	—
1980	—	—	—	—	—	—	—	—	—	—	—	—
1990	—	—	—	—	—	—	—	—	—	—	—	—

TABLE Aa5607-5707   South Carolina population by race, sex, age, nativity, and urban-rural residence: 1790-1990
Continued

						Population						
						White						
	Male, by age			Female, by age					Male, by age		Female, by age	
	16-25	26-44	45 and older	0-9	10-15	16-25	26-44	45 and older	0-15	16 and older	0-15	16 and older
	Aa5696	Aa5697	Aa5698	Aa5699	Aa5700	Aa5701	Aa5702	Aa5703	Aa5704	Aa5705	Aa5706	Aa5707
Year	Number	Number	Number	Number	Number	Number	Number	Number	Number	Number	Number	Number
1790	—	—	—	—	—	—	—	—	37,722	35,576	35,440	31,440
1800	17,761	19,344	10,244	34,664	15,857	18,145	17,236	9,437	—	—	—	—
1810	20,933	20,488	11,304	37,497	16,629	20,583	18,974	10,926	—	—	—	—
1820	23,984	22,115	13,919	39,891	18,741	23,662	20,939	13,273	—	—	—	—
1830	—	—	—	—	—	—	—	—	—	—	—	—
1840	—	—	—	—	—	—	—	—	—	—	—	—
1850	—	—	—	—	—	—	—	—	—	—	—	—
1860	—	—	—	—	—	—	—	—	—	—	—	—
1870	—	—	—	—	—	—	—	—	—	—	—	—
1880	—	—	—	—	—	—	—	—	—	—	—	—
1890	—	—	—	—	—	—	—	—	—	—	—	—
1900	—	—	—	—	—	—	—	—	—	—	—	—
1910	—	—	—	—	—	—	—	—	—	—	—	—
1920	—	—	—	—	—	—	—	—	—	—	—	—
1930	—	—	—	—	—	—	—	—	—	—	—	—
1940	—	—	—	—	—	—	—	—	—	—	—	—
1950	—	—	—	—	—	—	—	—	—	—	—	—
1960	—	—	—	—	—	—	—	—	—	—	—	—
1970	—	—	—	—	—	—	—	—	—	—	—	—
1980	—	—	—	—	—	—	—	—	—	—	—	—
1990	—	—	—	—	—	—	—	—	—	—	—	—

Sources
See the sources for Table Aa2244-2340.

Documentation
See the text for Table Aa2244-2340.

South Carolina was one of the original thirteen states, admitted to the Union in 1788.

TABLE Aa5708-5770   South Dakota population by race, sex, age, nativity, and urban-rural residence: 1860-1990
Contributed by Michael R. Haines

				Population								
					Race				Residence		Nativity	
	Area	Population density	Total	White	Nonwhite	Black	Other nonwhite		Urban	Rural	Native-born	Foreign-born
	Aa5708	Aa5709	Aa5710	Aa5711	Aa5712	Aa5713	Aa5714		Aa5715	Aa5716	Aa5717	Aa5718
Year	Square miles	Persons per square mile	Number	Number	Number	Number	Number		Number	Number	Number	Number
1860	312,094	0.02	4,837	2,576	2,261	0	2,261		0	4,837	3,063	1,774
1870	147,687	0.10	14,181	12,887	1,294	94	1,200		0	14,181	9,366	4,815
1880	147,687	0.92	135,177	133,147	2,030	401	1,629		9,901	125,276	83,382	51,795
1890 [1]	76,868	4.54	348,600	327,290	1,518	541	977		28,555	320,045	237,753	91,055
1900	76,868	5.22	401,570	380,714	20,856	465	20,391		40,936	360,634	313,062	88,508
1910	76,868	7.60	583,888	563,771	20,117	817	19,300		76,469	507,419	483,098	100,790
1920	76,868	8.28	636,547	619,147	17,400	832	16,568		101,872	534,675	554,013	82,534
1930	76,868	9.01	692,849	670,269	22,580	646	21,934		130,907	561,942	626,788	66,061
1940	76,536	8.40	642,961	619,075	23,886	474	23,412		158,087	484,874	598,837	44,124
1950	76,536	8.53	652,740	628,504	24,236	727	23,509		216,710	436,030	619,000	30,710
1960	75,956	8.96	680,514	653,098	27,416	1,114	26,302		267,180	413,334	661,937	18,577
1970	75,955	8.76	665,507	630,333	35,174	1,627	33,547		296,628	368,879	654,608	10,899
1980	75,952	9.09	690,768	639,669	51,099	2,144	48,955		320,777	369,991	681,169	9,599
1990	75,896	9.17	696,004	637,515	58,489	3,258	55,231		347,903	348,101	688,273	7,731

Note appears at end of table

(continued)

TABLE Aa5708–5770   South Dakota population by race, sex, age, nativity, and urban–rural residence: 1860–1990
Continued

	Population										
	Sex		Male, by age								
	Male	Female	0	1–4	5–9	10–14	15–19	20–29	20–24	25–29	30–39
	Aa5719	Aa5720	Aa5721	Aa5722	Aa5723	Aa5724	Aa5725	Aa5726	Aa5727	Aa5728	Aa5729
Year	Number	Number	Number	Number	Number	Number	Number	Number	Number	Number	Number
1860	2,797	2,040	30	337	372	381	201	628	—	—	415
1870	8,878	5,303	216	851	764	672	533	—	1,923	1,360	—
1880	82,296	52,881	2,208	7,821	7,924	6,134	5,195	—	11,707	11,630	—
1890 [1]	180,250	148,558	5,237	19,806	21,955	18,174	15,309	—	16,540	16,838	—
1900	216,164	185,406	6,018	22,054	26,346	24,396	20,718	—	19,555	17,049	—
1910	317,112	266,776	7,871	29,296	33,954	30,790	30,339	—	34,991	31,112	—
1920	337,120	299,427	7,672	32,896	37,869	33,810	30,319	—	28,918	29,020	—
1930	363,650	329,199	7,065	29,295	39,543	38,338	35,569	—	30,371	26,182	—
1940	332,514	310,447	5,675	23,477	29,602	31,703	32,811	—	27,766	24,404	—
1950	337,251	315,489	8,075	31,190	30,831	26,945	25,731	—	25,854	25,534	—
1960	344,271	336,243	8,613	33,715	39,721	34,284	26,098	—	19,564	18,778	—
1970	330,033	335,474	5,666	21,921	34,952	37,974	35,279	—	24,390	17,650	—
1980	340,683	350,085	6,628	23,142	26,810	27,743	34,616	—	33,789	29,122	—
1990	342,498	353,506	4,929	23,018	30,061	28,249	25,583	—	24,171	26,748	—

	Population										
	Male, by age										
	30–34	35–39	40–49	40–44	45–49	50–59	50–54	55–59	60–69	60–64	65–69
	Aa5730	Aa5731	Aa5732	Aa5733	Aa5734	Aa5735	Aa5736	Aa5737	Aa5738	Aa5739	Aa5740
Year	Number	Number	Number	Number	Number	Number	Number	Number	Number	Number	Number
1860	—	—	254	—	—	115	—	—	54	—	—
1870	839	587	—	359	260	—	202	120	—	96	51
1880	8,987	6,649	—	4,526	3,260	—	2,615	1,507	—	1,099	552
1890 [1]	16,799	13,192	—	9,680	7,627	—	6,132	4,487	—	3,487	2,178
1900	15,073	14,273	—	13,578	10,447	—	8,296	6,215	—	4,509	3,291
1910	24,557	20,626	—	16,792	14,688	—	13,655	9,684	—	6,887	4,935
1920	26,555	24,505	—	19,176	16,566	—	13,672	11,167	—	9,578	6,455
1930	25,088	25,603	—	23,923	20,645	—	17,064	13,345	—	10,639	8,520
1940	22,034	21,135	—	20,756	20,704	—	19,550	15,996	—	12,749	9,683
1950	23,266	21,621	—	19,782	18,545	—	18,426	17,030	—	15,204	11,903
1960	20,497	20,917	—	20,045	18,720	—	17,027	15,918	—	14,772	13,155
1970	15,421	15,947	—	18,015	18,382	—	17,594	16,063	—	14,261	12,012
1980	23,739	17,522	—	15,263	15,295	—	16,693	16,782	—	15,074	12,900
1990	28,250	26,797	—	21,861	16,856	—	14,197	14,033	—	14,848	14,197

	Population										
	Male, by age					Female, by age					
	70–79	70–74	75–79	80 and older	Unknown age	0	1–4	5–9	10–14	15–19	20–29
	Aa5741	Aa5742	Aa5743	Aa5744	Aa5745	Aa5746	Aa5747	Aa5748	Aa5749	Aa5750	Aa5751
Year	Number	Number	Number	Number	Number	Number	Number	Number	Number	Number	Number
1860	6	—	—	4	0	35	271	287	284	240	392
1870	—	25	13	7	0	207	777	726	628	482	—
1880	—	277	127	78	—	2,091	7,601	7,683	5,550	4,722	—
1890 [1]	—	1,395	604	300	510	5,066	19,064	21,472	16,820	14,402	—
1900	—	2,025	1,122	646	553	5,875	21,270	25,703	22,903	19,643	—
1910	—	2,910	1,858	1,114	1,053	7,647	28,675	32,979	29,231	28,303	—
1920	—	4,014	2,413	1,572	943	7,272	31,991	36,652	32,700	29,157	—
1930	—	6,340	3,605	2,284	231	6,797	28,167	38,418	37,054	34,040	—
1940	—	6,843	4,321	3,305	—	5,597	23,114	28,929	30,332	31,905	—
1950	—	8,223	5,868	3,223	—	7,710	29,738	29,741	26,145	25,448	—
1960	—	10,597	6,631	5,219	—	8,493	32,306	38,190	33,160	25,967	—
1970	—	10,068	7,359	7,079	—	5,338	21,333	33,683	36,531	34,710	—
1980	—	10,138	7,288	8,139	—	6,529	22,147	26,061	26,657	34,025	—
1990	—	11,162	8,398	9,140	—	4,651	21,906	28,734	27,188	24,988	—

Note appears at end of table

TABLE Aa5708–5770   South Dakota population by race, sex, age, nativity, and urban–rural residence: 1860–1990
Continued

	Population										
	Female, by age										
	20–24	25–29	30–39	30–34	35–39	40–49	40–44	45–49	50–59	50–54	55–59
	Aa5752	Aa5753	Aa5754	Aa5755	Aa5756	Aa5757	Aa5758	Aa5759	Aa5760	Aa5761	Aa5762
Year	Number	Number	Number	Number	Number	Number	Number	Number	Number	Number	Number
1860	—	—	279	—	—	157	—	—	72	—	—
1870	590	519	—	365	307	—	209	160	—	130	75
1880	5,779	4,877	—	4,041	3,093	—	2,133	1,711	—	1,299	865
1890 [1]	13,308	12,827	—	11,494	8,768	—	6,683	5,347	—	4,221	3,115
1900	16,425	13,715	—	11,930	11,018	—	9,589	7,454	—	5,904	4,627
1910	28,003	23,773	—	18,655	15,637	—	12,708	11,298	—	9,536	6,630
1920	27,787	26,084	—	22,905	19,731	—	15,298	12,533	—	10,394	8,505
1930	29,213	24,563	—	23,034	22,675	—	20,282	16,854	—	13,225	10,303
1940	27,102	24,060	—	21,564	20,341	—	18,995	18,457	—	16,509	13,231
1950	24,107	23,403	—	21,748	20,521	—	18,713	17,488	—	16,438	15,082
1960	19,601	19,045	—	20,081	19,925	—	19,369	18,163	—	16,674	15,302
1970	24,256	17,717	—	16,284	17,012	—	17,847	17,913	—	17,547	16,342
1980	32,764	27,746	—	22,220	17,729	—	15,918	16,104	—	16,876	16,785
1990	23,097	26,395	—	28,020	25,729	—	20,829	16,671	—	14,945	15,185

	Population							
	Female, by age							
	60–69	60–64	65–69	70–79	70–74	75–79	80 and older	Unknown age
	Aa5763	Aa5764	Aa5765	Aa5766	Aa5767	Aa5768	Aa5769	Aa5770
Year	Number	Number	Number	Number	Number	Number	Number	Number
1860	19	—	—	4	—	—	0	0
1870	—	70	29	—	20	6	3	0
1880	—	673	354	—	212	112	85	—
1890 [1]	—	2,401	1,613	—	957	494	305	201
1900	—	3,414	2,516	—	1,606	949	681	184
1910	—	4,910	3,640	—	2,278	1,447	1,106	320
1920	—	6,832	4,628	—	3,033	1,910	1,511	504
1930	—	8,263	6,691	—	4,718	2,689	2,068	145
1940	—	10,023	7,985	—	5,515	3,712	3,076	—
1950	—	13,128	10,336	—	7,110	5,336	3,297	—
1960	—	14,056	12,936	—	10,423	6,812	5,740	—
1970	—	14,995	13,196	—	11,561	9,081	10,128	—
1980	—	15,970	14,740	—	12,737	10,411	14,666	—
1990	—	15,734	15,269	—	13,843	11,909	18,413	—

[1] Includes 19,792 American Indians not counted in the general enumeration; see text for Table Aa2244–2340.

Sources
See the sources for Table Aa2244–2340.

Documentation
See the text for Table Aa2244–2340.

The portion of present-day South Dakota east of the Missouri River was part of Minnesota Territory in 1849 and the western portion was incorporated as part of Nebraska Territory in 1854. The population of the eastern portion is included with Minnesota Territory in Table Aa4242–4304. Minnesota statehood in 1858 left the portion of Minnesota Territory west of the present Minnesota state border as unorganized territory. When Dakota Territory was organized in 1861, it comprised the present area of North and South Dakota. In 1860, the census reported the population of "Dakota Territory" even though it was not organized at the time of the census. North and South Dakota became separate states in 1889. The data for the entire Dakota Territory for 1860–1880 are reported in this table as the population of "South Dakota."

TABLE Aa5771-5871 Tennessee population by race, sex, age, nativity, and urban-rural residence: 1790-1990

Contributed by Michael R. Haines

					Population							
					Race				Residence		Nativity	
	Area	Population density	Total	White	Nonwhite	Black	Other nonwhite	Urban	Rural	Native-born	Foreign-born
	Aa5771	Aa5772	Aa5773	Aa5774	Aa5775	Aa5776	Aa5777	Aa5778	Aa5779	Aa5780	Aa5781
Year	Square miles	Persons per square mile	Number	Number	Number	Number	Number	Number	Number	Number	Number
1790	46,977	0.76	35,691	31,913	3,778	3,778	—	0	35,691	—	—
1800	41,687	2.53	105,602	91,709	13,893	13,893	—	0	105,602	—	—
1810	41,687	6.28	261,727	215,875	45,852	45,852	—	0	261,727	—	—
1820	41,687	10.14	422,823	339,927	82,896	82,834	52	0	422,823	—	—
1830	41,687	16.36	681,904	535,746	146,158	146,158	—	5,566	676,338	—	—
1840	41,687	19.89	829,210	640,627	188,583	188,583	—	6,929	822,281	—	—
1850	41,687	24.05	1,002,717	756,836	245,881	245,881	—	21,983	980,734	997,064	5,653
1860	41,687	26.62	1,109,801	826,722	283,079	283,019	60	46,541	1,063,260	1,088,575	21,226
1870	41,687	30.19	1,258,520	936,119	322,401	322,331	70	94,237	1,164,283	1,239,204	19,316
1880	41,687	37.00	1,542,359	1,138,831	403,528	403,151	377	115,984	1,426,375	1,525,657	16,702
1890	41,687	42.40	1,767,518	1,336,637	430,881	430,678	203	238,394	1,529,124	1,747,489	20,029
1900	41,687	48.47	2,020,616	1,540,186	480,430	480,243	187	326,639	1,693,977	2,002,870	17,746
1910	41,687	52.41	2,184,789	1,711,432	473,357	473,088	269	441,045	1,743,744	2,166,182	18,607
1920	41,687	56.08	2,337,885	1,885,993	451,892	451,758	134	611,226	1,726,659	2,322,237	15,648
1930	41,687	62.77	2,616,556	2,138,644	477,912	477,646	266	896,538	1,720,018	2,603,305	13,251
1940	41,961	69.49	2,915,841	2,406,906	508,935	508,736	199	1,027,206	1,888,635	2,904,373	11,468
1950	41,797	78.75	3,291,718	2,760,257	531,461	530,603	858	1,452,602	1,839,116	3,271,980	14,305
1960	41,366	86.23	3,567,089	2,977,753	589,336	586,876	2,460	1,864,828	1,702,261	3,551,246	15,843
1970	41,328	94.94	3,923,687	3,293,930	629,757	621,261	8,496	2,318,458	1,605,229	3,904,702	19,024
1980	41,155	111.56	4,591,120	3,835,452	755,668	725,942	29,726	2,773,573	1,817,547	4,542,751	48,369
1990	41,220	118.32	4,877,185	4,048,068	829,117	778,035	51,082	2,969,948	1,907,237	4,818,071	59,114

						Population					
	Sex					Male, by age					
	Male	Female	0	1-4	5-9	10-14	15-19	20-29	20-24	25-29	30-39
	Aa5782	Aa5783	Aa5784	Aa5785	Aa5786	Aa5787	Aa5788	Aa5789	Aa5790	Aa5791	Aa5792
Year	Number	Number	Number	Number	Number	Number	Number	Number	Number	Number	Number
1790	—	—	—	—	—	—	—	—	—	—	—
1800	—	—	—	—	—	—	—	—	—	—	—
1810	—	—	—	—	—	—	—	—	—	—	—
1820	214,848	207,913	—	—	—	—	—	—	—	—	—
1830	347,612	334,292	—	—	—	—	—	—	—	—	—
1840	419,707	409,503	—	—	—	—	—	—	—	—	—
1850	504,132	498,585	15,212	70,839	79,601	72,773	58,181	86,253	—	—	50,566
1860	562,718	547,083	17,934	75,342	82,993	77,730	62,463	100,501	—	—	62,003
1870	623,347	635,173	20,063	82,144	84,986	89,106	70,663	—	61,714	42,560	—
1880	769,277	773,082	27,518	100,313	116,887	99,621	78,527	—	75,480	57,582	—
1890	891,585	875,933	26,421	99,009	125,478	119,577	102,523	—	83,507	61,204	—
1900	1,021,224	999,392	29,081	110,834	134,516	124,492	113,167	—	99,544	80,157	—
1910	1,103,491	1,081,298	31,839	118,382	136,096	124,001	119,086	—	101,009	85,375	—
1920	1,173,967	1,163,918	28,847	113,696	145,472	140,672	117,244	—	96,884	86,704	—
1930	1,304,559	1,311,997	28,775	114,046	155,034	142,070	138,143	—	118,178	95,622	—
1940	1,445,829	1,470,012	26,930	114,012	143,291	149,415	147,332	—	127,393	120,712	—
1950	1,623,107	1,668,611	36,697	156,065	164,130	145,675	134,059	—	127,151	128,987	—
1960	1,740,690	1,826,399	40,319	159,076	190,389	182,102	150,395	—	109,861	103,807	—
1970	1,897,674	2,026,013	34,259	131,344	191,909	201,743	192,255	—	153,688	129,227	—
1980	2,216,600	2,374,520	35,577	131,791	179,209	189,403	219,497	—	209,291	190,309	—
1990	2,348,928	2,528,257	29,879	140,834	173,189	173,968	188,380	—	183,450	197,983	—

TABLE Aa5771–5871   Tennessee population by race, sex, age, nativity, and urban–rural residence: 1790–1990
Continued

	Population										
	Male, by age										
	30–34	35–39	40–49	40–44	45–49	50–59	50–54	55–59	60–69	60–64	65–69
	Aa5793	Aa5794	Aa5795	Aa5796	Aa5797	Aa5798	Aa5799	Aa5800	Aa5801	Aa5802	Aa5803
Year	Number	Number	Number	Number	Number	Number	Number	Number	Number	Number	Number
1790	—	—	—	—	—	—	—	—	—	—	—
1800	—	—	—	—	—	—	—	—	—	—	—
1810	—	—	—	—	—	—	—	—	—	—	—
1820	—	—	—	—	—	—	—	—	—	—	—
1830	—	—	—	—	—	—	—	—	—	—	—
1840	—	—	—	—	—	—	—	—	—	—	—
1850	—	—	32,327	—	—	20,895	—	—	10,740	—	—
1860	—	—	38,071	—	—	25,311	—	—	13,074	—	—
1870	35,020	31,928	—	24,848	20,971	—	20,813	12,421	—	10,607	6,722
1880	45,378	37,155	—	27,669	25,573	—	26,198	17,116	—	13,195	9,295
1890	55,016	48,368	—	36,374	32,557	—	31,893	21,562	—	16,933	11,786
1900	62,834	53,862	—	44,526	39,706	—	42,567	27,843	—	20,176	15,010
1910	72,602	68,160	—	49,238	43,459	—	49,116	33,690	—	26,140	19,578
1920	73,278	76,791	—	59,342	59,800	—	53,990	35,845	—	31,093	22,634
1930	83,299	83,877	—	69,004	63,151	—	66,571	47,826	—	35,985	25,181
1940	109,773	96,465	—	82,364	74,966	—	68,236	55,074	—	43,822	40,246
1950	116,263	116,141	—	104,262	88,182	—	76,498	64,941	—	52,008	46,407
1960	109,505	114,140	—	106,289	103,377	—	92,355	77,850	—	61,324	53,543
1970	109,746	103,058	—	108,843	109,079	—	99,878	91,966	—	79,681	61,582
1980	175,239	140,666	—	119,172	110,242	—	110,846	106,819	—	90,901	79,489
1990	198,835	188,331	—	173,786	140,241	—	115,412	103,714	—	98,277	88,550

	Population										
	Male, by age					Female, by age					
	70–79	70–74	75–79	80 and older	Unknown age	0	1–4	5–9	10–14	15–19	20–29
	Aa5804	Aa5805	Aa5806	Aa5807	Aa5808	Aa5809	Aa5810	Aa5811	Aa5812	Aa5813	Aa5814
Year	Number	Number	Number	Number	Number	Number	Number	Number	Number	Number	Number
1790	—	—	—	—	—	—	—	—	—	—	—
1800	—	—	—	—	—	—	—	—	—	—	—
1810	—	—	—	—	—	—	—	—	—	—	—
1820	—	—	—	—	—	—	—	—	—	—	—
1830	—	—	—	—	—	—	—	—	—	—	—
1840	—	—	—	—	—	—	—	—	—	—	—
1850	4,797	—	—	1,832	116	14,939	69,278	78,007	69,484	60,079	86,098
1860	5,075	—	—	1,871	350	17,303	73,144	81,269	74,504	64,552	96,913
1870	—	4,445	2,212	2,124	0	19,355	79,033	82,067	84,662	73,029	—
1880	—	5,907	3,371	2,492	—	26,073	96,089	113,349	95,463	79,477	—
1890	—	7,767	4,441	3,420	3,749	24,926	94,166	120,887	113,246	103,193	—
1900	—	9,442	5,535	3,577	4,355	28,590	106,418	130,229	119,281	113,413	—
1910	—	11,960	7,007	4,613	2,140	30,564	113,806	132,923	119,327	118,586	—
1920	—	15,406	9,380	5,722	1,167	27,874	110,322	140,912	135,765	121,127	—
1930	—	18,108	10,501	7,375	1,813	27,560	111,437	151,595	138,108	138,294	—
1940	—	24,105	12,276	9,417	—	26,338	110,832	140,516	144,669	149,712	—
1950	—	31,671	22,582	11,388	—	35,946	151,094	158,899	140,928	136,350	—
1960	—	39,580	26,336	20,442	—	39,146	155,133	185,162	176,693	146,562	—
1970	—	43,970	28,661	26,785	—	32,425	126,705	184,401	193,995	185,699	—
1980	—	59,030	37,063	32,056	—	33,757	124,963	170,719	180,537	210,756	—
1990	—	64,921	46,459	42,719	—	28,174	134,528	164,179	165,130	178,186	—

(continued)

TABLE Aa5771–5871   Tennessee population by race, sex, age, nativity, and urban–rural residence: 1790–1990
Continued

	Population											
	Female, by age											
	20–24	25–29	30–39	30–34	35–39	40–49	40–44	45–49	50–59	50–54	55–59	60–69
	Aa5815	Aa5816	Aa5817	Aa5818	Aa5819	Aa5820	Aa5821	Aa5822	Aa5823	Aa5824	Aa5825	Aa5826
Year	Number	Number	Number	Number	Number	Number	Number	Number	Number	Number	Number	Number
1790	—	—	—	—	—	—	—	—	—	—	—	—
1800	—	—	—	—	—	—	—	—	—	—	—	—
1810	—	—	—	—	—	—	—	—	—	—	—	—
1820	—	—	—	—	—	—	—	—	—	—	—	—
1830	—	—	—	—	—	—	—	—	—	—	—	—
1840	—	—	—	—	—	—	—	—	—	—	—	—
1850	—	—	50,684	—	—	33,252	—	—	19,591	—	—	10,515
1860	—	—	58,969	—	—	37,174	—	—	23,199	—	—	12,691
1870	68,185	50,558	—	39,212	34,671	—	28,086	21,709	—	17,752	10,932	—
1880	79,656	59,368	—	46,758	41,734	—	33,746	28,209	—	23,693	15,166	—
1890	86,882	63,809	—	53,199	47,496	—	39,879	34,103	—	28,169	19,085	—
1900	104,861	81,741	—	61,856	53,066	—	45,443	39,229	—	34,145	24,987	—
1910	110,084	92,048	—	73,207	66,963	—	50,565	42,798	—	37,739	27,518	—
1920	110,188	96,022	—	79,054	77,994	—	62,008	54,078	—	42,263	30,457	—
1930	130,441	107,591	—	89,475	88,079	—	72,550	65,431	—	57,729	41,789	—
1940	137,545	129,133	—	115,780	104,023	—	85,480	76,195	—	67,139	53,969	—
1950	138,194	137,948	—	123,524	121,766	—	108,619	92,776	—	79,515	65,855	—
1960	119,174	114,758	—	120,807	124,887	—	114,264	109,194	—	97,683	84,614	—
1970	167,489	134,441	—	117,827	114,921	—	119,758	119,914	—	110,195	102,410	—
1980	214,122	197,678	—	181,397	147,004	—	126,999	121,034	—	123,244	123,488	—
1990	184,362	204,994	—	210,509	197,996	—	180,875	146,312	—	124,245	117,238	—

	Population											
								White				
	Female, by age									Male, by age		
	60–64	65–69	70–79	70–74	75–79	80 and older	Unknown age	Male	Female	0–4	5–9	10–14
	Aa5827	Aa5828	Aa5829	Aa5830	Aa5831	Aa5832	Aa5833	Aa5834	Aa5835	Aa5836	Aa5837	Aa5838
Year	Number	Number	Number	Number	Number	Number	Number	Number	Number	Number	Number	Number
1790	—	—	—	—	—	—	—	16,548	15,365	—	—	—
1800	—	—	—	—	—	—	—	47,180	44,529	—	—	—
1810	—	—	—	—	—	—	—	111,763	104,112	—	—	—
1820	—	—	—	—	—	—	—	173,600	166,327	—	—	—
1830	—	—	—	—	—	—	—	275,066	260,680	59,576	45,366	36,044
1840	—	—	—	—	—	—	—	325,434	315,193	67,182	53,821	44,489
1850	—	—	4,686	—	—	1,864	108	—	—	—	—	—
1860	—	—	5,102	—	—	2,022	241	—	—	—	—	—
1870	10,308	6,389	—	4,545	2,298	2,382	0	—	—	—	—	—
1880	12,807	8,785	—	6,014	3,479	3,216	—	—	—	—	—	—
1890	16,551	11,351	—	7,537	4,377	3,993	3,084	—	—	—	—	—
1900	19,839	14,125	—	9,292	5,388	4,072	3,417	—	—	—	—	—
1910	23,374	17,410	—	11,272	6,643	4,981	1,490	—	—	—	—	—
1920	26,820	19,649	—	13,821	8,326	6,251	987	—	—	—	—	—
1930	32,226	23,297	—	16,781	9,915	7,887	1,812	—	—	—	—	—
1940	42,947	38,899	—	23,176	13,061	10,598	—	—	—	—	—	—
1950	54,361	50,727	—	33,899	24,918	13,292	—	—	—	—	—	—
1960	69,362	61,603	—	47,335	32,449	27,573	—	—	—	—	—	—
1970	92,906	77,669	—	58,945	42,188	44,125	—	—	—	—	—	—
1980	108,872	101,443	—	83,065	60,230	65,212	—	—	—	—	—	—
1990	115,360	112,436	—	91,516	76,080	96,137	—	—	—	—	—	—

TABLE Aa5771–5871 Tennessee population by race, sex, age, nativity, and urban–rural residence: 1790–1990
Continued

	Population										
	White										
	Male, by age								Female, by age		
	15–19	20–29	30–39	40–49	50–59	60–69	70–79	80 and older	0–4	5–9	10–14
	Aa5839	Aa5840	Aa5841	Aa5842	Aa5843	Aa5844	Aa5845	Aa5846	Aa5847	Aa5848	Aa5849
Year	Number	Number	Number	Number	Number	Number	Number	Number	Number	Number	Number
1790	—	—	—	—	—	—	—	—	—	—	—
1800	—	—	—	—	—	—	—	—	—	—	—
1810	—	—	—	—	—	—	—	—	—	—	—
1820	—	—	—	—	—	—	—	—	—	—	—
1830	29,247	44,982	25,111	15,108	11,188	5,543	2,107	794	55,399	42,975	33,556
1840	34,218	51,112	31,323	19,369	12,755	7,140	3,039	986	62,684	51,013	42,327
1850	—	—	—	—	—	—	—	—	—	—	—
1860	—	—	—	—	—	—	—	—	—	—	—
1870	—	—	—	—	—	—	—	—	—	—	—
1880	—	—	—	—	—	—	—	—	—	—	—
1890	—	—	—	—	—	—	—	—	—	—	—
1900	—	—	—	—	—	—	—	—	—	—	—
1910	—	—	—	—	—	—	—	—	—	—	—
1920	—	—	—	—	—	—	—	—	—	—	—
1930	—	—	—	—	—	—	—	—	—	—	—
1940	—	—	—	—	—	—	—	—	—	—	—
1950	—	—	—	—	—	—	—	—	—	—	—
1960	—	—	—	—	—	—	—	—	—	—	—
1970	—	—	—	—	—	—	—	—	—	—	—
1980	—	—	—	—	—	—	—	—	—	—	—
1990	—	—	—	—	—	—	—	—	—	—	—

	Population										
	White										
	Female, by age								Male, by age		
	15–19	20–29	30–39	40–49	50–59	60–69	70–79	80 and older	0–9	10–15	16–25
	Aa5850	Aa5851	Aa5852	Aa5853	Aa5854	Aa5855	Aa5856	Aa5857	Aa5858	Aa5859	Aa5860
Year	Number	Number	Number	Number	Number	Number	Number	Number	Number	Number	Number
1790	—	—	—	—	—	—	—	—	—	—	—
1800	—	—	—	—	—	—	—	—	19,227	7,194	8,282
1810	—	—	—	—	—	—	—	—	44,494	17,170	19,486
1820	—	—	—	—	—	—	—	—	67,746	28,497	31,028
1830	30,616	42,970	23,545	15,264	9,279	4,541	1,855	680	—	—	—
1840	35,965	51,907	30,597	19,198	11,535	6,465	2,617	885	—	—	—
1850	—	—	—	—	—	—	—	—	—	—	—
1860	—	—	—	—	—	—	—	—	—	—	—
1870	—	—	—	—	—	—	—	—	—	—	—
1880	—	—	—	—	—	—	—	—	—	—	—
1890	—	—	—	—	—	—	—	—	—	—	—
1900	—	—	—	—	—	—	—	—	—	—	—
1910	—	—	—	—	—	—	—	—	—	—	—
1920	—	—	—	—	—	—	—	—	—	—	—
1930	—	—	—	—	—	—	—	—	—	—	—
1940	—	—	—	—	—	—	—	—	—	—	—
1950	—	—	—	—	—	—	—	—	—	—	—
1960	—	—	—	—	—	—	—	—	—	—	—
1970	—	—	—	—	—	—	—	—	—	—	—
1980	—	—	—	—	—	—	—	—	—	—	—
1990	—	—	—	—	—	—	—	—	—	—	—

(continued)

TABLE Aa5771–5871   Tennessee population by race, sex, age, nativity, and urban–rural residence: 1790–1990
Continued

	Population											
	White											
	Male, by age		Female, by age					Male, by age		Female, by age		
	26–44	45 and older	0–9	10–15	16–25	26–44	45 and older	0–15	16 and older	0–15	16 and older	
	Aa5861	Aa5862	Aa5863	Aa5864	Aa5865	Aa5866	Aa5867	Aa5868	Aa5869	Aa5870	Aa5871	
Year	Number	Number	Number	Number	Number	Number	Number	Number	Number	Number	Number	
1790	—	—	—	—	—	—	—	8,762	7,786	8,793	6,572	
1800	8,352	4,125	18,450	7,042	8,554	6,992	3,491	—	—	—	—	
1810	19,957	10,656	41,810	16,329	19,864	17,624	8,485	—	—	—	—	
1820	27,549	18,780	63,419	27,770	31,569	27,931	15,638	—	—	—	—	
1830	—	—	—	—	—	—	—	—	—	—	—	
1840	—	—	—	—	—	—	—	—	—	—	—	
1850	—	—	—	—	—	—	—	—	—	—	—	
1860	—	—	—	—	—	—	—	—	—	—	—	
1870	—	—	—	—	—	—	—	—	—	—	—	
1880	—	—	—	—	—	—	—	—	—	—	—	
1890	—	—	—	—	—	—	—	—	—	—	—	
1900	—	—	—	—	—	—	—	—	—	—	—	
1910	—	—	—	—	—	—	—	—	—	—	—	
1920	—	—	—	—	—	—	—	—	—	—	—	
1930	—	—	—	—	—	—	—	—	—	—	—	
1940	—	—	—	—	—	—	—	—	—	—	—	
1950	—	—	—	—	—	—	—	—	—	—	—	
1960	—	—	—	—	—	—	—	—	—	—	—	
1970	—	—	—	—	—	—	—	—	—	—	—	
1980	—	—	—	—	—	—	—	—	—	—	—	
1990	—	—	—	—	—	—	—	—	—	—	—	

Sources

See the sources for Table Aa2244–2340.

Documentation

See the text for Table Aa2244–2340.

Tennessee was originally part of North Carolina. In 1790, it was part of the "Territory South of the Ohio River," which also included Kentucky. It was admitted to the Union in 1796.

TABLE Aa5872–5934   Texas population by race, sex, age, nativity, and urban–rural residence: 1850–1990

Contributed by Michael R. Haines

			Population									
				Race				Residence		Nativity		
	Area	Population density	Total	White	Nonwhite	Black	Other nonwhite	Urban	Rural	Native-born	Foreign-born	
	Aa5872	Aa5873	Aa5874	Aa5875	Aa5876	Aa5877	Aa5878	Aa5879	Aa5880	Aa5881	Aa5882	
Year	Square miles	Persons per Square miles	Number	Number	Number	Number	Number	Number	Number	Number	Number	
1850	262,398	0.81	212,592	154,034	58,558	58,558	—	7,665	204,927	194,911	17,681	
1860	262,398	2.30	604,215	420,891	183,324	182,921	403	26,615	577,600	560,793	43,422	
1870	262,398	3.12	818,579	564,700	253,879	253,475	404	54,521	764,058	756,168	62,411	
1880	262,398	6.07	1,591,749	1,197,237	394,512	393,384	1,128	146,795	1,444,954	1,477,133	114,616	
1890 [1]	262,398	8.52	2,235,527	1,745,935	489,588	488,171	1,417	349,511	1,886,016	2,082,567	152,956	
1900	262,398	11.62	3,048,710	2,426,669	622,041	620,722	1,319	520,759	2,527,951	2,869,353	179,357	
1910	262,398	14.85	3,896,542	3,204,848	691,694	690,049	1,645	938,104	2,958,438	3,654,604	241,938	
1920	262,398	17.77	4,663,228	3,918,165	745,063	741,694	3,369	1,512,689	3,150,539	4,299,396	363,832	
1930	262,398	22.20	5,824,715	4,967,172	857,543	854,964	2,579	2,389,348	3,435,367	5,462,428	362,257	
1940	263,644	24.33	6,414,824	5,487,545	927,279	924,391	2,888	2,911,389	3,503,435	6,179,296	235,528	
1950	263,513	29.26	7,711,194	6,726,534	984,660	977,458	7,202	4,838,060	2,873,134	7,408,150	277,515	
1960	262,970	36.43	9,579,677	8,374,831	1,204,846	1,187,125	17,721	7,187,470	2,392,207	9,282,717	298,791	
1970	262,134	42.71	11,196,730	9,717,128	1,479,602	1,399,005	80,597	8,922,211	2,274,519	10,885,644	309,772	
1980	262,017	54.31	14,229,191	11,198,441	3,030,750	1,710,175	1,320,575	11,333,017	2,896,174	13,372,978	856,213	
1990	261,914	64.86	16,986,510	12,774,762	4,211,748	2,021,632	2,190,116	13,634,517	3,351,993	15,462,074	1,524,436	

Note appears at end of table

TABLE Aa5872–5934 Texas population by race, sex, age, nativity, and urban–rural residence: 1850–1990 *Continued*

Population

	Sex		Male, by age								
	Male	Female	0	1–4	5–9	10–14	15–19	20–29	20–24	25–29
	Aa5883	Aa5884	Aa5885	Aa5886	Aa5887	Aa5888	Aa5889	Aa5890	Aa5891	Aa5892
Year	Number	Number	Number	Number	Number	Number	Number	Number	Number	Number
1850	113,780	98,812	3,142	15,566	16,671	14,523	11,029	22,079	—	—
1860	320,167	284,048	10,173	43,743	45,820	39,979	32,477	61,502	—	—
1870	423,557	395,022	12,966	55,502	57,733	59,730	44,462	—	44,614	33,028
1880	837,840	753,909	30,821	112,094	125,997	97,894	73,309	—	86,783	75,326
1890 [1]	1,172,553	1,062,970	33,921	138,186	169,663	153,124	121,337	—	107,133	87,531
1900	1,578,900	1,469,810	47,778	182,053	219,170	194,483	166,042	—	152,315	127,360
1910	2,017,626	1,878,916	57,206	217,226	257,899	232,023	211,350	—	195,130	168,292
1920	2,409,222	2,254,006	54,936	216,086	289,795	276,424	243,169	—	229,348	204,228
1930	2,965,994	2,858,721	61,361	247,717	337,753	304,051	301,352	—	287,232	250,676
1940	3,221,103	3,193,721	56,610	234,594	300,309	316,967	316,825	—	276,847	277,239
1950	3,863,142	3,848,052	91,049	367,271	372,694	310,853	307,855	—	313,632	318,900
1960	4,744,981	4,834,696	119,974	470,343	545,405	474,859	381,506	—	309,756	307,169
1970	5,481,169	5,715,561	107,081	402,092	582,548	601,908	554,214	—	474,050	376,590
1980	6,998,723	7,230,468	130,688	466,747	596,734	602,487	691,034	—	721,080	657,264
1990	8,365,963	8,620,547	122,593	588,551	713,663	662,092	672,557	—	679,254	774,830

Population

	Male, by age										
	30–39	30–34	35–39	40–49	40–44	45–49	50–59	50–54	55–59	60–69	60–64
	Aa5893	Aa5894	Aa5895	Aa5896	Aa5897	Aa5898	Aa5899	Aa5900	Aa5901	Aa5902	Aa5903
Year	Number	Number	Number	Number	Number	Number	Number	Number	Number	Number	Number
1850	15,271	—	—	8,706	—	—	4,364	—	—	1,617	—
1860	39,680	—	—	23,370	—	—	12,329	—	—	5,362	—
1870	—	24,791	22,368	—	17,223	17,319	—	13,328	7,538	—	6,219
1880	—	60,174	44,649	—	31,976	32,604	—	22,815	13,588	—	14,254
1890 [1]	—	81,123	71,318	—	53,255	48,711	—	33,357	21,239	—	19,751
1900	—	97,984	83,089	—	74,521	72,310	—	54,240	33,300	—	27,749
1910	—	140,557	125,271	—	92,560	85,276	—	73,020	52,394	—	45,365
1920	—	170,445	166,074	—	127,880	126,258	—	87,690	61,487	—	59,099
1930	—	216,274	209,626	—	173,871	156,603	—	125,791	93,951	—	74,072
1940	—	260,513	240,867	—	207,071	185,586	—	154,267	121,510	—	95,430
1950	—	284,221	284,856	—	262,161	228,326	—	192,093	158,364	—	126,686
1960	—	318,788	318,841	—	282,679	272,327	—	241,146	206,087	—	159,012
1970	—	314,424	305,416	—	315,430	306,180	—	268,602	244,312	—	210,052
1980	—	562,178	437,868	—	355,987	333,884	—	328,145	306,388	—	249,336
1990	—	781,544	685,982	—	578,047	448,232	—	352,082	318,069	—	292,996

Population

	Male, by age						Female, by age				
	65–69	70–79	70–74	75–79	80 and older	Unknown age	0	1–4	5–9	10–14	15–19
	Aa5904	Aa5905	Aa5906	Aa5907	Aa5908	Aa5909	Aa5910	Aa5911	Aa5912	Aa5913	Aa5914
Year	Number	Number	Number	Number	Number	Number	Number	Number	Number	Number	Number
1850	—	468	—	—	163	181	3,052	15,028	15,878	13,566	11,539
1860	—	1,332	—	—	371	4,029	9,837	42,650	44,361	37,792	32,990
1870	3,256	—	1,984	787	709	0	12,434	53,735	55,134	56,102	46,072
1880	7,675	—	4,287	2,070	1,524	—	29,745	107,363	121,533	92,880	73,534
1890 [1]	12,017	—	7,424	3,848	2,915	6,700	32,330	131,814	164,854	146,462	123,917
1900	18,147	—	11,171	6,058	4,278	6,852	46,026	176,585	213,185	188,694	168,005
1910	27,582	—	16,115	9,199	6,269	4,892	55,237	209,315	250,755	224,769	211,920
1920	40,691	—	25,727	13,724	9,126	7,035	52,954	209,931	282,912	268,675	245,390
1930	49,416	—	37,014	21,925	15,088	2,221	60,735	241,355	327,807	295,352	305,717
1940	79,839	—	48,952	26,199	21,478	—	55,023	229,453	293,173	310,438	319,256
1950	102,197	—	68,538	49,827	23,619	—	88,643	354,310	361,031	300,925	293,432
1960	132,887	—	96,563	60,450	47,189	—	116,177	455,525	529,106	460,845	364,923
1970	162,904	—	114,381	74,213	66,772	—	103,703	387,633	562,702	580,801	538,538
1980	212,743	—	158,024	101,748	86,388	—	126,013	445,613	573,155	577,501	661,321
1990	258,436	—	184,088	130,581	122,366	—	117,238	561,672	682,510	632,261	639,134

Note appears at end of table

(continued)

TABLE Aa5872–5934   Texas population by race, sex, age, nativity, and urban–rural residence: 1850–1990   *Continued*

	Population										
	Female, by age										
	20–29	20–24	25–29	30–39	30–34	35–39	40–49	40–44	45–49	50–59	50–54
	Aa5915	Aa5916	Aa5917	Aa5918	Aa5919	Aa5920	Aa5921	Aa5922	Aa5923	Aa5924	Aa5925
Year	Number	Number	Number	Number	Number	Number	Number	Number	Number	Number	Number
1850	18,028	—	—	10,825	—	—	6,263	—	—	2,955	—
1860	50,331	—	—	30,626	—	—	17,631	—	—	8,954	—
1870	—	42,017	31,368	—	24,330	20,404	—	16,495	12,300	—	9,521
1880	—	77,575	59,513	—	46,708	38,812	—	30,506	23,969	—	18,989
1890 [1]	—	99,728	75,061	—	65,565	56,306	—	44,889	36,210	—	28,286
1900	—	152,432	117,242	—	85,672	72,198	—	64,248	52,020	—	42,233
1910	—	194,948	161,484	—	128,391	110,233	—	80,787	64,872	—	57,201
1920	—	226,845	199,688	—	163,446	149,740	—	118,375	94,088	—	69,349
1930	—	292,805	255,565	—	214,375	201,544	—	162,237	138,596	—	109,386
1940	—	291,590	291,323	—	266,010	242,719	—	200,835	175,280	—	143,272
1950	—	319,666	326,377	—	289,651	292,915	—	258,842	224,895	—	186,632
1960	—	315,902	317,453	—	332,656	331,508	—	289,867	280,651	—	245,151
1970	—	484,457	386,051	—	330,031	322,428	—	334,311	324,786	—	283,930
1980	—	699,278	644,790	—	562,305	442,361	—	367,015	347,507	—	352,130
1990	—	655,158	757,910	—	771,887	686,539	—	588,457	458,350	—	369,970

	Population								
	Female, by age								
	55–59	60–69	60–64	65–69	70–79	70–74	75–79	80 and older	Unknown age
	Aa5926	Aa5927	Aa5928	Aa5929	Aa5930	Aa5931	Aa5932	Aa5933	Aa5934
Year	Number	Number	Number	Number	Number	Number	Number	Number	Number
1850	—	1,174	—	—	325	—	—	146	33
1860	—	3,897	—	—	1,118	—	—	343	3,518
1870	5,164	—	4,622	2,372	—	1,581	602	769	0
1880	11,166	—	9,463	5,365	—	3,396	1,718	1,674	—
1890 [1]	18,171	—	15,312	9,316	—	5,797	3,086	2,826	3,040
1900	29,104	—	22,509	14,929	—	9,792	5,413	4,249	5,274
1910	40,973	—	33,251	22,490	—	14,300	8,241	6,605	3,144
1920	50,684	—	44,696	31,045	—	20,646	12,241	9,846	3,455
1930	80,217	—	62,044	42,727	—	31,696	19,121	15,472	1,970
1940	113,816	—	90,506	76,475	—	45,437	25,840	23,275	—
1950	155,008	—	126,486	110,702	—	74,035	54,866	29,636	—
1960	214,067	—	172,563	149,910	—	113,989	76,724	67,679	—
1970	266,164	—	236,237	199,139	—	151,334	108,057	115,259	—
1980	337,008	—	282,213	263,367	—	213,131	159,532	176,228	—
1990	343,521	—	334,835	312,833	—	242,882	203,433	261,957	—

[1] Includes four American Indians not counted in the general enumeration; see text for Table Aa2244–2340.

Sources
See the sources for Table Aa2244–2340.

Documentation
See the text for Table Aa2244–2340.

Texas became a state in 1845 after having been an independent republic during the period 1836–1845.

TABLE Aa5935–5997   Utah population by race, sex, age, nativity, and urban–rural residence: 1850–1990

Contributed by Michael R. Haines

			Population									
				Race				Residence		Nativity	
	Area	Population density	Total	White	Nonwhite	Black	Other nonwhite	Urban	Rural	Native-born	Foreign-born
	Aa5935	Aa5936	Aa5937	Aa5938	Aa5939	Aa5940	Aa5941	Aa5942	Aa5943	Aa5944	Aa5945
Year	Square miles	Persons per square mile	Number	Number	Number	Number	Number	Number	Number	Number	Number
1850	230,610	0.05	11,380	11,330	50	50	—	0	11,380	9,336	2044
1860	122,887	0.33	40,273	40,125	148	59	89	8,236	32,037	27,519	12754
1870	82,184	1.06	86,786	86,044	742	118	624	15,981	70,805	56,084	30702
1880	82,184	1.75	143,963	142,423	1,540	232	1,308	33,665	110,298	99,969	43994
1890 [1]	82,184	2.56	210,779	205,899	2,006	588	1,418	75,155	135,624	154,841	53064
1900	82,184	3.37	276,749	272,465	4,284	672	3,612	105,427	171,322	222,972	53777
1910	82,184	4.54	373,351	366,583	6,768	1,144	5,624	172,934	200,417	307,529	65822
1920	82,184	5.47	449,396	441,901	7,495	1,446	6,049	215,584	233,812	390,196	59200
1930	82,184	6.18	507,847	499,967	7,880	1,108	6,772	266,264	241,583	459,832	48015
1940	82,346	6.68	550,310	542,920	7,390	1,235	6,155	305,493	244,817	517,034	33276
1950	82,346	8.37	688,862	676,909	11,953	2,729	9,224	449,855	239,007	656,375	31025
1960	82,381	10.81	890,627	873,828	16,799	4,148	12,651	667,158	223,469	858,494	32133
1970	82,096	12.90	1,059,273	1,031,926	27,347	6,617	20,730	851,472	207,801	1,029,700	29573
1980	82,073	17.80	1,461,037	1,382,550	78,487	9,225	69,262	1,233,060	227,977	1,410,586	50451
1990	82,168	20.97	1,722,850	1,615,845	107,005	11,576	95,429	1,499,081	223,769	1,664,250	58600

			Population								
	Sex		Male, by age								
	Male	Female	0	1–4	5–9	10–14	15–19	20–29	20–24	25–29	30–39
	Aa5946	Aa5947	Aa5948	Aa5949	Aa5950	Aa5951	Aa5952	Aa5953	Aa5954	Aa5955	Aa5956
Year	Number	Number	Number	Number	Number	Number	Number	Number	Number	Number	Number
1850	6,046	5,334	220	877	699	685	663	1,268	—	—	764
1860	20,255	20,018	999	3,849	3,059	2,317	1,595	2,984	—	—	2,328
1870	44,121	42,665	1,811	6,739	6,842	5,881	4,074	—	3,315	2,861	—
1880	74,509	69,454	2,815	10,207	10,907	9,060	7,312	—	6,681	5,374	—
1890 [1]	110,463	97,442	3,093	12,401	15,222	12,428	10,634	—	10,580	9,988	—
1900	141,687	135,062	4,685	16,692	19,311	16,639	14,566	—	12,090	10,545	—
1910	196,863	176,488	5,484	21,093	23,277	20,312	18,844	—	19,778	18,782	—
1920	232,051	217,345	6,150	25,012	28,594	26,033	21,585	—	19,330	18,527	—
1930	259,999	247,848	5,911	24,322	31,673	29,856	26,481	—	23,111	18,881	—
1940	278,620	271,690	5,819	24,103	28,626	29,528	29,458	—	25,529	22,084	—
1950	347,636	341,226	9,881	38,173	38,765	31,484	28,151	—	27,291	27,722	—
1960	444,924	445,703	12,936	51,483	58,052	48,332	37,435	—	28,283	28,722	—
1970	523,265	536,008	12,722	44,578	59,530	63,062	58,215	—	46,185	35,966	—
1980	724,501	736,536	21,662	75,648	74,483	64,228	69,021	—	75,915	68,860	—
1990	855,759	867,091	15,963	70,926	94,404	94,416	76,321	—	68,439	69,370	—

Note appears at end of table

(continued)

TABLE Aa5935–5997   Utah population by race, sex, age, nativity, and urban–rural residence: 1850–1990 *Continued*

Population

	Male, by age										
	30–34	35–39	40–49	40–44	45–49	50–59	50–54	55–59	60–69	60–64	65–69
	Aa5957	Aa5958	Aa5959	Aa5960	Aa5961	Aa5962	Aa5963	Aa5964	Aa5965	Aa5966	Aa5967
Year	Number	Number	Number	Number	Number	Number	Number	Number	Number	Number	Number
1850	—	—	514	—	—	224	—	—	100	—	—
1860	—	—	1,587	—	—	958	—	—	430	—	—
1870	2,574	2,429	—	1,971	1,648	—	1,401	910	—	767	427
1880	4,487	3,820	—	3,307	2,909	—	2,341	1,718	—	1,540	906
1890 [1]	8,789	6,544	—	5,085	3,821	—	3,447	2,437	—	2,115	1,474
1900	9,665	8,666	—	7,350	5,396	—	4,619	3,239	—	2,661	2,031
1910	15,220	12,602	—	10,427	8,090	—	7,581	4,862	—	3,464	2,415
1920	17,190	16,449	—	12,792	10,833	—	9,115	6,755	—	5,443	3,495
1930	17,488	16,809	—	15,277	13,204	—	10,760	8,075	—	6,594	4,865
1940	19,677	17,253	—	15,615	14,411	—	12,875	10,532	—	8,304	6,029
1950	25,182	22,995	—	20,564	17,453	—	15,378	13,079	—	11,082	8,685
1960	28,046	27,205	—	25,255	22,640	—	19,389	16,063	—	13,204	10,725
1970	28,652	26,320	—	26,937	25,892	—	23,904	20,378	—	16,927	12,536
1980	53,430	39,561	—	31,574	28,201	—	27,594	25,604	—	22,152	17,636
1990	68,771	62,370	—	50,245	38,179	—	30,160	26,676	—	25,229	22,719

Population

	Male, by age					Female, by age					
	70–79	70–74	75–79	80 and older	Unknown age	0	1–4	5–9	10–14	15–19	20–29
	Aa5968	Aa5969	Aa5970	Aa5971	Aa5972	Aa5973	Aa5974	Aa5975	Aa5976	Aa5977	Aa5978
Year	Number	Number	Number	Number	Number	Number	Number	Number	Number	Number	Number
1850	31	—	—	1	0	212	867	670	689	670	897
1860	125	—	—	20	4	1,018	3,681	2,972	2,102	1,743	3,181
1870	—	276	119	75	1	1,734	6,412	6,733	5,739	4,098	—
1880	—	600	351	174	—	2,736	9,833	10,271	8,798	7,416	—
1890 [1]	—	1,063	556	356	430	3,128	12,172	14,662	12,145	10,664	—
1900	—	1,470	908	573	581	4,491	15,984	18,817	16,731	15,074	—
1910	—	1,749	1,103	826	954	5,401	20,720	22,598	19,758	18,620	—
1920	—	2,189	1,319	955	285	5,916	24,297	27,897	25,593	21,788	—
1930	—	3,504	1,884	1,169	135	5,719	23,309	30,566	29,528	26,281	—
1940	—	4,342	2,581	1,854	—	5,511	23,339	27,805	28,234	28,762	—
1950	—	5,802	3,890	2,059	—	9,289	35,964	36,641	30,782	28,940	—
1960	—	8,156	5,169	3,829	—	12,480	49,310	55,444	46,255	38,781	—
1970	—	9,387	6,125	5,949	—	11,950	42,548	57,649	60,510	58,392	—
1980	—	13,031	8,263	7,638	—	20,571	72,081	71,704	61,453	69,882	—
1990	—	17,770	12,218	11,583	—	14,956	67,788	89,270	89,430	76,134	—

Note appears at end of table

TABLE Aa5935–5997　Utah population by race, sex, age, nativity, and urban–rural residence: 1850–1990 *Continued*

	Population										
	Female, by age										
	20–24	25–29	30–39	30–34	35–39	40–49	40–44	45–49	50–59	50–54	55–59
	Aa5979	Aa5980	Aa5981	Aa5982	Aa5983	Aa5984	Aa5985	Aa5986	Aa5987	Aa5988	Aa5989
Year	Number	Number	Number	Number	Number	Number	Number	Number	Number	Number	Number
1850	—	—	600	—	—	405	—	—	205	—	—
1860	—	—	2,373	—	—	1,433	—	—	932	—	—
1870	3,182	2,814	—	2,502	2,173	—	1,838	1,482	—	1,278	933
1880	6,360	4,539	—	3,592	3,202	—	2,887	2,332	—	2,120	1,713
1890 [1]	8,845	7,207	—	6,414	4,692	—	3,701	3,140	—	2,852	2,131
1900	12,544	9,899	—	8,554	7,350	—	6,437	4,624	—	3,610	2,991
1910	17,241	14,983	—	12,196	10,033	—	8,332	6,856	—	5,892	4,092
1920	19,274	17,421	—	15,364	13,785	—	10,961	8,770	—	7,427	5,903
1930	22,961	18,452	—	16,479	15,663	—	13,436	11,489	—	9,502	7,155
1940	25,733	21,859	—	19,559	16,935	—	15,096	13,777	—	11,885	9,824
1950	28,496	27,325	—	24,892	22,477	—	19,901	16,541	—	14,706	12,627
1960	32,247	28,289	—	27,685	27,330	—	24,943	22,078	—	19,069	16,097
1970	51,674	36,201	—	29,142	27,238	—	27,053	26,619	—	24,568	20,848
1980	79,761	66,227	—	52,258	39,617	—	32,054	28,820	—	28,251	27,097
1990	69,383	67,951	—	68,806	61,839	—	50,218	38,969	—	31,173	28,254

	Population							
	Female, by age							
	60–69	60–64	65–69	70–79	70–74	75–79	80 and older	Unknown age
	Aa5990	Aa5991	Aa5992	Aa5993	Aa5994	Aa5995	Aa5996	Aa5997
Year	Number	Number	Number	Number	Number	Number	Number	Number
1850	94	—	—	22	—	—	3	0
1860	427	—	—	130	—	—	22	4
1870	—	779	457	—	295	134	81	1
1880	—	1,395	1,013	—	645	399	203	—
1890 [1]	—	2,002	1,473	—	1,098	561	384	171
1900	—	2,632	2,022	—	1,441	960	650	251
1910	—	3,145	2,427	—	1,834	1,157	858	345
1920	—	4,848	3,221	—	2,121	1,423	1,160	176
1930	—	5,977	4,638	—	3,342	1,872	1,391	88
1940	—	7,962	6,137	—	4,372	2,755	2,145	—
1950	—	10,663	8,820	—	6,098	4,501	2,563	—
1960	—	13,617	11,433	—	9,076	6,267	5,302	—
1970	—	18,052	14,484	—	11,768	8,401	8,911	—
1980	—	24,108	20,547	—	16,606	11,979	13,520	—
1990	—	27,252	25,957	—	21,741	17,048	20,922	—

[1] Includes 2,874 American Indians not counted in the general enumeration; see text for Table Aa2244–2340.

Sources

See the sources for Table Aa2244–2340.

Documentation

See the text for Table Aa2244–2340.

Utah was originally part of the Mexican Cession of 1848. It became a territory in 1850 and a state in 1896.

TABLE Aa5998–6098   Vermont population by race, sex, age, nativity, and urban–rural residence: 1790–1990

Contributed by Michael R. Haines

	Area	Population density	Population								
				Race				Residence		Nativity	
	Area	Population density	Total	White	Nonwhite	Black	Other nonwhite	Urban	Rural	Native-born	Foreign-born
	Aa5998	Aa5999	Aa6000	Aa6001	Aa6002	Aa6003	Aa6004	Aa6005	Aa6006	Aa6007	Aa6008
Year	Square miles	Persons per square mile	Number	Number	Number	Number	Number	Number	Number	Number	Number
1790	9,124	9.35	85,341	85,072	269	269	—	0	85,425	—	—
1800	9,124	16.93	154,465	153,908	557	557	—	0	154,465	—	—
1810	9,124	23.88	217,895	216,963	750	750	—	0	217,895	—	—
1820	9,124	25.86	235,981	234,846	1,135	903	15	0	235,981	—	—
1830	9,124	30.76	280,652	279,771	881	881	—	0	280,652	—	—
1840	9,124	32.00	291,948	291,218	730	730	—	0	291,948	—	—
1850	9,124	34.43	314,120	313,402	718	718	—	6,110	308,010	280,405	33,715
1860	9,124	34.54	315,098	314,369	729	709	20	6,213	308,885	282,355	32,743
1870	9,124	36.23	330,551	329,613	938	924	14	22,960	307,591	283,396	47,155
1880	9,124	36.42	332,286	331,218	1,068	1,057	11	33,367	298,919	291,327	40,959
1890	9,124	36.43	332,422	331,418	1,004	937	67	50,638	281,784	288,334	44,088
1900	9,124	37.66	343,641	342,771	870	826	44	75,831	267,810	298,894	44,747
1910	9,124	39.01	355,956	354,298	1,658	1,621	37	98,917	257,039	306,035	49,921
1920	9,124	38.63	352,428	351,817	611	572	39	109,976	242,452	307,870	44,558
1930	9,124	39.41	359,611	358,966	645	568	77	118,766	240,845	316,510	43,101
1940	9,278	38.72	359,231	358,806	425	384	41	123,239	235,992	327,478	31,753
1950	9,278	40.71	377,747	377,188	559	443	116	137,612	240,135	346,935	28,400
1960	9,274	42.04	389,881	389,092	789	519	270	149,921	239,960	366,545	23,336
1970	9,267	47.95	444,330	442,553	1,777	761	1,016	142,889	301,441	425,848	18,482
1980	9,273	55.16	511,456	506,736	4,720	1,135	3,585	172,735	338,721	490,461	20,995
1990	9,249	60.84	562,758	555,088	7,670	1,951	5,719	181,149	381,609	545,214	17,544

	Sex		Population								
				Male, by age							
	Male	Female	0	1–4	5–9	10–14	15–19	20–29	20–24	25–29	30–39
	Aa6009	Aa6010	Aa6011	Aa6012	Aa6013	Aa6014	Aa6015	Aa6016	Aa6017	Aa6018	Aa6019
Year	Number	Number	Number	Number	Number	Number	Number	Number	Number	Number	Number
1790	—	—	—	—	—	—	—	—	—	—	—
1800	—	—	—	—	—	—	—	—	—	—	—
1810	—	—	—	—	—	—	—	—	—	—	—
1820	117,748	118,001	—	—	—	—	—	—	—	—	—
1830	140,422	140,230	—	—	—	—	—	—	—	—	—
1840	146,742	145,206	—	—	—	—	—	—	—	—	—
1850	160,033	154,087	3,360	15,664	19,479	18,529	17,508	27,517	—	—	19,823
1860	158,786	156,312	3,342	15,458	17,861	17,288	17,174	25,857	—	—	19,238
1870	165,721	164,830	3,632	15,341	17,500	17,888	17,031	—	14,625	11,998	—
1880	166,887	165,399	3,499	13,940	17,412	17,221	15,887	—	14,958	12,565	—
1890	169,327	163,095	2,932	12,358	16,138	16,442	16,446	—	15,524	12,561	—
1900	175,138	168,503	3,454	13,082	16,074	15,331	15,735	—	14,962	14,188	—
1910	182,568	173,388	3,607	13,801	16,474	15,893	16,122	—	14,617	14,017	—
1920	178,854	173,574	3,341	14,161	16,827	16,620	14,880	—	13,277	12,594	—
1930	183,266	176,345	3,363	13,572	17,726	17,121	16,010	—	14,523	12,579	—
1940	182,224	177,007	2,968	12,290	15,400	16,521	16,691	—	15,059	13,452	—
1950	187,754	189,993	4,185	17,316	17,737	15,127	14,122	—	13,582	13,149	—
1960	191,743	198,138	4,601	18,017	20,658	19,472	15,886	—	11,063	10,369	—
1970	217,166	227,164	4,076	16,218	23,523	23,715	21,933	—	17,403	14,452	—
1980	249,080	262,376	3,978	14,502	19,507	21,930	25,552	—	23,975	21,997	—
1990	275,492	287,266	3,733	17,442	21,417	19,569	21,245	—	22,041	22,213	—

TABLE Aa5998–6098   Vermont population by race, sex, age, nativity, and urban–rural residence: 1790–1990
Continued

				Population							
				Male, by age							
	30–34	35–39	40–49	40–44	45–49	50–59	50–54	55–59	60–69	60–64	65–69
	Aa6020	Aa6021	Aa6022	Aa6023	Aa6024	Aa6025	Aa6026	Aa6027	Aa6028	Aa6029	Aa6030
Year	Number	Number	Number	Number	Number	Number	Number	Number	Number	Number	Number
1790	—	—	—	—	—	—	—	—	—	—	—
1800	—	—	—	—	—	—	—	—	—	—	—
1810	—	—	—	—	—	—	—	—	—	—	—
1820	—	—	—	—	—	—	—	—	—	—	—
1830	—	—	—	—	—	—	—	—	—	—	—
1840	—	—	—	—	—	—	—	—	—	—	—
1850	—	—	15,893	—	—	10,705	—	—	6,648	—	—
1860	—	—	16,037	—	—	12,333	—	—	8,763	—	—
1870	10,518	9,856	—	8,710	8,288	—	7,560	5,863	—	5,612	4,330
1880	10,933	10,016	—	9,144	8,295	—	7,417	6,442	—	5,942	4,589
1890	11,618	10,887	—	9,838	8,893	—	8,352	6,608	—	6,045	4,858
1900	12,961	11,678	—	10,790	9,831	—	8,737	7,460	—	6,469	4,911
1910	13,529	13,088	—	11,953	10,224	—	9,597	8,090	—	6,770	5,489
1920	11,710	12,149	—	11,369	11,448	—	10,217	8,217	—	7,107	5,778
1930	11,840	12,048	—	11,007	10,804	—	10,358	9,112	—	7,800	5,816
1940	12,915	11,898	—	11,025	10,840	—	9,847	8,893	—	7,825	6,540
1950	12,614	12,389	—	11,924	10,760	—	9,854	9,071	—	7,749	6,619
1960	11,177	11,621	—	11,338	11,081	—	10,414	9,144	—	7,884	6,956
1970	11,979	11,315	—	11,731	11,510	—	10,934	9,906	—	9,067	7,040
1980	21,186	16,283	—	12,511	11,769	—	11,788	11,143	—	9,803	8,499
1990	24,526	24,140	—	21,958	16,505	—	12,293	11,136	—	10,715	9,491

					Population						
	Male, by age					Female, by age					
	70–79	70–74	75–79	80 and older	Unknown age	0	1–4	5–9	10–14	15–19	20–29
	Aa6031	Aa6032	Aa6033	Aa6034	Aa6035	Aa6036	Aa6037	Aa6038	Aa6039	Aa6040	Aa6041
Year	Number	Number	Number	Number	Number	Number	Number	Number	Number	Number	Number
1790	—	—	—	—	—	—	—	—	—	—	—
1800	—	—	—	—	—	—	—	—	—	—	—
1810	—	—	—	—	—	—	—	—	—	—	—
1820	—	—	—	—	—	—	—	—	—	—	—
1830	—	—	—	—	—	—	—	—	—	—	—
1840	—	—	—	—	—	—	—	—	—	—	—
1850	3,529	—	—	1,352	26	3,234	15,391	18,674	17,639	16,818	25,736
1860	3,985	—	—	1,450	0	3,467	15,084	17,430	16,573	16,555	26,241
1870	—	3,490	1,944	1,533	2	3,496	14,894	16,937	17,058	16,693	—
1880	—	4,104	2,556	1,967	—	3,261	13,391	16,731	16,362	15,850	—
1890	—	4,320	2,651	2,395	461	2,830	11,753	15,238	15,202	15,509	—
1900	—	4,097	2,688	2,069	621	3,301	13,015	15,772	14,848	14,731	—
1910	—	4,432	2,750	1,975	140	3,626	13,137	16,183	15,558	15,039	—
1920	—	4,165	2,791	1,971	232	3,233	13,809	16,585	15,965	14,628	—
1930	—	4,637	2,890	2,002	58	3,180	13,117	17,039	16,592	15,361	—
1940	—	4,960	2,862	2,238	—	2,718	11,977	14,832	15,823	15,908	—
1950	—	5,234	3,980	2,342	—	4,006	16,434	16,697	14,387	14,572	—
1960	—	5,306	3,578	3,178	—	4,339	16,916	20,074	18,524	15,831	—
1970	—	5,355	3,613	3,396	—	3,899	15,465	22,382	21,937	22,464	—
1980	—	6,342	4,351	3,964	—	3,704	13,814	18,348	20,720	25,735	—
1990	—	7,102	5,092	4,874	—	3,516	16,570	20,372	18,421	20,454	—

(continued)

TABLE Aa5998–6098   Vermont population by race, sex, age, nativity, and urban–rural residence: 1790–1990
Continued

Population

	Female, by age										
	20–24	25–29	30–39	30–34	35–39	40–49	40–44	45–49	50–59	50–54	55–59
	Aa6042	Aa6043	Aa6044	Aa6045	Aa6046	Aa6047	Aa6048	Aa6049	Aa6050	Aa6051	Aa6052
Year	Number	Number	Number	Number	Number	Number	Number	Number	Number	Number	Number
1790	—	—	—	—	—	—	—	—	—	—	—
1800	—	—	—	—	—	—	—	—	—	—	—
1810	—	—	—	—	—	—	—	—	—	—	—
1820	—	—	—	—	—	—	—	—	—	—	—
1830	—	—	—	—	—	—	—	—	—	—	—
1840	—	—	—	—	—	—	—	—	—	—	—
1850	—	—	19,294	—	—	15,249	—	—	10,424	—	—
1860	—	—	19,265	—	—	15,471	—	—	12,277	—	—
1870	14,821	12,927	—	11,321	10,201	—	8,897	7,897	—	7,266	5,773
1880	14,872	12,447	—	10,995	10,832	—	9,557	8,343	—	7,441	6,559
1890	14,740	12,350	—	11,437	10,355	—	9,575	8,929	—	8,146	6,702
1900	14,499	13,520	—	12,116	11,119	—	10,118	9,028	—	8,394	7,436
1910	14,168	13,068	—	12,560	12,207	—	10,891	9,550	—	8,862	7,321
1920	13,276	12,708	—	11,699	11,600	—	11,007	10,319	—	9,271	7,556
1930	13,306	12,011	—	11,575	11,734	—	10,787	10,236	—	9,735	8,514
1940	13,881	12,760	—	12,175	11,438	—	10,915	10,467	—	9,841	8,571
1950	13,902	13,638	—	12,867	12,376	—	11,672	10,576	—	10,088	9,235
1960	11,350	10,674	—	11,726	12,261	—	11,793	11,144	—	10,524	9,604
1970	18,606	14,472	—	11,769	11,398	—	12,238	12,260	—	11,589	10,693
1980	24,662	22,848	—	21,139	16,088	—	12,512	11,849	—	12,368	12,359
1990	21,469	23,048	—	25,470	24,917	—	21,417	16,145	—	12,446	11,651

Population

	Female, by age									White	
	60–69	60–64	65–69	70–79	70–74	75–79	80 and older	Unknown age		Male	Female
	Aa6053	Aa6054	Aa6055	Aa6056	Aa6057	Aa6058	Aa6059	Aa6060		Aa6061	Aa6062
Year	Number	Number	Number	Number	Number	Number	Number	Number		Number	Number
1790	—	—	—	—	—	—	—	—		44,710	40,362
1800	—	—	—	—	—	—	—	—		79,328	74,580
1810	—	—	—	—	—	—	—	—		109,581	107,382
1820	—	—	—	—	—	—	—	—		117,310	117,536
1830	—	—	—	—	—	—	—	—		139,996	139,775
1840	—	—	—	—	—	—	—	—		146,378	144,840
1850	6,735	—	—	3,564	—	—	1,317	12		—	—
1860	8,202	—	—	4,169	—	—	1,577	1		—	—
1870	—	5,535	4,172	—	3,223	1,930	1,788	1		—	—
1880	—	5,797	4,544	—	3,780	2,523	2,114	—		—	—
1890	—	5,858	5,027	—	3,966	2,552	2,653	273		—	—
1900	—	6,358	5,180	—	3,762	2,643	2,421	242		—	—
1910	—	6,533	5,497	—	4,107	2,709	2,303	69		—	—
1920	—	6,785	5,421	—	4,226	2,881	2,461	144		—	—
1930	—	7,190	5,682	—	4,681	2,940	2,605	60		—	—
1940	—	7,809	6,609	—	5,274	3,194	2,815	—		—	—
1950	—	8,184	7,219	—	6,000	4,998	3,142	—		—	—
1960	—	8,655	8,016	—	6,681	4,943	5,083	—		—	—
1970	—	9,908	8,617	—	7,358	5,563	6,546	—		—	—
1980	—	11,220	10,081	—	8,851	6,861	9,217	—		—	—
1990	—	11,766	11,127	—	9,352	7,733	11,392	—		—	—

TABLE Aa5998–6098   Vermont population by race, sex, age, nativity, and urban–rural residence: 1790–1990
Continued

	Population								
	White								
	Male, by age								
Year	0–4	5–9	10–14	15–19	20–29	30–39	40–49	50–59	60–69
	Aa6063	Aa6064	Aa6065	Aa6066	Aa6067	Aa6068	Aa6069	Aa6070	Aa6071
	Number	Number	Number	Number	Number	Number	Number	Number	Number
1790	—	—	—	—	—	—	—	—	—
1800	—	—	—	—	—	—	—	—	—
1810	—	—	—	—	—	—	—	—	—
1820	—	—	—	—	—	—	—	—	—
1830	21,700	19,406	17,597	15,782	24,207	15,773	10,405	7,051	5,203
1840	21,786	19,069	17,551	16,999	23,006	17,596	12,817	7,982	5,454
1850	—	—	—	—	—	—	—	—	—
1860	—	—	—	—	—	—	—	—	—
1870	—	—	—	—	—	—	—	—	—
1880	—	—	—	—	—	—	—	—	—
1890	—	—	—	—	—	—	—	—	—
1900	—	—	—	—	—	—	—	—	—
1910	—	—	—	—	—	—	—	—	—
1920	—	—	—	—	—	—	—	—	—
1930	—	—	—	—	—	—	—	—	—
1940	—	—	—	—	—	—	—	—	—
1950	—	—	—	—	—	—	—	—	—
1960	—	—	—	—	—	—	—	—	—
1970	—	—	—	—	—	—	—	—	—
1980	—	—	—	—	—	—	—	—	—
1990	—	—	—	—	—	—	—	—	—

	Population								
	White								
	Male, by age		Female, by age						
Year	70–79	80 and older	0–4	5–9	10–14	15–19	20–29	30–39	40–49
	Aa6072	Aa6073	Aa6074	Aa6075	Aa6076	Aa6077	Aa6078	Aa6079	Aa6080
	Number	Number	Number	Number	Number	Number	Number	Number	Number
1790	—	—	—	—	—	—	—	—	—
1800	—	—	—	—	—	—	—	—	—
1810	—	—	—	—	—	—	—	—	—
1820	—	—	—	—	—	—	—	—	—
1830	2,203	669	21,334	18,632	16,870	15,753	25,180	16,264	11,034
1840	3,137	981	20,379	18,877	16,677	15,744	24,225	18,163	12,807
1850	—	—	—	—	—	—	—	—	—
1860	—	—	—	—	—	—	—	—	—
1870	—	—	—	—	—	—	—	—	—
1880	—	—	—	—	—	—	—	—	—
1890	—	—	—	—	—	—	—	—	—
1900	—	—	—	—	—	—	—	—	—
1910	—	—	—	—	—	—	—	—	—
1920	—	—	—	—	—	—	—	—	—
1930	—	—	—	—	—	—	—	—	—
1940	—	—	—	—	—	—	—	—	—
1950	—	—	—	—	—	—	—	—	—
1960	—	—	—	—	—	—	—	—	—
1970	—	—	—	—	—	—	—	—	—
1980	—	—	—	—	—	—	—	—	—
1990	—	—	—	—	—	—	—	—	—

(continued)

TABLE Aa5998–6098   Vermont population by race, sex, age, nativity, and urban–rural residence: 1790–1990
Continued

	Population								
	White								
	Female, by age				Male, by age				
	50–59	60–69	70–79	80 and older	0–9	10–15	16–25	26–44	45 and older
	Aa6081	Aa6082	Aa6083	Aa6084	Aa6085	Aa6086	Aa6087	Aa6088	Aa6089
Year	Number	Number	Number	Number	Number	Number	Number	Number	Number
1790	—	—	—	—	—	—	—	—	—
1800	—	—	—	—	29,420	12,046	13,242	16,544	8,076
1810	—	—	—	—	38,062	18,347	19,678	20,441	13,053
1820	—	—	—	—	35,708	19,241	24,137	22,035	16,189
1830	7,152	4,727	2,086	743	—	—	—	—	—
1840	8,612	5,423	2,875	1,058	—	—	—	—	—
1850	—	—	—	—	—	—	—	—	—
1860	—	—	—	—	—	—	—	—	—
1870	—	—	—	—	—	—	—	—	—
1880	—	—	—	—	—	—	—	—	—
1890	—	—	—	—	—	—	—	—	—
1900	—	—	—	—	—	—	—	—	—
1910	—	—	—	—	—	—	—	—	—
1920	—	—	—	—	—	—	—	—	—
1930	—	—	—	—	—	—	—	—	—
1940	—	—	—	—	—	—	—	—	—
1950	—	—	—	—	—	—	—	—	—
1960	—	—	—	—	—	—	—	—	—
1970	—	—	—	—	—	—	—	—	—
1980	—	—	—	—	—	—	—	—	—
1990	—	—	—	—	—	—	—	—	—

	Population								
	White								
	Female, by age					Male, by age		Female, by age	
	0–9	10–15	16–25	26–44	45 and older	0–15	16 and older	0–15	16 and older
	Aa6090	Aa6091	Aa6092	Aa6093	Aa6094	Aa6095	Aa6096	Aa6097	Aa6098
Year	Number	Number	Number	Number	Number	Number	Number	Number	Number
1790	—	—	—	—	—	22,305	22,405	21,327	19,035
1800	28,272	11,366	12,606	15,287	7,049	—	—	—	—
1810	36,613	17,339	21,181	20,792	11,457	—	—	—	—
1820	35,327	18,577	24,713	23,683	15,236	—	—	—	—
1830	—	—	—	—	—	—	—	—	—
1840	—	—	—	—	—	—	—	—	—
1850	—	—	—	—	—	—	—	—	—
1860	—	—	—	—	—	—	—	—	—
1870	—	—	—	—	—	—	—	—	—
1880	—	—	—	—	—	—	—	—	—
1890	—	—	—	—	—	—	—	—	—
1900	—	—	—	—	—	—	—	—	—
1910	—	—	—	—	—	—	—	—	—
1920	—	—	—	—	—	—	—	—	—
1930	—	—	—	—	—	—	—	—	—
1940	—	—	—	—	—	—	—	—	—
1950	—	—	—	—	—	—	—	—	—
1960	—	—	—	—	—	—	—	—	—
1970	—	—	—	—	—	—	—	—	—
1980	—	—	—	—	—	—	—	—	—
1990	—	—	—	—	—	—	—	—	—

Sources

See the sources for Table Aa2244–2340.

Documentation

See the text for Table Aa2244–2340.

Vermont became a state in 1791 from lands previously in New Hampshire and New York.

TABLE Aa6099–6199 Virginia population by race, sex, age, nativity, and urban–rural residence: 1790–1990 [Present boundaries]

Contributed by Michael R. Haines

					Population							
					Race				Residence		Nativity	
	Area	Population density	Total	White	Nonwhite	Black	Other nonwhite	Urban	Rural	Native-born	Foreign-born
	Aa6099	Aa6100	Aa6101	Aa6102	Aa6103	Aa6104	Aa6105	Aa6106	Aa6107	Aa6108	Aa6109
Year	Square miles	Persons per square mile	Number	Number	Number	Number	Number	Number	Number	Number	Number
1790	40,262	17.18	691,737	391,524	300,213	300,213	—	12,296	679,441	—	—
1800	40,230	20.07	807,557	447,780	359,777	359,777	—	21,155	786,402	—	—
1810	40,230	21.82	877,683	463,913	413,792	413,792	—	31,823	845,860	—	—
1820	40,230	23.32	938,261	489,398	448,863	448,657	210	35,453	902,808	—	—
1830	40,230	25.95	1,044,054	543,627	500,427	500,427	—	50,375	993,679	—	—
1840	40,230	25.48	1,025,227	544,573	480,654	480,654	—	70,968	954,259	—	—
1850	40,262	27.80	1,119,348	616,069	503,279	503,279	—	89,255	1,030,093	1,108,368	10,980
1860	40,262	30.29	1,219,630	691,773	527,857	527,763	94	115,879	1,103,751	1,201,117	18,513
1870	40,262	30.43	1,225,163	712,089	513,074	512,841	233	145,618	1,079,545	1,211,409	13,754
1880	40,262	37.57	1,512,565	880,858	631,707	631,616	91	189,079	1,323,486	1,497,869	14,696
1890	40,262	41.13	1,655,980	1,020,122	635,858	635,438	420	282,721	1,373,259	1,637,606	18,374
1900	40,262	46.05	1,854,184	1,192,855	661,329	660,722	607	340,067	1,514,117	1,834,723	19,461
1910	40,262	51.20	2,061,612	1,389,809	671,803	671,096	707	476,529	1,585,083	2,034,555	27,057
1920	40,262	57.35	2,309,187	1,617,909	691,278	690,017	1,261	673,984	1,635,203	2,277,482	31,705
1930	40,262	60.15	2,421,851	1,770,441	651,410	650,165	1,245	785,537	1,636,314	2,397,484	24,367
1940	39,899	67.11	2,677,773	2,015,583	662,190	661,449	741	944,675	1,733,098	2,654,335	23,438
1950	39,893	83.19	3,318,680	2,581,555	737,125	734,211	2,914	1,560,115	1,758,565	3,276,875	35,690
1960	39,841	99.57	3,966,949	3,142,443	824,506	816,258	8,248	2,204,913	1,762,036	3,906,244	48,185
1970	39,780	116.86	4,648,494	3,761,514	886,980	861,368	25,612	2,938,917	1,709,577	4,576,198	72,281
1980	39,704	134.67	5,346,818	4,229,798	1,117,020	1,008,668	108,352	3,529,423	1,817,395	5,169,500	177,318
1990	39,598	156.26	6,187,358	4,791,739	1,395,619	1,162,994	232,625	4,293,443	1,893,915	5,875,549	311,809

					Population							
	Sex		Male, by age									
	Male	Female	0	1–4	5–9	10–14	15–19	20–29	20–24	25–29	30–39
	Aa6110	Aa6111	Aa6112	Aa6113	Aa6114	Aa6115	Aa6116	Aa6117	Aa6118	Aa6119	Aa6120
Year	Number	Number	Number	Number	Number	Number	Number	Number	Number	Number	Number
1790	—	—	—	—	—	—	—	—	—	—	—
1800	—	—	—	—	—	—	—	—	—	—	—
1810	—	—	—	—	—	—	—	—	—	—	—
1820	474,480	463,575	—	—	—	—	—	—	—	—	—
1830	522,764	521,290	—	—	—	—	—	—	—	—	—
1840	512,739	512,488	—	—	—	—	—	—	—	—	—
1850	561,892	557,456	13,478	71,796	81,935	76,630	59,761	94,450	—	—	62,428
1860	613,892	605,738	17,603	76,457	85,737	82,282	66,329	103,677	—	—	69,852
1870	597,058	628,105	18,071	74,795	76,737	82,976	64,336	—	53,793	38,803	—
1880	745,589	766,976	24,607	93,783	110,804	95,361	71,757	—	69,712	52,816	—
1890	824,278	831,702	21,687	87,963	115,951	112,500	92,898	—	72,596	52,832	—
1900	925,897	928,287	26,372	98,775	121,310	111,517	101,156	—	87,803	68,373	—
1910	1,035,348	1,026,264	28,384	107,308	129,152	120,431	107,821	—	94,952	78,370	—
1920	1,168,492	1,140,695	27,911	111,212	142,876	134,603	118,424	—	104,395	88,479	—
1930	1,216,046	1,205,805	24,967	104,878	147,552	136,026	129,433	—	108,191	85,941	—
1940	1,349,004	1,328,769	22,850	100,717	127,633	136,874	143,759	—	129,210	115,483	—
1950	1,675,216	1,643,464	36,445	157,517	160,605	135,868	138,614	—	153,557	147,738	—
1960	1,979,372	1,987,577	46,768	185,534	214,330	196,572	167,614	—	152,056	128,171	—
1970	2,297,121	2,351,373	40,823	158,762	232,508	241,202	225,034	—	231,510	167,638	—
1980	2,618,310	2,728,508	39,582	145,156	198,256	219,464	259,129	—	272,928	236,875	—
1990	3,033,974	3,153,384	40,678	185,483	217,304	203,741	225,664	—	270,811	289,626	—

(continued)

TABLE Aa6099–6199   Virginia population by race, sex, age, nativity, and urban–rural residence: 1790–1990
[Present boundaries]   *Continued*

	Population										
	Male, by age										
	30–34	35–39	40–49	40–44	45–49	50–59	50–54	55–59	60–69	60–64	65–69
	Aa6121	Aa6122	Aa6123	Aa6124	Aa6125	Aa6126	Aa6127	Aa6128	Aa6129	Aa6130	Aa6131
Year	Number	Number	Number	Number	Number	Number	Number	Number	Number	Number	Number
1790	—	—	—	—	—	—	—	—	—	—	—
1800	—	—	—	—	—	—	—	—	—	—	—
1810	—	—	—	—	—	—	—	—	—	—	—
1820	—	—	—	—	—	—	—	—	—	—	—
1830	—	—	—	—	—	—	—	—	—	—	—
1840	—	—	—	—	—	—	—	—	—	—	—
1850	—	—	45,063	—	—	28,976	—	—	17,189	—	—
1860	—	—	49,665	—	—	32,011	—	—	19,706	—	—
1870	31,880	31,723	—	26,513	24,987	—	22,250	14,440	—	14,652	8,806
1880	41,915	37,499	—	32,012	27,600	—	24,549	16,261	—	18,884	11,882
1890	48,654	46,627	—	38,410	32,494	—	27,151	18,522	—	20,434	14,120
1900	55,117	48,776	—	47,092	39,458	—	35,572	24,607	—	21,112	15,239
1910	66,972	64,251	—	51,894	43,915	—	41,866	29,882	—	25,490	18,893
1920	72,954	77,475	—	63,268	63,528	—	47,870	32,978	—	30,517	22,267
1930	75,902	77,736	—	67,919	63,689	—	56,937	43,785	—	33,791	23,611
1940	100,762	89,722	—	79,392	71,855	—	62,585	50,373	—	41,568	34,722
1950	135,000	125,414	—	106,464	88,034	—	76,331	62,821	—	50,220	41,904
1960	135,546	142,589	—	130,717	116,628	—	95,860	78,651	—	60,708	50,702
1970	139,365	132,886	—	137,317	136,877	—	121,814	101,895	—	80,366	58,914
1980	221,884	181,620	—	147,602	133,359	—	132,543	126,807	—	103,377	81,048
1990	281,268	255,641	—	233,799	184,198	—	143,850	124,269	—	114,284	101,873

	Population										
	Male, by age					Female, by age					
	70–79	70–74	75–79	80 and older	Unknown age	0	1–4	5–9	10–14	15–19	20–29
	Aa6132	Aa6133	Aa6134	Aa6135	Aa6136	Aa6137	Aa6138	Aa6139	Aa6140	Aa6141	Aa6142
Year	Number	Number	Number	Number	Number	Number	Number	Number	Number	Number	Number
1790	—	—	—	—	—	—	—	—	—	—	—
1800	—	—	—	—	—	—	—	—	—	—	—
1810	—	—	—	—	—	—	—	—	—	—	—
1820	—	—	—	—	—	—	—	—	—	—	—
1830	—	—	—	—	—	—	—	—	—	—	—
1840	—	—	—	—	—	—	—	—	—	—	—
1850	7,274	—	—	2,850	62	13,780	70,748	79,737	73,667	61,390	94,694
1860	7,767	—	—	2,535	271	17,639	75,576	83,312	78,440	67,414	102,925
1870	—	6,315	3,120	2,861	0	17,731	72,872	74,901	79,460	69,408	—
1880	—	7,985	4,555	3,607	—	24,194	92,103	108,040	91,796	74,553	—
1890	—	9,675	5,342	4,134	2,288	20,656	84,959	112,830	108,499	96,431	—
1900	—	10,683	6,230	4,522	2,183	26,016	97,892	119,318	109,320	102,346	—
1910	—	12,360	6,813	4,892	1,702	27,784	105,349	127,338	117,132	109,451	—
1920	—	14,595	8,071	5,307	1,762	27,746	110,315	140,259	131,390	115,936	—
1930	—	17,678	10,210	7,198	602	24,399	102,894	144,323	133,600	126,324	—
1940	—	21,547	11,123	8,829	—	22,456	98,054	124,835	133,413	138,294	—
1950	—	28,567	20,408	9,709	—	35,540	151,976	155,805	131,744	127,756	—
1960	—	36,044	23,004	17,878	—	45,885	180,073	208,258	191,246	156,793	—
1970	—	40,940	26,138	23,132	—	38,913	153,595	224,450	233,080	215,838	—
1980	—	55,486	33,751	29,443	—	37,764	138,184	189,268	211,587	246,545	—
1990	—	72,674	47,823	40,988	—	38,791	178,203	207,057	194,790	212,892	—

TABLE Aa6099–6199   Virginia population by race, sex, age, nativity, and urban-rural residence: 1790–1990
[Present boundaries]   *Continued*

	Population										
	Female, by age										
	20–24	25–29	30–39	30–34	35–39	40–49	40–44	45–49	50–59	50–54	55–59
	Aa6143	Aa6144	Aa6145	Aa6146	Aa6147	Aa6148	Aa6149	Aa6150	Aa6151	Aa6152	Aa6153
Year	Number	Number	Number	Number	Number	Number	Number	Number	Number	Number	Number
1790	—	—	—	—	—	—	—	—	—	—	—
1800	—	—	—	—	—	—	—	—	—	—	—
1810	—	—	—	—	—	—	—	—	—	—	—
1820	—	—	—	—	—	—	—	—	—	—	—
1830	—	—	—	—	—	—	—	—	—	—	—
1840	—	—	—	—	—	—	—	—	—	—	—
1850	—	—	62,037	—	—	44,265	—	—	28,286	—	—
1860	—	—	69,004	—	—	48,324	—	—	31,286	—	—
1870	64,925	49,287	—	39,282	35,765	—	30,139	24,326	—	21,610	13,126
1880	77,000	58,015	—	46,480	42,821	—	36,160	28,855	—	25,940	16,589
1890	79,092	58,447	—	51,189	46,707	—	39,951	33,210	—	29,086	18,837
1900	94,256	71,927	—	56,425	49,972	—	45,863	37,701	—	33,959	23,931
1910	100,356	82,932	—	68,101	63,501	—	50,092	41,632	—	37,993	27,191
1920	107,770	91,520	—	74,995	75,725	—	61,922	52,721	—	42,221	29,561
1930	109,412	90,997	—	80,694	80,475	—	68,105	61,978	—	53,486	39,148
1940	124,110	113,432	—	99,871	91,545	—	80,066	71,330	—	61,434	49,265
1950	137,849	146,954	—	131,516	122,603	—	104,787	89,165	—	78,118	63,279
1960	132,702	128,956	—	138,948	148,325	—	130,154	115,838	—	97,483	83,022
1970	208,308	167,407	—	141,037	136,410	—	143,349	145,608	—	126,089	108,725
1980	258,040	241,037	—	228,068	184,490	—	149,173	138,201	—	141,804	141,082
1990	249,055	284,615	—	285,179	262,617	—	239,699	187,799	—	147,485	132,938

	Population									White	
	Female, by age										
	60–69	60–64	65–69	70–79	70–74	75–79	80 and older	Unknown age		Male	Female
	Aa6154	Aa6155	Aa6156	Aa6157	Aa6158	Aa6159	Aa6160	Aa6161		Aa6162	Aa6163
Year	Number	Number	Number	Number	Number	Number	Number	Number		Number	Number
1790	—	—	—	—	—	—	—	—		200,408	191,116
1800	—	—	—	—	—	—	—	—		227,462	220.318
1810	—	—	—	—	—	—	—	—		234,743	229,170
1820	—	—	—	—	—	—	—	—		245,635	243,763
1830	—	—	—	—	—	—	—	—		270,173	273,454
1840	—	—	—	—	—	—	—	—		270,019	274,554
1850	17,097	—	—	8,124	—	—	3,574	57		—	—
1860	19,727	—	—	8,373	—	—	3,462	256		—	—
1870	—	13,569	8,110	—	6,589	3,313	3,692	0		—	—
1880	—	16,664	10,262	—	8,236	4,560	4,708	—		—	—
1890	—	18,411	12,207	—	9,042	5,203	4,946	1,999		—	—
1900	—	21,484	14,605	—	10,439	5,974	5,154	1,705		—	—
1910	—	24,314	17,529	—	11,892	6,938	5,664	1,075		—	—
1920	—	27,570	20,233	—	14,349	8,422	6,764	1,276		—	—
1930	—	31,407	22,324	—	17,137	10,111	8,409	582		—	—
1940	—	41,941	34,050	—	21,868	11,927	10,878	—		—	—
1950	—	52,436	45,623	—	31,989	23,793	12,531	—		—	—
1960	—	68,552	59,496	—	44,936	30,039	26,871	—		—	—
1970	—	91,667	75,226	—	58,074	40,549	43,048	—		—	—
1980	—	117,689	101,927	—	79,835	57,725	66,089	—		—	—
1990	—	131,152	126,857	—	99,218	77,475	97,562	—		—	—

(continued)

TABLE Aa6099–6199   Virginia population by race, sex, age, nativity, and urban–rural residence: 1790–1990 [Present boundaries]   *Continued*

	Population								
	White								
	Male, by age								
	0–4	5–9	10–14	15–19	20–29	30–39	40–49	50–59	60–69
	Aa6164	Aa6165	Aa6166	Aa6167	Aa6168	Aa6169	Aa6170	Aa6171	Aa6172
Year	Number	Number	Number	Number	Number	Number	Number	Number	Number
1790	—	—	—	—	—	—	—	—	—
1800	—	—	—	—	—	—	—	—	—
1810	—	—	—	—	—	—	—	—	—
1820	—	—	—	—	—	—	—	—	—
1830	50,110	39,746	33,200	28,674	47,472	29,121	18,691	12,241	7,069
1840	49,248	38,431	33,293	28,203	45,468	30,290	20,574	12,747	7,342
1850	—	—	—	—	—	—	—	—	—
1860	—	—	—	—	—	—	—	—	—
1870	—	—	—	—	—	—	—	—	—
1880	—	—	—	—	—	—	—	—	—
1890	—	—	—	—	—	—	—	—	—
1900	—	—	—	—	—	—	—	—	—
1910	—	—	—	—	—	—	—	—	—
1920	—	—	—	—	—	—	—	—	—
1930	—	—	—	—	—	—	—	—	—
1940	—	—	—	—	—	—	—	—	—
1950	—	—	—	—	—	—	—	—	—
1960	—	—	—	—	—	—	—	—	—
1970	—	—	—	—	—	—	—	—	—
1980	—	—	—	—	—	—	—	—	—
1990	—	—	—	—	—	—	—	—	—

	Population								
	White								
	Male, by age		Female, by age						
	70–79	80 and older	0–4	5–9	10–14	15–19	20–29	30–39	40–49
	Aa6173	Aa6174	Aa6175	Aa6176	Aa6177	Aa6178	Aa6179	Aa6180	Aa6181
Year	Number	Number	Number	Number	Number	Number	Number	Number	Number
1790	—	—	—	—	—	—	—	—	—
1800	—	—	—	—	—	—	—	—	—
1810	—	—	—	—	—	—	—	—	—
1820	—	—	—	—	—	—	—	—	—
1830	2,835	1,014	47,653	38,389	32,612	32,008	49,691	29,568	19,372
1840	3,351	1,072	46,531	37,647	32,140	31,369	49,439	30,753	20,677
1850	—	—	—	—	—	—	—	—	—
1860	—	—	—	—	—	—	—	—	—
1870	—	—	—	—	—	—	—	—	—
1880	—	—	—	—	—	—	—	—	—
1890	—	—	—	—	—	—	—	—	—
1900	—	—	—	—	—	—	—	—	—
1910	—	—	—	—	—	—	—	—	—
1920	—	—	—	—	—	—	—	—	—
1930	—	—	—	—	—	—	—	—	—
1940	—	—	—	—	—	—	—	—	—
1950	—	—	—	—	—	—	—	—	—
1960	—	—	—	—	—	—	—	—	—
1970	—	—	—	—	—	—	—	—	—
1980	—	—	—	—	—	—	—	—	—
1990	—	—	—	—	—	—	—	—	—

TABLE Aa6099–6199 Virginia population by race, sex, age, nativity, and urban–rural residence: 1790–1990 [Present boundaries] *Continued*

	Population							
	White							
	Female, by age				Male, by age			
	50–59	60–69	70–79	80 and older	0–9	10–15	16–25	26–44	45 and older
	Aa6182	Aa6183	Aa6184	Aa6185	Aa6186	Aa6187	Aa6188	Aa6189	Aa6190
Year	Number	Number	Number	Number	Number	Number	Number	Number	Number
1790	—	—	—	—	—	—	—	—	—
1800	—	—	—	—	79,266	35,119	42,674	44,328	26,075
1810	—	—	—	—	80,483	35,597	43,576	45,349	29,738
1820	—	—	—	—	82,480	36,846	47,311	48,067	30,931
1830	12,690	7,227	3,192	1,052	—	—	—	—	—
1840	13,355	7,939	3,529	1,175	—	—	—	—	—
1850	—	—	—	—	—	—	—	—	—
1860	—	—	—	—	—	—	—	—	—
1870	—	—	—	—	—	—	—	—	—
1880	—	—	—	—	—	—	—	—	—
1890	—	—	—	—	—	—	—	—	—
1900	—	—	—	—	—	—	—	—	—
1910	—	—	—	—	—	—	—	—	—
1920	—	—	—	—	—	—	—	—	—
1930	—	—	—	—	—	—	—	—	—
1940	—	—	—	—	—	—	—	—	—
1950	—	—	—	—	—	—	—	—	—
1960	—	—	—	—	—	—	—	—	—
1970	—	—	—	—	—	—	—	—	—
1980	—	—	—	—	—	—	—	—	—
1990	—	—	—	—	—	—	—	—	—

	Population							
	White							
	Female, by age					Male, by age		Female, by age	
	0–9	10–15	16–25	26–44	45 and older	0–15	16 and older	0–15	16 and older
	Aa6191	Aa6192	Aa6193	Aa6194	Aa6195	Aa6196	Aa6197	Aa6198	Aa6199
Year	Number	Number	Number	Number	Number	Number	Number	Number	Number
1790	—	—	—	—	—	101,545	98,863	92,003	99,113
1800	74,771	33,975	44,982	42,320	24,270	—	—	—	—
1810	74,652	35,160	46,719	44,305	28,334	—	—	—	—
1820	78,211	37,250	51,338	46,958	30,006	—	—	—	—
1830	—	—	—	—	—	—	—	—	—
1840	—	—	—	—	—	—	—	—	—
1850	—	—	—	—	—	—	—	—	—
1860	—	—	—	—	—	—	—	—	—
1870	—	—	—	—	—	—	—	—	—
1880	—	—	—	—	—	—	—	—	—
1890	—	—	—	—	—	—	—	—	—
1900	—	—	—	—	—	—	—	—	—
1910	—	—	—	—	—	—	—	—	—
1920	—	—	—	—	—	—	—	—	—
1930	—	—	—	—	—	—	—	—	—
1940	—	—	—	—	—	—	—	—	—
1950	—	—	—	—	—	—	—	—	—
1960	—	—	—	—	—	—	—	—	—
1970	—	—	—	—	—	—	—	—	—
1980	—	—	—	—	—	—	—	—	—
1990	—	—	—	—	—	—	—	—	—

Sources

See the sources for Table Aa2244–2340.

Documentation

See the text for Table Aa2244–2340.

Virginia was one of the original thirteen states, joining the Union in 1788. This table excludes the counties that formed the state of West Virginia in 1863. To see the population of Virginia as constituted before 1863, it is necessary to add those counties back into these totals. Population figures for those counties are shown in Table Aa6312–6412. Virginia ceded the territory of the city of Alexandria and some surrounding rural areas to the District of Columbia in 1790. This was retroceded to Virginia in 1846.

Table Aa6099–6199 is based on Virginia's present boundaries. Table Aa6200–6248 is based on the historical boundaries (that is, Virginia without the West Virginia counties but excluding the territory in the District of Columbia for 1800–1846).

TABLE Aa6200–6248 Virginia population by race, sex, age, nativity, and urban–rural residence: 1790–1840
[Historical boundaries]

Contributed by Michael R. Haines

			Population							
					Race				Residence	
	Area	Population density	Total	White	Nonwhite	Black	Other nonwhite		Urban	Rural
	Aa6200	Aa6201	Aa6202	Aa6203	Aa6204	Aa6205	Aa6206		Aa6207	Aa6208
Year	Square miles	Persons per square mile	Number	Number	Number	Number	Number		Number	Number
1790	40,262	17.18	691,737	391,524	300,213	300,213	—		12,296	679,441
1800	40,262	19.91	801,608	443,386	358,222	358,222	—		16,184	785,424
1810	40,262	21.59	869,131	458,179	410,974	410,974	—		24,596	844,535
1820	40,262	23.06	928,558	482,842	445,716	445,510	210		27,235	901,323
1830	40,262	25.69	1,034,481	537,216	497,265	497,265	—		42,134	992,347
1840	40,262	25.22	1,015,260	537,842	477,418	477,418	—		62,509	952,751

	Population								
	Sex		White						
					Male, by age				
	Male	Female	Male	Female	0–4	5–9	10–14	15–19	20–29
	Aa6209	Aa6210	Aa6211	Aa6212	Aa6213	Aa6214	Aa6215	Aa6216	Aa6217
Year	Number	Number	Number	Number	Number	Number	Number	Number	Number
1790	—	—	200,408	191,116	—	—	—	—	—
1800	—	—	225,192	218,194	—	—	—	—	—
1810	—	—	231,804	226,375	—	—	—	—	—
1820	469,985	458,367	242,492	240,350	—	—	—	—	—
1830	518,409	516,072	267,170	270,046	49,599	39,355	32,787	28,305	46,935
1840	508,110	507,150	266,781	271,061	48,731	38,035	32,924	27,757	44,866

	Population									
	White									
	Male, by age						Female, by age			
	30–39	40–49	50–59	60–69	70–79	80 and older	0–4	5–9	10–14	15–19
	Aa6218	Aa6219	Aa6220	Aa6221	Aa6222	Aa6223	Aa6224	Aa6225	Aa6226	Aa6227
Year	Number	Number	Number	Number	Number	Number	Number	Number	Number	Number
1790	—	—	—	—	—	—	—	—	—	—
1800	—	—	—	—	—	—	—	—	—	—
1810	—	—	—	—	—	—	—	—	—	—
1820	—	—	—	—	—	—	—	—	—	—
1830	28,776	18,463	12,116	7,008	2,820	1,006	47,146	37,983	32,145	31,555
1840	29,867	20,348	12,584	7,276	3,325	1,068	46,009	37,270	31,752	30,899

	Population									
	White									
	Female, by age							Male, by age		
	20–29	30–39	40–49	50–59	60–69	70–79	80 and older	0–9	10–15	16–25
	Aa6228	Aa6229	Aa6230	Aa6231	Aa6232	Aa6233	Aa6234	Aa6235	Aa6236	Aa6237
Year	Number	Number	Number	Number	Number	Number	Number	Number	Number	Number
1790	—	—	—	—	—	—	—	—	—	—
1800	—	—	—	—	—	—	—	78,577	34,799	42,191
1810	—	—	—	—	—	—	—	79,610	35,145	43,012
1820	—	—	—	—	—	—	—	81,489	36,392	46,726
1830	49,070	29,147	19,115	12,528	7,156	3,153	1,048	—	—	—
1840	48,750	30,318	20,371	13,185	7,854	3,491	1,162	—	—	—

TABLE Aa6200–6248   Virginia population by race, sex, age, nativity, and urban–rural residence: 1790–1840 [Historical boundaries]   *Continued*

	Population										
	White										
	Male, by age		Female, by age					Male, by age		Female, by age	
	26–44	45 and older	0–9	10–15	16–25	26–44	45 and older	0–15	16 and older	0–15	16 and older
	Aa6238	Aa6239	Aa6240	Aa6241	Aa6242	Aa6243	Aa6244	Aa6245	Aa6246	Aa6247	Aa6248
Year	Number	Number	Number	Number	Number	Number	Number	Number	Number	Number	Number
1790	—	—	—	—	—	—	—	101,545	98,863	92,003	99,113
1800	43,771	25,854	74,101	33,662	44,503	41,847	24,081	—	—	—	—
1810	44,575	29,462	73,774	34,710	46,193	43,677	28,021	—	—	—	—
1820	47,317	30,568	77,249	36,786	50,573	46,159	29,583	—	—	—	—
1830	—	—	—	—	—	—	—	—	—	—	—
1840	—	—	—	—	—	—	—	—	—	—	—

Sources

See the sources for Table Aa2244–2340.

Documentation

See the text for Tables Aa2244–2340 and Aa6099–6199. Like Table Aa6099–6199, this table excludes the counties that formed the state of West Virginia in 1863.

TABLE Aa6249–6311   Washington population by race, sex, age, nativity, and urban–rural residence: 1850–1990

Contributed by Michael R. Haines

			Population									
				Race					Residence		Nativity	
	Area	Population density	Total	White	Nonwhite	Black	Other nonwhite		Urban	Rural	Native-born	Foreign-born
	Aa6249	Aa6250	Aa6251	Aa6252	Aa6253	Aa6254	Aa6255		Aa6256	Aa6257	Aa6258	Aa6259
Year	square mile	Persons per square mile	Number	Number	Number	Number	Number		Number	Number	Number	Number
1850	—	—	1,201	1,049	152	152	—		0	1,201	844	357
1860	183,254	0.06	11,594	11,138	456	30	426		0	11,594	8,450	3,144
1870	66,836	0.36	23,955	22,195	1,760	207	1,553		0	23,955	18,931	5,024
1880	66,836	1.12	75,116	67,199	7,917	325	7,592		7,121	67,995	59,313	15,803
1890 [1]	66,836	5.34	357,232	340,513	8,877	1,602	7,275		127,178	230,054	259,385	90,005
1900	66,836	7.75	518,103	496,304	21,799	2,514	19,285		211,477	306,626	406,739	111,364
1910	66,836	17.09	1,141,990	1,109,111	32,879	6,058	26,821		605,530	536,460	885,749	256,241
1920	66,836	20.30	1,356,621	1,319,777	36,844	6,883	29,961		742,801	613,820	1,091,329	265,292
1930	66,836	23.39	1,563,396	1,521,661	41,735	6,840	34,895		884,539	678,857	1,308,138	255,258
1940	66,977	25.92	1,736,191	1,698,147	38,044	7,424	30,620		921,969	814,222	1,525,812	210,379
1950	66,786	35.62	2,378,963	2,316,496	62,467	30,691	31,776		1,503,166	875,797	2,177,340	196,530
1960	66,663	42.80	2,853,214	2,751,675	101,539	48,738	52,801		1,943,249	909,965	2,674,556	178,658
1970	66,570	51.21	3,409,169	3,251,055	158,114	71,308	86,806		2,501,051	908,118	3,253,141	156,020
1980	66,511	62.13	4,132,156	3,779,170	352,986	105,574	247,412		3,037,014	1,095,142	3,893,096	239,060
1990	66,581	73.09	4,866,692	4,308,937	557,755	149,801	407,954		3,717,948	1,148,744	4,544,548	322,144

Note appears at end of table

(continued)

TABLE Aa6249-6311   Washington population by race, sex, age, nativity, and urban-rural residence: 1850-1990
Continued

		Population									
Sex		Male, by age									
Male	Female	0	1-4	5-9	10-14	15-19	20-29	20-24	25-29	30-39
Aa6260	Aa6261	Aa6262	Aa6263	Aa6264	Aa6265	Aa6266	Aa6267	Aa6268	Aa6269	Aa6270
Year	Number	Number	Number	Number	Number	Number	Number	Number	Number	Number	Number

Year	Male	Female	0	1-4	5-9	10-14	15-19	20-29	20-24	25-29	30-39
1850	926	275	2	58	64	34	43	465	—	—	178
1860	8,446	3,148	188	603	498	363	305	3,236	—	—	2,239
1870	14,990	8,965	343	1,499	1,537	1,261	851	—	1,210	1,520	—
1880	45,973	29,143	1,100	4,210	4,578	4,016	3,495	—	4,593	4,919	—
1890 [1]	217,562	131,828	4,131	15,363	18,103	14,734	14,025	—	26,402	31,823	—
1900	304,178	213,925	5,532	21,563	28,801	24,175	23,203	—	27,082	28,332	—
1910	658,663	483,327	11,234	44,198	50,645	46,962	52,025	—	72,568	77,896	—
1920	734,701	621,920	12,564	51,922	64,927	59,269	53,516	—	56,369	63,195	—
1930	826,392	737,004	10,992	47,505	69,285	70,264	69,658	—	67,163	62,494	—
1940	905,757	830,434	12,472	49,679	59,336	64,908	74,754	—	76,267	75,366	—
1950	1,223,851	1,155,112	26,518	107,459	104,097	81,262	85,088	—	92,158	97,636	—
1960	1,435,037	1,418,177	32,296	128,648	152,894	140,244	104,905	—	89,883	84,599	—
1970	1,693,747	1,715,422	29,724	113,242	167,944	178,369	168,828	—	148,646	120,729	—
1980	2,052,307	2,079,849	34,538	122,141	151,442	165,160	189,332	—	206,258	197,253	—
1990	2,413,747	2,452,945	32,888	154,950	190,090	173,528	165,818	—	181,447	209,117	—

	Population										
	Male, by age										
30-34	35-39	40-49	40-44	45-49	50-59	50-54	55-59	60-69	60-64	65-69
Aa6271	Aa6272	Aa6273	Aa6274	Aa6275	Aa6276	Aa6277	Aa6278	Aa6279	Aa6280	Aa6281
Year	Number	Number	Number	Number	Number	Number	Number	Number	Number	Number	Number

Year	30-34	35-39	40-49	40-44	45-49	50-59	50-54	55-59	60-69	60-64	65-69
1850	—	—	48	—	—	24	—	—	9	—	—
1860	—	—	690	—	—	229	—	—	75	—	—
1870	1,651	1,808	—	1,329	718	—	619	279	—	148	92
1880	4,504	3,752	—	3,233	2,413	—	2,416	1,245	—	747	390
1890 [1]	27,156	19,436	—	13,775	9,464	—	8,629	5,127	—	3,582	1,939
1900	29,449	30,055	—	25,048	17,172	—	13,909	8,980	—	6,527	4,496
1910	65,720	54,571	—	47,517	40,124	—	33,050	20,981	—	14,699	9,611
1920	65,966	67,495	—	54,460	48,008	—	40,831	32,931	—	25,083	16,198
1930	58,806	64,089	—	64,625	60,564	—	50,919	38,809	—	32,673	25,258
1940	69,716	65,085	—	61,024	61,728	—	61,433	53,417	—	42,668	31,303
1950	95,639	92,103	—	82,247	72,120	—	64,531	59,567	—	54,794	45,368
1960	89,190	97,817	—	95,132	89,389	—	77,202	65,782	—	53,987	47,683
1970	97,362	90,485	—	95,307	100,046	—	93,943	82,726	—	67,373	50,065
1980	178,753	138,715	—	108,450	97,405	—	97,453	98,323	—	86,540	70,295
1990	222,509	213,981	—	188,660	143,983	—	109,360	94,749	—	90,368	86,117

Note appears at end of table

TABLE Aa6249–6311   Washington population by race, sex, age, nativity, and urban–rural residence: 1850–1990
Continued

	Population										
	Male, by age					Female, by age					
	70–79	70–74	75–79	80 and older	Unknown age	0	1–4	5–9	10–14	15–19	20–29
	Aa6282	Aa6283	Aa6284	Aa6285	Aa6286	Aa6287	Aa6288	Aa6289	Aa6290	Aa6291	Aa6292
Year	Number	Number	Number	Number	Number	Number	Number	Number	Number	Number	Number
1850	0	—	—	1	0	2	58	46	34	26	59
1860	18	—	—	2	0	143	583	463	338	312	628
1870	—	42	27	14	42	340	1,427	1,475	1,124	812	—
1880	—	205	103	54	—	1,043	3,957	4,508	3,601	2,943	—
1890 [1]	—	968	500	278	2,127	3,869	14,836	17,449	14,218	12,261	—
1900	—	2,539	1,298	692	5,325	5,229	20,919	27,622	24,058	20,901	—
1910	—	5,962	3,351	2,036	5,513	10,845	42,479	49,033	45,840	47,622	—
1920	—	9,569	5,289	3,460	3,649	12,105	49,843	63,331	58,284	52,969	—
1930	—	17,243	9,108	5,661	1,276	10,666	45,691	66,728	68,129	68,264	—
1940	—	22,897	14,052	9,652	—	11,903	47,864	57,426	62,934	71,971	—
1950	—	30,913	20,641	11,710	—	25,765	103,584	99,689	78,433	72,607	—
1960	—	39,302	26,263	19,821	—	30,971	123,718	148,157	135,266	103,670	—
1970	—	36,523	25,829	26,606	—	28,661	108,815	160,453	170,523	161,075	—
1980	—	49,475	30,999	29,775	—	32,816	116,628	144,569	156,835	179,691	—
1990	—	67,230	46,832	42,120	—	31,336	147,606	181,003	164,134	156,893	—

	Population									
	Female, by age									
	20–24	25–29	30–39	30–34	35–39	40–49	40–44	45–49	50–59	50–54
	Aa6293	Aa6294	Aa6295	Aa6296	Aa6297	Aa6298	Aa6299	Aa6300	Aa6301	Aa6302
Year	Number	Number	Number	Number	Number	Number	Number	Number	Number	Number
1850	—	—	34	—	—	14	—	—	2	—
1860	—	—	386	—	—	191	—	—	78	—
1870	791	765	—	668	524	—	335	242	—	165
1880	2,600	2,301	—	2,074	1,848	—	1,342	1,027	—	782
1890 [1]	14,481	13,887	—	11,456	8,295	—	6,167	4,730	—	3,626
1900	19,321	17,761	—	17,669	16,313	—	12,815	8,855	—	6,845
1910	49,490	48,178	—	41,243	35,578	—	29,769	24,868	—	19,363
1920	54,645	57,226	—	53,480	50,092	—	41,345	33,756	—	28,620
1930	63,238	58,157	—	56,642	58,744	—	53,480	47,716	—	39,304
1940	72,600	71,228	—	65,041	59,905	—	57,501	55,981	—	51,482
1950	83,461	97,451	—	92,997	88,646	—	76,843	66,594	—	61,408
1960	83,921	81,777	—	90,709	100,678	—	94,059	86,682	—	73,293
1970	147,318	117,975	—	96,036	90,535	—	97,521	103,834	—	94,831
1980	194,284	192,744	—	175,892	134,667	—	105,382	96,068	—	101,095
1990	170,233	202,705	—	220,857	213,709	—	187,413	140,691	—	107,509

Note appears at end of table

(continued)

TABLE Aa6249–6311 Washington population by race, sex, age, nativity, and urban–rural residence: 1850–1990
Continued

	Population								
	Female, by age								
	55–59	60–69	60–64	65–69	70–79	70–74	75–79	80 and older	Unknown age
	Aa6303	Aa6304	Aa6305	Aa6306	Aa6307	Aa6308	Aa6309	Aa6310	Aa6311
Year	Number	Number	Number	Number	Number	Number	Number	Number	Number
1850	—	0	—	—	0	—	—	0	0
1860	—	21	—	—	5	—	—	0	0
1870	93	—	78	52	—	28	14	10	22
1880	432	—	279	194	—	121	54	37	—
1890 [1]	2,374	—	1,703	1,033	—	566	294	217	366
1900	5,147	—	3,880	2,699	—	1,622	809	526	934
1910	12,680	—	9,445	6,974	—	4,412	2,553	1,674	1,281
1920	22,122	—	17,269	11,100	—	7,078	4,467	3,050	1,138
1930	30,451	—	24,857	19,182	—	12,832	7,002	5,217	704
1940	43,281	—	34,901	26,660	—	19,046	11,895	8,815	—
1950	55,739	—	49,122	41,183	—	28,742	20,696	12,152	—
1960	63,221	—	56,079	50,976	—	41,636	28,624	24,740	—
1970	84,152	—	70,655	56,943	—	47,812	36,825	41,458	—
1980	105,663	—	92,497	81,029	—	62,548	46,410	61,031	—
1990	96,853	—	99,014	100,562	—	82,125	65,616	84,686	—

[1] Includes 7,842 American Indians not counted in the general enumeration; see text for Table Aa2244–2340.

Sources
See the sources for Table Aa2244–2340.

Documentation
See the text for Table Aa2244–2340.

The population in 1850 is that of Clark and Lewis Counties in the Oregon Territory. Washington and Oregon became part of the United States officially after the conclusion of a treaty with Great Britain in 1846. Washington became a territory in 1853 and a state in 1889.

TABLE Aa6312–6412 West Virginia population by race, sex, age, nativity, and urban–rural residence: 1790–1990
Contributed by Michael R. Haines

			Population								
				Race				Residence		Nativity	
	Area	Population density	Total	White	Nonwhite	Black	Other nonwhite	Urban	Rural	Native-born	Foreign-born
	Aa6312	Aa6313	Aa6314	Aa6315	Aa6316	Aa6317	Aa6318	Aa6319	Aa6320	Aa6321	Aa6322
Year	Square miles	Persons per square mile	Number	Number	Number	Number	Number	Number	Number	Number	Number
1790	24,022	2.33	55,873	50,593	5,280	5,280	—	0	55,873	—	—
1800	24,022	3.27	78,592	70,894	7,698	7,698	—	0	78,592	—	—
1810	24,022	4.39	105,469	93,355	12,114	12,114	—	0	105,469	—	—
1820	24,022	5.70	136,808	120,232	16,576	16,532	40	0	136,808	—	—
1830	24,022	7.37	176,924	157,084	19,840	19,840	—	0	176,924	—	—
1840	24,022	9.35	224,537	203,016	21,521	21,521	—	7,885	216,652	—	—
1850	24,022	12.58	302,313	278,731	23,582	23,582	—	11,435	290,878	290,308	12,005
1860	24,022	15.68	376,688	355,526	21,162	21,144	18	20,077	356,611	360,143	16,545
1870	24,022	18.40	442,014	424,033	17,981	17,980	1	36,009	406,005	424,923	17,091
1880	24,022	25.75	618,457	592,537	25,920	25,886	34	54,050	564,407	600,192	18,265
1890	24,022	31.75	762,794	730,077	32,717	32,690	27	81,365	681,429	743,911	18,883
1900	24,022	39.91	958,800	915,233	43,567	43,499	68	125,465	833,335	936,349	22,451
1910	24,022	50.83	1,221,119	1,156,817	64,302	64,173	129	228,242	992,877	1,163,901	57,218
1920	24,022	60.93	1,463,701	1,377,235	86,466	86,345	121	369,007	1,094,694	1,401,596	62,105
1930	24,022	71.98	1,729,205	1,614,191	115,014	114,893	121	491,504	1,237,701	1,677,340	51,865
1940	24,090	78.95	1,901,974	1,784,102	117,872	117,754	118	534,292	1,367,682	1,860,075	41,899
1950	24,080	83.29	2,005,552	1,890,282	115,270	114,867	403	694,487	1,311,065	1,965,925	33,910
1960	24,084	77.25	1,860,421	1,770,133	90,288	89,378	910	711,101	1,149,320	1,836,558	23,863
1970	24,070	72.47	1,744,237	1,673,480	70,757	67,342	3,415	681,555	1,062,682	1,727,574	16,662
1980	24,119	80.83	1,949,644	1,874,751	74,893	65,051	9,842	705,319	1,244,325	1,927,664	21,980
1990	24,087	74.46	1,793,477	1,725,523	67,954	56,295	11,659	648,184	1,145,293	1,777,765	15,712

TABLE Aa6312–6412   West Virginia population by race, sex, age, nativity, and urban–rural residence: 1790–1990
Continued

	Sex		Population — Male, by age								
	Male	Female	0	1–4	5–9	10–14	15–19	20–29	20–24	25–29	30–39
	Aa6323	Aa6324	Aa6325	Aa6326	Aa6327	Aa6328	Aa6329	Aa6330	Aa6331	Aa6332	Aa6333
Year	Number	Number	Number	Number	Number	Number	Number	Number	Number	Number	Number
1790	—	—	—	—	—	—	—	—	—	—	—
1800	—	—	—	—	—	—	—	—	—	—	—
1810	—	—	—	—	—	—	—	—	—	—	—
1820	70,869	65,895	—	—	—	—	—	—	—	—	—
1830	90,942	85,982	—	—	—	—	—	—	—	—	—
1840	115,592	108,945	—	—	—	—	—	—	—	—	—
1850	155,972	146,341	4,584	21,292	23,708	20,841	16,098	27,331	—	—	17,245
1860	192,209	184,479	5,988	27,008	28,687	25,727	20,628	30,688	—	—	21,260
1870	222,843	219,171	7,351	29,996	31,262	30,620	24,140	—	20,386	15,056	—
1880	314,495	303,962	10,787	39,871	46,187	40,853	31,538	—	30,480	23,516	—
1890	390,285	372,509	11,517	43,058	54,134	49,742	43,146	—	38,211	27,884	—
1900	499,242	459,558	15,433	53,990	61,846	56,708	53,073	—	50,232	42,419	—
1910	644,044	577,075	18,205	67,599	75,019	67,050	65,029	—	64,471	57,900	—
1920	763,100	700,601	19,526	79,626	93,331	82,933	71,418	—	65,686	60,408	—
1930	889,871	839,334	20,608	84,392	111,471	97,762	88,282	—	75,909	65,205	—
1940	968,582	933,392	18,546	81,183	97,484	104,122	102,895	—	85,373	78,264	—
1950	1,006,287	999,265	23,560	98,710	104,582	97,201	81,005	—	76,136	77,729	—
1960	915,035	945,386	19,539	80,437	101,781	102,862	78,033	—	49,255	46,577	—
1970	844,669	899,568	14,320	56,448	80,914	90,439	86,834	—	60,063	48,115	—
1980	945,408	1,004,236	15,628	59,109	78,350	81,004	88,174	—	85,141	80,019	—
1990	861,536	931,941	9,030	45,708	61,722	69,394	72,787	—	59,646	58,550	—

	Population — Male, by age										
	30–34	35–39	40–49	40–44	45–49	50–59	50–54	55–59	60–69	60–64	65–69
	Aa6334	Aa6335	Aa6336	Aa6337	Aa6338	Aa6339	Aa6340	Aa6341	Aa6342	Aa6343	Aa6344
Year	Number	Number	Number	Number	Number	Number	Number	Number	Number	Number	Number
1790	—	—	—	—	—	—	—	—	—	—	—
1800	—	—	—	—	—	—	—	—	—	—	—
1810	—	—	—	—	—	—	—	—	—	—	—
1820	—	—	—	—	—	—	—	—	—	—	—
1830	—	—	—	—	—	—	—	—	—	—	—
1840	—	—	—	—	—	—	—	—	—	—	—
1850	—	—	11,472	—	—	7,052	—	—	3,943	—	—
1860	—	—	14,773	—	—	9,044	—	—	5,548	—	—
1870	11,994	11,049	—	9,204	7,886	—	7,913	5,022	—	4,249	2,840
1880	18,781	16,110	—	12,454	9,941	—	10,576	7,173	—	6,197	4,242
1890	24,975	21,691	—	17,225	14,074	—	12,834	8,692	—	7,847	5,710
1900	34,172	28,471	—	24,376	19,467	—	17,639	12,624	—	9,459	6,933
1910	48,221	43,476	—	33,875	25,519	—	24,190	17,075	—	13,150	9,811
1920	53,328	55,454	—	42,362	39,176	—	30,220	21,000	—	17,574	12,752
1930	60,205	58,977	—	51,099	46,596	—	38,458	29,476	—	22,707	15,822
1940	68,942	62,409	—	55,948	50,506	—	44,015	36,871	—	29,131	23,816
1950	69,834	68,871	—	61,430	53,619	—	47,731	40,693	—	34,590	29,290
1960	55,046	58,429	—	55,760	55,158	—	49,186	42,532	—	36,462	30,988
1970	43,107	41,545	—	49,894	51,967	—	48,721	46,288	—	40,059	30,813
1980	72,479	54,825	—	47,757	44,093	—	49,542	49,342	—	42,084	37,071
1990	67,493	69,498	—	64,630	50,287	—	43,604	39,693	—	42,318	38,964

(continued)

TABLE Aa6312-6412   West Virginia population by race, sex, age, nativity, and urban-rural residence: 1790-1990
Continued

Population

	Male, by age					Female, by age					
	70-79	70-74	75-79	80 and older	Unknown age	0	1-4	5-9	10-14	15-19	20-29
	Aa6345	Aa6346	Aa6347	Aa6348	Aa6349	Aa6350	Aa6351	Aa6352	Aa6353	Aa6354	Aa6355
Year	Number	Number	Number	Number	Number	Number	Number	Number	Number	Number	Number
1790	—	—	—	—	—	—	—	—	—	—	—
1800	—	—	—	—	—	—	—	—	—	—	—
1810	—	—	—	—	—	—	—	—	—	—	—
1820	—	—	—	—	—	—	—	—	—	—	—
1830	—	—	—	—	—	—	—	—	—	—	—
1840	—	—	—	—	—	—	—	—	—	—	—
1850	1,651	—	—	611	144	4,466	20,327	22,880	19,758	16,262	24,998
1860	2,101	—	—	685	72	5,751	25,654	27,572	24,007	20,934	31,233
1870	—	2,006	1,017	852	0	7,003	28,372	29,606	29,202	24,598	—
1880	—	2,809	1,717	1,263	—	10,344	38,308	44,373	38,556	31,502	—
1890	—	4,063	2,250	1,664	1,568	10,687	40,992	52,868	47,905	42,681	—
1900	—	4,925	2,852	1,960	2,663	14,673	51,369	59,843	54,021	50,921	—
1910	—	6,028	3,523	2,435	1,468	17,524	65,790	73,160	63,977	60,116	—
1920	—	8,421	5,050	3,163	1,672	18,992	77,790	91,041	81,214	69,893	—
1930	—	11,197	6,730	4,575	400	20,099	81,988	108,895	95,503	87,552	—
1940	—	15,076	8,153	5,848	—	17,983	78,867	94,503	101,670	102,941	—
1950	—	19,729	14,647	6,930	—	22,645	95,192	100,808	93,778	85,435	—
1960	—	23,956	16,404	12,630	—	18,873	77,446	98,095	99,445	78,421	—
1970	—	23,689	15,968	15,485	—	13,620	53,861	77,724	86,432	85,552	—
1980	—	27,104	17,276	16,410	—	14,669	56,177	74,452	76,485	86,030	—
1990	—	28,456	20,811	18,945	—	8,537	43,384	58,152	65,419	69,268	—

Population

Female, by age

	20-24	25-29	30-39	30-34	35-39	40-49	40-44	45-49	50-59	50-54	55-59
	Aa6356	Aa6357	Aa6358	Aa6359	Aa6360	Aa6361	Aa6362	Aa6363	Aa6364	Aa6365	Aa6366
Year	Number	Number	Number	Number	Number	Number	Number	Number	Number	Number	Number
1790	—	—	—	—	—	—	—	—	—	—	—
1800	—	—	—	—	—	—	—	—	—	—	—
1810	—	—	—	—	—	—	—	—	—	—	—
1820	—	—	—	—	—	—	—	—	—	—	—
1830	—	—	—	—	—	—	—	—	—	—	—
1840	—	—	—	—	—	—	—	—	—	—	—
1850	—	—	15,454	—	—	10,277	—	—	6,283	—	—
1860	—	—	20,201	—	—	13,546	—	—	8,197	—	—
1870	21,858	16,485	—	12,985	11,231	—	9,444	7,817	—	6,422	4,407
1880	30,555	22,655	—	18,043	15,866	—	12,955	10,516	—	9,045	6,544
1890	36,714	26,836	—	23,363	19,913	—	16,249	13,866	—	11,599	8,317
1900	46,440	37,485	—	29,871	24,546	—	21,312	17,373	—	14,794	11,343
1910	57,043	49,425	—	40,117	35,045	—	27,392	21,840	—	19,244	14,054
1920	64,156	56,116	—	47,554	44,898	—	35,537	29,922	—	23,395	17,331
1930	77,578	65,388	—	56,598	53,168	—	43,546	38,802	—	32,270	24,072
1940	88,104	78,460	—	68,559	60,983	—	51,709	45,581	—	38,415	32,024
1950	83,414	81,069	—	72,539	68,815	—	60,546	52,483	—	45,132	38,121
1960	55,927	53,514	—	61,612	64,102	—	60,444	57,013	—	50,274	44,247
1970	68,590	50,097	—	46,998	48,075	—	55,396	56,486	—	53,592	49,981
1980	87,547	80,935	—	72,170	55,053	—	49,784	49,214	—	55,263	55,877
1990	60,521	63,594	—	72,066	71,685	—	65,291	51,084	—	46,343	45,572

TABLE Aa6312–6412   West Virginia population by race, sex, age, nativity, and urban–rural residence: 1790–1990
Continued

	Population								White	
	Female, by age									
	60–69	60–64	65–69	70–79	70–74	75–79	80 and older	Unknown age	Male	Female
	Aa6367	Aa6368	Aa6369	Aa6370	Aa6371	Aa6372	Aa6373	Aa6374	Aa6375	Aa6376
Year	Number	Number	Number	Number	Number	Number	Number	Number	Number	Number
1790	—	—	—	—	—	—	—	—	26,663	23,930
1800	—	—	—	—	—	—	—	—	36,937	33,957
1810	—	—	—	—	—	—	—	—	48,234	45,121
1820	—	—	—	—	—	—	—	—	62,239	57,993
1830	—	—	—	—	—	—	—	—	80,717	76,367
1840	—	—	—	—	—	—	—	—	104,432	98,584
1850	3,464	—	—	1,486	—	—	564	122	—	—
1860	4,710	—	—	1,937	—	—	675	62	—	—
1870	—	3,772	2,512	—	1,704	933	820	0	—	—
1880	—	5,413	3,798	—	2,583	1,622	1,284	—	—	—
1890	—	7,095	5,133	—	3,647	2,074	1,744	826	—	—
1900	—	8,877	6,481	—	4,405	2,705	1,975	1,124	—	—
1910	—	11,477	8,764	—	5,641	3,452	2,538	476	—	—
1920	—	14,894	11,073	—	7,409	4,822	3,450	1,114	—	—
1930	—	18,823	13,853	—	10,000	6,138	4,728	333	—	—
1940	—	25,512	20,746	—	13,122	7,777	6,436	—	—	—
1950	—	31,358	27,545	—	18,970	13,677	7,738	—	—	—
1960	—	37,435	31,801	—	24,711	17,379	14,647	—	—	—
1970	—	44,645	37,251	—	29,170	20,579	21,519	—	—	—
1980	—	50,573	45,882	—	37,241	26,996	29,888	—	—	—
1990	—	49,304	48,251	—	40,072	32,897	40,501	—	—	—

	Population										
	White										
	Male, by age										
	0–4	5–9	10–14	15–19	20–29	30–39	40–49	50–59	60–69	70–79	80 and older
	Aa6377	Aa6378	Aa6379	Aa6380	Aa6381	Aa6382	Aa6383	Aa6384	Aa6385	Aa6386	Aa6387
Year	Number	Number	Number	Number	Number	Number	Number	Number	Number	Number	Number
1790	—	—	—	—	—	—	—	—	—	—	—
1800	—	—	—	—	—	—	—	—	—	—	—
1810	—	—	—	—	—	—	—	—	—	—	—
1820	—	—	—	—	—	—	—	—	—	—	—
1830	16,194	12,450	10,500	8,642	13,976	7,763	4,918	3,145	1,963	854	312
1840	20,577	15,450	12,898	10,506	18,599	11,274	7,117	4,086	2,397	1,133	395
1850	—	—	—	—	—	—	—	—	—	—	—
1860	—	—	—	—	—	—	—	—	—	—	—
1870	—	—	—	—	—	—	—	—	—	—	—
1880	—	—	—	—	—	—	—	—	—	—	—
1890	—	—	—	—	—	—	—	—	—	—	—
1900	—	—	—	—	—	—	—	—	—	—	—
1910	—	—	—	—	—	—	—	—	—	—	—
1920	—	—	—	—	—	—	—	—	—	—	—
1930	—	—	—	—	—	—	—	—	—	—	—
1940	—	—	—	—	—	—	—	—	—	—	—
1950	—	—	—	—	—	—	—	—	—	—	—
1960	—	—	—	—	—	—	—	—	—	—	—
1970	—	—	—	—	—	—	—	—	—	—	—
1980	—	—	—	—	—	—	—	—	—	—	—
1900	—	—	—	—	—	—	—	—	—	—	—

(continued)

TABLE Aa6312–6412   West Virginia population by race, sex, age, nativity, and urban–rural residence: 1790–1990 *Continued*

	Population										
	White										
	Female, by age										
	0–4	5–9	10–14	15–19	20–29	30–39	40–49	50–59	60–69	70–79	80 and older
	Aa6388	Aa6389	Aa6390	Aa6391	Aa6392	Aa6393	Aa6394	Aa6395	Aa6396	Aa6397	Aa6398
Year	Number	Number	Number	Number	Number	Number	Number	Number	Number	Number	Number
1790	—	—	—	—	—	—	—	—	—	—	—
1800	—	—	—	—	—	—	—	—	—	—	—
1810	—	—	—	—	—	—	—	—	—	—	—
1820	—	—	—	—	—	—	—	—	—	—	—
1830	15,265	11,981	9,791	8,924	12,974	7,309	4,635	2,919	1,609	694	266
1840	19,277	14,994	12,244	11,576	17,047	9,764	6,557	3,680	2,132	977	336
1850	—	—	—	—	—	—	—	—	—	—	—
1860	—	—	—	—	—	—	—	—	—	—	—
1870	—	—	—	—	—	—	—	—	—	—	—
1880	—	—	—	—	—	—	—	—	—	—	—
1890	—	—	—	—	—	—	—	—	—	—	—
1900	—	—	—	—	—	—	—	—	—	—	—
1910	—	—	—	—	—	—	—	—	—	—	—
1920	—	—	—	—	—	—	—	—	—	—	—
1930	—	—	—	—	—	—	—	—	—	—	—
1940	—	—	—	—	—	—	—	—	—	—	—
1950	—	—	—	—	—	—	—	—	—	—	—
1960	—	—	—	—	—	—	—	—	—	—	—
1970	—	—	—	—	—	—	—	—	—	—	—
1980	—	—	—	—	—	—	—	—	—	—	—
1990	—	—	—	—	—	—	—	—	—	—	—

	Population						
	White						
	Male, by age					Female, by age	
	0–9	10–15	16–25	26–44	45 and older	0–9	10–15
	Aa6399	Aa6400	Aa6401	Aa6402	Aa6403	Aa6404	Aa6405
Year	Number	Number	Number	Number	Number	Number	Number
1790	—	—	—	—	—	—	—
1800	13,861	5,701	6,517	6,491	4,367	13,222	5,173
1810	18,167	7,774	8,461	7,992	5,840	16,941	7,497
1820	22,474	9,370	12,137	10,581	7,677	21,236	8,980
1830	—	—	—	—	—	—	—
1840	—	—	—	—	—	—	—
1850	—	—	—	—	—	—	—
1860	—	—	—	—	—	—	—
1870	—	—	—	—	—	—	—
1880	—	—	—	—	—	—	—
1890	—	—	—	—	—	—	—
1900	—	—	—	—	—	—	—
1910	—	—	—	—	—	—	—
1920	—	—	—	—	—	—	—
1930	—	—	—	—	—	—	—
1940	—	—	—	—	—	—	—
1950	—	—	—	—	—	—	—
1960	—	—	—	—	—	—	—
1970	—	—	—	—	—	—	—
1980	—	—	—	—	—	—	—
1990	—	—	—	—	—	—	—

TABLE Aa6312–6412   **West Virginia population by race, sex, age, nativity, and urban–rural residence: 1790–1990**
Continued

	Population						
	White						
	Female, by age			Male, by age		Female, by age	
	16–25	26–44	45 and older	0–15	16 and older	0–15	16 and older
	Aa6406	Aa6407	Aa6408	Aa6409	Aa6410	Aa6411	Aa6412
Year	Number	Number	Number	Number	Number	Number	Number
1790	—	—	—	14,590	12,073	11,520	12,410
1800	6,227	5,963	3,372	—	—	—	—
1810	8,706	7,486	4,491	—	—	—	—
1820	11,838	9,836	6,103	—	—	—	—
1830	—	—	—	—	—	—	—
1840	—	—	—	—	—	—	—
1850	—	—	—	—	—	—	—
1860	—	—	—	—	—	—	—
1870	—	—	—	—	—	—	—
1880	—	—	—	—	—	—	—
1890	—	—	—	—	—	—	—
1900	—	—	—	—	—	—	—
1910	—	—	—	—	—	—	—
1920	—	—	—	—	—	—	—
1930	—	—	—	—	—	—	—
1940	—	—	—	—	—	—	—
1950	—	—	—	—	—	—	—
1960	—	—	—	—	—	—	—
1970	—	—	—	—	—	—	—
1980	—	—	—	—	—	—	—
1990	—	—	—	—	—	—	—

Sources

See the sources for Table Aa2244–2340.

Documentation

See the text for Table Aa2244–2340.

West Virginia was originally part of Virginia, one of the original thirteen states, which was admitted to the Union in 1788. In 1863, the U.S. Congress recognized fifty counties of Virginia as a separate state named West Virginia. For 1790–1860, this table gives the population of the area that would become West Virginia.

TABLE Aa6413–6499   **Wisconsin population by race, sex, age, nativity, and urban–rural residence: 1840–1990**

Contributed by Michael R. Haines

			Population								
				Race				Residence		Nativity	
	Area	Population density	Total	White	Nonwhite	Black	Other nonwhite	Urban	Rural	Native-born	Foreign-born
	Aa6413	Aa6414	Aa6415	Aa6416	Aa6417	Aa6418	Aa6419	Aa6420	Aa6421	Aa6422	Aa6423
Year	Square miles	Persons per square mile	Number	Number	Number	Number	Number	Number	Number	Number	Number
1840	82,643	0.37	30,945	30,749	196	196	—	0	30,945	—	—
1850	55,256	5.53	305,391	304,756	635	635	—	28,623	276,768	194,914	110,477
1860	55,256	14.04	775,881	773,693	2,188	1,171	1,017	111,874	664,007	498,954	276,927
1870	55,256	19.09	1,054,670	1,051,351	3,319	2,113	1,206	207,099	847,571	690,171	364,499
1880	55,256	23.81	1,315,497	1,309,618	5,879	2,702	3,177	317,204	998,293	910,072	405,425
1890 [1]	55,256	30.65	1,693,330	1,680,473	6,407	2,444	3,963	562,286	1,131,044	1,167,681	519,199
1900	55,256	37.44	2,069,042	2,057,911	11,131	2,542	8,589	790,213	1,278,829	1,553,071	515,971
1910	55,256	42.24	2,333,860	2,320,555	13,305	2,900	10,405	1,004,320	1,329,540	1,820,995	512,865
1920	55,256	47.63	2,632,067	2,616,938	15,129	5,201	9,928	1,244,858	1,387,209	2,171,582	460,485
1930	55,256	53.19	2,939,006	2,916,255	22,751	10,739	12,012	1,553,843	1,385,163	2,550,707	388,299
1940	54,715	57.34	3,137,587	3,112,752	24,835	12,158	12,677	1,679,144	1,458,443	2,848,569	289,018
1950	54,705	62.78	3,434,575	3,392,690	41,885	28,182	13,703	1,987,888	1,446,687	3,203,470	216,965
1960	54,466	72.55	3,951,777	3,858,903	92,874	74,546	18,328	2,522,179	1,429,598	3,780,966	171,519
1970	54,464	81.11	4,417,731	4,258,959	158,772	128,224	30,548	2,910,418	1,507,313	4,287,062	130,669
1980	54,426	86.46	4,705,767	4,443,035	262,732	182,592	80,140	3,020,732	1,685,035	4,580,470	125,297
1990	54,314	90.07	4,891,769	4,512,523	379,246	244,539	134,707	3,211,956	1,679,813	4,770,222	121,547

Note appears at end of table

(continued)

TABLE Aa6413–6499 Wisconsin population by race, sex, age, nativity, and urban–rural residence: 1840–1990
Continued

		Population									
Sex		**Male, by age**									
Male	Female	0	1–4	5–9	10–14	15–19	20–29	20–24	25–29	30–39
Aa6424	Aa6425	Aa6426	Aa6427	Aa6428	Aa6429	Aa6430	Aa6431	Aa6432	Aa6433	Aa6434
Year	Number	Number	Number	Number	Number	Number	Number	Number	Number	Number	Number
1840	18,862	12,083	—	—	—	—	—	—	—	—	—
1850	164,716	140,675	5,294	20,871	21,815	17,596	14,549	32,003	—	—	26,172
1860	407,449	368,432	12,926	56,943	56,278	44,814	37,012	63,098	—	—	59,252
1870	544,886	509,784	15,946	63,808	73,529	71,193	55,157	—	44,185	36,152	—
1880	680,069	635,428	19,175	72,486	84,974	77,797	71,116	—	66,759	51,480	—
1890 [1]	874,951	811,929	21,990	87,885	107,108	94,732	85,868	—	79,523	72,519	—
1900	1,067,562	1,001,480	26,425	103,549	126,465	116,963	104,519	—	91,204	82,594	—
1910	1,208,578	1,125,282	26,354	103,156	125,159	124,858	122,493	—	113,445	100,325	—
1920	1,356,718	1,275,349	26,953	117,612	139,948	131,405	118,893	—	114,890	113,972	—
1930	1,510,815	1,428,191	26,894	111,596	147,403	144,945	137,500	—	123,712	114,879	—
1940	1,600,176	1,537,411	24,570	104,819	129,097	140,478	144,183	—	131,211	124,745	—
1950	1,726,842	1,707,733	38,359	151,935	151,858	131,410	118,810	—	119,906	127,227	—
1960	1,964,512	1,987,265	48,886	190,587	218,506	189,608	140,562	—	106,025	113,033	—
1970	2,167,373	2,250,358	37,946	157,443	235,102	242,456	218,148	—	158,146	135,126	—
1980	2,305,427	2,400,340	38,690	139,421	176,843	200,634	235,736	—	224,250	202,273	—
1990	2,392,935	2,498,834	32,334	152,418	192,535	181,775	177,063	—	181,812	199,600	—

	Population										
	Male, by age										
30–34	35–39	40–49	40–44	45–49	50–59	50–54	55–59	60–69	60–64	65–69
Aa6435	Aa6436	Aa6437	Aa6438	Aa6439	Aa6440	Aa6441	Aa6442	Aa6443	Aa6444	Aa6445
Year	Number	Number	Number	Number	Number	Number	Number	Number	Number	Number	Number
1840	—	—	—	—	—	—	—	—	—	—	—
1850	—	—	14,371	—	—	7,649	—	—	3,209	—	—
1860	—	—	39,915	—	—	22,295	—	—	10,747	—	—
1870	30,903	30,745	—	29,136	26,400	—	25,247	14,661	—	11,810	7,292
1880	41,922	36,320	—	30,660	27,907	—	29,349	22,902	—	19,493	12,384
1890 [1]	66,664	52,900	—	42,089	35,308	—	31,752	25,121	—	24,374	18,995
1900	76,358	72,464	—	64,084	49,158	—	40,381	31,692	—	25,228	21,163
1910	86,076	79,239	—	70,020	64,610	—	57,298	41,274	—	30,873	24,508
1920	104,692	97,060	—	79,662	74,137	—	63,821	54,171	—	45,107	30,634
1930	111,519	113,000	—	102,246	88,986	—	75,190	61,146	—	51,182	42,106
1940	117,628	111,494	—	108,091	105,443	—	96,056	77,291	—	62,139	48,755
1950	122,169	121,733	—	113,733	105,581	—	100,566	91,699	—	79,330	61,130
1960	122,797	123,993	—	119,688	116,274	—	105,800	95,558	—	83,903	72,531
1970	115,845	111,619	—	121,235	119,545	—	112,744	104,836	—	90,479	72,670
1980	174,497	134,821	—	114,330	108,401	—	114,761	110,278	—	96,830	84,318
1990	209,420	195,602	—	168,238	129,267	—	107,840	99,641	—	100,535	89,744

Note appears at end of table

TABLE Aa6413–6499   Wisconsin population, by race, sex, age, nativity, and urban–rural residence: 1840–1990
Continued

	Population										
	Male, by age					Female, by age					
	70–79	70–74	75–79	80 and older	Unknown age	0	1–4	5–9	10–14	15–19	20–29
	Aa6446	Aa6447	Aa6448	Aa6449	Aa6450	Aa6451	Aa6452	Aa6453	Aa6454	Aa6455	Aa6456
Year	Number	Number	Number	Number	Number	Number	Number	Number	Number	Number	Number
1840	—	—	—	—	—	—	—	—	—	—	—
1850	889	—	—	186	112	5,130	20,077	20,464	16,412	14,244	26,422
1860	3,349	—	—	698	122	12,776	55,210	54,393	42,713	36,767	59,647
1870	—	4,869	2,347	1,506	0	15,070	62,266	72,347	68,763	55,419	—
1880	—	7,901	4,422	3,022	—	18,369	71,263	83,518	75,750	71,987	—
1890 [1]	—	13,821	7,268	5,027	2,007	21,145	85,246	105,116	93,127	85,554	—
1900	—	15,801	10,536	7,144	1,834	26,097	100,663	124,687	115,149	104,419	—
1910	—	16,716	11,459	9,013	1,702	25,673	100,988	122,719	121,296	120,178	—
1920	—	20,066	12,652	9,265	1,778	26,185	114,292	137,510	128,302	119,239	—
1930	—	30,051	16,562	10,950	948	25,652	107,218	143,819	141,532	133,927	—
1940	—	35,217	22,720	16,239	—	23,768	100,623	124,108	134,769	140,622	—
1950	—	42,905	31,089	17,402	—	36,600	145,114	145,591	125,706	120,341	—
1960	—	55,688	34,353	26,720	—	47,012	183,020	209,761	181,723	143,315	—
1970	—	56,950	40,333	36,750	—	36,614	150,224	226,082	231,722	215,005	—
1980	—	62,950	43,289	43,105	—	36,629	132,200	167,961	191,613	230,876	—
1990	—	70,445	52,516	52,150	—	31,071	144,907	183,768	171,812	170,226	—

	Population										
	Female, by age										
	20–24	25–29	30–39	30–34	35–39	40–49	40–44	45–49	50–59	50–54	55–59
	Aa6457	Aa6458	Aa6459	Aa6460	Aa6461	Aa6462	Aa6463	Aa6464	Aa6465	Aa6466	Aa6467
Year	Number	Number	Number	Number	Number	Number	Number	Number	Number	Number	Number
1840	—	—	—	—	—	—	—	—	—	—	—
1850	—	—	18,684	—	—	10,445	—	—	5,580	—	—
1860	—	—	49,438	—	—	29,414	—	—	16,341	—	—
1870	43,246	34,371	—	30,416	29,219	—	26,346	21,702	—	17,123	11,178
1880	63,547	45,539	—	36,921	33,194	—	28,634	26,432	—	24,329	18,501
1890 [1]	76,198	65,083	—	57,405	44,511	—	36,455	31,797	—	27,721	23,156
1900	91,049	77,239	—	68,445	62,722	—	54,154	41,747	—	34,067	28,231
1910	108,652	91,645	—	77,851	70,424	—	61,949	55,788	—	48,209	34,957
1920	113,494	108,651	—	96,294	85,920	—	72,566	63,247	—	55,569	46,821
1930	120,392	110,454	—	105,767	104,780	—	92,635	79,772	—	67,797	54,819
1940	130,594	124,850	—	114,701	107,976	—	102,611	98,304	—	86,496	71,074
1950	124,815	129,361	—	125,637	122,851	—	111,309	102,518	—	97,054	88,286
1960	116,806	114,145	—	123,177	127,567	—	123,128	117,530	—	105,248	95,405
1970	178,952	137,620	—	117,856	114,402	—	122,990	124,178	—	119,464	111,082
1980	225,776	199,642	—	173,618	136,840	—	115,982	111,465	—	118,318	118,768
1990	181,587	201,745	—	211,450	193,906	—	166,871	131,237	—	110,538	105,006

Note appears at end of table

(continued)

TABLE Aa6413–6499   Wisconsin population, by race, sex, age, nativity, and urban–rural residence: 1840–1990
Continued

	Population								White		
	Female, by age								Male	Female	Male, by age
	60–69	60–64	65–69	70–79	70–74	75–79	80 and older	Unknown age			0–4
	Aa6468	Aa6469	Aa6470	Aa6471	Aa6472	Aa6473	Aa6474	Aa6475	Aa6476	Aa6477	Aa6478
Year	Number	Number	Number	Number	Number	Number	Number	Number	Number	Number	Number
1840	—	—	—	—	—	—	—	—	18,757	11,992	2,627
1850	2,341	—	—	654	—	—	142	80	—	—	—
1860	8,402	—	—	2,670	—	—	566	95	—	—	—
1870	—	9,017	5,928	—	4,168	1,893	1,312	0	—	—	—
1880	—	14,997	9,780	—	6,211	3,653	2,803	—	—	—	—
1890 [1]	—	21,132	16,324	—	10,519	5,974	4,407	1,059	—	—	—
1900	—	23,341	19,081	—	13,886	9,240	6,341	922	—	—	—
1910	—	27,354	22,009	—	15,433	10,584	8,915	658	—	—	—
1920	—	38,393	27,297	—	18,314	12,274	9,904	1,077	—	—	—
1930	—	46,549	37,841	—	27,127	15,586	11,836	688	—	—	—
1940	—	57,664	46,326	—	33,488	22,222	17,215	—	—	—	—
1950	—	75,159	60,731	—	43,285	33,390	19,985	—	—	—	—
1960	—	85,984	76,992	—	60,557	40,784	35,111	—	—	—	—
1970	—	98,005	83,141	—	71,309	53,887	57,825	—	—	—	—
1980	—	110,117	100,404	—	82,743	64,279	83,109	—	—	—	—
1990	—	108,344	105,565	—	92,665	78,780	109,356	—	—	—	—

	Population										Female, by age
	White										
	Male, by age										0–4
	5–9	10–14	15–19	20–29	30–39	40–49	50–59	60–69	70–79	80 and older	
	Aa6479	Aa6480	Aa6481	Aa6482	Aa6483	Aa6484	Aa6485	Aa6486	Aa6487	Aa6488	Aa6489
Year	Number	Number	Number	Number	Number	Number	Number	Number	Number	Number	Number
1840	1,793	1,303	1,344	6,328	3,348	1,191	554	201	55	13	2,528
1850	—	—	—	—	—	—	—	—	—	—	—
1860	—	—	—	—	—	—	—	—	—	—	—
1870	—	—	—	—	—	—	—	—	—	—	—
1880	—	—	—	—	—	—	—	—	—	—	—
1890 [1]	—	—	—	—	—	—	—	—	—	—	—
1900	—	—	—	—	—	—	—	—	—	—	—
1910	—	—	—	—	—	—	—	—	—	—	—
1920	—	—	—	—	—	—	—	—	—	—	—
1930	—	—	—	—	—	—	—	—	—	—	—
1940	—	—	—	—	—	—	—	—	—	—	—
1950	—	—	—	—	—	—	—	—	—	—	—
1960	—	—	—	—	—	—	—	—	—	—	—
1970	—	—	—	—	—	—	—	—	—	—	—
1980	—	—	—	—	—	—	—	—	—	—	—
1990	—	—	—	—	—	—	—	—	—	—	—

Note appears at end of table

TABLE Aa6413–6499   Wisconsin population, by race, sex, age, nativity, and urban–rural residence: 1840–1990
Continued

	Population									
	White									
	Female, by age									
	5–9	10–14	15–19	20–29	30–39	40–49	50–59	60–69	70–79	80 and older
	Aa6490	Aa6491	Aa6492	Aa6493	Aa6494	Aa6495	Aa6496	Aa6497	Aa6498	Aa6499
Year	Number	Number	Number	Number	Number	Number	Number	Number	Number	Number
1840	1,692	1,289	1,200	2,713	1,423	612	360	128	37	10
1850	—	—	—	—	—	—	—	—	—	—
1860	—	—	—	—	—	—	—	—	—	—
1870	—	—	—	—	—	—	—	—	—	—
1880	—	—	—	—	—	—	—	—	—	—
1890 [1]	—	—	—	—	—	—	—	—	—	—
1900	—	—	—	—	—	—	—	—	—	—
1910	—	—	—	—	—	—	—	—	—	—
1920	—	—	—	—	—	—	—	—	—	—
1930	—	—	—	—	—	—	—	—	—	—
1940	—	—	—	—	—	—	—	—	—	—
1950	—	—	—	—	—	—	—	—	—	—
1960	—	—	—	—	—	—	—	—	—	—
1970	—	—	—	—	—	—	—	—	—	—
1980	—	—	—	—	—	—	—	—	—	—
1990	—	—	—	—	—	—	—	—	—	—

[1] Includes 6,450 American Indians not counted in the general enumeration; see text for Table Aa2244–2340.

Sources
See the sources for Table Aa2244–2340.

Documentation
See the text for Table Aa2244–2340.
   Wisconsin was originally part of the Northwest Territory. It became a territory in 1836 and a state in 1848.

TABLE Aa6500–6550   Wyoming population by race, sex, age, nativity, and urban–rural residence: 1870–1990
Contributed by Michael R. Haines

			Population						
				Race				Residence	
	Area	Population density	Total	White	Nonwhite	Black	Other nonwhite	Urban	Rural
	Aa6500	Aa6501	Aa6502	Aa6503	Aa6504	Aa6505	Aa6506	Aa6507	Aa6508
Year	Square miles	Persons per square mile	Number	Number	Number	Number	Number	Number	Number
1870	97,594	0.09	9,118	8,726	392	183	209	0	9,118
1880	97,594	0.21	20,789	19,437	1,352	298	1,054	6,152	14,637
1890 [1]	97,594	0.64	62,555	59,275	1,430	922	508	21,484	41,071
1900	97,594	0.95	92,531	89,051	3,480	940	2,540	26,657	65,874
1910	97,594	1.50	145,965	140,318	5,647	2,235	3,412	43,221	102,744
1920	97,548	1.99	194,402	190,146	4,256	1,375	2,881	57,095	137,307
1930	97,548	2.31	225,565	221,241	4,324	1,250	3,074	70,097	155,468
1940	97,506	2.57	250,742	246,597	4,145	956	3,189	93,577	157,165
1950	97,506	2.98	290,529	284,009	6,520	2,557	3,963	144,618	145,911
1960	97,281	3.39	330,066	322,922	7,144	2,183	4,961	187,551	142,515
1970	97,203	3.42	332,416	323,024	9,392	2,568	6,824	201,111	131,305
1980	96,989	4.84	469,557	446,488	23,069	3,364	19,705	294,639	174,918
1990	97,105	4.67	453,588	427,061	26,527	3,606	22,921	294,635	158,953

Note appears at end of table

(continued)

TABLE Aa6500–6550   Wyoming population by race, sex, age, nativity, and urban–rural residence: 1870–1990
Continued

	Population								
	Nativity		Sex		Male, by age				
	Native-born	Foreign-born	Male	Female	0	1–4	5–9	10–14	15–19
	Aa6509	Aa6510	Aa6511	Aa6512	Aa6513	Aa6514	Aa6515	Aa6516	Aa6517
Year	Number	Number	Number	Number	Number	Number	Number	Number	Number
1870	5,605	3,513	7,219	1,899	81	278	210	143	257
1880	14,939	5,850	14,152	6,637	272	992	938	669	754
1890 [1]	45,792	14,913	39,343	21,362	624	2,899	3,145	2,312	2,557
1900	75,116	17,415	58,184	34,347	1,068	4,283	5,102	4,103	4,500
1910	116,945	29,020	91,670	54,295	1,618	6,157	6,635	5,530	6,464
1920	167,835	26,567	110,359	84,043	2,186	9,337	10,520	8,950	7,892
1930	202,222	23,343	124,785	100,780	2,245	9,156	12,278	11,140	10,549
1940	233,635	17,107	135,055	115,687	2,329	9,247	10,964	11,359	12,583
1950	275,925	13,390	154,853	135,676	3,584	13,999	14,131	11,627	12,501
1960	320,403	9,663	169,015	161,051	4,176	16,447	19,281	16,933	12,471
1970	325,427	6,989	166,775	165,641	3,126	11,515	17,125	18,792	16,872
1980	459,950	9,607	240,560	228,997	5,157	17,739	20,305	19,119	22,019
1990	445,941	7,647	227,007	226,581	2,998	14,810	20,702	20,102	18,126

	Population								
	Male, by age								
	20–24	25–29	30–34	35–39	40–44	45–49	50–54	55–59	60–64	65–69
	Aa6518	Aa6519	Aa6520	Aa6521	Aa6522	Aa6523	Aa6524	Aa6525	Aa6526	Aa6527
Year	Number	Number	Number	Number	Number	Number	Number	Number	Number	Number
1870	1,990	1,832	1,082	645	346	173	97	52	22	7
1880	2,302	2,603	2,060	1,495	860	469	358	177	127	42
1890 [1]	5,495	6,492	4,930	3,675	2,714	1,698	1,182	618	384	221
1900	6,894	7,373	6,286	5,967	4,333	2,961	2,142	1,300	837	468
1910	13,381	13,731	10,388	7,922	6,060	4,498	3,706	2,146	1,507	859
1920	9,373	11,488	11,250	10,855	7,752	6,190	4,737	3,533	2,576	1,508
1930	11,537	10,078	9,878	10,851	9,638	7,919	6,187	4,535	3,359	2,443
1940	12,842	11,551	10,559	9,363	8,893	9,025	8,108	6,347	4,592	3,165
1950	13,390	12,508	11,718	11,282	10,044	8,561	7,974	7,376	6,068	4,491
1960	9,520	10,438	11,748	11,510	10,702	10,016	8,807	7,179	6,347	5,304
1970	12,374	10,769	9,187	9,051	10,132	9,688	8,990	8,138	6,945	4,860
1980	26,748	26,229	20,982	15,360	12,170	10,490	10,893	9,517	7,715	6,085
1990	14,145	16,386	20,470	21,005	17,318	12,886	10,211	8,796	8,820	7,532

Note appears at end of table

TABLE Aa6500–6550   Wyoming population by race, sex, age, nativity, and urban–rural residence: 1870–1990
Continued

	Population										
	Male, by age				Female, by age						
	70–74	75–79	80 and older	Unknown age	0	1–4	5–9	10–14	15–19	20–24	25–29
	Aa6528	Aa6529	Aa6530	Aa6531	Aa6532	Aa6533	Aa6534	Aa6535	Aa6536	Aa6537	Aa6538
Year	Number	Number	Number	Number	Number	Number	Number	Number	Number	Number	Number
1870	2	1	1	0	75	224	191	135	161	323	317
1880	18	5	11	—	261	909	938	576	562	777	760
1890 [1]	110	37	20	230	654	2,717	2,911	2,148	2,023	2,292	2,262
1900	215	113	69	170	1,037	4,132	4,847	3,740	3,273	3,433	3,198
1910	487	257	132	192	1,547	6,009	6,414	5,299	5,024	5,992	5,802
1920	856	433	224	699	2,032	8,969	10,365	8,508	6,888	7,793	8,740
1930	1,627	779	462	124	2,218	8,876	11,819	10,610	9,613	8,908	8,411
1940	2,091	1,196	841	—	2,196	8,909	10,742	10,973	11,419	10,454	10,410
1950	2,768	1,875	956	—	3,412	13,302	13,411	11,076	9,987	10,745	11,842
1960	4,012	2,410	1,714	—	4,082	15,903	18,639	15,913	12,123	10,061	10,503
1970	3,908	2,831	2,472	—	2,901	10,830	16,732	17,773	16,357	12,433	10,729
1980	4,497	2,724	2,811	—	4,971	16,978	18,992	18,005	20,560	23,920	23,106
1990	5,444	3,822	3,434	—	2,899	14,073	19,915	18,815	16,681	13,645	16,882

	Population										
	Female, by age										
	30–34	35–39	40–44	45–49	50–54	55–59	60–64	65–69	70–74	75–79	80 and older	Unknown age
	Aa6539	Aa6540	Aa6541	Aa6542	Aa6543	Aa6544	Aa6545	Aa6546	Aa6547	Aa6548	Aa6549	Aa6550
Year	Number	Number	Number	Number	Number	Number	Number	Number	Number	Number	Number	Number
1870	196	111	76	40	23	12	6	1	4	1	3	0
1880	648	467	251	181	133	66	54	28	18	6	2	—
1890 [1]	1,895	1,465	997	716	497	306	194	133	65	41	21	25
1900	2,708	2,374	1,757	1,234	931	656	428	272	125	90	55	57
1910	4,705	3,852	2,772	2,126	1,738	1,119	774	482	313	160	106	61
1920	7,840	6,408	4,912	3,487	2,635	1,868	1,454	908	547	314	199	176
1930	8,252	7,957	6,643	5,094	4,056	2,823	2,050	1,545	965	557	329	54
1940	9,314	8,290	7,553	6,845	5,925	4,221	3,171	2,320	1,420	882	643	—
1950	10,977	10,243	8,690	7,247	6,614	5,573	4,482	3,356	2,265	1,522	932	—
1960	10,970	11,237	10,052	9,423	7,748	6,455	5,474	4,693	3,571	2,303	1,901	—
1970	9,443	9,406	9,705	9,650	8,909	8,059	6,581	5,308	4,223	3,242	3,360	—
1980	18,418	14,053	11,412	10,200	10,022	9,413	7,889	6,994	5,291	3,925	4,848	—
1990	20,558	19,909	15,967	12,380	10,020	9,097	8,777	8,187	6,596	5,285	6,895	—

[1] Includes 1,850 American Indians not counted in the general enumeration; see text for Table Aa2244–2340.

Sources
See the sources for Table Aa2244–2340.

Documentation
See the text for Table Aa2244–2340.

Wyoming became a territory in 1868 and a state in 1890. It was originally part of the Louisiana Purchase of 1803. In 1860 it had been part of Nebraska, Washington, and Utah Territories.

CHAPTER Ab
Vital Statistics

Editor: Michael R. Haines

VITAL STATISTICS

Michael R. Haines

Vital statistics are indicators of the two major dynamic biological forces that shape population change: births and deaths. Sociological factors that can have a profound effect on population dynamics, such as marriages and divorces, are often considered vital statistics, but in this work they are treated separately in Chapter Ae, on family and household composition. Economic forces regulating in-migration and out-migration are treated in Chapter Ad, on international migration. Political forces that result in annexation of new territory that has a resident population or that dictate a partition of a national territory can also affect the population of a nation. In the American experience, boundary changes have almost always resulted in the acquisition of new territory (see Chapters Cf, on geography and the environment, and Ef, on outlying areas).

The official census taken every ten years provides a snapshot of the American population. The Census Bureau literally attempts to count every resident within U.S. territory. Mandated by the Constitution, these static population counts are the responsibility of the federal government. The collection of vital statistics on births and deaths, however, was left to state and local governments. In consequence, vital registration was instituted unevenly. The legal requirement for registering births and deaths and issuing birth and death certificates did not apply to the entire United States until 1933. Although some cities (for example, Boston, New York, Philadelphia, Baltimore, New Orleans) began vital registration early in the nineteenth century, the first state in the United States to do so was Massachusetts in 1842. An official Death Registration Area consisting of ten states and the District of Columbia was established in 1900 and gradually enlarged until it was completed in 1933. A parallel Birth Registration Area was instituted in 1915 and also reached complete coverage in 1933. The coverage of the official registration areas is given in Table Ab31–37, and the dates of entry into the two areas are given in Table Ab38–39.

The U.S. Census enumerators attempted to collect mortality information in the Censuses of 1850–1900 by questioning each household about the deaths of any of its members during the preceding year. The responses in principle could also be combined with the census of individuals under 1 year of age at the time of the census to calculate information on the number of births. Nevertheless, there were significant problems regarding completeness.

Many households failed to report deaths, and many people died without leaving behind a household that could report. This census information on adult mortality did improve over time, and after 1880 it was merged with state registration data. A similar process was not undertaken for birth counts because the census of infant mortality was considered too weak and the number of states with birth registration systems too few.

A criterion for admission to the official U.S. Death Registration Area after 1900 and the Birth Registration Area after 1915 was that registration be 90 percent complete. As late as 1935, it was estimated that birth registration was about 91 percent complete overall but only 80 percent complete for the nonwhite population. No comprehensive study of death registration completeness has been done, but the data appear to have been less than fully inclusive even in the most compliant states of the Death Registration Area in 1900.

One consequence of the lack of vital registration data before the early part of the twentieth century has been a resort to special estimation techniques and indirect measures of fertility and mortality to gain insight into the demographic transition of the nineteenth century. Most of the statistics presented are simple tabulations or standard demographic rates. However, a number of the newer findings arise from application of rather sophisticated techniques (Preston and Haines 1991; Haines and Preston 1997; Haines 1998a). Estimation of demographic information is important for research in social, demographic, and economic history. Basic demographic structures and events, reflected in birth and death rates, population size and structure, growth rates, the composition and growth of the labor force, marriage rates and patterns, household composition, the levels and nature of migration flows, causes of death, urbanization, and spatial population distribution, determine the "human capital" of society. Demographic events are important both as indicators of social and economic change and as integral components of modern economic growth.

Many of the measures presented here are termed "rates," such as birth and death rates (for example, see Table Ab1–10). Rates are calculated as the number of events (deaths) that took place in a region during a set period (usually a year) divided by the size of the relevant population. Generally, demographers prefer that the relevant population, often called the "base population," be the number of people who could experience the event. In the case of death rates, the base population would be the number of people alive at the beginning of the period plus those who were born during the period. In the case of births, the fertility rate (or general fertility rate) is calculated by dividing the number of births by the number of women of childbearing age, conventionally defined as all

Acknowledgments

Michael R. Haines wishes to acknowledge the assistance and advice of Stephanie J. Ventura of the National Center for Health Statistics. The collection of data for this chapter was supported in part by a grant from the National Institute of Aging.

women ages 15–44 years. Sometimes, because of data limitations or other considerations, a different denominator is chosen. Thus, a "crude birth rate" is the number of births in a given year divided by the total midyear population of the region. However defined, once calculated a demographic rate is usually expressed per 1,000 in the base population. A general fertility rate of 70 means that 7 percent of all women ages 15–44 years gave birth during a given year.

One problem that arises in interpreting simple demographic rates is that their value can depend on the underlying age composition of the base population. Thus, a country with many old persons is likely to have a higher crude death rate than one with a preponderance of young adults simply because the probability of an adult dying increases with age. For this reason demographers often calculate age-specific measures, such as the probability of dying at the specific age of 36 years. Age-specific rates can be measured at every single year of age and arranged into what is commonly called a "life table." Life tables are usually presented for a cross section of the population at various ages measured at a single point in time. Calculated in this way it is called a "period life table," in contrast with a "cohort life table," which would follow an actual group of people born at the same time from birth through the death of the last survivor.

Some of the statistics discussed in this essay arise from age-specific measures that have been summarized to be useful and intuitively interpretable. The life table, for example, takes age-specific death rates and converts them into the expectation of life at any age, that is, the average number of years of life remaining if people of that age experienced the age-specific mortality rates embodied in the life table. For example, Table Ab644–655 presents the expectation of life at birth for the white and black populations from 1850 onward. Table Ab656–703 gives the expectation of life at various ages around census dates from 1850 to 1990. Another life table measure is the probability of an infant surviving from birth to the first birthday (exact age of 1 year), which is presented here as the infant mortality rate (infant deaths per 1,000 live births per annum). Table Ab912–927 has the infant mortality rate for the United States, along with the fetal death ratio (the number of stillbirths per 1,000 live births) and neonatal mortality rate (infant deaths in the first twenty-seven days of life per 1,000 live births). The infant mortality rate on an annual basis for Massachusetts for 1850–1998 is found in Table Ab928. Massachusetts is the state with the longest reliable series of annual birth and infant death data.

Similarly, age-specific fertility rates can be summarized. One instance, provided in Table Ab52–117, is the total fertility rate (TFR), which is the sum of age-specific births for all women ages 15–49 years. This can be seen as the average number of births a woman would have if she remained alive throughout her entire reproductive life and if she personally experienced rates of childbearing at each age of life displayed by the cross-sectional age-specific data. Extensions of the TFR, and the gross and net reproduction rates, may be found in Table Ab306–314. The gross reproduction rate is the TFR for female births only. The net reproduction rate (NRR) is the gross reproduction rate adjusted for the mortality of women between birth and their age at the birth of their daughters. An NRR of 1.0 indicates that over the long term a society is reproducing just a replacement number of individuals. A rate above 1.0 indicates positive long-term population growth, and a rate below 1.0 points to a long-term population decline from the natural processes of births and deaths.

Table Ab315–346 provides yet another measure of fertility known as the child/woman ratio, which is the number of surviving children ages 0–4 years per 1,000 women ages 20–44 years. It is a wholly census-based fertility rate, requiring no vital statistics. It is, in fact, the main direct source of information on fertility in the nineteenth century for the United States and is the basis for the early estimates of crude birth rate and TFR also given in Table Ab40–51. The child/woman ratio does have some serious drawbacks because it deals with surviving children at the time of census and not actual births in the preceding five years. It also suffers from relative differences in underenumeration of young children and adult women. It has the advantage of being available back to 1800 for the white population and to 1830 for the black population. Table Ab315–346 provides this measure for geographic divisions and rural–urban residence from 1800 to 1990.

Another measure of fertility available historically is based on a census question that asked each woman how many live births she had experienced. Data on children ever born are set forth in Table Ab536–625 for the whole United States from the Censuses of 1900, 1910, and 1940–1990, and for two state censuses that happened to ask such questions – New York State in 1865 and Massachusetts in 1885 (see Tables Ab626–643).

The Long-Term Decline of Fertility

The young republic was notable for its large families and early marriages. The TFR in Table Ab1–10 indicates an average number of births per woman of approximately seven in 1800, followed by a sustained decline in birth rates up until the late 1940s (see Figure Ab-A). The unusual aspect of the American experience is that the decline began before the nation had developed a substantially urban or industrial character. Both rural and urban birth rates declined in parallel, although rural fertility remained higher throughout the period considered here. Fertility decreased across regions, but the South lagged behind the Northeast and Midwest with regard to the timing and speed of the decline (Table Ab315–346). Even the fertility of the antebellum slave population showed signs of decline just prior to 1860, though family sizes of blacks were, on average, significantly larger than those of whites (Sutch 1975; Steckel 1982).

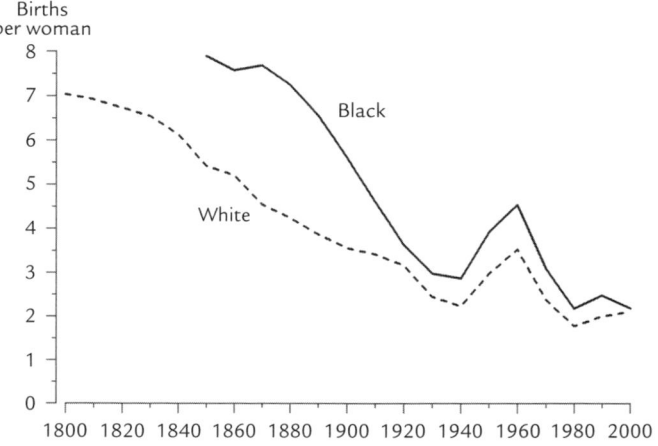

FIGURE Ab-A   Total fertility rate, by race: 1800–2000

Source

Series Ab5–6.

The fertility of the female population will be determined by the typical age at first sexual experience. As women come of childbearing age in their midteens, postponement of sexual activity until older ages will reduce the number of years during which a woman may become pregnant. Statisticians have very little historical evidence about this extremely private aspect of most people's lives, but demographers suspect that the state of matrimony is highly correlated with sexual activity. Thus, the fraction of women who are married – "nuptiality" – is of interest in the study of the general fertility of a population. Either because of a cultural taboo against premarital sex or because a woman would often marry soon after discovering her first pregnancy, the age at first marriage is also an important demographic variable.

We know relatively little about marriage in the early nineteenth century and what we do know is rather speculative. Around 1800, the age of women at first marriage was probably rather young, perhaps below twenty years. Men on average were several years older at marriage, and all but a relatively small proportion of both sexes eventually married (Haines 1996). The federal census did not include a question on marital status until 1880 and did not begin reporting results until 1890. Several state censuses did, however, ask these questions earlier. A sample of seven New York state counties from the manuscripts of the Census of 1865, for example, reveals an estimated age at first marriage of 23.8 years for women and 26.6 years for men. Percentages of individuals who never married by the ages of 45–54 years were 7.4 percent for women and 5.9 percent for men, pointing to quite low levels of lifetime unmarried status. Although the typical age at marriage was probably higher in New York than in the nation as a whole and although it had very likely risen by 1865, nuptiality was still rather extensive by European standards. The average age at first marriage for women was 25.4 years in England and Wales in 1861 and 26.3 years in Germany in 1871 (with German men having had an average age at marriage as late as 28.8 years).

In 1880, when the U.S. Census first asked a question on marital status, the average age for women at first marriage was 23.0 years, while that for men was 26.5 years. The proportions of individuals who never married by middle age were still relatively low, at 7 percent for both men and women. Age at marriage rose slightly up until 1890 and 1900 and thereafter began a long-term decline up to the 1950s (see Table Ae489–506 and Figure Ab-B). Recent work with the Integrated Public Use Microdata Samples (IPUMS) of the federal census has provided estimates of the median age at marriage for the white population back to 1850 by using imputed marital status for 1850–1870.[1] The median age at marriage is the age at which half of all ever-married women in a cohort are younger and half are older. Those results indicate that the median age at marriage was roughly stable over that period, at about 25 years for men and 21–22 years for women (Table Ae481–488). This is in sharp contrast to the late twentieth century, when the age at marriage rose to its highest point (26–28 years for men and 25–29 years for women). However, in the late twentieth century the link between marriage and childbearing was beginning to weaken. In 1998, about one third of all births were to unmarried women.

A decomposition of the fertility decline into the contributions of nuptiality and marital fertility found that, up to approximately 1850, half of the decline could be attributed to adjustments in marriage age and marriage incidence. Thereafter, most of the decline

[1] See the Guide to the Millennial Edition for information on IPUMS.

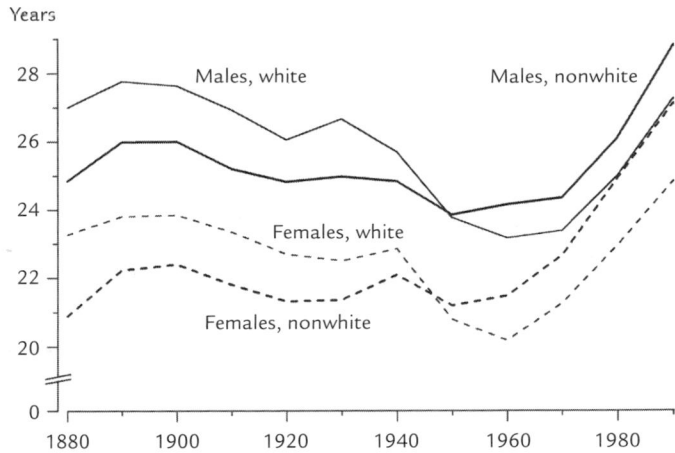

FIGURE Ab-B   Singulate mean age at first marriage, by sex and race: 1880–1990

Sources
Ae491–492 and Ae501–502.

originated in lower fertility within marriage (Sanderson 1979, pp. 339–58).

Such evidence as we have concerning fertility differentials between native-born and foreign-born women points to relatively small differences at midcentury but generally higher fertility for the foreign-born thereafter. The fertility of native white women continued to decline, while the successive cohorts of incoming migrants continued to produce large families. Birth rates of native-born women of foreign-born parentage were intermediate between those of native white women of native parentage and foreign-born white women, suggesting a form of convergence to native white demographic patterns. Data on children ever born (parity) from a sample of seven New York counties in 1865 revealed few differences between native-born and foreign-born women born near the beginning of the nineteenth century (Table Ab626–636). However, published data from the Massachusetts Census of 1885 showed substantially more births per ever-married foreign-born woman relative to the native-born (Table Ab637–643). Such differentials also appeared in the data from the federal censuses of 1900 and 1910 (Table Ab536–625). Much of the difference was due to the lower age at marriage and lower percentages of individuals remaining single among the foreign-born. However, fertility within marriage was also greater for foreign-born women in the late nineteenth and early twentieth centuries. Relatively few of them, for instance, remained permanently childless. The federal Census of 1910 reported that native white women ages 55–64 years (that is, those born in the years 1846–1855) had an average number of children ever born of 4.4 (4.8 for ever-married women). More than 17 percent of all native white women (and 9 percent of those who married) remained childless. Among the foreign-born enumerated at the same census, the average number of children was 5.5 for all women and 5.8 for ever-married women, with only 12 percent of all women, and 7 percent of ever-married women, remaining childless. Such differentials between native-born and foreign-born women had largely disappeared for those born at the end of the nineteenth century and enumerated in 1940.

The inexorable decline of American birth rates continued apace after the Civil War. However, most of the decline originated in adjustments in fertility within marriage. Recent work with data from the 1900, 1910, and 1940 federal censuses shows rapid reductions in marital fertility, especially among white urban women. In 1910, for example, more than half of native white urban women ages 45–49 years were estimated to have been effectively controlling fertility within marriage, and about a quarter of rural farm and nonfarm women were doing the same. Among younger women (ages 15–34 years) the proportions were much higher, rising to more than 70 percent for native white urban women and more than half for native white farm women. It could be said that the "two-child norm" was being established in the United States in this era. Some fascinating supporting evidence is furnished by a survey of the wives of professional and white-collar men over the period 1892–1920. Although the sample was small and nonrepresentative, it revealed extensive use of contraceptives and contraceptive practices and active strategies of family limitation. This was a preview of the rapid adoption of such behaviors in the twentieth century (David and Sanderson 1986, 1987).

The usual pattern of fertility transition is that women "stop" having children by lowering their age at last birth. By the 1890s, however, American women were also "spacing," that is, lengthening the intervals between births to reduce completed family size further. New estimates of age-specific fertility rates for the United States around the turn of the century point to low marital fertility at young ages, quite unlike the situation in Europe at the same time (Haines 1990).

The period after 1865 was also marked by reductions in fertility according to residence and race (Table Ab315–346). Rural fertility remained higher than urban fertility, but absolute differences diminished as both populations progressively limited family size. The absolute gap dropped from 474 more children ages 0–4 years per 1,000 women of childbearing age in rural than in urban areas in 1800 to 273 in 1920. As Table Ab1–10 shows, fertility differences by race also tended to converge after the middle of the nineteenth century. Whereas the TFR for blacks was 48 percent higher than that for whites in the 1850s, it was only 15 percent higher in 1920. Differentials in birth rates by race have persisted up to the present and actually widened somewhat after 1920 (Tables Ab40–117). Birth rates also varied across regions both before and after the Civil War, with the South and West having been areas of higher fertility relative to the Northeast and Midwest (Table Ab315–346).

Finally, although we know rather less about the fertility of different socioeconomic status groups, the evidence points to smaller families among higher socioeconomic status groups, such as professionals, proprietors, clerks, and other white-collar workers. This was true from at least the middle of the nineteenth century onward. Among proprietors, however, an exception was farmers who owned their own farms, who, throughout the century, typically had larger families than other groups. Fertility among unskilled workers tended to be closer to that of farmers, while skilled and semiskilled manual workers and craftsmen occupied an intermediate position. These socioeconomic fertility differences may have widened over the course of the nineteenth century before they eventually narrowed (Haines 1993).

One consequence of declining fertility has been the aging of the population. As Table Aa599–613 indicates, the median age of the American population rose from 16 in 1800 to over 20 in 1870, to over 25 in 1920, and finally to almost 33 in 1990. The reason is that births add people of age zero to the population but mortality, in contrast, affects all ages. As fertility declines, so does the proportion of children. The average age of the population rises.

The implications of this are great, changing the society from one oriented toward children to one centered on adults and the elderly.

Explaining the decline in fertility among Americans poses a series of difficult issues. Conventional demographic transition theory has placed great reliance on the changes in child costs and benefits associated with structural changes accompanying modern economic growth, such as urbanization, industrialization, the rise in literacy and education, and increased employment of women outside the home. The classic statement of the theory was made by Frank Notestein in 1953.

> The new ideal of the small family arose typically in the urban industrial society. It is impossible to be precise about the various causal factors, but apparently many were important. Urban life stripped the family of many functions in production, consumption, recreation, and education. In factory employment the individual stood on his own accomplishments. The new mobility of young people and the anonymity of city life reduced the pressure toward traditional behavior exerted by the family and community. In a period of rapidly developing technology, new skills were needed, and new opportunities for individual advancement arose. Education and a rational point of view became increasingly important. As a consequence the cost of child-rearing grew and the possibilities for economic contributions by children declined. Falling death-rates at once increased the size of the family to be supported and lowered the inducements to have many births. Women, moreover, found new independence from household obligations and new economic roles less compatible with childbearing.

But, of course, the fertility transition began in the United States well before many of these structural changes became important.

An early alternative theory to explain the American fertility decline for the antebellum period was the land availability hypothesis (Yasuba 1962; Forster and Tucker 1972). It was noted that in the period before the Civil War, an inverse relationship existed between population density and child/woman ratio. If high population density meant a scarcity of unoccupied agricultural land and high land prices, then the cost to farm families of endowing their children with a suitable means of earning a living in an agricultural society would be high. This may then be presumed to reduce the attractiveness of large families.

An intriguing alternative to the land availability–child bequest hypothesis has been proposed by Sundstrom and David (1988). They argue that smaller families resulted more from the development of nearby nonagricultural labor market opportunities than from the march of the frontier and the disappearance of inexpensive homesteads. With an active urban labor market, larger material inducements were necessary to keep children "down on the farm" once jobs were readily available within easy distance. A related model, that of Ransom and Sutch, emphasizes the westward migration of children who then "defaulted" on their implicit contracts to care for their parents in old age (Sutch 1990). In response, parents began accumulating real and financial assets as a substitute for offspring as retirement insurance, leading to smaller families. In general, however, the land availability, urban labor markets, and child default models are all consistent with the patterns of fertility decline across space and time. Such data do not allow us to discriminate between the models, which are, indeed, not mutually exclusive. Richard Steckel, using published state-level data from the 1850 and 1860 federal censuses, ran some tests on the competing hypotheses. Although he found modest support for the land availability view, the strongest predictors of marital fertility differentials just prior to the Civil War were the presence of financial intermediaries (banks) and labor force structure (that is, the ratio of nonagricultural to agricultural labor force) (Steckel 1992a). These findings tend to support the Ransom and Sutch and Sundstrom and David theories, respectively.

Recent work by D. S. Smith (1996) with the rich data from the 1915 Census of Iowa provides support for the importance of education. Women with more years of schooling and exposure to grammar school, as opposed simply to the common school with no grades, were more effective in controlling family size. Education would facilitate the transmission of contraceptive knowledge, which may also help to explain the appearance of spacing from early in childbearing that was characteristic of the American experience around the end of the nineteenth century (Haines 1990).

Most of the hypotheses about the American fertility transition can also be fit into the more general model offered by Caldwell (1982). His model focuses attention on the net flow of resources between parents and children over the entire life course. Family limitation sets in when this net flow starts to tilt away from parents and toward children – in other words, when parents typically are transferring more resources to their children than they are receiving from them. This signifies a rise in the net cost of childrearing (that is, benefits minus costs) and is accelerated by factors such as the introduction of mass education (implying more years in school and lower child labor contributions to the family), child labor laws, and a more positive view of the value of transmitting human capital, rather than financial assets or physical capital, from parents to their children.

Before the Civil War, fertility among blacks was heavily influenced by their condition as slaves. Despite the higher infant and child mortality rates among blacks, child/woman ratios for blacks were higher than those for whites, pointing to even larger differential fertility for blacks. Further, the regional pattern was the opposite of that for the white population, with higher black child/woman ratios in the Southeast and lower ratios in the Southwest. Selective movement of adult unmarried slaves to the West and the emphasis on slave reproduction in the Old South likely played a role, as did the quite harsh work regimen on the larger plantations of the New South specializing in cotton and sugar. After the Civil War, the decline in black fertility was more similar in nature to the white fertility transition, influenced by urbanization, industrial development, the growing shortage of good farmland, and changes in family norms. Differential fertility in urban areas actually reversed, with fertility for blacks lower than that for whites in the late nineteenth and early twentieth centuries.

The Baby Boom

Fertility decline continued in the twentieth century, but it was punctuated by one of the most interesting demographic phenomena of modern times – the post–World War II "baby boom." As seen in Figure Ab-A and Tables Ab40–117, birth rates reached a low point in the late 1930s, remained low during World War II, and thereafter rose dramatically until they reached a peak in the early 1960s. Thereafter, birth rates fell to a low point in the middle of the 1970s, followed by a gradual rise until they reached a plateau at about long-term replacement (that is, a TFR of about 2.1). The

white population is just about replacing itself, while the nonwhite population has fertility slightly above replacement levels.

The leading explanation for the baby boom and subsequent "baby bust" remains that of Richard Easterlin (1980). It involves an interaction of the small cohort size of young adults in the 1945–1962 period (caused by low birth rates in the 1920s and 1930s) and the prosperous post–World War II economy. These young adults in the peak childbearing years experienced high wages and incomes and low unemployment. They chose both higher consumption, especially housing, automobiles, home furnishings, and appliances, as well as more children. This was in part the result of tastes formed in the 1930s and early 1940s, when consumer goods were less available owing to Depression-era poverty and then war rationing. After about 1962 the process operated in reverse. Couples began experiencing relatively less favorable labor force outcomes and then chose to have fewer children.

The implications of the baby boom and subsequent baby bust are enormous. The large birth cohorts of 1946–1962 have influenced consumer spending, demand for housing, needs for schools and higher education, savings behavior, voting patterns, and many other aspects of the society and economy. The smaller cohort born in the late 1960s and the 1970s posed new challenges. The smaller size of the bust relative to the boom generation has thrown into question long-standing formulas defining Social Security benefits and Medicare. When the "boomers" retire, the smaller succeeding cohorts must assume the burden of paying for these benefits.

Since 1962 there has been what some have called a "second demographic transition" in terms of the family patterns described in Chapter Ae, on family and household composition. There has been a dramatic increase in cohabitation, along with a significant rise in divorce. The proportion of the population living alone has also risen notably, particularly among older individuals.

The Long-Term Decline of Mortality

We know less about the American mortality transition of the nineteenth century than we do about that for fertility. There are no ready census-based mortality measures such as the child/woman ratio, and vital statistics were absent or incomplete for most areas up until the early twentieth century. Demographers have tended to rely either on mortality data from states that had implemented death registration in the nineteenth century, such as Massachusetts, or on samples of genealogical data. Both techniques have disadvantages. Massachusetts began statewide civil vital statistics registration in 1842, but Massachusetts was not typical of the nation in the nineteenth century. It was more urban and industrial, was populated with a larger number of immigrants, and had lower fertility rates. The Massachusetts data reach reasonable quality by about 1860 and are reproduced here in Tables Ab928 and Ab1048–1058. Recent work with the genealogical data has concluded that adult mortality was relatively stable after about 1800 and then rose in the 1840s and 1850s before commencing long and slow improvement after the Civil War. This finding is surprising because we have evidence of rising real income per capita and of significant economic growth during the 1840–1860 period. However, income distribution may have worsened, and urbanization and immigration may have had more deleterious effects than hitherto believed. Further, the disease environment may have shifted in an unfavorable direction (Fogel 1986; Pope 1992; Haines, Craig, and Weiss 2003). It should be noted, however, that the genealogical records exist only for individuals whose ancestors compiled a family tree. They may be subject to biases that stem from inadequate records, systematic errors introduced when linking records, and the selectivity that determines whose family tree is thought worth researching and which families are not traced in this manner.

We have better information for the post–Civil War period. Rural mortality probably began its decline in the 1870s because of improvements in diet, nutrition, housing, and other quality-of-life aspects on the farm. There would have been little role for public health systems before the twentieth century in rural areas. Urban mortality probably did not begin to decline prior to 1880, but thereafter urban public health measures – especially construction of central water distribution systems to deliver pure water and sanitary sewers – were important in producing a rapid decline of infectious diseases and mortality in the cities that installed these improvements (Melosi 2000). There is no doubt that mortality declined dramatically in both rural and urban areas after about 1900 (Preston and Haines 1991).

Tables Ab644–703 provide data on the expectation of life at birth and the infant mortality rate (deaths in the first year of life per 1,000 live births) for the white population from 1850 onward. No information is given for the years prior to 1850 because of the difficulty of finding comprehensive, comparable, and reliable mortality estimates. Both the expectation of life at birth and the infant mortality rate show sustained improvement in mortality (that is, rising expectation of life or falling infant mortality or crude death rates) only from about the 1870s onward.

What is apparent is that serious fluctuations in mortality were less likely after the 1870s, and that this was integral in the process of the mortality transition. This also confirms one unusual aspect of the American demographic transition: the decline of fertility commenced substantially earlier than that of mortality. Although levels of mortality in the United States in the middle of the nineteenth century were comparable with those in western and northern Europe, significant mortality fluctuations were still occurring right up to the twentieth century. Consistent control of mortality in terms of both sustained decline and damping of mortality peaks started only after the 1870s.

The evidence of rising mortality in the antebellum period from genealogical data is bolstered by data on the stature of adults. Males were shorter in the birth cohorts from about 1830 to about 1870 than those who were born earlier or later (Steckel 1992b; Haines 1998b). This evidence strongly suggests a poorer disease environment in that period as well as deteriorating nutrition. Following the Civil War, the disease environment improved in what might be called an "epidemiological transition." A variety of factors can affect mortality; these may be conveniently grouped into ecobiological, public health, medical, and socioeconomic categories. These divisions are not mutually exclusive because, for example, economic growth can make resources available for public health projects, and advances in medical science can inform the effectiveness of public health. Ecobiological factors, those that change the virulence of a disease course or its transmission mechanism, were not likely to have been significant. The remaining factors – socioeconomic, medical, and public health – are often difficult to disentangle. For example, if the germ theory of disease (a medical/scientific advance of the later nineteenth century) contributed to better techniques of water filtration and purification in public health projects, then how should the roles of medicine versus public health be apportioned? Thomas McKeown (1976) has proposed that, prior to the twentieth century, medical science contributed little to reduced mortality in Europe and elsewhere. This conclusion was based particularly on the experience of England and Wales, where much of the mortality decline between the 1840s and the 1930s was attributable to reductions in deaths from respiratory tuberculosis, other respiratory infections (for example, bronchitis), and nonspecific gastrointestinal diseases (for example, diarrhea, gastroenteritis), when as yet no effective medical therapies were available for these infections until well into the twentieth century. If ecobiological, medical, and public health factors are eliminated, the mortality decline must have been due to socioeconomic factors, especially in McKeown's view – better diet and nutrition, and improved clothing and shelter.

It is true that medical science did have a rather limited direct role before the twentieth century. In terms of specific therapies, smallpox vaccination was known by the late eighteenth century, and diphtheria and tetanus antitoxin and rabies therapy by the 1890s. The germ theory of disease, advanced by Pasteur in the 1860s and greatly advanced by the work of Koch and others in the 1870s and 1880s, was only slowly accepted by what was at the time a very conservative medical profession. Even after Robert Koch conclusively identified the tuberculosis bacillus and the cholera vibrio in 1882 and 1883, various theories of miasmas and anticontagionist views were common among physicians in the United States and elsewhere. Hospitals, having originated as pesthouses and almshouses, were (correctly) perceived as generally unhealthy places to be. Surgery was also very dangerous before the advances made by William Halsted in the 1880s and 1890s. Major thoracic surgery was rarely risked, and if attempted, patients had a high probability of dying from infection, shock, or both. The best practice in amputations was to do them quickly to minimize risks. Although anesthesia had been introduced in America in the 1840s and the use of antisepsis in the operating theater had been advocated by the British surgeon Joseph Lister in the 1860s, surgery cannot be considered as reasonably safe until the twentieth century.

Although the direct impact of medicine on mortality in the United States over this period is questionable, public health did play an important role and thereby indirectly allowed medicine a part. After John Snow identified a polluted water source as the origin of a cholera outbreak in London in 1854, pure water and sewage disposal became important issues for municipal authorities. New York City constructed its forty-mile-long Croton Aqueduct in 1844, and Boston was also tapping various outside water sources by aqueduct before the Civil War. Chicago, which drew on Lake Michigan for its water, also had to cope with sewage disposal directly into its water supply from the Chicago River. At an early date, all buildings in the entire downtown area were raised by one story to facilitate gravity sewage flow. Water intakes were moved farther offshore in the 1860s, requiring tunnels several miles long driven through solid rock. But this was only a temporary solution. Finally, the city reversed the flow of the Chicago River, using locks, and sent the effluent down to the Illinois River and away from the water intakes in Lake Michigan. The project took eight years (1892–1900) and was called one of the "engineering wonders of the modern world." The bond issue to fund it was approved by an overwhelming vote of 70,958 to 242.

A pattern was emerging in the late nineteenth century – massive public works projects in larger metropolitan areas to provide clean water and proper sewage disposal. But progress was uneven.

Baltimore and New Orleans, for example, were rather late in constructing adequate sanitary sewage systems. Filtration and chlorination were added to remove or neutralize particulate matter and microorganisms as a consequence of advances in the new science of bacteriology. Public health officials were often more eager to embrace the findings from bacteriology than were physicians, who sometimes saw public health officials as a professional threat. Most public works and public health projects were locally funded, with the consequence of uneven and intermittent progress toward water and sewer systems, public health departments, and so forth. Indeed, one reason for the better mortality showing of the ten largest cities in 1900 as compared with remaining cities with populations greater than 25,000 was the capacity of the largest cities to secure the necessary financial resources (Preston and Haines 1991; Melosi 2000; see also Chapter Dh, on services and utilities).

Progress in public health was not confined to water and sewer systems, though they were among the most effective weapons in the fight to prolong and enhance human life. Other areas of public health activity from the late nineteenth century onward included vaccination against smallpox; use of diphtheria and tetanus antitoxins (from the 1890s); more extensive use of quarantine (as more diseases were identified as contagious); cleaning urban streets and public areas; physical examinations for schoolchildren; health education; improved child labor and workplace health and safety laws; legislation and enforcement efforts to reduce food adulteration and especially to obtain pure milk; measures to eliminate ineffective or dangerous medications (the Pure Food and Drug Act of 1906); increased knowledge of and education concerning nutrition; stricter licensing of physicians, nurses, and midwives; more rigorous medical education; building codes to improve heat, plumbing, and ventilation in housing; measures to alleviate air pollution in urban settings; and the creation of state and local boards of health to oversee and administer these programs.

Public health measures proceeded on a broad front, but not without delays and considerable unevenness in enforcement and effectiveness. The issue of milk purity is a case in point. It became apparent that pasteurization (heating the milk to a temperature below boiling for a period of time), known since the 1860s, was the only effective means of ensuring a bacteria-free product. Pasteurization was, however, resisted by milk sellers, and it came into practice only relatively late. In 1911, only 15 percent of the milk in New York City was pasteurized. In 1908 only 20 percent of Chicago's milk was so treated. Pasteurization did not become compulsory in Chicago until 1908 and in New York City until 1912.

Long-Term Changes in the Causes of Death

Reductions in death from infectious and parasitic diseases, both of the respiratory (usually air-borne) and gastrointestinal (usually water-borne) types, explain much of the decrease in mortality in the late nineteenth and early twentieth centuries. In a study of Philadelphia over the period 1870–1930, about two thirds of the decline in death rates came from reductions in deaths caused by various infectious diseases. Most impressive is a 22 percent decline in deaths from respiratory tuberculosis. Among children there were significant reductions in mortality from diphtheria and croup, scarlet fever, smallpox, and respiratory tuberculosis. Diphtheria antitoxin, water filtration, and quarantine helped, but an improved standard of living was also important, especially in controlling tuberculosis,

for which no specific therapy was available until the 1940s. Well-nourished individuals were better able to resist tuberculosis. As the population became increasingly well fed, the disease became a less frequent cause of death.

Reliable cause-of-death information for large areas of the nation became available in 1900 with the initiation of the Death Registration Area. The crude death rate declined (at least for the Death Registration Area) by 25 percent between 1900 and 1920 (see Tables Ab929–987). Of this decline, 70 percent was accounted for by a reduction in death from infectious and parasitic diseases. Of that reduction from infectious disease, 24 percent was attributable to reductions in mortality from respiratory tuberculosis. Over the longer period of 1900–1960, the crude death rate declined by 45 percent, while mortality from all infectious and parasitic diseases was reduced by 90 percent. Deaths from infectious and parasitic diseases declined from 57 percent of all deaths to only 8.8 percent. In addition, diagnosis and reporting were becoming more accurate, as deaths in the category "other and unknown" declined from 21 percent of all deaths to 9.3 percent. The decline in mortality from infectious disease actually exceeded that from all causes combined because mortality from chronic, degenerative diseases (cancer, cardiovascular disease) increased.

One of the great events in human history has been the prolongation of life and reduction in mortality in the modern era, attributable chiefly to great declines in death from epidemic and endemic infectious disease. Americans and most inhabitants of the developed world no longer live with the kind of fear and fatalism that characterized a world in which sudden and pervasive death from disease was a fact of life. For the United States, most of this improvement took place in the twentieth century.

Mortality Differentials

During the nineteenth century, both prior to and during the mortality transition commencing in the 1870s, significant differentials in mortality existed – by sex, rural–urban residence, race, region, origin (native versus foreign-born), and socioeconomic status. Male mortality usually exceeds female mortality at all ages. This was generally true in the United States in the nineteenth century. The relative differences were often smaller than those in the mid to late twentieth century, as a consequence of the hazards of childbearing, pervasive exposure to disease-causing organisms, and the effects of differential health behaviors. Sex differentials in mortality increased in the twentieth century as sex differentials in smoking rose.

It is clear that, before about 1920, urban mortality was much in excess of rural mortality and, in general, the larger the city, the higher the death rate (Haines 2001). A variety of circumstances contributed to the greater mortality in cities: greater density and crowding, leading to the more rapid spread of infection; a higher likelihood of contaminated air, water, and food; garbage, horse droppings, and carrion in streets; larger inflows of foreign migrants, both new foci of infection and new victims; and migrants from the countryside who had not been exposed to the harsher urban disease environment. Cities were the home of the poor.

According to the Death Registration Area life tables for 1900–1902, the expectation of life at birth was 48.2 years for white males overall – 44 years in urban areas and 54 years in rural places. The comparable results for females were similar: 51.1 years overall,

48 years in urban areas, and 55 years in rural areas. For the seven states with reasonable registration data in both 1890 and 1900, the ratio of urban to rural crude death rates reported in the 1890 Census was 1.27, and that in 1900 was 1.18. For young children (ages 1–4 years) the ratios were much higher, with urban mortality being 107 percent higher in 1890 and 97 percent higher in 1900. For infants the excess urban mortality was 63 percent in 1890 and 49 percent in 1900. Residence in cities – with poorer water quality, lack of refrigeration to keep food and milk fresh, and close proximity to a variety of pathogens – was very hazardous to the youngest inhabitants.

The higher urban mortality rates began to diminish after the turn of the century, especially as public health measures and improved diet, shelter, and general living standards took effect. The excess in expectation of life at birth for rural white males over that for urban white males was 10 years in 1900. This fell to 7.7 years in 1910, 5.4 years in 1930, and 2.6 years by 1940.

The black population of the United States certainly experienced higher death rates, both as slaves and then as a free population, than did whites. Table Ab1–10 provides a breakdown of the expectation of life at birth and the infant mortality rate by race (see Figure Ab-C). For the 1890s, based on estimates using the 1900 Census public use sample, the infant mortality rate was 111 infant deaths per 1,000 live births for the white population and 170 for the black population. The implied expectations of life at birth were 51.8 years for whites and 41.8 years for blacks (see Tables Ab644–911 and Ab952–987). The differential clearly had not disappeared by 1920, when the absolute difference in expectation of life at birth by race was 10.4 years, and the infant mortality rate for blacks was 60 percent higher than that for whites, despite the fact that blacks still lived in predominantly rural areas. Even in 1980, although some convergence had occurred, the difference in life expectancy was 6.3 years, and black infant mortality was 90 percent higher than white. The absolute difference had narrowed, but the relative

difference in infant survival had actually worsened. The disadvantaged status of the black population is apparent, as mortality is a sensitive indicator of socioeconomic well-being.

The mortality and health of the antebellum slave population has more recently been studied using plantation records and coastal shipping manifests that gave the heights of transported slaves. It has revealed very high mortality and very stunted stature among slave infants and young children, pointing to poor health conditions. For example, the infant mortality rate for slaves is estimated to have been as high as 350 infant deaths per 1,000 live births, in comparison to 197 for the entire American population in 1860. Death rates among slave children ages 1–4 years were also very high. A hypothesis for the high mortality and short stature of slave children is that they were not given much animal protein in their diets until about the age of ten years. In addition, pregnant and lactating women were often kept hard at field work, leading to lower birth weights, less breast-feeding, and early weaning (Steckel 1986a, 1986b).

Information on mortality differences between the native- and the foreign-born populations is ambiguous. In Massachusetts, for example, the crude death rate for the native population was higher (20.4 per 1,000 population) than that for the foreign-born (17.4) for the period 1888–1895. This difference disappears, however, once the results are adjusted for the younger age structure of the immigrant population. Using census samples to estimate the mortality of children of native- and foreign-born parents reveals the opposite: for seven New York counties in 1865, the probability of dying before age five years was 0.19 for children of native-born parents but 0.23 for children of foreign-born parents. The same calculation using the national sample of the 1900 Census gives a probability of death before age five years of 0.166 when both parents were native-born and 0.217 when both parents were immigrants. For the Death Registration Area life tables of 1900–1902, life expectancies at age 10 years were rather similar by origin: 51.6 years for native white males and 49.1 years for foreign-born white males. The results for 1909–1911 were 51.9 and 50.3 years, respectively. Differentials by origin were converging and had largely disappeared by the 1930s because the higher mortality of the foreign-born was largely attributable to lower socioeconomic status and a greater proportion living in large cities. As socioeconomic attainment narrowed between the groups and as the rural–urban mortality difference disappeared, the mortality penalty paid by the foreign-born also diminished.

Regional differences in mortality before the twentieth century are rather difficult to establish because of the incompleteness of geographic coverage of both vital statistics and local studies. In colonial times, especially in the seventeenth century, New England was the area with lowest mortality, while the region from the Chesapeake to the south had higher mortality. These differentials diminished in the eighteenth century, but the pattern continued into the first half of the nineteenth century, as is confirmed from estimates of adult mortality from genealogies for cohorts born in the late eighteenth and early nineteenth centuries. The Midwest also appeared as a relatively healthy region. For cohorts born in the middle of the century, however, these regional differences had dissipated. Indeed, the highest life expectation at age twenty years for white females born in the 1850s and 1860s was in the South Atlantic states. Regional differences, such as they were, converged into the twentieth century, but as late as 1950 the region with the lowest mortality was still the western portion of the Midwest, while the

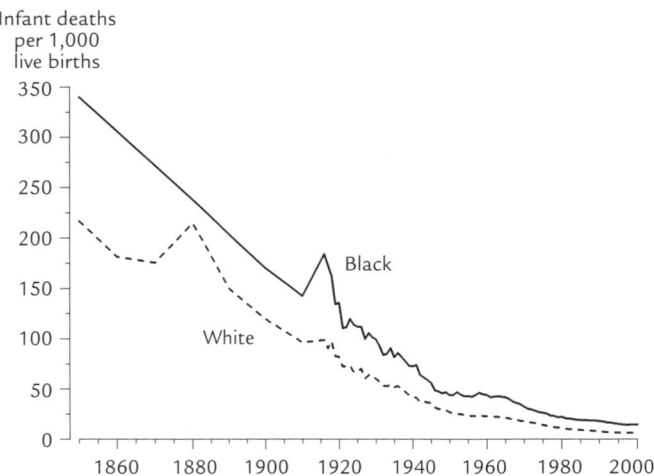

FIGURE Ab-C   Infant mortality rate, by race: 1850–2000

Sources
Series Ab921 and Ab923.

Documentation
For 1850–1910, the data are for ten-year intervals for the white population. For the black population, there are no data points between 1850 and 1900, and for 1900 and 1910, the series is for ten-year intervals. Beginning in 1915, both series represent annual data. For 1915–1932, the series are for the official Birth Registration Area (see Tables Ab31–39 for the composition of the Birth Registration Area).

highest death rates were found in the Mountain states. Regional areas of poverty (for example, West Virginia, New Mexico) have led to significant variation across states.

Differences in survival probabilities also existed across socioeconomic groups, although here too the information is sketchy. Estimates of child mortality according to the occupation and socioeconomic status of the father from the 1900 and 1910 U.S. Census public use samples indicate that children of white-collar workers, professionals, proprietors, and farmers did better than average, while children of laborers, including agricultural laborers, had worse than average survival chances. The advantage to professionals, such as physicians, teachers, and clergy, was not great in 1900 but was becoming more pronounced by 1910. Data from registered births in the 1920s classified by occupation of father point to a widening of these socioeconomic status differentials as the century progressed. For instance, in 1900 children of laborers had mortality about 1.2–1.3 times greater than children of fathers with professional and technical occupations. This ratio had risen to about 1.4 in 1910 and over 2.0 by 1929.

Higher income and better educated groups more easily assimilated advice and improvements in child care, hygiene, and health practices and so were "leaders" in the American mortality decline of the early twentieth century. Public health improvements led to a reduction in the level of mortality but did not lead to a reduction in relative differentials across class and occupation groups. Rural–urban differences did converge into the early twentieth century, but both relative and absolute mortality differences by race did not. The role of personal and household health behavior has been inadequately emphasized in the debate on the origins of the mortality transition. It was very likely central, although the precise contribution to differential child mortality is not easy to assess. For adults, the mortality gradient observed at the turn of the century from high mortality among laborers to intermediate levels among skilled manual workers to the most favorable mortality among white-collar workers persisted up to the middle of the twentieth century. There is some evidence from earlier in the nineteenth century that socioeconomic variables, such as wealth or income, occupation, and literacy, were less important in predicting mortality differentials. For the 1850s, for instance, survival probabilities differed little between the children of the poor and the wealthy. Rural versus urban residence and region made more of a difference.

Overall, the mortality transition in the United States was a delayed event. Perhaps this is not surprising. Given the relatively low mortality in the United States in the late eighteenth century and given that the public health system was not yet capable of coping with the growing problems of urban life and contagion from population mobility, it would have been difficult to have had significant declines in mortality as soon as the early nineteenth century. Indeed, an increase in mortality was evident prior to the Civil War. The sustained decline commenced nationally only in the 1870s. A damping of year-to-year mortality fluctuations also took place after midcentury. It is not easy to assign credit to various causal factors in the mortality transition, but the principal proximate cause was the control of both epidemic and endemic infectious diseases. By the later nineteenth century, public health certainly contributed much, with improvements in diet, housing, and standard of living also being significant. The direct role of medical intervention was rather limited before the twentieth century but then increased as the germ theory of disease was accepted and better diagnosis and effective therapies were developed. Though difficult to assess, changes in personal health behavior must be assigned importance, particularly after the turn of the twentieth century.

References

Caldwell, John C. 1982. *Theory of Fertility Decline*. Academic Press.

David, Paul, and Warren Sanderson. 1986. "Rudimentary Contraceptive Methods and the American Transition to Marital Fertility Control, 1855–1915." In Stanley L. Engerman and Robert E. Gallman, editors. *Long-Term Factors in American Economic Growth*. University of Chicago Press.

David, Paul, and Warren Sanderson. 1987. "The Emergence of a Two-Child Norm among American Birth Controllers." *Population and Development Review* 13 (1): 1–41.

Easterlin, Richard A. 1980. *Birth and Fortune: The Impact of Numbers on Personal Welfare*. Basic Books.

Fogel, Robert W. 1986. "Nutrition and the Decline in Mortality since 1700: Some Preliminary Findings." In Stanley L. Engerman and Robert E. Gallman, editors. *Long-Term Factors in American Economic Growth*. University of Chicago Press.

Forster, Colin, and G. S. L. Tucker. 1972. *Economic Opportunity and White American Fertility Ratios, 1800–1860*. Yale University Press.

Haines, Michael R. 1990. "Western Fertility in Mid-Transition: A Comparison of the United States and Selected Nations at the Turn of the Century." *Journal of Family History* 15 (1): 21–46.

Haines, Michael R. 1993. "Occupation and Social Class during Fertility Decline: Historical Perspectives." In John Gillis, David Levine, and Louis Tilly, editors. *The European Experience of Declining Fertility: 1850–1970*. Basil Blackwell.

Haines, Michael R. 1996. "Long Term Marriage Patterns in the United States from Colonial Times to the Present." *The History of the Family: An International Quarterly* 1 (1): 15–39.

Haines, Michael R. 1998a. "Estimated Life Tables for the United States, 1850–1910." *Historical Methods* 31 (4): 149–69.

Haines, Michael R. 1998b. "Health, Height, Nutrition, and Mortality: Evidence on the 'Antebellum Puzzle' from Union Army Recruits for New York State and the United States." In John Komlos and Joerg Baten, editors. *The Biological Standard of Living in Comparative Perspective*. Franz Steiner Verlag.

Haines, Michael R. 2001. "The Urban Mortality Transition in the United States, 1800 to 1940." *Annales de démographie historique* 1: 33–64.

Haines, Michael R., Lee A. Craig, and Thomas Weiss. 2003. "The Short and the Dead: Nutrition, Mortality, and the 'Antebellum Puzzle' in the United States." *Journal of Economic History* 63 (2): 385–416.

Haines, Michael R., and Samuel H. Preston. 1997. "The Use of the Census to Estimate Childhood Mortality: Comparisons from the 1900 and 1910 Public Use Samples." *Historical Methods* 30 (2): 77–96.

Haines, Michael R., and Richard H. Steckel, editors. 2000. *A Population History of North America*. Cambridge University Press.

McKeown, Thomas. 1976. *The Modern Rise of Population*. Academic Press.

Melosi, Martin V. 2000. *The Sanitary City: Urban Infrastructure in America from Colonial Times to the Present*. Johns Hopkins University Press.

Notestein, Frank W. 1953. "The Economics of Population and Food Supplies. I. The Economic Problems of Population Change." *Proceedings of the Eighth International Conference of Agricultural Economists*. Oxford University Press.

Pope, Clayne L. 1992. "Adult Mortality in America before 1900: A View from Family Histories." In Claudia Goldin and Hugh Rockoff, editors. *Strategic Factors in Nineteenth Century American Economic History: A Volume to Honor Robert W. Fogel*. University of Chicago Press.

Preston, Samuel H. 1970. "Older Male Mortality and Cigarette Smoking: A Demographic Analysis." Population Monograph No. 7. Institute of International Studies, University of California at Berkeley.

Preston, Samuel H., and Michael R. Haines. 1991. *Fatal Years: Child Mortality in Late Nineteenth Century America*. Princeton University Press.

Sanderson, Warren C. 1979. "Quantitative Aspects of Marriage, Fertility and Family Limitation in Nineteenth Century America: Another Application of the Coale Specifications." *Demography* 16 (3): 339–58.

Smith, Daniel Scott. 1996. "'The Number and Quality of Children': Education and Marital Fertility in Early Twentieth-Century Iowa." *Journal of Social History* 30 (2): 367–92.

Steckel, Richard. 1982. "The Fertility of American Slaves." *Research in Economic History* 7: 239–86.

Steckel, Richard H. 1986a. "A Peculiar Population: The Nutrition, Health, and Mortality of American Slaves from Childhood to Maturity." *Journal of Economic History* 46 (3): 721–41.

Steckel, Richard H. 1986b. "A Dreadful Childhood: Excess Mortality of American Slaves." *Social Science History* 10 (4): 427–65.

Steckel, Richard H. 1992a. "The Fertility Transition in the United States: Tests of Alternative Hypotheses." In Claudia Goldin and Hugh Rockoff, editors. *Strategic Factors in Nineteenth Century American Economic History*. University of Chicago Press.

Steckel, Richard H. 1992b. "Stature and Living Standards in the United States." In Robert E. Gallman and John Joseph Wallis, editors. *American Economic Growth and Standards of Living before the Civil War*. University of Chicago Press.

Sundstrom, William A., and Paul A. David. 1988. "Old-Age Security Motives, Labor Markets, and Farm Family Fertility in Antebellum America." *Explorations in Economic History* 25 (2): 164–97.

Sutch, Richard. 1975. "The Breeding of Slaves for Sale and the Westward Expansion of Slavery, 1850–1860." In Stanley L. Engerman and Eugene D. Genovese, editors. *Race and Slavery in the Western Hemisphere: Quantitative Studies*. Princeton University Press.

Sutch, Richard. 1990. "All Things Reconsidered: The Life-Cycle Perspective and the Third Task of Economic History." *Journal of Economic History* 51 (June): 1–18.

U.S. Bureau of the Census. 1975. *Historical Statistics of the United States from Colonial Times to 1970*. U.S. Government Printing Office.

Yasuba, Yasukichi. 1962. *Birth Rates of the White Population of the United States, 1800–1860: An Economic Analysis*. Johns Hopkins University Press.

GENERAL

Michael R. Haines

TABLE Ab1–10   Fertility and mortality, by race: 1800–2000

Contributed by Michael R. Haines

	Crude birth rate		Child–woman ratio		Total fertility rate		Expectation of life at birth		Infant mortality rate	
	White	Black	White	Black	White	Black	White	Black	White	Black
	Ab1	Ab2 [1]	Ab3	Ab4	Ab5	Ab6 [1]	Ab7	Ab8	Ab9	Ab10
Approximate year	Per 1,000	Per 1,000	Per 1,000	Per 1,000	Number	Number	Years	Years	Per 1,000	Per 1,000
1800	55.0	—	1,342	—	7.04	—	—	—	—	—
1810	54.3	—	1,358	—	6.92	—	—	—	—	—
1820	52.8	—	1,295	1,191	6.73	—	—	—	—	—
1830	51.4	—	1,145	1,220	6.55	—	—	—	—	—
1840	48.3	—	1,085	1,154	6.14	—	—	—	—	—
1850	43.3	58.6	892	1,087	5.42	7.90	39.5	23.0	216.8	340.0
1860	41.4	55.1	905	1,072	5.21	7.58	43.6	—	181.3	—
1870	38.3	55.4	814	997	4.55	7.69	45.2	—	175.5	—
1880	35.2	51.9	780	1,090	4.24	7.26	40.5	—	214.8	—
1890	31.5	48.1	685	930	3.87	6.56	46.8	—	150.6	—
1900 [2]	30.1	44.4	666	845	3.56	5.61	49.6	41.8	119.8	170.3
1910 [2]	29.2	38.5	631	736	3.42	4.61	54.6	46.2	96.5	142.6
1920	26.9	35.0	604	608	3.17	3.64	54.9	45.3	82.1	135.6
1930	20.6	27.5	506	554	2.45	2.98	61.4	48.1	60.1	99.5
1940	18.6	26.7	419	513	2.23	2.87	64.2	53.1	43.2	72.9
1950	23.0	33.3	580	663	2.98	3.93	69.1	60.8	26.8	43.9
1960	22.7	31.9	717	895	3.53	4.54	70.6	63.6	22.9	44.3
1970	17.4	25.3	507	689	2.39	3.10	71.7	64.1	17.8	32.6
1980	15.1	21.3	365	507	1.77	2.18	74.4	68.1	10.9	22.2
1990	15.8	22.4	355	458	2.00	2.48	76.1	69.1	7.6	18.0
2000 [3]	14.1	17.6	—	—	2.11	2.19	77.4	71.7	5.8	14.6

[1] For 1850–1880, the values are averages for the following periods: 1850–1859, 1860–1869, 1870–1879, and 1880–1884.

[2] For the expectation of life at birth and the infant mortality rate, the values for 1900 and 1910 are from approximately 1895 and 1904, respectively.

[3] Values for the infant mortality rate are for 1999.

Sources

Series Ab1–2. 1800–1990: from series Ab41–43. 2000: U.S. Bureau of the Census, *Statistical Abstract of the United States, 2002* (U.S. Government Printing Office, 2002), Table 68.

Series Ab3–4. From series Ab315–317, except that series Ab4, 1820–1850, is from W. S. Thompson and P. K. Whelpton, *Population Trends in the United States* (McGraw-Hill, 1933), Table 74, with adjustments described below.

Series Ab5–6. 1800–1990: from series Ab63 and Ab85, changed to a per-woman basis. 2000: *Statistical Abstract of the United States, 2002*, Table 71.

Series Ab7–8. 1850–1990: from series Ab647, Ab650, and Ab653, except that series Ab8, 1850, is based on Ansley J. Coale and Paul Demeny, *Regional Model Life Tables and Stable Populations* (Princeton University Press, 1966) and series Ab923; see below. 2000: *Statistical Abstract of the United States, 2002*, Table 91.

Series Ab9–10. 1850–1990: from series Ab921 and Ab923, except that series Ab10, 1850, is from Richard H. Steckel, "A Dreadful Childhood: The Excess Mortality of American Slaves," *Social Science History* (Winter 1986): 427–65. 1999: *Statistical Abstract of the United States, 2002*, Table 98.

Documentation

Series Ab1–2. Births per 1,000 population per annum. For series Ab2 the rates are for the total nonwhite population for 1920–1950.

Series Ab3–4. Children ages 0–4 years per 1,000 women ages 20–44 years. For series Ab4, 1820–1850, the values provided by the source were adjusted upward 47 percent for relative underenumeration of black children ages 0–4 years.

Series Ab5–6. Total number of births per woman if she experienced the current period age-specific fertility rates throughout her life.

Series Ab7–8. Expectation of life at birth for both sexes combined. Series Ab8 is for the total nonwhite population for 1920–1960. For 1850, series Ab8 is based on the implied expectation of life at birth in the Coale and Demeny West Model life table system for two sexes combined with an infant mortality rate of 340 infant deaths per 1,000 live births.

Series Ab9–10. Infant deaths per 1,000 live births per annum.

TABLE Ab11–30 Live births, deaths, infant deaths, marriages, and divorces, by race: 1909–1998[1]
Contributed by Michael R. Haines

	Live births						Deaths					
			Other races						Other races			
	Total	White	Total	Black	American Indian	Asian and Pacific Islander	Total	White	Total	Black	American Indian	Asian and Pacific Islander
	Ab11 [2,3]	Ab12	Ab13	Ab14	Ab15	Ab16	Ab17 [4]	Ab18	Ab19	Ab20	Ab21	Ab22
Year	Number	Number	Number	Number	Number	Number	Number	Number	Number	Number	Number	Number
1909	2,718,000	2,344,000	374,000	—	—	—	—	—	—	—	—	—
1910	2,777,000	2,401,000	376,000	—	—	—	—	—	—	—	—	—
1911	2,809,000	2,435,000	374,000	—	—	—	—	—	—	—	—	—
1912	2,840,000	2,467,000	373,000	—	—	—	—	—	—	—	—	—
1913	2,869,000	2,497,000	372,000	—	—	—	—	—	—	—	—	—
1914	2,966,000	2,588,000	378,000	—	—	—	—	—	—	—	—	—
1915	2,965,000	2,594,000	371,000	—	—	—	—	—	—	—	—	—
1916	2,964,000	2,599,000	365,000	—	—	—	—	—	—	—	—	—
1917	2,944,000	2,587,000	357,000	—	—	—	—	—	—	—	—	—
1918	2,948,000	2,588,000	360,000	—	—	—	—	—	—	—	—	—
1919	2,740,000	2,387,000	353,000	—	—	—	—	—	—	—	—	—
1920	2,950,000	2,566,000	383,000	—	—	—	—	—	—	—	—	—
1921	3,055,000	2,657,000	398,000	—	—	—	—	—	—	—	—	—
1922	2,882,000	2,507,000	375,000	—	—	—	—	—	—	—	—	—
1923	2,910,000	2,531,000	380,000	—	—	—	—	—	—	—	—	—
1924	2,979,000	2,577,000	401,000	—	—	—	—	—	—	—	—	—
1925	2,909,000	2,506,000	403,000	—	—	—	—	—	—	—	—	—
1926	2,839,000	2,441,000	398,000	—	—	—	—	—	—	—	—	—
1927	2,802,000	2,425,000	377,000	—	—	—	—	—	—	—	—	—
1928	2,674,000	2,325,000	349,000	—	—	—	—	—	—	—	—	—
1929	2,582,000	2,244,000	339,000	—	—	—	—	—	—	—	—	—
1930	2,618,000	2,274,000	344,000	—	—	—	—	—	—	—	—	—
1931	2,506,000	2,170,000	335,000	—	—	—	—	—	—	—	—	—
1932	2,440,000	2,099,000	341,000	—	—	—	—	—	—	—	—	—
1933	2,307,000	1,982,000	325,000	—	—	—	1,342,106	1,162,398	179,708	172,114	—	—
1934	2,396,000	2,058,000	338,000	—	—	—	1,396,903	1,207,197	189,706	182,075	—	—
1935	2,377,000	2,042,000	334,000	—	—	—	1,392,752	1,207,359	185,393	177,523	—	—
1936	2,355,000	2,027,000	328,000	—	—	—	1,479,228	1,278,379	200,849	192,748	—	—
1937	2,413,000	2,071,000	342,000	—	—	—	1,450,427	1,254,787	195,640	187,594	—	—
1938	2,496,000	2,148,000	348,000	—	—	—	1,381,391	1,195,431	185,960	178,573	—	—
1939	2,466,000	2,117,000	349,000	—	—	—	1,387,897	1,207,078	180,819	173,510	—	—
1940	2,559,000	2,199,000	360,000	—	—	—	1,417,269	1,231,223	186,046	178,743	—	—
1941	2,703,000	2,330,000	374,000	—	—	—	1,397,642	1,213,511	184,131	176,729	—	—
1942	2,989,000	2,605,000	384,000	—	—	—	1,385,187	1,209,944	175,243	168,244	—	—
1943	3,104,000	2,704,000	400,000	—	—	—	1,459,544	1,280,887	178,657	171,247	—	—
1944	2,939,000	2,545,000	394,000	—	—	—	1,411,338	1,238,829	172,509	165,180	—	—
1945	2,858,000	2,471,000	388,000	—	—	—	1,401,719	1,233,889	167,830	160,733	—	—
1946	3,411,000	2,990,000	420,000	—	—	—	1,395,617	1,232,337	163,280	156,493	—	—
1947	3,817,000	3,347,000	469,000	—	—	—	1,445,370	1,274,893	170,477	163,781	—	—
1948	3,637,000	3,141,000	495,000	—	—	—	1,444,337	1,270,589	173,748	167,046	—	—
1949	3,649,000	3,136,000	513,000	—	—	—	1,443,607	1,268,848	174,759	168,067	—	—
1950	3,632,000	3,108,000	524,000	—	—	—	1,452,454	1,276,085	176,369	169,606	—	—
1951	3,820,000	3,275,000	545,000	—	—	—	1,482,099	1,302,969	179,130	171,983	—	—
1952	3,909,000	3,356,000	553,000	—	—	—	1,496,838	1,315,022	181,816	174,695	—	—
1953	3,959,000	3,387,000	572,000	—	—	—	1,517,541	1,335,835	181,706	174,625	—	—
1954	4,071,000	3,472,000	599,000	—	—	—	1,481,091	1,306,989	174,102	167,241	—	—
1955	4,097,000	3,485,000	613,000	—	—	—	1,528,717	1,350,869	177,848	171,021	—	—
1956	4,210,000	3,570,000	640,000	—	—	—	1,564,476	1,380,915	183,561	176,341	—	—
1957	4,300,000	3,646,000	654,000	—	—	—	1,633,128	1,437,652	195,476	187,912	—	—
1958	4,246,000	3,595,000	651,000	—	—	—	1,647,886	1,451,077	196,809	189,341	—	—
1959	4,244,796	3,597,430	647,366	605,962	—	—	1,656,814	1,460,840	195,974	187,951	—	—
1960	4,257,850	3,600,744	657,106	602,264	21,114	—	1,711,982	1,505,335	206,647	196,010	—	—
1961	4,268,326	3,600,864	667,462	611,072	21,464	—	1,701,522	1,498,332	203,190	192,791	—	—
1962 [6]	4,167,362	3,394,068	641,580	584,610	21,698	—	1,756,720	1,488,113	206,583	195,598	—	—
1963 [6]	4,098,020	3,326,344	638,928	580,658	22,358	—	1,813,549	1,533,015	216,662	204,888	—	—
1964	4,027,490	3,369,160	658,330	607,556	24,382	—	1,798,051	1,578,674	219,377	209,065	—	—

Notes appear at end of table

TABLE Ab11–30 Live births, deaths, infant deaths, marriages, and divorces, by race: 1909–1998 *Continued*

	Live births						Deaths					
				Other races						Other races		
	Total	White	Total	Black	American Indian	Asian and Pacific Islander	Total	White	Total	Black	American Indian	Asian and Pacific Islander
	Ab11 [2,3]	Ab12	Ab13	Ab14	Ab15	Ab16	Ab17 [4]	Ab18	Ab19	Ab20	Ab21	Ab22
Year	Number	Number	Number	Number	Number	Number	Number	Number	Number	Number	Number	Number
1965	3,760,358	3,123,860	636,498	581,126	24,066	—	1,828,136	1,605,498	222,638	211,230	—	—
1966	3,606,274	2,993,230	613,044	558,244	23,014	—	1,863,149	1,634,461	228,688	216,736	—	—
1967 [7]	3,520,959	2,922,502	598,457	543,976	22,665	—	1,851,323	1,627,151	224,172	212,252	—	—
1968	3,501,564	2,912,224	589,340	531,152	24,156	—	1,930,082	1,689,559	240,523	227,682	—	—
1969	3,600,206	2,993,614	606,592	543,132	24,008	—	1,921,990	1,683,622	238,368	225,537	—	—
1970	3,731,386	3,091,264	640,122	572,362	25,864	—	1,921,031	1,682,096	238,935	225,647	—	—
1971	3,555,970	2,919,746	636,224	564,960	27,148	—	1,927,542	1,689,771	237,771	224,138	—	—
1972	3,258,411	2,655,558	602,853	531,329	27,368	—	1,963,944	1,721,468	242,476	228,450	—	—
1973	3,136,965	2,551,030	585,935	512,597	26,464	—	1,973,003	1,728,405	244,598	230,110	—	—
1974	3,159,958	2,575,792	584,166	507,162	26,631	—	1,934,388	1,697,295	237,093	222,948	—	—
1975	3,144,198	2,551,996	592,202	511,581	27,546	—	1,892,879	1,660,366	232,513	217,932	—	—
1976	3,167,788	2,567,614	600,174	514,479	29,009	—	1,909,440	1,674,989	234,451	219,442	—	—
1977	3,326,632	2,691,070	635,562	544,221	30,500	—	1,899,597	1,664,100	235,497	220,076	—	—
1978	3,333,279	2,681,116	652,163	551,540	33,160	—	1,927,788	1,689,722	238,066	221,340	—	—
1979	3,494,398	2,808,420	685,978	577,855	34,269	—	1,913,841	1,676,145	237,696	220,818	—	—
1980	3,612,258	2,936,351	675,907	568,080	29,389	74,355	1,989,841	1,738,607	251,234	233,135	6,923	11,071
1981	3,629,238	2,947,679	681,599	564,955	29,688	84,553	1,977,981	1,731,233	246,748	228,560	6,608	11,475
1982	3,680,537	2,984,817	695,720	568,506	32,436	93,193	1,974,797	1,729,085	245,712	226,513	6,679	12,430
1983	3,638,933	2,946,468	692,465	562,624	32,881	95,713	2,019,201	1,765,582	253,619	233,124	6,839	13,554
1984	3,669,141	2,967,100	702,041	568,138	33,256	98,926	2,039,369	1,781,897	257,472	235,884	6,949	14,483
1985	3,760,561	3,037,913	722,648	581,824	34,037	104,606	2,086,440	1,819,054	267,386	244,207	7,154	15,887
1986	3,756,547	3,019,175	737,372	592,910	34,169	107,797	2,105,361	1,831,083	274,278	250,326	7,301	16,514
1987	3,809,394	3,043,828	765,566	611,173	35,322	116,560	2,123,323	1,843,067	280,256	254,814	7,602	17,689
1988	3,909,510	3,102,083	807,427	638,562	37,088	129,035	2,167,999	1,876,906	291,093	264,019	7,917	18,963
1989	4,040,958	3,192,355	848,603	673,124	39,478	133,075	2,150,466	1,853,841	296,625	267,642	8,614	20,042
1990	4,158,212	3,290,273	867,939	684,336	39,051	141,635	2,148,463	1,853,254	295,209	265,498	8,316	21,127
1991	4,110,907	3,241,273	869,634	682,602	38,841	145,372	2,169,518	1,868,904	300,614	269,525	8,621	22,173
1992	4,065,014	3,201,678	863,336	673,633	39,453	150,250	2,175,613	1,873,781	301,832	269,219	8,953	23,660
1993	4,000,240	3,149,833	850,407	658,875	38,732	152,800	2,268,553	1,951,437	317,116	282,151	9,579	25,386
1994	3,952,767	3,121,004	831,763	636,391	37,740	157,632	2,278,994	1,959,875	319,119	282,379	9,637	27,103
1995	3,899,589	3,098,885	800,704	603,139	37,278	160,287	2,312,132	1,987,437	324,695	286,401	9,997	28,297
1996	3,891,494	3,093,057	798,437	594,781	37,880	165,776	2,314,690	1,992,966	321,724	282,089	10,127	29,508
1997	3,880,894	3,072,640	808,254	599,913	38,572	169,769	2,314,245	1,996,393	317,852	276,520	10,576	30,756
1998	3,941,553	3,118,727	822,826	609,902	40,272	172,652	2,337,256	2,015,984	321,272	278,440	10,845	31,987

	Infant deaths							
					Other races			
	Total	White	Total	Black	American Indian	Asian and Pacific Islander	Marriages	Divorces
	Ab23 [4]	Ab24	Ab25	Ab26	Ab27	Ab28	Ab29	Ab30 [5]
Year	Number	Number	Number	Number	Number	Number	Number	Number
1909	—	—	—	—	—	—	—	—
1910	—	—	—	—	—	—	—	—
1911	—	—	—	—	—	—	—	—
1912	—	—	—	—	—	—	—	—
1913	—	—	—	—	—	—	—	—
1914	—	—	—	—	—	—	—	—
1915	—	—	—	—	—	—	—	—
1916	—	—	—	—	—	—	—	—
1917	—	—	—	—	—	—	—	—
1918	—	—	—	—	—	—	—	—
1919	—	—	—	—	—	—	—	—
1920	—	—	—	—	—	—	1,274,476	170,505
1921	—	—	—	—	—	—	1,163,863	159,580
1922	—	—	—	—	—	—	1,134,151	148,815
1923	—	—	—	—	—	—	1,229,784	165,096
1924	—	—	—	—	—	—	1,184,574	170,952

Notes appear at end of table

(continued)

TABLE Ab11–30 Live births, deaths, infant deaths, marriages, and divorces, by race: 1909–1998 *Continued*

	Infant deaths							
				Other races				
Year	Total	White	Total	Black	American Indian	Asian and Pacific Islander	Marriages	Divorces
	Ab23 [4]	Ab24	Ab25	Ab26	Ab27	Ab28	Ab29	Ab30 [5]
	Number	Number	Number	Number	Number	Number	Number	Number
1925	—	—	—	—	—	—	1,188,334	175,449
1926	—	—	—	—	—	—	1,202,574	184,678
1927	—	—	—	—	—	—	1,201,053	196,292
1928	—	—	—	—	—	—	1,182,497	200,176
1929	—	—	—	—	—	—	1,232,559	205,876
1930	—	—	—	—	—	—	1,126,856	195,961
1931	—	—	—	—	—	—	1,060,914	188,003
1932	—	—	—	—	—	—	981,903	164,241
1933	120,887	94,749	26,138	21,035	—	—	1,098,000	165,000
1934	130,185	101,720	28,465	23,393	—	—	1,302,000	204,000
1935	120,138	97,907	22,231	20,905	—	—	1,327,000	218,000
1936	122,535	99,504	23,031	21,614	—	—	1,369,000	236,000
1937	119,931	97,064	22,867	21,513	—	—	1,451,296	249,000
1938	116,702	94,485	22,217	20,855	—	—	1,330,780	244,000
1939	108,846	87,841	21,005	19,755	—	—	1,403,633	251,000
1940	110,984	89,406	21,578	20,342	—	—	1,595,879	264,000
1941	113,949	90,874	23,075	21,834	—	—	1,695,999	293,000
1942	113,492	92,678	20,814	19,756	—	—	1,772,132	321,000
1943	118,484	97,229	21,255	19,967	—	—	1,577,050	359,000
1944	111,127	90,607	20,520	19,234	—	—	1,452,394	400,000
1945	104,684	85,295	19,389	18,228	—	—	1,612,992	485,000
1946	111,063	92,510	18,553	17,480	—	—	2,291,045	610,000
1947	119,173	98,547	20,626	19,420	—	—	1,991,878	483,000
1948	113,169	92,034	21,135	19,836	—	—	1,811,155	408,000
1949	111,531	89,007	22,524	21,213	—	—	1,579,798	397,000
1950	103,825	82,018	21,807	20,492	—	—	1,667,231	385,144
1951	106,702	83,678	23,024	21,665	—	—	1,594,694	381,000
1952	109,413	84,752	24,661	23,360	—	—	1,539,318	392,000
1953	108,405	84,041	24,364	23,009	—	—	1,546,000	390,000
1954	106,791	82,200	24,591	23,323	—	—	1,490,000	379,000
1955	106,903	81,682	25,221	24,046	—	—	1,531,000	377,000
1956	108,183	82,203	25,980	24,785	—	—	1,585,000	382,000
1957	112,094	84,412	27,682	26,360	—	—	1,518,000	381,000
1958	113,789	84,935	28,854	27,528	—	—	1,451,000	368,000
1959	112,008	83,493	28,515	27,164	—	—	1,494,000	395,000
1960	110,873	82,479	28,394	26,691	—	—	1,523,000	393,000
1961	107,956	80,781	27,175	25,573	—	—	1,548,000	414,000
1962 [6]	105,479	75,812	26,535	24,911	—	—	1,577,000	413,000
1963 [6]	103,390	73,727	26,511	24,824	—	—	1,654,000	428,000
1964	99,783	72,728	27,055	25,721	—	—	1,725,000	450,000
1965	92,866	67,198	25,668	24,320	—	—	1,800,000	479,000
1966	85,516	61,749	23,767	22,427	849	—	1,857,000	499,000
1967 [7]	79,028	57,533	21,495	20,372	697	—	1,927,000	523,000
1968	76,263	55,902	20,361	19,219	701	—	2,069,000	584,000
1969	75,073	55,108	19,965	18,882	619	—	2,145,000	639,000
1970	74,667	54,876	19,791	18,687	569	—	2,158,802	708,000
1971	67,981	49,842	18,139	17,131	547	—	2,190,481	773,000
1972	60,182	43,460	16,722	15,738	506	—	2,282,154	845,000
1973	55,581	40,239	15,342	14,411	501	—	2,284,108	915,000
1974	52,776	38,249	14,527	13,584	494	—	2,229,667	977,000
1975	50,525	36,173	14,352	13,409	491	—	2,152,662	1,036,000
1976	48,265	34,163	14,102	13,142	534	—	2,154,807	1,083,000
1977	46,975	33,199	13,776	12,863	476	—	2,178,367	1,091,000
1978	45,945	32,212	13,733	12,747	454	—	2,282,272	1,130,000
1979	45,665	32,079	13,586	12,586	522	—	2,331,337	1,181,000
1980	45,526	31,880	13,646	12,603	485	545	2,390,252	1,189,000
1981	43,305	30,478	12,827	11,757	435	619	2,422,145	1,213,000
1982	42,401	29,659	12,742	11,642	411	673	2,456,278	1,170,000
1983	40,627	28,301	12,326	11,242	443	627	2,445,604	1,158,000
1984	39,580	27,608	11,972	10,881	393	681	2,477,192	1,169,000

Notes appear at end of table

TABLE Ab11–30   Live births, deaths, infant deaths, marriages, and divorces, by race: 1909–1998   *Continued*

			Infant deaths					
					Other races			
	Total	White	Total	Black	American Indian	Asian and Pacific Islander	Marriages	Divorces
	Ab23 [4]	Ab24	Ab25	Ab26	Ab27	Ab28	Ab29	Ab30 [5]
Year	Number	Number	Number	Number	Number	Number	Number	Number
1985	40,030	27,864	12,166	11,063	389	701	2,412,625	1,190,000
1986	38,891	26,564	12,327	11,204	440	670	2,407,099	1,178,000
1987	38,408	25,810	12,598	11,461	431	693	2,403,378	1,166,000
1988	38,910	25,925	12,985	11,840	414	714	2,395,926	1,167,000
1989	39,655	25,794	13,861	12,527	491	829	2,403,268	1,157,000
1990	38,351	24,883	13,468	12,290	419	747	2,443,489	1,182,000
1991	36,766	23,657	13,109	11,994	405	691	2,371,000	1,187,000
1992	34,628	22,164	12,464	11,348	393	723	2,362,000	1,215,000
1993	33,466	21,497	11,969	10,887	361	721	2,334,000	1,187,000
1994	31,710	20,504	11,206	10,072	369	765	2,362,000	1,191,000
1995	29,583	19,490	10,093	9,118	304	671	2,336,000	1,169,000
1996	28,487	18,761	9,726	8,730	317	679	2,344,000	1,150,000
1997	28,045	18,539	9,506	8,496	317	693	2,384,000	1,163,000
1998	28,371	18,561	9,810	8,726	379	705	—	—

[1] Birth, marriage, and divorce figures represent estimates of all such events; death figures, the number of registered events. Data based on race of child through 1979, race of mother thereafter.

[2] 1959–1996, registered live births; 1909–1958, adjusted for underregistration.

[3] Based on a 50 percent sample for 1951–1954, 1956–1966, and 1968–1971; a 20–50 percent sample for 1967; and a 100 percent sample in selected states and a 50 percent sample in all other states for 1972–1984.

[4] Excludes fetal deaths.

[5] Includes reported annulments.

[6] Figures by race exclude New Jersey, which did not require reporting by race.

[7] Based on a 20–50 percent sample.

Sources
Births. U.S. Public Health Service, National Center for Health Statistics, *Vital Statistics of the United States, 1993*, volume 1, *Natality*, Table 1-2; *National Vital Statistics Reports*, volume 48, number 3, "Births: Final Data for 1998," Table 1.

Deaths and infant deaths. U.S. Public Health Service, National Center for Health Statistics, *Vital Statistics of the United States, 1992*, volume 2, part A, "Mortality," Tables 1-1 and 2-1; *National Vital Statistics Report*, volume 48, number 11, "Deaths: Final Data for 1998," Table 1. Infant deaths by specific ethnicity are from various issues of *Vital Statistics of the United States; National Vital Statistics Report*, volume 48, number 11, "Deaths: Final Data for 1998," Table 2; *Monthly and National Vital Statistics Reports*, various issues, 1993–1997.

Marriages and divorces. U.S. Public Health Service, National Center for Health Statistics, *Vital Statistics of the United States, 1988*, volume 3, *Marriage and Divorce*, pp. 1–2; *Monthly Vital Statistics Report*, volume 43, number 12, Supplement, "Advance Report of Final Marriage Statistics, 1989 and 1990," Table 1. U.S. Bureau of the Census, *Statistical Abstract of the United States: 1998* (U.S. Government Printing Office, 1998), Table 158.

Documentation
Vital statistics, including statistics of births, deaths, marriages, and divorces, are compiled for the country as a whole by the National Center for Health Statistics, successor in recent years to the former National Office of Vital Statistics. Beginning in 1900, the collection of these data was the responsibility of the Bureau of the Census. In July 1946, this function was transferred to the Federal Security Agency, which, in 1953, was reconstituted as the Department of Health, Education, and Welfare. The National Center for Health Statistics (NCHS) is currently a part of the Centers for Disease Control and Prevention of the Public Health Service in the Department of Health and Human Services. The data are published in the annual report from NCHS *Vital Statistics of the United States*, in certain reports of the *Vital and Health Statistics* series, and in the *National Vital Statistics Reports* (formerly *Monthly Vital Statistics Reports*). Reports in this field are also issued by various state and local bureaus of vital statistics. The annual report, *Vital Statistics of the United States*, presents final figures and an annual life table. A series of national summaries,

Vital Statistics – Special Reports, containing data on particular subjects, was issued each year from 1934 to 1959. This series was superseded by *Vital and Health Statistics*, Series 20, 21, and 22, and the *National Vital Statistics Reports* (formerly *Monthly Vital Statistics Reports*).

Data on fertility, age of persons at first marriage, and marital status and marital history are compiled by the U.S. Census Bureau in its Current Population Survey (CPS) and published in *Current Population Reports*, P-20 Series. Data on abortions are published by the Alan Guttmacher Institute, New York, and published in selected issues of *Family Planning Perspectives*.

The registration of births, deaths, fetal deaths, and other vital events is primarily a state and local governmental function. The civil laws of every state provide for a continuous and permanent birth and death registration system. Most (but not all) states also provide for marriage and divorce registration systems. Vital events occurring to U.S. residents outside the United States are not currently included in the data. The live birth, death, and fetal death statistics prepared by the National Center for Health Statistics are currently based on copies of vital records received from registration offices of all states, New York City, and the District of Columbia. Marriage and divorce statistics are based on information from two sources: (1) complete counts of events obtained from all states and the District of Columbia and (2) samples of marriage and divorce certificates obtained from states meeting certain reporting criteria. In the statistical tabulations, "United States" refers to the aggregate of the fifty states and the District of Columbia. Alaska and Hawai'i have been included in the United States totals since 1959 and 1960, respectively.

Although every state has adopted a law requiring the registration of births, deaths, and fetal deaths, these laws are not uniformly observed. One condition for admission to the national registration areas was a demonstration of registration completeness of at least 90 percent. On the basis of this criterion, all of the states were admitted to both the Birth and Death Registration Areas by 1933. It is recognized, however, that the methods then used in testing completeness were subject to considerable error.

The annual collection of mortality statistics for the national Death Registration Area began in 1900 with ten registration states and the District of Columbia; the collection of birth statistics for the national Birth Registration Area began in 1915, also with ten states and the District of Columbia. The two areas did not cover the entire United States until 1933. The organized territories of Hawai'i and Alaska were admitted to the registration areas in 1929 and 1950, respectively. The essay on vital statistics in this chapter contains information detailing the growth of the Death and Birth Registration Areas. The changing composition of the two registration areas makes it impossible to obtain geographically comparable birth and death data for the entire United States before 1933. Although the national Birth Registration Area was not started until 1915, annual estimates of births have been prepared for the period 1909–1934. These estimates include adjustments for

(continued)

TABLE Ab11–30 Live births, deaths, infant deaths, marriages, and divorces, by race: 1909–1998 *Continued*

underregistration and for states not in the Birth Registration Area before 1933. National statistics on fetal deaths were compiled for 1918 and annually since 1922.

Prior to 1951, birth statistics were the result of a complete count of the records received in the Public Health Service. Since 1951, they have been based on a 50 percent sample of all registered births (except for 1955 when they reverted to a complete count and for 1967 when they were based on a 20–50 percent sample). Beginning in 1972, they have been based on a complete count for states participating in the Vital Statistics Cooperative Program (VSCP) and on a 50 percent sample in other areas. (For details, see the technical appendix in *Vital Statistics of the United States*.) Beginning in 1986, all reporting areas participated in the VSCP.

Mortality data have been based on a complete count of records for each area, except for a 50 percent sample in 1972. Beginning in 1970, births to and deaths of nonresident aliens of the United States and U.S. citizens outside the United States have been excluded from the data. Fetal deaths and deaths among the armed forces overseas are excluded. Data based on samples are subject to sampling error.

Mortality statistics are compiled in accordance with World Health Organization regulations, which specify that member nations classify causes of death according to the *International Statistical Classification of Diseases, Injuries, and Causes of Death* (ICD). The ICD is revised about every ten years. The first ICD was put into effect in 1899. The current ICD is the "Ninth Revision International Classification of Diseases, Adapted for Use in the United States" and has been used since 1979. Deaths in prior years were classified according to the revision of the ICD in use at the time. Each revision of the ICD introduces a number of discontinuities in the mortality statistics. For a discussion of those between the Eighth and Ninth Revisions, see *Monthly Vital Statistics Report*, volume 28, number 11, Supplement.

A number of the tables present age-adjusted death rates in addition to the crude rates and the age-specific rates. The age-adjusted death rates were prepared using the method of direct standardization, in which the actual age-specific death rates for the population of interest are applied to a standard population distributed by age. The standard population is the whole U.S. population by age in 1940. Age-adjustment eliminates the differences in crude death rates that occur over time and across groups from differences in age composition.

Accurate measures of birth registration completeness on a nationwide basis were obtained for the first time in 1940, when studies were made in connection with the population census of that year. They showed that, for the United States as a whole, birth registration was 92.5 percent complete. A corresponding study ten years later indicated that registration had improved considerably, with 97.9 percent of the births in 1950 being recorded. Only in a few states was underregistration shown to be still a problem. The results of this study have been published in considerable detail (U.S. Bureau of the Census, *Infant Enumeration Study*, 1950) and provide a basis for adjusting registered birth data for underreporting and for making estimates of registration completeness in postcensal years. Birth registration has continued to improve since 1930 and, in 1968, 99.1 percent of the live births were registered. (See National Office of Vital Statistics, "Birth-Registration Completeness in the United States and Geographic Areas, 1950," parts 1, 2, and 3, and *Vital Statistics – Special Reports*, volume 39, numbers 2 and 4, and volume 45, number 9.)

Death registration is believed to be at least as complete as birth registration. However, quantitative information on the completeness with which deaths are reported is limited to that obtained years ago in applying the "90 percent" standard for entry in the Death Registration Area and to information obtained from occasional local area studies. Although underregistration for the country as a whole is negligible, local studies furnish evidence that in certain isolated places underreporting of deaths may still be a problem. Registration of fetal deaths is probably significantly incomplete in all areas.

The compilation of nationwide statistics on marriages and divorces in the United States began in 1887–1888, when the National Office of Vital Statistics prepared estimates for the years 1867–1886. (See Carroll D. Wright, "Marriage and Divorce in the United States, 1867 to 1886," *First Special Report of the United States Commissioner of Labor* (U.S.Government Printing Office, 1987).) Although periodic updates took place after 1888, marriage and divorce statistics were not collected and published annually until 1944

by the National Office of Vital Statistics. Estimates have been made for intervening years and for years in which collections were not complete. A Marriage Registration Area was established by the Public Health Service in 1957, and a Divorce Registration Area in 1958. Beginning in 1957, the Marriage Registration Area comprised thirty states, plus Alaska, Hawai'i, Puerto Rico, and the Virgin Islands. It currently includes forty-two states and the District of Columbia. The Divorce Registration Area, starting in 1958 with fourteen states, Alaska, Hawai'i, and the Virgin Islands, currently includes a total of thirty-one states and the Virgin Islands. Procedures for estimating the number of marriages and divorces are discussed in U.S. Public Health Service, National Center for Health Statistics, *Vital Statistics of the United States, 1988*, volume 3, "Marriage and Divorce." Total counts of events for registration and nonregistration states are gathered by collecting already summarized data on marriages and divorces reported by state offices of vital statistics and by county offices of registration. The National Center for Health Statistics (NCHS) has not published marriage and divorce statistics since the volume for 1988, although data have been made available by other means.

Vital statistics showing color and race are compiled from entries that appear on certificates filed with vital registration offices. The Census Bureau's CPS obtains information on race by asking respondents to classify their race as (1) white; (2) black; (3) American Indian, Eskimo, or Aleut; or (4) Asian or Pacific Islander. Data thus tabulated begin in 1980. Beginning with the 1989 data year, NCHS tabulated its birth data primarily by the race of the mother. In prior years, births were tabulated by the race of the child, which was determined from the race of the parents as entered in the birth certificate. Hispanic origin of the mother is reported and tabulated independently of race. Hispanic origin persons may be of any race. In 1994, 91 percent of women of Hispanic origin were reported as white. The classification "white" previously included persons reported as Mexican, Cuban, and Puerto Rican. The category "black" includes persons of mixed black and other ancestry. Prior to 1960, most vital statistics data were reported for "white" and "all other races." For a further discussion of race, see the text for Table Aa145–184. For births, the newborn child is ordinarily assigned to the race of the parents. If parents are of different races, the following applies: (1) when only one parent is white, the child is assigned the other parent's race; (2) when neither is white, the child is assigned the father's race.

Births are estimated for the entire United States for 1909–1932. Deaths are estimated for the Death Registration States for 1900–1932. This excludes certain cities that were in the Death Registration Area but outside of the states in the Death Registration Area. For 1910–1915, North Carolina is excluded from the series because it reported deaths only in municipalities with a population of 1,000 or more for that period. It was, however, included in the official series for the Death Registration States in the contemporary mortality sources. North Carolina reported deaths for the full population from 1916 onward and so is included. For 1917 and 1918, deaths of soldiers, sailors, and marines are included, although reported separately in the official sources.

Population statistics published or made available by the U.S. Bureau of the Census have been used in computing the vital rates shown here. Rates for 1940, 1950, 1960, 1970, 1980, and 1990 are based on the population enumerated in the censuses of those years that were taken as of April 1. Rates for all other years are based on midyear (July 1) estimates of population made by the U.S. Bureau of the Census. Except for 1941–1946, vital rates are based on the population residing in the contiguous United States. In those years, the transfer overseas of several million men precluded the computation of birth and divorce rates strictly comparable with such rates for prewar years. For 1941–1946, the birth and divorce rates are based on the population including the armed forces overseas. (For a discussion of the interpretation of rates during wartime, see "Summary of Natality and Mortality Statistics, United States, 1943," *Vital Statistics Special Reports*, volume 21, number 1, and "Marriage and Divorce in the United States, 1937 to 1945," *Vital Statistics Special Reports*, volume 23, number 9.)

The base populations used here for death rates are slightly different for the years 1940 and later. They are based on annual population estimates made at the U.S. Census Bureau. Those estimates and the methods are reported in Tables Aa6–8 and Aa110–144. The published age-adjusted death rates are taken directly from the official publications.

TABLE Ab31–37   Birth and death registration areas – population and number of states included: 1900–1933[1]

Contributed by Michael R. Haines

	Total U.S. population	Birth registration area			Death registration area		
		Population		States included	Population		States included
		Number	Percentage of total United States		Number	Percentage of total United States	
	Ab31	Ab32	Ab33	Ab34 [2]	Ab35	Ab36	Ab37 [2]
Year	Thousand	Thousand	Percent	Number	Thousand	Percent	Number
1900	76,094	—	—	—	19,965	26.2	11
1901	77,585	—	—	—	20,237	26.1	11
1902	79,160	—	—	—	20,583	26.0	11
1903	80,632	—	—	—	20,943	26.0	11
1904	82,165	—	—	—	21,332	26.0	11
1905	83,820	—	—	—	21,768	26.0	11
1906	85,437	—	—	—	33,782	39.5	16
1907	87,000	—	—	—	34,553	39.7	16
1908	88,709	—	—	—	38,635	43.6	18
1909	90,492	—	—	—	44,224	48.9	19
1910	92,407	—	—	—	47,470	51.4	21
1911	93,868	—	—	—	53,930	57.5	23
1912	95,331	—	—	—	54,848	57.5	23
1913	97,227	—	—	—	58,157	59.8	24
1914	99,118	—	—	—	60,963	61.5	25
1915	100,549	—	—	—	61,895	61.6	25
1916	101,966	32,944	32.3	12	66,971	65.7	27
1917	103,266	55,198	53.5	21	70,235	68.0	28
1918	103,203	55,154	53.4	21	79,008	76.6	31
1919	104,512	61,212	58.6	23	83,158	79.6	34
1920	106,466	63,597	59.7	24	86,079	80.9	35
1921	108,541	70,807	65.2	28	87,814	80.9	35
1922	110,055	79,561	72.3	31	92,703	84.2	38
1923	111,950	81,072	72.4	31	96,788	86.5	39
1924	114,113	87,000	76.2	34	99,318	87.0	40
1925	115,832	88,295	76.2	34	102,032	88.1	41
1926	117,399	90,401	77.0	36	103,823	88.4	42
1927	119,038	104,321	87.6	41	107,085	90.0	43
1928	120,501	113,636	94.3	45	113,636	94.3	45
1929	121,770	115,317	94.7	47	115,317	94.7	47
1930	123,077	116,545	94.7	47	117,238	95.3	48
1931	124,040	117,455	94.7	47	118,149	95.3	48
1932	124,840	118,904	95.2	48	118,904	95.2	48
1933	125,579	125,579	100.0	49	125,579	100.0	49

[1] Contiguous United States, midyear populations.

[2] Includes the District of Columbia.

Source

U.S. Bureau of the Census, *Historical Statistics of the United States* (1975), p. 44.

Documentation

The annual collection of mortality statistics for the national Death Registration Area began in 1900 with ten registration states and the District of Columbia; the collection of birth statistics for the national Birth Registration Area began in 1915, also with ten states and the District of Columbia. The changing composition of the two registration areas makes it impossible to obtain geographically comparable birth and death data for the entire United States before 1933. Although the national Birth Registration Area was not started until 1915, annual estimates of births were prepared for the period 1909–1934. These estimates include adjustments for underregistration and for states not in the Birth Registration Area before 1933 (see the text for Table Ab11–30). Beginning in 1933, the Birth and Death Registration Areas have comprised the entire United States, including Alaska beginning in 1959 and Hawai'i beginning in 1960. National statistics on fetal deaths were compiled for 1918 and annually since 1922. Also see Table Ab38–39 and the essay on vital statistics in this chapter.

TABLE Ab38–39   Birth and death registration areas – year of entry, by state: 1900–1933

Contributed by Michael R. Haines

State	Birth registration area Ab38 Year	Death registration area Ab39 Year	State	Birth registration area Ab38 Year	Death registration area Ab39 Year
Alabama	1927	1925	Nebraska	1920	1920
Arizona	1926	1926	Nevada	1929	1929
Arkansas	1927	1927	New Hampshire	1915	1900
California	1919	1906	New Jersey	1921	1900
Colorado	1928	1906	New Mexico	1929	1929
Connecticut	1915	1900	New York	1915	1900
Delaware	1921	1919	North Carolina	1917	1916 [4]
District of Columbia	1915	1900	North Dakota	1924	1924
Florida	1924	1919	Ohio	1917	1909
Georgia	1928	1922 [3]	Oklahoma	1928	1928
Idaho	1926	1922	Oregon	1919	1918
Illinois	1922	1918	Pennsylvania	1915	1906
Indiana	1917	1900	Rhode Island	1915 [1]	1900
Iowa	1924	1923	South Carolina	1919 [2]	1916
Kansas	1917	1914	South Dakota	1932	1930 [5]
Kentucky	1917	1911	Tennessee	1927	1917
Louisiana	1927	1918	Texas	1933	1933
Maine	1915	1900	Utah	1917	1910
Maryland	1916	1906	Vermont	1915	1900
Massachusetts	1915	1900	Virginia	1917	1913
Michigan	1915	1900	Washington	1917	1908
Minnesota	1915	1910	West Virginia	1925	1925
Mississippi	1921	1919	Wisconsin	1917	1908
Missouri	1927	1911	Wyoming	1922	1922
Montana	1922	1910			

[1] Withdrew from the Birth Registration Area (BRA), 1919–1920.

[2] Withdrew from the BRA, 1925–1927.

[3] Withdrew from the Death Registration Area (DRA), 1925–1927.

[4] Reported deaths in places with population of 1,000 and more, 1910–1915.

[5] Was briefly in the DRA, 1906–1909.

Source

Compiled from Forrest E. Linder and Robert D. Grove, *Vital Statistics Rates in the United States, 1900–1940* (U.S. Government Printing Office, 1947), Table AE, p. 97.

Documentation

See the text for Table Ab31–37.

BIRTHS AND FERTILITY

Michael R. Haines

TABLE Ab40–51   Crude birth rate and general fertility rate, by race: 1800–1998[1]

Contributed by Michael R. Haines

	Crude birth rate						General fertility rate					
			Other races						Other races			
	Total	White	Total	Black	American Indian	Asian and Pacific Islander	Total	White	Total	Black	American Indian	Asian and Pacific Islander
	Ab40	Ab41	Ab42	Ab43	Ab44	Ab45	Ab46	Ab47	Ab48	Ab49	Ab50	Ab51
Year	Per 1,000	Per 1,000	Per 1,000	Per 1,000	Per 1,000	Per 1,000	Per 1,000	Per 1,000	Per 1,000	Per 1,000	Per 1,000	Per 1,000
1800	—	55.0	—	—	—	—	—	278.0	—	—	—	—
1810	—	54.3	—	—	—	—	—	274.0	—	—	—	—
1820	55.2	52.8	—	—	—	—	—	260.0	—	—	—	—
1830	—	51.4	—	—	—	—	—	240.0	—	—	—	—
1840	51.8	48.3	—	—	—	—	—	222.0	—	—	—	—
1850	—	43.3	—	—	—	—	—	194.0	—	—	—	—
1855	—	42.8	—	58.6 [4]	—	—	—	—	—	—	—	—
1860	44.3	41.8	—	—	—	—	—	184.0	—	—	—	—
1865	—	35.4	—	55.1 [5]	—	—	—	—	—	—	—	—
1870	—	37.1	—	—	—	—	—	167.0	—	—	—	—
1875	—	36.8	—	55.4 [6]	—	—	—	—	—	—	—	—
1880	39.8	33.6	—	51.9 [7]	—	—	—	155.0	—	—	—	—
1890	—	31.2	—	48.1	—	—	—	137.0	—	—	—	—
1900	32.3	28.5	—	44.4	—	—	—	130.0	—	—	—	—
1909	30.0	29.2	—	—	—	—	126.8	123.6	—	—	—	—
1910	30.1	29.2	—	38.5	—	—	126.8	123.8	—	—	—	—
1911	29.9	29.1	—	—	—	—	126.3	123.6	—	—	—	—
1912	29.8	29.0	—	—	—	—	125.8	123.3	—	—	—	—
1913	29.5	28.8	—	—	—	—	124.7	122.4	—	—	—	—
1914	29.9	29.3	—	—	—	—	126.6	124.6	—	—	—	—
1915	29.5	28.9	—	34.4	—	—	125.0	123.2	—	—	—	—
1916	29.1	28.5	—	—	—	—	123.4	121.8	—	—	—	—
1917	28.5	27.9	32.9	—	—	—	121.0	—	—	—	—	—
1918	28.2	27.6	33.0	—	—	—	119.8	—	—	—	—	—
1919	26.1	25.3	32.4	—	—	—	111.2	—	—	—	—	—
1920	27.7	26.9	35.0	—	—	—	117.9	115.4	137.5	—	—	—
1921	28.1	27.3	35.8	—	—	—	119.8	117.2	140.8	—	—	—
1922	26.2	25.4	33.2	—	—	—	111.2	108.8	130.8	—	—	—
1923	26.0	25.2	33.2	—	—	—	110.5	108.0	130.5	—	—	—
1924	26.1	25.1	34.6	—	—	—	110.9	107.8	135.6	—	—	—
1925	25.1	24.1	34.2	—	—	—	106.6	103.3	134.0	—	—	—
1926	24.2	23.1	33.4	—	—	—	102.6	99.2	130.3	—	—	—
1927	23.5	22.7	31.1	—	—	—	99.8	97.1	121.7	—	—	—
1928	22.2	21.5	28.5	—	—	—	93.8	91.7	111.0	—	—	—
1929	21.2	20.5	27.3	—	—	—	89.3	87.3	106.1	—	—	—
1930	21.3	20.6	27.5	—	—	—	89.2	87.1	105.9	—	—	—
1931	20.2	19.5	26.6	—	—	—	84.6	82.4	102.1	—	—	—
1932	19.5	18.7	26.9	—	—	—	81.7	79.0	103.0	—	—	—
1933	18.4	17.6	25.5	—	—	—	76.3	73.7	97.3	—	—	—
1934	19.0	18.1	26.3	—	—	—	78.5	75.8	100.4	—	—	—
1935	18.7	17.9	25.8	—	—	—	77.2	74.5	98.4	—	—	—
1936	18.4	17.6	25.1	—	—	—	75.8	73.3	95.9	—	—	—
1937	18.7	17.9	26.0	—	—	—	77.1	74.4	99.4	—	—	—
1938	19.2	18.4	26.3	—	—	—	79.1	76.5	100.5	—	—	—
1939	18.8	18.0	26.1	—	—	—	77.6	74.8	100.1	—	—	—
1940	19.4	18.6	26.7	—	—	—	79.9	77.1	102.4	—	—	—
1941	20.3	19.5	27.3	—	—	—	83.4	80.7	105.4	—	—	—
1942	22.2	21.5	27.7	—	—	—	91.5	89.5	107.6	—	—	—
1943	22.7	22.1	28.3	—	—	—	94.3	92.3	111.0	—	—	—
1944	21.2	20.5	27.4	—	—	—	88.8	86.3	108.5	—	—	—

Notes appear at end of table

(continued)

TABLE Ab40–51   Crude birth rate and general fertility rate, by race: 1800–1998   *Continued*

	Crude birth rate						General fertility rate					
			Other races						Other races			
	Total	White	Total	Black	American Indian	Asian and Pacific Islander	Total	White	Total	Black	American Indian	Asian and Pacific Islander
	Ab40	Ab41	Ab42	Ab43	Ab44	Ab45	Ab46	Ab47	Ab48	Ab49	Ab50	Ab51
Year	Per 1,000	Per 1,000	Per 1,000	Per 1,000	Per 1,000	Per 1,000	Per 1,000	Per 1,000	Per 1,000	Per 1,000	Per 1,000	Per 1,000
1945	20.4	19.7	26.5	—	—	—	85.9	83.4	106.0	—	—	—
1946	24.1	23.6	28.4	—	—	—	101.9	100.4	113.9	—	—	—
1947	26.6	26.1	31.2	—	—	—	113.3	111.8	125.9	—	—	—
1948	24.9	24.0	32.4	—	—	—	107.3	104.3	131.6	—	—	—
1949	24.5	23.6	33.0	—	—	—	107.1	103.6	135.1	—	—	—
1950	24.1	23.0	33.3	—	—	—	106.2	102.3	137.3	—	—	—
1951	24.9	23.9	33.7	—	—	—	111.4	107.7	141.7	—	—	—
1952	25.1	24.1	33.4	—	—	—	113.8	110.0	142.7	—	—	—
1953	25.1	24.0	33.9	—	—	—	115.0	110.9	146.4	—	—	—
1954	25.3	24.2	34.7	—	—	—	117.9	113.5	152.2	—	—	—
1955	25.0	23.8	34.5	—	—	—	118.3	113.7	154.3	—	—	—
1956	25.2	24.0	35.1	—	—	—	121.0	115.9	159.7	—	—	—
1957	25.3	24.0	35.0	—	—	—	122.7	117.6	161.7	—	—	—
1958	24.5	23.3	34.0	—	—	—	120.0	114.8	159.1	—	—	—
1959	24.0	22.9	32.9	—	—	—	118.8	113.9	156.0	—	—	—
1960	23.7	22.7	32.1	31.9	—	—	118.0	113.2	153.6	153.5	—	—
1961	23.3	22.2	31.6	—	—	—	117.1	112.3	153.0	—	—	—
1962 [2]	22.4	21.4	30.5	—	—	—	112.0	107.5	147.8	—	—	—
1963 [2]	21.7	20.7	29.7	—	—	—	108.3	103.6	143.7	—	—	—
1964	21.1	20.0	29.2	29.5	—	—	104.7	99.8	140.0	142.6	—	—
1965	19.4	18.3	27.6	27.7	—	—	96.3	91.3	131.9	133.2	—	—
1966	18.4	17.4	26.1	26.2	—	—	90.8	86.2	123.5	124.7	—	—
1967 [3]	17.8	16.8	25.0	25.1	—	—	87.2	82.8	117.1	118.5	—	—
1968	17.6	16.6	24.2	24.2	—	—	85.2	81.3	111.9	112.7	—	—
1969	17.9	16.9	24.5	24.4	—	—	86.1	82.2	111.6	112.1	—	—
1970	18.4	17.4	25.1	25.3	—	—	87.9	84.1	113.0	115.4	—	—
1971	17.2	16.1	24.6	24.4	—	—	81.6	77.3	109.1	109.7	—	—
1972	15.6	14.5	22.8	22.5	—	—	73.1	68.9	99.5	99.9	—	—
1973	14.8	13.8	21.7	21.4	—	—	68.8	64.9	93.4	93.6	—	—
1974	14.8	13.9	21.2	20.8	—	—	67.8	64.2	89.8	89.7	—	—
1975	14.6	13.6	21.0	20.7	—	—	66.0	62.5	87.7	87.9	—	—
1976	14.6	13.6	20.8	20.5	—	—	65.0	61.5	85.8	85.8	—	—
1977	15.1	14.1	21.6	21.4	—	—	66.8	63.2	87.7	88.1	—	—
1978	15.0	14.0	21.6	21.3	—	—	65.5	61.7	87.0	86.7	—	—
1979	15.6	14.5	22.2	22.0	—	—	67.2	63.4	88.5	88.3	—	—
1980	15.9	15.1	21.3	21.3	20.7	19.9	68.4	65.6	83.9	84.7	82.7	73.2
1981	15.8	15.0	20.8	20.8	20.0	20.1	67.3	64.8	81.1	82.0	79.6	73.7
1982	15.9	15.1	20.7	20.7	21.1	20.3	67.3	64.8	80.3	80.9	83.6	74.8
1983	15.6	14.8	20.1	20.2	20.6	19.5	65.7	63.4	77.9	78.7	81.8	71.7
1984	15.6	15.0	20.0	20.1	20.1	18.8	65.5	63.2	77.0	78.2	79.8	69.2
1985	15.8	14.8	20.1	20.4	19.8	18.7	66.3	64.1	77.3	78.8	78.6	68.4
1986	15.6	14.9	20.1	20.5	19.2	18.0	65.4	63.1	76.8	78.9	75.9	66.0
1987	15.7	15.0	20.4	20.8	19.1	18.4	65.8	63.3	77.8	80.1	75.6	67.1
1988	16.0	15.4	21.0	21.5	19.3	19.2	67.3	64.5	80.3	82.6	76.8	70.2
1989	16.4	15.4	21.6	22.3	19.7	18.7	69.2	66.4	82.7	86.2	79.0	68.2
1990	16.7	15.8	21.7	22.4	18.9	19.0	70.9	68.3	83.2	86.8	76.2	69.6
1991	16.3	15.4	21.1	21.9	18.3	18.2	69.6	67.0	81.5	85.2	75.1	67.6
1992	15.9	15.0	20.5	21.3	18.4	18.0	68.9	66.5	79.5	83.2	75.4	67.2
1993	15.5	14.7	19.7	20.5	17.8	17.7	67.6	65.4	77.1	80.5	73.4	66.7
1994	15.2	14.4	18.9	19.5	17.1	17.5	66.7	64.9	74.4	76.9	70.9	66.8
1995	14.8	14.2	17.9	18.2	16.6	17.3	65.6	64.4	70.7	72.3	69.1	66.4
1996	14.7	14.1	17.5	17.8	16.6	17.0	65.3	64.3	69.6	70.7	68.7	65.9
1997	14.5	13.9	—	17.7	16.6	16.9	65.0	63.9	—	70.7	69.1	66.3
1998	14.6	14.0	—	17.7	17.1	16.4	64.6	71.0	—	71.0	70.7	64.0

[1] Based on a 50 percent sample of births for 1951–1954, 1956–1966, and 1968–1971; on a 20–50 percent sample for 1967; and on a 100 percent sample in selected states and a 50 percent sample in all other states for 1972–1984. Through 1958, births adjusted for underregistration; thereafter, they are registered live births. Data based on race of child through 1979, race of mother thereafter.

[2] Figures by race exclude New Jersey, which did not require reporting of race.

[3] Based on a 20–50 percent sample of births.

[4] 1850–1859.

[5] 1860–1869.

[6] 1870–1879.

[7] 1880–1884.

TABLE Ab40–51   Crude birth rate and general fertility rate, by race: 1800–1998   *Continued*

Sources

Series Ab40–51, 1909–1992. U.S. Public Health Service, National Center for Health Statistics, *Vital Statistics of the United States, 1993*, volume 1, *Natality*, Table 1-1. Reporting for the black population separately only began in 1960, was discontinued, and resumed in 1964. For 1994–1998 for all races, whites, all others, and blacks, and 1980–1998 for the American Indian and Asian and Pacific Islander populations: *National Vital Statistics Report*, volume 48, number 3, "Births: Final Data for 1998," Table 1.

Series Ab40. 1820–1900: Henry D. Sheldon, *The Older Population of the United States* (Wiley, 1955), p. 145.

Series Ab41 and Ab47. 1800–1850: Warren S. Thompson and P. K. Whelpton, *Population Trends in the United States* (McGraw-Hill, 1933), p. 263. 1855–1900: Ansley J. Coale and Melvin Zelnik, *New Estimates of Fertility and Population in the United States: A Study of Annual White Births from 1855 to 1960 and of Completeness of Enumeration in the Censuses from 1880 to 1960* (Princeton University Press, 1963), Table 1.

Series Ab43. 1855–1915: Ansley J. Coale and Norfleet W. Rives Jr., "A Statistical Reconstruction of the Black Population of the United States,

1880–1970: Estimates of True Numbers by Age and Sex, Birth Rates, and Total Fertility," *Population Index* 31 (4) (1973): 26.

Documentation

These data are based on estimated total live births per 1,000 population for the specified group. The base population is as of July 1 in each year, except in census years, when it is as of April 1.

Estimates for 1909–1934 were prepared by Pascal K. Whelpton. For 1915–1932, the figures include adjustments for states not in the Birth Registration Area. For years prior to 1915, figures are estimates based on the number of registered births in the ten original registration states for the same period.

Also see the text for Table Ab11–30.

Series Ab43. Figures for 1890–1930 are arithmetic averages for the two quinquennia surrounding the year.

Series Ab46–51. The general fertility rate (GFR) is computed by relating total births, regardless of the age of mother, to women ages 15–44.

TABLE Ab52–117   Total fertility rate and birth rate, by race and age: 1800–1998[1]

Contributed by Michael R. Haines

		All races									
		Birth rate, women aged									
	Total fertility rate	10–14	15–19	15–17	18–19	20–24	25–29	30–34	35–39	40–44	45–49
	Ab52	Ab53	Ab54	Ab55	Ab56	Ab57	Ab58	Ab59	Ab60	Ab61	Ab62 [2]
Year	Per 1,000	Per 1,000	Per 1,000	Per 1,000	Per 1,000	Per 1,000	Per 1,000	Per 1,000	Per 1,000	Per 1,000	Per 1,000
1800	—	—	—	—	—	—	—	—	—	—	—
1810	—	—	—	—	—	—	—	—	—	—	—
1820	—	—	—	—	—	—	—	—	—	—	—
1830	—	—	—	—	—	—	—	—	—	—	—
1840	—	—	—	—	—	—	—	—	—	—	—
1850	—	—	—	—	—	—	—	—	—	—	—
1860	—	—	—	—	—	—	—	—	—	—	—
1870	—	—	—	—	—	—	—	—	—	—	—
1880	—	—	—	—	—	—	—	—	—	—	—
1890	—	—	—	—	—	—	—	—	—	—	—
1900	—	—	—	—	—	—	—	—	—	—	—
1905 [3]	3,551	—	60.5	—	—	168.4	181.6	146.7	104.0	43.0	6.0
1910	—	—	—	—	—	—	—	—	—	—	—
1920	—	—	—	—	—	—	—	—	—	—	—
1930	—	—	—	—	—	—	—	—	—	—	—
1933	2,210	0.6	46.7	—	—	121.0	116.1	82.6	51.9	21.0	2.3
1934	2,274	0.6	49.0	—	—	126.9	119.8	85.0	50.7	20.7	2.2
1935	2,235	0.6	49.3	—	—	126.5	118.0	81.1	50.1	19.4	2.1
1936	2,193	0.5	48.6	—	—	126.5	116.3	78.9	47.7	18.0	2.1
1937	2,225	0.5	51.1	—	—	130.3	118.1	79.7	46.3	16.9	2.0
1938	2,280	0.7	53.2	—	—	134.5	121.5	81.7	46.3	16.5	1.9
1939	2,232	0.7	52.4	—	—	130.4	119.7	81.1	45.4	15.1	1.7
1940	2,301	0.7	54.1	—	—	135.6	122.8	83.4	46.3	15.6	1.9
1941	2,399	0.7	56.9	—	—	145.4	128.7	85.3	46.1	15.0	1.7
1942	2,628	0.7	61.1	—	—	165.1	142.7	91.8	47.9	14.7	1.6
1943	2,718	0.8	61.7	—	—	164.0	147.8	99.5	52.8	15.7	1.5
1944	2,568	0.8	54.3	—	—	151.8	136.5	98.1	54.6	16.1	1.4

Notes appear at end of table

(continued)

TABLE Ab52–117   Total fertility rate and birth rate, by race and age: 1800–1998   *Continued*

				All races							
					Birth rate, women aged						
	Total fertility rate	10–14	15–19	15–17	18–19	20–24	25–29	30–34	35–39	40–44	45–49
	Ab52	Ab53	Ab54	Ab55	Ab56	Ab57	Ab58	Ab59	Ab60	Ab61	Ab62 [2]
Year	Per 1,000	Per 1,000	Per 1,000	Per 1,000	Per 1,000	Per 1,000	Per 1,000	Per 1,000	Per 1,000	Per 1,000	Per 1,000
1945	2,491	0.8	51.1	—	—	138.9	132.2	100.2	56.9	16.6	1.6
1946	2,943	0.7	59.3	—	—	181.8	161.2	108.9	58.7	16.5	1.5
1947	3,274	0.9	79.3	—	—	209.7	176.0	111.9	58.9	16.6	1.4
1948	3,109	1.0	81.8	—	—	200.3	163.4	103.7	54.5	15.7	1.3
1949	3,110	1.0	83.4	—	—	200.1	165.4	102.1	53.5	15.3	1.3
1950	3,091	1.0	81.6	—	—	196.6	166.1	103.7	52.9	15.1	1.2
1951	3,269	0.9	87.6	—	—	211.6	175.3	107.9	54.1	15.4	1.1
1952	3,358	0.9	86.1	—	—	217.6	182.0	112.6	55.8	15.5	1.3
1953	3,424	1.0	88.2	—	—	224.6	184.1	113.4	56.6	15.8	1.0
1954	3,543	0.9	90.6	—	—	236.2	188.4	116.9	57.9	16.2	1.0
1955	3,580	0.9	90.5	—	—	242.0	190.5	116.2	58.7	16.1	1.0
1956	3,689	1.0	94.6	—	—	253.7	194.7	117.3	59.3	16.3	1.0
1957	3,767	1.0	96.3	—	—	260.6	199.4	118.9	59.9	16.3	1.1
1958	3,701	0.9	91.4	—	—	258.2	198.3	116.2	58.3	15.7	0.9
1959	3,670	0.9	89.1	—	—	257.5	198.6	114.4	57.3	15.3	0.9
1960	3,654	0.8	89.1	43.9	166.7	258.1	197.4	112.7	56.2	15.5	0.9
1961	3,620	0.9	88.6	43.8	155.2	251.9	197.5	113.3	55.6	15.6	0.9
1962 [4]	3,461	0.8	81.4	38.1	150.8	241.9	191.1	108.6	52.6	14.9	0.9
1963 [4]	3,319	0.9	76.7	36.9	147.8	229.1	185.1	105.8	51.2	14.2	0.9
1964	3,191	0.9	73.1	37.2	142.8	217.5	178.7	103.4	49.9	13.8	0.8
1965	2,913	0.8	70.5	36.6	124.5	195.3	161.6	94.4	46.2	12.8	0.8
1966	2,721	0.8	70.3	35.7	120.3	185.6	148.2	85.1	41.9	11.7	0.7
1967	2,558	0.9	67.5	35.3	116.7	172.9	142.1	78.7	38.3	10.6	0.7
1968	2,464	1.0	65.6	35.1	113.5	166.5	140.0	74.2	35.4	9.6	0.6
1969	2,456	1.0	65.5	35.7	112.4	165.7	143.0	73.5	33.1	8.8	0.5
1970	2,480	1.2	68.3	38.8	114.7	167.8	145.1	73.3	31.7	8.1	0.5
1971	2,267	1.1	64.5	38.2	105.3	150.1	134.1	67.3	28.7	7.1	0.4
1972	2,010	1.2	61.7	39.0	96.9	130.2	117.7	59.8	24.8	6.2	0.4
1973	1,879	1.2	59.3	38.5	91.2	119.7	112.2	55.6	22.1	5.4	0.3
1974	1,835	1.2	57.5	37.3	88.7	117.7	111.5	53.8	20.2	4.8	0.3
1975	1,774	1.3	55.6	36.1	85.0	113.0	108.2	52.3	19.5	4.6	0.3
1976	1,738	1.2	52.8	34.1	80.5	110.3	106.2	53.6	19.0	4.3	0.2
1977	1,790	1.2	52.8	33.9	80.9	112.9	111.0	56.4	19.2	4.2	0.2
1978	1,760	1.2	51.5	32.2	79.8	109.9	108.5	57.8	19.0	3.9	0.2
1979	1,808	1.2	52.3	32.3	81.3	112.8	111.4	60.3	19.5	3.9	0.2
1980	1,840	1.1	53.0	32.5	82.1	115.1	112.9	61.9	19.8	3.9	0.2
1981	1,812	1.1	52.2	32.0	80.0	112.2	111.5	61.4	20.0	3.8	0.2
1982	1,828	1.1	52.4	32.3	79.4	111.6	111.0	64.1	21.2	3.9	0.2
1983	1,799	1.1	51.4	31.8	77.4	107.8	108.5	64.9	22.0	3.9	0.2
1984	1,807	1.2	50.6	31.0	77.4	106.8	108.7	67.0	22.9	3.9	0.2
1985	1,844	1.2	51.0	31.0	79.6	108.3	111.0	69.1	24.0	4.0	0.2
1986	1,838	1.3	50.2	30.5	79.6	107.4	109.8	70.1	24.4	4.1	0.2
1987	1,872	1.3	50.6	31.7	78.5	107.9	111.6	72.1	26.3	4.4	0.2
1988	1,934	1.3	53.0	33.6	79.9	110.2	114.4	74.8	28.1	4.8	0.2
1989	2,014	1.4	57.3	36.4	84.2	113.8	117.6	77.4	29.9	5.2	0.2
1990	2,081	1.4	59.9	37.5	88.6	116.5	120.2	80.8	31.7	5.5	0.2
1991	2,073	1.4	62.1	38.7	94.4	115.7	118.2	79.5	32.0	5.5	0.2
1992	2,065	1.4	60.7	37.8	94.5	114.6	117.4	80.2	32.5	5.9	0.3
1993	2,046	1.4	59.6	37.8	92.1	112.6	115.5	80.8	32.9	6.1	0.3
1994	2,036	1.4	58.9	37.6	91.5	111.1	113.9	81.5	33.7	6.4	0.3
1995	2,019	1.3	56.8	36.0	89.1	109.8	112.2	82.5	34.3	6.6	0.3
1996	2,027	1.2	54.4	33.8	86.0	110.4	113.1	83.9	35.3	6.8	0.3
1997	2,033	1.1	52.3	32.1	83.6	110.4	113.8	85.3	36.1	7.1	0.4
1998	2,059	1.0	51.1	30.4	82.0	111.2	115.9	87.4	37.4	7.3	0.4

Notes appear at end of table

TABLE Ab52 117 Total fertility rate and birth rate, by race and age: 1800–1998 *Continued*

					White						
					Birth rate, women aged						
	Total fertility rate	10–14	15–19	15–17	18–19	20–24	25–29	30–34	35–39	40–44	45–49
	Ab63	Ab64	Ab65	Ab66	Ab67	Ab68	Ab69	Ab70	Ab71	Ab72	Ab73 [2]
Year	Per 1,000	Per 1,000	Per 1,000	Per 1,000	Per 1,000	Per 1,000	Per 1,000	Per 1,000	Per 1,000	Per 1,000	Per 1,000
1800	7,040	—	—	—	—	—	—	—	—	—	—
1810	6,920	—	—	—	—	—	—	—	—	—	—
1820	6,730	—	—	—	—	—	—	—	—	—	—
1830	6,550	—	—	—	—	—	—	—	—	—	—
1840	6,140	—	—	—	—	—	—	—	—	—	—
1850	5,420	—	—	—	—	—	—	—	—	—	—
1860	5,210	—	—	—	—	—	—	—	—	—	—
1870	4,550	—	—	—	—	—	—	—	—	—	—
1880	4,240	—	—	—	—	—	—	—	—	—	—
1890	3,870	—	—	—	—	—	—	—	—	—	—
1900	3,560	—	—	—	—	—	—	—	—	—	—
1905 [3]	3,443	—	55.6	—	—	161.2	180.3	144.8	100.0	41.5	5.0
1910	3,420	—	—	—	—	—	—	—	—	—	—
1920	3,170	—	—	—	—	—	—	—	—	—	—
1930	2,450	—	—	—	—	—	—	—	—	—	—
1933	2,116	0.2	39.7	—	—	115.4	114.7	80.4	50.4	20.3	2.1
1934	2,172	0.2	41.5	—	—	120.7	118.3	82.7	49.1	19.9	2.1
1935	2,171	0.3	42.6	—	—	122.5	118.1	80.5	49.1	19.0	1.9
1936	2,131	0.2	42.0	—	—	122.9	116.4	78.5	46.7	17.6	1.8
1937	2,156	0.2	43.8	—	—	126.4	118.1	79.3	45.2	16.4	1.7
1938	2,214	0.2	45.5	—	—	131.1	121.8	81.4	45.2	16.1	1.6
1939	2,161	0.2	44.3	—	—	126.5	119.7	80.8	44.4	14.7	1.5
1940	2,229	0.2	45.3	—	—	131.4	123.6	83.4	45.3	15.0	1.6
1941	2,328	0.2	47.6	—	—	141.6	130.1	85.2	45.1	14.3	1.4
1942	2,577	0.3	51.8	—	—	162.9	145.6	92.3	47.2	14.1	1.3
1943	2,664	0.3	52.1	—	—	161.1	150.7	100.2	52.2	15.0	1.3
1944	2,501	0.3	45.3	—	—	147.9	137.7	98.2	54.1	15.5	1.2
1945	2,421	0.3	42.1	—	—	134.7	133.1	100.5	56.3	16.0	1.4
1946	2,901	0.3	50.6	—	—	179.8	164.0	110.0	58.4	15.9	1.3
1947	3,230	0.4	69.8	—	—	207.9	179.1	113.0	58.4	16.1	1.2
1948	3,022	0.4	71.1	—	—	195.5	163.9	103.6	53.5	15.2	1.1
1949	3,009	0.4	72.1	—	—	194.6	165.2	101.5	52.2	14.6	1.1
1950	2,977	0.4	70.0	—	—	190.4	165.1	102.6	51.4	14.5	1.0
1951	3,157	0.4	75.9	—	—	206.0	174.2	106.5	52.6	14.6	1.0
1952	3,250	0.4	75.0	—	—	212.5	180.5	111.4	54.4	14.8	0.9
1953	3,306	0.4	77.2	—	—	219.6	181.5	111.9	55.1	15.0	0.9
1954	3,415	0.4	79.0	—	—	230.7	185.0	115.1	56.2	15.4	0.9
1955	3,446	0.3	79.2	—	—	236.0	186.8	114.1	56.7	15.4	0.8
1956	3,546	0.3	83.2	—	—	247.1	190.6	114.4	57.0	15.4	0.8
1957	3,625	0.5	85.2	—	—	253.8	195.8	115.9	57.4	15.4	0.8
1958	3,560	0.5	81.0	—	—	251.4	194.8	113.0	55.8	14.8	0.8
1959	3,544	0.4	79.2	—	—	251.7	195.5	111.3	55.1	14.7	0.9
1960	3,533	0.4	79.4	35.5	154.6	252.8	194.9	109.6	54.0	14.7	0.8
1961	3,497	0.4	79.2	35.3	143.8	246.7	194.2	110.1	53.1	14.8	0.9
1962 [4]	3,341	0.4	73.2	29.5	136.7	237.0	187.4	105.2	50.1	14.2	0.8
1963 [4]	3,194	0.3	68.2	28.4	133.2	223.5	181.1	102.6	48.8	13.4	0.8
1964	3,065	0.3	63.4	29.1	129.7	211.6	175.9	100.5	47.6	13.0	0.7
1965	2,783	0.3	60.6	27.8	111.9	189.0	158.4	91.6	44.0	12.0	0.7
1966	2,603	0.3	60.4	26.6	108.2	180.0	146.0	82.5	39.9	10.8	0.7
1967	2,447	0.3	56.9	25.7	104.0	167.9	141.0	76.4	36.5	9.8	0.6
1968	2,366	0.4	54.9	25.6	100.5	162.1	140.3	72.4	33.7	8.9	0.5
1969	2,360	0.4	54.7	26.4	99.2	161.3	143.7	71.9	31.5	8.1	0.5
1970	2,385	0.5	57.4	29.2	101.5	163.4	145.9	71.9	30.0	7.5	0.4
1971	2,161	0.5	53.6	28.5	92.3	144.9	134.0	65.4	26.9	6.4	0.4
1972	1,907	0.5	51.0	29.3	84.3	124.8	117.4	58.4	23.3	5.6	0.3
1973	1,783	0.6	49.0	29.2	79.3	114.4	112.3	54.4	20.7	4.9	0.3
1974	1,749	0.6	47.9	28.7	77.3	113.0	111.8	52.9	18.9	4.4	0.2

Notes appear at end of table

(continued)

TABLE Ab52–117 Total fertility rate and birth rate, by race and age: 1800–1998 *Continued*

White

	Total fertility rate	Birth rate, women aged									
		10–14	15–19	15–17	18–19	20–24	25–29	30–34	35–39	40–44	45–49
	Ab63	Ab64	Ab65	Ab66	Ab67	Ab68	Ab69	Ab70	Ab71	Ab72	Ab73 [2]
Year	Per 1,000	Per 1,000	Per 1,000	Per 1,000	Per 1,000	Per 1,000	Per 1,000	Per 1,000	Per 1,000	Per 1,000	Per 1,000
1975	1,686	0.6	46.4	28.0	74.0	108.2	108.1	51.3	18.2	4.2	0.2
1976	1,652	0.6	44.1	26.3	70.2	105.3	105.9	52.6	17.8	3.9	0.2
1977	1,703	0.6	44.1	26.1	70.5	107.7	110.9	55.3	18.0	3.8	0.2
1978	1,668	0.6	42.9	24.9	69.4	104.1	107.9	56.6	17.7	3.5	0.2
1979	1,716	0.6	43.7	24.7	71.0	107.0	110.8	59.0	18.3	3.5	0.2
1980	1,773	0.6	45.4	25.5	73.2	111.1	113.8	61.2	18.8	3.5	0.2
1981	1,748	0.5	44.9	25.4	71.5	108.3	112.3	61.0	19.0	3.4	0.2
1982	1,767	0.6	45.0	25.5	70.8	107.7	111.9	64.0	20.4	3.6	0.2
1983	1,741	0.6	43.9	25.0	68.8	103.8	109.4	65.3	21.3	3.6	0.2
1984	1,749	0.6	42.9	24.3	68.4	102.7	109.8	67.7	22.2	3.6	0.2
1985	1,787	0.6	43.3	24.4	70.4	104.1	112.3	69.9	23.3	3.7	0.2
1986	1,776	0.6	42.3	23.8	70.1	102.7	110.8	70.9	23.9	3.8	0.2
1987	1,805	0.6	42.5	24.6	68.9	102.3	112.3	73.0	25.9	4.1	0.2
1988	1,857	0.6	44.4	26.0	69.6	103.7	114.8	75.4	27.7	4.5	0.2
1989	1,931	0.7	47.9	28.1	72.9	106.9	117.8	78.1	29.7	4.9	0.2
1990	2,003	0.7	50.8	29.5	78.0	109.8	120.7	81.7	31.5	5.2	0.2
1991	1,996	0.8	52.8	30.7	83.5	109.0	118.8	80.5	31.8	5.2	0.2
1992	1,994	0.8	51.8	30.1	83.8	108.2	118.4	81.4	32.2	5.7	0.2
1993	1,982	0.8	51.1	30.3	82.1	106.9	116.6	82.1	32.7	5.9	0.3
1994	1,985	0.8	51.1	30.7	82.1	106.2	115.5	83.2	33.7	6.2	0.3
1995	1,989	0.8	50.1	30.0	81.2	106.3	114.8	84.6	34.5	6.4	0.3
1996	2,006	0.8	48.1	28.4	78.4	107.2	116.1	86.3	35.6	6.7	0.3
1997	2,009	0.7	46.3	27.1	75.9	106.7	116.6	87.8	36.4	6.9	0.4
1998	2,041	0.6	45.4	25.9	74.6	107.2	119.1	90.5	37.8	7.2	0.4

All nonwhite

	Total fertility rate	Birth rate, women aged									
		10–14	15–19	15–17	18–19	20–24	25–29	30–34	35–39	40–44	45–49
	Ab74	Ab75	Ab76	Ab77	Ab78	Ab79	Ab80	Ab81	Ab82	Ab83	Ab84 [2]
Year	Per 1,000	Per 1,000	Per 1,000	Per 1,000	Per 1,000	Per 1,000	Per 1,000	Per 1,000	Per 1,000	Per 1,000	Per 1,000
1800	—	—	—	—	—	—	—	—	—	—	—
1810	—	—	—	—	—	—	—	—	—	—	—
1820	—	—	—	—	—	—	—	—	—	—	—
1830	—	—	—	—	—	—	—	—	—	—	—
1840	—	—	—	—	—	—	—	—	—	—	—
1850	—	—	—	—	—	—	—	—	—	—	—
1860	—	—	—	—	—	—	—	—	—	—	—
1870	—	—	—	—	—	—	—	—	—	—	—
1880	—	—	—	—	—	—	—	—	—	—	—
1890	—	—	—	—	—	—	—	—	—	—	—
1900	—	—	—	—	—	—	—	—	—	—	—
1905 [3]	—	—	—	—	—	—	—	—	—	—	—
1910	—	—	—	—	—	—	—	—	—	—	—
1920	—	—	—	—	—	—	—	—	—	—	—
1930	—	—	—	—	—	—	—	—	—	—	—
1933	2,962	3.0	107.1	—	—	165.1	124.7	99.1	63.2	25.9	4.4
1934	3,099	3.4	113.7	—	—	176.3	129.1	102.7	63.7	26.4	4.5
1935	2,728	3.4	107.2	—	—	156.8	112.4	82.9	56.4	22.6	3.9
1936	2,660	3.1	106.3	—	—	153.6	110.8	78.7	54.8	21.1	3.7
1937	2,756	3.5	114.8	—	—	160.4	113.3	79.9	55.0	20.8	3.5
1938	2,790	3.7	119.9	—	—	160.7	115.2	80.6	54.5	19.9	3.3
1939	2,780	3.8	122.2	—	—	160.9	115.2	79.9	52.7	18.1	3.1

Notes appear at end of table

TABLE Ab52–117   Total fertility rate and birth rate, by race and age: 1800–1998   *Continued*

		All nonwhite									
		Birth rate, women aged									
	Total fertility rate	10–14	15–19	15–17	18–19	20–24	25–29	30–34	35–39	40–44	45–49
	Ab74	Ab75	Ab76	Ab77	Ab78	Ab79	Ab80	Ab81	Ab82	Ab83	Ab84 [2]
Year	Per 1,000	Per 1,000	Per 1,000	Per 1,000	Per 1,000	Per 1,000	Per 1,000	Per 1,000	Per 1,000	Per 1,000	Per 1,000
1940	2,870	3.7	121.7	—	—	168.5	116.3	83.5	53.7	21.5	5.2
1941	2,956	4.0	128.3	—	—	175.0	118.1	86.2	54.1	21.5	4.1
1942	3,022	3.9	131.8	—	—	182.3	119.6	88.1	54.0	20.8	4.0
1943	3,128	4.0	133.4	—	—	187.2	125.1	93.9	56.9	21.5	3.7
1944	3,075	3.9	121.5	—	—	182.4	126.8	97.3	58.4	21.5	3.2
1945	3,017	3.9	117.5	—	—	172.1	125.4	97.1	61.3	22.3	3.7
1946	3,238	3.7	121.9	—	—	197.3	139.2	99.3	61.0	21.8	3.5
1947	3,575	4.6	146.6	—	—	223.7	150.6	102.4	62.7	21.4	3.1
1948	3,742	4.9	157.3	—	—	237.0	159.6	104.1	62.5	20.4	2.8
1949	3,855	5.1	162.8	—	—	241.3	167.0	107.3	63.9	21.1	2.5
1950	3,928	5.1	163.5	—	—	242.6	173.8	112.6	64.3	21.2	2.6
1951	4,091	5.4	166.7	—	—	252.5	184.2	117.9	66.5	22.6	2.2
1952	4,147	5.2	162.9	—	—	254.0	194.2	122.0	66.6	21.9	2.2
1953	4,283	5.1	165.4	—	—	261.4	206.4	125.7	70.0	23.0	2.2
1954	4,474	4.9	170.3	—	—	274.7	215.7	131.3	72.9	22.5	2.1
1955	4,550	4.8	168.3	—	—	283.4	219.6	133.5	75.4	22.1	2.1
1956	4,730	4.7	172.5	—	—	299.1	225.9	139.4	78.8	23.6	2.0
1957	4,798	5.6	172.8	—	—	307.0	228.1	143.5	78.7	23.5	2.0
1958	4,727	4.3	167.3	—	—	305.2	224.2	142.3	78.4	21.8	1.9
1959	4,595	4.2	160.5	—	—	297.9	220.2	138.1	75.0	21.2	1.8
1960	4,522	4.0	158.2	103.1	251.8	294.2	214.6	135.6	74.2	22.0	1.7
1961	4,497	4.0	155.2	101.7	241.6	286.6	220.4	134.7	74.9	22.3	1.4
1962 [4]	4,340	3.9	147.1	92.9	230.2	276.9	215.2	130.0	71.8	21.8	1.5
1963 [4]	4,203	4.0	142.6	91.6	224.5	268.4	208.7	125.7	68.7	21.1	1.5
1964	4,070	4.0	141.5	93.7	233.8	258.6	198.0	122.7	66.8	20.9	1.6
1965	3,808	4.0	138.4	93.9	218.5	239.2	183.5	113.0	62.7	19.3	1.5
1966	3,532	4.0	136.4	92.7	210.9	224.7	163.0	102.1	56.3	18.4	1.4
1967	3,299	4.1	135.0	93.8	203.6	208.7	149.2	93.9	50.9	16.7	1.2
1968	3,108	4.3	132.3	92.8	197.5	197.7	138.6	85.9	46.9	14.8	1.2
1969	3,061	4.5	131.3	91.8	195.1	195.9	138.2	83.6	44.1	13.7	1.0
1970	3,067	4.8	133.4	95.2	195.4	196.8	140.1	82.5	42.2	12.6	0.9
1971	2,920	4.7	128.5	94.0	185.6	184.0	134.6	79.3	40.2	11.7	0.9
1972	2,628	4.7	123.8	93.8	173.3	163.4	119.3	68.9	34.8	9.9	0.7
1973	2,443	5.0	117.5	90.5	160.9	151.6	111.2	63.2	30.9	8.6	0.6
1974	2,339	4.6	111.3	84.9	153.1	145.5	109.5	59.9	28.8	7.6	0.5
1975	2,276	4.7	106.4	80.5	146.1	141.0	108.7	58.8	27.6	7.5	0.5
1976	2,223	4.3	99.9	75.5	137.2	138.9	107.6	59.5	26.9	6.9	0.5
1977	2,279	4.3	99.5	74.8	136.8	142.3	111.5	63.4	27.3	6.9	0.5
1978	2,265	4.0	96.0	70.4	134.4	142.1	111.9	65.2	26.9	6.4	0.4
1979	2,310	4.1	96.5	70.5	134.9	144.3	114.6	68.3	27.3	6.4	0.4
1980	2,199	3.8	91.4	66.7	127.7	136.5	108.5	66.7	26.3	6.2	0.4
1981	2,134	3.5	87.5	63.1	122.7	132.6	106.9	64.0	25.8	6.0	0.4
1982	2,132	3.5	87.1	63.1	120.8	132.0	106.7	64.4	26.4	5.8	0.5
1983	2,084	3.5	85.9	62.6	117.8	128.0	103.7	63.2	26.4	5.7	0.4
1984	2,079	3.7	85.1	61.4	118.0	127.1	103.4	63.7	26.8	5.5	0.4
1985	2,107	3.8	85.4	60.8	120.6	128.6	104.7	65.1	27.9	5.4	0.4
1986	2,115	3.9	84.8	60.4	121.6	129.5	105.0	66.1	27.5	5.7	0.4
1987	2,169	4.0	85.5	62.1	120.6	133.4	108.0	68.0	28.6	5.8	0.4
1988	2,265	4.1	89.2	64.7	125.2	138.9	112.3	71.5	30.2	6.3	0.4
1989	2,361	4.2	95.9	69.2	132.5	143.6	116.6	73.7	31.1	6.6	0.4
1990	2,398	4.0	96.3	69.1	132.4	145.4	117.7	76.3	32.8	6.7	0.4
1991	2,383	3.9	98.4	70.3	137.2	144.1	115.2	75.0	32.8	6.8	0.4
1992	2,343	3.8	95.4	67.9	135.7	140.8	113.1	74.8	33.4	6.9	0.4
1993	2,294	3.7	92.5	66.9	131.0	135.8	110.7	74.9	33.6	7.1	0.4
1994	2,300	—	—	—	—	—	—	—	—	—	—
1995	2,175	—	—	—	—	—	—	—	—	—	—
1996	2,149	—	—	—	—	—	—	—	—	—	—
1997	—	—	—	—	—	—	—	—	—	—	—
1998	—	—	—	—	—	—	—	—	—	—	—

Notes appear at end of table   (continued)

TABLE Ab52–117   Total fertility rate and birth rate, by race and age: 1800–1998   *Continued*

					Black						
					Birth rate, women aged						
	Total fertility rate	10–14	15–19	15–17	18–19	20–24	25–29	30–34	35–39	40–44	45–49
	Ab85	Ab86	Ab87	Ab88	Ab89	Ab90	Ab91	Ab92	Ab93	Ab94	Ab95 [2]
Year	Per 1,000	Per 1,000	Per 1,000	Per 1,000	Per 1,000	Per 1,000	Per 1,000	Per 1,000	Per 1,000	Per 1,000	Per 1,000
1800	—	—	—	—	—	—	—	—	—	—	—
1810	—	—	—	—	—	—	—	—	—	—	—
1820	—	—	—	—	—	—	—	—	—	—	—
1830	—	—	—	—	—	—	—	—	—	—	—
1840	—	—	—	—	—	—	—	—	—	—	—
1850	7,900 [5]	—	—	—	—	—	—	—	—	—	—
1860	7,580 [6]	—	—	—	—	—	—	—	—	—	—
1870	7,690 [7]	—	—	—	—	—	—	—	—	—	—
1880	7,260 [8]	—	—	—	—	—	—	—	—	—	—
1890	6,560	—	—	—	—	—	—	—	—	—	—
1900	5,610	—	—	—	—	—	—	—	—	—	—
1905 [3]	4,351	—	103.6	—	—	227.0	182.2	153.8	130.1	55.0	18.4
1910	4,610	—	—	—	—	—	—	—	—	—	—
1920	3,640	—	—	—	—	—	—	—	—	—	—
1930	2,980	—	—	—	—	—	—	—	—	—	—
1933	—	—	—	—	—	—	—	—	—	—	—
1934	—	—	—	—	—	—	—	—	—	—	—
1935	—	—	—	—	—	—	—	—	—	—	—
1936	—	—	—	—	—	—	—	—	—	—	—
1937	—	—	—	—	—	—	—	—	—	—	—
1938	—	—	—	—	—	—	—	—	—	—	—
1939	—	—	—	—	—	—	—	—	—	—	—
1940	2,870	—	—	—	—	—	—	—	—	—	—
1941	—	—	—	—	—	—	—	—	—	—	—
1942	—	—	—	—	—	—	—	—	—	—	—
1943	—	—	—	—	—	—	—	—	—	—	—
1944	—	—	—	—	—	—	—	—	—	—	—
1945	—	—	—	—	—	—	—	—	—	—	—
1946	—	—	—	—	—	—	—	—	—	—	—
1947	—	—	—	—	—	—	—	—	—	—	—
1948	—	—	—	—	—	—	—	—	—	—	—
1949	—	—	—	—	—	—	—	—	—	—	—
1950	3,930	—	—	—	—	—	—	—	—	—	—
1951	—	—	—	—	—	—	—	—	—	—	—
1952	—	—	—	—	—	—	—	—	—	—	—
1953	—	—	—	—	—	—	—	—	—	—	—
1954	—	—	—	—	—	—	—	—	—	—	—
1955	—	—	—	—	—	—	—	—	—	—	—
1956	—	—	—	—	—	—	—	—	—	—	—
1957	—	—	—	—	—	—	—	—	—	—	—
1958	—	—	—	—	—	—	—	—	—	—	—
1959	—	—	—	—	—	—	—	—	—	—	—
1960	4,542	4.3	156.1	—	—	295.4	218.6	137.1	73.9	21.9	1.1
1961	—	—	—	—	—	—	—	—	—	—	—
1962 [4]	—	—	—	—	—	—	—	—	—	—	—
1963 [4]	—	—	—	—	—	—	—	—	—	—	—
1964	4,139	4.3	147.6	98.7	242.4	264.7	198.5	123.5	66.8	20.8	1.5
1965	3,829	4.3	144.6	99.3	227.6	243.1	180.4	111.3	61.9	18.7	1.4
1966	3,545	4.2	142.7	97.9	219.2	227.9	159.0	100.3	55.4	18.2	1.4
1967	3,312	4.4	141.8	99.5	213.4	211.9	145.3	91.1	50.1	16.6	1.2
1968	3,100	4.7	138.7	98.2	206.1	199.8	133.1	82.2	45.8	14.5	1.2
1969	3,043	4.8	137.0	96.9	202.5	198.0	132.3	79.1	42.9	13.5	1.0
1970	3,100	5.2	140.7	101.4	204.9	202.7	136.3	79.6	41.9	12.5	1.0
1971	2,902	5.1	134.5	99.4	192.6	186.6	128.0	74.8	38.9	11.6	0.9
1972	2,601	5.1	129.8	99.5	179.5	165.0	112.4	64.0	33.4	9.8	0.7
1973	2,411	5.4	123.1	96.0	166.6	153.1	103.9	58.1	29.4	8.6	0.6
1974	2,299	5.0	116.5	90.0	158.7	146.7	102.2	54.1	27.0	7.6	0.6

Notes appear at end of table

TABLE Ab52–117   Total fertility rate and birth rate, by race and age: 1800–1998   *Continued*

Black

					Birth rate, women aged					
	Total fertility rate	10–14	15–19	15–17	18–19	20–24	25–29	30–34	35–39	40–44	45–49
	Ab85	Ab86	Ab87	Ab88	Ab89	Ab90	Ab91	Ab92	Ab93	Ab94	Ab95 [2]
Year	Per 1,000	Per 1,000	Per 1,000	Per 1,000	Per 1,000	Per 1,000	Per 1,000	Per 1,000	Per 1,000	Per 1,000	Per 1,000
1975	2,243	5.1	111.8	85.6	152.4	142.8	102.2	53.1	25.6	7.5	0.5
1976	2,187	4.7	104.9	80.3	142.5	140.5	101.6	53.6	24.8	6.8	0.5
1977	2,251	4.7	104.7	79.6	142.9	144.4	106.4	57.5	25.4	6.6	0.5
1978	2,218	4.4	100.9	75.0	139.7	143.8	105.4	58.3	24.3	6.1	0.4
1979	2,263	4.6	101.7	75.7	140.4	146.3	108.2	60.7	24.7	6.1	0.4
1980	2,177	4.3	97.8	72.5	135.1	140.0	103.9	59.9	23.5	5.6	0.3
1981	2,118	4.0	94.5	69.3	131.0	136.5	102.3	57.4	23.1	5.4	0.3
1982	2,107	4.0	94.3	69.7	128.9	135.4	101.3	57.5	23.3	5.4	0.3
1983	2,066	4.1	93.9	69.6	127.1	131.9	98.4	56.2	23.3	5.1	0.3
1984	2,071	4.4	94.1	69.2	128.1	132.2	98.4	56.7	23.3	4.8	0.2
1985	2,109	4.5	95.4	69.3	132.4	135.0	100.2	57.9	23.9	4.6	0.3
1986	2,136	4.7	95.8	69.3	135.1	137.3	101.1	59.3	23.8	4.8	0.3
1987	2,198	4.8	97.6	72.1	135.8	142.7	104.3	60.6	24.6	4.8	0.2
1988	2,298	4.9	102.7	75.7	142.7	149.7	108.2	63.1	25.6	5.1	0.3
1989	2,433	5.1	111.5	81.9	151.9	156.8	114.4	66.3	26.7	5.4	0.3
1990	2,480	4.9	112.8	82.3	152.9	160.2	115.5	68.7	28.1	5.5	0.3
1991	2,480	4.8	115.5	84.1	158.6	160.9	113.1	67.7	28.3	5.5	0.2
1992	2,442	4.7	112.4	81.3	157.9	158.0	111.2	67.5	28.8	5.6	0.2
1993	2,385	4.6	108.6	79.8	151.9	152.6	108.4	67.3	29.2	5.9	0.3
1994	2,300	4.6	104.5	76.3	148.3	146.0	104.0	65.8	28.9	5.9	0.3
1995	2,175	4.2	96.1	69.7	137.1	137.1	98.6	64.0	28.7	6.0	0.3
1996	2,144	3.6	91.4	64.7	132.5	136.8	98.2	63.3	29.1	6.1	0.3
1997	2,154	3.3	88.2	60.8	130.1	139.0	99.5	64.3	29.7	6.5	0.3
1998	2,171	2.9	85.4	56.8	126.9	141.9	101.8	64.7	30.5	6.7	0.3

American Indian

					Birth rate, women aged					
	Total fertility rate	10–14	15–19	15–17	18–19	20–24	25–29	30–34	35–39	40–44	45–49
	Ab96	Ab97	Ab98	Ab99	Ab100	Ab101	Ab102	Ab103	Ab104	Ab105	Ab106 [2]
Year	Per 1,000	Per 1,000	Per 1,000	Per 1,000	Per 1,000	Per 1,000	Per 1,000	Per 1,000	Per 1,000	Per 1,000	Per 1,000
1980 [9]	2,163	1.9	82.2	51.5	129.5	143.7	106.6	61.8	28.1	8.2	—
1981	2,090	2.1	78.4	49.7	121.5	141.2	105.6	58.9	25.2	6.6	—
1982	2,213	1.4	83.5	52.6	127.6	148.1	115.8	60.9	26.9	6.0	—
1983	2,181	1.9	84.2	55.2	121.4	145.5	113.7	58.9	25.5	6.4	—
1984	2,136	1.7	81.5	50.7	124.7	142.4	109.2	60.5	26.3	5.6	—
1985	2,128	1.7	79.2	47.7	124.1	139.1	109.6	62.6	27.4	6.0	—
1986	2,082	1.8	78.1	48.7	125.3	138.8	107.9	60.7	23.8	5.3	—
1987	2,099	1.7	77.2	48.8	122.2	140.0	107.9	63.0	24.4	5.6	—
1988	2,154	1.7	77.5	49.7	121.1	145.2	110.9	64.5	25.6	5.3	—
1989	2,247	1.5	82.7	51.6	128.9	152.4	114.2	64.8	27.4	6.4	—
1990	2,183	1.6	81.1	48.5	129.3	148.7	110.3	61.5	27.5	5.9	—
1991	2,169	1.6	85.0	52.7	134.3	144.9	106.9	61.9	27.2	5.9	0.4
1992	2,190	1.6	84.4	53.8	132.6	145.5	109.4	63.0	28.0	6.1	—
1993	2,141	1.4	83.1	53.7	130.7	139.8	107.6	62.8	27.6	5.9	—
1994	2,080	1.9	80.8	51.3	130.3	134.2	104.1	61.2	27.5	5.9	0.4
1995	2,034	1.8	78.0	47.8	130.7	132.5	98.4	62.2	27.7	6.1	—
1996	2,030	1.7	73.9	46.4	122.3	133.9	98.5	63.2	28.5	6.3	—
1997	2,048	1.7	71.8	45.3	117.6	134.9	100.8	64.2	29.3	6.4	0.4
1998	2,091	1.6	72.1	44.4	118.4	139.3	102.2	66.3	30.2	6.4	—

Notes appear at end of table

(continued)

TABLE Ab52–117   Total fertility rate and birth rate, by race and age: 1800–1998   *Continued*

Asian and Pacific Islander

		Birth rate, women aged									
	Total fertility rate	10–14	15–19	15–17	18–19	20–24	25–29	30–34	35–39	40–44	45–49
	Ab107	Ab108	Ab109	Ab110	Ab111	Ab112	Ab113	Ab114	Ab115	Ab116	Ab117 [2]
Year	Per 1,000	Per 1,000	Per 1,000	Per 1,000	Per 1,000	Per 1,000	Per 1,000	Per 1,000	Per 1,000	Per 1,000	Per 1,000
1980 [9]	1,954	0.3	26.2	12.0	46.2	93.3	127.4	96.0	38.3	8.5	0.7
1981	1,976	0.3	28.5	13.4	49.5	96.4	129.1	93.4	38.0	8.6	0.9
1982	2,016	0.4	29.4	14.0	50.8	98.9	130.9	94.4	39.2	8.8	1.1
1983	1,944	0.5	26.1	12.9	44.5	94.0	126.2	93.3	39.4	8.2	1.0
1984	1,892	0.5	24.2	12.6	40.7	86.7	124.3	92.4	40.6	8.7	1.0
1985	1,885	0.4	23.8	12.5	40.8	83.6	123.0	93.6	42.7	8.7	1.2
1986	1,836	0.5	22.8	12.1	38.8	79.2	119.9	92.6	41.9	9.3	1.0
1987	1,886	0.6	22.4	12.6	37.0	79.7	122.7	97.0	44.2	9.5	1.1
1988	1,984	0.6	24.2	13.6	39.6	80.7	128.0	104.4	47.5	10.3	1.0
1989	1,948	0.6	25.6	15.0	40.4	78.8	124.0	102.3	47.0	10.2	1.0
1990	2,003	0.7	26.4	16.0	40.2	79.2	126.3	106.5	49.6	10.7	1.1
1991	1,956	0.8	27.4	16.1	43.1	75.2	123.2	103.3	49.0	11.2	1.1
1992	1,942	0.7	26.6	15.2	43.1	74.6	121.0	103.0	50.6	11.0	0.9
1993	1,936	0.6	27.0	16.0	43.3	73.3	119.9	103.9	50.2	11.3	0.9
1994	1,943	0.7	27.1	16.1	44.1	73.1	118.6	105.2	51.3	11.6	1.0
1995	1,924	0.7	26.1	15.4	43.4	72.4	113.4	106.9	52.4	12.1	0.8
1996	1,908	0.6	24.6	14.9	40.4	70.7	111.2	109.2	52.2	12.2	0.8
1997	1,926	0.5	23.7	14.3	39.3	70.5	113.2	110.3	54.1	11.9	0.9
1998	1,868	0.4	23.1	13.8	38.3	68.8	110.4	105.1	52.8	12.0	0.9

[1] Based on a 50 percent sample of births for 1951–1954, 1956–1966, and 1968–1971; on a 20–50 percent sample for 1967; and on a 100 percent sample for selected states and a 50 percent sample for all other states for 1972–1984. Beginning in 1970, data exclude births to nonresidents of the United States. Through 1958, births adjusted for underregistration; thereafter, they are registered live births. Data based on race of child through 1979, race of mother thereafter.

[2] Beginning in 1997, rates computed by relating births to women ages 45–54 to those to women ages 45–49.

[3] 1905–1910.

[4] Figures by race exclude New Jersey, which did not require reporting of race.

[5] 1850–1859.

[6] 1860–1869.

[7] 1870–1879.

[8] 1880–1884.

[9] Data for American Indians and for Asians and Pacific Islanders are not available before 1980.

Sources

1800–1930, white population, total fertility rate. Ansley J. Coale and Melvin Zelnik, *New Estimates of Fertility and Population in the United States: A Study of Annual White Births from 1855 to 1960 and of Completeness of Enumeration in the Censuses from 1880 to 1960* (Princeton University Press, 1963), p. 36.

1800–1930, black population, total fertility rate. Ansley J. Coale and Norfleet W. Rives Jr., "A Statistical Reconstruction of the Black Population of the United States, 1880–1970: Estimates of True Numbers by Age and Sex, Birth Rates, and Total Fertility," *Population Index* 31 (4) (1973): 26.

1905–1910, total fertility rates and age–specific birth rates. Michael R. Haines, "American Fertility in Transition: New Estimates of Birth Rates in the United States, 1900–1910," *Demography* 26 (1) (1989), Table 1.

1933–1939. Forrest E. Linder and Robert D. Grove, *Vital Statistics Rates in the United States, 1900–1940* (U.S. Government Printing Office, 1947), Table 46. The rates are adjusted upward on the basis of the annual adjustments implied in *Vital Statistics of the United States, 1993*, volume 1, *Natality*, Tables 1–1 and 1–2.

1940–1959. U.S. Public Health Service, *Vital Statistics of the United States, 1968*, volume 1, Table 1.

1960–1997. U.S. Public Health Service, National Center for Health Statistics, *Vital Statistics of the United States, 1993*, volume 1, *Natality*, Table 1-9; *National Vital Statistics Report*, volume 48, number 3, "Births: Final Data for 1998," Table 4.

Documentation
Birth rates are live births per 1,000 women in the specified groups. Total fertility rates are the sums of birth rates, by age of mother, multiplied by 5. The total fertility rate is an age–adjusted rate because it is based on the assumption that there is the same number of women in each age group. The rate of 2,027 in 1996, for example, means that if a hypothetical group of 1,000 women were to have the same birth rate in each age group observed in the actual childbearing population in 1996, the women would have a total of 2,027 children by the time they reached the end of the reproductive period (taken here as age 50), assuming that all of the women survive to that age.

Also see the text for Table Ab11–30.

Series Ab63 and Ab85. Numbers for 1890–1930 are arithmetic averages for the two quinquennia surrounding the year.

TABLE Ab118–149   Birth rate, by race and live birth order: 1940–1998[1]

Contributed by Michael R. Haines

	All races									White		
	Total	First births	Second births	Third births	Fourth births	Fifth births	Sixth and seventh births	Eighth and later births		Total	First births	Second births
	Ab118	Ab119	Ab120	Ab121	Ab122	Ab123	Ab124	Ab125		Ab126	Ab127	Ab128
Year	Per 1,000	Per 1,000	Per 1,000	Per 1,000	Per 1,000	Per 1,000	Per 1,000	Per 1,000		Per 1,000	Per 1,000	Per 1,000
1940	79.9	29.3	20.0	10.9	6.4	4.1	4.8	4.3		77.1	29.4	20.0
1941	83.4	32.2	20.7	11.2	6.4	4.1	4.7	4.1		80.7	32.5	20.7
1942	91.5	37.5	22.9	11.9	6.6	4.1	4.6	3.9		89.5	38.3	23.1
1943	94.3	34.7	25.5	13.5	7.4	4.4	4.8	4.0		92.3	35.2	25.9
1944	88.8	30.2	23.8	13.8	7.6	4.5	4.9	4.0		86.3	30.4	24.2
1945	85.9	28.9	22.9	13.4	7.5	4.5	4.8	4.0		83.4	29.0	23.3
1946	101.9	38.5	27.9	14.5	7.8	4.5	4.7	3.8		100.4	39.5	28.5
1947	113.3	46.7	30.3	15.6	7.9	4.5	4.6	3.7		111.8	47.8	30.8
1948	107.3	39.6	30.9	16.1	8.0	4.5	4.6	3.6		104.3	39.9	31.1
1949	107.1	36.2	32.1	17.1	8.6	4.7	4.7	3.7		103.6	36.3	32.2
1950	106.2	33.3	32.1	18.4	9.2	4.8	4.7	3.6		102.3	33.3	32.3
1951	111.5	34.9	32.6	20.0	10.2	5.3	5.0	3.6		107.7	35.0	32.9
1952	113.9	34.0	32.7	21.3	11.3	5.8	5.2	3.6		110.0	34.1	33.1
1953	115.2	33.4	32.5	21.9	12.0	6.3	5.5	3.6		111.0	33.3	32.9
1954	118.1	33.6	32.4	22.7	12.8	6.8	6.0	3.8		113.6	33.3	32.8
1955	118.5	32.9	31.9	23.1	13.3	7.2	6.4	3.8		113.8	32.6	32.0
1956	121.2	33.5	31.9	23.6	13.9	7.6	6.8	4.0		116.0	33.2	31.9
1957	122.9	33.7	31.7	23.9	14.4	7.9	7.1	4.2		117.7	33.4	31.7
1958	120.2	32.2	30.6	23.3	14.4	8.1	7.3	4.2		114.9	31.9	30.6
1959	118.8	31.5	29.9	23.0	14.5	8.2	7.4	4.2		113.9	31.2	29.9
1960	118.0	31.1	29.2	22.8	14.4	8.3	7.6	4.3		113.2	30.8	29.2
1961	117.1	30.9	28.3	22.4	14.6	8.5	7.9	4.5		112.3	30.6	28.3
1962 [2]	112.0	29.9	26.9	21.0	13.8	8.2	7.6	4.5		107.5	29.6	26.8
1963 [2]	108.3	29.9	26.1	19.9	13.1	7.8	7.3	4.3		103.6	29.4	25.9
1964	104.7	30.3	25.1	18.7	12.2	7.3	6.9	4.1		99.8	29.8	24.8
1965	96.3	29.7	23.3	16.6	10.7	6.4	6.0	3.7		91.3	28.9	22.9
1966	90.8	30.9	22.4	14.7	9.1	5.4	5.2	3.1		86.2	30.0	21.9
1967	87.2	30.7	22.5	13.9	8.3	4.8	4.5	2.7		82.8	29.6	22.1
1968	85.2	31.9	22.4	13.1	7.5	4.2	3.9	2.3		81.3	30.8	22.0
1969	86.1	32.6	23.3	13.4	7.3	4.0	3.5	2.0		82.2	31.4	22.9
1970	87.9	34.2	24.2	13.6	7.2	3.8	3.2	1.8		84.1	32.9	23.7
1971	81.6	32.0	23.1	12.5	6.4	3.3	2.8	1.5		77.3	30.5	22.5
1972	73.1	29.8	21.4	10.6	5.3	2.6	2.2	1.2		68.9	28.1	20.9
1973	68.8	28.6	21.0	9.8	4.5	2.2	1.8	0.9		64.9	27.0	20.4
1974	67.8	28.7	21.4	9.5	4.1	1.9	1.5	0.8		64.2	27.2	20.8
1975	66.0	28.1	20.9	9.4	3.9	1.7	1.3	0.7		62.5	26.7	20.3
1976	65.0	27.5	20.8	9.5	3.8	1.6	1.2	0.6		61.5	26.3	20.2
1977	66.8	28.2	21.6	10.0	3.8	1.6	1.1	0.5		63.2	26.9	20.9
1978	65.5	27.8	21.1	9.8	3.8	1.5	1.0	0.4		61.7	26.6	20.2
1979	67.2	28.6	21.6	10.1	3.8	1.5	1.0	0.4		63.4	27.4	20.8
1980	68.4	29.5	21.8	10.3	3.9	1.5	1.0	0.4		65.6	28.8	21.3
1981	67.3	29.0	21.6	10.1	3.8	1.5	0.9	0.4		64.8	28.4	21.1
1982	67.3	28.6	22.0	10.2	3.8	1.4	0.9	0.3		64.8	28.0	21.6
1983	65.7	27.8	21.5	10.1	3.7	1.4	0.9	0.3		63.4	27.2	21.2
1984	65.5	27.4	21.7	10.1	3.7	1.4	0.9	0.3		63.2	26.8	21.4
1985	66.3	27.6	22.0	10.4	3.8	1.4	0.8	0.3		64.1	27.0	21.8
1986	65.4	27.2	21.6	10.3	3.8	1.4	0.8	0.3		63.1	26.6	21.3
1987	65.8	27.2	21.6	10.5	3.9	1.4	0.8	0.3		63.3	26.5	21.3
1988	67.3	27.6	22.0	10.9	4.1	1.5	0.9	0.3		64.5	26.8	21.6
1989	69.2	28.4	22.4	11.3	4.3	1.6	0.9	0.3		66.4	27.6	21.9
1990	70.9	29.0	22.8	11.7	4.5	1.7	1.0	0.3		68.3	28.4	22.4
1991	69.6	28.3	22.4	11.4	4.5	1.7	1.0	0.3		67.0	27.8	22.0
1992	68.9	27.8	22.3	11.3	4.4	1.7	1.0	0.3		66.5	27.3	22.0
1993	67.6	27.5	21.9	11.0	4.3	1.6	1.0	0.3		65.4	27.0	21.7
1994	66.7	27.5	21.5	10.7	4.2	1.6	1.0	0.3		64.9	27.0	21.4
1995	65.6	27.3	21.1	10.5	4.0	1.5	0.9	0.3		64.4	26.9	21.1
1996	65.3	26.8	21.1	10.5	4.1	1.5	0.9	0.3		64.3	26.6	21.2
1997	65.0	26.5	21.1	10.6	4.1	1.5	0.9	0.3		63.9	26.2	21.2
1998	65.6	26.4	21.4	10.8	4.2	1.5	0.9	0.3		64.9	26.1	21.5

Notes appear at end of table   (continued)

TABLE Ab118–149 Birth rate, by race and live birth order: 1940–1998 *Continued*

	White					All nonwhite					
	Third births	Fourth births	Fifth births	Sixth and seventh births	Eighth and later births	Total	First births	Second births	Third births	Fourth births	Fifth births
	Ab129	Ab130	Ab131	Ab132	Ab133	Ab134	Ab135	Ab136	Ab137	Ab138	Ab139
Year	Per 1,000	Per 1,000	Per 1,000	Per 1,000	Per 1,000	Per 1,000	Per 1,000	Per 1,000	Per 1,000	Per 1,000	Per 1,000
1940	10.5	5.9	3.6	4.1	3.5	102.4	28.6	19.6	14.1	10.5	7.8
1941	10.7	5.9	3.6	3.9	3.2	105.4	29.8	20.6	14.5	10.6	8.0
1942	11.5	6.1	3.6	3.8	3.1	107.6	31.0	21.1	14.9	10.8	8.1
1943	13.2	6.9	3.9	4.0	3.1	111.0	31.0	22.2	15.5	11.4	8.4
1944	13.6	7.1	4.0	4.1	3.1	108.5	28.7	21.1	15.6	11.7	8.6
1945	13.2	7.0	3.9	4.0	3.0	106.0	27.9	20.1	14.7	11.3	8.7
1946	14.4	7.3	4.0	3.9	2.8	113.9	31.1	23.4	16.0	11.8	8.7
1947	15.3	7.4	4.0	3.8	2.7	125.9	38.4	26.2	17.3	12.1	8.8
1948	15.7	7.4	3.9	3.7	2.6	131.6	37.3	29.5	19.4	12.9	9.2
1949	16.6	7.9	4.0	3.8	2.7	135.1	35.4	30.8	21.2	14.0	9.8
1950	17.9	8.4	4.1	3.7	2.5	137.3	33.8	30.3	22.9	15.3	10.4
1951	19.5	9.4	4.5	3.9	2.5	142.1	34.1	29.9	23.9	16.9	11.2
1952	21.0	10.4	5.0	4.0	2.5	143.3	33.1	29.2	24.0	18.1	12.4
1953	21.6	11.1	5.4	4.3	2.5	147.2	34.1	29.5	23.8	18.4	13.3
1954	22.6	12.0	5.9	4.6	2.5	153.2	35.6	29.7	24.4	19.1	14.2
1955	22.9	12.6	6.2	4.9	2.5	155.3	35.0	30.7	24.4	19.1	14.6
1956	23.4	13.1	6.6	5.2	2.6	160.9	35.9	31.7	25.2	19.7	15.0
1957	23.7	13.7	7.0	5.6	2.7	163.0	36.1	31.6	25.7	19.8	15.3
1958	23.1	13.8	7.2	5.7	2.7	160.5	34.7	31.0	25.4	19.5	14.9
1959	22.9	13.9	7.3	5.9	2.8	156.0	33.9	29.8	24.4	19.1	14.5
1960	22.7	14.1	7.5	6.1	2.8	153.6	33.6	29.3	24.0	18.6	14.1
1961	22.2	14.0	7.7	6.4	3.0	153.0	33.5	28.7	23.6	18.7	14.0
1962 [2]	20.8	13.3	7.5	6.3	3.0	147.8	32.9	27.8	22.7	17.7	13.6
1963 [2]	19.6	12.6	7.1	6.1	2.9	143.7	33.5	27.4	21.6	16.8	13.0
1964	18.4	11.7	6.7	5.7	2.7	140.0	34.4	27.1	20.9	15.8	12.0
1965	16.2	10.1	5.8	5.0	2.4	131.9	35.3	26.2	19.3	14.4	10.7
1966	14.3	8.6	4.9	4.3	2.1	123.5	36.6	25.5	17.7	12.6	9.2
1967	13.5	7.8	4.3	3.7	1.8	117.1	37.6	25.3	16.5	11.2	7.9
1968	12.8	7.1	3.8	3.2	1.6	111.9	39.5	24.6	15.3	10.1	6.8
1969	13.1	7.0	3.6	2.9	1.4	111.6	41.0	25.6	15.4	9.8	6.5
1970	13.3	6.8	3.4	2.7	1.2	113.0	42.4	26.9	15.9	9.7	6.1
1971	12.0	6.0	3.0	2.3	1.0	109.1	41.6	26.8	15.5	9.0	5.6
1972	10.1	4.9	2.3	1.8	0.8	99.5	40.6	25.0	13.7	7.7	4.6
1973	9.2	4.1	1.9	1.5	0.7	93.4	38.8	24.4	13.0	6.9	3.9
1974	9.0	3.8	1.7	1.2	0.6	89.8	37.7	24.7	12.5	6.3	3.3
1975	8.8	3.5	1.5	1.1	0.5	87.7	36.7	24.6	12.6	6.1	3.1
1976	8.9	3.4	1.4	1.0	0.4	85.8	35.2	24.7	12.8	6.0	3.0
1977	9.4	3.4	1.4	0.9	0.4	87.7	35.6	25.7	13.5	6.2	3.0
1978	9.2	3.3	1.3	0.8	0.3	87.0	35.0	25.8	13.8	6.3	2.9
1979	9.4	3.4	1.3	0.8	0.3	88.5	35.7	26.2	14.2	6.4	2.9
1980	9.6	3.4	1.3	0.8	0.3	83.9	33.5	24.8	13.7	6.3	2.8
1981	9.5	3.4	1.2	0.8	0.3	81.1	32.0	24.2	13.4	6.1	2.7
1982	9.6	3.4	1.2	0.7	0.3	80.3	31.5	24.0	13.4	6.1	2.7
1983	9.5	3.3	1.2	0.7	0.2	77.9	30.9	23.2	12.9	5.9	2.6
1984	9.6	3.3	1.2	0.7	0.2	77.0	30.5	23.0	12.8	5.8	2.5
1985	9.9	3.4	1.2	0.7	0.2	77.3	30.5	23.2	12.9	5.9	2.6
1986	9.8	3.4	1.2	0.7	0.2	76.8	30.3	23.0	12.6	5.8	2.5
1987	10.0	3.5	1.2	0.7	0.2	77.8	30.6	23.3	13.1	5.9	2.6
1988	10.4	3.6	1.2	0.7	0.2	80.3	31.3	24.1	13.6	6.2	2.7
1989	10.7	3.8	1.3	0.7	0.2	82.7	32.0	24.6	14.2	6.5	2.9
1990	11.1	4.0	1.4	0.8	0.2	83.2	31.7	24.7	14.4	6.7	3.0
1991	10.8	4.0	1.4	0.8	0.2	81.5	30.9	24.2	14.1	6.7	3.0
1992	10.8	4.0	1.4	0.8	0.2	79.5	30.1	23.6	13.7	6.5	3.0
1993	10.5	3.9	1.4	0.8	0.2	77.3	29.7	22.9	13.0	6.2	2.8
1994	10.4	3.8	1.3	0.8	0.2	—	—	—	—	—	—
1995	10.3	3.8	1.3	0.7	0.2	—	—	—	—	—	—
1996	10.4	3.8	1.3	0.8	0.2	—	—	—	—	—	—
1997	10.4	3.8	1.3	0.8	0.2	—	—	—	—	—	—
1998	10.7	3.9	1.3	0.8	0.2	—	—	—	—	—	—

Notes appear at end of table

TABLE Ab118–149   Birth rate, by race and live birth order: 1940–1998   *Continued*

	All nonwhite		Black								
	Sixth and seventh births	Eighth and later births	Total	First births	Second births	Third births	Fourth births	Fifth births	Sixth and seventh births	Eighth and later births
	Ab140	Ab141	Ab142	Ab143	Ab144	Ab145	Ab146	Ab147	Ab148	Ab149
Year	Per 1,000	Per 1,000	Per 1,000	Per 1,000	Per 1,000	Per 1,000	Per 1,000	Per 1,000	Per 1,000	Per 1,000
1940	10.4	11.3	—	—	—	—	—	—	—	—
1941	10.6	11.3	—	—	—	—	—	—	—	—
1942	10.5	11.1	—	—	—	—	—	—	—	—
1943	11.0	11.6	—	—	—	—	—	—	—	—
1944	11.3	11.6	—	—	—	—	—	—	—	—
1945	11.3	11.9	—	—	—	—	—	—	—	—
1946	11.3	11.7	—	—	—	—	—	—	—	—
1947	11.4	11.6	—	—	—	—	—	—	—	—
1948	11.7	11.6	—	—	—	—	—	—	—	—
1949	12.2	11.8	—	—	—	—	—	—	—	—
1950	12.6	12.0	—	—	—	—	—	—	—	—
1951	13.5	12.2	—	—	—	—	—	—	—	—
1952	14.2	12.4	—	—	—	—	—	—	—	—
1953	15.4	12.8	—	—	—	—	—	—	—	—
1954	16.5	13.5	—	—	—	—	—	—	—	—
1955	17.4	14.1	—	—	—	—	—	—	—	—
1956	18.7	15.0	—	—	—	—	—	—	—	—
1957	19.0	15.6	—	—	—	—	—	—	—	—
1958	19.1	15.9	—	—	—	—	—	—	—	—
1959	18.7	15.6	—	—	—	—	—	—	—	—
1960	18.4	15.6	153.5	33.6	29.3	24.0	18.6	14.1	18.4	15.6
1961	18.4	16.0	—	—	—	—	—	—	—	—
1962 [2]	17.5	15.6	—	—	—	—	—	—	—	—
1963 [2]	16.4	15.0	—	—	—	—	—	—	—	—
1964	15.6	14.3	142.6	35.0	27.3	21.1	16.1	12.3	16.1	14.7
1965	13.6	12.4	133.2	35.6	26.1	19.3	14.5	10.9	14.0	12.7
1966	11.4	10.5	124.7	36.9	25.5	17.7	12.7	9.4	11.7	10.8
1967	9.9	8.8	118.5	38.0	25.3	16.5	11.4	8.1	10.1	9.1
1968	8.3	7.2	112.7	39.8	24.4	15.3	10.2	7.0	8.5	7.5
1969	7.2	6.1	112.1	41.2	25.4	15.4	9.9	6.6	7.4	6.3
1970	6.7	5.3	115.4	43.3	27.1	16.1	10.0	6.4	7.0	5.6
1971	5.9	4.6	109.7	41.7	26.6	15.5	9.2	5.7	6.2	4.6
1972	4.6	3.4	99.9	40.7	24.6	13.7	7.9	4.7	4.8	3.6
1973	3.7	2.6	93.6	38.9	24.0	13.0	7.0	4.0	3.9	2.8
1974	3.1	2.1	89.7	37.7	24.2	12.6	6.5	3.4	3.3	2.2
1975	2.8	1.8	87.9	36.9	24.2	12.6	6.3	3.2	2.9	1.9
1976	2.5	1.5	85.8	35.2	24.4	12.9	6.2	3.1	2.6	1.5
1977	2.4	1.3	88.1	35.6	25.5	13.6	6.4	3.1	2.4	1.4
1978	2.2	1.1	86.7	34.6	25.4	13.9	6.5	3.0	2.3	1.1
1979	2.1	1.0	88.3	35.3	25.8	14.4	6.6	3.0	2.2	1.0
1980	2.0	0.9	84.9	33.7	24.7	14.0	6.5	2.9	2.1	0.9
1981	1.9	0.8	82.0	32.3	24.2	13.7	6.3	2.8	1.9	0.8
1982	1.8	0.7	80.9	31.7	23.9	13.8	6.3	2.7	1.8	0.7
1983	1.8	0.6	78.7	31.1	23.1	13.2	6.1	2.7	1.8	0.6
1984	1.7	0.6	78.1	30.9	23.0	13.2	6.0	2.6	1.7	0.6
1985	1.7	0.6	78.8	31.0	23.4	13.4	6.1	2.6	1.7	0.5
1986	1.7	0.6	78.9	31.0	23.4	13.5	6.1	2.6	1.7	0.5
1987	1.7	0.6	80.1	31.2	23.8	13.9	6.3	2.7	1.7	0.5
1988	1.8	0.6	82.6	31.8	24.6	14.4	6.6	2.8	1.8	0.5
1989	1.9	0.6	86.2	32.9	25.4	15.3	7.1	3.0	1.9	0.6
1990	2.0	0.7	86.8	32.4	25.6	15.6	7.4	3.2	2.0	0.6
1991	2.0	0.7	85.2	31.5	25.0	15.4	7.4	3.3	2.1	0.6
1992	2.0	0.7	83.2	30.6	24.3	15.0	7.2	3.3	2.2	0.6
1993	2.0	0.7	80.5	30.2	23.4	14.1	6.9	3.1	2.2	0.7
1994	—	—	76.9	29.8	22.2	13.1	6.3	2.9	2.0	0.6
1995	—	—	72.3	28.7	20.7	12.0	5.7	2.6	1.8	0.6
1996	—	—	70.7	27.6	20.5	12.0	5.6	2.6	1.8	0.6
1997	—	—	70.7	27.3	20.7	12.1	5.7	2.5	1.8	0.6
1998	—	—	71.0	27.0	21.1	12.3	5.7	2.6	1.7	0.6

Notes appear on next page

(continued)

TABLE Ab118–149   Birth rate, by race and live birth order: 1940–1998   *Continued*

[1] Based on a 50 percent sample of births for 1951–1954, 1956–1966, and 1968–1970; based on a 20–50 percent sample for 1967. Through 1958, births are adjusted for underregistration; thereafter, they are registered live births. Data are based on race of child through 1979 and race of mother thereafter. Figures for unknown live birth order have been distributed.

[2] Figures by race exclude New Jersey, which did not require reporting of race.

Sources

1940–1959: U.S. Public Health Service, *Vital Statistics of the United States, 1968*, volume 1, Table 1-8. 1960–1997: U.S. Public Health Service, National Center

for Health Statistics, *Vital Statistics of the United States, 1993*, volume 1, *Natality*, Table 1-11; *National Vital Statistics Report*, volume 48, number 3, "Births: Final Data for 1998," Table 5.

Documentation

Rates are live births per 1,000 women ages 15–44 in the specified group. Live birth order refers to the number of children born alive to the mother.

Also see the text for Table Ab11–30.

TABLE Ab150–215   First birth rate, by age and race: 1940–1998[1]

Contributed by Michael R. Haines

	All races, by age										
	15–44	10–14	15–19	15–17	18–19	20–24	25–29	30–34	35–39	40–44	45–49
	Ab150	Ab151	Ab152	Ab153	Ab154	Ab155	Ab156	Ab157	Ab158	Ab159	Ab160 [2]
Year	Per 1,000	Per 1,000	Per 1,000	Per 1,000	Per 1,000	Per 1,000	Per 1,000	Per 1,000	Per 1,000	Per 1,000	Per 1,000
1940	29.3	0.6	39.8	—	—	63.3	37.8	15.4	4.5	0.8	0.1
1941	32.2	0.7	42.4	—	—	71.6	42.0	16.8	4.9	0.8	0.1
1942	37.5	0.7	46.4	—	—	85.8	50.0	19.6	5.8	0.9	0.1
1943	34.7	0.8	46.2	—	—	77.8	44.1	18.7	6.3	1.0	0.1
1944	30.2	0.7	40.2	—	—	70.1	36.0	16.1	6.2	1.1	0.1
1945	28.9	0.8	38.5	—	—	67.1	34.4	15.7	6.4	1.2	0.1
1946	38.5	0.7	45.4	—	—	93.4	50.6	20.6	7.6	1.4	0.1
1947	46.7	0.9	63.2	—	—	114.2	57.5	22.8	8.2	1.5	0.1
1948	39.6	0.9	62.2	—	—	95.8	45.3	18.0	6.8	1.3	0.1
1949	36.2	0.9	60.1	—	—	87.3	40.9	16.0	6.2	1.3	0.1
1950	33.3	0.9	57.7	—	—	80.2	37.1	14.5	5.7	1.2	0.1
1951	34.9	0.9	62.7	—	—	86.8	38.1	14.4	5.4	1.2	0.1
1952	34.0	0.9	61.1	—	—	87.0	37.3	14.0	5.3	1.2	0.1
1953	33.4	0.9	62.7	—	—	86.8	35.5	13.0	5.0	1.2	0.1
1954	33.6	1.0	64.5	—	—	89.9	34.3	12.6	4.8	1.1	0.1
1955	32.9	0.9	63.7	—	—	90.5	33.0	11.5	4.5	1.1	0.1
1956	33.5	0.9	66.5	—	—	94.0	32.2	10.9	4.2	1.0	0.1
1957	33.7	0.9	67.7	—	—	94.5	31.7	10.5	4.0	1.0	0.1
1958	32.2	0.9	63.3	—	—	91.0	29.6	9.8	3.7	0.9	0.1
1959	31.7	0.9	62.4	—	—	89.1	27.9	9.3	3.5	0.8	(Z)
1960	31.1	0.8	61.4	37.3	105.4	87.9	26.6	8.6	3.2	0.8	(Z)
1961	30.9	0.8	61.3	35.5	99.5	85.7	25.6	8.1	3.0	0.7	(Z)
1962 [3]	29.9	0.8	56.1	30.9	96.5	82.5	24.6	7.4	2.7	0.7	(Z)
1963 [3]	29.9	0.8	53.8	30.3	95.7	81.2	24.3	7.2	2.6	0.6	(Z)
1964	30.3	0.8	52.3	30.7	94.1	80.4	25.2	7.7	2.9	0.7	(Z)
1965	29.7	0.8	51.6	30.5	85.2	75.4	24.6	7.2	2.7	0.6	(Z)
1966	30.9	0.8	52.7	30.1	85.3	77.5	25.7	7.1	2.6	0.6	(Z)
1967	30.7	0.8	50.8	29.8	82.9	74.8	26.4	6.5	2.2	0.5	(Z)
1968	31.9	0.9	50.5	30.1	82.5	76.1	29.6	7.3	2.4	0.5	(Z)
1969	32.6	1.0	50.8	30.9	82.2	76.8	30.1	7.0	2.1	0.5	(Z)
1970	34.2	1.1	53.7	33.8	84.9	78.2	31.2	7.3	2.1	0.4	(Z)
1971	32.0	1.1	50.7	33.3	77.6	68.9	30.2	7.0	1.9	0.4	(Z)
1972	29.8	1.2	49.1	34.5	71.9	60.6	29.2	7.0	1.8	0.3	(Z)
1973	28.6	1.2	47.3	34.2	67.5	56.0	29.7	7.2	1.7	0.3	(Z)
1974	28.7	1.2	45.6	33.0	64.9	55.8	31.5	7.7	1.8	0.3	(Z)
1975	28.1	1.2	43.9	32.0	61.8	54.0	31.4	8.0	1.9	0.3	(Z)
1976	27.5	1.2	41.4	30.1	58.2	52.9	31.7	8.7	1.9	0.3	(Z)
1977	28.2	1.2	41.3	29.8	58.4	54.1	34.2	9.7	2.0	0.3	(Z)
1978	27.8	1.1	40.2	28.3	57.7	53.1	34.8	10.8	2.2	0.3	(Z)
1979	28.6	1.2	40.9	28.4	59.0	55.0	36.5	11.8	2.4	0.3	(Z)
1980	29.5	1.1	41.4	28.5	59.7	57.3	38.2	12.8	2.6	0.3	(Z)
1981	29.0	1.0	40.7	28.0	58.2	55.9	38.6	13.3	2.8	0.4	(Z)
1982	28.6	1.1	40.7	28.2	57.4	54.8	38.4	14.6	3.3	0.4	(Z)
1983	27.8	1.1	38.9	27.8	56.1	52.7	37.9	15.4	3.7	0.4	(Z)
1984	27.4	1.1	39.1	27.0	55.8	52.1	38.1	16.3	4.1	0.5	(Z)

Notes appear at end of table

TABLE Ab150–215   First birth rate, by age and race: 1940–1998 *Continued*

	All races, by age										
	15–44	10–14	15–19	15–17	18–19	20–24	25–29	30–34	35–39	40–44	45–49
	Ab150	Ab151	Ab152	Ab153	Ab154	Ab155	Ab156	Ab157	Ab158	Ab159	Ab160 [2]
Year	Per 1,000	Per 1,000	Per 1,000	Per 1,000	Per 1,000	Per 1,000	Per 1,000	Per 1,000	Per 1,000	Per 1,000	Per 1,000
1985	27.6	1.2	39.4	27.0	57.2	52.7	38.9	17.0	4.5	0.5	(Z)
1986	27.2	1.2	38.8	26.6	57.1	52.3	39.0	17.7	4.7	0.6	(Z)
1987	27.2	1.3	39.0	27.5	55.9	52.1	40.1	18.6	5.3	0.7	(Z)
1988	27.6	1.3	40.5	28.9	56.6	52.5	41.5	19.4	5.7	0.8	(Z)
1989	28.4	1.4	43.5	31.1	59.5	54.0	42.8	20.2	6.3	0.9	(Z)
1990	29.0	1.3	45.1	31.9	62.0	55.2	44.1	21.2	6.7	1.0	(Z)
1991	28.3	1.3	48.5	32.9	65.3	54.7	43.1	20.9	6.8	1.0	(Z)
1992	27.8	1.3	45.2	32.0	64.7	53.4	42.8	21.2	6.9	1.1	(Z)
1993	27.5	1.3	45.3	32.5	64.4	52.9	42.5	21.7	7.1	1.2	0.1
1994	27.5	1.4	45.8	32.8	65.6	52.9	42.3	22.3	7.3	1.3	0.1
1995	27.3	1.3	44.6	31.6	64.8	52.7	42.6	22.9	7.5	1.4	0.1
1996	26.8	1.2	42.5	29.8	62.0	52.0	42.7	23.4	7.8	1.4	0.1
1997	26.5	1.1	40.8	28.3	60.2	51.2	42.7	24.0	8.0	1.5	0.1
1998	26.4	1.0	39.9	27.0	59.2	50.8	42.5	24.6	8.3	1.5	0.1

	White, by age										
	15–44	10–14	15–19	15–17	18–19	20–24	25–29	30–34	35–39	40–44	45–49
	Ab161	Ab162	Ab163	Ab164	Ab165	Ab166	Ab167	Ab168	Ab169	Ab170	Ab171 [2]
Year	Per 1,000	Per 1,000	Per 1,000	Per 1,000	Per 1,000	Per 1,000	Per 1,000	Per 1,000	Per 1,000	Per 1,000	Per 1,000
1940	29.4	0.2	34.6	—	—	65.8	41.0	16.6	4.8	0.8	0.1
1941	32.5	0.2	37.1	—	—	74.7	45.6	18.1	5.3	0.9	(Z)
1942	38.3	0.3	41.3	—	—	90.3	54.4	21.2	6.3	0.9	(Z)
1943	35.2	0.3	41.0	—	—	81.4	47.7	20.1	6.7	1.1	0.1
1944	30.4	0.3	35.4	—	—	73.1	38.6	17.1	6.6	1.2	0.1
1945	29.0	0.3	33.6	—	—	69.8	36.7	16.7	6.8	1.3	0.1
1946	39.5	0.3	40.9	—	—	98.2	54.5	22.0	8.1	1.4	0.1
1947	47.8	0.4	58.6	—	—	119.7	61.7	24.3	8.8	1.5	0.1
1948	39.9	0.4	57.0	—	—	99.5	48.0	19.0	7.2	1.4	0.1
1949	36.3	0.4	55.0	—	—	90.8	43.2	16.7	6.5	1.4	0.1
1950	33.3	0.4	52.4	—	—	83.5	39.1	15.1	5.9	1.3	0.1
1951	35.0	0.4	57.6	—	—	91.0	40.2	15.0	5.6	1.2	0.1
1952	34.1	0.3	56.2	—	—	91.4	39.2	14.5	5.5	1.2	0.1
1953	33.3	0.3	57.7	—	—	90.9	37.2	13.4	5.1	1.2	0.1
1954	33.3	0.4	59.1	—	—	93.9	35.8	13.0	4.9	1.2	0.1
1955	32.6	0.4	58.5	—	—	94.4	34.4	11.9	4.6	1.1	0.1
1956	33.2	0.4	61.5	—	—	98.0	33.6	11.2	4.3	1.0	0.1
1957	33.4	0.4	62.9	—	—	98.5	33.2	10.9	4.1	1.0	0.1
1958	31.9	0.4	58.8	—	—	94.8	31.0	10.1	3.8	0.9	0.1
1959	31.3	0.4	57.7	—	—	92.7	29.1	9.5	3.5	0.8	(Z)
1960	30.8	0.3	57.2	22.0	103.5	91.5	27.7	8.9	3.3	0.8	(Z)
1961	30.6	0.4	57.2	29.9	97.5	89.1	26.6	8.3	3.0	0.7	(Z)
1962 [3]	29.6	0.4	52.6	25.0	92.3	85.3	25.2	7.5	2.7	0.7	(Z)
1963 [3]	29.4	0.3	50.0	24.4	91.4	83.4	24.8	7.3	2.6	0.6	(Z)
1964	29.8	0.3	47.6	25.2	90.8	82.9	26.3	7.9	2.9	0.7	(Z)
1965	28.9	0.3	46.7	24.4	81.6	77.2	25.4	7.4	2.8	0.7	(Z)
1966	30.0	0.3	47.6	23.6	81.5	79.4	26.6	7.2	2.6	0.6	(Z)
1967	29.6	0.3	45.0	22.8	78.2	76.2	27.5	6.7	2.2	0.5	(Z)
1968	30.8	0.4	44.3	23.0	77.4	77.4	30.8	7.4	2.5	0.5	(Z)
1969	31.4	0.4	44.4	23.8	76.7	77.9	31.2	7.0	2.1	0.4	(Z)
1970	32.9	0.5	47.1	26.4	79.3	79.4	32.3	7.4	2.1	0.4	(Z)
1971	30.5	0.5	43.9	25.8	71.7	69.5	31.1	7.0	1.9	0.4	(Z)
1972	28.1	0.5	42.1	28.8	65.7	60.7	29.9	6.9	1.8	0.3	(Z)
1973	27.0	0.6	40.6	26.8	61.7	56.1	30.6	7.2	1.7	0.3	(Z)
1974	27.2	0.6	39.2	26.1	59.3	56.1	32.4	7.7	1.7	0.3	(Z)
1975	26.7	0.6	37.8	25.4	56.3	54.2	32.3	7.9	1.8	0.3	(Z)
1976	26.3	0.6	35.7	23.9	53.1	53.0	32.7	8.8	1.9	0.3	(Z)
1977	26.9	0.6	35.5	23.6	53.1	54.2	35.5	9.7	2.0	0.3	(Z)
1978	26.6	0.6	34.6	22.4	52.4	53.0	36.0	10.9	2.1	0.3	(Z)
1979	27.4	0.6	35.2	22.3	53.8	54.8	37.9	11.8	2.3	0.3	(Z)

Notes appear at end of table

(continued)

TABLE Ab150–215   First birth rate, by age and race: 1940–1998   *Continued*

	White, by age										
	15–44	10–14	15–19	15–17	18–19	20–24	25–29	30–34	35–39	40–44	45–49
	Ab161	Ab162	Ab163	Ab164	Ab165	Ab166	Ab167	Ab168	Ab169	Ab170	Ab171 [2]
Year	Per 1,000	Per 1,000	Per 1,000	Per 1,000	Per 1,000	Per 1,000	Per 1,000	Per 1,000	Per 1,000	Per 1,000	Per 1,000
1980	28.8	0.6	36.5	23.0	55.5	58.0	40.1	13.0	2.5	0.3	(Z)
1981	28.4	0.5	36.2	22.8	54.3	56.6	40.5	13.7	2.8	0.3	(Z)
1982	28.0	0.6	36.0	22.9	53.4	55.3	40.3	15.1	3.3	0.4	(Z)
1983	27.2	0.6	35.1	22.5	51.8	53.0	39.7	16.1	3.7	0.4	(Z)
1984	26.8	0.6	34.2	21.7	51.4	52.3	39.9	17.0	4.1	0.5	(Z)
1985	27.0	0.6	34.6	21.9	52.8	52.9	40.7	17.5	4.5	0.5	(Z)
1986	26.6	0.6	33.9	21.3	52.6	52.2	40.8	18.5	4.8	0.6	(Z)
1987	26.5	0.6	33.9	22.0	51.5	51.7	41.9	19.3	5.4	0.7	(Z)
1988	26.8	0.6	35.3	23.2	51.9	52.0	43.1	20.0	5.8	0.8	(Z)
1989	27.6	0.7	38.0	25.0	54.4	53.6	44.5	20.9	6.5	0.9	(Z)
1990	28.4	0.7	40.1	26.1	57.8	55.1	45.9	22.0	6.9	1.0	(Z)
1991	27.8	0.7	41.5	27.1	61.5	54.7	45.0	21.7	7.0	1.0	(Z)
1992	27.3	0.7	40.5	26.5	61.1	53.4	44.7	22.0	7.1	1.1	(Z)
1993	27.0	0.8	40.6	27.0	60.9	53.1	44.4	22.4	7.3	1.2	0.1
1994	27.0	0.8	41.1	27.6	61.8	53.2	44.3	23.0	7.5	1.3	0.1
1995	26.9	0.8	40.8	27.0	61.5	53.3	44.7	23.8	7.7	1.4	0.1
1996	26.6	0.7	38.7	25.6	58.8	52.8	45.0	24.3	8.0	1.5	0.1
1997	26.2	0.7	37.1	24.3	56.8	51.6	45.0	24.9	8.2	1.5	0.1
1998	26.1	0.6	36.4	23.4	55.8	51.0	44.8	25.7	8.4	1.6	0.1

	All nonwhite, by age										
	15–44	10–14	15–19	15–17	18–19	20–24	25–29	30–34	35–39	40–44	45–49
	Ab172	Ab173	Ab174	Ab175	Ab176	Ab177	Ab178	Ab179	Ab180	Ab181	Ab182 [2]
Year	Per 1,000	Per 1,000	Per 1,000	Per 1,000	Per 1,000	Per 1,000	Per 1,000	Per 1,000	Per 1,000	Per 1,000	Per 1,000
1940	28.6	3.5	79.4	—	—	44.5	12.9	5.2	1.8	0.5	0.2
1941	29.8	4.0	82.7	—	—	46.8	13.7	5.8	2.1	0.4	0.1
1942	31.0	3.9	85.5	—	—	50.1	14.8	6.2	2.3	0.4	0.1
1943	31.0	4.0	85.0	—	—	49.4	15.5	7.1	2.5	0.4	0.1
1944	28.7	3.9	76.1	—	—	46.9	15.4	7.5	2.8	0.5	0.1
1945	27.9	3.9	74.3	—	—	45.5	15.3	7.5	3.0	0.6	0.1
1946	31.1	3.4	77.5	—	—	55.8	19.3	8.4	3.3	0.7	0.1
1947	38.4	4.2	96.0	—	—	71.6	23.9	10.1	3.7	0.7	0.1
1948	37.3	4.4	98.9	—	—	66.1	23.1	9.4	3.7	0.8	0.1
1949	35.4	4.6	96.5	—	—	60.6	22.3	9.9	3.9	1.0	0.1
1950	33.8	4.7	95.1	—	—	56.0	21.4	9.6	3.9	0.8	0.1
1951	34.1	4.6	98.1	—	—	55.4	21.8	9.7	4.0	1.0	0.1
1952	33.1	4.4	94.8	—	—	55.3	22.1	9.5	3.9	0.8	0.1
1953	34.1	4.4	97.3	—	—	58.1	22.1	9.3	4.1	0.8	0.1
1954	35.6	4.8	101.7	—	—	62.2	22.4	9.4	3.9	0.8	0.1
1955	35.0	4.4	98.8	—	—	63.7	21.3	8.8	3.9	0.9	0.1
1956	35.9	4.7	101.1	—	—	66.7	21.1	8.6	3.7	0.8	0.1
1957	36.1	4.8	100.9	—	—	67.6	20.3	8.0	3.4	0.7	(Z)
1958	34.7	4.2	95.8	—	—	64.6	19.6	7.7	3.3	0.7	0.1
1959	34.9	4.2	96.3	—	—	64.4	19.5	7.6	3.2	0.7	0.1
1960	33.6	3.8	91.1	62.2	118.6	63.5	18.8	6.9	2.9	0.7	0.1
1961	33.5	3.8	90.0	74.5	115.1	62.4	18.8	6.6	2.7	0.6	(Z)
1962 [3]	32.9	3.7	85.2	67.9	109.5	61.4	18.1	6.2	2.4	0.6	(Z)
1963 [3]	33.5	3.7	84.5	67.6	109.3	62.4	18.3	6.0	2.5	0.5	0.1
1964	34.4	3.8	85.5	69.1	117.0	63.0	17.8	6.0	2.4	0.6	(Z)
1965	35.3	3.8	85.4	70.8	111.7	62.8	18.9	6.0	2.3	0.5	(Z)
1966	36.6	3.8	86.8	70.6	114.4	64.2	19.0	6.2	2.2	0.5	(Z)
1967	37.6	3.9	88.1	72.2	114.4	64.6	19.3	5.7	2.0	0.5	(Z)
1968	39.5	4.2	89.3	73.3	116.0	67.2	21.6	6.5	2.3	0.4	(Z)
1969	41.0	4.3	90.3	73.9	116.8	69.4	22.9	6.9	2.2	0.5	(Z)
1970	42.4	4.6	93.1	77.2	118.9	70.0	24.0	7.0	2.2	0.4	(Z)
1971	41.6	4.6	90.7	76.6	114.2	65.4	23.9	7.4	1.9	0.3	(Z)
1972	40.6	4.6	89.7	78.1	109.1	60.2	23.9	7.4	1.9	0.3	(Z)
1973	38.8	4.8	85.6	75.8	101.5	55.6	24.0	7.2	2.0	0.4	(Z)
1974	37.7	4.5	81.0	71.2	96.5	54.0	25.6	9.1	2.2	0.4	(Z)

Notes appear at end of table

TABLE Ab150–215   First birth rate, by age and race: 1940–1998   *Continued*

	All nonwhite, by age										
	15–44	10–14	15–19	15–17	18–19	20–24	25–29	30–34	35–39	40–44	45–49
	Ab172	Ab173	Ab174	Ab175	Ab176	Ab177	Ab178	Ab179	Ab180	Ab181	Ab182 [2]
Year	Per 1,000	Per 1,000	Per 1,000	Per 1,000	Per 1,000	Per 1,000	Per 1,000	Per 1,000	Per 1,000	Per 1,000	Per 1,000
1975	36.7	4.5	77.2	67.6	92.0	52.9	26.0	8.2	2.3	0.4	(Z)
1976	35.2	4.1	72.3	63.1	86.5	52.2	25.7	8.5	2.4	0.4	(Z)
1977	35.6	4.1	72.2	62.5	86.9	53.6	26.6	9.6	2.7	0.4	(Z)
1978	35.0	3.9	69.2	58.6	85.3	53.6	27.9	10.6	2.8	0.4	(Z)
1979	35.7	3.9	69.9	59.1	85.9	55.9	29.0	11.6	3.0	0.4	(Z)
1980	33.5	3.7	65.9	55.7	80.9	53.5	27.7	11.6	2.9	0.5	(Z)
1981	32.0	3.4	62.6	52.2	77.7	52.1	28.2	11.2	3.0	0.5	(Z)
1982	31.5	3.4	62.4	52.2	76.9	52.0	28.5	11.8	3.4	0.5	(Z)
1983	30.9	3.4	62.0	52.0	75.8	51.0	28.6	12.2	3.6	0.5	(Z)
1984	30.5	3.6	61.2	50.8	75.7	51.3	29.1	12.6	4.0	0.6	(Z)
1985	30.5	3.7	61.2	50.2	76.9	52.1	30.0	13.1	4.3	0.6	(Z)
1986	30.3	3.8	60.7	50.0	77.0	52.7	30.6	14.0	4.3	0.7	(Z)
1987	30.6	3.8	60.7	51.0	75.4	53.7	32.0	14.8	4.6	0.7	(Z)
1988	31.3	3.9	62.5	52.5	77.2	54.6	34.1	16.1	5.1	0.9	(Z)
1989	32.0	4.1	66.3	55.5	81.1	55.6	35.1	16.6	5.4	1.0	0.1
1990	31.7	3.8	65.2	54.7	79.1	55.5	35.8	17.4	5.7	1.0	(Z)
1991	30.9	3.7	65.9	55.4	80.5	54.7	34.8	17.3	5.8	1.1	0.1
1992	30.1	3.6	63.7	53.6	78.6	53.1	34.8	17.8	6.0	1.1	(Z)
1993	29.7	3.5	63.7	54.0	78.2	52.4	34.3	18.3	6.1	1.1	0.1
1994	—	—	—	—	—	—	—	—	—	—	—
1995	—	—	—	—	—	—	—	—	—	—	—
1996	—	—	—	—	—	—	—	—	—	—	—
1997	—	—	—	—	—	—	—	—	—	—	—
1998	—	—	—	—	—	—	—	—	—	—	—

	Black, by age										
	15–44	10–14	15–19	15–17	18–19	20–24	25–29	30–34	35–39	40–44	45–49
	Ab183	Ab184	Ab185	Ab186	Ab187	Ab188	Ab189	Ab190	Ab191	Ab192	Ab193 [2]
Year	Per 1,000	Per 1,000	Per 1,000	Per 1,000	Per 1,000	Per 1,000	Per 1,000	Per 1,000	Per 1,000	Per 1,000	Per 1,000
1940	—	—	—	—	—	—	—	—	—	—	—
1941	—	—	—	—	—	—	—	—	—	—	—
1942	—	—	—	—	—	—	—	—	—	—	—
1943	—	—	—	—	—	—	—	—	—	—	—
1944	—	—	—	—	—	—	—	—	—	—	—
1945	—	—	—	—	—	—	—	—	—	—	—
1946	—	—	—	—	—	—	—	—	—	—	—
1947	—	—	—	—	—	—	—	—	—	—	—
1948	—	—	—	—	—	—	—	—	—	—	—
1949	—	—	—	—	—	—	—	—	—	—	—
1950	—	—	—	—	—	—	—	—	—	—	—
1951	—	—	—	—	—	—	—	—	—	—	—
1952	—	—	—	—	—	—	—	—	—	—	—
1953	—	—	—	—	—	—	—	—	—	—	—
1954	—	—	—	—	—	—	—	—	—	—	—
1955	—	—	—	—	—	—	—	—	—	—	—
1956	—	—	—	—	—	—	—	—	—	—	—
1957	—	—	—	—	—	—	—	—	—	—	—
1958	—	—	—	—	—	—	—	—	—	—	—
1959	—	—	—	—	—	—	—	—	—	—	—
1960	33.6	4.1	90.0	—	—	63.8	19.0	7.0	2.9	0.7	(Z)
1961	—	—	—	—	—	—	—	—	—	—	—
1962 [3]	—	—	—	—	—	—	—	—	—	—	—
1963 [3]	—	—	—	—	—	—	—	—	—	—	—
1964	35.0	4.0	88.8	72.7	119.8	62.7	16.3	5.4	2.2	0.6	(Z)

Notes appear at end of table

(continued)

TABLE Ab150–215 First birth rate, by age and race: 1940–1998 *Continued*

					Black, by age					
	15–44	10–14	15–19	15–17	18–19	20–24	25–29	30–34	35–39	40–44	45–49
	Ab183	Ab184	Ab185	Ab186	Ab187	Ab188	Ab189	Ab190	Ab191	Ab192	Ab193 [2]
Year	Per 1,000	Per 1,000	Per 1,000	Per 1,000	Per 1,000	Per 1,000	Per 1,000	Per 1,000	Per 1,000	Per 1,000	Per 1,000
1965	35.0	4.1	88.7	74.6	114.7	61.8	16.1	5.0	2.0	0.5	(Z)
1966	36.9	4.1	90.2	74.3	117.3	63.0	15.9	5.1	1.9	0.4	(Z)
1967	38.0	4.2	92.0	76.4	118.3	63.4	15.9	4.6	1.7	0.4	(Z)
1968	39.8	4.5	93.2	77.2	119.6	65.8	17.5	5.1	1.9	0.4	(Z)
1969	41.2	4.6	93.7	77.8	119.8	67.9	18.5	5.4	1.9	0.4	(Z)
1970	43.3	5.0	92.6	82.0	123.1	69.8	19.8	5.6	1.8	0.3	(Z)
1971	41.7	4.9	94.4	80.8	116.9	63.8	18.7	5.1	1.6	0.3	(Z)
1972	40.7	4.9	93.6	82.5	111.8	58.5	18.6	5.3	1.4	0.2	(Z)
1973	38.9	5.2	89.2	80.1	103.7	54.0	18.6	5.2	1.5	0.3	(Z)
1974	37.7	4.9	84.4	75.3	98.9	52.5	20.1	5.9	1.6	0.3	(Z)
1975	36.9	4.9	80.8	71.7	95.1	51.9	20.8	6.0	1.7	0.3	(Z)
1976	35.2	4.5	75.5	66.9	88.6	51.0	20.9	6.3	1.8	0.3	(Z)
1977	35.6	4.5	75.5	66.2	89.7	52.7	21.8	7.1	2.0	0.3	(Z)
1978	34.6	4.3	72.4	62.3	87.6	52.1	22.2	7.6	2.1	0.3	(Z)
1979	35.3	4.4	73.3	63.3	88.3	54.6	23.4	8.3	2.3	0.3	(Z)
1980	33.7	4.2	70.3	60.5	84.9	53.1	22.7	8.4	2.2	0.3	(Z)
1981	32.3	3.9	67.3	57.1	82.0	52.0	23.2	8.3	2.2	0.4	(Z)
1982	31.7	3.9	67.3	57.4	81.2	51.7	23.2	8.6	2.5	0.3	(Z)
1983	31.1	4.0	67.5	57.6	81.1	51.1	23.3	8.8	2.7	0.4	(Z)
1984	30.9	4.2	67.4	57.2	81.4	51.8	23.9	9.2	2.9	0.4	(Z)
1985	31.0	4.4	68.1	57.1	83.7	53.2	24.9	9.5	3.1	0.4	(Z)
1986	31.0	4.5	68.3	57.3	84.7	54.2	25.5	10.4	3.1	0.5	(Z)
1987	31.2	4.6	69.0	59.0	84.0	55.5	26.8	11.0	3.3	0.6	(Z)
1988	31.8	4.7	71.6	61.3	86.8	56.7	28.2	11.6	3.6	0.7	(Z)
1989	32.9	5.0	76.6	65.6	91.7	58.3	29.7	12.4	3.9	0.7	(Z)
1990	32.4	4.7	75.7	64.9	89.9	58.4	29.9	12.9	4.0	0.7	(Z)
1991	31.5	4.6	76.6	65.9	91.2	58.0	28.9	12.9	4.2	0.7	(Z)
1992	30.6	4.5	74.3	63.8	89.6	56.5	28.7	13.2	4.4	0.8	(Z)
1993	30.2	4.4	74.2	64.2	89.2	55.6	28.3	13.5	4.4	0.8	(Z)
1994	29.8	4.5	73.9	62.7	91.3	54.7	27.6	13.9	4.7	0.9	(Z)
1995	28.7	4.1	69.7	58.5	87.2	52.8	27.1	13.9	4.8	0.9	(Z)
1996	27.6	3.5	65.9	54.4	83.7	51.3	26.5	13.8	5.1	0.9	(Z)
1997	27.3	3.2	64.0	51.3	83.5	52.0	26.2	14.1	5.3	1.0	(Z)
1998	27.0	2.8	62.1	48.4	82.1	52.5	25.7	14.3	5.5	1.1	0.1

					American Indian, by age					
	15–44	10–14	15–19	15–17	18–19	20–24	25–29	30–34	35–39	40–44	45–49
	Ab194	Ab195	Ab196	Ab197	Ab198	Ab199	Ab200	Ab201	Ab202	Ab203	Ab204 [2]
Year	Per 1,000	Per 1,000	Per 1,000	Per 1,000	Per 1,000	Per 1,000	Per 1,000	Per 1,000	Per 1,000	Per 1,000	Per 1,000
1992 [4]	24.6	1.5	60.7	45.3	85.0	49.1	20.1	8.2	2.4	0.4	—
1993	25.0	1.4	60.8	45.2	86.1	50.2	20.9	8.1	2.5	0.6	—
1994	25.4	1.8	61.4	45.0	88.9	49.6	21.6	8.7	2.7	0.4	—
1995	25.4	1.7	60.2	41.9	92.1	50.6	21.2	8.4	2.8	0.5	—
1996	24.9	1.7	57.6	41.4	86.1	49.5	20.0	9.3	3.1	0.6	—
1997	24.7	1.7	55.2	40.4	80.8	49.6	20.2	9.6	3.2	0.6	—
1998	25.0	1.6	55.1	39.3	81.7	50.1	20.3	9.5	3.3	0.5	—

Notes appear at end of table

TABLE Ab150–215 First birth rate, by age and race: 1940–1998 *Continued*

	Asian and Pacific Islander, by age										
	15–44	10–14	15–19	15–17	18–19	20–24	25–29	30–34	35–39	40–44	45–49
	Ab205	Ab206	Ab207	Ab208	Ab209	Ab210	Ab211	Ab212	Ab213	Ab214	Ab215 [2]
Year	Per 1,000	Per 1,000	Per 1,000	Per 1,000	Per 1,000	Per 1,000	Per 1,000	Per 1,000	Per 1,000	Per 1,000	Per 1,000
1992 [4]	29.4	0.7	19.8	12.6	30.2	41.5	60.4	36.0	12.4	2.3	0.1
1993	29.2	0.6	20.1	13.4	30.1	41.1	59.0	37.1	12.6	2.2	0.1
1994	29.8	0.6	20.9	13.6	32.1	41.3	59.3	38.8	13.3	2.4	0.2
1995	29.9	0.7	20.4	13.1	32.2	41.9	58.0	39.4	13.7	2.6	0.2
1996	29.7	0.6	19.4	12.8	30.2	41.6	56.9	40.4	13.6	2.6	0.1
1997	30.4	0.5	18.8	12.5	29.3	41.8	59.5	41.4	14.5	2.8	0.2
1998	29.4	0.4	18.6	12.2	29.0	41.1	57.8	39.9	14.7	2.9	0.2

(Z) Less than 0.05 births.

[1] Beginning in 1970, data exclude births to nonresidents of the United States. Based on a 50 percent sample of births for 1951–1954, 1956–1966, and 1968–1971; on a 20–50 percent sample for 1967; and on a 100 percent sample for selected states and a 50 percent sample for all other states for 1972–1984. For 1940–1959, births adjusted for underregistration; thereafter, they are registered live births. Data based on race of child through 1979 and race of mother thereafter.

[2] Beginning in 1997, rates computed by relating births to women ages 45–54 to those to women ages 45–49.

[3] Figures by race exclude New Jersey, which did not require reporting of race.

[4] Data for American Indians and for Asians and Pacific Islanders are not available before 1992.

Sources

1940–1959: Robert D. Grove and Alice Hetzel, *Vital Statistics Rates in the United States, 1940–1960* (National Center for Health Statistics, 1968), Public Health Service Publication number 1677, Table 13.

1960–1997: U.S. Public Health Service, National Center for Health Statistics, *Vital Statistics of the United States, 1993*, volume 1, *Natality*, Table 1–10; *Monthly Vital Statistics Reports* and *National Vital Statistics Reports* final birth (natality) data for 1994–1998.

Documentation

Birth rates are live births per 1,000 women in the specified groups. These rates are those for a woman's first birth only.

Also see the text for Table Ab11–30.

TABLE Ab216–263 Pregnancy, live birth, induced abortion, and fetal loss rates, by age and race: 1976–1996

Contributed by Michael R. Haines

	Pregnancies											
	All races											
		Age									White	Other races
	Total	Under 15	15–19	15–17	18–19	20–24	25–29	30–34	35–39	40 and over		
	Ab216	Ab217	Ab218	Ab219	Ab220	Ab221	Ab222	Ab223	Ab224	Ab225	Ab226	Ab227
Year	Per 1,000	Per 1,000	Per 1,000	Per 1,000	Per 1,000	Per 1,000	Per 1,000	Per 1,000	Per 1,000	Per 1,000	Per 1,000	Per 1,000
1976	102.7	3.2	101.4	69.4	148.9	166.1	150.8	82.2	35.3	9.9	92.8	161.6
1980	111.9	3.2	110.0	73.2	162.2	183.5	165.7	95.0	36.4	9.1	102.4	164.4
1981	110.5	3.1	109.2	72.6	159.6	180.0	164.3	94.8	36.8	8.8	101.3	159.9
1982	110.1	3.1	107.8	72.1	155.7	182.4	163.4	97.3	37.6	8.8	101.7	154.9
1983	108.0	3.3	107.2	72.2	153.5	177.8	160.0	98.4	39.0	8.6	99.6	151.9
1984	107.4	3.5	105.8	70.4	154.4	177.2	160.2	101.1	40.1	8.3	99.3	149.4
1985	108.3	3.6	106.9	71.1	158.3	179.4	163.0	103.7	41.8	8.4	99.9	150.9
1986	106.7	3.6	104.7	69.8	157.1	178.2	161.6	105.0	42.4	8.5	97.9	150.6
1987	106.8	3.5	104.8	70.9	154.8	178.9	163.6	107.7	45.1	9.0	97.5	152.0
1988	110.0	3.4	109.9	74.1	158.7	186.3	169.0	110.8	48.4	9.8	100.6	154.7
1989	111.8	3.4	113.0	76.9	159.3	190.8	173.0	114.2	51.0	10.3	102.4	156.2
1990	115.6	3.5	116.3	80.3	162.4	196.7	179.6	120.2	56.1	11.3	106.2	159.2
1991	113.0	3.4	116.5	79.8	167.2	195.7	177.0	118.1	56.2	11.1	103.4	156.2
1992	111.8	3.4	112.8	77.3	165.1	194.1	176.3	118.8	56.8	11.9	102.2	153.9
1993	109.8	3.3	110.4	76.8	160.6	191.1	174.0	119.4	57.3	12.2	100.4	150.8
1994	107.5	3.3	107.6	75.5	156.7	186.6	171.2	119.9	58.2	12.7	98.8	145.0
1995	105.1	3.0	102.7	71.7	150.8	182.2	168.7	120.5	58.9	12.9	97.5	137.4
1996	104.7	2.8	98.7	67.8	146.4	183.3	170.7	122.5	60.4	13.4	—	—

(continued)

TABLE Ab216–263   Pregnancy, live birth, induced abortion, and fetal loss rates, by age and race: 1976–1996
Continued

						Live births							
						All races							
						Age							
Year	Total	Under 15	15–19	15–17	18–19	20–24	25–29	30–34	35–39	40 and over	White	Other races
	Ab228	Ab229	Ab230	Ab231	Ab232	Ab233	Ab234	Ab235	Ab236	Ab237	Ab238	Ab239
	Per 1,000	Per 1,000	Per 1,000	Per 1,000	Per 1,000	Per 1,000	Per 1,000	Per 1,000	Per 1,000	Per 1,000	Per 1,000	Per 1,000
1976	65.0	1.2	52.8	34.1	80.5	110.3	106.2	53.6	19.0	4.5	62.2	82.0
1980	68.4	1.1	53.0	32.5	82.1	115.1	112.9	61.9	19.8	4.1	65.6	83.7
1981	67.3	1.1	52.2	32.0	80.0	112.2	111.5	61.4	20.0	4.0	64.8	81.1
1982	67.3	1.1	52.4	32.3	79.4	111.6	111.0	64.1	21.2	4.1	64.8	80.3
1983	65.7	1.1	51.4	31.8	77.4	107.8	108.5	64.9	22.0	4.0	63.4	77.9
1984	65.5	1.2	50.6	31.0	77.4	106.8	108.7	67.0	22.9	4.0	63.2	77.0
1985	66.3	1.2	51.0	31.0	79.6	108.3	111.0	69.1	24.0	4.1	64.1	77.3
1986	65.4	1.3	50.2	30.5	79.6	107.4	109.8	70.1	24.4	4.2	63.1	76.8
1987	65.8	1.3	50.6	31.7	78.5	107.9	111.6	72.1	26.3	4.6	63.3	77.9
1988	67.3	1.3	53.0	33.6	79.9	110.2	114.4	74.8	28.1	5.0	64.5	80.3
1989	69.2	1.4	57.3	36.4	84.2	113.8	117.6	77.4	29.9	5.3	66.4	82.7
1990	70.9	1.4	59.9	37.5	88.6	116.5	120.2	80.8	31.7	5.6	68.3	83.2
1991	69.6	1.4	62.1	38.7	94.4	115.7	118.2	79.5	32.0	5.7	67.0	81.5
1992	68.9	1.4	60.7	37.8	94.5	114.6	117.4	80.2	32.5	6.1	66.5	79.5
1993	67.6	1.4	59.6	37.8	92.1	112.6	115.5	80.8	32.9	6.3	65.4	77.3
1994	66.7	1.4	58.9	37.6	91.5	111.1	113.9	81.5	33.7	6.6	64.9	74.5
1995	65.6	1.3	56.8	36.0	89.1	109.8	112.2	82.5	34.3	6.8	64.4	70.8
1996	65.3	1.2	54.4	33.8	86.0	110.4	113.1	83.9	35.3	7.1	64.3	69.5

						Induced abortions							
						All races							
						Age							
Year	Total	Under 15	15–19	15–17	18–19	20–24	25–29	30–34	35–39	40 and over	White	Other races
	Ab240	Ab241	Ab242	Ab243	Ab244	Ab245	Ab246	Ab247	Ab248	Ab249	Ab250	Ab251
	Per 1,000	Per 1,000	Per 1,000	Per 1,000	Per 1,000	Per 1,000	Per 1,000	Per 1,000	Per 1,000	Per 1,000	Per 1,000	Per 1,000
1976	24.2	1.6	34.3	24.2	49.3	39.6	24.1	15.0	9.3	3.7	18.8	56.3
1980	29.4	1.7	42.7	30.1	60.6	51.6	31.0	17.2	9.4	3.5	24.4	57.0
1981	29.3	1.7	42.9	30.1	60.6	51.4	31.3	17.7	9.5	3.4	24.3	55.8
1982	28.8	1.6	42.7	30.0	59.7	51.1	31.5	17.8	9.3	3.3	23.8	55.3
1983	28.5	1.9	43.2	30.7	59.9	50.9	31.0	17.8	9.5	3.2	23.3	55.2
1984	28.1	2.0	42.9	29.9	60.8	51.6	31.0	17.9	9.6	2.9	23.2	53.8
1985	28.0	2.0	43.5	30.6	62.0	52.0	31.1	17.9	9.7	2.9	22.7	54.9
1986	27.4	2.0	42.3	29.9	60.8	51.8	31.1	18.0	9.7	2.8	21.8	55.1
1987	26.9	1.8	41.8	29.6	59.8	52.0	31.0	18.2	9.9	2.9	21.2	55.1
1988	27.4	1.7	43.5	30.2	62.0	53.6	32.0	18.4	10.0	3.0	21.3	56.2
1989	26.8	1.6	42.0	28.0	60.0	53.8	32.2	18.6	10.1	3.0	20.9	54.7
1990	27.4	1.5	40.3	26.5	57.9	56.7	33.9	19.7	10.8	3.2	21.6	54.6
1991	26.3	1.4	37.6	24.3	55.9	56.6	33.7	19.1	10.4	3.0	20.3	53.8
1992	25.9	1.5	35.5	23.1	53.8	56.3	33.9	19.0	10.4	3.2	19.6	53.9
1993	25.4	1.4	34.3	22.5	52.0	55.8	33.9	18.9	10.2	3.2	18.9	53.5
1994	24.1	1.3	32.2	21.4	48.8	53.0	33.1	18.4	10.0	3.2	17.9	51.1
1995	22.9	1.2	30.0	19.9	45.7	50.3	32.6	17.9	9.8	3.2	17.0	48.1
1996	22.9	1.1	29.2	19.0	44.9	50.7	33.6	18.2	9.9	3.2	—	—

TABLE Ab216–263 Pregnancy, live birth, induced abortion, and fetal loss rates, by age and race: 1976–1996
Continued

					Fetal losses							
					All races							
					Age							
	Total	Under 15	15–19	15–17	18–19	20–24	25–29	30–34	35–39	40 and over	White	Other races
	Ab252	Ab253	Ab254	Ab255	Ab256	Ab257	Ab258	Ab259	Ab260	Ab261	Ab262	Ab263
Year	Per 1,000	Per 1,000	Per 1,000	Per 1,000	Per 1,000	Per 1,000	Per 1,000	Per 1,000	Per 1,000	Per 1,000	Per 1,000	Per 1,000
1976	13.4	0.4	14.4	11.1	19.1	16.2	20.5	13.6	6.9	1.6	11.8	23.3
1980	14.1	0.4	14.3	10.6	19.5	16.9	21.8	15.8	7.2	1.5	12.4	23.7
1981	13.9	0.4	14.1	10.5	19.0	16.5	21.6	15.7	7.2	1.4	12.2	23.0
1982	14.1	0.3	12.7	9.8	16.7	19.7	20.9	15.5	7.1	1.4	13.1	19.3
1983	13.8	0.3	12.5	9.7	16.2	19.0	20.4	15.7	7.4	1.4	12.8	18.8
1984	13.8	0.4	12.3	9.5	16.2	18.9	20.5	16.2	7.7	1.4	12.9	18.6
1985	14.0	0.4	12.4	9.4	16.7	19.1	20.9	16.7	8.1	1.4	13.1	18.7
1986	13.9	0.4	12.3	9.3	16.7	19.0	20.7	16.9	8.2	1.4	12.9	18.7
1987	14.1	0.4	12.4	9.6	16.5	19.0	21.0	17.4	8.8	1.5	13.0	19.1
1988	15.4	0.4	13.5	10.3	16.8	22.5	22.7	17.7	10.4	1.8	14.8	18.2
1989	15.7	0.5	13.7	12.6	15.2	23.3	23.3	18.3	11.0	2.0	15.1	18.8
1990	17.2	0.5	16.1	16.2	15.9	23.5	25.5	19.7	13.6	2.4	16.4	21.3
1991	17.0	0.5	16.8	16.8	16.9	23.4	25.1	19.4	13.8	2.4	16.2	20.9
1992	17.0	0.5	16.6	16.4	16.9	23.2	25.0	19.6	13.9	2.6	16.2	20.5
1993	16.8	0.5	16.5	16.5	16.5	22.8	24.6	19.7	14.1	2.7	16.1	20.0
1994	16.7	0.6	16.5	16.5	16.4	22.4	24.2	19.9	14.5	2.8	16.1	19.3
1995	16.5	0.5	15.9	15.9	16.0	22.1	23.9	20.1	14.8	2.9	16.1	18.5
1996	16.5	0.5	15.2	15.0	15.5	22.3	24.1	20.5	15.2	3.1	—	—

Source

S. J. Ventura, W. D. Mosher, et al., "Trends in Pregnancies and Pregnancy Rates by Outcome: Estimates for the United States, 1976–1996," National Center for Health Statistics, *Vital and Health Statistics*, series 21, number 56 (January 2000), Table 3.

Documentation

A pregnancy necessarily results in one of three outcomes: a live birth, an induced abortion, or spontaneous fetal loss. The fetal loss rate measures spontaneous fetal losses from recognized pregnancies of all gestational periods as reported by women in the 1982, 1988, and 1995 National Survey of Family Growth conducted by the National Center for Health Statistics. The rate of fetal loss depends on the degree to which losses at very early gestations are detected. Rates for 1988–1992 have been revised on the basis of new information from the 1995 National Survey of Family Growth. These revised estimates differ from those previously published.

All rates are per 1,000 women with the specified characteristics. For women of all ages, the rates were computed by relating the number of events to women of all ages to those to women ages 15–44. For women younger than 15, the rates were computed by relating the number of events experienced by women younger than age 15 to those experienced by women ages 10–14. For women older than 40, the rates were computed by relating the number of events experienced by women older than 40 to those experienced by women ages 40–44.

Data are based on the race of the woman.

Due to rounding, figures may not add to totals.

TABLE Ab264–305   Birth rate and live births to unmarried women, by age and race: 1940–1998[1, 2]

Contributed by Michael R. Haines

		All races								
		Birth rate, by age								
	Total births	15–44	15–19	15–17	18–19	20–24	25–29	30–34	35–39	40–44
	Ab264	Ab265 [3]	Ab266	Ab267	Ab268	Ab269	Ab270	Ab271	Ab272	Ab273 [4]
Year	Number	Per 1,000	Per 1,000	Per 1,000	Per 1,000	Per 1,000	Per 1,000	Per 1,000	Per 1,000	Per 1,000
1940	89,500	7.1	7.4	—	—	9.5	7.2	5.1	3.4	1.2
1941	95,700	7.8	8.0	—	—	10.5	7.8	6.0	3.7	1.4
1942	95,500	8.0	8.2	—	—	11.0	8.4	6.3	3.8	1.2
1943	98,100	8.3	8.4	—	—	11.4	8.8	6.7	3.8	1.3
1944	105,200	9.0	8.8	—	—	13.1	10.1	7.0	4.0	1.3
1945	117,400	10.1	9.5	—	—	15.3	12.1	7.1	4.1	1.6
1946	125,200	10.9	9.5	—	—	17.3	15.6	7.3	4.4	1.8
1947	131,900	12.1	11.0	—	—	18.9	15.7	9.2	5.6	1.8
1948	129,700	12.5	11.4	—	—	19.8	16.4	10.0	5.8	1.6
1949	133,200	13.3	12.0	—	—	21.0	16.0	11.4	6.8	1.9
1950	141,600	14.1	12.6	—	—	21.3	19.9	13.3	7.2	2.0
1951	146,500	15.1	13.2	—	—	23.2	22.8	14.6	7.6	2.2
1952	150,300	15.8	13.5	—	—	25.4	24.8	15.7	8.2	1.9
1953	160,800	16.9	13.9	—	—	28.0	27.6	17.3	9.0	2.4
1954	176,600	18.7	14.9	—	—	31.4	31.0	20.4	10.3	2.5
1955	183,300	19.3	15.1	—	—	33.5	33.5	22.0	10.5	2.7
1956	193,500	20.4	15.6	—	—	36.4	35.6	24.6	11.1	2.8
1957	201,700	21.0	15.8	—	—	37.3	36.8	26.8	12.1	3.1
1958	208,700	21.2	15.3	—	—	38.2	40.5	27.5	13.3	3.2
1959	220,600	21.9	15.5	—	—	40.2	44.1	28.1	14.1	3.3
1960	224,300	21.6	15.3	—	—	39.7	45.1	27.8	14.1	3.6
1961	240,200	22.7	16.0	—	—	41.4	46.4	28.2	15.4	3.9
1962 [5]	245,100	21.9	14.8	—	—	40.7	46.6	29.6	15.6	4.1
1963 [5]	259,400	22.5	15.3	—	—	39.9	48.8	33.1	16.1	4.3
1964	275,700	23.0	15.9	—	—	39.5	49.9	36.9	16.3	4.4
1965	291,200	23.4	16.7	—	—	39.6	49.1	37.2	17.4	4.5
1966	302,400	23.3	17.5	13.1	25.6	39.0	45.1	32.7	16.3	4.1
1967	318,100	23.7	18.5	13.8	27.6	38.1	41.1	28.9	15.3	4.0
1968	339,200	24.3	19.7	14.7	29.6	37.2	38.3	27.8	14.8	3.8
1969	360,800	24.8	20.4	15.2	30.8	37.3	37.9	27.0	13.5	3.6
1970	398,700	26.4	22.4	17.1	32.9	38.4	37.0	27.1	13.6	3.5
1971	401,400	25.5	22.3	17.5	31.7	35.5	34.5	25.2	13.3	3.5
1972	403,200	24.8	22.8	18.5	30.9	33.2	30.8	22.6	12.0	3.1
1973	407,300	24.3	22.7	18.7	30.4	31.5	29.6	20.3	10.8	3.0
1974	418,100	23.9	23.0	18.8	31.2	30.5	27.9	18.4	10.0	2.6
1975	447,900	24.5	23.9	19.3	32.5	31.2	27.5	17.9	9.1	2.6
1976	468,100	24.3	23.7	19.0	32.1	31.7	26.8	17.5	9.0	2.5
1977	515,700	25.6	25.1	19.8	34.6	34.0	27.7	16.9	8.4	2.4
1978	543,900	25.7	24.9	19.1	35.1	35.3	28.5	16.9	8.2	2.2
1979	597,800	27.2	26.4	19.9	37.2	37.7	29.9	17.7	8.4	2.3
1980	665,747	29.4	27.6	20.6	39.0	40.9	34.0	21.1	9.7	2.6
1981	686,605	29.5	27.9	20.9	39.0	41.1	34.5	20.8	9.8	2.6
1982	715,227	30.0	28.7	21.5	39.6	41.5	35.1	21.9	10.0	2.7
1983	737,893	30.3	29.5	22.0	40.7	41.8	35.5	22.4	10.2	2.6
1984	770,355	31.0	30.0	21.9	42.5	43.0	37.1	23.3	10.9	2.5
1985	828,174	32.8	31.4	22.4	45.9	46.5	39.9	25.2	11.6	2.5
1986	878,477	34.2	32.3	22.8	48.0	49.3	42.2	27.2	12.2	2.7
1987	933,013	36.0	33.8	24.5	48.9	52.6	44.5	29.6	13.5	2.9
1988	1,005,299	38.5	36.4	26.4	51.5	56.0	48.5	32.0	15.0	3.2
1989	1,094,169	41.6	40.1	28.7	56.0	61.2	52.8	34.9	16.0	3.4
1990	1,165,384	43.8	42.5	29.6	60.7	65.1	56.0	37.6	17.3	3.6
1991	1,213,769	45.2	44.8	30.9	65.7	68.0	56.5	38.1	18.0	3.8
1992	1,224,876	45.2	44.6	30.4	67.3	68.5	56.5	37.9	18.8	4.1
1993	1,240,172	45.3	44.5	30.6	66.9	69.2	57.1	38.5	19.0	4.4
1994	1,289,592	46.9	46.4	32.0	70.1	72.2	59.0	40.1	19.8	4.7
1995	1,253,976	45.1	44.4	30.5	67.6	70.3	56.1	39.6	19.5	4.7
1996	1,260,306	44.8	42.9	29.0	65.9	70.7	56.8	41.1	20.1	4.8
1997	1,257,444	44.0	42.3	28.2	65.2	71.0	56.2	39.0	19.0	4.6
1998	1,293,567	44.3	41.5	27.0	64.5	72.3	58.4	39.1	19.0	4.6

Notes appear at end of table

TABLE Ab264–305   Birth rate and live births to unmarried women, by age and race: 1940–1998   *Continued*

		White									
		Birth rate, by age									
	Total births	15–44	15–19	15–17	18–19	20–24	25–29	30–34	35–39	40–44	35–44
	Ab274	Ab275 [3]	Ab276	Ab277	Ab278	Ab279	Ab280	Ab281	Ab282	Ab283	Ab284 [4]
Year	Number	Per 1,000	Per 1,000	Per 1,000	Per 1,000	Per 1,000	Per 1,000	Per 1,000	Per 1,000	Per 1,000	Per 1,000
1940	40,300	3.6	3.3	—	—	5.7	4.0	2.5	—	—	1.2
1941	41,900	—	—	—	—	—	—	—	—	—	—
1942	42,000	—	—	—	—	—	—	—	—	—	—
1943	42,800	—	—	—	—	—	—	—	—	—	—
1944	49,600	—	—	—	—	—	—	—	—	—	—
1945	56,400	—	—	—	—	—	—	—	—	—	—
1946	61,400	—	—	—	—	—	—	—	—	—	—
1947	60,500	—	—	—	—	—	—	—	—	—	—
1948	54,800	—	—	—	—	—	—	—	—	—	—
1949	53,500	—	—	—	—	—	—	—	—	—	—
1950	53,500	6.1	5.1	—	—	10.0	8.7	5.9	—	—	2.0
1951	52,600	—	—	—	—	—	—	—	—	—	—
1952	54,100	—	—	—	—	—	—	—	—	—	—
1953	56,600	—	—	—	—	—	—	—	—	—	—
1954	62,700	—	—	—	—	—	—	—	—	—	—
1955	64,200	7.9	6.0	—	—	15.0	13.3	8.6	—	—	2.8
1956	67,500	8.3	6.2	—	—	16.3	14.0	9.2	—	—	3.0
1957	70,800	8.6	6.4	—	—	16.6	14.6	10.5	—	—	3.0
1958	74,600	8.8	6.3	—	—	17.3	15.8	10.8	—	—	3.4
1959	79,600	9.2	6.5	—	—	18.3	17.6	10.7	—	—	3.6
1960	82,500	9.2	6.6	—	—	18.2	18.2	10.8	—	—	3.9
1961	91,100	10.0	7.1	—	—	19.7	19.4	11.3	—	—	4.2
1962 [5]	94,700	9.8	6.5	—	—	19.9	19.8	12.6	—	—	4.3
1963 [5]	104,600	10.5	7.0	—	—	20.7	21.9	14.2	—	—	4.6
1964	114,300	11.0	7.4	—	—	21.1	24.0	15.9	—	—	4.8
1965	123,700	11.6	7.9	—	—	22.0	24.3	16.6	—	—	4.9
1966	132,900	11.9	8.5	5.4	14.1	22.6	23.4	15.7	—	—	4.9
1967	142,200	12.5	8.9	5.6	15.3	23.0	22.7	14.0	—	—	4.7
1968	155,200	13.1	9.7	6.2	16.6	23.0	22.1	15.0	—	—	4.7
1969	163,700	13.4	9.9	6.6	16.6	23.0	22.5	15.1	7.6	2.0	—
1970	175,100	13.9	10.9	7.5	17.6	22.5	21.1	14.2	7.6	2.0	—
1971	163,800	12.5	10.3	7.4	15.8	18.7	18.5	13.2	7.2	1.9	—
1972	160,500	11.9	10.4	8.0	15.1	16.6	16.5	12.1	6.5	1.6	—
1973	163,000	11.8	10.6	8.4	14.9	15.5	15.9	10.6	5.9	1.7	—
1974	168,500	11.7	11.0	8.8	15.3	15.0	14.7	9.5	5.5	1.5	—
1975	186,400	12.4	12.0	9.6	16.5	15.5	14.8	9.8	5.4	1.5	—
1976	197,100	12.6	12.3	9.7	16.9	15.8	14.0	10.1	5.5	1.4	—
1977	220,100	13.5	13.4	10.5	18.7	17.4	14.4	9.3	4.9	1.4	—
1978	233,600	13.7	13.6	10.3	19.3	18.1	14.8	9.4	4.8	1.3	—
1979	263,000	14.9	14.6	10.8	21.0	20.3	15.9	10.0	5.1	1.4	—
1980	328,984	18.1	16.5	12.0	24.1	25.1	21.5	14.1	7.1	1.8	—
1981	346,541	18.6	17.2	12.6	24.6	25.8	22.3	14.2	7.2	1.9	—
1982	365,647	19.3	18.0	13.1	25.3	26.5	23.1	15.3	7.4	2.1	—
1983	381,276	19.8	18.7	13.6	26.4	27.1	23.8	15.9	7.8	2.0	—
1984	403,022	20.6	19.3	13.7	27.9	28.5	25.5	16.8	8.4	2.0	—
1985	445,595	22.5	20.8	14.5	31.2	31.7	28.5	18.4	9.0	2.0	—
1986	480,533	23.9	21.8	14.9	33.5	34.2	30.5	20.1	9.7	2.2	—
1987	513,984	25.3	23.2	16.2	34.5	36.6	32.0	22.3	10.7	2.4	—
1988	557,394	27.4	25.3	17.6	36.8	39.2	35.4	24.2	12.1	2.7	—
1989	613,543	30.2	28.0	19.3	40.2	43.8	39.1	26.8	13.1	2.9	—
1990	669,698	32.9	30.6	20.4	44.9	48.2	43.0	29.9	14.5	3.2	—
1991	707,502	34.6	32.8	21.8	49.6	51.5	44.6	31.1	15.2	3.2	—
1992	721,986	35.2	33.0	21.6	51.5	52.7	45.4	31.5	16.2	3.6	—
1993	742,129	35.9	33.6	22.1	52.4	54.2	46.7	32.2	16.4	3.9	—
1994	794,261	38.3	36.2	24.1	56.4	58.1	49.7	34.2	17.3	4.3	—
1995	784,992	37.5	35.5	23.6	55.4	58.0	48.7	34.2	16.9	4.2	—
1996	795,432	37.6	34.5	22.7	54.1	59.0	49.9	36.1	17.8	4.3	—
1997	793,202	37.0	34.2	22.4	53.6	59.2	49.3	34.4	16.7	3.9	—
1998	821,441	37.5	34.0	21.8	53.5	60.5	50.9	34.9	17.0	4.0	—

Notes appear at end of table   (continued)

TABLE Ab264-305   Birth rate and live births to unmarried women, by age and race: 1940-1998   *Continued*

		All nonwhite									
		Birth rate, by age									
	Total births	15-44	15-19	15-17	18-19	20-24	25-29	30-34	35-39	40-44	35-44
	Ab285	Ab286 [3]	Ab287	Ab288	Ab289	Ab290	Ab291	Ab292	Ab293	Ab294	Ab295 [4]
Year	Number	Per 1,000	Per 1,000	Per 1,000	Per 1,000	Per 1,000	Per 1,000	Per 1,000	Per 1,000	Per 1,000	Per 1,000
1940	49,200	35.6	42.5	—	—	46.1	32.5	23.4	—	—	9.3
1941	53,800	—	—	—	—	—	—	—	—	—	—
1942	53,500	—	—	—	—	—	—	—	—	—	—
1943	55,400	—	—	—	—	—	—	—	—	—	—
1944	55,600	—	—	—	—	—	—	—	—	—	—
1945	60,900	—	—	—	—	—	—	—	—	—	—
1946	63,800	—	—	—	—	—	—	—	—	—	—
1947	71,500	—	—	—	—	—	—	—	—	—	—
1948	74,900	—	—	—	—	—	—	—	—	—	—
1949	79,700	—	—	—	—	—	—	—	—	—	—
1950	88,100	71.2	68.5	—	—	105.4	94.2	63.5	—	—	20.0
1951	93,900	—	—	—	—	—	—	—	—	—	—
1952	96,200	—	—	—	—	—	—	—	—	—	—
1953	104,200	—	—	—	—	—	—	—	—	—	—
1954	113,900	—	—	—	—	—	—	—	—	—	—
1955	119,200	87.2	77.6	—	—	133.0	125.2	100.9	—	—	25.3
1956	126,000	92.1	79.6	—	—	143.5	132.7	113.7	—	—	27.0
1957	130,900	95.3	81.4	—	—	147.7	142.6	115.1	—	—	30.3
1958	134,100	97.8	80.4	—	—	153.2	161.2	110.5	—	—	32.5
1959	141,000	100.8	80.8	—	—	167.8	168.0	106.5	—	—	34.9
1960	141,800	98.3	76.5	—	—	166.5	171.8	104.0	—	—	35.6
1961	149,100	101.0	78.8	—	—	165.8	171.3	110.0	—	—	37.4
1962 [5]	150,400	97.6	75.3	—	—	158.5	171.3	113.2	—	—	35.5
1963 [5]	154,900	97.2	75.3	—	—	156.3	168.9	120.8	—	—	34.4
1964	161,300	97.2	75.5	—	—	158.2	164.9	127.0	—	—	34.4
1965	167,500	97.4	77.1	—	—	147.8	161.0	131.9	—	—	38.7
1966	169,500	92.1	77.4	61.2	113.3	137.0	138.0	113.3	—	—	33.3
1967	175,800	88.3	80.0	64.1	114.5	126.2	113.5	92.1	—	—	28.4
1968	183,900	85.1	82.1	66.2	115.4	116.4	100.0	75.8	—	—	24.6
1969	197,200	84.8	84.2	67.3	118.9	115.4	93.9	69.0	33.3	10.4	—
1970	223,600	89.9	90.8	73.3	126.5	121.0	93.8	69.8	32.0	10.7	—
1971	237,500	90.2	92.0	75.4	125.4	120.6	92.6	65.3	32.2	10.4	—
1972	242,700	86.2	91.8	77.6	119.3	112.4	83.3	55.7	29.0	8.2	—
1973	244,500	83.2	88.5	75.6	112.8	107.8	81.0	55.8	26.2	7.2	—
1974	249,600	80.3	87.3	73.2	113.4	103.0	77.0	50.9	23.2	6.6	—
1975	261,600	79.0	86.3	70.7	114.3	102.1	73.2	47.9	20.0	6.9	—
1976	271,000	76.4	82.5	67.5	108.9	101.1	74.0	43.4	18.7	6.9	—
1977	295,500	77.4	84.0	67.2	112.7	103.1	74.4	43.7	18.5	6.6	—
1978	310,200	76.5	81.2	63.2	111.6	104.9	76.4	43.6	18.2	5.6	—
1979	334,800	78.2	83.9	64.8	115.3	107.1	77.7	44.8	19.1	5.7	—
1980	336,763	75.2	80.2	62.1	109.3	103.5	76.4	45.2	18.5	5.4	—
1981	340,064	72.8	76.7	58.9	104.3	101.6	75.9	43.5	18.7	5.5	—
1982	349,580	71.5	76.7	59.1	103.0	100.1	75.4	42.4	19.2	5.1	—
1983	356,617	69.9	76.4	59.1	101.3	97.8	73.8	42.5	18.9	4.7	—
1984	367,333	68.8	76.1	58.0	102.2	97.5	72.7	43.0	19.3	4.4	—
1985	382,579	70.1	76.6	57.6	104.7	101.0	74.4	46.4	20.0	4.4	—
1986	397,944	71.4	76.6	57.4	106.3	104.0	78.5	48.5	20.1	4.6	—
1987	419,029	74.3	78.0	59.4	107.0	110.1	85.0	51.6	22.2	4.9	—
1988	447,905	77.3	81.6	61.9	111.8	116.7	89.9	54.9	23.5	5.0	—
1989	480,626	80.7	87.8	65.6	119.5	123.5	94.7	57.9	24.3	5.1	—
1990	495,686	79.7	88.3	65.0	120.6	124.3	94.3	57.8	24.6	5.2	—
1991	506,267	78.8	90.3	66.3	125.0	124.4	90.1	55.8	25.1	5.7	—
1992	502,890	76.1	87.9	64.2	123.9	121.2	86.9	53.6	25.4	5.7	—
1993	498,043	74.3	85.4	63.4	119.5	118.8	85.3	54.2	25.7	6.1	—
1994	495,331	—	—	—	—	—	—	—	—	—	—
1995	468,984	—	—	—	—	—	—	—	—	—	—
1996	464,874	—	—	—	—	—	—	—	—	—	—
1997	464,242	—	—	—	—	—	—	—	—	—	—
1998	472,126	—	—	—	—	—	—	—	—	—	—

Notes appear at end of table

TABLE Ab264–305   Birth rate and live births to unmarried women, by age and race: 1940–1998   *Continued*

		Black								
		Birth rate, by age								
	Total births	15–44	15–19	15–17	18–19	20–24	25–29	30–34	35–39	40–44
	Ab296	Ab297 [3]	Ab298	Ab299	Ab300	Ab301	Ab302	Ab303	Ab304	Ab305 [4]
Year	Number	Per 1,000	Per 1,000	Per 1,000	Per 1,000	Per 1,000	Per 1,000	Per 1,000	Per 1,000	Per 1,000
1969 [6]	189,400	90.6	90.3	72.0	128.4	125.3	99.5	70.1	34.3	10.1
1970	215,100	95.5	96.9	77.9	136.4	131.5	100.9	71.8	32.9	10.4
1971	229,000	96.1	98.6	80.7	135.2	130.6	99.6	68.6	32.7	10.1
1972	233,300	91.6	98.2	82.8	128.2	121.2	88.3	57.4	30.4	8.5
1973	234,500	88.6	94.9	81.2	120.5	116.0	84.5	57.8	27.6	7.7
1974	238,800	85.5	93.8	78.6	122.2	109.8	80.3	51.8	24.3	6.7
1975	249,600	84.2	93.5	76.8	123.8	108.0	75.7	50.0	20.5	7.2
1976	258,800	81.6	89.7	73.5	117.9	107.2	78.0	45.0	19.2	7.0
1977	281,600	82.6	90.9	73.0	121.7	110.1	78.6	45.7	19.0	6.6
1978	293,400	81.1	87.9	68.8	119.6	111.4	79.6	43.9	18.5	6.2
1979	315,800	83.0	91.0	71.0	123.3	114.1	80.0	44.8	19.3	5.9
1980	318,799	81.1	87.9	68.8	118.2	112.3	81.4	46.7	19.0	5.5
1981	321,383	79.4	85.0	65.9	114.2	110.7	83.1	45.5	19.6	5.6
1982	327,998	77.9	85.1	66.3	112.7	109.3	82.7	44.1	19.5	5.2
1983	333,183	76.2	85.5	66.8	111.9	107.2	79.7	43.8	19.4	4.6
1984	342,524	75.2	86.1	66.5	113.6	107.9	77.8	43.8	19.4	4.3
1985	356,205	77.0	87.6	66.8	117.9	113.1	79.3	47.5	20.4	4.3
1986	369,786	79.0	88.5	67.0	121.1	118.0	84.6	50.0	20.6	4.4
1987	387,468	82.6	90.9	69.9	123.0	126.1	91.6	53.1	22.4	4.7
1988	413,157	86.5	96.1	73.5	130.5	133.6	97.2	57.4	24.1	5.0
1989	442,395	90.7	104.5	78.9	140.9	142.4	102.9	60.5	24.9	5.0
1990	455,304	90.5	106.0	78.8	143.7	144.8	105.3	61.5	25.5	5.1
1991	463,750	89.5	108.5	80.4	148.7	147.5	100.9	60.1	25.6	5.4
1992	458,969	86.5	105.9	78.0	147.8	144.3	98.2	57.7	25.8	5.4
1993	452,476	84.0	102.4	76.8	141.6	142.2	94.5	57.3	25.9	5.8
1994	448,315	82.1	100.9	75.1	141.6	138.1	93.6	57.2	26.3	5.9
1995	421,489	75.9	92.8	68.6	131.2	127.7	84.8	54.3	25.6	6.0
1996	415,213	74.4	89.2	64.0	129.2	125.8	84.5	54.5	25.5	6.1
1997	415,054	73.4	86.4	60.6	127.2	127.8	85.2	52.3	24.7	6.5
1998	421,383	73.3	83.4	56.5	123.5	131.0	90.3	51.7	24.7	6.1

[1] Data for 1940–1979 are estimated. Data for 1980–1998 are reported or inferred. See text.

[2] Based on a 50 percent sample for 1951–1954, 1956–1966, and 1968–1971; on a 20–50 percent sample for 1967; and on a 100 percent sample from some states and a 50 percent sample from other states for 1972–1984. Data are based on the race of the child through 1988 and on the race of the mother thereafter. Beginning in 1970, data exclude births to nonresidents of the United States.

[3] Rates computed by relating total illegitimate births regardless of age of mother to women ages 15–44 years.

[4] Rates for ages 40–44 years computed by relating births to unmarried mothers age 40 and older to those to unmarried women ages 40–44. Rates by race for 1940–1968 were computed by relating births to unmarried mothers age 35 and older to those to women ages 35–44.

[5] Excludes New Jersey, which did not require reporting of race.

[6] Data for blacks are not available before 1969.

Sources

U.S. Public Health Service, National Center for Health Statistics, *Vital Statistics of the United States, 1991*, volume 1, *Natality*, Tables 1–76 and 1–77; *National Vital Statistics Report*, volume 48, number 3, "Births: Final Data for 1998," Tables 17 and 18.

Total births for 1994–1998 are taken from the annual *Monthly Vital Statistics Reports* and *National Vital Statistics Reports* for the *Births: Final Data* volumes for 1994–1998.

Documentation

These are estimated data based on certificates of live birth filed for each child born in the United States. Rates are live births to unmarried women per 1,000 unmarried women in the specified group. Figures for age of mother unknown are distributed. Data are based on the race of the child through 1988 and on the race of the mother thereafter.

During the 1930s almost all states had a query concerning legitimacy or illegitimacy on their certificates. During the 1940s, concern for confidentiality prompted a number of states to remove it. These data are based on reports of thirty-four states and the District of Columbia for 1940–1965 and on reports of forty states and the District of Columbia for 1966–1970. By 1990, marital status was reported directly on the birth certificates of forty-four states and the District of Columbia. In the remaining six states (California, Connecticut, Michigan, Nevada, New York, and Texas), lacking such an item, marital status was inferred from a comparison of the child's and parents' surnames. This procedure contrasts with that used for inference prior to 1980, which assumed that the incidence of births to unmarried women in states with no direct question on marital status was the same as the incidence in reporting states in the same geographic division (see below). By 1999, direct questions on the marital status of the mother were asked during the birth registration process in forty-eight states and the District of Columbia. Two states (Michigan and New York) continued to use inferential procedures to compile birth statistics by marital status.

In making estimates of the number of illegitimate births occurring in the country as a whole, the states were grouped into nine geographic divisions. The combined ratio of illegitimate births per 1,000 total live births for all reporting states in a single geographic division was then applied to all live births to residents of that division. This estimating procedure was separately applied for white persons and for blacks and other persons. The sum of these estimates for the nine geographic divisions represents the estimate for the United States. No adjustments were made for misstatements of legitimacy status on the birth record or for failure to register illegitimate births because the extent of such reporting problems is unknown. A birth with legitimacy status not recorded was considered to be legitimate. Data for states in which marital status was not reported have been inferred from other items on

(continued)

TABLE Ab264–305   Birth rate and live births to unmarried women, by age and race: 1940–1998   *Continued*

the birth certificate and included with the reporting states for 1980–1998. Births to unmarried women are estimated for the United States from data for registration areas in which marital status of mother was reported for 1940–1979.

The rates shown for the years 1951–1965 differ from those published in earlier issues of *Vital Statistics of the United States*. The rates shown here are based on a smoothed series of population estimates for unmarried women

by race and age that were not available when the rates previously published were computed. For details concerning these estimates and other data for illegitimate births, see U.S. Public Health Service, National Center for Health Statistics, "Trends in Illegitimacy, United States, 1940–1965," *Vital and Health Statistics*, Public Health Service Publication number 1000, series 21, number 15, February 1968.

Also see the text for Table Ab11–30.

TABLE Ab306–314   Total fertility rate, gross reproduction rate, and net reproduction rate, by race: 1905–1993[1]

Contributed by Michael R. Haines

	Total fertility rate			Gross reproduction rate			Net reproduction rate		
	All women	White	Other	All women	White	Other	All women	White	Other
	Ab306	Ab307	Ab308	Ab309	Ab310	Ab311	Ab312	Ab313	Ab314
Year(s)	Per 1,000	Per 1,000	Per 1,000	Per 1,000	Per 1,000	Per 1,000	Per 1,000	Per 1,000	Per 1,000
1905–1910	3,551	3,443	4,351	1,793	1,740	2,240	1,336	1,339	1,329
1930–1935	—	—	—	1,108	1,080	1,336	984	972	1,074
1935–1940	2,270	2,195	2,845	1,101	1,063	1,413	978	957	1,137
1935	2,235	2,171	2,728	1,091	1,059	1,350	975	958	1,433
1940	2,301	2,229	2,870	1,121	1,082	1,422	1,027	1,002	1,209
1941	2,399	2,328	2,956	1,168	1,131	1,458	1,075	1,052	1,242
1942	2,628	2,577	3,022	1,277	1,250	1,487	1,185	1,171	1,293
1943	2,718	2,664	3,128	1,323	1,294	1,543	1,228	1,211	1,348
1944	2,568	2,501	3,075	1,249	1,214	1,520	1,163	1,139	1,334
1945	2,491	2,421	3,017	1,212	1,175	1,493	1,132	1,106	1,323
1946	2,943	2,901	3,238	1,430	1,406	1,600	1,344	1,331	1,435
1947	3,274	3,230	3,575	1,593	1,568	1,766	1,505	1,492	1,594
1948	3,109	3,022	3,742	1,514	1,469	1,845	1,430	1,400	1,679
1949	3,110	3,009	3,855	1,515	1,462	1,906	1,439	1,397	1,743
1950	3,091	2,977	3,928	1,505	1,446	1,940	1,435	1,387	1,780
1951	3,269	3,157	4,091	1,593	1,534	2,027	1,521	1,472	1,865
1952	3,358	3,250	4,147	1,637	1,579	2,062	1,563	1,516	1,897
1953	3,424	3,306	4,283	1,668	1,607	2,118	1,597	1,546	1,959
1954	3,543	3,415	4,474	1,727	1,660	2,216	1,657	1,601	2,062
1955	3,580	3,446	4,550	1,746	1,675	2,255	1,676	1,617	2,101
1956	3,689	3,546	4,730	1,796	1,724	2,339	1,729	1,665	2,184
1957	3,767	3,625	4,798	1,837	1,764	2,371	1,765	1,701	2,206
1958	3,701	3,560	4,727	1,807	1,735	2,339	1,736	1,675	2,178
1959	3,670	3,544	4,595	1,791	1,725	2,271	1,722	1,667	2,118
1960	3,654	3,533	4,522	1,783	1,720	2,241	1,715	1,662	2,093
1961	3,629	3,502	4,533	1,770	1,704	2,240	1,704	1,648	2,100
1962 [2]	3,474	3,348	4,396	1,695	1,630	2,170	1,633	1,577	2,033
1963 [2]	3,333	3,201	4,269	1,623	1,556	2,102	1,564	1,506	1,973
1964	3,208	3,074	4,153	1,564	1,495	2,051	1,507	1,447	1,923
1965	2,928	2,790	3,891	1,428	1,357	1,919	1,376	1,314	1,802
1966	2,736	2,609	3,615	1,336	1,271	1,785	1,288	1,231	1,678
1967	2,573	2,453	3,385	1,255	1,193	1,676	1,213	1,158	1,582
1968	2,477	2,368	3,197	1,206	1,151	1,577	1,166	1,116	1,495
1969	2,465	2,360	3,148	1,201	1,147	1,554	1,161	1,113	1,473
1970	2,480	2,385	3,067	1,207	1,158	1,509	1,168	1,125	1,433
1971	2,267	2,161	2,920	1,105	1,051	1,438	1,071	1,022	1,369
1972	2,010	1,907	2,628	980	927	1,297	950	902	1,238
1973	1,879	1,783	2,443	916	867	1,204	889	844	1,152
1974	1,835	1,749	2,339	893	849	1,149	869	828	1,103
1975	1,774	1,686	2,276	864	819	1,120	841	800	1,076
1976	1,738	1,652	2,223	847	803	1,094	825	785	1,053
1977	1,790	1,703	2,279	872	827	1,122	851	809	1,082
1978	1,760	1,668	2,265	857	810	1,114	837	793	1,076
1979	1,808	1,716	2,310	881	834	1,137	861	817	1,099
1980	1,840	1,773	2,177	896	850	1,143	876	833	1,106
1981	1,812	1,748	2,118	883	839	1,111	864	823	1,078
1982	1,828	1,767	2,107	891	848	1,111	873	832	1,079
1983	1,799	1,741	2,066	877	834	1,088	859	819	1,058
1984	1,807	1,749	2,071	881	838	1,085	864	823	1,055

Notes appear at end of table

TABLE Ab306–314   Total fertility rate, gross reproduction rate, and net reproduction rate, by race: 1905–1993
Continued

	Total fertility rate			Gross reproduction rate			Net reproduction rate		
	All women	White	Other	All women	White	Other	All women	White	Other
	Ab306	Ab307	Ab308	Ab309	Ab310	Ab311	Ab312	Ab313	Ab314
Year(s)	Per 1,000	Per 1,000	Per 1,000	Per 1,000	Per 1,000	Per 1,000	Per 1,000	Per 1,000	Per 1,000
1985	1,844	1,787	2,109	898	855	1,101	881	841	1,072
1986	1,838	1,776	2,136	896	851	1,104	879	836	1,075
1987	1,872	1,805	2,198	913	864	1,137	896	849	1,106
1988	1,934	1,857	2,298	943	888	1,188	925	873	1,155
1989	2,014	1,931	2,433	982	922	1,241	964	907	1,207
1990	2,081	2,003	2,480	1,015	956	1,266	997	941	1,233
1991	2,073	1,996	2,480	1,013	953	1,261	995	939	1,229
1992	2,065	1,994	2,442	1,007	949	1,241	990	935	1,211
1993	2,046	1,982	2,385	988	965	1,127	980	950	1,098

[1] Based on a 50 percent sample of estimated total live births for 1951–1954, 1956–1966, and 1968–1971; on a 20–50 percent sample for 1967; and on a 100 percent sample in selected states and a 50 percent sample in all other states for 1972–1984. Beginning in 1970, data exclude births to nonresidents of the United States.

[2] Excludes New Jersey, which did not require reporting of race.

Sources

1905–1910 to 1935–1940: U.S. Bureau of the Census, "Differential Fertility, 1940 and 1910: Standardized Fertility Rates and Reproduction Rates," in *Sixteenth Census of the United States: 1940* (1944), Tables 7 and 8.

1935: U.S. Public Health Service, *Vital Statistics of the United States, 1950,* volume 1, p. 87.

1940–1993, U.S. Public Health Service, *Vital Statistics of the United States, 1993,* volume 1, *Natality,* Table 1–5.

Documentation

Total fertility rates are the sums of birth rates, by age of mother, multiplied by 5. Birth rates are live births per 1,000 women in the specified groups. The total fertility rate is an age-adjusted rate because it is based on the assumption that there is the same number of women in each age group. The rate of 2,046 in 1993, for example, means that if a hypothetical group of 1,000 women were to have the same birth rate in each age group observed in the actual childbearing population in 1993, the women would have a total of 2,046 children by the time they reached the end of the reproductive period (taken here as age 50), assuming that all of the women survive to that age.

Gross reproduction rates are the sums of birth rates, by five-year age groups of mother, multiplied by 5 and by the proportion of births that were female. Birth rates are live births per 1,000 women in the specified groups. The gross reproduction rate represents the number of daughters a hypothetical cohort of 1,000 women entering the childbearing period would have during their lives, if they were subject to the age-specific birth rates observed in a given time period, and if none of the cohort were to die before the childbearing period was completed. The age-specific birth rate is the ratio of number of births by age of mother to women in each age interval for a specified year. The gross reproduction rate is the sum of the age-specific birth rates of female infants per 1,000 women. It shows the maximum possible replacement of women that may be expected from the given set of age-specific birth rates. If no migration took place and if the gross rate remained below 1,000, no improvement in mortality alone could prevent the population from declining when a stable age distribution had been reached.

Net reproduction rates are the sums of birth rates, by five-year age groups of mother, multiplied by 5 and by the proportion of births that were female and by the probability (as determined from the life table for the year) of women surviving from birth to that specified age group. The net reproduction rate is based on the specific fertility and mortality conditions existing in a given time period. If the age-specific birth and death rates of a certain year (or years) were to continue until the population became stable, a net reproduction rate of 1,000 would mean that a cohort of 1,000 newly born girls would bear just enough daughters to replace themselves. Reproduction rates are useful in the analyses of fertility and mortality conditions of a given period, but they are not indicators of future population growth. They do not take into account such factors as nuptiality, marital duration, and size of family, and they assume the continuation of the age-specific rates in a given year throughout the lifetime of a cohort of women. Since the United States has experienced major changes in marriage and fertility rates over short periods of time, variations in reproduction rates should not be taken as indications of long-term movements in family formation and rates of fertility and mortality.

Also see the text for Table Ab11–30.

TABLE Ab315-346   Fertility ratios – children under age 5 per 1,000 women ages 20-44, by race, region, and urban–rural residence: 1800-1990[1]

Contributed by Michael R. Haines

	Adjusted, United States		Unadjusted, white population									
	White population	Black population	United States			New England			Middle Atlantic		
			Total	Urban	Rural	Total	Urban	Rural	Total	Urban	Rural
	Ab315	Ab316	Ab317	Ab318	Ab319	Ab320	Ab321	Ab322	Ab323	Ab324	Ab325
Year	Per 1,000	Per 1,000	Per 1,000	Per 1,000	Per 1,000	Per 1,000	Per 1,000	Per 1,000	Per 1,000	Per 1,000	Per 1,000
1800	1,342	—	1,281	845	1,319	1,098	827	1,126	1,279	852	1,339
1810	1,358	—	1,290	900	1,329	1,052	845	1,079	1,289	924	1,344
1820	1,295	—	1,236	831	1,276	930	764	952	1,183	842	1,235
1830	1,145	—	1,134	708	1,189	812	614	851	1,036	722	1,100
1840	1,085	—	1,070	701	1,134	752	592	800	940	711	1,006
1850	892	1,087	877	—	—	621	—	—	763	—	—
1860	905	1,072	886	—	—	622	—	—	767	—	—
1870	814	997	792	—	—	544	—	—	679	—	—
1880	780	1,090	754	—	—	498	—	—	624	—	—
1890	685	930	667	—	—	440	—	—	547	—	—
1900	666	845	644	—	—	478	—	—	549	—	—
1910	631	736	609	469	782	482	468	566	533	495	650
1920	604	608	581	471	744	518	500	602	539	501	680
1930	506	554	485	388	658	441	417	541	424	386	590
1940	419	513	400	311	551	347	321	443	320	286	457
1950	580	663	551	479	673	516	486	612	471	432	596
1960	717	895	667	636	747	664	636	755	602	574	720
1970	507	689	503	483	558	521	504	574	486	466	568
1980	365	507	363	339	427	318	300	368	329	309	398
1990	355	458	347	336	379	321	308	361	327	315	380

	Unadjusted, white population											
	East North Central			West North Central			South Atlantic			East South Central		
	Total	Urban	Rural	Total	Urban	Rural	Total	Urban	Rural	Total	Urban	Rural
	Ab326	Ab327	Ab328	Ab329	Ab330	Ab331	Ab332	Ab333	Ab334	Ab335	Ab336	Ab337
Year	Per 1,000	Per 1,000	Per 1,000	Per 1,000	Per 1,000	Per 1,000	Per 1,000	Per 1,000	Per 1,000	Per 1,000	Per 1,000	Per 1,000
1800	1,840	—	1,840	—	—	—	1,345	861	1,365	1,799	—	1,799
1810	1,702	1,256	1,706	1,810	—	1,810	1,325	936	1,347	1,700	1,348	1,701
1820	1,608	1,059	1,616	1,685	—	1,685	1,280	881	1,310	1,631	1,089	1,635
1830	1,467	910	1,484	1,678	1,181	1,703	1,174	767	1,209	1,519	863	1,529
1840	1,270	841	1,291	1,445	705	1,481	1,140	770	1,185	1,408	859	1,424
1850	1,022	—	—	1,114	—	—	937	—	—	1,099	—	—
1860	999	—	—	1,105	—	—	918	—	—	1,039	—	—
1870	869	—	—	990	—	—	811	—	—	903	—	—
1880	757	—	—	905	—	—	851	—	—	926	—	—
1890	653	—	—	781	—	—	777	—	—	850	—	—
1900	599	—	—	710	—	—	779	—	—	834	—	—
1910	555	470	672	630	426	760	760	485	894	817	469	922
1920	548	485	668	584	416	711	694	458	851	734	441	846
1930	458	400	605	495	365	614	593	401	744	655	414	781
1940	388	326	533	431	324	538	464	305	596	539	333	648
1950	552	491	679	600	514	702	572	450	677	631	494	720
1960	704	674	783	743	699	816	625	588	681	656	609	707
1970	530	510	585	530	497	597	469	443	514	490	453	537
1980	380	356	441	409	365	500	329	299	385	381	343	426
1990	355	344	392	373	352	431	325	315	347	333	323	354

Note appears at end of table

TABLE Ab315–346 Fertility ratios – children under age 5 per 1,000 women ages 20–44, by race, region, and urban–rural residence: 1800–1990 *Continued*

	Unadjusted, white population								
	West South Central			Mountain			Pacific		
	Total	Urban	Rural	Total	Urban	Rural	Total	Urban	Rural
	Ab338	Ab339	Ab340	Ab341	Ab342	Ab343	Ab344	Ab345	Ab346
Year	Per 1,000	Per 1,000	Per 1,000	Per 1,000	Per 1,000	Per 1,000	Per 1,000	Per 1,000	Per 1,000
1800	—	—	—	—	—	—	—	—	—
1810	1,383	727	1,557	—	—	—	—	—	—
1820	1,418	866	1,522	—	—	—	—	—	—
1830	1,359	877	1,463	—	—	—	—	—	—
1840	1,297	846	1,495	—	—	—	—	—	—
1850	1,046	—	—	886	—	—	901	—	—
1860	1,084	—	—	1,051	—	—	1,026	—	—
1870	935	—	—	967	—	—	888	—	—
1880	1,043	—	—	872	—	—	775	—	—
1890	968	—	—	757	—	—	587	—	—
1900	925	—	—	720	—	—	512	—	—
1910	845	504	977	661	466	810	460	360	640
1920	686	445	823	664	470	807	425	344	603
1930	584	410	723	582	428	712	360	306	507
1940	474	342	591	526	404	643	339	283	466
1950	607	542	703	663	584	754	539	478	652
1960	695	680	736	775	742	859	653	633	751
1970	512	500	547	542	525	596	482	474	537
1980	403	385	452	433	411	513	341	331	408
1990	369	365	400	389	383	424	353	354	388

[1] Adjusted data were standardized for the age structure of women, and allowance was made for undercount in censuses. See text.

Sources

Series Ab315–316, 1800–1940, and series Ab317–346, 1800–1840 and 1910–1950, Wilson H. Grabill, Clyde V. Kiser, and Pascal K. Whelpton, *The Fertility of American Women* (Wiley, 1958). Series Ab315–316, 1950–1970, and series Ab317–346, 1850–1900 and 1960–1970, U.S. Bureau of the Census, special computations from decennial census reports. For 1980, the basic data were obtained from published census reports by state and aggregated up to regions. For 1990, the national data and regional totals were calculated from published census reports. The data for the white population by rural and urban residence were taken from the Integrated Public Use Microdata Series (IPUMS) metro sample for the 1990 U.S. Census, weighted up by "perwt." See the Guide to the Millennial Edition for information on IPUMS.

Documentation

Figures for series Ab315–316 were adjusted for underreporting of children in 1800–1940 on the basis of factors obtained for 1925–1930 and for underreporting of both women and children in 1950–1990 on the basis of estimates derived by analytical methods. The ratios for white women for 1830–1970 have been standardized for age of women using the 1930 age distribution of women to offset the effect of changes in the age distribution of the female population. Therefore, the figures represent the fertility ratios of women having the same age distribution as those in 1930. Rates for 1800–1860 are partly estimated. The analytical estimates of census undercount for 1980 and 1990 were furnished by J. Gregory Robinson of the U.S. Bureau of the Census, Population Division. For methodology, see J. Gregory Robinson, B. Ahmed, P. Das Gupta, and K. A. Woodrow, "Estimation of Population Coverage in the 1990 United States Census Based on Demographic Analysis," *Journal of the American Statistical Association* 88 (423) (1993): 1061–71.

The urban–rural classification shown for 1800–1950 is based on the rules used in 1940. That shown for 1960–1970 is based on the rules used for those censuses. For definition of residence by old and new rules of classification, see text for Table Aa684–698. The change in rules is known to have relatively little effect on the fertility ratios for 1950 and probably has little effect on the comparability of the fertility ratios for 1969–1970 with those of earlier years.

See Table Ap-G in Appendix 2 regarding the composition of census regions and divisions.

TABLE Ab347–361   Median interval between births, by race: 1930–1979[1]

Contributed by Michael R. Haines

All races

Years	First marriage to first birth Ab347 Months	First birth to second birth Ab348 Months	Second birth to third birth Ab349 Months	Third birth to fourth birth Ab350 Months	Fourth birth to fifth birth Ab351 Months
1930–1934	15.5	27.6	27.0	23.8	28.4
1935–1939	16.8	28.3	29.2	28.6	31.9
1940–1944	18.5	29.7	30.2	28.8	34.3
1945–1949	18.1	30.0	30.3	29.1	32.5
1950–1954	18.1	30.4	29.5	28.6	32.4
1955–1959	15.7	27.8	30.8	29.6	30.9
1960–1964	14.2	26.4	30.1	30.3	31.4
1965–1969	14.0	29.1	33.9	33.9	36.2
1970–1974	16.6	32.8	35.7	37.3	36.1
1975–1979	23.5	36.0	39.3	39.5	36.8

White

Years	First marriage to first birth Ab352 Months	First birth to second birth Ab353 Months	Second birth to third birth Ab354 Months	Third birth to fourth birth Ab355 Months	Fourth birth to fifth birth Ab356 Months
1930–1934	15.9	28.0	27.3	24.0	29.3
1935–1939	17.6	28.8	31.2	29.3	32.5
1940–1944	19.2	30.7	31.7	29.6	35.5
1945–1949	19.1	30.9	31.9	29.5	33.2
1950–1954	18.9	31.3	30.5	29.6	33.4
1955–1959	16.4	28.2	31.9	30.5	31.5
1960–1964	14.9	26.6	31.7	31.7	32.0
1965–1969	15.2	29.6	34.9	35.2	38.3
1970–1974	18.6	33.2	36.2	39.4	39.0
1975–1979	25.0	35.7	40.1	42.2	41.0

Black

Years	First marriage to first birth Ab357 Months	First birth to second birth Ab358 Months	Second birth to third birth Ab359 Months	Third birth to fourth birth Ab360 Months	Fourth birth to fifth birth Ab361 Months
1930–1934	10.9	24.7	25.5	—[2]	—[2]
1935–1939	9.1	22.2	24.1	23.4	—[2]
1940–1944	10.7	23.7	24.7	24.6	—[2]
1945–1949	9.8	23.9	24.2	23.7	31.2
1950–1954	12.4	24.1	23.4	24.7	27.6
1955–1959	7.7	23.4	25.6	24.1	28.4
1960–1964	6.6	25.3	22.9	23.3	29.0
1965–1969	4.4	26.4	28.7	27.0	29.9
1970–1974	4.1	31.1	32.8	27.7	30.7
1975–1979	10.1	39.1	37.2	28.2	29.1

[1] Excludes Alaska and Hawai'i. Excludes institutional population. Based on sample data.

[2] Not shown. The base for the estimate is too small (number of children reported by women surviving to 1980 is less than 150,000).

Source

U.S. Bureau of the Census, *Current Population Reports*, series P-20, number 385, "Childspacing among Birth Cohorts of American Women: 1905 to 1979," February 1984, Tables 9 and 10.

Documentation

The median interval between two sets of events is an estimate of the length of time after the first set of events in which half of the second set takes place. If the first set of events is births of a first child and the second set is births of a second child and the estimate of the median interval is 32.2 months, the interpretation is that half of the second births occur within 32.2 months of the first births. Data on median intervals between births and first marriage and between births of successive orders are useful for comparing childspacing and family building patterns between subgroups within a population at a given point in time and between different cohorts either of women or (as in Table Ab315–346) of their children.

TABLE Ab362–389   Live births, crude birth rates, and general fertility rates, by Hispanic origin and race of mother: 1989–1998[1]

Contributed by Michael R. Haines

Live births

		Hispanic						Non-Hispanic		
	Total	Total	Mexican	Puerto Rican	Cuban	Central and South American	Other and unknown	Total	White	Black
	Ab362	Ab363	Ab364	Ab365	Ab366	Ab367	Ab368	Ab369	Ab370	Ab371
Year	Number	Number	Number	Number	Number	Number	Number	Number	Number	Number
1989	3,903,012	532,249	327,233	56,229	10,842	72,443	65,502	3,297,493	2,526,367	611,269
1990	4,092,994	595,073	385,640	58,807	11,311	83,008	56,307	3,457,417	2,626,500	661,701
1991	4,094,566	623,085	411,233	59,833	11,058	86,908	54,053	3,434,464	2,589,878	666,758
1992	4,049,024	643,271	432,047	59,569	11,472	89,031	51,152	3,365,862	2,527,207	657,450
1993	4,000,240	654,418	443,733	58,102	11,916	92,371	48,296	3,295,345	2,472,031	641,273
1994	3,952,767	665,026	454,536	57,240	11,889	93,485	47,876	3,245,115	2,438,855	619,198
1995	3,899,589	679,768	469,615	54,824	12,473	94,996	47,860	3,160,495	2,382,638	587,781
1996	3,891,494	701,339	489,666	54,863	12,613	97,888	46,309	3,133,484	2,358,989	578,099
1997	3,880,894	709,767	499,024	55,450	12,887	97,405	45,001	3,115,174	2,333,363	581,431
1998	3,941,553	734,661	516,011	57,349	13,226	98,226	49,849	3,158,975	2,361,462	593,127

Crude birth rate

		Hispanic					Non-Hispanic		
	All women	Total	Mexican	Puerto Rican	Cuban	Other and unknown [2]	Total	White	Black
	Ab372	Ab373	Ab374	Ab375	Ab376	Ab377	Ab378	Ab379	Ab380
Year	Per 1,000	Per 1,000	Per 1,000	Per 1,000	Per 1,000	Per 1,000	Per 1,000	Per 1,000	Per 1,000
1989	16.3	26.2	25.7	23.7	10.0	28.3	15.4	14.2	22.8
1990	16.7	26.7	28.7	21.6	10.9	27.5	15.7	14.4	23.0
1991	16.3	26.7	29.2	21.0	10.1	26.5	15.2	13.9	22.5
1992	15.9	26.5	27.8	23.2	10.1	27.9	14.8	13.5	21.9
1993	15.5	26.0	27.4	21.9	10.5	26.9	14.4	13.1	21.1
1994	15.2	25.5	27.0	21.4	10.8	25.7	14.0	12.8	20.0
1995	14.8	25.2	26.9	19.7	11.0	25.3	13.7	12.6	18.8
1996	14.7	24.8	27.4	17.9	10.7	23.4	13.5	12.4	18.3
1997	14.5	24.2	26.8	18.1	10.1	22.4	13.3	12.2	18.1
1998	14.6	24.3	26.4	19.0	10.0	23.2	13.4	12.3	18.2

General fertility rate

		Hispanic					Non-Hispanic		
	All women	Total	Mexican	Puerto Rican	Cuban	Other and unknown [2]	Total	White	Black
	Ab381	Ab382	Ab383	Ab384	Ab385	Ab386	Ab387	Ab388	Ab389
Year	Per 1,000	Per 1,000	Per 1,000	Per 1,000	Per 1,000	Per 1,000	Per 1,000	Per 1,000	Per 1,000
1989	69.2	104.9	106.6	86.6	49.8	95.8	65.7	60.5	84.8
1990	71.0	107.7	118.9	82.9	52.6	102.7	67.1	62.8	89.0
1991	69.6	108.1	121.6	80.9	49.1	99.3	65.4	61.0	87.6
1992	68.9	108.6	116.0	89.9	50.3	107.0	64.4	60.2	85.5
1993	67.6	106.9	114.8	82.5	55.5	105.0	63.1	59.0	82.7
1994	66.7	105.6	115.4	81.9	55.9	97.7	62.0	58.3	79.0
1995	65.6	105.0	117.0	75.7	55.1	94.5	60.8	57.6	74.5
1996	65.3	104.9	119.3	71.3	58.9	90.2	60.3	57.3	72.5
1997	65.0	102.8	116.6	71.7	57.4	87.6	60.1	57.0	72.4
1998	65.6	101.1	112.1	75.5	50.1	90.2	60.7	57.7	73.0

[1] Excludes Louisiana (1989), New Hampshire (1989–1992), and Oklahoma (1989–1990), which did not report Hispanic origin.

[2] The rate includes both the Central and South American population and the other and unknown population.

Source

S. J. Ventura, J. A. Martin, S. C. Curtin, T. J. Matthews, and M. M. Park, "Births: Final Data for 1998," *National Vital Statistics Reports*, volume 48, number 3 (National Center for Health Statistics, 2000), Table 6.

Documentation

Race and Hispanic origin are reported separately on both birth and death certificates. Persons of Hispanic origin may be of any race. In Tables Ab362–497 and Ab1059–1137 Hispanic persons are classified only by place of origin; non-Hispanic women are classified by race. Data for persons of Hispanic origin are not further classified by race because the vast majority of Hispanic deaths and births to Hispanic women are reported as white. Data

(continued)

TABLE Ab362–389   Live births, crude birth rates, and general fertility rates, by Hispanic origin and race of mother: 1989–1998   *Continued*

for non-Hispanic persons are classified according to the race of the mother because there are substantial differences between Hispanics and non-Hispanic white persons (for example, in fertility and in maternal and child health). Items asking for the Hispanic origin of the mother and the father have been included on the birth and death certificates of all states and the District of Columbia only since 1993.

The crude birth rate is live births per 1,000 population per annum in the specified group. The general fertility rate is live births per 1,000 women ages 15–44 in the specified group.

Series Ab362. Includes origin not stated.

Series Ab369. Includes races other than white and black.

TABLE Ab390–497   Total fertility rates, general fertility rates, and age-specific birth rates, by Hispanic origin and race of mother: 1989–1998[1]

Contributed by Michael R. Haines

			All women									
			Birth rate, for women ages									
	Total fertility rate	General fertility rate	10–14	15–19	15–17	18–19	20–24	25–29	30–34	35–39	40–44	45–49
	Ab390	Ab391	Ab392	Ab393	Ab394	Ab395	Ab396	Ab397	Ab398	Ab399	Ab400	Ab401
Year	Per 1,000	Per 1,000	Per 1,000	Per 1,000	Per 1,000	Per 1,000	Per 1,000	Per 1,000	Per 1,000	Per 1,000	Per 1,000	Per 1,000
1989	2,014.0	69.2	1.4	57.3	36.4	84.2	113.8	117.6	77.4	29.9	5.2	0.2
1990	2,081.0	70.9	1.4	59.9	37.5	88.6	116.5	120.2	80.8	31.7	5.5	0.2
1991	2,073.0	69.6	1.4	62.1	38.7	94.4	115.7	118.2	79.5	32.0	5.5	0.2
1992	2,065.0	68.9	1.4	60.7	37.8	94.5	114.6	117.4	80.2	32.5	5.9	0.3
1993	2,046.0	67.6	1.4	59.6	37.8	92.1	112.6	115.5	80.8	32.9	6.1	0.3
1994	2,036.0	66.7	1.4	58.9	37.6	91.5	111.1	113.9	81.5	33.7	6.4	0.3
1995	2,019.0	65.6	1.3	56.8	36.0	89.1	109.8	112.2	82.5	34.3	6.6	0.3
1996	2,027.0	65.3	1.2	54.4	33.8	86.0	110.4	113.1	83.9	35.3	6.8	0.3
1997	2,032.5	65.0	1.1	52.3	32.1	83.6	110.4	113.8	85.3	36.1	7.1	0.4
1998	2,058.5	65.6	1.0	51.1	30.4	82.0	111.2	115.9	87.4	37.4	7.3	0.4

			All Hispanic women									
			Birth rate, for women ages									
	Total fertility rate	General fertility rate	10–14	15–19	15–17	18–19	20–24	25–29	30–34	35–39	40–44	45–49
	Ab402	Ab403	Ab404	Ab405	Ab406	Ab407	Ab408	Ab409	Ab410	Ab411	Ab412	Ab413
Year	Per 1,000	Per 1,000	Per 1,000	Per 1,000	Per 1,000	Per 1,000	Per 1,000	Per 1,000	Per 1,000	Per 1,000	Per 1,000	Per 1,000
1989	2,903.5	104.9	2.3	100.8	—	—	184.4	146.6	92.1	43.5	10.4	0.6
1990	2,959.5	107.7	2.4	100.3	65.9	147.7	181.0	153.0	98.3	45.3	10.9	0.7
1991	3,002.5	108.1	2.4	106.7	70.6	158.5	186.3	152.8	96.1	44.9	10.7	0.6
1992	3,043.0	108.6	2.6	107.1	71.4	159.7	190.6	154.4	96.8	45.6	10.9	0.6
1993	3,020.5	106.9	2.7	106.8	71.7	159.1	188.3	154.0	96.4	44.7	10.6	0.6
1994	3,014.0	105.6	2.7	107.7	74.0	158.0	188.2	153.2	95.4	44.3	10.7	0.6
1995	3,019.5	105.0	2.7	106.7	72.9	157.9	188.5	153.8	95.9	44.9	10.8	0.6
1996	3,047.5	104.9	2.6	101.8	69.0	151.1	189.5	161.0	98.1	45.1	10.8	0.6
1997	2,999.5	102.8	2.3	97.4	66.3	144.3	184.2	161.7	97.9	45.0	10.8	0.6
1998	2,947.5	101.1	2.1	93.6	62.3	140.1	178.4	160.2	98.9	44.9	10.8	0.6

Notes appear at end of table

TABLE Ab390–497   Total fertility rates, general fertility rates, and age-specific birth rates, by Hispanic origin and race of mother: 1989–1998 *Continued*

Mexican women

							Birth rate, for women ages					
	Total fertility rate	General fertility rate	10–14	15–19	15–17	18–19	20–24	25–29	30–34	35–39	40–44	45–49
	Ab414	Ab415	Ab416	Ab417	Ab418	Ab419	Ab420	Ab421	Ab422	Ab423	Ab424	Ab425
Year	Per 1,000	Per 1,000	Per 1,000	Per 1,000	Per 1,000	Per 1,000	Per 1,000	Per 1,000	Per 1,000	Per 1,000	Per 1,000	Per 1,000
1989	2,916.5	106.6	2.0	94.5	—	—	184.3	153.7	96.1	41.0	11.1	0.6
1990	3,214.0	118.9	2.5	108.0	69.7	162.2	200.3	165.3	104.4	49.1	12.4	0.8
1991	3,317.5	121.6	2.6	117.3	75.9	178.4	209.9	168.2	103.3	49.1	12.3	0.8
1992	3,196.5	116.0	2.5	108.8	—	—	202.3	166.3	99.1	47.7	11.8	0.8
1993	3,174.0	114.8	2.6	108.7	71.6	164.9	196.6	168.2	100.5	46.1	11.3	0.8
1994	3,211.5	115.4	2.8	116.2	78.0	175.0	202.6	165.2	96.9	46.2	11.7	0.7
1995	3,273.5	117.0	2.8	124.6	84.4	185.3	208.9	160.5	98.5	46.8	11.9	0.7
1996	3,353.5	119.3	2.8	120.7	83.4	174.3	206.3	176.9	103.7	47.6	12.0	0.7
1997	3,307.5	116.6	2.5	112.4	77.3	165.1	204.9	176.3	104.2	49.0	11.6	0.6
1998	3,198.0	112.1	2.2	102.7	67.0	159.1	197.6	173.5	103.7	48.4	10.9	0.6

Puerto Rican women

							Birth rate, for women ages					
	Total fertility rate	General fertility rate	10–14	15–19	15–17	18–19	20–24	25–29	30–34	35–39	40–44	45–49
	Ab426	Ab427	Ab428	Ab429	Ab430	Ab431	Ab432	Ab433	Ab434	Ab435	Ab436	Ab437
Year	Per 1,000	Per 1,000	Per 1,000	Per 1,000	Per 1,000	Per 1,000	Per 1,000	Per 1,000	Per 1,000	Per 1,000	Per 1,000	Per 1,000
1989	2,421.0	86.6	3.8	112.7	—	—	171.0	98.0	65.2	26.9	6.3	0.3
1990	2,301.0	82.9	2.9	101.6	71.6	141.6	150.1	109.9	62.8	26.2	6.2	0.5
1991	2,276.0	80.9	2.5	102.7	75.2	143.0	149.4	107.5	61.4	25.7	5.7	0.3
1992	2,644.5	89.9	3.5	110.4	—	—	204.9	106.6	66.7	30.0	6.5	0.3
1993	2,523.5	82.5	3.1	110.0	73.4	181.0	193.1	108.4	56.3	27.1	6.2	0.5
1994	2,490.0	81.9	3.2	106.0	72.8	168.4	181.0	111.7	62.3	28.0	5.6	0.2
1995	2,245.5	75.7	3.0	89.0	61.2	139.2	151.5	107.2	64.8	27.7	5.6	0.3
1996	2,163.0	71.3	2.1	82.3	52.2	143.2	148.8	109.4	58.3	25.9	5.6	—
1997	2,164.0	71.7	1.8	74.9	48.9	120.0	154.0	109.3	59.1	27.0	6.2	0.5
1998	2,268.0	75.5	1.9	81.2	55.1	120.7	164.2	104.4	67.6	26.7	7.2	0.4

Cuban women

							Birth rate, for women ages					
	Total fertility rate	General fertility rate	10–14	15–19	15–17	18–19	20–24	25–29	30–34	35–39	40–44	45–49
	Ab438	Ab439	Ab440	Ab441	Ab442	Ab443	Ab444	Ab445	Ab446	Ab447	Ab448	Ab449
Year	Per 1,000	Per 1,000	Per 1,000	Per 1,000	Per 1,000	Per 1,000	Per 1,000	Per 1,000	Per 1,000	Per 1,000	Per 1,000	Per 1,000
1989	1,479.0	49.8	0.5	25.1	—	—	64.2	101.8	73.7	27.2	3.0	0.3
1990	1,459.5	52.6	—	30.3	18.2	46.1	64.6	95.4	67.6	28.2	4.9	—
1991	1,385.5	49.1	—	27.7	17.5	41.3	61.2	88.8	68.2	26.7	4.0	—
1992	1,485.5	50.3	1.0	26.3	—	—	51.6	98.4	86.2	28.9	4.7	(Z)
1993	1,632.5	55.5	—	33.0	20.4	49.7	68.9	102.0	86.9	31.0	4.7	—
1994	1,680.5	55.9	0.6	40.2	23.1	77.4	72.5	98.4	87.6	31.3	5.5	—
1995	1,705.5	55.1	—	29.2	16.6	51.2	77.0	110.6	88.0	29.8	6.0	—
1996	1,774.5	58.9	0.9	34.0	19.8	54.5	82.5	110.7	85.9	34.3	6.4	—
1997	1,814.5	57.4	1.0	38.3	25.3	53.4	82.7	123.5	75.7	35.1	6.3	0.3
1998	1,560.0	50.1	0.8	24.2	15.6	38.8	85.6	95.2	64.5	34.2	7.1	—

Notes appear at end of table

(continued)

TABLE Ab390–497   Total fertility rates, general fertility rates, and age-specific birth rates, by Hispanic origin and race of mother: 1989–1998 *Continued*

Other Hispanic women

						Birth rate, for women ages					
	Total fertility rate	General fertility rate	10–14	15–19	15–17	18–19	20–24	25–29	30–34	35–39	40–44	45–49
	Ab450	Ab451	Ab452	Ab453	Ab454	Ab455	Ab456	Ab457	Ab458	Ab459	Ab460	Ab461
Year	Per 1,000	Per 1,000	Per 1,000	Per 1,000	Per 1,000	Per 1,000	Per 1,000	Per 1,000	Per 1,000	Per 1,000	Per 1,000	Per 1,000
1989	2,683.0	95.8	1.7	66.4	—	—	159.2	150.4	85.1	60.3	12.7	0.8
1990	2,877.0	102.7	2.1	86.0	57.2	123.8	162.9	155.8	106.9	49.4	11.6	0.7
1991	2,817.0	99.3	2.1	88.1	58.9	128.8	161.1	150.6	101.5	48.2	11.2	0.6
1992	3,076.0	107.0	2.5	112.1	—	—	172.9	157.8	106.6	50.3	12.5	0.5
1993	3,038.5	105.0	2.7	106.9	78.2	141.7	175.2	147.1	110.4	52.4	12.5	0.5
1994	2,855.5	97.7	2.6	87.9	66.4	112.4	162.0	147.4	109.3	49.4	11.9	0.6
1995	2,834.0	94.5	2.4	77.5	54.8	107.8	158.3	161.8	103.7	50.9	11.6	0.6
1996	2,762.0	90.2	2.4	69.8	46.6	103.1	166.5	146.3	105.3	50.4	11.0	0.7
1997	2,653.5	87.6	2.0	72.1	48.3	106.8	146.4	147.9	104.4	45.4	11.8	0.7
1998	2,719.0	90.2	1.9	80.0	56.7	106.9	137.4	157.2	106.9	46.9	12.9	0.6

All non-Hispanic women

						Birth rate, for women ages					
	Total fertility rate	General fertility rate	10–14	15–19	15–17	18–19	20–24	25–29	30–34	35–39	40–44	45–49
	Ab462	Ab463	Ab464	Ab465	Ab466	Ab467	Ab468	Ab469	Ab470	Ab471	Ab472	Ab473
Year	Per 1,000	Per 1,000	Per 1,000	Per 1,000	Per 1,000	Per 1,000	Per 1,000	Per 1,000	Per 1,000	Per 1,000	Per 1,000	Per 1,000
1989	1,921.0	65.7	1.3	53.4	—	—	107.8	113.4	74.7	28.6	4.8	0.2
1990	1,979.5	67.1	1.3	54.8	33.8	81.4	108.1	116.5	79.2	30.7	5.1	0.2
1991	1,959.5	65.4	1.3	56.1	34.4	86.1	106.6	114.0	77.8	30.8	5.1	0.2
1992	1,941.0	64.4	1.2	54.4	33.2	85.5	104.7	112.7	78.4	31.2	5.4	0.2
1993	1,918.5	63.1	1.2	52.9	33.1	82.6	102.5	110.4	79.0	31.7	5.7	0.3
1994	1,905.0	62.0	1.2	52.0	32.5	81.8	100.4	108.6	79.9	32.6	6.0	0.3
1995	1,881.0	60.8	1.1	49.6	30.7	79.0	98.5	106.4	80.9	33.2	6.2	0.3
1996	1,881.0	60.3	1.0	47.3	28.7	76.2	98.4	106.5	82.0	34.2	6.5	0.3
1997	1,888.5	60.1	0.9	45.5	27.0	74.3	98.6	107.0	83.5	35.1	6.7	0.4
1998	1,919.5	60.7	0.8	44.3	25.4	72.8	99.9	109.3	85.7	36.5	7.0	0.4

Non-Hispanic white women

						Birth rate, for women ages					
	Total fertility rate	General fertility rate	10–14	15–19	15–17	18–19	20–24	25–29	30–34	35–39	40–44	45–49
	Ab474	Ab475	Ab476	Ab477	Ab478	Ab479	Ab480	Ab481	Ab482	Ab483	Ab484	Ab485
Year	Per 1,000	Per 1,000	Per 1,000	Per 1,000	Per 1,000	Per 1,000	Per 1,000	Per 1,000	Per 1,000	Per 1,000	Per 1,000	Per 1,000
1989	1,770.0	60.5	0.4	39.9	—	—	94.7	111.7	75.0	27.8	4.3	0.2
1990	1,850.5	62.8	0.5	42.5	23.2	66.6	97.5	115.3	79.4	30.0	4.7	0.2
1991	1,826.5	61.0	0.5	43.4	23.6	70.5	95.7	112.7	77.9	30.2	4.7	0.2
1992	1,810.5	60.2	0.5	41.7	22.7	69.8	93.9	111.5	78.7	30.5	5.1	0.2
1993	1,792.5	59.0	0.5	40.7	22.7	67.7	92.1	109.2	79.4	31.1	5.3	0.2
1994	1,792.0	58.3	0.5	40.4	22.8	67.4	90.9	107.9	80.7	32.1	5.7	0.2
1995	1,786.5	57.6	0.4	39.3	22.0	66.1	90.0	106.5	82.0	32.9	5.9	0.3
1996	1,795.5	57.3	0.4	37.6	20.6	63.7	90.1	107.0	83.5	34.0	6.2	0.3
1997	1,801.0	57.0	0.4	36.0	19.4	61.9	89.8	107.2	85.2	34.9	6.4	0.3
1998	1,837.0	57.7	0.3	35.2	18.4	60.6	90.7	109.7	88.0	36.4	6.7	0.4

TABLE Ab390–497   Total fertility rates, general fertility rates, and age-specific birth rates, by Hispanic origin and race of mother: 1989–1998 *Continued*

			Non-Hispanic black women									
			Birth rate, for women ages									
	Total fertility rate	General fertility rate	10–14	15–19	15–17	18–19	20–24	25–29	30–34	35–39	40–44	45–49
	Ab486	Ab487	Ab488	Ab489	Ab490	Ab491	Ab492	Ab493	Ab494	Ab495	Ab496	Ab497
Year	Per 1,000	Per 1,000	Per 1,000	Per 1,000	Per 1,000	Per 1,000	Per 1,000	Per 1,000	Per 1,000	Per 1,000	Per 1,000	Per 1,000
1989	2,424.0	64.8	5.2	111.9	—	—	156.3	113.8	65.7	26.3	5.3	0.3
1990	2,547.5	89.0	5.0	116.2	84.9	157.5	165.1	118.4	70.2	28.7	5.6	0.3
1991	2,551.0	87.6	4.9	118.9	86.7	163.1	166.1	116.3	69.3	28.9	5.6	0.2
1992	2,514.0	85.5	4.8	116.0	83.9	162.9	163.0	114.6	69.1	29.4	5.7	0.2
1993	2,454.5	82.7	4.7	112.2	82.5	156.7	157.4	111.5	69.0	29.8	6.0	0.3
1994	2,365.0	79.0	4.7	107.7	78.6	152.9	150.3	107.0	67.5	29.5	6.0	0.3
1995	2,245.0	74.5	4.3	99.3	72.1	141.9	141.7	102.0	65.9	29.4	6.1	0.3
1996	2,204.0	72.5	3.8	94.2	66.6	136.6	140.9	100.8	64.9	29.7	6.2	0.3
1997	2,210.5	72.4	3.4	90.8	62.6	134.0	143.0	101.9	65.8	30.3	6.6	0.3
1998	2,235.5	73.0	3.0	88.2	58.8	130.9	146.4	104.6	66.6	31.2	6.8	0.3

(Z) Fewer than 0.05 births.

[1] Excludes Louisiana (1989), New Hampshire (1989–1992), and Oklahoma (1989–1990), which did not report Hispanic origin.

Source

S. J. Ventura, J. A. Martin, S. C. Curtin, T. J. Matthews, and M. M. Park, "Births: Final Data for 1998," in *National Vital Statistics Reports*, volume 48, number 3 (National Center for Health Statistics, 2000), Table 9.

Documentation

See the text for Table Ab362–389.

Total fertility rates are sums of birth rates for five-year age groups multiplied by 5. General fertility rates are total live births, regardless of age of mother, per 1,000 women ages 15–44 in the specified group, enumerated as of April 1 for 1990, and estimated as of July 1 for all other years. Beginning in 1997, rates computed by relating births to women ages 45–54 to those to women ages 45–49.

Series Ab450–461. Includes Central and South American as well as other and unknown Hispanic origin.

Series Ab462–473. Includes races other than white and black.

Series Ab462–497. Includes persons for whom Hispanic origin was not stated.

TABLE Ab498–535   Ever-married women – percentage distribution, by number of children ever born, birth cohort, and race: 1835–1944

Contributed by Michael R. Haines

			All races							
			Percentage with							
	Census year	Age of women reporting	No births	1 or 2 births	3 or 4 births	5 or 6 births	7, 8, or 9 births	7 or more births	10 or more births	Children per 1,000 women
	Ab498	Ab499	Ab500	Ab501	Ab502	Ab503	Ab504	Ab505	Ab506	Ab507
Year of birth	—	Years	Percent	Percent	Percent	Percent	Percent	Percent	Percent	Number
1835–1839	1910	70–74	7.7	17.3	20.0	18.7	21.6	36.3	14.7	5,395
1840–1844	1910	65–69	7.9	17.9	20.1	18.1	21.6	35.9	14.3	5,364
1845–1949	1910	60–64	8.2	18.5	20.3	18.3	20.8	34.8	14.0	5,266
1850–1854	1910	55–59	8.3	18.8	20.8	17.8	20.4	34.3	13.9	5,218
1855–1859	1910	50–54	8.9	20.6	21.3	17.9	19.0	31.3	12.3	4,972
1860–1864	1910	45–49	9.5	22.4	22.0	17.3	17.6	28.8	11.2	4,744
1865–1869	1940	70–74	12.3	26.6	26.1	16.0	12.5	18.9	6.4	3,901
1870–1874	1940	65–69	13.9	28.4	25.1	15.2	11.6	17.4	5.8	3,700
1875–1879	1940	60–64	15.0	30.5	25.2	14.4	10.3	15.0	4.7	3,462
1880–1884	1940	55–59	16.7	30.7	24.7	14.1	9.6	13.8	4.2	3,301
1885–1889	1940	50–54	16.6	33.1	25.1	13.1	8.6	12.2	3.6	3,146
1890–1894	1940	45–49	16.8	35.3	25.0	12.2	7.7	10.8	3.1	2,998
1895–1899	1950	50–54	18.6	39.0	23.9	10.0	5.8	8.4	2.6	2,706
1900–1904	1950	45–49	20.4	41.5	22.4	8.4	5.0	7.2	2.2	2,492
1905–1909	1960	50–54	20.8	43.2	22.3	7.8	4.2	5.9	1.7	2,355
1910–1914	1960	45–49	18.1	44.2	24.7	7.8	3.8	5.3	1.5	2,402
1915–1919	1970	50–54	13.8	43.1	28.9	8.8	3.9	5.3	1.4	2,854
1920–1924	1970	45–49	10.6	39.9	32.8	10.7	4.5	6.0	1.5	2,701
1925–1929	1980	50–54	9.0	35.1	36.1	12.9	—	6.9	—	3,101
1930–1934	1980	45–49	7.4	32.2	39.1	14.4	—	6.8	—	3,229
1935–1939	1990	50–54	7.6	35.3	40.3	12.1	—	4.7	—	3,004
1940–1944	1990	45–49	8.9	45.4	35.9	7.7	—	2.1	—	2,556

(continued)

TABLE Ab498–535   Ever-married women – percentage distribution, by number of children ever born, birth cohort, and race: 1835–1944 *Continued*

			White							
			Percentage with							
	Census year	Age of women reporting	No births	1 or 2 births	3 or 4 births	5 or 6 births	7, 8, or 9 births	7 or more births	10 or more births	Children per 1,000 women
	Ab498	Ab499	Ab508	Ab509	Ab510	Ab511	Ab512	Ab513	Ab514	Ab515
Year of birth	—	Years	Percent	Percent	Percent	Percent	Percent	Percent	Percent	Number
1835–1839	1910	70–74	7.9	17.5	20.3	19.1	21.8	35.2	13.4	5,278
1840–1844	1910	65–69	8.0	18.2	20.6	18.5	21.7	34.7	13.0	5,237
1845–1949	1910	60–64	8.3	18.8	20.8	18.7	20.9	33.5	12.6	5,123
1850–1854	1910	55–59	8.4	19.1	21.3	18.2	20.5	33.0	12.5	5,082
1855–1859	1910	50–54	9.0	20.9	22.0	18.3	19.0	29.8	10.8	4,817
1860–1864	1910	45–49	9.6	22.9	22.7	17.7	17.4	27.2	9.8	4,594
1865–1869	1940	70–74	14.3	26.6	25.7	15.7	11.8	17.6	5.8	3,741
1870–1874	1940	65–69	15.7	28.3	25.0	14.6	11.2	16.4	5.2	3,558
1875–1879	1940	60–64	16.6	30.3	24.9	13.9	9.9	14.2	4.3	3,349
1880–1884	1940	55–59	16.7	31.4	24.7	13.7	9.2	13.4	4.2	3,270
1885–1889	1940	50–54	16.4	33.6	25.3	13.0	8.4	11.6	3.2	3,106
1890–1894	1940	45–49	16.3	36.0	25.5	12.1	7.4	10.1	2.7	2,968
1895–1899	1950	50–54	18.0	39.9	24.5	10.0	5.4	7.7	2.3	2,665
1900–1904	1950	45–49	19.5	42.7	23.0	8.3	4.6	6.5	1.9	2,456
1905–1909	1960	50–54	20.0	44.3	23.0	7.6	3.8	5.2	1.4	2,313
1910–1914	1960	45–49	17.1	45.4	25.6	7.6	3.3	4.4	1.1	2,354
1915–1919	1970	50–54	12.9	44.3	29.9	8.6	3.3	4.3	1.0	2,553
1920–1924	1970	45–49	9.9	40.9	33.9	10.5	3.8	4.8	1.0	2,791
1925–1929	1980	50–54	8.5	36.2	37.8	12.4	—	5.1	—	2,985
1930–1934	1980	45–49	7.0	33.1	41.0	13.9	—	5.0	—	3,113
1935–1939	1990	50–54	7.3	36.6	41.7	11.2	—	3.1	—	2,891
1940–1944	1990	45–49	8.9	45.4	35.9	7.7	—	2.1	—	2,466

			Black							
			Percentage with							
	Census year	Age of women reporting	No births	1 or 2 births	3 or 4 births	5 or 6 births	7, 8, or 9 births	7 or more births	10 or more births	Children per 1,000 women
	Ab498	Ab499	Ab516	Ab517	Ab518	Ab519	Ab520	Ab521	Ab522	Ab523
Year of birth	—	Years	Percent	Percent	Percent	Percent	Percent	Percent	Percent	Number
1835–1839	1910	70–74	5.4	12.4	14.1	11.3	21.4	56.8	35.4	6,947
1840–1844	1910	65–69	6.9	16.3	14.1	14.0	18.4	48.7	30.3	7,035
1845–1949	1910	60–64	5.9	13.9	13.8	14.2	21.3	52.2	30.9	6,883
1850–1854	1910	55–59	7.2	16.1	14.5	12.7	18.7	49.5	30.8	6,910
1855–1859	1910	50–54	7.8	16.4	14.0	13.6	19.5	48.2	28.7	6,580
1860–1864	1910	45–49	8.6	17.9	15.5	13.8	18.7	44.2	25.5	6,162
1865–1869	1940	70–74	12.8	18.1	22.6	15.1	17.6	31.4	13.8	4,892
1870–1874	1940	65–69	14.5	22.1	20.9	17.5	14.1	25.1	11.0	4,347
1875–1879	1940	60–64	17.0	23.0	21.3	16.5	13.0	22.2	9.2	4,046
1880–1884	1940	55–59	19.3	25.5	21.4	14.1	10.9	19.7	8.8	3,751
1885–1889	1940	50–54	20.1	25.6	22.1	14.2	10.7	18.0	7.3	3,594
1890–1894	1940	45–49	23.8	28.1	19.5	12.6	9.9	16.0	6.1	3,255
1895–1899	1950	50–54	25.5	30.9	17.4	10.9	8.8	15.3	6.5	3,085
1900–1904	1950	45–49	28.4	31.9	17.6	9.2	8.0	12.9	4.9	2,767
1905–1909	1960	50–54	28.5	34.0	16.0	8.9	7.6	12.6	5.0	2,696
1910–1914	1960	45–49	27.9	33.2	16.9	8.9	7.8	13.0	5.2	2,761
1915–1919	1970	50–54	23.0	33.0	18.9	10.9	8.8	14.2	5.4	3,030
1920–1924	1970	45–49	17.9	31.3	21.4	13.1	10.5	16.3	5.8	3,394
1925–1929	1980	50–54	13.8	28.3	23.5	15.6	—	18.8	—	3,796
1930–1934	1980	45–49	10.1	27.2	26.3	17.7	—	18.7	—	3,941
1935–1939	1990	50–54	9.2	28.5	31.8	16.9	—	13.6	—	3,613
1940–1944	1990	45–49	9.3	37.7	33.2	13.6	—	6.2	—	2,973

TABLE Ab498–535   Ever-married women – percentage distribution, by number of children ever born, birth cohort, and race: 1835–1944   *Continued*

			American Indian					
			Percentage with					Children per
	Census year	Age of women reporting	No births	1 or 2 births	3 or 4 births	5 or 6 births	7 or more births	1,000 women
	Ab498	Ab499	Ab524	Ab525	Ab526	Ab527	Ab528	Ab529
Year of birth	—	Years	Percent	Percent	Percent	Percent	Percent	Number
1835–1839	1910	70–74	—	—	—	—	—	—
1840–1844	1910	65–69	—	—	—	—	—	—
1845–1949	1910	60–64	—	—	—	—	—	—
1850–1854	1910	55–59	—	—	—	—	—	—
1855–1859	1910	50–54	—	—	—	—	—	—
1860–1864	1910	45–49	—	—	—	—	—	—
1865–1869	1940	70–74	—	—	—	—	—	—
1870–1874	1940	65–69	—	—	—	—	—	—
1875–1879	1940	60–64	—	—	—	—	—	—
1880–1884	1940	55–59	—	—	—	—	—	—
1885–1889	1940	50–54	—	—	—	—	—	—
1890–1894	1940	45–49	—	—	—	—	—	—
1895–1899	1950	50–54	—	—	—	—	—	—
1900–1904	1950	45–49	—	—	—	—	—	—
1905–1909	1960	50–54	—	—	—	—	—	—
1910–1914	1960	45–49	—	—	—	—	—	—
1915–1919	1970	50–54	12.4	27.4	23.1	15.0	22.1	4,034
1920–1924	1970	45–49	9.8	24.8	23.6	17.5	24.3	4,379
1925–1929	1980	50–54	8.3	24.3	27.7	19.0	20.8	4,250
1930–1934	1980	45–49	6.9	22.0	31.1	20.0	19.9	4,293
1935–1939	1990	50–54	6.1	30.3	41.4	14.4	7.8	3,368
1940–1944	1990	45–49	7.4	41.7	36.4	12.1	2.5	2,810

			Asian and Pacific Islander					
			Percentage with					
	Census year	Age of women reporting	No births	1 or 2 births	3 or 4 births	5 or 6 births	Children per 7 or more births	1,000 women
	Ab498	Ab499	Ab530	Ab531	Ab532	Ab533	Ab534	Ab535
Year of birth	—	Years	Percent	Percent	Percent	Percent	Percent	Number
1835–1839	1910	70–74	—	—	—	—	—	—
1840–1844	1910	65–69	—	—	—	—	—	—
1845–1949	1910	60–64	—	—	—	—	—	—
1850–1854	1910	55–59	—	—	—	—	—	—
1855–1859	1910	50–54	—	—	—	—	—	—
1860–1864	1910	45–49	—	—	—	—	—	—
1865–1869	1940	70–74	—	—	—	—	—	—
1870–1874	1940	65–69	—	—	—	—	—	—
1875–1879	1940	60–64	—	—	—	—	—	—
1880–1884	1940	55–59	—	—	—	—	—	—
1885–1889	1940	50–54	—	—	—	—	—	—
1890–1894	1940	45–49	—	—	—	—	—	—
1895–1899	1950	50–54	—	—	—	—	—	—
1900–1904	1950	45–49	—	—	—	—	—	—
1905–1909	1960	50–54	—	—	—	—	—	—
1910–1914	1960	45–49	—	—	—	—	—	—
1915–1919	1970	50–54	—	—	—	—	—	—
1920–1924	1970	45–49	—	—	—	—	—	—
1925–1929	1980	50–54	11.7	31.6	34.4	14.5	7.9	3,136
1930–1934	1980	45–49	11.9	34.1	36.2	12.5	5.3	2,894
1935–1939	1990	50–54	11.3	35.8	36.9	9.7	6.4	2,880
1940–1944	1990	45–49	10.0	46.2	33.3	7.5	3.1	2,523

(continued)

TABLE Ab498–535   Ever-married women – percentage distribution, by number of children ever born, birth cohort, and race: 1835–1944 *Continued*

Sources

U.S. Bureau of the Census, *Sixteenth Census Reports, Population, Differential Fertility, 1940 and 1910*, part 2; *U.S. Census of Population: 1950, Special Reports*, P-E, number 5C, Fertility; *U.S. Census of Population: 1960*, PC(2)3A, Women by Number of Children Ever Born; *U.S. Census of Population: 1970*, PC(2)3A, Women by Number of Children Ever Born; *U.S. Census of Population: 1980*, volume 1, *Characteristics of the Population*, Chapter C, "General Social and Economic Characteristics," part 1, United States Summary, PC80-1-C1, Table 270; Integrated Public Use Microdata Series (IPUMS), 1 percent Metro Sample of the Census of 1990, weighted up by "perwt" (ip9902). See the Guide to the Millennial Edition for information on IPUMS.

Census years 1910–1950, all races: Conrad and Irene Taeuber, *The Changing Population of the United States, 1790–1955* (Wiley, 1957), pp. 255–6.

Documentation

These data are based on an analysis of the decennial censuses. In each of these censuses women who had ever married were asked about the number of children they had ever borne. When these women are classified according to age, it is to suggest the trend in fertility among women who had completed their childbearing at each census.

Caution should be used in comparing the data from the 1910 Census with those from later censuses. The 1910 may have inadvertently obtained some stillbirths in the counts of children ever born, resulting in overstatements of fertility. Comparisons of the average number of children ever born to women ages 40–44 in 1910 with the average for those surviving to age 70–74 in 1940 show about 10 percent more children at the earlier date. In contrast, there is little difference when the average number of children ever born is compared for women who recently completed fertility in 1940 with the average for survivors at much older ages in the Censuses of 1950–1970, suggesting that the memory factor does not cause much undercount of children by women long past the childbearing ages.

Illegitimate births are represented in the data insofar as the women ever married included births before marriage (as they were supposed to do) in their reported total number of children ever born. Comparisons of cumulations of birth data from annual vital statistics (which include all illegitimate births) with recent census data on children ever born suggest that the census data may be short by about 5 percent for all races and about 3 percent for whites.

TABLE Ab536–625   Ever-married women – number of children ever born and percentage childless, by race and age: 1900–1990

Contributed by Michael R. Haines

	All races												
	Percentage childless, by age									Children ever born per 1,000, by age			
	15–44	15–19	20–24	25–29	30–34	35–39	40–44	45–49	50–59	15–44	15–19	20–24	25–29
	Ab536	Ab537	Ab538	Ab539	Ab540	Ab541	Ab542	Ab543	Ab544	Ab545	Ab546	Ab547	Ab548
Year	Percent	Percent	Percent	Percent	Percent	Percent	Percent	Percent	Percent	Per 1,000	Per 1,000	Per 1,000	Per 1,000
1900	17.4	49.8	28.1	18.4	12.8	11.2	9.8	9.3	10.1	3,005	657	1,400	2,256
1910	16.2	42.7	24.2	17.2	13.7	11.6	10.4	9.5	8.7	2,866	725	1,407	2,180
1940	26.5	54.6	39.9	30.1	23.3	19.9	17.4	16.8	16.6	1,904	572	987	1,463
1950	22.8	52.8	33.3	21.1	17.3	19.1	20.0	20.4	18.1	1,859	604	1,082	1,654
1960	15.0	43.6	24.2	12.6	10.4	11.1	14.1	18.1	20.7	2,314	792	1,441	2,241
1970	16.4	50.9	35.7	15.8	8.3	7.3	8.6	10.6	15.6	2,360	636	1,071	1,984
1980	20.2	52.5	41.9	27.3	14.4	8.8	7.1	7.4	10.0	1,927	583	904	1,392
1990	20.1	49.6	40.0	29.7	18.0	13.8	11.4	8.9	7.6	1,749	677	957	1,328

	All races					White									
	Children ever born per 1,000, by age					Percentage childless, by age									
	30–34	35–39	40–44	45–49	50–59	15–44	15–19	20–24	25–29	30–34	35–39	40–44	45–49	50–59
	Ab549	Ab550	Ab551	Ab552	Ab553	Ab554	Ab555	Ab556	Ab557	Ab558	Ab559	Ab560	Ab561	Ab562
Year	Per 1,000	Per 1,000	Per 1,000	Per 1,000	Per 1,000	Percent	Percent	Percent	Percent	Percent	Percent	Percent	Percent	Percent
1900	3,142	4,125	4,748	5,157	5,196	17.1	50.5	28.8	18.2	12.7	11.0	9.7	9.8	10.2
1910	2,956	3,781	4,383	4,744	5,076	15.9	43.5	24.2	16.8	13.4	11.5	10.4	9.6	8.8
1940	1,964	2,414	2,754	2,998	3,215	25.9	56.4	40.3	29.7	22.3	18.9	16.7	16.3	16.5
1950	2,059	2,247	2,364	2,492	2,822	21.8	55.4	34.0	20.1	15.8	17.5	18.9	19.5	17.5
1960	2,627	2,686	2,564	2,402	2,420	14.6	46.0	25.0	12.3	9.7	10.2	13.0	17.1	20.0
1970	2,806	3,170	3,097	2,854	2,520	16.7	53.7	37.5	16.1	8.1	6.9	8.1	9.9	14.7
1980	1,972	2,534	3,041	3,229	2,978	21.2	54.5	44.5	29.2	15.0	8.9	6.9	7.0	9.4
1990	1,768	2,006	2,185	2,556	3,111	21.1	50.6	42.1	31.2	18.8	14.7	11.9	9.0	7.3

TABLE Ab536–625   Ever-married women – number of children ever born and percentage childless, by race and age: 1900–1990   Continued

	White									Black				
	Children ever born per 1,000, by age									Percentage childless, by age				
	15–44	15–19	20–24	25–29	30–34	35–39	40–44	45–49	50–59	15–44	15–19	20–24	25–29	30–34
	Ab563	Ab564	Ab565	Ab566	Ab567	Ab568	Ab569	Ab570	Ab571	Ab572	Ab573	Ab574	Ab575	Ab576
Year	Per 1,000	Per 1,000	Per 1,000	Per 1,000	Per 1,000	Per 1,000	Per 1,000	Per 1,000	Per 1,000	Percent	Percent	Percent	Percent	Percent
1900	2,945	635	1,316	2,179	3,056	4,000	4,641	4,951	5,064	18.5	45.9	23.4	20.2	12.2
1910	2,806	699	1,344	2,099	2,880	3,683	4,263	4,594	4,929	18.7	39.7	24.2	19.6	16.5
1940	1,870	539	941	1,413	1,922	2,369	2,717	2,968	3,180	32.8	46.6	38.7	35.1	31.0
1950	1,828	548	1,028	1,620	2,034	2,218	2,329	2,456	2,786	30.8	38.0	28.9	30.0	30.8
1960	2,253	729	1,370	2,171	2,559	2,629	2,516	2,354	2,378	18.7	25.3	17.0	14.2	15.8
1970	2,285	579	1,006	1,922	2,734	3,086	3,012	2,791	2,470	13.8	32.2	20.7	12.6	9.4
1980	1,848	545	836	1,318	1,903	2,452	2,930	3,113	2,874	13.3	40.2	24.4	15.3	10.3
1990	1,682	648	898	1,266	1,708	1,932	2,104	2,466	2,989	14.1	52.8	29.8	19.9	13.4

	Black												
	Percentage childless, by age				Children ever born per 1,000, by age								
	35–39	40–44	45–49	50–59	15–44	15–19	20–24	25–29	30–34	35–39	40–44	45–49	50–59
	Ab577	Ab578	Ab579	Ab580	Ab581	Ab582	Ab583	Ab584	Ab585	Ab586	Ab587	Ab588	Ab589
Year	Percent	Percent	Percent	Percent	Per 1,000	Per 1,000	Per 1,000	Per 1,000	Per 1,000	Per 1,000	Per 1,000	Per 1,000	Per 1,000
1900	12.0	10.4	5.3	8.4	3,466	766	1,846	2,774	4,025	5,133	5,713	7,112	6,472
1910	13.3	10.5	8.6	7.4	3,237	834	1,696	2,645	3,532	4,515	5,484	6,162	6,709
1940	28.8	25.8	23.8	19.8	2,096	723	1,234	1,761	2,243	2,666	3,012	3,255	3,660
1950	32.3	30.1	28.4	25.1	2,089	921	1,474	1,931	2,250	2,450	2,619	2,767	3,175
1960	20.0	24.7	27.9	28.1	2,808	1,258	2,030	2,835	3,190	3,139	2,949	2,761	2,756
1970	9.8	13.0	17.9	24.4	2,976	1,026	1,631	2,541	3,395	3,839	3,795	3,394	2,938
1980	8.7	8.5	10.1	16.0	2,465	850	1,362	1,863	2,399	3,040	3,706	3,941	3,600
1990	8.9	9.3	9.3	9.4	2,103	768	1,298	1,675	2,044	2,321	2,555	2,973	3,754

	American Indian												
	Percentage childless, by age									Children ever born per 1,000, by age			
	15–44	15–19	20–24	25–29	30–34	35–39	40–44	45–49	50–59	15–44	15–19	20–24	25–29
	Ab590	Ab591	Ab592	Ab593	Ab594	Ab595	Ab596	Ab597	Ab598	Ab599	Ab600	Ab601	Ab602
Year	Percent	Percent	Percent	Percent	Percent	Percent	Percent	Percent	Percent	Per 1,000	Per 1,000	Per 1,000	Per 1,000
1900	—	—	—	—	—	—	—	—	—	—	—	—	—
1910	—	—	—	—	—	—	—	—	—	—	—	—	—
1940	—	—	—	—	—	—	—	—	—	—	—	—	—
1950	—	—	—	—	—	—	—	—	—	—	—	—	—
1960	—	—	—	—	—	—	—	—	—	—	—	—	—
1970	12.2	42.5	20.9	9.6	6.9	6.2	7.8	9.8	13.9 [1]	3,229	817	1,556	2,769
1980	13.8	40.2	24.7	15.4	8.8	6.7	6.4	6.9	8.9	2,470	777	1,326	1,908
1990	19.4	46.2	29.3	31.4	20.0	13.8	9.9	7.4	6.3	1,870	711	1,251	1,438

Note appears at end of table

(continued)

TABLE Ab536–625   Ever-married women – number of children ever born and percentage childless, by race and age: 1900–1990   Continued

	American Indian						Asian and Pacific Islander					
	Children ever born per 1,000, by age						Percentage childless, by age					
	30–34	35–39	40–44	45–49	50–59		15–44	15–19	20–24	25–29	30–34	35–39
	Ab603	Ab604	Ab605	Ab606	Ab607		Ab608	Ab609	Ab610	Ab611	Ab612	Ab613
Year	Per 1,000	Per 1,000	Per 1,000	Per 1,000	Per 1,000		Percent	Percent	Percent	Percent	Percent	Percent
1900	—	—	—	—	—		—	—	—	—	—	—
1910	—	—	—	—	—		—	—	—	—	—	—
1940	—	—	—	—	—		—	—	—	—	—	—
1950	—	—	—	—	—		—	—	—	—	—	—
1960	—	—	—	—	—		—	—	—	—	—	—
1970	3,774	4,521	4,589	4,379	4,007 [1]		—	—	—	—	—	—
1980	2,594	3,268	4,025	4,293	4,170		22.5	58.0	46.0	33.5	18.1	11.8
1990	1,784	2,104	2,342	2,810	3,598		22.0	55.2	50.1	37.0	20.6	12.8

	Asian and Pacific Islander											
	Percentage childless, by age			Children ever born per 1,000, by age								
	40–44	45–49	50–59	15–44	15–19	20–24	25–29	30–34	35–39	40–44	45–49	50–59
	Ab614	Ab615	Ab616	Ab617	Ab618	Ab619	Ab620	Ab621	Ab622	Ab623	Ab624	Ab625
Year	Percent	Percent	Percent	Per 1,000	Per 1,000	Per 1,000	Per 1,000	Per 1,000	Per 1,000	Per 1,000	Per 1,000	Per 1,000
1900	—	—	—	—	—	—	—	—	—	—	—	—
1910	—	—	—	—	—	—	—	—	—	—	—	—
1940	—	—	—	—	—	—	—	—	—	—	—	—
1950	—	—	—	—	—	—	—	—	—	—	—	—
1960	—	—	—	—	—	—	—	—	—	—	—	—
1970	—	—	—	—	—	—	—	—	—	—	—	—
1980	10.9	11.9	11.1	1,752	536	822	1,174	1,719	2,241	2,683	2,894	3,236
1990	12.1	10.0	11.7	1,727	695	770	1,170	1,661	2,064	2,199	2,523	3,080

[1] Ages 50–64.

Sources

1900: Integrated Public Use Microdata Series (IPUMS) for 1900 (ip9001). 1910 and 1940: U.S. Bureau of the Census, *Sixteenth Census of Population, Special Reports*, "Differential Fertility, 1940 and 1910 – Fertility for States and Large Cities," Tables 3 and 4; "Differential Fertility, 1940 and 1910 – Women by Number of Children Ever Born," Tables 9 and 12; and unpublished data. 1950: *U.S. Census of Population: 1950, Special Report FE No. 5C*, "Fertility," Tables 1, 2, and 12; and unpublished data. 1960: *U.S. Census of Population: 1960*, volume 1, *Characteristics of the Population*, part 1, U.S. Summary, Table 190, and *Final Report PC(2)-3A*, "Women by Number of Children Ever Born," Tables 2 and 8. 1970: *U.S. Census of Population: 1970*, part 1, "U.S. Summary," Tables 8 and 213. 1980: *U.S. Census of Population: 1980*, volume 1, *Characteristics of the Population*, Chapter C, "General Social and Economic Characteristics," part 1, United States Summary, PC80-1-C1, Table 270. 1990: Integrated Public Use Microdata Series (IPUMS), 1 percent Metro Sample of the Census of 1990, weighted up by "perwt" (ip9902). See the Guide to the Millennial Edition for information on IPUMS.

Documentation

These data are based on a one-in-750 sample in 1900, an 8.9 percent sample for 1910, a 3.3 percent sample for 1940, a 2.4 percent sample for 1950, a 25 percent sample for 1960 (except that the separate data for blacks are from a 5 percent sample), a 20 percent sample for 1970, an approximate one-in-six sample for 1980, and a 1 percent sample for 1990. The data shown for 1940 in Tables Ab498–625 include special adjustments to allow for the fertility of women with no original report on number of children ever born and therefore differ slightly from the data published in the "Differential Fertility, 1940 and 1910" reports.

Data are based on the age and race of the woman.

See the text for Table Ab498–535 for cautions regarding the comparability of data from the 1910 Census with data from later censuses, and possible minor shortages in counts of children ever born owing to underreporting of illegitimate births.

TABLE Ab626–636   Ever-married women – number of children ever born and percentage childless, by urban–rural residence, nativity, and age: 1865   [Seven New York counties]

Contributed by Michael R. Haines

	Age	Children ever born					Percentage childless				
		All	Rural	Urban	Native-born	Foreign-born	All	Rural	Urban	Native-born	Foreign-born
	Ab626	Ab627	Ab628	Ab629	Ab630	Ab631	Ab632	Ab633	Ab634	Ab635	Ab636
Year of birth	Years	Per 1,000	Per 1,000	Per 1,000	Per 1,000	Per 1,000	Percent	Percent	Percent	Percent	Percent
Before 1786	80+	6,860	6,524	7,182	6,833	7,000	4.7	4.8	4.5	5.6	0.0
1786–1790	75–79	6,517	6,650	6,250	7,000	5,188	3.3	5.0	0.0	2.3	6.3
1791–1795	70–74	6,288	6,895	5,738	6,569	5,067	5.0	5.3	4.8	4.6	6.7
1796–1800	65–69	6,574	6,373	6,857	6,584	6,500	4.0	3.4	4.8	3.4	8.3
1801–1805	60–64	6,050	6,480	5,380	6,088	5,907	7.4	6.5	8.9	6.9	9.3
1806–1810	55–59	5,656	5,784	5,444	5,643	5,702	4.2	4.5	3.7	3.0	8.5
1811–1815	50–54	5,240	5,690	4,664	5,325	4,948	5.8	5.5	6.2	4.0	12.1
1816–1820	45–49	4,918	5,073	4,707	4,614	6,000	7.3	7.3	7.3	8.7	2.6
1821–1825	40–44	4,808	4,730	4,892	4,452	5,829	5.9	5.2	6.7	5.5	5.7
1826–1830	35–39	3,824	3,863	3,777	3,493	4,689	8.2	7.3	9.3	8.8	6.7
1831–1835	30–34	3,114	3,112	3,116	2,802	3,838	8.9	7.5	10.7	9.3	8.1
1836–1840	25–29	2,083	2,038	2,137	1,944	2,577	16.4	17.1	15.6	17.7	11.7
1841–1845	20–24	1,173	1,197	1,141	1,147	1,321	28.7	30.0	27.0	30.9	16.0
1846–1850	15–19	529	476	607	534	500	52.9	57.1	46.4	51.7	58.3

Source

Sample of enumerators' manuscripts from the 1865 Census of the State of New York, as reported in Michael R. Haines and Avery M. Guest, "Fertility and Marriage in New York State in the Era of the Civil War," National Bureau of Economic Research, NBER Historical Working Paper number 70 (July 1995).

Documentation

The counties are: Allegany, Dutchess, Montgomery, Rensselaer, Steuben, Tompkins, and Warren. The sample of ever-married women is: all women (3,591), rural women (1,996), urban women (1,595), native-born women (2,764), and foreign-born women (827).

The figures for children ever born are reported per 1,000 by age group. Data are based on the age and origin of the woman.

TABLE Ab637–643   Ever-married women – number of children ever born and percentage childless, by nativity and age: 1885   [Massachusetts]

Contributed by Michael R. Haines

	Age	Children ever born			Percentage childless		
		All	Native-born	Foreign-born	All	Native-born	Foreign-born
	Ab637	Ab638	Ab639	Ab640	Ab641	Ab642	Ab643
Year of birth	Years	Per 1,000	Per 1,000	Per 1,000	Percent	Percent	Percent
Before 1806	80+	5,007	4,662	6,321	10.9	11.9	7.3
1806–1825	60–79	4,495	3,897	5,818	11.5	12.7	8.7
1826–1835	50–59	4,314	3,269	5,740	12.4	14.8	9.3
1836–1845	40–49	4,015	2,851	5,495	14.3	17.4	10.3
1846–1855	30–39	3,041	2,394	4,042	17.1	20.2	12.3
1856–1865	20–29	1,469	1,339	1,722	29.6	31.9	25.1
1866–1871	14–19	474	477	465	59.3	58.9	60.6

Source

Calculated from data in Massachusetts Bureau of Statistics of Labor, *The Census of Massachusetts: 1885*, volume 1, *Population and Social Statistics,* part 2 (Wright and Potter, 1888), pp. 1172–81.

Documentation

The figures for average children ever born are reported per 1,000 women by age group. Data are for age and origin (native or foreign-born) of the woman.

LIFE EXPECTANCY

Michael R. Haines

TABLE Ab644–655 Expectation of life at birth, by sex and race: 1850–1998

Contributed by Michael R. Haines

Year	All races			White			Nonwhite					
							Total			Black		
	Both sexes	Male	Female	Both sexes	Male	Female	Both sexes	Male	Female	Both sexes	Male	Female
	Ab644	Ab645	Ab646	Ab647	Ab648	Ab649	Ab650	Ab651	Ab652	Ab653	Ab654	Ab655
	Years	Years	Years	Years	Years	Years	Years	Years	Years	Years	Years	Years
1850	38.3	37.2	39.4	39.5	38.4	40.6	—	—	—	—	—	—
1860	41.8	41.6	42.2	43.6	43.2	44.1	—	—	—	—	—	—
1870	44.0	43.0	44.9	45.2	44.1	46.4	—	—	—	—	—	—
1880	39.4	39.7	39.1	40.5	40.4	40.6	—	—	—	—	—	—
1890	45.2	44.8	45.6	46.8	46.0	47.4	—	—	—	—	—	—
1900	47.8	47.1	48.4	49.6	48.5	50.7	—	—	—	41.8	40.4	43.3
1900 [1]	47.3	46.3	48.3	47.6	46.6	48.7	33.0	32.5	33.5	—	—	—
1901 [1]	49.1	47.6	50.6	49.4	48.0	51.0	33.7	32.2	35.3	—	—	—
1902 [1]	51.5	49.8	53.4	51.9	50.2	53.8	34.6	32.9	36.4	—	—	—
1903 [1]	50.5	49.1	52.0	50.9	49.5	52.5	33.1	31.7	34.6	—	—	—
1904 [1]	47.6	46.2	49.1	48.0	46.6	49.5	30.8	29.1	32.7	—	—	—
1905 [1]	48.7	47.3	50.2	49.1	47.6	50.6	31.3	29.6	33.1	—	—	—
1906 [1]	48.7	46.9	50.8	49.3	47.3	51.4	32.9	31.8	33.9	—	—	—
1907 [1]	47.6	45.6	49.9	48.1	46.0	50.4	32.5	31.1	34.0	—	—	—
1908 [1]	51.1	49.5	52.8	51.5	49.9	53.3	34.9	33.8	36.0	—	—	—
1909 [1]	52.1	50.5	53.8	52.5	50.9	54.2	35.7	34.2	37.3	—	—	—
1910	53.1	51.5	54.7	54.6	53.0	56.0	—	—	—	46.2	44.7	47.7
1910 [1]	50.0	48.4	51.8	50.3	48.6	52.0	35.6	33.8	37.5	—	—	—
1911 [1]	52.6	50.9	54.4	53.0	51.3	54.9	36.4	34.6	38.2	—	—	—
1912 [1]	53.5	51.5	55.9	53.9	51.9	56.2	37.9	35.9	40.0	—	—	—
1913 [1]	52.5	50.3	55.0	53.0	50.8	55.7	38.4	36.7	40.3	—	—	—
1914 [1]	54.2	52.0	56.8	54.9	52.7	57.5	38.9	37.1	40.8	—	—	—
1915 [1]	54.5	52.5	56.8	55.1	53.1	57.5	38.9	37.5	40.5	—	—	—
1916 [1]	51.7	49.6	54.3	52.5	50.2	55.2	41.3	39.6	43.1	—	—	—
1917 [1]	50.9	48.4	54.0	52.0	49.3	55.3	38.8	37.0	40.8	—	—	—
1918 [1]	39.1	36.6	42.2	39.8	37.1	43.2	31.1	29.9	32.5	—	—	—
1919 [1]	54.7	53.5	56.0	55.8	54.5	57.4	44.5	44.5	44.4	—	—	—
1920 [1]	54.1	53.6	54.6	54.9	54.4	55.6	45.3	45.5	45.2	—	—	—
1921 [1]	60.8	60.0	61.8	61.8	60.8	62.9	51.5	51.6	51.3	—	—	—
1922 [1]	59.6	58.4	61.0	60.4	59.1	61.9	52.4	51.8	53.0	—	—	—
1923 [1]	57.2	56.1	58.5	58.3	57.1	59.6	48.3	47.7	48.9	—	—	—
1924 [1]	59.7	58.1	61.5	61.4	59.8	63.4	46.6	45.5	47.8	—	—	—
1925 [1]	59.0	57.6	60.6	60.7	59.3	62.4	45.7	44.9	46.7	—	—	—
1926 [1]	56.7	55.5	58.0	58.2	57.0	59.6	44.6	43.7	45.6	—	—	—
1927 [1]	60.4	59.0	62.1	62.0	60.5	63.9	48.2	47.6	48.9	—	—	—
1928 [1]	56.8	55.6	58.3	58.4	57.0	60.0	46.3	45.6	47.0	—	—	—
1929 [1]	57.1	55.8	58.7	58.6	57.2	60.3	46.7	45.7	47.8	—	—	—
1930	59.7	58.1	61.6	61.4	59.7	63.5	48.1	47.3	49.2	—	—	—
1931	61.1	59.4	63.1	62.6	60.8	64.7	50.4	49.5	51.5	—	—	—
1932	62.1	61.0	63.5	63.2	62.0	64.5	53.7	52.8	54.6	—	—	—
1933	63.3	61.7	65.1	64.3	62.7	66.3	54.7	53.5	56.0	—	—	—
1934	61.1	59.3	63.3	62.4	60.5	64.6	51.8	50.2	53.7	—	—	—
1935	61.7	59.9	63.9	62.9	61.0	65.0	53.1	51.3	55.2	—	—	—
1936	58.5	56.6	60.6	59.8	58.0	61.9	49.0	47.0	51.4	—	—	—
1937	60.0	58.0	62.4	61.4	59.3	63.8	50.3	48.3	52.5	—	—	—
1938	63.5	61.9	65.3	65.0	63.2	66.8	52.9	51.7	54.3	—	—	—
1939	63.7	62.1	65.4	64.9	63.3	66.6	54.5	53.2	56.0	—	—	—
1940	62.9	60.8	65.2	64.2	62.1	66.6	53.1	51.5	54.9	—	—	—
1941	64.8	63.1	66.8	66.2	64.4	68.5	53.8	52.5	55.3	—	—	—
1942	66.2	64.7	67.9	67.3	65.9	69.4	56.6	55.4	58.2	—	—	—
1943	63.3	62.4	64.4	64.2	63.2	65.7	55.6	55.4	56.1	—	—	—
1944	65.2	63.6	66.8	66.2	64.5	68.4	56.6	55.8	57.7	—	—	—

Notes appear at end of table

TABLE Ab644–655   Expectation of life at birth, by sex and race: 1850–1998   *Continued*

	All races			White			Nonwhite					
							Total			Black		
	Both sexes	Male	Female	Both sexes	Male	Female	Both sexes	Male	Female	Both sexes	Male	Female
	Ab644	Ab645	Ab646	Ab647	Ab648	Ab649	Ab650	Ab651	Ab652	Ab653	Ab654	Ab655
Year	Years	Years	Years	Years	Years	Years	Years	Years	Years	Years	Years	Years
1945	65.9	63.6	67.9	66.8	64.4	69.5	57.7	56.1	59.6	—	—	—
1946	66.7	64.4	69.4	67.5	65.1	70.3	59.1	57.5	61.0	—	—	—
1947	66.8	64.4	69.7	67.6	65.2	70.5	59.7	57.9	61.9	—	—	—
1948	67.2	64.6	69.9	68.0	65.5	71.0	60.0	58.1	62.5	—	—	—
1949	68.0	65.2	70.7	68.8	66.2	71.9	60.6	58.9	62.7	—	—	—
1950	68.2	65.6	71.1	69.1	66.5	72.2	60.8	59.1	62.9	—	—	—
1951	68.4	65.6	71.4	69.3	66.5	72.4	61.2	59.2	63.4	—	—	—
1952	68.6	65.8	71.6	69.5	66.6	72.6	61.4	59.1	63.8	—	—	—
1953	68.8	66.0	72.0	69.7	66.8	73.0	62.0	59.7	64.5	—	—	—
1954	69.6	66.7	72.8	70.5	67.5	73.7	63.4	61.1	65.9	—	—	—
1955	69.6	66.7	72.8	70.5	67.4	73.7	63.7	61.4	66.1	—	—	—
1956	69.7	66.7	72.9	70.5	67.5	73.9	63.6	61.3	66.1	—	—	—
1957	69.5	66.4	72.7	70.3	67.7	73.7	63.0	60.7	65.5	—	—	—
1958	69.6	66.6	72.9	70.5	67.4	73.9	63.4	61.0	65.8	—	—	—
1959	69.9	66.8	73.2	70.7	67.5	74.2	63.9	61.3	66.5	—	—	—
1960	69.7	66.6	73.1	70.6	67.4	74.1	63.6	61.1	66.3	—	—	—
1961	70.2	67.1	73.6	71.0	67.8	74.6	64.5	62.0	67.1	—	—	—
1962 [2]	70.1	66.9	73.5	70.9	67.7	74.5	64.2	61.6	66.9	—	—	—
1963 [2]	69.9	66.6	73.4	70.8	67.4	74.4	63.7	61.0	66.6	—	—	—
1964	70.2	66.8	73.7	71.0	67.7	74.7	64.2	61.3	67.3	—	—	—
1965	70.2	66.8	73.8	71.1	67.6	74.8	64.3	61.2	67.6	—	—	—
1966	70.2	66.7	73.9	71.1	67.5	74.8	64.2	60.9	67.6	—	—	—
1967	70.5	67.0	74.3	71.4	67.8	75.2	64.9	61.4	68.5	—	—	—
1968	70.2	66.6	74.1	71.1	67.5	75.0	64.1	60.4	67.9	—	—	—
1969	70.5	66.8	74.4	71.4	67.7	75.3	64.5	60.6	68.6	—	—	—
1970	70.8	67.1	74.7	71.7	68.0	75.6	65.3	61.3	69.4	64.1	60.0	68.3
1971	71.1	67.4	75.0	72.0	68.3	75.8	65.6	61.6	69.8	64.6	60.5	68.9
1972	71.2	67.4	75.1	72.0	68.3	75.9	65.7	61.5	70.1	64.7	60.4	69.1
1973	71.4	67.6	75.3	72.2	68.5	76.1	66.1	62.0	70.3	65.0	60.9	69.3
1974	72.0	68.2	75.9	72.8	69.0	76.7	67.1	62.9	71.3	66.0	61.7	70.3
1975	72.6	68.8	76.6	73.4	69.5	77.3	68.0	63.7	72.4	66.8	62.4	71.3
1976	72.9	69.1	76.8	73.6	69.9	77.5	68.4	64.2	72.7	67.2	62.9	71.6
1977	73.3	69.5	77.2	74.0	70.2	77.9	68.9	64.7	73.2	67.7	63.4	72.0
1978	73.5	69.6	77.3	74.1	70.4	78.0	69.3	65.0	73.5	68.1	63.7	72.4
1979	73.9	70.0	77.8	74.6	70.8	78.4	69.8	65.4	74.1	68.5	64.0	72.9
1980	73.7	70.0	77.4	74.4	70.7	78.1	69.5	65.3	73.6	68.1	63.8	72.5
1981	74.1	70.4	77.8	74.8	71.1	78.4	70.3	66.2	74.4	68.9	64.5	73.2
1982	74.5	70.8	78.1	75.1	71.5	78.7	70.9	66.8	74.9	69.4	65.1	73.6
1983	74.6	71.0	78.1	75.2	71.6	78.7	70.9	67.0	74.7	69.4	65.2	73.5
1984	74.7	71.1	78.2	75.3	71.8	78.7	71.1	67.2	74.9	69.5	65.3	73.6
1985	74.7	71.1	78.2	75.3	71.8	78.7	71.0	67.0	74.8	69.3	65.0	73.4
1986	74.7	71.2	78.2	75.4	71.9	78.8	70.9	66.8	74.9	69.1	64.8	73.4
1987	74.9	71.4	78.3	75.6	72.1	78.9	71.0	66.9	75.0	69.1	64.7	73.4
1988	74.9	71.4	78.3	75.6	72.2	78.9	70.8	66.7	74.8	68.9	64.4	73.2
1989	75.1	71.7	78.5	75.9	72.5	79.2	70.9	66.7	74.9	68.8	64.3	73.3
1990	75.4	71.8	78.8	76.1	72.7	79.4	71.2	67.0	75.2	69.1	64.5	73.6
1991	75.5	72.0	78.9	76.3	72.9	79.6	71.5	67.3	75.5	69.3	64.6	73.8
1992	75.8	72.3	79.1	76.5	73.2	79.8	71.8	67.7	75.7	69.6	65.0	73.9
1993	75.5	72.2	78.8	76.3	73.1	79.5	71.5	67.3	75.5	69.2	64.6	73.7
1994	75.7	72.4	79.0	76.5	73.3	79.6	71.7	67.6	75.7	69.5	64.9	73.9
1995	75.8	72.5	78.9	76.5	73.4	79.6	71.9	67.9	75.7	69.6	65.2	73.9
1996	76.1	73.1	79.1	76.8	73.9	79.7	72.6	68.9	76.1	70.2	66.1	74.2
1997	76.5	73.6	79.4	77.1	74.3	79.9	73.4	69.8	76.7	71.1	67.2	74.7
1998	76.7	73.8	79.5	77.3	74.5	80.0	—	—	—	71.3	67.6	74.8

[1] Death Registration Area only.

[2] Excludes New Jersey, which did not require reporting of race.

Sources

For the whole United States, 1850–1910: Michael R. Haines, "Estimated Life Tables for the United States, 1850–1910," *Historical Methods* 31 (4) (1998): 149–69. For the total and white populations for 1850–1900, the U.S. Model life tables are used. For the total and white populations for 1910 and for the black population for 1900 and 1910, the West Model life tables are used. For the Death Registration Area, 1900–1928, and the whole United States,

1929–1997: National Center for Health Statistics. 1900–1993: *Vital Statistics of the United States, 1993*, preprint of volume 2, *Mortality,* part A, section 6, "Life Tables," Table 6.5. 1994–1997: U.S. Public Health Service, *National Vital Statistics Report,* volume 47, number 19, "Deaths: Final Data for 1997," Table 6. U.S. Public Health Service, *National Vital Statistics Report,* volume 48, number 11, "Deaths: Final Data for 1998," Table 6.

Documentation

See the text for Table Ab656–703.

TABLE Ab656–703   Expectation of life at specified ages, by sex and race: 1850–1998[1]

Contributed by Michael R. Haines

	All races											
	At birth		Age 5		Age 20		Age 40		Age 60		Age 70	
	Males	Females	Males	Females	Males	Females	Males	Females	Males	Females	Males	Females
	Ab656	Ab657	Ab658	Ab659	Ab660	Ab661	Ab662	Ab663	Ab664	Ab665	Ab666	Ab667
Years	Years	Years	Years	Years	Years	Years	Years	Years	Years	Years	Years	Years
1850	37.2	39.4	49.5	50.8	38.4	39.8	25.7	27.1	13.6	14.4	8.6	9.0
1860	41.6	42.2	51.9	52.2	40.3	40.9	26.8	27.7	14.1	14.6	8.9	9.2
1870	43.0	44.9	52.9	54.2	41.1	42.6	27.4	28.9	14.4	15.3	9.0	9.6
1880	39.7	39.1	51.0	51.3	39.6	40.3	26.5	27.5	14.0	14.7	8.8	9.2
1890	44.8	45.6	52.8	53.6	41.0	41.9	27.0	28.2	14.0	14.8	8.8	9.2
1900	47.1	48.4	53.2	54.3	41.1	42.3	26.9	28.2	13.7	14.6	8.5	9.0
1900–1902 [2]	47.9	50.7	54.2	55.8	42.0	43.6	27.6	29.1	14.3	15.2	9.0	9.6
1901–1910 [2]	—	—	—	—	—	—	—	—	—	—	—	—
1909–1911 [2]	49.9	53.2	55.1	57.4	42.5	40.7	27.3	29.2	14.0	14.9	8.8	9.4
1910	51.5	54.7	56.1	58.5	43.4	45.9	27.8	30.2	13.9	15.4	8.6	9.4
1919–1921 [3]	55.5	57.4	57.6	58.4	45.0	45.6	29.6	30.6	15.2	15.9	9.5	10.0
1929–1931	57.7	60.9	58.1	60.7	44.9	47.2	28.7	30.9	14.6	15.9	9.2	10.0
1939–1941	61.6	65.9	60.8	64.4	46.9	50.4	29.6	32.7	15.0	16.9	9.5	10.6
1949–1951	65.5	71.0	63.1	68.2	48.9	53.7	30.8	35.1	15.7	18.5	10.1	11.7
1955	66.7	72.8	63.9	69.7	49.6	55.1	31.4	36.2	15.9	19.2	10.4	12.3
1956	66.7	72.9	63.9	69.8	49.6	55.2	31.3	36.2	15.8	19.2	10.3	12.2
1957	66.4	72.7	63.6	69.6	49.3	55.0	31.0	36.0	15.6	19.0	10.2	12.1
1958	66.6	72.9	63.8	69.8	49.4	55.2	31.1	36.2	15.6	19.1	10.1	12.1
1959	66.8	73.2	63.9	70.0	49.5	55.4	31.2	36.4	15.7	19.3	10.2	12.2
1960	66.6	73.1	63.9	70.1	49.6	55.5	31.2	36.5	15.8	19.5	10.2	12.4
1961	67.0	73.6	64.3	70.5	49.9	55.9	31.5	36.9	16.0	19.8	10.5	12.6
1962 [4]	66.8	73.4	64.1	70.3	49.7	55.7	31.4	36.7	15.9	19.6	10.3	12.5
1963 [4]	66.6	73.4	63.9	70.3	49.5	55.6	31.2	36.7	15.7	19.6	10.2	12.5
1964	66.8	73.7	64.0	70.6	49.7	55.9	31.4	37.0	15.9	19.9	10.4	12.8
1965	66.8	73.8	64.0	70.6	49.6	56.0	31.3	37.0	15.9	20.0	10.4	12.8
1966	66.7	73.9	63.8	70.6	49.4	56.0	31.2	37.0	15.8	20.0	10.3	12.8
1967	67.0	74.2	63.9	70.9	49.6	56.3	31.4	37.3	16.0	20.2	10.4	13.0
1968	66.6	74.0	63.5	70.6	49.2	56.0	31.1	37.0	15.7	20.0	10.2	12.9
1969	66.8	74.4	63.7	70.9	49.4	56.3	31.4	37.3	15.9	20.3	10.4	12.1
1970	67.1	74.7	63.9	71.3	49.6	56.7	31.6	37.8	16.1	20.8	10.6	13.6
1971	67.4	75.0	64.1	71.3	49.8	56.7	31.7	37.7	16.1	20.6	10.6	13.4
1972	67.4	75.1	64.0	71.5	49.7	56.9	31.6	37.9	16.1	20.8	10.4	13.5
1973	67.6	75.3	64.2	71.7	49.9	57.1	31.8	38.0	16.2	20.9	10.4	13.6
1974	68.2	75.9	64.7	72.2	50.4	57.5	32.2	38.5	16.5	21.3	10.7	13.9
1975	68.8	76.6	65.1	72.8	50.8	58.1	32.6	39.0	16.8	21.8	10.9	14.4
1976	69.0	76.7	65.4	72.9	51.0	58.2	32.8	39.1	16.8	21.8	10.9	14.4
1977	69.5	77.2	65.6	73.2	51.3	58.6	33.1	39.5	17.0	22.1	11.1	14.7
1978	69.6	77.3	65.8	73.3	51.4	58.7	33.2	39.5	17.1	22.1	11.1	14.7
1979	69.9	77.6	66.1	73.7	51.8	59.1	33.6	39.9	17.4	22.4	11.4	15.0
1980	70.0	77.4	66.1	73.5	51.8	58.9	33.5	39.7	17.4	22.2	11.3	14.8
1981	70.4	77.9	66.6	73.9	52.1	59.2	33.8	40.0	17.6	22.5	11.5	15.1
1982	70.8	78.1	66.8	74.1	52.4	59.4	34.0	40.2	17.7	22.6	11.6	15.2
1983	71.0	78.1	67.0	74.2	52.6	59.5	34.1	40.2	17.8	22.6	11.5	15.2
1984	71.2	78.2	67.2	74.1	52.7	59.4	34.3	40.1	17.9	22.5	11.6	15.0
1985	71.2	78.2	67.2	74.1	52.7	59.3	34.3	40.1	17.9	22.4	11.5	14.9
1986	71.3	78.3	67.3	74.1	52.8	59.4	34.5	40.2	18.0	22.5	11.7	15.0
1987	71.5	78.4	67.4	74.2	53.0	59.5	34.7	40.3	18.2	22.5	11.8	15.1
1988	71.5	78.3	67.5	74.2	53.0	59.4	34.8	40.2	18.2	22.5	11.8	15.0
1989	71.8	78.6	67.8	74.4	53.3	59.7	35.1	40.5	18.6	22.7	12.1	15.2
1990	71.8	78.8	67.7	74.5	53.3	59.8	35.1	40.6	18.5	22.8	12.0	15.3
1991	72.0	78.9	67.9	74.7	53.4	59.9	35.3	40.7	18.7	22.9	12.2	15.4
1992	72.3	79.1	68.1	74.8	53.7	60.1	35.5	40.9	18.9	23.1	12.4	15.5
1993	72.2	78.8	68.0	74.6	53.5	59.8	35.4	40.6	18.8	22.8	12.2	15.3
1994	72.4	79.0	68.1	74.6	53.6	59.9	35.5	40.7	18.9	22.9	12.4	15.3
1995	72.5	78.9	68.3	74.6	53.8	59.9	35.6	40.7	19.1	22.9	12.4	15.3
1996	73.1	79.1	68.8	74.7	54.2	60.0	35.9	40.7	19.2	22.9	12.6	15.3
1997	73.6	79.4	69.3	75.0	54.7	60.2	36.2	40.9	19.4	23.1	12.7	15.5
1998	73.8	79.5	69.5	75.1	55.0	60.3	36.4	41.1	19.6	23.2	12.8	15.5

Notes appear at end of table

TABLE Ab656–703   Expectation of life at specified ages, by sex and race: 1850–1998   *Continued*

												White
	At birth		Age 5		Age 20		Age 40		Age 60		Age 70	
	Males	Females	Males	Females	Males	Females	Males	Females	Males	Females	Males	Females
	Ab668	Ab669	Ab670	Ab671	Ab672	Ab673	Ab674	Ab675	Ab676	Ab677	Ab678	Ab679
Year(s)	Years	Years	Years	Years	Years	Years	Years	Years	Years	Years	Years	Years
1850	38.4	40.6	50.1	51.4	38.8	40.2	25.9	27.3	13.7	14.5	8.6	9.1
1860	43.2	44.1	52.7	53.2	41.0	41.7	27.3	28.1	14.3	14.8	9.0	9.3
1870	44.1	46.4	53.6	55.1	41.8	43.3	27.8	29.3	14.6	15.5	9.2	9.7
1880	40.4	40.6	51.5	52.0	40.0	40.9	26.7	27.8	14.1	14.8	8.8	9.3
1890	46.0	47.4	53.7	54.7	41.7	42.8	27.6	28.7	14.3	15.1	8.9	9.4
1900	48.5	50.7	54.3	55.7	42.0	43.5	27.5	28.9	14.1	15.0	8.7	9.2
1900–1902 [2]	48.2	51.1	54.4	56.0	42.2	43.8	27.7	29.2	14.4	15.2	9.0	9.6
1901–1910 [2]	49.3	52.5	54.8	56.9	42.4	44.4	27.6	29.3	14.2	15.1	9.0	9.6
1909–1911 [2]	50.2	53.6	55.4	57.7	42.7	44.9	27.4	29.3	14.0	14.9	8.8	9.4
1910	53.0	56.2	56.9	59.4	44.1	46.7	28.2	30.7	14.1	15.6	8.7	9.5
1919–1921 [3]	56.3	58.5	58.3	59.4	45.6	46.5	29.9	30.9	15.3	15.9	9.5	9.9
1929–1931	59.1	62.7	59.4	62.2	46.0	48.5	29.2	31.5	14.7	16.1	9.2	10.0
1939–1941	62.8	67.3	61.7	65.6	47.8	51.4	30.0	33.3	15.1	17.0	9.4	10.5
1949–1951	66.3	72.0	63.4	69.1	49.5	54.6	31.2	35.6	15.8	18.6	10.1	11.7
1955	67.4	73.7	64.5	70.4	50.1	55.8	31.7	36.7	16.0	19.3	10.3	12.2
1956	67.5	73.9	64.4	70.5	50.1	55.9	31.6	36.7	15.9	19.3	10.3	12.2
1957	67.7	73.7	64.2	70.3	49.9	55.7	31.4	36.6	15.7	19.2	10.1	12.1
1958	67.4	73.9	64.3	70.5	50.0	55.9	31.5	36.7	15.7	19.2	10.1	12.0
1959	67.5	74.2	64.4	70.7	50.3	56.3	31.8	37.2	16.1	19.7	10.4	12.5
1960	67.4	74.1	64.4	70.8	50.1	56.2	31.6	37.1	15.9	19.7	10.2	12.4
1961	67.8	74.5	64.8	71.2	50.4	56.6	31.9	37.4	16.1	20.0	10.4	12.6
1962 [4]	67.7	74.5	64.6	71.1	50.2	56.4	31.7	37.3	16.0	19.9	10.3	12.5
1963 [4]	67.4	74.4	64.4	71.0	50.1	56.4	31.6	37.3	15.8	19.9	10.2	12.5
1964	67.7	74.7	64.6	71.3	50.2	56.6	31.8	37.5	16.0	20.1	10.4	12.8
1965	67.6	74.8	64.5	71.3	50.2	56.6	31.7	37.5	16.0	20.1	10.3	12.8
1966	67.5	74.8	64.4	71.3	50.1	56.7	31.6	37.5	15.9	20.2	10.3	12.8
1967	67.8	75.2	64.6	71.5	50.2	56.9	31.8	37.8	16.1	20.4	10.4	13.0
1968	67.5	74.9	64.3	71.3	49.9	56.7	31.6	37.6	15.8	20.2	10.2	12.9
1969	67.7	75.3	64.4	71.5	50.1	56.9	31.8	37.8	16.0	20.5	10.4	13.0
1970	68.0	75.6	64.6	72.0	50.3	57.4	31.9	38.3	16.2	21.0	10.5	13.6
1971	68.3	75.8	64.8	72.1	50.5	57.5	32.1	38.4	16.2	21.1	10.5	13.6
1972	68.3	75.9	64.7	72.1	50.4	57.5	32.0	38.4	16.1	21.0	10.4	13.6
1973	68.5	76.1	64.9	72.3	50.5	57.7	32.2	38.5	16.2	21.1	10.4	13.7
1974	68.9	76.6	65.3	72.7	51.0	58.1	32.6	38.9	16.5	21.4	10.6	13.9
1975	69.4	77.2	65.7	73.3	51.4	58.6	33.0	39.4	16.8	21.9	10.9	14.4
1976	69.7	77.3	66.0	73.4	51.6	58.7	33.1	39.5	16.9	22.0	10.9	14.4
1977	70.0	77.7	66.2	73.7	51.9	59.1	33.4	39.8	17.1	22.3	11.1	14.8
1978	70.2	77.8	66.3	73.8	52.0	59.1	33.6	39.9	17.2	22.3	11.1	14.8
1979	70.6	78.2	66.7	74.2	52.3	59.5	33.9	40.2	17.5	22.6	11.3	15.0
1980	70.7	78.1	66.8	74.0	52.4	59.4	34.0	40.1	17.5	22.4	11.3	14.8
1981	71.1	78.5	67.1	74.4	52.7	59.7	34.2	40.4	17.7	22.7	11.5	15.1
1982	71.5	78.8	67.5	74.6	53.0	59.9	34.5	40.6	17.9	22.8	11.6	15.3
1983	71.7	78.7	67.6	74.5	53.1	59.8	34.6	40.4	17.9	22.6	11.5	15.1
1984	71.8	78.7	67.8	74.5	53.3	59.8	34.7	40.5	18.0	22.6	11.6	15.1
1985	71.9	78.7	67.8	74.5	53.3	59.8	34.7	40.4	18.0	22.6	11.6	15.0
1986	72.0	78.8	67.8	74.6	53.4	59.9	34.9	40.5	18.2	22.6	11.7	15.1
1987	72.2	78.9	68.1	74.7	53.6	59.9	35.1	40.6	18.3	22.7	11.8	15.1
1988	72.3	78.9	68.1	74.6	53.6	59.9	35.2	40.6	18.4	22.6	11.8	15.0
1989	72.7	79.2	68.5	74.9	54.0	60.2	35.6	40.9	18.7	22.9	12.1	15.3
1990	72.7	79.4	68.5	75.0	54.0	60.3	35.6	41.0	18.7	23.0	12.1	15.4
1991	72.9	79.6	68.7	75.2	54.1	60.4	35.8	41.1	18.9	23.1	12.3	15.5
1992	73.2	79.8	68.9	75.4	54.3	60.6	36.0	41.2	19.1	23.2	12.4	15.6
1993	73.1	79.5	68.8	75.1	54.2	60.3	35.9	41.0	18.9	23.0	12.3	15.3
1994	73.3	79.6	68.9	75.2	54.4	60.4	36.0	41.1	19.1	23.1	12.5	15.4
1995	73.4	79.6	69.1	75.1	54.5	60.4	36.1	41.0	19.3	23.0	12.5	15.4
1996	73.9	79.7	69.5	75.2	54.9	60.4	36.4	41.1	19.4	23.0	12.6	15.4
1997	74.3	79.9	69.9	75.4	55.3	60.7	36.7	41.3	19.6	23.2	12.7	15.5
1998	74.5	80.0	70.1	75.5	55.5	60.8	36.8	41.4	19.7	23.3	12.8	15.6

Notes appear at end of table

(continued)

TABLE Ab656–703   Expectation of life at specified ages, by sex and race: 1850–1998   *Continued*

	Nonwhite											
	Total											
	At birth		Age 5		Age 20		Age 40		Age 60		Age 70	
	Males	Females	Males	Females	Males	Females	Males	Females	Males	Females	Males	Females
	Ab680	Ab681	Ab682	Ab683	Ab684	Ab685	Ab686	Ab687	Ab688	Ab689	Ab690	Ab691
Year(s)	Years	Years	Years	Years	Years	Years	Years	Years	Years	Years	Years	Years
1850	—	—	—	—	—	—	—	—	—	—	—	—
1860	—	—	—	—	—	—	—	—	—	—	—	—
1870	—	—	—	—	—	—	—	—	—	—	—	—
1880	—	—	—	—	—	—	—	—	—	—	—	—
1890	—	—	—	—	—	—	—	—	—	—	—	—
1900	—	—	—	—	—	—	—	—	—	—	—	—
1900–1902 [2]	—	—	—	—	—	—	—	—	—	—	—	—
1901–1910 [2]	—	—	—	—	—	—	—	—	—	—	—	—
1909–1911 [2]	—	—	—	—	—	—	—	—	—	—	—	—
1910	—	—	—	—	—	—	—	—	—	—	—	—
1919–1921 [3]	—	—	—	—	—	—	—	—	—	—	—	—
1929–1931	—	—	—	—	—	—	—	—	—	—	—	—
1939–1941	52.3	55.5	53.1	58.5	39.7	42.1	25.2	27.3	14.4	16.1	10.1	11.8
1949–1951	58.9	62.7	57.7	55.5	43.7	46.8	27.3	29.8	14.9	17.0	10.7	12.3
1955	61.4	66.1	59.7	64.0	45.5	49.6	28.6	32.0	15.4	18.1	11.7	13.8
1956	61.3	66.1	59.6	63.9	45.4	49.4	28.5	31.8	15.2	17.9	11.5	13.6
1957	60.7	65.5	58.9	63.4	44.7	48.9	27.8	31.3	14.5	17.4	11.1	13.2
1958	61.0	65.8	59.3	63.8	45.0	49.3	28.0	31.5	14.5	17.4	10.9	13.1
1959	61.3	66.5	59.5	64.4	45.8	50.2	28.8	32.4	15.5	18.2	11.2	13.0
1960	61.1	66.3	59.7	64.4	45.5	49.9	28.4	32.1	14.9	17.7	10.7	12.7
1961	62.0	67.1	60.3	65.0	46.0	50.5	29.0	32.6	15.3	18.0	11.2	13.0
1962 [4]	61.6	66.9	59.9	64.7	45.6	50.2	28.6	32.4	15.0	17.7	10.9	12.9
1963 [4]	61.0	66.6	59.3	64.5	45.1	50.0	28.1	32.1	14.6	17.5	10.7	12.8
1964	61.3	67.3	59.5	65.1	45.3	50.6	28.5	32.7	15.2	18.1	11.4	13.4
1965	61.2	67.6	59.3	65.3	45.1	50.8	28.3	32.8	15.1	18.2	11.2	13.5
1966	60.9	67.6	58.8	65.2	44.6	50.7	28.0	32.8	14.9	18.1	11.0	13.4
1967	61.4	68.5	59.0	65.8	44.8	51.3	28.3	33.4	15.3	18.7	11.2	13.9
1968	60.1	67.5	57.8	65.0	43.6	50.5	27.4	32.7	14.5	17.9	10.5	13.2
1969	60.5	68.4	58.0	65.7	43.9	51.2	27.8	33.3	14.9	18.5	10.9	13.7
1970	61.3	69.4	58.9	66.7	44.7	52.2	28.6	34.2	15.7	19.4	11.2	13.7
1971	61.6	69.8	59.0	66.8	44.9	52.3	28.8	34.3	15.7	19.4	11.0	13.5
1972	61.5	70.1	58.8	67.1	44.6	52.5	28.5	34.4	15.6	19.4	10.8	13.5
1973	62.0	70.3	59.1	67.1	44.9	52.6	28.7	34.4	15.6	19.3	10.7	13.2
1974	62.9	71.3	59.9	68.2	45.7	53.6	29.2	35.3	15.9	19.9	11.0	13.8
1975	63.6	72.3	60.6	69.2	46.3	54.7	29.8	36.2	16.3	20.7	11.3	14.4
1976	64.1	72.6	61.1	69.5	46.8	54.9	30.0	36.4	16.3	20.7	11.3	14.3
1977	64.6	73.1	61.5	69.8	47.2	55.2	30.2	36.7	16.5	21.0	11.4	14.5
1978	65.0	73.6	61.8	70.2	47.4	55.6	30.4	37.0	16.5	21.2	11.6	14.8
1979	65.5	74.2	62.2	70.8	47.8	56.2	30.9	37.6	17.0	21.6	11.9	15.2
1980	65.3	73.6	61.9	70.2	47.5	55.5	30.3	36.8	16.2	20.7	11.1	14.2
1981	66.1	74.5	62.6	70.9	48.2	56.2	30.9	37.5	16.7	21.3	11.5	14.7
1982	66.8	75.0	63.3	71.4	48.8	56.8	31.3	37.9	16.8	21.5	11.7	15.0
1983	67.2	74.9	63.6	71.3	49.1	56.6	31.5	37.7	16.8	21.3	11.5	14.6
1984	67.4	75.0	63.7	71.4	49.3	56.7	31.6	37.8	16.9	21.3	11.5	14.6
1985	67.2	75.0	63.6	71.2	49.1	56.5	31.6	37.7	16.9	21.1	11.4	14.4
1986	67.2	75.1	63.6	71.3	49.1	56.6	31.8	37.8	17.0	21.2	11.5	14.5
1987	67.3	75.2	63.6	71.4	49.2	56.7	32.0	38.0	17.2	21.3	11.6	14.6
1988	67.1	75.1	63.5	71.3	49.1	56.7	32.0	37.9	17.2	21.3	11.6	14.5
1989	67.1	75.2	63.5	71.6	49.2	56.9	32.1	38.2	17.5	21.4	11.8	14.6
1990	67.0	75.2	63.4	71.5	49.0	56.8	31.9	38.1	17.0	21.3	11.4	14.5
1991	67.3	75.5	63.6	71.7	49.3	57.0	32.2	38.3	17.3	21.5	11.6	14.6
1992	67.7	75.7	63.9	71.9	49.6	57.2	32.4	38.4	17.5	21.7	11.7	14.8
1993	67.3	75.5	63.6	71.6	49.2	56.9	32.2	38.2	17.3	21.4	11.5	14.5
1994	67.6	75.7	63.8	71.8	49.5	57.1	32.4	38.4	17.6	21.6	11.7	14.6
1995	67.9	75.7	64.0	71.7	49.6	57.0	32.4	38.3	17.6	21.5	11.7	14.5
1996	68.9	76.1	64.9	72.1	50.6	57.4	33.1	38.7	18.0	21.8	12.0	14.7
1997	69.8	76.7	—	—	—	—	—	—	—	—	—	—
1998	—	—	—	—	—	—	—	—	—	—	—	—

Notes appear at end of table

TABLE Ab656–703   Expectation of life at specified ages, by sex and race: 1850–1998   *Continued*

		Nonwhite										
		Black										
	At birth		Age 5		Age 20		Age 40		Age 60		Age 70	
	Males	Females	Males	Females	Males	Females	Males	Females	Males	Females	Males	Females
	Ab692	Ab693	Ab694	Ab695	Ab696	Ab697	Ab698	Ab699	Ab700	Ab701	Ab702	Ab703
Year(s)	Years	Years	Years	Years	Years	Years	Years	Years	Years	Years	Years	Years
1850	—	—	—	—	—	—	—	—	—	—	—	—
1860	—	—	—	—	—	—	—	—	—	—	—	—
1870	—	—	—	—	—	—	—	—	—	—	—	—
1880	—	—	—	—	—	—	—	—	—	—	—	—
1890	—	—	—	—	—	—	—	—	—	—	—	—
1900	40.4	43.3	49.8	51.8	38.3	40.7	24.5	27.0	12.4	13.6	7.7	8.4
1900–1902 [2]	32.5	35.0	45.1	46.0	35.1	36.9	23.1	24.4	12.6	13.6	8.3	9.6
1901–1910 [2]	32.6	35.7	44.1	45.8	33.8	36.2	22.3	23.8	12.0	13.2	8.4	9.6
1909–1911 [2]	34.1	37.7	44.2	46.4	33.5	36.1	21.6	23.3	11.7	12.8	8.0	9.2
1910	41.8	44.6	46.4	48.5	34.6	36.6	20.8	24.0	10.1	12.3	6.6	8.0
1919–1921 [3]	47.1	46.9	50.2	48.7	38.4	37.2	26.5	25.6	14.7	14.7	9.6	10.3
1929–1931	47.6	49.5	48.7	49.8	36.0	37.2	23.4	24.3	13.2	14.2	8.8	10.4
1939–1941	52.3	55.6	53.0	55.4	39.5	42.0	25.1	27.2	14.4	16.1	10.1	11.8
1949–1951	—	—	—	—	—	—	—	—	—	—	—	—
1955	—	—	—	—	—	—	—	—	—	—	—	—
1956	—	—	—	—	—	—	—	—	—	—	—	—
1957	—	—	—	—	—	—	—	—	—	—	—	—
1958	—	—	—	—	—	—	—	—	—	—	—	—
1959	—	—	—	—	—	—	—	—	—	—	—	—
1960	—	—	—	—	—	—	—	—	—	—	—	—
1961	—	—	—	—	—	—	—	—	—	—	—	—
1962 [4]	—	—	—	—	—	—	—	—	—	—	—	—
1963 [4]	—	—	—	—	—	—	—	—	—	—	—	—
1964	—	—	—	—	—	—	—	—	—	—	—	—
1965	—	—	—	—	—	—	—	—	—	—	—	—
1966	—	—	—	—	—	—	—	—	—	—	—	—
1967	—	—	—	—	—	—	—	—	—	—	—	—
1968	—	—	—	—	—	—	—	—	—	—	—	—
1969	—	—	—	—	—	—	—	—	—	—	—	—
1970	60.0	68.3	—	—	—	—	—	—	—	—	—	—
1971	60.5	68.9	—	—	—	—	—	—	—	—	—	—
1972	60.4	69.1	—	—	—	—	—	—	—	—	—	—
1973	60.9	69.3	—	—	—	—	—	—	—	—	—	—
1974	61.7	70.3	—	—	—	—	—	—	—	—	—	—
1975	62.4	71.3	—	—	—	—	—	—	—	—	—	—
1976	62.9	71.6	—	—	—	—	—	—	—	—	—	—
1977	63.4	72.0	—	—	—	—	—	—	—	—	—	—
1978	63.7	72.4	—	—	—	—	—	—	—	—	—	—
1979	64.0	72.7	60.8	69.4	46.4	54.8	29.6	36.2	15.9	20.4	10.7	13.9
1980	63.7	72.3	60.5	69.0	46.0	54.3	29.1	35.7	15.5	19.8	10.5	13.4
1981	64.4	73.0	61.0	69.6	46.6	54.9	29.5	36.3	15.8	20.3	10.8	13.9
1982	64.9	73.5	61.6	70.0	47.2	55.4	29.9	36.6	15.9	20.5	10.9	14.1
1983	65.4	73.6	62.1	70.1	47.6	55.4	30.2	36.7	16.0	20.5	10.9	14.1
1984	65.6	73.7	62.1	70.2	47.6	55.5	30.3	36.7	16.1	20.5	10.9	14.0
1985	65.3	73.5	61.9	70.0	47.4	55.3	30.2	36.6	16.0	20.3	10.8	13.8
1986	65.2	73.5	61.7	69.9	47.3	55.3	30.3	36.6	16.1	20.3	10.8	13.9
1987	65.2	73.6	61.7	70.0	47.3	55.3	30.4	36.7	16.2	20.4	10.9	13.9
1988	64.9	73.4	61.4	69.8	47.0	55.1	30.3	36.6	16.2	20.3	10.9	13.8
1989	64.8	73.5	61.4	70.0	47.1	55.3	30.4	36.8	16.4	20.4	11.0	13.9
1990	64.5	73.6	61.0	70.0	46.7	55.3	30.1	36.8	15.9	20.5	10.7	14.1
1991	64.6	73.8	61.1	70.1	46.9	55.4	30.3	36.9	16.2	20.6	10.9	14.1
1992	65.0	73.9	61.4	70.3	47.2	55.6	30.5	37.1	16.3	20.8	11.0	14.3
1993	64.6	73.7	61.0	70.0	46.8	55.3	30.2	36.9	16.2	20.6	10.8	13.9
1994	64.9	73.9	61.3	70.1	42.8	55.5	30.5	37.0	16.5	20.7	11.0	14.1
1995	65.2	73.9	61.5	70.1	47.2	55.4	30.5	36.9	16.4	20.6	11.0	13.9
1996	66.1	74.2	62.4	70.3	48.0	55.7	31.0	37.1	16.7	20.7	11.2	17.2
1997	67.2	74.7	63.4	70.9	49.0	56.2	31.6	37.5	17.0	21.0	11.5	14.3
1998	67.6	74.8	63.9	70.9	49.5	56.2	31.9	37.5	17.1	21.0	11.5	14.1

Notes appear on next page   (continued)

TABLE Ab656–703   Expectation of life at specified ages, by sex and race: 1850–1998   *Continued*

[1] Data for 1929–1931 to 1958 are for the conterminous United States; those for 1919–1921 are for death registration states of 1920 (thirty-four states and the District of Columbia); and those for 1900–1902, 1901–1910, and 1909–1911 are for death registration states of 1900 (ten states and the District of Columbia).

[2] For the Death Registration Area of 1900.

[3] For the Death Registration Area of 1920.

[4] Excludes New Jersey, which did not require reporting of race.

Sources

1850–1900 and 1910 (the whole United States): Michael R. Haines, "Estimated Life Tables for the United States, 1850–1910," *Historical Methods* 31 (4) (1998): 149–69. For the total and white populations for 1850–1900, the U.S. Model life tables were used. For the total and white populations for 1910 and for the black population for 1900 and 1910, the West Model life tables were used.

1900–1902, 1901–1910, and 1909–1911 (Death Registration Area of 1900): James W. Glover, *United States Life Tables, 1890, 1901, 1910, and 1901–10* (U.S. Government Printing Office, 1921).

1919–1921 (Death Registration Area of 1920) and 1929–1998 (the whole United States): 1919–1993, National Center for Health Statistics, *Vital Statistics of the United States, 1993*, preprint of volume 2, *Mortality*, part A, section 6, "Life Tables," Table 6.5. 1994–1997, U.S. Public Health Service, *National Vital Statistics Report*, volume 47, number 19, "Deaths: Final Data for 1997," Table 6. 1998, *National Vital Statistics Report*, volume 48, number 11, "Deaths: Final Data for 1998," Table 5. Also used for 1955–1992 were annual issues of *Vital Statistics of the United States*, volume 2, *Mortality*. For 1994–1996, files from the National Center for Health Statistics Internet site were used.

Documentation

The composition of the Death Registration Area can be seen in Tables Ab31–39. Derivation of estimates is described in T. N. E. Greville and G. E. Carlson, "Estimated Average Length of Life in the Death-Registration States," National Center for Health Statistics, *Vital Statistics – Special Reports*, volume 33, number 9 (1951). The expectation of life at any age is the average number of years that members of a hypothetical cohort would live from that age if they were subject throughout the remainder of their lives to the age-specific mortality rates observed at the time of their birth. This is the most usual measure of the comparative longevity of different populations. There is some objection to the use of the expectation of life at birth as a standard of comparison because the method of calculating it gives great weight to the relatively large number of deaths occurring in the first several years of life. This influence may be entirely eliminated by considering instead the average lifetime remaining to those members of the cohort surviving to age 5, or, in other words, the expectation of life at age 5. However, this objection is growing less valid as infant mortality decreases.

The expectations of life at birth may differ slightly from those in Table Ab644–655 owing to differences in life table construction. The values in this table for 1955–1992 reflect, in general, the unabridged life table values (that is, single years of age life tables) for each year.

The mortality estimates for the 1850–1890 period are based on estimates made using a collection of actual nineteenth- and early-twentieth-century American life tables (for various states and cities, as well as for the Death Registration Area) to construct a life table system. Census mortality data for older children and young adults were then fitted to this model system to produce the estimates presented here. For 1900 and 1910, the mortality data are based on indirect estimates made using data from the microsamples of the 1900 and 1910 Censuses on children ever born, children surviving, and duration of marriage (Michael R. Haines and Samuel H. Preston, "The Use of the Census to Estimate Childhood Mortality: Comparisons from the 1900 and 1910 Public Use Samples," *Historical Methods* 30 (2) (1997): 77–96). For 1920 and thereafter, official Death Registration Area data are used.

TABLE Ab704–911 Life table l(x) values at selected ages, by sex and race: 1850–1997
Contributed by Michael R. Haines

All races — Male

	Expectation of life		Number living at beginning of year of age											
	At birth	At age 10	0	1	2	3	4	5	10	15	20	25	30
	Ab704	Ab705	Ab706	Ab707	Ab708	Ab709	Ab710	Ab711	Ab712	Ab713	Ab714	Ab715	Ab716
Year(s)	Years	Years	Number	Number	Number	Number	Number	Number	Number	Number	Number	Number	Number
1850	37.23	46.16	100,000	75,908	71,604	69,779	68,646	67,805	65,527	64,156	62,078	59,103	56,003
1860	41.55	48.33	100,000	79,791	76,021	74,403	73,392	72,639	70,587	69,342	67,441	64,689	61,783
1870	43.03	49.23	100,000	80,791	77,212	75,673	74,711	73,993	72,033	70,843	69,021	66,378	63,576
1880	39.72	47.54	100,000	77,985	74,003	72,305	71,248	70,462	68,325	67,034	65,069	62,240	59,270
1890	44.82	49.14	100,000	83,666	80,256	78,766	77,828	77,125	75,194	74,011	72,189	69,519	66,657
1900	47.12	49.43	100,000	86,644	83,520	82,129	81,248	80,584	78,745	77,608	75,842	73,222	70,376
1900–1902	47.88	50.39	100,000	86,426	83,386	82,041	81,189	80,548	78,775	77,681	75,984	73,472	70,747
1901–1910	—	—	—										
1909–1911	49.86	51.07	100,000	87,505	84,984	83,876	83,200	82,718	81,249	80,261	78,792	76,675	74,378
1910	51.54	52.01	100,000	88,700	86,313	85,268	84,583	84,075	82,716	81,735	80,272	78,234	76,077
1919–1921	55.50	53.44	100,000	91,745	90,180	89,435	88,924	88,505	87,184	86,156	84,440	82,252	79,890
1920–1929	—	—	—										
1929–1931	57.71	53.73	100,000	93,440	92,429	91,921	91,581	91,294	90,346	89,561	88,220	86,359	84,346
1939–1941	61.60	56.12	100,000	94,762	94,238	93,965	93,776	93,624	93,054	92,508	91,617	90,385	89,009
1949–1951	65.47	58.35	100,000	96,661	96,425	96,279	96,169	96,077	95,726	95,366	94,695	93,791	92,861
1959–1961	66.80	59.27	100,000	97,087	96,911	96,800	96,714	96,643	96,375	96,107	95,491	94,631	93,826
1969–1971	67.04	58.98	100,000	97,755	97,625	97,533	97,458	97,395	97,151	96,904	96,126	95,040	94,072
1979–1981	70.11	61.41	100,000	98,607	98,508	98,436	98,379	98,333	98,160	97,972	97,316	96,361	95,430
1989–1991	71.83	62.81	100,000	98,961	98,884	98,830	98,789	98,754	98,627	98,464	97,854	97,049	96,166
1997	73.60	64.30	100,000	99,205	99,145	99,105	99,072	99,047	98,947	98,809	98,293	97,581	96,875

All races — Male

	Number living at beginning of year of age												Expectation of life in the last interval
	35	40	45	50	55	60	65	70	75	80	85	90	
	Ab717	Ab718	Ab719	Ab720	Ab721	Ab722	Ab723	Ab724	Ab725	Ab726	Ab727	Ab728	Ab729
Year(s)	Number	Number	Number	Number	Number	Number	Number	Number	Number	Number	Number	Number	Years
1850	52,735	49,283	45,692	41,780	37,450	32,306	26,603	20,273	13,920	7,989	—	—	4.22
1860	58,675	55,340	51,812	47,896	43,470	38,082	31,927	24,856	17,477	10,296	—	—	4.37
1870	60,567	57,324	53,875	50,024	45,641	40,255	34,034	26,782	19,079	11,423	—	—	4.44
1880	56,114	52,751	49,219	45,330	40,970	35,715	29,779	23,042	16,108	9,444	—	—	4.32
1890	63,551	60,169	56,537	52,444	47,746	41,931	35,179	27,306	19,016	10,964	—	—	4.41
1900	67,245	63,787	60,025	55,731	50,738	44,467	37,120	28,500	19,446	10,809	—	—	4.40
1900–1902	67,752	64,447	60,849	56,736	51,939	45,895	38,736	30,217	21,076	12,084	5,179	1,508	2.86
1901–1910													
1909–1911	71,614	68,297	64,518	60,118	54,970	48,343	40,264	31,023	21,213	11,942	5,059	1,502	3.01
1910	73,682	70,896	67,515	63,394	58,135	51,581	43,306	33,571	22,892	12,698	—	—	4.52

(continued)

TABLE Ab704–911 Life table l(x) values at selected ages, by sex and race: 1850–1997 Continued

All races — Male

Year(s)	35 Ab717	40 Ab718	45 Ab719	50 Ab720	55 Ab721	60 Ab722	65 Ab723	70 Ab724	75 Ab725	80 Ab726	85 Ab727	90 Ab728	Expectation of life in the last interval Ab729
	Number	Number	Number	Number	Number	Number	Number	Number	Number	Number	Number	Number	Years
1919–1921	77,314	74,432	71,244	67,553	62,965	56,917	49,218	39,668	28,316	17,128	7,920	2,527	3.21
1920–1929	—	—	—	—	—	—	—	—	—	—	—	—	—
1929–1931	82,075	79,357	75,882	71,518	65,981	58,909	50,154	39,516	27,718	16,172	7,107	2,283	3.06
1939–1941	87,371	85,246	82,336	78,254	72,627	65,142	55,776	44,588	31,864	18,995	8,693	2,787	3.17
1949–1951	91,760	90,207	87,819	84,158	78,781	71,246	61,566	49,950	36,756	25,237	11,750	4,197	3.30
1959–1961	92,889	91,572	89,492	86,199	81,039	73,887	64,177	52,244	38,950	25,300	12,845	4,609	3.18
1969–1971	92,997	91,541	89,369	86,070	81,139	73,958	64,318	52,296	38,797	24,921	13,168	5,107	3.60
1979–1981	94,501	93,345	91,649	89,007	84,936	79,012	70,646	59,681	46,272	31,810	18,020	7,732	3.89
1989–1991	95,091	93,761	92,139	89,865	86,492	81,378	73,971	64,107	51,385	36,749	21,815	9,878	3.89
1997	96,039	94,978	93,502	91,379	88,363	83,809	77,032	67,780	55,576	41,374	25,630	11,991	4.00

All races — Female

	Expectation of life		Number living at beginning of year of age											
Year(s)	At birth Ab730	At age 10 Ab731	0 Ab732	1 Ab733	2 Ab734	3 Ab735	4 Ab736	5 Ab737	10 Ab738	15 Ab739	20 Ab740	25 Ab741	30 Ab742
	Years	Years	Number	Number	Number	Number	Number	Number	Number	Number	Number	Number	Number
1850	39.43	47.48	100,000	78,288	74,063	72,205	71,037	70,155	67,847	66,441	64,228	61,267	58,101
1860	42.15	48.69	100,000	80,847	76,959	75,232	74,141	73,316	71,143	69,812	67,705	64,865	61,798
1870	44.92	50.62	100,000	82,276	78,766	77,204	76,217	75,469	73,496	72,286	70,364	67,762	64,937
1880	39.12	47.98	100,000	77,020	72,825	70,993	69,845	68,981	66,723	65,353	63,202	60,334	57,277
1890	45.60	49.96	100,000	84,235	80,768	79,204	78,210	77,454	75,447	74,208	72,230	69,532	66,579
1900	48.45	50.52	100,000	87,524	84,428	83,004	82,089	81,389	79,514	78,343	76,456	73,843	70,939
1900–1902	50.70	51.94	100,000	88,733	85,908	84,603	83,763	83,119	81,390	80,307	78,555	76,119	73,394
1901–1910	—	—	—	—	—	—	—	—	—	—	—	—	—
1909–1911	53.24	53.31	100,000	89,623	87,257	86,242	85,587	85,117	83,728	82,813	81,418	79,481	77,247
1910	54.68	54.43	100,000	90,512	88,160	87,098	86,407	85,879	84,501	83,451	81,971	80,077	77,965
1919–1921	57.40	54.16	100,000	93,383	91,945	91,260	90,774	90,380	89,186	88,247	86,556	84,135	81,463
1920–1929	—	—	—	—	—	—	—	—	—	—	—	—	—
1929–1931	60.99	56.16	100,000	94,728	93,819	93,363	93,046	92,789	92,008	91,364	90,116	88,328	86,398
1939–1941	65.89	59.73	100,000	95,848	95,379	95,147	94,981	94,848	94,402	94,000	93,293	92,322	91,182
1949–1951	70.96	63.38	100,000	97,406	97,197	97,076	96,982	96,908	96,652	96,431	96,066	95,583	94,933
1959–1961	73.24	65.35	100,000	97,744	97,589	97,498	97,429	97,371	97,173	97,016	96,756	96,418	95,996
1969–1971	74.64	66.31	100,000	98,254	98,139	98,064	98,005	97,955	97,784	97,636	97,331	96,966	96,544
1979–1981	77.62	68.75	100,000	98,880	98,796	98,740	98,699	98,666	98,544	98,432	98,184	97,883	97,551
1989–1991	78.81	69.67	100,000	99,172	99,105	99,063	99,031	99,006	98,911	98,814	98,597	98,325	98,013
1997	78.40	70.00	100,000	99,383	99,333	99,302	99,276	99,256	99,174	99,083	98,868	98,624	98,336

All races

Female

	Number living at beginning of year of age												Expectation of life in the last interval
	35	40	45	50	55	60	65	70	75	80	85	90	
	Ab743	Ab744	Ab745	Ab746	Ab747	Ab748	Ab749	Ab750	Ab751	Ab752	Ab753	Ab754	Ab755
Year(s)	Number	Number	Number	Number	Number	Number	Number	Number	Number	Number	Number	Number	Years
1850	54,850	51,613	48,288	44,713	40,586	35,623	30,048	23,641	16,820	10,263	—	—	4.37
1860	58,617	55,419	52,101	48,495	44,283	39,148	33,285	26,425	18,977	11,676	—	—	4.45
1870	61,988	59,000	55,874	52,443	48,386	43,362	37,504	30,459	22,528	14,392	—	—	4.62
1880	54,148	51,039	47,852	44,427	40,474	35,716	30,353	24,149	17,466	10,916	—	—	4.41
1890	63,473	60,307	56,977	53,307	48,954	43,553	37,266	29,756	21,438	13,158	—	—	4.55
1900	67,836	64,624	61,196	57,365	52,752	46,942	40,077	31,776	22,537	13,421	—	—	4.56
1900–1902	70,463	67,407	64,121	60,415	55,908	50,155	43,246	34,721	24,994	15,129	7,063	2,306	3.04
1901–1910	—	—	—	—	—	—	—	—	—	—	—	—	—
1909–1911	74,719	71,894	68,755	65,001	60,392	54,226	46,438	36,916	26,155	15,682	7,051	2,269	3.05
1910	75,633	73,070	70,242	66,993	62,806	57,489	50,271	41,127	29,905	18,058	—	—	4.85
1919–1921	78,713	75,907	72,954	69,452	65,099	59,438	52,126	42,741	31,344	19,613	9,515	3,314	3.23
1920–1929	—	—	—	—	—	—	—	—	—	—	—	—	—
1929–1931	84,304	81,927	79,041	75,456	70,832	64,795	56,924	46,774	34,600	21,578	10,322	3,656	3.24
1939–1941	89,810	88,092	85,856	82,828	78,708	73,093	65,523	55,449	42,425	27,524	13,972	5,044	3.39
1949–1951	94,206	93,101	91,469	89,075	85,694	80,890	74,119	64,873	52,111	36,486	20,668	8,548	3.54
1959–1961	95,409	94,560	93,265	91,327	88,451	84,430	78,462	70,100	58,394	43,063	25,269	10,056	3.25
1969–1971	95,966	95,097	93,793	91,852	89,066	85,139	79,698	71,955	61,107	46,445	29,538	14,160	4.14
1979–1981	97,140	96,531	95,570	94,060	91,760	88,414	83,520	76,720	67,186	54,372	37,772	20,578	4.66
1989–1991	97,596	97,033	96,222	94,932	92,881	89,742	85,075	78,522	69,287	56,986	41,115	23,666	4.73
1997	97,945	97,381	96,561	95,346	93,471	90,515	86,006	79,677	70,550	58,348	42,258	24,167	4.70

Whites

Male

	Expectation of life		Number living at beginning of year of age											
	At birth	At age 10	0	1	2	3	4	5	10	15	20	25	30
	Ab756	Ab757	Ab758	Ab759	Ab760	Ab761	Ab762	Ab763	Ab764	Ab765	Ab766	Ab767	Ab768
Year(s)	Years	Years	Number	Number	Number	Number	Number	Number	Number	Number	Number	Number	Number
1850	38.42	46.65	100,000	77,171	73,003	71,228	70,124	69,303	67,075	65,731	63,687	60,753	57,682
1860	43.17	49.08	100,000	81,227	77,649	76,107	75,141	74,421	72,451	71,253	69,418	66,751	63,920
1870	44.11	49.91	100,000	81,487	78,045	76,563	75,636	74,943	73,052	71,902	70,139	67,577	64,855
1880	40.44	47.94	100,000	78,564	74,674	73,012	71,977	71,206	69,111	67,843	65,911	63,126	60,196
1890	46.04	49.95	100,000	84,325	81,074	79,653	78,758	78,086	76,240	75,108	73,362	70,799	68,045
1900	48.51	50.43	100,000	87,216	84,270	82,960	82,129	81,503	79,767	78,693	77,023	74,543	71,842
1900–1902	48.23	50.56	100,000	86,655	83,669	82,343	81,499	80,864	79,109	78,037	76,376	73,907	71,219
1901–1910	49.33	50.85	100,000	87,262	84,628	83,464	82,730	82,195	80,605	79,544	77,957	75,679	73,222
1909–1911	50.24	51.32	100,000	87,674	85,201	84,117	83,449	82,972	81,519	80,549	79,116	77,047	74,810
1910	52.97	52.75	100,000	89,503	87,340	86,392	85,772	85,311	84,045	83,125	81,740	79,808	77,768

(continued)

TABLE Ab704–911   Life table l(x) values at selected ages, by sex and race: 1850–1997   Continued

Whites

Male

	Expectation of life		Number living at beginning of year of age										
	At birth	At age 10	0	1	2	3	4	5	10	15	20	25	30
	Ab756	Ab757	Ab758	Ab759	Ab760	Ab761	Ab762	Ab763	Ab764	Ab765	Ab766	Ab767	Ab768
Year(s)	Years	Years	Number	Number	Number	Number	Number	Number	Number	Number	Number	Number	Number
1919–1921	56.34	54.15	100,000	91,975	90,485	89,765	89,262	88,842	87,530	86,546	84,997	83,061	80,888
1920–1929	57.85	54.65	100,000	92,846	91,647	91,059	90,659	90,323	89,239	88,390	87,112	85,467	83,680
1929–1931	59.12	54.96	100,000	93,768	92,837	92,354	92,023	91,738	90,810	90,074	88,904	87,371	85,707
1939–1941	62.81	57.03	100,000	95,188	94,724	94,474	94,295	94,150	93,601	93,089	92,293	91,241	90,092
1949–1951	66.31	58.98	100,000	96,931	96,726	96,592	96,490	96,403	96,069	95,728	95,104	94,294	93,489
1959–1961	67.55	59.78	100,000	97,408	97,259	97,160	97,082	97,015	96,758	96,503	95,908	95,106	94,401
1969–1971	67.94	59.69	100,000	97,994	97,880	97,799	97,728	97,671	97,441	97,208	96,480	95,524	94,716
1979–1981	70.82	61.98	100,000	98,769	98,679	98,614	98,562	98,519	98,357	98,176	97,525	96,616	95,783
1989–1991	72.72	63.35	100,000	99,138	99,072	99,024	98,987	98,956	98,839	98,686	98,134	97,430	96,662
1997	74.30	65.00	100,000	99,333	99,280	99,244	99,216	99,193	99,103	98,973	98,507	97,893	97,281

Whites

Male

	Number living at beginning of year of age												Expectation of life in the last interval
	35	40	45	50	55	60	65	70	75	80	85	90	
	Ab769	Ab770	Ab771	Ab772	Ab773	Ab774	Ab775	Ab776	Ab777	Ab778	Ab779	Ab780	Ab781
Year(s)	Number	Number	Number	Number	Number	Number	Number	Number	Number	Number	Number	Number	Years
1850	54,430	50,980	47,374	43,425	39,029	33,775	27,908	21,345	14,707	8,464	—	—	4.25
1860	60,875	57,590	54,092	50,183	45,732	40,263	33,949	26,605	18,837	11,172	—	—	4.42
1870	61,923	58,753	55,369	51,575	47,235	41,868	35,615	28,251	20,325	12,319	—	—	4.49
1880	57,076	53,742	50,232	46,355	41,994	36,715	30,721	23,878	16,778	9,897	—	—	4.34
1890	65,047	61,771	58,237	54,237	49,616	43,851	37,086	29,091	20,526	12,030	—	—	4.48
1900	68,862	65,560	61,950	57,806	52,953	46,809	39,500	30,768	21,382	12,165	—	—	4.49
1900–1902	68,245	64,954	61,369	57,274	52,491	46,452	39,245	30,640	21,387	12,266	5,252	1,523	2.85
1901–1910	70,342	66,996	63,304	58,963	54,075	47,701	39,996	31,050	21,547	12,295	5,214	1,492	2.90
1909–1911	72,108	68,848	65,115	60,741	55,622	48,987	40,862	31,527	21,585	12,160	5,145	1,523	2.99
1910	75,500	72,847	69,594	65,569	60,369	53,797	45,418	35,445	24,375	13,675			4.58
1919–1921	78,441	75,733	72,696	69,107	64,574	58,498	50,663	40,873	29,205	17,655	8,154	2,568	3.18
1920–1929	81,683	79,167	76,110	72,220	67,171	60,631	51,958	41,260	28,996	16,792	7,478	2,222	2.94
1929–1931	83,812	81,457	78,345	74,288	68,981	61,933	52,964	41,880	29,471	17,221	7,572	2,356	3.03
1939–1941	88,713	86,880	84,285	80,521	75,156	67,787	58,305	46,739	33,404	19,860	9,013	2,812	3.06
1949–1951	92,543	91,173	89,002	85,601	80,496	73,172	63,541	51,735	38,104	24,005	12,015	4,209	3.27
1959–1961	93,589	92,427	90,533	87,424	82,463	75,485	65,834	53,825	40,207	25,993	13,065	4,600	3.16
1969–1971	93,843	92,631	90,725	87,690	83,001	75,969	66,343	54,138	40,324	25,885	13,527	5,125	3.49
1979–1981	94,980	93,984	92,494	90,105	86,303	80,625	72,393	61,384	47,712	32,788	18,538	7,891	3.83
1989–1991	95,731	94,588	93,167	91,124	88,022	83,182	75,962	66,181	53,308	38,245	22,720	10,214	3.85
1997	96,537	95,595	94,278	92,384	89,600	85,314	78,788	69,556	57,282	42,767	26,491	12,311	3.90

Whites

Female

	Expectation of life		Number living at beginning of year of age											
	At birth	At age 10	0	1	2	3	4	5	10	15	20	25	30
	Ab782	Ab783	Ab784	Ab785	Ab786	Ab787	Ab788	Ab789	Ab790	Ab791	Ab792	Ab793	Ab794
Year(s)	Years	Years	Number	Number	Number	Number	Number	Number	Number	Number	Number	Number	Number
1850	40.56	47.96	100,000	79,404	75,316	73,511	72,373	71,514	69,258	67,881	65,709	62,792	59,660
1860	44.10	49.62	100,000	82,485	78,842	77,215	76,184	75,402	73,337	72,068	70,051	67,317	64,347
1870	46.38	51.38	100,000	83,367	80,032	78,544	77,501	76,886	74,996	73,834	71,984	69,472	66,733
1880	40.59	48.61	100,000	78,473	74,447	72,680	71,570	70,732	68,540	67,205	65,103	62,289	59,275
1890	47.44	50.95	100,000	85,510	82,278	80,815	79,882	79,171	77,282	76,111	74,236	71,667	68,840
1900	50.71	51.86	100,000	88,794	85,988	84,692	83,858	83,219	81,502	80,426	78,686	76,266	73,559
1900–1902	51.08	52.14	100,000	88,939	86,168	84,890	84,061	83,426	81,723	80,680	78,978	76,588	73,887
1901–1910	52.54	52.88	100,000	89,449	86,996	85,899	85,188	84,668	83,143	82,129	80,581	78,437	76,009
1909–1911	53.62	53.57	100,000	89,774	87,455	86,456	85,812	85,349	83,979	83,093	81,750	79,865	77,676
1910	56.24	55.27	100,000	91,243	89,154	88,200	87,573	87,089	85,828	84,864	83,497	81,737	79,765
1919–1921	58.53	55.17	100,000	93,608	92,243	91,582	91,108	90,721	89,564	88,712	87,281	85,163	82,740
1920–1929	60.62	56.41	100,000	94,307	93,205	92,675	92,309	92,005	91,083	90,392	89,233	87,543	85,695
1929–1931	62.67	57.65	100,000	95,037	94,202	93,772	93,466	93,216	92,466	91,894	90,939	89,524	87,972
1939–1941	67.29	60.85	100,000	96,211	95,796	95,585	95,431	95,309	94,890	94,534	93,984	93,228	92,320
1949–1951	72.03	64.26	100,000	97,645	97,460	97,351	97,266	97,199	96,960	96,756	96,454	96,072	95,605
1959–1961	74.79	66.05	100,000	98,036	97,904	97,824	97,762	97,709	97,525	97,375	97,135	96,844	96,499
1969–1971	75.49	66.97	100,000	98,468	98,368	98,303	98,249	98,203	98,042	97,902	97,618	97,299	96,945
1979–1981	78.22	69.21	100,000	99,035	98,958	98,908	98,871	98,841	98,725	98,618	98,374	98,093	97,802
1989–1991	79.45	70.16	100,000	99,333	99,274	99,238	99,209	99,187	99,099	99,007	98,795	98,547	98,283
1997	79.90	70.50	100,000	99,464	99,420	99,393	99,370	99,353	99,283	99,198	98,986	98,764	98,516

Whites

Female

	Number living at beginning of year of age												Expectation of life in the last interval
	35	40	45	50	55	60	65	70	75	80	85	90	
	Ab795	Ab796	Ab797	Ab798	Ab799	Ab800	Ab801	Ab802	Ab803	Ab804	Ab805	Ab806	Ab807
Year(s)	Number	Number	Number	Number	Number	Number	Number	Number	Number	Number	Number	Number	Years
1850	56,430	53,201	49,871	46,274	42,101	37,056	31,351	24,748	17,665	10,807	—	—	4.40
1860	61,245	58,105	54,824	51,231	46,998	41,784	35,759	28,607	20,717	12,853	—	—	4.53
1870	63,860	60,937	57,864	54,473	50,440	45,407	39,486	32,284	24,068	15,511	—	—	4.69
1880	56,174	53,077	49,886	46,439	42,436	37,583	32,069	25,631	18,626	11,691	—	—	4.46
1890	65,850	62,782	59,535	55,930	51,617	46,211	39,838	32,106	23,382	14,520	—	—	4.63
1900	70,646	67,607	64,338	60,649	56,160	50,424	43,526	34,998	25,244	15,319	—	—	4.68
1900–1902	70,971	67,935	64,677	61,005	56,509	50,752	43,806	35,206	25,362	15,349	7,149	2,322	3.02
1901–1910	73,295	70,383	67,235	63,539	59,053	53,104	45,654	36,512	26,163	15,831	7,265	2,307	3.05
1909–1911	75,200	72,425	69,341	65,629	61,053	54,900	47,086	37,482	26,569	15,929	7,152	2,291	3.00
1910	77,573	75,142	72,423	69,252	65,129	59,842	52,611	43,323	31,776	19,399	—	—	4.94

(continued)

TABLE Ab704–911   Life table l(x) values at selected ages, by sex and race: 1850–1997   Continued

Whites

Female

					Number living at beginning of year of age							Expectation of life in the last interval
	35	40	45	50	55	60	65	70	75	80	85	90	
	Ab795	Ab796	Ab797	Ab798	Ab799	Ab800	Ab801	Ab802	Ab803	Ab804	Ab805	Ab806	Ab807
Year(s)	Number	Number	Number	Number	Number	Number	Number	Number	Number	Number	Number	Number	Years
1919–1921	80,206	77,624	74,871	71,547	67,323	61,704	54,299	44,638	32,777	20,492	9,909	3,372	3.16
1920–1929	83,742	81,457	78,848	75,537	71,104	65,382	57,393	46,986	34,348	20,945	9,866	3,032	2.92
1929–1931	86,248	84,256	81,780	78,572	74,321	68,462	60,490	49,932	37,024	23,053	10,937	3,719	3.17
1939–1941	91,211	89,805	87,920	85,267	81,520	76,200	68,701	58,363	44,685	28,882	14,487	5,061	3.24
1949–1951	94,977	94,080	92,725	90,685	87,699	83,279	76,773	67,545	54,397	38,026	21,348	8,662	3.51
1959–1961	96,026	95,326	94,228	92,522	89,967	86,339	80,739	72,507	60,461	44,676	26,046	10,219	3.23
1969–1971	96,474	95,762	94,649	92,924	90,383	86,726	81,579	74,101	63,290	48,182	30,490	14,406	4.05
1979–1981	97,445	96,913	96,065	94,710	92,594	89,451	84,764	78,139	68,712	55,770	38,774	20,996	4.59
1989–1991	97,939	97,472	96,768	95,608	93,730	90,789	86,339	79,984	70,834	58,454	42,274	24,270	4.69
1997	98,180	97,702	95,993	95,922	94,193	91,412	87,106	80,905	71,921	59,627	43,261	24,704	4.60

Blacks

Male

	Expectation of life		Number living at beginning of year of age											
	At birth	At age 10	0	1	2	3	4	5	10	15	20	25	30
	Ab808	Ab809	Ab810	Ab811	Ab812	Ab813	Ab814	Ab815	Ab816	Ab817	Ab818	Ab819	Ab820
Year(s)	Years	Years	Number	Number	Number	Number	Number	Number	Number	Number	Number	Number	Number
1850	—	—	—	—	—	—	—	—	—	—	—	—	—
1860	—	—	—	—	—	—	—	—	—	—	—	—	—
1870	—	—	—	—	—	—	—	—	—	—	—	—	—
1880	—	—	—	—	—	—	—	—	—	—	—	—	—
1890	—	—	—	—	—	—	—	—	—	—	—	—	—
1900	40.45	46.21	100,000	81,654	77,344	75,457	74,221	73,302	71,235	69,779	67,779	65,027	62,109
1900–1902	32.54	41.90	100,000	74,674	68,902	66,541	65,325	64,385	61,730	59,667	56,733	53,285	49,867
1901–1910	—	—	—	—	—	—	—	—	—	—	—	—	—
1909–1911	34.05	40.65	100,000	78,065	72,849	70,508	69,311	68,589	66,377	64,478	61,426	57,736	54,073
1910	44.72	48.54	100,000	84,598	80,991	79,411	78,377	77,608	75,801	74,517	72,720	70,236	67,599
1919–1921	47.14	45.99	100,000	89,499	87,218	86,227	85,625	85,195	83,768	82,332	79,057	74,540	70,344
1920–1929	—	—	—	—	—	—	—	—	—	—	—	—	—
1929–1931	47.55	44.27	100,000	91,268	89,755	89,094	88,702	88,412	87,311	86,152	83,621	79,516	75,083
1939–1941	52.26	48.34	100,000	91,772	90,912	90,520	90,276	90,082	89,393	88,610	86,968	84,227	80,979
1949–1951	—	—	—	—	—	—	—	—	—	—	—	—	—
1959–1961	—	—	—	—	—	—	—	—	—	—	—	—	—
1969–1971	60.00	52.79	100,000	96,394	96,178	96,025	95,918	95,826	95,497	95,161	94,053	91,904	89,584
1979–1981	64.10	56.01	100,000	97,703	97,558	97,451	97,368	97,300	97,061	96,826	96,132	94,827	93,125
1989–1991	64.47	56.09	100,000	98,023	97,891	97,808	97,741	97,688	97,501	97,268	95,301	94,809	93,070
1997	67.20	58.50	100,000	98,451	98,348	98,280	98,223	98,184	98,030	97,841	97,036	95,702	94,344

Male

Year(s)	Number living at beginning of year of age												Expectation of life in the last interval
	35	40	45	50	55	60	65	70	75	80	85	90	
	Ab821	Ab822	Ab823	Ab824	Ab825	Ab826	Ab827	Ab828	Ab829	Ab830	Ab831	Ab832	Ab833
	Number	Number	Number	Number	Number	Number	Number	Number	Number	Number	Number	Number	Years
1850	—	—	—	—	—	—	—	—	—	—	—	—	—
1860	—	—	—	—	—	—	—	—	—	—	—	—	—
1870	—	—	—	—	—	—	—	—	—	—	—	—	—
1880	—	—	—	—	—	—	—	—	—	—	—	—	—
1890	—	—	—	—	—	—	—	—	—	—	—	—	—
1900	58,905	55,323	51,207	46,626	41,218	35,128	28,012	20,392	12,840	6,388	—	—	4.12
1900–1902	46,541	42,989	39,230	34,766	29,987	24,194	19,015	13,829	8,892	4,831	2,030	634	3.21
1901–1910	—	—	—	—	—	—	—	—	—	—	—	—	—
1909–1911	49,865	45,414	40,563	35,427	29,754	23,750	17,806	12,295	7,494	3,894	1,747	595	4.01
1910	64,686	61,386	57,520	53,081	47,686	41,373	33,762	25,286	16,513	8,639	—	—	4.26
1919–1921	65,873	61,353	56,589	51,880	46,581	40,506	34,042	26,923	18,854	11,615	5,605	2,040	3.60
1920–1929	—	—	—	—	—	—	—	—	—	—	—	—	—
1929–1931	70,049	64,710	58,432	51,748	44,436	36,790	29,314	21,741	14,419	8,239	3,660	1,246	3.42
1939–1941	77,221	72,780	67,346	60,495	52,426	43,833	35,371	27,236	19,456	12,186	6,444	2,836	4.23
1949–1951	—	—	—	—	—	—	—	—	—	—	—	—	—
1959–1961	—	—	—	—	—	—	—	—	—	—	—	—	—
1969–1971	86,885	83,441	78,976	73,282	66,101	57,457	47,485	36,925	25,921	16,560	9,648	4,696	4.68
1979–1981	91,080	88,490	84,997	80,065	73,413	64,980	55,061	44,213	32,717	22,017	12,383	5,708	4.47
1989–1991	90,827	87,948	84,467	79,984	74,095	66,334	56,795	45,690	33,755	22,549	12,709	5,972	4.24
1997	92,798	90,799	87,999	83,835	78,389	71,218	61,787	51,882	39,419	27,469	16,051	7,483	4.50

Blacks

Female

Year(s)	Expectation of life		Number living at beginning of year of age										
	At birth	At age 10	0	1	2	3	4	5	10	15	20	25	30
	Ab834	Ab835	Ab836	Ab837	Ab838	Ab839	Ab840	Ab841	Ab842	Ab843	Ab844	Ab845	Ab846
	Years	Years	Number	Number	Number	Number	Number	Number	Number	Number	Number	Number	Number
1850	—	—	—	—	—	—	—	—	—	—	—	—	—
1860	—	—	—	—	—	—	—	—	—	—	—	—	—
1870	—	—	—	—	—	—	—	—	—	—	—	—	—
1880	—	—	—	—	—	—	—	—	—	—	—	—	—
1890	—	—	—	—	—	—	—	—	—	—	—	—	—
1900	43.27	48.27	100,000	84,343	79,960	77,996	76,727	75,766	73,540	71,854	69,658	66,968	64,056
1900–1902	35.04	43.02	100,000	78,525	73,010	70,432	69,079	68,056	65,111	62,384	59,053	55,795	52,773
1901–1910	—	—	—	—	—	—	—	—	—	—	—	—	—
1909–1911	37.67	42.84	100,000	81,493	76,697	74,819	73,632	72,768	70,508	68,218	64,764	61,430	58,281
1910	47.71	50.77	100,000	86,949	83,318	81,690	80,639	79,843	77,933	76,479	74,556	72,173	69,566

(continued)

TABLE Ab704–911   Life table l(x) values at selected ages, by sex and race: 1850–1997   Continued

Blacks

Female

Year(s)	Expectation of life: At birth (Ab834) Years	Expectation of life: At age 10 (Ab835) Years	Number living at beginning of year of age: 0 (Ab836)	1 (Ab837)	2 (Ab838)	3 (Ab839)	4 (Ab840)	5 (Ab841)	10 (Ab842)	15 (Ab843)	20 (Ab844)	25 (Ab845)	30 (Ab846)
1919–1921	46.92	44.54	100,000	91,251	89,149	88,236	87,623	87,149	85,607	83,954	80,154	75,359	70,633
1920–1929	—	—	—	—	—	—	—	—	—	—	—	—	—
1929–1931	49.51	45.33	100,000	92,796	91,462	90,854	90,479	90,185	89,201	88,088	85,078	81,067	76,816
1939–1941	55.56	50.75	100,000	93,416	92,672	92,327	92,099	91,906	91,308	90,594	88,736	86,198	83,384
1949–1951	—	—	—	—	—	—	—	—	—	—	—	—	—
1959–1961	—	—	—	—	—	—	—	—	—	—	—	—	—
1969–1971	68.32	60.85	100,000	97,076	96,886	96,735	96,666	96,598	96,369	96,172	95,729	95,035	94,114
1979–1981	72.88	64.65	100,000	98,073	97,948	97,862	97,798	97,751	97,590	97,450	97,180	96,754	96,150
1989–1991	73.73	65.26	100,000	98,356	98,244	98,176	98,126	98,087	97,946	97,818	97,566	97,140	96,514
1997	74.70	66.00	100,000	98,717	98,638	98,584	98,545	98,514	98,373	98,247	98,006	97,632	97,091

Blacks

Female

Year(s)	Number living at beginning of year of age: 35 (Ab847)	40 (Ab848)	45 (Ab849)	50 (Ab850)	55 (Ab851)	60 (Ab852)	65 (Ab853)	70 (Ab854)	75 (Ab855)	80 (Ab856)	85 (Ab857)	90 (Ab858)	Expectation of life in the last interval (Ab859) Years
1850	—	—	—	—	—	—	—	—	—	—	—	—	—
1860	—	—	—	—	—	—	—	—	—	—	—	—	—
1870	—	—	—	—	—	—	—	—	—	—	—	—	—
1880	—	—	—	—	—	—	—	—	—	—	—	—	—
1890	—	—	—	—	—	—	—	—	—	—	—	—	—
1900	60,904	57,581	54,132	50,493	46,036	40,747	33,946	26,183	17,583	9,574	—	—	4.32
1900–1902	49,567	46,146	42,279	37,681	33,124	27,524	21,995	16,140	11,066	6,708	3,567	1,492	4.01
1901–1910	—	—	—	—	—	—	—	—	—	—	—	—	—
1909–1911	54,595	50,568	45,947	40,886	35,415	28,908	22,302	15,871	10,657	6,324	3,029	1,206	4.50
1910	66,719	63,672	60,442	56,933	52,551	47,214	40,197	31,845	22,181	12,670	—	—	4.52
1919–1921	65,857	61,130	56,230	50,780	44,742	37,954	31,044	24,107	17,216	11,151	5,972	2,579	4.07
1920–1929	—	—	—	—	—	—	—	—	—	—	—	—	—
1929–1931	72,192	67,271	61,365	54,920	47,074	38,761	30,852	23,341	16,576	10,822	6,033	2,774	4.20
1939–1941	80,092	76,084	71,157	64,885	57,314	48,928	40,504	32,354	24,502	17,039	10,622	5,652	4.96
1949–1951	—	—	—	—	—	—	—	—	—	—	—	—	—
1959–1961	—	—	—	—	—	—	—	—	—	—	—	—	—
1969–1971	92,807	90,817	88,001	84,168	79,177	72,820	64,716	54,873	43,193	31,756	21,358	12,210	5.41
1979–1981	95,338	94,137	92,322	89,563	85,653	80,293	73,266	64,729	53,831	41,686	28,004	16,260	5.47
1989–1991	95,599	94,364	92,676	90,277	86,793	81,886	75,031	66,278	55,684	43,622	30,089	17,536	5.24
1997	96,337	95,189	93,579	91,258	88,022	83,469	77,014	69,197	57,959	45,859	31,664	17,786	5.10

Nonwhites

Male

	Expectation of life		Number living at beginning of year of age											
	At birth	At age 10	0	1	2	3	4	5	10	15	20	25	30
	Ab860	Ab861	Ab862	Ab863	Ab864	Ab865	Ab866	Ab867	Ab868	Ab869	Ab870	Ab871	Ab872
Year(s)	Years	Years	Number	Number	Number	Number	Number	Number	Number	Number	Number	Number	Number
1850	—	—	—	—	—	—	—	—	—	—	—	—	—
1860	—	—	—	—	—	—	—	—	—	—	—	—	—
1870	—	—	—	—	—	—	—	—	—	—	—	—	—
1880	—	—	—	—	—	—	—	—	—	—	—	—	—
1890	—	—	—	—	—	—	—	—	—	—	—	—	—
1900	—	—	—	—	—	—	—	—	—	—	—	—	—
1900–1902	—	—	—	—	—	—	—	—	—	—	—	—	—
1901–1910	—	—	—	—	—	—	—	—	—	—	—	—	—
1909–1911	—	—	—	—	—	—	—	—	—	—	—	—	—
1910	—	—	—	—	—	—	—	—	—	—	—	—	—
1919–1921	—	—	—	—	—	—	—	—	—	—	—	—	—
1920–1929	—	—	—	—	—	—	—	—	—	—	—	—	—
1929–1931	—	—	—	—	—	—	—	—	—	—	—	—	—
1939–1941	52.33	48.54	100,000	91,696	—	—	—	89,920	89,211	88,417	86,770	84,055	80,865
1949–1951	58.91	52.96	100,000	94,911	94,469	94,223	94,057	93,921	93,453	92,965	91,941	90,285	88,327
1959–1961	61.48	55.19	100,000	95,301	94,980	94,793	94,666	94,570	94,234	93,874	93,108	91,825	90,270
1969–1971	60.98	53.67	100,000	96,592	96,382	96,233	96,128	96,038	95,716	95,385	94,293	92,267	90,106
1979–1981	65.63	57.40	100,000	97,939	97,803	97,703	97,623	97,559	97,337	97,113	96,431	95,200	93,666
1989–1991	66.97	58.44	100,000	98,288	98,169	98,094	98,031	97,984	97,819	97,611	96,763	95,500	94,049
1997	—	—	—	—	—	—	—	—	—	—	—	—	—

Nonwhites

Male

	Number living at beginning of year of age												Expectation of life in the last interval
	35	40	45	50	55	60	65	70	75	80	85	90	
	Ab873	Ab874	Ab875	Ab876	Ab877	Ab878	Ab879	Ab880	Ab881	Ab882	Ab883	Ab884	Ab885
Year(s)	Number	Number	Number	Number	Number	Number	Number	Number	Number	Number	Number	Number	Years
1850	—	—	—	—	—	—	—	—	—	—	—	—	—
1860	—	—	—	—	—	—	—	—	—	—	—	—	—
1870	—	—	—	—	—	—	—	—	—	—	—	—	—
1880	—	—	—	—	—	—	—	—	—	—	—	—	—
1890	—	—	—	—	—	—	—	—	—	—	—	—	—
1900	—	—	—	—	—	—	—	—	—	—	—	—	—
1900–1902	—	—	—	—	—	—	—	—	—	—	—	—	—
1901–1910	—	—	—	—	—	—	—	—	—	—	—	—	—
1909–1911	—	—	—	—	—	—	—	—	—	—	—	—	—
1910	—	—	—	—	—	—	—	—	—	—	—	—	—

(continued)

TABLE Ab704–911   Life table l(x) values at selected ages, by sex and race: 1850–1997   *Continued*

Nonwhites

Male

	Number living at beginning of year of age												Expectation of life in the last interval
	35	40	45	50	55	60	65	70	75	80	85	90	
	Ab873	Ab874	Ab875	Ab876	Ab877	Ab878	Ab879	Ab880	Ab881	Ab882	Ab883	Ab884	Ab885
Year(s)	Number	Number	Number	Number	Number	Number	Number	Number	Number	Number	Number	Number	Years
1919–1921	—	—	—	—	—	—	—	—	—	—	—	—	—
1920–1929	—	—	—	—	—	—	—	—	—	—	—	—	—
1929–1931	—	—	—	—	—	—	—	—	—	—	—	—	—
1939–1941	77,185	72,830	67,514	60,766	52,867	44,370	35,912	27,688	19,765	12,352	6,492	—	5.08
1949–1951	85,940	82,832	78,686	72,891	65,122	55,535	45,198	35,018	25,472	16,904	9,898	4,642	3.78
1959–1961	88,331	85,744	82,075	77,239	70,351	61,669	51,392	39,914	29,064	19,994	11,620	5,174	3.42
1969–1971	87,597	84,378	80,163	74,748	67,808	59,396	49,607	39,025	27,789	17,999	10,811	5,366	4.75
1979–1981	91,891	89,645	86,578	82,153	76,019	68,093	58,517	47,796	36,191	24,969	14,454	6,793	4.48
1989–1991	92,223	89,884	87,058	83,347	78,312	71,352	62,435	51,653	39,493	27,391	16,144	7,809	4.25
1997	—	—	—	—	—	—	—	—	—	—	—	—	—

Nonwhites

Female

	Expectation of life		Number living at beginning of year of age											
	At birth	At age 10	0	1	2	3	4	5	10	15	20	25	30
	Ab886	Ab887	Ab888	Ab889	Ab890	Ab891	Ab892	Ab893	Ab894	Ab895	Ab896	Ab897	Ab898
Year(s)	Years	Years	Number	Number	Number	Number	Number	Number	Number	Number	Number	Number	Number
1850	—	—	—	—	—	—	—	—	—	—	—	—	—
1860	—	—	—	—	—	—	—	—	—	—	—	—	—
1870	—	—	—	—	—	—	—	—	—	—	—	—	—
1880	—	—	—	—	—	—	—	—	—	—	—	—	—
1890	—	—	—	—	—	—	—	—	—	—	—	—	—
1900	—	—	—	—	—	—	—	—	—	—	—	—	—
1900–1902	—	—	—	—	—	—	—	—	—	—	—	—	—
1901–1910	—	—	—	—	—	—	—	—	—	—	—	—	—
1909–1911	—	—	—	—	—	—	—	—	—	—	—	—	—
1910	—	—	—	—	—	—	—	—	—	—	—	—	—
1919–1921	—	—	—	—	—	—	—	—	—	—	—	—	—
1920–1929	—	—	—	—	—	—	—	—	—	—	—	—	—
1929–1931	—	—	—	—	—	—	—	—	—	—	—	—	—
1939–1941	55.51	50.83	100,000	93,318	—	—	—	91,170	91,092	90,363	88,505	85,961	83,147
1949–1951	62.70	56.17	100,000	95,913	95,541	95,335	95,176	95,055	94,679	94,343	93,544	92,336	90,799
1959–1961	66.47	59.72	100,000	96,172	95,894	95,741	95,631	95,543	95,265	95,057	94,660	94,005	93,070
1969–1971	69.05	61.49	100,000	97,235	97,051	96,925	96,838	96,772	96,546	96,353	95,917	95,427	94,370
1979–1981	74.00	65.64	100,000	98,261	98,143	98,065	98,003	97,958	97,806	97,669	97,404	96,996	96,441
1989–1991	75.39	66.75	100,000	98,572	98,471	98,410	98,364	98,330	98,202	98,086	97,848	97,474	96,947
1997	—	—	—	—	—	—	—	—	—	—	—	—	—

Nonwhites

Female

Year(s)	Number living at beginning of year of age												Expectation of life in the last interval
	35	40	45	50	55	60	65	70	75	80	85	90	
	Ab899	Ab900	Ab901	Ab902	Ab903	Ab904	Ab905	Ab906	Ab907	Ab908	Ab909	Ab910	Ab911
	Number	Number	Number	Number	Number	Number	Number	Number	Number	Number	Number	Number	Years
1850	—	—	—	—	—	—	—	—	—	—	—	—	—
1860	—	—	—	—	—	—	—	—	—	—	—	—	—
1870	—	—	—	—	—	—	—	—	—	—	—	—	—
1880	—	—	—	—	—	—	—	—	—	—	—	—	—
1890	—	—	—	—	—	—	—	—	—	—	—	—	—
1900	—	—	—	—	—	—	—	—	—	—	—	—	—
1900–1902	—	—	—	—	—	—	—	—	—	—	—	—	—
1901–1910	—	—	—	—	—	—	—	—	—	—	—	—	—
1909–1911	—	—	—	—	—	—	—	—	—	—	—	—	—
1910	—	—	—	—	—	—	—	—	—	—	—	—	—
1919–1921	—	—	—	—	—	—	—	—	—	—	—	—	—
1920–1929	—	—	—	—	—	—	—	—	—	—	—	—	—
1929–1931	—	—	—	—	—	—	—	—	—	—	—	—	—
1939–1941	79,879	75,908	71,061	64,886	57,419	49,102	40,718	32,579	24,668	17,157	10,658	—	6.38
1949–1951	88,805	86,052	82,257	77,007	70,196	61,758	52,358	42,612	32,981	23,712	15,550	8,590	4.13
1959–1961	91,670	89,676	86,793	82,979	77,362	69,941	60,825	51,274	40,540	30,315	19,744	9,675	3.52
1969–1971	93,123	91,247	88,608	84,964	80,162	73,984	66,064	56,375	44,841	33,373	22,763	13,151	5.44
1979–1981	95,719	94,646	93,009	90,523	86,951	82,000	75,382	67,147	56,499	44,378	30,543	18,029	5.49
1989–1991	96,187	95,165	93,785	91,757	88,731	84,389	78,246	70,122	59,932	47,781	33,621	19,914	5.25
1997													

Sources

1850–1910: Michael R. Haines, "Estimated Life Tables for the United States, 1850–1910," *Historical Methods* 31 (4) (1998): 149–69. Intervals 1900–1902 and 1909–1911: James W. Glover, *United States Life Tables, 1890, 1901, 1910, and 1901–10* (U.S. Government Printing Office, 1921). 1919–1921 and 1929–1931: Joseph A. Hill, *United States Life Tables, 1929 to 1931, 1920 to 1929, 1919 to 1921, 1909 to 1911, 1901 to 1910, 1900 to 1902* (U.S. Government Printing Office, 1936). 1939–1941: Thomas N. E. Greville, *United States Life Tables and Actuarial Tables, 1939–1941, Sixteenth Census of the United States: 1940* (U.S. Government Printing Office, 1946). 1949–1951: U.S. National Office of Vital Statistics, *Vital Statistics Special Reports, Life Tables for 1949–51,* volume 41, number 1, "United States Life Tables for 1949–51" (November 23, 1954). 1959–1961: National Center for Health Statistics, *Life Tables: 1959–61,* volume 1, number 1, "United States Life Tables: 1959–61." 1969–1971: National Center for Health Statistics, *U.S. Decennial Life Tables for 1969–71,* volume 1, number 1, PHS Publication number 1252 (December 1964). "United States Life Tables: 1969–71, DHEW Publication number (HRA) 75-1150 (May 1975). 1979–1981: National Center for Health Statistics, *U.S. Decennial Life Tables for 1979–81,* volume 1, number 1, "United States Life Tables," DHEW Publication number (PHS) 85-1150-1 (August 1985). 1989–1991: National Center for Health Statistics, *U.S. Decennial Life Tables for 1989–91,* volume 1, number 1, "United States Life Tables," DHHS Publication number (PHS) 98-1150-1 (October 1997). 1997: Robert N. Anderson, "United States Life Tables, 1997," *National Vital Statistics Reports,* volume 47, number 28 (1999).

Documentation

For an introduction to the life table, see U.S. Bureau of the Census, *The Methods and Materials of Demography,* by Henry S. Shryock, Jacob S. Siegel, and Associates (U.S. Government Printing Office, 1971), Chapter 15. The l(x) column is the number of survivors out of 100,000 born at exact age "x" in the stationary life table population. This information, together with the expectation of life for the last open interval, is sufficient to reconstruct any of the life tables in full.

Series Ab860–911. Nonwhites include the black population and all other nonwhites.

MORTALITY

Michael R. Haines

TABLE Ab912–927 Fetal death ratio, neonatal mortality rate, infant mortality rate, and maternal mortality rate, by race: 1850–1998[1, 2]

Contributed by Michael R. Haines

	Fetal death ratio				Neonatal mortality rate			
			Nonwhite				Nonwhite	
	Total	White	Total	Black	Total	White	Total	Black
	Ab912	Ab913	Ab914	Ab915	Ab916	Ab917	Ab918	Ab919
Year	Per 1,000	Per 1,000	Per 1,000	Per 1,000	Per 1,000	Per 1,000	Per 1,000	Per 1,000
1850	—	—	—	—	—	—	—	—
1860	—	—	—	—	—	—	—	—
1870	—	—	—	—	—	—	—	—
1880	—	—	—	—	—	—	—	—
1890	—	—	—	—	—	—	—	—
1900	—	—	—	—	—	—	—	—
1910	—	—	—	—	—	—	—	—
1915	—	—	—	—	44.4	—	—	—
1916	—	—	—	—	44.1	43.5	68.9	68.9
1917	—	—	—	—	43.4	42.6	58.0	—
1918	—	—	—	—	44.2	43.3	60.5	60.9
1919	—	—	—	—	41.5	40.3	55.2	58.6
1920	—	—	—	—	41.5	40.4	55.0	56.5
1921	—	—	—	—	39.7	38.7	50.3	51.3
1922	39.4	36.4	73.4	—	39.7	38.8	49.9	50.7
1923	38.9	35.9	71.8	—	39.5	38.6	49.9	51.4
1924	39.3	35.8	76.2	—	38.6	37.4	51.2	51.8
1925	38.1	35.1	73.1	—	37.8	36.8	49.5	50.3
1926	38.1	35.1	73.0	—	37.9	37.1	48.0	48.3
1927	38.8	34.8	74.8	—	36.1	35.0	46.1	46.3
1928	40.2	35.0	81.5	—	37.2	35.7	48.8	49.1
1929	39.5	34.4	79.7	—	36.9	35.6	47.3	47.5
1930	39.2	34.0	79.9	—	35.7	34.2	47.4	47.6
1931	38.2	33.4	74.1	—	34.6	33.2	45.2	45.4
1932	37.8	32.7	74.4	—	33.5	32.0 [5]	43.7 [5]	44.4
1933	37.0	32.2	71.1	—	34.0	32.1 [5]	45.8 [5]	45.7
1934	36.2	31.4	70.1	—	34.1	32.3 [5]	45.3 [5]	46.0
1935	35.8	31.1	68.7	—	32.4	31.0	42.7	42.7
1936	34.4	29.8	66.9	—	32.6	31.0	43.9	43.8
1937	33.4	29.2	63.2	—	31.3	29.7	42.1	42.2
1938	32.1	28.1	61.1	—	29.6	28.3	39.1	39.2
1939	32.0	28.2	59.0	—	29.3	27.8	39.6	39.7
1940	31.3	27.7	56.7	—	28.8	27.2	39.7	39.9
1941	29.9	26.5	54.0	—	27.7	26.1	39.0	39.3
1942	28.2	25.5	49.3	—	25.7	24.5	34.6	34.9
1943	26.7	24.2	46.2	—	24.7	23.7	32.9	33.1
1944	27.0	24.5	45.4	—	24.7	23.6	32.5	32.7
1945	23.9	21.4	42.0	—	24.3	23.3	32.0	32.2
1946	22.8	20.4	40.9	—	24.0	23.1	31.5	31.7
1947	21.1	18.7	39.6	—	22.8	21.7	31.0	31.1
1948	20.6	18.3	36.5	—	22.2	21.2	29.1	29.3
1949	19.8	17.5	34.6	—	21.4	20.3	28.6	28.8
1950	19.2	17.1	32.5	—	20.5	19.4	27.5	27.8
1951	18.8	16.7	32.1	—	20.0	18.9	27.3	27.6
1952	18.3	16.1	32.2	—	19.8	18.5	28.0	28.5
1953	17.8	15.9	29.6	—	19.6	18.3	27.4	27.8
1954	17.5	15.5	28.9	—	19.1	17.8	27.0	27.5
1955	17.1	15.2	28.4	—	19.1	17.7	27.2	27.8
1956	16.5	14.6	27.2	—	18.9	17.5	27.0	27.6
1957	16.3	14.5	26.8	—	19.1	17.5	27.8	28.5
1958	16.5	14.5	27.5	—	19.5	17.8	29.0	29.7
1959 [3]	16.2	14.2	27.3	—	19.0	17.5	27.7	28.4

Notes appear at end of table

TABLE Ab912–927   Fetal death ratio, neonatal mortality rate, infant mortality rate, and maternal mortality rate, by
race: 1850–1998   *Continued*

	Fetal death ratio				Neonatal mortality rate			
			Nonwhite				Nonwhite	
	Total	White	Total	Black	Total	White	Total	Black
	Ab912	Ab913	Ab914	Ab915	Ab916	Ab917	Ab918	Ab919
Year	Per 1,000	Per 1,000	Per 1,000	Per 1,000	Per 1,000	Per 1,000	Per 1,000	Per 1,000
1960	16.1	14.1	26.8	—	18.7	17.2	26.9	27.8
1961	16.1	14.1	27.0	—	18.4	16.9	26.2	27.1
1962 [4]	15.9	13.9	26.7	—	18.3	16.9	26.1	27.1
1963 [4]	15.8	13.7	26.7	—	18.2	16.7	26.1	27.0
1964	16.4	14.1	28.2	—	17.9	16.2	26.5	27.5
1965	16.2	13.9	27.2	—	17.7	16.1	25.4	26.5
1966	15.7	13.6	26.1	—	17.2	15.6	24.8	25.9
1967	15.6	13.5	25.8	—	16.5	15.0	23.8	25.0
1968	15.8	13.8	25.6	—	16.1	14.7	23.0	24.3
1969	14.1	12.4	22.5	—	15.6	14.2	22.5	23.9
1970	14.2	12.4	22.6	23.8	15.1	13.8	21.4	22.6
1971	13.4	11.8	21.2	22.3	14.2	13.0	19.6	21.0
1972	12.7	11.2	19.5	20.5	13.6	12.4	19.2	20.7
1973	12.2	10.8	18.6	19.7	13.0	11.8	17.9	19.3
1974	11.5	10.2	17.0	18.0	12.3	11.1	17.2	18.7
1975	10.7	9.5	16.0	17.0	11.6	10.4	16.8	18.3
1976	10.5	9.3	15.2	16.3	10.9	9.7	16.3	17.9
1977	9.9	8.8	14.8	15.9	9.9	8.7	14.7	16.1
1978	9.7	8.5	14.7	15.8	9.5	8.4	14.0	15.5
1979	9.4	8.4	13.8	15.0	8.9	7.9	12.9	14.3
1980	9.2	8.2	13.4	14.7	8.5	7.4	13.2	14.6
1981	9.0	8.0	12.8	14.0	8.0	7.0	12.5	14.0
1982	8.9	7.9	12.7	14.0	7.7	6.7	12.0	13.6
1983	8.5	7.5	12.4	13.7	7.3	6.3	11.4	12.9
1984	8.2	7.4	11.5	12.9	7.0	6.1	10.9	12.3
1985	7.9	7.0	11.3	12.7	7.0	6.0	11.0	12.6
1986	7.7	6.8	11.2	12.6	6.7	5.7	10.8	12.3
1987	7.7	6.7	11.5	13.0	6.5	5.4	10.7	12.3
1988	7.5	6.4	11.4	12.9	6.3	5.3	10.3	12.1
1989	7.5	6.4	11.7	13.3	6.2	5.1	10.3	11.9
1990	7.5	6.4	11.9	13.4	5.8	4.8	9.9	11.6
1991	7.3	6.2	11.4	13.0	5.6	4.5	9.5	11.2
1992	7.4	6.3	11.7	13.4	5.4	4.3	9.2	10.8
1993	—	—	—	—	5.3	4.3	9.0	10.7
1994	—	—	—	—	5.1	4.2	8.6	10.2
1995	—	—	—	—	4.9	4.1	8.1	9.8
1996	—	—	—	—	4.8	4.0	7.9	9.6
1997	—	—	—	—	4.8	4.0	7.7	9.4
1998	—	—	—	—	4.8	4.0	7.9	9.5

	Infant mortality rate				Maternal mortality rate			
			Nonwhite				Nonwhite	
	Total	White	Total	Black	Total	White	Total	Black
	Ab920	Ab921	Ab922	Ab923	Ab924	Ab925	Ab926	Ab927
Year	Per 1,000	Per 1,000	Per 1,000	Per 1,000	Per 100,000	Per 100,000	Per 100,000	Per 100,000
1850	228.9	216.8	—	340.0	—	—	—	—
1860	196.7	181.3	—	—	—	—	—	—
1870	184.5	175.6	—	—	—	—	—	—
1880	225.1	214.8	—	—	—	—	—	—
1890	160.4	150.6	—	—	—	—	—	—
1900	129.0	119.8	—	170.3	—	—	—	—
1910	104.2	96.5	—	142.6	—	—	—	—
1915	99.9	98.6	181.2	—	608.0	601.0	1,056.0	—
1916	101.0	99.0	184.9	184.3	622.0	608.0	1,179.0	—
1917	93.8	90.5	150.7	—	662.0	632.0	1,177.0	—
1918	100.9	97.4	161.2	162.5	916.0	889.0	1,393.0	—
1919	86.6	83.0	130.5	134.3	737.0	696.0	1,244.0	—

Notes appear at end of table   (continued)

TABLE Ab912–927   Fetal death ratio, neonatal mortality rate, infant mortality rate, and maternal mortality rate, by race: 1850–1998 *Continued*

	Infant mortality rate				Maternal mortality rate			
			Nonwhite				Nonwhite	
	Total	White	Total	Black	Total	White	Total	Black
	Ab920	Ab921	Ab922	Ab923	Ab924	Ab925	Ab926	Ab927
Year	Per 1,000	Per 1,000	Per 1,000	Per 1,000	Per 100,000	Per 100,000	Per 100,000	Per 100,000
1920	85.8	82.1	131.7	135.6	799.0	760.0	1,281.0	—
1921	75.6	72.5	108.5	110.7	682.0	644.0	1,077.0	—
1922	76.2	73.2	110.0	111.6	664.0	628.0	1,068.0	—
1923	77.1	73.5	117.4	119.9	665.0	626.0	1,095.0	—
1924	70.8	66.8	112.9	114.1	656.0	607.0	1,179.0	—
1925	71.7	68.3	110.8	112.0	647.0	603.0	1,162.0	—
1926	73.3	70.0	111.8	112.1	656.0	619.0	1,071.0	—
1927	64.6	60.6	100.1	99.9	647.0	594.0	1,133.0	—
1928	68.7	64.0	106.2	105.9	692.0	627.0	1,210.0	—
1929	67.6	63.2	102.2	101.5	695.0	631.0	1,199.0	—
1930	64.6	60.1	99.9	99.5	673.0	609.0	1,174.0	—
1931	61.6	57.4	93.1	92.7	661.0	601.0	1,114.0	—
1932	57.6	53.3 [5]	86.2 [5]	84.1	633.0	581.0 [5]	976.0 [5]	—
1933	58.1	52.8 [5]	91.3 [5]	85.4	619.1	554.9 [5]	1,073.7 [5]	999.7
1934	60.1	54.5 [5]	94.4 [5]	91.0	593.2	534.8 [5]	1,005.1 [5]	931.1
1935	55.7	51.9	83.2	81.9	582.1	530.6	945.7	954.8
1936	57.1	52.9	87.6	86.1	568.0	511.6	971.8	980.9
1937	54.4	50.3	83.2	82.0	488.8	436.1	858.5	862.2
1938	51.0	47.1	79.1	77.9	435.2	377.2	849.4	861.0
1939	48.0	44.3	74.2	73.2	403.9	352.8	762.1	771.3
1940	47.0	43.2	73.8	72.9	376.0	319.8	773.5	781.7
1941	45.3	41.2	74.8	74.1	316.5	266.0	678.1	690.2
1942	40.4	37.3	64.6	64.2	258.7	221.8	544.0	549.1
1943	40.4	37.5	62.5	61.5	245.2	210.5	509.9	512.8
1944	39.8	36.9	60.3	59.3	227.9	189.4	506.0	513.9
1945	38.3	35.6	57.0	56.2	207.2	172.1	454.8	456.7
1946	33.8	31.8	49.5	48.8	156.7	130.7	358.9	363.6
1947	32.2	30.1	48.5	47.7	134.5	108.6	334.6	336.2
1948	32.0	29.9	46.5	45.7	116.6	89.4	301.0	303.6
1949	31.3	28.9	47.3	46.8	90.3	68.1	234.8	237.6
1950	29.2	26.8	44.5	43.9	83.3	61.1	221.6	223.0
1951	28.4	25.8	44.8	44.3	75.0	54.9	201.3	204.2
1952	28.4	25.5	47.0	46.9	67.8	48.9	188.1	189.2
1953	27.8	25.0	44.7	44.5	61.1	44.1	166.1	168.3
1954	26.6	23.9	42.9	42.9	52.4	37.2	143.8	145.9
1955	26.4	23.6	42.8	43.1	47.0	32.8	130.3	134.3
1956	26.0	23.2	42.1	42.4	40.9	28.7	110.7	114.3
1957	26.3	23.3	43.7	44.2	41.0	27.5	118.3	121.6
1958	27.1	23.8	45.7	46.3	37.6	26.3	101.8	104.5
1959 [3]	26.4	23.2	44.0	44.8	37.4	25.8	102.1	105.0
1960	26.0	22.9	43.2	44.3	37.1	26.0	97.9	103.6
1961	25.3	22.4	40.7	41.8	36.9	24.9	101.3	105.4
1962 [4]	25.3	22.3	41.4	42.6	35.2	23.8	95.9	99.4
1963 [4]	25.2	22.2	41.5	42.8	35.8	24.0	96.9	101.1
1964	24.8	21.6	41.1	42.3	33.3	22.3	89.9	93.8
1965	24.7	21.5	40.3	41.7	31.6	21.0	83.7	88.3
1966	23.7	20.6	38.8	40.2	29.1	20.2	72.4	74.2
1967	22.4	19.7	35.9	37.5	28.0	19.5	69.5	72.6
1968	21.8	19.2	34.5	36.2	24.5	16.6	63.6	65.9
1969	20.9	18.4	32.9	34.8	22.2	15.5	55.7	59.5
1970	20.0	17.8	30.9	32.6	21.5	14.4	55.9	59.8
1971	19.1	17.1	28.5	30.3	18.8	13.0	45.3	48.3
1972	18.5	16.4	27.7	29.6	18.8	14.3	38.5	40.7
1973	17.7	15.8	26.2	28.1	15.2	10.7	34.6	38.4
1974	16.7	14.8	24.9	26.8	14.6	10.0	35.1	38.3
1975	16.1	14.2	24.2	26.2	12.8	9.1	29.0	31.3
1976	15.2	13.3	23.5	25.5	12.3	9.0	26.5	29.5
1977	14.1	12.3	21.7	23.6	11.2	7.7	26.0	29.2
1978	13.8	12.0	21.1	23.1	9.6	6.4	23.0	25.0
1979	13.1	11.4	19.8	21.8	9.6	6.4	22.7	25.1

Notes appear at end of table

TABLE Ab912-927 Fetal death ratio, neonatal mortality rate, infant mortality rate, and maternal mortality rate, by race: 1850-1998 *Continued*

	Infant mortality rate				Maternal mortality rate			
			Nonwhite				Nonwhite	
	Total	White	Total	Black	Total	White	Total	Black
	Ab920	Ab921	Ab922	Ab923	Ab924	Ab925	Ab926	Ab927
Year	Per 1,000	Per 1,000	Per 1,000	Per 1,000	Per 100,000	Per 100,000	Per 100,000	Per 100,000
1980	12.6	10.9	20.2	22.2	9.2	6.7	19.8	21.5
1981	11.9	10.3	18.8	20.8	8.5	6.3	17.3	20.4
1982	11.5	9.9	18.3	20.5	7.9	5.8	16.4	16.2
1983	11.2	9.6	17.8	20.0	8.0	5.9	16.3	18.3
1984	10.8	9.3	17.1	19.2	7.8	5.4	16.9	19.7
1985	10.6	9.2	16.8	19.0	7.8	5.2	18.1	20.4
1986	10.4	8.8	16.7	18.9	7.2	4.9	16.0	18.8
1987	10.1	8.5	16.5	18.8	6.6	5.1	12.0	14.2
1988	10.0	8.4	16.1	18.5	8.4	5.9	17.4	19.5
1989	9.8	8.1	16.3	18.6	7.9	5.7	15.4	17.5
1990	9.2	7.6	15.5	18.0	8.2	5.5	17.8	21.1
1991	8.9	7.3	15.1	17.6	7.9	5.9	14.5	17.2
1992	8.5	6.9	14.4	16.8	7.8	5.1	16.8	19.5
1993	8.4	6.8	14.1	16.5	7.5	4.8	17.6	20.5
1994	8.0	6.6	13.5	15.8	8.3	6.2	16.2	18.5
1995	7.6	6.3	12.6	15.1	7.1	4.2	18.5	22.1
1996	7.3	6.1	12.2	14.7	7.6	5.1	16.9	20.3
1997	7.2	6.0	11.8	14.2	8.4	5.8	18.3	20.8
1998	7.2	6.0	11.9	14.3	7.1	5.1	14.9	17.1

[1] The fetal death ratio is fetal deaths per 1,000 live births. The neonatal mortality rate is deaths of infants ages 0-27 days per 1,000 live births. The infant mortality rate is deaths in the first year of life per 1,000 live births. The maternal mortality rate is deaths attributable to childbirth per 100,000 live births.

[2] Prior to 1980, race for live births is the race of the fetus or child. From 1980 onward, race for live births is the race of the mother. For the maternal mortality rate, race of the child is used throughout.

[3] Figures by race exclude New Jersey. The state did not require reporting of race.

[4] Includes Alaska.

[5] Mexicans included with all other.

Sources

Fetal mortality ratio: U.S. Public Health Service, 1922-1944, *Vital Statistics of the United States, 1956*, volume 1, p. lxxxviii. 1946-1992: U.S. Public Health Service, National Center for Health Statistics, *Vital Statistics of the United States, 1992*, volume 2, *Mortality*, part A, Table 3-2.

Neonatal and infant mortality rates: 1915-1992: U.S. Public Health Service, *Vital Statistics of the United States, 1992*, volume 2, *Mortality*, part A, Table 2-2. 1993-1998: *National Vital Statistics Report*, volume 48, number 11, "Deaths: Final Data for 1998," Table 27. For the total and white populations for 1850-1910, and for the black population for 1900 and 1910, Michael R. Haines, "Estimated Life Tables for the United States, 1850-1910," *Historical Methods* 31 (4) (1998): 149-69. For the black population in 1850, Richard H. Steckel, "A Dreadful Childhood: The Excess Mortality of American Slaves," *Social Science History* 10 (4) (1986): 427-65.

Maternal mortality rate: 1940-1992: U.S. Public Health Service, *Vital Statistics of the United States, 1992*, volume 2, *Mortality*, part A, Table 1-16. *Monthly Vital Statistics Reports*, "Advance Report of Final Mortality Statistics, 1993, 1994, 1995." *National Vital Statistics Reports*, "Deaths: Final Data for 1996, 1997, 1998," Table 32.

Documentation

For 1915-1932, data are for the current Birth Registration Area only. For the composition of the Birth Registration Area, see the essay on vital statistics in this chapter.

Series Ab912-915. For 1945-1970, the fetal mortality ratio includes only deaths for which the period of gestation was given as twenty weeks or more or not stated. For earlier years, it includes all fetal deaths, regardless of gestation. In 1945 the ratios, based on all fetal deaths regardless of gestation, were: total, 266; white, 241; all other, 446. Lack of uniformity in requirements for registration and variation in completeness of registration influence the comparability of the data over the years, especially in the series based on all reported fetal deaths. Considering the probable total effect of these factors, as well as that of incompleteness of the registration area until 1933, it appears likely that the ratios understate any decline in fetal mortality. Changes in the regulations have more often been in the direction of broadening the base of fetal death reporting than in the other direction. With respect to completeness of reporting, the situation has probably improved because of the increases in the number of women receiving hospital and medical care at childbirth and also because of the general strengthening of the vital registration system.

Series Ab916-923. The infant mortality rate represents the number of deaths under age 1 (exclusive of fetal deaths) per 1,000 live births. The rates have been computed by the conventional method in which the infant deaths occurring in a specified period are related to the number of live births occurring during the same period. Rates computed in this way are influenced by changes in the number of births and will not be comparable if the birth rate fluctuates widely. Deaths under 1 year of age occurring during any calendar year are deaths not only of infants born during that year but also of infants born during parts of the previous year. An approximate correction of this error can be made by relating infant deaths during a specified year to the year in which these infants were born. See U.S. Bureau of the Census, "Effect of Changing Birth Rates upon Infant Mortality Rates," *Vital Statistics – Special Reports*, volume 19, number 21.

Series Ab924-927. The maternal mortality rate represents the number of deaths from deliveries and complications of pregnancy, childbirth, and the puerperium per 100,000 live births. Beginning in 1970, the rate excludes deaths to nonresidents of the United States. Deaths are classified according to the International Classification of Diseases in use at the time.

TABLE Ab928 Infant mortality rate for Massachusetts: 1851–1998

Contributed by Michael R. Haines

Year	Infant mortality rate Ab928 Per 1,000	Year	Infant mortality rate Ab928 Per 1,000	Year	Infant mortality rate Ab928 Per 1,000
1851	132.5	1900	156.7	1950	23.6
1852	125.8	1901	138.3	1951	22.1
1853	135.0	1902	139.5	1952	23.3
1854	130.9	1903	139.6	1953	22.1
1855	135.2	1904	133.2	1954	23.1
1856	122.7	1905	140.2	1955	21.9
1857	117.8	1906	138.4	1956	22.4
1858	121.7	1907	132.9	1957	22.7
1859	117.9	1908	133.5	1958	22.8
1860	133.7	1909	127.2	1959	22.3
1861	145.8	1910	132.9	1960	21.6
1862	130.6	1911	119.4	1961	21.6
1863	149.9	1912	116.5	1962	21.8
1864	154.1	1913	110.1	1963	20.6
1865	161.0	1914	105.9	1964	19.8 [1]
1866	137.9	1915	101.9	1965	22.2
1867	135.8	1916	99.8	1966	21.2
1868	149.8	1917	97.9	1967	20.0
1869	148.5	1918	113.2	1968	19.9
1870	162.2	1919	88.5	1969	18.3
1871	150.7	1920	91.2	1970	16.8
1872	194.1	1921	76.0	1971	16.7
1873	177.9	1922	81.3	1972	14.7
1874	164.1	1923	78.1	1973	15.3
1875	175.3	1924	67.7	1974	13.9
1876	159.0	1925	73.2	1975	13.5
1877	151.6	1926	73.4	1976	12.1
1878	150.1	1927	64.7	1977	11.9
1879	145.3	1928	64.7	1978	11.1
1880	162.6	1929	62.0	1979	10.9
1881	163.4	1930	60.3	1980	10.5
1882	163.0	1931	54.8	1981	9.7
1883	158.9	1932	53.1	1982	10.1
1884	159.1	1933	51.9	1983	9.1
1885	156.3	1934	49.2	1984	9.0
1886	154.5	1935	48.7	1985	9.1
1887	160.1	1936	46.6	1986	8.5
1888	161.6	1937	43.8	1987	7.2
1889	159.5	1938	39.1	1988	7.9
1890	166.6	1939	37.4	1989	7.7
1891	161.7	1940	37.5	1990	7.0
1892	161.8	1941	35.3	1991	6.6
1893	163.6	1942	32.0	1992	6.5
1894	162.8	1943	34.8	1993	6.2
1895	156.4	1944	33.4	1994	6.0
1896	162.6	1945	32.1	1995	5.2
1897	146.9	1946	32.0	1996	5.0
1898	150.6	1947	28.4	1997	5.2
1899	149.5	1948	27.1	1998	5.1
		1949	24.9		

[1] Excludes approximately 6,000 deaths registered in Massachusetts, primarily to residents of the state, covering all ages.

Sources

1851–1941: *Annual Reports of the Vital Statistics of Massachusetts*. 1942–1956: U.S. Bureau of the Census and U.S. Public Health Service, *Vital Statistics of the United States*, volume 1, annual issues. 1957–1992: U.S. Public Health Service, *Vital Statistics of the United States*, volume 2, part A, annual issues. 1993–1995: *Monthly Vital Statistics Reports*. 1996–1998: *National Vital Statistics Reports*.

Documentation

See the text for Table Ab1048–1058.

Figures are deaths under 1 year per 1,000 live births. Fetal deaths are excluded. The data for 1940–1968 are by place of residence and those for other years are by place of occurrence.

TABLE Ab929–951   Death rate, by cause: 1900–1998

Contributed by Michael R. Haines

Year	Tuberculosis, all forms	Syphilis and its sequella	Typhoid and paratyphoid fever	Scarlet fever and streptococcal sore throat	Hepatitis	Diphtheria	Whooping cough	Measles	Malignant neoplasms	Diabetes mellitus	Major cardio-vascular–renal diseases	Ischemic heart disease
	Ab929	Ab930 [1]	Ab931 [2]	Ab932	Ab933	Ab934	Ab935	Ab936	Ab937 [3]	Ab938	Ab939	Ab940
	Per 100,000	Per 100,000	Per 100,000	Per 100,000	Per 100,000	Per 100,000	Per 100,000	Per 100,000	Per 100,000	Per 100,000	Per 100,000	Per 100,000
1900	194.4	12.0	31.3	9.6	—	40.3	12.2	13.3	64.0	11.0	345.2	—
1901	189.9	12.5	27.6	13.6	—	33.5	8.7	7.4	66.4	11.6	347.7	—
1902	174.2	12.9	26.4	11.9	—	29.8	12.4	9.3	66.3	11.7	349.8	—
1903	177.2	13.2	24.6	12.3	—	31.1	14.3	8.8	70.0	12.7	364.4	—
1904	188.1	13.9	23.9	11.6	—	29.3	5.8	11.3	71.5	14.2	388.8	—
1905	179.9	13.8	22.4	6.8	—	23.5	8.9	7.4	73.4	14.1	384.0	—
1906	175.8	14.1	30.9	7.3	—	26.3	16.1	12.9	69.3	13.4	364.3	—
1907	174.2	12.4	28.2	9.3	—	24.2	11.3	9.6	71.4	14.2	389.8	—
1908	162.1	12.4	23.4	12.4	—	21.9	10.7	10.6	71.5	13.8	356.7	—
1909	156.3	12.9	20.2	11.1	—	19.9	10.0	10.0	74.0	14.1	362.0	—
1910	153.8	13.5	22.5	11.4	—	21.1	11.6	12.4	76.2	15.3	371.9	—
1911	155.1	15.3	20.1	8.6	—	18.4	11.0	9.9	74.2	15.1	366.5	—
1912	145.4	15.1	16.1	6.0	—	17.6	9.2	7.2	77.0	15.1	375.7	—
1913	143.5	16.2	17.5	7.7	—	18.1	10.1	12.8	78.5	15.4	370.6	—
1914	141.7	16.7	14.7	6.6	—	17.2	10.2	6.8	78.7	16.2	374.5	—
1915	140.1	17.7	11.8	3.6	—	15.2	8.2	5.2	80.7	17.6	383.5	—
1916	138.4	18.6	13.2	3.1	—	13.9	10.5	11.4	81.0	16.9	389.4	—
1917	143.5	19.1	13.3	3.5	—	15.6	10.5	14.1	80.8	16.9	396.4	—
1918	149.8	18.7	12.3	3.1	—	14.0	17.0	10.8	80.8	16.1	387.0	—
1919	125.6	16.2	9.2	2.8	—	14.9	5.6	3.9	81.0	15.0	348.6	—
1920	113.1	16.5	7.6	4.6	—	15.3	12.5	8.8	83.4	16.1	364.9	—
1921	97.6	17.5	8.8	5.3	—	17.7	9.1	4.2	85.5	16.7	351.2	—
1922	95.3	18.0	7.4	3.5	—	14.6	5.5	4.3	86.2	18.3	366.6	—
1923	91.7	17.9	6.7	3.5	—	12.0	9.6	10.7	88.4	17.7	380.8	—
1924	87.9	17.8	6.6	3.1	—	9.3	8.1	8.2	90.4	16.4	383.4	—
1925	84.8	17.3	7.8	2.7	—	7.8	6.7	2.3	92.0	16.8	391.5	—
1926	85.5	17.1	6.4	2.5	—	7.4	8.8	8.3	94.6	17.9	410.6	—
1927	79.6	16.4	5.3	2.3	—	7.7	6.8	4.1	95.2	17.4	398.3	—
1928	78.3	16.4	4.9	1.9	—	7.2	5.4	5.2	95.7	19.0	419.1	—
1929	75.3	15.6	4.2	2.1	—	6.5	6.2	2.5	95.8	18.8	418.9	—
1930	71.1	15.7	4.8	1.9	—	4.9	4.8	3.2	97.4	19.1	414.4	—
1931	67.8	15.4	4.5	2.2	—	4.8	3.9	3.0	99.0	20.4	407.1	—
1932	62.5	15.4	3.7	2.2	—	4.4	4.5	1.6	102.3	22.0	418.2	—
1933	59.6	15.1	3.6	2.0	—	3.9	3.6	2.2	102.3	21.4	413.6	—
1934	56.7	15.9	3.4	2.0	—	3.3	5.9	5.5	106.4	22.2	430.0	—
1935	55.1	15.4	2.8	2.1	—	3.1	3.7	3.1	108.2	22.3	431.2	—
1936	55.9	16.2	2.5	1.9	—	2.4	2.1	1.0	111.4	23.7	461.1	—
1937	53.8	16.1	2.1	1.4	—	2.0	3.9	1.2	112.4	23.7	454.6	—
1938	49.1	15.9	1.9	0.9	—	2.0	3.7	2.5	114.9	23.9	456.8	—
1939	47.1	15.0	1.5	0.7	—	1.5	2.3	0.9	117.5	25.5	466.3	—
1940	45.9	14.4	1.1	0.5	—	1.1	2.2	0.5	120.3	26.6	485.7	—
1941	44.5	13.3	0.8	0.3	—	1.0	2.8	1.7	120.1	25.4	475.3	—
1942	43.1	12.2	0.6	0.3	—	1.0	1.9	1.0	122.0	25.4	479.5	—
1943	42.5	12.1	0.5	0.3	—	0.9	2.5	1.0	124.3	27.1	510.8	—
1944	41.2	11.2	0.4	0.3	—	0.9	1.4	1.4	128.8	26.3	500.5	—
1945	39.9	10.6	0.4	0.2	—	1.2	1.3	0.2	134.0	26.5	508.2	—
1946	36.4	9.3	0.3	0.1	—	0.9	0.9	0.9	130.0	24.8	476.8	—
1947	33.5	8.8	0.2	0.1	—	0.6	1.4	0.3	132.3	26.2	491.0	—
1948	30.0	8.0	0.2	(Z)	—	0.4	0.8	0.6	134.9	26.4	488.0	—
1949	26.3	5.8	0.1	0.3	0.4	0.4	0.5	0.6	138.8	16.9	502.1	—
1950	22.5	5.0	0.1	0.2	0.4	0.3	0.7	0.3	139.8	16.2	510.8	—
1951	20.1	4.1	0.1	0.2	0.4	0.2	0.6	0.4	140.5	16.3	513.2	—
1952	15.8	3.7	0.1	0.2	0.5	0.1	0.3	0.4	143.3	16.4	511.9	—
1953	12.3	3.3	(Z)	0.1	0.5	0.1	0.2	0.3	144.7	16.3	514.8	—
1954	10.2	3.0	(Z)	0.1	0.5	0.1	0.1	0.3	145.6	15.6	495.1	—
1955	9.1	2.3	(Z)	0.1	0.5	0.1	0.3	0.2	146.5	15.5	506.0	—
1956	8.4	2.3	(Z)	0.1	0.5	0.1	0.2	0.3	147.8	15.7	510.5	—
1957	7.8	2.2	(Z)	0.1	0.5	(Z)	0.1	0.2	148.6	16.0	523.4	—
1958	7.1	2.0	(Z)	0.1	0.5	(Z)	0.1	0.3	146.8	15.9	523.5	—
1959	6.5	1.7	(Z)	0.1	0.5	(Z)	0.2	0.2	147.3	15.9	515.9	—

Notes appear at end of table

(continued)

TABLE Ab929–951   Death rate, by cause: 1900–1998   *Continued*

Year	Tuberculosis, all forms Ab929 Per 100,000	Syphilis and its sequella Ab930 [1] Per 100,000	Typhoid and paratyphoid fever Ab931 [2] Per 100,000	Scarlet fever and streptococcal sore throat Ab932 Per 100,000	Hepatitis Ab933 Per 100,000	Diphtheria Ab934 Per 100,000	Whooping cough Ab935 Per 100,000	Measles Ab936 Per 100,000	Malignant neoplasms Ab937 [3] Per 100,000	Diabetes mellitus Ab938 Per 100,000	Major cardiovascular– renal diseases Ab939 Per 100,000	Ischemic heart disease Ab940 Per 100,000
1960	6.1	1.6	(Z)	0.1	0.5	(Z)	0.1	0.2	149.2	16.7	521.8	—
1961	5.4	1.6	(Z)	0.1	0.5	(Z)	(Z)	0.2	149.4	16.4	511.4	—
1962	5.1	1.5	(Z)	(Z)	0.5	(Z)	(Z)	0.2	149.9	16.8	521.2	—
1963	4.9	1.4	(Z)	(Z)	0.5	(Z)	(Z)	0.2	151.3	17.2	527.3	—
1964	4.3	1.4	(Z)	(Z)	0.4	(Z)	(Z)	0.2	151.3	16.9	514.3	—
1965	4.1	1.3	(Z)	(Z)	0.4	(Z)	(Z)	0.1	153.5	17.1	516.4	—
1966	3.9	1.1	(Z)	(Z)	0.4	(Z)	(Z)	0.1	155.1	17.7	521.4	—
1967	3.5	1.2	(Z)	(Z)	0.4	(Z)	(Z)	(Z)	157.2	17.7	511.5	—
1968	3.2	0.3	(Z)	(Z)	0.4	(Z)	(Z)	(Z)	159.8	19.2	513.2	338.4
1969	2.8	0.3	(Z)	(Z)	0.5	(Z)	(Z)	(Z)	160.4	19.1	503.0	332.6
1970	2.6	0.2	(Z)	(Z)	0.5	(Z)	(Z)	(Z)	162.8	18.9	496.0	328.1
1971	2.2	0.2	(Z)	(Z)	0.4	(Z)	(Z)	(Z)	163.6	18.6	493.3	327.0
1972	2.1	0.2	(Z)	(Z)	0.3	(Z)	(Z)	(Z)	166.0	18.6	497.1	328.7
1973	1.8	0.2	(Z)	(Z)	0.3	(Z)	(Z)	(Z)	167.3	18.2	494.4	326.0
1974	1.7	0.1	(Z)	(Z)	0.3	(Z)	(Z)	(Z)	170.5	17.7	478.2	314.5
1975	1.6	0.1	(Z)	(Z)	0.3	(Z)	(Z)	(Z)	171.7	16.5	455.8	301.7
1976	1.5	0.1	(Z)	(Z)	0.3	(Z)	(Z)	(Z)	175.8	16.1	454.0	301.0
1977	1.4	0.1	(Z)	(Z)	0.2	(Z)	(Z)	(Z)	178.7	15.2	444.5	295.1
1978	1.3	0.1	(Z)	(Z)	0.2	(Z)	(Z)	(Z)	181.9	15.5	442.7	294.3
1979	0.9	0.1	(Z)	(Z)	0.3	(Z)	(Z)	(Z)	179.6	14.8	426.7	245.5
1980	0.9	0.1	(Z)	(Z)	0.4	(Z)	(Z)	(Z)	183.9	15.4	436.4	249.7
1981	0.8	0.1	(Z)	(Z)	0.4	0.0	(Z)	(Z)	183.9	15.1	424.0	241.9
1982	0.8	0.1	(Z)	(Z)	0.4	(Z)	(Z)	(Z)	187.3	14.9	417.8	238.6
1983	0.8	0.1	(Z)	(Z)	0.4	0.0	(Z)	(Z)	189.5	15.5	419.6	236.3
1984	0.7	(Z)	(Z)	(Z)	0.4	0.0	(Z)	(Z)	192.3	15.2	412.8	229.5
1985	0.7	(Z)	(Z)	(Z)	0.4	0.0	(Z)	(Z)	194.0	15.5	411.0	225.6
1986	0.7	(Z)	(Z)	(Z)	0.4	0.0	(Z)	(Z)	195.5	15.5	403.2	216.9
1987	0.7	(Z)	(Z)	(Z)	0.5	(Z)	(Z)	(Z)	196.8	15.9	397.7	211.4
1988	0.8	(Z)	0.0	(Z)	0.5	0.0	(Z)	(Z)	198.4	16.5	396.5	208.4
1989	0.8	(Z)	(Z)	(Z)	0.6	0.0	(Z)	(Z)	201.0	19.0	377.5	201.8
1990	0.7	(Z)	(Z)	(Z)	0.6	0.0	(Z)	(Z)	203.2	19.2	368.3	196.7
1991	0.7	(Z)	(Z)	(Z)	0.7	0.0	0.0	(Z)	204.1	19.4	363.4	192.5
1992	0.7	(Z)	(Z)	(Z)	0.8	(Z)	(Z)	(Z)	204.1	19.6	358.3	188.2
1993	0.6	(Z)	0.0	(Z)	1.0	0.0	(Z)	0.0	205.6	20.9	367.8	190.1
1994	0.6	(Z)	(Z)	(Z)	1.2	0.0	(Z)	0.0	205.2	21.8	361.3	184.9
1995	0.5	(Z)	0.0	(Z)	1.3	(Z)	(Z)	(Z)	204.9	22.6	362.1	183.2
1996	0.5	(Z)	(Z)	(Z)	1.4	0.0	(Z)	(Z)	203.4	23.3	358.2	179.5
1997	0.4	(Z)	0.0	(Z)	1.5	0.0	(Z)	(Z)	201.6	23.4	352.8	174.2
1998	0.4	(Z)	—	(Z)	1.8	—	(Z)	(Z)	200.3	24.0	348.0	170.1

Year	Cerebrovascular disease Ab941 Per 100,000	Influenza and pneumonia Ab942 [4] Per 100,000	Gastritis, duodenitis, enteritis, and colitis Ab943 [5] Per 100,000	Cirrhosis of liver and chronic liver disease Ab944 Per 100,000	Accidents Total Ab945 Per 100,000	Motor vehicle Ab946 [6] Per 100,000	All other Total Ab947 Per 100,000	All other Falls Ab948 Per 100,000	All other Other Ab949 [7] Per 100,000	Suicide Ab950 Per 100,000	Homicide and legal intervention Ab951 Per 100,000
1900	—	202.2	142.7	12.5	72.3	—	72.3	—	—	10.2	1.2
1901	—	197.2	118.5	13.1	83.8	—	83.8	—	—	10.4	1.2
1902	—	161.3	104.9	13.0	72.5	—	72.5	—	—	10.3	1.2
1903	—	169.3	100.3	13.5	81.4	—	81.4	—	—	11.3	1.1
1904	—	192.1	111.5	13.9	85.4	—	85.4	—	—	12.2	1.3
1905	—	169.3	118.4	14.0	81.3	—	81.3	—	—	13.5	2.1
1906	—	156.3	123.6	14.1	94.4	0.4	94.0	—	—	12.8	3.9
1907	—	180.0	115.0	14.8	94.8	0.7	94.1	—	—	14.5	4.9
1908	—	150.9	112.5	13.5	82.9	0.8	82.1	—	—	16.8	4.8
1909	—	148.1	101.8	13.4	78.7	1.2	77.5	—	—	16.0	4.2
1910	—	155.9	115.4	13.3	84.2	1.8	82.4	15.4	67.0	15.3	4.6
1911	—	145.4	86.8	13.6	83.6	2.1	81.5	15.0	66.5	16.0	5.5
1912	—	138.4	79.6	13.1	80.8	2.8	78.0	15.4	62.6	15.6	5.4
1913	—	140.8	86.7	12.9	83.7	3.8	79.9	15.4	64.5	15.4	6.1
1914	—	132.4	75.1	12.5	76.7	4.2	72.5	15.0	57.5	16.1	6.2

Notes appear at end of table.

TABLE Ab929–951 Death rate, by cause: 1900–1998 *Continued*

		Gastritis, duodenitis, enteritis, and colitis	Cirrhosis of liver and chronic liver disease	Accidents						Suicide	Homicide and legal intervention
	Cerebrovascular disease	Influenza and pneumonia			Total	Motor vehicle	All other				
							Total	Falls	Other		
	Ab941	Ab942 [4]	Ab943 [5]	Ab944	Ab945	Ab946 [6]	Ab947	Ab948	Ab949 [7]	Ab950	Ab951
Year	Per 100,000	Per 100,000	Per 100,000	Per 100,000	Per 100,000	Per 100,000	Per 100,000	Per 100,000	Per 100,000	Per 100,000	Per 100,000
1915	—	145.9	67.5	12.1	73.5	5.8	67.7	14.8	52.9	16.2	5.9
1916	—	163.3	75.5	11.8	81.6	7.1	74.5	15.1	59.4	13.7	6.3
1917	—	164.5	75.2	10.9	86.0	8.6	77.4	14.8	62.6	13.0	6.9
1918	—	588.5	72.2	9.6	81.5	9.3	72.2	12.7	59.5	12.3	6.5
1919	—	223.0	55.2	7.9	71.1	9.3	61.8	11.3	50.5	11.5	7.2
1920	—	207.3	53.7	7.1	70.0	10.3	59.7	11.8	47.9	10.2	6.8
1921	—	98.7	50.7	7.3	66.8	11.3	55.5	11.4	44.1	12.4	8.1
1922	—	132.3	38.9	7.4	68.3	12.4	55.9	12.1	43.8	11.7	8.0
1923	—	151.7	39.1	7.1	74.3	14.6	59.7	12.8	46.9	11.5	7.8
1924	—	115.2	33.7	7.3	73.8	15.3	58.5	13.1	45.4	11.9	8.1
1925	—	121.7	38.6	7.2	76.5	16.8	59.7	13.4	46.3	12.0	8.3
1926	—	141.7	32.9	7.2	77.2	19.9	57.3	14.0	43.3	12.6	8.4
1927	—	102.2	27.1	7.4	77.1	21.6	55.5	14.0	41.5	13.2	8.4
1928	—	142.5	26.4	7.5	78.1	23.2	54.9	14.1	40.8	13.5	8.6
1929	—	146.5	23.3	7.2	79.7	25.5	54.2	14.5	39.7	13.9	8.4
1930	—	102.5	26.0	7.2	79.8	26.7	53.1	14.7	38.4	15.6	8.8
1931	—	107.5	20.5	7.4	77.8	27.1	50.7	14.6	36.1	16.8	9.2
1932	—	107.3	16.1	7.2	70.8	23.6	47.2	14.8	32.4	17.4	9.0
1933	—	95.7	17.3	7.4	71.9	25.0	46.9	15.1	31.8	15.9	9.7
1934	—	96.9	18.4	7.7	79.4	28.6	50.8	18.8	32.0	14.9	9.5
1935	—	104.2	14.1	7.9	77.9	28.6	49.3	19.2	30.1	14.3	8.3
1936	—	119.6	16.4	8.3	85.4	29.7	55.7	20.8	34.9	14.3	8.0
1937	—	114.9	14.7	8.5	81.2	30.8	50.4	20.4	30.0	15.0	7.6
1938	—	80.4	14.3	8.3	71.8	25.1	46.7	19.5	27.2	15.3	6.8
1939	—	75.7	11.6	8.3	70.3	24.7	45.6	17.5	28.1	14.1	6.4
1940	—	70.3	10.3	8.6	73.2	26.2	47.0	17.2	29.8	14.4	6.2
1941	—	63.8	10.5	8.9	75.9	30.0	45.9	16.7	29.2	12.8	6.0
1942	—	55.7	8.8	9.4	71.2	21.1	50.1	16.6	33.5	12.0	5.8
1943	—	67.1	9.6	9.3	73.4	17.7	55.7	18.0	37.7	10.2	5.0
1944	—	61.6	9.9	8.6	71.3	18.3	53.0	17.0	36.0	10.0	4.9
1945	—	51.6	8.7	9.5	72.1	21.2	50.9	17.7	33.2	11.2	5.6
1946	—	44.5	5.8	9.6	69.8	23.9	45.9	16.1	29.8	11.5	6.3
1947	—	43.1	5.6	10.4	69.2	22.8	46.4	16.7	29.7	11.5	6.0
1948	—	38.7	6.0	11.3	66.9	22.1	44.8	16.6	28.2	11.2	5.8
1949	—	30.0	6.7	9.2	60.6	21.3	39.3	15.0	24.3	11.4	5.4
1950	—	31.3	5.1	9.2	60.6	23.1	37.5	13.8	23.7	11.4	5.3
1951	—	31.4	5.2	9.8	62.5	24.1	38.4	13.9	24.5	10.4	4.9
1952	—	29.7	5.6	10.2	61.8	24.3	37.5	13.5	24.0	10.0	5.2
1953	—	33.0	5.4	10.4	60.1	24.0	36.1	13.0	23.1	10.1	4.8
1954	—	25.4	4.9	10.1	55.9	22.1	33.8	12.3	21.5	10.1	4.8
1955	—	27.1	4.7	10.2	56.9	23.4	33.5	12.3	21.2	10.2	4.5
1956	—	28.2	4.5	10.7	56.7	23.7	33.0	12.1	20.9	10.0	4.6
1957	—	35.8	4.7	11.3	55.9	22.7	33.2	12.1	21.1	9.8	4.5
1958	—	33.1	4.5	10.8	52.2	21.3	30.9	10.5	20.4	10.7	4.5
1959	—	31.2	4.4	10.9	52.2	21.5	30.7	10.6	20.1	10.6	4.6
1960	—	37.3	4.4	11.3	52.3	21.3	31.0	10.6	20.4	10.6	4.7
1961	—	30.1	4.3	11.3	50.4	20.8	29.6	10.2	19.4	10.4	4.7
1962	—	32.3	4.4	11.7	52.3	22.0	30.3	10.5	19.8	10.9	4.8
1963	—	37.5	4.4	11.9	53.4	23.1	30.3	10.2	20.1	11.0	4.9
1964	—	31.1	4.3	12.1	54.2	24.5	29.7	9.9	19.8	10.8	5.1
1965	—	31.9	4.1	12.8	55.8	25.4	30.4	10.3	20.1	11.1	5.5
1966	—	32.5	3.9	13.6	58.0	27.1	30.9	10.2	20.7	10.9	5.9
1967	—	28.8	3.8	14.1	57.1	26.7	30.4	10.2	20.2	10.8	6.8
1968	106.0	36.9	1.5	14.6	57.6	27.5	30.1	9.3	20.7	10.7	7.4
1969	102.9	33.9	1.3	14.8	57.8	27.7	30.1	8.8	21.2	11.1	7.7
1970	101.9	30.9	1.3	15.5	56.4	26.9	29.5	8.3	21.2	11.6	8.3
1971	101.4	27.7	1.2	15.4	55.0	26.4	28.6	8.1	20.5	11.7	9.1
1972	102.5	30.1	1.1	15.6	55.4	27.0	28.4	8.0	20.4	12.0	9.4
1973	102.1	29.8	1.1	15.9	55.2	26.5	28.7	7.9	20.8	12.0	9.8
1974	98.1	25.9	1.1	15.8	49.5	22.0	27.5	7.7	19.8	12.1	10.2

Notes appear at end of table

(continued)

TABLE Ab929–951   Death rate, by cause: 1900–1998   *Continued*

				Accidents							
		Gastritis, duodenitis, enteritis, and colitis	Cirrhosis of liver and chronic liver disease				All other				Homicide and legal intervention
	Cerebrovascular disease	Influenza and pneumonia			Total	Motor vehicle	Total	Falls	Other	Suicide	
	Ab941	Ab942 [4]	Ab943 [5]	Ab944	Ab945	Ab946 [6]	Ab947	Ab948	Ab949 [7]	Ab950	Ab951
Year	Per 100,000	Per 100,000	Per 100,000	Per 100,000	Per 100,000	Per 100,000	Per 100,000	Per 100,000	Per 100,000	Per 100,000	Per 100,000
1975	91.1	26.1	0.9	14.8	48.3	21.5	26.8	7.0	19.8	12.7	10.0
1976	87.9	28.8	0.9	14.7	46.9	21.9	25.0	6.6	18.4	12.5	9.1
1977	84.1	23.7	0.9	14.3	47.7	22.9	24.8	6.4	18.4	13.3	9.2
1978	80.5	26.7	0.9	13.8	48.4	24.0	24.4	6.3	18.1	12.5	9.4
1979	75.5	20.1	0.3	13.2	46.9	23.8	23.1	5.9	17.2	12.1	10.0
1980	75.1	24.1	0.3	13.5	46.7	23.5	23.2	5.9	17.3	11.9	10.7
1981	71.3	23.4	0.3	12.8	43.9	22.4	21.5	5.5	16.0	12.0	10.3
1982	68.1	21.1	0.3	12.0	40.6	19.8	20.8	5.2	15.6	12.2	9.7
1983	66.6	23.9	0.3	11.7	39.6	19.0	20.6	5.1	15.5	12.1	8.6
1984	65.4	25.0	0.3	11.6	39.4	19.6	19.8	5.1	14.7	12.4	8.4
1985	64.3	28.5	0.3	11.3	39.3	19.3	20.0	5.0	15.0	12.4	8.4
1986	62.3	29.1	0.3	10.9	39.7	19.9	19.8	4.8	15.0	12.9	9.0
1987	61.8	28.6	0.3	10.8	39.2	19.9	19.3	4.8	14.5	12.7	8.7
1988	61.6	31.8	0.3	10.8	39.7	20.1	19.6	4.9	14.7	12.4	9.0
1989	59.0	31.0	0.3	10.8	38.5	19.3	19.2	4.9	14.3	12.2	9.3
1990	57.9	31.9	0.3	10.4	37.0	18.8	18.2	5.0	13.2	12.4	10.0
1991	56.9	30.9	0.3	10.1	35.4	17.3	18.1	5.0	13.1	12.2	10.5
1992	56.4	29.7	0.3	9.9	34.0	16.1	17.9	5.0	12.9	12.0	10.0
1993	58.2	32.1	0.2	9.8	35.1	16.3	18.8	5.1	13.7	12.1	10.1
1994	58.9	31.3	0.3	9.8	35.1	16.3	18.8	5.2	13.6	12.0	9.6
1995	60.1	31.5	0.3	9.6	35.5	16.5	19.0	5.3	13.7	11.9	8.7
1996	60.3	31.6	0.3	9.4	35.8	16.5	19.3	5.6	13.7	11.6	7.9
1997	59.7	32.3	0.4	9.4	35.7	16.2	19.5	5.8	13.7	11.4	7.4
1998	58.6	34.0	—	9.3	36.2	16.1	20.1	—	—	11.3	6.8

(Z) Fewer than 0.05 deaths per 100,000 population.

[1] 1900–1920, excludes aneurysm of the aorta.

[2] Includes cholera 1979–1997.

[3] Includes neoplasms of lymphatic and hematopoietic tissues.

[4] 1900–1970, excludes pneumonia of newborns; 1900–1920, excludes capillary bronchitis.

[5] 1900–1970, excludes diarrhea of newborns; 1900–1920, includes ulcer of duodenum.

[6] 1906–1925, excludes automobile collisions with trains and streetcars, and motorcycle accidents.

[7] 1900–1921, includes legal executions; 1900–1908, includes food poisoning; and 1900–1905, includes motor vehicle accidents.

Sources

U.S. Public Health Service. Series Ab929–930, Ab932–946, and Ab950: 1900–1978, *Vital Statistics of the United States* (volume 1 to 1954 and volume 2, part A, thereafter), various annual issues. Series Ab933: 1900–1920, *Vital Statistics of the United States, 1950*, volume 1, p. 218; 1921–1940, *Vital Statistics Rates in the United States*, 1900–1940, p. 266; 1941–1970, unpublished data. Series Ab948–949: U.S. Bureau of the Census, 1900–1933, *Mortality Statistics*, various annual issues; 1934–1938, *Vital Statistics of the United States, Special Reports, Deaths from Each Cause, United States* 1934–1988; 1939–1949, *Vital Statistics of the United States*, part 1; 1950–1978, *Vital Statistics of the United States*, volume 2, part A, various annual issues. Series Ab951: *Vital Statistics Rates in the United States*, 1900–1940, Table 16 (for 1900–1933, for the Death Registration States only); *Vital Statistics Rates in the United States*, 1940–1960, Table 62; *Vital Statistics of the United States*, volume 2, part A, various annual issues.

Series Ab947: 1900–1909, U.S. Bureau of the Census, *Mortality Statistics*, various annual issues. Thereafter it is the sum of accidental falls, series Ab948, and all other accidents, Series Ab949.

All series 1979–1997: National Center for Health Statistics, *Mortality Tables*, GMWK292A and GMWK291 at NCHS Internet site. 1998: U.S. Public Health Service, *National Vital Statistics Report*, volume 48, number 11, "Deaths: Final Data for 1998," Table 11.

Documentation

Death rates are the number of deaths, excluding fetal deaths, per 100,000 population. Prior to 1933, for the Death Registration States only; see the essay on vital statistics in this chapter.

Mortality data are classified according to the numbers and titles of the detailed International List of Causes of Death, currently under the jurisdiction of the World Health Organization. A large proportion of the death certificates filed annually in the United States report two or more diseases or conditions as joint causes of death. General statistical practice requires that cases involving more than one cause of death be changed to a single cause.

In the French edition of the International List (1900), certain principles for determining the single cause to be selected from the joint causes given were incorporated as a part of the general classification scheme. As an outgrowth of practices in this country after 1902, definite relationships among the various conditions represented by items in the International List were put in concrete form in the *Manual of Joint Causes of Death*, first published in 1914, and revised to conform to successive revisions of the International List. This manual, which was developed for use in the United States, was followed until 1949, when an international procedure for joint-cause selection was adopted. The new international rules place the responsibility on the medical practitioner to indicate the underlying cause of death. This change, in conjunction with the sixth revision of the International List in 1949, the seventh revision in 1958, the eighth revision in 1968, and the ninth revision in 1979, has introduced rather serious breaks in statistical continuity.

Time-trend studies of causes of death would be facilitated if the International List were maintained without change over a long period of years. However, if the list were rigidly fixed it would be inconsistent with current medical knowledge and terminology. To obtain the advantages of frequent revision and yet to retain a fixed list for a number of years, revisions are made at an international conference every ten years (although ICD-9, the ninth revision, has been in place since 1979). In the process of revision, discontinuities are introduced into the time trends of death rates for certain specific causes of death (see, for example, National Office of Vital Statistics, "The Effect of the Sixth Revision of the International List of Diseases and Causes of Death upon Comparability of Mortality Trends," *Vital Statistics – Special Reports*, volume 36, number 10). For more technical details, see National Center for Health Statistics, *Vital Statistics of the United States, 1992*, volume 2, *Mortality*, part A (Public Health Service, 1996), Technical Appendix, pp. 9–11, and *Vital Statistics of the United States, 1979*, volume 2, *Mortality*, part A (Public Health Service, 1984), Technical Appendix, pp. 8–15.

Improvement in diagnostic procedures and development of medical knowledge and facilities are other important factors in the study of changes in death rates for certain causes.

TABLE Ab952–987   Death rate, by sex and race: 1900–1998

Contributed by Michael R. Haines

	Death rate											
	All races			White			All nonwhite			Black		
	Both sexes	Male	Female	Both sexes	Male	Female	Both sexes	Male	Female	Both sexes	Male	Female
	Ab952	Ab953	Ab954	Ab955	Ab956	Ab957	Ab958	Ab959	Ab960	Ab961	Ab962	Ab963
Year	Per 100,000	Per 100,000	Per 100,000	Per 100,000	Per 100,000	Per 100,000	Per 100,000	Per 100,000	Per 100,000	Per 100,000	Per 100,000	Per 100,000
1900	1,719.1	1,791.1	1,646.9	1,702.4	1,774.8	1,629.7	2,504.0	2,565.3	2,443.8	—	—	—
1901	1,641.5	1,725.9	1,556.9	1,624.7	1,708.4	1,540.7	2,434.3	2,559.3	2,311.8	—	—	—
1902	1,548.1	1,635.3	1,460.5	1,530.9	1,617.5	1,443.9	2,356.1	2,480.8	2,234.1	—	—	—
1903	1,562.8	1,643.6	1,481.4	1,544.0	1,624.6	1,462.9	2,446.6	2,552.3	2,343.3	—	—	—
1904	1,640.0	1,727.6	1,551.8	1,619.5	1,706.2	1,532.0	2,610.5	2,755.9	2,468.4	—	—	—
1905	1,588.9	1,674.4	1,502.5	1,568.5	1,653.5	1,482.6	2,553.0	2,681.5	2,427.5	—	—	—
1906	1,571.8	1,672.6	1,467.3	1,545.8	1,647.3	1,440.7	2,417.0	2,468.4	2,360.1	—	—	—
1907	1,592.5	1,702.2	1,478.4	1,566.8	1,676.9	1,452.7	2,427.3	2,500.9	2,345.7	—	—	—
1908	1,468.2	1,552.4	1,379.8	1,445.7	1,530.5	1,356.8	2,243.1	2,277.8	2,203.9	—	—	—
1909	1,424.7	1,506.4	1,338.8	1,403.4	1,485.3	1,317.5	2,176.4	2,226.3	2,120.0	—	—	—
1910	1,468.0	1,556.4	1,374.3	1,448.8	1,537.2	1,355.3	2,172.4	2,233.2	2,102.8	—	—	—
1911	1,390.5	1,472.7	1,303.7	1,366.1	1,448.4	1,279.3	2,132.1	2,193.6	2,063.5	—	—	—
1912	1,359.7	1,448.6	1,265.9	1,336.6	1,425.3	1,243.0	2,056.1	2,129.3	1,974.4	—	—	—
1913	1,380.6	1,476.0	1,280.1	1,351.4	1,447.8	1,250.0	2,032.0	2,099.3	1,959.6	—	—	—
1914	1,330.2	1,419.0	1,236.6	1,299.6	1,388.8	1,205.9	2,016.9	2,091.0	1,937.1	—	—	—
1915	1,317.6	1,399.6	1,231.3	1,286.3	1,368.8	1,199.6	2,021.3	2,083.3	1,954.5	—	—	—
1916	1,381.1	1,475.4	1,282.7	1,344.5	1,440.3	1,244.3	1,914.7	1,989.6	1,837.5	—	—	—
1917	1,397.1	1,504.6	1,285.4	1,349.5	1,457.8	1,236.8	2,043.1	2,143.4	1,940.3	—	—	—
1918	1,810.0	1,980.5	1,638.7	1,751.1	1,925.7	1,575.8	2,558.6	2,673.5	2,441.9	—	—	—
1919	1,289.4	1,345.8	1,231.5	1,242.5	1,303.5	1,179.8	1,794.7	1,805.3	1,784.0	—	—	—
1920	1,298.9	1,338.1	1,258.2	1,256.1	1,298.1	1,212.6	1,767.5	1,780.6	1,754.2	—	—	—
1921	1,149.8	1,194.7	1,103.4	1,112.9	1,160.8	1,063.2	1,554.8	1,569.5	1,539.9	—	—	—
1922	1,169.3	1,226.3	1,110.7	1,132.5	1,191.4	1,072.0	1,524.6	1,567.0	1,481.8	—	—	—
1923	1,213.0	1,274.5	1,149.8	1,169.1	1,231.7	1,104.5	1,650.3	1,704.7	1,595.4	—	—	—
1924	1,159.0	1,230.4	1,085.5	1,104.4	1,175.6	1,030.9	1,708.1	1,789.1	1,626.7	—	—	—
1925	1,168.1	1,239.4	1,094.7	1,113.1	1,184.2	1,039.8	1,735.9	1,816.2	1,655.0	—	—	—
1926	1,211.0	1,285.7	1,134.0	1,155.9	1,229.7	1,079.8	1,777.4	1,869.3	1,685.0	—	—	—
1927	1,131.5	1,209.4	1,051.3	1,080.0	1,158.6	999.0	1,640.4	1,718.9	1,561.6	—	—	—
1928	1,198.6	1,283.4	1,111.4	1,142.2	1,227.3	1,054.5	1,706.4	1,798.5	1,615.2	—	—	—
1929	1,187.8	1,276.9	1,096.4	1,132.4	1,220.4	1,041.8	1,687.9	1,795.9	1,580.5	—	—	—
1930	1,132.1	1,225.3	1,036.7	1,076.8	1,169.6	981.4	1,665.0	1,775.0	1,556.0	—	—	—
1931	1,106.5	1,201.5	1,009.3	1,057.6	1,152.6	960.1	1,617.4	1,729.5	1,506.6	—	—	—
1932	1,087.7	1,172.9	1,000.7	1,048.2	1,133.0	961.2	1,504.3	1,605.9	1,404.1	—	—	—
1933	1,068.7	1,163.2	972.4	1,030.4	1,124.7	933.8	1,509.0	1,619.1	1,400.6	—	—	—
1934	1,105.4	1,212.4	996.5	1,063.4	1,168.7	955.7	1,572.2	1,710.4	1,436.6	—	—	—
1935	1,094.5	1,203.1	984.2	1,056.2	1,163.1	947.2	1,430.2	1,559.0	1,304.0	—	—	—
1936	1,155.2	1,274.4	1,034.4	1,111.4	1,227.2	993.5	1,538.1	1,693.3	1,386.4	—	—	—
1937	1,125.9	1,248.4	1,001.9	1,084.5	1,204.7	962.2	1,488.2	1,636.0	1,344.0	—	—	—
1938	1,064.0	1,172.5	954.5	1,025.3	1,133.5	915.6	1,403.0	1,519.6	1,289.5	—	—	—
1939	1,060.4	1,170.0	949.9	1,027.1	1,136.3	916.4	1,352.6	1,470.2	1,238.3	—	—	—
1940	1,072.7	1,192.1	952.2	1,037.9	1,156.9	917.2	1,378.8	1,508.9	1,252.9	—	—	—
1941	1,047.7	1,173.1	921.5	1,013.5	1,139.1	886.6	1,346.9	1,477.7	1,220.2	—	—	—
1942	1,027.1	1,154.6	899.1	1,000.0	1,127.9	871.0	1,263.6	1,392.4	1,139.0	—	—	—
1943	1,067.4	1,192.6	941.5	1,044.7	1,172.3	916.0	1,264.0	1,371.6	1,159.1	—	—	—
1944	1,019.8	1,138.5	900.4	999.0	1,120.9	876.1	1,199.0	1,292.5	1,107.1	—	—	—
1945	1,001.7	1,125.2	878.0	985.0	1,111.9	857.7	1,144.7	1,240.1	1,050.4	—	—	—
1946	987.1	1,112.4	862.0	973.7	1,101.8	845.5	1,101.5	1,203.2	1,001.5	—	—	—
1947	1,002.9	1,137.3	868.8	987.8	1,125.6	850.1	1,131.5	1,238.5	1,027.1	—	—	—
1948	985.0	1,122.6	848.2	967.6	1,106.7	828.9	1,133.9	1,260.2	1,011.3	—	—	—
1949	967.6	1,104.8	831.4	949.7	1,089.1	810.9	1,121.0	1,242.2	1,004.0	—	—	—
1950	953.9	1,091.3	817.4	938.4	1,077.9	799.5	1,082.8	1,204.7	965.2	—	—	—
1951	956.9	1,096.3	818.8	942.7	1,083.9	802.2	1,075.4	1,200.8	954.5	—	—	—
1952	950.1	1,089.6	812.0	935.8	1,076.2	796.3	1,067.9	1,202.0	938.8	—	—	—
1953	947.4	1,089.1	807.3	935.6	1,078.6	793.9	1,043.6	1,176.9	915.6	—	—	—
1954	908.5	1,044.9	773.8	900.2	1,038.3	763.4	976.3	1,099.8	857.8	—	—	—
1955	921.3	1,059.5	785.1	914.9	1,055.2	776.1	973.0	1,094.4	856.7	—	—	—
1956	926.3	1,066.3	788.4	919.6	1,061.9	779.1	979.5	1,102.2	862.2	—	—	—
1957	949.6	1,091.8	809.8	941.1	1,085.0	799.1	1,017.3	1,146.7	893.7	—	—	—
1958	942.3	1,081.7	805.5	935.0	1,076.1	796.0	999.9	1,126.5	879.2	—	—	—
1959	931.7	1,071.7	794.5	926.6	1,068.0	787.6	971.4	1,101.8	847.2	—	—	—

(continued)

TABLE Ab952–987   Death rate, by sex and race: 1900–1998   *Continued*

	Death rate											
	All races			White			All nonwhite			Black		
	Both sexes	Male	Female	Both sexes	Male	Female	Both sexes	Male	Female	Both sexes	Male	Female
	Ab952	Ab953	Ab954	Ab955	Ab956	Ab957	Ab958	Ab959	Ab960	Ab961	Ab962	Ab963
Year	Per 100,000	Per 100,000	Per 100,000	Per 100,000	Per 100,000	Per 100,000	Per 100,000	Per 100,000	Per 100,000	Per 100,000	Per 100,000	Per 100,000
1960	947.6	1,092.3	806.0	940.7	1,086.2	798.0	1,000.8	1,140.8	867.7	1,031.3	1,170.7	900.5
1961	926.3	1,065.5	790.4	921.9	1,062.4	784.2	960.3	1,090.0	837.3	991.9	1,122.2	869.7
1962 [1]	941.8	1,080.5	806.5	938.9	1,084.3	797.8	982.0	1,118.8	852.9	—	—	—
1963 [1]	958.3	1,101.5	819.1	954.3	1,102.7	810.3	1,007.3	1,153.8	869.4	—	—	—
1964	937.0	1,076.8	801.3	932.7	1,072.0	797.0	969.3	1,113.6	833.4	1,011.3	1,160.3	872.5
1965	940.9	1,082.7	803.4	937.8	1,078.6	800.8	963.9	1,114.2	822.6	1,002.8	1,155.7	860.6
1966	947.9	1,089.7	810.8	944.8	1,084.7	809.0	970.6	1,126.9	824.0	1,011.2	1,171.0	862.8
1967	931.7	1,072.1	796.2	931.4	1,069.7	797.5	933.4	1,089.6	787.4	974.5	1,133.6	827.3
1968	961.6	1,104.6	824.1	958.6	1,097.9	824.0	983.3	1,153.6	824.8	1,029.5	1,204.0	868.4
1969	948.3	1,088.7	813.5	947.0	1,082.9	815.9	957.5	1,131.1	796.4	1,005.5	1,183.0	842.2
1970	936.8	1,074.7	804.7	936.3	1,069.3	808.3	940.4	1,113.7	779.9	989.6	1,168.7	825.2
1971	928.2	1,060.7	801.4	930.2	1,057.8	807.3	914.6	1,081.1	760.7	964.5	1,136.9	806.4
1972	935.7	1,068.5	808.7	939.0	1,065.8	817.2	912.6	1,087.9	750.9	966.1	1,148.4	799.4
1973	931.1	1,059.6	808.3	935.4	1,058.4	817.3	901.7	1,068.3	748.3	957.6	1,130.3	799.9
1974	904.5	1,026.6	788.2	911.7	1,027.7	800.4	856.4	1,018.5	707.5	913.6	1,083.0	759.3
1975	876.4	997.3	761.3	884.9	999.7	774.9	820.3	981.0	673.0	879.6	1,048.4	725.9
1976	875.7	989.6	767.5	885.9	993.4	783.0	809.5	963.7	668.4	872.3	1,035.2	724.3
1977	862.5	974.7	755.8	872.9	979.2	771.1	795.9	945.2	659.4	861.0	1,019.0	717.7
1978	866.1	973.3	764.3	878.5	979.0	782.5	787.0	936.2	650.8	851.8	1,009.3	709.2
1979	850.4	953.6	752.5	863.6	959.9	771.6	767.8	913.0	635.4	835.9	991.7	694.9
1980	873.8	969.8	782.7	889.1	977.8	804.4	780.9	919.9	654.1	867.0	1,019.8	729.0
1981	860.1	950.2	774.7	878.8	961.8	799.5	748.6	879.1	629.4	838.6	984.3	707.0
1982	850.5	934.5	770.9	871.4	948.3	798.0	727.7	851.4	614.9	819.8	958.3	694.7
1983	861.8	939.4	788.1	883.7	954.3	816.2	735.0	850.7	629.3	832.9	963.3	715.1
1984	862.9	934.9	794.4	886.1	950.6	824.4	730.4	843.4	627.1	832.5	960.8	716.7
1985	874.9	944.6	808.7	898.6	960.0	839.8	742.1	855.7	638.2	851.1	981.6	733.3
1986	874.9	941.0	812.0	898.4	955.2	844.0	744.5	860.2	638.6	861.3	995.2	740.5
1987	874.5	935.6	816.3	898.4	949.4	849.5	744.3	858.7	639.5	865.4	999.0	744.8
1988	884.8	941.5	830.8	908.9	954.6	865.0	755.9	869.4	651.9	884.6	1,018.5	763.7
1989	869.4	922.8	818.5	891.6	933.4	851.5	752.4	865.9	648.3	884.1	1,019.1	762.2
1990	859.6	912.1	809.4	884.4	925.5	844.8	730.8	840.8	629.8	863.4	995.8	743.8
1991	858.8	908.6	811.1	884.3	922.6	847.4	728.0	835.4	629.3	862.3	992.6	744.5
1992	851.9	899.0	806.8	879.0	914.6	844.7	714.9	818.2	620.0	847.6	971.9	735.2
1993	879.0	920.5	839.2	907.8	936.2	880.4	735.3	840.3	638.9	874.7	1,001.7	759.8
1994	874.5	912.0	838.6	904.7	928.9	881.3	725.9	826.8	633.4	862.9	984.2	753.2
1995	879.0	911.1	848.3	910.5	929.2	892.5	725.3	820.3	638.2	863.8	978.6	759.9
1996	872.0	895.2	849.7	906.4	916.9	896.1	706.1	787.2	631.7	840.2	936.7	752.8
1997	863.8	879.3	849.0	901.2	904.9	897.6	685.4	753.6	622.9	813.1	891.4	742.3
1998	864.7	876.4	853.5	904.0	904.4	903.7	—	—	—	808.7	877.7	746.4

Note appears at end of table

TABLE Ab952–987 Death rate, by sex and race: 1900–1998 *Continued*

	Death rate						Age-adjusted death rate					
	American Indian			Asian and Pacific Islander			All races			White		
	Both sexes	Male	Female	Both sexes	Male	Female	Both sexes	Male	Female	Both sexes	Male	Female
	Ab964	Ab965	Ab966	Ab967	Ab968	Ab969	Ab970	Ab971	Ab972	Ab973	Ab974	Ab975
Year	Per 100,000	Per 100,000	Per 100,000	Per 100,000	Per 100,000	Per 100,000	Per 100,000	Per 100,000	Per 100,000	Per 100,000	Per 100,000	Per 100,000
1900	—	—	—	—	—	—	1,778.5	1,862.7	1,695.2	1,759.3	1,843.7	1,675.7
1901	—	—	—	—	—	—	1,721.2	1,820.2	1,623.0	1,702.0	1,800.2	1,604.6
1902	—	—	—	—	—	—	1,616.4	1,721.2	1,513.1	1,597.3	1,701.7	1,494.4
1903	—	—	—	—	—	—	1,645.5	1,745.3	1,546.9	1,624.7	1,724.3	1,526.2
1904	—	—	—	—	—	—	1,729.0	1,839.2	1,619.8	1,706.2	1,815.6	1,597.8
1905	—	—	—	—	—	—	1,673.5	1,779.6	1,567.9	1,650.9	1,756.7	1,545.7
1906	—	—	—	—	—	—	1,667.0	1,789.8	1,541.2	1,638.9	1,762.2	1,512.7
1907	—	—	—	—	—	—	1,710.0	1,846.0	1,569.8	1,681.9	1,818.4	1,541.6
1908	—	—	—	—	—	—	1,574.9	1,682.5	1,463.1	1,549.9	1,658.0	1,438.0
1909	—	—	—	—	—	—	1,530.1	1,636.2	1,420.0	1,506.2	1,612.3	1,396.5
1910	—	—	—	—	—	—	1,578.7	1,693.2	1,458.8	1,556.8	1,671.3	1,437.2
1911	—	—	—	—	—	—	1,513.5	1,617.9	1,403.6	1,486.2	1,590.7	1,376.4
1912	—	—	—	—	—	—	1,483.2	1,595.3	1,365.4	1,456.5	1,568.5	1,339.2
1913	—	—	—	—	—	—	1,495.4	1,611.8	1,373.1	1,461.8	1,579.7	1,338.3
1914	—	—	—	—	—	—	1,447.3	1,555.7	1,333.4	1,412.2	1,521.4	1,297.7
1915	—	—	—	—	—	—	1,443.4	1,544.0	1,337.9	1,406.8	1,508.5	1,300.1
1916	—	—	—	—	—	—	1,511.5	1,623.7	1,393.7	1,466.0	1,581.6	1,344.6
1917	—	—	—	—	—	—	1,527.0	1,650.1	1,397.8	1,470.1	1,596.1	1,338.1
1918	—	—	—	—	—	—	1,906.6	2,085.2	1,727.2	1,839.6	2,022.9	1,655.7
1919	—	—	—	—	—	—	1,404.1	1,466.1	1,339.6	1,346.3	1,415.3	1,274.7
1920	—	—	—	—	—	—	1,423.6	1,470.6	1,374.9	1,368.2	1,420.6	1,313.9
1921	—	—	—	—	—	—	1,266.4	1,317.8	1,212.9	1,217.6	1,274.8	1,158.3
1922	—	—	—	—	—	—	1,306.0	1,371.1	1,238.2	1,254.1	1,324.0	1,181.3
1923	—	—	—	—	—	—	1,352.1	1,423.1	1,277.8	1,292.2	1,367.2	1,213.9
1924	—	—	—	—	—	—	1,290.7	1,373.4	1,204.8	1,220.5	1,305.0	1,132.6
1925	—	—	—	—	—	—	1,299.9	1,383.0	1,213.6	1,229.0	1,313.6	1,141.0
1926	—	—	—	—	—	—	1,346.5	1,434.1	1,255.5	1,274.4	1,363.1	1,182.4
1927	—	—	—	—	—	—	1,256.9	1,347.9	1,162.6	1,188.3	1,281.8	1,091.4
1928	—	—	—	—	—	—	1,337.4	1,436.0	1,235.0	1,259.6	1,360.5	1,154.8
1929	—	—	—	—	—	—	1,320.0	1,423.0	1,213.1	1,241.2	1,344.8	1,133.7
1930	—	—	—	—	—	—	1,246.1	1,352.0	1,136.5	1,165.3	1,272.2	1,054.9
1931	—	—	—	—	—	—	1,210.9	1,319.3	1,099.4	1,132.9	1,242.1	1,020.6
1932	—	—	—	—	—	—	1,187.2	1,286.4	1,085.1	1,119.1	1,219.2	1,016.1
1933	—	—	—	—	—	—	1,164.1	1,272.4	1,052.8	1,092.4	1,201.7	980.2
1934	—	—	—	—	—	—	1,190.9	1,312.4	1,066.6	1,115.6	1,236.1	992.2
1935	—	—	—	—	—	—	1,165.8	1,288.6	1,040.4	1,105.3	1,228.2	980.0
1936	—	—	—	—	—	—	1,217.5	1,352.0	1,080.3	1,149.8	1,282.7	1,014.5
1937	—	—	—	—	—	—	1,171.9	1,308.9	1,032.8	1,107.3	1,243.6	968.9
1938	—	—	—	—	—	—	1,092.4	1,213.7	969.5	1,031.7	1,154.5	907.4
1939	—	—	—	—	—	—	1,074.8	1,197.7	950.6	1,018.9	1,143.3	893.4
1940	—	—	—	—	—	—	1,069.7	1,205.9	933.2	1,010.9	1,148.2	873.3
1941	—	—	—	—	—	—	1,028.4	1,169.0	888.3	971.1	1,113.1	829.5
1942	—	—	—	—	—	—	990.6	1,132.3	849.8	940.7	1,084.1	798.1
1943	—	—	—	—	—	—	1,010.8	1,152.5	870.6	963.8	1,109.3	820.1
1944	—	—	—	—	—	—	961.7	1,097.9	827.3	917.6	1,058.1	779.2
1945	—	—	—	—	—	—	933.6	1,073.7	795.9	893.1	1,037.1	751.9
1946	—	—	—	—	—	—	909.9	1,051.7	771.1	872.7	1,018.0	730.6
1947	—	—	—	—	—	—	895.1	1,044.9	749.4	856.4	1,010.4	706.9
1948	—	—	—	—	—	—	876.5	1,031.5	726.5	836.1	993.7	683.8
1949	—	—	—	—	—	—	851.9	1,007.3	702.2	811.6	970.3	659.1
1950	—	—	—	—	—	—	832.4	990.4	681.1	794.1	955.4	639.9
1951	—	—	—	—	—	—	824.8	986.1	670.9	787.5	951.9	631.0
1952	—	—	—	—	—	—	811.4	974.1	656.7	774.1	938.8	617.8
1953	—	—	—	—	—	—	800.2	967.1	642.7	764.9	933.8	605.5
1954	—	—	—	—	—	—	759.2	921.2	607.1	727.7	892.4	573.3
1955	—	—	—	—	—	—	761.0	927.9	605.1	730.5	900.6	571.8
1956	—	—	—	—	—	—	759.7	931.1	600.7	728.7	903.5	566.8
1957	—	—	—	—	—	—	772.7	949.4	609.8	739.3	918.9	573.8
1958	—	—	—	—	—	—	761.3	938.2	599.2	728.7	908.8	564.0
1959	—	—	—	—	—	—	748.2	927.6	584.7	717.2	899.4	551.4

(continued)

TABLE Ab952–987   Death rate, by sex and race: 1900–1998 *Continued*

	Death rate						Age-adjusted death rate					
	American Indian			Asian and Pacific Islander			All races			White		
	Both sexes	Male	Female	Both sexes	Male	Female	Both sexes	Male	Female	Both sexes	Male	Female
	Ab964	Ab965	Ab966	Ab967	Ab968	Ab969	Ab970	Ab971	Ab972	Ab973	Ab974	Ab975
Year	Per 100,000	Per 100,000	Per 100,000	Per 100,000	Per 100,000	Per 100,000	Per 100,000	Per 100,000	Per 100,000	Per 100,000	Per 100,000	Per 100,000
1960	—	—	—	—	—	—	756.2	943.4	586.9	722.5	912.0	551.5
1961	—	—	—	—	—	—	734.8	919.3	569.5	703.1	890.3	535.8
1962 [1]	—	—	—	—	—	—	744.7	934.3	576.4	711.7	903.2	541.5
1963 [1]	—	—	—	—	—	—	756.1	955.2	581.3	721.6	921.2	546.0
1964	—	—	—	—	—	—	738.6	936.6	565.5	704.4	903.4	531.2
1965	—	—	—	—	—	—	738.2	942.9	561.2	704.1	909.1	527.6
1966	—	—	—	—	—	—	741.2	951.0	560.9	706.1	915.2	527.1
1967	—	—	—	—	—	—	724.4	934.7	545.1	691.0	900.4	513.3
1968	—	—	—	—	—	—	742.6	961.6	557.1	705.2	921.6	522.9
1969	—	—	—	—	—	—	727.3	945.8	543.4	690.8	906.0	510.8
1970	—	—	—	—	—	—	712.2	929.1	531.1	676.7	889.9	499.8
1971	—	—	—	—	—	—	696.8	911.2	519.0	663.1	874.2	489.1
1972	—	—	—	—	—	—	697.4	916.5	516.6	663.5	878.1	487.6
1973	—	—	—	—	—	—	686.8	904.6	508.1	653.6	867.3	479.3
1974	—	—	—	—	—	—	659.1	869.7	487.0	628.7	835.1	461.0
1975	—	—	—	—	—	—	630.0	836.1	462.5	601.9	803.4	439.0
1976	—	—	—	—	—	—	618.1	820.0	455.0	591.0	788.5	432.4
1977	—	—	—	—	—	—	601.8	800.4	441.8	575.4	769.9	419.6
1978	—	—	—	—	—	—	594.7	790.6	437.4	569.2	760.4	416.4
1979	—	—	—	—	—	—	576.7	767.7	423.0	551.6	737.8	402.5
1980	482.1	589.4	376.8	287.9	362.9	216.5	582.7	772.8	430.4	556.8	741.6	409.2
1981	444.6	545.7	345.5	271.8	335.0	211.4	568.3	753.0	420.8	544.6	724.2	401.5
1982	433.5	521.0	347.8	270.7	336.9	207.4	554.4	733.5	411.9	532.0	706.2	393.6
1983	427.7	513.3	343.8	275.6	337.9	216.0	552.2	728.7	412.4	529.2	701.1	393.2
1984	419.0	501.3	338.2	275.4	335.3	218.1	547.8	720.9	410.4	524.9	693.0	391.7
1985	415.7	490.6	342.2	282.9	343.4	224.8	548.5	722.3	410.3	524.7	692.7	391.0
1986	408.7	493.4	325.7	275.7	334.0	219.9	544.5	715.5	407.6	519.8	684.3	388.1
1987	410.0	482.3	338.9	278.4	337.2	221.9	538.9	706.1	404.6	513.4	673.6	384.8
1988	411.0	483.5	339.8	281.5	337.9	227.4	539.6	705.4	406.1	512.6	670.7	385.3
1989	429.8	509.5	351.3	280.4	333.5	229.4	527.7	688.5	397.3	499.4	651.6	376.0
1990	400.4 ·	473.1	328.8	279.1	329.0	231.1	517.7	676.2	389.0	490.7	640.8	368.5
1991	408.1	471.8	345.3	279.7	328.0	233.4	513.2	668.5	386.3	486.0	632.8	365.9
1992	416.6	485.6	348.5	284.7	334.3	237.4	504.1	655.1	380.2	477.3	620.2	359.8
1993	438.3	500.8	376.6	292.3	343.3	243.8	512.9	663.5	388.4	485.0	626.6	367.9
1994	434.0	498.6	370.2	300.6	351.3	252.6	507.0	653.0	385.4	479.7	616.9	365.2
1995	443.6	498.1	389.8	302.4	350.7	256.8	503.3	644.5	385.1	476.6	609.3	365.0
1996	442.5	489.5	396.2	304.2	351.9	259.2	491.3	623.4	380.8	466.6	591.2	361.7
1997	455.1	518.6	392.6	306.3	351.0	264.3	479.0	602.5	375.7	456.4	573.5	358.0
1998	459.5	513.2	407.0	304.4	349.8	262.5	471.7	589.4	372.5	450.4	562.4	355.2

Note appears at end of table

TABLE Ab952–987 Death rate, by sex and race: 1900–1998 *Continued*

	Age-adjusted death rate											
	All nonwhite			Black			American Indian			Asian and Pacific Islander		
	Both sexes	Male	Female	Both sexes	Male	Female	Both sexes	Male	Female	Both sexes	Male	Female
	Ab976	Ab977	Ab978	Ab979	Ab980	Ab981	Ab982	Ab983	Ab984	Ab985	Ab986	Ab987
Year	Per 100,000	Per 100,000	Per 100,000	Per 100,000	Per 100,000	Per 100,000	Per 100,000	Per 100,000	Per 100,000	Per 100,000	Per 100,000	Per 100,000
1900	2,785.0	2,866.9	2,714.4	—	—	—	—	—	—	—	—	—
1901	2,694.9	2,838.0	2,554.4	—	—	—	—	—	—	—	—	—
1902	2,595.1	2,745.4	2,452.4	—	—	—	—	—	—	—	—	—
1903	2,718.3	2,853.2	2,589.6	—	—	—	—	—	—	—	—	—
1904	2,903.6	3,069.5	2,745.4	—	—	—	—	—	—	—	—	—
1905	2,827.0	2,970.3	2,689.1	—	—	—	—	—	—	—	—	—
1906	2,623.0	2,695.7	2,548.3	—	—	—	—	—	—	—	—	—
1907	2,660.1	2,749.6	2,565.6	—	—	—	—	—	—	—	—	—
1908	2,470.0	2,525.6	2,413.5	—	—	—	—	—	—	—	—	—
1909	2,406.9	2,480.2	2,331.0	—	—	—	—	—	—	—	—	—
1910	2,406.6	2,483.1	2,324.3	—	—	—	—	—	—	—	—	—
1911	2,370.0	2,443.0	2,289.4	—	—	—	—	—	—	—	—	—
1912	2,313.0	2,401.5	2,218.9	—	—	—	—	—	—	—	—	—
1913	2,269.9	2,336.1	2,201.5	—	—	—	—	—	—	—	—	—
1914	2,263.3	2,335.6	2,188.0	—	—	—	—	—	—	—	—	—
1915	2,306.1	2,352.9	2,262.0	—	—	—	—	—	—	—	—	—
1916	2,214.6	2,264.5	2,166.9	—	—	—	—	—	—	—	—	—
1917	2,342.6	2,414.5	2,272.8	—	—	—	—	—	—	—	—	—
1918	2,796.4	2,891.0	2,711.5	—	—	—	—	—	—	—	—	—
1919	2,051.3	2,026.2	2,086.8	—	—	—	—	—	—	—	—	—
1920	2,064.5	2,042.4	2,098.4	—	—	—	—	—	—	—	—	—
1921	1,826.0	1,803.6	1,859.6	—	—	—	—	—	—	—	—	—
1922	1,833.3	1,838.6	1,838.7	—	—	—	—	—	—	—	—	—
1923	1,980.6	2,001.1	1,971.1	—	—	—	—	—	—	—	—	—
1924	2,052.1	2,105.7	2,005.7	—	—	—	—	—	—	—	—	—
1925	2,087.1	2,143.2	2,036.3	—	—	—	—	—	—	—	—	—
1926	2,140.2	2,207.2	2,077.2	—	—	—	—	—	—	—	—	—
1927	1,980.8	2,037.7	1,926.6	—	—	—	—	—	—	—	—	—
1928	2,095.0	2,167.4	2,024.8	—	—	—	—	—	—	—	—	—
1929	2,096.1	2,193.0	2,001.1	—	—	—	—	—	—	—	—	—
1930	2,042.2	2,136.5	1,949.3	—	—	—	—	—	—	—	—	—
1931	1,969.6	2,068.0	1,873.5	—	—	—	—	—	—	—	—	—
1932	1,843.1	1,931.3	1,757.1	—	—	—	—	—	—	—	—	—
1933	1,830.2	1,924.1	1,738.2	—	—	—	—	—	—	—	—	—
1934	1,889.0	2,016.0	1,762.3	—	—	—	—	—	—	—	—	—
1935	1,725.6	1,846.6	1,605.1	—	—	—	—	—	—	—	—	—
1936	1,853.4	2,003.9	1,702.5	—	—	—	—	—	—	—	—	—
1937	1,775.6	1,921.7	1,628.8	—	—	—	—	—	—	—	—	—
1938	1,658.7	1,765.9	1,551.5	—	—	—	—	—	—	—	—	—
1939	1,596.8	1,706.3	1,487.5	—	—	—	—	—	—	—	—	—
1940	1,626.5	1,755.5	1,497.2	—	—	—	—	—	—	—	—	—
1941	1,562.4	1,691.5	1,433.3	—	—	—	—	—	—	—	—	—
1942	1,451.4	1,576.8	1,326.5	—	—	—	—	—	—	—	—	—
1943	1,444.1	1,548.1	1,340.1	—	—	—	—	—	—	—	—	—
1944	1,361.2	1,455.3	1,266.1	—	—	—	—	—	—	—	—	—
1945	1,293.3	1,393.4	1,192.7	—	—	—	—	—	—	—	—	—
1946	1,238.8	1,342.8	1,134.9	—	—	—	—	—	—	—	—	—
1947	1,246.9	1,352.6	1,141.9	—	—	—	—	—	—	—	—	—
1948	1,248.9	1,377.5	1,121.7	—	—	—	—	—	—	—	—	—
1949	1,223.7	1,343.5	1,105.8	—	—	—	—	—	—	—	—	—
1950	1,179.5	1,303.0	1,058.2	—	—	—	—	—	—	—	—	—
1951	1,158.6	1,287.2	1,033.0	—	—	—	—	—	—	—	—	—
1952	1,141.8	1,284.0	1,004.0	—	—	—	—	—	—	—	—	—
1953	1,112.1	1,256.9	972.8	—	—	—	—	—	—	—	—	—
1954	1,030.1	1,164.5	901.8	—	—	—	—	—	—	—	—	—
1955	1,020.4	1,154.1	893.3	—	—	—	—	—	—	—	—	—
1956	1,023.6	1,159.1	895.7	—	—	—	—	—	—	—	—	—
1957	1,057.7	1,203.7	920.4	—	—	—	—	—	—	—	—	—
1958	1,036.0	1,181.1	900.4	—	—	—	—	—	—	—	—	—
1959	1,004.3	1,155.8	863.1	—	—	—	—	—	—	—	—	—

(continued)

TABLE Ab952–987   Death rate, by sex and race: 1900–1998   *Continued*

	Age-adjusted death rate											
	All nonwhite			Black			American Indian			Asian and Pacific Islander		
	Both sexes	Male	Female	Both sexes	Male	Female	Both sexes	Male	Female	Both sexes	Male	Female
	Ab976	Ab977	Ab978	Ab979	Ab980	Ab981	Ab982	Ab983	Ab984	Ab985	Ab986	Ab987
Year	Per 100,000	Per 100,000	Per 100,000	Per 100,000	Per 100,000	Per 100,000	Per 100,000	Per 100,000	Per 100,000	Per 100,000	Per 100,000	Per 100,000
1960	1,038.6	1,202.7	886.5	1,066.1	1,239.3	910.0	—	—	—	—	—	—
1961	997.5	1,155.2	852.9	1,026.2	1,194.5	876.0	—	—	—	—	—	—
1962 [1]	1,026.9	1,196.2	873.4	—	—	—	—	—	—	—	—	—
1963 [1]	1,062.3	1,248.6	894.2	—	—	—	—	—	—	—	—	—
1964	1,014.3	1,203.5	845.0	1,054.2	1,260.7	874.2	—	—	—	—	—	—
1965	1,011.1	1,213.7	831.5	1,048.5	1,266.8	859.9	—	—	—	—	—	—
1966	1,022.3	1,238.9	831.8	1,062.3	1,296.4	861.4	—	—	—	—	—	—
1967	987.9	1,207.9	795.9	1,028.9	1,265.7	827.1	—	—	—	—	—	—
1968	1,042.9	1,286.6	831.2	1,089.4	1,353.2	865.9	—	—	—	—	—	—
1969	1,016.2	1,266.5	800.7	1,065.0	1,334.6	838.1	—	—	—	—	—	—
1970	990.8	1,241.3	776.3	1,040.2	1,311.9	812.6	—	—	—	—	—	—
1971	957.6	1,202.0	749.5	1,006.1	1,271.6	784.8	—	—	—	—	—	—
1972	957.4	1,219.1	736.8	1,008.2	1,292.6	773.2	—	—	—	—	—	—
1973	941.3	1,196.6	727.6	992.4	1,269.1	765.2	—	—	—	—	—	—
1974	888.4	1,138.9	680.2	939.4	1,212.1	717.1	—	—	—	—	—	—
1975	839.4	1,087.5	634.7	889.9	1,160.8	670.4	—	—	—	—	—	—
1976	817.8	1,061.0	618.2	869.4	1,135.9	654.4	—	—	—	—	—	—
1977	795.9	1,033.9	601.8	848.7	1,109.7	639.4	—	—	—	—	—	—
1978	779.2	1,018.2	585.3	830.8	1,091.8	622.6	—	—	—	—	—	—
1979	756.4	991.8	566.6	811.3	1,071.1	605.2	—	—	—	—	—	—
1980	766.3	1,004.0	576.9	836.4	1,103.9	626.8	564.1	732.5	414.1	315.6	416.6	224.6
1981	733.2	962.2	551.4	806.0	1,066.6	602.6	514.0	676.7	368.5	293.2	382.3	213.9
1982	708.2	929.1	533.8	781.3	1,033.4	585.7	494.3	634.6	371.6	293.6	389.2	212.8
1983	710.1	927.0	540.1	786.7	1,035.5	595.3	485.9	634.0	360.1	298.6	388.6	218.0
1984	702.8	919.7	533.2	782.4	1,033.1	589.9	476.9	614.2	347.3	299.4	386.0	223.0
1985	708.5	930.1	535.5	792.6	1,051.1	594.5	468.2	602.6	353.3	305.7	396.9	228.5
1986	705.6	929.9	530.6	795.9	1,059.6	594.0	451.4	591.6	328.4	296.7	385.3	220.3
1987	701.9	925.7	527.4	795.4	1,060.8	592.4	456.7	580.8	351.3	297.0	386.2	221.3
1988	709.4	935.9	532.6	808.6	1,080.1	600.9	456.3	585.7	343.2	300.2	385.4	226.5
1989	703.2	930.6	525.1	804.9	1,079.5	594.0	475.7	622.8	353.4	295.8	378.9	225.2
1990	680.9	901.2	508.6	784.2	1,052.7	578.8	445.1	573.1	335.1	297.8	377.8	228.9
1991	674.0	890.6	503.9	781.0	1,047.0	576.1	441.8	562.6	335.9	283.2	360.2	218.3
1992	658.9	868.5	494.3	765.7	1,022.9	567.6	453.1	579.6	343.1	285.8	364.1	220.5
1993	671.0	885.2	501.9	784.1	1,048.8	578.7	468.9	589.6	364.5	295.9	381.4	226.7
1994	659.1	866.1	494.8	771.5	1,026.9	572.5	460.7	585.9	350.8	299.2	386.5	229.3
1995	651.6	852.1	492.8	765.6	1,014.4	571.8	468.5	580.4	368.0	298.9	384.4	231.4
1996	626.7	811.0	481.2	737.2	965.0	560.4	456.7	555.9	367.7	277.4	355.8	214.4
1997	600.8	769.3	468.1	704.9	910.9	545.4	465.3	584.1	359.9	274.8	350.3	214.7
1998	—	—	—	690.9	884.5	540.9	458.1	564.9	363.3	264.6	336.2	207.4

[1] Excludes New Jersey for rates by race. That state did not require reporting of race.

Sources

Total deaths: 1900–1992, U.S. Public Health Service, National Center for Health Statistics, *Vital Statistics of the United States, 1992,* volume 2, *Mortality,* part A, Tables 1-2 and 1-3. 1993–1997, and data for the American Indian and Asian and Pacific Islander populations, 1980–1997: *National Vital Statistics Report,* volume 47, number 19, "Deaths: Final Data for 1997," Table 1.

Deaths by age, sex, and race are taken from the various annual issues of *Mortality Statistics of the United States* (1900–1936) and *Vital Statistics of the United States* (1937–1992). Deaths by age, sex, and race for 1993–1997 are obtained from the file GMWK291A found on the National Center for Health Statistics (NCHS) Internet site.

Population: Death Registration Area, 1900–1932, and United States, 1933–1939, Forrest Linder and Robert D. Grove, *Vital Statistics Rates in the United States, 1900*–1940 (U.S. Government Printing Office, 1948), pp. 997–1034, and unpublished tables made available by the Mortality Statistics Branch of the NCHS. United States, 1940–1997: Machine readable versions of the data were obtained from U.S. Bureau of the Census, 1900–1979, PE-11 (POP 3987); 1980–1990, PE-10 (POP 3988–3990); 1990–1997, PE-61 (POP 3991–3998). See Frederick W. Hollmann, Lisa B. Kuzmekus, R. Colby Perkins, and Elizabeth A. Weber, "U.S. Population by Age, Sex, Race,

and Hispanic Origin: 1990 to 1997," U.S. Bureau of the Census, PPL-91 and appendixes. The population by race for 1962 and 1963 excludes New Jersey, which did not report deaths by race in these years. The estimated population of the United States for whites and all other races was estimated and reported in *Vital Statistics of the United States, 1962,* volume 2, *Mortality,* part A, Technical Appendix, and *Vital Statistics of the United States, 1963,* volume 2, *Mortality,* part A, Technical Appendix. Age-adjusted death rates for the American Indian and Asian and Pacific Islander populations for 1980–1997 are taken from *National Vital Statistics Report,* volume 47, number 19, "Deaths: Final Data for 1997," Table 1. The other overall and age-adjusted rates will differ from the official NCHS published rates because of the use of slightly different base populations here. Overall and age-adjusted death rates for 1998 are taken from *National Vital Statistics Report,* volume 48, number 11, "Deaths: Final Data for 1998," Table 1. The rates for 1998 do not use the same base population estimates as for the period 1940–1997. The same standard is used for the age adjustment.

Documentation

The overall death rate is the number of deaths, excluding fetal deaths, per 100,000 population. Prior to 1933, this is given for the Death Registration States only. For 1910–1915, North Carolina is excluded because it provided only partial coverage. For 1917–1918, deaths of soldiers, sailors, and marines

TABLE Ab952–987   Death rate, by sex and race: 1900–1998   *Continued*

were added. The base population is as of July 1 in each year. For the composition of the Death Registration Area and States, see the essay on vital statistics in this chapter. Beginning in 1970, the mortality data exclude nonresidents of the United States. The age-adjusted death rates are also per 100,000 population and are calculated by weighting the age–sex–race specific death rates by a set of weights from a standard United States population. The standard population is the total enumerated population in 1940, both sexes and all races combined. See U.S. Public Health Service, National Center for Health Statistics, *Vital Statistics of the United States, 1992,* volume 2, *Mortality,* part A, Technical Appendix. The overall death rates include deaths reported with unknown ages. The age-adjusted death rates do not include deaths with

unknown ages. The age-adjusted death rate is a convenient summary index that "corrects" for differences in age composition. These rates were computed by taking the age distribution of the population in 1940 as the "standard" without regard to sex, color, or other characteristics. The age-specific death rates actually observed in a given year were applied to the age distribution of this standard population and the total death rate was computed. The age-specific death rate is the rate of deaths per 100,000 population in each age interval for a specified year. For a detailed description of the direct method by which these rates were computed, see Linder and Grove (1947), pp. 66–9.

TABLE Ab988–1047   Death rate, by sex and age: 1900–1998

Contributed by Michael R. Haines

		Both sexes										
						Age						
	Total	0	1–4	5–9	10–14	15–19	20–24	25–29	30–34	35–39	40–44	45–49
	Ab988 [1]	Ab989	Ab990	Ab991	Ab992	Ab993	Ab994	Ab995	Ab996	Ab997	Ab998	Ab999
Year	Per 100,000	Per 100,000	Per 100,000	Per 100,000	Per 100,000	Per 100,000	Per 100,000	Per 100,000	Per 100,000	Per 100,000	Per 100,000	Per 100,000
1900	1,719.1	16,244.8	1,983.8	466.1	298.3	484.8	680.6	787.9	855.7	964.2	1,092.7	1,319.0
1901	1,641.5	14,139.0	1,695.0	427.6	273.6	454.4	649.1	761.9	852.8	947.8	1,125.7	1,312.9
1902	1,548.1	13,887.7	1,655.7	403.3	252.5	421.5	601.8	698.6	800.2	888.1	1,044.4	1,223.7
1903	1,562.8	13,261.1	1,542.1	414.7	268.2	434.1	595.8	705.5	794.2	911.6	1,050.6	1,262.4
1904	1,640.0	13,922.7	1,591.5	425.0	305.2	471.4	622.8	728.0	836.7	963.0	1,088.1	1,326.0
1905	1,588.9	14,120.6	1,498.9	396.3	279.8	439.3	595.0	687.1	798.3	920.5	1,045.4	1,325.0
1906	1,571.8	14,484.8	1,580.0	377.4	272.2	445.2	610.5	698.6	802.4	929.2	1,034.9	1,316.8
1907	1,592.5	13,858.0	1,468.3	365.6	265.8	437.7	616.9	690.7	823.6	965.9	1,073.8	1,360.0
1908	1,468.2	13,320.7	1,396.8	354.2	247.9	397.7	550.7	619.6	725.0	841.2	962.7	1,236.5
1909	1,424.7	12,668.9	1,348.9	330.2	230.5	363.6	509.6	591.9	683.2	820.6	933.3	1,193.9
1910	1,468.0	13,176.3	1,397.3	348.4	235.9	371.9	531.4	612.3	702.6	831.1	977.7	1,207.8
1911	1,390.5	11,404.5	1,176.0	310.0	222.2	366.0	526.6	594.3	686.9	828.8	957.9	1,178.0
1912	1,359.7	11,105.5	1,094.1	287.5	202.2	347.2	500.5	572.4	654.2	790.0	947.2	1,150.7
1913	1,380.6	11,478.7	1,193.4	317.7	214.8	360.3	511.9	582.4	659.7	796.8	965.1	1,166.3
1914	1,330.2	10,716.8	1,024.2	291.6	207.2	340.5	495.6	559.8	642.3	768.8	944.8	1,134.1
1915	1,317.6	10,237.7	924.2	260.6	196.7	330.9	480.5	542.4	627.6	753.7	928.8	1,141.9
1916	1,381.1	10,565.9	1,111.5	282.4	205.1	355.8	518.6	573.5	665.8	790.6	981.8	1,198.3
1917	1,397.1	10,457.2	1,066.0	290.7	218.9	380.3	556.3	603.3	700.3	812.8	1,007.2	1,218.8
1918	1,810.0	11,167.2	1,573.5	447.9	375.1	777.4	1,383.0	1,663.7	1,621.7	1,369.8	1,302.4	1,406.6
1919	1,289.4	9,095.0	928.0	300.0	236.4	438.5	626.2	722.3	784.8	826.1	904.8	1,088.3
1920	1,298.9	9,226.4	987.2	295.2	229.9	402.9	573.2	634.5	726.4	779.1	849.6	1,066.0
1921	1,149.8	8,063.2	801.2	281.4	209.9	326.5	450.1	460.6	520.2	622.3	738.4	978.9
1922	1,169.3	7,757.0	742.0	239.6	186.6	319.6	444.5	470.0	538.9	656.7	775.0	1,031.3
1923	1,213.0	8,107.7	806.7	240.0	188.2	325.8	453.4	478.8	531.8	681.3	785.6	1,054.5
1924	1,159.0	7,676.0	683.2	221.7	179.8	313.5	443.6	461.0	493.0	660.1	768.4	1,033.7
1925	1,168.1	7,542.7	641.0	211.5	181.0	314.0	442.8	474.0	493.2	669.3	771.8	1,032.6
1926	1,211.0	7,788.2	723.4	213.8	171.4	307.5	438.6	479.5	499.4	681.8	796.8	1,072.3
1927	1,131.5	6,883.9	591.0	208.3	167.5	289.5	410.8	456.7	481.4	647.1	767.7	1,015.1
1928	1,198.6	7,307.7	647.5	213.1	173.8	307.8	434.7	479.2	515.7	675.1	827.4	1,074.5
1929	1,187.8	7,156.7	625.5	208.0	165.0	298.0	428.5	479.0	520.1	647.2	830.7	1,075.6
1930	1,132.1	6,900.4	563.6	189.8	152.8	277.8	394.4	439.7	493.9	596.5	780.2	1,034.4
1931	1,106.5	6,444.8	526.6	182.0	150.3	263.5	377.4	416.3	484.9	587.8	771.1	1,024.9
1932	1,087.7	6,132.4	461.9	165.9	142.2	237.5	342.1	387.8	448.6	551.2	729.5	983.3
1933	1,068.7	6,125.7	472.6	161.3	138.0	223.4	327.9	378.7	435.6	532.1	716.1	974.5
1934	1,105.4	6,678.1	507.7	165.1	141.5	224.0	330.1	380.3	436.7	531.8	725.5	995.0
1935	1,094.5	6,093.8	440.9	162.4	143.4	222.3	322.0	379.1	428.1	537.1	718.8	987.8
1936	1,155.2	6,288.1	439.8	154.6	141.0	230.4	329.4	385.4	436.0	557.1	755.1	1,023.9
1937	1,125.9	6,127.2	418.7	142.9	128.3	219.0	309.6	359.3	417.9	528.9	724.3	995.5
1938	1,064.0	5,804.5	383.8	128.8	113.8	192.3	266.6	311.5	362.7	471.0	647.7	907.6
1939	1,060.4	5,367.1	318.3	112.6	106.5	179.8	247.2	289.7	347.4	451.6	616.6	884.3

Note appears at end of table

(continued)

TABLE Ab988–1047   Death rate, by sex and age: 1900–1998   *Continued*

		Both sexes											
		Age											
	Total	0	1–4	5–9	10–14	15–19	20–24	25–29	30–34	35–39	40–44	45–49
	Ab988 [1]	Ab989	Ab990	Ab991	Ab992	Ab993	Ab994	Ab995	Ab996	Ab997	Ab998	Ab999
Year	Per 100,000	Per 100,000	Per 100,000	Per 100,000	Per 100,000	Per 100,000	Per 100,000	Per 100,000	Per 100,000	Per 100,000	Per 100,000	Per 100,000
1940	1,072.7	5,480.1	288.5	108.7	99.7	171.5	238.1	275.1	336.1	434.2	608.4	865.3
1941	1,047.7	5,258.7	279.9	103.8	94.7	168.5	232.4	262.7	321.8	415.4	590.4	845.6
1942	1,027.1	4,881.4	243.5	96.1	85.8	153.6	221.7	244.6	305.2	404.7	566.6	820.2
1943	1,067.4	4,400.2	256.4	103.1	90.6	159.8	229.1	236.3	293.9	396.3	560.9	813.8
1944	1,019.8	4,417.1	233.0	98.7	89.7	148.0	209.0	210.3	273.1	372.8	537.4	765.4
1945	1,001.7	4,249.3	203.0	93.6	86.8	141.4	185.1	200.1	263.2	366.3	525.2	764.0
1946	987.1	4,625.3	181.5	85.6	78.6	131.9	189.2	198.5	251.0	346.8	489.6	733.1
1947	1,002.9	3,452.0	160.8	73.3	67.9	123.8	177.1	187.5	233.5	329.7	485.5	730.5
1948	985.0	3,570.8	160.1	70.6	65.6	117.3	164.3	173.2	217.1	315.3	471.9	710.5
1949	967.6	3,518.7	150.2	68.3	63.6	110.3	149.5	162.6	203.7	298.1	449.2	703.3
1950	953.9	3,282.9	137.0	60.9	57.6	108.0	143.5	157.8	196.7	281.2	437.6	676.9
1951	956.9	3,218.7	136.3	61.4	56.2	107.1	139.1	156.5	191.8	275.2	434.5	656.5
1952	950.1	3,190.6	140.5	61.0	56.6	112.5	135.2	153.9	185.9	267.4	422.2	650.9
1953	947.4	3,056.8	129.4	55.9	52.9	105.3	130.8	142.6	177.0	253.2	411.2	635.3
1954	908.5	2,909.3	117.7	52.3	47.6	94.6	123.2	134.8	166.4	237.2	382.8	602.2
1955	921.3	2,830.1	112.8	50.4	46.3	95.5	128.5	133.2	161.1	236.3	377.4	589.9
1956	926.3	2,802.7	109.6	48.1	46.1	95.3	129.8	130.6	162.6	229.5	372.9	590.0
1957	949.6	2,777.9	111.2	49.8	47.2	98.4	127.6	132.2	168.0	237.1	377.4	595.0
1958	942.3	2,793.7	111.1	48.2	44.4	90.2	121.9	127.2	162.1	230.9	366.7	582.2
1959	931.7	2,733.6	106.5	49.2	45.6	91.6	121.6	127.5	162.8	228.2	360.1	579.3
1960	947.6	2,708.3	108.8	48.7	43.6	90.6	119.9	130.0	160.2	232.5	367.7	589.0
1961	926.3	2,587.0	101.7	45.8	41.8	87.4	117.4	124.8	158.0	228.0	358.5	570.8
1962	941.8	2,582.9	99.2	45.6	41.9	86.9	120.0	126.9	159.2	235.0	361.3	579.2
1963	958.3	2,576.7	101.5	45.3	41.2	89.9	120.9	130.9	161.9	239.5	365.3	588.1
1964	937.0	2,528.2	98.5	44.6	41.6	93.4	122.8	131.9	168.4	240.7	368.2	580.3
1965	940.9	2,463.3	95.9	43.9	40.5	94.7	123.4	132.7	166.6	241.0	368.9	582.2
1966	947.9	2,405.3	96.4	44.3	41.1	101.2	129.2	135.0	168.6	240.2	373.2	588.0
1967	931.7	2,290.7	89.4	42.9	40.5	101.2	128.1	135.2	166.6	243.4	368.9	581.3
1968	961.6	2,265.4	89.6	44.5	41.6	107.5	136.0	141.1	171.5	249.3	381.8	596.3
1969	948.3	2,199.9	88.0	44.0	41.3	112.7	141.3	143.3	172.7	250.7	383.3	585.9
1970	936.8	2,128.4	84.6	42.2	40.5	108.8	140.9	141.5	170.5	246.1	376.5	582.4
1971	928.2	1,887.8	82.3	42.0	39.9	109.9	140.2	143.3	167.9	241.2	366.8	567.4
1972	935.7	1,820.6	80.4	40.8	40.4	110.0	143.3	139.2	167.1	235.3	363.5	574.1
1973	931.1	1,776.7	79.0	41.1	40.3	110.6	143.3	140.7	163.6	234.0	354.5	563.1
1974	904.5	1,721.6	73.2	37.2	38.3	104.5	136.1	134.1	155.5	217.2	338.7	540.9
1975	876.4	1,602.8	69.9	35.2	35.3	99.9	134.6	133.2	148.2	208.6	325.3	512.2
1976	875.7	1,549.2	68.8	34.1	34.2	95.5	127.7	125.3	141.7	197.5	312.7	498.3
1977	862.5	1,432.7	67.6	33.3	34.6	99.5	129.5	127.4	137.7	194.6	304.0	482.4
1978	866.1	1,381.2	67.9	32.7	33.7	98.6	130.3	126.7	136.0	188.5	295.3	471.9
1979	850.4	1,332.8	64.2	31.1	31.8	98.5	129.8	129.4	135.8	184.1	282.7	452.7
1980	873.8	1,278.9	63.5	30.6	30.8	98.0	131.1	130.0	137.6	181.7	278.9	450.4
1981	860.1	1,200.4	60.6	29.1	29.5	89.8	121.7	127.4	135.3	180.1	270.5	441.7
1982	850.5	1,163.7	58.2	28.3	28.2	85.1	113.8	118.1	131.6	168.7	256.1	421.3
1983	861.8	1,113.3	56.1	26.5	27.3	80.9	107.0	113.7	128.6	164.0	249.3	406.3
1984	862.9	1,108.1	52.2	25.3	28.3	80.2	108.6	112.3	131.2	167.0	251.2	399.9
1985	874.9	1,088.2	51.8	25.0	28.0	80.3	106.5	113.4	134.9	172.4	250.7	398.3
1986	874.9	1,051.2	52.4	23.9	28.6	86.0	113.2	120.2	146.2	179.5	255.9	390.6
1987	874.5	1,037.1	52.1	24.7	27.1	83.3	109.9	120.6	148.2	186.9	246.7	387.1
1988	884.8	1,035.8	51.5	24.5	27.7	86.5	111.5	122.6	150.6	192.3	251.9	383.3
1989	869.4	1,027.8	49.8	24.1	27.4	85.7	107.6	124.2	154.4	194.1	253.5	378.7
1990	859.6	961.9	46.6	22.1	25.8	88.3	108.9	124.4	152.4	195.1	249.6	375.0
1991	858.8	917.1	47.5	21.6	25.8	88.7	109.2	122.3	153.5	197.1	253.2	380.1
1992	851.9	869.3	43.6	20.4	24.7	83.8	104.8	120.1	153.2	199.1	261.3	367.8
1993	879.0	855.9	44.8	21.3	25.7	86.3	108.1	122.4	159.5	204.8	268.9	371.8
1994	874.5	822.0	42.9	20.0	25.3	86.2	107.6	121.7	161.7	207.9	272.3	374.6
1995	879.0	775.0	40.7	19.8	25.6	83.1	105.6	119.3	160.2	208.2	275.2	375.6
1996	872.0	748.7	38.3	19.5	24.0	78.6	100.7	108.8	142.3	188.1	257.1	363.5
1997	863.8	738.7	35.8	18.5	23.2	74.8	98.2	101.8	126.3	168.4	239.5	352.3
1998	864.7	751.3	34.6	17.7	22.1	70.6	95.3	97.6	120.7	164.6	235.8	346.8

Note appears at end of table

TABLE Ab988–1047   Death rate, by sex and age: 1900–1998   *Continued*

	Both sexes									Males			
	Age									Total	Age		
	50–54	55–59	60–64	65–69	70–74	75–79	80–84	85 and over			0	1–4	5–9
	Ab1000	Ab1001	Ab1002	Ab1003	Ab1004	Ab1005	Ab1006	Ab1007		Ab1008 [1]	Ab1009	Ab1010	Ab1011
Year	Per 100,000	Per 100,000	Per 100,000	Per 100,000	Per 100,000	Per 100,000	Per 100,000	Per 100,000		Per 100,000	Per 100,000	Per 100,000	Per 100,000
1900	1,700.3	2,342.4	3,187.9	4,706.6	6,973.3	10,310.7	16,606.0	26,088.2		1,791.1	17,914.4	2,054.2	470.2
1901	1,717.6	2,351.8	3,296.2	4,730.0	6,909.1	10,315.2	17,009.1	26,082.7		1,725.9	15,637.5	1,769.3	439.1
1902	1,602.2	2,199.5	3,070.5	4,429.2	6,535.3	9,535.1	15,380.8	23,560.0		1,635.3	15,336.5	1,713.8	420.6
1903	1,626.6	2,312.6	3,220.3	4,631.8	6,766.2	10,143.1	16,165.6	25,369.4		1,643.6	14,660.8	1,590.7	420.8
1904	1,717.6	2,378.0	3,441.7	4,812.7	7,284.5	10,523.8	17,019.9	26,998.9		1,727.6	15,391.1	1,659.3	428.7
1905	1,628.4	2,306.6	3,345.8	4,740.7	6,891.0	10,438.7	16,039.0	26,151.4		1,674.4	15,662.5	1,577.3	404.4
1906	1,607.1	2,277.8	3,237.7	4,622.0	6,776.1	10,292.9	15,694.2	25,511.1		1,672.6	16,017.0	1,640.7	390.9
1907	1,676.8	2,393.9	3,425.3	4,919.5	7,281.7	10,881.9	17,048.7	26,911.0		1,702.2	15,291.2	1,527.3	376.1
1908	1,542.0	2,202.9	3,137.4	4,486.5	6,685.9	10,168.8	15,700.6	24,862.7		1,552.4	14,696.5	1,456.8	368.7
1909	1,497.2	2,140.8	3,081.0	4,547.9	6,630.5	10,203.7	15,253.1	24,492.2		1,506.4	13,985.4	1,406.1	341.4
1910	1,570.2	2,205.9	3,142.3	4,634.3	6,917.0	10,381.3	16,074.3	25,030.8		1,556.4	14,553.2	1,458.0	359.8
1911	1,549.9	2,182.8	3,070.3	4,543.3	6,922.7	10,181.4	15,847.4	24,641.4		1,472.7	12,593.8	1,222.6	322.4
1912	1,553.9	2,201.4	3,052.7	4,534.9	6,809.3	10,273.8	15,674.3	24,219.4		1,448.6	12,329.5	1,148.5	306.8
1913	1,560.6	2,189.7	2,987.8	4,465.8	6,825.3	10,007.5	15,574.7	23,593.3		1,476.0	12,757.4	1,247.8	339.5
1914	1,519.4	2,153.9	2,952.0	4,424.4	6,878.2	9,728.9	15,483.0	23,147.9		1,419.0	11,894.2	1,074.8	304.9
1915	1,505.1	2,219.3	2,961.2	4,502.0	7,138.8	10,138.6	16,028.5	24,028.6		1,399.6	11,450.1	968.7	277.5
1916	1,554.5	2,333.9	3,041.4	4,687.4	7,242.0	10,465.7	16,519.3	25,042.6		1,475.4	11,820.5	1,169.2	301.7
1917	1,582.8	2,342.9	3,082.9	4,706.2	7,243.0	10,450.9	16,532.9	24,593.6		1,504.6	11,736.4	1,119.3	309.7
1918	1,664.0	2,314.9	3,049.9	4,575.1	6,881.7	9,653.6	14,821.0	22,213.5		1,980.5	12,453.5	1,600.6	458.3
1919	1,393.1	1,971.7	2,716.5	4,143.3	6,259.1	9,271.3	13,994.2	22,225.0		1,345.8	10,190.2	973.5	318.0
1920	1,398.6	1,985.4	2,805.8	4,314.0	6,641.5	10,136.4	15,613.2	24,825.2		1,338.1	10,358.0	1,027.7	312.5
1921	1,281.6	1,809.9	2,693.0	3,996.5	6,254.7	9,462.8	14,638.6	23,914.5		1,194.7	9,012.9	842.4	302.7
1922	1,348.4	1,857.0	2,896.8	4,236.2	6,733.5	9,975.7	15,527.7	25,813.6		1,226.3	8,697.8	787.6	259.2
1923	1,413.9	1,894.8	3,023.5	4,307.0	6,943.7	10,396.9	16,478.7	27,967.3		1,274.5	9,022.9	846.0	257.8
1924	1,420.6	1,827.2	2,931.7	4,136.2	6,618.1	9,792.1	15,796.1	26,177.4		1,230.4	8,623.6	723.8	239.3
1925	1,437.7	1,862.6	2,949.2	4,265.2	6,597.9	9,981.3	16,030.2	27,226.8		1,239.4	8,457.6	673.2	231.0
1926	1,506.1	1,951.4	3,018.6	4,472.8	6,788.6	10,584.7	16,660.3	27,967.8		1,285.7	8,708.8	762.4	233.0
1927	1,435.4	1,878.3	2,837.4	4,288.4	6,364.2	9,878.3	15,162.8	25,012.1		1,209.4	7,747.0	624.1	229.0
1928	1,523.6	2,012.7	2,948.9	4,554.3	6,692.4	10,695.0	16,336.1	26,833.2		1,283.4	8,232.7	683.4	232.2
1929	1,495.7	2,057.0	2,941.6	4,530.9	6,629.9	10,439.3	15,928.5	25,431.7		1,276.9	8,003.5	660.3	227.1
1930	1,432.6	1,999.2	2,901.9	4,248.9	6,402.6	9,663.1	14,594.0	22,795.6		1,225.3	7,701.3	602.6	209.3
1931	1,401.5	1,971.7	2,831.5	4,072.6	6,306.4	9,479.1	14,314.0	22,277.8		1,201.5	7,217.7	561.6	199.3
1932	1,357.8	1,948.2	2,827.1	4,024.8	6,389.7	9,793.3	14,821.9	23,334.2		1,172.9	6,854.5	487.7	179.1
1933	1,339.9	1,908.7	2,820.7	3,976.4	6,233.5	9,574.3	14,357.8	22,228.5		1,162.8	6,828.2	503.0	175.5
1934	1,392.2	1,937.5	2,866.8	4,034.4	6,245.1	9,861.0	14,618.3	22,484.9		1,211.6	7,479.3	540.6	181.1
1935	1,360.3	1,933.8	2,789.4	4,072.5	6,028.4	9,861.0	14,325.7	22,457.9		1,202.1	6,885.1	469.2	177.0
1936	1,420.9	2,004.9	2,916.5	4,271.8	6,248.3	10,569.1	15,510.7	24,273.5		1,273.0	7,066.1	471.0	172.0
1937	1,393.3	1,958.6	2,838.5	4,149.6	5,993.6	10,125.4	14,984.7	22,720.1		1,246.8	6,874.4	446.3	159.3
1938	1,300.6	1,836.3	2,663.8	3,956.5	5,819.0	9,551.0	14,309.1	21,258.9		1,170.8	6,523.9	408.3	141.8
1939	1,288.0	1,853.5	2,659.7	3,911.3	5,913.1	9,461.9	14,997.3	22,331.3		1,168.2	6,031.9	342.6	126.6
1940	1,274.8	1,837.5	2,648.6	3,941.0	6,073.2	9,412.8	14,456.1	23,213.6		1,192.1	6,171.3	310.4	122.9
1941	1,239.8	1,788.7	2,553.4	3,794.2	5,820.6	8,838.8	13,967.6	21,870.7		1,173.1	5,858.3	299.4	117.1
1942	1,223.7	1,760.3	2,506.1	3,695.7	5,645.2	8,494.3	13,434.5	21,099.8		1,154.6	5,442.9	260.7	111.7
1943	1,248.2	1,813.1	2,559.2	3,751.0	5,875.4	8,988.9	14,220.5	23,035.5		1,192.6	4,926.1	276.9	117.8
1944	1,191.2	1,750.1	2,465.4	3,569.4	5,590.8	8,588.0	13,299.0	21,516.8		1,138.5	4,912.7	250.2	115.6
1945	1,166.2	1,734.6	2,424.2	3,482.6	5,386.4	8,450.2	12,573.5	20,973.0		1,125.2	4,756.7	219.3	108.0
1946	1,129.8	1,662.5	2,363.7	3,353.5	5,220.8	8,232.1	12,008.2	21,084.0		1,112.4	5,209.7	196.4	100.1
1947	1,137.7	1,682.0	2,410.4	3,421.0	5,348.1	8,401.6	12,179.0	21,675.4		1,137.3	3,883.2	175.3	85.7
1948	1,109.5	1,642.7	2,368.1	3,378.4	5,230.1	8,249.0	11,885.4	21,301.6		1,122.6	4,015.9	174.2	81.9
1949	1,054.3	1,586.8	2,334.2	3,351.3	5,130.6	8,056.9	11,632.7	20,317.9		1,104.8	3,961.8	163.6	80.0
1950	1,037.3	1,549.9	2,312.2	3,298.0	5,104.1	7,878.3	11,733.7	19,761.5		1,091.3	3,709.0	149.0	70.0
1951	1,052.9	1,545.4	2,272.7	3,294.5	5,024.3	7,805.4	11,885.3	19,390.3		1,096.3	3,647.9	146.9	70.5
1952	1,034.8	1,525.8	2,244.3	3,253.5	4,914.9	7,628.4	11,716.8	18,737.2		1,089.6	3,594.8	151.3	69.8
1953	1,018.6	1,498.8	2,222.2	3,260.2	4,889.1	7,558.8	11,870.6	18,923.9		1,089.1	3,456.6	141.0	65.1
1954	970.8	1,402.8	2,111.6	3,134.1	4,679.8	7,200.5	11,203.5	17,925.1		1,044.9	3,287.2	127.8	60.3
1955	943.7	1,402.8	2,093.2	3,160.5	4,688.8	7,353.4	11,444.2	18,772.4		1,059.5	3,193.5	122.5	58.9
1956	922.4	1,417.2	2,105.3	3,162.4	4,667.5	7,297.2	11,494.8	19,053.4		1,066.3	3,178.3	118.2	55.6
1957	954.2	1,429.5	2,169.7	3,253.0	4,759.2	7,298.4	11,565.5	19,641.0		1,091.8	3,133.9	119.1	57.8
1958	943.3	1,394.7	2,127.6	3,180.7	4,694.5	7,273.0	11,598.3	19,692.7		1,081.7	3,140.2	118.6	55.4
1959	924.6	1,382.7	2,088.3	3,107.6	4,602.9	7,089.6	11,393.1	19,348.1		1,071.7	3,088.3	115.7	57.2

Note appears at end of table

(continued)

TABLE Ab988–1047   Death rate, by sex and age: 1900–1998   *Continued*

	Both sexes								Males			
	Age									Age		
	50–54	55–59	60–64	65–69	70–74	75–79	80–84	85 and over	Total	0	1–4	5–9
	Ab1000	Ab1001	Ab1002	Ab1003	Ab1004	Ab1005	Ab1006	Ab1007	Ab1008 [1]	Ab1009	Ab1010	Ab1011
Year	Per 100,000	Per 100,000	Per 100,000	Per 100,000	Per 100,000	Per 100,000	Per 100,000	Per 100,000	Per 100,000	Per 100,000	Per 100,000	Per 100,000
1960	937.4	1,378.3	2,144.8	3,130.6	4,686.6	7,141.1	11,569.3	19,629.3	1,092.3	3,074.3	119.2	55.9
1961	910.8	1,320.7	2,100.9	3,064.9	4,501.5	6,955.5	11,135.7	19,629.6	1,065.5	2,929.2	110.5	52.4
1962	923.4	1,338.9	2,122.5	3,105.0	4,537.6	7,067.9	11,170.7	20,485.0	1,080.5	2,934.5	106.1	51.5
1963	930.4	1,367.8	2,161.1	3,134.3	4,614.0	7,190.6	11,275.4	20,982.4	1,101.5	2,925.3	110.1	51.8
1964	923.2	1,334.4	2,134.0	3,030.3	4,445.9	6,940.8	10,803.1	19,923.8	1,076.8	2,850.7	107.6	51.6
1965	923.5	1,334.8	2,120.9	3,045.1	4,420.8	6,980.7	10,815.4	20,073.5	1,082.7	2,786.9	104.3	50.8
1966	923.7	1,353.8	2,097.7	3,062.4	4,488.0	6,983.2	10,775.8	19,986.6	1,089.7	2,713.6	105.2	51.3
1967	904.6	1,340.8	2,043.7	2,986.9	4,413.5	6,777.7	10,404.5	19,219.3	1,072.1	2,586.6	99.4	49.7
1968	920.1	1,381.2	2,090.8	3,079.9	4,530.1	6,946.9	10,645.1	19,587.7	1,104.6	2,562.0	98.2	52.0
1969	892.0	1,361.1	2,012.9	3,016.6	4,414.6	6,727.4	10,462.1	18,814.8	1,088.7	2,483.9	95.5	51.7
1970	884.4	1,356.5	1,989.9	2,954.5	4,352.4	6,659.0	10,034.9	17,263.6	1,074.7	2,393.0	93.3	49.8
1971	861.4	1,322.5	1,952.5	2,858.6	4,294.6	6,531.8	9,833.0	17,566.9	1,060.7	2,121.6	90.6	49.1
1972	850.8	1,321.8	1,957.7	2,870.7	4,393.9	6,575.7	9,794.1	17,538.0	1,068.5	2,055.5	89.4	46.7
1973	832.9	1,306.1	1,923.8	2,796.0	4,297.8	6,475.3	9,632.3	17,681.8	1,059.6	2,001.2	88.2	47.9
1974	808.1	1,238.4	1,860.9	2,687.9	4,186.9	6,143.1	9,295.3	16,898.0	1,026.6	1,930.9	81.5	44.2
1975	785.0	1,187.4	1,801.4	2,563.8	4,045.1	5,848.5	8,890.6	15,654.6	997.3	1,785.8	76.8	41.4
1976	768.4	1,161.0	1,786.0	2,530.2	3,944.5	5,767.8	8,789.0	16,056.2	989.6	1,715.2	76.9	40.2
1977	755.2	1,122.0	1,742.8	2,467.4	3,840.6	5,595.6	8,554.4	15,371.5	974.7	1,600.0	75.2	39.7
1978	743.1	1,097.9	1,728.3	2,448.9	3,784.0	5,496.8	8,662.0	15,479.9	973.3	1,532.6	76.7	37.9
1979	720.6	1,067.4	1,655.6	2,390.0	3,644.0	5,331.2	8,411.7	14,963.0	953.6	1,482.1	71.0	36.7
1980	712.8	1,085.3	1,638.3	2,455.0	3,659.3	5,458.0	8,582.8	15,758.3	969.8	1,417.8	72.2	35.2
1981	695.8	1,070.5	1,605.5	2,403.8	3,586.4	5,276.8	8,368.2	15,430.9	950.2	1,324.8	67.7	34.3
1982	671.7	1,045.4	1,582.1	2,370.5	3,532.7	5,260.2	8,173.2	15,050.1	934.5	1,291.7	64.0	32.9
1983	666.5	1,045.5	1,587.6	2,354.8	3,560.8	5,300.4	8,259.9	15,460.5	939.4	1,229.7	63.5	30.8
1984	652.4	1,030.5	1,577.2	2,330.4	3,532.5	5,245.5	8,196.2	15,395.8	934.9	1,223.4	57.3	29.7
1985	648.4	1,025.9	1,570.5	2,319.9	3,538.0	5,265.0	8,247.0	15,710.8	944.6	1,219.7	58.5	28.5
1986	637.6	990.8	1,553.6	2,291.0	3,514.8	5,199.0	8,086.7	15,589.6	941.0	1,173.9	58.4	27.8
1987	632.3	980.9	1,537.1	2,261.0	3,458.3	5,131.6	8,002.0	15,559.5	935.6	1,150.4	58.0	29.6
1988	616.5	982.6	1,523.3	2,255.4	3,421.4	5,121.6	8,081.0	15,933.1	941.5	1,145.2	57.1	28.3
1989	601.2	963.3	1,481.1	2,199.3	3,317.3	4,997.7	7,795.2	15,411.0	922.8	1,133.5	54.8	27.4
1990	587.0	934.3	1,458.0	2,156.9	3,248.7	4,899.7	7,633.4	15,140.4	912.1	1,071.5	52.2	25.6
1991	575.4	926.3	1,431.8	2,139.1	3,204.8	4,808.7	7,574.8	14,988.0	908.6	1,024.7	52.1	24.6
1992	568.0	901.9	1,402.4	2,116.4	3,151.6	4,720.6	7,452.0	14,743.6	899.0	960.4	48.0	23.8
1993	569.7	901.8	1,418.7	2,131.3	3,185.9	4,830.6	7,657.1	15,400.9	920.5	946.8	49.5	23.3
1994	571.1	876.8	1,401.1	2,091.6	3,152.0	4,720.2	7,582.3	15,210.3	912.0	902.6	47.4	22.8
1995	567.0	871.3	1,381.9	2,059.5	3,133.3	4,718.1	7,536.3	15,344.8	911.1	851.4	44.9	22.6
1996	554.8	851.3	1,370.3	2,021.8	3,119.6	4,673.6	7,503.9	15,324.6	895.2	820.7	42.2	22.1
1997	526.2	834.6	1,331.2	1,995.1	3,084.9	4,612.5	7,425.9	15,345.2	879.3	812.8	39.7	20.2
1998	515.5	811.2	1,295.9	1,978.2	3,058.5	4,564.5	7,439.5	15,111.7	876.4	818.2	37.6	20.0

Note appears at end of table

TABLE Ab988–1047   Death rate, by sex and age: 1900–1998   *Continued*

						Males						
						Age						
	10–14	15–19	20–24	25–29	30–34	35–39	40–44	45–49	50–54	55–59	60–64	65–69
	Ab1012	Ab1013	Ab1014	Ab1015	Ab1016	Ab1017	Ab1018	Ab1019	Ab1020	Ab1021	Ab1022	Ab1023
Year	Per 100,000	Per 100,000	Per 100,000	Per 100,000	Per 100,000	Per 100,000	Per 100,000	Per 100,000	Per 100,000	Per 100,000	Per 100,000	Per 100,000
1900	290.3	486.4	697.1	783.2	869.5	1,002.4	1,144.1	1,391.4	1,777.7	2,470.0	3,375.7	5,011.2
1901	286.4	463.0	672.4	789.8	880.5	1,009.5	1,199.4	1,436.0	1,811.5	2,522.3	3,490.3	5,044.3
1902	257.2	425.0	616.3	709.2	828.6	952.4	1,124.4	1,330.8	1,724.0	2,388.7	3,310.9	4,770.2
1903	279.4	439.9	622.1	719.2	823.3	962.9	1,136.3	1,390.9	1,735.4	2,468.3	3,443.7	4,948.0
1904	306.4	465.5	629.1	727.3	880.9	1,037.5	1,195.3	1,461.9	1,840.4	2,584.8	3,768.7	5,162.6
1905	280.9	439.8	614.8	691.6	836.1	999.9	1,133.8	1,467.2	1,746.4	2,478.0	3,624.1	5,013.5
1906	280.9	472.9	653.5	731.1	851.0	1,033.8	1,161.1	1,457.0	1,759.0	2,494.0	3,510.6	4,939.0
1907	280.6	473.2	679.6	744.8	893.8	1,078.5	1,217.7	1,538.2	1,853.4	2,617.5	3,731.6	5,302.9
1908	252.3	415.0	587.7	644.7	763.9	911.7	1,063.4	1,376.6	1,678.5	2,420.4	3,379.2	4,726.1
1909	241.1	380.5	532.9	613.4	720.4	880.3	1,040.0	1,328.6	1,653.5	2,328.3	3,335.8	4,834.5
1910	240.8	393.7	567.1	638.9	754.3	915.7	1,087.7	1,351.6	1,724.7	2,418.1	3,433.3	4,931.9
1911	232.3	381.4	551.9	616.2	732.9	904.1	1,065.7	1,320.4	1,696.1	2,378.6	3,336.6	4,838.0
1912	212.4	358.7	536.9	605.3	698.0	867.7	1,051.1	1,294.4	1,721.3	2,432.0	3,302.9	4,868.6
1913	222.3	378.4	552.2	624.0	714.6	877.8	1,076.5	1,310.9	1,717.5	2,429.2	3,235.4	4,822.9
1914	218.0	354.7	525.0	590.3	690.4	838.9	1,062.3	1,251.8	1,674.2	2,363.6	3,207.3	4,752.3
1915	206.1	340.0	503.1	569.2	673.7	820.3	1,025.7	1,262.8	1,640.2	2,431.6	3,185.6	4,789.5
1916	218.1	365.5	542.2	605.4	719.3	865.0	1,098.7	1,327.7	1,723.7	2,574.4	3,293.4	5,011.2
1917	227.4	393.7	598.1	652.5	769.6	894.5	1,143.7	1,364.0	1,765.2	2,587.1	3,353.9	5,057.5
1918	369.3	850.0	1,647.0	1,923.9	1,880.9	1,563.2	1,485.6	1,561.2	1,801.6	2,521.8	3,292.5	4,899.8
1919	246.2	452.0	613.2	695.0	796.3	861.4	959.2	1,152.5	1,457.3	2,086.5	2,874.6	4,323.3
1920	244.8	414.2	543.3	590.3	701.2	778.6	873.7	1,100.5	1,452.5	2,080.4	2,921.6	4,495.4
1921	225.8	329.6	439.2	449.8	512.5	629.0	771.2	1,018.5	1,324.5	1,909.6	2,832.5	4,184.5
1922	201.0	322.6	436.4	459.9	542.2	672.8	818.6	1,102.8	1,411.3	1,990.8	3,089.7	4,492.2
1923	205.3	327.2	450.7	477.7	544.4	712.7	837.4	1,145.4	1,496.5	2,021.4	3,264.1	4,561.7
1924	197.9	319.6	437.3	458.9	507.9	700.1	821.4	1,124.5	1,520.2	1,980.1	3,183.1	4,489.0
1925	199.6	319.1	437.2	470.9	511.0	701.4	825.5	1,126.8	1,562.9	2,016.6	3,197.5	4,594.3
1926	189.0	313.9	437.4	473.0	517.2	719.9	861.6	1,176.5	1,641.7	2,105.6	3,268.2	4,830.1
1927	185.6	297.3	408.2	456.4	494.7	695.7	824.8	1,110.2	1,577.7	2,051.7	3,114.8	4,661.8
1928	192.3	320.7	437.2	488.4	531.9	717.0	893.9	1,190.0	1,684.4	2,207.9	3,219.2	4,952.7
1929	185.6	312.8	437.5	491.6	540.3	693.4	915.6	1,194.0	1,663.1	2,274.3	3,226.7	4,941.1
1930	169.5	291.5	412.3	455.8	523.9	643.7	861.0	1,151.6	1,603.0	2,221.9	3,209.7	4,658.7
1931	167.0	284.7	392.1	431.3	514.1	644.3	856.2	1,153.5	1,564.6	2,207.7	3,129.2	4,469.5
1932	158.6	253.3	354.0	397.2	468.6	592.6	802.6	1,098.4	1,513.6	2,187.2	3,129.9	4,410.6
1933	155.4	241.8	346.9	392.5	461.8	577.6	797.6	1,104.1	1,507.2	2,149.0	3,165.2	4,394.4
1934	158.1	245.8	356.8	399.1	470.9	586.1	815.0	1,143.8	1,586.2	2,204.0	3,233.0	4,500.7
1935	162.2	244.1	349.2	402.0	460.4	595.2	812.4	1,133.9	1,552.9	2,209.5	3,156.5	4,554.7
1936	159.5	254.5	359.9	408.5	474.2	620.3	868.7	1,194.3	1,646.7	2,322.7	3,326.0	4,795.9
1937	145.5	245.2	341.4	388.3	458.0	589.4	828.3	1,164.4	1,619.4	2,284.9	3,261.7	4,699.9
1938	128.7	211.8	290.4	333.7	394.8	519.1	733.5	1,049.9	1,507.4	2,121.7	3,046.2	4,473.4
1939	124.5	199.7	274.9	311.5	378.6	497.0	700.9	1,023.5	1,496.0	2,156.5	3,044.7	4,446.3
1940	113.8	189.3	267.0	304.6	370.3	483.9	693.9	1,012.3	1,508.1	2,184.8	3,108.3	4,523.0
1941	110.3	192.8	266.5	296.7	359.7	474.5	679.6	998.8	1,472.7	2,144.2	3,016.7	4,392.7
1942	103.2	179.9	257.4	278.5	346.8	464.9	657.2	982.2	1,471.2	2,133.7	2,971.4	4,306.4
1943	106.7	191.6	276.5	267.1	322.7	445.0	647.6	964.5	1,496.3	2,186.6	3,041.7	4,346.1
1944	108.8	179.0	245.8	230.3	292.9	413.8	620.1	915.5	1,435.4	2,130.6	2,952.6	4,163.9
1945	103.7	171.7	209.1	219.9	287.0	409.9	618.7	914.2	1,421.6	2,134.3	2,940.1	4,096.6
1946	94.5	161.1	225.7	228.7	285.4	397.7	575.9	880.2	1,391.4	2,052.5	2,875.6	3,964.5
1947	81.9	150.4	218.7	217.8	266.2	381.6	581.1	882.2	1,411.8	2,106.2	2,970.6	4,100.5
1948	78.7	145.2	208.5	207.3	253.9	367.8	566.4	870.9	1,395.2	2,068.6	2,936.7	4,093.0
1949	77.7	140.2	192.1	196.7	236.5	352.7	539.2	860.8	1,324.8	2,008.1	2,912.3	4,079.5
1950	70.2	138.9	187.4	194.0	232.7	331.0	525.6	833.8	1,308.3	1,973.5	2,886.3	4,075.2
1951	71.0	140.3	183.5	195.9	229.6	327.1	527.7	814.6	1,326.1	1,985.4	2,850.8	4,104.1
1952	68.5	149.4	180.3	195.2	224.2	316.9	515.5	816.0	1,313.4	1,975.6	2,858.0	4,064.0
1953	66.1	141.8	180.7	183.9	216.6	303.3	505.1	801.9	1,295.6	1,943.4	2,868.5	4,090.6
1954	59.5	130.4	170.6	177.2	204.7	284.8	466.3	761.1	1,235.9	1,828.9	2,732.4	3,966.2
1955	58.5	132.1	180.3	175.5	198.6	286.0	464.8	751.5	1,220.5	1,835.9	2,728.9	4,003.0
1956	57.7	132.1	185.7	172.1	201.6	278.3	460.3	750.9	1,199.8	1,856.9	2,771.2	4,035.7
1957	58.8	135.5	180.0	171.7	205.6	287.8	471.0	756.0	1,242.5	1,879.3	2,871.9	4,190.4
1958	55.4	125.5	173.8	165.8	200.6	283.0	459.4	740.6	1,236.4	1,842.4	2,818.5	4,128.6
1959	58.2	128.0	172.5	167.7	201.8	281.3	451.7	746.0	1,220.6	1,839.3	2,783.4	4,058.1

(continued)

TABLE Ab988–1047   Death rate, by sex and age: 1900–1998   *Continued*

	Males											
	Age											
	10–14	15–19	20–24	25–29	30–34	35–39	40–44	45–49	50–54	55–59	60–64	65–69
	Ab1012	Ab1013	Ab1014	Ab1015	Ab1016	Ab1017	Ab1018	Ab1019	Ab1020	Ab1021	Ab1022	Ab1023
Year	Per 100,000	Per 100,000	Per 100,000	Per 100,000	Per 100,000	Per 100,000	Per 100,000	Per 100,000	Per 100,000	Per 100,000	Per 100,000	Per 100,000
1960	54.5	126.9	170.2	171.1	198.7	286.5	457.6	758.9	1,245.4	1,845.8	2,857.7	4,132.0
1961	52.5	121.8	167.6	163.9	195.4	279.9	451.2	732.1	1,202.9	1,780.5	2,810.2	4,077.7
1962	52.8	120.5	169.6	165.6	197.2	288.0	451.3	743.1	1,224.1	1,807.0	2,840.6	4,161.1
1963	50.8	124.3	171.3	173.1	201.5	294.0	456.0	756.3	1,232.9	1,853.3	2,906.4	4,238.5
1964	52.2	130.9	174.6	177.1	211.0	297.5	464.3	746.7	1,214.1	1,814.8	2,894.7	4,097.8
1965	50.9	134.3	176.1	180.6	207.8	299.0	462.9	745.8	1,226.2	1,820.7	2,903.3	4,137.7
1966	51.5	142.6	186.7	183.7	212.4	300.9	471.3	756.7	1,231.8	1,858.9	2,899.2	4,173.0
1967	50.9	143.2	184.4	187.3	213.6	305.0	469.0	750.1	1,205.0	1,834.0	2,833.9	4,069.9
1968	52.6	153.2	198.1	196.5	223.0	313.2	483.8	770.0	1,224.4	1,887.0	2,902.1	4,224.9
1969	51.3	160.9	207.3	201.8	224.6	316.7	488.9	762.1	1,189.5	1,861.7	2,804.4	4,161.7
1970	51.2	154.9	206.5	196.8	225.3	310.6	482.6	753.8	1,172.3	1,851.2	2,769.1	4,095.9
1971	49.5	156.2	206.9	200.6	220.9	308.4	464.0	734.6	1,141.0	1,804.0	2,706.9	3,983.2
1972	50.4	157.4	212.5	196.7	220.8	301.0	461.5	748.9	1,138.9	1,805.3	2,734.6	3,990.3
1973	51.1	158.9	214.1	201.8	219.1	301.0	451.4	733.1	1,105.4	1,774.0	2,676.7	3,925.0
1974	48.3	151.8	204.1	191.4	209.9	281.5	429.4	709.3	1,075.5	1,685.6	2,569.9	3,787.6
1975	44.9	144.6	202.0	193.5	201.2	273.0	416.0	668.2	1,048.4	1,607.5	2,494.5	3,625.0
1976	43.3	137.0	191.2	180.3	191.6	258.1	402.6	649.4	1,022.6	1,569.8	2,462.6	3,573.8
1977	43.6	142.1	194.0	185.8	187.9	255.8	389.8	627.7	1,004.4	1,515.1	2,393.0	3,459.3
1978	42.9	141.4	194.7	183.5	187.1	250.4	379.0	610.7	987.7	1,479.7	2,370.9	3,425.7
1979	40.0	142.6	196.1	191.5	189.7	242.7	366.8	593.8	957.4	1,440.3	2,264.7	3,324.8
1980	38.3	141.1	199.3	192.5	192.4	241.7	361.1	585.3	943.5	1,461.7	2,218.0	3,382.7
1981	36.7	128.3	183.3	187.7	189.7	240.1	353.0	574.1	916.5	1,433.6	2,160.4	3,293.3
1982	34.9	122.8	170.3	173.1	185.5	225.4	331.2	546.0	884.6	1,395.3	2,118.4	3,241.2
1983	34.2	114.7	158.1	164.8	181.5	219.2	323.1	524.6	867.5	1,389.9	2,115.9	3,201.2
1984	34.8	112.9	160.8	163.7	185.0	223.7	326.2	515.5	850.5	1,363.6	2,102.3	3,141.4
1985	35.0	113.0	158.8	166.1	191.2	235.5	330.6	513.9	841.4	1,355.8	2,085.9	3,116.1
1986	36.3	122.2	169.3	176.8	211.1	249.4	336.8	504.9	823.7	1,307.3	2,051.8	3,052.5
1987	35.1	117.3	163.4	175.4	212.5	260.0	328.7	500.0	816.3	1,284.3	2,030.3	3,000.2
1988	34.4	123.0	166.2	178.4	217.8	269.4	337.8	497.3	793.2	1,275.0	2,003.1	2,994.4
1989	33.9	120.8	159.9	182.3	223.1	276.2	341.0	496.9	773.4	1,251.9	1,943.3	2,907.5
1990	31.4	127.6	163.6	183.8	221.0	277.3	339.2	487.8	752.5	1,209.4	1,902.2	2,844.5
1991	32.9	127.9	163.1	180.8	222.4	278.8	344.6	496.6	735.9	1,190.0	1,862.1	2,814.3
1992	30.8	121.4	156.9	176.8	223.0	281.7	358.3	485.1	727.7	1,156.4	1,815.7	2,777.1
1993	31.8	124.7	162.0	179.3	232.7	289.2	370.3	486.4	732.5	1,154.6	1,827.2	2,784.4
1994	31.3	125.3	161.0	177.1	234.7	291.8	376.1	490.7	735.8	1,119.0	1,804.6	2,711.6
1995	31.2	118.2	158.0	173.1	230.8	290.3	376.4	496.5	727.8	1,105.8	1,765.4	2,651.0
1996	28.9	111.1	150.2	154.6	198.9	255.4	344.0	475.0	705.8	1,081.3	1,745.3	2,587.6
1997	27.9	104.3	144.2	144.5	172.9	221.5	311.6	456.6	665.5	1,048.2	1,679.6	2,550.6
1998	26.9	98.7	142.3	139.4	163.1	213.5	305.3	450.8	654.1	1,022.4	1,634.0	2,508.6

TABLE Ab988–1047   Death rate, by sex and age: 1900–1998   *Continued*

	Males					Females							
	Age				Total		Age						
	70–74	75–79	80–84	85 and over		0	1–4	5–9	10–14	15–19	20–24	25–29
	Ab1024	Ab1025	Ab1026	Ab1027	Ab1028 [1]	Ab1029	Ab1030	Ab1031	Ab1032	Ab1033	Ab1034	Ab1035
Year	Per 100,000	Per 100,000	Per 100,000	Per 100,000	Per 100,000	Per 100,000	Per 100,000	Per 100,000	Per 100,000	Per 100,000	Per 100,000	Per 100,000
1900	7,243.1	10,843.0	17,142.9	26,877.2	1,646.9	14,541.2	1,912.3	462.0	306.4	483.3	665.3	792.6
1901	7,175.2	10,691.1	17,936.9	26,806.6	1,556.9	12,610.5	1,619.6	415.9	260.8	446.2	627.4	734.3
1902	6,919.7	10,138.0	16,230.9	24,862.0	1,460.5	12,409.9	1,596.8	385.8	247.7	418.0	588.3	688.0
1903	7,145.4	10,727.4	16,919.9	26,266.3	1,481.4	11,833.1	1,492.8	408.5	256.8	428.5	571.1	691.8
1904	7,643.0	11,131.9	17,878.3	28,074.7	1,551.8	12,423.9	1,522.6	421.3	304.1	477.2	616.8	728.8
1905	7,190.2	11,002.1	16,956.9	27,054.2	1,502.5	12,546.0	1,419.2	388.0	278.6	438.8	576.1	682.6
1906	7,128.9	10,897.3	16,444.6	26,155.4	1,467.3	12,916.0	1,518.2	363.7	263.5	417.9	567.7	664.2
1907	7,709.3	11,412.0	17,685.2	27,501.2	1,478.4	12,389.0	1,408.4	354.8	250.8	402.7	553.7	633.0
1908	7,011.9	10,852.4	16,366.3	25,149.6	1,379.8	11,909.0	1,335.7	339.5	243.5	380.5	512.7	592.2
1909	6,994.9	10,726.4	16,002.7	25,140.6	1,338.8	11,317.3	1,290.4	318.8	219.8	346.6	485.6	568.3
1910	7,288.3	10,907.2	16,725.3	25,579.4	1,374.3	11,762.1	1,335.3	336.8	231.0	350.0	494.1	582.9
1911	7,286.6	10,642.1	16,599.5	24,927.2	1,303.7	10,184.1	1,128.4	297.4	211.9	350.6	500.4	570.3
1912	7,184.2	10,782.5	16,380.3	24,865.1	1,265.9	9,849.4	1,038.5	269.9	189.8	330.8	467.9	540.8
1913	7,218.4	10,389.4	16,602.4	24,138.4	1,280.1	10,167.3	1,137.7	297.6	204.9	334.6	478.3	539.1
1914	7,335.2	10,111.8	16,594.2	23,686.4	1,236.6	9,509.9	972.5	278.0	196.1	326.3	465.8	527.2
1915	7,524.5	10,435.2	17,189.1	24,672.3	1,231.3	8,995.3	878.7	243.3	187.1	321.9	457.7	513.9
1916	7,668.3	10,883.3	17,495.4	25,546.4	1,282.7	9,281.2	1,052.3	262.7	191.9	346.1	495.3	540.2
1917	7,714.0	10,855.4	17,626.0	25,107.1	1,285.4	9,147.2	1,011.5	271.3	210.2	367.1	515.9	553.2
1918	7,296.6	10,140.9	15,650.3	22,756.1	1,638.7	9,850.9	1,545.8	437.4	381.0	707.5	1,173.4	1,433.8
1919	6,518.4	9,568.9	14,555.9	22,958.9	1,231.5	7,974.8	881.4	281.7	226.3	425.2	638.0	748.5
1920	6,906.5	10,479.5	16,122.8	25,300.9	1,258.2	8,067.3	945.7	277.6	214.7	391.6	601.9	678.4
1921	6,542.3	9,804.6	15,129.8	24,123.7	1,103.4	7,082.1	758.8	259.8	193.7	323.5	460.7	471.3
1922	7,115.1	10,380.9	16,213.1	25,784.6	1,110.7	6,787.3	695.0	219.7	172.1	316.7	452.4	480.0
1923	7,328.1	10,863.0	16,967.2	27,939.9	1,149.8	7,164.7	766.1	221.9	170.9	324.5	456.1	479.9
1924	7,053.7	10,403.5	16,492.6	26,376.0	1,085.5	6,699.8	641.3	203.8	161.5	307.5	449.8	463.1
1925	7,050.8	10,556.7	16,922.2	27,352.5	1,094.7	6,597.9	607.8	191.5	162.2	308.9	448.2	477.1
1926	7,223.5	11,228.4	17,531.8	28,129.2	1,134.0	6,838.3	683.2	194.2	153.7	301.1	439.8	485.9
1927	6,825.1	10,532.4	16,098.4	25,423.3	1,051.3	5,998.9	556.9	187.0	149.3	281.8	413.3	457.0
1928	7,165.9	11,372.2	17,317.6	27,146.5	1,111.4	6,356.4	610.3	193.6	155.0	295.0	432.2	470.0
1929	7,115.2	11,079.5	16,850.9	25,980.3	1,096.4	6,286.1	589.6	188.5	144.1	283.4	419.8	466.7
1930	6,905.6	10,299.9	15,430.5	23,671.2	1,036.7	6,073.8	523.3	169.9	135.7	264.1	377.0	424.0
1931	6,821.9	10,159.5	15,216.6	23,409.2	1,009.3	5,646.5	490.6	164.3	133.2	242.4	363.2	401.6
1932	6,839.8	10,444.5	15,736.3	24,233.7	1,000.7	5,386.2	435.4	152.3	125.5	221.8	330.6	378.6
1933	6,758.1	10,210.5	15,366.0	23,272.2	972.8	5,403.0	441.3	146.7	120.2	205.0	309.5	365.4
1934	6,784.9	10,654.3	15,627.5	23,512.0	997.2	5,853.6	474.0	148.8	124.4	202.3	304.3	362.0
1935	6,547.0	10,659.4	15,462.9	23,466.8	985.1	5,280.3	411.9	147.4	124.0	200.6	295.8	356.8
1936	6,789.6	11,386.7	16,708.2	25,267.1	1,035.5	5,489.6	407.8	136.7	122.0	206.3	300.0	363.0
1937	6,559.7	10,954.7	16,326.0	23,803.7	1,003.2	5,359.9	390.3	125.9	110.7	192.9	279.0	331.2
1938	6,384.7	10,276.0	15,395.5	22,215.5	955.9	5,065.5	358.8	115.3	98.4	172.8	243.7	290.0
1939	6,503.2	10,195.4	16,172.5	23,263.9	951.4	4,684.3	293.3	98.2	88.0	159.9	220.5	268.5
1940	6,764.9	10,311.0	15,574.1	24,257.2	952.2	4,764.8	265.9	94.0	85.2	153.5	209.7	246.5
1941	6,552.0	9,724.8	15,180.5	23,157.0	921.5	4,629.8	259.8	90.0	78.6	143.9	198.8	229.8
1942	6,331.8	9,365.4	14,608.7	22,170.6	899.1	4,291.5	225.6	80.2	67.8	127.3	186.0	211.9
1943	6,596.9	9,896.6	15,453.8	24,264.2	941.5	3,847.9	235.1	88.2	73.7	128.1	181.0	206.4
1944	6,287.6	9,488.8	14,357.5	22,513.5	900.4	3,897.4	215.2	81.4	70.0	116.6	171.8	190.7
1945	6,104.8	9,370.1	13,648.1	22,129.6	878.0	3,716.9	186.1	78.8	69.3	111.2	160.9	180.6
1946	5,902.1	9,139.2	12,973.5	22,132.6	862.0	4,014.1	166.1	70.7	62.0	103.2	152.7	169.0
1947	6,124.8	9,386.9	13,206.3	22,954.5	868.8	2,999.8	145.7	60.4	53.4	96.8	136.7	157.9
1948	6,045.9	9,260.5	12,972.8	22,681.0	848.2	3,104.0	145.5	59.0	52.0	89.1	120.9	140.1
1949	5,964.3	9,127.3	12,824.0	21,542.9	831.4	3,055.8	136.4	56.1	49.1	79.8	107.9	129.7
1950	6,005.8	8,932.1	13,008.8	21,083.7	817.4	2,841.0	124.5	51.6	44.6	76.7	100.4	122.9
1951	5,959.9	8,887.0	13,185.8	20,419.1	818.8	2,775.1	125.3	52.0	40.9	73.5	95.1	118.5
1952	5,823.2	8,706.0	13,213.5	19,311.0	812.0	2,771.4	129.2	51.8	44.2	75.1	90.4	113.9
1953	5,839.3	8,688.5	13,405.6	19,619.8	807.3	2,642.6	117.4	46.2	39.2	68.4	81.2	102.4
1954	5,658.2	8,308.3	12,720.5	18,482.1	773.8	2,518.2	107.2	43.9	35.2	58.3	76.1	93.5
1955	5,737.5	8,520.7	13,001.2	19,346.1	785.1	2,453.2	102.8	41.6	33.8	58.4	76.9	91.7
1956	5,739.9	8,509.0	13,093.1	19,833.4	788.4	2,413.9	100.8	40.3	34.0	58.0	74.0	89.7
1957	5,886.2	8,534.2	13,109.8	20,549.9	809.8	2,409.0	103.0	41.6	35.1	60.6	75.4	93.3
1958	5,809.2	8,573.0	13,159.3	20,711.6	805.5	2,434.6	103.2	40.7	32.9	54.1	70.1	89.1
1959	5,745.9	8,386.7	12,916.4	20,459.2	794.5	2,367.4	96.9	41.0	32.7	54.5	70.6	87.9

Note appears at end of table

(continued)

TABLE Ab988–1047   Death rate, by sex and age: 1900–1998   *Continued*

	Males				Females							
	Age				Total	Age						
	70–74	75–79	80–84	85 and over		0	1–4	5–9	10–14	15–19	20–24	25–29
	Ab1024	Ab1025	Ab1026	Ab1027	Ab1028 [1]	Ab1029	Ab1030	Ab1031	Ab1032	Ab1033	Ab1034	Ab1035
Year	Per 100,000	Per 100,000	Per 100,000	Per 100,000	Per 100,000	Per 100,000	Per 100,000	Per 100,000	Per 100,000	Per 100,000	Per 100,000	Per 100,000
1960	5,922.8	8,551.0	13,213.6	20,956.3	806.0	2,330.4	98.1	41.2	32.3	53.6	69.6	89.5
1961	5,688.0	8,387.2	12,796.7	21,099.0	790.4	2,233.5	92.6	38.9	30.8	52.1	67.2	86.2
1962	5,779.5	8,565.2	12,865.7	22,233.7	806.5	2,219.1	92.1	39.5	30.6	52.5	70.2	88.7
1963	5,964.7	8,812.3	13,136.5	22,954.5	819.1	2,215.5	92.6	38.5	31.3	54.6	70.3	89.3
1964	5,796.2	8,567.4	12,633.0	21,650.9	801.3	2,192.8	89.1	37.4	30.6	54.8	70.9	87.5
1965	5,833.9	8,699.5	12,807.6	22,108.6	803.4	2,128.5	87.1	36.8	29.7	53.9	70.4	85.7
1966	5,938.9	8,741.6	12,805.4	21,987.3	810.8	2,084.8	87.2	37.1	30.4	58.5	71.2	87.2
1967	5,913.7	8,575.5	12,454.6	21,344.5	796.2	1,983.6	78.9	35.9	29.7	57.9	71.2	84.2
1968	6,127.0	8,834.8	12,762.1	21,708.0	824.1	1,956.1	80.7	36.7	30.2	60.3	73.3	86.5
1969	5,962.5	8,638.9	12,673.5	20,876.0	813.5	1,903.6	80.2	35.9	31.0	63.1	74.4	85.8
1970	5,875.4	8,610.4	12,278.1	19,468.9	804.7	1,852.6	75.5	34.3	29.4	61.2	74.4	87.0
1971	5,823.1	8,516.9	12,139.9	19,902.4	801.4	1,642.8	73.8	34.7	30.0	62.1	72.7	86.7
1972	5,980.3	8,648.1	12,218.0	19,816.2	808.7	1,575.3	71.0	34.7	30.0	61.0	73.4	82.2
1973	5,876.4	8,538.6	12,092.8	20,064.2	808.3	1,542.2	69.4	34.1	29.0	60.7	71.7	80.0
1974	5,726.8	8,160.0	11,694.1	19,272.9	788.2	1,502.1	64.6	29.9	27.9	55.6	67.1	77.2
1975	5,564.8	7,852.3	11,343.0	18,141.5	761.3	1,410.9	62.7	28.6	25.3	53.8	66.1	73.1
1976	5,445.5	7,791.0	11,227.2	18,672.1	767.5	1,375.7	60.4	27.8	24.7	52.5	63.2	70.6
1977	5,332.5	7,611.3	11,054.1	18,068.2	755.8	1,256.9	59.7	26.5	25.1	55.5	63.9	69.4
1978	5,259.7	7,461.7	11,249.0	18,208.0	764.3	1,222.6	58.8	27.1	24.2	54.3	65.0	70.2
1979	5,065.1	7,242.5	10,963.3	17,605.4	752.5	1,176.4	57.0	25.3	23.3	52.7	62.3	67.5
1980	5,046.4	7,422.3	11,163.2	18,606.5	782.7	1,133.5	54.4	25.7	22.9	53.2	61.6	67.6
1981	4,952.5	7,223.2	10,930.8	18,253.8	774.7	1,070.1	53.1	23.6	22.0	49.7	59.0	67.0
1982	4,855.3	7,189.3	10,678.5	17,940.5	770.9	1,029.7	52.2	23.5	21.1	46.0	56.1	62.9
1983	4,886.9	7,274.9	10,879.4	18,386.7	788.1	991.3	48.4	22.0	20.2	45.8	54.5	62.2
1984	4,825.2	7,146.1	10,814.0	18,317.0	794.4	987.3	46.8	20.8	21.5	46.1	54.8	60.4
1985	4,836.3	7,170.2	10,937.5	18,605.7	808.7	950.4	44.8	21.4	20.6	46.2	52.4	60.1
1986	4,769.6	7,059.9	10,729.6	18,356.3	812.0	922.7	46.2	19.7	20.4	48.2	55.0	62.9
1987	4,683.2	6,941.9	10,598.0	18,206.9	816.3	918.5	45.8	19.6	18.8	47.7	54.3	64.9
1988	4,599.6	6,897.8	10,649.9	18,705.9	830.8	921.2	45.5	20.6	20.7	48.1	54.5	65.9
1989	4,424.3	6,670.7	10,246.6	18,015.7	818.5	917.1	44.5	20.6	20.6	48.7	52.8	65.1
1990	4,315.2	6,547.4	10,070.6	17,837.6	809.4	847.1	40.8	18.5	20.0	46.7	51.2	64.1
1991	4,224.3	6,371.5	10,003.6	17,704.0	811.1	804.4	42.8	18.4	18.3	47.2	52.5	62.8
1992	4,107.6	6,211.9	9,752.2	17,528.1	806.8	774.1	39.0	16.9	18.2	43.9	50.0	62.6
1993	4,136.1	6,298.0	9,967.0	18,053.8	839.2	760.4	39.9	19.1	19.3	45.5	51.4	64.8
1994	4,071.7	6,073.2	9,750.9	17,741.4	838.6	737.6	38.3	17.1	18.9	44.7	51.4	65.5
1995	4,031.1	6,034.5	9,609.5	17,714.9	848.3	695.0	36.3	16.8	19.7	45.7	50.4	64.7
1996	3,995.7	5,935.2	9,479.0	17,571.7	849.7	673.4	34.3	16.7	18.9	44.0	48.4	62.4
1997	3,941.9	5,824.6	9,313.5	17,461.9	849.0	661.1	31.8	16.6	18.3	43.3	49.4	58.6
1998	3,867.0	5,719.7	9,226.6	16,763.3	853.5	681.3	31.4	15.3	17.2	40.8	46.5	56.3

Note appears at end of table

TABLE Ab988–1047   Death rate, by sex and age: 1900–1998   *Continued*

	Females											
	Age											
	30–34	35–39	40–44	45–49	50–54	55–59	60–64	65–69	70–74	75–79	80–84	85 and over
	Ab1036	Ab1037	Ab1038	Ab1039	Ab1040	Ab1041	Ab1042	Ab1043	Ab1044	Ab1045	Ab1046	Ab1047
Year	Per 100,000	Per 100,000	Per 100,000	Per 100,000	Per 100,000	Per 100,000	Per 100,000	Per 100,000	Per 100,000	Per 100,000	Per 100,000	Per 100,000
1900	841.4	923.5	1,037.0	1,243.4	1,619.8	2,215.3	3,007.4	4,418.7	6,715.8	9,817.1	16,133.5	25,517.4
1901	823.8	883.0	1,046.3	1,183.9	1,619.5	2,181.8	3,110.0	4,433.0	6,656.0	9,968.2	16,197.6	25,557.1
1902	770.6	820.5	958.2	1,111.2	1,474.7	2,010.3	2,839.8	4,107.0	6,170.9	8,979.7	14,644.7	22,611.1
1903	763.8	857.8	958.3	1,127.2	1,512.1	2,156.4	3,005.8	4,332.5	6,408.7	9,608.0	15,514.7	24,713.2
1904	790.6	884.6	972.5	1,182.7	1,588.0	2,169.6	3,127.3	4,481.1	6,947.5	9,970.7	16,280.6	26,209.0
1905	758.8	837.2	950.3	1,175.1	1,503.5	2,133.3	3,077.5	4,481.8	6,610.7	9,929.9	15,250.2	25,486.5
1906	749.6	815.2	894.1	1,163.0	1,440.6	2,051.2	2,963.1	4,310.0	6,436.7	9,735.5	15,040.0	25,028.7
1907	747.1	843.2	913.4	1,164.3	1,482.9	2,158.3	3,115.7	4,541.4	6,871.5	10,396.1	16,494.6	26,467.2
1908	681.9	763.5	849.3	1,080.3	1,389.3	1,968.9	2,888.5	4,246.5	6,369.4	9,530.4	15,117.9	24,640.5
1909	642.0	754.8	813.8	1,044.6	1,322.9	1,938.4	2,818.0	4,259.6	6,276.2	9,716.2	14,598.2	23,986.1
1910	644.8	737.2	853.6	1,046.4	1,396.1	1,973.6	2,838.8	4,332.8	6,554.5	9,890.1	15,504.5	24,599.8
1911	636.0	745.2	837.1	1,018.0	1,384.3	1,966.6	2,789.3	4,241.7	6,564.3	9,745.6	15,191.6	24,415.1
1912	600.8	712.2	820.9	998.8	1,352.4	1,969.2	2,760.1	4,228.1	6,389.4	9,843.9	14,966.8	23,712.2
1913	597.7	710.3	837.4	1,013.2	1,371.5	1,946.0	2,698.4	4,146.4	6,369.0	9,681.0	14,645.2	23,168.9
1914	589.7	691.0	815.1	1,000.8	1,344.3	1,921.6	2,677.6	4,084.3	6,426.1	9,359.1	14,569.8	22,729.0
1915	577.3	679.5	822.2	1,004.4	1,352.6	1,984.5	2,719.5	4,203.6	6,757.5	9,853.5	15,079.7	23,532.4
1916	608.1	708.3	854.5	1,051.1	1,363.7	2,067.8	2,767.9	4,349.6	6,820.3	10,068.6	15,722.3	24,659.6
1917	626.5	722.8	859.7	1,053.5	1,376.8	2,072.8	2,787.9	4,337.9	6,775.2	10,066.9	15,634.5	24,205.2
1918	1,360.0	1,157.3	1,105.2	1,229.6	1,508.8	2,085.9	2,784.4	4,232.8	6,469.2	9,192.7	14,131.1	21,805.0
1919	772.9	787.2	846.3	1,014.3	1,320.8	1,844.8	2,542.5	3,952.5	6,000.2	8,990.5	13,523.5	21,676.0
1920	752.7	779.6	823.5	1,027.0	1,337.7	1,880.9	2,678.5	4,121.9	6,375.5	9,810.8	15,179.7	24,466.8
1921	528.1	614.9	702.9	934.8	1,233.0	1,700.6	2,541.7	3,797.8	5,967.1	9,137.5	14,221.3	23,756.1
1922	535.7	639.2	727.9	953.5	1,277.2	1,710.2	2,691.6	3,966.5	6,352.8	9,590.9	14,945.9	25,835.7
1923	519.0	647.5	729.1	956.9	1,320.0	1,754.8	2,768.5	4,038.0	6,558.2	9,952.9	16,062.0	27,988.4
1924	477.9	617.5	710.4	936.5	1,308.9	1,657.4	2,665.4	3,763.8	6,177.5	9,209.2	15,200.1	26,025.5
1925	475.2	635.5	712.9	930.8	1,299.3	1,691.2	2,686.2	3,919.1	6,138.1	9,431.4	15,266.2	27,130.3
1926	481.3	642.0	725.4	959.6	1,357.8	1,779.6	2,753.6	4,099.0	6,344.3	9,968.7	15,911.6	27,843.8
1927	467.8	596.7	705.0	911.7	1,280.7	1,685.1	2,541.7	3,899.1	5,890.7	9,249.3	14,356.0	24,696.0
1928	499.5	631.9	754.9	948.7	1,348.4	1,795.7	2,658.8	4,139.2	6,203.9	10,041.1	15,482.0	26,593.6
1929	499.8	599.6	738.6	946.5	1,313.0	1,817.6	2,635.8	4,104.6	6,129.1	9,817.4	15,123.5	25,015.9
1930	463.8	547.8	693.6	907.2	1,245.4	1,756.5	2,573.3	3,821.2	5,884.6	9,043.0	13,858.0	22,138.0
1931	455.7	529.7	680.1	885.9	1,222.9	1,715.3	2,514.7	3,660.3	5,777.5	8,818.1	13,521.2	21,428.5
1932	428.7	508.7	651.5	859.4	1,187.5	1,689.1	2,506.0	3,626.1	5,929.7	9,162.6	14,020.3	22,659.1
1933	409.5	485.7	629.6	835.4	1,157.2	1,648.3	2,455.6	3,545.2	5,697.4	8,956.7	13,470.8	21,442.3
1934	402.8	476.6	630.8	836.0	1,180.9	1,649.3	2,480.0	3,556.0	5,696.2	9,094.0	13,733.2	21,711.5
1935	396.1	478.4	620.2	832.4	1,150.9	1,636.3	2,403.1	3,580.1	5,503.8	9,092.3	13,332.0	21,698.5
1936	398.2	493.4	636.0	843.3	1,175.8	1,662.8	2,486.8	3,739.3	5,703.8	9,785.4	14,468.5	23,525.7
1937	378.2	468.1	615.8	817.2	1,148.5	1,608.2	2,395.9	3,593.3	5,427.5	9,334.2	13,822.1	21,904.6
1938	330.9	422.9	558.7	757.8	1,077.0	1,530.7	2,265.2	3,436.5	5,256.6	8,862.7	13,371.9	20,539.0
1939	316.6	406.3	529.7	738.2	1,063.3	1,529.6	2,259.4	3,375.8	5,330.4	8,769.3	13,988.2	21,629.4
1940	302.4	385.0	521.8	712.6	1,025.3	1,468.8	2,175.5	3,363.2	5,397.2	8,581.3	13,491.9	22,429.5
1941	284.7	357.2	500.6	687.4	992.7	1,413.7	2,077.8	3,202.6	5,110.5	8,025.5	12,931.8	20,903.4
1942	264.7	345.7	475.9	654.1	963.0	1,368.6	2,030.4	3,094.5	4,982.5	7,700.6	12,440.3	20,297.5
1943	265.8	348.7	474.2	660.1	988.7	1,423.8	2,067.9	3,167.8	5,183.1	8,167.7	13,185.2	22,120.3
1944	253.7	332.9	454.9	613.0	937.4	1,355.5	1,971.1	2,989.0	4,925.4	7,777.3	12,414.5	20,777.0
1945	240.0	323.8	432.5	612.2	902.6	1,322.6	1,902.9	2,885.8	4,704.3	7,626.5	11,678.9	20,121.5
1946	217.5	297.5	404.0	585.1	861.6	1,262.9	1,847.9	2,762.2	4,577.6	7,422.7	11,207.5	20,320.8
1947	201.8	279.4	390.8	578.3	858.7	1,249.8	1,846.7	2,767.0	4,620.1	7,525.7	11,330.0	20,756.6
1948	181.5	264.5	378.5	550.0	821.1	1,211.4	1,796.8	2,695.2	4,472.8	7,354.7	10,991.8	20,323.7
1949	172.0	245.3	360.1	546.1	783.1	1,162.4	1,753.1	2,659.0	4,363.1	7,115.9	10,661.2	19,457.8
1950	162.0	232.9	350.4	520.3	767.0	1,124.0	1,735.6	2,567.2	4,280.9	6,957.9	10,705.2	18,834.3
1951	155.4	224.9	342.6	499.3	781.3	1,106.6	1,697.9	2,536.5	4,176.7	6,868.5	10,857.8	18,658.2
1952	149.0	219.3	330.4	487.4	758.4	1,080.8	1,641.3	2,497.1	4,098.6	6,702.5	10,555.8	18,324.9
1953	139.0	204.5	319.1	471.1	744.2	1,061.8	1,594.8	2,487.7	4,041.9	6,595.2	10,698.3	18,422.6
1954	129.4	191.0	301.1	446.0	708.5	986.2	1,515.6	2,363.7	3,813.3	6,261.4	10,056.9	17,525.9
1955	125.1	188.1	292.2	431.6	670.3	981.2	1,489.1	2,385.3	3,766.3	6,371.1	10,275.7	18,365.2
1956	124.9	182.2	287.8	432.8	649.3	990.8	1,478.6	2,365.4	3,729.7	6,287.2	10,302.2	18,509.5
1957	131.7	188.3	286.2	437.8	671.5	994.7	1,515.0	2,405.6	3,778.1	6,278.0	10,419.2	19,020.0
1958	124.8	180.8	276.8	427.9	656.9	963.0	1,489.2	2,332.9	3,729.5	6,212.0	10,446.9	19,012.7
1959	125.0	177.3	271.5	417.2	636.3	943.7	1,450.5	2,265.5	3,619.3	6,040.4	10,275.8	18,621.1

(continued)

TABLE Ab988-1047   Death rate, by sex and age: 1900-1998   *Continued*

	Females											
	Age											
	30-34	35-39	40-44	45-49	50-54	55-59	60-64	65-69	70-74	75-79	80-84	85 and over
	Ab1036	Ab1037	Ab1038	Ab1039	Ab1040	Ab1041	Ab1042	Ab1043	Ab1044	Ab1045	Ab1046	Ab1047
Year	Per 100,000	Per 100,000	Per 100,000	Per 100,000	Per 100,000	Per 100,000	Per 100,000	Per 100,000	Per 100,000	Per 100,000	Per 100,000	Per 100,000
1960	122.9	180.7	281.0	423.9	638.1	930.3	1,494.3	2,251.2	3,632.7	6,012.0	10,376.9	18,782.3
1961	121.5	178.3	269.3	414.6	628.1	882.3	1,455.4	2,187.2	3,504.9	5,820.8	9,946.6	18,703.7
1962	121.9	184.1	275.1	420.8	633.6	895.4	1,470.4	2,202.0	3,511.3	5,897.5	9,975.2	19,408.1
1963	123.0	187.1	278.8	426.3	640.0	910.7	1,486.4	2,201.5	3,516.4	5,941.5	9,981.7	19,797.0
1964	126.5	186.0	276.5	421.0	645.0	885.0	1,447.7	2,137.2	3,367.0	5,706.2	9,546.4	18,901.1
1965	126.1	185.2	279.5	426.4	635.3	882.3	1,418.2	2,137.6	3,309.5	5,699.1	9,468.4	18,891.3
1966	125.6	181.7	279.9	427.9	631.5	885.5	1,381.5	2,146.2	3,365.0	5,694.4	9,424.0	18,846.3
1967	120.5	183.9	273.9	421.9	621.2	885.3	1,341.5	2,097.6	3,268.1	5,482.6	9,059.3	18,028.8
1968	121.3	187.6	285.0	432.9	634.5	915.3	1,373.5	2,145.4	3,327.0	5,611.2	9,278.5	18,420.6
1969	122.1	186.9	283.1	420.6	614.3	901.6	1,316.4	2,088.4	3,260.0	5,399.5	9,060.4	17,699.7
1970	117.2	183.9	275.7	422.0	616.8	903.8	1,307.0	2,033.0	3,227.9	5,323.7	8,648.2	16,091.4
1971	116.2	176.6	273.9	411.3	601.9	882.8	1,294.3	1,949.9	3,173.5	5,191.7	8,440.5	16,347.9
1972	114.7	172.1	269.5	410.8	583.8	881.7	1,282.0	1,971.1	3,235.6	5,196.9	8,359.5	16,372.2
1973	109.3	169.6	261.4	404.0	581.1	881.4	1,270.2	1,894.4	3,147.6	5,123.6	8,200.5	16,482.2
1974	102.4	155.4	251.4	382.9	561.4	834.4	1,245.0	1,814.6	3,063.7	4,843.0	7,918.8	15,722.0
1975	96.4	146.6	237.9	365.5	542.6	808.5	1,199.7	1,722.6	2,935.7	4,570.6	7,500.4	14,451.4
1976	92.9	139.1	226.1	355.6	535.0	792.6	1,198.8	1,704.1	2,847.2	4,489.9	7,418.2	14,828.1
1977	88.3	135.4	221.5	345.0	526.6	768.3	1,179.5	1,681.1	2,753.8	4,331.0	7,166.0	14,132.2
1978	85.8	128.4	214.8	340.6	518.2	755.4	1,171.9	1,673.1	2,713.7	4,263.2	7,249.7	14,246.8
1979	82.9	127.2	201.7	319.3	502.3	733.4	1,130.2	1,643.8	2,616.9	4,127.2	7,042.1	13,788.6
1980	83.6	123.4	199.9	322.7	499.6	749.0	1,138.2	1,712.8	2,655.9	4,225.5	7,210.1	14,519.2
1981	81.6	121.8	191.2	316.0	491.1	747.0	1,125.1	1,691.7	2,599.2	4,056.3	7,009.7	14,231.4
1982	78.4	113.4	183.8	302.5	473.7	733.9	1,116.8	1,672.7	2,576.7	4,050.7	6,848.3	13,845.9
1983	76.3	110.2	178.1	293.5	479.2	737.8	1,129.8	1,674.2	2,601.6	4,061.6	6,878.8	14,260.7
1984	78.0	111.6	178.8	289.4	467.2	731.6	1,122.3	1,676.5	2,597.0	4,051.9	6,820.0	14,215.1
1985	79.1	110.6	173.5	287.7	467.8	728.1	1,124.9	1,675.1	2,596.9	4,065.7	6,834.9	14,554.5
1986	81.8	111.0	177.5	281.0	463.1	704.0	1,124.3	1,672.1	2,602.8	4,023.8	6,700.7	14,492.1
1987	84.2	115.2	167.2	278.7	459.3	704.9	1,112.3	1,658.7	2,564.7	3,983.1	6,639.0	14,515.8
1988	83.6	116.4	168.4	273.7	449.9	716.1	1,109.0	1,654.1	2,556.5	3,989.2	6,728.6	14,850.4
1989	86.0	113.2	168.2	265.1	438.6	699.5	1,080.3	1,623.8	2,499.3	3,924.9	6,497.4	14,397.7
1990	84.0	114.0	162.0	266.3	430.8	682.6	1,070.5	1,599.2	2,454.9	3,835.7	6,337.6	14,099.8
1991	84.7	116.2	163.7	268.0	423.8	684.4	1,054.3	1,591.3	2,438.0	3,785.1	6,275.6	13,941.7
1992	83.4	117.2	166.5	254.6	417.0	668.0	1,038.1	1,579.0	2,427.1	3,732.3	6,206.5	13,670.3
1993	86.4	121.0	169.8	261.2	415.6	669.1	1,057.6	1,597.0	2,461.3	3,846.7	6,391.3	14,374.7
1994	88.7	124.5	170.7	262.5	415.1	653.7	1,043.2	1,581.1	2,447.5	3,802.0	6,377.7	14,224.7
1995	89.6	126.4	175.8	259.0	414.6	655.0	1,041.4	1,567.8	2,443.5	3,813.4	6,364.3	14,413.2
1996	85.8	121.1	171.7	255.7	411.9	639.0	1,036.4	1,548.1	2,445.6	3,795.9	6,366.8	14,433.5
1997	79.9	115.4	168.6	251.6	394.0	637.3	1,019.9	1,527.7	2,422.8	3,760.6	6,321.6	14,492.3
1998	79.0	116.1	167.7	246.7	384.4	616.2	993.4	1,530.2	2,427.8	3,744.2	6,377.9	14,427.4

[1] Age not reported is included in "Total" but not distributed among specified age groups.

Sources

Total deaths: 1900-1992, U.S. Public Health Service, National Center for Health Statistics, *Vital Statistics of the United States, 1992*, volume 2, *Mortality*, part A, Tables 1-2 and 1-3. 1993-1997, *National Vital Statistics Report*, volume 47, number 19, "Deaths: Final Data for 1997," Table 1.

Deaths by age and sex are taken from the various annual issues of *Mortality Statistics of the United States* (1900-1936) and *Vital Statistics of the United States* (1937-1992). Deaths by age and sex for 1993-1997 are obtained from the file GMWK291A found on the National Center for Health Statistics (NCHS) Internet site.

Population: Death Registration Area, 1900-1932, and United States, 1933-1939, Forrest Linder and Robert D. Grove, *Vital Statistics Rates in the United States, 1900-1940* (U.S. Government Printing Office, 1947), pp. 997-1034, and unpublished tables made available by the Mortality Statistics Branch of the NCHS. United States, 1940-1997, machine-readable versions of the data were obtained from U.S. Bureau of the Census, 1900-1979, PE-11 (POP 3987); 1980-1990, PE-10 (POP 3988-3990); 1990-1997, PE-61 (POP 3991-3998). See Frederick W. Hollmann, Lisa B. Kuzmekus,

R. Colby Perkins, and Elizabeth A. Weber, "U.S. Population by Age, Sex, Race, and Hispanic Origin: 1990 to 1997," U.S. Bureau of the Census, PPL-91 and appendixes. The other overall and age-specific rates will differ from the official NCHS published rates because of the use of slightly different base populations here. For 1998, death rates were not calculated and were taken directly from U.S. Public Health Service, *National Vital Statistics Report*, volume 48, number 11, "Deaths: Final Data for 1998," Table 2.

Documentation

The overall death rate is the number of deaths, excluding fetal deaths, per 100,000 population. Prior to 1933, this is given for the Death Registration States only. For 1910-1915, North Carolina is excluded because it provided only partial coverage. For 1917-1918, deaths of soldiers, sailors, and marines were added. The base population is as of July 1 in each year. For the composition of the Death Registration Area, see the essay on vital statistics. Beginning in 1970, the mortality data exclude nonresidents of the United States. The overall death rates include deaths reported with unknown ages. The age-specific death rates do not include distributed deaths with unknown ages.

See the text for Table Ab952-987.

TABLE Ab1048–1058   Death rate for Massachusetts, by sex and selected causes: 1855–1970[1]

Contributed by Michael R. Haines

	Sex			Cause								
	Both	Male	Female	Tuberculosis of the respiratory system	Diphtheria	Typhoid and paratyphoid fever	Measles	Smallpox	Malignant neoplasms	Heart and circulatory diseases	Stroke and related conditions
	Ab1048	Ab1049	Ab1050	Ab1051	Ab1052	Ab1053 [2]	Ab1054	Ab1055	Ab1056	Ab1057 [3]	Ab1058
Year	Per 100,000	Per 100,000	Per 100,000	Per 100,000	Per 100,000	Per 100,000	Per 100,000	Per 100,000	Per 100,000	Per 100,000	Per 100,000
1855	1,836.7	1,869.9	1,783.5	22,838.7	2,582.0	5,279.4	596.2	1,562.7	1,221.3	2,509.9	—
1856	1,799.7	1,823.7	1,754.7	22,672.9	2,503.1	4,630.1	839.2	675.2	1,046.6	2,778.0	—
1857	1,815.9	1,882.0	1,738.4	21,734.0	2,434.2	4,746.2	474.6	108.1	1,137.2	2,767.9	—
1858	1,743.6	1,789.8	1,687.6	22,015.8	2,478.8	4,336.7	1,448.8	57.8	1,391.0	2,801.3	—
1859	1,731.7	1,767.3	1,685.4	22,425.6	2,669.7	4,443.2	524.4	1,215.7	1,458.8	2,836.6	—
1860	1,873.8	1,917.8	1,820.3	19,754.6	3,628.4	4,061.9	971.0	1,447.9	1,452.2	3,069.2	—
1861	1,945.1	1,986.9	1,897.2	18,775.2	4,583.8	4,106.3	867.8	137.0	1,395.1	3,080.8	—
1862	1,844.6	1,982.7	1,709.0	18,581.9	4,992.6	4,940.4	1,606.2	174.1	1,388.5	3,094.8	—
1863	2,215.4	2,414.6	2,025.4	16,817.4	8,230.3	5,196.2	508.1	151.3	1,167.5	2,958.5	—
1864	2,279.9	2,490.1	2,079.0	16,478.1	6,959.6	4,679.2	1,114.1	842.5	1,148.9	2,694.7	—
1865	2,064.0	2,173.6	1,958.4	17,822.7	4,496.8	6,477.5	520.0	845.1	1,433.9	3,158.5	—
1866	1,811.1	1,864.0	1,758.1	19,461.0	3,511.4	4,615.6	461.1	596.5	1,760.0	3,574.9	—
1867	1,695.4	1,765.9	1,623.1	19,155.1	2,665.6	4,237.7	851.9	860.7	1,734.6	3,833.7	—
1868	1,853.6	1,941.1	1,767.7	17,330.0	3,054.3	3,499.6	1,121.0	78.1	1,738.1	3,843.3	—
1869	1,835.7	1,869.6	1,798.0	17,882.1	2,951.6	4,625.0	852.1	226.5	1,888.4	3,523.5	—
1870	1,875.3	1,946.5	1,804.5	18,306.6	2,473.6	4,877.6	984.3	479.3	1,888.1	3,589.6	—
1871	1,867.5	1,937.2	1,799.0	18,144.1	2,673.3	3,993.8	468.8	1,055.7	1,971.9	4,133.4	—
1872	2,281.1	2,394.1	2,170.1	15,865.7	2,150.3	4,863.1	1,222.2	2,938.4	1,547.7	3,492.4	—
1873	2,154.4	2,274.2	2,039.6	16,383.6	2,196.9	4,146.0	530.8	1,969.8	1,801.7	3,709.6	—
1874	1,976.9	2,049.8	1,904.4	16,571.0	2,863.2	3,597.1	504.9	81.5	1,834.6	4,083.2	—
1875	2,117.4	2,181.4	2,054.6	16,404.6	5,374.8	3,027.6	666.1	97.2	1,695.4	3,888.2	—
1876	1,977.5	2,042.3	1,913.9	16,051.9	9,925.9	2,654.7	141.6	93.4	1,979.8	4,143.3	—
1877	1,838.9	1,881.3	1,797.2	17,411.1	10,139.7	2,597.2	430.7	76.6	2,061.1	4,457.3	—
1878	1,808.8	1,835.2	1,780.6	17,039.9	8,040.8	2,169.1	974.3	6.4	2,578.0	4,820.6	—
1879	1,810.1	1,848.1	1,771.5	16,424.0	7,210.5	2,003.1	59.7	22.0	2,710.6	5,056.4	—
1880	1,979.3	2,030.0	1,930.7	15,567.3	6,783.4	2,499.1	668.7	107.7	2,629.5	5,162.6	—
1881	2,008.8	2,077.9	1,943.1	16,144.6	6,536.3	2,940.4	630.9	128.9	2,603.0	5,532.4	—
1882	1,991.9	2,067.1	1,921.6	15,944.0	4,814.5	2,933.3	184.9	122.3	2,683.2	5,806.7	—
1883	2,009.5	2,086.1	1,938.1	15,712.1	4,294.3	2,278.3	850.4	13.2	2,718.0	6,024.2	—
1884	1,936.3	2,006.3	1,871.0	15,674.5	4,449.9	2,365.5	202.8	8.1	2,865.6	6,077.3	—
1885	1,961.4	2,024.8	1,902.9	15,632.4	3,998.0	2,016.1	821.7	49.9	2,853.5	6,250.3	—
1886	1,860.8	1,928.2	1,798.2	15,833.4	4,183.2	2,148.0	349.0	0.0	2,964.2	6,629.3	—
1887	1,978.0	2,043.5	1,916.8	14,402.8	3,993.8	2,261.9	1,116.2	7.4	2,880.1	6,959.7	—
1888	1,985.5	2,070.0	1,906.3	13,606.7	4,349.5	2,240.1	520.2	19.0	3,028.7	7,271.3	—
1889	1,916.7	1,985.2	1,852.4	13,359.0	5,299.6	2,132.8	409.3	14.4	3,171.6	7,851.2	—
1890	1,944.1	2,001.2	1,890.2	13,304.1	3,735.5	1,918.3	261.9	2.3	3,186.5	7,850.1	—
1891	1,972.1	2,036.8	1,911.0	12,136.8	2,695.6	1,817.0	522.3	2.2	3,087.3	7,949.5	—
1892	2,080.8	2,164.5	2,001.7	11,769.4	2,983.9	1,696.0	180.5	4.1	2,875.2	7,655.6	—
1893	2,048.8	2,139.3	1,963.4	11,260.3	2,840.0	1,528.0	562.3	18.3	3,123.2	7,153.0	—
1894	1,911.4	2,000.2	1,827.6	11,675.3	3,849.0	1,598.6	209.4	70.5	3,351.1	7,334.7	—
1895	1,901.5	1,990.2	1,817.6	11,539.8	3,752.6	1,430.4	246.1	0.0	3,679.0	7,501.1	—
1896	1,928.0	2,018.9	1,842.1	11,210.8	3,396.0	1,464.1	277.4	0.0	3,641.1	7,419.9	—
1897	1,808.3	1,881.5	1,739.0	11,453.2	3,007.2	1,280.1	333.2	8.4	3,667.3	7,623.5	—
1898	1,742.7	1,843.4	1,647.1	11,308.6	1,509.8	1,417.8	175.4	0.0	4,078.2	7,737.2	—
1899	1,738.5	1,817.9	1,663.1	10,943.2	2,194.5	1,282.7	505.1	29.3	3,852.4	7,736.3	—
1900	1,823.5	1,896.5	1,754.1	10,163.0	2,883.3	1,235.4	645.1	5.9	3,905.7	7,494.7	—
1901	1,696.8	1,793.1	1,605.3	10,425.7	2,415.3	1,162.1	358.4	200.9	4,308.6	8,213.4	4,884.5
1902	1,646.3	1,722.2	1,574.3	9,865.0	1,838.2	1,132.8	701.2	598.0	4,508.2	8,096.3	5,251.5
1903	1,677.4	1,766.7	1,592.7	9,236.8	1,771.5	1,074.3	503.5	44.8	4,572.5	8,405.0	5,151.4
1904	1,635.7	1,713.8	1,561.6	10,055.3	1,441.8	955.0	330.0	18.6	4,993.6	9,112.7	5,666.0
1905	1,680.8	1,778.6	1,588.1	9,313.5	1,291.4	1,030.0	350.6	4.0	4,953.8	8,713.3	5,785.7
1906	1,645.7	1,745.6	1,550.5	9,102.4	1,467.7	942.2	410.9	0.0	5,141.8	8,719.2	5,791.7
1907	1,722.4	1,820.8	1,628.3	8,797.1	1,386.6	717.3	300.5	11.1	5,059.6	9,025.7	5,787.8
1908	1,607.7	1,696.8	1,522.1	8,583.1	1,442.4	998.3	639.1	5.8	5,433.7	8,453.7	5,895.2
1909	1,555.5	1,628.2	1,485.4	8,578.0	1,354.5	761.2	306.4	2.0	5,603.5	7,941.7	6,267.1

Notes appear at end of table

(continued)

TABLE Ab1048–1058   Death rate for Massachusetts, by sex and selected causes: 1855–1970   *Continued*

	Sex			Cause								
	Both	Male	Female	Tuberculosis of the respiratory system	Diphtheria	Typhoid and paratyphoid fever	Measles	Smallpox	Malignant neoplasms	Heart and circulatory diseases	Stroke and related conditions
	Ab1048	Ab1049	Ab1050	Ab1051	Ab1052	Ab1053 [2]	Ab1054	Ab1055	Ab1056	Ab1057 [3]	Ab1058
Year	Per 100,000	Per 100,000	Per 100,000	Per 100,000	Per 100,000	Per 100,000	Per 100,000	Per 100,000	Per 100,000	Per 100,000	Per 100,000
1910	1,616.2	1,707.2	1,528.1	8,276.5	1,248.0	755.4	441.1	0.0	5,565.5	7,399.8	6,098.5
1911	1,546.2	1,631.7	1,463.5	8,425.9	1,096.2	586.8	577.3	5.7	6,154.4	11,957.8	6,486.4
1912	1,498.4	1,572.6	1,426.6	8,394.3	949.3	514.8	754.1	3.8	6,520.6	12,488.0	6,495.7
1913	1,499.0	1,601.9	1,399.5	8,043.4	1,171.0	523.6	936.5	0.0	6,750.4	12,190.8	6,583.3
1914	1,460.3	1,547.1	1,376.5	8,107.2	1,241.2	520.3	376.5	1.9	6,903.9	12,642.4	6,921.0
1915	1,438.6	1,507.1	1,372.2	8,154.2	1,379.4	465.5	510.7	18.8	7,178.0	12,475.3	7,057.4
1916	1,513.1	1,614.9	1,414.6	8,158.0	1,105.4	306.9	841.0	0.0	7,205.2	12,895.2	6,672.9
1917	1,507.3	1,606.2	1,411.9	8,229.4	1,471.5	321.1	656.4	17.6	7,213.1	13,512.1	6,900.7
1918	2,081.0	2,240.9	1,926.3	6,710.9	763.3	198.0	658.5	1.3	5,307.1	10,556.1	5,160.9
1919	1,370.1	1,408.6	1,332.6	8,065.1	1,128.0	201.4	356.8	3.8	7,859.8	13,287.0	7,664.1
1920	1,392.2	1,408.7	1,376.1	7,022.7	1,095.4	177.6	663.6	3.7	8,353.6	14,148.2	7,512.4
1921	1,227.6	1,254.8	1,201.5	6,928.7	1,287.0	255.3	382.9	0.0	9,701.4	15,451.9	8,368.4
1922	1,300.0	1,333.0	1,268.2	6,367.2	1,167.6	172.4	438.8	0.0	9,084.5	15,798.4	8,447.8
1923	1,318.9	1,350.9	1,288.1	5,980.9	1,123.3	134.2	659.4	0.0	9,124.7	16,806.0	8,442.2
1924	1,233.2	1,293.6	1,175.3	6,159.1	1,071.8	141.8	346.4	4.1	10,235.4	16,558.6	9,052.2
1925	1,280.9	1,335.6	1,228.6	5,626.3	645.8	141.1	674.8	0.0	9,999.8	19,960.9	7,844.0
1926	1,292.9	1,347.8	1,240.4	5,653.7	474.9	112.1	761.8	0.0	10,093.5	20,641.0	7,773.9
1927	1,194.2	1,250.9	1,140.0	5,654.9	558.0	85.2	184.6	0.0	11,056.1	20,884.7	8,185.0
1928	1,233.6	1,281.5	1,187.9	5,280.8	491.8	68.6	544.7	0.0	10,898.6	21,940.3	8,312.1
1929	1,239.2	1,288.6	1,192.3	4,975.3	495.0	80.9	244.6	1.9	10,807.8	22,303.3	8,024.5
1930	1,164.9	1,218.4	1,113.9	4,923.7	368.9	77.0	287.8	0.0	11,728.5	24,302.2	8,410.2
1931	1,145.2	1,206.0	1,087.4	4,730.9	266.7	63.6	131.3	0.0	12,020.2	24,534.8	8,951.0
1932	1,161.9	1,218.6	1,107.9	4,120.7	216.0	50.5	129.2	0.0	12,422.5	26,761.0	8,418.0
1933	1,190.5	1,255.7	1,128.5	4,050.6	169.2	47.2	53.1	0.0	12,555.1	27,775.8	8,575.3
1934	1,187.0	1,274.9	1,103.4	3,747.0	98.5	27.6	179.3	0.0	13,150.1	28,650.5	8,410.2
1935	1,158.8	1,228.6	1,092.5	3,652.7	52.4	20.1	74.5	0.0	12,795.7	29,888.8	8,395.5
1936	1,199.0	1,280.9	1,121.1	3,421.6	51.9	21.1	69.2	0.0	13,006.2	30,490.7	8,230.2
1937	1,204.2	1,294.1	1,118.8	3,418.3	40.2	32.5	51.7	0.0	12,869.4	30,726.5	8,339.1
1938	1,145.3	1,226.9	1,067.8	3,179.1	40.3	28.2	26.2	0.0	13,998.3	34,818.4	8,625.0
1939	1,166.9	1,240.2	1,097.2	3,028.5	33.4	27.5	33.4	0.0	13,938.4	35,479.3	8,957.7
1940	1,174.5	1,249.1	1,103.6	2,963.5	17.6	15.6	23.5	0.0	14,297.4	36,988.8	9,130.9
1941	1,158.8	1,249.3	1,073.1	3,031.0	23.7	5.9	7.9	0.0	14,575.3	37,265.6	9,093.1
1942	1,162.2	1,262.4	1,067.2	2,941.1	13.7	5.9	29.4	0.0	14,454.5	37,120.9	9,077.9
1943	1,234.0	1,324.8	1,148.2	3,105.0	20.1	12.8	36.6	0.0	13,602.2	38,091.2	8,940.0
1944	1,157.3	1,252.5	1,067.4	3,126.5	21.3	0.0	40.6	0.0	14,715.2	38,716.9	9,153.0
1945	1,135.4	1,244.1	1,032.8	3,033.3	23.5	9.8	19.6	0.0	15,279.8	38,898.6	9,672.8
1946	1,131.9	1,229.6	1,039.7	3,041.0	73.9	3.9	31.1	0.0	15,097.9	39,252.5	9,243.6
1947	1,130.4	1,242.7	1,024.6	2,861.6	25.1	7.7	23.2	0.0	15,523.4	40,354.4	8,901.7
1948	1,139.8	1,252.3	1,034.0	2,427.2	57.0	7.6	34.2	0.0	16,131.6	41,056.1	9,273.7
1949	1,091.0	1,200.3	988.4	2,105.7	86.7	7.9	23.6	0.0	16,556.0	44,785.0	10,132.6
1950	1,052.9	1,158.1	954.2	1,915.5	18.2	2.0	4.0	0.0	17,059.5	45,233.5	10,681.2
1951	1,137.7	1,252.1	1,030.4	1,557.1	16.7	5.6	11.1	0.0	16,482.0	45,379.8	10,532.1
1952	1,078.7	1,195.0	969.8	1,316.2	3.9	0.0	38.8	0.0	16,765.9	45,108.3	10,570.5
1953	1,073.5	1,195.3	959.4	968.6	3.9	3.9	3.9	0.0	17,056.7	45,862.2	10,700.0
1954	1,061.9	1,174.1	956.7	906.2	3.9	0.0	11.6	0.0	17,848.6	45,395.3	10,355.2
1955	1,084.3	1,189.4	986.0	830.4	0.0	3.7	33.7	0.0	17,548.0	45,486.9	10,424.6
1956	1,070.1	1,185.4	962.3	779.1	5.6	1.9	1.9	0.0	17,538.3	45,668.6	10,360.4
1957	1,090.9	1,206.4	982.8	729.9	1.8	0.0	7.3	0.0	17,700.5	45,310.5	10,224.1
1958	1,119.6	1,223.7	1,022.4	574.0	0.0	1.8	7.1	0.0	17,158.2	46,467.7	10,687.0
1959	1,069.1	1,173.4	971.8	612.2	0.0	1.8	0.0	0.0	16,854.2	46,037.1	10,612.9
1960	1,104.0	1,228.4	987.8	541.9	0.0	7.0	12.3	0.0	16,723.0	45,761.6	9,618.6
1961	1,080.4	1,190.7	977.7	540.8	0.0	5.3	3.6	0.0	17,151.8	46,176.8	9,283.0
1962	1,075.0	1,181.6	975.9	442.4	0.0	3.5	8.8	0.0	16,989.3	46,112.3	9,652.8
1963	1,050.9	1,152.1	956.9	412.1	1.8	5.4	0.0	0.0	16,492.0	46,736.2	9,367.7
1964 [4]	947.3	1,044.2	857.6	348.3	0.0	3.9	3.9	0.0	17,550.2	45,942.5	9,260.1
1965	1,086.9	1,202.2	980.3	366.7	0.0	6.8	10.2	0.0	17,332.0	45,662.8	9,110.8
1966	1,055.2	1,168.3	950.9	309.9	0.0	12.1	0.0	0.0	17,488.6	46,043.4	8,817.0
1967	1,049.8	1,159.3	948.9	325.7	0.0	5.2	0.0	0.0	17,957.6	45,846.3	8,622.9
1968	1,064.9	1,179.4	959.7	262.5	0.0	1.7	0.0	0.0	17,305.2	55,839.3	10,145.9
1969	1,025.6	1,129.6	930.2	171.3	0.0	5.2	1.7	0.0	18,275.6	55,124.3	9,804.0
1970	1,006.8	1,122.1	901.2	192.0	0.0	3.5	1.7	0.0	18,377.0	54,897.2	9,956.7

TABLE Ab1048–1058   Death rate for Massachusetts, by sex and selected causes: 1855–1970   *Continued*

[1] Includes only deaths, excluding fetal deaths, occurring within Massachusetts, except for 1940–1970; for these years, data are for deaths occurring to residents of Massachusetts.

[2] Beginning in 1958, data include "other salmonella infections."

[3] Diseases of the heart for 1855–1937. Diseases of the circulatory system for 1938–1970.

[4] Excludes approximately 6,000 deaths registered in Massachusetts, primarily to residents of the state.

Sources

Population: Censuses of the United States (1850–1970) and Censuses of Massachusetts (1855–1925). Deaths by sex and cause: 1860–1899, computed from the *Annual Registration Reports for the Vital Statistics of Massachusetts;* 1900–1956, U.S. Bureau of the Census, *Mortality Statistics of the United States,* and U.S. Public Health Service, *Vital Statistics of the United States,* volume 1, annual issues; 1957–1970, U.S. Public Health Service, *Vital Statistics of the United States,* volume 2, part A, annual issues.

Documentation

Massachusetts was the first state in the United States to institute a comprehensive vital registration system in 1842. The system was producing ac-

ceptable mortality data by the middle of the 1850s. (See Robert Gutman, "The Accuracy of Vital Statistics in Massachusetts, 1842–1901," Ph.D. dissertation, Columbia University, 1956.) Cause of death information lacked a consistent reporting format until 1899, when the First International Classification of Diseases (ICD-1) was developed and accepted in the United States. From 1900, the data reflect this and subsequent lists. (The latest is ICD-9, issued in 1979.)

An effort was made at the French national statistical office in the early twentieth century to provide consistent classification of Massachusetts data from 1849 to 1910. A subsequent publication carried the effort to 1936. See France, "Statistique International du Mouvement de la Population d'après les Registres d'Etat Civil: Résumé Rétrospectif depuis l'Origine des Statistiques de l'Etat Civil jusqu'en 1905," in *Statistique Générale de la France* (Imprimerie National, 1905), pp. 867–8; "Statistique International du Mouvement de la Population d'après les Registres d'Etat Civil: Second Volume Années 1901 à 1910," in *Statistique Générale de la France* (Imprimerie National, 1913), p. 257. See also Henri Bunle, *Le Movement Naturel de la Population dans le Monde de 1906 à 1936* (I.N.E.D., 1954), pp. 152–5, 187, 522–4.

Rates are given per 100,000 population.
See the text for Table Ab929–951.

TABLE Ab1059–1137   Deaths, infant deaths, age-adjusted death rates, and infant mortality rates, by Hispanic origin and race of mother: 1989–1998[1]

Contributed by Michael R. Haines

				Deaths								
	All persons			Hispanic								
				Total			Mexican			Puerto Rican		
	Both sexes	Males	Females	Both sexes	Males	Females	Both sexes	Males	Females	Both sexes	Males	Females
	Ab1059	Ab1060	Ab1061	Ab1062	Ab1063	Ab1064	Ab1065	Ab1066	Ab1067	Ab1068	Ab1069	Ab1070
Year	Number	Number	Number	Number	Number	Number	Number	Number	Number	Number	Number	Number
1989	1,960,745	1,016,507	944,238	76,379	45,975	30,404	37,885	22,967	14,918	10,174	6,275	3,899
1990	1,970,337	1,021,783	948,554	68,673	41,012	27,661	40,624	24,642	15,982	5,159	3,146	2,013
1991	2,058,417	1,064,439	993,978	72,021	42,964	29,057	42,641	25,857	16,784	5,770	3,508	2,262
1992	2,136,558	1,102,513	1,034,045	82,395	49,434	32,961	44,483	26,971	17,512	10,481	6,452	4,029
1993	2,236,131	1,145,300	1,090,831	86,935	52,177	34,758	47,088	28,650	18,438	11,334	6,982	4,352
1994	2,246,695	1,146,309	1,100,386	90,109	54,104	36,005	48,598	29,529	19,069	13,690	8,358	5,332
1995	2,279,279	1,156,342	1,122,937	94,776	56,167	38,609	50,587	30,491	20,096	14,248	8,588	5,660
1996	2,281,571	1,147,085	1,134,486	94,957	55,217	39,740	51,637	30,657	20,980	13,531	8,025	5,506
1997	2,314,245	1,154,039	1,160,206	95,460	54,348	41,112	53,405	31,182	22,223	12,516	7,198	5,318
1998	2,337,256	1,157,260	1,179,996	98,406	55,821	42,585	55,104	32,188	22,916	12,965	7,218	5,547

				Deaths						
	Hispanic									Non-Hispanic
	Cuban			Central and South American			Other and unknown			Total
	Both sexes	Males	Females	Both sexes	Males	Females	Both sexes	Males	Females	Both sexes
	Ab1071	Ab1072	Ab1073	Ab1074	Ab1075	Ab1076	Ab1077	Ab1078	Ab1079	Ab1080
Year	Number	Number	Number	Number	Number	Number	Number	Number	Number	Number
1989	7,388	4,174	3,214	5,031	2,986	2,045	15,901	9,573	6,328	1,864,732
1990	7,181	4,063	3,118	4,122	2,417	1,705	11,587	6,744	4,843	1,887,983
1991	7,443	4,299	3,144	4,235	2,466	1,769	11,932	6,834	5,098	1,972,864
1992	8,109	4,563	3,546	6,080	3,524	2,556	13,242	7,924	5,318	2,026,890
1993	8,756	4,870	3,886	6,563	3,859	2,704	13,194	7,816	5,378	2,123,220
1994	8,891	5,032	3,859	7,314	4,322	2,992	11,616	6,863	4,753	2,146,659
1995	9,903	5,476	4,427	8,396	4,824	3,572	11,642	6,788	4,854	2,173,061
1996	9,929	5,354	4,575	8,093	4,480	3,613	11,767	6,701	5,066	2,176,851
1997	9,873	5,197	4,676	8,098	4,259	3,839	11,568	6,512	5,056	2,209,450
1998	10,389	5,472	4,917	8,307	4,315	3,992	11,841	6,628	5,213	2,230,127

Note appears at end of table

(continued)

TABLE Ab1059-1137   Deaths, infant deaths, age-adjusted death rates, and infant mortality rates, by Hispanic origin and race of mother: 1989-1998 *Continued*

Deaths

	Non-Hispanic								Origin not stated		
	Total		White			Black					
	Males	Females	Both sexes	Males	Females	Both sexes	Males	Females	Both sexes	Males	Females
	Ab1081	Ab1082	Ab1083	Ab1084	Ab1085	Ab1086	Ab1087	Ab1088	Ab1089	Ab1090	Ab1091
Year	Number	Number	Number	Number	Number	Number	Number	Number	Number	Number	Number
1989	959,297	905,435	1,612,878	820,893	791,985	225,626	123,074	102,552	19,634	11,235	8,399
1990	972,814	915,169	1,636,015	834,188	801,827	225,718	123,446	102,272	13,681	7,957	5,724
1991	1,013,900	958,964	1,701,137	864,703	836,434	244,057	133,313	110,744	13,532	7,575	5,957
1992	1,038,336	988,554	1,734,220	878,144	856,076	262,047	142,575	119,472	27,273	14,743	12,530
1993	1,079,354	1,043,866	1,815,608	911,188	904,420	274,696	149,338	125,358	25,976	13,769	12,207
1994	1,086,525	1,060,134	1,834,633	916,723	917,910	277,296	150,050	127,246	9,927	5,680	4,247
1995	1,093,758	1,079,303	1,856,052	922,471	933,581	280,666	150,871	129,795	11,442	6,417	5,025
1996	1,086,328	1,090,523	1,862,615	918,911	943,704	276,720	146,469	130,251	9,763	5,540	4,223
1997	1,094,541	1,114,909	1,895,461	929,703	965,758	273,381	142,241	131,140	9,335	5,150	4,185
1998	1,096,677	1,133,450	1,912,802	931,844	980,958	275,264	141,627	133,637	8,723	4,762	3,961

Infant deaths / Age-adjusted death rate

		Hispanic					Non-Hispanic				Age-adjusted death rate
	All persons	Total	Mexican	Puerto Rican	Cuban	Other and unknown	Total	White	Black	Origin not stated	All persons Both sexes
	Ab1092	Ab1093	Ab1094	Ab1095	Ab1096	Ab1097	Ab1098	Ab1099	Ab1100	Ab1101	Ab1102
Year	Number	Number	Number	Number	Number	Number	Number	Number	Number	Number	Per 100,000
1989	35,914	4,431	2,581	499	79	1,272	30,535	18,936	10,438	948	—
1990	35,030	4,228	2,952	363	81	832	30,231	18,745	10,465	571	—
1991	34,681	4,304	3,057	371	63	813	29,835	18,018	10,840	542	—
1992	34,117	4,376	2,925	466	71	914	28,921	16,996	10,903	820	—
1993	33,057	4,401	2,994	443	64	900	27,946	16,492	10,462	710	—
1994	31,322	4,340	2,984	497	54	805	26,562	15,751	9,784	420	506.6
1995	29,203	4,147	2,845	473	63	766	24,567	14,907	8,766	489	503.5
1996	28,093	4,102	2,858	426	64	754	23,549	14,239	8,404	442	491.1
1997	28,045	4,240	2,968	411	71	790	23,387	14,170	8,272	418	479.1
1998	28,371	4,371	3,059	422	61	829	23,563	14,105	8,447	437	471.7

Age-adjusted death rate

	All persons		Hispanic									Cuban
	Males	Females	Total Both sexes	Males	Females	Mexican Both sexes	Males	Females	Puerto Rican Both sexes	Males	Females	Both sexes
	Ab1103	Ab1104	Ab1105	Ab1106	Ab1107	Ab1108	Ab1109	Ab1110	Ab1111	Ab1112	Ab1113	Ab1114
Year	Per 100,000	Per 100,000	Per 100,000	Per 100,000	Per 100,000	Per 100,000	Per 100,000	Per 100,000	Per 100,000	Per 100,000	Per 100,000	Per 100,000
1989	—	—	—	—	—	—	—	—	—	—	—	—
1990	—	—	—	—	—	—	—	—	—	—	—	—
1991	—	—	—	—	—	—	—	—	—	—	—	—
1992	—	—	—	—	—	—	—	—	—	—	—	—
1993	—	—	—	—	—	—	—	—	—	—	—	—
1994	653.6	384.0	383.8	516.4	268.6	370.4	480.3	269.1	565.8	838.9	373.5	358.1
1995	545.5	384.9	386.8	515.0	274.4	362.4	469.2	264.0	582.9	847.5	395.5	387.4
1996	622.8	380.8	365.9	474.8	268.0	359.1	448.9	271.8	509.0	740.5	347.5	346.7
1997	602.8	375.7	350.3	447.7	263.4	365.2	442.3	289.3	419.7	558.9	306.9	302.6
1998	589.4	372.5	342.8	442.7	255.5	348.4	425.1	273.9	406.1	540.8	296.3	299.5

TABLE Ab1059–1137   Deaths, infant deaths, age-adjusted death rates, and infant mortality rates, by Hispanic origin and race of mother: 1989–1998   *Continued*

	Age-adjusted death rate										
	Hispanic					Non-Hispanic					
	Cuban		Other and unknown			Total			White		
	Males	Females	Both sexes	Males	Females	Both sexes	Males	Females	Both sexes	Males	Females
	Ab1115	Ab1116	Ab1117	Ab1118	Ab1119	Ab1120	Ab1121	Ab1122	Ab1123	Ab1124	Ab1125
Year	Per 100,000	Per 100,000	Per 100,000	Per 100,000	Per 100,000	Per 100,000	Per 100,000	Per 100,000	Per 100,000	Per 100,000	Per 100,000
1989	—	—	—	—	—	—	—	—	—	—	—
1990	—	—	—	—	—	—	—	—	—	—	—
1991	—	—	—	—	—	—	—	—	—	—	—
1992	—	—	—	—	—	—	—	—	—	—	—
1993	—	—	—	—	—	—	—	—	—	—	—
1994	507.9	225.8	354.0	496.1	245.0	510.5	656.8	389.7	478.1	613.4	366.1
1995	531.0	254.2	368.5	519.7	255.8	507.0	648.1	389.7	475.2	605.7	366.4
1996	451.8	247.7	332.2	478.0	238.4	496.2	628.1	386.3	466.7	589.5	364.1
1997	391.5	215.6	320.8	465.9	232.5	485.0	609.5	381.4	424.3	575.3	360.9
1998	421.9	203.1	325.0	469.2	235.1	478.0	595.9	379.0	452.7	563.6	359.1

	Age-adjusted death rate				Infant mortality rate								
	Non-Hispanic					Hispanic					Non-Hispanic		
	Black												
	Both sexes	Males	Females	All persons	Total	Mexican	Puerto Rican	Cuban	Other and unknown	Total	White	Black
	Ab1126	Ab1127	Ab1128	Ab1129	Ab1130	Ab1131	Ab1132	Ab1133	Ab1134	Ab1135	Ab1136	Ab1137
Year	Per 100,000	Per 100,000	Per 100,000	Per 1,000	Per 1,000	Per 1,000	Per 1,000	Per 1,000	Per 1,000	Per 1,000	Per 1,000	Per 1,000
1989	—	—	—	9.8	8.5	7.9	9.6	7.4	9.6	9.8	7.9	18.5
1990	—	—	—	9.1	7.8	7.7	10.2	7.6	7.2	9.3	7.4	17.9
1991	—	—	—	8.9	7.5	7.5	9.0	5.9	6.8	9.0	7.1	17.5
1992	—	—	—	8.5	6.8	6.8	7.8	6.2	6.5	8.7	6.8	16.7
1993	—	—	—	8.4	6.7	6.8	7.6	5.4	6.4	8.6	6.8	16.4
1994	791.8	1,057.3	586.3	8.0	6.5	6.6	8.7	4.5	5.7	8.3	6.5	15.9
1995	783.6	1,042.4	583.5	7.6	6.1	6.1	8.6	5.1	5.4	7.9	6.3	15.0
1996	758.4	995.5	575.4	7.3	5.9	5.9	7.8	5.1	5.3	7.6	6.1	14.7
1997	724.3	937.4	559.9	7.2	6.0	5.9	7.4	5.5	5.5	7.5	6.1	14.2
1998	710.7	911.1	555.8	7.2	5.9	5.9	7.4	4.6	5.6	7.5	6.0	14.2

[1] Excludes Connecticut (1989–1990), Louisiana (1989), Maryland (1989), New Hampshire (1989–1992), Oklahoma (1989–1996), New York City (1990–1991), and Virginia (1989), which did not report Hispanic origin.

Sources
1989–1994: National Center for Health Statistics, *Monthly Vital Statistics Report*, "Advance Report of Final Mortality Statistics." 1995: National Center for Health Statistics, *Monthly Vital Statistics Report*, "Report of Final Mortality Statistics." 1996–1998: National Center for Health Statistics, *National Vital Statistics Reports*, "Deaths: Final Data for 1996, 1997, 1998."

Documentation
See the text for Table Ab362–389.

The infant mortality rate is deaths younger than age 1 per 1,000 live births for the specified group. See the text for Table Ab952–987 for a discussion of age-adjusted death rates.

Series Ab1080–1082. Includes races other than white and black.

Series Ab1089–1091 and Ab1101. Includes deaths that occurred in areas that did not report Hispanic origin on the death certificate.

Series Ab1097. Includes Central and South American as well as other and unknown Hispanic.

Series Ab1117–1119 and Ab1134. Includes origin not stated.

CHAPTER Ac
Internal Migration

Editor: Joseph P. Ferrie

INTERNAL MIGRATION

Joseph P. Ferrie

Americans are an unusually peripatetic people, as both historical and contemporary observers have noted. Before the arrival of permanent European settlers at the start of the seventeenth century, the indigenous population roamed the North American continent after having arrived from Asia more than ten thousand years before (Thornton 2000, p. 9).[1] Soon after the arrival of Europeans, migration was of such concern that permission was required for travel among the early colonies; the ease with which obligations could be escaped through migration led to capital penalties for runaway indentured servants (Smith 1947, pp. 265–70). Two centuries later, Alexis de Tocqueville described Americans' comparative rootlessness: "Millions of men advance at once toward the same point on the horizon: their language, their religion, their mores differ, their goal is common. They were told that fortune is to be found somewhere toward the west, and they go off in haste to meet it" (2000, pp. 268–9). In the twentieth century, Americans were twice as likely to relocate during their lives as the British or Japanese (Greenwood 1997).

High rates of geographic mobility have had important consequences for American economic development. This mobility has facilitated the exploitation of natural resources at locations distant from the narrow band of initial settlement on the Atlantic coast. Farmers moved to more productive land in the Ohio River valley in the late eighteenth century and to the Great Plains by the middle of the nineteenth century. Migrants in the West and the Northwest worked mineral and timber resources. High rates of mobility also spurred the rapid integration of labor markets as transportation improvements – initially canals and riverboats and later railroads – lowered the cost of migration. By the Civil War, much of the gap in wages between the West and the East in the Northern states had been erased (Margo 2000, p. 154). The possibility of migration to cheaper western lands may have also overturned long-standing family support patterns, as children sought their fortunes far removed from parents who were forced to invest in resources other than their children to support themselves in their old age (Ransom and Sutch 1986). And migration from farms to towns and cities in the late nineteenth and early twentieth centuries provided much of the labor force for America's mills, factories, and offices. The migration out of central cities toward suburban counties made

possible by streetcars, commuter railroads, and highways has spawned new communities that in many places now compete with nearby central cities for economic supremacy.

Migration's impact can be seen well beyond these economic effects, however. The pressure of population growth in older regions and the need for new territory to which migration could be directed have caused conflict with the indigenous population since colonial times and conflict with other colonial powers (France, Britain, and Spain) over territorial expansion. Since the time of Frederick Jackson Turner, historians have debated the role of easy migration to the west in forging peculiarly American institutions. Though the importance of the frontier as a "safety valve" relieving pressure on eastern labor markets has been debated for more than a century, the role of migration generally, and of the occupational mobility with which it was often accompanied, in preventing the radicalization of the American labor movement has been remarked upon since the time of Marx. High rates of mobility have also influenced rates of civic participation and voting patterns: out-migration has left political power in the hands of a small number of persistent residents, while in-migration has tipped the balance in close elections (Winkle 1988). The shift in population from the Northeast and Midwest to the South and West in the second half of the twentieth century fundamentally realigned American national politics.

Measuring Migration

Conceptually, the measurement of migration is straightforward.[2] Ideally, data would identify where individuals were located at some date t, and where they were located at some subsequent date $t + n$, making it possible to calculate how many had changed locations in the interval $(t, t + n)$ and which places had lost and received population. For example, if the population of locations A and B at time t and time $t + n$ are known, along with how many people moved from A to B and from B to A in the interval $(t, t + n)$, we can easily calculate the gross rates of in-migration and out-migration for each location. Complication arises in the definition of a "location," the interval between dates, and the populations at the two dates.

The choice of what sorts of places among which migration will be measured will have a large influence on measured rates of migration. For example, if a great many individuals move very short distances (e.g., within the same county), but we are able to examine only moves that cross state boundaries, we will substantially underestimate migration. As long as some moves are over only short distances, the choice of progressively larger geographic units into

---

[1] Unfortunately, we know little more about the native population's geographic mobility, except for its forced removal from the path of advancing settlement to lands farther west and, eventually, to reservations.

[2] Many of these issues are addressed in Henry Shryock, Jacob S. Siegel, and Associates (1980).

which to partition the population will result in greater and greater understatement of the extent of migration.[3]

Similarly, the choice of the time interval $(t, t + n)$ over which to measure migration will influence how much of the actual migration will be captured in measured migration. This difficulty can occur for two reasons. The first is return migration: Suppose that among the population of individuals who move from location A to location B in the interval $(t, t + n)$, some fraction return to location A before time $t + n$. If individuals' locations are not observed continuously but are observed only at discrete dates (such as time t and time $t + n$), undercounts of both migration from location A and migration from location B will result. Use of smaller and smaller increments n between the initial and terminal dates can reduce this problem. The other difficulty in choosing the interval is that it may be defined imprecisely. For example, it may be possible only to compare each individual's location at date of birth time t with their location at some later date $t + n_i$, where n_i is the individual's age and differs across individuals in the population. If we compare the rate of "lifetime" mobility calculated in this way across two populations, we may get very misleading results if the age structures of the populations differ substantially: the younger population will have had fewer years over which to migrate than the older population.

Finally, the population for which migration information is available may not be representative of the general population, so the migration behavior observed may not reflect overall migration accurately. Also, information on the population may be inadequate to calculate separately how many have moved in and how many have moved out of each location even if the geographic units and time intervals are not a problem. For example, if it is not possible to identify where the population of a geographic unit was located at a previous date, but it is known that the geographic unit's population has increased since a previous date, net migration can be calculated as the difference between observed population growth and the natural increase of the population (the excess of birth over deaths). This will not reveal precisely how many people moved out and how many moved in; it will show only how the numbers moving in and out compare.

Data Sources

For the colonial period, the calculation of migration rates is limited by the available data. Only a handful of sources provide information on the location of individuals at more than one point in time. For example, colonial militia muster rolls from the French and Indian War and the Revolutionary War describe the place of birth and of enlistment for men of age for military service (Villaflor and Sokoloff 1982). However, this population may be unrepresentative of the entire colonial population, so inferences based on its experiences must be made with caution. Genealogies are another source of information on migrants, though their coverage, too, is narrow (Adams and Kasakoff 1985). For the period through 1790, rates of net migration can be calculated by comparing each colony's population with the predicted excess of births over deaths; the difference measures net total (domestic and international) migration.

For 1800–1860, similar techniques have been used to calculate net migration, but for this period it is possible to separate domestic and international migration (McClelland and Zeckhauser 1982). Applications for land promised in exchange for service in the War of 1812 provide information on the state of enlistment and the state of residence later in life for men who served in the war (Oberly 1986). However, the best information on nineteenth-century migration comes from the Seventh Census of the United States in 1850, which asked for the first time that each respondent give his or her state of birth. Using this information together with the information on the respondent's state of residence, it was possible to examine patterns of internal migration for the U.S. population. "Lifetime migration" (i.e., the migration undertaken between the individual's birth and the date at which the individual is observed in the census) could now be calculated (see Tables Ac1–52). By examining the change in the native-born population in each state together with information on births and deaths (from either separate counts of vital events or the data by age in the census itself), net migration could now be estimated as well (see Tables Ac53–413). Until the end of the Second World War, this was the only source of information available on internal migration for the entire nation. The introduction, in 1947, of the Current Population Survey (a joint project of the U.S. Bureau of the Census and the U.S. Bureau of Labor Statistics) provided additional information: in most years, respondents were asked whether they had moved to a different house, county, or state over a specified time interval (see Tables Ac419–436).

The greatest shortcoming generally in the nation's statistics on internal migration is the lack of pre-1935 data on migration over specified time intervals. Thus, for example, we do not know how many people made intercounty or interstate moves over the course of a year or five years or ten years for any time before 1935. The only information available for the nineteenth century is how many people had moved by the time of a given census out of the state in which they were born. Now we can use new microlevel data from most of the federal censuses from 1850 onward, which report each individual's age, place of birth, and place of residence, and get better results. It is possible to create what demographers refer to as synthetic cohorts and follow their internal migration. For example, we could use the 1850 Census to note the distribution of people born in New England between 1820 and 1830 (these people would show up in the 1850 microlevel data with ages between 20 and 30). We could then look for the same birth cohort in 1860 (when they would be between 30 and 40 years of age) and in 1870 (when they would be between 40 and 50 years of age). In this way, it is possible to say how the distribution of locations for these individuals who all started their lives in New England changed at regular ten-year intervals.[4]

Several studies centered on particular communities have attempted to identify out-migrants by comparing census manuscripts or census-like enumerations (city directories, tax lists, or voter lists) at different dates.[5] These studies, however, cannot distinguish out-migrations from deaths, as they do not observe individuals who do not appear in the second enumeration. Three studies have linked individuals across successive census manuscripts and made it possible for us to examine migration patterns over ten-year periods that

---

[3] This chapter focuses on migration among units within the boundaries of the United States. International migration into the United States is treated in Chapter Ad.

[4] This approach is taken in Hall and Ruggles (2004) and Rosenbloom and Sundstrom (2004).

[5] Several of these studies are summarized in Thernstrom (1973).

explicitly distinguish the experiences of out-migrants from those of decedents (Schaefer 1985; Steckel 1988; Ferrie 1996).

General Trends

For the colonial period, only a few broad generalizations are possible. By the end of the seventeenth century, New England was already sending more of its population to other places than it was receiving people from other colonies and from abroad; from 1680 to 1780, the region saw a net loss of 52,000 people (Gemery 2000, p. 171). It appears that geographic mobility rates increased over the last quarter of the eighteenth century. Between 1771 and 1798, the fraction of men in a sample of Massachusetts genealogies who had not moved from their place of birth fell from one half to one third, as the fraction moving 100 miles or more rose from one eighth to one third (Adams and Kasakoff 1985, p. 367). In militia muster rolls from the French and Indian and Revolutionary Wars, migration rates also seem to have increased over time: in the four colonies for which muster rolls were examined in both wars (New York, Pennsylvania, Maryland, and Virginia), the fraction of native-born recruits who enlisted in the county where they were born fell from the French and Indian War (1754–1763) to the Revolutionary War (1776–1783). Mobility was generally higher in the South, and a substantial urban-to-rural migration among the native-born can be seen (Villaflor and Sokoloff 1982, pp. 542, 562).

Between 1800 and 1860, migration rates appeared to increase further. The predominant trend was movement from east to west, with the Middle Atlantic states (New Jersey, and the eastern portions of New York and Pennsylvania) providing most of the migrants to the Northwest. East–west migration was greater in volume in the Northern states than in the Southern states, and there is evidence of some south–north migration in the decades prior to the Civil War (McClelland and Zeckhauser 1982, pp. 6–7).[6]

Despite their shortcomings, the data on internal migration over the century and a half since the first questions on place of birth were included in the 1850 Census of Population document several important general trends in internal migration. Figure Ac-A shows the fraction of the native-born population residing in the state of birth at each census from 1850 to 1990. The first regularity is the clear rise since 1900 in the fraction of the population located outside the state, division, and region where they were born. This fraction rises with only one interruption – in the 1930s, when it falls slightly. Before 1900, there is a decline, suggesting that before the era of increasing mobility in the post-1900 period, there was a decrease in mobility from the eve of the Civil War to 1900.

This measure of lifetime migration is somewhat misleading, however, if the age structure of the population changes over time. And the United States was clearly a population with more young people in the second half of the nineteenth century than in the second half of the twentieth. If attention is restricted to individuals of a particular age at each census, a somewhat different picture emerges. Among white native-born males of age 55 at the time of the census, the fraction residing outside the state of birth was 45 percent in 1850 (those born in 1795). By 1900 (for those born in 1845), this fraction had fallen to 40 percent, and it reached its

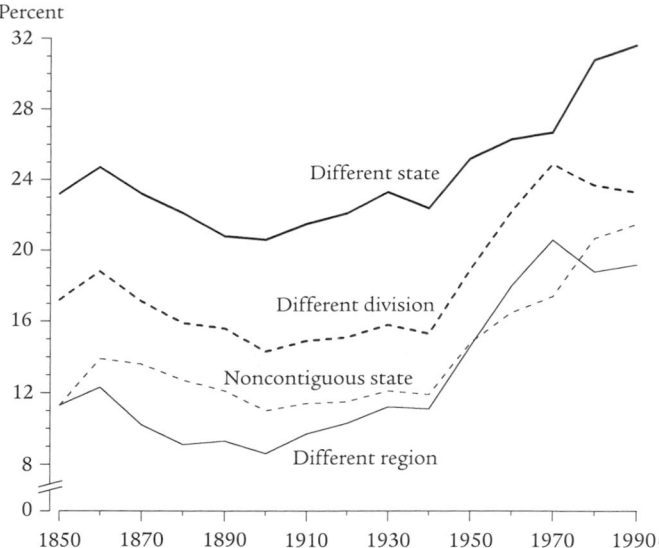

FIGURE Ac-A **Percentage of the native-born population living outside state of birth: 1850–1990**

Sources

1850–1860: series Ac19, Ac21, Ac26, and Ac28; thereafter, series Ac5, Ac7, Ac12, and Ac14.

Documentation

Note that the data cover only the white population for 1850–1860. See Table Ap-G in Appendix 2 regarding the composition of census regions and divisions.

nadir in 1940 (among those born in 1885) at 30 percent. By 1990, it had climbed to 39 percent, still substantially below its level in the 1850–1880 period. Lifetime interstate migration thus seems to be somewhat less common at the end of the twentieth century than in the second half of the nineteenth century (Hall and Ruggles 2004, Figure 3a; see also Rosenbloom and Sundstrom 2004, Figure 4).

Table Ac-B reports net migration by region for three eras (1850–1900, 1900–1940, and 1940–1990) for the native-born white and black populations. These were calculated using the "census survivor" technique.[7] The most striking patterns here are: (1) the persistent population losses among whites suffered by the New England and Middle Atlantic states, and even by the East North Central states (the old Northwest) from 1850 onward; (2) the large flows of white population into both the Pacific and South Atlantic states since 1940; and (3) the onset of the "Great Migration" out of the South seen in the data for blacks, with out-migration doubling in volume for the South Atlantic states and tripling in volume for the East South Central states between 1850–1900 and 1900–1940, and then nearly tripling again for the East South Central states and rising by a factor of six for the West South Central states between 1900–1940 and 1940–1990.

Since 1920, the U.S. Department of Agriculture has followed migration from farms to nonfarm locations (see Table Ac414–418). The rate of net migration away from farms in Figure Ac-C shows a great deal of year-to-year fluctuation that reflects economic

---

[6] These findings are supported by Oberly's (1986, p. 433) analysis of military bounty land warrant recipients from the War of 1812. By the 1850s, nearly 20 percent of those born in New York had relocated to the Northwest, representing a higher rate of migration to this region than from New England.

[7] This technique relies on the relationship $P_{t+n} - P_t = (B - D) + (M - X)$, where P is the population at each date, B and D are the numbers of births and deaths between those dates, and M and X are in-migration and out-migration. With information on P, B, and D, it is possible to estimate net migration, $M - X$.

TABLE Ac-B   Net migration of the native-born population, by region, race, and major time period: 1850–1990

	New England	Middle Atlantic	East North Central	West North Central	South Atlantic	East South Central	West South Central	Mountain	Pacific
	Thousand	Thousand	Thousand	Thousand	Thousand	Thousand	Thousand	Thousand	Thousand
White									
1850–1900	−283.5	−1,034.8	−753.9	1,137.2	−614.8	−1,022.3	1,018.3	414.6	638.4
1900–1940	−346.7	−587.7	−2.3	−2,190.1	73.6	−1,344.6	38.7	403.6	3,954.6
1940–1990	−753.7	−7,208.5	−5,621.2	−3,058.6	7,544.0	−1,059.7	934.0	2,670.2	6,604.2
Black									
1850–1900	32.8	170.0	128.5	39.9	−498.9	−221.8	325.5	0.0	0.0
1900–1940	32.6	764.5	677.4	114.3	−957.7	−658.5	−105.2	21.9	111.3
1940–1990	160.7	562.1	999.0	91.8	−1,015.0	−1,717.4	−642.2	210.0	1,321.5

Sources

Calculated from series Ac258–309 and Ac362–413.

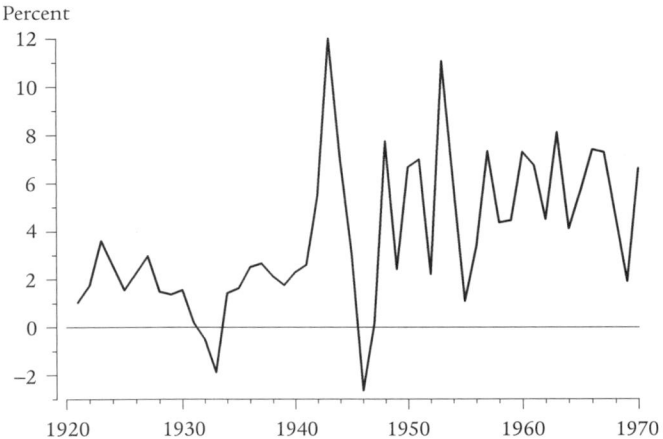

FIGURE Ac-C   Net outmigration from farms as a percentage of farm population: 1921–1970

Source

The negative of series Ac416 expressed as a percentage of series Ac414.

FIGURE Ac-D   Intercounty mobility – percentage of the population living in a different county at a later date: 1935–1999

Sources

Series Ac419, Ac424, Ac428, and Ac433.

Documentation

The years on the horizontal axis represent the beginning of given time intervals.

conditions in agriculture. In only three years – 1932, 1933, and 1946 – is the rate negative. The former reflects back-to-the-farm migration in the depths of the Depression, whereas the latter reflects the return of World War II veterans and those employed in wartime industries to the farm. The average rate of migration away from farms rises sharply from 2 to 3 percent per year before World War II to roughly 5 percent per year after the war.[8]

The Current Population Survey (from 1947 onward) and the Census of Population (from 1940 onward) provide more detailed information on short-distance migration. The percentages changing county since 1935 show remarkably little trend over time (see Figure Ac-D). The only substantial difference is between the 1940 figures for migration over five years (which report pre–World War II migration between 1935 and 1940) and the entire postwar period. If anything, the American population seems to have become slightly less mobile since the mid-1980s.

A large number of studies have been completed for specific communities in the United States that give us a sense of geographic mobility in the nineteenth century that is similar conceptually to that contained in the Current Population Survey and the censuses from 1940 onward. The ten-year nonpersistence rates (the fractions of individuals not located in the same county over a decade) for mid-nineteenth-century communities were 56 percent in eleven cities (1850–1880) and 64 percent in nine rural counties (1850–1880). Higher rates were observed for lower-class workers before World War I, but higher rates were then observed for white-collar workers after World War I (these studies are surveyed in Thernstrom 1973). These studies are unable to distinguish out-migration from deaths, however, and tell us nothing about where out-migrants have gone.

An alternative approach is to create data like that in the contemporary Current Population Survey by linking individuals across successive censuses. In one study, this has been done for 4,938 native-born males linked at 1850–1860 (see Ferrie 1996). Of the nearly five thousand males located in both 1850 and 1860, 47 percent changed counties between these dates (Ferrie 1996, Table 5).[9] Unfortunately, none of the intervals in the Current Population Survey series are as long as ten years. However, there are intervals of one and five years reported, as shown in Figure Ac-D. Based

---

[8] Migration from rural to urban places can be inferred from data on the population of rural and urban places given in Tables Aa684–698 through Aa716–775.

[9] Oberly (1986, p. 435) finds that a much higher fraction – 85 percent – of those born in Virginia had made an intercounty move by the 1850s.

TABLE Ac-E   Gross migration of the native-born population, by region: 1850–1860 and the late twentieth century

Period	Origin region	Destination Region								Observations
		New England	Middle Atlantic	East North Central	West North Central	South Atlantic	East South Central	West South Central	Mountain and Pacific	
		Percent	Percent	Percent	Percent	Percent	Percent	Percent	Percent	Number
1850–1860	New England	88.65	4.43	4.20	1.02	0.11	0.11	1.48	0.00	881
	Middle Atlantic	3.52	78.96	12.34	2.75	0.96	0.51	0.70	0.26	1,564
	East North Central	1.94	6.91	76.85	9.82	0.73	0.85	2.18	0.73	825
	West North Central	1.87	6.54	11.21	65.42	1.87	2.80	7.48	2.80	107
	South Atlantic	1.31	2.25	2.43	1.87	87.27	3.56	0.94	0.37	534
	East South Central	0.39	0.78	6.64	7.81	3.13	74.22	5.86	1.17	256
	West South Central	2.94	4.41	7.35	10.29	0.00	4.41	69.12	1.47	68
	Mountain and Pacific	11.11	7.41	14.81	3.70	0.00	7.41	3.70	51.85	27
Average of three periods:	New England	81.10	9.64	2.71	0.98	2.96	0.65	0.63	1.34	56,580
1965–1970, 1975–1980,	Middle Atlantic	2.12	86.94	2.54	0.74	5.28	0.89	0.61	0.88	165,416
1985–1990	East North Central	0.66	3.65	79.31	3.39	3.54	6.21	1.92	1.32	205,844
	West North Central	0.49	1.66	6.47	81.69	1.29	1.62	3.68	3.12	88,536
	South Atlantic	2.40	9.48	6.70	1.91	70.83	4.79	1.88	2.01	169,185
	East South Central	0.46	1.70	4.62	1.29	5.33	82.66	2.76	1.18	69,678
	West South Central	0.74	2.45	4.63	4.46	2.87	3.88	76.92	4.04	113,488
	Mountain and Pacific	2.07	6.37	10.20	10.79	3.24	2.27	8.15	56.91	204,797

Sources

Computed from the following: Integrated Public Use Microdata Series (IPUMS) for 1965–1970, 1975–1980, and 1985–1990; and a linked 1850–1860 Census sample described in Ferrie (1996). See the Guide to the Millennial Edition for information on IPUMS.

Documentation

The figures cover native-born males ages 15 and older in the base year. The percentages in each row may not sum to 100 percent owing to rounding.

on these rates, over a ten-year interval in the post–World War II period, roughly 37 percent of those present in the United States in both years would have changed county.[10] Another comparison is possible: among males age 20–29 in the 1850–1860 linked sample, 56 percent changed county over a decade; in the young men cohort of the National Longitudinal Survey, the rate of intercounty mobility among males age 20–29 was only 49 percent over the period 1971–1981. This suggests that intercounty migration rates may have been more than 25 percent higher in the 1850s than they were from the 1950s onward.

The availability of linked data for the nineteenth century makes possible a final comparison with more recent data: rates of *gross* migration among regions. Table Ac-E shows interregional flows for the 1850–1860 decade and interregional flows in the five years preceding the 1970, 1980, and 1990 Censuses. In both the 1850s and the last third of the twentieth century, New England is a region of low population turnover: even though it lost one tenth of its native-born adult male population in the 1850s and one fifth of it over a typical five-year period between 1965 and 1990, it experienced very little in-migration. The East North Central and West North Central states experienced high turnover in the 1850s (for example, with one quarter departing the East North Central states, but large inflows from the Middle Atlantic states and the West North Central states). By the twentieth century, these regions experienced much lower turnover. In the 1850s, in both the North and the South, rates of out-migration from east to west increased; by the twentieth century, this pattern was no longer apparent (e.g.,

New England lost more population over five years than the Middle Atlantic or West North Central states; the South Atlantic region lost more than any region except the Mountain and Pacific regions). Finally, gross flows reveal a somewhat surprising flow from south to north in the decade before the Civil War: a substantial fraction of those who began the 1850s in the East South Central and West South Central regions moved by 1860 into the East North Central and West North Central states. In the late twentieth century, this flow reversed direction: population moved from the Middle Atlantic to the South Atlantic, from the East North Central to the East South Central, and from the West North Central to the West South Central, though this latter flow was smaller than in the 1850s.

References

Adams, John, and Alice Kasakoff. 1985. "Wealth and Migration in Massachusetts and Maine: 1771–1798." *Journal of Economic History* 45 (June): 363–8.

Ferrie, Joseph P. 1996. "A New Sample of Americans Linked from the 1850 Public Use Micro Sample of the Federal Census of Population to the 1860 Federal Census Manuscript Schedules." *Historical Methods* 29 (Fall): 141–56.

Gemery, Henry A. 2000. "The White Population of the Colonial United States." In Michael Haines and Richard Steckel, editors. *A Population History of North America*. Cambridge University Press.

Greenwood, Michael J. 1997. "Internal Migration in Developed Countries." In M. R. Rosenzweig and O. Stark, editors. *Handbook of Population and Family Economics*. Elsevier.

Hall, Patricia Kelly, and Steven Ruggles. 2004. "'Restless in the Midst of Their Prosperity': New Evidence on the Internal Migration of Americans, 1850–2000." *Journal of American History* 91 (4): 829–46.

Margo, Robert A. 2000. *Wages and Labor Markets in the United States, 1820–1860*. University of Chicago Press.

McClelland, Peter D., and Richard J. Zeckhauser. 1982. *Demographic Dimensions of the New Republic: American Interregional Migration, Vital Statistics, and Manumissions, 1800–1860*. Cambridge University Press.

---

[10] This extrapolation is based on a linear regression using the years in which both one- and five-year migration rates are reported, with the intercounty migration rate as the dependent variable and the number of years in the migration question (one or five) as the independent variable. The estimated intercept is 3.6 and the coefficient on the number of years is 2.9. If the microlevel data from the Current Population Survey are made comparable to that in Ferrie (1996), these differences remain.

Oberly, James W. 1986. "Westward Who? Estimates of Native White Interstate Migration after the War of 1812." *Journal of Economic History* 46 (June): 431–40.

Ransom, Roger, and Richard Sutch. 1986. "Did Rising Out-Migration Cause Fertility to Decline in Antebellum New England? A Life-Cycle Perspective on Old-Age Security Motives, Child Default, and Farm-Family Fertility." Working Papers on the History of Saving number 5 (April).

Rosenbloom, Joshua L., and William A. Sundstrom. 2004. "The Decline and Rise of Interstate Migration in the United States: Evidence from the IPUMS, 1850–1900." In Alexander J. Field, editor. *Research in Economic History*, volume 22. Elsevier.

Schaefer, Donald. 1985. "A Statistical Profile of Frontier and New South Migration: 1850–1860." *Agricultural History* 59 (October): 563–78.

Shryock, Henry, Jacob S. Siegel, and associates. 1980. *The Methods and Materials of Demography*. U.S. Government Printing Office.

Smith, Abbott Emerson. 1947. *Colonists in Bondage: White Servitude and Convict Labor in America, 1607–1776*. University of North Carolina Press.

Steckel, Richard. 1988. "Census Matching and Migration: A Research Strategy." *Historical Methods* 21 (Spring): 52–60.

Thernstrom, Stephen. 1973. *The Other Bostonians*. Harvard University Press.

Thornton, Russell. 2000. "Population History of Native North Americans." In Michael Haines and Richard Steckel, editors. *A Population History of North America*. Cambridge University Press.

Tocqueville, Alexis de. 2000. *Democracy in America*. Translated by Harvey C. Mansfield and Delba Winthrop. Chicago: University of Chicago Press.

Villaflor, Georgia C., and Kenneth L. Sokoloff. 1982. "Migration in Colonial America: Evidence from the Militia Muster Rolls." *Social Science History* 6 (Fall): 539–70.

Winkle, Kenneth J. 1988. *The Politics of Community: Migration and Politics in Antebellum Ohio*. Cambridge University Press.

INTERNAL MIGRATION

Joseph P. Ferrie

TABLE Ac1–42 Interstate migration – native-born population, by race and residence within or outside the state of birth: 1850–1990[1,2]

Contributed by Joseph P. Ferrie

All races

	Total	Born in state of residence		Interstate migration status				Born in outlying areas	Born abroad or at sea	State of birth not reported	Born in division of residence		Born in region of residence	
				Born in another state										
				Contiguous to state of residence		Noncontiguous to state of residence								
	Ac1	Ac2	Ac3	Ac4	Ac5	Ac6	Ac7	Ac8	Ac9	Ac10	Ac11	Ac12	Ac13	Ac14
Year	Number	Number	Percent	Number	Percent	Number	Percent	Number	Number	Number	Number	Percent	Number	Percent
1850 [3]	—	—	—	—	—	—	—	—	—	—	—	—	—	—
1860 [3]	—	—	—	—	—	—	—	—	—	—	—	—	—	—
1870	32,991,142	25,321,340	76.8	3,182,563	9.6	4,474,757	13.6	51	169	12,262	27,363,803	82.9	29,634,393	89.8
1880 [4]	43,475,840	33,882,734	77.9	4,083,004	9.4	5,509,760	12.7	51	291	0	36,582,390	84.1	39,530,266	90.9
1890 [4]	53,372,703	41,872,656	78.5	4,628,768	8.7	6,464,295	12.1	322	10,010	396,652	45,022,600	84.4	48,398,175	90.7
1900	65,653,299	51,901,722	79.0	6,308,975	9.6	7,192,070	11.0	2,923	67,151	180,458	56,248,496	85.7	60,025,002	91.4
1910	78,456,380	61,185,305	78.0	7,959,860	10.1	8,950,254	11.4	7,365	67,911	285,685	66,746,379	85.1	70,864,304	90.3
1920	91,789,928	71,071,013	77.4	9,741,781	10.6	10,532,669	11.5	38,020	92,863	313,582	77,906,515	84.9	82,308,490	89.7
1930 [5]	108,570,897	82,677,619	76.2	12,200,290	11.2	13,187,810	12.1	136,032	130,677	238,469	91,382,402	84.2	96,447,180	88.8
1940	120,074,379	92,609,754	77.1	12,583,482	10.5	14,322,504	11.9	156,956	122,169	279,514	101,694,396	84.7	106,734,907	88.9
1950	139,868,715	102,788,395	73.5	14,589,035	10.4	20,695,175	14.8	329,970	96,355	1,369,785	113,477,925	81.1	119,490,525	85.4
1960	169,587,580	119,293,462	70.3	16,640,284	9.8	28,050,769	16.5	660,425	401,510	4,541,130	131,889,464	77.8	139,065,350	82.0
1970	193,454,051	131,296,419	67.9	18,081,446	9.3	33,577,139	17.4	873,241	744,155	8,881,651	145,349,492	75.1	153,603,453	79.4
1970 [6]	—	—	—	—	—	—	—	—	—	—	—	—	—	—
1980	212,861,712	145,268,860	68.2	21,445,004	10.1	44,066,020	20.7	1,088,269	993,559	0	162,403,336	76.3	172,897,262	81.2
1990	227,522,504	153,298,336	67.4	23,089,783	10.1	48,865,208	21.5	1,359,517	909,660	0	172,193,980	76.7	183,897,351	80.8

Notes appear at end of table

(continued)

TABLE Ac1–42 Interstate migration – native-born population, by race and residence within or outside the state of birth: 1850–1990 *Continued*

White

	Total	Born in state of residence		Interstate migration status						State of birth not reported	Born in division of residence		Born in region of residence	
				Born in another state				Born in outlying areas	Born abroad or at sea					
				Contiguous to state of residence		Noncontiguous to state of residence								
		Number	Percent	Number	Percent	Number	Percent	Number	Number	Number	Number	Percent	Number	Percent
	Ac15	Ac16	Ac17	Ac18	Ac19	Ac20	Ac21	Ac22	Ac23	Ac24	Ac25	Ac26	Ac27	Ac28
Year	Number	Number	Percent	Number	Percent	Number	Percent	Number	Number	Number	Number	Percent	Number	Percent
1850 [3]	17,772,270	13,624,902	76.7	2,105,724	11.9	2,006,033	11.3	—	—	35,611	14,707,719	82.8	15,765,010	88.7
1860 [3]	23,353,385	17,527,069	75.1	2,529,494	10.8	3,242,190	13.9	—	2,618	52,014	18,969,880	81.2	20,481,089	87.7
1870	28,095,665	21,355,242	76.0	2,779,526	9.9	3,951,487	14.1	38	160	9,212	23,130,521	82.3	24,914,093	88.7
1880	36,843,291	28,310,081	76.8	3,576,340	9.7	4,956,596	13.5	50	224	0	30,681,197	83.3	33,126,949	89.9
1890 [4]	45,862,023	35,524,287	77.5	4,064,121	8.9	5,926,722	12.9	279	9,543	337,071	38,315,138	83.5	41,227,682	89.9
1900	56,595,379	44,278,021	78.2	5,534,957	9.8	6,562,833	11.6	2,563	63,366	153,639	48,102,508	85.0	51,407,811	90.8
1910	68,386,412	52,806,091	77.2	7,018,331	10.3	8,245,872	12.0	6,413	64,356	245,349	57,703,559	84.4	61,361,087	89.7
1920	81,108,161	62,524,789	77.1	8,675,416	10.7	9,521,420	11.7	26,476	88,838	271,222	68,601,740	84.6	72,563,235	89.5
1930 [5]	95,497,800	72,821,481	76.2	10,824,966	11.3	11,452,788	12.0	71,582	125,060	201,923	80,492,581	84.3	85,075,201	89.1
1940	106,795,732	82,533,805	77.3	11,298,723	10.6	12,492,817	11.7	99,170	117,933	253,284	90,586,586	84.8	95,225,370	89.2
1950	124,382,950	91,984,045	74.0	13,195,215	10.6	17,629,435	14.2	289,435	88,065	1,196,755	101,491,060	81.6	107,061,715	86.1
1960	149,543,683	105,655,834	70.7	15,174,128	10.1	24,070,953	16.1	621,762	377,398	3,643,608	116,915,448	78.2	123,605,716	82.7
1970	169,273,531	115,156,268	68.0	16,633,079	9.8	29,039,976	17.2	790,751	680,042	6,973,415	127,824,055	75.5	135,541,644	80.1
1970 [6]	—	—	—	—	—	—	—	—	—	—	—	—	—	—
1980	183,207,102	124,762,766	68.1	19,259,430	10.5	37,516,616	20.5	968,935	699,355	0	139,769,737	76.3	149,345,360	81.5
1990	194,458,247	130,014,494	66.9	20,593,322	10.6	42,007,868	21.6	1,213,090	629,473	0	146,453,824	75.3	157,042,738	80.8

Black and other races

Year	Total	Born in state of residence		Interstate migration status — Born in another state				Born in outlying areas	Born abroad or at sea	State of birth not reported	Born in division of residence		Born in region	
				Contiguous to state of residence		Noncontiguous to state of residence								
	Ac29	Ac30	Ac31	Ac32	Ac33	Ac34	Ac35	Ac36	Ac37	Ac38	Ac39	Ac40	Ac41	Ac42
	Number	Number	Percent	Number	Percent	Number	Percent	Number	Number	Number	Number	Percent	Number	Percent
1850 [3]	—	—	—	—	—	—	—	—	—	—	—	—	—	—
1860 [3]	—	—	—	—	—	—	—	—	—	—	—	—	—	—
1870	4,895,477	3,966,098	81.0	403,037	8.2	523,270	10.7	13	9	3,050	4,233,282	86.5	4,720,300	96.4
1880	6,632,549	5,572,653	84.0	506,664	7.6	553,164	8.3	1	67	0	5,901,193	89.0	6,403,317	96.5
1890 [4]	7,510,680	6,348,369	84.5	564,647	7.5	537,573	7.2	43	467	59,581	6,707,462	89.3	7,170,493	95.5
1900	9,057,920	7,623,701	84.2	774,018	8.5	629,237	6.9	360	3,785	26,819	8,145,988	89.9	8,617,191	95.1
1910	10,069,968	8,379,214	83.2	941,529	9.3	704,382	7.0	952	3,555	40,336	9,042,820	89.8	9,503,217	94.4
1920	10,681,767	8,546,224	80.0	1,066,365	10.0	1,011,249	9.5	11,544	4,025	42,360	9,304,775	87.1	9,745,255	91.2
1930 [5]	13,073,097	9,856,138	75.4	1,375,324	10.5	1,735,022	13.3	64,450	5,617	36,546	10,889,821	83.3	11,371,979	87.0
1940	13,278,647	10,075,949	75.9	1,284,759	9.7	1,829,687	13.8	57,786	4,236	26,230	11,107,810	83.7	11,509,537	86.7
1950	15,485,765	10,804,350	69.8	1,393,820	9.0	3,065,740	19.8	40,535	8,290	173,030	11,986,865	77.4	12,428,810	80.3
1960	20,043,897	13,637,628	68.0	1,466,156	7.3	3,979,816	19.9	38,663	24,112	897,522	14,974,016	74.7	15,459,634	77.1
1970 [6]	24,180,520	16,140,151	66.7	1,448,367	6.0	4,537,163	18.8	82,490	64,113	1,908,236	17,525,437	72.5	18,061,809	74.7
1970	22,260,196	14,775,004	66.4	1,353,981	6.1	4,259,605	19.1	53,968	37,106	1,780,532	16,020,511	72.0	16,498,493	74.1
1980	29,654,610	20,506,094	69.1	2,185,574	7.4	6,549,404	22.1	119,334	294,204	0	22,633,599	76.3	23,551,902	79.4
1990	33,064,257	23,283,842	70.4	2,496,461	7.6	6,857,340	20.7	146,427	280,187	0	25,740,156	77.8	26,854,613	81.2

[1] Through 1950, Alaska and Hawai'i included in outlying areas.

[2] Based on a 20 percent sample (1950), 25 percent sample (1960), 5 percent sample (1970–1990).

[3] Free blacks included with whites: 434,495 in 1850; 487,970 in 1860.

[4] Excludes population of Indian Territory and Indian reservations, specially enumerated in 1890, with a native population of 117,368 white, and 208,083 Negro and other races, not distributed by state of birth.

[5] Mexicans classified under "other races."

[6] Black only.

Sources

1850–1970: Special compilations made by the University of Pennsylvania Studies of Population Redistribution and Economic Growth from the following U.S. Bureau of the Census reports. 1850, *The Seventh Census of the United States: 1850* (Robert Armstrong, public printer, 1853), pp. xxxvi-xxxviii.

1860, *Eighth Census of the United States: 1860* (U.S. Government Printing Office, 1864), Table 5 for each state, pp. 10–589 (various pages), 616–9.

1870, *Ninth Census Reports*, volume 1 (U.S. Government Printing Office, 1872), pp. 327–35.

1880, *Tenth Census Reports, Population* (U.S. Government Printing Office, 1883), pp. 484–91.

1890, *Eleventh Census Reports, Population* (U.S. Government Printing Office, 1895), part 1, pp. 564–7, 576–9.

1900, *Twelfth Census Reports, Population*, volume 1 (U.S. Government Printing Office, 1901), part 1, pp. 686–93, 702–5.

1910, *Thirteenth Census Reports, Population*, volume 1 (U.S. Government Printing Office, 1913), pp. 730–44.

1920, *Fourteenth Census Reports, Population*, volume 2 (U.S. Government Printing Office, 1922), pp. 626–40.

1930, *Fifteenth Census Reports, Population*, volume 2 (U.S. Government Printing Office, 1933), pp. 153–67.

1940, *Sixteenth Census Reports, State of Birth of the Native Population* (U.S. Government Printing Office, 1942), pp. 20–39.

1950, *U.S. Census of Population: 1950*, part 4, *Special Reports*, "State of Birth" (U.S. Government Printing Office, 1953), pp. 4A–24 to 4A-43.

1960, *U.S. Census of Population: 1960*, part 2, *Subject Reports*, Final Report PC(2)–2A, "State of Birth" (U.S. Government Printing Office, 1963).

1970, *U.S. Census of Population: 1970*, part 2, *Subject Reports*, Final Report PC(2)–2A, "State of Birth" (U.S. Government Printing Office, 1973).

1980 and 1990: Integrated Public Use Microdata Series (IPUMS), 5 percent Public Use Samples. See the Guide to the Millennial Edition for information about IPUMS.

TABLE Ac43–52 Native-born population, by race, division of residence, and division of birth: 1850–1990[1]

Contributed by Joseph P. Ferrie

							Division of residence				
			Total	New England	Middle Atlantic	East North Central	West North Central	South Atlantic	East South Central	West South Central	Mountain	Pacific
			Ac43	Ac44	Ac45	Ac46	Ac47	Ac48	Ac49	Ac50	Ac51	Ac52
Race	Census year	Division of birth	Number	Number	Number	Number	Number	Number	Number	Number	Number	Number
White	1850 [2]	Total	17,736,659	2,423,178	4,884,300	3,965,269	695,231	2,907,947	2,207,677	503,295	68,484	81,278
		New England	2,821,823	2,367,932	237,367	171,172	9,404	11,074	5,922	5,522	1,131	12,299
		Middle Atlantic	5,483,951	46,635	4,566,495	725,056	39,123	55,210	19,778	12,656	2,286	16,712
		East North Central	2,757,356	2,410	16,349	2,582,600	96,708	7,048	21,821	14,616	2,511	13,293
		West North Central	373,500	181	568	12,794	334,662	495	2,951	11,619	1,341	8,889
		South Atlantic	3,764,808	5,100	60,734	286,195	80,838	2,811,305	446,391	65,489	482	8,274
		East South Central	2,179,505	507	1,840	184,634	131,053	21,951	1,705,017	123,282	823	10,398
		West South Central	286,016	378	934	2,812	3,435	858	5,796	270,104	88	1,611
		Mountain	59,802	—	—	—	—	—	—	—	59,802	—
		Pacific	9,898	35	13	6	8	6	1	7	20	9,802
White	1860 [2]	Total	23,298,753	2,663,062	5,898,979	5,715,955	1,702,245	3,358,465	2,538,909	984,856	150,116	286,166
		New England	3,144,598	2,584,262	212,218	224,230	57,324	12,213	7,269	5,930	6,006	35,146
		Middle Atlantic	6,944,042	64,518	5,582,854	946,080	184,972	68,452	24,020	15,661	10,348	47,137
		East North Central	4,562,911	5,057	29,662	4,044,329	358,725	10,445	32,248	24,038	17,053	41,354
		West North Central	848,692	652	1,965	27,496	756,018	915	5,842	23,459	7,188	25,157
		South Atlantic	4,264,749	6,777	66,971	265,569	125,982	3,236,171	411,919	133,672	3,046	14,642
		East South Central	2,781,432	797	3,061	202,798	210,990	28,932	2,048,662	263,132	4,306	18,754
		West South Central	550,043	522	1,648	4,322	7,759	1,230	8,887	518,799	950	5,926
		Mountain	100,739	—	—	—	—	—	—	—	100,739	—
		Pacific	101,547	477	600	1,131	475	107	62	165	480	98,050
White	1870	Total	28,086,255	2,807,945	6,788,821	7,325,414	3,038,215	3,469,244	2,835,457	1,161,542	224,834	434,783
		New England	3,270,626	2,704,882	180,779	212,928	97,087	14,708	5,552	4,418	9,181	41,091
		Middle Atlantic	8,065,869	83,537	6,479,733	967,899	339,388	84,225	23,259	13,223	20,533	54,072
		East North Central	6,550,805	8,463	48,589	5,625,542	704,106	19,407	48,469	24,893	20,631	50,705
		West North Central	1,684,544	1,621	5,031	62,386	1,524,350	2,051	8,851	33,449	11,644	35,161
		South Atlantic	4,206,178	6,497	65,515	230,689	138,450	3,308,462	313,905	123,369	5,032	14,259
		East South Central	3,165,831	1,206	4,920	214,814	210,645	37,442	2,420,279	253,883	4,766	17,876
		West South Central	765,053	730	2,651	7,885	20,005	2,591	14,865	707,821	1,487	7,018
		Mountain	153,772	66	138	432	2,169	52	65	159	147,771	2,920
		Pacific	223,577	943	1,465	2,839	2,015	306	212	327	3,789	211,681
White	1880	Total	36,843,017	3,177,460	8,287,904	9,098,915	4,950,250	4,483,127	3,563,017	2,067,174	468,678	746,492
		New England	3,614,346	3,031,308	176,366	178,124	123,105	17,545	4,886	6,645	21,169	55,198
		Middle Atlantic	9,693,744	116,499	7,921,093	899,051	479,473	103,764	21,758	23,520	51,848	76,738
		East North Central	9,062,808	12,806	73,777	7,521,118	1,126,361	42,533	67,865	69,347	62,709	86,292
		West North Central	3,117,714	3,176	11,055	101,161	2,801,794	4,361	11,515	78,285	43,790	62,577
		South Atlantic	5,169,015	8,618	90,530	192,311	149,700	4,256,663	272,498	168,103	12,170	18,422
		East South Central	4,077,215	1,725	7,269	192,398	232,785	52,704	3,164,256	390,416	12,557	23,105
		West South Central	1,410,432	1,016	4,219	9,494	28,023	4,633	19,693	1,328,521	5,920	8,913
		Mountain	265,689	711	1,096	1,941	4,925	339	177	1,083	248,307	7,110
		Pacific	432,054	1,601	2,499	3,317	4,084	585	369	1,254	10,208	408,137

Division of residence

Race	Census year	Division of birth	Total	New England	Middle Atlantic	East North Central	West North Central	South Atlantic	East South Central	West South Central	Mountain	Pacific
			Ac43	Ac44	Ac45	Ac46	Ac47	Ac48	Ac49	Ac50	Ac51	Ac52
			Number	Number	Number	Number	Number	Number	Number	Number	Number	Number
White	1890 [3]	Total	45,515,130	3,498,667	9,620,523	10,679,859	7,053,073	5,376,140	4,186,475	2,937,889	856,949	1,305,555
		New England	3,869,022	3,308,754	157,962	141,909	126,561	21,469	5,802	7,058	28,966	70,541
		Middle Atlantic	11,026,901	149,620	9,222,526	769,746	507,162	115,883	24,664	29,588	84,419	123,293
		East North Central	11,459,737	18,588	95,477	9,280,356	1,464,505	57,949	94,521	112,084	138,062	198,195
		West North Central	5,083,535	5,555	16,549	137,664	4,511,678	8,284	14,461	121,395	113,722	154,227
		South Atlantic	5,988,960	9,927	107,554	159,824	151,969	5,101,959	232,107	177,366	20,095	28,159
		East South Central	4,794,666	2,026	9,597	171,757	238,208	62,460	3,790,050	466,533	20,572	33,463
		West South Central	2,138,369	1,275	5,167	11,125	36,260	6,446	23,931	2,019,570	15,988	18,607
		Mountain	452,657	756	1,664	3,155	10,025	523	341	2,074	417,647	16,472
		Pacific	701,283	2,166	4,027	4,323	6,705	1,167	598	2,221	17,478	662,598
White	1900	Total	56,375,811	4,063,335	11,764,269	13,037,883	8,501,171	6,487,097	4,947,654	4,494,019	1,281,152	1,799,231
		New England	4,304,088	3,782,347	175,529	117,475	95,473	21,464	4,972	7,981	27,658	71,189
		Middle Atlantic	12,994,778	213,818	11,203,366	725,710	410,130	152,668	24,477	39,005	88,623	136,981
		East North Central	13,990,407	31,065	162,945	11,539,208	1,424,563	83,300	119,432	192,025	180,312	257,557
		West North Central	7,211,362	11,316	33,376	267,723	6,142,945	15,230	22,391	305,129	190,402	222,850
		South Atlantic	7,028,299	14,206	152,680	154,152	125,802	6,105,309	221,912	197,884	24,638	31,716
		East South Central	5,696,181	3,111	16,105	195,986	209,595	95,892	4,515,686	597,479	26,407	35,920
		West South Central	3,330,565	1,888	7,950	18,745	58,754	9,877	36,961	3,143,786	28,208	24,396
		Mountain	765,078	1,716	4,543	9,280	21,396	1,446	823	6,401	685,356	34,117
		Pacific	1,055,053	3,868	7,775	9,604	12,513	1,911	1,000	4,329	29,548	984,505
White	1910	Total	68,070,294	4,641,157	14,003,037	14,791,593	9,682,750	7,765,765	5,657,676	6,344,580	2,063,208	3,120,528
		New England	4,867,376	4,305,759	215,838	97,016	73,131	28,394	5,221	11,024	30,999	99,994
		Middle Atlantic	15,123,715	247,999	13,264,960	652,982	337,132	191,251	26,602	60,485	110,309	231,995
		East North Central	16,287,667	37,814	211,088	13,239,961	1,411,304	111,408	129,227	309,955	291,913	544,997
		West North Central	9,210,184	13,453	48,916	323,844	7,410,156	22,494	26,257	484,944	378,359	501,761
		South Atlantic	8,273,219	19,347	201,618	167,764	109,371	7,244,553	220,304	204,527	42,174	63,561
		East South Central	6,631,841	4,461	24,205	250,933	196,661	145,352	5,198,232	686,321	52,956	72,720
		West South Central	4,909,800	3,879	13,329	27,218	91,459	15,183	48,275	4,563,489	84,119	62,849
		Mountain	1,206,525	3,876	11,416	17,638	36,206	3,417	2,055	15,963	1,024,876	91,078
		Pacific	1,559,967	4,569	11,667	14,237	17,330	3,713	1,503	7,872	47,503	1,451,573
White	1920	Total	80,721,625	5,420,554	16,651,261	17,641,695	10,798,750	9,311,926	6,286,445	7,615,242	2,730,830	4,264,922
		New England	5,613,387	5,003,487	251,361	103,025	53,349	49,436	5,803	13,680	25,804	107,442
		Middle Atlantic	17,754,221	305,384	15,714,467	746,504	252,354	264,186	27,434	74,672	99,028	270,192
		East North Central	18,836,603	48,079	273,633	15,606,106	1,292,533	179,169	136,431	306,576	319,171	674,905
		West North Central	11,077,968	17,259	72,434	462,835	8,699,489	50,549	32,428	534,721	529,090	679,163
		South Atlantic	9,605,593	24,111	246,672	232,580	90,706	8,487,281	222,844	180,365	45,179	75,855
		East South Central	7,445,580	5,815	36,076	377,338	179,126	234,259	5,791,383	663,654	63,268	94,661
		West South Central	6,358,200	4,562	21,272	53,305	141,216	30,900	64,080	5,791,839	133,956	117,070
		Mountain	1,785,103	4,997	15,165	32,948	62,656	7,714	3,300	34,621	1,442,878	180,824
		Pacific	2,244,970	6,860	20,181	27,054	27,321	8,432	2,742	15,114	72,456	2,064,810
White	1930 [4]	Total	95,099,235	6,204,011	19,780,421	20,990,462	11,778,688	11,025,521	7,158,480	8,906,478	2,999,731	6,255,443
		New England	6,535,693	5,752,888	392,102	114,311	36,849	65,025	6,084	12,825	19,829	135,780
		Middle Atlantic	20,610,693	321,693	18,427,461	834,310	[a] 179,234	314,394	27,532	69,246	78,751	358,072
		East North Central	21,523,034	53,302	362,359	18,167,867	1,102,154	229,645	151,942	278,633	275,415	901,717
		West North Central	13,113,754	21,386	106,542	760,889	9,918,618	68,103	39,461	558,788	562,360	1,077,607
		South Atlantic	11,319,720	29,326	353,731	322,548	72,008	9,955,907	271,607	166,797	42,096	105,700
		East South Central	8,531,783	7,315	52,209	596,959	153,991	326,357	6,563,867	635,683	61,895	133,507
		West South Central	8,039,544	5,401	34,716	101,431	202,164	44,638	90,120	7,117,591	179,510	263,973
		Mountain	2,317,079	5,090	22,734	53,880	82,608	10,884	4,219	47,331	1,699,814	390,519
		Pacific	3,107,935	7,610	28,567	38,267	31,062	10,568	3,648	19,584	80,061	2,888,568

(continued)

Notes appear at end of table

TABLE Ac43–52   Native-born population, by race, division of residence, and division of birth: 1850–1990   *Continued*

							Division of residence				
Race	Census year	Division of birth	Total	New England	Middle Atlantic	East North Central	West North Central	South Atlantic	East South Central	West South Central	Mountain	Pacific
			Ac43	Ac44	Ac45	Ac46	Ac47	Ac48	Ac49	Ac50	Ac51	Ac52
			Number	Number	Number	Number	Number	Number	Number	Number	Number	Number
White	1940	Total	106,325,345	6,788,754	21,562,277	22,892,971	12,296,354	12,766,703	7,936,741	10,255,758	3,698,071	8,127,716
		New England	7,091,608	6,292,313	410,907	101,637	25,600	91,015	6,952	12,776	16,803	133,605
		Middle Atlantic	22,321,593	340,901	20,113,804	765,363	123,075	440,461	30,373	64,963	66,229	376,424
		East North Central	23,255,752	62,294	393,318	20,031,073	896,605	301,011	155,711	238,290	242,314	935,136
		West North Central	14,401,132	25,609	120,901	818,929	10,705,594	102,722	45,398	516,685	633,440	1,431,854
		South Atlantic	12,601,815	35,011	360,021	314,513	54,368	11,290,451	246,371	135,018	39,439	126,623
		East South Central	9,333,222	9,258	59,151	616,381	133,904	432,330	7,336,524	531,150	59,299	155,225
		West South Central	10,085,283	7,189	43,268	142,119	237,853	69,671	105,050	8,669,708	270,484	539,941
		Mountain	3,089,040	6,431	26,562	59,659	85,530	18,445	5,519	61,359	2,271,873	553,662
		Pacific	4,145,900	9,748	34,345	43,297	33,825	20,597	4,843	25,809	98,190	3,875,246
White	1950	Total	122,808,695	7,765,220	23,667,205	26,038,680	12,848,660	15,490,860	8,652,720	11,564,885	4,543,490	12,236,975
		New England	8,123,805	7,040,420	445,570	130,600	31,000	185,885	16,245	35,245	30,575	208,265
		Middle Atlantic	25,133,805	456,510	21,967,895	883,575	119,430	800,840	61,425	124,225	113,220	606,685
		East North Central	26,253,590	90,555	434,780	22,344,070	801,785	498,185	208,910	292,995	314,300	1,268,010
		West North Central	15,804,720	40,080	142,145	925,255	11,186,855	180,270	66,485	532,565	697,650	2,033,415
		South Atlantic	14,808,625	66,925	434,560	461,355	70,370	12,976,725	326,755	174,420	63,965	233,550
		East South Central	10,389,290	19,555	82,350	908,915	132,160	613,630	7,795,585	523,035	75,205	238,855
		West South Central	12,022,265	18,830	69,435	223,550	314,375	141,435	150,350	9,699,470	357,420	1,047,400
		Mountain	3,945,625	11,210	34,890	79,265	109,840	36,690	10,845	98,400	2,721,865	842,620
		Pacific	6,326,970	21,135	55,580	82,095	82,845	57,200	16,120	84,530	169,290	5,758,175
White	1960	Total	144,900,915	8,860,751	26,514,136	30,582,096	14,065,699	18,980,114	9,132,225	13,395,232	6,126,688	17,243,974
		New England	9,379,371	7,867,550	501,445	161,376	41,355	339,937	27,450	54,718	53,109	332,431
		Middle Atlantic	28,792,297	563,705	24,484,595	996,389	131,702	1,292,957	90,898	172,495	180,074	879,482
		East North Central	30,831,621	130,905	503,605	25,809,611	771,484	876,755	269,049	356,533	451,384	1,662,295
		West North Central	17,598,319	56,135	163,403	1,017,835	12,224,504	286,651	87,599	555,159	849,164	2,357,869
		South Atlantic	17,490,468	114,501	526,613	736,366	100,832	14,879,459	377,346	242,667	112,871	399,813
		East South Central	11,416,161	30,940	104,069	1,288,476	138,456	859,016	8,028,843	533,910	104,099	328,352
		West South Central	14,333,384	35,774	95,707	330,036	393,228	245,390	197,496	11,188,447	483,802	1,363,504
		Mountain	5,241,623	19,514	46,859	104,479	138,863	68,215	20,095	145,481	3,605,164	1,092,953
		Pacific	9,817,671	41,727	87,840	137,528	125,275	131,734	33,449	145,822	287,021	8,827,275
White	1970	Total	160,829,323	9,988,571	28,254,639	33,326,277	14,654,554	22,102,985	9,719,571	14,938,789	7,158,450	20,685,487
		New England	10,491,117	8,639,976	518,674	198,334	57,232	474,328	34,980	77,014	79,605	410,974
		Middle Atlantic	31,485,397	727,930	25,946,240	1,097,309	166,661	1,813,354	118,221	237,659	256,491	1,121,532
		East North Central	34,048,261	196,779	587,629	28,014,272	783,411	1,256,454	360,325	437,381	560,130	1,851,880
		West North Central	18,187,380	71,586	182,941	1,055,465	12,598,459	399,709	107,802	602,993	897,031	2,271,394
		South Atlantic	19,609,673	163,267	594,163	889,657	136,850	16,389,562	454,197	306,955	152,724	522,298
		East South Central	11,892,067	37,328	109,618	1,297,743	135,052	1,025,285	8,305,511	517,380	111,518	352,632
		West South Central	15,776,495	49,641	116,093	397,803	409,795	367,518	243,510	12,291,853	492,089	1,408,193
		Mountain	6,235,092	27,654	60,032	143,989	180,791	119,593	30,607	215,004	4,174,510	1,282,912
		Pacific	13,103,841	74,410	139,249	231,705	186,303	257,182	64,418	252,550	434,352	11,463,672

Division of residence

Race	Census year	Division of birth	Total	New England	Middle Atlantic	East North Central	West North Central	South Atlantic	East South Central	West South Central	Mountain	Pacific
			Ac43	Ac44	Ac45	Ac46	Ac47	Ac48	Ac49	Ac50	Ac51	Ac52
			Number	Number	Number	Number	Number	Number	Number	Number	Number	Number
White	1980	Total	181,538,812	10,740,584	28,330,183	5,003,426	15,834,036	27,222,406	11,581,470	18,752,815	10,097,186	23,976,706
		New England	11,479,862	9,025,734	535,773	225,496	75,558	754,230	61,642	139,638	159,912	501,879
		Middle Atlantic	33,848,974	958,195	25,877,257	1,144,634	214,159	3,023,463	189,778	453,765	549,964	1,437,759
		East North Central	37,742,072	238,452	604,730	29,485,205	934,275	1,996,900	617,809	788,316	991,707	2,084,678
		West North Central	19,458,385	84,283	178,256	1,094,945	13,304,593	523,263	155,932	823,590	1,129,925	2,163,598
		South Atlantic	22,670,023	197,258	635,125	930,321	187,304	18,640,618	679,560	510,055	267,454	622,328
		East South Central	13,168,437	44,465	111,764	1,190,020	147,446	1,203,507	9,382,289	599,477	149,738	339,731
		West South Central	18,465,747	53,961	122,403	409,743	443,410	465,044	330,642	14,641,758	614,379	1,384,407
		Mountain	8,007,553	39,836	95,060	219,409	255,445	200,224	56,631	342,115	5,384,350	1,414,393
		Pacific	16,697,759	98,400	169,815	303,563	271,846	415,157	107,187	454,101	849,757	14,027,933
White	1990	Total	192,615,684	11,262,664	27,926,803	34,826,725	16,036,234	31,393,765	11,882,336	20,376,772	11,817,938	27,092,447
		New England	11,957,157	9,243,758	540,520	205,979	72,331	987,522	65,769	140,161	181,305	519,812
		Middle Atlantic	34,431,909	1,079,461	25,311,093	1,031,006	218,828	3,889,796	223,108	509,863	634,855	1,533,899
		East North Central	39,383,719	288,127	642,047	29,630,405	989,644	2,771,260	751,419	989,552	1,180,191	2,141,074
		West North Central	19,670,142	100,755	182,544	1,080,453	13,397,431	689,659	184,321	893,997	1,200,151	1,940,831
		South Atlantic	24,480,311	241,517	687,619	909,821	200,754	20,173,076	739,689	545,524	306,866	675,445
		East South Central	13,046,090	44,729	108,107	1,012,198	136,389	1,370,223	9,333,643	585,397	150,040	305,364
		West South Central	19,980,820	77,845	148,924	420,553	465,985	709,361	387,788	15,777,542	658,771	1,334,051
		Mountain	9,261,333	52,873	92,521	197,659	260,750	251,350	66,515	399,556	6,442,507	1,497,602
		Pacific	20,404,203	133,599	213,428	338,651	294,122	551,518	130,084	535,180	1,063,252	17,144,369
Black and other races	1870	Total	4,892,405	30,847	146,581	134,896	145,086	2,216,892	1,463,794	738,385	3,456	12,468
		New England	22,477	19,514	1,426	405	135	345	155	236	43	218
		Middle Atlantic	120,810	2,904	110,845	2,941	664	1,786	444	611	113	502
		East North Central	67,523	100	430	62,667	2,220	375	857	718	69	87
		West North Central	117,168	31	78	4,817	101,335	159	3,096	7,011	296	345
		South Atlantic	2,622,615	7,873	32,620	27,869	15,027	2,201,827	210,996	124,766	384	1,253
		East South Central	1,426,109	244	828	34,648	21,324	11,437	1,238,885	118,026	295	422
		West South Central	504,139	167	328	1,512	4,306	940	9,345	486,997	352	192
		Mountain	1,952	2	3	9	59	4	3	9	1,813	50
		Pacific	9,612	12	23	28	16	19	13	11	91	9,399
Black and other races	1880	Total	6,632,481	39,430	188,000	191,082	206,963	2,939,779	1,926,935	1,087,916	23,548	28,828
		New England	29,078	25,077	1,843	466	210	648	235	399	41	159
		Middle Atlantic	149,988	3,309	136,808	3,445	900	3,061	995	895	155	420
		East North Central	116,353	150	739	105,676	3,728	1,236	2,753	1,641	233	197
		West North Central	159,284	29	147	6,194	141,665	180	2,981	6,742	1,005	341
		South Atlantic	3,340,699	10,369	46,950	30,110	16,439	2,917,316	197,100	120,570	729	1,116
		East South Central	1,942,781	288	963	43,205	35,325	16,183	1,708,900	136,846	657	414
		West South Central	847,230	167	419	1,902	8,583	1,073	13,918	820,685	220	263
		Mountain	19,932	24	80	52	78	37	19	100	19,345	197
		Pacific	27,136	17	51	32	35	45	34	38	1,163	25,721
Black and other races	1890 [3]	Total	7,450,589	42,248	219,834	210,343	225,426	3,249,541	2,105,538	1,342,049	26,286	29,324
		New England	28,981	24,677	2,201	468	216	736	142	242	102	197
		Middle Atlantic	150,505	3,438	136,516	3,555	1,051	3,738	605	665	389	548
		East North Central	136,704	142	1,483	121,167	6,422	1,292	2,752	2,027	915	504
		West North Central	178,589	56	569	6,448	157,506	372	2,765	7,100	2,741	1,032
		South Atlantic	3,627,912	13,252	76,277	27,938	15,723	3,223,865	148,595	116,874	2,700	2,688
		East South Central	2,183,937	322	1,639	48,570	37,128	18,188	1,932,764	141,602	2,365	1,359
		West South Central	1,103,866	274	663	2,059	7,086	1,100	17,493	1,073,379	790	1,022
		Mountain	17,177	11	284	47	225	29	364	85	15,873	259
		Pacific	22,918	76	202	91	69	221	58	75	411	21,715

Notes appear at end of table

(continued)

TABLE Ac43–52   Native-born population, by race, division of residence, and division of birth: 1850–1990   *Continued*

			Total	New England	Middle Atlantic	East North Central	West North Central	South Atlantic	East South Central	West South Central	Mountain	Pacific
			Ac43	Ac44	Ac45	Ac46	Ac47	Ac48	Ac49	Ac50	Ac51	Ac52
Race	Census year	Division of birth	Number	Number	Number	Number	Number	Number	Number	Number	Number	Number
Black and other races	1900	Total	9,026,956	56,174	325,698	267,124	276,104	3,723,920	2,496,880	1,750,800	80,317	49,939
		New England	34,186	28,948	2,803	625	206	1,002	136	186	120	160
		Middle Atlantic	183,339	3,999	166,691	4,070	947	5,640	520	676	332	464
		East North Central	170,049	346	3,494	148,199	7,232	2,002	4,267	2,805	978	726
		West North Central	237,297	122	752	10,828	203,858	507	3,032	12,603	4,182	1,413
		South Atlantic	4,133,276	21,417	145,557	30,787	14,038	3,684,080	134,831	96,632	2,772	3,162
		East South Central	2,628,985	633	4,066	68,777	38,282	28,514	2,327,272	156,214	3,327	1,900
		West South Central	1,524,820	241	1,052	3,405	8,624	1,790	26,633	1,480,511	1,317	1,247
		Mountain	70,780	27	335	152	2,741	77	70	868	66,036	474
		Pacific	44,224	441	948	281	176	308	119	305	1,253	40,393
Black and other races	1910	Total	10,025,125	60,931	407,348	311,737	278,717	4,103,893	2,646,426	2,048,401	95,408	72,264
		New England	39,839	32,693	3,944	598	265	1,414	185	344	133	263
		Middle Atlantic	219,137	4,018	196,486	5,117	1,178	9,186	966	989	415	782
		East North Central	192,088	405	4,471	162,724	9,180	3,160	5,131	3,718	1,397	1,902
		West North Central	238,996	211	1,294	13,386	198,839	1,138	3,076	12,660	5,225	3,167
		South Atlantic	4,497,605	21,394	191,612	35,299	12,656	4,048,161	108,763	71,118	2,700	5,902
		East South Central	2,849,182	967	5,787	88,363	40,006	37,547	2,494,110	173,531	4,361	4,510
		West South Central	1,848,608	285	1,448	5,011	14,034	2,203	33,650	1,783,963	3,363	4,651
		Mountain	82,771	64	581	281	2,145	462	320	1,415	76,130	1,373
		Pacific	56,899	894	1,725	958	414	622	225	663	1,684	49,714
Black and other races	1920	Total	10,623,838	68,704	562,963	522,270	311,204	4,315,975	2,516,980	2,110,266	105,563	109,913
		New England	46,726	36,756	5,356	1,023	292	2,051	343	453	152	300
		Middle Atlantic	265,307	4,315	235,108	8,594	1,178	13,020	733	705	689	965
		East North Central	225,537	501	6,458	190,121	10,630	4,709	5,336	3,390	1,686	2,706
		West North Central	242,757	220	2,089	20,419	194,448	2,093	2,721	10,710	5,407	4,650
		South Atlantic	4,771,502	24,251	280,607	86,850	12,137	4,231,573	76,086	47,528	5,097	7,373
		East South Central	2,923,262	1,423	25,506	190,571	58,241	56,648	2,399,065	178,676	6,134	6,998
		West South Central	1,981,385	371	5,096	22,118	31,599	4,588	32,076	1,867,040	6,868	11,629
		Mountain	85,376	85	593	840	2,020	472	331	951	77,728	2,356
		Pacific	81,986	782	2,150	1,734	659	821	289	813	1,802	72,936
Black and other races	1930 [4]	Total	12,966,484	85,473	980,056	957,610	394,534	4,421,188	2,655,398	2,797,906	298,651	375,668
		New England	60,784	47,909	8,543	1,308	191	1,964	152	166	83	468
		Middle Atlantic	405,404	4,380	365,212	12,886	1,046	17,792	1,109	917	405	1,657
		East North Central	355,312	617	11,840	307,789	10,799	6,950	7,522	4,144	1,366	4,285
		West North Central	295,827	243	3,229	33,085	229,087	1,531	2,675	11,592	5,841	8,544
		South Atlantic	5,215,766	29,024	531,014	197,586	11,337	4,316,289	85,900	31,498	2,444	10,674
		East South Central	3,197,521	1,779	45,220	321,450	74,933	68,994	2,515,818	153,257	4,486	11,584
		West South Central	2,855,954	574	11,050	79,125	62,438	6,528	41,697	2,588,627	20,299	45,616
		Mountain	303,676	73	783	2,162	3,782	368	219	5,937	258,301	32,051
		Pacific	276,240	874	3,165	2,219	921	772	306	1,768	5,426	260,789

Division of residence

Race	Census year	Division of birth	Total Ac43	New England Ac44	Middle Atlantic Ac45	East North Central Ac46	West North Central Ac47	South Atlantic Ac48	East South Central Ac49	West South Central Ac50	Mountain Ac51	Pacific Ac52
			Number	Number	Number	Number	Number	Number	Number	Number	Number	Number
Black and other races	1940	Total	13,190,395	95,035	1,208,567	1,084,123	401,916	4,706,493	2,779,679	2,489,075	163,606	261,901
		New England	72,448	58,883	9,094	1,190	142	2,143	228	150	58	560
		Middle Atlantic	571,445	4,352	526,569	12,397	945	22,910	1,084	779	324	2,085
		East North Central	469,788	762	13,421	420,714	9,676	8,114	7,444	3,391	1,111	5,155
		West North Central	304,282	275	3,971	31,247	240,766	1,918	2,635	8,471	4,933	10,066
		South Atlantic	5,484,716	27,275	585,734	188,711	8,733	4,579,081	62,448	19,370	1,753	11,611
		East South Central	3,359,873	2,016	50,942	340,816	74,444	82,512	2,664,877	125,376	4,036	14,854
		West South Central	2,615,711	735	13,731	85,882	64,924	8,126	40,421	2,329,478	17,136	55,278
		Mountain	144,576	69	793	1,357	1,610	596	240	1,151	131,955	6,805
		Pacific	167,556	668	4,312	1,809	676	1,093	302	909	2,300	155,487
Black and other races	1950	Total	15,263,910	136,825	1,771,205	1,799,890	469,245	5,068,460	2,687,045	2,473,610	214,980	642,650
		New England	95,105	74,260	11,345	2,245	350	3,780	410	515	270	1,930
		Middle Atlantic	884,085	6,990	798,465	20,225	1,675	41,660	3,180	3,280	1,175	7,435
		East North Central	754,760	1,605	19,745	675,230	11,170	13,040	11,310	5,920	1,915	14,825
		West North Central	362,865	790	6,165	45,560	268,130	3,660	3,420	7,830	5,980	21,330
		South Atlantic	6,125,045	43,895	810,945	269,290	8,740	4,882,210	60,780	18,125	2,960	28,100
		East South Central	3,634,040	5,730	91,980	604,445	89,670	104,760	2,569,950	108,770	6,020	52,715
		West South Central	2,954,750	2,575	25,165	169,690	85,170	15,965	36,775	2,323,380	32,520	263,510
		Mountain	183,685	145	1,425	2,520	2,150	1,015	355	1,800	158,355	15,920
		Pacific	269,575	835	5,970	10,685	2,190	2,370	865	3,990	5,785	236,885
Black and other races	1960	Total	19,083,600	224,801	2,527,559	2,715,123	595,583	5,692,481	2,660,976	2,763,662	318,112	1,585,303
		New England	144,829	119,877	11,807	2,731	508	5,096	564	675	334	3,237
		Middle Atlantic	1,515,818	11,258	1,388,304	26,523	2,665	59,936	4,516	4,495	2,012	16,109
		East North Central	1,442,437	3,132	24,857	1,317,877	14,858	18,671	16,622	9,088	3,735	33,597
		West North Central	485,700	1,236	7,075	50,981	367,449	4,989	3,453	8,567	8,989	32,961
		South Atlantic	6,896,680	70,680	930,590	301,498	12,028	5,448,369	53,412	21,303	6,289	52,511
		East South Central	3,911,070	11,970	123,760	789,358	96,597	125,386	2,547,807	106,306	10,550	99,336
		West South Central	3,405,655	4,623	30,858	208,938	93,669	21,587	32,197	2,600,442	50,239	363,102
		Mountain	267,216	308	1,741	3,166	3,131	1,386	483	3,650	226,396	26,955
		Pacific	1,014,195	1,717	8,567	14,051	4,678	7,061	1,922	9,136	9,568	957,495
Black and other races	1970	Total	22,152,681	341,142	3,410,327	3,633,676	714,238	6,000,302	2,440,828	2,928,778	396,456	2,286,934
		New England	258,577	193,028	14,410	31,759	920	8,522	1,283	1,333	583	6,739
		Middle Atlantic	2,454,261	18,139	2,257,280	37,755	4,592	86,691	6,727	7,468	3,670	31,939
		East North Central	2,346,566	5,437	32,370	2,150,800	19,068	29,594	22,995	13,898	7,439	64,965
		West North Central	629,565	2,298	7,982	56,701	476,071	7,748	4,905	12,533	11,698	49,629
		South Atlantic	7,133,334	91,102	901,078	282,870	15,460	5,670,277	43,959	26,021	12,944	89,623
		East South Central	3,808,822	20,359	143,726	824,905	92,914	140,497	2,327,288	93,127	13,709	152,297
		West South Central	3,653,069	6,025	38,188	222,589	92,607	35,030	27,718	2,752,576	51,926	426,410
		Mountain	349,703	1,079	2,785	5,869	4,748	3,745	1,480	6,496	278,143	45,358
		Pacific	1,518,784	3,675	12,508	20,428	7,858	18,198	4,473	15,326	16,344	1,419,974
Black and other races	1980	Total	26,731,823	494,405	4,162,323	4,778,745	965,995	7,782,972	2,913,564	3,879,336	738,492	3,525,240
		New England	385,610	289,225	22,472	10,248	2,280	30,198	3,780	6,907	3,125	17,375
		Middle Atlantic	3,290,745	36,950	2,787,634	65,186	10,125	244,124	20,145	25,926	14,648	86,007
		East North Central	3,417,462	9,469	46,432	2,975,723	40,585	84,522	59,546	44,084	22,794	134,307
		West North Central	914,280	2,323	13,168	89,318	640,304	21,372	10,830	29,678	25,250	82,037
		South Atlantic	8,858,766	113,449	1,055,358	329,477	24,440	7,016,144	77,166	70,332	25,527	146,873
		East South Central	4,542,181	26,395	168,545	988,621	108,415	218,698	2,683,108	120,332	23,975	204,092
		West South Central	4,672,551	8,609	41,955	273,919	112,909	68,498	42,482	3,509,694	82,949	531,536
		Mountain	650,228	1,920	6,063	13,528	10,807	17,331	4,444	21,373	491,758	83,004
		Pacific	2,509,249	6,065	20,696	32,725	16,130	82,085	12,063	51,010	48,466	2,240,009

(continued)

Notes appear at end of table

TABLE Ac43–52   Native-born population, by race, division of residence, and division of birth: 1850–1990   Continued

| | | | Total | New England | Middle Atlantic | East North Central | West North Central | South Atlantic | East South Central | West South Central | Mountain | Pacific |
			Ac43	Ac44	Ac45	Ac46	Ac47	Ac48	Ac49	Ac50	Ac51	Ac52
Race	Census year	Division of birth	Number	Number	Number	Number	Number	Number	Number	Number	Number	Number
Black and	1990	Total	32,637,643	622,725	4,459,274	5,062,744	1,113,186	8,839,838	3,005,537	4,290,285	906,732	4,337,322
other races		New England	506,243	389,067	26,446	8,967	2,458	42,584	4,251	6,369	4,465	21,636
		Middle Atlantic	3,976,268	51,231	3,258,701	69,840	14,609	387,216	26,340	36,731	21,313	110,287
		East North Central	4,142,944	15,458	57,326	3,491,139	59,103	154,995	79,616	76,137	36,388	172,782
		West North Central	1,065,298	4,278	13,341	85,186	760,237	32,473	12,105	43,061	29,753	84,864
		South Atlantic	9,414,399	107,557	874,628	286,171	31,479	7,732,516	87,210	85,116	34,801	174,921
		East South Central	4,455,962	30,314	147,027	829,783	97,507	260,729	2,721,520	136,677	28,835	203,570
		West South Central	4,968,708	13,405	44,348	234,990	112,749	116,050	51,642	3,808,564	84,973	501,987
		Mountain	769,113	1,925	6,218	11,758	12,004	17,369	4,087	27,573	599,658	88,521
		Pacific	3,338,708	9,490	31,239	44,910	23,040	95,906	18,766	70,057	66,546	2,978,754

(column header group: Division of residence)

1 Based on a 20 percent sample (1950), 25 percent sample (1960), 5 percent sample (1970–1990).

2 Includes free blacks.

3 Excludes population of Indian Territory and Indian reservations, specially enumerated in 1890, with a native population of 117,368 white and 208,083 black and other races, not distributed by state of birth.

4 Mexicans classified under other races.

Sources

1850–1970: Special compilations made by the University of Pennsylvania Studies of Population Redistribution and Economic Growth based on U.S. Bureau of the Census reports shown in Table Ac1–42.

1980 and 1990: Integrated Public Use Microdata Series (IPUMS), 5 percent Public Use Samples. See the Guide to the Millennial Edition for information on IPUMS.

Documentation

Data exclude persons born outside the United States and persons for whom state of birth was not reported.

An error in the published data for 1970 was present in *Historical Statistics of the United States* (1975). The data included here are correctly oriented. See Table Ap-G in Appendix 2 regarding the composition of census regions and divisions.

TABLE Ac53–205   Net intercensal migration, by race and state: 1940–1990   [Components of change method]

Contributed by Joseph P. Ferrie

	White and black population											
	New England						Middle Atlantic			East North Central		
	Maine	New Hampshire	Vermont	Massachusetts	Rhode Island	Connecticut	New York	New Jersey	Pennsylvania	Ohio	Indiana	Illinois
	Ac53	Ac54	Ac55	Ac56	Ac57	Ac58	Ac59	Ac60	Ac61	Ac62	Ac63	Ac64
Period	Thousand	Thousand	Thousand	Thousand	Thousand	Thousand	Thousand	Thousand	Thousand	Thousand	Thousand	Thousand
1940–1950	−27	(Z)	−19	23	11	113	270	294	−355	245	97	75
1950–1960	−67	12	−38	−96	−26	234	210	578	−475	407	61	124
1960–1970	−69	69	15	74	13	214	−101	488	−378	−126	−16	−43
1970–1980	76	136	38	−136	−33	−52	−1,543	−114	−289	−544	−87	−410
1980–1990	45	117	17	19	20	18	−467	5	−368	−585	−283	−801

	White and black population											
	East North Central		West North Central							South Atlantic		
	Michigan	Wisconsin	Minnesota	Iowa	Missouri	North Dakota	South Dakota	Nebraska	Kansas	Delaware	Maryland	District of Columbia
	Ac65	Ac66	Ac67	Ac68	Ac69	Ac70	Ac71	Ac72	Ac73	Ac74	Ac75	Ac76
Period	Thousand	Thousand	Thousand	Thousand	Thousand	Thousand	Thousand	Thousand	Thousand	Thousand	Thousand	Thousand
1940–1950	336	−84	−173	−196	−190	−121	−79	−135	−91	21	270	49
1950–1960	155	−53	−98	−234	−134	−105	−95	−117	−44	63	321	−160
1960–1970	27	4	−25	−183	2	−94	−94	−73	−130	38	385	−100
1970–1980	−297	14	11	−58	16	−17	−26	−12	−19	8	55	−151
1980–1990	−585	−126	−29	−280	−64	−72	−50	−99	−62	29	244	−60

	White and black population											
	South Atlantic						East South Central				West South Central	
	Virginia	West Virginia	North Carolina	South Carolina	Georgia	Florida	Kentucky	Tennessee	Alabama	Mississippi	Arkansas	Louisiana
	Ac77	Ac78	Ac79	Ac80	Ac81	Ac82	Ac83	Ac84	Ac85	Ac86	Ac87	Ac88
Period	Thousand	Thousand	Thousand	Thousand	Thousand	Thousand	Thousand	Thousand	Thousand	Thousand	Thousand	Thousand
1940–1950	169	−235	−258	−230	−290	578	−366	−143	−342	−433	−415	−147
1950–1960	15	−446	−328	−222	−212	1,616	−390	−274	−369	−433	−433	−49
1960–1970	141	−265	−94	−149	51	1,326	−153	−45	−233	−267	−71	−130
1970–1980	353	113	395	272	443	2,716	209	394	176	85	232	188
1980–1990	431	−208	375	111	524	2,774	−171	38	−88	−143	−51	−412

	White and black population											
	West South Central		Mountain								Pacific	
	Oklahoma	Texas	Montana	Idaho	Wyoming	Colorado	New Mexico	Arizona	Utah	Nevada	Washington	Oregon
	Ac89	Ac90	Ac91	Ac92	Ac93	Ac94	Ac95	Ac96	Ac97	Ac98	Ac99	Ac100
Period	Thousand	Thousand	Thousand	Thousand	Thousand	Thousand	Thousand	Thousand	Thousand	Thousand	Thousand	Thousand
1940–1950	−434	73	−40	−27	−1	41	16	137	9	34	392	286
1950–1960	−219	121	−25	−40	−20	164	52	329	9	86	87	16
1960–1970	13	146	−58	−42	−39	215	−130	228	−11	144	249	159
1970–1980	295	1,779	33	130	96	446	141	712	149	257	474	396
1980–1990	−107	945	−53	−41	−75	71	37	610	−32	315	370	38

Note appears at end of table

(continued)

TABLE Ac53–205   Net intercensal migration, by race and state: 1940–1990   [Components of change method]
Continued

	White and black population			White population									
	Pacific			New England							Middle Atlantic		
	California	Alaska	Hawai'i	Maine	New Hampshire	Vermont	Massachusetts	Rhode Island	Connecticut		New York	New Jersey	Pennsylvania
	Ac101	Ac102	Ac103	Ac104	Ac105	Ac106	Ac107	Ac108	Ac109		Ac110	Ac111	Ac112
Period	Thousand	Thousand	Thousand	Thousand	Thousand	Thousand	Thousand	Thousand	Thousand		Thousand	Thousand	Thousand
1940–1950	2,658	—	—	−27	−1	−20	8	9	98		−6	231	−467
1950–1960	3,142	41	3	−69	11	−38	−122	−28	195		−72	466	−552
1960–1970	2,113	16	11	−69	68	14	23	4	166		−638	336	−423
1970–1980	2,078	36	76	72	131	36	−203	−38	−75		−1,626	−241	−290
1980–1990	3,354	52	14	—	—	—	—	—	—		—	—	—

	White population											
	East North Central					West North Central						
	Ohio	Indiana	Illinois	Michigan	Wisconsin	Minnesota	Iowa	Missouri	North Dakota	South Dakota	Nebraska	Kansas
	Ac113	Ac114	Ac115	Ac116	Ac117	Ac118	Ac119	Ac120	Ac121	Ac122	Ac123	Ac124
Period	Thousand	Thousand	Thousand	Thousand	Thousand	Thousand	Thousand	Thousand	Thousand	Thousand	Thousand	Thousand
1940–1950	110	57	−142	146	−96	−175	−198	−222	−119	−74	−139	−96
1950–1960	274	17	−64	28	−82	−102	−236	−161	−103	−90	−121	−49
1960–1970	−191	−58	−215	−124	−29	−39	−189	−25	−94	−92	−76	−139
1970–1980	−568	−114	−529	−417	−33	−32	−75	18	−18	−30	−19	−42
1980–1990	—	—	—	—	—	—	—	—	—	—	—	—

	White population											
	South Atlantic									East South Central		
	Delaware	Maryland	District of Columbia	Virginia	West Virginia	North Carolina	South Carolina	Georgia	Florida	Kentucky	Tennessee	Alabama
	Ac125	Ac126	Ac127	Ac128	Ac129	Ac130	Ac131	Ac132	Ac133	Ac134	Ac135	Ac136
Period	Thousand	Thousand	Thousand	Thousand	Thousand	Thousand	Thousand	Thousand	Thousand	Thousand	Thousand	Thousand
1940–1950	17	231	−14	194	−219	−95	−24	−49	564	−349	−97	−140
1950–1960	57	284	−213	85	−406	−121	−4	−8	1,516	−375	−217	−145
1960–1970	32	290	−137	206	−247	81	44	198	1,340	−158	1	−5
1970–1980	−3	−171	−21	229	109	317	214	308	2,533	118	346	183
1980–1990	—	—	—	—	—	—	—	—	—	—	—	—

	White population												
	East South Central	West South Central				Mountain							
	Mississippi	Arkansas	Louisiana	Oklahoma	Texas	Montana	Idaho	Wyoming	Colorado	New Mexico	Arizona	Utah	Nevada
	Ac137	Ac138	Ac139	Ac140	Ac141	Ac142	Ac143	Ac144	Ac145	Ac146	Ac147	Ac148	Ac149
Period	Thousand	Thousand	Thousand	Thousand	Thousand	Thousand	Thousand	Thousand	Thousand	Thousand	Thousand	Thousand	Thousand
1940–1950	−108	−259	−2	−361	173	−36	−28	−2	32	17	135	6	31
1950–1960	−110	−283	43	−193	147	−23	−41	−19	149	53	339	8	80
1960–1970	10	38	26	−4	92	−57	−44	−39	187	−120	248	−16	136
1970–1980	132	243	173	223	1,535	30	124	93	400	127	666	134	228
1980–1990	—	—	—	—	—	—	—	—	—	—	—	—	—

Note appears at end of table

TABLE Ac53–205   Net intercensal migration, by race and state: 1940–1990   [Components of change method]
Continued

	White population						Black population					
	Pacific						New England					
	Washington	Oregon	California	Alaska	Hawai'i		Maine	New Hampshire	Vermont	Massachusetts	Rhode Island	Connecticut
	Ac150	Ac151	Ac152	Ac153	Ac154		Ac155	Ac156	Ac157	Ac158	Ac159	Ac160
Period	Thousand	Thousand	Thousand	Thousand	Thousand		Thousand	Thousand	Thousand	Thousand	Thousand	Thousand
1940–1950	375	278	2,373	—	—		(Z)	(Z)	(Z)	12	1	15
1950–1960	69	10	2,788	42	55		2	1	(Z)	20	1	37
1960–1970	220	145	1,528	22	58		−2	(Z)	(Z)	33	2	38
1970–1980	383	359	1,178	30	16		2	4	2	58	3	18
1980–1990	—	—	—	—	—		—	—	—	—	—	—

	Black population											
	Middle Atlantic			East North Central					West North Central			
	New York	New Jersey	Pennsylvania	Ohio	Indiana	Illinois	Michigan	Wisconsin	Minnesota	Iowa	Missouri	North Dakota
	Ac161	Ac162	Ac163	Ac164	Ac165	Ac166	Ac167	Ac168	Ac169	Ac170	Ac171	Ac172
Period	Thousand	Thousand	Thousand	Thousand	Thousand	Thousand	Thousand	Thousand	Thousand	Thousand	Thousand	Thousand
1940–1950	266	61	107	131	39	203	186	14	4	2	31	(Z)
1950–1960	255	107	75	129	42	182	122	29	5	2	24	1
1960–1970	396	120	25	45	32	127	124	27	7	2	14	1
1970–1980	162	115	−23	7	16	104	107	39	34	12	−13	(Z)
1980–1990	—	—	—	—	—	—	—	—	—	—	—	—

	Black population											
	West North Central			South Atlantic								
	South Dakota	Nebraska	Kansas	Delaware	Maryland	District of Columbia	Virginia	West Virginia	North Carolina	South Carolina	Georgia	Florida
	Ac173	Ac174	Ac175	Ac176	Ac177	Ac178	Ac179	Ac180	Ac181	Ac182	Ac183	Ac184
Period	Thousand	Thousand	Thousand	Thousand	Thousand	Thousand	Thousand	Thousand	Thousand	Thousand	Thousand	Thousand
1940–1950	(Z)	4	4	4	37	61	−29	−17	−164	−208	−243	12
1950–1960	(Z)	4	2	6	31	51	−74	−41	−204	−218	−205	96
1960–1970	(Z)	2	−1	4	79	36	−79	−20	−175	−197	−154	−32
1970–1980	3	5	19	9	216	−130	115	(Z)	75	55	125	173
1980–1990	—	—	—	—	—	—	—	—	—	—	—	—

	Black population											
	East South Central				West South Central				Mountain			
	Kentucky	Tennessee	Alabama	Mississippi	Arkansas	Louisiana	Oklahoma	Texas	Montana	Idaho	Wyoming	Colorado
	Ac185	Ac186	Ac187	Ac188	Ac189	Ac190	Ac191	Ac192	Ac193	Ac194	Ac195	Ac196
Period	Thousand	Thousand	Thousand	Thousand	Thousand	Thousand	Thousand	Thousand	Thousand	Thousand	Thousand	Thousand
1940–1950	−18	−48	−204	−326	−158	−147	−47	−107	(Z)	(Z)	2	7
1950–1960	−16	−59	−224	−323	−150	−93	−21	−33	(Z)	(Z)	−1	13
1960–1970	1	−51	−231	−279	−112	−163	−3	−4	(Z)	(Z)	(Z)	16
1970–1980	14	40	−9	−53	−14	8	67	223	2	4	1	43
1980–1990	—	—	—	—	—	—	—	—	—	—	—	—

Note appears at end of table

(continued)

TABLE Ac53–205   Net intercensal migration, by race and state: 1940–1990   [Components of change method]
Continued

	Black population								
	Mountain				Pacific				
	New Mexico	Arizona	Utah	Nevada	Washington	Oregon	California	Alaska	Hawai'i
	Ac197	Ac198	Ac199	Ac200	Ac201	Ac202	Ac203	Ac204	Ac205
Period	Thousand	Thousand	Thousand	Thousand	Thousand	Thousand	Thousand	Thousand	Thousand
1940–1950	2	6	1	3	21	8	289	—	—
1950–1960	4	4	1	6	8	3	255	(Z)	(Z)
1960–1970	−4	−4	1	6	10	4	272	(Z)	1
1970–1980	14	43	13	29	87	33	865	7	58
1980–1990	—	—	—	—	—	—	—	7	—

(Z) Series Ac54, less than 1,000; other series, less than 500.

Sources

1940–1970: U.S. Bureau of the Census, Current Population Reports, Population Estimates and Projections, series P-25, number 72, p. 5; number 304, p. 12; and number 460, pp. 10, 14.

1970–1980: Michael J. White, Peter Mueser, and Joseph P. Tierney, *Net Migration of the Population of the United States by Age, Race and Sex, 1970–1980* (computer file) (Inter-university Consortium for Political and Social Research (distributor), 1990).

1980–1990: U.S. Bureau of the Census, Population Distribution Branch, "1981 to 1989 Intercensal Estimates of the Resident Population of States, and Year-to-Year Components of Change," Sept. 1995, available at the U.S. Bureau of the Census Internet site.

Documentation

The figures in this table include international immigration as well as domestic migration, whereas the figures in Table Ac206–413, using a different method, provide estimates of net domestic migration. The components of change technique employed in this table uses information on the population in each state at the beginning and end of each decade and information on the total number of births and deaths to estimate net migration into or out of the state. It uses the formula

$$P_{t+10} = P_t + (B_{\Sigma t, t+10} - D_{\Sigma t, t+10}) + R_{\Sigma t, t+10}$$

$$R = (P_{t+10} - P_t) - (B - D)$$

where P_{t+10} and P_t are the enumerated populations at time t and time $t+10$, B and D are births and deaths over the decade, and R is a residual with several components: net domestic migration, net international immigration, movement of the federal population (such as those in the armed forces), and "the error of closure" (what must be added to balance the equation because of differences in enumeration rates between two adjacent censuses).

Until 1965, net international immigration and federal population movements were quite small, and the error of closure was also small. The estimated residual was thus a good approximation to net domestic migration. With the large increase in immigration after 1965 and the substantial decline in the underenumeration rate between 1980 and 1990, this series exhibits a substantial discontinuity. Though the U.S. Census Bureau is now able to estimate separately the error of closure, net federal movements, net international immigration, and net domestic migration, it has not revised all of the pre-1990 data.

The 1970–1980 tabulations were performed separately from the U.S. Census Bureau's calculations for the total population. They were based on births, deaths, and population totals tabulated for all counties and reaggregated to the state level.

TABLE Ac206–413 Net intercensal migration, by race, nativity, and state: 1850–1990 [Survival rate method]
Contributed by Joseph P. Ferrie

	White and black population										
	New England						Middle Atlantic			East North Central	
	Maine	New Hampshire	Vermont	Massachusetts	Rhode Island	Connecticut	New York	New Jersey	Pennsylvania	Ohio	Indiana
	Ac206	Ac207	Ac208	Ac209	Ac210	Ac211	Ac212	Ac213	Ac214	Ac215	Ac216
Year	Thousand	Thousand	Thousand	Thousand	Thousand	Thousand	Thousand	Thousand	Thousand	Thousand	Thousand
1850–1860	−61.4	−37.3	−50.7	−127.1	−13.1	17.4	−323.7	−7.2	−163.1	−266.2	−3.5
1860–1870	−57.1	1.6	−17.4	16.6	−1.9	8.4	−401.7	69.3	−52.3	−175.5	16.0
1870–1880	−33.3	10.1	−26.2	140.2	27.9	22.4	61.7	48.4	19.1	−12.9	−70.2
1880–1890	−15.9	20.7	−13.3	295.7	42.5	72.9	395.4	151.3	285.1	41.9	−86.7
1890–1900	4.1	20.4	−2.4	334.9	45.9	90.8	604.8	218.3	262.0	77.7	33.4
1900–1910	10.6	3.2	−3.7	307.3	66.1	112.7	1,061.0	376.1	444.6	207.7	−54.4
1910–1920	−8.3	−3.6	−17.6	192.2	12.8	122.1	467.4	278.2	51.9	499.4	16.0
1920–1930	−39.3	−10.2	−20.6	22.1	11.4	64.1	1,062.1	442.3	−252.9	214.7	−0.9
1930–1940	−1.2	9.1	−18.7	−69.5	−2.3	39.2	396.3	−28.2	−301.0	−56.6	10.6
1940–1950	−35.8	−9.1	−23.8	−29.5	2.7	89.5	83.8	200.7	−447.2	151.6	56.7
1950–1960	−70.5	−2.1	−38.4	−154.0	−36.5	−172.7	1.2	409.9	−594.0	265.9	21.0
1960–1970	−80.2	53.4	3.3	−79.5	−4.2	95.2	−764.2	162.0	−566.1	−207.7	−40.2
1970–1980	44.5	96.0	17.5	−357.6	−70.2	−203.4	−2,388.1	−554.2	−627.7	−797.0	−209.4
1980–1990	27.0	94.8	6.4	−139.7	−20.3	−70.1	−1,215.3	−336.0	−449.7	−593.9	−265.2

	White and black population										
	East North Central			West North Central							
	Illinois	Michigan	Wisconsin	Minnesota	Iowa	Missouri	North Dakota	North and South Dakota	South Dakota	Nebraska	Kansas
	Ac217	Ac218	Ac219	Ac220	Ac221	Ac222	Ac223	Ac224	Ac225	Ac226	Ac227
Year	Thousand	Thousand	Thousand	Thousand	Thousand	Thousand	Thousand	Thousand	Thousand	Thousand	Thousand
1850–1860	334.1	149.0	111.7	—	266.1	76.4	—	—	—	—	—
1860–1870	203.8	136.4	−73.4	145.4	178.6	160.5	—	—	—	—	—
1870–1880	−59.0	161.4	9.0	156.2	85.1	−30.4	—	86.8	—	204.4	366.8
1880–1890	170.3	172.3	100.8	264.1	−5.6	56.4	—	243.4	—	362.5	159.7
1890–1900	340.0	62.0	84.3	148.4	21.7	−17.2	63.8	—	0.3	−153.9	−149.8
1900–1910	223.0	117.2	9.2	72.6	−207.5	−163.8	137.3	—	86.9	−28.8	20.0
1910–1920	255.6	465.2	37.6	59.1	−18.3	−134.7	−46.0	—	−31.2	−34.5	−74.5
1920–1930	414.0	549.6	−17.9	−106.2	−167.2	−98.7	−76.3	—	−45.0	−78.1	−83.1
1930–1940	−60.8	17.1	−10.9	36.0	−73.4	−20.8	−105.8	—	−101.4	−139.5	−163.8
1940–1950	−22.1	251.4	−95.1	−160.9	−178.8	−168.6	−109.4	—	−71.2	−123.0	−86.8
1950–1960	−10.1	88.0	85.2	−109.2	−220.7	−150.0	−91.0	—	−76.1	−102.4	−29.6
1960–1970	−320.5	−134.5	−37.2	−38.5	−181.9	−17.0	−82.5	—	−86.7	−65.1	−130.6
1970–1980	−813.5	−575.6	−70.0	−61.4	−91.0	−83.2	−23.7	—	−29.9	−24.3	−34.2
1980–1990	−900.4	−660.0	−122.8	−11.4	−249.1	−22.8	−56.3	—	−37.9	−81.3	−36.3

(continued)

TABLE Ac206–413   Net intercensal migration, by race, nativity, and state: 1850–1990   [Survival rate method]
Continued

White and black population

				South Atlantic						East South Central	
	Delaware	Maryland	District of Columbia	Virginia	West Virginia	North Carolina	South Carolina	Georgia	Florida	Kentucky	Tennessee
	Ac228	Ac229	Ac230	Ac231	Ac232	Ac233	Ac234	Ac235	Ac236	Ac237	Ac238
Year	Thousand	Thousand	Thousand	Thousand	Thousand	Thousand	Thousand	Thousand	Thousand	Thousand	Thousand
1850–1860	−3.1	−47.7	0.8	−115.6	—	−55.0	−91.1	−66.8	16.6	−109.2	−156.3
1860–1870	6.1	−20.8	29.9	−149.0	—	−53.3	−53.5	−32.9	28.4	−55.2	−38.7
1870–1880	−2.3	−11.2	18.1	−51.1	24.0	−14.4	25.7	−40.0	12.1	−47.2	−91.8
1880–1890	4.3	−10.7	36.1	−80.9	−4.8	−57.7	−35.9	−19.5	51.1	−96.8	−77.7
1890–1900	−1.2	8.2	34.3	−91.5	17.2	−88.8	−75.5	−56.1	36.9	−65.1	−95.4
1900–1910	2.7	−8.3	41.0	−73.7	46.1	−80.4	−80.6	−41.7	103.5	−177.8	−156.9
1910–1920	5.1	43.1	97.0	−27.7	−1.7	−74.3	−80.9	−98.1	101.6	−167.1	−131.2
1920–1930	−3.5	10.2	27.3	−231.6	−53.8	−7.9	−256.9	−414.9	297.6	−206.1	−113.8
1930–1940	16.0	87.0	157.8	0.2	−73.6	−85.4	−102.5	−134.1	280.3	−93.5	−14.9
1940–1950	14.5	213.3	78.5	152.0	−210.8	−202.8	−172.4	−224.3	510.9	−319.2	−102.8
1950–1960	51.1	231.1	−115.1	−2.0	−401.6	−277.6	−179.1	−169.7	1,385.6	−350.2	−252.6
1960–1970	29.8	290.3	−82.5	128.9	−248.8	−51.1	−134.1	39.2	1,136.0	−127.5	−30.6
1970–1980	−14.8	−143.8	−167.4	101.7	44.6	207.8	143.2	190.8	2,085.0	96.6	235.6
1980–1990	21.2	125.5	−34.0	293.0	−196.9	341.7	113.2	456.0	2,189.0	−154.6	36.4

White and black population

	East South Central		West South Central				Mountain				
	Alabama	Mississippi	Arkansas	Louisiana	Oklahoma	Texas	Montana	Idaho	Wyoming	Colorado	New Mexico
	Ac239	Ac240	Ac241	Ac242	Ac243	Ac244	Ac245	Ac246	Ac247	Ac248	Ac249
Year	Thousand	Thousand	Thousand	Thousand	Thousand	Thousand	Thousand	Thousand	Thousand	Thousand	Thousand
1850–1860	−34.6	12.3	99.9	−10.7	—	192.7	—	—	—	—	12.3
1860–1870	−76.9	−61.8	−21.2	−44.3	—	37.7	—	—	—	—	−19.6
1870–1880	−60.7	−5.6	84.0	−12.0	—	308.5	12.1	11.7	7.2	119.1	−3.3
1880–1890	−11.5	−60.6	75.1	−3.0	44.5	151.2	70.6	34.2	28.7	146.8	6.4
1890–1900	−40.4	−44.5	−82.8	1.4	501.3	147.7	63.5	39.8	15.6	51.9	1.2
1900–1910	−47.8	−46.4	−27.2	10.6	491.5	131.1	86.5	104.1	33.3	159.8	63.1
1910–1920	−113.9	−199.3	−74.7	−64.7	62.4	114.3	90.1	37.3	20.7	39.8	−20.2
1920–1930	−149.2	−101.6	−191.3	−23.2	−51.8	243.5	−72.9	−50.6	−1.2	−16.6	−22.9
1930–1940	−165.3	−90.3	−128.8	5.7	−269.4	−72.8	−19.3	−20.5	−0.1	1.0	18.6
1940–1950	−271.0	−349.9	−320.4	−112.1	−356.1	132.9	−42.2	−29.6	−4.6	32.4	9.8
1950–1960	−332.3	−369.6	−353.0	−39.0	−196.0	174.5	−25.3	−39.3	−18.7	132.4	51.7
1960–1970	−192.2	−236.3	−42.5	−115.6	17.6	71.7	−58.4	−43.9	−37.1	182.1	−111.0
1970–1980	45.8	−0.6	166.4	28.5	193.2	1,134.0	20.0	104.7	76.6	349.0	100.3
1980–1990	−61.8	−99.0	−28.1	−335.5	−54.8	600.1	−51.9	−47.5	−66.0	46.7	21.5

TABLE Ac206–413   Net intercensal migration, by race, nativity, and state: 1850–1990   [Survival rate method]
Continued

	White and black population								White population		
									Native-born		
	Mountain			Pacific					New England		
	Arizona	Utah	Nevada	Washington	Oregon	California	Alaska	Hawai'i	Maine	New Hampshire	Vermont
	Ac250	Ac251	Ac252	Ac253	Ac254	Ac255	Ac256	Ac257	Ac258	Ac259	Ac260
Year	Thousand	Thousand	Thousand	Thousand	Thousand	Thousand	Thousand	Thousand	Thousand	Thousand	Thousand
1850–1860	—	—	—	—	—	—	—	—	−40.2	−37.3	−19.1
1860–1870	—	−0.7	—	—	11.9	44.2	—	—	−55.2	1.6	−23.5
1870–1880	19.8	16.7	6.6	28.7	39.0	129.6	—	—	−46.5	−7.1	−24.7
1880–1890	10.9	17.9	−15.6	205.4	85.9	214.2	—	—	−40.8	−7.1	−21.9
1890–1900	21.4	8.9	−5.1	80.4	43.0	172.7	—	—	−20.6	−2.5	−10.9
1900–1910	50.7	24.9	32.9	464.7	189.9	694.1	—	—	−18.4	−15.7	−17.2
1910–1920	75.4	−0.2	−6.4	97.5	56.0	804.1	—	—	−22.7	−12.8	−19.7
1920–1930	23.5	−30.8	6.9	81.6	96.5	1,695.2	—	—	−46.6	−14.4	−25.2
1930–1940	−3.5	−30.5	12.5	109.2	94.1	974.6	—	—	−2.2	8.3	−14.6
1940–1950	117.4	6.4	28.8	351.3	244.0	2,339.1	—	—	−41.6	−12.6	−25.8
1950–1960	289.3	4.9	74.9	49.5	1.2	2,573.1	48.0	47.9	−71.4	−2.7	−38.1
1960–1970	187.5	−8.4	130.1	170.6	113.5	1,522.0	13.8	9.6	−70.8	51.4	5.9
1970–1980	591.5	98.1	206.5	273.9	289.5	378.9	26.1	−5.4	46.8	95.2	17.4
1980–1990	506.5	−13.5	235.7	201.7	−11.9	1,059.2	43.3	5.0	34.0	95.0	11.6

	White population										
	Native-born										
	New England			Middle Atlantic			East North Central				
	Massachusetts	Rhode Island	Connecticut	New York	New Jersey	Pennsylvania	Ohio	Indiana	Illinois	Michigan	Wisconsin
	Ac261	Ac262	Ac263	Ac264	Ac265	Ac266	Ac267	Ac268	Ac269	Ac270	Ac271
Year	Thousand	Thousand	Thousand	Thousand	Thousand	Thousand	Thousand	Thousand	Thousand	Thousand	Thousand
1850–1860	−52.8	−13.3	16.8	−182.4	−13.3	−72.2	−224.8	−25.3	220.6	97.2	86.4
1860–1870	13.2	9.7	−5.1	−218.1	26.3	−54.1	−125.1	(Z)	128.0	89.6	−32.2
1870–1880	13.5	4.1	−6.5	−167.4	−8.9	−105.2	−92.8	−101.2	−192.5	25.8	−78.8
1880–1890	31.9	2.4	2.8	−146.4	9.4	−70.0	−96.7	−120.4	−170.7	−19.7	−75.6
1890–1900	46.9	3.3	5.4	−18.6	46.3	−60.2	−29.6	−7.6	44.0	−26.8	−25.7
1900–1910	−23.3	5.1	−10.9	−74.9	71.4	−178.1	−40.4	−111.9	−198.9	−35.9	−103.3
1910–1920	−6.0	−10.5	18.7	−76.5	72.0	−199.4	233.4	−33.1	−36.2	181.5	−37.3
1920–1930	−101.7	−8.7	6.4	138.1	179.3	−380.2	58.2	−43.3	80.3	239.9	−53.2
1930–1940	−45.6	0.8	30.2	140.3	−18.8	−260.9	−58.6	7.1	−58.7	18.1	−10.0
1940–1950	−73.8	−0.2	49.0	−270.8	88.6	−531.3	28.5	15.0	−202.9	51.7	−110.3
1950–1960	−185.0	−34.2	106.6	−392.6	214.5	−657.9	116.8	−24.6	−229.6	−57.7	−120.8
1960–1970	−93.6	−5.7	83.6	−803.5	52.7	−549.3	−204.1	−66.7	−379.3	−145.9	−43.5
1970–1980	−309.8	−59.2	−150.7	−1,853.0	−482.1	−466.5	−677.4	−183.9	−742.7	−514.9	−73.9
1980–1990	−116.5	−9.0	−49.5	−946.8	−251.1	−359.4	−500.4	−223.7	−667.5	−542.8	−120.7

(continued)

TABLE Ac206–413   Net intercensal migration, by race, nativity, and state: 1850–1990   [Survival rate method]
Continued

				White population							
				Native-born							
		West North Central							South Atlantic		
	Minnesota	Iowa	Missouri	North Dakota	North and South Dakota	South Dakota	Nebraska	Kansas	Delaware	Maryland	District of Columbia
	Ac272	Ac273	Ac274	Ac275	Ac276	Ac277	Ac278	Ac279	Ac280	Ac281	Ac282
Year	Thousand	Thousand	Thousand	Thousand	Thousand	Thousand	Thousand	Thousand	Thousand	Thousand	Thousand
1850–1860	—	208.3	65.5	—	—	—	—	—	−1.4	−33.0	1.1
1860–1870	64.5	135.7	160.6	—	—	—	—	—	6.7	−6.7	8.4
1870–1880	38.2	2.7	−43.2	—	43.5	—	139.2	290.1	−2.6	−16.1	8.6
1880–1890	37.2	−108.2	2.4	—	126.0	—	244.3	106.3	−11.0	−29.4	18.1
1890–1900	25.9	−29.9	−50.0	20.4	—	−26.5	−159.2	−156.6	−3.7	−5.8	20.1
1900–1910	−61.4	−249.1	−228.1	81.8	—	59.6	−62.4	−18.2	−3.0	−26.9	22.2
1910–1920	−1.2	−45.9	−173.7	−46.3	—	−33.7	−53.2	−86.9	0.3	16.8	69.3
1920–1930	−113.6	−164.0	−141.4	−72.8	—	−46.1	−81.1	−84.6	−3.8	−4.5	5.5
1930–1940	27.1	−70.5	−36.8	−99.1	—	−96.8	−135.5	−156.2	12.8	72.2	101.2
1940–1950	−163.1	−180.9	−197.4	−103.6	—	−71.3	−125.9	−90.1	11.2	167.6	6.7
1950–1960	−111.1	−218.3	−173.7	−87.5	—	−74.0	−106.0	−33.6	43.6	187.6	−165.4
1960–1970	−55.1	−181.5	−24.5	−80.5	—	−83.6	−71.0	−124.0	20.3	224.9	−100.7
1970–1980	−51.8	−89.2	−47.4	−22.4	—	−28.4	−19.6	−24.3	−8.5	−231.4	−15.0
1980–1990	−19.7	−229.8	8.0	−50.0	—	−30.2	−71.2	−25.8	21.1	39.7	9.6

				White population							
				Native-born							
	South Atlantic						East South Central				West South Central
	Virginia	West Virginia	North Carolina	South Carolina	Georgia	Florida	Kentucky	Tennessee	Alabama	Mississippi	Arkansas
	Ac283	Ac284	Ac285	Ac286	Ac287	Ac288	Ac289	Ac290	Ac291	Ac292	Ac293
Year	Thousand	Thousand	Thousand	Thousand	Thousand	Thousand	Thousand	Thousand	Thousand	Thousand	Thousand
1850–1860	−49.4	—	−30.6	−47.9	−56.3	7.4	−90.5	−135.7	−43.3	−14.3	64.3
1860–1870	−86.2	—	−45.0	−22.8	−47.3	10.2	−9.5	−51.6	−59.8	−39.6	−18.5
1870–1880	−16.5	18.1	−7.6	9.1	−20.8	7.3	−39.6	−67.0	−25.9	−22.7	53.0
1880–1890	−33.6	−12.3	−19.8	−17.5	−35.1	24.8	−85.6	−64.9	−12.1	−47.7	25.3
1890–1900	−25.8	3.5	−41.7	−10.8	−31.4	10.1	−58.9	−76.7	−41.1	−35.8	−77.6
1900–1910	−35.6	−6.2	−54.4	−10.5	−30.8	46.6	−159.9	−127.3	−32.8	−19.0	−55.2
1910–1920	−9.5	−29.3	−47.7	−8.0	−27.4	84.5	−153.1	−103.2	−45.3	−70.3	−74.4
1920–1930	−111.7	−62.7	5.2	−52.4	−155.1	221.1	−188.4	−100.6	−69.7	−33.8	−144.4
1930–1940	33.7	−66.7	−27.1	−8.7	−44.2	208.4	−83.8	−24.4	−101.0	−32.0	−95.5
1940–1950	169.1	−193.0	−81.6	−15.7	−38.2	438.7	−299.1	−68.6	−108.6	−94.3	−207.1
1950–1960	58.4	−361.3	−109.9	−0.7	−10.8	1,152.8	−334.8	−201.6	−142.5	−104.8	−243.8
1960–1970	182.7	−221.6	99.0	24.6	159.7	878.6	−119.1	12.7	−10.7	−4.5	36.3
1970–1980	116.5	46.7	210.8	147.8	182.3	1,784.0	106.2	234.6	110.6	87.6	192.1
1980–1990	225.8	−179.5	309.3	119.3	351.1	1,887.8	−125.1	62.6	−16.4	−43.9	2.9

TABLE Ac206–413   Net intercensal migration, by race, nativity, and state: 1850–1990   [Survival rate method]
Continued

	White population										
	Native-born										
	West South Central			Mountain							
Year	Louisiana	Oklahoma	Texas	Montana	Idaho	Wyoming	Colorado	New Mexico	Arizona	Utah	Nevada
	Ac294	Ac295	Ac296	Ac297	Ac298	Ac299	Ac300	Ac301	Ac302	Ac303	Ac304
	Thousand	Thousand	Thousand	Thousand	Thousand	Thousand	Thousand	Thousand	Thousand	Thousand	Thousand
1850–1860	−10.2	—	120.4	—	—	—	—	12.3	—	—	—
1860–1870	−7.1	—	19.4	—	—	—	—	−19.6	—	−0.7	—
1870–1880	−11.8	—	233.9	8.2	8.5	5.5	86.7	−5.9	11.7	0.6	0.8
1880–1890	−12.2	39.6	90.9	39.8	24.6	19.1	101.1	2.7	7.2	2.7	−10.0
1890–1900	9.2	404.3	95.5	37.1	31.0	11.7	33.1	−2.3	15.1	−2.5	−3.9
1900–1910	15.8	414.2	60.5	51.0	81.9	19.8	108.8	52.7	25.7	2.8	21.5
1910–1920	−17.8	54.5	−28.4	75.4	31.5	19.9	29.2	−32.0	39.9	−7.6	−6.1
1920–1930	2.9	−51.2	197.5	−66.9	−49.5	−1.8	−17.6	−17.2	31.8	−31.5	5.1
1930–1940	15.3	−253.4	−1.7	−14.8	20.8	2.2	7.4	22.5	12.4	−27.5	13.8
1940–1950	−4.7	−319.5	134.4	−41.9	−30.7	−5.6	21.1	3.8	97.6	1.0	24.2
1950–1960	23.0	−179.5	155.3	−23.5	−39.5	−17.0	110.1	43.3	255.5	−2.0	66.0
1960–1970	−14.5	−3.9	119.3	−53.8	−47.7	−38.4	152.8	−92.5	196.4	−6.3	114.4
1970–1980	104.7	160.1	876.1	22.7	98.5	74.2	308.5	75.5	531.1	90.8	175.7
1980–1990	−246.4	−81.5	430.8	−44.3	−43.2	−58.3	70.8	28.3	455.4	2.6	194.5

	White population										
	Native-born					Foreign-born					
	Pacific					New England					
Year	Washington	Oregon	California	Alaska	Hawai'i	Maine	New Hampshire	Vermont	Massachusetts	Rhode Island	Connecticut
	Ac305	Ac306	Ac307	Ac308	Ac309	Ac310	Ac311	Ac312	Ac313	Ac314	Ac315
	Thousand	Thousand	Thousand	Thousand	Thousand	Thousand	Thousand	Thousand	Thousand	Thousand	Thousand
1850–1860	—	—	—	—	—	−21.1	— [1]	−31.5	−74.7	— [1]	— [1]
1860–1870	—	11.9	44.2	—	—	−1.9	— [1]	6.0	−1.3	−11.8	12.2
1870–1880	20.8	25.7	56.0	—	—	13.4	17.1	−1.4	123.7	22.9	28.1
1880–1890	133.2	57.4	109.6	—	—	25.0	27.9	8.6	259.3	38.9	69.0
1890–1900	54.0	29.2	96.3	—	—	24.4	22.7	8.6	278.0	41.1	82.9
1900–1910	311.4	132.0	425.2	—	—	28.9	18.9	12.7	324.8	60.3	123.2
1910–1920	51.9	38.2	537.7	—	—	14.3	9.2	3.0	191.3	22.7	98.1
1920–1930	49.2	74.3	1,244.5	—	—	7.5	4.0	4.7	120.9	21.0	52.5
1930–1940	100.3	90.4	899.5	—	—	0.8	1.0	−4.0	−26.6	−3.6	6.8
1940–1950	303.9	222.9	1,874.7	—	—	5.9	3.3	2.0	33.6	1.7	27.5
1950–1960	27.8	−4.5	1,964.6	41.1	44.5	−0.4	(Z)	−0.3	14.2	−2.6	37.6
1960–1970	155.7	97.3	962.6	15.2	50.3	−8.1	1.7	−3.0	−10.6	0.6	−26.0
1970–1980	249.6	270.8	−379.3	28.0	−13.5	−6.0	−2.1	−1.2	−55.6	−8.3	−37.4
1980–1990	196.9	−14.2	467.5	37.0	5.3	−9.3	−2.8	−7.0	−34.4	−10.6	−31.2

Notes appear at end of table

(continued)

TABLE Ac206–413   Net intercensal migration, by race, nativity, and state: 1850–1990   [Survival rate method]
Continued

	White population										
	Foreign-born										
	Middle Atlantic			East North Central					West North Central		
	New York	New Jersey	Pennsylvania	Ohio	Indiana	Illinois	Michigan	Wisconsin	Minnesota	Iowa	Missouri
	Ac316	Ac317	Ac318	Ac319	Ac320	Ac321	Ac322	Ac323	Ac324	Ac325	Ac326
Year	Thousand	Thousand	Thousand	Thousand	Thousand	Thousand	Thousand	Thousand	Thousand	Thousand	Thousand
1850–1860	−139.9	6.6	−90.0	−46.5	23.1	112.5	49.1	24.9	—	57.7	9.8
1860–1870	−195.2	39.4	−6.9	−57.7	0.2	58.1	43.3	−41.2	80.9	43.0	8.1
1870–1880	221.5	54.4	115.6	77.3	24.3	124.8	134.0	86.5	116.5	80.2	17.2
1880–1890	532.0	133.5	334.3	133.4	29.9	332.6	193.2	176.3	225.4	102.1	58.1
1890–1900	589.7	154.2	282.9	102.1	32.9	273.4	88.3	107.0	116.5	50.1	32.8
1900–1910	1,100.2	286.2	589.8	232.5	53.4	398.3	151.1	112.0	131.7	39.4	63.3
1910–1920	480.9	181.6	168.7	196.5	23.8	222.0	245.1	72.7	58.1	23.7	11.8
1920–1930	751.3	196.0	25.6	65.8	19.3	214.4	223.6	30.9	6.9	−1.3	6.7
1930–1940	120.1	−18.9	−60.4	−18.8	−5.0	−51.5	−29.0	−1.9	7.8	−2.6	−3.3
1940–1950	111.0	58.5	−5.5	16.5	9.5	1.0	36.4	3.4	−0.5	1.1	3.0
1950–1960	150.0	103.2	3.4	41.7	10.3	60.2	35.7	12.1	−1.7	−3.4	4.5
1960–1970	−225.1	4.2	−34.6	−51.5	−3.9	−47.0	−93.8	−16.4	7.5	−1.1	−8.3
1970–1980	−221.2	−58.2	−58.4	−73.2	−18.8	−38.8	−74.1	−20.8	−16.6	−5.4	−7.6
1980–1990	−170.5	−45.5	−50.0	−68.9	−29.3	−79.5	−92.8	−21.4	−16.6	−16.2	−25.2

	White population										
	Foreign-born										
	West North Central					South Atlantic					
	North Dakota	North and South Dakota	South Dakota	Nebraska	Kansas	Delaware	Maryland	District of Columbia	Virginia	West Virginia	North Carolina
	Ac327	Ac328	Ac329	Ac330	Ac331	Ac332	Ac333	Ac334	Ac335	Ac336	Ac337
Year	Thousand	Thousand	Thousand	Thousand	Thousand	Thousand	Thousand	Thousand	Thousand	Thousand	Thousand
1850–1860	—	—	—	—	—	—[1]	—[1]	—[1]	−8.9	—[1]	—[1]
1860–1870	—	—	—	—	—	—[1]	−3.5	—[1]	−5.9	—[1]	—[1]
1870–1880	—	43.0	—	64.1	62.0	1.7	12.4	3.3	2.9	3.8	1.1
1880–1890	—	117.4	—	110.9	50.7	5.1	26.2	4.7	6.2	4.0	0.6
1890–1900	38.6	—	12.7	7.7	7.4	3.1	20.6	5.5	5.1	8.0	1.5
1900–1910	55.2	—	27.0	32.0	35.6	6.0	30.0	9.1	11.3	37.0	2.3
1910–1920	0.3	—	2.5	13.4	7.0	5.3	19.4	9.3	9.0	12.1	2.2
1920–1930	−3.4	—	1.2	3.0	−4.4	−0.3	9.7	5.8	−2.7	−3.9	2.7
1930–1940	−6.6	—	−4.4	−4.6	−7.5	0.8	4.1	9.1	3.4	−2.8	1.6
1940–1950	−5.8	—	−0.2	−0.2	1.1	0.8	15.7	10.7	13.4	−1.1	6.1
1950–1960	−3.9	—	−2.2	(Z)	1.6	2.9	18.6	−0.9	10.7	−3.5	3.6
1960–1970	−2.9	—	−0.1	−1.5	−5.3	4.8	5.6	−18.8	15.0	−1.3	4.0
1970–1980	−0.1	—	−1.5	−2.4	−15.9	−6.8	−29.7	−10.2	−28.6	0.9	−7.3
1980–1990	−5.8	—	−3.0	−11.7	−9.6	−2.5	−4.9	7.3	−4.6	−9.3	−3.5

Notes appear at end of table

TABLE Ac206–413   Net intercensal migration, by race, nativity, and state: 1850–1990   [Survival rate method]
Continued

	White population										
	Foreign-born										
	South Atlantic			East South Central				West South Central			
	South Carolina	Georgia	Florida	Kentucky	Tennessee	Alabama	Mississippi	Arkansas	Louisiana	Oklahoma	Texas
	Ac338	Ac339	Ac340	Ac341	Ac342	Ac343	Ac344	Ac345	Ac346	Ac347	Ac348
Year	Thousand	Thousand	Thousand	Thousand	Thousand	Thousand	Thousand	Thousand	Thousand	Thousand	Thousand
1850–1860	— [1]	— [1]	— [1]	— [1]	— [1]	— [1]	— [1]	— [1]	−37.8	—	— [1]
1860–1870	— [1]	— [1]	— [1]	— [1]	— [1]	— [1]	— [1]	— [1]	−34.0	—	−3.0
1870–1880	0.9	1.1	3.4	5.5	−0.2	1.3	−0.6	5.6	1.2	—	53.6
1880–1890	0.3	3.3	10.5	11.2	5.9	6.3	0.3	5.1	5.8	2.7	47.6
1890–1900	0.7	2.5	3.4	6.0	0.4	2.4	1.7	2.6	13.8	17.8	45.0
1900–1910	2.0	5.4	16.2	4.4	4.7	7.0	3.4	5.5	10.9	22.6	80.8
1910–1920	1.6	4.0	13.9	2.7	1.3	2.2	0.7	0.8	4.3	7.1	137.5
1920–1930	−0.2	0.2	22.4	−1.0	0.7	1.1	1.1	−0.6	−0.6	−2.4	36.4
1930–1940	0.6	0.5	22.0	−0.7	1.0	−0.5	−0.2	(Z)	−1.1	−2.9	−76.1
1940–1950	2.3	5.1	65.0	2.7	4.0	3.0	2.5	2.8	6.4	2.3	65.8
1950–1960	2.5	6.2	152.9	1.2	1.0	1.8	−0.6	−0.6	4.3	2.2	38.7
1960–1970	−1.3	1.2	290.6	−3.4	0.7	3.6	3.1	0.4	10.2	6.4	−46.3
1970–1980	−2.9	−12.8	258.3	−8.3	−0.3	−6.2	−3.7	3.1	−18.9	−11.1	145.0
1980–1990	−14.7	4.7	272.0	−17.7	−16.7	−15.9	−10.1	−7.0	−22.2	−26.8	119.5

	White population										
	Foreign-born										
	Mountain								Pacific		
	Montana	Idaho	Wyoming	Colorado	New Mexico	Arizona	Utah	Nevada	Washington	Oregon	California
	Ac349	Ac350	Ac351	Ac352	Ac353	Ac354	Ac355	Ac356	Ac357	Ac358	Ac359
Year	Thousand	Thousand	Thousand	Thousand	Thousand	Thousand	Thousand	Thousand	Thousand	Thousand	Thousand
1850–1860	—	—	—	—	—	—	—	—	—	— [1]	— [1]
1860–1870	—	—	—	—	—	—	—	—	—	— [1]	— [1]
1870–1880	4.0	3.3	1.7	32.4	2.6	8.2	16.1	5.8	8.0	13.4	73.6
1880–1890	30.9	9.5	9.6	45.6	3.6	3.8	15.2	−5.7	72.2	28.5	104.7
1890–1900	26.4	8.9	4.0	18.7	3.5	6.4	11.4	−1.1	26.4	13.8	76.4
1900–1910	35.2	21.9	12.3	47.9	10.4	24.8	21.6	11.1	149.8	57.5	259.1
1910–1920	14.8	5.6	1.4	9.9	7.8	29.8	7.1	−0.2	44.4	17.2	250.3
1920–1930	−5.9	−0.9	0.6	0.3	−2.7	−10.2	1.0	1.6	32.3	22.1	414.2
1930–1940	−4.4	−0.3	−2.1	−7.3	−5.4	−19.4	−3.2	−1.5	7.7	3.3	33.8
1940–1950	−0.5	0.7	−0.3	5.1	3.7	13.0	4.2	1.7	29.6	14.3	265.4
1950–1960	−1.8	(Z)	−0.8	11.3	4.3	26.8	6.4	3.6	15.0	3.3	388.2
1960–1970	−5.4	4.3	−0.2	10.8	−9.8	3.3	−6.0	7.1	−3.6	11.9	232.1
1970–1980	−2.6	1.5	1.0	5.3	−0.4	23.7	0.9	13.3	−17.8	−0.8	447.7
1980–1990	−6.5	−3.7	−4.3	−30.1	3.9	33.1	−11.1	20.7	−23.4	−3.7	529.7

Notes appear at end of table

(continued)

TABLE Ac206–413   Net intercensal migration, by race, nativity, and state: 1850–1990   [Survival rate method]
Continued

	White population		Black population									
	Foreign-born		New England						Middle Atlantic		
	Pacific											
	Alaska	Hawai'i	Maine	New Hampshire	Vermont	Massachusetts	Rhode Island	Connecticut	New York	New Jersey	Pennsylvania
	Ac360	Ac361	Ac362	Ac363	Ac364	Ac365	Ac366	Ac367	Ac368	Ac369	Ac370
Year	Thousand	Thousand	Thousand	Thousand	Thousand	Thousand	Thousand	Thousand	Thousand	Thousand	Thousand
1850–1860	—	—	—[1]	—[1]	—[1]	0.4	0.2	0.6	−1.4	−0.6	−0.9
1860–1870	—	—	—[1]	—[1]	—[1]	4.7	0.3	1.3	11.7	3.5	8.7
1870–1880	—	—	−0.2	0.1	(Z)	3.0	0.8	0.8	7.6	2.9	8.7
1880–1890	—	—	−0.1	(Z)	(Z)	4.4	1.2	1.1	9.9	8.4	20.8
1890–1900	—	—	0.3	0.1	−0.1	9.9	1.5	2.5	33.8	17.7	39.2
1900–1910	—	—	0.2	(Z)	0.8	5.9	0.6	0.5	35.8	18.5	32.9
1910–1920	—	—	0.1	(Z)	−0.9	6.9	0.6	5.3	63.1	24.5	82.5
1920–1930	—	—	−0.2	0.2	(Z)	2.9	−0.7	5.2	172.8	67.0	101.7
1930–1940	—	—	0.2	−0.3	−0.2	2.7	0.6	2.2	135.9	9.5	20.3
1940–1950	—	—	−0.1	0.2	0.1	10.6	1.2	12.9	243.6	53.6	89.6
1950–1960	1.7	2.2	1.4	0.7	(Z)	16.8	0.3	28.5	243.8	92.2	60.4
1960–1970	2.1	4.4	−1.2	0.3	0.3	24.7	0.9	37.6	264.3	105.1	17.8
1970–1980	−3.8	−5.0	3.8	2.8	1.3	7.9	−2.7	−15.3	−313.9	−13.9	−102.8
1980–1990	−2.1	−8.9	2.3	2.6	1.8	11.1	−0.7	10.6	−98.0	−39.4	−40.4

	Black population										
	East North Central					West North Central					
	Ohio	Indiana	Illinois	Michigan	Wisconsin	Minnesota	Iowa	Missouri	North Dakota	North and South Dakota	South Dakota
	Ac371	Ac372	Ac373	Ac374	Ac375	Ac376	Ac377	Ac378	Ac379	Ac380	Ac381
Year	Thousand	Thousand	Thousand	Thousand	Thousand	Thousand	Thousand	Thousand	Thousand	Thousand	Thousand
1850–1860	5.1	−1.3	1.0	2.7	—[1]	—	—[1]	1.1	—	—	—
1860–1870	7.3	15.8	17.8	3.5	—[1]	—	—[1]	−8.3	—	—	—
1870–1880	2.6	6.6	8.7	1.6	1.3	1.5	2.3	−4.3	—	0.3	—
1880–1890	5.2	3.9	8.4	−1.2	0.1	1.5	0.4	−4.0	—	(Z)	—
1890–1900	5.2	8.1	22.7	0.4	3.0	5.9	1.6	(Z)	4.9	—	14.0
1900–1910	15.6	4.1	23.5	1.9	0.5	2.3	2.1	1.0	0.3	—	0.3
1910–1920	69.4	20.3	69.8	38.7	2.2	2.1	3.9	27.2	−0.1	—	(Z)
1920–1930	90.7	23.2	119.3	86.1	4.4	0.6	−1.9	35.9	−0.1	—	−0.2
1930–1940	20.7	8.6	49.4	28.0	1.0	1.0	−0.4	19.2	−0.1	—	−0.1
1940–1950	106.7	32.1	179.8	163.3	11.9	2.7	1.0	25.7	0.1	—	0.2
1950–1960	107.4	35.3	159.2	109.9	23.5	3.6	0.9	19.2	0.3	—	0.2
1960–1970	47.9	30.5	105.8	105.3	22.6	9.2	0.7	15.9	1.0	—	−2.9
1970–1980	−46.4	−6.7	−32.0	13.4	24.7	7.0	3.7	−28.1	−1.2	—	0.1
1980–1990	−24.6	−12.2	−153.4	−24.4	19.2	24.9	−3.1	−5.7	−0.6	—	−4.7

Notes appear at end of table.

TABLE Ac206–413   Net intercensal migration, by race, nativity, and state: 1850–1990   [Survival rate method]
Continued

| | West North Central | | South Atlantic | | | | | | | | |
| | Black population | | | | | | | | | | |

Year	Nebraska	Kansas	Delaware	Maryland	District of Columbia	Virginia	West Virginia	North Carolina	South Carolina	Georgia	Florida
	Ac382	Ac383	Ac384	Ac385	Ac386	Ac387	Ac388	Ac389	Ac390	Ac391	Ac392
	Thousand	Thousand	Thousand	Thousand	Thousand	Thousand	Thousand	Thousand	Thousand	Thousand	Thousand
1850–1860	—	—	−1.7	−14.7	−0.3	−57.2	—	−24.4	−43.2	−10.5	9.2
1860–1870	—	—	−0.7	−10.5	21.5	−56.8	—	−8.3	−30.7	14.4	18.3
1870–1880	1.2	14.7	−1.4	−7.5	6.2	−37.6	2.1	−7.9	15.7	−20.3	1.4
1880–1890	7.3	2.7	0.3	−7.5	13.4	−53.4	3.6	−38.4	−18.6	12.3	15.8
1890–1900	−2.3	−0.6	−0.7	−6.5	8.7	−70.8	5.8	−48.7	−65.5	−27.3	23.4
1900–1910	1.6	2.6	−0.4	−11.4	9.8	−49.3	15.3	−28.4	−72.0	−16.2	40.7
1910–1920	5.2	5.4	−0.6	7.0	18.3	−27.2	15.5	−28.9	−74.5	−74.7	3.2
1920–1930	(Z)	6.0	0.5	5.0	16.0	−117.2	12.8	−15.7	−204.3	−260.0	54.2
1930–1940	0.6	−0.1	2.4	10.7	47.5	−36.9	−4.1	−60.0	−94.4	−90.3	49.9
1940–1950	3.0	2.3	2.4	29.9	61.2	−30.6	−16.7	−127.3	−159.0	−191.2	7.2
1950–1960	3.6	2.4	4.6	24.9	51.3	−71.1	−36.8	−171.3	−180.8	−165.1	79.8
1960–1970	7.3	−1.4	4.6	59.8	37.0	−68.8	−25.8	−154.1	−157.4	−121.6	−33.3
1970–1980	−2.3	6.0	0.5	117.3	−142.2	13.9	−3.0	4.3	−1.7	21.3	42.7
1980–1990	1.5	−0.8	2.7	90.7	−50.9	71.7	−8.1	35.9	8.7	100.3	29.2

| | East South Central | | | | West South Central | | | | Mountain | | |
| | Black population | | | | | | | | | | |

Year	Kentucky	Tennessee	Alabama	Mississippi	Arkansas	Louisiana	Oklahoma	Texas	Montana	Idaho	Wyoming
	Ac393	Ac394	Ac395	Ac396	Ac397	Ac398	Ac399	Ac400	Ac401	Ac402	Ac403
	Thousand	Thousand	Thousand	Thousand	Thousand	Thousand	Thousand	Thousand	Thousand	Thousand	Thousand
1850–1860	−28.3	−20.6	8.7	26.7	35.6	37.2	—	72.3	—	—	—
1860–1870	−22.2	12.9	−17.1	−22.3	−2.7	−3.1	—	21.3	—	—	—
1870–1880	−13.1	−24.6	−36.1	17.6	25.4	−1.3	—	21.0	—	—	—
1880–1890	−22.4	−18.7	−5.8	−13.2	44.7	3.3	2.3	12.6	—	—	—
1890–1900	−12.2	−19.0	−1.7	−10.4	−7.9	−21.6	79.3	7.1	—	—	—
1900–1910	−22.3	−34.3	−22.1	−30.9	22.5	−16.1	54.8	−10.2	0.3	0.3	1.2
1910–1920	−16.6	−29.3	−70.8	−129.6	−1.0	−51.2	0.8	5.2	−0.1	0.3	−0.6
1920–1930	−16.6	−14.0	−80.7	−68.8	−46.3	−25.5	1.9	9.7	−0.2	−0.1	−0.1
1930–1940	−9.1	8.6	−63.8	−58.2	−33.3	−8.4	−13.0	4.9	(Z)	(Z)	−0.2
1940–1950	−22.8	−38.2	−165.4	−258.2	−116.1	−113.8	−38.9	−67.2	0.1	0.3	1.3
1950–1960	−16.6	−52.2	−191.6	−264.2	−108.6	−66.2	−18.8	−19.6	(Z)	0.1	−0.8
1960–1970	−5.1	−44.1	−185.2	−234.9	−79.2	−111.2	15.1	−1.3	0.7	−0.5	1.6
1970–1980	−1.3	1.2	−58.5	−84.5	−28.8	−57.4	44.3	113.0	−0.1	4.7	1.4
1980–1990	−11.8	−9.6	−29.5	−45.0	−24.1	−66.8	53.5	49.8	−1.1	−0.7	−3.4

Notes appear at end of table

(continued)

TABLE Ac206–413   Net intercensal migration, by race, nativity, and state: 1850–1990   [Survival rate method]
Continued

	Black population									
	Mountain					Pacific				
	Colorado	New Mexico	Arizona	Utah	Nevada	Washington	Oregon	California	Alaska	Hawai'i
	Ac404	Ac405	Ac406	Ac407	Ac408	Ac409	Ac410	Ac411	Ac412	Ac413
Year	Thousand	Thousand	Thousand	Thousand	Thousand	Thousand	Thousand	Thousand	Thousand	Thousand
1850–1860	—	—	—	—	—	—	—	—	—	—
1860–1870	—	—	—	—	—	—	—	—	—	—
1870–1880	—	—	—	—	—	—	—	—	—	—
1880–1890	—	—	—	—	—	—	—	—	—	—
1890–1900	—	—	—	—	—	—	—	—	—	—
1900–1910	3.1	—	0.2	0.5	0.4	3.4	0.5	9.8	—	—
1910–1920	0.7	4.1	5.8	0.4	−0.1	1.1	0.7	16.1	—	—
1920–1930	0.8	−2.9	1.9	−0.3	0.2	0.2	0.2	36.4	—	—
1930–1940	0.9	1.5	3.5	0.2	0.2	1.2	0.5	41.2	—	—
1940–1950	6.1	2.3	6.7	1.1	2.8	17.8	6.9	258.9	—	—
1950–1960	11.0	4.1	7.0	0.5	5.3	6.7	2.4	220.4	5.2	1.2
1960–1970	18.5	−8.8	−12.1	3.9	8.5	18.5	4.3	327.3	−3.5	−45.0
1970–1980	35.3	25.2	36.6	6.3	17.4	42.1	19.5	310.4	1.9	13.1
1980–1990	5.9	−10.7	18.1	−5.0	20.5	28.3	6.0	62.0	8.5	8.6

(Z) Fewer than 50.

[1] Insufficient sample size.

Sources

1850–1870, native and foreign-born white: Integrated Public Use Microdata Series (IPUMS) 1 percent samples. 1850–1860, black: Inter-university Consortium for Political and Social Research, Study 0003. 1860–1870, black: IPUMS 1 percent sample with black oversample.

1870–1950: Everett S. Lee, Ann Ratner Miller, et al., *Population Redistribution and Economic Growth: United States, 1870–1950* (American Philosophical Society, 1957), volume 1, pp. 107–231.

1950–1960: Hope T. Eldridge, "Net Intercensal Migration for States and Geographic Divisions of the United States, 1950–1960," Analytical and Technical Reports, number 5, Population Studies Center, University of Pennsylvania, Table A-1.

1960–1970: IPUMS 1 percent sample.

1970–1980: IPUMS 1 percent sample (Form 2, State Sample).

1980–1990: IPUMS 5 percent state samples.

Documentation

See the Guide to the Millennial Edition for information on IPUMS.

For the native population, the figures show the estimated amount of net internal migration. For the foreign-born, the figures represent the estimated net change attributable to direct movement into the state from abroad and the net gain or loss in the exchange of foreign-born residents with other states.

The estimates of net migration by the survival rate method were obtained by a residual method, using survival ratios derived from census data. The loss through mortality during an intercensal period was estimated on the basis of the ratios of appropriate age groups as enumerated in successive decennial censuses. The difference between the enumerated population at the end of the decennial period and the estimated survivors from the beginning to the end of the period was assumed to be net migration, using the identity

$$M = P_{t+10} - s P_t$$

where P_{t+10} and P_t are the state's population at time t and time $t + 10$, s is the fraction of the time t population that is predicted to survive to time $t + 10$, and M is net domestic migration. Computations were by age groups for each sex, the figures being summations for ages 10 years and older at the end of each intercensal period.

Series Ac245–257. For 1870–1890, only white population in Mountain and Pacific States; no estimates made for blacks.

Series Ac362–413. For 1850–1870, free blacks and slaves combined.

Series Ac231, Ac283, Ac335, and Ac387. West Virginia included with Virginia, 1850–1870.

TABLE Ac414–418   Change in the farm population through births, deaths, and migration: 1920–1970

Contributed by Joseph P. Ferrie

		Change in farm population			
		Net from births and deaths	Migration and reclassification of residence		
	Farm population		Net (to farms)	To farms	From farms
	Ac414	Ac415	Ac416	Ac417	Ac418
Year	Thousand	Thousand	Thousand	Thousand	Thousand
1920	31,974	—	—	—	—
1921	32,123	485	−336	560	896
1922	32,109	550	−564	759	1,323
1923	31,490	518	−1,137	1,115	2,252
1924	31,177	494	−807	1,355	2,162
1925	31,190	500	−487	1,581	2,068
1926	30,979	491	−702	1,336	2,038
1927	30,530	458	−907	1,427	2,334
1928	30,548	475	−457	1,705	2,162
1929	30,580	454	−422	1,698	2,120
1930	30,529	426	−477	1,604	2,081
1931	30,845	377	−61	1,985	2,046
1932	31,388	387	156	1,918	1,762
1933	32,393	398	607	1,826	1,219
1934	32,305	375	−463	970	1,433
1935	32,161	383	−527	783	1,310
1936	31,737	375	−799	825	1,624
1937	31,266	363	−834	719	1,553
1938	30,980	375	−661	872	1,533
1939	30,840	405	−545	823	1,368
1940	30,547	410	−703	819	—
1941	30,118	359	−788	—	—
1942	28,914	383	−1,587	—	—
1943	26,186	418	−3,145	—	—
1944	24,815	370	−1,740	—	—
1945	24,420	353	−748	—	—
1946	25,403	312	671	—	—
1947	25,829	470	−44	—	—
1948	24,383	443	−1,889	—	—
1949	24,194	397	−586	—	—
1950	23,048	392	−1,537	—	—
1951	21,890	373	−1,531	—	—
1952	21,748	341	−483	—	—
1953	19,874	328	−2,201	—	—
1954	19,019	296	−1,151	—	—
1955	19,078	268	−210	—	—
1956	18,712	261	−627	—	—
1957	17,656	239	−1,295	—	—
1958	17,128	220	−748	—	—
1959	16,592	203	−740	—	—
1960	15,635	184	−1,142	356	1,498
1961	14,803	168	−1,000	309	1,309
1962	14,313	156	−646	287	933
1963	13,367	140	−1,086	352	1,438
1964	12,954	121	−533	283	816
1965	12,363	112	−703	275	978
1966	11,595	90	−858	250	1,108
1967	10,875	73	−793	299	1,092
1968	10,454	60	−481	268	749
1969	10,307	51	−198	284	481
1970	9,712	47	−642	—	—

Sources

1920–1962: U.S. Department of Agriculture, Economic Research Service, Farm Population Estimates for 1910–1962, ERS-130, 1963. 1963–1970: Farm Population Estimates, annual issues.

Documentation

Data shown are as of April 1, or represent change since the preceding April.

Series Ac416–418. Includes persons who did not move but who were in or out of the farm population because agricultural operations on the places where they were living either ceased or began.

TABLE Ac419–427   Population mobility – nonmovers and movers, by type of move: 1940–2000[1]

Contributed by Joseph P. Ferrie

				Movers					
				Different house in the United States					Abroad at beginning of period
						Different county (migrants)			
Year	Total population	Nonmovers	Total	Total	Same county	Total	Within a state	Between states	
	Ac419	Ac420	Ac421	Ac422	Ac423	Ac424	Ac425	Ac426	Ac427
	Thousand	Thousand	Thousand	Thousand	Thousand	Thousand	Thousand	Thousand	Thousand
1940–1947 [2]	122,633	52,136	70,497	69,898	44,429	25,469	13,081	12,388	599
1947–1948	141,698	113,026	28,672	28,210	19,202	9,008	4,638	4,370	462
1948–1949	144,101	116,498	27,603	27,127	18,792	8,335	3,992	4,344	476
1949–1950	146,864	118,849	28,015	27,526	19,276	8,250	4,360	3,889	491
1950–1951	148,400	116,936	31,464	31,158	20,694	10,464	5,276	5,188	306
1951–1952	150,494	120,016	30,478	29,840	19,874	9,966	4,854	5,112	638
1952–1953	153,038	121,512	31,526	30,786	20,638	10,148	4,626	5,522	740
1953–1954	155,679	125,654	30,025	29,027	19,046	9,981	4,947	5,034	998
1954–1955	158,609	126,190	32,419	31,492	21,086	10,406	5,511	4,895	927
1955–1956	161,497	127,457	34,040	33,098	22,186	10,912	5,859	5,053	942
1956–1957	164,371	131,648	32,723	31,834	21,566	10,268	5,192	5,076	889
1957–1958	167,604	133,501	34,103	33,263	22,023	11,240	5,656	5,584	840
1958–1959	170,658	137,018	33,640	32,804	22,315	10,489	5,419	5,070	836
1959–1960	174,451	139,766	34,685	33,811	22,564	11,247	5,724	5,523	874
1960–1961	177,354	140,821	36,533	35,535	24,289	11,246	5,493	5,753	998
1961–1962	179,663	144,445	35,218	34,364	23,341	11,023	5,461	5,562	854
1962–1963	182,541	146,109	36,432	35,411	23,059	12,352	5,712	6,640	1,021
1963–1964	185,312	148,125	37,187	36,327	24,089	12,238	6,191	6,047	859
1964–1965	187,974	149,128	38,846	37,866	25,122	12,744	6,597	6,147	978
1965–1966	190,242	152,656	37,586	36,703	24,165	12,538	6,275	6,263	883
1966–1967	192,233	155,710	36,523	35,200	22,339	12,861	6,308	6,553	1,323
1967–1968	194,621	156,735	37,886	36,603	22,960	13,643	6,607	7,035	1,283
1968–1969	196,642	159,310	37,332	35,933	22,993	12,940	6,316	6,625	1,399
1969–1970	198,955	160,860	38,095	36,541	23,225	13,316	6,250	7,066	1,554
1970–1971	201,506	163,800	37,705	36,161	23,018	13,143	6,197	6,946	1,544
1970–1973 [2, 3]	195,519	124,940	70,578	62,457	37,924	24,533	12,237	12,297	8,121
1970–1974 [2, 3]	194,965	111,977	82,988	72,444	43,462	28,983	14,214	14,769	10,544
1970–1975 [2, 3]	193,511	99,651	93,860	79,837	46,834	33,003	16,349	16,654	14,023
1975–1976	208,069	171,276	36,793	35,645	22,399	13,246	7,106	6,140	1,148
1975–1977 [2]	206,419	149,789	56,630	54,620	33,258	21,362	11,417	9,946	2,010
1975–1978 [2]	204,883	132,106	72,777	70,080	41,947	28,134	15,095	13,030	2,697
1975–1979 [2]	203,437	118,598	84,840	81,824	47,168	34,656	18,220	16,435	3,016
1980–1981	221,641	183,442	38,200	36,887	23,097	13,789	7,614	6,175	1,313
1981–1982	223,719	185,592	38,127	37,039	23,081	13,959	7,330	6,628	1,088
1982–1983	225,874	188,465	37,408	36,430	22,858	13,572	7,403	6,169	978
1983–1984	228,232	188,853	39,379	38,300	23,659	14,641	8,198	6,444	1,079
1984–1985	230,333	183,863	46,470	45,043	30,126	14,917	7,995	6,921	1,427
1985–1986	232,998	189,760	43,237	42,037	26,401	15,636	8,665	6,971	1,200
1986–1987	235,089	191,396	43,693	42,551	27,196	15,355	8,762	6,593	1,142
1987–1988	237,431	195,258	42,174	40,974	26,201	14,772	7,727	7,046	1,200
1988–1989	239,793	197,173	42,620	41,153	26,123	15,030	7,949	7,081	1,467
1989–1990	242,208	198,827	43,381	41,821	25,726	16,094	8,061	8,033	1,560
1990–1991	244,884	203,345	41,539	40,154	25,151	15,003	7,881	7,122	1,385
1991–1992	247,380	204,580	42,800	41,545	26,587	14,957	7,853	7,105	1,255
1992–1993	250,210	208,162	42,048	40,743	26,212	14,532	7,735	6,797	1,305
1993–1994	255,774	212,939	42,835	41,590	26,638	14,952	8,226	6,726	1,245
1994–1995	258,175	215,870	42,306	41,528	27,900	13,627	7,886	5,741	778
1995–1996	260,406	217,868	42,538	41,177	26,696	14,481	8,009	6,472	1,361
1996–1997	262,976	219,585	43,391	42,088	27,740	14,348	7,960	6,389	1,303
1997–1998	265,209	222,702	42,507	41,304	27,082	14,222	7,867	6,355	1,203
1998–1999	267,934	225,298	42,636	41,207	25,268	15,939	8,423	7,516	1,429
1999–2000	270,219	226,831	43,387	41,641	24,399	17,242	8,814	8,428	1,746

[1] Data for all survey intervals exclude children who were born during the interval.

[2] Multiyear interval.

[3] "No Report on Mobility Status" included under series Ac419, Ac421, and Ac427.

Sources

One-year intervals 1947–1948 through 1998–1999. U.S. Census Bureau Internet site, Migration Table A-1, "Annual Geographic Mobility Rates"; the original data (including breakdowns by age, sex, and race) can be found in U.S. Census Bureau, Current Population Reports, Series P-20 (CPR). 1999–2000: U.S. Census Bureau, CPR number 538. Other intervals: 1940–1947, CPR number 14; 1970–1973, CPR number 262; 1970–1974, CPR number 273; 1970–1975, CPR number 285; 1975–1977, CPR number 320; 1975–1978, CPR number 331; and 1975–1979, CPR number 353.

TABLE Ac419–427   Population mobility – nonmovers and movers, by type of move: 1940–2000   *Continued*

Documentation

See Table Ac428–436 for mobility rates based on five-year time intervals.

Comparisons are April to April for 1940–1947 through 1954–1955, 1956–1957, 1958–1959, 1961–1962, 1935–1940, and 1975–1980. All other comparisons are March to March.

Members of the armed forces living on post without their families are excluded from all except 1935–1940 and 1975–1980.

Beginning in 1948, the Current Population Survey asked respondents in most years where they were living one year before the survey date (in the same house, county, or state). In addition to these "one-year-ago" questions, the Current Population Survey included a question covering a different interval in some years (e.g., in the 1970s, questions from 1972–1974 referred to residence in 1970, whereas questions from 1977–1980 referred to residence in 1975). Finally, the decennial census also contained a question on residence five years ago. The figures in this table and Table Ac428–436 contain questions from all the intervals used since 1947 (including the 1947 question on residence in 1940 that makes it possible to estimate internal migration over the Second World War).

Series Ac421. Equals the sum of series Ac422 and Ac427.

TABLE Ac428–436   Population mobility – nonmovers and movers, by type of move: 1935–1995   [Five-year intervals]

Contributed by Joseph P. Ferrie

				Movers					
				Different house in the United States					
						Different county (migrants)			
Year	Total population	Nonmovers	Total	Total	Same county	Total	Within a state	Between states	Abroad at beginning of period
	Ac428	Ac429	Ac430	Ac431	Ac432	Ac433	Ac434	Ac435	Ac436
	Thousand	Thousand	Thousand	Thousand	Thousand	Thousand	Thousand	Thousand	Thousand
1935–1940	117,932	47,480	70,452	68,945	55,516	13,429	6,929	6,500	1,507
1955–1960	156,308	79,167	77,141	75,150	47,837	27,313	13,165	14,148	1,991
1965–1970	175,395	97,522	77,873	75,167	43,347	31,820	15,616	16,204	2,705
1970–1975 [1]	193,511	99,651	93,860	79,837	46,834	33,003	16,349	16,654	14,023
1975–1980	210,418	112,939	97,478	93,553	52,625	40,928	20,580	20,348	3,926
1980–1985	216,108	125,982	90,126	86,269	47,858	38,411	19,629	18,782	3,857
1985–1990	230,446	122,797	107,649	102,540	58,676	43,864	22,279	21,585	5,109
1990–1995	241,805	135,189	147,614	142,413	60,417	40,998	21,311	19,687	5,201

[1] "No Report on Mobility Status" included under series Ac428, Ac430, and Ac436.

Sources

1935–1940, 1955–1960, 1965–1970, 1975–1980: calculated from 1 percent Integrated Public Use Microdata Series (IPUMS). See the Guide to the Millennial Edition for information on IPUMS.

1970–1975, U.S. Census Bureau, Current Population Reports, Series P-20, number 285.

1980–1985, U.S. Census Bureau, Current Population Reports, number 420.

1985–1990, U.S. Census Bureau, 1990 Census Summary Tape File 3 (STF3), File STF3C-1, available at the Census Bureau Internet site.

1990–1995, U.S. Census Bureau, Current Population Reports, Series P-23, number 200.

Documentation

See Table Ac419–427 for mobility rates based on shorter time intervals.

Data include persons 5 years of age and older at the end of the survey interval.

Comparisons are April to April for 1955–1960, 1965–1970, 1975–1980, and 1985–1990. All other comparisons are March to March.

Members of the armed forces living on post without their families are excluded from all except 1935–1940, 1955–1960, 1965–1970, 1975–1980, and 1985–1990.

CHAPTER Ad
International Migration

Editors: Robert Barde, Susan B. Carter, and Richard Sutch

INTERNATIONAL MIGRATION

Robert Barde, Susan B. Carter, and
Richard Sutch

Immigration is a recent development. Although people have moved from place to place throughout history, spreading, in the first instance, from Africa to many parts of the globe, most of these relocations are not immigration. Immigration, by definition, presupposes the existence of nation-states that have a desire and ability to control their borders (Torpey 2000). Thus, when Europeans moved to the Americas in the seventeenth and eighteenth centuries, they were *emigrating* from their home countries and *colonizing* the Americas. They were not *immigrating*. Enslaved peoples have been transported against their will as recently as the mid-nineteenth century and even into modern nation-states. This was not immigration either. Immigration refers to voluntary movement. Today when émigrés flee their home countries under duress, seeking freedom from political, religious, and racial persecution, it is better to think of their decision to flee as *emigration* because the term "immigration" is reserved to describe voluntary choice. Large-scale immigration therefore requires the worldwide development of effective constitutional guarantees of civil rights and personal liberties. As history vividly makes clear, large-scale immigration had to await improvements in income and reductions in transportation costs before such movement could be considered a possibility for more than a handful of the elite. For all these reasons, immigration could not have begun much earlier than the mid-nineteenth century.

Immigration is a central feature of the economic, social, and political history of the United States. It is arguably the defining feature. The United States is often called a "nation of immigrants" but this phrase should not be interpreted too literally. Since the U.S. Census Bureau began publishing statistics on the fraction of the population foreign-born in 1850, the foreign-born share has never exceeded 20 percent of the total (Table Ad354–443). Australia and Canada have long reported larger foreign-born shares than the United States. In addition, in the 1990s, many European countries achieved foreign-born shares that approach, and in some cases exceed, the U.S. levels (Organization for Economic Cooperation and Development 2001).

Still, the phrase "nation of immigrants" is a nice way of highlighting some distinctive and long-standing features of the American experience. From 1860, when statistics on the Native American population – American Indians, Eskimos, and Aleuts – were first published by the Census Bureau, their share has been less than 1 percent of the total, even though many of those enumerated as Native Americans are of mixed ancestry. The exception is Census 2000, in which people who trace their heritage to the aboriginal population account for 3 percent of the total (see Table Aa145–184). Because most American blacks are descendents of slaves who were brought to America against their will as part of the trans-Atlantic slave trade, few are descendents of immigrants (Passel and Edmonston 1994). Nonetheless, because the black population has never been more than one fifth of the total, it is still the case that the vast majority of Americans are either immigrants themselves or descended from immigrants.

Another reason to embrace the "nation of immigrants" label is that, over its history, the United States has absorbed more immigrants than other nations – indeed, more than all of the other immigrant-recipient nations combined. This is no small feat. Of the estimated fifty-five million immigrants who relocated during the hundred years or so preceding the 1920s, approximately 60 percent came to the United States (see Tables Ad25–79). Moreover, unlike Australia, where approximately four fifths of immigrants came from Britain, and unlike Argentina, where more than three quarters of immigrants came from Italy or Spain, the United States received immigrants from many different countries all around the world. Finally, the United States is one of only a handful of countries that have not experienced an extensive diaspora of its own people (Mitchell 1980, 1983). Estimates of emigration from the United States are shown in Tables Ad1–2 and Ad21–24. These numbers are small relative to those for other countries. Scholars suggest that most of these emigrants had recently arrived from another country, so their "emigration" is best thought of as a return to their native lands (Baines 1995).

The pace and pattern of international migration to the United States, the experience of immigrants in the United States, and the impact of immigrants on the growth and development of the

Acknowledgments

Robert Barde, Susan Carter, and Richard Sutch acknowledge the helpful comments of Barry Chiswick, Barry Edmonston, Henry Gemery, Marvin McInnis, Marian Smith, Matt Sobek, Jeffrey G. Williamson, and Gavin Wright on earlier drafts of the essay. Christopher Meissner, Victoria Nayak, Luong Lam, and Simone Pert provided research assistance for the data tables. Additional assistance with the creation of tables for this chapter was provided by Marian Smith, historian of the Immigration and Naturalization Service; Josiah Heyman, Department of Sociology and Anthropology, University of Texas at El Paso; and James Woodard, of the Budget Office of the Immigration and Naturalization Service. Financial assistance was provided by the National Science Foundation; the Institute of Business and Economic Research at the University of California, Berkeley; and the Center for Social and Economic Policy at the University of California, Riverside.

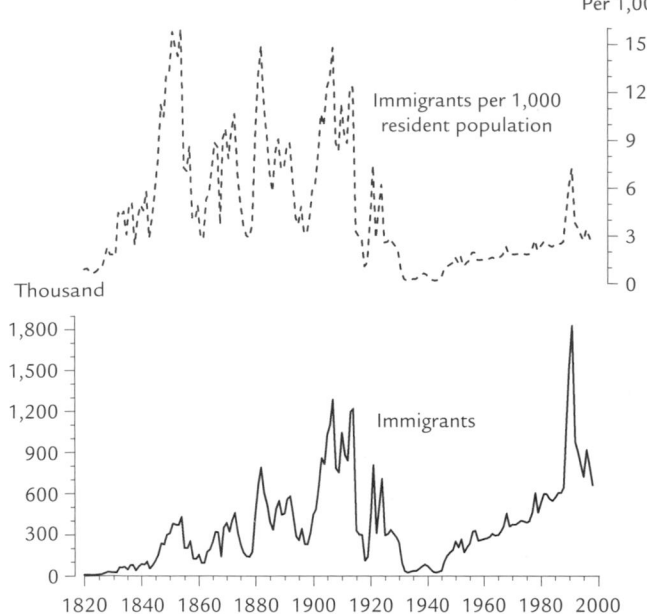

FIGURE Ad-A Immigrants to the United States – total and number per 1,000 of the resident population: 1820–1998

Sources

Series Aa7 and Ad1.

American economy have all been subjects of large scholarly literatures over the years.[1]

Immigrants, Emigrants, and Net Migration: The Statistical Record

The first systematic collection of data on immigration to the United States began in 1819, and the official estimates of annual immigration are presented in series Ad1 and Figure Ad-A.[2] In the nineteenth and early twentieth centuries the official immigrant series reveals strong cycles with successively higher peaks until the disruption of World War I from 1915 through 1919. After the war there was a brief recovery followed by a sharp decline in the mid-1920s and a virtual cessation during the 1930s. Beginning about 1950, there is a more or less smooth increase in the numbers over the last half of the twentieth century, except for a sharp spike in the early 1990s, reflecting legalizations authorized by the Immigration Reform and Control Act (IRCA) of 1986, which are discussed later. At the end of the twentieth century, the number of immigrants admitted annually (excluding the IRCA legalizations) approximates those in peak years in the late nineteenth century. Of course, the United States was a much larger country at the end of the twentieth century than it had been one hundred years earlier. To put the immigrant flows into perspective, the number of immigrants can be shown relative to the size of the resident population (also in Figure Ad-A). In proportionate terms, the current inflow of immigrants is rather modest by historical standards. If the IRCA legalizations are omitted,

---

[1] Key works of synthesis include Bailyn (1986) for the colonial period, Jones (1960) for the period through 1924, Bodnar (1985) for the period 1830–1930, Hatton and Williamson (1998) for 1850 through World War I, and Archdeacon (1983) up to 1980.

[2] For immigration history of the earlier period, see Chapters Aa, on population characteristics, and Eg, on colonial statistics.

then the late-twentieth-century flows are comparable to those in the *slowest* years from the period between 1840 and the onset of World War I.

Still another way to think about the size of the immigrant flows is to calculate the contribution of net immigration to American population growth, as shown in Figure Ad-B. During the period of mass immigration preceding World War I, immigration accounted for somewhere between one third and one half of U.S. population growth. At the end of the twentieth century, immigration again accounts for about one third of this growth, despite the fact that the number of immigrants arriving is smaller and the base population is larger today than it was in the decades immediately preceding World War I. The reason for the relatively large contribution of immigration to American population growth today is that the rate of natural increase (births minus deaths) is low.

Scholars divide the history of international migration to the United States into three phases. The first was an era of mass, largely unregulated migration that began in 1815, just before statistics were first collected, and proceeded, with enormous year-to-year variation, until the imposition of stringent numerical restrictions in the 1920s. The beginning year, 1815, witnessed the end of the War of 1812 between Britain and the United States, the conclusion of the Napoleonic Wars in Europe, and the beginning of massive economic, social, and political upheavals throughout the European continent. Beginning in England, Scotland, and Ireland, then moving east into Scandinavia and Germany, and then south and east into Spain, Italy, Eastern Europe, and Russia, traditional agricultural economies became market – and in some cases industrial – economies. The Industrial Revolution displaced handicraft industries, throwing artisans out of work. Commercial farming displaced self-sufficient agriculture, reducing the demand for labor in rural areas. The period was one of rapid population growth, and this meant that the contraction in employment opportunities coincided with an unprecedented surge in the number of young people looking for work. By contrast, in America and other New World countries, jobs were plentiful, wages high, and land cheap. Also, the U.S. Constitution guaranteed individual liberties and religious tolerance. It is no wonder that emigration proved so attractive to so many.

Between 1815 and 1924, an estimated fifty-five million people left Europe to make their homes in the New World countries of

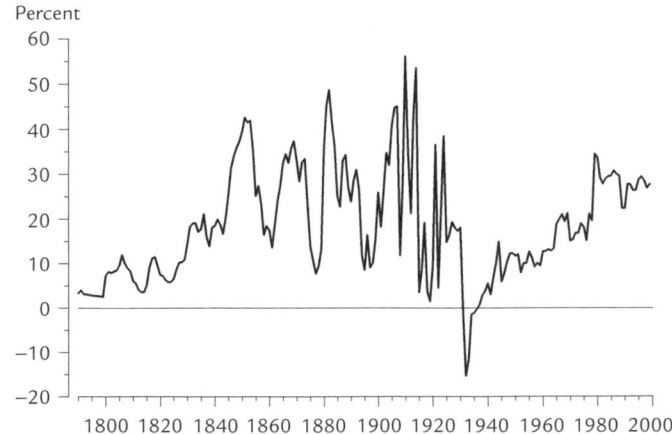

FIGURE Ad-B Net immigration as a percentage of population growth: 1790–1999

Source

Series Aa13 expressed as a percentage of series Aa10.

Argentina, Australia, Brazil, Canada, New Zealand, and the United States. The United States was the premier destination country and it received more immigrants than all the other destination countries combined (Tables Ad25–79). The United States offered economic opportunities and, for most of the period, it placed relatively few restrictions on immigrant entry.

The immigrant flows to the United States during this first period of relatively open borders display two distinct features. One is long-term growth. From 1820 through 1914 and the outbreak of World War I, the number of immigrants arriving in the United States in each successive decade is generally larger than in the previous one. Equally remarkable is the volatility – the sharp peaks and troughs in the annual flows. These peaks and troughs correspond to economic and political developments in both the United States and the countries from which people emigrated. Good economic conditions in the United States attracted immigrants, whereas depressions repelled them or at least led migrants to postpone their departure for America. Thus, years of economic prosperity are years of high immigration flows and vice versa. Wars, both in the United States and abroad, dampened the flow of migrants across international borders.

The second phase covers the period when the National Origins Quota Act was in effect, from 1924 through 1965. This Act severely limited the number of immigrants and restricted their admission to countries with low levels of out-migration. Passage of this Act had a major impact on the magnitude and character of the subsequent immigrant flows. As Figure Ad-A shows, this was a period of historically low levels of immigration. The 1920s through the 1940s was also a time of retreat from international integration on many other fronts, including more restricted flows of capital, reductions in the volume of international trade, and, of course, World War II (also see Table Ee1–21). It was a period of tremendous internal migration within the United States, as blacks moved out of the South and into northern industrial cities; as farmers moved off the farm and into cities in the 1920s and then back to the farm again in the Great Depression of the 1930s; and as the population moved to the West, especially to California. Immigration policy became an arm of foreign policy as the United States gave high priority to political asylees, especially those fleeing the Nazis during the 1930s and those fleeing Communist countries after the onset of the Cold War. It was a period during which many distinguished scientists and engineers left Europe and came to the United States to live and work. Another important development, which began during World War II and continued into the 1950s and 1960s, was the creation of a large migrant agricultural labor force that moved between Mexico and the United States. The policy of admitting Mexican farm laborers for temporary employment came be known as the "Braceros Program." Data on those engaged in this work during the war years are described in Table Ad1014–1022 and the number participating in the 1950s through 1964 is included in series Ad1022. During the peak years of the Braceros Program in the late 1950s, almost a half-million people entered the country under its auspices – more than the number who entered as immigrants during the same period.

The third phase of U.S. immigration history commenced in 1965 with the adoption of the Preference System that raised the limit on the number of immigrants and shifted the criterion of admission from country of origin to family reunification. The number of immigrants increased and, unexpectedly, the country of origin of immigrants shifted away from Europe toward Asia and Latin America. At the conclusion of the Braceros Program in 1964, the annual flow of migrant agricultural labor became an undocumented flow and the population of undocumented persons rose. By the mid-1980s, this population was so large as to prompt legislation that legalized the status of this group while implementing controls to slow the future stream of such workers.

Legal Context for Immigration

Immigration to the United States takes place within a complex framework of federal and state laws and executive decisions that has changed significantly over time. While the federal government has successfully asserted its primacy in deciding who is allowed to enter the territory of the United States, various states have periodically attempted to influence the level of immigration by enacting laws specifically designed to discourage certain groups from settling or remaining in a particular state. Examples include Massachusetts's Act to Prevent the Introduction of Paupers, from Foreign Ports or Places (1820), California's Alien Land Laws of 1913 and 1920 (aimed at legal Japanese and Chinese immigrants), and California's Proposition 187 of 1994 (the "Save Our State" initiative, which attempted to limit the presence of illegal or undocumented aliens).

Edward P. Hutchinson describes U.S. immigration law as one of the "largest and most complex bodies of legislation (in the United States), perhaps exceeded only by the tax code" (Hutchinson 1981, p. xiii). The complexity of the legal framework is magnified by the fact that all three branches of the federal government play important roles in its structure, administration, and execution. Congress makes immigration law. The president can authorize the admission of aliens for reasons of national interest and foreign policy and can negotiate treaties that have implications for immigration. Exercise of the presidential prerogative on admissions was especially important during the Cold War. The implications of international trade treaties, especially the North American Free Trade Agreement (NAFTA), for the admission of aliens to the United States have been enormous. The executive branch of the federal government has been responsible for administration and enforcement of immigration law since 1864 when Congress established the post of Commissioner of Immigration. Since its establishment in 1891, the Bureau of Immigration – later the Immigration and Naturalization Service (INS) – has had considerable latitude in its enforcement and has often played an active role in shaping legislation. Hutchinson (1981) provides an authoritative and detailed account of the major elements of U.S. immigration law and its development through 1965. The judicial branch has also been active. Individual federal judges made millions of case-by-case decisions to establish citizenship, and the Supreme Court decisions established a definition of "white" person for purposes of eligibility for naturalization. In cases such as *Yick Wo v. Hopkins* (1886), which attempted to discourage Chinese immigration by preventing Chinese launderers from doing business, the court reaffirmed federal primacy in matters of immigration by finding local statutes discriminatory (for a summary of major pieces of legislation, see Table Ad-C).[3]

---

[3] For a description and analyses of more recent developments, see Briggs 1984 and the annual issues of *Statistical Yearbook of the INS*. Michael LeMay and Elliott Barkan (1999) offer a compilation of major federal, as well as some state, legislative acts and executive orders affecting immigration.

TABLE Ad-C   Major legislation and social, political, and economic events relating to immigration: 1790–1996

1790	Act of March 26, 1790. Established uniform rule for naturalization by setting the residence requirement at two years. Asserted federal authority over immigration for the first time (in the pre-federal era, naturalization had been controlled by the states). Limited naturalization to free whites. No prohibitions on immigration were part of this Act.
1798	Aliens Act of June 25, 1798. First federal law relating to immigration. Authorized the president to arrest or deport any alien deemed dangerous to the United States. Required vessel captains to report the arrival of aliens on board. Expired two years after its enactment.
1819	Steerage Act of March 2, 1819. First significant federal law relating to immigration. Established the continuing reporting of immigration to the United States (see Table Ad1–2).
1838	Transatlantic Steamship Service. First regular transatlantic steamship service begun.
1843	Know-Nothings. Nativistic Know-Nothing political movement founded the American Republican Party to combat foreign influences and to uphold American values. Disbanded after the presidential election of 1856.
1845	Beginning of the Great Irish Potato Famine, 1845–1849. Stimulated the immigration of a large number of Irish to the United States.
1848	Treaty of Guadalupe Hidalgo. Peace treaty between the United States and Mexico that ended the Mexican War, confirmed the U.S. claims on Texas, and ceded to the United States land that includes the present-day states of California, Arizona, Nevada, and Utah, plus parts of New Mexico, Colorado, and Wyoming. Residents of these areas became U.S. citizens.
1849	California Gold Rush. Economic opportunities – in the gold fields, in sectors such as manufacturing, trade, and services that supported the miners, and in the expansion of the railroad system that was stimulated by the gold discoveries – attracted immigrants from around the world.
1853	Gadsden Purchase. Transferred to the United States ownership of the Mesilla Valley near the Rio Grande in southern New Mexico and Arizona. This thinly populated region was sought by the United States because it was the most practicable route for a southern railroad from the East to the Pacific Coast.
1864	Act of July 4, 1864. Congress established the post of Commissioner of Immigration; legalized immigrant contract labor whereby would-be immigrants would pledge their wages to pay for transportation to the United States.
1866	Fourteenth Amendment to the Constitution. Conferred citizenship on emancipated slaves.
1870	Naturalization Act of July 14, 1870. Extended the naturalization laws to aliens of African nativity and to persons of African descent. Overturned the 1790 restriction against the naturalization of nonwhites.
1882	Chinese Exclusion Act of May 6, 1882. Outlawed the immigration of Chinese laborers to the United States for a period of ten years, barred Chinese from naturalization, provided for the deportation of Chinese living illegally in the United States, and permitted the entry of Chinese students, teachers, merchants, and tourists. Continued in a series of laws and made "permanent" in 1904.
1882	Immigration Act of August 3, 1882. Broadened restrictions on immigration by adding to the classes of inadmissible aliens to include persons likely to become a public charge, as well as the mentally retarded. Introduced a head tax on each passenger brought to the United States.
1885	Act of February 26, 1885. First Contract Labor Law, making it unlawful to import aliens into the United States under contract for the performance of labor or services.
1887	Act of March 3, 1887. Restricted ownership of real estate in the United States to American citizens and those who had lawfully declared their intentions to become citizens.
1891	Immigration Act of March 3, 1891. Established Bureau of Immigration. Further restricted immigration by adding to the categories of inadmissible persons: those with any contagious disease; paupers, professional beggars, and vagrants; and the insane. Allowed the Secretary of the Treasury to prescribe rules for inspection along the borders of Canada and Mexico.
1892	Ellis Island. Opening of Ellis Island as the chief immigration station of the country and entry point for millions of immigrants. Ellis Island remained open until 1943. In 1965, Ellis Island was added to the Statue of Liberty National Monument, established in 1924.
1898	Treaty of Paris. United States acquired ownership of the Philippine Islands, Puerto Rico, and other possessions from Spain at the close of the Spanish-American War. The Philippines gained its independence in 1948; Puerto Rico remains a U.S. territory. Included a clause that conferred restricted U.S. citizenship on residents of these territories.
1898	Annexation of Hawai'i. Conferred U.S. citizenship on residents.
1906	Naturalization Act of June 29, 1906. Made knowledge of the English language a requirement for naturalization.
1907	Immigration Act of February 20, 1907. Major codifying act. Established distinction between immigrants and nonimmigrants, increased head tax on immigrants, and added to the excludable classes.
1907	Gentleman's Agreement between the United States and Japan. Under this agreement, Japan would halt the emigration of Japanese laborers to the United States and the United States would end discrimination against Japanese nationals living in the United States. The Quota Act of 1924 later excluded immigration from Japan.
1910	Opening of Angel Island Immigration Station as the chief immigration station on the West Coast, especially for Chinese. Angel Island remained open until 1940. In 1997, Angel Island was designated a National Historic Landmark.
1910	White Slave Traffic Act of June 25, 1910 (the Mann Act). Prohibited the importation and interstate transportation of women for immoral purposes.
1914	World War I. Prompted the emigration of European men of military age to the United States to escape conscription. After this event, the flow of immigrants to the United States slowed greatly.

TABLE Ad-C   Major legislation and social, political, and economic events relating to immigration: 1790–1996
Continued

1915	Sinking of the Lusitania, an unarmed British passenger ship, by a German submarine during World War I. Killed 1,195 persons and signaled a decline in the safety of transatlantic travel, further slowing the flow of immigrants to the United States.
1917	Immigration Act of February 5, 1917. Excluded illiterate immigrants from entry; expanded the list of aliens excluded for mental health and other reasons; further restricted the immigration of Asian persons, creating the "barred zone," known as the Asia-Pacific triangle, natives of which were declared inadmissible.
1920	Arrest of Nicola Sacco and Bartolomeo Vanzetti, immigrant anarchists, for murder in a bungled robbery. After a long trial, Sacco and Vanzetti were executed in 1927. Case stirred antiforeign feelings among Americans.
1921	Quota Law of May 19, 1921. First numerically restrictive immigration law. Limited the number of immigrants to 3 percent of the foreign-born persons of that nationality living in the United States in 1910. Exempted from this limitation aliens who had resided continuously for at least one year immediately preceding their application in one of the independent countries of the Western Hemisphere.
1924	Immigration Act of May 26, 1924. Established the National Origins Quota System. In conjunction with the Immigration Act of 1917, governed American immigration policy until 1952. This important law radically changed the level of immigration to the United States and the country of origin of immigrants (see Table Ad950–954).
1929	Great Depression of the 1930s. Poor economic conditions in the United States relative to the rest of the world slowed immigration to the United States.
1930s	Mexican and Filipino repatriations. A large number of Mexican and Filipino agricultural laborers who had migrated to the western United States to work in seasonal agriculture during the 1920s were unable to find work after the onset of the Great Depression. Strong anti-Mexican and anti-Filipino demonstrations by native-born whites prompted the federal government to pay for the transportation costs of returning these workers to their home countries.
1942	Japanese Internment. Internment of approximately 110,000 Japanese and Japanese Americans in relocation centers during World War II. Most were U.S. citizens, who remained interned through December 1944.
1943	Act of April 29, 1943. Provided for the importation of temporary agricultural laborers to the United States from North, South, and Central America to aid agriculture during World War II. Later extended through 1947.
1943	Act of December 17, 1943. Effective repeal of the Chinese Exclusion Act of 1882. At the time, China was an ally of the United States against Japan in World War II.
1944	Act of February 14, 1944. Provided for the importation of temporary workers from countries in the Western Hemisphere for employment in the war effort. Served as the legal basis of the Mexican "Braceros Program," which lasted through 1964.
1945	Displaced persons. President Truman's directive of December 22, 1945, facilitated the admission of displaced persons.
1945	War Brides Act of December 28, 1945. Waived visa requirements and provisions of immigration law when they concerned members of the American armed forces who, during World War II, had married nationals of foreign countries.
1946	Act of July 2, 1946. Amended the Immigration Act of 1917, granting the privilege of admission to the United States as quota immigrants and eligibility for naturalization to races indigenous to India and persons of Filipino descent.
1948	Displaced Persons Act of June 25, 1948. First expression of U.S. policy for admitting persons fleeing persecution (see Table Ad989–1004).
1949	Agricultural Act of October 31, 1949. Facilitated the entry of seasonal farm workers to meet labor shortages in the United States. Further extension of the Mexican Braceros Program.
1950	Internal Security Act of September 22, 1950. Amended various immigration laws with a view toward strengthening security screening in cases of aliens in the United States or applying for entry.
1951	Act of July 12, 1951. Amended Agricultural Act of 1949, serving as the basic framework under which the Mexican Braceros Program operated until 1964.
1952	Immigration and Nationality Act of June 27, 1952 (INA, or McCarren Act). Brought into one comprehensive statute the multiple laws that, before enactment of the INA, governed immigration and naturalization in the United States. Made all races eligible for naturalization, eliminating race as a barrier to immigration. Eliminated discrimination between sexes, and revised the national origins quota system of the Immigration Act of 1924 (see Table Ad950–954).
1959	Cuban revolution. Thousands of Cubans fleeing the government of Fidel Castro were granted nonimmigrant visas and entered the United States. Many were later granted permanent resident status with the passage of the Act of November 2, 1966.
1961	Vietnam War. U.S. military and economic aid treaty with South Vietnam and arrival of first U.S. support troops. Direct U.S. involvement in the war continued through 1972.
1965	Immigration and Nationality Act Amendments of October 3, 1965. Abolished the national origins quota system, eliminating national origin, race, or ancestry as a basis for immigration to the United States and established the Preference System (see Table Ad955–965).
1975	Indochina Migration and Refugee Assistance Act of May 23, 1975. Established a program of domestic resettlement assistance for refugees who had fled Cambodia and Vietnam. Laotians were made eligible in the following year.
1978	Boat people. United States agrees to admit 47,000 "boat people" fleeing Vietnam and Cambodia.
1980	Mariel Boat Lift. United States agrees to admit approximately 125,000 Cubans fleeing Castro's Cuba.
1980	Refugee Act of March 17, 1980. Provided the first permanent and systematic procedure for the admission and effective resettlement of refugees of special humanitarian concern to the United States.

(continued)

TABLE Ad-C   Major legislation and social, political, and economic events relating to immigration: 1790–1996
Continued

1986	Immigration Reform and Control Act of 1986 (IRCA). Comprehensive immigration legislation that authorized legalization for certain aliens who had resided in the United States in an unlawful status, and increased employer sanctions and border enforcement (see Table Ad955–965).
1990	Immigration Act of November 29, 1990. Major overhaul of immigration law. Increased total immigration. Revised all grounds for exclusion and deportation, established new nonimmigrant categories, and revised naturalization procedures and enforcement activities (see Table Ad966–975).
1993	North American Free Trade Agreement (NAFTA). Called for a free flow of goods among member countries by eliminating duties, tariffs, and trade barriers; facilitated investment among member countries; and established import preferences. One goal was to increase the flow of investment and final goods so as to reduce the incentive for labor migration.
1996	Illegal Immigration Reform and Immigrant Responsibility Act of September 30, 1996. Established measures to control U.S. borders and enforce employment restrictions and placed added restrictions on benefits for aliens.

Sources
1997 Yearbook of the Immigration and Naturalization Service, Appendix 1.

Edward P. Hutchinson, *Legislative History of American Immigration Policy, 1798–1965* (University of Pennsylvania Press, 1981).

Federal laws governing immigration developed out of English colonial policies that strongly promoted it (such as the Plantation Act: The British Naturalization Act of 1740). With sparse populations and abundant lands, the colonies and the Crown viewed immigrants as a source of strength, security, and wealth. In the early years, many colonies tried to attract potential settlers with offers of land grants, religious toleration, exemption from taxation, and travel assistance. The desire for immigrants was not unbounded, however, and even in the early days some colonies did not welcome Catholics and Quakers because of their religion. The colonies were also suspicious of immigrants who might not be able to support themselves, and they actively resisted the transportation of convicts.

Shortly after ratification of the U.S. Constitution, the new federal government asserted its authority over immigration by introducing the Act of March 26, 1790, which established a uniform rule for naturalization, the process by which aliens become citizens. A key provision of this law restricted naturalization to free white persons. In 1798, the federal government authorized the president to arrest and deport any alien deemed dangerous to the United States. Except for these prohibitions, however, immigration and naturalization were unrestricted.

Over the nineteenth century, the United States became increasingly selective regarding the characteristics of aliens whom it permitted to enter the country. From the earliest times, immigrants had been judged on a variety of criteria and declared "desirable" or "undesirable." These judgments developed into a selective immigration policy that progressed along two separate lines. There was a negative selection policy that excluded undesirables through restrictions on admission and through deportation of those defined as undesirable, and there was a positive selection policy that encouraged the entry of desirable immigrants. Negative selection policy has predominated.

At its beginnings in 1798, U.S. immigration policy excluded only persons suspected of being foreign agents entering the country for the purpose of overthrowing the U.S. government. By the late nineteenth and early twentieth centuries, the classes of excludable aliens had expanded in important ways. Over this period at least nine important broad categories of undesirables were added to the list of those excluded by law.

The first to be written into immigration law was the class of convicted criminals. Legislation to bar the entry of convicted criminals was first passed in 1875. It appears to have been a response to

actions of foreign governments that were allegedly pardoning convicted criminals who displayed a willingness to exile themselves abroad. The law was an effort to keep such people from coming to the United States.

A second class of undesirables was persons who were deemed likely to require public assistance because of a supposed inability or unwillingness to support themselves. Exclusion of immigrants likely to become "public charges" had deep roots in concerns that poor immigrants might become a financial burden on the resident community. Persons excluded under this heading were those who arrived in the United States without sufficient resources to support themselves while they looked for work and those with a physical or mental condition that, in the view of the authorities, would make it difficult to earn a living. The category was later extended to mandate the exclusion of unaccompanied minors younger than age 16.

So-called mental defectives and persons with health problems such as communicable diseases and serious physical defects were also excluded. The rationale for this exclusion was both the fear that these people would become public charges and a concern about public health. In the nineteenth century many medicines that now offer control for communicable diseases such as tuberculosis and leprosy were not available. In addition, many physical and mental conditions such as tuberculosis and mental retardation were thought to be of genetic origin. The eugenics movement of the era opposed the immigration of people with these conditions with the argument that their immigration would weaken the American genetic "stock" (Walker 1891).

Opponents of immigration from Southern and Eastern Europe attempted to erect additional barriers to such immigration. The National Quarantine Act of February 15, 1893, and its precursors were responses to "health emergencies," such as the 1892 typhus and cholera outbreaks in New York, attributed to "unhealthy" immigrants. Other legislative proposals, for example, sought to impose onerous conditions on steamship companies to deter them from carrying immigrants, or to impose health requirements likely to affect immigrants from particular geographical areas.

Persons deemed to be "immoral" were another undesirable class. Beginning in 1875, prostitutes, polygamists, and homosexuals were excluded under this rubric.

In the latter part of the nineteenth century, many mass-based organizations that challenged established governments in Europe and

Latin America appeared on the political scene. The Haymarket Riot in Chicago in 1886 was blamed on anarchists, as was the assassination of President William McKinley in 1901. In the wake of these political developments, U.S. immigration policy identified anarchists, and later socialists and then communists, as "undesirable."

In addition, Congress excluded certain classes of laborers thought to put American workers at an unfair competitive advantage. The principal category before 1924 was contract laborers – immigrants who pledged a portion of their wages to brokers in return for transportation to the United States. The argument was that because of their legal obligation to the agencies that sponsored their transportation, such workers could not offer their services on the open labor market. Contract labor was authorized in 1864 but was then outlawed in 1885.

From the beginning, American immigration laws were designed to control the racial and ethnic composition of the U.S. population. The 1790 law limited naturalization to free whites. Following the defeat of the South in the Civil War and the abolition of slavery, the Fourteenth Amendment to the U.S. Constitution authorized the naturalization of persons of African ancestry but implicitly left in place bars against the naturalization of Asians. After a surge of Chinese immigration in response to the California Gold Rush and railroad construction boom during the 1850s, Chinese laborers were barred from immigration in 1882. The same law explicitly barred Chinese naturalization. The prohibition of the immigration of Chinese was made permanent in 1904 by a law that also prohibited the entry of alien Chinese laborers from Hawai'i. This was an unusual step as Hawai'i was a U.S. territory at the time and citizens of Hawai'i were citizens of the United States. De facto exclusion of Japanese immigrants was accomplished by the Gentleman's Agreement of 1907–1908, according to which the Japanese agreed to prohibit emigration to the United States in return for a U.S. guarantee of better treatment of Japanese nationals already living in the country. In 1917 legislation identified a "barred zone" that included South Asia from Arabia to Indochina and the islands adjacent to Asia not possessed by the United States. It was drawn to allow for the admission of immigrants from the American possessions of the Philippines and Guam but to bar all other Asians.

Literacy was first proposed as a criterion for immigration in 1891, and although the implementing legislation was defeated, support remained strong. A literacy test requirement was finally passed in 1917 over the veto of President Woodrow Wilson. The literacy test requirement for immigration was a conscious effort by its proponents to limit immigration from Southern and Eastern Europe.

Limitations on immigration were also used as a weapon against the international traffic in narcotic drugs. The first act limiting the immigration of narcotic drug users was passed in 1952, although foreign-born violators of U.S. drug laws were subject to deportation at an earlier date.

As the complexity of America's immigration system increased, prohibitions on the immigration of persons found to have violated admission regulations were added. The first such act, passed in 1917, was directed against stowaways. In later years, the list of violators of admission regulations grew to include persons without proper documents, those found to have made false statements in their immigration application, and those found to have aided illegal immigration.

Generally speaking, once a criterion became a basis for exclusion from immigration to the United States, it remained in effect. Thus at any point in time, immigration law represents the accumulation of practices built up over many years. There were three major exceptions to this generalization. The prohibition against contract labor was repealed in 1952 and replaced with different regulations aimed at moderating the labor market implications of immigration. The ban against Chinese was removed during World War II, when China was a U.S. ally, and all racial criteria for admissions were removed in 1952. The bars against the immigration of unaccompanied minors were removed in the post–World War II era when Americans began adopting foreign-born children. The restrictions on the immigration of persons with certain illnesses and infirmities were modified over the years and the list of dangerous, communicable diseases has changed with medical advances in the ability to treat various afflictions.

A substantive and far-reaching change in U.S. policy toward immigrants from the Eastern Hemisphere (Europe, Asia, Africa, and Australia) occurred in the 1920s with the passage of the Quota Acts. After establishing temporary quotas through the Quota Act of 1921, a more permanent "Quota System" was officially established by the Immigration Act of 1924, which set an annual numerical quota for the total number of immigrants based on the representation of ethnic populations from each of these countries in the United States prior to the passage of the laws. The goal of this legislation was to reduce the overall level of immigration and to maintain the predominance of people from Northern and Western Europe in the U.S. population. Thus Great Britain and Northern Ireland had the largest annual quota – 65,361. Eastern Europe, Russia, and Italy – countries that had been sending large numbers of immigrants to the United States in the two decades just prior to the passage of the Quota Acts – were given much smaller quotas. The level of the overall annual quota is shown in series Ad950, and the rather complicated formula used to calculate each country's quota is described in the text for this table. The effect of these restrictions was profound and can be seen in the drop in the overall number of immigrants admitted, which fell from more than 800,000 in 1921 to less than 150,000 by the end of the 1920s. This drop in immigration is especially remarkable because the United States was enjoying economic prosperity at that time. In the absence of the numerical restrictions embodied in the Quota Acts, the annual number of immigrants would probably have been well in excess of 800,000.

The Quota Acts did not apply to immigration from the Western Hemisphere countries (North and South America). Scholars suggest that this exemption was partly a concession to ranchers and farmers in the Southwest who relied heavily on Mexican agricultural labor and, more important, that the exemption reflected the U.S. foreign policy goal of Pan-Americanism. Maldwyn Allen Jones writes:

> The restrictive immigration laws were essentially an expression of American revulsion from the Old World; and since, as a consequence of her isolationism, the United States tended to draw closer to other American countries, it was natural for her to place immigration from them upon a special footing. . . . But although Mexican immigration was checked by administrative action during the depression, every demand that immigration from the Americas should be placed on a quota basis was rejected in the interests of what eventually became known as the "Good Neighbor" policy. (Jones 1960, p. 289)

After the passage of the Quota Acts, immigrants from the Americas – Canada and Mexico in particular – grew as a share of the total.

During the 1930s, the overall level of immigration to the United States was negligible. Part of the explanation is that this was the period of the Great Depression, when the unemployed – those actively looking for work but unable to attain it – accounted for approximately one quarter of the entire work force. Such dismal employment prospects would be expected to reduce the inflow of immigrants because the prospects of employment were so poor. On the other hand, the rise of fascism in many countries, with its intended persecution of Jews, intellectuals, and other "enemies of the state," motivated many of those with the means to do so to seek refuge in the United States. The United States admitted approximately 250,000 refugees fleeing fascist regimes in Europe. These were primarily of middle-class origin and worked in business and the professions. Twelve of these immigrants had already received Nobel Prizes, most famously Albert Einstein. Many scientists who immigrated to the United States at this time went on to win Nobel Prizes after their arrival (see Table Ad938–949). Many less-well-connected refugees who wished to immigrate to the United States in order to flee fascism were not permitted to enter (Gemery 1994).

Far-reaching changes to American immigration law were made during and immediately following the conclusion of World War II. Wartime labor shortages in agriculture and other industries led the United States, in cooperation with Mexico, to initiate an organized recruitment of Mexican temporary workers. These nonimmigrants were authorized to come to the United States for a temporary period for work and were then expected to return to their home countries. The wartime program for agricultural workers was continued in the late 1940s and was finally regularized under the renewed urgency created by the Korean War in 1951. This wartime program formed the basis under which the Mexican Braceros Program operated through the end of 1964. Data on Mexicans admitted as nonimmigrant temporary workers, together with other nonimmigrant programs initiated during and immediately following World War II, are shown in Tables Ad1014–1029.

The inauguration of the Cold War led to the use of immigration policy or, more particularly, refugee policy, as an important arm of U.S. foreign policy. World War II had displaced millions of people from their home countries and many of these people believed that they faced high risk of political persecution if they returned. Although the United States had political reasons for wanting to assist these people, it was unable to easily grant them admission as immigrants because many of them did not have proper documents, were indigent, or possessed other characteristics that made them "excludable" under the immigration law prevailing at the time. Because the United States wanted to admit these people for geopolitical reasons, Congress passed a considerable body of legislation that facilitated the entry of select political refugees into the United States. Beginning in 1965, the president and the State Department became even more active in initiating offers of asylum. By 1978, thirteen separate presidential directives or pieces of legislation had been enacted to facilitate the entry of favored groups. In 1980, Congress, in an effort to regularize the process of approving requests for asylum and reduce the independence of the executive branch in this area, passed the Refugee Act. Nonetheless, all subsequent presidents have been actively involved in refugee policy, and the number of refugees and asylees admitted in each year has exceeded the cap of 50,000 mandated in the 1980 law (see series Ad989).

Gilbert Loescher and John Scanlon (1998) find that since the end of World War II, approximately 90 percent of all refugees admitted

to the United States under special circumstances arrived from communist-controlled countries. Refugees from countries ruled by fascistic governments, such as Chile in the 1970s and Haiti in the 1970s and 1980s, were not offered similar access to the United States (for details regarding Chilean and Haitian refugees, respectively, see Llambias-Wolff 1995 and Zucker and Zucker 1995). Table Ad989–1004 describes acts relating to the admission of refugees and asylees and displays the number of persons admitted under each program, and Table Ad1005–1013 displays the number of refugees and asylees admitted annually by continent of birth. In the 1940s and 1950s, an overwhelming majority of refugees admitted for permanent resident status in the United States came from Europe. Beginning in the mid-1960s, refugees from Latin America and then Asia predominated.

U.S. immigration law changed profoundly in 1965 with the adoption of amendments to the Immigration and Nationality Act that abolished the national origins quota system and replaced it with the Preference System, which heavily favored family reunification as the basis for admission. It established two broad classes of immigrants for purposes of admission. The first, which was admitted without numerical restriction, included immediate relatives of U.S. citizens, that is, spouses, young children, and parents. Ministers and other religious workers, and after 1981, graduates of foreign medical schools and "investors," were also admitted without limitation. A numerical "cap" limited all other immigrant admissions and a system of "preferences" selected among applicants subject to this numerical limitation. There were four types of preferences: relative preferences (for specified relatives of citizens and immediate family members of lawful permanent residents of the United States), occupational preferences, refugee preferences, and nonpreference immigrants. The last group could be used to fill the numerical limitation only after the other three preferences were filled. Initially, this fourfold preference system applied only to non–Western Hemisphere immigrants; those from the Western Hemisphere were admitted without limit on a first-come, first-served basis. Beginning on July 1, 1968, Western Hemisphere immigrants became subject to the numerical cap. (See the text for Table Ad955–965 for further details of the program.)

Because of the heavy weight given to family reunification, proponents of the new law expected that future immigrant streams would reflect the national origins of the 1965 population. As Michael Teitelbaum and Jay Winter point out, however, this is not what happened. Instead, the opposite of what was expected took place.

> "Pioneer" immigrants from Asia, admitted under a labor certification system as nurses, doctors, engineers, and scientists, began to use the family-preference categories while they were still resident aliens to petition for admission of their spouses and children. The aliens recognized the advantages of expeditious naturalization, too, since it permitted unlimited admission of immediate family members and petitions for the admission of extended family, such as adult brothers and sisters. Family-based immigration from Asia grew, at first gradually and later rapidly. (Teitelbaum and Winter 1998, pp. 140–1)

In the 1970s, Vietnamese, Laotian, and Cambodian refugees joined this migrant stream. Whereas in 1965, the year the Preference System was enacted, Asians accounted for less than 7 percent of all immigrants, by the early 1980s, they comprised more than half of the total (see Table Ad98–105).

Consequences of the temporary migrant labor programs established during World War II were also becoming apparent. Farmers in the Southwest had come to rely on these workers. The migrant workers had come to rely on the relatively high wages such jobs offered. When the wartime programs ended, the seasonal migration continued despite legal prohibitions. In 1986, the Immigration Reform and Control Act (IRCA), also known as the Simpson-Rodino Bill, was signed into law. It sought to reduce illegal immigration through two strategies. It legalized the status of undocumented aliens who had been living in the country for many years, and it sought to reduce future flows by imposing penalties on employers who hired undocumented aliens. IRCA provided a one-time amnesty for certain other undocumented aliens residing in the United States. Two classes of undocumented aliens were eligible for legalization: those who had resided continuously in an unlawful status since January 1, 1982; and "special agricultural workers" (SAWs) who had worked in perishable agricultural commodities at least ninety days in each of the three years preceding May 1, 1986, and "entered without inspection" (EWIs). For details on numbers admitted, see series Ad963 and Ad972. It is estimated that more than 90 percent of those legalized under the IRCA provisions were Mexican nationals. IRCA-sponsored immigration is the proximate cause of the prominent spike in the number of immigrants to the United States in the early 1990s.

There were two notable changes in immigration law in the 1990s. The Immigration Act of 1990 increased the number of authorized immigrants and revised the grounds for exclusion and deportation. The Illegal Immigration Reform and Immigrant Responsibility Act of 1996 established new, harsher measures to control U.S. borders, to enforce employment restrictions, and to limit benefits for both legal and illegal aliens. Through the initiative process, in 1994 California's Proposition 187 sought to limit illegal aliens' access to public services provided by that state.

Naturalization

Naturalization is the process by which aliens become citizens. Although the U.S. Constitution gives many rights to both citizens and resident noncitizens, there are some rights that the Constitution reserves exclusively for citizens. Among these are the rights to vote, carry a U.S. passport, and receive U.S. government assistance when traveling abroad. The process of naturalization involves taking an oath of allegiance, in the course of which an alien promises to give up prior allegiances to other countries, swear allegiance to the United States, support and defend the Constitution and laws of the United States, and serve the country when required to do so. Naturalized citizens have all of the rights and responsibilities of the native-born except for one – a naturalized citizen is ineligible to become President of the United States.

One of the first acts of the new federal government, shortly after ratification of the U.S. Constitution in 1789, was to establish a uniform rule for naturalization. The basic requirements – including evidence of good moral character, allegiance to the Constitution, a residency requirement, and a formal declaration of intention to naturalize – have remained part of the provisions to this day. A key provision of the law restricted naturalization to free white persons.

Aliens wishing to become American citizens presented their petitions for naturalization before a local judge who had wide latitude in decision making. The only automatic reason for denial would have been race. A considerable body of legislation was developed over the course of the nineteenth century in an effort to curb alleged abuses of the naturalization process by which judges' approval of naturalization petitions was done with an eye to affecting election outcomes. Passage of the Fourteenth Amendment to the Constitution in 1866, following the conclusion of the Civil War, made all persons born or naturalized in the United States American citizens. The Naturalization Act of 1870 lifted restrictions on the naturalization of persons of African ancestry and explicitly conferred U.S. citizenship on the newly freed slaves.

Over the years the requirements for naturalization were modified, generally in the direction of making them more stringent. Knowledge of the English language was made a requirement for naturalization in 1906. The current provisions for U.S. naturalization were set out in the Immigration and Nationality Act of 1952. All racial restrictions on naturalization were removed and a process for naturalization was laid out. According to this process, an alien applicant for naturalization must be at least eighteen years of age, have been lawfully admitted to the United States for permanent residence, and have resided in the United States continuously for at least five years. Additional requirements included the ability to speak, read, and write the English language, knowledge of the U.S. government and U.S. history, and good moral character. Special provisions exempted spouses and children of U.S. citizens and certain aliens who served in the U.S. armed forces from some of these requirements.

Because of the decentralized method of conferring naturalization during the nineteenth century, there was no systematic annual reporting of naturalizations. The first national data were collected in the federal census of 1890, which asked foreign-born males at least twenty-one years of age to report their citizenship status. Among those who responded, approximately two thirds reported U.S. citizenship. In 2000, only 40 percent were citizens. The data for 1890 and for other years when similar questions were asked by the federal census are reported in Table Ad280–318. The percentage for 2000 was computed from U.S. Census Bureau 2001, Table 1.1.

Annual data on the number of aliens naturalized were first reported in 1907 (see Table Ad1030–1037). This is when U.S. courts were first required to report naturalization proceedings to a central federal agency. Throughout most of the twentieth century, the vast majority of naturalizations were conducted under the general naturalization provisions. The number of such naturalizations each year, beginning in 1945, is shown in series Ad1031. In the period immediately following World War II, however, the special naturalization regulations developed for spouses of citizens were the predominant method of naturalization because this is the period when a large number of "war brides" became U.S. citizens. The annual numbers of persons naturalized under the special provisions for spouses and for children are shown in series Ad1032 and Ad1033, respectively.

Naturalizations under the special provisions for children of U.S. citizens reached a high in the early 1960s, when they accounted for more than 5 percent of all naturalizations. This was a period when family-based immigrant admissions accounted for a large share of total admissions. Aliens naturalized under the special provisions developed for those who served in the U.S. armed forces are shown in series Ad1034. These naturalizations accounted for more than half the total in the years immediately following World War I and more than 10 percent of the total in the years following World

War II. The Korean and Vietnam conflicts were also followed by bulges in naturalizations conducted under the special procedures developed for former U.S. military personnel.

The courts may deny petitions for naturalization by aliens who fail to meet the prerequisites. Reasons for denial include failure to establish lawful admission to the United States or to meet residence requirements, as well as failure to pass the U.S. history or government tests or tests for speaking, reading, and writing in the English language. Failure to establish evidence of good moral character or to show attachment to the Constitution of the United States is also grounds for denial of the petition to naturalize. Series Ad1037 shows the number of petitions for naturalization denied annually since 1907. Denials were unusually high during two different episodes. One was during the 1920s, when anti-immigration sentiment was strong and the quota system was first put in place. Scholars suggest that these rejections were a reflection of the anti-immigrant sentiment at the time, especially the public fear of socialists and anarchists. A second episode when a large fraction of naturalization petitions were denied occurred during the 1990s, when the threat of withdrawal of public services for noncitizens greatly increased the volume of applications for naturalization.

Although every immigrant admitted to the United States has the right to become a naturalized citizen after fulfilling the requirements, a large number never do. The term "naturalization rate" refers to the proportion of immigrants who have gained citizenship through naturalization. Casual observation suggests that immigrants from different nations differ dramatically in their propensity to become American citizens. Despite the potential importance of this issue, we know of no systematic, long-term study of such country-of-origin differences. The most probable reason for this gap is that the data required to properly measure naturalization rates are not available. The most precise way of calculating naturalization rates would be to compare the number of persons who naturalize with the number eligible to do so. Persons who become citizens in any given year would be drawn from the population of immigrants in all previous years who were alive, remained in the United States, had served the required waiting period of five years (or less for some categories of immigrants), and had not yet naturalized. However, the exact size of the total eligible population is very difficult to estimate. It is the result of many decades of immigrant experience, including immigrant arrivals, departures, and deaths. The required data for calculating the number eligible to naturalize and who have not yet done so are not available because the INS does not collect information on emigration or on immigrant mortality.

As an alternative to a comprehensive approach to calculating naturalization rates, the INS has recently begun following the naturalization experience of two immigration-year cohorts, those of 1977 and 1982. Estimates of the naturalization rates of these cohorts are derived by linking the statistical records of each arrival group with naturalization records starting in the year they became immigrants and for each subsequent year. Series Ad1051 displays the overall naturalization rate achieved in each year by the 1977 cohort. A perhaps surprising finding is that a large proportion of these immigrants had not yet naturalized after a relatively long period as permanent residents in the United States. Only about one third had naturalized ten years later; only a little more than half had naturalized after twenty years. Naturalization rates differ greatly depending on the immigrant's country of origin. Table Ad1051–1071

shows the naturalization rates for the 1977 cohort of immigrants from a number of different countries. It reveals high naturalization rates for immigrants from Cuba, the People's Republic of China, and the former Soviet Union – more than 60 percent by 1997 – a rate that is twice the rate among immigrants from Mexico, and three times the rate among immigrants from Canada and the UK. Other data not reported here suggest that the naturalization rates among immigrants reporting a professional specialty or a technical occupation are also high, suggesting that the highly skilled are more likely to naturalize than are immigrants generally. In addition, immigrants who arrive as young adults or who come as refugees also have a greater tendency to naturalize than others. Legislative efforts during the 1990s to restrict public social spending programs to citizens seem to have increased the propensity of all immigrants to naturalize.

The series presented in Table Ad1051–1071 display the cumulative percentage of the 1977 immigration-year cohort who have naturalized by a given date. Immigrants who fail to naturalize may be divided analytically into three categories: those who die before naturalizing, those who emigrate before naturalizing, and those who fail to apply. Failure to apply may in turn have several explanations: the fees may seem high, requirements for passing examinations in the English language and civics may seem daunting, and evidence of "good moral character" may be impossible for · persons with criminal records. Language may be a particular barrier for elderly immigrants, although the naturalization laws make some allowances for older persons. Another reason not to naturalize is that the perceived benefits are small or that the costs are great. Scholars estimate that the fraction of the world's population with dual or multiple national allegiances is growing and that such transnational citizens are playing an increasingly important role in international trade and politics (Schiller 1999).

Immigrants by Country of Origin

The geographic origin of immigrants to the United States has changed substantially over time. We have already mentioned the transition from Western and Northern Europe to Southern and Eastern Europe in the late nineteenth century and the shift from Europe to Latin America and Asia after 1965. Important shifts have also occurred among countries within continents. We have assembled and presented two measures of immigrants' "country of origin": one is "country of last residence," which has been collected and published since 1820, and the second is "country of birth," a measure available beginning in 1941 (see Tables Ad106–221). The tables classify migrants from particular areas by defining their boundaries according to the country in existence at the time of the migrant's move. Where country border changes were frequent and substantial, such as in Eastern Europe during the late nineteenth and early twentieth centuries, it may be impossible to use these data to measure migrant flows from a particular geographic area. Migration from Poland is perhaps the most notorious example. The tables document as clearly as possible the legal boundary changes. Users should exercise caution in interpreting the numbers.

For years beginning in 1941, both measures are available and they often display different patterns. For example, the number of immigrants who were born in Italy declined rather dramatically beginning in the early 1970s. By contrast, the number of immigrants for whom Italy was their last country of residence rose during the mid-1980s and displayed a sharp spike during the IRCA legalizations in the years surrounding 1990. The contrast provides a glimpse into the complicated pattern of international migration, in which migrants often live in one or more foreign countries before they settle in the United States. Scholars believe that international migration involving multiple countries was also common in the period before 1941.

Shifts over time in the country of origin of international migrants to the United States are the result of complicated processes acting within both the sending countries and the United States. The single most important factor that explains these shifts is change in the location of economic opportunities. Migrants' pursuit of economic opportunity has influenced the pattern of migration to the United States by country of origin in three different ways. One is that sharp changes in relative economic opportunities help explain the timing of the onset of immigration from individual countries. The massive movement of the Irish to the United States during the Great Potato Famine of 1845–1849 is a good example. For the Irish, migration to the United States was becoming common in the late eighteenth and early nineteenth centuries as rapid population increase, a stagnant economy, and political instability meant few economic opportunities for young people in Ireland. Young Irishmen moved to Scotland, England, and America in search of better prospects. In the United States they found work building canals and highways in the new nation. When the Great Potato Famine struck from 1845 to 1849, an estimated 1.6 million Irish moved to the United States in search of a better means of livelihood (Scally 1995).

English, Swedish, and German farmers immigrated to the United States in an effort to escape economic ruin when improvements in railroad and water transportation brought cheap grain from the United States, Russia, and India to their markets.

> Upon European farming the effect was immediate and catastrophic. Germany, now linked by rail to the Russian black earth zone, the Polish and Hungarian plains, and the Rumanian wheatlands, changed with a single decade – 1865–75 – from a grain-exporting to a grain-importing country. In England a searing agricultural depression in the seventies, originating in the competition of American wheat, spelled the doom of the old agrarian economy; between the sixties and the eighties the price of wheat and the acreage of land under wheat both fell by almost 50 percent. In Sweden, which turned to free trade in 1865, the agrarian crisis was heightened by disastrous crop failures between 1861 and 1869, which produced famine conditions in many areas. In each of the areas affected tens of thousands of farmers and agricultural laborers were driven to emigrate. (Jones 1960, pp. 193–4)

Mass emigration out of Italy took place in the aftermath of a war for national unification, which left farmlands in the south of the country in ruins and no alternative source of support either from the Church or from large landowners. These so-called push factors were augmented by economic "pull" from the United States. Peak years of immigration into the United States – such as 1882, 1907, and 1910 – were also peak years of performance for the U.S. economy (for the dates of business cycle peaks and troughs, see Table Cb5–8).

Economic considerations are important even in migrations that are motivated by the search for religious and political freedom. Although there is only one place a migrant can leave, there are many places where he or she can go. At the same time, the income differential between the United States and other parts of the world is not the only factor governing international migration. If this were the case, then migrants to the United States would be coming from the poorest countries of the world and from the poorest regions within these countries. This is not the case.

A second set of factors determining the pattern of immigration from any single country has to do with the way an initial migration changes the environment in which later potential migrants operate. These migration-induced changes help explain a widely observed pattern in international migration. That is, in the absence of stringent and effective regulations, immigration from any single country follows the pattern of an inverted U. There is an initial introductory phase that is often the result of a political or economic disjuncture in the home country. In the second phase, emigration from the country rises at an increasing pace. This is because family and friends of the initial migrants can benefit from the experience of the first movers. Immigrants in the first wave send money to help finance the travel of those who remained behind. They also provide temporary homes upon arrival, information about the country, and help in locating jobs. With the cost of migration reduced in these important ways, it is easier for others to follow. At some point, however, the migrant flows reach a saturation phase where the numbers level off. After this, they begin to decline. One reason for this leveling off is that the stock of potential migrants becomes depleted. There are fewer people left in the sending country, and, especially, many fewer with the ability and incentive to make such a move. Moreover, for those who remain, employment and other economic opportunities are often improved as a result of the exodus of their neighbors. There are relatively more jobs, more land, and, especially if the migrants send back remittances, more money. These factors also discourage further out-migration. In the absence of further disruption, then, large-scale migration would be expected to cease of its own accord. One can observe this inverted-U pattern in the immigration data for Ireland, Germany, Britain, and Scandinavia, four regions that more or less completed the full process before the United States imposed stringent general numerical restrictions on immigration in the 1920s (see Figure Ad-D) (see also Massey 1994; Hatton and Williamson 1998).

A final set of forces that affect migration from any country are the immigration laws of the United States and of the sending countries. Three examples of how such laws affect the level and timing of immigration are the histories of immigration from China, Japan, and Mexico.

The rapid expansion of immigration from China began under circumstances that were similar to those that sent thousands of Europeans across the Atlantic in search of economic opportunity.

> Large-scale Chinese immigration, like that of the Irish, originated in economic catastrophe; the great Taiping rebellion, beginning in 1848, paralyzed trade and industry in southeastern China and brought famine and ruin to millions. News of the high wages paid to laborers in gold rush California was thus all that was needed to start an exodus from the hard-hit province of Kwangtung. (Jones 1960, p. 204)

However, unlike the case of the Irish, Chinese immigration was brought to an abrupt halt in 1882 when the United States passed the Chinese Exclusion Act. It was not until 1943 that a change to the Alien Registration Act effectively repealed the Chinese Exclusion Act and authorized an annual inflow of 150 immigrants from

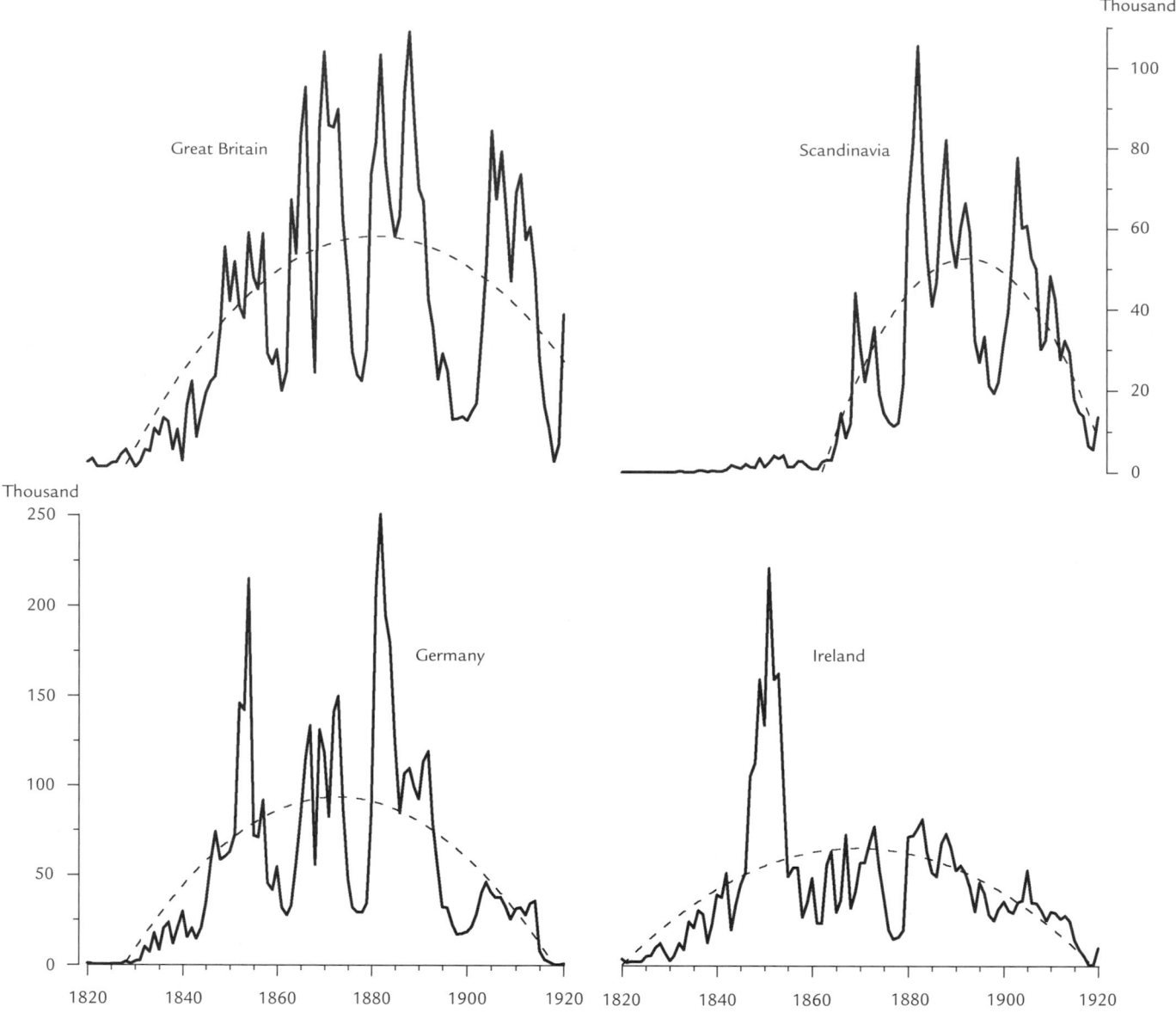

FIGURE Ad-D   Immigrants, by country of last residence – Great Britain, Scandinavia, Germany, and Ireland: 1820–1920

Sources

Series Ad107–109 and Ad111, along with quadratic trend lines fitted to the data over the period 1820–1920 for Great Britain, Germany, and Ireland and over the period 1860–1920 for Scandinavia.

China. Figures on immigrants whose country of last residence or country of birth was China do not display an immediate response to the passage of this law during wartime, though in 1947, following the conclusion of World War II, both figures soar to heights that greatly exceeded the official numerical quota of 150 (series Ad138 and Ad151). The vast majority of these Chinese immigrants were alien wives of American citizens admitted on a nonquota basis. Roger Daniels (1988, p. 199) estimates that almost ten thousand Chinese women were admitted under this program in the eight years following the conclusion of World War II. Nonetheless, the number of immigrants from China remained small until 1965, when the National Origins Quota Acts were abolished and the Preference System, which eliminated country of origin as a criterion for admission, was adopted. The fact that immigration from China soared

immediately following the abolition of the National Origins Quota Acts suggests that these Acts had served as a binding constraint on immigration (see Tables Ad151–152).

The history of immigration from Japan was also profoundly influenced by legal changes. Japanese immigration to the United States began in the 1860s and intensified in the 1880s and 1890s after the Japanese government lifted restrictions on the emigration of its nationals. Many Japanese also migrated to Hawai'i during this period, and when Hawai'i was annexed by the United States in 1898 these Japanese immigrants automatically became U.S. residents. For Japanese immigration to Hawai'i during the nineteenth century, see series Ad85. Japanese immigration was curtailed in 1907 with the so-called Gentleman's Agreement between the emperor of Japan and the president of the United States, according to which the Japanese emperor would not issue passports to unskilled laborers. In exchange, the United States promised better treatment of the Japanese population living in this country. Until 1924, wives of Japanese men living in the United States were allowed to migrate from Japan to the United States to join their husbands; however, the adoption of the Quota System severely curtailed even this migration.

Like Chinese Americans, Japanese Americans suffered intense discrimination in the United States. In 1913 and 1920, laws were passed in some states that prohibited Japanese from owning land and limited their ability to lease land. During World War II, an estimated 110,000 Japanese Americans, including 70,000 American-born U.S. citizens, living on the West Coast were obliged by President Franklin Roosevelt's Executive Order 9066 to liquidate their possessions and were forced into "relocation centers" for the duration of the war (Spicer [and others] 1969; Daniels 1972). Immigration from Japan resumed at the conclusion of World War II. Much of this migration comprised Japanese-born wives of U.S. servicemen who were stationed in Japan during the American occupation following the war. One scholar estimates that 45,000 of these so-called war brides were admitted to the United States between 1947 and 1975 (Kim 1977; see also Glenn 1986). If correct, it would mean that those war brides accounted for almost half of all Japanese immigrants to the United States during this period. Daniels's calculations (1988, p. 307) support this view. He shows that women accounted for 85.9 percent of Japanese immigrants to the United States between 1950 and 1960.

The Immigration Reform and Control Act (IRCA) shaped the immigration of Mexicans. Series Ad175 shows an almost fifteen-fold increase in Mexican immigration between 1986 and the peak of IRCA-enabled immigration in 1991. The total number of IRCA legalizations is shown in series Ad963 and Ad973. More than 80 percent of the immigrants admitted under IRCA were of Mexican birth. IRCA was a response to the flow of undocumented migrants from Mexico, which began in the late 1960s and grew during the 1970s and 1980s. By 1980, an estimated two to four million undocumented persons were living in the country (Edmonston, Passel, and Bean 1990, p. 27). IRCA was a compromise designed to meet two goals. One was to regularize the status of a large population, much of which had been living in the country for many years. The second was to stem this migratory tide by implementing sanctions against employers who hired undocumented workers (Bean, Edmonston, and Passel 1990).

Immigrant Characteristics

Data on immigrants' age, gender, and occupation were collected as part of the earliest efforts to count immigrants, which began in 1820. The figures are shown in Tables Ad222–255. These personal characteristics of immigrants are of great interest to policy makers because they help determine the impact of immigration on the U.S. economy and society. If immigrants are highly skilled young adults who migrate in order to work, then immigration will raise per capita income and earnings. If immigrants are less skilled than the average worker or if they are not engaged in paid labor, then average per capita income may fall, even though the income of each individual rises. This will be the case as long as immigrants' income in the United States is greater than that in their country of origin.

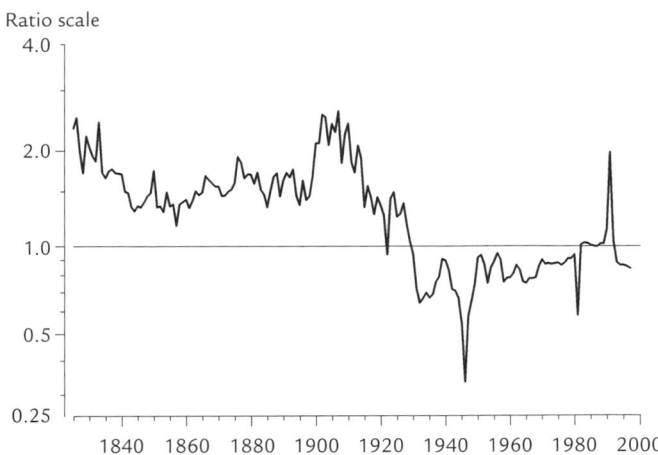

FIGURE Ad-E Male-to-female ratio among immigrants: 1825–1997

Sources
Series Ad223–224.

Perhaps the most consistent pattern revealed in these data is that the numerical restrictions on immigration that began in the 1920s profoundly altered the characteristics of immigrants who came to the United States. Prior to the numerical restrictions, immigrants were disproportionately young adult males. Around the turn of the twentieth century, males outnumbered females by more than two to one (see Figure Ad-E). Young adults outnumbered children and older persons and their share in the immigrant stream was more than four times greater than their share in the resident population. This predominance of young adult males is a characteristic of the entire period of uncontrolled immigration; however, it disappears within a decade following the imposition of numerical limitations. Prior to these restrictions, most immigrants came to the United States in order to work for wages. Men were more likely than women to be engaged in wage work and young adult males enjoyed a greater relative labor market advantage than did older ones. The new regime equalized the probabilities of males and females gaining admission and it increased the immigration of children and older adults. The one exception is the spike in the late 1980s and early 1990s, which is associated with the IRCA legalizations. The large proportion of males and young people suggests that a large share of the previously undocumented population that had come to the United States were similar in their motivation to temporary migrants at the turn of the twentieth century, when employment opportunities were of paramount importance in the migration decision.

The occupational distribution of immigrants is shown in Tables Ad231–255. These can be compared with distributions of the native- and foreign-born labor force across the same occupational categories (see Tables Ba1131–1158). There are many insights to be gained from a careful study of the trends in each table and from a comparison among them. As Matthew Sobek writes, "Occupations are among the most revealing and valuable pieces of socioeconomic information pertaining to individuals that survive in the historical record" (see the essay on occupations in Chapter Ba).

One example of what can be done is displayed in Figure Ad-F, which aggregates these data in a way that highlights skill differentials among three classes – newly arrived immigrants, all foreign-born workers, and native-born workers. For those who

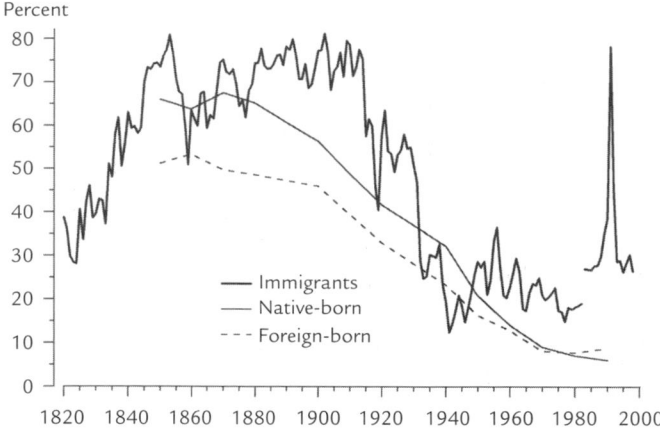

FIGURE Ad-F   Low-skill occupations as a percentage of known occupations among immigrants, native-born persons, and foreign-born persons: 1820–1998

Sources

Immigrants, through 1982: series Ad231, Ad233, Ad239, Ad241, and Ad244–245. Immigrants, beginning 1983: series Ad246, Ad252–253, and Ad255. Native-born persons: series Ba1131, Ba1133, Ba1140, and Ba1142–1144. Foreign-born persons: series Ba1145, Ba1147, Ba1154, and Ba1156–1158.

Documentation

In each case, the sum of the series for "low-skill" occupations is expressed as a percentage of the following: the total minus those with an unspecified occupation or no occupation reported.

Note that the figures for native-born and foreign-born persons exclude women in 1850 and slaves in 1850–1860.

reported an occupation, we added together those who defined themselves as farmers, farm laborers, nonfarm laborers, or domestic servants and then expressed that number as a share of the total. This is not a perfect measure of "low-skill" occupations because successful farming requires experience and specialized knowledge. Yet this is a standard measure and, in any case, it is the best we can do. In the era of mass migration, roughly 70 percent of immigrants who reported an occupation reported one that we have classified as low-skill. Such an occupational distribution is not particularly surprising because most of these immigrants came from rural backgrounds. As time passed and the American labor force was becoming more skilled, the low skills of immigrants were increasingly disparate from those of the native-born. It is also interesting to compare the occupations of newly arrived immigrants with those of all foreign-born workers. This differential is even greater than that vis-à-vis the native-born. The explanation for this surprising pattern is that the foreign-born were more likely than the native-born to live in cities and to work in manufacturing industries. Because very few immigrants had worked in factories in their home countries, their migration to the United States meant not only a change in country and occupation, but a change in industry as well.

The passage of the Quota Acts in the 1920s led to a change in the occupations of arriving immigrants, bringing them much more closely into line with the occupations of both the native- and foreign-born work force of the United States. The exception is the occupations of immigrants legalized by IRCA. This group is heavily concentrated in agricultural occupations, which is not surprising because the program specifically targeted agricultural workers.

Nonimmigrants

Nonimmigrants are aliens who come to the United States for a temporary period. The category "nonimmigrant" was first defined in the Immigration Act of 1819; however, the regular reporting of nonimmigrants did not begin until 1906. Prior to 1906, many of the so-called immigrants recorded in the official statistics were nonimmigrants by this more precise definition. Most of these early migrants came to the United States to work for a short time, save their earnings, and then return to their home countries. Between 40 and 60 percent of official immigrants who arrived during the period 1900–1906 had left the United States by 1920 (Carter and Sutch 1998, 1999). The Quota Act of 1924 first established a distinction among several different classes of nonimmigrants. The number of these classes has grown over time so that by the late 1990s, eighteen separate classes were being reported by the INS (see Tables Ad1014–1029). The number of nonimmigrants admitted to the United States in any year far exceeds the number of immigrants. In 1996, for example, the number of nonimmigrant admissions was more than twenty-five times larger than that of immigrants. The disproportion between nonimmigrants and immigrants was not always so great. In 1950, the number of nonimmigrants was less than twice as large as the flow of immigrants. What happened over the second half of the twentieth century is that nonimmigrant admissions grew rapidly. With the exception of the "special programs" category, which was discontinued in 1982 (series Ba4916), extremely rapid growth occurred in every category of nonimmigrant admissions.

"Visitors for pleasure" or tourists account for more than 90 percent of all nonimmigrant admissions today (series Ad1015). The rapid growth in the number of international tourists coming to the United States is a manifestation of the growth of international tourism worldwide. With the decline in transportation costs and worldwide improvements in standard of living, international tourism has moved from a luxury available only to the elite to an option for the broad middle class in many different countries around the world.

Temporary workers, though far less numerous than tourists, are a class of nonimmigrants with very important economic and political implications for the American economy. Temporary workers are migrants who move to the United States for a short period for the purpose of working, earning income, and accumulating assets. Their larger goal is to return to their home countries better prepared with the assets they need to establish themselves in careers (see Table Ad1023–1029).

In much of the world, temporary worker policy is a prominent political and economic issue. Temporary workers are usually attractive to the host country because their migration decisions are strongly motivated by labor market considerations. Temporary workers tend to move toward tight labor markets and leave loose ones. Their entry thus moderates wage increases during boom times and their exit softens domestic job loss during depressions. At the same time, the job skills and personal characteristics of temporary workers are often quite different from those of the native labor force. They tend to complement rather than compete with existing workers.

Despite these positive benefits, temporary workers and the policies that invite and regulate their flow are not without critics. The temporary workers who are most visible tend to live at the margins of their host country's economy and society, contributing little to the country's culture and repatriating a substantial fraction of the wages and salaries earned. Some temporary workers decide to become permanent residents and thus temporary flows lead to permanent stocks, perhaps in numbers unanticipated by or unwelcome to the host country. In some cases the transition from temporary to permanent residence is made without proper authorization.

Official statistics on temporary workers began in 1950; however, the flow of temporary workers began much earlier. As noted earlier, many of those recorded as immigrants prior to 1906 were, in fact, temporary workers. For the period 1906–1949, some temporary workers were recorded as nonimmigrants but many were not recorded at all. The Immigration Act of 1924 defined the term "immigrant" and placed temporary workers in the category of "nonimmigrant temporary visitors" along with tourists and other temporary visitors. There were no restrictions on the number or occupations of such nonimmigrants that could be admitted beyond those of the Chinese Exclusion Act and the Contract Labor Law. In 1943, the Contract Labor Law was amended to permit the contractual importation of temporary agricultural laborers from North, Central, and South America to relieve wartime labor shortages. Virtually all of those admitted under the Emergency Farm Labor Supply Program were Mexican nationals. The 1943 Act evolved through its various extensions into the Mexican Braceros Program, which lasted through 1964. Temporary workers admitted as agricultural workers were considered as neither immigrants nor nonimmigrants, and statistics on their numbers were maintained separately by the Department of Labor.

The Immigration and Nationality Act of 1952 restricted the admission of temporary workers to three classes: persons of "distinguished merit or ability" (called "specialty occupations" since fiscal 1992), persons performing "services unavailable in the United States" (defined to mean that unemployed residents capable of performing such labor cannot be found), and "industrial trainees" (when the training involved could not be obtained in the worker's home country). A new class of nonimmigrant admission was added by an act in 1970: intracompany transferees. These are persons employed by an international company who enter the United States temporarily in order to continue to work for the same employer (or a subsidiary or affiliate) in a capacity that is primarily managerial or executive or that involves special knowledge. At the same time, a special admission category for spouses and children of temporary workers was added. The U.S.-Canadian Free Trade Agreement of 1988 and the North American Free Trade Agreement of 1993 established provisions for temporary admission of professional business persons to work in the United States.

Temporary worker flows are large relative to the flow of immigrants and they have a different pattern over time. At their peak in the late 1950s, temporary worker admissions were almost twice as large as immigrant admissions. At their ebb in the late 1970s, temporary worker flows fell to less than 20 percent of the level of immigrant flows. Today, the flow of nonimmigrant temporary workers and their families is more than half as large as that of official legal immigrants.

Foreign student admissions have also grown rapidly (series Ad1017). Over the last quarter of the twentieth century, foreign-born students grew as a share of all students in American colleges and universities, especially within graduate programs in the fields of science and engineering (Table Bc537–564). In 1997, one fourth of all earned doctoral degrees awarded by American universities were bestowed on noncitizens holding temporary visas. In the field of engineering, the figure was almost 40 percent (National Science Board 2000, appendix Table 4-26). Many of these advanced-degree recipients later become permanent residents and citizens. They account for a significant share of the science and engineering work force of the United States.

Population of Foreign-Born Residents and Their Characteristics

The foreign-born population includes all residents born in a country other than the United States, whether or not they are citizens or are residing in the country legally. Because the flow of immigrants and emigrants has varied over time, so too has the size and relative share of the foreign-born population. Data on the size of the foreign-born white population are available beginning in 1850 and for the total foreign-born population beginning in 1870. These totals are shown in Table Ad354–443. As a consequence of the heavy immigrant flows beginning in the second third of the nineteenth century, the number of foreign-born grew to be a large share of the total population. In the years between 1860 and 1920, resident Americans born abroad accounted for between 13 and 15 percent of the total population. The passage of the Quota Acts with their stringent numerical controls precipitated a substantial fall in the foreign-born share from 1920 through 1970, at which point the foreign-born accounted for less than 5 percent of the population. The expansion of immigrant flows following the 1965 Act, combined with the fall in U.S. fertility, meant a rise in the foreign-born share of the population in the closing years of the twentieth century.

As noted earlier, immigrants tend to migrate as young adults, and prior to the imposition of quotas, males predominated in the immigrant stream. These characteristics would be expected to affect the characteristics of the stock of foreign-born residents, and this was the case. While the male-to-female ratio among native-born whites remained close to 1 throughout the long period for which data are available, this ratio shifts wildly for the population of foreign-born whites. During the period of mass immigration in the nineteenth and early twentieth centuries, males predominated by a substantial margin. The imposition of quotas gradually reduced the margin until, by 1950, the ratio was about equal to 1. After that, it fell through 1970 as the foreign-born population aged and the greater longevity of women gave them the edge. The relaxation of immigration controls in 1965 led to growth in the male share. The age structure of the foreign-born population also reflects the pace and pattern of immigrant flows. Among both males and females, the fraction of the foreign-born population in the prime working ages was substantially above that for the native-born population throughout the period of mass immigration, fell sharply with the curtailment of immigration, and is again on the rise. The distinctive gender and age structure of the foreign-born population is important because, to a large extent, it determines the impact of immigration on the rest of the economy.

If a larger fraction of the foreign- than native-born population is in the working-age groups and participates in the labor force, this will cause output per capita to rise even if the productivity of labor remains unchanged. In the last era of mass migration, immigrants were far more likely to participate in the labor force than the average American at the time. This was true for three reasons. Immigrants were predominantly male and, at the time, males were far more likely than females to participate. Immigrants were predominantly young adults, and young adults are more likely than the very young and the very old to participate. Finally, among the young adults, immigrants were more likely to be labor market participants than were their white native-born counterparts. These labor force participation rates by sex, race, and nativity are shown in Table Ad752–759. For these three reasons, then, immigration before the quota era tended to raise per capita income in the United States.

The characteristics of immigrants arriving in the renewed immigrant flows following the abolition of the Quota Acts in 1965 have changed. The male–female ratio is more balanced, there are relatively more children and older persons, and the labor force participation rate of these immigrants is actually somewhat below that for the native-born white population and, for women (but not for men), below that for the black population as well. The positive impact of this wave of immigrants on per capita income in the United States will be more muted.

Characteristics of the foreign-born population relative to those of the native-born population are sometimes used as a measure of immigrant assimilation. Assimilation refers to immigrants' absorption into the prevailing culture. The assumption underlying this approach is that the greater the similarity between foreign-born and native-born characteristics, the more fully have immigrants been absorbed into American culture. Thus, for example, the larger share of the foreign-born population with English language proficiency in 1990 compared with 1900 suggests greater immigrant assimilation at the later date (see Table Ad711–721).

Throughout American history, perhaps the most distinctive characteristic of the foreign-born population has been its geographic location. To a far greater extent than the native-born, the foreign-born have made their homes in cities. When data first became available in 1890, the share of the foreign-born living in urban places was more than 61 percent, almost double the share of the native-born (Table Ad707–710). Although the gap closed somewhat over time, the urban location of the foreign-born remains a distinctive trait. Because of their concentration in urban centers, the foreign-born are more highly concentrated across states than are the native-born. Table Ad696–706 displays a measure of this differential concentration. It compares each state's share of the foreign-born population with its share of the native-born population. Thus, for example, in 1990 California was home to 10.2 percent of the native-born but 32.7 percent of the foreign-born population. The table indicates that the native-born population showed a modest tendency to become more widely dispersed across the states over time. In 1990, the three states with the largest native-born populations accounted for a smaller fraction of the native-born population than in 1850. For the foreign-born population, the pattern is quite different. In each year, the degree of geographic concentration is greater and it shows a different pattern over time. The rise of mass migration in the late nineteenth century was initially accompanied by greater geographic dispersal, although this process was reversed after 1890. Perhaps the most spectacular development was the unprecedented surge in the geographic concentration of the foreign-born after 1970, leading to an all-time high rate in 1990. Over the 1990s, the geographic concentration of the foreign-born was reduced somewhat as some of the foreign-born began selecting their homes from a broader range of areas (Frey 2002).

Finally, until very recently, a disproportionate share of immigrants made their homes in the Northeast, Midwest, and Western portions of the country. This so-called avoidance of the South is thought to result from the potential labor market competition from slave labor up through 1860 and the relative absence of Southern

manufacturing and low Southern wages throughout the nineteenth century and continuing into the 1960s (Wright 1986). For those coming to the United States to work, the South offered far fewer opportunities than other regions of the country. Beginning in 1940, the share of the foreign-born population living in the South began to rise and in the 1960s growth accelerated (Table Ad696–706). Both reflect largely political developments, the first being the Braceros Program promoting the temporary migration of agricultural labor for Southwestern farms (especially Texas) and the second being the admission of Cuban refugees, a large proportion of whom settled in south Florida.

Appendix: A Note about Sources of Immigration Statistics

The primary source for quantitative measures of trends in immigration to the United States is the data collected by the federal office now known as the Immigration and Naturalization Service (INS), located in the U.S. Department of Justice until 2002, when it became part of the new Department of Homeland Security. The collection of data on immigrants began following the passage of the Act of March 2, 1819, which required the captain or master of a vessel arriving from abroad to deliver to the local collector of customs a list or manifest of all passengers taken on board. This original reporting requirement included a call for information on the age, sex, and occupation of each passenger, "the country to which they severally belonged," and the number that had died on the voyage. Copies of these manifests were to be transmitted to the Secretary of State, who was to report the information to Congress "at each and every session." Subsequently, the Act of 1855 prescribed that the Secretary of State report annually to Congress. Later acts expanded the range of data to be collected. Currently these data are collected, tabulated, and published by the INS in its *Statistical Yearbook*. Although the INS makes some effort to present continuous time series on various measures, the results are uneven. Important compilations of historical series relating to immigration include Bromwell ([1856] 1969), U.S. Bureau of the Census (1975), and Hutchinson (1958, 1981). Hutchinson prepared the chapter titled "International Migration and Naturalization," in U.S. Bureau of the Census (1975). For two recent evaluations of the official statistics on immigration, see Levine, Hill, and Warren (1985) and Edmonston (1996). Many of the statistics presented here update those that appear in U.S. Bureau of the Census (1975). Table Ad1–2 includes a detailed description of the underlying sources. For most of these series, the updating process required an examination of each of the *Statistical Yearbook*s of the INS published since 1970. In some cases – for example, country of last residence – we offer more detail than Hutchinson so as to better reflect the increasing importance of, and diversity within, immigration from Latin America and Asia since 1970. More detailed data in the form of microdata are available from the National Technical Information Service, through which the INS also distributes public use data sets. Such data sets contain demographic information on each individual immigrant, the only major exception being those legalized under the IRCA legislation.

Though the number of immigrants is presented as a continuous series from 1820 to 1998, the underlying definition of immigrant has changed over time with numerous year-to-year changes that are documented in the text for Table Ad1–2. There were three major conceptual shifts. From the beginning of the data collection process in 1820 and continuing through 1904, the data represent primarily the tabulations of reports by ship captains, who were required to provide a list, or manifest, of all passengers taken on board. The lists included passengers coming for brief stays as well as those who planned to settle permanently in the United States. The systematic reporting of persons who crossed into the United States over land borders with Canada and Mexico began in 1904 and was largely complete by 1908. It has been continued to the present. In 1906, arriving aliens were divided into two classes. "Immigrants" were defined as those who declared their intention to settle in the United States. Nonimmigrants were defined as aliens who stated that they did not intend to settle in the United States and also those aliens who were returning to their homes in the United States after a brief visit to their home country. In 1933, the definition of immigrants and nonimmigrants was changed to pertain not to physical movement, but to legal status. "Immigrant" was redefined as an alien accepted for legal permanent resident status. The shift in definition away from an emphasis on the geographic and toward an emphasis on the legal has a profound effect on the meaning of immigration data. Admission as an immigrant may occur on arrival in the United States; however, it may also take place many years after a person has begun living in the United States. For example, the IRCA legalizations did not represent the movement of individuals into the United States, but rather the adjustment of the status of people who had been living in the country for some time.

The primary source for statistical information on the foreign-born population of the United States is the decennial census conducted by the federal government. Beginning in 1850 and continuing through 2000, the Census asked respondents to report their country of birth. For the years 1880 through 1970, the Census also inquired about the country of birth of the respondent's parents. Recently, microdata samples from the manuscripts of the federal censuses have been put into electronic format and made available to the public as the Public Use Microdata Series (PUMS). To facilitate the public's use of the PUMS data for the analysis of time trends, Steven Ruggles and Matthew Sobek have standardized the coding of many PUMS variables, including the coding of country of birth, to create the Integrated Public Use Microdata Series (IPUMS; see the Guide to the Millennial Edition for information on the IPUMS).

Two important data collection efforts that attempted to document characteristics of immigrants during the period of mass immigration around the turn of the twentieth century deserve comment. One important source of systematic quantitative evidence on the foreign-born population was collected in a series of surveys of working-class households in the late nineteenth century that were motivated by an effort to better understand the cause of the social unrest that immigration seemed to prompt. Carroll D. Wright (1840–1909), the leader of this effort, began his work as Commissioner of the Massachusetts Bureau of Labor Statistics and within a short space of time was appointed Commissioner of the U.S. Bureau of Labor, where he organized and supervised large-scale studies of native- and foreign-born working-class families. These studies inspired labor commissioners in other states to conduct similar studies in the half-century that followed. For a description of this project see Carter, Ransom, and Sutch (1991). For an annotated bibliography of these surveys, see Williams and Zimmerman (1935). A second important source of information on immigrants

and their characteristics is the forty-two-volume report of the U.S. Immigration Commission of 1911, also known as the Dillingham Commission Report (see U.S. Congress, Senate (1911)).

Many countries around the world collect and publish data on immigration and emigration. An authoritative and influential compilation of such statistics through 1924 is Ferenczi and Willcox (1929). Tables Ad25–79 display summary statistics from this source. For the late twentieth century, immigration data from many different countries are collected and published by the Organization for Economic Cooperation and Development (2001). An impressive survey of international migration from ninety-five separate perspectives is Cohen (1995).

References

Archdeacon, Thomas J. 1983. *Becoming American: An Ethnic History.* Free Press.

Bailyn, Bernard. 1986. *The Peopling of British North America: An Introduction.* Knopf.

Baines, Dudley. 1995. *Emigration from Europe, 1815–1930.* Cambridge University Press.

Bean, Frank D., Barry Edmonston, and Jeffrey Passel, editors. 1990. *Undocumented Migration to the United States – IRCA and the Experience of the 1980s.* Rand Corporation and the Urban Institute.

Bodnar, John. 1985. *The Transplanted: A History of Immigrants in Urban America.* Indiana University Press.

Briggs, Vernon M., Jr. 1984. *Immigration Policy and the American Labor Force.* Johns Hopkins University Press.

Bromwell, William J. [1856] 1969. *History of Immigration to the United States, 1819–1855.* 1st edition, Redfield, 1856; reprinted by Augustus M. Kelley, 1969.

Carter, Susan B., Roger L. Ransom, and Richard Sutch. 1991. "The Historical Labor Statistics Project at the University of California." *Historical Methods* 24 (2): 52–65.

Carter, Susan B., and Richard Sutch. 1998. "Historical Background to Current Immigration Issues." In James P. Smith and Barry Edmonston, editors. *The Immigration Debate: Studies on the Economic, Demographic, and Fiscal Effects of Immigration.* National Academy Press.

Carter, Susan B., and Richard Sutch. 1999. "Historical Perspectives on the Economic Consequences of Immigration into the United States." In Charles Hirschman, Philip Kasinitz, and Josh DeWind, editors. *The Handbook of International Migration: The American Experience.* Russell Sage Foundation.

Cohen, Robin, editor. 1995. *The Cambridge Survey of World Migration.* Cambridge University Press.

Daniels, Roger. 1972. *Concentration Camps, U.S.A.: Japanese-Americans and World War II.* Rinehart and Winston.

Daniels, Roger. 1988. *Asian America: Chinese and Japanese in the United States since 1850.* University of Washington Press.

Edmonston, Barry, editor. 1996. "Committee on National Statistics and Committee on Population, National Research Council." *Statistics on U.S. Immigration: An Assessment of Data Needs for Future Research.* National Academy Press.

Edmonston, Barry, Jeffrey S. Passel, and Frank D. Bean. 1990. "Perceptions and Estimates of Undocumented Migration to the United States." In Frank D. Bean, Barry Edmonston, and Jeffrey Passel, editors. *Undocumented Migration to the United States – IRCA and the Experience of the 1980s.* Rand Corporation and the Urban Institute.

Ferenczi, Imre, and Walter F. Willcox. 1929. *International Migrations,* volume 1, *Statistics Compiled on Behalf of the International Labour Office, Geneva, with Introduction and Notes.* National Bureau of Economic Research.

Frey, William H. 2002. "U.S. Census Shows Different Paths for Domestic and Foreign-Born Migrants." *Population Today* (August/September). Available only online at the Web site of the Population Reference Bureau.

Gemery, Henry A. 1984. "European Emigration to North America, 1700–1820: Numbers and Quasi-Numbers." *Perspectives in American History* new series 1: 283–342.

Gemery, Henry A. 1994. "Immigrants and Emigrants: International Migration and the US Labor Market in the Great Depression." In Timothy J. Hatton and Jeffrey G. Williamson, editors. *Migration and the International Labor Market, 1850–1939.* Routledge.

Glenn, Evelyn Nakano. 1986. *Issei, Nisei, War Bride: Three Generations of Japanese American Women in Domestic Service.* Temple University Press.

Hatton, Timothy J., and Jeffrey G. Williamson. 1998. *The Age of Mass Migration: Causes and Economic Impact.* Oxford University Press.

Hutchinson, Edward P. 1958. "Notes on the Immigration Statistics of the United States." *Journal of the American Statistical Association* 55: 963–1025.

Hutchinson, Edward P. 1981. *Legislative History of American Immigration Policy, 1798–1965.* University of Pennsylvania Press.

Jones, Maldwyn Allen. 1960. *American Immigration.* University of Chicago Press.

Kim, Bok-Lim C. 1977. "Asian Wives of U.S. Servicemen: Women in the Shadows." *Amerasia Journal* 4: 98–100.

LeMay, Michael, and Elliott Barkan, editors. 1999. *U.S. Immigration and Naturalization Laws and Issues: A Documentary History.* Greenwood.

Levine, Daniel B., Kenneth Hill, and Robert Warren, editors. 1985. *Immigration Statistics: A Story of Neglect.* National Academy Press.

Llambias-Wolff, Jaime. 1995. "Chile's Exiles and Their Return: Two Faces of Expatriation." In Robin Cohen, editor. *The Cambridge Survey of World Migration.* Cambridge University Press.

Loescher, Gilbert D., and John A. Scanlon. 1998. *Calculated Kindness: Refugees and America's Half-Open Door, 1945 to the Present.* Free Press.

Massey, Douglas S. 1994. "An Evaluation of International Migration Theory: The North American Case." *Population and Development Review* 20: 699–751.

Mitchell, B. R. 1980. *European Historical Statistics: 1750–1975.* 2nd revised edition. Macmillan.

Mitchell, B. R. 1983. *International Historical Statistics: The Americas and Australasia.* Gale Research.

National Science Board. 2000. *Science and Engineering Indicators – 2000.* National Science Foundation.

Organization for Economic Cooperation and Development (OECD). 2001. *Trends in International Migration: Continuous Reporting System on Migration.* Annual Report 2000 edition. OECD.

Passel, Jeffrey S., and Barry Edmonston. 1994. "Immigration and Race: Recent Trends in Immigration to the United States." In Barry Edmonston and Jeffrey S. Passel, editors. *Immigration and Ethnicity: The Integration of America's Newest Arrivals.* Urban Institute Press.

Scally, Robert. 1995. "The Irish and the 'Famine Exodus' of 1847." In Robin Cohen, editor. *The Cambridge Survey of World Migration.* Cambridge University Press.

Schiller, Nina Glick. 1999. "Transmigrants and Nation-States: Something Old and Something New in the U.S. Immigrant Experience." In Charles Hirschman, Philip Kasinitz, and Josh DeWind, editors. *The Handbook of International Migration: The American Experience.* Russell Sage Foundation.

Spicer, Edward H., [and others]. 1969. *Impounded People: Japanese-Americans in the Relocation Centers.* University of Arizona Press.

Teitelbaum, Michael S., and Jay Winter. 1998. *A Question of Numbers: High Migration, Low Fertility, and the Politics of National Identity.* Hill and Wang.

Torpey, John. 2000. *The Invention of the Passport: Surveillance, Citizenship and the State.* Cambridge University Press.

U.S. Bureau of the Census. 1975. *Historical Statistics of the United States, Colonial Times to 1970.* Bicentennial edition. U.S. Government Printing Office.

U.S. Bureau of the Census. 2001. *Profile of the Foreign-Born Population in the United States: 2000.* Current Population Reports Special Studies number P23-206. U.S. Government Printing Office.

U.S. Congress, Senate. 1911. *Reports of the Immigration Commission.* Committee on Immigration, U.S. Senate, 61st Congress, 3rd Session. 5 December 1910. 42 volumes. U.S. Government Printing Office.

Walker, Francis Amasa. 1891. "Immigration and Degradation." *Forum* 11: 634–44.

Williams, Faith M., and Carle C. Zimmerman. 1935. "Studies of Family Living in the United States and Other Countries: An Analysis of Material and Method." U.S. Department of Agriculture, Miscellaneous Publication No. 223. U.S. Government Printing Office.

Wright, Gavin. 1986. *Old South, New South: Revolutions in the Southern Economy.* Basic Books.

Zucker, Naomi Flink, and Norman L. Zucker. 1995. "US Admissions Policies towards Cuban and Haitian Migrants." In Robin Cohen, editor. *The Cambridge Survey of World Migration.* Cambridge University Press.

IMMIGRANTS, EMIGRANTS, AND NET MIGRATION

Susan B. Carter and Richard Sutch

TABLE Ad1-2   U.S. immigrants and emigrants: 1820–1998[1, 2, 3]

Contributed by Susan B. Carter and Richard Sutch

Fiscal year	Immigrants to the United States — Ad1 Number	Emigrants from the United States — Ad2 Number	Fiscal year	Immigrants to the United States — Ad1 Number	Emigrants from the United States — Ad2 Number	Fiscal year	Immigrants to the United States — Ad1 Number	Emigrants from the United States — Ad2 Number
1820	8,385	—	1875	227,498	—	1930	241,700	50,661
1821	9,127	—	1876	169,986	—	1931	97,139	61,882
1822	6,911	—	1877	141,857	—	1932	35,576	103,295
1823	6,354	—	1878	138,469	—	1933	23,068	80,081
1824	7,912	—	1879	177,826	—	1934	29,470	39,771
1825	10,199	—	1880	457,257	—	1935	34,956	38,834
1826	10,837	—	1881	669,431	—	1936	36,329	35,817
1827	18,875	—	1882	788,992	—	1937	50,244	26,736
1828	27,382	—	1883	603,322	—	1938	67,895	25,210
1829	22,520	—	1884	518,592	—	1939	82,998	26,651
1830	23,322	—	1885	395,346	—	1940	70,756	21,461
1831	22,633	—	1886	334,203	—	1941	51,776	17,115
1832	60,482	—	1887	490,109	—	1942	28,781	7,363
(TQ)	7,303	—	1888	546,889	—	1943	23,725	5,107
1833	58,640	—	1889	444,427	—	1944	28,551	5,669
1834	65,365	—	1890	455,302	—	1945	38,119	7,442
1835	45,374	—	1891	560,319	—	1946	108,721	18,143
1836	76,242	—	1892	579,663	—	1947	147,292	22,501
1837	79,340	—	1893	439,730	—	1948	170,570	20,875
1838	38,914	—	1894	285,631	—	1949	188,317	24,586
1839	68,069	—	1895	258,536	—	1950	249,187	27,598
1840	84,066	—	1896	343,267	—	1951	205,717	26,174
1841	80,289	—	1897	230,832	—	1952	265,520	21,880
1842	104,565	—	1898	229,299	—	1953	170,434	24,256
1843 [4]	52,496	—	1899	311,715	—	1954	208,177	30,665
1844	78,615	—	1900	448,572	—	1955	237,790	31,245
1845	114,371	—	1901	487,918	—	1956	321,625	22,824
1846	154,416	—	1902	648,743	—	1957	326,867	23,933
1847	234,968	—	1903	857,046	—	1958	253,265	—
1848	226,527	—	1904	812,870	—	1959	260,686	—
1849	297,024	—	1905	1,026,499	—	1960	265,398	—
1850	310,004 [6]	—	1906	1,100,825	—	1961	271,344	—
(TQ)	59,976	—	1907	1,285,349	—	1962	283,763	—
1851	379,466 [6]	—	1908	782,870	395,073	1963	306,260	—
1852	371,603	—	1909	751,786	225,802	1964	292,248	—
1853	368,645	—	1910	1,041,570	202,436	1965	296,697	—
1854	427,833	—	1911	878,587	295,666	1966	323,040	—
1855	200,877	—	1912	838,172	333,262	1967	361,972	—
1856	200,436	—	1913	1,197,892	308,190	1968	454,448	—
1857	251,306	—	1914	1,218,480	303,338	1969	358,579	—
1858	123,126	—	1915	326,700	204,074	1970	373,326	—
1859	121,282	—	1916	298,826	129,765	1971	370,478	—
1860	153,640	—	1917	295,403	66,277	1972	384,685	—
1861	91,918	—	1918	110,618	94,585	1973	400,063	—
1862	91,985	—	1919	141,132	123,522	1974	394,861	—
1863	176,282	—	1920	430,001	288,315	1975	386,194	—
1864	193,418	—	1921	805,228	247,718	1976	398,613	—
1865	248,120	—	1922	309,556	198,712	(TQ)	103,676	—
1866 [5]	318,568	—	1923	522,919	81,450	1977	462,315	—
1867	315,722	—	1924	706,896	76,789	1978	601,442	—
1868	138,840	—	1925	294,314	92,728	1979	460,348	—
1869	352,768	—	1926	304,488	76,992	1980	530,639	—
1870	387,203	—	1927	335,175	73,366	1981	596,600	—
1871	321,350	—	1928	307,255	77,457	1982	594,131	—
1872	404,806	—	1929	279,678	69,203	1983	559,763	—
1873	459,803	—				1984	543,903	—
1874	313,339	—						

Notes appear at end of table   (continued)

TABLE Ad1-2   U.S. immigrants and emigrants: 1820-1998   *Continued*

	Immigrants to the United States	Emigrants from the United States		Immigrants to the United States	Emigrants from the United States		Immigrants to the United States	Emigrants from the United States
	Ad1	Ad2		Ad1	Ad2		Ad1	Ad2
Fiscal year	Number	Number	Fiscal year	Number	Number	Fiscal year	Number	Number
1985	570,009	—	1990	1,536,483	—	1995	720,461	—
1986	601,708	—	1991	1,827,167	—	1996	915,900	—
1987	601,516	—	1992	973,977	—	1997	798,378	—
1988	643,025	—	1993	904,292	—	1998	660,477	—
1989	1,090,924	—	1994	804,416	—			

(TQ) indicates transitional quarter.

[1] Through 1867, data exclude returning citizens and therefore do not agree with series Ad222, Ad226, and Ad231.

[2] Year ending September 30 (1820-1832, 1844-1850, and beginning 1977), December 31 (1833-1842 and 1851-1865), and June 30 (1867-1976).

[3] Beginning in 1906, arriving aliens were divided into two classes: "immigrants," defined as those who intended to settle in the United States, and "nonimmigrants," defined as those who declared an intention not to settle in the United States and all aliens returning to resume domiciles formerly acquired in the United States.

[4] First three quarters of 1843.

[5] Six months ending June 30.

[6] Data in the original source have been revised.

Sources

Immigration statistics were compiled by the Department of State for 1820-1870; by the Treasury Department, Bureau of Statistics, for 1867-1895; and by a separate Office or Bureau of Immigration, in the Immigration and Naturalization Service, between 1892 and 2003. In 2003, immigration statistics were moved to the Bureau of Citizenship and Immigration Services within the Department of Homeland Security. See U.S. Department of the Treasury, Bureau of Statistics, *Monthly Summary of Commerce and Finance of the U.S., June 1903.* For 1892-1932, the Bureau of Immigration issued annual reports. For 1933-1940, the data were summarized in the *Annual Report of the Secretary of Labor*; for 1941, they were issued in the *Annual Report of the Attorney General*; for 1942, no report was published; and for subsequent years, the statistics appeared in the *Annual Report of the Immigration and Naturalization Service* and then in the Immigration and Naturalization Service's *Statistical Yearbook.*

Documentation

The continuous record of immigration to the United States began in 1819, under the Steerage Act of 1819, which required the captain or master of a vessel arriving from abroad to deliver to the local collector of customs a list or manifest of all passengers taken on board. This list was to designate the name, age, sex, and occupation of each passenger, "the country to which they severally belonged," and the number that had died on the voyage. Copies of these manifests were to be transmitted to the Secretary of State, who reported the information periodically to Congress. Subsequently, the Act of 1855 prescribed quarterly reports to the Secretary of State and annual reports to Congress. Later acts have continued to require the collection of such information.

Although the reporting of alien arrivals was required by the Act of 1798, which expired two years later, the number arriving before 1819 is not known. William J. Bromwell, in *History of Immigration to the United States* (Redfield, 1856), pp. 18-9, estimated the number of passengers of foreign birth arriving in the United States during the period between the close of the Revolutionary War and 1819 at 250,000. This estimate was accepted by the Treasury's Bureau of Statistics when it later compiled the official statistics of immigration.

Since 1820, the official immigration data have undergone many changes in the reporting area covered. During the first decades only arrivals by vessel at Atlantic and Gulf ports were reported. Arrivals at Pacific ports were first included in 1850. During the Civil War, the only Southern ports that reported were those controlled by the federal government. Later, the reporting area was expanded to include arrivals at outlying possessions. Arrivals in Alaska were first reported in 1871, but only irregularly thereafter until 1904, after which Alaska was regularly included among the places of entry. Arrivals in Hawai'i were first included in 1901, Puerto Rico in 1902, and the Virgin Islands in 1942.

Counting arrivals at the land borders was not required by the early immigration acts, and the counting of such arrivals did not approach completeness until after 1904. For 1820-1823, a few arrivals by land borders were included. Complete reporting was attempted in 1855 with only partial success, was interrupted for several years by the Civil War, and was discontinued in 1885. Beginning in 1894, European immigrants who arrived at Canadian ports with the declared intention of proceeding to the United States were included in the immigration statistics. Some immigration was reported at land border stations established in 1904. More stations were opened in the following years, but reporting of land border arrivals was not fully established until 1908.

The statistical treatment of Canadian and Mexican immigrants at times has differed from that of other immigrants. When reporting of arrivals by land borders was discontinued in 1885, regular reporting of Canadian and Mexican arrivals by vessel was also discontinued; however, a few Canadian and Mexican immigrants were reported in most of the following years. Arrivals of Canadians and Mexicans by land borders began to be reported in 1906, and reporting was fully established in 1908 under authority of the Immigration Act of 1907, which provided for the inspection of Canadians and Mexicans at the land borders.

Not all aliens entering via the Canadian and Mexican borders are counted for inclusion in the immigration statistics. Before 1930, no count was made of residents of Canada, Newfoundland, or Mexico who had been living there for a year or longer and who planned to remain in the United States for less than six months. For 1930-1945, the following classes of aliens entering via the land borders were counted and included in the statistics of immigration: (1) those who had not been in the United States within six months, who came to stay for more than six months; (2) those for whom straight head tax was a prerequisite to admission, or for whom head tax was specially deposited and subsequently converted to straight head tax account; (3) those required by law or regulation to present an immigration visa or reentry permit, and those who surrendered either, regardless of whether they were required by law or regulation to do so; (4) those announcing an intention to depart via a seaport of the United States for Hawai'i or insular possessions of the United States, or for foreign countries, except arrivals from Canada intending to return thereto by water; and (5) those announcing an intention to depart across the other land boundary.

These classes were revised in 1945 so that the statistics of arriving aliens at land border ports of entry for 1945-1952 included (1) arriving aliens who came into the United States for thirty days or more and (2) returning alien residents who had been out of the United States for more than six months. Arriving aliens who came into the United States for nine days or less were not counted, except those certified by public health officials, aliens held for a board of special inquiry, aliens excluded and deported, and aliens in transit who announced an intention to depart across another land boundary or by sea.

Since 1953, all aliens arriving at land border ports of entry have been counted and included except Canadian citizens and British subjects resident in Canada who were admitted for six months or less, and Mexican citizens who were admitted for seventy-two hours or less to the United States. Persons who cross the land borders for brief periods (border crossers) are not included in the immigration and emigration statistics. The Immigration and Naturalization Service publishes statistics on alien and citizen border crossers in its *Annual Report*, however.

Arrivals in and departures from the Philippines were recorded in the port tables for 1910-1924, but were not included in the total immigration data.

TABLE Ad1–2   U.S. immigrants and emigrants: 1820–1998   *Continued*

For 1925–1931, such arrivals and departures were obtained annually from the Bureau of Insular Affairs, War Department, and published in separate tables. Since 1932, the Immigration Service has kept no records of arrivals in the Philippines or departures from the Philippines to foreign countries.

Data on aliens admitted to the conterminous United States from insular possessions were compiled from 1908 through 1964. Aliens admitted from the Virgin Islands were first recorded in 1917. The departure of aliens from the mainland to Puerto Rico was first recorded in 1918. Data on aliens from Guam began to be recorded in 1929; those on aliens from Samoa began to be recorded in 1932.

For 1820–1867, immigration totals (compiled by the Department of State) were shown as alien passenger arrivals; however, they may have included alien passengers who died before arrival, and they did include, for 1856–1867, temporary visitors among arriving alien passengers. For the twelve-year period, temporary visitors constituted about 1.5 percent of the alien passenger arrivals.

For 1868–1891, the Bureau of Statistics reported immigrant arrival figures (excluding temporary visitors). Since 1892, official immigration data have been compiled by the Office of Immigration (and its successors), and for 1892–1893, its totals were 7–8 percent lower than those of the Bureau of Statistics for that period. The difference is largely attributable to the limitation of the Office of Immigration figures to alien steerage passengers; cabin class passengers were not included as immigrants until 1904. A further difference was that the Bureau of Statistics figures were for arrivals and those of the Office of Immigration were for admissions.

For 1893–1897, the Office of Immigration resumed counting arrivals and the figures include the 2,419 aliens debarred in 1893, the 2,799 debarred in 1896, and 1,880 debarred in 1897. In later years, the immigration data were further refined to exclude aliens in transit through the United States (1904) and resident aliens returning from a visit abroad (1906).

In 1906, arriving aliens were divided into two classes: immigrants, or those who intended to settle in the United States; and nonimmigrants, or admitted aliens who declared an intention not to settle in the United States and all aliens returning to resume domiciles formerly acquired in the United States.

The official record of emigration began in 1907 and ended in 1957. It was made possible by the Immigration Act of 1907, which required all steamship companies carrying departing aliens to furnish manifests similar to those required for arriving aliens.

For 1908–1932, aliens arriving in or departing from the United States were classified as follows: Arriving aliens with permanent domicile outside the United States who intended to reside permanently in the United States were classed as immigrants; departing aliens with permanent residence in the United States who intended to reside permanently abroad were classed as emigrants; all alien residents taking temporary trips abroad and all aliens residing abroad making temporary trips to the United States were classed as nonimmigrants on the inward journey and nonemigrants on the outward. Permanent residence was defined as residence for one year or longer. (*Annual Report of the Commissioner General of Immigration, 1908*, p. 6.)

Since 1933, aliens arriving in the United States have been classified as immigrants or nonimmigrants. Immigrants are nonresident aliens admitted to the United States for permanent residence. Until July 1, 1968, they were further classified as quota or nonquota immigrants. Quota immigrants were those subject to the established quotas of Eastern Hemisphere countries and their dependencies. Nonquota immigrants included natives of the Western Hemisphere and their spouses and children, immediate relatives of U.S. citizens, and certain groups of special immigrants. Beginning July 1, 1968, immigrants have been classified as those subject to the numerical limitations of the Eastern Hemisphere, those subject to the numerical imitations of the Western Hemisphere, and those exempt from numerical limitations. Those who are exempt include immediate relatives (parents, spouses, and children) of U.S. citizens and various classes of special immigrants.

Nonimmigrants are nonresident aliens admitted to the United States for a temporary period. Included in this group are visitors for business and pleasure, students and their spouses and children, temporary workers and trainees and their spouses and children, foreign government officials, exchange visitors and their spouses and children, international representatives, treaty traders and investors, representatives of foreign information media, fiancés/fiancées of U.S. citizens and their children, intracompany transferees and their spouses and children, NATO officials, aliens in transit, and, for statistical purposes, permanent resident aliens returning after short trips abroad. Excluded are border crossers, crewmen, and insular travelers.

Data on emigrants were discontinued beginning in 1958.

The old definitions of immigrant, emigrant, nonimmigrant, and nonemigrant somewhat impaired the reliability of net immigration figures. Immigrants who were admitted for permanent residence could depart before the end of one year's residence, in which case they were counted as immigrants on arrival and nonemigrants on departure. Persons coming in temporarily as nonimmigrants, however, who failed to leave within a year were counted as emigrants on departure.

TABLE Ad3–15   Decennial net migration to English America, by region and race: 1630–1800

Contributed by Susan B. Carter

	White						Black						
	British North America					British West Indies	British North America					British West Indies	Net import of slaves to British North America
	Total	New England	Middle Colonies	Upper South	Lower South		Total	New England	Middle Colonies	Upper South	Lower South		
Decade beginning	Ad3	Ad4	Ad5	Ad6	Ad7	Ad8	Ad9	Ad10	Ad11	Ad12	Ad13	Ad14	Ad15
	Thousand	Thousand	Thousand	Thousand	Thousand	Thousand	Thousand	Thousand	Thousand	Thousand	Thousand	Thousand	Thousand
1630	22	11	0	11	0	41	—	—	—	—	—	—	1
1640	19	5	0	14	0	40	—	—	—	—	—	—	1
1650	21	3	0	18	0	33	1	0	0	1	0	39	2
1660	28	8	0	17	3	12	2	0	0	2	0	38	2
1670	23	1	4	15	3	15	2	0	0	2	0	53	3
1680	25	–1	13	9	4	11	8	0	0	7	1	59	11
1690	–7	–17	7	0	3	19	9	0	0	8	1	95	14
1700	21	–4	0	18	7	10	14	0	1	11	2	88	16
1710	52	20	10	21	1	18	21	1	3	7	10	93	23
1720	61	–2	15	38	10	16	19	1	1	6	11	126	20
1730	82	9	27	30	16	6	42	1	1	29	11	88	45
1740	2	–10	13	–17	16	9	59	0	0	47	12	115	63
1750	64	–9	40	20	13	11	22	–1	2	4	17	127	55
1760	47	6	9	–2	34	5	37	–1	–2	8	32	86	73
1770	15	–23	12	–25	51	11	–17	–5	–2	–19	9	81	33
1780	—	—	—	—	—	—	—	—	—	—	—	—	77
1790	—	—	—	—	—	—	—	—	—	—	—	—	71
1800	—	—	—	—	—	—	—	—	—	—	—	—	143

Sources

Series Ad3–14. David W. Galenson, "The Settlement and Growth of the Colonies: Population, Labor, and Economic Development," in Stanley L. Engerman and Robert E. Gallman, editors, *The Cambridge Economic History of the United States*, volume I, *The Colonial Era* (Cambridge University Press, 2000), Tables 4.5, 4.6, pp. 178, 180. Galenson draws on Henry Gemery, "Emigration from the British Isles to the New World, 1630–1700," *Research in Economic History* 5 (1980): 179–232.

Series Ad15. Robert William Fogel, Ralph A. Galantine, and Richard L. Manning, *Without Consent or Contract: Evidence and Methods* (Norton, 1992), Table 4.2, p. 55.

Documentation

Figures cover the decade beginning in the year shown.

New England includes Maine, New Hampshire, Vermont, Plymouth, Massachusetts, Rhode Island, and Connecticut. Middle Colonies include New York, New Jersey, Pennsylvania, and Delaware. Upper South includes Maryland and Virginia. Lower South includes Georgia, North Carolina, and South Carolina. West Indies includes Barbados, Jamaica, Antigua, Montserrat, Nevis, and St. Kitts.

Series Ad15. Covers the colonies that would become the United States.

TABLE Ad16–20   Net immigration – various estimates: 1774–1860

Contributed by Richard Sutch

Year	Net immigration (McClelland and Zeckhauser)			Gross immigration, free and slave (Blodget)	Net immigration (Schaefer)
	Total	Whites	Slaves		
	Ad16	Ad17	Ad18	Ad19	Ad20
	Number	Number	Number	Number	Number
1774	—	—	—	3,000	—
1784	—	—	—	5,000	—
1790	—	—	—	3,500	—
1791	—	—	—	4,000	—
1792	—	—	—	5,000	—
1793	—	—	—	3,500	—
1794	—	—	—	3,500	—
1795	—	—	—	3,900	—
1796	—	—	—	4,500	—
1797	—	—	—	3,500	—
1798	—	—	—	3,800	—
1799	—	—	—	4,000	—
1800	9,400	4,400	5,000	3,800	—
1801	13,800	8,800	5,000	4,000	—
1802	13,800	8,800	5,000	4,500	—
1803	13,800	8,800	5,000	3,900	—
1804	15,263	8,800	6,463	9,500	—
1805	15,948	8,800	7,148	10,000	—
1806	22,550	8,800	13,750	—	—
1807	27,611	8,800	18,811	—	—
1808	14,400	6,400	8,000	—	—
1809	23,440	8,000	15,440	—	—
1810	13,000	8,000	5,000	—	—
1811	13,000	8,000	5,000	—	—
1812	10,411	5,411	5,000	—	—
1813	7,498	2,498	5,000	—	—
1814	7,950	2,950	5,000	—	—
1815	7,879	2,879	5,000	—	—
1816	16,517	11,517	5,000	—	—
1817	28,688	23,688	5,000	—	—
1818	31,091	26,091	5,000	—	—
1819	32,079	27,079	5,000	—	—
1820	22,197	17,197	5,000	—	—
1821	20,688	15,688	5,000	—	—
1822	20,723	15,723	5,000	—	—
1823	18,017	13,017	5,000	—	—
1824	18,203	13,203	5,000	—	—
1825	19,980	14,980	5,000	—	—
1826	24,732	19,732	5,000	—	—
1827	35,330	30,330	5,000	—	—
1828	38,236	33,236	5,000	—	—
1829	37,018	32,018	5,000	—	—
1830	45,142	40,142	5,000	—	—
1831	63,269	58,269	5,000	—	—
1832	82,422	77,422	5,000	—	—
1833	74,346	69,346	5,000	—	—
1834	86,311	81,311	5,000	—	—
1835	56,075	51,075	5,000	—	—
1836	94,826	89,826	5,000	—	—
1837	94,307	89,307	5,000	—	—
1838	44,317	39,317	5,000	—	—
1839	74,810	69,810	5,000	—	—
1840	94,113	89,113	5,000	—	—
1841	88,256	83,256	5,000	—	—
1842	115,145	110,145	5,000	—	—
1843	79,199	74,199	5,000	—	—
1844	93,554	88,554	5,000	—	—
1845	130,068	125,068	5,000	—	—
1846	179,936	174,936	5,000	—	—
1847	244,897	239,897	5,000	—	—
1848	245,671	240,671	5,000	—	—
1849	298,243	293,243	5,000	—	—

(continued)

TABLE Ad16-20   Net immigration – various estimates: 1774–1860 *Continued*

	Net immigration (McClelland and Zeckhauser)			Gross immigration, free and slave (Blodget)	Net immigration (Schaefer)
	Total	Whites	Slaves		
	Ad16	Ad17	Ad18	Ad19	Ad20
Year	Number	Number	Number	Number	Number
1850	295,783	290,783	5,000	—	280,278
1851	378,324	373,324	5,000	—	380,612
1852	368,842	363,842	5,000	—	389,492
1853	365,505	360,505	5,000	—	369,469
1854	425,292	420,292	5,000	—	422,854
1855	201,671	196,671	5,000	—	193,965
1856	201,458	196,458	5,000	—	194,880
1857	252,031	247,031	5,000	—	244,159
1858	125,507	120,507	5,000	—	118,070
1859	123,011	118,011	5,000	—	116,654
1860	154,321	149,321	5,000	—	—

Sources

Series Ad16–18. Peter D. McClelland and Richard J. Zeckhauser, *Demographic Dimensions of the New Republic: American Interregional Migration, Vital Statistics, and Manumissions, 1800–1860* (Cambridge University Press, 1982), pp. 30–49.

Series Ad19. Samuel Blodget Jr., *Economica: A Statistical Manual for the United States of America* (privately printed, 1806; reprinted by Augustus M. Kelley, 1964), p. 58.

Series Ad20. Donald Schaefer, "U.S. Migration, 1850-59," in Thomas Weiss and Donald Schaefer, editors, *American Economic Development in Historical Perspective* (Stanford University Press, 1994), Table 3.1, p. 56.

Documentation

Table Ad21–24 presents various estimates for the period beginning in 1870. No net immigration estimates have been made for the Civil War decade.

Series Ad16–18. McClelland and Zeckhauser have estimated the net immigration of whites and slaves for the period 1800–1860 using available evidence on immigration, population counts from the decennial censuses, estimates of immigration from and emigration to Canada, and a rather complex demographic model. They report their figures as applying to calendar years.

Series Ad17. Immigration numbers for the period before 1820 can only be conjectural estimates based on very little and partial data. McClelland and Zeckhauser's figures for the years before 1820 are crude estimates made after reviewing the work of Samuel Blodget (series Ad19), Adam Seybert (*Statistical Annals of the United States of America* (Dobson, 1818)) and George Tucker (*Progress of the United States in Population and Wealth in Fifty Years as Exhibited by the Decennial Census from 1790 to 1840, with an Appendix Containing an Abstract of the Census of 1850* (Hunt's Merchant's Magazine, 1855; reprinted by Augustus M. Kelley, 1964), p. 82). Seybert made an investigation of passenger arrivals from records he obtained from the customhouses. George Tucker (1855) relied on Seybert's single observation of 22,240 for 1817, which he adjusted to 21,000, to estimate immigration for 1810–1820. McClelland and Zeckhauser also relied on Seybert's estimate of the number of immigrants in 1817 as 20,083 (1982, 38, pp. 96–7). Tucker assumed that no immigration took place during the three years of the War of 1812 and that the 1817 flow continued through 1820. He set the figures for the other years of the decade at 10,000 each. Although McClelland and Zeckhauser's estimates for the period 1800–1816 are very rough, they are considered the best available (McClelland and Zeckhauser 1982, Table A-12, p. 100). For the years covered by the official immigration statistics reported in series Ad1, McClelland and Zeckhauser made adjustments to eliminate tourists and aliens in transit and the double counting of aliens making a second passage. They also made estimates of the net immigration from Canada. They suggest that the effect of overland immigration from Mexico, aliens arriving by Pacific ports, and underenumeration of immigrants arriving at Atlantic ports was largely offset by aliens who died on shipboard and emigration of U.S. residents (McClelland and Zeckhauser 1982, Table A-24, p. 113).

Series Ad18. The slave trade was prohibited by federal law beginning January 1808. Before that date the trade was outlawed in every state except South Carolina for the period 1804–1807 and the Territory of Louisiana from 1803 to 1807 (before the Louisiana Purchase in 1803, slave trade into the territory had been allowed by Spain and France). McClelland and Zeckhauser base their estimates of slave imports for 1804–1807 on fragmentary evidence on the legal importations, their estimate for 1809 on fragmentary evidence of illegal importation of slaves from Cuba to New Orleans in that year, and a conjecture that illegal importation of slaves amounted to 5,000 per year throughout the entire period (except 1808, which they put at 8,000). This estimate of the illegal flow, although a guess, reflects their belief, supported by a careful review of the evidence, that slave smuggling was very limited. Their figure is higher than Philip Curtin's 1,000 per year (*The Atlantic Slave Trade: A Census* (University of Wisconsin Press, 1969), p. 74), broadly consistent with the estimates by Lewis Cecil Gray (*History of Agriculture in the Southern United States to 1860* (Carnegie Institution, 1933), volume II, p. 650) and Winfield H. Collins (*The Domestic Slave Trade of the Southern States* (Broadway Publishing, 1904), p. 20), but significantly below that of Noel Deerr (*The History of Sugar* (Chapman and Hall, 1949–1950), volume II, p. 282), who put the number at 17,500 per year.

Series Ad19. Samuel Blodget claimed that his estimates for selected years were based on "the best records and estimates at present attainable." Blodget also expressed the opinion that about half of the number arriving in those years soon left, either to Upper Canada or on "seafaring adventures, to every port of the globe" (p. 75). Thus, net immigration according to Blodget would be approximately one half of the numbers given. Seybert (1818, p. 28) thought Blodget's numbers were too low. He gave his own estimate as 10,000 for 1794 (pp. 28–9). McClelland and Zeckhauser obviously agree.

Series Ad19. William J. Bromwell, in his *History of Immigration to the United States* (Redfield, 1856; reprinted by Augustus M. Kelley, 1969, pp. 18–9), estimated the number of passengers of foreign birth arriving in the United States from the close of the Revolutionary War to 1819 at 250,000. This figure was accepted by Edward Young (1872, p. v) of the U.S. Bureau of Statistics and by the authors of the 1880 Census (volume I, p. 458). Ernest Rubin (*Immigration and the Economic Growth of the United States: 1790–1914*, National Bureau of Economic Research, Conference in Income and Wealth, 1957, p. 3) thought the number might be twice as high.

Series Ad20. Schaefer did not rely on the published official estimates of immigration but returned to the original reports of passenger arrivals by the Department of State to Congress. This allowed him to put the entire decade on a calendar year basis. Schaefer also corrected gaps in the original data by including estimates for female immigrants arriving at the Port of Galveston, Texas, and for arrivals in San Francisco in 1851–1853. He also adjusted the totals for 1850–1853 downward to remove aliens not intending to reside in the United States (pp. 64–6). Although Schaefer makes no adjustment for emigration, he treats his estimates as a measure of net immigration, implicitly assuming, as do McClelland and Zeckhauser, that emigration was relatively low and would be offset in the estimates by the underenumeration of arriving passengers and other downward biases in the State Department data.

TABLE Ad21–24   Net immigration – various estimates: 1870–1957
Contributed by Richard Sutch

	Net immigration of aliens		Arrivals of alien passengers	Departures of alien passengers
	Official INS figures	Kuznets and Rubin		
	Ad21	Ad22	Ad23	Ad24
Year	Number	Number	Number	Number
1870	—	366,000	403,000	37,000
1871	—	300,000	343,000	43,000
1872	—	379,000	423,000	44,000
1873	—	402,000	473,000	71,000
1874	—	245,000	328,000	83,000
1875	—	133,000	245,000	112,000
1876	—	100,000	190,000	90,000
1877	—	71,000	165,000	94,000
1878	—	89,000	158,000	69,000
1879	—	132,000	198,000	66,000
1880	—	424,000	484,000	60,000
1881	—	645,000	695,000	50,000
1882	—	752,000	816,000	64,000
1883	—	579,000	645,000	66,000
1884	—	474,000	561,000	87,000
1885	—	284,000	438,000	154,000
1886	—	250,000	358,000	108,000
1887	—	416,000	513,000	97,000
1888	—	438,000	567,000	129,000
1889	—	315,000	465,000	150,000
1890	—	328,000	476,000	148,000
1891	—	426,000	579,000	153,000
1892	—	480,000	644,000	164,000
1893	—	381,000	544,000	163,000
1894	—	137,000	347,000	210,000
1895	—	95,000	301,000	206,000
1896	—	205,000	363,000	158,000
1897	—	105,000	244,000	139,000
1898	—	121,000	250,000	129,000
1899	—	201,000	335,000	134,000
1900	—	385,000	519,000	134,000
1901	—	288,000	563,000	275,000
1902	—	386,000	731,000	345,000
1903	—	532,000	921,000	389,000
1904	—	530,000	841,000	311,000
1905	—	662,000	1,060,000	398,000
1906	—	697,000	1,166,000	469,000
1907	—	767,000	1,438,000	671,000
1908	387,797	210,000	925,000	715,000
1909	525,984	544,000	944,000	400,000
1910	839,134	818,000	1,198,000	380,000
1911	582,921	512,000	1,030,000	518,000
1912	504,910	402,000	1,017,000	615,000
1913	889,702	815,000	1,427,000	612,000
1914	915,142	769,000	1,403,000	634,000
1915	122,626	50,000	434,000	384,000
1916	169,061	126,000	367,000	241,000
1917	229,126	217,000	363,000	146,000
1918	16,033	19,000	212,000	193,000
1919	17,610	21,000	237,000	216,000
1920	141,686	194,000	622,000	428,000
1921	557,510	552,000	978,000	426,000
1922	110,844	87,000	432,000	345,000
1923	441,469	472,000	673,000	201,000
1924	630,107	662,000	879,000	217,000
1925	201,586	232,000	458,000	226,000
1926	227,496	268,000	496,000	228,000
1927	261,809	284,000	538,000	254,000
1928	229,798	227,000	501,000	274,000
1929	210,475	227,000	479,000	252,000

(continued)

TABLE Ad21–24   Net immigration – various estimates: 1870–1957   *Continued*

	Net immigration of aliens		Arrivals of alien passengers	Departures of alien passengers
	Official INS figures	Kuznets and Rubin		
	Ad21	Ad22	Ad23	Ad24
Year	Number	Number	Number	Number
1930	191,039	174,000	446,000	272,000
1931	35,257	−10,000	281,000	291,000
1932	−67,719	−113,000	175,000	288,000
1933	−57,013	−93,000	151,000	244,000
1934	−10,301	−13,000	164,000	177,000
1935	−3,878	−9,000	180,000	189,000
1936	512	−2,000	191,000	193,000
1937	23,508	8,000	232,000	224,000
1938	42,685	30,000	253,000	223,000
1939	56,347	66,000	268,000	202,000
1940	49,295	43,000	209,000	166,000
1941	34,661	64,000	152,000	88,000
1942	21,418	36,000	111,000	75,000
1943	18,618	46,000	105,000	59,000
1944	22,882	58,000	142,000	84,000
1945	30,677	109,000	202,000	93,000
1946	90,578	—	—	—
1947	124,791	—	—	—
1948	149,695	—	—	—
1949	163,731	—	—	—
1950	221,589	—	—	—
1951	179,543	—	—	—
1952	243,640	—	—	—
1953	146,178	—	—	—
1954	177,512	—	—	—
1955	206,545	—	—	—
1956	298,801	—	—	—
1957	302,934	—	—	—

Sources

Series Ad21. Calculated from series Ad1–2.

Series Ad22–24. Simon Kuznets and Ernest Rubin, "Immigration and the Foreign Born," Occasional Paper 46, National Bureau of Economic Research, 1954, Table B-1, pp. 95–6.

Documentation

This table presents the available estimates for the period 1870–1957. Table Ad16–20 presents various estimates for the period ending in 1860. No net immigration estimates have been made for the Civil War decade.

Series Ad21. The official record of the immigration of aliens is given in series Ad1, and the official count of emigrant alien departures is given in series Ad2 for the period 1908–1957. This series is calculated as the difference between the two.

Series Ad22–24. Kuznets and Rubin developed "an approximation to net immigration," series Ad22, by calculating the difference between arrivals and departures of alien passengers. They use the official data on arrivals and departures for the period beginning in 1908 and make estimates for the period before this year. For the period 1870–1890, they use the official data on arrivals, series Ad23. They estimate departures by starting with the official number of Americans returning from abroad (assuming that these Americans stay abroad for one year), some assumed mortality rate, and a guess that permanently departing citizens constituted 0.5 percent of all citizen departures (Kuznets and Rubin 1954, p. 57). For 1901–1907, they estimated emigration by extrapolating the 1908–1914 ratio of departures to arrivals using the official data on arrivals for 1900–1907 (p. 57). For the period 1908–1945, Kuznets and Rubin used the official data described above but reported the result rounded to the nearest thousand.

TABLE Ad25–50   Intercontinental emigration of citizens – annual averages, by country of departure: 1846–1925[1]

Contributed by Susan B. Carter

		From Europe							
		Lands governed by Austria and Hungary			British Isles				
	Total	As of 1924	As of 1846	Belgium	Intercontinental passengers	Intercontinental emigrants	Denmark	France	Germany
	Ad25 [2]	Ad26 [3]	Ad27 [4]	Ad28 [5]	Ad29	Ad30	Ad31	Ad32	Ad33
Years	Number	Number	Number	Number	Number	Number	Number	Number	Number
1846–1850	255,593	1,616	1,849	817	199,108	—	73	10,740	36505 [7]
1851–1855	342,171	4,027	20,137	376	231,733	—	254	11,418	74,926
1856–1860	201,115	2,241	11,204	601	123,497	—	496	3,893	49,386
1861–1865	223,199	2,177	10,886	485	143,559	—	1,049	3,045	43,535
1866–1870	345,657	5,747	28,734	1,060	170,807	—	3,942	6,141	83,356
1871–1875	371,801	10,471	52,357	910	193,907	—	4,682	8,325	78,963
1876–1880	283,286	11,773	58,864	720	141,876	—	3,038	2,974	46,231
1881–1885	686,293	34,645	173,223	1,959	258,462	—	7,725	5,098	171,457
1886–1890	778,936	52,500	262,498	5,012	253,245	—	8,598	18,747	97,027
1891–1895	728,970	67,551	337,754	3,019	195,715	—	7,533	5,443	80,513
1896–1900	601,603	77,249	386,243	1,390	152,843	—	2,769	4,800	24,859
1901–1905	1,052,731	203,025	1,015,127	3,807	234,168	—	7,356	4,800	28,382
1906–1910	1,388,788	265,411	1,327,055	4,836	334,125	—	7,327	5,823	26,449
1911–1915	1,345,483	243,629	730,886	5,526	357,991	268,842	7,058	4,300	15,820
1916–1920	431,138	11,453	57,265	2,270	129,484	101,118	3,263	2,130	2,387
1921–1925	774,924	57,220	228,880	2,078	287,517	204,426	5,831	1,598	58,142

	From Europe								
	Ireland	The Netherlands	Norway	Sweden	Switzerland	Finland	Poland (Russian, prewar)	Russia	Italy
	Ad34 [6]	Ad35	Ad36 [7]	Ad37	Ad38	Ad39	Ad40	Ad41 [8]	Ad42
Years	Number	Number	Number	Number	Number	Number	Number	Number	Number
1846–1850	—	2,418	2,400	1,834	377	—	—	66	240
1851–1855	—	1,943	4,054	2,549	4,019	—	—	4	738
1856–1860	—	1,225	3,160	831	1,534	—	—	117	4,202
1861–1865	—	987	4,710	3,963	1,539	—	—	163	8,027
1866–1870	—	3,107	14,881	20,526	4,569 [10]	—	—	423	18,714
1871–1875	—	2,250	9,028	8,411	3,630	57	—	6,080	23,329
1876–1880	35,009	1,248	8,049	12,089	3,517	44	—	5,505	28,899
1881–1885	73,595	5,627	21,141	29,524	10,098	1,126	—	12,879	64,043
1886–1890	66,389	4,001	16,197	35,977	6,835	4,394	—	44,650	134,235
1891–1895	46,494	3,529	12,203	28,376	4,870	5,201	10,431	55,852	150,226
1896–1900	34,619	1,255	6,767	12,527	2,053	6,608	7,637	40,349	165,692
1901–1905	33,117	2,375	20,639	25,949	3,752	16,211	16,854	84,083	320,604
1906–1910	28,659	3,226	17,533	18,859	3,764	15,555	40,431	98,058	402,436
1911–1915	22,576	2,074	8,910	12,672	3,640	10,134	44,386	140,215 [11]	312,246
1916–1920	4,402	2,271	3,394	4,532	2,506	3,336	9,883	—	126,572
1921–1925	13,243	3,557	9,466	12,457	5,400	7,056	33,960	3,356	167,887

Notes appear at end of table

(continued)

TABLE Ad25-50   Intercontinental emigration of citizens – annual averages, by country of departure: 1846–1925
Continued

		From Europe				From Asia		From Africa	
		Spain							
Years	Portugal	Intercontinental passengers	Intercontinental emigrants	Malta (British)		British India	Japan	St. Helena	Cape Verde
	Ad43 [9]	Ad44	Ad45	Ad46		Ad47	Ad48	Ad49	Ad50
	Number	Number	Number	Number		Number	Number	Number	Number
1846–1850	144	255	—	—		10,919	—	—	—
1851–1855	5,265	865	—	—		18,535	—	—	—
1856–1860	8,082	1,850	—	—		29,768	—	—	—
1861–1865	8,082	1,878	—	—		21,639	—	—	—
1866–1870	7,762	4,622	—	—		14,120	—	—	—
1871–1875	14,649	7,109	—	—		19,425	—	—	—
1876–1880	11,565	5,758	—	—		18,316	—	—	—
1881–1885	16,576	47,892	—	—		14,662	—	—	—
1886–1890	20,497	76,161	—	—		12,466	—	—	—
1891–1895	31,035	77,904	—	—		14,820	—	—	—
1896–1900	22,135	80,307	—	—		19,123	17,984	—	—
1901–1905	25,371	72,209	—	—		17,728	10,883	1,805	—
1906–1910	39,428	145,958	135,997	—		15,009	15,506	127	—
1911–1915	53,948	166,259	120,416	1,061		9,100	13,187	101	2,687
1916–1920	26,407	94,901	69,101	6,349		2,099	15,669	87	1,890
1921–1925	19,382	98,292	76,703	1,725		826	9,697	165	1,024

[1] Figures are annual averages covering the five-year intervals shown; multiply by 5 to obtain the total number of people who migrated over any five-year period.

[2] Excludes emigrants from the British Isles (1911–1924), Spain (1906–1924), Ireland (1876–1924), and Poland (1891–1915), as well as the third-class passengers from Portugal (1921–1924).

[3] For 1846–1870, figures are for Austria only. For 1871–1913, port statistics for Austria and Hungary are combined. For the territory of Austria-Hungary, the following are included: the emigrants from Austria, Hungary, and Czechoslovakia; 50 percent of the emigrants from Romania; 75 percent of the emigrants from the Serb, Croat, and Slovene state; and 33.3 percent of the emigrants from Poland.

[4] No data (1847–1848, 1914–1915, 1916–1919). Excludes Hungary (through 1850).

[5] Antwerp statistics.

[6] Emigrants from Irish ports only.

[7] Includes some aliens.

[8] Via German ports only. Through 1913, includes emigrants from Finland and Poland.

[9] Passport statistics. Port statistics for 1921 record 25,006 emigrants.

[10] 1868–1870.

[11] For 1899–1913, includes emigrants to the United Kingdom.

Source

Imre Ferenczi and Walter F. Willcox, *International Migrations,* volume 1, *Statistics Compiled on Behalf of the International Labour Office, Geneva, with Introduction and Notes* (National Bureau of Economic Research, 1929), Table 1, pp. 230–1, 349.

Documentation

The figures refer to migrants who moved to a country on an entirely different continent from the one in which they originally resided. Ferenczi and Wilcox adopted the broadest possible definition of emigrant and included "all persons going from one continent to another with a view to residing there for over a year, even if the destination was a colonial possession of a country to which the migrant belonged" (p. 56). In the nineteenth and early twentieth centuries, the period covered by these figures, the bulk of intercontinental emigration was out of Europe (and to a lesser degree out of Asia) and into the Americas, Australia, and New Zealand.

Records of emigration are, in general, much less complete than those of immigration. Many countries forbade the emigration of their residents, primarily because potential émigrés were overwhelmingly young-adult males who were subject to the military draft. Persons who circumvented the restrictions against emigration also circumvented enumeration. In countries where emigration was legal, governments tended to be less concerned with keeping records of these outward movements than they were with documenting inward movements.

Scholars' primary use of emigration statistics has been as a check on the coverage and reliability of immigration statistics, since one country's emigrants are another's immigrants. They have also been used to estimate reverse migration, the return of former emigrants back to their home countries. The extent of this return migration was increasing in the late nineteenth and early twentieth centuries as the cost of transportation was falling. See Dudley Baines, *Emigration from Europe, 1815–1930* (Cambridge University Press, 1995).

Ferenczi and Willcox assembled the series in this table, as well as those in Table Ad51-79, at the behest of the Social Science Research Council, which commissioned the National Bureau of Economic Research to assemble quantitative evidence on international migration from the official records of the many different countries around the world that had experienced extensive emigration, immigration, or both. The data-collection effort began in 1924 and was aided by the cooperation of the International Labour Office in Geneva, Switzerland. Tables Ad25-79 report summary statistics only. Ferenczi and Willcox report individual country statistics in considerable detail.

TABLE Ad51–79   Intercontinental immigration of aliens – annual averages, by country of destination: 1821–1925[1]

Contributed by Susan B. Carter

	Canada	New Brunswick (Brit.)	Nova Scotia (Brit.)	Newfoundland (Brit.)	Prince Edward Island (Brit.)	United States	Mexico	British West Indies	Cuba	Guadeloupe (Fr.)
	Ad51	Ad52 [2]	Ad53 [2]	Ad54 [2]	Ad55 [2]	Ad56 [3]	Ad57	Ad58 [4]	Ad59	Ad60 [5]
Years	Number	Number	Number	Number	Number	Number	Number	Number	Number	Number
1821–1825	900	—	—	—	611	7,851	—	—	—	—
1826–1830	18,126	—	—	—	211	19,418	—	—	—	—
1831–1835	33,443	—	—	—	84	46,493	—	—	—	—
1836–1840	16,512	—	—	—	93	66,963	—	2,146	—	—
1841–1845	27,941	4,639	1,225	560	36	87,829	—	6,504	—	—
1846–1850	41,177	6,584	662	501	—	238,299	—	10,241	—	—
1851–1855	38,281	2,884	222	180	—	342,655	—	5,226	—	—
1856–1860	17,255	419	151	248	—	164,510	—	7,335	—	1,276
1861–1865	20,404	719	358	73	—	153,389	—	11,335	—	1,134
1866–1870	36,259	—	—	—	—	309,292	—	8,910	—	1,510
1871–1875	29,719	—	—	—	—	308,417	—	10,769	—	970
1876–1880	14,237	—	—	—	—	176,335	—	8,802	—	1,916
1881–1885	38,994	—	—	—	—	516,194	—	6,857	—	1,674
1886–1890	32,846	—	—	—	—	454,186	—	6,284	—	—
1891–1895	25,979	—	—	—	—	424,643	—	7,585	—	—
1896–1900	23,749 [2]	—	—	—	—	312,060	—	4,563	—	—
1901–1905	67,785	—	—	784 [14]	—	764,121	—	11,202	24,581	—
1906–1910	138,062	—	—	885	—	949,182	—	39,019	23,939	—
1911–1915	170,549	—	—	712 [15]	—	804,570	13,013	50,979	27,345	—
1916–1920	40,428	—	—	—	—	150,355	8,393	46,760	46,043	—
1921–1925	81,559	—	—	—	—	426,090 [16]	18,492	63,593	39,236	—

	To the Americas					To Asia	To Oceania			
	Dutch Guiana	Argentina	Brazil	Paraguay	Uruguay	Philippines (U.S.)	Australia	New South Wales	Queensland	Victoria
	Ad61	Ad62 [6]	Ad63 [7]	Ad64	Ad65 [8]	Ad66	Ad67 [9,10]	Ad68	Ad69 [10]	Ad70 [10]
Years	Number	Number	Number	Number	Number	Number	Number	Number	Number	Number
1821–1825	—	—	207	—	—	—	—	—	—	—
1826–1830	—	—	1,278	—	—	—	—	—	—	—
1831–1835	—	—	—	—	—	—	—	—	—	—
1836–1840	—	—	568	—	2,820	—	—	—	—	—
1841–1845	—	—	374	—	8,770	—	—	—	—	—
1846–1850	—	—	985	—	—	—	—	—	—	—
1851–1855	—	—	7,816	—	—	—	—	—	—	—
1856–1860	77	5,000	16,534	—	—	—	—	—	—	—
1861–1865	—	9,375	10,194	—	—	—	—	—	6,663	—
1866–1870	463	22,539	9,320	—	17,031	—	—	—	3,231	9,183
1871–1875	—	29,719	16,263	—	14,565	—	—	—	7,708	6,622
1876–1880	696	22,438	27,563	—	7,296	—	—	—	8,434	10,022
1881–1885	—	51,037	27,096	165	10,408	—	—	—	15,875	16,964
1886–1890	881	117,187	79,085	905	17,662	—	—	—	9,248	22,219
1891–1895	1,498	47,250	133,274	323	9,505	—	—	—	1,998	9,286
1896–1900	1,057	82,415	95,506	222	8,460	—	—	—	2,648	13,707
1901–1905	1,054	105,206	57,606	318	7,117	—	46,478	16,454	1,922	11,328
1906–1910	1,954	247,615	80,218	970	—	—	76,632	23,760	4,779	7,205
1911–1915	1,587	202,367	121,633	929	9,758	3,573	124,880	44,569	9,959	19,118
1916–1920	1,670	38,617	36,802	315	5,536	7,500	59,596	17,984	2,894	4,125 [17]
1921–1925	1,256	145,588	60,306	294	7,569	7,754	95,465	30,961	5,332	—

Notes appear at end of table

(continued)

TABLE Ad51-79   Intercontinental immigration of aliens – annual averages, by country of destination: 1821-1925
Continued

Years	To Oceania				To Africa				
	New Zealand	Fiji (Brit.)	New Caledonia (Fr.)	Hawai'i (U.S.)	Mauritius (Brit.)	Seychelles (Brit.)	Natal	Cape of Good Hope	Union of South Africa
	Ad71 [10,11]	Ad72 [12]	Ad73	Ad74	Ad75 [13]	Ad76	Ad77	Ad78 [10]	Ad79 [4]
	Number	Number	Number	Number	Number	Number	Number	Number	Number
1821–1825	—	—	—	—	—	—	—	—	—
1826–1830	—	—	—	—	—	—	—	—	—
1831–1835	—	—	—	—	—	—	—	—	—
1836–1840	—	—	—	—	4,245 [20]	—	—	—	—
1841–1845	—	—	—	—	18,846	—	—	—	—
1846–1850	—	—	—	—	6,985	—	—	—	—
1851–1855	2,192	—	—	—	13,941	—	—	—	—
1856–1860	5,316	—	—	—	22,979	—	—	—	—
1861–1865	9,628	—	—	—	11,575	—	—	—	—
1866–1870	4,071	—	—	—	3,022	—	—	—	—
1871–1875	17,411	—	—	—	5,365	—	—	—	—
1876–1880	11,732	—	—	—	2,267	—	—	—	—
1881–1885	7,699	2,262 [19]	—	—	1,981	—	3,091	—	—
1886–1890	5,223	903	—	—	1,858	—	1,558	—	—
1891–1895	3,551	1,398	—	—	847	—	3,589	—	—
1896–1900	3,455	1,316	413	—	823	—	4,741	—	—
1901–1905	6,400	2,125	541	—	5,148	394	6,889	43,568	—
1906–1910	11,459	2,890	267	—	3,659	350	6,345	30,606	—
1911–1915	13,235	3,037	652	9,358	3,741	340	4,698 [21]	34,073	9,485
1916–1920	6,242	351	380	7,733	2,100	294	—	—	8,439
1921–1925	— [18]	1,844	811	12,321	3,371	304	—	—	15,555

[1] Figures are annual averages covering the five-year intervals shown; multiply by 5 to obtain the total number of people who migrated over any five-year period.

[2] Includes aliens in transit.

[3] 1821-1867, alien passengers arrived; 1868-1903, immigrants arrived; 1904-1906, aliens admitted; 1907-1924 immigrant aliens admitted.

[4] For 1834-1875, includes all British West Indian colonies; for 1876-1900, includes only British Guiana and Trinidad and Tobago; for 1901-1905, also includes Bermuda and Jamaica; for 1906-1924, also includes Barbados; for 1906-1914, also includes the Bahamas. The annual averages are the sums of the averages of the colonies in question. From 1902, and so far as data were available, the figures comprise not only the unskilled Asian laborers, but all immigrants, including those from continental Europe.

[5] East Indians introduced.

[6] Second- and third-class passengers by sea.

[7] For 1821-1907, includes a certain number of Brazilians and citizens of other South American countries; for 1908-1924, these have been excluded.

[8] Includes a certain number of citizens and continental immigrants through 1878; thereafter, series covers alien passengers by sea from abroad landing at the Port of Montevideo (all classes), citizens of any South American state.

[9] Includes Pacific Islanders, Papuans, and a small number of other immigrants from Oceania into Australia.

[10] Passengers.

[11] Arrivals, except those arriving from British possessions, 1853-1870, and those arriving from the Australian commonwealth, 1871-1919.

[12] East Indian and Polynesian laborers; 1901-1908, indentured East Indians only.

[13] For 1834-1875, immigration principally from East Indies; for 1876-1900, East Indian immigrants; for 1901-1924, immigrants from all countries.

[14] Intending settlers only.

[15] 1911-1913 only.

[16] Corresponding average for calendar years is 349,623.

[17] 1916 only.

[18] 11,651 intercontinental immigrants (data for other years in series are passengers).

[19] Except 1883.

[20] 1834-1839.

[21] Indentured East Indians only.

Source

Imre Ferenczi and Walter F. Willcox, *International Migrations*, volume I, *Statistics Compiled on Behalf of the International Labour Office, Geneva, with Introduction and Notes* (National Bureau of Economic Research, 1929), Table 6, pp. 236-8, 350.

Documentation

See the text for Table Ad25-50.

TABLE Ad80–81   Emigrants from the United States to Canada: 1881–1998

Contributed by Susan B. Carter and Richard Sutch

Year	U.S. emigrants to Canada Ad80 [1] Number	Canadians returning to Canada Ad81 Number	Year	U.S. emigrants to Canada Ad80 [1] Number	Canadians returning to Canada Ad81 Number	Year	U.S. emigrants to Canada Ad80 [1] Number	Canadians returning to Canada Ad81 Number
1881	21,822	—	1930	25,632	31,608	1970	24,474	—
1882	58,372	—	1931	15,195	20,352	1971	24,366	—
1883	78,508	—	1932	13,709	18,220	1972	22,618	—
1884	65,886	—	1933	8,500	10,209	1973	25,242	—
1885	57,506	—	1934	6,071	7,272	1974	26,541	—
1886	40,650	—	1935	5,291	6,378	1975	20,155	—
1887	41,046	—	1936	4,876	5,168	1976	17,315	—
1888	44,952	—	1937	5,555	5,167	1977	12,888	—
1889	67,896	—	1938	5,833	4,659	1978	9,946	—
1890	50,336	—	1939	5,649	4,610	1979	9,617	—
1891	52,516	—	1940	7,134	4,990	1980	9,900	—
1897	2,412	—	1941	6,594	3,564	1981	8,695	—
1898	9,119	—	1942	5,098	3,467	1982	9,360	—
1899	11,945	—	1943	4,401	2,333	1983	7,381	—
1900	8,543 [3]	—	1944	4,509	2,210	1984	6,922	—
1904	39,950	—	1945	6,394	2,689	1985	6,669	—
1905	39,935	—	1946	11,469	5,177	1986	7,275	—
1906	59,392	—	1947	9,440	8,970	1987	7,967	—
1907	51,584	—	1948	7,381	5,678	1988	6,537	—
1908	51,750	—	1949	7,744	4,050	1989	6,931	—
1909	80,409	—	1950	7,799	3,518	1990	6,084	—
1910	108,300	—	1951	7,732	3,635	1991	6,597	—
1911	112,028	—	1952	9,306	4,707	1992	7,537	—
1912	120,095	—	1953	9,379	4,606	1994 [2]	6,705	—
1913	97,712	—	1954	10,110	4,516	1995 [2]	5,851	—
1914	50,213	—	1955	10,392	3,942	1996 [2]	5,466	—
1915	24,297	—	1956	9,777	4,740	1997 [2]	5,462	—
1916	41,779	—	1957	11,008	5,426	1998 [2]	4,696	—
1917	65,737	—	1958	10,846	5,297			
1918	31,769	—	1959	11,338	5,243			
1919	42,129	—	1960	11,247	5,233			
1920	40,188	—	1961	11,516	—			
1921	23,888	—	1962	11,643	—			
1922	17,534	—	1963	11,736	—			
1923	16,716	—	1964	12,565	—			
1924	16,042	—	1965	15,143	—			
1925	17,717	39,987	1966	17,514	—			
1926	20,944	62,293	1967	19,038	—			
1927	23,818	42,078	1968	20,422	—			
1928	29,933	34,120	1969	22,785	—			
1929	31,852	30,479						

[1] Beginning in 1955, figures are for persons whose country of last residence was the United States.

[2] Year beginning July 1.

[3] Six months ended June 30.

Sources

Series Ad80. 1881–1900: Imre Ferenczi and Walter F. Willcox, *International Migrations*, volume 1, *Statistics Compiled on Behalf of the International Labour Office, Geneva, with Introduction and Notes* (National Bureau of Economic Research, 1929), Table II, p. 361. 1904–1954: M. C. Urquhart, editor, *Historical Statistics of Canada* (Cambridge University Press, 1965), series A337. 1955–1998: Statistics Canada Web site.

Series Ad81. 1925–1960: Urquhart (1965), series A337.

TABLE Ad82–89   Foreign-born arrivals to Hawai'i, by nationality: 1852–1899

Contributed by Susan B. Carter

	All nationalities	Chinese		German	Japanese	Portuguese	South Seas Islanders	Other nationalities
		Schmidt estimates	Glick estimates					
	Ad82	Ad83	Ad84	Ad85	Ad86	Ad87	Ad88	Ad89
Year	Number	Number	Number	Number	Number	Number	Number	Number
1852	293	293	293	0	0	0	0	0
1853	64	64	64	0	0	0	0	0
1854	12	12	12	0	0	0	0	0
1855	61	61	61	0	0	0	0	0
1856	23	23	23	0	0	0	0	0
1857	14	14	14	0	0	0	0	0
1858	13	13	13	0	0	0	0	0
1859	171	171	171	0	0	0	0	0
1860	21	21	21	0	0	0	0	0
1861	2	2	2	0	0	0	0	0
1862	13	13	13	0	0	0	0	0
1863	8	8	8	0	0	0	0	0
1864	9	9	9	0	0	0	0	0
1865	654	615	615	0	0	0	39	0
1866	117	117	117	0	0	0	0	0
1867	214	210	210	0	0	0	4	0
1868	199	51	51	0	148	0	0	0
1869	204	78	78	0	0	0	126	0
1870	327	305	305	0	0	0	22	0
1871	248	223	223	0	0	0	25	0
1872	61	61	61	0	0	0	0	0
1873	48	48	48	0	0	0	0	0
1874	69	62	62	0	0	0	7	0
1875	151	151	151	0	0	0	0	0
1876	1,283	1,283	1,283	0	0	0	0	0
1877	557	557	557	0	0	0	0	0
1878	2,858	2,464	2,464	0	0	180	214	0
1879	4,549	3,652	3,812	0	0	419	478	0
1880	3,547	2,422	2,505	0	0	332	793	0
1881	5,722	3,898	3,924	124	0	840	245	615 [1]
1882	3,927	1,367	1,362	183	0	2,356	21	0
1883	9,262	4,295	4,243	826	0	3,812	329	0
1884	4,363	2,693	2,708	18	0	1,532	120	0
1885	5,194	2,924	3,108	25	1,946	278	21	0
1886	1,784	338	1,766	0	979	467	0	0
1887	1,429	0	1,546	0	1,429	0	0	0
1888	4,554	0	1,526	0	4,211	343	0	0
1889	2,035	0	439	0	2,035	0	0	0
1890	3,764	0	654	0	3,764	0	0	0
1891	6,271	478	1,386	0	5,793	0	0	0
1892	3,129	0	1,802	0	3,129	0	0	0
1893	4,158	95	981	0	4,063	0	0	0
1894	5,428	1,414	1,459	0	3,647	367	0	0
1895	3,270	1,067	2,734	0	2,203	0	0	0
1896	8,656	4,140	5,280	0	4,516	0	0	0
1897	3,122	2,137	4,481	227	758	0	0	0
1898	10,274	0	3,100	0	9,888	0	0	386 [2]
1899	19,932	24	975	0	19,908	0	0	0

[1] Norwegians.

[2] 372 Galicians and 14 Americans.

Sources

Series Ad82–83 and Ad85–89. Robert C. Schmitt, *Historical Statistics of Hawaii* (University Press of Hawaii, 1977), Table 3.6, pp. 97–8.

Series Ad84. Clarence E. Glick, *Sojourners and Settlers: Chinese Migrants in Hawaii* (Hawaii Chinese History Center and University Press of Hawaii, 1980), p. 12.

Documentation

Figures include several thousand duplications of arrivals of persons who temporarily left the islands and then returned. Data for Europeans are limited to those who came to Hawai'i under the auspices of the Bureau of Immigration and as part of some organized scheme of immigration. There do not appear to be data on arrivals from the United States.

Robert Barde, Susan B. Carter, and Richard Sutch

TABLE Ad90-97   Immigrants, by continent of last residence: 1820-1997[1,2]

Contributed by Robert Barde, Susan B. Carter, and Richard Sutch

Fiscal year	Total Ad90 Number	Europe Ad91 Number	Asia Ad92 Number	North America Ad93 [3] Number	South America Ad94 Number	Africa Ad95 Number	Oceania Ad96 Number	Other or unknown Ad97 Number
1820	8,385	7,691	5	376	11	1	1	300
1821	9,127	5,936	0	295	8	2	0	2,886
1822	6,911	4,418	1	371	7	0	2	2,112
1823	6,354	4,016	0	362	20	0	0	1,956
1824	7,912	4,965	1	534	25	0	0	2,387
1825	10,199	8,543	1	779	67	1	0	808
1826	10,837	9,751	1	768	63	0	0	254
1827	18,875	16,719	1	526	54	4	79	1,492
1828	27,382	24,729	3	2,013	77	6	0	554
1829	22,520	12,523	2	3,226	73	1	0	6,695
1830	23,322	7,217	0	2,159	137	2	0	13,807
1831	22,633	13,039	1	2,152	42	2	1	7,396
1832	60,482	34,193	4	2,697	174	2	0	23,412
(TQ)	7,303	—	—	—	—	—	—	7,303
1833	58,640	29,111	3	3,255	27	1	0	26,243
1834	65,365	57,510	6	2,705	74	1	0	5,069
1835	45,374	41,987	17	3,167	145	14	3	41
1836	76,242	70,465	4	4,790	146	6	2	829
1837	79,340	71,039	11	3,537	91	2	0	4,660
1838	38,914	34,070	1	2,918	72	10	0	1,843
1839	68,069	64,148	0	3,568	49	10	1	293
1840	84,066	80,126	1	3,779	36	6	2	116
1841	80,289	76,216	3	3,210	219	14	3	624
1842	104,565	99,945	7	3,892	102	3	0	616
1843 [4]	52,496	49,013	11	2,792	62	6	5	607
1844	78,615	74,745	6	3,679	61	14	0	110
1845	114,371	109,301	6	4,955	80	4	0	25
1846	154,416	146,315	11	5,433	92	1	0	2,564
1847	234,968	229,117	12	5,161	70	0	1	607
1848	226,527	218,025	8	7,839	150	10	3	492
1849	297,024	286,501	11	8,714	190	3	0	1,605
1850	310,004 [6]	250,939 [6]	7	11,268 [6]	2,462 [6]	0	17	45,131 [6]
(TQ)	59,976	57,384	0	1,947	91	0	0	554
1851	379,466 [6]	369,510 [6]	2	9,644 [6]	59 [6]	5 [6]	0	143 [6]
1852	371,603	362,484	4	7,656	39	0	0	1,420
1853	368,645	361,576	47	5,992	38	8	0	984
1854	427,833	405,542	13,100	8,397	136	0	31	627
1855	200,877	187,729	3,540	9,069	191	14	12	322
1856	200,436	186,083	4,747	8,874	184	6	—	542
1857	251,306	216,224	5,945	6,728	83	25	—	22,301
1858	123,126	111,354	5,133	5,690	131	17	—	801
1859	121,282	110,949	3,461	5,311	155	11	—	1,395
1860	153,640	141,209	5,476	6,135	208	126	—	486
1861	91,918	81,200	7,528	2,666	97	47	—	380
1862	91,985	83,710	3,640	4,029	146	12	—	448
1863	176,282	163,733	7,216	4,053	94	3	—	1,183
1864	193,418	185,233	2,982	4,455	152	37	—	559
1865	248,120	214,048	2,947	22,630	148	49	—	8,298
1866 [5]	318,568	278,916	2,411	33,288	294	33	—	3,626
1867	315,722	283,751	3,961	24,491	224	25	—	3,270
1868	138,840	130,090	5,171	3,333	82	3	—	161
1869	352,768	315,963	12,949	23,676	91	72	—	17
1870	387,203	328,626	15,825	42,589	69	31	36	27
1871	321,350	265,145	7,240	48,739	96	24	21	85
1872	404,806	352,155	7,825	42,103	102	41	2,416	164
1873	459,803	397,541	20,325	40,169	166	28	1,414	160
1874	313,339	262,783	13,838	35,195	144	58	1,193	128

Notes appear at end of table

(continued)

TABLE Ad90–97   Immigrants, by continent of last residence: 1820–1997   *Continued*

Fiscal year	Total	Europe	Asia	North America	South America	Africa	Oceania	Other or unknown
	Ad90	Ad91	Ad92	Ad93 [3]	Ad94	Ad95	Ad96	Ad97
	Number	Number	Number	Number	Number	Number	Number	Number
1875	227,498	182,961	16,499	26,508	132	54	1,268	76
1876	169,986	120,920	22,943	24,530	156	89	1,312	36
1877	141,857	106,195	10,640	23,978	87	16	914	27
1878	138,469	101,612	9,014	27,116	88	18	606	15
1879	177,826	134,259	9,660	32,974	69	12	816	36
1880	457,257	348,691	5,839	101,604	88	18	954	63
1881	669,431	528,545	11,982	127,467	110	33	1,191	103
1882	788,992	648,186	39,629	100,038	91	60	889	99
1883	603,322	522,587	8,113	71,652	77	67	747	79
1884	518,592	453,686	510	63,274	65	59	900	98
1885	395,346	353,083	198	41,159	44	112	679	71
1886	334,203	329,529	317	2,780	246	122	1,136	73
1887	490,109	482,829	615	4,904	366	40	1,282	73
1888	546,889	538,131	843	4,962	440	65	2,387	61
1889	444,427	434,790	1,725	5,032	427	187	2,196	70
1890	455,302	445,680	4,448	3,395	438	112	1,167	62
1891	560,319	546,085	7,678	4,418	664	103	1,301	70
1892	579,663	570,876	— [7]	— [7]	— [7]	— [7]	267	8,520 [7]
1893	439,730	429,324	2,392	2,593	— [7]	— [7]	248	5,173 [7]
1894	285,631	277,052	4,690	3,512	39	24	244	70
1895	258,536	250,342	4,495	3,472	36	36	155	0
1896	343,267	329,067	6,764	7,268	35	21	112	0
1897	230,832	216,397	9,662	4,488	49	37	199	0
1898	229,299	217,786	8,637	2,588	39	48	201	0
1899	311,715	297,349	8,972	4,227	89	51	810	217
1900	448,572	424,700	17,946	5,331	124	30	428	13
1901	487,918	469,237	13,593	4,213	203	173	498	1
1902	648,743	619,068	22,271	6,361	337	37	566	103
1903	857,046	814,507	29,966	10,434	589	176	1,349	25
1904	812,870	767,933	26,186	14,753	1,667	686	1,555	90
1905	1,026,499	974,273	23,925	22,641	2,576	757	2,166	161
1906	1,100,825	1,018,365	22,300	21,856	2,757	712	1,733	33,102 [8]
1907	1,285,349	1,199,566	40,524	38,983	2,779	1,486	1,989	22
1908	782,870	691,901	28,365	57,682	2,315	1,411	1,179	17
1909	751,786	654,875	12,904	80,302	1,906	858	892	49
1910	1,041,570	926,291	23,533	87,383	2,151	1,072	1,097	43
1911	878,587	764,757	17,428	91,315	3,049	956	1,043	39
1912	838,172	718,875	21,449	92,937	2,989	1,009	898	15
1913	1,197,892	1,055,855	35,358	99,659	4,248	1,409	1,340	23
1914	1,218,480	1,058,391	34,273	116,826	5,869	1,539	1,446	136
1915	326,700	197,919	15,211	107,405	3,801	934	1,399	31
1916	298,826	145,699	13,204	133,138	4,286	894	1,574	31
1917	295,403	133,083	12,756	140,848	6,931	566	1,142	77
1918	110,618	31,063	12,701	62,075	3,343	299	1,090	47
1919	141,132	24,627	12,674	99,015	3,271	189	1,310	46
1920	430,001	246,295	17,505	158,554	4,112	648	2,185	702
1921	805,228	652,364	25,034	119,103	5,015	1,301	2,281	130
1922	309,556	216,385	14,263	74,780	2,668	520	915	25
1923	522,919	307,920	13,705	195,235	4,737	548	759	15
1924	706,896	364,339	22,065	309,585	9,270	900	679	58
1925	294,314	148,366	3,578	139,026	2,470	412	462	0
1926	304,488	155,562	3,413	141,286	3,107	529	591	0
1927	335,175	168,368	3,669	158,095	3,777	520	746	0
1928	307,255	158,513	3,380	140,115	4,166	475	606	0
1929	279,678	158,598	3,758	112,474	3,703	509	636	0
1930	241,700	147,438	4,535	84,802	3,302	572	1,051	0
1931	97,139	61,909	3,345	29,121	1,695	417	652	0
1932	35,576	20,579	1,931	11,875	702	186	303	0
1933	23,068	12,383	552	9,488	437	71	137	0
1934	29,470	17,210	600	11,054	355	104	147	0

Notes appear at end of table

TABLE Ad90–97   Immigrants, by continent of last residence: 1820–1997   *Continued*

Fiscal year	Total Ad90 Number	Europe Ad91 Number	Asia Ad92 Number	North America Ad93 [3] Number	South America Ad94 Number	Africa Ad95 Number	Oceania Ad96 Number	Other or unknown Ad97 Number
1935	34,956	22,778	745	10,701	473	118	141	0
1936	36,329	23,480	793	11,294	492	105	165	0
1937	50,244	31,863	1,149	16,165	738	155	174	0
1938	67,895	44,495	2,492	19,601	885	174	248	0
1939	82,998	63,138	2,281	16,224	915	218	222	0
1940	70,756	50,454	2,050	16,707	1,115	202	228	0
1941	51,776	26,541	1,971	20,229	2,216	564	255	0
1942	28,781	11,153	615	15,388	989	473	163	0
1943	23,725	4,920	342	17,469	693	141	160	0
1944	28,551	4,509	231	21,924	1,160	112	615	0
1945	38,119	5,943	461	28,037	1,609	406	1,663	0
1946	108,721	52,852	2,108	43,433	2,633	1,516	6,106	73
1947	147,292	83,535	6,733	49,659	3,094	1,284	2,960	27
1948	170,570	103,544	11,907	49,687	3,046	1,027	1,336	23
1949	188,317	129,592	7,595	46,218	3,107	995	776	34
1950	249,187	199,115	4,508	40,899	3,284	849	517	15
1951	205,717	149,545	7,149	44,035	3,596	845	527	20
1952	265,520	193,626	9,328	56,458	4,591	931	578	8
1953	170,434	82,352	8,231	72,139	5,511	989	782	430
1954	208,177	92,121	9,970	89,012	6,575	1,248	910	8,341
1955	237,790	110,591	10,935	102,782	7,654	1,203	1,028	3,597
1956	321,625	156,866	17,327	135,526	9,187	1,351	1,346	22
1957	326,867	169,625	20,008	123,309	10,851	1,600	1,458	16
1958	253,265	115,198	20,870	98,828	14,304	2,008	2,045	12
1959	260,686	138,191	25,259	80,196	12,865	1,992	2,162	21
1960	265,398	120,221	21,429	103,031	16,494	2,057	2,140	26
1961	271,344	108,598	19,264	120,485	19,095	2,016	1,881	5
1962	283,763	104,021	20,217	133,321	22,550	1,834	1,819	1
1963	306,260	109,097	23,211	142,207	27,759	1,982	1,977	27
1964	292,248	108,215	21,279	123,753	34,891	2,015	2,070	25
1965	296,697	101,468	20,040	137,262	33,757	1,949	2,199	22
1966	323,040	115,898	40,113	134,438	28,113	1,967	2,500	11
1967	361,972	128,775	57,574	151,673	18,562	2,577	2,811	0
1968	454,448	129,022	56,298	238,745	23,991	3,220	3,172	0
1969	358,579	114,052	72,959	138,503	25,542	4,460	3,061	2
1970	373,326	109,809	91,059	138,033	23,694	7,099	3,632	0
1971	370,478	91,509	98,062	149,002	22,678	5,844	3,383	0
1972	384,685	86,321	115,978	151,601	21,393	5,472	3,737	183
1973	400,063	91,183	119,984	157,181	22,423	5,537	3,755	0
1974	394,861	80,407	127,003	154,882	23,964	5,227	3,378	0
1975	386,194	72,774	129,196	150,549	24,183	5,868	3,624	0
1976	398,613	73,035	146,725	145,625	23,555	5,723	3,950	0
(TQ)	103,676	18,641	37,725	37,910	6,362	1,967	1,071	0
1977	462,315	74,048	150,842	189,503	33,671	9,612	4,639	0
1978	601,442	76,156	243,596	224,390	42,080	10,336	4,884	0
1979	460,348	64,173	182,970	161,408	35,715	11,212	4,870	0
1980	530,639	72,121	236,097	164,566	39,717	13,981	2,358	1,799
1981	596,600	66,695	264,343	210,427	35,913	15,029	2,055	2,138
1982	594,131	69,174	313,291	158,057	35,448	14,314	2,147	1,700
1983	559,763	58,867	277,701	168,487	36,087	15,084	1,984	1,553
1984	543,903	69,879	247,775	169,475	38,636	13,594	4,249	295
1985	570,009	69,526	255,164	185,467	40,052	15,236	4,552	12
1986	601,708	69,224	258,546	211,428	42,650	15,500	4,352	8
1987	601,516	67,967	248,293	220,244	44,782	15,730	4,437	63
1988	643,025	71,854	254,745	253,260	41,646	17,124	4,324	72
1989	1,090,924	94,338	296,420	612,827	59,812	22,485	4,956	86
1990	1,536,483	124,026	321,879	963,706	86,821	32,797	6,999	255
1991	1,827,167	146,671	342,157	1,217,272	80,308	33,542	7,061	156
1992	973,977	153,260	344,802	389,469	55,725	24,707	5,994	20
1993	904,292	165,711	345,425	307,399	54,077	25,532	6,144	4
1994	804,416	166,279	282,449	277,668	47,505	24,864	5,647	4
1995	720,461	132,914	259,984	236,207	46,063	39,818	5,472	3
1996	915,900	151,898	300,574	345,823	61,990	49,605	6,008	2
1997	798,378	122,358	258,561	307,019	52,600	44,668	4,855	8,317

Notes appear on next page

(continued)

TABLE Ad90-97 Immigrants, by continent of last residence: 1820-1997 *Continued*

(TQ) indicates transitional quarter.

[1] Fiscal year varies as follows: 1820-1832, year ending September 30; 1833-1842, year ending December 31; 1843-1850, year ending September 30; 1851-1865, year ending December 31; 1866-1976, year ending June 30; 1977-1997, year ending September 30.

[2] Beginning in 1906, aliens entering the United States were recorded by "country of last permanent residence"; prior to this date they were recorded by "country whence they came."

[3] Through 1907, includes only partial count of arrivals over land borders.

[4] Three quarters ending September 30.

[5] Six months ending June 30.

[6] Data in the original source have been corrected or revised.

[7] Data for Asia, North America, South America, and Africa included under series Ad97 when the value for the continent is not available.

[8] Includes 32,987 persons returning from abroad to their homes in the United States.

Sources

1820-1926: *Annual Report of the Commissioner General of Immigration, Report for 1926*, Table 74. 1820-1855 (Oceania): William J. Bromwell, *History of Immigration to the United States* (Redfield, 1856). 1927-1931: *Annual Report of the Commissioner General of Immigration, 1931*, Table 84. 1932: *Annual Report of the Commissioner General of Immigration, 1932*, Table 2. 1933: figures for Europe were derived by subtracting published figures for 1931-1932 and 1934-1940 from decadal total in *Annual Report of the Attorney General of the United States, for Fiscal Year Ended June 30, 1941*, Table X; 1933 non-European figures from U.S. Bureau of the Census, *Historical Statistics of the United States* (U.S. Government Printing Office, 1975), based on unpublished data from the U.S. Immigration and Naturalization Service. 1934-1937: *Annual Report of the Secretary of Labor, 1937*, "Immigrant Aliens Admitted and Emigrant Aliens Departed, Years Ended June 30, 1934-1937, by Countries of Last or Intended Future Permanent Residence." 1938-1940: *Annual Report of the Attorney General of the United States, for Fiscal Year Ended June 30, 1941*, Table VII. 1941-1971: *Annual Report of the INS*, various years. 1972-1977, 1979, 1986-1988: U.S. Immigration and Naturalization Service public use data files. 1978, 1980-1985, 1989-1997: *Statistical Yearbook of the INS*, various years.

Documentation

Series Ad90. Equals series Ad1.

TABLE Ad98-105 Immigrants, by continent of birth: 1941-1997[1]

Contributed by Robert Barde, Susan B. Carter, and Richard Sutch

	Total	Europe	Asia	North America	South America	Africa	Oceania	Other and unknown
	Ad98	Ad99	Ad100	Ad101	Ad102	Ad103	Ad104	Ad105
Fiscal year	Number	Number	Number	Number	Number	Number	Number	Number
1941	51,776	36,989	1,025	12,484	742	281	255	0
1942	28,781	14,881	432	12,569	572	142	129	56
1943	23,725	8,953	362	13,718	474	83	110	25
1944	28,551	8,694	364	17,961	899	75	533	25
1945	38,119	10,141	575	24,229	1,326	267	1,535	46
1946	108,721	64,877	1,921	33,125	1,755	1,098	5,746	199
1947	147,292	96,865	4,098	40,295	2,421	849	2,532	232
1948	170,570	115,750	7,626	42,270	2,768	840	1,110	206
1949	188,317	138,301	6,355	39,469	2,639	737	602	214
1950	249,187	206,341	4,821	34,004	2,777	689	443	112
1951	205,717	161,065	5,147	35,482	2,724	831	449	19
1952	265,520	202,749	9,456	48,092	3,902	847	451	23
1953	170,434	96,082	8,000	60,107	4,691	1,046	496	12
1954	208,177	110,944	11,854	77,772	5,523	1,367	706	11
1955	237,790	127,286	12,337	90,732	5,599	1,186	595	55
1956	321,625	175,119	17,974	119,417	6,846	1,441	800	28
1957	326,867	184,656	23,561	106,942	9,002	1,673	1,016	17
1958	253,265	137,796	20,382	80,788	11,039	2,040	1,210	10
1959	260,686	157,733	24,602	64,740	9,792	2,631	1,178	10
1960	265,398	138,785	24,956	85,075	13,048	2,319	1,179	36
1961	271,344	126,979	22,299	103,388	15,470	1,980	1,204	24
1962	283,763	118,778	23,019	121,226	17,592	1,931	1,203	14
1963	306,260	124,677	25,021	129,705	22,919	2,639	1,289	10
1964	292,248	122,104	21,845	112,973	31,102	2,887	1,325	12
1965	296,697	113,424	20,683	126,729	30,962	3,383	1,512	4
1966	323,040	123,469	41,432	127,340	25,836	3,137	1,820	6
1967	361,972	137,301	61,446	140,138	16,517	4,236	2,328	6
1968	454,448	137,754	58,989	228,060	21,976	5,078	2,588	3
1969	358,579	118,028	75,679	132,426	23,928	5,876	2,639	3

Notes appear at end of table

(continued)

TABLE Ad98–105   Immigrants, by continent of birth: 1941–1997   *Continued*

Fiscal year	Total	Europe	Asia	North America	South America	Africa	Oceania	Other and unknown
	Ad98	Ad99	Ad100	Ad101	Ad102	Ad103	Ad104	Ad105
	Number	Number	Number	Number	Number	Number	Number	Number
1970	373,326	116,039	94,883	129,114	21,973	8,115	3,198	4
1971	370,478	96,498	103,459	140,126	20,702	6,772	2,919	2
1972	384,685	89,993	121,058	144,377	19,359	6,612	3,284	2
1973	400,063	92,870	124,160	152,788	20,335	6,655	3,255	0
1974	394,861	81,212	130,662	151,445	22,307	6,182	3,051	2
1975	386,194	73,996	132,469	146,669	22,984	6,729	3,346	1
1976	398,613	72,411	149,881	142,307	22,699	7,723	3,591	1
(TQ)	103,676	18,166	39,184	36,807	6,209	2,322	988	0
1977	462,315	70,010	157,759	187,346	32,954	10,155	4,091	0
1978	601,442	73,198	249,776	220,784	41,764	11,524	4,396	0
1979	460,348	60,845	189,293	157,579	35,344	12,838	4,449	0
1980	530,639	72,121	236,094	164,772	39,717	13,981	3,954	0
1981	596,600	66,695	264,332	210,427	35,913	15,029	4,198	6
1982	594,131	69,174	313,272	158,057	35,448	14,314	3,852	14
1983	559,763	58,867	277,697	168,487	36,087	15,084	3,515	26
1984	543,903	64,076	256,272	166,706	37,460	15,540	3,818	31
1985	570,009	63,043	264,691	182,045	39,058	17,117	4,054	1
1986	601,708	62,512	268,248	207,714	41,874	17,463	3,894	3
1987	601,516	61,174	257,684	216,550	44,385	17,724	3,993	6
1988	643,025	64,797	264,465	250,009	41,007	18,882	3,339	26
1989	1,090,924	82,891	312,149	607,398	58,926	25,166	4,360	34
1990	1,536,483	112,401	338,581	957,558	85,819	35,893	6,182	49
1991	1,827,167	135,234	358,533	1,210,981	79,934	36,179	6,236	70
1992	973,977	145,392	356,955	384,047	55,308	27,086	5,169	20
1993	904,292	158,254	358,047	301,380	53,921	27,783	4,902	5
1994	804,416	160,916	292,589	272,226	47,377	26,712	4,592	4
1995	720,461	128,185	267,931	231,526	45,666	42,456	4,695	2
1996	915,900	147,581	307,807	340,540	61,769	52,889	5,309	5
1997	798,378	119,871	265,810	307,488	52,877	47,791	4,344	197

(TQ) indicates transitional quarter.

[1] Through 1976, fiscal year ending June 30; thereafter, fiscal year ending September 30.

Sources

1941: *Annual Report of the Attorney General of the United States, 1941.* 1942: *Annual Report of Lemuel B. Schofield, Special Assistant to the Attorney General in Charge of the Immigration and Naturalization Service, 1942.* 1943–1949: *U.S. Immigration and Naturalization Service Annual Report of 1952*, Table 13A. 1950: *INS Annual Report 1959*, Table 14. 1951: *INS Annual Report 1960*, Table 14. 1952: *INS Annual Report 1961*, Table 14. 1953–1955: *INS Annual Report 1962*, Table 14. 1956–1961: *INS Annual Report 1965*, Table 14. 1962–1969: *INS Statistical Yearbook 1971*, Table 14. 1970: *INS Statistical Yearbook 1970*, Table 6. 1971–1979: *INS Annual Report 1980*, Table 13. 1980–1983: *INS Statistical Yearbook 1984*, Table IMM 1.3. 1984–1990: *INS Statistical Yearbook 1992*, Table 3. 1991–1997: *INS Statistical Yearbook 1997*, Table 3.

Documentation

Series Ad98. Equals series Ad1.

TABLE Ad106–120 Immigrants, by country of last residence – Europe: 1820–1997[1]

Contributed by Robert Barde, Susan B. Carter, and Richard Sutch

	Total	Northwestern Europe				Central Europe			Eastern Europe		Greece	Italy	Portugal	Spain	Other
		Great Britain	Ireland	Scandinavia	Other	Germany	Poland[2]	Other	Former Soviet Union and Baltic states[3]	Other					
Fiscal year	Ad106	Ad107	Ad108	Ad109	Ad110	Ad111	Ad112	Ad113	Ad114	Ad115	Ad116	Ad117	Ad118[4]	Ad119[5]	Ad120
	Number	Number	Number	Number	Number	Number	Number	Number	Number	Number	Number	Number	Number	Number	Number
1820	7,691	2,410	3,614	23	452	968	5	0	14	1	0	30	35	139	0
1821	5,936	3,210	1,518	24	521	383	1	0	7	0	0	63	18	191	0
1822	4,418	1,221	2,267	28	522	148	3	0	10	4	0	35	28	152	0
1823	4,016	1,100	1,908	7	528	183	3	0	7	2	0	33	24	220	1
1824	4,965	1,264	2,345	20	671	230	4	0	7	2	5	45	13	359	0
1825	8,543	2,095	4,888	18	719	450	1	0	10	0	0	75	13	273	1
1826	9,751	2,319	5,408	26	968	511	0	0	4	2	4	57	16	436	0
1827	16,719	4,186	9,766	28	1,829	432	1	0	19	1	0	35	7	414	1
1828	24,729	5,352	12,488	60	4,700	1,851	1	0	7	6	7	34	14	209	0
1829	12,523	3,179	7,415	30	1,065	597	0	0	1	1	1	23	9	202	0
1830	7,217	1,153	2,721	19	1,305	1,976	2	0	3	2	3	9	3	21	0
1831	13,039	2,475	5,772	36	2,277	2,413	0	0	1	0	0	28	0	37	0
1832	34,193	5,331	12,436	334	5,695	10,194	34	0	52	0	1	3	5	106	2
1833	29,111	4,916	8,648	189	5,355	6,988	1	0	159	1	1	1,699	633	516	5
1834	57,510	10,490	24,474	66	4,468	17,686	54	0	15	1	0	105	44	107	0
1835	41,987	8,970	20,927	68	3,369	8,311	54	0	9	0	7	60	29	183	0
1836	70,465	13,106	30,578	473	5,189	20,707	53	0	2	3	28	115	29	180	2
1837	71,039	12,218	28,508	399	5,769	23,740	81	0	19	0	5	36	34	230	0
1838	34,070	5,420	12,645	112	3,839	11,683	41	0	13	0	4	86	24	202	1
1839	64,148	10,271	23,963	380	7,891	21,028	46	0	7	1	0	84	19	428	30
1840	80,126	2,613	39,430	207	7,978	29,704	5	0	0	1	3	60	12	136	0
1841	76,216	16,188	37,772	226	6,077	15,291	15	0	174	6	0	179	7	215	66
1842	99,945	22,005	51,342	588	5,361	20,370	10	0	28	2	1	100	15	122	1
1843[6]	49,013	8,430	19,670	1,777	4,364	14,441	17	0	6	5	4	117	32	145	5
1844	74,745	14,353	33,490	1,336	4,343	20,731	36	0	13	10	3	141	16	270	3
1845	109,301	19,210	44,821	982	9,466	34,355	6	0	1	3	2	137	14	304	0
1846	146,315	22,180	51,752	2,030	12,303	57,561	4	0	248	4	3	151	2	73	4
1847	229,117	23,302	105,536	1,320	24,336	74,281	8	0	5	2	0	164	5	158	0
1848	218,025	35,159	112,934	1,113	9,877	58,465	0	0	1	3	1	241	67	164	0
1849	286,501	55,132	159,398	3,481	7,634	60,235	4	0	44	9	0	209	26	329	0
1850	250,939[8]	41,679[8]	133,806[8]	1,373[8]	9,786[8]	63,182[8]	3[8]	0	31	13[8]	2	373[8]	366	325[8]	0
(TQ)	57,384[8]	9,406	30,198	216	1,684	15,714	2	0	0	2	0	58	0	104	0
1851	369,510[8]	51,487	221,253	2,438	20,905	72,482	10	0	1	2	0	447	50	435	0
1852	362,484	40,699	159,548	4,106	11,278	145,918	110	0	2	3	10	351	68	391	0
1853	361,576	37,576	162,649	3,396	14,205	141,946	33	0	3	15	12	555	95	1,091	0
1854	405,542	58,647	101,606	4,222	23,070	215,009	208	0	2	7	1	1,263	72	1,433	2
1855	187,729	47,572	49,627	1,349	14,571	71,918	462	0	13	9	0	1,052	205	951	0
1856	186,083	44,658	54,349	1,330	12,403	71,028	20	0	9	5	2	1,365	128	786	0
1857	216,224	58,479	54,361	2,747	6,879	91,781	124	0	25	11	4	1,007	92	714	0
1858	111,354	28,956	26,873	2,662	4,580	45,310	9	0	246	17	0	1,240	170	1,283	8
1859	110,949	26,163	35,216	1,590	3,727	41,784	106	0	91	10	1	932	46	1,283	0

Fiscal year	Total	Northwestern Europe				Central Europe			Eastern Europe						
		Great Britain	Ireland	Scandinavia	Other	Germany	Poland [2]	Other	Former Soviet Union and Baltic states [3]	Other	Greece	Italy	Portugal [4]	Spain [5]	Other
	Ad106	Ad107	Ad108	Ad109	Ad110	Ad111	Ad112	Ad113	Ad114	Ad115	Ad116	Ad117	Ad118	Ad119	Ad120
	Number	Number	Number	Number	Number	Number	Number	Number	Number	Number	Number	Number	Number	Number	Number
1860	141,209	29,737	48,637	840	5,278	54,491	82	0	65	4	1	1,019	122	932	1
1861	81,200	19,675	23,797	850	3,769	31,661	48	51	34	5	1	811	47	448	3
1862	83,710	24,639	23,351	2,550	4,386	27,529	63	111	79	11	5	566	72	348	0
1863	163,733	66,882	55,916	3,119	3,245	33,162	94	85	77	16	4	547	86	500	0
1864	185,233	53,428	63,523	2,961	5,621	57,276	165	230	256	11	5	600	240	917	0
1865	214,048	82,465	29,772	7,258	7,992	83,424	528	422	183	14	7	924	365	692	2
1866 [7]	278,916	94,924	36,690	14,495	13,648	115,892	412	93	287	18	10	1,382	344	718	3
1867	283,751	52,641	72,879	8,491	12,417	133,426	310	692	205	26	10	1,624	126	904	0
1868	130,090	24,127	32,068	11,985	4,293	55,831	0	192	141	4	0	891	174	384	0
1869	315,963	84,438	40,786	43,941	10,585	131,042	184	1,499	343	18	8	1,489	507	1,123	0
1870	328,626	103,677	56,996	30,742	9,152	118,225	223	4,425	907	6	22	2,891	697	663	0
1871	265,145	85,455	57,439	22,132	7,174	82,554	535	4,887	673	23	11	2,816	887	558	1
1872	352,155	84,912	68,732	28,575	15,614	141,109	1,647	4,410	1,018	20	12	4,190	1,306	595	15
1873	397,541	89,500	77,344	35,481	22,892	149,671	3,338	7,112	1,634	53	23	8,757	1,185	541	10
1874	262,783	62,021	53,707	19,178	15,998	87,291	1,795	8,850	4,073	62	36	7,666	1,611	485	10
1875	182,961	47,905	37,957	14,322	11,987	47,769	984	7,658	7,997	27	25	3,631	1,939	601	159
1876	120,920	29,291	19,575	12,323	10,923	31,937	925	6,276	4,775	38	19	3,015	1,277	518	28
1877	106,195	23,581	14,569	11,274	8,621	29,298	533	5,396	6,599	32	24	3,195	2,363	665	45
1878	101,612	22,150	15,932	12,254	6,929	29,313	547	5,150	3,048	29	16	4,344	1,332	457	111
1879	134,259	29,955	20,013	21,820	9,081	34,602	489	5,963	4,453	29	21	5,791	916	457	669
1880	348,691	73,273	71,603	65,657	15,042	84,638	2,177	17,267	5,014	35	23	12,354	808	389	411
1881	528,545	81,376	72,342	81,582	26,883	210,485	5,614	27,935	5,041	102	19	15,401	1,215	484	66
1882	648,186	102,991	76,432	105,326	27,796	250,630	4,672	29,150	16,918	134	126	32,159	1,436	378	38
1883	522,587	76,606	81,486	71,994	24,271	194,786	2,011	27,625	9,909	163	73	31,792	1,573	262	36
1884	453,686	65,950	63,344	52,728	18,768	179,676	4,536	36,571	12,689	388	37	16,510	1,927	300	262
1885	353,083	57,713	51,795	40,704	13,732	124,443	3,085	27,309	17,158	941	172	13,642	2,024	350	15
1886	329,529	62,929	49,619	46,735	11,737	84,403	3,939	28,680	17,800	670	104	21,315	1,194	344	60
1887	482,829	93,378	68,370	67,629	17,307	106,865	6,128	40,265	30,766	2,251	313	47,622	1,360	436	139
1888	538,131	108,692	73,513	81,924	23,251	109,717	5,826	45,811	33,487	1,393	782	51,558	1,625	526	26
1889	434,790	87,992	65,557	57,504	22,010	99,538	4,922	34,174	33,916	1,145	158	25,307	2,024	526	17
1890	445,680	69,730	53,024	50,368	20,575	92,427	11,073	56,199	35,598	723	524	52,003	2,600	813	23
1891	546,085	66,605	55,706	60,107	21,824	113,554	27,497	71,042	47,426	1,222	1,105	76,055	2,999	905	38
1892	570,876	42,215	51,383	66,295	21,731	119,168	40,536	76,937	81,511	1,331	660	61,631	3,400	4,078	0
1893	429,324	35,189	43,578	58,945	17,888	78,756	16,374	57,420	42,310	625	1,072	72,145	4,816	206	0
1894	277,052	22,520	30,231	32,400	9,514	53,989	1,941	38,638	39,278	1,027	1,356	42,977	2,190	920	71
1895	250,342	28,833	46,304	26,852	7,313	32,173	790	33,401	35,907	768	597	35,427	1,452	501	24
1896	329,067	24,565	40,262	33,199	7,611	31,885	691	65,103	51,445	954	2,175	68,060	2,766	351	0
1897	216,397	12,752	28,421	21,089	5,323	22,533	4,165	33,031	25,816	943	571	59,431	1,874	448	0
1898	217,786	12,894	25,128	19,282	4,698	17,111	4,726	39,797	29,828	1,076	2,339	58,613	1,717	577	0
1899	297,349	13,456	31,673	22,192	5,150	17,476	—	62,491	60,982	1,738	2,333	77,419	2,054	385	0
1900	424,700	12,509	35,730	31,151	5,822	18,507	—	114,847	90,787	6,852	3,771	100,135	4,234	355	0
1901	469,237	14,985	30,561	39,234	9,279	21,651	—	113,390	85,257	8,199	5,910	135,996	4,165	592	18
1902	619,068	16,898	29,138	54,038	10,322	28,304	—	171,989	107,347	8,234	8,104	178,375	5,307	975	37
1903	814,507	33,637	35,310	77,647	17,009	40,086	—	206,011	136,093	12,600	14,090	230,622	9,317	2,080	5
1904	767,933	51,448	36,142	60,096	23,321	46,380	—	177,156	145,141	12,756	11,343	193,296	6,715	3,996	143

Notes appear at end of table

(continued)

TABLE Ad106–120   Immigrants, by country of last residence – Europe: 1820–1997   Continued

		Northwestern Europe				Central Europe			Eastern Europe						
	Total	Great Britain	Ireland	Scandinavia	Other	Germany	Poland [2]	Other	Former Soviet Union and Baltic states [3]	Other	Greece	Italy	Portugal [4]	Spain [5]	Other
Fiscal year	Ad106	Ad107	Ad108	Ad109	Ad110	Ad111	Ad112	Ad113	Ad114	Ad115	Ad116	Ad117	Ad118	Ad119	Ad120
	Number	Number	Number	Number	Number	Number	Number	Number	Number	Number	Number	Number	Number	Number	Number
1905	974,273	84,189	52,945	60,625	24,693	40,574	—	275,693	184,897	11,022	10,515	221,479	5,028	2,600	13
1906	1,018,365	67,198	34,995	52,781	23,277	37,564	—	265,138	215,665	18,652	19,489	273,120	8,517	1,921	48
1907	1,199,566	79,037	34,530	49,965	26,512	37,807	—	338,452	258,943	36,510	36,580	285,731	9,608	5,784	107
1908	691,901	62,824	30,556	30,175	22,177	32,309	—	168,509	156,711	27,345	21,489	128,503	7,307	3,899	97
1909	654,875	46,793	25,033	32,496	17,756	25,540	—	170,191	120,460	11,659	14,111	183,218	4,956	2,616	46
1910	926,291	68,941	29,855	48,267	23,852	31,283	—	258,737	186,792	25,287	25,888	215,537	8,229	3,472	151
1911	764,757	73,384	29,112	42,285	25,549	32,061	—	159,057	158,721	21,655	26,226	182,882	8,374	5,074	377
1912	718,875	57,148	25,879	27,554	22,921	27,788	—	178,882	162,395	20,925	21,449	157,134	10,230	6,327	243
1913	1,055,855	60,328	27,876	32,267	28,086	34,329	—	254,825	291,040	18,036	22,817	265,542	14,171	6,167	371
1914	1,058,391	48,729	24,688	29,391	25,591	35,734	—	278,152	255,660	21,420	35,832	283,738	10,898	7,591	967
1915	197,919	27,237	14,185	17,883	12,096	7,799	—	18,511	26,187	2,892	12,592	49,688	4,907	2,762	1,180
1916	145,699	16,063	8,639	14,761	8,715	2,877	—	5,191	7,842	1,167	27,034	33,665	12,259	5,769	1,717
1917	133,083	10,735	5,406	13,771	6,731	1,857	—	1,258	12,716	369	23,974	34,596	9,975	10,232	1,463
1918	31,063	2,516	331	6,506	3,146	447	—	61	4,242	93	1,910	5,250	2,224	4,295	42
1919	24,627	6,797	474	5,590	5,126	52	—	53	1,403	51	386	1,884	1,222	1,573	16
1920	246,295	38,471	9,591	13,444	24,491	1,001	4,813	5,666	1,751	3,913	11,981	95,145	15,472	18,821	1,735
1921	652,364	51,142	28,435	22,854	29,317	6,803	95,089	77,069	10,193	32,793	28,502	222,260	19,195	23,818	4,894
1922	216,385	25,153	10,579	14,625	11,149	17,931	28,635	29,363	19,910	12,244	3,457	40,319	1,950	665	405
1923	307,920	45,759	15,740	34,184	12,469	48,277	26,538	34,038	21,151	16,082	3,333	46,674	2,384	841	450
1924	364,339	59,490	17,111	35,577	16,077	75,091	28,806	32,700	20,918	13,423	4,871	56,246	2,769	932	328
1925	148,366	28,382	25,440	16,810	8,548	46,068	5,341	4,701	3,364	1,645	826	6,203	619	275	144
1926	155,562	25,947	24,478	16,818	8,773	50,421	7,126	6,020	3,533	1,754	1,121	8,253	666	326	326
1927	168,368	24,160	28,054	16,860	9,134	48,513	9,211	6,559	3,156	1,951	2,089	17,297	567	429	388
1928	158,513	20,682	24,544	16,184	9,079	45,778	8,755	7,091	2,876	2,039	2,328	17,728	584	455	390
1929	158,598	23,576	17,672	17,379	9,091	46,751	9,002	8,081	2,654	2,482	2,266	18,008	623	547	466
1930	147,438	36,489	17,971	6,919	9,170	26,569	9,231	9,184	2,914	2,500	2,291	22,327	637	670	566
1931	61,909	10,294	6,121	3,133	4,420	10,401	3,604	4,500	1,472	1,414	1,763	13,399	542	476	370
1932	20,579	2,155	441	938	1,558	2,670	1,296	1,749	653	837	877	6,662	248	445	50
1933	12,383	979	338	510	1,041	1,919	1,332	981	458	399	532	3,477	90	198	129
1934	17,210	1,421	327	557	1,262	4,392	1,032	1,422	607	447	605	4,374	225	297	242
1935	22,778	1,553	314	688	1,783	5,201	1,504	2,357	418	576	877	6,566	366	333	242
1936	23,480	1,426	328	645	1,696	6,346	869	2,723	378	559	863	6,774	313	299	261
1937	31,863	1,845	412	971	2,433	10,895	1,212	3,763	629	664	875	7,192	301	315	356
1938	44,495	2,433	914	1,386	3,268	17,199 [9]	2,403	5,195 [9]	960	723	1,009	7,712	374	379	540
1939	63,138	3,146	1,101	1,175	5,086	33,515 [9]	3,072	5,334 [9]	1,021	779	907	6,570	422	257	753
1940	50,454	6,248	749	1,256	7,596	21,520 [9]	702	3,628 [9]	898	572	811	5,302	448	259	465
1941	26,541	7,775	211	1,131	8,815	4,028 [9]	451	786 [9]	665	259	268	450	1,101	300	301
1942	11,153	920	70	361	5,500	2,150 [9]	343	396 [9]	197	82	174	103	437	234	186
1943	4,920	1,007	132	229	1,521	248 [9]	394	206 [9]	159	48	229	49	395	254	49
1944	4,509	1,365	68	246	617	238 [9]	292	316 [9]	157	77	226	120	431	271	85
1945	5,943	3,331	125	149	361	172 [9]	195	206 [9]	98	81	176	213	570	156	110
1946	52,852	34,842	526	1,085	8,547	2,598	335	511	153	36	367	2,636	578	227	411
1947	83,535	24,917	1,445	4,814	14,465	13,900	745	4,622	761	144	2,370	13,866	633	260	593
1948	103,544	28,114	5,823	6,042	13,616	19,368	2,447	6,006	897	392	2,250	16,075	890	404	1,220
1949	129,592	23,275	6,552	6,562	12,170	55,284	1,673	7,411	694	177	1,734	11,695	1,282	409	674

Fiscal year	Total	Northwestern Europe				Central Europe			Eastern Europe		Greece	Italy	Portugal	Spain	Other
		Great Britain	Ireland	Scandinavia	Other	Germany	Poland[2]	Other	Former Soviet Union and Baltic states[3]	Other			[4]	[5]	
	Ad106	Ad107	Ad108	Ad109	Ad110	Ad111	Ad112	Ad113	Ad114	Ad115	Ad116	Ad117	Ad118	Ad119	Ad120
	Number	Number	Number	Number	Number	Number	Number	Number	Number	Number	Number	Number	Number	Number	Number
1950	199,115	13,760	4,837	5,539	10,793	128,592	696	17,792	526	168	1,179	12,454	1,106	383	1,290
1951	149,545	15,450	2,592	5,387	10,922	87,755	98	10,365	555	230	4,459	8,958	1,078	442	1,254
1952	193,626	22,928	2,775	5,284	12,386	104,236	235	23,529	548	137	6,996	11,342	953	481	1,796
1953	82,352	17,550	3,393	5,398	11,068	27,329	136	2,885	609	86	1,296	8,432	1,077	814	2,279
1954	92,121	17,642	3,685	5,324	11,794	33,098	67	2,873	475	104	1,154	13,145	1,455	542	763
1955	110,591	16,559	4,424	5,018	10,646	29,596	129	4,133	523	134	6,182	30,272	1,293	802	880
1956	156,866	20,092	4,744	5,512	15,254	44,409	263	10,284	643	401	11,216	40,430	1,322	576	1,720
1957	169,625	25,368	7,084	6,009	25,109	60,353	571	15,498	663	575	5,326	19,624	1,457	748	1,240
1958	115,198	24,435	9,134	5,740	11,364	29,498	1,470	3,508	641	677	2,733	23,115	1,556	899	428
1959	138,191	18,531	6,595	5,931	14,217	32,039	2,800	30,738	775	730	4,612	16,804	2,631	1,193	595
1960	120,221	20,875	6,010	6,013	17,163	29,452	4,216	9,073	873	741	3,634	13,369	6,766	1,397	639
1961	108,598	19,483	4,974	4,776	14,593	25,815	6,254	2,911	1,019	586	3,124	18,956	3,832	1,737	538
1962	104,021	18,895	4,289	4,556	13,061	21,477	5,660	2,533	719	716	4,408	20,119	3,622	3,353	613
1963	109,097	23,656	4,798	5,060	11,886	24,727	6,785	3,244	508	960	4,744	16,175	2,911	2,969	674
1964	108,215	26,859	4,954	5,311	11,052	24,494	7,097	3,248	658	793	3,998	12,769	2,006	4,069	907
1965	101,468	24,988	4,334	5,680	11,441	22,432	7,093	3,693	522	830	3,016	10,874	1,937	3,929	699
1966	115,898	19,439	2,603	4,415	8,990	17,654	8,490	3,972	615	821	8,236	26,447	8,482	4,944	790
1967	128,775	23,778	1,991	4,095	9,831	16,595	4,356	5,116	748	856	14,194	28,487	13,400	4,562	766
1968	129,022	26,752	2,268	4,070	9,807	16,590	3,676	5,659	878	840	12,185	25,882	11,827	7,904	684
1969	114,052	15,486	1,567	1,971	5,909	10,380	2,115	8,889	254	1,167	16,634	27,033	15,785	5,929	933
1970	109,809	14,484	1,188	1,867	6,919	10,632	2,013	10,411	360	520	15,430	27,369	12,263	5,263	1,090
1971	91,509	12,302	1,173	1,549	5,625	8,646	1,928	6,432	686	735	15,002	22,818	10,545	3,661	407
1972	86,321	11,521	1,423	1,719	5,404	7,760	3,770	6,645	806	402	10,452	22,440	9,465	4,284	230
1973	91,183	11,860	1,588	1,537	4,721	7,565	4,136	8,720	1,200	1,417	10,348	22,286	10,019	5,538	248
1974	80,407	11,661	1,306	1,579	4,296	7,238	3,492	6,899	1,212	1,348	10,590	15,071	10,696	4,704	315
1975	72,774	12,244	1,069	1,326	3,702	5,861	3,482	4,270	4,952	920	9,799	10,970	11,291	2,573	315
1976	73,035	12,970	962	1,385	4,210	6,642	3,192	3,657	7,700	1,802	8,553	8,000	11,031	2,758	173
(TQ)	18,641	3,328	265	415	1,208	1,959	820	891	1,808	364	2,198	2,034	2,692	625	34
1977	74,048	14,040	967	1,467	5,060	7,414	3,331	3,522	5,690	1,655	7,792	7,372	9,977	5,568	193
1978	76,156	16,425	923	1,568	5,418	7,567	4,495	3,795	5,044	1,804	6,994	7,034	10,517	4,266	306
1979	64,173	15,537	808	1,728	5,551	7,166	3,863	3,390	2,253	1,332	5,942	5,974	7,068	3,285	276
1980	72,121	15,485	1,006	1,675	4,236	6,595	4,725	4,370	11,034	2,131	4,699	5,467	8,408	1,879	411
1981	66,695	14,997	902	1,669	3,830	6,552	5,014	3,789	9,645	2,109	4,361	4,662	7,049	1,711	405
1982	69,174	14,559	949	1,679	4,258	6,726	5,874	3,359	15,920	3,354	3,472	3,644	3,510	1,586	304
1983	58,867	14,830	1,101	1,792	4,460	7,185	6,427	3,393	5,613	2,766	2,997	3,225	3,231	1,507	340
1984	69,879	16,516	1,096	2,083	6,250	9,375	7,229	4,943	3,586	3,096	3,311	6,334	3,800	2,168	92
1985	69,526	15,591	1,288	2,142	6,555	10,028	7,409	4,726	1,792	3,908	3,487	6,353	3,811	2,278	158
1986	69,224	16,129	1,757	2,241	6,951	9,853	6,540	5,107	1,284	3,964	3,497	5,712	3,804	2,232	153
1987	67,967	15,889	3,032	2,150	6,968	9,923	5,818	4,909	1,447	2,889	4,087	4,667	4,009	2,056	123
1988	71,854	14,667	5,121	2,330	6,447	9,748	7,298	5,983	1,786	3,077	4,690	5,333	3,290	1,972	112
1989	94,338	16,961	6,983	2,426	7,131	10,419	13,279	6,576	4,570	3,535	4,588	11,089	3,861	2,179	741
1990	124,026	19,054	9,740	2,604	7,895	12,108	18,364	8,089	14,779	3,496	3,887	16,246	4,066	2,744	954
1991	146,671	16,768	4,608	2,425	6,985	10,887	17,106	7,882	31,557	6,786	2,929	30,316	4,576	2,663	1,183
1992	153,260	21,924	12,035	3,065	8,439	12,875	24,491	7,549	37,523	5,541	2,168	11,962	2,774	2,041	873
1993	165,711	20,422	13,396	3,015	7,540	9,965	27,288	6,487	60,438	5,963	2,460	3,899	2,075	1,791	972
1994	166,279	17,666	16,525	2,443	6,755	8,940	27,597	6,065	65,551	4,798	2,539	2,664	2,163	1,756	817
1995	132,914	14,207	4,851	1,730	6,275	7,896	13,570	11,075	54,768	7,475	2,404	2,594	2,611	1,664	1,794
1996	151,898	15,564	1,611	2,810	7,595	8,365	15,504	14,379	63,455	11,296	2,394	2,755	3,024	1,970	1,176
1997	122,358	11,950	932	2,024	6,139	6,941	11,729	13,046	—	—	1,483	2,190	1,690	1,607	—

(continued)

Notes appear on next page

TABLE Ad106–120   Immigrants, by country of last residence – Europe: 1820–1997   *Continued*

(TQ) indicates transitional quarter.

[1] Fiscal year varies as follows: 1820–1832, year ending September 30; 1833–1842, year ending December 31; 1843–1850, year ending September 30; 1851–1865, year ending December 31; 1866–1976, year ending June 30; 1977–1997, year ending September 30.

[2] Included with Austria-Hungary, Germany, and Russia, 1899–1999. Includes Danzig 1925–1932.

[3] Excludes former USSR in Asia, 1931–1950; thereafter, includes all of former USSR, Estonia, Finland, Latvia, and Lithuania, including former USSR in Asia.

[4] Includes Sardinia and Sicily 1869–1972. Includes the Cape Verde Islands 1869–1972; thereafter, they are listed separately and included in Africa.

[5] Includes the Azores Islands beginning 1869.

[6] Three quarters ending September 30.

[7] Six months ending June 30.

[8] Data from original source were revised.

[9] Austria included with Germany.

Sources

1820–1926: *Annual Report of the Commissioner General of Immigration, Report for 1926*, Table 74. 1927–1931: *Annual Report of the Commissioner General of Immigration, 1931*, Table 84. 1932: *Annual Report of the Commissioner General of Immigration, 1932*, Table 2. 1933: Figures for Europe were derived by subtracting published figures for 1931–1932 and 1934–1940 from decadal total in *Annual Report of the Attorney General of the United States, for Fiscal Year Ended June 30, 1941*, Table X. 1934–1937: *Annual Report of the Secretary of Labor, 1937*, "Immigrant Aliens Admitted and Emigrant Aliens Departed, Years Ended June 30, 1934–1937, by Countries of Last or Intended Future Permanent Residence." 1938–1940: *Annual Report of the Attorney General of the United States, for Fiscal Year Ended June 30, 1941*, Table VII. 1941–1945: *Annual Report of the Immigration and Naturalization Service, 1945*, Table 13. 1946–1947: *Annual Report of the INS, 1947*, Table 13. 1948–1950: *Annual Report of the INS, 1951*, Table 13. 1951–1956: *Annual Report of the INS, 1956*, Table 4. 1957–1959: *Annual Report of the INS, 1959*, Table 13. 1960–1971: *Annual Report of the INS*, Table 6A. 1972–1977: INS Public Use Tapes. 1978: *Statistical Yearbook of the INS*, Table 6A. 1979: INS Public Use Tapes. 1980: *Statistical Yearbook of the INS, 1981*, Table 2. 1981–1983: *Statistical Yearbook of the INS, 1985*,

Table IMM1. 1984: *Statistical Yearbook of the INS, 1984*, Table IMM2.4. 1985: *Statistical Yearbook of the INS, 1985*, Table IMM2.4. 1986–1988: INS Public Use Tapes. 1989–1991: *Statistical Yearbook of the INS*, Table 8. 1992–1997: *Statistical Yearbook of the INS*, Table 9.

Documentation

Series Ad107. Includes separate data published for Northern Ireland, 1925–1932, 1934–1957, and 1972–1979. For 1901–1951, "United Kingdom not specified" was included in "other Europe."

Series Ad108. Comprises the entire island of Ireland 1820–1924; thereafter, the Republic of Ireland. Data for Northern Ireland were included with United Kingdom and have been published separately for most years since 1924.

Series Ad109. Comprises Denmark, Iceland (separate data for Iceland published in 1972–1979 and 1984–1988), Norway, and Sweden.

Series Ad110. Comprises Belgium, France, Luxembourg (separate data published only in 1925–1932, 1956–1959, and 1971–1985), Netherlands, and Switzerland.

Series Ad111. Includes the German Democratic Republic (East Germany), for which separate data were published only for 1984–1988.

Series Ad113. Comprises Hungary (since 1861), Austria (since 1861), Czechoslovakia (since 1920), Hungary, and Yugoslavia (since 1920). In 1920, a separate enumeration was made for the Kingdom of Serbs, Croats, and Slovenes; after 1922, the kingdom was reported as Yugoslavia.

Series Ad114. Comprises Russia (former USSR), Estonia, Finland, Latvia, and Lithuania.

Series Ad115. Excludes the Baltic states.

Series Ad117. Comprises Albania (separate data published for 1924–1946, 1951, 1956–1959, 1969–1984, and 1994–), Bulgaria (reported separately since 1920), Latvia (1994, 1996), Lithuania (1994–), Romania (reported separately since 1906), and Turkey in Europe (1820–1937 and 1952–1969).

Series Ad118. Includes separate data published for San Marino in 1972–1979 and 1984–1988.

TABLE Ad121–135   Immigrants, by country of birth – Europe: 1941–1997[1]

Contributed by Robert Barde, Susan B. Carter, and Richard Sutch

		Northwestern Europe				Central Europe			Eastern Europe						
		United Kingdom	Ireland	Scandinavia	Other	Germany	Poland	Other	Former Soviet Union and Baltic states	Other	Greece	Italy	Portugal	Spain	Other
	Total	Ad122	Ad123	Ad124	Ad125	Ad126 [2]	Ad127	Ad128	Ad129	Ad130	Ad131	Ad132	Ad133	Ad134	Ad135
Fiscal year	Ad121														
	Number	Number	Number	Number	Number	Number	Number	Number	Number	Number	Number	Number	Number	Number	Number
1941	36,989	4,361	358	1,119	5,166	13,307	4,688	2,782	2,690	454	284	731	371	372	306
1942	14,881	1,515	182	364	2,053	4,945	2,376	1,030	1,172	331	216	69	190	243	195
1943	8,953	1,556	227	378	1,060	1,295	1,647	641	782	241	309	81	301	318	117
1944	8,694	1,631	146	404	634	1,360	1,420	746	704	272	292	177	429	291	188
1945	10,141	3,582	286	289	480	1,260	1,222	605	612	245	235	320	562	238	205
1946	64,877	34,314	1,387	997	7,662	4,010	4,806	3,317	1,893	461	578	3,886	554	402	610
1947	96,865	24,045	2,446	4,734	11,601	14,674	8,156	7,992	4,007	686	2,056	14,557	636	302	973
1948	115,750	25,814	7,651	6,037	11,619	21,365	8,020	9,308	4,293	902	1,964	15,801	890	509	1,577
1949	138,301	21,475	8,585	6,301	10,349	23,844	23,744	10,138	16,995	1,127	1,759	11,157	1,235	503	1,089
1950	206,341	13,437	6,501	5,505	9,503	31,225	52,851	22,962	40,980	3,599	1,242	9,839	1,075	463	7,159
1951	161,065	12,491	3,739	5,022	9,153	26,369	37,484	19,816	27,334	2,351	4,447	7,348	1,048	510	3,953
1952	202,749	17,631	3,796	5,304	9,705	50,283	33,211	35,090	20,842	4,915	7,084	9,306	1,013	536	4,033
1953	96,082	19,230	4,655	5,455	9,387	27,305	4,395	6,110	3,054	468	1,603	9,701	1,141	991	2,587
1954	110,944	19,309	5,232	5,553	10,156	32,935	5,663	6,902	3,391	666	2,127	15,201	1,636	964	1,209

Notes appear at end of table

TABLE Ad121–135   Immigrants, by country of birth – Europe: 1941–1997   *Continued*

		Northwestern Europe				Central Europe			Eastern Europe						
	Total	United Kingdom	Ireland	Scandinavia	Other	Germany	Poland	Other	Former Soviet Union and Baltic states	Other	Greece	Italy	Portugal	Spain	Other
	Ad121	Ad122	Ad123	Ad124	Ad125	Ad126 [2]	Ad127	Ad128	Ad129	Ad130	Ad131	Ad132	Ad133	Ad134	Ad135
Fiscal year	Number	Number	Number	Number	Number	Number	Number	Number	Number	Number	Number	Number	Number	Number	Number
1955	127,286	17,849	5,975	5,345	9,930	29,603	4,697	7,682	3,159	988	6,311	31,925	1,366	1,134	1,322
1956	175,119	21,582	6,483	5,867	12,660	38,390	8,453	17,922	4,661	2,328	10,531	39,789	1,396	964	4,093
1957	184,656	27,570	9,124	6,200	19,916	45,230	11,225	26,197	5,332	2,573	4,952	19,061	1,537	1,009	4,730
1958	137,796	27,613	10,383	6,101	10,714	32,145	6,607	8,004	2,852	805	3,079	24,479	1,635	1,354	2,025
1959	157,733	20,954	7,371	6,013	11,420	31,422	8,301	39,615	3,561	1,345	4,507	16,251	2,694	1,528	2,751
1960	138,785	24,643	7,687	6,379	12,285	31,768	7,949	14,360	3,226	993	3,797	14,933	6,968	1,737	2,060
1961	126,979	22,717	6,541	5,378	11,361	29,048	9,281	7,168	3,041	813	3,392	20,652	3,960	1,812	1,815
1962	118,778	21,189	5,486	5,092	10,868	24,008	8,098	6,536	2,968	784	4,702	21,442	3,730	2,148	1,647
1963	124,677	25,916	6,178	5,593	10,589	26,887	9,546	7,940	2,668	854	4,825	16,588	2,975	2,187	1,931
1964	122,104	29,108	6,307	5,733	9,810	26,739	8,884	8,222	2,496	1,391	3,909	13,245	2,077	2,252	1,931
1965	113,424	27,358	5,463	6,051	10,113	24,045	8,465	7,966	2,522	1,644	3,002	10,821	2,005	2,200	1,769
1966	123,469	21,441	3,241	4,620	7,802	18,239	9,404	8,053	1,881	1,938	8,265	25,154	8,713	2,954	1,764
1967	137,301	24,965	2,624	4,262	8,126	16,041	5,976	10,402	1,619	2,457	14,905	26,565	13,927	3,620	1,812
1968	137,754	28,586	3,004	4,278	8,269	15,920	5,995	11,773	1,819	1,833	13,047	23,593	12,212	5,260	2,165
1969	118,028	15,014	1,989	1,993	4,438	9,289	4,052	14,728	931	2,545	17,724	23,617	16,528	3,916	1,264
1970	116,039	14,158	1,562	1,863	5,507	9,684	3,585	15,753	912	2,794	16,464	24,973	13,195	4,139	1,450
1971	96,498	10,787	1,614	1,699	4,439	7,519	2,897	10,039	1,274	2,058	15,939	22,137	11,692	4,121	283
1972	89,993	10,078	1,780	1,689	4,106	6,848	4,797	10,004	1,509	1,726	11,021	21,427	10,343	4,386	279
1973	92,870	10,638	2,000	1,524	3,786	6,600	4,927	11,286	1,735	2,293	10,751	22,151	10,751	4,134	294
1974	81,212	10,710	1,572	1,544	3,583	6,320	4,046	8,204	1,620	1,862	10,824	15,884	11,302	3,390	351
1975	73,996	10,807	1,285	1,337	3,068	5,154	3,947	5,333	5,485	1,345	9,984	11,552	11,845	2,549	305
1976	72,411	11,392	1,171	1,370	3,428	5,836	3,808	4,576	8,638	2,429	8,417	8,380	10,511	2,254	201
(TQ)	18,166	3,020	302	416	930	1,695	961	1,145	1,964	527	2,144	2,035	2,455	532	40
1977	70,010	12,477	1,238	1,475	3,650	6,372	4,010	4,619	6,154	2,299	7,838	7,510	9,657	2,487	224
1978	73,198	14,245	1,180	1,601	4,163	6,739	5,050	4,773	5,661	2,307	7,035	7,415	10,445	2,297	287
1979	60,845	13,907	982	1,735	3,930	6,314	4,418	4,164	3,018	1,781	5,090	6,174	7,085	1,933	314
1980	72,121	15,485	1,006	1,861	4,236	6,595	4,725	4,370	11,034	2,131	4,699	5,467	8,408	1,879	225
1981	66,695	14,997	902	1,845	3,830	6,552	5,014	3,789	9,645	2,109	4,361	4,662	7,049	1,711	229
1982	69,174	14,539	949	1,805	4,258	6,726	5,874	3,359	15,920	3,354	3,472	3,644	3,510	1,586	178
1983	58,867	14,830	1,101	1,975	4,460	7,185	6,427	3,393	5,613	2,766	2,997	3,225	3,231	1,507	157
1984	64,076	13,949	1,223	1,979	4,553	6,875	9,466	4,054	6,443	4,261	2,865	3,130	3,779	1,393	106
1985	63,043	13,408	1,397	2,032	4,688	7,235	9,464	4,312	3,882	5,482	2,579	3,214	3,781	1,413	156
1986	62,512	13,657	1,839	2,139	5,100	7,127	8,481	4,598	2,991	5,472	2,512	3,089	3,766	1,591	150
1987	61,174	13,497	3,060	2,008	5,164	7,318	7,519	4,661	2,790	4,104	2,653	2,784	3,912	1,578	126
1988	64,797	13,228	5,058	2,203	5,071	6,755	9,507	5,164	3,428	4,174	2,458	2,949	3,199	1,483	120
1989	82,891	14,090	6,961	2,277	5,143	6,845	15,101	5,182	11,587	4,909	2,491	2,910	3,758	1,550	87
1990	112,401	15,928	10,333	2,493	5,831	7,493	20,537	6,570	26,025	5,153	2,742	3,287	4,035	1,886	88
1991	135,234	13,903	4,767	2,284	4,975	6,509	19,199	5,992	57,579	8,861	2,079	2,619	4,524	1,849	94
1992	145,392	19,973	12,226	3,048	6,702	9,888	25,504	5,790	45,105	8,231	1,858	2,592	2,748	1,631	96
1993	158,254	18,783	13,590	2,900	5,937	7,312	27,846	5,449	60,503	8,030	1,884	2,487	2,081	1,388	64
1994	160,916	16,326	17,256	2,345	5,371	6,992	28,048	5,658	65,588	5,914	1,440	2,305	2,169	1,418	86
1995	128,185	12,427	5,315	2,072	5,166	6,237	13,824	10,899	56,593	8,088	1,309	2,231	2,615	1,321	88
1996	147,581	13,624	1,731	2,519	6,191	6,748	15,772	14,980	65,475	11,874	1,452	2,501	2,984	1,659	71
1997	119,871	10,708	1,001	1,878	5,272	5,723	12,038	13,396	51,159	12,694	1,049	1,982	1,665	1,241	65

(TQ) indicates transitional quarter.

[1] Through 1976, fiscal year ending June 30; thereafter, fiscal year ending September 30.

[2] Includes Austria 1941–1945; includes East Germany 1982–1990.

Sources

1941: *Annual Report of the Attorney General of the United States, 1941.* 1942: *Annual Report of Lemuel B. Schofield, Special Assistant to the Attorney General in Charge of the Immigration and Naturalization Service, 1942.* 1943–1949: *INS Annual Report of 1952,* Table 13A. 1950: *INS Annual Report 1959,* Table 14. 1951: *INS Annual Report 1960,* Table 14. 1952: *INS Annual Report 1961,* Table 14. 1953–1955: *INS Annual Report 1962,* Table 14. 1956–1961: *INS Annual Report 1965,* Table 14. 1962–1969: *INS Statistical Yearbook 1971,* Table 14. 1970: *INS Statistical Yearbook 1970,* Table 6. 1971–1979: *INS Annual Report 1980,* Table 13. 1980–1983: *INS Statistical Yearbook 1984,* Table IMM 1.3. 1984–1990: *INS Statistical Yearbook 1992,* Table 3. 1991–1997: *INS Statistical Yearbook 1997,* Table 3.

Documentation

Series Ad124. Includes Denmark, Iceland, Norway, and Sweden.

Series Ad125. Includes Belgium, France, Luxembourg, Netherlands, and Switzerland.

Series Ad128. Includes Austria (1946–), Czechoslovakia, Hungary, and Yugoslavia.

Series Ad129. Includes USSR, Estonia, Finland, Latvia, and Lithuania.

Series Ad130. Includes Albania, Bulgaria, and Romania.

TABLE Ad136–148   Immigrants, by country of last residence – Asia: 1820–1997[1]

Contributed by Robert Barde, Susan B. Carter, and Richard Sutch

| | Total | Arab states | China | Hong Kong | India | Iran | Israel | Japan | Korea | Philippines | Southeast Asia | Turkey | Other |
| | Ad136 | Ad137 | Ad138 | Ad139 | Ad140 | Ad141 | Ad142 | Ad143 | Ad144 | Ad145 | Ad146 | Ad147 | Ad148 |
Fiscal year	Number	Number	Number	Number	Number	Number	Number	Number	Number	Number	Number	Number	Number
1820	5	—	1	—	1	—	—	—	—	—	—	—	3
1821	0	—	0	—	0	—	—	—	—	—	—	—	0
1822	1	—	0	—	1	—	—	—	—	—	—	—	0
1823	0	—	0	—	0	—	—	—	—	—	—	—	0
1824	1	—	0	—	1	—	—	—	—	—	—	—	0
1825	1	—	1	—	0	—	—	—	—	—	—	—	0
1826	1	—	0	—	1	—	—	—	—	—	—	—	0
1827	1	—	0	—	1	—	—	—	—	—	—	—	0
1828	3	—	0	—	3	—	—	—	—	—	—	—	0
1829	2	—	1	—	1	—	—	—	—	—	—	—	0
1830	0	—	0	—	0	—	—	—	—	—	—	—	0
1831	1	—	0	—	1	—	—	—	—	—	—	—	0
1832	4	—	0	—	4	—	—	—	—	—	—	—	0
1833	3	—	0	—	3	—	—	—	—	—	—	—	0
1834	6	—	0	—	6	—	—	—	—	—	—	—	0
1835	17	—	8	—	8	—	—	—	—	—	—	—	1
1836	4	—	0	—	4	—	—	—	—	—	—	—	0
1837	11	—	0	—	11	—	—	—	—	—	—	—	0
1838	1	—	0	—	1	—	—	—	—	—	—	—	0
1839	0	—	0	—	0	—	—	—	—	—	—	—	0
1840	1	—	0	—	1	—	—	—	—	—	—	—	0
1841	3	—	2	—	1	—	—	—	—	—	—	—	0
1842	7	—	4	—	2	—	—	—	—	—	—	—	1
1843 [2]	11	—	3	—	2	—	—	—	—	—	—	—	6
1844	6	—	3	—	1	—	—	—	—	—	—	—	2
1845	6	—	6	—	0	—	—	—	—	—	—	—	0
1846	11	—	7	—	4	—	—	—	—	—	—	—	0
1847	12	—	4	—	8	—	—	—	—	—	—	—	0
1848	8	—	0	—	6	—	—	—	—	—	—	—	2
1849	11	—	3	—	8	—	—	—	—	—	—	—	0
1850	7	—	3	—	4	—	—	—	—	—	—	—	0
(TQ)	0	—	0	—	0	—	—	—	—	—	—	—	0
1851	2	—	0	—	2	—	—	—	—	—	—	—	0
1852	4	—	0	—	4	—	—	—	—	—	—	—	0
1853	47	—	42	—	5	—	—	—	—	—	—	—	0
1854	13,100	—	13,100	—	0	—	—	—	—	—	—	—	0
1855	3,540	—	3,526	—	6	—	—	—	—	—	—	—	8
1856	4,747	—	4,733	—	13	—	—	—	—	—	—	—	1
1857	5,945	—	5,944	—	1	—	—	—	—	—	—	—	0
1858	5,133	—	5,128	—	5	—	—	—	—	—	—	—	0
1859	3,461	—	3,457	—	2	—	—	—	—	—	—	—	2
1860	5,476	—	5,467	—	5	—	—	—	—	—	—	—	4
1861	7,528	—	7,518	—	6	—	—	1	—	—	—	—	3
1862	3,640	—	3,633	—	5	—	—	0	—	—	—	—	2
1863	7,216	—	7,214	—	1	—	—	0	—	—	—	—	1
1864	2,982	—	2,975	—	6	—	—	0	—	—	—	—	1
1865	2,947	—	2,942	—	5	—	—	0	—	—	—	—	0
1866 [3]	2,411	—	2,385	—	17	—	—	7	—	—	—	—	2
1867	3,961	—	3,863	—	2	—	—	67	—	—	—	—	29
1868	5,171	—	5,157	—	0	—	—	0	—	—	—	—	14
1869	12,949	—	12,874	—	3	—	—	63	—	—	—	2	7
1870	15,825	—	15,740	—	24	—	—	48	—	—	—	0	13
1871	7,240	—	7,135	—	14	—	—	78	—	—	—	4	9
1872	7,825	—	7,788	—	12	—	—	17	—	—	—	0	5
1873	20,325	—	20,292	—	15	—	—	9	—	—	—	3	6
1874	13,838	—	13,776	—	17	—	—	21	—	—	—	6	18
1875	16,499	—	16,437	—	19	—	—	3	—	—	—	1	39
1876	22,943	—	22,781	—	25	—	—	4	—	—	—	8	125
1877	10,640	—	10,594	—	17	—	—	7	—	—	—	3	19
1878	9,014	—	8,992	—	8	—	—	2	—	—	—	7	5
1879	9,660	—	9,604	—	15	—	—	4	—	—	—	31	6

Notes appear at end of table

TABLE Ad136–148   Immigrants, by country of last residence – Asia: 1820–1997   *Continued*

Fiscal year	Total	Arab states	China	Hong Kong	India	Iran	Israel	Japan	Korea	Philippines	Southeast Asia	Turkey	Other
	Ad136	Ad137	Ad138	Ad139	Ad140	Ad141	Ad142	Ad143	Ad144	Ad145	Ad146	Ad147	Ad148
	Number	Number	Number	Number	Number	Number	Number	Number	Number	Number	Number	Number	Number
1880	5,839	—	5,802	—	21	—	—	4	—	—	—	4	8
1881	11,982	—	11,890	—	33	—	—	11	—	—	—	5	43
1882	39,629	—	39,579 [4]	—	10	—	—	5	—	—	—	—	35
1883	8,113	—	8,031	—	9	—	—	27	—	—	—	—	46
1884	510	—	279	—	12	—	—	20	—	—	—	—	199
1885	198	—	22	—	34	—	—	49	—	—	—	—	93
1886	317	—	40	—	17	—	—	194	—	—	—	15	51
1887	615	—	10	—	32	—	—	229	—	—	—	208	136
1888	843	—	26	—	20	—	—	404	—	—	—	273	120
1889	1,725	—	118	—	59	—	—	640	—	—	—	593	315
1890	4,448	—	1,716	—	43	—	—	691	—	—	—	1,126	872
1891	7,678	—	2,836	—	42	—	—	1,136	—	—	—	2,488	1,176
1892 [5]	—	—	—	—	—	—	—	—	—	—	—	—	—
1893	2,392	—	472	—	—	—	—	1,380	—	—	—	—	540
1894	4,690	—	1,170	—	—	—	—	1,931	—	—	—	—	1,589
1895	4,495	—	539	—	—	—	—	1,150	—	—	—	2,767	39
1896	6,764	—	1,441	—	—	—	—	1,110	—	—	—	4,139	74
1897	9,662	—	3,363	—	—	—	—	1,526	—	—	—	4,732	41
1898	8,637	—	2,071	—	—	—	—	2,230	—	—	—	4,275	61
1899	8,972	—	1,660	—	17	—	—	2,844	—	—	—	4,436	15
1900	17,946	—	1,247	—	9	—	—	12,635	—	—	—	3,962	93
1901	13,593	—	2,459	—	22	—	—	5,269	—	—	—	5,782	61
1902	22,271	—	1,649	—	93	—	—	14,270	—	—	—	6,223	36
1903	29,966	—	2,209	—	94	—	—	19,968	—	—	—	7,118	577
1904	26,186	—	4,309	—	261	—	—	14,264	—	—	—	5,235	2,117
1905	23,925	—	2,166	—	190	—	—	10,331	—	—	—	6,157	5,081
1906	22,300	—	1,544	—	216	—	—	13,835	—	—	—	6,354	351
1907	40,524	—	961	—	898	—	—	30,226	—	—	—	8,053	386
1908	28,365	—	1,397	—	1,040	—	—	15,803	—	—	—	9,753	372
1909	12,904	—	1,943	—	203	—	—	3,111	—	—	—	7,506	141
1910	23,533	—	1,968	—	1,696	—	—	2,720	—	—	—	15,212	1,937
1911	17,428	—	1,460	—	524	—	—	4,520	—	—	—	10,229	695
1912	21,449	—	1,765	—	175	—	—	6,114	—	—	—	12,788	607
1913	35,358	—	2,105	—	179	—	—	8,281	—	—	—	23,955	838
1914	34,273	—	2,502	—	221	—	—	8,929	—	—	—	21,716	905
1915	15,211	—	2,660	—	161	—	—	8,613	—	—	—	3,543	234
1916	13,204	—	2,460	—	112	—	—	8,680	—	—	—	1,670	282
1917	12,756	—	2,237	—	109	—	—	8,991	—	—	—	393	1,026
1918	12,701	—	1,795	—	130	—	—	10,213	—	—	—	43	520
1919	12,674	—	1,964	—	171	—	—	10,064	—	—	—	19	456
1920	17,505	—	2,330	—	300	—	—	9,432	—	—	—	5,033	410
1921	25,034	—	4,009	—	511	—	—	7,878	—	—	—	11,735	901
1922	14,263	—	4,406	—	360	—	—	6,716	—	—	—	1,998	783
1923	13,705	—	4,986	—	257	—	—	5,809	—	—	—	2,183	470
1924	22,065	—	6,992	—	183	—	—	8,801	—	—	—	2,820	3,269
1925	3,578	670	1,937	—	65	32	—	723	—	—	—	38	113
1926	3,413	679	1,751	—	93	56	—	654	—	—	—	21	159
1927	3,669	1,054	1,471	—	102	33	—	723	—	—	—	60	226
1928	3,380	1,058	1,320	—	102	50	—	550	—	—	—	59	241
1929	3,758	1,069	1,446	—	103	37	—	771	—	—	—	57	275
1930	4,535	1,199	1,589	—	110	33	—	837	—	—	—	105	662
1931	3,345	630	1,150	—	123	25	—	653	—	—	—	139	625
1932	1,931	439	750	—	87	41	—	526	—	—	14	43	31
1933	552	—	148	—	44	—	—	75	—	—	—	27	258
1934	600	230	187	—	28	—	—	86	—	3	—	22	44
1935	745	258	229	—	32	—	—	88	—	63	—	31	44
1936	793	273	273	—	13	—	—	91	—	72	—	20	51
1937	1,149	505	293	—	47	—	—	132	—	84	—	13	75
1938	2,492	1,518	613	—	34	—	—	93	—	116	—	11	107
1939	2,281	1,273	642	—	36	—	—	102	—	119	—	15	94

Notes appear at end of table

(continued)

TABLE Ad136–148   Immigrants, by country of last residence – Asia: 1820–1997 *Continued*

	Total	Arab states	China	Hong Kong	India	Iran	Israel	Japan	Korea	Philippines	Southeast Asia	Turkey	Other
	Ad136	Ad137	Ad138	Ad139	Ad140	Ad141	Ad142	Ad143	Ad144	Ad145	Ad146	Ad147	Ad148
Fiscal year	Number	Number	Number	Number	Number	Number	Number	Number	Number	Number	Number	Number	Number
1940	2,050	961	643	—	52	—	—	102	—	137	—	7	148
1941	1,971	282	1,003	—	94	—	—	289	—	170	—	16	117
1942	615	174	179	—	36	—	—	44	—	51	—	31	100
1943	342	116	65	—	71	—	—	20	—	8	—	36	26
1944	231	53	50	—	41	—	—	4	—	4	—	15	64
1945	461	151	71	—	103	—	—	1	—	19	—	13	103
1946	2,108	573	252	—	425	—	—	14	—	475	—	16	353
1947	6,733	1,272	3,191	—	432	—	—	131	—	910	—	22	775
1948	11,907	1,150	7,203	—	263	—	—	423	44	1,168	—	16	1,640
1949	7,595	421	3,415	—	175	—	—	529	39	1,157	—	40	1,819
1950	4,508	168	1,280	—	121	—	378	100	24	729	—	13	1,695
1951	7,149	164	335	—	109	—	968	271	21	3,228	—	3	2,050
1952	9,328	34	263	—	123	—	485	3,814	47	1,179	—	12	3,371
1953	8,231	—	528	—	104	—	1,344	2,579	75	1,074	—	13	2,514
1954	9,970	—	254	—	144	—	1,778	3,846	175	1,234	—	33	2,506
1955	10,935	—	568	—	194	—	1,525	4,150	263	1,598	—	54	2,583
1956	17,327	—	1,386	—	185	—	2,175	5,967	579	1,792	—	48	5,195
1957	20,008	—	2,098	—	196	—	2,600	6,829	577	1,874	—	77	5,757
1958	20,870	—	1,143	1,458	323	454	4,788	6,847	1,470	2,034	—	197	2,156
1959	25,259	—	1,702	3,734	351	561	5,335	6,248	1,614	2,503	—	229	2,982
1960	21,429	1,154	1,380	1,760	244	459	4,478	5,699	1,410	2,791	302	200	1,552
1961	19,264	1,313	900	2,039	292	3,774	488	4,955	1,442	2,628	274	296	863
1962	20,217	1,382	1,356	2,490	390	3,015	647	4,519	1,463	3,354	111	304	1,186
1963	23,211	1,637	1,605	2,825	965	3,466	753	4,605	2,560	3,483	51	307	954
1964	21,279	1,703	2,684	2,166	488	2,320	830	4,367	2,329	2,862	72	331	1,127
1965	20,040	1,790	1,611	2,249	467	2,002	898	4,119	2,139	2,963	353	365	1,084
1966	40,113	3,520	2,948	13,803	2,293	1,846	1,122	4,058	2,414	5,894	354	365	1,496
1967	57,574	4,656	7,118	15,737	4,129	2,565	1,254	4,623	3,845	10,336	604	491	2,216
1968	56,298	4,629	4,851	9,838	4,165	3,706	1,240	4,506	3,592	16,086	1,574	325	1,786
1969	72,959	6,411	5,264	14,140	5,205	3,739	1,368	4,792	5,854	20,263	2,712	556	2,655
1970	91,059	6,777	6,427	9,720	8,795	1,739	3,169	5,561	8,888	30,507	3,792	1,339	4,345
1971	98,062	6,503	7,597	7,960	13,056	2,270	2,308	5,819	13,706	27,688	6,427	1,147	3,581
1972	115,978	8,559	8,511	10,916	15,592	2,880	2,995	6,451	18,110	28,690	9,067	1,531	2,676
1973	119,984	7,988	9,153	10,283	11,977	2,853	2,879	6,339	22,313	30,248	10,990	1,447	3,514
1974	127,003	9,482	10,038	10,696	11,704	2,491	2,891	5,473	27,495	32,461	9,457	1,433	3,382
1975	129,196	9,318	9,201	12,547	14,336	2,209	3,509	4,826	28,100	31,323	8,731	1,071	4,025
1976	146,725	10,403	9,925	13,740	16,143	2,623	5,170	4,808	30,577	36,773	11,164	956	4,443
(TQ)	37,725	3,152	3,031	3,209	4,127	1,051	1,233	1,222	6,864	9,622	2,745	262	1,207
1977	150,842	11,561	12,513	12,272	16,865	4,191	4,446	4,557	30,665	38,507	9,721	991	4,553
1978	243,596	10,616	14,455	11,145	19,145	5,861	4,460	4,503	28,796	36,599	95,004	1,022	11,990
1979	182,970	11,754	12,251	16,838	18,632	8,297	4,304	4,509	28,692	40,759	30,482	1,306	5,146
1980	236,097	—	27,651	—	22,607	—	—	4,225	—	—	—	2,233	179,381 [6]
1981	264,343	7,780	25,803	4,055	21,522	11,105	3,542	3,896	32,663	43,772	88,984	2,766	18,455
1982	313,291	6,452	36,984	4,971	21,738	10,314	3,356	3,903	31,724	45,102	128,087	2,864	17,796
1983	277,701	5,659	42,475	5,948	25,451	11,163	3,239	4,092	33,339	41,546	85,217	2,263	17,309
1984	247,775	11,217	29,109	12,290	23,617	11,131	4,136	4,517	32,537	46,985	60,917	1,652	9,667
1985	255,164	10,841	33,095	10,795	24,536	12,327	4,279	4,552	34,791	53,137	55,079	1,690	10,042
1986	258,546	11,340	32,389	9,930	24,808	12,031	5,124	4,444	35,164	61,492	48,893	1,975	10,956
1987	248,293	11,034	32,669	8,785	26,394	10,323	4,753	4,711	35,397	58,315	42,606	2,080	11,226
1988	254,745	12,025	34,300	11,817	25,312	9,846	4,544	5,085	34,151	61,017	44,015	2,200	10,533
1989	296,420	14,275	39,284	15,257	28,599	13,027	5,494	5,454	33,016	66,119	58,044	2,538	15,313
1990	321,879	16,717	40,639	14,367	28,809	14,905	5,906	6,431	30,964	71,279	69,031	3,205	19,626
1991	342,157	16,546	39,922	15,895	42,707	9,927	5,116	5,600	25,430	68,750	72,482	3,466	36,316
1992	344,802	19,469	47,589	16,802	34,841	6,995	5,938	11,735	18,734	63,478	97,146	3,203	18,872
1993	345,425	19,098	73,532	14,026	38,653	8,908	5,216	7,673	17,320	63,406	76,814	3,487	17,292
1994	282,449	17,083	58,867	11,953	33,173	6,998	3,982	6,974	15,417	52,832	54,791	3,880	16,499
1995	259,984	17,786	41,112	10,699	33,060	5,646	3,188	5,556	15,053	49,696	54,102	4,806	19,280
1996	300,574	22,063	50,981	11,319	42,819	7,299	4,029	6,617	17,380	54,588	53,354	5,573	24,552
1997	258,561	17,091	44,356	7,974	36,092	6,291	2,951	5,640	13,626	47,842	46,727	4,596	25,374

(TQ) indicates transitional quarter.

[1] Fiscal year varies as follows: 1820–1832, year ending September 30; 1833–1842, year ending December 31; 1843–1850, year ending September 30; 1851–1865, year ending December 31; 1866–1976, year ending June 30; 1977–1997, year ending September 30.

[2] Three quarters ending September 30.

[3] Six months ending June 30.

[4] The large increase in the number of Chinese immigrants in 1882 is due to the imminent passage of the Chinese Exclusion Act.

TABLE Ad136–148   Immigrants, by country of last residence – Asia: 1820–1997   *Continued*

[5] Data for 1892 included in series Ad97.

[6] Because the data on immigrants by country of last residence are limited in this year, the residual category, "other Asia," is large.

Sources

1820–1926: *Annual Report of the Commissioner General of Immigration, Report for 1926*, Table 74. 1927–1931: *Annual Report of the Commissioner General of Immigration, 1931*, Table 84. 1932: *Annual Report of the Commissioner General of Immigration, 1932*, Table 2. 1933: U.S. Bureau of the Census, *Historical Statistics of the United States* (U.S. Government Printing Office, 1975), based on unpublished data from the U.S. Immigration and Naturalization Service. 1934–1937: "Immigrant Aliens Admitted and Emigrant Aliens Departed, Years Ended June 30, 1934–1937, by Countries of Last or Intended Future Permanent Residence," *Annual Report of the Secretary of Labor, 1937*. 1938–1940: *Annual Report of the Attorney General of the United States, for Fiscal Year Ended June 30, 1941*, Table VII. 1941–1945: *Annual Report of the INS, 1945*, Table 13. 1946–1947: *Annual Report of the INS, 1947*, Table 13. 1948–1950: *Annual Report of the INS, 1951*, Table 13. 1951–1956: *Annual Report of the INS, 1956*, Table 4. 1957–1959: *Annual Report of the INS, 1959*, Table 13. 1960–1971: *Annual Report of the INS*, Table 6A. 1972–1977: INS Public Use Tapes. 1978: *Statistical Yearbook of the INS*, Table 6A. 1979: INS Public Use Tapes. 1980: *Statistical Yearbook of the INS, 1981*, Table 2. 1981–1983: *Statistical Yearbook of the INS, 1985*, Table IMM1. 1984: *Statistical Yearbook of the INS, 1984*, Table IMM2.4. 1985: *Statistical Yearbook of the INS, 1985*, Table IMM2.4. 1986–1988: INS Public Use Tapes. 1990–1991: *Statistical Yearbook of the INS*, Table 8. 1991–1996: *INS Statistical Yearbook*, Table 9.

Documentation

Series Ad137. Includes Bahrain (1974–1979, 1984–1988), Iraq (1961–1979, 1984–), Jordan (1960–1979, 1981–), Kuwait (1972–1979, 1984–), Lebanon (1960–1979, 1981–), Oman (1972–1979, 1984–1996), Palestine (1925–1932, 1934–1952), Qatar (1974–1979, 1984–1996), Saudi Arabia (1972–1979, 1984–), Syria (1925–1932, 1934–1946, 1963–1979, 1984–), United Arab Emirates (1972–1979, 1984–), and Yemen (1972–).

Series Ad138. Includes Formosa/Taiwan, for which separate data have been published since 1984.

Series Ad140. Data for India for 1933–1957 were obtained from previously unpublished U.S. Immigration and Naturalization Service (INS) data cited in "Immigrants by Country (India), 1820 to 1970," in U.S. Bureau of the Census (1975), series C-105, p. 197.

Series Ad142. Prior to 1948, included in Palestine.

Series Ad143. Includes separate data published for Ryuku Islands for 1970–1979.

Series Ad144. Data for Korea for 1948–1957 obtained from previously unpublished INS data cited in "Immigrants by Country (Korea), 1820 to 1970," in U.S. Bureau of the Census (1975), series C-107, p. 197.

Series Ad145. Prior to 1934, the Philippines were recorded in separate tables as insular travel.

Series Ad146. Includes Brunei (1972–1979, 1984–1985), Burma (1971–1979, 1984–), Cambodia (1972–1979, 1981–), Indonesia (1960–1979, 1984–), Laos (1972–1979, 1981–), Malaysia (1972–1979, 1984–), Singapore (1972–1979, 1984–), Thailand (1932, 1968–1979, 1981–), and Vietnam (1966–1979, 1981–).

Series Ad147. Data for Turkey for 1933–1957 obtained from previously unpublished INS data cited in "Immigrants by Country (Turkey in Asia), 1820 to 1970," in U.S. Bureau of the Census (1975), series C-103.

TABLE Ad149–161   Immigrants, by country of birth – Asia: 1941–1997[1]

Contributed by Robert Barde, Susan B. Carter, and Richard Sutch

Fiscal year	Total	Arab states	China	Hong Kong	India	Iran	Israel	Japan	Korea	Philippines	Southeast Asia	Turkey	Other
	Ad149	Ad150	Ad151	Ad152	Ad153	Ad154	Ad155	Ad156	Ad157	Ad158	Ad159	Ad160	Ad161
	Number	Number	Number	Number	Number	Number	Number	Number	Number	Number	Number	Number	Number
1941	1,025	126	357	—	101	—	—	103	—	91	—	—	247
1942	432	62	88	—	0	—	—	20	—	0	—	—	262
1943	362	47	56	—	40	—	—	16	—	9	—	—	194
1944	364	35	72	—	43	—	—	9	—	15	—	—	190
1945	575	52	109	—	95	—	—	3	—	15	—	—	301
1946	1,921	193	337	—	407	—	—	17	—	293	—	—	674
1947	4,098	363	1,407	—	375	—	—	82	—	739	—	—	1,132
1948	7,626	376	3,987	—	239	—	—	371	—	1,122	—	—	1,531
1949	6,355	234	2,823	—	166	—	—	508	—	1,068	—	—	1,556
1950	4,821	226	1,494	—	153	245	110	76	10	595	—	206	1,706
1951	5,147	504	1,821	—	134	237	261	198	32	760	96	516	588
1952	9,456	463	1,421	54	153	223	206	4,517	127	1,066	112	441	673
1953	8,000	690	1,536	98	155	160	421	2,432	115	1,160	115	269	849
1954	11,854	832	2,770	177	308	249	515	3,882	254	1,633	217	519	498
1955	12,337	846	2,705	160	332	219	471	4,089	315	1,784	185	566	665
1956	17,974	1,552	4,450	418	314	227	857	5,712	703	1,873	525	764	579
1957	23,561	1,783	5,425	546	337	328	1,275	6,554	648	1,996	3,184	771	714
1958	20,382	1,318	3,213	342	513	433	1,681	6,752	1,604	2,236	455	1,046	789
1959	24,602	1,517	5,722	844	506	409	2,057	6,159	1,720	2,633	1,080	1,068	887

Notes appear at end of table   (continued)

TABLE Ad149–161   Immigrants, by country of birth – Asia: 1941–1997   *Continued*

	Total	Arab states	China	Hong Kong	India	Iran	Israel	Japan	Korea	Philippines	Southeast Asia	Turkey	Other
	Ad149	Ad150	Ad151	Ad152	Ad153	Ad154	Ad155	Ad156	Ad157	Ad158	Ad159	Ad160	Ad161
Fiscal year	Number	Number	Number	Number	Number	Number	Number	Number	Number	Number	Number	Number	Number
1960	24,956	2,526	3,681	475	391	429	1,608	5,843	1,507	2,954	4,657	885	0
1961	22,299	2,624	3,213	625	421	471	1,318	4,684	1,534	2,738	3,901	770	0
1962	23,019	2,744	4,017	652	545	601	1,127	4,268	1,538	3,437	3,176	914	0
1963	25,021	2,889	4,658	712	1,173	705	1,325	4,390	2,580	3,618	1,709	1,262	0
1964	21,845	2,998	5,009	639	634	754	940	4,142	2,362	3,006	401	960	0
1965	20,683	2,952	4,057	712	582	804	882	3,857	2,165	3,130	637	905	0
1966	41,432	4,636	13,736	3,872	2,458	1,085	939	3,863	2,492	6,093	704	1,554	0
1967	61,446	6,348	19,741	5,355	4,642	1,414	1,481	4,315	3,956	10,865	470	2,213	646
1968	58,989	6,263	12,738	3,696	4,682	1,280	1,989	4,138	3,811	16,731	1,228	1,760	673
1969	75,679	8,774	15,440	5,453	5,963	1,352	2,049	4,476	6,045	20,744	2,055	2,058	1,270
1970	94,883	6,973	14,093	3,863	10,114	1,825	1,980	5,106	9,314	31,203	4,101	2,067	4,244
1971	103,459	7,420	14,417	3,204	14,317	2,411	1,739	5,326	14,297	28,471	7,163	1,748	2,946
1972	121,058	8,438	17,339	4,391	16,929	3,059	2,099	5,777	18,876	29,376	9,399	1,986	3,389
1973	124,160	8,120	17,297	4,359	13,128	2,998	1,917	5,676	22,930	30,799	11,277	1,899	3,760
1974	130,662	9,496	18,056	4,629	12,795	2,608	1,998	4,917	28,028	32,857	9,750	1,867	3,661
1975	132,469	9,224	18,536	4,891	15,785	2,337	2,125	4,293	28,362	31,751	9,199	1,592	4,374
1976	149,881	10,886	18,823	5,766	17,500	2,700	2,982	4,275	30,803	37,281	12,084	1,676	5,105
(TQ)	39,184	3,662	5,034	1,493	4,572	1,031	845	1,142	6,887	9,738	3,022	479	1,279
1977	157,759	13,729	19,764	5,632	18,636	4,261	3,008	4,192	30,917	39,111	11,590	1,758	5,161
1978	249,776	12,355	21,331	5,158	20,772	5,861	3,276	4,028	29,288	37,216	102,959	1,578	5,954
1979	189,293	13,247	24,264	4,119	19,717	8,476	3,093	4,063	29,248	41,300	34,046	1,764	5,956
1980	236,097	12,692	27,651	3,860	22,607	10,410	3,517	4,225	32,320	42,316	67,687	2,233	6,579
1981	264,343	13,587	25,803	4,055	21,522	11,105	3,542	3,896	32,663	43,772	92,545	2,766	9,087
1982	313,291	12,903	36,984	4,971	21,738	10,314	3,356	3,903	31,724	45,102	131,550	2,864	7,882
1983	277,961	10,796	42,475	5,948	25,451	11,163	3,239	4,092	33,339	41,546	88,384	2,263	9,265
1984	256,273	11,400	35,841	5,465	24,964	13,807	3,066	4,043	33,042	42,768	69,349	1,793	10,735
1985	264,691	11,251	39,682	5,171	26,026	16,071	3,113	4,086	35,253	47,978	63,504	1,691	10,865
1986	268,248	11,456	38,530	5,021	26,227	16,505	3,790	3,959	35,776	52,558	60,981	1,753	11,692
1987	257,684	11,970	37,772	4,706	27,803	14,426	3,699	4,174	35,849	50,060	53,944	1,596	11,685
1988	264,465	13,105	38,387	8,546	26,268	15,246	3,640	4,512	34,703	50,697	56,872	1,642	10,847
1989	312,149	16,113	46,246	9,740	31,175	21,243	4,244	4,849	34,222	57,034	70,442	2,007	14,834
1990	338,581	18,257	46,966	9,393	30,667	24,977	4,664	5,734	32,301	63,756	80,452	2,468	18,946
1991	358,533	17,842	46,299	10,427	45,064	19,569	4,181	5,049	26,518	63,596	81,484	2,528	35,976
1992	356,955	20,890	55,251	10,452	36,755	13,233	5,104	11,028	19,359	61,022	102,852	2,488	18,521
1993	358,047	21,147	79,907	9,161	40,121	14,841	4,494	6,908	18,026	63,457	80,658	2,204	17,123
1994	292,589	19,690	64,017	7,731	34,921	11,422	3,425	6,093	16,011	53,535	57,668	1,840	16,236
1995	267,931	19,227	44,840	7,249	34,748	9,201	2,523	4,837	16,047	50,984	56,205	2,947	19,123
1996	307,807	22,478	55,129	7,834	44,859	11,084	3,126	6,011	18,185	55,876	55,191	3,657	24,377
1997	265,810	17,082	47,892	5,577	38,071	9,642	2,448	5,097	14,239	49,117	48,694	3,145	24,806

(TQ) indicates transitional quarter.

[1] Through 1976, fiscal year ending June 30; thereafter, fiscal year ending September 30.

Sources

1941: *Annual Report of the Attorney General of the United States, 1941.* 1942: *Annual Report of Lemuel B. Schofield, Special Assistant to the Attorney General in Charge of the Immigration and Naturalization Service, 1942.* 1943–1949: *Immigration and Naturalization Service Annual Report of 1952,* Table 13A. 1950: *INS Annual Report 1959,* Table 14. 1951: *INS Annual Report 1960,* Table 14. 1952: *INS Annual Report 1961,* Table 14. 1953–1955: *INS Annual Report 1962,* Table 14. 1956–1961: *INS Annual Report 1965,* Table 14. 1962–1969: *INS Statistical Yearbook 1971,* Table 14. 1970: *INS Statistical Yearbook 1970,* Table 6. 1971–1979: *INS Annual Report 1980,* Table 13. 1980–1983: *INS Statistical Yearbook 1984,* Table IMM 1.3. 1984–1990: *INS Statistical Yearbook 1992,* Table 3. 1991–1997: *INS Statistical Yearbook 1997,* Table 3.

Documentation

Series Ad150. Arab states in Asia (Arab Middle East) comprise Bahrain (1971–1979 and 1986–1997), Iraq (1953–), Jordan (1950–), Kuwait (1971–), Lebanon (1951–), Oman (1971–1979 and 1986–1997), Palestine (1941–1949), Qatar (1974–1979 and 1986–1997), Saudi Arabia (1971–1979; 1984–), Syria (1956–), United Arab Emirates (1966–1969; 1971–1979; 1984–), Yemen (1991–), South Yemen-Aden (1971–1990), and North Yemen-Sana'a (1960–1969; 1971–1990).

Series Ad151. China includes data for Formosa/Taiwan (published separately for 1982–) and Mongolia (published separately for 1991–).

Series Ad153. India includes Portuguese India.

Series Ad156. Japan includes data for Ryuku Islands (published separately for 1953–1969), Bonin Islands, and Okinawa.

Series Ad159. Southeast Asia comprises Brunei (1971–1979 and 1986–1997), Burma (1971–), Cambodia (1951–), Indonesia (1951–, including Irian Barat and Portuguese Timor), Laos (1971–), Malaysia (1956–1966; 1971–), Singapore (1971–), Thailand (1968–), and Vietnam (1970–).

Series Ad160. Data for Turkey were originally listed by the U.S. Immigration and Naturalization Service as part of Europe for the period 1950–1970.

TABLE Ad162–172   Immigrants, by country of last residence – North America: 1820–1997[1]

Contributed by Robert Barde, Susan B. Carter, and Richard Sutch

			Central America			Caribbean					Other
	Total	Canada	Mexico	El Salvador	Other	Cuba	Dominican Republic	Haiti	Jamaica	Other	
	Ad162	Ad163	Ad164 [2]	Ad165	Ad166	Ad167	Ad168	Ad169	Ad170	Ad171	Ad172
Fiscal year	Number	Number	Number	Number	Number	Number	Number	Number	Number	Number	Number
1820	376	209	1	—	2	—	—	—	—	164	—
1821	295	184	4	—	0	—	—	—	—	107	—
1822	371	204	5	—	3	—	—	—	—	159	—
1823	362	167	35	—	0	—	—	—	—	160	—
1824	534	155	110	—	10	—	—	—	—	259	—
1825	779	314	68	—	8	—	—	—	—	389	—
1826	768	223	106	—	12	—	—	—	—	427	—
1827	526	165	127	—	7	—	—	—	—	227	—
1828	2,013	267	1,089	—	5	—	—	—	—	652	—
1829	3,226	409	2,290	—	10	—	—	—	—	517	—
1830	2,159	189	983	—	50	—	—	—	—	937	—
1831	2,152	176	692	—	3	—	—	—	—	1,281	—
1832	2,697	608	827	—	6	—	—	—	—	1,256	—
1833	3,255	1,194	779	—	18	—	—	—	—	1,264	—
1834	2,705	1,020	885	—	9	—	—	—	—	791	—
1835	3,167	1,193	1,032	—	4	—	—	—	—	938	—
1836	4,790	2,814	798	—	0	—	—	—	—	1,178	—
1837	3,537	1,279	627	—	4	—	—	—	—	1,627	—
1838	2,918	1,476	211	—	0	—	—	—	—	1,231	—
1839	3,568	1,926	353	—	0	—	—	—	—	1,289	—
1840	3,779	1,938	395	—	0	—	—	—	—	1,446	—
1841	3,210	1,816	352	—	0	—	—	—	—	1,042	—
1842	3,892	2,078	403	—	1	—	—	—	—	1,410	—
1843 [3]	2,792	1,502	398	—	12	—	—	—	—	880	—
1844	3,679	2,711	197	—	0	—	—	—	—	771	—
1845	4,955	3,195	498	—	21	—	—	—	—	1,241	—
1846	5,433	3,855	222	—	5	—	—	—	—	1,351	—
1847	5,161	3,827	62	—	21	—	—	—	—	1,251	—
1848	7,839	6,473	24	—	4	—	—	—	—	1,338	—
1849	8,714	6,890	518	—	233	—	—	—	—	1,073	—
1850	11,268	7,796 [5]	498	—	71	—	—	—	—	2,903	—
(TQ)	1,947	1,580	99	—	0	—	—	—	—	268	—
1851	9,644	7,438 [5]	181	—	96	—	—	—	—	1,929	—
1852	7,656	6,352	72	—	0	—	—	—	—	1,232	—
1853	5,992	5,424	162	—	0	—	—	—	—	406	—
1854	8,397	6,891	446	—	24	—	—	—	—	1,036	—
1855	9,069	7,761	420	—	1	—	—	—	—	887	—
1856	8,874	6,493	741	—	303	—	—	—	—	1,337	—
1857	6,728	5,670	133	—	2	—	—	—	—	923	—
1858	5,690	4,603	429	—	11	—	—	—	—	647	—
1859	5,311	4,163	265	—	4	—	—	—	—	879	—
1860	6,135	4,514	229	—	8	—	—	—	—	1,384	—
1861	2,666	2,069	218	—	21	—	—	—	—	358	—
1862	4,029	3,275	142	—	27	—	—	—	—	585	—
1863	4,053	3,464	96	—	2	—	—	—	—	491	—
1864	4,455	3,636	99	—	2	—	—	—	—	718	—
1865	22,630	21,586	193	—	0	—	—	—	—	851	—
1866 [4]	33,288	32,150	239	—	4	—	—	—	—	895	—
1867	24,491	23,379	292	—	3	—	—	—	—	817	—
1868	3,333	2,785	129	—	0	—	—	—	—	419	—
1869	23,676	21,120	320	—	3	—	—	—	—	2,233	—
1870	42,589	40,414	463	—	33	—	—	—	—	1,679	—
1871	48,739	47,164	402	—	4	—	—	—	—	1,169	—
1872	42,103	40,204	569	—	8	—	—	—	—	1,322	—
1873	40,169	37,891	606	—	38	—	—	—	—	1,634	—
1874	35,195	33,020	386	—	12	—	—	—	—	1,777	—
1875	26,508	24,097	610	—	11	—	—	—	—	1,790	—
1876	24,530	22,505	631	—	12	—	—	—	—	1,382	—
1877	23,978	22,137	445	—	6	—	—	—	—	1,390	—
1878	27,116	25,592	465	—	40	—	—	—	—	1,019	—
1879	32,974	31,286	556	—	9	—	—	—	—	1,123	—

Notes appear at end of table

(continued)

TABLE Ad162–172 Immigrants, by country of last residence – North America: 1820–1997 *Continued*

			Central America			Caribbean					
	Total	Canada	Mexico	El Salvador	Other	Cuba	Dominican Republic	Haiti	Jamaica	Other	Other
	Ad162	Ad163	Ad164 [2]	Ad165	Ad166	Ad167	Ad168	Ad169	Ad170	Ad171	Ad172
Fiscal year	Number	Number	Number	Number	Number	Number	Number	Number	Number	Number	Number
1880	101,604	99,744	492	—	17	—	—	—	—	1,351	—
1881	127,467	125,450	325	—	12	—	—	—	—	1,680	—
1882	100,038	98,366	366	—	15	—	—	—	—	1,291	—
1883	71,652	70,274	469	—	6	—	—	—	—	903	—
1884	63,274	60,626	430	—	10	—	—	—	—	2,208	—
1885	41,159	38,336	323	—	23	—	—	—	—	2,477	—
1886	2,780	—	—	—	29	—	—	—	—	2,734	17 [9]
1887	4,904	—	—	—	19	—	—	—	—	4,876	9 [9]
1888	4,962	—	—	—	67	—	—	—	—	4,880	15 [9]
1889	5,032	28	—	—	81	—	—	—	—	4,923	0
1890	3,395	183	—	—	142	—	—	—	—	3,070	0
1891	4,418	234	—	—	278	—	—	—	—	3,906	0
1892 [6]	—	—	—	—	—	—	—	—	—	—	—
1893	2,593	— [6]	—	—	— [6]	—	—	—	—	2,593	— [6]
1894	3,512	194	109	—	— [6]	—	—	—	—	3,177	32
1895	3,472	244	116	—	16	—	—	—	—	3,096	0
1896	7,268	278	150	—	12	—	—	—	—	6,828	0
1897	4,488	291	91	—	5	—	—	—	—	4,101	0
1898	2,588	352	107	—	5	—	—	—	—	2,124	0
1899	4,227	1,322	161	—	159	—	—	—	—	2,585	0
1900	5,331	396	237	—	42	—	—	—	—	4,656	0
1901	4,213	540	347	—	130	—	—	—	—	3,176	20
1902	6,361	636	709	—	254	—	—	—	—	4,711	51
1903	10,434	1,058	528	—	597	—	—	—	—	8,170	81
1904	14,753	2,837	1,009	—	605	—	—	—	—	10,193	109
1905	22,641	2,168	2,637	—	1,072	—	—	—	—	16,641	123
1906	21,856	5,063	1,997	—	1,140	—	—	—	—	13,656	0
1907	38,983	19,918	1,406	—	970	—	—	—	—	16,689	0
1908	57,682	38,510	6,067	—	1,217	—	—	—	—	11,888	0
1909	80,302	51,941	16,251	—	930	—	—	—	—	11,180	0
1910	87,383	56,555	18,691	—	893	—	—	—	—	11,244	0
1911	91,315	56,830	19,889	—	1,193	—	—	—	—	13,403	0
1912	92,937	55,990	23,238	—	1,242	—	—	—	—	12,467	0
1913	99,659	73,802	11,926	—	1,473	—	—	—	—	12,458	0
1914	116,826	86,139	14,614	—	1,622	—	—	—	—	14,451	0
1915	107,405	82,215	12,340	—	1,252	—	—	—	—	11,598	0
1916	133,138	101,551	18,425	—	1,135	—	—	—	—	12,027	0
1917	140,848	105,399	17,869	—	2,073	—	—	—	—	15,507	0
1918	62,075	32,452	18,524	—	2,220	—	—	—	—	8,879	0
1919	99,015	57,782	29,818	—	2,589	—	—	—	—	8,826	0
1920	158,554	90,025	52,361	—	2,360	—	—	—	—	13,808	0
1921	119,103	72,317	30,758	—	2,254	—	—	—	—	13,774	0
1922	74,780	46,810	19,551	—	970	—	—	—	—	7,449	0
1923	195,235	117,011	63,768	—	1,275	—	—	—	—	13,181	0
1924	309,585	200,690	89,336	—	2,000	—	—	—	—	17,559	0
1925	139,026	102,753	32,964	—	1,199	1,430	—	—	—	676	4
1926	141,286	93,368	43,316	—	1,374	2,281	—	—	—	941	6
1927	158,095	84,580	67,721	—	1,771	3,020	—	—	—	999	4
1928	140,115	75,281	59,016	—	1,751	3,012	—	—	—	1,046	9
1929	112,474	66,451	40,154	—	1,557	3,026	—	—	—	1,280	6
1930	84,802	65,254	12,703	—	1,618	3,132	—	—	—	2,093	2
1931	29,121	22,183	3,333	—	1,107	1,174	—	—	—	1,322	2
1932	11,875	8,003	2,171	73	599	675	77	34	—	243	0
1933	9,488	6,187	1,936	—	503	—	—	—	—	862	0
1934	11,054	7,945	1,801	—	443	—	—	—	—	861	4
1935	10,701	7,782	1,560	—	427	—	—	—	—	931	1
1936	11,294	8,121	1,716	—	470	—	—	—	—	985	2
1937	16,165	12,011	2,347	—	484	—	—	—	—	1,322	1
1938	19,601	14,404	2,502	—	582	—	—	—	—	2,110	3
1939	16,224	10,813	2,640	—	530	—	—	—	—	2,231	10
1940	16,707	11,078	2,313	—	639	—	—	—	—	2,675	2
1941	20,229	11,473	2,824	—	1,239	—	—	—	—	4,687	6

Notes appear at end of table

TABLE Ad162–172 Immigrants, by country of last residence – North America: 1820–1997 *Continued*

			Central America			Caribbean					Other
	Total	Canada	Mexico	El Salvador	Other	Cuba	Dominican Republic	Haiti	Jamaica	Other	Other
	Ad162	Ad163	Ad164 [2]	Ad165	Ad166	Ad167	Ad168	Ad169	Ad170	Ad171	Ad172
Fiscal year	Number	Number	Number	Number	Number	Number	Number	Number	Number	Number	Number
1942	15,388	10,599	2,378	—	805	—	—	—	—	1,599	7
1943	17,469	9,761	4,172	—	1,218	—	—	—	—	2,312	6
1944	21,924	10,143	6,598	—	1,985	—	—	—	—	3,198	0
1945	28,037	11,530	6,702	—	3,423	—	—	—	—	5,452	930
1946	43,433	21,344	7,146	—	2,338	—	—	—	—	5,878	6,727
1947	49,659	24,342	7,558	—	3,386	—	—	—	—	6,728	7,645
1948	49,687	25,485	8,384	—	2,671	—	—	—	—	6,932	6,215
1949	46,218	25,156	8,083	—	2,431	—	—	—	—	6,733	3,815
1950	40,899	21,885	6,744	—	2,169	—	—	—	—	6,206	3,895
1951	44,035	25,880	6,153	—	2,011	—	—	—	—	5,902	4,089
1952	56,458	33,354	9,079	—	2,637	—	—	—	—	6,672	4,716
1953	72,139	36,283	17,183	—	3,016	—	—	—	—	8,628	7,029
1954	89,012	34,873	30,645	—	3,300	—	—	—	—	8,411	11,783
1955	102,782	32,435	43,702	—	3,667	—	—	—	—	12,876	10,102
1956	135,526	42,363	61,320	—	4,916	—	—	—	—	19,512	7,415
1957	123,309	46,354	49,321	—	5,731	—	—	—	—	18,362	3,541
1958	98,828	45,143	26,791	—	6,718	11,701	—	—	—	5,282	3,193
1959	80,196	34,599	22,909	—	6,036	6,901	—	—	—	5,208	4,543
1960	103,031	46,668	32,708	—	6,719	8,126	—	—	—	5,510	3,300
1961	120,485	47,470	41,476	—	7,272	11,239	—	—	—	9,281	3,747
1962	133,321	44,272	55,805	1,337	8,302	6,534	4,476	1,248	5,619	3,040	2,688
1963	142,207	50,509	55,986	1,737	8,969	5,073	10,657	1,675	2,883	2,663	2,055
1964	123,753	51,114	34,448	1,676	10,153	9,561	7,567	1,861	2,089	2,989	2,295
1965	137,262	50,035	40,686	1,742	10,994	13,160	9,451	3,301	2,175	3,054	2,664
1966	134,438	37,273	47,217	1,411	8,478	11,567	16,574	3,553	2,789	3,516	2,060
1967	151,673	34,768	43,034	1,028	7,586	30,869	11,560	3,317	10,072	6,169	3,270
1968	238,745	41,716	44,716	1,596	9,162	95,724 [7]	9,298	6,429	16,690	12,686	728
1969	138,503	29,303	45,748	1,731	8,126	10,177	10,445	5,903	15,672	10,993	405
1970	138,033	26,850	44,821	1,711	7,283	14,632	10,367	6,285	14,160	11,170	754
1971	149,002	22,709	50,324	1,773	7,097	21,741	12,646	7,036	13,816	11,313	547
1972	151,601	18,596	64,209	1,995	6,412	19,885	10,839	5,491	12,730	11,442	2
1973	157,181	14,800	70,411	2,036	7,089	22,537	14,011	4,641	9,615	12,033	8
1974	154,882	12,301	71,863	2,264	7,167	17,402	15,722	3,780	12,174	12,206	3
1975	150,549	11,215	62,552	2,426	7,370	25,611	14,090	4,955	10,867	11,412	51
1976	145,625	11,439	58,354	2,405	7,692	28,433	12,473	5,266	8,743	10,819	1
(TQ)	37,910	3,591	16,095	675	2,185	6,616	2,552	1,230	2,059	2,907	0
1977	189,503	18,003	44,646	4,424	12,468	66,057	11,621	5,213	11,359	15,709	3
1978	224,390	23,495	92,681	5,858	14,333	27,539	19,460	6,079	18,496	13,919	2,530
1979	161,408	20,181	52,479	4,479	13,230	13,988	17,476	6,104	18,748	14,617	106
1980	164,566	13,609	56,680	—	20,968	—	—	—	—	73,296 [8]	13
1981	210,427	11,191	101,268	8,210	16,299	10,858	18,220	6,683	23,569	13,971	158
1982	158,057	10,786	56,106	7,107	16,519	8,209	17,451	8,779	18,711	14,229	160
1983	168,487	11,390	59,079	8,596	16,005	8,978	22,058	8,424	19,535	14,311	111
1984	169,475	15,659	57,820	8,753	18,873	5,699	23,207	9,554	18,997	10,911	2
1985	185,467	16,354	61,290	10,093	18,354	17,115	23,861	9,872	18,277	10,249	2
1986	211,428	16,060	66,753	10,881	19,205	30,787	26,216	12,356	18,916	10,252	2
1987	220,244	16,741	72,511	10,627	19,739	27,363	24,947	14,643	22,430	11,232	11
1988	253,260	15,821	95,170	12,043	19,268	16,610	27,195	34,858	20,474	11,812	9
1989	612,827	18,294	405,660	57,628	43,645	9,523	26,744	13,341	23,572	14,417	3
1990	963,706	24,642	680,186	79,601	66,642	9,436	42,136	19,869	23,667	17,527	0
1991	1,217,272	19,931	947,923	46,923	63,897	9,474	41,422	47,046	22,977	17,672	7
1992	389,469	21,541	214,128	26,077	31,772	10,890	41,948	10,756	18,280	14,071	6
1993	307,399	23,898	126,642	26,794	31,872	12,976	45,464	9,899	16,761	13,085	8
1994	277,668	22,243	111,415	17,669	22,587	14,216	51,221	13,166	13,909	11,238	4
1995	236,207	18,117	90,045	11,670	20,350	17,661	38,493	13,872	16,061	9,934	4
1996	345,823	21,751	163,743	17,847	26,489	26,166	36,284	18,185	18,732	16,624	2
1997	307,019	15,788	146,680	17,741	25,710	29,913	24,966	14,941	17,585	13,690	5

(TQ) indicates transitional quarter.

[1] Fiscal year varies as follows: 1820–1832, year ending September 30; 1833–1842, year ending December 31; 1843–1850, year ending September 30; 1851–1865, year ending December 31; 1866–1976, year ending June 30; 1977–1997, year ending September 30.

[2] No record of immigration for 1886–1893.

[3] Three quarters ending September 30.

[4] Six months ending June 30.

[5] Data in original source were revised.

(continued)

TABLE Ad162–172   Immigrants, by country of last residence – North America: 1820–1997   *Continued*

[6] Included with series Ad97.

[7] Includes 91,509 persons admitted under the Cuban Refugees Act of November 2, 1966.

[8] The large number for "other Caribbean" reflects the absence of country-specific information for Cuba, Dominican Republic, Haiti, and Jamaica in this year.

[9] Includes only Bermuda and British Honduras.

Sources

1820–1926: *Annual Report of the Commissioner General of Immigration, Report for 1926*, Table 74. 1927–1931: *Annual Report of the Commissioner General of Immigration, 1931*, Table 84. 1932: *Annual Report of the Commissioner General of Immigration, 1932*, Table 2. 1933: U.S. Bureau of the Census, *Historical Statistics of the United States* (U.S. Government Printing Office, 1975), based on unpublished data from the U.S. Immigration and Naturalization Service. 1934–1937: "Immigrant Aliens Admitted and Emigrant Aliens Departed, Years Ended June 30, 1934–1937, by Countries of Last or Intended Future Permanent Residence," *Annual Report of the Secretary of Labor, 1937*. 1938–1940: *Annual Report of the Attorney General of the United States, for Fiscal Year Ended June 30, 1941*, Table VII. 1941–1945: *Annual Report of the INS, 1945*, Table 13. 1946–1947: *Annual Report of the INS, 1947*, Table 13. 1948–1950: *Annual Report of the INS, 1951*, Table 13. 1951–1956: *Annual Report of the INS, 1956*, Table 4. 1957–1959: *Annual Report of the INS, 1959*, Table 13. 1960–1971: *Annual Report of the INS*, Table 6A. 1972–1977: INS Public Use Tapes. 1978: *Statistical Yearbook of the INS*, Table 6A. 1979: INS Public Use Tapes. 1980: *Statistical Yearbook of the INS, 1981*, Table 2. 1981–1983: *Statistical Yearbook of the INS, 1985*, Table IMM1. 1984: *Statistical Yearbook of the INS, 1984*, Table IMM2.4. 1985: *Statistical Yearbook of the INS, 1985*, Table IMM2.4. 1986–1988: INS Public Use Tapes. 1990–1991: *Statistical Yearbook of the INS*, Table 8. 1991–1997: *INS Statistical Yearbook*, Table 9.

Documentation

Series Ad163. Prior to 1905, Canada and Newfoundland were recorded as British North America.

Series Ad166. Includes separate data published for Belize (1925–1932, as British Honduras; 1967–1968; 1984–), Canal Zone (1932), Costa Rica (1932, 1962–1979, 1984–), Guatemala (1932, 1962–1979, 1981–), Honduras (1932, 1962–1979, 1984–), Nicaragua (1932, 1962–1979, 1984–), and Panama (1932, 1962–1979, 1981–).

Series Ad171. Includes separate data for Anguilla (1984–1985, 1990–), Antigua-Barbuda (1984–1994), Bahamas (1984–), Barbados (1967–1979, 1984–1989, 1995), Bermuda (1984–1987), British Virgin Islands (1984–1987), Cayman Islands (1970–1979, 1984–1985), Dominica (1984–), Grenada (1984–), Guadeloupe (1932, 1984–1985), Martinique (1984–1985), Montserrat (1984–1985), Netherlands Antilles (1932, 1984–1985), St. Kitts and Nevis (1967–1978, 1984–1993), St. Lucia (1984–1994), St. Vincent and the Grenadines (1984–1994), Trinidad and Tobago (1967–1979, 1981–), and Turks and Caicos Islands (1984–1985).

Series Ad172. Includes separate data published in 1984–1985 for Greenland and for St. Pierre and Miquelon.

TABLE Ad173–190   Immigrants, by country of birth – North America: 1941–1997[1]

Contributed by Robert Barde, Susan B. Carter, and Richard Sutch

				Central America						
	Total	Canada	Mexico	Total	El Salvador	Guatemala	Honduras	Nicaragua	Panama	Other
	Ad173	Ad174	Ad175	Ad176	Ad177	Ad178	Ad179	Ad180	Ad181	Ad182
Fiscal year	Number	Number	Number	Number	Number	Number	Number	Number	Number	Number
1941	12,484	8,635	2,068	659	—	—	—	—	—	659
1942	12,569	8,698	2,182	711	—	—	—	—	—	711
1943	13,718	7,429	3,985	1,181	—	—	—	—	—	1,181
1944	17,961	7,386	6,399	1,876	—	—	—	—	—	1,876
1945	24,229	9,379	6,455	3,395	—	—	—	—	—	3,395
1946	33,125	18,627	6,805	2,171	—	—	—	—	—	2,171
1947	40,295	22,008	7,775	3,470	—	—	—	—	—	3,470
1948	42,270	22,612	8,730	2,884	—	—	—	—	—	2,884
1949	39,469	21,515	7,977	2,493	—	—	—	—	—	2,493
1950	34,004	18,043	6,841	2,151	—	—	—	—	—	2,151
1951	35,482	20,809	6,372	1,970	—	—	—	—	—	1,970
1952	48,092	28,141	9,600	2,642	—	—	—	—	—	2,642
1953	60,107	28,967	18,454	3,056	566	323	498	696	551	422
1954	77,772	27,055	37,456	3,488	457	412	457	630	946	586
1955	90,732	23,091	50,772	3,683	383	394	454	789	1,024	639
1956	119,417	29,533	65,047	4,981	496	565	591	1,203	1,372	754
1957	106,942	33,203	49,154	5,780	690	779	750	1,200	1,439	922
1958	80,788	30,055	26,712	6,573	757	644	1,016	1,326	1,744	1,086
1959	64,740	23,082	23,061	5,808	679	510	879	1,129	1,571	1,040
1960	85,075	30,990	32,684	6,661	1,091	627	755	1,301	1,722	1,165
1961	103,388	32,038	41,632	6,817	1,007	662	905	1,306	1,875	1,062
1962	121,226	30,377	55,291	8,405	1,289	939	1,154	1,083	2,098	1,842
1963	129,705	36,003	55,253	10,275	1,695	1,228	1,504	1,430	2,184	2,234
1964	112,973	38,074	32,967	11,500	1,684	1,436	1,776	1,531	1,750	3,323
1965	126,729	38,327	37,969	12,423	1,768	1,613	2,355	1,332	1,933	3,422
1966	127,340	28,358	45,163	9,658	1,415	1,584	1,958	984	1,594	2,123
1967	140,138	23,442	42,371	8,709	1,045	1,469	1,550	729	1,676	2,240
1968	228,060	27,662	43,563	10,862	1,625	2,148	1,720	646	1,976	2,747
1969	132,426	18,582	44,623	9,692	1,762	2,291	1,286	419	1,585	2,349

Notes appear at end of table

TABLE Ad173–190   Immigrants, by country of birth – North America: 1941–1997   *Continued*

				Central America						
	Total	Canada	Mexico	Total	El Salvador	Guatemala	Honduras	Nicaragua	Panama	Other
	Ad173	Ad174	Ad175	Ad176	Ad177	Ad178	Ad179	Ad180	Ad181	Ad182
Fiscal year	Number	Number	Number	Number	Number	Number	Number	Number	Number	Number
1970	129,114	13,804	44,469	9,343	1,698	2,130	1,263	670	1,630	1,952
1971	140,126	13,128	50,105	8,628	1,776	2,194	1,146	566	1,497	1,449
1972	144,377	10,776	64,040	8,110	2,001	1,640	964	606	1,517	1,382
1973	152,788	8,951	70,141	8,842	2,042	1,759	1,330	670	1,612	1,429
1974	151,445	7,654	71,586	9,237	2,278	1,638	1,390	942	1,664	1,325
1975	146,669	7,308	62,205	9,696	2,416	1,859	1,357	947	1,694	1,423
1976	142,307	7,638	57,863	9,913	2,363	1,970	1,310	934	1,699	1,637
(TQ)	36,807	2,458	16,001	2,797	659	585	288	326	463	476
1977	187,346	12,688	44,079	19,485	4,426	3,599	1,626	1,850	2,390	5,594
1978	220,784	16,863	92,367	20,153	5,826	3,996	2,727	1,888	3,108	2,608
1979	157,579	13,772	52,096	17,547	4,479	2,583	2,545	1,938	3,472	2,530
1980	164,772	13,609	56,680	20,968	6,101	3,751	2,552	2,337	3,572	2,655
1981	210,427	11,191	101,268	24,509	8,210	3,928	2,358	2,752	4,613	2,648
1982	158,057	10,786	56,106	23,626	7,107	3,633	3,186	3,077	3,320	3,303
1983	168,487	11,390	59,079	24,601	8,596	4,090	3,619	2,983	2,546	2,767
1984	166,706	10,791	57,557	24,088	8,787	3,937	3,405	2,718	2,276	2,965
1985	182,045	11,385	61,077	26,302	10,156	4,389	3,726	2,786	2,611	2,634
1986	207,714	11,039	66,533	28,380	10,929	5,158	4,532	2,826	2,194	2,741
1987	216,550	11,876	72,351	29,296	10,693	5,729	4,751	3,294	2,084	2,745
1988	250,009	11,783	95,039	30,715	12,045	5,723	4,302	3,311	2,486	2,848
1989	607,398	12,151	405,172	101,034	57,878	19,049	7,593	8,830	3,482	4,202
1990	957,558	16,812	679,068	146,202	80,173	32,303	12,024	11,562	3,433	6,707
1991	1,210,981	13,504	946,167	111,093	47,351	25,527	11,451	17,842	4,204	4,718
1992	384,047	15,205	213,802	57,558	26,191	10,521	6,552	8,949	2,845	2,500
1993	301,380	17,156	126,561	58,162	26,818	11,870	7,306	7,086	2,679	2,403
1994	272,226	16,068	111,398	39,908	17,644	7,389	5,265	5,255	2,378	1,977
1995	231,526	12,932	89,932	31,814	11,744	6,213	5,496	4,408	2,247	1,706
1996	340,540	15,825	163,572	44,289	17,903	8,763	5,870	6,903	2,560	2,290
1997	307,488	11,609	146,865	43,676	17,969	7,785	7,616	6,331	1,981	1,994

			The Caribbean					
	Total	Cuba	Dominican Republic	Haiti	Jamaica	Trinidad and Tobago	Other	Other
	Ad183	Ad184	Ad185	Ad186	Ad187	Ad188	Ad189	Ad190
Fiscal year	Number	Number	Number	Number	Number	Number	Number	Number
1941	1,122	701	—	—	—	—	421	—
1942	978	—	—	—	—	—	978	—
1943	1,116	—	—	—	—	—	1,116	7
1944	2,299	—	—	—	—	—	2,299	1
1945	4,660	—	—	—	—	—	4,660	340
1946	4,876	—	—	—	—	—	4,876	646
1947	6,299	—	—	—	—	—	6,299	743
1948	6,994	—	—	—	—	—	6,994	1,050
1949	6,518	—	—	—	—	—	6,518	966
1950	6,093	2,179	—	—	—	—	3,914	3,027
1951	5,553	1,893	—	—	—	—	3,660	778
1952	6,723	2,536	—	—	—	—	4,187	986
1953	8,875	3,509	1,666	266	243	—	3,191	755
1954	8,999	5,527	435	493	997	—	1,547	774
1955	12,499	9,294	606	433	901	—	1,265	687
1956	19,022	14,943	874	620	1,018	—	1,567	1,093
1957	18,056	13,733	1,004	405	1,123	—	1,791	1,093
1958	16,762	11,581	1,168	766	1,342	—	1,905	1,028
1959	12,218	7,021	873	543	1,695	—	2,086	913

Notes appear at end of table

(continued)

TABLE Ad173–190   Immigrants, by country of birth – North America: 1941–1997   *Continued*

Fiscal year	Total Ad183 Number	Cuba Ad184 Number	The Caribbean Dominican Republic Ad185 Number	Haiti Ad186 Number	Jamaica Ad187 Number	Trinidad and Tobago Ad188 Number	Other Ad189 Number	Other Ad190 Number
1960	14,047	8,283	756	931	1,340	—	2,737	1,055
1961	22,258	14,287	3,045	1,025	1,283	415	2,203	956
1962	26,472	16,254	4,603	1,322	1,573	388	2,332	1,116
1963	27,600	10,587	10,683	1,851	1,880	448	2,151	1,054
1964	29,960	15,808	7,537	2,082	1,762	413	2,358	1,066
1965	37,583	19,760	9,504	3,609	1,837	485	2,388	938
1966	43,804	17,355	16,503	3,801	2,743	756	2,646	898
1967	65,273	33,321	11,514	3,567	10,483	2,160	4,228	501
1968	145,751	99,312	9,250	6,806	17,470	5,266	7,647	409
1969	59,395	13,751	10,670	6,542	16,947	6,833	4,652	558
1970	61,403	16,334	10,807	6,932	15,033	7,350	4,947	95
1971	68,189	21,615	12,624	7,444	14,571	7,130	4,805	76
1972	61,373	20,045	10,760	5,809	13,427	6,615	4,717	78
1973	64,769	24,147	13,921	4,786	9,963	7,035	4,917	85
1974	62,959	18,929	15,680	3,946	12,408	6,516	5,480	9
1975	67,430	25,955	14,066	5,145	11,076	5,982	5,206	30
1976	66,839	29,233	12,526	5,410	9,026	4,839	5,805	54
(TQ)	15,528	6,763	2,562	1,281	2,074	1,201	1,647	23
1977	114,011	69,708	11,655	5,441	11,501	6,106	9,600	83
1978	91,361	29,754	19,458	6,470	19,265	5,973	10,441	40
1979	74,074	15,585	17,519	6,433	19,714	5,225	9,598	90
1980	73,296	15,054	17,245	6,540	18,970	5,154	10,333	219
1981	73,301	10,858	18,220	6,683	23,569	4,599	9,372	158
1982	67,379	8,209	17,451	8,779	18,711	3,532	10,697	160
1983	73,306	8,978	22,058	8,424	19,535	3,156	11,155	111
1984	74,265	10,599	23,147	9,839	19,822	2,900	7,958	5
1985	83,281	20,334	23,787	10,165	18,923	2,831	7,241	0
1986	101,632	33,114	26,175	12,666	19,595	2,891	7,191	130
1987	102,899	28,916	24,858	14,819	23,148	3,543	7,615	128
1988	112,357	17,558	27,189	34,806	20,966	3,947	7,891	115
1989	88,932	10,046	26,723	13,658	24,523	5,394	8,588	109
1990	115,351	10,645	42,195	20,324	25,013	6,740	10,434	125
1991	140,139	10,349	41,405	47,527	23,828	8,407	8,623	78
1992	97,413	11,791	41,969	11,002	18,915	7,008	6,728	69
1993	99,438	13,666	45,420	10,094	17,241	6,577	6,440	63
1994	104,804	14,727	51,189	13,333	14,349	6,292	4,914	48
1995	96,788	17,937	38,512	14,021	16,398	5,424	4,496	60
1996	116,801	26,466	39,604	18,386	19,089	7,344	5,912	53
1997	105,299	33,587	27,053	15,057	17,840	6,409	5,353	39

(TQ) indicates transitional quarter.

[1] Through 1976, fiscal year ending June 30; thereafter, fiscal year ending September 30.

Sources

1941: *Annual Report of the Attorney General of the United States,* 1941. 1942: *Annual Report of Lemuel B. Schofield, Special Assistant to the Attorney General in Charge of the Immigration and Naturalization Service,* 1942. 1943–1949: *Immigration and Naturalization Service Annual Report of 1952,* Table 13A. 1950: *INS Annual Report 1959,* Table 14. 1951: *INS Annual Report 1960,* Table 14. 1952: *INS Annual Report 1961,* Table 14. 1953–1955: *INS Annual Report 1962,* Table 14. 1956–1961: *INS Annual Report 1965,* Table 14. 1962–1969: *INS Statistical Yearbook 1971,* Table 14. 1970: *INS Statistical Yearbook 1970,* Table 6. 1971–1979: *INS Annual Report 1980,* Table 13. 1980–1983: *INS Statistical Yearbook 1984,* Table IMM 1.3. 1984–1990: *INS Statistical Yearbook 1992,* Table 3. 1991–1997: *INS Statistical Yearbook 1997,* Table 3.

Documentation

Series Ad182. Includes data published separately for Belize (1967–1968; 1971–) and for the Canal Zone (1977).

Series Ad189. Includes data published separately for Anguilla (1977–1979), Antigua (1971–1994), Bahamas (1969–), Barbados (1967–), Bermuda (1971–1979), British Virgin Islands (1971–1979), Cayman Islands (1971–1979), Dominica (1971–), Grenada (1971–), Guadeloupe (1971–1979), Martinique (1971–1979), Montserrat (1971–1979), Netherlands Antilles (1971–1979), Puerto Rico (1971–1973), St. Kitts and Nevis (1967–1968; 1971–1994), St. Lucia (1971–), St. Vincent and the Grenadines (1971–1994), Turks and Caicos Islands (1971–1979), and the U.S. Virgin Islands (1971–1973).

Series Ad190. Includes data published separately in 1971–1979 for Greenland, for St. Pierre and Miquelon, and for the United States.

TABLE Ad191–195   Immigrants, by country of last residence – South America: 1820–1997[1]

Contributed by Robert Barde, Susan B. Carter, and Richard Sutch

Fiscal year	Total Ad191 Number	Argentina Ad192 Number	Colombia Ad193 Number	Ecuador Ad194 Number	Other Ad195 Number	Fiscal year	Total Ad191 Number	Argentina Ad192 Number	Colombia Ad193 Number	Ecuador Ad194 Number	Other Ad195 Number
1820	11	—	—	—	11	1880	88	—	—	—	88
1821	8	—	—	—	8	1881	110	—	—	—	110
1822	7	—	—	—	7	1882	91	—	—	—	91
1823	20	—	—	—	20	1883	77	—	—	—	77
1824	25	—	—	—	25	1884	65	—	—	—	65
1825	67	—	—	—	67	1885	44	—	—	—	44
1826	63	—	—	—	63	1886	246	—	—	—	246
1827	54	—	—	—	54	1887	366	—	—	—	366
1828	77	—	—	—	77	1888	440	—	—	—	440
1829	73	—	—	—	73	1889	427	—	—	—	427
1830	137	—	—	—	137	1890	438	—	—	—	438
1831	42	—	—	—	42	1891	664	—	—	—	664
1832	174	—	—	—	174	1892 [4]	—	—	—	—	—
1833	27	—	—	—	27	1893 [4]	—	—	—	—	—
1834	74	—	—	—	74	1894	39	—	—	—	39
1835	145	—	—	—	145	1895	36	—	—	—	36
1836	146	—	—	—	146	1896	35	—	—	—	35
1837	91	—	—	—	91	1897	49	—	—	—	49
1838	72	—	—	—	72	1898	39	—	—	—	39
1839	49	—	—	—	49	1899	89	—	—	—	89
1840	36	—	—	—	36	1900	124	—	—	—	124
1841	219	—	—	—	219	1901	203	—	—	—	203
1842	102	—	—	—	102	1902	337	—	—	—	337
1843 [2]	62	—	—	—	62	1903	589	—	—	—	589
1844	61	—	—	—	61	1904	1,667	—	—	—	1,667
1845	80	—	—	—	80	1905	2,576	—	—	—	2,576
1846	92	—	—	—	92	1906	2,757	—	—	—	2,757
1847	70	—	—	—	70	1907	2,779	—	—	—	2,779
1848	150	—	—	—	150	1908	2,315	—	—	—	2,315
1849	190	—	—	—	190	1909	1,906	—	—	—	1,906
1850	2,462	—	—	—	2,462	1910	2,151	—	—	—	2,151
(TQ)	91	—	—	—	91	1911	3,049	—	—	—	3,049
1851	59	—	—	—	59	1912	2,989	—	—	—	2,989
1852	39	—	—	—	39	1913	4,248	—	—	—	4,248
1853	38	—	—	—	38	1914	5,869	—	—	—	5,869
1854	136	—	—	—	136	1915	3,801	—	—	—	3,801
1855	191	—	—	—	191	1916	4,286	—	—	—	4,286
1856	184	—	—	—	184	1917	6,931	—	—	—	6,931
1857	83	—	—	—	83	1918	3,343	—	—	—	3,343
1858	131	—	—	—	131	1919	3,271	—	—	—	3,271
1859	155	—	—	—	155	1920	4,112	—	—	—	4,112
1860	208	—	—	—	208	1921	5,015	—	—	—	5,015
1861	97	—	—	—	97	1922	2,668	—	—	—	2,668
1862	146	—	—	—	146	1923	4,737	—	—	—	4,737
1863	94	—	—	—	94	1924	9,270	—	—	—	9,270
1864	152	—	—	—	152	1925	2,470	—	—	—	2,470
1865	148	—	—	—	148	1926	3,107	—	—	—	3,107
1866 [3]	294	—	—	—	294	1927	3,777	—	—	—	3,777
1867	224	—	—	—	224	1928	4,166	—	—	—	4,166
1868	82	—	—	—	82	1929	3,703	—	—	—	3,703
1869	91	—	—	—	91	1930	3,302	—	—	—	3,302
1870	69	—	—	—	69	1931	1,695	—	—	—	1,695
1871	96	—	—	—	96	1932	702	124	154	36	388
1872	102	—	—	—	102	1933	437	—	—	—	437
1873	166	—	—	—	166	1934	355	—	—	—	355
1874	144	—	—	—	144	1935	473	—	—	—	473
1875	132	—	—	—	132	1936	492	—	—	—	492
1876	156	—	—	—	156	1937	738	—	—	—	738
1877	87	—	—	—	87	1938	885	—	—	—	885
1878	88	—	—	—	88	1939	915	—	—	—	915
1879	69	—	—	—	69						

Notes appear at end of table

(continued)

TABLE Ad191–195   Immigrants, by country of last residence – South America: 1820–1997   *Continued*

Fiscal year	Total Ad191 Number	Argentina Ad192 Number	Colombia Ad193 Number	Ecuador Ad194 Number	Other Ad195 Number	Fiscal year	Total Ad191 Number	Argentina Ad192 Number	Colombia Ad193 Number	Ecuador Ad194 Number	Other Ad195 Number
1940	1,115	—	—	—	1,115	1970	23,694	3,989	6,738	4,243	8,724
1941	2,216	—	—	—	2,216	1971	22,678	2,539	6,463	4,995	8,681
1942	989	—	—	—	989	1972	21,393	2,451	5,225	4,354	9,363
1943	693	—	—	—	693	1973	22,423	2,869	5,287	4,178	10,089
1944	1,160	—	—	—	1,160	1974	23,964	2,883	5,852	4,782	10,447
1945	1,609	—	—	—	1,609	1975	24,183	2,778	6,434	4,726	10,245
1946	2,633	—	—	—	2,633	1976	23,555	2,650	5,701	4,484	10,720
1947	3,094	—	—	—	3,094	(TQ)	6,362	586	1,456	1,143	3,177
1948	3,046	—	—	—	3,046	1977	33,671	3,129	8,194	5,249	17,099
1949	3,107	—	—	—	3,107	1978	42,080	4,087	10,907	5,665	21,421
1950	3,284	—	—	—	3,284	1979	35,715	3,110	10,539	4,368	17,698
1951	3,596	—	—	—	3,596	1980	39,717	—	—	—	39,717
1952	4,591	—	—	—	4,591	1981	35,913	2,236	10,335	5,129	18,213
1953	5,511	—	—	—	5,511	1982	35,448	2,065	8,608	4,127	20,648
1954	6,575	—	—	—	6,575	1983	36,087	2,029	9,658	4,243	20,157
1955	7,654	—	—	—	7,654	1984	38,636	2,287	10,897	4,244	21,208
1956	9,187	—	—	—	9,187	1985	40,052	1,925	11,802	4,601	21,724
1957	10,851	—	—	—	10,851	1986	42,650	2,318	11,213	4,518	24,601
1958	14,304	3,552	2,977	—	7,775	1987	44,782	2,192	11,482	4,656	26,452
1959	12,865	2,674	2,624	1,189	6,378	1988	41,646	2,556	10,153	4,736	24,201
1960	16,494	3,652	3,081	1,570	8,191	1989	59,812	3,766	14,918	7,587	33,541
1961	19,095	4,510	3,674	1,819	9,092	1990	86,821	5,953	23,783	12,474	44,611
1962	22,550	3,766	4,624	2,703	11,457	1991	80,308	4,231	19,272	9,962	46,843
1963	27,759	5,519	5,987	4,365	11,888	1992	55,725	4,083	12,885	7,322	31,435
1964	34,891	8,336	10,762	3,870	11,923	1993	54,077	2,972	12,597	7,400	31,108
1965	33,757	7,120	11,171	4,333	11,133	1994	47,505	2,474	10,653	5,943	28,435
1966	28,113	5,118	9,736	4,077	9,182	1995	46,063	2,239	10,641	6,453	26,730
1967	18,562	3,013	4,679	2,709	8,161	1996	61,990	2,878	14,078	8,348	36,686
1968	23,991	3,928	6,999	3,631	9,433	1997	52,600	2,055	12,795	7,763	29,987
1969	25,542	4,422	7,658	5,030	8,432						

(TQ) indicates transitional quarter.

[1] Fiscal year varies as follows: 1820–1832, year ending September 30; 1833–1842, year ending December 31; 1843–1850, year ending September 30; 1851–1865, year ending December 31; 1866–1976, year ending June 30; 1977–1997, year ending September 30.

[2] Three quarters ending September 30.

[3] Six months ending June 30.

[4] Included in Series Ad97.

Sources

1820–1926: *Annual Report of the Commissioner General of Immigration, Report for 1926,* Table 74. 1927–1931: *Annual Report of the Commissioner General of Immigration, 1931,* Table 84. 1932: *Annual Report of the Commissioner General of Immigration, 1932,* Table 2. 1933: U.S. Bureau of the Census, *Historical Statistics of the United States* (U.S. Government Printing Office, 1975), based on unpublished data from the U.S. Immigration and Naturalization Service. 1934–1937: "Immigrant Aliens Admitted and Emigrant Aliens Departed, Years Ended June 30, 1934–1937, by Countries of Last or Intended Future Permanent Residence," *Annual Report of the Secretary of Labor, 1937.* 1938–1940: *Annual Report of the Attorney General of the United States, for Fiscal Year Ended*

June 30, 1941, Table VII. 1941–1945: *Annual Report of the INS, 1945,* Table 13. 1946–1947: *Annual Report of the INS, 1947,* Table 13. 1948–1950: *Annual Report of the INS, 1951,* Table 13. 1951–1956: *Annual Report of the INS, 1956,* Table 4. 1957–1959: *Annual Report of the INS, 1959,* Table 13. 1960–1971: *Annual Report of the INS,* Table 6A. 1972–1977: INS Public Use Tapes; *1978: Statistical Yearbook of the INS,* Table 6A. 1979: INS Public Use Tapes. 1980: *Statistical Yearbook of the INS, 1981,* Table 2. 1981–1983: *Statistical Yearbook of the INS, 1985,* Table IMM1. 1984: *Statistical Yearbook of the INS, 1984,* Table IMM2.4. 1985: *Statistical Yearbook of the INS, 1985,* Table IMM2.4. 1986–1988: INS Public Use Tapes. 1990–1991: *Statistical Yearbook of the INS,* Table 8. 1991–1997: *INS Statistical Yearbook,* Table 9.

Documentation

Series Ad191. Equals series Ad94.

Series Ad195. Total includes separate listings for Bolivia (1932; 1965–1971; 1984–), Brazil (1932; 1960–1979; 1981–), Chile (1932; 1962–1979; 1984–), French Guiana (1984), Guyana (1932; 1968–1979; 1981–), Paraguay (1932; 1984–), Peru (1932; 1960–1979; 1981–), Suriname (1932; 1984–1985), Uruguay (1932; 1969–1979; 1984–1994), and Venezuela (1960–1979; 1984–).

TABLE Ad196–205   Immigrants, by country of birth – South America: 1941–1997[1]

Contributed by Robert Barde, Susan B. Carter, and Richard Sutch

	Total	Argentina	Brazil	Chile	Colombia	Ecuador	Guyana	Peru	Venezuela	Other
	Ad196	Ad197	Ad198	Ad199	Ad200	Ad201	Ad202	Ad203	Ad204	Ad205
Fiscal year	Number	Number	Number	Number	Number	Number	Number	Number	Number	Number
1941	742	—	—	—	—	—	—	—	—	742
1942	572	—	—	—	—	—	—	—	—	572
1943	474	—	—	—	—	—	—	—	—	474
1944	899	—	—	—	—	—	—	—	—	899
1945	1,326	—	—	—	—	—	—	—	—	1,326
1946	1,755	—	—	—	—	—	—	—	—	1,755
1947	2,421	—	—	—	—	—	—	—	—	2,421
1948	2,768	—	—	—	—	—	—	—	—	2,768
1949	2,639	—	—	—	—	—	—	—	—	2,639
1950	2,777	364	412	—	592	278	—	250	289	592
1951	2,724	423	359	—	750	363	—	211	173	1,188
1952	3,902	506	465	—	1,140	691	—	349	195	1,565
1953	4,691	691	501	—	1,322	945	—	379	220	1,733
1954	5,523	932	590	—	1,202	1,061	—	515	300	2,328
1955	5,599	961	773	—	1,226	839	—	622	347	2,573
1956	6,846	1,282	970	436	1,576	739	—	780	458	3,249
1957	9,002	2,058	1,274	715	1,961	1,002	—	824	411	3,981
1958	11,039	2,665	1,360	636	2,891	1,193	—	888	572	4,290
1959	9,792	1,948	1,180	689	2,524	1,130	211	907	678	4,190
1960	13,048	2,878	1,399	924	2,989	1,576	195	1,607	779	5,605
1961	15,470	3,591	1,443	1,120	3,559	1,826	169	2,086	895	6,494
1962	17,592	2,985	1,560	1,137	4,391	2,562	268	2,667	1,037	7,654
1963	22,919	4,624	1,973	1,153	5,733	4,283	273	2,528	1,169	8,279
1964	31,102	7,114	2,416	1,509	10,446	3,917	296	2,585	1,250	9,625
1965	30,962	6,124	2,869	1,872	10,885	4,392	233	1,953	969	9,561
1966	25,836	4,414	2,397	1,260	9,504	4,111	377	1,474	824	7,807
1967	16,517	2,477	1,676	836	4,556	2,719	857	1,670	539	6,765
1968	21,976	3,425	2,525	965	6,902	3,663	1,148	1,426	698	7,986
1969	23,928	3,938	1,713	860	7,627	5,086	1,615	1,180	599	7,277
1970	21,973	3,443	1,919	832	6,724	4,410	1,763	909	348	7,396
1971	20,702	1,992	1,413	956	6,440	4,981	2,115	1,086	507	7,289
1972	19,359	1,819	1,089	857	5,173	4,337	2,826	1,443	485	8,030
1973	20,335	2,034	1,213	1,139	5,230	4,139	2,969	1,713	640	8,932
1974	22,307	2,077	1,114	1,285	5,837	4,795	3,241	1,942	604	9,598
1975	22,984	2,227	1,070	1,111	6,434	4,727	3,169	2,256	527	9,596
1976	22,699	2,267	1,038	1,266	5,742	4,504	3,326	2,640	530	10,186
(TQ)	6,209	522	265	415	1,470	1,128	1,171	716	191	3,089
1977	32,954	2,787	1,513	2,596	8,272	5,302	5,718	3,903	736	16,593
1978	41,764	3,732	1,923	3,122	11,032	5,732	7,614	5,243	990	21,268
1979	35,344	2,856	1,450	2,289	10,637	4,383	7,001	4,135	841	17,468
1980	39,717	2,815	1,570	2,569	11,289	6,133	8,381	4,021	1,010	19,480
1981	35,913	2,236	1,616	2,048	10,335	5,129	6,743	4,664	1,104	18,213
1982	35,448	2,065	1,475	1,911	8,608	4,127	10,059	4,151	1,336	20,648
1983	36,087	2,029	1,503	1,970	9,658	4,243	8,980	4,384	1,508	20,157
1984	37,460	2,141	1,847	1,912	11,020	4,164	8,412	4,368	1,721	20,135
1985	39,058	1,844	2,272	1,992	11,982	4,482	8,531	4,181	1,714	20,750
1986	41,874	2,187	2,332	2,243	11,408	4,516	10,367	4,895	1,854	23,763
1987	44,385	2,106	2,505	2,140	11,700	4,641	11,384	5,901	1,694	25,938
1988	41,007	2,371	2,699	2,137	10,322	4,716	8,747	5,936	1,791	23,598
1989	58,926	3,301	3,332	3,037	15,214	7,532	10,789	10,175	2,099	32,879
1990	85,819	5,437	4,191	4,049	24,189	12,476	11,362	15,726	3,142	43,717
1991	79,934	3,889	8,133	2,842	19,702	9,958	11,666	16,237	2,622	46,385
1992	55,308	3,877	4,755	1,937	13,201	7,286	9,064	9,868	2,340	30,944
1993	53,921	2,824	4,604	1,778	12,819	7,324	8,384	10,447	2,743	30,954
1994	47,377	2,318	4,491	1,640	10,847	5,906	7,662	9,177	2,427	28,306
1995	45,666	1,762	4,558	1,534	10,838	6,397	7,362	8,066	2,627	26,669
1996	61,769	2,456	5,891	1,706	14,283	8,321	9,489	12,871	3,468	36,709
1997	52,877	1,964	4,583	1,443	13,004	7,780	7,257	10,853	3,328	30,129

Notes appear on next page

(continued)

TABLE Ad196–205   Immigrants, by country of birth – South America: 1941–1997   *Continued*

(TQ) indicates transitional quarter.

[1] Through 1976, fiscal year ending June 30; thereafter, fiscal year ending September 30.

Sources

1941: *Annual Report of the Attorney General of the United States, 1941.* 1942: *Annual Report of Lemuel B. Schofield, Special Assistant to the Attorney General in Charge of the Immigration and Naturalization Service, 1942.* 1943–1949: *INS Annual Report of 1952,* Table 13A. 1950: *INS Annual Report 1959,* Table 14. 1951: *INS Annual Report 1960,* Table 14. 1952: *INS Annual Report 1961,* Table 14. 1953–1955: *INS Annual Report 1962,* Table 14. 1956–1961:

INS Annual Report 1965, Table 14. 1960–1961: *Annual Report of the INS 1969,* Table 14. 1962–1970: *INS Statistical Yearbook 1971,* Table 14. 1971–1979: *INS Annual Report 1980,* Table 13. 1980–1986: *INS Statistical Yearbook 1990,* Table 3. 1987–1997: *INS Statistical Yearbook 1997,* Table 3.

Documentation

Series Ad196. Equals series Ad102.

Series Ad205. Includes data published separately for Bolivia (1956–), Falkland Islands (1977–1985), French Guiana (1971–1985), Paraguay (1971–), Suriname (1971–1985), and Uruguay (1962–).

TABLE Ad206–213   Immigrants, by country of last residence – Africa, Oceania, and other: 1820–1997[1]

Contributed by Robert Barde, Susan B. Carter, and Richard Sutch

	Africa				Oceania			
	Total	North	Sub-Saharan	Not specified	Total	Australia and New Zealand	Other	Other and unknown
	Ad206	Ad207	Ad208	Ad209	Ad210	Ad211	Ad212	Ad213
Fiscal year	Number	Number	Number	Number	Number	Number	Number	Number
1820	1	—	—	1	1	0	1	300
1821	2	—	—	2	0	0	0	2,886
1822	0	—	—	0	2	2	0	2,112
1823	0	—	—	0	0	0	0	1,956
1824	0	—	—	0	0	0	0	2,387
1825	1	—	—	1	0	0	0	808
1826	0	—	—	0	0	0	0	254
1827	4	—	—	4	79	0	79	1,492
1828	6	—	—	6	0	0	0	554
1829	1	—	—	1	0	0	0	6,695
1830	2	—	—	2	0	0	0	13,807
1831	2	—	—	2	1	0	1	7,396
1832	2	—	—	2	0	0	0	23,412
(TQ)	—	—	—	—	—	—	—	7,303
1833	1	—	—	1	0	0	0	26,243
1834	1	—	—	1	0	0	0	5,069
1835	14	—	—	14	3	0	3	41
1836	6	—	—	6	2	0	2	829
1837	2	—	—	2	0	0	0	4,660
1838	10	—	—	10	0	0	0	1,843
1839	10	—	—	10	1	1	0	293
1840	6	—	—	6	2	2	0	116
1841	14	—	—	14	3	0	3	624
1842	3	—	—	3	0	0	0	616
1843 [2]	6	—	—	6	5	0	5	607
1844	14	—	—	14	0	0	0	110
1845	4	—	—	4	0	0	0	25
1846	1	—	—	1	0	0	0	2,564
1847	0	—	—	0	1	0	1	607
1848	10	—	—	10	3	0	3	492
1849	3	—	—	3	0	0	0	1,605
1850	0	—	—	0	17	0	17	45,131 [4]
(TQ)	0	—	—	0	0	—	—	554
1851	5 [4]	—	—	5 [4]	0	0	0	143 [4]
1852	0	—	—	0	0	0	0	1,420
1853	8	—	—	8	0	0	0	984
1854	0	—	—	0	31	11	20	627
1855	14	—	—	14	12	4	8	322
1856	6	—	—	6	—	—	—	542
1857	25	—	—	25	—	—	—	22,301
1858	17	—	—	17	—	—	—	801
1859	11	—	—	11	—	—	—	1,395

Notes appear at end of table

TABLE Ad206–213   Immigrants, by country of last residence – Africa, Oceania, and other: 1820–1997   *Continued*

	Africa				Oceania			Other and unknown
	Total	North	Sub-Saharan	Not specified	Total	Australia and New Zealand	Other	
	Ad206	Ad207	Ad208	Ad209	Ad210	Ad211	Ad212	Ad213
Fiscal year	Number	Number	Number	Number	Number	Number	Number	Number
1860	126	—	—	126	—	—	—	486
1861	47	—	—	47	—	—	—	380
1862	12	—	—	12	—	—	—	448
1863	3	—	—	3	—	—	—	1,183
1864	37	—	—	37	—	—	—	559
1865	49	—	—	49	—	—	—	8,298
1866 [3]	33	—	—	33	—	—	—	3,626
1867	25	—	—	25	—	—	—	3,270
1868	3	—	—	3	—	—	—	161
1869	72	—	—	72	—	—	—	17
1870	31	—	—	31	36	36	—	27
1871	24	—	—	24	21	18	3	85
1872	41	—	—	41	2,416	2,180	236	164
1873	28	—	—	28	1,414	1,135	279	160
1874	58	—	—	58	1,193	960	233	128
1875	54	—	—	54	1,268	1,104	164	76
1876	89	—	—	89	1,312	1,205	107	36
1877	16	—	—	16	914	912	2	27
1878	18	—	—	18	606	606	0	15
1879	12	—	—	12	816	813	3	36
1880	18	—	—	18	954	953	1	63
1881	33	—	—	33	1,191	1,188	3	103
1882	60	—	—	60	889	878	11	99
1883	67	—	—	67	747	554	193	79
1884	59	—	—	59	900	502	398	98
1885	112	—	—	112	679	449	230	71
1886	122	—	—	122	1,136	522	614	73
1887	40	—	—	40	1,282	528	754	73
1888	65	—	—	65	2,387	697	1,690	61
1889	187	—	—	187	2,196	1,000	1,196	70
1890	112	—	—	112	1,167	699	468	62
1891	103	—	—	103	1,301	777	524	70
1892	— [5]	—	—	— [5]	267	267	— [5]	8,520 [6]
1893	— [5]	—	—	— [5]	248	248	— [5]	5,173 [6]
1894	24	—	—	24	244	244	— [5]	70
1895	36	—	—	36	155	155	—	0
1896	21	—	—	21	112	87	25	0
1897	37	—	—	37	199	139	60	0
1898	48	—	—	48	201	153	48	0
1899	51	—	—	51	810	456	354	217
1900	30	—	—	30	428	214	214	13
1901	173	—	—	173	498	325	173	1
1902	37	—	—	37	566	384	182	103
1903	176	—	—	176	1,349	1,150	199	25
1904	686	—	—	686	1,555	1,461	94	90
1905	757	—	—	757	2,166	2,091	75	161
1906	712	—	—	712	1,733	1,682	51	33,102 [7]
1907	1,486	—	—	1,486	1,989	1,947	42	22
1908	1,411	—	—	1,411	1,179	1,098	81	17
1909	858	—	—	858	892	839	53	49
1910	1,072	—	—	1,072	1,097	998	99	43
1911	956	—	—	956	1,043	984	59	39
1912	1,009	—	—	1,009	898	794	104	15
1913	1,409	—	—	1,409	1,340	1,229	111	23
1914	1,539	—	—	1,539	1,446	1,336	110	136
1915	934	—	—	934	1,399	1,282	117	31
1916	894	—	—	894	1,574	1,484	90	31
1917	566	—	—	566	1,142	1,014	128	77
1918	299	—	—	299	1,090	925	165	47
1919	189	—	—	189	1,310	1,234	76	46

Notes appear at end of table

(continued)

TABLE Ad206-213   Immigrants, by country of last residence – Africa, Oceania, and other: 1820-1997   *Continued*

	Africa				Oceania			Other and unknown
	Total	North	Sub-Saharan	Not specified	Total	Australia and New Zealand	Other	
	Ad206	Ad207	Ad208	Ad209	Ad210	Ad211	Ad212	Ad213
Fiscal year	Number	Number	Number	Number	Number	Number	Number	Number
1920	648	—	—	648	2,185	2,066	119	702
1921	1,301	—	—	1,301	2,281	2,191	90	130
1922	520	—	—	520	915	855	60	25
1923	548	—	—	548	759	711	48	15
1924	900	—	—	900	679	635	44	58
1925	412	142	—	270	462	416	46	0
1926	529	214	—	315	591	556	35	0
1927	520	228	—	292	746	712	34	0
1928	475	215	—	260	606	578	28	0
1929	509	264	—	245	636	619	17	0
1930	572	277	—	295	1,051	1,026	25	0
1931	417	193	—	224	652	616	36	0
1932	186	58	81	47	303	291	12	0
1933	71	—	—	71	137	122	15	0
1934	104	—	—	104	147	130	17	0
1935	118	—	—	118	141	132	9	0
1936	105	—	—	105	165	147	18	0
1937	155	—	—	155	174	145	29	0
1938	174	—	—	174	248	228	20	0
1939	218	—	—	218	222	213	9	0
1940	202	—	—	202	228	207	21	0
1941	564	—	—	564	255	194	61	0
1942	473	—	—	473	163	120	43	0
1943	141	—	—	141	160	120	40	0
1944	112	—	—	112	615	577	38	0
1945	406	—	—	406	1,663	1,625	38	0
1946	1,516	—	—	1,516	6,106	6,009	97	73
1947	1,284	—	—	1,284	2,960	2,821	139	27
1948	1,027	—	—	1,027	1,336	1,218	118	23
1949	995	—	—	995	776	661	115	34
1950	849	—	—	849	517	460	57	15
1951	845	—	—	845	527	490	37	20
1952	931	—	—	931	578	545	33	8
1953	989	—	—	989	782	742	40	430
1954	1,248	—	—	1,248	910	845	65	8,341
1955	1,203	—	—	1,203	1,028	932	96	3,597
1956	1,351	—	—	1,351	1,346	1,171	175	22
1957	1,600	—	—	1,600	1,458	1,228	230	16
1958	2,008	—	—	2,008	2,045	1,783	262	12
1959	1,992	—	—	1,992	2,162	1,878	284	21
1960	2,057	862	379	816	2,140	1,892	248	26
1961	2,016	873	404	739	1,881	1,556	325	5
1962	1,834	725	380	729	1,819	1,427	392	1
1963	1,982	722	441	819	1,977	1,642	335	27
1964	2,015	590	558	867	2,070	1,767	303	25
1965	1,949	577	505	867	2,199	1,803	396	22
1966	1,967	633	449	885	2,500	1,894	606	11
1967	2,577	826	593	1,158	2,811	2,128	683	0
1968	3,220	1,165	586	1,469	3,172	2,374	798	0
1969	4,460	2,444	411	1,605	3,061	2,278	783	2
1970	7,099	4,112	576	2,411	3,632	2,693	939	0
1971	5,844	2,794	806	2,244	3,383	2,357	1,026	0
1972	5,472	2,150	3,322	0	3,737	2,550	1,187	183
1973	5,537	2,157	3,380	0	3,755	2,466	1,289	0
1974	5,227	1,770	3,457	0	3,378	1,978	1,400	0
1975	5,868	1,595	3,847	426	3,624	1,779	1,845	0
1976	5,723	1,679	4,044	0	3,950	2,133	1,817	0
(TQ)	1,967	686	1,280	1	1,071	606	465	0
1977	9,612	3,473	6,139	0	4,639	2,544	2,095	0
1978	10,336	3,341	4,912	2,083	4,884	2,452	2,432	0
1979	11,212	3,526	7,686	0	4,870	2,476	2,394	0

Notes appear at end of table

TABLE Ad206-213   Immigrants, by country of last residence – Africa, Oceania, and other: 1820-1997   *Continued*

	Africa				Oceania			Other and unknown
	Total	North	Sub-Saharan	Not specified	Total	Australia and New Zealand	Other	
	Ad206	Ad207	Ad208	Ad209	Ad210	Ad211	Ad212	Ad213
Fiscal year	Number	Number	Number	Number	Number	Number	Number	Number
1980	13,981	—	—	13,981	2,358	2,209	149	1,799
1981	15,029	—	—	15,029	2,055	1,947	108	2,138
1982	14,314	—	—	14,314	2,147	2,009	138	1,700
1983	15,084	—	—	15,084	1,984	1,879	105	1,553
1984	13,594	3,033	10,561	0	4,249	2,328	1,921	295
1985	15,236	3,260	11,976	0	4,552	2,501	2,051	12
1986	15,500	3,452	12,048	0	4,352	2,423	1,929	8
1987	15,730	3,909	11,821	0	4,437	2,312	2,125	63
1988	17,124	3,730	13,394	0	4,324	2,514	1,810	72
1989	22,485	4,213	15,727	2,545	4,956	2,948	2,008	86
1990	32,797	4,800	24,778	3,219	6,999	3,384	3,615	255
1991	33,542	6,762	23,718	3,062	7,061	3,275	3,786	156
1992	24,707	4,421	17,526	2,760	5,994	4,053	1,941	20
1993	25,532	4,315	18,104	3,113	6,144	4,454	1,690	4
1994	24,864	4,147	18,086	2,631	5,647	3,999	1,648	4
1995	39,818	7,572	29,196	3,050	5,472	3,195	2,277	3
1996	49,605	8,578	37,451	3,576	6,008	3,408	2,600	2
1997	44,668	7,165	32,014	5,489	4,855	2,794	2,061	8,317

(TQ) indicates transitional quarter.

[1] Fiscal year varies as follows: 1820-1832, year ending September 30; 1833-1842, year ending December 31; 1843-1850, year ending September 30; 1851-1865, year ending December 31; 1866-1976, year ending June 30; 1977-1997, year ending September 30.

[2] Three quarters ending September 30.

[3] Six months ending June 30.

[4] Data in original source revised.

[5] Included in series Ad213.

[6] Includes data for Asia, North America, and South America, as well as for Africa and Oceania from 1892 and for South America for 1893.

[7] Includes 32,987 persons returning to their homes in the United States.

Sources

1820-1926: *Annual Report of the Commissioner General of Immigration, Report for 1926*, Table 74. 1820-1855 for Oceania: William J. Bromwell, *History of Immigration to the United States* (Redfield, 1856). 1927-1931: *Annual Report of the Commissioner General of Immigration, 1931*, Table 84. 1932: *Annual Report of the Commissioner General of Immigration, 1932*, Table 2. 1933: U.S. Bureau of the Census, *Historical Statistics of the United States* (U.S. Government Printing Office, 1975), based on unpublished data from the U.S. Immigration and Naturalization Service. 1934-1937: "Immigrant Aliens Admitted and Emigrant Aliens Departed, Years Ended June 30, 1934-1937, by Countries of Last or Intended Future Permanent Residence," *Annual Report of the Secretary of Labor, 1937*. 1938-1940: *Annual Report of the Attorney General of the United States, for Fiscal Year Ended June 30, 1941*, Table VII. 1941-1945: *Annual Report of the INS, 1945*, Table 13. 1946-1947: *Annual Report of the INS, 1947*, Table 13. 1948-1950: *Annual Report of the INS, 1951*, Table 13. 1951-1956: *Annual Report of the INS, 1956*, Table 4. 1957-1959: *Annual Report of the INS, 1959*, Table 13. 1960-1971: *Annual Report of the INS*, Table 6A. 1972-1977: INS Public Use Tapes. 1978: *Statistical Yearbook of the INS*, Table 6A. 1979: INS Public Use Tapes. 1980: *Statistical Yearbook of the INS, 1981*, Table 2. 1981-1983: *Statistical Yearbook of the INS, 1985*, Table IMM1. 1984: *Statistical Yearbook of the INS, 1984*, Table IMM2.4. 1985: *Statistical Yearbook of the INS, 1985*, Table IMM2.4. 1986-1988: INS Public Use Tapes. 1990-1991: *Statistical Yearbook of the INS*, Table 8. 1991-1997: *INS Statistical Yearbook*, Table 9.

Documentation

Series Ad206. Equals series Ad95.

Series Ad207. Includes separate data published for Algeria (1962-1966, 1972-1979, 1984-1985, 1995-), Egypt (1925-1932, 1960-1979, 1984-), Libya (1972-1979, 1984-1985), Morocco (1932, 1960-1979, 1984-1985, 1987-), Tunisia (1961-1964, 1972-1979, 1984-1985), and Western Sahara (1977-1979, 1985).

Series Ad208. Includes separate data published for Angola (1972-1979, 1984-1985), Benin (1972-1979, 1984-1985), Botswana (1972-1979, 1984-1985), Burkina Faso (1972-1979, 1984-1985), Burundi (1972-1979, 1984-1985, 1991), Cameroon (1972-1979, 1984-1985, 1996), Cape Verde (1972-1979, 1984-), Central African Republic (1972-1979, 1984-1985), Chad (1972-1979, 1984), Comoros (1973-1979), Congo (1972-1979, 1984-1985), Djibouti (1972-1979, 1984-1985), Equatorial Guinea (1972-1979, 1985), Ethiopia (1972-1979, 1984-), French Southern and Antarctic Lands (1973-1979, 1987-1988), Gabon (1984-1985), Gambia (1972-1979, 1984-1985), Ghana (1972-1979, 1984-), Guinea (1972-1979, 1984-1985), Guinea-Bissau (1972-1979, 1984-1985), Ivory Coast (1972-1979, 1984-1985, 1992, 1994-), Kenya (1972-1979, 1984-), Lesotho (1972-1979, 1984-1985), Liberia (1972-1979, 1932, 1984-), Madagascar (1972-1979, 1984-1985), Malawi (1972-1979, 1984-1985), Mali (1972-1979, 1984-1985), Mauritania (1972-1979, 1984), Mauritius (1972-1979, 1984-1985), Mozambique (1972-1979, 1984-1985), Namibia (1972-1979, 1984-1985), Niger (1972-1979, 1984-1985), Nigeria (1964-1966, 1971-1979, 1984-1997), Rwanda (1972-1979, 1984-1985), St. Helena (1972-1979, 1984), São Tomé and Príncipe (1972-1979, 1984-1985), Senegal (1972-1979, 1984-1985, 1990-1991, 1995-), Seychelles (1972-1979, 1984-1985), Sierra Leone (1972-1979, 1984-1985, 1987-), Somalia (1972-1979, 1984-1988, 1991-), South Africa (1932, 1960-1979, 1984-), Sudan (1972-1979, 1984-), Swaziland (1972-1979, 1984-1985), Tanzania (1972-1979, 1984-1985, 1988, 1990), Togo (1972-1979, 1984-1985), Uganda (1972-1979, 1984-1985), Zaire (1972-1979, 1984-1985), Zambia (1972-1979, 1984-1985), and Zimbabwe (1972-1979, 1984-1985).

Series Ad210. Equals series Ad96.

Series Ad212. Separate figures were published for New Zealand for 1925-1932, 1934-1945, 1960-1979, and 1984-.

TABLE Ad214–221   Immigrants, by country of birth – Africa, Oceania, and other: 1941–1997[1]

Contributed by Robert Barde, Susan B. Carter, and Richard Sutch

	Africa				Oceania			Other and unknown
	Total	North	Sub-Saharan	Not specified	Total	Australia and New Zealand	Other Oceania	
	Ad214	Ad215	Ad216	Ad217	Ad218	Ad219	Ad220	Ad221
Fiscal year	Number	Number	Number	Number	Number	Number	Number	Number
1941	281	—	—	281	255	194	61	0
1942	142	—	—	142	129	129	—	56
1943	83	—	—	83	110	110	—	25
1944	75	—	—	75	533	533	—	25
1945	267	—	—	267	1,535	1,535	—	46
1946	1,098	—	—	1,098	5,746	5,746	—	199
1947	849	—	—	849	2,532	2,532	—	232
1948	840	—	—	840	1,110	—	—	206
1949	737	—	—	737	602	—	—	214
1950	689	—	—	689	443	443	—	112
1951	831	411	131	289	449	390	59	19
1952	847	340	136	371	451	416	35	23
1953	1,046	424	147	475	496	450	46	12
1954	1,367	741	210	416	706	605	101	11
1955	1,186	654	187	345	595	474	121	55
1956	1,441	623	229	589	800	602	198	28
1957	1,673	758	266	649	1,016	756	260	17
1958	2,040	916	294	830	1,210	937	273	10
1959	2,631	1,643	308	680	1,178	870	308	10
1960	2,319	1,472	353	494	1,179	912	267	36
1961	1,980	969	399	612	1,204	865	339	24
1962	1,931	941	370	620	1,203	808	395	14
1963	2,639	1,372	521	746	1,289	942	347	10
1964	2,887	1,471	580	836	1,325	1,008	317	12
1965	3,383	1,915	528	940	1,512	1,066	446	4
1966	3,137	1,630	545	962	1,820	1,202	618	6
1967	4,236	2,160	—	2,076	2,328	1,661	422	6
1968	5,078	2,566	—	2,512	2,588	1,799	421	3
1969	5,876	4,000	—	1,876	2,639	1,878	761	3
1970	8,115	5,412	575	2,128	3,198	2,280	918	4
1971	6,772	4,312	2,460	0	2,919	1,870	1,049	2
1972	6,612	3,215	3,397	0	3,284	2,048	1,236	2
1973	6,655	2,968	3,687	0	3,255	1,890	1,365	0
1974	6,182	2,513	3,669	0	3,051	1,645	1,406	2
1975	6,729	2,306	4,423	0	3,346	1,500	1,846	1
1976	7,723	2,418	5,305	0	3,591	1,796	1,795	1
(TQ)	2,322	656	1,666	0	988	517	471	0
1977	10,155	2,961	7,194	0	4,091	1,986	2,105	0
1978	11,524	3,614	7,910	0	4,396	2,184	2,212	0
1979	12,838	4,068	8,770	0	4,449	1,999	2,450	0
1980	13,981	3,728	10,253	0	3,954	2,209	1,745	0
1981	15,029	4,326	10,703	0	4,198	1,947	2,251	6
1982	14,314	3,731	10,583	0	3,852	2,009	1,843	14
1983	15,084	3,594	11,490	0	3,515	1,879	1,636	26
1984	15,540	3,648	11,892	0	3,818	1,903	1,915	31
1985	17,117	3,909	13,208	0	4,054	2,041	2,013	1
1986	17,463	4,134	13,329	0	3,894	1,964	1,930	3
1987	17,724	4,487	13,237	0	3,993	1,844	2,149	6
1988	18,882	4,227	14,655	0	3,839	2,024	1,815	26
1989	25,166	5,266	19,900	0	4,360	2,335	2,025	34
1990	35,893	6,113	29,780	0	6,182	2,583	3,599	49
1991	36,179	8,061	28,118	0	6,236	2,471	3,765	70
1992	27,086	5,801	21,285	0	5,169	3,205	1,964	20
1993	27,783	5,602	22,181	0	4,902	3,372	1,530	5
1994	26,712	5,145	21,567	0	4,592	2,967	1,625	4
1995	42,456	8,429	34,027	0	4,695	2,478	2,217	2
1996	52,889	9,509	43,380	0	5,309	2,750	2,559	5
1997	47,791	8,441	39,350	0	4,344	2,285	2,059	197

TABLE Ad214–221   Immigrants, by country of birth – Africa, Oceania, and other: 1941–1997   *Continued*

(TQ) indicates transitional quarter.

[1] Through 1976, fiscal year ending June 30; thereafter, fiscal year ending September 30.

Sources

1941: *Annual Report of the Attorney General of the United States, 1941.* 1942: *Annual Report of Lemuel B. Schofield, Special Assistant to the Attorney General in Charge of the Immigration and Naturalization Service, 1942.* 1943–1949: *INS Annual Report of 1952,* Table 13A. 1950: *INS Annual Report 1959,* Table 14. 1951: *INS Annual Report 1960,* Table 14. 1952: *INS Annual Report 1961,* Table 14. 1953–1955: *INS Annual Report 1962,* Table 14. 1956–1961: *INS Annual Report 1965,* Table 14. 1962–1969: *INS Statistical Yearbook 1971,* Table 14. 1970: *INS Statistical Yearbook 1970,* Table 6. 1971–1979: *INS Annual Report 1980,* Table 13. 1980–1983: *INS Statistical Yearbook 1984,* Table IMM 1.3. 1984–1985: *INS Statistical Yearbook 1992,* Table 3. 1986: *INS Statistical Yearbook 1996,* Table 3. 1987–1997: *INS Statistical Yearbook 1997,* Table 3.

Documentation

Series Ad214. Equals series Ad103.

Series Ad215. Includes data published separately for Algeria (1955–1966; 1971–), Egypt (1951–), Libya (1971–), Morocco (1951–), Tunisia (1954–1955; 1960–1964; 1971–), and Western Sahara (1971–).

Series Ad216. Includes data published separately for Angola (1971–), Benin (1971–), Botswana (1971–), Burkina Faso (1971–), Burundi (1971–), Cameroon (1971–), Cape Verde (1971–), Central African Republic (1971–1975; 1977–), Chad (1971–1976; 1977–), Comoros Islands (1973–1974; 1977–), Congo 1971–1976; 1977–), Djibouti (1972–1976; 1977–), Equatorial Guinea (1971–1975; 1977–), Ethiopia (1971–), French Somaliland (1976; 1977–1983), Gabon (1973–1975; 1977–), Gambia (1971–), Ghana (1971–), Guinea (1971–), Guinea-Bissau (1971–), Ivory Coast (1971–), Kenya (1971–), Lesotho (1971–), Liberia (1971–), Madagascar (1971–), Malawi (1971–), Mali (1971–), Mauritania (1971–), Mauritius (1971–), Mozambique (1971–), Namibia (1971–), Niger (1971–), Nigeria (1956–1966; 1971–), Reunion (1971–), Rwanda (1971–), St. Helena (1972–), São Tomé (1972–), Senegal (1971–), Seychelles (1971–), Sierra Leone (1971–), Somalia (1971–), South Africa (1951–1966; 1971–), Sudan (1971–), Swaziland (1971–), Tanzania (1971–), Togo (1971–), Uganda (1971–), Zaire (1971–), Zambia (1971–), and Zimbabwe (1971–).

Series Ad218. Equals series Ad104.

Series Ad219. Includes data published separately for Fiji (1967–1968; 1980–) and Tonga (1980–).

Robert Barde, Susan B. Carter, and Richard Sutch

TABLE Ad222–225   Immigrants, by sex: 1820–1997[1]
Contributed by Robert Barde, Susan B. Carter, and Richard Sutch

	Total	Male	Female	Sex not recorded		Total	Male	Female	Sex not recorded
	Ad222	Ad223 [2]	Ad224 [2]	Ad225		Ad222	Ad223 [2]	Ad224 [2]	Ad225
Fiscal year	Number	Number	Number	Number	Fiscal year	Number	Number	Number	Number
1820	8,385	4,871	2,393	1,121	1875	227,498	139,950	87,548	0
1821	9,127	4,651	1,636	2,840	1876	169,986	111,786	58,200	0
1822	6,911	3,816	1,013	2,082	1877	141,857	92,033	49,824	0
1823	6,354	3,598	848	1,908	1878	138,469	86,259	52,210	0
1824	7,912	4,706	1,393	1,813	1879	177,826	111,882	65,944	0
1825	10,199	6,917	2,959	323	1880	457,257	287,623	169,634	0
1826	10,837	7,702	3,078	57	1881	669,431	410,729	258,702	0
1827	18,875	11,803	5,939	1,133	1882	788,992	498,814	290,178	0
1828	27,382	17,261	10,060	61	1883	603,322	363,863	239,459	0
1829	22,520	11,303	5,112	6,105	1884	518,592	308,509	210,083	0
1830	23,322	6,439	3,135	13,748	1885	395,346	226,382	168,964	0
1831	22,633	14,909	7,724	0	1886	334,203	200,704	133,499	0
1832	53,179	34,596	18,583	0	1887	490,109	306,658	183,451	0
(TQ)	7,303	4,691	2,512	100	1888	546,889	345,375	201,514	0
1833	58,640	41,546	17,094	0	1889	444,427	263,024	181,403	0
1834	65,365	38,796	22,540	4,029	1890	455,302	281,853	173,449	0
1835	45,374	28,196	17,027	151	1891	560,319	354,059	206,260	0
1836	76,242	47,865	27,553	824	1892	579,663	361,864	217,799	0
1837	79,340	48,837	27,653	2,850	1893	439,730	280,344	159,386	0
1838	38,914	23,474	13,685	1,755	1894	285,631	169,274	116,357	0
1839	68,069	42,932	25,125	12	1895	258,536	149,016	109,520	0
1840	84,066	52,883	31,132	51	1896	343,267	212,466	130,801	0
1841	80,289	48,082	32,031	176	1897	230,832	135,107	95,725	0
1842	104,565	62,277	41,907	381	1898	229,299	135,775	93,524	0
1843 [3]	52,496	30,069	22,424 [6]	3	1899	311,715	195,277	116,438	0
1844	78,615	44,431	34,184	0	1900	448,572	304,148	144,424	0
1845	114,371	65,015	48,115	1,241	1901	487,918	331,055	156,863	0
1846	154,416	87,777	65,742	897	1902	648,743	466,369	182,374	0
1847	234,968	136,086	97,917	965	1903	857,046	613,146	243,900	0
1848	226,527	133,906	92,149	472	1904	812,870	549,100	263,770	0
1849	297,024	177,232	119,280	512	1905	1,026,499	724,914	301,585	0
1850	310,004 [6]	196,331	112,635	1,038	1906 [5]	1,100,735	764,463	336,272	0
(TQ)	59,976	32,990	26,805	181	1907	1,285,349	929,976	355,373	0
1851	379,466 [6]	217,181	162,219	66	1908	782,870	506,912	275,958	0
1852	371,603	212,469	157,696	1,438	1909	751,786	519,969	231,817	0
1853	368,645	207,958	160,615	72	1910	1,041,570	736,038	305,532	0
1854	427,833	256,177	171,656	0	1911	878,587	570,057	308,530	0
1855	200,877	115,307	85,567	3	1912	838,172	529,931	308,241	0
1856	200,436	115,852	84,584	—	1913	1,197,892	808,144	389,748	0
1857	251,306	135,454	115,852	—	1914	1,218,480	798,747	419,733	0
1858	123,126	71,167	51,959	—	1915	326,700	187,021	139,679	0
1859	121,282	70,586	50,696	—	1916	298,826	182,229	116,597	0
1860	153,640	90,033	63,607	—	1917	295,403	174,479	120,924	0
1861	91,918	52,485	39,433	—	1918	110,618	61,880	48,738	0
1862	91,985	53,719	38,266	—	1919	141,132	83,272	57,860	0
1863	176,282	105,945	70,337	—	1920	430,001	247,625	182,376	0
1864	193,418	114,890	78,528	—	1921	805,228	449,422	355,806	0
1865	248,120	148,624	99,496	—	1922	309,556	149,741	159,815	0
1866 [4]	318,568	199,742	118,826	—	1923	522,919	307,522	215,397	0
1867	315,722	195,747	119,975	—	1924	706,896	423,186	283,710	0
1868	138,840	—	—	138,840	1925	294,314	163,252	131,062	0
1869	352,768	214,865	137,903	0	1926	304,488	170,567	133,921	0
1870	387,203	235,612	151,591	0	1927	335,175	194,163	141,012	0
1871	321,350	190,428	130,922	0	1928	307,255	165,977	141,278	0
1872	404,806	240,170	164,636	0	1929	279,678	142,132	137,546	0
1873	459,803	275,792	184,011	0					
1874	313,339	189,225	124,114	0					

Notes appear at end of table

TABLE Ad222–225   Immigrants, by sex: 1820–1997   *Continued*

	Total	Male	Female	Sex not recorded		Total	Male	Female	Sex not recorded
	Ad222	Ad223 [2]	Ad224 [2]	Ad225		Ad222	Ad223 [2]	Ad224 [2]	Ad225
Fiscal year	Number	Number	Number	Number	Fiscal year	Number	Number	Number	Number
1930	241,700	117,026	124,674	0	1965	296,697	127,171	169,526	0
1931	97,139	40,621	56,518	0	1966	323,040	141,456	181,584	0
1932	35,576	13,917	21,659	0	1967	361,972	158,324	203,648	0
1933	23,068	9,219	13,849	0	1968	454,448	199,732	254,716	0
1934	29,470	12,101	17,369	0	1969	358,579	165,472	193,107	0
1935	34,956	14,010	20,946	0	1970	373,326	176,990	196,336	0
1936	36,329	14,776	21,553	0	1971	370,478	172,528	197,950	0
1937	50,244	21,664	28,580	0	1972	384,685	179,715	204,970	0
1938	67,895	29,959	37,936	0	1973	400,063	186,320	213,743	0
1939	82,998	39,423	43,575	0	1974	394,861	184,518	210,343	0
1940	70,756	33,460	37,296	0	1975	386,194	180,741	205,453	0
1941	51,776	23,519	28,257	0	1976	398,613	184,863	213,750	0
1942	28,781	12,008	16,773	0	(TQ)	103,676	48,283	55,393	0
1943	23,725	9,825	13,900	0	1977	462,315	216,424	245,891	0
1944	28,551	11,410	17,141	0	1978	601,442	286,374	315,068	0
					1979	460,348	219,536	240,812	0
1945	38,119	13,389	24,730	0	1980	530,639	192,660 [7]	205,436 [7]	132,543 [7]
1946	108,721	27,275	81,446	0	1981	596,600	130,351 [7]	224,184 [7]	242,065 [7]
1947	147,292	53,769	93,523	0	1982	594,131	287,874	284,576	21,681
1948	170,570	67,322	103,248	0	1983	559,763	271,966	264,975	22,822
1949	188,317	80,340	107,977	0	1984	543,903	274,896	269,007	0
1950	249,187	119,130	130,057	0	1985	570,009	286,141	283,868	0
1951	205,717	99,327	106,390	0	1986	601,708	300,777	300,931	0
1952	265,520	123,609	141,911	0	1987	601,516	300,238	301,278	0
1953	170,434	73,073	97,361	0	1988	643,025	324,521	318,504	0
1954	208,177	95,594	112,583	0	1989	1,090,924	550,176	540,661	87
1955	237,790	112,032	125,758	0	1990	1,536,483	818,443	717,764	276
1956	321,625	156,410	165,215	0	1991	1,827,167	1,213,767	613,166	234
1957	326,867	155,201	171,666	0	1992	973,977	496,724	477,062	191
1958	253,265	109,121	144,144	0	1993	904,292	424,475	479,771	46
1959	260,686	114,367	146,319	0	1994	804,416	372,691	431,684	41
1960	265,398	116,687	148,711	0	1995	720,461	333,859	386,582	20
1961	271,344	121,380	149,964	0	1996	915,900	422,740	493,142	18
1962	283,763	131,575	152,188	0	1997	798,378	365,484	432,699	195
1963	306,260	139,297	166,963	0					
1964	292,248	126,214	166,034	0					

(TQ) indicates transitional quarter.

[1] Fiscal year varies as follows: 1820–1832, year ending September 30; 1833–1842, year ending December 31; 1843–1850, year ending September 30; 1851–1865, year ending December 31; 1866–1976, year ending June 30; 1977–1997, year ending September 30.

[2] Figures for 1856–1867 estimated based on male share of alien plus native-born arrivals for whom sex was recorded.

[3] Three quarters ending September 30.

[4] Six months ending June 30.

[5] Includes 32,897 persons returning to their homes in the United States.

[6] Data in the original source have been revised.

[7] Calculated from the U.S. Immigration and Naturalization Service public use tapes.

Sources

1820–1855: William J. Bromwell, *History of Immigration to the United States, 1819–1855* (Redfield, 1856). 1856–1868 and 1904–1910: 61st Congress, Doc. No. 756. 1869–1903: U.S. Department of Treasury, Bureau of Statistics, *Monthly Summary of Commerce and Finance of the United States, January 1903, No. 7: Series 1902–1903* (U.S. Government Printing Office, 1903), p. 4347. 1911–1931: *Annual Report of the Commissioner General of Immigration*, 1931. 1932: U.S. Immigration and Naturalization Service, *Annual Report of the Commissioner General of Immigration*, 1932. 1933–1939: unpublished data as reported in U.S. Bureau of the Census, *Historical Statistics of the United States, Colonial Times to 1970, Bicentennial Edition*, two volumes (U.S. Government Printing Office, 1975). 1940–1997: U.S. Immigration and Naturalization Service, *Annual Report* and *Statistical Yearbook*, annual issues.

Documentation

In the period 1820–1867, the sex of many immigrants was not recorded. For the years 1820 through 1855, male immigrants and female immigrants refer to those enumerated as such in the ship manifests. The number whose sex was not noted in the ship manifests is shown in series Ad225. For the years 1856 through 1867, the actual number of immigrants recorded as male, female, or not recorded is not available. For these years, the figures shown in series Ad223–224 are the estimates of the Immigration Commission of 1911, which based its calculations on the assumption that the male share of all immigrants was the same as the male share of immigrants for whom sex was recorded.

In 1868, all evidence on the sex of immigrants was lost. In 1980 and 1981, evidence on the sex of an unusually high number of immigrants was lost.

TABLE Ad226–230   Immigrants, by age classification: 1820–1997[1]

Contributed by Robert Barde, Susan B. Carter, and Richard Sutch

Fiscal year	Total Ad226 [2] Number	Youthful Ad227 [3] Number	Mid-age Ad228 [4] Number	Older Ad229 [5] Number	Age not recorded Ad230 Number	Fiscal year	Total Ad226 [2] Number	Youthful Ad227 [3] Number	Mid-age Ad228 [4] Number	Older Ad229 [5] Number	Age not recorded Ad230 Number
1820	10,311	1,313	6,064	1,518	1,416	1880	457,257	87,154	327,662	42,441	0
1821	11,644	170	7,047	1,396	3,031	1881	669,431	153,480	454,495	61,456	0
1822	8,549	51	5,430	956	2,112	1882	788,992	171,021	540,677	77,294	0
1823	8,265	17	5,314	984	1,950	1883	603,322	143,865	390,406	69,051	0
1824	9,627	94	6,550	1,106	1,877	1884	518,592	123,562	335,572	59,458	0
1825	12,858	1,825	9,392	1,151	490	1885	395,346	92,880	257,551	44,915	0
1826	13,908	2,261	10,025	1,281	341	1886	334,203	66,188	232,118	35,897	0
1827	21,777	3,905	14,089	2,148	1,635	1887	490,109	94,278	345,575	50,256	0
1828	30,184	8,117	18,397	3,036	634	1888	546,889	97,287	396,990	52,612	0
1829	24,513	3,686	11,603	1,764	7,460	1889	444,427	92,534	303,835	48,058	0
1830	24,837	2,878	6,347	1,173	14,439	1890	455,302	86,404	315,054	53,844	0
1831	23,880	7,040	13,598	1,863	1,379	1891	560,319	95,879	405,843	58,597	0
1832	54,351	16,485	31,069	4,273	2,524	1892	623,084	89,167	491,839	42,078	0
(TQ)	7,303	1,946	3,774	425	1,158	1893	502,917	57,392	419,701	25,824	0
1833	59,925	17,425	35,002	4,855	2,643	1894	314,467	41,755	258,162	14,550	0
1834	67,948	15,383	42,811	6,818	2,936	1895	279,948	33,289	233,543	13,116	0
1835	48,716	10,635	32,412	5,431	238	1896	343,267	52,741	254,519	36,007	0
1836	80,972	16,665	54,738	8,141	1,428	1897	230,832	38,627	165,181	27,024	0
1837	84,959	16,014	54,312	8,421	6,212	1898	229,299	38,267	164,905	26,127	0
1838	45,159	8,822	28,713	5,748	1,876	1899	311,715	43,983	248,187	19,545	0
1839	74,666	15,167	51,063	7,201	1,235	1900	448,572	54,624	370,382	23,566	0
1840	92,207	21,727	62,461	7,556	463	1901	487,918	62,562	396,516	28,840	0
1841	87,805	19,732	58,864	8,590	619	1902	648,743	74,063	539,254	35,426	0
1842	110,980	25,516	74,499	9,709	1,256	1903	857,046	102,431	714,053	40,562	0
1843 [6]	56,529	14,930	34,606	5,197	1,796	1904	812,870	109,150	657,155	46,565	0
1844	84,764	19,913	54,745	8,655	1,451	1905	1,026,499	114,668	855,419	56,412	0
1845	119,896	26,182	79,448	12,059	2,207	1906	1,100,735 [8]	136,273	913,955	50,507	0
1846	158,649	36,878	103,263	17,160	1,348	1907	1,285,349	138,344	1,100,771	46,234	0
1847	239,482	57,161	156,627	20,800	4,894	1908	782,870	112,148	630,671	40,051	0
1848	229,483	53,213	151,148	23,066	2,056	1909	751,786	88,393	624,876	38,517	0
1849	299,683	67,331	200,899	30,679	774	1910	1,041,570	120,509	868,310	52,751	0
1850	315,334	62,543	181,468	26,085	45,238	1911	878,587	117,837	714,709	46,041	0
(TQ)	65,570	13,825	43,699	7,621	425	1912	838,172	113,700	678,480	45,992	0
1851	408,828	89,241	274,359	44,072	1,156	1913	1,197,892	147,158	986,355	64,379	0
1852	397,343	90,274	246,076	43,394	17,599	1914	1,218,480	158,621	981,692	78,167	0
1853	400,982	87,331	267,876	44,558	1,217	1915	326,700	52,982	244,472	29,246	0
1854	460,474	100,013	312,301	47,377	783	1916	298,826	47,070	220,821	30,935	0
1855	230,476	53,045	151,440	25,155	836	1917	295,403	47,467	214,616	33,320	0
1856	224,496	42,732	141,986	19,905	19,873	1918	110,618	21,349	76,098	13,171	0
1857	271,982	50,548	177,093	22,808	21,533	1919	141,132	26,373	97,341	17,418	0
1858	144,906	25,914	102,921	15,545	526	1920	430,001	81,890	307,589	40,522	0
1859	155,509	24,670	114,110	16,115	614	1921	805,228	146,613	587,965	70,650	0
1860	179,691	28,620	133,919	16,795	357	1922	309,556	63,710	210,164	35,682	0
1861	112,702	18,878	81,515	11,221	1,088	1923	522,919	91,816	383,960	47,143	0
1862	114,463	20,641	80,725	12,888	209	1924	706,896	132,264	513,788	60,844	0
1863	199,811	37,433	142,009	20,108	261	1925	294,314	50,722	213,980	29,612	0
1864	221,535	41,912	151,711	27,778	134	1926	304,488	47,347	228,527	28,614	0
1865	287,399	46,524	175,501	32,190	33,184	1927	335,175	51,689	254,574	28,912	0
1866 [7]	185,892	27,011	112,692	18,034	28,155	1928	307,255	49,680	230,832	26,743	0
1867	342,162	65,335	236,017	40,810	0	1929	279,678	47,935	207,990	23,753	0
1868	282,189	57,637	188,359	36,193	0	1930	241,700	40,777	177,059	23,864	0
1869	352,768	79,803	232,397	40,568	0	1931	97,139	17,320	67,100	12,719	0
1870	387,203	89,129	250,965	47,109	0	1932	35,576	6,781	22,905	5,890	0
1871	321,350	71,148	210,366	39,836	0	1933	23,068	4,131	15,033	3,904	0
1872	404,806	90,510	263,213	51,083	0	1934	29,470	5,389	18,987	5,094	0
1873	459,803	104,672	288,272	66,859	0	1935	34,956	6,893	22,557	5,506	0
1874	313,339	63,578	199,840	49,921	0	1936	36,329	6,925	23,391	6,013	0
1875	227,498	44,254	154,621	28,623	0	1937	50,244	8,326	33,907	8,011	0
1876	169,986	27,875	121,734	20,377	0	1938	67,895	10,181	47,068	10,646	0
1877	141,857	23,754	100,366	17,737	0	1939	82,998	12,204	54,235	16,559	0
1878	138,469	24,285	95,938	18,246	0						
1879	177,826	34,554	122,731	20,541	0						

Notes appear at end of table

TABLE Ad226–230   Immigrants, by age classification: 1820–1997   *Continued*

Fiscal year	Total Ad226 [2] Number	Youthful Ad227 [3] Number	Mid-age Ad228 [4] Number	Older Ad229 [5] Number	Age not recorded Ad230 Number	Fiscal year	Total Ad226 [2] Number	Youthful Ad227 [3] Number	Mid-age Ad228 [4] Number	Older Ad229 [5] Number	Age not recorded Ad230 Number
1940	70,756	9,602	45,026	16,128	0	1970	373,326	104,880	221,534	46,902	10
1941	51,776	7,982	30,747	13,047	0	1971	370,478	95,908	227,466	47,102	2
1942	28,781	3,710	17,529	7,542	0	1972	384,685	97,503	238,397	48,780	5
1943	23,725	3,179	15,282	5,264	0	1973	400,063	103,606	244,360	52,097	0
1944	28,551	4,092	18,511	5,948	0	1974	394,861	103,330	241,444	50,087	0
1945	38,119	5,645	25,482	6,992	0	1975	386,194	98,415	232,939	54,840	0
1946	108,721	11,092	85,797	11,832	0	1976	398,613	95,427	240,837	62,349	0
1947	147,292	18,831	101,459	27,002	0	(TQ)	103,676	25,379	61,850	16,447	0
1948	170,570	24,095	112,453	34,022	0	1977	462,315	99,319	275,419	87,577	0
1949	188,317	32,728	123,340	32,152	97	1978	601,442	141,632	370,008	89,802	0
1950	249,187	50,468	152,358	46,347	14	1979	460,348	102,526	285,300	72,522	0
1951	205,717	44,023	121,823	39,861	10	1980	530,639	—	—	—	530,639
1952	265,520	64,513	159,788	41,211	8	1981	596,600	—	—	—	596,600
1953	170,434	37,016	110,860	22,541	17	1982	594,131	135,563	371,116	87,452	0
1954	208,177	45,105	135,731	27,299	42	1983	559,763	121,281	359,138	79,344	0
1955	237,790	51,829	156,001	29,925	35	1984	543,903	114,893	347,379	81,631	0
1956	321,625	74,429	206,770	40,367	59	1985	570,009	115,474	366,643	87,892	0
1957	326,867	80,140	207,664	38,894	169	1986	601,708	120,639	381,303	99,766	0
1958	253,265	60,124	162,240	30,813	88	1987	601,516	114,173	384,990	102,283	70
1959	260,686	58,826	165,366	36,438	56	1988	643,025	113,780	411,669	117,551	25
1960	265,398	59,895	170,084	35,389	30	1989	1,090,924	163,684	750,138	176,952	150
1961	271,344	64,544	170,881	35,908	11	1990	1,536,483	180,895	1,119,109	236,289	190
1962	283,763	64,531	182,464	36,741	27	1991	1,827,167	152,515	1,424,334	249,945	373
1963	306,260	72,510	197,506	36,237	7	1992	973,977	169,551	636,267	168,024	135
1964	292,248	70,444	186,821	34,970	13	1993	904,292	180,217	558,340	165,632	103
1965	296,697	72,431	188,652	35,614	0	1994	804,416	164,995	482,345	157,005	71
1966	323,040	89,715	189,526	43,775	24	1995	720,461	157,325	423,223	139,856	57
1967	361,972	97,598	207,434	56,935	5	1996	915,900	186,362	551,678	177,760	100
1968	454,448	111,794	262,598	80,054	2	1997	798,378	157,089	477,120	163,993	176
1969	358,579	98,167	210,681	49,729	2						

(TQ) indicates transitional quarter.

[1] Fiscal year varies as follows: 1820–1832, year ending September 30; 1833–1842, year ending December 31; 1843–1850, year ending September 30; 1851–1865, year ending December 31; 1866–1976, year ending June 30; 1977–1997, year ending September 30.

[2] Through 1867, includes U.S. citizens returning from abroad; thereafter, includes alien immigrants only.

[3] Through 1899, less than age fifteen; 1900–1917, less than age fourteen; 1918–1970, less than age sixteen; thereafter, less than age fifteen.

[4] Through 1899, age 15–40; 1900–1917, age 14–44; 1918–1939, age 16–44; 1940–1944, age 16–45; 1945–1970, age 16–44; thereafter, age 15–44.

[5] Through 1899, age forty-one and older; 1900–1939, age forty-five and older; 1940–1944, age forty-six and older; thereafter, age forty-five and older.

[6] Three quarters ending September 30.

[7] Six months ending June 30.

[8] Includes 32,897 persons returning to their homes in the United States.

Sources

1820–1855: William J. Bromwell, *History of Immigration to the United States,*

1819–1855 (Redfield, 1856). 1856–1868 and 1904–1910: 61st Congress, Doc. No. 756. 1869–1903: U.S. Department of Treasury, Bureau of Statistics, *Monthly Summary of Commerce and Finance of the United States, January 1903, No. 7, Series 1902–1903* (U.S. Government Printing Office, 1903), p. 4347. 1911–1931: *Annual Report of the Commissioner General of Immigration, 1931.* 1932: U.S. Immigration and Naturalization Service, *Annual Report of the Commissioner General of Immigration, 1932.* 1933–1939: unpublished data as reported in U.S. Bureau of the Census, *Historical Statistics of the United States, Colonial Times to 1970, Bicentennial Edition,* two volumes (U.S. Government Printing Office, 1975). 1940–1997: U.S. Immigration and Naturalization Service, *Annual Report* and *Statistical Yearbook,* annual issues.

Documentation

For the years 1820 through 1866, the age of many immigrants was not recorded. For fiscal years 1980 and 1981 data processing problems at the Immigration and Naturalization Service led to the loss of all data on the age of immigrants.

TABLE Ad231–245   Immigrants, by occupation at time of arrival: 1820–1982[1]
Contributed by Susan B. Carter, Matthew Sobek, and Richard Sutch

						Craftsmen, foremen, operatives, and kindred		
	Total	Professional, technical, and kindred	Farmers and farm managers	Managers, officials, and proprietors	Clerical, sales, and kindred	Total	Craftsmen, foremen, and kindred	Operatives and kindred
	Ad231	Ad232	Ad233	Ad234	Ad235	Ad236	Ad237	Ad238
Fiscal year	Number	Number	Number	Number	Number	Number	Number	Number
1820	10,311	105	874	933	63	1,027	514	513
1821	11,644	204	1,249	1,441	114	1,419	777	642
1822	8,549	151	834	1,431	74	1,323	575	748
1823	8,265	179	800	1,427	85	1,183	604	579
1824	9,627	187	918	1,926	88	1,149	514	635
1825	12,858	204	1,647	1,841	51	1,365	586	779
1826	13,908	190	1,382	1,943	75	2,054	1,000	1,054
1827	21,777	262	2,071	2,076	86	2,970	1,719	1,251
1828	30,184	331	2,542	2,328	106	3,762	2,277	1,485
1829	24,549	252	1,264	2,661	108	2,507	1,462	1,045
1830	24,837	136	1,424	1,427	32	1,713	1,167	546
1831	23,880	183	2,685	2,368	65	2,318	1,647	671
1832 [2]	61,654	176	8,502	5,424	56	10,277	7,112	3,165
1833	59,925	459	6,618	4,913	18	12,782	7,168	5,614
1834	67,948	561	7,160	3,021	182	7,008	5,084	1,924
1835	48,716	487	6,117	3,875	171	5,834	4,820	1,014
1836	80,972	472	8,770	3,379	73	8,806	7,860	946
1837	84,459	522	10,835	3,893	124	7,859	7,338	521
1838	45,159	459	6,667	4,005	173	5,502	4,650	852
1839	74,666	584	12,410	5,692	208	9,818	8,892	926
1840	92,207	481	18,476	5,311	73	10,738	9,484	1,254
1841	87,805	541	12,343	5,267	86	11,025	9,916	1,109
1842	110,980	744	12,966	4,976	101	14,452	13,129	1,323
1843 [3]	56,529	578	8,031	3,226	18	6,075	5,168	907
1844	84,764	755	9,831	3,960	78	9,398	8,514	884
1845	119,896	542	19,349	5,049	57	10,800	9,875	925
1846	158,649	592	27,944	4,189	107	13,143	12,234	909
1847	239,482	703	43,594	4,218	56	25,839	25,073	766
1848	229,583	517	31,670	3,407	42	24,763	23,928	835
1849	299,683	972	39,675	3,508	263	31,758	29,982	1,776
1850	315,334	918	42,873	6,400	203	26,166	23,579	2,587
1851 [2]	474,398	938	59,095	14,983	161	36,136	31,981	4,155
1852	397,343	572	58,023	11,502	131	27,045	24,337	2,708
1853	400,982	722	56,322	12,782	154	20,652	17,225	3,427
1854	460,474	699	87,188	15,173	158	36,310	32,199	4,111
1855	230,476	780	34,693	14,759	242	17,221	15,288	1,933
1856	224,496	462	24,722	11,101	135	18,662	9,991	8,671
1857	271,982	570	34,702	12,114	271	25,791	18,600	7,191
1858	144,906	662	20,506	10,217	259	18,483	12,576	5,907
1859	155,509	858	16,323	12,495	194	24,434	13,578	10,856
1860	179,691	792	21,742	11,207	200	19,142	13,697	5,445
1861	112,701	667	11,668	7,683	121	11,472	8,162	3,310
1862	114,463	788	9,265	7,774	658	11,315	7,390	3,925
1863	199,810	1,172	12,348	7,590	1,277	22,849	15,210	7,639
1864	221,531	1,116	13,837	9,473	1,574	24,940	15,271	9,669
1865	287,398	1,742	20,012	12,700	2,775	33,716	22,119	11,597
1866 [4]	359,956	2,241	30,302	15,827	2,731	38,306	25,974	12,332
1867	342,152	2,287	32,626	14,706	2,957	41,064	28,559	12,505
1868	282,195	1,395	23,046	8,556	1,479	30,690	21,568	9,122
1869	352,768	1,700	28,102	8,837	1,651	31,634	22,141	9,493
1870	387,201	1,829	35,656	7,139	1,611	34,015	24,305	9,710
1871	321,305	2,202	27,042	5,553	1,720	31,560	24,107	7,453
1872	404,710	1,809	38,159	7,156	2,159	41,989	28,953	13,036
1873	459,670	2,847	36,983	7,593	2,370	45,656	31,151	14,505
1874	313,285	2,422	28,775	5,641	1,597	36,540	24,526	12,014
1875	227,409	2,337	16,447	5,029	1,568	31,596	21,055	10,541
1876	169,881	2,294	14,536	4,963	1,474	22,150	15,525	6,625
1877	141,759	1,788	13,188	4,667	1,362	19,170	13,349	5,821
1878	138,443	1,484	14,843	4,475	1,437	14,742	9,765	4,977
1879	177,765	1,578	19,907	5,202	1,829	19,132	12,379	6,753

Notes appear at end of table

TABLE Ad231–245   Immigrants, by occupation at time of arrival: 1820–1982   *Continued*

| | | | | | | Craftsmen, foremen, operatives, and kindred | | |
	Total	Professional, technical, and kindred	Farmers and farm managers	Managers, officials, and proprietors	Clerical, sales, and kindred	Total	Craftsmen, foremen, and kindred	Operatives and kindred
	Ad231	Ad232	Ad233	Ad234	Ad235	Ad236	Ad237	Ad238
Fiscal year	Number	Number	Number	Number	Number	Number	Number	Number
1880	457,229	1,745	47,204	7,916	3,044	46,260	32,360	13,900
1881	669,291	2,672	58,028	9,371	3,445	61,646	45,627	16,019
1882	788,910	2,910	61,888	10,102	3,594	67,675	48,189	19,486
1883	603,262	2,390	39,048	8,280	3,543	57,427	39,287	18,140
1884	518,517	2,209	42,050	7,691	3,680	49,999	33,695	16,304
1885	395,289	2,040	27,585	6,707	3,526	35,321	23,712	11,609
1886	334,154	2,029	20,600	6,237	3,156	32,488	21,167	11,321
1887	490,007	2,780	30,932	8,032	3,477	47,826	29,869	17,957
1888	546,780	3,251	29,335	7,597	4,056	54,342	35,040	19,302
1889	444,796	2,685	28,962	7,859	4,163	44,826	28,516	16,310
1890	455,197	3,131	29,296	7,802	3,805	39,382	26,167	13,215
1891	560,129	3,241	36,398	11,340	3,889	49,478	33,321	16,157
1892	569,884	2,519	31,563	9,835	3,339	45,547	29,954	15,593
1893	461,274	2,536	26,779	9,154	3,293	43,036	26,878	16,158
1894	265,029	1,679	16,452	7,939	2,303	30,486	19,042	11,444
1895	231,413	1,894	11,001	5,251	2,728	28,564	18,010	10,554
1896	343,220	2,277	29,251	6,174	2,273	42,560	26,582	15,978
1897	230,789	1,689	22,560	7,159	1,799	29,755	19,783	9,972
1898	229,299	1,347	16,243	5,959	2,078	29,619	20,059	9,560
1899	311,715	1,972	3,973	6,815	2,473	38,608	—	—
1900	448,572	2,392	5,433	7,216	2,870	54,793	—	—
1901	487,918	2,665	3,035	8,294	3,197	57,346	—	—
1902	648,743	2,937	8,168	9,340	3,836	71,131	—	—
1903	857,046	6,999	13,363	15,603	7,226	110,644	—	—
1904	812,870	12,195	4,507	26,914	11,055	133,748	—	—
1905	1,026,499	12,582	18,474	27,706	12,759	159,442	—	—
1906 [5]	1,100,735	13,015	15,288	23,515	12,226	156,902	—	—
1907	1,285,349	12,016	13,476	20,132	12,735	169,394	—	—
1908	782,870	10,504	7,720	16,410	11,523	106,943	—	—
1909	751,786	7,603	8,914	11,562	8,467	75,730	—	—
1910	1,041,570	9,689	11,793	14,731	12,219	121,847	—	—
1911	878,587	11,275	9,709	15,416	14,723	128,717	—	—
1912	838,172	10,913	7,664	14,715	13,782	107,893	—	—
1913	1,197,892	12,552	13,180	19,094	15,173	139,091	—	—
1914	1,218,480	13,454	14,442	21,903	17,933	149,515	—	—
1915	326,700	11,453	6,518	10,728	9,377	45,591	—	—
1916	298,826	9,024	6,840	8,725	9,907	36,086	—	—
1917	295,403	7,499	7,764	8,329	10,554	38,660	—	—
1918	110,618	3,529	2,583	3,940	4,239	17,501	—	—
1919	141,132	5,261	3,933	4,247	6,524	21,671	—	—
1920	430,001	10,540	12,192	9,654	14,054	55,991	—	—
1921	805,228	12,852	22,282	18,286	18,922	109,710	—	—
1922	309,556	9,696	7,676	9,573	10,055	40,309	—	—
1923	522,919	13,926	12,503	12,086	17,931	87,899	—	—
1924	707,256	20,926	20,320	15,668	27,373	123,923	—	—
1925	294,314	8,942	13,875	5,508	15,363	36,927	—	—
1926	304,488	9,203	9,720	5,374	19,086	38,682	—	—
1927	335,175	9,883	10,324	5,772	20,140	42,394	—	—
1928	307,255	9,332	8,773	5,287	16,344	42,765	—	—
1929	279,678	8,792	8,309	4,709	15,354	36,437	—	—
1930	241,700	8,585	8,375	4,620	14,414	32,474	—	—
1931	97,139	4,120	2,743	2,384	4,229	9,555	—	—
1932	35,576	2,100	403	1,331	919	2,053	—	—
1933	23,068	1,615	292	690	600	1,821	—	—
1934	29,470	2,101	425	1,207	933	2,267	—	—
1935	34,956	2,244	593	1,347	1,024	2,689	—	—
1936	36,329	2,564	535	1,782	1,449	2,490	—	—
1937	50,244	4,130	852	3,422	2,126	3,996	—	—
1938	67,895	5,418	1,508	5,408	3,119	5,697	—	—
1939	82,998	7,199	1,186	8,929	4,794	6,532	—	—

Notes appear at end of table   (continued)

TABLE Ad231–245   Immigrants, by occupation at time of arrival: 1820–1982   *Continued*

	Total	Professional, technical, and kindred	Farmers and farm managers	Managers, officials, and proprietors	Clerical, sales, and kindred	Craftsmen, foremen, operatives, and kindred		
						Total	Craftsmen, foremen, and kindred	Operatives and kindred
	Ad231	Ad232	Ad233	Ad234	Ad235	Ad236	Ad237	Ad238
Fiscal year	Number	Number	Number	Number	Number	Number	Number	Number
1940	70,756	6,802	847	7,415	4,361	5,710	—	—
1941	51,776	6,232	356	5,640	2,837	3,513	—	—
1942	28,781	3,518	254	2,305	1,638	2,061	—	—
1943	23,725	2,695	235	988	1,840	2,587	—	—
1944	28,551	2,616	349	894	2,368	3,533	—	—
1945	38,119	2,852	497	1,457	3,715	4,511	—	—
1946	108,721	6,198	947	3,616	8,378	8,826	—	—
1947	147,292	10,891	3,462	5,886	13,961	19,306	—	—
1948	170,570	12,619	4,884	6,207	15,298	23,816	—	—
1949	188,317	13,884	8,937	6,014	14,797	27,964	—	—
1950	249,187	20,502	17,642	6,396	16,796	41,450	—	—
1951	205,717	15,269	10,214	5,493	14,098	34,041	—	—
1952	265,520	16,496	10,566	5,968	16,724	42,315	—	—
1953	170,434	12,783	3,393	5,025	15,171	26,975	—	—
1954	208,177	13,817	3,846	5,296	16,018	32,151	—	—
1955	237,790	14,109	4,446	5,114	18,060	34,218	—	—
1956	321,625	18,995	5,727	5,814	23,413	44,950	—	—
1957	326,867	24,489	3,506	6,127	25,897	46,338	—	—
1958	253,265	22,482	2,221	4,646	22,140	31,518	—	—
1959	260,686	23,287	2,187	4,688	21,475	36,552	—	—
1960	265,398	21,940	3,050	5,309	24,386	34,135	—	—
1961	271,344	21,455	3,002	5,363	25,198	30,967	—	—
1962	283,763	23,710	1,589	5,554	26,304	30,148	—	—
1963	306,260	27,930	1,776	5,986	28,094	32,444	—	—
1964	292,248	28,756	1,732	6,822	30,015	31,811	—	—
1965	296,697	28,790	1,833	7,090	29,779	31,676	—	—
1966	323,040	30,039	2,964	6,773	22,676	30,725	—	—
1967	361,972	41,652	3,276	7,974	19,783	34,596	—	—
1968	454,448	48,753	2,727	9,436	29,090	56,819	—	—
1969	358,579	40,427	3,687	5,356	17,448	43,266	—	—
1970	373,326	46,151	3,839	5,829	16,517	46,622	—	—
1971	370,478	48,850	1,215	6,254	14,667	40,752	—	—
1972	384,685	48,887	161	7,748	14,921	37,963	—	—
1973	400,063	41,147	118	9,185	15,897	40,275	—	—
1974	394,861	35,483	238	9,206	16,165	38,025	—	—
1975	386,194	38,491	927	10,012	17,552	41,922	—	—
1976	398,613	41,068	1,354	11,635	18,756	42,786	—	—
(TQ)	99,619	10,411	464	3,576	986	10,716	—	—
1977	462,315	45,000	630	17,398	26,056	55,904	—	—
1978	601,442	48,908	474	20,898	33,847	75,067	—	—
1979	460,348	39,466	814	18,853	26,037	51,493	—	—
1980 [6]	—	—	—	—	—	—	—	—
1981 [6]	—	—	—	—	—	—	—	—
1982	606,104	44,899	11,973	19,841	26,432	53,490	—	—

Notes appear at end of table

TABLE Ad231–245 Immigrants, by occupation at time of arrival: 1820–1982 *Continued*

	Private household workers	Service, except private household	Laborers			Unspecified occupation	No occupation or not stated
			Total	Farm laborers and foremen	Laborers, except farm and mine		
	Ad239	Ad240	Ad241	Ad242	Ad243	Ad244	Ad245
Fiscal year	Number	Number	Number	Number	Number	Number	Number
1820	139	0	334	—	—	—	6,836
1821	94	0	453	—	—	—	6,670
1822	20	0	414	—	—	—	4,302
1823	6	0	338	—	—	—	4,247
1824	13	0	381	—	—	—	4,965
1825	69	0	650	—	—	—	7,031
1826	70	0	716	—	—	—	7,478
1827	136	0	1,761	—	—	—	12,415
1828	421	0	2,628	—	—	—	18,066
1829	337	0	1,885	—	—	—	15,535
1830	22	0	720	—	—	—	19,363
1831	115	0	928	—	—	—	15,218
1832 [2]	56	0	3,323	—	—	—	33,840
1833	82	0	4,109	—	—	—	30,944
1834	1,236	0	2,874	—	—	—	45,906
1835	599	0	2,897	—	—	—	28,736
1836	39	0	8,749	—	—	—	50,684
1837	120	0	9,095	—	—	—	52,011
1838	42	0	3,684	—	—	—	24,627
1839	99	0	7,870	—	—	—	37,985
1840	183	0	9,640	—	—	—	47,305
1841	923	0	11,423	—	—	—	46,197
1842	1,264	0	15,951	—	—	—	60,526
1843 [3]	413	0	5,346	—	—	—	32,842
1844	1,174	0	9,725	—	—	—	49,843
1845	2,492	0	16,552	—	—	—	65,055
1846	3,349	0	18,193	—	—	—	91,132
1847	3,198	0	35,869	—	—	—	126,005
1848	4,433	0	46,223	—	—	—	118,528
1849	3,671	0	62,179	—	—	—	157,657
1850	3,203	0	46,640	—	—	—	188,931
1851 [2]	3,733	0	101,976	—	—	—	257,376
1852	942	0	75,267	—	—	—	223,861
1853	3,938	0	83,022	—	—	—	223,390
1854	3,357	0	82,373	—	—	—	235,216
1855	2,598	0	42,580	—	—	—	117,603
1856	1,748	0	37,019	—	—	—	130,647
1857	1,322	0	43,249	—	—	—	153,963
1858	1,142	0	22,317	—	—	—	71,320
1859	1,281	0	21,696	—	—	—	78,228
1860	1,415	0	31,268	—	—	—	93,925
1861	739	29	19,417	—	—	145	60,760
1862	3,683	21	17,761	—	—	338	62,860
1863	9,103	16	46,214	—	—	202	99,039
1864	15,623	22	48,052	—	—	238	106,656
1865	9,231	27	45,267	—	—	348	161,580
1866 [4]	8,883	47	58,662	—	—	501	202,456
1867	7,715	43	57,476	—	—	484	182,794
1868	6,561	27	59,175	—	—	283	150,983
1869	10,265	25	88,727	—	—	374	181,453
1870	14,261	94	84,651	—	—	771	207,174
1871	13,814	122	66,187	—	—	890	172,215
1872	11,108	339	86,662	—	—	1,370	213,959
1873	16,259	521	105,192	—	—	2,942	239,307
1874	12,427	407	66,395	—	—	3,959	155,122
1875	10,579	524	47,345	—	—	5,261	106,723
1876	6,493	387	39,299	—	—	7,174	71,111
1877	5,158	299	25,851	—	—	6,960	63,316
1878	6,157	354	26,939	—	—	5,390	62,622
1879	6,804	367	37,191	—	—	3,983	81,772

Notes appear at end of table

(continued)

TABLE Ad231–245   Immigrants, by occupation at time of arrival: 1820–1982   *Continued*

	Private household workers	Service, except private household	Laborers			Unspecified occupation	No occupation or not stated
			Total	Farm laborers and foremen	Laborers, except farm and mine		
	Ad239	Ad240	Ad241	Ad242	Ad243	Ad244	Ad245
Fiscal year	Number	Number	Number	Number	Number	Number	Number
1880	18,580	468	105,449	—	—	9,117	217,446
1881	19,342	859	149,259	—	—	8,999	355,670
1882	23,010	1,017	210,834	—	—	5,045	402,835
1883	27,988	988	137,266	—	—	4,014	322,318
1884	24,249	766	107,555	—	—	3,266	277,052
1885	20,213	683	83,748	—	—	3,736	211,730
1886	20,198	669	87,425	—	—	3,400	157,952
1887	27,510	953	141,595	—	—	2,829	224,073
1888	27,310	1,597	171,292	—	—	4,100	243,900
1889	30,220	1,072	112,755	—	—	3,493	208,761
1890	28,625	1,126	140,185	—	—	6,075	195,770
1891	32,596	1,303	168,174	—	—	5,075	248,635
1892	38,969	1,473	177,260	—	—	3,547	255,832
1893	36,043	956	127,195	—	—	2,515	209,767
1894	28,763	1,287	60,188	—	—	2,685	113,247
1895	30,346	1,405	55,023	—	—	3,008	92,193
1896	38,926	2,577	91,902	—	—	4,084	123,196
1897	23,739	2,089	46,677	—	—	3,698	91,624
1898	23,656	1,868	52,985	—	—	4,975	90,569
1899	34,120	4,580	109,795	17,343	92,452	—	109,379
1900	40,311	4,406	196,210	31,949	164,261	—	134,941
1901	42,027	5,352	217,316	54,753	162,563	—	148,686
1902	69,913	6,298	323,961	80,562	243,399	—	153,159
1903	92,686	11,482	399,342	77,518	321,824	—	199,701
1904	104,937	6,400	298,422	85,850	212,572	—	214,692
1905	125,473	5,849	432,196	142,187	290,009	—	232,018
1906 [5]	115,984	10,439	467,906	239,125	228,781	—	285,460
1907	121,587	13,578	617,722	323,854	293,868	—	304,709
1908	89,942	10,367	286,784	138,844	147,940	—	242,677
1909	64,568	5,849	347,800	171,310	176,490	—	221,293
1910	96,658	8,977	505,654	288,745	216,909	—	260,002
1911	107,153	11,051	334,521	176,003	158,518	—	246,022
1912	116,529	13,580	322,026	184,154	137,872	—	231,070
1913	140,218	17,609	543,787	320,105	223,682	—	297,188
1914	144,409	19,621	516,988	288,053	228,935	—	320,215
1915	39,774	11,976	74,343	24,723	49,620	—	116,940
1916	29,258	10,989	83,231	26,250	56,981	—	104,766
1917	31,885	11,784	74,510	22,328	52,182	—	104,418
1918	7,816	6,367	19,680	4,538	15,142	—	44,963
1919	6,277	11,571	23,334	4,412	18,922	—	58,314
1920	37,197	18,487	98,753	15,257	83,496	—	173,133
1921	102,478	24,298	195,259	32,400	162,859	—	301,141
1922	44,531	12,340	44,326	10,529	33,797	—	131,050
1923	52,223	22,244	112,522	25,905	86,617	—	191,585
1924	51,680	29,621	139,836	27,492	112,344	—	277,909
1925	26,924	15,399	52,632	16,022	36,610	—	118,744
1926	30,587	14,340	62,589	17,390	45,199	—	114,907
1927	31,344	10,070	79,687	23,698	55,989	—	125,561
1928	28,751	8,846	62,065	24,161	37,904	—	125,092
1929	31,841	6,820	47,722	19,849	27,873	—	119,694
1930	29,073	6,749	31,816	13,736	18,080	—	105,594
1931	9,740	3,128	8,228	3,422	4,806	—	53,012
1932	1,232	1,063	1,411	254	1,157	—	25,064
1933	550	933	1,021	134	887	—	15,546
1934	805	1,216	1,387	233	1,154	—	19,129
1935	1,418	1,390	1,763	408	1,355	—	22,488
1936	1,944	1,056	1,519	324	1,195	—	22,990
1937	3,213	1,426	2,282	378	1,904	—	28,797
1938	5,919	1,794	3,020	609	2,411	—	36,012
1939	5,420	1,979	2,485	415	2,070	—	44,474

Notes appear at end of table

TABLE Ad231-245 Immigrants, by occupation at time of arrival: 1820-1982 *Continued*

			Laborers				
	Private household workers	Service, except private household	Total	Farm laborers and foremen	Laborers, except farm and mine	Unspecified occupation	No occupation or not stated
	Ad239	Ad240	Ad241	Ad242	Ad243	Ad244	Ad245
Fiscal year	Number	Number	Number	Number	Number	Number	Number
1940	2,891	949	2,372	252	2,120	—	39,409
1941	1,503	829	861	129	732	—	30,005
1942	872	740	585	92	493	—	16,808
1943	770	707	845	164	681	—	13,058
1944	1,125	811	1,233	203	1,030	—	15,622
1945	1,495	1,047	1,111	225	886	—	21,434
1946	2,464	2,153	1,662	189	1,473	—	74,477
1947	4,922	3,882	3,273	442	2,831	—	81,709
1948	6,389	4,350	5,772	946	4,826	—	91,235
1949	6,990	3,937	7,125	933	6,192	—	98,669
1950	8,900	4,970	9,669	3,976	5,693	—	122,862
1951	7,243	5,292	10,453	4,972	5,481	—	103,614
1952	9,653	6,418	15,258	6,289	8,969	—	142,122
1953	6,852	4,390	6,907	1,538	5,369	—	88,938
1954	8,096	5,203	11,683	1,622	10,061	—	112,067
1955	11,824	6,512	23,004	5,486	17,518	—	120,503
1956	15,347	7,922	36,857	9,050	27,807	—	162,600
1957	11,457	8,761	26,411	4,585	21,826	—	173,881
1958	7,521	7,362	13,611	2,511	11,100	—	141,764
1959	7,465	9,641	14,666	2,729	11,937	—	140,725
1960	8,173	8,812	16,752	3,914	12,838	—	142,841
1961	8,811	8,399	20,493	4,799	15,694	—	147,656
1962	9,690	9,414	28,415	10,801	17,614	—	148,939
1963	9,522	9,392	25,525	9,463	16,062	—	165,591
1964	8,451	10,396	13,115	3,988	9,127	—	161,150
1965	9,706	10,743	11,194	2,638	8,556	—	165,886
1966	10,558	10,541	14,057	4,227	9,830	—	194,707
1967	17,406	12,832	15,406	5,277	10,129	—	209,047
1968	25,419	16,411	20,376	6,002	14,374	—	245,417
1969	16,822	10,461	18,286	5,224	13,062	—	202,826
1970	10,479	9,272	18,480	4,332	14,148	—	216,137
1971	10,586	12,182	18,616	5,479	13,137	—	217,356
1972	10,498	15,403	21,660	6,403	15,257	—	227,444
1973	8,798	16,472	24,585	6,221	18,364	—	243,586
1974	8,789	18,135	25,227	6,912	18,315	—	243,593
1975	5,919	15,510	19,272	6,281	12,991	—	236,589
1976	6,811	13,956	18,292	6,224	12,068	—	243,955
(TQ)	1,751	3,259	4,655	1,629	3,026	—	63,801
1977	8,469	16,794	19,127	6,891	12,236	—	272,937
1978	10,548	24,969	34,052	11,111	22,941	—	352,679
1979	8,568	16,269	23,445	9,644	13,801	—	275,403
1980 [6]	—	—	—	—	—	—	—
1981 [6]	—	—	—	—	—	—	—
1982	— [7]	29,895	28,883	11,973	16,910	—	390,691

(TQ) indicates transitional quarter.

[1] For 1820-1831, years ending September 30; 1832-1842, years ending December 31; 1843-1850, years ending September 30; 1851-1865, years ending December 31; 1866-1976, years ending June 30; 1977-1982, years ending September 30.

[2] Fifteen months ending December 31.

[3] Nine months ending September 30.

[4] Six months ending June 30.

[5] Includes 32,897 persons returning to their homes in the United States.

[6] No data are available for 1980 and 1981 due to data processing problems at the INS.

[7] Included with other service workers, series Ad240.

Sources

1820-1898: U.S. Department of Treasury, Bureau of Statistics, *Monthly Summary of Commerce and Finance, June, 1903*. 1899-1970: U.S. Bureau of the Census, *Historical Statistics of the United States, Colonial Times to 1970* (U.S. Government Printing Office, 1975). For 1899-1944, the underlying source is unpublished U.S. Immigration and Naturalization Service (INS) data; for 1945-1970, the underlying sources are *Annual Report of the Immigration and*

Naturalization Service, annual issues, and unpublished data. 1971-1972: *1972 Statistical Yearbook of the INS*, Table 10A. 1973-1976: *1976 Statistical Yearbook of the INS*, Table 10A. 1977-1982: *1982 Statistical Yearbook of the INS*, Table IMM 4.2.

Documentation

This table displays data on the occupations of immigrants at the time of their immigration to the United States. The data are categorized according to the major groupings of the 1950 occupational classification system. Because of limitations in the source, the classification of the pre-1899 data is imperfect. For comparably categorized occupations of the foreign-born after their arrival in the United States, see Tables Ad802-873.

The original instructions for collecting statistics on the occupations of immigrants specified that the occupation should be described as precisely as possible, and the original statistical sources provide more detailed occupational information than is shown here.

For 1820-1898, the authors have classified the detailed occupations from the source to correspond as closely as possible with the 1950 groupings. From

(continued)

TABLE Ad231–245   Immigrants, by occupation at time of arrival: 1820–1982   *Continued*

1945 to 1951, the INS applied the major occupation groups as shown in the *Sixteenth Census of the United States, Alphabetical Index of Occupations and Industries*, 1950. It also grouped occupations of immigrants for 1899–1944 (compiled in unpublished records) as closely as possible into the new groups. From 1952 to 1961, occupations were coded and grouped in accordance with the definitions in *U.S. Census of Population: 1950, Alphabetical Index of Occupations and Industries*. Sources for subsequent years used more modern classifications, but they were quite similar to the 1950 groupings. The authors combined some categories to make the data compatible with the earlier groupings.

The occupation figures include all immigrants, those with and without work experience. The figures through 1867 are for all passengers who arrived

in the United States, including returning citizens; beginning in 1868 the data are for immigrants only.

See Table Ad246–255 for more recent immigrant occupation data grouped according to a different classification system.

Series Ad231. The "total" series is calculated from the sum of the components and consequently may not always agree with the sources.

Series Ad245. Includes housewives, the unemployed, retired persons, students, children less than fourteen years of age, aliens with no occupation, and occupation unknown or not reported.

TABLE Ad246–255   Immigrants, by occupation at time of arrival: 1983–1998

Contributed by Robert Barde, Susan B. Carter, and Richard Sutch

Fiscal year	Total	Professional or technical specialty	Executive, administrative, or managerial	Sales	Administrative support	Precision production, craft, or repair	Operator, fabricator, or laborer	Farming, forestry, or fishing	Service worker	No occupation or occupation not reported
	Ad246	Ad247	Ad248	Ad249	Ad250	Ad251	Ad252	Ad253	Ad254	Ad255
	Number	Number	Number	Number	Number	Number	Number	Number	Number	Number
1983	559,763	39,020	19,675	8,483	19,797	24,967	47,740	8,738	40,421	350,922
1984	543,903	38,595	20,247	10,542	17,703	25,472	46,157	10,715	41,961	332,511
1985	570,009	41,770	20,511	11,908	19,105	26,305	48,639	10,870	42,765	348,136
1986	601,708	42,104	21,269	12,255	19,706	26,773	53,252	11,606	47,142	367,601
1987	601,516	42,307	21,792	12,331	20,989	27,181	55,448	12,025	49,999	359,444
1988	643,025	45,188	20,014	12,027	25,452	28,460	68,269	15,513	65,158	362,944
1989	1,090,924	55,434	35,305	22,123	45,748	70,263	168,241	31,173	142,494	520,143
1990	1,536,483	67,655	46,684	34,211	58,050	112,969	245,168	101,070	230,553	640,123
1991	1,827,167	58,921	27,945	19,726	31,435	52,891	100,304	932,606	96,095	507,244
1992	973,977	74,205	30,985	15,226	24,348	33,475	66,027	133,070	61,203	535,438
1993	904,292	78,905	30,855	14,436	23,667	27,669	71,679	21,814	56,586	578,681
1994	804,416	67,286	26,931	13,024	21,590	24,518	67,486	15,606	50,646	517,329
1995	720,461	59,015	24,850	11,609	18,322	18,395	51,532	12,517	46,637	477,584
1996	915,900	75,267	31,850	15,317	21,698	23,867	76,843	14,575	62,126	594,357
1997	798,378	62,674	26,353	14,291	18,345	20,460	71,718	13,402	53,301	517,834
1998	660,477	45,088	18,429	10,507	12,623	12,186	33,174	11,589	24,759	492,122

Source

Statistical Yearbook of the Immigration and Naturalization Service, various years.

Documentation

The data correspond to the 1980 Census occupational classification. These occupational groupings are different from the occupational groupings reported in Table Ad231–245.

FOREIGN-BORN POPULATION AND ITS CHARACTERISTICS

Susan B. Carter, Michael R. Haines, and Matthew Sobek

TABLE Ad256–279   Population, by sex, nativity, and citizenship status: 1920–1990[1]

Contributed by Michael R. Haines

	Both sexes		Foreign-born						Male		Foreign-born	
						Not a citizen						
	Total	Native-born	Total	Naturalized	Total	Having first papers	Having no papers	Citizenship status unknown	Total	Native-born	Total	Naturalized
	Ad256	Ad257	Ad258	Ad259	Ad260	Ad261	Ad262	Ad263	Ad264	Ad265	Ad266	Ad267
Year	Number	Number	Number	Number	Number	Number	Number	Number	Number	Number	Number	Number
1920	105,710,620	91,789,928	13,920,692	6,489,883	6,629,333	1,222,553	5,406,780	801,476	53,900,431	46,224,996	7,675,435	3,449,547
1930	122,775,046	108,570,897	14,204,149	7,919,536	5,784,760	1,266,419	4,518,341	499,853	62,137,080	54,489,990	7,647,090	4,365,403
1940	131,669,275	120,074,379	11,594,896	7,280,265	3,479,652	924,524	2,555,128	834,979	66,061,592	59,939,945	6,121,647	4,137,027
1950	150,216,110	139,868,715	10,347,395	7,562,970	2,052,640	—	—	731,785	74,200,085	68,941,830	5,258,255	4,033,070
1960	179,325,657	169,587,566	9,738,091	—	—	—	—	—	88,303,167	83,542,735	4,760,432	—
1970	203,193,774	193,454,051	9,739,723	6,198,173	3,541,550	—	—	—	98,896,402	94,424,109	4,472,293	2,918,753
1980	226,545,805	212,465,899	14,079,906	7,110,475	6,969,431	—	—	—	110,047,513	103,466,419	6,581,094	—
1990	248,709,873	228,942,557	19,767,316	7,996,998	11,770,318	—	—	—	121,239,418	111,568,557	9,670,861	3,719,976

	Male	Foreign-born			Female		Foreign-born					
	Not a citizen								Not a citizen			
	Total	Having first papers	Having no papers	Citizenship status unknown	Total	Native-born	Total	Naturalized	Total	Having first papers	Having no papers	Citizenship status unknown
	Ad268	Ad269	Ad270	Ad271	Ad272	Ad273	Ad274	Ad275	Ad276	Ad277	Ad278	Ad279
Year	Number	Number	Number	Number	Number	Number	Number	Number	Number	Number	Number	Number
1920	3,832,063	1,137,021	2,695,042	393,825	51,810,189	45,564,932	6,245,257	3,040,336	2,797,270	85,532	2,711,738	407,651
1930	3,037,652	955,942	2,081,710	244,035	60,637,966	54,080,907	6,557,059	3,554,133	2,747,108	310,477	2,436,631	255,818
1940	1,589,782	581,711	1,008,071	394,836	65,607,683	60,134,434	5,473,249	3,143,238	1,889,868	342,811	1,547,057	440,143
1950	875,720	—	—	349,465	76,016,025	70,926,885	5,089,140	3,529,900	1,176,920	1,176,920	1,176,920	382,320
1960	—	—	—	—	91,022,490	86,044,831	4,977,659	—	—	—	—	—
1970	1,553,540	—	—	—	104,297,372	99,029,942	5,267,430	3,279,420	1,988,010	1,988,010	1,988,010	—
1980	—	—	—	—	116,498,292	108,999,480	7,498,812	—	—	—	—	—
1990	5,950,885	—	—	—	127,470,455	117,374,000	10,096,455	4,177,022	5,919,433	5,919,433	5,919,433	—

[1] Beginning 1950, figures are based on sample data.

Sources

U.S. Bureau of the Census. 1890–1940, total, native, and total foreign-born population, and 1930–1940, citizenship status of foreign-born and persons twenty-one years of age and older: *Sixteenth Census Reports, Population*, volume II, part 1. 1890–1920, data on persons twenty-one years of age and older, and 1920, citizenship status of foreign born: *Fifteenth Census Reports, Population*, volume II. 1950: *U.S. Census of Population: 1950*, volume II, part 1. 1960: *U.S. Census of Population: 1960*, volume I, part 1. 1970: *U.S. Census of Population: 1970*, volume II, *Subject Reports*. 1980: *U.S. Census of Population: 1980*, volume I, part 1, "Detailed Population Characteristics," "United States Summary," PC80-1 D1-A. U.S. 1990: *U.S. Census of Population: 1990*, volume I, *Subject Reports*, "Ancestry of the Population in the United States," 1990 CP-3-2.

Documentation

Information on citizenship was used to classify the population into two major categories, citizens and aliens. Citizens are further classified as native or naturalized. "Native" includes all persons born in the United States, Puerto Rico, the Canal Zone, Guam, American Samoa, or the Virgin Islands and persons born abroad or at sea to American parents. It was assumed that all natives were citizens. See also the text for Table Aa1896–1921. In 1970, when information on citizenship was missing, it was assigned on the basis of related information. These statistics relate to the citizenship status of the population at the date of the specified decennial census.

Figures for 1950–1990 therefore differ from those for 1890–1940, which are based on complete counts. 1950 figures are based on a 20 percent sample; 1960 figures are based on a 25 percent sample; and 1970 figures are based on a 5 percent sample. Figures for 1980 and 1990 are based on a one-in-six sample, except in governmental units estimated to be less than 2,500 persons, which used a 50 percent sample.

TABLE Ad280–318   Population, by sex, nativity, and citizenship status: 1890–1990   [Persons at least 18 or 21 years of age][1]

Contributed by Michael R. Haines

	Age 21 years and older									
	Both sexes								Male	
			Foreign-born							
					Not a citizen					
	Total	Native-born	Total	Naturalized	Total	Having first papers	Having no papers	Citizenship status unknown	Total	Native-born
	Ad280	Ad281	Ad282	Ad283	Ad284	Ad285	Ad286	Ad287	Ad288	Ad289
Year	Number	Number	Number	Number	Number	Number	Number	Number	Number	Number
1890	—	—	—	—	—	—	—	—	16,940,311	12,591,852
1900	—	—	—	—	—	—	—	—	21,134,299	16,124,013
1910	—	—	—	—	—	—	—	—	26,999,151	20,218,937
1920	60,886,520	48,200,127	12,686,393	6,218,801	5,727,454	1,197,698	4,529,756	740,138	31,403,370	24,339,776
1930	72,943,624	59,607,271	13,336,353	7,681,681	5,183,431	1,237,255	3,946,176	471,241	37,056,757	29,837,780
1940	83,996,629	72,703,808	11,292,821	7,159,643	3,335,392	910,416	2,424,976	797,786	42,004,816	36,035,228
1950	96,732,900	86,712,450	10,020,450	7,466,445	1,879,900	—	—	674,105	47,137,460	42,045,230
1960	108,051,172	99,071,648	8,979,524			—	—	—	52,147,983	47,765,139
1970	122,597,202	114,076,804	8,520,398	5,795,027	2,725,371	—	—	—	57,992,895	54,128,061
1980	149,747,265	138,013,427	11,733,838	6,484,569	5,249,269	—	—	—	70,850,521	65,486,773
1990	173,597,245	156,805,934	16,791,311	7,463,506	9,327,805	—	—	—	82,689,266	74,593,299

	Age 21 years and older									
	Male						Female			
	Foreign-born								Foreign-born	
			Not a citizen							
	Total	Naturalized	Total	Having first papers	Having no papers	Citizenship status unknown	Total	Native-born	Total	Naturalized
	Ad290	Ad291	Ad292	Ad293	Ad294	Ad295	Ad296	Ad297	Ad298	Ad299
Year	Number	Number	Number	Number	Number	Number	Number	Number	Number	Number
1890	4,348,459	2,545,753	1,425,513	236,061	1,189,452	377,193	—	—	—	—
1900	5,010,286	2,848,807	1,426,490	412,271	1,014,219	734,989	—	—	—	—
1910	6,780,214	3,038,303	2,961,947	571,521	2,390,426	779,964	—	—	—	—
1920	7,063,594	3,320,226	3,379,292	1,119,982	2,259,310	364,076	29,483,150	23,860,351	5,622,799	2,898,575
1930	7,218,977	4,247,704	2,740,170	939,875	1,800,295	231,103	35,886,867	29,769,491	6,117,376	3,433,977
1940	5,969,588	4,076,207	1,517,151	574,296	942,855	376,230	41,991,813	36,668,580	5,323,233	3,083,436
1950	5,092,230	3,981,895	790,300	—	—	320,035	49,595,440	44,667,220	4,928,220	3,484,550
1960	4,382,844	—		—	—	—	55,903,189	51,306,509	4,596,680	
1970	3,864,834	2,719,383	1,145,451	—	—	—	64,604,307	59,948,743	4,655,564	3,075,644
1980	5,363,748	2,920,723	2,443,025	—	—	—	78,896,744	72,526,654	6,370,090	3,563,846
1990	8,095,967	3,439,722	4,656,245	—	—	—	90,907,979	82,212,635	8,695,344	4,023,784

Note appears at end of table

TABLE Ad280–318   Population, by sex, nativity, and citizenship status: 1890–1990   [Persons at least 18 or 21 years of age]   *Continued*

	Age 21 years and older				Aged 18 years and older						
	Female				Both sexes					Male	
	Foreign-born						Foreign-born				
	Not a citizen										
	Total	Having first papers	Having no papers	Citizenship status unknown	Total	Native-born	Total	Naturalized	Not a citizen	Total	Native-born
	Ad300	Ad301	Ad302	Ad303	Ad304	Ad305	Ad306	Ad307	Ad308	Ad309	Ad310
Year	Number	Number	Number	Number	Number	Number	Number	Number	Number	Number	Number
1890	—	—	—	—	—	—	—	—	—	—	—
1900	—	—	—	—	—	—	—	—	—	—	—
1910	—	—	—	—	—	—	—	—	—	—	—
1920	2,348,162	77,716	2,270,446	376,062	—	—	—	—	—	—	—
1930	2,443,261	297,380	2,145,881	240,138	—	—	—	—	—	—	—
1940	1,818,241	336,120	1,482,121	421,556	—	—	—	—	—	—	—
1950	1,089,600	—	—	354,070	—	—	—	—	—	—	—
1960	—	—	—	—	—	—	—	—	—	—	—
1970	1,579,920	—	—	—	133,313,480	124,526,125	8,787,355	5,900,350	2,887,005	63,277,575	59,283,513
1980	2,806,244	—	—	—	162,753,486	150,393,150	12,360,336	6,666,541	5,693,795	77,404,802	71,706,758
1990	4,671,560	—	—	—	185,103,329	167,428,473	17,674,856	7,656,964	10,017,892	88,553,487	79,968,905

	Age 18 years and older							
	Male			Female				
	Foreign-born					Foreign-born		
	Total	Naturalized	Not a citizen	Total	Native-born	Total	Naturalized	Not a citizen
	Ad311	Ad312	Ad313	Ad314	Ad315	Ad316	Ad317	Ad318
Year	Number	Number	Number	Number	Number	Number	Number	Number
1890	—	—	—	—	—	—	—	—
1900	—	—	—	—	—	—	—	—
1910	—	—	—	—	—	—	—	—
1920	—	—	—	—	—	—	—	—
1930	—	—	—	—	—	—	—	—
1940	—	—	—	—	—	—	—	—
1950	—	—	—	—	—	—	—	—
1960	—	—	—	—	—	—	—	—
1970	3,994,062	2,770,610	1,223,452	70,035,905	65,242,612	4,793,293	3,129,740	1,663,553
1980	5,698,044	3,012,853	2,685,191	85,348,678	78,686,386	6,662,292	3,653,688	3,008,604
1990	8,584,582	3,543,661	5,040,921	96,549,842	87,459,568	9,090,274	4,113,303	4,976,971

[1] Prior to 1920, the citizenship inquiry of the Population Census was restricted to males twenty-one years of age and older. Beginning in 1950, figures are based on sample data.

Sources

U.S. Bureau of the Census. 1890–1940, total, native, and total foreign-born population, and 1930–1940, citizenship status of foreign-born and persons twenty-one years of age and older: *Sixteenth Census Reports, Population*, volume II, part 1. 1890–1920, data on persons twenty-one years of age and older, and 1920, citizenship status of foreign-born: *Fifteenth Census Reports, Population*, volume II. 1950: *U.S. Census of Population: 1950*, volume II, part 1. 1960: *U.S. Census of Population: 1960*, volume I, part 1. 1970: *U.S. Census of Population: 1970*, volume II, *Subject Reports*. U.S. 1980: *U.S. Census of Population: 1980*, volume I, part 1, "Detailed Population Characteristics," "United States Summary," PC80-1 D1-A. U.S. 1990: *U.S. Census of Population:* 1990, volume I, *Subject Reports*, "Ancestry of the Population in the United States," 1990 CP-3-2. Campbell Gibson and Emily Lennon, "Historical Census Statistics on the Foreign-Born Population of the United States: 1850 to 1990," U.S. Bureau of the Census, Population Division, Working Paper No. 29 (Feb. 1999).

Documentation

See the text for Table Ad256–279.

Starting with the 1930 Census, data on citizenship status have been published by sex for all ages as well as for the voting age population. For years prior to 1940, when age was not reported, the data on citizenship status by age assume that all individuals for whom age was not reported were twenty-one years of age and older. In 1960, a question on citizenship status was not included on the general census questionnaire (although it was included on the questionnaire used in New York state).

TABLE Ad319–353 Native-born population of foreign parentage, by parents' country of origin: 1900–1970[1]

Contributed by Michael R. Haines

		Europe									
				Ireland							
	Total	England and Wales	Scotland	Total	Northern Ireland	Ireland (Eire)	Norway	Sweden	Denmark	The Netherlands	Belgium
	Ad319	Ad320	Ad321	Ad322	Ad323	Ad324	Ad325	Ad326	Ad327 [2]	Ad328	Ad329
Year	Number	Number	Number	Number	Number	Number	Number	Number	Number	Number	Number
1900	15,646,017	1,695,558	447,524	3,375,546	—	—	478,531	542,032	187,844	—[3]	—[3]
1910	18,897,837	1,822,264	484,699	3,304,015	—	—	609,068	752,695	256,175	188,015	46,222
1920	22,686,204	1,864,345	514,436	3,122,013	—	—	701,096	888,497	320,410	249,339	68,961
1930	25,902,383	1,890,051	545,268	2,858,879	517,167	2,341,712	752,246	967,453	349,668	280,833	82,897
1940	23,157,580	1,466,900	446,540	2,109,740	270,820	1,838,920	662,600	856,320	305,640	261,320	76,400
1950	23,589,485	1,443,230	463,325	1,921,385	29,890	1,891,495	652,380	864,695	318,710	272,535	85,500
1960	24,312,263	1,409,159	455,453	1,621,574	186,984	1,434,590	622,056	832,451	314,290	280,243	89,972
1970	23,955,930	1,268,643	411,121	1,298,032	99,187	1,198,845	517,406	679,068	264,151	273,139	89,238

	Europe											
	Switzerland	France	Germany	Poland	Czechoslovakia	Austria	Hungary	Yugoslavia	Russia/USSR	Lithuania	Finland	Romania
	Ad330	Ad331	Ad332	Ad333	Ad334	Ad335	Ad336	Ad337	Ad338	Ad339	Ad340	Ad341
Year	Number	Number	Number	Number	Number	Number	Number	Number	Number	Number	Number	Number
1900	178,691	214,592	5,340,147	326,764	—[3]	391,636	81,897	—[5]	288,098	—[6]	—[6]	—[3]
1910	217,459	226,059	5,670,611	725,924	—[3]	716,753	215,295	—[5]	775,654	—[6]	85,672	26,934
1920	257,341	288,350	5,346,004	1,303,351	—[3]	1,235,097 [4]	538,518 [4]	—[5]	1,508,604	—[6]	152,161	64,776
1930	260,993	336,373	5,264,289	2,073,615	890,441	583,734	316,318	257,979	1,516,214	245,589	178,058	147,060
1940	205,680	246,120	3,998,840	1,912,380	664,620	781,340	371,840	222,300	1,569,360	229,040	167,080	131,760
1950	215,660	253,665	3,742,615	1,925,015	705,890	816,465	437,080	239,920	1,647,420	249,825	172,370	130,100
1960	201,486	240,099	3,330,849	2,032,276	690,212	794,123	456,385	282,705	1,599,669	281,371	173,203	149,230
1970	168,976	237,982	2,789,070	1,826,137	598,628	761,311	420,432	293,526	1,479,733	254,976	158,327	146,116

	Europe						Americas					
								Canada				
	Greece	Italy	Spain	Portugal	Other Europe	Asia	Total	French Canada	Other	Mexico	Other Americas	All other
	Ad342	Ad343	Ad344	Ad345	Ad346	Ad347	Ad348	Ad349	Ad350	Ad351	Ad352	Ad353
Year	Number	Number	Number	Number	Number	Number	Number	Number	Number	Number	Number	Number
1900	—[3]	254,550	—[3]	—[3]	—	—[3]	1,389,470	456,030	933,440	—[3]	—[3]	453,137
1910	9,985	771,645	—[7]	—[7]	74,548	—[3]	1,650,821	562,709	1,088,112	162,959	30,169	74,196
1920	52,083	1,751,091	—[7]	—[7]	137,284	—[3]	1,841,605	562,360	1,279,245	253,176	51,259	176,407
1930	129,225	2,756,453	52,305	97,917	101,652	152,347	2,058,924	735,307	1,323,617	583,422	75,220	96,960
1940	163,420	2,971,200	61,700	114,060	75,660	183,260	1,866,040	635,020	1,231,020	699,220	91,980	245,220
1950	195,235	3,143,405	69,490	117,675	128,030	239,525	1,987,820	519,495	1,468,325	891,980	101,240	157,300
1960	219,419	3,286,936	81,164	148,602	121,984	642,520	2,228,551	—	—	1,160,090	248,272	317,919
1970	257,296	3,232,246	97,668	149,532	168,082	920,475	2,222,135	—	—	1,579,440	479,439	913,605

[1] 1940 figures based on a 5 percent sample; 1950 figures based on a 20 percent sample; 1960 figures based on a 25 percent sample; and 1970 figures based on a 15 percent sample.

[2] Includes Iceland prior to 1930.

[3] Included with "all other."

[4] Areas as defined in 1910.

[5] Included with Austria and Hungary.

[6] Included with Russia/USSR.

[7] Included with other Europe.

Sources

U.S. Bureau of the Census. 1900–1940: *Sixteenth Census Reports, Population, Country of Origin of Foreign Stock*. 1950: *U.S. Census of Population: 1950*, volume 4, *Special Reports, Nativity and Parentage*. 1960: *U.S. Census of Population: 1960*, volume 1, part 1. 1970: *U.S. Census of Population: 1970*, volume 2, *Subject Reports*.

Documentation

Figures are the native-born population with one or both parents born in the specified country or region (that is, including persons of mixed parentage).

The category "native" comprises persons born in the United States, in the Commonwealth of Puerto Rico, in an outlying area of the United States, or at sea. Also included in this category is the small number of persons who, although they were born in a foreign country, have at least one native American parent. When information on place of birth was missing, nativity was assigned on the basis of related information. In previous censuses, persons for whom nativity was not reported were generally classified as native. The rules for determining the nativity of parents are generally the same as those for determining the nativity of the person him- or herself.

Information on birthplace of parents is used to classify the native population into two categories: native of native parentage and native of foreign or mixed parentage. The category "native of native parentage" comprises

TABLE Ad319–353   Native-born population of foreign parentage, by parents' country of origin: 1900–1970
Continued

native persons with both parents born in the United States. The category "native of foreign or mixed parentage" includes native persons with one or both parents foreign-born. The definition of country of birth of parents is similar to that used in Table Ad354–443, with one important exception. The classification by country of birth of parents for 1930 and later years is made on the basis of boundaries existing at the date of the specified decennial census. This is the same procedure used for all of the years in Table Ad354–443. However, the 1920 data on country of birth of parents shown in this table are based on pre–World War I boundaries because of the difficulty of obtaining correct replies on the basis of postwar boundaries for parents of persons enumerated.

See also the text for Tables Aa1896–2025 and Aa2078–2092.

TABLE Ad354–443   Foreign-born population, by country of birth: 1850–1990[1]
Contributed by Michael R. Haines

			Europe								
				Northern Europe							
							Great Britain				
	Total	Total reporting specific country or region	Total, Europe	Total, Northern and Western Europe	Total, Northern Europe	Total, British Isles	Total	England	Scotland	Wales	Great Britain not elsewhere classified
	Ad354	Ad355	Ad356	Ad357	Ad358	Ad359	Ad360	Ad361	Ad362	Ad363	Ad364
Year	Number	Number	Number	Number	Number	Number	Number	Number	Number	Number	Number
1850 [9]	2,244,602	2,202,625	2,031,867	2,022,195	1,358,887	1,340,812	379,093	278,675	70,550	29,868	—
1860 [9]	4,138,697	4,134,809	3,807,062	3,773,347	2,271,661	2,199,079	587,775	431,692	108,518	45,763	1,802
1870	5,567,229	5,563,637	4,941,049	4,845,679	2,867,926	2,626,241	770,414	550,924	140,835	74,533	4,122
1880	6,679,943	6,675,875	5,751,823	5,499,889	3,212,431	2,772,169	917,598	662,676	170,136	83,302	1,484
1890	9,249,547	9,243,535	8,030,347	7,288,917	4,056,160	3,122,911	1,251,402	908,141	242,231	100,079	951
1900	10,341,276	10,330,534	8,881,548	7,204,649	3,917,815	2,783,082	1,167,623	840,513	233,524	93,586	—
1910	13,515,886	13,506,272	11,810,115	7,306,325	3,953,947	2,573,534	1,221,283	877,719	261,076	82,488	—
1920	13,920,692	13,911,767	11,916,048	6,241,916	3,501,149	2,172,723	1,135,489	813,853	254,570	67,066	—
1930	14,204,149	14,197,553	11,784,010	5,850,256	3,415,551	2,147,733	1,224,091	809,563	354,323	60,205	—
1940 [10]	11,594,896	—	—	—	—	—	—	—	—	—	—
1950 [11]	10,420,908	10,331,217	8,286,871	—	—	1,351,855	—	—	—	—	—
1960 [11]	9,738,091	9,678,201	7,256,311	3,334,971	1,694,430	1,171,777	764,893	528,205	213,219	23,469	—
1970 [11]	9,619,302	9,303,570	5,740,891	2,629,200	1,271,591	937,474	645,262	458,114	170,134	17,014	—
1980 [11]	14,079,906	13,192,563	5,149,572	2,384,257	1,083,499	866,966	649,318	442,499	142,001	13,528	51,290
1990 [11]	19,767,316	18,959,158	4,350,403	2,058,853	968,271	809,972	623,614	405,588	104,168	10,638	103,220

		Europe							
		Northern Europe							
	Ireland			Scandinavia					
	Total	Northern Ireland	Ireland (Eire)	Total	Denmark	Finland	Iceland	Norway	Sweden
	Ad365	Ad366 [2]	Ad367	Ad368	Ad369 [3]	Ad370	Ad371 [3]	Ad372	Ad373
Year	Number	Number	Number	Number	Number	Number	Number	Number	Number
1850 [9]	961,719	—	—	18,075	1,838	—	—	12,678	3,559
1860 [9]	1,611,304	—	—	72,582	9,962	—	—	43,995	18,625
1870	1,855,827	—	—	241,685	30,107	—	—	114,246	97,332
1880	1,854,571	—	—	440,262	64,196	—	—	181,729	194,337
1890	1,871,509	—	—	933,249	132,543	—	—	322,665	478,041
1900	1,615,459	—	—	1,134,733	153,690	62,641	—	336,388	582,014
1910	1,352,251	—	—	1,380,413	181,649	129,680	—	403,877	665,207
1920	1,037,234	—	—	1,328,426	189,154	149,824	—	363,863	625,585
1930	923,642	178,832	744,810	1,267,818	179,474	142,478	2,764	347,852	595,250
1940 [10]	—	—	—	—	—	—	—	—	—
1950 [11]	—	—	505,285	—	107,982	95,686	—	202,448	325,118
1960 [11]	406,884	68,162	338,722	522,653	85,060	67,624	2,780	152,698	214,491
1970 [11]	292,212	40,837	251,375	334,117	61,410	45,499	2,895	97,243	127,070
1980 [11]	217,648	19,831	197,817	216,533	42,732	29,172	4,156	63,316	77,157
1990 [11]	186,358	16,531	169,827	158,299	34,999	22,313	5,071	42,240	53,676

Notes appear at end of table

(continued)

TABLE Ad354–443   Foreign-born population, by country of birth: 1850–1990   *Continued*

		Europe								
		Western Europe								
		The Low Countries								Other Western Europe
	Total	Total	The Netherlands	Belgium	Luxembourg	Switzerland	France	Germany	Austria	
	Ad374	Ad375	Ad376 [4]	Ad377	Ad378	Ad379	Ad380	Ad381	Ad382	Ad383
Year	Number	Number	Number	Number	Number	Number	Number	Number	Number	Number
1850 [9]	663,308	11,161	9,848	1,313	—	13,358	54,069	583,774	946	—
1860 [9]	1,501,686	37,353	28,281	9,072	—	53,327	109,870	1,276,075	25,061	—
1870	1,977,753	65,157	46,802	12,553	5,802	75,153	116,402	1,690,533	30,508	—
1880	2,287,458	86,461	58,090	15,535	12,836	88,621	106,971	1,966,742	38,663	—
1890	3,232,757	107,349	81,828	22,639	2,882	104,069	113,174	2,784,894	123,271	—
1900	3,286,834	127,719	94,931	29,757	3,031	115,593	104,197	2,663,418	275,907	—
1910	3,352,378	172,534	120,063	49,400	3,071	124,848	117,418	2,311,237 [12]	6,26,341 [12]	—
1920	2,740,767	207,038	131,766	62,687	12,585	118,659	153,072	1,686,108	575,627	263
1930	2,434,705	206,375	133,133	64,194	9,048	113,010	135,592	1,608,814	370,914	—
1940 [10]	—	—	—	—	—	—	—	—	—	—
1950 [11]	—	—	102,224	—	—	71,636	108,547	991,321	409,043	—
1960 [11]	1,640,541	173,069	118,415	50,294	4,360	61,568	111,582	989,815	304,507	—
1970 [11]	1,357,609	155,513	110,570	41,412	3,531	49,732	105,385	832,965	214,014	—
1980 [11]	1,300,758	142,748	103,136	36,487	3,125	42,804	120,215	849,384	145,607	—
1990 [11]	1,090,582	132,617	96,198	34,366	2,053	39,130	119,233	711,929	87,673	—

		Europe								
	Total, Southern and Eastern Europe	Eastern Europe								
		Total	Albania	Bulgaria	Czechoslovakia	Estonia	Hungary	Latvia	Lithuania	Poland
	Ad384	Ad385	Ad386	Ad387	Ad388	Ad389	Ad390	Ad391	Ad392	Ad393
Year	Number	Number	Number	Number	Number	Number	Number	Number	Number	Number
1850 [9]	9,672	1,520	—	—	—	—	—	—	—	—
1860 [9]	32,312	10,586	—	—	—	—	—	—	—	7,298
1870	93,824	63,408	—	—	40,289	—	3,737	—	—	14,436
1880	248,620	182,371	—	—	85,361	—	11,526	—	—	48,557
1890	728,851	512,464	—	—	118,106	—	62,435	—	—	147,440
1900	1,674,648	1,134,680	—	—	156,891	—	145,714	—	—	383,407
1910	4,500,932	2,956,783	— [13]	11,498	219,214	—	495,609	—	—	937,884 [12]
1920	5,670,927	3,731,327	5,608	10,477	362,438	—	397,283	—	135,068	1,139,979
1930	5,918,982	3,785,890	8,814	9,399	491,638	3,550	274,450	20,673	193,606	1,268,583
1940 [10]	—	—	—	*	—	—	—	—	—	—
1950 [11]	—	—	—	—	278,438	—	268,183	—	147,872	861,655
1960 [11]	3,907,020	2,365,579	9,618	8,223	227,618	13,991	245,252	50,681	121,475	747,750
1970 [11]	3,090,991	1,727,796	9,180	8,609	160,899	12,163	183,236	41,707	76,001	548,107
1980 [11]	2,748,547	1,411,742	7,381	8,463	112,707	12,169	144,368	34,349	48,194	418,128
1990 [11]	2,285,513	1,231,372	5,627	8,579	87,020	9,210	110,337	26,179	29,745	388,328

Notes appear at end of table

TABLE Ad354–443   Foreign-born population, by country of birth: 1850–1990   *Continued*

	Europe										
	Eastern Europe					Southern Europe					
									Portugal		
	Romania	Russia/USSR	Turkey in Europe	Yugoslavia	Other Eastern Europe	Total	Greece	Italy	Total	Portugal	Azores
	Ad394	Ad395 [5,6]	Ad396 [7]	Ad397	Ad398	Ad399	Ad400	Ad401	Ad402	Ad403	Ad404
Year	Number	Number	Number	Number	Number	Number	Number	Number	Number	Number	Number
1850 [9]	—	1,414	106	—	—	8,152	86	3,679	1,274	1,274	—
1860 [9]	—	3,160	128	—	—	21,726	328	11,677	5,477	4,116	1,361
1870	—	4,644	302	—	—	30,416	390	17,157	8,973	4,542	4,431
1880	—	35,722	1,205	—	—	66,249	776	44,230	15,650	8,138	7,512
1890	—	182,644	1,839	—	—	216,387	1,887	182,580	25,735	15,996	9,739
1900	15,032	423,726	9,910	—	—	539,968	8,515	484,027	40,376	30,608	9,768
1910	65,923	1,184,412 [12]	32,230 [13]	—	10,013	1,544,149	101,282	1,343,125	77,634	59,360	18,274
1920	102,823	1,400,495	5,284	169,439	2,433	1,939,600	175,976	1,610,113	103,976	69,981	33,995
1930	146,393	1,153,628	2,257	211,416	1,483	2,133,092	174,526	1,790,429	108,775	73,164	35,611
1940 [10]	—	—	—	—	—	—	—	—	—	—	—
1950 [11]	85,230	896,000	—	144,076	—	—	169,335	1,427,952	—	56,591	—
1960 [11]	84,575	690,598	—	165,798	—	1,541,441	159,167	1,256,999	80,276	57,690	22,586
1970 [11]	70,687	463,462	—	153,745	—	1,363,195	177,275	1,008,533	119,899	91,034	28,865
1980 [11]	66,994	406,022	—	152,967	—	1,336,805	210,998	831,922	209,968	177,437	32,531
1990 [11]	91,106	333,725	—	141,516	—	1,054,141	177,398	580,592	210,122	180,466	29,656

	Europe			Asia					
	Southern Europe								
	Spain	Other Southern Europe	Europe not elsewhere classified	Total	Armenia	China	Japan	India	Korea
	Ad405	Ad406	Ad407	Ad408	Ad409 [6]	Ad410	Ad411	Ad412	Ad413
Year	Number	Number	Number	Number	Number	Number	Number	Number	Number
1850 [9]	3,113	—	—	1,135	—	758	—	—	—
1860 [9]	4,244	—	1,403	36,796	—	35,565	—	—	—
1870	3,764	132	1,546	64,565	—	63,042	73	586	—
1880	5,121	472	3,314	107,630	—	104,468	401	1,707	—
1890	6,185	—	12,579	113,396	—	106,701	2,292	2,143	—
1900	7,050	—	2,251	120,248	—	81,534	24,788	2,031	—
1910	22,108	—	2,858 [14]	191,484	— [15]	56,756	67,744	4,664	—
1920	49,535	—	3,205	237,950	36,628	43,560	81,502	4,901	—
1930	59,362	—	14,772	275,665	32,166	46,129	70,993	5,850	—
1940 [10]	—	—	—	—	—	—	—	—	—
1950 [11]	—	—	185,685	275,990	—	—	—	—	—
1960 [11]	44,999	—	14,320	490,996	—	99,735	109,175	12,296	11,171
1970 [11]	57,488	—	20,700	824,887	—	172,132	120,235	51,000	38,711
1980 [11]	73,735	10,182	16,768	2,539,777	—	286,120	221,794	206,087	289,885
1990 [11]	76,415	9,614	6,037	4,979,037	—	529,837	290,128	450,406	568,397

Notes appear at end of table

(continued)

TABLE Ad354–443   Foreign-born population, by country of birth: 1850–1990   *Continued*

	Asia						America			
				Turkey				Northern America		
									Canada	
Year	Palestine	Philippines	Syria	Total	Turkey in Asia	Other Asia	Total	Total	Total	French Canada
	Ad414	Ad415	Ad416	Ad417	Ad418 [7]	Ad419 [6]	Ad420	Ad421	Ad422	Ad423
	Number	Number	Number	Number	Number	Number	Number	Number	Number	Number
1850 [9]	—	—	—	106	—	377	168,484	147,711	147,711	—
1860 [9]	—	—	—	128	—	1,231	288,285	249,970	249,970	—
1870	—	—	—	302	—	864	551,335	493,467	493,464	—
1880	—	—	—	1,205	—	1,054	807,230	717,286	717,157	—
1890	—	—	—	1,839	—	2,260	1,088,245	980,938	980,938	302,496
1900	—	—	—	9,910	—	11,895	1,317,380	1,179,922	1,179,922	395,126
1910	— [15]	—	— [15]	91,959	59,729	2,591	1,489,231	1,209,717	1,209,717	385,083
1920	3,203	—	51,901	16,303	11,019	5,236	1,727,017	1,138,174	1,138,174	307,786
1930	6,137	—	57,227	48,911	46,654	10,509	2,102,209	1,310,369	1,310,369	370,852
1940 [10]	—	—	—	—	—	—	—	—	—	—
1950 [11]	—	—	—	—	—	—	1,655,324 [17]	1,003,038	1,003,038	—
1960 [11]	— [16]	104,843	16,717	52,228	52,228	84,831 [16]	1,860,809	952,500	952,500	—
1970 [11]	— [16]	184,842	14,962	48,085	48,085	194,920 [16]	2,616,391	812,421	812,421	—
1980 [11]	— [16]	501,440	22,081	51,915	51,915	960,455 [16]	5,225,914	853,427	842,859	—
1990 [11]	21,070	912,674	36,782	55,087	55,087	2,114,656	9,161,754	753,917	744,830	—

	America									
	Northern America			Latin America						
	Canada				Caribbean					
Year	Newfoundland	Other	Other Northern America	Total	Total	Cuba	Other Caribbean	Mexico	Central America	South America
	Ad424 [8]	Ad425	Ad426	Ad427	Ad428	Ad429	Ad430	Ad431	Ad432	Ad433
	Number	Number	Number	Number	Number	Number	Number	Number	Number	Number
1850 [9]	—	—	—	20,773	5,772	—	5,772 [18]	13,317	141	1,543
1860 [9]	—	—	—	38,315	7,353	—	7,353 [18]	27,466	233	3,263
1870	—	—	3	57,871	11,570	5,319	6,251	42,435	301	3,565
1880	—	—	129	90,073	16,401	6,917	9,484	68,399	707	4,566
1890	—	678,442	—	107,307	23,256	—	23,256 [18]	77,853	1,192	5,006
1900	—	784,796	—	137,458	25,435	11,081	14,354	103,393	3,897	4,733
1910	5,080	819,554	—	279,514	47,635	15,133	32,502	221,915	1,736	8,228
1920	13,249	817,139	—	588,843	78,962	14,872	64,090	486,418	4,912	18,551
1930	23,980	915,537	—	791,840	106,241	18,493	87,748	641,462	10,514	33,623
1940 [10]	—	—	—	—	—	—	—	—	—	—
1950 [11]	—	—	—	—	—	—	—	454,417	—	—
1960 [11]	—	—	—	908,309	193,922	79,150	114,772 [19]	575,902	48,949	89,536
1970 [11]	—	—	—	1,803,970	675,108	439,048	236,060 [19]	759,711	113,913	255,238
1980 [11]	—	—	10,568	4,372,487	1,258,363	607,814	650,549	2,199,221	353,892	561,011
1990 [11]	—	—	9,087	8,407,837	1,938,348	736,971	1,201,377	4,298,014	1,133,978	1,037,497

Notes appear at end of table

TABLE Ad354–443　Foreign-born population, by country of birth: 1850–1990　*Continued*

	Africa			Oceania				All other countries	Country not specified	At sea
	Total	Excluding Atlantic islands	Atlantic islands	Total	Australia	Sandwich Islands	Other Oceania			
	Ad434	Ad435	Ad436	Ad437	Ad438	Ad439	Ad440	Ad441	Ad442	Ad443
Year	Number	Number	Number	Number	Number	Number	Number	Number	Number	Number
1850 [9]	551	551	—	588	—	588	—	—	41,977	—
1860 [9]	526	526	—	2,140	1,419	435	286	—	1,366	2,522
1870	2,657	2,657	—	4,028	3,118	584	326	—	954	2,638
1880	2,204	2,204	—	6,859	4,906	1,147	806	—	—	4,068
1890	2,207	2,207	—	9,353	5,984	1,304	2,065	—	479	5,533
1900	2,538	2,538	—	8,820	6,807	—	2,013	—	2,546	8,196
1910	3,992	3,992	—	11,450	9,035	—	2,415	—	2,687	6,927
1920	16,126	5,781	10,345	14,626	10,914	—	3,712	—	3,589	5,336
1930	18,326	8,859	9,467	17,343	12,816	—	4,527	—	1,588	5,008
1940 [10]	—	—	—	—	—	—	—	—	—	—
1950 [11]	—	—	—	—	—	—	—	202,723 [17]	89,691	—
1960 [11]	35,355	27,053	8,302	34,730	22,209	—	12,521 [20]	—	59,890	—
1970 [11]	80,143	61,463	18,680	41,258	24,271	—	16,987 [20]	—	315,732	—
1980 [11]	199,723	189,266	10,457	77,577	36,120	—	41,457	—	887,343	—
1990 [11]	363,819	349,451	14,368	104,145	42,267	—	61,878	—	808,158	—

[1] Data given for each country for all census years since 1850 for which figures are available.

[2] Through 1920, included with Ireland.

[3] Through 1920, Iceland included with Denmark.

[4] Listed as Holland prior to 1910.

[5] Includes Russia, Finland, Estonia, Latvia, and Lithuania (1850–1890); Russia, Estonia, Latvia, and Lithuania (1900–1910); and USSR, Estonia, and Latvia (1920).

[6] For 1920–1950, Armenian foreign-born included with other Asia; beginning 1960, with USSR.

[7] For 1850–1900, Turkey in Asia included with Turkey in Europe; beginning 1950, Turkey in Europe included with Turkey in Asia.

[8] Newfoundland included with Canada prior to 1910.

[9] Data refer to whites and free blacks only; data on nativity were not collected for slaves.

[10] There were 11,594,896 total foreign-born persons in 1940; data by country of birth are not available.

[11] Based on complete count (1950), 25 percent sample (1960 and 1980), and 15 percent sample (1970 and 1990).

[12] Persons of Polish mother tongue born in Austria, Germany, and USSR have been deducted from their respective countries and combined as Poland.

[13] Albania included with Turkey in Europe.

[14] Includes persons born in Serbia and Montenegro, which became part of Yugoslavia in 1918.

[15] Included with Turkey in Asia.

[16] Palestine included with other Asia.

[17] Includes countries for which figures are not shown separately.

[18] Excludes U.S. outlying areas.

[19] Includes "other Atlantic islands" and excludes the Azores.

[20] Includes New Zealand and Trust Territories of the Pacific Islands, but excludes outlying areas of the United States.

Sources

U.S. Bureau of the Census. 1850–1930, total foreign born: *Fifteenth Census Reports, Population*, volume II, p. 233. 1940: *U.S. Census of Population: 1940*, "Population," Second Series, "Characteristics of the Population," "United States Summary," Table 4. 1950: *U.S. Census of Population: 1950*, volume IV, *Special Reports, Nativity and Parentage*, p. 3A-71 and volume IV, *Special Reports, Nonwhite Population by Race*, p. 3B-82, and unpublished data. 1960: *U.S. Census of Population: 1960*, volume I, part 1. 1970: *U.S. Census of Population: 1970*, volume II, *Subject Reports*. 1980: *U.S. Census of Population: 1980*, volume 1, Chapter D, part 1, section A, PC80-1-D1-A, Table 254. 1990: *U.S. Census of Population: 1990*, "The Foreign-Born Population in the United States," 1990 CP-3-1, Table 1. Campbell Gibson and Emily Lennon, "Historical Census

Statistics on the Foreign-Born Population of the United States: 1850 to 1990" U.S. Bureau of the Census, Population Division, Working Paper No. 29 (Feb. 1999).

Documentation

The foreign-born population comprises all persons born outside the United States, Puerto Rico, or an outlying area of the United States, except those persons with at least one American parent. Persons born in any of the outlying areas, and American citizens born abroad or at sea, are regarded as native.

The statistics on country of birth are generally based on the political boundaries of foreign nations existing at the date of the specified decennial census. Because of boundary changes following World War I and World War II, accurate comparisons over the entire period, 1850–1950, can be made for relatively few countries. These countries include England, Scotland, Wales, Norway, Sweden, Netherlands, Switzerland, Spain, Portugal, Canada (total of Canada-French, Canada-other, and Newfoundland), and Mexico. For several other countries – for example, Italy, France, and Belgium – the figures are slightly affected by boundary changes; but these changes have not been so great as to destroy entirely the value of comparative figures. The boundaries of other countries – for example, USSR, Austria, Hungary, Romania, and Greece – have been so changed that comparisons over time are subject to a large margin of error.

Statistics on country of birth of the foreign-born have generally been restricted to those countries that were a separate political entity at the time of the census. For 1860–1900, however, an exception was made in the case of Poland. Although Poland was not restored to its original status as an independent country until the end of World War I, its historical position was such that Polish immigrants generally regarded Poland as their country of birth regardless of the political sovereignty over their birthplace. For 1860–1890, persons reported as born in Poland were so tabulated without qualification. In the Census of 1900, an attempt was made to distinguish Austrian, German, and Russian Poland, and separate statistics for each were presented. In the Census of 1910, persons reported as born in Poland were assigned either to Russia, Germany, or Austria. The figures for 1910, however, have been adjusted on the basis of mother tongue data to conform as nearly as possible to the conditions in 1930.

Since World War I, the greatest difficulties encountered in the country-of-birth statistics have been the classification of persons born in the former Austro-Hungarian Empire. Many persons born within the prewar boundaries of this empire could not or did not give the census enumerator the information needed for the determination of their country of birth on the basis of postwar geography. It is therefore quite possible that some persons were assigned to Austria who were born within the present areas of either Czechoslovakia or Yugoslavia, and that persons were assigned to Hungary

(continued)

TABLE Ad354–443   Foreign-born population, by country of birth: 1850–1990   *Continued*

who were born within the present areas of Romania or Yugoslavia. Similarly, it is possible that some persons born in Latvia, Estonia, or Lithuania were assigned to Russia. Persons for whom Austria-Hungary was reported in the 1950 Census were allocated on the basis of surname to the various countries created out of the territory of the old empire after World War I. Even with this procedure, however, there appears to be some indication that Austria and Hungary are overreported at the expense of Yugoslavia and Czechoslovakia.

In 1950, the situation was further complicated by the fact that, although there were extensive de facto boundary changes as a result of World War II, only a small number of these changes were officially recognized by the United States at that time.

Since 1950, persons have been allocated to a specific country based on mother-tongue data.

See also the text for Tables Aa1896–1921.

TABLE Ad444–514   Foreign-born white population, by country of birth: 1910–1990[1]

Contributed by Michael R. Haines

		Europe									
			Northern and Western Europe								
					British Isles						
					Great Britain				Ireland		
	Total	Total	Total	Total	Total	England	Scotland	Wales	Total	Northern Ireland	Ireland (Eire)
	Ad444	Ad445	Ad446	Ad447	Ad448	Ad449	Ad450	Ad451	Ad452	Ad453	Ad454
Year	Number	Number	Number	Number	Number	Number	Number	Number	Number	Number	Number
1910	13,345,545	10,263,944	4,237,373	2,572,123	1,219,968	876,455	261,034	82,479	1,352,155	— [9]	—
1920	13,712,754	9,975,210	3,828,876	2,171,694	1,134,461	812,828	254,567	67,066	1,037,233	— [9]	—
1930	13,983,405	9,649,704	3,726,844	2,146,854	1,223,212	808,684	354,323	60,205	923,642	178,832	744,810
1940	11,419,138	7,803,858	2,825,671	1,615,103	936,656	621,975	279,321	35,360	678,447	106,416	572,031
1950 [7]	10,158,854	6,561,460	2,326,887	1,349,244	828,885	554,625	244,200	30,060	520,359	15,398	504,961
1960 [7]	9,293,992	5,694,688	1,968,797	1,169,023	762,590	526,157	213,026	23,407	406,433	68,083	338,350
1970 [7]	8,733,770	4,350,870	1,528,092	931,632	640,407	453,867	169,636	16,904	291,225	40,733	250,492
1980 [8]	11,698,993	5,512,398	1,403,686	665,185	644,717	482,766	147,959	13,992	221,877	20,468	201,409
1990 [8]	22,269,799	9,362,468	1,541,490	487,907	473,372	367,432	96,117	9,823	162,309	14,535	147,774

				Europe					
				Northern and Western Europe					
	Norway	Sweden	Denmark	Iceland	The Netherlands	Belgium	Luxembourg	Switzerland	France
	Ad455	Ad456	Ad457	Ad458	Ad459	Ad460	Ad461	Ad462	Ad463
Year	Number	Number	Number	Number	Number	Number	Number	Number	Number
1910	403,858	665,183	181,621	— [10]	120,053	49,397	3,068	124,834	117,236
1920	363,862	625,580	189,154	— [10]	131,766	62,686	12,585	118,659	152,890
1930	347,852	595,250	179,474	2,764	133,133	64,194	9,048	113,010	135,265
1940	262,088	445,070	138,175	2,104	111,064	53,958	6,886	88,293	102,930
1950 [7]	202,294	324,944	107,897	2,455	102,133	52,891	5,590	71,515	107,924
1960 [7]	152,644	214,313	84,989	2,769	118,160	50,210	4,335	61,490	110,864
1970 [7]	96,938	126,843	61,307	2,868	109,709	41,259	3,498	49,547	104,491
1980 [8]	65,565	79,436	43,949	6,130	104,981	38,755	3,344	45,778	149,154
1990 [8]	54,994	66,567	44,904	9,726	216,730	82,773	5,677	96,343	328,095

				Europe				
				Central and Eastern Europe				
	Total	Germany	Poland	Czechoslovakia	Austria	Hungary	Yugoslavia	Russia/USSR
	Ad464	Ad465	Ad466	Ad467	Ad468	Ad469	Ad470	Ad471
Year	Number	Number	Number	Number	Number	Number	Number	Number
1910	6,013,720	2,311,085 [11]	937,884 [11]	—	845,506 [11]	495,600	—	1,184,382 [11,12]
1920	6,134,825	1,686,102	1,139,978	362,436	575,625	397,282	169,437	1,400,489 [13]
1930	5,897,795	1,608,814	1,268,583	491,638	370,914	274,450	211,416	1,153,624
1940	4,958,368	1,237,772	993,479	319,971	479,906	290,228	161,093	1,040,884
1950 [7]	4,218,903	984,331	861,184	278,268	408,785	268,022	143,956	894,844
1960 [7]	3,711,725	986,564	747,250	227,467	304,192	244,945	165,658	689,462 [14]
1970 [7]	2,802,546	830,498	547,010	160,672	213,501	182,681	153,020	461,444 [14]
1980 [8]	2,657,518	1,083,381	421,921	115,417	145,680	144,036	154,454	397,169 [14]
1990 [8]	5,244,571	2,282,285	856,336	201,642	209,523	248,515	319,689	731,356 [14]

Notes appear at end of table

TABLE Ad444–514   Foreign-born white population, by country of birth: 1910–1990   *Continued*

	Europe							
	Central and Eastern Europe							
							Turkey	
	Latvia	Estonia	Lithuania	Finland	Romania	Bulgaria	Total	Turkey in Europe
	Ad472	Ad473	Ad474	Ad475	Ad476	Ad477	Ad478	Ad479 [2]
Year	Number	Number	Number	Number	Number	Number	Number	Number
1910	— [11]	— [11]	— [11]	129,669	65,920	11,453	91,923	32,221 [3]
1920	—	—	135,068	149,824	102,823	10,477	16,298	5,284
1930	20,673	3,550	193,606	142,478	146,393	9,399	48,908	2,257
1940	18,636	4,178	165,771	117,210	115,940	8,888	56,891	4,412
1950 [7]	31,590	10,085	147,765	95,506	84,952	9,615	71,730	—
1960 [7]	50,658	13,974	121,349	67,540	84,471	8,195	51,887	—
1970 [7]	41,558	12,130	75,806	45,372	70,364	8,490	47,705	—
1980 [8]	33,733	11,917	47,193	29,674	64,672	8,271	57,666	—
1990 [8]	62,483	20,193	71,523	26,410	196,295	18,321	135,011	—

	Europe						
	Southern Europe						
	Total	Greece	Albania	Italy	Spain	Portugal	Other Europe
	Ad480	Ad481	Ad482 [3]	Ad483	Ad484	Ad485	Ad486
Year	Number	Number	Number	Number	Number	Number	Number
1910	1,523,934	101,264	—	1,343,070	21,977	57,623	12,851 [15]
1920	1,902,781	175,972	—	1,610,109	49,247	67,453	11,509
1930	2,093,976	174,526	—	1,790,424	59,033	69,993	25,065 [3]
1940	1,896,886	163,252	—	1,623,580	47,707	62,347	19,819 [3]
1950 [7]	1,706,640	169,083	10,510	1,427,145	45,565	54,337	15,670 [16]
1960 [7]	1,525,251	158,894	9,572	1,255,812	44,815	56,158	14,166
1970 [7]	1,337,283	176,025	8,895	1,005,687	56,866	89,810	20,232
1980 [8]	1,375,023	212,232	7,429	856,246	86,529	212,587	76,171
1990 [8]	2,458,781	396,694	12,942	1,389,034	208,198	451,913	117,626

	Asia									
	Total	Palestine	Syria	Turkey in Asia	China	Japan	India	Korea	Philippines	Other Asia
	Ad487	Ad488	Ad489	Ad490 [2]	Ad491	Ad492	Ad493	Ad494	Ad495	Ad496
Year	Number	Number	Number	Number	Number	Number	Number	Number	Number	Number
1910	64,314	—	—	59,702 [14, 18]	333	198	2,078	—	—	2,003
1920	110,450	3,202	51,900	11,014	716	278	2,532	—	—	40,808 [14]
1930	157,580	6,135	57,227	46,651	2,279	632	3,300	—	—	41,356 [14]
1940	149,909	7,047	50,859	52,479	—	—	—	—	—	39,524 [14]
1950 [7]	179,900	—	35,325	71,730	11,985	4,650	5,370	—	—	50,840 [14]
1960 [7]	201,330	— [17]	16,566	51,887	12,858	11,686	6,414	2,681	15,624	83,614 [17]
1970 [7]	273,598	— [17]	14,840	47,705	11,839	6,085	41,412	2,094	11,187	138,436 [17]
1980 [8]	633,326	68,423	22,260	57,666	17,327	92,382	15,642	14,858	37,350	307,418
1990 [8]	1,641,326	229,414	76,198	135,011	19,661	113,907	42,491	21,592	36,911	966,141

Notes appear at end of table   (continued)

TABLE Ad444–514   Foreign-born white population, by country of birth: 1910–1990 *Continued*

		America								
		Canada								
	Total	Total	French Canada	Newfoundland	Other	Cuba	Other West Indies	Mexico	Central America	South America
	Ad497	Ad498	Ad499	Ad500	Ad501	Ad502	Ad503 [4]	Ad504	Ad505	Ad506
Year	Number	Number	Number	Number	Number	Number	Number	Number	Number	Number
1910	1,453,186	1,201,146	385,083	5,076	810,987	12,869	10,300	219,802	1,507	7,562
1920	1,656,801	1,131,120	307,786	13,242	810,092	12,843	13,526	478,383	4,074	16,855
1930	2,011,224	1,302,483	370,852	23,971	907,660	16,089	15,511	639,017	7,791	30,333
1940	1,509,855	1,065,480	273,366	21,361	770,753	15,277	15,257	377,433	7,638	28,770
1950 [7]	1,564,139	994,562	238,409	—	756,153	29,295	22,735	450,562	23,475	43,510
1960 [7]	1,743,058	941,906	—	—	—	74,921	30,876	572,564	38,773	84,018
1970 [7]	2,360,490	798,782	—	—	—	425,974	5,388	746,327	145,251	238,768
1980 [8]	4,641,612	907,648	—	—	—	593,274	184,223	2,131,650	307,763	517,054
1990 [8]	10,292,871	1,813,179	—	—	—	1,558,814	614,966	4,541,089	764,399	1,000,424

				All other				
					Oceania		Country not specified	At sea
	Total	Africa	Atlantic islands	Total	Australia	Pacific islands		
	Ad507	Ad508	Ad509 [5]	Ad510	Ad511	Ad512 [6]	Ad513	Ad514
Year	Number	Number	Number	Number	Number	Number	Number	Number
1910	40,167	3,518	15,795	11,282	8,938	2,344	2,687	6,885
1920	67,512	5,222	38,984	14,444	10,801	3,643	3,560	5,302
1930	70,921	7,868	39,485	17,087	12,720	4,367	1,518	4,963
1940	58,630	—	28,983	—	10,998	—	17,638	1,011
1950 [7]	146,715	13,260	30,620	25,660	19,900	5,760	77,175	—
1960 [7]	129,665	16,545	27,416	29,725	22,060	7,665	55,979	—
1970 [7]	411,529	48,021	37,537	26,269	23,699	2,570	299,702	—
1980 [8]	911,657	130,967	14,958	62,498	41,666	20,832	702,263	971
1990 [8]	973,134	182,545	26,353	74,917	53,557	21,360	688,713	606

[1] Data given for each country for all census years since 1850 for which figures are available.

[2] For 1850–1900, Turkey in Asia included with Turkey in Europe; beginning 1950, Turkey in Europe included with Turkey in Asia.

[3] For 1910, Albania included with Turkey in Europe; for 1920–1940, Albania included with other Europe.

[4] Excludes U.S. outlying areas, 1950–1990.

[5] Includes the Azores and "other Atlantic Islands."

[6] Includes New Zealand and Trust Territories of the Pacific Islands; however, excludes outlying areas of the United States, 1950–1990.

[7] Based on a 20 percent sample (1950), 25 percent sample (1960), and 15 percent sample (1970).

[8] Based on 7 percent (1980) and 9 percent (1990) samples from the Integrated Public Use Microdata Series.

[9] Included with Ireland.

[10] Included with Denmark.

[11] Persons of Polish mother tongue born in Austria, Germany, and USSR have been deducted from their respective countries and combined as Poland.

[12] Includes Estonia, Latvia, and Lithuania.

[13] Includes Estonia and Latvia.

[14] Armenian white foreign-born population included with Turkey in Asia (1910), other Asia (1920–1950), and USSR thereafter.

[15] Includes persons born in Serbia and Montenegro, which became part of Yugoslavia in 1918.

[16] Includes countries for which figures are not shown separately.

[17] Palestine included with "other Asia."

[18] Includes Palestine and Syria.

Sources

U.S. Bureau of the Census. 1910–1940, foreign-born white: 1940, *U.S. Census of Population, Sixteenth Census Reports, Population,* volume 2, part 1, p. 43. 1950: *U.S. Census of Population: 1950,* volume 4, *Special Reports, Nativity and Parentage,* p. 3A-71, and volume 4, *Special Reports, Nonwhite Population by Race,* p. 3B-82, and unpublished data. 1960: *U.S. Census of Population: 1960,* volume 1, part 1. 1970: *U.S. Census of Population: 1970,* volume 2, *Subject Reports.*

Documentation

See the text for Tables Ad354–443 and Aa1896–1921.

TABLE Ad515–695 Foreign-born population, by country or area of birth: 1960–1990[1]

Contributed by Michael R. Haines

			Europe												
						Northern Europe									
								United Kingdom							
									Great Britain						
	Total	Total reporting specific country or region	Total, Europe	Total, Northern and Western Europe	Total, Northern Europe	Total, British Isles	Total	Total	England	Scotland	Wales	Great Britain not elsewhere classified	Northern Ireland	Ireland
	Ad515	Ad516 [2]	Ad517	Ad518	Ad519	Ad520	Ad521	Ad522	Ad523	Ad524	Ad525	Ad526	Ad527	Ad528
Year	Number	Number	Number	Number	Number	Number	Number	Number	Number	Number	Number	Number	Number	Number
1960	9,738,091	9,678,201	7,256,311	3,334,971	1,694,430	1,171,777	833,055	764,893	528,205	213,219	23,469	—	68,162	338,722
1970	9,619,302	9,303,570	5,740,891	2,629,200	1,271,591	937,474	686,099	645,262	458,114	170,134	17,014	—	40,837	251,375
1980	14,079,906	13,192,563	5,149,572	2,384,257	1,083,499	866,966	669,149	649,318	442,499	142,001	13,528	51,290	19,831	197,817
1990	19,767,316	18,959,158	4,350,403	2,058,853	968,271	809,972	640,145	623,614	405,588	104,168	10,638	103,220	16,531	169,827

	Europe											
	Northern Europe						Western Europe					
	Scandinavia						The Low Countries					
	Total	Denmark	Finland	Iceland	Norway	Sweden	Total	Total	Belgium	Luxembourg	The Netherlands	Austria
	Ad529	Ad530	Ad531	Ad532	Ad533	Ad534	Ad535	Ad536	Ad537	Ad538	Ad539	Ad540
Year	Number	Number	Number	Number	Number	Number	Number	Number	Number	Number	Number	Number
1960	522,653	85,060	67,624	2,780	152,698	214,491	1,640,541	173,069	50,294	4,360	118,415	304,507
1970	334,117	61,410	45,499	2,895	97,243	127,070	1,357,609	155,513	41,412	3,531	110,570	214,014
1980	216,533	42,732	29,172	4,156	63,316	77,157	1,300,758	142,748	36,487	3,125	103,136	145,607
1990	158,299	34,999	22,313	5,071	42,240	53,676	1,090,582	132,617	34,366	2,053	96,198	87,673

	Europe											
	Western Europe				Southern Europe							
									Portugal			
	France	Germany	Switzerland	Total, Southern and Eastern Europe	Total	Greece	Italy	Malta	Total	Portugal	The Azores	Spain
	Ad541	Ad542	Ad543	Ad544	Ad545	Ad546	Ad547	Ad548	Ad549	Ad550	Ad551	Ad552
Year	Number	Number	Number	Number	Number	Number	Number	Number	Number	Number	Number	Number
1960	111,582	989,815	61,568	3,907,020	1,541,441	159,167	1,256,999	—	80,276	57,690	22,586	44,999
1970	105,385	832,965	49,732	3,090,991	1,363,195	177,275	1,008,533	—	119,899	91,034	28,865	57,488
1980	120,215	849,384	42,804	2,748,547	1,336,805	210,998	831,922	10,182	209,968	177,437	32,531	73,735
1990	119,233	711,929	39,130	2,285,513	1,054,141	177,398	580,592	9,614	210,122	180,466	29,656	76,415

	Europe													Europe not elsewhere classified
	Eastern Europe													
	Total	Albania	Bulgaria	Czechoslovakia	Estonia	Hungary	Latvia	Lithuania	Poland	Romania	USSR	Yugoslavia	
	Ad553	Ad554	Ad555	Ad556	Ad557	Ad558	Ad559	Ad560	Ad561	Ad562	Ad563	Ad564	Ad565
Year	Number	Number	Number	Number	Number	Number	Number	Number	Number	Number	Number	Number	Number
1960	2,365,579	9,618	8,223	227,618	13,991	245,252	50,681	121,475	747,750	84,575	690,598	165,798	14,320
1970	1,727,796	9,180	8,609	160,899	12,163	183,236	41,707	76,001	548,107	70,687	463,462	153,745	20,700
1980	1,411,742	7,381	8,463	112,707	12,169	144,368	34,349	48,194	418,128	66,994	406,022	152,967	16,768
1990	1,231,372	5,627	8,579	87,020	9,210	110,337	26,179	29,745	388,328	91,106	333,725	141,516	6,037

Notes appear at end of table   (continued)

TABLE Ad515–695 Foreign-born population, by country or area of birth: 1960–1990 *Continued*

Asia

	Total	Eastern Asia							South Central Asia			
		Total	China	Hong Kong	Japan	Korea (total)	Macau	Taiwan	Total	Afghanistan	Bangladesh	India
	Ad566	Ad567	Ad568	Ad569	Ad570	Ad571	Ad572	Ad573	Ad574	Ad575	Ad576	Ad577
Year	Number	Number	Number	Number	Number	Number	Number	Number	Number	Number	Number	Number
1960	490,996	—	99,735 [4]	—	109,175	11,171	—	—	—	—	—	12,296
1970	824,887	—	172,132 [4]	—	120,235	38,711	—	—	—	—	—	51,000
1980	2,539,777	956,491	286,120	80,380	221,794	289,885	2,959	75,353	373,535	3,760	4,989	206,087
1990	4,979,037	1,784,702	529,837	147,131	290,128	568,397	5,107	244,102	819,378	28,444	21,414	450,406

Asia

	South Central Asia				Southeastern Asia							
	Iran	Nepal	Pakistan	Sri Lanka	Total	Burma	Cambodia	Indonesia	Laos	Malaysia	Philippines	Singapore
	Ad578	Ad579	Ad580	Ad581	Ad582	Ad583	Ad584	Ad585	Ad586	Ad587	Ad588	Ad589
Year	Number	Number	Number	Number	Number	Number	Number	Number	Number	Number	Number	Number
1960	—	—	1,708	—	—	—	—	—	—	—	104,843	—
1970	—	—	6,182	—	—	—	—	—	—	—	184,842	—
1980	121,505	844	30,774	5,576	919,646	11,236	20,175	29,920	54,881	10,473	501,440	5,598
1990	210,941	2,262	91,889	14,022	1,968,210	19,835	118,833	48,387	171,577	33,834	912,674	12,889

Asia

	Southeastern Asia		Western Asia									
	Thailand	Vietnam	Total	Cyprus	Iraq	Israel	Jordan	Kuwait	Lebanon	Palestine	Saudi Arabia	Syria
	Ad590	Ad591	Ad592	Ad593	Ad594	Ad595	Ad596	Ad597	Ad598	Ad599	Ad600	Ad601
Year	Number	Number	Number	Number	Number	Number	Number	Number	Number	Number	Number	Number
1960	—	—	132,697	—	—	17,724	—	—	22,217	—	—	16,717
1970	—	—	174,053	—	—	35,858	—	—	22,396	—	—	14,962
1980	54,803	231,120	281,426	8,806	32,121	66,961	21,587	4,337	52,674	—	17,317	22,081
1990	106,919	543,262	400,313	10,060	44,916	86,048	31,871	8,889	86,369	21,070	12,632	36,782

Asia / Africa

	Asia					Africa						
	Western Asia						Eastern Africa					
	Turkey	United Arab Emirates	Yemen	Middle East not elsewhere classified	Asia not elsewhere classified	Total	Total	Ethiopia	Kenya	Somalia	Tanzania	Uganda
	Ad602	Ad603	Ad604	Ad605	Ad606	Ad607	Ad608	Ad609	Ad610	Ad611	Ad612	Ad613
Year	Number	Number	Number	Number	Number	Number	Number	Number	Number	Number	Number	Number
1960	52,228	—	—	23,811	19,371	35,355	—	—	—	—	—	—
1970	48,085	—	—	52,752	77,732	80,143	—	—	—	—	—	—
1980	51,915	534	3,093	—	8,679	199,723	26,036	7,516	6,250	691	3,246	3,804
1990	55,087	1,656	4,933	—	6,434	363,819	72,300	34,805	14,371	2,437	6,282	6,684

Africa

	Eastern Africa		Middle Africa				Northern Africa					
	Zambia	Zimbabwe	Total	Angola	Cameroon	Zaire	Total	Algeria	Egypt	Libya	Morocco	Sudan
	Ad614	Ad615	Ad616	Ad617	Ad618	Ad619	Ad620	Ad621	Ad622	Ad623	Ad624	Ad625
Year	Number	Number	Number	Number	Number	Number	Number	Number	Number	Number	Number	Number
1960	—	—	—	—	—	—	15,903	—	8,316	—	—	—
1970	—	—	—	—	—	—	32,396	—	20,666	—	—	—
1980	1,346	3,183	3,719	1,094	1,214	1,411	69,777	3,853	43,424	6,427	9,896	2,711
1990	2,954	4,767	8,800	2,252	3,161	3,387	99,044	4,629	66,313	4,037	15,541	4,423

Notes appear at end of table

TABLE Ad515–695   Foreign-born population, by country or area of birth: 1960–1990   *Continued*

	Africa										
	Northern Africa			Western Africa							Africa not elsewhere classified
	Tunisia	Northern Africa not elsewhere classified	South Africa	Total	Cape Verde	Ghana	Liberia	Nigeria	Senegal	Sierra Leone	
	Ad626	Ad627	Ad628	Ad629	Ad630 [3]	Ad631	Ad632	Ad633	Ad634	Ad635	Ad636
Year	Number	Number	Number	Number	Number	Number	Number	Number	Number	Number	Number
1960	—	7,587	5,394	—	8,302	—	—	—	—	—	5,756
1970	—	11,730	7,667	—	18,680	—	—	—	—	—	21,400
1980	3,466	—	16,103	50,002	10,457	7,564	3,728	25,528	762	1,963	34,086
1990	4,101	—	34,707	111,566	14,368	20,889	11,455	55,350	2,287	7,217	37,402

	Oceania								America			
				Pacific islands						Latin America		
											Caribbean	
	Total	Australia	New Zealand	Total	Fiji	Tonga	Western Samoa	Other Pacific islands	Total	Total	Total	Antigua and Barbuda
	Ad637	Ad638	Ad639	Ad640	Ad641	Ad642	Ad643	Ad644	Ad645	Ad646	Ad647	Ad648
Year	Number	Number	Number	Number	Number	Number	Number	Number	Number	Number	Number	Number
1960	34,730	22,209	5,826	6,695	—	—	—	—	1,860,809	908,309	193,922	—
1970	41,258	24,271	8,117	8,870	—	—	—	—	2,616,391	1,803,970	675,108	—
1980	77,577	36,120	11,413	30,044	7,538	5,619	12,582	4,305	5,225,914	4,372,487	1,258,363	3,920
1990	104,145	42,267	15,415	46,463	15,935	10,668	11,408	8,452	9,161,754	8,407,837	1,938,348	12,022

	America											
	Latin America											
	Caribbean											
	Aruba	Bahamas	Barbados	Cuba	Dominica	Dominican Republic	Grenada	Haiti	Jamaica	Montserrat	The Netherlands Antilles	St. Kitts–Nevis
	Ad649	Ad650	Ad651	Ad652	Ad653	Ad654	Ad655	Ad656	Ad657	Ad658	Ad659	Ad660
Year	Number	Number	Number	Number	Number	Number	Number	Number	Number	Number	Number	Number
1960	—	—	—	79,150	—	11,883	—	4,816	24,759	—	—	—
1970	—	—	—	439,048	—	61,228	—	28,026	68,576	—	—	—
1980	2,597	13,993	26,847	607,814	3,296	169,147	7,101	92,395	196,811	1,212	5,123	1,903
1990	3,363	21,633	43,015	736,971	19,529	347,858	17,730	225,393	334,140	3,493	3,426	7,447

	America											
	Latin America											
	Caribbean							Central America				
					Other Caribbean							
	St. Lucia	St. Vincent and the Grenadines	Trinidad and Tobago	Total	West Indies not elsewhere classified	Other West Indies	Mexico	Total	Belize	Costa Rica	El Salvador	Guatemala
	Ad661	Ad662	Ad663	Ad664	Ad665	Ad666	Ad667	Ad668	Ad669	Ad670	Ad671	Ad672
Year	Number	Number	Number	Number	Number	Number	Number	Number	Number	Number	Number	Number
1960	—	—	—	73,314	73,314	—	575,902	48,949	2,780	5,425	6,310	5,381
1970	—	—	20,673	57,557	57,557	—	759,711	113,913	8,860	16,691	15,717	17,356
1980	1,901	4,044	65,907	54,352	—	54,352	2,199,221	353,892	14,436	29,639	94,447	63,073
1990	6,959	12,824	115,710	26,835	18,509	8,326	4,298,014	1,133,978	29,957	43,530	465,433	225,739

Notes appear at end of table

(continued)

TABLE Ad515–695   Foreign-born population, by country or area of birth: 1960–1990   *Continued*

	America											
	Latin America											
	Central America				South America							
	Honduras	Nicaragua	Panama	Central America not elsewhere classified	Total	Argentina	Bolivia	Brazil	Chile	Colombia	Ecuador	Guyana
	Ad673	Ad674	Ad675	Ad676	Ad677	Ad678	Ad679	Ad680	Ad681	Ad682	Ad683	Ad684
Year	Number	Number	Number	Number	Number	Number	Number	Number	Number	Number	Number	Number
1960	6,503	9,474	13,076	—	89,536	16,579	2,168	13,988	6,259	12,582	7,670	—
1970	19,118	16,125	20,046	—	255,238	44,803	6,872	27,069	15,393	63,538	36,663	—
1980	39,154	44,166	60,740	8,237	561,011	68,887	14,468	40,919	35,127	143,508	86,128	48,608
1990	108,923	168,659	85,737	6,000	1,037,497	92,563	31,303	82,489	55,681	286,124	143,314	120,698

	America										
	Latin America						Northern America				Region or country of birth not reported
	South America										
	Paraguay	Peru	Suriname	Uruguay	Venezuela	South America not elsewhere classified	Total	Canada	Bermuda	Northern America not elsewhere classified	
	Ad685	Ad686	Ad687	Ad688	Ad689	Ad690	Ad691	Ad692	Ad693	Ad694	Ad695
Year	Number	Number	Number	Number	Number	Number	Number	Number	Number	Number	Number
1960	595	7,102	—	1,170	6,851	14,572	952,500	952,500	—	—	59,890
1970	—	21,663	—	5,092	11,348	22,797	812,421	812,421	—	—	315,732
1980	2,858	55,496	1,433	13,278	33,281	17,020	853,427	842,859	8,844	1,724	887,343
1990	6,057	144,199	2,860	20,766	42,119	9,324	753,917	744,830	7,972	1,115	808,158

[1] Based on a 25 percent sample (1960 and 1980); otherwise, based on a 15 percent sample.

[2] Includes countries for which figures are not shown separately.

[3] Data for 1960 and 1970 are for other Atlantic Islands.

[4] Includes Taiwan.

Source

Campbell Gibson and Emily Lennon, "Historical Census Statistics on the Foreign-Born Population of the United States: 1850 to 1990," U.S. Bureau of the Census, Population Division, Working Paper number 29 (February 1999).

Documentation

The foreign-born population comprises all persons born outside the United States, Puerto Rico, or an outlying area of the United States, except those with at least one American parent. A person born in any of the outlying areas and American citizens born abroad or at sea are regarded as native.

The countries or areas of birth included in this table are those for which data are available for 1990. Prior to 1960, the earliest year included in this table, census data were published for only a small number of countries outside of Europe, reflecting the small number of non-European countries that were numerically important sources of immigration to the United States. Tables Ad354–514 show data for the 1850–1990 period for a less detailed list of countries.

The six regions of the world shown in Table 3 of Gibson and Lennon (1999) are the "macro regions" used by the United Nations in its annual *Demographic Yearbook*. These regions are Europe, Asia, Africa, Oceania,

Latin America, and Northern America (United Nations, 1997, pp. 30–1). In general, the subregions are the "component regions" used in the same publication. The differences lie in Oceania and Europe. For Oceania, the component regions of Melanesia, Micronesia, and Polynesia are combined and shown here as Pacific islands. For Europe, the component regions of Northern, Western, Southern, and Eastern Europe are modified to reflect historical groupings and patterns of immigration to the United States: Albania and Yugoslavia are included in Eastern Europe rather than in Southern Europe; and Estonia, Latvia, and Lithuania are included in Eastern Europe rather than in Northern Europe. Table Ad515–695 includes various subtotals of historical interest within regions (for example, within Northern Europe, subtotals are shown for the British Isles and for Scandinavia).

Data on country of birth are generally based on the political boundaries of foreign countries existing at the date of the specified decennial census. Changes in political boundaries are less of a concern for the 1960–1990 period covered in this table than for the entire 1850–1990 period for which data on country of birth are available – shown in Tables Ad354–514.

In this table, the term "country or area of birth" is used (rather than just "country of birth") because the foreign geographic areas of birth for which data are available have not always reflected the United States's diplomatic relations at the date of each census. For example, the United States has recognized People's Republic of China since 1979. Taiwan is officially considered part of the People's Republic of China; however, data for Taiwan are available for 1980 and 1990. Statistics on country of birth of the foreign-born have generally been restricted to those countries that had at the time of the census a separate political entity.

See the text for Table Aa1896–1921.

TABLE Ad696–706 Geographic concentration of the foreign-born population – top three states and the South: 1850–1990

Contributed by Susan B. Carter

	First			Second			Third			The South's share of U.S. population	
	State	State's share of U.S. population		State	State's share of U.S. population		State	State's share of U.S. population			
	State	Foreign-born	Native-born	State	Foreign-born	Native-born	State	Foreign-born	Native-born	Foreign-born	Native-born
	Ad696	Ad697	Ad698	Ad699	Ad700	Ad701	Ad702	Ad703	Ad704	Ad705	Ad706
Year	—	Percent	Percent	—	Percent	Percent	—	Percent	Percent	Percent	Percent
1850	New York	29.2	11.7	Pennsylvania	13.5	9.6	Ohio	9.7	8.4	10.8	41.7
1860	New York	24.2	10.5	Pennsylvania	10.4	9.1	Ohio	7.9	7.4	9.5	39.3
1870	New York	20.4	9.8	Pennsylvania	9.8	9.0	Illinois	9.3	6.1	7.2	36.0
1880	New York	18.1	8.9	Pennsylvania	8.8	8.5	Illinois	8.7	5.7	6.7	37.0
1890	New York	17.0	8.3	Pennsylvania	9.1	8.3	Illinois	9.1	5.6	5.7	36.2
1900	New York	18.4	8.2	Pennsylvania	9.5	8.1	Illinois	9.3	5.9	5.5	36.5
1910	New York	20.3	8.1	Pennsylvania	10.7	7.9	Illinois	8.9	5.7	5.5	36.5
1920	New York	20.3	8.2	Pennsylvania	10.0	8.0	Illinois	8.7	5.7	6.2	35.1
1930	New York	23.0	8.6	Illinois	8.7	5.9	Pennsylvania	8.7	7.7	5.8	34.1
1940	New York	25.2	8.8	Pennsylvania	8.4	7.4	Illinois	1.0	2.8	5.5	34.2
1950	New York	24.9	8.7	California	10.2	6.8	Illinois	9.4	5.0	7.4	33.1
1960	New York	23.5	8.5	California	13.8	8.5	Illinois	7.0	5.5	9.9	31.8
1970	New York	21.9	8.3	California	18.3	9.4	New Jersey	6.6	3.4	13.7	31.8
1980	California	25.4	9.5	New York	17.0	7.1	Florida	7.5	4.1	20.6	34.1
1990	California	32.7	10.2	New York	14.4	6.6	Florida	8.4	4.9	23.2	35.3

Source

Campbell J. Gibson and Emily Lennon, "Historical Census Statistics on the Foreign-Born Population of the United States: 1850–1990," U.S. Bureau of the Census, Population Division, Population Division Working Paper number 29 (February 1999), derived from Table 13.

Documentation

Series Ad705–706. The South is defined by the U.S. Census Bureau as follows: Delaware, Maryland, District of Columbia, West Virginia, Virginia, North Carolina, South Carolina, Georgia, Florida, Kentucky, Tennessee, Alabama, Mississippi, Arkansas, Louisiana, Oklahoma, and Texas.

TABLE Ad707–710 Percentage of foreign- and native-born persons living in urban and rural locations: 1890–1990

Contributed by Susan B. Carter

	Percentage of native-born population living in places of		Percentage of foreign-born population living in places of	
	Fewer than 2,500 persons	2,500 or more persons	Fewer than 2,500 persons	2,500 or more persons
	Ad707	Ad708	Ad709	Ad710
Year	Percent	Percent	Percent	Percent
1890	68.4	31.6	38.6	61.4
1900	63.9	36.1	33.7	66.3
1910	58.1	41.9	27.9	72.1
1920	52.3	47.7	24.6	75.4
1930	46.9	53.1	20.8	79.2
1940	45.7	54.3	20.0	80.0
1960	31.1	68.9	12.6	87.4
1970	27.4	72.6	9.3	90.7
1980	27.5	72.5	8.3	91.7
1990	26.4	73.6	6.4	93.6

Source

Campbell J. Gibson and Emily Lennon, "Historical Census Statistics on the Foreign-Born Population of the United States: 1850–1990," U.S. Bureau of the Census, Population Division, Population Division Working Paper number 29 (February 1999), derived from Table 18.

TABLE Ad711–721   Percentage of foreign-born persons able to speak English, by region of birth: 1900–1990[1]

Contributed by Matthew Sobek

	North America outside the United States	Central America and Caribbean	South America	Europe				Asia	Africa	Outlying areas of the United States	Other non-U.S. areas
				Northern	Western	Eastern	Southern				
	Ad711	Ad712	Ad713	Ad714	Ad715	Ad716	Ad717	Ad718	Ad719	Ad720	Ad721
Year	Percent	Percent	Percent	Percent	Percent	Percent	Percent	Percent	Percent	Percent	Percent
1900	92.7	32.2	—	97.0	92.4	64.5	58.8	53.1	—	—	—
1910	93.3	23.8	—	96.1	87.8	55.9	44.1	55.7	—	—	—
1920	96.5	40.2	—	98.3	97.0	83.2	76.9	81.5	—	—	—
1980	99.8	82.5	94.1	100.0	99.9	97.9	94.2	96.3	99.3	92.8	95.0
1990	99.7	84.4	94.8	100.0	99.9	97.2	96.8	96.7	99.5	94.9	91.7

[1] Data pertain to noninstitutionalized persons ages 16–64.

Source

Calculated from the Integrated Public Use Microdata Series (IPUMS). See the Guide to the Millennial Edition for information on IPUMS.

Documentation

Percentages in 1900 and 1920 are based on the number of persons with interpretable responses; they exclude foreign-born persons for whom ability to speak English could not be determined. Northern Europe includes the United Kingdom and Ireland; Western Europe includes Germany.

The 1980 and 1990 samples record degree of English-speaking ability ("well," "not well"). This table interprets all responses other than "not at all" as the ability to speak English.

TABLE Ad722–739   Native-born children of foreign-born parents, by parents' citizenship status – United States and selected states: 1920–1990[1,2]

Contributed by Matthew Sobek

	United States				Percentage					
	With foreign-born parents		With alien parents		California		Florida		Illinois	
					With foreign-born parents	With alien parents	With foreign-born parents	With alien parents	With foreign-born parents	With alien parents
	Number	Percentage	Number	Percentage						
	Ad722	Ad723	Ad724	Ad725	Ad726	Ad727	Ad728	Ad729	Ad730	Ad731
Year	Number	Percent	Number	Percent	Percent	Percent	Percent	Percent	Percent	Percent
1920	4,524,297	16.4	1,789,124	6.5	20.1	10.5	3.8	2.3	14.5	9.1
1940	2,918,986	9.8	656,553	2.2	13.3	8.5	1.9	1.3	9.2	2.0
1950	1,039,066	3.5	112,684	0.4	4.7	2.1	1.0	0.3	2.9	0.2
1970	850,324	1.6	174,820	0.3	3.0	1.2	1.3	0.5	1.4	0.4
1980	1,519,995	3.2	577,593	1.2	9.3	4.7	4.9	1.5	2.6	1.4
1990	2,531,659	5.6	1,123,520	2.5	17.7	9.6	8.1	3.3	4.3	2.9

	Percentage							
	New Jersey		New York		Pennsylvania		Texas	
	With foreign-born parents	With alien parents	With foreign-born parents	With alien parents	With foreign-born parents	With alien parents	With foreign-born parents	With alien parents
	Ad732	Ad733	Ad734	Ad735	Ad736	Ad737	Ad738	Ad739
Year	Percent	Percent	Percent	Percent	Percent	Percent	Percent	Percent
1920	14.5	19.1	18.7	17.0	11.9	11.3	4.8	3.3
1940	14.9	4.1	17.8	4.2	9.7	2.6	4.5	3.6
1950	5.7	0.2	9.0	0.5	3.1	0.1	2.6	1.6
1970	2.0	0.4	2.7	0.6	0.7	0.1	1.3	0.6
1980	4.1	1.5	5.2	2.3	1.0	0.3	4.2	2.1
1990	6.5	2.7	6.9	4.1	1.3	0.4	8.2	4.1

[1] Data pertain to noninstitutionalized persons ages 5–17.

[2] All percentages are expressed relative to the total number of native-born school-age children.

Source

Calculated from the Integrated Public Use Microdata Series (IPUMS). See the Guide to the Millennial Edition for information on IPUMS.

Documentation

Persons born in U.S. outlying areas are considered native-born. The states included in this table were among the top three in foreign-born population in at least one of the years, with the exception of Texas. Determinations of alien-parent status require that all parents present in the household are aliens. Determinations of foreign-born-parent status require that all parents present in the household are foreign-born. The 1940 and 1950 Census samples include categories for indeterminate responses for nativity, parental nativity, and parental citizenship. All percentages are calculated using only cases in which all relevant items of information are known.

Determinations of parental nativity and alien status require coresident parents. By default, children without a resident parent are considered not to have foreign or alien parents.

TABLE Ad740-743   Home ownership rates, by race and nativity of household head: 1900-1997[1]

Contributed by Matthew Sobek

	Native-born			
	White	Black	Other race	Foreign-born
	Ad740	Ad741	Ad742	Ad743
Year	Percent	Percent	Percent	Percent
1900	62.3	30.6	—	57.0
1910	63.7	35.4	—	55.2
1920	62.5	33.1	—	55.5
1940	56.9	32.3	—	50.4
1960	71.5	46.7	61.3	60.1
1970	75.9	51.0	65.7	60.8
1980	81.6	58.7	71.3	62.3
1990	81.7	58.2	71.5	62.1
1997	82.2	60.3	74.0	63.6

[1] Data pertain to household heads ages 45-64 not living in group quarters.

Sources

1900-1990: Calculated from the Integrated Public Use Microdata Series (IPUMS). See the Guide to the Millennial Edition for information on IPUMS. 1997: Calculated from the U.S. Census Bureau, *Current Population Survey, 1997 October Supplement* [computer file].

Documentation

Persons born in U.S. outlying areas are considered foreign-born. Household heads were referred to as "householders" in the 1980 and 1990 Censuses, and as the "reference person" in the 1997 Current Population Survey. The home ownership rate is the percentage of households that own their housing unit. Subtracting the ownership rate from 100 yields the home rental rate for each group.

TABLE Ad744-751   Children ever born per woman, by race and nativity: 1900-1995[1]

Contributed by Matthew Sobek

	Ever-married women				All women			
	Native-born				Native-born			
	White	Black	Other race	Foreign-born	White	Black	Other race	Foreign-born
	Ad744	Ad745	Ad746	Ad747	Ad748	Ad749	Ad750	Ad751
Year	Number	Number	Number	Number	Number	Number	Number	Number
1900	4.7	6.7	4.6	5.5	—	—	—	—
1910	4.4	6.4	6.6	5.3	—	—	—	—
1940	2.9	3.3	5.3	3.4	—	—	—	—
1950	2.6	2.9	4.3	2.6	—	—	—	—
1960	2.3	2.8	3.8	2.2	—	—	—	—
1970	2.7	3.2	3.4	2.5	2.5	3.1	3.2	2.4
1980	3.1	3.9	3.7	3.0	3.0	3.7	3.5	2.9
1990	2.7	3.3	3.2	2.8	2.6	3.2	3.0	2.7
1995	2.3	2.8	2.8	2.6	2.2	2.7	2.7	2.6

[1] Data pertain to women ages 45-54.

Sources

1900-1990: Calculated from the Integrated Public Use Microdata Series (IPUMS). See the Guide to the Millennial Edition for information on IPUMS. 1995: Calculated from the U.S. Census Bureau, *Current Population Survey, 1995 June Supplement* [computer file].

Documentation

Race and nativity pertain to the women, not the children. Persons born in U.S. outlying areas are considered foreign-born.

TABLE Ad752–759 Labor force participation rate, by sex, race, and nativity: 1850–1997[1]

Contributed by Matthew Sobek

	Male				Female			
	Native-born				Native-born			
Year	White	Black	Other race	Foreign-born	White	Black	Other race	Foreign-born
	Ad752	Ad753	Ad754	Ad755	Ad756	Ad757	Ad758	Ad759
	Percent	Percent	Percent	Percent	Percent	Percent	Percent	Percent
1850	89.6	79.5 [3]	—	91.2	—	—	—	—
1860	86.9	84.0 [3]	—	92.1	10.0	32.7 [3]	—	17.1
1870	89.8	94.6	—	94.8	10.4	39.4	—	16.9
1880	90.7	95.3	79.4	94.9	12.3	42.2	22.1	17.3
1900	91.0	94.3	78.6	93.3	18.9	44.2	27.4	21.3
1910 [2]	91.1	95.6	77.8	93.7	22.0	59.6	20.0	22.5
1920	89.7	93.5	74.8	92.2	22.6	43.6	15.8	19.4
1940	88.2	89.9	75.7	91.7	28.5	42.3	22.7	23.2
1950	88.2	86.4	77.5	90.7	32.5	41.5	29.8	29.2
1960	88.9	83.5	79.7	90.3	39.2	47.9	40.8	39.2
1970	85.4	77.1	77.2	86.3	47.1	52.4	49.2	45.9
1980	85.1	73.5	78.5	83.5	58.8	59.1	58.8	55.1
1990	85.7	75.0	76.8	84.9	69.2	67.0	65.1	61.8
1997	85.4	73.1	72.4	85.5	72.9	69.0	64.4	61.6

[1] Data pertain to civilian noninstitutionalized persons ages 16–64.

[2] The wording of the census occupation question elicited high participation rates for women.

[3] Excludes slaves.

Sources

1850–1990: Calculated from the Integrated Public Use Microdata Series (IPUMS). See the Guide to the Millennial Edition for information on IPUMS. 1997: Calculated from the U.S. Census Bureau, *Current Population Survey, 1997 March Supplement* [computer file].

Documentation

Persons born in U.S. outlying areas are considered foreign-born. Before 1940, labor force participation means gainful employment (that is, whether a person claimed an occupation). Starting in 1940, labor force participation was formalized to mean working or seeking work in the week prior to the census. The switch from gainful employment to the labor force definition has implications for new, seasonal, part-time, and female workers. The 1850 Census did not address the occupation question to women.

TABLE Ad760–771 Female labor force participation rate, by marital status, race, and nativity: 1880–1997[1]

Contributed by Matthew Sobek

	Married				Widowed, divorced, or separated				Never-married			
	Native-born				Native-born				Native-born			
Year	White	Black	Other race	Foreign-born	White	Black	Other race	Foreign-born	White	Black	Other race	Foreign-born
	Ad760	Ad761	Ad762	Ad763	Ad764	Ad765	Ad766	Ad767	Ad768	Ad769	Ad770	Ad771
	Percent	Percent	Percent	Percent	Percent	Percent	Percent	Percent	Percent	Percent	Percent	Percent
1880	2.1	29.3	17.7	3.6	15.9	54.0	—	21.4	29.6	64.9	—	65.8
1900	3.3	26.1	15.2	3.8	34.2	66.0	—	28.4	42.0	66.6	37.5	74.6
1910 [2]	6.1	49.4	16.2	7.1	30.4	73.9	—	24.4	49.3	73.9	31.3	79.4
1920	6.4	32.3	10.5	7.8	29.8	66.8	—	22.5	54.7	58.6	22.0	76.7
1940	14.5	34.1	14.3	14.5	46.5	61.8	—	31.5	56.9	53.1	32.3	71.2
1950	22.3	33.7	21.7	20.7	56.2	58.3	—	44.2	60.1	45.0	44.1	74.6
1960	32.1	43.4	36.8	31.7	63.3	70.0	50.0	53.0	57.0	45.0	47.5	70.9
1970	41.8	53.5	47.7	40.1	66.7	58.6	55.6	57.2	55.0	44.1	50.0	62.8
1980	53.5	64.7	57.4	51.8	71.2	62.2	64.1	62.8	66.3	50.9	58.3	60.4
1990	66.3	72.9	66.7	59.6	76.1	68.5	68.4	67.9	72.1	61.3	61.3	63.9
1997	72.2	75.8	64.2	59.8	77.8	68.5	63.4	68.1	71.2	64.8	64.9	61.7

[1] Data pertain to civilian noninstitutionalized women ages 16–64.

[2] The wording of the census occupation question elicited high participation rates for women.

Sources

1900–1990: Calculated from the Integrated Public Use Microdata Series (IPUMS). See the Guide to the Millennial Edition for information on IPUMS. 1997: Calculated from the U.S. Census Bureau, *Current Population Survey, 1997 March Supplement* [computer file].

Documentation

Persons born in U.S. outlying areas are considered foreign-born. Before 1940, labor force participation means gainful employment (that is, whether a person claimed an occupation). Starting in 1940, labor force participation was formalized to mean working or seeking work in the week prior to the census. The switch from gainful employment to the labor force definition has implications for new, seasonal, part-time, and female workers. 1940 and 1950 had small residual categories of persons with unknown nativity; they are excluded from these statistics. The category "separated," included in series Ad764–767, was not an available response prior to 1950. Separated women are included with married women from 1880 to 1940.

TABLE Ad772–781   Percentage of nonagricultural workers who were self-employed, by sex, race, and nativity: 1910–1990[1]

Contributed by Matthew Sobek

	Male					Female				
		Native-born						Native-born		
	All	White	Black	Other race	Foreign-born	All	White	Black	Other race	Foreign-born
	Ad772	Ad773	Ad774	Ad775	Ad776	Ad777	Ad778	Ad779	Ad780	Ad781
Year	Percent	Percent	Percent	Percent	Percent	Percent	Percent	Percent	Percent	Percent
1910	16.0	17.3	6.0	—	15.3	16.1	14.3	26.1	—	13.7
1920	14.3	14.6	6.1	—	15.7	10.6	8.9	18.9	—	11.5
1940	12.3	11.9	5.6	13.9	18.2	6.1	5.4	8.1	21.1	9.1
1950	12.2	12.3	4.1	14.8	18.7	5.2	5.2	3.2	10.5	8.6
1960	10.2	10.6	3.8	12.3	14.4	4.1	4.2	2.3	3.0	5.5
1970	9.1	9.5	4.0	8.2	10.8	3.7	3.9	1.7	3.9	4.2
1980	9.8	10.4	3.6	7.6	10.3	3.9	4.3	1.3	3.3	4.3
1990	10.4	11.1	4.1	7.7	10.8	5.9	6.4	2.3	4.8	6.9

[1] Data pertain to civilian noninstitutionalized persons ages 16–64 in the labor force.

Source

Calculated from the Integrated Public Use Microdata Series (IPUMS). See the Guide to the Millennial Edition for information on IPUMS.

Documentation

Persons born in U.S. outlying areas are considered foreign-born. Self-employed persons own their own business or contract out their own labor. The converse of self-employment is wage and salary work. The self-employment rate is the number of self-employed divided by the total number of persons in the labor force (that is, persons working or seeking work in the week prior to the census for 1940–1990; or claiming an occupation for 1910–1920).

TABLE Ad782–791   Unemployment rate, by sex, race, and nativity: 1940–1997[1]

Contributed by Matthew Sobek

	Male					Female				
		Native-born						Native-born		
	All	White	Black	Other race	Foreign-born	All	White	Black	Other race	Foreign-born
	Ad782	Ad783	Ad784	Ad785	Ad786	Ad787	Ad788	Ad789	Ad790	Ad791
Year	Percent	Percent	Percent	Percent	Percent	Percent	Percent	Percent	Percent	Percent
1940	9.7	9.5	10.7	14.1	10.6	9.7	9.6	11.1	8.6	8.1
1950	4.1	3.7	6.6	6.8	5.1	3.7	3.2	6.6	5.9	4.6
1960	5.0	4.5	8.9	8.3	4.9	5.5	4.9	8.8	7.2	6.4
1970	3.8	3.6	6.3	6.4	3.8	5.2	4.8	8.0	5.8	5.6
1980	6.5	5.9	12.5	9.4	6.4	6.5	5.7	11.5	7.8	7.7
1990	6.5	5.4	14.2	10.5	7.4	6.2	4.9	12.4	9.0	8.7
1997	5.9	4.9	12.1	10.2	6.6	5.2	4.0	9.7	10.6	7.7

[1] Data pertain to civilian noninstitutionalized persons ages 16–64 in the labor force.

Sources

1940–1990: Calculated from the Integrated Public Use Microdata Series (IPUMS). See the Guide to the Millennial Edition for information on IPUMS. 1997: Calculated from the U.S. Census Bureau, *Current Population Survey, 1997 March Supplement* [computer data file].

Documentation

Persons born in U.S. outlying areas are considered foreign-born. Unemployed status means that a person is currently without a job (at the time of the census) but is looking for work. The unemployment rate is the number of unemployed divided by the total number of persons in the labor force (that is, persons working or seeking work in the week prior to the census).

TABLE Ad792–801   Median earned income of full-time workers, by sex, race, and nativity: 1949–1989[1]

Contributed by Matthew Sobek

	Male					Female				
		Native-born						Native-born			
	All	White	Black	Other race	Foreign-born	All	White	Black	Other race	Foreign-born
	Ad792	Ad793	Ad794	Ad795	Ad796	Ad797	Ad798	Ad799	Ad800	Ad801
Year	Dollars	Dollars	Dollars	Dollars	Dollars	Dollars	Dollars	Dollars	Dollars	Dollars
1949	3,050	3,150	1,950	2,350	3,100	2,050	2,150	1,150	1,850	2,050
1959	5,350	5,550	3,450	5,050	5,150	3,150	3,350	2,050	3,450	3,050
1969	8,950	9,050	6,050	8,550	8,450	5,050	5,050	4,050	5,350	5,050
1979	18,005	18,985	13,805	17,005	16,005	10,155	10,405	9,885	11,005	10,005
1989	30,000	30,000	23,000	29,000	25,500	20,000	20,000	18,050	20,900	19,000

[1] Data pertain to noninstitutionalized employed persons ages 25–64. All figures are for full-time workers – persons who worked thirty-five or more hours in the previous week and fifty or more weeks in the previous year.

Source

Calculated from the Integrated Public Use Microdata Series (IPUMS). See the Guide to the Millennial Edition for information on IPUMS.

Documentation

Original data are from the decennial U.S. censuses and pertain to earnings in the year prior to the census. Persons born in U.S. outlying areas are considered foreign-born. Earned income includes wages and salaries, income from a farm, or earnings from working in one's own unincorporated business.

TABLE Ad802–849   Occupational distribution, by sex and nativity: 1850–1990[1, 2]

Contributed by Matthew Sobek

	Male											
	Native-born white											
	Professionals	Proprietors	Managers and officials	Clerical workers	Sales workers	Craft workers	Operatives	Service workers	Domestic workers	Laborers	Farmers	Farm laborers
	Ad802	Ad803	Ad804	Ad805	Ad806	Ad807	Ad808	Ad809	Ad810	Ad811	Ad812	Ad813
Year	Percent	Percent	Percent	Percent	Percent	Percent	Percent	Percent	Percent	Percent	Percent	Percent
1850	3.4	4.8	—	0.3	2.2	15.9	7.8	0.5	0.1	8.3	51.0	5.8
1860	3.9	5.6	—	0.8	2.7	14.4	7.8	0.5	0.3	7.2	42.1	14.7
1870	3.6	6.2	—	1.7	3.0	12.8	9.9	0.8	0.2	6.3	36.3	19.3
1880	3.8	5.7	—	2.4	3.5	11.5	11.1	1.0	0.5	9.2	34.8	16.6
1900	4.0	7.2	—	4.8	3.8	13.6	11.8	2.1	0.5	11.7	25.8	14.7
1910	4.0	5.7	3.9	5.9	4.8	14.6	13.3	2.4	0.4	8.3	21.6	15.0
1920	4.9	4.4	5.0	6.9	4.7	18.1	13.7	2.5	0.1	10.0	21.2	8.6
1940	5.7	4.3	5.7	7.9	5.7	15.6	18.9	4.6	0.1	11.6	12.6	7.4
1950	8.0	5.1	7.0	7.3	5.9	20.2	21.1	4.6	0.0	7.0	9.6	4.1
1960	11.4	3.9	9.2	7.5	6.0	22.0	21.4	4.8	0.0	6.2	5.4	2.2
1970	15.5	2.7	10.2	7.4	5.7	21.8	19.6	6.8	0.0	6.0	2.8	1.4
1980	16.5	2.9	12.8	7.0	5.0	20.8	17.3	7.9	0.0	6.6	2.0	1.1
1990	18.5	2.6	15.2	7.3	5.3	19.1	14.5	8.7	0.0	6.7	1.4	0.7

Notes appear at end of table

TABLE Ad802–849 Occupational distribution, by sex and nativity: 1850–1990 *Continued*

Male

Foreign-born

Year	Professionals	Proprietors	Managers and officials	Clerical workers	Sales workers	Craft workers	Operatives	Service workers	Domestic workers	Laborers	Farmers	Farm laborers
	Ad814	Ad815	Ad816	Ad817	Ad818	Ad819	Ad820	Ad821	Ad822	Ad823	Ad824	Ad825
	Percent	Percent	Percent	Percent	Percent	Percent	Percent	Percent	Percent	Percent	Percent	Percent
1850	1.8	5.0	—	0.3	2.5	22.3	16.0	1.7	0.6	26.7	17.5	5.6
1860	2.0	5.8	—	0.5	2.7	20.5	16.7	1.8	1.0	22.9	17.7	8.6
1870	1.9	7.1	—	0.9	2.4	18.4	20.7	2.1	1.1	19.9	17.6	7.8
1880	2.1	7.0	—	1.2	2.7	17.5	20.6	2.3	1.6	18.6	19.9	6.4
1900	2.5	7.5	—	2.4	3.1	19.0	19.0	3.0	1.7	22.0	13.9	5.9
1910	2.1	7.9	2.2	2.2	2.5	17.7	22.1	3.9	1.4	23.5	8.6	5.8
1920	2.7	7.0	2.9	2.6	3.0	21.8	21.6	5.0	0.4	20.5	8.4	3.9
1940	4.3	8.4	4.1	3.8	4.1	21.5	21.2	8.8	0.5	14.4	5.3	3.5
1950	6.1	9.9	5.4	3.9	4.1	22.5	21.4	10.3	0.3	9.3	3.4	3.3
1960	10.2	5.6	6.5	5.3	4.7	22.1	21.5	10.3	0.2	7.5	1.9	4.1
1970	16.7	3.0	7.1	6.8	4.4	20.8	20.3	11.5	0.1	6.3	0.6	2.3
1980	16.6	3.1	9.2	7.1	3.1	18.1	19.6	12.6	0.1	7.2	0.4	2.8
1990	16.8	2.8	10.2	7.8	3.3	16.1	16.9	14.3	0.1	8.5	0.4	2.8

Female

Native-born white

Year	Professionals	Proprietors	Managers and officials	Clerical workers	Sales workers	Craft workers	Operatives	Service workers	Domestic workers	Laborers	Farmers	Farm laborers
	Ad826	Ad827	Ad828	Ad829	Ad830	Ad831	Ad832	Ad833	Ad834	Ad835	Ad836	Ad837
	Percent	Percent	Percent	Percent	Percent	Percent	Percent	Percent	Percent	Percent	Percent	Percent
1850	—	—	—	—	—	—	—	—	—	—	—	—
1860	12.0	2.3	—	0.1	0.5	4.6	33.1	2.1	28.6	1.5	13.1	2.3
1870	11.5	1.0	—	0.8	1.2	3.5	29.5	2.2	42.6	0.6	3.7	3.4
1880	14.0	1.3	—	0.7	2.2	3.1	32.4	2.7	33.5	1.8	4.0	4.4
1900	12.3	2.3	—	6.9	4.8	2.5	25.9	3.1	31.6	1.6	6.2	2.9
1910	14.9	1.1	0.9	14.0	7.0	1.7	25.8	5.7	16.2	1.4	3.3	8.0
1920	16.2	1.1	1.3	27.4	8.0	2.0	21.1	6.8	8.5	2.2	2.5	2.9
1940	14.0	1.9	12.2	26.8	8.2	1.4	21.1	11.2	9.9	1.1	0.9	1.3
1950	13.7	1.9	2.8	33.2	9.4	1.6	19.7	11.2	3.1	0.6	0.5	2.2
1960	14.5	1.2	3.4	35.9	8.8	1.3	16.9	13.0	3.2	0.5	0.5	1.0
1970	17.0	0.7	3.4	37.7	7.4	1.8	14.1	14.6	1.7	0.9	0.2	0.5
1980	18.9	0.8	7.4	36.5	5.8	1.9	10.2	15.5	0.7	1.3	0.3	0.5
1990	23.6	0.9	12.0	32.6	5.0	1.8	6.8	14.8	0.6	1.4	0.3	0.3

Female

Foreign-born

Year	Professionals	Proprietors	Managers and officials	Clerical workers	Sales workers	Craft workers	Operatives	Service workers	Domestic workers	Laborers	Farmers	Farm laborers
	Ad838	Ad839	Ad840	Ad841	Ad842	Ad843	Ad844	Ad845	Ad846	Ad847	Ad848	Ad849
	Percent	Percent	Percent	Percent	Percent	Percent	Percent	Percent	Percent	Percent	Percent	Percent
1850	—	—	—	—	—	—	—	—	—	—	—	—
1860	1.7	2.2	—	0.0	0.4	4.5	24.8	3.0	57.6	2.0	3.5	0.3
1870	2.4	2.5	—	0.2	0.9	2.4	25.9	3.8	60.1	0.7	0.7	0.4
1880	3.0	3.8	—	0.2	1.3	2.9	29.1	3.8	51.8	1.6	1.7	0.7
1900	3.0	2.7	—	1.7	1.6	4.0	23.7	3.8	54.2	1.7	2.9	0.7
1910	5.5	2.8	0.5	3.4	3.2	2.0	31.1	9.0	35.3	2.6	1.8	2.8
1920	6.2	2.7	0.9	9.5	4.9	2.7	32.5	11.0	22.8	3.3	1.9	1.6
1940	8.4	4.0	2.0	11.1	6.8	2.0	30.6	14.3	17.6	1.2	0.9	1.0
1950	8.4	3.5	2.6	14.2	7.3	2.2	35.0	14.8	9.4	0.9	0.4	1.3
1960	9.5	1.7	2.7	20.9	7.8	1.5	31.5	15.2	7.2	0.7	0.3	0.9
1970	13.9	0.7	2.7	27.2	6.2	2.2	26.3	15.4	3.6	0.9	0.1	0.8
1980	15.7	1.0	5.3	26.8	4.6	2.4	21.7	17.3	2.2	1.6	0.1	1.2
1990	18.9	1.2	8.1	24.9	4.1	2.2	15.2	19.6	2.7	1.8	0.1	1.2

(continued)

TABLE Ad802–849   Occupational distribution, by sex and nativity: 1850–1990   *Continued*

[1] Data pertain to civilian noninstitutionalized persons in the labor force with an occupation, ages 16–64.

[2] Managers and officials are included with proprietors through 1900.

Source

Calculated from the Integrated Public Use Microdata Series (IPUMS). See the Guide to the Millennial Edition for information on IPUMS.

Documentation

Persons born in U.S. outlying areas are considered foreign-born. Before 1940, labor force participation means gainful employment (that is, whether a person claimed an occupation). Starting in 1940, labor force participation was formalized to mean working or seeking work in the week prior to the census. The switch from gainful employment to the labor-force definition has implications for seasonal, part-time, and female workers. The 1850 Census did not address the occupation question to women. In 1940 and 1950 there were small residual categories of persons with unknown nativity; they are excluded from these statistics.

TABLE Ad850–873   Occupational distribution of recent immigrants, by sex: 1900–1990[1]

Contributed by Matthew Sobek

	Male											
	Professionals	Proprietors	Managers and officials	Clerical workers	Sales workers	Craft workers	Operatives	Service workers	Domestic workers	Laborers	Farmers	Farm laborers
	Ad850	Ad851	Ad852	Ad853	Ad854	Ad855	Ad856	Ad857	Ad858	Ad859	Ad860	Ad861
Year	Percent	Percent	Percent	Percent	Percent	Percent	Percent	Percent	Percent	Percent	Percent	Percent
1900 [2]	2.7	1.8	—	1.6	2.3	12.8	19.9	2.3	3.1	41.8	3.5	8.2
1910	1.3	2.5	0.8	1.1	1.5	13.2	25.1	3.5	1.7	40.3	1.4	7.7
1920	3.4	3.3	1.8	3.0	3.0	13.9	19.7	5.8	0.9	31.9	2.5	10.6
1970	22.8	0.8	4.4	6.9	2.6	16.9	22.3	13.1	0.2	7.1	0.2	3.0
1980	15.8	1.8	7.3	6.8	2.5	13.9	22.4	15.8	0.2	8.6	0.3	4.8
1990	14.4	1.2	7.3	7.8	2.8	13.4	18.0	18.8	0.2	11.3	0.4	4.4

	Female											
	Professionals	Proprietors	Managers and officials	Clerical workers	Sales workers	Craft workers	Operatives	Service workers	Domestic workers	Laborers	Farmers	Farm laborers
	Ad862	Ad863	Ad864	Ad865	Ad866	Ad867	Ad868	Ad869	Ad870	Ad871	Ad872	Ad873
Year	Percent	Percent	Percent	Percent	Percent	Percent	Percent	Percent	Percent	Percent	Percent	Percent
1900 [2]	2.4	0.7	—	1.0	2.1	2.8	20.1	1.7	64.9	2.4	0.7	1.0
1910	3.7	0.8	0.2	1.6	1.9	2.6	35.7	6.7	42.3	3.2	0.1	1.2
1920	6.5	0.9	0.7	9.2	4.2	1.8	30.2	10.7	26.4	3.6	0.2	5.6
1970	15.7	0.3	1.3	22.8	3.2	1.8	32.4	13.6	6.8	1.0	0.1	1.1
1980	13.9	0.6	3.1	22.3	3.3	2.3	27.3	18.9	4.2	2.2	0.1	1.8
1990	16.0	0.5	4.5	21.5	3.9	2.0	16.9	24.6	5.9	2.4	0.1	1.7

[1] Data pertain to civilian noninstitutionalized persons in the labor force, ages 16–64.

[2] Managers and officials included with proprietors.

Source

Calculated from the Integrated Public Use Microdata Series (IPUMS). See the Guide to the Millennial Edition for information on IPUMS.

Documentation

Data pertain to persons who immigrated within the previous five years.

TABLE Ad874–937 Industrial distribution of workers, by sex and nativity: 1910–1990[1]

Contributed by Matthew Sobek

	Male									
	Native-born white									
					Manufacturing			Trade		
	Agriculture	Forestry and fishing	Mining	Construction	Durable	Nondurable	Transportation and communications	Wholesale	Retail	Finance, insurance, real estate
	Ad874	Ad875	Ad876	Ad877	Ad878	Ad879	Ad880	Ad881	Ad882	Ad883
Year	Percent	Percent	Percent	Percent	Percent	Percent	Percent	Percent	Percent	Percent
1910	36.8	0.3	2.8	7.0	11.0	8.4	10.7	2.4	9.5	2.1
1920	30.0	0.2	3.5	5.9	13.9	9.7	11.6	3.6	8.3	2.5
1940	20.7	0.5	3.0	10.7	13.1	10.9	8.3	3.0	12.7	2.8
1950	14.1	0.3	2.6	8.8	16.7	11.2	9.6	4.3	13.6	2.8
1960	8.0	0.2	1.8	9.5	20.5	11.8	8.9	4.3	13.2	3.5
1970	4.7	0.2	1.4	9.6	20.1	9.9	8.4	5.1	14.0	4.0
1980	3.8	0.3	1.8	10.7	18.4	8.3	8.4	5.4	14.0	4.3
1990	3.4	0.2	1.2	11.4	14.5	7.5	8.0	5.6	15.2	5.1

	Male											
	Native-born white						Foreign-born					
	Service										Manufacturing	
	Business	Personal	Educational	Other professional	Entertainment	Government	Agriculture	Forestry and fishing	Mining	Construction	Durable	Nondurable
	Ad884	Ad885	Ad886	Ad887	Ad888	Ad889	Ad890	Ad891	Ad892	Ad893	Ad894	Ad895
Year	Percent	Percent	Percent	Percent	Percent	Percent	Percent	Percent	Percent	Percent	Percent	Percent
1910	1.3	2.0	0.9	2.4	0.6	2.0	14.5	0.3	7.2	9.8	17.8	15.3
1920	3.1	1.9	0.8	2.3	0.6	2.3	12.4	0.1	5.8	6.6	20.8	16.6
1940	2.5	2.4	1.8	2.6	1.2	3.9	9.3	0.5	3.0	11.0	17.2	14.0
1950	3.4	2.1	1.9	2.9	1.0	4.9	7.1	0.4	1.6	8.7	19.4	14.1
1960	3.4	1.9	3.0	3.6	0.9	5.6	6.4	0.2	0.6	8.5	22.3	13.8
1970	3.9	1.7	5.3	4.3	1.1	6.2	3.6	0.2	0.4	8.4	21.8	11.6
1980	5.1	1.4	5.2	5.6	1.3	6.2	4.4	0.1	0.6	8.5	19.9	10.3
1990	6.5	1.5	5.0	7.0	2.0	5.8	5.5	0.2	0.4	10.6	13.7	8.7

	Male									
	Foreign-born									
		Trade			Service					
	Transportation and communications	Wholesale	Retail	Finance, insurance, real estate	Business	Personal	Educational	Other professional	Entertainment	Government
	Ad896	Ad897	Ad898	Ad899	Ad900	Ad901	Ad902	Ad903	Ad904	Ad905
Year	Percent	Percent	Percent	Percent	Percent	Percent	Percent	Percent	Percent	Percent
1910	11.6	1.8	12.3	1.1	1.2	4.2	0.4	1.4	0.4	0.8
1920	10.0	3.1	13.1	1.3	2.0	4.2	0.4	1.5	0.6	1.2
1940	7.6	2.9	17.3	2.9	1.9	5.9	1.0	2.4	1.1	1.9
1950	8.1	4.3	18.0	3.0	2.3	5.1	1.2	3.2	1.0	2.5
1960	6.8	4.0	15.3	3.2	2.9	4.8	2.5	4.9	1.0	2.7
1970	6.3	4.7	15.2	4.2	4.1	3.7	5.2	6.5	1.2	3.1
1980	6.0	4.7	15.7	4.4	5.6	2.9	4.4	7.6	1.3	3.5
1990	5.9	5.1	18.3	4.5	7.2	3.3	4.4	7.4	1.7	3.1

Notes appear at end of table

(continued)

TABLE Ad874–937 Industrial distribution of workers, by sex and nativity: 1910–1990 *Continued*

Female

Native-born white

Year	Agriculture	Forestry and fishing	Mining	Construction	Manufacturing Durable	Manufacturing Nondurable	Transportation and communications	Trade Wholesale	Trade Retail	Finance, insurance, real estate	Service Business	Service Personal
	Ad906	Ad907	Ad908	Ad909	Ad910	Ad911	Ad912	Ad913	Ad914	Ad915	Ad916	Ad917
	Percent	Percent	Percent	Percent	Percent	Percent	Percent	Percent	Percent	Percent	Percent	Percent
1910	11.4	0.0	0.2	0.3	3.2	18.6	3.2	1.1	14.0	1.9	0.9	27.2
1920	5.5	0.0	0.1	0.4	6.4	18.9	5.9	1.8	15.3	3.7	4.3	17.6
1940	2.4	0.0	0.2	0.6	6.1	19.2	3.7	1.9	19.6	4.4	0.9	17.4
1950	2.8	0.0	0.2	0.7	9.3	16.5	5.2	2.9	22.4	5.5	1.4	8.6
1960	1.7	0.0	0.2	0.8	10.3	14.0	4.2	2.5	21.2	6.8	2.1	7.9
1970	1.0	0.0	0.2	1.0	9.7	10.7	4.0	2.7	20.7	7.0	2.9	6.1
1980	1.3	0.1	0.3	1.3	8.8	7.8	3.6	2.8	20.9	8.4	4.0	4.2
1990	1.2	0.1	0.2	1.5	6.3	6.1	3.6	3.0	20.0	9.2	5.3	4.0

Female

	Native-born white Service Educational	Native-born white Service Other professional	Native-born white Entertainment	Native-born white Government	Foreign-born Agriculture	Foreign-born Forestry and fishing	Foreign-born Mining	Foreign-born Construction	Foreign-born Manufacturing Durable	Foreign-born Manufacturing Nondurable	Foreign-born Transportation and communications
	Ad918	Ad919	Ad920	Ad921	Ad922	Ad923	Ad924	Ad925	Ad926	Ad927	Ad928
Year	Percent	Percent	Percent	Percent	Percent	Percent	Percent	Percent	Percent	Percent	Percent
1910	12.0	4.3	0.7	0.9	4.8	0	0.3	0.2	2.7	24.5	1.0
1920	12.3	5.1	0.8	2.0	3.6	0	0.0	0.3	5.1	27.3	2.1
1940	10.7	7.7	1.0	4.1	2.1	0	0.1	0.4	4.7	24.7	1.4
1950	9.3	9.3	1.0	4.9	2.1	0	0.1	0.4	8.3	27.0	1.9
1960	11.0	11.6	1.0	4.7	1.4	0	0.1	0.5	10.0	24.5	2.3
1970	15.3	13.5	1.0	4.3	1.1	0	0.1	0.7	10.8	18.8	2.8
1980	13.9	16.3	1.3	5.0	1.6	0	0.2	0.8	11.5	15.1	3.0
1990	14.4	18.6	1.7	4.6	1.7	0	0.1	1.0	8.0	10.8	3.0

Female

Foreign-born

Year	Trade Wholesale	Trade Retail	Financial, insurance, real estate	Service Business	Service Personal	Service Educational	Service Other professional	Entertainment	Government
	Ad929	Ad930	Ad931	Ad932	Ad933	Ad934	Ad935	Ad936	Ad937
	Percent	Percent	Percent	Percent	Percent	Percent	Percent	Percent	Percent
1910	0.6	11.0	1.0	1.1	44.8	3.2	4.6	0.1	0.1
1920	1.3	13.6	1.7	2.3	34.1	3.3	4.5	0.6	0.4
1940	1.4	19.7	3.8	0.7	27.5	4.4	7.0	0.8	1.3
1950	2.6	20.5	4.0	1.1	16.9	4.5	8.3	0.9	1.7
1960	2.6	18.8	5.5	1.9	12.9	5.5	11.0	1.0	2.0
1970	3.0	17.6	6.7	3.0	9.0	9.2	13.8	0.9	2.3
1980	2.9	16.7	7.9	3.8	7.3	8.6	16.4	1.0	3.3
1990	3.5	18.1	8.0	5.7	8.6	9.4	17.5	1.4	3.1

[1] Data pertain to civilian noninstitutionalized persons in the labor force reporting an industry, ages 16–64.

Documentation
Persons born in U.S. outlying areas are considered foreign-born.

Source
Calculated from the Integrated Public Use Microdata Series (IPUMS). See the Guide to the Millennial Edition for information on IPUMS.

TABLE Ad874–937   Industrial distribution of workers, by sex and nativity: 1910–1990[1]

Contributed by Matthew Sobek

Male

Native-born white

| | | | | Manufacturing | | | Trade | | |
	Agriculture	Forestry and fishing	Mining	Construction	Durable	Nondurable	Transportation and communications	Wholesale	Retail	Finance, insurance, real estate
	Ad874	Ad875	Ad876	Ad877	Ad878	Ad879	Ad880	Ad881	Ad882	Ad883
Year	Percent	Percent	Percent	Percent	Percent	Percent	Percent	Percent	Percent	Percent
1910	36.8	0.3	2.8	7.0	11.0	8.4	10.7	2.4	9.5	2.1
1920	30.0	0.2	3.5	5.9	13.9	9.7	11.6	3.6	8.3	2.5
1940	20.7	0.5	3.0	10.7	13.1	10.9	8.3	3.0	12.7	2.8
1950	14.1	0.3	2.6	8.8	16.7	11.2	9.6	4.3	13.6	2.8
1960	8.0	0.2	1.8	9.5	20.5	11.8	8.9	4.3	13.2	3.5
1970	4.7	0.2	1.4	9.6	20.1	9.9	8.4	5.1	14.0	4.0
1980	3.8	0.3	1.8	10.7	18.4	8.3	8.4	5.4	14.0	4.3
1990	3.4	0.2	1.2	11.4	14.5	7.5	8.0	5.6	15.2	5.1

Male

| Native-born white | | | | | | Foreign-born | | | | Manufacturing | |
| | | Service | | | | | | | | | |
Business	Personal	Educational	Other professional	Entertainment	Government	Agriculture	Forestry and fishing	Mining	Construction	Durable	Nondurable
Ad884	Ad885	Ad886	Ad887	Ad888	Ad889	Ad890	Ad891	Ad892	Ad893	Ad894	Ad895
Percent	Percent	Percent	Percent	Percent	Percent	Percent	Percent	Percent	Percent	Percent	Percent
1.3	2.0	0.9	2.4	0.6	2.0	14.5	0.3	7.2	9.8	17.8	15.3
3.1	1.9	0.8	2.3	0.6	2.3	12.4	0.1	5.8	6.6	20.8	16.6
2.5	2.4	1.8	2.6	1.2	3.9	9.3	0.5	3.0	11.0	17.2	14.0
3.4	2.1	1.9	2.9	1.0	4.9	7.1	0.4	1.6	8.7	19.4	14.1
3.4	1.9	3.0	3.6	0.9	5.6	6.4	0.2	0.6	8.5	22.3	13.8
3.9	1.7	5.3	4.3	1.1	6.2	3.6	0.2	0.4	8.4	21.8	11.6
5.1	1.4	5.2	5.6	1.3	6.2	4.4	0.1	0.6	8.5	19.9	10.3
6.5	1.5	5.0	7.0	2.0	5.8	5.5	0.2	0.4	10.6	13.7	8.7

(Note: Year column for above: 1910, 1920, 1940, 1950, 1960, 1970, 1980, 1990)

Male

Foreign-born

| | Trade | | | Service | | | | | |
Transportation and communications	Wholesale	Retail	Finance, insurance, real estate	Business	Personal	Educational	Other professional	Entertainment	Government
Ad896	Ad897	Ad898	Ad899	Ad900	Ad901	Ad902	Ad903	Ad904	Ad905
Percent	Percent	Percent	Percent	Percent	Percent	Percent	Percent	Percent	Percent
11.6	1.8	12.3	1.1	1.2	4.2	0.4	1.4	0.4	0.8
10.0	3.1	13.1	1.3	2.0	4.2	0.4	1.5	0.6	1.2
7.6	2.9	17.3	2.9	1.9	5.9	1.0	2.4	1.1	1.9
8.1	4.3	18.0	3.0	2.3	5.1	1.2	3.2	1.0	2.5
6.8	4.0	15.3	3.2	2.9	4.8	2.5	4.9	1.0	2.7
6.3	4.7	15.2	4.2	4.1	3.7	5.2	6.5	1.2	3.1
6.0	4.7	15.7	4.4	5.6	2.9	4.4	7.6	1.3	3.5
5.9	5.1	18.3	4.5	7.2	3.3	4.4	7.4	1.7	3.1

(Note: Year column for above: 1910, 1920, 1940, 1950, 1960, 1970, 1980, 1990)

Notes appear at end of table   (continued)

TABLE Ad874-937   Industrial distribution of workers, by sex and nativity: 1910-1990 *Continued*

Female

Native-born white

					Manufacturing			Trade			Service	
Year	Agriculture	Forestry and fishing	Mining	Construction	Durable	Nondurable	Transportation and communications	Wholesale	Retail	Finance, insurance, real estate	Business	Personal
	Ad906	Ad907	Ad908	Ad909	Ad910	Ad911	Ad912	Ad913	Ad914	Ad915	Ad916	Ad917
	Percent	Percent	Percent	Percent	Percent	Percent	Percent	Percent	Percent	Percent	Percent	Percent
1910	11.4	0.0	0.2	0.3	3.2	18.6	3.2	1.1	14.0	1.9	0.9	27.2
1920	5.5	0.0	0.1	0.4	6.4	18.9	5.9	1.8	15.3	3.7	4.3	17.6
1940	2.4	0.0	0.2	0.6	6.1	19.2	3.7	1.9	19.6	4.4	0.9	17.4
1950	2.8	0.0	0.2	0.7	9.3	16.5	5.2	2.9	22.4	5.5	1.4	8.6
1960	1.7	0.0	0.2	0.8	10.3	14.0	4.2	2.5	21.2	6.8	2.1	7.9
1970	1.0	0.0	0.2	1.0	9.7	10.7	4.0	2.7	20.7	7.0	2.9	6.1
1980	1.3	0.1	0.3	1.3	8.8	7.8	3.6	2.8	20.9	8.4	4.0	4.2
1990	1.2	0.1	0.2	1.5	6.3	6.1	3.6	3.0	20.0	9.2	5.3	4.0

Female

Native-born white				Foreign-born						
Service								Manufacturing		
Year	Educational	Other professional	Entertainment	Government	Agriculture	Forestry and fishing	Mining	Construction	Durable	Nondurable	Transportation and communications
	Ad918	Ad919	Ad920	Ad921	Ad922	Ad923	Ad924	Ad925	Ad926	Ad927	Ad928
	Percent	Percent	Percent	Percent	Percent	Percent	Percent	Percent	Percent	Percent	Percent
1910	12.0	4.3	0.7	0.9	4.8	0	0.3	0.2	2.7	24.5	1.0
1920	12.3	5.1	0.8	2.0	3.6	0	0.0	0.3	5.1	27.3	2.1
1940	10.7	7.7	1.0	4.1	2.1	0	0.1	0.4	4.7	24.7	1.4
1950	9.3	9.3	1.0	4.9	2.1	0	0.1	0.4	8.3	27.0	1.9
1960	11.0	11.6	1.0	4.7	1.4	0	0.1	0.5	10.0	24.5	2.3
1970	15.3	13.5	1.0	4.3	1.1	0	0.1	0.7	10.8	18.8	2.8
1980	13.9	16.3	1.3	5.0	1.6	0	0.2	0.8	11.5	15.1	3.0
1990	14.4	18.6	1.7	4.6	1.7	0	0.1	1.0	8.0	10.8	3.0

Female

Foreign-born

	Trade			Service					
Year	Wholesale	Retail	Financial, insurance, real estate	Business	Personal	Educational	Other professional	Entertainment	Government
	Ad929	Ad930	Ad931	Ad932	Ad933	Ad934	Ad935	Ad936	Ad937
	Percent	Percent	Percent	Percent	Percent	Percent	Percent	Percent	Percent
1910	0.6	11.0	1.0	1.1	44.8	3.2	4.6	0.1	0.1
1920	1.3	13.6	1.7	2.3	34.1	3.3	4.5	0.6	0.4
1940	1.4	19.7	3.8	0.7	27.5	4.4	7.0	0.8	1.3
1950	2.6	20.5	4.0	1.1	16.9	4.5	8.3	0.9	1.7
1960	2.6	18.8	5.5	1.9	12.9	5.5	11.0	1.0	2.0
1970	3.0	17.6	6.7	3.0	9.0	9.2	13.8	0.9	2.3
1980	2.9	16.7	7.9	3.8	7.3	8.6	16.4	1.0	3.3
1990	3.5	18.1	8.0	5.7	8.6	9.4	17.5	1.4	3.1

[1] Data pertain to civilian noninstitutionalized persons in the labor force reporting an industry, ages 16–64.

Source

Calculated from the Integrated Public Use Microdata Series (IPUMS). See the Guide to the Millennial Edition for information on IPUMS.

Documentation

Persons born in U.S. outlying areas are considered foreign-born.

TABLE Ad938–949 Nobel prizes awarded to American citizens, by field and country of birth: 1906–2000

Contributed by Susan B. Carter

	Physics		Chemistry		Medicine or physiology	
	Name	Country of birth	Name	Country of birth	Name	Country of birth
Year	Ad938	Ad939	Ad940	Ad941	Ad942	Ad943
1906	—	—	—	—	—	—
1907	Albert A. Michelson	Germany	—	—	—	—
1912	—	—	—	—	Alexis Carrel	France
1914	—	—	Theodore W. Richards	United States	—	—
1923	Robert A. Millikan	United States	—	—	—	—
1925	James Franck	Germany	—	—	—	—
1927	A. Holly Compton	United States	—	—	—	—
1930	—	—	—	—	Karl Landsteiner	Austria
1932	—	—	Irving Langmuir	United States	—	—
1933	—	—	—	—	Thomas H. Morgan	United States
1934	—	—	Harold C. Urey	United States	George H. Whipple	United States
1934	—	—	—	—	George R. Minot	United States
1934	—	—	—	—	William P. Murphy	United States
1936	Carl D. Anderson	United States	—	—	—	—
1937	Clinton J. Davisson	United States	—	—	—	—
1939	Ernest O. Lawrence	United States	—	—	—	—
1943	Otto Stern	Germany	—	—	Edward Doisy	United States
1944	Isidor I. Rabi	Austria	—	—	Joseph Erlanger	United States
1944	—	—	—	—	Herbert S. Gasser	United States
1945	Wolfgang Pauli	Austria	—	—	—	—
1946	Percy W. Bridgman	United States	James B. Sumner	United States	Herman J. Muller	United States
1946	—	—	John H. Northrop	United States	—	—
1946	—	—	Wendell M. Stanley	United States	—	—
1947	—	—	—	—	Carl F. Cori	Czechoslovakia
1947	—	—	—	—	Gerty T. Cori	Czechoslovakia
1949	—	—	William F. Giauque	Canada	—	—
1950	—	—	—	—	Philip S. Hench	United States
1950	—	—	—	—	Edward C. Kendall	United States
1951	—	—	Edwin M. McMillan	United States	Max Theiler	South Africa
1951	—	—	Glenn T. Seaborg	United States	—	—
1952	Felix Bloch	Switzerland	—	—	Selman A. Waksman	Russia
1952	Edward M. Purcell	United States	—	—	—	—
1953	—	—	—	—	Fritz A. Lipmann	Germany
1954	—	—	Linus C. Pauling	United States	John F. Enders	United States
1954	—	—	—	—	Thomas H. Weller	United States
1954	—	—	—	—	Frederick C. Robbins	United States
1955	Polykarp Kusch	Germany	Vincent Du Vigneud	United States	—	—
1955	Willis Eugene Lamb	United States	—	—	—	—
1956	William B. Shockley	Britain	—	—	Andre F. Cournand	France
1956	John Bardeen	United States	—	—	Dickinson W. Richards	United States
1956	Walter H. Brattain	China	—	—	—	—
1957	Tsung-Dao Lee	China	—	—	—	—
1957	Chen Ning Yang	China	—	—	—	—
1958	—	—	—	—	George W. Beadle	United States
1958	—	—	—	—	Edward L. Tatum	United States
1958	—	—	—	—	Joshua Lederberg	United States
1959	Emilio G. Segre	Italy	—	—	Severo Ochoa	Spain
1959	Owen Chamberlain	United States	—	—	Arthur Kornberg	United States
1960	Donald A. Glaser	United States	Willard F. Libby	United States	—	—
1961	Robert Hofstadter	Germany	Melvin Calvin	United States	Georg von Bekesy	Hungary
1962	—	—	—	—	James D. Watson	United States
1963	Eugene P. Wigner	Hungary	—	—	—	—
1963	Maria G. Mayer	Germany	—	—	—	—
1964	Charles H. Townes	United States	—	—	Konrad E. Bloch	Germany
1965	Richard P. Feynman	United States	Robert B. Woodward	United States	—	—
1966	—	—	Robert S. Mulliken	United States	Charles B. Huggins	Canada
1966	—	—	—	—	Francis Peyton Rous	United States
1967	Hans A. Bethe	Germany	—	—	Haldan K. Hartline	United States
1967	—	—	—	—	George Wald	United States
1968	Luis W. Alvarez	United States	Lars Onsager	Norway	Robert W. Holley	United States

(continued)

TABLE Ad938–949   Nobel prizes awarded to American citizens, by field and country of birth: 1906–2000   *Continued*

Year	Physics Name Ad938	Physics Country of birth Ad939	Chemistry Name Ad940	Chemistry Country of birth Ad941	Medicine or physiology Name Ad942	Medicine or physiology Country of birth Ad943
1968	—	—	—	—	H. Gobind Khorana	India
1968			—	—	Marshall W. Nirenberg	United States
1969	Murray Gell-Mann	United States	—	—	Max Delbruck	Germany
1969	—	—	—	—	Alfred D. Hershey	United States
1969	—	—	—	—	Salvador E. Luria	Italy
1970	—	—	—	—	Julius Axelrod	United States
1971	—	—	—	—	Earl W. Sutherland Jr.	United States
1972	John Bardeen	United States	Christian B. Anfinsen	United States	Gerald M. Edelman	United States
1972	Leon N. Cooper	United States	Stanford Moore	United States	—	—
1972	John R. Schrieffer	United States	William H. Stein	United States	—	—
1973	Ivar Glaever	Norway	—	—	—	—
1974	—	—	Paul J. Flory	United States	George E. Palade	Romania
1974	—	—	—	—	Christian De Duve	Great Britain
1975	L. James Rainwater	United States	—	—	David Baltimore	United States
1975	—	—	—	—	Howard M. Temin	United States
1976	Burton Richter	United States	William N. Lipscomb	United States	Baruch S. Blumberg	United States
1976	Samuel C. C. Ting	United States	—	—	D. Carleton Gajdusek	United States
1977	Philip W. Anderson	United States	—	—	Roger C. L. Guillemin	France
1977	John H. Van Vleck	United States	—	—	Andrew V. Schally	Poland
1977	—	—	—	—	Rosalyn S. Yalow	United States
1978	Arno Allan Penzias	Germany	—	—	Daniel Nathans	United States
1978	Robert W. Wilson	United States	—	—	Hamilton O. Smith	United States
1979	Sheldon L. Glashow	United States	Herbert C. Brown	Britain	Allan M. Cormack	South Africa
1979	Steven Weinberg	United States	—	—	—	—
1980	James W. Cronin	United States	Paul Berg	United States	Baruj Benacerraf	Venezuela
1980	Val L. Fitch	United States	Walter Gilbert	United States	Geroge D. Snell	United States
1981	Nicholass Bloembergen	The Netherlands	Roald Hoffmann	Poland	Roger W. Sperry	United States
1981	Arthur L. Schawlow	United States	—	—	David H. Hubel	Canada
1981	—	—	—	—	Torsten N. Wiesel	Sweden
1982	Kenneth G. Wilson	United States	—	—	—	—
1983	S. Chandrasekhar	India	Henry Taube	Canada	Barbara McClintock	United States
1983	William A. Fowler	United States	—	—	—	—
1984	—	—	R. B. Merrifield	United States	—	—
1985	—	—	Herbert A. Hauptman	United States	Michael S. Brown	United States
1985	—	—	Jerome Karle	United States	Joseph Goldstein	United States
1986	—	—	Dudley R. Herschbach	United States	Stanley Cohen	United States
1986	—	—	Yuan Tseh Lee	Taiwan	—	—
1987	—	—	Donald J. Cram	United States	—	—
1987	—	—	Charles J. Pederson	Korea	—	—
1988	Leon Max Lederman	United States	Johann Deisenhofer	Bavaria	George H. Hitchings	United States
1988	Melvin Schwartz	United States	—	—	Gertrude B. Elion	United States
1989	Hans G. Dehmelt	Germany	Sidney Altman	Canada	J. Michael Bishop	United States
1989	Norman F. Ramsey Jr.	United States	Thomas R. Cech	United States	Harold Varmus	United States
1990	Jerome I. Friedman	United States	Elias James Corey	United States	Joseph E. Murray	United States
1990	Henry W. Kendall	United States	—	—	E. Donnall Thomas	United States
1990	Richard E. Taylor	Canada	—	—	—	—
1991	—	—	—	—	—	—
1992	—	—	Rudolph A. Marcus	Canada	Edmond H. Fischer	China
1992	—	—	—	—	Edwin G. Krebs	United States
1993	Joseph H. Taylor Jr.	United States	Kary B. Mullis	United States	Phillip A. Sharp	United States
1993	Russell A. Hulse	United States	—	—	Richard J. Roberts	Great Britain
1994	Clifford G. Shull	United States	George A. Olah	Hungary	Alfred G. Gilman	United States
1994	—	—	—	—	Martin Rodbell	United States
1995	Martin L. Perl	United States	Mario Molina	Mexico	Edward B. Lewis	United States
1995	Frederick Reines	United States	F. Sherwood Rowland	United States	Eric F. Wieschaus	United States
1996	David M. Lee	United States	Robert F. Curl Jr.	United States	Peter C. Doherty	Australia
1996	Douglas D. Oshcroff	United States	Richard E. Smalley	United States	—	—
1996	Robert C. Richardson	United States	—	—	—	—
1997	Steven Chu	United States	Paul D. Boyer	United States	Stanley B. Prusiner	United States
1997	William Phillips	United States	—	—	—	—

TABLE Ad938–949   Nobel prizes awarded to American citizens, by field and country of birth: 1906–2000   *Continued*

	Physics		Chemistry		Medicine or physiology	
	Name	Country of birth	Name	Country of birth	Name	Country of birth
Year	Ad938	Ad939	Ad940	Ad941	Ad942	Ad943
1998	Robert B. Laughlin	United States	Walter Kohn	United States	Robert F. Furghott	United States
1998	Horst L. Stormer	Germany	John A. Pople	Great Britain	Louis J. Ignarro	United States
1998	Daniel C. Tsui	United States	—	—	Ferid Murad	United States
1999	Martinus J. G. Veltman	The Netherlands	Aluned H. Zewail	Egypt	Gunter Blobel	Germany
2000	Jack S. Kilby	United States	Alan J. Heeger	United States	Paul Greengard	United States
2000	Herbert Kroemer	Germany	Alan G. MacDiarmid	United States	Eric R. Kandel	United States

	Literature		Peace		Economic science	
	Name	Country of birth	Name	Country of birth	Name	Country of birth
Year	Ad944	Ad945	Ad946	Ad947	Ad948	Ad949
1906	—	—	Theodore Roosevelt	United States	—	—
1912	—	—	Elihu Root	United States	—	—
1919	—	—	T. Woodrow Wilson	United States	—	—
1925	—	—	Charles G. Dawes	United States	—	—
1929	—	—	Frank B. Kellogg	United States	—	—
1930	H. Sinclair Lewis	United States	—	—	—	—
1931	—	—	Jane Addams	United States	—	—
1931	—	—	Nicholas Murray Butler	United States	—	—
1936	Eugene G. O'Neill	United States	—	—	—	—
1938	Pearl S. Buck	United States	—	—	—	—
1945	—	—	Cordell Hull	United States	—	—
1946	—	—	Emily Greene Balch	United States	—	—
1946	—	—	John R. Mott	United States	—	—
1947	—	—	American Friends Service Committee	United States	—	—
1949	William H. Faulkner	United States	—	—	—	—
1953	—	—	George C. Marshall	United States	—	—
1954	Ernest M. Hemingway	United States	—	—	—	—
1962	John E. Steinbeck	United States	Linus C. Pauling	United States	—	—
1964	—	—	Martin Luther King Jr.	United States	—	—
1970	—	—	Norman E. Borlaug	United States	Paul A. Samuelson	United States
1971	—	—	—	—	Simon S. Kuznets	Russia
1972	—	—	—	—	Kenneth J. Arrow	United States
1973	—	—	Henry A. Kissinger	Germany	Wassily Leontief	Russia
1975	—	—	—	—	Tjalling C. Koopmans	The Netherlands
1976	Saul Bellow	Canada	—	—	Milton Friedman	United States
1978	Isaac Bashevis Singer	Poland	—	—	Herbert A. Simon	United States
1979	—	—	—	—	Theodore W. Schultz	United States
1979	—	—	—	—	Sir Arthur Lewis	St. Lucia
1980	Czeslaw Milosz	Lithuania	—	—	Lawrence R. Klein	United States
1981	—	—	—	—	James Tobin	United States
1982	—	—	—	—	George J. Stigler	United States
1983	—	—	—	—	Gerard Debreu	France
1985	—	—	—	—	Franco Modigliani	Italy
1986	—	—	Elie Wiesel	Romania	James M. Buchanan Jr.	United States
1987	Joseph Brodsky	Russia	—	—	Robert M. Solow	United States
1990	—	—	—	—	Harry M. Markowitz	United States
1990	—	—	—	—	Merton H. Miller	United States
1990	—	—	—	—	William F. Sharpe	United States
1991	—	—	—	—	Ronald H. Coase	Great Britain
1992	—	—	—	—	Gary S. Becker	United States
1993	Toni Morrison	United States	—	—	Robert W. Fogel	United States
1993	—	—	—	—	Douglass C. North	United States
1994	—	—	—	—	John C. Harsanyi	Hungary
1994	—	—	—	—	John F. Nash	United States
1995	—	—	—	—	Robert E. Lucas Jr.	United States

(continued)

TABLE Ad938–949   Nobel prizes awarded to American citizens, by field and country of birth: 1906–2000   *Continued*

Year	Literature		Peace		Economic science	
	Name	Country of birth	Name	Country of birth	Name	Country of birth
	Ad944	Ad945	Ad946	Ad947	Ad948	Ad949
1996	—	—	—	—	William Vickrey	Canada
1997	—	—	International Campaign to Ban Landmines	United States	Robert C. Merton	United States
1997	—	—	Jody Williams	United States	Myron S. Scholes	Canada
1999	—	—	—	—	Robert A. Mundell	Canada
2000	—	—	—	—	James J. Heckman	United States
2000	—	—	—	—	Daniel L. McFadden	United States

Source

Internet site of the Nobel Foundation, viewed May 19, 2000.

Documentation

The Nobel Prize is presented by the Nobel Foundation, a private institution established in 1900 on the basis of the will of Alfred Nobel and awarding prizes in physics, chemistry, physiology or medicine, literature, and peace.

In 1969 the Nobel Foundation added the Bank of Sweden Prize in Economic Sciences in memory of Alfred Nobel.

American prizewinners were U.S. residents when their award was conferred. If a prize was shared between an American and non-American resident, only the American's name is listed.

Also see Table Cg212–235.

ALIEN ADMISSIONS, BY PROGRAM

Robert Barde, Susan B. Carter, and Richard Sutch

TABLE Ad950-954 Immigrants admitted under the Quota System: 1925–1968[1]

Contributed by Robert Barde, Susan B. Carter, and Richard Sutch

		Immigrants admitted under the Quota System			
	Annual immigrant quota	Natives of Eastern Hemisphere countries	Natives of Western Hemisphere countries	Immediate relatives of U.S. citizens	Other
	Ad950	Ad951	Ad952	Ad953 [2]	Ad954
Fiscal year	Number	Number	Number	Number	Number
1925	164,667	145,971	139,389	7,159	1,795
1926	164,667	157,432	134,305	11,061	1,690
1927	164,667	158,070	147,399	18,361	11,345
1928	164,667	153,231	123,534	25,678	4,812
1929	164,667	146,918	97,548	30,245	4,967
1930	153,714	141,497	63,147	32,105	4,951
1931	153,714	54,118	21,287	17,264	4,470
1932	153,831	12,983	9,461	9,490	3,642
1933	153,831	8,220	7,549	6,658	641
1934	153,774	12,483	8,237	7,891	859
1935	153,774	17,207	7,747	9,228	774
1936	153,774	18,675	8,066	8,824	764
1937	153,774	27,762	12,152	9,536	794
1938	153,774	42,494	14,379	10,262	760
1939	153,774	62,402	12,223	7,043	1,330
1940	153,774	51,997	11,985	5,474	1,300
1941	153,774	36,220	12,586	2,122	848
1942	153,774	14,597	12,596	1,262	326
1943	153,774	9,045	13,522	875	283
1944	153,774	9,394	17,614	1,302	241
1945	153,879	11,623	22,828	3,078	590
1946	153,879	29,095	29,502	49,267	857
1947	153,929	70,701	35,640	38,739	2,212
1948	153,929	92,526	37,968	36,830	3,246
1949	153,929	113,046	36,394	35,854	3,023
1950	154,206	197,460	33,238	16,275	2,214
1951	154,277	156,547	35,274	11,462	2,434
1952	154,277	194,247	48,408	19,315	3,550
1953	154,657	84,175	61,099	22,543	2,617
1954	154,657	94,098	80,526	30,689	2,864
1955	154,657	82,232	94,274	30,882	30,402
1956	154,657	89,310	124,032	31,742	76,541
1957	154,857	97,178	113,488	32,359	83,842
1958	154,957	102,153	88,575	35,320	27,217
1959	154,857	97,657	68,196	36,402	58,431
1960	154,887	101,373	91,701	34,215	38,109
1961	156,487	96,104	112,836	32,551	29,853
1962	156,687	90,319	133,505	30,316	29,623
1963	156,987	103,036	147,744	30,606	24,874
1964	158,161	102,844	139,284	33,669	16,451
1965	158,561	99,381	153,199	32,714	11,403
1966	158,561	126,310	147,906	39,231	9,593 [3]
1967	158,261	153,079	151,034	46,903	10,956 [3]
1968	158,261	156,212	245,449	43,677	9,110 [3]

[1] Fiscal years ending June 30.

[2] Beginning in 1966, includes parents of adult U.S. citizens.

[3] Does not agree with source; adjusted to conform to definitions used in later years.

Sources

U.S. Immigration and Naturalization Service, *Annual Report of Immigration and Naturalization Service*, annual issues; presidential proclamations on quotas; and unpublished data as reported in U.S. Bureau of the Census, *Historical Statistics of the United States* (1975).

Documentation

The Quota System was established by the Immigration Act of 1924 (also known as the Johnson-Reed Act). This system is remarkable for its establishment of an annual quota based on national origins for certain immigrants. The level of the annual quota is shown in series Ad950. Immediate relatives of U.S. citizens and natives of Western Hemisphere countries were not subject to the quota and were admitted without limitation.

(continued)

TABLE Ad950–954   Immigrants admitted under the Quota System: 1925–1968   *Continued*

For the years 1925 through 1929, the annual quota on natives of Eastern Hemisphere countries was 164,667, a number that equals 2 percent of the number of foreign-born residents from the Eastern Hemisphere in the United States as shown in the 1890 Census. The quota for individual countries was also set at 2 percent of foreign-born residents from that country recorded in the 1890 Census.

For the years 1930 through 1965, a new, rather complicated "national origin" formula was used to set the annual quota. An overall quota was first set by taking one sixth of 1 percent of the difference between the number of white inhabitants in the United States in 1920 and the number of Western Hemisphere immigrants and their descendants. This number was found to be approximately 150,000. Quotas for Eastern Hemisphere nations were determined by first calculating the share of the 1920 U.S. resident population born in that nation and then multiplying this fraction by 150,000. Thus, for example, a nation that accounted for 1 percent of the U.S. resident population in 1920 would be allowed an annual quota of 1,500 immigrants to the United States. The country with the largest quota under this law was Great Britain and Northern Ireland, with an annual quota of 65,361. The law also set a minimum quota of 100 for any nation. The Act of 1943 that repealed the Chinese Exclusion Act established a quota of 150 for Chinese. Changes in territorial boundaries and the emergence of new countries led to other adjustments to the overall quota from year to year.

The Immigration and Nationality Act of October 3, 1965 – an amendment to the Immigration and Nationality Act of 1952 – abolished the Quota System and in its place set up an annual numerical limitation of 170,000 immigrants from the Eastern Hemisphere, with no more than 20,000 immigrants allowed to come from any one country. From December 1, 1965, through June 30, 1968, countries retained their old quotas, but unused visa numbers from each year went into a general pool of numbers available on a first-come, first-served basis during the next year. On July 1, 1968, the new law and its system of numerical limitations went fully into effect. Also at that time, a numerical limitation of 120,000 per year was imposed on Western Hemisphere immigration, which had previously been unrestricted.

Series Ad952. Data include Cuban refugees adjusting their immigrant status and the spouses and children of natives of Western Hemisphere countries.

Series Ad953. Includes spouses and children of U.S. citizens. Parents of adult U.S. citizens are included beginning 1966.

TABLE Ad955–965   Immigrants admitted under the Preference System: 1966–1991[1]

Contributed by Robert Barde, Susan B. Carter, and Richard Sutch

		Immigrant admissions									
		Subject to numerical cap				Not subject to numerical cap					
	Numerical cap under Preference System	Total	Family-sponsored preferences	Employment-based preferences	Other preferences	Total	Immediate relatives of U.S. citizens	Natives of Western Hemisphere countries	IRCA legalizations	Refugees and asylees	Others
	Ad955	Ad956	Ad957	Ad958	Ad959	Ad960	Ad961	Ad962	Ad963	Ad964	Ad965
Fiscal year	Number	Number	Number	Number	Number	Number	Number	Number	Number	Number	Number
1966	170,000	126,310	54,935	10,525	60,850	196,730	39,231	147,906	—	8,828	765
1967	170,000	153,079	79,671	25,365	48,043	208,893	46,903	125,282	—	35,615	1,093
1968	170,000	156,212	68,384	26,865	60,963	298,236	43,677	153,929	—	100,822	−192
1969	290,000	290,995	92,458	31,763	166,774	67,584	60,016	—	—	16,864	−9,296
1970	290,000	287,283	92,432	34,016	160,835	86,043	79,222	—	—	22,215	−15,394
1971	290,000	280,626	82,191	34,563	163,872	89,852	83,486	—	—	26,403	−20,037
1972	290,000	283,666	83,165	33,714	166,787	101,019	93,160	—	—	28,795	−20,936
1973	290,000	282,911	92,054	26,767	164,090	117,152	109,229	—	—	30,907	−22,984
1974	290,000	274,131	94,915	28,482	150,734	120,730	112,729	—	—	25,650	−17,649
1975	290,000	281,561	95,945	29,334	156,282	104,633	96,561	—	—	34,665	−26,593
1976	290,000	284,773	102,007	26,361	156,405	113,840	107,033	—	—	48,576	−41,769
(TQ)	72,500	72,511	28,382	5,621	38,508	31,165	29,303	—	TQ	—	1,862
1977	290,000	276,500	130,784	23,585	122,131	185,815	111,555	—	—	78,485	−4,225
1978	290,000	341,104	190,297	30,877	119,930	260,338	131,825	—	—	132,781	−4,268
1979	290,000	279,478	213,729	37,709	28,040	180,870	142,825	—	—	45,128	−7,083
1980	280,000	289,479	216,856	44,369	28,254	241,160	157,743	—	—	88,057	−4,640
1981	270,000	330,409	226,576	44,311	59,522	266,191	152,359	—	—	107,573	6,259
1982	270,000	259,749	206,065	51,182	2,502	334,382	168,398	—	—	156,601	9,383
1983	270,000	269,213	213,488	55,468	257	290,550	177,792	—	—	102,685	10,073
1984	270,000	262,016	212,324	49,521	171	281,887	183,247	—	—	92,127	6,513
1985	270,000	264,208	213,257	50,895	56	305,801	204,368	—	—	95,040	6,393
1986	270,000	266,968	212,939	53,625	404	334,740	223,468	—	—	104,383	6,889
1987	270,000	271,135	211,809	53,873	5,453	330,381	218,575	—	—	91,840	19,966
1988	270,000	264,148	200,772	53,607	9,769	378,877	219,340	—	—	81,719	77,818
1989	270,000	280,275	217,092	52,755	10,428	810,649	217,514	—	478,814	84,288	30,033
1990	270,000	298,306	214,550	53,729	30,027	1,238,177	231,680	—	880,372	97,364	28,761
1991	295,000	293,846	216,088	54,949	22,809	1,533,321	237,103	—	1,123,162	139,079	33,977

(TQ) indicates transitional quarter.

[1] Through 1976, fiscal year ending June 30; thereafter, fiscal year ending September 30.

Source

U.S. Immigration and Naturalization Service, *Statistical Yearbook*, various years.

Documentation

The Preference System was established in 1965 by a set of amendments to the Immigration and Nationality Act of 1952. These amendments ended the national origin quota system and put in its place a new, two-class system for immigrant admissions. One class was admitted without numerical

TABLE Ad955–965   Immigrants admitted under the Preference System: 1966–1991   *Continued*

restriction; the other was limited by a fixed "cap." Immediate relatives of U.S. citizens – that is, spouses, children younger than twenty-one years of age (including adopted children), and parents of citizens twenty-one years of age and older – were not subject to numerical limitation. In addition, ministers and other religious workers – and after 1981, graduates of foreign medical schools and "investors" – were also admitted without limitation.

Admissions of all other immigrants were limited by a numerical "cap." A system of "preferences" selected among applicants subject to this numerical limitation. The new law provided for four types of preferences: relative preferences (for specified relatives of citizens and immediate family members of lawful permanent residents of the United States), occupational preferences, refugee preferences, and nonpreference immigrants. The last group could be used to fill the numerical limitation only after the other three preferences were filled. Initially, this fourfold preference system applied only to non–Western Hemisphere immigrants; those from the Western Hemisphere were admitted without limit on a first-come, first-served basis. Beginning July 1, 1968, Western Hemisphere immigrants were subject to the numerical cap.

The Refugee Act of 1980 reclassified refugees, permitting them to enter without any restrictions on their number. The Act established procedures for an annual consultation with Congress to establish the number of refugees of special humanitarian concern to the United States in need of resettlement. At the same time, the worldwide cap was lowered. The Refugee Act also distinguished between "refugees" and "asylees." Although both are individuals unable or unwilling to return to their country of nationality because of persecution or a well-founded fear of persecution, a refugee is outside of the United States at the time of application, whereas an asylee is already in the United States or at a U.S. port of entry. The number of asylee admissions was limited to 5,000 annually. This cap on asylee admissions is separate from the overall cap.

The Immigration Reform and Control Act of 1986 (IRCA) provided for a one-time amnesty for certain "undocumented" aliens residing in the United States. Two classes of undocumented aliens were eligible for legalization: those who had resided continuously in an unlawful status since January 1, 1982, and "Special Agricultural Workers" (SAWs) who had worked in perishable agricultural commodities at least ninety days in each of three years preceding May 1, 1986.

Series Ad955. The numerical cap is the total of the separate maximums allowable in each of the four subcategories for the fiscal year. The cap refers to the maximum number of immigrant *visas* that can be issued. The actual number of immigrants *admitted* may differ from this number because some who were issued visas decided not to immigrate and others who were issued visas used them in a subsequent year. Still others may have entered with a visa issued in some previous year. The initial cap was set at 170,000. Beginning July 1, 1968, a separate cap of 120,000 was imposed on the admission of Western Hemisphere immigrants. In addition to the overall numerical cap on preference admissions, each non–Western Hemisphere country had a numerical cap. During a transition period lasting through June 30, 1968, those limitations were the same as under the previous National Origins Quota Law. After that date, no more than 20,000 visas were available to any one country (and no more than 200 for "dependent areas" such as colonies). Beginning in October 1976, the country cap of 20,000 was extended to countries of the Western Hemisphere and the dependent area cap was raised to 600. Also beginning in October 1976, admissions from Western Hemisphere countries

were shifted from first-come, first-served to the preference system. After September 1978, separate limitations for the Western Hemisphere and the rest of the world were dropped and a worldwide numerical limitation of 290,000 was established. In 1991, the numerical cap was raised by 25,000, with 15,000 of these visas designated for aliens from countries "adversely affected" by the Immigration and Nationality Act Amendments of 1965 and 10,000 for aliens from "underrepresented" countries.

Series Ad956. The total of family-sponsored, employment-based, and other preference-based immigrant admissions.

Series Ad957. Includes family members of citizens and legal residents not admissible as immediate relatives of U.S. citizens. Relationships that qualify as family-sponsored preferences include sons and daughters of U.S. citizens and their spouses and children; the spouses, children, and unmarried sons and daughters of permanent resident aliens; and the adult brothers and sisters of U.S. citizens together with their spouses and children.

Series Ad958. Employment-based immigration subject to numerical limitation included two general categories: professional or highly skilled immigrants and "needed skilled or unskilled workers."

Series Ad959. Between 1965 and 1980, the major groups included in the "other" category were refugees and nonpreference immigrants. The Refugee Act of 1980 removed refugees from the groups subject to the numerical cap. After fiscal year 1990, immigrants from "underrepresented countries" were included.

Series Ad960. The total of immediate relatives of U.S. citizens before fiscal year 1993, Western Hemisphere admissions for fiscal years 1966, 1967, and 1968, and IRCA legalizations since fiscal year 1989.

Series Ad961. Immediate relatives are defined as spouses of citizens, children younger than twenty-one years of age of citizens, parents of citizens twenty-one years of age or older, and orphans adopted by citizens who are at least twenty-one years of age.

Series Ad962. During the transition period spanning fiscal years 1966, 1967, and 1968, immigrants from independent countries in the Western Hemisphere were not subject to a numerical limitation. A limit of 120,000 was placed on this flow effective in fiscal year 1969.

Series Ad963. The Immigration Reform and Control Act of 1986 authorized the legalization of aliens who had resided in the United States in an unlawful status since January 1, 1982, and agricultural workers who had worked at least ninety days in each of three years preceding May 1986.

Series Ad964. Refugees and asylees are aliens who are unable or unwilling to return to their country of nationality because of persecution or a well-founded fear of persecution. Refugee status is conferred before entry to the United States; asylee status is conferred on those already in the United States. Both groups are eligible to adjust to immigrant status after one year of continuous presence in the United States. There is an annual limit of 10,000 asylee admissions per year. The number of refugee admissions is set annually by the president. Limitations on the number of refugee and asylee admissions are separate from limitations in the "numerical cap" shown in series Ad955.

Series Ad965. A numerically significant group in this residual category is Amerasian children born in Vietnam (Act of 1987).

TABLE Ad966–975   Immigrants admitted or legalized, by program: 1992–1997

Contributed by Robert Barde, Susan B. Carter, and Richard Sutch

		Admitted under the Immigration Act of 1990						Legalized under Immigration Reform and Control Act (IRCA) of 1986		
	Total	Preference immigrants			Immediate relatives of U.S. citizens	Refugees and asylees	Other immigrants	Total	Residents since 1982	Special Agricultural Workers (SAWs)
		Total	Family-sponsored	Employment-based						
	Ad966	Ad967	Ad968	Ad969	Ad970	Ad971	Ad972	Ad973	Ad974	Ad975
Fiscal year	Number	Number	Number	Number	Number	Number	Number	Number	Number	Number
1992	973,977	329,321	213,123	116,198	235,484	117,037	810,635	163,342	46,962	116,380
1993	904,292	373,788	226,776	147,012	255,059	127,343	880,014	24,278	18,717	5,561
1994	804,416	335,252	211,961	123,291	249,764	121,434	798,394	6,022	4,436	1,586
1995	720,461	323,458	238,122	85,336	220,360	114,664	716,194	4,267	3,124	1,143
1996	915,900	411,673	294,174	117,499	300,430	128,565	911,265	4,635	3,286	1,349
1997	798,378	303,938	213,331	90,607	321,008	112,158	795,830	2,548	1,439	1,109

Source

U.S. Immigration and Naturalization Service, *1997 Statistical Yearbook*, Table 4.

Documentation

The Immigration Act of 1990 revised the Preference System in 1992. It permitted increased total immigration to the United States under an overall flexible cap that ranged between 421,000 and 675,000, depending on the number of admissions in the previous year. It continued preferential immigration status for persons with a close family relationship with a U.S. citizen or legal permanent resident and persons with needed job skills. It continued to authorize admission categories exempt from the numerical cap. The major exempt categories are immediate relatives of U.S. citizens, refugees and asylees, and former illegal aliens who gained permanent resident status through the legalization provisions of the Immigration Reform and Control Act (IRCA) of 1986.

Series Ad967–969. Subject to the numerical cap. Family-sponsored preference immigrants include unmarried adult sons and daughters of U.S. citizens; spouses, children, and unmarried adult sons and daughters of permanent resident aliens; married sons and daughters of U.S. citizens together with their spouses and unmarried children; and adult siblings of U.S. citizens. Series Ad969 includes priority workers (persons of extraordinary ability, outstanding professors and researchers, and certain multinational executives and managers), professionals with advanced degrees or aliens with exceptional ability, skilled workers, needed unskilled workers, and investors.

Series Ad970. Includes spouses, unmarried children, and parents. They were admitted without reference to the numerical cap, though these admissions reduced the following year's cap.

Series Ad971. Refugees and asylees were not subject to the numerical cap, though these admissions are subject to separate limitations. See the text for Table Ad989–1004.

Series Ad972. Numerically large groups within this residual category are diversity and diversity transition immigrants, together with the dependents of IRCA legalizations.

Series Ad973–975. IRCA legalizations are not subject to the numerical cap.

TABLE Ad976–988   Immigrant-orphan admissions, by sex and place of birth: 1962–1997[1]

Contributed by Robert Barde, Susan B. Carter, and Richard Sutch

		Born in								Top two countries by number of immigrant-orphan admissions			
		Europe		Asia		Western Hemisphere		Other		First		Second	
	Total	Total	Female	Total	Female	Total	Female	Total	Female	Country	Number	Country	Number
	Ad976	Ad977	Ad978	Ad979	Ad980	Ad981	Ad982	Ad983	Ad984	Ad985	Ad986	Ad987	Ad988
Fiscal year	Number	Number	Number	Number	Number	Number	Number	Number	Number	—	Number	—	Number
1962	358	—	—	—	—	—	—	—	—	—	—	—	—
1963	1,312	—	—	—	—	—	—	—	—	—	—	—	—
1964	1,651	—	—	—	—	—	—	—	—	—	—	—	—
1965	1,448	—	—	—	—	—	—	—	—	—	—	—	—
1966	1,679	—	—	—	—	—	—	—	—	—	—	—	—
1967	1,905	—	—	—	—	—	—	—	—	—	—	—	—
1968	1,612	—	—	—	—	—	—	—	—	—	—	—	—
1969	2,080	—	—	—	—	—	—	—	—	—	—	—	—
1970	2,409	—	—	—	—	—	—	—	—	—	—	—	—
1971	2,724	—	—	—	—	—	—	—	—	—	—	—	—
1972	3,023	—	—	—	—	—	—	—	—	—	—	—	—
1973	4,015	—	—	—	—	—	—	—	—	—	—	—	—
1974	4,770	—	—	—	—	—	—	—	—	—	—	—	—
1975	5,633	—	—	—	—	—	—	—	—	—	—	—	—
1976	6,552	196	—	5,044	—	1,276	—	36	—	Korea	3,859	Colombia	554
(TQ)	1,998	70	—	1,489	—	428	—	11	—	Korea	988	Vietnam	323
1977	6,493	159	—	4,920	—	1,369	—	45	—	Korea	3,858	Colombia	575
1978	5,315	141	—	3,759	—	1,382	—	33	—	Korea	3,045	Colombia	599
1979	4,864	141	—	3,139	—	1,559	—	25	—	Korea	2,406	Colombia	626
1980	5,139	114	—	3,434	—	1,564	—	27	—	Korea	2,683	Colombia	653
1981	4,868	96	—	3,216	—	1,536	—	20	—	Korea	2,444	Colombia	628
1982	5,749	71	—	4,189	—	1,475	—	14	—	Korea	3,254	Colombia	534
1983	7,127	96	—	5,334	—	1,676	—	21	—	Korea	4,412	Colombia	608
1984	8,327	79	—	6,251	—	1,980	—	17	—	Korea	5,157	Colombia	595
1985	9,286	91	—	6,991	—	2,184	—	20	—	Korea	5,694	Colombia	622
1986	9,945	103	61	7,679	4,478	2,120	1,039	43	23	Korea	6,188	Philippines	634
1987	10,097	122	64	7,614	4,384	2,336	1,172	25	17	Korea	5,910	India	807
1988	9,120	99	51	6,484	3,613	2,494	1,276	43	26	Korea	4,942	Colombia	699
1989	7,948	120	66	5,112	2,742	2,667	1,346	49	25	Korea	3,552	Colombia	735
1990	7,088	232	129	3,823	1,989	2,973	1,499	60	31	Korea	2,603	Colombia	628
1991	9,008	2,761	1,495	3,194	1,675	2,996	1,578	57	32	Romania	2,552	Korea	1,817
1992	6,536	874	444	3,030	1,727	2,554	1,303	76	32	Korea	1,787	Soviet Union	432
1993	7,348	1,521	827	3,163	1,784	2,604	1,337	60	39	Korea	1,765	Russia	695
1994	8,200	2,370	1,262	3,689	2,285	2,052	1,064	91	49	Korea	1,757	Russia	1,324
1995	9,384	2,660	1,383	4,792	3,450	1,768	915	113	66	China	2,049	Russia	1,684
1996	11,316	3,568	1,776	6,097	4,661	1,555	747	93	52	China	3,318	Russia	2,328
1997	12,596	4,916	2,510	5,901	4,560	1,640	951	139	81	Russia	3,626	China	3,295

(TQ) indicates transitional quarter.

[1] Through 1976, fiscal year ending June 30; thereafter, fiscal year ending September 30.

Source

Figures for 1976–1981 are reported in U.S. Immigration and Naturalization Service, *1981 Statistical Yearbook of the Immigration and Naturalization Service*. Figures for earlier and later dates are reported in the current-year *Yearbook*. Revised and newly available data are also published in this annual volume.

Documentation

An "orphan" is a child, younger than age 16 at the time a petition is filed on his or her behalf, whose parents have died or disappeared, or who has been abandoned or otherwise separated from both parents. An orphan may also be a child whose parent is incapable of providing that child with proper care and who has, in writing, irrevocably released the child for emigration and adoption. The data in series Ad976 correspond to the U.S. Immigration and Naturalization Service (INS) category "immigrant orphans adopted by U.S. citizens." The INS title is misleading insofar as it suggests that the *action* taking place in the reference year is adoption. In fact, the action is the immigration of the alien child. Some children are adopted abroad and then immigrate. Others immigrate first and are then adopted by their U.S. parents. "Immigration" is recorded in the year in which the child is adjusted to permanent resident status.

The immigration of orphans was first made possible by legislation passed in 1961 under the Quota System. Data on country of birth of immigrant-orphans were first published in 1976; data on gender of immigrant-orphans were first published in 1986.

Series Ad985–988. Figures refer to the country of birth of the immigrant-orphans, not necessarily the country from which they emigrated.

TABLE Ad989–1004   Refugees and asylees granted permanent resident status, by legislative act: 1946–1997[1]

Contributed by Robert Barde, Susan B. Carter, and Richard Sutch

Fiscal year	Total	Presidential Directive of December 22, 1945	Displaced Persons Act of June 25, 1948	Orphans Act of July 29, 1953	Refugee Relief Act of August 7, 1953	Refugee Escapee Act of September 11, 1957	Hungarian Refugees Act of July 25, 1958	Azores and Netherlands Refugees Act of September 2, 1958
	Ad989	Ad990	Ad991	Ad992	Ad993	Ad994	Ad995	Ad996
	Number	Number	Number	Number	Number	Number	Number	Number
1946	2,551	2,551	—	—	—	—	—	—
1947	17,018	17,018	—	—	—	—	—	—
1948	20,755	20,755	0	—	—	—	—	—
1949	40,213	—	40,213	—	—	—	—	—
1950	132,810	—	132,810	—	—	—	—	—
1951	98,555	—	98,555	—	—	—	—	—
1952	121,964	—	121,964	—	—	—	—	—
1953	6,792	—	6,792	—	—	—	—	—
1954	7,302	—	6,082	399	821	—	—	—
1955	31,684	—	2,615	67	29,002	—	—	—
1956	75,958	—	485	—	75,473	—	—	—
1957	82,538	—	94	—	82,444	—	—	—
1958	3,956	—	76	—	1,012	2,868	—	—
1959	41,344	—	6	—	198	15,716	25,424	—
1960	13,408	—	0	—	43	5,679	5,067	1,187
1961	12,776	—	0	—	9	3,441	122	8,870
1962	7,115	—	3	—	15	1,520	51	5,472
1963	7,018	—	1	—	3	193	20	4,796
1964	6,041	—	—	—	1	29	17	1,888
1965	4,419	—	—	—	0	9	18	—
1966	8,828	—	—	—	0	7	18	—
1967	35,615	—	—	—	0	—	2	—
1968	100,822	—	—	—	0	—	7	—
1969	16,864	—	—	—	0	—	3	—
1970	22,215	—	—	—	0	—	0	—
1971	26,403	—	—	—	0	—	0	—
1972	28,795	—	—	—	0	—	2	—
1973	30,907	—	—	—	0	—	0	—
1974	25,650	—	—	—	0	—	0	—
1975	34,665	—	—	—	0	—	0	—
1976	48,576	—	—	—	0	—	0	—
1977 [2]	78,485	—	—	—	0	—	0	—
1978	132,781	—	—	—	1	—	0	—
1979	45,128	—	—	—	1	—	0	—
1980	88,057	—	—	—	0	—	0	—
1981	107,573	—	—	—	1	—	0	—
1982	156,601	—	—	—	0	—	1	—
1983	102,685	—	—	—	1	—	0	—
1984	92,127	—	—	—	—	—	0	—
1985	95,040	—	—	—	—	—	0	—
1986	104,383	—	—	—	—	—	0	—
1987	91,840	—	—	—	—	—	0	—
1988	81,719	—	—	—	—	—	0	—
1989	84,288	—	—	—	—	—	0	—
1990	97,364	—	—	—	—	—	0	—
1991	139,079	—	—	—	—	—	0	—
1992	117,037	—	—	—	—	—	0	—
1993	127,343	—	—	—	—	—	0	—
1994	121,434	—	—	—	—	—	0	—
1995	114,664	—	—	—	—	—	0	—
1996	128,565	—	—	—	—	—	0	—
1997	112,164	—	—	—	—	—	6	—

Notes appear at end of table

TABLE Ad989–1004 Refugees and asylees granted permanent resident status, by legislative act: 1946–1997
Continued

Fiscal year	Refugees Relatives Act of September 22, 1959	Fair Share Refugee Act of July 14, 1960	Refugees Conditional Entrants Act of October 3, 1965	Cuban Refugees Act of November 2, 1966	Indochinese Refugees Act of October 28, 1977	Refugee Parolees Act of October 5, 1978	Refugees Act of March 17, 1980	Asylees Act of March 17, 1980
	Ad997	Ad998	Ad999	Ad1000	Ad1001	Ad1002	Ad1003	Ad1004
	Number	Number	Number	Number	Number	Number	Number	Number
1946	—	—	—	—	—	—	—	—
1947	—	—	—	—	—	—	—	—
1948	—	—	—	—	—	—	—	—
1949	—	—	—	—	—	—	—	—
1950	—	—	—	—	—	—	—	—
1951	—	—	—	—	—	—	—	—
1952	—	—	—	—	—	—	—	—
1953	—	—	—	—	—	—	—	—
1954	—	—	—	—	—	—	—	—
1955	—	—	—	—	—	—	—	—
1956	—	—	—	—	—	—	—	—
1957	—	—	—	—	—	—	—	—
1958	—	—	—	—	—	—	—	—
1959	—	—	—	—	—	—	—	—
1960	1,432	—	—	—	—	—	—	—
1961	334	—	—	—	—	—	—	—
1962	54	—	—	—	—	—	—	—
1963	—	2,005	—	—	—	—	—	—
1964	—	4,106	—	—	—	—	—	—
1965	—	4,392	—	—	—	—	—	—
1966	—	2,359	6,444	—	—	—	—	—
1967	—	3,210	6,651	25,752	—	—	—	—
1968	—	2,637	6,658	91,520	—	—	—	—
1969	—	985	9,533	6,343	—	—	—	—
1970	—	20	9,863	12,332	—	—	—	—
1971	—	36	6,436	19,931	—	—	—	—
1972	—	4	9,801	18,988	—	—	—	—
1973	—	0	9,311	21,596	—	—	—	—
1974	—	0	8,722	16,928	—	—	—	—
1975	—	0	9,090	25,575	—	—	—	—
1976	—	0	14,080	34,496	—	—	—	—
1977 [2]	—	0	9,575	68,910	—	—	—	—
1978	—	29	10,309	28,296	94,146	—	—	—
1979	—	4	13,079	11,378	20,666	—	—	—
1980	—	9	12,222	6,021	22,497	46,058	—	1,250
1981	—	0	329	3,961	19,589	15,756	66,439	1,498
1982	—	2	—	1,965	13,666	48,826	90,282	1,859
1983	—	0	—	3,274	3,122	13,409	79,965	2,914
1984	—	0	—	3,460	875	7,657	74,528	5,607
1985	—	0	—	14,288	166	3,766	71,820	5,000
1986	—	0	—	30,152	136	1,720	67,375	5,000
1987	—	0	—	26,869	83	866	59,022	5,000
1988	—	1	—	10,993	42	437	64,801	5,445
1989	—	0	—	5,206	40	381	73,516	5,145
1990	—	0	—	5,730	33	153	86,511	4,937
1991	—	0	—	5,486	22	69	110,838	22,664
1992	—	1	—	5,365	29	82	100,902	10,658
1993	—	—	—	6,976	24	53	108,486	11,804
1994	—	—	—	8,316	11	20	107,104	5,983
1995	—	—	—	9,579	10	22	97,216	7,837
1996	—	—	—	20,131	5	9	98,383	10,037
1997	—	—	—	27,967	3	3	74,079	10,106

[1] Through 1976, fiscal year ending June 30; beginning 1977, fiscal year ending September 30.

[2] Fifteen-month period ending September 30.

Sources

1946–1985: *Statistical Yearbook of the INS, 1985*, Table REF 4.1. Figures for other years were obtained by subtracting annual cumulative totals from those of the previous year. Sources are: 1986: *Statistical Yearbook of the INS, 1986*, Table 34; 1987: *Statistical Yearbook of the INS, 1987*, Table 37; 1988: *Statistical Yearbook of the INS, 1988*, Table 37; 1989: *Statistical Yearbook of the INS, 1989*, Table 38; 1990: *Statistical Yearbook of the INS, 1990*, Table 26; 1991: *1991 Statistical Yearbook of the INS*, Table 29; 1992: *1992 Statistical Yearbook of the INS*, Table 32; 1993: *1993 Statistical Yearbook of the INS*, Table 32; 1994: *1994 Statistical Yearbook of the INS*, Table 32; 1995: *1995 Statistical Yearbook of the INS*, Table 31; 1996: *1996 Statistical Yearbook of the*

(continued)

TABLE Ad989–1004   Refugees and asylees granted permanent resident status, by legislative act: 1946–1997 *Continued*

INS, Table 31; *1997 Statistical Yearbook of the INS*, Table 31, and U.S. Immigration and Naturalization Service, *An Immigrant Nation: United States Regulation of Immigration, 1798–1991* (1991).

Documentation

A refugee is a person residing outside of his or her country of nationality who is unable or unwilling to return because of persecution or well-founded fear of persecution. Persecution or fear of persecution may be based on the alien's race, religion, nationality, political opinion, or membership in a particular social group. A refugee may be so designated before actually arriving in the United States. An asylee is a refugee located in the United States or at a U.S. port of entry. Refugees and asylees become eligible to adjust to lawful permanent residence status after one year of continuous residence in the United States. Refugees and asylees are classified as nonimmigrants when they are initially admitted to the United States, although they are not included in the official nonimmigrant admissions total (series Ad1014). These series display the number of refugees and asylees who adjust to permanent resident status in a given year. This is different from the number who arrive in the United States.

The United States first recognized refugees as a category for alien entry in 1946. Series Ad989 shows the total number of refugees and asylees granted permanent resident status annually beginning in that year.

The first refugee and asylee programs resulted from legislative acts passed in response to specific international events. These situation-specific programs, and the number of refugees and asylees admitted annually under them, are shown in series Ad990–1004.

Series Ad990, Presidential Directive of December 22, 1945. Allowed the president to admit more refugees than indicated by their home-country immigrant quotas, as established under the Quota Acts of 1924 and 1929.

Series Ad991, Displaced Persons Act of June 25, 1948. Sought to coordinate the Presidential Directive of 12/22/45 with the Quota Acts by allowing the president to "mortgage" individual country immigrant quotas into the future. By doing so, it allowed the immediate entry of refugees and asylees from war-ravaged areas with the proviso that countries with oversubscribed quotas would "repay" with low admissions at some time in the future. Many of the oversubscribed quotas, however, were later overlooked. The Displaced Persons Act was extended until 1952 and enabled 400,000 refugees to enter.

Series Ad992, Orphans Act of July 29, 1953. Allowed the adoption of alien orphans.

Series Ad993, Refugee Relief Act of August 7, 1953. Initiated a new policy whereby refugee admissions were not counted against the country quotas. Most visas issued under this law went to European refugees and so-called escapees from Communist countries.

Series Ad994, Refugee Escapee Act of September 11, 1957. Redefined a refugee-escapee as any alien who has fled from any Communist area or from the Middle East because of persecution on account of race, religion, or political opinion and established a program for their admission.

Series Ad995, Hungarian Refugees Act of July 25, 1958. In 1956, the U.S. witnessed the influx of a large number of Hungarians fleeing from Communist persecution after the Soviets crushed the Hungarian Revolution. The number of Hungarian escapees exceeded the number of visas available under the Refugee Relief Act of 1953. The Hungarian escapees were initially admitted as "parolees," that is, persons who do not qualify for admission under other provisions but are allowed into the United States for humanitarian reasons or because their entry is deemed to be in the public interest. The passage of the Hungarian Refugees Act reclassified them as permanent residents.

Series Ad996, Azores and Netherlands Refugees Act of September 2, 1958. Permitted visas to be made available to Portuguese unable to return to the Azores because of volcanic eruptions on that island and nationals of the Netherlands who were displaced from Indonesia.

Series Ad997, Refugees Relatives Act of September 22, 1959. Amended the Immigration and Naturalization Act of 1952, specifying five preference categories for the admittance of immigrants into the United States. The first preference earmarked up to 50 percent of the quotas for immigrants with special skills or abilities. The next two categories applied to family members of U.S. citizens, and the last two categories incorporated residual groups. This Act put more family members into preference portions of the immigration quotas in an effort to reunite families.

Series Ad998, Fair Share Refugee Act of July 14, 1960. Enabled the United States to participate in the World Refugee Year. The Act allowed World War II refugees and displaced persons who remained in camps under the mandate of the United Nations High Commissioner for Refugees to be allowed into the United States.

Series Ad999, Refugees Conditional Entrants Act of October 3, 1965. Passed in the wake of the Immigration and Naturalization Act of 1965, which expanded the number of preference categories to eight and reordered the priorities for admittance. Under the Immigration and Naturalization Act of 1965, categories one, two, four, and five admitted relatives of U.S. citizens; categories three and six admitted persons with special skills or with skills in short supply in the United States; and category seven allowed conditional entrants or persons fleeing racial, religious, or political persecution from any Communist or Communist-dominated country or from any country within the general area of the Middle East. The Act allocated 6 percent of the Eastern Hemisphere ceiling of 170,000 visas to these conditional entrants, half of which could be used for aliens currently residing in the United States who wished to adjust to permanent resident status.

Series Ad1000, Cuban Refugees Act of November 2, 1966. Passed in response to Fidel Castro's 1959 overthrow of the Cuban government, which produced a large number of Cuban refugees. Because no other mechanism existed for dealing with this large influx, the president admitted all Cuban refugees seeking refuge in the United States. The Attorney General exercised his authority to "parole" Cuban aliens into the United States. The Cuban Refugee Act allowed Cuban refugees to adjust to permanent resident status.

Series Ad1001, Indochinese Refugees Act of October 28, 1977. After the military collapse of South Vietnam and Cambodia in 1975, a large number of nationals from these countries and also from Laos were admitted to the United States as parolees. The Indochinese Refugee Act authorized these "parolees" to adjust their status and become permanent residents.

Series Ad1002, Refugee Parolees Act of October 5, 1978. Allowed the retroactive adjustment of the status of refugees who were paroled into the United States.

Series Ad1003–1004, Refugees Act of March 17, 1980 and Asylees Act of March 17, 1980. Two general laws that gave the president the authority to respond to worldwide political developments without special legislation. The president, in consultation with Congress, reviews the worldwide refugee situation before the beginning of each fiscal year, directing special attention to individuals who are of humanitarian concern to the United States, and then authorizing a number for admission in each category during the following year.

TABLE Ad1005–1013   Refugees and asylees admitted and granted permanent resident status, by continent of birth: 1948–1997[1]

Contributed by Robert Barde, Susan B. Carter, and Richard Sutch

		Granted permanent resident status							
		Total	Continent of birth						Country unknown or not reported
	Admitted		Europe	Asia	Africa	North America	South America	Oceania	
	Ad1005	Ad1006	Ad1007	Ad1008	Ad1009	Ad1010	Ad1011	Ad1012 [2]	Ad1013
Fiscal year	Number	Number	Number	Number	Number	Number	Number	Number	Number
1948 [3]	—	42,669	42,397	221	4	33	6	1	7
1955 [4]	—	49,237	45,615	3,342	177	83	7	8	6
1963 [5]	—	6,020	2,911	2,857	219	53	4	—	—
1965	—	4,419	3,076	208	1,134	0	0	1	68
1966	—	8,828	4,210	3,912	705	0	1	—	0
1967	—	35,615	7,596	2,323	805	24,874	15	—	2
1968	—	100,822	9,887	1,158	944	88,765	68	—	0
1969	—	16,864	9,410	547	720	6,182	5	—	0
1970	—	22,215	9,414	318	303	12,037	19	—	0
1971	—	26,403 [8]	5,967	645	269	19,505	13	—	5
1972	—	28,795	6,583	4,088	252	17,834	36	—	2
1973	—	30,907	6,679	3,193	326	20,673	35	—	1
1974	—	25,650	5,990	3,186	292	16,131	50	—	1
1975	—	34,665	5,571	3,637	144	25,228	84	—	1
1976 [6]	—	48,576	9,637	4,494	176	34,124	145	—	0
1977	—	78,485	6,520	3,451	85	68,171	258	—	0
1978	—	132,781	7,257	96,659	227	28,473	150	—	14
1979	—	45,128	4,353	28,070	414	12,240	50	1	0
1980	—	88,057	13,304	63,260	806	10,247	423	17	0
1981	—	107,573	11,306	89,362	1,643	5,030	227	2	3
1982	93,252	156,601	19,475	131,089	1,659	4,125	242	2	9
1983	57,064	102,685	10,226	85,298	2,456	4,547	156	2	0
1984	67,750	92,127	16,068	68,399	2,322	5,146	178	5	9
1985	62,477	95,040	14,008	62,035	3,201	15,667	124	5	0
1986	58,329	104,383	11,868	58,685	2,547	31,086	195	1	1
1987	66,803	91,840	9,684	52,600	1,719	27,677	155	3	2
1988	80,382	81,719	11,418	56,006	2,121	11,912	260	1	1
1989	98,563 [7]	84,288	18,348	56,751	2,269	6,740	175	1	4
1990	109,078 [7]	97,364	33,111	51,867	2,212	9,910	264	0	0
1991	96,587 [7]	139,079	62,946	49,762	4,731	21,317	320	1	2
1992	114,498 [7]	117,037	42,721	53,422	4,480	15,962	442	9	1
1993	107,926 [7]	127,343	53,195	51,783	5,944	15,926	461	34	0
1994	106,593 [7]	121,434	54,978	45,768	6,078	14,204	383	23	0
1995	98,520 [7]	114,664	46,998	43,314	7,527	16,265	497	63	0
1996	74,791	128,565	51,977	42,076	5,464	28,070	922	56	0
1997	69,276	112,158	39,795	30,835	7,651	32,898	890	59	30

[1] Through 1975, fiscal year ending June 30; thereafter, fiscal year ending September 30.

[2] Data for 1966–1978 included with other countries and country of birth unknown.

[3] Figures are the annual average for the five-year period 1946 through 1950.

[4] Figures are the annual average for the ten-year period 1951 through 1960.

[5] Figures are the annual average for the four-year period 1961 through 1964.

[6] Fifteen months ending September 30.

[7] Derived from the U.S. Department of State, Bureau of Refugee Services, as presented in the *1996 Statistical Yearbook of the Immigration and Naturalization Service*, Table 24.

Earlier issues of the *Yearbook* presented data derived from the Nonimmigrant Information System of the U.S. Immigration and Naturalization Service.

[8] Component series do not sum to total because of an error in the original that could not be corrected.

Sources

Annual figures not available before 1965. Figures for 1965 through 1978 calculated by subtraction from figures in the following volumes: *Annual Report of the Immigration and Naturalization Service* and *Statistical Yearbook of the Immigration and Naturalization Service*, various years.

TABLE Ad1014–1022   Nonimmigrants admitted, by class of admission: 1925–1996[1]

Contributed by Robert Barde, Susan B. Carter, and Richard Sutch

	Nonimmigrant admissions								Aliens admitted under special programs
	Total	Temporary visitor	Transit alien	Student	Foreign government and international official	Returning resident alien	Exchange visitor	Other	
	Ad1014 [2]	Ad1015	Ad1016	Ad1017	Ad1018	Ad1019 [3]	Ad1020	Ad1021	Ad1022
Fiscal year	Number	Number	Number	Number	Number	Number	Number	Number	Number
1925	164,121	35,326	22,697	1,397	1,930	64,617	—	38,154	—
1926	191,618	56,614	25,574	1,878	5,638	83,744	—	18,170	—
1927	202,826	60,508	28,312	524	4,769	95,502	—	13,211	—
1928	193,376	64,581	27,257	517	5,340	94,368	—	1,313	—
1929	199,649	64,310	27,776	561	5,273	100,879	—	850	—
1930	204,514	70,823	27,991	552	5,326	99,056	—	766	—
1931	183,540	55,636	32,169	272	3,951	91,201	—	311	—
1932	139,295	40,465	28,678	147	2,966	66,879	—	160	—
1933	127,660	36,899	22,693	877	4,053	62,460	—	678	—
1934	134,434	49,833	23,687	1,048	4,363	54,928	—	575	—
1935	144,765	61,633	24,931	1,377	5,194	50,885	—	745	—
1936	154,570	73,313	26,571	1,515	5,312	47,166	—	693	—
1937	181,640	89,455	31,822	1,828	6,493	51,223	—	819	—
1938	184,802	79,840	45,146	2,451	6,221	50,266	—	878	—
1939	185,333	88,309	44,115	2,182	7,777	42,196	—	754	—
1940	138,032	65,325	36,304	2,044	7,448	26,105	—	806	—
1941	100,008	34,660	18,749	1,766	9,269	35,246	—	318	—
1942	82,457	25,135	28,305	1,368	12,038	15,462	—	149	—
1943	81,117	27,700	31,906	1,021	16,328	4,102	—	60	—
1944	113,641	48,689	34,856	1,643	23,630	4,745	—	78	—
1945	164,247	107,729	28,174	2,866	18,054	6,896	—	528	—
1946	203,469	134,826	31,124	5,855	17,689	13,306	—	669	—
1947	366,305	214,558	96,825	11,003	20,320	22,818	—	781	—
1948	476,006	284,983	124,780	11,914	20,881	32,464	—	984	—
1949	447,272	299,083	81,615	10,481	18,445	36,984	—	664	—
1950	426,837	287,794	68,640	9,744	18,985	40,903	—	771	122,676
1951	465,106	314,205	72,027	7,355	26,407	44,212	—	900	130,630
1952	516,082	356,351	77,899	8,613	27,404	44,980	—	835	235,316
1953	485,714	306,715	67,684	13,533	30,614	50,397	12,584	1,166	192,132
1954	566,613	353,754	78,526	25,425	28,696	55,887	15,260	1,586	221,709
1955	620,946	401,090	71,301	27,192	32,291	61,442	16,077	1,803	351,191
1956	686,259	471,969	65,214	28,013	32,299	52,136	17,204	2,347	431,985
1957	758,858	537,760	107,399	30,760	34,904	10,617	17,849	2,713	466,713
1958	847,764	596,004	99,190	34,848	36,046	32,747	20,349	4,178	433,704
1959	1,024,945	689,416	116,814	35,583	38,308	85,915	24,293	5,277	464,128
1960	1,140,736	779,205	118,291	35,415	39,967	97,895	25,233	6,251	447,207
1961	1,220,315	858,472	106,888	35,072	40,087	103,931	24,346	7,256	312,991
1962	1,331,383	928,021	110,276	41,202	43,120	112,261	26,977	11,918	303,634
1963	1,507,091	1,067,444	105,815	38,991	45,961	135,701	30,002	19,700	243,120
1964	1,744,808	1,249,948	119,360	44,952	47,519	165,429	33,371	23,759	237,700
1965	2,075,967	1,498,979	142,686	50,435	52,570	203,235	33,768	26,425	155,761
1966	2,341,923	1,674,188	177,827	55,716	55,696	238,013	35,253	29,382	64,881
1967	2,608,193	1,848,999	204,936	63,370	61,302	284,330	38,630	36,616	57,720
1968	3,200,336	2,300,466	232,731	73,303	65,146	373,252	45,320	41,149	50,782
1969	3,645,328	2,682,008	210,543	90,486	64,896	441,082	47,175	46,186	43,527
1970	4,431,880	3,345,169	231,891	98,179	74,241	493,522	50,817	52,007	47,483
1971	4,403,761	3,460,771	225,736	102,984	75,346	363,513	69,821	36,110	42,142
1972	5,171,460	3,835,114	265,309	106,090	92,941	682,592	64,551	46,973	38,752
1973	5,977,324	4,528,471	264,577	100,012	87,292	789,410	63,568	59,700	37,294
1974	6,908,708	5,326,332	296,483	119,918	105,037	842,264	69,233	56,370	33,908
1975	7,083,937	5,587,410	272,987	117,960	101,050	799,951	63,378	51,528	25,434
1976	7,654,491	6,065,933	263,769	133,013	114,089	844,296	62,765	87,791	22,124
(TQ)	2,673,652	2,077,012	79,178	74,308	40,569	323,775	30,478	20,482	6,534
1977	8,036,916	6,381,436	252,124	171,004	109,451	897,719	71,503	64,679	21,671
1978	9,343,710	7,443,337	273,123	206,697	127,828	1,053,602	75,097	72,737	18,679
1979 [4]	7,060,082	5,731,091	176,338	120,614	75,988	798,878	42,332	48,952	18,213
1980	—	—	—	—	—	—	—	—	16,548
1981 [5]	11,756,903	10,650,592	214,218	271,861	138,933	—	108,023	253,352	16,190
1982 [5]	11,779,559	10,627,557	189,519	294,641	146,063	—	115,354	261,501	10,334
1983 [5]	9,849,458	8,532,257	269,009	318,186	151,421	—	118,543	272,239	—
1984 [6]	9,292,732	8,217,996	238,411	256,465	145,914	—	120,927	129,835	—

Notes appear at end of table

TABLE Ad1014–1022   Nonimmigrants admitted, by class of admission: 1925–1996   *Continued*

	Nonimmigrant admissions								Aliens admitted under special programs
	Total	Temporary visitor	Transit alien	Student	Foreign government and international official	Returning resident alien	Exchange visitor	Other	
	Ad1014 [2]	Ad1015	Ad1016	Ad1017	Ad1018	Ad1019 [3]	Ad1020	Ad1021	Ad1022
Fiscal year	Number	Number	Number	Number	Number	Number	Number	Number	Number
1985	9,539,880	8,405,409	236,537	285,496	147,393	—	141,213	129,449	—
1986	10,470,900	9,279,917	243,859	288,230	153,104	—	163,007	135,696	—
1987 [6]	12,272,286	11,019,343	264,138	288,006	148,982	—	183,029	148,472	—
1988 [6]	14,591,735	13,196,729	299,138	337,903	157,874	—	202,926	162,373	—
1989	16,144,576	14,667,303	293,364	360,771	162,963	—	217,458	176,665	—
1990	17,574,055	16,079,666	306,156	355,207	158,138	—	214,644	183,528	—
1991	18,962,520	17,385,990	364,187	314,392	162,281	—	224,157	279,907	—
1992	20,973,847	19,238,240	345,610	401,287	172,630	—	231,950	396,716	—
1993	21,566,404	19,879,443	331,208	403,272	174,876	—	239,405	184,381	—
1994	22,118,706	20,318,933	330,936	427,721	180,021	—	259,171	187,622	—
1995	22,640,539	20,886,867	320,333	395,480	175,588	—	240,364	173,916	—
1996	24,842,503	22,880,338	325,538	459,388	197,685	—	256,725	193,442	—

(TQ) indicates transitional quarter.

[1] Through 1976, fiscal year ending June 30; thereafter, fiscal year ending September 30.

[2] Through 1979, includes returning resident aliens; thereafter, excludes returning resident aliens.

[3] Classified as "immigrants" and included in series Ad1 prior to 1925.

[4] Data for first three quarters of fiscal year only.

[5] Excludes an unknown number of nonimmigrant admissions for which records were lost (see text).

[6] Figures excludes parolees, withdrawals and stowaways, and refugees processed as "nonimmigrants."

Sources

Series Ad 1014–1021: 1925–1970: U.S. Immigration and Naturalization Service (INS), *Annual Report* annual issues; 1971: *1971 INS Annual Report*, Table 16; 1972: *1972 INS Annual Report*, Table 16; 1973: *1973 INS Annual Report*, Table 16; 1974: *1974 INS Annual Report*, Table 16; 1975: *1975 INS Annual Report*, Table 16; 1976: *1976 INS Annual Report*, Table 16; 1977: *INS 1977 Statistical Yearbook*, Table 16; 1978: *INS 1978 Statistical Yearbook*, Table 16; 1979: *INS 1979 Statistical Yearbook*, Table 16; 1981: *INS 1981 Statistical Yearbook*, Table 64; 1982: *INS 1982 Statistical Yearbook*, Table NIM 1; 1983: *INS 1983 Statistical Yearbook*, Table NIM 2.1; 1984–1987: *INS 1987 Statistical Yearbook*, Table 43; 1988–1992: *INS 1992 Statistical Yearbook*, Table 40; 1993–1996: *INS 1997 Statistical Yearbook*, Table 39. Series Ad 1022: 1950–1955: *1955 INS Annual Report*, Table 17-A; 1956–1963: *1963 INS Annual Report*, Table 18; 1964–1970: *1970 INS Annual Report*, Table 18; 1971–TQ1976: *1976 INS Annual Report*, Table 18; 1977–1982, *INS 1982 Statistical Yearbook*, Table NIM 2.

Documentation

Nonimmigrants are aliens seeking temporary entry to the United States for some specific, authorized purpose. Series Ad1014 shows the total of these official nonimmigrant alien admissions. Before 1921, such aliens were admitted freely except for the two prohibitions that limited the free entry of all aliens. Chinese laborers were excluded by the Chinese Exclusion Act of 1882 and its extensions, which lasted until its repeal in 1943. Laborers under contract were barred by the Prohibition of Contract Labor Act of February 26, 1885. This law was repealed in 1952. The Emergency Quota Act of 1921 applied numerical limitations to the admission of nonimmigrants from countries outside the Western Hemisphere. These quotas applied to both temporary visitors and to those intending to make the United States their permanent home.

Data for the period beginning in the fourth quarter of fiscal year 1979 (July 1 through September 30, 1979) and running through the first quarter of fiscal year 1983 (October 1 through December 31, 1982) were lost by the U.S. Immigration and Naturalization Service (INS) because of data processing problems. Figures for the fourth quarter of fiscal year 1979 and all of fiscal year 1980 were never recovered. For fiscal years 1981 and 1982, data on the class of admission of nonimmigrants were reconstructed by the INS from administrative records for most (but not all) admissions. Where this information could not be reconstructed, class of admission was listed as unknown. For 1983, the INS provided data for the calendar year instead of the fiscal year. The INS described its change in the reporting period as an effort to cover its loss of data for the period October 1 through December 31, 1982. For fiscal year 1984, the INS returned to a reporting of data for fiscal years ending September 30. This resulted in a double printing of data for October 1 through December 31, 1983 (once in calendar year 1983 and then again in fiscal year 1984). If the number of admissions and their distribution across categories was not very different in the periods October 1 through December 31 of 1982 and 1983, then the official figures do not distort the overall trends.

Series Ad1015–1021. Provides the annual number of admissions according to the major legal classifications of nonimmigrants. These series show admissions, not persons. The same person will be counted several times if he or she makes repeat trips.

Series Ad1015. Includes both "temporary visitors for pleasure" (tourists) and "temporary visitors for business."

Series Ad1016. Primarily those who enter the United States while in transit to another destination.

Series Ad1017. Aliens pursuing a full-time course of study in the United States.

Series Ad1018. Ambassadors, public ministers, career diplomatic and consular officers, other accredited officials and their attendants, servants and personal employees, plus foreign government representatives to international organizations. Includes spouses and children.

Series Ad1019. Aliens with permanent resident status returning to the United States after a trip abroad. Prior to 1925, returning resident aliens were counted as immigrants. Beginning in 1981, the INS discontinued its recording of these arrivals.

Series Ad1020. Aliens coming to the United States for a temporary stay under the auspices of one of the training programs approved by the Secretary of State. They bring aliens as teachers, researchers, and trainees. Includes spouses and children.

Series Ad1021. Some numerically important categories in this residual group are "treaty traders and investors," together with their families. These are aliens who come to the United States under the provisions of some treaty of navigation or commerce to conduct substantial trade or to direct the operations of a personally owned business enterprise.

Series Ad1022. Aliens admitted under special programs were almost exclusively agricultural laborers admitted temporarily to relieve perceived labor shortages. From fiscal years 1942 to 1982, temporary workers entering under special programs were classified neither as official immigrants nor as official "nonimmigrants." They were counted separately and are not included in Series Ad 1014 or Series Ad1021. These special programs had their origins early in World War II with the Emergency Farm Labor Supply Program

(continued)

TABLE Ad1014–1022   Nonimmigrants admitted, by class of admission: 1925–1996   *Continued*

(Wayne D. Rasmussen, "A History of the Emergency Farm Labor Supply Program: 1943–47," *Agricultural Monograph* number 123, U.S. Department of Agriculture, September 1951). This program began with the admission of Mexican agricultural workers in 1942 under an informal agreement between the government of Mexico and the U.S. State Department and with the (retroactive) authority of the Farm Labor Supply Appropriation Act of 1943. The 1943 Act evolved through various extensions into the Mexican Braceros Program that lasted through the end of calendar year 1964.

During World War II, temporary agricultural workers were also admitted from Jamaica, Canada, the Bahamas, Barbados, and Newfoundland. A small number of temporary workers were admitted during the war as railroad track workers and "laborers in industries essential to the war effort" (U.S. Immigration and Naturalization Service, *Annual Report,* 1947, p. 14). The wartime programs for nonagricultural workers were closed in 1946. The program for agricultural workers, however, was continued (under a provision of the Immigration Act of 1917) and, with the renewed urgency created by the Korean War, was regularized with Public Law 78 of July 12, 1951, and the international Migrant Labor Agreement of 1951. Public Law 78 became the basis under which the Mexican Braceros Program operated. Although the overwhelming majority of farm workers admitted before end of the Braceros Program were from Mexico, there were significant flows from Canada (Newfoundland became part of Canada in 1949) and the British West Indies (an independent country that included Jamaica and Barbados from 1958 to 1962). After the Braceros Program ended in 1964, West Indian and Canadian agricultural workers predominated. Very small numbers were admitted from British Honduras (1952–1954, 1960, and 1962), British Guiana (1952, 1959, 1961–1963), the French West Indies (1956–1963), the Dutch West Indies (1963), Japan (1957–1965), and the Philippines (1958 and 1963). There was also a small special program for the admission of Basque sheepherders from Spain (1958–1982).

Beginning with fiscal year 1963, nonagricultural laborers were once again admitted under special programs. Most of these were Canadian "woodsmen," but there were also smaller flows of nonfarm workers into the U.S. Virgin Islands and Guam.

Fiscal year data on the number admitted under these programs for 1942 through 1949 seem not to exist. Calendar year data are presented in a special report to Congress (U.S. Department of Labor, "Admission of Aliens into the United States for Temporary Employment," U.S. House of Representatives, Committee on the Judiciary, Subcommittee 1, Administrative Publications (III) special series number 11, 1963, Table 2, p. 109; Table 8, p. 112; and Table 1, p. 132) as follows.

| Calendar Year | Number of Agricultural Workers Admitted | |
	Total	From Mexico
1942	4,203	4,203
1943	65,624	52,098
1944	84,419	62,170
1945	73,422	49,454
1946	51,347	32,043
1947	30,775	19,632
1948	44,916	35,345
1949	112,765	107,000
1950	76,525	67,500
1951	203,640	192,000
1952	210,210	197,100
1953	215,321	201,380
1954	320,737	309,033
1955	411,966	398,650
1956	459,850	445,197
1957	452,205	436,049
1958	447,513	432,857
1959	455,420	437,643
1960	334,729	315,846
1961	310,375	291,420
1962	217,028	194,978

Fiscal year data by country of origin are available in the original sources for series Ad 1022.

TABLE Ad1023–1029   Nonimmigrant workers admitted, by category: 1953–1996[1]

Contributed by Robert Barde, Susan B. Carter, and Richard Sutch

	Total	Temporary workers and industrial trainees		Intracompany transfers		Free-trade-agreement workers	
		Admissions	Spouses and children	Admissions	Spouses and children	Admissions	Spouses and children
	Ad1023	Ad1024	Ad1025	Ad1026	Ad1027	Ad1028	Ad1029
Fiscal year	Number	Number	Number	Number	Number	Number	Number
1953	3,021	3,021	—	—	—	—	—
1954	7,479	7,479	—	—	—	—	—
1955	9,750	9,750	—	—	—	—	—
1956	17,077	17,077	—	—	—	—	—
1957	16,856	16,856	—	—	—	—	—
1958	24,402	24,402	—	—	—	—	—
1959	29,339	29,339	—	—	—	—	—
1960	38,479	38,479	—	—	—	—	—
1961	44,263	44,263	—	—	—	—	—
1962	57,608	57,608	—	—	—	—	—
1963	63,477	63,477	—	—	—	—	—
1964	60,470	60,470	—	—	—	—	—
1965	67,869	67,869	—	—	—	—	—
1966	75,848	75,848	—	—	—	—	—
1967	70,010	70,010	—	—	—	—	—
1968	68,969	68,969	—	—	—	—	—
1969	62,952	62,952	—	—	—	—	—
1970	86,054	85,688	833	188	178	—	—
1971	69,480	54,686	7,658 [5]	3,618	3,518 [5]	—	—
1972	77,890	56,944	9,711	6,098	5,137	—	—
1973	84,294	57,023	9,873	8,893	8,505	—	—
1974	93,071	60,371	11,373	12,478	8,849	—	—
1975	89,673	56,766	10,568	12,570	9,769	—	—
1976	82,835	47,387	9,161	15,112	11,175	—	—
(TQ)	27,850	14,019	3,330	5,847	4,654	—	—
1977	89,000	45,000	9,000	20,000	15,000	—	—
1978	91,289	42,979	8,294	21,495	18,521	—	—
1979 [2]	65,889	32,942	5,285	16,423	11,239	—	—
1981 [3]	119,924	44,770	10,110	38,595	26,449	—	—
1982 [3]	144,924	52,482	11,453	47,893	33,096	—	—
1983 [3,4]	187,803	72,411	10,781	62,025	42,586	—	—
1984	183,184	68,730	10,831	62,359	41,264	—	—
1985	194,383	74,869	12,632	65,349	41,533	—	—
1986	207,087	85,359	13,710	66,925	41,093	—	—
1987	220,316	97,334	16,211	65,673	41,098	—	—
1988	234,792	113,424	19,673	63,849	37,846	—	—
1989	266,052	138,703	23,807	62,390	38,335	2,677	140
1990	276,716	139,587	28,687	63,180	39,375	5,293	594
1991	231,606	161,291	34,803	70,505	42,529	8,123	777
1992	314,177	163,137	40,009	75,315	45,464	12,531	1,271
1993	353,819	162,976	39,704	82,606	49,537	16,610	2,386
1994	414,302	185,988	43,207	98,189	56,048	24,837	6,033
1995	447,991	196,760	46,380	112,124	61,621	23,904	7,202
1996	529,455	227,440	53,572	140,457	73,305	26,987	7,694

(TQ) indicates transitional quarter.

[1] Through 1976, fiscal year ending June 30; thereafter, fiscal year ending September 30, except where noted.

[2] First three quarters only.

[3] Figures exclude an unknown number of admissions in this category whose records were lost (see text).

[4] Calendar year.

[5] Figures are incomplete.

Sources

1953–1970: U.S. Immigration and Naturalization Service, *Annual Report* annual issues. 1971: *1971 INS Annual Report*, Table 16. 1972: *1972 INS Annual Report*, Table 16. *1973: 1973 INS Annual Report*, Table 16. 1974: *1974 INS Annual Report*, Table 16. 1975: *1975 INS Annual Report*, Table 16. 1976: *1976 INS Annual Report*, Table 16. 1977: *INS 1977 Statistical Yearbook*, Table 16. 1978: *INS 1978 Statistical Yearbook*, Table 16. 1979: *INS 1979 Statistical Yearbook*, Table 16. 1981: *INS 1981 Statistical Yearbook*, Table 64. 1982: *INS 1982 Statistical Yearbook*, Table NIM 1. 1983: *INS 1983 Statistical Yearbook*, Table NIM 2.1. 1984–1987: *INS 1987 Statistical Yearbook*, Table 43. 1988–1992: *INS 1992 Statistical Yearbook*, Table 40. 1993–1996: *INS 1996 Statistical Yearbook*, Table 39, *INS 1997 Statistical Yearbook*, Table 39.

Documentation

Nonimmigrant workers are aliens admitted to the United States for a limited period of time to take up some specified employment. At the end of the employment period, these workers are expected to return to their home countries. At the completion of one employment period, nonimmigrant workers may apply for another. They may bring their immediate family members (spouses and unmarried dependent children) with them.

(continued)

TABLE Ad1023–1029 Nonimmigrant workers admitted, by category: 1953–1996 *Continued*

Temporary workers, defined broadly to include all aliens coming to the United States for a relatively brief period of work and then returning to their home countries, have been an important feature of foreign migration throughout U.S. history. Before 1921, such temporary workers were admitted freely except for the two prohibitions that limited the free entry of all aliens: Chinese laborers were excluded by the Chinese Exclusion Act of 1882 and its extensions, which lasted until the Act's repeal in 1943, and laborers under contract were barred by the Contract Labor Law of 1885, which was repealed in 1952. The Emergency Quota Act of 1921 applied numerical limitations on admission from countries outside the Western Hemisphere, and these quotas applied to both temporary workers and those intending to become permanent residents, although actors, artists, lecturers, singers, nurses, ministers, professors, domestic servants, and practitioners of other recognized, learned professions were admitted for temporary work periods on a nonquota basis.

In 1924, the Immigration Act defined the term "immigrant" and placed temporary workers in the category of "nonimmigrant temporary visitors" along with tourists and other temporary visitors (see series Ad1014). There were no restrictions on the number or occupations of such nonimmigrants who could be admitted, beyond those of the Chinese Exclusion Act and the Contract Labor Law.

In 1943, the Contract Labor Law was amended to permit the contractual importation of temporary agricultural laborers from North, Central, and South America to relieve wartime labor shortages (see series Ad1022).

Series Ad1023. Sum of temporary workers and industrial trainees, intracompany transfers, free-trade (NAFTA) workers and their spouses and families. Excludes officials of foreign governments, representatives to international organizations, and their families (see series Ad1027). The unit of observation is the *event* of entering the United States, not the number of different persons who enter. A single person will be counted several times if he or she makes repeat trips. Data for the period beginning in the fourth quarter of fiscal year 1979 (July 1 through September 30, 1979) and running through the first quarter of fiscal year 1983 (October 1 through December 30, 1982) were lost by the U.S. Immigration and Naturalization Service (INS) because of data processing problems. Figures for the fourth quarter of fiscal year 1979 and all of fiscal year 1980 were never recovered. For fiscal years 1981 and 1982, data on the class of admission were reconstructed from administrative records for most admissions. Where this information could not be reconstructed, class of admission was listed as unknown. For 1983, the INS provided data for the calendar year instead of the fiscal year. The INS de-

scribed its change in the reporting period as an effort to cover its loss of data for the period October 1 through December 31, 1982. For fiscal year 1984, the INS returned to a reporting of data for fiscal years ending September 30. This resulted in a double printing of data for October 1 through December 31, 1983 (once in calendar year 1983 and then again in fiscal year 1984). If the number of admissions and its distribution across categories were not very different in the periods October 1 through December 31 of 1982 and 1983, then the official figures do not distort the overall trends.

Series Ad1024. Alien workers coming to the United States to work for a temporary period. The provisions regarding the entry of temporary workers were established by the Immigration and Nationality Act of 1952, which restricted the admission of temporary workers to three classes: persons of "distinguished merit or ability" (called "specialty occupations" since fiscal 1992), persons performing "services unavailable in the United States" (defined to mean that unemployed residents capable of performing such labor cannot be found), and "industrial trainees" (when the training involved could not be obtained in the worker's home country). Nonimmigrants in these three categories were granted H1, H2, and H3 visas, respectively. Beginning in 1988, the official category was expanded to include agricultural workers (who were issued H2A visas). Such workers were previously admitted and counted separately (see series Ad1022). Revised by the Immigration Reform and Control Act of 1986 (IRCA), the Immigration Nursing Relief Act of 1989, and the Immigration Act of 1990 to create new classes of nonimmigrant admission.

Series Ad1025. This class (H4 and L2 visas) was added in 1970. Kin of temporary workers and intracompany transfers have been separately recorded since 1970 although the figures for fiscal year 1971 are incomplete. Prior to 1970, the accompanying family members were included with temporary visitors and no estimates of their numbers are available.

Series Ad1026–1027. Employees of international companies who enter the United States temporarily to provide managerial or specialized services. This new class of nonimmigrant admissions was added by an act in 1970. Before 1970, intracompany transfers were classified as temporary workers.

Series Ad1028–1029. Includes workers admitted under the U.S.-Canadian Free-Trade-Agreement of 1988 and the North American Free Trade Agreement of 1993 (NAFTA). Family members were permitted to accompany these persons and their entries are recorded in the totals. Free-trade-agreement workers were issued TC and TN visas; their spouses and children were issued TB and TD visas.

NATURALIZATION

Robert Barde, Susan B. Carter, and Richard Sutch

TABLE Ad1030–1037   Aliens naturalized, by provision: 1907–1997[1]

Contributed by Robert Barde, Susan B. Carter, and Richard Sutch

	Aliens naturalized							Petitions for naturalization denied
	Total	Under general naturalization provisions	Because of marriage to U.S. citizens	As children of U.S. citizens	As military	For other reasons	For reasons not reported	
	Ad1030	Ad1031	Ad1032	Ad1033	Ad1034	Ad1035	Ad1036	Ad1037
Fiscal year	Number	Number	Number	Number	Number	Number	Number	Number
1907	7,941	—	—	—	—	—	—	250
1908	25,975	—	—	—	—	—	—	3,330
1909	38,374	—	—	—	—	—	—	6,341
1910	39,448	—	—	—	—	—	—	7,781
1911	56,683	—	—	—	—	—	—	9,017
1912	70,310	—	—	—	—	—	—	9,635
1913	83,561	—	—	—	—	—	—	10,891
1914	104,145	—	—	—	—	—	—	13,133
1915	91,848	—	—	—	—	—	—	13,691
1916	87,831	—	—	—	—	—	—	11,927
1917	88,104	—	—	—	—	—	—	9,544
1918	151,449	—	—	—	63,993	87,456	—	12,182
1919	217,358	—	—	—	128,335	89,023	—	13,119
1920	177,683	—	—	—	51,972	125,711	—	15,586
1921	181,292	—	—	—	17,636	163,656	—	18,981
1922	170,447	—	—	—	9,468	160,979	—	29,076
1923	145,084	—	—	—	7,109	137,975	—	24,884
1924	150,510	—	—	—	10,170	140,340	—	18,324
1925	152,457	—	—	—	0	152,457	—	15,613
1926	146,331	—	—	—	92	146,239	—	13,274
1927	199,804	—	—	—	4,311	195,493	—	11,946
1928	233,155	—	—	—	5,149	228,006	—	12,479
1929	224,728	—	—	—	531	224,197	—	11,848
1930	169,377	—	—	—	1,740	167,637	—	9,068
1931	143,495	—	—	—	3,224	140,271	—	7,514
1932	136,600	—	—	—	2	136,598	—	5,478
1933	113,363	—	—	—	995	112,368	—	4,703
1934	113,669	—	—	—	2,802	110,867	—	1,133
1935	118,945	—	—	—	0	118,945	—	2,765
1936	141,265	—	—	—	481	140,784	—	3,124
1937	164,976	—	—	—	2,053	162,923	—	4,042
1938	162,078	—	—	—	3,936	158,142	—	4,854
1939	188,813	—	—	—	3,638	185,175	—	5,630
1940	235,260	—	—	—	2,760	232,500	—	6,549
1941	277,294	—	—	—	1,547	275,747	—	7,769
1942	270,364	—	—	—	1,602	268,762	—	8,348
1943	318,933	—	—	—	37,474	281,459	—	13,656
1944	441,979	—	—	—	49,213	392,766	—	7,297
1945	231,402	137,729	69,526	182	22,695	1,270	—	9,782
1946	150,062	93,346	40,190	118	15,213	1,195	—	6,575
1947	93,904	46,339	27,066	245	16,462	3,792	—	3,953
1948	70,150	34,347	28,898	419	1,070	5,416	—	2,887
1949	66,594	24,566	35,131	448	2,456	3,993	—	2,271
1950	66,346	19,403	40,684	499	2,067	3,693	—	2,276
1951	54,716	14,864	36,433	487	975	1,957	—	2,395
1952	88,655	26,920	58,027	760	1,585	1,363	—	2,163
1953	92,051	46,793	42,088	698	1,575	897	—	1,122
1954	117,831	86,166	15,977	1,208	13,745	735	—	2,084
1955	209,526 [2]	173,954	20,460	2,600	11,958 [2]	554	—	4,571
1956	145,885	117,161	18,224	2,865	7,204	431	—	3,935
1957	138,043	114,827	18,212	3,779	845	380	—	2,948
1958	119,866	94,380	19,353	4,966	916	251	—	2,688
1959	103,931	77,230	19,512	5,632	1,308	249	—	2,208

Notes appear at end of table

(continued)

TABLE Ad1030–1037 Aliens naturalized, by provision: 1907–1997 *Continued*

		Aliens naturalized						Petitions for naturalization denied
	Total	Under general naturalization provisions	Because of marriage to U.S. citizens	As children of U.S. citizens	As military	For other reasons	For reasons not reported	
	Ad1030	Ad1031	Ad1032	Ad1033	Ad1034	Ad1035	Ad1036	Ad1037
Fiscal year	Number	Number	Number	Number	Number	Number	Number	Number
1960	119,442	91,548	19,799	6,149	1,594	352	—	2,277
1961	132,450	104,341	18,674	7,416	1,719	300	—	3,175
1962	127,307	98,739	17,379	8,723	2,335	131	—	3,557
1963	124,178	93,325	19,048	9,136	2,560	109	—	2,436
1964	112,234	82,621	17,867	9,056	2,605	85	—	2,309
1965	104,299	76,630	16,602	7,914	3,085	68	—	2,059
1966	103,059	76,214	16,448	7,695	2,561	141	—	2,029
1967	104,902	78,544	16,778	6,740	2,691	149	—	2,008
1968	102,726	76,377	17,156	6,579	2,438	176	—	1,962
1969	98,709	73,489	14,346	5,271	5,458	145	—	2,043
1970	110,399	79,761	14,899	5,023	10,616	100	—	1,979
1971	108,407	79,491	14,162	5,116	9,554	84	—	2,028
1972	116,215	89,475	13,211	4,961	8,476	92	—	1,837
1973	120,740	94,039	13,380	5,461	7,796	64	—	1,708
1974	131,655	103,450	14,768	6,511	6,848	78	—	2,210
1975	141,537	113,289	15,416	6,568	6,214	50	—	2,300
1976	142,504	114,653	15,138	7,038	5,632	43	—	2,231
(TQ)	48,218	40,261	4,374	2,054	1,513	16	—	568
1977	159,873	131,331	15,394	7,787	5,305	56	—	2,845
1978	173,535	143,133	16,207	9,035	5,126	34	—	3,894
1979	164,150	132,533	15,293	10,408	5,875	41	—	3,987
1980	157,938	129,404	13,904	9,960	4,595	75	—	4,370
1981	166,317	139,909	14,147	8,083	4,090	88	—	4,316
1982	173,688	146,785	14,929	8,333	3,617	24	—	3,994
1983	178,948	154,990	13,146	7,485	3,196	57	74	3,160
1984	197,023	168,720	14,201	9,126	2,965	66	1,945	3,373
1985	244,717	214,831	14,461	9,059	3,266	43	3,057	3,610
1986	280,623	251,035	14,416	9,859	2,901	42	2,370	5,980
1987	227,008	204,250	12,349	7,428	2,402	73	506	6,771
1988	242,063	219,480	13,338	6,644	2,296	79	226	4,304
1989	233,777	210,673	14,346	6,087	1,954	92	625	5,200
1990	270,101	225,319	15,126	6,339	1,630	61	21,626	6,516
1991	308,058	269,594	21,833	7,901	1,804	45	6,881	6,268
1992	240,252	197,559	19,151	5,743	5,702	66	12,031	19,293
1993	314,681	273,857	22,392	6,759	7,069	203	4,401	39,931
1994	434,107	367,960	25,935	7,848	6,194	307	25,863	40,561
1995	488,088	445,835	23,384	4,709	3,862	241	10,057	46,067
1996	1,044,689	890,949	28,501	6,948	1,261	83	116,947	229,842
1997	598,225	513,139	21,139	439	538	39	62,931	130,676

(TQ) indicates transitional quarter.

[1] Through 1976, fiscal year ending June 30; thereafter, fiscal year ending September 30.

[2] Includes aliens in U.S. armed forces naturalized abroad.

Sources

1907–1930: U.S. Bureau of Naturalization, *Annual Report of the Commissioner of Naturalization*. 1931–1997: U.S. Immigration and Naturalization Service, *Annual Reports* and *Statistical Yearbooks*, annual issues.

Documentation

The Basic Naturalization Act of 1906 required all courts conducting naturalization proceedings to file with a central federal agency a copy of each declaration of intention and petition of naturalization filed and of each certificate of naturalization issued. Prior to that time, individual courts kept records of naturalizations, but no national data were compiled. The data reported here refer to naturalizations that take place in court ceremonies or at administrative hearings. They do not include the naturalizations of children whose parents request a certificate of citizenship or those of aliens who become U.S. citizens through the legislative process. One example of the legislative process occurred after the dissolution of the Trust Territory of the Pacific through which the Northern Mariana Islands became a commonwealth of the United States, making its residents U.S. citizens.

In the early laws, the right to become naturalized was limited to white persons and petitions of persons of ineligible races were denied. Gradually, such restrictions were removed with respect to blacks, Filipinos, races indigenous to North and South America and adjacent islands, Chinese, and Guamanians. In 1952, the Immigration and Nationality Act removed all racial restrictions to naturalization.

Series Ad1031. The general naturalization provisions set the basic requirements concerning age, admission, residency, skill, and character required for naturalization.

Series Ad1032. The Married Woman's Act of September 22, 1922 ("Cable Act") legalized the judicial naturalization of married women and established a special, shorter residence requirement for women married to U.S. citizens. Prior to the passage of this law, married women were ineligible for judicial naturalization. A May 24, 1934, act extended the special consideration to husbands of U.S. citizens.

Series Ad1033. The Act of October 14, 1940, was the first to make special provisions for the naturalization of the minor children of U.S. citizens. The data include adopted children.

TABLE Ad1030–1037   Aliens naturalized, by provision: 1907–1997   *Continued*

Series Ad1034. Special provisions for the naturalization of certain aliens who had served in the U.S. armed forces were first allowed by the Act of May 9, 1918. Subsequent amendments provided for streamlined naturalization procedures for veterans of World War I and prior conflicts and, later, gave special consideration to those serving in World War II and the Korean and Vietnam conflicts.

Series Ad1035. Includes special provisions for persons who perform ministerial or priestly functions of a religious order in the United States, persons who served on certain U.S. vessels, former U.S. citizens who lost citizenship by marriage, and other categories.

Series Ad1036. In 1996 and 1997 the "not reported" category for naturalization was unusually large. These naturalizations took place in areas that were still recording their data manually. The INS did not transfer all of the

detail from these handwritten records into its computerized Central Index System (CIS).

Series Ad1037. Statistics on petitions denied have been compiled since 1907. The Basic Naturalization Act of 1906 and subsequent naturalization laws specified the eligibility requirements for naturalization. Petitions may be denied by the courts at the final naturalization hearing for aliens who fail to meet the prerequisites. Included among the reasons for denial are lack of knowledge and understanding of the history, principles, and form of government of the United States, failure to establish good moral character, lack of attachment to the Constitution of the United States, inability to speak (read, write) the English language, failure to establish lawful admission to the United States or to meet residence requirements, and so forth.

TABLE Ad1038–1050   Aliens naturalized, by sex and country of former allegiance: 1923–1997[1]

Contributed by Robert Barde, Susan B. Carter, and Richard Sutch

				Country of former allegiance			
				In Northwestern Europe	In Central Europe	In Eastern Europe	In Southern Europe
	Total	Male	Female				
	Ad1038	Ad1039	Ad1040	Ad1041	Ad1042	Ad1043	Ad1044
Year	Number	Number	Number	Number	Number	Number	Number
1923	145,084	139,073 [4]	6,011 [4]	29,107	56,112	22,897	28,392
1924	150,510	135,739	14,771	28,780	55,915	23,348	32,232
1925	152,457	133,881	18,576	29,006	55,262	23,154	31,671
1926	146,331	121,561	24,770	28,317	49,696	23,158	33,750
1927	199,804	165,833	33,971	37,293	65,592	27,399	55,924
1928	233,155	181,875	51,280	46,059	72,111	34,962	63,989
1929	224,728	167,665	57,063	50,554	72,267	33,652	53,234
1930	169,377	120,572	48,805	38,915	56,540	24,046	37,481
1931	143,495	106,715	36,780	38,465	48,041	17,428	27,793
1932	136,600	95,901	40,699	39,123	43,334	14,884	24,851
1933	113,363	78,293	35,070	40,795	37,068	12,544	19,498
1934	113,669	82,465	31,204	39,481	38,859	11,476	20,349
1935	118,945	82,182	36,763	44,605	39,554	11,825	21,171
1936	141,265	86,777	54,488	54,852	47,289	14,781	22,194
1937	164,976	97,696	67,280	58,002	55,789	18,970	29,169
1938	162,078	92,041	70,037	55,359	51,359	19,809	32,235
1939	188,813	113,934	74,879	62,430	59,636	22,209	40,452
1940	235,260	132,406	102,854	78,357	75,024	29,146	47,236
1941	277,294	136,348	140,946	96,375	86,122	35,844	51,819
1942	270,364	112,040	158,324	117,607	71,762	41,586	31,047
1943	318,933 [3]	157,663 [5]	161,270 [5]	122,708	86,365	42,012	51,758
1944	441,979 [3]	202,698 [5]	239,281 [5]	114,801	139,304	48,382	122,638
1945	231,402 [3]	116,691 [5]	114,711 [5]	57,997	82,195	23,948	51,629
1946	150,062 [3]	76,296	73,766	41,772	46,802	14,481	30,336
1947	93,904 [3]	52,998	40,906	27,017	24,220	7,281	15,661
1948	70,150	33,147	37,003	18,834	17,495	6,150	13,059
1949	66,594	27,865	38,729	20,782	14,471	5,244	11,716
1950	66,346	25,745	40,601	20,260	13,946	4,300	12,200
1951	54,716	18,711	36,005	17,069	11,864	3,485	8,503
1952	88,655	28,597	60,058	23,688	25,933	5,392	13,360
1953	92,051	34,657	57,394	23,238	26,676	5,440	13,507
1954	117,831 [3]	54,477	63,354	31,085	28,341	7,848	16,024
1955	209,526 [3]	95,850	113,676	46,253	62,557	22,795	23,955
1956	145,885 [3]	64,962	80,923	28,183	47,186	21,017	14,200
1957	138,043	60,289	77,754	25,878	47,656	18,062	15,762
1958	119,866	51,350	68,516	23,992	42,358	11,520	13,725
1959	103,931	43,719	60,212	21,842	32,594	7,975	12,202
1960	119,442	50,896	68,546	22,978	33,796	8,094	20,248
1961	132,450	58,791	73,655	22,168	34,858	8,908	27,188
1962	127,307	60,988	66,319	21,586	34,841	6,155	25,720
1963	124,178	58,303	65,875	23,861	37,789	4,952	18,338
1964	112,234	51,408	60,826	20,807	29,180	3,878	17,771

Notes appear at end of table

(continued)

TABLE Ad1038–1050   Aliens naturalized, by sex and country of former allegiance: 1923–1997   *Continued*

				Country of former allegiance			
	Total	Male	Female	In Northwestern Europe	In Central Europe	In Eastern Europe	In Southern Europe
	Ad1038	Ad1039	Ad1040	Ad1041	Ad1042	Ad1043	Ad1044
Year	Number	Number	Number	Number	Number	Number	Number
1965	104,299	48,495	55,804	19,205	26,734	3,461	16,620
1966	103,059	46,536	56,523	18,391	23,837	2,736	17,446
1967	104,902	46,014	58,888	18,487	23,059	2,832	17,156
1968	102,726	45,102	57,624	17,734	22,054	3,258	15,221
1969	98,709	45,177	53,532	16,065	18,822	2,725	14,235
1970	110,399	52,679	57,720	14,976	18,002	2,678	13,122
1971	108,407	51,072	57,335	13,621	16,164	2,692	12,588
1972	116,215	55,416	60,799	12,174	14,609	2,399	15,752
1973	120,740	56,901	63,839	12,940	14,529	2,123	18,143
1974	131,655	60,823	70,832	13,332	13,950	1,693	19,039
1975	141,537	66,587	74,950	12,971	14,870	2,015	20,412
1976	142,504	66,007	76,497	12,878	13,979	1,888	20,577
(TQ)	48,218	22,244	25,974	3,725	3,679	544	5,101
1977	159,873	73,377	86,496	13,663	12,961	1,920	18,936
1978	173,535	78,746	94,789	13,122	13,382	2,328	18,801
1979	164,150	74,706	89,444	11,396	10,662	2,265	17,437
1980	157,938	70,653	87,285	10,028	8,875	2,620	13,668
1981	166,317	—	—	10,476	8,262	3,642	11,836
1982	173,688	—	—	10,877	8,187	4,343	12,238
1983	178,948	83,446	95,344	10,391	8,321	3,763	10,416
1984	197,023	92,416	104,228	10,167	8,306	5,169	10,286
1985	244,717	115,114	124,425	11,972	9,732	10,335	12,388
1986	280,623	133,982	140,087	11,760	9,859	11,186	10,695
1987	227,008	109,548	108,583	9,748	8,006	9,185	8,689
1988	242,063	120,528	119,599	10,002	9,543	7,678	9,128
1989	233,777	—	—	10,730	10,140	5,540	8,669
1990	270,101	—	—	11,443	11,749	6,147	7,925
1991	308,058	—	—	13,694	11,102	6,759	6,253
1992	240,252	120,430	114,273	10,966	9,418	4,484	5,913
1993	314,681	155,910	157,980	14,098	11,755	5,899	10,410
1994	434,107	205,671	221,367	21,519	15,532	11,400	15,464
1995	488,088	230,754	253,698	20,362	16,022	21,585	11,036
1996	1,044,689	457,273	522,101	28,017	23,130	42,083	15,736
1997	598,225	257,587	303,497	15,900	12,812	29,320	8,818

				Country of former allegiance			
	In Asia	Canada	Mexico	Cuba	In the Americas not elsewhere classified	Countries not elsewhere classified
	Ad1045	Ad1046 [2]	Ad1047	Ad1048	Ad1049	Ad1050
Year	Number	Number	Number	Number	Number	Number
1923	— [6]	6,546	—	—	— [6]	2,030
1924	— [6]	5,765	—	—	270	4,200
1925	— [6]	7,013	—	—	290	6,061
1926	— [6]	5,078	—	—	283	6,049
1927	— [6]	5,237	—	—	455	7,904
1928	1,334	7,712	—	—	506	6,482
1929	1,445	8,223	—	—	664	4,689
1930	993	7,566	—	—	651	3,185
1931	822	7,173	—	—	989	2,784
1932	676	10,144	—	—	721	2,867
1933	706	—	—	—	780	1,972
1934	703	—	—	—	896	1,905
1935	760	—	—	—	987	43
1936	901	—	—	—	1,220	28
1937	1,290	—	—	—	1,710	46
1938	1,311	—	—	—	1,976	29
1939	1,331	—	—	—	2,709	46

Notes appear at end of table

TABLE Ad1038–1050   Aliens naturalized, by sex and country of former allegiance: 1923–1997   *Continued*

	Country of former allegiance					
	In Asia	Canada	Mexico	Cuba	In the Americas not elsewhere classified	Countries not elsewhere classified
	Ad1045	Ad1046 [2]	Ad1047	Ad1048	Ad1049	Ad1050
Year	Number	Number	Number	Number	Number	Number
1940	1,523	—	—	—	3,930	44
1941	1,844	—	—	—	5,249	41
1942	2,075	—	—	—	6,247	40
1943	6,133	—	—	—	9,866	91
1944	5,592	—	—	—	11,099	163
1945	2,545	—	—	—	8,590	4,498
1946	3,450	—	—	—	7,144	6,077
1947	11,741	—	—	—	4,676	3,308
1948	7,201	3,860	—	—	3,183	368
1949	4,993	5,347	—	—	3,607	434
1950	4,802	5,882	—	—	4,133	823
1951	2,886	5,872	—	—	3,827	1,210
1952	3,749	10,004	—	—	4,548	1,981
1953	4,966	10,303	—	—	5,181	2,740
1954	12,170	13,062	—	—	7,210	2,091
1955	16,000	18,151	—	—	15,321	4,494
1956	10,412	11,539	—	—	10,795	2,553
1957	7,548	10,891	—	—	8,977	3,269
1958	7,496	10,211	—	—	8,463	2,101
1959	8,313	10,324	—	—	8,804	1,877
1960	11,071	10,215	—	—	10,606	2,434
1961	12,308	10,033	—	—	14,178	2,809
1962	14,573	9,272	—	—	12,533	2,627
1963	15,253	9,944	—	—	11,602	2,439
1964	15,724	9,479	—	—	12,442	2,953
1965	14,680	8,489	—	—	12,273	2,837
1966	14,369	8,579	—	—	14,858	2,843
1967	14,259	8,120	—	—	17,542	3,447
1968	14,980	6,984	—	—	19,264	3,231
1969	15,362	6,387	—	—	22,202	2,911
1970	16,466	6,340	—	—	36,032	2,783
1971	17,839	5,915	6,361	19,754	10,624	2,849
1972	28,097	4,835	5,850	18,397	11,206	2,896
1973	30,349	4,739	5,507	17,415	12,232	2,763
1974	37,804	4,084	5,206	18,394	14,945	3,208
1975	44,942	3,548	5,781	15,546	16,641	4,811
1976	46,772	3,384	5,602	15,138	17,316	4,970
(TQ)	15,072	1,077	1,505	11,137	5,098	1,280
1977	56,473	3,759	6,301	20,506	20,821	4,533
1978	65,418	3,594	8,662	16,053	27,857	4,318
1979	63,688	3,085	8,046	13,317	30,538	5,180
1980	67,402	2,823	9,341	12,717	26,969	4,733
1981	73,516	2,662	9,545	11,329	30,398	4,651
1982	80,189	2,672	11,423	9,551	29,164	5,044
1983	84,555	2,937	12,594	10,365	28,902	6,704
1984	87,261	3,403	14,575	15,756	34,166	7,934
1985	113,084	3,824	23,042	10,487	39,635	10,218
1986	134,695	3,787	27,807	13,818	45,412	11,604
1987	113,392	2,919	21,999	6,738	37,083	9,249
1988	114,849	2,947	22,085	11,228	45,808	8,795
1989	111,488	2,922	18,520	9,514	47,501	8,753
1990	124,675	3,644	17,564	10,291	52,779	23,884
1991	160,367	4,441	22,066	9,554	56,705	17,117
1992	121,965	4,067	12,880	7,763	51,982	10,814
1993	145,318	6,662	23,630	15,109	68,814	12,986
1994	186,963	9,128	46,186	16,421	93,361	18,133
1995	182,570	7,949	79,614	17,481	105,527	25,942
1996	267,334	10,324	217,418	62,168	244,962	133,517
1997	169,658	6,094	134,494	12,860	143,054	65,215

Notes appear on next page

(continued)

TABLE Ad1038–1050   Aliens naturalized, by sex and country of former allegiance: 1923–1997   *Continued*

(TQ) indicates transitional quarter.

[1] For years ending June 30.

[2] For 1933–1947, included in Northwestern Europe as part of British Empire.

[3] Includes naturalizations in various theaters of war or areas occupied by U.S. forces.

[4] "Male" series includes data for both male and female for the first quarter of the year when sexes were not reported separately.

[5] Data are obtained from unpublished data of the U.S. Immigration and Naturalization Service and do not agree with source quoted. Source excludes armed forces overseas whereas the data shown here include them.

[6] Included with series Ad1050.

Sources

1923–1970: U.S. Bureau of the Census, *Historical Statistics of the United States, Colonial Times to 1970*, Bicentennial Edition (U.S. Government Printing Office, 1975), series C172–C179. 1971–1997: U.S. Immigration and Naturalization Service, *Statistical Yearbook*, annual issues.

Documentation

"Country of former allegiance or nationality" is the country of which the alien was a citizen or subject at the time. Data on the number of aliens naturalized, by country or region of former allegiance, have been compiled since 1922. Owing to changes in the list of countries separately reported and to changes in boundaries, data for certain countries are not comparable throughout. The principal changes in reporting since 1923 are shown for individual series below.

Series Ad1041. Includes the British Empire, Norway, Sweden, Denmark, Netherlands, Belgium, Luxembourg, Switzerland, France, and, beginning 1948, Iceland. Beginning in 1948, Ireland has been reported separately. Australia has been reported separately from 1951 and is included in series Ad1050. For earlier years, Ireland and Australia are included under the British Empire.

Series Ad1042. Includes Germany, Poland, Czechoslovakia, Austria, Hungary, and Yugoslavia. For 1938–1947, Austria was included with Germany.

Series Ad1043. Includes the former USSR, Latvia, Estonia, Lithuania, Finland, Romania, Bulgaria, and Turkey. For 1923–1927, Lithuania comprised portions of Russia and Germany. European and Asiatic Turkey are included in Eastern Europe.

Series Ad1044. Includes Greece, Italy, Spain, Portugal, and, for 1929–1970, "other Europe," which comprises Albania, the Free City of Danzig, Liechtenstein, San Marino, Monaco, Andorra, and, for the years 1950–1959, Trieste. For 1923–1928, "other Europe" was recorded under the "miscellaneous" group of countries and is included with series Ad1050.

Series Ad1045. Note that until 1953, racial restrictions on naturalization limited the naturalization of aliens who were citizens or subjects of countries located in Asia (see text for series Ad1037).

Series Ad1049. Includes the West Indies and Central and South America. Excludes Cuba and Mexico beginning in 1971.

Series Ad1050. From 1923–1928 and 1979–1987 includes individuals reported in the "other Europe" category.

TABLE Ad1051–1071   Naturalization rate for immigrants admitted in 1977, by country of birth: 1990–1997

Contributed by Robert Barde, Susan B. Carter, and Richard Sutch

Year	Total	Canada	China (People's Republic)	Colombia	Cuba	Dominican Republic	Ecuador	Germany	Greece	Guyana	Haiti
	Ad1051	Ad1052	Ad1053	Ad1054	Ad1055	Ad1056	Ad1057	Ad1058	Ad1059	Ad1060	Ad1061
	Percent	Percent	Percent	Percent	Percent	Percent	Percent	Percent	Percent	Percent	Percent
1990	37.4	11.1	57.2	32.0	33.8	19.6	20.5	12.9	29.2	52.6	34.3
1991	38.7	12.1	58.1	34.0	34.6	20.5	22.2	13.4	29.9	53.9	35.4
1992	39.6	12.9	58.7	36.1	36.0	21.7	23.3	13.9	30.5	54.7	36.4
1993	41.5	14.5	60.9	40.5	39.8	24.3	25.3	14.7	31.6	55.8	38.2
1995	45.9	18.1	65.5	50.9	46.8	28.6	32.5	16.8	33.6	59.3	43.1
1997	52.8	21.9	69.0	61.2	61.3	38.1	47.2	19.0	36.0	62.6	52.4

Year	India	Italy	Jamaica	Korea	Mexico	Philippines	Portugal	Former USSR	Trinidad and Tobago	United Kingdom
	Ad1062	Ad1063	Ad1064	Ad1065	Ad1066	Ad1067	Ad1068	Ad1069	Ad1070	Ad1071
	Percent	Percent	Percent	Percent	Percent	Percent	Percent	Percent	Percent	Percent
1990	48.0	14.7	35.8	53.2	15.1	59.5	22.0	61.7	22.0	15.8
1991	49.8	15.1	37.6	54.3	16.2	60.7	22.7	62.4	25.0	17.0
1992	51.3	15.7	38.8	54.7	16.6	61.3	23.3	62.8	27.1	17.9
1993	53.7	16.7	40.5	55.8	17.6	62.0	25.0	63.3	29.9	19.3
1995	59.1	19.4	45.4	59.2	22.2	63.4	29.5	65.4	38.1	22.6
1997	64.6	21.8	52.0	64.8	32.2	65.5	33.5	68.5	47.8	26.1

Sources

1990: *1991 Statistical Yearbook of the INS*, Tables K and 53. 1991: *1992 Statistical Yearbook of the INS*, Tables L and 57. 1992: *1993 Statistical Yearbook of the INS*, Tables L, M, and 57. 1993: *1994 Statistical Yearbook of the INS*, Tables K, L, and 57. 1995: *1996 Statistical Yearbook of the INS*, Tables M, N, and 56. 1997: *1997 Statistical Yearbook of the INS*, Tables J and K.

Documentation

The series reported in this table derive from a study undertaken by the U.S. Immigration and Naturalization Service (INS) to examine the naturalization experience of a single immigration-year cohort, that of 1977. This study involves linking the records of the 1977 immigrants with their naturalization records in 1977 and subsequent years. Record linkages have been completed for all years through 1997, and the naturalization rates based on these linked records form the basis for the rates reported here. The calculations omit persons who were younger than age 16 in 1977. Because children younger than 16 may automatically derive U.S. citizenship based on the naturalization of their parents, many children are likely to have become citizens without appearing in the naturalization database.

Errors in either the immigration or naturalization record may have prevented a successful match, so some people who did naturalize may be classified as not having done so. This would cause the calculated naturalization rates to be understated. The rates are also understated to the extent that immigrants die before naturalizing. However, when age-specific U.S. death rates are applied to the 1977 immigrant cohort, a preliminary analysis indicates that mortality has an estimated effect of only about 3 percentage points on the calculated naturalization rate overall. This relatively small effect is due to the young age structure of the immigrant cohort, implying few expected deaths in the time frame of this analysis. This analysis covers only one cohort, and it is possible that immigrants arriving in earlier or later years behave differently with regard to naturalizations, although the patterns of the 1977 immigrant cohort are consistent with patterns seen in the annual naturalization tables.

The INS did not report these data in 1994 and 1996.

BORDER CONTROL

Robert Barde, Susan B. Carter, and Richard Sutch

TABLE Ad1072–1075   Deportable aliens located, and aliens expelled: 1892–1998[1]

Contributed by Robert Barde, Susan B. Carter, and Richard Sutch

Fiscal year	Deportable aliens located		Aliens expelled		Fiscal year	Deportable aliens located		Aliens expelled	
	Total	Mexican nationals	By formal removal	By voluntary departure		Total	Mexican nationals	By formal removal	By voluntary departure
	Ad1072 [2]	Ad1073 [2]	Ad1074 [3]	Ad1075		Ad1072 [2]	Ad1073 [2]	Ad1074 [3]	Ad1075
	Number	Number	Number	Number		Number	Number	Number	Number
1892	—	—	2,801	—	1945	69,164	63,602	13,611	69,490
1893	—	—	1,630	—	1946	99,591	91,456	17,317	101,945
1894	—	—	1,806	—	1947	193,657	182,986	23,434	195,880
1895	—	—	2,596	—	1948	192,779	179,385	25,276	197,184
1896	—	—	3,037	—	1949	288,253	278,538	23,874	276,297
1897	—	—	1,880	—	1950	468,339	458,215	10,199	572,477
1898	—	—	3,229	—	1951	509,040	500,000	17,328	673,169
1899	—	—	4,061	—	1952	528,815	543,538	23,125	703,778
1900	—	—	4,602	—	1953	885,587	865,318	22,482	885,391
1901	—	—	3,879	—	1954	1,089,583	1,075,168	30,264	1,074,277
1902	—	—	5,439	—	1955	254,096	242,608	17,695	232,769
1903	—	—	9,316	—	1956	87,696	72,442	9,006	80,891
1904	—	—	8,773	—	1957	59,918	44,451	5,989	63,379
1905	—	—	12,724	—	1958	53,474	37,242	7,875	60,600
1906	—	—	13,108	—	1959	45,336	30,196	8,468	56,610
1907	—	—	14,059	—	1960	70,684	29,651	7,240	52,796
1908	—	—	12,971	—	1961	88,823	29,817	8,181	52,383
1909	—	—	12,535	—	1962	92,758	30,272	8,025	54,164
1910	—	—	26,965	—	1963	88,712	39,124	7,763	69,392
1911	—	—	25,137	—	1964	86,597	43,844	9,167	73,042
1912	—	—	18,513	—	1965	110,371	55,349	10,572	95,263
1913	—	—	23,399	—	1966	138,520	89,751	9,680	123,683
1914	—	—	37,651	—	1967	161,608	108,327	9,728	142,343
1915	—	—	26,675	—	1968	212,057	151,705	9,590	179,952
1916	—	—	21,648	—	1969	283,557	201,636	11,030	240,958
1917	—	—	17,881	—	1970	345,353	277,377	17,469	303,348
1918	—	—	8,866	—	1971	420,126	348,178	18,294	370,074
1919	—	—	16,694	—	1972	505,949	430,213	16,883	450,927
1920	—	—	14,557	—	1973	655,968	576,823	17,346	568,005
1921	—	—	18,296	—	1974	788,145	709,959	19,413	718,740
1922	—	—	18,076	—	1975	766,600	680,392	24,432	655,814
1923	—	—	24,280	—	1976	875,915	781,474	29,226	765,094
1924	—	—	36,693	—	(TQ)	221,824	198,622	9,245	190,280
1925	7,488	—	34,885	—	1977	1,042,215	954,778	31,263	867,015
1926	12,735	—	31,454	—	1978	1,057,977	976,667	29,277	975,515
1927	16,393	—	31,417	15,012	1979	1,076,418	998,830	26,825	966,137
1928	23,566	—	30,464	19,946	1980	910,361	817,479	18,013	719,211
1929	32,711	—	31,035	25,888	1981	975,780	874,433	17,379	823,875
1930	20,880	—	24,864	11,387	1982	970,246	887,481	15,216	812,572
1931	22,276	—	27,886	11,719	1983	1,251,357	1,172,306	19,211	931,600
1932	22,735	—	26,490	10,775	1984	1,246,981	1,170,769	18,696	909,833
1933	20,949	—	25,392	10,347	1985	1,348,749	1,266,999	23,105	1,041,296
1934	10,319	—	14,263	8,010	1986	1,767,400	1,671,458	24,592	1,586,320
1935	11,016	—	13,877	7,978	1987	1,190,488	1,139,606	24,336	1,091,203
1936	11,728	—	16,195	8,251	1988	1,008,145	949,722	25,829	911,790
1937	13,054	—	16,905	8,788	1989	954,243	865,292	34,427	830,890
1938	12,851	—	17,341	9,278	1990	1,169,939	1,092,258	30,039	1,022,533
1939	12,037	—	14,700	9,590	1991	1,197,875	1,131,510	33,189	1,061,105
1940	10,492	—	12,254	8,594	1992	1,258,482	1,205,817	43,671	1,105,829
1941	11,294	—	7,336	6,531	1993	1,327,259	1,269,294	42,469	1,243,334
1942	11,784	—	5,542	6,904	1994	1,094,717	1,040,302	45,621	1,029,052
1943	11,175	8,189	5,702	11,947	1995	1,394,554	1,340,458	50,873	1,313,711
1944	31,174	26,689	8,821	32,270	1996	1,649,986	1,598,016	69,588	1,573,372
					1997	1,536,520	1,478,782	114,292	1,440,580
					1998	1,679,439	1,614,308	172,547	1,569,817

TABLE Ad1072–1075   Deportable aliens located, and aliens expelled: 1892–1998   *Continued*

(TQ) indicates transitional quarter.

[1] Through 1976, fiscal year beginning July 1; thereafter, fiscal year beginning October 1.

[2] Through 1960, apprehensions only; thereafter, includes all deportable aliens located by the Border Patrol.

[3] Through 1960, deportations and exclusions only; thereafter, deportations, exclusions, and removals.

Sources

Series Ad1072. 1925–1960: *INS Yearbook*, various issues. 1961–1998: *1998 Yearbook of the INS*, Table 56.

Series Ad1073. *INS Yearbook*, various issues.

Series Ad1074. 1892–1960: calculated as the sum of series C159 and C161 in U.S. Bureau of the Census, *Historical Statistics of the United States* (U.S. Government Printing Office, 1975). 1961–1998: *1998 Yearbook of the INS*, Table 61.

Series Ad1075. 1927–1960: U.S. Bureau of the Census (1975), series C160; 1961–1998: *1998 Yearbook of the INS*, Table 61.

Documentation

Series Ad1072–1073. Includes deportable aliens located by either Border Patrol agents or U.S. Immigration and Naturalization Service (INS) Investigations special agents. Prior to 1960, all of the deportable aliens located, reported here, were also apprehended, that is, arrested. Beginning in 1960, the data include nonwillful crewman violators who were not apprehended. Deportable aliens are located and apprehended attempting an illegal entry, after successfully completing an illegal entry, or after entering legally but then losing their legal status, usually because their visas have expired. The number of aliens apprehended was first recorded in 1925. Beginning in 1943, the INS identified the nationality of the deportable aliens it apprehended. Series Ad1073 shows the number of these who were Mexican nationals.

Series Ad1074. "Formal removal" is the expulsion of an alien from the ᴜnited States. Formal removal may be accomplished by deportation or eᵪᴄlusion.

"Deportation" is ordered by an immigration judge without any punishment being imposed or contemplated. "Exclusion" refers to the denial of an alien's entry into the United States. Prior to the passage of the Illegal Immigration Reform and Immigrant Responsibility Act of 1996, deportation and exclusion were separate removal procedures. Beginning April 1, 1997, these procedures were consolidated as "removal" procedures, with "voluntary departure" (series Ad1075) continuing as an option at government convenience. The Illegal Immigration Reform and Immigrant Responsibility Act of 1996 also authorized "expedited removals." Under expedited removals, an immigration officer may determine that an arriving alien is inadmissible because the alien engaged in fraud or misrepresentation or because the alien lacks proper documents. The officer can order the alien removed without further hearing or review unless the alien states a fear of persecution or an intention to apply for asylum. Officers refer aliens who make such pleas to an asylum officer and the case may eventually be argued before an immigration judge. The penalties associated with formal removal include not only the removal but possible fines, imprisonment for up to ten years, and a bar to future legal entry (the bar is permanent for aggravated felons and up to twenty years for other aliens). The imposition and extent of these penalties depend on the circumstances of the case.

Series Ad1075. In some cases, an apprehended alien may be offered voluntary departure. This procedure is common with noncriminal aliens who are apprehended by the Border Patrol during an attempted illegal entry. They agree that their entry was illegal, waive their right to a hearing, remain in custody, and are removed under supervision. Some aliens apprehended within the United States agree to voluntarily depart and pay the expense of departing. These departures may be granted by an immigration judge or, in some circumstances, by an INS district director. Aliens who have agreed to a voluntary departure can be legally admitted in the future without penalty. Although such departures are called "voluntary departures," they are required and verified. Voluntary departures include departures by aliens under "docket control," an INS mechanism for tracking the case status of potentially removable aliens.

TABLE Ad1076–1084   Immigration and Naturalization Service and the Border Patrol – expenditures, force, and interdiction: 1922–1998[1]

Contributed by Robert Barde, Susan B. Carter, and Richard Sutch

Year	Immigration and Naturalization Service		Border Patrol		Smugglers of aliens located	Aliens located who were smuggled into the United States	Seizures		
	Expenditures	Force	Expenditures	Force			Conveyances	Narcotics	Non-narcotics
	Ad1076 [2,3]	Ad1077 [4]	Ad1078	Ad1079 [5]	Ad1080	Ad1081	Ad1082	Ad1083	Ad1084 [6]
	Thousand dollars	Number	Thousand dollars	Number	Number	Number	Number	Thousand dollars	Thousand dollars
1922	3,845	1,968	—	—	—	—	—	—	—
1923	4,077	1,972	—	—	—	—	—	—	—
1924	4,337	2,195	—	—	—	—	—	—	—
1925	5,761	2,590	1,000	472	—	—	—	—	—
1926	6,273	2,672	1,150	632	—	—	—	—	—
1927	6,984	2,975	1,500	731	—	—	—	—	—
1928	7,291	3,117	1,593	738	—	—	—	—	—
1929	8,601	3,236	1,809	787	—	—	—	—	—
1930	9,495	3,642	1,865	828	—	—	—	—	—
1931	10,215	3,975	1,595	836	—	—	—	—	—
1932	12,755	4,245	2,155	1,021	—	—	—	—	—
1933	10,903	4,125	1,792	983	—	—	—	—	—
1934	10,384	3,961	1,619	934	—	—	—	—	—
1935	8,594	3,661	1,734	916	—	—	—	—	—
1936	9,716	3,862	1,808	916	—	—	—	—	—
1937	,155	3,785	1,975	866	—	—	—	—	—
1938	,870	3,775	1,738	850	—	—	—	—	—
1939	9,892	3,771	1,728	850	—	—	—	—	—
1940	10,119	3,796	—	856	—	—	—	—	—
1941	19,254	6,360	3,579	1,465	—	—	—	—	—
1942	21,650	6,556	3,072	—	—	—	—	—	—
1943	27,932	8,348	4,445	—	—	—	—	—	—
1944	28,956	8,100	3,884	—	—	—	—	—	—
1945	28,300	7,513	4,275	1,246	136	—	90	—	79
1946	26,192	7,233	4,385	1,052	220	—	178	—	111
1947	29,596	6,956	5,616	1,315	227	—	229	—	153
1948	28,537	6,557	5,520	—	—	—	—	—	—
1949	31,916	6,784	6,335	—	635	—	250	—	222
1950	32,643	6,805	6,613	—	713	—	184	—	171
1951	35,633	7,564	6,683	—	811	—	261	—	261
1952	42,633	7,729	7,057	—	1,122	—	310	—	324
1953	40,959	7,461	6,519	—	1,540	—	284	—	417
1954	42,572	7,309	7,133	—	1,822	—	348	—	953
1955	43,781	7,557	11,531	—	928	—	257	—	679
1956	45,995	7,280	12,168	—	765	—	327	—	683
1957	50,033	7,170	12,815	—	405	—	300	—	764
1958	53,782	7,045	14,755	—	402	—	325	172	618
1959	55,327	6,887	15,067	—	321	—	183	145	538
1960	57,206	7,046	16,255	—	330	—	60	52	286
1961	64,549	7,282	18,411	—	284	—	88	26	239
1962	65,458	7,375	17,662	—	349	—	118	13	475
1963	68,401	7,363	18,317	—	348	—	187	12	234
1964	68,998	7,164	17,676	—	513	—	176	252	387
1965	75,433	7,189	18,829	—	525	1,814	90	393	201
1966	77,559	7,155	20,029	—	959	3,813	65	382	91
1967	81,515	7,354	20,248	—	1,219	5,671	84	1,719	174
1968	88,890	7,402	21,126	—	1,210	6,662	117	688	158
1969	93,321	6,921	23,476	—	2,048	11,784	198	1,208	475
1970	110,367	7,202	30,142	—	3,298	18,747	320	3,865	682
1971	127,210	7,591	35,121	—	3,814	19,765	423	5,379	774
1972	130,934	8,063	39,627	—	4,564	24,918	709	11,709	1,253
1973	137,468	8,020	42,902	—	6,355	41,589	1,250	23,464	2,490
1974	155,161	8,436	45,810	—	8,074	83,114	1,041	45,056	2,154
1975	181,320	8,526	56,231	—	6,860	90,385	917	26,302	2,353
1976	214,609	9,379	64,818	—	9,600	82,910	701	16,035	1,984
(TQ)	54,690	9,983	17,772	—	2,478	22,577	197	4,728	584
1977	244,515	10,689	70,644	2,427	12,405	138,805	736	17,071	2,486
1978	283,087	11,453	72,231	2,480	13,306	159,191	564	6,251	2,097
1979	309,285	10,969	71,021	2,731	15,280	172,688	421	8,448	1,519

Notes appear at end of table

TABLE Ad1076–1084 Immigration and Naturalization Service and the Border Patrol – expenditures, force, and interdiction: 1922–1998 *Continued*

Year	Immigration and Naturalization Service		Border Patrol		Smugglers of aliens located	Aliens located who were smuggled into the United States	Seizures		
	Expenditures	Force	Expenditures	Force			Conveyances	Narcotics	Non-narcotics
	Ad1076 [2,3]	Ad1077 [4]	Ad1078	Ad1079 [5]	Ad1080	Ad1081	Ad1082	Ad1083	Ad1084 [6]
	Thousand dollars	Number	Thousand dollars	Number	Number	Number	Number	Thousand dollars	Thousand dollars
1980	340,742	10,311	84,815	2,915	13,076	112,647	1,920	110,272	5,843
1981	366,017	10,353	86,048	2,872	12,643	90,084	2,441	10,236	7,112
1982	446,461	10,620	98,744	2,890	11,777	80,350	4,033	5,242	783
1983	500,972	10,659	110,174	2,865	13,393	86,294	5,807	28,729	1,596
1984	518,058	11,268	114,088	2,857	13,435	91,722	6,456	42,940	1,566
1985	599,001	11,656	141,902	3,695	14,666	95,741	7,327	119,822	2,185
1986	594,415	12,413	150,418	3,693	19,275	114,665	10,512	161,737	3,370
1987	882,888	14,773	194,624	5,541	11,560	59,268	7,512	582,395	8,243
1988	1,010,300	17,021	205,276	5,530	10,373	50,122	6,643	700,524	20,690
1989	1,135,307	16,265	246,437	5,485	13,794	50,638	10,789	1,191,505	21,219
1990	1,171,185	16,190	261,129	4,848	21,901	71,049	17,275	797,768	45,794
1991	1,317,790	16,925	295,517	4,929	18,826	64,170	14,693	910,146	40,053
1992	1,472,453	18,425	325,784	4,948	17,237	69,538	11,391	1,216,834	31,105
1993	1,551,194	18,299	354,473	4,863	15,266	80,835	10,995	1,337,766	45,132
1994	1,628,437	18,673	374,450	5,434	14,143	92,934	9,134	1,555,732	42,322
1995	1,827,000	20,629	393,985	5,423	12,796	102,591	9,327	1,965,311	46,457
1996	2,327,000	25,617	479,168	6,383	13,458	122,233	11,129	1,208,779	46,600
1997	3,136,000	—	636,686	7,383	12,523	124,605	11,792	1,046,293	48,296
1998	—	—	—	—	13,908	174,514	14,401	1,340,000	64,000

(TQ) indicates transitional quarter.

[1] Through 1976, fiscal year ended June 30; thereafter, fiscal year ended September 30.

[2] From 1922–1933, separate budgets were reported for the Bureau of Immigration and for the Bureau of Naturalization. Beginning 1936, a single budget was presented for the Immigration and Naturalization Service (INS).

[3] Beginning 1987, actual expenditures of the INS included a number of fee-funded programs, such as immigration legalization fees, immigration user fees, and immigration examination fees.

[4] "Force" is defined as permanent positions from 1922 to 1977. Beginning in 1978, the figures are for full-time equivalents, permanent and nonpermanent, working in either directly funded programs or in fee-funded or reimbursable programs.

[5] For 1948–1976, the data refer to the authorized, not the actual, force.

[6] Through 1957, includes the value of narcotics seizures.

Sources

Series Ad1076–1077. Budget of the United States, including direct obligations, reimbursable expenditures, and fee-based programs.

Series Ad1078. 1925–1928: *Annual Report of the Immigration and Naturalization Service.* 1929–1976: *Budget of the United States*, compiled from published data by Josiah Heyman (University of Texas, El Paso). 1977–1998 Immigration and Naturalization Service (INS) Congressional budget request.

Series Ad1079. 1925–1928: *Annual Report of the Immigration and Naturalization Service.* 1929–1939: *Budget of the United States.* 1940–1947: *Annual Report of the Immigration and Naturalization Service.* 1977–1998: INS Congressional budget request.

Series Ad1080–1084. Annual issues of the *Statistical Yearbook of the INS.*

Documentation

Where the budget of the United States is cited as the source, those compilations were provided by Josiah Heyman, Department of Sociology and Anthropology, University of Texas, El Paso. The INS's Congressional budget requests were furnished by James Woodard of the INS Budget Office.

TABLE Ad1085–1088 Public attitudes regarding number of immigrants admitted: 1955–1997

Contributed by Robert Barde

Year	Want more immigrants allowed Ad1085 Percent	Want number of immigrants allowed to stay the same Ad1086 Percent	Want fewer immigrants allowed Ad1087 Percent	No opinion Ad1088 Percent
1955	13	37	39	11
1964	6	46	38	10
1977	7	37	42	14
1982	4	23	66	7
1986	8	35	51	6
1990	9	29	48	14
1992	9	21	55	15
1993	7	27	61	5
1994	6	27	63	4
1995	6	30	55	9
1996	8	35	50	7
1997	10	39	46	5

Sources

Roper Center for Public Opinion Research, University of Connecticut, Internet site. Sources for the following years indicate the month in which the poll was conducted, the sponsoring organization, and, if different, the organization carrying out the survey. 1955: April, Foreign Affairs; 1964: September, Gallup/Hopes and Fears; 1977: March, Gallup; 1982: March, Roper Report; 1986: May, U.S. News/Roper; 1990: May, Federation for American Immigration Reform/Roper; 1992: April, Federation for American Immigration Reform/Roper; 1993: June, CBS/NY Times; 1994: September, CBS/NY Times; 1995: September, CBS/NY Times; 1996: October, CBS; 1997: August, Columbus Day Survey: Looking for America/Princeton Survey Research Associates.

Documentation

A discussion of national polls of public opinion on immigrants can be found in Rita Simon and Susan Alexander, *The Ambivalent Welcome: Print Media, Public Opinion and Immigration* (Praeger, 1993), pp. 29–48. Efforts to survey the public for its opinions on various aspects of immigration date back to the 1930s. Survey questions asked whether aliens on relief should be returned to their own countries (Gallup 1937), if aliens should be eligible for relief (Gallup 1939), whether people of certain countries should be allowed to live and work in the United States (Roper 1942), whether Jews should be given the same opportunities to immigrate to the United States as non-Jews (National Opinion Research Center 1944), whether Poles, Jews, and other displaced persons should be allowed to enter the United States (Gallup 1946 and 1947, Roper 1948), and if escapees from Russian-controlled countries should be allowed to enter the United States and become citizens (Gallup 1949, 1951, 1952).

This table presents survey responses to questions about the general level of immigration. Although the questions posed by the selected polling organizations varied slightly over the years, there is enough similarity in the wording

to rule out large framing effects. The exact questions put to those surveyed were as follows:

1955: "Do you think the United States is letting too many immigrants come into this country, or not enough?"

1964: "Do you think the number of immigrants allowed to enter the U.S. each year should be increased somewhat, decreased somewhat, or kept at about the present level?"

1977: "Should immigration be kept at its present level, increased or decreased?"

1982: "In recent years, there has been a lot of discussion about the number of immigrants allowed into our country. On the whole, would you say that you would like to see the number of immigrants allowed to enter our country increased, or would you like to see the number decreased, or do you think we are letting in about the right number now?"

1986: "At the present time our law allows about a half million immigrants a year into the United States. Would you like to see the number of immigrants LEGALLY ALLOWED to enter our country increased, or would you like to see the number decreased, or do you think we're letting in about the right number now?"

1990 and 1992: "Is it your impression that the current immigration laws allow too many immigrants, too few immigrants, or about the right number of immigrants into this country each year?"

1993, 1994, and 1995: "Should immigration be kept at its present level, increased or decreased?"

1996: "Should legal immigration into the United States be kept at its present level, increased or decreased?"

1997: "I have some questions about immigrants – people who come from other countries to live here in the United States. In your view, should immigration be kept at its present level, increased, decreased, or stopped altogether?"

CHAPTER Ae
Family and Household Composition

Editor: Steven Ruggles

FAMILY AND HOUSEHOLD COMPOSITION

Steven Ruggles

Household and family composition in the United States is in rapid flux, and historical data are essential to put current trends into perspective. Nevertheless, the previous edition of *Historical Statistics of the United States* included no long-run statistical series describing family and household composition. The Census Bureau published minimal statistics on families and households until 1940, focusing mainly on the size distribution of households. Even for the period since 1940, the official published statistics on the subject are minimal. Consequently, until recently most scholarly discussions of long-run changes in the living arrangements of Americans focused on isolated fragments of inconsistently tabulated data for particular localities.[1]

During the past two decades, new microdata samples of historical censuses have become available. These data are collected in the Integrated Public Use Microdata Series (IPUMS), a coherent national database describing the characteristics of 55 million Americans in thirteen census years spanning the period from 1850 through 1990.[2] The IPUMS allows us for the first time to construct detailed and consistent statistical series on family and household composition for the past 150 years.

This essay briefly surveys the comparability issues posed by measurement of long-run changes in family and household composition and then presents selected summary statistics on key changes in American living arrangements since 1850.

Data

The IPUMS combines census microdata files produced by the Census Bureau for the period since 1960 with new historical census samples produced at the University of Minnesota and elsewhere. By putting the samples in the same format, imposing consistent variable coding, and carefully documenting changes in variables over time, the IPUMS is designed to facilitate the use of the census samples as a time series. The IPUMS allows us to circumvent most of the incompatibilities and errors in published census tabulations and to create new series on household and family composition over the last 150 years.

A key innovation of the IPUMS is a set of consistently constructed family interrelationship variables for all years. These variables identify the location within the household of each individual's spouse, mother, and father. The family interrelationship pointers provide the building blocks to construct virtually any standard measures of household composition. Because the family interrelationship variables were designed to be as compatible as possible across census years, the resulting measures of household and family composition are more useful for the study of long-run change than are the tabulations generated by the Census Bureau.

Comparability Issues

The construction of consistent long-run series requires close attention to changing census definitions and procedures. To maximize comparability over time, scholars should account for changes in the census concepts of households and group quarters and should be aware of shifts in the criteria for distinguishing the boundaries of households. This section briefly describes the most important comparability issues.[3]

The census concepts of household and group quarters did not emerge in their modern form until 1930, and their definitions have shifted significantly since then. Until 1920, the permanent residents of large dwelling units such as institutions, hotels, and boarding houses were enumerated as if they were simply very large households.[4] From 1930 onward, such units were classified as group quarters and excluded from the count of households. In all periods since then, the group quarters category included residents of correctional institutions, asylums, homes for the aged or needy, convents and monasteries, worker's dormitories, crew quarters

---

[1] Before the mid-1990s, only a few studies attempted long-term comparisons of family and household composition at the national level. These included Kobrin (1976), Smith (1986), Ruggles (1988), and Sweet and Bumpass (1987).

[2] See the Guide to the Millennial Edition for more information about the IPUMS.

[3] For further detail, see Ruggles and Brower (2003).

[4] Before 1940, these units were called "census families" rather than households. In this discussion, we use the term "household" for all census years to avoid confusion with the modern census concept of "family." In 1930 and 1940, the term for group quarters was "quasi-households"; to simplify the discussion, we use the term "group quarters" throughout. The Census Bureau implemented an early version of the group quarters concept for the 1900 Census, by excluding from the count of households hotels, boarding houses, schools, institutions, work camps, ships, military posts, and "miscellaneous groups of persons lodging together but having no family relationship" (U.S. Bureau of the Census 1902, p. clviii). We have ignored this count of private households because the

Acknowledgments
Steven Ruggles thanks Susan Brower for contributing the tables for this chapter. He also thanks Catherine Fitch for helpful comments and suggestions.

This work was supported in part by grants from the National Science Foundation and the National Institutes of Health.

TABLE Ae-A   Estimates of the number of households and group quarters residents: 1850–1990

	Households			Group quarters residents	
Year	Published by Census	1950–1970 definition	1980–1990 definition	1950–1970 definition	1980–1990 definition
1850	3,598,240	3,539,847	3,581,172	808,353	361,720
1860	5,210,934	5,143,703	5,194,160	844,999	347,386
1870	7,579,363	7,471,754	7,549,028	1,339,846	586,931
1880	9,945,946	9,824,573	9,907,583	1,656,167	802,140
1890	12,690,152	12,530,206 [1]	12,638,749 [1]	—	—
1900	15,963,965	15,977,199	16,119,014	2,604,683	1,974,006
1910	20,255,555	19,984,021	20,165,673	3,508,773	1,793,064
1920	24,351,676	24,073,793	24,233,961	3,135,649	1,827,598
1930	29,904,663	29,798,665 [1]	29,904,663 [2]	—	—
1940	34,948,666	34,904,634	34,948,666 [2]	2,807,103	—
1950	42,857,335	42,857,335	—	4,075,907	—
1960	53,021,061	53,023,935	—	2,881,383	—
1970	63,573,042	63,637,721	—	3,659,644	—
1980	80,389,673	80,351,102	80,389,673	3,500,854	3,242,871
1990	91,947,410	91,873,988	91,947,410	3,806,303	3,363,726

[1] 1890 and 1930 group quarters residence interpolated.

[2] 1930–1940 definition (10 or fewer unrelated).

Sources

Households, published by census. U.S. Bureau of the Census. 1850–1880: *Twelfth Census Special Reports, A Century of Population Growth, 1790–1900*. 1900: *Twelfth Census of the United States, Population*, part 2. 1890 and 1910–1950: *U.S. Census of Population: 1950*, volume 4, *Special Reports, General Char-*

acteristics of Families. 1960: *Census of Population and Housing: 1960 Final Report PC (2)-4A, Subject Reports: Families*. 1970: *Census of Population: 1970, Detailed Characteristics, Final Report PC(1)-D1, United States Summary*. 1980: *Census of Population: 1980, General Population Characteristics*, part 1, *U.S. Summary*. 1990: *Census of Population: 1990, General Population Characteristics*, part 1 (CP-1-1).

Households, other series, and group quarters: series Ae1–2 and Ae114–115.

on inland vessels, college dormitories and fraternities, hospitals, hotels, missions, flophouses, camps, and large lodging houses. In each census year since 1930, the Census Bureau also classified as group quarters any unit with more than a specified number of persons unrelated to the householder. The threshold number of unrelated persons for classification as group quarters was eleven in 1930 and 1940, fell to five in 1950–1970, and then rose to ten in 1980 and 1990.

Ruggles and Brower developed a procedure for estimating the number of households and group quarters residents under constant definitions (Ruggles and Brower 2003). These methods form the basis of the statistical series on the number of households and group quarters residents under both the 1950–1970 and 1980–1990 group quarters definitions (Tables Ae1–28 and Ae97–127). The main results are summarized in Table Ae-A. The aggregate impact of variations in the group quarters definition on the total number of households is small. In no case does the difference between the published total number of households and the number of households under 1950–1970 definitions exceed 2 percent, and in the 1980–1990 period, the effect of differences between the two definitions is trivial. The effect of definitional changes is much greater, however, for size of the group quarters population. Indeed, in the 1850–1890 period, the number of people residing in non-institutional group quarters is twice as large under the 1950–1970 group quarters definition as under the 1980–1990 definition. Thus, long-run comparisons of the group quarters population are meaningless unless we impose a standard definition of group quarters.

The introduction and modification of the group quarters concept is not the only definitional change that affects census-based measures of family and household composition. The criteria for

distinguishing one household from the next have also shifted over time. For most measures, these changes have had marginal effects, but for certain kinds of living arrangements the potential effects of changing household definitions can be significant.

In the mid-nineteenth century, the definition of the household was a preindustrial one: the household was an economic unit that depended on "one common means of support" and resided together in a house or part of a house. This definition was altered in 1870 by an instruction to enumerators to distinguish the number of separate households within a dwelling according to the number of separate eating tables. Since multihousehold dwellings were comparatively rare in the nineteenth century, this change probably had minor effects.

From 1870 through 1940, the definition of household was subtly modified several times, but the changes seem to have had insignificant consequences for the identification of households in the census. Throughout this period, the instructions stressed shared housekeeping, dining tables, or cooking facilities. Moreover, before 1950 the instructions made it clear that single rooms in apartment hotels should not be counted as independent households; rather, the entire hotel should be counted as a single group quarters unit.

In 1950, the enumeration instructions introduced a new criterion: a unit could be distinguished as a separate household if it had at least two rooms and direct access to the outside by means of a common hallway. This concept was expanded in 1960, when even single-room units without separate cooking facilities could qualify as separate households if they had direct access to a common hallway. The common hallway criterion meant that many single-room occupancy units that had previously been regarded as hotels or boarding houses were reclassified as independent households.

Ruggles and Brower estimate that this definitional change added between 240,000 and 400,000 additional single-room households in each census year from 1960 to 1980 (Ruggles and Brower 2003). The change had only a small effect on the total number

definition is incompatible with later census years; instead we followed the same procedures for 1900 as for the other early census years. All enumerator instructions for the period 1850–1990 are available online at the IPUMS Internet site.

of households, which stood at about 53 million in 1960, but it did have important consequences for the number of nonfamily households, which are defined as households in which the household head or householder has no coresident relatives. For example, the relaxation of the definition of household between 1950 and 1960 accounts for approximately 28 percent of the increase in male nonfamily householders during that decade. In most instances, the IPUMS microdata allow researchers focusing on this period to make adjustments for these definitional changes.

One additional change in census procedures should be noted. In 1940 and before, the census enumerated college students at their "usual place of abode," which meant that those students who lived in dormitories were usually counted as part of their parental family. In 1950, the census began to enumerate college students in the community where they attended college. Because of this change, 45.5 percent of college students were unrelated to the household head in 1950, compared to only 10.6 percent in 1940. Because the college population was small in 1940, the overall effects of the change are modest, but analysts should nevertheless use caution when assessing the living arrangements of the college-aged in the mid-twentieth century (Ruggles 1988).

In addition to problems caused by shifting census definitions, statistical series can also be distorted by changes in census processing. In particular, Ruggles and Brower argue that because of errors in tabulation procedures, published statistics on subfamilies from both the census and the Current Population Surveys are unreliable.[5] Accordingly, the statistics relating to subfamilies that are presented here are derived entirely from the IPUMS (Table Ae38–78).

Trends in American Living Arrangements

During the past century and a half, American families have become dramatically smaller and simpler. In the mid-nineteenth century, the aged ordinarily lived with their children, divorce was exceedingly rare, and births to unmarried women were infrequent. Today, most of the elderly reside alone, about half of all marriages will end in divorce, and about one in three babies are born to unmarried mothers (Cherlin 1992; Bramlett and Mosher 2001). Pundits, politicians, and scholars have debated and analyzed these changes in countless publications and speeches, but they still disagree about exactly what happened and why. Past discussions of the transformation of the family have involved guesswork because, until recently, we had only fragmentary information on family structure for the period before 1960. IPUMS data allow researchers to construct high-precision, closely comparable series describing national changes in the family over the very long run. The sections that follow describe two key changes in American living arrangements: the decline of multigenerational families and the rise of single-parent families.

Decline of the Multigenerational Family

Figure Ae-B presents the living arrangements of the population ages 65 or older between 1850 and 1990. In the mid-nineteenth century, about 70 percent of individuals and couples ages 65 or older lived with their children. In addition, about a tenth of the aged lived with other relatives – mainly grandchildren, siblings, nephews, and nieces. Another tenth lived with nonrelatives; some

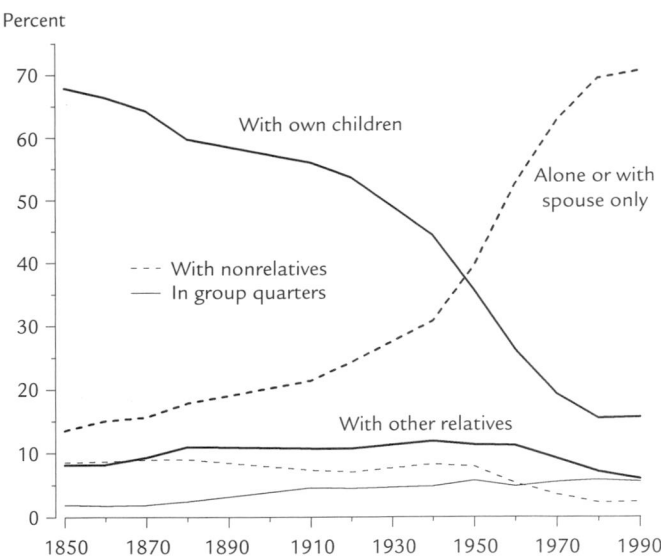

FIGURE Ae-B   Living arrangements of individuals and married couples age 65 or older: 1850–1990

Sources
Computed from series Ae245–269.

of these were household heads who kept boarders or servants, but most were boarders in other people's households. Only 11 percent of the aged in 1850 lived alone or with only their spouses, and only 1.5 percent lived in institutions such as almshouses and homes for the aged.

After 1850, residence with children began to decline. Increasingly, the elderly began to live alone, with their spouses only, or in old-age homes. The trend was gradual until 1920, but then it began to accelerate. The decline in residence with children was most rapid during the period from 1940 to 1980, when more than half the total change took place. By 1990, only 16 percent of the aged lived with their children, while 6.5 percent lived in institutions, and 70 percent lived alone or with their spouses only.

The high percentage of aged who resided with children in the nineteenth century is especially striking when we consider that not all the aged population had the possibility of residing with their children. About 7 percent of the elderly never married, and with few exceptions, this meant that they had no children with whom to reside. Another 8 percent married but remained childless. Some 5 percent of the aged had outlived all their children. Taking all this into account, then, somewhere on the order of 20 percent of the elderly in the mid-nineteenth century had no living children; thus, as near as we can measure, living with children must have been almost universal among the aged population that had living children (Ruggles 2001).

The decline of coresidence between the aged and their children is the single most dramatic change in the American family during the past two centuries. Contemporary observers were well aware of the decline of the multigenerational family, and they had little doubt as to the cause. Thomas H. Eliot, the chief drafter of the Social Security Act of 1935, put it this way:

> In the old days, the old-age assistance problem was not so great so long as most people lived on farms, had big families, and at least some of the children stayed on the farm. It was customary when the old people got too old to do their share of the work they would stay on the farm and the sons or daughters would keep them there

[5] Ruggles and Brower (2003). See also Bianchi (1995), Graham and Beller (1985), London (1998), and Sweet and Bumpass (1987).

in the home. That pattern changed slowly but continuously from the early part of the century as more and more of the young, rural population left the farms. The three generation household (aged parents, children, and grandchildren), perfectly common 50 years ago, had begun to become very rare indeed. By the time people got old, the children had already left and gone to the city. There was no one to take care of them. Hence, an increase in the problem of the needy aged. (Eliot 1961)

This interpretation makes sense. In preindustrial America, the economy was based on farming and wealth derived from the land. Land was concentrated in the hands of men, who inherited it from their fathers and passed it on to their sons. Those men who did not work in farming – such as merchants, artisans, and craftsmen – were also frequently self-employed. This system was destroyed between 1850 and 1950 by a fundamental transformation of the economy. Agriculture and crafts ceased to be the dominant occupations; they were eclipsed by the enormous growth of jobs in commerce and industry, which shifted millions of workers from self-employment to wage labor. This shift in the economy undermined the logic of the preindustrial family.

With the growth of new job opportunities in the nineteenth and early twentieth centuries, many young men left the farm in favor of the high wages, independence, and excitement offered by town life. The declining importance of farming, in turn, meant that fewer and fewer parents could offer the incentive of agricultural inheritance to keep their grown children from leaving home. Moreover, without the labor demands of the farm, fewer and fewer aged had reason to try to keep their children at home. Many of the other traditional self-employed village occupations – such as blacksmiths, cabinetmakers, and shoemakers – were rendered obsolete by industrialization, and the disappearance of such businesses reinforced the effects of declining agricultural employment.

Historians of the family, however, do not agree with this interpretation. Virtually all scholars writing on this subject in recent years regard nineteenth-century coresidence of the aged and their children as a form of old-age support. They maintain that the aged in the nineteenth century lived with their children when they were infirm or impoverished and had no other good alternatives.[6] In this scenario, the increase of aged living alone resulted from increasing income of the aged, a consequence of the Social Security program and the growth of private pensions.

There are several problems with the hypothesis that declining coresidence of the aged resulted from rising income. First, census evidence clearly shows that in the nineteenth century the needy and sick aged were the group least likely to reside with their children (Ruggles 2003). Moreover, most studies have found that even in the recent past the rising income of the aged has been insufficient to account for the entire shift in living arrangements.[7] There are also problems with the timing of change: the shift to independent residence began well before Social Security had a significant

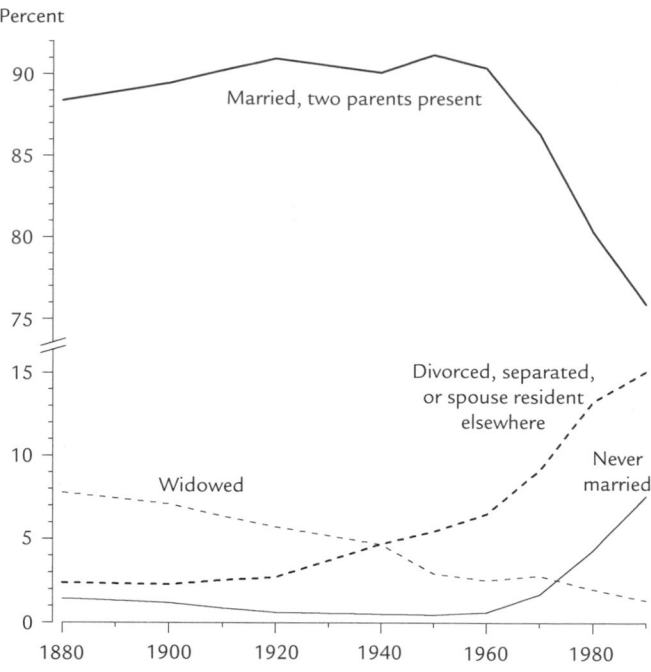

FIGURE Ae-C   Marital status of mothers with children younger than age 18: 1880–1990

Sources
Computed from series Ae223–228.

impact on the resources of the aged. Judging from the commentary of Thomas Eliot and the other creators of the Social Security legislation, the changing living arrangements of the aged were as much a cause of Social Security as they were a consequence.

After 1940, the pace of change in the household composition of the aged accelerated. There can be little doubt that, in this period, rising incomes were an important contributor to the increase in independent residence of the aged. It is also likely that changing norms reinforced the decline of the multigenerational family. Nevertheless, I am persuaded by Eliot and other contemporaries that the key to understanding the transformation of the living arrangements of the aged lies with the rise of wage labor and the destruction of the preindustrial family economy.

Rise of Single Parenthood

The changing marital status of mothers with children under 18 years old is summarized in Figure Ae-C. From 1880, when marital status was first recorded in the census, until 1950, the overall percentage of young children without married mothers declined slightly from 11.6 to 8.8 percent. The percentage of children with divorced or separated mothers more than doubled during this period, but that increase was canceled out by a dramatic decline in

---

[6] See, for example, Hareven (1994, 1996), Smith (1979, 1981, 1986), Costa (1997), Elman (1998), Elman and Uhlenberg (1995), McGarry and Schoeni (2000), Kramarow (1995), Wall (1995), Hammel (1995), and Schoeni (1998). The implicit assumption that the aged have always preferred residential autonomy owes much to Laslett's (1972) finding that extended families were rare in northwestern Europe before industrialization; see Ruggles (1987, 1994, 2001).
[7] My own analysis suggests that about a fourth of the change in the percentage of aged residing with children between 1950 and 1990 can be attributed to income effects (Ruggles 1996a, 2001). This result was obtained by decomposing the

effects of changing income distribution using the method proposed by Das Gupta (1978), controlling for age in five-year groups, eight income categories, sex, and currently married status. This estimate is somewhat lower than has been found by most other investigators; although there is some disagreement, most studies suggest that about half of the recent shift toward living alone can be explained by rising income. See Beresford and Rivlin (1966); Chevan and Korson (1972); Carliner (1975); Davis and van den Oever (1981); Michael, Fuchs, and Scott (1980); Pampel (1983); and Ruggles (1988, 1996a, 1996b). Also relevant are Angel and Tienda (1982), Troll (1971), and King (1988).

the percentage of children with widowed mothers. From 1950 to 1990, however, the percentage of children residing with never-married mothers rose sixteen-fold. Simultaneously, the percentage of children with divorced or separated mothers continued to rise. By 1990, about one quarter of all children was residing with a single mother.

The increase in single parenthood is a consequence of the rapid rise of divorce, separation, and unmarried fertility (Table Ae507–513). The causes of these changes have been vigorously debated. The traditional explanation is that rising female labor force participation weakened marriage. Writing in 1893, Emile Durkheim pointed to the sexual division of labor as a source of interdependence between men and women, producing what he called "organic solidarity." Durkheim warned that if the sexual division of labor receded, "conjugal society would eventually subsist in sexual relations preeminently ephemeral" (Durkheim 1960 [1893], p. 60). More recently, scholars have argued that the rise in economic opportunities for women encouraged both the increase of marital instability and the decline of marriage rates (Cherlin 1980, 1992; Degler 1980; Fitch and Ruggles 2000; Goldscheider and Waite 1986; Mare and Winship 1991; McLanahan 1991; McLanahan and Casper 1995; Preston and Richards 1975; Ross and Sawhill 1975; Ruggles 1997b; Waite and Spitze 1981). According to this interpretation, women in the past who lacked independent means of support were often trapped in bad marriages; as the opportunities for female wage labor expanded, women were increasingly able to escape and live on their own. Hence, the rising economic power of women undermined patriarchal authority and made separate residence as a divorced or never-married parent feasible.

Following the publication of Charles Murray's *Losing Ground* in 1984, many commentators blamed the rise of single parenthood on the Aid to Families with Dependent Children (AFDC) program. From 1936 to 1996, AFDC provided a federal entitlement to economic support for single parents with children younger than age 18 who fell below a threshold of assets and income. Murray argued explicitly that the growth of female-headed families during the 1960s and 1970s was the result of increasing generosity and availability of AFDC. His proposed solution was radical: the elimination of welfare benefits to unmarried mothers and their children. Murray's argument was ultimately endorsed by Congress, but few scholars were persuaded. Dozens of separate investigations involving the impact of AFDC benefit levels on family structure were carried out from the 1970s to the 1990s (Moffitt 1992; Ellwood and Bane 1985; Groenveld, Hannan, and Tuma 1983; Ruggles 1997a). The results of these studies uniformly suggest that the impact of welfare on single parenthood is small and often insignificant. As Robert Moffitt concludes, "the failure to find strong benefit effects is the most notable characteristic of this literature" (Moffitt 1992, p. 31).

A third line of argument contends that both unmarried fertility and marital instability were encouraged by stagnant and declining economic opportunity for young men between the early 1970s and the mid-1990s (Oppenheimer 1994; Oppenheimer, Kalmijn, and Lim 1997; Oppenheimer and Lew 1995; Wilson and Neckerman 1987). There is evidence that a shortage of young men with sufficient earnings to support a family contributed to the large increase in marriage age during the past three decades, especially among blacks (Cready, Fossett, and Kiecolt 1997; James 1998; Fossett and Kiecolt 1993; Lichter, LeClere, and McLaughlin 1991; Lichter, McLaughlin, et al. 1992; Lloyd and South 1996; Testa and Krogh 1995). By reducing the pool of desirable husbands, declining real

wages and labor force participation of young men probably contributed to both the dramatic growth of unmarried fertility and the increase of divorce and separation.

Although economic theories predominate, some scholars have also emphasized cultural explanations for rising marital instability and unmarried fertility (Cherlin and Walters 1981; May 1980; Thornton 1985, 1989; Riley 1991). The social stigmas associated with divorce and illegitimacy have greatly diminished, and the legal barriers to divorce have virtually disappeared. The rise of individualism associated with urbanization and industrialization has meant increasing emphasis on self-fulfillment and growing intolerance of unsuccessful marriages. In essence, the cultural argument suggests that marriages in the past were governed more by social norms and less by rational calculation to maximize individual happiness.

Decline of the Patriarchal Family

There can be little doubt that the transformation of the American family could not have occurred without changes in attitudes. That does not, however, mean that we should assume that the changes in the family were driven by shifting cultural values. The destruction of the nineteenth-century patriarchal family system was simultaneously an economic and a cultural change.

The American family in the mid-nineteenth century was organized according to patriarchal tradition. The household head held near absolute authority. In most states, wives could not own property, the husband owned any earnings of his wife and children, fathers had veto power over the marriage of their daughters, and disobedience could be met with corporal punishment. Today, patriarchal authority has diminished to the point that the very concept of "household head" is obsolete; in recognition of shifting attitudes, the U.S. Census Bureau abandoned the term in 1980 (Ruggles and Brower 2003; Shammas 2002).

Within the preindustrial family economy, older-generation men exercised control over the means of production. Women and younger-generation men provided labor in exchange for food, shelter, and economic security. The decline of farming, the rise of wage labor, and the growth of mass education fundamentally shifted the balance of power within American families. First, the rise of wage labor among men reduced the importance of agricultural and occupational inheritance by providing opportunity for young men. Second, the rise of wage labor among women curbed the control that husbands and fathers exercised over their wives and daughters.

These changes undermined the patriarchal authority at the heart of the nineteenth-century family. Power within the family shifted from fathers toward sons, and from husbands toward wives. The increasing economic independence of sons and wives was essential for the decline of multigenerational families and the increase in single parenthood. Most wage-labor jobs available before the mid-nineteenth century – farm labor and domestic service were the most important ones – simply did not pay enough to support independent residence. Hence, the transformation of the economy made the transformation of the family possible. The changes in the family were not, however, purely economic; little would have happened had there not also been profound attitudinal changes. It is not especially useful to debate whether the economic or cultural changes were primary; both were essential.

In the second half of the twentieth century, rising incomes of the aged further encouraged independent residence, and declining economic opportunities of young men probably accelerated the rise of single parenthood. It would be a mistake, however, to devote too much weight to these comparatively recent effects. The decline of the multigenerational family and the rise of single parenthood clearly predate these shifts in the age patterns of income. If the same economic changes had occurred a hundred years earlier, they would no doubt have had very different consequences. In the nineteenth-century context, increased income of the aged and reduced opportunity for young men would probably only have strengthened the patriarchal authority structure of the family.

This brief survey can only hint at the complexity of the transformation of the American family. Much work remains to be done. The availability of consistent census microdata has stimulated a surge of new research on changes in American households and families.[8] Nevertheless, the field is in its infancy; scholars are just beginning to grasp the dimensions of change in American living arrangements from childhood to old age. The statistical series in this volume illustrate the sort of dramatic trends and differentials that are virtually invisible using previously available published statistics. But thousands of other measures of household and family composition are possible, and researchers now have the means to tailor their measures to the particular research question at hand.

References

Angel, R., and M. Tienda. 1982. "Determinants of Extended Family Structure: Cultural Pattern or Economic Need?" *American Journal of Sociology* 87: 1360–83.

Beresford, John C., and Alice M. Rivlin. 1966. "Privacy, Poverty, and Old Age." *Demography* 3: 247–58.

Bianchi, Suzanne M. 1995. "The Changing Demographic and Socioeconomic Characteristics of Single Parent Families." *Marriage and Family Review* 20: 71–97.

Bramlett, M. D., and W. D. Mosher. 2001. "First Marriage Dissolution, Divorce and Remarriage: United States." *Advance Data from Vital and Health Statistics,* number 323. National Center for Health Statistics.

Carliner, Geoffrey. 1975. "Determinants of Household Headship." *Journal of Marriage and the Family* 37: 28–38.

Cherlin, A. 1980. "Postponing Marriage: The Influence of Young Women's Work Expectations." *Journal of Marriage and the Family* 42: 355–65.

Cherlin, A. 1992. *Marriage, Divorce, Remarriage.* Revised and enlarged edition. Harvard University Press.

Cherlin, A. J., and P. B. Walters. 1981. "Trends in United States Men's and Women's Sex-role Attitudes: 1972 to 1978." *American Sociological Review* 46: 453–60.

Chevan, A., and J. H. Korson. 1972. "The Widowed Who Live Alone: An Examination of Social and Demographic Factors." *Social Forces* 51: 45–53.

Costa, Dora. 1997. "Displacing the Family: Union Army Pensions and Elderly Living Arrangements." *Journal of Political Economy* 6: 1269–92.

Cready, C. M., M. A. Fossett, and K. J. Kiecolt. 1997. "Mate Availability and African American Family Structure in the U.S. Nonmetropolitan South, 1960–1990." *Journal of Marriage and the Family* 59: 192–203.

Das Gupta, Prithwis. 1978. "A General Method for Decomposing a Difference between Two Rates into Components." *Demography* 15: 99–112.

Davis, Kingsley, and Pietronella van den Oever. 1981. "Age Relations and Public Policy in Advanced Industrial Societies." *Population and Development Review* 7: 1–18.

Degler, Carl N. 1980. *At Odds: Women and the Family in America from the Revolution to the Present.* Oxford.

Durkheim, Emile. 1960 [1893]. *The Division of Labor in Society.* Free Press.

Eliot, Thomas H. 1961. "The Legal Background of the Social Security Act." Paper presented at a general staff meeting at Social Security Administration Headquarters, Baltimore, Maryland, on February 3, 1961. Accessed at the Internet site of the Social Security Administration, July 12, 2002.

Ellwood, David T., and Mary Jo Bane. 1985. "The Impact of AFDC on Family Structure and Living Arrangements." In R. Ehrenberg, editor. *Research in Labor Economics,* volume 7. JAI Press.

Elman, Cheryl. 1998. "Intergenerational Household Structure and Economic Change at the Turn of the Twentieth Century." *Journal of Family History* 4: 417–40.

Elman, Cheryl, and Peter Uhlenberg. 1995. "Co-Residence in the Early Twentieth Century: Elderly Women in the United States and Their Children." *Population Studies* 49 (3): 501–17.

Fitch, C. A., and S. Ruggles. 2000. "Historical Trends in Marriage Formation." In L. Waite, C. Bachrach, et al., editors. *Ties That Bind: Perspectives on Marriage and Cohabitation.* Aldine de Gruyter.

Fossett, Mark A., and K. Jill Kiecolt. 1993. "Mate Availability and Family Structure among African Americans in U.S. Metropolitan Areas." *Journal of Marriage and the Family* 55: 288–302.

Goldscheider, F. K., and L. J. Waite. 1986. "Sex Differences in the Entry to Marriage." *American Journal of Sociology* 92: 91–109.

Graham, John W., and Andrea H. Beller. 1985. "A Note on the Number and Living Arrangements of Women with Children under 21 from an Absent Father: Revised Estimates from the April 1979 and 1982 Current Population Surveys." *Journal of Economic and Social Measurement* 13: 209–14.

Groenveld, Lyle, Michael Hannan, and Nancy Tuma. 1983. "Income and Marital Events: Review of Previous Research." In *Final Report of the Seattle–Denver Income Maintenance Experiment,* volume 1. SRI International.

Hammel, E. A. 1995. "The Elderly in the Bosom of the Family: *La Famille Souche* and Hardship Reincorporation." In David I. Kertzer and Peter Laslett, editors. *Aging in the Past: Demography, Society and Old Age.* University of California Press.

Hareven, Tamara K. 1994. "Intergenerational Supports for the Old in the United States: A Historical Life Course Perspective." *Annual Review of Sociology* 20: 442.

Hareven, Tamara K., editor. 1996. *Aging and Generational Relations over the Life Course: A Historical and Cross-Cultural Perspective.* Aldine de Gruyter.

James, A. 1998. "What's Love Got to Do with It? Economic Viability and the Likelihood of Marriage among African American Men." *Journal of Comparative Family Studies* 29: 373–86.

King, Miriam L. 1988. *Changes in the Living Arrangements of the Elderly: 1960–2030.* Special Study, Congressional Budget Office. U.S. Government Printing Office.

Kobrin, Frances. 1976. "The Fall in Household Size and the Rise of the Primary Individual in the United States." *Demography* 13: 127–38.

Kramarow, Ellen. 1995. "Living Alone among the Elderly in the United States: Historical Perspectives on Household Change." *Demography* 32: 335–52.

Laslett, Peter. 1972. "Introduction." In Peter Laslett and Richard Wall, editors. *Household and Family in Past Time.* Cambridge University Press.

Lichter, D. T., F. B. LeClere, and D. K. McLaughlin. 1991. "Local Marriage Markets and the Marital Behavior of Black and White Women." *American Journal of Sociology* 96: 843–67.

Lichter, D. T., D. K. McLaughlin, et al. 1992. "Race and the Retreat from Marriage: A Shortage of Marriageable Men?" *American Sociological Review* 57: 781–99.

Lloyd, K. M., and S. J. South. 1996. "Contextual Influences on Young Men's Transition to First Marriage." *Social Forces* 74: 1097–119.

London, Rebecca A. 1998. "Trends in Single Mothers' Living Arrangements from 1970 to 1995: Correcting the Current Population Survey." *Demography* 35: 125–31.

Mare, R. D., and C. Winship. 1991. "Socioeconomic Change and the Decline of Marriage for Blacks and Whites." In Christopher Jencks and Paul E. Peterson, editors. *The Urban Underclass.* Brookings Institution Press.

May, Elaine Tyler. 1980. *Great Expectations: Marriage and Divorce in Post-Victorian America.* University of Chicago Press.

McGarry, Kathleen, and Robert Schoeni. 2000. "Social Security, Economic Growth, and the Rise in Elderly Widows' Independence in the Twentieth Century." *Demography* 37 (2): 221–36

McLanahan, Sara S. 1991. "The Two Faces of Divorce: Women's and Children's Interests." In Joan Huber, editor. *Macro–Micro Linkages in Sociology.* Sage.

---

[8] See the IPUMS Internet site for a current listing.

McLanahan, S., and L. Casper. 1995. "Growing Diversity and Inequality in the American Family." In R. Farley, editor. *State of the Union: America in the 1990s*, volume 2. Russell Sage Foundation.

Michael, R. T., V. R. Fuchs, and S. R. Scott. 1980. "Changes in the Propensity to Live Alone, 1950–1976." *Demography* 17: 39–53.

Moffitt, Robert. 1992. "Incentive Effects of the U.S. Welfare System: A Review." *Journal of Economic Literature* 30: 1–61.

Murray, Charles. 1984. *Losing Ground: American Social Policy, 1950–1980.* Basic Books.

Oppenheimer, V. K. 1994. "Women's Rising Employment and the Future of the Family in Industrial Societies." *Population and Development Review* 20: 293–342.

Oppenheimer, V. K., and V. Lew. 1995. "American Marriage Formation in the Eighties: How Important Was Women's Economic Independence?" In K. O. Mason and A. Jenson, editors. *Gender and Family Change in Industrialized Countries.* Clarendon Press.

Oppenheimer, V. K., M. Kalmijn, and N. Lim. 1997. "Men's Career Development and Marriage Timing during a Period of Rising Inequality." *Demography* 34: 311–30.

Pampel, Fred C. 1983. "Changes in the Propensity to Live Alone: Evidence from Consecutive Cross-Sectional Surveys." *Demography* 23: 433–47.

Preston, S. H., and A. T. Richards. 1975. "The Influence of Women's Work Opportunities on Marriage Rates." *Demography* 12: 209–22.

Riley, Glenda. 1991. *Divorce: An American Tradition.* Oxford University Press.

Ross, Heather L., and Isabel V. Sawhill. 1975. *Time of Transition: The Growth of Families Headed by Women.* Urban Institute.

Ruggles, Steven. 1987. *Prolonged Connections: The Rise of the Extended Family in Nineteenth Century England and America.* University of Wisconsin Press.

Ruggles, Steven. 1988. "The Demography of the Unrelated Individual, 1900–1950." *Demography* 25: 521–36.

Ruggles, Steven. 1994. "The Transformation of American Family Structure." *American Historical Review* 99: 103–28.

Ruggles, Steven. 1996a. "The Effects of Demographic Change on Multigenerational Family Structure: United States Whites 1880–1980." In Alain Bideau, A. Perrenoud, et al., editors. *Les systèmes démographiques du passé.* Centre Jacques Cartier.

Ruggles, Steven. 1996b. "Living Arrangements of the Elderly in America, 1880–1980." In Tamara K. Hareven, editor. *Aging and Generational Relations over the Life Course: A Historical and Cross-Cultural Perspective.* Aldine de Gruyter.

Ruggles, Steven. 1997a. "The Effects of AFDC on American Family Structure, 1940–1990." *Journal of Family History* 22: 307–25.

Ruggles, Steven. 1997b. "The Rise of Divorce and Separation in the United States, 1880–1990." *Demography* 34: 455–66.

Ruggles, Steven. 2001. "Living Arrangements and Economic Well-Being of the Aged in the Past." *Population Bulletin of the United Nations* 42/43: 111–61.

Ruggles, Steven. 2003. "Multigenerational Families in Nineteenth Century America." *Continuity and Change* 18: 139–65.

Ruggles, Steven, and Susan Brower. 2003. "Measurement of Household and Family Composition in the United States, 1850–2000." *Population and Development Review* 29 (1): 73–101.

Schoeni, Robert. 1998. "Reassessing the Decline in Parent–Child Old-Age Coresidence during the Twentieth Century." *Demography* 35: 307–13.

Shammas, Carole. 2002. *A History of American Household Government.* University Press of Virginia.

Smith, Daniel Scott. 1979. "Life Course, Norms, and the Family System of Older Americans in 1900." *Journal of Family History* 4: 285–98.

Smith, Daniel Scott. 1981. "Historical Change in the Household Structure of the Elderly in Economically Developed Countries." In R. W. Fogel and J. G. March, editors. *Aging: Stability and Change in the Family.* Academic Press.

Smith, Daniel Scott. 1986. "Accounting for Change in the Families of the Elderly in the United States, 1900–Present." In David Van Tassel and Peter N. Stearns, editors. *Old Age in a Bureaucratic Society: The Elderly, the Experts, and the State in American History.* Greenwood Press.

Sweet, James A., and Larry Bumpass. 1987. *American Families and Households.* Russell Sage Foundation.

Testa, M., and M. Krogh. 1995. "The Effect of Employment on Marriage among Black Males in Inner-City Chicago." In M. B. Tucker and C. Mitchell-Kernan, editors. *The Decline in Marriage among African-Americans: Causes, Consequences, and Policy Implications.* Russell Sage Foundation.

Thornton, Arland. 1985. "Changing Attitudes towards Separation and Divorce: Causes and Consequences." *American Journal of Sociology* 90: 856–72.

Thornton, Arland. 1989. "Changing Attitudes toward Family Issues in the United States." *Journal of Marriage and the Family* 51: 873–93.

Troll, L. E. 1971. "The Family of Later Life: A Decade Review." *Journal of Marriage and the Family* 33: 263–90.

U.S. Bureau of the Census. 1902. *Twelfth Census of the United States, Population, Part II.* U.S. Government Printing Office.

Waite, L., and G. D. Spitze. 1981. "Young Women's Transition to Marriage." *Demography* 18: 681–94.

Wall, Richard. 1995. "Elderly Persons and Members of Their Households in England and Wales from Preindustrial Times to the Present." In David I. Kertzer and Peter Laslett, editors. *Aging in the Past: Demography, Society and Old Age.* University of California Press.

Wilson, W. J., and K. Neckerman. 1987. "Poverty and Family Structure: The Widening Gap between Evidence and Public Policy." In W. J. Wilson, editor. *The Truly Disadvantaged: The Inner City, the Underclass, and Public Policy.* University of Chicago Press.

FAMILY AND HOUSEHOLD COMPOSITION

Steven Ruggles

TABLE Ae1–28   Households, by race and sex of householder and household type: 1850–1990[1]
[Census enumerations]

Contributed by Susan Brower and Steven Ruggles

		Households under 1950–1970 definition								
		All races								
			Family				Nonfamily			
								All nonfamily		
					Householder, no spouse present			Householder, no relatives present		Single-person nonfamily
	Households under 1980–1990 definition	Total	Total	Married couple	Male	Female	Total	Male	Female	
	Ae1	Ae2	Ae3	Ae4	Ae5	Ae6	Ae7	Ae8	Ae9	Ae10
Year	Number	Number	Number	Number	Number	Number	Number	Number	Number	Number
1850 [2]	3,581,172	3,539,847	3,425,104	2,927,930	204,373	283,384	124,160	85,069	39,091	74,834
1860 [2]	5,194,160	5,143,703	4,921,809	4,211,562	284,463	414,641	233,037	165,175	67,862	151,341
1870	7,549,028	7,471,754	7,147,728	6,023,073	380,208	721,547	346,926	221,763	125,164	242,539
1880	9,907,583	9,824,573	9,296,707	7,881,300	442,403	954,305	546,565	339,752	206,813	412,759
1890	12,638,749	12,530,206	—	—	—	—	—	—	—	—
1900	16,119,014	15,977,199	14,914,385	12,537,530	814,617	1,555,386	1,069,666	653,220	416,446	958,515
1910	20,165,673	19,984,021	18,678,011	15,868,181	956,584	1,790,755	1,368,501	807,931	560,570	1,024,858
1920	24,233,961	24,073,793	22,517,148	19,193,669	1,199,235	2,054,887	1,626,003	904,763	721,240	1,263,895
1930	29,904,663	29,798,665	—	—	—	—	—	—	—	—
1940	34,948,666 [3]	34,904,634	31,549,857	26,629,353	1,517,604	3,274,715	3,482,962	1,612,075	1,870,887	2,737,584
1950	—	42,857,335	37,914,998	32,989,943	1,338,966	3,434,892	5,093,534	2,016,295	3,077,239	4,193,497
1960	—	53,023,935	45,108,529	39,620,933	1,288,678	4,155,498	7,958,826	2,984,031	4,974,795	7,063,284
1970	—	63,637,721	51,189,513	43,870,603	1,618,924	5,651,744	12,496,449	4,599,928	7,896,521	11,184,758
1980	80,389,673	80,351,102	59,269,952	48,978,367	1,973,236	8,167,176	21,232,323	8,939,962	12,292,361	18,217,377
1990	91,947,410	91,873,988	64,957,602	51,197,074	2,939,422	10,566,590	27,170,903	11,493,516	15,677,387	22,640,489

		Households under 1950–1970 definition							
		White							
		Family				Nonfamily			
							All nonfamily		
					Householder, no spouse present			Householder, no relatives present		Single-person nonfamily
	Total	Total	Married couple	Male	Female	Total	Male	Female	
	Ae11	Ae12	Ae13	Ae14	Ae15	Ae16	Ae17	Ae18	Ae19
Year	Number	Number	Number	Number	Number	Number	Number	Number	Number
1850 [2]	3,462,272	3,355,327	2,878,205	199,918	268,293	115,856	80,612	35,244	69,670
1860 [2]	5,043,897	4,834,836	4,153,747	275,808	395,135	219,206	156,718	62,489	143,382
1870	6,512,213	6,255,743	5,340,443	313,628	583,568	274,574	175,587	98,987	192,367
1880	8,530,119	8,114,531	6,944,729	385,346	770,161	429,883	266,133	163,750	325,736
1890	—	—	—	—	—	—	—	—	—
1900	14,100,523	13,276,011	11,248,606	722,496	1,300,341	829,081	501,712	327,368	738,486
1910	17,712,607	16,646,171	14,247,238	854,810	1,494,987	1,115,572	656,280	459,291	851,279
1920	21,572,278	20,276,921	17,386,727	1,075,969	1,762,154	1,347,427	754,755	592,672	1,062,027
1930	—	—	—	—	—	—	—	—	—
1940	31,640,780	28,733,959	24,482,392	1,359,961	2,799,481	2,998,946	1,368,021	1,630,925	2,396,808
1950	39,038,813	34,660,417	30,488,355	1,190,524	2,875,275	4,484,659	1,751,861	2,732,798	3,750,634
1960	47,866,136	40,868,261	36,444,173	1,113,083	3,284,787	7,024,093	2,559,359	4,464,734	6,291,808
1970	56,780,259	45,800,220	40,173,505	1,358,950	4,234,267	11,013,537	3,933,365	7,080,172	9,892,619
1980	70,226,590	51,821,118	44,433,374	1,563,811	5,701,940	18,527,466	7,620,038	10,907,428	15,884,837
1990	79,364,900	55,901,105	46,206,291	2,309,117	7,165,536	23,683,957	9,882,070	13,801,887	19,690,893

Notes appear at end of table

TABLE Ae1–28   Households, by race and sex of householder and household type: 1850–1990
[Census enumerations]   *Continued*

				Households under 1950–1970 definition					
				Black					
		Family				Nonfamily			
							All nonfamily		
				Householder, no spouse present			Householder, no relatives present		Single-person nonfamily
	Total	Total	Married couple	Male	Female	Total	Male	Female	
	Ae20	Ae21	Ae22	Ae23	Ae24	Ae25	Ae26	Ae27	Ae28
Year	Number	Number	Number	Number	Number	Number	Number	Number	Number
1850 [2]	77,575	69,777	49,726	4,455	15,091	8,304	4,457	3,847	5,164
1860 [2]	88,765	78,915	53,836	5,971	18,410	10,548	5,574	4,975	7,064
1870	945,362	883,998	679,238	63,083	137,179	65,863	40,284	25,578	48,572
1880	1,269,100	1,166,903	925,412	55,490	182,870	105,328	63,147	42,181	83,012
1890	—	—	—	—	—	—	—	—	—
1900	1,786,075	1,582,034	1,242,482	87,553	249,715	206,325	121,816	84,509	192,621
1910	2,169,124	1,949,954	1,553,923	94,467	290,225	230,509	131,246	99,263	161,743
1920	2,411,438	2,169,352	1,747,828	116,529	288,510	258,571	131,812	126,759	186,886
1930	—	—	—	—	—	—	—	—	—
1940	3,141,679	2,715,443	2,067,571	147,940	464,579	461,589	224,860	236,729	323,096
1950	3,667,647	3,129,720	2,398,884	138,934	548,330	581,499	241,278	340,221	424,151
1960	4,777,518	3,932,316	2,917,125	160,697	837,891	861,804	370,449	491,355	710,847
1970	6,189,991	4,849,507	3,249,107	232,889	1,353,370	1,354,625	594,043	760,582	1,185,924
1980	8,391,740	6,116,111	3,480,528	340,887	2,269,513	2,300,811	1,104,328	1,196,484	2,007,132
1990	9,881,800	7,021,884	3,422,766	486,821	3,085,986	2,886,227	1,284,223	1,602,004	2,495,245

[1] As of June for 1850–1880 and 1900; as of January for 1920; as of April for other years.

[2] Excludes slave population.

[3] Excludes households with eleven or more persons unrelated to householder.

Sources

U.S. Bureau of the Census. Total households, 1850–1880: *Twelfth Census Special Reports, A Century of Population Growth, 1790–1900*. Total households, 1900: *Twelfth Census of the United States, Population*, part 2. Total households, 1890 and 1910–1950: *U.S. Census of Population: 1950*, volume 4, *Special Reports, General Characteristics of Families*. Total households, 1960: *Census of Population and Housing: 1960 Final Report PC (2)-4A, Subject Reports: Families*. Total households, 1970: *Census of Population: 1970, Detailed Characteristics, Final Report PC(1)-D1, United States Summary*. Total households, 1980: *Census of Population: 1980, General Population Characteristics*, part 1, *U.S. Summary*. Total Households, 1990: *Census of Population: 1990, General Population Characteristics*, part 1 (CP-1-1).

Adjustments to exclude group quarters from published household totals for 1850–1920 and tabulations of household types for 1850–1990 were tabulated from the Integrated Public Use Microdata Series (IPUMS); see the Guide to the Millennial Edition.

Documentation

Family households, which were termed "primary families" in the previous edition of *Historical Statistics of the United States* (1975), are households that include one or more persons related by birth, marriage, or adoption to the householder or household head. The concept of household head was replaced with the householder concept in 1980, but for the purposes of this table, the two may be considered identical. Married-couple family households have a married-spouse-present household head or householder; male-householder family households have a male householder residing with a child or other relatives, but no spouse; and female-householder family households have a female householder residing with a child or other relatives, but no spouse. Nonfamily households are composed of householders with no related persons but may include persons unrelated to the householder, such as boarders, servants, or roommates. Single person households, a subset of nonfamily households, contain only one person.

According to the 1990 Census Bureau definition, a household consists of all the persons who occupy a housing unit. A housing unit is a house, an apartment, a mobile home, a group of rooms, or a single room that is occupied as separate living quarters. Separate living quarters are those in which the occupants live and eat separately from any other persons in the building and have direct access from the outside of the building or through a common hall. A household may consist of a single family, one person living alone, two or more families living together, or any other group of related or unrelated person who share living arrangements.

The count of households given in Table Ae1–28 excludes group quarters. The Census Bureau first distinguished between private households and group quarters in 1930, when the count of households excluded "quasi-households," defined as living arrangements for institutional inmates, regardless of the number of inmates, or for other groups containing eleven or more persons unrelated to the household head. This definition of group quarters remained virtually unchanged from 1930 until 1990, except for adjustments in the number of persons unrelated to the head (or the householder) required for classification as group quarters. In 1930 and 1940, units had to contain eleven persons unrelated to the head before they were classified as group quarters; from 1950 through 1970, the threshold was five unrelated persons; and since 1980 the cutoff has been ten unrelated persons. When the 1940 public use microdata sample was designed in the late 1970s, it imposed the then-contemporary criterion of five persons unrelated to the head, so in that year the microdata are incompatible with the published statistics. For an extended discussion of group quarters issues, see Steven Ruggles and Susan Brower, "The Measurement of Family and Household Composition in the United States, 1850–2000," *Population and Development Review* 29 (1) (2003): 73–101.

Most household and group quarters tables in this edition of *Historical Statistics of the United States* use the IPUMS to adjust the count of households and group quarters residents for changes in census definitions. For 1850, 1860, 1870, 1880, 1910, and 1920, the proportion of all units (households and group quarters) that were households under the 1950–1970 and the 1980–1990 definitions was estimated from the IPUMS, and that proportion was multiplied by the total published number of enumerated units to estimate the number of households. For 1890 and 1900, the same procedure was followed, except that the proportion of all units that were households was estimated by interpolation because it could not be tabulated from the IPUMS in those years. The number of households under 1950–1970 definitions in 1930 was calculated by interpolating the effect of

(continued)

TABLE Ae1–28   Households, by race and sex of householder and household type: 1850–1990 [Census enumerations] *Continued*

the definitional shift in the surrounding census years. For 1940, the number of households under 1950–1970 definitions was estimated directly from the IPUMS. For 1980 and 1990, the number of households under 1950–1970 definitions was estimated by calculating the proportion of households in the IPUMS under the 1980–1990 definition that would have been counted as group quarters under the earlier definition and then by deflating the published totals accordingly.

Most of the household statistics in this chapter use the 1950–1970 group quarters definition, which counts units with five or more persons unrelated to the head or householder as group quarters because that definition can be constructed for most census years. In addition, we provide the count of

households according to the 1980–1990 definition in series Ae1. The differences between series Ae1 and Ae2 are modest. Nevertheless, the number of households in this edition of *Historical Statistics of the United States* differs slightly from that in previous editions.

In addition to changes in the definition of group quarters, the number of households is affected by changes in the definition of a separate housing unit (Ruggles and Brower 2003). Moreover, the distinction between group quarters and household and the classification of household type is based on inferred family relationships in the 1850–1870 period, which reduces the reliability of the statistics in those years.

TABLE Ae29–37   Households, by sex of householder and household type: 1947–2002[1]   [Current Population Surveys]

Contributed by Susan Brower, Steven Ruggles, and Richard Sutch

		Family				Nonfamily			
				Householder, no spouse present			All nonfamily		
								Householder, no relatives present		Single-person nonfamily
	Total	Total	Married couple	Male	Female	Total	Male	Female	
	Ae29	Ae30	Ae31	Ae32	Ae33	Ae34	Ae35	Ae36	Ae37
Year	Thousand	Thousand	Thousand	Thousand	Thousand	Thousand	Thousand	Thousand	Thousand
1947	39,107	34,964	30,612	1,129	3,223	4,143	1,388	2,755	2,894
1948	40,532	36,629	31,900	1,020	3,709	3,903	1,198	2,705	—
1949	42,182	38,080	33,257	1,197	3,626	4,102	1,308	2,794	—
1950	43,554	38,838	34,075	1,169	3,594	4,716	1,668	3,048	3,954
1951	44,673	39,502	34,391	1,154	3,957	5,171	1,732	3,439	—
1952	45,538	40,235	35,164	1,119	3,952	5,303	1,757	3,546	—
1953	46,385	40,540	35,577	1,206	3,757	5,845	1,902	3,943	—
1954	46,962	40,998	35,926	1,315	3,757	5,964	1,925	4,039	5,025
1955	47,874	41,732	36,251	1,328	4,153	6,142	2,059	4,083	5,221
1956	48,902	42,593	37,047	1,408	4,138	6,309	2,058	4,250	5,428
1957	49,673	43,262	37,718	1,241	4,304	6,411	2,038	4,374	5,464
1958	50,474	43,426	37,911	1,278	4,237	7,047	2,329	4,718	6,107
1959	51,435	43,971	38,410	1,285	4,276	7,464	2,449	5,015	6,327
1960	52,799	44,905	39,254	1,228	4,422	7,895	2,716	5,179	6,917
1961	53,557	45,383	39,620	1,199	4,564	8,174	2,779	5,395	7,112
1962	54,764	46,262	40,404	1,268	4,590	8,502	2,932	5,570	7,473
1963	55,270	46,872	40,888	1,295	4,689	8,398	2,838	5,560	7,501
1964	56,149	47,381	41,341	1,204	4,836	8,768	2,965	5,803	7,821
1965	57,436	47,838	41,689	1,167	4,982	9,598	3,277	6,321	8,631
1966	58,406	48,399	42,263	1,163	4,973	10,007	3,299	6,708	9,093
1967	59,236	49,086	42,743	1,190	5,153	10,150	3,419	6,731	9,200
1968	60,813	50,012	43,507	1,195	5,310	10,801	3,658	7,143	9,802
1969	62,214	50,729	44,086	1,221	5,422	11,485	3,890	7,595	10,401
1970	63,401	51,456	44,728	1,228	5,500	11,945	4,063	7,882	10,851
1971	64,778	52,102	44,928	1,254	5,920	12,676	4,403	8,273	11,446
1972	66,676	53,163	45,724	1,331	6,108	13,513	4,839	8,674	12,189
1973	68,251	54,264	46,297	1,432	6,535	13,986	5,129	8,858	12,635
1974	69,859	54,917	46,787	1,421	6,709	14,942	5,654	9,288	13,368
1975	71,120	55,563	46,951	1,485	7,127	15,557	5,912	9,645	13,939
1976	72,867	56,056	47,297	1,424	7,335	16,811	6,548	10,263	14,983
1977	74,142	56,472	47,471	1,461	7,540	17,669	6,971	10,698	15,532
1978	76,030	56,958	47,357	1,564	8,037	19,071	7,811	11,261	16,715
1979	77,330	57,498	47,662	1,616	8,220	19,831	8,064	11,767	17,201
1980 [2]	80,776	59,550	49,112	1,733	8,705	21,226	8,807	12,419	18,296
1981	82,368	60,309	49,294	1,933	9,082	22,059	9,279	12,780	18,936
1982	83,527	61,019	49,630	1,986	9,403	22,508	9,457	13,051	19,354
1983	83,918	61,393	49,908	2,016	9,469	22,525	9,514	13,011	19,250
1984 [3]	85,290	62,015	50,081	2,038	9,896	23,276	9,689	13,587	19,954

Notes appear at end of table

TABLE Ae29–37   Households, by sex of householder and household type: 1947–2002   [Current Population Surveys]
Continued

		Family				Nonfamily			
							All nonfamily		
				Householder, no spouse present				Householder, no relatives present		
	Total	Total	Married couple	Male	Female	Total	Total	Male	Female	Single-person nonfamily
	Ae29	Ae30	Ae31	Ae32	Ae33	Ae34	Ae35	Ae36	Ae37
Year	Thousand	Thousand	Thousand	Thousand	Thousand	Thousand	Thousand	Thousand	Thousand
1985	86,789	62,706	50,350	2,228	10,129	24,082	10,114	13,968	20,602
1986	88,458	63,558	50,933	2,414	10,211	24,900	10,648	14,252	21,178
1987	89,479	64,491	51,537	2,510	10,445	24,988	10,652	14,336	21,128
1988 [4]	91,124	65,204	51,675	2,834	10,696	25,919	11,282	14,637	21,889
1989	92,830	65,837	52,100	2,847	10,890	26,994	11,874	15,120	22,708
1990	93,347	66,090	52,317	2,884	10,890	27,257	11,606	15,651	22,999
1991	94,312	66,322	52,147	2,907	11,268	27,990	12,150	15,840	23,590
1992	95,699	67,173	52,547	3,025	11,692	28,496	12,428	16,068	23,974
1993 [5]	96,426	68,216	53,090	3,065	12,061	28,210	12,297	15,914	23,558
1994	97,107	68,490	53,171	2,913	12,406	28,617	12,462	16,155	23,611
1995	98,990	69,305	53,858	3,226	12,220	29,686	13,190	16,496	24,732
1996	99,627	69,594	53,567	3,513	12,514	30,033	13,348	16,685	24,900
1997	101,018	70,241	53,604	3,847	12,790	30,777	13,707	17,070	25,402
1998	102,528	70,880	54,317	3,911	12,652	31,648	14,133	17,516	26,327
1999	103,874	71,535	54,770	3,976	12,789	32,339	14,368	17,971	26,606
2000	104,705	72,025	55,311	4,028	12,687	32,680	14,641	18,039	26,724
2001 [6]	108,209	73,767	56,592	4,275	12,900	34,442	15,345	19,097	28,207
2002 [6]	109,297	74,329	56,747	4,438	13,143	34,969	15,579	19,390	28,775

[1] As of March except for 1947–1949 and 1951–1955, which are as of April.

[2] Revised using population controls based on the 1980 Census.

[3] Revised to incorporate Spanish-origin population controls.

[4] Revised based on 1988 reprocessing.

[5] Revised using population controls based on the 1990 Census.

[6] Data for 2001 and later based on population controls based on the 2000 Census.

Sources

U.S. Bureau of the Census, *Current Population Reports*, Series P20, numbers 176, 251, and 515. U.S. Census Bureau Internet site, Tables HH-1 and HH-4, release date June 12, 2003.

Documentation

See the text for Table Ae1–28 for definitions of household types.

The figures presented in Table Ae29–37, which are based on published Current Population Survey (CPS) data, are less reliable than the decennial statistics presented in Table Ae1–28. This is chiefly because they are subject to greater sampling error and because of Census Bureau processing errors; see the essay in this chapter. Moreover, unlike the statistics in Table Ae1–28, the series in Table Ae29–37 make no adjustment for change in the definition of group quarters. Like the decennial census, the CPS twice altered its definition of households. Until 1951 the CPS defined households as units with ten or fewer persons unrelated to the head. The threshold was then four or fewer until 1983, when it was raised to nine or fewer.

TABLE Ae38–78   Related and unrelated subfamilies, by race and sex of reference person and subfamily type: 1850–1990[1]
Contributed by Susan Brower and Steven Ruggles

		Related subfamilies					Unrelated subfamilies					
		Married couple						Married couple				
Year	Total	Total	With children	Without children	Other male-headed	Other female-headed	Total	Total	With children	Without children	Other male-headed	Other female-headed
	Ae38	Ae39	Ae40	Ae41	Ae42	Ae43	Ae44	Ae45	Ae46	Ae47	Ae48	Ae49
	Number	Number	Number	Number	Number	Number	Number	Number	Number	Number	Number	Number
1850 [2]	266,058	130,442	49,223	81,219	31,506	104,110	48,612	28,457	6,483	21,973	4,861	15,293
1860 [2]	338,061	174,199	68,462	104,592	37,217	131,677	64,565	40,948	10,545	30,227	6,664	17,921
1870	522,093	255,977	98,659	156,416	51,493	218,921	121,484	66,402	16,690	49,560	8,308	47,808
1880	500,883	263,946	122,815	141,131	43,950	192,987	78,210	35,727	10,376	25,350	9,586	32,898
1900	842,775	440,802	193,370	247,432	90,595	311,378	—	—	—	—	—	—
1910	1,059,645	611,195	264,276	346,919	94,229	354,220	179,147	110,107	27,461	82,646	16,126	52,914
1920	1,367,007	872,303	328,744	543,558	103,740	390,965	216,536	148,479	28,045	120,434	22,114	45,943
1940	2,129,254	1,468,836	640,742	828,094	131,444	528,974	315,239	237,366	45,448	191,918	18,369	59,504
1950	2,399,499	1,660,177	817,470	842,707	121,674	617,649	312,102	241,120	55,560	185,560	13,709	57,273
1960	1,672,095	900,919	422,346	478,573	117,841	653,335	85,737	44,833	8,209	36,623	7,298	33,606
1970	1,474,120	608,759	264,804	343,955	96,678	768,683	75,033	26,175	3,909	22,265	5,719	43,139
1980	1,758,138	620,513	260,654	359,859	112,298	1,025,327	231,095	33,879	8,096	25,784	17,279	179,937
1990	2,415,929	693,734	293,404	400,330	244,841	1,477,354	440,435	60,824	13,460	47,364	33,682	345,929

White

		Related subfamilies					Unrelated subfamilies					
		Married couple						Married couple				
Year	Total	Total	With children	Without children	Other male-headed	Other female-headed	Total	Total	With children	Without children	Other male-headed	Other female-headed
	Ae50	Ae51	Ae52	Ae53	Ae54	Ae55	Ae56	Ae57	Ae58	Ae59	Ae60	Ae61
	Number	Number	Number	Number	Number	Number	Number	Number	Number	Number	Number	Number
1850 [2]	257,347	127,708	47,704	80,004	30,492	99,147	45,673	27,343	6,180	21,163	4,759	13,571
1860 [2]	327,708	169,747	66,670	101,962	36,023	126,816	60,082	39,227	9,847	29,215	6,465	15,286
1870	429,724	223,190	84,871	137,544	41,794	168,283	81,988	51,262	11,990	39,162	6,307	25,111
1880	425,497	240,655	110,289	130,365	37,980	146,863	54,815	27,794	8,318	19,476	7,923	19,099
1900	706,502	401,214	172,055	229,159	82,221	223,067	—	—	—	—	—	—
1910	895,122	554,509	238,076	316,433	81,633	258,980	142,611	92,973	23,429	69,544	13,101	36,537
1920	1,203,841	796,303	302,202	494,101	91,680	315,858	172,410	115,711	23,425	92,286	19,400	37,299
1940	1,831,872	1,324,882	573,781	751,101	101,881	405,109	218,699	161,343	33,482	127,861	14,633	42,723
1950	1,981,014	1,450,833	700,362	750,471	86,347	443,835	199,093	150,597	36,739	113,858	9,313	39,184
1960	1,245,312	744,262	334,014	410,248	74,522	426,528	50,914	23,817	4,103	19,715	4,396	22,700
1970	1,039,167	494,895	204,716	290,179	63,681	480,592	53,566	18,553	2,607	15,946	3,914	31,100
1980	1,131,630	510,703	211,885	298,818	73,440	547,487	187,928	28,681	6,896	21,786	13,782	145,464
1990	1,548,873	549,605	240,453	309,152	150,101	849,167	365,746	47,141	10,778	36,363	26,314	292,291

Black

Year	Related subfamilies Total (Ae62)	Married couple Total (Ae63)	With children (Ae64)	Without children (Ae65)	Other male-headed (Ae66)	Other female-headed (Ae67)	Unrelated subfamilies Total (Ae68)	Married couple Total (Ae69)	With children (Ae70)	Without children (Ae71)	Other male-headed (Ae72)	Other female-headed (Ae73)	Secondary individuals Total (Ae74)	Male White (Ae75)	Male Black (Ae76)	Female White (Ae77)	Female Black (Ae78)
1850 [2]	8,711	2,734	1,519	1,215	1,014	4,963	2,939	1,114	304	811	102	1,722	951,082	534,229	29,617	361,461	25,775
1860 [2]	8,961	3,948	1,792	2,126	896	4,253	4,484	1,721	698	1,011	199	2,635	1,322,454	759,441	27,996	503,896	31,121
1870	91,570	32,384	13,588	18,672	9,600	50,334	39,496	15,141	4,700	10,398	2,001	22,697	1,701,245	808,968	154,473	615,452	122,352
1880	73,916	22,311	12,035	10,276	5,970	45,635	23,101	7,933	2,058	5,875	1,468	13,701	2,253,245	1,081,747	224,796	754,814	166,447
1900	128,659	33,497	18,269	15,228	8,374	86,788	—	—	—	—	—	—	—	—	—	—	—
1910	158,729	53,916	25,445	28,471	11,840	92,973	36,283	16,882	3,780	13,102	3,025	16,377	3,589,186	1,975,832	294,445	1,077,850	205,289
1920	157,738	72,782	25,134	47,647	11,557	73,399	42,517	31,461	4,319	27,143	2,613	8,443	3,095,421	1,687,570	247,557	958,870	174,984
1940	287,638	138,602	63,990	74,612	28,187	120,849	95,690	75,274	11,787	63,487	3,736	16,680	3,480,692	1,540,874	281,363	1,380,996	256,045
1950	402,292	198,495	110,871	87,624	34,143	169,654	111,013	88,954	18,364	70,589	4,225	17,835	2,812,771	1,219,228	273,764	1,067,709	228,466
1960	400,570	139,850	78,833	61,017	41,119	219,602	33,622	20,315	4,006	16,309	2,703	10,605	2,383,985	966,373	280,432	867,409	228,934
1970	403,054	96,207	51,063	45,144	31,393	275,453	19,761	6,921	1,002	5,918	1,605	11,235	2,745,683	1,092,350	250,353	1,111,101	210,286
1980	544,481	61,450	31,781	29,668	34,166	448,865	35,575	2,899	600	2,299	2,997	29,679	5,179,837	2,118,173	404,082	2,145,304	298,253
1990	706,183	51,770	24,884	26,886	83,458	570,956	51,477	3,863	327	3,536	5,497	42,117	8,344,556	3,510,182	684,403	3,279,249	451,147

[1] As of June for 1850–1880 and 1900; as of January for 1920; as of April for other years.

[2] Excludes slave population.

Source

Tabulated from the Integrated Public Use Microdata Series (IPUMS); see the Guide to the Millennial Edition.

Documentation

A subfamily is a married couple with or without children or a single parent with one or more own never-married children less than 18 years old. A subfamily does not maintain its own household, but lives in the home of someone else. Related subfamilies are those in which the reference person is related to the householder. Unrelated subfamilies, formerly called secondary families, are those in which the reference person is not related to the householder. Secondary individuals are persons unrelated to the householder who are not members of unrelated subfamilies.

Historical Statistics of the United States (1975) provided a series on subfamilies based on published sources; that series is inaccurate, for reasons explained in the essay in this chapter. The IPUMS tabulations shown here were adjusted to conform to the adjusted published count of households in each census year; see the text for Table Ae1–28. Also see Steven Ruggles and Susan Brower, "Measurement of Household and Family Composition in the United States, 1850–2000," *Population and Development Review* 29 (1) (2003): 73–101.

TABLE Ae79–81   Households, by farm–nonfarm residence: 1850–1990[1]   [Decennial series]

Contributed by Susan Brower and Steven Ruggles

	Total	Nonfarm	Farm
	Ae79	Ae80	Ae81
Year	Number	Number	Number
1850 [2]	3,539,847	1,762,642	1,777,205
1860 [2]	5,143,703	2,873,305	2,270,398
1870	7,471,754	4,614,753	2,857,001
1880	9,824,573	5,899,482	3,925,091
1890	12,530,206	7,823,112	4,707,094
1900	15,977,199	10,326,637	5,650,562
1910	19,984,021	13,869,016	6,115,004
1920	24,073,793	17,287,727	6,786,067
1930	29,798,665	23,217,438	6,581,227
1940	34,904,634	27,756,816	7,147,818
1950	42,857,335	37,049,735	5,807,600
1960	53,023,935	48,786,802	4,237,133
1970	63,637,721	61,139,912	2,497,809
1980	80,351,102	78,493,361	1,857,742
1990	91,873,988	90,468,456	1,405,532

[1] As of June for 1850–1880 and 1900; as of January for 1920; as of April for other years.

[2] Excludes slave population.

Sources

1850–1880, 1900–1920, 1940–1990: Tabulated from the Integrated Public Use Microdata Series (IPUMS); see the Guide to the Millennial Edition. 1890 and 1930: U.S. Census Bureau, *U.S. Census of Population: 1950*, volume 4, *Special Reports: General Characteristics of Families*, P-E number 2A.

Documentation

The tabulations are based on the 1950–1970 household definition. The number of households was adjusted to conform to the adjusted published count of households in each census year; see the text for Table Ae1–28.

Between 1850 and 1880 a household was coded as a farm household if one or more persons in the household reported "farmer" as occupation. In 1900 the census counted a household as a farm if a member of the household operated a farm. The household did not necessarily live on or operate the farm during these years. For 1910–1930 enumerators defined a farm household as any household located either on a tract of three or more acres used for any agricultural operations, regardless of the amount of labor or produce involved, or households on fewer than three acres that either yielded at least $250 in produce sales the previous year or employed at least one full-time farmer or agricultural laborer. In 1940 and 1950 enumerators simply asked respondents whether or not the house in which they lived was located on a farm. For 1960 and 1970 a farm was either a household on ten or more acres that yielded at least $50 in produce, or a household on fewer than ten acres that yielded at least $250 in produce. For 1980 and 1990 a farm was any household on one or more acres that yielded $1,000 or more in produce. Families that paid cash rent were considered farm households if the parcel of land they farmed met these criteria. Those that paid no cash rent were enumerated the same way as owner-occupied farms. For both years, vacant units and those on urban lands could not be farms. The 1980 census excluded households on suburban lots, and 1990 excluded multiple dwelling units.

TABLE Ae82–84   Households, by farm–nonfarm residence: 1900–1992[1]   [Annual series]

Contributed by Susan Brower, Steven Ruggles, and Richard Sutch

	Total	Nonfarm	Farm		Total	Nonfarm	Farm		Total	Nonfarm	Farm
	Ae82	Ae83	Ae84		Ae82	Ae83	Ae84		Ae82	Ae83	Ae84
Year	Thousand	Thousand	Thousand	Year	Thousand	Thousand	Thousand	Year	Thousand	Thousand	Thousand
1900	15,992	—	—	1935	31,892	24,665	7,227	1970	62,874	60,150	2,724
1901	16,345	—	—	1936	32,454	25,253	7,201	1971	64,374	61,723	2,651
1902	16,716	—	—	1937	33,088	25,917	7,171	1972	66,676	63,785	2,891
1903	17,108	—	—	1938	33,683	26,518	7,165	1973	68,251	65,365	2,886
1904	17,521	—	—	1939	34,409	27,249	7,160	1974	69,859	66,970	2,889
1905	17,939	—	—	1940	35,153	28,001	7,152	1975	71,120	68,382	2,738
1906	18,394	—	—	1941	35,929	28,786	7,143	1976	72,867	70,365	2,503
1907	18,863	—	—	1942	36,445	29,433	7,012	1977	74,142	71,656	2,485
1908	19,294	—	—	1943	36,833	30,206	6,627	1978	76,030	73,505	2,524
1909	19,734	—	—	1944	37,115	30,722	6,393	1979	77,330	74,934	2,396
1910	20,183	13,989	6,194	1945	37,503	31,158	6,345	1980	80,776	78,857	1,919
1911	20,620	14,358	6,262	1946	38,370	31,944	6,426	1981	82,368	80,527	1,841
1912	21,075	14,727	6,348	1947	39,107	32,673	6,434	1982	83,527	81,708	1,819
1913	21,606	15,187	6,419	1948	40,532	34,116	6,416	1983	83,918	82,071	1,847
1914	22,110	15,630	6,480	1949	42,182	35,687	6,495	1984	85,407	83,589	1,818
1915	22,501	15,949	6,552	1950	43,554	37,279	6,275	1985	86,789	—	—
1916	22,926	16,291	6,635	1951	44,673	38,602	6,071	1986	88,458	86,653	1,805
1917	23,323	16,643	6,680	1952	45,538	39,584	5,954	1987	89,479	87,775	1,704
1918	23,519	16,846	6,673	1953	46,385	40,548	5,837	1988	91,066	89,382	1,684
1919	23,873	17,307	6,566	1954	46,962	41,460	5,502	1989	92,830	91,224	1,606
1920	24,467	17,668	6,799	1955	47,874	42,319	5,555	1990	93,347	91,710	1,637
1921	25,119	18,255	6,864	1956	48,902	43,239	5,663	1991	94,312	92,670	1,642
1922	25,687	18,780	6,907	1957	49,673	44,441	5,232	1992	95,669	94,104	1,565
1923	26,298	19,492	6,806	1958	50,474	45,289	5,185				
1924	26,941	20,182	6,759	1959	51,435	46,028	5,407				
1925	27,540	20,745	6,795	1960	52,799	48,708	4,091				
1926	28,101	21,325	6,776	1961	53,464	49,715	3,749				
1927	28,632	21,941	6,691	1962	54,652	50,890	3,762				
1928	29,124	22,416	6,708	1963	55,189	51,725	3,464				
1929	29,582	22,851	6,731	1964	55,996	52,651	3,345				
1930	29,997	23,268	6,729	1965	57,251	53,899	3,350				
1931	30,272	23,476	6,796	1966	58,092	54,875	3,214				
1932	30,439	23,541	6,898	1967	58,845	55,910	2,934				
1933	30,802	23,653	7,149	1968	60,444	57,501	2,944				
1934	31,306	24,118	7,188	1969	61,805	58,935	2,870				

[1] As of July for 1900–1946; as of April for 1951–1955; and as of March for 1950 and 1956–1992.

Sources

U.S. Bureau of the Census, *Current Population Reports*: 1900–1950, series P-20, number 92; 1951–1968, series P-20, numbers 59 and 176; 1950–1970, series P-20, numbers 176, 200, and 218; 1971–1992, series P-20, numbers 233, 311, 326, 352, 411, 439, 472, and 479, and series P-27, number 58.

Documentation

For the definition of household types, see the text for Table Ae1–28.

The annual series for 1947–1992 is based on published statistics from the Current Population Survey (CPS) and should be considered less reliable than the decennial series given in Table Ae79–81; see the text for Table Ae29–37.

The data in series Ae82 for 1961–1971, 1984, 1988, and 1992 have been revised; see series Ae29 for the revised numbers. However, the farm/nonfarm breakdown has not been revised for these years.

In the CPS, farm households as currently defined consist of households in rural territory on one or more acres that yielded $1,000 or more in produce. Before 1978, farm households were in rural areas either on ten or more acres with $50 or more in produce, or on fewer than ten acres with $250 or more in produce. The definition of rural territory has been modified each decade based on the decennial census; see source notes for series A43–72 in *Historical Statistics of the United States* (1975). Before 1960 the definition of farms varied as described in the text for Table Ae79–81.

The annual number of households for 1900–1946 was estimated by the Census Bureau in 1959. These figures should be regarded as approximations. The Census Bureau first estimated the number of married couples through a combination of decennial census data and annual data on marriages, divorces, and net immigration of married people. The number of married couples was then adjusted by extrapolating backwards the proportion of married couples not residing in their own household and the proportion of households not headed by a married couple. In some cases, the error of the estimate may be a substantial proportion of the indicated annual change in the number of households. The estimates by residence for this period were made by subdividing the total into farm and nonfarm components, using estimates of the average size of farm households in conjunction with annual estimates of the farm population (see joint report of Bureau of the Census and Bureau of Agricultural Economics, *Estimates of the Farm Population: 1910 to 1950*, series Census-BAE, number 16A). The remaining households were classified as nonfarm. The annual farm household series for 1900–1946 relates to the total farm population, whereas that for the period since 1947 relates to the rural-farm population. There were 88,000 urban-farm households in 1940 and 96,000 in 1950.

TABLE Ae85–96   Population in households, by household size: 1790–1990[1]

Contributed by Susan Brower and Steven Ruggles

Year	Total	1 person	2 persons	3 persons	4 persons	5 persons	6 persons	7 persons	8 persons	9 persons	10 persons	11 or more persons
	Ae85	Ae86	Ae87	Ae88	Ae89	Ae90	Ae91	Ae92	Ae93	Ae94	Ae95	Ae96
	Number	Number	Number	Number	Number	Number	Number	Number	Number	Number	Number	Number
1790 [2]	2,358,631	15,353	63,958	144,348	226,460	285,855	324,312	323,204	295,456	240,183	173,560	265,942
1850 [2]	19,090,077	74,690	712,032	1,497,504	2,126,756	2,578,225	2,765,040	2,567,642	2,261,008	1,731,942	1,240,190	1,535,048
1860 [2]	26,555,861	152,601	1,108,706	2,329,380	3,448,716	4,066,840	3,917,622	3,499,685	2,921,528	2,097,657	1,397,640	1,615,486
1870	37,026,062	243,644	1,812,728	3,657,495	5,093,808	5,654,240	5,589,576	4,807,271	3,825,736	2,794,077	1,634,980	1,912,507
1880	48,186,043	420,632	2,615,732	4,915,827	6,673,684	7,475,565	7,217,436	6,225,289	4,850,496	3,430,845	2,105,480	2,255,057
1900	70,282,838	955,517	5,248,880	8,704,332	10,691,956	11,338,630	9,990,756	8,112,328	6,077,744	4,098,276	2,390,710	2,673,709
1910	87,339,262	1,024,683	6,880,110	11,488,524	13,882,332	13,900,785	12,207,240	9,731,288	7,244,600	4,842,441	3,042,810	3,094,449
1920	101,339,121	1,268,712	9,279,462	14,501,499	17,330,692	16,444,005	13,721,928	10,318,672	7,464,736	4,880,862	2,959,810	3,168,743
1940	127,565,781	2,737,584	17,189,038	23,389,245	25,487,756	20,276,145	14,209,644	9,356,543	6,086,616	3,815,388	2,312,140	2,705,682
1950	145,048,103	4,246,403	24,649,192	29,531,835	31,745,080	22,215,675	13,433,184	7,763,014	4,647,832	2,832,624	1,698,200	2,285,064
1960	174,397,661	7,032,951	29,680,248	29,920,476	36,310,240	29,185,345	18,643,656	9,994,257	5,704,456	3,452,409	1,950,440	2,523,183
1970	197,471,798	11,165,872	37,612,422	32,768,475	39,245,492	31,036,345	20,400,990	13,447,378	5,084,624	2,903,013	1,610,130	2,197,057
1980	220,526,012	18,218,371	50,212,978	41,815,341	49,655,612	31,454,955	15,678,726	8,553,608	2,301,336	1,202,157	689,440	743,488
1990	240,874,565	22,405,065	58,800,800	48,139,920	55,136,748	31,863,515	13,426,158	6,458,858	2,072,664	1,158,030	558,630	854,177

[1] As of August for 1790; as of June for 1850–1880 and 1900; as of January for 1920; as of April for 1910 and 1940–1990.

[2] Excludes slave population.

Sources

1790: *Twelfth Census Special Reports, A Century of Population Growth, 1790–1900.*
1850–1990: Tabulated from the Integrated Public Use Microdata Series (IPUMS); see the Guide to the Millennial Edition.

Documentation

For 1790 the definition of household is imprecise, but the source specifies that "all households which were obviously institutions, or of a public or semipublic character, were excluded." In addition, the 1790 data exclude New Jersey, Delaware, Virginia, Georgia, Kentucky, and Tennessee. For the remaining census years, the tabulations are based on the 1950–1970 household definition. It is likely that the 1790 definition is somewhat broader and includes some large units that would have been classified as group quarters under 1950–1970 definitions. The number of households in the 1850–1990 period was adjusted to conform to the adjusted published count of households in each census year; see the text for Table Ae1–28.

TABLE Ae97–127 Population in institutions and other group quarters, by sex, age, and race: 1850–1990[1]

Contributed by Susan Brower and Steven Ruggles

Population in institutions

	Total	Correctional institutions	Mental institutions	Homes for the aged and dependent	Other institutions	Male Total	Male Age 0–17	Male 18–64	Male 65 and above	Male White	Male Black	Female Total	Female Age 0–17	Female 18–64	Female 65 and above	Female White	Female Black
	Ae97	Ae98	Ae99	Ae100	Ae101	Ae102	Ae103	Ae104	Ae105	Ae106	Ae107	Ae108	Ae109	Ae110	Ae111	Ae112	Ae113
Year	Number	Number	Number	Number	Number	Number	Number	Number	Number	Number	Number	Number	Number	Number	Number	Number	Number
1850 [2]	81,856	15,265	5,254	3,437	57,900	49,017	13,443	31,329	4,245	46,491	2,526	32,839	8,384	20,513	3,942	31,121	1,718
1860 [2]	86,406	24,067	12,539	2,509	47,291	54,379	14,552	37,014	2,813	50,764	2,713	32,027	14,760	14,653	2,614	30,120	1,506
1870	153,751	34,197	23,019	6,732	89,803	87,394	25,994	57,287	4,113	77,058	8,329	66,357	31,943	30,796	3,618	63,444	2,913
1880	288,103	72,546	49,774	10,778	155,005	174,494	43,602	114,733	16,159	149,644	22,956	113,609	33,109	69,025	11,475	103,736	9,674
1900	711,897	141,921	86,521	56,919	426,536	388,579	112,321	235,275	40,983	337,733	47,051	323,318	59,960	238,314	25,044	311,934	11,384
1910	720,915	163,216	102,770	75,816	379,113	450,129	78,593	291,433	80,103	382,633	63,968	270,786	68,011	169,270	33,505	257,685	12,597
1920	790,138	119,386	255,616	83,572	331,564	464,099	97,880	291,648	74,571	400,926	58,735	326,039	79,107	192,539	54,393	306,164	15,943
1940	1,296,107	288,607	573,667	234,054	199,779	833,560	99,804	612,130	121,626	703,039	127,186	462,547	71,826	281,930	108,791	419,619	40,807
1950	1,566,846	264,557	613,628	296,783	391,878	933,658	122,851	649,170	161,637	770,381	154,801	633,188	92,873	325,560	214,755	571,278	59,630
1960	1,886,967	346,015	630,046	469,717	441,189	1,093,452	143,748	713,646	236,058	873,663	204,175	793,515	89,682	350,140	353,693	717,008	70,186
1970	2,126,719	328,020	433,890	927,514	437,295	1,119,763	166,215	652,305	301,243	867,148	236,525	1,006,956	91,389	281,681	633,886	914,644	84,319
1980	2,506,777	466,371	245,029	1,426,731	368,646	1,227,381	117,859	738,173	371,348	909,610	289,615	1,279,396	48,661	248,544	982,192	1,162,454	104,269
1990	3,334,018	1,115,111	128,530	1,772,032	318,345	1,827,923	112,873	1,269,663	445,387	1,185,697	594,235	1,506,095	36,154	267,029	1,202,912	1,333,811	153,668

Population in other group quarters

	Total, 1990 definition of group quarters	Total, 1970 definition of group quarters	Male Total	Male Age 0–17	Male 18–64	Male 65 and above	Male White	Male Black	Female Total	Female Age 0–17	Female 18–64	Female 65 and above	Female White	Female Black
	Ae114	Ae115	Ae116	Ae117	Ae118	Ae119	Ae120	Ae121	Ae122	Ae123	Ae124	Ae125	Ae126	Ae127
Year	Number	Number	Number	Number	Number	Number	Number	Number	Number	Number	Number	Number	Number	Number
1850 [2]	361,720	808,353	508,377	107,159	396,570	4,648	494,121	14,256	299,976	107,169	188,764	4,043	289,462	10,514
1860 [2]	347,386	844,999	539,054	105,754	427,278	6,022	523,525	12,023	305,945	98,896	199,624	7,425	295,720	9,325
1870	586,931	1,339,846	831,504	165,533	649,593	16,378	727,419	81,776	508,342	165,033	330,562	12,747	436,548	70,092
1880	802,140	1,656,167	1,109,716	163,657	928,701	17,358	946,502	95,276	546,451	164,443	363,950	18,058	473,759	70,502
1900	1,974,006	2,604,683	1,787,307	200,365	1,552,790	34,152	1,580,875	146,476	817,376	185,936	604,118	27,322	731,611	73,622
1910	1,793,064	3,508,773	2,467,404	265,262	2,147,986	54,156	2,227,570	144,099	1,041,369	228,470	771,850	41,049	942,878	89,423
1920	1,827,598	3,135,649	2,125,214	198,703	1,847,301	79,210	1,890,069	180,043	1,010,435	186,792	782,483	41,160	908,508	90,018
1940	—	2,807,103	1,664,470	134,810	1,410,417	119,243	1,491,255	143,369	1,142,633	119,934	939,205	83,494	1,010,603	127,282
1950	—	4,075,907	2,546,046	181,800	2,177,445	186,801	2,179,256	323,230	1,529,861	174,544	1,218,240	137,077	1,250,803	267,951
1960	—	2,881,383	1,965,616	118,641	1,777,425	69,550	1,747,445	177,804	915,767	68,150	779,279	68,338	806,963	95,542
1970	—	3,659,644	2,341,255	89,325	2,207,422	44,509	2,068,211	219,127	1,318,389	46,887	1,208,782	62,720	1,192,305	106,927
1980	3,242,871	3,500,854	2,059,699	104,004	1,908,648	47,047	1,664,631	305,944	1,441,154	65,993	1,273,829	101,332	1,224,401	165,537
1990	3,363,726	3,806,303	2,212,071	124,889	2,039,728	47,454	1,752,582	347,058	1,594,232	112,789	1,403,137	78,306	1,275,581	229,248

Notes appear on next page   (continued)

TABLE Ae97–127   Population in institutions and other group quarters, by sex, age, and race: 1850–1990   *Continued*

[1] As of June for 1850–1880 and 1900; as of January for 1920; as of April for other years. There are no data for 1890 because the original census manuscripts were destroyed in a fire. There are no data for 1930 because the 1930 Census records were not publicly available when this table was prepared.

[2] Excludes slave population.

Sources

Number of group quarters residents, 1850–1960, tabulated from the Integrated Public Use Microdata Series (IPUMS; see the Guide to the Millennial Edition); 1970, U.S. Bureau of the Census, *Census of Population: 1970, Subject Reports PC(2)-4E, Persons in Institutions and Other Group Quarters*, p. 503; 1980, *Census of Population: 1980, Summary PC80-1-D1-A, Detailed Population Characteristics, United States*, p. 88; 1990, *Census of Population: 1990, General Population Characteristics: United States*, 1990 CP 1-1, p. 48. Number of institutional inmates, 1850–1940, tabulated from the IPUMS and *U.S. Census of Population: 1950*, volume 4, part 2, chapter C, "Institutional Population," pp. 15–17; 1960, *U.S. Census of Population: 1960, Final Report PC(2)-8A, Inmates of Institutions*, pp. 3–5, 7, and 12; 1970, *U.S. Census of Population: 1970, Final Report PC(2)-4E, Persons in Institutions and Other Group Quarters*, pp. 2–3, 5, 7, 11, 21, and 503. 1980, *1980 Census of Population, Summary PC80-1-D1-A, Detailed Population Characteristics, United States*, p. 88; 1990, *Census of Population: 1990, General Population Characteristics: United States*, 1990 CP 1-1, p. 48. Characteristics of group quarters residents and institutional inmates, 1850–1990, tabulated from the IPUMS.

Documentation

For the definition of group quarters, see the text for Table Ae1–28. The number of group quarters residents was adjusted to conform to published totals in the period since 1970. In the 1990 Census, inmates of institutions were defined as persons under formally authorized, supervised care or custody in institutions at the time of enumeration. Such persons are classified as patients or inmates of an institution regardless of the availability of nursing or medical care, their length of stay, or the number of people in the institution. There has been little change in the definition of institutions since 1950. The published tabulations for institutions in 1940 are incompatible with those of subsequent census years, and there are no published tabulations on institutions before 1940. For the period 1850–1940, therefore, the statistics are tabulated from the IPUMS. The statistics on institutions are probably more complete in the recent period – especially since 1950 – than they are in earlier years. In all periods, the data on the characteristics of inmates and types of institutions were tabulated from the IPUMS, but the number of inmates in the period since 1950 was adjusted to conform to published totals. Although data on types of institutions are generally comparable for each year shown, it should be noted that the use of progressively refined techniques to identify types of institutions over the past century has resulted in more inclusive and definitive classification of these types.

TABLE Ae128–190   Living arrangements of children, by age and race: 1850–1990[1]

Contributed by Susan Brower and Steven Ruggles

						All races						
		Both parents present					Mother only present				Father only present	
	Total	Age 0–4	Age 5–9	Age 10–14	Age 15–17	Age 0–4	Age 5–9	Age 10–14	Age 15–17	Age 0–4	Age 5–9
	Ae128	Ae129	Ae130	Ae131	Ae132	Ae133	Ae134	Ae135	Ae136	Ae137	Ae138
Year	Number	Number	Number	Number	Number	Number	Number	Number	Number	Number	Number
1850 [2]	9,503,589	2,631,638	2,367,739	1,920,444	864,763	155,665	189,622	211,567	124,453	68,132	91,984
1860 [2]	12,725,438	3,841,982	3,080,752	2,445,799	1,165,498	192,913	246,667	293,373	187,731	95,806	115,851
1870	17,558,453	4,905,125	4,031,773	3,625,599	1,590,349	371,721	431,724	524,161	288,168	121,857	142,022
1880	22,026,804	6,337,618	5,593,784	4,539,216	1,888,034	385,145	483,633	554,244	346,988	90,261	160,924
1900	30,783,580	8,481,171	7,795,898	6,509,493	3,129,919	442,453	607,924	758,948	500,904	106,256	251,964
1910	34,997,020	9,875,724	8,657,688	7,462,673	3,883,538	444,595	633,497	799,738	592,174	101,762	242,318
1920	39,535,156	10,809,245	10,146,201	8,897,997	4,268,149	477,002	666,218	858,651	586,424	147,434	307,257
1940	40,434,693	9,553,082	9,493,105	9,776,140	5,581,844	508,134	746,255	1,112,951	819,020	113,296	220,844
1950	46,506,074	14,695,053	11,631,255	9,320,547	4,717,955	873,652	923,984	990,839	663,053	124,103	170,560
1960	64,622,690	18,449,418	16,582,060	14,505,818	6,652,682	1,479,662	1,494,655	1,534,826	883,226	168,838	203,117
1970	70,390,948	14,592,583	17,088,646	17,259,261	9,144,604	1,995,272	2,421,679	2,601,599	1,471,242	251,633	385,738
1980	64,293,006	13,143,119	13,141,189	14,175,570	9,089,120	2,665,387	2,985,883	3,296,993	2,131,120	306,244	336,079
1990	63,565,880	13,378,347	13,238,314	12,260,751	6,878,564	3,722,436	3,746,231	3,526,454	2,015,313	708,748	639,971

Notes appear at end of table

TABLE Ae128–190 Living arrangements of children, by age and race: 1850–1990 *Continued*

All races

	Father only present		Both parents absent							
			Living with other relatives				Living with nonrelatives			
	Age 10–14	Age 15–17	Age 0–4	Age 5–9	Age 10–14	Age 15–17	Age 0–4	Age 5–9	Age 10–14	Age 15–17
	Ae139	Ae140	Ae141	Ae142	Ae143	Ae144	Ae145	Ae146	Ae147	Ae148
Year	Number	Number	Number	Number	Number	Number	Number	Number	Number	Number
1850 [2]	100,372	58,013	61,251	90,860	144,765	127,561	17,479	30,530	99,065	147,686
1860 [2]	126,609	75,952	64,613	102,543	172,681	163,258	19,458	39,021	113,885	181,046
1870	175,458	90,976	95,703	164,719	254,450	223,013	22,806	53,356	191,336	254,137
1880	199,481	110,924	116,302	176,848	238,239	232,392	25,933	61,456	194,294	291,088
1900	312,679	191,255	100,940	202,636	283,088	312,683	53,885	101,698	234,514	405,272
1910	328,465	246,356	112,343	227,208	339,307	397,994	49,876	97,231	192,451	312,082
1920	421,495	277,501	155,088	293,060	371,866	401,024	40,267	70,232	144,204	195,841
1940	362,290	295,854	155,943	253,761	383,413	434,246	88,826	113,512	194,154	228,023
1950	225,232	172,317	224,203	289,752	334,373	415,076	157,062	141,913	189,588	245,557
1960	248,820	159,462	306,197	326,333	386,292	519,179	117,859	140,079	198,708	265,459
1970	451,546	285,889	243,175	367,617	489,810	586,392	97,469	152,058	228,586	276,149
1980	424,119	338,004	266,601	326,306	427,739	554,613	86,625	99,209	170,056	329,030
1990	639,159	420,320	374,214	380,282	460,404	444,658	134,947	126,467	170,184	300,116

White

	Both parents present					Mother only present				Father only present	
	Total	Age 0–4	Age 5–9	Age 10–14	Age 15–17	Age 0–4	Age 5–9	Age 10–14	Age 15–17	Age 0–4	Age 5–9
	Ae149	Ae150	Ae151	Ae152	Ae153	Ae154	Ae155	Ae156	Ae157	Ae158	Ae159
Year	Number	Number	Number	Number	Number	Number	Number	Number	Number	Number	Number
1850 [2]	9,307,614	2,592,020	2,336,207	1,895,378	854,653	140,708	175,777	201,967	120,407	66,011	90,670
1860 [2]	12,488,984	3,795,594	3,042,519	2,410,786	1,151,156	178,258	234,020	283,033	180,908	93,096	111,741
1870	15,138,955	4,314,390	3,560,010	3,239,615	1,432,309	229,511	321,547	428,648	239,729	91,133	113,193
1880	18,643,231	5,477,095	4,833,554	3,966,512	1,679,295	218,642	328,806	433,248	288,822	67,620	128,798
1900	26,604,858	7,481,657	6,888,964	5,790,771	2,792,183	262,588	436,403	566,938	387,822	91,835	214,778
1910	30,387,409	8,758,589	7,642,804	6,642,510	3,498,132	271,029	434,234	617,373	489,909	81,112	195,225
1920	34,947,182	9,766,419	9,099,906	7,996,325	3,860,948	343,095	497,776	677,002	477,948	121,303	258,611
1940	35,538,309	8,536,807	8,494,615	8,849,692	5,130,038	345,866	541,002	861,293	666,952	81,186	172,939
1950	40,774,956	13,272,951	10,518,238	8,388,926	4,261,035	560,855	646,760	741,455	515,933	87,247	130,022
1960	55,779,518	16,348,345	14,789,164	13,115,960	6,050,299	862,769	916,028	1,068,400	660,836	117,133	142,357
1970	59,835,207	12,970,575	15,197,519	15,418,630	8,248,355	1,163,345	1,495,494	1,676,327	1,005,725	189,942	300,219
1980	52,614,403	11,542,829	11,505,887	12,451,867	8,028,509	1,461,147	1,779,361	2,042,473	1,358,803	206,245	237,283
1990	51,106,689	11,844,562	11,602,107	10,662,583	5,984,361	2,098,930	2,286,284	2,185,717	1,261,747	513,652	477,544

White

	Father only present		Both parents absent							
			Living with other relatives				Living with nonrelatives			
	Age 10–14	Age 15–17	Age 0–4	Age 5–9	Age 10–14	Age 15–17	Age 0–4	Age 5–9	Age 10–14	Age 15–17
	Ae160	Ae161	Ae162	Ae163	Ae164	Ae165	Ae166	Ae167	Ae168	Ae169
Year	Number	Number	Number	Number	Number	Number	Number	Number	Number	Number
1850 [2]	98,046	57,204	57,412	86,413	138,498	125,136	16,166	27,195	87,744	140,002
1860 [2]	122,796	74,647	61,300	98,022	164,453	157,736	18,156	36,012	102,942	171,809
1870	145,223	76,918	65,985	117,610	188,845	170,179	17,073	40,186	137,903	208,948
1880	168,961	96,665	58,751	108,620	168,606	181,718	20,245	42,698	141,338	233,237
1900	270,177	170,006	58,441	122,185	195,052	252,727	42,501	76,654	179,110	324,066
1910	280,360	213,611	55,924	132,249	226,971	303,038	43,579	79,600	160,462	260,698
1920	357,616	239,655	98,077	201,835	259,541	306,266	36,633	61,455	123,922	162,849
1940	300,701	255,044	81,785	141,947	245,353	318,895	70,249	93,034	165,751	185,160
1950	178,406	142,293	106,559	166,927	204,079	300,108	96,302	105,886	151,411	199,563
1960	185,873	125,003	115,040	147,432	205,884	388,990	73,027	96,638	149,998	220,342
1970	359,795	225,993	119,778	204,847	286,296	416,647	67,316	108,888	169,976	209,540
1980	321,716	263,575	128,511	162,571	235,107	395,047	57,251	70,528	117,697	247,996
1990	474,443	320,937	189,757	197,589	241,935	283,980	77,303	79,831	109,435	213,992

Notes appear at end of table

(continued)

TABLE Ae128–190 Living arrangements of children, by age and race: 1850–1990 *Continued*

Black

	Total	Both parents present				Mother only present				Father only present	
		Age 0–4	Age 5–9	Age 10–14	Age 15–17	Age 0–4	Age 5–9	Age 10–14	Age 15–17	Age 0–4	Age 5–9
	Ae170	Ae171	Ae172	Ae173	Ae174	Ae175	Ae176	Ae177	Ae178	Ae179	Ae180
Year	Number	Number	Number	Number	Number	Number	Number	Number	Number	Number	Number
1850 [2]	—	—	—	—	—	—	—	—	—	—	—
1860 [2]	—	—	—	—	—	—	—	—	—	—	—
1870	—	—	—	—	—	—	—	—	—	—	—
1880	3,348,864	852,437	753,950	566,923	206,746	166,204	154,327	119,298	57,666	22,443	31,629
1900	4,035,277	960,806	877,334	701,265	333,182	174,552	163,172	186,697	107,769	13,662	36,427
1910	4,326,952	1,030,479	943,841	774,057	365,249	168,023	192,964	175,564	99,745	19,642	43,063
1920	4,336,510	958,575	986,658	864,033	389,144	129,366	164,406	176,503	106,154	23,507	45,818
1940	4,666,893	960,491	944,118	880,438	426,177	157,392	199,726	244,845	148,071	30,254	45,307
1950	5,474,470	1,339,497	1,058,094	889,081	435,965	306,356	271,088	243,491	143,551	35,190	39,248
1960	8,133,471	1,886,886	1,617,262	1,254,357	544,610	594,880	560,693	449,682	214,317	48,422	56,877
1970	9,612,213	1,404,466	1,668,178	1,628,286	794,485	802,878	894,921	893,814	447,391	57,486	79,708
1980	9,606,724	1,113,676	1,179,803	1,301,934	836,867	1,119,808	1,124,897	1,169,198	719,662	84,316	81,714
1990	9,557,933	915,456	1,000,516	1,011,934	575,015	1,482,409	1,331,400	1,219,905	676,732	157,264	131,478

Black

	Father only present		Both parents absent							
			Living with other relatives				Living with nonrelatives			
	Age 10–14	Age 15–17	Age 0–4	Age 5–9	Age 10–14	Age 15–17	Age 0–4	Age 5–9	Age 10–14	Age 15–17
	Ae181	Ae182	Ae183	Ae184	Ae185	Ae186	Ae187	Ae188	Ae189	Ae190
Year	Number	Number	Number	Number	Number	Number	Number	Number	Number	Number
1850 [2]	—	—	—	—	—	—	—	—	—	—
1860 [2]	—	—	—	—	—	—	—	—	—	—
1870	—	—	—	—	—	—	—	—	—	—
1880	30,121	13,661	57,351	67,530	69,233	49,976	5,489	18,359	50,860	54,661
1900	41,743	21,249	41,740	79,692	85,000	57,680	9,866	21,249	47,814	74,378
1910	46,341	30,477	53,901	92,943	108,558	88,406	6,045	13,854	26,195	47,605
1920	59,237	33,909	55,397	88,095	107,985	91,426	3,432	7,061	16,850	28,954
1940	58,218	38,743	73,380	108,358	135,807	112,103	18,304	18,946	25,777	40,438
1950	45,177	28,784	115,418	119,583	126,124	111,261	59,020	31,602	33,335	42,605
1960	57,569	31,869	184,283	172,929	173,737	123,519	41,742	38,759	42,136	38,942
1970	87,439	54,987	117,789	155,054	192,102	159,731	26,344	37,860	51,697	57,597
1980	86,222	62,139	123,804	148,653	171,352	133,798	22,582	22,884	42,064	61,351
1990	131,241	76,644	165,282	162,203	190,730	129,404	46,533	40,000	49,275	64,512

[1] As of June for 1850–1880 and 1900; as of January for 1920; as of April for other years. There are no data for 1890 because the original census manuscripts were destroyed in a fire. There are no data for 1930 because the 1930 Census records were not publicly available when this table was prepared.

[2] Excludes slave population.

Source

Tabulated from the Integrated Public Use Microdata Series (IPUMS); see the Guide to the Millennial Edition.

TABLE Ae191–220   Living arrangements of unmarried mothers with children, by race: 1850–1990[1]

Contributed by Susan Brower and Steven Ruggles

All races

		Living with relatives					Living with nonrelatives			
			Householders		Nonhouseholders					Total living with own children only
	Total	Total	Parent present	Other relative present	Parent present	Other relative present	Total	Householders	Nonhouseholders	
	Ae191	Ae192	Ae193	Ae194	Ae195	Ae196	Ae197	Ae198	Ae199	Ae200
Year	Number	Number	Number	Number	Number	Number	Number	Number	Number	Number
1850 [2]	—	—	—	—	—	—	—	—	—	—
1860	—	—	—	—	—	—	—	—	—	—
1870	—	—	—	—	—	—	—	—	—	—
1880	679,739	230,487	17,157	68,322	107,212	37,796	91,364	61,541	29,823	357,888
1900	891,760	327,101	33,393	73,619	176,832	43,257	—	—	—	528,987
1910	970,764	389,423	30,479	104,285	185,391	69,268	131,237	86,142	45,095	450,104
1920	1,015,398	422,740	36,219	119,086	199,319	68,116	121,603	83,763	37,840	471,055
1940	1,164,859	483,447	49,789	134,655	233,123	65,880	105,594	72,669	32,925	575,818
1950	1,595,415	726,138	73,132	150,772	407,785	94,449	127,224	78,644	48,580	742,053
1960	2,133,633	773,542	89,458	188,459	408,949	86,676	104,515	74,041	30,474	1,255,576
1970	3,471,663	995,316	108,122	273,280	511,781	102,133	144,689	99,519	45,170	2,331,658
1980	5,869,910	1,497,570	123,980	436,331	802,184	135,075	582,104	402,654	179,450	3,790,236
1990	7,243,828	1,964,790	146,120	518,655	1,154,289	145,726	1,114,841	785,074	329,767	4,164,197

White

		Living with relatives					Living with nonrelatives			
			Householders		Nonhouseholders					Total living with own children only
	Total	Total	Parent present	Other relative present	Parent present	Other relative present	Total	Householders	Nonhouseholders	
	Ae201	Ae202	Ae203	Ae204	Ae205	Ae206	Ae207	Ae208	Ae209	Ae210
Year	Number	Number	Number	Number	Number	Number	Number	Number	Number	Number
1850 [2]	293,343	136,762	5,660	33,762	62,569	34,771	37,906	19,813	18,093	118,675
1860	409,309	175,431	11,540	41,028	78,330	44,533	49,680	29,402	20,278	184,198
1870	575,264	234,624	15,962	50,232	118,026	50,404	73,830	41,999	31,831	266,810
1880	504,844	170,523	13,565	49,870	79,470	27,618	66,932	48,874	18,058	267,389
1900	658,766	227,681	28,080	50,090	123,710	25,801	—	—	—	404,520
1910	736,506	287,898	23,928	77,836	135,256	50,878	101,265	69,773	31,492	347,343
1920	809,940	331,301	30,367	87,095	159,145	54,694	99,807	69,133	30,674	378,832
1940	946,718	373,194	41,685	96,967	183,131	51,411	85,110	59,446	25,664	488,414
1950	1,199,669	507,874	57,805	94,908	293,458	61,703	89,291	55,715	33,576	602,504
1960	1,511,335	480,387	70,133	99,823	259,434	50,997	73,334	53,121	20,213	957,614
1970	2,318,925	556,266	77,787	126,090	296,519	55,870	98,921	66,669	32,252	1,663,738
1980	3,749,956	742,744	74,025	176,853	424,428	67,438	428,617	284,043	144,574	2,578,595
1990	4,645,987	1,047,829	86,841	233,837	647,018	80,133	845,654	566,715	278,939	2,752,504

Notes appear at end of table

(continued)

TABLE Ae191–220   Living arrangements of unmarried mothers with children, by race: 1850–1990   *Continued*

		Black								
		Living with relatives					Living with nonrelatives			
			Householders		Nonhouseholders					
	Total	Total	Parent present	Other relative present	Parent present	Other relative present	Total	Householders	Nonhouseholders	Total living with own children only
	Ae211	Ae212	Ae213	Ae214	Ae215	Ae216	Ae217	Ae218	Ae219	Ae220
Year	Number	Number	Number	Number	Number	Number	Number	Number	Number	Number
1850 [2]	—	—	—	—	—	—	—	—	—	—
1860	—	—	—	—	—	—	—	—	—	—
1870	185,387	73,812	4,519	17,181	26,612	25,500	36,150	8,736	27,414	75,425
1880	173,597	59,465	3,592	18,152	27,742	9,979	24,232	12,567	11,665	89,900
1900	226,922	97,143	5,313	22,011	53,122	16,697	—	—	—	122,190
1910	230,229	99,510	6,299	26,197	48,876	18,138	29,217	15,866	13,351	101,502
1920	201,826	89,825	5,650	31,587	39,266	13,322	21,493	14,428	7,065	90,508
1940	211,370	107,295	7,865	36,776	48,531	14,123	19,901	12,741	7,160	84,174
1950	388,251	214,028	14,928	54,710	112,350	32,040	37,537	22,766	14,771	136,686
1960	603,270	284,789	18,828	85,750	145,231	34,980	30,881	20,820	10,061	287,600
1970	1,109,761	425,827	28,832	143,386	208,648	44,961	43,364	31,347	12,017	640,570
1980	1,977,075	713,563	44,259	246,991	360,073	62,240	137,102	107,021	30,081	1,126,410
1990	2,381,815	849,530	53,198	264,633	472,880	58,819	228,769	188,570	40,199	1,303,516

[1] As of June for 1850–1880 and 1900; as of January for 1920; as of April for other years. There are no data for 1890 because the original census manuscripts were destroyed in a fire. There is no data for 1930 because the 1930 Census records were not publicly available at the time this table was prepared.

[2] Excludes slave population.

Source

Tabulated from the Integrated Public Use Microdata Series (IPUMS); see the Guide to the Millennial Edition.

Documentation

Data cover unmarried mothers with children younger than age 18.

TABLE Ae221–244   Marital status of mothers with children, by race: 1880–1990[1]

Contributed by Susan Brower and Steven Ruggles

		All races						
		Women with children under age 18						
				No spouse present				
	Total women of childbearing age	Total	Married, spouse present	Total	Never married	Married, spouse absent	Divorced	Widowed
	Ae221	Ae222	Ae223	Ae224	Ae225	Ae226	Ae227	Ae228
Year	Number	Number	Number	Number	Number	Number	Number	Number
1880	11,334,786	7,059,704	6,239,841	819,863	101,933	139,825	27,716	550,389
1900	17,810,156	10,221,471	9,139,971	1,081,500	122,193	197,328	35,671	726,308
1910	21,841,582	12,392,644	11,179,293	1,213,351	108,814	239,815	75,067	789,655
1920	24,807,943	14,335,555	13,034,432	1,301,123	89,057	290,294	98,379	823,393
1940	32,111,339	17,410,797	15,686,560	1,724,237	90,888	559,378	259,006	814,965
1950	34,250,964	21,125,347	19,257,649	1,867,698	96,391	716,082	433,375	621,850
1960	36,141,966	26,369,799	23,828,534	2,541,265	164,180	1,051,569	658,123	667,393
1970	42,328,180	28,708,331	24,790,928	3,917,403	488,488	1,397,182	1,220,466	811,267
1980	52,785,374	31,211,743	25,089,136	6,122,607	1,357,888	1,492,557	2,646,915	625,247
1990	58,121,826	31,781,847	24,145,162	7,636,685	2,412,480	1,676,450	3,122,898	424,857

Note appears at end of table

TABLE Ae221–244   Marital status of mothers with children, by race: 1880–1990   *Continued*

White

Women with children under age 18

| | | | | No spouse present | | | | |
	Total women of childbearing age	Total	Married, spouse present	Total	Never married	Married, spouse absent	Divorced	Widowed
	Ae229	Ae230	Ae231	Ae232	Ae233	Ae234	Ae235	Ae236
Year	Number	Number	Number	Number	Number	Number	Number	Number
1880	9,857,877	6,113,029	5,505,659	607,370	50,247	102,227	20,136	434,760
1900	15,679,038	9,040,555	8,224,686	815,869	62,996	163,174	27,323	562,376
1910	19,270,535	11,016,557	10,097,167	919,390	58,430	181,624	58,437	620,899
1920	22,003,517	12,927,315	11,890,735	1,036,580	51,115	232,075	82,350	671,040
1940	28,638,767	15,851,407	14,488,751	1,362,656	54,677	415,938	233,826	658,215
1950	30,411,933	19,252,842	17,833,819	1,419,023	46,034	482,359	388,505	502,125
1960	31,855,653	23,705,999	21,879,072	1,826,927	56,892	663,670	571,866	534,499
1970	36,799,445	25,159,471	22,481,851	2,677,620	169,958	861,987	1,018,324	627,351
1980	44,491,594	26,206,010	22,286,995	3,919,015	469,881	898,758	2,116,453	433,923
1990	48,019,464	26,193,941	21,288,786	4,905,155	1,022,080	1,081,206	2,504,479	297,390

Black

Women with children under age 18

| | | | | No spouse present | | | | |
	Total women of childbearing age	Total	Married, spouse present	Total	Never married	Married, spouse absent	Divorced	Widowed
	Ae237	Ae238	Ae239	Ae240	Ae241	Ae242	Ae243	Ae244
Year	Number	Number	Number	Number	Number	Number	Number	Number
1880	1,456,455	936,004	725,208	210,796	51,586	37,199	7,580	114,431
1900	2,048,393	1,134,619	878,855	255,764	59,197	32,636	7,589	156,342
1910	2,444,844	1,294,214	1,009,070	285,144	49,376	54,915	15,875	164,978
1920	2,673,451	1,356,920	1,096,435	260,485	37,536	57,002	16,029	149,918
1940	3,359,829	1,490,513	1,138,695	351,818	35,628	140,448	23,747	151,995
1950	3,699,502	1,786,650	1,348,109	438,541	49,773	228,840	43,461	116,467
1960	3,934,827	2,427,885	1,739,948	687,937	105,296	374,546	81,675	126,420
1970	4,895,670	3,159,117	1,972,338	1,186,779	311,015	512,753	188,216	174,795
1980	6,677,680	4,052,530	2,006,704	2,045,826	853,940	548,544	473,804	169,538
1990	7,595,673	4,229,514	1,745,532	2,483,982	1,319,900	523,464	535,265	105,353

[1] As of June for 1880 and 1900; as of January for 1920; as of April for other years. There are no data for 1890 because the original census manuscripts were destroyed in a fire. There are no data for 1930 because the 1930 Census records were not publicly available at the time this table was prepared.

Documentation
Women of childbearing age are 15–44 years old.

Source
Tabulated from the Integrated Public Use Microdata Series (IPUMS); see the Guide to the Millennial Edition.

TABLE Ae245–319 Living arrangements of population age 65 and older, by race, sex, and marital status: 1850–1990[1]

Contributed by Susan Brower and Steven Ruggles

All races — Male

Year	Total	Total	Living with children and other relatives — No spouse present	Living with children and other relatives — Spouse present	Living with children only — No spouse present	Living with children only — Spouse present	Living with other relatives only — No spouse present	Living with other relatives only — Spouse present	Living with nonrelatives only — No spouse present	Living with nonrelatives only — Spouse present	No spouse present, living alone	Living with spouse only	Living in group quarters
	Ae245	Ae246	Ae247	Ae248	Ae249	Ae250	Ae251	Ae252	Ae253	Ae254	Ae255	Ae256	Ae257
	Number	Number	Number	Number	Number	Number	Number	Number	Number	Number	Number	Number	Number
1850[2]	515,786	258,232	47,307	48,410	14,657	65,589	7,681	11,119	13,040	8,083	4,953	32,239	5,154
1860[2]	700,534	350,464	64,300	61,030	22,372	83,084	10,524	16,654	18,257	11,941	8,330	47,645	6,327
1870	1,173,459	593,318	103,242	101,316	33,252	142,908	16,677	30,229	31,230	20,894	14,258	86,561	12,751
1880	1,731,728	866,283	108,417	131,226	42,392	245,073	32,929	45,581	39,801	33,133	23,242	141,242	23,247
1910	3,954,009	1,975,613	255,651	235,014	121,413	458,980	78,593	86,404	98,244	54,160	98,483	369,026	119,645
1920	4,967,934	2,512,649	306,988	274,788	153,290	547,306	122,504	98,281	122,011	62,870	145,311	540,751	138,549
1940	9,009,213	4,420,459	453,508	413,448	225,873	788,898	251,685	187,497	241,800	129,950	368,295	1,118,636	240,869
1950	12,259,626	5,804,795	494,375	442,092	229,796	757,329	312,167	244,731	287,665	147,791	566,170	1,973,831	348,848
1960	16,036,970	7,233,123	401,643	328,325	197,055	777,125	360,878	311,679	251,328	104,492	844,304	3,333,731	322,563
1970	20,293,422	8,567,602	284,268	230,593	185,947	768,778	399,352	281,165	239,115	60,380	1,241,830	4,508,665	367,509
1980	25,439,684	10,235,968	226,522	241,581	176,877	852,504	328,249	289,655	191,849	43,564	1,443,360	6,032,945	408,862
1990	31,428,197	12,586,525	214,438	336,533	237,997	1,119,852	317,743	312,472	294,007	46,660	1,886,634	7,342,668	477,521

All races — Female

Year	Total	Living with children and other relatives — No spouse present	Living with children and other relatives — Spouse present	Living with children only — No spouse present	Living with children only — Spouse present	Living with other relatives only — No spouse present	Living with other relatives only — Spouse present	Living with nonrelatives only — No spouse present	Living with nonrelatives only — Spouse present	No spouse present, living alone	Living with spouse only	Living in group quarters
	Ae258	Ae259	Ae260	Ae261	Ae262	Ae263	Ae264	Ae265	Ae266	Ae267	Ae268	Ae269
	Number	Number	Number	Number	Number	Number	Number	Number	Number	Number	Number	Number
1850[2]	257,554	96,740	25,667	25,582	26,078	16,478	6,773	17,889	5,051	10,918	21,627	4,751
1860[2]	350,070	131,746	36,740	37,226	28,390	19,164	10,935	22,667	7,923	17,654	31,800	5,825
1870	580,141	210,056	57,741	56,643	48,806	42,972	19,088	39,779	13,266	26,724	55,827	9,239
1880	865,445	270,777	69,789	91,766	74,920	84,997	26,726	62,640	20,558	53,459	90,755	19,058
1910	1,978,396	563,723	129,214	268,517	182,140	207,320	50,382	107,313	30,480	146,109	231,240	61,958
1920	2,455,285	677,417	140,154	339,559	222,391	254,800	53,175	132,581	31,286	183,138	337,238	83,546
1940	4,588,754	998,710	224,489	559,518	333,879	517,284	108,409	296,330	76,350	562,055	719,445	192,285
1950	6,454,831	1,190,726	253,187	656,830	349,464	677,123	145,029	437,461	91,684	1,013,635	1,287,315	352,377
1960	8,803,847	1,185,287	193,870	735,799	387,897	926,253	186,874	422,506	66,233	2,009,973	2,241,720	447,435
1970	11,725,820	1,095,030	127,151	822,924	387,121	994,738	178,331	374,964	39,356	3,750,237	3,212,573	743,395
1980	15,203,716	1,008,655	137,673	866,451	417,556	986,388	194,649	309,238	31,372	5,637,656	4,545,685	1,068,393
1990	18,841,672	1,004,607	213,792	1,121,783	647,791	1,028,441	219,787	371,664	32,119	7,087,400	5,862,936	1,251,352

White — Male

Year	Total (Ae270)	Total (Ae271)	Living with children and other relatives — No spouse present (Ae272)	Living with children and other relatives — Spouse present (Ae273)	Living with children only — No spouse present (Ae274)	Living with children only — Spouse present (Ae275)	Living with other relatives only — No spouse present (Ae276)	Living with other relatives only — Spouse present (Ae277)	Living with nonrelatives only — No spouse present (Ae278)	Living with nonrelatives only — Spouse present (Ae279)	No spouse present, living alone (Ae280)	Living with spouse only (Ae281)	Living in group quarters (Ae282)
1850 [2]	501,329	251,863	46,498	47,602	14,353	64,781	7,074	10,916	12,333	7,981	4,346	30,926	5,053
1860 [2]	682,664	341,626	63,395	59,824	21,368	81,980	10,324	16,554	16,751	11,739	7,025	46,639	6,027
1870	1,052,540	532,964	92,998	93,285	28,627	131,556	13,557	26,015	26,616	19,687	11,049	78,030	11,544
1880	1,551,602	779,013	102,732	117,765	39,002	220,138	30,236	38,798	32,715	31,135	18,853	126,585	21,054
1910	3,643,675	1,813,898	238,525	207,308	114,863	427,495	73,556	71,293	87,913	50,382	84,629	342,069	115,865
1920	4,614,227	2,321,709	286,901	250,770	144,609	515,316	112,411	84,758	109,291	58,735	125,935	504,225	128,758
1940	8,358,739	4,090,189	420,346	374,610	211,560	739,538	231,806	157,253	215,047	120,199	333,345	1,059,341	227,144
1950	11,370,611	5,370,286	458,273	392,005	211,348	714,190	286,386	204,869	252,334	134,074	517,163	1,874,845	324,799
1960	14,796,923	6,655,152	364,088	273,138	178,534	723,653	324,122	257,099	206,814	93,235	762,813	3,171,121	300,535
1970	18,541,016	7,784,681	252,023	183,545	162,318	688,270	337,061	226,506	186,650	48,868	1,094,431	4,267,938	337,071
1980	23,038,835	9,250,705	186,051	173,638	145,500	739,989	267,792	233,212	143,188	32,973	1,252,530	5,702,536	373,296
1990	28,286,627	11,347,256	158,289	229,813	190,640	965,542	249,400	244,184	235,784	38,334	1,649,235	6,961,276	424,759

White — Female

Year	Total (Ae283)	Living with children and other relatives — No spouse present (Ae284)	Living with children and other relatives — Spouse present (Ae285)	Living with children only — No spouse present (Ae286)	Living with children only — Spouse present (Ae287)	Living with other relatives only — No spouse present (Ae288)	Living with other relatives only — Spouse present (Ae289)	Living with nonrelatives only — No spouse present (Ae290)	Living with nonrelatives only — Spouse present (Ae291)	No spouse present, living alone (Ae292)	Living with spouse only (Ae293)	Living in group quarters (Ae294)
1850 [2]	249,466	93,606	25,262	25,077	25,775	15,568	6,671	16,271	5,051	10,514	21,122	4,549
1860 [2]	341,038	129,237	36,339	36,523	28,189	18,161	10,835	20,561	7,923	16,752	31,195	5,323
1870	519,576	184,044	55,030	52,527	47,801	35,139	16,476	33,048	13,065	23,104	50,304	9,038
1880	772,589	238,661	64,309	85,676	70,427	74,126	22,836	50,479	19,460	47,374	82,977	16,264
1910	1,829,777	512,592	119,895	256,174	174,835	188,174	44,088	96,229	28,465	134,519	216,123	58,683
1920	2,292,518	624,728	131,379	324,733	214,623	235,725	46,315	120,071	29,672	166,486	319,377	79,409
1940	4,268,550	905,550	208,445	525,408	319,909	466,930	95,181	270,589	72,358	530,029	690,250	183,901
1950	6,000,325	1,077,271	233,181	618,157	335,625	608,552	125,412	400,951	85,499	946,654	1,236,349	332,674
1960	8,141,771	1,055,705	169,264	684,097	367,684	814,053	154,509	377,367	60,557	1,885,252	2,144,969	428,314
1970	10,756,335	962,173	105,324	746,210	353,374	857,762	142,490	318,177	33,546	3,475,679	3,052,455	709,145
1980	13,788,130	837,904	103,702	748,459	371,701	808,855	155,477	256,475	23,581	5,167,925	4,306,506	1,007,545
1990	16,939,371	759,773	152,129	935,875	569,773	807,949	172,240	313,394	26,355	6,466,043	5,570,509	1,165,331

Notes appear at end of table

(continued)

TABLE Ae245–319   Living arrangements of population age 65 and older, by race, sex, and marital status: 1850–1990   Continued

Black — Male

Year	Total	Living with children and other relatives			Living with children only		Living with other relatives only		Living with nonrelatives only		No spouse present, living alone	Living with spouse only	Living in group quarters
		Total	No spouse present	Spouse present	No spouse present	Spouse present	No spouse present	Spouse present	No spouse present	Spouse present			
	Ae295	Ae296	Ae297	Ae298	Ae299	Ae300	Ae301	Ae302	Ae303	Ae304	Ae305	Ae306	Ae307
	Number	Number	Number	Number	Number	Number	Number	Number	Number	Number	Number	Number	Number
1850 [2]	—	—	—	—	—	—	—	—	—	—	—	—	—
1860 [2]	—	—	—	—	—	—	—	—	—	—	—	—	—
1870	119,915	60,053	10,244	7,931	4,524	11,252	3,120	4,214	4,614	1,207	3,209	8,531	1,207
1880	178,334	86,175	5,685	13,362	3,390	24,735	2,693	6,584	6,888	1,998	4,290	14,657	1,893
1910	291,440	151,387	15,867	25,690	5,794	29,721	4,785	14,608	8,819	3,778	13,351	25,950	3,024
1920	328,577	174,589	19,178	23,111	8,176	29,467	8,985	13,220	11,609	3,832	16,752	34,709	5,550
1940	625,356	315,151	32,072	36,924	13,505	46,254	17,752	29,234	25,628	9,650	33,031	57,982	13,119
1950	853,871	410,891	34,162	46,868	17,548	38,753	24,398	38,465	33,351	13,471	47,046	97,027	19,802
1960	1,158,844	530,049	32,476	48,118	17,524	46,799	34,463	52,786	41,829	10,858	72,618	153,443	19,135
1970	1,592,488	697,604	26,635	40,840	21,424	69,393	56,984	51,657	46,461	10,712	132,583	215,787	25,128
1980	2,052,256	821,107	29,575	48,663	27,377	88,139	52,762	49,851	41,466	9,291	167,653	277,358	28,972
1990	2,568,173	983,507	37,919	68,923	39,059	107,239	56,619	58,232	51,234	6,003	211,308	300,767	46,204

Black — Female

Year	Total	Living with children and other relatives		Living with children only		Living with other relatives only		Living with nonrelatives only		No spouse present, living alone	Living with spouse only	Living in group quarters
		No spouse present	Spouse present	No spouse present	Spouse present	No spouse present	Spouse present	No spouse present	Spouse present			
	Ae308	Ae309	Ae310	Ae311	Ae312	Ae313	Ae314	Ae315	Ae316	Ae317	Ae318	Ae319
	Number	Number	Number	Number	Number	Number	Number	Number	Number	Number	Number	Number
1850 [2]	—	—	—	—	—	—	—	—	—	—	—	—
1860 [2]	—	—	—	—	—	—	—	—	—	—	—	—
1870	59,862	25,711	2,711	4,015	1,005	7,532	2,612	6,731	201	3,620	5,523	201
1880	92,159	32,017	5,281	6,090	4,493	10,771	3,691	12,061	1,098	6,085	7,778	2,794
1910	140,053	48,611	8,563	11,335	7,053	18,390	6,042	10,329	2,015	10,582	13,858	3,275
1920	153,988	49,762	8,171	14,422	7,061	18,065	6,759	11,907	1,513	16,147	16,650	3,531
1940	310,205	90,272	14,871	33,302	13,061	49,165	12,622	25,438	3,891	31,217	27,982	8,384
1950	442,980	110,233	18,805	38,091	12,864	66,385	18,922	35,345	6,157	66,327	50,148	19,703
1960	628,795	121,112	21,716	48,414	18,423	109,312	30,470	43,242	5,577	121,135	91,171	18,223
1970	894,884	119,634	18,320	70,005	29,440	130,367	33,640	53,685	5,410	258,439	144,396	31,548
1980	1,231,149	133,789	24,381	105,798	38,463	164,943	35,573	48,966	6,991	417,270	202,221	52,754
1990	1,584,666	171,843	38,809	161,001	55,323	193,921	40,152	51,196	4,391	557,598	235,282	75,150

1 As of June for 1850–1880 and 1900; as of January for 1920; as of April for other years. There are no data for 1890 because the original census manuscripts were destroyed in a fire. There are no data for 1930 because the 1930 Census records were not publicly available at the time this table was prepared.

2 Excludes slave population.

Source
Tabulated from the Integrated Public Use Microdata Series (IPUMS); see the Guide to the Millennial Edition.

TABLE Ae320–480 Household status – population, by age, sex, race, and relationship to head of household: 1850–1990[1]

Contributed by Susan Brower and Steven Ruggles

All ages

Male

Year	Total	Head/householder	Spouse	Child	Child-in-law	Parent	Parent-in-law	Sibling	Sibling-in-law	Grandchild	Other relatives	Partner, friend, visitor	Other nonrelatives	Institutional inmates
	Ae320	Ae321	Ae322	Ae323	Ae324	Ae325	Ae326	Ae327	Ae328	Ae329	Ae330	Ae331	Ae332	Ae333
	Number	Number	Number	Number	Number	Number	Number	Number	Number	Number	Number	Number	Number	Number
1850 [2]	10,239,794	3,251,410	—	5,164,374	63,679	42,147	26,580	178,109	84,701	169,506	165,066	—	1,040,659	49,017
1860 [2]	14,068,720	4,744,160	—	7,012,751	82,473	59,589	37,916	230,767	109,655	208,107	198,414	—	1,324,091	54,379
1870	19,402,293	6,713,817	—	9,515,544	114,001	87,205	63,758	280,510	131,698	313,197	262,005	—	1,816,905	87,394
1880	25,551,807	8,934,234	—	12,692,143	92,663	87,565	54,160	292,436	113,027	394,765	251,996	18,451	2,444,463	159,352
1900	38,788,930	14,150,533	—	18,352,096	168,485	179,872	116,878	473,578	223,888	605,623	397,681	84,999	3,696,053	328,620
1910	47,326,853	17,828,442	—	21,048,394	259,190	213,607	173,544	603,787	359,439	680,846	502,786	134,528	5,109,201	413,089
1920	53,963,568	21,556,147	—	24,062,432	371,377	245,323	220,608	698,158	435,040	759,608	564,504	22,195	4,501,193	490,952
1940	65,950,138	29,759,032	—	26,744,669	630,236	332,402	297,177	764,722	488,686	1,244,579	700,334	84,204	4,070,537	833,560
1950	74,897,011	36,803,807	—	27,592,359	743,815	357,857	362,875	680,506	480,689	1,484,920	756,366	101,971	4,595,491	936,355
1960	88,075,636	43,705,143	—	35,650,027	307,081	288,871	315,406	564,271	366,832	1,357,424	973,842	108,291	3,317,051	1,121,397
1970	98,720,864	50,085,148	—	40,264,535	235,608	236,496	207,362	571,187	271,905	1,282,157	606,530	444,069	3,369,932	1,145,935
1980	109,816,985	58,185,645	1,735,671	39,797,320	231,806	313,033	127,487	948,428	216,933	1,382,316	747,859	1,585,613	3,325,277	1,219,597
1990	120,503,835	62,238,555	3,605,781	40,409,504	190,575	361,193	75,093	1,305,410	159,733	2,165,813	1,220,637	3,491,603	3,474,366	1,805,572

Female

Year	Total	Head/householder	Spouse	Child	Child-in-law	Parent	Parent-in-law	Sibling	Sibling-in-law	Grandchild	Other relatives	Partner, friend, visitor	Other nonrelatives	Institutional inmates
	Ae334	Ae335	Ae336	Ae337	Ae338	Ae339	Ae340	Ae341	Ae342	Ae343	Ae344	Ae345	Ae346	Ae347
	Number	Number	Number	Number	Number	Number	Number	Number	Number	Number	Number	Number	Number	Number
1850 [2]	9,747,765	334,387	2,953,330	4,921,146	42,049	120,686	77,736	189,747	95,116	164,662	159,416	—	656,651	32,839
1860 [2]	13,420,958	500,364	4,279,236	6,705,925	47,971	164,065	114,784	225,829	125,698	190,057	190,899	—	844,103	32,027
1870	19,121,470	880,589	6,093,225	9,220,804	74,219	246,301	171,550	305,319	174,458	308,258	302,467	—	1,277,923	66,357
1880	24,603,241	1,226,265	8,101,344	11,903,649	137,227	294,437	187,616	327,972	172,678	379,367	305,830	9,277	1,456,938	100,641
1900	37,210,258	2,024,101	12,617,463	17,298,626	185,177	534,294	316,470	566,935	300,542	593,481	459,157	14,421	2,111,370	188,221
1910	44,643,849	2,408,102	16,025,938	20,083,455	213,859	548,350	445,603	656,155	376,316	683,152	558,483	37,032	2,365,591	241,813
1920	51,748,505	2,886,203	19,391,562	22,717,391	303,955	664,449	561,705	786,197	449,493	751,806	628,100	30,276	2,293,811	283,557
1940	65,718,853	5,145,602	26,629,252	24,604,162	528,196	881,084	749,890	930,457	508,183	1,172,001	754,911	92,556	3,260,012	462,547
1950	75,797,823	6,594,289	33,405,790	25,560,541	533,073	1,067,356	976,052	901,338	501,496	1,400,806	818,090	154,562	3,246,042	638,388
1960	91,225,906	9,091,083	39,448,890	33,828,666	274,145	990,591	970,155	870,101	356,824	1,268,981	1,133,049	143,647	2,084,138	765,636
1970	104,581,963	13,446,989	43,817,989	38,108,657	269,235	1,008,131	849,221	934,369	316,757	1,255,128	734,090	560,185	2,267,567	1,013,645
1980	116,724,731	22,208,416	47,249,566	36,441,402	211,198	1,134,921	497,976	1,078,075	233,403	1,270,557	800,214	1,758,126	2,569,594	1,271,283
1990	127,508,294	29,511,435	47,760,553	36,429,163	169,521	1,278,368	282,134	1,106,056	158,015	1,991,269	1,203,541	3,465,613	2,664,947	1,487,679

Notes appear at end of table

(continued)

TABLE Ae320–480 Household status – population, by age, sex, race, and relationship to head of household: 1850–1990 *Continued*

All ages
White
Male

Year	Total	Head/householder	Spouse	Child	Child-in-law	Parent	Parent-in-law	Sibling	Sibling-in-law	Grandchild	Other relatives	Partner, friend, visitor	Other nonrelatives	Institutional inmates
	Ae348	Ae349	Ae350	Ae351	Ae352	Ae353	Ae354	Ae355	Ae356	Ae357	Ae358	Ae359	Ae360	Ae361
	Number	Number	Number	Number	Number	Number	Number	Number	Number	Number	Number	Number	Number	Number
1850 [2]	10,030,172	3,192,684	—	5,086,261	62,162	41,035	26,176	173,962	83,488	162,230	158,497	—	993,044	46,491
1860 [2]	13,801,296	4,668,209	—	6,913,185	80,570	58,286	37,313	218,125	107,649	201,876	191,488	—	1,268,016	50,764
1870	16,946,898	5,913,498	—	8,421,521	98,839	78,962	59,244	219,125	112,927	256,252	195,639	—	1,503,394	77,058
1880	22,137,410	7,836,968	—	11,071,701	83,287	82,879	51,866	256,849	98,957	298,281	203,199	12,469	1,997,490	132,401
1900	34,248,934	12,609,112	—	16,287,002	152,549	167,728	114,601	415,137	200,360	461,434	316,474	57,677	3,176,184	283,846
1910	42,060,348	15,937,261	—	18,803,556	234,253	200,761	165,483	540,811	327,965	498,970	393,472	106,310	4,504,908	345,590
1920	48,457,482	19,453,270	—	21,751,374	342,515	231,494	210,006	622,862	397,001	596,819	454,301	19,775	3,929,798	421,821
1940	59,382,121	27,210,374	—	24,212,951	579,100	306,195	282,189	668,089	435,888	942,410	523,362	68,607	3,449,917	703,039
1950	67,198,911	33,852,574	—	24,822,776	665,320	326,792	343,214	576,081	413,577	1,058,343	527,849	85,340	3,754,381	772,664
1960	78,125,010	39,944,336	—	31,424,258	260,088	259,591	290,401	460,870	295,691	822,853	632,237	94,044	2,748,346	892,295
1970	86,769,256	45,458,583	—	34,840,288	195,461	207,747	187,946	442,410	216,123	760,421	360,001	380,202	2,833,194	886,880
1980	94,315,680	52,177,555	1,460,588	33,203,634	192,731	251,187	108,401	671,457	167,470	790,033	433,133	1,334,422	2,621,227	903,842
1990	101,962,008	55,467,404	3,062,357	33,114,931	158,411	267,334	58,910	913,411	125,176	1,273,359	804,565	2,828,854	2,716,097	1,171,199

All ages
White
Female

Year	Total	Head/householder	Spouse	Child	Child-in-law	Parent	Parent-in-law	Sibling	Sibling-in-law	Grandchild	Other relatives	Partner, friend, visitor	Other nonrelatives	Institutional inmates
	Ae362	Ae363	Ae364	Ae365	Ae366	Ae367	Ae368	Ae369	Ae370	Ae371	Ae372	Ae373	Ae374	Ae375
	Number	Number	Number	Number	Number	Number	Number	Number	Number	Number	Number	Number	Number	Number
1850 [2]	9,520,028	314,879	2,904,206	4,835,226	41,241	116,847	75,917	184,289	92,591	159,099	151,228	—	613,384	31,121
1860 [2]	13,148,213	474,273	4,221,142	6,602,568	46,663	159,353	112,677	217,600	122,688	183,029	183,576	—	794,524	30,120
1870	16,617,426	708,459	5,408,987	8,124,520	68,498	208,539	150,671	243,830	147,258	248,614	222,503	—	1,022,103	63,444
1880	21,239,224	987,235	7,146,718	10,331,506	125,058	253,738	164,375	288,088	152,924	289,900	245,572	7,384	1,158,158	88,568
1900	32,719,607	1,674,984	11,337,880	15,265,429	166,962	465,228	293,704	503,183	275,496	430,317	354,426	10,626	1,763,017	178,355
1910	39,452,866	2,002,057	14,411,814	17,820,715	191,947	480,594	408,322	588,154	343,570	503,556	432,527	33,003	2,009,909	226,698
1920	46,313,568	2,445,638	17,571,074	20,442,552	277,117	594,825	519,815	706,472	404,787	593,672	499,624	26,746	1,968,071	263,175
1940	58,901,016	4,430,406	24,488,016	22,114,769	474,372	777,029	691,449	814,964	445,882	882,758	560,443	83,508	2,717,801	419,619
1950	67,765,148	5,678,825	30,878,008	22,848,616	464,008	941,545	899,535	779,467	425,728	1,000,687	568,632	143,604	2,560,499	575,994
1960	80,612,354	7,716,241	36,263,463	29,618,860	223,048	872,362	888,460	729,025	287,789	743,849	756,762	129,397	1,695,080	688,018
1970	91,444,390	11,219,968	40,094,836	32,683,939	213,574	876,872	769,922	774,161	257,566	744,907	469,526	484,874	1,930,413	923,832
1980	99,530,705	18,083,747	42,922,201	30,020,198	172,737	919,113	433,734	804,825	181,540	716,989	472,083	1,541,480	2,106,976	1,155,082
1990	106,875,557	23,733,442	43,137,654	29,485,146	140,472	969,482	234,779	770,942	122,105	1,112,139	788,520	2,953,375	2,109,999	1,317,502

All ages — Black — Male

Year	Total	Head/householder	Spouse	Child	Child-in-law	Parent	Parent-in-law	Sibling	Sibling-in-law	Grandchild	Other relatives	Partner, friend, visitor	Other nonrelatives	Institutional inmates
	Ae376	Ae377	Ae378	Ae379	Ae380	Ae381	Ae382	Ae383	Ae384	Ae385	Ae386	Ae387	Ae388	Ae389
	Number	Number	Number	Number	Number	Number	Number	Number	Number	Number	Number	Number	Number	Number
1850 [2]	209,622	58,726	—	78,113	1,517	1,112	404	4,147	1,213	7,276	6,569	—	47,615	2,526
1860 [2]	228,710	65,924	—	92,442	1,803	703	603	5,519	1,406	5,526	5,320	—	46,148	2,713
1870	2,386,029	785,371	—	1,086,206	15,061	8,042	4,414	57,064	18,069	56,645	64,559		276,449	8,329
1880	3,274,833	1,067,945	—	1,604,283	9,176	4,686	2,294	34,789	13,870	95,887	47,897	2,192	361,968	24,557
1900	4,287,263	1,459,453	—	2,008,928	15,177	9,867	2,277	57,682	21,251	140,394	73,619	13,662	440,939	40,979
1910	4,897,185	1,790,419	—	2,131,721	23,677	12,090	7,306	56,426	30,718	174,821	105,030	12,596	487,402	63,971
1920	5,240,684	2,011,850	—	2,234,065	27,652	12,921	9,895	73,075	37,332	157,845	107,073	2,218	492,181	65,093
1940	6,246,648	2,440,371	—	2,401,988	49,174	23,753	14,720	92,648	51,320	292,666	169,137	11,166	572,519	127,186
1950	7,303,505	2,814,158	—	2,631,042	75,283	27,031	18,386	97,781	64,664	412,591	219,623	11,154	776,598	155,194
1960	9,084,327	3,433,463	—	3,854,477	42,116	23,901	21,119	93,049	65,164	510,161	315,194	8,970	503,450	213,263
1970	10,688,505	4,077,540	—	4,901,708	35,338	22,737	14,310	117,863	48,067	497,814	227,508	49,852	452,137	243,631
1980	12,504,600	4,695,495	239,708	5,405,673	28,083	35,168	8,593	218,315	29,778	543,529	266,179	187,851	558,450	287,778
1990	13,951,153	4,835,923	436,754	5,543,345	17,343	44,082	4,717	274,680	15,636	798,228	318,461	488,033	586,982	586,969

All ages — Black — Female

Year	Total	Head/householder	Spouse	Child	Child-in-law	Parent	Parent-in-law	Sibling	Sibling-in-law	Grandchild	Other relatives	Partner, friend, visitor	Other nonrelatives	Institutional inmates
	Ae390	Ae391	Ae392	Ae393	Ae394	Ae395	Ae396	Ae397	Ae398	Ae399	Ae400	Ae401	Ae402	Ae403
	Number	Number	Number	Number	Number	Number	Number	Number	Number	Number	Number	Number	Number	Number
1850 [2]	227,737	19,508	49,124	85,920	808	3,839	1,819	5,458	2,525	5,563	8,188	—	43,267	1,718
1860 [2]	253,787	24,584	53,480	97,238	1,208	4,210	1,906	6,625	2,910	6,223	6,121	—	47,776	1,506
1870	2,486,677	170,725	680,024	1,090,558	5,621	37,361	20,779	60,783	26,999	59,344	79,462		252,108	2,913
1880	3,327,206	236,633	941,760	1,559,376	11,572	40,401	22,941	39,485	19,456	88,970	58,858	1,693	294,187	11,874
1900	4,351,001	338,491	1,240,116	1,982,345	15,179	66,790	22,766	59,198	24,287	160,128	103,213	3,036	325,586	9,866
1910	4,979,126	398,488	1,544,091	2,157,939	20,905	65,236	35,266	66,240	31,739	175,314	123,185	3,274	343,090	14,359
1920	5,263,485	434,208	1,757,414	2,202,386	25,022	67,304	40,678	78,819	43,797	153,086	125,951	3,328	312,724	18,768
1940	6,569,149	701,308	2,064,695	2,368,165	52,095	100,032	57,041	111,945	60,720	280,170	190,142	9,048	532,981	40,807
1950	7,737,532	899,761	2,425,497	2,593,702	65,906	119,589	74,001	116,873	73,525	388,986	242,386	10,411	666,788	60,107
1960	9,816,275	1,323,538	2,906,290	3,855,555	45,421	107,567	76,314	133,707	64,847	502,225	355,278	11,951	362,140	71,442
1970	11,846,910	2,104,145	3,225,584	4,920,317	46,552	113,135	67,882	148,396	52,782	487,887	247,044	58,690	291,990	82,506
1980	14,061,806	3,702,797	3,161,169	5,307,484	24,978	152,559	39,072	226,589	30,677	510,007	285,774	157,589	359,503	103,608
1990	15,790,784	5,058,786	2,930,249	5,314,785	12,148	186,232	18,118	249,389	14,961	786,243	317,738	342,843	407,503	151,789

Notes appear at end of table

(continued)

TABLE Ae320–480 Household status – population, by age, sex, race, and relationship to head of household: 1850–1990 Continued

Age 0–17

	Male											Female		
	Total	Head/householder	Child	Child-in-law	Sibling	Sibling-in-law	Grandchild	Other relatives	Partner, friend, visitor	Other nonrelatives	Institutional inmates	Total	Head/householder	Spouse
	Ae404	Ae405	Ae406	Ae407	Ae408	Ae409	Ae410	Ae411	Ae412	Ae413	Ae414	Ae415	Ae416	Ae417
Year	Number	Number	Number	Number	Number	Number	Number	Number	Number	Number	Number	Number	Number	Number
1850 [2]	4,805,120	4,143	4,255,751	303	50,239	21,534	157,374	106,234	—	195,998	13,443	4,698,469	1,718	27,589
1860 [2]	6,413,574	5,422	5,764,475	300	57,103	30,799	191,964	124,800	—	224,159	14,552	6,311,864	2,405	38,848
1870	8,850,806	11,343	7,858,636	200	84,148	38,483	292,093	175,932	—	363,877	25,994	8,707,647	9,645	45,206
1880	11,162,247	12,365	10,134,171	100	56,452	23,638	362,560	146,661	1,892	381,205	42,904	10,864,457	5,089	55,649
1900	15,549,294	9,866	14,168,040	1,518	75,891	28,081	550,981	224,643	6,831	401,481	81,962	15,175,844	3,795	88,041
1910	17,616,299	9,319	16,096,885	502	81,374	50,374	616,109	257,683	4,284	418,412	81,357	17,291,532	1,764	98,239
1920	19,909,780	9,888	18,388,392	404	82,044	42,889	692,912	283,167	3,735	299,582	106,767	19,500,333	3,126	105,557
1940	20,409,224	9,518	18,440,016	1,459	62,243	43,928	1,091,746	314,622	4,113	341,775	99,804	20,024,812	3,274	97,235
1950	23,684,901	9,729	21,378,647	1,395	45,845	37,432	1,352,127	349,754	3,737	382,745	123,490	22,820,248	3,847	131,192
1960	32,720,181	24,304	30,539,609	3,884	33,551	32,974	1,246,949	392,980	5,975	292,352	147,603	31,902,309	8,864	177,021
1970	35,743,387	77,203	33,645,027	4,910	63,086	45,050	1,109,625	304,331	50,872	280,482	162,801	34,471,040	23,321	161,516
1980	32,818,328	26,978	30,537,446	5,798	147,882	25,180	1,169,705	377,354	48,852	361,021	117,112	31,468,581	29,571	117,894
1990	32,564,969	17,742	29,575,545	1,440	123,327	9,499	1,767,727	406,098	85,175	466,195	111,493	31,000,165	22,240	37,400

Age 0–17 — Female (continued)

	Child	Child-in-law	Sibling	Sibling-in-law	Grandchild	Other relatives	Partner, friend, visitor	Other nonrelatives	Institutional inmates
	Ae418	Ae419	Ae420	Ae421	Ae422	Ae423	Ae424	Ae425	Ae426
Year	Number	Number	Number	Number	Number	Number	Number	Number	Number
1850 [2]	4,116,029	4,042	52,567	22,242	150,912	105,540	—	209,446	8,384
1860 [2]	5,612,130	5,317	56,261	28,197	176,114	125,392	—	252,440	14,760
1870	7,635,064	6,126	85,370	47,513	284,648	184,340	—	377,792	31,943
1880	9,788,329	5,187	54,366	38,116	352,250	161,092	1,598	369,368	33,413
1900	13,726,281	10,624	68,305	58,436	543,392	249,686	3,795	377,950	45,539
1910	15,709,618	11,842	81,362	66,241	622,442	276,592	5,039	349,873	68,520
1920	17,850,415	20,592	79,123	64,591	691,151	310,309	6,455	292,930	76,084
1940	17,971,924	27,271	59,383	56,884	1,061,618	334,886	4,129	336,382	71,826
1950	20,419,124	29,005	45,758	46,024	1,299,044	365,828	5,701	380,962	93,763
1960	29,645,236	26,604	41,431	38,252	1,197,628	432,843	7,771	235,225	91,434
1970	32,319,483	25,739	74,689	49,979	1,114,836	347,890	54,281	212,892	86,414
1980	29,177,621	19,676	152,971	24,875	1,106,500	391,061	61,942	338,118	48,352
1990	28,110,901	6,234	110,984	9,355	1,697,583	412,594	89,886	467,276	35,712

Age 18–64 — Male

	Total	Head/householder	Spouse	Child	Child-in-law	Parent
	Ae427	Ae428	Ae429	Ae430	Ae431	Ae432
Year	Number	Number	Number	Number	Number	Number
1850 [2]	5,176,442	3,051,803	—	908,522	63,275	14,655
1860 [2]	7,304,682	4,476,957	—	1,248,176	82,073	19,452
1870	9,958,069	6,257,800	—	1,656,807	113,600	27,533
1880	13,522,877	8,250,288	—	2,557,572	92,264	18,052
1900	21,659,514	12,973,414	—	4,184,056	165,449	37,189
1910	27,738,217	16,381,306	—	4,950,249	257,680	59,952
1920	31,545,983	19,702,663	—	5,672,829	370,165	63,473
1940	41,120,354	26,406,325	—	8,296,322	625,846	81,907
1950	45,406,580	32,348,019	—	6,208,413	739,146	77,856
1960	48,122,232	37,687,127	—	5,101,658	300,708	58,265
1970	54,409,675	42,573,680	—	6,569,428	227,186	43,053
1980	66,759,389	49,305,289	1,411,226	9,244,182	219,415	89,521
1990	75,351,948	51,321,821	3,057,015	10,815,923	184,790	130,407

Age 18–64

	Male									Female						
	Parent-in-law	Sibling	Sibling-in-law	Grandchild	Other relatives	Partner, friend, visitor	Other nonrelatives	Institutional inmates	Total	Head/householder	Spouse	Child	Child-in-law	Parent	Parent-in-law	Sibling
	Ae433	Ae434	Ae435	Ae436	Ae437	Ae438	Ae439	Ae440	Ae441	Ae442	Ae443	Ae444	Ae445	Ae446	Ae447	Ae448
Year	Number	Number	Number	Number	Number	Number	Number	Number	Number	Number	Number	Number	Number	Number	Number	Number
1850 [2]	12,430	126,152	62,460	12,132	57,922	—	831,418	31,329	4,791,742	282,017	2,849,436	804,813	38,007	58,323	40,536	133,743
1860 [2]	18,259	171,559	77,654	16,143	71,912	—	1,079,065	37,014	6,759,024	428,935	4,139,756	1,093,694	42,654	78,363	58,403	164,049
1870	27,809	192,248	91,307	21,104	83,360		1,413,857	57,287	9,833,682	754,940	5,876,890	1,585,236	67,992	114,187	83,971	207,501
1880	16,261	227,702	85,898	32,005	94,856	16,459	2,014,477	102,283	12,873,040	1,023,196	7,787,972	2,114,721	131,941	118,401	85,699	255,651
1900	36,429	383,266	189,735	54,642	152,546	75,891	3,199,705	198,085	20,503,640	1,618,075	12,096,064	3,570,827	174,553	204,155	139,640	464,476
1910	57,426	506,543	299,744	64,737	223,946	126,718	4,546,195	261,957	25,375,685	1,875,579	15,360,671	4,370,815	202,017	214,601	178,601	522,401
1920	74,580	589,270	379,436	66,595	247,936	16,644	4,027,241	304,267	29,794,097	2,227,066	18,562,604	4,865,462	282,959	261,053	236,253	640,776
1940	89,837	634,454	414,246	152,328	334,139	75,088	3,397,732	612,130	41,104,630	3,654,420	25,156,507	6,620,827	500,117	318,126	277,700	718,368
1950	96,699	546,997	402,731	132,587	337,695	90,254	3,775,365	650,818	46,522,281	4,522,152	31,265,405	5,132,163	503,530	354,474	348,030	645,294
1960	67,956	441,055	290,938	110,475	476,480	94,742	2,764,176	728,652	50,519,650	5,888,080	36,298,673	4,165,102	247,442	273,082	277,227	566,866
1970	41,948	401,345	189,397	172,331	244,730	367,068	2,913,612	665,897	58,384,602	8,454,394	39,787,225	5,720,672	241,293	254,130	206,393	562,183
1980	32,269	694,223	167,066	211,112	317,045	1,513,181	2,821,368	733,492	70,049,637	14,910,783	42,138,439	7,233,906	189,325	314,222	105,094	630,737
1990	21,327	1,088,385	139,110	398,086	737,894	3,311,577	2,891,475	1,254,138	77,666,104	20,145,701	41,277,267	8,284,121	160,690	406,370	67,021	750,950

Age 18–64

	Female					
	Sibling-in-law	Grandchild	Other relatives	Partner, friend, visitor	Other nonrelatives	Institutional inmates
	Ae449	Ae450	Ae451	Ae452	Ae453	Ae454
Year	Number	Number	Number	Number	Number	Number
1850 [2]	71,357	13,750	49,729	—	429,518	20,513
1860 [2]	95,796	13,943	62,599	—	566,179	14,653
1870	124,536	23,610	108,085		855,938	30,796
1880	128,584	26,917	112,411	6,981	1,024,614	55,952
1900	229,962	50,089	170,766	9,867	1,656,770	118,396
1910	291,937	60,458	218,659	27,711	1,920,495	131,740
1920	364,816	59,847	237,060	20,288	1,879,400	156,513
1940	411,320	109,447	312,602	79,760	2,663,506	281,930
1950	393,826	101,489	307,387	127,285	2,491,921	329,325
1960	248,131	71,353	485,711	114,862	1,568,393	314,728
1970	199,789	139,190	258,036	451,728	1,845,038	264,531
1980	161,273	161,359	268,975	1,657,416	2,031,140	246,968
1990	132,407	293,686	562,792	3,282,067	2,039,268	263,764

Age 65 and older

	Male									
	Total	Head/householder	Spouse	Child	Child-in-law	Parent	Parent-in-law	Sibling	Sibling-in-law	Other relatives
	Ae455	Ae456	Ae457	Ae458	Ae459	Ae460	Ae461	Ae462	Ae463	Ae464
Year	Number	Number	Number	Number	Number	Number	Number	Number	Number	Number
1850 [2]	258,232	195,464	—	—	—	27,492	14,150	1,718	707	910
1860 [2]	350,464	261,781	—	—	—	40,137	19,657	2,105	1,202	1,702
1870	593,418	444,674	—	400	—	59,672	35,949	4,114	1,908	2,713
1880	866,483	671,581	—	—	299	69,513	37,899	8,282	3,491	10,479
1900	1,580,122	1,167,253	—	—	1,518	142,683	80,449	14,421	6,072	20,492
1910	1,974,353	1,437,817	—	1,260	1,008	153,655	116,118	15,870	9,321	21,157
1920	2,507,502	1,843,596	—	1,211	808	181,648	146,028	26,844	12,715	33,401
1940	4,420,055	3,343,189	—	8,331	2,931	250,495	207,340	68,025	30,512	51,573
1950	5,804,862	4,446,059	—	5,299	3,274	279,772	265,943	87,664	40,526	68,917
1960	7,233,123	5,993,712	—	8,760	2,489	230,506	247,450	89,665	42,920	104,382
1970	8,567,401	7,434,265	—	50,080	3,512	193,443	165,214	106,756	37,458	57,469
1980	10,234,469	8,853,378	323,445	15,692	6,593	223,512	91,918	106,323	24,687	53,460
1990	12,586,525	10,898,992	548,038	18,036	4,345	230,786	53,373	93,698	11,124	76,645

Notes appear at end of table

(continued)

TABLE Ae320–480 Household status – population, by age, sex, race, and relationship to head of household: 1850–1990 *Continued*

Age 65 and older

	Male			Female												
	Partner, friend, visitor	Other nonrelatives	Institutional inmates	Total	Head/householder	Spouse	Child	Child-in-law	Parent	Parent-in-law	Sibling	Sibling-in-law	Other relatives	Partner, friend, visitor	Other nonrelatives	Institutional inmates
	Ae465	Ae466	Ae467	Ae468	Ae469	Ae470	Ae471	Ae472	Ae473	Ae474	Ae475	Ae476	Ae477	Ae478	Ae479	Ae480
Year	Number	Number	Number	Number	Number	Number	Number	Number	Number	Number	Number	Number	Number	Number	Number	Number
1850 [2]	—	13,243	4,245	257,554	50,652	76,305	—	—	62,363	37,200	3,437	1,517	4,147	—	17,687	3,942
1860 [2]	—	20,867	2,813	350,070	69,024	100,632	—	—	85,702	56,381	5,519	1,705	2,908	—	25,484	2,614
1870	—	39,171	4,113	580,141	116,004	171,129	—	—	132,114	87,579	12,448	2,409	10,042	—	44,193	3,618
1880	100	48,781	14,165	865,444	197,980	257,723	599	99	175,936	101,917	17,955	5,978	32,327	698	62,956	11,276
1900	2,277	94,867	48,573	1,530,774	402,231	433,358	1,518	—	330,139	176,830	34,154	12,144	38,705	759	76,650	24,286
1910	3,526	144,594	69,775	1,976,380	530,759	567,028	3,022	—	333,749	267,002	52,392	18,138	63,232	4,282	95,223	41,553
1920	1,816	174,370	79,918	2,452,964	656,011	723,401	1,514	404	403,194	325,351	66,298	20,086	80,731	3,533	121,481	50,960
1940	5,003	331,030	121,626	4,587,818	1,487,908	1,375,510	11,411	808	562,857	471,634	152,706	39,979	107,423	8,667	260,124	108,791
1950	7,980	437,381	162,047	6,454,558	2,068,290	2,009,193	9,254	538	712,631	627,810	210,286	61,646	144,875	21,576	373,159	215,300
1960	7,574	260,523	245,142	8,803,847	3,194,139	2,973,196	18,328	99	717,409	692,928	261,804	70,441	214,495	21,014	280,520	359,474
1970	26,129	175,838	317,237	11,724,718	4,969,274	3,869,248	68,502	2,203	753,901	642,427	297,497	66,989	128,164	54,176	209,637	662,700
1980	23,580	142,888	368,993	15,201,018	7,268,062	4,993,233	29,875	2,197	820,599	390,185	294,367	47,255	140,178	38,768	200,336	975,963
1990	94,851	116,696	439,941	18,841,672	9,343,494	6,445,886	34,141	2,597	871,998	214,760	244,122	16,253	228,155	93,660	158,403	1,188,203

[1] As of June for 1850–1880 and 1900; as of January for 1920; as of April for other years. There are no data for 1890 because the original census manuscripts were destroyed in a fire. There are no data for 1930 because the 1930 Census records were not publicly available at the time this table was prepared.

[2] Excludes slave population.

Source

Tabulated from the Integrated Public Use Microdata Series (IPUMS); see the Guide to the Millennial Edition.

Documentation

This table gives the number of persons reporting thirteen categories of relationship to householder or household head. In the period 1850 to 1870, relationships are inferred. The shift from the household head to the householder concept between 1970 and 1980 can affect some categories; see Steven Ruggles and Susan Brower, "Measurement of Household and Family Composition in the United States, 1850–2000," *Population and Development Review* 29 (1) (2003): 73–101.

TABLE Ae481–488   Median age at first marriage, by sex and race: 1850–1999

Contributed by Catherine Fitch and Michael R. Haines

	Census and CPS data		Vital Statistics		Census data			
					Native whites		Blacks	
	Male	Female	Male	Female	Male	Female	Male	Female
	Ae481	Ae482 [1]	Ae483 [2]	Ae484 [2]	Ae485 [3]	Ae486 [3]	Ae487 [3]	Ae488 [3]
Year	Years	Years	Years	Years	Years	Years	Years	Years
1850	—	—	—	—	25.3	21.3	—	—
1860	—	—	—	—	25.0	21.4	—	—
1870	—	—	—	—	25.0	21.2	23.1	19.9
1880	—	—	—	—	25.4	21.8	23.3	20.0
1890	26.1	22.0	—	—	—	—	—	—
1900	25.9	21.9	—	—	26.0	22.1	23.9	20.3
1910	25.1	21.6	—	—	25.2	21.7	23.0	20.2
1920	24.6	21.2	—	—	24.8	21.5	22.4	19.5
1930	24.3	21.3	—	—	—	—	—	—
1940	24.3	21.5	—	—	24.5	21.5	22.4	20.1
1947	23.7	20.5	—	—	—	—	—	—
1948	23.3	20.4	—	—	—	—	—	—
1949	22.7	20.3	—	—	—	—	—	—
1950	22.8	20.3	—	—	22.8	20.1	22.4	19.5
1951	22.9	20.4	—	—	—	—	—	—
1952	23.0	20.2	—	—	—	—	—	—
1953	22.8	20.2	—	—	—	—	—	—
1954	23.0	20.3	—	—	—	—	—	—
1955	22.6	20.2	—	—	—	—	—	—
1956	22.5	20.1	—	—	—	—	—	—
1957	22.6	20.3	—	—	—	—	—	—
1958	22.6	20.2	—	—	—	—	—	—
1959	22.5	20.2	—	—	—	—	—	—
1960	22.8	20.3	—	—	22.2	19.9	22.5	20.4
1961	22.8	20.3	—	—	—	—	—	—
1962	22.7	20.3	—	—	—	—	—	—
1963	22.8	20.5	—	—	—	—	—	—
1964	23.1	20.5	22.4	20.4	—	—	—	—
1965	22.8	20.6	22.5	20.4	—	—	—	—
1966	22.8	20.5	22.6	20.3	—	—	—	—
1967	23.1	20.6	22.6	20.5	—	—	—	—
1968	23.1	20.8	22.4	20.6	—	—	—	—
1969	23.2	20.8	22.4	20.6	—	—	—	—
1970	23.2	20.8	22.5	20.6	22.4	20.7	22.5	21.1
1971	23.1	20.9	22.5	20.5	—	—	—	—
1972	23.3	20.9	22.4	20.5	—	—	—	—
1973	23.2	21.0	22.5	20.6	—	—	—	—
1974	23.1	21.1	22.5	20.6	—	—	—	—
1975	23.5	21.1	22.7	20.8	—	—	—	—
1976	23.8	21.3	22.9	21.0	—	—	—	—
1977	24.0	21.6	23.0	21.1	—	—	—	—
1978	24.2	21.8	23.2	21.4	—	—	—	—
1979	24.4	22.1	23.4	21.6	—	—	—	—
1980	24.7	22.0	23.6	21.8	23.9	22.0	25.4	24.3
1981	24.8	22.3	23.9	22.0	—	—	—	—
1982	25.2	22.5	24.1	22.3	—	—	—	—
1983	25.4	22.8	24.4	22.5	—	—	—	—
1984	25.4	23.0	24.6	22.8	—	—	—	—
1985	25.5	23.3	24.8	23.0	—	—	—	—
1986	25.7	23.1	25.1	23.3	—	—	—	—
1987	25.8	23.6	25.3	23.6	—	—	—	—
1988	25.9	23.6	25.5	23.7	—	—	—	—
1989	26.2	23.8	25.7	23.9	—	—	—	—
1990	26.1	23.9	25.9	24.0	25.8	23.6	28.6	27.3
1991	26.3	24.1	—	—	—	—	—	—
1992	26.5	24.4	—	—	—	—	—	—
1993	26.5	24.5	—	—	—	—	—	—
1994	26.7	24.5	—	—	—	—	—	—

Notes appear at end of table

(continued)

TABLE Ae481–488 Median age at first marriage, by sex and race: 1850–1999 *Continued*

	Census and CPS data		Vital Statistics		Census data			
					Native whites		Blacks	
	Male	Female	Male	Female	Male	Female	Male	Female
	Ae481	Ae482 [1]	Ae483 [2]	Ae484 [2]	Ae485 [3]	Ae486 [3]	Ae487 [3]	Ae488 [3]
Year	Years	Years	Years	Years	Years	Years	Years	Years
1995	26.9	24.5	—	—	—	—	—	—
1996	27.1	24.8	—	—	—	—	—	—
1997	26.8	25.0	—	—	—	—	—	—
1998	26.7	25.0	—	—	—	—	—	—
1999	—	—	—	—	26.6	24.5	—	—

[1] Based on census population data by age, sex, and marital status; for 1947–1994 they are based on sample population data from Current Population Survey. See text for method of computation.

[2] Based on vital registration data. The Marriage Registration Area does not cover the entire United States.

[3] Based on census data samples from the Integrated Public Use Microdata Series (IPUMS) of the U.S. censuses; see the Guide to the Millennial Edition.

Sources

Series Ae481–482. U.S. Bureau of the Census, *Current Population Reports*, series P-20, number 484, "Marital Status and Living Arrangements: March 1994," Table A-2; series P-20, number 514, "Marital Status and Living Arrangements: March 1998 (Update)," Table MS-2.

Series Ae483–484. U.S. National Center for Health Statistics, "First Marriages, United States, 1968–1976," Data from the National Vital Statistics System, series 21, number 35, PHS 79-1913 (September 1979), Table 4. U.S. National Center for Health Statistics, "Advance Report of Final Marriage Statistics, 1989 and 1990," *Monthly Vital Statistics Report*, volume 43, number 12, Supplement (July 14, 1995), Table 9.

Series Ae485–488. Catherine A. Fitch and Steven Ruggles, "Historical Trends in Marriage Formation, United States: 1850-1990," in Linda Waite, Christine Bachrach, et al., editors, *Ties That Bind: Perspectives on Marriage and Cohabitation* (de Gruyter, 2000), pp. 59–88.

Documentation

The median age at first marriage is simply the age at which half of the never-married population (either from census or vital registration) is older and half is younger.

Series Ae481–482. The median age at first marriage in these series is an approximation derived indirectly from tabulations of marital status and age. (See source for detailed explanation of computation procedures.) These estimates differ from those based on annual marriage records or census questions on age at first marriage. The median age at first marriage shown here can be interpreted as applying to the cohort born *n* years earlier, where *n* is the median age at first marriage. Estimates from 1947 to 1970 are subject to sampling variability.

Series Ae483–484. The median age at first marriage in these series is based on vital registration in the Marriage Registration Area. The Marriage Registration Area was formed in 1957 and included thirty states and the District of Columbia, Alaska, Hawai'i, Puerto Rico, and the Virgin Islands. It now comprises forty-two states and the District of Columbia, although the remaining states do contribute data, which is sometimes incomplete.

Series Ae485–488. Recent work with the Integrated Public Use Microdata Series (IPUMS) of the U.S. censuses allows estimation of medians beyond the first appearance in 1890 of the published data on population by age, sex, marital status, race, and nativity. The results for 1850–1870 are based on imputed marital status in IPUMS files. Series Ae485–488 are based on the median age for ever-married women at each census. The results for the native white population for 1999 are based on Current Population Survey (*Basic Monthly Survey*, January–July 1999).

TABLE Ae489–506   **Singulate mean age at first marriage, by sex, race, and nativity: 1880–1990**

Contributed by Michael R. Haines

	White												Nonwhite				Spanish origin	
							Native-born				Foreign-born				Black			
							Native parentage		Foreign or mixed parentage									
	Male	Female	Male	Female	Male	Female	Male	Female	Male	Female	Male	Female	Male	Female	Male	Female	Male	Female
	Ae489	Ae490	Ae491	Ae492	Ae493	Ae494	Ae495	Ae496	Ae497	Ae498	Ae499	Ae500	Ae501	Ae502	Ae503	Ae504	Ae505	Ae506
Year	Years	Years	Years	Years	Years	Years	Years	Years	Years	Years	Years	Years	Years	Years	Years	Years	Years	Years
1880	26.80	23.08	27.00	23.27	26.44	23.28	25.96	23.09	28.48	23.44	28.18	23.48	24.85	20.89	24.15	20.85	—	—
1890	27.57	23.61	27.77	23.81	27.65	23.71	27.14	23.02	28.81	25.40	28.31	23.94	25.99	22.24	25.54	22.25	—	—
1900	27.43	23.65	27.64	23.85	27.61	23.88	26.95	23.07	28.91	25.57	27.89	23.57	26.01	22.40	25.77	22.48	—	—
1910	26.73	23.14	26.93	23.35	26.75	23.41	26.19	22.75	28.23	25.02	27.51	22.83	25.20	21.81	25.14	21.84	—	—
1920	25.92	22.50	26.06	22.70	25.86	22.82	25.44	22.43	27.02	23.93	26.87	21.64	24.82	21.32	24.72	21.36	—	—
1930	25.56	22.32	26.67	22.51	25.46	22.40	25.07	22.10	26.52	23.26	27.19	22.91	24.98	21.37	24.54	21.40	—	—
1940	25.60	22.74	25.70	22.86	—	—	—	—	—	—	—	—	24.84	22.10	—	—	—	—
1950	23.79	20.83	23.78	20.80	—	—	—	—	—	—	—	—	23.86	21.21	—	—	—	—
1960	23.38	20.33	23.18	20.18	—	—	—	—	—	—	—	—	24.16	21.49	—	—	—	—
1970	23.51	21.46	23.39	21.27	—	—	—	—	—	—	—	—	24.36	22.67	24.19	22.70	23.09	21.22
1980	25.20	23.32	25.00	22.95	—	—	—	—	—	—	—	—	26.11	24.92	26.63	25.84	24.56	22.47
1990	27.60	25.36	27.26	24.84	—	—	—	—	—	—	—	—	28.81	27.12	29.73	28.72	27.02	24.33

Source

Michael R. Haines, "Long-Term Marriage Patterns in the United States from Colonial Times to the Present," *The History of the Family: An International Quarterly* 1 (1) (1996), Table 2.

Documentation

The original data were taken from the U.S. Census of Population: 1880, public use micro sample of the 1880 U.S. Census. U.S. Bureau of the Census; 1890–1950, U.S. Census of Population: 1950, volume 2, part 1, pp. 179–81; 1960, U.S. Census of Population: 1960, volume 1, part 1, pp. 424–5; 1970, U.S. Census of Population: 1970, volume 1, part 1, section 2, pp. 640–1; 1980, U.S. Census of Population: 1980, volume 1, chapter D, part 1 (PC80-1-D1-A), pp. 67–79; 1990, U.S. Census of Population: 1990, volume 1 (CP-1-1), pp. 45–7.

The procedure for calculating singulate mean age at first marriage is described in U.S. Bureau of the Census, *The Methods and Materials of Demography*, by Henry S. Shryock, Jacob S. Siegel, et al. (U.S. Government Printing Office, 1971), pp. 294–5. The method was developed by John Hajnal, "Age at Marriage and Proportions Marrying," *Population Studies* 7 (2) (1953): 111–36.

TABLE Ae507–513   Marriage and divorce rates: 1920–1995[1]

Contributed by Michael R. Haines

	Marriage rate		Divorce				
			Rate				
Year	Per 1,000 population	Per 1,000 unmarried females	Per 1,000 population	Per 1,000 married females	Median duration of marriage	Percentage of spouses separated	Divorced persons per 1,000 persons married, spouse present
	Ae507	Ae508	Ae509	Ae510 [2]	Ae511	Ae512	Ae513 [3]
	Per 1,000	Per 1,000	Per 1,000	Per 1,000	Years	Percent	Per 1,000
1920	12.0	92.0	1.6	8.0	—	—	—
1921	10.7	83.0	1.5	7.2	—	—	—
1922	10.3	79.7	1.4	6.6	—	—	—
1923	11.0	85.2	1.5	7.1	—	—	—
1924	10.4	80.3	1.5	7.2	—	—	—
1925	10.3	79.2	1.5	7.2	—	—	—
1926	10.2	78.7	1.6	7.5	—	—	—
1927	10.1	77.0	1.6	7.8	—	—	—
1928	9.8	74.1	1.7	7.8	—	—	—
1929	10.1	75.5	1.7	8.0	—	—	—
1930	9.2	67.6	1.6	7.5	—	—	—
1931	8.6	61.9	1.5	7.1	—	—	—
1932	7.9	56.0	1.3	6.1	—	—	—
1933	8.7	61.3	1.3	6.1	—	—	—
1934	10.3	71.8	1.6	7.5	—	—	—
1935	10.4	72.5	1.7	7.8	—	—	—
1936	10.7	74.0	1.8	8.3	—	—	—
1937	11.3	78.0	1.9	8.7	—	—	—
1938	10.3	69.9	1.9	8.4	—	—	—
1939	10.7	73.0	1.9	8.5	—	—	—
1940	12.1	82.8	2.0	8.8	—	—	—
1941	12.7	88.5	2.2	9.4	—	—	—
1942	13.2	93.0	2.4	10.1	—	—	—
1943	11.7	83.0	2.6	11.0	—	—	—
1944	10.9	76.5	2.9	12.0	—	—	—
1945	12.2	83.6	3.5	14.4	—	—	—
1946	16.4	118.1	4.3	17.9	—	—	—
1947	13.9	106.2	3.4	13.6	—	—	—
1948	12.4	98.5	2.8	11.2	—	—	33.0
1949	10.6	86.7	2.7	10.6	—	—	29.0
1950	11.1	90.2	2.6	10.3	5.8	1.8	29.0
1951	10.4	86.6	2.5	9.9	6.0	1.5	29.0
1952	9.9	83.2	2.5	10.1	6.1	1.4	29.0
1953	9.8	83.7	2.5	9.9	6.1	1.5	31.0
1954	9.2	79.8	2.4	9.5	6.4	1.7	33.0
1955	9.3	80.9	2.3	9.3	6.4	1.8	31.0
1956	9.5	82.4	2.3	9.4	6.5	1.8	32.0
1957	8.9	78.0	2.2	9.2	6.7	1.6	31.0
1958	8.4	72.0	2.1	8.9	6.4	1.8	32.0
1959	8.5	73.6	2.2	9.3	7.0	1.9	33.0
1960	8.5	73.5	2.2	9.2	7.2	1.8	35.0
1961	8.5	72.2	2.3	9.6	7.1	1.9	37.0
1962	8.5	71.2	2.2	9.4	7.3	1.9	37.0
1963	8.8	73.4	2.3	9.6	7.5	1.8	39.0
1964	9.0	74.6	2.4	10.0	7.4	1.9	41.0
1965	9.3	75.0	2.5	10.6	7.2	2.0	41.0
1966	9.5	75.6	2.5	10.9	7.1	1.9	43.0
1967	9.7	76.4	2.6	11.2	7.1	1.8	43.0
1968	10.4	79.1	2.9	12.4	7.0	1.8	45.0
1969	10.6	80.0	3.2	13.4	6.9	1.9	46.0
1970	10.6	76.5	3.5	14.9	6.7	1.8	47.0
1971	10.6	76.2	3.7	15.8	6.7	3.1	51.3
1972	10.9	77.9	4.0	17.0	6.7	3.3	52.1
1973	10.8	76.0	4.3	18.2	6.6	3.3	55.8
1974	10.5	72.0	4.6	19.3	6.5	3.3	63.0

Notes appear at end of table

TABLE Ae507–513   Marriage and divorce rates: 1920–1995   *Continued*

	Marriage rate		Divorce				
			Rate		Median duration of marriage	Percentage of spouses separated	Divorced persons per 1,000 persons married, spouse present
	Per 1,000 population	Per 1,000 unmarried females	Per 1,000 population	Per 1,000 married females			
	Ae507	Ae508	Ae509	Ae510 [2]	Ae511	Ae512	Ae513 [3]
Year	Per 1,000	Per 1,000	Per 1,000	Per 1,000	Years	Percent	Per 1,000
1975	10.0	66.9	4.8	20.3	6.5	3.6	68.7
1976	9.9	65.2	5.0	21.1	6.5	3.7	75.1
1977	9.9	63.6	5.0	21.1	6.6	3.7	83.7
1978	10.3	64.1	5.1	21.9	6.6	3.8	90.2
1979	10.4	63.6	5.3	22.8	6.8	3.9	91.5
1980	10.6	61.4	5.2	22.6	6.8	3.8	99.6
1981	10.6	61.7	5.3	22.6	7.0	4.0	108.6
1982	10.6	61.4	5.0	21.7	7.0	4.1	114.4
1983	10.5	59.9	4.9	21.3	7.0	3.9	114.4
1984	10.5	59.5	5.0	21.5	6.9	3.9	121.0
1985	10.1	57.0	5.0	21.7	6.8	4.0	128.0
1986	10.0	56.2	4.9	21.2	6.9	4.0	131.1
1987	9.9	55.7	4.8	20.8	7.0	4.0	130.4
1988	9.7	54.6	4.8	20.7	7.1	4.0	132.7
1989	9.7	54.2	4.7	20.4	7.2	3.9	137.6
1990	9.8	54.5	4.7	20.9	7.2	4.1	142.0
1991	9.4	54.2	4.7	20.9	—	4.2	148.2
1992	9.3	53.3	4.8	21.2	—	4.3	152.5
1993	9.0	52.3	4.6	20.5	—	4.0	153.7
1994	9.1	51.5	4.6	20.5	—	4.1	160.1
1995	8.9	50.8	4.4	19.8	—	4.2	160.6

[1] Persons 15 and older, except where noted.

[2] Persons 14 and older.

[3] Includes Alaska.

Sources

Series Ae507–511. 1920–1988: National Center for Health Statistics, *Vital Statistics of the United States*, volume 3, annual issues. 1989–1990: Sally C. Clarke, "Advance Report of Final Marriage Statistics, 1989 and 1990," *Monthly Vital Statistics Report*, volume 43, number 12, Supplement (National Center for Health Statistics, 1995); Sally C. Clarke, "Advance Report of Final Divorce Statistics, 1989 and 1990," *Monthly Vital Statistics Report*, volume 43, number 9, Supplement (National Center for Health Statistics, 1995). 1991–1995: U.S. Bureau of the Census, *Statistical Abstract of the United States: 1998* (118th edition) (U.S. Government Printing Office, 1998), Tables 156 and 159.

Series Ae512–513. Calculated from data reported from the annual March segment of the Current Population Survey. U.S. Bureau of the Census, *Current Population Reports*, series P-20, "Marital Status and Living Arrangements, March."

See also: U.S. Commissioner of Labor, *A Report on Marriage and Divorce in the United States, 1867 to 1886*; U.S. Bureau of the Census, *Marriage and Divorce, 1867–1906*; *Vital Statistics – Special Reports*, volume 9, number 60, "A Review of Marriage and Divorce Statistics: United States: 1887–1937"; U.S. Bureau of the Census, *Marriage and Divorces*, 1916 and annual issues for 1922–1932; S. A. Stouffer and L. M. Spencer, "Recent Increases in Marriage and Divorce," *American Journal of Sociology* 44 (4) (1939): 551–4 (for the years 1933–1936); U.S. Bureau of the Census, *Vital Statistics – Special Reports*, volume 15, numbers 13 and 18, "Estimated Number of Marriages by State: United States, 1937–1940" and "Estimated Number of Divorces by State: United States, 1937–1940," respectively. For exact population base figures, see *Vital Statistics – Special Reports*, volume 46, number 12, p. 330.

Documentation

Marriage and divorce records are filed only at the county level in some states, but gradually the various states are requiring by law that such events be recorded at the state level. The completeness of reporting to the state offices varies, but there has been no nationwide test. A Marriage Registration Area covering thirty states and five independent areas was established by the National Office of Vital Statistics in 1957. A major criterion for admission of a state to the registration area was agreement with the National Office of Vital Statistics to conduct a test of marriage registration completeness. By 1971, the Marriage Registration Area covered forty states and three independent areas. In 1990, it still covered forty states and the District of Columbia. A Divorce Registration Area with fourteen states and three independent areas was inaugurated in 1958. By 1971, it covered twenty-nine states and one independent area. It had expanded to thirty-one states and the District of Columbia by 1990.

Figures are for population enumerated as of April 1 for 1940, 1950, and 1960, and estimated as of July 1 for all other years. They include armed forces abroad for 1941–1946.

See the text for Table Ab11–30.

Series Ae508 and Ae510. Rates are based on those segments of the female population that may be considered as subject to possible marriage and divorce.

Series Ae511. At time of divorce decree.

Series Ae512. For 1971–1995, calculated as the number of separated persons as a percent of all married males and females, whether spouse present or absent.

Series Ae513. For 1971–1995, calculated as the number of divorced persons per 1,000 of all married persons with spouse present.

CHAPTER Af

Cohorts

Editor: Susan B. Carter
Associate Editor: Matthew Sobek

COHORTS

Susan B. Carter

A cohort is a group of people born at about the same time. Thus, one can speak of the birth cohort of 1951–1960 to refer to people born in that ten-year period. A cohort can also be defined in terms of other significant demographic events. A marriage cohort is a group of people married around the same time; a schooling cohort is a group of people who experienced some educational milestone such as starting the first grade or graduating from high school or college at the same time (for example, the "Class of 2000"); a migration cohort is a group of people who entered or left a country at about the same time; and so forth. However, the most common cohort considered in demographic, social, and economic analysis is the birth cohort (see Whelpton 1954; Ryder 1968; Shryock, Siegel, and Associates 1976, pp. 550–3).

In technical analyses conducted by demographers, birth cohorts are generally defined in terms of some standardized period of time, such as a decade between censuses, but in the social sciences generally it is more common to define birth cohorts in terms of events that were important enough to have shaped the lives of a generation. Thus, the "Depression-era generation" refers to those born in the years from about 1910 through about 1925, who came of age during the Great Depression of the 1930s and fought in World War II. The baby boom generation, or "boomers," includes those born in the ten to fifteen years of historically high fertility beginning in 1946. Generation "X" – sometimes called the "baby busters" – are those born during the period of unusually low fertility beginning about 1965 and extending through 1980.[1]

It is common to categorize people according to their birth cohort and to identify differences in the attitudes and behavior of different cohorts – "generation gaps." This is because unique events such as war, famine, economic depression, political struggles, legislative change, and even the advent of television seem to have a lifelong impact on those coming of age at the time they occur. Moreover, behavior is often influenced by what others are doing at the same time. For example, in the 1950s, employed mothers with young children often had to defend their decision to work to family and friends. In the 1990s, it was the "stay-at-home moms" who more often felt on the defensive. The combination of changed circumstances and the social tendency to adjust one's behavior to coordinate with that of one's neighbors means that in our history we sometimes observe radical differences in the behavior of people born just a few years apart from one another. These behavioral differences can show up in a variety of areas including health, educational attainment, marriage and divorce, fertility, employment, and worldview. In some cases, such cohort differences in behavior and attitude characterize a lifetime. A number of recent books attempt to highlight generational differences in attitudes and values. For a detailed depiction of the generation that came of age during the Great Depression and World War II, see Tom Brokaw's *The Greatest Generation*. William Strauss and Neil Howe propose a larger historical generational cycle, with four generations to a cycle, each of which displays a distinctive world outlook. Meredith Bagby offers a sketch of "Generation X." Thomas Schelling discusses the implications of the fact that in many situations individuals' behavior depends on the behavior of those around them (Schelling 1978; Strauss and Howe 1990, 1993, 1997; Bagby 1998; Brokaw 1998; Howe and Strauss 2000).

This chapter presents data arranged so as to illustrate some of the major differences in the life experience of distinct birth cohorts in American history. As such, it is a reworking of data presented elsewhere. There is great value, however, in presenting data in cohort format, because cohort differences are often invisible in conventionally displayed statistics. Discussion in the other chapters of *Historical Statistics of the United States* is conducted in terms of what demographers call "period analysis." Period analysis focuses on some aggregate of the behavior of people of all ages at one particular point in time – for example, daily newspaper circulation per household. One reason for the predominance of period analysis in *Historical Statistics* is that most economic and social statistics are collected and presented as a characterization of the entire population or economy at some point in time. For many issues, period analysis is the appropriate research strategy. For example, the most salient characteristic of the Great Depression of the 1930s was the

---

[1] Here the terms "birth cohort" and "generation" are used interchangeably to refer to people born about the same time. Sometimes, however, the term generation is used to refer to people who occupy the same relationship within a family, say, grandchild. According to this usage, members of a single generation may be of many different ages. Generation is also a measure of time, thought of as the average age of mothers at the time they give birth – about twenty-five years.

Acknowledgments
Richard A. Easterlin, Richard Sutch, Gavin Wright, and Matt Sobek provided valuable comments on the essay. This work was made possible in part by funding from the James A. Shannon Director's Award from the National Institute on Aging and the support of the College of Humanities, Arts, and Sciences at the University of California, Riverside.

massive failure of the macroeconomy. The Great Depression lasted a full decade and at its depth nearly a fourth of the labor force was unemployed (see Chapter Cb, on business fluctuations and cycles). It had a sizable and permanent effect on people of all ages and all birth cohorts, and it is appropriate to focus on the many differences between this period and the adjacent periods of American history.

For other issues, however, period analysis is inappropriate. Take the example of newspaper readership. Ever since Alexis de Tocqueville wrote in the early nineteenth century, social observers have commented on the connection between newspaper readership and civic engagement. Recently, Robert Putnam has argued that newspaper readership remains a mark of "substantial civic engagement." For this reason, it is important to understand the marked decline in newspaper readership that began about 1950. Newspaper circulation per household was 1.24 per day in 1950 and has declined steadily since then, reaching 0.55 in 1998 (series Ae29 and Dg268). Was the decline the result of some force that affected all age groups, much like the Great Depression, or was it something else? Putnam argues as follows:

> Newspaper reading is a lasting habit established early in adult life. If we start young, we generally continue. Virtually none of the precipitous decline in newspaper circulation over the last half century can be traced to declining readership by individuals. Virtually all of the decline is due to the by now familiar pattern of general succession.... [T]hree out of every four Americans born in the first third of the twentieth century continue to read a daily newspaper as the century closes just as that generation did decades ago. Fewer than half of their boomer children are carrying on the tradition, however, a fraction that has dwindled to one in four among their X'er grandchildren. Since more recent cohorts show no sign of becoming newspaper readers as they age, circulation continues to plunge as the generation of readers is replaced by the generation of nonreaders. (Putnam 2000, pp. 218–9)

Overall, then, the downward trend in the period data results from successively lower newspaper-readership rates among consecutive birth cohorts. This means that the public policy implications are more serious than they would be if the decline in readership affected all age groups. As Putnam concludes, "reversing that slump will not be easy, since each year the ground is slipping away beneath our feet."

In principle, one could observe differences in newspaper readership across birth cohorts by studying "cross-sectional" data with a disaggregation by age. Cross-sectional means that data for a single year are disaggregated in a way that allows the user to observe differences in the behavior of people of different ages at one point in time. These cross-sectional data for many different years are another type of data found in many chapters in *Historical Statistics of the United States*. Like period data, cross-sectional data are useful for many purposes. Putnam's observation, described in the previous paragraph, is one example.

Despite their usefulness, however, period and even cross-sectional data can obscure changes in behavior across cohorts. To illustrate this point, consider Figures Af-A and Af-B, both of which are derived from the same underlying data. Figure Af-A displays cross-sectional data on the proportion of women in the labor force, by age, at seven different census years beginning in 1920. It is tempting to view one of these cross-sections as if it represented the experience of a typical individual as she aged. In this case, a

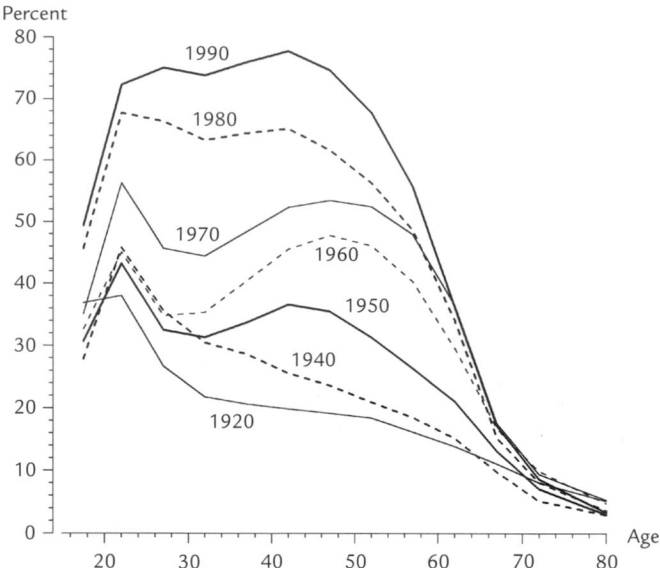

FIGURE Af-A   Female labor force participation rate, by age and census year: 1920–1990

Sources
Table Ba404–416.

Documentation
For display purposes the means of the age ranges are used and 80 is the value assigned to the category "75 and older."

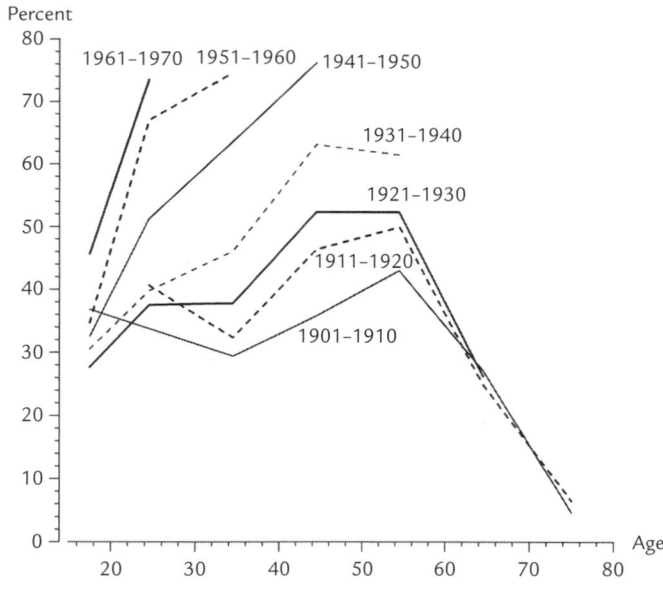

FIGURE Af-B   Female labor force participation rate, by age and birth cohort: 1901–1970

Sources
Series Af8–14.

Documentation
For display purposes the means of the age ranges are used and 75 is the value assigned to the category "70 and older."

"synthetic cohort" approach would seem to imply one constancy and two dramatic changes in the overall level and life-cycle pattern of women's labor force participation over the twentieth century. The constancy is the rising pattern of women's labor force participation with increases in participation from the teens to the midtwenties and then a decline into the retirement years evident in every census year. One change is an increase in the level of employment at almost every age over the course of the twentieth century. The other is the disappearance of a dip in female labor force participation during the key child-rearing years in a woman's midtwenties through her midforties. In 1920 and 1940, the cross-sectional data seem to imply that women entered the labor force after completion of their schooling, withdrew when they married and had children, and then reentered after their children were in school or had left home. By 1990, the "withdrawal" is virtually eliminated. It seems as if those women participating in the labor force in their midtwenties stick with it for a good thirty years, but begin retiring at a relatively early age (50 years old).

However, as Claudia Goldin (1990) has shown, an entirely different view of change in female labor force participation across the life cycle emerges when the data are rearranged in a way that highlights the actual experience of different cohorts as they aged, as in Figure Af-B. For example, the labor force experience of the cohort born in 1931–1940 is assembled by considering the participation rates of 20- to 29-year-olds in 1960, 30- to 39-year-olds in 1970, and so forth.

In Figure Af-B it is clear that no group of women born in the twentieth century displayed a consistent decline in participation before the age of fifty-five. The apparent withdrawal of women's participation in the labor force during the peak child-bearing years that is so striking in the synthetic cohort does not represent the actual experience of a true cohort. Although the cohorts of 1901 through 1920 exhibit a decline in their middle years, they show the highest participation rates of their lives in their fifties, after their children were grown. For the cohort of 1921–1930, the labor force participation withdrawal during the child-rearing years disappears completely. For the cohorts of 1931–1940 and younger, there is a clear and pronounced pattern of increasing participation at every age, up to the age of fifty-five.

The moral of this story is that in a rapidly changing economy, the synthetic cohort approach based on cross-sectional data can be misleading. Synthetic cohorts give an accurate picture of life course only if cohorts do not differ radically from one another in their behavior. Where cohort effects are strong – that is, where the behavior of one cohort differs substantially from that of earlier and later ones – they can confound true life-cycle patterns. In the case of women's labor force participation rates, marked increases in participation at each age across successive cohorts raised the rates of young workers relative to older workers so much as to make it appear in the cross section that participation rates were falling at older ages. Cohort data make it clear that the opposite is the case.

This chapter presents a small number of data tables arranged to draw attention to differences in the experiences of successive cohorts as they age and also to show what cohort data look like. These tables focus on three different areas of life experience: labor force participation, education, and marital status. The essay also points to shifts in the behavior and experience of different cohorts that can be detected in data displayed in other chapters of *Historical Statistics of the United States*. These thumbnail sketches are meant as illustrations of the enormous range of intercohort variation in life experience. A full descriptive effort would require the development of many new data series and, therefore, is beyond the scope of this project. Fortunately, the technique for translating cross-sectional data disaggregated by age into cohort data can be applied to many different series.[2] Even where cross-sectional data by age are not available, one can often guess the cohort patterns by remembering that changed circumstances often have their greatest impact on people who are young adults at the time. For reasons that will become clear, young adults are the ones most likely to embrace new attitudes and behavior.

Occupation and Industry

In a dynamic economy such as that of the United States, the demand for labor is constantly shifting across occupations and industries. Technological and organizational changes mean new products (the automobile in the 1920s), new methods of production (the tractor in the 1920s and 1930s), and shifts in the demand for inputs (more college-educated labor in the 1980s and 1990s). Increase in the sheer size of the economy makes it profitable for some to make a full-time occupation out of an activity that in an earlier era was carried out as a sideline. Real estate services are a recent example. Wars, natural disasters, and mineral discoveries are other developments that can alter labor demand in ways that are difficult or impossible to reverse. One example is the destruction of the American merchant marine during the Civil War (1860–1865). The fleet was owned by Northerners; the Confederate Navy conducted successful raids (Table Eh59–94). As a consequence, shipping business moved to foreign fleets. The American fleet never recovered (see Tables Df606–611 and Df736–741). Changing tastes are also a factor. Americans' growing preference for athletic shoes and "casual Fridays" in the latter part of the twentieth century reduced the demand for shoe shines. There are many other examples (see, for example, the essay and tables on occupations in Chapter Ba).

Occupational shifts tend to have strong cohort effects because, as in the case of newspaper readership, occupational choices tend to be made at young adult ages and to remain relatively fixed for life. There is a good reason for this. Most occupations require costly and specialized training before a novice becomes proficient. Even where this training takes place on the job and involves no out-of-pocket expense, it often takes several years of experience to achieve full proficiency. For these reasons, older workers who have already achieved proficiency in an industry or occupation tend to stay with it, even when prospects worsen. Even if relative returns in the industry itself may have fallen, the first industry to which they are attached may offer superior rewards given the costly learning needed to excel at some other occupation. By contrast, new labor market entrants have every reason to select occupations and industries that pay high wages and where future prospects seem good. Thus, shifts in occupational and industrial demand tend to create disjunctures in the experiences of different cohorts.

---

[2] This method provides a measure of *net* changes in experience of a cohort as it ages. It is a net change because some women who leave the labor force at a given age are offset by others who enter at that age. The aggregate statistic thus indicates the net change in labor force participants. This technique is a simplification of the intercensal cohort-component method for measuring net changes, also known as the census survival method; see Shryock, Siegel, and Associates (1976, pp. 357–8). Sutch (1975, pp. 199–210) gives an example of the method used to estimate geographical net migration. Sutch's appendix provides a detailed description of the procedure and discusses the accuracy and sensitivity of the method. Carter and Sutch (1996) use this method to study the retirement behavior of men before the advent of government-sponsored Social Security.

The decline from cohort to cohort in the share of the workforce engaged in farming is one example. At the beginning of the eighteenth century, agriculture accounted for almost the entirety of the American workforce; at the end of the twentieth century the share was about 2 percent (Tables Da–C and Ba1033–1046.) This decline in the agricultural workforce presents one of the great paradoxes in the history of the American economy. Whereas the industrial side of economic life is widely acknowledged to be dynamic and increasingly productive, the quantitative record suggests that productivity growth in agriculture was even more impressive. It is ironic that agriculture's relative success in this regard was precisely the reason it shrank as a share of the total economy. While farm productivity and farm output were rising, farm prices were falling. Farm incomes could not keep pace with those in other sectors. Farmers' children discovered more lucrative careers in industry, services, and the professions.

The cohort-to-cohort change in the occupations of women is another dimension of long-term change that is large enough to be visible even in the aggregate data. In 1870, more than 40 percent of both black and white women workers were employed as domestic servants. Among white women, improvements in education – in particular the high school movement – and the expansion of white-collar clerical jobs meant that by 1920 fewer than 10 percent of white working women were employed in domestic service whereas almost one quarter (23.4 percent) worked as clerks and typists. When educational opportunities for black women expanded following the Great Migration, black women also moved into clerical work and their domestic service work declined proportionately (see Tables Ba1103–1130).

To observe other changes that may have had similar, dramatic impacts on the life experience of adjacent cohorts, one needs to take a closer look at the detailed occupational data presented in Tables Ba652–813 and Ba1159–4206. It is an exercise that can be both revealing and enjoyable. For example, most people would not be surprised to observe the rise through 1900 and the subsequent decline in the number of blacksmiths. However, not many people are aware that there were more than one million miners in the 1920 workforce, or that in 1900 more than 2.5 percent of the workforce was engaged in the hand production of clothing and hats. Today, the share is about one tenth of 1 percent. No one will be surprised at the meteoric growth in the number of economists over the last half of the twentieth century, but they may be startled at the rapid increase in occupations associated with security, law enforcement, legal matters, religious observance, insurance, and real estate. For most workers in these occupations, the occupational shifts at the national level represent a generational shift as well.

International Immigration to the United States

Immigration can affect the size and demographic structure of cohorts. Because the number of immigrants and their characteristics have fluctuated substantially over the course of U.S. history, immigration has had an uneven impact across the different cohorts (see Chapter Ad, on international migration).

People tend to migrate as young adults. Thus, one way to display the relative importance of immigrants across cohorts is to show the share of the foreign-born among those in their twenties. Data in Tables Aa185–286 and Aa2026–2077 suggest that immigration had a substantial impact on cohorts born in the mid- to late nineteenth century. For these cohorts, the foreign-born account for

about one sixth of the total when these cohorts are in their twenties. The passage of the Quota Acts in the 1920s and then the Great Depression of the 1930s brought immigration virtually to a halt. Indeed, during some years of the Great Depression, more American residents emigrated from the United States than foreigners immigrated to the country. This dramatic cessation of immigration is reflected in an equally dramatic reduction in the impact of immigration on the cohorts born during the early years of the twentieth century. At the nadir, the foreign-born accounted for only about 2 percent of these cohorts when they were in their twenties. The post–World War II baby boom cohort was also only slightly affected by migration from abroad, but the situation is quite different for the small birth cohorts that followed. For the cohort born about 1965, the foreign-born account for approximately one tenth of the total. This resumption of immigration after years of relatively small flows partially offsets the small number of births in the "baby bust" generation born after 1965.

Abolition of Slavery, Reconstruction, and the Great Migration

For nearly two and a half centuries, black slave labor was an integral part of the economic, social, and political life of the American South. The most profound consequences of the abolition of slavery were naturally felt by the former slaves themselves – the freedmen. On the eve of the Civil War, in 1860, there were more than four million slaves in the United States. Almost 90 percent of the black population and more than one third of the total population of the Southern states was enslaved (Tables Aa2093–2188). Slaves accounted for almost half of the taxable wealth in the Southern states (Table Eh50–58).

The Fourteenth Amendment to the Constitution, passed in 1865, made these four million people suddenly free. For the first time in their lives, freedmen could retain their labor earnings and dispose of them as they pleased. Following Emancipation, freedmen reduced the labor of young children and women (Tables Ba11–24 and Ba50–63). Children were enrolled in school instead of being sent to the fields (Table Bc438–446). Fertility fell (Table Ab52–117) and more young children were cared for by their own mothers and fathers (Table Ae128–190). The improvements in quality of life were substantial.[3]

At the same time, opportunities for the black population remained far more limited than those for whites. Roger L. Ransom and Richard Sutch (1977) blame this failure on the character of the economic and social institutions constructed in the years immediately following the Civil War. Further progress required either a change in these institutions or the departure of blacks from the South. The Great Migration, the movement of blacks from the rural South into the urban North from 1910 to 1950, helped to accomplish both. In the forty years following Emancipation, only slightly more than a half million blacks left the South for the North. In the forty years beginning in 1910, more than 3.5 million did so. This figure refers to net migration, that is, the excess of out-migration over return migration.

In 1900, fewer than 5 percent of blacks born in the South lived in other regions of the country. By 1950, the figure was more than

---

[3] For a description of other changes in the lives of freedmen immediately following Emancipation, see Ransom and Sutch (1977).

20 percent (Table Ac1–42) (Eldridge and Thomas 1964; Collins 1997). Because these migrants were overwhelmingly young adults, the impact on the lives of the cohorts who came of age in those years was far greater than these numbers suggest.

The Great Migration expanded opportunities for black Americans in two ways. First, by getting out of the relatively impoverished rural South, blacks gained access to better-paying jobs for themselves and to better education for their children. Virtually all of the decline in the relative importance of farm and farm laborer occupations for black men and women displayed in Tables Ba1089–1102 and Ba1117–1130 is due to the movement of blacks out of the rural South and into the great cities of the North, Midwest, and West. Much of the improvement in the education of black children over the same years is due to their parents' move away from the South (Margo 1990).

Another consequence of the Great Migration is that it forced Southern whites to improve the quality of the schools and jobs they offered to blacks. With the onset of the migratory flow, blacks suddenly had a new option in life. If conditions at home were unattractive, they could move to the North. Robert A. Margo (1990) documents the substantial improvement in the quality of schools for blacks relative to those for whites in the South following the initiation of the Great Migration.

Mortality

The size and quality of life of a cohort are affected by its experience of mortality. Across the span of American history, cohorts have had different experiences in this regard. Evidence on mortality experience by cohort is presented in Table Ab656–703.

Two points stand out. One is the huge gulf between life expectancy at birth and life expectancy at age five years in the nineteenth and early twentieth centuries, and the much more rapid improvements in life expectancy at birth relative to improvements at other ages over time. In the nineteenth century, the United States had exceptionally high child mortality levels – approximately one in five children died before reaching the age of five years. Samuel Preston and Michael Haines (1991) show that children of the well-to-do together with those of the poor suffered this plight. Improvements resulted from advances in the medical understanding of infectious disease and from better public health efforts such as sewage systems and water filtration plants to control disease spread. The second point is that year-to-year fluctuations in mortality are much greater for earlier cohorts. Before the development of detailed knowledge about communicable diseases and the ability to control their spread, there were periodic epidemics that killed large numbers of people (see Chapter Ab, on vital statistics). People did not know, from year to year, what risks they might face. Historians have argued that this uncertainty led to a mindset characterized by fear and fatalism. The control of disease nourished confidence and optimism. The transition was accomplished in less than fifty years – and was experienced within the lifetime of cohorts born around the turn of the twentieth century.

Military Service

Because the United States maintains a relatively small peacetime army and goes to war only infrequently, it has had relatively few veterans in the population relative to the experience of many other countries. Nonetheless the major wars, especially World War II, involved a large share of draft-age males. These circumstances mean that military experience and veterans' status differ dramatically from one cohort to another. One measure of these differences can be obtained from series Aa228–229 and Ed234–235, which can be used to calculate veterans 30–39 years of age as a share of all males of that age group according to their year of birth. This measure records only those who survived their military combat and for this reason understates the impact of wartime experience on affected generations (for combat deaths see Table Ed82–119). Nonetheless, the cohort-to-cohort differences are stark. About half of the men born around 1840 experienced military service (in the Civil War); among the cohorts born between about 1850 and 1880, very few did. The experience of their younger brothers and sons was quite different. Survivors of the U.S. involvement in World War I from the cohorts born in the 1890s represented about one third of this population. Cohorts born in the early twentieth century were most involved. Virtually all men born in the years immediately following the conclusion of World War I had some military experience. Although there was a decline from this high peak, a full generation later, among the cohorts born in the early years of the baby boom, fully half of all men served in the military. Then it ended. Among the cohorts born between 1960 and 1980, military experience was the exception. Fewer than 10 percent of men had been involved by the time they reached their thirties.

The Post–World War II Baby Boom

The term "baby boom" refers to the temporary reversal in the long-term decline of the crude birth rate following the conclusion of World War II. The baby boom is clearly visible in series Ab40, which displays data for the crude birth rate for two centuries beginning from 1800. The crude birth rate dropped well below the long-term trend during the difficult years of the Great Depression and then rose during the 1950s to levels that had not been experienced since the early 1920s. It is the combination of an unusually small number of births during the 1930s, an unusually large number in the 1950s, followed by a small number again in the 1970s that gives the baby boom its name.

The large baby boom cohort is easy to spot in Table Aa185–286, which displays population by age at each of the decennial censuses beginning in 1850. The substantial long-term decline in fertility (and mortality) reduced the relative importance of successive cohorts at young ages (0–9 years) from almost 30 percent of the total in 1850 to only 16 percent by 1940. As a result of the baby boom, the size of this young age group rose to almost 22 percent by 1960. The continuing numerical importance of the baby boom cohort through the twentieth century is evident in the disproportionate size of the 10- to 19-year-old age group in 1970, the 20- to 29-year-old age group in 1980, and the 30- to 39-year-old age group in 1990. Population projections indicate that the baby boom generation will be a distinct feature of the U.S. population structure through the first half of the twenty-first century.

The direct and indirect consequences of the unusually large baby boom generation were first and most famously analyzed by Richard Easterlin (1962, 1968, 1980). Many are readily apparent in data series that appear throughout *Historical Statistics of the United States*. For example, the statistics on elementary and secondary school enrollments show pronounced expansions and then contractions as the baby boom generation moved through these institutions (Table Bc7–18). Even college and university enrollments reveal the impact of the baby boom cohort, although the effect is muted because of the rapid rise in college enrollment rates among the generations that preceded and followed the baby boomers (Table Bc523–536).

Employment measures also reflect the labor force entry of the baby boom generation and its maturation over time (Tables Ba470–506). Young male and female workers were especially numerous in the late 1960s and the 1970s. In the 1980s and 1990s, middle-age workers predominated in the labor force. In the early decades of the twenty-first century it will be older workers, both at retirement age and beyond, who will form the largest share. It is especially remarkable that the sheer size of the baby boom cohort predominates even in the case of female workers. As noted earlier, successive cohorts of women have exhibited higher labor force participation rates at each and every age. Others things being equal, such a trend in participation would have meant that successively younger cohorts would outnumber their older sisters. This is not what happened.

Easterlin analyzed the negative consequences of its large size for the baby boom generation itself. To the extent to which young and older workers are poor labor market substitutes, membership in a large cohort will mean more intense labor market competition, lower wages, and higher unemployment than would otherwise be the case. From the point of view of the economy, however, having a large fraction of the total population in the working age groups is a good thing because these are the people who support the young and the old. Development economists measure the importance of the population in the working age groups relative to the total population with the "dependency ratio." The dependency ratio is calculated by dividing the sum of people 0–14 years of age and those 65 years of age and older by the number of people 15–64 years of age. The dependency ratio for the United States can be calculated from the population-by-age data from the federal Censuses of 1850 through 1990 (Table Aa185–286) and from the annual population-by-age data for the period 1900 through 1998 (Table Aa125–144). Such calculations reveal a dependency ratio that drops from 0.79 in 1850 to 0.48 by 1940, rises to a local maximum of 0.68 in 1961, after which it falls, reaching a nadir of 0.50 in 1986. Thus, the increase in per capita income between the early 1960s and the late 1980s was in part due to reductions in the dependency ratio. With the aging of the baby boom generation, the dependency ratio will rise again. Improvements in worker productivity will be required to forestall reductions in per capita income.

Conclusion

Although there is a small number of explicit cohort tables in *Historical Statistics of the United States*, the imaginative and industrious user can apply the approach described in this essay to many of the more standard data series and identify cohort differences across a broad spectrum of American life. The examples presented here were chosen in part because they illustrate a variety of techniques of analysis. They are also great stories. There are other great stories in the data, including some that still await their storyteller.

References

Bagby, Meredith. 1998. *Rational Exuberance: The Influence of Generation X on the New American Economy.* Dutton.

Brokaw, Tom. 1998. *The Greatest Generation.* Random House.

Carter, Susan B., and Richard Sutch. 1996. "Myth of the Industrial Scrap Heap: A Revisionist View of Turn-of-the-Century American Retirement." *Journal of Economic History* 56 (1): 5–37.

Collins, William J. 1997. "When the Tide Turned: Immigration and the Delay of the Great Black Migration." *Journal of Economic History* 57 (3): 607–32.

Easterlin, Richard A. 1962. "The American Baby Boom in Historical Perspective." Occasional Paper 79, National Bureau of Economic Research.

Easterlin, Richard A. 1968. *Population, Labor Force, and Long Swings in American Economic Growth.* National Bureau of Economic Research.

Easterlin, Richard A. 1980. *Birth and Fortune: The Impact of Numbers on Personal Welfare.* Basic Books.

Eldridge, Hope T., and Dorothy Swaine Thomas. 1964. *Population Redistribution and Economic Growth, United States, 1870–1950,* volume 3, *Demographic Analyses and Interrelations.* American Philosophical Society.

Goldin, Claudia. 1990. *Understanding the Gender Gap: An Economic History of American Women.* Oxford University Press.

Howe, Neil, and William Strauss. 2000. *Millennials Rising: The Next Great Generation.* Vintage Books.

Margo, Robert A. 1990. *Race and Schooling in the South, 1880–1950: An Economic History.* University of Chicago Press.

Preston, Samuel H., and Michael R. Haines. 1991. *Fatal Years: Child Mortality in Late Nineteenth-Century America.* Princeton University Press.

Putnam, Robert D. 2000. *Bowling Alone: The Collapse and Revival of American Community.* Simon & Schuster.

Ransom, Roger L., and Richard Sutch. 1977. *One Kind of Freedom: The Economic Consequences of Emancipation.* Cambridge University Press.

Ryder, Norman B. 1968. "Cohort Analysis." In David Sills, editor. *The International Encyclopedia of the Social Sciences,* volume 2. Macmillan.

Schelling, Thomas C. 1978. *Micromotives and Macrobehavior.* Norton.

Shryock, Harry S., Jacob S. Siegel, and Associates. 1976. *The Methods and Materials of Demography.* Condensed edition by Edward G. Stockwell. Academic Press.

Strauss, William, and Neil Howe. 1990. *Generations: The History of America's Future, 1584 to 2069.* Morrow.

Strauss, William, and Neil Howe. 1993. *Thirteenth Gen: Abort, Retry, Fail, Ignore?* Vintage Books.

Strauss, William, and Neil Howe. 1997. *The Fourth Turning: An American Prophecy.* Broadway Books.

Sutch, Richard. 1975. "The Breeding of Slaves for Sale and the Westward Expansion of Slavery, 1850–1860." In Stanley L. Engerman and Eugene D. Genovese, editors. *Race and Slavery in the Western Hemisphere: Quantitative Studies.* Princeton University Press.

Whelpton, P. K. 1954. *Cohort Fertility: Native White Women in the United States.* Princeton University Press.

LABOR FORCE

Matthew Sobek

TABLE Af1–14   Labor force participation rate, by cohort, age, and sex: 1801–1980

Contributed by Matthew Sobek

	Male							Female						
	16–19	20–29	30–39	40–49	50–59	60–69	70 and older	16–19	20–29	30–39	40–49	50–59	60–69	70 and older
	Af1	Af2	Af3	Af4	Af5	Af6	Af7	Af8	Af9	Af10	Af11	Af12	Af13	Af14
Birth year	Percent	Percent	Percent	Percent	Percent	Percent	Percent	Percent	Percent	Percent	Percent	Percent	Percent	Percent
1801–1810	—	—	—	—	—	—	71.1	—	—	—	—	—	—	6.0
1811–1820	—	—	—	—	—	90.5	34.9	—	—	—	—	—	8.9	10.7
1821–1830	—	—	—	—	96.5	—	54.3	—	—	—	—	10.8	—	8.8
1831–1840	—	—	—	97.4	—	86.3	47.1	—	—	—	11.8	—	14.2	7.1
1841–1850	—	—	97.4	—	94.5	81.5	52.2	—	—	13.2	—	18.1	13.7	6.8
1851–1860	—	93.5	—	97.0	95.2	84.5	12.8	—	21.6	—	16.3	18.2	12.5	2.1
1861–1870	76.1	—	97.4	97.6	94.3	—	28.3	29.0	—	17.9	21.1	17.6	—	3.8
1871–1880	—	93.3	98.1	97.3	—	71.2	27.3	—	27.9	22.7	19.4	—	12.6	4.9
1881–1890	74.5	96.0	97.7	—	90.3	70.8	20.3	32.5	33.5	21.3	—	19.6	17.2	6.1
1891–1900	76.4	93.5	—	94.0	89.3	62.5	14.8	38.7	32.4	—	24.4	28.7	23.3	5.3
1901–1910	66.3	—	96.0	94.5	90.0	58.1	12.8	36.8	—	29.4	35.9	43.0	27.2	4.7
1911–1920	—	92.2	95.1	94.9	89.2	46.2	14.1	—	40.7	32.4	46.4	50.0	24.9	6.6
1921–1930	48.9	87.0	95.8	94.0	84.6	42.1	—	27.7	37.6	37.9	52.4	52.3	26.3	—
1931–1940	50.8	90.0	95.1	92.9	83.7	—	—	30.5	39.8	46.1	63.1	61.5	—	—
1941–1950	50.2	86.3	94.3	91.8	—	—	—	32.6	51.2	63.6	76.2	—	—	—
1951–1960	47.0	87.2	92.2	—	—	—	—	34.7	67.0	74.6	—	—	—	—
1961–1970	52.7	85.9	—	—	—	—	—	45.7	73.5	—	—	—	—	—
1971–1980	51.8	—	—	—	—	—	—	49.3	—	—	—	—	—	—

Source

Tabulated from the Integrated Public Use Microdata Series (IPUMS); see the Guide to the Millennial Edition.

Documentation

Prior to 1940, labor force participation means gainful employment (that is, whether a person claimed an occupation). The requirements for claiming an occupation were never entirely systematized and they varied over time; consequently, the pre-1940 figures are less consistent than more recent statistics. Starting in 1940, labor force participation was formalized to mean working or seeking work in the week prior to the census. The switch from the gainful employment to the labor force definition has significant implications for new, seasonal, part-time, and female workers.

For a discussion of the implications of the gainful worker definition on the measured labor force participation of older men, see Roger L. Ransom and Richard Sutch, "The Labor of Older Americans: Retirement of Men On and Off the Job, 1870–1937," *Journal of Economic History* 46 (1986): 379–90.

The unique wording of the occupation question in 1910 yielded high labor force participation rates for women in that census. The census year from which a particular statistic was derived can be determined using the combination of birth year and age.

TABLE Af15–42 Labor force participation rate, by cohort, age, sex, and race: 1801–1980

Contributed by Matthew Sobek

Male

Birth year	White 16–19 Af15 Percent	20–29 Af16 Percent	30–39 Af17 Percent	40–49 Af18 Percent	50–59 Af19 Percent	60–69 Af20 Percent	70 and older Af21 Percent	Nonwhite 16–19 Af22 Percent	20–29 Af23 Percent	30–39 Af24 Percent	40–49 Af25 Percent	50–59 Af26 Percent	60–69 Af27 Percent	70 and older Af28 Percent
1801–1810	—	—	—	—	—	—	69.7	—	—	—	—	—	—	83.0
1811–1820	—	—	—	—	—	89.8	31.0	—	—	—	—	—	96.8	56.2
1821–1830	—	—	—	—	96.3	—	52.1	—	—	—	—	97.8	—	77.3
1831–1840	—	—	—	97.4	—	85.8	44.7	—	—	—	97.2	—	91.5	76.2
1841–1850	—	—	97.5	—	94.2	80.3	50.8	—	—	96.8	—	97.3	93.9	69.4
1851–1860	—	93.1	—	97.2	94.9	83.7	12.4	—	95.8	—	95.2	98.1	93.6	18.5
1861–1870	74.2	—	97.5	97.6	94.0	—	27.9	88.8	—	95.8	98.2	97.4	—	32.9
1871–1880	—	93.4	98.1	97.2	—	71.0	27.2	—	92.8	98.3	97.7	—	73.1	29.1
1881–1890	72.8	95.9	97.8	—	90.3	71.1	20.4	85.4	97.0	97.1	—	90.0	67.3	19.4
1891–1900	75.2	93.4	—	94.2	89.6	63.0	15.0	85.8	94.2	—	91.3	86.1	56.1	13.0
1901–1910	65.2	—	96.3	95.0	90.7	58.8	12.9	74.5	—	93.2	90.6	83.8	51.5	11.7
1911–1920	—	92.4	95.6	95.5	90.0	46.6	14.2	—	90.9	90.3	89.3	81.5	43.0	12.8
1921–1930	47.7	87.4	96.5	94.8	85.7	42.5	—	59.7	83.4	89.5	87.4	75.2	38.5	—
1931–1940	49.8	90.8	95.9	93.9	84.7	—	—	57.3	84.5	89.1	86.2	76.8	—	—
1941–1950	51.2	87.1	95.4	93.0	—	—	—	42.2	79.8	87.0	83.9	—	—	—
1951–1960	48.9	88.8	93.9	—	—	—	—	34.9	77.8	82.8	—	—	—	—
1961–1970	55.7	87.9	—	—	—	—	—	37.7	75.3	—	—	—	—	—
1971–1980	54.9	—	—	—	—	—	—	39.0	—	—	—	—	—	—

Female

Birth year	White 16–19 Af29 Percent	20–29 Af30 Percent	30–39 Af31 Percent	40–49 Af32 Percent	50–59 Af33 Percent	60–69 Af34 Percent	70 and older Af35 Percent	Nonwhite 16–19 Af36 Percent	20–29 Af37 Percent	30–39 Af38 Percent	40–49 Af39 Percent	50–59 Af40 Percent	60–69 Af41 Percent	70 and older Af42 Percent
1801–1810	—	—	—	—	—	—	3.9	—	—	—	—	—	—	21.9
1811–1820	—	—	—	—	—	6.1	9.1	—	—	—	—	—	32.8	20.8
1821–1830	—	—	—	—	7.6	—	7.1	—	—	—	—	38.9	—	25.2
1831–1840	—	—	—	8.4	—	12.7	5.4	—	—	—	38.3	—	31.9	26.8
1841–1850	—	—	9.5	—	15.0	10.7	5.7	—	—	39.5	—	47.9	50.1	21.4
1851–1860	—	18.0	—	13.4	14.5	10.7	1.9	—	44.1	—	42.1	58.2	39.0	4.8
1861–1870	25.3	—	15.0	17.3	15.3	—	3.6	53.4	—	43.1	58.1	44.5	—	7.6
1871–1880	—	25.7	18.4	16.7	—	11.7	4.8	—	43.5	57.7	45.8	—	24.1	6.7
1881–1890	29.7	29.7	18.6	—	18.4	16.8	6.0	49.2	60.2	45.5	—	35.3	22.4	7.6
1891–1900	35.7	30.9	—	22.6	27.9	22.9	5.1	59.6	43.4	—	42.9	38.3	27.5	7.1
1901–1910	36.5	—	27.5	34.7	42.5	26.9	4.6	38.9	—	45.9	46.6	48.4	29.7	6.0
1911–1920	—	40.1	30.6	45.2	49.6	24.7	6.5	—	45.2	46.9	57.1	53.2	27.2	7.5
1921–1930	27.3	37.1	36.0	51.5	52.0	26.2	—	30.4	40.8	52.2	59.1	54.9	27.8	—
1931–1940	31.7	39.0	44.4	62.6	61.5	—	—	22.5	45.6	57.4	66.7	61.5	—	—
1941–1950	33.8	50.5	62.4	76.3	—	—	—	23.6	56.2	70.7	76.0	—	—	—
1951–1960	36.3	67.6	74.5	—	—	—	—	24.7	64.4	75.2	—	—	—	—
1961–1970	48.6	74.7	—	—	—	—	—	31.4	68.3	—	—	—	—	—
1971–1980	51.9	—	—	—	—	—	—	38.4	—	—	—	—	—	—

Source

Tabulated from the Integrated Public Use Microdata Series (IPUMS); see the Guide to the Millennial Edition.

Documentation

See the text for Table Af1–14.

TABLE Af43–63 Labor force participation rate, by cohort, age, nativity, and race – males: 1801–1980

Contributed by Matthew Sobek

	Native-born										
	All							White			
Birth year	16–19	20–29	30–39	40–49	50–59	60–69	70 and older	16–19	20–29	30–39	40–49
	Af43	Af44	Af45	Af46	Af47	Af48	Af49	Af50	Af51	Af52	Af53
	Percent	Percent	Percent	Percent	Percent	Percent	Percent	Percent	Percent	Percent	Percent
1801–1810	—	—	—	—	—	—	73.3	—	—	—	—
1811–1820	—	—	—	—	—	91.3	38.2	—	—	—	—
1821–1830	—	—	—	—	96.4	—	59.0	—	—	—	—
1831–1840	—	—	—	97.2	—	87.1	50.4	—	—	—	97.2
1841–1850	—	—	97.1	—	94.8	82.8	55.4	—	—	97.2	—
1851–1860	—	92.9	—	96.9	95.4	85.6	13.9	—	92.5	—	97.2
1861–1870	75.4	—	96.9	97.6	94.5	—	30.0	73.4	—	97.1	97.5
1871–1880	—	92.9	97.9	97.3	—	72.0	28.5	—	93.0	97.8	97.2
1881–1890	73.4	95.3	97.6	—	90.4	71.3	21.2	71.4	95.1	97.7	—
1891–1900	75.0	93.1	—	93.9	89.3	62.6	15.0	73.4	92.9	—	94.2
1901–1910	65.5	—	96.0	94.6	89.9	58.0	12.9	64.3	—	96.3	95.0
1911–1920	—	92.3	95.2	94.8	89.0	45.9	14.0	—	92.4	95.7	95.4
1921–1930	48.9	87.1	95.8	94.0	84.4	41.3	—	47.6	87.5	96.6	94.8
1931–1940	50.8	90.1	95.2	92.9	83.3	—	—	49.8	90.8	96.0	93.9
1941–1950	50.1	86.4	94.5	91.8	—	—	—	51.2	87.2	95.6	93.1
1951–1960	47.1	87.7	92.4	—	—	—	—	48.9	89.1	94.1	—
1961–1970	53.0	86.1	—	—	—	—	—	55.9	88.0	—	—
1971–1980	52.1	—	—	—	—	—	—	54.8	—	—	—

	Native-born			Foreign-born						
	White									
Birth year	50–59	60–69	70 and older	16–19	20–29	30–39	40–49	50–59	60–69	70 and older
	Af54	Af55	Af56	Af57	Af58	Af59	Af60	Af61	Af62	Af63
	Percent	Percent	Percent	Percent	Percent	Percent	Percent	Percent	Percent	Percent
1801–1810	—	—	71.7	—	—	—	—	—	—	64.1
1811–1820	—	90.3	34.0	—	—	—	—	—	88.6	26.2
1821–1830	96.2	—	56.3	—	—	—	—	96.6	—	45.2
1831–1840	—	86.5	47.3	—	—	—	97.9	—	84.7	39.9
1841–1850	94.4	81.3	53.7	—	—	98.0	—	93.7	78.4	44.4
1851–1860	95.0	84.7	13.4	—	96.4	—	97.1	94.6	81.4	9.9
1861–1870	94.1	—	29.8	83.0	—	98.6	97.8	93.7	—	23.1
1871–1880	—	71.8	28.4	—	95.6	98.7	97.1	—	68.7	23.6
1881–1890	90.5	71.8	21.4	86.2	98.3	97.8	—	89.8	69.2	17.3
1891–1900	89.6	63.4	15.3	90.9	96.1	—	94.3	89.5	61.8	14.0
1901–1910	90.6	58.8	13.1	78.4	—	96.3	94.2	91.0	58.7	12.0
1911–1920	89.9	46.3	14.1	—	91.0	92.4	95.7	91.1	50.1	15.4
1921–1930	85.6	42.0	—	50.6	84.1	96.1	94.4	87.5	50.6	—
1931–1940	84.5	—	—	50.4	88.9	94.3	93.1	87.0	—	—
1941–1950	—	—	—	52.8	83.4	91.9	91.5	—	—	—
1951–1960	—	—	—	46.2	81.3	90.5	—	—	—	—
1961–1970	—	—	—	48.4	83.9	—	—	—	—	—
1971–1980	—	—	—	48.5	—	—	—	—	—	—

Source

Tabulated from the Integrated Public Use Microdata Series (IPUMS); see the Guide to the Millennial Edition.

Documentation

See the text for Table Af1–14.

Persons born in outlying areas and territories of the United States are classified as foreign-born.

TABLE Af64–84 Labor force participation rate, by cohort, age, nativity, and race – females: 1801–1980

Contributed by Matthew Sobek

	Native-born										
	All							White			
Birth year	16–19	20–29	30–39	40–49	50–59	60–69	70 and older	16–19	20–29	30–39	40–49
	Af64	Af65	Af66	Af67	Af68	Af69	Af70	Af71	Af72	Af73	Af74
	Percent	Percent	Percent	Percent	Percent	Percent	Percent	Percent	Percent	Percent	Percent
1801–1810	—	—	—	—	—	—	6.2	—	—	—	—
1811–1820	—	—	—	—	—	9.2	12.1	—	—	—	—
1821–1830	—	—	—	—	11.4	—	9.0	—	—	—	—
1831–1840	—	—	—	12.0	—	16.0	7.7	—	—	—	7.1
1841–1850	—	—	13.0	—	19.5	15.4	7.4	—	—	8.0	—
1851–1860	—	20.2	—	16.8	19.6	13.4	2.3	—	15.8	—	13.2
1861–1870	27.0	—	18.2	22.3	18.2	—	4.1	22.6	—	14.5	17.4
1871–1880	—	26.7	23.5	20.2	—	13.3	5.0	—	23.8	18.2	16.9
1881–1890	30.2	33.3	22.1	—	20.6	17.8	6.4	26.7	28.7	18.7	—
1891–1900	36.3	32.7	—	24.8	29.3	24.0	5.5	32.7	31.1	—	22.8
1901–1910	35.5	—	29.6	36.1	43.3	27.6	4.8	34.9	—	27.5	34.8
1911–1920	—	40.5	32.3	46.4	50.0	25.0	6.6	—	39.9	30.5	45.1
1921–1930	27.4	37.6	37.8	52.4	52.3	26.3	—	27.1	37.2	35.8	51.5
1931–1940	30.4	39.7	46.4	63.4	61.9	—	—	31.6	38.9	44.6	63.0
1941–1950	32.4	51.5	64.1	77.0	—	—	—	33.7	50.8	63.0	77.2
1951–1960	34.7	67.7	75.7	—	—	—	—	36.3	68.1	75.5	—
1961–1970	46.0	74.7	—	—	—	—	—	48.9	75.8	—	—
1971–1980	50.1	—	—	—	—	—	—	52.6	—	—	—

	Native-born			Foreign-born						
	White									
Birth year	50–59	60–69	70 and older	16–19	20–29	30–39	40–49	50–59	60–69	70 and older
	Af75	Af76	Af77	Af78	Af79	Af80	Af81	Af82	Af83	Af84
	Percent	Percent	Percent	Percent	Percent	Percent	Percent	Percent	Percent	Percent
1801–1810	—	—	3.5	—	—	—	—	—	—	5.2
1811–1820	—	5.3	10.0	—	—	—	—	—	7.9	7.1
1821–1830	6.7	—	6.4	—	—	—	—	9.4	—	8.2
1831–1840	—	14.0	5.4	—	—	—	11.4	—	10.2	5.6
1841–1850	15.2	11.2	5.9	—	—	13.9	—	14.8	9.5	5.4
1851–1860	14.8	10.9	2.1	—	31.1	—	14.4	13.7	9.9	1.6
1861–1870	15.4	—	3.8	51.7	—	16.7	17.1	15.3	—	2.9
1871–1880	—	12.2	4.9	—	35.2	19.7	16.1	—	10.0	4.5
1881–1890	19.1	17.3	6.3	57.8	34.6	18.2	—	16.0	14.8	4.8
1891–1900	28.4	23.7	5.3	67.2	29.9	—	22.3	26.0	19.4	4.3
1901–1910	42.7	27.4	4.6	57.9	—	27.8	33.6	41.1	24.1	4.2
1911–1920	49.6	24.8	6.5	—	44.0	33.6	46.2	49.4	23.8	6.4
1921–1930	52.1	26.2	—	37.3	36.2	38.5	51.9	52.4	27.3	—
1931–1940	62.0	—	—	36.5	41.2	43.0	60.8	58.4	—	—
1941–1950	—	—	—	39.3	46.4	58.9	69.9	—	—	—
1951–1960	—	—	—	34.9	58.8	66.2	—	—	—	—
1961–1970	—	—	—	39.3	63.7	—	—	—	—	—
1971–1980	—	—	—	40.1	—	—	—	—	—	—

Source

Tabulated from the Integrated Public Use Microdata Series (IPUMS); see the Guide to the Millennial Edition.

Documentation

See the text for Table Af1–14.

Persons born in outlying areas and territories of the United States are classified as foreign-born.

TABLE Af85–126   Labor force participation rate, by cohort, age, marital status, and race – females: 1801–1980

Contributed by Matthew Sobek

	All races										
	Unmarried							Married			
Birth year	16–19	20–29	30–39	40–49	50–59	60–69	70 and older	16–19	20–29	30–39	40–49
	Af85	Af86	Af87	Af88	Af89	Af90	Af91	Af92	Af93	Af94	Af95
	Percent	Percent	Percent	Percent	Percent	Percent	Percent	Percent	Percent	Percent	Percent
1801–1810	—	—	—	—	—	—	7.2	—	—	—	—
1811–1820	—	—	—	—	—	15.8	10.9	—	—	—	—
1821–1830	—	—	—	—	24.5	—	9.9	—	—	—	—
1831–1840	—	—	—	34.6	—	24.8	8.1	—	—	—	5.0
1841–1850	—	—	43.1	—	42.5	21.8	8.6	—	—	5.8	—
1851–1860	—	43.7	—	53.1	39.6	21.6	2.1	—	6.9	—	5.8
1861–1870	32.1	—	61.6	57.8	41.0	—	4.2	9.7	—	6.0	10.5
1871–1880	—	56.9	67.8	57.5	—	20.5	5.6	—	5.7	11.0	8.9
1881–1890	36.5	64.9	69.7	—	43.0	26.7	6.7	8.1	12.4	9.8	—
1891–1900	42.7	69.0	—	62.5	53.2	33.2	5.7	14.9	10.8	—	14.9
1901–1910	41.3	—	74.3	69.6	64.6	35.5	4.8	12.8	—	18.9	26.8
1911–1920	—	75.2	73.2	73.8	67.1	30.5	7.4	—	20.2	24.2	40.2
1921–1930	30.1	73.6	73.8	72.2	65.1	31.3	—	13.2	24.2	31.9	47.7
1931–1940	33.1	72.4	70.7	75.1	69.3	—	—	20.8	29.1	41.0	59.6
1941–1950	33.8	70.6	79.3	81.9	—	—	—	27.2	41.9	58.3	73.8
1951–1960	34.6	75.7	81.8	—	—	—	—	35.5	59.5	71.2	—
1961–1970	45.7	76.8	—	—	—	—	—	45.6	69.4	—	—
1971–1980	49.4	—	—	—	—	—	—	47.1	—	—	—

	All races			White						
	Married			Unmarried						
Birth year	50–59	60–69	70 and older	16–19	20–29	30–39	40–49	50–59	60–69	70 and older
	Af96	Af97	Af98	Af99	Af100	Af101	Af102	Af103	Af104	Af105
	Percent	Percent	Percent	Percent	Percent	Percent	Percent	Percent	Percent	Percent
1801–1810	—	—	3.1	—	—	—	—	—	—	5.0
1811–1820	—	2.7	9.1	—	—	—	—	—	11.7	9.3
1821–1830	4.3	—	5.1	—	—	—	—	19.7	—	8.2
1831–1840	—	4.1	3.8	—	—	—	29.0	—	22.8	6.4
1841–1850	5.5	6.2	2.4	—	—	38.3	—	38.4	18.3	7.5
1851–1860	8.7	4.4	2.2	—	40.3	—	48.7	35.4	19.0	2.0
1861–1870	6.9	—	2.6	28.5	—	58.5	53.8	38.1	—	4.0
1871–1880	—	5.6	2.9	—	54.8	64.6	54.7	—	19.6	5.5
1881–1890	10.1	8.7	4.2	33.7	63.0	67.8	—	42.1	26.8	6.6
1891–1900	18.3	15.2	4.1	40.1	68.8	—	61.9	53.4	33.5	5.5
1901–1910	34.5	20.7	4.4	41.0	—	74.6	70.7	66.0	36.1	4.7
1911–1920	43.6	21.1	5.3	—	76.0	75.0	75.1	69.0	31.0	7.4
1921–1930	47.7	23.1	—	29.8	76.3	75.7	74.4	67.3	32.0	—
1931–1940	58.1	—	—	34.2	75.5	74.1	78.1	71.9	—	—
1941–1950	—	—	—	35.2	73.0	82.0	83.9	—	—	—
1951–1960	—	—	—	36.4	78.9	84.4	—	—	—	—
1961–1970	—	—	—	48.8	79.5	—	—	—	—	—
1971–1980	—	—	—	52.2	—	—	—	—	—	—

(continued)

TABLE Af85–126 Labor force participation rate, by cohort, age, marital status, and race – females: 1801–1980
Continued

	White							Nonwhite				
	Married							Unmarried				
	16–19	20–29	30–39	40–49	50–59	60–69	70 and older	16–19	20–29	30–39	40–49	50–59
	Af106	Af107	Af108	Af109	Af110	Af111	Af112	Af113	Af114	Af115	Af116	Af117
Birth year	Percent	Percent	Percent	Percent	Percent	Percent	Percent	Percent	Percent	Percent	Percent	Percent
1801–1810	—	—	—	—	—	—	1.5	—	—	—	—	—
1811–1820	—	—	—	—	—	1.3	7.2	—	—	—	—	—
1821–1830	—	—	—	—	2.0	—	3.4	—	—	—	—	56.1
1831–1840	—	—	—	2.4	—	3.3	2.4	—	—	—	68.0	—
1841–1850	—	—	2.7	—	3.6	3.7	1.5	—	—	69.5	—	68.2
1851–1860	—	2.7	—	4.0	5.6	3.3	1.7	—	69.2	—	79.6	73.6
1861–1870	3.5	—	3.7	7.2	5.3	—	2.3	58.8	—	81.0	84.5	68.2
1871–1880	—	2.5	6.7	6.6	—	4.9	2.7	—	75.1	89.4	77.1	—
1881–1890	3.9	6.5	7.1	—	9.1	8.3	4.1	54.5	81.1	83.6	—	50.9
1891–1900	7.1	7.7	—	13.2	17.6	14.7	3.9	63.0	71.1	—	66.2	51.2
1901–1910	9.5	—	16.8	25.9	33.9	20.2	4.2	43.7	—	72.6	64.3	56.6
1911–1920	—	18.2	22.7	39.2	43.1	20.6	5.1	—	68.0	65.7	68.4	57.8
1921–1930	10.9	23.5	30.5	46.9	47.1	22.7	—	32.2	58.9	67.9	64.4	56.2
1931–1940	21.6	28.2	39.4	58.8	57.6	—	—	24.6	60.1	62.0	67.1	60.7
1941–1950	27.6	40.8	56.8	73.5	—	—	—	23.5	60.2	71.3	75.5	—
1951–1960	36.0	58.8	70.6	—	—	—	—	23.8	63.9	74.8	—	—
1961–1970	46.4	69.4	—	—	—	—	—	31.0	67.8	—	—	—
1971–1980	47.3	—	—	—	—	—	—	38.2	—	—	—	—

	Nonwhite								
	Unmarried		Married						
	60–69	70 and older	16–19	20–29	30–39	40–49	50–59	60–69	70 and older
	Af118	Af119	Af120	Af121	Af122	Af123	Af124	Af125	Af126
Birth year	Percent	Percent	Percent	Percent	Percent	Percent	Percent	Percent	Percent
1801–1810	—	22.1	—	—	—	—	—	—	20.9
1811–1820	42.0	21.0	—	—	—	—	—	19.0	19.2
1821–1830	—	27.9	—	—	—	—	26.9	—	18.1
1831–1840	45.9	28.2	—	—	—	26.4	—	15.3	21.9
1841–1850	58.2	22.1	—	—	29.4	—	28.7	40.3	18.8
1851–1860	51.1	4.2	—	31.0	—	24.7	48.0	22.9	10.4
1861–1870	—	7.5	34.1	—	27.8	46.4	28.7	—	8.2
1871–1880	29.2	6.8	—	25.2	47.6	33.4	—	17.3	6.1
1881–1890	26.1	8.0	26.4	49.3	34.5	—	25.3	16.3	5.7
1891–1900	31.0	7.0	47.7	31.4	—	33.5	27.8	22.8	7.3
1901–1910	31.7	5.9	25.5	—	37.6	37.2	42.1	26.9	6.4
1911–1920	27.5	7.5	—	34.5	38.9	51.3	49.6	26.7	7.4
1921–1930	28.1	—	24.2	30.4	45.1	56.1	53.9	27.3	—
1931–1940	—	—	15.5	36.3	54.9	66.4	62.3	—	—
1941–1950	—	—	23.8	52.4	70.1	76.6	—	—	—
1951–1960	—	—	31.9	65.2	75.6	—	—	—	—
1961–1970	—	—	39.0	69.6	—	—	—	—	—
1971–1980	—	—	45.3	—	—	—	—	—	—

Source

Tabulated from the Integrated Public Use Microdata Series (IPUMS); see the Guide to the Millennial Edition.

Documentation

See the text for Table Af1–14.

MARITAL STATUS

Matthew Sobek

TABLE Af127–147 Percentage married, by cohort, age, and sex: 1801–1980

Contributed by Matthew Sobek

	Both sexes							Male			
	16–19	20–29	30–39	40–49	50–59	60–69	70 and older	16–19	20–29	30–39	40–49
	Af127	Af128	Af129	Af130	Af131	Af132	Af133	Af134	Af135	Af136	Af137
Birth year	Percent	Percent	Percent	Percent	Percent	Percent	Percent	Percent	Percent	Percent	Percent
1801–1810	—	—	—	—	—	—	49.5	—	—	—	—
1811–1820	—	—	—	—	—	67.5	26.2	—	—	—	—
1821–1830	—	—	—	—	77.2	—	41.2	—	—	—	—
1831–1840	—	—	—	81.1	—	63.2	41.1	—	—	—	85.1
1841–1850	—	—	78.9	—	74.0	64.0	44.5	—	—	77.6	—
1851–1860	—	49.0	—	79.7	75.2	64.2	25.5	—	38.3	—	81.3
1861–1870	7.8	—	75.6	79.0	74.7	—	39.5	1.3	—	72.9	80.3
1871–1880	—	46.2	76.3	79.9	—	64.0	40.3	—	35.7	73.6	81.2
1881–1890	7.8	48.9	78.3	—	76.3	64.1	41.3	1.2	38.7	76.0	—
1891–1900	7.8	53.3	—	81.8	76.1	66.7	41.2	1.3	43.3	—	83.6
1901–1910	9.3	—	80.3	81.9	77.8	67.6	45.3	2.6	—	79.6	85.0
1911–1920	—	54.1	83.8	84.2	78.9	69.5	55.0	—	45.0	84.3	86.8
1921–1930	8.2	65.2	85.5	83.5	78.1	69.6	—	2.2	57.0	85.3	86.1
1931–1940	12.3	68.0	83.9	79.9	74.7	—	—	3.9	60.4	85.1	82.7
1941–1950	11.6	62.5	75.6	73.0	—	—	—	4.5	57.3	76.4	75.7
1951–1960	9.0	48.2	67.2	—	—	—	—	4.5	43.1	66.3	—
1961–1970	6.3	38.9	—	—	—	—	—	3.1	33.5	—	—
1971–1980	3.8	—	—	—	—	—	—	2.1	—	—	—

	Male			Female						
	50–59	60–69	70 and older	16–19	20–29	30–39	40–49	50–59	60–69	70 and older
	Af138	Af139	Af140	Af141	Af142	Af143	Af144	Af145	Af146	Af147
Birth year	Percent	Percent	Percent	Percent	Percent	Percent	Percent	Percent	Percent	Percent
1801–1810	—	—	69.6	—	—	—	—	—	—	29.3
1811–1820	—	81.2	43.8	—	—	—	—	—	52.6	11.2
1821–1830	85.8	—	58.8	—	—	—	—	67.5	—	23.8
1831–1840	—	74.7	58.7	—	—	—	77.0	—	51.3	24.4
1841–1850	81.5	75.4	61.4	—	—	80.2	—	65.8	51.7	28.2
1851–1860	80.4	74.6	42.2	—	60.1	—	77.9	69.2	52.6	11.7
1861–1870	80.0	—	56.5	14.0	—	78.6	77.6	68.7	—	24.2
1871–1880	—	74.6	58.7	—	56.6	79.3	78.3	—	53.3	25.2
1881–1890	81.2	75.3	63.2	14.4	59.8	80.7	—	71.1	53.2	25.4
1891–1900	82.1	79.5	67.4	14.3	63.0	—	79.9	70.0	55.3	25.0
1901–1910	84.3	81.0	72.1	15.7	—	81.0	78.9	71.6	56.2	29.0
1911–1920	85.3	82.6	77.0	—	62.8	83.4	81.7	73.0	58.6	39.8
1921–1930	83.6	80.6	—	14.2	73.0	85.7	81.0	73.1	60.4	—
1931–1940	80.2	—	—	20.5	75.2	82.7	77.1	69.7	—	—
1941–1950	—	—	—	18.7	67.4	74.7	70.3	—	—	—
1951–1960	—	—	—	13.5	53.3	68.0	—	—	—	—
1961–1970	—	—	—	9.5	44.3	—	—	—	—	—
1971–1980	—	—	—	5.6	—	—	—	—	—	—

Source

Tabulated from the Integrated Public Use Microdata Series (IPUMS); see the Guide to the Millennial Edition.

TABLE Af148–175   Percentage married, by cohort, age, sex, and race: 1801–1980

Contributed by Matthew Sobek

Male

Birth year	White							Nonwhite						
	16–19	20–29	30–39	40–49	50–59	60–69	70 and older	16–19	20–29	30–39	40–49	50–59	60–69	70 and older
	Af148	Af149	Af150	Af151	Af152	Af153	Af154	Af155	Af156	Af157	Af158	Af159	Af160	Af161
	Percent	Percent	Percent	Percent	Percent	Percent	Percent	Percent	Percent	Percent	Percent	Percent	Percent	Percent
1801–1810	—	—	—	—	—	—	69.3	—	—	—	—	—	—	72.2
1811–1820	—	—	—	—	—	81.0	40.8	—	—	—	—	—	83.0	60.7
1821–1830	—	—	—	—	85.8	—	58.6	—	—	—	—	85.2	—	60.8
1831–1840	—	—	—	85.2	—	75.1	58.3	—	—	—	84.6	—	70.8	63.4
1841–1850	—	—	77.5	—	81.8	75.2	61.7	—	—	78.6	—	79.6	77.9	58.5
1851–1860	—	36.6	—	81.7	80.6	74.6	41.8	—	49.6	—	77.9	78.1	74.6	47.4
1861–1870	1.1	—	72.6	80.5	80.0	—	56.6	2.3	—	75.0	78.8	80.0	—	54.8
1871–1880	—	34.6	73.6	81.3	—	74.7	58.9	—	43.2	74.0	80.2	—	72.5	55.5
1881–1890	1.1	37.3	75.8	—	81.5	76.0	63.7	2.5	48.8	77.8	—	77.9	66.7	56.8
1891–1900	1.2	42.1	—	83.9	82.7	80.5	68.5	2.2	52.4	—	80.6	75.3	68.3	56.3
1901–1910	2.3	—	79.7	85.9	85.4	82.5	73.6	5.3	—	78.2	77.0	73.3	66.9	58.0
1911–1920	—	44.0	85.2	87.9	86.6	84.3	78.5	—	54.0	76.5	76.0	72.6	67.4	62.4
1921–1930	2.0	57.5	86.6	87.5	85.4	82.3	—	4.0	52.9	74.2	74.2	68.9	66.4	—
1931–1940	3.8	61.5	86.5	84.4	82.1	—	—	4.8	52.1	73.7	70.6	67.1	—	—
1941–1950	4.6	58.5	78.2	77.5	—	—	—	4.2	48.3	64.6	64.4	—	—	—
1951–1960	4.5	45.0	68.8	—	—	—	—	4.4	31.9	52.1	—	—	—	—
1961–1970	3.3	35.7	—	—	—	—	—	2.0	22.1	—	—	—	—	—
1971–1980	2.2	—	—	—	—	—	—	1.5	—	—	—	—	—	—

Female

Birth year	White							Nonwhite						
	16–19	20–29	30–39	40–49	50–59	60–69	70 and older	16–19	20–29	30–39	40–49	50–59	60–69	70 and older
	Af162	Af163	Af164	Af165	Af166	Af167	Af168	Af169	Af170	Af171	Af172	Af173	Af174	Af175
	Percent	Percent	Percent	Percent	Percent	Percent	Percent	Percent	Percent	Percent	Percent	Percent	Percent	Percent
1801–1810	—	—	—	—	—	—	30.2	—	—	—	—	—	—	22.2
1811–1820	—	—	—	—	—	54.0	10.9	—	—	—	—	—	40.2	13.0
1821–1830	—	—	—	—	68.5	—	23.4	—	—	—	—	58.9	—	27.6
1831–1840	—	—	—	77.8	—	51.7	24.5	—	—	—	71.4	—	45.9	23.2
1841–1850	—	—	80.9	—	67.3	52.2	28.6	—	—	74.9	—	51.5	45.4	21.8
1851–1860	—	59.2	—	78.9	70.0	53.3	11.8	—	65.7	—	68.3	60.1	43.2	10.5
1861–1870	12.9	—	79.4	78.4	69.5	—	24.5	21.6	—	71.1	69.4	59.9	—	19.6
1871–1880	—	55.7	79.7	79.0	—	54.1	25.5	—	63.2	75.9	71.5	—	42.8	19.6
1881–1890	13.6	58.9	81.1	—	71.9	54.4	25.8	18.8	65.6	77.6	—	61.0	37.9	20.2
1891–1900	13.2	62.1	—	80.7	71.3	56.4	25.4	21.9	69.7	—	71.2	55.2	43.0	19.6
1901–1910	14.2	—	81.6	80.4	73.2	57.7	29.8	26.2	—	76.2	65.0	56.8	41.6	20.9
1911–1920	—	62.1	85.0	83.5	75.0	60.5	41.2	—	68.0	70.1	66.3	55.8	42.3	27.2
1921–1930	13.2	74.2	87.9	83.3	75.6	62.9	—	22.4	63.4	69.2	63.5	54.2	41.7	—
1931–1940	20.2	77.3	85.6	80.5	72.8	—	—	22.9	61.0	64.2	56.7	50.7	—	—
1941–1950	18.9	69.7	78.0	73.4	—	—	—	17.2	51.4	55.4	53.0	—	—	—
1951–1960	13.8	56.4	71.9	—	—	—	—	11.7	37.1	49.1	—	—	—	—
1961–1970	10.4	47.9	—	—	—	—	—	5.5	27.9	—	—	—	—	—
1971–1980	6.3	—	—	—	—	—	—	3.1	—	—	—	—	—	—

Source

Tabulated from the Integrated Public Use Microdata Series (IPUMS); see the Guide to the Millennial Edition.

TABLE Af176–196   Percentage divorced, by cohort, age, and sex: 1801–1980

Contributed by Matthew Sobek

	Both sexes							Male			
	16–19	20–29	30–39	40–49	50–59	60–69	70 and older	16–19	20–29	30–39	40–49
	Af176	Af177	Af178	Af179	Af180	Af181	Af182	Af183	Af184	Af185	Af186
Birth year	Percent	Percent	Percent	Percent	Percent	Percent	Percent	Percent	Percent	Percent	Percent
1801–1810	—	—	—	—	—	—	0.25	—	—	—	—
1811–1820	—	—	—	—	—	0.42	0.61	—	—	—	—
1821–1830	—	—	—	—	0.43	—	0.17	—	—	—	—
1831–1840	—	—	—	0.37	—	0.41	0.41	—	—	—	0.31
1841–1850	—	—	0.40	—	0.54	0.77	0.67	—	—	0.27	—
1851–1860	—	0.26	—	0.62	0.86	0.80	0.55	—	0.12	—	0.66
1861–1870	0.05	—	0.41	0.84	0.89	—	1.02	0.01	—	0.43	0.73
1871–1880	—	0.29	0.72	0.93	—	1.43	1.28	—	0.12	0.57	0.99
1881–1890	0.01	0.44	0.93	—	1.92	2.18	2.04	0.00	0.23	0.75	—
1891–1900	0.05	0.55	—	2.18	2.97	2.98	2.72	0.02	0.37	—	1.96
1901–1910	0.08	—	2.03	3.24	3.58	4.03	3.75	0.01	—	1.43	2.69
1911–1920	—	1.02	2.71	3.55	4.61	5.45	5.02	—	0.61	2.18	2.90
1921–1930	0.14	1.73	2.85	4.82	7.39	7.91	—	0.05	1.31	2.28	3.86
1931–1940	0.34	1.83	4.21	9.06	12.00	—	—	0.22	1.42	3.20	7.62
1941–1950	0.28	2.75	10.01	14.37	—	—	—	0.12	2.12	8.59	12.41
1951–1960	0.28	5.39	11.16	—	—	—	—	0.17	4.27	9.95	—
1961–1970	0.29	4.50	—	—	—	—	—	0.11	3.56	—	—
1971–1980	0.20	—	—	—	—	—	—	0.10	—	—	—

	Male			Female						
	50–59	60–69	70 and older	16–19	20–29	30–39	40–49	50–59	60–69	70 and older
	Af187	Af188	Af189	Af190	Af191	Af192	Af193	Af194	Af195	Af196
Birth year	Percent	Percent	Percent	Percent	Percent	Percent	Percent	Percent	Percent	Percent
1801–1810	—	—	0.24	—	—	—	—	—	—	0.27
1811–1820	—	0.44	0.80	—	—	—	—	—	0.39	0.45
1821–1830	0.33	—	0.26	—	—	—	—	0.54	—	0.08
1831–1840	—	0.57	0.66	—	—	—	0.44	—	0.25	0.17
1841–1850	0.58	0.94	1.02	—	—	0.53	—	0.50	0.60	0.33
1851–1860	0.78	0.92	0.80	—	0.40	—	0.58	0.95	0.68	0.35
1861–1870	0.99	—	1.30	0.09	—	0.39	0.97	0.78	—	0.76
1871–1880	—	1.63	1.66	—	0.45	0.89	0.86	—	1.23	0.96
1881–1890	1.93	2.51	2.30	0.03	0.67	1.11	—	1.90	1.85	1.86
1891–1900	2.88	2.94	2.66	0.09	0.72	—	2.40	3.07	3.01	2.75
1901–1910	3.08	3.66	3.54	0.14	—	2.62	3.78	4.07	4.35	3.87
1911–1920	3.77	4.64	4.46	—	1.40	3.21	4.17	5.38	6.13	5.41
1921–1930	6.33	6.93	—	0.22	2.13	3.38	5.72	8.35	8.73	—
1931–1940	10.32	—	—	0.47	2.22	5.17	10.43	13.56	—	—
1941–1950	—	—	—	0.43	3.35	11.39	16.26	—	—	—
1951–1960	—	—	—	0.39	6.49	12.35	—	—	—	—
1961–1970	—	—	—	0.47	5.45	—	—	—	—	—
1971–1980	—	—	—	0.31	—	—	—	—	—	—

Source

Tabulated from the Integrated Public Use Microdata Series (IPUMS); see the Guide to the Millennial Edition.

Documentation

Figures are the percentage of persons in the age/cohort group who were currently divorced at the time of the relevant census (that is, they are not the percentage of persons who had ever been divorced).

TABLE Af197–224   Percentage divorced, by cohort, age, sex, and race: 1801–1980

Contributed by Matthew Sobek

Male

	White							Nonwhite						
	16–19	20–29	30–39	40–49	50–59	60–69	70 and older	16–19	20–29	30–39	40–49	50–59	60–69	70 and older
	Af197	Af198	Af199	Af200	Af201	Af202	Af203	Af204	Af205	Af206	Af207	Af208	Af209	Af210
Birth year	Percent	Percent	Percent	Percent	Percent	Percent	Percent	Percent	Percent	Percent	Percent	Percent	Percent	Percent
1801–1810	—	—	—	—	—	—	0.27	—	—	—	—	—	—	0.00
1811–1820	—	—	—	—	—	0.46	0.00	—	—	—	—	—	0.29	5.20
1821–1830	—	—	—	—	0.31	—	0.29	—	—	—	—	0.57	—	0.00
1831–1840	—	—	—	0.30	—	0.63	0.60	—	—	—	0.40	—	0.00	1.42
1841–1850	—	—	0.26	—	0.58	1.01	1.02	—	—	0.35	—	0.55	0.15	1.03
1851–1860	—	0.10	—	0.68	0.80	0.90	0.85	—	0.21	—	0.39	0.67	1.08	0.11
1861–1870	0.01	—	0.47	0.74	1.00	—	1.33	0.00	—	0.14	0.65	0.83	—	1.01
1871–1880	—	0.10	0.51	0.99	—	1.69	1.69	—	0.25	1.06	1.04	—	1.00	1.29
1881–1890	0.00	0.20	0.71	—	1.94	2.54	2.28	0.00	0.44	1.06	—	1.82	2.13	2.46
1891–1900	0.02	0.34	—	1.99	2.88	2.94	2.54	0.06	0.63	—	1.68	2.87	2.95	3.89
1901–1910	0.01	—	1.45	2.69	3.00	3.55	3.30	0.00	—	1.22	2.62	3.77	4.75	5.79
1911–1920	—	0.61	2.14	2.82	3.62	4.34	4.15	—	0.63	2.56	3.66	5.23	7.40	7.32
1921–1930	0.05	1.31	2.17	3.70	5.92	6.52	—	0.06	1.31	3.24	5.23	9.79	10.33	—
1931–1940	0.22	1.46	3.10	7.29	9.88	—	—	0.20	1.07	3.99	9.89	13.38	—	—
1941–1950	0.13	2.15	8.42	12.22	—	—	—	0.10	1.87	9.68	13.68	—	—	—
1951–1960	0.17	4.40	10.00	—	—	—	—	0.20	3.53	9.70	—	—	—	—
1961–1970	0.12	3.80	—	—	—	—	—	0.08	2.30	—	—	—	—	—
1971–1980	0.10	—	—	—	—	—	—	0.08	—	—	—	—	—	—

Female

	White							Nonwhite						
	16–19	20–29	30–39	40–49	50–59	60–69	70 and older	16–19	20–29	30–39	40–49	50–59	60–69	70 and older
	Af211	Af212	Af213	Af214	Af215	Af216	Af217	Af218	Af219	Af220	Af221	Af222	Af223	Af224
Birth year	Percent	Percent	Percent	Percent	Percent	Percent	Percent	Percent	Percent	Percent	Percent	Percent	Percent	Percent
1801–1810	—	—	—	—	—	—	0.22	—	—	—	—	—	—	0.63
1811–1820	—	—	—	—	—	0.40	0.52	—	—	—	—	—	0.32	0.00
1821–1830	—	—	—	—	0.56	—	0.06	—	—	—	—	0.39	—	0.28
1831–1840	—	—	—	0.41	—	0.27	0.18	—	—	—	0.69	—	0.00	0.00
1841–1850	—	—	0.49	—	0.48	0.62	0.33	—	—	0.85	—	0.66	0.35	0.37
1851–1860	—	0.34	—	0.52	0.94	0.66	0.38	—	0.81	—	1.08	1.05	0.89	0.00
1861–1870	0.08	—	0.33	0.89	0.76	—	0.78	0.18	—	0.87	1.74	1.10	—	0.56
1871–1880	—	0.42	0.78	0.80	—	1.22	0.97	—	0.69	1.79	1.44	—	1.36	0.86
1881–1890	0.03	0.54	1.01	—	1.95	1.86	1.81	0.00	1.57	2.01	—	1.27	1.71	2.49
1891–1900	0.07	0.65	—	2.42	3.11	3.01	2.70	0.22	1.21	—	2.21	2.58	2.97	3.33
1901–1910	0.11	—	2.60	3.79	4.02	4.30	3.77	0.33	—	2.76	3.66	4.53	4.77	4.89
1911–1920	—	1.36	3.10	4.00	5.18	5.92	5.26	—	1.70	4.15	5.64	7.19	7.90	6.82
1921–1930	0.21	2.09	3.16	5.43	7.91	8.39	—	0.32	2.47	5.07	7.94	11.70	11.23	—
1931–1940	0.48	2.18	4.83	9.77	12.92	—	—	0.44	2.52	7.39	14.44	17.39	—	—
1941–1950	0.46	3.30	10.93	15.62	—	—	—	0.22	3.71	14.05	19.88	—	—	—
1951–1960	0.39	6.63	12.21	—	—	—	—	0.41	5.73	13.04	—	—	—	—
1961–1970	0.51	5.75	—	—	—	—	—	0.31	4.06	—	—	—	—	—
1971–1980	0.34	—	—	—	—	—	—	0.16	—	—	—	—	—	—

Source

Tabulated from the Integrated Public Use Microdata Series (IPUMS); see the Guide to the Millennial Edition.

Documentation

Figures are the percentage of persons in the age/cohort group who were currently divorced at the time of the relevant census (that is, they are not the percentage of persons who had ever been divorced).

TABLE Af225-245   Percentage widowed, by cohort, age, and sex: 1801–1980

Contributed by Matthew Sobek

	Both sexes							Male			
	16–19	20–29	30–39	40–49	50–59	60–69	70 and older	16–19	20–29	30–39	40–49
	Af225	Af226	Af227	Af228	Af229	Af230	Af231	Af232	Af233	Af234	Af235
Birth year	Percent	Percent	Percent	Percent	Percent	Percent	Percent	Percent	Percent	Percent	Percent
1801–1810	—	—	—	—	—	—	44.36	—	—	—	—
1811–1820	—	—	—	—	—	26.07	68.97	—	—	—	—
1821–1830	—	—	—	—	15.96	—	53.68	—	—	—	—
1831–1840	—	—	—	9.23	—	29.11	51.92	—	—	—	4.32
1841–1850	—	—	4.51	—	17.56	27.92	47.98	—	—	2.48	—
1851–1860	—	1.47	—	8.65	15.10	26.55	64.99	—	0.79	—	5.40
1861–1870	0.20	—	4.20	7.78	14.39	—	49.90	0.11	—	2.56	4.69
1871–1880	—	1.36	3.73	7.01	—	24.70	48.81	—	0.74	2.18	4.07
1881–1890	0.18	1.31	3.37	—	12.11	23.59	47.36	0.03	0.68	2.11	—
1891–1900	0.15	1.38	—	5.70	10.99	21.04	47.55	0.02	0.78	—	2.71
1901–1910	0.20	—	2.33	4.31	8.74	19.51	43.89	0.05	—	1.05	1.64
1911–1920	—	0.66	1.39	3.26	8.16	18.04	33.99	—	0.32	0.50	1.10
1921–1930	0.13	0.48	1.05	3.06	6.99	15.99	—	0.08	0.25	0.39	1.12
1931–1940	0.20	0.32	1.18	2.33	5.73	—	—	0.15	0.15	0.41	0.75
1941–1950	0.06	0.55	0.73	1.69	—	—	—	0.03	0.23	0.25	0.60
1951–1960	0.18	0.22	0.56	—	—	—	—	0.08	0.09	0.23	—
1961–1970	0.03	0.20	—	—	—	—	—	0.01	0.09	—	—
1971–1980	0.09	—	—	—	—	—	—	0.05	—	—	—

	Male			Female						
	50–59	60–69	70 and older	16–19	20–29	30–39	40–49	50–59	60–69	70 and older
	Af236	Af237	Af238	Af239	Af240	Af241	Af242	Af243	Af244	Af245
Birth year	Percent	Percent	Percent	Percent	Percent	Percent	Percent	Percent	Percent	Percent
1801–1810	—	—	25.08	—	—	—	—	—	—	63.73
1811–1820	—	12.56	50.87	—	—	—	—	—	40.77	84.42
1821–1830	7.17	—	36.13	—	—	—	—	25.86	—	71.02
1831–1840	—	17.17	34.28	—	—	—	14.27	—	41.55	68.61
1841–1850	9.51	16.02	30.97	—	—	6.67	—	26.26	40.66	64.37
1851–1860	8.87	15.43	48.17	—	2.17	—	12.48	22.42	39.04	78.84
1861–1870	8.29	—	32.69	0.28	—	6.00	11.30	21.31	—	65.45
1871–1880	—	13.56	30.37	—	1.97	5.45	10.31	—	35.94	63.92
1881–1890	6.13	11.69	25.37	0.33	1.98	4.71	—	18.53	35.28	63.30
1891–1900	4.69	8.28	21.89	0.28	1.97	—	8.75	17.38	32.48	63.48
1901–1910	3.00	6.64	17.85	0.35	—	3.58	6.93	14.23	30.42	59.71
1911–1920	2.63	5.87	12.99	—	0.98	2.25	5.32	13.22	28.13	48.55
1921–1930	2.21	5.69	—	0.18	0.70	1.66	4.87	11.31	24.62	—
1931–1940	1.83	—	—	0.24	0.49	1.91	3.82	9.33	—	—
1941–1950	—	—	—	0.09	0.86	1.19	2.75	—	—	—
1951–1960	—	—	—	0.28	0.35	0.88	—	—	—	—
1961–1970	—	—	—	0.06	0.30	—	—	—	—	—
1971–1980	—	—	—	0.13	—	—	—	—	—	—

Source

Tabulated from the Integrated Public Use Microdata Series (IPUMS); see the Guide to the Millennial Edition.

Documentation

Figures are the percentage of persons in the age/cohort group who were currently widowed at the time of the relevant census (that is, they are not the percentage of persons who had ever been widowed).

TABLE Af246–273   Percentage widowed, by cohort, age, sex, and race: 1801–1980

Contributed by Matthew Sobek

	Male													
	White							Nonwhite						
	16–19	20–29	30–39	40–49	50–59	60–69	70 and older	16–19	20–29	30–39	40–49	50–59	60–69	70 and older
	Af246	Af247	Af248	Af249	Af250	Af251	Af252	Af253	Af254	Af255	Af256	Af257	Af258	Af259
Birth year	Percent	Percent	Percent	Percent	Percent	Percent	Percent	Percent	Percent	Percent	Percent	Percent	Percent	Percent
1801–1810	—	—	—	—	—	—	25.44	—	—	—	—	—	—	22.15
1811–1820	—	—	—	—	—	12.73	55.00	—	—	—	—	—	11.23	28.07
1821–1830	—	—	—	—	7.06	—	36.65	—	—	—	—	8.09	—	30.85
1831–1840	—	—	—	4.26	—	16.61	34.55	—	—	—	4.75	—	22.87	31.12
1841–1850	—	—	2.35	—	9.11	16.01	30.77	—	—	3.47	—	12.95	16.10	33.39
1851–1860	—	0.64	—	5.15	8.53	15.16	48.33	—	1.79	—	7.77	12.17	18.79	45.96
1861–1870	0.12	—	2.45	4.41	7.96	—	32.50	0.04	—	3.63	7.34	11.89	—	35.25
1871–1880	—	0.58	1.92	3.81	—	13.11	30.11	—	1.75	4.32	6.36	—	18.95	33.70
1881–1890	0.03	0.50	1.95	—	5.80	11.08	25.02	0.00	2.09	3.65	—	10.18	19.26	29.38
1891–1900	0.01	0.68	—	2.43	4.30	7.59	21.28	0.12	1.60	—	5.59	9.04	15.83	28.27
1901–1910	0.03	—	0.90	1.39	2.65	5.90	17.01	0.19	—	2.47	3.95	6.30	13.63	25.77
1911–1920	—	0.25	0.41	0.91	2.26	5.26	12.30	—	0.89	1.30	2.89	6.15	11.46	19.42
1921–1930	0.07	0.20	0.30	0.95	1.87	5.23	—	0.13	0.62	1.15	2.64	5.15	9.54	—
1931–1940	0.15	0.13	0.35	0.64	1.56	—	—	0.16	0.34	0.95	1.58	3.76	—	—
1941–1950	0.03	0.19	0.20	0.49	—	—	—	0.03	0.51	0.61	1.27	—	—	—
1951–1960	0.07	0.07	0.19	—	—	—	—	0.11	0.21	0.44	—	—	—	—
1961–1970	0.01	0.08	—	—	—	—	—	0.00	0.16	—	—	—	—	—
1971–1980	0.04	—	—	—	—	—	—	0.07	—	—	—	—	—	—

	Female													
	White							Nonwhite						
	16–19	20–29	30–39	40–49	50–59	60–69	70 and older	16–19	20–29	30–39	40–49	50–59	60–69	70 and older
	Af260	Af261	Af262	Af263	Af264	Af265	Af266	Af267	Af268	Af269	Af270	Af271	Af272	Af273
Birth year	Percent	Percent	Percent	Percent	Percent	Percent	Percent	Percent	Percent	Percent	Percent	Percent	Percent	Percent
1801–1810	—	—	—	—	—	—	62.56	—	—	—	—	—	—	72.73
1811–1820	—	—	—	—	—	39.29	84.66	—	—	—	—	—	53.23	82.89
1821–1830	—	—	—	—	24.73	—	71.29	—	—	—	—	35.59	—	68.49
1831–1840	—	—	—	13.44	—	40.81	68.16	—	—	—	20.70	—	50.32	73.80
1841–1850	—	—	5.79	—	24.36	39.79	63.78	—	—	13.02	—	44.26	51.12	72.26
1851–1860	—	1.62	—	11.14	21.32	38.15	78.40	—	5.61	—	24.62	34.33	51.51	84.83
1861–1870	0.23	—	4.94	10.06	20.25	—	64.83	0.59	—	15.15	23.14	34.27	—	74.63
1871–1880	—	1.59	4.52	9.21	—	34.80	63.26	—	4.63	12.98	21.01	—	50.76	73.97
1881–1890	0.18	1.30	3.97	—	17.32	33.94	62.77	1.24	6.70	11.13	—	33.56	52.12	70.00
1891–1900	0.15	1.49	—	7.59	16.23	31.34	63.10	1.24	5.49	—	20.53	30.62	44.88	68.05
1901–1910	0.27	—	2.69	5.92	13.28	29.27	59.13	0.91	—	10.98	16.00	23.39	41.18	65.51
1911–1920	—	0.71	1.79	4.68	12.29	27.01	47.59	—	3.19	6.06	10.85	21.60	37.72	57.17
1921–1930	0.14	0.58	1.36	4.30	10.45	23.29	—	0.49	1.56	3.97	9.35	17.84	34.48	—
1931–1940	0.22	0.40	1.57	3.19	8.33	—	—	0.41	1.10	4.14	7.68	15.31	—	—
1941–1950	0.07	0.75	0.93	2.38	—	—	—	0.22	1.60	2.68	4.81	—	—	—
1951–1960	0.27	0.30	0.75	—	—	—	—	0.32	0.64	1.47	—	—	—	—
1961–1970	0.05	0.28	—	—	—	—	—	0.09	0.42	—	—	—	—	—
1971–1980	0.11	—	—	—	—	—	—	0.21	—	—	—	—	—	—

Source

Tabulated from the Integrated Public Use Microdata Series (IPUMS); see the Guide to the Millennial Edition.

Documentation

Figures are the percentage of persons in the age/cohort group who were currently widowed at the time of the relevant census (that is, they are not the percentage of persons who had ever been widowed).

EDUCATION

Matthew Sobek

TABLE Af274–294 High school noncompletion rate, by cohort, age, and sex: 1831–1980
Contributed by Matthew Sobek

	Both sexes							Male			
	19	20–29	30–39	40–49	50–59	60–69	70 and older	19	20–29	30–39	40–49
	Af274	Af275	Af276	Af277	Af278	Af279	Af280	Af281	Af282	Af283	Af284
Birth year	Percent	Percent	Percent	Percent	Percent	Percent	Percent	Percent	Percent	Percent	Percent
1831–1840	—	—	—	—	—	—	93.5	—	—	—	—
1841–1850	—	—	—	—	—	—	90.1	—	—	—	—
1851–1860	—	—	—	—	—	—	87.6	—	—	—	—
1861–1870	—	—	—	—	—	—	85.8	—	—	—	—
1871–1880	—	—	—	—	—	84.5	82.4	—	—	—	—
1881–1890	—	—	—	—	82.3	80.3	79.7	—	—	—	—
1891–1900	—	—	—	77.7	74.6	77.3	71.2	—	—	—	79.2
1901–1910	—	—	69.9	66.9	68.2	65.7	59.1	—	—	72.1	69.6
1911–1920	—	58.7	55.8	55.5	52.5	50.5	42.5	—	60.9	57.3	57.0
1921–1930	57.0	47.1	44.7	41.9	38.5	32.3	—	61.8	50.0	46.7	43.7
1931–1940	47.4	37.9	33.4	28.3	23.1	—	—	51.9	39.1	33.4	27.9
1941–1950	39.3	23.5	18.3	14.0	—	—	—	42.1	23.4	17.8	14.0
1951–1960	28.4	16.6	11.6	—	—	—	—	31.1	17.4	12.2	—
1961–1970	24.1	13.0	—	—	—	—	—	27.3	14.3	—	—
1971–1980	18.2	—	—	—	—	—	—	21.2	—	—	—

	Male			Female						
	50–59	60–69	70 and older	19	20–29	30–39	40–49	50–59	60–69	70 and older
	Af285	Af286	Af287	Af288	Af289	Af290	Af291	Af292	Af293	Af294
Birth year	Percent	Percent	Percent	Percent	Percent	Percent	Percent	Percent	Percent	Percent
1831–1840	—	—	92.8	—	—	—	—	—	—	93.9
1841–1850	—	—	91.7	—	—	—	—	—	—	88.8
1851–1860	—	—	88.7	—	—	—	—	—	—	86.7
1861–1870	—	—	87.3	—	—	—	—	—	—	84.4
1871–1880	—	85.7	85.0	—	—	—	—	—	83.4	80.4
1881–1890	83.6	82.0	82.8	—	—	—	—	80.8	78.7	77.5
1891–1900	76.0	79.1	74.9	—	—	—	76.1	73.2	75.6	68.9
1901–1910	70.5	68.4	62.1	—	—	67.8	64.4	65.9	63.5	57.4
1911–1920	53.7	51.1	42.6	—	56.7	54.3	53.9	51.4	50.0	42.4
1921–1930	39.6	33.4	—	52.3	44.4	42.9	40.3	37.5	31.3	—
1931–1940	23.1	—	—	43.1	36.8	33.5	28.7	23.1	—	—
1941–1950	—	—	—	36.7	23.6	18.8	13.9	—	—	—
1951–1960	—	—	—	25.9	15.9	11.0	—	—	—	—
1961–1970	—	—	—	20.7	11.7	—	—	—	—	—
1971–1980	—	—	—	15.1	—	—	—	—	—	—

Source

Tabulated from the Integrated Public Use Microdata Series (IPUMS); see the Guide to the Millennial Edition.

Documentation

Persons who completed grade 12 but did not receive a diploma are classified as graduates. These series were calculated from individuals' own reports of highest grade completed, first asked in the 1940 Census. The 1940 Census is thought to overstate the high school graduation rate of older Americans. See the essay in Chapter Bc, on education.

TABLE Af295–336 High school noncompletion rate, by cohort, age, sex, race, and nativity: 1831–1980
Contributed by Matthew Sobek

	Male										
	Native- and foreign-born										
	White							Nonwhite			
	19	20–29	30–39	40–49	50–59	60–69	70 and older	19	20–29	30–39	40–49
	Af295	Af296	Af297	Af298	Af299	Af300	Af301	Af302	Af303	Af304	Af305
Birth year	Percent	Percent	Percent	Percent	Percent	Percent	Percent	Percent	Percent	Percent	Percent
1831–1840	—	—	—	—	—	—	89.2	—	—	—	—
1841–1850	—	—	—	—	—	—	90.4	—	—	—	—
1851–1860	—	—	—	—	—	—	88.1	—	—	—	—
1861–1870	—	—	—	—	—	—	86.7	—	—	—	—
1871–1880	—	—	—	—	—	84.9	84.3	—	—	—	—
1881–1890	—	—	—	—	82.7	81.0	82.0	—	—	—	—
1891–1900	—	—	—	77.8	74.4	77.9	73.5	—	—	—	93.5
1901–1910	—	—	69.9	67.4	68.6	66.3	60.1	—	—	92.2	90.0
1911–1920	—	57.8	54.6	54.4	51.1	48.5	40.2	—	88.8	82.3	81.6
1921–1930	58.6	46.6	43.9	41.0	37.2	31.0	—	88.4	78.5	70.8	66.6
1931–1940	48.0	36.0	30.9	25.7	21.4	—	—	81.2	62.8	53.1	43.0
1941–1950	38.7	21.1	16.4	12.9	—	—	—	68.7	40.8	27.8	21.5
1951–1960	28.1	15.9	11.4	—	—	—	—	51.2	26.2	16.4	—
1961–1970	24.9	13.8	—	—	—	—	—	40.4	17.2	—	—
1971–1980	19.7	—	—	—	—	—	—	28.0	—	—	—

	Male									
	Native- and foreign-born			Foreign-born						
	Nonwhite									
	50–59	60–69	70 and older	19	20–29	30–39	40–49	50–59	60–69	70 and older
	Af306	Af307	Af308	Af309	Af310	Af311	Af312	Af313	Af314	Af315
Birth year	Percent	Percent	Percent	Percent	Percent	Percent	Percent	Percent	Percent	Percent
1831–1840	—	—	100.0	—	—	—	—	—	—	100.0
1841–1850	—	—	98.5	—	—	—	—	—	—	95.6
1851–1860	—	—	96.2	—	—	—	—	—	—	92.8
1861–1870	—	—	95.7	—	—	—	—	—	—	91.5
1871–1880	—	94.9	94.1	—	—	—	—	—	90.8	88.0
1881–1890	93.8	94.5	92.0	—	—	—	—	89.3	85.9	86.7
1891–1900	92.1	92.1	88.9	—	—	—	86.3	81.3	83.8	78.2
1901–1910	88.6	88.0	81.1	—	—	78.3	73.7	74.6	70.4	64.2
1911–1920	78.8	74.1	65.0	—	63.9	60.5	62.0	56.7	54.4	45.9
1921–1930	60.8	53.5	—	59.5	54.4	54.7	49.7	46.3	42.1	—
1931–1940	35.1	—	—	53.2	54.6	45.3	40.9	36.1	—	—
1941–1950	—	—	—	58.1	35.8	34.3	30.3	—	—	—
1951–1960	—	—	—	47.8	32.9	29.2	—	—	—	—
1961–1970	—	—	—	40.6	31.5	—	—	—	—	—
1971–1980	—	—	—	36.3	—	—	—	—	—	—

TABLE Af295–336   High school noncompletion rate, by cohort, age, sex, race, and nativity: 1831–1980   *Continued*

	Female										
	Native- and foreign-born										
	White							Nonwhite			
	19	20–29	30–39	40–49	50–59	60–69	70 and older	19	20–29	30–39	40–49
	Af316	Af317	Af318	Af319	Af320	Af321	Af322	Af323	Af324	Af325	Af326
Birth year	Percent	Percent	Percent	Percent	Percent	Percent	Percent	Percent	Percent	Percent	Percent
1831–1840	—	—	—	—	—	—	87.4	—	—	—	—
1841–1850	—	—	—	—	—	—	86.5	—	—	—	—
1851–1860	—	—	—	—	—	—	86.0	—	—	—	—
1861–1870	—	—	—	—	—	—	83.6	—	—	—	—
1871–1880	—	—	—	—	—	82.4	79.5	—	—	—	—
1881–1890	—	—	—	—	79.7	77.4	76.4	—	—	—	—
1891–1900	—	—	—	74.5	71.8	74.2	67.5	—	—	—	92.1
1901–1910	—	—	65.1	61.7	63.7	61.2	55.3	—	—	90.0	88.5
1911–1920	—	53.1	51.2	51.0	48.6	47.3	39.8	—	84.5	80.6	79.4
1921–1930	48.8	40.6	39.7	37.2	34.6	28.7	—	81.4	73.8	67.1	64.4
1931–1940	39.4	33.8	30.6	26.2	20.9	—	—	71.3	57.8	52.3	44.0
1941–1950	33.0	21.4	17.2	12.6	—	—	—	61.6	38.9	28.2	21.2
1951–1960	23.0	14.5	10.0	—	—	—	—	44.2	23.0	15.7	—
1961–1970	18.9	11.1	—	—	—	—	—	30.0	14.4	—	—
1971–1980	14.2	—	—	—	—	—	—	19.5	—	—	—

	Female									
	Native- and foreign-born			Foreign-born						
	Nonwhite									
	50–59	60–69	70 and older	19	20–29	30–39	40–49	50–59	60–69	70 and older
	Af327	Af328	Af329	Af330	Af331	Af332	Af333	Af334	Af335	Af336
Birth year	Percent	Percent	Percent	Percent	Percent	Percent	Percent	Percent	Percent	Percent
1831–1840	—	—	100.0	—	—	—	—	—	—	100.0
1841–1850	—	—	99.0	—	—	—	—	—	—	91.0
1851–1860	—	—	96.7	—	—	—	—	—	—	93.7
1861–1870	—	—	96.1	—	—	—	—	—	—	91.6
1871–1880	—	96.5	94.3	—	—	—	—	—	92.5	88.3
1881–1890	94.5	93.7	91.5	—	—	—	—	91.1	87.4	87.5
1891–1900	90.5	91.3	85.5	—	—	—	88.3	83.8	86.1	79.5
1901–1910	86.8	84.9	78.3	—	—	81.2	72.9	77.0	73.4	66.5
1911–1920	76.8	73.0	65.7	—	65.4	57.9	62.6	59.3	57.4	52.3
1921–1930	59.2	50.6	—	53.3	50.0	53.2	49.9	48.0	43.8	—
1931–1940	35.9	—	—	52.3	54.6	48.3	42.7	38.5	—	—
1941–1950	—	—	—	57.7	38.4	35.5	30.7	—	—	—
1951–1960	—	—	—	45.4	32.5	28.2	—	—	—	—
1961–1970	—	—	—	35.0	26.2	—	—	—	—	—
1971–1980	—	—	—	26.8	—	—	—	—	—	—

Source

Tabulated from the Integrated Public Use Microdata Series (IPUMS); see the Guide to the Millennial Edition.

Documentation

Persons who completed grade 12 but did not receive a diploma are classified as graduates. Persons born in outlying areas and territories of the United States are classified as foreign-born.

TABLE Af337–354   College graduation rate, by cohort, age, and sex: 1831–1970

Contributed by Matthew Sobek

Birth year	Both sexes						Male		
	23–29	30–39	40–49	50–59	60–69	70 and older	23–29	30–39	40–49
	Af337	Af338	Af339	Af340	Af341	Af342	Af343	Af344	Af345
	Percent	Percent	Percent	Percent	Percent	Percent	Percent	Percent	Percent
1831–1840	—	—	—	—	—	1.33	—	—	—
1841–1850	—	—	—	—	—	2.24	—	—	—
1851–1860	—	—	—	—	—	2.64	—	—	—
1861–1870	—	—	—	—	—	2.84	—	—	—
1871–1880	—	—	—	—	3.28	3.38	—	—	—
1881–1890	—	—	—	3.76	4.09	3.94	—	—	—
1891–1900	—	—	4.54	5.30	4.58	5.86	—	—	5.28
1901–1910	—	6.03	6.94	6.75	7.36	8.83	—	7.08	7.97
1911–1920	5.72	7.35	7.67	8.54	9.49	10.11	6.76	8.71	9.24
1921–1930	7.29	10.19	11.44	12.80	13.59	—	8.68	13.84	15.21
1931–1940	10.78	14.03	16.75	18.41	—	—	13.76	18.41	21.69
1941–1950	16.19	23.16	25.63	—	—	—	18.80	27.86	29.73
1951–1960	20.49	24.99	—	—	—	—	21.58	26.05	—
1961–1970	21.28	—	—	—	—	—	20.53	—	—

Birth year	Male			Female					
	50–59	60–69	70 and older	23–29	30–39	40–49	50–59	60–69	70 and older
	Af346	Af347	Af348	Af349	Af350	Af351	Af352	Af353	Af354
	Percent	Percent	Percent	Percent	Percent	Percent	Percent	Percent	Percent
1831–1840	—	—	0.00	—	—	—	—	—	2.11
1841–1850	—	—	3.14	—	—	—	—	—	1.59
1851–1860	—	—	3.51	—	—	—	—	—	1.93
1861–1870	—	—	3.56	—	—	—	—	—	2.19
1871–1880	—	4.01	4.07	—	—	—	—	2.54	2.82
1881–1890	4.48	4.78	4.45	—	—	—	3.00	3.45	3.57
1891–1900	6.08	5.22	6.57	—	—	3.78	4.55	4.01	5.43
1901–1910	7.64	8.25	10.21	—	4.99	5.97	5.89	6.61	7.99
1911–1920	10.20	11.64	12.79	4.73	6.07	6.16	7.03	7.71	8.26
1921–1930	16.91	17.95	—	6.02	6.73	7.92	9.09	9.94	—
1931–1940	23.07	—	—	7.93	9.90	12.06	14.11	—	—
1941–1950	—	—	—	13.72	18.60	21.69	—	—	—
1951–1960	—	—	—	19.42	23.96	—	—	—	—
1961–1970	—	—	—	22.04	—	—	—	—	—

Source

Tabulated from the Integrated Public Use Microdata Series (IPUMS); see the Guide to the Millennial Edition.

Documentation

For figures derived from censuses prior to 1990, college graduation means having completed sixteen or more years of school. In the 1990 Census, college graduation means having actually received a bachelor's or higher degree, regardless of number of years of school.

TABLE Af355–390   College graduation rate, by cohort, age, sex, race, and nativity: 1831–1970

Contributed by Matthew Sobek

	Male											
	Native- and foreign-born											
	White						Nonwhite					
	23–29	30–39	40–49	50–59	60–69	70 and older	23–29	30–39	40–49	50–59	60–69	70 and older
	Af355	Af356	Af357	Af358	Af359	Af360	Af361	Af362	Af363	Af364	Af365	Af366
Birth year	Percent	Percent	Percent	Percent	Percent	Percent	Percent	Percent	Percent	Percent	Percent	Percent
1831–1840	—	—	—	—	—	0.00	—	—	—	—	—	0.00
1841–1850	—	—	—	—	—	3.77	—	—	—	—	—	0.00
1851–1860	—	—	—	—	—	3.65	—	—	—	—	—	1.64
1861–1870	—	—	—	—	—	3.74	—	—	—	—	—	1.20
1871–1880	—	—	—	—	4.22	4.31	—	—	—	—	1.46	1.05
1881–1890	—	—	—	4.73	5.07	4.70	—	—	—	1.44	1.17	1.53
1891–1900	—	—	5.63	6.49	5.55	6.96	—	—	1.68	1.69	1.59	2.52
1901–1910	—	7.66	8.63	8.22	8.87	10.84	—	1.84	1.92	2.19	2.40	4.32
1911–1920	7.38	9.39	9.89	10.87	12.28	13.44	1.25	2.48	3.31	3.81	5.84	6.64
1921–1930	9.43	14.88	16.27	17.88	18.97	—	2.33	4.98	5.95	8.74	9.33	—
1931–1940	14.86	19.61	22.67	24.02	—	—	5.19	8.92	14.73	16.45	—	—
1941–1950	20.20	29.26	31.00	—	—	—	7.66	18.49	21.49	—	—	—
1951–1960	22.98	27.16	—	—	—	—	13.12	19.81	—	—	—	—
1961–1970	21.59	—	—	—	—	—	14.93	—	—	—	—	—

	Male						Female					
	Foreign-born						Native- and foreign-born					
							White					
	23–29	30–39	40–49	50–59	60–69	70 and older	23–29	30–39	40–49	50–59	60–69	70 and older
	Af367	Af368	Af369	Af370	Af371	Af372	Af373	Af374	Af375	Af376	Af377	Af378
Birth year	Percent	Percent	Percent	Percent	Percent	Percent	Percent	Percent	Percent	Percent	Percent	Percent
1831–1840	—	—	—	—	—	0.00	—	—	—	—	—	4.37
1841–1850	—	—	—	—	—	2.22	—	—	—	—	—	1.95
1851–1860	—	—	—	—	—	2.31	—	—	—	—	—	1.98
1861–1870	—	—	—	—	—	2.41	—	—	—	—	—	2.30
1871–1880	—	—	—	—	2.79	3.50	—	—	—	—	2.69	2.94
1881–1890	—	—	—	2.88	3.58	2.90	—	—	—	3.16	3.67	3.73
1891–1900	—	—	3.66	4.81	3.96	5.36	—	—	4.02	4.80	4.25	5.63
1901–1910	—	6.02	6.84	6.63	7.74	9.36	—	5.40	6.32	6.24	6.95	8.32
1911–1920	7.63	8.86	10.70	12.26	13.68	14.50	5.12	6.43	6.48	7.34	7.97	8.59
1921–1930	10.62	15.79	16.68	18.62	18.11	—	6.42	7.04	8.26	9.37	10.21	—
1931–1940	15.18	22.42	24.66	24.56	—	—	8.31	10.34	12.37	14.42	—	—
1941–1950	20.65	29.16	29.52	—	—	—	14.49	19.22	22.25	—	—	—
1951–1960	20.01	27.15	—	—	—	—	20.43	24.85	—	—	—	—
1961–1970	19.66	—	—	—	—	—	23.18	—	—	—	—	—

(continued)

TABLE Af355–390   College graduation rate, by cohort, age, sex, race, and nativity: 1831–1970 *Continued*

	Female											
	Native- and foreign-born						Foreign-born					
	Nonwhite											
Birth year	23–29	30–39	40–49	50–59	60–69	70 and older	23–29	30–39	40–49	50–59	60–69	70 and older
	Af379	Af380	Af381	Af382	Af383	Af384	Af385	Af386	Af387	Af388	Af389	Af390
	Percent	Percent	Percent	Percent	Percent	Percent	Percent	Percent	Percent	Percent	Percent	Percent
1831–1840	—	—	—	—	—	0.00	—	—	—	—	—	0.00
1841–1850	—	—	—	—	—	0.00	—	—	—	—	—	2.25
1851–1860	—	—	—	—	—	1.18	—	—	—	—	—	1.03
1861–1870	—	—	—	—	—	0.63	—	—	—	—	—	1.16
1871–1880	—	—	—	—	0.64	1.10	—	—	—	—	0.95	1.46
1881–1890	—	—	—	1.03	0.76	1.56	—	—	—	1.27	1.76	1.54
1891–1900	—	—	1.35	1.70	1.47	2.95	—	—	1.50	1.87	1.65	2.35
1901–1910	—	1.62	2.72	2.52	3.46	4.62	—	2.13	3.23	2.84	3.23	4.61
1911–1920	1.63	3.10	3.39	4.28	5.46	5.30	3.99	6.14	4.81	5.90	7.02	6.04
1921–1930	2.84	4.37	5.19	6.91	7.94	—	5.91	6.16	7.72	8.71	8.66	—
1931–1940	5.28	7.00	10.20	12.20	—	—	7.41	9.27	12.56	13.26	—	—
1941–1950	8.33	15.00	18.51	—	—	—	12.94	18.34	19.72	—	—	—
1951–1960	14.12	19.57	—	—	—	—	17.26	23.06	—	—	—	—
1961–1970	16.65	—	—	—	—	—	20.60	—	—	—	—	—

Source

Tabulated from the Integrated Public Use Microdata Series (IPUMS); see the Guide to the Millennial Edition.

Documentation

See the text for Table Af337–354.

Persons born in outlying areas and territories of the United States are classified as foreign-born.

CHAPTER Ag
American Indians

Editor: C. Matthew Snipp

Susan B. Carter and Richard Sutch

The U.S. Census Bureau defines American Indians and Alaska Natives as people whose ancestry derives from any of the original peoples of North and South America, and who maintain tribal affiliation or community attachment. The Census presently counts as an Indian anyone who declares himself or herself to be an Indian. Native Hawaiians and other Pacific Islanders are not considered "Indians" under U.S. law and are enumerated separately in the Census. See Chapter Aa on population characteristics and Chapter Ef on outlying areas for information on Hawaiians and other Pacific Islanders.

From the perspective of historical ethnography, an Indian tribe is a body of people bound together by a common ancestry and continuity in culture and social organization. Tribal members occupied a defined territory and spoke a common language or dialect. Many precontact tribes have disappeared or were absorbed into other tribes. Today, there are more than 550 federally recognized tribes in the United States, including 223 village groups in Alaska.

"Federally recognized" means these tribes and groups have a special, legal relationship with the U.S. government. That special relationship is based on four principles:

1. Tribes are thought of as separate sovereign nations to be dealt with on a government-to-government basis.
2. As separate nations, the internal affairs of tribes are the responsibility of the tribal entity.
3. Relations with tribes are considered to be between two nations and are handled by the central government.
4. Indians are U.S. citizens but are also members of their respective tribes and thus have dual citizenship.

Relations with the tribes are codified in treaties ratified by Congress, judicial opinions, and by executive orders issued by the President and by the Secretary of the Interior. The U.S. Bureau of Indian Affairs (BIA) is the principal agent of the United States in carrying out the government-to-government relationship that exists. It also acts as the principal agent of the U.S. government in carrying out the responsibilities the United States has as a trustee for property it holds for federally recognized tribes and individual American Indians. A number of Indian groups do not have a federally recognized status, although some are recognized by the states in which they are located. This means they have no relations

with the BIA or the programs it operates. A special program at the BIA, however, works with groups seeking federal status. Of the 150 petitions for federal recognition the BIA has received since 1978, twelve groups have received acknowledgment through the BIA process, two had their status clarified by the Department of the Interior through other means, and seven were restored or recognized by Congress.

In 1924 Congress granted American citizenship to all Indians born in the territorial limits of the United States. Before that date, however, citizenship had been conferred upon approximately two thirds of the Indian population through treaty agreements, statutes, naturalization proceedings, and by service in the armed forces during World War I. No single federal or tribal criterion establishes a person's identity as an Indian. Tribes have varying eligibility criteria for membership.

In the essay that follows, C. Matthew Snipp uses – for editorial convenience – the term "American Indian" consistently in lieu of the more cumbersome "American Indian and Alaska Native," and in lieu of other equally appropriate nomenclature, such as "Native American."

C. Matthew Snipp

American Indians occupy a position in American society that is unmatched by any other group. Legally, politically, and culturally, American Indians represent a unique segment of the American population. No other group, for example, is explicitly recognized in the Constitution of the United States. The so-called commerce clause in the American Constitution specifically recognizes American Indians and delegates to Congress the authority to oversee affairs with them. This recognition has evolved into a special kind of dual citizenship buttressed by a long and tangled history of treaties, court decisions, and legal agreements. The unique status of American Indians is further manifest in volume 25 of the Code of Federal Regulations (CFR) devoted entirely to American Indian law, two Congressional committees – for the House and for the Senate – that oversee relations with American Indians, an agency within the executive branch responsible solely for American Indians (the Bureau of Indian Affairs (BIA) within the Department of the Interior), and special "Indian Desks" too numerous to mention scattered throughout the federal bureaucracy.

In light of the long and extensive relationship that has existed between American Indians and the federal government, one might also assume that an equally extensive set of records would exist, charting and documenting in great detail the special circumstances

Acknowledgments
Matthew Snipp thanks Thomas Hall and Clifford Trafzer for their comments.

of American Indians. Such an assumption would be greatly in error. To shorten a long and complex story, for decades the U.S. government has regarded American Indians as belonging to nations apart, and to some extent continues to do so today. As a result, in the early years of the country's history, the federal government made no more effort to systematically collect information about American Indians than it did for other foreign governments. To the extent this information exists, it reflects the activities of the federal bureaucracy in its dealings with various groups of American Indians.

Consequently, data that span the entire history of the United States for American Indians are virtually nonexistent. For example, the decennial census did not systematically enumerate American Indians until 1860, and devoted almost no attention to American Indian population characteristics until 1890.[1] The census, in particular, illustrates the peculiar status that American Indians have occupied throughout this country's history. In the first census that counted American Indians, a distinction was made between "Indians taxed" and "Indians not taxed." Indians taxed were individuals who had settled in or near Anglo communities, had adopted Anglo livelihoods and lifestyles, and had more or less assimilated themselves into Anglo-American society. They resembled Anglo-Americans enough to be considered "citizens" and they could be taxed. Indians not taxed were precisely the opposite. They were Indians who lived among their kinsmen in tribal communities and refused to adopt Euro-American customs, and from whom taxes were not collected because they were not citizens of the United States (Snipp 1989). This distinction between Indians taxed and those not taxed was eventually discarded as they were settled on reservations, and was officially abolished when in 1924 the Indian Citizenship Act made all American Indians eligible for taxation.

Sources of Historical Statistics on American Indians

As the tables in this chapter show, the disappointing lack of data for American Indians does not mean that such information is missing altogether. Indeed, the history of data for American Indians begins with a small number of sources, which slowly increases over time, to the present in which data for American Indians are available from a large number of sources within the federal government. For scholars interested in American Indians during the early years of this nation's history, there are three basic sources of statistical information: Congressional acts, especially appropriation bills; reports of the Commissioner of Indian Affairs; and unofficial records such as diaries, letters, and other documents of priests, explorers, travelers, and others who had an opportunity to observe or have dealings with American Indians.

Unofficial records do not contribute much to the tables that accompany this essay, because the amount of usable statistical data in these records is usually small or nonexistent. Unofficial records such as letters, diaries, and business receipts, although often extensive in volume, are also difficult to access and, by definition, are unsystematic and unorganized. For statistical purposes, this material is not very useful and little else needs to be said about it. In comparison, much more useful data can be gleaned from federal sources. These data vary considerably with respect to their content, quality, and historical coverage.

Some of the earliest federal data detailing the federal government's dealings with American Indians can be found in a body of annual legislation generically known as the Indian Appropriation Acts. Each year, usually in the spring, Congress passed a bill authorizing the expenditure of federal funds for American Indians. This included money paid for a wide variety of goods and services, as well as payments made directly to American Indian tribes. These expenditures paid the salaries and expenses of Indian agents, doctors, teachers, and missionaries working in Indian communities, and also paid for food, clothing, blankets, tools, farm implements, and other items that were provided directly to American Indians. These goods and services were provided in exchange for land cessions and reservation settlement, to meet the terms of treaties, and for other agreements made with American Indians.

The types of data available in the Indian Appropriations Acts offer a glimpse of how the federal government managed its affairs with American Indians. In particular, these Acts itemize in detail the quantities and costs of goods and services allocated to various tribes, agencies, and reservations. It is important to understand, however, that corruption was widespread in the Indian Service throughout the nineteenth century. Thus, the goods and services appropriated by Congress were not necessarily equal to the goods and services received by Indians. Nonetheless, these data still offer useful insights into the nature of the financial transactions that took place between American Indians and the federal government, as well as the kinds of goods bargained for and consumed by American Indians.

Reports of the Commissioner of Indian Affairs provide an even more detailed and comprehensive view of the federal government's dealings with American Indians. In the early years of the United States, the Secretary of War was responsible for overseeing Indian affairs. However, as these duties expanded in scope and complexity, Secretary of War John C. Calhoun established an Office of Indian Affairs in 1824. In 1832, Congress granted statutory authority to the Office of Indian Affairs, and in subsequent years the Commissioner of Indian Affairs was responsible for submitting an annual report of this agency's activities (Taylor 1984).

Reports of the Commissioner of Indian Affairs, though issued regularly, did not follow a consistent format, and their content varied from one year to the next. In some years, for example, there is detailed reporting about population counts, health conditions, and school attendance. Other years provide only cursory details about the activities of Indian agents and little else. Unfortunately, these reports represent the single largest source of federal information about American Indians in the first half of the nineteenth century.

In the latter part of the nineteenth century, two developments occurred that vastly increased the quality and quantity of statistical data for American Indians. One was the emergence and growing influence of modern social science, especially anthropology. Empirical observation, systematic record keeping, and comparability are the hallmarks of social scientific methods that gradually infiltrated federal recordkeeping systems.

The rise of modern anthropology was especially important for information about American Indians collected by the federal government in the late nineteenth century. Anthropologists of this era were convinced, as were many others, that American Indians were destined for extinction. Guided by this belief, anthropologists in the late nineteenth century set out to observe, document, and collect every conceivable detail connected with the lifestyles and

---

[1] In some states, American Indians were identified as such during the process of enumeration for censuses before 1860.

cultures of American Indians. This effort has come to be known as "salvage ethnography."

The federal government sponsored a great deal of the salvage ethnography undertaken in the late nineteenth and early twentieth centuries. This work was overseen by the Smithsonian Institution's Bureau of American Ethnology (BAE). During the course of its existence, the BAE issued hundreds (perhaps thousands) of reports detailing the material and symbolic culture of American Indians. Although these reports are primarily qualitative in content, some statistical information can be gleaned from them. For example, in a 1910 BAE bulletin the anthropologist James Mooney reported the first systematic estimate of the precontact (circa 1600) American Indian population (Thornton 1987) (Table Ag1–16).

The growing professionalization of the Census Bureau in the mid-to-late nineteenth century was the second development to enhance federal statistics for American Indians. The Census Bureau issued its first major report devoted to American Indians in 1894, as part of the eleventh decennial census in 1890. The report, titled *Report on Indians Taxed and Not Taxed in the United States, Except Alaska* (volume 17), was a remarkable document for at least two reasons. One is that it was the Census Bureau's first significant effort to enumerate and collect data on the characteristics of American Indians. The other is that this document was clearly an exercise in salvage ethnography. As such, this report also includes maps, drawings, photographs, and narrative accounts of tribal culture in addition to statistical data. Never before and never since has the Census Bureau produced a document such as this 1894 report.

In 1902, Congress established the Census Bureau as a permanent agency with duties that extended beyond conducting the decennial census (Anderson 1988). The creation of the bureau as a permanent entity rapidly propelled it toward becoming the nation's principal repository of statistical data. It also immeasurably improved census procedures in the collection and tabulation of statistical data, in ways consonant with scientific standards. The presence of statisticians and social scientists in the Census Bureau had a tremendous impact on federal data for American Indians, making the designation of "American Indian" a more or less regular feature in federal statistical systems, most notably the decennial census.

Historical Statistics for American Indians in the Twentieth Century

The permanent establishment of the Census Bureau reflects the burgeoning federal statistical system that grew rapidly throughout the twentieth century. Not surprisingly, data for American Indians also grew more detailed and systematic through the century. However, it is not true that it became more accessible during this time. In fact, there is a great deal of data available for American Indians at the century's end, somewhat less at the beginning of the century, and precious little for the midcentury decades. The reasons for this midcentury lapse and late-century recovery are extraordinarily complex and far beyond the scope of this discussion. Suffice it to say that popular opinion, public policy, and political considerations have had a profound impact on how American Indians are embedded within federal data collection efforts.

In the twentieth century the Census Bureau became the federal government's preeminent source of information about the American Indian population. No other source contains as much information for the American Indian population in its entirety – urban and reservation – for so many different characteristics. In the early part of the century, the Census Bureau published two special reports devoted to American Indians – one in 1915 and another in 1937, based on the 1910 and 1930 decennial Censuses, respectively. These reports also contained a small amount of information about Alaska Natives.

In 1940, American Indians were enumerated in the census but virtually disappeared in most Census Bureau publications, subsumed within the "other races" category of the bureau's racial classification.[2] Data for American Indians did not appear in the main publications for states and other localities. During these decades, data for American Indians appeared in special reports for the "nonwhite population" published in 1943, 1953, and 1963, derived from the 1940, 1950, and 1960 Censuses.

Likewise, American Indians were missing from most of the reports produced from the 1970 Census. However, the Census Bureau produced a special report devoted exclusively to American Indians and, to a lesser extent, Alaska Natives. The publications from the 1980 Census were the first to include American Indians and Alaska Natives throughout its data for racial characteristics. In 1983 the Census Bureau also produced a special subject report for American Indians and Alaska Natives, resembling the 1970 special report, though containing much more detail. In addition to the regular census, a special supplementary questionnaire was distributed to reservation households. The results of this survey were published in yet another special report. The Census Bureau did not sponsor a special reservation survey in the 1990 Census. However, it did publish two special reports, one tabulated for reservations and another tabulated for tribes and languages, in addition to including American Indians in all of its tabulations for racial characteristics.

For the first time, the Census of 2000 gave respondents the opportunity to select one or more categories for their racial heritage. Preliminary reports indicate that 4.1 million people, or 1.5 percent of the population, reported themselves as "American Indian or Alaska Native" either alone or in combination with other races. 2.5 million people, or 0.9 percent of the population, reported their race only as American Indian or Alaska Native. Among those who reported American Indian in combination with another race, the most common admixture was American Indian or Alaska Native and white, followed by American Indian or Alaska Native and black (Crieco and Cassidy 2000, Table 6).

The Census Bureau is not the only source of data for American Indians in the twentieth century. The BIA produces a copious amount of information in the course of carrying out its duties. Its information is more limited because the scope of BIA activities does not ordinarily include urban American Indians (now about half of the total Indian population). Nonetheless, statistics available from the BIA range in topic from natural resources on reservation lands, to enrollments at BIA-administered schools, to estimates of unemployment and labor force participation on reservations.

It is fair to say that unlike the Census Bureau, the BIA's principal mission is not data collection and distribution. This may explain why the quality of BIA data is more variable than that of Census Bureau data. For some purposes, BIA data can be highly accurate, or at least bear the appearance of accuracy. For example, the amount of land under its jurisdiction is reported in one-hundredths of acres. In contrast, the BIA regularly disclaims the accuracy of its

---

[2] One likely reason is that the onset of World War II in 1941 curtailed the Census Bureau's publication program.

estimates of reservation labor force participation and unemployment. These data are based on "guesstimates." They are reasonably accurate for small reservations with concentrated settlements, where the employment status of local residents is easy to observe. By the same token, they are very poor for large reservations with dispersed populations.

The Indian Health Service (IHS) is another important source of information about American Indians. In 1955, IHS was placed in the Public Health Service (PHS) agency in the Department of Health, Education, and Welfare (now the Department of Health and Human Services). This move was accompanied by heightened efforts to observe and monitor the health status of American Indians, especially those living in areas served by the IHS. As a result of these efforts, the data and publications produced by the IHS represent the single largest source of information about American Indian health conditions: morbidity, mortality, leading causes of death, incidence and prevalence of certain diseases, as well as operational data from IHS clinics and hospitals (for example, expenditures and numbers of patients treated).

The most significant limitation of IHS data is that in most instances they are based on populations residing within IHS service areas. IHS service areas roughly correspond to geographic regions on and around reservations with access to an IHS hospital or clinic. American Indians living outside these areas, especially in cities, are not incorporated into most IHS data systems. However, some data produced for IHS by other agencies employ national record systems and cover the entire American Indian population. Users of these data should pay close attention to the geography from which this information is obtained.

There are numerous sources of data for American Indians other than the Census, the BIA, and the IHS. For example, the Senate and House committees that deal with American Indian issues occasionally commission studies that require the collection of statistical data. However, these studies are highly topical and reflect congressional preoccupations more than anything else. Furthermore, they are not well publicized and to access them, one must know of the existence of a particular study and more or less the date of its publication as a congressional report.

Since the 1960s the amount of information about American Indians produced by a variety of federal agencies has increased dramatically. Few of these agencies produce data in serial format as the IHS does; however, they do produce special reports devoted to American Indians. For example, the Department of Education periodically produces a report about American Indians in higher education. Similarly, the Department of Housing and Urban Development has produced reports about the conditions of the housing in which American Indians reside. In fact, most agencies that serve American Indians in one capacity or another – including the Department of Justice, the Department of Agriculture, the Environmental Protection Agency, and the Small Business Administration, to name only a few – have produced reports for American Indians or include them in their recordkeeping systems. Although these data and reports now have limited utility as "historical" documents, if these practices continue there is no doubt they will be valuable to future generations of historians.

Statistical Overview

The tables that follow this essay are necessarily a small sampling of the kinds of data that are available for American Indians. The content areas are also not exhaustive of the subject matter that is available for American Indians. There are other, much more voluminous sources of information that interested readers can consult (see Stuart 1987; Reddy 1995). However, these tables and the subject matter they represent were chosen for the purpose of charting the position of American Indians within the larger context of American society at the turn of the millennium.

In particular, they begin with a presentation of data for American Indians that predate or roughly coincide with the arrival of Europeans. This is followed by more recent population statistics. Health and labor statistics reflect the well-being, and lack thereof, for American Indians. The remaining topics focus on the natural resources still held by American Indians, and the government relations that characterize the special status of American Indians.

Early Population History

James Mooney was an anthropologist employed by the Smithsonian Institution in the early years of the twentieth century. As mentioned, he was responsible for pioneering work estimating the size of American Indian populations at the time of contact with Europeans. He painstakingly assembled the records of explorers, traders, priests, and other visitors to Native America, and determined dates of contact that varied through the seventeenth and eighteenth centuries, for different groups of American Indians. He also used this information to determine the likely population size for each tribe that he could identify. His approach to this work was largely educated guesswork and, for this reason, his method has been described as "dead reckoning" (Thornton 1987). The results of Mooney's efforts are shown in Tables Ag17–264.

In a brief 1910 article Mooney estimated that the North American indigenous population numbered around 1.15 million roughly at the time of contact with Europeans, 1600 and later (Snipp 1989). Map Ag-A shows the geographic distribution of American Indian tribes around 1600. Mooney's number proved to be enormously influential and stood for decades as the benchmark for the pre-Columbian population of North America. It suggested that Native North Americans lived in small and relatively primitive societies. However, this image was not entirely consistent with a growing body of archaeological knowledge. Furthermore, critics of this number pointed out that Mooney had failed to take into account the devastating epidemics that swept through the continent after Europeans arrived. Smallpox was an especially deadly disease for American Indians lacking immunity to this newly imported pathogen (Tables Ag493–495).

Others pointed out that the arrival of Europeans also created massive cultural change, disrupted or destroyed food resources (Table Ag685), and proved to be a demographic disaster likely unprecedented in human history (Thornton 1987). The outcome of this catastrophe was the wholesale destruction of entire cultures throughout the Americas, shown in Table Ag1–16. Those tribes occupying what is now the eastern half of the United States were virtually annihilated in the eighteenth and nineteenth centuries.

The realization that Mooney had seriously underestimated the size of the North American Native population sparked a debate in the mid-1960s that has continued unresolved up to the present: how many people were present in North America when Columbus sailed into what is now known as the Caribbean Sea? There is no agreement about an exact number, and indeed it seems doubtful that one will ever be known, but it was probably at least 3 million,

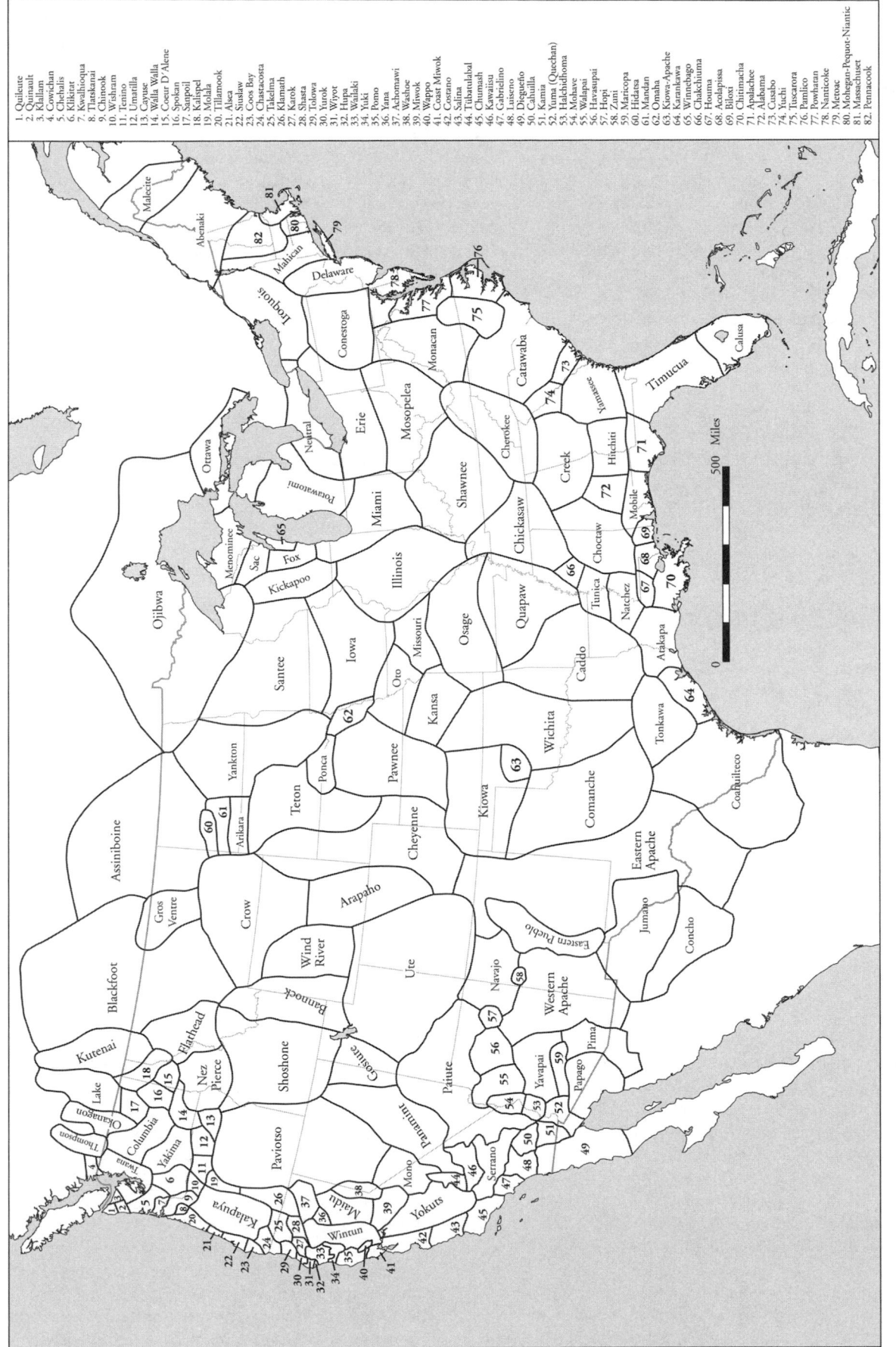

MAP Ag-A   American Indian tribes: circa 1600

Legend:

1. Quileute
2. Quinault
3. Klallam
4. Cowichan
5. Chehalis
6. Klikitar
7. Kwalhioqua
8. Tlatskanai
9. Chinook
10. Wishram
11. Tenino
12. Umatilla
13. Cayuse
14. Walla Walla
15. Coeur D'Alene
16. Spokan
17. Sanpoil
18. Kalispel
19. Molala
20. Tillamook
21. Alsea
22. Siuslaw
23. Coos Bay
24. Chastacosta
25. Takelma
26. Klamath
27. Karok
28. Shasta
29. Tolowa
30. Yurok
31. Wiyot
32. Hupa
33. Wailaki
34. Yuki
35. Pomo
36. Yana
37. Achomawi
38. Washoe
39. Miwok
40. Wappo
41. Coast Miwok
42. Costano
43. Salina
44. Tübatulabal
45. Chumash
46. Kawaiisu
47. Gabrielino
48. Luiseno
49. Degueño
50. Cahuilla
51. Kamia
52. Yuma (Quechan)
53. Halchidhoma
54. Mohave
55. Walapai
56. Havasupai
57. Hopi
58. Zuni
59. Maricopa
60. Hidatsa
61. Mandan
62. Omaha
63. Kiowa-Apache
64. Karankawa
65. Winnebago
66. Chakchiuma
67. Houma
68. Acolapissa
69. Biloxi
70. Chitimacha
71. Apalachee
72. Alabama
73. Cusabo
74. Yuchi
75. Tuscarora
76. Pamlico
77. Powhatan
78. Nanticoke
79. Metoac
80. Mohegan-Pequot-Niantic
81. Massachuset
82. Pennacook

Sources

C. Matthew Snipp, *American Indians: The First of This Land* (Russell Sage, 1989), Map 2.2, insert following p. 36. Adapted and corrected by Matthew Snipp from George Peter Murdock and Timothy J. O'Leary, *Ethnographic Bibliography of North America*, 4th edition (Human Relations Area Press, 1975). Also see Stephan Thernstrom, editor, *Harvard Encyclopedia of American Ethnic Groups* (Harvard University Press, 1980).

Documentation

These boundaries are in most cases approximate. The actual boundaries between tribes circa 1600 are only imperfectly known and even at the time were rarely sharp lines. Border regions often contained uninhabited "no-man's land." Murdock and O'Leary's work was based on and extends John Reed Swanton, *The Indian Tribes of North America*, Smithsonian Institution, Bureau of Ethnography, Bulletin 145 (U.S. Government Printing Office, 1952). The Smithsonian book was the culmination of nearly fifty years of work by anthropologists at the museum to systematically document the size and location of American Indians in the United States (the title is a misnomer) circa 1600.

perhaps 5–7 million, possibly (but unlikely) as many as 12 million or more. Most experts have given up trying to find a single number and have instead focused their attention on the processes that decimated the American Indian population from the time of European arrival to the late nineteenth century.

Population Statistics

Toward the end of the nineteenth century, it was widely believed that American Indians would become extinct, joining the buffalo and passenger pigeon as casualties of Western "progress." This expectation was, in fact, well grounded in empirical experience. The American Indian population had spiraled downward in size from the time that Europeans had first arrived. By 1890, barely 228,000 American Indians were alive (Thornton 1987). To observers, this small number coupled with past trends seemed to predestine American Indians for extinction. The American Indian population would dwindle and then disappear altogether sometime, possibly in the early years of the coming twentieth century.

Tables Ag265–492 and Ag700–703 show the size and distribution of the American Indian population since 1890. These tables make it abundantly clear that, contrary to most expectations, the American Indian population grew steadily throughout the twentieth century. From barely a quarter million at the beginning of the century, the American Indian population numbered nearly two million by the century's end. By 1990, the number of American Indians was greater than at any time in the preceding 150 years. A number of factors contributed to this remarkable comeback.

One factor is that by 1890, hostilities ceased between the United States and various Indian tribes. The twentieth century was a period in which American Indians were allowed to live relatively undisturbed, albeit in desperate poverty. Another factor is that public health measures and sanitation improved on reservations, as did access to health care provided by the IHS. The third factor is that American Indians adapted to the changing world around them, learning new skills and modifying their cultures to confront the new realities of living in an industrialized world.

For the first half of the twentieth century, population growth was relatively slow. In fact, there was a slight decline between 1910 and 1920, followed by another recovery in 1930. A massive influenza epidemic may account for this decline. However, there were also special reports for American Indians in the 1910 and 1930 Censuses, which may have led to better enumeration coverage in these years than in 1920.

The largest amount of growth in the American Indian population took place after 1950. In 1960, the Census Bureau altered its enumeration procedures and allowed respondents to report their race. In earlier censuses, it was the job of enumerators to observe and report the racial characteristics of a household. Undoubtedly, there were many American Indians whose race had been misclassified in earlier censuses. This change was a significant improvement over past practices.

In the decades after 1960, the American Indian population grew at a spectacular and unprecedented rate. Many factors contributed to this growth. Some of it is due to birth rates that are higher than death rates. However, most of this growth is attributable to persons who had been counted as white, black, or some other race in an earlier census switching their identity to American Indian in a subsequent census. Not much is known about "ethnic switching" behavior, but some of it may be due to declining levels of stigma attached to nonwhite racial ancestries and to the ethnic pride associated with being an American Indian.

In addition to the massive growth of the American Indian population, the other major development that took place during the twentieth century was the urbanization of American Indians. Historically, American Indians were moved to reservations and other places far from the mainstream of American society. In 1930, barely 10 percent of the American Indian population could be found in cities. At this time about half of all Americans lived in urban areas. However, by 1970 nearly half of the American Indian population was living in metropolitan locations.

There are many reasons why the American Indian population urbanized so rapidly. World War II was an important influence. After American Indians were discharged from military service, many settled in places like Los Angeles or New York. The GI Bill of Rights provided money for mortgages and college scholarships, and this induced many to leave their reservation homes, where they could find jobs and buy houses. The BIA also was an influence. Throughout the 1950s and 1960s, the BIA actively encouraged American Indians to move to cities by offering relocation assistance, job training, and other inducements. Finally, as all of America urbanized after World War II, American Indians also were not immune to the complex social conditions driving the growth of cities around the nation.

Health

The data in Tables Ag496–541 pertain to the mortality and morbidity of the American Indian population. These statistics are taken from regularly published series produced by the IHS. As noted, the IHS was placed under the administration of the PHS in 1955. The PHS has been credited with improving the quality of health care offered by the IHS. In particular, the PHS instituted policies and practices consistent with the standards of scientific medicine. Among those practices was the collection of statistical data to monitor the health status of American Indians. This resulted in a long series of statistical reports about American Indian health. Similarly, this is why almost no data exist for American Indian health in the years prior to 1955.

The IHS is not beyond reproach, but its existence certainly has coincided with major improvements in the health of American Indians. One important measure of these improvements can be seen in the numbers for infant mortality, shown in Table Ag496–497. Before the advent of the modern IHS, infant mortality was more than three times higher for American Indians than for other Americans. By 1960, infant mortality had declined by nearly 65 percent. However, it was still nearly twice as high as infant mortality in the rest of the nation. In subsequent years, American Indians have continued to lag behind the rest of the nation in terms of reducing infant mortality rates, but the gap has narrowed significantly.

The IHS cannot be credited with all of these improvements. Nevertheless, it undoubtedly played a role in uncoupling the historic and well-documented connection between socioeconomic status and infant mortality. American Indians have continued to be one of the poorest groups in American society, yet they have enjoyed unprecedented reductions in infant mortality. Other groups of poor Americans cannot report a parallel experience.

It is well known that infant survival rates can be improved with public health measures such as sanitation, safe drinking water, improved nutrition, prenatal care, and so forth. Other diseases are less amenable to this kind of intervention and this is reflected in the major causes of death for American Indians, shown in Table Ag498–538. Heart disease and accidents are the most typical causes of death for American Indians, as they are for other Americans. However, American Indians differ from the rest of American society in their susceptibility to diabetes and suicide-related deaths (Young 1994). In spite of these health problems, and higher than average mortality rates, American Indians have enjoyed significant improvements in their longevity and especially in their life expectancy at birth, shown in Table Ag539–541. Owing largely to improvements in infant survival rates, life expectancy at birth for American Indians has increased by nearly twenty years.

Labor

Increases in American Indian life expectancy also reflect gradual improvements in the material living conditions of American Indians. The statistics in Tables Ag726–1113 show the extent to which American Indians have become attached to and integrated into the national economy. For decades the federal government has enacted a variety of policies aimed at assimilating American Indians into the mainstream of American society – first through the adoption of Euro-American agriculture and later through urban relocation. For a variety of complicated reasons, these programs worked poorly, yielding few benefits and arguably doing more harm than good. As the data in these tables show, American Indians have not been fully embraced by the mainstream economy. Similarly, American Indians are among the poorest groups in American society.

These data reflect a long-standing deficit of human capital that is no doubt connected to the historic socioeconomic disadvantages that have plagued American Indians throughout the twentieth century. Although these data are fairly unambiguous about the disadvantaged position of American Indians, they are also somewhat difficult to interpret. This is because over time, definitions of labor force participation, and especially industrial and occupational classifications, have changed significantly. When examining these tables, readers should pay close attention to the table documentation indicating changes over time that would affect comparability.

One reason why American Indians are heavily disadvantaged in the labor market is their historic low levels of education. It is ironic that the federal government invested heavily in education for American Indians during the latter part of the nineteenth century and in the early years of the twentieth century. However, education was offered mainly in the confines of boarding schools, with curriculums designed less for education and much more for cultural indoctrination. Education was an instrument of cultural repression and a means of persecuting the personal identities of schoolchildren. Ultimately, the experiences of these children with federal boarding schools evolved into lasting misgivings about the value of education that persists into the present in some communities. Table Ag915–1097 shows that school attendance was a common experience for most children in most parts of the country. However, it continues to be the case that American Indians are one of the least educated groups in modern society.

Low levels of schooling have not been an insurmountable barrier to employment for American Indians. Limited schooling notwithstanding, it might be a surprise to some that American Indians, even in the early decades of this century, were accustomed to working for a living. This is perhaps contrary to the popular stereotypes of American Indians as hunters and gatherers. However, by the twentieth century, the reservation system was well established and American Indians were more or less regular participants in the cash economy of the United States. Between 1900 and 1930, 60–65 percent of American Indian men were "gainfully employed."

The special report published by the Census Bureau in 1915 suggests that in the 1910 Census the true number of gainfully employed American Indians was smaller than reported, but it offers no clear explanation why this should be the case. Overstated or not, it is doubtful that these workers were paid much for their labor. There is very little information published before 1970 about the monetary incomes American Indians received. So, unfortunately, we can only speculate about how much or how little American Indians actually earned.

Nevertheless, agricultural labor provided many jobs for American Indians, especially before the introduction of mechanized farming. For example, in the early decades of the twentieth century, about two thirds of American Indian men were employed in agriculture, either as farmers or as laborers. By 1990, this figure was about 10 percent. There can be little doubt that the slow decline of agriculture in the American economy, and the rise of mechanized farming, contribute to the extraordinarily high levels of unemployment that plague reservations.

Natural Resources

The economic hardships many American Indians face today are ironic considering that American Indians once claimed possession of all of the territory that is now the United States. In the wake of a long, complex history, by the late twentieth century American Indians possessed a little over 45 million acres of land. The title to this land is held in trust by the federal government, under the administration of the BIA (see Tables Ag547–684). The amount of land owned by American Indians reached a low point in the early 1930s, about 33 million acres. Since then, tribes have used land claims, court cases (see Table Ag544–546), and in some instances purchases in the open market to increase their holdings.

Land ownership is especially complicated for American Indians. Some land is held in trust by the federal government and collectively owned by the membership of a federally recognized tribe. In the late nineteenth century, the federal government assigned ("allotted") reservation lands to individuals and families. A great deal of this land passed into the private market, but land that was not sold is also held in trust. In some cases this land was not sold into the private market because the individuals or families who owned it did not want it sold. In other cases, this land cannot be sold because of unresolved heirship claims. Finally, on many if not most reservations, there is some amount of privately owned land often described as "fee land," an abbreviated term for fee simple title. This is privately owned land that may or may not belong to American Indians. The federal government does not monitor or have responsibility for this land, so statistics about it are not readily available.

Reservations are extremely varied in size, geography, location, and the resources found on them. Some reservations are blessed with an abundance of natural resources. Others are arid, barren places. Farmland, water, fisheries, timber, and minerals are among the natural resources reservations possess. Few, if any, can claim an abundance of all of these resources; most have some of these commodities, and a sizable number have virtually nothing because their reservation is too small or is in a barren location. Map Ag-B shows the present-day location of these reservations.

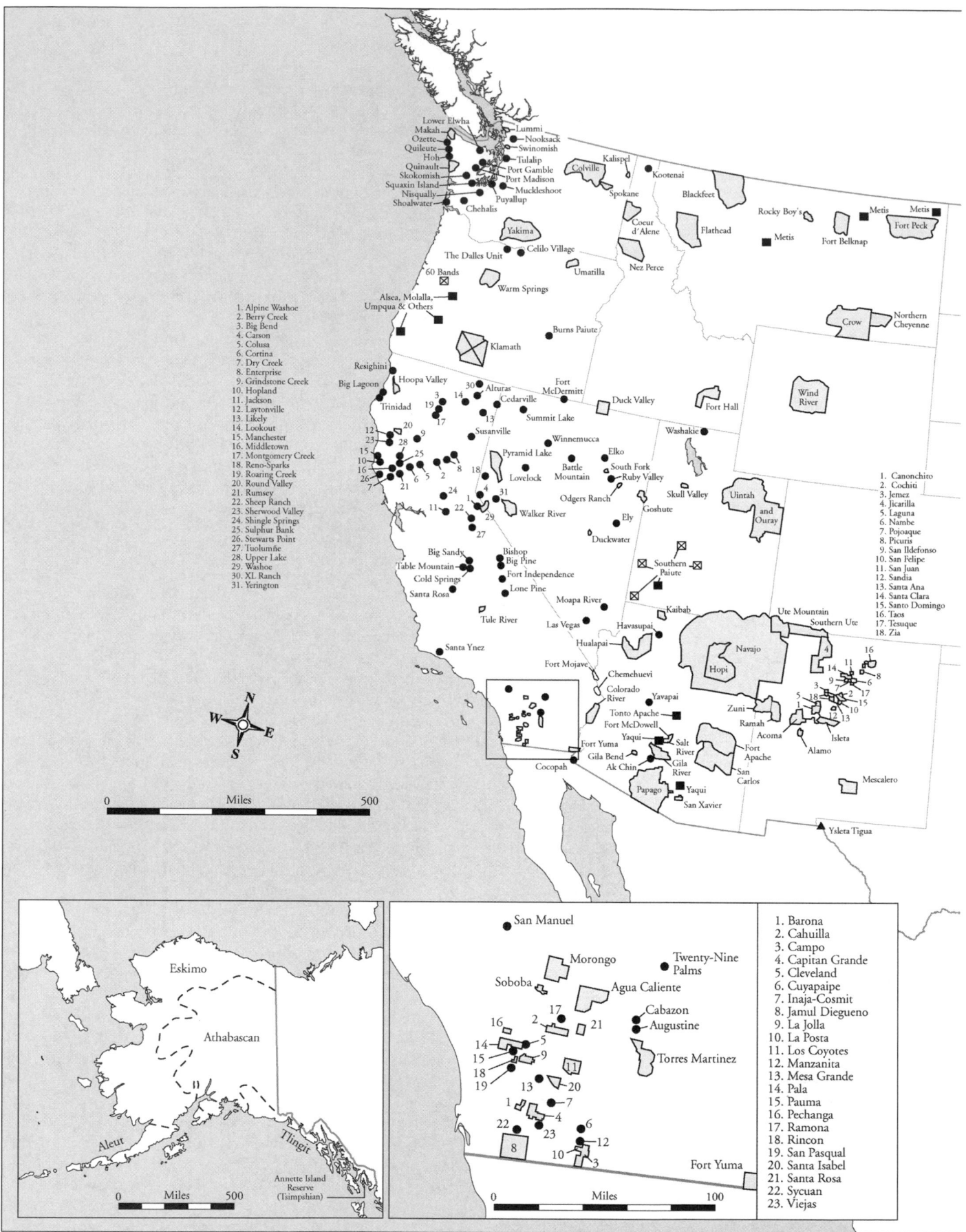

MAP Ag-B   Indian lands and communities: 1995

Source

C. Matthew Snipp, *American Indians: The First of This Land* (Russell Sage, 1989), Map 3.2, insert following p. 36, using unpublished information supplied by the Council of Energy Resource Tribes, with subsequent corrections and updates based on Veronica E. Velarde Tiller, *American Indian Reservations and Indian Trust Areas* (U.S. Economic Development Administration, October 1995). For

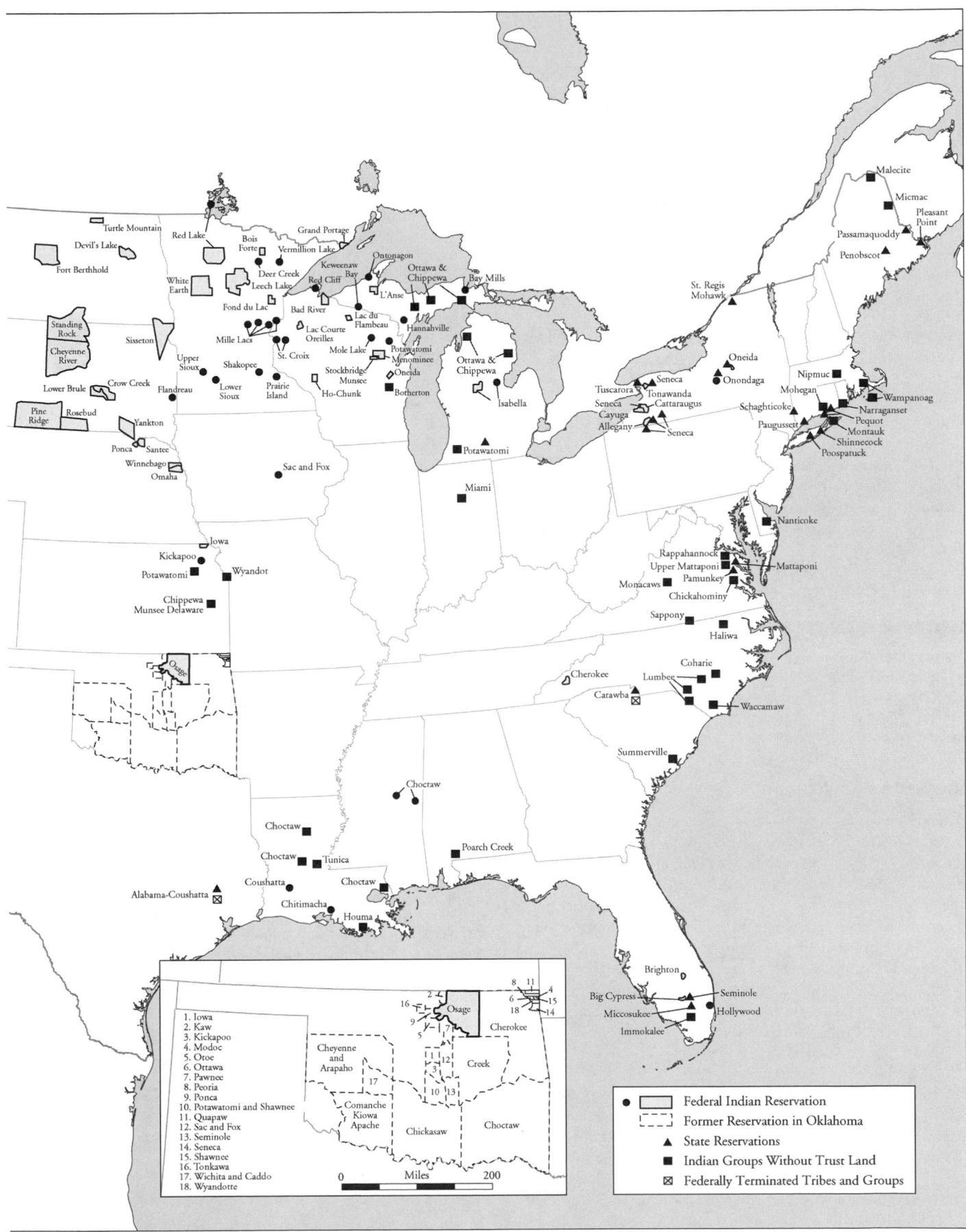

Turtle Mountain
Devil's Lake
Fort Berthhold
Red Lake
Bois Forte
Grand Portage
Vermillion Lake
White Earth
Deer Creek
Leech Lake
Ontonagon
Keweenaw Bay
Red Cliff
Ottawa & Chippewa
Bay Mills
Fond du Lac
Bad River
L'Anse
Standing Rock
Cheyenne River
Sisseton
Mille Lacs
Lac Courte Oreilles
Lac du Flambeau
Hannahville
Ottawa & Chippewa
Upper Sioux
Shakopee
St. Croix
Mole Lake
Potawatomi
Menominee
Lower Brule
Crow Creek
Flandreau
Lower Sioux
Prairie Island
Stockbridge Munsee
Ho-Chunk
Oneida
Botherton
Isabella
Pine Ridge
Rosebud
Yankton
Ponca
Santee
Winnebago
Omaha
Sac and Fox
Potawatomi
Miami
Iowa
Kickapoo
Potawatomi
Wyandot
Chippewa Munsee Delaware
Osage

Malecite
Micmac
Pleasant Point
Passamaquoddy
Penobscot
St. Regis Mohawk
Tuscarora
Seneca
Tonawanda
Cattaraugus
Seneca
Cayuga
Allegany
Seneca
Oneida
Onondaga
Nipmuc
Mohegan
Wampanoag
Schaghticoke
Paugussett
Narraganset
Pequot
Montauk
Shinnecock
Poospatuck
Nanticoke
Rappahannock
Upper Mattaponi
Pamunkey
Monacaws
Chickahominy
Mattaponi
Sappony
Haliwa
Cherokee
Coharie
Catawba
Lumbee
Waccamaw
Summerville
Choctaw
Choctaw
Poarch Creek
Choctaw
Tunica
Coushatta
Alabama-Coushatta
Choctaw
Chitimacha
Houma
Brighton
Seminole
Big Cypress
Miccosukee
Hollywood
Immokalee

Cheyenne and Arapaho
Comanche Kiowa Apache
Osage
Cherokee
Creek
Chickasaw
Choctaw
Seminole

1. Iowa
2. Kaw
3. Kickapoo
4. Modoc
5. Otoe
6. Ottawa
7. Pawnee
8. Peoria
9. Ponca
10. Potawatomi and Shawnee
11. Quapaw
12. Sac and Fox
13. Seminole
14. Seneca
15. Shawnee
16. Tonkawa
17. Wichita and Caddo
18. Wyandotte

0   Miles   200

● ▭ Federal Indian Reservation
▯ Former Reservation in Oklahoma
▲ State Reservations
■ Indian Groups Without Trust Land
⊠ Federally Terminated Tribes and Groups

the spelling of tribal names see U.S. Census Bureau, Census 2000 Summary File 1, at the Census Internet site.

Documentation

Alaska has more than 200 Native communities. Shown here are only the general locations of the Eskimos, the Aleuts, and the Athabascan and Tlingit Indians. There are also many small groups in the contiguous forty-eight states that are not shown. Oklahoma, in particular, has many small communities that are remnants of former reservations.

The BIA is responsible for managing, or helping manage, the natural resources on reservation lands. It is responsible, for example, for overseeing leases of timber lands and oil or natural gas reserves. It is required to enforce the terms of lease agreements and to ensure that market prices are being paid for these resources. Over the years the BIA has been harshly criticized for being inept and occasionally fraudulent in the management of these leases. Increasingly, these arrangements are being handled by the tribes themselves, with the assistance of BIA staff. However, a class action suit filed in 1997 as *Cobell v. Babbitt* and subsequently as *Cobell v. Norton* has accused the BIA and the Department of the Interior of gross negligence in the management of hundreds of millions, possibly billions, of dollars belonging to more than 500,000 American Indians. The department's inability to rectify this situation has led the federal judge hearing this case, Royce C. Lamberth, to find Secretaries of the Interior Bruce Babbitt (Clinton administration) and Gale Norton (George W. Bush administration) guilty of fraud and litigation misconduct, and to cite them for civil contempt in September 2002.

Timber and mineral resources are two especially valuable resources found on reservations. According to one source, reservations in the 1970s possessed 40 percent of all uranium and 30 percent of all strippable coal (Jorgensen, Clemmer, et al. 1978). Tables Ag686–694 show the economic value of these resources. Despite the seemingly large value of these commodities, it is not true that they have made American Indians wealthy. On the contrary, even tribes with relatively large amounts of these resources remain relatively poor. One possible reason is that the cost of managing these leases is relatively high, diluting the funds actually received by tribes. Another more plausible reason is that on a per capita basis, they do not represent vast amounts of money. Indeed, there are many explanations for the persistent poverty of reservations.

Government Relations

In addition to managing the land and natural resources, the BIA is responsible for a variety of other obligations involving American Indians. And the BIA is not the only federal agency with a special interest in American Indians. The federal government has, in recent years, affirmed its commitment to conducting what amounts to a "government-to-government" relationship with federally recognized tribes – under the rubric of self-determination. In practice, this means that the federal government acknowledges the limited rights of self-government granted by the legal doctrine of tribal sovereignty. Prior to the inception of this doctrine in the early 1970s, the federal government was involved in the everyday lives of American Indians in almost every conceivable way, ranging from child rearing to road maintenance.

Tables Ag542–543, Ag695–699, Ag704–717, and Ag721–725 touch upon several different domains in which there has been an historic connection between American Indians and the federal government. First and foremost, American Indians were the original occupants of North America. In the early years of the United States, the federal government sought to purchase land (see Table Ag542–543) for settlement before adopting a much more aggressive (and hostile) program under the guise of "manifest destiny." Ultimately, this policy led to the creation of the reservation system, under the administration of the BIA (see Tables Ag695–699 and Ag721).

As mentioned, it was widely believed that American Indians would eventually disappear from American society and the so-called Indian problem would simply take care of itself by vanishing from sight. This belief persisted into the early years of the twentieth century, and it would cause the noted anthropologist Evon Vogt (1957, p. 137) to observe, "By the mid-twentieth century, it has become apparent to social scientists studying the American Indian . . . [the population] is markedly increasing and . . . the rate of basic acculturation to white American ways of life is incredibly slower than our earlier assumptions led us to believe."

By midcentury, the tenacity of American Indians made it obvious to most observers that the "Indian problem" was not going to solve itself. In response, shortly after World War II, the federal government initiated a policy known as "termination and relocation" that was intended to unilaterally dissolve reservation boundaries. In doing so, it would end the historic relationship that it had established with American Indians throughout U.S. history. This policy was enacted over the vigorous objections of American Indians and their supporters. It was finally reversed by the policy of self-determination articulated by the Nixon administration in 1970. In the years after 1970, beginning with the Menominee reservation in Wisconsin, terminated reservations slowly regained their federal recognition (see Table Ag722–725).

Today, Public Law 93-638, also known as the American Indian Self-Determination and Education Assistance Act, mandates federal authorities to work closely with tribal leaders in making decisions that affect Indian communities. This law affects a wide range of issues, including law enforcement, conservation, and social services. Initially, it did not include the IHS but it was subsequently amended to include these services. As the population of persons receiving health care has increased in recent years (see Table Ag704–717), the number of tribally operated clinics funded by the IHS has also grown.

Conclusion

The ancestors of today's American Indians reached North America sometime around 15,000 to 25,000 years ago. Experts disagree about this date, but there can be no disagreement that the descendants of these people continue to be a vital and dynamic part of modern American society. Once the "Vanishing American," today's American Indian population is larger and more heterogeneous than at any time in the past.

It is fitting that American Indians are represented in a document devoted to statistics for the United States. American Indians have been an enduring presence in American society, predating the founding of this nation. Historical documents bridge the past with the future. And just as American Indians have been an integral part of this nation's past, it seems certain that they will also be a part of its future.

References

Anderson, Margo J. 1988. *The American Census: A Social History*. Yale University Press.

Crieco, Elizabeth M., and Rachel C. Cassidy. 2000. "Overview of Race and Hispanic Origin, 2000." U.S. Census Bureau, Census 2000 Brief, C2KBR/01-1.

Jorgensen, Joseph G., Richard O. Clemmer, et al. 1978. *Native Americans and Energy Development*. Anthropology Resource Center.

Reddy, Marlita A., editor. 1995. *Statistical Record of Native North Americans.* 2nd edition. Gale Research.

Snipp, C. Matthew. 1989. *American Indians: The First of This Land.* Russell Sage.

Stuart, Paul. 1987. *Nations within a Nation: Historical Statistics of American Indians.* Greenwood Press.

Taylor, Theodore W. 1984. *The Bureau of Indian Affairs.* Westview Press.

Thornton, Russell. 1987. *American Indian Holocaust and Survival.* University of Oklahoma Press.

Vogt, Evon Z. 1957. "The Acculturation of American Indians." *Annals* 311: 137–46.

Young, T. Kue. 1994. *The Health of Native Americans: Towards a Biocultural Epidemiology.* Oxford University Press.

POPULATION AND TRIBES

C. Matthew Snipp

TABLE Ag1–16   American Indian population – number of tribes, average size, and number extinct, by region: 1600–1990

Contributed by C. Matthew Snipp

	Characteristics at European contact				Characteristics in 1907			
			Tribes		Population		Tribes	
	Year of contact	Population	Number	Mean population	Number	As a percent of year-of-contact population	Number	Mean population
	Ag1	Ag2	Ag3	Ag4	Ag5	Ag6	Ag7	Ag8
Region	Year	Number	Number	Number	Number	Percent	Number	Number
U.S.	—	952,000	367	—	313,918	33.0	269	—
North Atlantic	1600	55,600	24	2,317	21,900	39.4	10	2,190
South Atlantic	1600	52,200	35	1,491	2,170	4.2	15	145
Gulf States	1650	114,400	39	2,933	62,700	54.8	12	5,225
Central States	1650	75,300	12	6,275	46,126	61.3	10	4,613
Northern Plains	1780	100,800	20	5,040	50,477	50.1	19	2,657
Southern Plains	1690	41,000	12	3,417	2,861	7.0	7	409
Columbia Region	1780	88,800	95	935	15,261	17.4	83	211
Central Mountains	1845	19,300	6	3,217	11,544	59.8	6	1,924
New Mexico and Arizona	1680	72,000	25	2,880	53,772	74.8	19	2,833
California	1769	260,000	45	5,778	18,797	7.2	36	696
Alaska	1740	72,600	54	1,344	28,310	39.0	52	544

	Characteristics in 1907			Characteristics in 1990				
	Tribes			Population		Tribes		
	Number extinct	Number near extinction	Percent extinct or near extinction	Number	As a percent of year-of-contact population	Number	Mean population	Number without report
	Ag9	Ag10	Ag11	Ag12	Ag13	Ag14	Ag15	Ag16
Region	Number	Number	Percent	Number	Percent	Number	Number	Number
U.S.	98	76	—	1,628,502	171.1	142	—	225
North Atlantic	14	6	83.3	72,433	130.3	10	7,243	14
South Atlantic	20	14	97.1	8,461	16.2	7	1,209	28
Gulf States	27	4	79.5	548,728	479.7	11	49,884	28
Central States	2	1	25.0	156,932	208.4	8	19,617	4
Northern Plains	1	1	10.0	217,183	215.5	16	13,574	4
Southern Plains	5	0	41.7	20,157	49.2	6	3,360	6
Columbia Region	12	40	54.7	60,145	67.7	31	1,940	64
Central Mountains	0	0	0.0	32,959	170.8	6	5,493	0
New Mexico and Arizona	6	1	28.0	358,049	497.3	19	18,845	6
California	9	9	40.0	43,891	16.9	24	1,829	21
Alaska	2	0	4.0	109,564	150.9	4	27,391	50

Source

Russell Thornton, *We Shall Live Again: The 1870 and 1890 Ghost Dance Movements as Demographic Revitalization* (Cambridge University Press, 1986), Table 4.1, p. 22; U.S. Bureau of the Census, *Characteristics of American Indians by Tribe and Language, 1990*, CP-3-7 (1994), Table 1.

Documentation

Thornton constructed this table from Mooney's 1928 publication (see Table Ag17–129) and two other anthropological publications. There seems to be a perpetual dispute among historical demographers about the robustness of these numbers, and indeed their relative magnitude. Although not exact, they are probably indicative of the relative magnitudes of the populations they purport to measure.

Thornton appears to have classified as "nearly extinct" any group numbering 100 or less, consisting mostly of mixed-race persons.

TABLE Ag17–129   Estimated population of American Indians, by region, state, and tribe: 1600–1990
[Atlantic, Gulf, and Central States]
Contributed by C. Matthew Snipp

					North Atlantic					
					New England					
Year	Total	Total	Abenaki (including Passamaquoddy)	Pennacook	Massachuset	Nipmuc	Pocomtuc	Wampanoag	Nauset	Nantucket
	Ag17	Ag18	Ag19	Ag20	Ag21	Ag22	Ag23	Ag24	Ag25	Ag26
	Number	Number	Number	Number	Number	Number	Number	Number	Number	Number
1600	55,600	25,100	3,000	2,000	3,000	500	1,200	2,400	1,200	1,500
1650	—	—	—	—	—	—	—	—	—	—
1907	21,900	1,630	1,400	0	0	0	0	0	50	0
1990	72,433	11,022	4,015	—	—	434	—	2,334	—	—

					North Atlantic					
					New England					
Year	Martha's Vineyard	Narraganset and Eastern Niantic	Pequot	Mohegan	Western Niantic	Podunk	Quinnipiac	Paugussett and Wepawaug	Tunxis	Wengunk
	Ag27	Ag28	Ag29	Ag30	Ag31	Ag32	Ag33	Ag34	Ag35	Ag36
	Number	Number	Number	Number	Number	Number	Number	Number	Number	Number
1600	1,500	4,000	2,200	600	250	300	250	400	400	400
1650	—	—	—	—	—	—	—	—	—	—
1907	50	30	25	75	0	0	0	0	0	0
1990	—	2,564	679	996	—	—	—	—	—	—

		North Atlantic							South Atlantic		
		New York				New Jersey and Pennsylvania			Maryland and Delaware		
Year	Total	Iroquois (excluding Tuscarora)	Mahican	Wappinger	Metoac	Total	Delaware and Munsee	Conestoga	Total	Total	Conoy, Piscataway, and Patuxent
	Ag37	Ag38	Ag39	Ag40	Ag41	Ag42	Ag43	Ag44	Ag45	Ag46	Ag47
	Number	Number	Number	Number	Number	Number	Number	Number	Number	Number	Number
1600	17,500	5,500	3,000	3,000	6,000	13,000	8,000	5,000	51,500	4,700	2,000
1650	—	—	—	—	—	—	—	—	—	—	—
1907	18,420	17,630	760	0	30	1,850	1,850	0	2,170	100	0
1990	51,611	49,312	2,219	—	80	9,800	9,800	—	8,461	2,391	824

					South Atlantic					
	Maryland and Delaware			Virginia						
Year	Tocwogh and Ozinies	Nanticoke	Wicomico	Total	Powhatan	Monacan	Manahoac	Nottoway	Occaneechi	Meherrin
	Ag48	Ag49	Ag50	Ag51	Ag52	Ag53	Ag54	Ag55	Ag56	Ag57
	Number	Number	Number	Number	Number	Number	Number	Number	Number	Number
1600	700	1,600	400	14,400	9,000	1,200	1,500	1,500	1,200	700
1650	—	—	—	—	—	—	—	—	—	—
1907	0	80	20	500	500	0	0	0	0	0
1990	—	1,529	38	795	795	—	—	—	—	—

(continued)

Table Ag17–129   Estimated population of American Indians, by region, state, and tribe: 1600–1990
[Atlantic, Gulf, and Central States]   *Continued*

		South Atlantic									
		North Carolina									
	Total	Yeopim and Pasquotank	Chowanoc	Machapunga	Pamptico and Bear River	Neus and Corree	Tuscarora	Woccon	Sara	Keyaunee	Eno, Shoccoree, and Adshusheer
	Ag58	Ag59	Ag60	Ag61	Ag62	Ag63	Ag64	Ag65	Ag66	Ag67	Ag68
Year	Number	Number	Number	Number	Number	Number	Number	Number	Number	Number	Number
1600	17,300	800	1,500	1,200	1,000	1,000	5,000	600	1,200	500	1,500
1650	—	—	—	—	—	—	—	—	—	—	—
1907	1,280	0	80	0	0	0	700	0	0	500 [1]	0 [1]
1990	3,245	—	—	—	—	—	3,245	—	—	—	—

	South Atlantic									
	North Carolina			South Carolina						
	Sissiphaw	Cape Fear	Waxhaw and Sugaree	Total	Catawba	Pedee	Waccamaw, Winya, and Hook	Sewee	Santee	Congaree
	Ag69	Ag70	Ag71	Ag72	Ag73	Ag74	Ag75	Ag76	Ag77	Ag78
Year	Number	Number	Number	Number	Number	Number	Number	Number	Number	Number
1600	800	1,000	1,200	15,100	5,000	600	900	800	1,000	800
1650	—	—	—	—	—	—	—	—	—	—
1907	0 [1]	0 [1]	0 [1]	290	90	200 [2]	0 [2]	0 [2]	0 [2]	0
1990	—	—	—	2,030	964	—	1,066	—	—	—

	South Atlantic						Gulf States			
	South Carolina						Georgia, Alabama, and Tennessee			
	Wateree	Etiwaw	Edisto	Westo and Stono	Cusso	Cusabo	Total	Total	Cherokee	Yuchi
	Ag79	Ag80	Ag81	Ag82	Ag83	Ag84	Ag85	Ag86	Ag87	Ag88
Year	Number	Number	Number	Number	Number	Number	Number	Number	Number	Number
1600	1,000	600	1,000	1,600	600	1,200	—	—	—	—
1650	—	—	—	—	—	—	114,100	45,500	22,000	1,500
1907	0	0	0	0	0	0	62,700	38,900	25,000	700
1990	—	—	—	—	—	—	548,728	430,851	369,035	380

	Gulf States										
	Georgia, Alabama, and Tennessee			Florida							
	Creek and Seminole	Yamassee	Mobile and Tohome	Total	Apalachee	Potano	Yustaga	Timucua	Tocobaga	Caloosa	Ais and Tagesta
	Ag89	Ag90	Ag91	Ag92	Ag93	Ag94	Ag95	Ag96	Ag97	Ag98	Ag99
Year	Number	Number	Number	Number	Number	Number	Number	Number	Number	Number	Number
1600	—	—	—	—	—	—	—	—	—	—	—
1650	18,000	2,000	2,000	24,000	7,000	3,000	1,000	8,000	1,000	3,000	1,000
1907	13,200	0	0	0	0	0	0	0	0	0	0
1990	61,436	—	—	0	—	—	—	—	—	—	—

Notes appear at end of table

Table Ag17–129   Estimated population of American Indians, by region, state, and tribe: 1600–1990
[Atlantic, Gulf, and Central States]   *Continued*

	Gulf States							Arkansas	
	Mississippi								
Year	Total	Chickasaw	Choctaw	Natchez	Tunica, Yazoo, Koroa, and Ofogoula	Chachiuma, Ibitoupa, Toposa, and Tiou	Biloxi, Pascagoula, and Moctobi	Total	Quapaw
	Ag100	Ag101	Ag102	Ag103	Ag104	Ag105	Ag106	Ag107	Ag108
	Number	Number	Number	Number	Number	Number	Number	Number	Number
1600	—	—	—	—	—	—	—	—	—
1650	31,700	8,000	15,000	4,500	2,000	1,200	1,000	2,500	2,500
1907	23,075	5,000	18,000	25	50	0	0	290	290
1990	108,005	21,522	86,231	70	44	—	138	1,438	1,438

	Gulf States								Central States	
	Louisiana									
Year	Total	Houma	Chitimacha	Atakapa	Acolapissa	Bayogoula, Mugulasha, and Quinipissa	Chawasha, Washa, and Opelousa	Taensa	Total	Erie
	Ag109	Ag110	Ag111	Ag112	Ag113	Ag114	Ag115	Ag116	Ag117	Ag118
	Number	Number	Number	Number	Number	Number	Number	Number	Number	Number
1600	—	—	—	—	—	—	—	—	—	—
1650	10,400	1,000	3,000	1,500	1,500	1,500	1,400	500	75,300	4,000
1907	435	350	60	25	0	0	0	0	46,126	0
1990	8,434	7,809	625	—	—	—	—	—	156,932	—

	Central States										
Year	Fox	Illinois	Kickapoo	Mascouten	Menominee	Miami	Ojibwa	Potawatomi	Sauk	Shawnee	Winnebago
	Ag119	Ag120	Ag121	Ag122	Ag123	Ag124	Ag125	Ag126	Ag127	Ag128	Ag129
	Number	Number	Number	Number	Number	Number	Number	Number	Number	Number	Number
1600	—	—	—	—	—	—	—	—	—	—	—
1650	3,000	8,000	2,000	1,500	3,000	4,500	35,000	4,000	3,500	3,000	3,800
1907	345	50	830	0	1,375	530	36,000	2,555	608	1,500	2,333
1990	—	—	3,576	—	8,064	4,580	105,988	16,719	4,774	6,640	6,591

[1]   Population given for the Keyaunee tribe also includes the Eno, Shoccoree, Adshusheer, Sissiphaw, Cape Fear, Waxhaw, and Sugaree tribes.

[2]   Population given for the Pedee tribe also includes the Waccamaw, Winya, Hook, Sewee, and Santee tribes.

Sources

James Mooney, *The Aboriginal Population of America North of Mexico,* Smithsonian Miscellaneous Collections, volume 80, number 7 (Smithsonian Institution, 1928); U.S. Bureau of the Census, *Characteristics of American Indians by Tribe and Language, 1990,* CP-3-7 (1994), Table 1.

Documentation

The early numbers are estimates produced by the noted Smithsonian Institution anthropologist James Mooney. Mooney was the first to attempt to produce comprehensive estimates for the American Indian population at contact. He produced them by inspecting a variety of sources, mostly documentary material, and by "dead reckoning" estimated the likely population size. The accuracy of these figures has been the subject of much controversy over the last seventy years, but they are nonetheless still the most complete set of figures available. In any event, they have historic merit above and beyond their accuracy as statistical data.

A value of zero indicates that the tribe was believed to be extinct at the time of the enumeration. In some cases, however, tribes believed to be extinct were subsequently identified in later enumerations.

Series Ag117–129. Central States include Minnesota, Iowa, Wisconsin, Illinois, Missouri, Indiana, Ohio, Michigan, and Western Kentucky.

Table Ag130–264   Estimated population of American Indians, by region, state, and tribe: 1680–1990   [Plains and Pacific States]
Contributed by C. Matthew Snipp

Northern Plains

	Total	Arapaho	Arikara	Assiniboin	Atsina	Blackfoot	Cheyenne	Crow	Hidatsa	Iowa	Kansa	Kiowa	Kiowa-Apache	Mandan	Missouri
	Ag130	Ag131	Ag132	Ag133	Ag134	Ag135	Ag136	Ag137	Ag138	Ag139	Ag140	Ag141	Ag142	Ag143	Ag144
Year	Number	Number	Number	Number	Number	Number	Number	Number	Number	Number	Number	Number	Number	Number	Number
1680	—	—	—	—	—	—	—	—	—	—	—	—	—	—	—
1690	—	—	—	—	—	—	—	—	—	—	—	—	—	—	—
1740	—	—	—	—	—	—	—	—	—	—	—	—	—	—	—
1769	—	—	—	—	—	—	—	—	—	—	—	—	—	—	—
1780	112,845	3,000	3,000	10,000	15,000	15,000	3,500	4,000	2,500	1,200	3,000	2,000	300	3,600	1,000
1845	—	—	—	—	—	—	—	—	—	—	—	—	—	—	—
1907	50,477	1,774	389	2,080	553	4,560	3,351	1,787	468	339	196	1,220	156	263	0
1990	217,183	6,918	1,671	5,521	—	37,992	11,809	9,394	1,539	1,555	—	9,460	—	1,273	—

Northern Plains

	Omaha	Osage	Oto	Pawnee	Panca	Sioux
	Ag145	Ag146	Ag147	Ag148	Ag149	Ag150
Year	Number	Number	Number	Number	Number	Number
1680	—	—	—	—	—	—
1690	—	—	—	—	—	—
1740	—	—	—	—	—	—
1769	—	—	—	—	—	—
1780	2,800	6,200	900	10,000	845	25,000
1845	—	—	—	—	—	—
1907	1,246	2,156	390	644	845	28,060
1990	4,363	10,430	1,762	3,387	2,788	107,321

Southern Plains

	Total	Akokisa	Aranama	Bidai	Caddo including Hasanai	Comanche	Karankawa	Kichai	Lipan
	Ag151	Ag152	Ag153	Ag154	Ag155	Ag156	Ag157	Ag158	Ag159
Year	Number	Number	Number	Number	Number	Number	Number	Number	Number
1680	—	—	—	—	—	—	—	—	—
1690	41,000	500	200	500	8,500	7,000	2,800	500	500
1740	—	—	—	—	—	—	—	—	—
1769	—	—	—	—	—	—	—	—	—
1780	—	—	—	—	—	—	—	—	—
1845	2,861	0	0	0	555	1,430	0	30	25
1907	—	—	—	—	—	—	—	—	—
1990	20,157	—	—	—	2,984	11,437	—	—	30

Columbia Region

Year	Mescalero Ag160 Number	Coahuiltecan Ag161 Number	Tonkawa Ag162 Number	Wichita Ag163 Number	Total Ag164 Number	Total Ag165 Number	Makah Ag166 Number	Chimakum Ag167 Number	Quileute and Hoh Ag168 Number	Klallam Ag169 Number	Quinault and Quaitso Ag170 Number	Chehalis and Cowlitz, including Humptulip Ag171 Number	Lummi, Samish, and Nooksak Ag172 Number	Skagit and Swinomish Ag173 Number	Snohomish, Snoqualmu, and Tulalip Ag174 Number
	Southern Plains				Western Washington										
1680	—	—	—	3,200	—	—	—	—	—	—	—	—	—	—	—
1690	700	15,000	1,600	—	—	—	—	—	—	—	—	—	—	—	—
1740	—	—	—	—	—	—	—	—	—	—	—	—	—	—	—
1769	—	—	—	—	—	—	—	—	—	—	—	—	—	—	—
1780	—	—	—	—	86,100	22,750	2,000	400	500	2,000	1,500	1,000	1,000	1,200	1,200
1845	—	—	—	—	15,261	3,943									
1907	466	0	45	310			438	0	295	327	196	170	614	273	200
1990	4,144	—	321	1,241	60,145	20,446	1,661	14	723	1,522	2,513	1,118	4,240	1,139	3,113

Columbia Region

Year	Suquamish and Dwamish Ag175 Number	Nisqually and Puyallup Ag176 Number	Skokomish, Toanho, and Squaxon Ag177 Number	Echeloot Ag178 Number	Chiluktkwa and Smackshop Ag179 Number	Shoto Ag180 Number	Quathlapotle Ag181 Number	Callamaks Ag182 Number	Wahkiakum Ag183 Number	Chinook Ag184 Number	Killaxthokle Ag185 Number	Kwalhioqua Ag186 Number	Klikitat and Taitinapam Ag187 Number	Total Ag188 Number	Lake Ag189 Number
	Western Washington												Eastern Washington		
1680	—	—	—	—	—	—	—	—	—	—	—	—	—	—	—
1690	—	—	—	—	—	—	—	—	—	—	—	—	—	—	—
1740	—	—	—	—	—	—	—	—	—	—	—	—	—	—	—
1769	—	—	—	—	—	—	—	—	—	—	—	—	—	—	—
1780	1,200	1,200	1,000	1,500	3,000	600	1,300	250	300	600	200	200	600	17,500	500
1845	—	—	—	—	—	—	—	—	—	—	—	—	—	—	—
1907	210	780	290	150[1]	0[1]	0[1]	0[1]	0[1]	0[1]	0[1]	0[1]	0	0	4,403	268
1990	850	1,449	1,226	—	—	—	—	—	—	878	—	—	—	16,856	—

Notes appear at end of table

(continued)

Table Ag130–264   Estimated population of American Indians, by region, state, and tribe: 1680–1990   [Plains and Pacific States]   *Continued*

Columbia Region

	Eastern Washington												Western Montana and Northern Idaho			
	Colville	Sanpoil	Spokan	Okinagan	Methow and Isle de Pierre	Piskwau	Palus	Wanapum	Channapum	Yakima	Tapanash and Atanum	Total	Salish or Flathead	Kalispel or Pend d'Oreille	Skitswish or Coeur d'Alene	Nez Perce
Year	Ag190	Ag191	Ag192	Ag193	Ag194	Ag195	Ag196	Ag197	Ag198	Ag199	Ag200	Ag201	Ag202	Ag203	Ag204	Ag205
	Number	Number	Number	Number	Number	Number	Number	Number	Number	Number	Number	Number	Number	Number	Number	Number
1680	—	—	—	—	—	—	—	—	—	—	—	—	—	—	—	—
1690	—	—	—	—	—	—	—	—	—	—	—	—	—	—	—	—
1740	—	—	—	—	—	—	—	—	—	—	—	—	—	—	—	—
1769	—	—	—	—	—	—	—	—	—	—	—	—	—	—	—	—
1780	1,000	—	1,400	1,000	800	1,400	1,800	1,800	1,800	3,000	2,200	6,800	600	1,200	1,000	4,000
1845	—	—	—	—	—	—	—	—	—	—	—	—	—	—	—	—
1907	334	358	769	348	324	2,002 [2]	0 [2]	0 [2]	0 [2]	0 [2]	0 [2]	3,635	623	943	506	1,563
1990	7,057	—	2,042	—	—	—	—	—	—	7,757	—	12,358	7,123	175	1,057	4,003

Columbia Region

Western Oregon

| | Total | Skilloot | Clatsop | Cathlamet | Wappatoo | Clackamas | Charcowa | Cushook | Shahala, Wasco, Tillamook, Nestuca, Salmon River, and Siletz | Tlatskanai | Luckton, Yaquina, Alsea, and Siuslaw | Coos, Mulluk (lower Coquille) | Takelma and Latgawa | Chocreleatan (upper Coquille), Cosuthenten, Euquachee, Yashute, Chetlessentun, Wishtenatin, Chetco, Tototin, Machinotin, and Shistakoostee | Umpqua, Nahakhuotane', Taltushtuntude', and Dakubetede' |
| Year | Ag206 | Ag207 | Ag208 | Ag209 | Ag210 | Ag211 | Ag212 | Ag213 | Ag214 | Ag215 | Ag216 | Ag217 | Ag218 | Ag219 | Ag220 |
	Number	Number	Number	Number	Number	Number	Number	Number	Number	Number	Number	Number	Number	Number	Number
1680	—	—	—	—	—	—	—	—	—	—	—	—	—	—	—
1690	—	—	—	—	—	—	—	—	—	—	—	—	—	—	—
1740	—	—	—	—	—	—	—	—	—	—	—	—	—	—	—
1769	—	—	—	—	—	—	—	—	—	—	—	—	—	—	—
1780	39,050	3,000	300	450	3,600	2,500	300	900	1,500	1,600	6,000	2,000	500	5,600	3,200
1845	3,280	0	0	0	10	18	0	0	0	0	100	50	0	250	100
1990	10,485	—	32	—	—	—	—	—	1,819	—	48	201	—	341	—

| | Columbia Region | | | | | | Central Mountain Region | | | | | | | New Mexico and Arizona | |
| | Western Oregon | | | | | | | | | | | | | | |
Year	Atfalati, Calapooya, Lakmiut, Mary's River, Santiam, Yamhill, and Yonkalla Ag221 Number	Walla-Walla, and Umatilla Ag222 Number	Tenino, Tilquini (Warmspring), Tai-aq, Tukspush, and Waiam Ag223 Number	Cayuse Ag224 Number	Klamath Ag225 Number	Modoc Ag226 Number	Total Ag227 Number	Bannock Ag228 Number	Shoshoni Ag229 Number	Ute Ag230 Number	Paiute Ag231 Number	Washo Ag232 Number	Jicarilla Ag233 Number	Total Ag234 Number	Chemehuevi Ag235 Number
1680	—	—	—	—	—	—	—	—	—	—	—	—	—	63,000	—
1690	—	—	—	—	—	—	—	—	—	—	—	—	—	—	—
1740	—	—	—	—	—	—	—	—	—	—	—	—	—	—	—
1769	—	—	—	—	—	—	—	—	—	—	—	—	—	—	—
1780	3,000	1,500	1,400	500	800	400	—	—	—	—	—	—	—	—	—
1845	—	—	—	—	—	—	19,300	1,000	4,500	4,500	7,500	1,000	800	—	—
1907	49	612	750	405	665	271	11,544	530	2,265	2,068	5,605	300	776	53,772	144
1990	52	1,512	2,685	161	3,113	521	32,959	187	9,506	7,658	11,369	1,489	2,750	358,049	640

| | New Mexico and Arizona | | | | | | | | | | | | | | |
Year	Havasupai Ag236 Number	Yavapai Ag237 Number	Walapai Ag238 Number	Mohave Ag239 Number	Maricopa Ag240 Number	Quigyuma Ag241 Number	Cajuenche Ag242 Number	Alchedoma Ag243 Number	Sobaipuri Ag244 Number	Pima Ag245 Number	Papago Ag246 Number	Apache Ag247 Number	Navajo Ag248 Number	Hopi Ag249 Number	Zuni Ag250 Number
1680	300	600	700	3,000	2,000	2,000	3,000	3,000	600	4,000	6,000	5,000	8,000	2,800	2,500
1690	—	—	—	—	—	—	—	—	—	—	—	—	—	—	—
1740	—	—	—	—	—	—	—	—	—	—	—	—	—	—	—
1769	—	—	—	—	—	—	—	—	—	—	—	—	—	—	—
1780	—	—	—	—	—	—	—	—	—	—	—	—	—	—	—
1845	—	—	—	—	—	0	0	—	0	—	—	—	—	—	—
1907	172	655	525	1,309	383	—	—	—	—	4,037	5,800	4,500	25,000	1,970	1,682
1990	557	686	1,205	1,321	744	—	—	—	—	15,074	16,876	46,406	225,298	11,791	8,281

Notes appear at end of table   (continued)

Table Ag130–264 Estimated population of American Indians, by region, state, and tribe: 1680–1990 [Plains and Pacific States] *Continued*

New Mexico and Arizona

Year	Tano	Nambe, San Ildefonso, San Juan, Santa Clara, Tesuque, and Hano	Isleta and Sandia	Taos and Picuris	Pecos	Jemez	Cochiti, San Felipe, Santa Ana, San Domingo, and Sia	Acoma and Laguna
	Ag251	Ag252	Ag253	Ag254	Ag255	Ag256	Ag257	Ag258
	Number	Number	Number	Number	Number	Number	Number	Number
1680	4,000	2,500	3,000	1,500	2,000	2,500	2,500	1,500
1690	—	—	—	—	—	—	—	—
1740	—	—	—	—	—	—	—	—
1769	—	—	—	—	—	—	—	—
1780	—	—	—	—	—	—	—	—
1845	—	—	—	—	—	—	—	—
1907	0	1,215	1,108	590	0	521	1,971	2,190
1990	—	3,197	3,597	2,120	—	2,238	7,656	10,362

Year	California	Alaska				
		Total	Eskimo	Aleut	Athapascans	Tlingit
	Ag259	Ag260	Ag261	Ag262	Ag263	Ag264
	Number	Number	Number	Number	Number	Number
1680	—	—	—	—	—	—
1690	—	—	—	—	—	—
1740	—	72,600	40,000	16,000	6,600	10,000
1769	260,000	—	—	—	—	—
1780	—	—	—	—	—	—
1845	—	—	—	—	—	—
1907	18,797	28,310	16,850	1,890	4,135	5,435
1990	43,891	109,564	57,152	23,797	14,198	14,417

1 Population given for the Echeloot tribe also includes the Chiluktkwa, Smackshop, Shoto, Quathlapotle, Callamaks, Wahkiakum, Chinook, and Killaxthokle tribes.

2 Population given for the Piskwau tribe also includes the Palus, Wanapum, Channapum, Yakima, Tapanash, and Atanum tribes.

Sources

See the sources for Table Ag17–129.

Documentation

See the text for Table Ag17–129.

Series Ag130–150. Northern Plains include North Dakota, South Dakota, Nebraska, Kansas, northern Oklahoma, Texas panhandle, eastern Colorado, eastern Wyoming, and eastern Montana.

Series Ag151–163. Southern Plains include Texas (except panhandle) and southeastern New Mexico.

Series Ag164–226. Columbia region does not include Alaska or California.

Series Ag227–233. Central Mountain region includes Nevada, Utah, western Colorado, western Wyoming, southern Idaho, southeast Oregon, and southwest Montana.

Series Ag259. The 1990 California Indian tribes include the Cahuilla, Chumash, Costanoan, Cupeno, Diegueno, Gabrieleno, Hupa, Juaneno, Konkow, Luiseno, Maidu, Mission, Modoc, Mono, Pit River, Pomo, Salinan, Serrano, Shasta, Tolowa, Wintu, Wiwok, Yokuts, Yurok, and other California tribes.

Table Ag265–330 Population of American Indians, by sex and age: 1910–1990

Contributed by C. Matthew Snipp

Population — Both sexes

Year	All ages	Under 5	5–9	10–14	15–19	20–24	25–29	30–34	35–39	40–44	45–49	50–54	55–59	60–64	65–69	70–74
	Ag265	Ag266	Ag267	Ag268	Ag269	Ag270	Ag271	Ag272	Ag273	Ag274	Ag275	Ag276	Ag277	Ag278	Ag279	Ag280
	Number	Number	Number	Number	Number	Number	Number	Number	Number	Number	Number	Number	Number	Number	Number	Number
1910	265,683	40,384	36,541	31,393	28,486	21,844	18,137	15,243	14,834	11,961	9,887	9,343	7,171	6,524	4,482	3,382
1920	244,437	33,346	34,166	30,173	25,417	20,009	16,537	13,474	13,707	11,618	10,806	8,728	6,573	5,953	4,655	3,455
1930	332,397	46,680	46,736	39,456	36,219	28,843	23,491	19,309	17,941	15,090	13,416	11,623	9,236	7,551	5,840	4,190
1940	333,969	47,151	43,486	39,719	36,010	29,376	24,946	20,490	18,895	15,414	13,629	11,180	8,967	7,632	11,383	5,691 [1]
1950	342,226	51,988	44,301	43,575	33,829	30,122	23,510	19,574	18,917	15,489	14,340	11,551	9,292	7,694	7,185	4,517
1960	546,228	91,287	75,947	63,499	49,897	39,667	33,026	30,122	28,389	22,929	21,711	20,767	31,560	11,830	9,975	6,857
1970	763,594	91,456	102,105	98,129	84,105	65,147	51,878	46,591	39,486	36,144	31,822	27,922	24,986	20,021	17,239	11,121
1980	1,420,400	149,275	146,647	155,992	170,215	149,154	124,932	107,219	84,179	69,370	58,089	51,593	44,897	33,919	28,310	19,893
1990	1,959,234	201,950	199,446	188,000	180,516	165,549	175,577	170,668	150,182	126,154	96,817	76,714	61,819	51,389	42,710	29,270

Population — Both sexes (continued)

Year	75 and over	75–79	80–84	85 and over	Unknown age
	Ag281	Ag282	Ag283	Ag284	Ag285
	Number	Number	Number	Number	Number
1910	5,122	—	—	—	949
1920	5,029	—	—	—	791
1930	6,327	—	—	—	449
1940	—	—	—	—	—
1950	6,342	—	—	—	—
1960	8,765	—	—	—	—
1970	15,442	7,468	4,234	3,740	—
1980	26,716	13,760	7,085	5,871	—
1990	42,473	21,152	12,116	9,205	—

Population — Males

Year	All ages	Under 5	5–9	10–14	15–19	20–24	25–29	30–34	35–39	40–44	45–49	50–54
	Ag286	Ag287	Ag288	Ag289	Ag290	Ag291	Ag292	Ag293	Ag294	Ag295	Ag296	Ag297
	Number	Number	Number	Number	Number	Number	Number	Number	Number	Number	Number	Number
1910	135,133	20,202	18,349	16,199	14,612	11,265	9,237	7,756	7,721	6,126	5,103	4,914
1920	125,068	16,591	16,931	15,225	12,710	10,413	8,558	6,963	7,213	6,071	5,987	4,764
1930	170,350	23,447	23,434	20,028	18,154	14,697	12,127	10,032	9,404	7,881	7,131	6,272
1940	171,427	23,476	21,475	19,983	18,143	15,068	12,659	10,602	9,950	8,281	7,442	6,151
1950	178,172	26,386	22,295	23,321	16,912	16,257	12,080	9,929	9,709	8,044	7,799	6,360
1960	273,526	45,926	37,784	32,132	25,615	20,032	16,312	14,630	14,054	11,559	10,878	10,310
1970	375,384	46,017	51,043	49,088	41,963	31,934	25,693	22,665	18,833	17,624	15,337	13,300
1980	702,228	75,803	74,182	78,988	86,202	74,828	61,559	52,407	41,131	33,759	27,932	24,979
1990	967,186	102,628	101,188	95,747	93,058	85,043	87,474	82,744	72,594	61,194	46,993	36,888

Note appears at end of table

(continued)

Table Ag265–330 Population of American Indians, by sex and age: 1910–1990   Continued

Population

	Males									Females							
	55–59	60–64	65–69	70–74	75 and over	75–79	80–84	85 and over	Unknown age	All ages	Under 5	5–9	10–14	15–19	20–24	25–29	30–34
	Ag298	Ag299	Ag300	Ag301	Ag302	Ag303	Ag304	Ag305	Ag306	Ag307	Ag308	Ag309	Ag310	Ag311	Ag312	Ag313	Ag314
Year	Number	Number	Number	Number	Number	Number	Number	Number	Number	Number	Number	Number	Number	Number	Number	Number	Number
1910	3,706	3,332	2,259	1,561	2,310	—	—	—	481	130,550	20,182	18,192	15,194	13,874	10,579	8,900	7,487
1920	3,594	3,136	2,429	1,748	2,335	—	—	—	400	119,369	16,755	17,235	14,948	12,707	9,596	7,979	6,511
1930	5,118	4,060	3,104	2,153	3,079	—	—	—	229	162,047	23,233	23,302	19,428	18,065	14,146	11,364	9,277
1940	4,987	4,180	6,176	2,854 [1]	—	—	—	—	—	162,542	23,675	22,011	19,736	17,867	14,308	12,287	9,888
1950	5,216	4,263	3,846	2,431	3,324	—	—	—	—	164,054	25,602	22,006	20,254	16,917	13,865	11,430	9,645
1960	15,066	6,080	5,181	3,524	4,443	—	—	—	—	272,702	45,361	38,163	31,367	24,282	19,635	16,714	15,492
1970	11,627	9,558	8,242	5,260	7,200	3,507	2,037	1,656	—	388,210	45,439	51,062	49,041	42,142	33,213	26,185	23,926
1980	21,471	16,010	12,847	8,848	11,282	6,099	2,872	2,311	—	718,172	73,472	72,465	77,004	84,013	74,326	63,373	54,812
1990	29,354	24,192	19,298	12,500	16,291	8,460	4,557	3,274	—	992,048	99,322	98,258	92,253	87,458	80,506	88,103	87,924

Population

	Females												
	35–39	40–44	45–49	50–54	55–59	60–64	65–69	70–74	75 and over	75–79	80–84	85 and over	Unknown age
	Ag315	Ag316	Ag317	Ag318	Ag319	Ag320	Ag321	Ag322	Ag323	Ag324	Ag325	Ag326	Ag327
Year	Number	Number	Number	Number	Number	Number	Number	Number	Number	Number	Number	Number	Number
1910	7,113	5,835	4,784	4,429	3,465	3,192	2,223	1,821	2,812	—	—	—	468
1920	6,494	5,547	4,819	3,964	2,979	2,817	2,226	1,707	2,694	—	—	—	391
1930	8,537	7,209	6,285	5,351	4,118	3,491	2,736	2,037	3,248	—	—	—	220
1940	8,945	7,133	6,187	5,029	3,980	3,452	5,207	2,837 [1]	—	—	—	—	—
1950	9,208	7,445	6,541	5,191	4,076	3,431	3,339	2,086	3,018	—	—	—	—
1960	14,335	11,370	10,833	10,457	16,494	5,750	4,794	3,333	4,322	—	—	2,084	—
1970	20,653	18,520	16,485	14,622	13,359	10,463	8,997	5,861	8,242	3,961	2,197	3,560	—
1980	43,048	35,611	30,157	26,614	23,426	17,909	15,463	11,045	15,434	7,661	4,213	5,931	—
1990	77,588	64,960	49,824	39,826	32,465	27,197	23,412	16,770	26,182	12,692	7,559		—

Median age

	Overall	Males	Females
	Ag328	Ag329	Ag330
Year	Number	Number	Number
1910	18.7	18.8	18.6
1920	19.3	19.9	18.7
1930	19.1	19.5	18.6
1940	19.6	20.4	18.9
1950	19.1	19.6	18.7
1960	19.2	19.1	19.4
1970	20.4	19.9	20.9
1980	22.8	22.3	23.4
1990	26.2	25.3	27.2

[1] Includes persons ages 75 and older.

Sources

U.S. Bureau of the Census, *The Indian Population of the United States and Alaska* (1937), Table 16; U.S. Bureau of the Census, *Characteristics of the Nonwhite Population by Race* (1943), Table 3; Paul Stuart, *Nations within a Nation* (Greenwood Press, 1987), Tables 3.14, 3.15, 3.16, 3.17; U.S. Bureau of the Census, *General Population Characteristics, United States*, CP-1-1 (1992), Table 19.

Table Ag331–391 Population of American Indians, by region and state: 1890–1990

Contributed by C. Matthew Snipp

		New England							Middle Atlantic				East North Central		
	Total	Total	Maine	New Hampshire	Vermont	Massachusetts	Rhode Island	Connecticut	Total	New York	New Jersey	Pennsylvania	Total	Ohio	Indiana
	Ag331	Ag332	Ag333	Ag334	Ag335	Ag336	Ag337	Ag338	Ag339	Ag340	Ag341	Ag342	Ag343	Ag344	Ag345
Year	Number	Number	Number	Number	Number	Number	Number	Number	Number	Number	Number	Number	Number	Number	Number
1890	273,607	1,445	559	16	34	428	180	228	7,209	6,044	84	1,081	16,202	206	343
1900	266,732	1,600	798	22	5	587	35	153	6,959	5,257	63	1,639	15,027	42	243
1910	291,014	2,076	892	34	26	688	284	152	7,717	6,046	168	1,503	18,255	127	279
1920	270,995	1,715	839	28	24	555	110	159	5,940	5,503	100	337	15,695	151	125
1930	362,380	2,466	1,012	64	36	874	318	162	7,709	6,973	213	523	19,817	435	285
1940	366,427	2,483	1,251	50	16	769	196	201	9,303	8,651	211	441	19,732	338	223
1950	377,273	3,545	1,522	74	30	1,201	385	333	12,402	10,640	621	1,141	22,223	1,146	438
1960	551,636	6,044	1,879	135	57	2,118	932	923	20,312	16,491	1,699	2,122	31,560	1,910	948
1970	827,273	10,872	2,195	361	229	4,475	1,390	2,222	38,594	28,355	4,706	5,533	57,732	6,654	3,887
1980	1,420,400	21,597	4,087	1,352	984	7,743	2,898	4,533	57,441	39,582	8,394	9,465	105,907	12,239	7,836
1990	2,015,143	34,692	6,392	2,433	2,215	12,585	4,267	6,800	89,704	59,081	14,647	15,976	159,561	22,331	14,494

	East North Central			West North Central								South Atlantic			
	Illinois	Michigan	Wisconsin	Total	Minnesota	Iowa	Missouri	North Dakota	South Dakota	Nebraska	Kansas	Total	Delaware	Maryland	District of Columbia
	Ag346	Ag347	Ag348	Ag349	Ag350	Ag351	Ag352	Ag353	Ag354	Ag355	Ag356	Ag357	Ag358	Ag359	Ag360
Year	Number	Number	Number	Number	Number	Number	Number	Number	Number	Number	Number	Number	Number	Number	Number
1890	98	5,625	9,930	46,822	10,096	457	128	8,174	19,854	6,431	1,682	2,359	4	44	25
1900	16	6,354	8,372	42,339	9,182	382	130	6,968	20,225	3,322	2,130	6,585	9	3	22
1910	188	7,519	10,142	41,406	9,053	471	313	6,486	19,137	3,502	2,444	9,054	5	55	68
1920	194	5,614	9,611	37,263	8,761	529	171	6,254	16,384	2,888	2,276	13,673	2	32	37
1930	469	7,080	11,548	48,245	11,077	660	578	8,387	21,833	3,256	2,454	19,060	5	50	40
1940	624	6,282	12,265	51,618	12,528	733	330	10,114	23,347	3,401	1,165	25,076	14	73	190
1950	1,443	7,000	12,196	54,609	12,533	1,084	547	10,766	23,344	3,954	2,381	7,500	—	314	330
1960	4,704	9,701	14,297	67,071	15,496	1,708	1,723	11,736	25,794	5,545	5,069	47,538	597	1,538	587
1970	11,413	16,854	18,924	93,555	23,128	2,992	5,405	14,369	32,365	6,624	8,672	67,126	656	4,239	956
1980	16,283	40,050	29,499	142,486	35,016	5,455	12,321	20,158	44,968	9,195	15,373	118,726	1,328	8,021	1,031
1990	24,077	58,934	39,725	191,140	49,507	7,811	22,334	25,305	50,369	12,564	23,250	186,949	2,199	14,258	1,559

(continued)

Table Ag331–391 Population of American Indians, by region and state: 1890–1990 *Continued*

	South Atlantic						East South Central					West South Central				
	Virginia	West Virginia	North Carolina	South Carolina	Georgia	Florida	Total	Kentucky	Tennessee	Alabama	Mississippi	Total	Arkansas	Louisiana	Oklahoma	Texas
	Ag361	Ag362	Ag363	Ag364	Ag365	Ag366	Ag367	Ag368	Ag369	Ag370	Ag371	Ag372	Ag373	Ag374	Ag375	Ag376
Year	Number	Number	Number	Number	Number	Number	Number	Number	Number	Number	Number	Number	Number	Number	Number	Number
1890	349	9	1,516	173	68	171	3,396	71	146	1,143	2,036	66,042	250	628	64,456	708
1900	354	12	5,687	121	19	358	2,590	102	108	177	2,203	65,574	66	593	64,445	470
1910	539	36	7,851	331	95	74	2,612	234	216	909	1,253	76,767	460	780	74,825	702
1920	824	7	11,824	304	125	518	1,623	57	56	405	1,105	60,618	106	1,066	57,337	2,109
1930	779	18	16,579	959	43	587	2,106	22	161	465	1,458	95,670	408	1,536	92,725	1,001
1940	198	25	22,546	1,234	106	690	2,756	44	114	464	2,134	66,307	278	1,801	63,125	1,103
1950	1,056	160	3,742	554	333	1,011	4,003	234	339	928	2,502	57,447	533	409	53,769	2,736
1960	2,155	181	38,129	1,098	749	2,504	5,424	391	638	1,276	3,119	74,606	580	3,587	64,689	5,750
1970	4,853	751	44,406	2,241	2,347	6,677	10,363	1,531	2,276	2,443	4,113	123,733	2,014	5,294	98,468	17,957
1980	9,454	1,610	64,652	5,757	7,616	19,257	22,477	3,610	5,104	7,583	6,180	231,027	9,428	12,065	169,459	40,075
1990	16,391	3,099	82,606	8,935	15,283	42,619	46,570	6,946	12,473	18,295	8,856	356,735	14,320	20,075	252,468	69,872

	Mountain									Pacific					
	Total	Montana	Idaho	Wyoming	Colorado	New Mexico	Arizona	Utah	Nevada	Total	Washington	Oregon	California	Alaska	Hawai'i
	Ag377	Ag378	Ag379	Ag380	Ag381	Ag382	Ag383	Ag384	Ag385	Ag386	Ag387	Ag388	Ag389	Ag390	Ag391
Year	Number	Number	Number	Number	Number	Number	Number	Number	Number	Number	Number	Number	Number	Number	Number
1890	72,002	11,206	4,223	1,844	1,092	15,044	29,981	3,456	5,156	58,130	11,181	4,971	16,624	25,354	—
1900	66,155	11,343	4,226	1,686	1,437	13,144	26,480	2,623	5,216	59,903	10,039	4,951	15,377	29,536	—
1910	75,338	10,745	3,488	1,486	1,482	20,573	29,201	3,123	5,240	57,789	10,997	5,090	16,371	25,331	—
1920	76,899	10,956	3,098	1,343	1,383	19,512	32,989	2,711	4,907	57,569	9,061	4,590	17,360	26,558	—
1930	102,083	14,798	3,638	1,845	1,395	28,941	43,726	2,869	4,871	65,224	11,253	4,776	19,212	29,983	—
1940	122,031	16,841	3,537	2,349	1,360	34,510	55,076	3,611	4,747	67,121	11,394	4,594	18,675	32,458	—
1950	142,098	16,606	3,800	3,237	1,567	41,901	65,761	4,201	5,025	73,446	13,816	5,820	19,947	33,863	—
1960	188,004	21,181	5,231	4,020	4,288	56,255	83,387	6,961	6,681	111,077	21,076	8,026	39,014	42,489	472
1970	235,439	27,130	6,687	4,980	8,836	72,788	95,812	11,273	7,933	189,859	33,386	13,510	91,018	50,819	1,126
1980	364,381	37,270	10,521	7,094	18,068	106,119	152,745	19,256	13,308	356,358	60,804	27,314	201,369	64,103	2,768
1990	484,304	47,769	14,677	9,921	28,544	134,035	204,589	24,371	20,398	465,488	83,212	41,626	248,929	86,125	5,596

Source

1890–1930: U.S. Bureau of the Census, *The Indian Population of the United States and Alaska* (1937), Tables 1 and 2. 1940–1990: Campbell Gibson and Kay Jung, "Historical Census Statistics on Population Totals by Race, 1790 to 1990, and by Hispanic Origin, 1790–1990, for the United States, Regions, Divisions, and States," U.S. Census, *Population Division Working Paper*, number 56 (2002).

Table Ag392–433 Population of selected American Indian tribes: 1910–1990

Contributed by C. Matthew Snipp

Year	United States Ag392 Number	Total Reported in table Ag393 Number	Table total as a percentage of U.S. total Ag394 Percent	Apache Ag395 Number	Arapaho Ag396 Number	Blackfeet Ag397 Number	Chemhuevi Ag398 Number	Cherokee Ag399 Number	Cheyenne Ag400 Number	Chickasaw Ag401 Number	Ojibwa Ag402 Number	Choctaw Ag403 Number	Colville Ag404 Number	Comanche Ag405 Number
1910	265,683	205,291	77.3	4,973	1,419	2,367	355	31,489	3,055	4,204	20,214	15,917	785	1,171
1930	332,397	256,798	77.3	6,537	1,241	3,145	—	45,238	2,695	4,745	21,549	17,757	—	1,423
1970	776,454	521,269	67.1	22,993	2,993	9,921	—[2]	66,150	6,872	5,616	41,946	23,562[3]	3,180[4]	4,250
1980	1,356,297	983,358	72.5	35,861	4,423	21,964	467	232,080	9,918	10,317	73,602	50,220	5,456	9,037
1990	1,937,391	1,446,278	74.7	53,330	6,918	37,992	640	369,035	11,089	21,522	105,988	86,231	7,057	11,437

Year	Creek Ag406 Number	Crow Ag407 Number	Delaware Ag408 Number	Salish-Kootenai Ag409 Number	Iroquois Ag410[1] Number	Kaw Ag411 Number	Kiowa Ag412 Number	Lumbee Ag413 Number	Menominee Ag414 Number	Navajo Ag415 Number	Omaha Ag416 Number	Osage Ag417 Number	Paiute Ag418 Number	Tohono O'Odham Ag419 Number
1910	7,341[5]	1,799	985	486	8,190	238	1,126	6,195[8]	1,422	22,455	1,105	1,373	5,631[9]	3,798
1930	9,083	1,674	971	—	7,219	318	1,050	12,975[8]	1,969	39,064	1,103	2,344	5,060[9]	5,205
1970	17,004[5]	3,779	2,926[6]	3,702	21,473	6,849[7]	4,337	27,520	4,307	96,743	—[7]	—[7]	—[2]	16,690[10]
1980	28,278	7,074	5,381	4,948	38,218	677	7,386	28,818	6,044	158,633	3,090	6,884	9,253	13,297
1990	45,872	9,394	9,800	7,868	52,557	1,166	9,460	51,065	8,064	225,298	4,363	10,430	11,369	16,876

Year	Pima Ag420 Number	Ponca Ag421 Number	Potawatomi Ag422 Number	Pueblo Ag423 Number	Quapaw Ag424 Number	Seminole Ag425 Number	Shoshone Ag426 Number	Sioux Ag427 Number	Stockbridge Ag428 Number	Tlingit-Haida Ag429 Number	Ute Ag430 Number	Winnebago Ag431 Number	Yakima Ag432 Number	Yuman Ag433 Number
1910	4,236	875	2,440	10,843	231	1,729	3,840	22,778	533	—	2,244	1,820	1,362	4,267
1930	4,382	939	1,854	12,047	222	2,048	3,994	25,934	—	5,050	1,980	1,446	—	4,537
1970	—[10]	—[7]	4,626	30,971	—[7]	5,055	14,248[2]	47,875	—[6]	7,543	3,815	2,832	3,856	7,635
1980	11,722	2,056	9,715	42,522	929	10,363	9,830	78,608	1,547	10,943	5,821	5,165	6,506	6,611
1990	15,074	2,788	16,719	55,330	1,438	15,564	9,506	107,321	2,219	16,353	7,658	6,591	7,577	7,319

1 Includes Cayuga, Mohawk, Oneida, Onondaga, Seneca, Tuscarora, and Wyandotte.
2 Paiute and Chemhuevi included with Shoshone.
3 Includes Houma.
4 Includes Lakes.
5 Includes Alabama and Coushatta.
6 Delaware included with Stockbridge.
7 Omaha, Osage, Ponca, and Quapaw included with Kaw.
8 Virginia–Carolina Algonquian and Croatan.
9 Includes Mono and Pviotso.
10 Pima combined with Tohono O'Odham.

Sources

Paul Stuart, *Nations within a Nation* (Greenwood Press, 1987), p. 58, Table 3.8; C. Matthew Snipp, *American Indians: The First of This Land* (Russell Sage, 1989), pp. 324–32, Table A1.1; U.S. Bureau of the Census, *Characteristics of Americans Indians by Tribe and Language* (1994), Table 1, pp. 1–37.

Documentation

Series Ag393. Equals the sum of series Ag395–433.

Series Ag394. Equals series Ag393 expressed as a percentage of series Ag392.

Table Ag434–475 Population of American Indians, by region and urban–rural residence: 1910–1990

Contributed by C. Matthew Snipp

United States total and Northeast

	United States			Northeast			New England			Middle Atlantic		
	Urban	Rural	Percentage urban	Urban	Rural	Percentage urban	Urban	Rural	Percentage urban	Urban	Rural	Percentage urban
	Ag434	Ag435	Ag436	Ag437	Ag438	Ag439	Ag440	Ag441	Ag442	Ag443	Ag444	Ag445
Year	Number	Number	Percent	Number	Number	Percent	Number	Number	Percent	Number	Number	Percent
1910	11,925	253,758	4.5	1,625	8,168	16.6	800	1,276	38.5	825	6,892	10.7
1920	15,219	229,218	6.2	1,627	5,983	21.8	766	949	44.7	906	5,034	15.3
1930	32,816	299,581	9.9	3,222	6,953	31.7	1,041	1,425	42.2	2,181	5,528	28.3
1950	55,909	286,317[1]	16.3	6,707	8,495[1]	44.1	—	—[1]	—	—	—[1]	—
1960	165,922	380,306[1]	30.4	23,028	11,878[1]	66.0	—	—[1]	—	—	—[1]	—
1970	340,367	424,227[1]	44.5	32,808	12,912[1]	71.8	7,459	2,903[1]	72.0	25,349	10,009[1]	71.7
1980	719,047	664,986	52.0	54,960	22,470	71.0	14,339	6,769	67.9	40,621	15,701	72.1
1990	1,058,315	820,379	56.3	92,523	29,028	76.1	22,262	9,724	69.6	70,261	19,304	78.4

Midwest

	Midwest			East North Central			West North Central		
	Urban	Rural	Percentage urban	Urban	Rural	Percentage urban	Urban	Rural	Percentage urban
	Ag446	Ag447	Ag448	Ag449	Ag450	Ag451	Ag452	Ag453	Ag454
Year	Number	Number	Percent	Number	Number	Percent	Number	Number	Percent
1910	2,948	56,713	4.9	1,319	16,936	7.2	1,629	39,777	3.9
1920	3,449	49,509	6.5	1,634	14,061	10.4	1,815	35,448	4.9
1930	7,319	60,743	10.8	3,822	15,995	19.3	3,497	44,748	7.2
1950	13,966	62,679[1]	18.2	—	—[1]	—	—	—[1]	—
1960	39,160	65,888[1]	37.3	—	—[1]	—	—	—[1]	—
1970	72,596	71,658[1]	50.3	34,937	19,641[1]	64.0	37,659	52,017[1]	42.0
1980	130,692	115,653	53.1	67,273	37,274	64.3	63,419	78,379	44.7
1990	184,495	149,503	55.2	94,437	52,962	64.1	90,058	96,541	48.3

South

	South			South Atlantic			East South Central			West South Central		
	Urban	Rural	Percentage urban	Urban	Rural	Percentage urban	Urban	Rural	Percentage urban	Urban	Rural	Percentage urban
	Ag455	Ag456	Ag457	Ag458	Ag459	Ag460	Ag461	Ag462	Ag463	Ag464	Ag465	Ag466
Year	Number	Number	Percent	Number	Number	Percent	Number	Number	Percent	Number	Number	Percent
1910	4,857	83,576	5.5	131	8,923	1.4	137	2,475	5.2	4,589	72,178	6.0
1920	5,599	70,315	7.4	196	13,477	1.4	51	1,572	3.1	5,352	55,266	8.8
1930	15,425	101,411	13.2	218	18,842	1.1	99	2,007	4.7	15,108	80,562	15.8
1950	15,721	52,880[1]	22.9	—	—[1]	—	—	—[1]	—	—	—[1]	—
1960	39,668	92,908[1]	29.9	—	—[1]	—	—	—[1]	—	—	—[1]	—
1970	89,064	106,342[1]	45.6	20,289	46,078[1]	30.6	3,817	4,891[1]	43.8	64,958	55,373[1]	54.0
1980	186,024	183,579	50.3	50,098	67,359	42.7	9,827	12,337	44.3	126,099	103,883	54.8
1990	294,210	265,704	52.5	79,700	89,854	47.0	17,027	23,193	42.3	197,483	152,657	56.4

West

	West			Mountain			Pacific		
	Urban	Rural	Percentage urban	Urban	Rural	Percentage urban	Urban	Rural	Percentage urban
	Ag467	Ag468	Ag469	Ag470	Ag471	Ag472	Ag473	Ag474	Ag475
Year	Number	Number	Percent	Number	Number	Percent	Number	Number	Percent
1910	2,495	105,391	2.3	1,272	74,066	1.7	1,223	31,325	3.8
1920	4,499	103,411	4.2	1,772	75,127	2.3	2,727	28,284	8.8
1930	6,850	130,474	5.0	2,677	99,406	2.6	4,173	31,068	11.8
1950	19,515	161,733[1]	10.8	—	—[1]	—	—	—[1]	—
1960	64,066	209,632[1]	23.4	—	—[1]	—	—	—[1]	—
1970	145,899	233,315[1]	38.5	49,889	179,780[1]	21.7	96,010	53,535[1]	64.2
1980	347,371	323,284	51.8	125,660	237,539	34.6	221,711	85,745	72.1
1990	489,787	376,144	56.6	208,011	270,487	43.5	281,776	105,657	72.7

Table Ag434–475   Population of American Indians, by region and urban–rural residence: 1910–1990   *Continued*

[1] Includes rural farm and nonfarm populations.

Sources

U.S. Bureau of the Census, *The Indian Population of the United States and Alaska, 1930* (1937), Table 5; U.S. Bureau of the Census, *Special Report: Nonwhite Population by Race* (1953), Table 3; U.S. Bureau of the Census, *Nonwhite Population by Race*, Subject Report PC(2)-1C (1963), Table 3; U.S. Bureau of the Census, *American Indians*, Subject Report PC(2)-1F (1973), Table 1; U.S. Bureau of

the Census, *Characteristics of the Population, U.S. Summary*, PC80-1-B1 (1983), Table 38; U.S. Bureau of the Census, *General Population Characteristics, States*, PC80-1-2 to 52 (1992), Table 3.

Documentation

See Table Ap-G in Appendix 2 regarding the composition of census regions and divisions.

Table Ag476–492   Population of American Indians in selected metropolitan areas: 1890–1990

Contributed by C. Matthew Snipp

	Reported in table								
		As a percentage of total U.S. Indian population	Albuquerque, New Mexico	Anaheim, Santa Ana, and Garden Grove, California	Dallas and Ft. Worth, Texas	Detroit, Michigan	Los Angeles and Long Beach, California	Minneapolis and St. Paul, Minnesota	New York, New York
	Total								
	Ag476	Ag477	Ag478	Ag479	Ag480	Ag481	Ag482	Ag483	Ag484
Year	Number	Percent	Number	Number	Number	Number	Number	Number	Number
1890 [1]	6,354	2.6	3,469	5	14	11	144	52	144
1910	13,376	4.8	1,192	21	16	41	97	37	343
1930	18,376	5.4	1,106	125	53	460	997	373	391
1940	4,237	1.3	—	—	61	434	914	205	1,064
1960	61,368	11.7	3,378	730 [2]	2,120	2,195	8,839	3,285	4,366
1970	135,389	17.1	5,839	3,920	6,632	5,683	24,509	9,852	12,160
1980	259,989	19.1	20,721	12,782	11,076	12,372	47,234	15,831	13,440
1990	350,113	18.6	16,201	11,834	18,608	17,731	43,899	23,621	28,387

	Oklahoma City, Oklahoma	Phoenix, Arizona	Riverside, San Bernardino, and Ontario, California	San Diego, California	San Francisco and Oakland, California	Seattle and Everett, Washington	Tucson, Arizona	Tulsa, Oklahoma
	Ag485	Ag486	Ag487	Ag488	Ag489	Ag490	Ag491	Ag492
Year	Number	Number	Number	Number	Number	Number	Number	Number
1890 [1]	2	1	399	478	56	675	904	—
1910	112	3,099	2,163	1,516	87	1,157	3,495	1,381
1930	698	3,845	1,795	1,722	333	1,173	5,305	3,674
1940	303	—	—	143	329	222	—	623
1960	6,453	8,136	3,566	3,293	3,883	3,817	7,307	7,608
1970	13,033	11,159	6,378	5,880	12,011	9,496	8,837	15,519
1980	24,695	22,788	17,107	14,355	17,546	15,162	14,880	38,463
1990	45,623	37,708	24,460	19,564	20,436	21,810	20,231	48,116

[1] Enumeration included only American Indians residing outside of reservation areas.

[2] Data for Orange County, not a Standard Metropolitan Statistical Area (SMSA) in 1960.

Sources

Paul Stuart, *Nations within a Nation* (Greenwood Press, 1987), Tables 4.16 and 4.17; U.S. Bureau of the Census, *General Population Characteristics: United States*, CP-1-1 (1992).

Documentation

The Census Bureau first designated Metropolitan Areas in 1950. For earlier years, Stuart used central-city counties as proxies for Metropolitan Areas. Data for years after 1950 are for Metropolitan Areas. The boundaries and criteria of Census Metropolitan Areas have changed over time. This table is an attempt to present the data as simply as possible, essentially assuming that these are the same areas over time.

Series Ag476. Equals the sum of series Ag478–492.

HEALTH AND VITAL STATISTICS

C. Matthew Snipp

Table Ag493–494   Infectious disease epidemics among American Indians: 1531–1918
Contributed by C. Matthew Snipp

Period	Epidemic Ag493	People affected Ag494
1531–1533	Measles	New Spain, probably beyond the colony, northward including Pueblos and beyond
1545–1548	Bubonic Plague	New Spain to Pueblos and perhaps beyond
1559	Influenza	Southeastern peoples
1576	Bubonic Plague	New Spain
1586	Typhus	Tidewater Carolina tribes to Florida Timucua and Alalachee; probably Creek; extending to southern New England tribes
1592–1593	Measles	Sinaloa
1601–1602	Diphtheria	Central New Spain to Sinaloa
1602	Measles	Sinaloa
1611	Typhus	Sinaloa
1612–1619	Bubonic Plague	New Spain to Florida and New England
1633–1634	Measles	New England, New France, and Great Lakes groups; Native Americans near Boston and Plymouth to Mohawks, Oneidas, Hurons, Montagnais, New Narragansetts, Delawares, etc.
1647	Influenza	New England tribes
1658–1659	Measles	Canadian tribes; Florida peoples to Mexico City – with diphtheria
1659	Diphtheria	New England and Canadian tribes
1675	Influenza	Iroquois and New England tribes
1692–1693	Measles	Illinois peoples; Oneidas
1696–1698	Influenza	Possible component with smallpox epidemic among Gulf Coast and southeastern peoples
1713–1715	Measles	New England tribes to Illinois
1720	Typhus	"Marseilles Fever" among Naskapi
1727–1728	Measles	Mexico City to California tribes; Florida peoples; possibly New England groups
1742	Typhus	Lower California tribes; possibly Choctaw
1746	Influenza	Possible component with smallpox epidemic among northeastern tribes
1759–1760	Measles	Possibly southeastern peoples
1761	Influenza	All Native Americans in North America
1767	Bubonic Plague	Louisiana peoples
1776–1778	Measles	Possibly in Plains, Hudson Bay, and Texas tribes
1779–1783	Influenza	Possible accompaniment to continental smallpox pandemic
1784–1787	Diphtheria	New Spain
1803	Measles	Caddoan tribes
1819	Measles	Lac Seul Ojibwa
1832–1834	Cholera	Potawatomi, Winnebago, Menominee, Ojibwa, Mexican tribes, Panya
1837	Measles	Florida Seminoles
1849	Cholera	Kiowa, Pawnee, Ojibwa, Menominee, Brule, Sioux, Maricopa, Pima, Papago
1867	Cholera	Plains tribes, Wichita, Caddo, Pima
1880–1889 [1]	Diphtheria	Kutchin of Arctic Canada
1887	Measles	Walapai
1889–1890	Influenza	Indian Territory reservation tribes
1892	Measles	Indian Territory reservation tribes
1892	Influenza	Indian Territory reservation tribes
1918	Influenza	All Native Americans in North America

[1] The original source did not indicate exact dates, stating only that the epidemic occurred in the 1880s. It is unlikely the epidemic spanned the entire decade.

Source

Henry Dobyns, *Their Number Become Thinned* (University of Tennessee Press, 1983), pp. 17–21.

Documentation

This table covers probable epidemics of infectious diseases in the post-European contact period.

Table Ag495   Smallpox epidemics among American Indians: 1520–1899

Contributed by C. Matthew Snipp

Period	People or place affected Ag495
1520–1524	From Chile across present-day United States
1592–1593	Central Mexico to Sinaloa; southern New England; eastern Great Lakes
1602	Sinaloa and northward
1639	French and British northeastern North America
1646–1648	New Spain to Nuevo Leon tribes and western Sierra Madre to Florida
1649–1650	Northeastern tribes; Montagnais-Neskapi to Quebec, Huron, and Iroquois; Florida
1655	Florida chiefdoms
1662–1663	Iroquois, Delaware; Canadian tribes; Central Mexico
1665–1667	Florida chiefdoms to Virginia tribes
1669–1670	French and British northeastern North America
1674–1675	Coahuiltecan tribes of Texas; northeastern New Spain
1677–1679	French and British northeastern North America
1687–1691	Northeastern tribes on British and French frontiers; Texas tribes
1696–1699	Southeastern and Gulf Coast chiefdoms
1701–1703	Northeastern tribes to Illinois
1706	Coahuiltecan tribes of Texas and northeastern New Spain
1755–1760	From Canada, New England, and Great Lakes to Virginia, Carolinas, and Texas
1762–1766	From Central Mexico through Texas and the Southeast to Iroquois, Potawatomi, Wea, Kickapoo, Miami, Shawnee, Arikira, and Northwest Coast
1779–1783	From Central Mexico across all of North America
1785–1787	Alaskan coastal tribes across northern Canada
1788	New Mexico Pueblos
1793–1797	New Spain
1799	Ottawa tribe
1801–1802	Columbia River peoples; Great Plains to Gulf of Mexico
1810–1811	Leech Lake Dakota to Lake Superior tribes
1815–1816	Rio Grande Pueblos and Plains tribes
1828	California tribes; Osage
1831–1834	Plains tribes; Great Lakes tribes
1836–1840	Alaskan, Columbia River, California, Plains, Plateau, and Mackenzie Yukon tribes; Pueblos
1843–1846	Aleuts to Plains Crow tribe
1848–1850	Plains tribes, Coeur d'Alene; Kutchin
1852–1853	Columbia River peoples; western Pueblos
1854–1857	Plains tribes
1860–1867	Iroquois and Great Lakes tribes in 1860–1862; southern Plains to Northwest Coast; 1863 to Southwestern and southern California tribes; 1864 to southern Plains tribes; 1865–1867 to northern Plains and Great Lakes tribes
1876–1878	Lower St. Lawrence River tribes to Northwest Coast tribes and to Southwestern tribes
1896–1899	California to Rio Grande Pueblos; Navajos; Jicarilla Apaches; Indian Territory tribes

Source

Henry Dobyns, *Their Number Become Thinned* (University of Tennessee Press, 1983), pp. 15–16.

Documentation

This table covers probable epidemic episodes of smallpox among Native Americans in North America.

Table Ag496–497   American Indian infant mortality rate: 1944–1993[1,2]

Contributed by C. Matthew Snipp

Year	American Indians and Alaska Natives Ag496 Per 1,000	All races Ag497 Per 1,000	Year	American Indians and Alaska Natives Ag496 Per 1,000	All races Ag497 Per 1,000
1944 [3]	135.3	41.4	1973	22.2	17.7
1950 [3]	85.1	29.2	1974	21.4	16.7
1955	62.7	26.4	1975	21.6	16.1
1956	60.7	26.0	1976	20.5	15.2
1957	59.2	26.3	1977	19.2	14.1
1958	55.8	27.1	1978	17.9	13.8
1959	52.5	26.4	1979	16.5	13.1
1960	48.0	26.0	1980	15.4	12.6
1961	46.3	25.3	1981	13.2	11.9
1962	44.1	25.3	1982	12.3	11.5
1963	41.8	25.2	1983	11.5	11.2
1964	40.0	24.8	1984	11.1	10.8
1965	38.5	24.7	1985	11.1	10.6
1966	36.8	23.7	1986	11.1	10.4
1967	34.0	22.4	1987	11.1	10.1
1968	30.0	21.8	1988	11.0	10.0
1969	27.1	20.9	1989	10.6	9.8
1970	24.6	20.0	1990	10.2	9.2
1971	22.7	19.1	1991	9.4	8.9
1972	21.3	18.5	1992	8.8	8.5
			1993	8.7	8.4

[1] Beginning in 1973, the Indian Health Service altered its procedures for collecting data for infant mortality; thus, data for earlier years are not strictly comparable.

[2] Rates based on three-year averages centered on the year reported, for example, 1993 is based on an average for 1992–1994.

[3] American Indians only; does not include Alaska Natives.

Source

1944–1950: William A. Brophy and Sophie D. Aberle, compilers, *The Indian, America's* *Unfinished Business: Report of the Commission on the Rights, Liberties, and Responsibilities of the American Indian* (University of Oklahoma Press, 1966). 1955–1972: U.S. Indian Health Service, *Chart Series Book* (1988), Table 3.5, p. 22. 1973–1993: U.S. Indian Health Service, *Trends in Indian Health* (1997), Table 3.8, p. 48.

Documentation

Rates are per 1,000 live births.

Table Ag498–538 Deaths in Indian Health Service areas, by cause: 1951–1994[1]

Contributed by C. Matthew Snipp

Deaths

Period	All causes Ag498 Number	Heart disease Ag499 Number	Accidents Ag500 Number	Influenza and pneumonia Ag501 Number	Tuberculosis Ag502 Number	Early infancy diseases Ag503 Number	Malignant neoplasms Ag504 Number	Liver disease Ag505 Number	Cerebrovascular disease Ag506 Number	Congenital malformations Ag507 Number	Homicide Ag508 Number	Diabetes mellitus Ag509 Number	Suicide Ag510 Number	Other Ag511 Number
1951–1953	—	—	—	—	—	—	—	—	—	—	—	—	—	—
1972–1974	13,385	2,265	2,972	687	142	364	1,127	738	678	160	361	354	352	3,185
1982–1984	19,633	4,462	3,278	662	36	382	2,528	915	949	—	594	622	555	4,650
1992–1994 [2]	23,917	5,297	3,467	863	24	—	3,544	1,071	992	—	576	1,252	708	6,123

Rate

Period	All causes Ag512 Per 100,000	Heart disease Ag513 Per 100,000	Accidents Ag514 Per 100,000	Influenza and pneumonia Ag515 Per 100,000	Tuberculosis Ag516 Per 100,000	Early infancy diseases Ag517 Per 100,000	Malignant neoplasms Ag518 Per 100,000	Liver disease Ag519 Per 100,000	Cerebrovascular disease Ag520 Per 100,000	Congenital malformations Ag521 Per 100,000	Homicide Ag522 Per 100,000	Diabetes mellitus Ag523 Per 100,000	Suicide Ag524 Per 100,000	Other Ag525 Per 100,000
1951–1953	—	—	—	—	—	—	—	—	—	—	—	—	—	—
1972–1974	896.3	151.7	199.0	46.0	9.5	24.4	75.5	49.4	45.4	10.7	24.2	23.7	23.6	213.2
1982–1984	480.5	109.2	80.2	16.2	3.3	9.3	61.9	22.4	23.2	—	14.5	15.2	13.6	111.5
1992–1994 [2]	612.4	135.6	88.8	22.1	2.3	—	90.7	24.1	25.4	—	14.7	32.1	18.1	158.2

Percentage of all causes

Period	Heart disease Ag526 Percent	Accidents Ag527 Percent	Influenza and pneumonia Ag528 Percent	Tuberculosis Ag529 Percent	Early infancy diseases Ag530 Percent	Malignant neoplasms Ag531 Percent	Liver disease Ag532 Percent	Cerebrovascular disease Ag533 Percent	Congenital malformations Ag534 Percent	Homicide Ag535 Percent	Diabetes mellitus Ag536 Percent	Suicide Ag537 Percent	Other Ag538 Percent
1951–1953	14.2	14.1	10.5	8.1	7.1	5.9	—	4.3	1.6	1.6	—	—	32.6
1972–1974	16.9	22.2	5.1	1.1	2.7	8.4	5.5	5.1	1.2	2.7	2.6	2.6	23.9
1982–1984	22.7	16.7	3.4	0.2	1.9	12.9	4.7	4.8	—	3.0	3.2	2.8	23.7
1992–1994 [2]	22.1	14.5	3.6	0.1	—	14.8	4.5	4.1	—	2.4	5.2	3.0	25.6

Documentation

An Indian Health Service area is a catchment area served by an IHS clinic or hospital.

Series Ag508, Ag522, and Ag535. Includes legal executions.

[1] Data for years subsequent to 1973 are not strictly comparable to earlier years due to changes in the Indian Health Service (IHS) statistical collection systems. Later years are based on a different geographic definition.

[2] Numbers and rates adjusted to compensate for miscoding of Indian race on death certificates. This problem was discovered in studies undertaken in the late 1980s.

Sources

U.S. Congress, Office of Technology Assessment, *Indian Health Care*, OTA-H-290 (1986), Table 4.8; U.S. Indian Health Service, *Selected Vital Statistics for Indian Health Service Areas and Service Units, 1972 to 1977* (1979), Table 20; U.S. Indian Health Service, *Chart Series Book* (1987, 1997), Tables 4.6 and 4.8.

Table Ag539–541   Life expectancy at birth for American Indians, by sex: 1940–1993

Contributed by C. Matthew Snipp

Year	Both sexes Ag539 Years	Males Ag540 Years	Females Ag541 Years
1940	51.6	51.3	51.9
1950	60.0	58.1	62.2
1960	61.7	60.0	65.7
1970	65.1	60.7	71.2
1980	71.1	67.1	75.1
1993	71.1 [1]	—	—

[1] Adjusted for misclassification of American Indians on death certificates; unadjusted estimate is higher.

Sources

C. Matthew Snipp, *American Indians: The First of This Land* (Russell Sage Foundation, 1989), Table 3.1; U.S. Indian Health Service, *Chart Series Book* (1997), Table 4.51.

Documentation

This table covers American Indians and Alaska Natives.

LAND AND RESOURCES

C. Matthew Snipp

Table Ag542–543   Lands purchased by the United States from American Indian tribes: 1795–1838

Contributed by C. Matthew Snipp

Year	Lands purchased Ag542 Acres	Consideration in money or land Ag543 Dollars	Year	Lands purchased Ag542 Acres	Consideration in money or land Ag543 Dollars
1795	11,808,499	210,000	1825	85,699,680	2,451,400
1801	2,641,920	— [1]	1826	4,132,480	5,938,000
1802	853,760	2,201	1827	1,337,780	533,748
1803	10,950,250	16,000	1828	1,285,120	63,741
1804	11,841,920	26,234	1829	990,720	189,795
1805	9,167,360	155,600	1830	6,695,760	1,143,401
1806	1,209,600	44,000	1831	24,092,000	23,409,661
1807	7,862,400	100,400	1832	8,326,397	16,440,767
1808	50,269,440	60,000	1833	19,122,280	6,958,187
1809	3,395,840	20,700	1834	4,128,640	549,576
1814	14,284,800	120,000	1835	5,113,920	7,631,649
1816	2,814,080	77,000	1836	22,652,720	9,257,646
1817	4,807,680	561,830	1837	4,698,240	1,082,083
1818	51,925,120	482,600	1838	18,250,000	3,738,000
1819	8,060,800	67,000			
1820	4,510,240	5,000			
1821	5,500,000	150,000			
1823	—	106,000			
1824	11,000,000	79,900			

[1] Included in figure for 1802.

Source

Secretary of War, "Indians Removed to West Mississippi from 1789," 25th Congress, 3rd session, *House Documents*, number 147, serial 347 (February 5, 1839), p. 9.

Documentation

Series Ag543. Compensation in land cessions was paid in the form of goods, cash annuities, and reserved land. That is, when Indians were resettled to a reservation, the value of the land to which they were resettled was considered part of their compensation. It is easy to put a dollar figure on goods and annuities, but the value of frontier land was more ambiguous. The federal government valued it at $1.25 an acre.

Table Ag544–546   Indian land claims decided – number and awards: 1883–1978[1]

Contributed by C. Matthew Snipp

	By dismissals	By decisions or awards	Amount of awards		By dismissals	By decisions or awards	Amount of awards
	Ag544	Ag545	Ag546		Ag544	Ag545	Ag546
Year	Number	Number	Dollars	Year	Number	Number	Dollars
1883	1	—	—	1938	9	2 [2]	372,817
1884	1	—	—	1939	5	1 [2]	—
1885	1	—	—	1940	16	—	—
1886	—	1	2,858,799	1941	14	4 [2]	2,022,367
1887	—	1	240,165	1942	13	1	5,024,847
1891	—	2	816,113	1943	3	—	—
1892	—	1	104,626	1944	4	—	—
1893	—	1	205,265	1945	5	1 [2]	—
1894	—	1	168,605	1946	9	—	—
1895	—	1	903,365	1949	7	—	—
1899	1	—	—	1950	12	—	—
1900	—	1	15,145	1951	7	2	3,489,844
1901	1	—	—	1952	8	3	2,998,220
1902	—	1 [2]	—	1953	7	—	—
1903	1	—	—	1954	8	1	927,688
1904	—	2	4,371,598	1955	4	1	864,108
1905	—	2 [2]	1,134,248	1956	1	3	1,515,495
1906	—	1	1,998,844	1957	12	1	433,014
1907	—	1	131,189	1958	10	4	6,860,239
1909	1	—	—	1959	12	2	3,288,975
1910	—	1	3,516,231	1960	7	13	21,588,008
1912	1	—	—	1961	5	5	14,926,255
1916	—	1	711,828	1962	5	2	18,063,860
1917	1	1 [2]	—	1963	9	8	18,319,187
1918	—	1	117,735	1964	7	9	15,796,255
1920	—	1	312,811	1965	7	27	57,019,353
1923	1	—	—	1966	2	12	38,701,570
1924	1	—	—	1967	2	7	21,497,767
1926	1	—	—	1968	3	23	43,576,733
1927	2	—	—	1969	23	24	32,025,817
1928	2	1	100,000	1970	2	14	44,254,099
1929	—	1	254,633	1971	4	20	46,621,561
1930	3	1	2,169,169	1972	11	14	33,078,112
1931	5	—	—	1973	11	32	40,837,122
1932	8	—	—	1974	11	24	46,409,564
1933	4	2	766,572	1975	3	9	35,945,459
1934	2	—	—	1976	—	15	63,055,867
1935	7	2	4,418,543	(TQ)	—	5	27,825,466
1936	7	—	—	1977	—	11	67,604,270
1937	6	1	5,313,347	1978	4	31	110,648,723

(TQ) indicates transitional quarter.

[1] Claims were decided by U.S. federal courts through 1946, and by the Indian Claims Commission thereafter. Also associated with this change was a switch in the reporting of data from a calendar to fiscal year basis.

[2] Amount of monetary compensation, if any, was not indicated for one or more cases.

Sources

1883–1946: Compiled from data in U.S. Congress, House of Representatives, Committee on Interior and Insular Affairs, "Investigation of the Bureau of Indian Affairs," 83rd Congress, 2nd session, *House Report*, number 2608, serial 11747, pp. 1563–71.

1947–1978: U.S. Indian Claims Commission, *Final Report: August 13, 1946 to September 30, 1978* (U.S. Government Printing Office, 1979), p. 125.

Documentation

Indian claims were heard in the U.S. Court of Claims, 1881–1946 and beginning 1979. In 1946, the Indian Claims Commission was established as an independent agency and it heard Indian claims until it was abolished in 1978. The U.S. Court of Federal Claims heard appeals of decisions of the Indian Claims Commission.

A dismissal occurs when a legal claim is denied by the court. An award takes place when the court rules in favor of the plaintiff. Land awarded is valued in monetary terms.

Series Ag544–545. Number of dockets completed.

Table Ag547–654 American Indian lands, by state: 1936–1996
Contributed by C. Matthew Snipp

	United States			Alabama			Alaska			Arizona		
	Total	Tribal	Allotted to individuals	Total	Tribal	Allotted to individuals	Total	Tribal	Allotted to individuals	Total	Tribal	Allotted to individuals
	Ag547	Ag548	Ag549	Ag550	Ag551	Ag552	Ag553	Ag554	Ag555	Ag556	Ag557	Ag558
Year	Acres	Acres	Acres	Acres	Acres	Acres	Acres	Acres	Acres	Acres	Acres	Acres
1936	51,399,536	33,104,060	18,295,476	—	—	—	—	—	—	19,088,602	18,915,802	172,800
1953	57,463,155	42,788,394	14,674,761	—	—	—	2,993,729	2,987,682	6,047	23,821,458	22,986,732	834,726
1962	50,617,234	38,854,074	11,763,160	—	—	—	96,947	87,636	9,311	19,649,468	19,389,073	260,395
1974	51,017,416	40,772,934	10,244,482	—	—	—	106,116	86,741	19,375	19,758,410	19,505,283	253,127
1983	52,611,213	42,385,033	10,226,180	—	—	—	792,204	86,759	705,445	19,809,213	19,556,806	252,407
1996	55,379,401	45,266,584	10,112,817	2,934	2,934	0	1,140,410	83,880	1,056,530	20,627,741	20,370,975	256,766

	California			Colorado			Connecticut			Florida		
	Total	Tribal	Allotted to individuals	Total	Tribal	Allotted to individuals	Total	Tribal	Allotted to individuals	Total	Tribal	Allotted to individuals
	Ag559	Ag560	Ag561	Ag562	Ag563	Ag564	Ag565	Ag566	Ag567	Ag568	Ag569	Ag570
Year	Acres	Acres	Acres	Acres	Acres	Acres	Acres	Acres	Acres	Acres	Acres	Acres
1936	568,548	507,865	60,683	435,583	396,143	39,440	—	—	—	26,741	26,741	0
1953	593,374	481,230	112,144	865,955	851,585	14,370	—	—	—	78,933	78,933	0
1962	553,343	467,168	86,175	751,551	746,420	5,131	—	—	—	78,974	78,974	0
1974	543,868	469,601	74,267	781,731	777,525	4,206	—	—	—	79,014	79,014	0
1983	569,227	501,388	67,839	786,946	783,903	3,043	—	—	—	79,495	79,495	0
1996	591,884	520,328	71,556	800,295	797,595	2,700	5,028	5,028	0	165,267	165,267	0

	Idaho			Iowa			Kansas			Louisiana		
	Total	Tribal	Allotted to individuals	Total	Tribal	Allotted to individuals	Total	Tribal	Allotted to individuals	Total	Tribal	Allotted to individuals
	Ag571	Ag572	Ag573	Ag574	Ag575	Ag576	Ag577	Ag578	Ag579	Ag580	Ag581	Ag582
Year	Acres	Acres	Acres	Acres	Acres	Acres	Acres	Acres	Acres	Acres	Acres	Acres
1936	517,882	57,369	460,513	3,480	3,480	0	38,058	863	37,195	—	—	—
1953	676,374	239,884	436,490	3,476	3,476	0	35,577	1,717	33,860	422	262	160
1962	831,049	440,448	390,601	4,105	4,105	0	28,204	1,784	26,420	262	262	(Z)
1974	786,445	440,189	346,256	4,133	4,133	0	26,155	2,669	23,486	262	262	0
1983	792,499	462,395	330,104	4,164	4,164	0	29,653	7,355	22,298	416	416	0
1996	721,112	450,270	270,842	7,271	7,271	0	34,176	10,841	23,335	2,528	2,528	0

Note appears at end of table

(continued)

Table Ag547–654 American Indian lands, by state: 1936–1996 *Continued*

	Maine			Massachusetts			Michigan			Minnesota		
	Total	Tribal	Allotted to individuals	Total	Tribal	Allotted to individuals	Total	Tribal	Allotted to individuals	Total	Tribal	Allotted to individuals
	Ag583	Ag584	Ag585	Ag586	Ag587	Ag588	Ag589	Ag590	Ag591	Ag592	Ag593	Ag594
Year	Acres	Acres	Acres	Acres	Acres	Acres	Acres	Acres	Acres	Acres	Acres	Acres
1936	—	—	—	—	—	—	13,635	683	12,952	742,857	565,003	177,854
1953	—	—	—	—	—	—	22,527	7,818	14,709	829,047	678,090	150,957
1962	—	—	—	—	—	—	17,243	7,816	9,427	725,719	670,525	55,194
1974	—	—	—	—	—	—	17,181	7,939	9,242	734,618	683,420	51,198
1983	221,633	221,633	0	—	—	—	21,496	12,230	9,266	765,377	714,118	51,259
1996	265,234	265,234	0	467	467	0	25,167	15,898	9,269	1,025,932	975,715	50,217

	Mississippi			Missouri			Montana			Nebraska		
	Total	Tribal	Allotted to individuals	Total	Tribal	Allotted to individuals	Total	Tribal	Allotted to individuals	Total	Tribal	Allotted to individuals
	Ag595	Ag596	Ag597	Ag598	Ag599	Ag600	Ag601	Ag602	Ag603	Ag604	Ag605	Ag606
Year	Acres	Acres	Acres	Acres	Acres	Acres	Acres	Acres	Acres	Acres	Acres	Acres
1936	2,609	2,609	0	—	—	—	6,054,808	958,758	5,096,050	67,947	7,317	60,630
1953	16,620	16,212	408	—	—	—	6,130,736	1,413,596	4,717,140	71,179	14,431	56,748
1962	16,479	16,270	209	373	0	373	5,253,484	1,613,201	3,640,283	67,053	14,235	52,818
1974	17,382	17,381	1	375	0	375	5,156,682	1,946,482	3,210,200	61,461	18,080	43,381
1983	17,654	17,635	19	374	0	374	5,222,711	2,256,358	2,966,353	64,535	23,389	41,146
1996	22,772	22,772	0	374	0	374	5,384,824	2,534,379	2,850,445	66,462	23,174	43,288

	Nevada			New Mexico			New York			North Carolina		
	Total	Tribal	Allotted to individuals	Total	Tribal	Allotted to individuals	Total	Tribal	Allotted to individuals	Total	Tribal	Allotted to individuals
	Ag607	Ag608	Ag609	Ag610	Ag611	Ag612	Ag613	Ag614	Ag615	Ag616	Ag617	Ag618
Year	Acres	Acres	Acres	Acres	Acres	Acres	Acres	Acres	Acres	Acres	Acres	Acres
1936	1,039,448	1,024,382	15,066	5,739,449	5,385,122	354,327	—	—	—	63,211	63,211	0
1953	1,336,310	1,254,158	82,152	3,147,982	3,054,796	93,186	—	—	—	56,115	56,115	0
1962	1,142,576	1,062,316	80,260	6,536,025	5,886,887	649,138	—	—	—	56,414	56,414	0
1974	1,143,430	1,064,622	78,808	7,149,155	6,468,353	680,802	—	—	—	56,444	56,444	0
1983	1,220,068	1,141,501	78,567	7,173,731	6,499,030	674,701	—	—	—	56,461	56,461	0
1996	1,228,021	1,149,492	78,529	8,169,407	7,500,567	668,840	53,188	53,188	0	51,166	51,166	0

North Dakota, Oklahoma, Oregon, Rhode Island

Year	North Dakota Total	Tribal	Allotted to individuals	Oklahoma Total	Tribal	Allotted to individuals	Oregon Total	Tribal	Allotted to individuals	Rhode Island Total	Tribal	Allotted to individuals
	Ag619	Ag620	Ag621	Ag622	Ag623	Ag624	Ag625	Ag626	Ag627	Ag628	Ag629	Ag630
	Acres	Acres	Acres	Acres	Acres	Acres	Acres	Acres	Acres	Acres	Acres	Acres
1936	3,184,716	117,142	3,067,574	2,881,703	78,543	2,803,160	1,572,792	1,197,192	375,600	—	—	—
1953	1,544,391	235,086	1,309,305	2,393,727	59,775	2,333,952	1,671,184	1,321,483	349,701	—	—	—
1962	866,251	130,075	736,176	1,697,236	58,627	1,638,609	691,677	496,062	195,615	—	—	—
1974	843,616	181,062	662,554	1,298,773	63,757	1,235,016	761,079	612,369	148,710	—	—	—
1983	842,282	210,116	632,166	1,199,401	87,635	1,111,766	759,148	622,297	136,851	2,335	2,335	0
1996	864,968	245,630	619,338	1,061,496	104,291	957,205	796,572	666,106	130,466			

South Carolina, South Dakota, Tennessee, Texas

Year	South Carolina Total	Tribal	Allotted to individuals	South Dakota Total	Tribal	Allotted to individuals	Tennessee Total	Tribal	Allotted to individuals	Texas Total	Tribal	Allotted to individuals
	Ag631	Ag632	Ag633	Ag634	Ag635	Ag636	Ag637	Ag638	Ag639	Ag640	Ag641	Ag642
	Acres	Acres	Acres	Acres	Acres	Acres	Acres	Acres	Acres	Acres	Acres	Acres
1936	—	—	—	4,823,828	661,775	4,162,053	—	—	—	3,071	3,071	0
1953	4,249	4,249	0	4,860,483	2,010,109	2,850,374	—	—	—	4,181	4,181	0
1962	—	—	—	4,853,712	1,933,166	2,920,546	—	—	—	11	0	11
1974	—	—	—	4,869,652	2,231,155	2,638,497	—	—	—	—	—	—
1983	—	—	—	5,092,335	2,636,292	2,456,043	—	—	—	—	—	—
1996	720	720	0	4,999,411	2,617,895	2,381,516	168	168	0	5,250	5,250	0

Utah, Washington, Wisconsin, Wyoming

Year	Utah Total	Tribal	Allotted to individuals	Washington Total	Tribal	Allotted to individuals	Wisconsin Total	Tribal	Allotted to individuals	Wyoming Total	Tribal	Allotted to individuals
	Ag643	Ag644	Ag645	Ag646	Ag647	Ag648	Ag649	Ag650	Ag651	Ag652	Ag653	Ag654
	Acres	Acres	Acres	Acres	Acres	Acres	Acres	Acres	Acres	Acres	Acres	Acres
1936	1,666,688	1,583,280	83,408	1,724,339	749,135	975,204	419,752	273,574	146,178	719,789	525,000	194,789
1953	1,127,465	1,049,628	77,837	2,688,759	1,772,677	916,082	431,199	289,807	141,392	2,057,703	1,914,682	143,021
1962	2,115,449	2,045,157	70,292	2,550,307	1,827,842	722,465	146,063	60,015	86,048	1,887,259	1,759,596	127,663
1974	2,276,074	2,233,675	42,399	2,498,780	1,958,767	540,013	161,548	80,069	81,479	1,885,032	1,783,942	101,090
1983	2,283,149	2,249,726	33,423	2,505,119	2,027,475	477,644	414,756	333,615	81,141	1,887,166	1,792,841	94,325
1996	2,331,007	2,297,770	33,237	2,602,094	2,170,346	431,748	435,484	352,515	82,969	1,888,236	1,794,589	93,647

(Z) Less than 1 acre.

Sources

Paul Stuart, *Nations within a Nation* (Greenwood Press, 1987), Tables 2.10, 2.11, 2.12, 2.13, 2.15; U.S. Department of the Interior, *Lands under Jurisdiction of the Bureau of Indian Affairs* (1996).

Documentation

States that do not appear in this table contain no Indian lands.

Table Ag655–680   Land under the jurisdiction of the Office of Indian Affairs, by state: 1881–1940

Contributed by C. Matthew Snipp

Year: type	Total Ag655 Acres	Arizona Ag656 Acres	Arkansas Ag657 Acres	California Ag658 Acres	Colorado Ag659 Acres	Florida Ag660 Acres	Idaho Ag661 Acres	Iowa Ag662 Acres	Kansas Ag663 Acres	Michigan Ag664 Acres	Minnesota Ag665 Acres	Mississippi Ag666 Acres	Montana Ag667 Acres
1881: total	155,632,312	3,092,720	—	415,841	12,467,200	—	2,748,981	692	137,747	66,332	5,026,447	—	29,356,800
1890: total	104,314,349	6,603,191	—	494,045	1,094,400	—	2,273,421	1,258	102,026	27,319	2,254,781	—	10,591,360
1900: total	78,372,185	15,150,757	—	496,305	483,750	23,062	1,364,500	2,965	28,279	8,317	1,566,707	—	9,500,700
1911: total	71,646,796	17,358,746	—	437,629	556,561	23,542	770,706	3,251	273,408	153,910	1,480,647	3,863 [6]	6,263,151
1933: total	52,651,393	18,657,984	80	625,354	443,751	125,880	803,239	3,361	34,821	20,233	549,320	9,347	6,055,009
1940: total	55,406,412 [1,2,3,4]	19,224,717 [3,4]	80	666,817 [4]	666,533	60,574	817,659	3,386 [5]	35,678	26,872	652,746	9,347	6,454,953
1940: trust-allotted	17,573,936 [1]	263,945	80	198,368	42,198	—	458,845	55	33,653	16,455	141,424	—	5,117,418
1940: tribal	36,046,660	18,953,098 [3]	—	458,934 [4]	622,512	60,574	355,802	3,253 [5]	1,015	3,081	491,972	—	1,214,907
1940: government-owned	1,785,816	7,674	—	9,515	1,823	—	3,012	78	1,010	7,336	19,350	9,347	122,628

Year: type	Nebraska Ag668 Acres	Nevada Ag669 Acres	New Mexico Ag670 Acres	New York Ag671 Acres	North Carolina Ag672 Acres	North Dakota Ag673 Acres	Oklahoma Ag674 Acres	Oregon Ag675 Acres	South Dakota Ag676 Acres	Utah Ag677 Acres	Washington Ag678 Acres	Wisconsin Ag679 Acres	Wyoming Ag680 Acres
1881: total	436,252	885,015	7,228,731	86,366	65,211	—	41,100,915	3,853,800	36,616,448	2,039,040	7,079,348	586,026	2,342,400
1890: total	136,947	954,135	10,002,525	87,677	65,211	5,861,120	39,156,040	2,075,240	11,661,360	3,972,480	4,045,284	512,129	2,342,400
1900: total	74,592	954,135	1,667,485	87,677	98,211	3,701,724	26,397,237	1,300,225	8,991,791	2,039,040	2,333,574	381,051	1,810,000
1911: total	344,375	696,749	4,520,652	87,677	63,211	2,786,162	22,736,473	1,719,561	7,221,939	292,101	2,948,708	590,094	318,543
1933: total	69,280	866,176	6,188,964	—	57,705	1,034,123	2,919,886	1,718,510	5,544,424	1,571,020	2,712,915	395,919	2,249,576
1940: total	75,950 [7]	1,127,171	7,153,109	—	56,849	1,036,292	2,844,431 [8]	1,736,794 [9]	5,864,604	1,693,160	2,739,830	445,443	2,013,409
1940: trust-allotted	64,428 [7]	88,841	933,687	—	—	987,035	2,744,786 [8]	401,634 [9]	4,662,210	95,087	1,000,041	144,804	178,942
1940: tribal	11,580	1,036,491	4,873,487	—	56,464	33,725	70,180	1,327,350	1,041,641	1,591,400	1,734,950	276,013	1,828,281
1940: government-owned	—	1,839	1,345,935	—	385	15,532	29,455	7,810	160,753	6,673	4,839	24,626	6,186

1 Includes 399,193 acres of taxable trust land.

2 Includes 3,212 acres of taxable tribal land.

3 Does not include 495,578 acres of land in litigation which was apparently lost to the Atchison, Topeka, and Santa Fe railroad.

4 Includes Santa Ynez reservation containing 75 acres belonging to the Catholic Church.

5 Includes 3,219 acres of taxable tribal land.

6 Reservation established 1918.

7 Includes 27,642 acres of taxable trust land.

8 Includes 370,285 acres of taxable trust land.

9 Includes 1,266 acres of taxable restricted land.

Source

U.S. Department of the Interior, *Statistical Supplement to the Annual Report of the Commissioner of Indian Affairs for the Fiscal Year Ended June 20, 1940* (1941).

Table Ag681–684   Land under the jurisdiction of the Bureau of Indian Affairs: 1881–1985

Contributed by Michelle L. Butler and Myron P. Gutmann

Year	Indian Total Ag681 Thousand acres	Trust-allotted Ag682 Thousand acres	Tribal Ag683 Thousand acres	Government-owned Ag684 Thousand acres	Year	Indian Total Ag681 Thousand acres	Trust-allotted Ag682 Thousand acres	Tribal Ag683 Thousand acres	Government-owned Ag684 Thousand acres
1881	155,632	—	155,632	—	1930	32,097	—	32,097	—
1882	143,526	—	143,526	—	1932	46,795	—	46,795	—
1884	137,767	—	137,767	—	1933	52,651	—	47,398	—
					1934	49,388	—	49,388	—
1885	137,725	—	137,725	—					
1886	135,978	—	135,978	—	1935	50,696	—	50,696	—
1887	136,395	—	136,395	—	1936	51,057	—	51,057	—
1888	118,484	—	118,484	—	1937	34,620	—	34,620	—
1889	116,386	—	116,386	—	1939	54,839	17,594	35,402	1,842
1890	104,314	—	104,314	—	1940	55,406	17,574	36,047	1,786
1891	91,146	—	91,146	—	1941	55,392	17,762	36,276	1,354
1892	92,478	—	92,478	—	1942	55,410	17,503	36,602	1,305
1893	85,873	—	85,873	—	1943	55,657	17,441	36,957	1,258
1894	85,581	—	85,581	—	1944	56,577	17,474	37,233	1,869
1895	84,571	—	84,571	—	1945	55,363	16,796	37,251	1,317
1896	83,405	—	83,405	—	1946	56,567	17,143	37,524	1,901
1897	82,770	—	82,770	—	1949	56,005	16,534	38,608	863
1900	84,602	6,737	77,865	—	1953	55,406	14,251	40,178	977
1901	76,117	—	—	—	1954	54,108	13,652	39,882	574
1902	75,149	—	75,149	—	1955	53,771	13,662	39,487	622
1903	83,426	8,823	74,603	—	1956	53,376	13,328	39,465	583
1904	72,392	—	72,392	—	1957	53,331	13,223	39,549	558
1905	58,202	—	58,202	—	1958	57,023	12,896	42,304	1,823
1906	55,831	—	55,831	—	1959	56,870	12,560	39,676	4,634
1907	53,549	—	53,549	—	1960	58,080	12,235	41,226	4,618
1908	52,013	—	52,013	—	1961	57,107	11,958	40,538	4,612
1909	49,566	—	49,566	—	1962	55,247	11,763	38,814	4,669
1910	72,146	31,094	41,052	—	1963	55,196	11,607	38,877	4,713
1911	72,535	32,272	40,263	—	1964	55,134	11,450	38,975	4,709
1912	71,917	32,414	39,503	—	1965	55,319	11,287	39,097	4,935
1913	72,147	33,571	38,576	—	1966	55,294	11,121	39,251	4,922
1914	69,900	34,072	35,828	—	1967	55,413	11,019	39,443	4,951
1915	68,103	34,768	33,334	—	1968	55,427	10,894	39,586	4,947
1916	71,978	35,565	36,413	—	1969	55,351	10,757	39,641	4,952
1917	71,306	35,740	35,566	—	1970	55,408	10,698	39,642	5,068
1918	71,094	36,861	34,233	—	1974	53,175	51,017	40,773	2,158
1919	72,546	36,986	35,560	—	1975	51,845	50,950	40,822	896
1920	72,661	37,159	35,502	—	1976	51,834	51,373	41,334	461
1921	35,502	—	35,502	—	1978	52,250	51,789	41,679	461
1922	34,979	—	34,979	—	1981	52,473	52,022	42,033	451
1923	34,988	—	34,988	—	1982	52,511	52,061	42,138	450
1924	34,948	—	34,948	—	1983	53,054	52,611	42,385	443
1925	31,582	—	31,582	—	1984	53,887	53,446	43,237	441
1926	81,791	—	31,791	—	1985	54,051	53,634	43,450	417
1927	31,420	—	31,420	—					
1928	30,262	—	30,262	—					
1929	32,015	—	32,015	—					

Sources

U.S. Department of the Interior: 1881–1897, 1900, 1903, 1910–1920, 1953–1958, *Annual Report of the Secretary of the Interior*, various issues; 1901, 1902, 1904–1909, 1939, 1940, 1942–1946, 1949, *Annual Report of the Commissioner of Indian Affairs* and *Statistical Supplements*, various issues; 1921–1930, 1932–1937, 1941, compiled by the Commissioner of Indian Affairs; 1959–1970, *Annual Real Property Management Report*, various issues; 1974–1988, *Annual Report of Indian Lands*, various issues.

Documentation

Indian lands are the private landholdings of individual Indians or Indian tribes that are subject to special restrictive provisions of federal law administered by the Bureau of Indian Affairs. They have been set aside for Indian use by treaties, congressional acts, and executive orders. Although most of these lands are in reservations for specific tribes, there are groups of scattered off-reservation allotments in individual ownership and other small tracts of land occupied by Indian groups. The *Annual Report of Indian Lands* was discontinued in 1988, and the last available data are for fiscal year 1985.

Table Ag685   Buffalo population: 1800–1983

Contributed by C. Matthew Snipp

Year	Buffalo Ag685 Number	Year	Buffalo Ag685 Number
1800	40,000,000	1885	20,000
1850	20,000,000	1889	1,091
1865	15,000,000	1895	— [1]
1870	14,000,000	1902	1,940
1875	1,000,000	1983	50,000
1880	395,000		

[1] Fewer than 1,000.

Source

Russell Thornton, *American Indians Holocaust and Survival* (University of Oklahoma Press, 1987), Table 3-1, p. 52.

Documentation

Thornton constructed this table from an Interior Department publication and two other reference works about North American animal populations. As for all such figures produced before the advent of modern methods for studying wildlife ecology, these data are speculative.

The buffalo population in aboriginal times is estimated at 60 million.

Table Ag686–688   Timber cut on Indian land: 1910–1998[1]

Contributed by C. Matthew Snipp

Year	Amount Ag686 Thousand board feet	Value Total Ag687 Dollars	Value Per thousand board feet Ag688 Dollars per thousand board feet	Year	Amount Ag686 Thousand board feet	Value Total Ag687 Dollars	Value Per thousand board feet Ag688 Dollars per thousand board feet
1910	141,532	900,612	6.36	1935	277,795	903,933	3.25
1911	137,208	752,303	5.48	1936	337,951	1,056,042	3.12
1912	123,472	739,699	5.99	1937	493,493	1,604,737	3.25
1913	170,766	1,028,184	6.02	1938	457,504	1,239,456	2.71
1914	143,426	780,856	5.44	1939	510,957	1,437,610	2.81
1915	138,624	773,483	5.58	1940	531,965	1,423,627	2.68
1916	167,602	726,483	4.33	1941	608,366	1,792,951	2.95
1917	205,312	715,453	3.48	1942	577,360	1,890,767	3.27
1918	323,131	1,253,651	3.88	1943	504,117	1,905,147	3.78
1919	291,164	1,303,840	4.48	1944	528,472	2,326,228	4.40
1920	398,485	1,585,812	3.98	1945	475,662	2,113,884	4.44
1921	348,300	1,390,436	3.99	1946	497,972	2,262,791	4.54
1922	216,583	808,551	3.73	1947	512,469	2,574,117	5.02
1923	493,563	1,856,323	3.76	1948	597,662	4,816,437	8.06
1924	510,314	1,937,245	3.80	1949	573,236	5,411,061	9.44
1925	467,779	1,921,157	4.11	1950	688,791	6,067,847	8.81
1926	579,958	2,446,455	4.22	1951	719,076	7,720,989	10.74
1927	627,365	2,953,752	4.71	1952	658,728	8,369,011	12.71
1928	639,244	2,676,779	4.19	1953	696,189	9,567,608	13.74
1929	660,257	2,818,317	4.27	1954	638,156	9,002,699	14.11
1930	541,014	2,273,820	4.20	1955	778,413	11,715,027	15.05
1931	315,366	1,240,817	3.93	1956	740,033	14,430,583	19.50
1932	121,509	393,151	3.24	1957	539,628	9,234,767	17.11
1933	99,047	290,292	2.93	1958	620,770	11,106,861	17.89
1934	167,992	452,195	2.69	1959	715,997	12,633,751	17.64

Note appears at end of table

Table Ag686–688   Timber cut on Indian land: 1910–1998   *Continued*

Year	Amount Ag686 Thousand board feet	Total Ag687 Dollars	Per thousand board feet Ag688 Dollars per thousand board feet	Year	Amount Ag686 Thousand board feet	Total Ag687 Dollars	Per thousand board feet Ag688 Dollars per thousand board feet
1960	669,333	11,649,548	17.40	1980	845,508	89,919,452	106.35
1961	625,483	8,466,873	13.54	1981	803,415	75,546,488	94.03
1962	651,447	8,616,658	13.23	1982	672,207	43,126,777	64.16
1963	764,947	10,429,272	13.63	1983	757,357	61,580,094	81.31
1964	885,739	13,023,283	14.70	1984	787,016	61,856,891	78.60
1965	922,906	13,398,940	14.52	1985	646,479	48,132,215	74.45
1966	889,819	15,596,609	17.53	1986	762,753	58,085,592	76.15
1967	993,079	18,401,933	18.53	1987	865,998	68,780,222	79.42
1968	1,090,731	27,195,639	24.93	1988	837,027	73,974,960	88.38
1969	964,378	33,541,375	34.78	1989	756,248	82,025,992	108.46
1970	843,408	23,020,591	27.29	1990	803,000	84,934,000	105.77
1971	939,995	32,464,238	34.54	1991	785,000	96,701,000	123.19
1972	1,040,868	45,680,770	43.89	1992	719,000	114,000,000	158.55
1973	1,017,190	71,112,876	69.91	1993	633,282	136,613,771	215.72
1974	1,005,166	75,816,021	75.43	1994	655,363	164,668,463	251.26
1975	914,033	51,622,969	56.48	1995	658,855	143,365,429	217.60
1976	1,005,166	76,394,275	76.00	1996	659,900	132,885,600	201.37
1977	1,013,886	90,548,839	89.31	1997	686,627	143,519,589	209.02
1978	1,015,603	105,740,137	104.12	1998	672,830	117,829,852	175.13
1979	926,838	119,350,108	128.77				

[1] Calendar years through 1976; fiscal years thereafter.

Sources

Alan S. Newell, *A Forest in Trust: Three-Quarters of a Century of Indian Forestry, 1910–1986* (U.S. Bureau of Indian Affairs, Division of Forestry, 1986), Table 7.3; U.S. Bureau of Indian Affairs, Division of Forestry, unpublished data provided in personal communication with Bill Downes.

Table Ag689–694   Sales value and royalties received from leasable minerals on Indian lands: 1937–1998[1]

Contributed by C. Matthew Snipp

Year(s)	Total Sales value Ag689 Dollars	Total Royalties Ag690 Dollars	Oil and gas operations Sales value Ag691 Dollars	Oil and gas operations Royalties Ag692 Dollars	Mining operations Sales value Ag693 Dollars	Mining operations Royalties Ag694 Dollars
1937–1945	315,506,576	30,578,831	126,576,610	14,697,376	188,929,966	15,881,455
1946	29,100,021	2,784,762	19,549,681	2,257,035	9,550,340	527,727
1947	43,578,531	4,317,775	31,519,492	3,640,684	12,059,039	677,091
1948	61,658,481	6,212,113	46,672,972	5,361,384	14,985,509	850,729
1949	43,916,662	4,817,825	37,474,196	4,287,522	6,442,466	530,303
1950	49,326,320	5,269,148	38,281,811	4,392,287	11,044,509	876,861
1951	55,316,469	5,813,223	41,843,174	4,749,297	13,473,295	1,063,926
1952	53,684,040	5,704,966	40,654,689	4,612,642	13,029,351	1,092,324
1953	59,536,505	6,645,156	48,038,668	5,522,898	11,497,837	1,122,258
1954	65,309,464	7,401,102	50,931,731	5,958,121	14,377,733	1,442,981
1955	72,685,996	8,071,732	51,276,267	5,854,292	21,409,729	2,217,440
1956	87,104,289	9,812,547	55,971,039	6,418,870	31,133,250	3,393,677
1957	97,873,284	11,018,753	69,479,204	7,989,914	28,394,080	3,028,839
1958	154,649,503	18,055,618	126,341,443	15,167,706	28,308,060	2,887,912
1959	203,892,663	24,389,782	176,850,081	21,589,345	27,042,582	2,800,437
1960	196,686,844	24,102,820	168,509,591	21,151,044	28,177,253	2,951,776
1961	175,098,066	21,837,268	147,742,396	19,117,152	27,355,670	2,720,116
1962	159,031,587	20,264,891	136,512,664	18,002,610	22,518,923	2,262,281
1963	160,657,629	20,305,255	134,779,958	17,833,451	25,877,671	2,471,804
1964	142,951,900	17,629,304	115,521,788	15,013,867	27,430,112	2,615,437

Notes appear at end of table

(continued)

Table Ag689–694   Sales value and royalties received from leasable minerals on Indian lands: 1937–1998   *Continued*

Year(s)	Total		Oil and gas operations		Mining operations	
	Sales value	Royalties	Sales value	Royalties	Sales value	Royalties
	Ag689	Ag690	Ag691	Ag692	Ag693	Ag694
	Dollars	Dollars	Dollars	Dollars	Dollars	Dollars
1965	134,989,800	16,900,856	109,663,086	14,593,704	25,326,714	2,307,152
1966	134,367,834	16,602,900	106,826,872	14,272,026	27,540,962	2,330,874
1967	160,657,786	19,966,871	126,638,644	16,952,321	34,019,142	3,014,550
1968	143,339,955	18,085,138	110,940,205	15,159,309	32,399,750	2,925,829
1969	150,004,002	18,666,567	111,859,351	15,220,945	38,144,651	3,445,622
1970	169,348,291	20,588,951	120,457,129	16,105,829	48,891,162	4,483,122
1971	180,106,151	21,977,541	123,900,674	16,854,455	56,205,477	5,123,086
1972	177,464,803	21,679,278	121,259,326	16,556,192	56,205,477	5,123,086
1973	196,710,449	23,857,512	134,253,337	18,387,463	62,457,112	5,470,049
1974	317,127,941	39,623,445	235,389,278	33,410,808	81,738,663	6,212,637
1975	379,135,124	47,920,982	272,611,184	39,203,536	106,523,940	8,717,446
1976 [2]	560,469,942	62,884,499	304,908,208	44,372,088	255,561,734	18,512,411
1977	558,007,033	70,005,831	330,544,539	47,713,146	227,462,494	22,292,685
1978	562,206,769	70,948,769	346,852,323	50,237,457	215,354,446	20,711,312
1979	779,499,668	88,868,467	469,169,649	67,284,003	310,330,019	21,584,464
1980	1,002,185,112	119,201,383	669,418,876	97,912,151	332,766,236	21,289,232
1981	1,337,628,354	161,473,757	973,470,089	140,799,715	364,158,265	20,674,042
1982	1,454,560,378	162,726,747	985,905,263	146,938,198	468,655,115	15,788,549
1983	1,446,426,252	156,373,198	943,242,064	140,015,543	503,184,188	16,357,655
1984	1,233,235,553	128,386,900	895,451,328	113,268,170	337,784,225	15,118,730
1985	1,306,459,744	139,424,708	824,112,541	110,879,143	482,347,203	28,545,565
1986	978,840,191	105,018,658	522,547,105	69,684,355	456,293,086	35,334,303
1987	997,632,684	104,787,583	504,382,287	68,054,095	493,250,397	36,733,488
1988	967,868,524	112,282,668	422,367,727	58,538,720	545,500,797	53,743,948
1989	1,038,077,572	122,429,802	460,334,417	65,468,865	577,743,155	56,960,937
1990	1,156,002,555	151,992,888	550,184,767	81,958,260	605,817,788	70,034,628
1991	1,108,172,340	145,185,355	493,571,772	73,654,730	614,600,568	71,530,625
1992	1,151,963,524	156,397,215	528,466,810	81,016,719	623,496,714	75,380,496
1993	1,298,354,801	166,371,356	585,470,892	88,388,887	712,883,909	77,982,469
1994	1,183,045,371	160,252,886	541,270,592	80,231,967	641,774,779	80,020,919
1995	1,083,248,776	146,401,447	469,560,236	69,954,064	613,688,540	76,447,383
1996	1,229,957,257	168,181,612	631,325,538	95,689,407	598,631,719	72,492,205
1997	1,471,638,220	205,226,131	852,127,552	128,948,168	619,510,668	76,277,963
1998	1,276,873,496	175,792,659	710,994,441	106,532,874	565,879,055	69,259,785

[1] Fiscal years through 1976; calendar years thereafter.

[2] Data apply to an eighteen-month period, July 1975 through December 1976.

Sources

1937–1971: Conservation Division, U.S. Geological Survey, *Federal and Indian Lands: Coal, Phosphate, Potash, Sodium, and Other Mineral Production, Royalty Income, and Related Statistics, 1920–1972* (U.S. Department of the Interior, 1973), p. 36.

1972–1998: Royalty Management Program, Minerals Management Service, *Mineral Revenues 1980–89: Report on Receipts from Federal and Indian Leases*, Table 14; *Mineral Revenues 1993: Report on Receipts from Federal and Indian Leases*, Table 25; *Mineral Revenues 1996: Report on Receipts from Federal and Indian Leases*, Table 28; *Mineral Revenues 1998: Report on Receipts from Federal and Indian Leases*, Table 28. Data available at the Internet site of the Minerals Management Service.

Documentation

Series Ag689, Ag691, and Ag693. Figures reflect the total value of the extracted resource.

Series Ag690, Ag692, and Ag694. Figures represent the royalties paid for the extraction rights.

RESERVATIONS AND FEDERAL EXPENDITURES

C. Matthew Snipp

Table Ag695–699   Selected American Indian reservations – land area, population, and year established: 1990

Contributed by C. Matthew Snipp

Reservation	State	Total area	Population	American Indian population	Year established
	Ag695	Ag696	Ag697	Ag698	Ag699
	—	Acres	Number	Number	Year
Poarch Creek	AL	230	212	149	1984
Ak-Chin (Maricopa)	AZ	21,840	446	405	1912
Camp Verde	AZ	640	618	569	1871
Cocopah	AZ	6,009	515	436	1917
Colorado River	AZ–CA	269,921	7,865	2,345	1865
Fort Apache	AZ	1,664,972	10,394	9,825	1871
Fort McDowell	AZ	24,680	640	560	1903
Fort Yuma	AZ–CA	43,942	2,084	1,160	1884
Gila Bend	AZ	10,404	0	0	1882
Gila River	AZ	371,933	9,540	9,516	1859
Havasupai	AZ	188,077	423	400	1880
Hopi	AZ	1,561,213	7,360	7,061	1882
Hualapai	AZ	992,463	822	802	1883
Kaibab	AZ	120,840	165	102	1913
Navajo	AZ–NM–UT	16,224,896	148,451	143,405	1868
Pascua Yaqui	AZ	892	2,412	2,284	1978
Payson Community	AZ	85	102	97	1974
Salt River	AZ	52,729	4,852	3,533	1879
San Carlos	AZ	1,853,841	7,294	7,110	1871
San Juan Southern Paiute	AZ	0	204	204	1989
San Xavier	AZ	71,095	1,172	1,073	1874
Tohono O'Odham (Papago)	AZ	2,774,370	8,730	8,480	1874
Yavapai	AZ	1,409	176	134	1935
Alturas Rancheria	CA	20	5	5	1906
Aqua Caliente	CA	31,610	20,206	117	1876
Augustine	CA	502	0	0	1891
Barona Rancheria	CA	5,904	537	373	1875
Benton Paiute	CA	163	63	52	1915
Berry Creek Rancheria	CA	65	2	2	1916
Big Bend Rancheria	CA	40	3	3	1916
Big Lagoon Rancheria	CA	20	22	19	1918
Big Pine	CA	279	452	331	1912
Big Sandy	CA	228	51	38	1909
Bishop	CA	875	1,408	935	1912
Blue Lake Rancheria	CA	31	58	30	1983
Bridgeport Indian Colony	CA	40	49	37	1974
Buena Vista	CA	0	1	1	1974
Cabazon	CA	1,706	819	20	1876
Cahuilla	CA	18,884	104	82	1875
Campo	CA	16,512	281	143	1893
Capitain Grande	CA	15,753	0	0	1875
Cedarville Rancheria	CA	20	8	6	1906
Chemehuevi	CA	30,653	358	95	1970
Chicken Ranch Rancheria	CA	3	73	10	—
Cold Springs Rancheria	CA	155	192	159	1961
Colusa Rancheria	CA	573	22	19	1907
Cortina Rancheria	CA	640	30	22	1907
Coyote Valley Rancheria	CA	58	135	122	1976
Cuyapaipe	CA	4,103	0	0	1891
Dry Creek Rancheria	CA	75	75	38	1915

(continued)

Table Ag695–699 Selected American Indian reservations – land area, population, and year established: 1990 *Continued*

Reservation	State	Total area	Population	American Indian population	Year established
	Ag695	Ag696	Ag697	Ag698	Ag699
	—	Acres	Number	Number	Year
Elk Valley Rancheria	CA	105	77	32	1906
Enterprise Rancheria	CA	40	5	5	1906
Fort Bidwell	CA	3,335	118	107	1879
Fort Mojave	CA–AZ–NV	41,884	758	592	1911
Fort Independence	CA	352	69	38	1915
Greenville Rancheria	CA	51	24	7	1983
Grindstone Rancheria	CA	120	103	102	1906
Hoopa Valley	CA	85,446	2,143	1,733	1876
Hopland Rancheria	CA	63	189	142	1907
Jackson Rancheria	CA	331	21	13	1895
Jamul Indian Village	CA	6	0	0	1981
Karuk Tribe	CA	243	421	33	1979
La Jolla	CA	8,541	152	121	1875
La Posta	CA	3,556	10	3	1893
Laytonville Rancheria	CA	200	142	129	1906
Likely Rancheria	CA	1	0	0	1922
Lone Pine	CA	237	244	168	1912
Lookout Rancheria	CA	40	17	12	1913
Los Coyotes Rancheria	CA	25,050	58	42	1900
Manchester Point Rancheria	CA	363	200	178	1909
Manzanita	CA	3,579	84	47	1893
Mesa Grande	CA	1,000	96	72	1875
Middletown Rancheria	CA	109	79	18	1910
Montgomery Creek Rancheria	CA	72	11	9	1915
Morongo	CA	32,362	1,072	1,070	1908
North Fork Rancheria	CA	80	4	0	1983
Pala	CA	11,893	1,070	563	1875
Pauma and Yulma	CA	5,877	148	137	1892
Pechanga	CA	4,394	398	289	1882
Picayune Rancheria	CA	29	32	15	1983
Pinoleville Rancheria	CA	99	130	77	1906
Potter Valley Rancheria	CA	10	1	1	1909
Quartz Valley Rancheria	CA	174	124	19	1983
Ramona	CA	560	0	0	1893
Redding Rancheria	CA	31	101	79	1985
Redwood Valley Rancheria	CA	177	142	14	1909
Resighini Rancheria	CA	228	28	26	1938
Rincon	CA	4,276	1,352	379	1875
Roaring Creek Rancheria	CA	80	18	18	1915
Robinson Rancheria	CA	113	139	113	1908
Rohnerville Rancheria	CA	60	8	8	1983
Round Valley	CA	30,538	1,183	577	1858
Rumsey Rancheria	CA	185	8	4	1907
San Manuel	CA	658	80	56	1891
San Pasqual	CA	1,380	512	212	1910
Santa Rosa Rancheria	CA	170	323	284	1921
Santa Rosa	CA	11,093	50	37	1907
Santa Ynez	CA	99	50	37	1901
Santa Ysabel	CA	15,527	169	150	1875
Sheep Ranch Rancheria	CA	1	0	0	1916
Sherwood Valley Rancheria	CA	356	15	9	1908
Shingle Springs Rancheria	CA	160	18	7	1916
Soboba	CA	5,916	369	308	1883
Stewart's Point Rancheria	CA	40	91	86	1936
Sulphur Bank Rancheria	CA	50	93	90	1949
Susanville Rancheria	CA	151	454	154	1923
Sycuan Rancheria	CA	640	4	0	1875
Table Bluff Rancheria	CA	0	48	43	1916
Table Mountain Rancheria	CA	61	51	48	1916
Timbi-Sha West Shoshone	CA	40	55	55	1982

Table Ag695–699   Selected American Indian reservations – land area, population, and year established: 1990   *Continued*

Reservation	State Ag695	Total area Ag696	Population Ag697	American Indian population Ag698	Year established Ag699
	—	Acres	Number	Number	Year
Torres-Martinez	CA	24,024	4,462	143	1876
Trinidad Rancheria	CA	47	78	59	1917
Tule River	CA	55,356	798	745	1873
Tuolumne Rancheria	CA	336	135	107	1910
Twenty-Nine Palms	CA	402	0	0	1891
Upper Lake Rancheria	CA	119	76	28	1907
Viejas	CA	1,609	411	227	1875
XL Ranch	CA	9,255	35	27	1938
Yurok Tribe	CA	56,585	1,357	463	1891
Southern Ute	CO	818,000	7,804	1,044	1863
Ute Mountain	CO	595,787	1,320	1,264	1863
Mashantucket Pequot	CT	2,000 [1]	83	55	1655
Mohegan	CT	244	—	—	1995
Big Cypress	FL	42,739	484	447	1930 [3]
Brighton	FL	35,805	524	402	1930 [3]
Hollywood	FL	480	1,394	481	1930 [3]
Immolakee	FL	600	—	—	1993
Miccosukee	FL	75,145	94	94	1930 [3]
Omaha	IA–NE	26,792	5,227	1,908	1854
Sac and Fox	IA	4,300	577	564	1856
Coeur d'Alene	ID	345,000	5,802	749	1873
Duck Valley	ID	289,819	1,101	1,022	1877
Fort Hall	ID	544,000	5,114	3,035	1868
Kootenai	ID	250	65	61	1855
Nez Perce	ID	750,000	16,160	1,863	1855
Iowa	KS	1,619	172	83	1836
Kickapoo	KS	4,879	478	370	1862
Potawatomi	KS	22,764	279	502	1846
Sac and Fox	KS–NE	7,924	210	49	1842
Chitimacha	LA	283	286	212	1935
Coushatta	LA	154	36	33	1771
Tunica-Biloxi	LA	154	29	16	1981
Gay Head	MA	485	—	—	1987
Aroostook Band of Mic-Mac	ME	100	—	—	1991
Houlton Maliseet	ME	800	—	—	1980
Indian Township	ME	23,000	617	541	1794
Penobscot	ME	148,525	517	430	1786
Pleasant Point	ME	212	572	523	1794
Bay Mills	MI	2,209	461	403	1855
Grand Traverse	MI	450	228	208	1984
Hannahville Community	MI	4,025	181	173	1913
Isabella	MI	138,240	22,944	795	1864
Lac Vieux Desert	MI	250	124	119	1988
L'Anse	MI	54,561	3,293	724	1854
Sault Ste. Marie	MI	1,265	768	554	1974
Bois Forte (Nett Lake)	MN	105,284 [2]	358	346	1866
Deer Creek	MN	— [2]	186	6	1866
Fond du Lac	MN	100,000	3,229	1,106	1854
Grand Portage	MN	47,000	306	207	1854
Leech Lake	MN	602,880	8,669	3,390	1854
Lower Sioux Community	MN	1,743	259	225	1887
Mille Lacs	MN	61,000	470	428	1855
Prairie Island Community	MN	400	60	56	1887
Red Lake	MN	837,736	3,699	3,602	1863
Sandy Lake	MN	—	37	36	—
Shakopee	MN	1,500	203	153	1888
Upper Sioux Community	MN	755	49	43	1938
Vermillion Lake	MN	— [2]	91	87	1866
White Earth	MN	837,120	8,727	2,759	1867
Mississippi Choctaw	MS	20,683	4,073	3,932	1830

Notes appear at end of table

(continued)

Table Ag695–699   Selected American Indian reservations – land area, population, and year established: 1990 *Continued*

Reservation	State	Total area	Population	American Indian population	Year established
	Ag695	Ag696	Ag697	Ag698	Ag699
	—	Acres	Number	Number	Year
Blackfeet	MT	1,525,712	8,849	7,025	1888
Crow	MT	2,235,093	6,370	4,724	1888
Flathead	MT	1,244,000	21,259	5,130	1855
Fort Belknap	MT	654	2,508	2,338	1888
Fort Peck	MT	2,093,318	10,595	5,782	1888
Northern Cheyenne	MT	450,000	3,923	3,542	1884
Rocky Boy's	MT	120,000	1,954	1,882	1916
Santee Sioux	NE	9,358	758	425	1866
Winnebago	NE	27,537	2,341	1,156	1865
Eastern Cherokee	NC	56,688	6,527	5,388	1925
Devil's Lake Sioux	ND	245,141	3,588	2,676	1867
Fort Berthold	ND	1,000,000	5,395	2,999	1851
Turtle Mountain	ND	140,107	7,106	6,772	1882
Acoma Pueblo	NM	378,114	2,590	2,551	1877
Alamo (Navajo)	NM	63,109	1,271	1,228	1868
Canoncito	NM	76,813	1,189	1,177	1868
Cochiti Pueblo	NM	50,681	1,342	666	1864
Isleta Pueblo	NM	211,045	2,915	2,699	1864
Jemez Pueblo	NM	89,619	1,750	1,738	1864
Jicarilla Apache	NM	870,580	2,617	2,375	1887
Laguna Pueblo	NM	533,000	3,731	3,634	1864
Mescalero Apache	NM	460,679	2,695	2,516	1852
Nambe Pueblo	NM	19,120	1,402	329	1864
Picuris Pueblo	NM	14,980	1,882	147	1864
Pojoaque Pueblo	NM	11,602	2,556	177	1864
Ramah Community	NM	146,953	194	191	1868
Sandia Pueblo	NM	22,890	3,971	358	1864
San Felipe Pueblo	NM	48,930	2,434	1,859	1864
San Ildefonso	NM	26,198	1,499	347	1864
San Juan Pueblo	NM	12,237	5,209	1,276	1864
Santa Ana Pueblo	NM	61,935	593	481	1883
Santa Clara Pueblo	NM	45,969	10,193	1,246	1909
Santo Domingo	NM	71,331	2,992	2,947	1864
Taos Pueblo	NM	95,341	4,745	1,212	1864
Tesuque Pueblo	NM	16,813	697	232	1864
Zia Pueblo	NM	121,611	637	637	1864
Zuni Pueblo	NM	463,271	7,412	7,073	1864
Battle Mountain	NV	683	—	—	1917
Carson Colony	NV	160	248	235	1916
Dresslerville Colony	NV	39	152	144	1917
Duck Valley	NV	289,819	1,101	1,022	1877
Duckwater	NV	3,914	135	115	1940
Elko Colony	NV	193	—	—	1918
Ely Colony	NV	100	59	52	1931
Fallon Colony	NV	5,540	546	506	1930
Fort McDermitt	NV	35,326	396	387	1867
Las Vegas Colony	NV	3,867	80	72	1911
Lovelock Colony	NV	20	94	80	1907
Moapa River	NV	71,954	375	190	1875
Pyramid Lake	NV	476,689	1,388	959	1874
Reno-Sparks Colony	NV	2,004	264	262	1917
South Fork	NV	13,049	—	—	1941
Summit Lake	NV	10,863	7	6	1913
Walker River	NV	323,406	802	620	1871
Washoe	NV	63,400	157	65	1936
Wells Colony	NV	80	—	—	1977
Winnemucca Colony	NV	360	67	61	1917
Yerington	NV	1,632	428	324	1917
Yomba	NV	4,718	95	88	1937
Allegany	NY	30,189	7,315	1,062	1794

Table Ag695–699 Selected American Indian reservations – land area, population, and year established: 1990 _Continued_

Reservation	State	Total area	Population	American Indian population	Year established
	Ag695	Ag696	Ag697	Ag698	Ag699
	—	Acres	Number	Number	Year
Cattaraugus	NY	21,680	2,178	2,051	1794
Oil Springs	NY	640	5	0	1794
Onondaga	NY	6,100	771	2	1788
St. Regis Mohawk	NY	14,648	1,978	1,923	1796
Tonawanda	NY	7,549	501	453	1857
Tuscarora	NY	5,700	772	310	1784
Osage	OK	1,470,559	41,465	6,161	1871
Burns Paiute	OR	11,465	163	151	1863
Coquille Tribal Community	OR	925	—	—	1989
Coos, Lower Umpqua, Siuslaw	OR	10	4	1	1940
Cow Creek	OR	47	58	11	1982
Grand Ronde	OR	10,300	57	1	1857
Klamath	OR	372	—	—	1864
Siletz	OR	4,014	5	0	1980
Umatilla	OR	172,140	2,502	1,029	1855
Warm Springs	OR	643,570	3,076	2,820	1855
Narragansett	RI	1,943	31	17	1983
Cheyenne River	SD	1,419,504	7,743	5,100	1868
Crow Creek	SD	122,531	1,756	1,531	1868
Flandreau Santee Sioux	SD	2,356	279	249	1868
Lake Traverse-Sisseton	SD–ND	107,245	10,733	2,821	1867
Lower Brule	SD	240,000	1,123	994	1868
Pine Ridge	SD–NE	1,771,082	12,215	11,182	1868
Rosebud	SD	954,751	9,696	8,043	1868
Standing Rock	SD–ND	847,799	7,956	4,870	1889
Yankton	SD	434,932	6,269	1,994	1858
Alabama-Coushatta	TX	4,503	478	477	1854
Kickapoo	TX	125	—	—	1984
Tigua	TX	76	292	211	1968
Goshute	UT	112,085	99	98	1914
Paiute	UT	3,236	645	323	1903
Skull Valley	UT	17,444	32	32	1917
Uintah and Ouray	UT	2,100,000	17,224	2,650	1861
Chehalis	WA	4,215	491	308	1864
Colville	WA	1,400,000	6,957	3,788	1872
Hoh	WA	443	96	74	1893
Jamestown Klallam	WA	12	22	4	1874
Kalispel	WA	4,629	100	91	1914
Lower Elwah	WA	443	137	130	1968
Lummi	WA	21,000	3,147	1,594	1855
Makah	WA	27,950	1,214	940	1855
Muckleshoot	WA	3,840	3,841	864	1857
Nisqually	WA	4,800	578	365	1854
Nooksack	WA	2,500	556	412	1973
Port Gamble	WA	1,301	552	377	1936
Port Madison	WA	7,486	4,834	388	1855
Puyallup	WA	103	32,406	937	1885
Quileute	WA	700	381	303	1889
Quinault	WA	208,150	1,216	943	1873
Saul-Suiattle	WA	23	124	69	1975
Shoalwater	WA	335	131	66	1866
Skokomish	WA	5,000	614	431	1859
Spokane	WA	154,898	1,502	1,229	1881
Squaxin Island	WA	1,979	157	127	1855
Stillaquamish	WA	21	113	96	1855
Swinomish	WA	7,169	2,282	585	1873
Tulalip	WA	11,500	7,103	1,204	1855
Upper Skagit	WA	250	180	162	1974
Yakima	WA	1,372,000	27,668	6,307	1855
Bad River	WI	60,985	1,070	868	1854

(continued)

Table Ag695–699 Selected American Indian reservations – land area, population, and year established: 1990 *Continued*

Reservation	State Ag695 —	Total area Ag696 Acres	Population Ag697 Number	American Indian population Ag698 Number	Year established Ag699 Year
Ho-Chunk (Winnebago)	WI	8,333	700	570	1963
Lac Courte Oreilles	WI	79,000	2,408	1,771	1837
Lac du Flambeau	WI	44,919	2,434	1,432	1854
Menominee	WI	235,000	3,397	3,182	1854
Oneida	WI	7,658	18,033	2,447	1838
Potawatomi	WI	11,692	1,082	266	1913
Red Cliff	WI	14,541	857	727	1854
St. Croix	WI	3,145	505	462	1938
Sokaogon Chippewa	WI	1,750	357	311	1938
Stockbridge	WI	46,000	581	447	1938
Wind River	WY	2,268,008	21,851	5,676	1863

[1] 2,000 acres or more.

[2] The total land area of the Bois Forte reservation includes the combined areas of the Nett Lake, Deer Creek, and Vermillion reservations.

[3] Seminole reservations were created in a series of land consolidations that took place throughout the 1930s.

Sources

Veronica E. Velarde Tiller, *American Indian Reservations and Indian Trust Areas: Washington* (Economic Development Administration, 1996); Marlita A. Reddy, *Statistical Record of Native North Americans* (Gale Research, 1995), Table 804; National Native American Cooperative, *Native American Directory* (National Native American Cooperative, 1996); Confederation of American Indians, *Indian Reservations: A State and Federal Handbook* (McFarland, 1986); U.S. Department of Commerce, *Federal and State Indian Reservations and Indian Trust Areas* (1974).

Documentation

This table covers selected federal- and state-recognized American Indian reservations. See Map Ag-B for the locations of many of the reservations.

Table Ag700–703 Population on reservations – Bureau of Indian Affairs and Census estimates: 1860–1995

Contributed by C. Matthew Snipp

Year	Bureau of Indian Affairs estimates			Census	Year	Bureau of Indian Affairs estimates			Census
	Total U.S. Ag700 Number	U.S. except Alaska Ag701 Number	Alaska Ag702 Number	Ag703 Number		Total U.S. Ag700 Number	U.S. except Alaska Ag701 Number	Alaska Ag702 Number	Ag703 Number
1860	—	—	—	339,421	1939	381,861	351,878	29,983	—
1865	—	294,574	—	—	1940	—	—	—	333,969
1870	—	288,646	—	383,712	1945	426,372	393,622	32,750	—
1875	305,168	279,337	25,831 [3]	—	1950	—	—	—	343,410
1880	—	256,127	—	306,543	1953 [1]	403,071	368,401	34,670	—
1885	—	259,244	—	—	1960	—	—	—	509,147
1890	—	243,534	—	248,253	1962	367,179	328,857	38,332	—
1895	—	248,340	—	—	1970	—	—	—	776,454
1900	—	270,544	—	237,196	1980	—	—	—	1,356,297
1905	—	284,079	—	—	1983	755,201	690,231	64,970	—
1910	—	304,950	—	265,683	1990	—	—	—	1,878,285
1915	—	330,010	—	—	1995	1,260,106	1,174,847	85,259	—
1920	—	336,337	—	244,437					
1925	—	349,595	—	—					
1930	—	340,541 [2]	—	332,397					

[1] Includes persons on tribal rolls only (that is, those officially recognized as tribal members).

[2] Includes an estimated 118,773 American Indians not enumerated.

[3] Excludes 1,500 "half-breeds or creoles."

Sources

Paul Stuart, *Nations within a Nation* (Greenwood Press, 1987), Table 3.3; U.S. Bureau of Indian Affairs, "Indian Service Population and Labor Force Estimates" (1995), Table 3.

Documentation

The Bureau of Indian Affairs (BIA) figures are based on administrative records, while census numbers are obtained from the decennial census. Before 1950, the BIA figures may be more accurate than those from the Census Bureau.

These figures are for American Indians only; in some instances, they include Alaska Natives.

Series Ag702. Data for Alaska include Eskimos, Aleuts, and American Indians.

Table Ag704–717   Population of American Indians residing in Indian Health Service areas: 1972–2000
Contributed by C. Matthew Snipp

Year	Total Ag704	Aberdeen Ag705	Alaska Ag706	Albuquerque Ag707	Bemidji Ag708	Billings Ag709	California Ag710	Nashville Ag711	Navajo Ag712	Oklahoma Ag713	Phoenix Ag714	Portland Ag715	Tucson Ag716	Growth factor Ag717
	Number	Number	Number	Number	Number	Number	Number	Number	Number	Number	Number	Number	Number	Number
1972	479,349	45,714	52,168	34,653	21,994	28,058	—	9,236	94,057	106,051	51,273	25,903	10,242	—
1973	488,839	46,505	53,093	35,425	22,148	28,523	—	9,384	95,309	109,438	52,289	26,314	10,411	—
1974	525,134	47,931	53,906	36,205	24,724	28,982	—	11,721	117,060	112,995	53,255	27,931	10,424	—
1975	586,078	52,617	64,121	41,720	28,635	32,733	65,757	12,807	122,964	119,602	66,169	31,527	13,183	—
1976	606,275	53,647	66,252	43,202	29,546	33,765	67,132	13,180	128,000	123,204	69,158	32,621	13,700	—
1977	626,688	54,537	68,620	44,692	30,474	34,822	68,676	13,547	132,895	126,881	72,232	33,804	14,184	—
1980	828,609	63,253	64,047	46,610	42,686	35,708	65,757	26,731	145,162	172,636	74,020	75,769	16,230	—
1981	849,504	64,971	65,784	47,707	43,653	37,165	67,132	27,174	149,234	176,422	76,323	77,359	16,580	2.52
1982	872,436	66,761	67,625	48,849	45,676	38,658	68,676	28,119	153,424	180,435	78,249	79,006	16,958	2.58
1983	902,701	68,571	69,493	49,992	45,745	40,147	70,181	30,309	157,600	185,229	80,256	87,795	17,383	3.62
1984	936,942	70,449	71,499	51,186	46,882	41,687	71,962	35,430	161,994	189,395	82,417	96,249	17,792	3.79
1985	961,881	73,296	73,599	52,413	48,068	42,851	73,893	35,972	166,511	193,661	84,709	98,693	18,215	2.66
1986	986,551	75,298	75,798	53,673	49,424	44,058	75,973	36,527	171,152	198,038	87,123	100,836	18,651	2.56
1987	1,011,837	77,348	78,088	54,966	50,603	45,295	78,208	37,098	175,915	202,519	89,661	103,036	19,100	2.56
1988	1,038,121	79,455	80,478	56,297	51,959	46,569	80,595	37,686	180,802	207,105	92,319	105,293	19,563	2.60
1989	1,073,886	81,617	82,960	59,848	54,107	47,878	83,128	42,468	185,812	211,799	96,626	107,606	20,037	3.45
1990	1,207,236	74,789	86,251	67,504	61,349	47,008	104,828	48,943	180,959	262,517	120,707	127,774	24,607	—
1991	1,242,482	81,066	88,554	68,989	62,680	48,188	107,031	54,264	185,588	267,309	123,445	130,337	25,031	2.92
1992	1,269,163	83,187	90,842	70,500	64,013	49,346	109,250	55,121	190,158	272,171	126,172	132,948	25,455	2.15
1993	1,298,090	85,312	93,119	72,032	65,351	50,494	113,590	56,002	194,699	277,110	128,417	136,086	25,878	2.23
1994	1,338,500	87,416	95,382	73,574	67,100	51,618	116,675	69,145	199,100	282,172	131,188	138,829	26,301	3.11
1995	1,373,408	89,462	97,633	75,134	76,149	52,730	118,976	70,263	203,489	287,304	133,908	141,638	26,722	2.61
1996	1,402,062	92,626	99,870	76,710	77,656	53,819	121,298	71,433	207,818	292,567	136,625	144,498	27,142	2.09
1997	1,429,801	94,709	102,094	78,304	79,168	54,898	123,630	72,629	212,091	297,944	139,350	147,424	27,560	1.98
1998	1,457,621	96,772	104,305	79,914	80,696	55,953	125,974	73,854	216,298	303,404	142,071	150,401	27,979	1.95
1999	1,485,553	98,812	106,506	81,544	82,237	56,992	128,329	75,113	220,449	308,948	144,789	153,437	28,397	1.92
2000 [1]	1,513,618	100,839	108,695	83,189	83,787	58,013	130,696	76,406	224,535	314,598	147,511	156,535	28,814	1.89

[1] The year 2000 data are estimated from a growth factor extrapolated from the preceding three years.

Source
U.S. Indian Health Service, *Chart Book Series, Chart Series Book,* and *Trends in Indian Health,* published annually, Table 2.1.

Documentation
An Indian Health Service (IHS) area is a catchment area served by an IHS clinic or hospital. Intercensal years are estimated by the IHS using vital events data. Decennial census years show actual counts. Estimates for years preceding 1975 are based on linear interpolation from the 1960 and 1970 Censuses.

Series Ag710. California was not designated an IHS service area until 1978.

Series Ag717. The growth factor is obtained using linear regression techniques based on ten years of birth and death data provided by the National Center for Health Statistics. The natural change (estimated number of births minus the estimated number of deaths) is applied to each decennial enumeration after 1970. For the years before 1980, the IHS used a set of different and unspecified forecasting methods.

Table Ag718–720   Federal expenditures for American Indians in urban and reservation areas: 1950–1980

Contributed by C. Matthew Snipp

	Total	Urban areas	Reservation areas		Total	Urban areas	Reservation areas
	Ag718	Ag719	Ag720		Ag718	Ag719	Ag720
Year	Thousand 1982 dollars	Thousand 1982 dollars	Thousand 1982 dollars	Year	Thousand 1982 dollars	Thousand 1982 dollars	Thousand 1982 dollars
1950	174,402	0	174,402	1970	799,095	49,852	749,243
1951	216,765	1,048	215,717	1971	922,944	40,482	882,462
1952	236,173	2,259	233,914	1972	1,173,026	32,280	1,140,746
1953	275,170	2,185	272,985	1973	1,390,081	44,335	1,345,746
1954	277,312	2,198	275,114	1974	1,419,795	52,624	1,367,171
1955	314,463	2,540	311,923	1975	1,505,430	91,545	1,413,885
1956	279,189	3,463	275,726	1976	1,680,150	110,830	1,569,320
1957	307,543	9,646	297,897	1977	1,990,306	101,639	1,888,667
1958	335,219	10,333	324,886	1978	1,911,535	94,731	1,816,804
1959	330,480	9,178	321,302	1979	2,094,211	99,911	1,994,300
1960	345,065	8,472	336,593	1980	1,979,488	95,594	1,883,894
1961	374,077	9,429	364,648				
1962	391,097	21,734	369,363				
1963	430,074	24,753	405,321				
1964	450,444	27,720	422,724				
1965	476,050	34,269	441,781				
1966	521,746	34,694	487,052				
1967	582,228	42,755	539,473				
1968	599,873	56,907	542,966				
1969	644,116	60,055	584,061				

Source

Joane Nagel, *American Indian Ethnic Renewal* (Oxford University Press, 1996), Table 10, p. 128.

Table Ag721   Employees of the Bureau of Indian Affairs: 1852–1999

Contributed by C. Matthew Snipp

	BIA employees		BIA employees
	Ag721		Ag721
Year	Number	Year	Number
1852	108	1985	13,915
1888	1,725	1986	13,580
1911	6,000	1987	13,251
1933	5,000	1988	12,924
1934	12,000	1989	13,146
1975	14,576	1990	12,652
1976	14,115	1991	12,605
1977	13,797	1992	13,013
1978	13,778	1993	13,074
1979	13,486	1994	12,876
1980	13,412	1995	12,488
1981	16,868	1998 [1]	10,900
1982	15,054	1999 [1]	10,496
1983	14,854		
1984	14,572		

[1] Number of employees in January.

Sources

Theodore W. Taylor, *The Bureau of Indian Affairs* (Westview Press, 1984), Table 2.1; Marlita A. Reddy, *Statistical Record of Native North Americans* (Gale Research, 1995), Tables 858, 859; U.S. Office of Personnel Management, *Employment and Trends* (1998, 1999), Table 15.

Documentation

Data for 1975–1995 are full-time equivalents for fiscal years.

Table Ag722–725   Terminated American Indian tribes – year of termination and restoration, and 1990 population: 1954–1994

Contributed by C. Matthew Snipp

	State	Year of tribe		Population in 1990
		Termination	Restoration	
	Ag722	Ag723	Ag724	Ag725
Tribe or reservation	—	Year	Year	Number
Alexander Valley [1]	CA	1958	—	—
Auburn	CA	1958	1994	—
Big Sandy	CA	1958	1983	36
Big Valley	CA	1958	1983	31
Blue Lake	CA	1958	1983	25
Buena Vista	CA	1958	1983	—
Cache Creek [1]	CA	1958	—	—
Chicken Ranch	CA	1958	1983	0
Chico [1]	CA	1958	—	—
Cloverdale	CA	1958	1983	—
Coyote Valley Ranch	CA	1957	1976	124
Elk Valley	CA	1958	1983	50
Graton [1]	CA	1958	—	—
Greenville	CA	1958	1983	0
Guidiville [1]	CA	1958	—	—
Hopland	CA	1958	1982	160
Indian Ranch [1]	CA	1958	—	—
Lytton [1]	CA	1958	—	—
Mark West [1]	CA	1958	—	—
Mooretown	CA	1958	1983	—
Nevada City [1]	CA	1958	—	—
North Fork	CA	1958	1983	0
Paskenta	CA	1958	1994	—
Picayune	CA	1958	1983	0
Pinoleville	CA	1958	1983	51
Potter Valley	CA	1958	1983	—
Quartz Valley	CA	1958	1983	0
Redding	CA	1958	1983	44
Redwood Valley	CA	1958	1983	0
Robinson	CA	1958	1975	125
Rohnerville	CA	1958	1983	0
Ruffey's [1]	CA	1958	—	—
Scott's Valley [1]	CA	1958	—	—
Smith River	CA	1958	1983	96
Strawberry Valley [1]	CA	1958	—	—
Table Bluff	CA	1958	1981	39
Table Mountain	CA	1958	1983	35
Upper Lake	CA	1958	1984	—
Wilton [1]	CA	1958	—	—
Ponca	NE	1962	1990	0
Ottawa	OK	1956	1978	—
Peoria	OK	1956	1978	—
Wyandotte	OK	1956	1978	—
Modoc	OR–OK	1954	1978	—
Alsea [1]	OR	1954	—	—
Applegate Creek [1]	OR	1954	—	—
Calapooya [1]	OR	1954	—	—
Chaftan [1]	OR	1954	—	—
Chempho [1]	OR	1954	—	—
Chetco [1]	OR	1954	—	—
Chetlessington [1]	OR	1954	—	—
Chinook [1]	OR	1954	—	—
Clackamas [1]	OR	1954	—	—
Clatskanie [1]	OR	1954	—	—
Clatsop [1]	OR	1954	—	—
Clowwewalla [1]	OR	1954	—	—
Coos [2]	OR	1954	1987	0
Cow Creek	OR	1954	1982	25
Euchees [1]	OR	1954	—	—
Galic Creek [1]	OR	1954	—	—

Notes appear at end of table   (continued)

Table Ag722–725   Terminated American Indian tribes – year of termination and restoration, and 1990 population: 1954–1994   *Continued*

	State	Year of tribe		Population in 1990
		Termination	Restoration	
	Ag722	Ag723	Ag724	Ag725
Tribe or reservation	—	Year	Year	Number
Grand Ronde [3]	OR	1954	1988	2
Grave [1]	OR	1954	—	—
Joshua [1]	OR	1954	—	—
Karok [1]	OR	1954	—	—
Kathlamet [1]	OR	1954	—	—
Klamath	OR	1954	1986	1,814
Kusotony [1]	OR	1954	—	—
Kwatami [1]	OR	1954	—	—
Lakmiut [1]	OR	1954	—	—
Long Tom Creek [1]	OR	1954	—	—
Lower Coquille	OR	1954	1989	0
Lower Umpqua [2]	OR	1954	1987	—
Mackanotin [1]	OR	1954	—	—
Maddy [1]	OR	1954	—	—
Mary's River [1]	OR	1954	—	—
Multnomah [1]	OR	1954	—	—
Munsel Creek [1]	OR	1954	—	—
Naltunnetunne [1]	OR	1954	—	—
Nehalem [1]	OR	1954	—	—
Nestucca [1]	OR	1954	—	—
Northern Molalla [3]	OR	1954	—	—
Port Orford [1]	OR	1954	—	—
Pudding River [1]	OR	1954	—	—
Rogue River [3]	OR	1954	—	—
Salmon River [1]	OR	1954	—	—
Santiam [1]	OR	1954	—	—
Scoton [1]	OR	1954	—	—
Shasta [3]	OR	1954	—	—
Shasta Costa [1]	OR	1954	—	—
Siletz [4]	OR	1954	1977	0
Siuslaw [2]	OR	1954	1987	—
Skiloot [1]	OR	1954	—	—
Southern Molalla [1]	OR	1954	—	—
Takelma [1]	OR	1954	—	—
Tillamook [1]	OR	1954	—	—
Tolowa [1]	OR	1954	—	—
Tualatin [1]	OR	1954	—	—
Tututui [1]	OR	1954	—	—
Upper Coquille	OR	1954	1989	5,354
Upper Umpqua [3]	OR	1954	—	—
Willamette Tumwater [1]	OR	1954	—	—
Yamhill [1]	OR	1954	—	—
Yaquina [1]	OR	1954	—	—
Yoncalla [1]	OR	1954	—	—
Catawba	SC	1959	1993	111
Alabama-Coushatta	TX	1954	1986	477
Mixed Blood Utes [1]	UT	1954	—	—
Southern Paiute	UT	1954	1980	285
Menominee	WI	1954	1973	3,182

[1] Terminated; not restored.

[2] Coos reservation includes Coos, Lower Umpqua, and Siuslaw tribes.

[3] Grand Ronde includes the Shasta, Kalapuya, Rogue River, Molalla, and Umpqua tribes, as well as descendants of the Chinook and Clackamas tribes.

[4] Siletz consists of approximately twenty-four tribes including the Rogue River, Umpqua, Calapooya, Shasta, Scoton, Kalapuya, and Molalla.

Sources

Marlita A. Reddy, *Statistical Record of Native North Americans* (Gale Research, 1995), Table 100; Mary B. Davis, *Native America in the Twentieth Century* (Garland Publishing, 1994); U.S. Bureau of the Census, *General Population Characteristics, American Indian and Alaska Native Areas*, CP-1-1A (1992), Table 2.

Documentation

Sometimes, the names listed in this table are tribes, sometimes they are reservations, and sometimes they are both. This is because some tribes reside on more than one reservation, some reservations have more than one tribe, and in other cases, the tribe and the reservation have the same name. Sometimes Congress terminated tribes, and sometimes they terminated reservations (and by implication the tribes residing on them). The names in the table are consistent with the way they have appeared in legal documents and legislation.

Termination occurred when Congress withdrew federal recognition of these tribes or reservations. Restoration occurred when recognition was reestablished.

EMPLOYMENT AND OCCUPATIONS

C. Matthew Snipp

Table Ag726–734 American Indians gainfully employed, by sex: 1900–1930

Contributed by C. Matthew Snipp

	Both sexes			Males			Females		
	Total	Gainfully employed		Total	Gainfully employed		Total	Gainfully employed	
		Number	Percent		Number	Percent		Number	Percent
	Ag726	Ag727	Ag728	Ag729	Ag730	Ag731	Ag732	Ag733	Ag734
Year	Number	Number	Percent	Number	Number	Percent	Number	Number	Percent
1900	171,552	62,934	36.7	86,504	51,218	59.2	85,048	11,716	13.8
1910	188,758	73,916	39.2	96,582	59,206	61.3	92,176	14,710	16.0
1920	176,925	63,326	35.8	91,546	53,478	58.4	85,379	9,848	11.5
1930	238,981	98,148	41.1	123,469	80,306	65.0	115,512	17,842	15.4

Source

U.S. Bureau of the Census, *The Indian Population of the United States and Alaska* (1937), Table 55.

Documentation

Data are for persons age 10 and older.

Table Ag735–758 Labor force participation of American Indians, by sex: 1950–1990[1]

Contributed by C. Matthew Snipp

	Both sexes							Males				
	Total	In labor force	Percentage in labor force	Civilian labor force				Not in labor force	Total	In labor force	Percentage in labor force	Civilian labor force	
				Total	Employed	Unemployed	Percentage unemployed					Total	Employed
	Ag735	Ag736	Ag737	Ag738	Ag739	Ag740	Ag741	Ag742	Ag743	Ag744	Ag745	Ag746	Ag747
Year	Number	Number	Percent	Number	Number	Number	Percent	Number	Number	Number	Percent	Number	Number
1950	210,609	86,635	41.1	84,996	74,697	10,299	12.1	123,974	110,451	69,619	63.0	68,019	59,209
1960	326,289	138,692	42.5	134,545	115,000	19,545	14.5	187,597	163,337	97,197	59.5	93,178	78,100
1970	491,117	224,252	45.7	216,410	192,265	24,145	11.2	266,865	239,005	140,880	58.9	133,310	117,683
1970	452,938	221,733	49.0	213,897	190,233	23,664	11.1	231,205	219,672	139,339	63.4	131,775	116,467
1980	1,022,411	598,626	58.6	584,479	507,614	76,865	13.2	423,785	497,737	346,419	69.6	333,571	286,687
1990	1,395,009	865,703	62.1	851,312	728,953	122,359	14.4	529,306	680,355	472,266	69.4	459,892	388,911

Note appears at end of table

(continued)

Table Ag735–758   Labor force participation of American Indians, by sex: 1950–1990   *Continued*

	Males			Females						
	Civilian labor force		Not in labor force	Total	In labor force	Percentage in labor force	Total	Civilian labor force			Not in labor force
	Unemployed	Percentage unemployed						Employed	Unemployed	Percentage unemployed	
	Ag748	Ag749	Ag750	Ag751	Ag752	Ag753	Ag754	Ag755	Ag756	Ag757	Ag758
Year	Number	Percent	Number	Number	Number	Percent	Number	Number	Number	Percent	Number
1950	8,810	13.0	40,832	100,158	17,016	17.0	16,977	15,488	1,489	8.8	83,142
1960	15,078	16.2	66,140	162,952	41,495	25.5	41,367	36,900	4,467	10.8	121,457
1970	15,627	11.7	98,125	252,112	83,372	33.1	83,100	74,582	8,518	10.3	168,740
1970	15,308	11.6	80,333	233,266	82,394	35.3	82,122	73,766	8,356	10.2	150,872
1980	46,884	14.1	151,318	524,674	252,207	48.1	250,908	220,927	29,981	11.9	272,467
1990	70,981	15.4	208,089	714,654	393,437	55.1	391,420	340,042	51,378	13.1	321,217

[1] American Indians, 14 and older (1950, 1960, and the first set of data for 1970); American Indians, 16 and older (the second set of data for 1970); American Indians and Alaska Natives, 16 and older (thereafter).

Sources

1950: U.S. Bureau of the Census, *U.S. Census of Population: 1950, Special Reports, Nonwhite Population by Race*, P-E number 3B (1953), p. 3B-32.

1960: U.S. Bureau of the Census, *U.S. Census of Population: 1960, Subject Reports, Nonwhite Population by Race*, Final Report PC (2)-1C (1963), p. 104.

1970: U.S. Bureau of the Census, *Census of Population: 1970, Subject Reports, American Indians*, Final Report PC (2)-1F (1973), p. 86.

1980: U.S. Bureau of the Census, *1980 Census of Population, Characteristics of the Population, General Social and Economic Characteristics, United States Summary*, PC 80-1-C1 (1983), p. 159.

1990: U.S. Bureau of the Census, *Social and Economic Characteristics, United States*, CP-2-1 (1993), Table 126.

Table Ag759–806   Occupations of American Indian workers, by sex: 1910–1930

Contributed by C. Matthew Snipp

	Both sexes												
	Total	Professionals	Proprietors, managers, and officials				Clerks and kindred workers	Skilled workers and foremen	Semi-skilled workers			Unskilled workers	
			Total	Farmers (owners, tenants)	Wholesale and retail dealers	Other			Total	Manufacturing	Other	Total	Agricultural laborers
	Ag759	Ag760	Ag761	Ag762	Ag763	Ag764	Ag765	Ag766	Ag767	Ag768	Ag769	Ag770	Ag771
Year	Number	Number	Number	Number	Number	Number	Number	Number	Number	Number	Number	Number	Number
1910	73,916	1,284	23,013	21,997	520	496	1,027	2,056	8,052	6,728	1,324	38,484	26,490
1920	63,326	1,004	22,824	22,181	342	301	997	2,164	5,850	4,202	1,648	30,487	17,849
1930	98,148	2,355	29,280	28,038	625	617	2,494	4,228	11,755	8,016	3,739	48,036	28,245

Both sexes

	Unskilled workers					Proprietors, managers, and officials					
	Factory and building construction laborers	Other laborers	Servant classes	Total	Professionals	Total	Farmers (owners, tenants)	Wholesale and retail dealers	Other	Clerks and kindred workers	Skilled workers and foremen
Year	Ag772	Ag773	Ag774	Ag775	Ag776	Ag777	Ag778	Ag779	Ag780	Ag781	Ag782
	Number	Number	Number	Number	Number	Number	Number	Number	Number	Number	Number
1910	3,656	4,873	3,465	59,206	927	21,765	20,841	482	442	859	2,021
1920	3,923	6,304	2,411	53,478	665	21,684	21,097	322	265	700	2,097
1930	7,084	8,323	4,384	80,306	1,531	27,615	26,521	569	525	1,630	4,204

Males

	Semi-skilled workers			Unskilled workers				
	Total	Manufacturing	Other	Total	Agricultural laborers	Factory and building construction laborers	Other laborers	Servant classes
Year	Ag783	Ag784	Ag785	Ag786	Ag787	Ag788	Ag789	Ag790
	Number	Number	Number	Number	Number	Number	Number	Number
1910	1,511	673	838	32,123	23,293	3,571	4,772	487
1920	1,887	824	1,063	26,445	16,000	3,826	6,244	375
1930	4,278	1,632	2,646	41,048	25,124	6,973	8,277	674

Females

	Proprietors, managers, and officials		Farmers (owners, tenants)	
	Total	Professionals	Total	
Year	Ag791	Ag792	Ag793	Ag794
	Number	Number	Number	Number
1910	14,710	357	1,248	1,156
1920	9,848	339	1,140	1,084
1930	17,842	824	1,665	1,517

	Proprietors, managers, and officials		Clerks and kindred workers	Skilled workers and foremen	Semi-skilled workers			Unskilled workers				
	Wholesale and retail dealers	Other			Total	Manufacturing	Other	Total	Agricultural laborers	Factory and building construction laborers	Other laborers	Servant classes
Year	Ag795	Ag796	Ag797	Ag798	Ag799	Ag800	Ag801	Ag802	Ag803	Ag804	Ag805	Ag806
	Number	Number	Number	Number	Number	Number	Number	Number	Number	Number	Number	Number
1910	38	54	168	35	6,541	6,055	486	6,361	3,197	85	101	2,978
1920	20	36	297	67	3,963	3,378	585	4,042	1,849	97	60	2,036
1930	56	92	864	24	7,477	6,384	1,093	6,988	3,121	111	46	3,710

Source

U.S. Bureau of the Census, *The Indian Population of the United States and Alaska, 1930* (1937), Table 58, p. 202.

Documentation

Data are for gainfully employed workers, age 10 and older.

Table Ag807–848 Occupations of American Indian workers, by sex: 1950–1970

Contributed by C. Matthew Snipp

Both sexes

Year	Total Ag807	Professional, technical, and kindred workers Ag808	Farmers and farm managers Ag809	Managers, officials, and proprietors (except farm) Ag810	Clerical and kindred workers Ag811	Sales workers Ag812	Craftsmen, foremen, and kindred workers Ag813	Operatives and kindred workers Ag814	Private household workers Ag815	Service workers (except private household) Ag816	Farm laborers (unpaid family workers) Ag817	Farm laborers and farm foremen Ag818	Laborers (except farm and mine) Ag819	Occupation not reported Ag820
	Number	Number	Number	Number	Number	Number	Number	Number	Number	Number	Number	Number	Number	Number
1950	74,697	2,225	14,327	1,306	3,130	—	6,376	11,257	2,341	4,880	5,776	8,319	10,052	4,708
1960	115,000	5,823	6,999	2,406	6,185	2,002	10,557	18,751	4,908	11,176	—	11,462	13,798	20,933
1970	190,233	18,938	3,084	7,623	25,132	5,712	27,303	41,631	5,119	31,448	—	7,925	16,318	—

Males

Year	Total Ag821	Professional, technical, and kindred workers Ag822	Farmers and farm managers Ag823	Managers, officials, and proprietors (except farm) Ag824	Clerical and kindred workers Ag825	Sales workers Ag826	Craftsmen, foremen, and kindred workers Ag827	Operatives and kindred workers Ag828	Private household workers Ag829	Service workers (except private household) Ag830	Farm laborers (unpaid family workers) Ag831	Farm laborers and farm foremen Ag832	Laborers (except farm and mine) Ag833	Occupation not reported Ag834
	Number	Number	Number	Number	Number	Number	Number	Number	Number	Number	Number	Number	Number	Number
1950	59,209	1,418	13,499	1,090	1,754	—	6,129	7,289	141	2,020	4,599	7,854	9,902	3,514
1960	78,100	3,270	6,247	1,859	2,222	989	10,214	14,491	211	3,952	—	9,279	13,334	12,032
1970	116,467	10,754	2,645	5,871	6,609	2,798	25,725	27,872	164	12,047	—	6,655	15,327	—

Females

Year	Total Ag835	Professional, technical, and kindred workers Ag836	Farmers and farm managers Ag837	Managers, officials, and proprietors (except farm) Ag838	Clerical and kindred workers Ag839	Sales workers Ag840	Craftsmen, foremen, and kindred workers Ag841	Operatives and kindred workers Ag842	Private household workers Ag843	Service workers (except private household) Ag844	Farm laborers (unpaid family workers) Ag845	Farm laborers and farm foremen Ag846	Laborers (except farm and mine) Ag847	Occupation not reported Ag848
	Number	Number	Number	Number	Number	Number	Number	Number	Number	Number	Number	Number	Number	Number
1950	15,488	807	828	216	1,376	—	247	3,968	2,200	2,860	1,177	465	150	1,194
1960	36,900	2,553	752	547	3,963	1,013	343	4,260	4,697	7,224	—	2,183	464	8,901
1970	73,766	8,184	439	1,752	18,523	2,914	1,578	13,759	4,955	19,401	—	1,270	991	—

Documentation

Data are for workers in the civilian labor force – age 14 and older for 1950 and 1960, and age 16 and older for 1970.

When not available separately, sales workers are included under clerical and kindred workers, and farm laborers (unpaid family workers) are included under farm laborers and foremen.

Sources

1950: U.S. Bureau of the Census, *U.S. Census of Population: 1950. Special Reports. Nonwhite Population by Race*, P-E number 3B (1953), p. 3B-32.

1960: U.S. Bureau of the Census, *U.S. Census of Population: 1960. Subject Reports. Nonwhite Population by Race*, Final Report PC (2)-1C (1963), p. 104.

1970: U.S. Bureau of the Census, *Census of Population: 1970. Subject Reports. American Indians*, Final Report PC (2)-1F (1973), p. 86.

Table Ag849–869   Occupations of American Indian workers, by sex: 1980–1990

Contributed by C. Matthew Snipp

Both sexes

Year	Total	Managerial and professional specialty occupations	Technical, sales, and administrative support	Service	Farming, forestry, and fishing	Precision production, craft, and repair	Operators, fabricators, and laborers
	Ag849	Ag850	Ag851	Ag852	Ag853	Ag854	Ag855
	Number	Number	Number	Number	Number	Number	Number
1980	507,614	81,840	122,676	91,813	18,614	76,107	116,564
1990	728,953	133,555	195,096	134,744	24,405	99,782	141,371

Males

Year	Total	Managerial and professional specialty occupations	Technical, sales, and administrative support	Service	Farming, forestry, and fishing	Precision production, craft, and repair	Operators, fabricators, and laborers
	Ag856	Ag857	Ag858	Ag859	Ag860	Ag861	Ag862
	Number	Number	Number	Number	Number	Number	Number
1980	286,687	42,517	37,480	36,050	16,066	69,074	85,500
1990	388,911	59,707	60,603	55,101	20,665	89,173	103,662

Females

Year	Total	Managerial and professional specialty occupations	Technical, sales, and administrative support	Service	Farming, forestry, and fishing	Precision production, craft, and repair	Operators, fabricators, and laborers
	Ag863	Ag864	Ag865	Ag866	Ag867	Ag868	Ag869
	Number	Number	Number	Number	Number	Number	Number
1980	220,927	39,323	85,196	55,763	2,548	7,033	31,064
1990	340,042	73,848	134,493	79,643	3,740	10,609	37,709

Sources

1980: U.S. Bureau of the Census, *1980 Census of Population, Characteristics of the Population, Detailed Population Characteristics, United States Summary*, PC80-1-D1-A (1984), Table 278, pp. 196–205.

1990: U.S. Bureau of the Census, *Social and Economic Characteristics, United States*, CP-2-1 (1993), Table 110.

Documentation

Data are for workers in the civilian labor force age 16 and older. They include Alaska Natives.

Table Ag870–914   American Indian workers, by industry and sex: 1960–1990

Contributed by C. Matthew Snipp

Both sexes

Year	Total	Agriculture, forestry, and fisheries	Mining	Construction	Durable goods manufacturing	Nondurable goods manufacturing	Transportation, communications, and other public utilities	Wholesale and retail trade	Finance, insurance, and real estate	Business and repair services	Personal services	Entertainment and recreation services	Professional and related services	Public administration	Other
	Ag870	Ag871	Ag872	Ag873	Ag874	Ag875	Ag876	Ag877	Ag878	Ag879	Ag880	Ag881	Ag882	Ag883	Ag884
	Number	Number	Number	Number	Number	Number	Number	Number	Number	Number	Number	Number	Number	Number	Number
1960	115,000	20,241	2,208	9,254	11,990	5,946	5,792	9,478	839	1,509	8,684	617	12,359	5,921	20,162
1970	190,188	13,612	2,832	15,425	27,079	17,281	10,859	26,495	4,160	5,470	12,620	1,416	36,175	16,764	—
1980	507,614	17,839	11,133	42,592	62,559	35,354	35,483	79,655	17,129	20,583	18,363	5,057	102,589	59,278	—
1990	728,953	25,445	8,386	61,635	72,455	44,934	50,969	142,189	28,700	33,516	27,692	12,491	162,069	58,472	—

Males

Year	Total	Agriculture, forestry, and fisheries	Mining	Construction	Durable goods manufacturing	Nondurable goods manufacturing	Transportation, communications, and other public utilities	Wholesale and retail trade	Finance, insurance, and real estate	Business and repair services	Personal services	Entertainment and recreation services	Professional and related services	Public administration	Other
	Ag885	Ag886	Ag887	Ag888	Ag889	Ag890	Ag891	Ag892	Ag893	Ag894	Ag895	Ag896	Ag897	Ag898	Ag899
	Number	Number	Number	Number	Number	Number	Number	Number	Number	Number	Number	Number	Number	Number	Number
1960	—	—	—	—	—	—	—	—	—	—	—	—	—	—	—
1970	116,467	11,522	—	—	20,703	9,391	9,186	14,773	—	—	2,666	—	—	—	48,226
1980	286,687	14,631	9,780	39,618	44,730	19,033	27,082	40,829	6,399	13,454	4,762	2,956	31,727	31,686	—
1990	388,911	20,293	7,219	56,330	50,596	23,755	36,542	69,974	10,610	21,678	7,420	6,328	48,270	29,896	—

Females

Year	Total	Agriculture, forestry, and fisheries	Mining	Construction	Durable goods manufacturing	Nondurable goods manufacturing	Transportation, communications, and other public utilities	Wholesale and retail trade	Finance, insurance, and real estate	Business and repair services	Personal services	Entertainment and recreation services	Professional and related services	Public administration	Other
	Ag900	Ag901	Ag902	Ag903	Ag904	Ag905	Ag906	Ag907	Ag908	Ag909	Ag910	Ag911	Ag912	Ag913	Ag914
	Number	Number	Number	Number	Number	Number	Number	Number	Number	Number	Number	Number	Number	Number	Number
1960	—	—	—	—	—	—	—	—	—	—	—	—	—	—	—
1970	73,721	2,090	—	—	6,376	7,890	1,673	11,722	—	—	9,954	—	—	—	34,016
1980	220,927	3,208	1,353	2,974	17,829	16,321	8,401	38,826	10,730	7,129	13,601	2,101	70,862	27,592	—
1990	340,042	5,152	1,167	5,305	21,859	21,179	14,427	72,215	18,090	11,838	20,272	6,163	113,799	28,576	—

Documentation

Data are for employed workers age 14 and older in 1960, age 16 and older in subsequent years. Data for 1980 and 1990 include Alaska Natives.

Sex-specific data are not available for 1960; only partial data are available for 1970.

Sources

U.S. Bureau of the Census, *Nonwhite Population by Race, Final Report*, PC(2)-1C (1963), Table 38; U.S. Bureau of the Census, *American Indians*, PC (2)-1F (1973), Table 10; U.S. Bureau of the Census, *General Social and Economic Characteristics, United States Summary*, PC80-1-C1 (1983), Table 146; U.S. Bureau of the Census, *Social and Economic Characteristics, United States*, CP-2-1 (1993), Table 46.

EDUCATION AND VETERANS

C. Matthew Snipp

Table Ag915–1097   American Indian school-age population and school attendance, by region and state: 1900–1990

Contributed by C. Matthew Snipp

Year	United States			New England			Maine			New Hampshire			Vermont			Massachusetts			Rhode Island			Connecticut			Middle Atlantic			New York		
	School-age population	In school		School-age population	In school		School-age population	In school		School-age population	In school		School-age population	In school		School-age population	In school		School-age population	In school		School-age population	In school		School-age population	In school		School-age population	In school	
	Ag915	Ag916	Ag917	Ag918	Ag919	Ag920	Ag921	Ag922	Ag923	Ag924	Ag925	Ag926	Ag927	Ag928	Ag929	Ag930	Ag931	Ag932	Ag933	Ag934	Ag935	Ag936	Ag937	Ag938	Ag939	Ag940	Ag941	Ag942	Ag943	Ag944
	Number	Number	Percentage	Number	Number	Percentage	Number	Number	Percentage	Number	Number	Percentage	Number	Number	Percentage	Number	Number	Percentage	Number	Number	Percentage	Number	Number	Percentage	Number	Number	Percentage	Number	Number	Percentage
	Number	Number	Percent	Number	Number	Percent	Number	Number	Percent	Number	Number	Percent	Number	Number	Percent	Number	Number	Percent	Number	Number	Percent	Number	Number	Percent	Number	Number	Percent	Number	Number	Percent
1900	89,632[2]	36,243[2]	40.4	—	—	—	—	—	—	—	—	—	—	—	—	—	—	—	—	—	—	—	—	—	—	—	—	1,784	880	49.3
1910	88,741	50,065	56.4	577	398	69.0	259	163	62.9	9	8	88.9	4	3	75.0	191	149	78.0	81	54	66.7	33	21	63.6	2,746	2,040	74.3	1,855	1,239	66.8
1930	128,656	78,321	60.9	789	540	68.4	364	232	63.7	24	15	62.5	14	8	57.1	262	208	79.4	90	58	64.4	35	19	54.3	2,558	1,811	70.8	2,377	1,691	71.1
1970[1]	—	—	—	—	—	—	—	—	—	—	—	—	—	—	—	—	—	—	—	—	—	—	—	—	—	—	—	6,651	6,038	90.8
1980	500,037	421,532	84.3	7,412	6,468	87.3	1,441	1,189	82.5	328	276	84.1	337	265	78.6	2,923	2,632	90.0	1,014	901	88.9	1,369	1,205	88.0	18,957	16,167	85.3	13,045	11,277	86.4
1990	564,768	493,477	87.4	8,354	7,290	87.3	1,758	1,537	87.4	509	426	83.7	716	588	82.1	3,143	2,793	88.9	969	856	88.3	1,259	1,090	86.6	20,422	17,733	86.8	14,088	12,488	88.6

Notes appear at end of table

(continued)

Table Ag915–1097 American Indian school-age population and school attendance, by region and state: 1900–1990 *Continued*

Middle Atlantic

	New Jersey			Pennsylvania		
	School-age population	In school		School-age population	In school	
		Number	Percentage		Number	Percentage
	Ag945	Ag946	Ag947	Ag948	Ag949	Ag950
Year	Number	Number	Percent	Number	Number	Percent
1900	—	—	—	—	—	—
1910	54	25	46.3	837	776	92.7
1930	57	40	70.2	124	80	64.5
1970 [1]						
1980	2,835	2,308	81.4	3,077	2,582	83.9
1990	2,949	2,422	82.1	3,385	2,823	83.4

South Atlantic

	Maryland			Delaware		
	School-age population	In school		School-age population	In school	
		Number	Percentage		Number	Percentage
	Ag957	Ag958	Ag959	Ag954	Ag955	Ag956
Year	Number	Number	Percent	Number	Number	Percent
1900	—	—	—	—	—	—
1910	29	22	75.9	4	4	100.0
1930	16	12	75.0	0	0	0.0
1970 [1]						
1980	2,600	2,216	85.2	378	343	90.7
1990	3,031	2,500	82.5	368	324	88.0

South Atlantic

	West Virginia			North Carolina			South Carolina		
	School-age population	In school		School-age population	In school		School-age population	In school	
		Number	Percentage		Number	Percentage		Number	Percentage
	Ag966	Ag967	Ag968	Ag969	Ag970	Ag971	Ag972	Ag973	Ag974
Year	Number	Number	Percent	Number	Number	Percent	Number	Number	Percent
1900	—	—	—	2,287	621	27.2	—	—	—
1910	17	14	82.4	2,668	1,608	60.3	115	62	53.9
1930	1	0	0.0	7,363	4,028	54.7	419	181	43.2
1970 [1]				15,381	13,215	85.9			
1980	526	449	85.4	21,641	18,135	83.8	1,919	1,537	80.1
1990	755	631	83.6	23,258	19,635	84.4	2,016	1,652	81.9

South Atlantic

	District of Columbia			Virginia		
	School-age population	In school		School-age population	In school	
		Number	Percentage		Number	Percentage
	Ag960	Ag961	Ag962	Ag963	Ag964	Ag965
Year	Number	Number	Percent	Number	Number	Percent
1900	—	—	—	—	—	—
1910	18	14	77.8	192	57	29.7
1930	14	12	85.7	332	136	41.0
1970 [1]						
1980	196	181	92.3	2,619	2,080	79.4
1990	221	170	76.9	3,434	2,946	85.8

South Atlantic

	Georgia			Florida		
	School-age population	In school		School-age population	In school	
		Number	Percentage		Number	Percentage
	Ag975	Ag976	Ag977	Ag978	Ag979	Ag980
Year	Number	Number	Percent	Number	Number	Percent
1900	—	—	—	—	—	—
1910	29	11	37.9	19	5	26.3
1930	11	1	9.1	228	24	10.5
1970 [1]						
1980	2,749	2,118	77.0	5,813	4,611	79.3
1990	3,393	2,750	81.0	8,763	7,326	83.6

East North Central

				Ohio			Indiana		
	School-age population	In school		School-age population	In school		School-age population	In school	
		Number	Percentage		Number	Percentage		Number	Percentage
	Ag981	Ag982	Ag983	Ag984	Ag985	Ag986	Ag987	Ag988	Ag989
Year	Number	Number	Percent	Number	Number	Percent	Number	Number	Percent
1900	—	—	—	—	—	—	—	—	—
1910	5,942	3,883	65.3	40	26	65.0	111	66	59.5
1930	7,440	4,962	66.7	129	89	69.0	78	57	73.1
1970 [1]									
1980	38,975	33,322	85.5	4,062	3,364	82.8	2,522	2,074	82.2
1990	42,182	36,529	86.6	4,892	4,193	85.7	3,539	2,959	83.6

East North Central

Year	Illinois — School-age population (Ag990)	Illinois — In school, Number (Ag991)	Illinois — In school, Percentage (Ag992)	Michigan — School-age population (Ag993)	Michigan — In school, Number (Ag994)	Michigan — In school, Percentage (Ag995)	Wisconsin — School-age population (Ag996)	Wisconsin — In school, Number (Ag997)	Wisconsin — In school, Percentage (Ag998)
1900	—	—	—	2,234	963	43.1	3,072	1,268	41.3
1910	44	32	72.7	2,303	1,448	62.9	3,444	2,311	67.1
1930	95	52	54.7	2,478	1,625	65.6	4,660	3,139	67.4
1970 [1]	2,519	2,182	86.6	4,786	4,374	91.4	6,848	6,247	91.2
1980	5,372	4,431	82.5	15,883	13,940	87.8	11,136	9,513	85.4
1990	5,237	4,391	83.8	16,751	14,562	86.9	11,763	10,424	88.6

West North Central

Year	School-age population (Ag999)	In school, Number (Ag1000)	In school, Percentage (Ag1001)	Minnesota — School-age population (Ag1002)	Minnesota — In school, Number (Ag1003)	Minnesota — In school, Percentage (Ag1004)
1900	—	—	—	3,357	1,072	31.9
1910	13,361	8,728	65.3	3,094	2,259	73.0
1930	18,313	11,808	64.5	4,360	2,831	64.9
1970 [1]	—	—	—	8,530	7,640	89.6
1980	53,587	45,454	84.8	14,052	11,702	83.3
1990	60,437	52,366	86.6	15,632	13,383	85.6

West North Central

Year	Iowa — School-age pop. (Ag1005)	Iowa — No. (Ag1006)	Iowa — % (Ag1007)	Missouri — School-age pop. (Ag1008)	Missouri — No. (Ag1009)	Missouri — % (Ag1010)	North Dakota — School-age pop. (Ag1011)	North Dakota — No. (Ag1012)	North Dakota — % (Ag1013)	South Dakota — School-age pop. (Ag1014)	South Dakota — No. (Ag1015)	South Dakota — % (Ag1016)	Nebraska — School-age pop. (Ag1017)	Nebraska — No. (Ag1018)	Nebraska — % (Ag1019)
1900	—	—	—	—	—	—	2,474	746	30.2	6,561	3,819	58.2	1,365	822	60.2
1910	111	54	48.6	100	68	68.0	2,258	1,421	62.9	5,543	3,326	60.0	1,224	754	61.6
1930	226	114	50.4	194	115	59.3	3,303	2,028	61.4	8,068	5,278	65.4	1,277	855	67.0
1970 [1]	—	—	—	—	—	—	5,353	4,724	88.2	11,607	10,497	90.4	—	—	—
1980	2,232	1,907	85.4	3,820	3,051	79.9	7,712	6,449	83.6	17,811	14,717	82.6	3,367	2,831	0.8
1990	2,305	1,925	83.5	5,180	4,373	84.4	8,916	8,052	90.3	17,973	15,651	87.1	4,068	3,440	84.6

West North Central

Year	Kansas — School-age population (Ag1020)	Kansas — In school, Number (Ag1021)	Kansas — In school, Percentage (Ag1022)
1900	1,069	777	72.7
1910	1,031	846	82.1
1930	885	587	66.3
1970 [1]	—	—	—
1980	5,129	4,261	83.1
1990	6,363	5,542	87.1

East South Central

Year	School-age pop. (Ag1023)	No. (Ag1024)	% (Ag1025)	Kentucky — School-age pop. (Ag1026)	Kentucky — No. (Ag1027)	Kentucky — % (Ag1028)	Tennessee — School-age pop. (Ag1029)	Tennessee — No. (Ag1030)	Tennessee — % (Ag1031)	Alabama — School-age pop. (Ag1032)	Alabama — No. (Ag1033)	Alabama — % (Ag1034)
1900	—	—	—	—	—	—	—	—	—	—	—	—
1910	907	211	23.3	92	16	17.4	76	35	46.1	320	112	35.0
1930	849	298	35.1	5	4	80.0	58	14	24.1	222	83	37.4
1970 [1]	—	—	—	—	—	—	—	—	—	—	—	—
1980	7,699	6,107	79.3	1,160	768	66.2	1,581	1,277	80.8	2,575	2,187	84.9
1990	12,943	11,164	86.3	1,420	1,194	84.1	2,727	2,266	83.1	5,978	5,295	88.6

Notes appear at end of table

(continued)

Table Ag915–1097 American Indian school-age population and school attendance, by region and state: 1900–1990 *Continued*

East South Central / West South Central

Year	Mississippi — School-age pop. (Ag1035)	Miss. In school, Number (Ag1036)	Miss. In school, Percent (Ag1037)	West South Central — School-age pop. (Ag1038)	W.S.C. In school, Number (Ag1039)	W.S.C. In school, Percent (Ag1040)	Arkansas — School-age pop. (Ag1041)	Ark. In school, Number (Ag1042)	Ark. In school, Percent (Ag1043)	Louisiana — School-age pop. (Ag1044)	La. In school, Number (Ag1045)	La. In school, Percent (Ag1046)	Oklahoma — School-age pop. (Ag1047)	Okla. In school, Number (Ag1048)	Okla. In school, Percent (Ag1049)
1900	931	47	5.0	—	—	—	—	—	—	—	—	—	27,413	11,625	42.4
1910	419	48	11.5	27,765	18,525	66.7	167	104	62.3	321	56	17.4	27,060	18,288	67.6
1930	564	197	34.9	40,279	27,318	67.8	156	87	55.8	643	224	34.8	39,143	26,829	68.5
1970 [1]	—	—	—	—	—	—	—	—	—	—	—	—	30,591	27,281	89.2
1980	2,383	1,875	78.7	77,771	66,509	85.5	3,431	2,790	81.3	4,061	3,175	78.2	56,979	49,673	87.2
1990	2,818	2,409	85.5	103,808	90,827	87.5	3,526	2,991	84.8	5,842	4,910	84.0	78,368	68,931	88.0

West South Central (Texas) / Mountain

Year	Texas — School-age pop. (Ag1050)	Tex. In school, Number (Ag1051)	Tex. In school, Percent (Ag1052)	Mountain — School-age pop. (Ag1053)	Mtn. In school, Number (Ag1054)	Mtn. In school, Percent (Ag1055)	Montana — School-age pop. (Ag1056)	Mont. In school, Number (Ag1057)	Mont. In school, Percent (Ag1058)	Idaho — School-age pop. (Ag1059)	Idaho In school, Number (Ag1060)	Idaho In school, Percent (Ag1061)	Wyoming — School-age pop. (Ag1062)	Wyo. In school, Number (Ag1063)	Wyo. In school, Percent (Ag1064)
1900	—	—	—	23,947	7,433	31.0	3,889	1,640	42.2	1,204	374	31.1	503	294	58.4
1910	217	77	35.5	24,276	8,516	35.1	3,292	1,519	46.1	875	382	43.7	437	289	66.1
1930	337	178	52.8	38,498	18,746	48.7	5,556	3,623	65.2	1,170	788	67.4	610	449	73.6
1970 [1]	4,302	3,627	84.3	—	—	—	10,226	9,129	89.3	—	—	—	—	—	—
1980	13,300	10,871	81.7	136,294	112,661	82.7	13,741	11,636	84.7	3,797	3,229	85.0	2,783	2,379	85.5
1990	16,072	13,995	87.1	151,750	133,378	87.9	15,499	13,730	88.6	4,354	3,792	87.1	3,264	2,859	87.6

Mountain (*continued*)

Year	Colorado — School-age pop. (Ag1065)	Colo. In school, Number (Ag1066)	Colo. In school, Percent (Ag1067)	New Mexico — School-age pop. (Ag1068)	N.M. In school, Number (Ag1069)	N.M. In school, Percent (Ag1070)	Arizona — School-age pop. (Ag1071)	Ariz. In school, Number (Ag1072)	Ariz. In school, Percent (Ag1073)	Utah — School-age pop. (Ag1074)	Utah In school, Number (Ag1075)	Utah In school, Percent (Ag1076)	Nevada — School-age pop. (Ag1077)	Nev. In school, Number (Ag1078)	Nev. In school, Percent (Ag1079)
1900	716	373	52.1	5,160	1,541	29.9	10,020	2,671	26.7	867	173	20.0	1,588	367	23.1
1910	588	403	68.5	6,749	1,799	26.7	10,039	3,366	33.5	870	101	11.6	1,426	657	46.1
1930	468	283	60.5	11,460	5,055	44.1	16,598	7,167	43.2	1,087	472	43.4	1,549	909	58.7
1970 [1]	—	—	—	27,226	24,315	89.3	36,089	31,154	86.3	4,382	3,989	91.0	4,417	3,989	—
1980	6,572	5,500	83.7	38,539	30,578	79.3	58,024	48,451	83.5	8,421	7,221	85.7	4,417	3,667	83.0
1990	7,082	5,940	83.9	42,239	37,216	88.1	66,305	58,472	88.2	8,266	7,259	87.8	4,741	4,110	86.7

Notes appear at end of table

Pacific

Year	School-age population Ag1080 Number	In school Number Ag1081	In school Percentage Ag1082	Alaska School-age population Ag1083 Number	Alaska In school Number Ag1084	Alaska In school Percentage Ag1085	Washington School-age population Ag1086 Number	Washington In school Number Ag1087	Washington In school Percentage Ag1088	Oregon School-age population Ag1089 Number	Oregon In school Number Ag1090	Oregon In school Percentage Ag1091	California School-age population Ag1092 Number	California In school Number Ag1093	California In school Percentage Ag1094	Hawai'i School-age population Ag1095 Number	Hawai'i In school Number Ag1096	Hawai'i In school Percentage Ag1097
1900	—	—	—	—	—	—	3,142	1,408	44.8	1,745	1,024	58.7	4,996	2,035	40.7	—	—	—
1910	10,076	5,967	59.2	—	—	—	3,264	1,710	52.4	1,714	1,349	78.7	5,098	2,908	57.0	—	—	—
1930	11,546	8,444	73.1	—	—	—	3,928	2,455	62.5	1,202	1,691	140.7	6,416	4,298	67.0	—	—	—
1970 [1]	—	—	—	6,090	5,472	89.9	10,807	9,689	89.7	4,570	4,043	88.5	24,659	22,475	91.1	—	—	—
1980	120,901	103,174	85.3	22,758	19,822	87.1	20,566	17,328	84.3	10,031	8,282	82.6	66,851	57,227	85.6	695	515	74.1
1990	120,972	104,917	86.7	25,536	22,307	87.4	23,132	19,733	85.3	11,451	9,696	84.7	59,546	52,034	87.4	1,307	1,147	87.8

[1] Data for states with fewer than 10,000 American Indians were not reported.

[2] Includes all states.

Source

U.S. Bureau of the Census, *Indian Population in the United States and Alaska, 1910* (1915), Tables 77, 80; U.S. Bureau of the Census, *The Indian Population of the United States and Alaska* (1937), Table 33; U.S. Bureau of the Census, *American Indians, Final Report, PC(2)-1F* (1973), Tables 2, 3; U.S. Bureau of the Census, *General Social and Economic Characteristics*, PC80-1-C, Parts 2-52 (1983), Tables 73, 76; U.S. Bureau of the Census, *Social and Economic Characteristics*, CP-2, parts 2-52 (1993), Tables 45, 47.

Documentation

The population covered by this table varies: for 1900 and 1930, American Indians ages 5–20; for 1910, American Indians ages 6–19; for 1970, American Indians ages 5–17; and for 1980–1990, American Indians and Alaska Natives ages 5–19.

Table Ag1098–1113　American Indian veterans, by sex and period of service: 1980–1990

Contributed by C. Matthew Snipp

	Veterans																Nonveterans
	Conflict or period									Both sexes		Males		Females		
Year	May 1975 or later only Ag1098 Number	Vietnam era Ag1099 Number	February 1955 to July 1964 only Ag1100 Number	Both Vietnam era and Korean conflict Ag1101 Number	Korean conflict Ag1102 Number	Both Korean conflict and World War II Ag1103 Number	World War II Ag1104 Number	World War I Ag1105 Number	Other Ag1106 Number	Number Ag1107 Number	As a percentage of the civilian population Ag1108 Percent	Number Ag1109 Number	As a percentage of civilian males Ag1110 Percent	Number Ag1111 Number	As a percentage of civilian females Ag1112 Percent	Ag1113 Number
1980	10,721	57,950	18,963	3,853	21,521	3,968	38,474	1,187	2,448	159,085	15.8	151,365	31.2	7,720	1.5	849,179
1990	37,560	72,458	20,151	3,575	23,084	3,751	31,712	162	1,058	193,511	14.0	181,439	27.2	12,072	1.7	1,201,498

Sources

U.S. Bureau of the Census, *General Social and Economic Characteristics, United States Summary*, PC80-1-C1 (1983), Table 147; U.S. Bureau of the Census, *Social and Economic Characteristics, United States*, CP-2-1 (1993), Table 43.

Documentation

This table covers American Indians and Alaska Natives, age 16 and older.

INDEX

Note: The number before the colon is the volume; the number after the colon is the page. A number range indicates inclusive pages in the same volume. Numbers in italics refer to pages in essays; numbers not in italics refer to pages in statistical tables.

Numbers in italics refer to pages in essays; numbers not in italics refer to pages in statistical tables.

Numbers in italics refer to pages in essays; numbers not in italics refer to pages in statistical tables.

Numbers in italics refer to pages in essays; numbers not in italics refer to pages in statistical tables.

Numbers in italics refer to pages in essays; numbers not in italics refer to pages in statistical tables.

Numbers in italics refer to pages in essays; numbers not in italics refer to pages in statistical tables.

Numbers in italics refer to pages in essays; numbers not in italics refer to pages in statistical tables.

Numbers in italics refer to pages in essays; numbers not in italics refer to pages in statistical tables.

Numbers in italics refer to pages in essays; numbers not in italics refer to pages in statistical tables.

Numbers in italics refer to pages in essays; numbers not in italics refer to pages in statistical tables.

Numbers in italics refer to pages in essays; numbers not in italics refer to pages in statistical tables.

Numbers in italics refer to pages in essays; numbers not in italics refer to pages in statistical tables.

Natural resources, *3:333, 3:341*
  belonging to American Indians, *1:721–4,*
    1:747–56
  definition, *3:333*
  government expenditures for, 3:365
    federal, 4:252, 5:106–8
  industries, *4:275–84,* 4:285–394
    energy, 4:335–57
    fisheries, 4:358–75
    forestry, 4:376–94
    mining, 4:285–334
Naturalization, *1:531,* 1:641–7. *See also*
    Citizenship status; Immigration
  alien, 1:641–7
Naval vessels, 4:912–13
Navy, 3:453–5. *See also* Armed forces
NCAA. *See* National Collegiate Athletic
    Association
Near East, U.S. government foreign grants and
    credits, 5:483–97
Nebraska. *See* State data
Nectarines, acreage, price, and production,
    4:131–4
Nepal, U.S. population born in, 1:610
Net worth, *3:295,* 3:314–16
Netherlands
  investment in United States, by industry,
    5:479–82
  U.S. population born in, 1:602, 1:606, 1:609
Nevada. *See* State data
New Alliance Party, 5:172–9
New Deal
  banking reforms, *3:591–2, 3:621–2*
  farm policies, *4:34–5*
New England. *See also* Regional data
  charitable and voluntary organizations, 2:852
  codfish prices, 5:675–6
  incorporations, business, *3:483,* 3:548
  towns settled and incorporated, 5:665–8
  turnpike mileage and cost, 4:783
New Hampshire, 5:658. *See also* State data
New Haven. *See also* Metropolitan areas
  college foundings and failures, 2:875
  nonprofit and voluntary institutions per capita,
    2:851
New Jersey. *See also* State data
  business incorporations, *3:483,* 3:539–47
  colonial agriculture, 5:700
  colonial population, 5:662
New Mexico. *See* State data
New Orleans. *See also* Metropolitan areas
  cotton freight rates, 4:884
  price indexes, 3:197–8
  steamboat trade, 4:878
  travel times to, 4:779
New York. *See also* State data
  business incorporations, 3:539–47
  canals, 4:881, 4:885
  charitable giving, 2:929
  colonial population, 5:660–1
  cotton freight rates, 4:884
  foundations, 2:855–7
  household manufacturing, 2:365
  manufacturing companies chartered in, 3:549
  poor relief expenditures, 2:729–31
  public relief, *2:697–8,* 2:732–3
New York City. *See also* Metropolitan areas
  colonial population, 5:655
  homicides, number, indictments, and rates,
    5:248–9
  poor relief, 2:720–1, 2:729–31
  public relief recipients, 2:732–3
  rental housing, price indexes, 3:168
  travel times, 4:779
  vessels clearing, in colonial foreign commerce,
    5:720–2

New York Stock Exchange sales, 3:770. *See also*
    Stock market
New Zealand
  immigration from, 1:583–5
  U.S. population born in, 1:611
Newport, Rhode Island, colonial population,
    5:655. *See also* Metropolitan areas
Newspapers, *4:984–5,* 4:1050–9. *See also*
    Magazines and newspapers
  advertising, 4:752–8
  circulation, 4:915–53, 4:1055
  daily, number and circulation, *4:984*
  newsprint consumption, 4:1059
  number, 4:1055–8
  pages per issue, 4:1059
Newsprint, 4:391–3, 4:1059
Nicaragua
  immigration from, 1:574–6
  U.S. population born in, 1:612
Nickel, 4:318–20
Nigeria, U.S. population born in, 1:611
NIPA. *See* National income and product accounts
Nitrogen oxide emissions, 4:852
Nobel prizes
  American recipients, by field and country of
    birth, 1:623–6
  by category, 3:457
  by recipient's country of residence, 3:457
Nonaccelerating inflation rate of unemployment
    (NAIRU), 3:84–8
Non-Hodgkin's lymphoma, 2:568–71
Nonmetals, nonfuel imports and exports, 4:333–4
Nonprofit arts, humanities, and cultural
    institutions, 2:885–7. *See also* Nonprofit
    institutions
Nonprofit institutions, *2:837–48,* 2:851–84
  assets, *3:295*
  benevolent, 2:851, 2:865–7
  business, 2:851
  charitable, *2:841–2,* 2:859–60
  definition, *2:837, 2:838–9*
  employee compensation, 2:857–9
  employment, 2:857–9
  endowment income, 2:853–4
  farmers' cooperatives, 2:861–3
  flow of funds balance sheets, 3:799–804
  grant expenditures, 2:853–4
  gross domestic product, as component of,
    3:50–2
  net worth, *3:295,* 3:314–6
  noncharitable, *2:841–2*
  nonexempt charitable trusts, 2:861–3
  number, 2:853–4, 2:857–9
  per capita, 2:851
  personal saving, 3:304–6
  public/private, *2:840–1*
  religious, 2:851 (*see also* Religious institutions;
    specific religions)
  revenue, philanthropic, 2:923–5
  secular, 2:851
  schools, 2:871–5
  tax-exempt organizations, 2:861–4, 2:867–70
  women's, 2:851
  youth, 2:851
Nonresidential structures
  net stock, 4:414–19
    composition, *4:396*
  value of new construction, by type, 4:455–60
North America
  emigration from, 1:555–8, 1:571–6
  immigration to, 1:551
  map of, *5:629*
  refugees and asylees from, 1:635
  U.S. population born in, 1:604, 1:612
North American Industry Classification System
    (NAICS), 4:5

North Atlantic Treaty Organization (NATO), 5:371
North Carolina, 5:751. *See also* State data
North Central States. *See* Regional data
North Dakota. *See* State data
Northern Ireland. *See also* Ireland
  immigration from, *1:534*
  U.S. population born in, 1:601, 1:606, 1:609
Northern Mariana Islands. *See also* Outlying
    areas
  consumer price indexes, 5:619–20
  education, 5:599–603
  employment, 5:605–7
  exports, 5:610–12
  government revenues and expenditures, 5:624–5
  gross domestic product, 5:604–5
  imports, 5:612–14
  infant mortality, 5:597–8
  population, 1:39, 5:594–5
  telephones in, 5:617–18
  unemployment, 5:607
  visitor arrivals, 5:615–16
Norway, U.S. population born in, 1:601, 1:606,
    1:609. *See also* Scandinavia
Nuclear fuel and waste inventory, 3:370–1
Nuclear power
  energy consumption, 4:337–9
  energy production, 4:335–7
  plants, 4:353
Nuclear weapons, 5:404–5, *5:335–6*
  U.S. strategic, 5:404
Nullifiers Party, 5:172–9
Nursery school, 2:431
Nurses, 2:541–5
Nursing facilities
  Medicaid recipients and days of care, 2:560
  nonprofit, 2:881–3
Nursing homes
  consumer expenditures, 3:243–66
  U.S. Department of Veterans Affairs, 5:435
Nutrient consumption. *See also* Food and
    beverages; Nutrition
  daily, 2:576–7
  per capita, 2:572–3
Nutrition, *2:499–507,* 2:572–81. *See also* Food
    and beverages; Nutrient consumption
  calorie consumption, 2:576–7
  carbohydrate consumption, 2:576–7
  child, public expenditures for, 2:749–50
  cholesterol consumption, 2:576–7
  diet, *2:506–7*
  fat consumption, 2:576–7
  lifestyle choices, *2:506*
  nutrient consumption, 2:572–3, 2:576–7
  protein consumption, 2:576–7
Nuts, tree, 4:122–4. *See also specific nuts*

OASDHI. *See* Old-Age, Survivors, Disability, and
    Health Insurance
Oats, acreage, price, and production, *4:16,* 4:92–6
Occupations, *1:693–4, 2:35–40,* 2:133–253. *See
    also* Employment; *specific occupations*
  of American Indians, 1:767–72
  blue collar, *2:38*
  consumer expenditures by occupation class,
    3:286
  distribution, *2:38*
  earnings, 2:271–2
  of economically active population, 2:232–53
  employment, cost indexes, 2:295–300
  groups, major, 2:133
  immigrants by, *1:536,* 1:590–6, 1:618–20
  by nativity, 2:212–131, 2:253
  by race, 2:136–9, 2:172–211, 2:253
  by sex, 1:618–20, 1:770, 2:134–9, 2:152–211,
    2:253
  skill differential, *2:42*

Numbers in italics refer to pages in essays; numbers not in italics refer to pages in statistical tables.

Numbers in italics refer to pages in essays; numbers not in italics refer to pages in statistical tables.

Numbers in italics refer to pages in essays; numbers not in italics refer to pages in statistical tables.

Numbers in italics refer to pages in essays; numbers not in italics refer to pages in statistical tables.

Numbers in italics refer to pages in essays; numbers not in italics refer to pages in statistical tables.

Numbers in italics refer to pages in essays; numbers not in italics refer to pages in statistical tables.

Numbers in italics refer to pages in essays; numbers not in italics refer to pages in statistical tables.

Numbers in italics refer to pages in essays; numbers not in italics refer to pages in statistical tables.

Numbers in italics refer to pages in essays; numbers not in italics refer to pages in statistical tables.